CANADIAN CONTRIBUTORS

Barbara J. Astle RN, MN
Sessional Instructor
Faculty of Nursing
University of Calgary
Calgary, Alberta
Chapter 24: Documenting and Reporting

Cyndee Blake, RN, MN
Instructor
Faculty of Nursing
University of Calgary
Calgary, Alberta
Chapter 26: Nurse-Patient Relationship

Christine Ceci, RN, PhD (c)
Doctoral Candidate
Faculty of Nursing
University of Calgary
Calgary, Alberta
Chapter 1: Historical and Contemporary Nursing Practice
Chapter 4: Nursing Philosophies, Theories, Concepts, Frameworks, and Models

Roberta deJong RN, MN
Clinical Nurse Specialist
Hypertension and Cholesterol Clinic
University of Calgary
Medical Clinic
Calgary, Alberta
Chapter 31: Vital Signs

Margaret Edwards RN, PhD
Professor, Coordinator
Graduate Programs Centre for Nursing and Health Studies
Athabasca University
Athabasca, Alberta
Chapter 25: Nursing Informatics

Bonnie Friesen RN, MN
Nursing Skills Clinician
Faculty of Nursing
University of Calgary
Calgary, Alberta
Chapter 31: Vital Signs
Chapter 32: Asepsis

Sandra P. Hirst RN, PhD GNC(C)
Associate Professor
Faculty of Nursing
University of Calgary
Calgary, Alberta
Chapter 1: Historical and Contemporary Nursing Practice
Chapter 2: Nursing Education in Canada
Chapter 3: Nursing Research in Canada
Chapter 5: The Individual—the Client of Care
Chapter 13: Spirituality
Chapter 17: Home Care
Chapter 19: Concepts of Growth and Development
Chapter 20: Development from Conception through Adolescence
Chapter 21: Development from Young Through Older Adulthood
Chapter 35: Fecal Elimination
Chapter 36: Urinary Elimination
Chapter 43: Activity and Exercise
Chapter 46: Self-Concept

Dorothy Hughes RN, PhD
Associate Professor
Associate Dean, Graduate Programs
Faculty of Nursing
University of Calgary
Calgary, Alberta
Chapter 11: Holistic Healing Modalities

Carol McDonald RN, PhD (c)
Doctoral Candidate
Faculty of Nursing
University of Calgary
Calgary, Alberta
Chapter 12: Sexuality

Meg McDonagh RN, MN
Instructor
Faculty of Nursing
University of Calgary
Calgary, Alberta
Chapter 18: Rural Health Care

Marjorie McIntyre RN, PhD
Associate Professor
Faculty of Nursing
University of Calgary
Chapters 1: Historical and Contemporary Nursing Practice
Chapter 4: Nursing Philosophies, Theories, Concepts, Frameworks, and Models
Chapter 12: Sexuality

Nancy J. Moules RN, PhD
Assistant Professor
Faculty of Nursing
University of Calgary
Calgary, Alberta
Chapter 48: Loss, Grieving, and Death

Florence Myrick RN, PhD
Associate Professor
Acting Dean, Faculty of Nursing
University of Calgary
Calgary, Alberta
Chapter 22: Critical Thinking

Kathleen Oberle RN, PhD
Associate Professor
Faculty of Nursing
University of Calgary
Calgary, Alberta
Chapter 7: Ethics, Morality, and Values
Chapter 8: Legal Aspects of Nursing

Heather L. Orstead RN, BN, ET
Clinical Specialist
Skin and Wound Management Care in the Community
Calgary Health Region
Chapter 37: Skin Integrity and Wound Care

Harry Plummer, RN, PhD (c)
Instructor
Faculty of Nursing
University of Calgary
Calgary, Alberta
Chapter 45: Pain

D. Shelley Raffin Bouchal RN, PhD
Assistant Professor
Faculty of Nursing
University of Calgary
Calgary, Alberta
Chapter 8: Legal Aspects of Nursing
Chapter 24: Documenting and Reporting
Chapter 33: Safety
Chapter 34: Hygiene
Chapter 44: Clients Having Surgery: Promoting Healthy Recovery
Chapter 48: Loss, Grieving, and Death

James A. Rankin RN, ANCP, PhD
Associate Professor
Faculty of Nursing
University of Calgary
Calgary, Alberta
Chapter 27: Health Assessment
Chapter 28: Medications
Chapter 39: Oxygenation
Chapter 40: Fluid, Electrolyte, and Acid-Base Balance

Sandra M. Reilly
Associate Professor
Faculty of Nursing
University of Calgary
Calgary, Alberta
Chapter 9: Health, Wellness, and Illness

Marlene Reimer, RN, PhD, NNC(C)
Associate Professor
Associate Dean, Research Faculty of Nursing
University of Calgary
Calgary, Alberta
Chapter 23: The Nursing Process
Chapter 41: Sensory Perception
Chapter 42: Rest and Sleep

Dianne M. Tapp RN, PhD
Associate Professor
Faculty of Nursing
University of Calgary
Calgary, Alberta
Chapter 6: Ethics, Morality, and Values

Sandra C. Tenove RN, PhD
Associate Professor
Faculty of Nursing
University of Calgary
Calgary, Alberta
Chapter 10: Health Promotion
Chapter 15: Health Care Delivery Systems

Karen L. Then RN, CCn(C), ACNP, PhD
Associate Professor
Faculty of Nursing
University of Calgary
Calgary, Alberta
Chapter 27: Health Assessment
Chapter 28: Medications
Chapter 39: Oxygenation
Chapter 40: Fluid, Electrolyte, and Acid-Base Balance

Elizabeth Thomlinson RN, PhD
Associate Professor
Faculty of Nursing
University of Calgary
Calgary, Alberta
Chapter 14: Culture and Ethnicity
Chapter 18: Rural Health Care
Chapter 30: Leading, Managing, and Influencing Change
Chapter 47: Stress and Coping

Ardene Robinson Vollman RN, PhD
Associate Professor (Retired)
Faculty of Nursing
University of Calgary
Calgary, Alberta
Chapter 16: Community-Based Nursing

Lorraine Watson RN, PhD
Associate Professor
Faculty of Nursing
University of Calgary
Calgary, Alberta
Chapter 38: Nutrition

Leanne Wyrostok RN, MN
Nursing Skills Clinician
Faculty of Nursing
University of Calgary
Calgary, Alberta
Chapter 37: Skin Integrity and Wound Care

We dedicate this book to

The memory of Barbara's parents, the late Luella and Bertie Blackwood

The memory of Glen's twin sister; the late Valerie Nicholson, and her husband, the late Peter Nicholson — with warm thoughts and feelings

The memory of Audrey's father, Jack L. Berman, MD, and to the hundreds of pracitsing nurses who, as students, taught me how to teach

The loving memory of Karen's grandson, Aiden, her parents, Lila and Willie Raihala, And her father-in-law, Brad Burke

Shelley's family for their support, love, and inspiration

Sandra's family, Martin, Rebecca, and Brittany for a thousand different reasons, but especially for their love

Fundamentals of Nursing

The Nature of Nursing Practice in Canada Canadian Edition

Fundamentals of Nursing

The Nature of Nursing Practice in Canada

Canadian Edition

Barbara Kozier, RN, MN

Glenora Erb, RN, BSN

Audrey Jean Berman, PhD, RN, AOCN
Associate Dean, Nursing Academic Affairs
Samuel Merritt College
Oakland, California

Karen Burke, RN, MS
Director of Health Occupations
Clatsop Community College
Astoria, Oregon

D. Shelly Raffin Bouchal, RN, PhD
Assistant Professor, Faculty of Nursing
University of Calgary
Calgary, Alberta

Sandra P. Hirst, RN, PhD, GNC(C)
Associate Professor, Faculty of Nursing
University of Calgary
Calgary, Alberta

PRENTICE HALL HEALTH

Toronto

National Library of Canada Cataloguing in Publication

Fundamentals of nursing: the nature of nursing practice in Canada/Barbara Kozier ...[et al.]. — 1st Canadian ed.

Includes index.
ISBN 0-13-062268-0

1. Nursing. I. Kozier, Barbara

RT41.K72 2004 610.73 C2003-900024-9

Care has been taken to confirm the accuracy of information presented in this book. The authors, editors, and the publisher, however, cannot accept any responsibility for errors or omissions or for the consequences from application of the information in this book and make no warranty, expressed or implied, with respect to its contents. In view of ongoing research and changes in government regulations, the reader is especially urged to check the package inserts of all drugs for any change in indications of dosage and for added warnings and precautions.

ISBN 0-13-062268-0
10 9 8 7 6 5 4 3 2 CKV 08 07 06 05

Statistics Canada information is used with the permission of the Minister of Industry, as Minister responsible for Statistics Canada. Information on the availability of the wide range of data from Statistics Canada can be obtained from Statistics Canada's Regional Offices, its World Wide Web site at http://www.statcan.ca, and its toll-free access number 1-800-263-1136.

Vice President, Editorial Director: Michael J. Young
Executive Acquisitions Editor: Samantha Scully
Executive Marketing Manager: Cas Shields
Supervising Developmental Editor: Maurice Esses
Production Editor: Judith Scott
Copy Editor: Rohini Herbert
Production Coordinator: Janette Lush
Photo and Permissions Research: Nicola Wynn-Stanley
Page Layout: ArtPlus Design & Communications
Art Director: Julia Hall
Interior Design: The ArtPlus Group
Cover Design: Amy Harnden
Cover Image: The Stock Illustration Source

Printed and bound in the USA.

PRENTICE HALL HEALTH

CANADIAN CONTRIBUTORS

Barbara J. Astle RN, MN
Sessional Instructor
Faculty of Nursing
University of Calgary
Calgary, Alberta
Chapter 24: Documenting and Reporting

Cyndee Blake, RN, MN
Instructor
Faculty of Nursing
University of Calgary
Calgary, Alberta
Chapter 26: Nurse-Patient Relationship

Christine Ceci, RN, PhD (c)
Doctoral Candidate
Faculty of Nursing
University of Calgary
Calgary, Alberta
Chapter 1: Historical and Contemporary Nursing Practice
Chapter 4: Nursing Philosophies, Theories, Concepts, Frameworks, and Models

Roberta deJong RN, MN
Clinical Nurse Specialist
Hypertension and Cholesterol Clinic
University of Calgary
Medical Clinic
Calgary, Alberta
Chapter 31: Vital Signs

Margaret Edwards RN, PhD
Professor, Coordinator
Graduate Programs Centre for Nursing and Health Studies
Athabasca University
Athabasca, Alberta
Chapter 25: Nursing Informatics

Bonnie Friesen RN, MN
Nursing Skills Clinician
Faculty of Nursing
University of Calgary
Calgary, Alberta
Chapter 31: Vital Signs
Chapter 32: Asepsis

Sandra P. Hirst RN, PhD GNC(C)
Associate Professor
Faculty of Nursing
University of Calgary
Calgary, Alberta
Chapter 1: Historical and Contemporary Nursing Practice
Chapter 2: Nursing Education in Canada
Chapter 3: Nursing Research in Canada
Chapter 5: The Individual—the Client of Care
Chapter 13: Spirituality
Chapter 17: Home Care
Chapter 19: Concepts of Growth and Development
Chapter 20: Development from Conception through Adolescence
Chapter 21: Development from Young Through Older Adulthood
Chapter 35: Fecal Elimination
Chapter 36: Urinary Elimination
Chapter 43: Activity and Exercise
Chapter 46: Self-Concept

Dorothy Hughes RN, PhD
Associate Professor
Associate Dean, Graduate Programs
Faculty of Nursing
University of Calgary
Calgary, Alberta
Chapter 11: Holistic Healing Modalities

Carol McDonald RN, PhD (c)
Doctoral Candidate
Faculty of Nursing
University of Calgary
Calgary, Alberta
Chapter 12: Sexuality

Meg McDonagh RN, MN
Instructor
Faculty of Nursing
University of Calgary
Calgary, Alberta
Chapter 18: Rural Health Care

Marjorie McIntyre RN, PhD
Associate Professor
Faculty of Nursing
University of Calgary
Chapter 1: Historical and Contemporary Nursing Practice
Chapter 4: Nursing Philosophies, Theories, Concepts, Frameworks, and Models
Chapter 12: Sexuality

Nancy J. Moules RN, PhD
Assistant Professor
Faculty of Nursing
University of Calgary
Calgary, Alberta
Chapter 48: Loss, Grieving, and Death

Florence Myrick RN, PhD
Associate Professor
Acting Dean, Faculty of Nursing
University of Calgary
Calgary, Alberta
Chapter 22: Critical Thinking

Kathleen Oberle RN, PhD
Associate Professor
Faculty of Nursing
University of Calgary
Calgary, Alberta
Chapter 7: Ethics, Morality, and Values
Chapter 8: Legal Aspects of Nursing

Heather L. Orstead RN, BN, ET
Clinical Specialist
Skin and Wound Management Care in the Community
Calgary Health Region
Chapter 37: Skin Integrity and Wound Care

Harry Plummer, RN, PhD (c)
Instructor
Faculty of Nursing
University of Calgary
Calgary, Alberta
Chapter 45: Pain

D. Shelley Raffin Bouchal RN, PhD
Assistant Professor
Faculty of Nursing
University of Calgary
Calgary, Alberta
Chapter 8: Legal Aspects of Nursing
Chapter 24: Documenting and Reporting
Chapter 33: Safety
Chapter 34: Hygiene
Chapter 44: Clients Having Surgery: Promoting Healthy Recovery
Chapter 48: Loss, Grieving, and Death

James A. Rankin RN, ANCP, PhD
Associate Professor
Faculty of Nursing
University of Calgary
Calgary, Alberta
Chapter 27: Health Assessment
Chapter 28: Medications
Chapter 39: Oxygenation
Chapter 40: Fluid, Electrolyte, and Acid-Base Balance

Sandra M. Reilly
Associate Professor
Faculty of Nursing
University of Calgary
Calgary, Alberta
Chapter 9: Health, Wellness, and Illness

Marlene Reimer, RN, PhD, NNC(C)
Associate Professor
Associate Dean, Research Faculty of Nursing
University of Calgary
Calgary, Alberta
Chapter 23: The Nursing Process
Chapter 41: Sensory Perception
Chapter 42: Rest and Sleep

Dianne M. Tapp RN, PhD
Associate Professor
Faculty of Nursing
University of Calgary
Calgary, Alberta
Chapter 6: Ethics, Morality, and Values

Sandra C. Tenove RN, PhD
Associate Professor
Faculty of Nursing
University of Calgary
Calgary, Alberta
Chapter 10: Health Promotion
Chapter 15: Health Care Delivery Systems

Karen L. Then RN, CCn(C), ACNP, PhD
Associate Professor
Faculty of Nursing
University of Calgary
Calgary, Alberta
Chapter 27: Health Assessment
Chapter 28: Medications
Chapter 39: Oxygenation
Chapter 40: Fluid, Electrolyte, and Acid-Base Balance

Elizabeth Thomlinson RN, PhD
Associate Professor
Faculty of Nursing
University of Calgary
Calgary, Alberta
Chapter 14: Culture and Ethnicity
Chapter 18: Rural Health Care
Chapter 30: Leading, Managing, and Influencing Change
Chapter 47: Stress and Coping

Ardene Robinson Vollman RN, PhD
Associate Professor (Retired)
Faculty of Nursing
University of Calgary
Calgary, Alberta
Chapter 16: Community-Based Nursing

Lorraine Watson RN, PhD
Associate Professor
Faculty of Nursing
University of Calgary
Calgary, Alberta
Chapter 38: Nutrition

Leanne Wyrostok RN, MN
Nursing Skills Clinician
Faculty of Nursing
University of Calgary
Calgary, Alberta
Chapter 37: Skin Integrity and Wound Care

U.S. CONTRIBUTORS

Ruth Alteneder, RN, PhD, CNM
Medical College of Ohio
Toledo, Ohio
Chapter 12: Sexuality

Suzanne Beyea, RN, CS, PhD
Co-Director Perioperative Nursing Research
Denver, Colorado
Revised and Updated Procedures

Kathleen Blais, RN, EdD
Florida International University
Miami, Florida
Chapter 13: Spirituality
Chapter 29: Teaching
Chapter 41: Sensory Perception
Chapter 47: Stress and Coping

Janet Brown, RN, MSN, CS
California State University
Chico, California
Chapter 26 Nurse-Patient Relationship
Chapter 45 Pain

Wendy Earl
Medical Writer/Editor
San Francisco, California
Revised Procedures and Checklists

Jane Freeman, RN, EdD
Jacksonville State University
Jacksonville, Alabama
Chapter 11: Holistic Healing Modalities

Carol J. Green-Nigro, RN, PhD
Johnson County Community College
Overland Park, Kansas
Focus on Critical Thinking boxes

Diana Hankes, RN, PhD, CS
Carroll College
Columbia College of Nursing
Milwaukee, Wisconsin
Chapter 33: Safety

Pat Jamerson, RNC, BSN, MSN, PhD
South Dakota State University
Brookings, South Dakota
Chapter 30: Leading, Managing, and Influencing Change

Penny Marshall-Chura, RN, PhD
Johnson County Community College
Overland Park, Kansas
Nursing Care Plans

Dawna Martich, RN, BSN, MSN
Highmark Diabetes Management Program
Pittsburgh, Pennsylvania
Chapter 17: Home Care

Vince Salyers, RN, MSN
Dominican College
San Rafael, California
Chapter 15: Health Care Delivery Systems
Chapter 28: Medications

Judith Wilkinson, PhD, RNC, ARNP
Johnson County Community College
Overland Park, Kansas
Chapter 5: Values, Ethics, and Advocacy
Chapter 23: The Nursing Process
Chapter 24: Documenting and Reporting

Sharon Wisneski, RN, MSN
Delaware State College University
Dover, Delaware
Chapter 14: Culture and Ethnicity
Chapter 46: Self-Concept

CANADIAN REVIEWERS

L. Dawn Ansell, RN
Instructor, Practical Nurse Careers
NorQuest College
Edmonton, Alberta

Christine A. Ateah, RN, PhD
Faculty of Nursing
University of Manitoba
Winnipeg, Manitoba

Madeleine Buck, MSc(A)
Faculty Lecturer
School of Nursing
McGill University
Montreal, Quebec

Sharon G. Card, RN, BScN, Med
Professor of Nursing
Okanagan University College
North Kelowna Campus
Kelowna, British Columbia

R. Marjorie Drury, MN
Nursing Faculty
Trinity Western University
Langley, British Columbia

Elizabeth C. Edwards, RN, BScN, MSN
Collaborative Nursing Program
Loyalist College of Applied Science and Technology
Belleville, Ontario

Cheryl Anne Fenton, RN, BHSc (Nursing)
Professor
Mohawk College of Applied Arts and Technology
Hamilton, Ontario

Catherine Pugnaire Gros, RN, MSc(A)
School of Nursing
McGill University
Montreal, Quebec

Janice Marshall Henty, RN, BScN, MEd
Nursing Professor
George Brown College
Toronto, Ontario

Diane Jensen, RN, BScN, MN
Nursing Division
Saskatchewan Institute of Applied Science and Technology
Nursing Education Program of Saskatchewan
Saskatoon, Saskatchewan

Manon Lemonde, RN, PhD
School of Nursing
Laurentian University
Sudbury, Ontario

Nicole Letourneau, RN, MN, PhD
Centre for Health Promotion Studies
University of Alberta
Edmonton, Alberta

Lisa Little, RN, BScN
Ottawa, Ontario

Sandra Madorin, RN, BScN, MScN
Assistant Pofessor
School of Nursing
University of Western Ontario
London, Ontario

Carrie Mines, RN, MSc(T)
Mohawk College of Applied Arts and Technology
Hamilton, Ontario

Linda J. Patrick, RN, BScN, MA, MSc, PhD(c)
Assistant Professor
Faculty of Nursing
University of Windsor
Windsor, Ontario

Judith Pearce, RN, BN, MSc(A), EdD
School of Nursing
Ryerson University
Toronto, Ontario

Frances Ross, RN, SScN, MScN
Nursing Professor
George Brown College
Toronto, Ontario

Mary Elizabeth Roth, RN, BScN
Nursing Professor
Conestoga College
Kitchener, Ontario

Janet L. Storch, RN, BScN, MHSA, PhD
Professor
School of Nursing
University of Victoria
Victoria, British Columbia

Lorna M. Weisbrod, RN, BScN
Nursing Division
Saskatchewan Institute of Applied Science and Technology
Nursing Education Program of Saskatchewan
Regina, Saskatchewan

CONTENTS

SECTION 1 Conceptual Foundations of Nursing *1*

UNIT 1 The Nature of Nursing *2*

CHAPTER 1
Historical and Contemporary Nursing Practice *2*
- Changing Contexts of Nursing in Canada *3*
- Selected Themes in Nursing History *6*
- Contemporary Nursing Practice *7*
- Roles and Functions of the Nurse *12*
- Nursing Profession *15*
- Factors Influencing Contemporary Nursing Practice *17*
- Nursing Organizations *18*

CHAPTER 2
Nursing Education in Canada *23*
- Nursing Education *24*
- Types of Educational Programs *24*
- Nursing Associations and Their Influence upon Education *26*
- Issues Facing Nursing Education *27*

CHAPTER 3
Nursing Research in Canada *31*
- Nursing Research *32*

CHAPTER 4
Nursing Philosophies, Theories, Concepts, Frameworks, and Models *45*
- What Is Philosophy? *46*
- Philosophy's Three Primary Areas of Inquiry *46*
- Paradigms or World Views *46*
- Philosophy in Nursing *47*
- Overview of Selected Nursing Philosophies *48*
- Concepts and Theories *49*
- Overview of Selected Nursing Theories *50*

CHAPTER 5
The Individual—The Client of Care *59*
- Individual Health *60*
- Cultural Factors *64*
- Applying Theoretical Frameworks to Individuals *65*

CHAPTER 6
Nursing Care of Families *71*
- What Is "Family?" *72*
- Family Nursing *72*
- Development of Family Nursing *73*
- Shifting Focus to Family Involvement in Health Care *74*
- Canadian Families: A Demographic Snapshot *75*
- Understanding Families *77*
- Nursing Care of Families *81*
- Evaluating Nursing Care of Families *87*

CHAPTER 7
Ethics, Morality, and Values *90*
- Morality and Ethics *91*
- Values *92*
- Moral Development *92*
- Ethical Theory *92*
- Nursing Code of Ethics *95*
- Ethical Decision Making *95*
- Clinical Application: Ethics and Cultural Diversity at the End of Life *98*
- Some Ethical Issues in Nursing *100*
- Nursing and Advocacy *102*
- Enhancing Ethical Practice *103*

CHAPTER 8
Legal Aspects of Nursing 108
Relationship of Nurses and the Law 109
Contractual Arrangements in Nursing 114
Selected Legal Aspects of Nursing Practice 116
Areas of Potential Liability in Nursing 119
Legal Protections in Nursing Practice 122
Reporting Crimes, Torts, and Unsafe Practices 125
Legal Responsibilities of Students 126

UNIT 2 Health, Beliefs, and Practices 130

CHAPTER 9
Health, Wellness, and Illness 130
Introduction 131
Personal Definition of Health 132
Health 132
Health Models 133
Health Belief Models 137
Illness and Disease 138
Canadian Approaches to Health 140

CHAPTER 10
Health Promotion 146
The Canadian Initiative 147
Defining Health Promotion 149
Types of Health-Promotion Programs 150
Sites for Health-Promotion Activities 151
Pender's Health Promotion Model 151
Stages of Health Behaviour Change 153
The Nurse's Role in Health Promotion 154
The Nursing Process and Health Promotion 154
Assessing the Health of Families, Groups, and Communities 159

CHAPTER 11
Holistic Healing Modalities 163
Concepts of Holism and Holistic Nursing 164
Concepts of Healing 164
Healing Modalities 166
Complementary Medical Therapies 175

CHAPTER 12
Sexuality and Sexual Health Practices 180
Sexuality 181
Sexual Orientation 181
Sexual Health 182
Sexuality throughout Life 183
Factors Influencing Sexuality 184
Sexual Desire and Pleasure 187
Interference with Sexual Desire, Pleasure, and Performance 188

CHAPTER 13
Spirituality 206
Spirituality, Religion, and Faith 207
Spiritual Development 208
Spiritual Well-Being 208
Spiritual Distress 210
Religious Practices Affecting Nursing Care 210
Spiritual Health and the Nursing Process 212

CHAPTER 14
Culture and Ethnicity 221
Canadian Culture 222
Concepts Related to Culture 227
Culture and Health Care 230
Culturally Sensitive Care 232
Selected Cultural Parameters for Nursing 233
Providing Culturally Competent Care 239

UNIT 3 Health-Care Environment 245

CHAPTER 15
Health-Care Delivery Systems 245
Categories of Health Care 246
Rights and Health Care 248
Types of Health-Care Settings 250
Providers of Health Care 254
Factors Affecting Health-Care Delivery 256
Contemporary Frameworks for Care 258
Models for the Delivery of Nursing 259
Health-Care Economics 262

CHAPTER 16
Community-Based Nursing *264*
Health-Care Reform *265*
Community-Based Health Care *267*
Community-Based Nursing *270*
Continuity of Care *272*

CHAPTER 17
Home Care *279*
Home Health Nursing *280*
The Home Health-Care System *281*
Roles of the Home Health Nurse *282*
Perspectives of Home Care Clients *283*
Selected Dimensions of Home Health Nursing *283*
Applying the Nursing Process in the Home *285*
Trends Influencing Home Care *286*
The Future of Home Health Care *287*

CHAPTER 18
Rural Health Care *291*
Definition of "Rural" *292*
Factors in Rural Health Consideration *292*
Health of Rural Residents *294*
Mental Health Issues *298*
Health-Care Delivery *299*

SECTION 2
Human Functioning and Development *307*

CHAPTER 19
Concepts of Growth and Development *308*
Factors Influencing Growth and Development *309*
Stages of Growth and Development *309*
Growth and Development Theories *310*
Applying Growth and Development Concepts to Nursing Practice *318*

CHAPTER 20
Development from Conception through Adolescence *322*
Conception and Prenatal Development *323*
Neonates and Infants (Birth to 1 Year) *324*
Toddlers (1 to 3 Years) *329*
Preschoolers (4 and 5 Years) *331*
School-Age Children (6 to 12 Years) *335*
Adolescence (12 to 18 Years) *339*

CHAPTER 21
Development from Young through Older Adulthood *347*
Young Adults (20 to 40 Years) *348*
Middle-Aged Adults (40 to 65 Years) *351*
Older Adults (Over 65 Years) *356*

SECTION 3
Nature of Nursing Practice 371

UNIT 1 Professional Practice Knowledge 372

CHAPTER 22
Critical Thinking 372
Critical Thinking 373
Skills in Critical Thinking 375
Attitudes that Foster Critical Thinking 376
Elements and Standards of Critical Thinking 378
Applying Critical Thinking to Nursing Practice 379
Developing Critical-thinking Attitudes and Skills 382

CHAPTER 23
The Nursing Process 387
Overview of the Nursing Process 388
Assessing 391
Diagnosing 405
Planning 415
Implementing 431
Nursing Process Summarized 439

CHAPTER 24
Documenting and Reporting 443
Ethical and Legal Considerations 444
Purposes of Client Records 444
Documentation Systems 446
Documenting Nursing Activities 451
Long-Term Care Documentation 455
Home Care Documentation 459
Guidelines for Recording 459
Reporting 462
Conferring 464

CHAPTER 25
Nursing Informatics 467
Nursing Informatics Applications in Clinical Nursing Practice 468
Nursing Informatics Applications in Nursing Education 473
Nursing Informatics Applications in Nursing Administration 474
Nursing Informatics Applications in Nursing Research 475
Conclusion 476

UNIT 2 Professional Practice Skills 480

CHAPTER 26
Nurse-Patient Relationship 480
Caring 481
Comforting 482
Communicating 483
The Helping Relationship 491
Group Communication 498
Communication and the Nursing Process 501

CHAPTER 27
Health Assessment 509
Physical Health Assessment 510
General Survey 518
The Integument 520
Head 527
Breasts and Axillae 554
Thorax and Lungs 558
Cardiovascular and Peripheral Vascular Systems 567
Abdomen 575
Muskuloskeletal System 583
Neurological System 586
Female Genitals and Inguinal Lymph Nodes 595
Male Genitals and Inguinal Area 599
Rectum, Anus, and Prostate 603

CHAPTER 28
Medications 607

Drug Standards 609
Legal Aspects of Drug Administration 609
Effects of Drugs 610
Drug Misuse 612
Actions of Drugs on the Body 612
Factors Affecting Medication Action 614
Routes of Administration 615
Medication Prescription 617
Systems of Measurement 621
Administering Medications Safely 623
Oral Medications 626
Nasogastric and Gastrostomy Medications 630
Parenteral Medications 630
Respiratory Inhalation 660
Irrigations 662

CHAPTER 29
Teaching 667

Learning 668
Teaching 673
Teaching Guidelines 674

CHAPTER 30
Leading, Managing, and Influencing Change 691

The Nurse as Leader and Manager 692
Leadership 692
Management 696
Change 699

SECTION 4
Nursing Therapeutics 707

CHAPTER 31
Vital Signs 708

Body Temperature 709
Pulse 719
Respirations 727
Blood Pressure 731

CHAPTER 32
Asepsis 743

Types of Organisms Causing Infections 745
Types of Infections 745
Nosocomial Infections 745
Chain of Infection 745
Body Defences Against Infection 748
Factors Increasing Susceptibility to Infection 750
Isolation Precautions 761
Isolation Practices 762
Sterile Technique 768
Infection Control for Health-Care Workers 770
Role of the Infection Control Nurse 777

CHAPTER 33
Safety 782

Factors Affecting Safety 783
Safety Concerns for Health-Care Workers 795

CHAPTER 34
Hygiene 806

Skin 807
Nails 824
Mouth 825
Hair 834
Eyes 841
Ears 845
Nose 847
Supporting a Hygienic Environment 847

CHAPTER 35
Fecal Elimination 856
Physiology of Defecation 857
Factors That Affect Defecation 860
Common Fecal Elimination Problems 861
Bowel Diversion Ostomies 864

CHAPTER 36
Urinary Elimination 891
Physiology of Urinary Elimination 892
Factors Affecting Voiding 894
Altered Urine Production 896
Altered Urinary Elimination 897

CHAPTER 37
Skin Integrity and Wound Care 934
Skin Function and Integrity 935
Classification of Wounds 935
Pressure Ulcers 936
Wound Healing 939
Wound Management 951
Heat and Cold 965

CHAPTER 38
Nutrition 972
Essential Nutrients 973
Macronutrients 973
Micronutrients 975
Energy Balance 975
Factors Affecting Nutrition 977
Nutritional Variations Throughout the Life Cycle 981
Standards for a Healthy Diet 985
Vegetarian Diets 986
Altered Nutrition 987
The Nursing Care Process 988
Laboratory Tests 993

CHAPTER 39
Oxygenation 1018
Physiology of the Respiratory System 1019
Respiratory Regulation 1022
Physiology of the Cardiovascular System 1023
Lifespan Considerations 1026
Factors Affecting Respiratory and Cardiovascular Function 1026
Alterations in Function 1028

CHAPTER 40
Fluid, Electrolyte, and Acid-Base Balance 1071
Body Fluids and Electrolytes 1072
Acid-Base Balance and pH 1080
Factors Affecting Body Fluid, Electrolytes, and Acid-Base Balance 1081
Disturbances in Fluid Volume, Electrolyte, and Acid-Base Balances 1082

CHAPTER 41
Sensory Perception 1132
Components of the Sensory Experience 1133
Sensory Alterations 1133
Factors Affecting Sensory Function 1135

CHAPTER 42
Rest and Sleep 1150
Physiology of Sleep 1151
Functions of Sleep 1153
Normal Sleep Patterns and Requirements 1153
Factors Affecting Sleep 1155
Common Sleep Disorders 1157

CHAPTER 43
Activity and Exercise 1170
Normal Movement 1171
Exercise 1178
Factors Affecting Body Alignment and Activity 1180
Effects of Immobility 1181

CHAPTER 44
Clients Having Surgery: Promoting Healthy Recovery 1230
Types of Surgery 1231
Preoperative Phase 1233
Postoperative Phase 1244

CHAPTER 45
Pain Management 1268
The Nature of Pain 1269
Physiology of Pain 1271
Barriers to Pain Management 1283
Key Factors in Pain Management 1283
Pharmacological Pain Management 1284
WHO Three-Step Ladder Approach 1288
Administration of Placebos 1288
Routes for Opiate Delivery 1288
Patient-Controlled Analgesia 1290
Nonpharmacological Pain Management 1291
Nonpharmacological Invasive Therapies 1292

CHAPTER 46
Self-Concept 1301
Self-Concept 1302
Formation of Self-Concept 1302
Components of Self-Concept 1304
Factors That Affect Self-Concept 1306

CHAPTER 47
Stress and Coping 1318
Concept of Stress 1319
Models of Stress 1319
Indicators of Stress 1323
Coping 1327

CHAPTER 48
Loss, Grieving, and Death 1340
Loss and Grief 1341
Dying and Death 1347

Appendix A 1366

Glossary 1393

Credits 1424

Index 1427

PREFACE

"I learn a great deal by merely observing you, and letting you talk as long as you please, and taking note of what you do not say." — *T. S. Eliot*

Nurses today must be able to grow and evolve in order to meet the demands of a dramatically changing health-care system. They need skills in communication and interpersonal relations to become effective members of a collaborative health-care team. They need to think critically and be creative in implementing nursing strategies with clients of diverse cultural backgrounds in increasingly diverse settings. They need skills in teaching, leading, and managing. They need to be prepared to provide home-based as well as community-based nursing care. They need to understand holistic healing modalities and complementary therapies. And, they need to continue their unique role that demands a blend of nurturance, sensitivity, caring, empathy, commitment, and skill based on a broad base of knowledge.

Fundamentals of Nursing: The Nature of Nursing Practice in Canada addresses the concepts of contemporary professional nursing. These concepts include but are not limited to the following: caring, wellness, health promotion, disease prevention, families, holistic care, multiculturalism, nursing theories, nursing informatics, nursing research, and ethics. Thus, for example, throughout the book we have emphasized wellness and the registered nurse's role in health promotion.

This text has been designed so that it can be used with a variety of nursing theories and conceptual frameworks. In the clinically oriented chapters, we have used the nursing process as the main framework.

The Canadian Edition

One of our principal aims in preparing this edition is to provide a book that thoroughly meets the needs of Canadian nursing students and instructors. Therefore, in addition to updating all the material in light of the latest nursing research and theory, the authors and contributors have carefully revised *all the chapters* to reflect the Canadian context in which nurses currently practise.

Throughout the book, we have placed more emphasis on multiculturalism, critical thinking, wellness, and home-based and community-based care. The Canadian perspective is especially evident in the following chapters:

- Chapter 2 — Nursing Education in Canada
- Chapter 3 — Nursing Research in Canada
- Chapter 8 — Legal Aspects of Nursing
- Chapter 14 — Culture and Ethnicity

NEW CHAPTERS AND NEW FEATURES

For the Canadian edition of *Fundamentals of Nursing: The Nature of Nursing Practice in Canada*, we have included two brand new chapters:

- **Chapter 6 — Nursing Care of Families.** We have created a new chapter on families, separate from Chapter 5 on The Individual — The Client of Care. Families play a particularly prominent role in current Canadian models of nursing.
- **Chapter 18 — Rural Health Care.** We have devoted an entire chapter to this topic to reflect the importance of nursing in rural and remote areas in Canada.

To further highlight the Canadian perspective, we have also added the following features:

- **Canadian Society Notes**. In thirty of the chapters, a special box focuses on data about Canadian society and their implications for nursing.

Canadian Society Notes

Fact	Implications for Nursing Practice
In 1971, the Federal Government announced	This policy promotes a cultural mosaic whereby persons are encouraged to

- **Annotated Weblinks**. Each chapter concludes with a list of Annotated Weblinks that make it easier for users to explore various topics.

WEBLINKS

Canadian Nurses Association
http://www.cna-nurses.ca
The Canadian Nurses Association is a federation of 11 provincial and territorial nursing associations representing more than 110,000 registered nurses. The CNA Web site includes multiple resources including online publications that support its vision of registered nurses collectively contributing to the health of Canadians and the advancement of nursing. The CNA's mission is to advance the quality of nursing in the interest of the public.

Canadian Nursing Index
http://www.nursingindex.com
The Canadian Nursing Index is your Canadian guide to nursing resources on the Internet. This site will be of interest to staff nurses, nurse managers, nurse educators, nurse researchers and nursing students. The site includes links to special areas of interest to nurses.

Ordre des infirmières et infirmiers du Québec
http://www.oiiq.org/
The Web site for a consortium of professional and educational organizations of interest to Quebec nurses and/or French-speaking nurses.

Canadian Association for the History of Nursing (CAHN)
http://www.ualberta.ca/jhibberd
This Web site was established by CAHN and is an excellent resource for those interested in the promotion of interest in the history of nursing and to developing scholarship in the field. CAHN promotes the preservation of historical nursing materials; hosts forums for discussion of nursing history; supports innovations in teaching nursing history; advances historical research; and is an affiliate group of the Canadian Nurses Association.

- **Focus on Critical Thinking**. In contrast to the U.S. edition, our first Canadian edition contains a Focus on Critical Thinking Box in *every* chapter. These case studies with their questions are designed to encourage the learner to develop and apply important critical thinking skills such as analysis, comparison, interpretation, and evaluation. These activities can be used by individual students or by groups of students in classroom settings or in clinical conferences with instructors. There are no absolute right or wrong answers to the critical thinking questions. Suggested answers to all the questions, along with additional activities, are provided in Appendix A near the back of the book.

FOCUS ON CRITICAL THINKING

Mrs. Chu is a 42-year-old professional whose father recently died following a prolonged illness from diabetes and hypertension. She voices concern that she will develop the same diseases and wants to make lifestyle changes to avoid that possibility. She admits to a 13-kilogram weight gain over the past two years, increased stress at work, and a fairly sedentary lifestyle. She considers herself healthy and is conscientious about her yearly physical and dental exams, breast self-examinations, and Pap smears. Last week, she began walking 30 minutes every day and purchased a book on low-fat cooking. Currently, her blood glucose levels and blood pressure are normal. She is seeking your assistance to determine if there are other things she can do to meet her goal.

1. On the basis of the limited data provided, speculate whether Mrs. Chu's activities represent health promotion, health prevention, or both.
2. What additional activities could you suggest to Mrs. Chu that are "health promoting?"
3. What evidence is there that Mrs. Chu will achieve and maintain the lifestyle changes she wants to make?
4. In what ways might you (the nurse) be able to assist Mrs. Chu?
5. Devise a plan to intervene with a client who is knowledgeable about the benefits of healthful behaviours and wants to make behavioural changes but has been unable to do so.

See Appendix A for answers to these questions.

- **Canadian Case Studies**. A special Canadian Case Study, associated with a CBC video segment, is provided at the end of each of Section 1, Unit 2; Section 1, Unit 3; Section 3, Unit 2; and Section 4. These Canadian Case Studies have been designed so that they can be completed even without viewing the accompanying videos. (The videos are available on the *Companion Website*.) With or without the videos, these cases readily lend themselves to classroom discussion. (Model answers are provided in the *Instructor's Manual*.)

CBC

Canadian Case Study — Does Betty Two-Trees Need an Advocate?

Betty Two-Trees is from a First Nations tribe of Algonquian stock called the Maliseet. She lives on a reserve in New Brunswick. There are approximately 600 reserves in Canada for over 200,000 aboriginal people. On many of them, the social conditions are horrifying, and even where conditions have improved in recent years, the wounds of over a hundred years of government rules and regulations are still fresh and painful. Unemployment, suicide rates, health problems, and housing shortages are at epidemic levels on most reserves. Aboriginal women rank among the most severely disadvantaged in Canadian society. They are worse off economically than both aboriginal men and Canadian women, and although they live longer than aboriginal men, their life expectancy does not approach that of Canadian women generally.

With two long braids hanging down her back, Betty was working on a child's beaded vest with the coffee perking and three young children playing throughout the house, when the community health nurse visited. She was coming to talk to Betty about immunizations for the youngest grandchild. Born in 1953 and married in 1972, Betty had four children before her husband left her. "I

language because my parents and grandparents spoke it, but I usually answered back in English. The old people here would always make me answer back in our language or they would not listen to me. I don't think many of them understood English. We have our own way of talking. You never say please in our language because we don't need to. So when my people say something in English, it sounds like a demand."

"Some people say that traditionally Maliseet women had the final say in the family. It was true for us. My grandmother always had the say and my grandfather always honoured it. It was not the same for my mother. I remember one day, perhaps grade 1 or 2 and I was called dirty brown Indian and not understanding what it meant. I felt embarrassed but I didn't know why. Today, I would call it prejudice. I remember other examples of prejudice from my childhood, but I did not do anything about it because I didn't have a name for it or an understanding of it."

Browne and Fiske's (2001) research examined mainstream health-care encounters from the viewpoint of First Nations women from a reserve commu-

Hallmark Special Features

For this Canadian edition of *Fundamentals of Nursing: The Nature of Nursing Practice in Canada*, we have retained many of the features that have been well received by users of the U.S. editions of this text.

- A set of learning **Objectives** at the beginning of each chapter clarifies the skills and knowledge to be learned in that chapter.
- **Key terms** are boldfaced where they are introduced in the body of the text. For convenience, all the key terms with their definitions are collated in a **Glossary** near the end of the book.
- Boxed **Research Notes** describe particular research studies and show how they are relevant to clinical practice.

RESEARCH NOTE

Who are Home Care Clients and What Is the Cost of Providing Care?

The goals of the Ontario-based study were to describe home care clients and their care providers; to determine the competencies required to provide their care; to determine the costs of the formal care providers; and to determine the burden of care for informal care providers. Structured interviews, documentation review, and a burden tool were used to collect the data from a variety of stakeholders. Of the clients who participated, almost half were over the age of 70 years, and slightly over half required acute care. The most common medical diagnoses related to cardiac function. Costs varied, depending upon the amount and type of care required and upon the coping ability of both the client and the family.

Implications: The study suggests the competencies required by registered nurses working with home care clients include pharmaceutical knowledge and strong assessment skills.

Source: Alcock, D., Danbrook, C., Walker, D., & Hunt, C. (1998). Home care clients, providers and costs. *Canadian Journal of Public Health, 89,* 297–300. Reproduced with permission of the Canadian Journal of Public Health.

- **Procedures** provide step-by-step directions, along with their rationales, for performing particular clinical procedures. Each Procedure includes a purpose statement, an assessment focus, a list of equipment, and an evaluation focus box. Some Procedures also include special *Lifespan Considerations* or *Home Care Considerations.*

PROCEDURE 27.4 Assessing the Nails *continued*

ASSESSMENT	NORMAL FINDINGS	DEVIATIONS FROM NORMAL
Inspect tissues surrounding nails.	Intact epidermis	Hangnails; paronychia (inflammation)
Perform blanch test to test capillary refill. Press two or more nails between your thumb and index finger; look for blanching and return of usual colour to nail bed.	Prompt return of pink or usual colour	Delayed return of pink or usual colour (may indicate circulatory impairment)

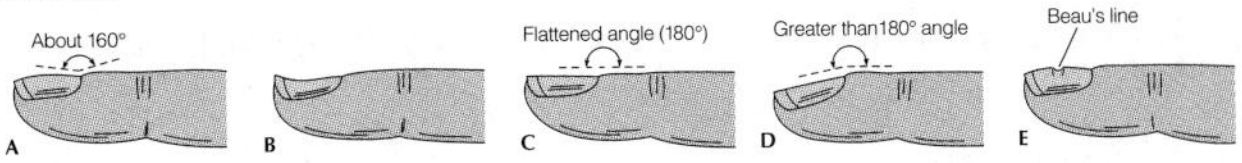

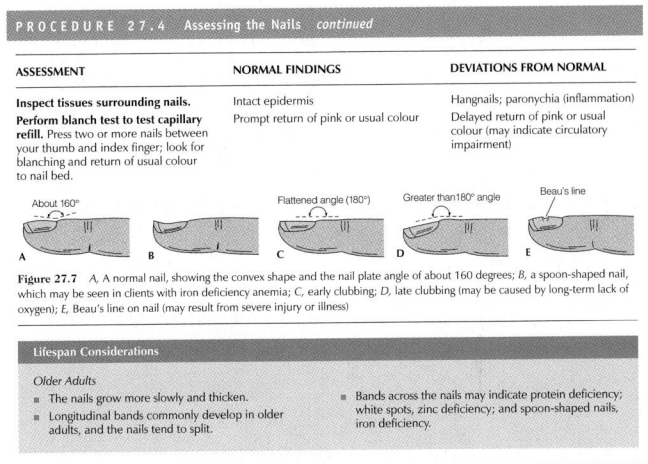

Figure 27.7 *A,* A normal nail, showing the convex shape and the nail plate angle of about 160 degrees; *B,* a spoon-shaped nail, which may be seen in clients with iron deficiency anemia; *C,* early clubbing; *D,* late clubbing (may be caused by long-term lack of oxygen); *E,* Beau's line on nail (may result from severe injury or illness)

Lifespan Considerations

Older Adults

- The nails grow more slowly and thicken.
- Longitudinal bands commonly develop in older adults, and the nails tend to split.
- Bands across the nails may indicate protein deficiency; white spots, zinc deficiency; and spoon-shaped nails, iron deficiency.

- **Clinical Guidelines** — provide concise summaries of clinical do's and don'ts.

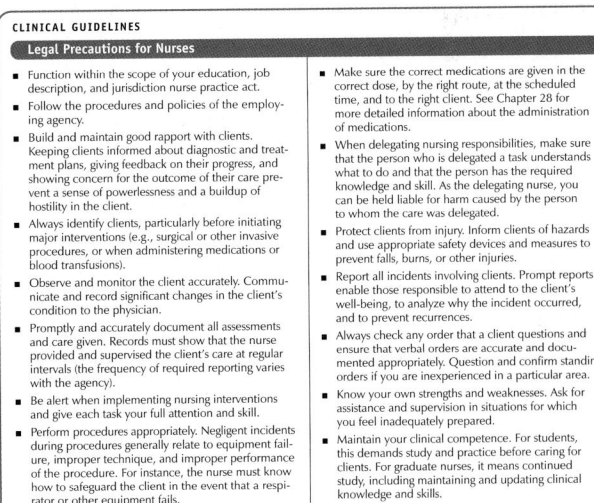

CLINICAL GUIDELINES

Legal Precautions for Nurses

- Function within the scope of your education, job description, and jurisdiction nurse practice act.
- Follow the procedures and policies of the employing agency.
- Build and maintain good rapport with clients. Keeping clients informed about diagnostic and treatment plans, giving feedback on their progress, and showing concern for the outcome of their care prevent a sense of powerlessness and a buildup of hostility in the client.
- Always identify clients, particularly before initiating major interventions (e.g., surgical or other invasive procedures, or when administering medications or blood transfusions).
- Observe and monitor the client accurately. Communicate and record significant changes in the client's condition to the physician.
- Promptly and accurately document all assessments and care given. Records must show that the nurse provided and supervised the client's care at regular intervals (the frequency of required reporting varies with the agency).
- Be alert when implementing nursing interventions and give each task your full attention and skill.
- Perform procedures appropriately. Negligent incidents during procedures generally relate to equipment failure, improper technique, and improper performance of the procedure. For instance, the nurse must know how to safeguard the client in the event that a respirator or other equipment fails.
- Make sure the correct medications are given in the correct dose, by the right route, at the scheduled time, and to the right client. See Chapter 28 for more detailed information about the administration of medications.
- When delegating nursing responsibilities, make sure that the person who is delegated a task understands what to do and that the person has the required knowledge and skill. As the delegating nurse, you can be held liable for harm caused by the person to whom the care was delegated.
- Protect clients from injury. Inform clients of hazards and use appropriate safety devices and measures to prevent falls, burns, or other injuries.
- Report all incidents involving clients. Prompt reports enable those responsible to attend to the client's well-being, to analyze why the incident occurred, and to prevent recurrences.
- Always check any order that a client questions and ensure that verbal orders are accurate and documented appropriately. Question and confirm standing orders if you are inexperienced in a particular area.
- Know your own strengths and weaknesses. Ask for assistance and supervision in situations for which you feel inadequately prepared.
- Maintain your clinical competence. For students, this demands study and practice before caring for clients. For graduate nurses, it means continued study, including maintaining and updating clinical knowledge and skills.

- **Sample Care Plans** provide assessment data, nursing diagnoses, client goals, desired outcomes, and nursing interventions relevant to the scenario presented.

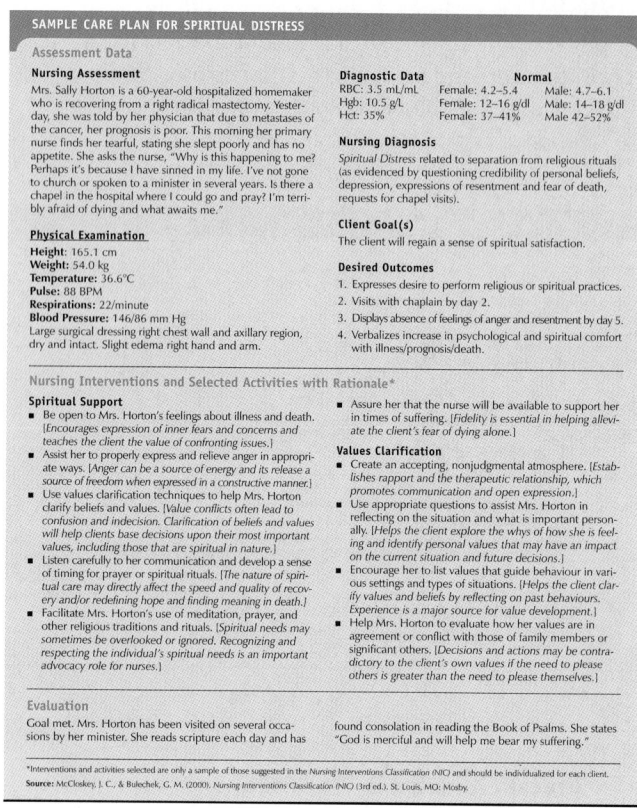

SAMPLE CARE PLAN FOR SPIRITUAL DISTRESS

Assessment Data

Nursing Assessment

Mrs. Sally Horton is a 60-year-old hospitalized homemaker who is recovering from a right radical mastectomy. Yesterday, she was told by her physician that due to metastases of the cancer, her prognosis is poor. This morning her primary nurse finds her tearful, stating she slept poorly and has no appetite. She asks the nurse, "Why is this happening to me? Perhaps it's because I have sinned in my life. I've not gone to church or spoken to a minister in several years. Is there a chapel in the hospital where I could go and pray? I'm terribly afraid of dying and what awaits me."

Physical Examination

Height: 165.1 cm
Weight: 54.0 kg
Temperature: 36.6°C
Pulse: 88 BPM
Respirations: 22/minute
Blood Pressure: 146/86 mm Hg
Large surgical dressing right chest wall and axillary region, dry and intact. Slight edema right hand and arm.

Diagnostic Data	Normal	
RBC: 3.5 mL/mL	Female: 4.2–5.4	Male: 4.7–6.1
Hgb: 10.5 g/L	Female: 12–16 g/dl	Male: 14–18 g/dl
Hct: 35%	Female: 37–41%	Male 42–52%

Nursing Diagnosis

Spiritual Distress related to separation from religious rituals (as evidenced by questioning credibility of personal beliefs, depression, expressions of resentment and fear of death, requests for chapel visits).

Client Goal(s)

The client will regain a sense of spiritual satisfaction.

Desired Outcomes

1. Expresses desire to perform religious or spiritual practices.
2. Visits with chaplain by day 2.
3. Displays absence of feelings of anger and resentment by day 5.
4. Verbalizes increase in psychological and spiritual comfort with illness/prognosis/death.

Nursing Interventions and Selected Activities with Rationale*

Spiritual Support

- Be open to Mrs. Horton's feelings about illness and death. [*Encourages expression of inner fears and concerns and teaches the client the value of confronting issues.*]
- Assist her to properly express and relieve anger in appropriate ways. [*Anger can be a source of energy and its release a source of freedom when expressed in a constructive manner.*]
- Use values clarification techniques to help Mrs. Horton clarify beliefs and values. [*Value conflicts often lead to confusion and indecision. Clarification of beliefs and values will help clients base decisions upon their most important values, including those that are spiritual in nature.*]
- Listen carefully to her communication and develop a sense of timing for prayer or spiritual rituals. [*The nature of spiritual care may directly affect the speed and quality of recovery and/or redefining hope and finding meaning in death.*]
- Facilitate Mrs. Horton's use of meditation, prayer, and other religious traditions and rituals. [*Spiritual needs may sometimes be overlooked or ignored. Recognizing and respecting the individual's spiritual needs is an important advocacy role for nurses.*]
- Assure her that the nurse will be available to support her in times of suffering. [*Fidelity is essential in helping alleviate the client's fear of dying alone.*]

Values Clarification

- Create an accepting, nonjudgmental atmosphere. [*Establishes rapport and the therapeutic relationship, which promotes communication and open expression.*]
- Use appropriate questions to assist Mrs. Horton in reflecting on the situation and what is important personally. [*Helps the client explore the whys of how she is feeling and identify personal values that may have an impact on the current situation and future decisions.*]
- Encourage her to list values that guide behaviour in various settings and types of situations. [*Helps the client clarify values and beliefs by reflecting on past behaviours. Experience is a major source for value development.*]
- Help Mrs. Horton to evaluate how her values are in agreement or conflict with those of family members or significant others. [*Decisions and actions may be contradictory to the client's own values if the need to please others is greater than the need to please themselves.*]

Evaluation

Goal met. Mrs. Horton has been visited on several occasions by her minister. She reads scripture each day and has found consolation in reading the Book of Psalms. She states "God is merciful and will help me bear my suffering."

*Interventions and activities selected are only a sample of those suggested in the *Nursing Interventions Classification (NIC)* and should be individualized for each client.
Source: McCloskey, J. C., & Bulechek, G. M. (2000). *Nursing Interventions Classification (NIC)* (3rd ed.). St. Louis, MO: Mosby.

- **Assessment Interview** boxes provide examples of interview questions to help elicit relevant information from the client in the assessment stage.

- **Developmental Assessment Guidelines** boxes in Section 2 provide important questions to consider when assessing the development and growth of a client.

DEVELOPMENTAL ASSESSMENT GUIDELINES

The Adolescent

In these three developmental areas, does the adolescent do the following?

1. **Physical Development**
   - Exhibit physical growth (weight, height) within normal range for age and gender
   - Demonstrate male or female sexual development consistent with standards
   - Manifest vital signs within normal range for age and gender
   - Exhibit vision and hearing abilities within normal range
2. **Psychosocial Development**
   - Interact well with parents, teachers, peers, siblings, and persons in authority
   - Like self
   - Think and plan for the future, such as university or a career
   - Choose a lifestyle and interests that fit own identity
   - Determine own beliefs and values
   - Begin to establish a sense of identity in the family
   - Seek help from appropriate persons about problems
3. **Development in Activities of Daily Living**
   - Demonstrate knowledge of physical development, menstruation, reproduction, birth control, and methods for the prevention of sexually transmitted diseases
   - Exhibit healthy lifestyle practices in nutrition, exercise, recreation, sleep patterns, and personal habits
   - Demonstrate concern for personal cleanliness and appearance

- **Health Promotion Guidelines**, also given in Section 2, provide guidelines for promoting the health of clients at various stages of their development.

Health Promotion Guidelines for Infants

Health Examinations
- At two weeks and at 2, 4, 6, and 12 months

Protective Measures
- Immunizations: diphtheria tetanus pertussis (acellular) vaccine (DTaP), inactivated poliovirus vaccine (IPV), measles-mumps-rubella vaccine (MMR), *Haemophilus influenzae* type B vaccine (Hib), hepatitis B vaccine (Hep B), varicella, pneumococcal conjugate vaccine, and meningococcal C conjugate vaccine; other vaccines as recommended
- Immunization schedules may vary from province to province
- Fluoride supplements, if there is inadequate water fluoridation (less than 0.7 part per million)
- Screening for tuberculosis
- Screening for phenylketonuria (PKU)
- Prompt attention for illnesses
- Appropriate skin hygiene and clothing
- Positional therapy

Infant Safety
- Importance of supervision
- Car seat, crib, playpen, bath, and home environment safety measures
- Feeding measures (e.g., avoid propping bottle)
- Providing toys with no small parts or sharp edges

Nutrition
- Breast-feeding and bottle-feeding techniques
- Formula preparation
- Feeding schedule
- Introduction of solid foods
- Need for iron supplements at four to six months

Elimination
- Characteristics and frequency of stool and urine elimination
- Diarrhea and its effects

Rest/Sleep
- Usual sleep and rest patterns

Sensory Stimulation
- Touch: holding, cuddling, rocking
- Vision: colourful, moving toys
- Hearing: soothing voice tones, music, singing
- Play: toys appropriate for development

- **Home Care Assessments** direct the nurse to assess the client, the family/ caregiver, and the available community resources. With the expansion in home health care delivery in Canada, there is a growing need for early discharge planning and continuity of care in the home.

HOME CARE ASSESSMENT

Mobility and Activity Problems

Client and Environment
- *Capabilities or tolerance for required and desired activities:* Self-care (feeding, bathing, toileting, dressing, grooming, home maintenance, shopping, cooking); recreational activities
- *Mobility aids required:* Cane, walker, crutches, wheelchair, transfer boards
- *Equipment required if immobilized:* Special bed, side rails, pressure-reducing mattress
- *Current level of knowledge:* Body mechanics for use of mobility aids; specific exercises prescribed
- *Home mobility hazard appraisal:* Adequacy of lighting; presence of handrails; safety of pathways and stairs; congested areas; unanchored rugs, mats, or electrical cords; and any other obstacles to safe movement (see "Home Hazard Appraisal" in Chapter 17); structural adjustments needed for wheelchair access

Family or Caregiver
- *Caregiver availability, skills, and willingness:* Primary people able to assist client with self-care, movement, shopping, and so on; physical and emotional status to assist with care; learning needs
- *Family role changes and coping:* Effect on financial status, parenting and spousal roles, social roles
- *Availability of caregiver support:* Other support people available for occasional duties, such as shopping, transportation, housekeeping, cooking, budgeting, respite care

Community
- *Resources:* Availability and familiarity with sources of medical equipment, financial assistance, homemaker services, hygienic care, and other services; Meals on Wheels; religious counsellors and visitors; sources of respite for caregiver

- **Home Care Teaching Guides** are designed to help clients facilitate self-care, monitor problems, understand medication effects, perform prescribed therapies, and alter lifestyle patterns.

HOME CARE TEACHING GUIDE

Healthy Nutrition

- Instruct clients about the content of a healthy diet based on *Canada's Food Guide to Healthy Eating*.
- Encourage clients, particularly older clients, to reduce dietary fat (see Wellness Teaching: Reducing Dietary Fat, page 992).
- Instruct strict vegetarians, as needed, about proper protein complementation and additional vitamin and mineral supplementation.
- Discuss foods high in specific nutrients required, such as protein, iron, calcium, vitamin C, fibre, and so on.
- Discuss importance of properly fitted dentures and dental care.
- Discuss safe food preparation and preservation techniques as appropriate.

Dietary Alterations

- Explain the purpose of the diet.
- Discuss allowed and prohibited foods.
- Explain the importance of reading food labels when selecting foods.
- Include family or significant others as appropriate.
- Reinforce information provided by the dietitian or nutritionist as appropriate.
- Discuss herbs and spices as alternatives to salt and substitutes for sugar.

For Overweight Clients

- Discuss physiological, psychological, and lifestyle factors that predispose to weight gain.
- Provide information about normal weight range and recommended calorie intake.
- Discuss principles of a well-balanced diet (see *Canada's Food Guide to Healthy Eating* or other food guidelines) and high- and low-calorie foods.
- Encourage intake of low-calorie, caffeine-free beverages and plenty of water.
- Discuss ways to adapt eating practices by using smaller plates, smaller servings, chewing each bit a specified number of times, and putting fork down between bites.
- Discuss ways to control the desire to eat by taking a walk, drinking a glass of water, or doing slow deep-breathing exercises.
- Discuss the importance of exercise and help the client plan an exercise program.
- Discuss stress-reduction techniques (see Chapters 11 and 47).
- Provide information about available community resources (e.g., weight-loss groups, dietary counselling, exercise programs, self-help groups).

For Underweight Clients

- Discuss factors contributing to inadequate nutrition and weight loss.
- Discuss recommended calorie intake and normal weight range.
- Provide information about the content of a balanced diet based on the *Canada's Food Guide to Healthy Eating*.
- Provide information about ways to increase calorie intake (e.g., high-protein or high-calorie foods and supplements).
- Discuss ways to manage, minimize, or alter the factors contributing to malnourishment.
- If appropriate, discuss ways to purchase low-cost nutritious foods.
- Provide information about community agencies that can assist in providing food (e.g., Meals-On-Wheels).

For Clients Requiring Enteral/Parenteral Nutrition

(See Client Teaching for Home Nutritional Therapy later in this chapter.)

- **Client Teaching** boxes focus on the learning needs of clients.

CLIENT TEACHING

Controlling Postural Hypotension

- Sleep with the head of the bed elevated 20–30 degrees. This position makes the position change on rising less severe.
- Avoid sudden changes in position. Arise from bed in three stages:
  a. Sit up in bed for at least one minute (or until symptoms subside).
  b. Sit on the side of the bed with legs dangling for at least one minute.
  c. Stand with care, holding onto the edge of the bed or another nonmovable object for at least one minute. Gradual changes in position stimulate renin (a kidney enzyme that has a role in regulating blood pressure), which prevents a dramatic drop in pressure.
- Never bend down all the way to the floor or stand up too quickly after stooping. Baroreceptors (sensory nerve endings in the walls of blood vessels) cannot accommodate rapid change.
- Postpone activities, such as shaving and hair grooming, for at least one hour after rising. Baroreceptor reflexes are slow to respond after a night of recumbency during sleep.
- Wear elastic stockings at night to inhibit venous pooling in the legs.
- Be aware that the symptoms of hypotension are most severe at the following times:
  a. 30 to 60 minutes after a heavy meal
  b. One to two hours after taking an antihypertension medication
- Get out of a warm bath very slowly because warm temperatures can lead to venous pooling. Avoid hot water for bathing.
- Use a rocking chair to improve circulation in the lower extremities. Even mild leg conditioning can strengthen muscle tone and enhance circulation.
- Refrain from any strenuous activity that results in holding the breath and bearing down. This Valsalva maneuver slows the heart rate, leading to subsequent lowering of blood pressure.

- **Wellness Teaching** boxes focus on wellness information in order to enable nurses help clients live healthier lives.

WELLNESS TEACHING

Promoting Fluid and Electrolyte Balance

- Consume 200 to 2500 mL of water daily, unless contraindicated
- Avoid excess amounts of foods or fluids high in salt, sugar, and caffeine.
- Eat a well-balanced diet. Include adequate amounts of milk or milk products to maintain bone calcium levels.
- Limit alcohol intake, as it has a diuretic effect.
- Increase fluid intake before, during, and after strenuous exercise, particularly when the environmental temperature is high, and replace lost electrolytes from excessive perspiration, as needed, with commercial electrolyte solutions.
- Maintain normal body weight.
- Learn about and monitor side effects of medications that affect fluid and electrolyte balance (e.g., diuretics) and ways to handle side effects.
- Recognize possible risk factors for fluid and electrolyte imbalance, such as prolonged or repeated vomiting, frequent watery stools, or inability to consume fluids because of illness.
- Seek prompt professional health care for noticeable signs of fluid imbalance, such as sudden weight gain or loss, decreased urine volume, swollen ankles, shortness of breath, dizziness, or confusion.

- **Chapter Highlights** summarize the important points of the chapter.
- The **Readings and References** section near the end of each chapter includes an annotated list of **Suggested Readings** to help guide users to other valuable sources.
- A robust **Index** at the back of the book includes references to material in the Boxes, Tables, and Figures.

Complete Teaching/Learning Package

A comprehensive set of supplements has been carefully prepared to assist instructors and students in using this edition.

For the Instructor

The following supplements are designed to aid instructors in presenting classes, fostering classroom discussion, and encouraging learning.

- An ***Instructor's Manual*** provides a list of key terms, a chapter outline, discussion questions, classroom activities, and clinical activities for each chapter of the textbook.
- A ***Test Item File*** provides over 1000 multiple-choice questions. Each question is accompanied by the correct answer and is coded by the cognitive level tested, the relevant nursing process, and the client need involved.
- An ***Instructor's Resource CD-ROM*** provides an electronic version of the **Instructor's Manual**, a set of **PowerPoint Slides** that illuminate and build upon key concepts in the text, and the **Pearson TestGen**. Pearson TestGen is a special computerized version of the Test Item File that enables instructors to view and edit the existing questions, add questions, generate tests, and print the tests in a variety of formats. Powerful search and sort functions make it easy to locate questions and arrange them in any order desired. TestGen also enables instructors to administer tests on a local area network, have the tests graded electronically, and have the results prepared in electronic or printed reports.
- The ***CBC/Pearson Education Canada Video Library for Nursing*** is available on cassettes for instructors and on the Companion Website for students. The CBC and Pearson Education Canada have combined their expertise in educational publishing and global reporting to create a special video ancillary to the text. The library consists of 6 video segments from the CBC programs *The National* and *The Health Show*. The segments have been chosen to supplement the Canadian Case Studies in the book.
- ***The Companion Website*** (**www.pearsoned.ca/kozier**) includes a password-protected section from which instructors can download some of the text's supplements.

For the Student

The following supplements are designed for students to facilitate active learning.

- The Student CD-ROM packaged with the book includes innovative animations and special videos to reinforce important concepts and skills.
- The free ***Companion Website*** (**www.pearsoned.ca/kozier**) includes self-test questions for each chapter of the textbook. (The questions do not duplicate any of those in the *Test Item File*.) Students can try the questions, send the answers to the electronic grader, and receive instant feedback. The Companion Website also provides links to valuable Internet resources and hosts the *CBC/Pearson Education Canada Video Library for Nursing*.

Acknowledgements

We wish to extend a sincere thank you to the many talented people involved in the Canadian Edition. We are especially grateful to the following:

- The Canadian Contributors (listed in the inside of the front cover), who provided content in their areas of expertise.
- The many Canadian Reviewers (listed on the pages immediately preceding the Table of Contents), who provided so many helpful comments for improving the manuscript.
- Our colleagues, who provided many valuable suggestions for this edition.
- Our nursing students, who continue to inspire us with their questioning minds.
- Samantha Scully, Maurice Esses, and Judith Scott of Pearson Education Canada. Their expertise, commitment to an excellent book, understanding, and very gentle pushes in developing this edition and carrying it through to completion are evident in the final product.

Shelley Raffin Bouchal

Sandi Hirst

SPECIAL FEATURES

Canadian Society Notes

1 Historical and Contemporary Nursing Practice *11*
2 Nursing Education in Canada *29*
3 Nursing Research in Canada *35*
4 Nursing Philosophies, Theories, Concepts, Frameworks, and Models *49*
5 The Individual—The Client of Care *60*
6 Nursing Care of Families *78*
7 Ethics, Morality, and Values *101*
8 Legal Aspects of Nursing *112*
9 Health, Wellness, and Illness *141*
10 Health Promotion *147*
11 Holistic Healing Modalities *176*
12 Sexuality and Sexual Health Practices *185*
12 Sexuality and Sexual Health Practices *200*
13 Spirituality *217*
14 Culture and Ethnicity *227*
15 Health-Care Delivery Systems *258*
16 Community-Based Nursing *274*
17 Home Care *288*
18 Rural Health Care *294*
19 Concepts of Growth and Development *319*
20 Development from Conception through Adolescence *342*
21 Development from Young through Older Adulthood *365*
22 Critical Thinking *384*
23 The Nursing Process *388*
24 Documenting and Reporting *462*
25 Nursing Informatics *476*
26 Nurse-Patient Relationship *489*
29 Teaching *669*
30 Leading, Managing, and Influencing Change *695*
33 Safety *783*
42 Rest and Sleep *1151*
48 Loss, Grieving and Death *1346*

Focus on Critical Thinking

1 Historical and Contemporary Nursing Practice *13*
2 Nursing Education in Canada *26*
3 Nursing Research in Canada *40*
4 Nursing Philosophies, Theories, Concepts, Frameworks, and Models *55*
5 The Individual—The Client of Care *69*
6 Nursing Care of Families *85*
7 Ethics, Morality, and Values *102*
8 Legal Aspects of Nursing *127*
9 Health, Wellness, and Illness *133*
10 Health Promotion *159*
11 Holistic Healing Modalities *177*
12 Sexuality and Sexual Health Practices *203*
13 Spirituality *218*
14 Culture and Ethnicity *241*
15 Health-Care Delivery Systems *257*
16 Community-Based Nursing *273*
17 Home Care *288*
18 Rural Health Care *301*
19 Concepts of Growth and Development *320*
20 Development from Conception through Adolescence *343*
21 Development from Young through Older Adulthood *367*
22 Critical Thinking *384*
23 The Nursing Process *434*
24 Documenting and Reporting *464*
25 Nursing Informatics *477*
26 Nurse-Patient Relationship *504*
27 Health Assessment *605*
28 Medications *663*
29 Teaching *687*
30 Leading, Managing, and Influencing Change *702*
31 Vital Signs *740*
32 Asepsis *779*
33 Safety *803*
34 Hygiene *853*
35 Fecal Elimination *888*
36 Urinary Elimination *929*
37 Skin Integrity and Wound Care *965*
38 Nutrition *1014*
39 Oxygenation *1067*
40 Fluid, Electrolyte, and Acid-Base Balance *1126*
41 Sensory Perception *1147*
42 Rest and Sleep *1168*
43 Activity and Exercise *1226*
44 Clients Having Surgery: Promoting Healthy Recovery *1264*
45 Pain Management *1297*
46 Self-Concept *1314*
47 Stress and Coping *1336*
48 Loss, Grieving and Death *1360*

Canadian Case Studies

14 Does Betty Two-Trees Need an Advocate? *244*
18 Should Jacob Remain at Home? *305*
30 How Do We Get to know Mrs. M.? *706*
48 How Does Jackie View Her Role as a Registered Nurse? *1365*

Research Notes

3 Quantitative Study *36*
3 Qualitative Study *37*
3 Examples of Research Journals in Nursing *40*
7 Ethics in Nursing Practice *91*
10 How Do Employees Who Participate in Worksite Wellness Programs Differ from Those Who Do Not? *152*
11 Do Parents Use Complementary Therapies for Their Children with Cancer? *176*
12 To What Extent Do Cardiac Nurses Assess Sexual Concerns and Provide Teaching to Clients with Myocardial Infarction? *201*
13 The Problem of Theodicy and Religious Response to Cancer *217*
14 Cross-Cultural Hospital Care as Experienced by Mi'kmaq Clients *229*
16 What Are the Learning Needs of Nurses Preparing to Change from Acute to Community-Based Care? *271*
17 Who are Home Care Clients and What Is the Cost of Providing Care? *282*
18 "We're It": Issues and Realities in Rural Nursing Practice *300*
22 How Do Nurses Make Clinical Decisions? *383*
23 Are Hospital Nurses Expected to Use Nursing Diagnoses? *415*
24 Can "Charting by Exception" Save Nurses' Time? *450*
25 Does an Automated Documentation System in a Hospital Save Nurses' Time? *477*
26 How Can Nurses Show Caring While They Are Implementing Care? *481*
28 What Kind of Discharge Medication Instructions Provide a Higher Level of Medication Knowledge? *625*
29 Clients' Use of Health Teaching Materials at Three Readability Levels *677*
30 Organizational trust and empowerment: Effects on staff nurse commitment. *698*
31 How Do Different Sites and Methods of Temperature Measurement Differ in Clients with Fevers? *715*
32 How Do Nurses Determine the Effectiveness of Infection Control Practices? *758*
33 Does a Fall Prevention Program Help Older Women Decrease Their Incidence of Falls, and Is a Group Teaching or One-to-One Strategy More Effective? *792*
34 What Are the Effects of Hydrogen Peroxide Rinses on the Normal Oral Mucosa? *835*
34 Using Massage to Reduce Agitation *847*
35 Is Power Pudding an Effective Natural Laxative Therapy? *877*
36 Is Bladder Training Effective to Treat Urinary Incontinence? *912*
37 Best Practices *936*
37 Does the Degree of Lateral Positioning Make a Difference in Oxygenation of Tissues? *951*
41 Does a Telephone Follow-Up Program Make a Difference for Patients Recently Discharged from an Ophthalmic Unit? *1146*
44 Can Staff Nurses Prevent Postoperative Tape Blisters? *1256*
45 Can Nurses Assist Clients with Pain Relief and a Sense of Control Postoperatively? *1287*
46 Understanding the Persistence of Self *1304*
47 Use of a Projective Technique to Assess Young Children's Appraisal and Coping Responses to a Venipuncture *1335*
48 What Factors Account for Bereavement Outcome Among Spouses and Children of People Who Have Died from Cancer? *1343*

Assessment Interview

13 Spirituality *213*
29 Learning Needs and Characteristics *675*
32 Clients at Risk for Infections *751*
34 Skin Hygiene *810*
34 Foot Hygiene *822*
34 Nail Hygiene *825*
34 Oral Hygiene *827*
34 Hair Care *836*
34 Eyes *842*
35 Fecal Elimination *866*
36 Urinary Elimination *899*
39 Oxygenation *1031*
40 Fluid, Electrolyte, and Acid-Base Balance *1092*
41 Sensory-Perceptual Functioning *1136*
42 Sleep Disturbances *1160*
43 Activity and Exercise *1187*
45 Pain History *1278*
46 Personal Identity *1308*
46 Body Image *1308*
46 Role Relationships *1309*
47 Stress and Coping Patterns *1328*
48 Loss and Grieving *1345*

Developmental Assessment Guidelines

20 The Infant *328*
20 The Toddler *332*
20 The Preschooler *335*
20 The School-Age Child *338*
20 The Adolescent *343*
21 The Young Adult *350*
21 The Middle-Aged Adult *355*
21 The Older Adult *366*
48 The Dying Individual *1353*

Health Promotion Guidelines

20 Health Promotion Guidelines for Infants *329*
20 Health Promotion Guidelines for Toddlers *332*
20 Health Promotion Guidelines for Preschoolers *336*
20 Health Promotion Guidelines for School-Age Children *339*
20 Health Promotion Guidelines for Adolescents *344*
21 Health Promotion Guidelines for Young Adults *351*
21 Health Promotion Guidelines for Middle-Aged Adults *356*
21 Health Promotion Guidelines for Older Adults *367*

Home Care Assessment

34 Hygiene *811*
35 Fecal Elimination *869*
36 Urinary Elimination *908*
37 Wound Prevention and Care *948*
38 Nutrition *998*
39 Oxygenation *1041*
40 Fluid, Electrolyte, and Acid-Base Balance *1099*
41 Sensory-Perceptual Alterations *1140*
43 Mobility and Activity Problems *1195*
44 Surgical Clients *1250*
45 Pain *1283*
47 Stress and Coping *1332*

Client Teaching

12 Preventing Transmission of STIs *196*
12 Breast Self-Examination *197*
12 Breast screening centres *198*
12 Mammography *198*
12 Testicular Self-Examination (TSE) *199*
28 Using a Metered-Dose Inhaler *661*
28 Administering the Medication *661*
32 Home Care Teaching Guide *753*
33 Preventing Poisoning *794*
34 Skin Problems and Care *820*
34 Dry Skin *820*
34 Skin Rashes *820*
34 Acne *820*
34 Foot Care *824*
35 Assessing Stool for Occult Blood *868*
35 Managing Diarrhea *872*
36 Kegel Exercises *913*
36 Intermittent Self-Catheterization *925*
37 Home Care Teaching Guide *948*
38 Home Nutrition Therapy *1013*
39 Abdominal (Diaphragmatic) and Pursed-Lip Breathing *1044*
39 Controlled and Huff Coughing *1044*
39 Using Cough Medications *1044*
39 Using an Incentive Spirometer *1045*
41 Preventing Sensory Impairments *1141*
43 Active ROM Exercises *1214*
43 Controlling Postural Hypotension *1218*
43 Using Canes *1219*
43 Using Walkers *1220*
43 Using Crutches *1221*

Wellness Teaching

32 Preventing Infections in the Home *754*
34 Measures to Prevent Tooth Decay *829*
35 Healthy Defecation *871*
38 Nutrition for Older Adults *985*
38 Reducing Dietary Fat *985*
39 Promoting Healthy Breathing *1043*
39 Promoting a Healthy Heart *1043*
40 Promoting Fluid and Electrolyte Balance *1100*
42 Promoting Rest and Sleep *1164*
43 Preventing Back Injuries *1198*

Homecare Teaching

35 Fecal Elimination *871*
36 Urinary Elimination *909*
38 Healthy Nutrition *999*
39 Oxygenation *1041*
40 Fluid, Electrolyte, and Acid-Base Balance *1101*
43 Activity and Exercise *1196*
45 Monitoring Pain *1284*

Clinical Guidelines

8 Legal Precautions for Nurses *124*
10 Enhancing Behaviour Change *160*
23 Communication During an Interview *398*
28 Administering Medications by Nasogastric or Gastrostomy Tube *631*
28 Applying Skin Preparations *654*
28 Guidelines for Administering an Eye and Ear Irrigation *663*
28 Eye Irrigation *663*
32 Recommendations on Hand Washing (LCDC, 1998, revised 1999) *758*
32 Removing Disposable Gloves *765*
32 Gowning *766*
32 Using Disposable Masks *766*
32 Removing Soiled Personal Protective Equipment *767*
32 Steps to Follow after Exposure to Blood-borne Pathogens *778*
33 Preventing Falls in Health-Care Agencies *791*
33 Applying Restraints *802*
34 Bed-Making *848*
35 Giving and Removing a Bedpan *875*
36 Maintaining Normal Voiding Habits *911*
36 Bladder Training *912*
36 Preventing Catheter-Associated Urinary Infections *923*
37 Assessing Common Pressure Sites *944*
37 Acute Wounds *945*
37 Treating Pressure Ulcers *953*
37 Cleaning Wounds *953*
37 Applying Wet-to-Damp Dressings *957*
37 Bandaging *961*
37 Assessing before Applying Bandages or Binders *961*
40 Facilitating Fluid Intake *1102*
40 Helping Clients Restrict Fluid Intake *1102*
40 Vein Selection *1104*
40 Caring for Clients with a Venous Access Device *1107*
43 Wheelchair Safety *1209*
43 Safe Use of Stretchers *1210*
43 Providing Passive ROM Exercises *1215*
44 Assessing Surgical Wounds *1256*
44 Shortening a Drain *1259*
44 Removing and Emptying a Jackson Pratt Drain *1260*
45 Individualizing Care for Clients with Pain *1285*

Sample Care Plan

13 Sample Care Plan for Spiritual Distress *215*
23 Care Plan for Amanda Aquilini *426*
35 Sample Care Plan for Altered Bowel Elimination *873*
36 Sample Care Plan for Urinary Elimination *907*
38 Sample Care Plan for Nutrition *996*
39 Sample Care Plan for Ineffective Airway Clearance *1039*
40 Sample Care Plan for Fluid Volume Deficit *1127*
41 Sample Care Plan for Sensory-Perceptual Alteration *1144*
42 Sample Care Plan for Rest and Sleep *1163*
43 Sample Care Plan for Activity and Exercise *1193*
45 Sample Care Plan for Acute Pain *1294*
47 Sample Care Plan for Ineffective Individual Coping *1330*

Critical Pathway

15 Critical Pathway for Client Following Laparoscopic Cholecystectomy *260*
46 Critical Pathway for Client Following Total Mastectomy *1310*

Procedures

PROCEDURE 27.1 Assessing General Appearance and Mental Status *518*

PROCEDURE 27.2 Assessing the Skin *522*

PROCEDURE 27.3 Assessing the Hair *525*

PROCEDURE 27.4 Assessing the Nails *526*

PROCEDURE 27.5 Assessing the Skull and Face *527*

PROCEDURE 27.6 Assessing the Eye Structures and Visual Acuity *530*

PROCEDURE 27.7 Assessing the Ears and Hearing *538*

PROCEDURE 27.8 Assessing the Nose and Sinuses *543*

PROCEDURE 27.9 Assessing the Mouth and Oropharynx *545*

PROCEDURE 27.10 Assessing the Neck *551*

PROCEDURE 27.11 Assessing the Breasts and Axillae *554*

PROCEDURE 27.12 Assessing the Thorax and Lungs *562*

PROCEDURE 27.13 Assessing the Heart and Central Vessels *570*

PROCEDURE 27.14 Assessing the Peripheral Vascular System *573*

PROCEDURE 27.15 Assessing the Abdomen *577*

PROCEDURE 27.16 Assessing the Musculoskeletal System *584*

PROCEDURE 27.17 Assessing Motor Function *591*

PROCEDURE 27.18 Assessing Sensory Function *592*

PROCEDURE 27.19 Assessing the Female Genitals and Inguinal Lymph Nodes *596*

PROCEDURE 27.20 Assessing the Male Genitals and Inguinal Area *600*

PROCEDURE 27.21 Assessing the Rectum and the Anus *604*

PROCEDURE 28.1 Administering Oral Medications *626*

PROCEDURE 28.2 Preparing Medications from Ampules *635*

PROCEDURE 28.3 Preparing Medications from Vials *636*

PROCEDURE 28.4 Mixing Medications Using One Syringe *637*

PROCEDURE 28.5 Administering a Subcutaneous Injection *640*

PROCEDURE 28.6 Administering an Intramuscular Injection *645*

PROCEDURE 28.7 Adding Medications to Intravenous Fluid Containers *648*

PROCEDURE 28.8 Administering Intravenous Medications Using IV Push *651*

PROCEDURE 28.9 Administering Ophthalmic Instillations *654*

PROCEDURE 28.10 Administering Otic Instillations *656*

PROCEDURE 28.11 Administering Vaginal Instillations *658*

PROCEDURE 31.1 Assessing Body Temperature *716*

PROCEDURE 31.2 Assessing a Peripheral Pulse *722*

PROCEDURE 31.3 Assessing an Apical Pulse *724*

PROCEDURE 31.4 Assessing an Apical-Radial Pulse *726*

PROCEDURE 31.5 Assessing Respirations *730*

PROCEDURE 31.6 Assessing Blood Pressure *737*

PROCEDURE 32.1 Hand Washing *756*

PROCEDURE 32.2 Establishing and Maintaining a Sterile Field *771*

PROCEDURE 32.3 Donning and Removing Sterile Gloves (Open Method) *774*

PROCEDURE 32.4 Donning a Sterile Gown and Sterile Gloves (Closed Method) *776*

PROCEDURE 33.1 Using A Bed or Chair Exit Safety Monitoring Device *793*

PROCEDURE 33.2 Applying Restraints *800*

PROCEDURE 34.1 Bathing an Adult or Pediatric Client *814*

PROCEDURE 34.2 Providing Perineal-Genital Care *818*

PROCEDURE 34.3 Providing Foot Care *821*

PROCEDURE 34.4 Brushing and Flossing the Teeth *830*

PROCEDURE 34.5 Cleaning Artificial Dentures *832*

PROCEDURE 34.6 Providing Special Oral Care *833*

PROCEDURE 34.7 Providing Hair Care for African-Canadian Clients *838*

PROCEDURE 34.8 Shampooing the Hair of a Client Confined to Bed *839*

PROCEDURE 34.9 Removing, Cleaning, and Inserting a Hearing Appliance *846*

PROCEDURE 34.10 Changing an Unoccupied Bed *849*

PROCEDURE 34.11 Changing an Occupied Bed *852*

PROCEDURE 35.1 Administering an Enema *878*

PROCEDURE 35.2 Changing a One-Piece, Drainable Bowel Diversion Ostomy Appliance *883*

PROCEDURE 36.1 Collecting a Urine Specimen for Culture and Sensitivity by Clean Catch *901*

PROCEDURE 36.2 Applying a Condom Catheter *913*

PROCEDURE 36.3 Female Urinary Catheterization Using a Straight Catheter *917*

PROCEDURE 36.4 Male Urinary Catheterization Using a Straight Catheter *919*

PROCEDURE 36.5 Inserting a Retention (Indwelling) Catheter *921*

PROCEDURE 36.6 Irrigating a Catheter or Bladder (Closed System) *926*

PROCEDURE 37.1 Obtaining a Specimen of Wound Drainage *946*

PROCEDURE 37.2 Irrigating a Wound *956*

PROCEDURE 37.3 Applying a Moist Transparent Wound Barrier Dressing *958*

PROCEDURE 37.4 Applying a Hydrocolloid Dressing *959*

PROCEDURE 38.1 Inserting a Nasogastric Tube *1003*

PROCEDURE 38.2 Removing a Nasogastric Tube *1006*

PROCEDURE 38.3 Administering a Tube Feeding *1008*

PROCEDURE 38.4 Administering a Gastrostomy or Jejunostomy Feeding *1010*

PROCEDURE 39.1 Using a Pulse Oximeter *1032*

PROCEDURE 39.2 Administering Oxygen by Cannula, Face Mask, or Face Tent *1049*

PROCEDURE 39.3 Providing Tracheostomy Care *1055*

PROCEDURE 39.4 Suctioning Oropharyngeal and Nasopharyngeal Cavities *1058*

PROCEDURE 39.5 Suctioning a Tracheostomy or Endotracheal Tube *1060*

PROCEDURE 39.6 Applying a Sequential Compression Device *1064*

PROCEDURE 40.1 Starting an Intravenous Infusion *1109*

PROCEDURE 40.2 Monitoring a Peripheral Intravenous Infusion *1115*

PROCEDURE 40.3 Changing an Intravenous Container, Tubing, and Dressing *1116*

PROCEDURE 40.4 Discontinuing a Peripheral Intravenous Infusion *1118*

PROCEDURE 40.5 Changing a Peripheral Intravenous Catheter to an Intermittent Infusion Lock *1118*

PROCEDURE 40.6 Initiating, Maintaining, and Terminating a Blood Transfusion Using a Y-Set *1123*

PROCEDURE 42.1 Providing a Back Massage *1166*

PROCEDURE 43.1 Moving a Client up in Bed *1205*

PROCEDURE 43.2 Turning a Client to a Lateral or Prone Position in Bed *1206*

PROCEDURE 43.3 Logrolling a Client *1207*

PROCEDURE 43.4 Moving a Client to a Sitting Position on the Edge of the Bed *1208*

PROCEDURE 43.5 Transferring a Client between a Bed and a Chair *1210*

PROCEDURE 43.6 Transferring a Client between a Bed and a Stretcher *1212*

PROCEDURE 43.7 Using a (Electronic Operated) Hydraulic Lift to Transfer Clients from Bed to Chair *1213*

PROCEDURE 43.8 Assisting a Client to Walk *1216*

PROCEDURE 44.1 Teaching Moving, Leg Exercises, Deep Breathing, and Coughing *1238*

PROCEDURE 44.2 Applying Anti-embolism Stockings *1241*

PROCEDURE 44.3 Managing Gastrointestinal Suction *1253*

PROCEDURE 44.4 Cleaning a Sutured Wound and Applying a Sterile Dressing *1256*

PEARSON Education Canada | The Pearson Education Canada **COMPANION WEBSITE**

A Great Way to Learn and Instruct Online

The Pearson Education Canada Companion Website is easy to navigate and is organized to correspond to the chapters in this textbook. Whether you are a student in the classroom or a distance learner you will discover helpful resources for in-depth study and research that empower you in your quest for greater knowledge and maximize your potential for success in the course.

Companion Website

[www.pearsoned.ca/kozier]

Enter

PEARSON Prentice Hall

Jump to... http://www.pearsoned.ca/Kozier

Home | Search | Help | Profile

Companion Website

Home >

PH Companion Website

Fundamentals of Nursing: The Nature of Nursing Practice in Canada, Canadian Edition, by Kozier, Erb, Berman, Burke, Bouchal, and Hirst

Student Resources

The modules in this section provide students with tools for learning course material. These modules include:

- Self-Test Questions
- Essay Questions
- Internet Exercises
- Case Studies
- Destinations

For the self-test questions, students can send answers to the grader and receive instant feedback on their progress through the Results Reporter. Coaching comments and references to the textbook may be available to ensure that students take advantage of all available resources to enhance their learning experience.

Instructor Resources

The modules in this password-protected section provide instructors with downloadable versions of the Instructor's Manual and the PowerPoint slides.

SECTION 1

Conceptual Foundations of Nursing

UNIT 1 The Nature of Nursing

CHAPTER 1
Historical and Contemporary Nursing Practice

CHAPTER 2
Nursing Education in Canada

CHAPTER 3
Nursing Research in Canada

CHAPTER 4
Nursing Philosophies, Theories, Concepts, Frameworks, and Models

CHAPTER 5
The Individual—The Client of Care

CHAPTER 6
Nursing Care of Families

CHAPTER 7
Ethics, Morality, and Values

CHAPTER 8
Legal Aspects of Nursing

UNIT 2 Health, Beliefs, and Practices

CHAPTER 9
Health, Wellness, and Illness

CHAPTER 10
Health Promotion

CHAPTER 11
Holistic Healing Modalities

CHAPTER 12
Sexuality and Sexual Health Practices

CHAPTER 13
Spirituality

CHAPTER 14
Culture and Ethnicity

UNIT 3 Health-Care Environment

CHAPTER 15
Health-Care Delivery Systems

CHAPTER 16
Community-Based Nursing

CHAPTER 17
Home Care

CHAPTER 18
Rural Health Care

CHAPTER 1

Historical and Contemporary Nursing Practice

OBJECTIVES

After completing this chapter, you will be able to:

- Identify the importance of reading about nursing's past.
- Discuss historical and contemporary factors influencing the evolution of nursing.
- Analyze the influence of changing social, political, and economic conditions over time.
- Describe the scope and standards of nursing practice.
- Examine the roles of nurses in primary health care.
- Evaluate the expanded career goals and their functions.
- Examine the criteria of a profession and the professionalization of nursing.

Nursing has developed similarly in most Western industrialized nations. Industrialization, urbanization, world wars, cycles of economic depression and expansion, and the changing status of women created conditions which changed social structures and relations. Developments in scientific and technological knowledge and the consolidation of the medical profession altered the health and illness patterns of populations. These events occurred in context-specific ways throughout the Western world, and as this world changed, nursing both influenced and was influenced by these changes and events. Creating understanding of the relationships between nursing and changing social, political, and economic conditions is the focus or substance of many inquiries into nursing history. Knowledge of the past and of the ways in which nursing has developed in specific contexts or sets of circumstances enables nurses to better understand their present situation and particularly to see how current concerns might relate to larger social structural conditions. So, we read nursing history not only to learn about nursing's past but also to help us interpret our experience of nursing's present.

The intent of this section is to create some understanding of how we might situate nursing historically, that is, in relation to changing social, political, and economic conditions over time. Early writers of nursing history tended to concern themselves mainly with questions of professionalization, education, and leadership or to consider nursing history only as an aspect of medical history and the history of health-care services. However, since the 1980s, nurse historians have undertaken to locate nursing history within a larger social context. The significance of this approach is that we can begin to appreciate the complexity of nursing's position in society in terms of issues of gender, race, ethnicity, and class, rather than a history of unambiguous progress and advancement. Nursing has played a central role in defining the nature of health-care services in Canada. However, a fuller understanding of nursing can be achieved when nursing history is understood as being related to wider issues of social, economic, political, and cultural changes. In this broader view, we are encouraged to question the social arrangements and relations of power, the values and beliefs about women and about work, and particularly about the value of women's work that have influenced the position of nurses and nursing in Canadian society.

Changing Contexts of Nursing in Canada

As in many Western countries, the late 19th century marks the transformation of Canadian nursing from unpaid care to wage labour. In Canada, however, a distinctive feature of nursing was its roots in both the French tradition of nursing sisterhoods and the secular British model established by Florence Nightingale (Allemang, 1995; McPherson, 1996). Prior to the establishment of nursing in Canada as wage labour, nursing care was provided primarily by women within their families and communities and by organized groups of religious sisters (see Figure 1.1). The first group of European nuns arrived in what is now Quebec in 1639 with a mission to provide care for both the bodies and souls of European settlers and native inhabitants. These women with their strong beliefs in Christian charity cared for the sick and destitute, founding and managing hospitals to respond to health needs which arose consequent to war, epidemics of infectious diseases, and the hazards of pioneer life. As immigrants to Canada secured footholds in eastern regions, the nursing sisters followed the frontier west to continue their missionary and health-care work. Often, skilled nursing care was the only therapeutic intervention available, and these early nurses demonstrated through their practices that such care could improve health outcomes (Kerr, 1998).

Early Canadian towns and cities were plagued by inadequate sanitation and sewage systems, and waves of infectious diseases, such as typhus, influenza, and smallpox, regularly devastated both native and immigrant populations. Life chances improved in the late 19th century with public health innovations, such as those which protected food and water supplies from contamination, and with strategies for containing outbreaks of infectious disease. Trained nurses were instrumental both in implementing these innovations, which were based in the newly postulated scientific theory of germs, and in educating populations as to their need. The first training school for nurses

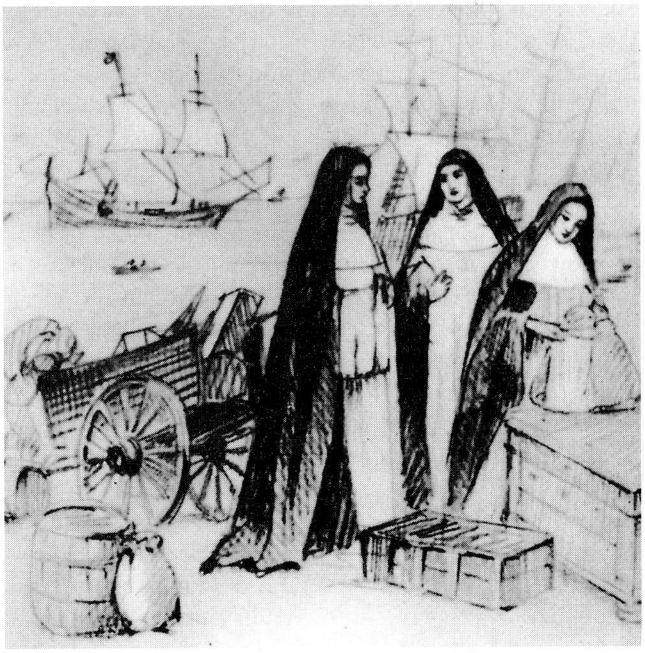

Figure 1.1 Arrival of the first three Augustinian Sisters at Quebec, 1639

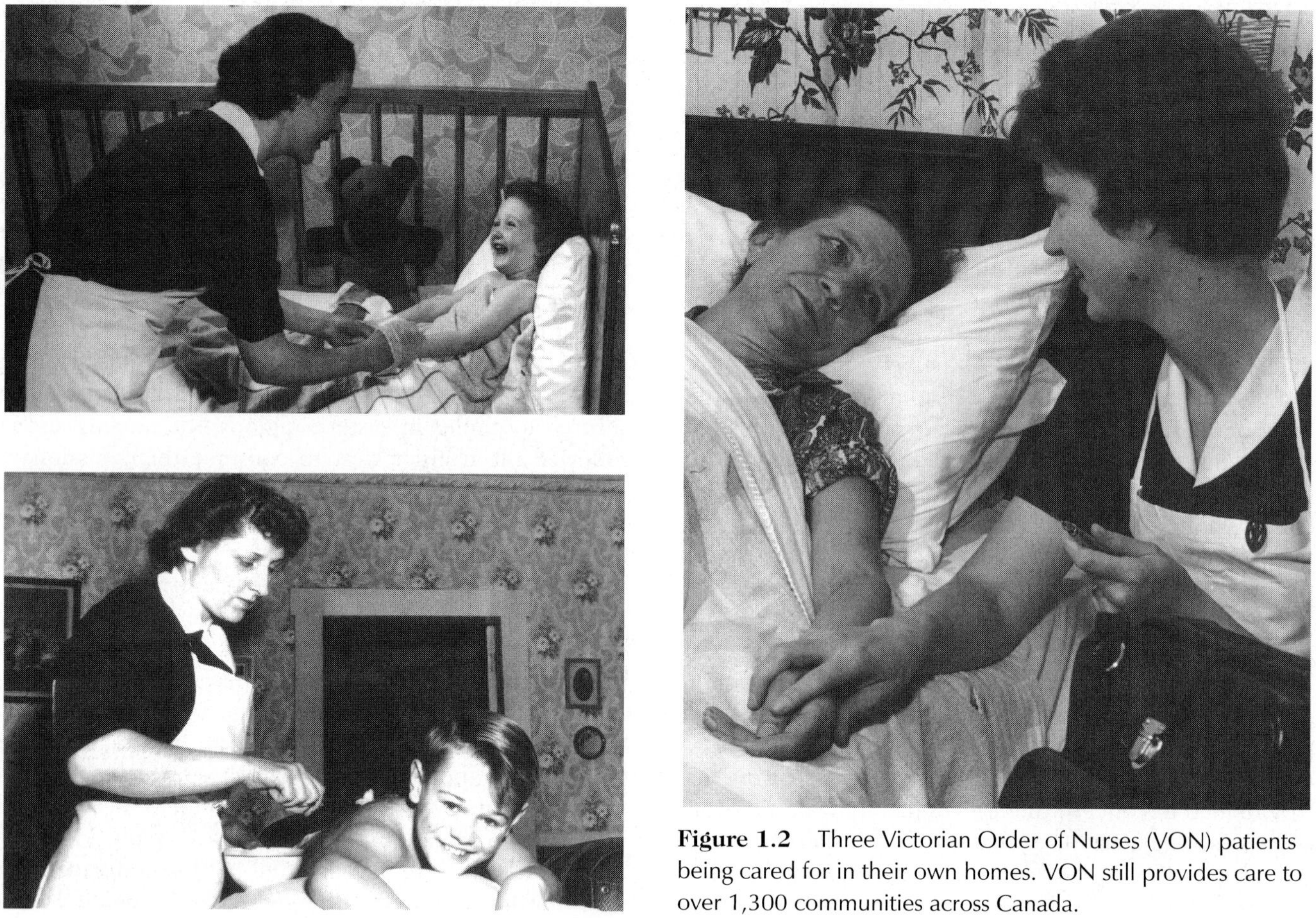

Figure 1.2 Three Victorian Order of Nurses (VON) patients being cared for in their own homes. VON still provides care to over 1,300 communities across Canada.

was established in 1874 at St. Catharines, Ontario, and the number of nurses in Canada rose dramatically from 300 trained nurses at the turn of the century to 20,000 by the end of the First World War (McPherson,1996). Early training schools were based on the Nightingale model, a philosophy of nursing which emphasized the nurse's role in facilitating the healing powers of nature. Though Nightingale's model of nursing was rigorously grounded in the scientific thinking of her times, nursing in Canada, as elsewhere, has also been thoroughly immersed in both religious and cultural ideals of womanly, selfless devotion to duty and service. The integration of scientific ideals with those of a particular conceptualization of respectable femininity facilitated the extension of women's caring roles from the home and the care of kin to the hospital and the care of strangers (see Figure 1.2).

Though the majority of medical and nursing care in the late 19th century was provided to patients in their homes, changing social conditions, such as the separation of families through migration and increasing urbanization, as well as changes in medical thinking and practice, contributed to a perceived need for centralized hospital care. Trained nursing was essential to the development of the modern hospital, to both its respectability as an institution and its therapeutic effectiveness. As a result, the nursing school became a standard feature of all large and small hospitals. Until the 1940s, most hospitals were almost exclusively staffed by student nurses, and until the 1970s, hospital apprenticeship programs remained the primary means of training nurses. Though such apprenticeship training was often exploitative, it was also a means through which nurses developed a shared work culture and nursing identity, one often closely aligned and loyal to the institutions in which nurses trained (McPherson, 1996).

Several events in the early decades of the 20th century were central factors in the gradual transformation in societal thinking about health care. Until this time, health had been generally conceived of as primarily a private affair and an individual or family responsibility. However, community experiences with recurrent epidemics of infectious diseases had highlighted the social effects of individual diseases, and the particularly devastating Spanish influenza epidemic of 1917–1918 revealed the uncoordinated and inadequate nature of Canada's health services (Allemang, 1995). Medical examination of army recruits prior to World War I also revealed the generally poor health status of the population, and it was clear to many reformers that the general level of health of Canadians needed attention. Reform and improvement in health

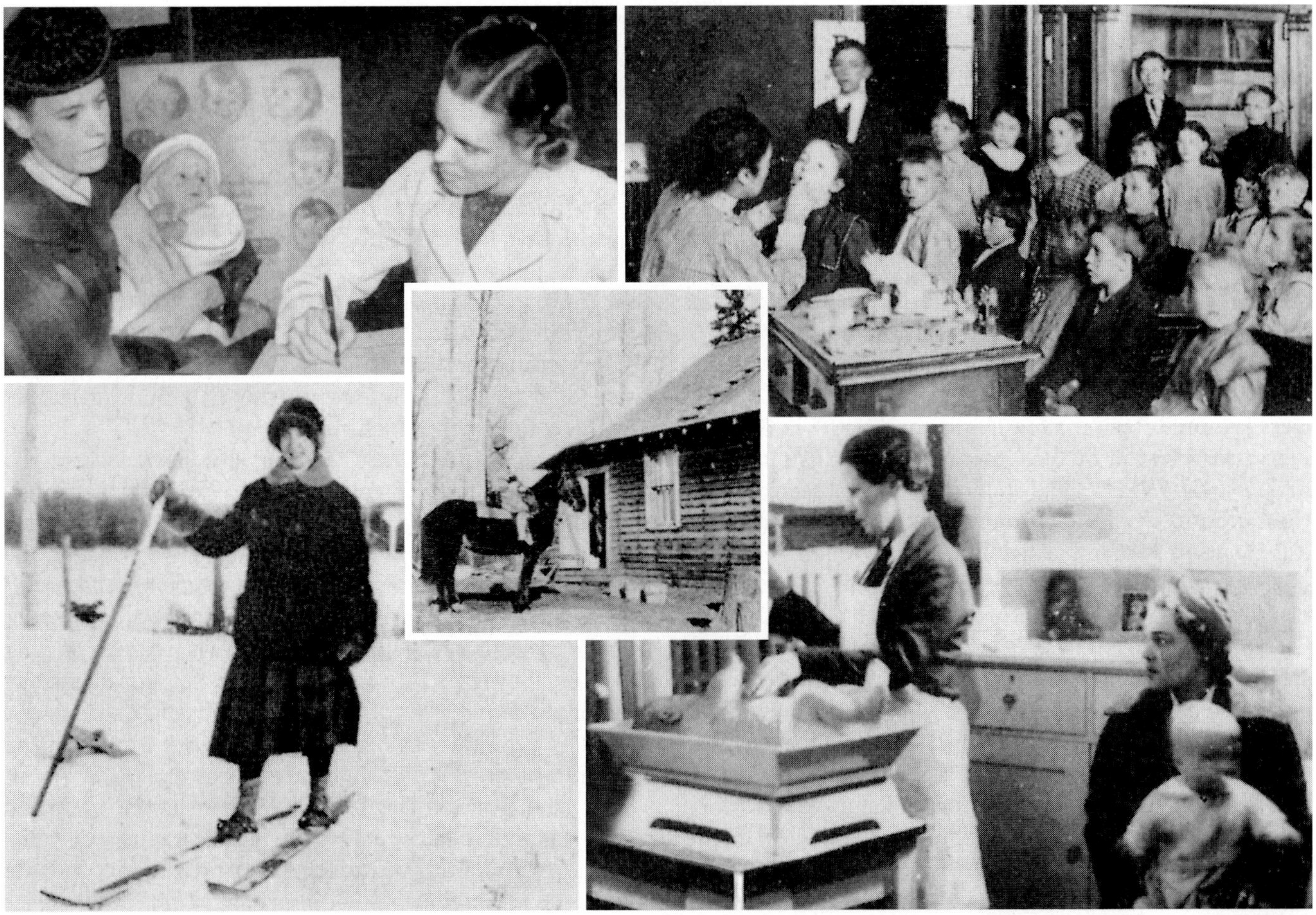

Figure 1.3 *Upper left*—Hastings Baby Clinic, 1940
Upper right— Early School of Nursing in Toronto
Centre—District Nurse at Old Pendryl Cottage, Alberta
Lower left—District Nurse at Griffin Creek, Alberta, 1922
Lower right—Well-Baby Clinic in Manitoba

status was undertaken primarily through federally and provincially sponsored public health programs in which specially trained nurses translated and enacted the new scientific theories of health, including ideas of social and mental hygiene, for families and communities. In homes and schools across the nation, public health nurses were responsible for health teaching, case finding, and the "Canadianizing" of new immigrants. In the more sparsely populated regions of Canada, district nurses expanded their scope of practice to meet the needs of those unserved by other care providers (see Figure 1.3). Where physicians were unable or unwilling to be available, nurses took on advanced roles, which suggests that the content of nursing has always been amenable to change and connected to the authority structure of various locations of practice (Kerr, 1998).

The conduct of nurses during the years of the First World War in response to crises both at home and abroad consolidated the position of nurses as valued and legitimate members of the health care team (McPherson,

Canada's Nursing Sisters' Legacy of Military Service

Canada's Nursing Sisters have a proud legacy of military service. The first nurses to serve in war were women who belonged to religious orders—hence the designation of "Nursing Sister" and the traditional white veil. (*Facts on Canadian Sisters*, Veterans Affairs Canada, 1998. Retrieved from http://www.vac-acc.gc.ca/general/sub.cfm?source=history/other/nursing.)

The legacy of providing care includes the following:

- Northwest Rebellion (1885)
- Northwest Mounted Police—the gold rush (1898)
- Great War (WW1) (1914–1918)—Canadian nurses volunteered
- Second World War (1939–1945)—Canadian nurses volunteered
- During United Nations operations in Korea, in the 1950s, Nursing Sisters served in both Korea and Japan (p. 2).
- In more recent times, Nursing Officers (as they are now called) have served in the Gulf War and in peace-keeping missions in Bosnia-Herzegovnia, Rwanda, and Somalia.

Source: Government of Canada, Veteran Affairs, *www.vac-acc.gc.ca*

1996), yet for many nurses, the years between the wars were very difficult. The rapid increase in the utilization of hospitals as the site of diagnosis and treatment and the reliance of hospitals on student labour meant that a continuous supply of students was required to meet the staffing needs of hospitals. This practice resulted in the oversupply and underemployment of graduate nurses, the largest number of whom still sought employment in the shrinking private-duty market. These conditions contributed to the hardship of many nurses, hardship that was merely exacerbated by the economic depression of the 1930s.

With the Second World War, the problem of oversupply was abruptly transformed to one of shortage. Nurses were required for war time service, and at the same time, new discoveries in medical therapeutics contributed to a dramatic increase in the demand for hospital services, and these advances called for more skilled and knowledgeable nursing care. Nursing leadership began to achieve success in weaning hospital administrators from their dependence on student labour, and most graduate nurses began to be employed in hospital settings. In these years, nursing articulated a relationship with science, which, in part at least, helped differentiate nursing work from the work of less skilled auxiliary workers whose positions were developed to help address the shortage of trained nurses (McPherson, 1994). Nursing's relationship with science was not without its tensions, however. Articles in the *Canadian Nurse* during the 1930s and 1940s include discussions both of nursing as a knowledge-based profession and of the scientific nurse being in danger of losing her most significant attribute—her womanliness.

Since the Second World War, the hospital has become firmly established as the therapeutic setting of choice, and it is the location in which approximately 60 percent of nurses work. Changes in medical therapeutics, such as drug therapies and surgical advances, have altered the health and illness patterns of populations and, at the same time, have been central forces in defining the nature and scope of nursing practices. The development of knowledge and technologies, and the delegation of medical tasks to nursing personnel, has led to an increasingly specialized nursing workforce both inside and outside of hospital settings. As the health and welfare of the population became a legitimate domain of federal/provincial interest and involvement, a position inscribed in Medicare legislation in 1968, Canadians have come to expect the presence of knowledgeable and skilled nurses as necessary to complete health care.

Selected Themes in Nursing History

There are many different perspectives through which one can interpret nursing history, such as consideration of gender or women's issues, analysis of labour force issues and working conditions, the drive for professional status, including emphasis on improving education, and a focus on nursing leadership. Different views on nursing history reflect an author's work of selecting and interpreting historical data, activities that create a particular point of view on nursing. The result is sometimes seemingly contradictory accounts of nursing history that may prompt us to ask: Which accounts should we believe? However, it may not be that the truth lies in one or another account of nursing history but, rather, that many accounts are necessary in order to bring the fullness of nursing history into view. McPherson (1996) has observed that nursing is premised on many paradigms and that a single explanation or explanatory framework simply cannot do justice to the complexity of nursing history.

Nursing is often described as having been constructed through the integration or blending of four paradigms: (1) domestic nurturing, (2) religious devotion, (3) military duty and discipline, and (4) scientific medicine. Additionally, the changing role and status of women in society has also influenced who would become a nurse and why. Though nurses have almost always been women, the ways in which nursing as women's work has been valued have changed over time. Certainly, the creators of the modern nurse had a particular ideal of femininity in mind as they set out to reform the nursing profession in the late 19th century. This was an ideal analogous to the role of women in the Victorian English, middle-class family. The modern nurse was to be wife to the doctor and mother to the patient, and the work she would do would be simply a natural extension of the woman's work in the home. This particular view of the nurse and of nursing work is sometimes held to explain why nurses have been unable to alter their subordinate position in health-care systems. That is, despite changes in nursing's role and advances in nursing knowledge, nursing remains firmly connected to a particular ideology of womanhood and ideas of women's proper sphere.

Some historians suggest that a comprehensive understanding of the complexity of nursing history requires an analysis of the ways in which nursing has occupied a social position defined not only by relations of gender but also by particular relations of class, race, and ethnicity. So, for example, though Canadian nurses have almost always been women, not all women were equally welcome recruits to nursing. The conception of respectable femininity on which Canadian nursing was founded was a femininity almost always exclusively white and Canadian-born (McPherson, 1996). Women of colour were trained as nurses primarily to serve their own communities. Nurses have, for the most part, been subordinate within health-care systems. However, relative to the status of other women workers, they have often been in positions of privilege. In our social worlds, power is based on gender, race, and class ideologies. Nurses as women of particular races and class backgrounds cannot therefore be understood simply on their own terms. In particular historical eras, nursing has partic-

Figure 1.4 Considered the founder of modern nursing, **Florence Nightingale** (1820–1910) was influential in developing nursing education, practice, and administration. Her 1859 publication, *Notes on Nursing: What It Is, and What It Is Not,* was intended for all women.

ipated in and challenged the social, political, and economic contexts which have created both possibilities and limitations for women. The conflicting forces in nursing histories and nursing ideologies call for continued study, not only to further our understanding of nursing itself, but perhaps more importantly to further our understanding of nursing's effects in the world.

Florence Nightingale (1820–1910)

Florence Nightingale's contributions to nursing are well documented. Her achievements in improving the standards for the care of war casualties in the Crimea earned her the title "Lady with the Lamp." Her efforts in reforming hospitals and in producing and implementing public health policies also made her an accomplished political nurse; she was the first nurse to exert political pressure on government. Through her contributions to nursing education—perhaps her greatest achievement—she is also recognized as nursing's first scientist-theorist for her work *Notes on Nursing: What It Is, and What It Is Not.* (See Figure 1.4.)

Nightingale's vision of nursing, which included public health and health promotion roles for nurses, was only partially addressed in the early days of nursing, when the focus tended to be on developing the profession within hospitals.

Contemporary Nursing Practice

An in-depth study of contemporary nursing practice includes a look at selected definitions of nursing, a framework for the Canadian health system, goals of the nurse within this system, the acts that legislate health care and nursing practice, and scope and standards of practice.

Definitions of Nursing

To understand what nursing is, one must first define the word. Many definitions exist, some of which misrepresent the complex knowledge and skill of professional nursing. Common dictionary definitions, for example, still refer to the nurse as "a person, usually a woman, trained to care for the sick" (*The New Lexicon Webster's Dictionary of the English Language*). Today, however, many men are choosing to become nurses, and nurses also provide preventive and health-promoting care to well clients. This section gives several definitions of nursing, and Chapter 4 provides other definitions by nursing theorists.

Florence Nightingale defined nursing over 50 years ago as "the act of utilizing the environment of the patient to assist him in his recovery" (Nightingale, 1860). Nightingale considered a clean, well-ventilated, and quiet environment essential for recovery. Often considered the first nurse-theorist, Nightingale raised the status of nursing through education. Nurses were no longer untrained housekeepers but people educated in the care of the sick.

Virginia Henderson was one of the first modern nurses to define nursing. In 1960, she wrote, "The unique function of the nurse is to assist the individual, sick or well, in the performance of those activities contributing to health or its recovery (or to peaceful death) that he would perform unaided if he had the necessary strength, will, or knowledge, and to do this in such a way as to help him gain independence as rapidly as possible" (Henderson, 1966, p. 3). Like Nightingale, Henderson described nursing in relation to the client and the client's environment. Unlike Nightingale, Henderson saw the nurse as concerned with both well and ill individuals, acknowledged that nurses interact with clients even when recovery may not be feasible, and mentioned the teaching and advocacy roles of the nurse.

Professional nursing associations have also examined nursing and developed their definitions of it. The Canadian Nurses Association (CNA) published a definition in 1984 that serves as the professional standard for nurses in Canada:

> *"Nursing" or "the practice of nursing" means the identification and treatment of human responses to actual or potential health problems and includes the practice of and supervision of functions and services that, directly or indirectly, in collaboration with a client or providers of health care other than nurses, have as their objectives the promotion of health, prevention of illness, alleviation of suffering, restoration of health and optimum development of health potential and includes all aspects of the nursing process.*
> (CNA Connection, 1984, p. 8)

In 1987, the CNA described nursing practice as a dynamic, caring, helping relationship in which the nurse assists the client to achieve and maintain optimal health (CNA, 1987). In the latter half of the 20th century, a number of nurse theorists developed their own theoretical

Themes Common to Definitions

- Nursing is caring.
- Nursing is an art.
- Nursing is a science.
- Nursing is client centred.
- Nursing is holistic.
- Nursing is adaptive.
- Nursing is concerned with health promotion, health maintenance, and health restoration.
- Nursing is a helping profession.

definitions of nursing. Theoretical definitions are important because they go beyond simplistic common definitions. They describe what nursing is and the interrelationship between nurses, nursing, the client, and the intended client outcome—health. See Chapters 5 and 26.

Caring is described as the "essence of nursing" (Leininger, 1984). It is a complex concept that has multiple aspects: affective, cognitive, and ethical. Research to explore the meaning of caring in nursing has been increasing because nursing, more than any other profession, has "the distinction of being responsible for the caring that clients receive in the health-care system" (Miller, 1995, p. 29). Details about caring are discussed in Chapter 26. See also Watson's "Assumptions of Caring" in Chapter 4.

Recipients of Nursing

The recipients of nursing are sometimes called *consumers*, sometimes *patients*, and sometimes *clients*. A **consumer** is an individual, a group of people, or a community that uses a service or commodity. People who use health-care products or services are consumers of health care.

A **patient** is a person who is waiting for or undergoing medical treatment and care. The word *patient* comes from a Latin word meaning "to suffer" or "to bear." Traditionally, the person receiving health care has been called a patient. Usually, people become patients when they seek assistance because of illness or for surgery. Some nurses believe that the word *patient* implies passive acceptance of the decisions and care of health professionals. Additionally, with the emphasis on health promotion and prevention of illness, many recipients of nursing care are not ill. Moreover, nurses interact with family members and significant others to provide support, information, and comfort in addition to caring for the client.

For these reasons, nurses increasingly refer to recipients of health care as clients. A **client** is a person who engages the advice or services of another who is qualified to provide this service. The term *client* presents the receivers of health care as collaborators in the care, that is, as people who are also responsible for their own health. Thus, the health status of a client is the responsibility of the individual in collaboration with health professionals. In this book, *client* is the preferred term, although *consumer* and *patient* are used in some instances.

Scope of Nursing

Nurses provide care for four types of clients—individuals, families, groups, and communities. Theoretical frameworks applicable to these client types, as well as assessments of individual, family, and community health are discussed in detail in Chapters 5, 6, and 16.

Nursing practice involves four areas: promoting health and wellness, preventing illness, restoring health, and care of the dying.

Promoting Health and Wellness

Wellness is a state of well-being. It means engaging in attitudes and behaviour that enhance the quality of life and maximize personal potential (Anspaugh et al., 1991). Nurses promote wellness in clients who are both healthy and ill. This may involve individual and community activities to *enhance* healthy lifestyles, such as improving nutrition and physical fitness; preventing drug and alcohol abuse; avoiding smoking; and preventing accidents and injury in the home and workplace.

Preventing Illness

The goal of illness prevention programs is to *maintain* optimal health by preventing disease. Nursing activities that prevent illness include immunizations, prenatal and infant care, and prevention of sexually transmitted diseases.

Restoring Health

Restoring health focuses on the ill client and extends from early detection of disease through helping the client during the recovery period. Nursing activities include the following:

- Providing direct care to the ill person, such as administering medications, baths, and specific procedures and treatments
- Performing diagnostic and assessment procedures, such as measuring blood pressure and examining feces for occult blood
- Consulting with other health-care professionals about client problems
- Teaching clients about recovery activities, such as exercises that will hasten recovery after a stroke
- Rehabilitating clients to their optimal functional level following physical or mental illness, injury, or chemical addiction

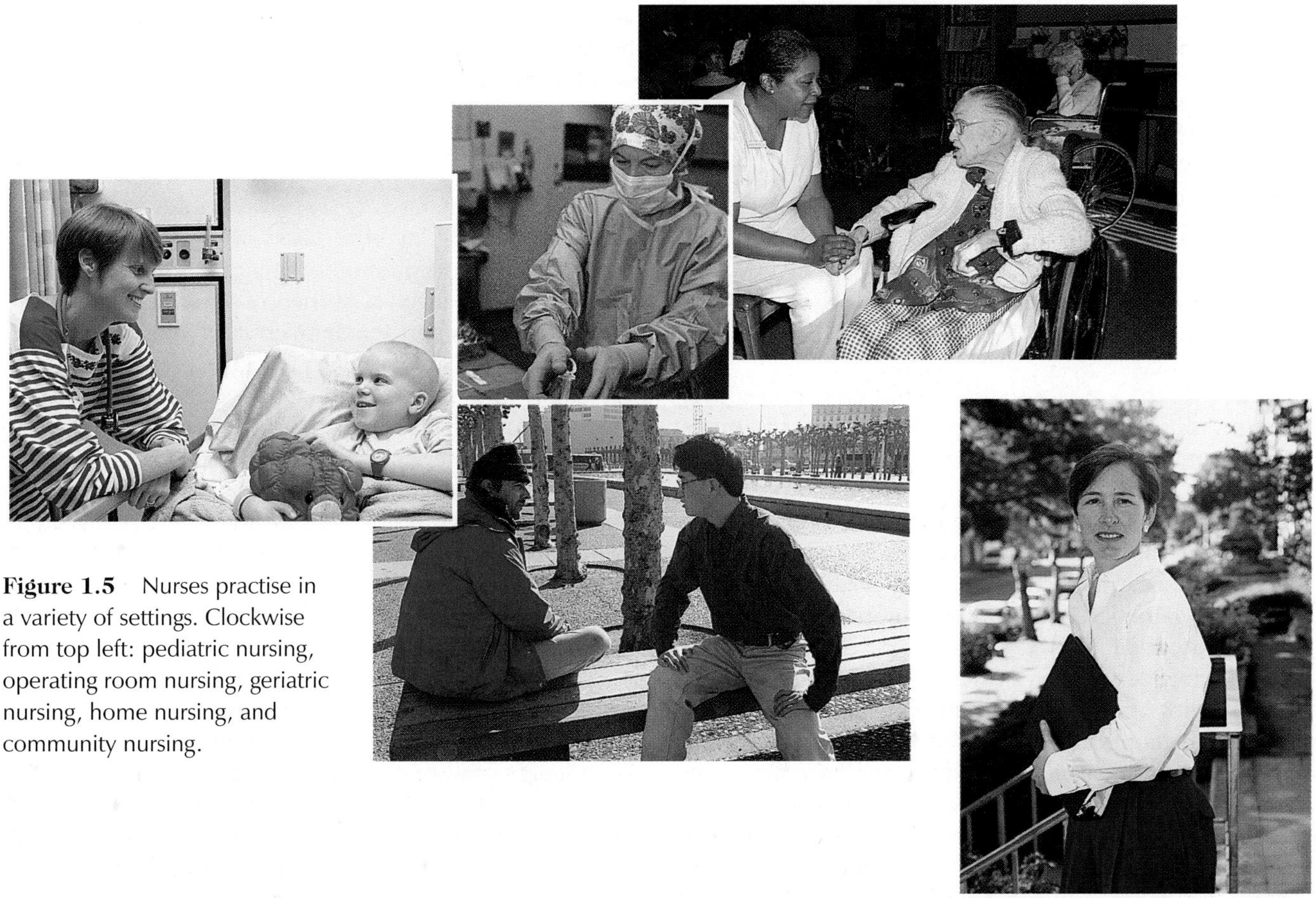

Figure 1.5 Nurses practise in a variety of settings. Clockwise from top left: pediatric nursing, operating room nursing, geriatric nursing, home nursing, and community nursing.

Care of the Dying

This area of nursing practice involves comforting and caring for people of all ages who are dying. It includes helping clients live as comfortably as possible until death and helping support persons close to the patient cope with death. Nurses carrying out these activities work in homes, hospitals, and extended-care facilities. Some agencies, called hospices, are specifically designed for this purpose.

Settings for Nursing

In the past, the acute-care hospital was the primary practice setting open to most nurses. In 1998, approximately 60 percent of nurses worked in hospitals, but increasingly they work in clients' homes, community agencies, ambulatory clinics, and nursing practice centres. Figure 1.5 shows nurses in a variety of settings.

Nurses have different degrees of nursing autonomy and nursing responsibility in the various settings. They may provide direct care, teach clients and support persons, serve as nursing advocates and agents of change, and help determine health policies affecting consumers in the community and in hospitals. For information about the models for delivery of nursing, see Chapter 4.

The CNA maintains that an individual's health affects the quality of that person's life. Health is influenced not only by the health-care system but also by human biology, lifestyle choices, and the environment. With this in mind, CNA advocates a framework to provide direction for the Canadian health-care system that includes (1) the *conditions* of the Canada Health Act; and, (2) the *principles* of primary health care.

The Canada Health Act (1984) lists the conditions or national standards which provincial/territorial health insurance plans must respect in order to receive federal cash contributions. The five conditions listed in the Canada Health Act are public administration, accessibility, comprehensiveness, universality, and portability. The CNA believes that these conditions are essential to Canada's health-care system.

1. *Universal coverage* means all Canadians are entitled to essential health services, regardless of gender, culture, income, language, education, marital status, or age.
2. *Comprehensiveness* means that federal and provincial or territorial health insurance acts together should cover the full continuum of health services for all Canadians, including health promotion, the prevention of disease and disability, the treatment of disease and disability, restoration, rehabilitation, and support.
3. *Accessibility* means the health-care system must ensure that Canadians have reasonable access to essential

health services, with no financial barriers, such as user fees, to impede access to services.

4. *Portability* means that Canadians should be covered equally for health services wherever they are in Canada.

5. *Public administration* means that federal, provincial, and territorial health insurance programs should be non-profit programs operated by public authorities who are appointed by government (CNA, 1988).

Primary Health Care

Primary health care is essential (promotive, preventive, curative, rehabilitative, and supportive) care that focuses on preventing illness and promoting health. It is both a philosophy of health care and an approach to providing health services. Primary health care has been adopted by the World Health Organization and by Canada as the key to a healthy society. Clients of primary health care can be individuals, families, groups, communities, and populations (CNA, 1988; WHO, 1987).

The principles of primary health care are accessibility, public participation, health promotion, appropriate technology, and cooperation. *Accessibility* means that essential health care is universally available to all clients in an acceptable and affordable way, regardless of geographical location. *Public participation* means clients should be encouraged to participate in making decisions about their own health. *Health promotion* means that the health-care system should increase its emphasis on helping clients stay well, rather than treating clients when they are ill. *Appropriate technology* means that technology and modes of care should be appropriately adapted to the community's social, economic, and cultural development. *Intersectoral collaboration* recognizes that health activities must be undertaken concurrently with measures aimed at improving economic and social development (CNA, 1995).

Taken together, the conditions of the Canada Health Act and the principles of primary health care serve as a solid framework for health-care delivery and the future development of Canada's health-care system. The conditions outlined in the Canada Health Act and the principles required for primary health care are congruent with the CNA's beliefs about nursing practice. All nurses, therefore, play a vital role in the implementation of the conditions of the Canada Health Act and the principles of primary health care (CNA, 1995; WHO, 1987).

Primary Care and Primary Nursing

Primary health care should not be confused with "primary care" or "primary nursing." Primary care "is a medical concept referring to a situation where the physician provides diagnosis, treatment, and follow-up for a specific disease or problem." Primary nursing is a system of delivering nursing services whereby a nurse is responsible for planning the 24-hour care of a specific patient. Both these concepts are illness-oriented concepts (Registered Nurses Association of British Columbia [RNABC], 1990, p. 2).

The Role of the Nurse

The goal of nursing is to improve the health of clients through partnerships with clients, with other health-care providers, related community agencies, and government. Nursing practice involves a variety of roles, including direct-care provider, educator, administrator, consultant, policy advisor, and researcher. The principles of primary health care apply to nurses in all these roles (CNA, 1995).

To ensure that Canadians have *reasonable access* to essential health services, nurses provide more options for accessing health services by (1) acting as an entry point for clients into the health-care system; (2) providing nursing care and treatment for health problems; (3) helping clients to identify and use health resources, both formal and informal; and (4) acting as a source of health information for clients (CNA, 1995).

Nurses increase public participation in planning and making decisions about their own health care by (1) involving clients in decisions about their own health; (2) encouraging clients to take action for their own health; (3) involving clients in identifying their health-care needs; (4) involving clients in planning, using, and evaluating their own health-care services; and (5) encouraging and utilizing community development approaches (CNA, 1995).

Health Promotion

In keeping with a health system's focus that helps clients stay well, nurses are able to play a leadership role in health promotion and initiate health education and other activities that assist, promote, and support clients as they strive to achieve the highest possible level of health (CNA Policy Statement on Health Promotion, March 1992).

Health promotion implies a commitment to dealing with the challenges of reducing inequities, extending the scope of prevention, and helping people cope with their circumstances. It means fostering public participation, strengthening community health services, and coordinating public health policy. Moreover, it means creating environments conducive to health in which people are better able to take care of themselves, and to offer each other support in solving and managing collective health problems (CNA, 1995).

Health status is influenced by social norms, cultural values, economic and environmental conditions and policies, as well as life practices, such as food and exercise choices, following safety precautions, and the abuse of tobacco, alcohol, and other drugs. The CNA believes that consideration of these influences is essential in the development of effective health promotion initiatives.

Health promotion initiatives must be widely targeted and begin with the very young and extend throughout their lifespan. The CNA supports the concept that health promotion strategies should be initiated collaboratively by a variety of appropriate bodies, including health, social, and educational agencies, to meet identified needs of individuals, families, and communities. It is the belief of the CNA that emphasis on health promotion strengthens and complements the health-care system (1992).

Nurses must provide leadership for health promotion. This should be done through positive role modelling and personal demonstration of healthy life practices, as well as by assisting, promoting, and supporting clients, individuals, groups, and communities in self-help activities to understand and achieve their highest possible level of health. Educational curricula for nurses should emphasize the importance of this leadership role and provide the opportunity for related skill development (1995).

As part of the goal to ensure that *technology* and *modes of care* are based on health needs and are appropriate to the community's social, economic, and cultural development, nurses (1) strive to provide cost-effective care that is based on client needs, research evidence, and measurable health outcomes; and (2) participate with other health-care professionals in developing, implementing, and evaluating technology and modes of care to ensure their appropriateness and cost-effectiveness (CNA, 1995).

In cooperation with clients, with each other, with professionals from other sectors, and with governments, nurses coordinate client care and strive to integrate health services. Nurses participate with clients in designing public health policies and will continue to do so to achieve health for all. Nurses will continue to work with clients and other health providers to implement the principles of primary health care. The CNA will support them in this endeavour and will monitor the progress of primary health care in Canada (CNA, 1995).

Canadian Society Notes

Fact	Implications for Nursing Practice
Canadian nursing history is rooted in the French tradition of nursing sisters and the secular British model.	Understanding history provides registered nurses with an appreciation of present issues, conflicts, and ideologies.
The CNA is a federation of 11 provincial and territorial registered nurses associations. The membership of approximately 110,000 registered nurses is broad and diverse, reflecting the face of nursing today.	Strength for changes to health care is often achieved through the large membership of the CNA.
Ordre des infirmières et infirmiers du Quebec speaks for registered nurses within that province.	Registration practices differ within Canada, which may influence the employment pattern of nurses.
Nurses in Canada are regulated through title control.	Only nurses who are currently registered with a nursing regulatory body may use the title "RN."

Nurse Practice Acts

Nurse practice acts, or legal acts for professional nursing practice, regulate the practice of nursing in the United States and Canada. Each province/territory in Canada has its own act. Although nurse practice acts differ in various jurisdictions, they all have a common purpose—to protect the public.

One of the ways that the public is protected is through regulation. The primary purpose of regulation is to protect the public from professionals who are "unqualified, incompetent, or unethical" (RNABC, 1999). Professions can be regulated in one of two ways: by the government or by the profession itself. In Canada, in all provinces except Ontario, which has a separate regulatory body, professional organizations are self-regulating. Self-regulation means provincial and territorial governments delegate to professional bodies, by legislative acts, "the power to regulate its peers." Self-regulation is a privilege granted by governments to professional organizations, and "to maintain this privilege, a profession must maintain the trust of the public." (p. 6).

One of the ways nurses in Canada are regulated is through title control. "The use of such titles as 'registered nurse,' 'RN,' and 'nurse' is protected by legislation. Only individuals who are currently registered with a nursing regulatory body may use these titles" (CNA, 2000, p. 6).

Nursing regulatory bodies including the International Council of Nurses (ICN), the Canadian Nurses Association (CNA), and the provincial and territorial professional organizations work together to develop frameworks for regulatory matters, such as standards of practice, scope of practice, and continuing competence. *Standards of practice* "reflect the values of the nursing profession, clarify what the profession expects of its members, define the expectations of the public/employers, and provide a benchmark below which performance is unacceptable" (CNA, 2000, p. 6). The *scope of practice* describes what activities nurses are educated and legislated to perform. Historically, what nurses can and are prepared to do has changed in response to the changing needs of the public. More recently, "the profession has moved toward broader scope of practice statements with an increased emphasis on standards" (p. 6). Professional organizations design *continuing competence* programs "to promote safe, ethical, and competent practices by nurses and to ensure that nurses have the opportunity to pursue and achieve professional growth throughout their careers" (p. 7).

Differences in the regulation of professionals in Canada can often be traced to the differences in provincial and territorial legislation. Other health-care workers, such as licensed practical nurses (LPNs) and registered psychiatric nurses (RPNs), are regulated under separate legislation. Non-regulated workers also work in the health-care system.

Nursing Practice Standards

Nursing Practice Standards are mandatory for a self-regulating profession. The overall purpose of practice standards is to provide a guideline for determining the quality of nursing care a patient/client receives.

The **Nursing Practice Standards** provide criteria "against which the practice of all registered nurses will be measured by the public, clients, employers, colleagues, and themselves. Nursing Practice Standards reflect the values of the profession and clarify what professional organizations expect of its members" (AARN, 1998, p. 3). For example, practice standards for Alberta nurses were developed by the professional organization and include the following: (1) professional responsibility, (2) knowledge-based practice, and (3) provision of service to the public (Alberta Association of Registered Nurses, 1998).

Roles and Functions of the Nurse

Nurses assume a number of roles when they provide care to clients. Often, nurses carry out these roles concurrently, not exclusively of one another. For example, the nurse may act as a counsellor while providing physical care and teaching aspects of that care. The roles required at a specific time depend on the needs of the client and aspects of the particular environment.

Caregiver

The caregiver role has traditionally included those activities that assist the client physically and psychologically while preserving the client's dignity. The required nursing actions may involve full care for the completely dependent client, partial care for the partially dependent client, and supportive-educative care to assist clients in attaining their highest possible level of health and wellness. Caregiving encompasses the physical, psychosocial, developmental, and spiritual levels. A nurse may provide care directly or delegate it to other caregivers.

Communicator

Communication is integral to all nursing roles. Nurses communicate with the client, support persons, other health professionals, and people in the community.

Nurses identify client problems and then communicate these verbally and/or in writing to other members of the health team. The quality of a nurse's communication is an important factor in nursing care. The nurse must be able to communicate clearly and accurately in order for a client's health-care needs to be met. See Chapter 26.

Teacher

As a teacher, the nurse helps clients learn about health and the health-care procedures they need to perform to restore or maintain health. The nurse determines the client's learning needs and readiness to learn, sets specific learning goals and teaching strategies, enacts teaching strategies, and measures learning. Nurses also teach other health-care providers to whom they delegate care, and they share their expertise with other nurses and health-care professionals. See Chapter 29 for additional details about the teaching/learning process.

Client Advocate

A client advocate acts to protect the client. In this role, the nurse may represent the client's needs and wishes to other health-care professionals, such as relaying the client's wishes for information to the physician. They also assist clients in exercising their rights and help them speak up for themselves. See Chapter 8.

Counsellor

Counselling is the process of helping a client recognize and cope with stressful psychological or social problems, develop improved interpersonal relationships, and promote personal growth. It involves providing emotional, intellectual, and psychological support. In contrast to the psychotherapist, who counsels individuals with identified problems, the nurse counsels primarily healthy individuals with normal adjustment difficulties. The nurse focuses on helping the person develop new attitudes, feelings, and behaviours, rather than on promoting intellectual growth. The nurse encourages the client to look at alternative behaviours, recognize the choices, and develop a sense of control.

FOCUS ON CRITICAL THINKING

It is only relatively recently that registered nurses have become aware of their ability to influence change at a federal policy level in Canada. Today, the Canadian Nurses Association works with its provincial and territorial associations to advance the role of registered nurses in promoting the health and well-being of all Canadians.

1. How does the Canadian Nurses Association influence national health-care policy?
2. What is the role of an individual nurse within the mandate of the CNA?
3. What changes are occurring across Canada that influence the discipline of nursing?

See Appendix A for answers to these questions.

Change Agent

The nurse acts as a change agent when assisting others, that is, clients, to make modifications in their own behaviour. Nurses also often act to make changes in a system, such as clinical care, if it is not helping a client return to health. Nurses are continually dealing with change in the health-care system. Technological change, change in the age of the client population, and changes in medications are just a few of the changes nurses deal with daily. See Chapter 30 for additional information about change.

Leader

The leadership role can be employed at different levels: individual client, family, groups of clients, colleagues, or the community. Effective leadership is a learned process requiring an understanding of the needs and goals that motivate people, the knowledge to apply the leadership skills, and the interpersonal skills to influence others. The leadership role of the nurse is discussed in Chapter 30.

Manager

The nurse manages the nursing care of individuals, families, and communities. The nurse-manager also delegates nursing activities to ancillary workers and other nurses and supervises and evaluates their performance. Managing requires knowledge about organizational structure and dynamics, authority and accountability, leadership, change theory, advocacy, delegation, and supervision and evaluation. See Chapter 30 for additional details.

Canada's chief executive nurses (CENs) are defined by the CNA and provide leadership in delivering quality, effective nursing services. The advanced educational preparation of the CEN optimizes the quality of nursing services in any health organization. With the support of management and nurses, the CEN creates and maintains a nursing practice. This quality nursing care is theory based and attains measurable client outcomes. The CEN also promotes collaborative and interdisciplinary management and care processes to enhance client care, provides a visionary leadership in the organization and the profession of nursing in order to fulfill the organization's mission, and supports a professional practice environment through reporting to the organization's mission, reporting to the organization's chief executive officer, and being an advisor at meetings of the governing body. As an equal member of the senior management team, the CEN is responsible for quality nursing services and has the authority and resources to ensure that nursing standards are met.

In collaboration with educational institutions, the CEN contributes to the quality of nursing education by exposing students to the continuum of service provision, such as the links between hospital, long-term, and community services. As a variety of new organizational structures are implemented in health-care settings, the CEN's leadership in supporting quality nursing care must be retained (CNA, 1993).

Research Consumer

Nurses often use research to improve client care. In a clinical area, nurses need to (1) have some awareness of the process and language of research; (2) be sensitive to issues related to protecting the rights of human subjects; (3) participate in the identification of significant researchable problems; and (4) be discriminating consumers of research findings.

Expanded Career Roles

Nurses are fulfilling expanded career roles, such as those of nurse practitioner, clinical nurse specialist, nurse midwife, nurse educator, and nurse researcher that allow greater independence and autonomy. See the accompanying box.

In Canada, the clinical nurse specialist (CNS) is a registered nurse who holds a master's or doctoral degree in

Selected Expanded Career Roles for Nurses

Nurse Practitioner

This is a nurse who has an advanced education and is a graduate of a nurse practitioner program.

Core Competencies

- Direct patient care focus, advanced assessments, appropriate diagnosis, and intervention skills
- Ability to work in a collaborative health-care delivery environment
- Make appropriate consultations and referrals; health promotion
- Ability to deal with multiple-system levels simultaneously
- Critical analysis of research literature and other forms of evidence
- Work to enhance the visibility and understanding of the nurse practitioner role

Clinical Nurse Specialist

The clinical nurse specialist has an advanced degree or expertise in a specialized area of practice (e.g., gerontology, oncology) and provides direct client care, educates others, consults, conducts research, and manages care.

Nurse Midwife

The nurse midwife is a registered nurse who has completed a program in midwifery and is certified. The nurse gives prenatal and postnatal care and manages deliveries in normal pregnancies. The midwife practises in association with a health-care agency and can obtain medical services if complications occur.

Nurse Researcher

Nurse researchers investigate nursing problems to improve nursing care and to refine and expand nursing knowledge. They are employed in academic institutions, teaching hospitals, and research centres. Nurse researchers usually have advanced education at the doctoral level.

Nurse Administrator

The nurse administrator manages client care, including the delivery of nursing service. The administrator may have a middle-management position, such as nurse manager or supervisor, or a more senior management position, such as director of nursing services. The functions of nurse administrators include budgeting, staffing, and planning programs. The educational preparation for nurse administrator positions is at least a baccalaureate degree in nursing and frequently a master's or doctoral degree.

Nurse Educator

Nurse educators are employed in nursing programs, at educational institutions, and in hospital staff education.

nursing with expertise in a clinical nursing specialty. An expert practitioner, the CNS provides direct care, education, and consultation to the health-care team. As health-care technology and the treatment of disease become increasingly complex, the demands upon nurses to provide complex care have also increased. This reality has created a trend toward specialization in nursing. The CNS nurse is prepared at the graduate level in a clinical specialty, such as mental health or cardiovascular nursing. These advanced practitioners provide expert care in complex client situations either through direct care or consultation. The CNS promotes excellence in nursing practice and acts as a role model.

There are five components of the CNS role. The balance of these components will vary in practice depending upon the needs of the clients and the setting. The CNS acts in the interrelated roles of practitioner, educator, consultant, researcher, and leader. As a *practitioner*, the CNS is prepared to assess and intervene in complex health-care problems within the selected clinical specialty and provides expert client care based upon an in-depth knowledge of nursing and other relevant sciences. The clients may be individuals, families, groups, or communities. The foundation of the CNS role is advanced clinical practice.

The focus of the *educator role* is clients and their families. The CNS also promotes a learning environment in the practice setting for nurses, students, and other health-care professionals and functions as a resource person, program planner, preceptor, teacher, and client educator. In the *consultant role*, the CNS shares specialized knowledge and provides consultation to clients, nurses, and other health-care professionals, health-care institutions, organizations, and policy makers. The CNS consults with others to improve client care and to deal with complex and challenging situations. The *research role* strengthens the link between clinical nursing and research. The CNS has expertise in research methodology, conducts nursing research, and participates in interdisciplinary research. The CNS encourages nurses to identify research questions, to participate in research, and to apply the findings to practice. In the *role of leader*, the CNS promotes quality care through the development of policies, standards of care, and clinical programs and services; directs nursing care activities, as well as plans, implements, and evaluates changes in clinical practice; and provides clinical leadership by acting as a resource, facilitator, coordinator, role model, and advocate (CNA, 1993b).

Nursing Profession

Nursing is gaining recognition as a profession. **Profession** has been defined as an occupation that requires extensive education or a calling that requires special knowledge, skill, and preparation. A profession is generally distinguished from other kinds of occupations by (1) its requirement of prolonged, specialized training to acquire a body of knowledge pertinent to the role to be performed, and (2) an orientation of the individual toward service, either to a community or to an organization. The standards of education and practice for the profession are determined by the members of the profession, rather than by outsiders. The education of the professional involves a complete socialization process, more far-reaching in its social and attitudinal aspects and its technical features than is usually required in other kinds of occupations.

Self-regulation is based on the belief that the profession of nursing has the special knowledge required to set standards of practice and to assess the conduct of its members through peer review. As members of the nursing profession, nurses are bound by the ethical values of the profession (Table 1.1) to base their practice on relevant and current knowledge. Although not all professional organizations use the same criteria for identifying a profession, most include that the profession holds its practitioners accountable; possesses a specialized body of knowledge; emphasizes the competent application of knowledge; abides by a code of ethics; has a tradition of service to the public; and engages in self-regulation (RNABC, 1999).

TABLE 1.1 Canadian Nurses Association Code of Ethics for Registered Nurses

The CNA Code of Ethics for Registered Nurses outlines the values that should guide Canadian nursing practice. Each value is accompanied by an itemized list of responsibilities. Values include:

- Safe, competent, and ethical care: Nurses value the ability to provide safe, competent, and ethical care that allows them to fulfill their ethical and professional obligations to the people they serve.
- Health and well-being: Nurses value health promotion and well-being and assisting persons to achieve their optimum level of health in situations of normal health, illness, injury, disability, or at the end of life.
- Choice: Nurses respect and promote the autonomy of persons and help them to express their health needs and values and also to obtain desired information and services so they can make informed decisions.
- Dignity: Nurses recognize and respect the inherent worth of each person and advocate for respectful treatment of all persons.
- Confidentiality: Nurses safeguard information learned in the context of a professional relationship, and ensure it is shared outside the health-care team only with the person's informed consent, or as may be legally required, or where the failure to disclose would cause significant harm.
- Justice: Nurses uphold principles of equity and fairness to assist persons in receiving a share of health services and resources proportionate to their needs and in the promotion of social justice.
- Accountability: Nurses are answerable for their practice, and they act in a manner consistent with their professional responsibilities and standards of practice.
- Quality practice environments: Nurses value and advocate for practice environments that have the organizational structures and resources necessary to ensure safety, support, and respect for all persons in the work setting.

Source: Reprinted with permission of Canadian Nurses Association. (2002). *Code of Ethics for Registered Nurses.* Ottawa: Author.

Criteria of a Profession

Specialized Education

Specialized education is an important aspect of professional status. In modern times, the trend in education for professions has shifted toward programs in colleges and universities. Many nursing educators believe that the undergraduate nursing curriculum should include liberal arts education in addition to the biological and social sciences and the nursing discipline.

The Canadian Nurses Association recommends the baccalaureate degree as the level of education required for entry to practice.

Specialized Body of Knowledge

As a profession, nursing is establishing a well-defined body of knowledge and expertise. A number of nursing conceptual frameworks (discussed in Chapter 4) contribute to the knowledge base of nursing and give direction to nursing practice, education, and ongoing research.

Increasing research in nursing is contributing to nursing practice. In the 1980s, increased federal funding and professional support helped establish centres for nursing research. Most early research was directed to the study of nursing education. In the 1960s, studies were often related to the nature of the knowledge base underlying nursing practice. Since the 1970s, nursing research has focused on practice-related issues. Nursing research as a dimension of the nurse's role is discussed further in Chapter 3.

Code of Ethics

Nurses have traditionally placed a high value on the worth and dignity of others. The nursing profession requires integrity of its members; that is, a member is expected to do what is considered right.

Ethical codes change as the needs and values of society change. Nursing has developed its own codes of ethics and, in most instances, has set up means to monitor the professional behaviour of its members. See Chapter 7 for additional information on ethics.

Autonomy

A profession is autonomous if it regulates itself and sets standards for its members. Providing autonomy is one of the purposes of a professional association. If nursing is to have professional status, it must function autonomously in the formation of policy and in the control of its activity. To be autonomous, a professional group must be granted legal authority to define the scope of its practice, describe its particular functions and roles, and determine its goals and responsibilities in delivery of its services.

To practitioners of nursing, autonomy means independence at work, responsibility, and accountability for one's actions.

Autonomy is more easily achieved and maintained from a position of authority. Therefore, some nurses seek administrative positions, rather than expanded clinical competence, as a means to ensure their autonomy in the workplace.

Service Orientation

A service orientation differentiates nursing from an occupation pursued primarily for profit. Many consider altruism (selfless concern for others) the hallmark of a profession. Nursing has a tradition of service to others. This service, however, must be guided by certain rules, policies, or codes of ethics. Today, nursing is also an important component of the health-care delivery system.

Professional Organization

Operation under the umbrella of a professional organization differentiates a profession from an occupation. In nursing, the CNA in Canada, in addition to the provincial/territorial nursing organizations, performs the self-regulatory functions.

Socialization to Nursing

Socialization can be defined simply as the process by which people (1) learn to become members of groups and society, and (2) learn the social rules defining relationships into which they will enter. Socialization involves learning to behave, feel, and see the world in a manner similar to other persons occupying the same role as oneself (Hardy & Conway, 1988). The goal of professional socialization is to instill in individuals the norms, values, attitudes, and behaviours deemed essential for the survival of the profession.

Various models of the socialization process have been developed. Benner's model (1984) describes five levels of proficiency in nursing based on the Dreyfus general model of skill acquisition. The five stages, which have implications for teaching and learning, are novice, advanced beginner, competent, proficient, and expert. Benner writes that experience is essential for the development of professional expertise. See the accompanying box.

One of the most powerful mechanisms of professional socialization is interaction with fellow students (Hardy & Conway, 1988). Within this student culture, students col-

Benner's Stages of Nursing Expertise

Stage I, Novice

No experience (e.g., nursing student). Performance is limited, inflexible, and governed by context-free rules and regulations, rather than experience.

Stage II, Advanced Beginner

Demonstrates marginally acceptable performance. Recognizes the meaningful "aspects" of a real situation. Has experienced enough real situations to make judgements about them.

Stage III, Competent Practitioner

Has two or three years of experience. Demonstrates organizational and planning abilities. Differentiates important factors from less important aspects of care. Coordinates multiple complex care demands.

Stage IV, Proficient Practitioner

Has three to five years of experience. Perceives a situation as a whole, rather than in terms of parts, as in Stage II. Uses maxims as guides for what to consider in a situation. Has holistic understanding of the client, which improves decision making. Focuses on long-term goals.

Stage V, Expert Practitioner

Performance is fluid, flexible, and highly proficient; no longer requires rules, guidelines, or maxims to connect an understanding of the situation to appropriate action. Demonstrates highly skilled intuitive and analytical abilities in new situations. Is inclined to take a certain action because "it feels right."

Source: *Novice to Expert: Excellence and Power in Clinical Nursing Practice,* by P. Benner, 1984, Menlo Park, CA: Addison-Wesley Nursing, p. 21–34. Reprinted with permission.

lectively set the level and direction of their scholastic efforts. They develop perspectives about the situation in which they are involved, the goals they are trying to achieve, and the kinds of activities that are expedient and proper, and they establish a set of practices congruent with all of these. Students become bound together by feelings of mutual cooperation, support, and solidarity.

Critical Values of Nursing

It is within the nursing educational program that the nurse develops, clarifies, and internalizes professional values. Specific professional nursing values are stated in nursing codes of ethics (see Chapter 7), in standards of nursing practice (discussed earlier in this chapter), and in the legal system itself (see Chapter 8). Values essential to the professional nurse have been identified and published by the CNA (see Table 1.1).

Factors Influencing Contemporary Nursing Practice

To understand nursing as it is practised today and as it will be practised tomorrow requires an understanding of some of the social forces currently influencing this profession. These forces usually affect the entire health-care system, and as a major component of that system, nursing cannot avoid the effects.

Economics

Greater financial support provided through public and private health insurance programs has increased the demand for nursing care. Health-care services, such as emergency room care, mental health counselling, and preventive physical examinations, are increasingly being used by people who could not afford them in the past.

These changes present challenges to nurses. Currently, the health-care industry is shifting its emphasis from inpatient care to outpatient care with pre-admission testing, increased outpatient same-day surgery, post-hospitalization rehabilitation, home health care, health maintenance, physical fitness programs, and community health education programs. As a result, more nurses are being employed in community-based health settings, such as home health agencies, hospices, and community clinics. These changes in employment for nurses have implications for nursing education, nursing research, and nursing practice.

Consumer Demands

Consumers of nursing services (the public) have become an increasingly effective force in changing nursing practice. On the whole, people are better educated and have more knowledge about health and illness than in the past. Consumers also have become more aware of others' needs for care. The ethical and moral issues raised by poverty and neglect have made people more vocal about the needs of minority groups and the poor.

The public's concepts of health and nursing have also changed. Most now believe that health is a right of all people, not just a privilege of the rich. The media emphasize the message that individuals must assume responsibility for their own health by obtaining a physical examination regularly, checking for the seven danger signals of cancer, and maintaining their mental well-being by balancing work and recreation. Interest in health and nursing services is therefore greater than ever. Furthermore, many people now want more than freedom from disease—they want energy, vitality, and a feeling of wellness.

Increasingly, the consumer has become an active participant in making decisions about health and nursing care. Planning committees concerned with providing nursing services to a community usually have active consumer membership. Recognizing the legitimacy of public input, many federal, provincial, and territorial nursing associations and regulatory agencies have consumer representatives on their governing boards.

Family Structure

New family structures are influencing the need for and provision of nursing services. More people are living away from the extended family and the nuclear family, and the family breadwinner is no longer necessarily the husband. Today, many single men and women rear children, and in many two-parent families, both parents work. It is also common for young parents to live at great distances from their own parents. These young families need support services, such as day-care centres. For additional information about the family, see Chapter 6.

Adolescent mothers also need specialized nursing services, both while they are pregnant and after their babies are born. These young mothers usually have the normal needs of teenagers as well as those of new mothers. Many teenage mothers are raising their children alone with little, if any, assistance from the child's father. This type of single-parent family is especially vulnerable because motherhood compounds the difficulties of adolescence. As well, because many of these families live in poverty, the infants often are at increased risk for nutritional and other health problems.

Science and Technology

Advances in science and technology affect nursing practice. For example, people with *acquired immune deficiency syndrome (AIDS)* are receiving new drug therapies to prolong life and delay the onset of AIDS-associated diseases. Nurses must be knowledgeable about the action of such drugs and the needs of clients receiving them. Nurses acquire knowledge and skills as they adapt to meet the new needs of clients.

In some settings, technological advances have required that nurses become highly specialized. Nurses frequently have to use sophisticated computerized equipment to provide care for clients. As technologies change, nursing education changes, and nurses require more advanced education to provide effective, safe nursing practice.

The space program has developed advanced technologies for space travel based on the need for long-distance monitoring of astronauts and spacecraft, lighter materials, and miniaturization of equipment. Health care has benefited as this new technology has been adapted in such health-care aids as Viewstar (an aid for the visually impaired), the insulin infusion pump, the voice-controlled wheelchair, magnetic resonance imaging, laser surgery, filtering devices for intravenous fluid control devices, and monitoring systems for intensive care.

Demography

Demography is the study of population, including statistics about distribution by age and place of residence, mortality (death), and morbidity (incidence of disease). From demographic data, needs of the population for nursing services can be assessed. For example:

- The total population in Canada is increasing. The proportion of older adults has also increased, creating a growing need for nursing services for this group.
- The population is shifting from rural to urban settings. This shift signals increased needs for nursing related to problems caused by pollution and other effects on the environment by concentrations of people.
- Mortality and morbidity studies reveal the presence of "risk factors." Many of these risk factors (e.g., smoking) are major causes of death and disease that can be prevented through changes in lifestyle. The nurse's role in assessing risk factors and helping clients make healthy lifestyle changes is discussed in Chapter 9.

The Women's Movement

The women's movement has brought public attention to human rights. People are seeking equality in all areas, particularly educational, political, economic, and social equality. Because the majority of nurses are women, this movement has altered nurses' perspectives on economic and educational needs. As a result, nurses are increasingly asserting themselves as professional people who have a right to equality with men in health professions and are demanding more autonomy in client care.

The women's movement has empowered nurses to identify "the commonality and interconnectedness of nurses' experiences as women and men and as health-care workers." This enables nurses to develop a greater sense of autonomy and group consciousness that can lead to greater empowerment and involvement in effective political action (Mason, Backer, & Georges, 1993, p. 107). Recently, because of research initiatives, a new concern for women's health has emerged.

Nursing Organizations

As nursing has developed, an increasing number of nursing organizations have been formed at the local, provincial/territorial, national, and international levels. The organizations that involve most Canadian nurses are the CNA, the International Council of Nurses (ICN), and the Canadian Nurse Specialists Association (CNSA). There are also an ever-increasing number of nursing specialty organizations, for example, the Canadian Association of Nurses in Oncology. Participation in the activities of nursing associations enhances the growth of involved individuals and helps nurses collectively influence policies affecting nursing practice.

Canadian Nurses Association

The CNA is a federation of 11 provincial and territorial nursing associations representing more than 110,000 registered nurses. The CNA's mission is to advance the quality of nursing in the interests of the public. Toward this end, it promotes high standards of practice, education, research, and administration.

The CNA is the national nursing association of Canada. Nurses do not join the CNA independently, but obtain membership by paying a fee to the provincial/territorial organizations. In November 1985, the Ordre des infirmières et infirmiers du Quebec (the Quebec Nurses Association) withdrew from the CNA.

The CNA has developed national standards and a code of ethics, and it offers support to all provincial/territorial organizations. Through the National Testing Services, the CNA prepares licensure examinations. These examinations are available to all provinces and territories and provide a national standard for licensure of registered nurses. Through the Canadian Nurses Foundation, research grants, fellowships, and scholarships are offered to Canadian nurses. The official journal of the CNA, *Canadian Nurse*, is published monthly and sent to each nurse member.

The CNA believes that the goal of health promotion must be to promote positive self-esteem of individuals, families, and communities; to help people understand the determinants of health; and to empower them to increase control over the determinants of health and well-being. The Association believes that nurses must be involved in research, planning, implementation, and evaluation of health promotion strategies in a variety of institutional and community settings (CNA, 2000).

International Council of Nurses

The ICN was established in 1899. Nurses from the United Kingdom, the United States, and Canada were among the founding members. The council is a federation of national nurses' associations, such as the the American Nurses Association (ANA) and the CNA. In 1993, 111 national nurses' associations representing 1.4 million nurses worldwide were affiliated with the ICN.

The ICN provides an organization through which member national associations can work together to promote the health of people and the care of the sick. The objectives of the ICN are (1) to improve the standards and status of nursing, (2) to promote the development of strong national nurses' associations, and (3) to serve as the authoritative voice for nurses and the nursing profession worldwide (Backus, 1990). The official journal of the ICN is *International Nursing Review.*

International Honour Society: Sigma Theta Tau

Sigma Theta Tau, the international honour society in nursing, was founded in 1922 and is headquartered in Indianapolis, Indiana. The Greek letters stand for the Greek words *storga, tharos,* and *tima,* meaning "love," "courage," and "honour." The society is a member of the association of college honour societies. The society's purpose is professional, rather than social. Membership is attained through academic achievement. Nursing students in baccalaureate programs and in master's, doctoral, and postdoctoral programs are eligible to be selected for membership.

The official journal of Sigma Theta Tau, *Image: Journal of Nursing Scholarship,* is published quarterly. The journal publishes scholarly articles of interest to nurses. The society also publishes *Reflections,* a quarterly newsletter that provides information about the organization and its various chapters.

CHAPTER HIGHLIGHTS

- Historical perspectives of nursing practice reveal recurring themes or influencing factors. For example, women have traditionally cared for others, but often in subservient roles. Religious orders left an imprint on nursing by instilling such values as compassion, devotion to duty, and hard work. Wars created an increased need for nurses and medical specialties. Societal attitudes have influenced nursing's image. Visionary leaders have made notable contributions to improve the status of nursing.
- There are many definitions and descriptions of nursing, but the essence of nursing is caring for and caring about people as holistic beings.
- The scope of nursing practice is outlined by the professional associations (or organizations) of each province and/or territory. It describes what it is that nurses in a particular province or territory have the legislated authority to do.
- Although traditionally the majority of nurses were employed in hospital settings, today the numbers of nurses working in home health care, ambulatory care, and community health settings are increasing.
- Nurse practice acts vary among provinces, and nurses are responsible for knowing the act that governs their practice.
- Standards of clinical nursing practice reflect the values of the profession and clarify what professional organizations expect of their members.
- Every nurse may function in a variety of roles that are not exclusive of one another; in reality, they often occur together and serve to clarify the nurse's activities. These roles include caregiver, communicator, teacher, client advocate, counsellor, change agent, leader, and research consumer.
- With advanced education and experience, nurses can fulfill advanced practice roles, such as clinical nurse specialist, nurse practitioner, midwife, educator, administrator, and researcher.
- A desired goal of nursing is professionalism, which necessitates specialized education; a unique body of knowledge, including specific skills and abilities; ongoing research; a code of ethics; autonomy; a service orientation; and a professional organization.
- Socialization is a lifelong process by which people become functioning participants of a society or a group. It is a reciprocal learning process that is brought about by interaction with other people and established boundaries of behaviour. Socialization to professional nursing practice is the process whereby the values and norms of the nursing profession are internalized into the nurse's own behaviour and self-concept. The nurse acquires the knowledge, skill, and attitudes characteristic of the profession.

- Although several models of the socialization process have been developed, Benner's five stages of novice, advanced beginner, competent, proficient, and expert may serve as guidelines to establish the phase and extent of an individual's socialization.
- Socialization for nursing requires the development of critical values, such as the provision of safe, competent care, confidentiality, choice, dignity, and accountability.
- Contemporary nursing practice is influenced by economics, changing demands for nurses, consumer demand, family structure, science and technology, legislation, demographic and social changes, the women's movement, collective bargaining, and the work of nursing associations.
- Both professional and non-professional nursing organizations and associations fulfill essential functions for the nursing profession and for individual nurses.
- Participation in the activities of nursing associations enhances the growth of involved individuals and helps nurses collectively influence policies affecting nursing practice.

READINGS AND REFERENCES

Suggested Readings

Allemang, M. (1995). The development of community health nursing in Canada. In M. Stewart (Ed.), *Community nursing: Promoting Canadian's health* (pp. 2–36). Toronto: W.B. Saunders.
The author provides a historical overview of the development of community health nursing in Canada with specific focus on the evolution of health promotion as central to community nursing practice.

Bishop, A. H. (1997, March/April). Nursing as a practice rather than an art or a science. *Nursing Outlook, 45*, 82–85.
The authors write that nursing cannot be strictly called a science or an art but it does involve science and the art of nursing. They state that having a dominant moral sense is a characteristic of a practice and nursing is a practice in that it intends to encourage healing and wellness.

Canadian Nurses Association. (1988). *Health for All Canadians: A Call for Health-Care Reform.* Ottawa: CNA.
Authors appeal to the Canadian Government for the reform of the Canadian health-care system to support the tenets of the Canada Health Act. (1986). *Achieving Health for All: A Framework for Health Promotion.* Ottawa: Health and Welfare Canada.
The authors offer a framework for health promotion that could provide health care for all Canadians through a change in focus from illness care to health promotion.

Kerr, J. R. (1998). *Prepared to care: Nurses and nursing in Alberta, 1859-1996.* Edmonton: University of Alberta.
The author provides a historical overview of nursing, nursing education, health, and medical care in Alberta. This author highlights how nurses have been central to the development of health care and to the growth of hospitals from the early settlement of Alberta.

Laskowski-Jones, L. (1998, September). Reaching beyond the rules. Understanding—and influencing—your scope of practice. *Nursing, 98, 28* (9), 42–45.
Laskowski-Jones outlines the hierarchy of authorities that make the rules governing nursing practice. In her experience, few nurses understand the bodies that make these rules, where they are located, and how to make inquiries for the purpose of initiating change, if appropriate. A table outlines the four sources of practice rules, examples of issues covered, where rules are documented, and how to initiate change. She uses a clinical example of manipulating a pulmonary artery catheter to explain how nurses can function as change agents.

World Health Organization. (1987). *Primary Health Care: Report of the International Conference on Primary Health Care.* Alma-Ata, USSR. Geneva: WHO.
Report of the meeting in Alma-Ata, September 12, 1978, expressing the need for urgent action by all governments, all health and development workers, and the world community to protect and promote the health of all the people of the world. The Conference strongly reaffirmed that health, which is a state of complete physical, mental and social well-being, and not merely the absence of disease or infirmity, is a fundamental human right and that the attainment of the highest possible level of health is a most important world wide social goal whose realization requires the action of many other social and economic sectors in addition to the health sector.

Selected References

Aiken, L., & Fagin, C. (1992). *Charting nursing's future: Agenda for the 1990s.* Philadelphia: Lippincott.

Anspaugh, D. J., Hamrick, M. H., & Rosata, F. D. (1991). *Wellness: Concepts and applications.* St. Louis: Mosby Year Book.

Backus, K. (1990). *Medical and health information directory* (5th ed.). Vol. 1: *Organizations, Agencies, and Institutions.* Detroit: Gale Research.

Benner, P. (1984). *From novice to expert: Excellence and power in clinical nursing practice.* Menlo Park, CA: Addison-Wesley Nursing.

Boykin, A., & Schoenhofer, S. (1993). *Nursing as caring: A model for transforming practice.* New York: NLN.

Calkin, J. D. (1992). Specialization issues. In A. J. Baumgart & J. Larsen (Eds.), *Canadian nursing faces the future* (2nd ed.). (pp. 327–342). Toronto: Mosby.

Canadian Nurses Association. (1987). *A definition of nursing practice: Standards for nursing practice.* Ottawa: Author.

Chitty, K. K. (1993). *Professional nursing: Concepts and challenges.* Philadelphia: Saunders.

CNA. (2001). Issues and trends in Canadian nursing: Self-regulation: safeguarding the privilege. *Nursing Now, 10*, 5–8.

CNA. (2000). Fact Sheet: "The primary health care approach." Ottawa, ON: Author.

CNA. (1995). *The Role of the Nurse in Primary Health Care.* Ottawa, ON: Author.

CNA. (1993a). Chief Executive Nurse. Ottawa, ON: Author.

CNA. (1993b). Policy Statement: "Clinical Nurse Specialist." Ottawa, ON: Author.

CNA Connection. (1984, April). Canada Health Act: CNA appears before Commons committee. *Canadian Nurse, 80*, 8–9.

D'Anonio, P. (1999). Revisiting and rethinking the rewriting of nursing history. *Bulletin of the History of Medicine, 73*, 268–290.

Davies, C. (1996, November 13). A new vision of professionalism. *Nursing Times, 92*(46), 54–56.

Davies, C. (Ed.). (1980). *Rewriting nursing history.* London: Croom Helm.

Dickens, C. (1896). *Martin Chuzzlewit.* Boston: Estes and Lauriat.

Dolan, J. A., Fitzpatrick, M. L., & Herrmann, E. K. (1983). *Nursing in society: A historical perspective* (15th ed.). Philadelphia: Saunders.

Dreyfus, S. E., & Dreyfus, H. L. (1980, February). A five-stage model of the mental activities involved in directed skill acquisition. [Unpublished report supported by the Air Force Office of Scientific Research (AFSC), USAF (Contract F49620-79-C-0063)], University of California at Berkeley.

Halldórsdóttir, S., & Hamrin, E. (1997). Caring and uncaring encounters within nursing and health care from the cancer patient's perspective. *Cancer Nursing, 20*, 120–128.

Hamilton, P. M. (1996). *Realities of contemporary nursing* (2nd ed.). Menlo Park, CA: Addison-Wesley.

Hamric, A. B., & Spross, J. A. (1989). *The clinical nurse specialist in theory and practice* (2nd ed.). Philadelphia & Toronto: W.B. Saunders.

Hardy, M. E., & Conway, M. E. (1988). *Role theory: Perspectives for healthy professionals* (2nd ed.). Norwalk, CT: Appleton & Lange.

Henderson, V. (1966). *The nature of nursing: A definition and its implications for practice, research, and education.* New York: Macmillan.

Innes, J. (1987, September). Primary Health Care in Perspective. *Canadian Nurse/L'infirmiere canadienne.*

International Council of Nurses. (1988). *Nursing and primary health care: A unified force.* Geneva: ICN.

Kelly, L. Y., & Joel, L. A. (1995). *Dimensions of professional nursing* (7th ed.). New York: McGraw-Hill.

Kerr, J. R. (1998). *Prepared to care: Nurses and nursing in Alberta, 1859–1996.* Edmonton: U of A Press.

Kitson, A. L. (1997, Second Quarter). Johns Hopkins address: Does nursing have a future? *Image: Journal of Nursing Scholarship, 29*, 111–115.

Kowalski, K., Burton, L., & Rehwaldt, M. (1997, September/October). Revisioning, re-educating, regenerating, and recommitting nursing for the twenty-first century. *Nursing Outlook, 45*, 220–223.

Lagemann, E. (Ed.). (1983). *Nursing history: New perspectives, new possibilities.* New York: Teachers College Press.

Leininger, M. (1984). *Care: The essence of nursing and health.* Thorofare, NJ: Slack.

Mangold, A. (1991, March). Senior nursing students and professional nurses' perceptions of effective caring behaviors: A comparative study. *Journal of Nursing Education, 30*, 134–139.

Mason, D. J., Backer, B. A., & Georges, C. A. (1993, Spring). Feminism and nursing: Toward a feminist model for the political empowerment of nurses. *Revolution: The Journal of Nurse Empowerment, 3*, 62–65, 68, 70–71, 106–107.

McPherson, K. (1996). *Bedside matters: The transformation of Canadian nursing, 1900–1990.* Toronto: Oxford University Press.

McPherson, K., & Stuart, M. (1994). Writing nursing history in Canada: Issues and approaches. *Canadian Bulletin of Medical History, 11*, 3–22.

Melosh, B. (1982). *"The physician's hand": Work, culture, and conflict in American nursing.* Philadelphia: Temple University Press.

Miller, K. L. (1995). Keeping the care in nursing care: Our biggest challenge. *JONA, 25*(11), 29–32.

Nightingale, F. (1860). *Notes on nursing: What it is, and what it is not.* Commemorative Edition. Philadelphia: Lippincott.

Noddings, N. (1984). *Caring: A feminine approach to ethics and moral education.* Berkeley, CA: University of California Press.

Phillips, P. (1993). A deconstruction of caring. *Journal of Advanced Nursing, 18*, 1554–1558.

Rafferty, A., Robinson, J., & Elkan, R. (Eds.). (1997). *Nursing history and the politics of welfare.* London: Routledge.

Registered Nurses Association of British Columbia. (1990, May). *Primary Health Care: A Discussion Paper* (p. 2). Vancouver: RNABC.

Registered Nurses Association of British Columbia. (1994). *Position statement on the clinical nurse specialist.* Vancouver: RNABC.

Registered Nurses Association of Nova Scotia. (1991). *Position statement on advanced nursing practice.* Dartmouth: RNANS.

Registered Nurses Association of British Columbia. (1999). *Nursing Self-Regulation; Nurses Governing Nurses in the Public Interest.* Vancouver, B.C.: Author.

Reverby, S. (1987). *Ordered to care: the dilemmas of American nursing, 1850–1945.* London: Cambridge University Press.

Schuyler, C. B. (1992). Florence Nightingale. In F. Nightingale, *Notes on nursing: What it is, and what it is not* (pp. 3–17). Commemorative Edition. Philadelphia: Lippincott.

Stuart, M. (1994). Shifting professional boundaries: Gender conflict in public health, 1920–1925. In D. Dodd & D. Gorham (Eds.), *Caring and curing: Historical perspectives on women and healing in Canada* (pp. 49–70). Ottawa: University of Ottawa Press.

Stuart, M. (1999). War and peace: Professional identities and nurses' training, 1914–1930. In E. Smyth, S. Acker, P. Bourne, & A. Prentice (Eds.), *Challenging professions: Historical and contemporary perspectives on women's professions* (pp. 171–193). Toronto: U of T Press.

Styles, M. M. (1983). The anatomy of a profession. *Heart and Lung, 12*, 570–575.

The New Lexicon Webster's Dictionary of the English Language, S.V. "nursing."

Tracy, J., Samarel, N., & DeYoung, S. (1995, April). Professional role development in baccalaureate nursing education. *Journal of Nursing Education, 34*, 180–182.

World Health Organization, Division of Health Manpower Development. (1982). Report of a meeting on "Nursing in support of the goal Health for All by the Year 2000", 16-20 November, 1981. Geneva: WHO.

Wuest, J. (1994, November/December). Professionalism and the evolution of nursing as a discipline: A feminist perspective. *Journal of Professional Nursing, 10*, 357–367.

Zerwekh, J., & Claborn, J. C. (1997). *Nursing today: Transition and trends* (2nd ed.). Philadelphia: Saunders.

WEBLINKS

Canadian Nurses Association
http://www.cna-nurses.ca
The Canadian Nurses Association is a federation of 11 provincial and territorial nursing associations representing more than 110,000 registered nurses. The CNA Web site includes multiple resources including online publications that support its vision of registered nurses collectively contributing to the health of Canadians and the advancement of nursing. The CNA's mission is to advance the quality of nursing in the interest of the public.

Canadian Nursing Index
http://www.nursingindex.com
The Canadian Nursing Index is your Canadian guide to nursing resources on the Internet. This site will be of interest to staff nurses, nurse managers, nurse educators, nurse researchers and nursing students. The site includes links to special areas of interest to nurses.

Ordre des infirmières et infirmiers du Québec
http://www.oiiq.org/
The Web site for a consortium of professional and educational organizations of interest to Quebec nurses and/or French-speaking nurses.

Canadian Association for the History of Nursing (CAHN)
http://www.ualberta.ca/jhibberd
This Web site was established by CAHN and is an excellent resource for those interested in the promotion of interest in the history of nursing and to developing scholarship in the field. CAHN promotes the preservation of historical nursing materials; hosts forums for discussion of nursing history; supports innovations in teaching nursing history; advances historical research; and is an affiliate group of the Canadian Nurses Association.

CHAPTER 2

Nursing Education in Canada

OBJECTIVES

After completing this chapter, you will be able to:

- Describe the different types of educational nursing programs.
- Identify aspects of the baccalaureate level for entry to professional nursing practice.
- Explain the importance of continuing nursing education.
- Describe the role of national nursing associations in shaping nursing education in Canada.
- Analyze issues influencing nursing education in Canada.

Nursing education is controlled from within the profession through provincial organizations of nursing and national accrediting bodies. The traditional focus of nursing education was to teach the knowledge and skills to enable the nurse to practise in the hospital setting.

In Canada, the first training program for nurses was offered at the General and Marine Hospital in St. Catharines, Ontario. It became the norm that hospitals had their own schools of nursing. The training programs of the 1920s, 1930s, and the 1940s were characterized by limited coordination of classroom and clinical teaching, long hours, night duty without supervision, and numerous housekeeping chores (Baumgart & Larsen, 1992). The medical staff and the nursing supervisors did the instruction.

Today, as nursing responds to new scientific knowledge and technological, cultural, political, and socioeconomic changes in society, nursing education curricula are continually being revised to meet the needs of nurses working in a changing environment. Programs of nursing study are increasingly based on a broad knowledge of biological, social, and physical sciences as well as the liberal arts and humanities. Nursing curricula now have a greater focus on critical thinking and the application of nursing and supporting knowledge to health promotion, health maintenance, and health restoration as provided in college and university settings.

Nursing Education

At the present time, provincial laws in Canada recognize three types of nurses: the *registered nurse (RN), the licensed practical nurse (LPN)*, and the *registered psychiatric nurse (RPN)*. These designations have been used since licensure laws were first enacted. Responsibilities differ for the three levels.

Currently, there are two *major* educational routes leading to RN licensure: diploma and baccalaureate programs. There are also *generic* master's and doctoral programs leading to RN licensure. For example, the students entering a generic master's program already have a baccalaureate degree from a discipline other than nursing. Upon completion of the program, generally two years in length, the graduates obtain their initial professional degree in nursing. Graduates of these master's programs demonstrate the same entry-level competencies as do graduates from baccalaureate programs and are eligible to take the licensure examinations to become RNs.

In Canada, nursing education is offered through colleges, which are non–degree-granting institutions whose mandate varies across the provinces, and through universities. Universities offer BN and BScN degree education at the undergraduate level. There are currently 32 university baccalaureate degrees, as identified by the **Canadian Nurses Association (CNA)** in their listing of nursing programs in Canada, and 25 colleges offering degrees in partnerships with universities. In addition, there are 70 colleges providing diploma education, many of which are in Quebec. In some provinces, such as Ontario, polytechnical institutes can provide undergraduate degrees.

Although all of these RN programs may vary, graduates of all programs take the same licensing examinations and, if successful, are licensed as registered nurses. The Canadian Nurses Registration Licensure Examination (RN Exam) is a criterion-referenced, multiple-choice test and results are reported to candidates as pass or fail. In Canada, except for Quebec, graduates take the RN Exam in either French or English. These national examinations are administered by the provincial/territorial regulatory authorities. The successful candidate becomes licensed in that province, even though the examinations are of national origin. To practise nursing in another province, the nurse must receive reciprocal licensure by applying to that province's or territory's professional association. Nurses from other countries are granted registration after successfully completing these examinations. Both licensure and registration must be renewed on an annual basis to remain valid.

The legal right to practise nursing requires not only a passing grade in licensing examinations but also verification that the graduate has completed a prescribed course of study from an approved program in nursing.

Minimum standards for basic nursing education are established in each province and monitored by the provincial nursing associations (or the College of Nurses in Ontario). Schools that meet these minimum standards are granted provincial approval. In addition to provincial approval in Canada, the Canadian Association of Schools of Nursing (CASN) grants accreditation that is concerned with optimum, rather than minimum, standards.

In 2001, there were 252,913 registered nurses in Canada. Of these, 231,512 (91.5 percent) were practising registered nurses.

The highest level of education in nursing reported by all registered nurses was:

74.2%	Diploma
24.0%	Baccalaureate
1.7%	Master's
0.1%	Doctorate

Source: Nursing Policy Division, CNA, June 2002. Reprinted with permission from the Canadian Nurses Association.

Types of Educational Programs

Hospital Diploma Programs

After Florence Nightingale established the school of nursing (the Nightingale Training School for Nurses) at St. Thomas's Hospital in England in 1860, the concept travelled quickly to North America. Hospital administrators welcomed the idea of training schools as a source of free or inexpensive staffing for the hospital. Nursing education in the early years largely took the form of apprenticeships. With little formal classroom instruction, students learned by doing, that is, by providing care to clients in hospitals. There was no standardization of curriculum and no accreditation. Programs were designed to meet the service needs of the hospital, not the educational needs of the students.

In Canada, The Mack Training School at the General and Marine Hospital in St. Catharines, Ontario, opened in 1874 as the first Canadian school of nursing patterned after the Nightingale school. The number of diploma programs rose quickly after these initial programs.

College Diploma Programs

Mussalem (1960) identified the problems in hospital-based diploma programs in nursing caused by the hospital's control over education. Students were used as the primary service providers, and their education was controlled by the hospital. Community college nursing education programs began to appear in the 1960s, also offering diploma preparation. It was not until the mid-1970s that most diploma nursing programs had moved into community colleges (Baumgart & Larsen, 1992). Today, the majority of colleges are in partnership with universities to provide a common curriculum leading to a baccalaureate degree in nursing.

Baccalaureate Degree Programs

In 1919, the first baccalaureate degree program in nursing in the British Empire was established at the University of British Columbia in Vancouver, Canada (Street, 1973). With the establishment of this program, nursing moved into the university sector. Baccalaureate education is an efficient way of providing each graduate with the wide range of knowledge and skills required for professional nursing practice. Undergraduate preparation also gives each nurse the foundation and flexibility for pursuing increased employment responsibility, promotion, and graduate study (CNA, 1993). The 1950s saw the greatest expansion of university schools of nursing. Students enrolled in the university for one year for non-nursing courses and then moved to a hospital-based model for the practical experience. A fifth year at the university completed what was labelled a "sandwich" program. The university had control over the academic courses and awarded the degree, while the hospital monitored the clinical practice of the nursing student.

In 1932, the CNA and the Canadian Medical Association (CMA) commissioned Dr. George Weir to conduct a study of nursing education in Canada. He found that education was secondary to hospital service as a priority in the schools. Dr. Weir recommended, in the *Survey of Nursing Education in Canada*, that nurses be given a liberal education in addition to a technical one and that university training programs award degrees. Today, universities and colleges have control over all components of education, and nursing students receive a liberal education combined with a professional one. The majority of these programs are four academic years in length, an academic year being eight calendar months. Many educational institutions offer students the opportunity for accelerated completion of the program. Requirements for university admission include a high-school diploma with specific prerequisites.

It was not until the 1960s that the number of students enrolled in these baccalaureate programs increased markedly. The curricula offer courses in the liberal arts, sciences, humanities, and nursing. Graduates must fulfill both the degree requirements of the college or university and the nursing program before being awarded a baccalaureate degree. The usual degree awarded is a bachelor of science in nursing (BScN) or a BN.

Most baccalaureate programs also admit registered nurses who have diplomas. Some programs have special curricula to meet the needs of these students. Some universities also offer nursing students the opportunity to pursue a self-paced or independent study program. Many programs offer online courses which can be accessed by nursing students. Many accept transfer credits from other accredited colleges and universities and offer students the opportunity to take challenge examinations when the students believe they have the knowledge or skills taught in a course. These programs are referred to as BScN completion, BSN transition, 2 + 2, or post-diploma programs.

Because of changes in the practice environment, the nurse who holds a baccalaureate degree is beginning to reap the rewards of greater autonomy, responsibility, participation in institutional decision making, and career advancement. These changes provide an incentive for nurses with diplomas to continue their formal preparation in baccalaureate completion (transition) programs.

Graduate Nursing Education

Most graduate programs are conducted by departments within the graduate school of a university, and the applicant must first meet requirements established by the graduate school. Although graduate schools differ, common requirements for admission to graduate programs in nursing include the following:

- The applicant must be a registered nurse and licensed or eligible for licensure within the program's province or territory.
- The applicant generally must hold a baccalaureate degree in nursing from an approved university.

FOCUS ON CRITICAL THINKING

The number of nurses with a baccalaureate degree in Canada is increasing; however, this number remains small compared with those nurses who hold a diploma. There is also an increase in the number of nurses holding Master's and Doctoral degrees in nursing. May is 23 years old and has been in the general workforce since high school. She is thinking about becoming a registered nurse. As part of her decision making, she has researched both diploma and university programs.

1. Identify the major components of basic nursing education that will prepare graduates to work as registered nurses. Provide reasons for your answer.
2. Explain why the Canadian Nurses Association has recommended the baccalaureate degree as entry level for professional practice.
3. Identify the difference between an undergraduate and graduate degree in nursing.

See Appendix A for answers to these questions.

- The applicant must give evidence of scholastic ability.
- Letters of recommendation from supervisors, nursing faculty, or nursing colleagues indicating the applicant's ability to do graduate study are required.

Master's Programs

The growth of university nursing programs encouraged the development of graduate study in nursing. In Canada, the first master's program in nursing was established at the University of Western Ontario in London in 1959. This was followed by a program at McGill University in Montreal in 1961.

Today, master's programs generally take from one and a half to two years to complete. Degrees granted are the Master of Arts (MA), Master in Nursing (MN), Master of Science in Nursing (MSN), and Master of Science (MS).

Master's degree programs provide specialized knowledge and skills that enable nurses to assume advanced roles in practice, education, administration, and research.

Doctoral Programs

Doctorally and post-doctorally prepared nurses are needed in both academic and practice settings to educate nurses at the baccalaureate and master's levels. The number of these programs is increasing in Canada. One of the primary benefits of doctorally prepared nurses is that they can undertake research, which advances nursing knowledge and evidence-based practice. As of 1996, less than 0.1 percent of registered nurses reported being educated at the doctorate level and even less at the post-doctoral level. Until recently, nurses were limited in their choice of doctoral programs in nursing and many completed a Doctor of Philosophy (PhD) degree in other disciplines, such as sociology or education. Doctoral programs in nursing, which award PhDs, began in the 1960s in the United States. These programs further prepare the nurse for advanced clinical practice, administration, education, and research. Today, doctoral education for nurses within their own discipline is available at Canadian universities.

Content and approach vary among doctoral programs. Some focus on the usual clinical areas, such as medical-surgical nursing, and others emphasize such non-traditional areas as transcultural nursing. Some programs emphasize theory development, but all emphasize research.

Licensed Practical Nursing Programs

Approved practical nursing programs are provided by community colleges, vocational schools, hospitals, or other independent health agencies. These programs are usually 10 to 24 months in length and provide both classroom and clinical experiences. Licensed practical nurses (LPNs) are autonomous practitioners who care for clients with less complex needs and more predictable outcomes. They work in collaboration with the registered nurse (RN) and other members of the health team. Licensed practical nurses are employed in a variety of settings including hospitals, nursing homes, rehabilitation centres, doctors' offices, and home health agencies.

In Canada, LPNs are also referred to as registered practical nurses (RPNs).

Nursing Associations and Their Influence upon Education

Several national nursing associations have influenced nursing education in Canada through their funding of research, pilot education projects, and policy development.

Canadian Nurses Association

The CNA has influenced nursing education in Canada in several key areas. Its co-sponsorship of the Weir report is one example. In addition, in 1948, the CNA, with financing from the Red Cross, established the Metropolitan School of Nursing in Windsor, Ontario. This demonstration school was Canada's first independent school of nursing, separated financially and physically from the hospital. This pioneer project led to the establishment of the first nursing education program in an educational setting in Canada at the Ryerson Institute of Technology in 1963. The growth of similar independent schools of nursing in Canada was delayed until the community college was developed in the 1970s and 1980s.

Another influence of the CNA on nursing education is **certification,** which is a voluntary and periodic process (recertification) by which an organized speciality group verifies that a registered nurse has demonstrated competence in a nursing specialty by having met identified standards of that specialty. Certification was initiated by a CNA membership request in June 1980 through a biennial resolution that directed the Board of Directors to study the feasibility of developing examinations for certification in major nursing specialities. In 1982, the Board of Directors adopted a policy in accreditation in nursing as well as a recommendation that the CNA promote the development of certification in nursing specialities (CNA, 1982). The first certification was offered in occupational health nursing. Currently, certification is offered in 12 specialty areas, including neuroscience, occupational health, nephrology, emergency care, critical care, psychiatric/mental health, perioperative care, oncology, gerontology, perinatal care, critical care–pediatrics, and cardiovascular nursing. In 2004, certification will be offered in palliative care and gastroenterology.

The purpose of certification is threefold:

1. To promote excellence in nursing care for the people of Canada through the establishment of national standards of practice in nursing specialty areas
2. To provide an opportunity for practitioners to confirm their competence in a specialty
3. To identify, through a recognized credential, those nurses meeting the national standards of their specialty

The Canadian Association of Schools of Nursing

In 1957, the Canadian Association of Schools of Nursing (CASN) published *Desirable General Standards for Canadian University Schools of Nursing*. At the time, there were few standards in place to guide the curricula of degree programs. Since then, university schools of nursing have initiated a national program of voluntary accreditation through the CASN. More recently, some provincial nursing associations have been legislated to approve new nursing programs, such as in Alberta.

The goals of the CASN are:

1. Canadian nursing education will work in partnership with other stakeholders as a positive force in the renewal of the Canadian health-care system.
2. Nursing will be seen as a desirable career choice.
3. Canadian nursing education will have full funding and infrastructure support.
4. Canada will have sufficient numbers of well-prepared nurse educators.
5. Canadian nursing education leaders will be among those nursing leaders involved in policy discussions and decisions that affect the profession and the education of nurses.

Issues Facing Nursing Education

Nursing education is facing a number of formidable and complex issues, partly because of changes that are generally occurring within Canadian society and education that have implications for professional nursing practice. Nurses must be knowledgeable about both the changes and the issues facing education. They must be able to use critical thinking skills to dialogue about these issues so that they can actively engage in addressing them, for their resolution will help to shape the nursing profession.

Changes in Health-Care Needs

There are shifts occurring within health care in Canada today. One is the shift away from acute-care services toward primary health care. The second is the shift toward community care, including home-care services, for clients. Clients are being discharged from hospital with higher acuity levels and more complex care needs. A third shift is the aging of the Canadian population. Partly because of these shifts, nurses are involved in new roles, such as case manager, program manager, or community developer. These new roles are in addition to the administrative functions that many nurses are currently performing, such as participating on boards, chairing committees, and preparing budgets. These shifts influence the content of nursing education programs, for students require skills to support these roles.

Entry to Practice

In 1982, the CNA approved the following policy statement in regard to future educational requirements for Registered Nurses:

> *The Canadian Nurses Association believes that by the year 2000 the minimum educational requirement for entry into the practice of nursing should be the successful completion of a baccalaureate degree in nursing.*

Their position was based on an examination of the future health needs of the country and the type of nursing services that would be required to meet them. Nurses' associations in every province and territory supported this policy. As the requirement changes, diploma graduates who are already practising will be able to continue without mandatory upgrading.

In 1991, Premier McKenna of New Brunswick became the first premier to commit his government to support the baccalaureate degree as entry point into nursing by the year 2000. The following year, 1992, Prince Edward Island became the first province to achieve the goal of a baccalaureate degree as the minimal level of entry into nursing. However, in March 2000, Manitoba's government announced a 23-month diploma program as part of their five-point plan to address the nursing shortage. This move was in direct opposition to the CNA entry-to-practice position. A month earlier, Saskatchewan nurses saw a compromise reached between the provincial government, the Saskatchewan Registered Nursing Association (SRNA), and the Nursing Education Program of Saskatchewan (NEPS) that protected the nursing degree but offered options regarding accelerated completion of the nursing program. There had been strong protests from RNs and nursing students over the provincial government's plan to restore diploma education as the entry-level requirement. As of January 1, 2005, in Ontario, all initial RNs will require a four-year baccalaureate degree in nursing.

A Shortage Crisis

The number of places for nursing students in educational facilities across Canada has risen slightly in recent years, yet the number of graduates remains inadequate to replace those nurses who are leaving the profession and to meet the health needs of clients. The number of nursing graduates peaked in the early 1970s and has substantively decreased since then. In 1971, there were 10,058 graduates from basic nursing programs; by 1998, there were only 5,302. By the end of 2001, the CNA estimated that 3,564 graduates would write the Canadian Registered Nurse Examination, and about a 1,000 more will write the Quebec registration exam. The number of graduates remains low.

There are a number of initiatives that are addressing this trend. The CNA assumed a lead role with other nursing and non-nursing groups as the secretariat of the study entitled, *The Nursing Labour Market in Canada: An Occupational Sector Study* (CNA, 1999). The goal of the study was to produce an integrated labour market strategy for the three regulated occupational groups in Canada (licensed practical nurses, registered psychiatric nurses, and registered nurses). Another initiative announced in 2000 was the National Nursing Forum. The Forum is an annual brainstorming session that permits nursing leaders from across the country to examine current issues and articulate strategies to address them.

Changing Demographics in Nursing Programs

Student populations in nursing programs are changing. There is a growth in program enrolment of non-traditional students, including older students, male students, and students with disabilities. In addition, more students are working throughout their programs to obtain the funds required for tuition and living expenses. These changes mean that nurse educators have to address the needs of a different group of learners, and nursing programs will have to continue to change. More options are being explored that permit part-time study and allow students to work while attending school. Many programs are now offering online courses as an alternative to traditional modes of learning.

Until recently, few aboriginal people from Northern Canada entered the nursing profession. To provide for Inuit nurses, Nunavut Arctic College in Iqaluit and the School of Nursing at Dalhousie University collaborated on a four-year baccalaureate program. The program admitted its first class of Inuit students in October 1999.

The average age of nurse educators in Canada is moving toward retirement, and active efforts to recruit more are underway. There are serious questions being asked of nursing programs as to where they will recruit future faculty members and how they will be prepared to teach.

Technological Advancements

The growth of technology is influencing nursing education. Advances in Web-based technology and computer-assisted instruction offer the potential for flexible, self-directed, interactive learning activities for students in on-site nursing programs. Computer-mediated distance education also makes it possible for nursing programs to offer courses over a large geographic area through the use of a computer network or the Internet. This method is a relative newcomer to nursing education. Some programs may also include video conferencing and other means of distance learning. For nurses who already hold a degree, computer-mediated instruction supports continuing education opportunities.

Continuing Education to Maintain Competency

To provide competent nursing care, a registered nurse must continuously enhance the knowledge, skills, and critical thinking required to meet client needs in a changing health-care system. Continuing education is a strategy to achieve this goal. The CNA interprets continuing nursing education as consisting of planned learning experiences undertaken following a basic nursing education. Acknowledging the need to ensure safe practice, the CNA published *A National Framework for Continuing Competency Programs for Registered Nurses* in September of 2000. The framework represents a consensus of nursing regulatory bodies in all provinces, including Quebec.

Canadian Society Notes

Fact	Implications for Nursing Practice
The baccalaureate requirement as entry-to-practice has been adopted throughout Canada by all provincial and territorial nurses' associations.	Students and registered nurses need to be aware that more career opportunities and graduate study will be open to those with a baccalaureate degree in nursing.
Nurses in Canada can obtain a PhD within their discipline at a number of Canadian universities.	PhD preparation supports nurses becoming educators and researchers by providing the theoretical knowledge and the practical experience for the roles.
Nursing specialty certification is offered through the CNA certification program.	Employment and personal satisfaction at work may be supported by certification.

Continuing education is the responsibility of each practising nurse. The CNA advocates the voluntary participation of nurses in continuing education in which they select learning activities based on their own experiences, learning styles, and practice requirements. Constant updating and growth are essential to keep abreast of scientific and technological changes as well as changes within the nursing profession. A variety of educational and health-care institutions conduct continuing education programs. They are usually designed to meet one or more of the following needs: (1) to keep nurses abreast of new techniques and knowledge; (2) to help nurses attain expertise in a specialized area of practice, such as intensive care nursing; and (3) to provide nurses with information essential to nursing practice, for example, knowledge about the legal aspects of nursing.

Mandatory versus voluntary continuing education has been a topic of interest to practising nurses, educators, administrators, professional and regulatory associations and unions, and governments.

Educational Support for Competent Nursing Practice

The competence of registered nurses is an essential element of safe and quality nursing practice. Competence is one of the main aspects to consider when evaluating quality of care (Canadian Council on Health Services Accreditation). To practise safely and competently, registered nurses comply with professional standards, base their practice on relevant knowledge, and, in adherence with the *Code of Ethics for Registered Nurses*, acquire new skills and knowledge in their area of practice on a continuing basis.

Provincial/territorial associations are currently at various stages of development in their continuing competency programs. To date, none of the regulatory bodies in Canada has specific education requirements for practising registered nurses. Nurses do maintain records of participation in continuing education for purposes of maintaining specialty certification, and in British Columbia, Alberta, and Ontario, for continuing competency programs.

In-Service Education

An **in-service education** program is administered by an employer; it is designed to upgrade the knowledge or skills of employees. For example, an employer might offer an in-service program to inform nurses about a new piece of equipment, about specific isolation practices, or about methods of implementing a nurse theorist's conceptual framework for nursing. Some in-service programs are mandatory, such as cardiopulmonary resuscitation and fire safety programs.

In-Service Programs

- May address client needs and emerging trends
- Usually conducted within a facility
- Attendance may be mandatory

CHAPTER HIGHLIGHTS

- Nursing education has changed dramatically since the mid-1800s. Early apprenticeship programs established in the 1800s were designed to meet the service needs of the hospital, not the educational needs of the students. Today, nursing education is provided primarily in college and university settings independent of hospitals' needs—a concept proposed by Florence Nightingale.
- Although baccalaureate programs began in the early 1900s, baccalaureate education began to take hold only after the release of the Weir report. Master's and doctoral programs in nursing grew significantly in the latter part of the 20th century. Admission requirements, lengths of programs, curricula, and costs for these programs vary considerably.
- Nursing education curricula are continually being revised in response to new scientific knowledge and technological, cultural, political, and socioeconomic changes in society.
- Continuing education is the responsibility of each practising nurse to keep abreast of scientific and technological changes as well as changes within the nursing profession.

READINGS AND REFERENCES

Suggested Readings

CAN press release. (1932). Some features of the report on the survey of nursing education in Canada. *Canadian Nurse, XXVII*, 127–131.

This summary of the Survey of Nursing Education in Canada, commonly called the Weir report, was released to the press in February of 1932. It provides a brief historical overview of the status of nursing education in Canada and the focus on hospital training. It is considered a key stimulus for the movement of nursing education into academic facilities.

Gillespie, M. (2002). Student-teacher connection in clinical nursing education. *Journal of Advanced Nursing, 37*(6), 566–576.

A qualitative research study was conducted to describe undergraduate nursing students' experiences of connection within the student–teacher relationship and the effects of student–teacher connections on students' learning experiences in clinical nursing education. Eight undergraduate nursing students participated in unstructured interviews and a focus group. Data were analyzed using a process of constant comparative analysis and revealed four primary themes that formed a description of the students' experience of student–teacher connection. Both the nature of student–teacher connection and the influence of teachers and other factors on the formation of student–teacher connection are discussed.

Selected References

Baumgart, A. J., & Larsen, J. (Eds.). (1992). *Canadian nursing faces the future* (2nd ed.). Toronto: C. V. Mosby.

Canadian Nurses Association. (1968). *The leaf and the lamp.* Ottawa: Author.

Canadian Nurses Association. (1982). *The definition and purposes of the CNA certification program.* Ottawa: Author.

Canadian Nurses Association. (1998). *Policy statement: Educational support for competent nursing practice.* Ottawa: Author.

Canadian Nurses Association. (1999). *The nursing labour market in Canada: An occupational sector study*. Ottawa: CNA.

Canadian Nurses Association. (2000). *A national framework for continuing competency programs for registered nurses.* Ottawa: Author.

Canadian Association of University Schools of Nursing. (1991). *Student and Faculty Statistical Summary for Canadian University Schools of Nursing (1990–1997)*. Ottawa: Author.

Canadian Nurses Association. (1985, February). *CNA position statements.* Ottawa: Author.

Canavan, K. (1997). Issues update: Nurses' CE options expand with distance learning. *American Journal of Nursing, 97*, 59–60.

Donahue, M. P. (1985). *Nursing: The finest art.* St. Louis, MO: Mosby.

French, S. E. (1992). Reform in higher education for nurses: Comparative comments from Canada. *Contemporary Nurse, 1*(2), 54–67.

Fitzpatrick, M. (1983). *Prologue to professionalism.* Bowie, MD: Robert J. Brady.

Mussalem, H. (1960). *Spotlight on nursing education.* Ottawa: Canadian Nurses Association.

Orem, D. E. (1971). *Nursing: Concepts of practice.* New York: McGraw-Hill.

Street, M. M. (1973). *Watch-fires on the mountains: The life and writings of Ethel Johns.* Toronto: University of Toronto Press.

Weir, G. M. (1932). *Survey of nursing education in Canada.* Toronto: University of Toronto Press.

Woodham-Smith, C. (1950). *Florence Nightingale.* London, U.K.: Constable & Co. (Classic).

WEBLINKS

Canadian Association of Schools of Nursing
http://www.casn.ca
CASN is a voluntary association representing all universities and colleges that offer undergraduate and graduate programs in nursing.

Canadian Nurses Association
http://www.cna-nurses.ca/default.htm
This is the Web site for the national nursing association in Canada.

Canadian Nursing Students' Association
http://www.cnsa.ca/
The site is host to the national association for nursing students in Canada.

CHAPTER 3

Nursing Research in Canada

OBJECTIVES

After completing this chapter, you will be able to:

- Identify the concepts and language of research.
- Identify common research methods used in clinical inquiries.
- Describe the way that theory, research, and practice interrelate to each other.
- State the significance of research to the practice of nursing.
- Identify ways the nurse can participate in research activities in practice.
- Describe the quantitative approach and the qualitative approach in nursing research.
- Analyze the nurse's role in protecting the rights of human subjects in research.
- Identify the steps of the research process.

Nursing Research

Today, nurses are actively generating, publishing, and applying research in practice to improve client care and enhance nursing's scientific knowledge base. The use of research has three main benefits for clients: it helps nurses understand the client's situation more thoroughly, assess more accurately, and intervene more effectively. Nursing research findings not only improve client care but also affect the health-care system itself. For example, research studies have demonstrated the cost-effectiveness of registered nurses as health-care providers.

The Canadian Nurses Association (CNA) is committed to promoting research as the foundation for clinical practice. Reading research, evaluating the results of research studies, and, where appropriate, integrating new findings into practice are necessary competencies of professional nursing practice. Nurses who base their clinical decisions on current, scientifically obtained evidence are being professionally accountable. Research-based nursing practice simply means nursing practice that is based on valid and reliable research findings obtained from scientific investigations. The term evidence-based practice, or evidence-based decision making, is gaining popularity in nursing and, in some cases, is preferred to research-based practice. Much of nursing practice today is still based on knowledge derived from trial-and-error experiences or opinions and methods passed from one generation to the next through books, articles, conferences, and workshops. However, nurses are increasingly realizing that such practices are no longer sufficient to provide quality care to clients.

When nurses have a question they want to answer to provide better care to their clients, they can do nursing research. Nursing research is the systematic, objective investigation of phenomena (experiences, events, or circumstances) of importance to nursing, with the goal of improving practice. Research may be classified, according to the purpose of the study, as basic or applied; the former is concerned with generating knowledge. Basic research is sometimes called pure research. The latter, applied research, is concerned with using knowledge to solve immediate problems. Nurse researchers employ a variety of research approaches to substantiate existing knowledge and to discover new knowledge. The two primary approaches are termed *qualitative* and *quantitative*.

Research is different from problem solving. Problem solving is specific to a given situation and is designed for immediate action, whereas knowledge gained from research is transferable to other situations (see Chapters 22 and 23). The body of knowledge called nursing science and the growth and development of professional nursing depend on research undertaken by nurses.

Although the focus for *all* nurses is the use of research findings in practice, the level of participation in research depends on the nurse's educational level, position, experience, and practical environment.

Policy Statement of Canadian Nurses Association—The Role of Nurses in Research

Registered nurses play key roles in nursing research and interdisciplinary health research that enhances the quality, the efficiency, and the effectiveness of health care.

Registered nurses' decisions about client care must be based on a foundation of solid research. Research is a systematic investigation that uses a range of approaches to refine or confirm existing knowledge, to uncover new knowledge, or to do both. This knowledge provides evidence that can be used to improve client outcomes. Research in nursing builds knowledge about the practice and the discipline of nursing, and contributes to the broad base of health-care research.

Registered nurses assume various roles in both nursing and interdisciplinary research, depending upon their education and experience. Roles range from evaluating the research of others, to being part of a research team or conducting an independent study. Nurses demonstrate professional responsibility related to research by:

- supporting an environment where research is accepted, encouraged, and facilitated;
- evaluating research that is relevant to their practice;
- incorporating appropriate research results into their practice;
- ensuring that research is ethically sound;
- participating in research projects or conducting independent studies;
- lobbying for adequate funding to develop structures for nursing research, to educate nurses about research, and to support research studies;
- seeking fair and equitable peer review for their research proposals; and
- sharing research findings.

Canadian Nurses Association, November 1993

The History

As early as 1854, Florence Nightingale demonstrated the importance of research in the delivery of nursing care. When Nightingale arrived in the Crimea in November of 1854, she found the military hospital barracks overcrowded, filthy, rat- and flea-infested, and lacking in food, drugs, and essential medical supplies. As a result of these conditions, men died from starvation and such diseases as dysentery, cholera, and typhus (Woodham-Smith, 1950). By systematically collecting, organizing, and reporting data, Nightingale was able to institute sanitary reforms and significantly reduce mortality rates from contagious diseases.

Although the Nightingale tradition influenced the establishment of Canadian nursing schools, the research approach did not take hold until the beginning of the 20th century.

Nursing research has become a significant activity in Canada. The First National Nursing Research Conference was held in 1971 in Ottawa. It was organized by the University of British Columbia School of Nursing and supported by the Federal Department of Health and Welfare. Only one of the invited speakers, Dr. Faye Abdellah, was a nurse. This international nursing leader offered a historical perspective of nursing research in the United States. As a result of the conference, the first Centre for Nursing Research in Canada was established at McGill University, in Montreal, with monies from the federal government.

Two studies have helped document the emergence of nursing research activities in Canada. In a 1985 study of nursing research activities in Canadian teaching hospitals, 84 institutions were surveyed (Thurston, Tenove, & Church, 1987). The researchers documented 170 completed studies: 118 focused on nursing care, 44 focused on nursing-care delivery, and eight focused on other areas. Almost one-third of these studies had received external funding. The commitment of administration was identified as an important factor in encouraging nursing research. In a later study, 45 teaching hospitals were surveyed to determine the extent of nursing research within them (Thurston, Tenove, & Church, 1990). Results indicated that the presence of a nurse researcher position and research review committees supported nursing research.

Development of research activity in nursing has occurred slowly as the result of a gradual increase in the number of nurses with research expertise. Since nurses were not prepared to conduct research, many early studies in nursing were conducted by members of other disciplines. Today, most nursing research is initiated in university settings because of faculty members' preparation as researchers.

Figure 3.1 Computer-assisted research is popular in individual nursing courses and within programs

Linking Theory, Practice, and Research

There is an interrelationship among nursing research, theory, and practice. Research can be used to demonstrate that one nursing practice intervention is more effective than another. Examples of changes in nursing practice motivated by research include:

- Changes to the colour of nursing uniforms in working with older adults to promote mental functioning
- Inclusion of patients in the decision-making process to increase compliance with treatment
- Implementation of multiple strategies to enhance patient learning
- Earlier ambulation of patients following surgery to facilitate respiratory functioning
- Development of patient-education material to promote successful post-operative pain management

Research ideas, while often born in practice, also come from the nursing literature and nursing theory. Published articles about nursing research may stimulate questions, which lead to interest in further studies. Nursing theorists also generate research questions, since they piece together ideas that explain why something happens. Their explanations are tested, through research, to see if they are credible enough to be useful in clinical practice.

Hospitals and health-care agencies have begun to formally define the link between nursing research and practice. Strategies include the cross-appointment of faculty among hospitals, health-care agencies, and universities; the implementation of programs to develop staff nurses as users of research in their practice; the establishment of ethics committees to review research proposals; the appointment of unit research coordinators; the establishment of nursing research committees; the development of strategic plans for nursing research; and the use of evidence-based decision-making models in practice settings.

Support for Nursing Research

Nursing research costs money. Computer and library services, data collection, statistical consultation, employment of research assistants, and release time for researchers from their regular work responsibilities can be expensive. While funding sources have developed, financial support is still difficult to obtain, especially for new researchers. Collaborative, interdisciplinary studies have a greater chance of receiving financial support than research conducted by only registered nurses. Insufficient funds to support research is an obstacle for nursing research.

One of the earliest funding sources for nurse researchers was the Alberta Foundation for Nursing Research (AFNR), established by the Alberta government in the 1980s. It existed for a decade and was the only Canadian Foundation specifically designed to fund nursing research.

Evidence-Based Decision Making and Nursing Practice

The utilization of evidence-based[1] decision making by registered nurses is an important element of quality[2] nursing practice.[3]

Background

Nursing practice is based on values, theories, and evidence. Although evidence is an important element in decision making in nursing, decisions are also influenced by individual values, client choice, clinical judgement, experiential knowledge, ethics, legislation, as well as the pressures and working conditions within given organizations and work environments.

Responsibility for Evidence-Based Practice

Individual nurses, professional associations, schools of nursing, organizations that employ nurses, accreditation councils, and governments share the responsibility for developing and funding strategies that facilitate evidence-based decision making and evidence-based practice. These responsibilities extend to identifying the barriers and enhancing the factors within organizational structures that facilitate and promote evidence-based practice.

- Individual nurses have the primary responsibility for evaluating and promoting evidence in the context of their practice to ensure that nursing practice maximizes health and quality of life from the client's perspective.
- Professional and regulatory nursing associations have the responsibility to encourage and support evidence-based practice.
- Nursing educators and educational institutions have the responsibility to assist nurses in developing the skills and abilities to assess, interpret, and incorporate evidence into their practice on a continuing basis; to ensure that researchers communicate their findings in language that is familiar to practitioners; and to ensure that nursing curricula are evidence-based.
- Employers of registered nurses have the responsibility to provide: an environment supportive of evidence-based practice, the tools necessary to implement evidence into practice, and continuing education to assist nurses in developing the skills and abilities to assess and incorporate evidence into practice.
- Governments have the responsibility to provide the necessary funding to support nursing research and its dissemination and the development of health information systems that support evidence-based nursing practice.

Competencies for the Utilization of Evidence in Practice

Competencies in evidence-based decision making must be developed through basic and continuing nursing education programs, should be applied through critical analysis, and must be reinforced within practice environments.

The Need for Further Research

Dissemination of research, evaluation, synthesis of the results of research, and quality improvement findings require planned targeted strategies to reach those who require the information. Ongoing research is needed to explore the concepts of evidence, evidence dissemination, and utilization in nursing practice. Outcomes of evidence-based nursing practice need to be regularly evaluated and disseminated. Evidence-based practice can facilitate the identification of knowledge gaps and thereby help establish research priorities.

Data Collection in Nursing

The data generated through research, evaluation, and quality improvement require analysis and interpretation to become usable information, and that information, to become knowledge, requires synthesis and application in practice.

Data about nursing practice must be collected, stored, maintained, and retrieved in broader health information systems. There is a need for consistent data collections using standardized languages to aggregate and compare data across and between sites.

The inclusion of nursing data in health information systems is essential to support evidence-based decision making by registered nurses. To be effective, these health information systems should be designed to be comprehensive, integrated, and relational.

References

Canadian Council on Health Services Accreditation. (1995). *Standards of care for acute care organizations: A client-centred approach*. Ottawa: CCHSA.

Canadian Nurses Association. (1997). *Code of ethics for registered nurses*. Ottawa: CNA.

National Forum on Health. (1998). *Canada health action: Building on the legacy*, vol. 5, Making decisions: Evidence and information. Quebec: Editions MultiMondes.

Approved by the Board of Directors,
Canadian Nurses Association
November 1998

[1] Evidence is information based on historical or scientific evaluation of a practice that is accessible to decision makers in the Canadian health-care system. The types of evidence include: experimental (randomized clinical trials, meta-analysis, and analytic studies); nonexperimental (quasi-experimental, observational); expert opinion (consensus, commission reports); and historical and experimental (National Forum on Health, 1998). Evidence-based decision making is the explicit, conscientious, and judicious consideration of the best available evidence in the provision of health care. Evidence-based practice is the implementation of evidence-based decisions.

[2] Aspects of quality that are considered when evaluating care include safety, competence, acceptability, effectiveness, appropriateness, efficiency, and accessibility. (Canadian Council on Health Services Accreditation [CCHSA] Standards of Care for Acute Care organizations).

[3] The term "nursing practice" encompasses the various domains of nursing, including direct care, education, research, and administration.

It served as the model for subsequent research funding for nurses and was instrumental in the development of graduate programs, especially doctoral programs, in this country.

Today, funds for nursing research come from several nursing sources. At the provincial (territorial) level, research funding varies a great deal from one province to another. A few provincial nursing associations have developed some capacity for the funding of nursing research. Nationally, the Canadian Nurses Foundation funds research. Specialty groups, such as the Canadian Gerontological Nursing Association, also provide financial assistance for their members to conduct research.

Several non-nursing provincial (territorial) and federal agencies accept proposals that meet their funding guidelines when submitted by qualified nurse researchers. These include the Social Sciences and Humanities Research Council and the Canadian Institutes of Health Research (CIHR). The CIHR was established by an Act of Parliament in 2000 and is Canada's foremost federal agency for health research. Its predecessor was the Medical Research Council. Its goal is to excel in the creation of new knowledge and its translation into improved health for Canadians. The CIHR's goal is based on a broader definition of health and includes biomedical and clinical research, health systems and services research, and population health research. These areas are of interest to nurse researchers.

There are other recent funding endeavours. The Canadian Foundation for Innovation (CFI) is a not-for-profit corporation funded by the federal government in 1997 to enable Canada's research community to conduct research and technology development. The Canadian Health Services Research Foundation (CHSRF) was founded by Industry Canada under the Canada Corporation Act. Its mandate is to sponsor applied health systems research and to facilitate its use in evidence-based decision making. While not composed solely of nurses, it has strong relevance to the profession since it administers the Nursing Research Fund. The fund's objectives are to develop nursing's research capacity, to sponsor research on nursing issues, and to disseminate nursing research knowledge.

The CHSRF and the Canadian Nurses Association (CNA) have allocated significant funds for the development of the Canadian Nursing Knowledge Network (CNKN). This initiative is to enhance the CNA's capacity to disseminate relevant research to nurses. Foundations and voluntary associations, such as the Canadian Cancer Society and the Kidney Foundation of Canada, are other sources of funds for nurse researchers.

Canadian Society Notes

Fact	Implications for Nursing Practice
The Canadian Association for Nursing Research (CANR) is a national organization with representation from every province and territory.	Nurses need to participate in associations that promote the use of research in practice.
The Canadian Health Services Research Foundation (1) funds management and policy research in health services and nursing; (2) supports the synthesis and dissemination of research results; and (3) supports the use of research results by managers and decision makers.	Nurses interested in research need to be aware of funding opportunities.
In 1969, Moyra Allen of McGill University founded the first Canadian scholarly nursing journal. Initially known as *Nursing Papers*, the journal is now known as the *Canadian Journal of Nursing Research*.	The reading of research studies promotes knowledge of Canadian nursing and how to meet the health-care needs of clients.

Approaches to Nursing Research

The two predominant research approaches are qualitative and quantitative. *Quantitative research* is generally considered objective and uses data-gathering techniques that can be verified by others. *Qualitative research* is more subjective, which means that qualitative researchers study things in their natural settings, attempting to make sense of phenomena in terms of the meanings people bring to them. While today both approaches are valued within the nursing research community, in the past, nurse researchers primarily conducted quantitative research.

These approaches originate from different philosophical perspectives and use different methods for collection and analysis of data.

Quantitative Research

Quantitative research is defined as "the study of phenomena that lend themselves to precise measurement and quantification, often involving a rigorous and controlled design" (Polit, Beck, & Hungler, 2001, p. 468). The quantitative approach is most frequently associated with *logical positivism*, a philosophical doctrine that asserts that scientific knowledge is the only kind of factual knowledge. Quantitative research is often viewed as "hard" science and tends to emphasize deductive reasoning and the *measurable* attributes of human experience. Data are usually collected using structured methods and procedures and are analyzed using a number of statistical procedures.

The following are examples of research questions that lend themselves to a quantitative approach:

- What is the effect of nurse home visits on the parenting ability of teen mothers?
- Does rocking in older adults elicit the physiologic changes of the relaxation response?
- What is the effect of social support intervention on coping in nurses working in intensive care units?

Qualitative Research

Qualitative research is defined as "the investigation of phenomena, typically in an in-depth and holistic fashion, through the collection of rich narrative material using a flexible research design" (Polit, Beck, & Hungler, 2001, p. 468).This approach is most often associated with the naturalistic paradigm that began as a countermovement to positivism. This perspective assumes there are multiple perspectives of reality, each existing within a context.

The qualitative approach allows for exploration of the subjective experiences of human beings, a more holistic view that places value on the perceptions of clients and nurses in the nursing context (Taylor, 1993). In the qualitative approach, no formal instruments are used; instead, loosely structured narrative data are collected. Using the inductive method, data are analyzed by identifying themes and patterns that emerge from the data.

The qualitative approach would be appropriate for the following types of research questions:

- What is the nature of the bereavement process in spouses of clients with terminal cancer?
- What is the nature of adjustment after a radical prostatectomy?
- What is the process of family caregiving for older family relatives with Alzheimer's dementia as experienced by the caregiver?

RESEARCH NOTES

Quantitative Study

The researcher distributed a survey on violence in the workplace to registered nurses practising in 210 hospitals in Alberta and British Columbia. Findings related to the frequency of violence against nurses, reported as the number of times they had experienced a violent incident in the workplace. Nearly half (46%) of those surveyed had experienced one or more types of violence in their last five shifts worked. Interestingly, 70 percent of those who had experienced violence identified they had not reported it. Patients comprised the primary source of all types of violence. Frequency varied by type: emotional abuse 38 percent, threat of assault 19 percent, physical assault 18 percent, verbal sexual harassment 7.6 percent, and sexual assault 0.6 percent. These findings suggest that working in health-care facilities may threaten the well-being of nurses and other health-care staff.

The most prevalent type, emotional abuse, was further explored for its possible determinants, since it was the type of violence most evenly distributed among sources (patients, families, co-workers, physicians). Multiple regression modelling using the individual nurse as the unit of analysis explained the significant predictors of emotional abuse to be age, casual job status, quality of care, degree of hospital restructuring, type of nursing unit, relationships among hospital staff, nurse-to-patient ratios, and violence-prevention measures. When using the hospital as the unit of analysis, the predictors were quality of care, age, relationships with hospital staff, presence of violence-prevention measures, and province. These findings illustrate important differences in models that use the individual and the institution as the unit of analysis.

Implications for practice: To reduce the potential for workplace violence, prevention strategies need to be designed and targeted at the individual nurse and at the hospital.

Source: Duncan, S. M., Hyndman, K., Estabrooks, C. A., Hesketh, K., Humphrey, C. K., Wong, J. S., Acorn, S., & Giovannetti, P. (2001). Nurses' experience of violence in Alberta and British Columbia hospitals. *Canadian Journal of Nursing Research, 32*(4), 57–78.

The Research Process

Polit, Beck, and Hungler (2001) defined research as the "systematic inquiry that uses orderly scientific methods to answer questions or solve problems" (p. 470). Whether a quantitative or qualitative approach is used, all research must be meticulously planned, systematically implemented, and carefully analyzed. To achieve this goal, researchers adhere to a formal course of action known as the research process. The formulation of the research problem is the first step of the process, and the communication of the research is the final one; however, there is sometimes variation in the terms given to the other steps.

State a Research Question or Problem

The investigator's initial task is to narrow a broad area of interest to a circumscribed problem that specifies exactly the intent of the study. The ideas for research may arise from recurrent problems encountered in practice, questions that

RESEARCH NOTES

Qualitative Study

Patient comfort is a desired goal in the provision of nursing care. The purpose of this qualitative exploratory study was to describe nurse comforting strategies as well as the outcomes of nurse comforting strategies from the perspective of emergency department (ED) patients. The study took place in a rural Canadian acute-care hospital. A volunteer sample of 14 hospitalized patients who had received initial treatment in the ED were interviewed on two occasions. Participants were nine females and five males ranging from 20 to 75 years of age.

The initial interview was tape recorded and transcribed. Content analysis was done on the transcripts. The second interview gave participants the opportunity of making corrections or additions to the transcript. Participants described the nurses' comforting strategies under these categories: immediate and competent technical/physical care, positive talk, vigilance, attending to physical discomforts, and including and attending to family.

Implications for practice: The comforting strategies used by nurses have the potential to impact the physical and emotional well-being of patients.

Source: Hawley, M. P. (2000). Nurse comforting strategies: Perceptions of emergency department patients. *Clinical Nursing Research, 9*(4), 441–459.

are difficult to resolve because of contradictions in the literature, or areas in which minimal or no research has been done.

In formulating a research problem, Polit, Beck, and Hungler (1995) suggest that three criteria be used: significance, researchability, and feasibility. A research problem has *significance* if it has the potential to contribute to nursing science by enhancing client care, testing or generating a theory, or resolving a day-to-day clinical problem. The question "So what?" must be answered adequately to determine if a research problem is significant.

Researchability means that the problem can be subjected to scientific investigation. Many significant problems that produce ambiguity and uncertainty in clinical situations may not be amenable to research. For instance, "Should nurses support voluntary euthanasia?" is a relevant, timely, and difficult question, but it cannot be answered through research.

Feasibility pertains to the availability of time as well as the material and human resources needed to investigate a research problem or question. Conducting a study involves the use of space, money, equipment, supplies, computers, subjects, research assistants, and consultants.

In quantitative approaches, research problems contain dependent and independent variables, except for descriptive research, which has no dependent variables. The **dependent variable** is the behaviour, characteristic, or outcome that the researcher wishes to explain or predict. The **independent variable** is the presumed cause of, or influence on, the dependent variable. Qualitative studies do not contain variables.

Define the Study's Purpose or Rationale

The statement of the study's purpose indicates what the researcher intends to do with the research problem identified. The study purpose includes *what* the researcher will do, *who* the subjects will be, and *where* the data will be collected.

Review the Literature

Before progressing with the development of the research design, the investigator determines what is known and what is not known about the problem. A thorough review of the literature provides the foundation on which to build new knowledge. Through a literature review, a researcher may also acquire information about available techniques, instruments, and methods of data analysis that have been used in prior research, as well as potential flaws or problems and how to avoid them.

Formulate the Research Question or Hypothesis

Once nurse researchers have identified a research problem and are knowledgeable of the literature, they formulate a research question. The question may be stated in one of three ways: a statement, a question, or a hypothesis. If researchers are going to describe something, they may make a statement, such as: "The purpose of this study is to identify gender differences in the nursing care of patients admitted to rehabilitation units." They could also ask a question, such as: "What are the communication styles of nurses that indicate client satisfaction with nursing care?" If conducting an experiment, researchers must have a hypothesis as to what the outcome will be so that hypothesis-testing statistics may be applied. For example, "Family members of palliative care patients attending support groups will demonstrate more positive coping strategies than those who do not" is a testable hypothesis. In whichever way a research question is stated, it must be clearly expressed.

Select a Research Design

A research design is the "overall plan for answering the research questions and for testing the research hypothesis" (Polit, Beck, & Hungler, 2001, p. 169). The choice of design depends on the nature of the problem. Quantitative, qualitative, or a combination of approaches may be used. The research design includes the study setting, the sample, and the type of data to be collected, as well as strategies to reduce bias.

There are three categories of quantitative research design:

1. *Experimental design.* The investigator manipulates the independent variable by administering an experimental treatment to some subjects while withholding it from others.

2. *Quasi-experimental design.* The investigator manipulates the independent variable but without either the randomization or control that characterizes true experiments.
3. *Nonexperimental design.* The investigator does not manipulate the independent variable.

Qualitative designs seek to derive meaning and understanding from human experience. In such disciplines as nursing, where it is necessary to know what the participant is experiencing, a qualitative design may be the preferred method of identifying data. A qualitative design differs from a quantitative design in the following ways: the phenomenon studied, the data collection and analysis procedures, and the interpretation of the data. Often, data collection and analysis are done simultaneously. Qualitative designs do not have identifiable measurable variables, and data are not processed through statistical analysis.

Ethnography, grounded theory, and phenomenology are some of the commonly used qualitative methods. In addition, LoBiondo-Wood and Haber (1998) include the case study as having the characteristics of qualitative research. Ethnographic research is used to describe culture and lifestyle from the participant's viewpoint. Studies related to the nursing care or health practices of a particular culture would be examples of ethnographic nursing research. Grounded theory research is used to develop nursing theory from collected data. Theory may be generated for relatively new areas, where very little is known, or for more familiar areas, where a fresh viewpoint is sought. Phenomenology is a philosophical research method, which regards each human as having a unique experience. The researcher attempts to derive meaning from individuals' descriptions of their experiences.

In selecting the approach, the researcher should try to identify factors that may affect the study's results. Sometimes, these factors are called limitations. The researcher should acknowledge the limitations of the study, as much as possible, before the data are collected.

Select the Population, Sample, and Setting

At this stage, the researcher chooses the study population, selects a sample, and decides on the setting where the sample can be found. The **population** includes all possible members of the group who meet the criteria for the study. The **sample** is the segment of the population from whom the data will actually be collected.

Conduct a Pilot Study

In quantitative studies, a pilot study is a "dress rehearsal" before the actual study begins. A trial run of the research procedure is conducted on a few subjects for the following purposes (Polit & Hungler, 1995):

- To examine the feasibility of the proposed study
- To test whether the subject recruitment plan is adequate
- To assess whether the data collection tools to be used are valid and reliable

By identifying any problems or flaws during the pilot study, the investigators can refine the proposed plan and strengthen the research methodology.

Collect the Data

When designing a study, researchers must consider how the data will be collected. The most commonly used methods of collecting data in nursing are questionnaires, rating scales, interviews, observation, and biophysical measures.

In quantitative designs, the validity and reliability of measurement tools need to be established prior to the start of data collection. **Validity** is the degree to which an instrument measures what it is supposed to measure. If a nurse measures anxiety, how would the nurse be sure that what is being measured is not fear or stress, which are related concepts? **Reliability** is the degree of consistency with which an instrument measures a concept or variable. If an instrument is reliable, repeated measurements of the same variable should yield similar or nearly similar results.

Analyze the Data

In this step, the collected data are organized, coded, and analyzed for the purpose of answering the research question or testing the hypothesis. Even before data collection is initiated, there must be a systematic plan for analyzing the results. Measurement is a critical part of the research process. Measurement is not a feature of qualitative designs; the discussion here is relevant to quantitative designs. Variables are important components of measurement. The identified research question helps the researcher identify the variables and possible relationships among them. The variables must be clearly defined, observable, and measurable to permit the results of a study to be interpretable. Regardless of the method of measurement used, there must be evidence of objectivity. This means that the system of measurement must be so clear that anyone following the prescribed rules will assign the same or similar score to what was observed.

Data analysis may involve descriptive or inferential statistics. **Descriptive statistics,** procedures that summarize large volumes of data, are used to describe and synthesize data, showing patterns and trends. Descriptive statistics include measures of central tendency and measures of variability.

Measures of central tendency describe the centre of a distribution of data, denoting where most of the subjects lie. These include the *mean*, *median*, and *mode*. **Measures of variability** indicate the degree of dispersion or spread of the data. These include the *range*, *variance*, and *standard deviation*. See the accompanying box for definitions of these measures. Typically, in a research report, the mean (a measure of central tendency) and standard deviation (a measure of variability) are reported together to give the reader an idea of the nature of the data distribution.

The following is an example:

Systolic blood pressure
130 ± 30

The two statistics reported are the mean and the standard deviation. The number 130 indicates the mean systolic blood pressure, whereas 30 represents 1 standard deviation (SD) from the mean. Hence, 1 SD from the mean would include blood pressure from 100 mm Hg to 160 mm Hg (1 SD below to 1 SD above the mean).

Nurse researchers attempt to determine (after data have been analyzed) whether the results are *statistically significant*. Underlying this statement is the notion of probability. By convention, p (probability) less than 0.05 is considered the acceptable level of significance. A p value greater than 0.05 is considered statistically insignificant. In research, the desire is to generalize beyond the sample; so, there is a need to determine the probability that the results were due to chance or a "fluke," rather than a true occurrence in the population. Hence, a p value of 0.05 means that the probability of the findings being caused by chance alone is 5 in 100 (Polit & Hungler, 1997).

In qualitative studies, data analysis is often done simultaneously with data collection, which enables the researcher to focus and shape the study as it proceeds. The researcher consistently reflects upon the data, works to organize it, and tries to discover meaning in it.

Definitions of Measures of Central Tendency and Variability

Central Tendency

mean A measure of central tendency, computed by summing all scores and dividing by the number of subjects; commonly symbolized as $\bar{X}$ or *M*.

median A measure of central tendency, representing the exact middle score or value in a distribution of scores; the median is the value above and below which 50 percent of the scores lie.

mode The score or value that occurs most frequently in a distribution of scores.

Variability

range A measure of variability, consisting of the difference between the highest and the lowest values in a distribution of scores.

variance A measure of variance or dispersion, equal to the square of the standard deviation.

standard deviation The most frequently used measure of variability, indicating the average to which scores deviate from the mean; commonly symbolized as SD or *S*.

Interpret the Findings

In either quantitative or qualitative research, when interpreting the results of the data analysis, the researcher first reports the findings directly related to the research question. Sometimes, the researcher uncovers unexpected findings, and these are also reported. Hirst (2000) articulated a definition of resident abuse as perceived by those living and working within long-term care institutions and unexpectedly found that older adults were devalued in these same facilities.

Conclusions are then drawn. What do these findings mean? At this point, researchers can be subjective and insert some of their own thinking into the research report. The results of the current research are compared with previous studies that investigated the same or similar phenomena. The researcher should discuss any problems encountered in the course of the study or any limitations that may have influenced the findings.

After the findings are interpreted, the researcher should indicate the implications for nursing. Implications are suggestions for ways of thinking about the phenomenon in the future. In nursing research, there may be indications for changes to nursing practice, administration, or education. For example, in research conducted to describe nursing students' experience of being immersed in a different cultural setting, findings suggested that they acquire cultural sensitivity from such experiences. An implication is that nurse educators need to provide culturally diverse opportunities for students. In a study examining what percentage of clients had post-operative pain at home and what impact pain had on their activity, the findings identified that clients had received no information on how to cope with pain and were not knowledgeable about analgesic use. These findings indicate a need for educational resources on the management of post-operative pain following discharge from hospital to be distributed to clients.

Communicate the Research

Implicit in conducting research is the requirement to share with others the knowledge generated, either through publication in professional journals or by reporting the results verbally at professional conferences. Interpreting the results, communicating the findings, and suggesting directions for further study conclude the research process.

In Canada, nursing research findings can be communicated in numerous ways. At the local, provincial (territorial), and national levels, nursing associations and special interest groups use their newsletters, publications, annual meetings, and conferences to promote nursing research and to disseminate findings. The best method of reaching a large number of nurses is through publication in nursing journals. The *Canadian Nurse* (*L'infirmière Canadienne*) publishes news items on research activities, abstracts of Canadian research articles, and articles that report research findings.

RESEARCH NOTES

Examples of Research Journals in Nursing

Canadian Journal of Nursing Research
Western Journal of Nursing Research
Canadian Journal of Nursing Administration
Canadian Journal of Public Health
Canadian Nurse/L'Infirmiére Canadienne
Clinical Nursing Research
Nursing Research
International Journal of Nursing Studies
Scholarly Inquiry for Nursing Practice

Developing Research-Based Practice

The nurse needs to be research minded, which conveys awareness and openness to nursing research. Nurses should critically read, interpret, and evaluate research evidence for applicability to their nursing practice. When reviewing research articles or reports, consider the philosophical view taken in the study; for example, where does knowledge exist? Does it exist in patients' experiences (qualitative) or in logical reasoning of the researcher (quantitative)? There are possibilities for both in nursing.

Research-based practice enables nurses to provide high-quality, cost-effective care. Through clinical practice, nurses can identify nursing problems that need to be investigated. Nurses can participate in the implementation of research studies by helping principal researchers collect data in clinical settings. They can also help disseminate research-based knowledge by sharing useful findings with colleagues.

Locating Nursing Research Findings

The journal *Nursing Research* was established in 1952 in the United States to serve as a vehicle to communicate nurses' research and scholarly productivity (Donahue, 1985). The publication of many other nursing research journals followed, some devoted to research and others combining clinical, theory, and research publications. Journals are available in the libraries of academic institutions and large hospitals. In this country, the *Canadian Journal of Nursing Research* is one of the premier research journals.

One way of keeping up with new research is to regularly scan the tables of contents of journals. Another way is through print-based indexes, which list articles published within a variety of journals. Indexes are located in libraries. Searches are conducted by using key terms to locate research articles. These indexes include the Cumulative Index to Nursing and Allied Health Literature (CINAHL), International Nursing Index, Medline, and Index Medicus.

The most effective way to search the literature is to use a database of nursing research articles. Computerized searchers are available in health-care libraries; the trick to finding relevant articles is to identify the key words to be used for the search. It may take several computer searches using different key terms and databases to locate the articles. Increasingly, these searches can be done through the World Wide Web. The Canadian Research Information Database (CRID) is a resource for researchers and others interested in accessing the results of research in Canada on the Web. In searching the Web, be aware of the credibility of the source and when the site was last updated.

Critiquing Research

If nurses are to use research, they must first learn to conduct a critical appraisal of research reports published in the literature. A research critique enables the nurse as a research consumer to evaluate the scientific merit of the study and decide how the results may be useful in practice. Critiquing involves intensive scrutiny of a study, including its strengths and weaknesses, statistical and clinical significance, as well as the generalizability of the results. See Table 3.1.

Polit, Beck, and Hungler (2001) proposed that the following elements be considered in conducting a research critique: substantive and theoretical dimensions, method-

FOCUS ON CRITICAL THINKING

A research study is being implemented on the unit as Jamie, a third-year student, starts his adult health course rotation. He participates in the orientation session held by the researchers to inform the staff about their study. The purpose of the study was to understand the pre-surgical experiences of the patients. Jamie is interested in working with the researchers.

1. Identify responsibilities of beginning nurses in relation to nursing research.
2. What questions might Jamie ask of the researchers as he explores his possible interest in the study?
3. How might Jamie ensure that he protects the rights of his patients, if they decide to participate in the study?

See Appendix A for answers to these questions.

ologic dimensions, ethical dimensions, interpretive dimensions, and presentation and stylistic dimensions.

- *Substantive and theoretical dimensions.* For these dimensions, the nurse needs to evaluate the significance of the research problem, the appropriateness of the conceptualizations and the theoretical framework of the study, and the congruence between the research question and the methods used to address it.
- *Methodologic dimensions.* The methodologic dimensions pertain to the appropriateness of the research design, the size and representativeness of the study sample as well as the sampling design, validity and reliability of the instruments, adequacy of the research procedures, and the appropriateness of data analytic techniques used in the study.
- *Ethical dimensions.* The nurse must determine whether the rights of human subjects were protected during the course of the study and whether any ethical problems compromised the scientific merit of the study or the well-being of the subjects.
- *Interpretive dimensions.* For these dimensions, the nurse needs to ascertain the accuracy of the discussion, conclusions, and implications of the study results. The findings must be related back to the original hypotheses and the conceptual framework of the study. The implications and limitations of the study should be reviewed, together with the potential for replication or generalizability of the findings to similar populations.
- *Presentation and stylistic dimensions.* The manner in which the research plan and results are communicated refers to the presentation and stylistic dimensions. The research report must be detailed, logically organized, concise, and well written.

Protecting the Rights of Human Subjects

When research is conducted on human participants, the researcher and the nurse have a responsibility to protect the research participant from harm that may be a result of participation in the study. The nurse, as client advocate, must ensure that clients' rights are protected.

All institutions in which research is conducted should have, or have access to, a committee of qualified individuals called a Research Ethics Board (REB) to approve the research activity and to ensure that the rights of participants are protected. The principle of protecting rights is enforced to some extent by major granting agencies, such as the CIHR and the SSHRC, who make their funding contingent on REB review. REBs have the authority to require modifications to proposed research and can terminate research that is not conducted according to specific requirements. Also offering guidance to nurse researchers in Canada is the Tri-Council Policy Statement on Ethical Conduct for Research Involving Humans (1997) and the Canadian Nurses Association Code of Ethics for Registered Nurses (2000). The CNA has updated the Code and its document "Ethical Guidelines for Nurses Involved in Research."

All nurses who practise in settings where research is being conducted with human subjects, or who participate in such research as data collectors or collaborators, play an important role in safeguarding the following rights.

Right to Informed Consent

Obtaining informed consent is the responsibility of the principal investigator. It is a contract between the investigator and the participant. All clients must be informed about the consequences of consenting to serve as research participants. The client needs to be able to judge whether there is a reasonable balance between the risks of participating in the study and the potential benefits.

Informed consent may appear to be straightforward and easy to implement, but this is not always true. Sometimes, researchers avoid informed consent, believing that the client's knowledge of being observed could alter behaviour and distort the findings. It is the nurse's responsibility to safeguard participants' human rights and ensure that informed consent takes place prior to their involvement in any research study.

Informed consent includes written and oral explanations. It should be in the participant's preferred language and at an appropriate educational level. Documenting informed consent by obtaining a participant's consent in writing is important. Participants who can only give oral permission must have their consent witnessed by a third person. If the participant is a minor, or is not capable of consenting because of mental or physical disability, a legally authorized representative, such as a parent or guardian, may sign the consent. There must be voluntary and informed consent and no additional risk, discomfort, or invasion of privacy to that stated in the consent document. In addition, the participant must be guaranteed that refusal to take part in the study will not jeopardize quality of nursing care.

Right Not to Be Harmed

Risk of harm to a research subject is defined as exposure to the possibility of injury going beyond everyday situations. The risk can be physical, emotional, legal, financial, or social. For instance, withholding standard care from a client in labour for the purpose of studying the course of natural childbirth clearly poses a potential physical danger. Risks can be less overt and involve psychologic factors, such as exposure to stress or anxiety, or social factors, such as loss of confidentiality or loss of privacy.

Right to Full Disclosure

Even though it may be possible to collect data about a client as part of everyday care without the client's particular

TABLE 3.1 How to Read a Nursing Research Article

Critically evaluate the written content of a research article. Do not assume anything about what is not written.

Ask Yourself:	You Might:
Does the content look interesting?	Read the abstract.
Is the content related to my practice?	
When was the research done? Is it classic, current, or outdated?	Identify the publication date.
What is the research question?	Read the problem statement.
What is the research approach: quantitative, qualitative, or a combination?	Read the method section.
How was the group selected?	Read the section on sample selection. Look at any tables that describe the participant group.
How were the rights of the human participants protected?	Read the statements about ethics.
What are the characteristics of the group studied?	Read the method and findings sections.
What is the setting in which the data were collected?	Read the data collection section. Read the findings section.
What data were collected?	Review the tables and figures.
What methods of data analysis were used?	
What are the research findings?	
Do I agree with the researcher's conclusions?	Think about whether the findings would be useful in your own nursing practice.

knowledge or consent, to do so is considered unethical. **Full disclosure** is a basic right. It means that deception, either by withholding information about a client's participation in a study or by giving the client false or misleading information about what participating in the study will involve, will not occur.

Right of Self-Determination

Many clients in dependent positions, such as people in nursing homes, feel pressured to participate in studies. They feel that they must please the doctors and nurses who are responsible for their treatment and care. The **right of self-determination** means that subjects should feel free from constraints, coercion, or any undue influence to participate in a study. Masked inducements, for instance, suggesting to potential participants that by taking part in the study they might become famous, make an important contribution to science, or receive special attention, must be strictly avoided. Nurses must be assertive in advocating for this essential right.

Right of Privacy and Confidentiality

Privacy enables a client to participate without worrying about later embarrassment. The anonymity of a study participant is ensured if even the investigator cannot link a specific subject to the information reported. **Confidentiality** means that any information a subject relates will not be made public or available to others without the subject's consent. Investigators must inform research subjects about the measures that provide for these rights. Such measures may include the use of pseudonyms or code numbers or reporting only aggregate or group data in published research.

CHAPTER HIGHLIGHTS

- Nurses are now generating new knowledge and applying research in practice to improve client care.
- Nurses at all levels are participating in nursing research activities. All nurses practising in settings where research is conducted have a role in safeguarding the clients' rights.
- The use of research will help nurses to understand the client's situation more thoroughly, to assess more accurately, and to intervene more effectively.
- The Canadian Nurses Association is a leader in the promotion of evidence-based nursing practice.
- Most nursing research is initiated in university settings because of the preparation of faculty members as researchers.
- In Canada today, there exist both capabilities and constraints for the ongoing development of nursing research.
- The nurse has a duty to protect the rights of the research participants.
- There is a need for nursing research on a wide range of nursing questions.
- Qualitative and quantitative methods are employed in nursing research.

READINGS AND REFERENCES

Suggested Readings

Davis, B., & Logan, J. (1997). *Reading research* (2nd ed.). Ottawa: Canadian Nurses Association.
Written for registered nurses, this booklet provides a brief overview of easy steps for the review of nursing research studies. It also provides a worksheet to complete as a learning activity for the reader.

Forbes, D., & Phillipchuk, D. (2001). The dissemination and use of nursing research. *Canadian Nurse, 97*(7), 18–22.
The authors describe a project of the Alberta Association of Registered Nurses to identify how research findings could be more effectively disseminated and used in clinical practice. From a series of five workshops, participants identified that they often had insufficient time to read research articles and implement new ideas. They also identified that sharing of ideas and successful approaches to using research in practice contributed to their own evidence-based practice.

Stajduhar, K. I., Bidgood, D., Meagher, C., Morris, V., Shaw, A. L., Showler, C., & Short, S. J. (2002). Bringing nursing research alive in the practice setting. *Canadian Nurse, 98*(10), 14–18.
The authors present the benefits and challenges that arose from front-line nurses in implementing a study on injection drug use. They identify their research informs their practice, and the value of doing research to learn about research. They describe their greatest challenge as overcoming their own bias towards research.

Selected References

Canadian Nurses Association. (1994). *Ethical guidelines for nurses in research involving human participants*. Ottawa: Author.

Canadian Nurses Association. (1993). *Policy statement: The role of nurses in research*. Ottawa: Author.

Clamp, C. G. L., & Gough, S. (1999). *Resources for nursing research: An annotated bibliography*. Thousand Oaks, CA: Sage.

Collins, M., & MacDonald, V. (2000). Managing postoperative pain at home. *Canadian Nurse, 96*(7), 26–29.

Davies, B., & Logan, J. (1993). *Reading Research: A user-friendly guide for nurses and other health professionals*. Ottawa: Canadian Nurses Association.

Dempsey, P. A. (2000). *Using nursing research: Process, critical evaluation, and utilization* (5th ed.). Baltimore, MD: Lippincott.

Donahue, M.P. (1985). *Nursing: The finest art*. St. Louis: Mosby.

Duncan, S. M., Hyndman, K., Estabrooks, C. A., Hesketh, K., Humphrey, C. K., Wong, J. S., Acorn, S., & Giovannetti, P. (2001). Nurses' experience of violence in Alberta and British Columbia hospitals. *Canadian Journal of Nursing Research, 32*(4), 57–78.

Granger, B. B. (1999). *Research strategies for clinicians*. Stamford, CT: Appleton & Lange.

Hawley, M. P. (2000). Nurse comforting strategies: Perceptions of emergency department patients. *Clinical Nursing Research, 9*, 441–459.

Health Canada. (1997). National Forum on Health. Ottawa: Author.

Hirst, S. (2000). Resident abuse: An insider's perspective. *Geriatric Nursing, 21*, 38–42.

Kerr, J. R. (1996). The financing of nursing research in Canada. In J. R. Kerr & J. MacPhail (Eds.), *Canadian nursing issues and perspectives* (3rd ed.) (pp. 135–145). St. Louis, MO: Mosby.

LoBiondo-Wood, G., & Haber, J. (1998). *Nursing Research: Methods, critical appraisal, and utilization* (4th ed.). St. Louis, MO: Mosby.

Nateo, M., & Kirchhoff, K. (1991). *Conducting and using nursing research in the clinical setting*. Baltimore: Williams and Wilkins.

Polit, D., & Hungler, B. P. (1995). *Nursing Research: Principles and Methods*. Philadelphia: Lippincott.

Polit, D.F., & Hungler, B. P. (1997) *Essentials of nursing research: Methods, appraisal, and utilization* (4th ed.). Philadelphia: Lippincott.

Polit, D. F., Beck, C. T., & Hungler, B. P. (2001). *Essentials of nursing research: Methods, appraisal, and utilization* (5th ed.). Philadelphia, PA: Lippincott.

Simpson, B. (1996). Evidence-based nursing practice: The state of the art. *The Canadian Nurse, 92*(12), 22–25.

Talbot, L. A. (1995). *Principles and practice of nursing research.* St. Louis, MO: Mosby.

Taylor, B. (1993). Phenomenology: One way to understand nursing practice. *International Journal of Nursing Studies, 30,* 171–179.

Thurston, N. E., Tenove, S., & Church, J. (1987). *Nursing research in Canadian teaching hospitals.* Calgary: Department of Nursing, Foothills Provincial General Hospital and Faculty of Nursing, University of Calgary.

Thurston, N. E., Tenove, S., & Church, J. (1990). Hospital nursing research is alive and flourishing. *Nursing Management, 21*(5), 50–54.

Woodham-Smith, C. (1950). *Florence Nightingale.* London, U.K.: Constable & Co. (Classic).

WEBLINKS

Canadian Nurses Association
http://www.cna-nurses.ca
Through its search mechanism, CNA provides access to research initiatives specific to the practice of nursing.

Canadian Institutes of Health Research
http://www.cihr-irsc.gc.ca
A primary funding source for Canadian nurse researchers.

Canadian Consortium for Health Promotion Research
http://www.utoronto.ca/chp/chp/consort/index.htm
The focus of the Consortium is to improve health promotion research, policy, and practice in Canada through linking research, capacity development, and information dissemination.

Canadian-International Nurse Researcher Database
http://NurseResearcher.com/
The site provides an interactive database for nurse researchers in Canada.

Canadian Cochrane Centre
http://hiru.mcmaster.ca/cochrane/centres/canadian
The Centre's mandate is to promote health-care decisions based on accurate knowledge (evidence-based health care), through the dissemination and application of systematic reviews of health-care interventions. This site provides evidence-based resources.

Cancer Care Ontario Program in Evidence-Based Care
http://hiru.mcmaster.ca/ccopgi/
The site focuses on oncology-specific, evidence-based care information for patients, families, and health-care providers.

CHAPTER 4

Nursing Philosophies, Theories, Concepts, Frameworks, and Models

OBJECTIVES

After completing this chapter, you will be able to:

- Identify the purposes and essential elements of theories in nursing.
- Examine the purposes and benefits of philosophies in nursing.
- Describe three main areas of philosophical inquiry and two research traditions.
- Compare selected philosophical approaches in relation to the questions they pose for nursing.
- Identify selected theoretical works in terms of how nursing is conceptualized and the assumptions underpinning these conceptualizations.
- Define the terms *philosophy*, *paradigm*, *assumption*, *concept*, *conceptual framework*, *conceptual model*, and *theory*.

Philosophical thinking is an indispensable feature of our everyday lives. When we reflect on the meaning of our experiences or consider how we might evaluate the *truth* of an observation, or try to determine what might be the *best* course of action in a particular situation, we are engaging in philosophical thought. The word *philosophy*, translated from its original Greek, means simply love of wisdom. Philosophical thinking is also what we draw upon to make our way, as wisely as we can, through our lives. To be wise means, in part, to use knowledge well. Therefore, as nurses, we should be committed to using philosophical thinking to improve our understanding of the particular values, beliefs, and assumptions that inform our thinking and influence what we say and do.

Philosophical thinking provides the foundation for the development and analysis of the concepts (including conceptual models and conceptual frameworks) and theories used to articulate knowledge of the discipline. **Concept** is another word for idea. Nurses make use of concepts to highlight the ideas that are important to the discipline. A conceptual *framework*, viewed simply, is a cluster of related concepts around a particular topic. A conceptual *model* is a diagram or illustration showing graphically how concepts within a particular cluster are positioned in relationship to each other. A *theory* goes beyond conceptual models and frameworks to show the nature and significance of relationships between and among concepts. Theories offer ways of looking at (conceptualizing) a discipline—such as nursing—in clear explicit terms that can be communicated to others.

Philosophical and theoretical thinking support the discipline's professionalism and collegial status with other health professionals. Nurses must communicate clearly what makes their place in the interdisciplinary team important. To achieve this clarity, concepts and theories are used to organize and analyze nursing knowledge. To use this knowledge wisely, the philosophical beliefs and assumptions that are the foundation for the creation and use of this knowledge must be made clear.

What Is Philosophy?

Though "philosophy" has an ordinary, everyday meaning, in the sense that we can say we each have our own *philosophy* or set of beliefs and assumptions about the world and our place in it, philosophy is also a scientific discipline. By science we mean the systematic formulation of a body of knowledge. In a formal sense, philosophy is a scientific discipline that raises, explores, and attempts to answer questions bearing upon "our ideas about our experience, the universe, and human affairs" (Fry, 1992, p. 87). In philosophy, we use critical analysis in pursuit of our goals.

Philosophical thinking can assist us to:

- identify and question assumptions,
- clarify how concepts are used and how they have meaning, and
- assess arguments made to defend or critique particular ways of thinking.

Philosophy's Three Primary Areas of Inquiry

Philosophy's three primary areas of inquiry are *ontology*, *epistemology*, and *ethics*. Though these particular terms may be unfamiliar, they refer to areas of inquiry somewhat familiar to most of us. **Ontology** investigates the nature of being. It asks such questions as: What is the nature of reality? What is the meaning and purpose of our existence? What does it mean to be a person? **Epistemology** investigates the nature of knowledge. How do we know something? What are the limits of our knowledge? On what grounds can we say something is true? What is the difference between what is believed to constitute knowledge and what is described as opinion? **Ethics** explores the nature of moral conduct and judgement. What is good? How should one behave or react in particular circumstances? How should we judge the actions of others? The ways in which we answer these kinds of ontological, epistemological, and ethical questions reflect our basic assumptions and beliefs about the world.

Paradigms or World Views

A **paradigm** (or world view) is a particular way of thinking based on a specific set of beliefs, values, and assumptions. The world view that we each hold influences how we perceive, comprehend, and interpret our worlds. It shapes our understanding of events and the means we use to seek knowledge. Nevertheless, we are often unaware of our underlying beliefs, values, and assumptions. In particular, **assumptions** often operate unconsciously and are beliefs that are taken for granted without evidence that has been systematically generated.

Many of our social arrangements rest solely on assumptions. For example, the idea that nursing is "women's work" relies on an assumption that particular kinds of work are best suited for women and other kinds of work are more appropriate for men. This assumption is often based on other unexamined beliefs about what is sometimes described as women's "natural" capacity for caring and nurturing. To critique this assumption, one might examine particular beliefs and values: notions such as caring, men and women's "proper" position in society, the difference between men and women, and the social value attributed to various kinds of work. This kind of inquiry might suggest that women's historical association with activities of care is not so much a reflection of women's essential nature but rather of the ways in which social roles and responsibilities have been allocated throughout history. Philosophical inquiry would help to make explicit what underlies the assumption that nursing is "women's work."

Empiricist and Interpretive Traditions

Though there are many world views or paradigms, two ways of understanding the world have been particularly influential in nursing: the *empiricist* and the *interpretive* traditions. According to the **empiricist tradition,** there is a single reality that exists independently of our knowledge of it. The world exists out there separate from human knowers. Knowledge can be obtained by observation and experiment—in others words, by means of the **scientific method.** Truth can be determined by comparing our knowledge claims against this independently existing reality. In making discoveries about this world as it really is, scientists can and should prevent subjective biases and beliefs from influencing their perceptions. According to this tradition, it is possible to produce objective knowledge of the world.

By contrast, according to the **interpretive tradition,** there is no single fixed reality against which knowledge can be measured. Knowledge of the world independent of our theorizing about it is not possible. Our knowledge of the world is always mediated through our assumptions. In fact, some scholars in the interpretive tradition argue that the nature of human understanding is itself interpretive and that it is our nature as human beings to create meaning from our experiences.

Each of these two philosophical traditions includes many variations. People who work in one of these traditions often express their beliefs and assumptions somewhat differently. Therefore, simply labelling a work as "empiricist" or "interpretive" is of limited use. It is much more fruitful to consider the specific beliefs and assumptions that underlie a particular work.

Both the empiricist and the interpretive traditions have their strong adherents. But the point here is not to suggest the rightness or wrongness of either tradition. Rather, we need to recognize that world views provide a general orientation to the world, a way to organize perceptions and experience. In knowledge-generating activities, paradigmatic views influence directions for research and study, problem identification, and guidelines for inquiry and action. Because writers often do not make their world views explicit, we as readers of nursing research and theory should carefully consider exactly what assumptions are at play as we read.

Philosophy in Nursing

Philosophy is an essential feature of all scientific disciplines, and nursing is no exception. The study of philosophy in nursing enables us to further our understanding of the values, beliefs, assumptions, and knowledge which constitute our discipline. Generally speaking, the study of philosophy in nursing can be understood as the "philosophical inquiry about nursing's social and humanitarian roles, its form of thought, nature, scope, purpose, methods, language, moral presuppositions, and knowledge claims" (Fry, 1999, p. 6). Philosophy in nursing involves consideration of the same sorts of ontological, epistemological, and ethical questions that we mentioned earlier in the chapter. But here, we formulate how these questions are studied in relation to the art, science, and practice of nursing. Thus, an ontological inquiry will consider the nature of nursing; an epistemological inquiry will consider nursing knowledge; and ethical inquiry will consider the moral questions that arise in nursing. Nurses use philosophy to think, to examine assumptions, to analyze concepts, and to carefully consider arguments. In this sense, philosophy in nursing is an invaluable practical activity in which all nurses should participate.

Developing a particular philosophy of nursing involves careful clarification and reflection on what, as nurses, we are trying to do, why we do it, and what knowledge we use. A useful philosophy of nursing will help accomplish these goals. First, it will identify what we believe to be the central phenomena of the discipline. Second, it will relate nursing to a particular world view or philosophical tradition. Third, it will offer some criterion concerning knowledge development in the discipline (Salsberry, 1994). Formulating a philosophy of nursing is about making our frame of reference for being in the world explicit (Smith, 1994).

Scientific inquiry is still the predominant mode of inquiry in nursing. However, there are nursing questions that science cannot answer (Kikuchi, 1992). Scientific inquiry is directed toward the material world, to that which can be measured or is observable through the senses. Thus, techniques of science cannot answer some questions concerning the nature of nursing, the moral ground of nursing practice, or the particular meanings of nurse–patient relationships. Interpretive approaches as well as empiricist approaches are important in nursing philosophy.

Philosophical thinking in nursing has developed on many fronts, and nurses have used philosophy in many different ways. Since the 1980s, nurses have published many articles and books about nursing philosophy, and they have organized many conferences around philosophical themes. In 1988, the Institute for Philosophical Nursing Research was founded at the University of Alberta. If we understand philosophy of nursing as simply an activity that uses philosophical methods and raises certain kinds of questions about the discipline of nursing, we can appreciate the necessity to support within nursing a number of different approaches to philosophy.

Overview of Selected Nursing Philosophies

A perusal of the work of selected nurse philosophers demonstrates the ways in which philosophy can be used in nursing and the kinds of questions a philosophical perspective might address. In the survey that follows, we have organized selected nurse philosophers into four groups according to the types of topics they might address (see Table 4.1). This survey is, of necessity, a partial one, but we have included a range of philosophical positions.

Some nurse philosophers directly address nursing philosophy itself as a topic for discussion. For example, Kikuchi and Simmons (1992) argue for a place for philosophical inquiry in nursing by reasoning that science cannot answer all of nursing's questions. In a later paper, Kikuchi and Simmons (1994) present a philosophical argument against the appropriateness of particular philosophies for nursing. Salsberry (1994) claims that a philosophy of nursing will identify what are to be believed the central phenomena of the discipline and that it will relate nursing to a particular world view or philosophical tradition. Smith (1994) asserts that arriving at a philosophy of nursing makes explicit our frame of reference for being in the world. Edwards (1997) explores what constitutes a philosophy of nursing, considering not only what should be included under this heading but also how it should be included. For Edwards, a philosophy of nursing should include an analysis of the concepts deemed to be central to the discipline. Such analysis would include ontological and epistemological values and logic. Johnson (1994) takes up the question of what is meant by the art of nursing using a philosophical method of argument to arrive at a definition of nursing as an art associated with expressive, creative, and intuitive abilities. Beginning from a different philosophical perspective, Bishop and Scudder (1999) use an interpretive approach to articulate a meaning of nursing from the point of view of practising nurses. They offer an interpretation of the meaning of nursing that focuses on nursing as the practice of caring, as a way of being for others, and as a relationship. In all these papers, the authors do not insist that they are offering "correct" knowledge as one might find in a scientific paper. Rather, they present arguments, defend positions, and invite readers to consider the persuasiveness of their analyses and conclusions.

A second group of nurse philosophers use philosophy to address nursing research questions. Often, these inquiries take a phenomenological approach, which means that the researcher investigates and describes particular phenomena as they are consciously experienced in nursing practice. Topics of this kind of research range from experiences of illness or grief to experiences of homelessness. For example, Cameron (1992) considers the meanings that the question "How are you?" can have in the context of a nurse–patient relationship, thereby showing that we should not take our understanding of these words for granted. Bergum (1989) philosophically explores women's experiences of becoming a mother. These kinds of philosophical writings stimulate nurses to reflect on the meanings of experiences and phenomena that we sometimes assume we already understand. In other words, these types of philosophical inquiries expand our thinking by giving us more to think about.

A third group of nurse philosophers ask epistemological questions about the practice of nursing. Some of these writers explicitly draw upon other philosophers or philosophical traditions to explicate nursing practice. Purkis (1997) uses ideas from the writings of the French philosopher Michel Foucault (1924–1984), such as the disciplined and disciplining gaze (how nurses communicate what counts as health and its promotion) of the nurse, to reflect on the implications of health promotion dis-

TABLE 4.1 Selected Nurse Philosophers

Topics They Might Address	Writers	Approach to Inquiry
Argument	Kikuchi and Simmons (1992)	Philosophical Analysis
	Johnson (1994)	Philosophical Analysis
Epistemology	Edwards (1998)	Philosophical Analysis
Research	Bergum (1989)	Interpretive phenomenology
	Cameron (1992)	Interpretive phenomenology
Ethics	Gadow (1994)	Relational ethics
	Storch (1993)	Bioethics

Canadian Society Notes

Fact	Implications for Nursing
In 1988, the Institute for Philosophical Nursing Research was founded at the University of Alberta.	The aim of the institute is to provide leadership in the pursuit of philosophical nursing knowledge that underlies the advancement of the nursing practice.
Philosophical methods raise certain kinds of questions about the discipline of nursing.	We can appreciate the necessity to support within nursing a number of different approaches to philosophy.
Techniques of science cannot answer some questions concerning the nature of nursing, the moral ground of nursing practice, or the particular meanings of nurse–patient relationships.	The CNA's (2002) position statement *Evidence-based Decision-making and Nursing Practice* provides directive to nurses concerning the need for scientific evidence to underlie practice.

Source: Canadian Nurses Association. (2002). *Evidence-based Decision-making and Nursing Practice*. Ottawa: Author.

courses and practice. Lawler (1997) also draws on Foucault's writings to suggest that the disciplines of science and economics have influenced how we speak and think about nursing. In particular, the world views that prevail in science and economics do not recognize the importance of relationship and contexts; concepts which nurses consider central to the practice of nursing.

In the area of ethics, a fourth group of nurse philosophers address ethical questions about the practice of nursing. Gadow (1994) suggests that the inability of patients to determine the meaning of their own experiences is a moral issue for nursing. Liaschenko (1997) suggests that serious ethical dilemmas may arise for nurses because of the systems and structures that contribute to the powerlessness that some nurses experience in practice.

Even this abbreviated discussion of nurse philosophers reveals that there are many ways to approach nursing philosophy. We should note that, although they are often not stated, philosophical ideas are an integral component of nursing practice, research, and theory development. By foregrounding or making explicit philosophical thinking, we can further our understanding of current nursing practices and develop our profession more effectively for the future.

Concepts and Theories

Philosophical thinking provides the foundation for the development and critical analysis of nursing knowledge. Nursing knowledge is organized and communicated using concepts, models, frameworks, and theories. A theory of nursing will address the subject matter of the discipline of nursing in accordance with a particular philosophical world view. For example, a theory of nursing will include some conceptualization of the nature of nursing, its scope, and purpose. It will identify and describe the central nursing concepts, such as person, health, nursing, and environment, and also propose how these phenomena can be known. It may also address ethical concerns by specifying how we might understand moral phenomena encountered in nursing practice. The building blocks of theories are *concepts*.

Concepts are abstract ideas or mental images of phenomena. They are words that bring forth mental pictures of the properties and meanings of objects, events, or things. Concepts may be (1) readily observable, or *concrete*, ideas, such as thermometer, rash, and lesion; (2) indirectly observable, or *inferential*, ideas, such as pain and temperature; or (3) non-observable, or *abstract*, ideas, such as equilibrium, adaptation, stress, and powerlessness. Many concepts apply to nursing: concepts about human beings, health, helping relationships, and communication. Nursing theories address and specify relationships among four major abstract concepts referred to as the **metaparadigm** of nursing—the most global philosophical or conceptual framework of a profession. A metaparadigm is a higher level of abstraction than a paradigm. It identifies the concepts central to the discipline without relating this to the assumptions of a particular world view. Although there is consensus that the following four concepts make up nursing's metaparadigm (Fawcett, 1984), others have proposed an alternative metaparadigm (Newman, Syme, & Cocorian-Perry, 1981; Parse, 1986).

1. *Person* or *client*, the recipient of nursing care (includes individuals, families, groups, and communities).
2. *Environment*, the internal and external surroundings that affect the client. This includes people in the physical environment, such as families, friends, and significant others.
3. *Health*, the degree of wellness or well-being that the client experiences.
4. *Nursing*, the attributes, characteristics, and actions of the nurse providing care on behalf of, or in conjunction with, the client.

Each nurse theorist's definitions of nursing's major concepts vary in accordance with their world view, their philosophy, and their experience in nursing. Nursing theories serve several purposes. See the box below.

The terms *theory* and *conceptual framework* are often used interchangeably in nursing literature. Strictly speaking, they differ in their levels of abstraction; conceptual framework is more abstract than theory. A **conceptual framework,** viewed simply, is a group of related concepts. It provides an overall view or orientation to focus thoughts. A conceptual framework can be visualized as an umbrella under which many concepts can exist. A **conceptual model,** a term also used interchangeably with *conceptual framework,* is a graphic illustration or diagram of a conceptual framework.

A **theory** is a supposition or system of ideas that is proposed to explain a given phenomenon. For example, Newton proposed his theory of gravity to explain why objects always fall from a tree to the ground. A *theory* goes one step beyond a *conceptual framework;* a theory relates concepts by using definitions that state significant relationships between concepts.

The major purpose of a conceptual framework is to give clear and explicit direction to the three areas of nursing: practice, education, and research. A theory, in contrast, is more limited in scope. Its primary purpose is to generate knowledge in a field. A theory explores phenomena, expresses relationships among facts, generates a hypothesis, and predicts future events and relationships.

Because the primary purpose of nursing theory is to generate scientific knowledge, nursing theory and nursing research are closely related. Nursing knowledge is generated within empiricist and interpretive research traditions. Empiricist approaches can be theory generating or theory testing, whereas interpretive approaches expose understandings of an experience. Scientific knowledge is derived from testing hypotheses (assumptions) generated by theories for nursing. Research determines the utility of those hypotheses, and research findings may be developed into theories for nursing. In the research process, comparisons are made between the observed outcomes of research and the relationship predicted by the hypotheses.

Overview of Selected Nursing Theories

Theory development gained momentum in the 1960s and has progressed markedly since then. Because opinions on the nature and structure of nursing vary, theories continue to be developed. Each theory bears the name of the person or group who developed it and reflects the beliefs of the developer.

The following nursing theories vary considerably (1) in their level of abstraction; (2) in their conceptualization of the client, health/illness, and nursing; and (3) in their ability to describe, explain, or predict. Some theories are broad in scope; others are limited.

Only brief summaries of the theorist's central theme and basic assumptions are included here.

Purposes of Nursing Theories and Conceptual Frameworks

Provide direction and guidance for (1) structuring professional nursing practice, education, and research; and (2) differentiating the focus of nursing from other professions.

In Practice

- Assist nurses to describe, explain, and predict everyday experiences.
- Serve to guide assessment, intervention, and evaluation of nursing care.
- Provide a rationale for collecting reliable and valid data about the health status of clients, which are essential for effective decision making and implementation.
- Help establish criteria to measure the quality of nursing care.
- Help build a common nursing terminology to use in communicating with other health professionals. Ideas are developed and words defined.
- Enhance autonomy (independence and self-governance) of nursing by defining its own independent functions.

In Education

- Provide a general focus for curriculum design.
- Guide curricular decision making.

In Research

- Offer a framework for generating knowledge and new ideas.
- Assist in discovering knowledge gaps in the specific field of study.
- Offer a systematic approach to identify questions for study, select variables, interpret findings, and validate nursing interventions.

TABLE 4.2 Selected Nurse Theorists' Conceptualization of Nursing

Nightingale (1860)	Nursing is the act of utilizing the environment of the patient to assist in his/her recovery.
Peplau (1952)	Nursing is a therapeutic relationship between the nurse and the client.
Henderson (1966)	Nursing is assisting sick or well individuals to gain independence in meeting their fundamental needs.
Roy (1976)	Nursing is assisting persons to use conscious awareness and choice to create human and environmental integration.
Watson (1979)	Nursing is caring, the unifying focus of practice.
Parse (1981)	Nursing is creating a situation in which clients choose and bear responsibility for patterns of health.
Leininger (1985)	Care is the essence and the dominant, distinctive, and unifying feature of nursing.
Allen (1986)	Nursing is the professional response to the person's natural response to healthy living.
Campbell (1987)	Nursing's unique function is to nurture individuals experiencing critical periods in their life cycles to assist them to reach optimal health.
Roach (1992)	Nursing is conceptualized as competence, compassion, confidence, consciousness, and commitment.

Nightingale's Environmental Theory

Florence Nightingale, often considered the first nurse theorist, defined nursing over 100 years ago as "the act of utilizing the environment of the patient to assist him in his recovery" (Nightingale, 1860). She linked health with five environmental factors: (1) pure or fresh air, (2) pure water, (3) efficient drainage, (4) cleanliness, and (5) light, especially direct sunlight. Deficiencies in these five factors produced lack of health, or illness.

These environmental factors attain significance when one considers that sanitation conditions in hospitals of the mid-1800s were extremely poor and that women working in the hospitals were often unreliable, uneducated, and incompetent to care for the ill.

In addition to those factors, Nightingale also stressed the importance of keeping the client warm, maintaining a noise-free environment, and attending to the client's diet in terms of assessing intake, timeliness of the meal, and its effect on the person.

Nightingale set the stage for further work in the development of nursing theories. Her general concepts about ventilation, cleanliness, quiet, warmth, and diet remain integral parts of nursing and health care today.

Peplau's Interpersonal Relations Model

Hildegard Peplau, a psychiatric nurse, introduced her interpersonal concepts in 1952. Central to Peplau's theory is the use of a therapeutic relationship between the nurse and the client.

Nurses enter into a personal relationship with an individual when a felt need is present. The nurse–client relationship evolves in four phases:

1. *Orientation.* During this phase, the client seeks help, and the nurse assists the client to understand the problem and the extent of the need for help.
2. *Identification.* During this phase, the client assumes a posture of dependence, interdependence, or independence in relation to the nurse (relatedness). The nurse's focus is to assure the person that the nurse understands the interpersonal meaning of the client's situation.
3. *Exploitation.* In this phase, the client derives full value from what the nurse offers through the relationship. The client uses available services on the basis of self-interest and needs. Power shifts from the nurse to the client.
4. *Resolution.* In this final phase, old needs and goals are put aside and new ones adopted. Once older needs are resolved, newer and more mature ones emerge.

To help clients fulfill their needs, nurses assume many roles: stranger, teacher, resource person, surrogate, leader, and counsellor. Peplau's model continues to be used by clinicians when working with individuals who have psychological problems.

Henderson's Definition of Nursing

In 1966, Virginia Henderson formulated a definition of the unique function of nursing. This definition was a major stepping-stone in the emergence of nursing as a discipline separate from medicine. Like Nightingale, Henderson described nursing in relation to the client and the client's environment. Unlike Nightingale, Henderson saw the nurse as concerned with both well and ill individuals, acknowledged that nurses interact with clients even when recovery may not be feasible, and mentioned the teaching and advocacy roles of the nurse.

Henderson conceptualized the nurse's role as assisting sick or well individuals to gain independence in meeting 14 fundamental needs (Henderson, 1966):

1. Breathing normally
2. Eating and drinking adequately
3. Eliminating body wastes
4. Moving and maintaining a desirable position
5. Sleeping and resting
6. Selecting suitable clothes
7. Maintaining body temperature within normal range by adjusting clothing and modifying the environment
8. Keeping the body clean and well groomed to protect the integument
9. Avoiding dangers in the environment and avoiding injuring others
10. Communicating with others in expressing emotions, needs, fears, or opinions
11. Worshipping according to one's faith
12. Working in such a way that one feels a sense of accomplishment
13. Playing or participating in various forms of recreation
14. Learning, discovering, or satisfying the curiosity that leads to normal development and health, and using available health facilities

Henderson has published many works and continues to be cited in current nursing literature. Her emphasis on the importance of nursing's independence from, and interdependence with, other health-care disciplines is well recognized.

Watson's Assumptions of Caring

- Human caring in nursing is not just an emotion, concern, attitude, or benevolent desire. *Caring* connotes a personal response.
- Caring is an intersubjective human process and is the moral ideal of nursing.
- Caring can be effectively demonstrated only interpersonally.
- Effective caring promotes health and individual or family growth.
- Caring promotes health more than does curing.
- Caring responses accept a person not only as they are now but also for what the person may become.
- A caring environment offers the development of potential while allowing the person to choose the best action for the self at a given point in time.
- Caring occasions involve action and choice by nurse and client. If the caring occasion is transpersonal, the limits of openness expand, as do human capacities.
- The most abstract characteristic of a caring person is that the person is somehow responsive to another person as a unique individual, perceives the other's feelings, and sets one person apart from another.
- Human caring involves values, a will and a commitment to care, knowledge, caring actions, and consequences.
- The ideal and value of caring is a starting point, a stance, and an attitude that has to become a will, an intention, a commitment, and a conscious judgement that manifests itself in concrete acts.

Roy's Adaptation Model

Sister Callista Roy's adaptation model was first published in book form in 1976. She defines *adaptation* as "the process and outcome whereby the thinking and feeling person uses conscious awareness and choice to create human and environmental integration" (Roy, 1997, p. 44).

In recent years, Roy has restated her scientific and philosophical assumptions for the 21st century. These assumptions focus on the increasing complexity of person and environment, self-organization, and the relationship between and among persons, the universe, and what can be considered a supreme being or God. Her philosophical assumptions have been refined using major characteristics of "creation spirituality"—a view that "persons and the earth are one, and that they are in God and of God" (Roy, 1997, p. 46).

Roy focuses on the individual as a biopsychosocial adaptive system that employs a feedback cycle of input (stimuli), throughput (control processes), and output (behaviours or adaptive responses). Both the individual and the environment are sources of stimuli that require modification to promote adaptation, an ongoing purposive response. Adaptive responses contribute to health, which she defines as the process of being and becoming integrated; ineffective or maladaptive responses do not contribute to health. Each person's adaptation level is unique and constantly changing.

Individuals respond to needs (stimuli) in one of four modes:

1. The *physiologic mode* involves the body's basic physiologic needs and ways of adapting in regard to fluid and electrolytes, activity and rest, circulation and

oxygen, nutrition and elimination, protection, the senses, and neurologic and endocrine functions.

2. The *self-concept mode* includes two components: the *physical* self, which involves sensation and body image, and the *personal* self, which involves self-ideal, self-consistency, and the moral-ethical self.
3. The *role function mode* is determined by the need for social integrity and refers to the performance of duties based on given positions within society.
4. The *interdependence mode* involves one's relations with significant others and support systems that provide help, affection, and attention.

The goal of Callista Roy's model is to enhance life processes through adaptation in the four adaptive modes.

Watson's Human Caring Theory

Jean Watson (1979) believes the practice of caring is central to nursing; it is the unifying focus for practice. Her major assumptions about caring are shown in the box opposite. Nursing interventions related to human care are referred to as *carative factors*, a guide Watson refers to as the "Core of Nursing." Watson outlines the following 10 factors:

1. Forming a humanistic-altruistic system of values
2. Instilling faith and hope
3. Cultivating sensitivity to one's self and others
4. Developing a helping-trust (human care) relationship
5. Promoting and accepting the expression of positive and negative feelings
6. Systematically using the scientific problem-solving method for decision making
7. Promoting interpersonal teaching-learning
8. Providing a supportive, protective, or corrective mental, physical, sociocultural, and spiritual environment
9. Assisting with the gratification of human needs
10. Allowing for existential-phenomenologic forces

Watson's theory of human caring has received worldwide recognition and is a major force in redefining nursing as a *caring-healing health* model.

Parse's Human Becoming Theory

Parse first published her theory in 1981 in *Man-Living-Health: A Theory for Nursing* and has since retitled her theory as human becoming theory, substituting the term *human* for *man* and *becoming* for *health*.

Parse proposes three assumptions about human becoming (1995):

1. Human becoming is freely choosing personal *meaning* in situations in the intersubjective process of relating value priorities.
2. Human becoming is co-creating *rhythmic patterns* or relating in mutual process with the universe.
3. Human becoming is *co-transcending* multidimensionally with the emerging possibilities.

These three assumptions focus on meaning, rhythmicity, and co-transcendence.

- *Meaning* arises from a person's interrelationship with the world and refers to happenings to which the person attaches varying degrees of significance.
- *Rhythmicity* is the movement toward greater diversity.
- *Co-transcendence* is the process of reaching out beyond the self.

Parse's model of human becoming emphasizes how individuals choose and bear responsibility for patterns of personal health. Parse contends that the client, not the nurse, is the authority figure and decision maker. The nurse's role involves helping individuals and families in choosing the possibilities for changing the health process. Specifically, the nurse's role consists of illuminating meaning (uncovering what was and what will be), synchronizing rhythms (leading through discussion to recognize harmony), and mobilizing transcendence (dreaming of possibilities and planning to reach them).

The Parse nurse uses "true presence" in the nurse–client process. "In true presence, the nurse's whole being is immersed with the client as the other illuminates the meanings of his or her situation and moves beyond the moment" (Parse, 1994b, p. 18).

Leininger's Cultural Care Diversity and Universality Theory

Madeleine Leininger, a well-known nurse anthropologist, first published her cultural care diversity and universality theory in 1985 in the journal *Nursing and Health Care*, and explained it further in 1988 and then in 1991, in her book *Culture Care Diversity and Universality: A Theory of Nursing*.

Leininger states that *care* is the essence of nursing and the dominant, distinctive, and unifying feature of nursing. She emphasizes that human caring, although a universal phenomenon, varies among cultures in its expressions, processes, and patterns; it is largely culturally derived. Leininger's definitions of culture, culture care, culture care diversity, culture care universality, generic care, professional care, and her sunrise model to depict her theory are discussed in Chapter 14. In order for nurses to assist people of diverse cultures, Leininger also presents three intervention modes:

- Culture care preservation and maintenance
- Culture care accommodation, negotiation, or both
- Culture care restructuring and repatterning

Campbell's UBC (University of British Columbia) Model of Nursing

Margaret Campbell (1987) developed the UBC Model of Nursing. Campbell guided nurse practitioners, researchers, and educators to look to the following elements of a model to guide their practice: "the view of the client" or "the recipient of care" and "the role and function of nursing in relation to the recipient of care and as a distinct and separate member of the team of health care professionals" (p. 5). In the UBC Model, the major theme is a behavioural system with interacting and interdependent subsystems, each representing a basic human need. Campbell viewed persons as having nine basic human needs, constantly striving to satisfy these needs by using a range of coping behaviours, both innate and acquired. According to this model, environment is that which lies outside the boundary of the system. The nurse is seen as nurturing "individuals experiencing critical periods so that they may develop and use a range of coping behaviours that will permit them to satisfy their basic human needs, to achieve stability and to reach optimum health" (Campbell, 1987, p.10).

Margaret Campbell developed this model on the basis of several assumptions about Canadian society. She assumed that society views optimal health as a desirable goal for all of its members and that members of society would assume responsibility for utilizing behaviours that promote and maintain positive health. She further assumed that society expects its members will behave in ways that will not be harmful to themselves or others in the satisfaction of their needs. She assumed that society expects health-care professionals to function competently and ethically. Lastly, Campbell assumed that society expected the UBC Model for Nursing, or any model for nursing, to be congruent with the values of that society. It was these assumptions about the values that Canadians hold and the beliefs about nursing she identified that guided her to conceptualize the UBC Model in a particular way.

The UBC Model in Figure 4.1 shows the nine subsystems that make up the behavioural system, with each subsystem representing one basic need. This illustration also shows how each of these subsystems relates to each other and how they interrelate to the system as whole, a feature of significance to nursing. For example, whatever happens to one subsystem (including nursing interventions) can influence the system as a whole. Figure 4.2 shows the structure of each of the subsystems. Each subsystem is responsible for the satisfaction of one of the basic needs. Each subsystem consists of (1) an inner region which includes the need and the abilities to meet that need, and (2) an outer region that includes the need-related goal and the forces influencing attainment of that goal. Figure 4.3 shows how the parts of a subsystem relate to each other. The determinants of coping behaviours are both cognitive (knowing what to do) and executive (carry the needed

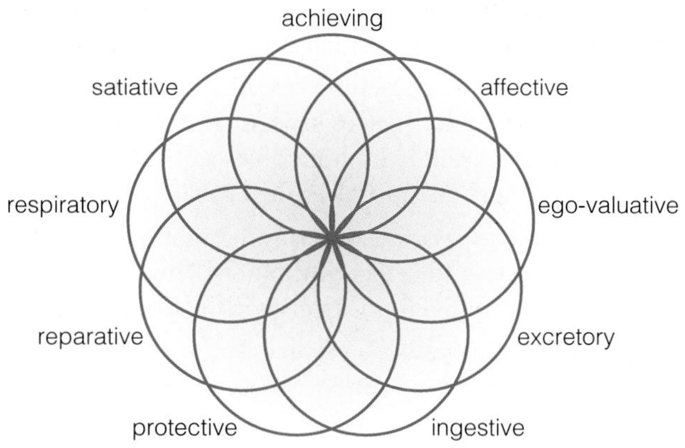

Figure 4.1 The nine basic needs of the individual
Source: Campbell, 1987, p. 32.

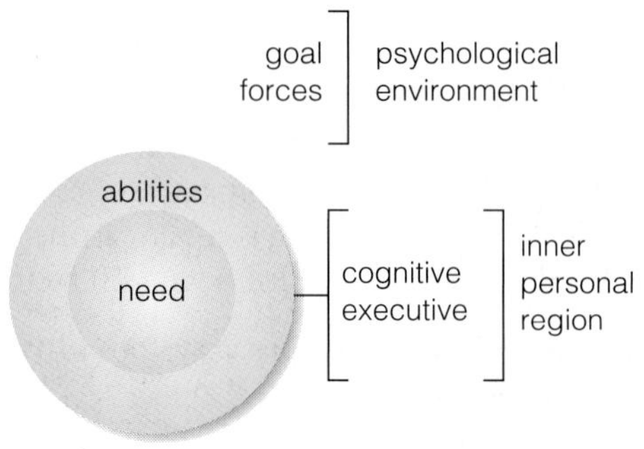

Figure 4.2 Structure of a subsystem: The parts
Source: Campbell, 1987, p. 33.

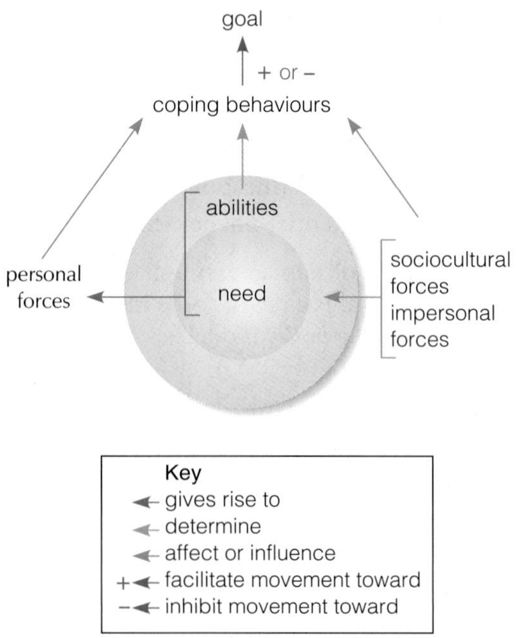

Figure 4.3 Structure of a subsystem: Interrelationship of the parts
Source: Campbell, 1987, p. 34.

action out). Forces influence movement toward or away from desired goals. It is in understanding the detailed structure and function of a particular subsystem, and its interrelation with other subsystems and with the behavioural system as a whole, that guides the nurse in making decisions relative to providing care.

Allen's McGill Model of Nursing (1986)

Another example of a nursing model is the McGill Model (1986) developed by Moyra Allen. In this model, the theme for nursing is the nature of healthy living. This model serves as the curriculum model for the McGill School of Nursing. Allen sees the search for healthy living as a quest. The focus of this model is the family or other social group in which learning is initiated, nurtured, and directed. The environment is the context in which this learning takes place. This context could be at home, the workplace, community group, the hospital or clinic. Health, according to Allen, is something that can be measured and can be modified. In Allen's model, nursing is a professional response to the person's natural response to healthy living. The goal of nursing is to assist people to enhance their problem-solving skills in dealing with health matters.

The McGill Model of Nursing has been credited with developing a unique role for nurses on an interdisciplinary team: providing a framework for the conceptualizing of the nurse's role; the assessment of families' needs; and the development of a nursing knowledge base (Feeley & Gerez-Lirette, 1992). The McGill Model of Nursing has been identified as appropriate to community health nursing in that it concentrates on health promotion and brings together elements underlying a family-development view of care. In more recent years, there has been increasing interest in shifting the focus of clinical practice with families from a deficit to a strengths-based perspective, a perspective that is central to the McGill Model of Nursing (Feeley & Gottlieb, 2000).

Sister Simone Roach's Attributes of Professional Caring

In her 1992 book *The Human Act of Caring*, Dr. Simone Roach puts forth the notion that "caring is an essential ingredient in human development and survival" (p. 2). Roach claims that nurses' professional caring has five important attributes: compassion, competence, confidence, conscience, and commitment (see box below for a description of each).

Roach's Attributes of Professional Caring

Compassion—a sensitivity to the pain and brokenness of the other; a quality of presence that allows one to share with and make room for the other

Competence—having the knowledge, judgement, skills, energy, experience, and motivation required to respond adequately to the demands of one's professional responsibilities

Confidence—the kind that fosters trusting relationships

Conscience—a state of moral awareness that grows with experience

Commitment—a complex, affective response characterized by convergence between one's desires and one's obligations and by the deliberate choice to act in accordance with them

Source: Roach (1992). *The Human Art of Caring: A Blueprint for the Health Professions*. Ottawa: Canadian Hospital Association Press.

FOCUS ON CRITICAL THINKING

The foundation of any profession, including nursing, is the development of a specialized body of knowledge. Nursing, like other disciplines, depends on philosophical thought, theories, frameworks, and models to organize its body of knowledge and, in so doing, provide direction for practice. Consider the following questions.

1. Thinking *philosophically* has changed the way nurses think about their practice. What do we mean by philosophical thought? Give at least three examples of how philosophical thought has influenced the evolution of nursing knowledge.
2. A *concept* is another word for an idea. Nurses make use of concepts to highlight the ideas that are important to the discipline. Discuss at least four concepts that you would consider central to the discipline and give your reasons for each concept you select.

See Appendix A for answers to these questions.

CHAPTER HIGHLIGHTS

- As an increasingly emerging profession, nursing is now deeply involved in identifying its own unique knowledge base—that is, the body of knowledge essential to nursing practice, or a so-called nursing science.
- Nurses must communicate exactly what makes their place in the interdisciplinary team unique and important.
- Theories offer ways of conceptualizing a discipline in clear, explicit terms that can be communicated to others.
- Because opinions about the nature and structure of nursing vary, theories continue to be developed. Each nursing theory bears the name of the person or group who developed it and reflects the beliefs of the developer.
- The theories vary considerably in (1) their level of abstraction; (2) their conceptualization of the client, health/illness, and nursing; and (3) their ability to describe, explain, or predict. Some theories are broad in scope; others are limited.
- Nursing theories serve several essential purposes, some of which are to differentiate the focus of nursing from other professions; to structure professional nursing practice, education, and research; to help build a common nursing terminology to use in communicating with other health professionals; and to enhance autonomy of nursing through defining its own independent functions.
- Because the primary purpose of nursing theory is to generate scientific knowledge, nursing theory and nursing research are closely related. Scientific knowledge is derived from testing hypotheses generated by theories for nursing. Research determines the utility of those hypotheses, and research findings may be developed into theories for nursing.
- The major distinction between a theory and a conceptual framework or model is the level of abstraction, with the conceptual framework being more abstract than the theory. A conceptual model is a system of related concepts or a conceptual diagram. Its major purpose is to give clear and explicit direction to the three areas of nursing: practice, education, and research. A theory generates knowledge in a field.
- Nursing theories address and specify relationships among four major concepts, the building blocks of theory: person or client, environment, health/illness, and nursing.
- Each nurse theorist's definitions of these four major concepts vary in accordance with personal philosophy, scientific orientation, experience in nursing, and how that experience has affected the theorist's view of nursing.
- Conceptual models for nursing relate to the nursing process in that they are operationalized or made real by the use of the nursing process. How nurses view human beings influences how they assess and intervene.
- In the 21st century, models for nursing will be refined in accordance with societal needs and with their tested usefulness.

READINGS AND REFERENCES

Suggested Readings

Arndt, M. J. (1995, Summer). Parse's theory of human becoming in practice with hospitalized adolescents. *Nursing Science Quarterly, 8*(2), 86–90.

This author applies Parse's theory of human becoming to the care of hospitalized adolescents and their families. Four scenarios are included to illustrate the practice methodology of this theory: an 18-year-old boy with Hirschsprung's disease; a 17-year-old boy with acute myelogenous leukemia; an 18-year-old girl with acute myeloblastic leukemia; and a 15-year-old girl admitted for surgery for an abdominal mass.

Gless, P. A. (1995, January/February). Applying the Roy adaptation model to the care of clients with quadriplegia. *Rehabilitation Nursing, 20*(1), 11–16.

Gless states that clients with quadriplegia can benefit from a holistic approach to care that focuses on promoting positive coping and adaptation, an approach that the Roy adaptation model delineates. This article discusses major assumptions of Roy's adaptation model and offers a case study to show the effectiveness of using the nursing process within the model's guidelines to help a client with quadriplegia adapt to living in a long-term care facility. Roy's five steps of the nursing process (assessment of stimuli, nursing diagnosis, goal setting, nursing interventions, and evaluation) are applied to the physiologic, self-concept, role-function, and interdependent adaptive modes.

Marckx, B. B. (1995, July). Watson's theory of caring: A model for implementation in practice. *Journal of Nursing Care Quality, 9*(4), 43–54.

Marckx introduces Jean Watson's theory of human caring in nursing as an innovative approach to improving care for residents in a special dementia unit. Specific examples of ways that Watson's model can be applied in typical nurse–client situations are presented. Implementation strategies with creative visual aids are included, and research tools for the evaluation of outcomes are described.

Wright, P. S., Piazza, D., Holcombe, J., & Foote, A. (1994, January). A comparison of three theories of nursing used as a guide for the nursing care of an 8-year-old child with leukemia. *Journal of Pediatric Oncology Nursing, 11*, 14–19.

These authors evaluate three nursing theories that can be used to provide a framework for holistic pediatric oncology nursing practice: *the Roy adaptation model, the Neuman systems model,* and *the Orem general theory of nursing.* The authors compare each theory in terms of the metaparadigm of nursing and present a critique. Four comparative tables are included. The decision of which theory to use is left to the individual nurse.

Related Research

Parse, R. R. (1996, Fall). Quality of life for persons living with Alzheimer's disease: The human becoming perspective. *Nursing Science Quarterly, 9*, 126–133.

Selected References

Bishop, A., & Scudder, J. (1999). A philosophical interpretation of nursing. *Scholarly Inquiry for Nursing Practice, 13*(1), 17–27.

Bergum, V. (1989). *Woman to mother: A Transformation*. Granby, MA: Bergin & Garvey.

Campbell, M. (1987). *The UBC Model for Nursing: Directions for Practice*. Vancouver: University of British Columbia School of Nursing.

Cameron, B. (1992). The nursing "how are you?" *Phenomenology &Pedagogy, 10*, 173–185.

Edwards, S. (1997). What is philosophy of nursing? *Journal of Advanced Nursing, 25*, 1089–1093.

Faucett, J. (1984). *Analysis and evaluation of conceptual models.* Philadelphia: F. A. Davis.

Feely, M. (1997, August). Using Peplau's theory in nurse-patient relations. *International Nursing Review, 34*(4), 115–120.

Feeley N., & Gerez-Lirette T. (1992). Development of professional practice based on the McGill model of nursing in an ambulatory care setting. *Journal of Advanced Nursing, 17*(7): 801–8.

Feeley, N., & Gottlieb, L. N. (2000). Nursing approaches for working with family strengths and resources. *Journal of Family Nursing, 6*(1): 9–24.

Fry, S. (1992). Neglect of philosophical inquiry in nursing: Cause and effect. In J. Kikuchi & H. Simmons (Eds.), *Philosophic Inquiry in Nursing* (pp. 85–96). Newbury Park, CA: Sage.

Fry, S. (1999). The philosophy of nursing. *Scholarly Inquiry for Nursing Practice, 13*(1), 5–15.

Gadow, S. (1994). Whose body? Whose Story? The question about narrative in women's health care. *Soundings*, 77 (3/4), 295–307.

George, J. B. (Ed.). (1995). *Nursing theories: The base for professional nursing practice* (4th ed.). Norwalk, CT: Appleton & Lange.

Henderson, V. (1966). *The nature of nursing: A definition and its implications for practice, research, and education.* Riverside, NJ: Macmillan.

Henderson, V. A. (1991). *The nature of nursing: Reflections after 25 years.* New York: National League for Nursing Press. Pub. No. 15-2346.

Johnson, J. A. (1994). Dialectical examination of nursing art. *Advances in Nursing Science, 17*(1), 1–14.

Kikuchi, J. (1992). Nursing questions that science cannot answer. In J. Kikuchi & H. Simmons (Eds.), *Philosophic inquiry in nursing* (pp. 26–37). Newbury Park, CA: Sage.

Kikuchi, J. & Simmons, H. (1994). A pragmatic philosophy of nursing: Threat or promise? In J. Kikuchi & H. Simmons (Eds.), *Developing a philosophy of nursing* (pp. 79–94). Thousand Oaks, CA: Sage.

Lawler, J. (1997). *The body in nursing*. Melbourne, Australia: Churchill Livingstone.

Leininger, M. M. (1978). *Transcultural nursing: Concepts, theories, and practices.* New York: Wiley.

Leininger, M. M. (1980). Caring: A central focus of nursing and health care services. *Nursing and Health Care, 1*(3), 135–143.

Leininger, M. M. (1984). *Care: The essence of nursing and health.* Thorofare, NJ: Charles B. Slack.

Leininger, M. M. (1985). Transcultural care diversity and universality: A theory of nursing. *Nursing and Health Care, 6*, 208–212.

Leininger, M. M. (1988). Leininger's theory of nursing: Cultural care, diversity and universality. *Nursing Science Quarterly, 1*(4), 152–160.

Leininger, M. M. (Ed.). (1991). *Culture care diversity and universality: A theory of nursing.* New York: National League for Nursing Press. Pub. No. 15-2402.

Leininger, M. (1996). Culture care theory, research, and practice. *Nursing Science Quarterly, 9*(2), 71–78.

Leininger, M. (1996). Major directions for transcultural nursing: A journey into the 21st century. *Journal of Transcultural Nursing*, 7(2), 28–31.

Liaschenko, J. (1997). Ethics and the geography of nurse-patient relationship: Spatial vulnerabilities and gendered space. *Scholarly Inquiry for Nursing Practice, 11*(1), 45–59.

Nightingale, F. (1957). *Notes on nursing.* Philadelphia, PA: Lippincott. (Original work published 1860).

Parse, R. R. (1981). *Man-living-health: A theory of nursing.* New York: Wiley.

Parse, R. R. (1987). *Nursing science: Major paradigms, theories, and critiques.* Philadelphia, PA: Saunders.

Parse, R. R. (1989). Man-living-health: A theory of nursing. In J. Riehl-Sisca (Ed.), *Conceptual models for nursing practice* (3rd ed.) (pp. 253–257). Norwalk, CT: Appleton & Lange.

Parse, R. R. (1994). Quality of life: Sciencing and living the art of human becoming. *Nursing Science Quarterly*, 7(1), 16–21.

Parse, R. R. (Ed.). (1995). *Illumination: The human becoming theory in practice and research.* New York: National League for Nursing Press. Pub. No. 15-2670.

Parse, R. R. (1996). The human becoming theory: Challenges in practice and research. *Nursing Science Quarterly, 9*(2), 55–60.

Parse, R. R. (1997). The human becoming theory: The was, is, and will be. *Nursing Science Quarterly, 10*(1), 32–37.

Peplau, H. E. (1952). *Interpersonal relations in nursing.* New York: Putnam.

Peplau, H. E. (1963). Interpersonal relations and the process of adaptations. *Nursing Science, 1*(4), 272–279.

Peplau, H. E. (1980). The Peplau developmental model for nursing practice. In J. P. Riehl & C. Roy (Eds.), *Conceptual models for nursing practice* (2nd ed.) (pp. 53–75). New York: Appleton-Century-Crofts.

Purkis, M.E. (1997). The "social determinants" of practice: A critical analysis of the discourse of health promotion. *Canadian Journal of Nursing Research, 29*(1), 47–62.

Roach, Sr. S. (1992). *The Human act of caring: A blueprint for the health professions*. Ottawa: Canadian Hospital Association Press.

Roy, C. (1970). Adaptation: A conceptual framework in nursing. *Nursing Outlook, 18*, 42–45.

Roy, C. (1976). *Introduction to nursing: An adaptation model.* Englewood Cliffs, NJ: Prentice-Hall.

Roy, C. (1984). *Introduction to nursing: An adaptation model* (2nd ed.). Englewood Cliffs, NJ: Prentice-Hall.

Roy, C. (1997, Spring). Future of the Roy model: Challenge to redefine adaptation. *Nursing Science Quarterly, 10*(1), 42–48.

Roy, C., & Andrews, H. A. (1991). *The Roy adaptation model: The definitive statement.* Norwalk, CT: Appleton & Lange.

Salsberry, P. (1994). A philosophy of nursing: What it is? What it is not? In J. Kikuchi & H. Simmons (Eds.), *Developing a philosophy of nursing* (pp. 11–19). Thousand Oaks, CA: Sage.

Simmons, H. (1992). Philosophic and scientific inquiry: The interface. In J. Kikuchi & H. Simmons (Eds.), *Philosophic Inquiry in Nursing* (pp. 9–25). Newbury Park, CA: Sage.

Simpson, J., & Taylor, D. (2002). Do conceptual models of nursing work today? *Canadian Nurse 98*(2), 24–26.

Smith, M. (1994). Arriving at a philosophy of nursing: Discovering? Constructing? Evolving? In J. Kikuchi & H. Simmons (Eds.), *Developing a philosophy of nursing* (pp. 43–59). Thousand Oaks, CA: Sage.

Watson, J. (1979). *Nursing: The philosophy and science of caring.* Boston: Little, Brown.

Watson, J. (1985). *Nursing: Human science and human care: A theory of nursing.* Norwalk, CT: Appleton-Century-Crofts.

Watson, J. (1988). *Nursing: Human science and human care: A theory of nursing.* New York: National League for Nursing Press. Pub. No. 15-2236.

Watson, J. (1997, Spring). The theory of human caring: retrospective and prospective. *Nursing Science Quarterly, 10*, 49–52.

Wesley, R. L. (1995). *Nursing theories and models* (2nd ed.). Springhouse, PA: Springhouse.

WEBLINKS

The Nursing Theory Page
http://www.ualberta.ca/~jrnorris/nt/theory.html
This site was developed by the Faculty of Nursing, University of Alberta and provides an overview of a number of different nursing theorists.

Clayton College and State University Department of Nursing—Nursing Theories Link Page
http://healthsci.clayton.edu/eichelberger/nursing.htm
This site provides access to the writings of a number of different nursing theorists.

College of Nursing Valdosta State University
http://www.valdosta.edu/nursing/history_theory/theory.html
A number of different nursing theorists are introduced and access to their works is available through this site.

CHAPTER 5

The Individual—The Client of Care

OBJECTIVES

After completing this chapter, you will be able to:

- Explain the relationship of individuality and holism to nursing practice.
- Identify four main characteristics of homeostatic mechanisms.
- Describe the components of individual health assessment.
- Identify common risk factors regarding an individual's health.
- Analyze theoretical frameworks used in individual health promotion.
- Identify Maslow's characteristics of the self-actualized person.
- Describe the concept of individuality as it relates to client care.

Nurses assess and plan health care for individuals. Care of the individual is enhanced when the nurse understands the concepts of individuality, holism, homeostasis, human needs, and systems theory. The beliefs and values of each person and the support they receive come in large part from the family and are reinforced by the community. Thus, an understanding of family dynamics and the context of the community assists the nurse in planning care. For additional information on the family and community, see Chapters 6 and 16. To assist clients towards health, nurses must understand them as individuals.

Individual Health

Concept of Individuality

To help clients attain, maintain, or regain an optimal level of health, nurses need to understand clients as individuals. Each individual is a unique being who is different from every other human being, with a different genetic makeup, life experiences, and environmental interactions.

Dimensions of individuality include the person's total character, self-identity, and perceptions. The person's *total character* encompasses behaviours, emotional states, attitudes, values, motives, abilities, habits, and appearances. The person's *self-identity* encompasses perception of self as a separate and distinct entity, alone and in interactions with others. Identity is often threatened by actual or perceived alterations in wellness. Some changes are minor and may be considered merely inconveniences; others may compromise existence in profound ways. The person's *perceptions* encompass the way the person interprets the environment or situation, directly affecting how the person thinks, feels, and acts in any given situation.

Nurses' and clients' perceptions determine their subjective realities at the time of their interaction. There may be differences in the two views of reality that will influence communication, acceptance of one another, and whether the client's health-care needs are being met. Sometimes, the views of nurses and clients differ because of their own unique experiences.

When providing care, nurses need to focus on the client within both a total-care and an individualized-care context. In the total-care context, the nurse considers all the principles and areas that apply when taking care of any client of that age and condition. In the individualized-care context, the nurse becomes acquainted with the client as an individual, referring to the total care principles and using those principles that apply to this person at this time. For example, a nurse who is advising the mother of a preschooler understands that the child's desire to explore the world is a developmental stage that all preschoolers experience. However, the preschooler diagnosed with attention deficit disorder with hyperactivity may have an increased risk of accidents and injuries when interacting with the environment, due to impulsivity and poor self-control.

Canadian Society Notes

Fact	Implications for Nursing Practice
The Census counted 30,007,094 people in Canada on May 15, 2001, compared with 28,846,761 in 1996.	The demand for nursing services will increase.
Canada is a mosaic of cultures, languages, and ethnic groups.	Nurses require knowledge of the numerous cultural groups within Canada in order to provide quality care.
In 1929, less than 4 percent of women worked outside the family home. In 1999, 55 percent of women had paid work, compared with 67 percent of men. (Source: http://www.communication.gc.ca/facts/women_e.html)	Nurses need to acknowledge the changes within Canadian society as they provide care, support policy changes, and address health-care concerns.

Concept of Holism

Nurses are concerned with the individual as a whole, complete, or holistic person, not as an assembly of parts and processes. The terms **holistic** and **holism** are derived

Factors Influencing the Impact of Illness on the Individual

- The meaning of the illness to the individual
- The nature of the illness, which can range from minor to life threatening
- The duration of the illness, which ranges from short to long term
- The residual effects of the illness, including none to permanent disability
- The financial and social impact of the illness upon the individual's ability to work
- The impact of the illness upon the individual's family

from the Greek word meaning "whole." The term *holism* itself was coined by Jan Smuts, a South African statesman, in his book *Holism and Evolution* (1926). In holistic theory, a living organism is seen as an interacting, unified whole that is more than the mere sum of its parts. Viewed in this light, any disturbance in one part is a disturbance of the whole system; in other words, the disturbance affects the whole being.

When applied in nursing, the concept of holism emphasizes that nurses must keep the whole person in mind and strive to understand how one area of concern relates to the whole person. The nurse must also consider the relationship of the individual to the external environment and to others. For example, in helping a man who is grieving over the death of his spouse, the nurse explores the impact of the loss on the whole person (i.e., on the man's appetite, rest and sleep patterns, energy level, sense of well being, mood, usual activities, family relationships, and relationships with others). Nursing interventions are directed toward restoring overall harmony, so they depend on the man's sense of purpose and meaning of his life. For additional information about holistic practices, see Chapter 11.

Concept of Homeostasis

The concept of homeostasis was first introduced by Cannon (1939) to describe the relative constancy of the internal processes of the body, such as blood oxygen and carbon dioxide levels, blood pressure, body temperature, blood glucose, and fluid and electrolyte balance. To Cannon, the word *homeostasis* did not imply something stagnant, set, or immobile; it meant a condition that might vary but remained relatively constant. Cannon viewed the human being as separate from the external environment and constantly endeavouring to maintain physiologic **equilibrium,** or balance, through adaptation to that environment. **Homeostasis,** then, is the tendency of the body to maintain a state of balance or equilibrium while continually changing.

Physiologic Homeostasis

Physiologic homeostasis means that the internal environment of the body is relatively stable and constant. All cells of the body require a relatively constant environment to function; thus, the body's internal environment must be maintained within narrow limits. Homeostatic mechanisms have four main characteristics:

1. They are self-regulating.
2. They are compensatory.
3. They tend to be regulated by negative feedback systems.
4. They may require several feedback mechanisms to correct only one physiologic imbalance.

Self-regulation means that homeostatic mechanisms come into play automatically in the healthy person. However, if a person is ill or if an organ, such as a lung, is injured, the homeostatic mechanisms may not be able to respond to the stimulus as they would normally. Homeostatic mechanisms are **compensatory** (counterbalancing) because they tend to counteract conditions that are abnormal for the person. An example is a sudden drop in temperature. The compensatory mechanisms are that the peripheral blood vessels constrict, thereby diverting most of the blood internally; and increased muscular activity and shivering occur to create heat. Through these mechanisms the body temperature remains stable, despite the cold.

Feedback is the mechanism by which some of the output of a system is "fed back" into the system as input. This input influences the behaviour of the system and its future output. **Negative feedback** inhibits change; **positive feedback** stimulates change. Most biologic systems are controlled by negative feedback to bring the system back to stability. This type of feedback system senses and counteracts any deviations from normal. The deviations may be greater or less than the normal level or range. Negative feedback is a common control mechanism for hormone levels. For example, an increase in the production of parathyroid hormone is stimulated by a drop in blood calcium, but when additional parathyroid hormone raises the level of blood calcium, the hormone's production is then inhibited. Several negative feedback systems may be required to correct one physiologic imbalance. For example, with hypoxia (shortage of oxygen), the concentration of red blood cells increases and the heart rate becomes faster to transport the blood and available oxygen around the body adequately.

The two major homeostatic regulators are the autonomic nervous system and the endocrine system. In addition, the cardiovascular system, the renal system, the respiratory system, and the gastrointestinal system are important in maintaining homeostasis. See Figure 5.1.

Psychologic Homeostasis

The term *psychologic homeostasis* refers to emotional or psychologic balance or a state of mental well-being. It is maintained by a variety of mechanisms. Each person has certain psychologic needs, such as the need for love, security, and self-esteem, that must be met to maintain psychologic homeostasis. When one or more of these needs is not met or is threatened, certain coping mechanisms are activated to protect the person and provide psychologic homeostasis.

Psychologic homeostasis is acquired or learned through the experience of living and interacting with others. In addition, societal norms and culture influence behaviour. Some prerequisites for a person to develop psychologic homeostasis can be summarized as follows:

- *A stable physical environment in which the person feels safe and secure.* For example, the basic needs for food, shelter, and clothing must be met consistently from birth onward.

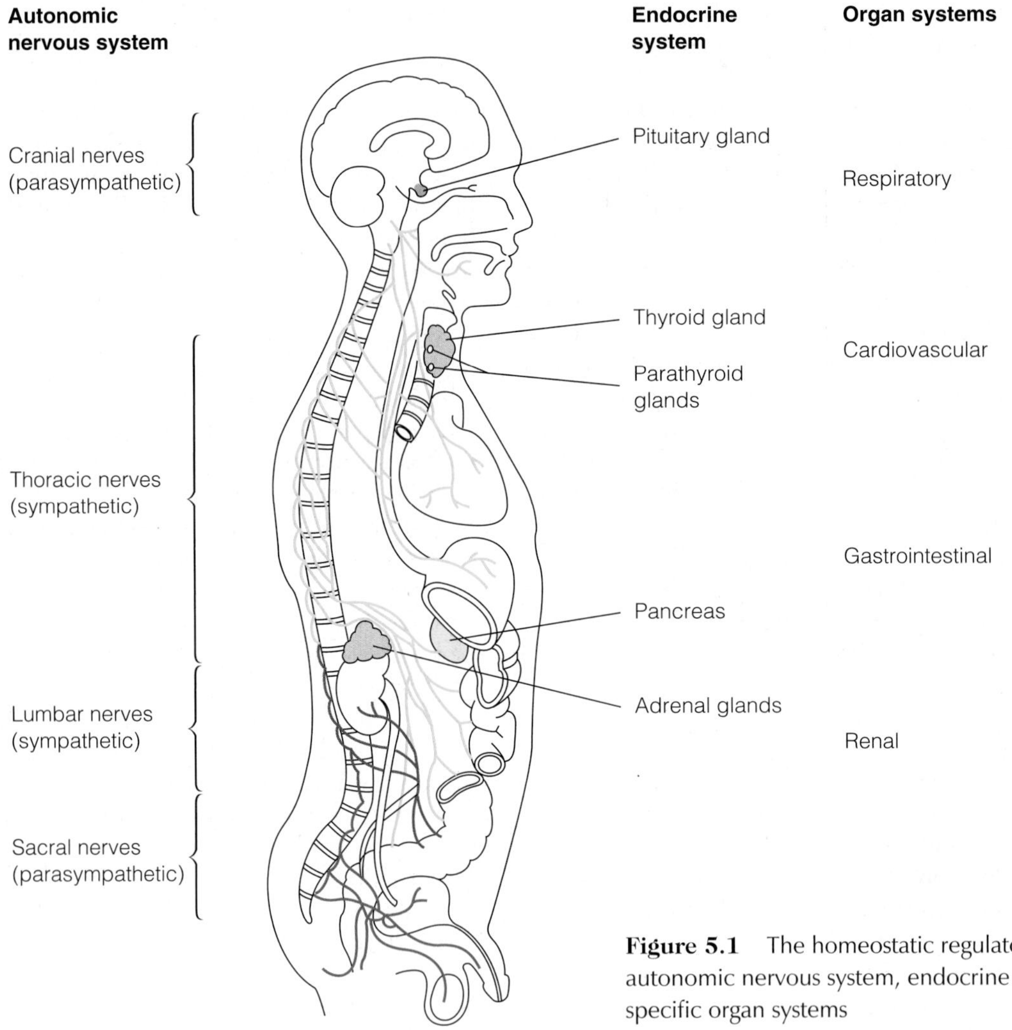

Figure 5.1 The homeostatic regulators of the body: autonomic nervous system, endocrine system, and specific organ systems

- *A stable psychologic environment from infancy onward, so that feelings of trust and love develop.* Growing children and adolescents also need kind but firm and consistent discipline, encouragement, and support to be their own unique selves.
- *A social environment that includes adults who are healthy role models.* Children learn the customs and values of society from these individuals.
- *A life experience that provides satisfactions.* Throughout life, people encounter many frustrations. They deal with these better if enough satisfying experiences have occurred to counterbalance the frustrating ones. See also unconscious ego defence mechanisms in Chapter 46.

Assessing the Health of Individuals

A thorough assessment of the individual's health status is basic to health promotion. Components of this assessment are the health history and physical examination, physical fitness assessment, lifestyle assessment, health risk appraisal, health beliefs review, and life-stress review. Details about these assessments are discussed in Chapter 9 and Chapter 27.

Health Appraisal

The *health appraisal* begins with a complete health history. The health history is one of the most effective ways of identifying existing or potential health problems (see Chapter 27). If further evaluation is indicated, a referral is made to the appropriate health-care professional. When the focus is on health, the appraisal includes information on lifestyle behaviours and health beliefs. The nurse uses data from the health appraisal to formulate a health profile. The health profile provides the data necessary to determine wellness or to establish a nursing diagnosis and to plan appropriate nursing interventions to promote optimal health through lifestyle modification.

Figure 5.2 Registered nurses intervene to promote the health and well-being of individuals of diverse ages and backgrounds

Health Beliefs

To promote health, the nurse must understand the health beliefs of individuals. Health beliefs may reflect a lack of information or misinformation about health or disease. They may also include folklore and practices from different cultures. There have been many advances in medicine and health care during the last few decades, but many clients may have outdated information about health, illness, treatment, and prevention. The nurse is frequently in a position to give the latest information or correct misconceptions. This function is an important component of the nursing care plan. For additional information on health beliefs, see Chapters 9 and 10.

Coping Mechanisms

Individual coping mechanisms are the behaviours individuals use to deal with stress or changes. Coping mechanisms can be viewed as an active method of problem solving developed to meet life's challenges. The coping mechanisms individuals develop reflect their own resourcefulness. Individuals may use the same coping patterns rather consistently over time or may change their coping strategies when new demands are made upon them. Coping is a basic function that helps the individual meet demands imposed from both within and without.

Nurses working with individuals realize the importance of assessing coping mechanisms as a way of determining how individuals relate to stress. Also important are the resources available to the individual. Internal resources, such as knowledge, skills, effective communication patterns, and a sense of purpose, assist in the problem-solving process. Age and the individual's developmental stage often bring with them experiences that may or may not support positive coping strategies. In addition, external support systems promote coping and adaptation. These external systems may be extended family, friends, religious affiliation, health-care professionals, or social services.

Health-Promoting Coping Mechanisms

- Problem solving
- Using positive thinking
- Sense of personal control over one's life
- Good health behaviours, e.g., exercise, good nutrition
- Social support relationships

Risk for Health Problems

Risk assessment helps the nurse identify individuals at higher risk than the general population of developing specific health problems, such as stroke, diabetes, and lung cancer. The vulnerability of individuals to health problems may be based on age, heredity or genetic factors, gender or race, sociological factors, and lifestyle practices.

Developmental Factors Individuals at both ends of the age continuum are at risk of developing health problems. Young children lack knowledge, skills, and experience to establish a repertoire of coping strategies. Many older adults feel a lack of purpose and decreased self-esteem. These feelings, in turn, reduce their motivation to engage in health-promoting behaviours, such as exercise or community and family involvement.

Hereditary Factors Individuals born into families with a history of certain diseases, such as diabetes or cardiovascular disease, are at greater risk of developing these conditions. A detailed individual and family history, including genetically transmitted disorders, is essential to the identification of individuals at risk. These data are used not only to monitor the health of individuals but also to recommend modifications in health practices that potentially reduce the risk, minimize the consequences, or postpone the development of genetically related conditions.

Gender or Race Some individuals may be at risk of developing a disease by reason of gender or race. Males, for example, are at greater risk of having cardiovascular disease at an earlier age than females, and females are at greater risk of developing osteoporosis, particularly after menopause. Although it is sometimes difficult to separate genetic factors from cultural ones, certain risk factors seem to be related to race. Some diseases are more common among whites than blacks and vice versa. Sickle-cell anemia, for example, is a hereditary disease limited to people of African descent. Indigenous people seem more susceptible to certain diseases, such as diabetes, than the general population.

Cultural Factors

Culture creates an atmosphere that influences the health beliefs and practices of an individual. To provide culturally sensitive care, nurses need to recognize and understand a broad spectrum of cultural values, beliefs, and practices (see Table 5.1)

Sociological Factors The individual's health is influenced by a variety of sociological factors. One of the most noteworthy is poverty. Poverty is a major problem that affects the health of the individual. If an individual is born into a single-parent family headed by a female, then the risk of poverty increases. Other factors include the person's roles within society, at work, and in the community, and personal interests and activities.

Lifestyle Factors It has become clear that many diseases are preventable; the effects of some diseases can be minimized, or the onset of disease can be delayed, through lifestyle modifications. Cancer, cardiovascular disease, adult-onset diabetes, and tooth decay are among lifestyle diseases. The incidence of lung cancer, for example, would be greatly reduced if people stopped smoking. Good nutrition, dental hygiene, and use of fluoride—in

TABLE 5.1 Cultural Variables and Their Implications for Nursing Practice

Cultural Variable	Example	Implications for Nursing Practice
Decision-making practices	Among the Chinese, the eldest son makes decisions for parents	Seek input of oldest son or son-in-law
Gender preference	In Kenya, there is a preference for the female gender because of the economic value of females	Ensure that parents are educated regarding nutritional needs regardless of newborn's gender
Health-care practices	In Africa, families often move into hospital to care for a family member	Ascertain needs of family as care providers to individual member

the water supply, in toothpaste, as topical supplements—have been shown to reduce dental decay, or caries.

Other important lifestyle considerations are exercise, stress management, and rest. Today, nurses have the knowledge to prevent or minimize the effects of some of the main causes of disease, disability, and death. The challenge is to disseminate information about prevention and to motivate individuals to make lifestyle changes prior to the onset of illness.

Nursing Process

Nurses committed to individualized care involve the client in the nursing process. The process is discussed in Chapter 23. Data gathered during an individual assessment may lead to different nursing diagnoses. Planned nursing interventions needed to assist the individual to health and which enhance personal well-being are identified on the basis of a diagnosis. Evaluation determines whether the planned interventions have led to the achievement of the established goals and outcomes.

Applying Theoretical Frameworks to Individuals

A variety of theoretical frameworks provide the nurse with a holistic overview of health promotion for the individual across the lifespan. Major theoretical frameworks that nurses use in promoting the health of the *individual* are needs theories, developmental stage theories, and systems theories. Major theoretical frameworks that nurses use in promoting the health of the *family* are developmental stage theories, systems theories, and structural-functional theories.

Needs Theories

In needs theories, human needs are ranked on an ascending scale according to how essential the needs are for survival. Abraham Maslow, perhaps the most renowned needs theorist, ranks human needs on five levels. The five levels in ascending order are physiological needs, safety and security needs, love and belonging needs, self-esteem needs, and the need for self-actualization (1970). See Figure 5.3 below and the associated box on the following page.

- *Physiologic needs.* Such needs as air, food, water, shelter, rest, sleep, activity, and temperature maintenance are crucial for survival.
- *Safety and security needs.* The need for safety has both physical and psychological aspects. The person needs to feel safe, both in the physical environment and in relationships.
- *Love and belonging needs.* The third level of needs includes giving and receiving affection, attaining a place in a group, and maintaining the feeling of belonging.
- *Self-esteem needs.* The individual needs both self-esteem (i.e., feelings of independence, competence, and self-respect) and esteem from others (i.e., recognition, respect, and appreciation).
- *Self-actualization.* When the need for self-esteem is satisfied, the individual strives for self-actualization, the innate need to develop one's maximum potential and realize one's abilities and qualities.

Kalish's Hierarchy of Needs

Richard Kalish (1977) has adapted Maslow's hierarchy of needs into six levels, rather than five. He suggests an additional category of needs between the physiological needs and the safety and security needs. This category, referred

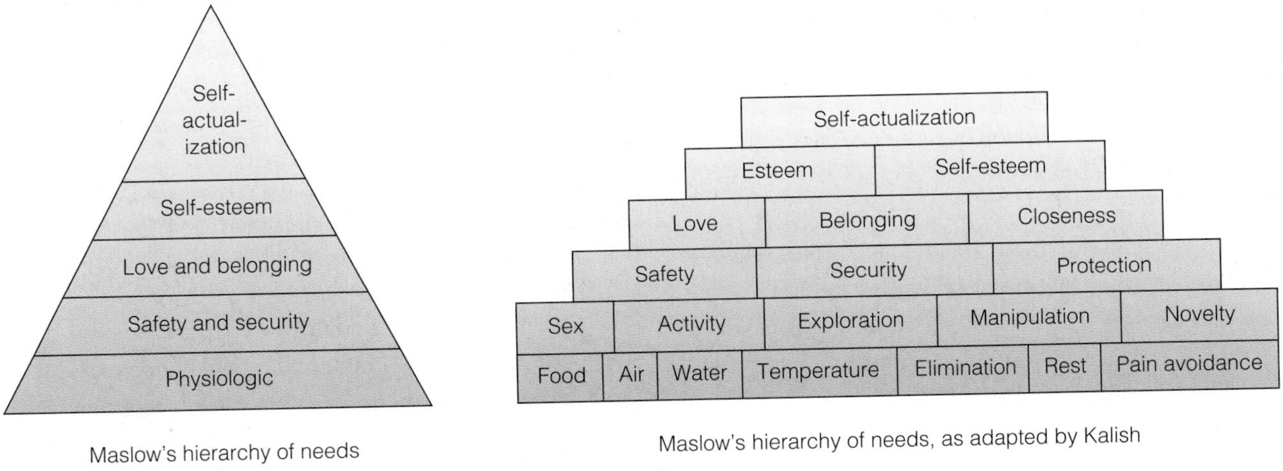

Figure 5.3 Maslow's needs

Source: R. A. Kalish, *The Psychology of Human Behavior*, 5th ed. Copyright © 1983 by Wadsworth, Inc. Reprinted by permission of Brooks/Cole Publishing Company, Monterey, CA 93940.

to as "stimulation needs," includes sex, activity, exploration, manipulation, and novelty. See Figure 5.3. Kalish emphasizes that children need to explore and manipulate their environments to achieve optimal growth and development. He notes that adults, too, often seek novel adventures or stimulating experiences before considering their safety or security needs. Maslow, by contrast, includes the pursuit of knowledge and aesthetic needs in the category of self-actualization needs.

Characteristics of Basic Needs

All people have the same basic needs; however, each person's needs are modified by that person's culture. A person's perception of a need varies according to learning and the standards of the culture. For example, professional achievement may be important in one culture or subculture and unimportant in another.

- People meet their own needs relative to their own priorities. For example, during a drought, a mother might give up her share of water and die so that her child might have sufficient water to live.
- Although basic needs generally must be met, some needs can be deferred. An example is the need for independence, which an ill person can defer until well.
- Failure to meet needs results in one or more homeostatic imbalances, which can eventually result in illness.
- A need can make itself felt by either external or internal stimuli. An example is the need for food. A person may experience hunger as a result of thinking about food (internal stimulation) or as a result of seeing a beautiful cake (external stimulation).
- A person who perceives a need can respond in several ways to meet it. The choice of response is largely a result of learned experiences, lifestyle, and the values of the culture. For example, the professional woman who comes home from work feeling tired may meet the need for relaxation by walking around the park. Many people's food choices at mealtimes and snack times are based on past experiences, lifestyle, and culture.
- Needs are interrelated. Some needs cannot be met unless related needs are also met. The need for hydration can be seriously altered if the need for elimination of urine is not also met. Likewise, the need for security can be markedly altered if the need for oxygen is threatened by a respiratory obstruction.

Needs can be satisfied in healthy and unhealthy ways. Ways of meeting basic needs are considered healthy when they are not harmful to others or to self, conform to the individual's sociocultural values, and are within the law. Conversely, unhealthy behaviour has one or more of the following characteristics: it may be harmful to others or to self, does not conform to the individual's sociocultural values, or is not within the law. Maslow found that people who satisfy their basic needs appropriately are healthier, happier, and more effective than those whose needs are frustrated (Goble, 1970).

Throughout their lifetime, individuals strive to meet needs. A person's perception of a need and his or her response to satisfy a need may be influenced by ethnocultural standards, by external and internal stimuli (e.g., hunger), and by self-determined priorities (e.g., stopping smoking). Positive factors that affect the satisfying of needs

Maslow's Characteristics of a Self-Actualized Person

- Is realistic, sees life clearly, and is objective about observations
- Judges people correctly
- Has superior perception, is more decisive
- Has clear notion of right and wrong
- Is usually accurate in predicting future events
- Understands art, music, politics, and philosophy
- Possesses humility, listens to others carefully
- Is dedicated to some work, task, duty, or vocation
- Is highly creative, flexible, spontaneous, courageous, and willing to make mistakes
- Is open to new ideas
- Is self-confident and has self-respect
- Has low degree of self-conflict; personality is integrated
- Respects self, does not need fame, possesses a feeling of self-control
- Is highly independent, desires privacy
- Can appear remote and detached
- Is friendly, loving, and governed more by inner directives than by society
- Can make decisions contrary to popular opinion
- Is problem centred rather than self-centred
- Accepts the world for what it is

Source: Based on Chapter 3, "The Study of Self-Actualization," from *The Third Force: The Psychology of Abraham Maslow,* by Frank Goble.

are an individual's healthy position on the wellness–illness continuum, the presence of supportive relationships, a good self-concept, and the satisfactory achievement of developmental stages. For example, if an infant achieves the developmental task of learning to trust, then the basic needs of feeling loved and secure are readily resolved.

Knowledge of the theoretical bases of human needs assists nurses in responding therapeutically to a client's behaviours and in understanding themselves and their own responses to needs. Human needs serve as a framework for assessing behaviours, assigning priorities to desired outcomes, and planning nursing interventions. For example, an adult with poor self-esteem would have difficulty in accomplishing self-actualization. Therefore, nursing interventions would focus on increasing the client's self-esteem.

Developmental Stage Theories

Developmental stage theories related to individuals categorize a person's behaviours or tasks into approximate age ranges or in terms that describe the features of an age group. The age ranges of the stages do not take into account individual differences; however, the categories do describe characteristics associated with the majority of individuals at periods when distinctive developmental changes occur and with the specific tasks that must be accomplished. Because human development is highly complex and multifaceted, developmental stage theories describe only one aspect of development, such as cognitive, psychosexual, psychosocial, moral, or faith development. Stage theories emphasize a definite, predictable sequence of development that is orderly and continuous. Each stage is affected by those stages preceding it and affects those stages that follow. For example, an adolescent who is unable to establish a stable sense of personal identity may have difficulty in later developmental stages with adult roles and career aspirations. See Chapter 19 for further information about developmental stages.

Developmental stage theories allow nurses to describe typical behaviours of an individual within a certain age group, explain the significance of those behaviours, predict behaviours that might occur in a given situation, and provide a rationale to control behavioural manifestations. Individuals can be compared with a representative group of people at the same point in time or compared at different points in time. During care, the nurse's knowledge of stage theories can be used in parental and client education, counselling, and anticipatory guidance.

Developmental stage theories view *families* as ever changing and growing. Crucial, yet predictable, tasks occur at each level or stage of development. Achievement of tasks appropriate at one level is a prerequisite for successfully achieving the tasks expected at the next level. A major task of the family, from a developmental perspective, is to create an environment where the family can master critical developmental tasks. This ensures orderly progression through the stages of the family life cycle.

Systems Theories

General systems theory explains the breaking of whole things into parts and the working together of those parts in systems. The theory explains the relationship between wholes and parts, describes concepts about them, and predicts how the parts will behave and react.

The basic concepts of systems theory were proposed in the 1950s. One of its major proponents, Ludwig von Bertalanffy (1969) introduced systems theory as a universal theory that could be applied to many fields of study. Nurses are increasingly using systems theory to understand not only biological systems but also systems in families, communities, and nursing and health care. General systems theory provides a way of examining interrelationships and deriving principles.

A **system** is a set of interacting identifiable parts or components. A system can be an individual, a family, or a community. The fundamental components of a system are matter, energy, and communication. Without any one of these, a system does not exist. The individual is a human system with matter (the body), energy (chemical or thermal), and communication (e.g., the nervous system). The **boundary** of a system, such as the skin in the human system, is a real or imaginary line that differentiates one system from another system or a system from its environment.

Systems may be complex and, therefore, are often studied as *subsystems*. Each subsystem belongs to a higher system. In the individual or human system, the subsystems (or lower level systems) are the organ systems, such as the respiratory system and the digestive system; the *suprasystems* are the family systems. See Figure 5.4 for a hierarchy of the human system.

Because all the parts of a system are interrelated, the whole system responds to changes in one of its parts. This interrelatedness is the basis for nursing's holistic view of the client. For example, a tumour of the liver affects the whole individual, that is, the person may be nauseated, tired, anxious, and so on. A psychological problem, such as stress or anxiety, may also manifest itself by physiological symptoms, such as sleeplessness, nausea, or changes in cardiac function.

There are two general types of systems: closed and open. A **closed system** does not exchange energy, matter, or information with its environment; it receives no input from the environment and gives no output to the environment. An example of a closed system is a chemical reaction that takes place in a test tube. In reality, outside the laboratory, no closed systems exist. In an **open system,** energy, matter, and information move into and out of the system through the system boundary. All living systems, such as plants, animals, people, families, and communities, are open systems, since their survival depends

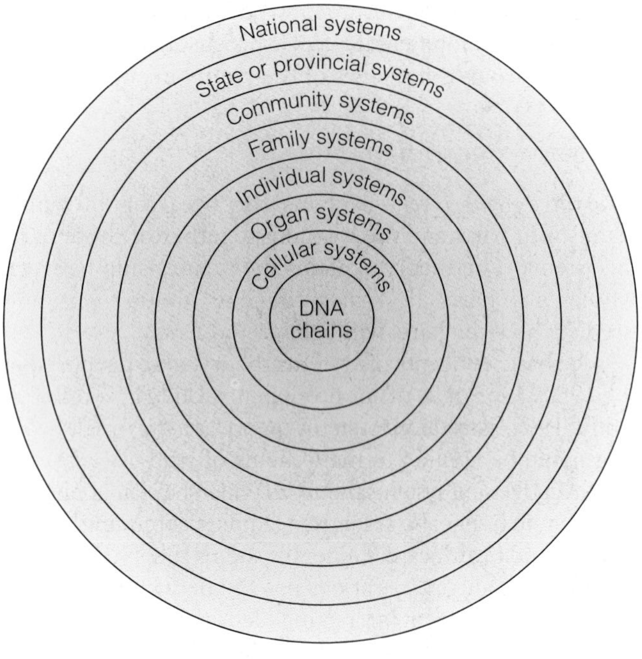

Figure 5.4 A common system hierarchy

on a continuous exchange of energy. They are, therefore, in a constant state of change.

Because humans are biopsychosocial beings, their biological, psychological, social, and spiritual components can be regarded as systems with hierarchic subsystems.

The *biological system* can be subdivided into the neurological, musculoskeletal, respiratory, circulatory, gastrointestinal, and urinary subsystems, among others. Each subsystem can, in turn, be subdivided. For example, the urinary system consists of the kidneys, the ureters, and the bladder; the circulatory system consists of the heart and the blood vessels; the neurological system consists of the brain, the spinal cord, and the nerves. The biological system can also be subdivided into categories of needs or functional health patterns or activities of daily living, such as nutrition and hydration, sleep/rest, activity/exercise, elimination, and so on.

The *psychological* and *social systems* consist of subsystems that include thinking, feeling, and interaction patterns. Names of the psychological and social subsystems vary considerably according to individual nurse theorists. For example, Dorothy Johnson (1980), who describes the human system in terms of behaviours, lists the following psychological subsystems: attachment-affiliative, dependence, achievement, and aggressive.

For its functioning, an open system depends on the quality and quantity of its input, output, and feedback. **Input** consists of information, material, or energy that enters the system. After the input is absorbed by the system, it is processed in a way useful to the system. This transformation is called **throughput.** For example, food is input to the digestive system; it is digested (throughput) so that it can be used by the body. **Output** from a system is energy, matter, or information given out by the system as a result of its processes. Output from the digestive system is feces, nutrients, and caloric energy.

Feedback, as discussed for homeostasis in an individual, is a process that enables a system to regulate itself by redirecting the output of a system to affect the input of the same system, thus forming a feedback loop (Figure 5.5). Numerous examples of this feedback mechanism are found within individual, family, and community systems. In the individual, for example, the autonomic nervous system relies on a feedback system to balance the effects of the sympathetic and parasympathetic centres, which modify heart and respiratory rates. In the family system, parents provide feedback to children to modify behaviour. In the community, laws, rules, and regulations guide the behaviour of citizens.

Human systems theories assert that the individual is an open system in constant interaction with a changing environment. People interact with the environment by adjusting themselves to it or adjusting it to themselves. Constant input into the system and feedback to it maintain the system in a state of dynamic equilibrium (homeostasis). This premise directs the nurse to look at environmental factors influencing the system and to plan nursing interventions to help the client maintain homeostasis. For example, the individual who is experiencing severe anxiety may be taught a variety of stress management techniques.

The family unit can also be viewed as a system. Its members are interdependent, working toward specific purposes and goals. Many families are described as *open systems*, for they are continually interacting with and influenced by other systems in the community. Boundaries regulate the input from other systems that interact with the family system; they also regulate output from the family system to the community or to society. Boundaries protect the family from the demands and influences of other systems. Open families are likely to welcome input from without, encouraging individual members to adapt beliefs and practices to meet the changing demands of society. Such families are more likely to seek out health-care information and use community resources. These families are adaptable and, therefore, better prepared to cope with changes in lifestyle needed to restore, maintain, or promote health.

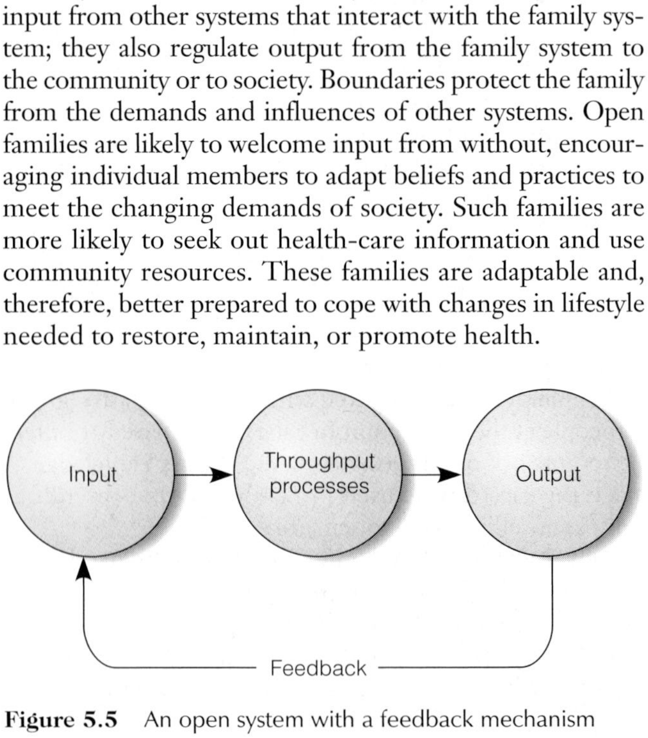

Figure 5.5 An open system with a feedback mechanism

FOCUS ON CRITICAL THINKING

Linda is a young mother of three children who has developed a severe arthritic condition that has affected her ability to work and adequately care for her family. Her illness has created a financial hardship for the family and has strained their roles. She has given up her position as a secretary. Linda and her husband have custody of their children from previous marriages as well as a daughter of their own. She is reluctant to seek assistance from outside sources because she fears interference from her ex-spouse in regard to her children.

1. What type of assessment data might you collect?
2. When dealing with Linda's physical problem, why must the nurse be concerned about the other issues occurring in Linda's life?
3. Explore Linda's situation from the perspective of Maslow.
4. What suggestions might you give Linda to help her cope with her condition?

See Appendix A for answers to these questions.

CHAPTER HIGHLIGHTS

- Nursing involves viewing the client as an individual and in a holistic way.
- To ensure holistic health care, the nurse considers all the components of health (health promotion, health maintenance, health education and illness prevention, and restorative-rehabilitative care) and recognizes that disturbance in one part of a person affects the whole being.
- Homeostasis is the tendency of the body to maintain a state of relative balance or constancy in response to a changing internal and external environment.
- Physiological homeostasis is maintained by coordinated functioning of the autonomic nervous, endocrine, respiratory, cardiovascular, renal, and gastrointestinal systems.
- Homeostatic mechanisms regulate hormone secretion, fluid and electrolyte levels, the functions of body viscera, and metabolic processes that provide energy for the body.
- Psychological homeostasis, or emotional well-being, is acquired or learned through the experience of living and interacting with others.
- Although each individual has unique characteristics, certain needs are common to all people.
- A variety of social, psychological, and nursing theoretical frameworks provide the nurse with a holistic overview of health promotion of individuals and families across the lifespan.
- Maslow's hierarchy of human needs consists of five categories: physiological (survival) needs, safety needs, love and belonging needs, self-esteem needs, and self-actualization needs.
- People vary in how they rank their needs at any given moment.
- Needs satisfaction can be altered by illness, significant relationships, self-concept, and developmental levels.

READINGS AND REFERENCES

Suggested Readings

Bruyere, J., & Garro, L. C. (2000). "He travels in the body." *Canadian Nurse, 96*(6), 25–28.
The authors explored the knowledge held by Ojibwas of Manitoba of type II diabetes. They found that participants, because of their cultural and belief background, viewed their condition differently from many health-care professionals. The implication is that nurses need to blend cultural factors into individualized nursing care.

Gerrish, K. (2000). Individualized care: Its conceptualization and practice within a multiethnic society. *Journal of Advanced Nursing, 32*, 91–99.
Gerrish's research examined nurses' conceptualization of individualized care. The author documents the finding from a large ethnographic study of the provision of individualized care by district nurses to patients from different ethnic backgrounds. Six principles underlying the philosophy of individualized care—respecting individuality, holistic care, focusing on nursing needs, promoting independence, partnership and negotiation of care, and equity and fairness—are examined as to how they are implemented in practice. Implications for nursing practice, including working with different ethnic groups, are explored. Nurses' conceptualization of individualized care and subsequent practice was strongly influenced by policy changes affecting both health and social care.

Perry, B. (2002). Growth and satisfaction. *Canadian Nurse, 98*(10), 19–22.
The author collected personal stories from nurses about experiences that gave them satisfaction in their daily work. Many nurses talked about the opportunity to provide individualized care. They gained satisfaction from helping others and treating them with respect and dignity.

Related Research

Coker, E. (1998). Does your care plan tell my story? Documenting aspects of personhood in long-term care. *Journal of Holistic Nursing, 16*, 435–452.

Redfern, S. (1996). Individualised patient care: Its meaning and practice in a general setting. *NT Research, 1*, 22–33.

Waters, K., & Easton, N. (1999). Individualised care: Is it possible to plan and carry out. *Journal of Advanced Nursing, 29*, 79–87.

Selected References

Bertalanffy, L. (1968). *General Systems Theory: Foundation, Development, Applications*. New York: Braziller.

Cannon, W. B. (1939). *The wisdom of the body.* (2nd ed.). New York: Norton.

Deheny, J. A. (1990). Anticipatory guidance. In M. J. Craft & J. A. Deheny (Eds.), *Nursing interventions for infants and children* (pp. 53–67). Philadelphia, PA: Saunders.

Erikson, E. (1963). *Childhood and society* (2nd ed.). New York: Norton.

Gertis, M., Edgman-Levitan, S., Daley, J., & Delbanco, T. (Eds.). (1993). *Through the patient's eyes.* San Francisco, CA: San Jossey-Bass.

Goble, F. G. (1970). *The third force: The psychology of Abraham Maslow.* Richmond Hill: Simon & Schuster.

Hegyvary, S. T. (1990). Education: Redefining community. *Journal of Professional Nursing, 6*, 7.

Jenny, J., & Logan, J. (1992). Knowing the patient: One aspect of clinical knowledge. *Journal of Nursing Scholarship, 24*, 254–258.

Johnson, D. E. (1980). The behavioral system model for nursing. In J. P. Riehl & C. Roy (Eds.), *Conceptual models for nursing practice* (2nd ed.) (pp. 207–216). New York: Appleton-Century-Crofts.

Kalish, R. (1977). *The later years: Social applications of gerontology.* Montery, CA: Brooks/Cole.

Kalish, R. A. (1983). *The psychology of human behavior* (5th ed.). Monterey, CA: Brooks/Cole.

Maslow, A. H. (1968). *Toward a psychology of being* (2nd ed.). New York: Van Nostrand Reinhold. (Classic.)

Maslow, A. H. (1970). *Motivation and personality.* (2nd ed.). New York: Harper & Row. (Classic.)

Maslow, A. H. (1971). *The farther reaches of human nature.* New York: Penguin Books. (Classic.)

McCloskey, J. C., & Bulechek, G. M. (1996). *Iowa Intervention Project: Nursing interventions classification (NIC)* (2nd ed.). St. Louis, MO: Mosby.

Ryan, M., Twibell, R., Brighman, C., & Bennett, P. (2000). Learning to care for clients in their world, not mine. *Journal of Nursing Education, 39*, 401–408.

Smuts, J. (1926). *Holism and evolution.* New York: Macmillan.

Spradley, B. W., & Allender, A. (1996). *Community health nursing: Concepts and practice* (4th ed.). Philadelphia, PA: Lippincott.

Wallace, T., Robertson, E., Millar, C., & Frisch, S. R. (1999). Perceptions of care and services by the clients and families: A personal experience. *Journal of Advanced Nursing, 29*, 1144–1153.

WEBLINKS

Canadian Health Network
http://www.canadian-health-network.ca/customtools/homee.html
This site provides health promotive information that is Canadian, current, and peer reviewed.

Statistics Canada
http://www.statcan.ca
This site provides a variety of federal government statistics related to Canadians, e.g., workplace injuries, education levels.

Government of Canada
http://www.canada.gc.ca/
The starting point for access to sites of the federal and provincial government departments and agencies.

Canadian Heritage
http://www.pch.gc.ca/
Canada Heritage, a department of the federal government, operates this site.

CHAPTER 6

Nursing Care of Families

OBJECTIVES

After completing this chapter, you will be able to:

- Define "family" in a way that accounts for diverse forms of structure and relationship.
- Describe factors influencing a shift in nursing perspective from the individual to the person in the context of the family.
- Outline historical developments in the history of family nursing.
- Discuss the impact of trends in health-care services on family involvement.
- Propose possible family member expectations for their involvement in care.
- Analyze demographic trends in Canadian families that influence health and family structure.
- Identify questions to be posed during a genogram and ecomap inquiry.
- Formulate questions aimed at exploring the reciprocal influences between health/illness and the family.
- Describe relational practices that foster a collaborative stance with family members.
- Explain at least five relational practices that can be integrated when providing nursing care with families.

Whenever concerns related to health and illness arise, not only are individual persons affected but also the people who are involved in their daily lives. Usually (though not always) these "others" are family members. Nurses encounter family members in every practice setting, including home care, community clinics, outpatient services, and acute-care hospitals. As health-care services have been shifting away from institutional care with shorter hospital stays, family members are increasingly called upon to provide care at home, including supportive and emotional care, symptom monitoring, and technical procedures, ranging from dressing changes to dialysis and intravenous therapies. Family members can be a tremendous resource to nurses through their knowledge of patient preferences and usual patterns of response to difficulties. Nurses are challenged to involve family members in decision making, to provide information and emotional support, and to prepare family members for caregiving roles.

Types of Families in Today's Society

- Traditional — both parents reside in the home with children; mother assumes nurturing role and father provides economic necessities
- Two career — both husband and wife are employed
- Single parent
- Adolescent — an infant is born to adolescent parents
- Blended — existing families who join together to form a new one
- Cohabiting — unrelated individuals or families who live under one roof
- Gay and Lesbian — same sex couple
- Single

What Is "Family?"

Expected norms of family structure and development have shifted dramatically over the past three decades. Couples are more likely to postpone childbearing in order to follow prolonged periods of education or establishment of careers. Rising rates of divorce and remarriage have resulted in increased numbers of blended families and single-parent families. Increased mobility of families has shifted the roles of extended family members. These changes challenge static definitions of family based on assumptions of even the recent past. Persons choosing to define themselves as family may or may not be bound by blood or legal status. The following definition attempts to be open and respectful of the many different ways that families may organize themselves:

> *Any combination of two or more persons who are bound together over time by ties of mutual consent, birth and/or adoption, or placement and who, together, assume responsibilities for variant combinations of some of the following:*
>
> - *Physical maintenance and care of group members*
> - *Addition of new members through procreation or adoption*
> - *Socialization of children*
> - *Social control of members*
> - *Production, consumption, distribution of goods and services*
> - *Affective nurturance—love.* (Vanier Institute of the Family, 2000)

In clinical practice, what may be most helpful to the nurse is to understand how the members of a particular family prefer to identify themselves in relation to each other. Who is in *this* family? How do *these* family members view their relationships, priorities, concerns, responsibilities, and preferences? To establish a therapeutic relationship with a family, nurses need to be respectful of the ways that families describe themselves, and to appreciate that "the family is who they say they are" (Wright & Leahey, 2000, p. 70).

Family Nursing

When "nursing families," one is inevitably engaging in dialogue and relationship with family members. While this is true of nursing in a general sense, it is especially so when providing nursing care to families. There are no technical procedures or psychomotor skills that are inherent in family nursing practices. **Family nursing** refers to those relational practices which involve family members in care, respond to their concerns, provide them with information, and/or offer emotional support. Whether in an intensive care unit or in a public health clinic, care of family members calls for nursing practices that occur in conversation and relationship.

Nurses encounter families in their day-to-day practice, and each encounter affords a possibility for nursing of families. Family members may be present when the home care nurse makes a visit to change a dressing. They may be maintaining a rotating vigil at the bedside of an ill family member, and the nurse may have several brief conversations with them over a particular shift, perhaps lasting only a few minutes during each contact. The nurse may conduct a more formal family assessment interview upon the patient's admission to an outpatient clinic or inpatient facility. The nurse may be involved in a family conference that gathers family and other health-care team members to facilitate decision making, treatment planning, or discharge. In some situations, the nurse has little or no direct contact with family members of the individual client, yet there may still be attention to the needs and concerns of family members in their absence. This, too, is nursing of families.

For decades, it has been a commonly accepted practice for health-care systems in Canada to be organized around provision of services to individuals. Typically, the individual is the focus of care, the identified patient for whom diagnosis and treatment services are coordinated. The extent to which family members are encouraged to be involved in health-care encounters varies greatly. In recent years, many agencies are providing structural supports that make it possible to include family members and to value their presence and contribution to care. These supports include flexible visiting hour policies; comfortable waiting rooms and access to overnight facilities, refreshments, and telephones; and increased access to information from health-care professionals.

These changes have made it both possible and necessary for nurses to change their practices to include family members. Nursing of families challenges nurses to shift their perspective from thinking of the client as an individual to "thinking family" or "thinking interactionally" (Wright & Leahey, 2000, p. 15). This means that the nurse must forge a collaborative relationship not only with the patient but also with the other persons who are involved with the patient during the health-care encounter (wherever that occurs). In doing so, the attention of the nurse is directed toward consideration of the impact of illness or health concerns on the other people in the patient's life and the impact on relationships between family members. Involvement of family members helps the nurse better understand the meaning of illness to the patient and family, and the possibilities for support during recovery, health maintenance, or health promotion.

In many practice settings, the "client" is conceptualized as the **person in the context of the family.** In this instance, the individual person is viewed as the primary focus of nursing concern, and the family is viewed as a significant contextual influence in health, illness, and recovery. Family nursing focuses on *both* individuals (foreground) and families (background). Family members are viewed as connected to the person, relevant to the health concerns of the individual, and a significant influence for the person and his or her environment. For example, participation of family members in decisions related to discharge planning is desirable because they can provide emotional support and instrumental assistance during the individual's recovery upon returning home. Family members can be a valuable resource to both the patient and the health-care team. Additionally, though the individual is the focus of care, there may also be varying degrees of intent to nurse family members by attending to the impact of the health situation on others in the family. Other family members may also be included in discharge planning because these decisions affect family members and may make demands on their time, energy, and health when the patient returns home. There is simultaneously a concern for the impact of these demands on the family caregiver. Friedemann (1995) offered the provocative idea that "all nursing is family nursing and is practised in all clinical settings" (p. 34). She proposed that nurses cannot contribute to the healing of persons without attention to the contexts and relationships in which they live.

Alternatively, practice may focus on the family unit as the client of care. As above, there is simultaneous attention to both the individual and the family, but in this instance, the family is foreground. There is intent to create a context for changes in family relationships and processes in relation to the difficulties they are encountering and to assist the family by facilitating changes within the family unit (Wright, Watson, & Bell, 1996). There is heightened attention to reciprocity within relationships between family members, between the family and the nurse, and between illness and the family. This work typically requires advanced practice skills, and nurses are often employed as clinical specialists with educational preparation at the graduate level (Hanson & Boyd, 1996). Family systems nursing (Wright & Leahey, 1990) is an example of family nursing specialization that is based on advanced preparation in family systems theory and clinical practice. Systems-focused family nursing addresses the complexity of the functioning of the family unit and shifts nursing attention between various family subsystems (such as the parent-child relationship or the marital relationship) and other higher systems levels (such as health-care agencies, schools, community clinics) as needed (Friedemann, 1995).

Development of Family Nursing

Historically, nurses have encountered family members by virtue of their shared presence in homes, communities, and hospitals. The interest in the family as a focus of nursing care extends back to the earliest traditions of modern nursing (Whall & Fawcett, 1991). During the early decades of the 20th century, there was interest in both clinical practice and nursing curricula on nursing care of families in their own homes by public health nurses and private duty nurses. There was emphasis on assisting families to care for their ill family members at home and providing family with respite from caregiving activities. Public health nurses have a longstanding tradition of educating families to address the health needs of all family members. In Canada, by the 1920s, there was a growing reliance on hospital services and reduced demand for health care provided at home by private duty nurses (McPherson, 1996). By the 1940s and 1950s, private duty nursing declined dramatically and was coupled with federal and provincial legislation that increased construction of public hospitals across the country. This was followed by the advent of the Canadian system of Medicare, which provided public health-care insurance for medical and hospital services. Illness care became increasingly entrenched within hospitals.

Focus on Individuals in Hospital Care

The rise of scientific biomedicine and the organizational efficiencies of hospital care contributed to a focus on the individual. The client was viewed as the individual patient, with a particular pathology, requiring diagnosis and treatment. As medicine focused on curing disease, nurses contributed greatly to the achievement of organizational efficiencies of the hospitals which supported these activities (MacPherson, 1996). Families were significantly overlooked as less relevant influences in health and recovery, with little entitlement to involvement in hospital care. In recent years, there has been renewed attention to the psychosocial aspects of health and illness, including recognition of the influence of family. As health-care services have been challenged to reconsider the importance of family, many changes in practice and policy have been guided by nurses' responsiveness to the needs, requests, and expectations of families.

Family Care Traditions in Public Health, Maternal-Child, and Pediatric Nursing

Throughout these developments, public health nurses, maternal-child nurses, and pediatric nurses have had an enduring interest in family care. It is understandable that maternal-child nursing and pediatric nursing would emphasize parent-child relationships as significant to the maintenance and recovery of health. Hospitals were challenged within these practice settings to provide structural support for family involvement. In labour and delivery settings, couples demanded the presence of fathers in the delivery room. Mothers objected to separation from their newborns during postpartum care, which led to "rooming-in" practices that allowed babies to be cared for extensively at the mother's bedside, rather than in large nurseries. In pediatric settings, parents desired access to their children round the clock through flexible visiting policies and availability of sleeping cots for their comfort and convenience during overnight stays. Nursing research in the 1970s and 1980s addressed such topics as parent-infant bonding, maternal role attainment, childbearing/childrearing and transitions in the family life cycle, and the impact of pediatric illness on family members. While much of this early work focused on maternal-child relationships, in recent years, there has been increased emphasis on the significant roles that fathers and husbands play.

Family Nursing in Critical Care Settings

During the last four decades of the 20th century, acute-care hospitals introduced specialized critical care units across the human life span, from neonates to adults. Nurses recognized the significant impact of implementation of highly invasive and technological procedures under tenuous life-and-death circumstances on family members. Due to the nature of the seriousness of their patients' conditions, it was more common for nurses to work intensively with one or two patients at a time, perhaps allowing increased contact with family members. Nursing research reflected a desire to understand and offer assistance regarding the emotional distress, uncertainty, and informational needs of family members under these extraordinary circumstances (Hickey, 1990; Hickey & Lewandowski, 1988). Again, nurses were challenged to humanize these environments on behalf of family members by finding ways to enable family access to patients and information and to facilitate family involvement in decision making.

Shifting Focus to Family Involvement in Health Care

During the 1990s, Canadian hospitals changed dramatically with increasing political pressure for fiscal restraint within the public health-care system. Length of hospital stays was dramatically reduced. Hospitalization typically signals high patient acuity, management of acute episodic events, urgent diagnostic assessment, and treatment requiring intensive physiological monitoring. Outpatient services, homecare, and community service have increased as an alternative to inpatient monitoring and assessment. These changes have been coupled with the shifting demographics of the Canadian population. The average life expectancy is increasing, and the main causes of death and disability have shifted to chronic illnesses, such as heart disease, cancer, and respiratory diseases. These changes suggest a need to shift illness care to respond not only to acute episodic events but also to address health concerns across the complete trajectory of chronic illnesses (Thorne, 1993).

At this juncture, more than at any time in the past, family members are implicitly expected to be involved in the complex ongoing medical management of an ill family member at home. Health-care providers rely on family members to assist with administration of complex medication regimes, ongoing symptom monitoring and management, recognition of complications, dressing changes, and even technical procedures, such as intravenous therapies, feeding systems, respiratory ventilators, and home dialysis. Health-care providers need the support and active involvement of family members.

Thus, our ability to nurse families has a chequered history. A focus on individuals has often been fostered within health-care delivery systems, sometimes resulting in exclusion of family members, inadvertent neglect of family needs, and limited involvement of family in health-care decision making. Family involvement and support have often occurred only when they have been demanded by family members. There have been many indications that while health-care professionals may now expect family

Expectations of Family Members

- Opportunity to communicate with health-care professionals about the family member's condition
- To be able to trust that the family member will be given good care and treated compassionately
- Recognition that they are part of what is happening to the patient
- Information and training to prepare them to feel confident about care they will provide at home

Source: Levine, C. (1998). *Rough crossings: Family caregivers' odysseys through the health care system*. New York: United Hospital Fund.

members to be involved, they may have been less sensitive to the expectations that family members may have of them. It is also possible that family members do not expect nurses to attend to their needs and prefer that nurses focus on caring for their ill family member.

Family Expectations for Involvement in Care

Levine's (1998) research offered many examples of family's hopes and expectations for involvement in care (see the box above). Family members want to be able to communicate with health-care professionals about the ill person's condition. They want access to information about test results, diagnosis, treatment plans, and prognosis. Family members want to be able to trust that the ill person will be given good care and treated compassionately. They may feel compelled to be present and vigilant to protect the ill family member at a time of vulnerability, when the patient cannot prevent errors in treatment or speak persuasively. Family members want recognition that they are a part of what is happening to the patient. Their emotional attachment to the ill person may be a powerful motive for their own ongoing involvement in providing care, but they expect recognition that they also experience emotional distress (Levine, 1998). Finally, family members want information and preparation for their roles at home so that they can provide ongoing physical and emotional care with confidence.

Canadian Contributions to the Field of Family Nursing

As nurses have been striving to change practice and policy, Canadian nurses have made significant contributions to the field of family nursing (Bell, 1996). The "Calgary Family Assessment Model" (Wright & Leahey, 2000) was first published in 1984 and has been updated and complemented by "The Calgary Family Intervention Model" in subsequent editions of the landmark text *Nurses and Families: A Guide to Family Assessment and Intervention.* The first International Family Nursing Conference was held in Calgary, Alberta in 1989 and continues to meet every three years. This forum gathers an international community of clinicians, educators, and researchers with an interest in family nursing and provides opportunities to share and further their work. The *Journal of Family Nursing* was first published in 1995 under the editorship of Dr. Janice Bell at the University of Calgary, providing opportunities for dissemination of family nursing knowledge. Nursing education programs are increasingly offering family nursing content in undergraduate programs, and nurses have many opportunities to specialize in family nursing in master's and doctoral programs in Canadian universities.

Canadian Families: A Demographic Snapshot

Canadian families are influenced by diverse ethnic, religious, and cultural traditions. The following depiction of Canadian demographics is based on an analysis of data from the Statistics Canada 1996 Census reported by The Vanier Institute of the Family (2000).

Cultural Diversity

Almost 3 percent of the total Canadian population identified themselves as having First Nations origins (i.e., North American Indians 66.2 percent, Metis 25.5 percent, and Inuit 5 percent). More than four out of five First Nations people live west of Quebec, and nearly half of them live on reserves. Proportionate to the population, they have resided more commonly in the prairie provinces and northern territories. First Nations people comprise more than 11 percent of the populations of Manitoba and Saskatchewan; 84 percent of Nunavut, 48 percent of Northwest Territories, 20 percent of Yukon; 3.8 percent of British Columbia; and 1.3 percent of Ontario.

Until the Second World War, Canadian culture was powerfully shaped by European immigration. In 1996, the largest proportions of Canadians not born in Canada were from the United Kingdom (13%), Italy (7%), United States (5%), Hong Kong (5%), India (5%), and China (5%). Canada's declining fertility rate of 1.6 children per woman is below the replacement rate of 2.1, as Canadians generally have chosen to bear fewer children. Population growth in the future will continue to be strongly influenced by immigration. New Canadians are more likely to move to large cities, such as Toronto and Vancouver. Four out of 10 people living in Toronto were not born in Canada. Seven out of 10 immigrants to British Columbia live in Vancouver, contributing to one-third of the residents in that city.

Mobility

Canadian families are also characterized by high mobility. Between 1991 and 1996, nearly half of all Canadian residents moved to a different location. Slightly more than half moved to a new location within their municipality, while one-third moved farther within their province. This is noteworthy since mobility can contribute to family stress, as "families join new communities, create new friendships, find new schools for the children, search for new employment for a relocated spouse, or handle a long-distance relationship with an elderly parent. Many young families experience difficulty getting new jobs when they are unable to call on their parents or grandparents for informal childcare" (Vanier Institute, 2000, p. 18).

Parenting

Sixty-five percent of all Canadian families have children living at home (Figure 6.1). Fifteen percent are single-parent families, and eight out of 10 single parents are mothers. More than 60 percent of female single parents with children under 16 years were employed. However, they tended to fare worse economically with more than half (56%) living in poverty, compared with all other groups including male single parents (24%), two-parent families (12%), couples without children (11%), and the elderly (7%).

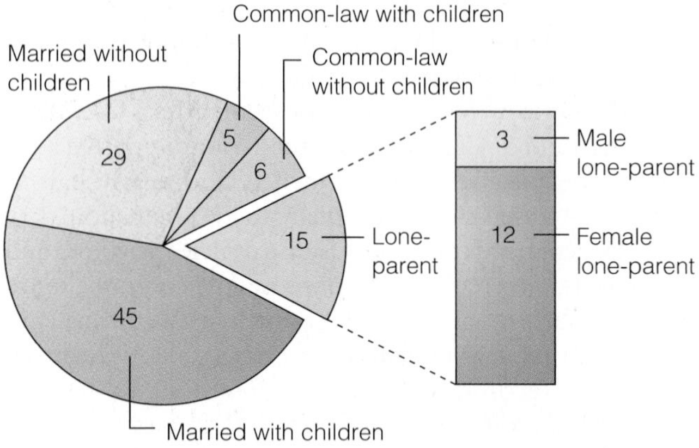

Figure 6.1 Types of families "Out of 100 Families" (1996)

Source: With permission from The Vanier Institute of the Family. (2000). *Profiling Canada's Families II* (p. 31). Nepean, Ontario, Canada.

Income

Seven out of 10 married or common-law couples with children were dual-income families, relying on two wages to make ends meet (Figure 6.2). In 1997, the median family income was $48,862, and over a quarter of Canadian families had incomes of less than $30,000. Nearly one out of 10 Canadians received social assistance or welfare and was living on an income well below the poverty line due to unemployment, disablity, or being a single parent.

Marriage, Divorce, Remarriage, and Common-Law Relationships

In recent years, the number of marriages, divorces, and remarriages has been declining. The average age of first marriages has been rising (30.9 years for brides, and 33.5 years for grooms). More people are choosing to live together in common-law relationships as a trial stage before marriage or as a preferred pattern of family formation. Common-law unions comprise 13.5% of all conjugal unions. Interestingly, senior couples over age 65 years were more likely to be married, but there were more seniors than teenagers living in common-law unions. Data are not available for same-sex unions. On the basis of 1996 divorce rates, 37% of marriages could be expected to result in divorce. Declining divorce rates reflect lower marriage rates, increasing common-law partnerships, and the drop which followed a peak subsequent to the 1985 changes to the Divorce Act. In 1995, one-tenth of Canadian families were "stepfamilies" or "blended families," in which at least one of the children was being raised by a biological or adoptive parent and a step-parent (Figure 6.3).

Families Providing Care to Persons with Disabilities

As perhaps has been expected in the past, families provide much of the care required for aging or disabled family members. "More than nine out of 10 individuals with special needs or disabilities lived with their families—typically in their own, their parents', or their children's home. While many persons with disabilities were capable of caring for themselves and carrying out household activities, when they did require assistance, they most often turned to their families" (Vanier Institute, 2000, p. 176). More than eight out of 10 Canadians over the age of 85 years had some form of disability, and women between the ages of 35 and 54 years

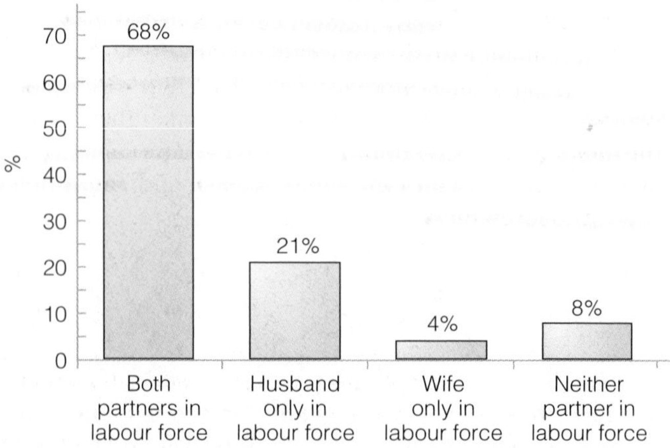

Figure 6.2 Labour force status of couples with children (1996)

Source: With permission from The Vanier Institute of the Family. (2000). *Profiling Canada's Families II* (p. 89). Nepean, Ontario, Canada.

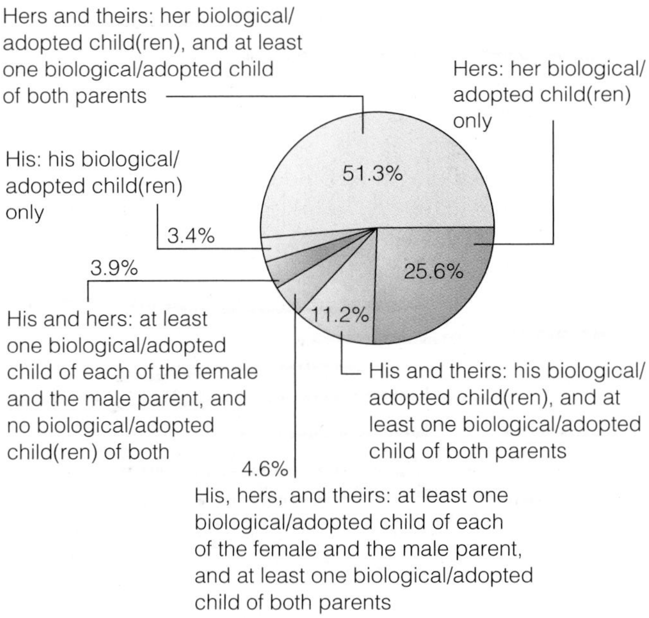

Figure 6.3 Distribution of children 0 to 11 years in step-families, by step-family type (1994–1995)

Source: With permission from The Vanier Institute of the Family. (2000). *Profiling Canada's Families II* (p. 67). Nepean, Ontario, Canada.

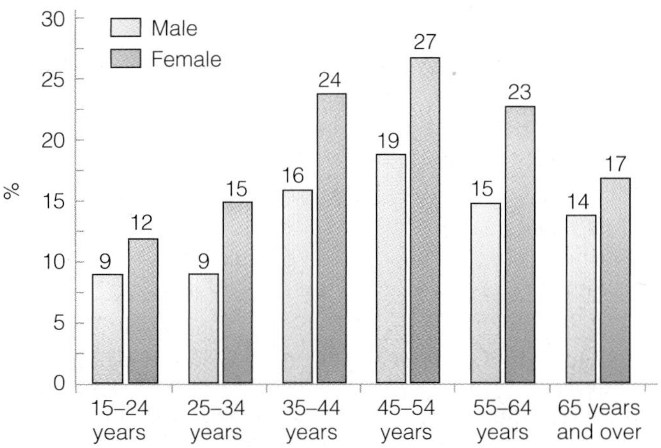

Figure 6.4 Percentage of population providing unpaid assistance* to seniors, by age (1996)

*Hours spent providing unpaid assistance to seniors for the week prior to Census day in 1996. Unpaid assistance includes such things as providing personal care, visiting, helping with shopping, baking, or giving medicines.

Source: With permission from The Vanier Institute of the Family. (2000). *Profiling Canada's Families II* (p. 177). Nepean, Ontario, Canada.

are far more likely than younger people or men to provide unpaid care to seniors (Figure 6.4). Women, in general, are more likely to provide informal care to relatives in addition to other career and family responsibilities.

Understanding Families

Nursing care of families begins with understanding the family's situation at a particular point in time, that is, who is involved in the family situation, and how they are involved. It is not realistic to expect that the nurse will necessarily "fix" all the past, present, or future problems confronting the family. However, it is reasonable to expect the nurse to assist the family to navigate their way through a particular difficulty with a health problem or life transition. The focus of these encounters is the family's hopes and expectations for the present situation and the ways that the nurse can help them deal with the reciprocal influences between the health/illness concern and the family members (Figure 6.5).

The nurse sustains a focus on the family situation and concerns by asking questions which explore both the impact of the health concern or illness on the family, and the influence of family members on the health concern.

Illness affects the family, and the family affects the illness. By exploring both segments of this reciprocal loop in clinical conversation, the nurse can uncover many areas of inquiry that inform the nurse and that create openings for addressing concerns of family members.

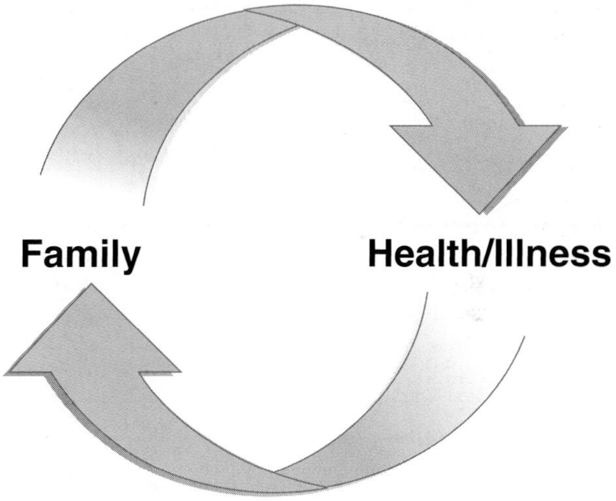

Figure 6.5 Reciprocal influence between family and health/illness

Who Is Involved in the Situation?

If the nurse intends to develop collaborative relationships with the patient *and* the other people who are involved, then efforts must be made to find out who these other people are. They may be present with the patient in the clinic, at the bedside, or in the home when the nurse encounters the patient. They may be unable to be present because of work commitments, transportation difficulties, child-care responsibilities, economic constraints, or their own poor health. Family members may not wish to be involved in the situation, or the patient may not wish to have them involved. If the nurse does not engage family members in

Canadian Society Notes

Fact	Implications for Nursing Practice
The average age of first marriages has been rising (30.9 years for women, 33.5 years for men).	Assess impact of family developmental tasks on health maintenance routines and practices.
Changes to the Divorce Act in 1985 resulted in a peak in divorce rates in the decade that followed. Divorce rates are currently declining (37% in 1996 data from Statistics Canada) due to lower marriage rates and increasing common-law partnerships.	Genogram inquiries should routinely include consideration of step-parenting and blended family arrangements.
More than nine out of 10 individuals with special needs or disabilities live with their families.	Nurses should routinely assess the need for respite care and home care support for family members who are willing and able to fulfill ongoing caregiving responsibilities.
Canadian families are highly mobile—between 1991 and 1996, nearly half of all Canadian residents moved to a different location.	Explore accessibility of family members to provide emotional and instrumental assistance during health difficulties.

conversation when encountering them, or does not ask about them in their absence, it will be impossible to understand the possibilities for family support or the constraints and limits for family involvement.

At a minimum, the nurse must acknowledge the presence of family members. Introducing oneself to family members, demonstrating an interest in who they are, inquiring about how they are managing, and inviting their questions and concerns convey the nurse's willingness to include family members. Unfortunately, much of this information is lost because it is not documented or communicated when individual nurses change shift or when nursing continuity cannot be assured over time because of organizational staffing patterns. More structured documentation about the family can be facilitated by a genogram inquiry (Hanson & Boyd, 1996; Wright & Leahey, 1990). The **genogram** is a concise visual depiction of family structure and relevant information about the family situation that is increasingly being used in health-care agencies as a tool to summarize and communicate pertinent family information. Some agencies use genogram forms, but these diagrams can also be sketched on nursing admission forms, progress notes, or Kardex® cards.

A brief genogram can be sketched in a few minutes, though a detailed diagram could be the focus of an entire family assessment interview. Patients and family members may have little experience with health-care providers who are openly interested in the needs and concerns of family members. It is important to offer them an explanation for the genogram inquiry. For example, the nurse should explain that it is helpful to understand who else might be involved during the hospitalization, clinic appointments, or home care visits; who else the patient would like to have access to new information; and who will be helping with discharge planning. Figure 6.6 illustrates an example of a detailed genogram and common conventions for constructing these diagrams.

After introducing the genogram, the nurse can increase the family's comfort with this inquiry by beginning with basic questions about individuals' ages, interests, and occupations. Age-appropriate questions to young children can elicit information about school, friends, and favourite games or toys. It is most helpful to demonstrate an interest in all family members by asking questions of each person present and also to inquire about family members who are unable to be present. Beginning questions usually focus on the family members currently residing together or who are involved in some way in the health-care situation. However, inquiry should explore any other family relationships which seem to be relevant to the current situation. For example, in Figure 6.6, the genogram inquiry uncovered the eight-year-old daughter's worries about her father's health, Ron's significant family history with heart disease, and Elaine's caregiving responsibilities for her aging mother. The genogram inquiry may reveal recent losses in the family or significant family events that may contribute to concurrent stress or difficulties confronted by the family. Asking questions about relationships with previous marital partners who are involved in ongoing co-parenting responsibilities may also be very important. For example, the nurse could ask Ron how his ex-wife, Susan, believes that Scott and Evan have been reacting to the news of his heart attack. This discussion could offer understanding regarding not only his relationship with the two sons but also the nature of his relationship with his ex-wife. The genogram inquiry can provide the nurse with relevant information about present family structure, recent life cycle transitions in family development (marriages, divorces, births, deaths, launching of young adults), and important family relationships. It is important that the genogram questions explore and focus on family concerns and the impact of the health problem on family members and their relationships. As they explore the genogram information together, the

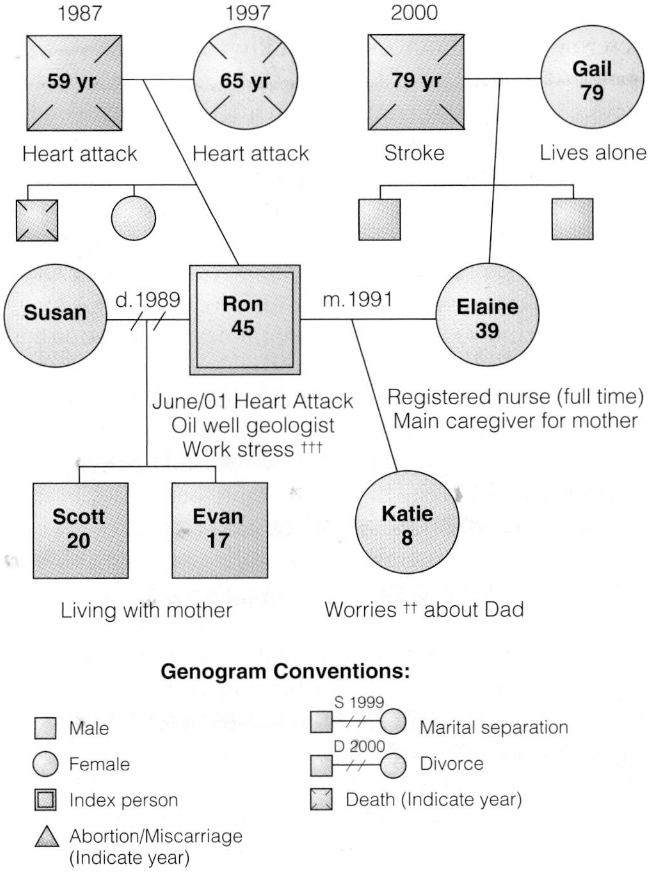

Figure 6.6 Family genogram

Source: Adapted from Wright & Leahey (2002). *Nurses and families: A guide to family assessment and intervention* (p. 87–94). Philadelphia: F. A. Davis. Reprinted with permission from F. A. Davis Company, PA.

nurse and family members can become more engaged and committed to working together. Initiating a genogram inquiry can be an intervention on the part of the nurse, which encourages one to "think family" and to consider the impact of the situation on all family members.

The context and external environment of the family can similarly be explored by sketching an **ecomap** (Figure 6.7). This diagram depicts the family's connections to larger systems, including community agencies, health-care providers, work, church, friends, and other meaningful activities in their lives (Bomar, 1996; Hanson & Boyd, 1996; Wright & Leahey, 2000). The genogram of family members sharing a household is sketched at the centre of the diagram. Ecomap questions could include the following examples:

- Are there any other clinics, health-care professionals, or community agencies that are involved with your family regarding this health concern?
- Which of these contacts have been most or least helpful to you?
- Are there any other religious groups, self-help groups, or personal relationships outside your family that have been either supportive to you or have contributed to your stress?

The ecomap can also depict the nature of relationships and stressors with extended family members, work colleagues, or friends. For example, Figure 6.7 helps highlight many external demands upon Elaine. In addition to coping with her husband's heart attack, she does shift-work and is a caregiver for her mother. She is dealing with the often difficult transition of placing her mother in a nursing home, with little apparent support from her brothers.

Each circle on the ecomap represents an outside contact with either an individual or the entire family. Straight lines are drawn to indicate the intensity of helpful relationships; dotted lines indicate ambivalent relationships; and slashed (or jagged) lines indicate difficult or stressful relationships. The ecomap can heighten the nurse's awareness of the possibility of social isolation or of family overload with multiple overlapping connections with health-care professionals or agencies. The number of identified contacts in the social network should not be assumed to indicate that support is provided or received or that such contacts are easily accessible (Bomar, 1996). The ecomap inquiry provides an opportunity to explore the nature and quality of these networks.

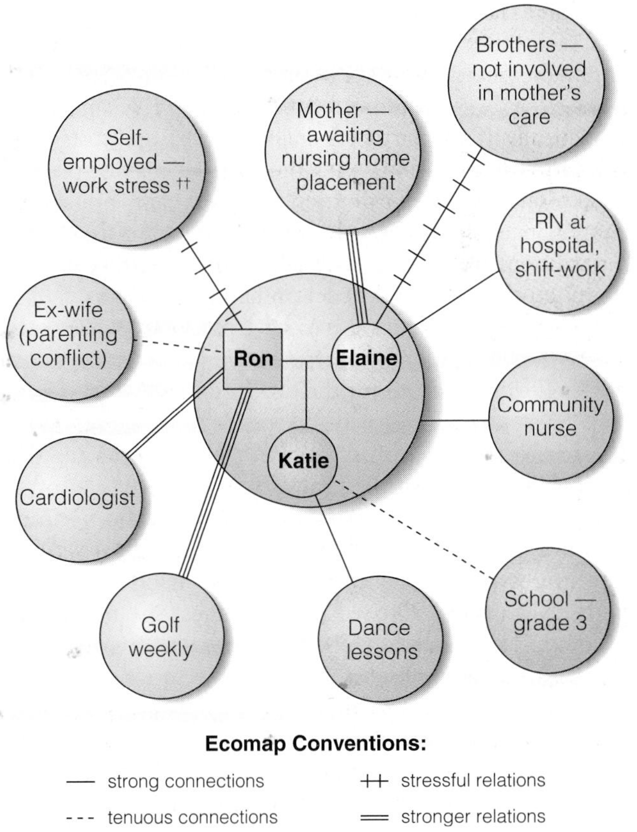

Figure 6.7 Family ecomap

Source: Adapted from Wright & Leahey. (2000). *Nurses and families: A guide to family assessment and intervention* (p. 95). Philadelphia, PA: F. A. Davis. Reprinted with permission from F. A. Davis Company, Philadelphia, PA.

How Does Illness Affect the Family?

Exploring the impact of illness on the family increases the nurse's appreciation of the distress and suffering of all family members, including the person who is experiencing the health problem (Wright & Leahey, 2000). The long-term impact of illness demands will differ when the family is confronted with recovery from an acute illness episode, rather than facing these responsibilities on an ongoing basis, as with a chronic or debilitating illness (Rolland, 1994). There may be a significant impact on instrumental functioning of the family (i.e., activities of daily living). If caring for an ill or recovering person at home, family members may need to assist with hygiene or mobilization, medication administration, changes in meal preparation, or follow-up visits to doctors and clinics.

Illness may have a huge impact on expressive functioning and communications within the family. Anxiety, depression, and uncertainty can cause great distress not only for the person diagnosed with an illness but may be an even greater difficulty for others in the family. There may be great concern regarding the loss of physical functioning, the implications of a poor prognosis, or the possibility of premature death. It may be difficult for family members to discuss their distress and worries. Communication patterns may shift as family members either work out these concerns with each other or conceal these worries from each other. Family members often feel compelled to maintain an optimistic attitude regarding the future. Family roles may shift dramatically. If one partner is unable to work and struggling with physical limitations, the other partner may be pressed to take on new responsibilties for child care, household maintenance, or employment. Every new diagnosis, change in treatment plan, or contact with a new health-care setting potentially has an impact on family members.

Nurses need to find ways to have productive conversations that explore family understandings of the impact of illness. It can be useful for the nurse to initiate these conversations in the presence of several family members at the same time. Listening to each other's concerns and discussing the impact of the illness on each other can often help family members be mutually supportive. Sometimes, the nurse can help the family by exploring topics that they might have been constrained to bring up among themselves (Tapp, 2001). At other times, the nurse may decide that it is more appropriate to meet privately with a particular family member. These conversations may also help family members to anticipate how their lives will be affected by illness in the future. Examples of questions that may be helpful to explore the impact of illness on the family are provided in the box to the right.

How Does the Family Affect the Illness?

Just as the illness has an influence on each family member, each family member also has an influence on the illness. This does not mean that they can control the illess or determine health outcomes. Family members cope with the illness and respond to the illness in many different ways. Therapeutic conversation in this domain helps uncover the ways that family members have found to manage the demands of the illness in their daily lives. They may view a health concern as a challenge and embrace changes necessitated by health maintenance or illness management. They may be overwhelmed by illness demands that compound other concurrent life stressors. A new diagnosis may challenge family members to seek out new information and to figure out what this means for their lives. Family members may develop expertise in their vigilance for the return of troublesome symptoms or potential complications.

Family members typically attempt to offer help and encouragement to the ill or recovering person while they are attempting to manage their own distress. On occasion, family offers of support are seen by the ill person as intrusive or as a limitation to their independence. Conversations about these attempts to influence illness can help family members to explore how they would most prefer to be involved, to limit the caregiving burden, and to enable family members to show their caring in a manner that is experienced as supportive. In some instances, the illness may compound other life stressors. Marital discord, difficulties with parenting of teenagers, unemployment, and conflict within the extended family are just a few examples of adverse circumstances that can interfere with family coping and increase the complexity of family involvement during health-care encounters.

Often, conversations that explore family responses to illness reveal incredible capability and competency on the part of family members. Learning about the family's

Examples of Questions that Explore Impact of Illness on the Family

- What do you think has been the most difficult change that each of you has had to deal with since your heart attack?
- Of all your family members, who do you think is worrying the most about what this new diagnosis means?
- Of all the things that both of you are confronting as you prepare for discharge, which ones are you thinking that we could try to address today?
- What do you anticipate will cause the most difficulty for your husband/wife/partner/son/daughter when you return home?
- Between the two of you, who is most likely to initiate discussions of difficulties or concerns as they arise at home?

Examples of Questions that Explore the Impact of the Family on Illness

- What has been the most helpful thing that your family has done for you that has made a difference to this hospitalization?
- What have each of you learned about limiting stress that will be most useful to you when you return home?
- How has your spouse/partner been most helpful to you as you have been preparing for discharge?
- Of all of the lifestyle changes that have been recommended to you, which ones do you believe you/your husband/your partner will be able to implement most successfully?
- How would you like your husband/wife/children to be involved in your recovery at home?

resourcefulness provides the nurse with opportunities to help the family recognize their own capability and explore other possible ways of coping based on the family's knowledge. These conversations help the nurse understand the family's usual ways of coping with difficulties and introduce ideas that may be different from those that the family has already attempted. Exploration of family strengths in illness management is an often-neglected domain of inquiry. Examples of questions that explore family influence on the illness are posed in the box above.

Nursing Care of Families

As stated earlier, nursing care of families is exercised almost exclusively through relational practices. Even if there are only one or two family members directly involved in the health-care encounter, the nurse-family relationship is more complex than when working with individual clients. The nurse needs to engage and get to know each family member. Questions will elicit each person's concerns and invite their questions. Family members and patients may hold very similar or very different perspectives and may require different kinds of support. The nurse needs to not only appreciate these multiple perspectives but also attempt to respond in ways that account for these similarities or differences. The following box summarizes examples of family nursing practices.

Family Nursing Practices

- Engaging in a collaborative relational stance
- Asking reflective questions
- Enabling access to the patient
- Eliciting illness narratives
- Commending family and individual strengths
- Offering information
- Creating and encouraging family support
- Suggesting respite from caregiving

Engaging in a Collaborative Relational Stance

Relational practices are influenced by nurses' beliefs about the kinds of obligations we have toward family members, about our expectations of family members, and about the skills and knowledge that nurses bring to family encounters. Many of these ideas are taken for granted in nursing practice, for example, the idea that recovery from an acute episode of illness will affect family members. However, ideas about whether nurses are responsible to nurse family members and how they ought to do so may be less clear. The nurse's stance toward the family is influenced by the habits, practices, concerns, and skills the nurse brings to the situation (Stannard, 1997). In family nursing, **relational stance** refers to the thoughtful and purposeful choices that nurses make in clinical practice about the ways that they will engage and involve families and respond to their concerns (Robinson, 1996; Tapp, 2000). These assumptions show up when nurses ask themselves questions about their relational practices, such as those summarized in the box below.

It has often been assumed that having a good nursing relationship with the patient and family will increase the effectiveness of their work together. Robinson's (1996)

Questions Inviting Nursing Reflection on Relational Stance

- To what extent am I imposing my beliefs on the family?
- To what extent did I elicit the patient's and family members' expectations, hopes, questions, and ideas?
- How frequently are decisions about the patient's health care made mutually by the patient, family, and myself?
- Do my actions and comments acknowledge the strengths and abilities of this family?
- What can I learn from this family about their experiences in living with this health problem?

Source: Leahey, M., & Harper-Jaques, S. (1996). Family-nurse relationships: Core assumptions and clinical implications. *Journal of Family Nursing, 2*(2), 133–151.

Family Assessment Guide

Family Structure

- Size and type: nuclear, extended, or other alternative family
- Age and sex of family members

Family Roles and Functions

- Family members working outside the home; type of work and satisfaction with it
- Household roles and responsibilities and how tasks are distributed
- Ways childrearing responsibilities are shared
- Major decision maker and methods of decision making
- Family members' satisfaction with roles, the way tasks are divided, and the way decisions are made

Physical Health Status

- Current physical health status of each member
- Perceptions of own health and other family members' health
- Preventive health practices (e.g., status of immunizations, oral hygiene practices, regularity and frequency of visits to the dentist, regularity of visual examinations)
- Routine health care, when and why physician last seen

Interaction Patterns

- Ways of expressing affection, love, sorrow, anger, and so on
- Most significant family member in person's life
- Openness of communication with all family members

Family Values

- Cultural and religious orientations; degree to which cultural practices are followed
- Use of leisure time and whether leisure time is shared with total family unit
- Family's view of education, teachers, and the school system
- Health values: how much emphasis is put on exercise, diet, preventive health care

Coping Resources

- Degree of emotional support offered to one another
- Availability of support persons and affiliations outside the family (e.g., friends, church memberships)
- Methods of handling stressful situations and conflicting goals of family members
- Financial ability to meet current and future needs

research challenged nurses to reconsider relational practices as not only creating a context or climate in which "interventions" can be more effective but that these relational practices in themselves *are* interventive. This research described examples of relational practices that were noticed by family members in this study of women and families experiencing chronic illnesses. They described the nurse as a *curious listener*, who found a balance between listening and asking good questions that focused conversation and brought out in the open significant differences in family perspectives. They viewed the nurse as a *compassionate stranger*, someone who was deeply interested in the family's situation, yet who had some objectivity and could offer a new point of view that was impartial to various family members. Families valued the nurse as a *nonjudgmental collaborator* whose avoidance of blaming and criticism helped family members speak with less reservation. This collaborative stance helped families realize what they needed to do and then to do it together. Families appreciated the nurse as a *mirror for family strengths*, whose positive orientation toward strengths, resources, and possibilities fostered family confidence and capability. Collaboration entails working with the family to co-evolve shared understandings of the difficulties they are encountering. Together, the family and the nurse generate other possibilities for dealing with health concerns or illness. A **collaborative relational stance** is one that values the multiple ideas and perspectives that are inevitably encountered within the family and that demonstrates respect for family strengths and capabilities in addressing health concerns and living with illness.

Asking Reflective Questions

In a series of studies conducted at the Family Nursing Unit, University of Calgary, Alberta, families consistently suggested that one of the ways that nurses were helpful to them was by asking good questions (Robinson, 1996; Tapp, 1997; Wright, Watson, & Bell, 1996). They described these questions as useful because they made them think about different possibilities for their present and future. These questions enabled them to think differently about themselves, about other family members, and about health and illness. Wright et al. (1996) have described this practice as "asking questions that invite reflection" (p. 116). Reflective questions are richly contextualized by understanding the events and relationships of everyday life. Wright and Leahey (2000) describe **reflective questions** as interventive

TABLE 6.1 Types of Reflective Questions

Types of Question	Examples
Difference Question Explores differences among people, relationships, time, ideas, or beliefs	Who do you think will be most affected by this new diagnosis of heart disease as you return home? What impact has this experience with heart attack had on your relationship as a couple?
Behavioural Effect Question Explores the effect of one family member's behaviour on another	When your daughter Katie is worried about her Dad's health, what do you tell her? How does Ron show his stress when his work is demanding? What impact does this have on you, Elaine? What impact does it have on Katie?
Hypothetical/Future-Oriented Question Explores family options and alternative actions or implications in the future	What do you predict will be the most difficult change for you as you try to implement lifestyle changes? How do you anticipate your family's daily routine to be different when you are discharged home?
Triadic Question Posed to a third person about the relationship between the other two people	Ron, what impact has this hospitalization had on Elaine's relationship with Katie? Elaine, how are you hoping Ron's relationship with Katie might be different since the heart attack?

Source: Adapted from Wright & Leahey. (2000). *Nurses and families: A guide to family assessment and intervention.* Philadelphia, PA: F.A. Davis. Reprinted with permission from F. A. Davis Company, Philadelphia, PA.

because they not only provide information to the nurse but they also facilitate changes in the family as new information emerges in conversations. Family members come to understand each other, their difficulties, and possible solutions differently as they listen to each other's responses to reflective questions. Table 6.1 summarizes examples of reflective questions including **difference questions, behavioural effect questions, hypothetical/future-oriented questions,** and **triadic questions** (Wright & Leahey, 2000).

Enabling Access to the Hospitalized Patient

Within inpatient practice settings, an issue that is commonly encountered by families is that of visiting hours (Hanson & Boyd, 1996). Hospital policies regarding visiting hours may impose significant constraints for family members who wish to be present at the patient's bedside. Reasons for limiting family access may include concerns for patient rest and privacy, infection control, limited space at the bedside, patient instability, and the possible impact of viewing procedures on family members. Nurses may not be comfortable when family members observe their performance of bedside care or technical procedures and may prefer to have the family wait outside. Nurses may believe that the impact of an emotionally distraught family member at the bedside can upset the patient. Sometimes, it is the patient who requests limitations to family visiting.

Family members may want to be present to provide emotional support to the ill person, to protect the ill person from harm through possible mistakes or careless treatment by health-care providers, or to quell their own emotional distress (Levine, 1998). Access to the patient often means access to information. Family members who are present at the bedside may have more opportunities to consult directly with physicians, physiotherapists, and other health-care providers. Benner et al. (1999) suggested that when family members are able to access the patient, they also have more access to understanding their loved one's condition. This could help family members to grasp the seriousness of the patient's condition and prepare for pending difficulties and loss or perhaps to gain more confidence as they see the patient progress in strength and recovery.

Importantly, nurses interpret hospital policy and unit guidelines and often have discretion to flex visiting rules when warranted in particular situations or to collectively generate a unit culture that is more family friendly. Family presence in hospitals has changed dramatically in recent years and is noticeable in most practice settings.

The importance of this practice is now recognized not only in such areas as pediatrics and labour and delivery but also in highly technical areas, such neonatal intensive care, adult critical care, and emergency rooms. Family presence may be facilitated even during resuscitation and life-and-death situations (Eichorn, Meyers, & Mitchell, 1996). In these situations, there is a need for adequate preparation of the family, availability of support personnel to help the family through a crisis situation, and family debriefing and support following a crisis (Benner et al., 1999). There is a need for further research that explores the impact of these practices on family members.

Eliciting Illness Narratives

Nurses access the beliefs and meanings that people hold about their day-to-day experience of illness through illness narratives, rather than medical narratives (Frank, 1998; Morris, 1998; Wright et al., 1996). **Medical narratives** provide clinicians with information relevant to the nature and course of physical symptoms, diagnosis and treatment of a disease process, and concurrent or past illness problems for the person or other family members. In contrast, **illness narratives** seek understanding of the person/family's experience of illness in the ordinary acts of everyday living; the influence of illness on relationships with family, friends, and workmates; the persons' ability to gain influence over the impact of illness in their lives; and the telling stories of encounters with the health-care system. Both medical and illness narratives are important and useful, and nurses must be able to conduct both forms of inquiry. Table 6.2 offers examples of questions that illustrate differences between medical and illness narratives.

Eliciting illness narratives with families is an important relational practice not only because these stories help the nurse understand family strengths and difficulties but also because they help the patients and their families sort out and make sense of their own experiences. In the telling of these stories, people come to a new understanding of their experiences with illness. Family members are more able to appreciate what is happening to each other and to realize that their experiences are both similar and different. Family members may describe the telling of illness stories as therapeutic in itself. There are many constraints against having illness conversations. Family members may want to maintain privacy or may not want to burden friends or other family members. People are very familiar with the expectation to tell health-care professionals their medical story. They are often surprised that health-care professionals are interested in illness stories, and they often tell of encounters with health-care systems that contributed to difficult illness experiences.

When nurses elicit illness stories, they are drawn into the richly contextualized lives of the people that they encounter. It becomes much more difficult to objectify or depersonalize people. It becomes much easier to appreciate how the family has managed other problems in the past and to be more aware of their strengths, resourcefulness, and capabilities. It is through illness stories that nurses will be able to offer family commendations to acknowledge their efforts to maintain health or manage illness.

Commending Family and Individual Strengths

Nurses can adopt the stance that patients and families have strengths and capabilities, that they have solved problems before and are resourceful and only temporarily in need of assistance from health-care professionals (McElheran & Harper-Jaques, 1994). This stance heightens the nurse's ability to recognize and elicit examples of the family's resourceful-

TABLE 6.2 Examples of Questions to Elicit Medical and Illness Narratives

Medical Narrative	Illness Narrative
Could you describe the onset of the chest pain?	What does it mean to you when the chest pains come and are so unpredictable?
Have you had any acute health problems or chronic illnesses in the past?	Of all of the health problems that you have encountered in the past, what has been the most difficult thing you have had to deal with?
Does your extended family have any previous history of heart disease?	What have you learned from your parents' experiences with heart disease that might be helpful during your own recovery?
Have you had any cardiac diagnostic tests done in the past?	Based on the diagnostic tests that you have had done, what are your predictions about your health in the future?
Which of the following cardiac risk factors would apply to you? (e.g., smoker, sedentary lifestyle, high-fat diet)	Tell me how it has been for you and your family as you have tried to incorporate the lifestyle changes that have been recommended.

ness throughout their work together. Examples of strength and capability show up in the illness narratives as persons and families tell of the ways that they have been able to manage or live with a health problem or illness. Other examples may be evident in the day-to-day situations and conversations that occur as nurses and families work together. When nurses strive to acknowledge strengths by verbalizing them directly to the family, the practice of offering commendations emerges. This practice can help families recognize their own strengths and to realize that their capability and expertise are valued by other health-care professionals.

Commendations are statements of praise that "highlight strengths, support movement of the nurse-patient-family system in ways that meet the family's needs and assist the nurse in engaging the patient and family at levels of interaction that are not problem saturated, but are resource focused" (McElheran & Harper-Jaques, 1994, p. 7). When health problems occur, families may be overwhelmed by difficulties and may feel unable to cope with the uncertainty or transitions they are facing. Commendations can help change the view that families have of themselves or their situations and support their confidence in each other. Commendations support the idea that the patient and the family are active participants who are in charge of their health or life situation and can offer hope for the future (McElheran & Harper-Jaques, 1994). This practice can encourage families to continue seeking further options to discover their own solutions to problems (Wright & Leahey, 2000). Commendations can also enhance connection in the family–nurse relationship as the nurse conveys respect and appreciation for the family's contributions and efforts as they deal with difficult situations.

Commendations should echo the family's own language and fit with their values and perceptions of their experiences. When the nurse does not know the family well, commendations can be offered as "beginning impressions" of what they have been doing well. Commendations can be introduced by such comments as: "What I've noticed about your family (or about what you've told me) is that ....," "I'm really impressed by the way that ...," "I appreciate how you have been able to ...," "I'm wondering if your talent in this situation is the way that you ...." It may be helpful to offer a commendation prior to offering an opinion or idea that might be difficult for family members to accept. Commendations that are offered at the end of a conversation can help highlight change or support family choices that have become more evident through the discussion.

Offering Information

Families indicate that having information about the health situation greatly assists them to make decisions, to cope more effectively, and to be able to support their ill family member appropriately (Levine, 1998). Nurses play an important role in providing information for health promotion, recovery, and health maintenance, and during acute episodes of illness. Health promotion messages within the media and public domain are often confusing and sometimes contradictory. Illness care operates within an increasingly technical biomedical domain with a specialized jargon of its own. Nurses are positioned in the middle of these public and biotechnical discourses and can help families interpret this information. Also, nurses typically know the health-care system well and can offer information that helps people access appropriate services effectively.

Family members other than the ill individual may play an important role in garnering information about diagnosis, treatment, and health maintenance issues. The ill person may be vulnerable and less able to seek out or comprehend new information because of illness, effects of medications, or invasive diagnostics and treatment. By informing and educating family members, the nurse helps family members understand illness events, anticipate likely events on a trajectory of illness, and prepare for their caregiving roles (Levine, 1998).

Nurses often make assumptions about the kind of information that would be most helpful to particular persons/

FOCUS ON CRITICAL THINKING

At the morning change of shift report on the medical unit where you work, you are warned about Mr. Black's "demanding family." He has been hospitalized for the past week for diagnostic tests that have attempted to locate the cause for his progressive neurological deficits. Test results have been inconclusive. Each morning, his wife (Joan, age 49) and son (Alex, age 23 and a pre-med student) arrive and question the nurse about his progress overnight and the plan of action for the day. Their approach to the nurses has been described by others as the "morning interrogation." You see them coming toward you down the hall as you begin your shift.

1. How would you engage this family to foster a more productive and collaborative relationship?
2. How would you attempt to address their concerns?
3. What is the relationship between the health problem and the family members?

See Appendix A for answers to these questions.

families. Often, these assumed essentials concern the details of the disease process, medication management, and activity guidelines. However, it is important to discuss with the family the kind of information that *they* believe would be most helpful to them. Other concerns may be far more pressing, such as how to provide emotional support at home or how to arrange for transportation to a follow-up appointment. Nurses often believe that more information will result in decreased anxiety. While this may be the case, it is not necessarily so. Nurses can be very helpful to families by assisting them to locate other sources of information, such as availability of self-help or support groups, public service groups, Web sites, or community resource centres.

Creating and Encouraging Family Support

When nurses are "thinking family" (Wright & Leahey, 2000), they are more likely to be aware that all family members may be in need of support. In health care literature, **family support** has often been conceptualized as a form of social support, which entails provision of emotional, instrumental, informational, and appraisal assistance that helps to buffer stress. The number of contacts within a social network are less important than the perceived quality of social relationships and the extent to which they are experienced as supportive (Bomar, 1996). Ornish (1998) proposed an alternative definition of social support, that it is the experience of being "cared for and loved, esteemed, and a member of a network of mutual obligations" (p. 29). This conceptualization invites the nurse to appreciate the mutuality of relationships. Family members may be simultaneously contending with their own needs and distress even as they are attempting to be supportive for each other. Social support is not a unidirectional concept, and the focus should not be limited to either the ill person or their primary caregiver, but on the **reciprocity** in their attempts to be supportive to each other.

Nurses provide family support as they involve family members in care and respond to their concerns and questions. Nurses can assist family members to listen to each other's concerns and feelings and increase possibilities for them to be supportive of each other (Wright & Leahey, 2000). Offering family support is implicit in nurses' efforts to help families make meaning of illness and health-care encounters through eliciting, listening to, and witnessing illness stories.

Family members may seek guidance from the nurse about how they can be supportive of the ill person. These needs typically arise at times when family members are not only trying to be supportive of others but are experiencing significant distress, concern, and need for emotional support themselves. Nurses can help family members discuss their preferences about the kind of assistance or support they desire from each other (Tapp, 1997). For example, following an acute episode of illness, the ill person may want to regain a sense of independence in day-to-day life. Family members may recognize a desire for self-reliance and have difficulty gauging how much assistance is desired and appropriate. If the ill person views asking for help or needing help as a sign of weakness, offers of assistance from other family members may be experienced as unwanted or intrusive.

For example, following a heart attack, family members frequently attempt to be helpful through their vigilance for signs of complications or through their watchful monitoring of activity or diet. These gestures may be motivated by caring and a concern about the future, as they want to contribute to prevention of a recurrent heart attack. The ill person may find reminders to be unhelpful or intrusive, especially if they have lost some of their self-confidence in recovery. It can be very hurtful or frustrating to family members when their well-intended efforts are declined. This is especially the case when family members view the ill person as not attending responsibly to health maintenance activities.

Family members often find these to be very difficult issues to discuss with each other. The ill person may be so self-absorbed with the experience of illness and recovery that there may be less awareness of the impact on other family members. Illness conversations may be constrained by a desire to maintain a positive attitude. Family members may be reluctant to engage in conversations about their own needs or frustrations, especially if their distress is motivated by worries about the future or prognosis. They may believe that conversation about these difficulties would hamper hope for the future or imply pessimism, which may be unhelpful to the ill person. In some instances, these difficulties contribute to significant family conflict. The nurse can offer assistance by helping family members explore their various concerns and discuss how each of them would prefer to both receive and offer assistance.

Suggesting Respite from Caregiving

Families differ greatly in their desire to be directly involved in caregiving activities. For example, Benner (1999) suggested that family members of chronically ill patients who are hospitalized may wish to participate in their familiar caregiving rituals (such as grooming, assisting with meals, comfort measures) to maintain connection and continuity. Others may be exhausted from caregiving at home and welcome respite from the demands of these usual caregiving activities. It is important to encourage family participation in caregiving to the extent that they desire, but this should be facilitated following careful exploration of both patient and family preferences in this regard.

A study by Ward-Griffin (1999) explored transitions in caregiving between community nurses and family members caring for an older person at home. Initially, family members were encouraged to be involved and were grateful to be of assistance. Family members became very knowledgeable and skillful in these activities as the nurse shifted care to the family caregiver at a pace they could manage. However, family members gradually reported feeling overwhelmed as nurses reduced their time and involvement with the family. Eventually, many family caregivers reported that the amount of care they were expected to provide led to physical and emotional exhaustion, social isolation, and strained family relationships. This report heightens sensitivity to the potential for caregiver burden when these responsibilities are faced for prolonged periods of time.

Financial constraints may make it very difficult for families to secure respite from caregiving. Household income may be reduced due to the ill person's inability to work, or family members may be forfeiting income in order to be available to provide assistance to an ill family member at home. Finances may limit options to compensate a suitable replacement caregiver or to be able to take a vacation. It may be difficult for family members to allow themselves to take respite from caregiving without significant guilt (Wright & Leahey, 2000). The ill person may be reluctant to accept an alternative caregiver. A primary caregiver may be reluctant to request assistance from other extended family members. Each of these possible constraints should be explored with the family.

There are many possible options for **respite care.** Obtaining a few hours away from the house on a regular basis to see a movie or visit with friends may be sufficient in some instances. Others may prefer an extended vacation for a couple of weeks. Some may desire respite for a brief one- or two-day period to build confidence that they could be away for longer. Respite programs may be available either to provide care in home or to provide a temporary inpatient placement for this purpose.

Evaluating Nursing Care of Families

Finally, relational practices are also inherent in nurses' efforts to evaluate their clinical practice with families. Every day and every encounter with persons and their families provide opportunities for the nurse to invite their views about the contact between the nurse and the family. The nurse can reflect upon the extent to which information was communicated to families, how families were involved in decision making, and the ways that patient and family expectations, hopes, questions, and ideas were discussed (Leahey & Harper-Jaques, 1996). The nurse can also solicit feedback on an ongoing basis from the patient and family about their experience of the family-nurse relationship (see box below). Their comments and suggestions may provide the most useful opportunities for fostering an ongoing development in clinical skills that enable nursing care of families to be provided in a respectful and healing manner.

Evaluating the Nursing Care of Families

- Of all the things that we have talked about today, which of these ideas, if any, seemed most useful to you? In what way is it useful?
- What else could we have talked about that would be more helpful?
- Which family member do you think has benefited most from our conversation? How?
- If I were to encounter another family in a similar situation tomorrow, what do you think I should be sure to talk with them about?
- What advice would you give to me about working with other families who might run into this situation?
- Is there anything in our work together that supported your confidence in dealing with this difficulty?

CHAPTER HIGHLIGHTS

- Definitions of "family" should take into account shifting social norms in family structure and each particular family's mode of describing themselves.
- Nursing care of families is based upon relational practices that involve family members in care, respond to their concerns, provide them with information, and/or offer emotional support.
- Nursing the person in the context of their family focuses nursing attention on both the individual person with a health concern and their family members.
- In advanced clinical practice, when the family unit is viewed as the client of care, there is simultaneous attention to both the individual and the family and to complex relationships among family members, the family and the nurse, the illness and the family, and larger systems within health care and the community.
- The evolution of hospitals contributed to a focus on individuals in provision of illness care.
- More recently, fiscal restraint and reduced length of hospital stay have increased expectations that family members will provide follow-up care during early recovery.

- Family roles in health maintenance include providing emotional support, assisting with medication administration, symptom monitoring and management, recognition of complications, and implementation of technical procedures.
- Family expectations of health-care providers may include a desire for access to information about diagnosis and treatment, to be able to trust that their ill family member will receive good care and be treated compassionately, recognition for their own involvement in care, and preparation for their roles at home.
- Canadian families can be characterized by diverse cultural traditions, high mobility, increasing age of first marriage, declining divorce rates, and increasing common-law partnerships.
- The genogram inquiry helps the nurse demonstrate a concern for all family members, to document relevant information about those involved in the health situation, to appreciate developmental transitions in the family, and to begin to understand family relationships.
- The ecomap inquiry helps the nurse understand sources of family support or stress by tracing external connections to employment, health-care services, and recreational and religious communities.
- Illness and health concerns affect both instrumental and expressive functioning of the family.
- Family members develop unique ways of gaining influence over the impact of illness and health concerns in their day-to-day lives.
- The nurse's collaborative relational stance addresses the concerns and perspectives of all family members and demonstrates respect for family strengths and capabilities.
- Reflective questions invite family members to think differently about themselves, health and illness concerns, and options for addressing concerns.
- In hospital settings, enabling access to the patient may assist family members to provide emotional support to the ill person, to obtain information, and to prepare for either pending difficulties or readiness for discharge.
- By eliciting illness narratives, nurses can more fully understand the reciprocal influences between health and the family and can assist families to make sense of the illness experience.
- The nurse can acknowledge and convey respect for family capability and strengths by offering commendations.
- By informing and educating family members, the nurse helps them interpret illness situations, anticipate likely events on a trajectory of illness, and prepare for caregiving roles.
- Family support reflects a network of mutual obligations in which all family members are simultaneously contending with their own needs and distress even while they are learning how to be supportive of each other.
- Families vary greatly in their desire to be directly involved in caregiving activities and may need encouragement to take a respite from prolonged caregiving.
- Nurses can evaluate nursing care of families by reflecting on their efforts to invite family questions and concerns and to involve them in decision making and by asking the family directly about their experience of the family-nurse relationship.

READINGS AND REFERENCES

Suggested Readings

Parsons, K. (1997). The male experience of caregiving for a family member with Alzheimer's disease. *Qualitative Health Research*, 7(3), 391–407.

This study explores the experiences of men and sons who were primary caregivers to a partner or parent diagnosed with Alzheimer's disease. The difficulties faced by these men as they endured caregiving over time included vigilance, loss, aloneness and loneliness, taking away, and overstepping the normal boundaries. The person suffering with the disease was not perceived as the "real" sufferer or the one who suffered the most. This research challenges at least two common assumptions about such caregiving: firstly, that it is done by women and, secondly, that it is primarily a negative experience.

Robinson, C. A. (1998). Women, families, chronic illness, and nursing interventions: From burden to balance. *Journal of Family Nursing*, 4(3), 271–290.

This article describes a qualitative study that outlines a four-stage theory of women's relationships when someone within the family has a chronic illness. Women carried the greatest share of illness responsibility and illness work, regardless of which family member was ill. The growing illness burden led to exhaustion and isolation, until eventually other stressors tipped the balance and led to "falling down and falling apart," often leading to the discovery that support was not available from other family members. Helpful nursing practices related to therapeutic conversations were described in the study as the women found ways to recruit other family members to address caregiving burden, and when they sought assistance from health-care professionals. Strengthening supportive family relationships was a powerful influence on the women's well being as they "took charge of one's life" to regain a balance within family relationships and in their relationship with chronic illness.

Selected References

Becvar, D. S., & Becvar, R. J. (2000). *Family therapy: A systemic integration* (4th ed.). Boston, MA: Allyn and Bacon.

Bell, J. M. (1996). Signal events in family nursing. *Journal of Family Nursing, 2*(4), 347–349.

Benner, P., Hooper-Kyriakidis, P., & Stannard, D. (1999). *Clinical wisdom and interventions in critical care: A thinking-in-action approach.* Philadelphia, PA: W.B. Saunders.

Bomar, P. J. (Ed.). (1996). *Nurses and family health promotion.* Philadelphia, PA: Saunders.

Eichorn, D. J., Meyers, T. A., & Mitchell, T. G. (1996, July). Opening the doors: Family presence during resuscitation. *The Journal of Cardiovascular Nursing, 10*(4), 59–70.

Frank, A.W. (1998). Just listening: Narrative and deep illness. *Families, Systems, and Health, 16*(3), 197–212.

Friedemann, M. (1995). *The framework of systemic organization: A conceptual approach to families and nursing.* Thousand Oaks, CA: Sage.

Hanson, S. M. H., & Boyd, S. T. (1996). *Family health care nursing: Theory, practice, research.* Philadelphia, PA: F.A. Davis.

Hickey, M. (1990). What are the needs of families of critically ill patients? A review of the literature since 1976. *Heart & Lung, 19*(4), 401–415.

Hickey, M., & Lewandowski, L. (1988). Critical care nurses' role with families: A descriptive study. *Heart & Lung, 17*(6), 670–676.

Leahey, M., & Harper-Jaques, S. (1996). Family-nurse relationships: Core assumptions and clinical implications. *Journal of Family Nursing, 2*(2), 133–151.

Levine, C. (1998). *Rough crossings: Family caregivers' odysseys through the health care system.* New York: United Hospital Fund of New York.

McElheran, N., & Harper-Jaques, S. (1994). Commendations: A resource intervention for clinical practice. *Clinical Nurse Specialist, 8*(1), 7–10.

McPherson, K. (1996). *Bedside matters: The transformation of Canadian nursing, 1900–1990.* Toronto: Oxford University Press.

Morris, D. B. (1998). *Illness and culture in the postmodern age.* Berkeley, CA: University of California Press.

Ornish, D. (1998). *Love and intimacy: 8 pathways to intimacy and health.* New York: Harper Perennial.

Parsons, K. (1997). The male experience of caregiving for a family member with Alzheimer's disease. *Qualitative Health Research,* 7(3), 391–407.

Robinson, C. A. (1996). Health care relationships revisited. *Journal of Family Nursing, 2*(2), 152–173.

Robinson, C. A. (1998). Women, families, chronic illness, and nursing interventions: From burden to balance. *Journal of Family Nursing, 4*(3), 271–290.

Rolland, J. (1994). *Families, illness and disabities: An integrative treatment model.* New York: Basic Books.

Stannard, D. (1997). *Reclaiming the house: An interpretive study of nurse-family interactions and activities in critical care.* Unpublished doctoral dissertation, University of California at San Francisco, San Francisco.

Tapp, D. M. (1997). *Exploring therapeutic conversations between nurses and families experiencing ischemic heart disease.* Unpublished doctoral dissertation, University of Calgary, Calgary, Alberta.

Tapp, D. M. (2000). The ethics of relational stance in family nursing: Resisting the view of "nurse as expert." *Journal of Family Nursing, 6*(1), 69–91.

Tapp, D. M. (2001). Conserving the vitality of suffering: Addressing family constraints to illness conversations. *Nursing Inquiry, 8*(4), 254–263.

Thorne, S. (1993). *Negotiating health care: The social context of chronic illness.* Newbury Park, CA: Sage.

The Vanier Institute of the Family. (2000). *Profiling Canada's Families II.* Nepean, ON: Author.

Ward-Griffin, C. (1999, Nov/Dec). Nurse-family caregiver relationships: Moving beyond the rhetoric of shared care. *Registered Nurse,* 8–10.

Whall, A. L., & Fawcett, J. (1991). The family as a focal phenomenon in nursing. In A. L. Whall & J. Fawcett (Eds.), *Family theory development in nursing: State of the science and art* (pp. 7–29). Philadelphia, PA: F.A. Davis.

Wright, L. M., & Leahey, M. (1990). Trends in nursing of families. *Journal of Advanced Nursing, 15,* 148–154.

Wright, L. M., & Leahey, M. (2000). *Nurses and families: A guide to family assessment and intervention* (3rd ed.). Philadelphia, PA: F.A. Davis.

Wright, L. M., Watson, W. L., & Bell, J. M. (1996). *Beliefs: The heart of healing in famlies and illness.* New York: Basic Books.

WEBLINKS

The Vanier Institute of the Family
http://www.vifamily.ca
The Vanier Institute is a national charitable organization dedicated to promoting the well-being of Canadian families through research, consultation, and policy development. The Web site accesses online publications related to contemporary family trends and such issues as aging, divorce, employment, and family income.

Department of Justice Canada
http://www.canada.justice.gc.ca/en/ps/sup/stat.htm
This Government of Canada Web site provides information about legal issues, programs and services of interest to families (such as child custody, access, and support), fact sheets on family violence and child abuse, and links to research publications on these topics.

Canadian Council on Social Development
http://www.ccsd.ca
The Web site of this national nonprofit organization provides information and publications relevant to the social and economic security of Canadian families.

Family Nursing Resources
http://www.eFamilyNursing.com
This Web site markets educational products (books and videotapes) to family nursing educators and students.

CHAPTER 7

Ethics, Morality, and Values

OBJECTIVES

After completing this chapter, you will be able to:

- Explain how cognitive development, values, moral frameworks, and codes of ethics affect moral decisions.
- Explain how nurses can use their knowledge of values and values clarification to facilitate the ethical decision making of clients.
- Identify the moral issues and principles involved when presented with an ethical situation.
- Explain the uses and limitations of professional codes of ethics.
- Analyze some common ethical issues currently facing health-care professionals.
- Describe ways in which nurses can enhance their ethical decision making and practice.
- Discuss the advocacy role of the nurse.

Ethics is about right and wrong in how humans conduct themselves in relation to one another. In their daily work, nurses deal with intimate and fundamental human events, such as birth, death, and suffering. The relationship between nurse and client is based on a moral commitment of nurse to client (Storch, 1999). Because of the special nurse–client relationship, nurses provide support for clients and families facing hard choices and for those living out the consequences of the choices that others make for and about them. This inevitably leads to questions of ethics and morality. The nurse is frequently faced with decisions about what would be the *right* thing to do in any given situation. Therefore, it is essential that the nurse have a strong sense of ethics and a sound approach to ethical decision making.

The present cost-driven environment of health care tends to give highest priority to business values (Rodney & Varcoe, 2001). This creates new moral problems and intensifies old ones, making it more critical than ever for nurses to make sound moral decisions. Therefore, nurses need to (1) develop sensitivity to the ethical dimensions of nursing practice, (2) examine their own values, (3) understand how values influence their decisions, (4) think ahead about the kinds of moral problems they are likely to face in nursing, and (5) develop a framework for ethical decision making. The purpose of this chapter is to introduce the concepts of nursing ethics, thus helping the student begin to develop ethical sensitivity and decision-making skills.

Morality and Ethics

Morality refers to private, personal standards of what is right or wrong in conduct, character, and attitude. Morals are similar to ethics, and many use the terms interchangeably. However, the term **ethics** has several meanings in common use. It refers to (1) a method of inquiry that helps people understand the morality of human behaviour (i.e., it is the study of morality), (2) the practices or beliefs of a certain group (e.g., medical ethics, nursing ethics), and (3) formal statements about expected standards of moral behaviour of a particular group. Thus, it is generally used to refer to a broader understanding of moral life through the application of theories and sets of principles that give structure to morality (Yeo, 1996).

Nurses are often faced with moral quandaries in practice, that is, with decisions about *ought*, *should*, *good*, and *bad*. For example, the nurse might have to decide about whether or not to use physical restraints on clients who are confused and in danger of hurting themselves. The question is whether taking away a person's free choice is truly in that person's best interests and, therefore, whether the nurse *ought* or *ought not* to do it. The nurse's action will be guided by the individual belief system (morality) and by the broadly accepted standards of the society and the profession (as articulated in ethics theory and codes of ethics). A **code of ethics** is a formalized statement of a group's beliefs.

When faced with difficult decisions, it is important that the nurse be able to distinguish between *ethics* and *law*. Laws do reflect the moral values of a society, and they offer guidance in determining what is moral. However, an action can be legal but not moral. For example, an order for full resuscitation of a dying client is legal, but one could still question whether the act is moral. On the other hand, an action can be moral but illegal. If a child at home stops breathing, it is moral but not legal to exceed the speed limit when driving to the hospital. The legal aspects of nursing practice are covered in Chapter 8.

RESEARCH NOTE

Ethics in Nursing Practice

The author of this study carried out a survey of 229 oncology nurses working in the United States. Participants in the study were mostly female (98.3%) and had an average of 18 years experience as a nurse. Of them, 38.6% had a baccalaureate degree, while 37.7% had a master's degree. Participants completed a moral reasoning questionnaire in which they indicated ethical problems they had experienced, and how they had dealt with the problems. They also completed a "ways of coping" inventory, and a demographic data sheet.

Results indicated that nurses had experienced an average of 32 different types of ethical problems in the past year. The top five problem areas identified were: (1) pain management, (2) cost containment, (3) decisions in the best interests of the patient, (4) quality-of-life decisions, and (5) patient–physician–nurse relationships. Participants used a variety of support resources, with other nurses, clinical nurse specialists, and social workers being cited as most helpful. Eight ways of coping with ethical issues were identified and included (1) problem solving, (2) seeking social support, (3) self-controlling, (4) confronting coping, (5) positive reappraisal, (6) distancing, (7) escape-avoidance, and (8) accepting responsibility/blame.

The author concludes that nurses can use a number of strategies to create an ethical environment for patient care. These include talking with other nurses, discussing their reasoning on specific issues, and increasing their understanding of how others perceive the ethical problem.

Source: Raines, M.L. (2000). Ethical decision making in nurses. Relationships among moral reasoning, coping style and ethics stress. *JONA'S Healthcare Law, Ethics and Regulation, 2*(1), 29–45.

Values

Morality and ethics are based on values. Even though they may be unspoken and perhaps even unconsciously held, questions of value underlie all moral decisions. Of course, not all values are moral values. For example, people hold values about work, family, religion, politics, money, and relationships, to name just a few. **Values** are freely chosen, *enduring* beliefs or attitudes about the worth of a person, object, idea, or action. Values are often taken for granted. In the same way that people are not aware of their breathing, they usually do not think about their values; they simply accept them and act on them.

A **value set** is the small group of values held by an individual. People organize their sets of values internally along a continuum from most important to least important, forming a **value system.** Value systems are basic to a way of life, give direction to life, and form the basis of behaviour—especially behaviour that is based on decisions or choices.

Although values consist of freely chosen and enduring beliefs and attitudes, beliefs and attitudes are related, but not identical, to values. People have many different beliefs and attitudes but only a small number of values. **Beliefs** are interpretations or conclusions that people accept as true. They may be based more on faith than fact and do not necessarily endure. Beliefs do not necessarily involve values. For example, the statement, "I believe I will get a good grade if I study hard" expresses a belief that does not involve a value. By contrast, the statement, "Good grades are really important to me. I believe I must study hard to obtain good grades" involves both a belief and a value.

The beliefs and value set that a person holds determine what that person believes to be right or wrong in any given situation. The priorities a person holds (value system) help determine how that person will act. For example, a nurse might believe that it is wrong to withhold information from a client but the doctor has ordered that the patient not be told the diagnosis. What the nurse tells the client when asked about the diagnosis depends on whether the nurse gives a higher priority to the value of truth telling or to following doctors' orders. Therefore, it is important that nurses reflect on and clarify their own values as they enter patient-care situations.

Moral Development

Moral development is the process of learning to tell the difference between right and wrong and of learning what ought or ought not to be done. That is, it is the way in which one develops a value system. Values are learned through observation and experience. As a result, they are heavily influenced by a person's sociocultural environment—that is, by societal traditions; by cultural, ethnic, and religious groups; and by family and peer groups. For example, if a parent consistently demonstrates honesty in dealing with others, the child will probably begin to value honesty.

Although people derive values from society and their subgroups of society, they internalize some or all of these values and perceive them as **personal values.** People need societal values to feel accepted, and they need personal values to have a sense of individuality. Nurses also develop **professional values** that are acquired during socialization into nursing—from codes of ethics, nursing experiences, teachers, and peers. Watson (1981) outlined four important values of nursing:

1. Strong commitment to service
2. Belief in the dignity and worth of each person
3. Commitment to education
4. Professional autonomy

In comparison, a project by the American Association of Colleges of Nursing (AACN, 1986) identified seven values essential for the professional nurse: (1) altruism, (2) equality, (3) esthetics, (4) freedom, (5) human dignity, (6) justice, and (7) truth.

Ethical Theory

What Is Ethical Theory?

Generally speaking, within a culture, there are certain widely accepted beliefs about right and wrong. For instance, there are beliefs about such things as whether it is acceptable to lie or to harm others deliberately. Not everyone shares the same beliefs because each person has a different personal history. As an example, one person might believe that it is never acceptable to lie, while another might think that lying is all right if one does it to protect another's sensitive feelings. Attitudes, beliefs, and values are shaped in a number of ways and may result in different decisions by different individuals.

Across the ages, philosophers have tried to find ways of structuring our thinking about morality in an effort to achieve some consistency and to help people make decisions about "right" actions. They have looked at how people think about right and wrong and have tried to articulate value systems as **ethical theories** that present a rational approach to moral decision making. Having an understanding of ethical theory can help the nurse articulate personal beliefs and values in discussing problems with others.

Kinds of Ethical Theory

Traditionally, two types of ethical theories have been widely used, differentiated by their emphasis on either (1) consequences, or (2) duties and rights.

Consequence-based theories look to the consequences of an action in judging whether that action is right or wrong. **Utilitarianism,** one form of consequentialist theory, views a good act as one that brings the most good and the least harm to the greatest number of people. This approach is often used in making decisions about the funding and delivery of health care (Yeo, 1996).

Rights- or duties-based (deontological) theories emphasize individual rights, duties, and obligations. The morality of an action is determined not by its consequences but by whether it is done according to an impartial, objective rule. Generally speaking, deontologists accept that if a rule applies, for example "Do not kill," it should apply in all cases. There are many deontological theories; each justifies the rules of acceptable behaviour differently. For example, some state that the rules are known by divine revelation, while others refer to a natural law or social contract (Yeo, 1996).

These theories and the differences between them have been widely debated. One could argue that it would make our lives much easier if everyone used the same approach to making ethical decisions. However, no single theory is agreed on by everyone. In fact, individuals are seldom totally consistent even within themselves. For example, in health care, a nurse might use a deontological framework in deciding that it is wrong to ever lie to another. In that case, it would be impossible for the nurse to go along with a request to deceive a patient about a diagnosis. The same nurse might use utilitarian-based thinking to justify immunizing a child, despite the child's violent objections, reasoning that eradicating an infectious disease, such as whooping cough, serves the greatest good for the greatest number. One reason for this lack of consistency is that the theories do not give clear direction in all cases. The rules in deontological theories are very broad and the obligations often unclear, and utilitarian theories are limited by a problem in defining "greatest good."

Bioethics and Principles

In the early 1970s, it became evident that health-care decisions were becoming increasingly complex and that traditional ethics theories were not adequate guides for practitioners facing specific health-care situations. Therefore, a group of ethics scholars set about to define a new theory that they called **bioethics**.

In it, they specified a number of principles that could be used in decision making. Their idea was that when health-care providers encountered an ethical problem, they would examine the situation, decide which ethical principle(s) applied, and use that to make a decision. Their belief was that principles would be useful because even if people disagreed about which action was right in a situation, they might be able to agree on the principles that applied. Such an agreement could serve as the basis for a solution that was acceptable to all parties. For example, most people would agree to the principle that nurses are obligated to respect their clients, even if they disagree as to whether the nurse should deceive a particular client about the prognosis. The original principles of bioethics were *autonomy*, *beneficence*, *nonmaleficence*, and *justice* (Beauchamp & Childress, 2001). Later, principles of *fidelity* and *veracity* were added, and autonomy was expanded to *respect for persons*. These principles are very useful in discussion about ethical dimensions of particular care situations in nursing.

The principle of **autonomy (respect for persons)** states that individuals have the right to make choices about their own lives. It also means showing respect for others and accepting them as unique individuals with personal histories that influence their decision making. In health care, this means that health-care providers must honour the person's right to choose methods or approaches to diagnosis and treatment. Choices must be free and informed, that is, made without coercion and with the benefit of all necessary information. Some patients are unable to make their own decisions (for example, cognitively impaired elderly persons; young children; or comatose patients), in which case, health-care professionals are obligated to try to make decisions that, to the best of their knowledge, the persons would make for themselves. Usually, the nurse gains information about the patients' preferences from their families.

Nonmaleficence is the duty to do no harm. Although this would seem to be a simple principle to follow, in reality, it is complex. Harm can mean intentional harm, risk of harm, and unintentional harm. In nursing, intentional harm is never acceptable; nurses must not deliberately harm patients. However, nurses sometimes inflict harm during a nursing intervention that is intended to be helpful. Causing such harm would not be unethical as such. For example, a nurse may be required to carry out treatments that cause pain or discomfort, such as administering anti-cancer chemotherapy that has the side effects of severe nausea and vomiting. If the principle of nonmaleficence were taken on the surface, it would appear to dictate that the nurse should not carry out such actions. On reflection, however, the nurse would realize that failure to administer the drugs would cause the patient greater harm by allowing the cancer to progress unchecked. Similarly, nurses are often in the position of trying to mobilize patients after surgery, even when they are in pain and resist movement. Again, the nurse must realize that the effects of immobility are potentially more harmful than the increased discomfort. The nurse must consider the risk of harm from various sources and consider which action would be the most beneficial to the patient. Thus, the nurse must examine potential harms *and* benefits in considering whether the acts of harm were unethical. Unintentional harm is often unpredictable and could result from a lack of specific knowledge about a patient or from unexpected consequences of certain actions. Harm of that nature would be an error but would not necessarily have ethical implications, as the intent was positive.

Beneficence means the obligation to "do good." Nurses have a duty to implement actions that benefit their clients, that is, to act in the client's best interests. However, what is considered "good" in any situation is not always clear. Is it better, for instance, to tell a patient the truth about the diagnosis of a terminal disease or withhold the information? Which would be of greater benefit? An important question that arises in discussions of benefit is, "Who defines 'good'?" Should it be the health professional or the patient/family? For example, a nurse might believe that it is in a patient's best interests to get up and walk, whereas the patient might believe otherwise. The nurse must then consider whose beliefs should prevail in this instance. When health-care providers make decisions for clients without seeking their input, it is called **paternalism**. In the past, a paternalistic attitude was accepted; people expected doctors and nurses to make decisions for them. Today, clients are respected as having the ability to make decisions for themselves, and paternalism is not considered ethical. Often, nurses want to make decisions for patients "in their best interests" and must question themselves whether they are being paternalistic.

Justice is often referred to as fairness. In health care, justice issues arise most often in deciding how the scarce resources should be used. Such questions as who should get a heart for transplantation, whether a patient should be discharged to make room for another patient who seems more ill, or whether funding should be directed to heart health programs or home care for the elderly require justice-based decisions. Nurses make justice decisions all the time in prioritizing care on any given day. For example, a nurse making home visits finds one client tearful and depressed and knows that staying for 30 minutes more to talk would help. However, that would take time from another client, who is diabetic and needs a great deal of teaching and observation. Many factors must be weighed in the decision, and a nurse must be prepared to do some "hard thinking" in making such decisions.

Fidelity means to be faithful to agreements and promises. Nurses often make promises to patients, such as "I'll be right back with your pain medication," or "I'll find out for you." Clients take such promises seriously. As professional caregivers, nurses have responsibilities to clients, employers, government, and society, as well as to themselves. Sometimes, these responsibilities are in conflict, as when institutional policy suggests one thing, and the nurse believes the patient would benefit from something else. Nurses need to be prepared to make decisions about where their primary responsibilities lie.

Veracity refers to telling the truth. Although this seems straightforward, in practice, choices are not always clear. Should a nurse tell the truth when it is known that it will cause harm? Does a nurse tell a lie when it is known that the lie will relieve anxiety and fear? These kinds of decisions form the basis for many moral dilemmas in nursing.

Bioethics principles are meant to help the health-care provider make decisions. Unfortunately, it is probably apparent that it is never quite as simple as deciding which principle applies in any one case. Often, several principles apply, and the principles may conflict with each other. If a nurse working in community health observes a young mother exhibiting inappropriate parenting practices, does the nurse respect the mother's autonomy and right to care for her child as she sees fit (respecting autonomy), or does the nurse intervene and insist that changes be made (beneficence)? Does a nurse restrain confused elderly patients to keep them from hurting themselves (nonmaleficence) or let them wander and risk a serious fall (respecting autonomy)? Such questions are very difficult and require active reflection. The nurse who is insensitive to or unaware of ethical dimensions of such practice decisions is less likely to choose the most ethically sound course of action.

Nursing Ethics and Relational Ethics

Bioethics theory is useful in helping individuals make decisions in difficult cases. However, as seen above, it does not provide a clear answer in many situations. Moreover, it has been suggested that it may not be sufficient as a framework for nursing ethics. Some authors believe that nursing's ethical foundation must be based on caring and, therefore, nursing is better served by an approach that takes into account the relationship between nurse and patient (Benner, 1991; Bergum, 1994, 1999; Bishop & Scudder, 1996). Some also suggest that caring is a **virtue,** that is, a highly valued personality characteristic that predisposes a person to act in a certain way, and that nurses must possess the virtue of caring if they are to make ethical decisions in practice (Benner, 1997; Salsberry, 1992; van Hooft, 1999).

Ethical theories coming from these perspectives are called **relational ethics theories** or **ethics of care.** These theories suggest that we have a moral obligation to others simply because we are human and that we ought to act in others' best interests. Actions are judged according to whether they demonstrate caring and responsibility. Bioethics theory tends to consider situations more in the abstract, whereas relational theories take into account the individual's personal story or "narrative." Thus, they are more concrete and rooted in the client's own reality.

Relational ethics theory seems to fit well with the caring concepts that are central to nursing, as it demands that clients be affirmed as persons, not objects (Marck, 2000a, 2000b). However, it is important to remember that caring is not unique to nursing and that some have criticized the caring perspective for (1) reinforcing the stereotype of women as caretakers, and (2) overlooking other important moral principles, such as fairness and autonomy (Bowden, 1995). Nonetheless, nursing scholars seem to

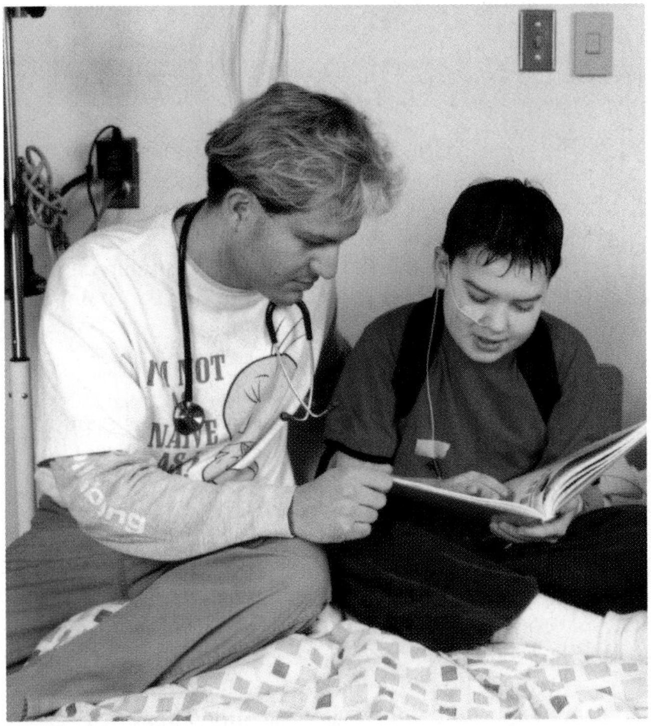

Figure 7.1 Relational caring: A professional relationship

be in agreement that the commitment to others that is reflected in an attitude of caring is the basis, if not the whole, of nursing ethics (Marck, 2000b).

Nursing Code of Ethics

No single theory of ethical decision making seems to be universally applicable to nursing. However, within the profession, there are norms of practice that can be used to help the nurse make moral decisions. These norms are reflected in a professional **code of ethics,** which is a set of ethical principles that (1) is shared by members of the group, (2) reflects their moral judgements over time, and (3) serves as a standard for their professional actions. Codes of ethics usually have higher requirements than legal standards. Nursing codes of ethics have the following purposes:

1. To inform the public about the minimum standards of the profession and help them understand professional nursing conduct.
2. To provide a sign of the profession's commitment to the public it serves.
3. To outline the major ethical considerations of the profession.
4. To provide general guidelines for professional behaviour.
5. To guide the profession in self-regulation.
6. To remind nurses of the special responsibility they assume when caring for clients.

Codes of ethics for nursing have been developed at the international level by the International Council of Nurses (ICN), and at the national level by different countries, including the United States and Canada. The Canadian Nurses Association (CNA) Code of Ethics for Registered Nurses articulates the value system held by the nursing profession in Canada and, as such, serves as a blueprint for ethical practice by Canadian nurses. However, the Code cannot provide answers to particular care decisions. Instead, the Code reflects the mandate of professional nursing and the elements that must be considered in making ethical practice decisions. Nurses are responsible for being familiar with the code that governs their practice. The most recent revisions of the ICN, Canadian, and American Codes of ethics are shown in the following boxes.

Ethical Decision Making

In this chapter, we have discussed several types of ethics theory (consequentialist, deontological, bioethics, and relational ethics). In addition, we have discussed codes of ethics and the impact of personal and professional values on decision making. How can these various parts be brought together to help a nurse develop a plan to enhance ethical practice? First, it should be fairly obvious that providing ethical care requires considerable thought and reflection. Ethical decision making can be enhanced if nurses have an understanding of the values that drive their practice.

Values Clarification

Clarifying Nurse Values

In preparing for practice, nurses and nursing students need to examine the values they hold about life, health, illness, and death. They need to think about whether they have some fundamental beliefs that would apply across all situations. For example, do they believe that individual rights are more or less important than the greater good (utilitarianism)? Are there certain rules that are basic to their belief system, such as, "Do not lie" (deontology)? Self-reflection, values clarification exercises, and discussions with other nurses can help nurses identify their values.

Once those basic values have been identified, the nurse must examine those values against those articulated in the CNA Code of Ethics and think about how they might be played out in practice. For example, nurses might ask whether they truly value clients' autonomy and how that affects their actions. Are there any circumstances under which they would be willing to take away a client's right to free choice? Would they, for example, be willing to support a mother's right to use cocaine during pregnancy? How highly do they value a client's confidentiality? Would that mean that they would not give information to a social worker if there were potential for harm to

The ICN Code of Ethics for Nurses

An international code of ethics for nurses was first adopted by the International Council of Nurses (ICN) in 1953. It has been revised and reaffirmed at various times since, most recently with this review and revision completed in 2000. The ICN Code of Ethics is also available in French [pdf file], Spanish [pdf file], and German.

Preamble

Nurses have four fundamental responsibilities: to promote health, to prevent illness, to restore health, and to alleviate suffering. The need for nursing is universal.

Inherent in nursing is respect for human rights, including the right to life, to dignity, and to be treated with respect. Nursing care is unrestricted by considerations of age, colour, creed, culture, disability or illness, gender, nationality, politics, race, or social status.

Nurses render health services to the individual, the family, and the community and co-ordinate their services with those of related groups.

The Code

The ICN Code of Ethics for Nurses has four principal elements that outline the standards of ethical conduct.

Elements of the Code

1. **Nurses and People**
   The nurse's primary professional responsibility is to people requiring nursing care.
   In providing care, the nurse promotes an environment in which the human rights, values, customs and spiritual beliefs of the individual, family, and community are respected.
   The nurse ensures that the individual receives sufficient information on which to base consent for care and related treatment.
   The nurse holds in confidence personal information and uses judgement in sharing this information.
   The nurse shares with society the responsibility for initiating and supporting action to meet the health and social needs of the public, in particular those of vulnerable populations.
   The nurse also shares responsibility to sustain and protect the natural environment from depletion, pollution, degradation, and destruction.
2. **Nurses and Practice**
   The nurse carries personal responsibility and accountability for nursing practice and for maintaining competence by continual learning.
   The nurse maintains a standard of personal health such that the ability to provide care is not compromised.
   The nurse uses judgement regarding individual competence when accepting and delegating responsibility.
   The nurse at all times maintains standards of personal conduct which reflect well on the profession and enhance public confidence.
   The nurse, in providing care, ensures that use of technology and scientific advances are compatible with the safety, dignity, and rights of people.
3. **Nurses and the Profession**
   The nurse assumes the major role in determining and implementing acceptable standards of clinical nursing practice, management, research, and education.
   The nurse is active in developing a core of research-based professional knowledge.
   The nurse, acting through the professional organization, participates in creating and maintaining equitable social and economic working conditions in nursing.
4. **Nurses and Co-workers**
   The nurse sustains a cooperative relationship with co-workers in nursing and other fields.
   The nurse takes appropriate action to safeguard individuals when their care is endangered by a co-worker or any other person.

Source: © 2000 International Council of Nurses, *ICN Code of Ethics for Nurses*. Reprinted with permission of the ICN, Geneva.

a child? How strongly would they be willing to advocate for a safer work environment? Would they be willing to put their own jobs on the line by refusing to accept new admissions to the nursing unit if they were understaffed?

Another important element of reflection involves thinking about relationships with patients (relational ethics). Each nurse needs to think about what personal commitment can be willingly made to patients and how boundaries on "caring" will be set. What does the nurse see as an obligation to clients? What would it mean to show "respect and caring" for another? The CNA Code of Ethics for Registered Nurses puts "health and well-being" as a primary value. Can a nurse promote well-being in the absence of knowledge about what matters to the client? Is the nurse committed to making the effort to "connect" with clients in an effort to find out what really does matter to them?

Values translate into motives for action. The nurse must make an effort to examine his or her motives in providing care and must guard against paternalism by constantly asking the questions, "Whose needs are being met here?" and "Why am I taking this course of action?" Nurses

Canadian Nurses Association Code of Ethics for Registered Nurses

The CNA Code of Ethics for Registered Nurses outlines the values that should guide Canadian nursing practice. Each value is accompanied by an itemized list of responsibilities. Values include:

- *Safe, competent, and ethical care:* Nurses value the ability to provide safe, competent, and ethical care that allows them to fulfill their ethical and professional obligations to the people they serve.
- *Health and well-being:* Nurses value health promotion and well-being and assisting persons to achieve their optimum level of health in situations of normal health, illness, injury, disability, or at the end of life.
- *Choice:* Nurses respect and promote the autonomy of persons and help them express their health needs and values and also obtain desired information and services so they can make informed decisions.
- *Dignity:* Nurses recognize and respect the inherent worth of each person and advocate for respectful treatment of all persons.
- *Confidentiality:* Nurses safeguard information learned in the context of a professional relationship and ensure it is shared outside the health-care team only with the person's informed consent, or as may be legally required, or where the failure to disclose would cause significant harm.
- *Justice:* Nurses uphold principles of equity and fairness to assist persons in receiving a share of health services and resources proportionate to their needs and in the promotion of social justice.
- *Accountability:* Nurses are answerable for their practice, and they act in a manner consistent with their professional responsibilities and standards of practice.
- *Quality practice environments:* Nurses value and advocate for practice environments that have the organizational structures and resources necessary to ensure safety, support, and respect for all persons in the work setting.

Source: Reprinted with permission from American Nurses Association, Code of Ethics for Nurses with Interpretive Statements, 82001 American Nurses Publishing, American Nurses Association, Washington, DC.

might (and should) ask themselves such questions as "Why did I do that? Was I truly acting in the client's best interests? Was I motivated by other things, such as a need to look like the 'expert' or a need to be in control?"

Examining these values requires a great deal of thought and can often be done most effectively in dialogue with other nurses. Therefore, nurses should seek to engage in conversations about practice with nurses who have shared similar experiences and are willing to discuss values and value systems.

American Nurses Association Code of Ethics for Nurses

1. The nurse, in all professional relationships, practises with compassion and respect for the inherent dignity, worth, and uniqueness of every individual, unrestricted by considerations of social or economic status, personal attributes, or the nature of health problems.
2. The nurse's primary commitment is to the patient, whether an individual, family, group, or community.
3. The nurse promotes, advocates for, and strives to protect the health, safety, and rights of the patient.
4. The nurse is responsible and accountable for individual nursing practice and determines the appropriate delegation of tasks consistent with the nurse's obligations to provide optimum patient care.
5. The nurse owes the same duties to self as to others, including the responsibility to preserve integrity and safety, to maintain competence, and to continue personal and professional growth.
6. The nurse participates in establishing, maintaining, and improving health-care environments and conditions of employment conducive to the provision of quality health care and consistent with the values of the profession through individual and collective action.
7. The nurse participates in the advancement of the profession through contributions to practice, education, administration, and knowledge development.
8. The nurse collaborates with other health professionals and the public in promoting community, national, and international efforts to meet health needs.
9. The profession of nursing, as represented by associations and their members, is responsible for articulating nursing values, for maintaining the integrity of the profession and its practice, and for shaping social policy.

Source: American Nurses Association (2001). Retrieved from Web site: http://nursingworld.org/ethics/chcode.htm

Clarifying Client Values

In order to plan effective and ethical care and to support clients and families in making difficult decisions about their care, nurses need to identify clients' values as they influence and relate to particular health concerns. The nurse needs to ask such questions as, "What really matters to you in this situation?", "What would have to happen to make this seem like a good experience for you?", "What do you think you want to have happen here?", "Who do you want to make decisions for you?", "What do you want from me as a nurse?" The reflective nurse will soon recognize that without an understanding of the values held by the client, it is impossible to answer the questions. Therefore, having an understanding of the client's values is foundational for ethical practice.

Clarifying Values and Obligation in Care Situations

Nurses need to understand their own values in the broader sense, but they also need to identify values that are relevant in individual care situations. They need to ask, "What factors are working in this situation that might impact on how I think about 'right' action?", "Are there particular contextual features that might change my views?" For example, the nurse might value autonomy as a general rule but might question this value if it means supporting a client's decision to commit suicide.

Because of their unique position in the health-care hierarchy, nurses often experience conflicts among their loyalties and obligations to clients, families, physicians, employing institutions, and licensing bodies. Client needs may conflict with institutional policies, physician preferences, needs of the client's family, or even laws. According to the Code of Ethics, the nurse's first loyalty is to the client. However, it is not always easy to determine which action best serves the client's needs. For instance, a nurse may think that a client needs to be provided with the most current evidence-based information, but that information may conflict with the physician's advice, going against which may damage the physician–client relationship. The nurse will then have to decide what the greater good is in the situation.

Ethical Obligations

Making a commitment to treat others with respect and to uphold the values of well-being, choice, and dignity are fundamental to nursing. However, despite such clear moral commitments, nurses may still face situations in which the right action is not easily identified (Oberle & Hughes, 2001; Redman & Fry, 2000). A good decision is one that is in the client's best interests and at the same time preserves the integrity of all involved. Nurses have ethical obligations to their clients, to the agency that employs them, and to other health-care professionals. (See the following box for examples of nurses' obligations in ethical decision making.) Unfortunately, there will be times when some of these obligations appear to be in conflict, as when the nurse feels a strong duty to follow institutional policy but at the same time feels that the policy does not serve the best interests of the client. For example, in a study of ethical issues in Canadian public health nursing, one participant described a situation in which there was a teen-aged client who was pregnant and already had another small child. She was booked for a prenatal visit with her doctor but had no means of transportation and had no money for taxi fare. The nurse was expecting to drive past the clinic and would have been pleased to take the client to her appointment but was aware of the rule prohibiting nurses from using their own cars to transport patients. She felt conflicted by the obligation to be a "good employee" and the obligation to meet the client's needs (Oberle & Tenove, 2000). Making choices between conflicting values and obligations can be a significant source of stress for nurses (Oberle, 1993).

Examples of Nurses' Obligations in Ethical Decisions

- Maximize the client's well-being
- Balance the client's need for autonomy with family members' responsibilities for the client's well-being
- Support each family member and enhance the family support system
- Carry out agency policies
- Protect other clients' well-being
- Protect the nurse's own standards of care

Decision Making in Practice

A decision-making framework can help the nurse in making ethical decisions. Frameworks must take into account the facts, beliefs, and values inherent in the situation. Knowing the kinds of questions to ask in a situation is essential if the nurse is to get the necessary information. In the box below are examples of questions a nurse might ask in gathering data. The box that follows it shows examples of two decision-making frameworks that might be used.

Clinical Application: Ethics and Cultural Diversity at the End of Life

In a recent situation at one Canadian acute-care hospital, nurses expressed concern with a care situation. The patient was a 98-year-old woman of Asian origin. She had been in

Questions for Ethical Decision Making

- How can this situation be explored by applying ethical principles?
- How does a focus on relationship assist our ethical understanding of the situation?
- What are the goals of care? Are these goals shared by the client? The nurse? Other health-care professionals?
- How would everyone (client, family, caregivers, institutions, organization, society) be affected by a decision?
- What other external conditions must be considered?
- What (and whose) other values must be considered?

Ethical Decision-Making Frameworks

Storch (1992)

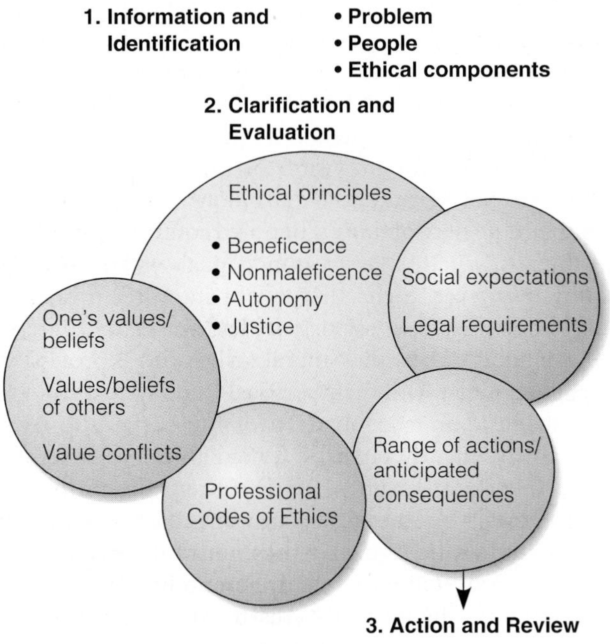

Cassells and Redman (1989)

- Identify the moral aspects of nursing care.
- Gather relevant facts related to a moral issue.
- Clarify and apply personal values.
- Understand ethical theories and principles (e.g., autonomy and justice).
- Utilize competent interdisciplinary resources (e.g., clergy, literature, family, other caregivers, and consultants).
- Propose alternative actions.
- Apply nursing codes of ethics to help guide actions.
- Choose and implement resolutive action.
- Participate actively in resolving the issue.
- Apply laws governing nursing practice.
- Evaluate the action taken.

Sources: J. Storch. (1992). Ethical issues. In A.J. Baumgart and J. Larsen, (eds.), *Canadian Nursing Faces the Future*. St. Louis: Mosby; and J. Cassells & B. Redman. (1989, June). Preparing students to be moral agents in clinical nursing practice. *Nursing Clinics of North America, 24*(2), 463–473. Used with permission.

a nursing home for a number of years and had been bedridden because of severe arthritis. As a result, she had numerous contractures that made it difficult to position her, and her skin had broken down in several areas. She was responding only to painful stimuli, and the nurses observed indications of considerable pain whenever she was moved. She had a pulmonary infection and was receiving triple antibiotic therapy. The antibiotics gave her severe diarrhea, which necessitated more frequent moving and bathing. The antibiotics had not been effective, and the order was due for renewal. The nurses expressed the view that the antibiotics ought to be discontinued and that further aggressive care should be terminated. In their view, continuing treatment was robbing the patient of the possibility of a dignified death. Nurses wanted a DNR (do not resuscitate) order instituted. The patient's daughter adamantly disagreed, saying that it was her obligation to see that her mother got every possible treatment. In their culture, she argued, it was a demonstration of respect to try to preserve life at all costs.

What could the nurses do? They wanted to respect the daughter's wishes, but they believed that treatment was causing harm to the patient and that it was wrong to continue to use scarce resources trying to preserve life in this futile situation. They felt constrained by the desire to respect cultural differences but felt strongly that the patient was being harmed, even tortured, by nursing actions. Because of their distress, they were putting pressure on the physician to have the DNR order instituted and discontinue therapy. The physician was reluctant to do it because of the felt need to respect the beliefs of the patient's daughter. A consultation with the clinical ethics committee was called by the unit manager.

Clinical ethics committees are present in many Canadian health-care institutions and may be accessed by health-care professionals and patients or their families when ethics concerns arise. In general, an ethics committee does not make the decision for the health-care providers. The role of the ethics committee is to ensure that all sides of the story are heard and to bring ethics theory and literature to bear on the situation. In this instance, the ethics committee heard from the nurses about their distress. The committee then asked for the daughter's viewpoint. It soon became evident that what the daughter had declared a cultural value, that is, "preservation of life," was, in fact, more of a personal belief. Indeed, the cultural value was respect for elders, but that was not necessarily to be translated into heroic actions in the face of certain death. What became clear was that the daughter was very close to her mother and was distraught at the prospect of losing her. It was also apparent that the daughter was in need of care and support. As the nurses described their concerns, they realized that the daughter had customarily been asked to leave whenever the patient was being positioned or when any painful procedures were being carried out. She was only permitted to come back to the bedside when her mother was settled and comfortable. Therefore, she was not aware of her mother's distress. It was also pointed out by the ethics committee that the prevailing viewpoint is that health-care providers are not obligated to continue treatment in futile situations. When the issue of resources was raised, the daughter first became angry but gradually began to realize that the main intent was not to deprive her mother of needed care but to preserve her dignity. She had understood that stopping active therapy would mean that her mother would receive no care at all. When she was assured that her mother would be kept comfortable, she agreed that medications and aggressive treatment could be stopped.

Some Ethical Issues in Nursing

In the past, nurses did not consider themselves to be moral agents. They expected simply to follow doctors' orders. With changes in the profession, nurses' awareness of ethical issues in practice is growing. Nurses are beginning to realize that many problems at the institutional level are really ethical issues. For example, resource allocation becomes an ethical issue for nurses when a unit is insufficiently staffed to enable them to uphold the values of well-being and respect. When nurses are too rushed to listen to patients or to employ comfort strategies, then professional values are being violated. This is becoming more evident in Canada as cost constraints are being introduced. Often, cost-saving measures are directed toward reducing the number of available registered nurses, which can lead to a significant erosion of quality of care (Oberle & Grant, 1994). Rodney and Varcoe (2001) argue that such problems *must* be examined from an ethics perspective and that nurses must begin to understand that striving for better working conditions is part of nursing's moral imperative. If working conditions are unsatisfactory, and the standard of care is compromised, the nurses' moral base is eroded.

Developing and maintaining a trusting, caring, and supportive relationship with a client is the foundation of nursing ethics (Gastmans, Dierckx de Casterle, & Schotsmans, 1998). The CNA Code of Ethics for Registered Nurses indicates the values held by the profession. However, the Code acknowledges that "there is room within the profession for disagreement among nurses about the relative weight of different ethical values and principles. More than one proposed intervention may be ethical and reflective of good practice" (p. 7). Thus, it points again to the need for nurses to have a clear understanding of their own values.

Nurses must consider how their values might affect the care they give to clients. Certainly, every caregiving situation has moral components and will be affected by the values, beliefs, and attitudes of all those involved. However, some kinds of care situations cause nurses to pay particular attention to their own values. Abortion, end-of-life issues, and withdrawing and withholding food and fluids are examples of issues where values are central.

Abortion may become an issue for nurses when they are required to assist in the procedure or provide care for the individual who has had the abortion. If the nurse has a deeply held value of sanctity of life, it may be very difficult to work in that situation. The CNA Code of Ethics indicates that nurses value choice, but what does that mean? Is the nurse required to provide care? Certainly, the nurse can make a decision about whether to work in an area where abortions are performed, but what about when the situation is encountered unexpectedly? In this instance, there are legal obligations for provision of care by professionals. Nurses are not permitted to "abandon" patients; to do so would be a neglect of duty. They are required by the Code of Ethics (CNA, 2002) to treat individuals with respect and dignity. However, each nurse might interpret this somewhat differently. It is important that nurses have a clear understanding of how their moral obligations as professionals might conflict with their personal value systems.

Euthanasia and termination of life-sustaining treatment are frequently cited by Canadian nurses as ethical issues (Oberle & Hughes, 2001). Often, the problem is that the family or the physician wants care to continue, whereas nurses believe that the client's dignity is being eroded by continued treatment. Sometimes, the opposite applies; nurses believe that treatment should continue, and others want it to be terminated. Either way, the situation can cause the nurse moral distress, particularly if one feels powerless to impact on the decision making. Redman and Fry (2000) analyzed numerous published reports of studies of ethical conflict in nursing and determined that the most common concerns are around disagreements with decisions about medical treatment of patients. In situations where such disagreement exists, communication and problem-solving skills are particularly important. The nurse can use a framework to analyze the problem on the basis of understanding the patient's and family's wishes and can use values cited in the CNA Code of Ethics (2002) to develop an argument for approaching the problem from a nursing ethics perspective. Nurses need to be prepared to explore, with the physician, patient, and family, why they all believe that a particular pathway should be followed and work with them to come to a common understanding that is acceptable to all. Sometimes, agreement is not possible, and nurses must look carefully at their own frame of reference and why they believe the treatment decisions are incorrect. The question that must be asked in every instance is, "Whose needs are being met?" If the nurses place priority on their own values above those of the patients (which may be contrary to the CNA Code of Ethics for Nurses), they may be unable to resolve the dilemma and may continue to experience moral distress. Thus, the importance of values clarification again becomes evident. Discussion with clients and other health-care providers about differences in values can help ease the tension that such situations produce (Pike, 1991).

Canadian Society Notes

Fact	Implications for Nursing Practice
The Canadian Human Rights Act provides that every individual should have an equal opportunity to make the life that the individual is able and wishes to have, consistent with the duties and obligations of that individual as a member of society, and, in order to secure that opportunity, establishes the Canadian Human Rights Commission to redress any proscribed discrimination, including discrimination on the basis of race, national or ethnic origin, or colour. **Source:** Canadian Multiculturalism Act R.S., 1985, c. 24 (4th Supp.)	Nurses need to examine their own practices in order to support clients. In other words, they need to examine the values and beliefs that govern their relationships with clients. Do they discriminate against certain clients in the ways they act or in the care they give? Is the client's well-being their first motivation? Are their actions designed to promote clients' dignity and preserve their integrity?
The Canadian Nurses Association Code of Ethics for Registered Nurses (CNA, 2002) includes statements of values and guidelines that apply to Canadian registered nurses in professional practice.	Nurses have a moral obligation to respect basic ethical principles, as reflected in the Code of Ethics. This Code serves as a standard against which professional nursing practice is measured. Nurses must be aware of the values expressed in the Code and the stated obligations to patients/clients. They must examine their practices to determine if they are acting in accordance with the Code of Ethics. This requires ongoing reflection.
Security and liberty of the person are enshrined in the Canadian Charter of Rights and Freedoms.	Nurses have a legal duty to provide "necessaries" of medical care and to use "reasonable" knowledge, skills, and care for clients who are helpless by virtue of physical or mental illness, or age. For example, patients who are incarcerated in a forensic unit may have committed crimes that are abhorrent to nurses. If that patient is admitted to the nursing unit, the nurse has an obligation to ensure that the patient receives the necessary care, despite a difference in values. If the nurse has difficulty providing care for the patient, he/she is nonetheless obligated to provide care until another nurse can accept responsibility for care.

The recent legalization of advance directives in several Canadian provinces has made it easier in some instances to make end-of-life or treatment decisions because health-care professionals are legally bound to respect the patient's wishes as outlined in the directive. Recent research in Quebec indicates that nurses have a strong intention of complying with written directives, but problems arise in the interpretation of patients' wishes (Blondeau et al., 2000). The authors point out that written directives are not a substitute for a trusting relationship with patient and family, as trust is essential to effective communication and problem solving.

Withdrawing and withholding foods and fluids is another issue of concern. It is generally accepted that providing food and fluids is part of ordinary nursing practice and, therefore, a moral duty. However, when food and fluids are administered by tube to a dying patient or are given over a long period of time to a patient who is unconscious and not expected to improve, then some consider it to be an extraordinary, or heroic, measure. A nurse might apply the principle of nonmaleficence in considering this situation. Is it more harmful to continue treatment or to discontinue it? In this case, it is important for the nurse to have the facts about how clients usually respond to withdrawal of food and fluids. Does withdrawal of food and fluids increase suffering? What evidence is there? It is also important to know if there are legal or policy statements supporting the withdrawal. Facts are helpful, but such situations still raise strong feelings in nurses and others. These kinds of situations generally require considerable dialogue among the health-care team and the patient/family.

When one thinks about ethics in health care, it is usually the kinds of dramatic issues described above that are brought to mind. However, ethics in nursing is "every day" and occurs in every care encounter. Nurses may not be required to make the "big E" ethics decisions, such as

FOCUS ON CRITICAL THINKING

The Smithers have been caring for their 28-year-old son at home since he became comatose after being injured in a car accident at age 9 years. While they have used some formal nursing care services, they have performed most of the caregiving on their own. While they love their son very much, they sometimes wonder about the value of what they are doing. They are now considering stopping tube feedings, which would result in his death.

1. How can the nurse best help the Smithers make this decision?
2. How would the nurse resolve the ethical problem in the situation?

See Appendix A for answers to these questions.

whether or not to discontinue treatment, but they do have to make daily decisions about how they will treat the individuals under their care. For example, a nurse might make a decision to spend less time conversing with colleagues and more time sitting with a patient who needs comfort. Or the nurse might become sensitive to the potential for disrespect in such practices as calling elderly patients "sweetie" or "cutie" instead of calling them by their names. These kinds of ethical considerations are the essence of nursing practice.

Most of the issues considered above are centred in acute-care settings. It is important to recognize that nurses in other areas of practice also experience ethical issues, although the problems may not be as obviously "dramatic" as the life-and-death concerns of acute-care nurses (Oberle & Tenove, 2000). MacPhail (1996) examined ethics in community nursing and found relationship, trust, and advocacy to be central to community health nursing practice. For example, nurses in the study talked about difficulties in working with individuals who had chosen to adopt self-destructive lifestyles, such as drug abuse and prostitution. How could they provide support for the person without appearing to condone or support the lifestyle? How could they honour autonomy and at the same time try to change the individuals' behaviours? How could they maintain trust while adhering to legal requirements to report certain practices, such as child abuse? This study demonstrated that community health nursing is rooted in relationships and that the nurses who fail to attend to the ethical dimensions of relationships will be unable to provide effective care.

Nursing and Advocacy

It is often said that the nurse is the client's **advocate.** An advocate is one who expresses and defends the cause of another. An overall goal of a client advocate is to protect clients' rights. An advocate informs clients about their rights, supports them in their decisions, and mediates or intervenes on their behalf.

Nurses are frequently placed in an advocacy role when clients and families are unable, or unwilling, to speak up for themselves. Nurses must ensure that clients and families have the necessary information to enable them to consider options and must provide them with support when they make decisions. Sometimes, the nurse must defend the client's/family's views when others are trying to coerce them into making a different decision. This is often a difficult role for the nurse because it may cast the nurse in a role against other members of the health-care team. However, the nurse must be guided by the professional code, which places choice, dignity, and well-being as the highest values. To be an effective advocate involves:

- Recognizing that the rights and values of clients and families must take precedence when they conflict with those of health-care providers.
- Being aware that conflicts may arise over issues that require consultation, confrontation, or negotiation.
- Being assertive and using excellent communication techniques.

Advocacy may be required at the broader, systems level as well. For example, the CNA Code of Ethics (2002) articulates a value of quality practice environments, that is, environments conducive to safe, competent, and ethical care. Nurses may have to be involved in political action when underfunding threatens the integrity of the health-care system. It is a nurse's moral obligation to work to ensure that the best possible conditions exist for the clients' health care needs to be met. This is another demanding role for nurses, one with which many nurses are unfamiliar. Nurses may choose not to act because it is too much trouble, or they are reluctant to engage with unfamiliar administrative personnel or agencies. However, providing ethical care for clients is not an easy task, and nurses must be prepared to take whatever action is necessary to ensure quality care.

Advocacy is an important role for nurses. Nonetheless, nurses must be careful not to suggest (or believe) that they are the only advocates for the client. The term "advocacy" is potentially divisive; that is, it could cause conflict in itself because it suggests that the client needs to be "protected." Not all clients feel the need for protection, and the nurse must honour their right to self-determination. As well, other health-care providers, such as physicians, may resent the implication that clients need to be protected from them. Physicians, too, consider themselves to be client advocates, as do many other concerned professionals, such as social workers and physiotherapists. The nurse has a moral obligation to the client, but there is also an obligation to keep the health-care team functioning cohesively. Therefore, the nurse must be sensitive to the implications of such terms as "**advocacy**," and use them carefully.

Enhancing Ethical Practice

It should be noted that decisions about a client's care are not made by nurses alone. Although the nurse's input is important, in reality, several people are usually involved in making an ethical decision. Therefore, collaboration, communication, and compromise are important skills for health professionals. When nurses do not have the autonomy to act on their moral or ethical choices, compromise becomes essential. Integrity-preserving compromises are most likely to be produced by collaborative decision making. The following mnemonic device, "LEARN," can remind nurses to work toward collaboration in ethical decisions (Berlin & Fowkes, 1983):

L isten to others.
E xplain your perceptions.
A cknowledge and discuss differences.
R ecommend alternatives.
N egotiate agreement.

As should be evident from the preceding discussion, excellent ethical decision-making skills require considerable reflection and practice. Rodney and Starzomski (1993), Davis and Aroskar (1991), and Wilkinson (1996) describe a number of strategies to help nurses overcome possible organizational and social constraints that may hinder the ethical practice of nursing. These include:

- Becoming aware of your own values and the ethical aspects of nursing.
- Being familiar with the Code of Ethics that is to guide your practice.
- Learning about and respecting the values, opinions, and responsibilities of other health-care professionals.
- Participating in or establishing ethics rounds. Ethics rounds, using hypothetical or real cases, incorporate the traditional teaching approach for clinical rounds but focus on the ethical dimensions of client care, rather than the client's clinical diagnosis and treatment.
- Serving on institutional ethics committees.

In addition, they stress the importance of striving for collaborative practice in which nurses function effectively in cooperation with clients and other health-care professionals. Ethical practice does not just "happen"—it takes a great deal of work. Every nurse has an obligation to understand the ethical foundations of practice and to make a conscious effort to examine and reflect on the ethical dimensions of each caregiving encounter. It is only with an understanding of the ethical components of a situation that nurses can meet their obligation to act in the best interests of the client.

CHAPTER HIGHLIGHTS

- Morality refers to personal standards of right and wrong in conduct.
- Ethics is the study of morality and refers to theories or codes of conduct.
- In health care, ethics and morality form the basis for decision making about questions of value and about *ought* and *ought not*.
- Ethics and law may be similar, but they may also conflict.
- Values form the basis of ethics and morality. They are based on beliefs and give direction to life and guide a person's behaviour.
- A value set is a small group of values held by an individual. A value system is the way individuals have given priority to their own values.
- Moral development begins in childhood and continues through life. It is the way in which people develop a value system and is influenced by many factors.
- Ethical theory gives structure to morality and seeks to provide a rational basis for decision making.
- Two prominent ethical theories are consequentialist (utilitarian) and rights- or duties-based (deontological).
- Bioethics theory was developed in response to a need for an ethical guide for health-care providers.
- Bioethics is based on principles of autonomy, beneficence, nonmaleficence, justice, fidelity, and veracity. These principles can help nurses understand the ethical dimensions of a problem and assist in decision making.
- Relational ethics is another ethics theory that takes into account the nurse's relationship with the client. It is congruent with the caring values of nursing.

- Codes of Ethics are formalized statements of the group's ideals and values. Codes of Ethics have been developed to help nurses in different countries make ethical decisions.
- The CNA Code of Ethics for Registered Nurses sets out the values that are the foundation for Canadian nursing.
- Making ethical decisions in practice requires nurses to have a clear understanding of their own values and how congruent they are with the values set out in the Code of Ethics. They also need to have knowledge of the values held by the clients and their families. Values clarification exercises are important in determining values.
- Nurses will experience situations in which values conflict, and they will have to make choices about whose values should take priority. This may require considerable reflection.
- Nurses can find help in making ethical decisions by using a framework for decision making.
- Ethics are inherent in every nursing situation. However, some issues, such as abortion, euthanasia, and withholding and withdrawing treatment, may cause nurses particular moral distress.
- Nurses in community practice often experience different kinds of ethical problems from those of nurses in acute-care settings.
- Nurses are said to be client advocates, and as such, they assist in protecting patients' rights. However, the term "advocacy" can be divisive within the health-care team and must be used with caution.
- Nurses are responsible for determining their own actions and for supporting clients who are making moral decisions or for whom decisions are being made by others.
- Nursing ethics require a commitment to upholding the dignity, respect, and well-being of clients in the health-care system. Failure to do so is a breach of nursing ethics. Sometimes, the system makes it impossible for nurses to provide the kind of care they believe clients deserve, and nurses are then obligated to speak out against the system.
- Integrity-preserving moral compromise requires that the different "players" in the situation speak the same moral language, that is, have the same understanding of ethical terms and concepts. It also requires mutual respect and recognition that not everyone sees things the same way. Moral situations are always complex, and those involved in the situation need to strive for awareness of the different facets—knowledge, beliefs, and values—that influence understandings and decision making.
- Nurses can enhance their ethical decision making by recognizing their responsibility in ethical decisions, learning the language of ethical communication, speaking out, and working collaboratively.
- Nurses can enhance their ethical practice and client advocacy by clarifying their own values, understanding the values of other health-care professionals, becoming familiar with nursing codes of ethics, and participating in discussions about ethics and values.

READINGS AND REFERENCES

Suggested Readings

Alberta Association of Registered Nurses. (1996). *Ethical decision-making for Registered Nurses in Alberta: Guidelines and recommendations*. Edmonton: Author.

This document was produced by a provincial subcommittee and is an excellent practical guide to clinical ethics in nursing. Scenarios are used to illustrate different approaches to ethical decision making.

Canadian Nurses Association. (1998). *Everyday ethics: Putting the Code into practice*. Ottawa: Author.

This document was developed as a study guide to be used as an adjunct to the 1997 CNA Code of Ethics. It provides the nurse with clear explanations and examples of how the Code might be used in practice. A revised edition will be forthcoming based on the 2002 Code of Ethics, but the 1998 edition is still worth reading.

Canadian Nurses Association. (series). *Ethics in practice*. Ottawa: Author.

This is a series of articles available on the Canadian Nurses Association Web site. Various issues are addressed in a clear, readable, and practical format. Some topics include "Whistle-blowing," "Advance Directives," and "Use of Restraints."

Canadian Nurses Association. (2002). Ethical research guidelines for registered nurses. Ottawa: Author.

This publication was prepared by the CNA in response to a need identified by nurses in practice for guidance around ethics in research. It details a nurse's obligations with respect to supporting and conducting research with patients or clients, and includes a series of case studies to demonstrate practical applications.

Related Research

deCasterle, B. D., Janssen, P. J., & Grypdonck, M. (1996). The relationship between education and ethical behavior of nursing students. *Western Journal of Nursing Research, 18*, 330–350.

Kelly, B. (1998). Preserving moral integrity: A follow-up study with new graduates. *Journal of Advanced Nursing, 28*, 1134–1145.

Oberle, K., & Tenove, S. (2000). Ethical issues in public health nursing. *Nursing Ethics, 7*, 425–438.

Oberle, K., & Hughes, D. (2001). Doctors' and nurses' perceptions of ethical problems in end-of-life decisions. *Journal of Advanced Nursing, 33*, 707–715.

Selected References

Aiken, T. D., & Catalano, J. T. (1994). *Legal, ethical, and political issues in nursing*. Philadephia, PA: Davis.

American Association of Colleges of Nursing. (1986). *Essentials of college and university education for professional nursing*. Washington, D.C.: Author.

Aroskar, M. A. (1995). An ethical perspective. Managed care and nursing values: A reflection ... *Journal of Nursing Law*, 2(4), 63–70.

Baylis, F. (1994). *The health care ethics consultant*. Totowa, NJ: Humana Press.

Beauchamp, T. L., & Childress, J. F. (2001). *Principles of biomedical ethics* (5th ed.). New York: Oxford University Press.

Benjamin, M., & Curtis, J. (1992). *Ethics in nursing* (3rd ed.). New York: Oxford University Press.

Benner, P., & Wrubel, J. (1989). *The primacy of caring*. Redwood City, CA: Addison-Wesley Nursing.

Benner, P. (1991). The role of experience, narrative, and community in skilled ethical comportment. *Advances in Nursing Science, 14*, 1–21.

Benner, P. (1997). A dialogue between virtue ethics and care ethics. *Theoretical Medicine, 18*, 47–61.

Benner, P. (2000). The roles of embodiment, emotion and lifeworld for rationality and agency in nursing practice. *Nursing Philosophy, 1*, 5–19.

Bergum, V. (1994). Knowledge for ethical care. *Nursing Ethics, 1*, 71–79.

Bergum, B. (1999). Ethics as question. In T. Kohn & R. McKechnie (Eds.), *expanding the boundaries of care. medical ethics and caring practices*. New York: Berg Publishers Inc.

Berlin, E. A., & Fowkes, W. C. (1983). A teaching framework for cross-cultural health care. *The Western Journal of Medicine, 139*(b), 934–938.

Bishop, A. C. H., & Scudder, J. R. (1996). *Nursing ethics: Therapeutic caring presence*. Boston, MA: Jones & Bartlett.

Blondeau, D., Lavioe, M., Valois, P., Keyserlingk, E.W., Hebert, M., & Marineau, I. (2000). The attitude of Canadian nurses towards advance directives. *Nursing Ethics, 7*, 399–411.

Bok, S. (1992). *Moral choice in public and private life*. New York: Pantheon Books. As cited in J. R. Ellis and C. L. Hartley. (1992). *Nursing in today's world* (4th ed.). Philadelphia, PA: Lippincott.

Bowden, P. L. (1995). The ethics of nursing care and "the ethic of care." *Nursing Inquiry*, 2(1), 10–21.

Breault, A. J., & Polifroni, E. C. (1992, January). Caring for people with AIDS. *Journal of Advanced Nursing, 17*, 21–27.

Canadian Nurses Association. (2002). Code of Ethics for Registered Nurses. Ottawa, Ontario: Author.

Cassells, J., & Redman, B. (1989, June). Preparing students to be moral agents in clinical nursing practice. *Nursing Clinics of North America, 24*, 463–473.

Chubon, S. J. (1994). Ethical dilemmas encountered by home care nurses: Caring for patients with acquired immune defieciency syndrome. *Home Healthcare Nurse, 12*(5), 12–17, 61–63.

Curtin, L. L. (1994). Ethical concerns of nutritional life support. *Nursing Management, 25*(1), 14–16.

Curtin, L. L. (1995). Abortion: The limits of moral repugnance. *Nursing Management, 25*(10), 22, 24.

Davis, A., Aroskar, M., Liaschenko, J., & Drought, T. (1997). *Ethical dilemmas and nursing practice* (4th ed.). Stamford, CT: Appleton & Lange.

Erlen, J. A., Mellors, M. P., & Koren, A. M. (1996). Ethics: Ethical issues and the new staff mix. *Orthopaedic Nursing, 15*(2), 73–77.

Esterhuizen, P. (1996). Is the professional code still the cornerstone of clinical nursing practice? *Journal of Advanced Nursing, 23*(1), 25–31.

Fry, S. (1989). The ethics of compromise. *Nursing Outlook, 37*, 152.

Gadow, S. (1989). Clinical subjectivity: Advocacy with silent patients. *Nursing Clinics of North America, 24*, 535–541.

Gadow, S. (1999). Relational narrative: The postmodern turn in nursing ethics. *Scholarly Inquiry for Nursing Practice: An International Journal, 13*, 57–67.

Gastmans, C., Dierckx de Casterle B., & Schotsmans, P. (1998). Nursing considered as moral practice: A philosophical-ethical interpretation on nursing. *Kennedy Institute of Ethics, 8*, 43–69.

Garrand, E. (1996). Ethic. Palliative care and the ethics of resource allocation. *International Journal of Palliative Nursing, 2*(2), 91–94.

Heitman, L. K., & Robinson, B. E. S. (1997). Developing a nursing ethics roundtable. *American Journal of Nursing, 97*(1), Nurse Practioner Extra Edition, 36–38.

Hussey, T. (1996). Nursing ethics and codes of professional conduct. *Nursing Ethics: An International Journal for Health Care Professionals, 3*, 250–258.

Husted, G. L., & Husted, J. H. (1995). *Ethical decision-making in nursing* (2nd ed.). St. Louis, MO: Mosby-Year Book.

International Council of Nurses. (1973). *ICN code for nurses: Ethical concepts applied to nursing*. Geneva, Switzerland: Imprimeries Populaires.

Jameton, A. (1984). *Nursing practice: The ethical issues*. Englewood Cliffs, NJ: Prentice Hall.

Joint Commission on Accreditation of Healthcare Organizations. (1996). *1997 Accreditation manual for hospitals*. Oakbrook Terrace, IL: Author.

Kelly, B. (1998). Preserving moral integrity: A follow-up study with new graduate nurses. *Journal of Advanced Nursing, 28*, 1134–1145.

Kluge, E. (1993). *Readings in biomedical ethics: A Canadian focus*. Scarborough: Prentice Hall.

Kohnke, M. F. (1982). *Advocacy: Risk and reality*. St. Louis, MO: Mosby.

Leddy, S., & Pepper, J. M. (1993). *Conceptual bases of professional nursing* (3rd ed.). Philadelphia, PA: Lippincott.

Liaschenko, J. (1996). A question of ethics. Safety first? Beyond duty. *Home Care Provider, 1*, 105–106.

Lipp, A. (1998). An enquiry into a combined approach for nursing ethics. *Nursing Ethics, 5*, 122–138.

MacPhail, S. (1996). *Ethical issues in community nursing*. Unpublished doctoral dissertation, University of Alberta.

Mallick, M., & McHale, J. (1995, January 25). Support for advocacy, *Nursing Times, 91*(4), 28–30.

Mandel, C., Boyle, P., & O'Donohoe, J. (1994). Ethical issues relevant to health promotion. In C. Edelman, & C. Mandel, (Eds.), *Health promotion through the lifespan*. St. Louis, MO: Mosby.

Marck, P. (2000a). Recovering ethics after "technics": Developing critical text on technology. *Nursing Ethics*, 7(1), 5–14.

Marck, P. (2000b). Nursing in a technological world: Searching for healing communities. *Advances in Nursing Science, 23*, 63–81.

Millette, B. E. (1994). Using Gilligan's framework to analyze nurses' stories of moral choices. *Western Journal of Nursing Research, 16*, 660–674.

Mohr, W. K. (1996). Ethics, nursing, and health care in the age of "re-form." *N & HC: Perspectives on Community, 17*(1), 16–21.

Moss, M. T. (1995). Principles, values, and ethics set the stage for managed care nursing. *Nursing Economics, 13*(5), 276–284.

Oberle, K., & Grant, N. (1994). Impact of health care cuts: Nurses' stories. *AARN Newsletter, 50*(4), 9–10.

Pence, T. (1994). Nursing's most pressing moral issue. *Bioethics Forum, 10*(1), 3–9.

Pike, A.W. (1991). Moral outrage and moral discourse in nurse-physician collaboration. *Journal of Professional Nursing*, 7, 351–363.

Pinch, W. J., Dougherty, C. J., & McCarthy, V. (1995). Ethics in nursing practice: Confidentiality for women and their children with HIV/AIDS. *Medsurg Nursing, 4*, 452–457.

Raines, D. A. (1994). Moral agency in nursing. *Nursing Forum, 29*(1), 5.

Raines, D. A. (1996). Parents' values: A missing link in the neonatal intensive care equation. *Neonatal Network: Journal of Neonatal Nursing, 15*(3), 7–12.

Ray, M. A., Didominic, V. A., Dittman, P. W., Hurst, P. A., Seaver, J. B., Sorbello, B. C., & Ross, M. A. S. (1995). The edge of chaos: Caring and the bottom line. *Nursing Management, 26*(9), 48–50.

Redman, B. K., & Fry, S. (2000). Nurses' ethical conflicts: What is really known about them? *Nursing Ethics*, 7, 360–366.

Rodney, P. (1998). Towards ethical decision-making in nursing practice. *Canadian Journal of Nursing Administration, 11*(4), 34–45.

Rodney, P., & Starzomski, R. (1993, October). Constraints on the moral agency of nurses. *Canadian Nurse, 89*, 23–26.

Rodney, P., & Starzomski, R. (1994). Responding to ethical challenges. *Nursing BC, 26*(2), 10–13.

Rodney, P., & Varcoe, C. (2001). Towards ethical inquiry in the economic evaluation of nursing practice. *Canadian Journal of Nursing Research, 33*(1), 35–57.

Rushton, C. (1994). The voice of nurses on ethics committees. *Bioethics Forum, 10*(4), 30.

Salladay, S. A. (1994). Organ donation: Family affair. *Nursing 94, 24*, 28–29.

Salladay, S. A. (1996). Ethical problems: Confidentiality: A chilling tale. *Nursing 96, 26*(2), 22, 25.

Salladay, S. A. (1998). *Ethical Problems: Nursing 98, 28*(8), 72–73.

Salsberry, P. (1992). Caring, virtue theory, and a foundation for nursing ethics. *Scholarly Inquiry for Nursing Practice: An International Journal, 6*, 155–167.

Sarvimaki, A. (1995). Aspects of moral knowledge in nursing. *Scholarly Inquiry for Nursing Practice, 9*, 343–353, 355–358.

Scanlon, C. (1995, October). *Ethical issues on the national level.* Presentation at the Fourth Annual Clinical Ethics Institute for Nurses, conducted by Midwest Bioethics Center, Kansas City, MO.

Sellin, S. C. (1996). Client advocacy in the home. *Home Care Provider, 1*(4), 208–209.

Smith, K. V. (1996). Ethical decision-making by staff nurses. *Nursing Ethics: An International Journal for Health Care Professionals, 3*(1), 17–25.

Storch, J. (1999). Is practical nursing experience necessary in administration, education, and research? *Western Journal of Nursing Research, 21*(1), 83–93.

Taylor, S.L. (1995). Quandary at the crossroads: Paternalism versus advocacy surrounding end-of-treatment decisions. *The American Journal of Hospice and Palliative Care, 12*(4), 43–46.

Taylor, P., & Ferszt, G. (1998, August). The nurse as patient advocate. *Nursing 98, 28*(8), 70–71.

Toulson, S. (1996). The right to die: The dilemma for A & E nurses. *Professional Nurse, 11*, 435–436.

van Hooft, S. (1990, February). Moral education for nursing decisions. *Journal of Advanced Nursing, 15*, 210–215.

van Hooft, S. (1999). Acting for the virtue of caring in nursing. *Nursing Ethics, 6*, 189–201.

Van Weel, H. (1995). Euthanasia: Mercy, morals and medicine. *Canadian Nurse, 91*, 35–40.

Vergara, M., & Lynn-McHale, D. J. (1995, November). Ethical issues. Withdrawing life support: Who decides? *American Journal of Nursing, 95*, 47–49.

Viney, C. (1996). A phenomenological study of ethical decision-making experiences among senior intensive care nurses and doctors concerning withdrawal of treatment. *Nursing in Critical Care, 1*, 182–187.

Warelow, P. J. (1996). Is caring the ethical ideal? *Journal of Advanced Nursing, 24*, 655–661.

Watson, J. (1981). Socialization of the nursing student in a professional nursing education programme. *Nursing Papers, 13*, 19–24.

Watson, J. (1985). *Nursing: Human science and human care.* Norwalk, CT: Appleton-Century-Crofts.

Watson, J. (1988). *Nursing: Human science and human care: A theory of nursing.* New York: National League for Nursing.

Wilkinson, J. M. (1987/88). Moral distress in nursing practice: Experience and effect. *Nursing Forum, 23*, 16–29.

Wilkinson, J. M. (1993). All ethics problems are not created equal. *The Kansas Nurse, 68*(1), 4–6.

Wilkinson, J. M. (1996). *Toward a context-sensitive theory of nursing ethics: Classification and comparison of nurses' narratives from four time periods (1934, 1979, 1989 and 1995).* Doctoral dissertation. University of Kansas, Kansas City, MO.

Winslow, B. J., & Winslow, G. R. (1991). Integrity and compromise in nursing ethics. *The Journal of Medicine and Philosophy, 16*, 307–323.

Wocial, L. D. (1996). Achieving collaboration in ethical decision making: Strategies for nurses in clinical practice. *Dimensions of Critical Care Nursing, 25*, 150–159.

Wood, L. C., & DelPapa, L. A. (1996). Nurses' attitudes, ethical reasons, and knowledge of the law concerning advance directives. *Image: Journal of Nursing Scholarship, 28*(4), 371.

Yeo, M. (1996). A primer in ethical theory. In M. Yeo, & A. Moorhouse, (Eds.), *concepts and cases in nursing ethics* (2nd ed.). Peterborough: Broadview Press.

WEBLINKS

Nursing Ethics.ca
http://www.nursingethics.ca/
A site for Canadian resources related to ethical practice.

Canadian Nurses Association—Code of Ethics
http://www.cna-nurses.ca/pages/ethics/ethicsframe.htm
Provides access to the Code of Ethics for the Association in addition to providing links to provincial Web sites for related documentation.

Centre for Applied Ethics
http://www.ethics.ubc.ca/newsletter/index.html
The Centre was established in 1993 by the University of British Columbia. It is an interdisciplinary research centre that studies a variety of topics, including health-care practices. Their newsletter is available on the site.

Provincial Health Ethics Network (Alberta)
http://www.phen.ab.ca/acgm/acgm01speaker.html
The Provincial Health Ethics Network (PHEN) is a nonprofit association that provides resources to Albertans to support analysis of ethical issues in the health-care system.

Canadian Bioethics Society
http://www.bioethics.ca/
The Canadian Bioethics Society was established in 1988 by the union of the Canadian Society of Bioethics and the Canadian Society for Medical Bioethics. Its members include health-care administrators, lawyers, nurses, philosophers, physicians, theologians, and others interested in the ethical dimensions of health care.

CHAPTER 8

Legal Aspects of Nursing

OBJECTIVES

After completing this chapter, you will be able to:

- Describe the history and sources of Canadian law.
- Discuss ways standards of care, agency policies, and nurse practice acts affect the scope of nursing practice.
- Analyze how privileged communication applies to the nurse–client relationship.
- Identify the purpose and essential elements of informed consent.
- Analyze the purpose of the Good Samaritan Act/Emergency Medical Aid Act, Human Rights legislation/Canadian Charter of Rights and Freedoms.
- Discuss provincial/territorial regulation of nursing practice in Canada.
- Discuss the problem of nurses and substance misuse.
- Identify the nurse's legal responsibilities regarding wills and advance directives.
- Analyze the elements of negligence.
- Identify examples of assault/battery, false imprisonment, invasion of privacy.
- Describe the elements of torts and give examples in nursing.
- Discriminate between professional misconduct and negligence.
- Identify information that needs to be included in an incident report.
- Identify ways nurses and nursing students can minimize their chances of liability.

Nursing practice is governed by many legal concepts. It is important for nurses to know the basics of the Canadian legal system and its relationship to the profession of nursing. Accountability is an essential concept of professional nursing practice and the law. Knowledge of laws that regulate and affect nursing practice is needed for two reasons:

1. To ensure that the nurse's decisions and actions are consistent with current legal principles.
2. To protect the nurse from liability.

Relationship of Nurses and the Law

Law can be defined as "those rules made by humans which regulate social conduct in a formally prescribed and legally binding manner" (Bernzweig, 1996, p. 3).

Functions of the Law in Nursing

The law serves a number of functions in nursing:

- It provides a framework for establishing which nursing actions in the care of clients are legal.
- It outlines responsibilities that govern nursing practice and nurses' relationships with physicians, other health-care practitioners, and the care system.
- It helps establish the boundaries of independent nursing action.
- It assists nurses in ensuring that they are consistent, competent, and safe in providing quality care that serves society while preserving individual rights and human dignity.

History and Source of Canada's Laws

Historically, Canadian law is derived from two distinct systems: one, from early Roman times, that has become the civil law in Quebec; and, two, from English common law, which forms the basis of the legal system in all other provinces. Dias (1973) noted that "the two traditions have much in common in terms of the legal rules they apply. Their essential difference has to do with culturally conditioned attitudes about the relation of law to society, the limits on government in using law, and the techniques and intellectual law for making, interpreting applying, and teaching law" (p. 4).

The Civil Law System

The civil law system of Quebec was based on the Roman civil law system still prevalent in most western European countries, and having its origin in the 12 tables of Rome in 450 B.C. These tables were codified by the Corpus Juris Civilis and were adopted by France in 1804 as the Napoleonic Code. By 1859, this Code became the legal system of Quebec and set out the rights and responsibilities of individuals (Philpot, 1985). Individual cases in court are since then decided in accordance with these basic tenets.

The Common Law System

The common law system evolved from the so called "common laws" of early Britain (Philpot, 1985). In Canada, English common law forms the basis of the legal system of all provinces, except Quebec. Unlike the system practised in civil law, the majority of common law is not written down or codified as statute law. Statute law is a formal written set of rules passed by parliament or any other legislative body regulating a particular area. In contrast, the common law approach is to scrutinize the judgements of previous cases and extract general principles to be applied to different problems at hand. This difference in approach helps explain the different manners in which the two systems regard the doctrine of *stare decisis.*

Sources of Legal Authority

Stare Decisis. This means "to stand by things decided" and refers to a custom where earlier cases would serve as precedents for the deciding of later cases having similar facts and legal issues. In contrast, however, in the civil law system, the codified principles, and not the cases, were supreme. In the common law system, the custom of deciding like cases alike (*stare decisis*) was intended to ensure a measure of predictability in the legal outcome. In reality, there are never two perfectly identical fact situations before the court where the first case necessarily applies to the second dispute. It is often the case that the courts "distinguish" the current case and refuse to apply the particular precedent if the case is sufficiently different.

In Canada, there is a hierarchy of courts, including the trial court or court of the first instance, the appeal court of the particular province, and the Supreme Court of Canada. The lower court (trial court) is subordinate in that it is bound to follow the decisions and precedents of the higher one. The application of precedent in common law strives to achieve two purposes. First, the law needs to be consistent. "Consistency is achieved by judges and the legal profession applying the same legal principles in the same circumstances in a similar manner over time" (Keatings & Smith, 2000, p. 55).

Secondly, the common law strives to be predictable. Philosophical tenets of common law declare that if lower courts were not bound to follow precedents of higher ones, then the outcome of a given case would be unpredictable. A court would be free to decide the case on the basis of any legal principle of its choosing, regardless of existing legal principles and rules established in case law, and thus, consistency of law would not be upheld (Keatings & Smith, 2000).

Legislative Authority. The Canadian Parliament and the provincial legislatures are a second source of Canadian law. Laws enacted by any legislative body are called statutory laws. These laws are formal written laws and regulations passed by legislature or cabinet that set forth rules and principles governing a particular subject. In Canada, the power to make laws rests with the parliament and, in the case of the provinces, the legislative assembly, which makes statute laws or "Acts." The bodies have the power to create, amend, and repeal these statutes.

The regulation of nursing is a function of provincial law (e.g., in Alberta, The Health Professions Act). "Acts," however, must be consistent with constitutional and federal provisions. Examples of federal statutes that are enacted by parliament and apply throughout the country are the Narcotic Control Act and the Food and Drug Act. These two acts control the manufacture, distribution, and sale of drugs in Canada.

Regulatory Law or Administrative Law. This guides nursing practice. Nurses have been granted an exclusivity of practice (a right of self-government or self-regulation) and an obligation to monitor and discipline their own membership. The legislature permits the professional associations to establish rules and regulations that uphold professional nursing practice. The law prohibits individuals from declaring themselves as *nurses* or *registered nurses* unless they are registered with a provincial nursing body. Writing the Registered Nurse licensing examination in all provinces, except Quebec, is the first step to becoming a Registered Nurse and continues with life-long continuing education and professional standards portfolios.

The laws regulating nursing in the provinces and territories of Canada (other than Ontario and Quebec) are fairly uniform. Several provinces have umbrella legislation containing general provisions pertaining to all recognized health professionals within the province, as well as companion legislation relating to each province. In Ontario, the Regulated Health Professions Act and the Nursing Act govern the nursing profession (Keatings & Smith, 2000). This legislation enables the College of Nurses of Ontario as the governing body responsible for the regulation of nursing in the province. Section II of the Nursing Act prohibits anyone from declaring oneself as competent to practice as a registered nurse unless the College of Nurses of Ontario has certified that person.

In other provinces, such as Manitoba, an independent, self-contained statute sets the standards for self-regulation of each health profession. The Registered Nurses Act has designated the Manitoba Association of Registered Nurses to be the governing body for nurses in that province. The Act claims that all will practise or declare themselves registered nurses only when their names appear in the register of the Association (see examples of the legislation for each province listed in Table 8.1).

TABLE 8.1 Nursing Legislation in Canadian Provinces and Territories

Province	Health Care/ Nursing Legislation
British Columbia	Nurses (Registered) Act
Alberta	Health Professions Act and Nursing Act
Yukon Territory	Registered Nurses Profession Act
Northwest Territories	Nursing Profession Act
Saskatchewan	The Registered Nurses Act
Manitoba	The Registered Nurses Act
New Brunswick	Nurses Act
Nova Scotia	Registered Nurses Act 2001
Prince Edward Island	Regulated Health Professions Act and Nursing Act
Newfoundland	The Newfoundland Registered Nurses Act
Ontario	Regulated Health Professions Act and Nursing Act
Quebec	Health Professions Act and Nurses Act

Source: Adapted from Keatings & Smith, 2000.

Professional associations value the role that public representatives play in helping regulate the nursing profession. Public representatives in Alberta are appointed by the Minister of Health to the Alberta Association of Registered Nursing (AARN) Provincial Council, and to the Professional Conduct, Appeals, and Practice Review committees. "They share decisions made at the council table and in hearings to investigate the conduct of registered nurses" (AARN, July/August, 1999, p. 2).

Credentialling

Credentialling is the process of determining and maintaining competence in nursing practice. The credentialling process is one way in which the nursing profession maintains standards of practice and accountability for the educational preparation of its members. Credentialling includes licensure, registration, certification, and accreditation.

Registration and Licensure

Registration/licensing is a mechanism that acts to protect the public from unsafe practitioners and to assure employers that the nurse has met certain minimum requirements for entry to practice. The term **registration** means the listing of an individual's name on an official roster. In

Canada, practising nurses in all provinces and territories are required by law to be registered or hold a valid permit with their provincial nursing association. Registration usually occurs every year. Only those who are registered are entitled to call themselves registered nurses or use the initials "RN." In order to be registered, the nurse must have completed a basic course of nursing studies in an approved program of the registering body and have passed the national qualifying exams with an acceptable grade.

Each provincial nursing body has a mechanism in place to review the conduct of its members to ensure safe and ethical nursing practice. They are required to investigate complaints against registered nurses and discipline those members who fail to meet the high standards of the profession. Written complaints related to practice or conduct of an RN are submitted to the associated province and are investigated by an investigations officer, who prepares a report. On the basis of the report, the association has the authority to dismiss the complaint, reprimand the nurse, require counselling, suspend registration, impose conditions for practice, or cancel registration. Administrative law governs any formal hearings conducted by an administrative tribunal. If a nurse loses the licensure and the case involves either civil or criminal wrongs, there is a possibility that further legal consequences may follow.

Nurse Practice Acts

In Canada, each province has enacted its own laws to control the practice of nursing, generally termed **nurse practice acts**. Nurse practice acts protect the nurse's professional capacity and legally control nursing practice through licensing. Nurse practice acts legally define and describe the scope of nursing practice, which the law seeks to regulate, thereby protecting the public as well. Recently, awareness about the need to standardize laws concerning the changing roles, scope, and complexity of practice of registered nurses has become increasingly evident.

In the province of Alberta, the Alberta Legislative Assembly in 1999 passed the Health Professions Act (HPA). The HPA or Bill 45 was passed with an amendment that was adopted by the Alberta Association of Registered Nurses (AARN) that allows the professions to more tightly define who can perform restricted activities and under what circumstances. The AARN's next step involves drafting the nursing profession regulations to the act, a process that will take the next few years to be proclaimed and become law. The AARN suggests that the Health Professions Act (1) expands the legal definition of nursing practice, (2) allows the profession the freedom to decide how its regulations and bylaws are approved by members of its profession and, (3) allows RNs to expand their practice into virtually any area through regulation, rather than the more difficult process of legislative amendments (AARN, July/August 1999). The Health Professions Act also requires that all members develop and meet requirements for a continuing competence program. The AARN oversees the program, and the amendment to the HPA, allowing greater protection to the public and nurses as employees.

The advanced nursing practice role, and development of policy and legislation, is a prominent issue in Canada. Diverse models have been used across Canada to provide authority to registered nurses performing extended/expanded roles. Diagnostic and treatment functions have been delegated by government to the medical profession through legislation (2002).The Canadian Nurses Association (CNA) has formed a committee of provincial and territorial representatives to establish a framework to guide the development and implementation of legislation dealing with nursing roles requiring additional regulation (i.e., primary care functions). This committee is also focusing on identifying the basic standards and competencies required in the role. If these standards/competencies are accepted by all jurisdictions, they would be used to highlight the essential components of education programs preparing registered nurses for primary-care roles. There exist key features which must be considered from a global perspective across Canada. Among these elements are title, scope of practice, and education (CNA 2002).

Certification

Certification is the voluntary practice of validating that an individual nurse has met minimum standards of nursing competence in speciality areas, such as perinatal nursing, pediatrics, mental health, gerontology, or critical care nursing. Certification enhances a nurse's confidence and competence of knowledge and skill in a speciality area. Certification is a commitment to the leading edge in national health-care standards. It gives national scope to the principle of continued competence encouraged by provincial and territorial quality assurance programs. The CNA offers certification in 11 speciality areas.

Accreditation/Approval of Basic Nursing Education Programs

Minimum standards for basic nursing education programs have been established in each province in Canada. In Alberta, the Nursing Education Program and Approval Board (NEPAB) of the Alberta Association of Registered Nurses (AARN) approves nursing programs, using the Entry to Practice Competencies (2000) as a guideline for evaluation.

Accreditation/Approval of Schools of Nursing

The Canadian Association of Schools of Nursing (CASN) is concerned with optimum, rather than minimum, standards. In other words, voluntary accreditation by the CASN certifies that an educational program has not only met minimum standards but is also considered "good" by national standards. The CASN believes that the basic function of standards is to promote a high quality of professional education and to encourage the creativity of individual organizational units. For this reason, it has selected four criteria that are dynamic in nature and are judged to be worthwhile in a program of nursing and against which a program could be evaluated. These qualities are: (1) relevance (how valid the mission and goals of the program are), (2) accountability (the extent to which the program places emphasis on "responsibility to the client that is the community group, family, person"), (3) relatedness (the extent to which the program supports, levels, and builds on other parts) and, (4) uniqueness (capitalizes on the unique characteristics of its resources).

Standards of Practice

The establishment of Nursing Practice Standards is essential for a self-regulating profession. In assessing the quality of care provided by nurses, it is essential to have objective criteria by which to judge whether the care given is good, adequate, or unsafe. Nursing Practise Standards are generally broad in nature to capture the varied roles and practice settings in which nurses practise. The following is an example of the AARN (July/August, 1999) Nursing Practice Standards (criteria against which the practice of all registered nurses will be measured by the public, employers, colleagues, and themselves):

- *Professional Responsibility.* The registered nurse is personally responsible and accountable for ensuring that her/his nursing practice and conduct meet the standards of the profession and legislative requirements.
- *Knowledge-Based Practice.* The registered nurse continually strives to acquire knowledge and skills to provide competent, evidence-based nursing practice.
- *Ethical Practice.* The registered nurse complies with the Canadian Nurses Association's *Code of Ethics for Registered Nurses* (1997).
- *Provision of Service to the Public.* The registered nurse provides nursing service in collaboration with the client, significant others, and health professionals.

Source: AARN, November 1999 Nursing Practice Standards, p. 4–7.

Limits on Power: The Constitution Act, 1982

The law has become increasingly complex, and it is important for all citizens to be aware of the laws that govern everyday life. On a daily basis, nurses are at great risk of violating the legal rights of others. The public expects that nurses will be knowledgeable and competent in the practice of their profession, as well as being aware of and respecting legal rights of their clients.

In November 1981, the federal and provincial governments, with the exception of Quebec, reached an agreement on a formula for repatriating (returning) the Constitution to Canada. Entrenched in the Constitution is a ***Canadian Charter of Rights and Freedoms.*** This charter guarantees such protections as *Fundamental Freedoms*, (freedom of religion and conscience, freedom of thought and expression, freedom of the press, freedom of peaceful assembly, and freedom of association), *Democratic Rights* (the right to vote), *Mobility Rights* (the right to enter, remain in, and leave Canada, as well as to move and take up residence in any other province to pursue the gaining of a livelihood), *Legal Rights* (right to life, liberty, and security of the person, the right to be secure against unreasonable search and seizure, and the right not to be arbitrarily detained or imprisoned), and *Equality Rights* (intended to protect individuals against discrimination based on race, national or ethnic origin, colour, religion, gender, age, mental or physical disability). Any governmental action or law that breaches the Constitution or a person's rights is itself illegal and invalid. These are rights the government cannot infringe upon, unless it has a justifiable reason.

Types of Laws

Laws govern the relationship of private individuals with government and with each other.

Public law refers to the body of law that deals with relationships between individuals and the government and includes constitutional, taxation, administrative, and

Canadian Society Notes

Fact	Implications for Nursing Practice
In Canada, the Charter of Human Rights and Freedoms and the Criminal Code are laws enforceable through the judicial process.	Nurses require skill in recognizing possible infringements upon the legal rights of clients under their care.
The right to client confidentiality is embedded in provincial hospital acts.	Nurses who fail to uphold client confidentiality are subject to allegations of professional misconduct. Nurses must also be aware of exceptions to the laws of confidentiality.
Some provinces have a patient's bill of rights enacted in legislation.	Nurses need to be aware of the legislation under which they practice.

criminal laws. An important segment of public law is **criminal law,** which deals with any actions against the safety and welfare of the public. Examples are manslaughter, infanticide, criminal negligence, criminal assault, and theft. No one has the authority to commit a criminal offence with protection from possible prosecution if the offence comes to the notice of the Crown (Philpot, 1985).

Private law, or **civil law,** is the body of law that deals with relationships between private individuals. It is categorized as contract law and tort law. **Contract law** involves the enforcement of agreements among private individuals or the payment of compensation for failure to fulfill the agreement. **Tort law** defines and enforces duties and rights among private individuals that are not based on contractual agreements, for example, a personal duty of care owed by the professional to the patient. Historically, common law has assigned a duty of care to professional persons who hold themselves as having particular knowledge and skill on which the patient relies. The duty of care owed by the registered nurse to the assigned patient is to exercise the knowledge, skill, and care that the reasonable prudent nurse would provide. If the nurse's practices are carried out in such a way that results in a breach of that duty of care and a patient injury, the patient may well have a cause to pursue the tort of negligence. If patients consider that they have been tested without a legally effective consent, they may pursue a remedy in battery. Some examples of tort laws applicable to nurses are negligence and malpractice, invasion of privacy, and assault and battery. See Table 8.2 for selected categories of laws affecting nurses.

TABLE 8.2 Selected Categories of Laws Affecting Nurses

Category	Examples
Constitutional	Due process Equal protection
Statutory (legislative)	Nurse practice acts Good Samaritan/ Emergency Medical Aid Acts Child and adult abuse laws Living wills Sexual harassment laws
Criminal (public)	Murder, manslaughter Theft Arson Active euthanasia Sexual assault Illegal possession of controlled drugs
Contracts (private/civil)	Nurse and client Nurse and employer Nurse and insurance Client and agency
Torts (private/civil)	Negligence Libel and slander Invasion of privacy Assault and battery False imprisonment Abandonment

Civil Law as Distinct from Criminal Law

There are many meanings attached to **civil law,** as suggested by lawyers and the courts. As previously discussed on page 109, civil law refers to a set of codified principles and rules, serving as the primary source of law. Civil law also refers to a body of rules and legal principles that govern relations, rights, and obligations among individuals in society; for example, a man may file a suit against a person who he believes cheated him. Civil actions that are of concern to nurses include the torts and contracts listed in Table 8.2. Civil law is separate and distinct from **criminal law,** which is chiefly concerned with relations between the individual and society as a whole that breach criminal statutes. The major difference between criminal and civil law is the potential outcome for the defendant. If found guilty in a civil action, such as malpractice, the defendant will have to pay a sum of money. If found guilty in a criminal action, the defendant may have to pay money and/or be jailed. Nurses face the possibility of losing their licence. The action of a lawsuit is called **litigation,** and lawyers who participate in lawsuits may be referred to as "litigators."

The Process of Action (Lawsuit)

In Canada, a court action, or a **lawsuit,** is not usually the first step in an attempt to resolve contractual, tort, or other legal disputes (Keatings & Smith, 2000). Resolving the problem often begins with informal discussions between the parties; complaint mechanisms, such as mediation or arbitration, may occur later. Engaging in discussion early may prevent the need for going to court. If court action is initiated, the following steps will occur:

1. The beginning actions are controlled by a code usually referred to as the **rule of civil procedures** (Keatings & Smith, 2000) or the rules of court (regulating how court action occurs). The procedure is initiated by filing of a **statement of claim,** or writ of summons, by a lawyer on behalf of the plaintiff. This document claims that the person's legal rights have been infringed upon by one or more persons, referred to as **defendants.**
2. In turn, the defendant has the right to respond or file a **statement of defence** to the plaintiff's claim within a specified time. This statement is necessary for the defendant to participate in the action. This statement

of defence is served to the plaintiff and filed in court. Collectively, the statements of claim and defence are known as **pleadings** (Keatings & Smith, 2000).

3. Both parties engage in pretrial activities, referred to as examination of **discovery,** in an effort to gain all the facts of the situation.
4. A civil action may be tried by judge alone, or by judge and jury, according to the wishes of either one of the parties. However, depending on the type of actions (based on nature or complexity), the action may involve a judge alone (Keatings and Smith, 2000). During the trial, a plaintiff must offer evidence of the defendant's wrongdoing. This duty of proving an assertion is the **burden of proof.** The defendant has opportunities to make counterclaims or provide justification for actions.
5. The judge renders a decision, or the jury renders a verdict. If the outcome is not acceptable to one of the parties, an appeal can be made for another trial.

Nurses as Witnesses

A nurse may be called to testify in a legal action for a variety of reasons. The nurse may be a defendant in a malpractice or negligence action or may have been a member of the health team that provided care to the plaintiff. *It is advisable that any nurse who is asked to testify in such a situation seek the advice of a lawyer before providing testimony.*

In most cases, the lawyer for the employer will provide support and counsel during the legal case. If the nurse is the defendant, however, it is advisable for the nurse to contact the Canadian Nurses Protective Society and retain a lawyer to protect the nurse's own interests.

A nurse may also be asked to provide testimony as an expert witness. An **expert witness** has special training, experience, or skill in a relevant area and is allowed by the court to offer an opinion on some issue within the nurse's area of expertise. Such a witness is usually called to help a judge or jury understand evidence pertaining to the extent of damage or the standard of care.

Contractual Arrangements in Nursing

Legal Roles of Nurses

Nurses have three separate, interdependent legal roles, each with rights and associated responsibilities: (1) provider of service, (2) employee or contractor for service, and (3) citizen.

Provider of Service

The nurse is expected to provide safe and competent care so that harm (physical, psychological, or material) to the recipient of the service is prevented. Implicit in this role are several legal concepts: liability, standard of care, and contractual obligations.

Liability is the quality or state of being legally responsible for one's obligations and actions and making financial restitution for wrongful acts. A nurse, for example, has an obligation to practise and direct the practice of others under the nurse's supervision so that harm or injury to the client is prevented and standards of care are maintained. When **delegating care** to others, the nurse is responsible to ensure that this delegation is appropriate and that those delegated to (e.g., family, other health-care members, students) are competent to fulfill the delegated functions (CNA, 2002). Nurses are obligated to follow physicians' orders, unless they believe that these orders have the potential to harm or injure the patient. The nurse must then carefully assess the situation and obtain further clarification from the physician, if necessary. If the physician confirms the order and the nurse still believes the order to be unsafe, informing the supervisor is the next responsibility. The nurse also needs to carefully document, in chronological order, the steps taken. At this point, resolving the problem of the questionable order should be the supervisor's responsibility. It is imperative that a nurse speaks out and investigates orders that are believed to be unsafe, as the nurse who carries out the order could be held legally responsible for any harm suffered by the patient.

The **standards of care** by which a nurse acts or fails to act are legally defined by nurse practice acts and by the rule of reasonable and prudent action—what a reasonable and prudent professional with similar preparation and experience would do in similar circumstances. **Contractual obligations** refer to the nurse's duty of care, that is, duty to render care, established by the presence of an expressed or implied contract discussed earlier.

Employee or Contractor for Service

Nurses, whether in independent practice or as employees, have employment contracts. A contract is defined as "an agreement between two or more persons which creates an obligation to do or not to do a particular thing" (Black, 1979, p. 291). For a contract to exist (Parisi, 1999), the following conditions must be met:

- Each contract must have a lawful purpose.
- Each party entering the contract must be competent and understand the subject matter.
- Each party must understand the obligations of the contract.
- Each party member must have obligations and benefits derived from the contract.
- At minimum, all employment contracts must meet the standards set forth in provincial, territional, and federal labour standards and codes.

Employment contracts may be oral, written, or implied. If a union is not involved, the nurse and the employer may negotiate an individual employment contract that sets

TABLE 8.3 Legal Protection in an Employee–Employer Relationship

- Nurses should seek written confirmation of their employment status and professional liability coverage.
- Nurses should ensure that the employer is notified immediately if they are sued or involved in a potential liability situation.
- Nurses should be aware of the process and cooperate with the employer's insurer and lawyer representing them in a legal suit.
- Nurses who practise as independent practitioners should contract their insurer, if they have one, and CNPs to discuss their existing liability protection.

Source: Excerpted from CNPS' *infoLAW®* Vol. 7, No. 1, April 1998, Vicarious Liability, Reprinted with permission of Canadian Nurses Protective Society (CNPS).

forth the rights and obligations of each party. A nurse who is employed directly by a client (a nurse in private practice) usually has a written contract with that client in which the nurse agrees to provide professional services for a certain fee. In a unionized organization, the terms and conditions of employment are those of the union contract with the employer. Verbal employment contracts can be problematic because of the inability in providing proof of terms negotiated. It is suggested that nurses who agree to verbal contract should at the very least have conditions such as duration of the contract, probation issues, negotiated time off, notice of job termination, and job description in writing. Employment is regulated by federal and provincial employment statutes, common law, industry standards, accreditation standards, human rights legislation, and institutional policies, as well as employment and union contracts.

Contractual relationships vary among practice settings. An independent nurse practitioner is a contractor for service, whose contractual relationship with the client is an independent one. The nurse employed by a hospital functions within an employer–employee relationship, in which the nurse represents and acts for the hospital and, therefore, must function within the policies of the employing agency (see Table 8.3). If an employee commits a wrongful action, employers are normally held legally responsible because of a doctrine called vicarious liability. This principle does not usually apply to independent practitioners (Canadian Nurses Protective Society, 1998). Nurses need to be familiar with their terms of employment and the laws that dictate who would be responsible if a lawsuit is initiated. The nurse found liable in a civil lawsuit would usually be covered by the employer's liability insurer, who would cover the payment of legal fees, court costs, and damages (Canadian Nurses Protective Society, 1998). This type of legal relationship creates the ancient legal doctrine known as **respondent superior** ("let the master answer"). In other words, the master (employer) assumes responsibility for the conduct of the servant (employee) and can also be held responsible for malpractice by the employee. For example, in the case of *Joseph Brant Memorial Hospital v. Koziol* (1978), a patient died from aspiration following back surgery. In this case, the nurse did not rouse him to cough or deep breathe, and the record did not document care. The nursing care was found to be below the standard and the hospital was held vicariously liable.

This doctrine does not imply that the nurse cannot be held liable as an individual. Nor does it imply that the doctrine will prevail if the employee's actions are extraordinarily inappropriate, that is, beyond those expected or foreseen by the employer. For example, if the nurse hits a client in the face, the employer could disclaim responsibility because this behaviour is beyond the bounds of expected behaviour. Criminal acts, such as taking tranquilizers from a client's supply for personal use, would also be considered extraordinarily inappropriate behaviour. Nurses can be held liable for failure to act as well. For example, a nurse who sees another nurse hitting a client and fails to do anything to protect the client may also be considered negligent. See Table 8.3 for information on legal protection for nurses.

The nurse in the role of employee or contractor for service has obligations to the employer, the client, and other personnel. The nursing care provided must be within the limitations and terms specified. The nurse has an obligation to contract only for those responsibilities that the nurse is competent to discharge.

The nurse is expected to respect the rights and responsibilities of other health-care participants. For example, although the nurse has a responsibility to explain nursing activities to a client, the nurse does not have the right to comment on medical practice in a way that disturbs the client or denounces the physician. At the same time, the nurse has the right to expect reasonable and prudent conduct from other health professionals.

Citizen

The rights and responsibilities of the nurse in the role of citizen are the same as those of any individual under the legal system. Rights of citizenship protect clients from harm and ensure consideration for their personal property rights, rights to privacy, confidentiality, and other rights discussed later in this chapter. These same rights apply to nurses.

Nurses move in and out of these roles when carrying out professional and personal responsibilities. An understanding of these roles and the rights and responsibilities associated with them promotes legally responsible conduct and practice by nurses. **Rights** are privileges or fundamental powers to which an individual is entitled, unless they are revoked by law or given up voluntarily; **responsibilities** are the obligations associated with these rights. See Table 8.4 for examples of the responsibilities and rights associated with each role.

TABLE 8.4 Legal Roles, Rights, and Responsibilities

Role	Responsibilities	Rights
Provider of service	To provide safe and competent care commensurate with nurse's preparation, experience, and circumstances	Right to adequate and qualified assistance as necessary
	To inform clients of the consequences of various alternatives and outcomes of care	Right to reasonable and prudent conduct from clients, e.g., provision of accurate information as required
	To provide adequate supervision and evaluation of others for whom the nurse is responsible	
	To remain competent	
Employee or contractor for service	To fulfill the obligations of contracted service with the employer	Right to adequate working conditions (e.g., safe equipment and facilities)
	To respect the employer	Right to compensation for services rendered
	To respect the rights and responsibilities of other health-care providers	Right to reasonable and prudent conduct by other health-care providers
Citizen	To protect the rights of the recipients of care	Right to respect of the nurse's own rights and responsibilities by others
		Right to physical safety

Collective Bargaining

Collective bargaining is the formalized decision-making process between representatives of management and representatives of unions to negotiate wages and conditions of employment, including work hours, working environment, and fringe benefits of employment (e.g., vacation time, sick leave, and personal leave). Through a written agreement, both employer and employees legally commit themselves to observe the terms and conditions of employment. Labour laws vary in each province/territory; it is important that nurses understand the employment laws where they work.

By accepting a job, the nurse enters into an agreement with the employer, committing to perform professional duties competently by adhering to the policies and procedures of the institution. The employer, in return, not only pays for services rendered but also ensures that the environment and equipment enable the nurse to carry out duties in a safe competent manner. The collective agreement and the written policies and procedures are interpreted by the nurse as the terms of agreement (contract) that have to be abided by.

Collective bargaining is more than the negotiation of salary terms and hours of work; it is a continuous process in which day-to-day working problems and relationships can be handled in an orderly and democratic manner. Day-to-day difficulties or grievances are handled through the grievance procedure, a formal plan established in the contract that outlines the channels for handling and settling grievances through progressively higher levels of administration. A **grievance** is any dispute, difference, controversy, or disagreement arising out of the terms and conditions of employment.

Selected Legal Aspects of Nursing Practice

Confidentiality

Fundamental to the nurse–patient relationship is the professional obligation to respect patient confidentiality. Confidentiality posits both moral and legal obligations for nurses. Whenever possible, nurses uphold confidentiality, except when harm might result to the patient or others or when statute law or legislature requires disclosure (i.e., suspected child abuse, infectious disease, releasing information to workers compensation boards, or a court order). The CNA Code of Ethics (2002) states: "Nurses safeguard information learned in the context of a professional relationship and ensure it is shared outside the health-care team only with the person's informed consent, or as may be legally required, or where failure to disclose would cause significant harm" (p. 14). Legally, the betrayal of a patient's confidence is covered under the area of professional misconduct and may result in discipline by the provincial/territorial conduct committee of one's professional nursing association.

Informed Consent

Informed consent is an autonomous authorization by a patient to accept a course of treatment or intervention. Patients are entitled to make decisions about their medical care and have the right to be given all available information relevant to such decisions. Obtaining consent is not a discrete event; rather, it is a process that should occur throughout the relationship between the patient and all health-care providers.

Consent has three components: (1) disclosure, (2) capacity, and (3) voluntariness. *Disclosure* refers to the provision of information, including the risks of treatment, alternative treatment and associated facts and risks, and the effects and risks of no treatment. *Capacity* refers to the patient's ability to understand the relevant information and appreciate those consequences of his/her decision that might reasonably be foreseen. *Voluntariness* refers to the patient's right to come to a decision without force, coercion, or manipulation from others (Etchells et al., 1999).

There are two types of consent: expressed and implied. **Expressed consent** is a clear statement of consent by the patient and may be either oral or written. "It is important to remember that the patient has the right to withdraw consent or revoke a previously given consent at any time, even orally, provided he/she is mentally competent to do so" (Keatings & Smith, 2000, p. 186). **Implied consent** exists when the individual's nonverbal behaviour indicates a willingness. Examples of implied consent include the following:

- During an emergency when the individual cannot provide consent
- During surgery when additional procedures are needed that are consistent with the procedure already consented to
- When persons continue to participate in therapy without removing previous consent

In such situations, the Canadian Nurses Protective Society (1994) suggests that provincial/territorial legislation, including hospital or institutional policies and procedures, be followed.

For treatments that entail risk or more than mild discomfort, expressed rather than implied consent should be obtained (Etchells et al, 1999).

Obtaining Consent/Disclosing Information

Obtaining consent to medical/nursing care is a legal requirement. Under common law, treating a patient without consent, or if the patient has refused, constitutes **battery**, whereas treating a patient on the basis of failure to adequately inform, constitutes **negligence** (Parisi, 1999).

Obtaining informed consent for specific *medical* and *surgical* treatments is the responsibility of a physician. Although this responsibility is delegated to nurses in some agencies and no laws prohibit the nurse from being part of the information-giving process, the practice, nevertheless, is highly undesirable. The nurse does not perform direct medical procedures and may not have the detailed medical knowledge of the physician performing the procedure. Also, it is not the nurse's responsibility to "supply the gaps or deficiencies in the physician's dialogue with the patient"; however, it is the responsibility of the nurse to "respond appropriately and ensure that when information gaps occur the physician is alerted in time to put things right" (Sneiderman, Irvine, & Osborne, 1995 p. 164). Often, the nurse's responsibility is to witness the giving of informed consent for medical procedures. This involves the following:

- Witnessing the exchange between the client and the physician
- Establishing that the client really did understand, that is, was truly informed

Obtaining informed consent for *nursing* procedures is the responsibility of the nurse. This applies, in particular, to nurse-midwives and nurse practitioners in performing procedures in their advanced practices. However, it also applies to other nurses performing direct care, such as insertion of nasogastric tubes or starting an intravenous infusion. It can be a challenge to determine the amount and type of information required for the client to make an informed decision. General guidelines include:

- The purposes of the treatment
- What the client can expect to feel or experience
- The intended benefits of the treatment
- Possible risks or negative outcomes of the treatment
- Advantages and disadvantages of possible alternatives to the treatment (including no treatment)

Voluntariness/Capacity

To give informed consent voluntarily, the client must not feel coerced. Sometimes, fear of disapproval by a health professional can be the motivation for giving consent; such consent is not voluntarily given.

It is also important that the client understands all the information. Technical words and language barriers can inhibit understanding. If a client cannot read, the consent form must be read to the client before it is signed. If the client does not speak the same language as the health professional who is providing the information, the help of an interpreter must be acquired.

If given sufficient information, a competent adult is assumed to be able to make decisions regarding health. A competent adult is a person over 18 years of age (ages vary across provinces/territories) who is conscious and oriented. A client who is confused, disoriented, or sedated is not considered functionally competent.

Informed consent regulations were originally written with acute-care settings in mind. Nonetheless, ensuring informed consent is equally important in providing nursing care in the home and community. Because the provision of home care often occurs over an extended period of time, the nurse has multiple opportunities to ensure that the client agrees to the plan of treatment. A challenge to informed consent in the home, however, is that the plan may affect other members of the family, and if so, they need to be consulted.

There are many areas in health-care law with respect to *capacity*, where consent becomes a confusing issue. The first is related to minors. In Canadian common law, there is not a stated age below which a person is not presumed capable (Etchells et al., 1999). Some provinces have legislation which may reduce the age of consent below 18 years. A minor can give consent if it is determined that the person has adequate knowledge and judgement (is able to reasonably foresee consequences of a decision or lack of a decision) (Sharpe, 1993). Some provinces have legislation that establishes the age of consent to treatment; health-care providers should be aware of the legislative requirements of their own provinces/territories.

It is also important to remember that capacity can change over time. A patient who is confused, disoriented, or sedated is not considered functionally competent; however, this may be temporary and requires careful skilled assessment. Individuals who are unconscious or injured in such a way that they are unable to give consent require substitute consent from another individual. The substitute decision maker(s) should be the person(s) with the best knowledge of the patient's specific wishes or of the patient's values and beliefs as they pertain to the present situation. In general, close relatives are preferred as substitute decision makers as they "know the patient best" and are able to make a decision that would be as close to the patients as possible if they were capable. Most jurisdictions have enacted legislation to deal with the substitute consent and the ability to create a legally valid personal or advance directive or to appoint a health-care agent (Downie and Caulfield, 1999). Although not all provinces have enacted comprehensive legislation, the courts are likely to apply many of the principles embodied in existing legislation (Morris 1999).

In the case of a mentally ill patient, *capacity* to consent may or may not be valid, depending on whether the mental illness makes that patient unable to appreciate the nature, quality, and consequences of the proposed treatment. In this case, patients who refuse treatment may have their capacity questioned by the clinician. The patients require careful assessment to screen for incapacity (beyond the scope of this text). If the clinician remains unsure, expert assessments can go further to hospital ethics committees or legal review boards (Etchells et al., 1999). Provincial/Territorial Mental Health Acts or similar statutes generally provide direction and specify the rights of the mentally ill under the law as well as the rights of the professionals caring for such patients.

Controlled Substances

The Controlled Drugs and Substances Act (1997) regulates the distribution and use of controlled substances, such as narcotics, depressants, stimulants, and hallucinogens. Misuse of controlled substances may lead to criminal penalties. See Chapter 28 for the legal aspects of drug administration.

Substance Misuse and Chemical Dependency

Substance misuse and/or chemical dependency are serious problems, endangering the safety of the public and the health of nurses. Many factors in the workplace may be linked to nurses' substance misuse. Shift work, stress, long working hours, and access to a large variety of pharmacological substances all contribute to the risk of substance misuse (RNABC, 1990). Prevention, early recognition, and effective treatment programs are essential to promote the health of nurses and ensure public safety.

Registered nurses have a professional responsibility to protect patients from harm. Education and prevention of substance misuse must begin in schools of nursing and nurses' workplaces to heighten awareness and promote early detection. Denying that there is a problem is a common first sign of substance misuse. Admitting there is a problem may be the hardest step. It is not uncommon for co-workers to explain or excuse unacceptable behaviour, rather than consider the possibility of a drug or alcohol problem (AARN, 2002). Nurses need to be aware of signs of a potential problem (see accompanying box). Consultation with licensing bodies is available to help deal with suspected problems. Guidance to registered nurses is also provided by the CNA Code of Ethics (2002); nurses must adhere to the reporting requirements of the licensing bodies.

Employers must have sound policies and procedures for identifying and intervening in situations involving a possibly impaired nurse. The primary concern is for the protection of clients, but it is also critically important that the nurse's problem be identified quickly so that appropriate treatment may be instituted. The following box lists behaviours that may be seen in the impaired nurse. The guidelines presented in the box can be used to report the nurse suspected of chemical impairment.

A variety of programs have been developed to help nurses recover from a substance abuse problem. Nurses need the same caring attitude from peers as that shown to patients. The goal is to have nurses enter rehabilitative treatment. Employee and family assistance programs can provide support and direction for nurses who require assistance to deal

Behavioural Indicators of Chemical Abuse

- Increasing isolation from colleagues, friends, and family
- Frequent reports of illness, minor accidents, and emergencies
- Complaints about poor work performance
- Inability to meet schedules and deadlines
- Tendency to avoid new and challenging assignments
- Mood swings, irritability, and depression
- Request for night shifts
- Social avoidance of staff
- Illogical and sloppy charting
- Excessive errors
- Increasing carelessness about personal appearance
- Medication "errors" that require many changes in charting
- Arriving on duty early or staying late for no reason
- Volunteering to administer client medications, especially pain medications

Source: Adapted from Springhouse. (1996). *Nurse's legal handbook.* (3rd ed.). Springhouse, PA: Springhouse, p. 338–339.

with their substance involvement. Rehabilitation is a complex process. A work re-entry plan can assist nurses to return to their job to provide safe and competent care.

Wills

A **will** is a declaration by a person about how the person's property is to be disposed of after death. The person making the will is called the testator. A will usually is in writing and signed by the testator. In order for a will to be valid, the following conditions must be met:

- The person making the will must be of sound mind, that is, able to understand and retain mentally the general nature and extent of the person's property, the relationship of the beneficiaries and of relatives to whom none of the estate will be left, and the disposition being made of the property. Therefore, a person who is seriously ill and unable to carry out usual roles may still be able to direct preparation of a will.
- The person must not be unduly influenced by anyone else. Sometimes, a client may be persuaded by someone who is close at that particular time to make that person a beneficiary. Clients sometimes are persuaded to leave their estates to persons looking after them, rather than to their relatives. Frequently, the relatives contest the will in such situations and take the matter to court, claiming undue influence.

Nurses may be requested from time to time to witness a will, in the capacity of someone who has no conflict of interest (a neutral party). In most provinces, the law requires a will to be signed in the presence of two or three competent witnesses. In some situations, a mark can suffice if the person making the will cannot write a signature. When witnessing a will, the nurse (1) attests that the client signed a document that is stated to be the client's last will, and (2) attests that the client appears to be mentally sound and appreciates the significance of his/her actions (Bernzweig, 1996). If the will has already been signed, the witness should either ask the testator to sign again or to declare that this is the testator's will and signature and that the testator was competent to sign.

If a nurse witnesses a will, the nurse should note on the client's chart the fact that a will was made and the nurse's perception of the physical and mental condition of the client. This record provides the nurse with accurate information if called as a witness later. The record may also be helpful if the will is contested. If a nurse does not wish to act as a witness, for example, if, in the nurse's opinion, undue influence has been brought on the client, then it is the nurse's right to refuse to act in this capacity.

A **living will** is a form of what is called an *advance directive*, in which an individual writes down personal preferences for treatment in the event that later it may not be possible to make that decision. Advance directives are becoming increasingly common, although at present, in Canada, living wills do not have legal sanction in all provinces. It is legally recognized in Ontario (Substitute Decisions Act, 1992), Manitoba (Health Care Directives Act), Nova Scotia (Medical Consent Act), and Alberta (pursuant to the Personal Directives Act) (Keatings & Smith, 2000), and Saskatchewan (The Health Care Directives and Substitute Decision Makers Act, 1997). A detailed discussion of the *advance directives* is given in Chapter 48.

Areas of Potential Liability in Nursing

Tort Law

Tort law is the basis for claims of negligence and malpractice. A **tort** is a civil wrong committed against a person or a person's property. Torts are usually litigated in court by civil action between individuals. In other words, the person or persons claimed to be responsible for the tort are sued for damages. Tort liability almost always is based on fault, that is, something that was done incorrectly (an unreasonable act of commission) or something that should have been done but was not (act of omission).

Torts may be classified as intentional or unintentional.

Unintentional Torts

Negligence and malpractice are examples of unintentional torts that may occur in the health-care setting. **Negligence** is misconduct or practice that is below the standard expected of an ordinary, reasonable, and prudent practitioner. Such conduct places another person at risk for harm. Both lay and professional persons can be liable for negligent acts. Negligence may involve *lacking in due care or carelessness*, extreme lack of knowledge, skill, or decision making that the person clearly should have known would put others at risk for harm. **Malpractice** is "professional negligence," that is, negligence that occurred while the person was performing as a professional. Malpractice applies to physicians, dentists, lawyers, and nurses. Four elements must be present in a negligence lawsuit against a nurse:

1. *Duty.* The nurse must have (or should have had) a relationship with the client that involves providing care. Such duty is evident when the nurse has been assigned to care for a client in the home, hospital, or community by virtue of employment. In contrast, a nurse in private practice may have the option of deciding whether to accept a patient for care; thus, the duty is incurred when the patient is accepted.
2. *Breach.* There must be a standard of care that is expected in the specific situation but that the nurse did not observe. This is the failure to act as a reasonable, prudent nurse under the circumstances. The practice is measured against that of similar nurses, unless the nurse undertakes a practice outside of the usual nursing role. In such an instance, the nurse may be held to a higher standard based on advanced training. The standard can come from documents published by national or professional organizations, provincial/territorial nursing practice standards, institutional policies and procedures, textbooks or journals, or it may be stated by expert witnesses.
3. *Harm.* The patient must have sustained injury, damage, or harm. The plaintiff will be asked to document physical injury, medical costs, loss of wages, "pain and suffering," and any other damages.
4. *Causation.* It must be proved that the harm occurred as a *direct result* of the nurse's failure to follow the standard and the nurse could have (or should have) known that failure to follow the standard could result in such harm.

To avoid charges of malpractice, nurses need to recognize those nursing situations in which negligent actions are most likely to occur and to take measures to prevent them. See the accompanying box. A common situation is the *medication error.* Because of the large number of medications taken by patients, and the numerous commercial names commonly used for the various drugs, safety precautions assume greater importance in ensuring that the patient receives the right drug, in the proper dose, at the right time, and in the proper manner. Medication errors include failing to read the medication label, misreading or incorrectly calculating the dosage, failing to identify the client correctly, preparing the wrong concentration, or administering a medication by the wrong route (e.g., intravenously instead of intramuscularly). Nurses always need to check medications very carefully. Even after checking, the nurse would be wise to recheck the medication order and the medication before administering it if the client states, for example, "I did not have a green pill before."

A nurse's responsibility for adverse effects and critical incidents (National Steering Committee on Patient Safety, 2002) will be weighed in accordance with the provincial/territorial body governing professional nursing standard. Health-care employers often have policies and procedures for medication administration and standards for documentation, which include the steps to follow once an error has been discovered. Such standards also include the requirement to keep up to date with the latest professional and technological developments, such as new intravenous tubing or intravenous pumps. Additional education should be taken as required to maintain expertise to the appropriate standard.

A nurse must administer medications according to the five *"rights"* of medication administration (right drug, dose, patient, route, and time). Nurses are often unaware that they also can be liable for contributing to a medication error even if they did not perform the act of giving the medication. In *Bugden v. Harbour View Hospital,* a physician asked a nurse to obtain novocaine to inject into a patient's thumb. The nurse, going to a different area to find the medication, asked another nurse for the drug and was given a vial that she gave to the physician who injected the medication. Unfortunately, the vial contained adrenalin, and the patient later died. Neither the nurses nor the physician checked the vial. As a result, both nurses were found negligent. The court ruled that the physician was not negligent because he had been justified in relying on the competency of the nurses to check the label to identify the "right" drug.

Clients often fall accidentally, sometimes with resultant injury. Some falls can be prevented by elevating the side rails on the cribs, beds, and stretchers of babies, small children, and, when necessary, adults. If a nurse leaves the rails down or leaves a baby unattended on a bath table, that nurse is guilty of malpractice if the client falls and is injured as a direct result. Most hospitals and nursing homes have policies regarding the use of safety devices, such as side rails and restraints. The nurse needs to be familiar with these policies and to take indicated precautions to prevent accidents. Information about providing a safe environment for the client can be found in Chapter 33.

In some instances, ignoring a client's complaints can constitute malpractice. This type of malpractice is termed *failure to observe and take appropriate action.* The nurse who does not

Basic Nursing Care Errors Resulting in Negligence

Assessment Errors

Failing to

- Gather and chart client information adequately.
- Recognize the significance of certain information (e.g., laboratory values, vital signs).

Planning Errors

Failing to

- Chart each identified problem.
- Use language in the care plan that other caregivers understand.
- Ensure continuity of care by ignoring the care plan.
- Give discharge instructions that the client understands.

Intervention Errors

Failing to

- Interpret and carry out a doctor's orders.
- Perform nursing tasks correctly.
- Pursue the physician if the physician doesn't respond to calls or notify the nurse-manager if the physician is unavailable.

report a client's complaint of acute abdominal pain is negligent and may be found guilty of malpractice for ensuing appendix rupture and death. By failing to take the blood pressure and pulse and to check the dressing of a client who has just had abdominal surgery, a nurse omits important assessments. If the client hemorrhages and dies, the nurse may be held responsible for the death as a result of this malpractice.

The case of *Downey v. Rothwell* (Alberta, 1974) is a good example of a nursing negligence, illustrating duty of care. In this case, a 35-year-old plaintiff who had a history of grand mal epileptic seizures and recently had discontinued her anticonvulsant prescription for phenobarbital, suffered a severe arm injury after falling off an examining room table. Mrs. Downey was under the care of a registered nurse (of 40 years experience) who had worked in this doctor's clinic for the past 22 years. The patient informed the nurse that she was experiencing the sensation ("aura") of having an epileptic seizure. The nurse remained in the room with the patient for about a half an hour. When nothing happened, however, the nurse left the room to locate Mrs. Downey's file, leaving her unattended. During this time, the patient experienced a severe seizure, fell onto the floor, and broke her arm. The nurse, having the knowledge about epileptic seizures, should have recognized an aura and remained with the patient, ensuring her safety on the examination table.

In this case, there was an undertaking of the nurse to provide care, a reliance on the RN by the patient, and a foreseeable risk which was not attended to. The judge concluded that the nurse's behaviour had fallen short of the standard expected for a registered nurse at that time. A nursing instructor as an expert witness, and textbook material were unanimous in stating that the nurse in this situation should have remained with the patient. The nurse was found to be negligent, and for that negligence, her employers were made vicariously liable.

Intentional Torts

There are several differences between unintentional torts and intentional torts. One difference is that harm is a required element in negligence. No harm need be caused by intentional torts for liability to exist. Also, since no standard is involved, no expert witnesses are needed. Another difference is that with intentional torts, the defendant executed the act on purpose. Intentional torts related to nursing will be discussed: assault/battery, false imprisonment, invasion of privacy, and libel/slander.

Assault can be described as an attempt or threat to touch another person unjustifiably. Assault precedes battery; it is the act that causes the person to believe a battery is about to occur. For example, the person who threatens someone by making a menacing gesture with a club or a closed fist is guilty of assault. In nursing, a nurse who threatens a client with an injection after the client refuses to take the medication orally would be committing assault.

Battery is the willful touching of a person (or the person's clothes, or even something the person is carrying), that may or may not cause harm, without consent. To be actionable at law, however, the touching must be wrong in some way, for example, done without permission, embarrassing, or causing injury. In the previous example, if the nurse followed through on the threat and gave the injection without the client's consent, the nurse would be committing battery. Liability applies even though the physician ordered the medication or the activity and even if the client benefits from the nurse's action.

Consent is required before procedures are performed. Battery exists when there is no consent, even if the plaintiff was not asked for consent. Unless there is implied consent, such as in life-threatening emergencies, a procedure performed on an unconscious client without informed consent is battery. Another requirement for consent is that the client be competent to give consent. It can be very difficult to determine if clients who are elderly, who have specific mental disorders, or who take particular medications are competent to agree to treatments. If the nurse is uncertain whether a client refusing a treatment is competent, the supervisor and physician should be consulted in order that ethical treatment that does not constitute battery can be provided. Determination of competency is not a medical decision; it is one made through court hearings.

False imprisonment is the restraint of movement or detention of another person without his or her consent. A nurse who pushes a patient into an examining room, or one who force-feeds a gerontological patient by holding the patient's head, commits a battery if there is no consent. False imprisonment accompanied by forceful restraint or threat of restraint is battery.

Although nurses may suggest under certain circumstances that a client remain in the hospital room or in bed, the client must not be detained against the client's will. The client has a right to insist upon leaving, even though it may be detrimental to health.

If the patient insists on leaving, most institutions require that the patient sign a release stating that the agency will not be held responsible for any resulting harm. As with all situations, the nurse should try and inform the patient of potential risks and alternative courses of actions. The use of force to detain someone against their will, or even the threat of restraint made in order to detain the patient, is considered assault. The nurse must be cautious with the use of restraints (see Chapter 33).

Invasion of privacy is a direct wrong of a personal nature. It injures the feelings of the person and does not take into account the effect of revealed information on the standing of the person in the community. Under Canadian law, the right to privacy is the right of individuals to withhold themselves and their lives from public scrutiny. It can also be described as the right to be left alone. Liability can result if the nurse breaches confidentiality by passing along confidential client information to others who are not directly involved in care of that client or intruding into the client's private domain.

In this context, there is a delicate balance between the need of a number of people to contribute to the diagnosis and treatment of a client and the client's right to confidentiality. In most situations, necessary discussion about a client's medical condition is considered appropriate, but unnecessary discussions and gossip are considered a breach of confidentiality. Necessary discussion involves only those engaged in the client's care.

Most provinces have a variety of statutes that impose a duty to report certain confidential client information. Four major categories are (1) vital statistics, such as births and deaths, (2) infections and communicable diseases, such as diphtheria, syphilis, and typhoid fever, (3) child or elder abuse, and (4) violent incidents, such as gunshot wounds and knife wounds.

There are four types of invasion from which the client must be protected.

1. *Use of the client's name or likeness for profit, without consent.* This refers to use of identifiable photographs or names as advertising for the health-care agency or provider without the client's permission.
2. *Unreasonable intrusion.* Observation of client care (such as by nursing students) or taking of photographs for any purpose, without the client's consent.
3. *Public disclosure of private facts.* Private information, normally considered offensive, is given to others who have no legitimate need for that information.
4. *Putting a person in a false light.* This kind of invasion involves publishing information that is normally considered offensive but that is not true.

Legal Protections in Nursing Practice

Professional Liability Insurance

All nurses are advised to have professional liability insurance. Despite the high level of competence promoted and maintained, excellent communication with clients, and increasing awareness of the risks involved in giving care, a lawsuit may still be initiated by a client. "Nurses who are employees are covered by their employer's insurance through the operation of vicarious liability. Vicarious liability means that the employer is responsible for the actions of its employees in the course of the employment relationship" (CNPS, 1995, p. 2). Nurses in independent practice do not have this protection and are held directly accountable for their practice, thus requiring their own insurance.

In Canada, legal support and liability protection insurance can be obtained through the Canadian Nurses Protective Society (CNPS), a nonprofit society established in 1988. As a member in good standing in most provincial associations, nurses are able to obtain the services of the CNPS free of charge. Nurses in British Columbia and Quebec are not included in the CNPS and are covered by other insurance agents. *CNPS Plus* offers additional insurance to all registered nurses at an annual premium. This added insurance originally designed for independent practitioners, nurse practitioners, and independent contractors, offers insurance for malpractice coverage, business protection, professional discipline costs, and directors and officers liability coverage (CNPS Web site).

Nurses often provide nursing services outside of employment-related activities, such as being available for first aid at children's sport or social activities or providing health screening and education at health fairs. Neighbours or friends may seek advice about illnesses or treatment for themselves or family members. In the latter situation, the nurse may be tempted to give advice; however, it is always advisable for the nurse to refer the friend or neighbour to the family physician.

Nurses may also act as **Good Samaritans,** by providing emergency assistance at an accident scene. This type of professional activity is not covered by an employer's insurance policy because the care given was not the responsibility of the employer. The Good Samaritan/Emergency Medical Aid Acts are designed to protect persons to help those acting reasonably, without gross negligence. While there is no legal duty for nurses to act as Good Samaritans, the Code of Ethics for Registered Nurses (2002) under the value *Health and Well-Being* states: "Nurses should provide the best care circumstances present, even when the need arises in an emergency outside an employment situation" (p. 10).

To encourage citizens to be Good Samaritans, most provinces have now enacted legislation releasing a Good Samaritan from legal liability for injuries caused under such circumstances, even if the injuries resulted from negligence of the person offering emergency aid. The Alberta Emergency Medical Act (1980) protects physicians and other registered health discipline members, including registered nurses, unless gross negligence is involved. The Act covers persons who render help in an emergency, at a level that would be provided by a reasonably prudent person under similar circumstances (Philips, 1999b). Manitoba, Ontario, New Brunswick, and Nunavut do not have Good Samaritan legislation, although New Brunswick does protect from liability physicians who render voluntary first aid or emergency treatment outside of a hospital or doctor's office under the Medical Act of 1981 (Phillips, 1999b).

Liability insurance coverage usually defrays costs of defending a nurse, including the costs of retaining a lawyer. The insurance also covers all costs incurred by the nurse up to the face value of the policy, including a settlement made out of court. In return, the insurance company may have the right to make the decisions about the claim and the settlement.

Carrying Out a Physician's Orders

Nurses are expected to analyze procedures and medications ordered by the physician. It is the nurse's responsibility to seek clarification of ambiguous or seemingly erroneous orders from the prescribing physician or covering on-call physician.

Nurses are not absolved of responsibility for their actions simply because they are following a physician's order. The law states that nurses must understand the cause and effect of the treatment that is undertaken. If nurses carry out treatment they know is wrong, they are guilty of negligence.

If the order is neither ambiguous nor apparently erroneous, the nurse is responsible for carrying it out. For example, if the physician orders oxygen to be administered at four litres per minute, the nurse must administer oxygen at that rate, and not at two or six litres per minute. If the orders state that the client is not to have solid food after a bowel resection, the nurse must ensure that no solid food is given to the client.

There are several categories of orders that nurses must question to protect themselves legally:

1. *Question any order a client questions.* For example, if a client who has been receiving an intramuscular injection tells the nurse that the doctor changed the order from an injectable to an oral medication, the nurse should recheck the order before giving the medication.
2. *Question any order if the client's condition has changed.* The nurse is considered responsible for notifying the physician of any significant changes in the client's condition, whether the physician requests notification or not. For example, if a client who is receiving an intravenous infusion suddenly develops a rapid pulse, chest pain, and a cough, the nurse must notify the physician immediately and question continuance of the ordered rate of infusion. If a client who is receiving morphine for pain develops severely depressed respirations, the nurse must withhold the medication and notify the physician.
3. *Question and record verbal orders to avoid miscommunications.* In addition to recording the time, the date, the physician's name, and the orders, the nurse documents the circumstances that occasioned the call to the physician, reads the orders back to the physician, and documents that the physician confirmed the orders as the nurse read them back.
4. *Question any order that is illegible, unclear, or incomplete.* Misinterpretations in the name of a drug or in dose, for example, can easily occur with handwritten orders. The nurse is responsible for ensuring that the order is interpreted the way it was intended and that it is a safe and appropriate order.

Providing Safe, Competent Nursing Care

Competent practice is a major legal safeguard for nurses. Nurses need to provide care that is within the legal boundaries of their practice and within the boundaries of agency policies and procedures. Nurses, therefore, must be familiar with their various job descriptions, which may be different from agency to agency. All nurses are responsible for ensuring that their various educational qualifications and experiences are adequate to meet the responsibilities delineated in their job description.

Competency also involves care that protects clients from harm. Nurses need to anticipate sources of client injury, educate clients about hazards, and implement measures to prevent injury.

Application of the nursing process is another essential aspect of providing safe and effective client care. Clients need to be assessed and monitored appropriately and involved in care decisions. All assessments and care must be documented accurately. Effective communication can also protect the nurse from negligence claims. Nurses need to approach every client with sincere concern and include the client in conversations. In addition, nurses should always acknowledge when they do not know the answer to a client's questions, telling the client they will find out the answer and then follow through.

Methods of legal protection are summarized in the accompanying Clinical Guidelines box.

Record Keeping

The client's medical record is a legal document and can be produced in court as evidence. Often, the record is used to remind a witness of events surrounding a lawsuit because several months or years usually elapse before the suit goes to trial. The effectiveness of a witness's testimony can depend on the accuracy of such records. Nurses, therefore, need to keep accurate and complete records of nursing care provided to clients. Failure to keep proper records can constitute negligence and be the basis for tort liability. Insufficient or inaccurate assessments and documentation can hinder proper diagnosis and treatment and result in injury to the client. See Chapter 24 for types of records and facts about recording.

Figure 8.1 The chart is a legal document

CLINICAL GUIDELINES

Legal Precautions for Nurses

- Function within the scope of your education, job description, and jurisdiction nurse practice act.
- Follow the procedures and policies of the employing agency.
- Build and maintain good rapport with clients. Keeping clients informed about diagnostic and treatment plans, giving feedback on their progress, and showing concern for the outcome of their care prevent a sense of powerlessness and a buildup of hostility in the client.
- Always identify clients, particularly before initiating major interventions (e.g., surgical or other invasive procedures, or when administering medications or blood transfusions).
- Observe and monitor the client accurately. Communicate and record significant changes in the client's condition to the physician.
- Promptly and accurately document all assessments and care given. Records must show that the nurse provided and supervised the client's care at regular intervals (the frequency of required reporting varies with the agency).
- Be alert when implementing nursing interventions and give each task your full attention and skill.
- Perform procedures appropriately. Negligent incidents during procedures generally relate to equipment failure, improper technique, and improper performance of the procedure. For instance, the nurse must know how to safeguard the client in the event that a respirator or other equipment fails.
- Make sure the correct medications are given in the correct dose, by the right route, at the scheduled time, and to the right client. See Chapter 28 for more detailed information about the administration of medications.
- When delegating nursing responsibilities, make sure that the person who is delegated a task understands what to do and that the person has the required knowledge and skill. As the delegating nurse, you can be held liable for harm caused by the person to whom the care was delegated.
- Protect clients from injury. Inform clients of hazards and use appropriate safety devices and measures to prevent falls, burns, or other injuries.
- Report all incidents involving clients. Prompt reports enable those responsible to attend to the client's well-being, to analyze why the incident occurred, and to prevent recurrences.
- Always check any order that a client questions and ensure that verbal orders are accurate and documented appropriately. Question and confirm standing orders if you are inexperienced in a particular area.
- Know your own strengths and weaknesses. Ask for assistance and supervision in situations for which you feel inadequately prepared.
- Maintain your clinical competence. For students, this demands study and practice before caring for clients. For graduate nurses, it means continued study, including maintaining and updating clinical knowledge and skills.

Telephone Advice

Nurses are often asked in their professional practice to provide telephone advice. There is increased likelihood of occurrence especially in expanded areas of practice, such as home care, community care, case management and consulting in workers compensation, and advance practice clinics. This practice poses particular skill and challenge in the areas of conducting assessments, giving appropriate advice, referring to appropriate person(s), and developing a therapeutic relationship with a patient and their familiy.

A nurse should be very careful when giving telephone information, and referrals, to a patient and family. A relationship over the phone establishes legal accountability for the nurse. If the patient suffers injuries as a result of a nurse's inappropriate advice, the end result could be one of the following: (1) discipline by the nurse's employer; (2) sanctions by the nurse's professional association or licensing body; and (3) the nurse may be held liable in a court of law if the patient initiates a civil lawsuit (Canadian Nurses Protective Society, 1997).

The most common allegations of negligence in this area are: providing inappropriate advice; improper referrals; and failure to refer (Canadian Nurses Protective Society, 1997). When in doubt about a patient's condition, referral to the appropriate caregiver, or arrangements to meet, should be conducted immediately for further assessment in person (Keatings & Smith, 2000). The process of documentation is also critical. Documentation should include: the date and time of the call; the name, telephone number, and address of the caller; information received; advice or information given; referral and follow-up information; and the name and designation of the person taking the call (Canadian Nurses Protective Society, 1997).

The Incident Report

An incident report is an agency record of an accident or unusual occurrence. Incident reports are tools of both quality assurance and risk management. Incident reports are used to make all the facts available to agency personnel, to contribute to statistical data about accidents or incidents, and to help health personnel prevent future incidents or accidents. Most agencies have policies requiring that such reports be completed following any unusual occurrence. The box on the right lists the information to be included in an incident report. The report should be completed as soon as possible, and filed according to agency policy. As incident reports are not part of the client's medical record, the facts of the incident should also be noted in the medical record.

The incident report should be completed by the person involved or witnessing the event—in other words, by the person with first-hand knowledge of the incident. For example, the nurse who discovers that an incorrect medication has been administered completes the form even if it was another nurse who administered the medication. In addition, all witnesses to an incident, such as a client fall, are listed on the incident form even if they were not directly involved.

Incident reports are often reviewed by an agency risk management committee, which decides whether to investigate the incident further. Nurses may be required to answer such questions as what they believe precipitated the accident, how it could have been prevented, and whether any equipment should be adjusted.

When an accident occurs, the nurse should first assess the client and intervene to prevent injury. If a client is injured, nurses must take steps to protect the client, themselves, and their employer. Most agencies have policies regarding accidents. It is important to follow these policies and not to assume one is negligent. Although negligence may be involved, accidents can and do happen even when every precaution has been taken to prevent them.

Reporting Crimes, Torts, and Unsafe Practices

Nurses may need to report nursing colleagues or other health professionals for practices that endanger the health and safety of clients. For instance, alcohol and drug use, theft from a client or agency, and unsafe nursing practice should be reported. Reporting a colleague is not easy. The person reporting may feel disloyal, incur the disapproval of others, or perceive chances for promotion are endangered. When reporting an incident or series of incidents, the nurse must be careful to describe observed behaviour only and not make inferences as to what might be happening. The box on the next page outlines guidelines for reporting a crime, tort, or unsafe practice. Reporting these events is referred to as "whistle-blowing."

Information to Include in an Incident Report

- Identify the person by name, initials, and hospital or identification number.
- Give the date, time, and place of the incident.
- Describe the facts of the incident. Avoid any conclusions or blame. Describe the incident as you saw it even if your impressions differ from those of others.
- Identify all witnesses to the incident.
- Identify any equipment by number and any medication by name and number.
- Document any circumstances surrounding the incident, for example, that another client was experiencing cardiac arrest.

"Whistleblowers are people who expose negligence, abuses, dangers, such as professional misconduct or incompetence in the organization in which they work" (Hardingham, 1999, p. 1). The decision to carry out the act is never an easy one, unless there is a legal obligation (such as in the cases of child abuse or the abuse of vulnerable adults in some provincial/territorial jurisdictions). To report it should be considered a step one takes when all else has failed. Nurses may be the first to come upon unsafe practice or to identify actual or potential hazards. It can be a difficult situation, where the nurse is caught between the values and standards of the profession and the values and norms of the employing organization. The Code of Ethics (2002) can be used as a guideline. Five values in the code are especially relevant to nurses deciding whether to blow the whistle.

- Health and well-being (especially Statements 1 & 3)
- Dignity (Statements 1, 5, & 7)
- Confidentiality (Statements 3 & 5)
- Accountability (Statements 3, 4, 6, 8, & 9)
- Quality Practice Environments (Statements 4 & 5)

Legal Responsibilities of Students

Nursing students are responsible for their own actions and liable for their own acts of negligence committed during the course of clinical experiences. When they perform duties that are within the scope of professional nursing, such as administering an injection, they generally share the responsibility with the instructor, health-care facility, and university.

In cases arising from negligent acts by nursing students, the student has traditionally been treated as an employee of the hospital, which was held liable under the doctrine of *respondent superior*. Today, nursing students are not usually considered employees of the agencies in which they receive clinical experience because nursing programs usually contract with agencies to provide clinical experiences for students. In cases of negligence involving such students, the hospital or agency (e.g., public health agency) and the educational institution will be held potentially liable for negligent actions by students.

Students in clinical situations must be assigned activity within their capabilities and be given reasonable guidance and supervision. Nursing instructors are responsible for assigning students to the care of clients and for providing reasonable supervision. Failure to provide reasonable supervision or the assignment of a client to a student who is not prepared and competent can be a basis for liability.

To fulfill responsibilities to clients and to minimize chances for liability, nursing students need to:

- Make sure they are prepared to carry out the necessary care for assigned clients.
- Ask for additional help or supervision in situations for which they feel inadequately prepared.
- Comply with the policies of the agency in which they obtain their clinical experience.
- Comply with the policies and definitions of responsibility supplied by the school of nursing.

Students who work as part-time or temporary nursing assistants or aides must also remember that legally they can perform only those tasks that appear in the job description of a nurse's aide or assistant. Even though a student may have received instruction and acquired competence in administering injections or suctioning a tracheostomy tube, the student cannot legally perform these tasks while employed as an aide or assistant. While acting as a paid worker, the student is covered for negligent acts by the employer, not the school of nursing.

Guidelines for Reporting a Crime, Tort, or Unsafe Practice

- Write a clear description of the situation you believe you should report.
- Make sure that your statements are accurate.
- Make sure you are credible. Obtain support from at least one trustworthy person before filing the report.
- Report the matter starting at the lowest possible level in the agency hierarchy.
- Assume responsibility for reporting the individual by being open about it. Sign your name to the letter.
- See the problem through once you have reported it.

FOCUS ON CRITICAL THINKING

The physician has determined that Mrs. Jiminez is not progressing well following extensive surgery for cancer. The physician elects to place a subclavian catheter in order to administer total parenteral nutrition. The physician telephones the nursing unit and requests that the nurse obtain the client's informed consent for this invasive procedure. The nurse completes the procedural permit and goes to Mrs. Jiminez's room and informs Mrs. Jiminez that the physician plans to place a catheter into her subclavian vein so that additional nutrients can be administered to her. The nurse further explains that such nutrients will help Mrs. Jiminez heal and regain her strength. Mrs. Jiminez asks, "Will it hurt? I'm so tired of all this pain, I'm not sure I want anything else done." The nurse replies, "Oh, don't worry, we'll make sure you don't feel a thing. Your doctor will be here shortly and he is expecting this permit to be signed, so will you please sign it now?"

1. How can you be certain that Mrs. Jiminez has given informed consent for this invasive procedure?
2. What is the difference between informed consent and signing a consent form?
3. Evaluate the nurse's approach to Mrs. Jiminez in regard to this invasive procedure.
4. When obtaining informed consent for a nursing treatment, such as insertion of a subclavian catheter for administration of total parenteral nutrition, what factors must the nurse consider in order to ensure informed consent from the client?
5. How is performing an invasive procedure without informed consent similar to battery?

See Appendix A for answers to these questions.

CHAPTER HIGHLIGHTS

- Accountability is an essential concept of professional nursing practice.
- Nurses need to understand laws that regulate and affect nursing practice to ensure that the nurses' actions are consistent with current legal principles and to protect the nurses from liability.
- Nurse practice acts legally define and describe the scope of nursing practice.
- Competence in nursing practice is determined and maintained by various credentialling methods, such as licensure, registration, certification, and accreditation, which protect the public's welfare and safety.
- Standards of practice published by provincial/territorial nursing associations and agency policies, procedures, and job descriptions further delineate the scope of a nurse's practice.
- The nurse has specific legal obligations and responsibilities to clients and employers. As a citizen, the nurse has the rights and responsibilities shared by all individuals in the society.
- Collective bargaining is one way nurses can improve their working conditions and economic welfare.
- Nurses can be held liable for intentional torts, such as invasion of privacy, assault and battery; and for unintentional torts, such as negligence and malpractice.
- Negligence or malpractice of nurses can be established when (1) the nurse (defendant) owed a duty to the client, (2) the nurse failed to carry out that duty according to standards, (3) the client (plaintiff) was injured, and (4) the client's injury was caused by the nurse's failure to follow the standard.
- When a client is accidentally injured or involved in an unusual situation, the nurse's first responsibility is to take steps to protect the client and then to notify appropriate agency personnel.
- The nurse is responsible for ensuring that the informed consent of a client is in the medical record before treatment regimens and procedures begin.
- Informed consent implies that (1) the consent was given voluntarily, (2) the client had the capacity and competency to understand, and (3) the client was given enough information on which to make an informed decision.
- Good Samaritan/Emergency Medical Aid acts protect health professionals from claims of malpractice when they offer assistance at the scene of an emergency, provided that there is no willful wrongdoing or gross departure from normal standards of care.
- Nurses can obtain professional liability insurance through the Canadian Nurses Protective Society (CNPS).

- Substance misuse and chemical dependency in health-care workers has become a problem because of the high levels of stress involved in many health-care settings and the easy access to addictive drugs. Chemical impairment includes abuse of alcohol and addictive drugs. The nurse needs to know the proper reporting of nursing colleagues whose practice is chemically impaired.
- Nursing students need to make certain that they are prepared to provide the necessary care to assigned clients and to ask for help or supervision in situations for which they feel inadequately prepared.
- Telephone advice is a challenging skill that requires complete and accurate assessment, appropriate referrals, and meeting in person, when necessary.

READINGS AND REFERENCES

Suggested Readings

Canadian Nurses Association. (2001). *Position statement: The role of the nurse in telepractice.* Ottawa, Canada: Author.

Cutshall, P. (1998). Regulating nursing: A new chapter begins. *Nursing BC, 30*(3), 35–38.

Kerr, L., & Ross-Kerr, J. (2003). The practising nurse and the law. In J. Ross-Kerr & M. Wood (Eds.), *Canadian nursing: Issues and perspectives* (4th ed.). Toronto, ON: Mosby. This chapter provides an overview of the law and the principal areas of nurses' involvement in the legal system, emphasizing areas of concern related to legal issues in Canada.

Selected References

Alberta Association of Registered Nurses. (2000, June). *Entry to practice competencies.* Edmonton: Author.

Alberta Association of Registered Nurses. (2001, January/February). Continuing competence: Make it your program. *AARN, 57*(1), 15.

Alberta Association of Registered Nurses. (1999, July/August). Health professions act: What are the gains for the nursing profession. *AARN, 55*(4), 4.

Alberta Association of Registered Nurses. (1999, November). *Alberta Association of Registered Nurses: Setting standards you trust.* Edmonton: Author.

Alberta Law Reform Institute. (1991). *Advance directives and sustitute decision-making in health care.* Edmonton: The Institute Report for discussion no 11.

Bernzweig, F. P. (1996). *The nurse's liability for malpractice: A programmed course* (6th ed.). St. Louis: Mosby.

Black's law dictionary. (1979). (5th ed.). St Paul, MN: West Publishing.

Bugden v. Harbour View Hospital. (1947). 2 D.L.R. 338 (N.S.S.C.).

Canadian Nurses Association. (2002). *Code of Ethics for Registered Nurses.* Ottawa: Author.

Canadian Nurses Association. (2002, April). Position statement on advanced nursing practice. Ottawa: Author.

Canadian Nurses Protective Society. (1994, December). Consent to treatment: The role of the nurse. *InfoLaw 3*(2), Ottawa: Author.

Canadian Nurses Protective Society. (1995, September). Independent Practice: Legal considerations. *InfoLaw 4*(1), Ottawa: Author.

Canadian Nurses Protective Society. (1997, September). Telephone Advice. *InfoLaw, 6*(1), Ottawa: Author.

Canadian Nurses Protective Society. (1998, April). Vicarious liability. *InfoLaw, 7*(1), Ottawa: Author.

Controlled Drug & Substances Act, s.c. 1996, c.19.

Dias, E. (1973). Canadian law: An overview. In S. R. Good & J. C. Kerr (Eds.), *Contemporary issues in Canadian law for nurses* (pp. 3–14). Toronto: Rinehart & Winston.

Downey v. Rothwell. (1974). 5W.W.R. 311, 49 D.L.R. (3d) 82 (Alta, S.C.).

Downey, J., & Caulfield, T. (1999). *Canadian health law and policy.* Toronto: Butterworths.

Etchells, E., Sharpe, G., Walsh, P., Williams, J., & Singer, P. (1999). Consent. In P. Singer (Ed.), *Bioethics at the bedside: A clinician's guide* (pp. 1–7). Ottawa: Canadian Cataloguing in Publication Data.

Etchells, E., Sharpe, G., Elliott, C., & Singer, P. (1999). Capacity. In P. Singer (Ed.), *Bioethics at the bedside: A clinician's guide* (pp. 17–24). Ottawa: Canadian Cataloguing in Publication Data.

Hardingham, L. (1999, October). I See and I am silent/I see and speak out: The ethical dilemma of whistleblowing. In *Ethics in Practice.* Ottawa: Canadian Nurses Association.

Joseph Brant Memorial Hospital v. Koziol. (1979). 2 C.C.L.T. 170 (S.C.C.).

Keatings, M., & Smith, O. (2000). The Canadian legal system. In M. Keatings & O. Smith (Eds.), *Ethical and legal issues in Canadian nursing* (pp. 51–94). Toronto: W.B. Saunders.

Morris, J., Ferguson, M., & Dykeman, M. (1999). *Canadian Nurses and the law.* Toronto: Butterworths.

National Steering Committee. (2002). *Building a Safer System: A National Integrated Strategy for Improving Patient Safety in Canadian Health Care.* Ottawa, Ontario: Author.

Parisi, L. (1999). Legal framework for health-care services. In J. Hibbard & D. Smith (Eds.), *Nursing management in Canada* (2nd ed.). Toronto: W.B. Saunders.

Phillips, E. (1999b). Is there a risk in being a Good Samaritan? *Canadian Nurse, 95*(8), 43–44.

Philpot, M. (1985). *Legal liability and the nursing process.* Toronto: W.B. Saunders Co.

Picard, E., & Robertson, G. (1996). *Legal liability of doctors and hospitals in Canada.* (3rd ed.). Toronto: Carswell.

Registered Nurses of British Columbia. (1990). *Substance abuse and the nursing profession: A guide for recognition and intervention.* Vancouver: Author.

Sharpe, G. (1993). Consent and minors. *Health Law Canada, 13*, 197–207.

Sneiderman, B., Irvine, J., & Osborne, P. (1995). Nursing Liability. In B. Sniderman, J. Irvine, & P. Osborne (Eds.), *Canadian medical law: An introduction for physicians, nurses and other health care professionals* (2nd ed.), (pp. 158–183). Scarborough: Carswell Thomson Professional Publishing.

The Centre for Nursing Studies in collaboration with The Institute for the Advancement of Public Policy, Inc. (2001). *The nature of extended/expanded nursing role in Canada: A project of the advisory committee on health human resources.* (Report No. NA 321). St. Johns: Author.

WEBLINKS

Canadian Nurses Protective Society
http://www.cnps.ca/
The Canadian Nurses Protective Society Web site offers information about several legal issues and liability protection for nurses who are members in a provincial/territorial nursing association in Canada.

Canadian Nurses Association: Certification
http://www.206.191.29.104/pages/certification_frame
This portion of the Canadian Nurses Association Web site offers a historical perspective of certification in Canada through the Canadian Nurses Association.

CASN Accreditation Program
http://www.casn.org/new/accredprogramprint.html
This Web site offers information about the accreditation standards and policies of the Canadian Association Schools of Nursing.

University of Toronto Joint Centre for Bioethics
http://www.utoronto.ca/jcb/jcblw.htm
This Web site allows you to download a blank living will (which includes legal information specific to each province, as well as further information on personal care decisions).

CHAPTER 9

Health, Wellness, and Illness

OBJECTIVES

After completing this chapter, you will be able to:

- Define in distinct terms health, wellness, and well-being.
- Describe the five dimensions of wellness.
- Analyze various models of health.
- Discuss the changes to the Canadian approaches to health.
- Differentiate illness from disease and acute illness from chronic illness.
- Identify Parson's four aspects of the sick role.
- Describe the effects of illness on the roles and functions of individuals and families.

Introduction

The concept of health remains largely misunderstood by the public and professional communities. The confusion regarding its meaning largely derives from the esteem people give to medical science. Many believe that "health" is what people receive from practitioners, who minister to the sick and ill. This belief contributes to the notion that health is a remedy for what ails people. By placing "health" along a continuum, opposite "disease," "health" becomes absent when illness or disease is present. Obviously *reactive* in its approach, such thinking reduces health to a commodity that practitioners dispense as needed.

What Makes Canadians Healthy or Unhealthy?

This deceptively simple story speaks to the complex set of factors or conditions that determine the level of health of every Canadian.

Why is Jason in the hospital?
Because he has a bad infection in his leg.

But why does he have an infection?
Because he has a cut on his leg, and it got infected.

But why does he have a cut on his leg?
Because he was playing in the junk yard next to his apartment building, and there was some sharp, jagged steel there that he fell on.

But why was he playing in a junk yard?
Because his neighbourhood is kind of run down. A lot of kids play there, and there is no one to supervise them.

But why does he live in that neighbourhood?
Because his parents can't afford a nicer place to live.

But why can't his parents afford a nicer place to live?
Because his Dad is unemployed and his Mom is sick.

But why is his Dad unemployed?
Because he doesn't have much education and he can't find a job.

But why ...?

As this story suggests, health, illness, and early death depend on a variety of factors or "determinants" that surround individuals, families, and nations. Getting to the root cause of Jason's illness and the other major health problems that we face in Canada today requires action on the broader determinants of health. It also requires that we continue to provide high-quality health services that will help Jason heal.

Source: Federal, Provincial, and Territorial Advisory Committee on Population Health. (1999). *Toward a healthy future: Second report on the health of Canadians* ©, p. vii–viii. Adapted and Reproduced with the permission of the Minister of Public Works and Government Services Canada, 2003. *Health Canada assumes no responsibility of any errors or omissions which may have occurred in the adaptation of its material.*

As this chapter endeavours to make clear, such thinking is wrongheaded. First of all, health is not a commodity. No one produces health; no one controls it; and no one brings it into existence. Nor is health something that exists in the absence of illness and disease. Whatever the popular belief, neither medicine, nursing nor any of the other professions delivers health. Science regularly devises new measures to diagnose, prevent, cure, and forestall disease, but science on its own cannot produce health.

Only a clear understanding of these facts can help explain the confusion surrounding the meaning of "health." It then becomes incumbent on nurses, when interacting with individuals, families, and communities, to convey the true meaning of health to those outside the profession. With their special knowledge and experiences, nurses, who understand the meaning of health, have something constructive to contribute to the dialogue. Speaking with conviction, they can effect the movers of society, such as legislators and policymakers who enact societal rules, or teachers and school administrators who determine educational practices. Similarly, they can prompt others with far less authority, especially marginalized people, such as the homeless and the chronically un- and underemployed, to act more on their own behalf.

Due to the complexity of this topic, the discussion opens with a clear statement as to the meaning of health.

> *Health includes the entire human ecological system; therefore, everything in nature and society ultimately contributes something to the health of individuals, families and communities. Nurses then have to concern themselves with everything in the world if they are to help their clients lead "socially and economically satisfying lives."* Mahler, H. (1979, November). *What is health for all?* (World Health, *p. 3–5)*

Such a mandate demands that nurses maintain a spirit of inquiry and inquisitiveness about the world. In other words, if they have not already done so, they have to become upstream thinkers.

Upstream thinkers differ from downstream thinkers in one important respect. The former concentrate on the underlying factors that contribute to an event, whereas the latter focus on the event itself. To understand the difference, imagine standing on the edge of a swift-running river. You hear a child's cry for help coming from the river. You jump in and save the drowning child. Shortly afterwards, you hear another cry for help, jump in again, and save yet another child. This is repeated several more times but not always with the same success. Although busy with your efforts to rescue these children, there are intervals when you have no one to rescue. Rather than go upstream to find out why these children fall into the stream, you occupy yourself doing other things. Consequently, because of your inaction, you never find out that the children who fell in the river slipped on the riverbank while playing dangerously close to the water. Families and the community apparently have no idea about the danger. And without you, they have even less of a chance to find out. That is, if you had travelled upstream, found out, and brought the facts to the community's attention, it is possible that fewer children would fall into the stream. However, the situation persists because you remained downstream.

What does this metaphor say to nurses about the meaning of health? Like all analogies, it teaches us something but not everything. That is, although the metaphor speaks about the role of a community in safeguarding the health of individuals and their families, it also tells us to look beyond the immediate event when studying health. For example, like most practice scientists, nurses usually work on individual cases and with families. In doing so, as in the analogy of drowning children, nurses make a difference every day in the lives of "drowning" patients with medical problems. The emphasis, however, is usually on episodic nursing care. Like downstream thinkers, these nurses focus on the immediate problem at hand and act to correct it. Alternatively, if nurses examined problems from a wider ecological perspective, they resemble upstream thinkers. In brief, if they become advocates for health, nurses invest not only in the biological but also in the psychological and sociological factors associated with health.

Some readers will immediately recognize themselves as upstream thinkers, and they will want to skip ahead to the next chapter which examines prevention and promotion. They will hopefully return to this chapter once they appreciate the complexity of health as a concept. Others will continue reading this chapter because they remain curious as to how they will employ health as a concept in their nursing practice. In any case, all readers in both groups will benefit if they look at Chapter 13 in Pender (1996). It will make clear how health operates at individual, family, and community levels.

Personal Definition of Health

Health is an individual matter. When reading the following vignette, think of answering one question. How would you describe Bob's health? In your answer, indicate whether you consider him well.

Bob, age 54 and divorced, spends his evenings and nights at a recently opened men's shelter in Calgary. During the day, which begins at 0600 hours, Bob hurries about with his shopping cart collecting discarded bottles and containers. Depending on luck and the vagaries of the weather, he earns about $15 a day. Together with his military pension, he manages, as he puts it, "to keep body and soul together."

Much of Bob's income goes to the shelter and a diner where he has his one full meal of the day. He also spends some on a variety of nutritious snack foods and all of the rest on alcohol and cigarettes for himself and his girlfriend.

Perhaps because of the distance he walks each day and his sparse but nutritious diet, Bob is lean and apparently fit. He presents with no disease.

If asked, he admits that he has some health worries. His underemployment bothers him because he sees it as socially unacceptable. He worries that his heart will someday "give out"—both his parents died of heart attacks in their early fifties, and his twin brother has a history of mini-strokes.

Otherwise, Bob confesses that his life has "lots of advantages." He enjoys the independent lifestyle and his street-friends, on whom he depends and who depend on him. If he could change anything, it is to have some dental care and more money so that he can put "something away when he can no longer collect empties."

Health

What is health? It is nearly axiomatic that people generally believe that, even if they cannot define it, they can identify "health" (the noun) or "healthy" (the adjective) when they see it. Like the public, nurses have no universally accepted definition. This leaves individual nurses in the enviable position of having to choose or devise their own definitions of health. When doing so, Fawcett (1995) cautions nurses to remember that "the discipline of nursing is concerned with the wholeness or health of human beings, recognizing that they are in continuous interaction with their environments" (p. 7). Of course, although an individual matter,

Developing a Personal Definition of Health

The following questions can help nurses develop a personal definition of health:

- Is a person more than a biophysiological system?
- Is health more than the absence of disease symptoms?
- Is health the ability of an individual to perform work?
- Is health the ability of an individual to adapt to the environment?
- Is health a condition of a person's actualization?
- Is health a state or a process?
- Is health the effective functioning of self-care activities?
- Is health static or changing?
- Are health and wellness the same?
- Are disease and illness different?
- Are there levels of health?
- Are wellness, health, and illness separate entities or points along a continuum?
- Is health socially determined?
- How do you rate your health, and why?

Concepts of Wellness

- Wellness is a choice—a decision you make to move toward optimal health.
- Wellness is a way of life—a lifestyle you design to achieve your highest potential for well-being.
- Wellness is a process—a developing awareness that there is no end point, but that health and happiness are possible in each moment, here and now.
- Wellness is an efficient channeling of energy—energy received from the environment, transformed within you, and sent on to affect the world outside.
- Wellness is the integration of body, mind, and spirit—the appreciation that everything you do, and think, and feel, and believe has an impact on your state of health.
- Wellness is the loving acceptance of yourself.

Source: Reprinted with permission, *Wellness Workbook,* Travis & Ryan, Ten Speed Press, Berkeley, CA. © 1981, 1988 by John W. Travis, MD.

nurses are bound, as practice scientists, to construct definitions that fit with the needs of society. Not to do so reduces the endeavour to a merely philosophical exercise.

To begin with, let us agree that languages, or the words in language, illuminate how we conceptualize the world. If so, a worthwhile way to begin any discussion about the meaning of health is to prepare a list of words used interchangeably to describe it. Some analogous words and synonyms to describe the positive appearance of good health include: *healthy, sound, wholesome, robust, hale, well, vigorous, energetic, hearty, strenuous, strong, sturdy, stalwart, tough,* and *tenacious* (Webster, 1978, p. 397). Contrarily, there are also words that speak about the negative appearance of health: *unhealthy, weak, feeble, frail, fragile, infirmed, decrepit, debilitated, weakened, enfeebled, disabled, sapped, impaired, ill,* and *damaged* (Webster, 1978, p. 870). The subtle differences or nuances in meaning among all these synonyms and antonyms tell us that health is a complex concept. In effect, these words testify as to why "health," as a concept, requires deconstruction or analysis as to its exact meaning.

Health Models

Smith (1981) organizes the different approaches around four models that describe common, broad theories of health. They are the eudaimonistic, adaptive, role-performance, and clinical models. Each, with its own outcomes, provides a unique dimension of health, which nurses and other practitioners select, depending on the thinking of different theorists who subscribe to a particular model. Before discussing each model, some general comments seem in order.

As stated, each model focuses on different outcomes. Do not take this to mean that the models are mutually exclusive in terms of practice. The choice is not always an "either-or" alternative. Sometimes it is a "both-and." As the double-sided arrows in Figure 9.1 indicate, practitioners can move between and among the models as the clients' needs change. As such, circumstances determine which model will work more efficaciously. For example, the clinical model emphasizes physiological needs, whereas role-performance structures nursing interventions around social relations. Nevertheless, both largely work to restore equilibrium for patients. On the other hand, the other two models, adaptive and eudaimonistic, focus on growth throughout the changes in people's lives. We begin with the most comprehensive—the eudaimonistic model.

FOCUS ON CRITICAL THINKING

Jerry and Joe have both suffered heart attacks. Jerry, upon advice from his physician, started exercising, changed his dietary intake, entered stress reduction classes, and returned to work 6 weeks after his heart attack. He has a positive outlook, is doing well, and talks about being "well." Joe also changed his dietary habits and started exercising; however, he has been unable to quit smoking even though he wants to and has been advised to do so. Joe is frequently despondent, very fearful of having another heart attack, has not yet returned to work, and frequently talks about being "ill."

1. How does Jerry's psychological dimension of health status differ from Joe's?
2. Both Jerry and Joe have heart disease. Jerry considers himself "well" whereas Joe considers himself "ill." Explain this phenomenon based on the health locus of control model.
3. What external factors may have influenced Jerry's decision to implement positive health behaviours?
4. What factors may have prevented Joe from developing the same positive outlook and actions that Jerry was able to take in regard to his illness?
5. What nursing interventions would be most beneficial to Joe in regard to his smoking problem?

See Appendix A for answers to these questions.

Figure 9.1 Definitions of health for each of Smith's four models

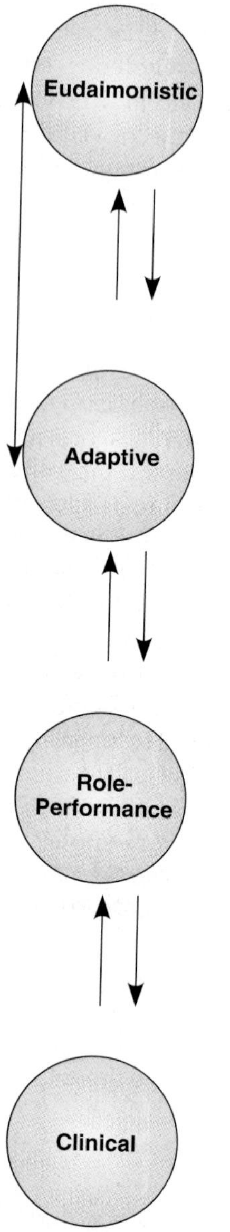

Eudaimonistic In the eudaimonistic model, "health is the condition of actualization or realization of ... [intrinsic] potential. Illness ... is a condition that impedes or prevents self-actualization .... A health professional ... has to attempt to assist the individual toward self-fulfillment." (p. 45).

Adaptive In the adaptive model, "health is the condition of the organism in which it can engage in effective interaction with its physical and social environments. ... Disease is a failure in adaptation: it is a breakdown in the ability of the organism to cope with certain changes in its environment." (p. 45).

Role-Performance In the role-performance model, "adequate role-performance [is the] ... common-sense criterion of health ... [S]ickness is an incapacity that prevents people from 'doing their jobs.'" (p. 46).

Clinical In the clinical model, "... health ... is the absence of [the] signs or symptoms of disease or disability as identified by medical science. Conversely, conspicuous presence of these signs or symptoms is a model indicator of the illness extreme." (p. 46).

Source: Smith, J. A. (1981). The idea of health: A philosophical inquiry. *Advances in Nursing Science, 3*(3), p. 45–46.

Eudaimonistic Model

This model "...comprises several views of human nature that extends the idea of health to general well-being and self-realization" (Smith, 1981, p. 44). Exemplified by Maslow (1954, 1962a, 1962b, and 1970), this approach measures health as the "fulfillment" and "complete development" of individuals. Instead of looking for isolated actions and employing a linear, causal framework for explaining health, the model takes a holistic view, where the characteristics of wholeness, unity, and individuality become assumptions on which the nature of humanity is explained" (Smith, 1981, p. 45).

The term "humanism," if you needed one word, defines this model. It assumes that every individual is unique, rational, capable of self-determination, and a social being who benefits from collective participation. For its part, society—each of us individually and collectively—owes every person mutual respect and tolerance.

An obvious example of humanist philosophy has to include Maslow (1962) as well as Labonte (1993). Since most nurses have a nodding familiarity with Maslow, let us consider the well-known Canadian health theorist, Ronald Labonte.

Labonte (1993), particularly well known for his leadership on public health issues, has a conceptualization of health (Figure 9.2). It represents the aforementioned humanistic principles as they relate to the three principal dimensions of health.

Using the research of Blaxter (1990) and the Registered Nurses Association of British Columbia (RNABC, 1990) on how people describe health, Labonte categorizes the findings into six groups.

1. Feeling vital, full of energy
2. Having good social relationships
3. Experiencing a sense of control over one's life and one's living conditions
4. Being able to do things one enjoys
5. Having a sense of purpose in life
6. Experiencing a connectedness to "community"

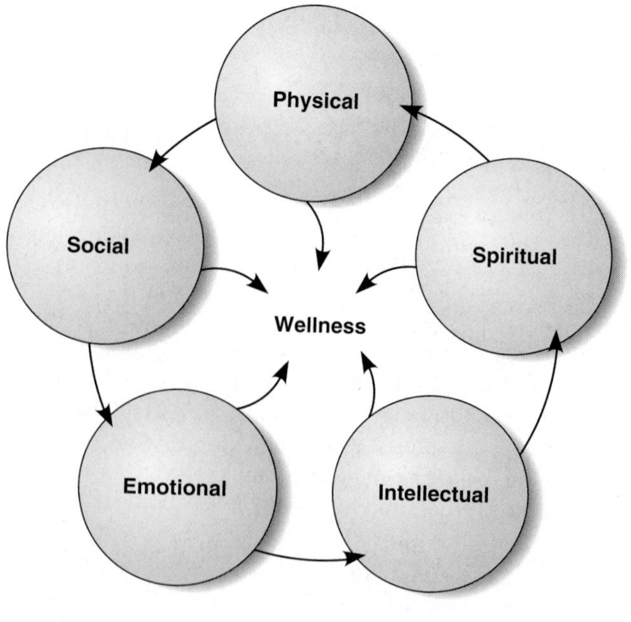

Figure 9.2 Dimensions of health and well-being

He then consolidates the groupings further in order to align them with the physical, mental, and social dimensions of health. To explain his positive conceptualization of health or well-being, Labonte also provides three summary statements.

1. We need a degree of physical vitality and a certain connectedness to others (groups, communities) to enjoy good social relationships.
2. We need a degree of physical vitality and a sense of meaning and purpose both to know and to act upon what we enjoy.
3. We need a sense of meaning and purpose and a certain connectedness to others (groups, communities) to experience a sense of control over our lives and living conditions.

If one accepts his formula for health, his conceptualization fits comfortably with the eudaimonistic thrust of the Canadian approach to health. How this works is a later topic for discussion.

Adaptive Model

Derived from the work of Dubos (1959, 1965), this model expands on the medical approach to injury or disease and includes human interaction with the physical and social environment. Due to the importance given to effective interaction, this model focuses on adaptive behaviour. That is, "... disease is a failure in adaptation; it is a breakdown in the ability of the organism to cope with certain changes in the environment" (Smith, 1981, p. 45). Unlike the clinical model, with its emphasis on the eradication of disease or repair of the body, the adaptive model focuses on restoration so the body will adapt to environmental dangers in the future. As such, it speaks to a more complex understanding of what constitutes well-being.

Adaptation is the cornerstone of Roy and Andrew's (1991) conceptual model of nursing (Figure 9.3). It holds that the person and environment constantly interact and, thereby, demand "the person to make adaptive responses. For human beings, life is never the same. It is constantly changing and presenting new challenges" (p. 18). In response, human beings behave in two ways. Their behaviour either contributes or fails in contributing to adaptation. Adaptive responses include "...those that promote the integrity of the person in terms of the goals of adaptation: survival, growth, reproduction, and mastery" (p. 12). In Figure 9.3, see the arrow, labelled "behaviour," that stays within the outer circle. Ineffective responses consist of "...those that neither promote integrity nor contribute to the goals of adaptation. That is, they may, in the immediate situation if continued over a long time, threaten the person's survival, growth, reproduction, or mastery" (p. 12). See the arrow, labelled "behaviour," that lies outside the circle. Health, in this scheme, is "a state and process of being and becoming an integrated and whole person" (p. 19). This model, being more complex, directs nurses to increase adaptive and decrease ineffective responses among patients.

Like Dubos, then, Roy and Andrews accept adaptability as an essential human characteristic. They imply that the integrity of the individual, even when the person is dying, is the ultimate goal of existence. In doing so, they avoid the fallacy that adaptation is a goal unto itself. Clearly, as positive an experience as it is, adaptation for the sake of adaptation holds out little promise and even has an air of futility without a higher purpose.

Role-Performance Model

This model adopts a sociological approach, using the research of Parsons (1972), DiCicco and Apple (1960), Nisbet (1970), and Twaddle (1974). Quite simply, the model, as its name implies, singles out role performance as the primary measure of wellness. As Smith (1981) states: "If nothing in a person's condition impedes the effective performance of his or her role, then he or she is in a healthy condition" (p. 46). Equating health with performance, the model assumes that individuals in optimal health function at optimal capacity. Yet, we know that people daily perform multiple roles, which often interfere with one another. Consequently, the model fails to address role conflict and the relative importance of different roles.

Such issues notwithstanding, the role-performance model, with its emphasis on individuals as social beings, has its adherents.

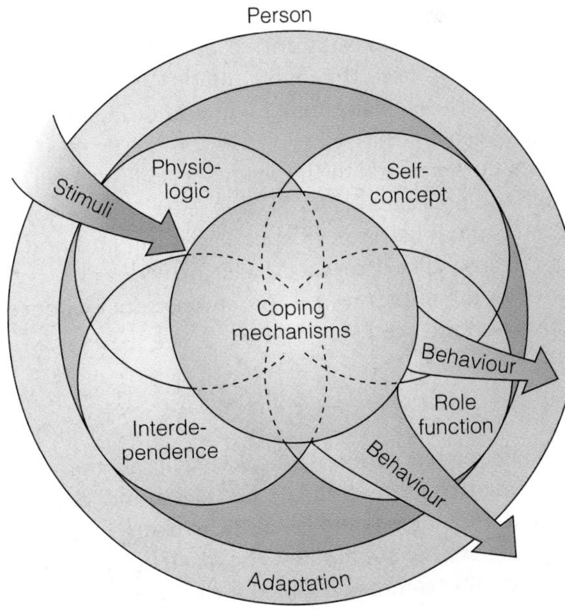

Figure 9.3 The person as an adaptive system

Source: Roy, C. & Andrews, H. A. (1991). *The Roy adaptation model: The definitive statement*, p. 17., Norwalk, CT: Appleton & Lange

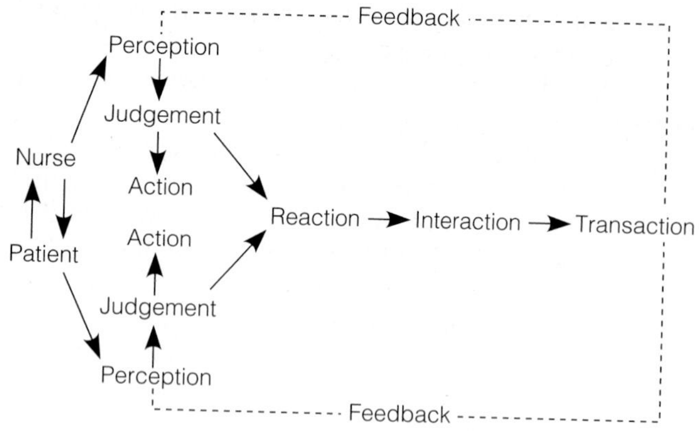

Figure 9.4 King's Transaction process model

Transaction Process Model

Models and theories represent knowledge and suggest ways of using knowledge relative to an individual's role in a profession such as nursing. Concepts such as communication, interaction, perception and role are examples of knowledge used by nurses in providing care for individuals and families. King designed a transaction process model within her theory of goal attainment (King, 1981, p. 145). This process explains how nurses react purposefully with health care consumers to mutually set goals, explore and agree to means to use to attain goals. When a transaction is made, goals are attained in most situations. The critical variable in King's model is mutual goal setting between nurse and patient/family. The concepts in this model (perception, communication, interaction, and transaction) provide substantive knowledge as nurses internationally use the Yura and Walsh "Nursing Process" of assess, plan, implement and evaluate patients (Yura & Wash 1978).

When nurses record the mutually set goals with patients/families and goals are achieved, this represents outcomes. Outcomes demonstrate evidence based nursing practice. King's Transaction Process Model provides theoretical knowledge for nurses to use to demonstrate evidence of effective nursing care.

Clinical Model

Closely associated with a medical viewpoint, the clinical model endeavours to eliminate the signs and symptoms associated with injury and disease. Looking at the body from a mechanistic standpoint, the model concerns itself with the body's restoration. Since the model currently has little, if any, interest in those "...considerations which transcend medicine and have to do with a lifestyle" (Smith, 1981, p. 47), the model has a minimal interest in improving the body's ultimate performance.

The simplest of all health models, the clinical model teaches that because health is the opposite of disease, the presence of one denies the existence of the other. Although it treats health as a commodity, controlled by medicine, it has, by the rigorous pursuit of knowledge by means of the scientific method and sizeable amounts of money, significantly increased knowledge about the human body. Physicians control access to this knowledge and its diagnostic or therapeutic benefits, whether surgical or pharmaceutical.

Leavell and Clark (1965), writing when they did, advocated what Smith (1981) describes as the clinical model (Figure 9.5). It serves to treat illness rather than promote wellness, although identification of risk factors that result from the interactions of agent, host, and environment are helpful in maintaining health.

The model has three dynamic interactive elements (see Figure 9.5):

1. *Agent.* Any environmental factor or stressor (biological, chemical, mechanical, physical, or psychosocial) that by its presence or absence (e.g., lack of essential nutrients) can lead to illness or disease.
2. *Host.* Includes person(s) who may or may not be at risk of acquiring a disease. Family history, age, and lifestyle habits influence the host's reaction to an agent.
3. *Environment.* Includes all factors external to the host that may or may not predispose the person to the development of the disease. Physical environment includes climate, living conditions, sound (noise) levels, and economic level. Social environment includes interactions with others and life events, such as the death of a spouse.

Because each of the agent-host-environment factors constantly interacts with the others, health is an ever-changing state. When the variables are in balance, health is maintained; when variables are not in balance, disease occurs.

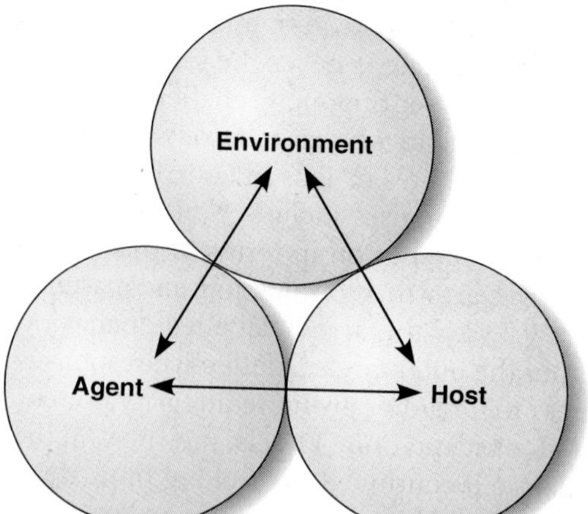

Figure 9.5 The agent-host-environment triangle

Health Belief Models

Several theories or models of health beliefs and behaviours have been developed to help determine whether an individual is likely to participate in disease prevention and health-promotion activities. These models prove useful tools in developing programs for helping people change to healthier lifestyles and develop a more positive attitude toward preventive health measures. See also Chapter 10, "Health Promotion."

Health Locus of Control Model

Locus of control (LOC) is a concept from social learning theory that nurses can use to determine whether clients are likely to take action regarding health, that is, whether clients believe that their health status is under their own or others' control. People who believe that they have a major influence on their own health status—that health is largely self-determined—are called *internals*. People who exercise internal control are more likely than others to take the initiative on their own health care, be more knowledgeable about their health, and adhere to prescribed health-care regimens, such as taking medication, making and keeping appointments with physicians, maintaining diets, and giving up smoking. By contrast, people who believe their health is largely controlled by outside forces (e.g., chance or powerful others) are referred to as *externals*.

Externally controlled people may need assistance to take more control internally if behaviour changes are to be successful. The results of a study by Lewis (1982) suggest that greater personal control over one's life is associated with higher levels of self-esteem, greater purpose in life, and decreased self-reports of anxiety—a general improvement in well-being.

Locus of control is a measurable concept that can be used to predict which people are most likely to change their behaviour. Measurement instruments are available to assess LOC. One example is the Multidimensional Health Locus of Control (MHLC) Scale (Wallston et al., 1978). Nurses can use LOC results to plan internal reinforcement training, if necessary, in order to improve client efforts toward better health.

Rosenstock's and Becker's Health Belief Models

In the 1950s, Rosenstock (1974) proposed a health belief model (HBM) intended to predict which individuals would or would not use such preventive measures as screening for early detection of cancer. Becker (1974) modified the health belief model to include these components: *individual perceptions*, *modifying factors*, and *variables likely to affect initiating action*.

The health belief model (Figure 9.6) is based on motivational theory. Rosenstock assumed that good health is an objective common to all people. Becker added "positive health motivation" as a consideration.

Individual Perceptions

Individual perceptions include the following:

- *Perceived susceptibility.* A family history of a certain disorder, such as diabetes or heart disease, may make the individual feel at high risk.
- *Perceived seriousness.* The question here is: In the perception of the individual, does the illness cause death or have serious consequences? Concern about the spread of acquired immune deficiency syndrome (AIDS) reflects the general public's perception of the seriousness of this illness.
- *Perceived threat.* According to Becker, perceived susceptibility and perceived seriousness combine to determine the total perceived threat of an illness to a specific individual. For example, a person who perceives that many individuals in the community have AIDS may not necessarily perceive a threat of the disease; if the person is a drug addict or a homosexual, however, the perceived threat of illness is likely to increase because the susceptibility is combined with seriousness.

Modifying Factors

Factors that modify a person's perceptions include the following:

- *Demographic variables.* Demographic variables include age, gender, race, and ethnicity. An infant, for example, does not perceive the importance of a healthy diet; an adolescent may perceive peer approval as more important than family approval and participate as a consequence in hazardous activities or adopt unhealthy eating and sleeping patterns.
- *Sociopsychological variables.* Social pressure or influence from peers or other reference groups (e.g., self-help or vocational groups) may encourage preventive health behaviours even when individual motivation is low. Expectations of others may motivate people, for example, not to drive an automobile after drinking alcohol.
- *Structural variables.* Knowledge about the target disease and prior contact with it are structural variables that are presumed to influence preventive behaviour. Becker found higher compliance rates with prescribed treatments among mothers whose children had frequent ear infections and occurrences of asthma.
- *Cues to action.* Cues can be either internal or external. Internal cues include feelings of fatigue, uncomfortable symptoms, or thoughts about the condition of an ill person who is close.

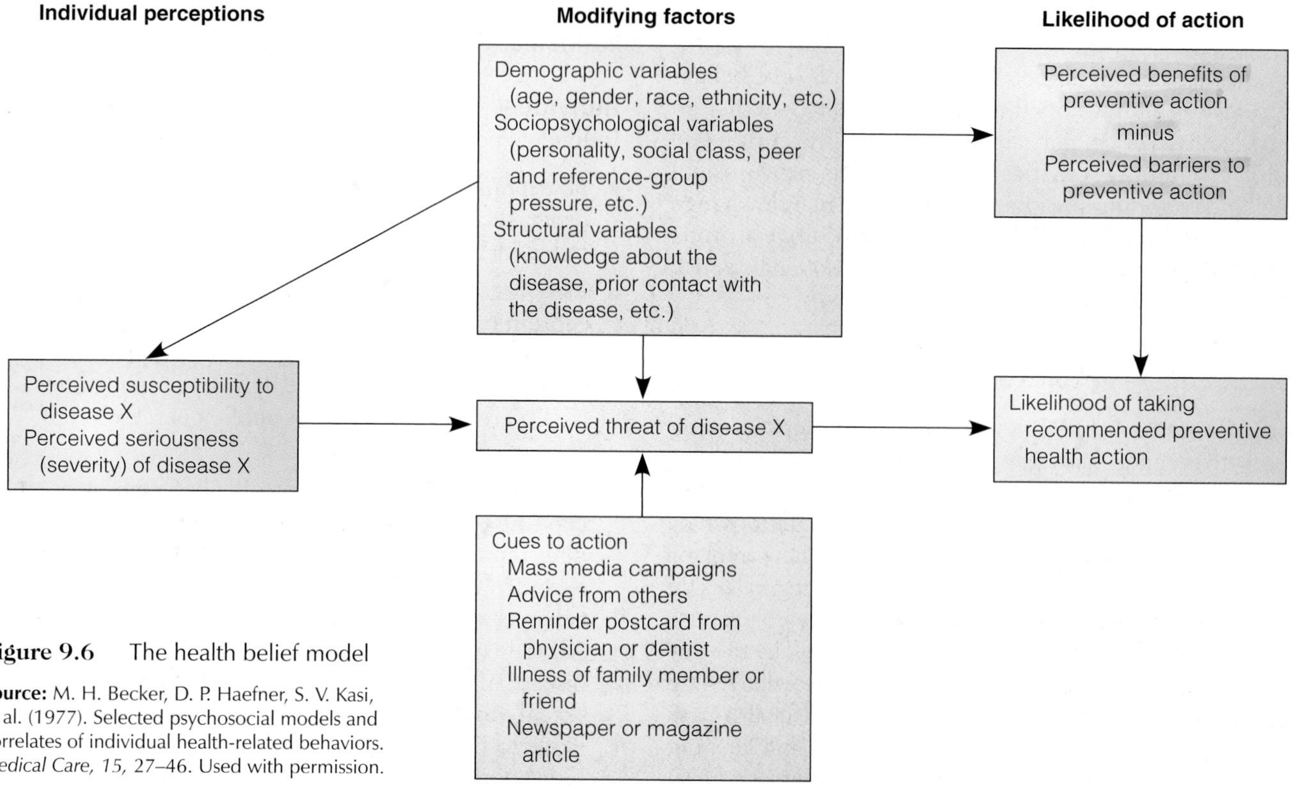

Figure 9.6 The health belief model

Source: M. H. Becker, D. P. Haefner, S. V. Kasi, et al. (1977). Selected psychosocial models and correlates of individual health-related behaviors. *Medical Care, 15,* 27–46. Used with permission.

Likelihood of Action

The likelihood of a person taking recommended preventive health action depends on the perceived benefits of the action minus the perceived barriers to the action.

- *Perceived benefits of the action.* Examples include refraining from smoking to prevent lung cancer, and eating nutritious foods and avoiding snacks to maintain weight.
- *Perceived barriers to action.* Examples include cost, inconvenience, unpleasantness, and lifestyle changes.

Nurses play a major role in helping clients implement healthy behaviours. They help clients monitor health, they supply anticipatory guidance, and they impart knowledge about health. Nurses can also reduce barriers to action (e.g., by minimizing inconvenience or discomfort) and can support positive actions.

Pender (1996) has modified this health belief model (HBM) to develop a health promotion model. According to Pender, HBM explains health-protecting or preventive behaviours but does not emphasize health-promoting behaviours. See Pender's health promotion model in Chapter 10.

Illness and Disease

Illness is a highly personal state in which the person's physical, emotional, intellectual, social, developmental, or spiritual functioning is thought to be diminished. It is not synonymous with disease and may or may not be related to disease. An individual could have a disease, for example, a growth in the stomach, and not feel ill. By the same token, a person can feel ill, that is, feel uncomfortable, yet have no discernible disease. Illness is highly subjective; only the individual person can say he or she is ill.

Disease can be described as an alteration in body functions, resulting in a reduction of capacities or a shortening of the normal lifespan. Traditionally, intervention by physicians has the goal of eliminating or ameliorating disease processes. Primitive people thought disease was caused by "forces" or spirits. Later, this belief was replaced by the single-causation theory. Today, multiple factors are considered to interact in causing disease and determining an individual's response to treatment.

The causation of a disease is called its **etiology.** A description of the etiology of a disease includes the identification of all causal factors that act together to bring about the particular disease. For example, the tubercle bacillus is designated as the biologic agent of tuberculosis. However, other etiological factors, such as age, nutritional status, and even occupation, are involved in the development of tuberculosis and influence the course of infection. There are many diseases for which the cause is unknown (e.g., multiple sclerosis).

Nurses have traditionally taken a holistic view of people and base their practice on the multiple-causation theory of health problems.

There are many ways to classify illness and disease; one of the most common is as acute or chronic. **Acute illness** is typically characterized by severe symptoms of relatively short duration. The symptoms often appear abruptly and subside quickly and, depending upon the cause, may or may not require intervention by health-care professionals. Some acute illnesses are serious (for example, appendicitis may require surgical intervention), but many acute illnesses, such as colds, subside without medical intervention or with the help of over-the-counter medications. Following an acute illness, most people return to their normal level of wellness.

A **chronic illness** is one that lasts for an extended period, usually six months or longer, and often for the person's life. Chronic illnesses usually have a slow onset and often have periods of **remission,** when the symptoms disappear, and **exacerbation,** when the symptoms reappear.

Examples of chronic illnesses are arthritis, heart and lung diseases, and diabetes mellitus. Nurses are involved in caring for chronically ill individuals of all ages in all types of settings—homes, nursing homes, hospitals, clinics, and other agencies. Care needs to be focused on promoting the highest level of independence, sense of control, and wellness that is possible. Clients often need to modify their activities of daily living, social relationships, and perception of self and body image. In addition, many must learn how to live with increasing physical limitations and discomfort.

Effects of Illness

Illness brings about changes in both the involved individual and in the family. The changes vary depending on the nature, severity, and duration of the illness, attitudes associated with the illness by the client and others, the financial demands, the lifestyle changes incurred, adjustments to usual roles, and so on.

Impact on the Client

Ill clients may experience behavioural and emotional changes, changes in self-concept and body image, and lifestyle changes. Behavioural and emotional changes associated with short-term illness are generally mild and short lived. The individual, for example, may become irritable and lack the energy or desire to interact in the usual fashion with family members or friends. More acute responses are likely with severe, life-threatening, chronic, or disabling illnesses. Anxiety, fear, anger, withdrawal, denial, a sense of hopelessness, and feelings of powerlessness are all common responses to severe or disabling illness. For example, a client who has experienced a heart attack fears for his life and the financial burden it may place on his family. Another client informed about a diagnosis of cancer, AIDS, or a crippling neurologic disease may, over time, experience episodes of denial, anger, fear, and hopelessness.

Certain illnesses can also change the client's body image or physical appearance, especially if there is severe scarring or loss of a limb or special sense organ. The client's self-esteem and self-concept may also be affected. Many factors can play a part in low self-esteem and a disturbance in self-concept: loss of body parts and function, pain, disfigurement, dependence on others, unemployment, financial problems, inability to participate in social functions, strained relationships with others, and spiritual distress. Nurses need to help clients express their thoughts and feelings, and to provide care that helps the client effectively cope with change.

Ill individuals are also vulnerable to loss of autonomy (**autonomy** is the state of being independent and self-directed without outside control). Family interactions may change so that clients may no longer be involved in making family decisions or even decisions about their own health care. Nurses need to support clients' right to self-determination and autonomy as much as possible by providing them with sufficient information to participate in decision-making processes and to maintain a feeling of being in control.

Illness also often necessitates a change in lifestyle. In addition to participating in treatments and taking medications, the ill person may need to change diet, activity and exercise, and rest and sleep patterns.

Nurses can help clients adjust their lifestyle by:

- Providing explanations about necessary adjustments
- Making arrangements, wherever possible, to accommodate the client's lifestyle
- Encouraging other health professionals to become aware of the person's lifestyle practices and to support healthy aspects of that lifestyle
- Reinforcing desirable changes in practices with a view to making them a permanent part of the client's lifestyle

Impact on the Family

A person's illness affects not only the person who is ill but also the family or significant others. The kind of effect and its extent depend chiefly on three factors: (1) the member of the family who is ill, (2) the seriousness and length of the illness, and (3) the cultural and social customs the family follows.

The changes that can occur in the family include the following:

- Role changes
- Task reassignments and increased demands on time
- Increased stress due to anxiety about the outcome of the illness for the client and conflict about unaccustomed responsibilities
- Financial problems
- Loneliness as a result of separation and pending loss
- Change in social customs

See Chapter 6 for further information about the effects of illness on the family.

Canadian Approaches to Health

Every discussion about the meaning of health likely begins with one coined by the World Health Organization (WHO), in 1947. It states: "Health is a state of complete physical, mental, and social well-being and not merely the absence of disease and infirmity." Well received by public health and community health practitioners, the definition also has its detractors (Rootman & Raeburn, 1994). For one thing, they state that the encyclopedic character of the definition places any- and everything under one umbrella. Also, by not delimiting what health includes, it is planetary in scope and, therefore, impractical. Lastly, by describing health as a "state," it implies that it is fixed and measurable, when health more closely resembles an ongoing unique "process."

To appreciate how Canadian policymakers and planners define health, one wants to study the shift in thinking that occurred over the last five years. This requires an examination, albeit briefly, of four documents or papers.

Lalonde Report (1974)

A medical approach to health dominated thinking for much of the 20th century. It changed when Lalonde, then Minister of Health in the Trudeau government, proposed that "future improvements [in health]... lie mainly in improving the environment, modifying self-imposed risks, and adding to our knowledge of human biology" (p. 31). Lalonde conceptualized his expanded view of health as a "health field concept" and included four components which would determine health including:

1. *Biology*, which referred to an individual's genetic makeup, family history, the processes of maturation and aging, and the physical or mental health challenges acquired during life.
2. *Lifestyle*, also referred to as behaviour, included individual responses to internal stimuli or external conditions, as demonstrated through the decisions by individuals that affect their risks and their subsequent health status.
3. *Environment*, both physical and social, which surround individuals and shape behaviour, positively or negatively, and over which they exert variable control.
4. *Health-care organization*, the human and physical resources that affect access and provision of health-care services.

Lalonde's report made two substantial contributions to the discussion of health. First, he asserted the discussion had to recognize that lifestyles, shaped by social experiences, directly influence individuals. Second, these influences directly affect health.

Fortuitously, at about the time of the report's publication, North Americans also became interested in the benefits of physical activity and healthy lifestyles. The success of the ParticipACTION program in Canada certainly attests to this.

Even the most successful ideas, however, have their downside. In the case of the Lalonde Report, it came when lifestyle, more so than the environment, received most of the attention from the public and policymakers. They translated lifestyle to mean that individuals at risk for disease largely had themselves to blame. This victim blaming led to an obvious conclusion. If individuals are responsible for their health, then health is an individual concern.

As in most things, when societal thinking moves too far in one direction, you can reasonably anticipate a shift in direction. Nurses did not have to wait long.

Ottawa Charter (1986)

If the Lalonde Report represents a shift from a medical to a behavioural approach, then the Ottawa Charter takes Canadian policymakers in another direction. As if in response to the question, "Where does the responsibility for health lie?" the charter suggests a balance between a medical, behavioural, and socio-environmental or ecological approach.

In 1986, Health and Welfare Canada, the Canadian Public Health Association, and the WHO met in Ottawa to develop a health promotion plan. It ultimately changed the way Canadian policymakers thought. That is, it emphasized the interrelationship between personal health behaviour and the environment. By defining health as "a resource for everyday living," it displayed the conviction that the health sector does not have jurisdiction over health. Only the coordinated actions of individuals from all sectors of society, including government and nongovernmental organizations, can properly address health issues. Certainly, the Charter's full definition of health implies as much:

> *Health is created and lived by people within the settings of their everyday life; where they learn, work, play, and love. Health is created by caring for oneself and others, by being able to make decisions and have control over one's life circumstances, and by ensuring that the society one lives in creates conditions that allow the attainment of health by all its members.* (Ottawa Charter for Health Promotion, p.4)

Unlike other definitions arrived at by international bodies, the Ottawa Charter takes a new direction. It goes beyond the 1947 WHO definition of health, which singled out the physical, mental, and social dimensions of health but confined it to some expert-driven, measurable absolute. Instead, the Ottawa Charter definition implies that health is a dynamic social process owned by everyone, not only experts, and represents an entitlement for all the world's people.

Epp Report (1986)

Formally known as *Achieving Health for All: A Framework for Health Promotion*, this report appeared during the tenure of another Canadian Minister of Health and Welfare, Jake Epp. Building on the principles of the Ottawa Charter, the Epp Report focused on three challenges to the health of Canadians. They included:

1. Reducing inequities
2. Increasing prevention
3. Enhancing coping

In this regard, the report displayed more specificity than earlier documents. That is, it earmarked for action specific problems that compromised the health of Canadians. More exactly, it singled out various social inequities, preventable illnesses and injuries as well as the resultant disabilities, and stress, the increasingly prevalent disorder of modern society. As importantly, the report also described various strategies for addressing these problems. They included:

- Fostering public participation
- Strengthening community health services
- Coordinating healthy public policy

The intentional appeal to public participation in implementing social health programs made an important point. The government had concluded that in matters pertaining to health, community action had become paramount. In less than 50 years, decisions about health no longer belonged exclusively to the experts. Health had become the prerogative of the community.

Canadian Society Notes

Fact	Implications for Nursing Practice
The National Forum on Health was launched in 1994 to inform Canadians and to advise the federal government on innovative ways to improve the health and the health care of Canadians.	Completed in 1997, these studies provide nurses with answers to crucial questions such as: what is good health, how can it be promoted, where is the Canadian health care system going today?
In 1996, 82% of all seniors living at home had a chronic health condition as diagnosed by a medical practitioner; 28% were limited in at least some activities because of the health condition.	The implementation of nursing activities to promote client health may be influenced by the presence of chronic conditions.
Released in September 1999, the Second Report on the Health of Canadians contains a wealth of information.	Nurses have a role in helping individuals change health inhibiting behaviours through educational interventions.

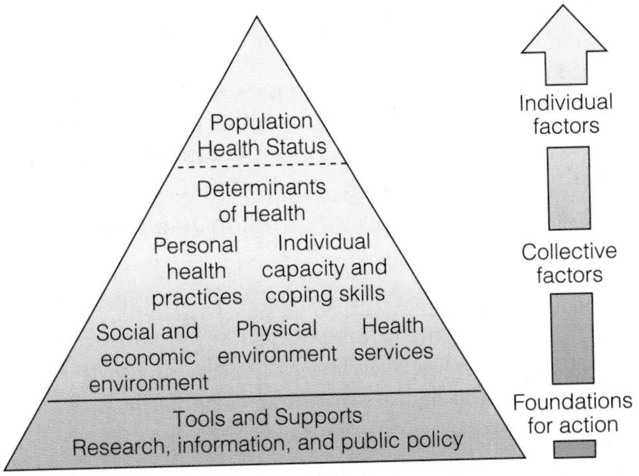

Figure 9.7 Framework for population health

Source: Population Health Approach: Underlying Premises and Evidence Table, 2002 © Adapted and Reproduced with the permission of the Minister of Public Works and Government Services Canada, 2003. *Health Canada assumes no responsibility for any errors or omissions which may have ocurred in the adaptation of its material.*

Strategies for Population Health (1994)

As a term, population health has come to mean that the health of a people improves only when society tackles all the medical, behavioural, and socio-environmental factors that determine health. These determinants, which now comprise 12 factors or classes, include all "...the things that make and keep people healthy" (Federal, Provincial, and Territorial Advisory Committee on Population Health, 1994, p. 1). Some encompass behaviours under the control of individuals; others lie outside their immediate control.

Although strategies or interventions on behalf of population health lie outside the purview of this chapter, a brief discussion seems in order. Doing so explains how the various elements combine synergistically to increase the health status of a population (Figure 9.7).

Information and research, sometimes referred to as community action research, lie at the basis of all population health initiatives. Tracking results and outcomes is critical in order to understand the broad, long-term effects of large-scale health initiatives. In this way, public policy remains informed, thereby rendering decisions based on science and not merely on expediency.

The determinants of health, not surprisingly, lie at the centre of the framework. They lend direction to all the initiatives. The *Strategies for Population Health* (1994) divides the determinants into five groups. They are:

- *Social & Economic Environment* (income, employment, social status, social support networks, education, and social factors in the workplace)
- *Physical Environment* (physical factors in the workplace, as well as other aspects of the natural and human-built physical environment)

- *Personal Health Practices* (behaviours that enhance or create risks to health)
- *Individual Capacity and Coping Skills* (psychological characteristics of the person such as personal competence, coping skills, and sense of control and mastery; and genetic and biologic characteristics)
- *Health Services* (services to promote, maintain, and restore health)

To the complexity of the undertaking, Table 9.1 outlines the underlying premises and supporting evidence for some of the determinants of health, currently identified by the Canadian government. The list has, over the years, undergone revision and now includes:

- Income and social status
- Social support networks
- Education
- Employment/Working conditions
- Social environments
- Physical environments
- Biology and genetic endowment
- Personal health practices and coping skills
- Healthy child development
- Health services
- Gender
- Culture

Source: Health Canada, Population Health Approach (May 25, 2000).

TABLE 9.1 Determinants that Influence Health, with Premises and Evidence Included

Key Determinant	Underlying Premises	Evidence
Income and Social Status	Health status improves at each step up the income and social hierarchy. High income determines living conditions such as safe housing and ability to buy sufficient food. The healthiest populations are those in societies which are prosperous and have an equitable distribution of wealth.	Only 47% of Canadians in the lowest income bracket rate their health as very good or excellent, compared with 73% of Canadians in the highest income group. At each rung up the income ladder, Canadians have less sickness, longer life expectancies, and improved health.
Social Support Networks	Support from families, friends, and communities is associated with better health. Such social support networks could be very important in helping people solve problems and deal with adversity, as well as maintaining a sense of mastery and control over life circumstances.	An extensive study in California found that for men and women, the more social contacts people have, the lower were their premature death rates. Another American study found that low availability of emotional support and low social participation were associated with all-cause mortality.
Education	Health status improves with level of education. Education is closely tied to socioeconomic status, and effective education for children and lifelong learning for adults are key contributors to health and prosperity for individuals, and for the country.	Canadians with low literacy skills are more likely to be unemployed and poor, to suffer poorer health, and to die earlier than Canadians with high levels of literacy. In the 1996–1997 National Population Health Survey (NPHS), only 19% of respondents with less than a high-school education rated their health as "excellent" compared with 30% of university graduates.
Employment/ Working Conditions	Unemployment, underemployment, and stressful or unsafe work are associated with poorer health. People who have more control over their work circumstances and fewer stress-related demands of the job are healthier and often live longer than those in more stressful or riskier work and activities.	Between 1991 and 1995, the proportion of Canadian workers who were "very satisfied" with their work declined and was more pronounced among female workers, dropping from 58% to 49%. Women aged 20 to 24 were almost three times as likely to report high work stress than the average Canadian worker.

TABLE 9.1 Determinants that Influence Health, with Premises and Evidence Included *continued*

Key Determinant	Underlying Premises	Evidence
Social Environments	The importance of social support also extends to the broader community. Civic vitality refers to the strength of social networks within a community, region, province, or country. It is reflected in the institutions, organizations and informal giving practices that people create to share resources and build attachments with others. In addition, social stability, recognition of diversity, safety, good working relationships, and cohesive communities provide a supportive society that reduces or avoids many potential risks to good health.	Family violence has a devastating effect on the health of women and children in both the short and long terms. In 1996, family members were accused in 24% of all assaults against children; among very young children, the proportion was much higher. Women who were assaulted often suffer severe physical and psychological health problems, some are even killed. In 1997, 80% of victims of spousal homicide were women, and 19 women were killed by boyfriends or ex-boyfriends.
Physical Environments	At certain levels of exposure, contaminants in our air, water, food, and soil can cause a variety of adverse health effects, including cancer, birth defects, respiratory illness, and gastrointestinal ailments. In our built environment, factors related to housing, indoor air quality, and the design of communities and transportation systems can significantly influence our physical and psychological well-being.	The prevalence of childhood asthma has increased sharply over the last two decades, especially among the age group 0 to 5. It was estimated that some 13% of boys and 11% of girls aged 0 to 19 (more than 890,000 children and young people) suffered from asthma in 1996–1997. Air pollution, including exposure to second-hand smoke, has a significant association with health. A study in southern Ontario found a consistent link between hospital admissions for respiratory illness in the summer months and levels of sulphates and ozone in the air.
Personal Health Practices and Coping Skills	Refers to those actions by which individuals can prevent diseases and promote self-care, cope with challenges, develop self-reliance, solve problems, and make choices that enhance health. Definitions of *lifestyle* include not only individual choices but also the influence of social, economic, and environmental factors on the decisions people make about their health.	In Canada, smoking is estimated to be responsible for at least one-quarter of all deaths among adults between the ages of 35 and 84. Rates of smoking have increased substantially among adolescents and youth, particularly among young women. Diet, in general, and the consumption of fat, in particular, are linked to some of the major causes of death, including cancer and coronary heart disease. The proportion of overweight men and women in Canada increased steadily between 1985 and 1996–1997 (from 22% to 34% among men and from 14% to 23% among women).
Healthy Child Development	New evidence on the effects of early experiences on brain development, school readiness, and health in later life has sparked a growing consensus about early child development as a powerful determinant in its own right.	Experiences from conception to age six have the most important influence of any time in the life cycle on the connecting and sculpting of the brain's neurons. Positive stimulation early in life improves learning, behaviour, and health into adulthood.
Biology and Genetic Endowment	The basic biology and organic makeup of the human body are a fundamental determinant of health.	Genetic endowment

Source: Strategies for population Health: Investing in the Health of Canadians, Health Canada, 1994 © Reproduced with the permission of the Minister of Public Works and Government Services Canada, 2003.

CHAPTER HIGHLIGHTS

- Nurses need to clarify their understanding of health because their definitions of health largely determine the scope and nature of nursing practice.
- The perspective on health has changed; instead of the absence of disease, health has come to mean the fulfillment of one's maximum potential for physical, psychosocial, and spiritual functioning.
- Wellness is an active, five-dimensional process of becoming aware of and making choices toward a higher level of well-being. The five dimensions of wellness are physical, social, emotional, intellectual, and spiritual.
- Well-being is considered a subjective perception of balance, harmony, and vitality. It is a state, rather than a process.
- Because notions of health are highly individual, the nurse determines a client's perception of health in order to provide meaningful assistance. Nurses need to be aware of their own personal definitions of health.
- Most people describe health as freedom from symptoms of disease, the ability to be active, and a state of being in good spirits.
- Various models explain health. Smith's four models generally classify them as clinical, role performance, adaptive, and eudaimonistic.
- The health status of a person (individual, family, or community) is affected by many factors over which the person has varying degrees of control.
- Health belief and behaviour models have been developed to help determine whether an individual is likely to participate in disease prevention and health promotion activities. These models are Health Locus of Control (LOC) and Rosenstock's and Becker's Health Belief Models (HBM).
- Illness is usually associated with disease but sometimes occurs independently. Illness is a highly personal experience in which the person feels unhealthy or ill. Disease alters body functions and results in a reduction of capacities or a shortened lifespan.
- An individual's usual pattern of behaviour changes with hospitalization, which disrupts a person's privacy, autonomy, lifestyle, roles, and finances.
- Nurses know that the illness of one member of a family affects all other members.
- Nurses also know that various determinants significantly impact on the health of individuals, families, and communities.

READINGS AND REFERENCES

Suggested Readings

Butterfield, P. G. (1990). Thinking upstream: Nurturing a conceptual understanding of the societal context of health behavior. *Advances in Nursing Science, 12*(20), 1–8.

Labonte, R. (2000). Health promotion and the common good: Toward a politics of practice. In D. Callahan (Ed.), *Promoting healthy behavior: How much freedom? Whose responsibility?* (pp. 95–115). Washington, D.C.: Georgetown University Press.

Seedhouse, D. (1986). *Health: The foundations for achievement.* Chichester, NY: John Wiley & Sons.

Selected References

Anspaugh, D. J., Hamrick, M. H., & Rosata, F. D. (1991). *Wellness: Concepts and applications.* St. Louis: Mosby-Year Book.

Becker, M. (Ed.). (1974). *The health belief model and personal health behavior.* Thorofare, NJ: Charles B. Slack.

Becker, M. H., Haefner, D. P., Kasi, S. V., et al. (1977). Selected psychosocial models and correlates of individual health-related behaviours. *Medical Care, 15*, 27–46.

Blaxter, M. (1990). *Health and lifestyles.* New York: Routledge.

DiCicco, L., & Apple, D. (1960). Health needs and opinions of older adults. In D. Apple (Ed.), *Sociological studies of health and illness.* New York: McGraw-Hill.

Dubos, R. (1959). *Mirage of health.* Garden City, NY: Doubleday & Co.

Dubos, R. (1965). *Man adapting.* New Haven: Yale University Press.

Epp, J. (1986). *Achieving health for all: A framework for health promotion.* Ottawa: Health and Welfare Canada.

Evans, R., Barer, M., & Marmor, T. (Eds.). (1994). Why are some people healthy and others not? *The determinants of health of populations.* New York: Aldine De Gruyter.

Fawcett, J. (1995). *Analysis and evaluation of conceptual models of nursing.* Philadelphia, PA: F. A. Davis.

Federal, Provincial, and Territorial Advisory Committee on Population Health. (1994). *Strategies for population health: Investing in the health of Canadians.* Ottawa: Minister of Supply and Services Canada.

Federal, Provincial, and Territorial Advisory Committee on Population Health. (1999). *Toward a healthy future: Second report on the health of Canadians.* Ottawa: Minister of Public Works and Government Services Canada.

King, I. M. (1971). *Toward a theory for nursing: General concepts of human behavior.* New York: John Wiley & Sons.

King, I. M. (1981). *A theory for nursing: Systems, concepts, process.* New York: John Wiley & Sons.

King, I. M. (1992). King's theory of goal attainment. *Nursing Science Quarterly,* 7(1),19–26.

Labonte, R. (1993). *Health promotion and empowerment: Practice frameworks. Issues in health promotion, series 3.* Toronto: Centre for Health Promotion, University of Toronto and ParticipACTION.

Labonte, R. (1996). Community health promotion strategies. In Pan American Health Organization (WHO) *Health promotion: An anthology*. Washington, D.C.: Pan American Health Organization (Scientific Publication # 557).

Lalonde, M. (1974). *A new perspective on the health of Canadians*. Ottawa: Government of Canada.

Leavell, H. R., & Clark, E. G. (1965). *Preventive medicine for the doctor in his community* (3rd ed.). New York: McGraw-Hill.

Leddy, S., & Pepper, J. M. (1998). *Conceptual bases of professional practice* (4th ed.). Philadelphia, PA: Lippincott.

Mahler, H. (1977, November). *What is health for all?* Geneva, Switzerland: World Health Organization.

Maslow, A. (1954). Normality, health and values. *Main Currents, 10*, 75–81.

Maslow, A. (1962). Health as transcendence of the environment. *Journal of Humanistic Psychology, 2*, 1–7.

Maslow, A. (1962). *Toward a psychology of being*. Princeton, NJ: Van Nostrand.

Maslow, A. (1970). *Motivation and personality* (2nd ed.). New York: Harper & Row.

Nisbet, R. (1970). *The social bond*. New York: Alfred Knopf.

Pan American Health Organization, Regional Office of the World Health Organization. (2000, June). Fifth global conference on health promotion: Final report. *The fifth global conference on health promotion: Bridging the equity gap. Mexico City*. Washington, DC: Pan American Sanitary Bureau Regional Office of the World Health Organization.

Parsons, T. (1972). Definitions of health and illness in the light of American values and social structure. In E. Jaco (Ed.), *Patients, physicians and illness*. New York: Free Press.

Pender, N. J. (1996). *Health promotion in nursing practice* (3rd ed.). Norwalk, CT: Appleton & Lange.

Registered Nurses Association of British Columbia. (1990). New directions for health care. Vancouver: RNABC.

Rootman, I., & Raeburn, J. (1994). The concept of health. In A. Pederson, M. O'Neill, & I. Rootman (Eds.), *Health promotion in Canada: Provincial, national, & international perspectives*. Toronto: W. B. Saunders.

Rosenstock, I. M. (1974). Historical origins of the health belief model. In M. H. Becker (Ed.), *The health belief model and personal health behavior*. Thorofare, NJ: Charles B. Slack.

Roy, C., & Andrews, H. A. (1991). *The Roy adaptation model: The definitive statement*. Norwalk, CT: Appleton & Lange.

Smith, J. A. (1981). The idea of health: A philosophical inquiry. *Advances in Nursing Science, 3*(3), 43–50.

Travis, J.W., & Ryan, R. S. (1988). *Wellness workbook* (2nd ed.). Berkeley, CA: Ten Speed Press.

Twaddle, A. (1974). The concept of health status. *Social Science & Medicine, 9*, 29–38.

Wallston, K. A., Wallston, B. S., & DeVellis. R. (1978, Spring). Development of the Multidimensional Locus of Control (MHLC) scales. *Health Education Monograms, 6*, 164–165.

Webster's New Dictionary of Synonyms. (1978). Springfield, MA: G&C Merriam Co.

World Health Organization. (1947). *Constitution of the World Health Organization: Chronicle of the World Health Organization 1*. Geneva, Switzerland: Author.

World Health Organization (WHO), Health & Welfare Canada (HWC), & Canadian Public Health Association (CPHA). (1986). *Ottawa charter for health promotion*. Ottawa: Canadian Public Health Association.

Yura, H., & Walsh, M. (1978). *The Nursing Process*. N.Y.: Appleton Century Crofts.

WEBLINKS

The Canadian Health Network
www.canadian-health-network.ca
Funded by and in partnership with Health Canada, this Web site links to a wide range of complementary and alternative health information, including the Natural Health Products Directorate.

Canadian Association of Chiropractic
www.ccachiro.org
This site provides the general public with information on the role of chiropractic in the health-care system, including its history, training, and scientific research.

The Canadian Holistic Nurses Association
www.chna.ca
This site presents the philosophy and objectives of the Canadian Holistic Nurses Association (CHNA) and information on the levels of training for a Holistic Nursing Specialty.

Healing Touch Canada Inc.
www.healingtouchcanada.net
This site provides a listing of course offerings of Healing Touch Canada Inc., a practitioner roster by province, and an extensive recommended reading list.

Health Canada, Population Health Approach, Determinants of Health
www.hc-sc.gc.ca/hppb/phdd/determinants/e_determinants.html

The Integrative Health Institute
www.integrativehealth.ca
The Integrative Health Institute, Calgary, provides evidence-based integrative health education to the public and health professionals. Its services include library facilities, personalized health education, research activities, and workshops.

The Canadian Naturopathic Association
www.naturopathicassoc.ca
This site provides information on ethics, standards, and a roster of Naturopathic Doctors who are members of the Canadian Naturopathic Association.

The Canadian Reiki Association
www.reiki.ca
This site presents the Code of Ethics of the Canadian Reiki Association (CRA), describes educational standards, membership criteria, and provides a list of Registered Teachers.

The Tzu Chi Institute
www.tzu-chi.bc.ca
The Tzu Chi Institute, based in Vancouver, offers an integrated approach to health care by helping clients combine complementary and mainstream health practices. The Web site offers information on its clinical treatment programs, research activities, and education and information services.

CHAPTER 10

Health Promotion

OBJECTIVES

After completing this chapter, you will be able to:

- Differentiate health preventive or protective care from health promotion.
- Discuss essential components of health promotion.
- Examine initiatives of the Canadian government toward health promotion.
- Identify various types and sites of health-promotion programs.
- Discuss Pender's health-promotion model.
- Explain Labonte's concept of health promotion.
- Discuss Prochaska and DiClemente's five-stage model of behaviour change.
- Analyze the nurse's role in health promotion.
- Assess the health of individuals, families, groups, and communities.
- Develop, implement, and evaluate plans for health promotion.

Health promotion is an important component of nursing practice. It is a way of thinking that revolves around a philosophy of wholeness, wellness, and well-being. In the past two decades, the public has become increasingly aware of and interested in health promotion. Many people are aware of the relationship between lifestyle and illness and are developing health-promoting habits, such as getting adequate exercise, rest, and relaxation; maintaining good nutrition; and controlling the use of tobacco, alcohol, and other drugs.

The term "health promotion" has been used by practitioners of various disciplines, including nursing. Early nursing theorists identified "health," rather than "illness," as the goal of nursing practice. Thus, nursing intervention focused on promoting health. History indicates a long tradition of health promotion beginning with Nightingale and the early public health movements in Canada, exemplified in the works of the Victorian Order of Nurses (MacDonald, 2002).

The Canadian Initiative

Around the middle of the 1980s, a new and widely disseminated vision of health promotion emerged within Canada. The highlight was in 1986, when the first international conference on health promotion was held in Ottawa. From this conference, the Ottawa Charter for Health Promotion (WHO, 1986) was adopted. Canada was chosen for the conference, since at that time, it was seen as a forerunner in health promotion with the publication in 1974 of the widely respected Lalonde Report. In addition, at the end of the conference, another visionary document, *Achieving Health for All*, or the Epp Report (1986), was released.

The Lalonde Report is one of the founding documents in health promotion in Canada. The document outlined a conceptual framework for health (called the "Health Field Concept"), suggesting that health should be looked at in terms of a health-fields approach, comprising four main elements: human biology, environment, lifestyle, and health-care organization.

- *Human biology*: "Those aspects of health, both physical and mental, which are developed within the human body as a consequence of the basic biology of man and the organic makeup of the individual." It includes genetic makeup, the process of development and aging, and the internal organs of the body.
- *Environment*: "All those matters related to health which are external to the human body and over which the individual has little or no control."
- *Lifestyle*: "The aggregation of decisions by individuals which affect their health and over which they more or less have control ... Personal decisions and habits that are bad, from a health point of view, may create self-imposed risks."

Canadian Society Notes

Fact	Implications for Nursing Practice
A New Perspective on the Health of Canadians (1974), also known as the Lalonde Report, is often cited as the beginning of health promotion.	Nurses need to appreciate the history of health promotion in Canada so that they understand its current status.
A World Health Organization meeting in Canada in 1986 produced the Ottawa Charter for Health Promotion. The most important component of the Charter is a shift from treatment and prevention methods of health care to health promotion strategies that feature empowerment.	Nurses, in their intervention strategies, need to focus on health as a positive concept to help individuals and or groups realize their aspirations and satisfy their needs; and on the other hand, to change and or cope with the environment.
Achieving Health for All: A Framework for Health Promotion, developed under the direction of Jake Epp (1986), incorporated concepts from the Charter and becameCanada's blueprint for achieving the WHO goal of health for all by 2000.	There is a need to emphasize health promotion within nursing interventions. These interventions are to enhance people's experience of well-being. Health promotion interventions are actions taken to enhance one's quality of life, encompassing the whole person.
The Canada Health Act (1984) ensures accountability, portability, comprehensiveness, and universality of hospital and medical services.	Nurses play a role in ensuring that clients seeking care are treated fairly at all levels of the health-care system. Nurses ensure that clients receive cost-effective and efficient care.

- *Health-care organization*: "The quantity, quality, arrangement, nature, and relationships of people and resources in the provision of health care." Included in this element are health-care facilities and personnel. (LaLonde, 1994)

This innovative framework gave momentum to national and international initiatives in knowledge development, health promotion, health protection, and health care, which have contributed to both the health of Canadians and global health initiatives.

In 1974, a federal publication of the Lalonde report, entitled *A New Perspective on the Health of Canadians*, put forward the view that people's health was influenced by a broad range of factors: human biology, lifestyle, the organization of health care, and the social and physical environments in which people live. The *New Perspective* document put considerable emphasis on the importance of lifestyle as a contributing factor in the leading causes of death in Canada (heart disease, cancer, stroke, accidents). Although this report favourably impacted the health of Canadians, its usefulness was limited, as it failed to take into perspective the socioeconomic environment on health.

In response to this report, The World Health Organization (WHO) recommended at the Alma Ata conference in 1978 that the prerequisites for health go beyond medical and behavioural health determinants to include economic, social, psychological, and environmental responsibilities of communities. Further consideration by the Ottawa Charter for Health Promotion (WHO, 1986) led to the vision of *Health for All* by the year 2000, and all countries were urged to work toward the goal through means that best suited their situations.

In Canada, two studies, *National Health Survey (1977–1979)* and *Health Promotion Survey (1985)*, fostered a greater understanding of the role of poverty, unemployment, and pollution and their impact on health. These findings led to the development of Health and Welfare's discussion paper entitled *Achieving Health for All: A Framework for Health Promotion*, known as the Epp Report.

The Epp Report (1986), identified three major health challenges facing Canadians:

1. Disadvantaged groups have significantly lower life expectancy, poorer health, and a higher prevalence of disability than the average Canadian.
2. Various forms of preventable diseases and injuries continue to undermine the health and quality of life of many Canadians.
3. Many thousands of Canadians suffer from chronic disease, disability, or various forms of emotional stress, and lack adequate community support to help them cope and live meaningful, productive, and dignified lives.

To address these challenges, Epp proposed *The Framework for Health Promotion*, a model which connected the ideas and actions that the Canadian government regarded as essential to the achievement of health for all. Other elements of the framework are a set of health promotion mechanisms and a series of implementation strategies (Figure 10.1). Three mechanisms intrinsic to health promotion were identified:

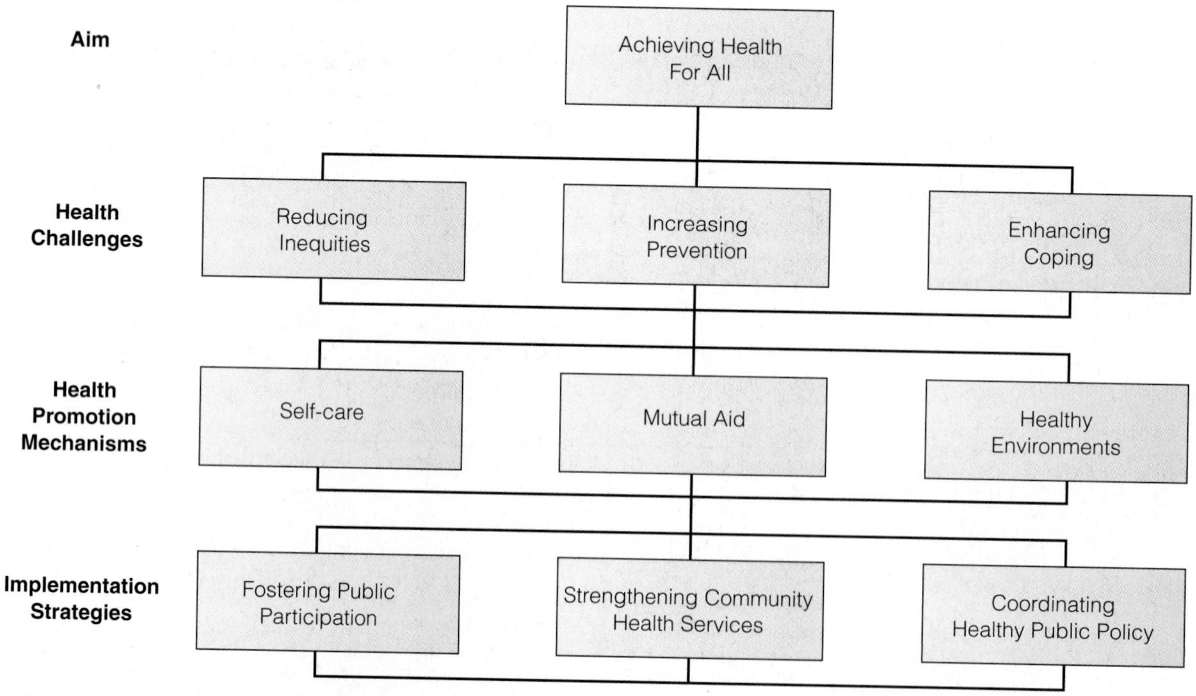

Figure 10.1 A framework for health promotion

Source: *Achieving Health for All: A Framework for Health Promotion*, Health Canada, 1986 © Reproduced with the permission of the Minister of Public Works and Government Services Canada, 2003.

1. Self-care, or the decisions and actions individuals take in the interest of their own health
2. Mutual aid, or the actions people take to help each other cope
3. Healthy environments, or the creation of conditions and surroundings conducive to health

The implementation strategies were:

- Fostering public participation
- Strengthening community health services
- Coordinating healthy public policy

Of particular importance is the emphasis on public participation, as nurses alone cannot address all the health needs of Canadians. The most important elements of these reports, beginning with the Ottawa Charter, is a shift from treatment and prevention methods of health care to a health promotion strategy that features empowerment. Labonte (1993) defines empowerment as the process "that describes the means through which internal feelings of powerlessness are transformed, and group actions initiated to change the physical and social living conditions that create or reinforce inequalities in power" (p. 101). This strategy opens possibilities for individual and or collective action on health-related concerns.

Defining Health Promotion

Health promotion is difficult to define. The term "health promotion" has often been used interchangeably with primary prevention, health protection, and illness prevention. This ambiguity contributes to considerable conceptual confusion. While it has been viewed that health promotion and disease prevention are complementary, it is important to note that the goal of health promotion has a broader focus. Health-promoting activities strive to increase one's state of health, whereas disease prevention strives to maintain the status quo (King, 1994).

Leavell and Clark (1965) define three levels of prevention: primary, secondary, and tertiary. Five steps describe these levels: **Primary prevention** focuses on (1) health promotion and (2) protection against specific health problems. **Secondary prevention** focuses on (1) early identification of health problems and (2) prompt intervention to alleviate health problems. **Tertiary prevention** focuses on restoration and rehabilitation to an optimal level of functioning. See Table 10.1 for examples of activities for each level of prevention.

Pender (1996, p. 7) considers health promotion to be distinct from primary prevention. She defines health promotion as "activities directed toward increasing the level of well-being," and primary prevention as "activities directed toward decreasing the probability of specific illnesses." In this instance, health promotion is considered to be an approach behaviour, whereas primary prevention is considered avoidance behaviour. Health promotion is not disease oriented; that is, no specific problem is being avoided. By contrast, primary prevention activities are geared toward avoiding specific problems (Pender, 1996).

Ronald Labonte (1993), a noted Canadian activist, defined health promotion as "any activity or program designed to improve social and environmental living conditions such that people's experience of well-being is increased" (p. 99). He identified five essential principles of community development that support health promotion: (1) empowering services (direct care is applied with dignity and cultural sensitivity), (2) connective processes (bringing people together into a sympathetic group working together for a common purpose), (3) organizational actions (groups organized to act as agents for change within community structures), (4) collaborative strategies (individuals, groups, and organizations work together), and (5) advocacy that challenges control.

The difficulty in separating the terms *health promotion*, *health prevention*, and *health protection* lies in the fact that an activity may be carried out for numerous reasons. For example, a 40-year-old male may begin a program of walking three miles each day. If the goal of his program is to "decrease the risk of heart disease," then the activity would be considered prevention. By contrast, if his walking regimen is instituted to "increase his overall health and feeling of well-being," then the activity would be considered health-promotion behaviour.

Health promotion can be offered to all clients regardless of their health, illness status, or age. For example, weight-control measures can benefit both overweight clients without disease and clients with cardiac or joint disease. Age-specific health-promotion activities are discussed in Chapters 19, 20, and 21. See the box below for examples of health-promotion topics for well or ill older adults.

Health-Promotion Topics for Older Adults

- Adequate sleep
- Appropriate use of alcohol
- Dental/oral health
- Drug management
- Exercise
- Foot health
- Health screening recommendations
- Hearing aid use
- Immunizations
- Medication instruction
- Nutrition
- Physical fitness
- Preventive health services
- Safety precautions
- Smoking cessation
- Weight control

TABLE 10.1 Levels of Prevention

Level and Description	Examples
Primary prevention Generalized health promotion and specific protection against disease. It precedes disease or dysfunction and is applied to generally healthy individuals or groups.	▪ Health education about accident and poisoning prevention, standards of nutrition and growth and development for each stage of life, exercise requirements, stress management, protection against occupational hazards, and so on ▪ Immunizations ▪ Risk assessments for specific disease ▪ Family planning services and marriage counselling ▪ Environmental sanitation and provision of adequate housing, recreation, and work conditions
Secondary prevention Emphasizes early detection of disease, prompt intervention, and health maintenance for individuals experiencing health problems. It includes prevention of complications and disabilities.	▪ Screening surveys and procedures of any type (e.g., Denver Developmental Screening Test, hypertension screening) ▪ Encouraging regular medical and dental checkups ▪ Teaching self-examination for breast and testicular cancers ▪ Assessing the growth and development of children ▪ Nursing assessments and care provided in home, hospital, or other agency to prevent complications (e.g., maintaining skin integrity; turning, positioning, and exercising clients; ensuring adequate rest, food, and fluid intake; promoting fecal and urinary elimination; administering medical therapies such as medications; and so on)
Tertiary prevention Begins after an illness, when a defect or disability is fixed, stabilized, or irreversible. Its focus is to help rehabilitate individuals and restore them to an optimum level of functioning within the constraints of the disability.	▪ Referring a client who has had a colostomy to a support group ▪ Teaching a client who has diabetes to identify and prevent complications ▪ Referring a client with a spinal cord injury to a rehabilitation centre to receive training that will maximize use of remaining abilities

Types of Health-Promotion Programs

A variety of programs can be used for the promotion of health, including (1) information dissemination, (2) health risk appraisal and wellness assessment, (3) lifestyle and behaviour changes, and (4) environmental control programs.

Information dissemination is the most basic type of health-promotion program. This method makes use of a variety of media to offer information to the public about the risk of particular lifestyle choices and personal behaviours, as well as the benefits of changing that behaviour and improving the quality of life. Billboards, posters, brochures, newspaper features, books, and health fairs all offer opportunities for the dissemination of health-promotion information. Alcohol and drug abuse, driving under the influence of alcohol, hypertension, and the need for immunizations are some of the topics frequently discussed. Since the 1980s, information about acquired immune deficiency syndrome (AIDS), including how it is transmitted, techniques for prevention, and the issue of sexual responsibility, has been disseminated. The intent is to reduce unjustified fear, correct misinformation, and educate the public about this disease. Information dissemination is a useful strategy for raising the level of knowledge and awareness of individuals and groups about health habits.

Health risk appraisal and *wellness assessment programs* are used to apprise individuals of the risk factors that are inherent in their lives in order to motivate them to reduce specific risks and develop positive health habits. Wellness assessment programs are focused on more positive methods of enhancement, in contrast to the risk-factor approach used in health appraisal. A variety of tools are available to facilitate these assessments. Some of these tools are computer based and can therefore be offered to educational institutions and industries at a reasonable cost.

Lifestyle and behaviour change programs require the participation of the individual and are geared toward enhancing the quality of life and extending the lifespan. Individuals generally consider lifestyle changes after they have been informed of the need to change their health behaviours and have become aware of the potential benefits of the process. Many programs are available to the public, both on group and individual bases, some of which address stress management, nutrition awareness, weight control, smoking cessation, and exercise.

Environmental control programs have been developed in response to the recent growth in the number of contaminants of human origin that have been introduced into our environment. The amounts of contaminants that are already present in the air, food, and water will affect the health of several future generations. The most common concerns of community groups are toxic and nuclear wastes, nuclear power plants, air and water pollution, and herbicide and pesticide spraying.

Sites for Health-Promotion Activities

Health-promotion programs are found in many settings. Programs and activities may be offered to individuals and families in the home or in the community setting and at schools, hospitals, or worksites. Some individuals may feel more comfortable having the nurse, diet counsellor, or fitness expert come to their home for teaching and follow up on individual needs. This type of program, however, is not cost effective for most individuals. Many people prefer the group approach, find it more motivating, and enjoy the socializing and group support. Most programs offered in the community are group oriented.

Community programs are frequently offered by cities and towns. The type of program depends on the current concerns and the expertise of the sponsoring department or group. Program offerings may include health promotion, specific protection, and screening for early detection of disease. Public health services may offer a townwide immunization program or blood pressure screening. The fire department may disseminate fire prevention information; the police department may offer a bicycle safety program for children or a safe-driving campaign for young adults.

Hospitals began the emphasis on health promotion and prevention by focusing on the health of their employees. Because of the stress involved in caring for the sick and the various shifts that nurses and other health-care workers must work, the lifestyles and health habits of health-care employees were given priority.

Programs offered by health-care organizations initially began with a specific focus on prevention. Examples include infection control, fire prevention and fire drills, limiting exposure to X-rays, and the prevention of back injuries. Gradually, issues related to the health and lifestyle of the employee were addressed with programs on such topics as smoking cessation, exercise and fitness, stress reduction, and time management. Increasingly, agencies have offered a variety of these programs and others (e.g., women's health) to the community as well as to their employees. Such community activities enhance the public image of the agency, increase the health of the surrounding population, and generate some additional income.

School health-promotion programs may serve as a foundation for children of all ages to gain basic knowledge about personal hygiene and issues in the health sciences. Because school is the focus of a child's life for so many years, the school provides a cost-effective and convenient setting for health-focused programs. The school nurse may teach programs about basic nutrition, dental care, activity and play, drug and alcohol abuse, domestic violence, child abuse, and issues related to sexuality and pregnancy. Classroom teachers may include health-related topics in their lesson plans, for example, the way the normal heart functions or the need for clean air and water in the environment.

Worksite programs for health promotion have developed out of the need for businesses to control the rising cost of health care and employee absenteeism. Many industries feel that both employers and employees can benefit from healthy lifestyles and behaviour. The convenience of the worksite setting makes these programs particularly attractive to many adults who would otherwise not be aware of them or motivated to attend them. Health-promotion programs may be held in the company cafeteria so that employees can watch a film or have a discussion group during their lunch break. Worksite programs may include programs that address air quality standards for the office, classroom, or plant; programs aimed at specific populations, such as accident prevention for the machine worker or back-saver programs for the individual involved in heavy lifting; programs to screen for high blood pressure; or health enhancement programs, for example, fitness information and relaxation techniques. Benefits to the worker may include an increased feeling of well-being, fitness, weight control, and decreased stress. Benefits to the employer may include an increase in employee motivation and productivity, an increase in employee morale, a decrease in absenteeism, and a lower rate of employee turnover, all of which may decrease business and health-care costs.

Pender's Health Promotion Model

Nola Pender's health promotion model (1996) is similar to Becker's health belief model (see discussion in Chapter 9). However, Pender's health promotion model focuses on *health-promoting* behaviours, rather than health-protecting or preventive behaviours (Figure 10.2). Determinants of health-promoting behaviours are categorized into (1) cognitive-perceptual factors, (2) modifying factors, and (3) cues to action.

Cognitive-Perceptual Factors

Cognitive-perceptual factors are considered to be the *primary motivational mechanisms* for acquiring and maintaining health-promoting behaviours. They include the following:

- *The importance of health.* Placing a high value on health results in information-seeking behaviour, such as reading health-related pamphlets.

RESEARCH NOTE

How Do Employees Who Participate in Worksite Wellness Programs Differ from Those Who Do Not?

This researcher examined select demographic characteristics (i.e., age, employment status, marital status, gender, race, and number of times of exercise per week) and lifestyle health behaviours of 200 individuals who belonged to a university wellness program and 200 individuals who did not belong. The mean age of the sample was 44.9 years with an age range from 22 to 70 years. All participants completed a demographic sheet and the Health Promotion Lifestyle Profile (HPLP), which focused on well-being, rather than illness prevention. The 48-statement HPLP instrument included six subscales: (1) self-actualization, (2) health responsibility, (3) exercise, (4) nutrition, (5) interpersonal support, and (6) stress management.

Study findings revealed that men used self-actualization and exercise behaviours more frequently than women. Women practised more health responsibility behaviours than men. Employees who were members of the wellness program more frequently practised health responsibility and exercise behaviours than nonmembers. Overall, wellness program members used a greater number of the total health-related behaviours than other employees. University employees who exercised on a regular basis had the most healthy lifestyles.

Implications: These findings support the establishment and maintenance of a wellness worksite program to assist employees in participating in exercise programs and practising other healthy lifestyle behaviours in their daily living.

Source: Worksite wellness programs and lifestyle behaviours, by J. L. O'Quinn. *Journal of Holistic Nursing* (1995, December) *13*(4), 346–360.

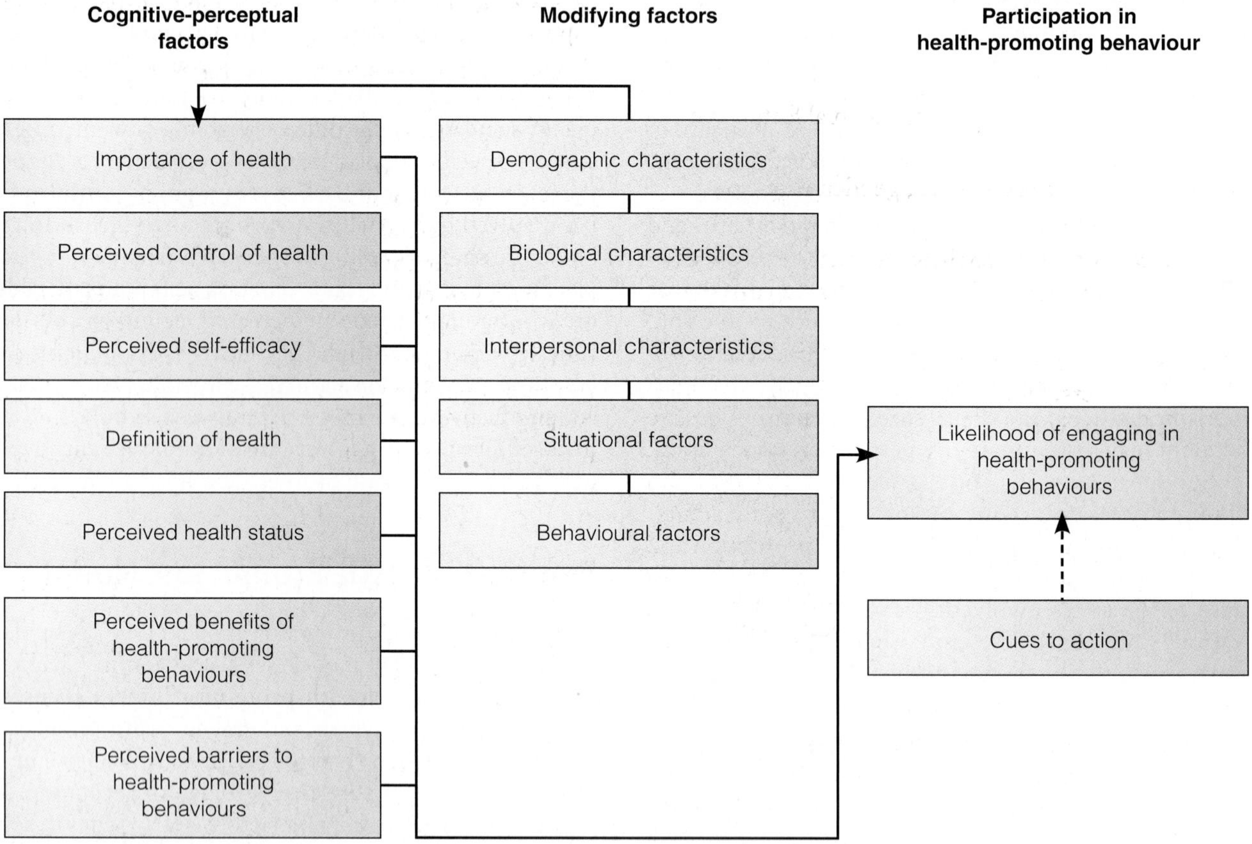

Figure 10.2 Health promotion model
Source: N. J. Pender. *Health Promotion in nursing* (3rd ed.) (1996). Norwalk, CT: Appleton & Lange, p. 52. Reprinted with permission.

- *Perceived control.* People who perceive that they have control over their own health are more likely to use preventive services than people who feel powerless. Control over health can relate to such behaviours as not smoking and using seat belts in automobiles.
- *Perceived self-efficacy.* This concept refers to the conviction that a person can successfully carry out the behaviour necessary to achieve a desired outcome, such as maintaining an exercise program to lose weight. Often, people who have serious doubts

about their capabilities decrease their efforts and give up, whereas those with a strong sense of efficacy exert greater effort to master problems or challenges.

- *Definition of health.* A person's definition of health may influence the extent to which the person engages in health-promoting behaviours.
- *Perceived health status.* Perceived health status may affect the frequency and intensity of health-promoting behaviours.
- *Perceived benefits of health-promoting behaviours.* Perceived benefits (e.g., physical fitness, psychological well-being, and stress reduction) affect the person's level of participation in health-promoting behaviours and may facilitate continued practice. Repetition of such behaviour itself can strengthen and reinforce beliefs about benefits.
- *Perceived barriers.* A person's perceptions about available time, access to facilities, and difficulty performing the activity may act as barriers (imagined or real) to health-promoting behaviours.

Modifying Factors

Factors that modify the cognitive-perceptual factors include the following:

- *Demographic factors,* such as age, gender, race, ethnicity, education, and income
- *Biological characteristics,* such as percentage of body fat and total body weight, which are related to exercise adherence
- *Interpersonal characteristics,* such as expectations of significant others, family patterns of health care, and interactions with health professionals
- *Situational factors,* such as easy access to healthy alternatives and availability of environmental options (e.g., vending machines and restaurant menus that provide healthful options)
- *Behavioural factors,* such as previous experience, knowledge, and skill in health-promoting actions

Cues to Action

The likelihood that a person will take health-promoting action may depend on (1) cues of *internal origin,* such as personal awareness of the potential for growth or increased feelings of well-being; and (2) cues of *external origin,* such as conversations with others about their health behaviour patterns and mass media information about personal and family health and environmental concerns.

Stages of Health Behaviour Change

Health behaviour change is a cyclic phenomenon in which people progress through several stages. In the first stage, individuals do not think seriously about changing a behaviour; by the time they reach the final stage, they are successfully maintaining the change in behaviour. Several behaviour change models have been proposed. The stage model proposed by Prochaska and DiClemente (1982, 1992) is discussed here. The stages are (1) precontemplation, (2) contemplation, (3) preparation, (4) action, and (5) maintenance. If the person does not succeed in changing behaviour, relapse occurs.

In the *precontemplation stage,* the person does not think about changing behaviour, nor is the person interested in information about the behaviour. The negative aspects of making the change outweigh the benefits. Some people may believe the behaviour is not under their control and may become defensive when confronted with information.

During the *contemplative stage,* the person seriously considers changing a specific behaviour, actively gathers information, and verbalizes plans to change the behaviour in the near future. Belief in the value of the change and self-confidence in the ability to change both increase in this phase. It is common for a person to feel some ambivalence when weighing the losses against the rewards of changing the behaviour. Some people may stay in the contemplative stage for months or years.

The *preparation stage* occurs when the person undertakes cognitive and behavioural activities in preparation for change. At this stage, the person believes that the advantages of changing the behaviour outweigh the disadvantages and makes specific plans to accomplish the change. Some people in this stage change small aspects of the behaviour, such as cutting out sugar in their coffee.

The *action stage* occurs when the person actively implements behavioural and cognitive strategies to interrupt previous behaviour patterns and adopt new ones. To prevent recurrences of previous behaviour, the action stage needs to continue for several weeks or months.

During the *maintenance stage,* the person integrates newly adopted behaviour patterns into the lifestyle. This stage lasts until the person no longer experiences temptation to return to previous unhealthy behaviours.

These five stages are cyclical; people generally move through one stage before progressing to the next. However, at any point, a person may regress to any previous stage. Sudden or gradual relapses to previous behaviour patterns may occur during the action or maintenance stages, for example. Individuals who relapse may return to the stage of precontemplation, contemplation, or preparation before their next attempt to change. To identify whether the client is in the precontemplative or contemplative stage, ask whether the client is thinking about changing a behaviour in the next six months or a year. Those in precontemplation will answer, no; those in contemplation or preparation will answer, yes.

The Nurse's Role in Health Promotion

Individuals and communities seeking to increase their responsibility for personal health and self-care require health education. The trend toward health promotion has created the opportunity for nurses to strengthen the profession's influence on health promotion, disseminate information that promotes an educated public, and assist individuals and communities to change longstanding health behaviours. Health-promotion activities involve collaborative relationships with both clients and health-care workers. The role of the nurse is to work *with* people, not *for* them—that is, to act as a facilitator of the process of assessing, evaluating, and understanding health. The nurse may act as advocate, consultant, teacher, or coordinator of services. For examples of the nurse's role in health promotion, see the box below.

In these roles, the nurse may work with individuals of all age groups and diverse family units or concentrate on a specific population, such as new parents, school-age children, or older adults. In any case, the nursing process is a basic tool for the nurse in a health-promotion role. Although the process is the same, the nurse emphasizes teaching the client (who can be either an individual, family, group, or community) self-care responsibility. Adult clients decide the goals, determine the health-promotion plans, and take the responsibility for the success of the plans.

The Nurse's Role in Health Promotion

- Model healthy lifestyle behaviours and attitudes.
- Facilitate client involvement in the assessment, implementation, and evaluation of health goals.
- Teach clients self-care strategies to enhance fitness, improve nutrition, manage stress, and enhance relationships.
- Assist individuals, families, and communities to increase their levels of health.
- Educate clients to be effective health-care consumers.
- Assist clients, families, and communities to develop and choose health-promoting options.
- Guide clients' development in effective problem solving and decision making.
- Reinforce clients' personal and family health-promoting behaviours.
- Advocate in the community for changes that promote a healthy environment.

The Nursing Process and Health Promotion

Assessing the Health of Individuals

A thorough assessment of the individual's health status is basic to health promotion. Components of this assessment are the health history and physical examination, physical fitness assessment, health risk appraisal, lifestyle assessment, health beliefs review, and life stress review. As nurses move toward greater autonomy in providing client care, expanded assessment skills are essential to provide the meaningful data needed for health planning.

Health History and Physical Examination

The health history and physical examination discussed in Chapter 27 provide a means for detecting any existing problems. The age of the individual must be considered when collecting data. For example, an environmental safety assessment and immunization history must be appropriate to the person's age. A nutritional assessment is an important part of the health history. The nurse must consider both age and body build of the client when gathering information on dietary patterns.

Lifestyle Assessment

Lifestyle assessment focuses on the personal lifestyle and habits of the client as they affect health. Categories of lifestyle generally assessed are physical activity, nutritional practices, stress management, and such habits as smoking, alcohol consumption, and drug use. Other categories may be included. The goals of lifestyle assessment tools are to provide:

1. An opportunity for clients to assess the impact of their present lifestyle on their health.
2. A basis for decisions related to desired behaviour and lifestyle change.

Several tools are available to assess lifestyle, ranging up to 100-item tools. A concise form for self-assessment of lifestyle is shown in Figure 10.3.

Health Risk Appraisal

A **health risk appraisal (HRA)** or **health hazard appraisal (HHA)** is an assessment and educational tool that indicates a client's risk for disease or injury over the next 10 years by comparing the client's risk with the mortality risk of the corresponding age, gender, and racial group. The client's health behaviour and demographic data are compared with behaviours of and data about a large national sample. The principle behind risk appraisal is that each person, as a member of a specific group, faces certain quantifiable health hazards and that average risks are applicable to a client if the health professional knows the client's characteristics and the mortality of a large group of cohorts with similar characteristics (Pender, 1996). The objectives of most HRAs are twofold:

Health-Style: A Self-Test

All of us want good health. But many of us do not know how to be as healthy as possible. Health experts now describe *life-style* as one of the most important factors affecting health. In fact, it is estimated that as many as seven of the ten leading causes of death could be reduced through common-sense changes in life-style. That's what this brief test, developed by the Public Health Service, is all about. Its purpose is simply to tell you how well you are doing to stay healthy. The behaviours covered in the test are recommended for most North Americans. Some of them may not apply to people with certain chronic diseases or disabilities, or to pregnant women. Such people may require special instructions from their physicians.

Cigarette Smoking

If you never smoke, enter a score of 10 for this section and go to the next section on *Alcohol and Drugs*.

	almost always	sometimes	almost never
1. I avoid smoking cigarettes.	2	1	0
2. I smoke only low tar and nicotine cigarettes *or* I smoke a pipe or cigars.	2	1	0

Smoking score: ______

Al[illegible]Drugs

	almost always	sometimes	almost never
1. I avo[illegible]holic beverages *or* I dri[illegible] one or two drinks a day[illegible]	4	1	0
2. I avoid using a[illegible] drugs (especially illegal [illegible] of handling stressful s[illegible] problems in my life.	2	1	0
3. I am careful not to drink a[illegible] taking certain medicines (for e[illegible] medicine for sleeping, pain, colds, [illegible] allergies), or when pregnant.	[illegible]	1	0
4. I read and follow the label directions when using prescribed and over-the-counter drugs.	[illegible]	[illegible]	0

Alcohol and drugs score: ______

Eating Habits

	almost always	sometimes	almost never
1. I eat a variety of foods each day, such as fruits and vegetables, whole grain breads and cereals, lean meats, dairy products, dry peas and beans, and nuts and seeds.	4	1	0
2. I limit the amount of fat, saturated fat, and cholesterol I eat (including fat on meats, eggs, butter, cream, shortenings, and organ meats such as liver).	2	1	0
3. I limit the amount of salt I eat by cooking with only small amounts, not adding salt at the table, and avoiding salty snacks.	2	1	0
4. I avoid eating too much sugar (especially frequent snacks of sticky candy or soft drinks).	2	1	0

Eating habits score: ______

Exercise and Fitness

	almost always	sometimes	almost never
1. I maintain a desired weight, avoiding overweight and underweight.	2	1	0
2. I do vigorous exercises for 15 to 30 minutes at least three times a week (examples include running, swimming, brisk walking).	3	1	0
3. I do exercises that enhance my muscle tone for 15 to 30 minutes at least three times a week (examples include yoga and calisthenics).	2	1	0
4. I use part of my leisure time participating in individual, family, or team activities that increase my level of fitness (such as gardening, bowling, golf, and baseball).	2	1	0

Exercise/fitness score: ______

Stress Control

	almost always	sometimes	almost never
1. I have a job or do other work that I enjoy.	2	1	0
2. I find it easy to relax and express my feelings freely.	2	1	0
3. I recognize early, and prepare for, events or situations likely to be stressful for me.	2	1	0
4. I have close friends, relatives, or others whom I can talk to about personal matters and call on for help when [illegible].	2	1	0
5. [illegible]te in group activities (such [illegible] community [illegible] hobbies that I enjoy.	2	1	0

[illegible] control score: ______

Safety

	almost always	sometimes	almost never
1. I wear a seat belt [illegible]ar.	2	1	0
2. I avoid driving while [illegible]ce of alcohol and other dru[illegible]	2	1	0
3. I obey traffic rules and the [illegible] when driving.	2	1	0
4. I am careful when using potentia[illegible] harmful products or substances (suc[illegible] as household cleaners, poisons, and electrical devices).	[illegible]	1	0
5. I avoid smoking in bed.	[illegible]	1	0

Safety score: ______

(continued)

Figure 10.3 Health-style: A self-test

Source: National Health Information Clearinghouse. P.O. Box 1133, Washington, DC 20013.

Health-Style: A Self-Test *(continued)*

What Your Scores Mean to You

Scores of 9 and 10
Excellent! Your answers show that you are aware of the importance of this area to your health. More important, you are putting your knowledge to work for you by practising good health habits. As long as you continue to do so, this area should not pose a serious health risk. It's likely that you are setting an example for your family and friends to follow. Because you got a very high test score on this part of the test, you may want to consider other areas where your scores indicate room for improvement.

Scores of 6 to 8
Your health practices in this area are good, but there is room for improvement. Look again at the items you answered with "Sometimes" or "Almost never." What changes can you make to improve your score? Even a small change can often help you achieve better health.

Scores of 3 to 5
Your health risks are showing! Would you like more information about the risks you are facing and about why it is important for you to change these behaviours? Perhaps you need help in deciding how to successfully make the changes you desire. In either case, help is available.

Scores of 0 to 2
Obviously, you were concerned enough about your health to take the test, but your answers show that you may be taking serious and unnecessary risks with your health. Perhaps you are unaware of the risks and what to do about them. You can easily get the information and help you need to improve, if you wish. The next step is up to you.

Where Do You Go from Here

Start by asking youself a few frank questions: *Am I really doing all I can to be as healthy as possible? What steps can I take to feel better? Am I willing to begin now?* If you scored low in one or more sections of the test, decide what changes you want to make for improvement. You might pick that aspect of your life-style where you feel you have the best chance for success and tackle that one first. Once you have improved your score there, go on to other areas.

If you already have tried to change your health habits (to stop smoking or exercise regularly, for example), don't be discouraged if you haven't yet succeeded. The difficulty you have encountered may be due to influences you've never really thought about—such as advertising—or to a lack of support and encouragement. Understanding these influences is an important step toward changing the way they affect you.

There's help available. In addition to personal actions you can take on your own, there are community programs and groups (such as the YMCA or the Canadian Heart and Stroke Foundation).

1. To assess risk factors that may lead to health problems: A **risk factor** is a phenomenon (e.g., age or lifestyle behaviour) that increases a person's chance of acquiring a specific disease, such as cancer. The concept of at-risk aggregate is increasingly being used in community nursing practice. An *at-risk aggregate* is a subgroup within the community or population that is at greater risk of illness or poor recovery.
2. To change health behaviours that place the client at risk of developing an illness

Many HRA instruments are available today. Recently, HRAs have begun to reflect a broader approach to health. The new focus is on the assessment of lifestyle factors and health behaviours. Risk factors may be categorized according to (1) age, (2) genetic factors, (3) biological characteristics, (4) personal health habits, (5) lifestyle, and (6) environment. Clients cannot control some of the risk factors appraised, such as age, gender, and family history; others, such as blood pressure, stress, and cigarette smoking, can be partially or totally controlled.

Health Care Beliefs

Clients' health care beliefs need to be clarified, particularly those beliefs that determine how they perceive control of their own health care status. Locus of control (see Chapter 9) is a measurable concept that can be used to predict which people are most likely to change their behaviours. Several instruments are available that assess perceptions of health control. Two instruments are the Multi-Dimensional Health Locus of Control (MHLC) instrument (Wallston, Wallston, & DeVellis, 1978) and the Health Self-Determination Index (HSDI) instrument (Cox, Cowell, Marion, & Miller, 1990). Assessment of clients' health care beliefs provides the nurse with an indication of how much the clients believe they can influence or control health through personal behaviours.

Life Stress Review

There is abundant literature about the impact of stress on mental and physical well-being. A variety of stress-related instruments have been found in the literature. For example, Holmes and Rahe (1967) developed a Life-Change Index, a tool that assigns numerical values to life events (e.g., divorce, pregnancy). Studies have shown that a high score is associated with an increased possibility of illness in an individual.

Validating Assessment Data

Following the collection of assessment data, the nurse and client need to review, validate, and summarize the information. This step is carried out jointly by the nurse and the client. During this process, the nurse verbally reviews the current practices and attitudes of the client. This allows validation of the information by the client and may increase awareness of the need to change behaviour. The nurse and client need to consider:

- Any existing health problems
- The client's perceived degree of control over health status
- Level of physical fitness and nutritional status
- Illnesses for which the client is at risk
- Current positive health practices
- Ability to handle stress
- Information needed to enhance health care practices

Diagnosing

Wellness nursing diagnoses, or *strength-oriented diagnoses,* can be applied at all levels of prevention but are particularly useful in primary-care settings, such as schools, industries, clinics, and community health facilities. When the nurse and client conclude that the client has positive function in a certain pattern area, such as adequate nutrition or effective coping, the nurse can use this information to help the client reach a higher level of functioning.

Nursing diagnoses accepted by NANDA (North American Nursing Diagnosis Association) have generally focused on altered health patterns or problems. However, some NANDA wellness diagnoses may be used for clients seeking a higher level of wellness. These include:

- Health-seeking behaviour (specify)
- Family coping: Potential for growth
- Effective breastfeeding
- Anticipatory grieving

The diagnosis of *health-seeking behaviour* needs to be specified (e.g., physical fitness). In lieu of these diagnoses, the nurse may write wellness diagnoses by using the words "potential for enhanced" followed by the wellness behaviour, as follows:

- Potential for enhanced nutritional status
- Potential for enhanced physical fitness
- Potential for enhanced family functioning
- Potential for enhanced coping patterns
- Potential for enhanced parenting skills
- Potential for enhanced use of safety precautions
- Potential for enhanced relationship with peers

Planning

Health-promotion plans need to be developed according to the needs, desires, and priorities of the client. The client decides on health-promotion goals, the activities or interventions to achieve those goals, the frequency and duration of the activities, and the method of evaluation. During the planning process, the nurse acts as a resource person, rather than as an adviser or counsellor. The nurse provides information when asked, emphasizes the importance of small steps to behavioural change, and reviews the client's goals and plans to make sure they are realistic, measurable, and acceptable to the client.

Steps in Planning

Pender (1996) outlines several steps in the process of planning health promotion, which are carried out jointly by the nurse and the client:

1. *Identify health care goals.* The client selects two or three top priority goals or areas of improvement. Common goals may include:
   - To reduce the risk of cardiovascular disease
   - To achieve or maintain a desired weight
   - To increase knowledge of safety practices in the home
2. *Identify behavioural or health outcomes.* For each of the selected goals or areas in step 1, determine what specific behavioural changes are needed to bring about the desired outcome. For example, to reduce the risk of cardiovascular disease, the client may need to change behaviours, such as stop smoking, lose weight, and increase activity level.
3. *Develop a behaviour change plan.* A constructive program of change is based on client "ownership" of the behaviour changed (Pender, 1996, p. 153). Clients may need to be assisted in examining value-behaviour inconsistencies and in selecting behavioural options that are most appealing and that they are most willing to try. The client's priorities will reflect personal values, activity preferences, and expectations for success.
4. *Reiterate benefits of change.* The benefits will probably need to be reiterated even though the client is committed

to the change. The health-related and non–health-related benefits should be kept before the client as central motivating factors.

5. *Address environmental and interpersonal facilitators and barriers to change.* Environmental and interpersonal factors that support positive change should be used to reinforce the client's efforts to change lifestyle. All people experience barriers, some of which can be anticipated and planned for, thereby making the change more likely to occur.
6. *Determine a time frame for implementation.* By developing a time frame, the appropriate knowledge and skills can be developed before a new behaviour is implemented. The time frame may be several weeks or months. Scheduling short-term goals and rewards can offer encouragement to achieve long-term objectives. Clients may need help to be realistic and to deal with one behaviour at a time.
7. *Make a commitment to goals of behaviour change.* In the past, commitments to changing behaviours have usually been verbal. Increasingly, a formal, written behavioural contract is being used to motivate the client to follow through with selected actions. Motivation to follow through is provided by a positive reinforcement or reward stated in the contract. Contracting is based on the belief that all people have the potential for growth and the right of self-determination, even though their choices may be different from the norm.

Exploring Available Resources

Another essential aspect of planning is identifying support resources available to the client. These may be community resources, such as a fitness program at a local gymnasium, or educational programs, such as stress management, breast self-examination, nutrition, smoking cessation, and health lectures. The nurse, too, may meet some of the client's educational needs. A major nursing role is to support and educate the client. The nurse can contact the client or be available at specified intervals to review the contract and to assist with problem solving.

Implementing

Implementing is the "doing" part of behaviour change. Self-responsibility is emphasized for implementing the plan. Depending on the client's needs, the nursing strategies may include supporting, teaching, consulting, coordinating, facilitating, counselling, and enhancing the behaviour change.

Providing and Facilitating Support

A vital component of lifestyle change is ongoing support that focuses on the desired behaviour change and is provided in a nonjudgmental manner. Support can be offered by the nurse on an individual basis or in a group setting. The nurse can also facilitate the development of support networks for the client, such as family members and friends.

Individual Counselling Sessions Counselling sessions may be routinely scheduled as part of the plan or may be provided if the client encounters difficulty in carrying out interventions or meets insurmountable barriers to change. In a counselling relationship, the nurse and client share ideas. In this sharing relationship, the nurse acts as a facilitator, promoting the client's decision making in regard to the health-promotion plan.

Telephone Counselling Regular telephone sessions may be provided to the client to help in answering questions, reviewing goals and strategies, and reinforcing progress. The client may find that scheduling a weekly telephone session is helpful or may wish to initiate a call if a problem occurs. The client is asked, "Is your plan working?" If the plan is not working, the nurse asks, "What would you like to do?" The client may wish to continue or may wish to change the plan to a more realistic one. Telephone support is efficient for the busy client who may not have the time for regular, in-person sessions.

Group Support Group sessions provide an opportunity for participants to learn the experiences of others in changing behaviour. Group contact gives individuals a renewed commitment to their goals. Groups can be scheduled at monthly or less frequent intervals for over a year.

Facilitating Social Support Social networks, such as family and friends, can facilitate or impede the efforts directed toward health promotion and prevention. The nurse's role is to assist the client to assess, modify, and develop the social support necessary to achieve the desired change. To provide the necessary support, families must communicate effectively, be aware of and support each other's needs and goals, and provide help and assistance to one another to achieve those goals. The client may wish the nurse to meet with the family or significant others and help enlist their understanding and support.

Providing Health Education

Health education programs on a variety of topics discussed earlier can be provided to groups, individuals, or communities. Group programs need to be planned carefully before they are implemented. The decision to establish a health-promotion program must be based on the health needs of the people; also, specific health-promotion goals must be set. After the program is implemented, outcomes must be evaluated.

FOCUS ON CRITICAL THINKING

Mrs. Chu is a 42-year-old professional whose father recently died following a prolonged illness from diabetes and hypertension. She voices concern that she will develop the same diseases and wants to make lifestyle changes to avoid that possibility. She admits to a 13-kilogram weight gain over the past two years, increased stress at work, and a fairly sedentary lifestyle. She considers herself healthy and is conscientious about her yearly physical and dental exams, breast self-examinations, and Pap smears. Last week, she began walking 30 minutes every day and purchased a book on low-fat cooking. Currently, her blood glucose levels and blood pressure are normal. She is seeking your assistance to determine if there are other things she can do to meet her goal.

1. On the basis of the limited data provided, speculate whether Mrs. Chu's activities represent health promotion, health prevention, or both.
2. What additional activities could you suggest to Mrs. Chu that are "health promoting?"
3. What evidence is there that Mrs. Chu will achieve and maintain the lifestyle changes she wants to make?
4. In what ways might you (the nurse) be able to assist Mrs. Chu?
5. Devise a plan to intervene with a client who is knowledgeable about the benefits of healthful behaviours and wants to make behavioural changes but has been unable to do so.

See Appendix A for answers to these questions.

Enhancing Behaviour Change

Whether people will make and maintain changes to improve health or prevent disease depends on many interrelated factors. See the section on assessing health care beliefs, earlier in this chapter. Murphy (1982) says that the distances between wanting to change, attempting to change, and being able to change can be enormous. She emphasizes this statement by pointing out the difficulty many people have in acquiring regular dental flossing habits.

To help clients succeed in implementing behaviour changes, the nurse needs to understand the process of change and the nature of the client's motivation or the client's current situation. An application of Lewin's stages of change (Lewin, 1951) can help the nurse recognize the client's needs. See Chapter 30 for additional information on Lewin's stages. Guidelines for assisting the client toward behaviour change are offered in the following box.

Modelling

Through observing a model, the client acquires ideas for behaviour and coping strategies for specific problems. The client is not expected to mimic the sequence of actions or behaviour patterns of the model. The nurse and client should mutually select models with whom the client can identify, since the cultural and ethnic backgrounds of the nurse and client often differ. Models should be frequently available during the early learning and change stages of unfreezing and moving. Models should also be people the client respects. Nurses should also serve as models of wellness. In order to model effectively, nurses need to have a philosophy and lifestyle that demonstrate good health habits.

Evaluating

Evaluation takes place on an ongoing basis, both during the attainment of short-term goals and after the completion of long-term goals. During evaluation, the client may decide to continue with the plan, reorder priorities, change strategies, or revise the health-promotion contract. Evaluation of the plan is a collaborative effort between the nurse and the client. Goals are written during the planning phase and a date determined for attaining the specific results or behaviours that are desired to promote health or prevent illness.

Assessing the Health of Families, Groups, and Communities

Clearly, there is a need for nurses to move beyond the individual level to the family, group, and community in assessing and promoting health. Nurses are at the forefront of influencing health promotion. Health promotion activities are possible within a wide range of facilities within Canadian communities that include homes, schools, work settings, religious centres, and public health agencies. The shift requires nurses to have knowledge of families, groups, and communities (see Chapters 6 and 16). Such a shift requires interdisciplinary collaboration.

CLINICAL GUIDELINES

Enhancing Behaviour Change

- Recognize that motivation is the basis of all behaviour, whether it is healthy or unhealthy, good or bad.
- Recognize that people are motivated by their needs.
- Avoid labelling people as unmotivated. The label simply means that the person does not comply with the wishes of the nurse who applies the label.
- Focus on the sources or factors that motivate the person's behaviour, rather than on the presence or absence of motivation.
- Remember that resistance is a normal part of change and a healthy response to a threat.
- Understand that a client may choose to keep unhealthy habits for many reasons.
  a. The habit may be a culturally learned response, such as cigarette smoking and alcohol consumption. In North America, these habits were once associated with a glamorous or sophisticated lifestyle and a certain kind of satisfaction.
  b. The client may be directing all available energies to meet other needs. A person who is grieving the loss of a loved one, or a recently divorced person, for example, may not have the energy to follow a weight-loss diet.
  c. The conditions required to change may be absent. For example, clients need help first to "unlearn" or "unfreeze" old habits and recognize the benefits of new habits before they can consider or undertake action.
- Cast aside the idea that the client *must* change. This attitude is not conducive to a helping relationship with the client and does not convey respect for the client. The client who does not change is entitled to the nurse's interest and nonjudgmental response.
- Measure your competence in terms of how well you understand clients' needs and implement clients' care, rather than by the extent to which clients change their behaviour.

Source: Adapted from M. M. Murphy. (1982). Why won't they shape up? Resistance to the promotion of health. *Canadian Journal of Public Health, 73,* 427–430.

CHAPTER HIGHLIGHTS

- The goal of health promotion is to raise the level of health of an individual, family, group, and community.
- Three key documents have influenced health promotion in Canada: Ottawa Charter for Health Promotion, the Lalonde Report, and *Achieving Health for All*, or the Epp Report.
- Health-promotion activities are directed toward developing client resources that maintain or enhance well-being. Health protection activities are geared toward preventing specific diseases, such as obtaining immunization to prevent poliomyelitis.
- A variety of programs can be used for health promotion, including (1) information dissemination, (2) health appraisal and wellness assessment, (3) lifestyle and behaviour change, and (4) environmental control programs. These programs are found in many settings—in the home, schools, community centres, hospitals, and worksites.
- Pender's (1996) health promotion model categorizes determinants of health-promoting behaviours as cognitive-perceptual factors, modifying factors, and variables affecting the likelihood of action. Cognitive-perceptual factors, the primary motivational factors, include the person's perception of the importance of health, perceived control, perceived self-efficacy, definition of health, perceived health status, perceived benefits of health-promoting behaviours, and perceived barriers. These factors may be modified by demographic factors, biological characteristics, interpersonal influences, situational factors, and behavioural factors. Cues to action may be of either internal origin or external origin.
- Prochaska and DiClemente (1982) propose a five-stage model for health behaviour change. The stages are (1) precontemplation, (2) contemplation, (3) preparation, (4) action, and (5) maintenance. If the person is not successful in changing behaviour, relapse may occur during the action or maintenance stages. However, at any point in these stages, people may move to any previous stage. An understanding of these stages enables the nurse to provide appropriate nursing interventions.
- Labonte (1993) advocated community development as a means of health promotion.

- The nurse's role in health promotion is to act as a facilitator of the process of assessing, evaluating, and understanding health.
- A complete and accurate assessment of the individual's health status is basic to health promotion. Wellness and lifestyle assessment tools give clients the opportunity to assess the impact of their present lifestyle behaviours on their health and to make decisions about specific lifestyle changes. Health risk or hazard appraisals provide the data that often spur the individual to adopt healthier life behaviours.
- Organizing assessment data from individual and family assessment enables the nurse to make wellness-oriented nursing diagnoses that identify client strengths, recognize self-care abilities, and enhance health-promotion goals.
- Health-promotion activities are directed toward developing the resources of the individual that maintain or enhance well-being.
- The nurse provides ongoing support and supplies additional information and education in order to help individuals change their lifestyles or health behaviours.
- During the evaluation phase of the health-promotion process, the nurse assists clients in determining whether they will continue with the plan, reorder priorities, or revise the plan.
- As role models for their clients, nurses should develop attitudes and behaviours that reflect healthy lifestyles.

READINGS AND REFERENCES

Suggested Readings

Camiletti, Y. A., & Marchuk, B. (1998). How men learn about health. *Canadian Nurse, 94*(1), 29–31.
Focus groups held with men to explore their views on health promotion activities and programs found that they wanted to learn more about health and suggested ways that this might be done. They also suggested that a macho image might prevent them from seeking information.

Dillon, D. L., & Sternas, K. (1997). Designing a successful health fair to promote individual, family, and community health. *Journal of Community Health Nursing, 14*(1), 1–14.
Dillon and Sternas discuss the steps in planning, implementing, and evaluating a health fair. A *health fair* is defined as a voluntary, community-based, cost-effective event used to detect health problems, identify risk factors, and provide educational information and supportive resources to promote healthy lifestyles of its participants. These authors present a list of topics for exhibits and a Health Fair Evaluation Questionnaire to use to measure outcomes of a health fair on participants' health beliefs and practices.

Landis, B. J., & Brykczynski, K. A. (1997). Employing prevention in practice. *American Journal of Nursing, 97*, 40–47.
This continuing education article incorporates a wide range of prevention efforts nurses can implement into their practice. The authors include in their discussion why prevention is so important, overcoming obstacles to prevention, setting priorities, mapping out strategies, developing protocols for delivering preventive services, and tailoring care to client's needs.

Pender, N. J. (1996). *Health-promotion in nursing practice* (3rd ed.). Norwalk, CT: Appleton & Lange.
Nola Pender has written extensively in the nursing and health-related literature about health-promotion issues. She developed a model for health-promoting behaviour (described in her book) that has been used as a theoretical framework for research studies. She discusses the nurse's role in the quest for health as well as nursing strategies for preventing illness and injury and promoting the health of individuals, families, and communities. Dr. Pender's leadership in health-promotion issues has enhanced the competence of nurses who are assisting clients in moving toward their maximum health potential.

Related Research

Choudhry, U. K. (1998). Health promotion among immigrant women from India living in Canada. *Image: Journal of Nursing Scholarship, 30*, 269–274.

Clark, M. B., & Olson, J. (2000). *Nursing within a faith community: Promoting health in times of transition*. Thousand Oaks, CA: Sage.

Epp, J. (1986). *Achieving health for all: A framework for health promotion*. Ottawa: Health and Welfare Canada.

Frye, B. A. (1995). Use of cultural themes in promoting health among Southeast Asian refugees. *American Journal of Health Promotion, 9*, 269–280.

Kilpatrick, D. (1999). A storefront approach to health promotion. *Canadian Nurse, 95*(7), 34–36.

King, P. (1994). Health promotion: The emerging frontier in nursing. *Journal of Advanced Nursing, 20*, 209–218.

Labonte, R. (1993). Health promotion and empowerment: Practice frameworks. *Issues in health promotion #3*. Toronto: University of Toronto/ParticipACTION.

MacDonald, M. (2002). Health promotion: Historical, philosophical, and theoretical perspectives. In L. Young & V. Hayes (Eds.), *Transforming health promotion practice: Concepts issues and applications*. Philadelphia, PA: F. A. Davis.

Stamler, L. L., Thomas, B., Lafreniere, K., & Charbonneau-Smith, R. (2001). Women's perceptions of breast cancer screening and educational opportunities in Canada. *Canadian Nurse, 97*(9), 23–27.

Stewart, M. J. (Ed.). (2000). *Community nursing: Promoting Canadians' health*. Toronto: W. B. Saunders.

Selected References

Byham, L. D., & Vickery, C. E. (1988, July/August). Compliance and health promotion. *Health Values, 12*(4), 5–12.

Conn, V. S. (1994, July). A stage-based approach to helping people change health behaviours. *Clinical Nurse Specialist, 8*, 187–193.

Cox, C. L., Cowell, J., Marion, L., & Miller, E. (1990, July/August). The health self-determination index for children. *Research in Nursing and Health, 13*(4), 237–246.

Health Canada. (1984). *Canada Health Act*, c.6, s.1.

Holmes, T. H., & Rahe, R. H. (1967, August). The social readjustment rating scale. *Journal of Psychosomatic Research, 11*, 213–218.

Lalonde, M. (1974). *A new perspective on the health of Canadians.* Ottawa: Government of Canada.

Leavell, H. R., & Clark, E. G. (1965). *Preventive medicine for the doctor in the community* (3rd ed.). New York: McGraw-Hill.

Lewin, K. (1948). *Field theory in social science.* New York: Harper and Row.

Murphy, M. M. (1982, November/December). Why don't they shape up? Resistance to the promotion of health. *Canadian Journal of Public Health, 73*, 427–430.

North American Nursing Diagnosis Association. (1999). *NANDA Nursing Diagnosis: Definitions and Classification 1999–2000.* Philadelphia, PA: Author.

O'Quinn, J. L. (1995). Worksite wellness programs and lifestyle behaviours. *Journal of Holistic Nursing, 13*, 346–350.

Pender, N. J. (1996). *Health promotion in nursing practice* (3rd ed.). Norwalk, CT: Appleton & Lange.

Prochaska, J., & DiClemente, C. (1982). Toward a more integrative model of change. *Psychotherapy: Theory, research, and practice, 19*, 276–288.

Wallston, K. A., Wallston, B. S., & DeVellis, R. (1978, Spring). Development of the Multi-dimensional Health Locus of Control (MHLC) scales. *Health Education Monographs, 6*, 164–165.

World Health Organization. (1984). *Report of the working group on the concept and principles of health promotion.* Copenhagen: Author.

World Health Organization. (1986). *Framework for health promotion training.* Copenhagen: Author.

WEBLINKS

Health Promotion Links
http://www.camacdonald.com/healthpromotion.htm
This Web site provides several links throughout Canada and the United States to reports, conference abstracts, research, and programs related to health promotion.

Canadian Fitness and Lifestyle Research Institute
http://www.cflri.ca/
The mission of the Canadian Fitness and Lifestyle Research Institute is to enhance the well-being of Canadians through research and communication of information about physically active lifestyles.

Health Canada, Population Health Approach, Determinants of Health
http://www.hc-sc.gc.ca/hppb/phdd/determinants/e-determinants.html
This site provides access to issues related to population health.

Health Canada—Health Promotion Online
http://www.hc-sc.gc.ca/hppb/hpo/
Health Promotion Online is a Web site providing many useful health professional resources and guides that will aid health-care professionals and community leaders.

CHAPTER 11

Holistic Healing Modalities

OBJECTIVES

After completing this chapter, you will be able to:

- Explain the concepts of holism and holistic nursing.
- Elucidate various healing modalities discussed within this chapter.
- Identify essential aspects of complementary medical therapies.
- Discuss nursing interventions related to the various healing modalities.
- Explain the role of the nurse as a healer.
- Identify the healing practices discussed within this chapter that you can add to your life.
- Analyze the attitudes and behaviours that nurses need in order to assist clients with the various healing modalities.

Today, many people are pursuing alternative methods of health care. Nurses therefore have an opportunity to play a major role in providing healing interventions that complement Western medical therapies.

Nurses have always been concerned with the client as a whole, and they are increasingly embracing the practice of holistic healing. Nurses are learning how to become "healing" nurses and seeing themselves as "healers." They are incorporating into their practice such healing techniques as massage, imagery, meditation, acupressure, art and music therapy, breathing exercises, biofeedback, reflexology, tai chi exercises, therapeutic touch, prayer, humour, and others.

Keegan (1994) contends that nursing centres will be primary sites for future health-care delivery. These will become healing centres staffed by nurses who view illness as an opportunity for growth for the patient. These centres will house modern technological equipment such as biofeedback devices, flotation tanks, light and colour therapy units, and quadraphonic sound relaxation units. Holistic health care centres will emerge to help clients seek alternative healthy, self-fulfilling behaviours and mobilize inner healing capacities.

Most provincial nursing associations have developed position statements on the provision of holistic therapies by nurses in agencies or as independent practitioners.

Concepts of Holism and Holistic Nursing

The term **holism** was coined by Jan Smuts, a South African statesman, in his book *Holism and Evolution* (1926). Smuts theorized that nature tends to bring things together to form whole organisms and that the determining factors in nature and evolution are wholes, not their constituent parts. The concept attracted further interest in the 1940s and 1950s, when Dunbar (1945), a pioneer in psychosomatic medicine, published studies that related stress and personality type to physical illness, and Hans Selye (1956) published his theory about the psycho-physiology of stress. Nurse theorist Martha Rogers (1970) introduced her philosophy in the work *Science of Unitary Human Beings*, a landmark work that set the stage for such holistic nursing theories as those of Parse (1995), Newman (1994), and Watson (1999). These nursing theories are discussed in Chapter 4.

In these holistic or unitary theories, all living organisms are seen as interacting, unified wholes that are more than the mere sum of their parts. Viewed in this light, any disturbance in one part is a disturbance of the whole system; in other words, the disturbance affects the whole being. Thus, the nurse must keep the whole person in mind when assessing one part of an individual and consider how that part relates to all others. The nurse must also consider how the individual interacts with and relates to the external environment and to others.

A *holistic health belief view* holds that the forces of nature must be maintained in balance or harmony. Human life is one aspect of nature that must be in harmony with the rest of nature. When the natural balance or harmony is disturbed, illness may result. **Holistic health,** then, involves the total person: the whole of the person's being and the overall quality of life. **Holistic health care** considers all the components of health: health promotion, health maintenance, health education and illness prevention, and restorative-rehabilitative care. All these components are equally important when identifying a client's needs, planning and implementing care, and evaluating the results.

Holistic nursing is described by the Canadian Holistic Nurses Association as nursing practice that uses noninvasive modalities and strategies to promote health and wellness. Holistic nurses believe in the body's inherent ability to heal and to achieve internal balance in harmony with the environment. They recognize and emphasize the integrating nature (bio-psycho-social-spiritual) of each person and incorporate therapies that provide support for health promotion, disease prevention, and illness states. Therapies offered by holistic nurses are considered complementary to conventional medical treatment plans.

Holistic health practitioners focus on *whole-brain thinking*, a blending of linear thought processes regulated by the left hemisphere of the brain and intuitive thought processes regulated by the right hemisphere. The left brain has consistently been referred to as the dominant hemisphere and valued by Western medicine because it regulates reason, logic, and verbal, mathematical, and calculative aspects of thinking. Intuitive processes, or right-brain functions, regulate creativity, artistry, poetry, and "knowing-without-knowing-why" aspects of cognition (Keegan, 1994, p. 218). Examples of beliefs underlying holistic practice are shown in the box on the following page.

It must be kept in mind that some clients do not endorse the practices based on the holistic paradigm. This calls for a careful assessment of the client's perspective before initiating any complementary therapy.

Concepts of Healing

Until recently, the idea of curing, rather than healing, has dominated the Western mode of health care, with emphasis on technology, power, analysis, and the repair of damaged parts. Curing also implies that the person who offers the cure is active, whereas the person who receives the cure is passive. Healing, on the other hand, requires that both the healer and the person receiving the healing work in partnership toward inner and outer harmony and balance.

Dossey's Eras of Medicine

The concept of healing has broadened dramatically in the 20th century. Dr. Larry Dossey, prolific author and editor of

Beliefs Underlying Holistic Practice

- The mind, body, and spirit are interdependent. They share one consciousness.
- The human spirit is the core of the person.
- A person's attitude and beliefs toward life are major etiological factors in health and disease.
- The self is empowered with the ability to create or maintain health or disease.
- Human beings are energy fields. These energy fields can become unbalanced in response to stress in any of the three domains: body, mind, and spirit.
- Each individual is an open system with the environment.
- Health means feeling whole with regard to body, mind, and spirit.
- Spiritual health is essential for physical, mental, and emotional well-being.
- Wellness is increasing openness (acceptance of diversity) and increasing harmony (coherent energy fields).
- Changes in health occur through experiential learning—learning that occurs as a result of living through an activity, situation, or event.
- Health involves a transformational change that encompasses the whole person.
- The client-practitioner relationship is a partnership, although the responsibilities of each partner may differ.

Source: Adapted from *The Nurse as healer* by L. Keegan, 1994, Albany, NY: Delmar, p. 211–212; and *Caring as healing: Renewal through hope* by D. A. Gaut and A. Boykin (Eds.), 1994, New York: National League for Nursing Press, Pub. no. 14-2607, p. 16–17.

the journal *Alternative Therapies in Health and Medicine*, categorizes three different eras of medicine according to their approach to health, illness, and healing (Dossey, 1999).

Era I refers to "physical medicine," which originated in the late 1860s and remains influential and effective even today. It focuses on the effects of "things" on the body and includes Western medical therapies, such as drugs, surgery, radiation, and so on. Era I is guided by classical laws of matter and energy; the universe and body are viewed as vast clocklike mechanisms that function according to causal, deterministic principles.

Era II refers to "mind-body" medicine, which arose in the mid-1950s and is still developing. Dossey marks the mid-1950s as the beginning of Era II medicine because it was then that mind-body approaches first began to spark attention among researchers. Perceptions, thoughts, emotions, attitudes, and images were found to affect the body profoundly and gained recognition as being therapeutic and important to healing. Mind-body therapies focus on helping individuals use their minds to heal their own bodies and include relaxation techniques, most types of imagery therapies, biofeedback, hypnosis, and counselling.

Era III refers to "nonlocal" or "transpersonal" medicine. Dossey differentiates Era III therapies from Era II therapies as follows: Era I and Era II therapies are "local" in emphasis. They adhere to a classical time-space framework in which the mind is seen as localized to points in *space* (that is, the brain) and *time* (the present moment). In contrast, Era III medicine does not regard the "mind" or "consciousness" as localized within the individual brain and confined to the present moment; rather, it claims that the mind can escape the confines of the body and the present moment and can move through time and space. Thus, Era III medicine involves mind-to-mind connection: the mind is seen as a factor that can effect healing *between* persons, regardless of the distance between them. Era III therapies always involve a sender (healer) and a receiver (person being healed). Therapies include noncontact therapeutic touch, intercessory prayer, transpersonal imagery, some types of shamanic healing, and all forms of distant healing. Noncontact therapeutic touch and intercessory prayer are discussed later in this chapter. Era III healing practices are not separate from those of Era I and Era II but are integrated with them.

Bodymind Healing

Barbara Dossey and colleagues use the term *bodymind* to refer to a state of integration that includes body, mind, and spirit (Dossey et al., 1995). The limbic-hypothalamic system, located within the brain and biochemically interconnected with all other parts of the body, is the primary connecting link between body and mind. Questions arise as to where the mind is located. Traditionally, the mind was believed to be located within the anatomic structure of the brain; Dossey and colleagues propose, however, that memories, thoughts, and behaviour processes are stored throughout the body (Dossey et al., 1995).

Theoretical bases for bodymind healing are complex; they include, but are not limited to, information transduction and mind modulation of the autonomic, endocrine, immune, and neuropeptide systems (Dossey et al., 1995).

Information transduction is the conversion or transformation of information or energy from one form to another. The mind is seen as nature's way of receiving, generating, and transducing information. Information (an idea or event) that is novel—challenging, intriguing, or mysterious—has the highest information value. Such information evokes changes in the body and mind that prompt neural pathways and consciousness to connect to bring about information transduction. Two examples of transduction are the use of relaxation techniques and imagery. Relaxation techniques can effect decreases in blood pressure, heart rate, respiratory rate, and pain. Imagery transforms images or ideas into an act of relaxation and physiological healing.

Mind modulation refers to the process by which the brain converts *neural messages* (thoughts, attitudes, feelings, and emotions) into neurohormonal *messenger molecules* and communicates them to all body systems that evoke states of health or illness (Dossey et al., 1995). The mind modulates cellular biochemical activities within all major organ systems, that is, the autonomic nervous system, endocrine system, immune system, and the neuropeptide system. All these systems are closely related; none is separate from the other. Activity of any one of these systems can modulate the activity of the other systems.

Mind modulation through the autonomic nervous system is used in holistic therapies, such as relaxation, imagery, meditation, and music therapy. These therapies encourage bodymind healing by decreasing a person's sympathetic response to stress, thus enabling the calming effect of the parasympathetic system to dominate (see the box below).

Mind modulation via the *immune system* involves receptor sites on the surface of T and B lymphocytes that are able to activate, direct, and modify immune function. Research has revealed a direct correlation among relaxation, imagery, and the function of the immune system.

Neuropeptides, amino acid messenger molecules with receptor sites on cells in tissues throughout the body, are another key to understanding our inseparable bodymind system. This unified neuropeptide-receptor system, or "psychosomatic network," is associated with emotional processing; transmitting messages across organs, tissues, and into the cells. Our biological system (body) is therefore flooded by our cognitions and our emotions (mind). Pert (1998) suggests that bodymind interventions that facilitate emotional expression can result in improved immune function and/or physiological healing.

Healing Modalities

To become effective holistic nursing practitioners or nurse healers, nurses need to develop certain attitudes and behaviours. Awareness of and development of one's own holism are important parts of integrating holism into clinical practice.

To facilitate the process of healing in others, nurses need to become conscious of the healers within themselves, that is, practice personal care. Nurses themselves do not create changes in others; they participate in the process. It is the person receiving the treatment or healing modality, be it medication, surgery, or "alternative" treatment, who does the healing. Nurses as healers, therefore, have a twofold responsibility: (1) to understand a bio-psycho-social-spiritual approach to care that facilitates a client's growth toward wholeness of mind, body, and spirit; and (2) to care for themselves to reveal the healers within (Wells-Federman, 1996). The box on the following page lists methods nurses can use to foster their personal health and well-being.

Nurses use many healing modalities to enhance healing of self and others. These include various touch therapies, mind-body therapies, aromatherapy, and transpersonal therapies. Nurses need specialized education to perform many of these therapies. Regardless of the strategy, the nurse's healing intention and genuine concern for the one to be healed are key factors.

Effects of the Autonomic Nervous System

Parasympathetic Branch (Relaxation)	Sympathetic Branch (Activation)
Decreased pupil size	Increased pupil size
Decreased lacrimal secretion	Increased lacrimal gland secretion
Increased salivary flow	Decreased salivary flow
Decreased heart rate	Increased heart rate
Vasodilation	Vasoconstriction
Bronchoconstriction	Bronchodilation
Increased gastric motility and secretion	Decreased gastric motility and secretion
Increased pancreatic secretion	Decreased pancreatic secretion
	Increased adrenal secretions (epinephrine and cortisol)*
Increased intestinal motility	Decreased intestinal motility

*Increased adrenal secretions bring about the fight-or-flight response and/or the general adaptation syndrome.

Self-Healing Methods for Nurses

- *Clarify values and beliefs.* Identify those things that are important, meaningful, and valuable to you, and assess whether your actions are consistent with your beliefs. For example, do you value time spent with your children and time reading or listening to music?
- *Set realistic goals.* Identify long-term goals, and then the short-term goals that will help you meet the long-term goals. For example, a long-term goal might be to experience an increase in emotional and physical comfort and a short-term goal to take a 30-minute walk each evening.
- *Challenge the belief that others always come first.* Overinvolvement with clients leads to overwork and overly solicitous helping that neglects the client's responsibilities, autonomy, and resources. It leaves little time for fulfillment of personal needs. Identify behaviours that indicate overinvolvement, such as saying "yes" much too often, a tendency to avoid conflict whenever possible, feeling selfish when not responding to someone else's needs, and always listening to others who need emotional support but seldom asking anyone to pay attention to your emotional needs. Assess whether you need to adjust your perspective and behaviour. Learn to ask for what you need; acknowledge that you are doing the best you can; and affirm that you can meet your own needs as well as care for others.
- *Learn to manage stress.* Stress management requires the following:
  1. Acknowledge the mind-body connection, that is, the relationship among thoughts, feelings, behaviours, and the physiological response to stress.
  2. Monitor stress warning signals and invoke the relaxation response on a regular basis, such as once a day for 20 minutes or twice a day for 10 minutes. "Mini-relaxations" (e.g., taking several deep breaths and thinking about something pleasant, such as your pet) throughout the day can also be used to counter the tension and anxiety associated with stress.
  3. Develop the skill of *personal presence* (physically "being there" and psychologically "being with" a client or other person). To be available to others in this way requires practising the skill of being present to yourself. Avoid allowing yourself to be hurried, distracted, or fragmented. Focus full attention on the activity you are doing at the moment.
- *Maintain and enhance physical health.* Eat healthy, balanced meals; exercise regularly; and obtain adequate rest.
- *Develop a support network.* Fellow nurses can often provide perspectives and insights to help cope with commonly shared experiences.

Source: Adapted from "Awakening the healer within" by C. L. Wells-Federman. 1996. *Holistic Nursing Practice, 10,* 13–29.

Touch Therapies

Healing through touch goes back to early civilization. One of the earliest written documents on this subject originated in Asia 5,000 years ago. Also, Hippocrates wrote about the effects of therapeutic massage and manipulation when Greek civilization was at its height. Although most cultures have developed some type of touch therapy, attitudes toward touch vary widely from culture to culture.

Touch rituals involve various parts of the body, and touch is an important part of healing. One possible explanation is that touch stimulates the production of certain chemicals in the immune system that promote healing.

There are a number of touch therapies. Three of the most common are therapeutic massage, foot reflexology, and acupressure. For nurses to become skilled in these therapies, special courses of study are required.

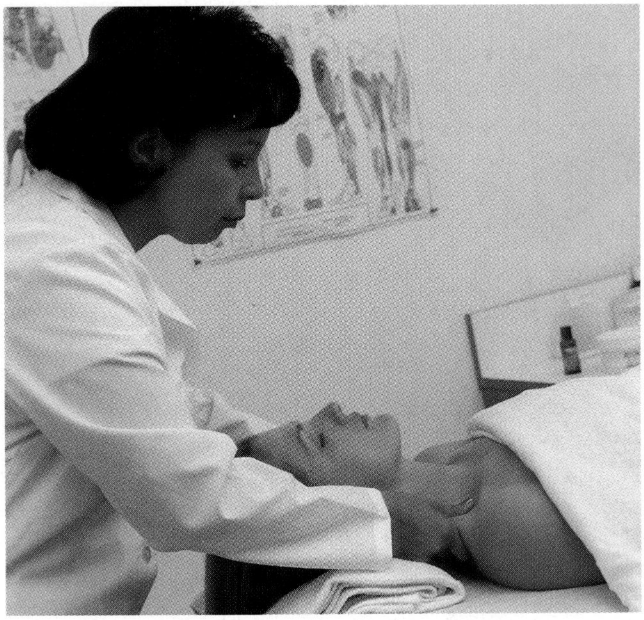

Figure 11.1 Touch is an importat part of healing

Therapeutic Massage

Over the centuries, nurses have provided back massage. It was thought to improve the circulation of the blood and assist in relaxation. More recently, the benefits have been more precisely identified and categorized as physical, mental-emotional, and spiritual.

Physically, massage relaxes muscles and releases the build-up of lactic acid that accumulates during exercise. It can also improve the flow of blood and lymph, stretch joints, and relieve pain and congestion. Massage is thought to release body toxins and stimulate the immune system, thereby helping the body combat disease (Horrigan, 1995).

In the mental-emotional area, massage can relieve anxiety and provide a sense of relaxation and well-being. Spiritually, it provides a sense of harmony and balance (Horrigan, 1995). The individuals receiving a massage may enter a meditative state, thus relaxing their minds and expanding their awareness.

A variety of massage strokes or movements may be used singly or in combination, depending on the outcome desired. These include **effleurage** (stroking), friction, pressure, and **petrissage** (kneading, or large, quick pinches of the skin, subcutaneous tissue, and muscle).

Reflexology

Reflexology, or zone therapy, can trace its origins to ancient times. Reflexology was introduced to the West in the early 1900s by William Fitzgerald, an American physician. His theory was that there are 10 equal longitudinal zones that run the length of the body from the top of the head to the tips of the toes and five closely associated zones on each arm (Lynn, 1996). Each great toe is the start of a line that runs up the medial aspect of the body through the centre of the face ending at the top of the head. Each zone (five on each side of the body) has a reflex area on the hand and the foot. Blockages in any part of the zone can affect the entire zone.

Reflexology is based on the principle that the hands and feet are mirrors of the body and that they have reflex points which correspond to each of the body's glands, structures, and organs. See Figure 11.2. Following assessment for areas of tenderness or sensitivity on the foot or hand, finger-thumb pressure is applied in a circular motion to release tension in the corresponding organs in that zone. This is thought to improve blood supply and promote overall relaxation (Mackey, 2001).

In the 1930s, Eunice Ingham expanded and refined Fitzgerald's work, mapping specific reflex zones on the feet, hands, and ears. At this time, limited research exists to validate the theory of the healing properties of reflexology. However, the effects of reflexology have been examined in various settings and for various conditions—from the relief of headaches and postoperative pain to the promotion of lactation in new mothers and quality of life in terminal illness. Although reflexology is a relatively safe procedure, experienced reflexologists need to be consulted when there are circulatory disorders of the extremities.

Acupressure

Acupressure is a form of healing in which the therapist exerts finger pressure on specific sites. According to the theory that underlies acupressure, 657 designated points can be massaged. These points are similar to those used in acupuncture and shiatsu massage. The points run along 12

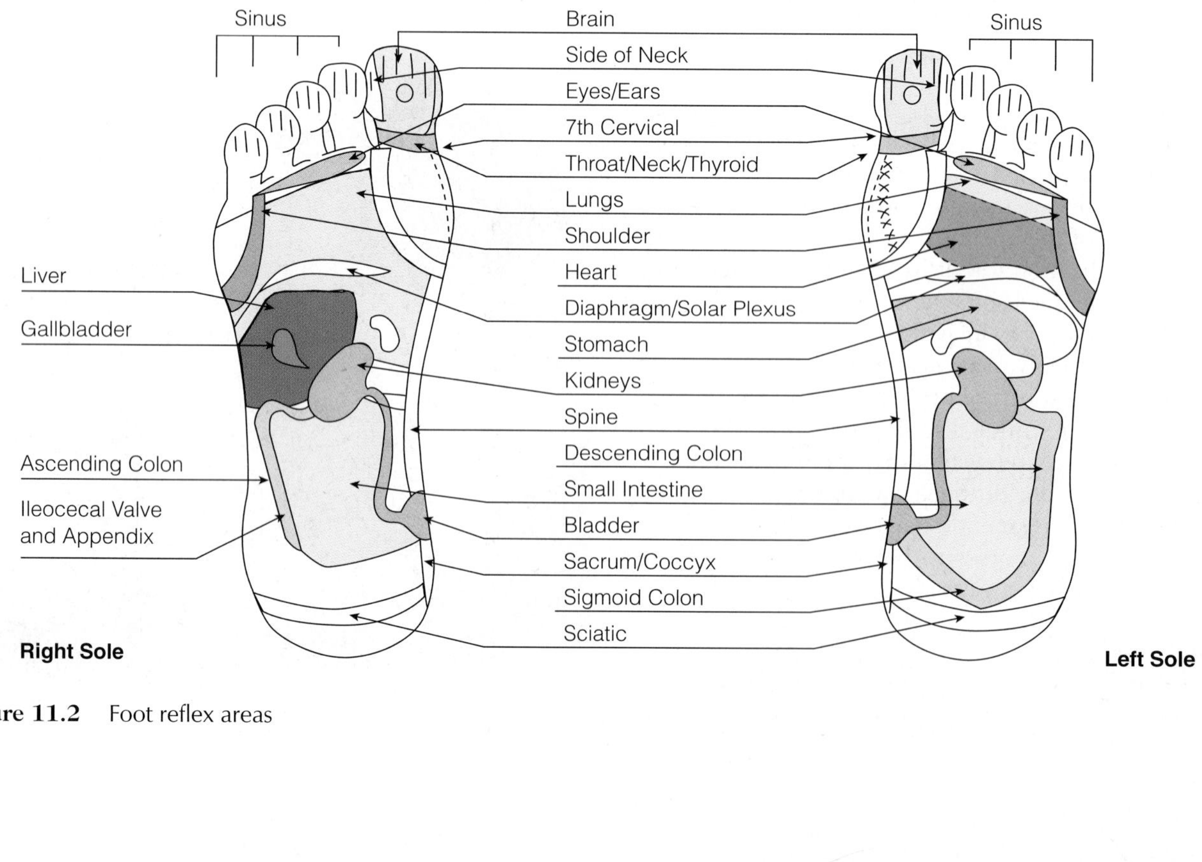

Figure 11.2 Foot reflex areas

pathways, or meridians, that connect the points on each half of the body. The application of finger or thumb pressure is thought to restore balance in the flow of energy (*Ki*), and when energy can flow freely, the body can heal itself.

Acupressure is used to both diagnose and treat ailments. With the application of acupressure, the body is theoretically kept in harmony, thus terminating many minor ailments and preventing them from becoming major diseases.

In shiatsu, pressure is applied to the same spots using the points of the thumbs and fingers and also the heel of the hand. Shiatsu's main purpose is to maintain health, rather than treat illness.

Mind-Body Therapies

In mind-body therapies, individuals use their minds to heal their bodies. These therapies include progressive relaxation, biofeedback, imagery, yoga, meditation, prayer, music therapy, humour and laughter, and hypnosis.

Progressive Relaxation

Relaxation techniques have been used extensively to reduce high levels of stress and chronic pain. Using relaxation techniques enables the client to exert control over the body's responses to tension and anxiety. For many years, nurses on maternity units have encouraged women in labour to relax and breathe rhythmically.

Progressive relaxation requires that the client (1) tense and then relax successive muscle groups, and (2) focus attention on discriminating between the feelings experienced when the muscle group is relaxed and when it was tense. Jacobsen (1938), the originator of the progressive relaxation technique, found that tensing a muscle group before relaxing it actually achieves a greater degree of relaxation than simply commanding oneself to relax. This technique can result in decreased body oxygen consumption, metabolism, respiratory rate, cardiac rate, muscle tension, and systolic and diastolic blood pressures.

Three requisites to relaxation are correct posture, a mind at rest, and a quiet environment. The client must be positioned comfortably, with all body parts supported, joints slightly flexed, and no strain or pull on muscles (e.g., arms and legs should not be crossed). To rest the mind, the client is asked to gaze slowly around the room (e.g., across the ceiling, down the wall, along a window curtain, around the fabric pattern, and back up the wall). This exercise focuses the mind outside of the body and creates a second centre of concentration.

Procedures for teaching progressive relaxation vary. The method for relaxing muscle groups, the specific muscle groups to be relaxed, the number of sessions involved, and the role of the instructor (taped versus live instructions) may differ. Tensing of muscle groups is often maintained for five to seven seconds and is followed by relaxation of the muscle group at a predetermined cue. To achieve maximum relaxation, various positive and affirmative phrases are used, such as, "Let all the tension go" and "Enjoy the feelings as your muscles become relaxed and loose." Guidelines for progressive relaxation are outlined in the accompanying box.

Guidelines for Progressive Relaxation

- Sit comfortably in a chair, with your feet flat on the ground.
- Tense and tighten your right fist. Focus on the feeling of tension as you do so.
- Allow the muscles in your right fist to relax. Contrast the difference in feeling from tension to relaxation.
- Repeat the preceding two steps for the left fist.
- Now tense and relax both your left and right fists.
- Focus on and relish the feeling of relaxation.
- Now tighten the muscles in both fists and both arms. Feel the tension, fully relax the muscles, and again focus on the sensation of relaxation.
- Progressively tighten and relax each muscle group in the body: toes, ankles, knees, buttocks and groin, stomach and lower back muscles, chest and upper back muscles, shoulders, forehead, jaw muscles.
- Couple deep breathing with progressive relaxation. While relaxing your muscles, inhale deeply, send the breath to the fist (or other muscle group), and exhale.
- The entire exercise should last a minimum of 10 minutes.

Source: Adapted from *The Nurse as healer* by L. Keegan, 1994, Albany, NY: Delmar, p. 156.

Biofeedback

Biofeedback is a technique that brings under conscious control bodily processes normally thought to be beyond voluntary command. In the past, physiological processes, such as muscle tension, heartbeat, blood flow, peristalsis, and skin temperature, were considered involuntary. However, studies show that these processes are partially subject to voluntary control. The feedback is usually provided through temperature meters that indicate skin temperature changes or an electromyogram (EMG) that shows the electric potential created by the contraction of muscles. Reduced EMG activity reflects muscle relaxation. Biofeedback teaches clients to achieve a generalized state of relaxation, which is characterized by parasympathetic dominance, in opposition to the pattern of physiological arousal manifested in stress-related disorders.

Imagery

Imagery is the internal experience of memories, dreams, fantasies, and visions that serves as a bridge connecting body, mind, and spirit (Dossey et al., 1995). Imagery enables people to open their minds to mental ideas of positive creative images that can foster self-healing and bring about desired achievements. In brief, individuals create a mental picture of how they want things to be—physically fit, healthy, mentally alert, or spiritually attuned. Images are evoked from memories, dreams, fantasies, and hopes. Although imagery is often thought of as visualization, it can employ all the senses—seeing, hearing, feeling, touching, or even tasting the created image.

Images can be either *concrete* or *symbolic.* A concrete image is one that is biologically correct; for example, a concrete image of body cells would resemble the way cells appear under a microscope. A person can also form symbolic images, which often replace concrete images. For example, a person receiving chemotherapy may visualize a dragon (representing the chemotherapeutic agent) travelling throughout the bloodstream eating the cancer cells.

Imagery can assist clients to heal by moving them in a step-by-step process toward a specific goal; this is called *process imagery* (Dossey, 1995). Process imagery is often concrete. It can be used to decrease anxiety about a medical procedure or treatment by having the client mentally rehearse for the event. It can also be used to focus on the healing process. In this situation, the nurse helps the client form biologically correct images. For example, following a client's acute myocardial infarction, the nurse assists the client to form images of the normal evolution from heart damage to building collateral blood flow to healthy scar formation, and includes information about medications, rest, and commitment to the healthy lifestyle needed for recovery (Dossey, 1995).

End-state imagery is imagining the healed final state. Achterberg, Dossey, and Kolkmeier (1994) advise that end-state imagery be used after other process imagery. For example, a client with a fractured femur might visualize walking unaided.

Table 11.1 describes several types of imagery that can be performed independently by clients or with the assistance of a skilled helper. When imagery is assisted, it is referred to as *guided imagery.* It is used by nurses to facilitate the relief of pain, anxiety, nausea, and various other symptoms (Eller, 1999).

Yoga

The word **yoga,** derived from the Sanskrit root *yug,* meaning "to bind" or "to yoke," is the uniting of all the powers of the body, mind, and spirit. Yoga is an approach to living a balanced life based on ancient teachings found in Hindu spiritual treatises (the *Upanishads*) written in 800–400 B.C. The great yogi Patanjali (500 B.C.) classified the teachings of the *Upanishads* into eight ways of being, referred to as Ashtanga yoga, meaning integrated or eight-limbed yoga. The

TABLE 11.1 Selected Types of Imagery

Type	Description	Example
Active	The conscious formation of an image that is directed to a body part or activity	A client visualizes a dragon eating up his tumour cells.
Correct biological	Images that are biologically correct and appear as they do in real life as they would under a microscope	A client visualizes white blood cells engulfing bacteria or having normal blood flow to the hands and feet.
Customized	Images that contain personalized, unique information	A client visualizes her heart bypass grafts as violet cylinders through which her blood flows without obstruction.
End-state	Images of a final healed state	A client who has an injured shoulder visualizes playing tennis.
Generalized healing	Image of an event, light, sense of unity, universal power, or spirit	A client describes being bathed with the warmth of the sun, or a white light penetrating the core of his being, or "an angel hovering over me."
Receptive	Images that enter the conscious mind but are not deliberately created; unexpected reception of an image	A client describes feelings of tension in the back of the neck as a huge knot.

Source: Adapted from *Holistic nursing: A handbook for practice* (2nd ed.) by B. M. Dossey, L. Keegan, C. E. Guzzetta, & L. G. Kolkmeier, 1995, Gaithersburg, MD: Aspen.

first two stages are the foundation of yoga. If a person does not practise them, the following six stages become meaningless. The remaining six stages set out practices that help a person master the first two stages. The eight stages follow:

1. *Yama* (universal moral commandments). This refers to improvement in social behaviour and is achieved by five noble practices: nonviolence (both physical and psychological); truthfulness; refraining from stealing; self-restraint in every sphere of life; and refraining from hoarding.
2. *Niyama* (rules for daily conduct). These refer to improvement in personal behaviour and are achieved by maintaining a purity of body and mind, developing a habit of contentment, practising austerity in every sphere of life, studying relevant literature, and practising dedication to God daily.
3. *Asanas* (physical postures). These consist of a series of 84 main postures (e.g., cobra posture and plough posture) intended to improve body health. The bending, stretching, and holding properties of the postures are designed to relax and tone the muscles and improve the function of various organs of the endocrine and nervous systems. People may assume 10 to 15 yogic postures, including stationary exercises, for all parts of the body for a period of about 15 minutes daily.
4. *Pranayama* (breath control). This stage includes eight main breath control techniques. Through the practice of various exercises, an individual learns not only to control breathing but also to restrain and quiet the flow of life force energy (*prana*). According to yogic philosophy, there is a direct relationship between life force activity and the rate of breathing. When the life force is operating smoothly, breathing is calm and regular, but when it is excited, breathing becomes erratic. Breath control is designed to still the mind and achieve transcendental awareness by controlling the life force. This is done by regulating and harmonizing breathing in particular patterns.
5. *Pratyahara* (controlling the senses). This aspect of yoga involves restraining the activities of all the sense organs with the ultimate goal of restraining the mind. It is achieved by minimizing the stimulation of the sense organs and leading as simple a life as possible.
6. *Dharana* (concentration of the mind on one point). Learning to avoid all distractions and concentrate on an object of one's choice involves tremendous perseverance and will power. The concentration helps to calm mental excitement and to induce tranquillity and serenity of the mind.
7. *Dhayana* (meditation). This stage refers to meditation that occurs when a person's concentration has become one-pointed, enabling the person to unify consciousness completely and experience a state of transcendental awareness.
8. *Samadhi* (supraconsciousness). This stage refers to extension of conscious control over successively deeper realms of consciousness.

There are many different schools of yoga, including Hatha yoga and Kundalini yoga, but the system of Ashtanga yoga is the core from which all other schools have evolved. Each school stresses a different technique, but all have as their goal the mastery of the self. For example, Hatha yoga is a series of gentle stretching exercises using specific *asanas* (postures) and *pranayama* (breathing techniques). Translated, *Ha-Tha* means "sun/moon," a symbolic representation of the male and female energies in the body. The goal of Hatha yoga is to attain and maintain a balance between the sun and the moon, the masculine and the feminine, the sympathetic and the parasympathetic, the day and the night, and the warm and the cool. Kundalini yoga is a more forceful, highly energizing form that focuses on pushing oneself to the limits. The breathing technique most commonly used in this type of yoga is the "breath of fire," a deep, hard, and fast nostril breath.

Individuals interested in beginning yoga are advised to explore the specific program offered to ensure that it includes the techniques most suited to their needs.

Meditation

Meditation is a technique used to quiet the mind and focus it in the present and to release fears, worries, anxieties, and doubts concerning the past and the future (Pettinati, 2001). It produces a state of deep peace and rest combined with mental alertness. Originally, meditation was viewed as a religious practice and is still practised by many as a form of prayer. However, one does not need to be religious to meditate or to receive the benefits of meditation.

Meditation involves both relaxation and focused attention. Skill in meditation is enhanced when the person first masters the skills of breathing, progressive relaxation, and imagery (Pettinati, 2001).

Because many types of meditation exist, the techniques used to achieve the desired outcome vary widely. In one type of meditation, referred to as *concentrative meditation*, the person visualizes and focuses attention on one particular object (e.g., a candle or a flower) or repeats the words of a mantra so that all other objects and stimuli in the environment are excluded. The Sanskrit word *om* or *aum*, meaning "one," is a commonly used mantra. Hindus believe that *om* is the universal sound and that its vibrational sound quality enhances a feeling of peace and deep meditation. People may, however, choose a word or phrase meaningful to them such as *shalom*, *peace*, or "I am at one with God."

In another type of meditation, referred to as *"opening up"* or *"mindfulness" meditation*, the person attempts to remain open to all stimuli. Various types of meditation integrate elements of both techniques. For example, a person may focus on a breathing pattern (Zen meditation) or on a mantra (transcendental meditation) but be willing to allow other thoughts to "come up," watch those thoughts, and then return to the original focus.

The following are some of the guidelines for meditation:

1. Create a special time and place for meditation. Ideally, choose the early morning or evening, and wait at least two hours after eating so that complete energy is devoted to meditation, rather than to digestive demands. A quiet, comfortable place, devoid of distractions, is essential.
2. Sit either cross-legged on the floor or upright in a straight-backed chair, keeping the spine straight and the body relaxed. Avoid a lying position; this increases the tendency to fall asleep.
3. Support the palms on the thighs, and close the eyes.
4. Follow deep-breathing and/or progressive relaxation exercises.
5. Focus attention completely on either breathing or a chosen mental image. If using a mantra, repeat the word or phrase either aloud or silently while exhaling. When distracting thoughts appear, allow them to drift into and out of your mind without giving them undue attention; then refocus on your breathing or your mantra.
6. Practise this process daily for 10- to 15-minute periods.

Prayer

Prayer is similar to meditation but is intended to be communication with God, a saint, or some other being who answers the prayer. Prayer may be conducted individually or in groups and may even be conducted at a distance by individuals unknown to the person for whom the prayers of healing are made. (See the discussion of intercessory prayer later in this chapter.)

Music Therapy

The human body has a fundamental vibrating pattern, according to music therapists. Thus, musical vibrations that closely relate to the body's fundamental frequency or vibrating pattern can have a profound healing effect on the entire human body, mind, and spirit, bringing about changes in emotions, organs, hormones, enzymes, cells, and atoms. Theoretically, carefully selected music helps restore regulatory functions that are out of tune during times of stress and illness. Music aligns the body, mind, and spirit with its own fundamental frequency (White, 2001). Our brain converts vibrations and rhythms to neural impulses, sensations, feelings, emotions, and then to aesthetic, spiritual, social, and healing meanings.

Music therapy consists of listening, rhythm, body movement, and singing. It is used for a variety of reasons. Music can serve as a vehicle for altering ordinary levels of consciousness to achieve the mind's fullest potential. Individuals can move through various stages of consciousness: normal waking, expanded sensory threshold, daydreaming, trance, and meditative states.

Using music therapy, people can also shift their perception of time from actual time of hours, minutes, and seconds (which is perceived in the left cerebral hemisphere) to *experiential time*—that which is perceived through memory. Listeners can actually lose track of time for extended periods, enabling them to reduce anxiety, fear, and pain. Because music is nonverbal in nature, it appeals to the right cerebral hemisphere, which regulates the intuitive, creative, imaging way of processing information. It recognizes pitch, rhythm, style, and melody. Music does not need logic or analysis from the left brain. However, as a person's knowledge of music increases, left-brain functioning may dominate; musicians, for example, critique compositional techniques and other features of the music. To benefit from music therapy, a person needs to learn to let go of conditioned responses to integrate the functioning of both hemispheres of the brain.

Music therapy can be used in a variety of practice settings. Quiet, soothing music without words is often used to induce relaxation. Musical selections without words are preferred because clients may concentrate on the messages and meaning of words, rather than allowing themselves to flow with the music. Music recordings are often used to relax and distract clients in perioperative holding areas, cardiac care units, birthing rooms, counselling rooms, rehabilitation and physical therapy units, and sleep induction units.

For individualized therapy, the nurse needs knowledge of the effects that particular types of music produce. Therapeutic music can include mood, choral, classical, romantic, impressionist, country, soft rock, opera, or New Age music. To select the appropriate music, the nurse needs to consider the client's preferences as well as the goals of therapy. Additionally, the nurse must consider appropriate times for use and length of therapy sessions. For example, some people may wish to have a music session after a morning shower to balance the body-mind for the day's events. The usual duration of a session is about 20 minutes. Clients are encouraged to let the body respond to the music as it wishes; that is, to relax the muscles, lie down, hum, clap, or dance. Some clients may wish to make their own recording of musical selections they find appealing. The healing capabilities of music are intimately bound with personal experience and what can achieve inner quietness or other desired qualities within that person.

Humour and Laughter

Health-care professionals recently have focused on the positive effects of humour and laughter on health and disease. Humour involves the ability to discover, express, or appreciate the comical or absurdly incongruous, to be amused by one's own imperfections or the whimsical aspects of life, and to see the funny side of an otherwise serious situation. The use of humour in nursing is defined as helping the client "to perceive, appreciate, and express what is funny, amusing, or ludicrous in order to establish relationships, relieve tension, release anger, facilitate learning, or cope with painful feeling" (Bulechek & McCloskey, 1999, p. 704). Elaboration of these functions of humour in nursing situations follows:

- *Establishing relationships.* Humour decreases the social distance between persons and assists in putting persons at ease. When tension is decreased, people can focus on the message and on other people rather than on their own feelings. Use of humour helps the nurse establish rapport with clients, an important factor in achieving success in nursing interventions.
- *Relieving tension and anxiety.* Freud, in 1905, stated that laughter releases psychic energy previously used to block expression of socially or personally unacceptable impulses. The effective use of humour relieves the tension of emotionally charged events. The personal nature of humour, for example, helps clients deal with the impersonal nature of wearing a hospital gown and a numbered ID band and with embarrassing questions and uncomfortable tests. People can also use humour prophylactically to decrease stress.
- *Releasing anger and aggression.* Humour helps individuals act out impulses or feelings in a safe and nonthreatening manner. It dissipates feelings of anger and aggression by focusing on the comic elements of a situation.
- *Facilitating learning.* Many lectures and presentations begin with a joke or cartoon. Humour not only reduces the presenter's anxiety but also gains the audience's attention. People learn more when humour is used and anxiety levels are reduced. People also recall more information when they associate information with a joke. Use of humour in instruction, however, needs to be carefully planned so that it will contribute to learning.
- *Coping with painful feelings.* People may use humour to blunt the immediate effect of situations that are too painful, such as the effect of a threatening diagnosis or treatment. Humour diminishes anxiety and fear and reduces tension, thus enabling the person to confront and deal with the situation.

Humour also has physiological benefits that involve alternating states of stimulation and relaxation. Laughter stimulates increases in respiratory rate, heart rate, muscular tension, and oxygen exchange. A state of relaxation follows laughter, during which heart rate, blood pressure, respiration, and muscle tension decrease. Humour stimulates the production of catecholamines and hormones. It also releases endorphins, thereby increasing pain tolerance.

According to Cousins (1989), humour brings out and integrates people's "positive emotions": hope, faith, will to live, festivity, purpose, and determination. It therefore has healing properties.

To use humour effectively, nurses need to be aware of their own feelings as well as the feelings of others and cultural variations in what people consider humourous. Humour can be misinterpreted or perceived as demeaning if not used appropriately (Struthers, 1999).

Many health-care settings are now interested in providing humour as a caring skill and have recognized that "laughter is the best medicine." "Humour rooms" that are supplied with games, funny audiotapes and videotapes, humorous books, collections of cartoons, and so on are being created for clients and staff.

Hypnosis

Hypnosis is an altered state of consciousness in which an individual's concentration is focused and distraction is minimized. Hypnosis can be used to control pain, alter body functions, and change lifestyle habits. Scientists do not understand exactly how hypnosis relieves pain; however, one theory is that it prevents pain stimuli in the brain from penetrating the conscious mind. Another theory is that hypnosis works by activating nerve pathways in the brain that cause the release of natural morphine-like substances called enkephalins and endorphins. These opioids modify behaviour and the perception of pain (Rosenfeld, 1996).

Hypnosis requires a client's active participation; clients can even learn to invoke their own hypnotic state. Hypnosis does not take away a person's self-control; in fact, people under hypnosis cannot be made to do anything that they consider immoral or dangerous. In a hypnotic trance, the client does not fall asleep but does become so sharply focused that minor distractions are ignored. A number of hypnosis techniques are used, depending on the type of pain and the preference of the client and the therapist. One of the most commonly used is symptom suppression, in which the client's awareness of the symptom (i.e., pain) is blocked and the client is distanced from it. The effectiveness of this type of hypnosis depends on the severity of the symptom and the client's ability to concentrate.

Aromatherapy

Aromatherapy was first used by the early Egyptians to ease pain. As a more recent example, in the 1800s, rosemary leaves were burned in hospitals for fumigation. Today, aromatherapists believe scents can improve mood and promote good health (Rosenfeld, 1996). They have used aroma to treat such conditions as edema, acne, allergies, bruising, and stress.

Although there is little evidence that scent plays an important role in the management of serious disease, some scientifically valid studies have shown that scent can help with less profound problems. One experiment was performed on clients undergoing magnetic resonance imaging (MRI) who often complained of claustrophobia in the magnetic capsule. After exposure to the aroma of vanilla, 63 percent of the clients reported that they felt less claustrophobic and the increased heart rates they experienced in earlier MRI sessions did not occur. It is believed that the clients' anxieties were lessened either by pleasant associations they made with vanilla—a purely psychological phenomenon—or by some undiscovered physiological response. Different aromas can influence the heart rate, blood pressure, breathing, and possibly the immune system (Rosenfeld, 1996).

Aromas are detected by the olfactory receptor cells in the nares. The stimuli travel along the olfactory nerve (cranial nerve I) to the olfactory bulb and then to the brain. From there, they are thought to play a role in a variety of body functions, emotions, and memory.

The essential oils that are used in aromatherapy are plant oils distilled from flowers, roots, bark, leaves, wood resins, and lemon or orange rinds. About 300 essential oils are currently used in aromatherapy. These oils can be sprayed into the air and inhaled, massaged on the body, applied as hot or cold compresses, or added to bath water (Rosenfeld, 1996). Examples are shown in Table 11.2.

Nurses should caution people who are considering aromatherapy to be aware that aromatic oils vary in quality and their production is not regulated. The skin should always be tested for allergies by applying a very small amount of the diluted oil before a whole treatment is tried (Rosenfeld, 1996). Essential oils should not be used near the eyes and should always be diluted in a suitable oil or water prior to application to the skin. These oils are not for internal use and should be stored in dark-coloured glass bottles and kept away from sunlight and heat. If the client is pregnant, she should be advised not to use the essential oils.

TABLE 11.2 Selected Essential Oils and Some of Their Uses

Oil	Use
Birch	Anti-inflammatory agent, decongestant, relief for arthritis
Geranium	Mood modifier, antidiarrheal agent
Lavender	Relief for headache, stress, and insomnia
Peppermint	Relief for nausea, antipyretic, respiratory aid

Source: Adapted from "The Sweet Smell of Health" by C. Kostiuk, October 1994, *Canadian Nurse, 90*(9), p. 45.

Transpersonal Therapies

Transpersonal therapies are therapies that effect healing *between* persons. Three therapies are discussed in this chapter: noncontact therapeutic touch, Reiki, and intercessory prayer.

Noncontact Therapeutic Touch

Noncontact **therapeutic touch (TT)** is a process by which practitioners believe they can transmit energy to a person who is ill or injured to potentiate the healing process. It is derived from, but not the same as, the "laying on of hands" associated with some religious philosophies. Delores Krieger (1979), who coined the term *therapeutic touch*, refers to TT as a healing meditation.

Basic to therapeutic touch are the concepts that the human being is an energy field, known as a human field, and that energy can be intentionally channelled from one person to another. The human field extends beyond the level of the skin and is perceptible to the trained sense (primarily touch) of a healer. This energy field can be most clearly "felt" within several feet of the body. An everyday experience that may demonstrate this field phenomenon is the feeling of having one's space invaded when someone stands too close in a crowded elevator, even though there is no physical contact.

The body and the environment are considered open systems that constantly exchange energy and matter. The pattern and organization of the human field are constantly affected by the flow of energy to and from the environment. In a healthy person, there is an equilibrium between the inward and outward flow of energy. In situations of disease, illness, or pain, the pattern and organization of the field are disrupted; there may be a loss of energy, a disruption in the flow, an accumulation, or a blockage of energy flow.

The therapeutic touch process requires specialized education. It consists of the following four steps (Fontaine, 2000):

1. *Centring* is a meditative step in which the person directs attention inward to achieve a sense of detachment, sensitivity, and balance.
2. *Assessing* is a head-to-toe scanning process in which the nurse holds the palms of both hands two to six inches over the client's skin surface. This process can be performed by one nurse or two. One nurse scans the client's front, while the second nurse scans the client's back. The purpose of the assessment is to detect asymmetric differences in the client's energy flow, such as heat, cold, tingling, congestion, pressure, emptiness, or other sensations.
3. *Unruffling*, or *mobilizing*, is a process in which an identified congestive energy field is "unruffled," or mobilized, to make the client's energy field more receptive and to enhance the transfer of energy from

the nurse to the client. The nurse accomplishes this step by moving the hands (palms facing the client) in a sweeping motion from the area where pressure was perceived down along the long bones of the body.

4. *Transferring energy* is the process in which the actual transfer of energy from the nurse to the client occurs. The nurse must know which form of energy to use, how to modulate energy, and where to apply energy. This assists clients to repattern their energy. The form of energy has different effects and is related to colours: blue energy is sedating; yellow energy is stimulating and energizing; and green energy is harmonizing. The nurse modulates these energy forms by mentally visualizing the colour, for example, by visualizing light through a blue stained-glass window. The nurse may apply energy directly over an identified area of congestion or to one of the *chakras* (special channels that serve as entry areas for energy from the environment, located in the thoracic or solar plexus). Energy transference helps restore the balance of the energy field and provides additional energy to promote self-healing.

To date, the energy fields and energy flow of TT have not been measured directly. No one has been able to demonstrate that real energy passes between the therapist and the client. Research into the efficacy of TT has shown mixed results due to inadequate sample sizes and differences among studies in the procedure used (Winstead-Fry & Kijek, 1999). Some believe that the real power of TT is in the considerable psychological boost of receiving a therapy from a practitioner who is compassionate and honestly believes that it can heal (Ball & Alexander, 1998).

Healing Touch is a group of noninvasive energy-based techniques that incorporate therapeutic touch. Research suggests that Healing Touch can be helpful in promoting relaxation, reducing pain, and managing stress. Used in combination with conventional medicine, it may be effective in speeding tissue and bone healing and strengthening the immune system. To be certified as a Healing Touch practitioner, a person completes a multi-levelled series of courses. The Healing Touch program is endorsed by the Canadian Holistic Nursing Association.

Reiki

Reiki (ray-key), a Japanese word for Universal Life Force, is a healing technique that channels life energy (*ki*) to someone through the hands. It is a stress reduction and relaxation technique that taps into the client's own life force energy to improve health and enhance quality of life. The ability to use Reiki—in other words, to access the life force—is transferred to the student by a Reiki Master. A set of *hand positions* are taught, which, in a Reiki session, give good coverage over the recipient's entire body (head, torso, legs). There are three levels of Reiki training. With mentorship and practice, one can advance to the level of Reiki Master.

Intercessory Prayer

Intercessory prayer refers to prayer offered in favour of another. The praying people are referred to as intercessors. In a chapter titled "Prayer and Healing: Reviewing the Research," Dossey (1995) describes a study designed by cardiologist Randolph Byrd to evaluate the role of prayer in healing.

In 1988, a study of 393 coronary care clients at San Francisco General Hospital revealed that clients for whom prayers were made daily did better on average than clients who did not receive prayers. The researcher randomly assigned half the clients to be prayed for to born-again Christians. To eliminate the placebo effect, the clients were not told of the experiment. Findings revealed that there were fewer deaths in the prayer group; those who were prayed for were five times less likely to need antibiotics and three times less likely to develop complications (Wallis, 1996). Since publication, Byrd's work has come under sharp criticism for design flaws. Controlled studies in intercessory prayer pose unique challenges due to a range of difficulties in using the conventional scientific approach (Dossey, 1997). Much more research is required to explore the benefits of intercessory prayer and healing.

Complementary Medical Therapies

Interest in alternative or complementary medical therapy is rapidly increasing as the public demands more choice in health care. Not only do alternative therapies appeal to people whose health care needs have not been met through traditional medicine, but some people believe they should have the freedom to choose for themselves the type of therapy they undergo.

In response to these concerns, some traditional medical practitioners offer alternative medical modalities, such as acupuncture and herbal and homeopathic therapies.

Acupuncture

Acupuncture is an ancient Chinese practice based on a principle that energy is channelled through the body along specific pathways. In acupuncture, needles are inserted into the body at specific points along these internal channels, which are called meridians. The needles can be heated, attached to a mild electric current, or twirled continuously with the hand. The internal organs are believed to be connected to the skin points and to the meridians; the acupuncture helps balance the energy that flows within them. It is therefore considered helpful in healing and for pain.

Studies have shown that acupuncture is effective for pain management. It is believed to exert its effects by releasing endogenous opioids that are produced in various parts of the central nervous system. These opioids combat the pain and promote deep muscle relaxation.

Canadian Society Notes

Fact	Implications for Nursing Practice
Over 50% of Canadians consume natural health products in the form of herbs, vitamin and mineral supplements, or traditional Chinese, Ayurvedic, and homeopathic preparations.	By understanding the interaction between natural and pharmaceutical products, nurses can offer informed advice to clients around self-care decisions.
Surveys have shown that many Canadians use complementary/alternative therapies for a wide range of diseases and conditions.	Nurses need to be aware of their provincial nursing guidelines around alternative/complementary therapies to ensure their advice is ethically sound and their services fall within the scope of practice.
The costs of complementary/alternative therapies are rarely covered by provincial or private health insurance plans.	Nurses need to know how to access information on the credentials of the therapists and costs of these therapies.

Chiropractic Therapy

Chiropractic therapy was founded by Canadian D. D. Palmer in 1895. Chiropractic doctors focus on the spine and its relation to the component bone structures, muscles, and nerves. Manipulation or adjustment of the spine will have a beneficial effect on problems in other areas of the body, such as the respiratory and gastrointestinal systems. Chiropractors believe that displacements of the spine can result in a variety of symptoms that can be treated by spinal manipulation. They are also concerned with maintaining the self-regulatory systems of the body. Chiropractors emphasize allowing the body to heal itself, rather than intervening in the body's processes.

Practitioners study at a university for three years before being admitted to a four-year course of studies in chiropractic medicine. Chiropractic doctors must pass both national and provincial exams in order to practise in Canada. In some provinces, chiropractic fees are partially covered by the provincial health plans.

Herbal Medicine

Herbs have been used by man since antiquity for the prevention and treatment of illness. During the last decade, North Americans have shown an increased interest in the use of herbs and herbal tonics. The reasons for this increased interest in herbal medicine vary from a search for a more natural way of life to dissatisfaction with the treatment offered by the medical profession (Gray, 1996).

Herbs have been defined as plants that are valued for their medicinal properties, flavour, scent, and so on. Over 10,000 herbs have been identified as useful for medicinal purposes. In 1995, Americans purchased $1.5 billion of herbs, and sales have been growing at a rate of 12 to 18 percent per year (Gray, 1996). See the accompanying box for some of the more commonly used herbs.

RESEARCH NOTE

Do Parents Use Complementary Therapies for Their Children with Cancer?

There is considerable research showing that use of complementary or alternative therapies is high among adult cancer patients; however, minimal research exists on the use of such therapies for cancer in children. The purpose of the study was to estimate the prevalence of use of unconventional therapy among children with cancer in Saskatchewan, to identify the most commonly used therapies, and to describe the experiences of different families.

Researchers conducted semi-structured telephone interviews with the parents of children who had been diagnosed with cancer as identified through the provincial cancer agencies.

Of the 44 families participating, 36 percent reported using some form of unconventional therapy for dealing with their child's cancer and another 21 percent considered it. The most frequently used were herbal remedies (47 percent). Other therapies included reflexology, aromatherapy, colour therapy, massage, relaxation techniques, music, and acupuncture. The reasons given for using these therapies included complementing medical treatment, coping with side effects, making the child stronger, and stopping the spread of cancer. The parents' satisfaction with these therapies was generally positive. A strong relationship existed between dissatisfaction with their child's medical experience and parents choosing to use unconventional therapies.

Implications: Unconventional therapies play a substantial complementary role in cancer care for children; therefore, parents and health professionals need better and more accessible information to make quality care decisions for children. This requires more research about the therapies' effectiveness and more training for health professionals in understanding unconventional therapies.

Source: Bold, J., & Leis, A. (2001, Jan-Feb). Unconventional therapy use among children with cancer in Saskatchewan. *Journal of Pediatric Oncology Nursing, 18*(1), 16–25, with permission of Elsevier. http://www2.us.elsevierhealth.com/scripts/om.dll/serve?action=searchDB&searchDBfor=home&id=jpon.

Popular Herbal Preparations

Echinacea	Supports the immune system
Ginseng	Improves physical endurance Reduces cholesterol
Gingko biloba	Enhances memory Acts as an antioxidant
St. John's wort	Reduces depression
Milk thistle	Acts as an antioxidant Revitalizes the liver

In 1995, Health Canada issued its current policy on traditional herbal medicines (Health Canada, 1995). The Drugs Directorate of Health Canada has authorized the marketing of several hundred herbal medicines for use in the treatment of minor conditions that can be safely self-diagnosed and treated by consumers. Unfortunately, a number of herbal products are being sold without the approval of Health Canada.

The determination of the safety and efficacy of herbal products presents a challenge, as herbal experts often disagree on how to interpret the varying evidence available for many types of herbal remedies. Herbs may be sold to manufacturers as whole plants or plant parts, cut pieces, or finely ground particles. The only definitive way to truly know the purity and concentration of a particular product is to perform assays.

Most herbs are consumed without untoward reactions when they are taken in small amounts. It is when the product is consumed in excess amounts that problems arise.

Although a healthy lifestyle is the primary promoter of good health, and conventional medicine may offer the best solutions for many problems, selected herbal therapies may have a place among options for health and illness management. With the current proliferation of lay literature on herbal remedies and the wide availability of such products in health food stores, more people are relying on herbal and other less conventional therapies for a wide variety of problems.

Health-care professionals must become aware of the use of herbs by their clients. The client's ingestion of unconventional medicines must be assessed when taking a medication history, since these therapies may be causing or exacerbating ill health (Youngkin & Israel, 1996).

Naturopathy

Naturopathic medicine involves botanical medicine, homeopathy, clinical nutrition, hydrotherapy, naturopathic manipulation, traditional Chinese medicine/acupuncture, and prevention and lifestyle counselling. In Canada, practitioners of naturopathic medicine are primary-care physicians trained at accredited medical colleges in a four-year, full-time program. Some provinces require that naturopathic doctors pass licensing board exams in order to practise.

Homeopathy

Homeopathy was founded in the late 18th century by a German physician, Samuel Hahnemann. It is based on the theory that the cure for the disease lies in the disease itself, much like the principle underlying vaccination. Therefore, the sick are treated with highly diluted amounts of substances that would produce the same symptoms as the disease were they given in more concentrated amounts (e.g., taking Belladonna, which creates cold-like symptoms, for a cold; or introducing minute quantities of a suspected allergen into the body to treat an allergy).

FOCUS ON CRITICAL THINKING

"In many cases, therapies that are termed "complementary" or "alternative" in Canada have been accepted practice in other cultures, perhaps even for centuries, as in the case of Chinese herbal medicine." This statement is from the July 1999 issue of *Nursing Now*, a series of papers that explore issues and trends in Canadian nursing. Mr. Chou, a 67-year-old Chinese man has been in the hospital for two weeks due to congestive heart failure. His family believes strongly in traditional Chinese medicine, and you notice that they are bringing in herbal teas for Mr. Chou. They would like to bring in an acupuncturist next week.

1. What are your attitudes toward methods of healing that are different from Western contemporary medicine?
2. How would you find out if the herbal teas were effective or detrimental to Mr. Chou's present condition?
3. What do you know about the benefits of acupuncture?
4. How would you deal with this situation with Mr. Chou? With the family? With the agency?

See Appendix A for answers to these questions.

CHAPTER HIGHLIGHTS

- Healing is a concept that is gaining increased recognition.
- Holistic nursing practice encompasses all nursing practice that has healing the whole person as its goal.
- Holistic nurses recognize and emphasize the biopsychosocial and spiritual dimensions of each person and the integrity of these dimensions. They incorporate various healing therapies in all areas of nursing to treat the psychological, social, and spiritual sequelae of all illness.
- The theoretical bases for bodymind healing include information transduction and mind modulation of the autonomic, endocrine, and immune systems.
- The limbic-hypothalamic system, located within the brain and biochemically interconnected with all other parts of the body, is considered the primary connecting link between body and mind.
- Healing modalities include touch therapies, mind-body therapies, aromatherapy, and transpersonal therapies.
- Touch therapies have been used for centuries and include therapeutic massage, acupressure, and foot reflexology.
- In mind-body therapies, individuals use their minds to heal their bodies. These therapies include relaxation techniques, biofeedback, imagery, yoga, meditation, prayer, music therapy, humour, and hypnosis.
- Aromatherapy has been used to improve mood and promote health. In the past few years, there has been a resurgence of interest in aromatherapy.
- Transpersonal therapies, those that effect healing between persons, include noncontact therapeutic touch and intercessory prayer.
- Complementary medical therapies are receiving increasing acceptance. These therapies are chosen either to complement Western medical therapies or to replace them.
- Alternative medical therapies include acupuncture, chiropractic therapy, herbal medicine, naturopathic medicine, and homeopathic medicine.
- Holistic nursing modalities can be used to complement both Western medicine and alternative medical therapies.
- As healers, nurses need to develop specific healing attitudes and behaviours.
- The development of a holistic self is a vital beginning.

READINGS AND REFERENCES

Suggested Readings

Geddes, N., & Henry, J. K. (1997). Nursing and alternative medicine: Legal and practice issues. *Journal of Holistic Nursing, 15*(3), 271–281.

This article presents a definition of alternative medicine and an overview of related research. Legal and practice considerations for professional nursing are also discussed. The article reports that the language of the current nurse practice acts neither prohibits nor actively promotes alternative medicine practices. Nurses must continually check for changes in the practice acts that will affect holistic health care.

Giedt, J. F. (1997). Guided imagery: A psychoneuroimmunological intervention in holistic nursing practice. *Journal of Holistic Nursing, 15*(2), 49–56.

This article discusses the use of guided imagery as an independent nursing intervention that uses psychneuroimmunology (PNI) principles to assist an individual in the management of distressing symptoms. PNI concepts and research are examined. Nursing research on guided imagery is reviewed.

Gray, M. (1996). Herbs: Multicultural folk medicines. *Orthopaedic Nursing, 15*(2), 49–56.

This article examines some of the cultural roots and general uses of herbs, which can be helpful to the nurse in conducting an interview to determine the client's past and current herbal uses. Although many herbs can be beneficial, others can be life threatening.

Related Research

Bold, J., & Leis, A. (2001). Unconventional therapy use among children with cancer in Saskatchewan. *Journal of Pediatric Oncology Nursing, 18*(1), 16–25.

Fawcett, J., Sidney, J., Riley-Lawless, K., & Hanson, M. (1996). Therapeutic touch with adolescent psychiatric patients. *Journal of Holistic Nursing, 14*(1), 6–23.

Weber, S. (1996). The effects of relaxation exercises on anxiety levels in psychiatric inpatients. *Journal of Holistic Nursing, 14*(3), 196–205.

Selected References

Achterberg, J., Dossey, B., & Kolkmeier, L. (1994). *Rituals of healing: Using imagery for health and wellness.* New York: Bantam Books.

Ball, T. S., & Alexander, D. D. (1998). Catching up with eighteenth century science in the evaluation of therapeutic touch. *Skeptical Inquirer, 22*(4), 31–34.

Bulechek, G., & McCloskey, J. (1999). *Nursing Interventions: Effective Nursing Treatments* (3rd ed.). Philadelphia, PA: WB Saunders.

Canadian Nurses Association. (July, 1999). "Complementary therapies: Find the right balance." *Nursing Now,* 6. Ottawa: Author.

Cousins, N. (1989). *Head first.* New York: Penguin.

Dossey, B. M. (1995). Using imagery to help your patient heal. *American Journal of Nursing, 95,* 41–46.

Dossey, B. M., Keegan, L., Guzzetta, C. E., & Kolkmeier, L. G. (1995). *Holistic nursing: A handbook for practice* (2nd ed.). Gaitherburg, MD: Aspen.

Dossey, L. (1993). *Healing Words: The power of prayer and the practice of medicine*. San Francisco: Harper.

Dossey, L. (1997). Notes on the journey: the return of prayer. *Alternative Therapies in Health & Medicine, 3*(6),10–17, 113–119.

Dossey, L. (1999). *Reinventing medicine*. San Francisco: Harper.

Dunbar, F. (1945). *Psychosomatic diagnosis*. New York: Paul B. Haebar.

Eller, L. (1999). Guided imagery interventions for symptom management. *Annual Review of Nursing Research, 17*, 57–84.

Fontaine, K. L. (2000). *Healing Practices: Alternative Therapies for Nursing*. Saddle River, NJ: Prentice Hall.

Gray, M. (1996). Herbs: Multicultural folk medicines. *Orthopaedic Nursing, 15*, 112–127.

Health Canada. (1995). *Drug Directorate Guideline, Traditional Herbal Medicines*. Ottawa: Author.

Horrigan, C. (1995). Massage. In D. Rankin-Box (Ed.), *The nurses' handbook of complementary therapies* (pp. 125–131). Edinburgh: Churchill Livingstone.

Jacobsen, E. (1938). *Progressive relaxation*. Chicago: University of Chicago Press. (Classic.)

Keegan, L. (1994). *The nurse as healer.* Albany, NY: Delmar.

Lynn, J. (1996). Using complementary therapies: Reflexology. *Professional Nurse, 11*, 321–322.

Mackey, B. (2001). Massage therapy and reflexology awareness. *Nursing Clinics of North America, 36*(1), 159–169.

Newman, M. A. (1994). *Health as expanding consciousness* (2nd ed.). Boston, MA: Jones & Bartlett.

Parse, R. R. (Ed.). (1995). Illuminations: *The human becoming theory in practice and research*. New York: National League for Nursing Press.

Pert, C. B., Dreher, H. E., & Ruff, M. R. (1998). The psychosomatic network: foundations of mind-body medicine. *Alternative Therapies in Health & Medicine, 4*(4), 30–41.

Pettinati, P. (2001). Meditation, yoga, and guided imagery. *Nursing Clinics of North America, 36*(1), 20.

Rogers, M. E. (1970). *An introduction to the theoretical basis of nursing*. Philadelphia, PA: F. A. Davis.

Rosenfeld, I. (1996). *Dr. Rosenfeld's guide to alternative medicine: what works, what doesn't - - - and what's right for you*. New York, NY: Random House.

Selye, H. (1956). *The stress of life*. New York: McGraw-Hill.

Smuts, J. (1926). *Holism and evolution*. New York: Macmillan. (Classic.)

Struthers, J. (1999). An investigation into community psychiatric nurses' use of humour during client interactions. *Journal of Advanced Nursing, 29*, 1197–1204.

Wallis, C. (1996, June). Faith & healing. *Time, 147*, 58–63.

Watson, J. M. (1999). *Postmodern nursing and beyond*. New York: Churchill Livingstone.

Wells-Federman, C. L. (1996). Awakening the nurse-healer within. *Holistic Nursing Practice, 10*, 13–29.

White, J. (2001). Music as intervention: a notable endeavour to improve patient outcomes. *Nursing Clinics of North America, 36*(1), 20.

Winstead-Fry, P., & Kijek, J. (1999). An integrative review and meta-analysis of therapeutic touch research. *Alternative Therapies in Health & Medicine, 5*(6), 58–60, 62–67.

Youngkin, E., & Israel, D. (1996). A review and critique of common herbal alternative therapies. *Nurse Practitioner, 21*(10), 42–45.

WEBLINKS

Canadian Health Network
www.canadian-health-network.ca
Funded by and in partnership with Health Canada, this Web site links to a wide range of complementary and alternative health information including the Natural Health Products Directorate.

Canadian Chiropractic Association
www.ccachiro.org
This site provides the general public with information on the role of chiropractic in the health care system, including its history, training, and scientific research.

Canadian Holistic Nurses Association
www.chna.ca
This site presents the philosophy and objectives of The Canadian Holistic Nurses Association (CHNA) and information on the levels of training for a Holistic Nursing Specialty.

Healing Touch Canada Inc.
www.healingtouchcanada.net
This site provides a listing of course offerings of Healing Touch Canada Inc., a practitioner roster by province, and an extensive recommended reading list.

The Integrative Health Institute
www.integrativehealth.ca
The Integrative Health Institute, Calgary, provides evidence-based integrative health education to the public and health professionals. Its services include library facilities, personalized health education, research activities, and workshops.

Canadian Naturopathic Association
www.naturopathicassoc.ca
This site provides information on ethics, standards, and a roster of Naturopathic Doctors who are members of the Canadian Naturopathic Association.

Canadian Reiki Assosiation
www.reiki.ca
This site presents the Code of Ethics of the Canadian Reiki Association (CRA), describes educational standards and membership criteria, and provides a list of Registered Teachers.

The Tzu Chi Institute
www.tzu-chi.bc.ca
The Tzu Chi Institute, based in Vancouver, offers an integrated approach to health care by helping clients combine complementary and mainstream health practices. The Web site offers information on its clinical treatment programs, research activities, and education and information services.

CHAPTER 12

Sexuality and Sexual Health Practices

OBJECTIVES

After completing this chapter, you will be able to:

- Differentiate between sex, sexuality, and gender.
- Understand how cultural, sociopolitical, and historical contexts influence sexual health.
- Identify ways of expressing sexual identity.
- Appreciate the scope and diversity of human sexual experience.
- Describe influences on and changes in sexual health throughout a person's life.
- Discuss potential interference with sexual desire, pleasure, and performance.
- Outline a plan for health promotion and nursing practices involved in compiling a sexual history.
- Formulate a plan for health promotion and education that supports sexual health practices.
- Understand the importance of client involvement in the generation of goals for desirable sexual practices.

Sexuality

A chapter on sexuality must begin with a discussion of what we understand to be sex and how we assume sexuality is experienced and expressed. The word "sex" can be used to describe the anatomical differences between men and women. A complicating factor, however, is the same word "sex" is used to describe specific sexual behaviour, such as sexual intercourse. The words "sex" and "gender" are sometimes used interchangeably and often incorrectly to denote different aspects of sexual being.

Gender refers to the ways in which a person lives life that demonstrate or reflect masculinity and femininity. Gender is understood to define the notions of "woman" and "man" that are formed in response to a particular culture's expectation of the role. That is, the roles of woman and man (gender) are not biologically determined but socially constructed. Social construction means that ideas, concepts, and roles are understood to be formed through the agreed upon ideologies of a society. Ideologies, in this sense, are not merely ideas, they are imbued with power. They become the authoritative voice in society through which we come to understand ourselves. Ideologies tell us who we are, what we are to think, and how we are to behave (Althusser, 1971). While there is undoubtedly some interrelationship between biological sex and gender, we can consider gender as distinct from the categories of biological sex.

According to Masters, Johnson, and Kolodny (1995, p. 3), "the word sexuality … refers to all aspects of being sexual. Sexuality means a dimension of personality instead of referring to a person's capacity for erotic response alone." Sexuality is subject to lifelong dynamic change. Although normal developmental changes and health status may necessitate adaptations to sexual expression, individuals continue to express sexuality in a variety of ways throughout their lives.

Sexual Orientation

Beliefs about the determinants of a person's sexual orientation are varied. Some note that homosexual and heterosexual identities often begin in childhood. There is discrepancy between the understanding of sexual orientation having a genetic basis and the understanding of sexual orientation as being a result of social constructions, role training, and societal norms.

Although there have been many attempts to categorize lesbian women and gay men on the basis of their perceived commonalties, it could be argued that the differences between and among homosexual persons is as pervasive as the differences between and among heterosexual persons. Health professionals should be aware of the stereotypes that are attributed to both heterosexual and homosexual appearances and behaviours. As advocates for sexual health, nurses have a responsibility to convey and to teach others to convey a nonjudgmental attitude regarding the expression of sexuality.

There is excellent research about what it is like to live as a lesbian or gay person in our society. Many of these accounts include experiences of persons not disclosing their sexual orientation to health-care providers for fear of being judged or of not receiving the treatment they would otherwise be entitled to (Stevens, 1995). Homophobia, a form of fear, and heterosexism, a form of prejudice, are

Sexuality

The term sexuality is used here in the broad sense intended by the World Health Organization:

> "Sexuality is an integral part of the personality of everyone: man, woman, and child. It is a basic need and aspect of being human that cannot be separated from other aspects of life."

In this view, sexuality encompasses the physical, physiological, social, emotional, cultural, and ethical dimensions of sex and gender.

> "Sexuality influences thoughts, feelings, actions and interactions, and thereby our mental and physical health. Since health is a fundamental human right, so must sexual health also be a basic human right." (WHO, 1975; Langfeldt and Porter, 1986)

Source: Health Canada, Canadian guidelines for sexual health education. http://www.hc-sc.gc.ca/hpb/lcdc/publicat/sheguide/defin_e.html

Figure 12.1 Many gay and lesbian relationships are often based on long-term mutuality

two ways that health professionals' attitudes can interfere with the adequate delivery and assessment of health care. Lesbian and gay persons must also contend with the heteronormative (privileging heterosexuality as the norm) assumptions that underlie the health-care system.

The health experiences of lesbian, gay, and bisexual persons are like those of heterosexual persons, formed through the unique experiences of their individual lives. This means that experiences of sexual expression cannot be thought of as the same for each lesbian, gay, bisexual, or heterosexual client. Assumptions of particular sexual behaviour should not be drawn from the category of orientation that a client identifies with. Some persons who currently identify themselves as gay or lesbian may have or have had previous sexual relationships with persons of the opposite sex. Persons who call themselves heterosexual may also engage in sexual behaviour with persons of the same sex. There are individuals who identify themselves as heterosexual or homosexual who are celibate.

In interactions with clients, our assumptions about sexuality and the construction of families are apparent in the language that we use. The use of gender-neutral language and the recognition of and inclusion of partners promotes the discussion of sexual health for all persons (see box below).

Sexual Health

Like "health" itself, sexual health is difficult to define. Although this chapter uses the World Health Organization definition of sexual health (see box at right), any attempt to define health for another can be seen as problematic. It is unlikely that any single definition of sexual health can capture the diversity of expressions of sexuality.

One limitation to our understanding of sexual health is that sexuality often comes to our attention as impairment, dysfunction, or illness. Although the focus on impairment of sexuality is an important part of a nurse's practice, it is inadequate to account for the range of experiences that might be thought of as relevant to sexual health.

Reducing Heteronormative Bias

Questions that reduce heteronormative bias include:

- Are you in a relationship or a partnership? Who is that with, and what is your relationship with that person?
- Who do you consider your immediate family?
- Over your lifetime, have your sexual partners been women, men, both, or neither?
- How would you like your partner or family to be involved in your care?

Secondly, drawing on the influences of prevailing social discourses and the representation of these discourses, for example, in the media, we tend to approach sexual health with a normative attitude. This means that we compare the sexual health and behaviour of individuals with some perceived norm of health, without recognizing the influences of different social and cultural practices on the construction of these norms. For example, in some cultures, sexual activity is presumed to imply only heterosexual intercourse, a conceptualization that narrows our understanding of what constitutes "normal" sexual activity.

As nurses, our professional opinions of sexual health are at risk of being shaped by our particular social position, values, and ethics. The influence of personal values on our understanding of sexual health carries particular consequences when "health" is used as a term of authority or truth. This is problematic when health professionals, under the guise of talking about sexual health, express disapproval of sexual behaviour that does not comply with their normative and socially constructed definition of sexual health.

Because sexuality and sexual functioning are aspects of health and well-being, they are a part of nursing care and may need to be assessed. Nurses should make their assessment nonjudgmentally, encouraging clients to discuss their concerns and offering suggestions to assist the return of sexual health.

Research indicates that clients prefer health-care professionals to initiate a discussion about sexual concerns, but many nurses expect clients to do this (Waterhouse & Metcalfe, 1991). When no one introduces the topic of sexuality, the client is often left to resolve sexual concerns alone.

Sexual Health

The term "sexual health" is defined by the World Health Organization as:

"[Sexual health is]...the integration of the physical, emotional, intellectual, and social aspects of sexual being, in ways that are positively enriching and that enhance personality, communication and love."

"[Sexual health involves]... a capacity to enjoy and control sexual and reproductive behaviour in accordance with a social and personal ethic."

"[Sexual health involves] ... freedom from fear, shame, guilt, false beliefs, and other psychological factors inhibiting sexual responses and impairing sexual relationships."

"[Sexual health involves] ... freedom from organic disorders, diseases, and deficiencies that interfere with sexual and reproductive function."

(WHO, 1975; Langfeldt & Porter, 1986)

Source: Health Canada, Canadian guidelines for Sexual Health Education. http://www.hc-sc.gc.ca/hpb/lcdc/publicat/sheguide/defin_e.html

Nurses require the following knowledge and skills to help clients in the area of sexuality:

- Self-knowledge and comfort with their own sexuality.
- Acceptance of sexuality as an important area for nursing intervention and a willingness to work with clients expressing their sexuality in a variety of ways.
- Knowledge of basic sexuality, including how certain health problems and treatments may affect sexuality.
- Ability to recognize the need of the client and family members to have the topic of sexuality introduced in verbal conversation, as well as through written or audiovisual materials.
- Ability to create a safe and comfortable environment in which clients can discuss their sexual health.

Sexuality throughout Life

Sexuality begins with conception and continues throughout life. Every society holds expectations about acceptable forms of sexual expression. Our understanding of what is appropriate or not appropriate sexual behaviour is socially constructed. These expectations are culturally and temporally specific, meaning they have developed in a particular culture at a particular point in time. Expectations of appropriate sexual behaviour are not universal and may vary considerably with the cultural and ethnic background of individual clients.

For the purposes of organizing nursing practices, it is convenient to cluster knowledge according to chronological age categories. It is, however, important to be aware of ageist attitudes which could lead to the assumption of "age-appropriate sexual expression." Sexual expression is always grounded in the lived life of the individual, regardless of chronological age. For example, the beginning and the ending of sexual desire is highly variable among cultures and among people within a culture.

Childhood

From birth, infants are assigned the biological sex of female or male and, by three years of age, begin to develop a gendered sense of themselves. Preschoolers become increasingly aware of their own and others' bodies. Body exploration and genital touching is normal and may begin in early childhood. Negative reaction to exploration of genitals and masturbation can lead to feelings of confusion about sexuality.

Adolescence

During early adolescence (12 to 13 years), primary and secondary sex characteristics develop. In boys, the testes and scrotum increase in size, the skin over the scrotum becomes darker, pubic hair grows, and axillary sweating begins. Development of the genitals to adult size takes five to six years. In girls, the pelvis and hips broaden, breast tissues develop, pubic hair grows, axillary sweating begins, vaginal secretions become milky and change from alkaline to an acid pH, and vaginal flora change.

Young women should be taught about menstruation prior to adolescence. The mean age of menarche has declined from 14.8 years in the 1890s to 12.5 years in 1988 (Maticka-Tyndale, 2001). Teenage women may have irregular menstruation initially. They can be taught to be aware of subtle signs of impending menstruation, such as breast tenderness, water retention or bloating, or the appearance of skin eruptions or pimples. Young women should be counselled regarding the variety of feminine hygiene products available (e.g., tampons and sanitary pads) so that they can make intelligent choices. Young women should be advised to wash their hands before inserting tampons, to change tampons frequently, and to use pads at night to decrease the chances of infection.

Adolescence is the time when biological maturity occurs; it is also the time when many people become sexually active. Maticka-Tyndale points out that "sexual activity in the teenage years is not something new. It has been relatively common throughout history and continues to be common if we look across cultures" (2001, p. 2). In most of the developed nations, the first experience of sexual intercourse is sometime during adolescence. Although there has been a gradual reduction in the age of first intercourse for Canadians, the mean age for first intercourse has been 17 years for both men and women since the 1960s (Maticka-Tyndale, 2001). In Canada, men under the age of 16 years are less likely than young men in other countries to have first intercourse. Canadian adolescents who are having intercourse at a younger age are likely to be "youth who are not in school, are from lower income households, and are born in Canada, rather than immigrants to Canada" (Maticka-Tyndale, 2001). It is suggested by researchers that this group forms a particular subset of youth, who are marginalized in a number of ways that may contribute to early sexual activity.

Given the fact that half the Canadian youth are sexually active by the age of 17, it is imperative that adolescents have accurate and complete information regarding sexual health. This includes education regarding the negotiation of sexual relationships, contraception, and prevention of sexually transmitted infections.

Gay, lesbian, and bisexual youth are likely to remain "closeted" (not disclosing their sexual orientation) in their interactions with friends, family, and in school throughout adolescence. These young people continue to face rejection if they "come out" (disclose their orientation), with parental "rejection as extreme as being kicked out of the house and left to live on the streets" (Maticka-Tyndale, 2001, p.13). During adolescence, many young people deal with issues of self-esteem, belonging, and identity; for lesbian, gay, and bisexual youth, these struggles are increased with the tensions of living in a heteronormative society and few visible role models for their development. In writing about the risks for youth who are nonheterosexual, McWhorter (1999) cites a 1996 Canadian study reporting that "gay and bisexual male youth are nearly 14 times more at risk than their heterosexual contemporaries of making a serious attempt on their own lives" (p. 5). She also notes that in the United States, up to 25 percent of adolescents living on the street are nonheterosexual youth who are no longer welcomed in their parent's homes.

Adulthood

During early adulthood, many people form emotional/sexual relationships and cohabitate with partners. Individuals establish their own value systems and develop lifestyles that reflect these personal values. While some young adults partner in heterosexual marriages and start to raise children, others cohabitate with sexual partners, live alone, or live with persons with whom they are not sexually involved.

Sexual activity is common throughout adulthood and includes not only sexual intercourse, but touching, masturbation, oral sex, sexual fantasies, and other sources of pleasure. Difficulties may arise in relationships because of differences in sexual desire and sexual response between individuals. Couples need to communicate their sexual needs to one another to support the growth and development of a successful intimate relationship. "Good sex means knowing what you want, what your partner wants, and how to talk about it comfortably—and never being forced to do anything that you don't want to do" (www.sexualityandu.ca).

Sexual desire and response are affected by social circumstances and biological changes throughout adulthood. During pregnancy, for example, some women and men express concerns about sexual intercourse. The Canadian Association of Gynecologists and Obstetricians suggests that intercourse is generally safe in a healthy pregnancy up to the last month before delivery (www.sexualityandu.ca). The sexual lives of young adults are also affected by the demands of raising young children and the fatigue and stress of busy schedules.

During middle adulthood, both men and women experience decreased hormone production, causing the climacteric, usually called menopause in women. Most women experience menopause in the fifth decade of life. Women who report symptoms during the perimenopausal period may experience hot flashes, vasomotor instability, sleep disturbances, vaginal dryness, mood changes, or skin, hair, and nail changes. The incidence of osteoporosis and cardiovascular lipid changes also increases following menopause. An extensive literature review conducted by Daniluk reported that "only a small percentage of women indicate that the cessation of menstruation and the secondary menopausal symptoms are particularly disruptive or debilitating. In fact, some women report a renewed sense of energy and creativity… like other transitions that occur throughout life, for most women, menopause is associated with both losses and gains. Each woman must incorporate these into her understanding of herself, as a woman, and as a sexual person" (1998, p. 272). Given this information on menopause, it is more helpful to view menopause as a normal occurrence in the lives of women than to frame menopause as a disorder that always requires medical intervention.

Troubling symptoms of menopause may, however, require intervention. Some changes in a woman's body can be effectively managed with nonprescription interventions, such as vaginal lubricants or moisturizers that increase lubrication and facilitate comfortable sexual contact. Vaginal lubrication and responsiveness to sex is also improved with continuing sexual activity. Administration of exogenous hormonal replacement therapy (HRT) is used to manage symptoms of menopause. Either oral or transdermal administration results in sustained estrogen blood levels. The decision to intervene with HRT should be made for each particular woman with consideration for the severity of her symptoms and should include a discussion of potential side effects of pharmacological intervention.

Andropause is the phase in men's lives in which they experience a gradual reduction in the production of testosterone and sperm by the testes. Physical changes in men are less dramatic than in women. Men may, however, experience enlargement of the prostate leading to problems with voiding, a general loss of physical strength, and changes in the sexual response cycle. Although men may remain fertile into older adulthood, the ability to obtain and sustain an erection is affected by aging and the reduction in testosterone levels associated with aging.

Both women and men remain capable of and interested in sexual activity well into old age. Older women remain capable of multiple orgasms, although as with men, the phases of the sexual response cycle may require longer to occur. As people age, there is an increased potential for obstacles to sexual intimacy, including chronic health conditions, such as diabetes or arthritis. These obstacles may require creative adaptation to facilitate a sexually satisfying relationship. Older adults are likely to experience social and relationship losses that impact their sexuality. These significant losses include the death of partners and the loss of privacy for those who eventually live with family or in long-term care facilities.

Factors Influencing Sexuality

Many factors influence a person's sexuality: developmental level (discussed above), culture, religious values, personal ethics, disease processes, and medications.

Culture

Sexuality is structured and regulated by the individual's culture. For example, culture influences the sexual nature of dressing, rules about marriage, expectations of role behaviour and social responsibilities, and specific sex practices. Societal attitudes vary widely. Attitudes about childhood sexual play with the self or children of the same or opposite sex may be restrictive or permissive. Premarital and extramarital coitus may be unacceptable or tolerated. Polygamy (several partners) or monogamy (one partner) may be the norm.

Specific sex practices include puberty rites, body beautification, and female circumcision and genital mutilation. Puberty rites of adolescent males in native African and Australian cultures include circumcision (removal of the foreskin of the penis). Female body beautification carried out in some cultures (e.g., Belgian Congo) to make the body more decorative involves the formation of keloids (scars) at four to five years of age from above the chest to the groin. Female circumcision or female genital mutilation (FGM), practised in Africa even today, involves either excision of the clitoris, the labia minora, and the labia majora, or closure of the vagina (infibulation). The reasons for sexual mutilation vary. Infibulation may be done to guarantee the bride's virginity. Excision of the clitoris reduces sexual desire and vulnerability to temptation. In 1980, the World Health Organization and the United Nations Children's Fund (UNICEF) unanimously recommended that all forms of female circumcision be abolished.

Because clients (and colleagues) may differ in their approaches to sexuality, nurses must be aware of and consider cultural factors when approaching sexual issues in health care. See Chapter 14 for additional information about culture.

Religious Ideologies

Religious beliefs influence sexual expression. They provide guidelines for sexual behaviour and acceptable circumstances for the behaviour, as well as prohibited sexual behaviour and the consequences of breaking the sexual rules. The guidelines or rules may be detailed and rigid or broad and flexible. For example, some religious ideologies dictate that forms of sexual expression other than male-female intercourse are unnatural and hold sexual activity before marriage to be unacceptable.

Some religious values conflict with the more liberal values of Canadian society. See Chapter 13 for additional information about religious values.

Personal Ethics

Although ethics is integral to religion, ethical thought and ethical approaches to sexuality can be viewed separately from religion. Many individuals and groups have developed written or unwritten codes of conduct based on ethical principles. What one person views as bizarre, perverted, or wrong may be completely natural and right to another. Examples include masturbation, oral or anal intercourse, and cross-dressing. Many people accept sexual

Canadian Society Notes

Cultural Influences on Experiences and Expression of Sexuality

Each person's experience and expression of their sexuality is influenced by a unique combination of multiple factors that must be considered by the health-care provider during assessment of sexual health.

Consideration of difference:

- Race and ethnicity
- Socioeconomic class
- Religious belief systems
- Adherence to "traditional beliefs"
- Acceptance of a "modern technological health system"

Reflective questions for the health-care provider:

- How does this person's race or ethnic origin influence the expression of sexuality?
- Do beliefs arising from ethnic, cultural, or religious ideologies create tension for this person in the experience with the modern Western health-care system?
- How does this person's location in a particular socioeconomic class influence experience or expression of sexual health?
- Does this person feel able to talk openly with me about particular sexual identity and health?

Clinical example:

In an assessment interview, a young aboriginal woman discloses that she is "two-spirited."

Within some cultures, there are recognized gender roles beyond the binary system of man and woman. These other gender roles can be referred to as third or fourth gender. In many aboriginal groups, these persons are called "two-spirited." While the term is often used in reference to a gay or lesbian sexual orientation, the reference may also have a spiritual element to it. Historically called "berdache," two-spirited people have held an important place in aboriginal history.

Rather than assuming the meaning of the young aboriginal woman's disclosure of being "two-spirited," the interviewer should seek to understand the meaning that this holds for the client. The interviewer might ask about the client's expression of her sexuality as a two-spirited person, how this experience is lived in her daily life and relationships, or if she experiences difficulties in her life in a dominantly heterosexual culture.

expression of various forms if it is performed by consenting adults, is practised in privacy, and is not harmful. Couples need to explore and communicate about various types of sexual expression to prevent domination of sexual decision making by one member of the couple.

Health and Illness Situations

Healthy minds, bodies, and emotions are necessary for sexual wellness. Many health factors can interfere with a person's expression of sexuality.

Heart Disease

Heart disease frequently influences sexual expression. Clients experiencing, or at risk for, myocardial infarction are often anxious about their sexuality and sexual activity. Concerns about the effect of sexual activity on the heart may cause people to restrict or avoid sexual activity. Education by health professionals can alleviate client fears following heart surgery or hospitalization for alterations in heart function. Suggestions as to when to resume activity based on reactions to exercise, avoiding sexual intercourse after large meals or consumption of alcoholic beverages, positions to assume, and signs of distress can provide the couple with information that will help them make sexual activity decisions.

Diabetes Mellitus

Many men with long-term diabetes mellitus develop erectile dysfunction related to neurologic changes associated with the disease process. Women who have diabetes may experience orgasmic dysfunction (loss of ability for orgasm), difficulty experiencing arousal, loss of vaginal lubrication, and painful intercourse related to a *Monilia* infection of the vagina. The latter commonly occurs with diabetes.

Spinal Cord Injury

Because the level of the injury to the spinal cord determines the effect on sexual functioning, individuals may be capable of erection and ejaculation and be fertile, may have psychogenic or reflexogenic genital arousal, or may have no physiological genital responses.

Surgical Procedures

Any surgical procedure has the potential to alter a person's body image, especially when the surgery involves mutilating, removing, or altering parts of the body. Examples include amputation of a leg, radical neck surgery, excision of large portions of the lower jaw, and ostomies. The impact is even greater when the surgery alters or removes body parts linked directly with sexual functioning (e.g., mastectomy, hysterectomy, and vaginal excision in women; orchiectomy [removal of the testicles] and penectomy in men). Feelings of ugliness and loss of masculinity or femininity are common after these surgeries.

Research has indicated that many people also have concerns about their reactions to their partners' surgical procedures. Having discussions with both individuals will provide facts in place of potentially erroneous beliefs about surgical procedures altering sexual behaviours (Bernhard, 1992).

Many men fear that prostatectomy can cause impotence and may delay seeking medical advice and treatment. Most surgical approaches for prostatectomy, however, do *not* result in impotence. Because of anatomic changes in the posterior urethra following a prostatectomy, retrograde ejaculation sometimes results; after ejaculation, the seminal fluid enters the bladder and is excreted in the urine. This affects fertility. In most instances, the man may resume sexual activity in six to eight weeks. The client needs to know that the ejaculate will be decreased or absent and that the urine is often cloudy.

Some radical prostatectomies (e.g., radical perineal prostatectomy) performed for cancer of the prostate may cause impotence because of damage to the nerves responsible for producing erections. However, surgeons are now performing nerve-sparing radical prostatectomies that maintain sexual function in certain clients (Moore et al., 1992).

Joint Disease

Joint disease may indirectly affect sexual function because of pain, stiffness, loss of joint motion, and fatigue. Such symptoms influence sexual motivation as well as sexual positioning and methods.

Chronic Pain

Chronic pain that accompanies many chronic illnesses often decreases sexual motivation. Altered positions for coitus may be necessary, and alternative ways to express sexual stimulation and warmth may need to be emphasized.

Sexually Transmitted Infections (STIs)

There are numerous sexually transmitted infections (STIs). See Table 12.5 later in this chapter. The presence of an STI in one partner induces fear of transmission in the other, often resulting in abstinence of sexual contact. In some situations, the presence of an STI is unknown and transmission occurs.

Mental Health and Illness

A positive sexual self-concept (how one values oneself as a sexual being) enables an individual to form intimate relationships throughout life. A negative sexual self-concept may prevent or impede the formation of relationships. A high self-esteem enables an individual to be comfortable seeking pleasure and asking another to help satisfy sexual desires.

Body image, a central part of the sense of self, is constantly changing. Pregnancy, aging, trauma, disease, and therapies can alter an individual's appearance and functioning, which can affect body image. People who feel good about their bodies are likely to be comfortable with and enjoy sexual activity. People who have a poor body image may respond negatively to sexual arousal. A major influence on body image is the media focus on a particular representation of physical attractiveness: slim, fit, and "youthful" bodies. Both women and men are vulnerable to the pressure to seek medical/surgical intervention to alter their "attractiveness" to align more closely to the images represented in media, such as large breasts, low body fat, and full heads of hair.

Because the mind and thought processes are involved in sexual functioning, any impairment of the mind may affect sexual expression. For example, depression lowers libido and can affect both the depressed and nondepressed partner. Some clients with mental disorders or brain injury may behave in an inappropriate sexual manner, such as touching their genitals, removing their clothing, or seeking frequent sexual activity. Other clients, such as those with Alzheimer's disease, may not remember any previous sexual contact with their partners.

Medications

Many prescription medications have side effects that affect sexual functioning. See "Effects of Medications on Sexual Function" later in this chapter. Some people also take drugs to enhance sexual motivation. Amphetamines and cocaine enhance sexual motivation for some people for short periods. Lysergic acid diethylamide (LSD) and marijuana increase libido in some but inhibit it in others.

Sexual Desire and Pleasure

The sexual response is preceded by a period when **sexual desire,** more commonly known as **libido,** is dominant, perhaps as the result of environmental stimuli, and the individual becomes receptive for sexual activity. Sexually arousing stimuli, often called **erotic** stimuli, may be real or symbolic. In the right circumstances, imagination (sexual fantasy), sight, hearing, smell, and touch can all invoke sexual arousal. Libido fluctuates within each person and varies from person to person. The range of fluctuation in each individual is broad and is considered a problem only when the client (or someone interacting with the client) identifies it as interfering with the ability to have satisfying sexual interactions.

Sexual desire may be enhanced by various conditions and circumstances. Both males and females experience increased sexual motivation during puberty and adolescence as a result of hormonal and body changes. Certain drugs also increase libido (see the previous section).

Several factors can also decrease sexual desire. Pregnancy can affect sexual desire if it is associated with physical discomfort, fear of injury to the fetus, or perceived loss of attractiveness. For about four weeks following delivery, libido is often reduced due to decreased vaginal lubrication, thinner vaginal walls, pain or fear of pain after an episiotomy, and a slower response to stimulation.

Desire generally diminishes with general ill health, chronic diseases that cause disability or pain, and depression. Many prescription medications can also diminish sexual desire. See "Effects of Medications on Sexual Function" later in this chapter.

Sexual Arousal

Sexual arousal is enhanced by physical stimulation that involves touch or pressure to parts of the body and may be applied by oneself, by another's body contact, or by inanimate objects. Examples include kissing, stroking, hugging, squeezing, breast stimulation, manual stimulation of the genitals, oral-genital stimulation, and anal stimulation. Any of these may be engaged in for sexual pleasure on their own or as a prelude to genital intercourse. Physical stimulation used as a prelude to intercourse is called **foreplay** or **precoital stimulation.** Physical stimulation used for sexual pleasure is called **sex play.** Wide variations exist in the amount and types of physical stimulation used.

Manual self-stimulation is called **masturbation.** Reciprocal manual stimulation is called *mutual masturbation.* Stimulation of the penis generally produces a more erotic response than stimulation of the scrotum. The most common form of male masturbation is firm gripping and stroking of the shaft and glans of the penis. Light rubbing or tugging at the *frenulum* (the fold of tissue that connects the lower surface of the glans to the prepuce) can also produce sexual excitement. Whatever method is used, as sexual excitement increases, manipulation often becomes more rapid and intense, until **ejaculation** (expulsion of seminal fluid and sperm) occurs. After ejaculation, the glans penis is often hypersensitive to touch.

Stimulation of the *clitoris* is usually a major erotic focus for females. This highly sensitive area rarely requires direct stimulation. Rubbing pressure on the *mons pubis (mons veneris),* pulling or rubbing the clitoral hood (prepuce), or pulling on the labia stimulate the clitoral shaft and produce intensely erotic responses. Some women use external manipulation as well as insertion of fingers into the vagina to produce sexual excitement.

Manual stimulation of the genitals may be used to produce **orgasm** (climax of sexual excitement) or as a prelude to sexual intercourse.

There are three forms of oral-genital stimulation: cunnilingus, fellatio, and soixante-neuf. **Cunnilingus** is oral stimulation (kissing, licking, or sucking) of the female genitals, including the mons pubis, vulva, clitoris, labia, and vagina. **Fellatio** is oral stimulation of the penis by licking and sucking. **Soixante-neuf** ("69") is simultaneous oral-genital stimulation by two persons. These practices, like other physical stimulation, may be engaged in for the pleasure they give, including orgasm, or as a prelude to genital intercourse. As with masturbation, there is no evidence that oral-genital contact is harmful.

Anal stimulation can be a source of sexual pleasure because the anus is richly innervated. Oral-anal stimulation is called **anilingus.** Stimulation may also be applied by hands or by sex aids, such as vibrators. Because the anus is associated with feces, many people do not include anal stimulation in their sexual repertoire.

Sexual Intercourse

The most common form of sexual activity with a heterosexual partner is genital intercourse, also known as **coitus** or **copulation.** Penile-vaginal intercourse can be both physically and emotionally satisfying. There are a variety of positions for this kind of intercourse; the most common is lying face to face (with female or male on top). Side-lying, standing, sitting, and rear-entry positions are also used. Side-lying, female-on-top, and rear-entry positions facilitate clitoral stimulation, either by penile or manual contact. The choice of intercourse positions and activities depends on physical comfort and beliefs, values, and attitudes about different practices.

During intercourse, the man moves the penis back and forth along the vaginal walls by rhythmic thrusting movements of his hips. At the same time the woman may move her own body to match the partner's hip movements. Movements continue until orgasm is achieved by one or both partners. Simultaneous orgasm is difficult to achieve. After coitus, caressing, hugging, and kissing can increase the shared intimacy. The other form of genital intercourse is **anal intercourse,** during which the penis is inserted into the anus and rectum of the partner. Anal intercourse is most commonly practised by gay men, but some heterosexual couples engage in it as well. Positions for anal intercourse are similar to those for penile-vaginal intercourse, with minor differences due to the position of the anus.

Current practice dictates the use of a condom in both forms of intercourse to prevent the transmission of disease. Because anorectal tissue is not self-lubricating, a lubricant must be used on the condom. Also, since normal bacterial flora from the bowel can produce infection in other parts of the body, the used condom should be removed and another applied before inserting the penis into other body orifices. (Condoms are used for contraception as well as for preventing sexually transmitted diseases. See the discussion of sexual health teaching later in this chapter.)

Sexual Response Cycle

During sexual arousal, two primary physiological changes occur: **vasocongestion** (congestion of the blood vessels in the genital area) and **myotonia** (increased muscle tension). One model of physiological response identifies four phases of physiological changes: excitement, plateau, orgasm, and resolution (Masters & Johnson, 1966). Table 12.1 summarizes the physiological changes associated with each of the phases of the sexual response cycle in both males and females. It is important to remember that many individual variations in this cycle fall within the norm.

Alternative Forms of Sexual Expression

Alternative forms of sexual expression, which may be illegal and harmful to others, include **voyeurism** (seeking sexual arousal by observing the body of another); **sadomasochistic bondage** (heterosexual or homosexual activities that involve inflicting pain or experiencing pain during sexual stimulation; can involve being tied up, hitting, whipping, pinching, scratching, and other activities); and **pedophilia** (sexual acts with children).

Nurses may also care for clients who act out sexually or who are sexually aggressive toward or harass other clients or the nurse. Such behaviours infringe on the rights of others or are harmful to others. Nurses need to recognize this behaviour as unacceptable but also recognize it as a possible expression of a sexual concern or problem that the client may be experiencing.

Interference with Sexual Desire, Pleasure, and Performance

The ability to engage in genital intercourse is of great importance to most people. Many people experience transient problems with their ability to respond to sexual stimulation or to maintain the response. A smaller percentage of people experience long-standing problems.

Male Dysfunction

Three male dysfunctions are erectile dysfunction, premature ejaculation, and retarded ejaculation. **Erectile dysfunction,** more commonly referred to as **impotence,** is the inability to achieve or maintain an erection sufficient for sexual satisfaction for oneself or one's partner. Erectile dysfunction can be caused by physiological or psychological factors. Physiological factors include (1) *neurologic disorders* created by spinal cord injuries, injury to the genitals or perineal nerves, extensive surgery, such as abdominal-perineal bowel resections or radical perineal prostatectomy, diabetes mellitus, multiple sclerosis, and Parkinson's disease; and (2) *prolonged use of drugs,* such as alcohol, sedatives, heroin, antidepressants, antipsychotics (phenothiazines), and antihypertensives.

Psychological factors are often signalled by a sudden, rather than a gradual, onset. They may include the following:

TABLE 12.1 Physiological Changes Associated with the Sexual Response Cycle

Phase of the Sexual Response Cycle	Signs Present in Both Sexes	Signs Present in Males Only	Signs Present in Females Only
Excitement	Increased muscle tension Moderate increase in heart rate, respiration, and blood pressure Sex flush (less prevalent in men than in women; present in 75 percent of women) Nipple erection (60 percent of men and most women)	Penile erection Tensing, thickening, and elevation of the scrotum Partial elevation and increase in size of testicles	Enlargement of the clitoral glans Vaginal lubrication Widening and lengthening of vaginal barrel Separation and flattening of the labia majora Reddening of the labia minora and vaginal wall Breast tumescence (enlargement) and enlarged areolae
Plateau	Increased voluntary and involuntary myotonia Abdominal, intercostal, anal, and facial muscle contraction Accelerated heart rate and respiratory rate, and increased blood pressure Sex flush (appearance in some men late in the phase; spread over the entire body in women)	Increase in penile circumference at the coronal ridge (base of the prepuce), and deepening of colour 50 percent increase in testicular size, and elevation close to the perineum Appearance of a few drops of mucoid secretions from the bulbo-urethral glands at tip of penis; may contain sperm	Retraction of the clitoris under the hood Appearance of the orgasmic platform (increase in the size of the outer one-third of the vagina and the labia minora) Slight increase in the width and depth of the inner two-thirds of the vagina Further reddening of the labia minora Appearance of a few drops of mucoid secretion from the Bartholin's glands to lubricate inner labia Further increase in breast size and areolar enlargement
Orgasm	Involuntary spasms of muscle groups throughout the body Diminished sensory awareness Involuntary contractions of the anal sphincter	Rhythmic, expulsive contractions of the penis at 0.8-second intervals Emission of seminal fluid into the prostatic urethra from contraction of the vas deferens and accessory organs (stage 1 of the expulsive process)	Approximately 5–12 contractions in the orgasmic platform at 0.8-second intervals Contraction of the muscles of the pelvic floor and the uterine muscles

(1) doubts about one's ability to perform or about one's masculinity; (2) fatigue, anger, or stress; (3) traumatic early sexual experiences (e.g., rejection); and (4) boredom associated with the specific partner.

Premature ejaculation occurs when a man is unable to delay ejaculation long enough to satisfy his partner. This usually means that ejaculation occurs after only very limited stimulation of the penis. Often, the ejaculation occurs either during penetration (of the vagina, mouth, or anus) or immediately thereafter. The condition may develop when the need for rapid orgasm or performance demands continue over time. To address the problem of

TABLE 12.1 *continued*

Phase of the Sexual Response Cycle	Signs Present in Both Sexes	Signs Present in Males Only	Signs Present in Females Only
Orgasm *continued*	Peak heart rate (110–180 BPM), respiratory rate (40/min or greater), and blood pressure (systolic 30–80 mm Hg and diastolic 20–50 mm Hg above normal)	Closing of the internal bladder sphincter just before ejaculation to prevent retrograde ejaculation into bladder Orgasm may occur without ejaculation Ejaculation of semen through the penile urethra and expulsion from the urethral meatus. The force of ejaculation varies from man to man and at different times but diminishes after the first two to three contractions (stage 2 of the expulsive process)	Varied patterns of orgasms, including minor surges and contractions, multiple orgasms, or a simple intense orgasm similar to that of the male
Resolution	Reversal of vasocongestion in 10–30 min; disappearance of all signs of myotonia within 5 min Genitals and breasts return to their pre-excitement states Sex flush disappears in reverse order of appearance Heart rate, respiratory rate, and blood pressure return to normal Other reactions include sleepiness, relaxation, and emotional outbursts, such as crying or laughing	A **refractory period** during which the body will not respond to sexual stimulation; varies, depending on age and other factors, from a few moments to hours or days	

premature ejaculation, many sex therapists advise couples to increase sexual communication and responsiveness and to decrease performance demands. The couple together practise *sensate exercises* (learning to enjoy the sensation of touch without attempting intercourse) and then work together to establish satisfying coitus.

Retarded ejaculation, or **ejaculatory incompetence,** is either the inability to ejaculate into the vagina or a delayed ejaculation. Like erectile dysfunction, retarded ejaculation may have physical or psychological origins.

TABLE 12.2 Effects of Medications on Sexual Function

Medication	Possible Effects*
Alcohol	Moderate amounts: increased sexual functioning; chronic use: decreased sexual desire, orgasmic dysfunction, and impotence
Alpha-blockers	Ejaculatory failure
Antianxiety agents	Decreased sexual desire; orgasmic dysfunction in women; delayed ejaculation
Anticonvulsants	Decreased sexual desire; reduced sexual response
Antidepressants	Decreased sexual desire; orgasmic delay or dysfunction in women; delayed or failed ejaculation; painful erection
Antihistamines	Decreased vaginal lubrication; decreased desire
Antihypertensives	Decreased sexual desire; erectile failure; ejaculation dysfunction
Antipsychotics	Decreased sexual desire; orgasmic dysfunction in women; delayed ejaculation; ejaculatory failure
Barbiturates	In low doses, increased sexual pleasure; in large doses, decreased sexual desire, orgasmic dysfunction, and impotence
Beta-blockers	Decreased sexual desire
Cardiotonics	Decreased sexual desire
Cocaine	Increased intensity of sexual experience; with chronic use, decreased sexual desire and sexual dysfunction
Diuretics	Decreased vaginal lubrication; decreased sexual desire; erectile dysfunction
Marijuana	As above for cocaine, but prolonged use reduces testosterone levels and reduces sperm production
Narcotics	Inhibited sexual desire and response; erectile and ejaculatory dysfunctions

*Nurses and clients must familiarize themselves with the specific medication prescribed or used, as effects vary in each category of drug.

Sources: Fogel, C. I., & Lauver, D. (1990). *Sexual health promotion.* Philadelphia, PA: Saunders, p. 487–488; and Crooks, R., & Baur, K. (1996). *Our sexuality* (6th ed.). Pacific Grove: Brooks/Cole, p. 430.

Female Dysfunction

Four female dysfunctions are orgasmic dysfunction, vaginismus, dyspareunia, and vulvodynia. **Orgasmic dysfunction** is the inability of a woman to achieve orgasm. Orgasmic dysfunction can be caused by drugs, alcohol, aging, and anatomic abnormalities of the genitals. However, most cases have psychological causes, including hostility between partners, fear or guilt about enjoying the sexual act, and concern about performance. Therapy usually involves helping both partners to establish new attitudes about sex. Pelvic muscle exercises (Kegel exercises) can also increase the woman's capacity to achieve orgasm by increasing the strength of the pubococcygeal muscle.

Vaginismus is the irregular and involuntary contraction of the muscles around the outer third of the vagina when coitus is attempted—that is, the vagina closes before penetration. Its causes can be severe sexual inhibition, often associated with early learning, or rape, incest, and painful intercourse.

Treatment often involves sensate focus exercises and therapy to bring about psychological changes. In some instances, graduated vaginal dilators are used.

Dyspareunia describes pain experienced by a woman during intercourse as a result of inadequate lubrication, scarring, vaginal infection, or hormonal imbalance. Treatment—such as applying additional lubrication before intercourse—may correct the underlying cause.

Vulvodynia is a chronic vulvar discomfort or pain that is characterized by complaints of burning, stinging, irritation, or rawness of the female genitalia, affecting one's ability to engage in sexual activity. Neither the cause nor the cure is known.

Effects of Medications on Sexual Function

Many prescription medications and social drugs can affect sexual desire and response (see Table 12.2). These include central nervous system depressants, such as narcotics; antianxiety agents, such as barbiturates and benzodiazepines; anticholinergic agents, such as atropine; cardiovascular agents, such as antiarrhythmics, antihypertensives, diuretics, and beta-blocking agents; antidepressants and antipsychotics; and social drugs, such as alcohol and marijuana.

Assessing

Information about a client's sexual health status should always be an integral part of a nursing assessment. The amount and kind of data collected depend on the context of the assessment, that is, the client's reason for seeking health care and how the client's sexuality interacts with other problems. The nurse's professional preparation also influences the level of sexual health assessment.

Generally, the nurse conducts a sexual history as part of a complete assessment, or:

- when a client is receiving care for pregnancy, infertility, contraception, or STI;
- when the client's illness or therapy will affect sexual functioning (e.g., clients with diabetes, gynecological problems, heart disease); or
- if the client is currently experiencing a sexual problem (e.g., erectile dysfunction).

Nursing History

Many aspects of sexuality are integrated into the nursing history. For example, the need to collect data about erectile dysfunction in a male who has diabetes may be indicated in the review of the cardiovascular, neurological, and genitourinary systems.

The screening process of the systems review allows the nurse and client to identify problem areas. For example, answers to the question "Do you have any concerns about the amount or regularity of your menstrual flow?" can give clues to the presence of problems not otherwise identified. A useful approach to psychosexual assessment is a review of sexual self-concept. Manner of dress, tone of voice, and comments about self and relationships with others can all give the nurse opportunities to explore issues of sexual self-concept more fully. Because illnesses and other health concerns can have a strong influence on sexual self-concept, assessment of these areas often provides the first clues to client concerns.

The Assessment Guidelines box below provides questions that the nurse can ask as part of the health history. Note that lead-in questions are asked before the questions about sexuality.

Physical Examination

Physical examination of the female genitals and reproductive tract and the male genitals is part of a routine physical examination in some agencies. Check agency protocol. See Chapter 27 for details of the examination. If the client

ASSESSMENT GUIDELINES

Sexual Health History

Women

- When did your menstrual periods first begin, and when did you have your last menstrual period?
- What is the usual length of your period in days and usual amount of bleeding?
- Do you have any concerns about the amount or regularity of your menstrual flow?
- If periods are irregular, problematic, or have stopped: Have you been evaluated for this change or done anything yourself to deal with it?
- Are you having any burning with urination, any vaginal itching or discharge, midcycle spotting, pain with intercourse, or any other problems?
- Have you ever been pregnant? (Explore number and outcome of pregnancies, including miscarriages and induced abortions.)
- Do you know how to do a breast self-examination?
- How often do you do breast self-examination?
- Is there a history of breast or ovarian cancer in your family?
- Do you have regular Pap test and mammogram?
- When was this last done?

Men

- Are you having any difficulty with initiating urination, urinary frequency, or frequent urination at night?
- Are you having any itching or discharge from your penis?
- Do you know how to do testicular self-examination?
- How often do you do testicular self-examination?
- Is there a history of testicular cancer in your family?

Men and Women

- Are you currently sexually active?
- What do you do to protect yourself from infection when you are sexually active?
- Have you ever had a sexually transmitted disease?
- Has any disease, injury, surgery, medication, or other situation affected your sexual health and happiness or your feelings about yourself as a woman or man?
- Do you have any questions about your sexual health or functioning, or is there anything else we have discussed that you would like clarified or explained?
- The language used in taking a sexual health history should not assume heterosexual partnering, leaving space for disclosure of sexual orientations (e.g., lesbian, gay, or bisexual).

has not been examined within one year, or if data from the recent nursing history indicate a need, the nurse performs a physical examination. Nursing history data indicating the need for a physical examination include the following:

- Suspicion of infertility, pregnancy, or an STI
- Reports of discharge, presence of a lump, or change in colour, size, and shape of a genital organ
- Changes in urinary function
- Need for Papanicolaou test
- Request for birth control

Identifying Clients at Risk

Clients at risk for altered sexual patterns include those experiencing:

- Altered body structure or function due to trauma, pregnancy, recent childbirth, anatomic abnormalities of the genitals, or disease (see "Health and Illness Situations" earlier in this chapter for common diseases affecting sexuality)
- Physical, psychosocial, or sexual abuse; sexual assault
- Disfiguring conditions, such as burns, skin conditions, birthmarks, scars (e.g., mastectomy), and ostomies
- Specific medication therapy that decreases sexual drive or causes erectile or ejaculatory dysfunction (see Table 12.2)
- Temporary or long-term impaired physical ability to perform grooming and maintain sexual attractiveness
- Value conflicts between personal beliefs and religious doctrine
- Loss of a partner
- Lack of knowledge or misinformation about sexual functioning and expression

Diagnosing

The NANDA nursing diagnoses relating specifically to sexuality include the following:

- *Altered Sexuality Patterns:* the state in which a person expresses concern regarding his or her sexuality.
- *Sexual Dysfunction:* the state in which a person experiences a change in sexual function that is viewed as unsatisfying, unrewarding, or inadequate.

Defining characteristics and contributing factors of these diagnoses were discussed earlier. Clinical applications of these diagnoses are shown in Table 12.3.

Nurses frequently diagnose a risk of one of the preceding two conditions because of risk factors in the client's database or because the client's illness, surgery, or therapies are associated with a high incidence of sexual concerns and problems.

Sexual problems can also be the etiology of other diagnoses, including the following:

- *Knowledge deficit* (e.g., about conception, STIs, contraception, or normal sexual changes over the lifespan) related to misinformation and sexual myths
- *Pain* related to inadequate vaginal lubrication or effects of genital surgery
- *Anxiety* related to loss of sexual desire or functioning
- *Fear* related to history of sexual abuse or dyspareunia
- *Body image disturbance* (mastectomy) related to perceived sexual rejection by spouse

Planning

Goals to meet clients' sexual needs include the following:

- Maintain, restore, or improve sexual health
- Increase knowledge of sexuality and sexual health
- Prevent the occurrence of sexually transmitted diseases

TABLE 12.3 Clinical Application: Assessment Data Clusters and Related Nursing Diagnoses for Clients with Sexuality Problems

Data Cluster	Nursing Diagnosis
Marsha Ogilvy, 55 years old, reports vaginal burning and pain whenever she and her husband make love. Her last menses was 14 months ago. She says her husband is concerned about the lack of her usual response to lovemaking.	***Sexual Dysfunction*** related to painful intercourse from inadequate vaginal lubrication
Georgina Honey, 49 years old, had a total mastectomy two weeks ago. She says, "I'm sure not going to be sexually appealing to my husband anymore. How on earth will he ever want to make love to me again? I feel like a lopsided oddity."	***Sexuality Pattern, Ineffective*** related to body image disturbance secondary to mastectomy
Larry Stogryn, 52 years old, has a history of hypertension for which he has been taking an antihypertensive (reserpine [Serpasil]). He says he has lost interest in sex in the past few months, and when he does have sex, he has trouble keeping an erection.	***Sexuality Pattern, Ineffective*** related to altered body function secondary to use of antihypertensive medication

- Prevent the spread of an existing STI
- Increase satisfaction with the level of sexual functioning
- Improve sexual self-concept

Examples of specific desired outcomes related to some of these goals, although established in this phase, are provided in Table 12.6 in the "Evaluating" section of this chapter. Nursing interventions to promote sexual health and function focus largely on the nurse's teaching role. For example, clients need to be taught about normal sexual function, the effects of medications on sexual function, preventing sexually transmitted diseases, and performing breast and testicular self-examinations. In addition to teaching, nurses can do the following to help clients maintain a healthy sexual self-concept:

- Provide privacy during intimate body care.
- Involve the client's partner in physical care.
- Give attention to the client's appearance and dress.
- Give clients privacy to meet their sexual needs alone or with a partner within physically safe limits.

Implementing

The interventions the nurse selects are based on the data obtained from the client and the identified nursing diagnoses. Many interventions are directed at preventing problems the client is at risk for and providing information about changes and how to adapt to those changes.

Providing Sexual Health Teaching

Providing education for sexual health is an important component of nursing implementation. Many sexual problems exist as a result of sexual ignorance; many others can be prevented with effective sexual health teaching. Examples of important areas of teaching include (1) sex education, (2) responsible sexual behaviour, and (3) self-examination.

Sex Education

Nurses can assist clients to understand their anatomy and how their bodies function. For example, understanding the anatomy of the genitals may help women learn how their bodies respond to sexual stimulation. Both men and women need to learn the kind of stimulation that is pleasing and causes arousal. The importance of open communication between partners should also be encouraged. Women may also benefit from learning *Kegel exercises.* These exercises involve contraction and relaxation of the pubococcygeal muscle, the muscle that contracts when a person prevents urine flow. The benefits of Kegel exercises include increased pelvic floor muscle tone; increased vaginal lubrication during sexual arousal; increased sensation during intercourse; increased genital sensitivity; stronger gripping of the base of the penis; earlier postpartum recovery of the pelvic floor muscle; and increased flexibility of episiotomy scars (Crooks & Baur, 1996; May & Mahlmeister, 1994). The steps to perform Kegel exercises are discussed in Chapter 36 because these exercises are also used in bladder retraining.

Adolescent Sex Education

- School-based programs are an important source of sexual health education.
- Canadian guidelines for sexual health education include promoting sexual health enhancement and the prevention of sexual health problems, such as unplanned pregnancies, transmission of infections, sexual exploitation, and abuse.
- A 1997 survey of adolescents in Ontario (McKay & Holowaty) found that 89 percent of students felt that it was important for them to receive sexual education and that school was identified as their preferred source of information.
- Health Canada's (1994) Canadian Guidelines for Sexual Health Education suggest that educational programs should acknowledge and address the diverse needs of all students, including those who are gay, lesbian, or bisexual.
- Surveys of Canadian parents and students themselves support the inclusion of education in which such issues as homophobia and discrimination based on sexual orientation can be addressed.

Source: McKay, A. (2000). Common questions about sexual health education. *The Canadian Journal of Human Sexuality, 9,* 2.

Details about physiological changes that occur during major developmental crises should be provided as part of general health care. For example, the nurse needs to discuss the effects of puberty, pregnancy, menopause, and the male climacteric on sexual function. When clients experience illness or surgery that alters sexual function, the nurse needs to discuss effects of treatment (e.g., medications) and any changes that need to be undertaken to ensure safe sex (e.g., position changes or a safe time to resume sexual intercourse after a heart attack).

Parents often need assistance to learn ways to answer questions and what information to provide for their children starting in the preschool years. Parents need to be the primary educators of children at an early age; however, peers, teachers, media, and toys also teach about sexual issues. See box on "Adolescent Sex Education."

Although there is an increasing awareness today of sexuality and sexual functioning, some people still hold certain myths and misconceptions about sexuality. Many of these are handed down in families and are part of the beliefs in a particular culture. It is highly important that nurses learn about the beliefs clients hold and provide up-to-date information. See Table 12.4 for some common sexual myths and misconceptions.

TABLE 12.4 Common Sexual Misconceptions

Misconception	Fact
Nearly all men over 70 years old are impotent.	Sexual desire and ability decrease very little after middle age.
Masturbation causes certain mental instabilities.	Masturbation is totally harmless.
Sexual activity weakens a person.	There is no evidence that sexual activity weakens a person.
Women who have experienced orgasm are more likely to become pregnant.	Conceiving is not related to experiencing orgasm.
A large penis provides greater sexual satisfaction to women than a small penis.	There is no evidence that a large penis provides greater satisfaction.
Alcohol is a sexual stimulant.	Alcohol is a relaxant and central nervous system depressant. Chronic alcoholism is associated with impotence.
Intercourse during menstruation is dangerous, i.e., it will cause vaginal tissue damage.	There is no physiological basis for abstinence during menses.
The face-to-face coital position is the moral or proper one.	The position that offers the most pleasure and is acceptable to both partners is the correct one.

Responsible Sexual Behaviour

Responsible sexual behaviour involves the prevention of sexually transmitted infections (STIs) and the prevention of unplanned pregnancy.

STI Prevention The prevention of STIs is an essential part of sexual health teaching. (See box on STIs among Canadians.) Note that *Trichomonas* and *Candida* infections can also be acquired nonsexually. Increases in these diseases are due to two factors: (1) changing sexual mores that permit increased sexual activity, and (2) an increase in the number of sexual partners. Because the term *sexually transmitted infections* elicits feelings of guilt, shame, and fear, people frequently do not seek medical help as early as they should. Clients need education about these diseases, preventive measures, and early treatment. Many STIs can be treated quickly and effectively. Others may have serious consequences. For example, women may develop pelvic inflammatory disease (PID) resulting in damage to the reproductive structures and possible infertility. AIDS has no long-term effective treatment. The anxiety about AIDS transmission has caused many individuals to alter their sexual behaviour, such as using a condom during intercourse.

Table 12.5 lists the common signs of STIs for which people should seek medical care. Methods for decreasing exposure to STIs are described in the Client Teaching box on page 196.

Prevention of Unplanned Pregnancies Prevention of unwanted pregnancies must be addressed not only with adolescents but also with couples who are planning the time of their first birth and want to space children and limit family size. Nurses need to be familiar with various contraceptive methods and their advantages, disadvantages, contraindications, effectiveness, safety, and cost. It is beyond the scope of this text to discuss contraceptives in detail. The various methods are outlined in the box on "Unplanned Pregnancies" on page 197.

Sexually Transmitted Infections among Canadians

- In 1997, epidemiological trends indicated that many of the reportable sexually transmitted infections (STIs) were either declining or close to elimination.
- Since 1997, there has been a gradual but broad-based increase in the rates of chlamydia and gonorrhea in Canada. The infection rate is greatest among the 15- to 24-year-olds.
- Both chlamydia and gonorrhea can lead to pelvic inflammatory disease, a leading cause of tubal infertility and ectopic pregnancy.
- Herpes simplex virus (HSV) is the second most prevalent viral STI worldwide. Symptoms may be very subtle so that many persons carrying the serologic markers of HSV-2 remain undiagnosed. Perinatal transmission is a particular concern for undiagnosed women.
- Infectious syphilis was on the brink of elimination in Canada in 1997. Several localized outbreaks have occurred since then, particularly among socially marginalized persons, such as those residing in the downtown eastside neighbourhood of Vancouver.

Source: Patrick, D., Wong, T. & Jordan, R. (2000). Sexually transmitted infections in Canada: Recent resurgence threatens national goals. *The Canadian Journal of Human Sexuality*, 9, 3.

TABLE 12.5 Clinical Signs of Sexually Transmitted Infections

Disease	Male	Female
Gonorrhea	Painful urination; urethritis with watery white discharge, which may become purulent	May be asymptomatic; or vaginal discharge, pain, and urinary frequency may be present
Syphilis	Chancre, usually on glans penis, which is painless and heals in 4–6 weeks; secondary symptoms—skin eruptions, low-grade fever, inflammation of lymph glands—in 6 weeks to 6 months after chancre heals	Chancre on cervix or other genital areas, which heals in 4–6 weeks; symptoms same as for male
Genital warts (condyloma acuminatum)	Single lesions or clusters of lesions growing beneath or on the foreskin, at external meatus, or on the glans penis; On dry skin areas, lesions are hard and yellow-gray; On moist areas, lesions are pink or red and soft with a cauliflowerlike appearance	Lesions appear at the bottom part of the vaginal opening, on the perineum, the vaginal lips, inner walls of the vagina, and the cervix
Herpes genitalis (Herpes simplex of the genitals)	Primary herpes involves the presence of painful sores or large, discrete vesicles that last for weeks; vesicles rupture; Recurrent herpes is itchy rather than painful; it lasts for a few hours to 10 days	Same as for males
Chlamydial urethritis	Urinary frequency; watery, mucoid urethral discharge	Commonly a carrier; vaginal discharge, dysuria, urinary frequency
Trichomoniasis	Slight itching; moisture on top of penis; slight, early morning urethral discharge. Many males are asymptomatic.	Itching and redness of vulva and skin inside thighs; copious watery, frothy vaginal discharge
Candidiasis	Itching, irritation, discharge, plaque of cheesy material under foreskin	Red and excoriated vulva; intense itching of vaginal and vulvar tissues; thick, white, cheesy or curdlike discharge
Acquired immune deficiency syndrome (AIDS)	Symptoms can appear anytime from several months to several years after acquiring the virus. The person has reduced immunity to other diseases. Symptoms include any of the following for which there is no other explanation: persistent heavy night sweats; extreme fatigue; severe weight loss; enlarged lymph glands in neck, axillae, or groin; persistent diarrhea; skin rashes; blurred vision or chronic headache; harsh, dry cough; thick gray-white coating on tongue or throat.	

CLIENT TEACHING

Preventing Transmission of STIs

- Limit the number of sexual partners.
- Use condoms in nonmonogamous and homosexual relationships or other relationships that have the potential for STI transmission.
- Talk openly with sexual partners about how to have "safe sex" and be honest about any history of an STI.
- Abstain from sexual activity with a partner *known* to have or *suspected* of having an STI.
- Report to a health-care facility for examination whenever in doubt about possible exposure or when signs of an STI are evident.
- When an STI is diagnosed, notify all partners and encourage them to seek treatment.

Teaching Self-Examination

The importance of monthly **breast self-examination (BSE)** for women and monthly **testicular self-examination (TSE)** for men cannot be overemphasized. Early detection of cancer results in a greater chance of cure and less complex treatment. Clients need to be assured that most lumps discovered are not cancerous but that it is essential that all lumps or other detected abnormalities be checked by the client's physician for accurate diagnosis. All nursing history assessments of clients need to include the client's understanding and practice of BSE or TSE. Self-examination involves both inspection and palpation procedures and should be conducted once a month.

For BSE, a regular time is best—such as one week following menstruation, when breast tenderness and fullness caused by fluid retention have subsided, or on the same day of the month, if postmenopausal. Women who examine themselves regularly become familiar with the shape and texture of their breasts. Women clients should also be informed about mammogram screening.

The best time for TSE is after a warm bath or shower when the scrotal sac is relaxed. Men should also be taught to inspect and palpate their breasts because they have some glandular tissue beneath each nipple, a potential site for malignancy.

Methods of Contraception

- Abstinence
- Coitus interruptus (withdrawal of the penis before ejaculation)
- Fertility awareness (identification of the days of the month when conception could take place and abstaining during that time)
- Mechanical barriers: vaginal diaphragm, cervical cap, condom
- Chemical barriers: insertion of spermicidal foams, creams, jellies, or suppositories into the vagina before intercourse
- Intrauterine devices (IUDs)
- Hormonal: oral contraceptives (birth control pills), subdermal implants of synthetic progestin
- Surgical sterilization: tubal ligation and vasectomy
- Abortion

Unplanned Pregnancies

Unplanned pregnancies can cause emotional distress for both partners. Some women find themselves alone dealing with a difficult decision-making process, often unable to seek support from family or friends. Unplanned pregnancies happen for a number of reasons including the failure of birth control measures. Health-care providers should avoid making assumptions about the cause of unplanned pregnancies and offer support and guidance to community resources. Options to consider include:

- The partners may decide to raise the child together.
- One partner may decide to raise the child.
- A family member may be able to raise the child until a parent is able to take over care.
- Adoption options including open or closed arrangements may be considered.
- Abortion in Canada is legal, safe, and accessible through the medical system.

CLIENT TEACHING

Breast Self-Examination

What is BSE?
BSE, or Breast Self-Examination, is a way of using your eyes and hands to get to know your breasts, and to help you identify any changes in your breasts at the earliest possible opportunity.

Breast Self-Examination is done in the privacy of your own home.

Who should do BSE?
BSE is an important practice for every woman. Every woman from the age of 20 years and over should examine her breasts every month.

Why do BSE?
Breasts have a normal amount of lumpiness that can be due to hormonal changes linked to the menstrual cycle and menopause. BSE will help you recognize these normal lumps so you will more easily recognize anything out of the ordinary.

With regular BSE, you can find a lump one to three years earlier than you could by waiting for it to grow large enough to find by chance.

You could save your breast; you could save your life. Breast cancer can be cured—especially when found early.

How to do BSE
There are three steps involved. It is important to do all the steps every month.

I. Visual Check

II. Hand Check—Standing

III. Hand Check—Lying Down

1. Visual Check
   a. Stand in front of a mirror and look at your breasts carefully—first face forward and then turn slowly from side to side.
   b. Lift your arms above your head and behind your ears. If you have pendulous breasts you may need to lift them up to see the lower halves.
   c. Lower your hands part-way and squeeze your palms together.

2. Hand Check—Standing. Use the opposite hand for each breast.
   a. Use a flat hand. Bend your wrist, not your fingers, to go over curves. Apply moderate pressure and keep constant contact with your skin.

CLIENT TEACHING

Breast Self-Examination *continued*

- **b.** Move back and forth across the breast in a straight line pattern, making constant small circles. Slide your hand down one finger width for each pass. Cover the full area indicated.
- **c.** Check the area under your arm. Relax your arm, place your hand under it, making the same small circular movements as before.

3. Hand Check—Lying Down
In the last step of BSE, lie down on a firm surface. Use exactly the same steps used when standing. It is not necessary to check your underarm while lying down.

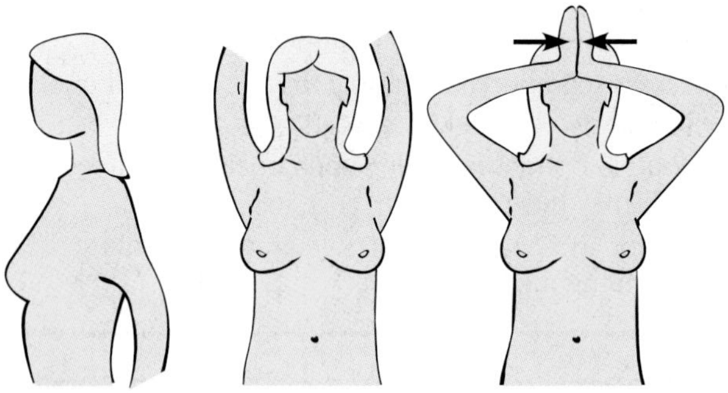

Look for:
Overall changes in shape, size, or contour; obvious lumps, dimpling, flattening, reddening; nipple flattening, indrawing, or pointing in a new direction. Also look for sores or rashes.

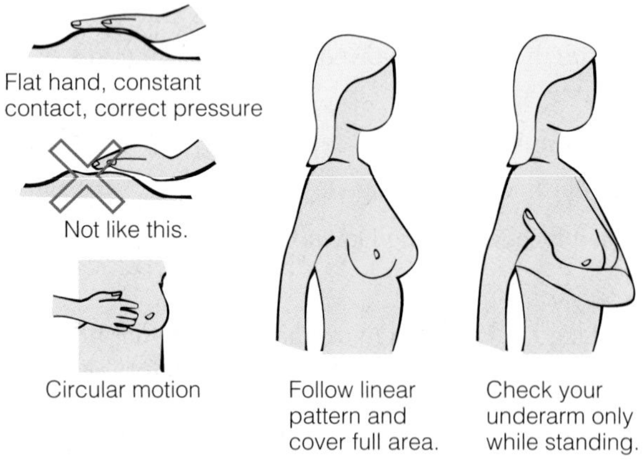

Flat hand, constant contact, correct pressure
Not like this.
Circular motion
Follow linear pattern and cover full area.
Check your underarm only while standing.

What changes are you checking for?
Anything that is a different texture or movement from what you have felt before. Remember that it may be normal for your breasts to be lumpy—you are checking for something that was not there last month. If you feel or see any changes, that is the time to consult your doctor.

Source: The Canadian Cancer Society, 2003. www.cancer.ca

CLIENT TEACHING

Mammography

Mammography is a type of x-ray that can see changes inside your breasts that are too small to feel. Mammography also gives you and your doctor information about changes in your breasts that you find during breast self-examination or that a health professional finds during a physical examination of the breasts.

All women should discuss the risks and benefits of mammography with their doctor. Women between 50–69 years should have a mammogram every 2 years. If you are under age 50 or over 69 and are at a higher risk for breast cancer, you should discuss with your doctor when mammography may be appropriate for you.

Breast screening programs vary between provinces. All provinces have breast cancer screening programs for women age 50–69. You can make an appointment at a screening centre without a doctor's referral.

Breast screening centres
To find out more about breast screening centres in your province, call the number below or ask your doctor to refer you to a Canadian Association of Radiologists (CAR) accredited facility.

British Columbia	1 800 663-9203
Yukon	1 867 393-8740
Alberta	1 800 667-0604
Northwest Territories	Call your doctor or health clinic
Saskatchewan	1 800 667-0017
Manitoba	1 800 903-9290
Ontario	1 800 668-9304
Nunavut	1 867 975 9700
Quebec	Call your doctor or Info-Santé
New Brunswick	Call your doctor or local hospital
Nova Scotia	1 800 565-0548
Prince Edward Island	1 888 858-2915
Newfoundland & Labrador	1 800 414-3443

Source: Canadian Cancer Society, 2003. www.cancer.ca

Counselling for Altered Sexual Function

One technique nurses can use to help clients with altered sexual function is the PLISSIT model, developed by Annon (1974) for this purpose. The model involves four progressive levels represented by the acronym PLISSIT:

P Permission giving
LI Limited information
SS Specific suggestions
IT Intensive therapy

CLIENT TEACHING

Testicular Self-Examination (TSE)

Testicular self-examination (TSE) is a simple 3-step process that can help you detect testicular cancer early. All men should perform a TSE once each month from the time they are 15 years old.

Ideally, you should examine your testicles after a hot bath or shower because the warmth will cause your testicles to descend and the skin of your scrotum to relax, making it easier to feel any lumps, growths, or tenderness.

- Stand in front of the mirror. Look for any swelling on the skin of your scrotum.
- Examine each testicle one at a time, placing your index and middle fingers of both hands on the underside of your testicle and your thumbs on the top side. Firmly roll your testicle between your fingers and thumbs, carefully feeling for any lumps, growths, or sensations of tenderness that don't feel normal. It is normal for one of your testicles to be larger than the other. At the back of each testicle there is a soft cord. This is the tube that collects and carries your sperm. It is a normal part of your scrotum. After you have examined one testicle and cord, check the opposite side. Some men find that comparing the 2 sides is helpful.
- Become familiar with how your scrotum feels so you will be able to tell if there are any changes over time. Testicular cancer may not always create a noticeable lump on your testicle. Other clues to look for include:
  - any change in size, shape, tenderness, or sensation of your testicles or scrotum
  - a change in the consistency or swelling of your testicles or scrotum
  - pain in your testicles or scrotum
  - a dull ache or heaviness in your lower abdomen
  - abnormal and persistent backache
  - unexplained weight loss
  - breast development

Three important things that you can do:

1. Check your testicles every month.
2. Have regular medical checkups that include a testicular exam.
3. See your doctor right away if you notice any symptoms.

Regular testicular self-examination is an important health habit, but it can't replace a doctor's examination. Your doctor should check your testicles when you have a physical exam. You can also ask your doctor to teach you how to do testicular self-examination.

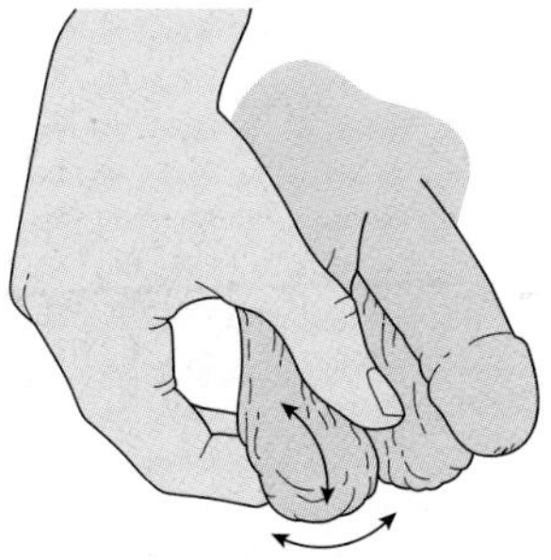

Source: Canadian Cancer Society, 2003. www.cancer.ca

At each level, the nurse provides additional guidance and information to the client and, therefore, requires more specialized and specific knowledge and skill. All professional nurses should be able to function at the first three levels.

Permission Giving

Clients may feel that they need permission to be sexual beings, to ask questions, to show affection, and to express themselves sexually. Giving permission means that the nurse, by attitude or word, lets the client know that sexual thoughts, fantasies, and behaviours between informed consenting adults are allowed. Giving permission begins when the nurse acknowledges the client's spoken and unspoken sexual concerns and conveys the attitude that sexual concerns and needs are important to health and recovery.

For example, the nurse might ask a client recuperating from a heart attack the following questions:

"Now that you're recuperating and you've had some time to sort out your feelings, have you thought about how your heart attack might alter your sex life?"
"Have you and your partner discussed how you both feel about it?"

Limited Information

Clients need accurate but concise information. The nurse might explain what is normal; how some medical conditions, treatments, injuries, or surgeries may affect sexuality and functioning; or how aging may affect sexuality and functioning.

Continuing with the preceding example, the nurse shares information and informs the client about how the heart attack might affect the client's sex life, including the following:

> *"Your heart attack will not alter your capacity for sexual response. Most people can resume intercourse in four to six weeks, but this should be confirmed by your doctor."*
>
> *"Many postcoronary clients fear sexual intercourse because of increased heart and respiratory rates associated with it. However, your prescribed program of progressive physical activity will also increase your tolerance for sexual activity."*

Many clients recuperating from childbirth, for example, or specific illness or disease (e.g., heart attack) need instructions about safe sexual activities and the effects that therapy may have on sexual functioning. The following topics need to be considered:

- When sexual activity is safe
- Specific sexual activities that are unsafe, and why
- Adaptations needed for resuming a satisfactory sexual life
- The side effects of prescribed medications on sexual functioning, and the need to notify the physician for possible dose or medication adjustment should problems develop

Specific Suggestions

At this level, the nurse requires specialized knowledge and skill about how sexuality and functioning may be affected by a disease process or therapy and what interventions might be effective. The nurse offers suggestions to help the client adapt sexual activity to promote optimal functioning, such as what measures might be used to alleviate vaginal dryness, safe positions for intercourse following a total hip replacement, safe and unsafe sexual practices following a heart attack, and ways to handle ostomy appliances, Foley catheters, casts, or other devices (e.g., prostheses) during sexual activity. Similarly, nurses on a cardiac unit need specialized knowledge about sexual readjustment during cardiac rehabilitation, and nurses working with clients with spinal cord injuries need information about the sexual consequences of spinal injuries at various levels.

Using the example of the client recuperating from a heart attack, the nurse may offer the following suggestion:

> *"Many people express concern about the stress of certain positions for intercourse, but you may use whatever position is comfortable for you and your partner, or try side-lying or partner-on-top positions."*

Canadian Society Notes

Fact	Implications for Nursing Practice
A Canadian survey showed that staff activities and behaviours in addressing sexuality are influenced by explicit expectation (policies, job descriptions) and implicit expectations (accepted practices and the organizational culture) (Pyke, Rabin, Moffs, & Balbirnie, 2002).	Implicit and explicit expectations of particular workplaces will influence the degree to which clients' sexual health issues and educational needs are addressed by nursing staff.
Chlamydia is the most frequently reported communicable disease in Canada. Although reported rates in Canada fell from 162 per 100,000 in 1992 to 123 per 100,000 in 1995, reported rates increased by 30 percent between 1997 and 2000 (Patrick, Wong, & Jordan, 2000).	Nurses need to remain vigilant to fluctuating changes in reported rates of sexually transmitted infections and to continue to educate clients about the use of safe sexual practices.
In Canada, the reported rates of newly acquired HIV infection decreased between 1995 and 1997, although this trend has not continued from 1998 to 2000.The rate of decline of cases of AIDS has declined since the peak of 1,859 new cases in 1993 to 644 reported cases in 2000. Differences between the rates of newly acquired HIV infection and AIDS is effected by the impact of antiretroviral therapy in preventing development of AIDS among those who are HIV positive (Patrick, Wong, & Jordan, 2000).	Nurses should be attentive to the shifting demographics of those contracting HIV, including heterosexual women. Complacency regarding the transmission of HIV, related to the decline of infection rates in Canada during the 1990s and the presence of new therapies, should be assessed and discussed with clients.

RESEARCH NOTE

To What Extent Do Cardiac Nurses Assess Sexual Concerns and Provide Teaching to Clients with Myocardial Infarction?

The study examined the assessment of sexual concerns and the practice of sexual counselling with myocardial infarction (MI) clients in a convenience sample of 171 cardiac nurses from three hospitals in the Midwest. Seventy-five percent of nurses had offered to discuss sexual concerns with less than 2 percent of their clients in the preceding year, and 71 percent of nurses had never referred clients to another professional for sexual counselling. Analysis of 17 items on the practice index indicated that nurses are not assessing sexual concerns, and specific information relevant to MI clients is largely not being taught for the most part.

Implications: Efforts need to be directed at increasing the comfort and knowledge level of nurses so that sexual counselling is implemented. Ideally, this would occur through both formal and informal educational methods. Client needs could be better addressed if education for both practicing nurses and nursing students included sexuality and how to include sexual information in their assessments and interventions. Nurses need to provide sexual counselling for clients with MI as part of their routine assessment and intervention to maintain the sexual integrity of the individual.

Source: Steinke, E. E., & Patterson, P. (1995). Sexual counseling of MI patients by cardiac nurses. *Journal of Cardiovascular Nursing, 10*(1), 81–87.

Intensive Therapy

Intensive therapy, provided by a clinical nurse specialist or sex therapist, is used when the first three levels of counselling are ineffective. It may involve such issues as sexual motivation, marriage, or self-concept.

Dealing with Inappropriate Sexual Behaviour

Nurses may encounter a variety of sexually inappropriate behaviours for a variety of reasons. The behaviour may be either aggressive or nonaggressive. Clients may act out sexually by:

- Exposing themselves.
- Asking the nurse to provide intimate physical care, such as bathing genital areas, when they are capable of doing this themselves.
- Touching or grabbing the nurse (e.g., on the breasts or buttocks); trying to pull the nurse into bed.
- Making blatant sexual statements to the nurse.
- Offering sex to the nurse.
- Whistling; making comments about the nurse's attractiveness or desirability.
- Making sexual comments to another client in the same room or to visitors about the "sexy" nurse or what they would like to do sexually with the nurse.

Possible reasons for this inappropriate behaviour are:

- Fear or anxiety over future ability to function sexually.
- Unmet need for intimacy and sexual closeness because of hospitalization, injury, illness, treatment, lack of a partner, lack of privacy.
- Misinterpretation of the nurse's behaviour as sexual or provocative.
- Need for reassurance that they are still sexual beings and still sexually attractive.
- Need for attention.
- Confusion: Neurologic impairment or trauma can lead clients to use profane sexual language, engage in masturbation, expose themselves, or inappropriately touch or grab at the nurse.
- Need to control: Clients may be experiencing loss of control over their lives because of hospitalization, injury, or illness.
- Need for power.
- Belief that flirtatious behaviour is expected due to media portrayal of nurses as sexy, available, and experienced.

Before implementing any nursing interventions, the nurse should first ensure that the behaviour *is* inappropriate and not an attempt to communicate a physical need. For example, clients may expose themselves if they are febrile, pull at the penis if a catheter is uncomfortable or irritating, or reach for the nurse if unable to communicate verbally. Nursing strategies to deal with inappropriate sexual behaviour are shown in the box on the following page.

Evaluating

The goals established during the planning phase are evaluated according to specific desired outcomes also established during that phase. Examples of these are shown in Table 12.6. If any outcomes have *not* been achieved, the nurse should explore the reasons with questions such as the following:

- Were risk factors correctly identified?
- Did the client convey all significant fears and concerns about sexuality?
- Was the client more comfortable following discussions about sexual matters?
- Did the client understand the nurse's teaching?
- Was the health teaching compatible with the client's culture and religious values?
- Was the client ready to deal with sexuality problems?

Nursing Strategies for Inappropriate Sexual Behaviour

- Communicate that the behaviour is not acceptable by saying, for example, "I really do not like the things you are saying," or "I see you are not dressed. I will be back in 10 minutes and will help you with breakfast when you get your clothes on."
- Tell the client how the behaviour makes you feel: "When you act like that toward me, I don't even want to come into your room. It makes it hard for me to give you the kind of nursing care you need."
- Identify the behaviour you expect: "Please call me by my name, not 'honey'," or "I expect you to keep yourself covered when I am in the room. If you are feeling hot or something is uncomfortable, let me know, and I will try to make you more comfortable."
- Set firm limits: Take the client's hand and move it away, use direct eye contact, and say, "Don't do that!"
- Try to refocus clients from the inappropriate behaviour to their real concerns and fears; offer to discuss sexuality concerns: "All morning you have been making very personal sexual comments about yourself. Sometimes people talk like that when they are concerned about the sexual part of their life and how their illness will affect them. Are there things that you have questions about or would like to talk about?"
- Report the incident to your nursing instructor, charge nurse, or clinical nurse specialist. Discuss the incident, your feelings, and possible interventions.
- Ensure health team members relate to the client in a consistent manner, confronting the behaviour.
- Clarify the consequences of continued inappropriate behaviour (avoidance, withdrawal of services, no chance to help resolve underlying concerns of client).

TABLE 12.6 Evaluation Goals and Outcomes: Sexuality

Goal	Examples of Desired Outcomes
Increase knowledge of sexuality and sexual health	Describes male and female sexual anatomy and function accurately
	Identifies signs of STIs
	Identifies factors related to altered sexuality pattern or dysfunction due to disease condition
	Describes alternative modes of sexual expression required for disease condition or therapy
Prevent the occurrence of sexually transmitted infection	Identifies STI exposure risks
	Describes ways to avoid STIs
	Uses appropriate methods to control STI transmission
	Inquires about partner's STI status before sexual activity
	Is free of STI
Prevent the spread of existing STIs	Recognizes the signs and symptoms of an STI
	Takes appropriate actions to control the STI
	Participates in screening for STI
	Uses available health service for STI treatment and complies with recommended treatment
	Notifies sexual partner(s) if STI infection exists
Increase satisfaction with level of sexual functioning	Verbalizes concerns about altered pattern of sexual functioning (e.g., body image, desirability as sexual partner, sexual stimulation pattern, sexual response)
	Reports satisfaction with sexual functioning
	Reports satisfaction with level of sexual relationship

Consider...

What actions would you take if the client did *not* meet the following outcome criterion?

- "Takes appropriate actions to control an existing STI." (Data reveal that the client refuses to use a condom, fails to notify sexual partners of STI infection, and failed to report to a health service for treatment.)

FOCUS ON CRITICAL THINKING

Mr. Curry is a 50-year-old male who suffered a heart attack three weeks ago. He is doing well and is in a cardiac rehabilitation program. His only medications consist of a daily aspirin and an antihypertensive medication. During a routine checkup you inquire how he is feeling and whether he is doing well on his medications. Reluctantly, he admits that he is having some sexual problems. You encourage further discussion of the matter by displaying interest and explaining that it is okay for him to share his concerns with you. Mr. Curry states that he is having some difficulty achieving erections but is more concerned that he will have another heart attack if he engages in sexual activities.

1. Speculate about Mr. Curry's reluctance to discuss his sexual concerns.
2. What factors influence nurses' abilities to discuss sexual concerns with their clients?
3. What is the relationship between health and sexual function?
4. How can you best intervene to help Mr. Curry?

See Appendix A for answers to these questions.

CHAPTER HIGHLIGHTS

- Sexuality is important in developing self-identity, interpersonal relationships, intimacy, and love.
- In its broad sense, sexuality involves physical, emotional, social, and ethical aspects of being and behaving.
- An understanding of the structure and function of the male and female genitals is essential for nurses.
- The components that contribute to the development of sexuality are numerous; both biological and psychological components exist at all ages.
- In adults, many secondary sexual problems are related to illnesses, injuries, and medical therapies.
- During the middle and later years, the genitals undergo physical changes. However, the desire and ability to maintain satisfying sexual relationships can remain.
- Assessing risk for, or actual, sexual problems is part of the initial nursing assessment. Assessment should also be carried out when clients or support people present cues that problems exist or when clients have an illness that could cause sexual problems.
- Nurses assess attitudes toward sexuality, including factors that affect attitudes and behaviours.
- An understanding of sexual stimuli and response patterns can help individuals have satisfying sexual relationships. This understanding is also vital for nurses to help clients with psychological problems, such as feelings of inadequacy, or medical problems, such as spinal cord injuries or myocardial infarctions.
- Common sexual problems of healthy adults are changes in libido, erectile dysfunction, premature ejaculation, retarded ejaculation, orgasmic dysfunction, vaginismus, dyspareunia, and vulvodynia.
- Illnesses that commonly affect sexuality include myocardial infarction and diabetes mellitus. Many surgical procedures, including mastectomy, hysterectomy, orchiectomy, and enterostomy, may also affect sexual abilities and sexual self-image.
- Nursing diagnoses for clients with sexual problems are related to many contributing factors, including altered body structure or function, lack of knowledge or misinformation about sexual matters, physical or psychological abuse, value conflicts, and loss or lack of a partner.
- Before assisting clients with sexual problems, nurses must acquire accurate information about sexuality, identify and accept their own sexual values and behaviours as well as those of others, and be comfortable acquiring and disseminating information about sexuality.

- Nursing interventions focus on teaching clients about sexual function and sexuality; responsible sexual behaviour that includes the prevention of STIs and unplanned pregnancies; and self-examination of the breasts and testicles.
- Counselling clients with altered sexual functions can be facilitated by using the PLISSIT model: permission giving (P); limited information (LI); and specific suggestions (SS). Intensive therapy (IT) requires intervention by clinical nurse specialists or sex therapists.

READINGS AND REFERENCES

Suggested Readings

Alteneder, R. R. (1997). Addressing couples' sexuality concerns during the childbearing period: Use of the PLISSIT model. *JOGNN, 26*(6), 651–658.

Alteneder describes the use of the PLISSIT model as a framework for developing interventions regarding sexuality changes during pregnancy and the postpartum period. This time in the lifespan provides a couple the opportunity for learning to cope with changes in sexual interest, sexual functioning, and emotional fluctuations. The author discusses how these changes are experienced during each trimester to assist the nurse in applying the PLISSIT model and recognizing when referral is necessary.

Doyle, D., Bisson, D., Janes, N., Lynch, H., & Martin, C. (1999, January). Human sexuality in long-term care. *Canadian Nurse, 95*(1), 26–29.

These authors define sexuality broadly and describe a three-part process they developed at a 577-bed, chronic-care hospital to acknowledge and support appropriate sexual expression of the residents. The process involves (1) a team meeting of staff members who are guided to answer six questions about the nature of the relationship, (2) a family meeting, and (3) ongoing assessment.

MacLaren, A. (1995). Primary care for women. Comprehensive sexual health assessment. *Journal of Nurse-Midwifery, 40*(2), 104–119.

MacLaren discusses the fundamentals of sexual functioning and describes the elements of a comprehensive, developmentally relevant sexual health assessment. Personal barriers that may prevent clinicians from comfortably addressing sexual issues are discussed, and useful strategies for facilitating effective, reciprocal communication during a sexual health history are presented. A therapeutic intervention model for counselling, referral, and sexual health assessment of women in the primary care setting is also included.

Related Research

Ettinger, B., Friedman, G. D., Bush, T., & Quesenberry, C. P. (1996). Reduced mortality associated with long-term postmenopausal estrogen therapy. *Obstetrics & Gynecology, 87*(1), 6–12.

Hyde, J. S., DeLamater, J. D., Plant, E. A., & Byrd, J. M. (1996). Sexuality during pregnancy and the year postpartum. *Journal of Sex Research, 33*, 143–151.

Steinke, E. E., & Patterson, P. (1995). Sexual counseling of MI patients by cardiac nurses. *Journal of Cardiovascular Nursing, 10*(1), 81–87.

Selected References

Althusser, L. (1971). Ideology and ideological state apparatuses. In *Lenin and philosophy and other essays* (pp. 123–173). London: NLB.

Annon, J. (1974). *The behavioural treatment of sexual problems.* Vol. 1. *Brief therapy.* New York: Harper & Row.

Bernhard, I. A. (1992). Men's views about hysterectomies and women who have them. *Image: Journal of Nursing Scholarship, 24*, 177–181.

Carpenito, L. J. (2002). *Handbook of nursing diagnosis* (9th ed.). Philadelphia, PA: Lippincott.

Crooks, R., & Baur, K. (1996). *Our sexuality* (6th ed.). Pacific Grove, CA: Brooks/Cole.

Daniluk, J. (1998). *Women's sexuality across the life span: Challenging myths, creating meanings.* New York: Guilford Press.

Fogel, C. I., & Lauver, D. (1990). *Sexual health promotion.* Philadelphia, PA: Saunders.

Health Canada. Canadian guidelines for sexual health education. http://www.hcsc.gc.ca/hpb/lcdc/publicat/sheguide/defin_ehtml

Masters, W. H., Johnston, V. E., & Kolodny, R. C. (1995). *Human sexuality* (5th ed.). New York: HarperCollins College.

Maticka-Tyndale, E. (2001). Sexual health and Canadian youth: How do we measure up? *The Canadian Journal of Human Sexuality, 10*(1-2), 1–17.

May, K. A., & Mahlmeister, L. R. (1994). *Comprehensive maternity nursing* (3rd ed.). Philadelphia, PA: Lippincott.

McKay, A. (2000).Common questions about sexual health education. *The Canadian Journal of Human Sexuality, 9*, 129–137.

McWhorter, L. (1999). *Bodies and pleasures: Foucault and the politics of sexual normalization.* Indianapolis, IN: Indiana University Press.

Moore, S., Kubrik, M., Shea, L., & Kubrik, N. (1992). Nerve-sparing prostatectomy. *American Journal of Nursing, 92*, 59–64.

Patrick, D., Wong, T., & Jordan, R. (2000). Sexually transmitted infections in Canada: Recent resurgence threatens national goals. *The Canadian Journal of Human Sexuality, 9*, 149–165.

Pyke J., Rabin K., Phillips J., Moffs, J., & Balbirnie, M. (2002). Sexuality and the mental health client. *Canadian Nurse, 98*, 18–23.

Stevens, P. (1995). Structural and interpersonal impact of heterosexual assumptions of lesbian health care clients. *Nursing Research, 44*(1), 25–30.

Waterhouse, J., & Metcalfe, M. (1991). Attitudes toward nurses discussing sexual concerns with patients. *Journal of Advanced Nursing, 16*, 1048–1054.

WEBLINKS

Canadian Health Network—Sexuality and Reproductive Health
http://www.hc-sc.gc.ca?pphp-dgspsp/publicat/cgshe-Idnemss/index.html
A Health Canada site that provides access to a range of health promotion information.

Health Canada—Canadian Guidelines for Sexual Health Education
http://www.hc-sc.gc.ca/hpb/lcdc/publicat/sheguide/
A federal government site related to education.

Health Canada—Division of Sexual Health Promotion
http://www.hc-sc.gc.ca/pphb-dgspsp/std-mts/
A site hosted by the federal government.

Planned Parenthood Federation of Canada
http://www.ppfc.ca/
A site sponsored by a national association advocating freedom of choice.

Sex Information and Education Council of Canada
http://www.sieccan.org/
A nonprofit association established to promote education about human sexuality.

The Society of Obstetricians and Gynaecologists of Canada
http://www.sexualityandu.ca
A site hosted by a specialty group of the Canadian Medical Association.

CHAPTER 13

Spirituality

OBJECTIVES

After completing this chapter, you will be able to:

- Compare and contrast the concepts of spirituality and religion as they relate to nursing and health care.
- Describe the spiritual development of the individual across the life span.
- List characteristics of spiritual well-being.
- Recognize factors associated with spiritual distress and manifestations of it.
- Discuss nursing interventions to support clients' spiritual beliefs and religious practices.
- Identify desired outcomes for evaluating the client's spiritual well-being.
- Analyze the influence of spiritual and religious beliefs about diet, dress, prayer and meditation, and birth and death on health care.
- Assess the spiritual needs of clients and plan nursing care to assist clients with spiritual needs.

In holistic nursing, the nurse provides care not only for the physical body and mind but also for the client's spirit or soul. Meeting the client's spiritual needs can decrease suffering and aid in physical and mental healing.

To implement spiritual care, nurses need to be skilled in establishing trusting nurse-client relationships. Because involvement in the meeting of spiritual needs is personal for both the nurse and the client, nurses need to communicate with sensitivity and empathy and have a good understanding of their own values. They also need to develop a broad concept of spirituality. Nurses cannot rely solely on their own spiritual practices; they need to be knowledgeable about various religious traditions and spiritual expressions that express clients' spirituality. Sensitivity in providing care is essential to meet the various levels and depths of clients' spiritual expressions and needs. A client's relationship with a higher power is complex and individual. Thus, individual clients need to be approached in light of their unique needs. Many clients have spiritual strengths that the nurse can nurture to help them attain or maintain a feeling of spiritual well-being, to recover from illness, and to face death peacefully.

Spirituality, Religion, and Faith

Spirituality, religion, and faith are separate entities, yet the words are often used interchangeably. The word *spiritual* derives from the Latin word *spiritus*, which means "to blow" or "to breathe," and has come to mean that which gives life or essence to the soul. **Spirituality** or spiritual belief, is a belief in or relationship with some higher power, creative force, divine being, or infinite source of energy. For example, a person may believe in "God," "Allah," the "Creator," or a "Higher Power." Spirituality includes the following aspects (Burkhardt, 1993):

- Dealing with the unknown or uncertainties in life
- Finding meaning and purpose in life
- Being aware of and able to draw upon inner resources and strength
- Having a feeling of connectedness with oneself and with God or a Higher Being

"The spiritual dimension tries to be in harmony with the universe, strives for answers about the infinite, and especially comes into focus or sustaining power when the person faces emotional stress, physical illness, or death. It goes outside a person's own power" (Murray & Zentner, 1997, p. 107). Characteristics of spirituality are listed in the accompanying box.

Religion is an organized system of worship. It offers a way of spiritual expression that provides guidance for believers in responding to life's questions and challenges. According to Vardey (1995), the organized religions offer (1) a sense of community bound by common beliefs, (2) the collective study of scripture (the Torah, Bible, Koran, or others), (3) the performance of ritual, (4) the use of disciplines and practices, commandments, and sacraments, and (5) ways of taking care of the person's soul (such as fasting, prayer, and meditation). Many traditional religious practices and rituals are related to such life events as birth, transition from childhood to adulthood, marriage, illness, and death. Religious rules of conduct may also apply to matters of daily life, such as dress, food, social interaction, menstruation, and sexual relationships.

Religious development of an individual refers to the acceptance of specific beliefs, values, rules of conduct, and rituals.

Religious development may or may not parallel spiritual development. For example, a person may follow certain religious practices and yet not internalize the symbolic meaning behind the practices. An **agnostic** is a person who doubts the existence of God or a supreme being or believes the existence of God has not been proved. An **atheist** denies the existence of God. **Monotheism** is the belief in

Characteristics of Spirituality

Relationship with Self

Inner strength/self-reliance

- Self-knowledge (who one is, what one can do)
- Attitudes (trust in self, trust in life and the future, peace of mind, harmony with self)

Relationship with Nature

Harmony

- Knowing about plants, trees, wildlife, weather
- Communing with nature (gardening, walking, being outside); preserving nature

Relationship with Others

- Sharing time, knowledge, and resources; reciprocating
- Caring for children, elderly, sick
- Reaffirming the living and the dead (visiting, photos, cemetery meetings)

Relationship with Deity

Religious or nonreligious

- Prayer-meditation
- Religious articles
- Being in nature
- Church participation

Source: M. Burkhardt. (1993). Characteristics of spirituality in the lives of women in a rural Appalachian community. *Journal of Transcultural Nursing, 4*, 12–18. Used with permission.

TABLE 13.1 Westerhoff's Four Stages of Faith

Stage	Age	Behaviour
Experienced faith	Infancy and early adolescence	Experiences faith through interaction with others who are living a particular faith tradition
Affiliative faith	Late adolescence	Participates in activities that characterize a particular faith tradition; experiences awe and wonderment; feels a sense of belonging
Searching faith	Young adulthood	Through a process of questioning and doubting own faith, acquires a cognitive as well as an affective faith
Owned faith	Middle adulthood and old age	Puts faith into personal and social action and is willing to stand up for beliefs even against the nurturing community

Source: Adapted from Westerhoff, J. (1976). *Will our children have faith?* (p. 79–103). New York: Seabury Press.

the existence of one God who created and rules the universe. **Polytheism** is the belief in more than one god. The moral and ethical codes of agnostics and atheists are not derived from theistic beliefs.

Spiritual Development

Faith is the complete and unquestioning acceptance of a belief that cannot be demonstrated or proven by the process of logical thought. According to Fowler and Keen (1985), faith is universal—a feature of living, acting, and self-understanding. To have faith is to believe in or be committed to something or someone. Fowler (1974) describes faith as being present in both religious and nonreligious people. Faith gives life meaning, providing the individual with strength in times of difficulty.

Westerhoff (Table 13.1) describes faith as a way of being and behaving that evolves from a faith guided by parents and others during infancy and childhood to an owned faith that is internalized in adulthood and serves as a directive for action. For the client who is ill, faith—whether in a higher authority (e.g., God, Allah, Jehovah), in oneself, in the health-care team, or in a combination of all—provides strength and trust.

Hope is a concept that also has a spiritual dimension. **Hope** is defined by Post-White and colleagues (1996) as a multidimensional concept that includes perceiving realistic expectations and goals, having motivation to achieve goals, anticipating outcomes, establishing trust and interpersonal relationships, relying on internal and external resources, having determination to endure, and being oriented to the future.

Hope is necessary for the individual to survive illness or other difficult times. Grimm (1991, p. 511) states that hope "is an interpersonal process that is created through trust and is nurtured by trusting relationships with others, including God." Whereas faith is the belief in someone or something, hope is the belief that things will get better. Stotland (1969, p. 1) states that "without hope, the individual is often dull, listless, and moribund." In the absence of hope, the client gives up, and illness—especially terminal illness—may progress more rapidly. Table 13.2 summarizes spiritual and religious behaviours during different life stages.

Spiritual Well-Being

Spiritual health, or **spiritual well-being,** is a feeling of being "generally alive, purposeful, and fulfilled" (Ellison, 1983, p. 332). According to Pilch (1988, p. 31), spiritual wellness is "a way of living, a lifestyle that views and lives life as purposeful and pleasurable, that seeks out life-sustaining and life-enriching options to be chosen freely at every opportunity, and that sinks its roots deeply into spiritual values and/or specific religious beliefs." Characteristics indicating spiritual well-being are shown in the box on page 210.

People enhance or nurture their spirituality in many ways. Some of these focus on development of one's inner self or world; others focus on the expression of their spiritual energy to others or the outer world. Relating to one's inner self or soul may be achieved through inner dialogue with a higher power or with oneself; prayer or meditation; analyzing dreams; communion with nature through walks in a park, in the woods, or by the sea; listening quietly to music; or experiencing the inspiration of art, drama, or dance. The expression of a person's spiritual energy to others is manifested in loving relationships with and service to others; joy and laughter; participation in religious services and associated fellowship gatherings and activities; and by revealing expressions of compassion, empathy, forgiveness, and hope.

TABLE 13.2 Summary of Spiritual Development

Developmental Stage	Characteristics
Infants and toddlers	Infants and toddlers have no sense of right or wrong, spiritual beliefs, or convictions to guide activities. Toddlers may follow rituals (e.g., bedtime prayers) in imitation of their parents. Toddlers may attend a church nursery school, but emphasis is on enhancing their positive self-image.
Preschoolers	Parental attitudes toward moral codes and religion convey to children what is considered good and bad. Preschoolers copy what they see, rather than what they are told. If what they see and what they are told are contradictory, problems arise. They often ask questions about morality and religion (e.g., "Why is [some action or word] wrong?" and "What is heaven?"). They believe that their parents are omnipotent. Two methods of spiritual education are used with preschool children: indoctrinating them and letting them choose their own way. Preschoolers follow a religion not because they understand it but because it is part of daily life. Five-year-olds often make up prayers themselves. They believe that a god or humans are responsible for such natural events as rain and wind. Many go to church school and participate in religious holidays. They ask the meaning of the holidays and need explanations, but they are more occupied with rituals than with the reason behind the holiday. When children begin to question myths, they are ready for a more sophisticated explanation.
School-age children	Young school-age children expect that their prayers will be answered, good rewarded, and bad punished. During the prepuberty stage, children become aware of spiritual disappointments. They realize that their prayers are not always answered on their own terms, and they begin to reason, rather than accept a faith blindly. Some children drop or modify certain religious practices (e.g., praying for tangible benefits); others continue to follow religious practices because of dependence on their parents. During adolescence, children compare the standards of their parents with others and determine which ones they want to incorporate into their own behaviour. Adolescents also compare the scientific viewpoint with the religious viewpoint and try to bring the two together. By 16 years, many adolescents have decided whether or not to accept the family religion. They may experience personal religious awakenings, such as being saved or converted, either suddenly or gradually. Adolescents with parents of different faiths may choose one faith over the other or no faith. For some, a firm faith provides strength during these turbulent years.
Adults	Young adults who need to answer the religious questions of their own children may find that the teachings of their own early childhood are more acceptable to them now than during adolescence. During the middle years, adults often find that they have more time for religious activities because their children are older. Older adults who have developed religious values often endeavour to broaden them and to understand the newer values of younger people. Older adults who do not have a well-developed faith may experience a feeling of deprivation as they become less active (e.g., because of retirement). During later years, people face death (their own, their spouse's, and their friends'). This recognition may make them despondent. The development of faith can often help older people face reality, participate in life, have feelings of self-worth, and accept death as inevitable.

Spiritual Distress

Spiritual distress refers to a disturbance in or a challenge to a person's belief or value system that provides strength, hope, and meaning to life. Many factors may be associated with a person's spiritual distress: physiological problems, treatment-related concerns, or situational concerns. Physiological problems include having a medical diagnosis of a terminal or debilitating disease, or experiencing pain, the loss of a body part or function, or a miscarriage or stillbirth. Treatment-related factors include the recommendation for blood transfusions, abortion, surgery, dietary restrictions, amputation of a body part, or isolation. Situational factors are the death or illness of a significant other, or barriers to or embarrassment at practising one's spiritual rituals (Carpenito, 2002).

Manifestations or defining characteristics of spiritual distress include:

- Experiencing a disturbance in one's personal belief system.
- Questioning the meaning of life, death, or suffering.
- Questioning the credibility of one's personal belief system.
- Demonstrating discouragement or despair.
- Choosing not to practise usual religious rituals.
- Having ambivalent feelings (doubts) about beliefs.
- Expressing not having a reason for living.
- Feeling a sense of spiritual emptiness.
- Showing emotional detachment for self and others.
- Expressing concern (e.g., anger, resentment, fear) over the meaning of life, suffering, or death.
- Requesting spiritual assistance for a disturbance in belief system.

Characteristics Indicative of Spiritual Well-Being

Sense of inner peace
Compassion for others
Reverence for life
Gratitude
Appreciation of both unity and diversity
Humour
Wisdom
Generosity
Ability to transcend the self
Capacity for unconditional love

Source: Carson, V. B. (1989). *Spiritual dimensions of nursing practice.* Philadelphia, PA: Saunders.

Religious Practices Affecting Nursing Care

The most common practices affecting the nursing care of clients include holy days, sacred writings, spiritual symbols, prayer, meditation, and those associated with diet, nutrition, dress, birth, and death.

Holy Days

A **holy day** is a day set aside for special religious observance. Most Christians observe Sunday as the Sabbath, while Jews, Muslims, and some Christians observe Saturday as the day of the week devoted to rest and worship. This observance is in response to the biblical commandment to "remember the Sabbath day and keep it holy." Holy days can also be special days of celebration and feasting that occur once a year, such as Christmas and Easter (Christian), and Sukkoth or the Feast of Tabernacles (Jewish). Solemn religious observances throughout the year may be referred to as high holy days and may include fasting, reflection, and prayer. Examples of such holy days are Rosh Hashanah and Yom Kippur (Jewish), Good Friday (Christian), and the month-long observance of Ramadan (Islam). Many religions require fasting, extended prayer, and reflection or ritual observances on sacred days; however, believers who are seriously ill are often exempted from such requirements. Many hospitals and health organizations facilitate ritual observances for clients and staff on holy days. For example, a hospital may provide fish or another nonmeat entree on Good Friday for Catholic clients. As many religions follow calendars that are different from the Gregorian calendar, a multifaith calendar can be used to identify the holy days of the various religious groups (Griffith, 1996).

Sacred Writings

Each religion has its sacred writings or scriptures believed to be the thought or word of the Supreme Being and written by the appointed prophets or disciples. Usually, the rules or commandments for living are contained in the scriptures. For example, the Torah contains the body of wisdom and law for Jews, and the Christian Bible contains the Ten Commandments. Religious laws or commandments are often used as the basis for secular law, such as laws regarding committing murder or stealing. Religious law may affect a client's willingness to accept treatment suggestions. For example, blood transfusions are in conflict with the religious law of Seventh-Day Adventists. A religion's sacred writings also frequently tell the stories of the religion's leaders, kings, and heroes, such as the stories of Abraham and Solomon in both Jewish and Christian scriptures.

People often gain strength and hope from reading religious writings when they are ill or in crisis. Examples of

Sacred Writings

Christianity	Bible
Judaism	Torah Talmud
Islam/Muslim	Koran (Qur'an)
Hindu	Ramayana Mahabharata Vedas Upanishads
Sikh	Granth
Buddhism	Vedas
Zoroastrianism	Avesta Sacred Writings

scriptural stories that may give comfort to clients are Job's suffering in both the Jewish and Christian scriptures and, in the Bible, Jesus healing people who were physically or mentally ill. See the accompanying box for a list of sacred writings.

Sacred Symbols

Sacred symbols include jewellery, medals, amulets, icons, totems, or body ornamentation (e.g., tattoos) that carry religious or spiritual significance. They may be worn to pronounce one's faith, to provide spiritual protection, or to be a source of comfort or strength. People may wear religious medals at all times, and they may wish to wear them when they are undergoing diagnostic studies, medical treatment, or surgery. People who are Catholic may carry a rosary for prayer, and a person who is Muslim may carry prayer beads.

People may have religious icons or statues in their homes, cars, or places of work as personal reminders of their faith or as part of personal places of worship or meditation. Hospitalized clients or long-term care residents may wish to have their spiritual icons or statues with them as a source of comfort.

Prayer and Meditation

Prayer or meditation is a part of every religion. **Prayer** is a communication with God, Allah, Jehovah, or other Supreme Being in word or in thought. Prayers may be said in thankfulness (e.g., for health or healing), in supplication or request (e.g., relief from pain and suffering, for cure), or as communion or reflection. Dossey (1993) identifies seven forms of prayer (see the accompanying box), all of which may be used when someone is experiencing illness or healing. Some religions have prescribed prayers that are printed in a prayer book, such as the Anglican or Episcopal Book of Common Prayer or the Catholic Missal. Some religious prayers are attributed to the source of faith: for example, the Lord's Prayer for Christians is attributed to Jesus, and the first sutra for Muslims is attributed to Mohammed.

Forms of Prayer

Petition	Asking something for oneself
Intercession	Asking something for others
Confession	The repentance of wrongdoing and the asking of forgiveness
Lamentation	Crying in distress and asking for vindication
Adoration	Giving honour and praise
Invocation	Summoning the presence of the Almighty
Thanksgiving	Offering gratitude

Source: Adapted from Dossey, L. (1993). *Healing words: The power of prayer and the practice of medicine.* New York: HarperSanFrancisco, p. 5.

Some religions require daily prayers or dictate specific times for prayer and worship, such as the five daily prayers, or Salat, of the Muslims (performed facing east toward Mecca at dawn, noon, midafternoon, sunset, and evening); the daily Kaddish of the Jews; or the seven canonical prayers of the Catholics. People who are ill may want to continue or increase their prayer practices (Moschella et al., 1997). They may need uninterrupted quiet time and want to have their prayer books, rosaries, prayer beads, or other icons available to them.

Meditation is the act of focusing one's thoughts or engaging in self-reflection or contemplation. Some people believe that through deep meditation, one can influence or control physical and psychological functioning and the course of illness. See Chapter 11 for more discussion of meditation.

Beliefs Affecting Diet and Nutrition

Many religions have proscriptions regarding diet. There may be rules about which foods and beverages are allowed and which are prohibited. For example, Orthodox Jews may not eat shellfish or pork, and Muslims may not drink alcoholic beverages or eat pork. Mormons, or members of the Church of Jesus Christ of Latter-Day Saints, may not drink caffeinated or alcoholic beverages. Older Catholics may choose not to eat meat on Fridays because of previous Catholic religious doctrine. Religious law may also dictate how food is prepared. For example, many Jewish people require **kosher** food, that is, food prepared according to Jewish law.

Some solemn religious observances are marked by fasting, which is the abstinence from food for a specified period of time. Some religions also restrict beverages; others allow drinking of water or other sustaining beverages on fast days. Examples of religions that observe fasting include Islam, Judaism, and Catholicism. During the month of Ramadan, devout Muslims eat no food and avoid beverages during daylight hours; the fast can be broken after sunset. Members of Jewish synagogues fast on Yom Kippur, the Day of Atonement, and devout Catholics may fast on Good Friday. Most religions lift the fasting requirements for seriously ill clients and believers for whom fasting may be a detriment to health, such as diabetic clients. Some religions may exempt nursing mothers or menstruating women from fasting requirements.

It is important for health-care providers to prescribe diet plans with an awareness of the client's dietary and fasting beliefs.

Beliefs Related to Dress

Many religions have laws or traditions that dictate dress. For example, Orthodox and Conservative Jewish men believe that it is important to have their head covered at all times and, therefore, wear a "yarmulke." Orthodox Jewish women may wear a wig or scarf to cover their hair as a sign of respect. Muslim women may also cover their hair with a scarf in compliance with religious law.

Some religions require that women dress in a conservative manner, which may include not wearing sleeveless or low-cut tops and skirts that are above the knees. Some religions, for example, Islam, may require that the body (torso, arms, and legs) be covered. Hospital gowns may make women who wish to comply with religious dress codes uneasy and uncomfortable. Clients may be especially disconcerted when undergoing diagnostic tests or treatments, such as mammography, that require body parts to be bared.

Beliefs Related to Birth

For all religions, the birth of a child is an important event giving cause for celebration. Many religions have specific ritual ceremonies that consecrate the new child to God.

When a Muslim child is born, "someone recites the call to prayer in the infant's ear." On the seventh day after birth, the child is named, and a tuft of hair is shaved from the head (Denny, 1993, p. 682).

In the Christian faith, baptism and christening ceremonies may take place after the birth of a child to confirm that the "infant [was] born into a Christian family as part of the organism of the church" (Frankiel, 1993, p. 556). Christian parents of seriously ill infants may want baptism performed at birth by the chaplain.

In the Jewish religion, the ritual circumcision conducted on male children on the eighth day after birth is an expression of the religious bond between the prophet Abraham, his descendants, and their God. Following the circumcision by the ritually trained surgeon, called a mohel, the child is named. Girls are named in the synagogue on the Sabbath after the birth (Fishbane, 1993).

When nurses are aware of the religious needs of families and their infants, they can assist families in fulfilling their religious obligations. This is especially important when the newborn infant is seriously ill or in danger of dying, as some people believe that if religious obligations are not fulfilled, the infant will not be accepted into the community of the faithful after death.

Beliefs Related to Death

Spiritual and religious beliefs play a significant role in the believer's approach to death just as they do in other major life events. Many believe that the person who dies transcends this life for a better place or being.

Some religions have special rituals surrounding dying and death that must be observed by the faithful. Observance of these rituals provides comfort to the dying person and their loved ones. Some rituals are carried out while the person is still alive and can include special prayers, such as the Sacrament of the Sick (previously referred to as the Last Rites), singing or chants, and reading of sacred scriptures. Muslims who are dying will want their body or head turned toward Mecca (Denny, 1993).

There may also be special religious observances that must be followed after death. Griffith (1996, p. 18) suggests that "during a terminal illness, the client and family should be asked if any special procedures follow death." Some religions require that the body of the deceased be touched only by members of that faith. In both the Muslim (Denny, 1993) and the Jewish (Fishbane, 1993) religions, devout believers may require that a ritual bath be given after death either by a family member or by a ritual burial society. Many religions may require that a family member or other believer stay with the body at all times until it is buried or cremated. Religious symbols or objects should be treated with respect and kept with the body (Griffith, 1996). The nurse can support the family of the deceased by providing an environment conducive to the performance of death rituals.

Spiritual Health and the Nursing Process

Assessing

Data about a client's spiritual beliefs are obtained from the client's general history (religious preferences or orientation); through a nursing history; and by clinical observa-

ASSESSMENT INTERVIEW

Spirituality

- Are any particular religious practices important to you? If so, could you please tell me about them?
- Will being here interfere with your religious practices?
- Do you feel your faith is helpful to you? In what ways is it important to you right now?
- In what ways can I help you carry out your faith? For example, would you like me to read your prayer book to you?
- Would you like a visit from your spiritual counsellor or the chaplain?
- What are your hopes and your sources of strength right now?

tions of the client's behaviour, verbalizations, mood, and so on. Nurses should never assume that a client follows all the practices of the client's stated religion.

Nursing History

The spiritual assessment is best taken at the end of the assessment process or following the psychosocial assessment, once the nurse has developed a relationship with the client and/or support person and feels that it is appropriate to discuss spiritual matters. The questions provided in the accompanying box may be suitable. Remember, however, that all people have a right not to discuss their spiritual beliefs with others. In general, the nurse obtains data about the client's concept of God, deity, or creative force; sources of hope and strength; religious practices and rituals; and any relationship perceived between spiritual beliefs and state of health.

Clinical Assessment

Cues to spiritual and religious preferences, strengths, concerns, or distress may be revealed by one or more of the following (Shelley & Fish, 1988; Sumner, 1998):

1. *Environment.* Does the client have a Bible, Torah, Koran, other prayer book, devotional literature, religious medals, rosary, cross, Star of David, or religious get-well cards in the room? Does a church send altar flowers or Sunday bulletins?
2. *Behaviour.* Does the client appear to pray before meals or at other times or read religious literature? Does the client have nightmares and sleep disturbances, or express anger at religious representatives or a deity?
3. *Verbalization.* Does the client mention God or a Higher Power, prayer, faith, the church, synagogue, temple, a spiritual or religious leader, or religious topics? Does the client ask about a visit from the clergy? Does the client express fear of death, concern with the meaning of life, inner conflict about religious beliefs, concern about a relationship with the deity, questions about the meaning of existence, the meaning of suffering, or the moral or ethical implications of therapy?
4. *Affect and attitude.* Does the client appear lonely, depressed, angry, anxious, agitated, apathetic, or preoccupied?
5. *Interpersonal relationships.* Who visits? How does the client respond to visitors? Do clergy visit? How does the client relate to other clients and nursing personnel?

Diagnosing

Spiritual Problems as the Diagnostic Label

The North American Nursing Diagnosis Association (NANDA) includes the following diagnostic label for clients with problems of spirituality:

- ***Spiritual Distress:*** "The state in which the individual or group experiences or is at risk of experiencing a disturbance in the belief or value system that provides strength, hope, and meaning to life" (Carpenito, 2002, p. 432). Defining characteristics and etiologies of this diagnostic label are discussed earlier on page 210. Clinical examples of assessment data clusters and related nursing diagnoses are shown in Table 13.3.

Carpenito (2002) includes a wellness diagnosis as follows:

- ***Spiritual Well-Being, Readiness for Enhanced:*** An individual experiences affirmation of life in a relationship with a higher power (as defined by the person), self, community, and environment that nurtures and celebrates wholeness.

The nursing diagnosis ***Spiritual Well-Being, Readiness for Enhanced*** is a diagnosis of positive functioning that does not warrant related factors (Carpenito, 2002). Some people will respond to adversity through an increased spiritual strength that provides hope and comfort.

Spiritual Distress as the Etiology

Spiritual distress may affect other areas of functioning and indicate other diagnoses. In these instances, spiritual distress becomes the etiology. Examples include:

- ***Fear*** related to apprehension about soul's future after death and unpreparedness for death

TABLE 13.3 Clinical Application: Assessment Data Clusters and Related Nursing Diagnoses for Clients with Spiritual Distress

Data Cluster	Nursing Diagnosis
Marilyn Eckhardt, 72 years old, is crying, fingering her rosary, and voicing concern that she has not seen her priest for confession since being admitted to the hospital. She states that she is afraid to die without confessing her sins. She also states that she does not want to see the hospital chaplain, but rather her own priest, whose parish is about 18 kilometres away. The hospital record indicates that Ms. Eckhardt is Roman Catholic.	***Spiritual Distress*** related to inability to practise spiritual ritual (confession with parish priest)
John Ames, 42 years old, is in a terminal state with an AIDS-related condition. He has become withdrawn but states to the nurse, "What have I done that God has punished me so?" The nurse observes religious literature on his bedside cabinet.	***Spiritual Distress*** related to crisis of illness and impending death

- ***Self-Esteem, Disturbed*** related to failure to live within the precepts of one's faith
- ***Sleep Pattern, Disturbed*** related to spiritual distress
- ***Coping, Ineffective Individual*** related to feelings of abandonment by God and loss of religious faith
- ***Decisional Conflict*** related to conflict between treatment plan and spiritual beliefs

Planning

In the planning phase, the nurse identifies interventions to help the client achieve the overall goal of maintaining or restoring spiritual well-being so that spiritual strength, serenity, and satisfaction are realized. For example, goals may include the following:

- Maintains meaningful personal relationship with deity
- Maintains harmonious supportive relationships with others

Examples of desired outcomes to achieve each of these goals, although developed in the planning phase, are provided in Table 13.4 in the Evaluating section later in this chapter.

Planning in relation to spiritual needs should be designed to do one or more of the following:

- Help the client fulfill religious obligations
- Help the client draw on and use inner resources more effectively to meet the present situation
- Help the client maintain or establish a dynamic, personal relationship with a Supreme Being in the face of unpleasant circumstances
- Help the client find meaning in existence and the present situation
- Promote a sense of hope
- Provide spiritual resources otherwise unavailable

Implementing

Nursing actions to help clients meet their spiritual needs include (1) providing presence, (2) supporting religious practices, (3) assisting clients with prayer, (4) referring clients for spiritual counselling, and (5) parish nursing.

Providing "Presence"

"Probably the greatest tool available to nurses for meeting spiritual needs is their own presence and an ability to touch another, both physically and spiritually" (Carson, 1989, p. 164). Being present means to be willing to suffer with another, to offer and share oneself, and to gain insight into the client's meaning and purpose in life, sickness, and health. The nurse provides presence through the development of a personal relationship with the client, a relationship that enables the nurse to experience the client's uniqueness. The client, in turn, experiences the nurse's uniqueness. In providing presence, the nurse communicates a willingness to care, to listen, and to be available to the client. "Presence itself touches the client's spirit, just as a cool hand might soothe a fevered brow" (Carson, 1989, p. 165).

The act of being present for clients involves qualities considered to be humanistic: compassion, kindness, honesty, love, gentleness, and patience.

Supporting Religious Practices

During the assessment of the client, the nurse will have obtained specific information about the client's religious preference and religious practices. Nurses need to consider specific religious practices that will affect nursing care, such as the client's beliefs about birth, death, dress, diet, prayer, sacred symbols, sacred writings, and holy days discussed earlier in this chapter. The accompanying box on page 216 outlines ways the nurse can help clients to continue their usual spiritual practices.

SAMPLE CARE PLAN FOR SPIRITUAL DISTRESS

Assessment Data

Nursing Assessment

Mrs. Sally Horton is a 60-year-old hospitalized homemaker who is recovering from a right radical mastectomy. Yesterday, she was told by her physician that due to metastases of the cancer, her prognosis is poor. This morning her primary nurse finds her tearful, stating she slept poorly and has no appetite. She asks the nurse, "Why is this happening to me? Perhaps it's because I have sinned in my life. I've not gone to church or spoken to a minister in several years. Is there a chapel in the hospital where I could go and pray? I'm terribly afraid of dying and what awaits me."

Physical Examination

Height: 165.1 cm
Weight: 54.0 kg
Temperature: 36.6°C
Pulse: 88 BPM
Respirations: 22/minute
Blood Pressure: 146/86 mm Hg
Large surgical dressing right chest wall and axillary region, dry and intact. Slight edema right hand and arm.

Diagnostic Data	Normal	
RBC: 3.5 mL/mL	Female: 4.2–5.4	Male: 4.7–6.1
Hgb: 10.5 g/L	Female: 12–16 g/dl	Male: 14–18 g/dl
Hct: 35%	Female: 37–41%	Male 42–52%

Nursing Diagnosis

Spiritual Distress related to separation from religious rituals (as evidenced by questioning credibility of personal beliefs, depression, expressions of resentment and fear of death, requests for chapel visits).

Client Goal(s)

The client will regain a sense of spiritual satisfaction.

Desired Outcomes

1. Expresses desire to perform religious or spiritual practices.
2. Visits with chaplain by day 2.
3. Displays absence of feelings of anger and resentment by day 5.
4. Verbalizes increase in psychological and spiritual comfort with illness/prognosis/death.

Nursing Interventions and Selected Activities with Rationale*

Spiritual Support

- Be open to Mrs. Horton's feelings about illness and death. [*Encourages expression of inner fears and concerns and teaches the client the value of confronting issues.*]
- Assist her to properly express and relieve anger in appropriate ways. [*Anger can be a source of energy and its release a source of freedom when expressed in a constructive manner.*]
- Use values clarification techniques to help Mrs. Horton clarify beliefs and values. [*Value conflicts often lead to confusion and indecision. Clarification of beliefs and values will help clients base decisions upon their most important values, including those that are spiritual in nature.*]
- Listen carefully to her communication and develop a sense of timing for prayer or spiritual rituals. [*The nature of spiritual care may directly affect the speed and quality of recovery and/or redefining hope and finding meaning in death.*]
- Facilitate Mrs. Horton's use of meditation, prayer, and other religious traditions and rituals. [*Spiritual needs may sometimes be overlooked or ignored. Recognizing and respecting the individual's spiritual needs is an important advocacy role for nurses.*]
- Assure her that the nurse will be available to support her in times of suffering. [*Fidelity is essential in helping alleviate the client's fear of dying alone.*]

Values Clarification

- Create an accepting, nonjudgmental atmosphere. [*Establishes rapport and the therapeutic relationship, which promotes communication and open expression.*]
- Use appropriate questions to assist Mrs. Horton in reflecting on the situation and what is important personally. [*Helps the client explore the whys of how she is feeling and identify personal values that may have an impact on the current situation and future decisions.*]
- Encourage her to list values that guide behaviour in various settings and types of situations. [*Helps the client clarify values and beliefs by reflecting on past behaviours. Experience is a major source for value development.*]
- Help Mrs. Horton to evaluate how her values are in agreement or conflict with those of family members or significant others. [*Decisions and actions may be contradictory to the client's own values if the need to please others is greater than the need to please themselves.*]

Evaluation

Goal met. Mrs. Horton has been visited on several occasions by her minister. She reads scripture each day and has found consolation in reading the Book of Psalms. She states "God is merciful and will help me bear my suffering."

*Interventions and activities selected are only a sample of those suggested in the *Nursing Interventions Classification (NIC)* and should be individualized for each client.

Source: McCloskey, J. C., & Bulechek, G. M. (2000). *Nursing Interventions Classification (NIC)* (3rd ed.). St. Louis, MO: Mosby.

Supporting Religious Practices

In Hospital or Other Care Centre

- Inform the client about religious services provided in the agency. Many agencies provide nondenominational religious services or several services for different denominations.
- Ensure opportunities for privacy for the client and family for prayer, meditation, or counsel. Many agencies have quiet areas for these purposes.
- Support the client's desire to have spiritual icons, statues, jewellery, or other religious items with them and protect them from damage or loss.
- With the client's permission, facilitate arrangements for the client's minister, priest, rabbi, or other spiritual adviser or healer to visit. Many hospitals also provide the services of an agency chaplain or a list of clergy to call when needed. Hospital chaplains can also be used as a resource for finding representatives for various religious groups.
- If sacraments or other rituals are to be performed by spiritual leaders or healers, prepare the client's room appropriately. For example, clear the bedside table or stand, draw the bed curtains, and make sure there is a seat near the bedside for the religious counsellor.
- Make arrangements with the dietitian for dietary practices to be met. If the agency cannot accommodate the client's needs, ask the family to bring in their own food.
- Consult with the client, family, or spiritual adviser before removing special amulets, garments, or body hair for tests, treatments, or surgery. For example, Sikhism requires that men wear a turban for 24 hours a day and have uncut hair. Some Sikhs, therefore, may refuse to have any body hair cut (e.g., for electrodes or an intravenous infusion).

In the Home

- Explore resources available, such as audiotapes of weekly religious services, taped meditations or inspirational music, televised religious services, and clergy who routinely make home visits.
- Consult with family members to consider ways to help the client, such as reading scriptures on a regular basis, having prayer sessions, providing inspirational literature, and so on.

Assisting Clients with Prayer

Prayer involves a sense of love, connection, and a reaching out. It has many health benefits and healing properties (Dossey, 1996). It offers a means to:

- Have someone to talk to.
- Promote a sense of being loved unconditionally.
- Provide a sense of serenity and connection with something greater.
- Develop compassionate behaviour.

Clients may choose to participate in private prayer or want group prayer with family, friends, or clergy. In such situations, the nurse's major responsibility is to ensure a quiet environment and privacy. Nursing care may need to be adjusted to accommodate periods for prayer.

Illness can interfere with some clients' ability to pray. Feelings such as anxiety, fear, guilt, grief, despair, and isolation can produce barriers to relationships in general, and in the relationship the person has with their deity. In these instances, the client may ask the nurse to pray with them. Prayers with clients should only be done when there is mutual agreement between the clients and those praying with them. Because prayer can take various forms, Carson (1989) offers the following guidelines:

- Ask the client if there is a special prayer that has personal significance. The client may be comforted by reciting such a prayer with the nurse or with the nurse present.
- Use a conversational type of prayer that reflects the client's concerns and needs. For example:

  Please comfort Mrs. Wilson as she enters surgery. Lift her fear and in its place give her peace and strength. Let her know you are with her...
- Tell the client that you will say a private prayer if you are not comfortable praying out loud or if the client is uncomfortable with the spoken prayer.
- Offer to be with clients during private prayer or personal meditation.

Nurses who are unaccustomed to praying aloud or in public may find it helpful to have a formal prayer or a religious

Canadian Society Notes

Fact	Implications for Nursing Practice
About 61% of Canadians say the religion they identify with is important to them. Most say that they know the basic traditions of their church (70%) and hold to them. Source: Bibby, R. W. (1995). *The Bibby Report: Social Trends Canadian Style*. Toronto: Stoddard Publishing.	Consider the need to include pastoral care professionals as part of the health-care team.
Gail Brimbecom is the founding member of the Canadian Association for Parish Ministry established in 1998, which fosters parish nursing education, supports parish nurses, and provides information for parish nursing itself.	Nurses have the opportunity to embrace faith and health, offer health promotion and illness prevention education, counsel, and refer and train volunteers for parish communities.
A group of Canadian nurses in their practice identified the following spiritual interventions to help restore hope and joy: communication, connectedness, bibliotherapy, music therapy, and prayer.	Nurses may implement these spiritual interventions in fostering to restore meaning in the lives of clients and bring about the associated outcomes of hope, well-being, joy, love, trust, and peace.

Source: Mayerhoff, H., VanHofwegen, L.,Harwood, C., Drury, M., & Emblen, J. (2002). Spiritual nursing interventions. *Canadian Nurse, 98*(3), 21–24.

passage readily available. Because prayer can evoke deep feelings, the nurse needs to spend time with the client following a prayer to enable the client to express these feelings.

Referring Clients for Spiritual Counselling

There are times when spiritual care is best referred to other members of the health-care team. Referrals can be made for hospitalized clients and their families through the hospital chaplain's office if one is available. Nurses in home and community health settings can identify spiritual resources by checking directories of community service agencies, telephone directories, or religious directories that describe available spiritual counsellors and the services provided through the religious community.

Many religious counsellors will provide assistance to members of their faith who are not members of their specific religious community. For example, a priest may attend a client in the hospital or at home even though the person is not a member of the priest's parish.

Referrals may be necessary when the nurse makes a diagnosis of spiritual distress. In this situation, the nurse and religious counsellor can work together to meet the client's needs. One situation the nurse may encounter is client refusal of necessary medical intervention because of religious tenets. In this case, the nurse encourages the client, physician, and spiritual adviser to discuss the conflict and consider alternative methods of therapy. The nurse's major role is to provide information the client needs to make an informed decision and to support the client's decision.

RESEARCH NOTE

The Problem of Theodicy and Religious Response to Cancer

The researchers studied the religious response to cancer in a group of 45 clients of a hematology/oncology clinic. Of the 45 clients, 67 percent ($n = 30$) increased their amount of prayer, 51 percent ($n = 23$) gained faith, and 16 percent ($n = 7$) increased the frequency of church attendance in response to their illness. The majority of clients across all levels of religious belief endorse theodicy, a belief that God is good and omnipotent in the face of evil and suffering and that God has a reason for their suffering but this reason cannot be explained or understood. The authors conclude that "religious cancer clients intensify their religious belief and practice in response to their illness. Despite the elusiveness of an explanation for their suffering in religious terms, clients remain confident in their faith."

Implications: Nurses must understand the importance of a client's spiritual beliefs as they relate to the client's potential for healing or acceptance of their illness or injury. With this understanding, nurses can better support clients in their spiritual practices.

Source: Moschella, V. D., Pressman, K. R., Pressman, P., Weissman, D. E. (1997, Spring). The problem of theodicy and religious response to cancer. *Journal of Religion & Health, 36*(1), 17–20.

Parish nurses are registered nurses who function as members of a congregation's ministry team, combining nursing and health expertise with theological concepts. They believe that spiritual health is the core of an individual's wellness and that it influences all aspects of well-being. Parish nurses build on the strengths of individuals, families, and the community, assisting and empowering them to become more active in their own health. They work in partnership with pastoral staff and congregation members to enable the faith community to become a place of health and healing.

Evaluating

Using the measurable desired outcomes developed during the planning stage, the nurse collects data needed to judge whether client goals and outcomes have been achieved. Examples of client goals and related outcomes are shown in Table 13.4.

TABLE 13.4 Evaluation Goals and Outcomes: Spiritual Well-Being

Goal	Examples of Desired Outcomes
Maintains meaningful personal relationships with deity	■ Verbalizes satisfaction with relationship with deity ■ Carries out usual religious practices using resources available ■ Expresses feelings of inner peace and spiritual fulfillment ■ States faith provides strength to understand and endure suffering
Maintains harmonious, supportive relationships with others	■ Conveys warmth and compassion to family, friends, and others ■ Shares thoughts, feelings, and faith with others

FOCUS ON CRITICAL THINKING

Terry is a 32-year-old male who received several units of blood following an automobile accident 10 years ago. Five years ago he was diagnosed with AIDS (acquired immune deficiency syndrome) and is now in the hospital with pneumonia and severe diarrhea. He is very ill and very discouraged. While you are caring for Terry, he comments, "I might as well die right now because I'm not going to get well. My folks were United, but I guess I'm being punished because I'm not very religious."

See Appendix A for answers to these questions.

1. Terry stated that he was "not very religious." Does that mean that he is not spiritual? Explain.
2. What data suggest that Terry may be experiencing spiritual distress?
3. How might illness affect one's spiritual beliefs? Religious beliefs?
4. How would you feel and respond if Terry were to ask you to pray with him?
5. How might a spiritual assessment be of benefit to both you and Terry?

CHAPTER HIGHLIGHTS

- Clients have a right to receive care that respects their individual spiritual and religious values.
- The spiritual needs of clients and support persons often come into focus at a time of illness. Spiritual beliefs often help people accept illness and plan for the future.
- Spirituality and religion are separate entities: *Religion* is an organized system of worship that offers a way of spiritual expression; *spirituality* is a broader concept that encompasses a relationship with a Higher Power but also a person's relationship with self, with nature, and with others. Both spiritual and religious beliefs influence lifestyle, attitudes, and feelings about illness and death.
- *Spiritual well-being* is described as a feeling of being generally alive, purposeful, and fulfilled. It is manifested by a person's communication that reveals meaning and purpose to one's existence, inner peace, trusting relationships, and an inner strength that is directed toward ultimate values of love, meaning, hope, beauty, and truth.
- *Spiritual distress* refers to a disturbance in or a challenge to a person's belief or value system that provides strength, hope, and meaning to life. Possible factors in spiritual distress include physiological problems, treatment-related concerns, and situational concerns. Spiritual distress may be reflected in a number of behaviours, including depression, anxiety, verbalizations of unworthiness, and fear of death.
- Because spiritual beliefs and practices are highly personal, nurses must respect the rights of people to hold their own spiritual beliefs and to communicate or not communicate these to others.
- A spiritual assessment is best obtained after the nurse has developed a relationship with the client. Information may be elicited about the client's concept of the deity or creative force, the client's source of hope and strength, the significance of religious practices and rituals, and the relationship the client perceives between health and spiritual beliefs.
- Home health nurses can observe cues in the home that may indicate client spiritual beliefs and practices. Nurses in community settings should be aware of spiritual and religious resources in the community and what services they provide.
- To implement spiritual care, nurses need to be skilled in establishing a trusting nurse-client relationship.
- Nurses can support clients' religious practices if they understand needs related to holy days, sacred writings, spiritual symbols, prayer and meditation, diet practices, dress requirements or prohibitions, birth rituals, and death rituals.
- Nursing interventions that promote spiritual well-being include offering a supportive presence, supporting the client's religious practices, praying with a client, and referring the client to a religious counsellor.
- Nurses need to be aware of their own spiritual beliefs in order to be comfortable assisting others.

READINGS AND REFERENCES

Suggested Readings

Andrews, M. M., & Hanson, P. A. (1995). Religion, culture, and nursing. In M. M. Andrews & J. S. Boyle (Eds.). *Transcultural concepts in nursing care* (2nd ed.). Philadelphia, PA: Lippincott. pp. 353–410.
The authors discuss the beliefs and religious practices, holy days, sacraments, religious beliefs related to healing, and religious beliefs about diet, medications, medical treatment, and surgical procedures of major world religions. Health issues that may be controversial within the religious group, the religious support system for ill believers, and religion-specific issues related to death and dying are also discussed.

Callister, L. C., Semenic, S., & Foster, J. C. (1999).Cultural and spiritual meanings of childbirth: Orthodox Jewish and Mormon women. *Journal of Holistic Nursing, 17*, 280–295.
The researchers used a descriptive, phenomenological approach to study how 30 Canadian Orthodox Jewish and 30 American Mormon women perceived the cultural and spiritual meanings of the childbirth experience. Participants expressed the importance of bearing children in accordance with religious principles. They also voiced the value of personal connectedness with others and with God, the significance of childbearing, and the spiritual and emotional dimensions of their childbirth experiences. Findings suggest that religious beliefs help women understand the meaning of childbirth and may offer coping strategies for them to deal with the experience and associated stresses.

Solari-Twadell, P., & Parish McDermott, M. A. (Eds.). (1999). *Parish nursing: Promoting whole person health within faith communities.* Thousand Oaks, CA: Sage.
Two chapters of importance are "The Canadian Experience" and "Perspectives on a Suburban Parish Nurse Practice." Both offer unique perspectives of the experience of being a parish nurse.

Sumner, H. (1998). Recognizing and responding to spiritual distress. *American Journal of Nursing, 98*, 26–31.
This continuing education article includes the scope of spiritual distress, a spiritual needs assessment guide, barriers to spiritual care, and points to consider in providing care that respects the individual spiritual values of clients.

Related Research

Harrington, A. (1995). Spiritual care: What does it mean to RNs? *Australian Journal of Advanced Nursing, 12*(4), 5–14.

Post-White, J., Ceronsky, C., Kreitzer, M. J., Nickelson, K., Drew, D., Mackey, K. W., Koopmeiners, L., & Gutknecht, S. (1996). Hope, spirituality, sense of coherence, and quality of life in patients with cancer. *Oncology Nursing Forum, 23*, 1571–1579.

Sherman, D. W. (1996). Nurses' willingness to care for AIDS patients and spirituality, social support, and death anxiety. *IMAGE: Journal of Nursing Scholarship, 28*, 205–213.

Selected References

Burkhardt, M. (1993). Characteristics of Spirituality in the lives of women in a rural Appalachian Community. *Journal of Transcultural Nursing, 4*, 12–18.

Carpenito, L. J. (2002). *Handbook of nursing diagnosis.* Philadelphia, PA: Lippincott.

Carson, V. B. (1989). *Spiritual dimensions of nursing practice.* Philadelphia, PA: Saunders. (Classic.)

Denny, F. M. (1993). Islam and the Muslim community. In H. Byron Earhart (Ed.), *Religious traditions of the world* (pp. 603–712). New York: HarperSanFrancisco.

Dossey, L. (1993). *Healing words: The power of prayer and the practice of medicine.* New York: HarperSanFranciso.

Dossey, L. (1996). *Prayer is good medicine. How to reap the benefits of prayer.* New York: Harper Collins.

Ellison, C. W. (1983). Spiritual well-being: Conceptualization and measurement. *Journal of Psychology and Theology, 11*, 330–340.

Fishbane, M. (1993). Judaism: Revelation and traditions. In H. Byron Earhart (Ed.), *Religious traditions of the world* (pp. 373–484). New York: HarperSanFrancisco.

Fowler, J. W. (1974). Toward a developmental perspective on faith. *Religious Education, 69*, 207–219. (Classic.)

Fowler, J., & Keen, S. (1985). *Life maps: Conversations in the journey of faith.* Waco, TX: Word Books. (Classic.)

Frankiel, S. S. (1993). Christianity: A way of salvation. In H. Byron Earhart (Ed.), *Religious traditions of the world* (pp. 484–601). New York: HarperSanFrancisco.

Griffith, J. K. (1996). *The religious aspects of nursing care.* Vancouver: Author.

Grimm, P. M. (1991). Hope. In J. L. Creasia & B. Parker (Eds.), *Conceptual foundations of professional nursing practice.* St. Louis, MO: Mosby-Year Book.

Mayerhoff, H., VanHofwegen, L., Harwood, C., Drury, M., & Emblen, J. (2002). Spiritual nursing interventions. *Canadian Nurse, 98*(3), 21–24.

McCloskey, J. C., & Bulechek, G. M. (2000). *Nursing Interventions Classification (NIC)* (3rd ed.). St. Louis, MO: Mosby.

Moschella, V. D., Pressman, K. R., Pressman, P., & Weissman, D. E. (1997, Spring). The problem of theodicy and religious response to cancer. *Journal of Religion & Health, 36*(1), 17–20.

Murray, R. B., & Zentner, J. B. (1997). *Nursing assessment and health promotion strategies through the life span* (6th ed.). Norwalk, CT: Appleton & Lange.

Pilch, J. J. (1988, May/June). Wellness spirituality. *Health Values, 12*, 28–31.

Post-White, J., Ceronsky, C., Kreitzer, M. J., Nickelson, K., Drew, D., Mackey, K. W., Koopmeiners, L., & Gutknecht, S. (1996). Hope, spirituality, sense of coherence, and quality of life in patients with cancer. *Oncology Nursing Forum, 23*, 1571–1579.

Shelley, J. A., & Fish, S. (1988). *Spiritual care: The nurse's role* (3rd ed.). Downers Grove, IL: Inter Varsity Press. (Classic.)

Stotland, E. (1969). *The psychology of hope.* San Francisco, CA: Jossey-Bass.

Westerhoff, J. (1976). *Will our children have faith?* New York: Seabury Press. (Classic.)

WEBLINKS

Nechi Training, Research and Health Promotions Institute
http://www.nechi.com/index.html
Nechi is an aboriginal movement committed to respond to the training, research, and health promotion needs of aboriginal people, organizations, and communities.

The United Church of Canada Exchange Magazine
http://www.uccan.org/exchange/spring9901.htm
By using the search option, several Canadian articles on parish nursing on this site can be accessed.

Parish Nurse Institute
http://www.mcmaster.ca/divinity/parishnursing.html
An overview of the requirements for the parish nursing institute offered by McMaster University.

CHAPTER 14

Culture and Ethnicity

OBJECTIVES

After completing this chapter, you will be able to:

- Describe the concept of culture.
- Identify concepts pertaining to cultural diversity in nursing.
- Differentiate cultural awareness, cultural sensitivity, and cultural competence.
- Discuss components of culture pertinent to nursing care.
- List components of Leininger's Sunrise Model.
- Recognize the value of guidelines to foster culturally sensitive health care.
- Describe ways to overcome cultural barriers to health care.
- Explain what is meant by cultural competence as it relates to transcultural nursing.
- Analyze the different health views of culturally diverse clients: magico-religious, biomedical, and holistic.
- Differentiate traditional healing from biomedical care.
- Identify factors related to communication with culturally diverse clients and colleagues.
- Assess clients from a cultural perspective and plan culturally competent client care.

Nurses need to become informed about and sensitive to culturally diverse subjective meanings of health, illness, caring, and healing practices. A transcultural care perspective is now considered essential for nurses and other health-care professionals to deliver quality health care to all clients. North America is a continent of many cultural groups. In addition to the aboriginal people, there is much diversity in immigrant groups in North America.

Canadian Culture

Canada is vast; there are natural and social barriers separating one part of the country from another, and there are significant differences in population, ethnic background, language, and resources as one travels from east to west and south to north. Canadian culture can be discussed from a number of perspectives, including: demographics, immigration patterns, ethnic diversity, language, religion, multicultural policy, and health-care issues.

Demographic Profile

A demographic profile of Canada includes statistical descriptions and analysis of its population; for example, the number of people in the country or in a region, or the number of people who speak both official languages. According to Statistics Canada, results of its 2001 census identify that:

- Canada's population doubled in the past 50 years from just over 14 million in 1951 to 30,007,094 enumerated residents in 2001.
- Canada's population climbed by 4 percent in the last five years of the 20th century due to immigration.
- Immigration outpaced natural population increase for the first time since the Second World War, for a total gain of almost 1.2 million people.
- National median age reached an all-time high of 37.6 years in 2001, up from 35.3 years in 1996.
- Canada's workforce is older than those in most industrialized countries, with a median age of 41.2 in the core working group aged 20 to 64 years.
- Chinese is the most common language spoken at home after English and French.

Immigration Patterns

The peopling of Canada is a history of migrations. It is believed by some that the first arrivals to Canada were the ancestors of the First Nations people, who migrated to America most likely from Northeast Asia. The Athapaskan peoples and the ancestors of the Inuit probably followed them. These groups were as distinct in language, culture, and ethnicity as are more recent immigrants to Canada.

The next group of settlers was the French between 1608 and 1759. They settled primarily in Quebec, New Brunswick, and Nova Scotia. They also moved westward, establishing settlements in Ontario, the Prairie provinces, and British Columbia. The defeat of Montcalm in 1769 put Canada under British rule. From the 1780s onward, English speakers, including American refugees who followed immigrants from Great Britain, arrived in Canada, along with persons from other European countries.

Not all settlers who came to Canada, especially to the West, stayed. Many immigrants and Canadians decided to settle in the accessible and attractive American frontier. In 1891, Canada's population growth lagged behind that of the United States. Canada's population of 4.8 million persons was distributed unevenly across its vast territory. The majority of this small population was concentrated in Ontario, Quebec, and the Maritimes.

It was not until 1896 that the tide of immigration began to turn to Canada. One reason was the completion of the transcontinental railway in 1885, which eased the passage west for settlers and provided a means for farmers to export their grain. In addition, the dispossession of Native land rights through the signing of the seven numbered treaties in the 1870s enabled the federal government to open up the West to agricultural settlement. The closing of the American frontier meant that Canada could attract immigrants from the United States, Great Britain, and Europe.

During the 20th century, there were three major waves of immigration that helped shape the present composition of the Canadian population (Figure 14.1). The first occurred between 1901 and 1912, when almost three million people arrived, mainly from Great Britain and other European countries. By 1911, immigrants accounted for 22 percent of the population, compared with 13 percent in 1901. Between 1919 and 1931, only 1.2 million immigrants arrived in Canada. There were several reasons for this decline.

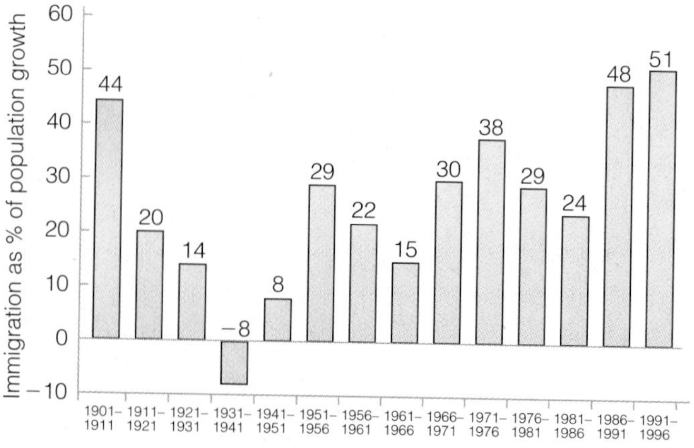

Figure 14.1 Immigration—an important contributor to total population growth throughout the 20th century

Canadians were involved in social policies that influenced the character of the country, including its immigration policy. The period between the First and Second World Wars was a period of immigration restriction and reduction. The Canadian government increased the sanctions against certain immigrant groups, and the war-torn conditions of Europe left many without the means to emigrate.

The second wave of immigration came after the Second World War, when hundreds of thousands of people were displaced from their homelands or were refugees. Over a million immigrants arrived in Canada between 1946 and 1955, with most of them still coming from Great Britain and other European countries. The third wave started in 1977 and continues today. Between 1991 and 2001, more than one million immigrants were accepted into this country. The largest group came from Asia. (See Figure 14.2.)

Currently, Canada takes in about twice as many people, in proportion to its population, as does the United States and four times as many as the United Kingdom. Consequently, the proportion of foreign-born in Canada is more than 20 percent, while the rate in the United States is between 9 and 10 percent. Only Israel and Australia rival Canada in the proportion of first-generation immigrants. More than 90 percent of all immigrants, according to 2001 census figures, live in Ontario, British Columbia, and Quebec. The Atlantic provinces are the only areas where people of British origin are the majority ethnic group, while Quebec retains French as the dominant ethnic origin of its population. New immigrants migrate toward the areas where others from their homelands live. In a new country, the presence of others from a familiar linguistic, religious, and cultural background makes the transition to a new way of life easier. Today, most immigrants live in urban areas, with more than one-half in the large cities of Toronto, Montreal, and Vancouver.

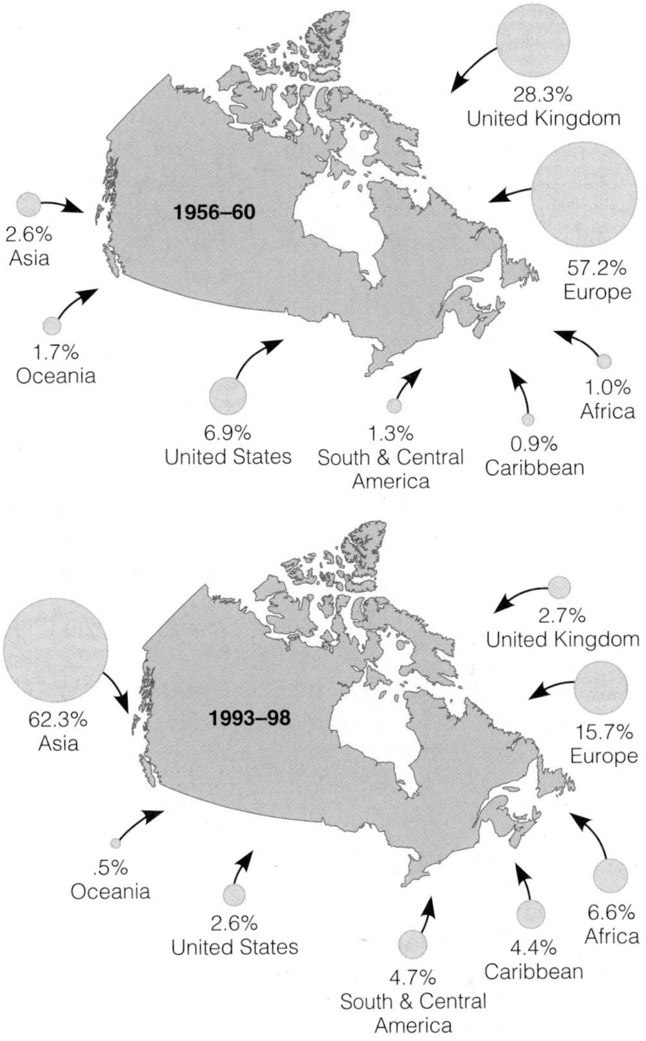

Figure 14.2 Immigration streams according to region of last residence, 1956–1960 and 1993–1998

Refugees

Since the end of World War II, a substantial proportion of immigrants, in excess of half a million in total, have been refugees. They came from Hungary in 1956, Czechoslovakia in 1968, and recently, from Southeast Asia, the Middle East, South and Central America, Africa, and, more recently, from Bosnia and Somalia. They face similar problems of adjustment as do immigrants but they also face other problems. Refugees have a sense of dignity and pride in the fact that they have upheld their personal convictions in the face of hostile governments, a situation that might not be understood by the residents in their host country, such as Canada.

Ethnic Diversity

In the Canadian experience, ethnicity refers to a person's ancestral roots or racial origin; culture refers to the beliefs, values, and life patterns of groups of people. Any given ethnic population may contain numerous subcultures, each with its own beliefs, values, and patterns of behaviour. In 1881, approximately 88 percent of Canadians identified with British or French ethnic origins. This is a reflection of British and French colonization in North America. All the societies in the New World are products of colonization, but only Canada has a history of two European charter groups intermingling and confronting one another, with no final assimilation of one group by the other.

Of the remaining 12 percent of the population in 1881, half identified themselves as German. The Germans, including large numbers of Mennonites, were the largest non-British and non-French ethnic group in Canada. Other groups, which composed the remaining 6 percent of the population, included First Nations (3%), Dutch (1%), and small groups of Italians, Jews, Russians, Scandinavians, Chinese, and African Canadians.

In 1891, the majority of the population was born in Canada. The foreign-born population, which constituted 13 percent of Canada's population, was distributed unevenly across the country. Whereas Quebec and the Maritime provinces contained small numbers of foreign-born residents, significant proportions of the foreign-born population resided in Ontario and Western Canada. Canada's population was still primarily of British and French origins. In 1921, ethnically British persons constituted a greater percentage of the population than they had in 1891. High birth rates in Quebec contributed to the stability of the French-speaking population.

Foreign immigration was making inroads in the ethnic diversity of Canada. In 1921, approximately 16 percent of the population did not identify ethnically with either British or French origins. Those recognized as Indians under the Indian Act constituted 1 percent of the total population.

Aboriginal People of Canada

The aboriginal population in Canada comprises the First Nations population, the Inuit, and the Métis. Within the First Nations population, the major cultural regions are the Woodland First Nations, First Nations of Southeastern Ontario, First Nations of the Plains, First Nations of the Plateau, Pacific Coast First Nations, and the First Nations of the Mackenzie and Yukon River Basins (Indian and Northern Affairs Canada, 2001). The aboriginal population is not a single, homogeneous group. They are extremely ethnically diverse and have long thought of themselves as quite distinct people.

The small bands of "Indians," now known as the First Nations people, who originally found their way across the Bering Sea, flourished, growing to an estimated 200,000 in Canada by the time the first French settlers arrived. Their numbers dwindled considerably during the 18th and 19th centuries due, in large part, to the new diseases the Europeans brought with them. During the past half century, the population has begun to grow again as infant and child mortality rates have declined. Many belong to one of about 600 bands and fall under the jurisdiction of the Indian Act or have been admitted to a general register kept by the Department of Indian Affairs and Northern Development. About one-third of the bands are in British Columbia.

Today, the growth rate of the First Nations peoples is greater than the overall Canadian rate. In the 1996 Canada census data, the most recent data available for this group, approximately one million people reported that they were Registered or Status Indians, Métis, or Inuit (Statistics Canada, 1996). The aboriginal population includes the approximately 41,000 Inuit who live mainly in the Arctic, a little more than half a million First Nations members (status or single origin), and more than 200,000 Métis (of mixed ethnic origin). There are also those who identify another ethnic group as their primary origin but claim some First Nations people among their ancestors (Statistics Canada, 1996). Each category encompasses various subgroups (see Table 14.1).

The Inuit people comprise the Inuvialuit of the western Arctic and the Inuit of the eastern Arctic and Labrador. They occupy small native communities north of the tree line in Canada, stretching from the Mackenzie River Delta, through the Arctic Islands and Baffin Island, along the coast of Hudson Bay and Ungava Bay in Quebec, to the east coast of Labrador. The Inuit have remained unique because of their limited access to mainstream Canadian culture.

The French

The first French colonists arrived on Canadian shores in the early 1600s. The large sizes of the families common in Quebec until the 1960s helped ensure continuation of the French language and culture in Canada. The current low birth rate in Quebec causes concern as it is below replacement levels. In 1991, the population reporting their ethnic origin as French was an estimated 17 percent of the total population, down from 24 percent in 1986. Outside of Quebec, the next largest group is in New Brunswick, although communities of ethnic French people are found in almost all provinces (Statistics Canada, 1996).

The British

The British conquest of Canada in 1769 marked the beginning of wide-scale settlements by people from England, Ireland, Scotland, and Wales. Over a century ago, at the time of Confederation, 61.5 percent of the estimated 5.7 million people in Canada were of British origin, including both single origin and multiple origins; this has now dwindled to 21 percent reporting British only or British and Canadian.

Visible Minorities

In Canada, non-British, non-French immigrants remained on the fringes of mainstream society until into the middle of the 20th century. The 1996 census collected information on people who are members of a visible minority group in Canada, defined by the Employment Equity Act as "persons, other than aboriginal people who are non-Caucasian in race, or non-white in colour" (Statistics Canada, 1997). In 1996, 3.2 million persons identified themselves as visible minorities, representing 11.2 percent of the Canadian population. Ontario and British Columbia together accounted for almost three-fourths of the visible minority population.

There has been a three-fold increase in the numbers of persons who identify themselves as visible minorities between the last two census reports (Statistics Canada, 2003). The largest visible minority population remains the Chinese (3.7% of Canada's total population). The next largest groups were South Asians (3.1%) and Blacks (2.2%). Other visible minority populations include Filipinos, Southeast Asians, Latin Americans, Japanese, Koreans, Arabs, and West Asians (Figure 14.3). Almost all visible minority persons lived in urban areas, with Toronto, Vancouver, and Calgary having the largest numbers.

TABLE 14.1 Population by Aboriginal Group, 1996 Census

Region	Total population	Aboriginal population (see definition)				Non-Aboriginal population
		Total[1]	North American Indian[2, 3]	Métis[2]	Inuit[2]	
Canada	**28,528,125**	**799,010**	**554,290**	**210,190**	**41,080**	**27,729,115**
Newfoundland	547,155	14,200	5,430	4,685	4,265	532,955
Prince Edward Island	132,855	950	825	120	15	131,905
Nova Scotia	899,965	12,380	11,340	860	210	887,585
New Brunswick	729,630	10,250	9,180	975	120	719,380
Quebec	7,045,080	71,415	47,600	16,075	8,300	6,973,665
Ontario	10,642,795	141,520	118,830	22,790	1,300	10,501,275
Manitoba	1,100,295	128,680	82,990	46,195	360	971,615
Saskatchewan	976,615	111,245	75,205	36,535	190	865,370
Alberta	2,669,195	122,835	72,645	50,745	795	2,546,360
British Columbia	3,689,755	139,655	113,315	26,750	815	3,550,100
Yukon	30,650	6,175	5,530	565	110	24,475
Northwest Territories[4]	64,120	39,690	11,400	3,895	24,600	24,430
Northwest Territories	39,460	19,000	x	x	x	20,460
Nunavut	24,665	20,690	x	x	x	3,975

x Data unavailable, not applicable, or confidential.

Source: Adapted from Statistics Canada Web site, http://www.statcan.ca/english/Pgdb/demo39a.htm

DEFINITIONS

Aboriginal population: There are different ways to define the aboriginal population. Data presented in this table are for those who identified with one or more aboriginal groups (North American Indian, Métis, or Inuit). Also included are those who did not identify with an aboriginal group but who reported that they were Registered/Treaty Indians or Band/First Nation members. The 1996 Census also provides information on those who reported aboriginal ethnic origin/ancestry. For more information, contact your local Statistics Canada regional office.

North American Indian population: Includes persons who identified as North American Indian and/or those who reported being a member of an Indian Band/First Nation and/or those who reported being a Treaty Indian or a Registered Indian as defined by the Indian Act of Canada.

NOTES

1. The sum of North American Indian, Métis, and Inuit is more than the total Aboriginal population because 6,415 persons reported identifying with more than one group.
2. Single and multiple response have been combined.
3. Users should note that depending on the geographic area under study, the counts for North American Indian may be affected by the incomplete enumeration of 77 Indian reserves and settlements in the 1996 Census.
4. Includes Nunavut.

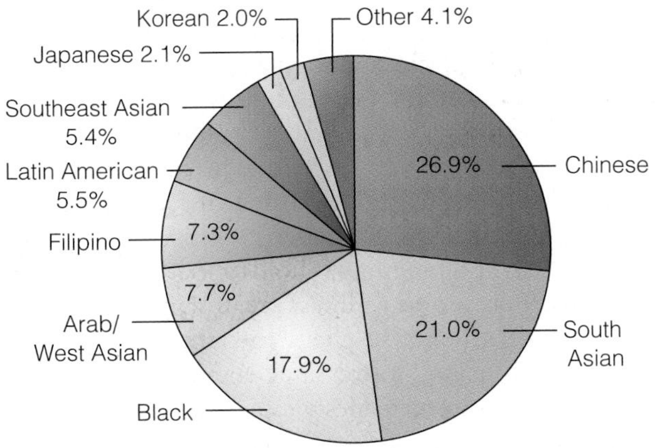

Figure 14.3 Changes in the visible minority population in Canada between 1996 and 2001

Source: Adapted from Statistics Canada. *The Daily*, Catalogue 11-001, February 17, 1998.

Language

Language and language conflict are defining characteristics of Canadian society. During the census in 1996 and 2001 Canadians were asked to identify their mother tongue, defined as "the first language that a person learned at home in childhood and still understands" (Statistics Canada, 2001). A total of 126 languages were reported, including 23 aboriginal languages. English was the most common language, with nearly 60 percent of the population reporting it as either their mother tongue or one of their mother tongues. The second most common was French, reported by 24 percent of the population. A single mother tongue other than English or French was reported by 16 percent of the population. Almost 10 percent of the people in Canada were allophones (i.e., spoke a language other than English or French most of the time). Chinese

TABLE 14.2 Visible minority population by place of origin, 1996 Census and 2001 Census

Total population	28,528,125	29,639,030
Total visible minority population	3,197,480	3,983,845
Black	573,860	662,200
South Asian	670,590	199,192
Chinese	860,150	1,029,400
Korean	64,840	119,515
Japanese	68,135	79,676
Southeast Asian	172,765	199,192
Filipino	234,195	318,707
Arab/West Asian	244,665	318,707
Latin American	176,975	199,192
Visible minority, n.i.e.[1]	69,745	
Multiple visible minority[2]	61,575	

1 not identified
2 several different places of origin

Source: Adapted from Statisitics Canada Web site, http://www.statcan.ca/english/Pgdb/demo41.htm

was the most common, followed by Italian and Punjabi (Statistics Canada, 2001).

According to the 1996 census, almost half a million people over the age of five years were unable to speak either one of the two official languages (Statistics Canada, 2001). This is a larger number than at any other time in the 20th century, a situation that puts a strain on certain services, such as English/French language training and translation services, and can cause problems in the delivery of health care. Most of these individuals are women who live in large households in urban centres, where there are large ethnic communities.

Religion

Canadians identified more than 100 denominations under religious affiliation in the 1991 census. Historically, the major religious denominations in Canada have been Christians, either Catholic or Protestant. A 1990 General Survey conducted by Statistics Canada identified that 46.5 percent of the population identified themselves as Roman Catholic and 30 percent as Protestant. The most common other religions cited were Judaism, Islam, Hinduism, Sikhism, and Buddhism. About 12 percent reported that they had no religious affiliation.

Multicultural Policy

Much of the dynamism of Canadian society has its origins in the ethnic diversity of the population. The multicultural policy in Canada was initiated in 1971 as a guideline for federal government policy and serves as a framework for discourse on the construction of Canadian society. In 1988, the Multiculturalism Act was passed, guaranteeing multicultural legal status and affirming its importance to Canada. As a policy promoting tolerance and diversity, multiculturalism was to be the opposite of assimilation, for to assimilate is to lose those characteristics which distinguish a group from the culture which surrounds it. Canada has been called a mosaic or an ethnically plural society because of the way it has absorbed immigrants. It has enabled its people to retain a distinct sense of cultural identity. This policy was formalized and included into legislation in the Canadian Multicultural Act (1985). This is in contrast to the melting pot of the United States, where immigrants are assimilated into the mainstream of that culture.

The policy of multiculturalism does raise issues for some Canadians. For French Canadians, immigration is a concern. In the early days of Canada, the fear was that immigrants, even those coming to Quebec, would overwhelmingly choose to become Anglophones, thus reducing the Francophones there to minority status. It was a justifiable fear, since English gave the children of newcomers more mobility in a country where most people speak that language. Until the 1970s, most immigrants to Quebec sent their children to English schools. Quebec Nationalists feared that integrating large numbers of immigrants into the French-speaking community would change its fundamental character, and they were right. Since Bill 22 and Bill 101 were passed in Quebec in the 1970s, mandating that the children of immigrants to the province be educated in French, the future of the French language in the province is secure. However, the future of traditional Quebecois nationalism is in doubt. Nontraditional Francophones are a cultural and political phenomenon in the province and have the ability to shape the future of Quebec.

Health-Care Concerns

In Canada, with its diverse population, nurses must consider cultural and ethnic factors in providing quality nursing care. Ethnicity is not the same as culture; just because people belong to the same ethnic group, it should not be assumed that they all share the same cultural characteristics. A group's worldview shapes its health culture—the values, beliefs, and practices it holds about health promotion, disease prevention, illness treatment, and expectations that guide the nurse-client encounter.

People who belong to the same ethnic group may have little in common in their lifestyles, beliefs, and values. For example, a Canadian of East Indian ancestry could be a third-generation Canadian who cannot speak a word of Hindi, a recently arrived lawyer from New Delhi, or an ethnic refugee from a small mountain village in northern India. This example illustrates the importance of not stereotyping people on the basis of their ethnic origin. Socioeconomic status, lengths of time people have been in Canada, educational level, age, gender, and country of origin will influence perspectives of health and health behaviours. However, there are genetically acquired biological traits that may have a bearing on a person's health. There are differences in skin pigmentation, body build, facial structure, and metabolism.

It is important for nurses to explore the cultural and ethnic beliefs and the health-care practices of all Canadians. The Canadian health-care system is rooted in Western biomedical principles, in which outcome is orientated toward the effective diagnosis and treatment of disease. Ethnic members may view nurses of a dominant culture as a threat to their traditional ways of dealing with health-care concerns. For example, a young woman may be perceived by an elderly Asian male as an inappropriate person to provide personal nursing care because of status difference. Language differences may present another barrier to effective nursing care. Ethnic minority immigrants may not be able to read and write in either official language of Canada. Written instructions from a nurse may be misunderstood or not fully understood.

Health-care professionals are not expected to know and understand *all* cultures of the world; it is possible, however, for them to develop an in-depth understanding of three or four cultures and to learn about other cultures through time (Leininger 1993). It is also important for nurses to understand their own cultural beliefs and biases.

Nurses need to be aware that although people from a given ethnic group share certain beliefs, values, and experiences, often there is also widespread intra-ethnic diversity. Major differences within ethnic groups may be due to such factors as age, gender, level of education, socioeconomic status, religious affiliation, and area of origin in the home country (rural or urban). Such factors influence the client's beliefs about health and illness, health and illness practices, help-seeking behaviours, and expectations of health professionals (Anderson et al., 1990). For these reasons, nurses should make special effort to avoid ethnic stereotyping.

Canadian Society Notes

Fact	Implications for Nursing Practice
In 1971, the Federal Government announced its policy of multiculturalism.	This policy promotes a cultural mosaic whereby persons are encouraged to retain their cultural beliefs and practices rather than being assimilated into the mainstream culture. This means that nurses need to be culturally sensitive and incorporate appropriate assessment measures into health-care assessment and care delivery.
In 1996, about 3 percent of Canadians belonged to aboriginal populations: First Nations, Métis, Inuit.	Nurses need to be aware of the multiplicity of differences that exist within these populations and not make assumptions that all persons have the same beliefs and practices.
Approximately two-fifths of the Canadian population have one origin other than British, French, or aboriginal.	The fact that the Canadian population is increasing in diversity has implications for how nurses incorporate the changes in practice needed to address this diversity. Nurses also need to be aware of the knowledge, skills, and attitudes about culture that are included in the 1999 CNA Blueprint for the Registered Nurse Examination.

Concepts Related to Culture

All groups of people face similar issues in adapting to their environment: providing nutrition and shelter, caring for and educating children, division of labour, social organization, controlling disease, and maintaining health. Humans adapt to varying environments by developing cultural solutions to meet these needs. Understanding the cultural dimension of people is the focus of the field of anthropology. Cultural anthropologists attempt to understand culture by studying both similarities and differences among human groups. Nurses can use the cultural information gained by cultural anthropologists to understand and help clients (individuals, their families, groups, or communities) to achieve optimum health.

Culture is a universal experience, but no two cultures are exactly alike. Two important terms identify the differences and similarities among peoples of different cultures. **Culture-universals** are the commonalities of values, norms of behaviour, and life patterns among different cultures. **Culture-specifics** are those values, beliefs, and patterns of behaviour that tend to be unique to a designated culture, rather than shared with members of other cultures. For example, most cultures have ceremonies to celebrate the passage from childhood to adulthood; this practice is a culture-universal. However, different cultural groups celebrate this important life event in very

Figure 14.4 Celebrations of the passage to adulthood: the Jewish bar mitzvah and the Latino or Hispanic "quince" or "quinceañero" party

different ways (Figure 14.4). In Latin or Hispanic cultures, the "quince" or "quinceañero" party, which celebrates a girl's 15th birthday, signifies that the young girl has now become a woman. In the Jewish tradition, the bar mitzvah (for boys) and the bat mitzvah (for girls) are celebrations of the passage to adulthood.

Anthropologists have also traditionally divided culture into material and nonmaterial culture. **Material culture** refers to objects (such as dress, art, religious artifacts, or eating utensils) and the ways these are used. **Nonmaterial culture** refers to beliefs, customs, languages, and social institutions.

The terms *culture*, *diversity*, *ethnicity*, and *race* are often used interchangeably, but they are not synonymous. **Culture** is defined as "the learned, shared, and transmitted values, beliefs, norms, and lifeway practices of a particular group that guide thinking, decisions, and actions in patterned ways" (Leininger, 1988, p. 158).

Because cultural patterns are learned, it is important for nurses to note that members of a particular group may not share identical cultural experiences. Thus, individual members of a cultural group will be somewhat different from their own cultural counterparts (Waxler-Morrison et al., 1990). For example, white Roman Catholics will have cultural patterns and beliefs different from those of white Seventh-Day Adventists. Third-generation Japanese Canadians, or *Sansei*, will differ in cultural understandings from first-generation Japanese, or *Issei*.

Large cultural groups often have cultural subgroups or subsystems. A **subculture** is usually composed of people who have a distinct identity and yet are also related to a larger cultural group. A subcultural group generally shares ethnic origin, occupation, or physical characteristics with the larger cultural group. Examples of cultural subgroups include occupational groups (e.g., nurses), societal groups (e.g., feminists), and ethnic groups (e.g., Métis, who are descendants of First Nations and European parents).

Bicultural is used to describe a person who crosses two cultures, lifestyles, and sets of values (Giger & Davidhizar, 1995). For example, a young man whose father is Cree and whose mother is European Canadian may maintain his traditional Cree heritage while also being influenced by his mother's cultural values.

Diversity refers to the "fact or state of being different" (Steinmetz & Braham, 1993, p. 141). Many factors account for differences: race, gender, sexual orientation, culture, ethnicity, socioeconomic status, educational attainment, religious affiliation, and so on. Diversity, therefore, occurs not only between cultural groups but also within a cultural group.

The term **ethnic** refers to a group of people who share a common and distinctive culture and who are members of a specific group. The **ethnic group** shares a common social and cultural heritage that is passed on to successive generations (Giger & Davidhizar, 1995). The characteristics of the group give an individual a sense of **cultural identity**. **Ethnicity** has been defined as "a consciousness of belonging to a group that is differentiated from others by symbolic markers (culture, biology, territory). It is rooted in bonds of a shared past and perceived ethnic interest" (Sprott, 1993, p. 190). Other factors that help define ethnicity are religion and the geographic background of the family.

Race is the classification of people according to shared biologic characteristics, genetic markers, or features. They have common characteristics, such as skin colour, bone structure, facial features, hair texture, and blood type. Different ethnic groups can belong to the same race, and different cultures can be found within the same ethnic group. For example, the terms *Caucasian* and *European Canadian* describe the race of people whose origins are in Europe. Whereas British Canadians are a subgroup of European Canadians, Scottish Canadians (an ethnic subgroup of British Canadians) may have cultural practices different from other British Canadians. It is important to understand that not all people of the same race have the same culture. Culture should not be confused with either race or ethnic group.

It is helpful to differentiate the terms *acculturation* and *ethnic identity*. **Acculturation** or **assimilation** is the assumption of the values, attitudes, beliefs, or practices of a dominant group in society by a minority group. It is often defined in terms of such observable factors as dress, food, and language. Individuals who are acculturated may no longer eat foods associated with their culture or always wear traditional dress (Lynam, 1992). **Ethnic identity,** in contrast, refers to a subjective perspective of the person's heritage and to a sense of belonging to a group that is distinguishable from other groups. Thus, people may be visibly acculturated to the mainstream culture but may retain an identity that differs from the mainstream.

The cultural beliefs and practices regarding health and illness of North America's many different ethnic and cultural groups are important considerations for nurses in planning nursing care. The study of anthropology by nurses, which looks at the origin, the behaviour, and the physical, social, and cultural development of human beings, is an important contribution to nursing (Leininger, 1970). Leininger defines **transcultural nursing** as a "field of nursing [that] focus[es] on the comparative study and analysis of different cultures and subcultures in the world with respect to their caring behaviors, nursing care, and health-illness values, beliefs, and patterns of behaviors with the goal of developing a scientific and humanistic body of knowledge in order to provide culture-specific and culture-universal nursing care practice" (p. 8).

Cultural awareness and cultural sensitivity are prerequisites to the provision of culturally competent nursing care. **Cultural awareness** is the conscious and informed recognition of the differences and similarities between different cultural or ethnic groups. Cultural awareness is not knowledge derived solely from myths and stereotypes. **Cultural sensitivity** is the respect and appreciation for cultural behaviours based on an understanding of the other person's perspective. **Cultural competence** is "knowing, utilizing, and appreciating the culture of another in assisting with the resolution of a problem" (DeSantis & Lowe, 1992, p. 1). The culturally competent nurse, therefore, works within the cultural belief system of the client to respond effectively in cross-cultural situations (Campbell & Campbell, 1996). To provide culturally competent care, nurses need data about the client's personal and cultural views regarding health and illness. To make valid assessments, nurses need to try to see and hear the world as their clients do. When developing care plans, nurses need to consider the client's world and daily experiences. Although a client's needs and behaviours can be better understood when participants' cultural health norms are identified, nurses must take care to avoid stereotyping clients by culture norms. This allows for individualized care.

Culture shock can occur when members of one culture are abruptly moved to another culture or setting. **Culture shock** is the state of being disoriented or unable to respond to a different cultural environment because of its sudden strangeness, unfamiliarity, and incompatibility to the stranger's perceptions and expectations (Leininger, 1978). For example, when immigrants first enter Canada or the United States, language and behaviour differences may initially cause them difficulty in carrying out normal activities. People can also experience culture shock when they are abruptly thrust into the health-care subculture. Nursing students, for example, may experience culture shock when they enter nursing school and must learn

RESEARCH NOTE

Cross-Cultural Hospital Care as Experienced by Mi'kmaq Clients

Members of First Nations communities may find that when they are hospitalized, health-care providers and other patients hold different values, beliefs, and customs. This study examined how Mi'kmaq from the Big Cove community in New Brunswick described their experiences with caregivers during recent hospitalization. Interviews with 10 participants were analyzed using an interpretive interaction method. Themes that evolved were misunderstanding, being misunderstood, and feeling understood. Participants identified the dichotomy of "our ways" and "their ways" as the source of the misunderstanding.

Implications: When working with clients, nurses need to be aware of two distinct contexts for cross-cultural caregiving: (1) nurses may be providing care in a cultural community that is different from their own, and/or (2) the care recipient may be receiving care surrounded by those of another culture. Participants valued caregivers with a nondiscriminatory and accepting attitude. Further studies with other cultural groups in other settings are recommended.

Source: Baker, C., & Daigle, M. C. (2000). Cross-cultural hospital care as experience by Mi'kmaq clients. *Western Journal of Nursing Research, 22*(1), 8–28.

medical terminology (a new language) and provide care for clients in clinical environments with which they are unfamiliar. Expressions of culture shock can range from silence and immobility to agitation.

Characteristics of Culture

Culture exhibits several characteristics.

- *Culture is learned.* It is neither instinctive nor innate. It is learned through life experiences from birth.
- *Culture is taught.* It is transmitted from parents, extended family, and peers to children over successive generations. All animals can learn, but only humans can pass along culture. Verbal and nonverbal communication patterns are the transmitters of culture.
- *Culture is social.* It originates and develops through the interactions of people: families, groups, and communities.
- *Culture is adaptive.* Customs, beliefs, and practices change as people adapt to the social environment and as the biological and psychological needs of people change. Some traditional forms in a culture may cease to provide satisfaction and are eliminated. For example, in many cultures, it is customary for family members of different generations to live together (extended family); however, education and employment considerations may require children to leave their parents and move to other parts of the country. In such cases, the extended family norm may change.
- *Culture is satisfying.* Cultural habits persist only as long as they satisfy people's needs. Gratification strengthens habits and beliefs. Once they no longer bring gratification, they may disappear.
- *Culture is difficult to articulate.* Members of a specific cultural group often find it difficult to explain their own culture. Many of the values and behaviours are habitual and are carried out subconsciously.
- *Culture exists at many levels.* Culture is most easily identified at the material level. For example, art, tools, and clothes usually reveal aspects of a culture relatively readily. It is often more difficult to find out about the more abstract concepts, such as values, beliefs, and traditions. Nurses may need to ask culture-sensitive questions of the client or support people to obtain this information.

Components of Culture

Cultures are complex. Their facets relate to all aspects of life: language, art, music, values systems (beliefs, morals, rules), religion, philosophy, family interaction, patterns of behaviour, childrearing practices, rituals or ceremonies, recreation and leisure activities, festivals and holidays, nutrition, food preferences, and health practices. Many facets of culture (e.g., health and illness practices, attitudes about touch, territory and privacy, childbirth, and death and dying practices) affect nursing practice.

Religious values are part of the cultural values of groups that have one dominant religion. For example, the roles of men and women in Islamic cultures are clearly defined by the Koran. The tenets of Roman Catholicism dictate the value placed on life and family and influence both laws and customs in many Roman Catholic cultures around the world. Culture and religion are deeply intertwined among many Jews, most notably in the nation of Israel, which is founded on Jewish beliefs and traditions.

Religious values associated with any culture influence many facets of life, including dietary restrictions, family planning, use of blood transfusions, and death-related practices, such as autopsy, organ donation, cremation, and prolonging life.

Culture and Health Care

Two transcultural health-care systems generally exist side by side with limited awareness by practitioners in both systems: an indigenous health-care system and a professional health-care system (Leininger, 1993). The *indigenous health-care system* refers to traditional folk methods of health care, such as folk medicines and other home treatments. The more recent *professional health-care system* refers to a structured system maintained by individuals who have engaged in a formal program of study. The indigenous system is the older system and has often provided health care long before a professional system enters the culture. According to Leininger, few professional health-care workers are knowledgeable about the indigenous health-care system or its practitioners. Some professionals regard the indigenous system as unscientific or "primitive," or even as "quackery." Leininger emphasizes that the goal of health care should be to use the best of both systems and that health professionals need to consider ways to interface with the two systems for the benefit of the people served. "Every culture has health, caring, and caring processes, techniques, and practices viewed as important to the people" (Leininger, 1993, p. 38).

Leininger's Sunrise Model

Leininger produced the Sunrise Model to depict her theory of cultural care diversity and universality (Figure 14.5). This model emphasizes that health and care are influenced by elements of the social structure, such as technology, religious and philosophical factors, kinship and social systems, cultural values, political and legal factors, economic factors, and educational factors. These social factors are addressed within environmental contexts, language expressions, and ethnohistory. Each of these systems is part of the social structure of any society; health-care expressions, patterns, and practices are also integral parts of these aspects of social structure (Leininger, 1993).

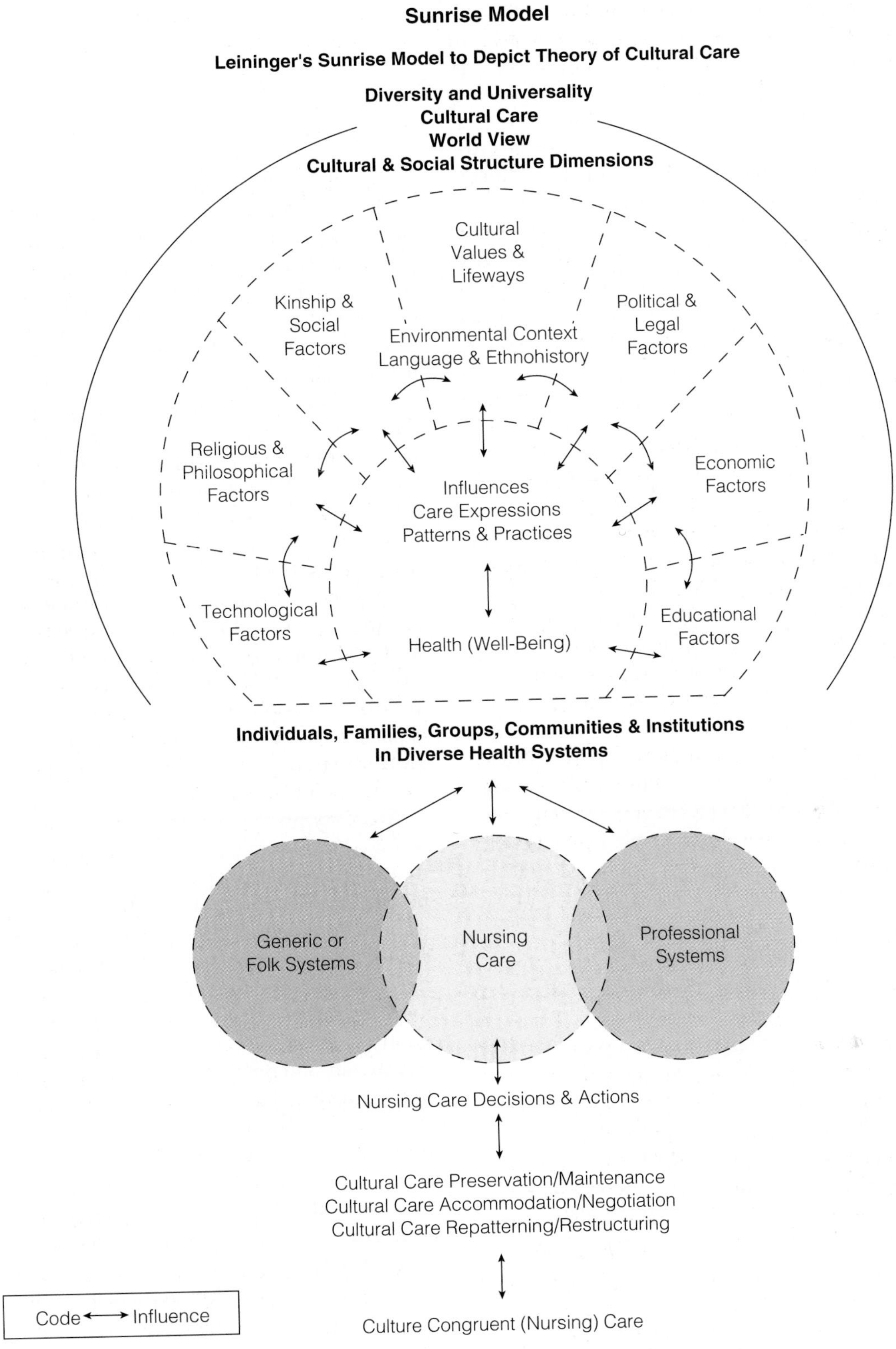

Figure 14.5 Leininger's Sunrise Model

Source: M. Leininger. (1991). *Culture care diversity and universality: A theory of nursing.* New York: National League for Nursing Pub. No. 15-2402, p. 43. Reprinted with permission.

Technological factors, such as the availability of technical and electrical equipment, greatly determine what health equipment will be used. For example, many European Canadians regard resuscitative equipment as essential. The *economic* system determines the quality of health care within a culture, for example, the availability of funds for health-care services materially affects the health of the culture's infants and aged. The *political* system is a major determinant of what health programs will be available and which health practitioners may provide health services. *Legal* aspects govern the roles, functions, and standards of health professionals within cultures. *Kinship* and the *social system* often influence who will or will not receive health care and how promptly it will be provided. For example, in some cultures, a person of high status (e.g., tribal leader, CEO, or king) may receive prompt care; a person of lower status (e.g., a peasant, housewife, or child) may experience a considerable waiting period for care. Because of male dominance in many cultures, men may receive care before a wife or female child. *Cultural, educational, religious,* and *philosophical* factors are closely related. They influence the type, quality, and quantity of health care considered desirable, appropriate, or acceptable to the culture. *Environmental* and *demographic* factors relate to the health needs of the culture and which strategies of care can be used in the setting.

Since the development of Leninger's Sunrise Model, several other models have been developed. These include the following: The Felder Cultural Diversity Practice Model (CDPM) (Felder, 1995); The Purnell Conceptual Model for Cultural Competence (Purnell & Paulanka, 1998); and the Model for Developing Cultural Sensitivity (Baldwin et al., 1996).

Culturally Sensitive Care

Kittler and Sucher (1990) suggest a four-step process to improve cultural sensitivity:

1. *Become aware of one's own cultural heritage.* Nurses should identify their own cultural values and beliefs. For example, does the nurse value stoic behaviour in relation to pain? Are the rights of the individual valued over and above the rights of the family? Only by knowing one's own culture (values, practices, and beliefs) can a person be ready to learn about another's.
2. *Become aware of the client's culture as described by the client.* It is important to avoid assuming that all people of the same ethnic background have the same cultural beliefs and values. When the nurse has a knowledge of the client's culture, mutual respect between client and nurse is more likely to develop.
3. *Become aware of adaptations the client made to live in a North American culture.* During this interview, a nurse can also identify the client's preferences in health practices, diet, hygiene, and so on.
4. *Develop nursing care plans with the clients that incorporate their culture.* In this way, cultural values, practices, and beliefs can be incorporated with care and judgement.

Barriers to Cultural Sensitivity

Many factors can be barriers to providing culturally sensitive or culturally congruent care to clients and their support people. These factors can also affect communication and working relationships with other health-care personnel. Ethnocentrism, stereotyping, prejudice, and discrimination are some of these factors.

Ethnocentrism refers to the view that the beliefs and values of one's own culture are superior to those of other cultures. In health care, ethnocentrism can include the view that the only valid health-care beliefs and practices are those held by the professionals in the health-care system. Nurses who take a transcultural view, however, value their own beliefs and practices while respecting the beliefs and practices of others. It is important for nurses to realize that although many people of differing racial and religious backgrounds have combined their traditional health practices with Western health practices, other people may be unable to do so.

Most people are gradually exposed to their culture's beliefs, values, and practices over a period of years starting at birth. Ethnocentrism is thought to result from lack of exposure or knowledge of cultures other than one's own. **Ethnorelativity** is the ability to appreciate and respect the viewpoints of other cultures.

Stereotyping is assuming that all members of a culture or ethnic group are alike. For example, a nurse may assume that all Italians express pain volubly or that all Chinese people like rice. Stereotyping may be based on generalizations founded in research, or it may be unrelated to reality. For example, research indicates that Italians are likely to express pain verbally; however, an Italian client may not verbalize pain. Stereotyping that is unrelated to reality may be either positive or negative and is frequently an outcome of racism or discrimination. Nurses need to realize that not all people of a specific group have the same health beliefs, practices, and values. It is, therefore, essential to identify a specific client's beliefs, needs, and values rather than assuming they are the same as those attributable to the larger group.

Prejudice is a strongly held opinion about some topic or group of people. A prejudice may be positive or negative. A positive prejudice often stems from a strong sense of ethnocentrism (Eliason, 1993). Prejudice may also derive from ignorance, misinformation, past experience, or fear. Other types of negative prejudice are ageism, which includes negative attitudes toward older adults; sexism, meaning negative attitudes toward women; and homophobia, which is negativism toward lesbians and gay men.

Banks and Banks (1989, p. 37) define **discrimination** as "the differential treatment of individuals or groups based on categories such as race, ethnicity, gender, social class, or exceptionality." For example, a nurse takes a child who is waiting in an emergency department ahead of another child. The child taken ahead appears clean, is neatly dressed, and is smiling; the other child appears dirty, is wearing worn clothes, and is angry. **Racism** is a form of discrimination related to ethnocentrism in which a person believes that race is the primary determinant of human traits and capacities and that racial differences result in an inherent superiority of a particular race.

Conveying Cultural Sensitivity

It is important for nurses to be culturally sensitive and to convey this sensitivity to clients, support people, and other health-care personnel. Some ways to do so include:

- Always address clients by their last names (e.g., Mrs. Aylia, Dr. Rush) until they give you permission to use other names. In some cultures, the more formal style of address is a sign of respect, whereas the informal use of first names may be considered disrespect. It is important to ask clients how they wish to be addressed.
- When meeting a person for the first time, introduce yourself by your full name, and when appropriate, explain your position. This helps establish a relationship and provides an opportunity for clients and nurses to learn the pronunciation of one another's names.
- Be genuine with people, and be honest about the knowledge you lack about their culture.
- Use language that is culturally sensitive; for example, say "gay," "lesbian," or "bisexual," rather than "homosexual"; do not use "man" or "mankind" when referring to a woman; "African Canadian" and "Latin American" are currently preferred over "black" or "Hispanic." "Asian" is more acceptable than "Oriental" (Eliason, 1993). In Canada, use the term "Aboriginal" to refer to First Nations, Inuit, and Métis members. Even better, ask the person what term they prefer. Older members of some ethnic groups may prefer the appellation of "black" or "Oriental."
- Find out what the clients know about their health problems, illnesses, and treatments. Assess whether this information is congruent with the dominant health-care culture. If the beliefs and practices are incongruent, establish whether this will have a negative effect on the client's health.
- Do not make any assumptions about the client, and always ask about anything you do not understand.
- Respect the clients' values, beliefs, and practices, even if they differ from your own or from those of the dominant culture. If you don't agree with them, it is important to respect the clients' rights to hold these beliefs.
- Show respect for the clients' support people. In some cultures, men in the family make decisions affecting the client, while in other cultures women make the decisions.
- Make a concerted effort to obtain the client's trust, but do not be surprised if it develops slowly or not at all.

Selected Cultural Parameters for Nursing

This section outlines selected cultural and ethnic phenomena of significance to nursing.

Health Beliefs and Practices

Andrews and Boyle (2003) describe three views of health beliefs: magico-religious, scientific, and holistic. In the **magico-religious health belief view,** health and illness are controlled by supernatural forces. The client may believe that illness is the result of "being bad" or opposing God's will. Getting well is also viewed as dependent on God's will. The client may make statements such as, "If it is God's will, I will recover," or "What did I do wrong to be punished with cancer?" Some cultures believe that magic can cause illness. A sorcerer or witch may put a spell or hex on the client. Some people view illness as possession by an evil spirit. Although these beliefs are not supported by empirical evidence, clients who believe that such things can cause illness may, in fact, become ill as a result. Such illnesses may require magical treatments in addition to scientific treatments. The fear of ridicule by health-care providers may prevent Haitian Canadians who continue to use voodoo practices from admitting their belief in these traditional practices (Boyle, 1999).

The **scientific** or **biomedical health belief** is based on the belief that life and life processes are controlled by physical and biochemical processes that can be manipulated by humans (Andrews & Boyle, 1995). The client with this view will believe that illness is caused by germs, viruses, bacteria, or a breakdown of the human machine, the body. This client will expect a pill, treatment, or surgery to cure health problems.

The **holistic health belief** holds that the forces of nature must be maintained in balance or harmony. Human life is one aspect of nature that must be in harmony with the rest of nature. When the natural balance or harmony is disturbed, illness results. The Medicine Wheel is an ancient symbol used by First Nations members of North and South America to express many concepts. For health and wellness, the Medicine Wheel teaches the four aspects of the individual's nature: the physical, the mental, the emotional, and the spiritual. The four dimensions must be in balance to be healthy. The Medicine Wheel can also be used to express the individual's relationship with the environment as a dimension of wellness.

The concept of yin and yang in the Chinese culture and the hot-cold theory of illness in many Spanish cultures are examples of holistic health beliefs. When a Chinese client has a yin illness or a "cold" illness, the treatment may include a yang or "hot" food (e.g., hot tea). For example, a Chinese client who has been diagnosed with cancer, a yin disease, will want to eat cultural foods that have yang properties.

What is considered hot or cold varies considerably across cultures. In many cultures, the mother who has just delivered a baby should be offered warm or hot foods and kept warm with blankets because childbirth is seen as a "cold" condition. Conventional scientific thought recommends cooling the body to reduce a fever. The physician may order liquids for the client and cool compresses to be applied to the forehead, the axillae, or the groin. Galanti (1991) states that many cultures believe that the best way to treat a fever is to "sweat it out." Clients from these cultures may want to cover up with several blankets, take hot baths, and drink hot beverages. Giger and Davidhizar (1995) state that the nurse must keep in mind that a treatment strategy that is consistent with the client's beliefs may have a better chance of being successful. For example, the Latin American client who avoids "hot" foods when experiencing a stomach disturbance may be eating foods consistent with the bland diet that is normally prescribed by physicians.

Sociocultural forces, such as politics, economics, geography, religion, and the predominant health-care system, can influence the client's health status and health-care behaviour. For example, people who have limited access to scientific health care may turn to traditional medicine or healing. **Traditional medicine** is defined as those beliefs and practices relating to illness prevention and healing that derive from cultural traditions, rather than from modern medicine's scientific base. Many students can recall special teas or "cures" used by older family members to prevent or treat colds, fevers, indigestion, and other common health problems. People also continue to use chicken soup as a treatment for "flu."

Why do individuals use these traditional healing methods? Traditional medicine, in contrast to biomedical health care, is thought to be more humanistic. The consultation and treatment takes place in the community of the recipient, frequently in the home of the healer. It is less expensive than scientific or biomedical care because the health problem is identified primarily through conversation with the client and the family. The healer often prepares the treatments, for example, teas to be ingested, poultices to be applied, or charms or amulets to be worn. A frequent component of treatment is some ritual practice on the part of the healer or the client to cause healing to occur. Because traditional healing practices are more they are culturally based, they are often more comfortable and less frightening for the client.

It is important for the nurse to obtain information about traditional healing practices that may have been used prior to the client seeking Western medical treatment. Often, clients are reluctant to share home remedies with health-care professionals for fear of being laughed at or rebuked. The nurse should remember that treatments once considered to be traditional treatments, including acupuncture, therapeutic touch, and massage, are now being investigated for their therapeutic effect.

Family Patterns

The family is the basic unit of society. Cultural values can determine communication within the family group, the norm for family size, and the roles of specific family members. In some families, the man is considered the provider and decision maker. The woman may need to consult her husband prior to making decisions about her medical treatment or the treatment of her children (Galanti, 1991). Some families are matriarchal; that is, the mother or grandmother is viewed as the leader of the family and is usually the decision maker. The nurse needs to identify who has the "authority" to make decisions in a client's family. If the decision maker is someone other than the client, the nurse needs to include that person in health-care discussions.

The value placed on children and older people within a society is culturally derived. In some cultures, elderly people are considered the holders of the culture's wisdom and are, therefore, highly respected. Responsibility for caring for elder relatives is determined by cultural practices. In many cultures, older relatives who cannot live independently often live with a married son or daughter and his/her family.

Cultural gender-role behaviour may also affect nurse–client interaction. In some countries, men dominate and women have little status. Men from these countries may not accept instruction from a female nurse or physician but are receptive to the same instruction given by a male physician or nurse (Galanti, 1991). Some cultures have a prevailing concept of machismo, or male superiority. The aspects of machismo require that the adult man provide for and protect his family, including extended family members. The woman is expected to maintain the home and raise the children.

Cultural family values may also dictate the extent of the family's involvement in the hospitalized client's care. In some cultures, the nuclear and the extended family will want to visit for long periods and participate in care. In other cultures, the entire clan may want to visit and participate in the client's care (Galanti, 1991). This can cause concern on nursing units with strict visiting policies. The nurse should evaluate the positive benefits of family participation in the client's care and modify visiting policies as appropriate.

Cultures that value the needs of the extended family as much as those of the individual may hold the belief that personal and family information must stay within the family. Some cultural groups are very reluctant to disclose family information to outsiders, including health-care professionals. This attitude can present difficulties for health-care professionals who require knowledge of family interaction patterns to help clients with emotional problems.

Naming systems in many cultures differ from those in North America. In some cultures (e.g., Japanese and Vietnamese), the family name comes first and the given name second. One or two names may or may not be added between the family and given names. Other nomenclature may be used to delineate gender and child or adult status. For example, in traditional Japanese culture, adults address other adults by their surname followed by *san*, meaning *Mr.*, *Mrs.*, or *Miss*. An example is "Maurakami san." The children are referred to by their first names followed by *kun* for boys and *chan* for girls. Sikhs and Hindus traditionally have three names. Hindus have a personal name, a complimentary name, and then a family name. Sikhs have a personal name, then the title *Singh* for men and *Kaur* for women, and lastly the family name. Names by marriage also vary. In Central America, a woman who marries retains her father's name and takes her husband's. For example, if Louisa Viccario marries Carlos Gonzales she becomes Louisa Viccario de Gonzales. The connecting *de* means "belonging to." Their son is Pedro Gonzales Viccario. Nurses need to become familiar with appropriate ways to address clients.

Communication Style

Communication and culture are closely interconnected. Through communication, the culture is transmitted from one generation to the next, and knowledge about the culture is transmitted within the group and to those outside the group. Communicating with clients of various ethnic and cultural backgrounds is critical to providing culturally competent nursing care. There can be cultural variations in both verbal and nonverbal communication.

Verbal Communication

The most obvious cultural difference is in verbal communication: vocabulary, grammatical structure, voice qualities, intonation, rhythm, speed, pronunciation, and silence (Giger & Davidhizar, 1995). In North America, the dominant language is English; however, immigrant groups who speak English still encounter language differences because English words can have different meanings in different English-speaking cultures. For example, in Canada a boot is a type of footwear that comes to the ankle or higher; in England, a boot can also be the trunk of a car. Similarly, great differences exist between the French spoken in Canada and that spoken in France. In Canada, the French language has evolved, assimilating First Nations and English terms. In Quebec, nurses must meet the French language requirements and need to be aware of the language diversity that exists within the province.

Initiating verbal communication may be influenced by cultural values. The busy nurse may want to complete nursing admission assessments quickly. The client, however, may be offended when the nurse immediately asks personal questions. In some cultures, it is believed that social courtesies should be established before business or personal topics are discussed. Discussing general topics can convey that the nurse is interested in the client and has time for the client. This enables the nurse to develop a rapport with the client before progressing to more personal discussion.

Verbal communication becomes even more difficult when an interaction involves people who speak different languages. Both clients and health professionals experience frustration when they are unable to communicate verbally with each other. For clients who have limited knowledge of English, the nurse should avoid slang words, medical terminology, and abbreviations. Augmenting spoken conversation with gestures or pictures can increase the client's understanding. The nurse should speak slowly, in a respectful manner, and at a normal volume. Speaking loudly does not help the client understand and may be offensive. The nurse must also frequently validate the client's understanding of what is being communicated. The nurse must be wary of interpreting a client's smiling and nodding to mean that the client understands; the client may only be trying to please the nurse while not understanding what is being said.

For the client who speaks a different language, an interpreter may be necessary. Galanti (1991) notes that cultural rules often dictate who can discuss what with whom. Guidelines for using an interpreter are shown in the accompanying box. Whenever possible, professional health-care interpreters should be used.

Interpreters should be objective individuals who can provide accurate interpretation of the client's information and of the health professional's questions, information, and instruction. Many institutions that are located in culturally diverse communities have interpreters available on staff or maintain a list of employees who are fluent in other languages. Embassies, consulates, ethnic churches, ethnic clubs, or telephone companies may also be able to provide interpretation services. Nursing and other health personnel can use pictures and gestures to augment verbal communication.

Nurses who speak a second language may be asked to interpret for others. Some nursing schools and health-care institutions do not permit nursing students to interpret for a procedure consent because a lack of knowledge about the procedure may lead the student to give inaccurate information. The student should check the institu-

Using an Interpreter

- Avoid asking a member of the client's family, especially a child or spouse, to act as interpreter. Some clients, not wishing family members to know about their problems, may not provide complete or accurate information.
- Be aware of gender and age differences; it is preferable to use an interpreter of the same sex as the client to avoid embarrassment and faulty translation of sexual matters.
- Avoid an interpreter who is politically or socially incompatible with the client. For example, a Bosnian Serb may not be the best interpreter for a Muslim, even if he speaks the language.
- Address the questions to the client, *not* to the interpreter.
- Ask the interpreter to interpret as closely as possible the words used by the nurse.
- Speak slowly and distinctly. Do *not* use metaphors, for example, "Does it swell like a grapefruit?" or "Is the pain stabbing like a knife stab?"
- Observe the facial expressions and body language that the client assumes when listening and talking to the interpreter.

tion's policy prior to agreeing to interpret for institutional staff and physicians.

Nurses and other health-care providers must remember that clients for whom English is a second language may lose command of their English when they are in stressful situations. Clients who have used English comfortably for years in social and business communication may forget and revert back to their primary language when they are ill or distressed. It is important for the nurse to assure the client that this is normal and to promote behaviours to facilitate verbal communication.

Nonverbal Communication

To communicate effectively with culturally diverse clients, the nurse needs to be aware of two aspects of nonverbal communication behaviours: (1) what nonverbal behaviours mean to the client, and (2) what specific nonverbal behaviours mean in the client's culture. It is not required that the nurse be knowledgeable about the nonverbal behaviour patterns of all cultures; however, before assigning meaning to nonverbal behaviour, the nurse must consider the possibility that the behaviour may have a different meaning for the client and the family. Furthermore, to provide safe and effective care, nurses who work with specific cultural groups should learn more about cultural behaviour and communication patterns within these cultures.

Nonverbal communication can include the use of silence, touch, eye movement, facial expressions, and body posture. Some cultures are quite comfortable with long periods of silence, whereas others consider it appropriate to speak before the other person has finished talking. Many people value silence and view it as essential to understanding a person's needs or use silence to preserve privacy. Some cultures view silence as a sign of respect, whereas to other people, silence may indicate agreement (Davidhizar & Giger, 1998).

Touching involves learned behaviours that can have both positive and negative meanings. In the American culture, a firm handshake is a recognized form of greeting that conveys character and strength (Davidhizar & Giger, 1998). In some European cultures, greetings may include a kiss on one or both cheeks along with the handshake. In some societies, touch is considered magical, and because of the belief that the soul can leave the body on physical contact, casual touching is forbidden. Vietnamese Canadians may find touching of the head or shoulders to be anxiety producing because there is the belief that the soul can leave the body on physical contact (Davidhizar & Giger, 1998). Nurses should, therefore, touch a client's head only with permission. The gender of the person touching and being touched often has cultural significance.

Cultures also dictate what forms of touch are appropriate for individuals of the same sex and opposite sex. In many cultures, for example, a kiss is not appropriate for a public greeting between persons of the opposite sex, even those who are family members; however, a kiss on the cheek is acceptable as a greeting among individuals of the same sex. The nurse should watch interaction among clients and families for cues to the appropriate degree of touch in that culture. The nurse can also assess the client's response to touch when providing nursing care, for example, by noting the client's reaction to the physical examination or the bath.

Facial expression can also vary between cultures. Davidhizar and Giger (1998) state that Italian, Jewish, black, and Spanish-speaking persons are more likely to smile readily and use facial expression to communicate feelings, whereas Irish, English, and northern European people tend to have less facial expression and are less open in their response, especially to strangers. Facial expressions can also convey a meaning opposite to what is felt or understood.

Eye movement during communication has cultural foundations. In Western cultures, direct eye contact is regarded as important and generally shows that the other is attentive and listening. It conveys self-confidence, openness, interest, and honesty. Lack of eye contact may be interpreted as secretiveness, shyness, guilt, lack of interest, or even a sign of mental illness. However, other cultures may view eye contact as impolite or an invasion of privacy. For Cree Nation members, continuous direct eye contact is considered impolite and an invasion of privacy (Yonge & Bernard, 1998). The nurse should not misinterpret the character of the client who avoids eye contact.

Body posture and gesture are also culturally learned. Finger pointing, the V sign with the index and middle fingers, and the thumbs-up sign may have different meanings. For example, the V sign means victory in some cultures, but it is an offensive gesture in other cultures (Galanti, 1991). In the Hmong culture, bowing the head slightly when entering the room where an elder is present and using both hands to give something to someone are considered signs of respect (Rairdan & Higgs, 1992).

Communication is an essential part of establishing a relationship with clients and their families. It is also important for developing effective working relationships with health-care colleagues. To enhance their practice, nurses can observe the communication patterns of clients and colleagues and be aware of their own communication behaviours.

Space Orientation

Space is a relative concept that includes the individual, the body, the surrounding environment, and objects within that environment. The relationship between the individual's own body and objects and persons within space is learned and is influenced by culture. For example, in nomadic societies space is not owned; it is occupied temporarily until the tribe moves on. In Western societies, people tend to be more territorial, as reflected in such phrases as "This is my space" or "Get out of my space." In Western cultures, spatial distances are defined as the intimate zone, the personal zone, and the social and public zones. See Chapter 26. The size of these areas may vary with the specific culture. Nurses move through all three zones as they provide care for clients. The nurse needs to be aware of the client's response to movement toward the client. The client may physically withdraw or back away if the nurse is perceived as being too close. The nurse will need to explain to the client why there is a need to be close to the client. To assess the lungs with a stethoscope, for example, the nurse needs to move into the client's intimate space. The nurse should first explain the procedure and await permission to continue.

Clients who reside in long-term care facilities, or who are hospitalized for an extended time, may want to personalize their space. They may want to arrange their room differently or control the placement of objects on their bedside cabinet or over-bed table. The nurse should be responsive to clients' needs to have some control over their space. When there are no medical contraindications, clients should be permitted and encouraged to wear their own clothing and have objects of personal significance. Wearing cultural dress or having personal and cultural items in one's environment can increase self-esteem by promoting not only one's individuality but also one's cultural identity. Of course, the nurse should caution the client about responsibility for loss of personal items.

Time Orientation

Time orientation refers to an individual's focus on the past, the present, or the future (Galanti, 1991). Most cultures combine all three time orientations, but one orientation is more likely to dominate. The North American focus on time tends to be directed to the future, emphasizing time and schedules (Smith, 1992). Nursing students know what times they "must" be in class or clinical. They know what courses they will take in future semesters. European Canadians often plan for next week, their vacation, or their retirement. Other cultures may have a different concept of time. Members of First Nations communities have been taught to be present oriented and to not be concerned with the future. Only what is needed for today should be used, and sharing what one has is to be respected. There is potential for those with a present orientation to not focus on health promotion efforts.

The culture of nursing and health care values time. Appointments are scheduled, and treatments are prescribed with time parameters (e.g., changing a dressing once a day). Medication orders include how often the medicine is to be taken and when (e.g., Digoxin 0.25 mg, once a day, in the morning). Nurses need to be aware of the meaning of time for clients. Giger and Davidhizar (1995) state that when caring for clients who are "present-oriented," it is important to avoid fixed schedules. The nurse can offer a time range for activities and treatments. For example, instead of telling the client to take Digoxin every day at 10:00 a.m., the nurse might tell the client to take it every day in the morning, or every day after getting out of bed.

Nutritional Patterns

Most cultures have staple foods, that is, foods that are plentiful or readily accessible in the environment. For example, the staple food of most Asians is rice; of Italians, pasta; and of Eastern Europeans, wheat. Even clients who have been in Canada for several generations often continue to eat the foods of their cultural homelands.

The way food is prepared and served is also related to cultural practices. For example, in the United States, a traditional food served for the Thanksgiving holiday is stuffed turkey; however, in different regions of the country, the contents of the stuffing may vary. In Southern states, the stuffing may be made of cornbread; in New England, of seasoned bread and chestnuts.

The ways in which staple foods are prepared also varies. For example, some Asian cultures prefer steamed rice; others prefer boiled rice. Southern Asians from India prepare unleavened bread from wheat flour, rather than the leavened bread of European Canadians.

Food-related cultural behaviours can include whether to breastfeed or bottle-feed infants and when to introduce solid foods to them. Food can also be considered part of the remedy for illness. Foods classified as "hot" foods or foods that are hot in temperature may be used to treat illnesses that are classified as "cold" illnesses. For example, corn meal (a "hot" food) may be used to treat arthritis (a "cold" illness). Each culture group defines what it considers to be hot and cold entities.

Religious practice associated with specific cultures also affects diet. Some Roman Catholics avoid meat on certain days, such as Ash Wednesday and Good Friday, and some Protestant faiths prohibit meat, tea, coffee, or alcohol. Both Orthodox Judaism and Islam prohibit the ingestion of pork or pork products. Orthodox Jews observe kosher customs, eating certain foods only if they are inspected by a rabbi and prepared according to dietary laws. For example, the eating of milk products and meat products at the same meal is prohibited. Some Buddhists, Hindus, and Sikhs are strict vegetarians. The nurse must be sensitive to such religious dietary practices.

Pain Responses

It has been demonstrated that beliefs about and responses to pain vary among ethnic and racial groups. Cultural response to pain must be viewed in relation to both the actual perception of pain and to the meaning or significance of pain to the client and family. In some cultures, pain may be considered a punishment for bad deeds; the individual is, therefore, to tolerate pain without complaint in order to atone for sins. In other cultures, self-infliction of pain is a sign of mourning or grief. In other groups, pain may be anticipated as a part of the ritualistic practices of passage ceremonies, and therefore, tolerance of pain signifies strength and endurance. In some cultures, boys especially are taught "to take pain like a man" and "big boys don't cry," but in other cultures, the expression of pain elicits attention and sympathy.

Calvillo and Flaskerud (1991) found that nurses and clients assess pain differently. In a study of Latin American clients experiencing pain, they found that nurses and physicians tend to underestimate and undertreat their client's pain in relation to the client's expression of pain. Client responses to pain should be assessed within the context of their culture. If the client does not complain of pain, it should not be assumed that the client is not experiencing pain. The nurse must be aware of what conditions are likely to cause pain and offer clients pain relief, as appropriate.

Treatment for pain may also vary with culture. In European Canadian cultures, medication is typically used for pain relief. In other cultures, heat, cold, relaxation, or other techniques and treatments may be used.

Death and Dying Practices

Death is a universal experience, and people want to die with dignity. Various cultural and religious traditions and practices associated with death, dying, and the grieving process help people cope with these experiences. Nurses are often present through the dying process and at the moment of death, especially when it occurs in a health-care facility. Knowledge of the client's religious and cultural heritage helps nurses provide individualized care to clients and their families, even though they may not participate in the rituals associated with death.

Balzer-Riley (1996) tells about a nurse caring for the dying king of a gypsy tribe. The nurse learned that the tribe had a ritual to honour the king but that only members of the tribe could touch and prepare the body after his death. So, as the client is nearing death, it is important for the nurse to ask the family if any special customs or practices are required after the death of the client.

Dying in solitude is unacceptable in most cultures. In many cultures, people prefer a peaceful death at home rather than in the hospital. Some ethnic groups may request that health professionals not reveal the prognosis to dying clients. They believe the person's last days should be free of worry and pain. People in other cultures prefer that a family member (preferably a male in some cultures) be told the diagnosis so that the client can be tactfully informed by a family member in gradual stages or not told at all. Nurses also need to determine whom to call, and when, as the client's death draws near.

Beliefs and attitudes about death, its cause, and the soul also vary among cultures. Unnatural deaths, or "bad deaths," are sometimes distinguished from "good deaths." In some cultures, the death of a person who has behaved well in life is considered less threatening because that person will be reincarnated into a good life next time.

Beliefs about preparation of the body, autopsy, organ donation, cremation, and prolonging life are closely allied to the person's religion. *Autopsy*, for example, may be prohibited, opposed, or discouraged by Eastern Orthodox religions, Muslims, Jehovah's Witnesses, and Orthodox Jews. Some religions prohibit the removal of body parts and dictate that all body parts be given appropriate burial. *Organ donation* is prohibited by Jehovah's Witnesses and Muslims, whereas Buddhists in America consider it an act of mercy and encourage it. *Cremation* is discouraged, opposed, or prohibited by the Mormon, Eastern Orthodox, Islamic, and Jewish faiths. Hindus, in contrast, prefer cremation and cast the ashes in a holy river. *Prolongation of life* is generally encouraged; however, some religions, such as Christian Science, are unlikely to use medical means to prolong life, and the Jewish faith generally opposes prolonging life after irreversible brain damage. In hopeless illness, Buddhists may permit euthanasia.

Nurses also need to be knowledgeable about the client's death-related rituals, such as last rites and administration of Holy Communion, chanting at the bedside, and other rituals, such as special procedures for washing, dressing, positioning, and shrouding the dead. For example, certain immigrants may wish to retain their native customs, in which family members of the same sex wash and prepare the body for burial and cremation. Muslims also customarily turn the body toward Mecca. Nurses need to ask family members about their preference and verify who will carry out these activities. Burial clothes and other cultural or religious items are often important symbols for the funeral. For example, faithful Mormons are often dressed in their "temple clothes." Some First Nations people may be dressed in elaborate apparel and jewellery and wrapped in new blankets with money. The nurse must ensure that any ritual items present in the health-care agency are given to the family or to the funeral home.

Providing Culturally Competent Care

Students in Canadian nursing programs are expected to learn about cultural diversity, and all nurses are expected to provide care, regardless of the culture of the client. The Canadian Nurses Association (CNA) notes that "cultural effectiveness is essential to the accurate assessment of client health status, needs and goals" (CNA, 2000, p. 2). Competencies expected of Canadian nurses include "... demonstrating consideration for client diversity, providing culturally sensitive care (e.g., openness, sensitivity, recognizing culturally based practices and values); and incorporating cultural practices into health promotion activities" (CNA, 2000, p. 1).

All phases of the nursing process are affected by the client's and the nurse's cultural values, beliefs, and behaviours. As the client's-culture and the nurse's culture come together in the nurse-client relationship, a unique cultural environment is created that can improve or impair the client's outcome. Self-awareness of personal biases can enable nurses to develop modifying behaviours or (if they are unable to do so) to remove themselves from situations where care may be compromised. Nurses can become more aware of their own culture through a values clarification (see Chapter 7). The nurse must also consider the cultural values of the health-care setting because those too may influence the client's outcome.

To obtain cultural assessment data, the nurse uses broad statements and open-ended questions that encourage clients to express themselves fully. See the accompanying box for examples. The important principle to remember when conducting an assessment is that "the client is the teacher and expert regarding his or her culture, and the nurse is the learner" (Rosenbaum, 1995, p. 188). At this stage, the nurse makes no conclusions but obtains information from the client.

Many cultural assessment tools are available. The nurse needs to use a tool appropriate to the situation and adapt it as required. For example, a nurse in an emergency department of an urban hospital may need a different format than a nurse working in a home-care setting. Tripp-Reimer et al. (1984) note that it is unnecessary to complete a total cultural assessment for every client. Instead, nurses need to collect enough basic cultural data to identify patterns of behaviour that may either facilitate or interfere with a nursing strategy or treatment plan.

Anderson et al. (1990) emphasize the following points relevant to cultural assessment:

- A cultural assessment takes time and usually needs to extend over several time periods.
- Recognition of one's own ethnicity and social background is essential. Even when the nurse and client share the same ethnic background, the nurse should expect differences in beliefs and values.
- The *process* of assessment is important. How and when questions are asked requires sensitivity and clinical judgement.
- The timing and phrasing of questions need to be adapted to the individual. Timing is important in introducing questions. Sensitivity is needed in phrasing questions.
- Trust must be established before clients can be expected to volunteer and share sensitive information. The nurse, therefore, needs to spend time with clients, introduce some social conversation, and convey a genuine desire to understand their values and beliefs.

Before a cultural assessment begins, the nurse determines what language the client speaks and the client's degree of fluency in the English language. The nurse can also learn about the client's communication patterns and space orientation by observing both verbal and nonverbal communication. For example, does the client do the speaking or defer to another? What nonverbal communication behaviours does the client exhibit (e.g., touching, eye contact)? What significance do these behaviours have for the nurse-client interaction? What is the client's proximity to other people and objects within the environment? How does the client react to the nurse's movement toward the client? What cultural objects within the environment have importance for health promotion or health maintenance?

To provide *culturally congruent care* that benefits, satisfies, and is meaningful to the people nurses serve, Leininger (1991) conceptualizes three major modes to guide nursing judgements, decisions, and actions:

1. *Cultural care preservation and/or maintenance.* The nurse accepts and complies with the client's cultural beliefs. For example, the nurse provides herbal tea to ease a "nervous stomach," a practice the client says has worked well in the past.

Examples of Open-Ended Questions for a Cultural Assessment

Cultural Affiliation

I am interested in learning about your cultural heritage. Can you tell me about your cultural group, where you were born, and how long you have lived in this country?

Beliefs about Current Illness

What do you call your problem? What name do you give it? What do you think has caused it? Why did it start when it did? What does your sickness do to your body? How severe is it? What do you fear most about your sickness? What are the chief problems your sickness has caused for you personally, for your family, and at work?

Health-Care Practices

What kinds of things do you do to maintain health? For example, what types of food do you eat to maintain health? What foods do you eat during illness, and how is food prepared? What other activities do you or your family do to keep people healthy (e.g., wearing amulets, religious or spiritual practices)? How do you know when you are healthy?

Illness Beliefs and Care Practices

What kinds of things do you do to treat illness? Do you use traditional healers (shaman, curandero, priest, spiritualist, minister, monk)? Who determines when a person is sick? How would you describe your past experiences with cultural healers and Western health professionals? What special remedies are generally used for the illness you have? What remedies are you currently using (e.g., herbal remedies, potions, massage, wearing of talismans, copper bracelets, or charms)? What remedies have you used in the past, and which did you find helpful? What remedies or treatments are you considering now, and how can we help?

Family Life and Support System

I would like to learn about your family. Who are the members of your family? What family duties do women and men usually perform in your culture? Whom do you consult when making health-care decisions (e.g., other family member, cultural or religious leader)? Who will be able to help you during and after treatment? Do you need help to contact these people?

Sources: Andrews, M. M. & Boyle, J. S. (1999). *Transcultural concepts in nursing care* (3rd ed.) (p. 539–544). Philadelphia, PA: Lippincott; Waxler-Morrison, N., Anderson, J. and Richardson, E. (Eds.). (1990). *Cross cultural caring: A handbook for health professionals in Western Canada* (p. 245–267). Vancouver, BC: UBC Press; J. N. Rosenbaum. (1991). "A cultural assessment guide: Learning cultural sensitivity" *Canadian Nurse, 88*, p. 32–33; and Kleinman, A., Eisenberg, L., and Good B. (1978). "Culture, illness and care" *Annals of Internal Medicine, 88*, p. 251–258.

2. *Cultural care accommodation and/or negotiation.* The nurse plans, negotiates, and accommodates the client's culturally specific food preferences, religious practices, kinship needs, child-care practices, and treatment practices.
3. *Cultural care repatterning or restructuring.* The nurse is knowledgeable about culture care and develops ways to repattern or restructure nursing care.

Cultural care preservation may involve the use of cultural health-care practices, such as giving herbal tea, chicken soup, or "hot foods" to the ill client. Accommodating the client's viewpoint and negotiating appropriate care require expert communication skills, such as responding empathetically, validating information, and effectively summarizing content.

Negotiation is a collaborative process. It acknowledges that the nurse-client relationship is reciprocal and that differences exist between the nurse and client about notions of health, illness, and treatment. The nurse attempts to bridge the gap between the nurse's (scientific) and the client's (cultural) perspectives. During the negotiation process, the nurse first elicits the client's views and acknowledges these views and then, if appropriate, provides relevant scientific information. If the client's views reveal that certain behaviours would not affect the client's condition adversely, then the nurse incorporates these views in planning care. If the client's views can lead to harmful behaviours, then the nurse attempts to shift the client's perspectives to the scientific view.

Negotiation, therefore, occurs when cultural treatment practices conflict with those of the health-care system and when the cultural practices are considered harmful to the client's well-being. The nurse must determine precisely how the client is managing the illness, what practices could be harmful, and which practices can be safely combined with Western medicine. For example, reducing dosages of an antihypertensive medication or replacing insulin therapy with herbal measures may be detrimental. In situations where harm may occur, the nurse needs to inform the client about possible outcomes.

When a client chooses to follow only cultural practices and refuses all prescribed medical or nursing interventions, nursing goals for the client need to be adjusted. Anderson and colleagues (1990) point out that monitoring the client's condition to identify changes in health state and to recognize impending crises before they become irreversible may be all that is realistically achievable. At a time of crisis, the nurse may then have the opportunity to renegotiate the original care approach.

Transcultural nursing care is challenging. It requires discovery of the meaning of the client's behaviour, flexibility, creativity, and knowledge to adapt nursing interventions. For example, a culturally sensitive nurse knows that a Chinese woman who has just given birth and refuses to eat fruit and vegetables, refuses to drink the cold water at her bedside, stays in bed, and refuses to take sitz baths, baths, or showers needs to increase the return of yang forces. The nurse will make plans to adapt nursing interventions accordingly.

Nurses also need to identify community resources that are available to assist clients of different cultures. Nurses should try to learn from each transcultural nursing situation they encounter to improve the delivery of culture-specific care to future clients. The accompanying box offers suggestions for providing culturally competent nursing care.

Providing Culturally Competent Care to Families

- Learn the rituals, customs, and practices of the major cultural groups with whom you come into contact. Learn to appreciate the richness of diversity as an asset, rather than a hindrance, in your practice.
- Identify personal biases, attitudes, prejudices, and stereotypes.
- Include cultural assessment of the client and family as part of overall assessment.
- Recognize that it is the client's (or family's) right to make their own health-care choices.
- Convey respect and cooperate with traditional helpers and caregivers.

FOCUS ON CRITICAL THINKING

Rachel was born to a Jewish couple and is Jewish by race and religion. Her father died when she was 10 years old and her mother remarried three years later. Rachel was legally adopted by her Italian stepfather, who was a devout Catholic. Although the family participated in Catholic-Italian traditions, Rachel's mother taught her many Jewish traditions as well so that her heritage would be preserved. Rachel is now 58 years old, practises traditions from both her Jewish and Italian upbringing, and is dying of cancer. You are the nurse caring for Rachel during her final days.

1. Differentiate between Rachel's culture, ethnicity, and race.
2. How may Rachel's mixed cultural background pose a dilemma for you as her nurse or for her family?
3. How may Rachel's culture affect her approach to death and the care of her body following her death?
4. Of what benefit would a cultural assessment be to Rachel or her family since she is dying?
5. How could nurses' race, culture, or religion influence their care of clients who are racially or culturally different?

See Appendix A for answers to these questions.

CHAPTER HIGHLIGHTS

- Canadians come from a variety of ethnic and cultural backgrounds, and many Canadians retain at least some of their traditional values, beliefs, and practices.
- Many groups in Canada are bicultural; that is, they embrace two cultures: their original ethnic culture and a Canadian culture.
- An individual's ethnic and cultural background can influence beliefs, values, and practices.
- Through acculturation, most ethnic and cultural groups in Canada modify some of their traditional cultural characteristics.
- Personal characteristics also modify an individual's cultural values, beliefs, and practices.
- Health beliefs and practices, family patterns, communication style, space and time orientation, nutritional patterns, pain response, death and dying practices, and childbirth and perinatal care influence the relationship between the nurse and the client who have different cultural backgrounds.
- When assessing a client, the nurse considers the client's cultural values, beliefs, and practices related to health and health care.

READINGS AND REFERENCES

Suggested Readings

Abdullah, S. N. (1995). Towards an individualized client's care: Implications for education. The transcultural approach. *Journal of Advanced Nursing, 22*, 715–720.
Individualized care cannot be achieved without considering the factors associated with the personal being, such as culture, beliefs, and traditions. This article has nurses look at their own values as a step to providing unbiased nursing care.

Baker, C., & Daigle, M. C. (2000). Cross-cultural hospital care as experienced by Mi'kmaq clients. *Western Journal of Nursing Research, 22*, 8–28.
Qualitative inquiry was used in this research study to investigate the experiences of Mi'kmaq patients with caregivers in a cross-cultural setting. Issues revolved around misunderstanding, being misunderstood, and feeling understood.

Indian and Northern Affairs Canada. (2001). *First Nations in Canada*. Ottawa: Author. Retrieved October 23, 2001 from http://www.ainc-inac.gc.ca/pr/pub/fnc/index_e.html.
This publication, which is available online, describes the First Nations peoples and their cultures, the diverse cultural regions, contact with European migrants, and the progress being made by the First Nations to gain control of education, the land claims, and self-government. The Indian Act, the Oka Crisis, and the Royal Commission on Aboriginal Peoples are among some of the other topics addressed in the publication.

Spector, R. E. (2000). *Cultural diversity in health & illness* (5th ed.). Upper Saddle River, NJ: Prentice Hall Health.
This useful text begins with sections on creating self-awareness in providers of their own and their familial beliefs and practices regarding health and illness. The author discusses general information on health traditions and health care. Specific views of specific cultural groups are outlined. A guide to heritage assessment and health traditions is included.

Spruhan, J. B. (1996). Beyond traditional nursing care: Cultural awareness and successful home healthcare nursing. *Home Healthcare Nurse, 14*, 445–449.
With the increase in home health care, nurses need to be aware of the many factors, especially cultural ones, that can affect a client's life. This article offers various case studies about how a client's health-care beliefs, values, and practices can affect their nursing care.

Related Research

Green, N. L. (1995). Development of the perceptions of racism scale. *Image: Journal of Nursing Scholarship, 27*, 141–146.

Morris, R. I. (1996). Bridging cultural boundaries: The African-American and transcultural caring. *Advanced Practice Nursing Quarterly, 2*, 31–38.

Selected References

Alexander, J. E., Beagle, C. J., Butler, P., Dougherty, D. A., Andrews Robards, K. D., Solotkin, D. C., & Velotta, C. (1994). Madeleine Leininger: Cultural care theory. In A. Marriner-Tomey (Ed.), *Nursing theorists and their work* (pp. 423–444). St. Louis, MO: Mosby.

Anderson, J. M. (1990). Health care across the cultures. *Nursing Outlook, 38*, 136–139.

Anderson, J. M., Waxler-Morrison, N., Richardson, E., Herbert, C., & Murphy, M. (1990). Delivering culturally-sensitive health care. In N. Waxler-Morrison, J. Anderson, & E. Richardson, (Eds.), *Cross cultural caring: A handbook for health professionals in western Canada* (pp. 245–267). Vancouver, BC: UBC Press.

Andrews, M. M., & Boyle, J. S. (2003). *Transcultural concepts in nursing care* (4th ed.). Philadelphia, PA: Lippincott.

Baldonado, A. A. (1996). Transcending the barriers of cultural diversity in health care. *Journal of Cultural Diversity, 3*, 20–22.

Baldwin, D., Cotanch, P., Johnson, P., & Williams, J. (1996). *An Afrocentric approach to breast and cervical cancer early detection and screening.* Washington, DC: ANA.

Balzer-Riley, J. W. (1997). *Communications in nursing: Communicating, assertively and responsibly in nursing: A guidebook* (3rd ed.). St. Louis, MO: Mosby.

Banks, J., & Banks, C. (1989). *Multicultural education and perspectives.* Boston, MA: Allyn & Bacon.

Baye, A. L. (1995, Summer/Fall). A lesson in culture. *Minority Nurse*, 35–38.

Bhimani, R., & Acorn, S. (1998). Managing within a culturally diverse environment. *Canadian Nurse, 94*, 32–36.

Boyd, M., & Vickes, M. (2000, Autumn). 100 years of immigration in Canada. *Canadian Societal Trends*, Statistics Canada 11-008, 22–32.

Boyle, J. S. (1999). Transcultural perspectives in the nursing care of middle-aged adults. In M. M. Andrews & J. S. Boyle (Eds.), *Transcultural concepts in nursing care* (3rd ed.). (p. 161–188). Philadelphia, PA: Lippincott.

Calvillo, E. R., & Flaskerud, J. H. (1991). Review of literature on culture and pain of adults with focus on Mexican Americans. *Journal of Transcultural Nursing, 2*, 16–23.

Campbell, J., & Campbell, D. (1996). Cultural competence in the care of abused women. *Journal of Nurse-Midwivery, 41*(6), 457–461.

Canadian Multiculturalism Act. RS 1985, c.24 (4th Supp). *Statutes of Canada*. Ottawa: Queen's Printer. pp. 835–41.

Canadian Nurses Association. (1999). *Blueprint for the Canadian Registered Nurse Examination*. Ottawa, ON: Author.

Canadian Nurses Association. (2000). Cultural diversity—Changes and challenges. *Nursing Now: Issues and Trends in Canadian Nursing*. Ottawa: Author. Retrieved January 23, 2001 from: http://www.cna-nurses.ca/pages/issuestrends/nrgrow/cultural_diversity.htm

Clark, W. (2000). Patterns of religious attendance. *Canadian Societal Trends.* Statistics Canada 11-008. pp. 23–27.

Crow, K. (1993). Multiculturalism and pluralistic thought in nursing education: Native American world view and the nursing academic world view. *Journal of Nursing Education, 32*, 198–204.

Davidhizar, R. E., & Giger, J. N. (1998). *Canadian transcultural nursing: Assessment and intervention*. St. Louis, MO: Mosby.

DeSantis, L., & Lowe, J. (1992). Moving from cultural sensitivity to cultural competence in nursing practice: Pitfalls and progress. Paper presented at the 18th Annual Transcultural Nursing Society Conference, Miami, FL, October 22–24, 1992.

Doswell, W. M., & Erlen, J. A. (1998, June). Multicultural issues and ethical concerns in the delivery of nursing care interventions. *Nursing Clinics of North America, 33*, 353–361.

Eliason, M. J. (1993, September/October). Ethics and transcultural nursing care. *Nursing Outlook, 4*, 225–228.

Felder, E. (1995). Integrating culturally diverse theoretical concepts into the education preparation of the advanced practice nurse: The cultural diversity practice model. *Journal of Cultural Diversity, 2*, 88–92.

Galanti, G. (1991). *Caring for patients from different cultures.* Philadelphia, PA: University of Pennsylvania Press.

Giger, J. N., & Davidhizar, R. (1990). Transcultural nursing assessment: A method for advancing nursing practice. *International Nursing Review, 37*, 199–202.

Giger, J. N., & Davidhizar, R. (1999). *Transcultural nursing: Assessment and interventions* (3rd ed.). St. Louis, MO: Mosby-Year Book.

Grossman, D., & Taylor, R. (1995). Working with people: Cultural diversity on the unit. *American Journal of Nursing, 95*, 64, 65–67.

Kittler, P. G., & Sucher, K. P. (1990). Diet counseling in a multicultural society. *Diabetes Educator, 16*, 127–134.

Lea, A. (1994). Nursing in today's multicultural society: A transcultural perspective. *Journal of Advanced Nursing, 20*, 307–313.

Leininger, M. M. (1970). *Nursing and anthropology: Two worlds to blend.* New York: Wiley.

Leininger, M. M. (1978). *Transcultural nursing: Concepts, theories, and practices.* New York: Wiley.

Leininger, M. M. (1988). Leininger's theory of nursing: Cultural care diversity and universality. *Nursing Science Quarterly, 14*, 152–160.

Leininger, M. M. (Ed.). (1991). *Culture care diversity and universality: A theory of nursing.* New York: National League for Nursing Press, Pub. No. 15-2402.

Leininger, M. M. (1993). Towards conceptualization of transcultural health care systems: Concepts and a model. *Journal of Transcultural Nursing, 4*, 32–40.

Lester, N. (1988). Cultural competence: A nursing dialogue. Part 1. *American Journal of Nursing, 98*(8), 26–33; Part 2. *American Journal of Nursing, 98*(9), 36–43.

Lipson, J., & Bauwens, E. (1988). Use of anthropology in nursing. *Practicing Anthropology, 10*, 4–5.

Lynam, M. J. (1992). Towards the goal of providing culturally sensitive care: Principles upon which to build nursing curricula. *Journal of Advanced Nursing, 17*, 149–157.

Purnell, L., & Paulanka, B. (1998). *Transcultural health care: A culturally competent approach.* Philadelphia, PA: Davis.

Rairdan, B., & Higgs, Z. R. (1992). When your patient is a Hmong refugee. *American Journal of Nursing, 92*, 52–55.

Rosenbaum, J. N. (1991). A cultural assessment guide: Learning cultural sensitivity. *Canadian Nurse, 88*, 32–33.

Rosenbaum, J. N. (1995). Teaching cultural sensitivity. *Journal of Nursing Education, 34*, 188–189.

Smith, S. (1992). *Communications in nursing* (2nd ed.). St. Louis, MO: Mosby-Year Book.

Spector, R. E. (1991). *Cultural diversity in health and illness* (3rd ed.). Norwalk, CT: Appleton-Century-Crofts.

Sprott, J. (1993). The black box in family assessments: Cultural diversity. In S. Feetham, S. Meister, J. Bell, & C. Gilliss (Eds.), *The nursing of families: Theory, research, education, practice* (pp. 189–199). Beverly Hills, CA: Sage Publications.

Statistics Canada. (1991). Statistics Canada, 1991 Census. Ottawa, ON: Government of Canada.

Statistics Canada. (1996). Statistics Canada, 1996 Census. Ottawa: Government of Canada.

Statistics Canada. (2001). 2001 Census. Ottawa, ON: Government of Canada.

Statistics Canada. (2003). Canada's ethnocultural portrait: The changing mosaic. 2001 census: Analysis series Catalogue no.96F0030XIE2001008. Ottawa: Author.

Steinmetz, S., & Braham, C. G. (Eds.). (1993). *Random House Webster's Dictionary.* New York: Ballantine Reference Library.

Tripp-Reimer, T., Brink, P. J., & Saunders, J. M. (1984). Cultural assessment: Content and process. *Nursing Outlook, 32*, 78–82.

Waxler-Morrison, N., Anderson, J., & Richardson, E. (Eds.). (1990). *Cross cultural caring: A handbook for health professionals in Western Canada.* Vancouver, BC: UBC Press.

Wenger, A. F. Z. (1993). Cultural meaning of symptoms. *Holistic Nursing Practice, 7*, 22–23.

Wong, F. K. Y. (1998). The integration of traditional Chinese health practices in nursing. *Reflections, 24(2)*, 20–21.

Yonge, O., & Bernard, M. (1998). The Cree living in urban settings. In R. E. Davidhizar & J. N. Giger (Eds.), *Canadian transcultural nursing: Assessment and intervention* (pp. 179–196). St. Louis, MO: Mosby.

WEBLINKS

Canadian Heritage Multiculturalism
http://www.pch.gc.can/multi/policy/framework_e.shtml
This site has multiple links to governmental, non-governmental, Canadian, and international organizations.

Virtual Museum Canada
http://www.virtualmuseum.ca/English/index_flash.html
This site is the result of a partnership between Canada's museum community and the Department of Canadian Heritage. Through the Internet, the user can celebrate the stories and treasures that have helped to define Canada.

Indian and Northern Affairs Canada
http://www.ainc-inac.gc.ca
This site describes the First Nations peoples and their cultures. The Indian Act, the Oka Crisis, and the Royal Commission on Aboriginal Peoples are among some of the other topics addressed through the publications available on the site.

CBC

Canadian Case Study — Does Betty Two-Trees Need an Advocate?

Betty Two-Trees is from a First Nations tribe of Algonquian stock called the Maliseet. She lives on a reserve in New Brunswick. There are approximately 600 reserves in Canada for over 200,000 aboriginal people. On many of them, the social conditions are horrifying, and even where conditions have improved in recent years, the wounds of over a hundred years of government rules and regulations are still fresh and painful. Unemployment, suicide rates, health problems, and housing shortages are at epidemic levels on most reserves. Aboriginal women rank among the most severely disadvantaged in Canadian society. They are worse off economically than both aboriginal men and Canadian women, and although they live longer than aboriginal men, their life expectancy does not approach that of Canadian women generally.

With two long braids hanging down her back, Betty was working on a child's beaded vest with the coffee perking and three young children playing throughout the house, when the community health nurse visited. She was coming to talk to Betty about immunizations for the youngest grandchild. Born in 1953 and married in 1972, Betty had four children before her husband left her. "I was 15 when I had my first baby. My middle child came back to live with me when her husband left her and these three are hers." She expressed discomfort with the immunizations but recognized that they were the "white man's ways" of protecting the children. Betty and the nurse were well acquainted because she visited her sometimes to help monitor her diabetes using some traditional health-care practices. Waldram, Whiting, Korner, and Habbick (2000) assessed the cultural understandings of diabetes and the use of traditional medicine among aboriginal people with diabetes in Saskatoon. Data was obtained from 60 individuals interviewed at the start of a diabetes education project and from 36 of the same individuals at its conclusion. While there was no evidence of a uniquely aboriginal view of diabetes etiology and symptomatology, many participants believed in the effectiveness of traditional aboriginal treatments for diabetes and used them periodically.

She commented to the nurse upon the differences in growing up for these young children. "The reserve was a beautiful place to live, especially for the children." You could swim in the river all day long and nobody drowned. Then, what they called progress started coming in, with the dam in the early sixties. You cannot even swim in the river today, and the fish are mostly gone. I understand my language because my parents and grandparents spoke it, but I usually answered back in English. The old people here would always make me answer back in our language or they would not listen to me. I don't think many of them understood English. We have our own way of talking. You never say please in our language because we don't need to. So when my people say something in English, it sounds like a demand."

"Some people say that traditionally Maliseet women had the final say in the family. It was true for us. My grandmother always had the say and my grandfather always honoured it. It was not the same for my mother. I remember one day, perhaps grade 1 or 2 and I was called dirty brown Indian and not understanding what it meant. I felt embarrassed but I didn't know why. Today, I would call it prejudice. I remember other examples of prejudice from my childhood, but I did not do anything about it because I didn't have a name for it or an understanding of it."

Browne and Fiske's (2001) research examined mainstream health-care encounters from the viewpoint of First Nations women from a reserve community in northwestern Canada. Guided in-depth interviews were conducted with ten First Nations women. Their narratives identified that their encounters were shaped by racism, discrimination, and structural inequities that contribute to their marginalization from mainstream society.

Betty is active in the self-government movement of the Maliseet that has gained increasing momentum in the past decade, as Canada's First Nations seek to gain greater decision-making powers for themselves.

QUESTIONS

1. Are cultural factors more or less important for Betty considering her lifestyle choices?
2. What strategies can nurses implement to promote equity within health-care environments?
3. How can the nurse advocate for Betty and those important to her?

VIDEO RESOURCE

Series Title: The Magazine/National
Segment Title: Medical Refugees
Telecast Date: March 1, 2000
Running Time: 22:15

Sources: Browne, A., & Fiske, J. (2001). First Nations women's encounters with mainstream health care services. *Western Journal of Nursing Research, 23* (2), 126-47. Jacobs, P., & Blanchard, J.F., James, R.C., & Depew, N. (2000). Excess costs of diabetes in the Aboriginal population of Manitoba, Canada. *Canadian Journal of Public Health*, 91 (4), 298-301. Silverman, B.E., Goodine, W. M., Ladouceur, M.G., & Quinn, J. (2001). Learning needs of nurses working in Canada's First Nations communities and hospitals. *Journal of Continuing Education in Nursing, 32* (1), 38-47. Waldram, J.B., Whiting, J., Lornder, N., & Habbick, B. (2000). Cultural understandings and the use of traditional medicine among urban Aboriginal people with diabetes in Saskatoon, Canada. *Canadian Journal of Diabetes Care, 24* (2), 31-8.

CHAPTER 15

Health-Care Delivery Systems

OBJECTIVES

After completing this chapter, you will be able to:

- Differentiate primary, secondary, and tertiary health-care delivery services.
- Discuss the essentials of the Patient's Bill of Rights.
- Describe the functions and purposes of the health-care agencies outlined in this chapter.
- List the elements that comprise Canada's social safety net.
- Name the principles of the Canada Health Act.
- Identify the roles of various health-care professionals.
- Analyze the social, political, and technological factors that affect health-care delivery and reform.
- Describe the contemporary frameworks for care.

A **health-care system** is the totality of services offered by all health disciplines. Health care is one of the largest industries in Canada. Traditionally, the primary purpose of a health-care system was to provide care to the ill and injured. However, with increasing awareness of health promotion, illness prevention, and levels of wellness, health-care delivery services are changing, as are the roles of nurses in these areas.

The British North America Act (1867) established Canada as a country and laid out the respective jurisdictions of the federal and provincial governments. Responsibility for health, education, and social services was delegated to the provinces.

As Canada grew by immigration and industrialization, the population became more urbanized. Poor housing and sanitation, crowded living conditions, and a volatile economy led to high rates of morbidity and mortality.

In response, the provinces enacted public health legislation to deal with infectious diseases, maternal-child health, workplace safety, and environmental sanitation. Churches and charities provided hospital care (as they did prior to Confederation), and voluntary organizations began to emerge. Some of these continue to serve the health of the public to this day (e.g., Children's Aid Societies, Canadian Mental Health Association). Municipal governments also became involved, particularly in serving those who were poverty stricken. The Union Movement and fraternal brotherhoods established benevolent funds into which members contributed and could access in the event they were unable to work. These funds were the precursors to today's employment insurance program (1941) and worker's compensation (Ontario, 1914).

The war years created demand for services for soldiers' widows, children, and elderly parents who lost their sources of support. In 1927, the federal government implemented a cost-sharing pension program for elderly persons in need. Rural municipalities were given the power by the Government of Canada to levy taxes (Municipality Act, 1916) to pay for physicians. This right was extended in 1939 to include hospital services (Municipal Medical and Hospital Services Act).

The Family Allowance Act (1945) was the first universal social program in Canada. It provided every Canadian family with a stipend for each child without regard to their income. Other universal programs that form the Canadian Social Safety Net include Old Age Security (OAS, 1951, 1975) and the Canada Pension Plan (CPP, 1966). Today, a comprehensive net of social and health programs are in place. Each province now has a health insurance plan which is governed by the Canada Health Act (1984). The Act provides for federal cost-sharing, provided five conditions are met: public administration, comprehensiveness, universality, portability, and accessibility (See Table 15.1).

With this social safety net in place, costs began to rise, and the provinces began to restructure their health services to accommodate changing views of how health is determined and disease and injury prevented. Intersectoral collaboration and public participation are strategies being used to create more equitable distribution of scarce health and social resources and services. Efforts are being made to curb costs and make more effective use of health personnel and infrastructure by such initiatives as regionalization, integration, and devolution of hospital care to communities and families. Increasingly, Canadians are contributing to supplementary health insurance plans that cover enhanced (i.e., nonessential) services; prescription drugs and supplies; vision, hearing, and dental care; and complementary therapies.

Categories of Health Care

Health-care services are commonly categorized according to type and level.

Types of Health Care

Four types of services are often described: (1) health promotion and illness prevention, (2) diagnosis and treatment, (3) rehabilitation and health restoration, and (4) palliative care.

Health Promotion and Illness Prevention

On the basis of the notion of maintaining an optimum level of wellness, the World Health Organization (WHO) developed a goal that by the year 2000, all persons would be able to lead socially and economically productive lives (1981). The overall goal is to ensure health for all individuals by increasing access to and distribution of health-care services; however, health care is not guaranteed under this goal.

Health promotion was slow to develop until the 1980s. Since that time, more and more people are recognizing the advantages of staying healthy and avoiding illness. Health-promotion programs address determinants of health, such as lifestyle, human biology, and physical, psychological, and social environments. Health-promotion activities emphasize the important role clients play in maintaining their own health and encourage them to maintain the highest level of wellness they can achieve. Recent transitions in health care also reflect a growing support for community-based nursing and health care that capitalizes on health-promotion activities.

The health-care delivery system also offers illness and injury prevention programs. These may be directed at the client or the community and involve such practices as providing immunizations, identifying risk factors for illnesses (e.g., cardiovascular disease), and helping people take measures to prevent these illnesses from occurring. Illness prevention also includes environmental programs that can reduce the incidence of illness or disability. For

TABLE 15.1 Canada Health Act (2003)

1. Public Administration	The public administration criterion, set out in section 8 of the Canada Health Act, applies to provincial and territorial health care insurance plans. The intent of the public administration criterion is that the provincial and territorial health care insurance plans be administered and operated on a non-profit basis by a public authority, accountable to the provincial or territorial government for decision making on benefit levels and services, and whose records and accounts are publicly audited.
2. Comprehensiveness	The comprehensiveness criterion of the Canada Health Act requires that, in order to be eligible for federal cash transfer payments, the health care insurance plan of a province or territory "must insure all insured health services provided by hospital, medical practitioners or dentists (i.e. surgical-dental services which require a hospital setting) and, where the law of the province so permits, similar or additional services rendered by other health care practitioners."
3. Universality	Under the universality criterion, all insured residents of a province or territory must be entitled to the insured health services provided by the provincial or territorial health care insurance plan on uniform terms and conditions. Provinces and territories generally require that residents register with the plans to establish entitlement. Newcomers to Canada, such as landed immigrants or Canadians returning from other countries to live in Canada, may be subject to a waiting period by a province or territory, not to exceed three months, before they are entitled to receive insured health care services.
4. Portability	Residents moving from one province or territory to another must continue to be covered for insured health care services by the "home" jurisdiction during any waiting period imposed by the new province or territory of residence. The waiting period for eligibility to a provincial or territorial health care insurance plan must not exceed three months. After the waiting period, the new province or territory of residence assumes responsibility for health care coverage. Residents who are temporarily absent from their home province or territory or from Canada must continue to be covered for insured health care services during their absence. This allows individuals to travel or be absent from their home province or territory, within a prescribed duration, while retaining their health insurance coverage. The portability criterion does not entitle a person to seek services in another province, territory or country, but is intended to permit one to receive necessary services in relation to an urgent or emergent need when absent on a temporary basis, such as on business or vacation. If insured persons are temporarily absent in another province or territory, the portability criterion requires that insured services be paid at the host province's rate. If insured persons are temporarily out of the country, insured services are to be paid at the home province's rate. Prior approval by the health care insurance plan in a person's home province or territory may also be required before coverage is extended for elective (non-emergency) services to a resident while temporarily absent from their province or territory.
5. Accessibility	The intent of the accessibility criterion is to ensure that residents of a province or territory have reasonable access to insured hospital, medical, and surgical-dental services on uniform terms and conditions, unprecluded or unimpeded, either directly or indirectly, by charges (user charges or extra-billing) or other means (e.g., discrimination on the basis of age, health status, or financial circumstances). In addition, the health care insurance plans of the province or territory must provide reasonable compensation to physicians and dentists for all the insured health care services they provide; and payment to hospitals to cover the cost of insured health care services. Reasonable access in terms of physical availability of medically necessary services has been interpreted under the Canada Health Act using the "where and as available" rule. Thus, residents of a province or territory are entitled to have access on uniform terms and conditions to insured health care services at the setting "where" the services are provided and "as" the services are available in that setting.

Source: *Canada Health Act Annual Report 2001–2002,* 2002 © Adapted and Reproduced with the permission of the Minister of Public Works and Government Services Canada, 2003. *Health Canada assumes no responsibility for any errors or omissions which may have occurred in the adaptation of its material.*

example, steps to decrease air pollution include requiring inspection of automobile exhaust systems to ensure acceptable levels of fumes. Environmental protective measures are frequently legislated by governments and lobbied for by citizens' groups. (See further issues of Safety, Chapter 33.)

Diagnosis and Treatment

Traditionally, the largest segment of the health-care delivery system has been dedicated to the diagnosis and treatment of illnesses. Hospitals and physicians' offices were the major agencies offering these services. More recently, however, community-based agencies have been instrumental in providing these services. For example, community health centres may provide maternal-child care, mental health services, care of clients with chronic health conditions (e.g., diabetes mellitus) as well as acute symptoms. Limited diagnostic technology may be available, but referrals for laboratory or diagnostic imaging services are offered. Voluntary human immunodeficiency virus (HIV) testing and counselling is another example of the shift in services from traditional health-care settings to community-based agencies. Some shopping malls and shopping centres have walk-in clinics that provide a wide range of services.

Rehabilitation and Health Restoration

Rehabilitation is a process of restoring ill or injured people to optimum and functional levels of wellness. Rehabilitative care emphasizes the importance of assisting clients to function adequately in the physical, mental, social, economic, and vocational areas of their lives. The goal of rehabilitation is to help people move to their previous level of health (i.e., to their previous capabilities) or the highest level they are capable of given their current health status. Rehabilitation may begin in the hospital but will eventually lead clients back out into the community for further treatment and follow-up once health has been restored.

Palliative Care

Nurses who provide palliative care may do so within the home, local health-care facilities, or within hospice settings. The term "palliative care" refers to the provision of humane, compassionate care to the dying. (See Chapter 48.)

Levels of Health Care

Health-care delivery services can also be categorized according to the complexity or level of the services provided: primary, secondary, or tertiary. See Table 15.2 for the levels of care and the kinds of services provided at each level. Also see "Levels of Prevention" in Chapter 9. Services provided within a level of care can be coordinated and implemented in many different health-care settings besides hospitals. Nurses play a key role in health-promotion activities and in providing primary health care, whether in the hospital or in the community.

TABLE 15.2 Types of Health-Care Service Classified According to Increasing Complexity

Level	Nursing Services
Primary	Health promotion Preventive care, e.g., immunization Health education Environmental protection Early detection and treatment
Secondary	Emergency care Diagnosis and treatment (complex) Acute care
Tertiary	Long-term care Care of the dying Rehabilitation

Rights and Health Care

The movement for clients' rights in health care arose in the late 1960s. At that time, the broad goals of the movement were to improve the quality of health care and to make the health-care system more responsive to clients' needs. Today, clients are also seeking more self-determination and control over their own bodies when they are ill. Informed consent, confidentiality, and the right of the client to refuse treatment are all aspects of this self-determination. The need for clients' rights is largely the result of two circumstances: (1) the vulnerability of the client because of illness, and (2) the complexity of the relationships in the health-care setting.

When people are ill, they are frequently unable to assert their rights as they would if they were healthy. Asserting rights requires energy and an underlying awareness of one's rights in the situation.

Today, the goals of health include the return of autonomy and independence to the client and the acceptance of good health as a responsibility of the client, the care providers, and society. These goals cannot be met unless clients accept active responsibility for their health and health care and unless clients and care providers have mutual respect.

In 1972 (and revised in 1989), the Consumers' Association of Canada published the *Consumer Rights to Health Care*. See Table 15.3. Included in this statement are the rights of clients to considerate and respectful care; consideration of privacy for clients, including confidentiality of all records and communications regarding their care; and the right to make decisions about their care, including the right to refuse a treatment or plan of care. In addition, clients have a right to make a statement, such as a living will, which should be followed by the agency as permitted by law.

POSITION STATEMENT

Framework for Canada's Health System

CNA Position

Canada's health system affects the well-being of Canadians. The health system reflects government policies and priorities, both economic and social. CNA believes provincial and federal governments together must ensure a congruent, effective, and sustainable health system. CNA will work with others in the health sector to influence government decisions that impact the health system and the delivery of quality health services. Accessibility and comprehensiveness of health and professional standards of care are of particular interest and relevance to nurses.

CNA believes that the health system must provide a broad range of services. The range of services must be included within the scope of provincial health insurance programs. Further, CNA believes that multi-year predictable financial support is integral to the sustainability of Canada's national health care system.

CNA endorses the primary health care approach to providing health services.[1] The principles of the primary health care approach, together with the national conditions established by the *Canada Health Act*[2] for publicly funded health services, provide the framework for Canada's health system for the twenty-first century.

Background

Canada's health system includes services covered by health insurance programs, administered by provincial governments and supplemented by other services paid for by a mixture of private insurance, government programs, and personal out-of pocket expenses.

Over the past two decades, there has been an erosion of public confidence in the health system in Canada. The public is concerned about the accessibility of quality health services, both now and in the future. This concern has sparked research on specific components and aspects of the system (e.g., waiting lists). It also triggered the creation of the National Forum on Health to look comprehensively at the national health system. The forum[3] reached some important conclusions:

- Canadians value the health system and its underlying principles of public ownership/administration, accessibility, comprehensiveness, portability and universality;
- To keep up with technological developments and innovations in delivery, the health system must continuously adapt and reform;
- Reform is needed in "how" and "where" funds for health are spent; reform should realign the scope of provincial health insurance programs to focus on health care rather than on providers and sites;
- Canadians recognize the importance of social and economic determinants of health.

In April 2000, the Canadian Institute for Health Information (CIHI), in cooperation with Statistics Canada, released the first annual report on Health Care in Canada.[4] The report offers evidence of the variations in the organization and delivery of health care across the country, among provinces, within provinces, and between rural/remote areas and urban centres. The report describes the differences, and in some cases the overlap, among skills and roles of the 30 provincially regulated health professions. The report highlights the challenges of public accountability with regard to tracking health spending.

The CIHI report indicates a need to facilitate information-sharing on best practices, on risks and benefits, on organ donations, etc. It presents the potential for improved efficiencies and effectiveness, with the implementation of mechanisms to integrate and coordinate the various elements of the health system.

International evidence from New Zealand[5] and from the UK,[6] points to the value of multidisciplinary teams to the effectiveness and efficiency of delivering health services. Further, public participation has been invaluable in streamlining and optimizing the design and delivery of health services in New Zealand. Both of these strategies (multidisciplinary teams and public participation) must become key elements of the Canadian health system framework.

Taken together, public concern and research results point to the need to improve and transform Canada's health system. They confirm the merit of delivering health services outside of hospital settings, and of ensuring appropriate recruitment and roles among health professions. They confirm the wisdom of providing a range of health services and ensuring the coherence of those services. In short, they confirm the validity of the principles of the primary health care approach and the conditions of the *Canada Health Act*, and the need to ensure those principles and conditions frame the evolution of Canada's health system. *June 2000*

Replaces:

- *A Framework for Health Care Delivery (1995)*
- *The Comprehensiveness of Canada's Health Care System (1996)*
- *Health Promotion (1992)*
- *The Role of the Nurse in Primary Health Care (1995)*

References:

1 See CNA fact sheet on the Primary Health Care Approach.
2 See CNA fact sheet on *Canada Health Act*.
3 *Canada Health Action: Building the Legacy*, final report from the National Forum on Health, 1997.
4 *Health Care in Canada 2000*, Canadian Institute of Health Information, April 2000.
5 New Zealand National Commission.
6 *British Medical Journal*, April 2000.

Canadian Nurses Association, 50 Driveway, Ottawa ON K2P 1E2
Tel: (613) 237-2133 or 1-800-361-8404 Fax: (613) 237-3520
Web site: www.cna-nurses.ca E-mail: prr@cna-nurses.ca

TABLE 15.3 Consumer Rights to Health Care

1. Right to be informed	(a) about preventative health care, including education on nutrition, drug use, birth control, appropriate education (b) about the health-care system, including the extent of government insurance coverage for services, supplemental insurance plans, the referral system to auxiliary health and social facilities and services in the community (c) about the individual's own diagnosis and specific treatment program, including prescribed surgery and medication, options, effects, and side effects (d) about the specific costs of procedures, services, and professional fees undertaken on behalf of the individual consumer
2. Right to be respected as the individual with the major responsibility for their own health care	(a) right that confidentiality of health records be maintained (b) right to refuse experimentation, undue painful prolongation of life, or participation in teaching programs (c) right of adult to refuse treatment, right to die with dignity
3. Right to participate in decision making affecting their health	(a) through consumer representation at each level of government in planning and evaluating the system of health services, the types and qualities of service and the conditions under which health services are delivered (b) with the health professionals and the personnel involved in their direct health care
4. Right to equal access to health care (health education, prevention, treatment and rehabilitation) regardless of the individual's economic status, gender, age, creed, ethnic origin, and location	(a) right to access to adequately qualified health personnel (b) right to a second opinion (c) right to prompt response in emergencies

Source: Consumers' Association of Canada (1972; 1989).

Clients have the right to review all their medical records and have them explained; to receive requested care and services, provided these are reasonable; and to be informed of any business arrangements among institutions or people involved in their care. In addition, clients have the right to be informed of resources that can be used to resolve a dispute or grievance and of hospital policies and practices that relate to client care, treatment, and responsibilities, and to be informed of hospital charges and available payment methods. Furthermore, clients have the right to refuse to participate in any research study, to expect a reasonable continuity of care, and to have options explained when hospital care is no longer appropriate.

Health-care agencies are obliged to advise clients of their rights to make informed choices about their treatment. The client should be asked about any advance directive (e.g., not to be resuscitated in the event of a cardiac arrest), and this information must be on the client's record. If the hospital's policy limits its ability to implement any advance directive, the client has a right to be informed of this before any problem arises. See details about Advance Directives in Chapter 48.

If a client lacks decision-making capacity, is legally incompetent, or is a minor, these rights can be exercised on the client's behalf by a designated surrogate or proxy decision maker.

Types of Health-Care Settings

Health-care agencies and settings in Canada are both varied and numerous. Some agencies provide a number of services; for example, a hospital may provide acute inpatient services, outpatient or ambulatory care services, and emergency services. In addition, the same services may be found in other community-based agencies. For example, hospice services may be provided in the hospital, in the home, or in another agency within the community.

A client may be categorized as an inpatient or an outpatient. An *inpatient* is a person who enters a setting, such as a hospital, and remains for at least 24 hours. An *outpatient* is a person who requires health care but does not need to stay in an institution, such as a hospital. Examples of services used by outpatients are diagnostic tests, minor surgical procedures, medications, and so on.

Because the array of health-care services and agencies is so great, nurses often need to help clients choose the services that best suit their needs. Clients may be seen in any number of these agencies, depending on their care needs and supplementary insurance coverage. Traditional nursing roles and responsibilities are also changing in response to the movement of client care from the hospital into the community.

Public Health

Government (official) agencies are established at the local, provincial or territorial, and federal levels to provide public health services. Health agencies at the provincial/territorial, rural, or urban level vary according to the need of the area. Local health departments traditionally have responsibility for developing programs to meet the health needs of the people, providing the necessary staff and facilities to carry out these programs, continually evaluating the effectiveness of the programs, and monitoring changing needs. Federal health services are responsible for assisting the provincial health departments. In some remote areas, Health Canada also provides direct services to First Nations people.

The Health Promotion and Programs Branch is an official department at the federal level. Its functions include conducting research and providing training in the health field, providing assistance to communities in planning and developing health facilities, and assisting regional and local communities through provision of trained personnel. Also, at the national level in Canada are research institutions, such as the Canada Institutes of Health. The Laboratory Centre for Disease Control (LCDC) administers a broad program related to surveillance of diseases. By means of laboratory and epidemiological investigations, data are made available to the appropriate authorities. The LCDC also publishes recommendations about the prevention and control of infections and administers a national health program. The federal government also administers a number of Veterans health services in Canada.

Physicians' Offices

In North America, the physician's office is a traditional primary-care setting. The majority of physicians either have their own offices or work with several other physicians in a group practice. Clients usually go to a physician's office for routine health screening, illness diagnosis, and treatment. People often seek consultation from physicians when they are experiencing symptoms of illness or when a significant other considers the person to be ill.

Nurses employed in physician's offices have a variety of roles and responsibilities. Some nurses carry out traditional functions including client registration, preparing the client for an examination, obtaining health information, and providing information. Other functions may include obtaining specimens, assisting with procedures, and providing some treatments. Nurse practitioners and clinical nurse specialists may be employed in a physician's office and are responsible for providing primary care to clients in stable health.

Community Health Centres

Such centres are being used more frequently in many communities. Most ambulatory care centres have diagnostic and treatment facilities providing medical, nursing, laboratory, and radiological services, and they may or may not be attached to or associated with an acute-care hospital. Some ambulatory care centres provide services to people who require minor surgical procedures that can be performed outside the hospital. After surgery, the client returns home, often the same day. These centres offer two advantages: (1) they permit the client to live at home while obtaining necessary health care, and (2) they free costly hospital beds for seriously ill clients. Nurses in community care centres may have specialized knowledge and skills to enable them to assist physicians with procedures. The term *community care centre* has replaced the term *clinic* in many places.

General Clinics

The term *clinic* can refer to a department inside or outside the hospital, managed by a group of physicians or by nurses. Some may provide a specialized type of health service, such as breastfeeding support, diabetes care, or hypertension treatment services. Traditionally, a hospital clinic was called an outpatient clinic, serving only outpatients as opposed to inpatients (those admitted to the hospital). Nurses in clinics perform many of the same functions as nurses employed in a physician's office.

Occupational Health Clinics

The occupational health clinic is gaining importance as a setting for employee health care. Employee health has long been recognized as important to productivity. Today, more companies recognize the value of healthy employees and encourage workplace wellness by providing exercise facilities and coordinating health-promotion activities.

Community nurses in the occupational health setting have a variety of roles. Worker safety has been a traditional concern of occupational health nurses. Today, nursing functions in occupational health care include work safety and health education, pre-employment and annual employee health screening for tuberculosis, hearing, and vision, and providing immunization information. Other functions may include screening for such health problems as hypertension and obesity, disability management and return to work, and counselling.

In Canada, occupational health nurses are registered nurses holding a minimum of a diploma or degree in nursing. They may also have a certificate, diploma, or degree in Occupational Health and Safety from a community college or university. Nurses who are certified in occupational health nursing have met specific eligibility requirements, passed a written examination, and have met a national standard of competency in Occupational Health. In Canada, expertise unique to this speciality is recognized with the initials COHN(C), granted by the Canadian Nurses Association. (See Chapters 1 and 2 for more information on certification and competency.)

Hospitals

Hospitals traditionally have provided restorative care to the ill and injured. They vary in size from the small rural hospital to the very large metropolitan hospital.

Military hospitals provide care to military personnel and their dependents. Although hospitals are chiefly viewed as institutions that provide care, they have other functions, such as providing sources for health-related research and teaching.

Hospitals can be classified by the services they provide. General hospitals admit clients requiring a variety of services, such as medical, surgical, obstetric, pediatric, and psychiatric services. Other hospitals offer only specialty services, such as psychiatric or pediatric care. Hospitals can be further described as acute-care or chronic-(long-term) care facilities. An acute-care hospital provides assistance to clients who are acutely ill or whose illness and need for hospitalization are relatively short term, for example, two days. In some instances, clients only require overnight observation following minor surgery. In this case, the client is admitted to the hospital for 24 hours to be monitored by nursing staff. Long-term care hospitals provide services for longer periods, sometimes for years or the remainder of the client's life.

The variety of health-care services hospitals provide usually depends on their size and location. The large urban hospitals usually have inpatient beds, emergency services, diagnostic facilities, ambulatory surgery centres, pharmacy services, intensive- and coronary-care services, and multiple outpatient services provided by clinics. Some large hospitals have other specialized services, such as spinal cord injury and burn units, oncology services, and infusion and dialysis units. In addition, some hospitals have substance abuse treatment units and health promotion units. Small rural hospitals often are limited to inpatient beds, radiology and laboratory services, and basic emergency services. The number of services a rural hospital provides is usually directly related to its size and its distance from an urban centre.

Hospitals in Canada have undergone massive changes. Some hospitals have merged with other hospitals or have been redesigned for other purposes, such as health centres or specialty services, e.g., auxiliary health-care centres that offer step-down care from hospitals to home or long-term care institutions. Within some provinces, regional health authorities (RHA) have been given the responsibility for such amalgamations. Other hospitals are providing innovative services, such as fitness classes, day care for older people, and nutrition classes. Some hospitals have even established alternative birth centres (ABCs) to attract new families.

Another change relates to the client population. Most clients in hospitals are seriously ill and require complex nursing care; others are less ill and may be treated on an outpatient basis. With the increasing acuity (severity) of illness among clients, general hospitals have virtually become complex-care centres.

Nurses in hospitals have multiple responsibilities, including the coordination of client care, assessing and monitoring client health, and providing direct care.

Extended-Care (Long-Term Care) Facilities

Traditionally, many extended-care facilities were called nursing homes. Extended-care facilities now include skilled nursing facilities (intermediate care) and extended-care facilities (long-term care) that provide personal care for those who are chronically ill or are unable to care for themselves without assistance. Traditionally, extended-care facilities only provided care for elderly clients, but now they provide care to clients of all ages who require rehabilitation or custodial care. As clients are being discharged earlier from acute-care hospitals, some clients may still require supplemental care in an extended-care facility before they return home.

Because long-term illness occurs most often in the elderly, long-term care facilities have programs that are oriented to the needs of this age group. These facilities are intended for people who require not only personal services (bathing, hygiene, assistance with daily activities, and so on) but also some regular nursing care and occasional medical attention. However, the type of care provided varies considerably. Some facilities admit and retain only residents who are able to dress themselves and are ambulatory. Other extended-care facilities provide bed care for clients who are more incapacitated. These facilities can, in effect, become the client's home, and consequently, the people who live there are frequently referred to as residents, rather than patients or clients.

Specific guidelines govern the admission procedures for clients admitted to an extended-care facility. Treatment needs and nursing care requirements must all be assessed beforehand. Many skilled nursing facilities exist as units within a hospital but are regulated to make sure they are meeting the requirements for a long-term care facility. If a client in a hospital needs to be transferred to such a unit, the client is discharged from the hospital and then admitted to the long-term care unit. Extended-care and skilled nursing facilities are becoming increasingly popular means for managing the health-care needs of clients who require additional care but do not meet the criteria for remaining in the hospital. Often, these extended-care facilities have client waiting lists for admission. Nurses in extended-care facilities assist clients with their daily activities, provide care when necessary, and coordinate rehabilitation activities.

Retirement and Assisted-Living Centres

Retirement or assisted-living centres consist of separate houses, condominiums, or apartments for residents. Residents live relatively independently; however, many of these facilities offer meals, laundry services, nursing care, transportation, and social activities. Some centres have a separate hospital to care for residents with short-term or long-term illnesses. Often, these centres also work collaboratively with other community services, including case managers, social services, and a hospice, to meet the needs of the residents who live there. The retirement or assisted-living centre is intended to meet the needs of people who are unable to remain at home but do not require hospital or nursing-home care. Nurses in retirement and assisted-living centres provide limited care to residents, usually related to the administration of medications and minor treatments.

Rehabilitation Centres

Rehabilitation centres usually are independent community centres or special units. However, because rehabilitation ideally starts the moment the client enters the health-care system, nurses who are employed on pediatric, psychiatric, or medical/surgical units of hospitals also help to rehabilitate clients. Rehabilitation centres play an important role in assisting clients to restore their health and recuperate. Drug and alcohol rehabilitation centres, for example, help free clients of drug and alcohol dependence and assist them to re-enter the community and function to the best of their abilities. Today, the concept of rehabilitation is applied to all illnesses (physical and mental), to injuries, and to chemical addictions. Nurses in the rehabilitation setting coordinate client activities and ensure that clients are complying with their treatments. This type of nursing often requires specialized skills and knowledge.

Home Health-Care Agencies

The implementation of earlier discharge of clients from hospitals has made home care an essential aspect of the health-care delivery system. As concerns about the cost of health care have escalated, the use of the home as a care delivery site has increased. In addition, the scope of services offered in the home has broadened. Home health-care agencies offer education to clients and families, as well as provide comprehensive care to acute, chronic, and terminally ill clients. See Chapter 17.

Day-Care Centres

Day-care centres serve many functions and many age groups. Some day-care centres provide care for infants and children while parents work. Other centres provide care for adults who cannot be left at home alone but do not need to be in an institution. Elder care centres often provide care involving socializing, exercise programs, and stimulation. Some centres provide counselling and physical therapy. Nurses who are employed in day-care centres may provide medications, treatments, and counselling, thereby facilitating continuity between day care and home care.

Rural Primary Care

Rural primary-care hospitals (RPCH) were created in some provinces during the process of health system reform in the 1990s. They provide emergency care to clients in rural areas who require stabilization before transfer to a larger hospital. Usually, basic laboratory and radiological services are also available.

Hospice Services

Traditionally, a hospice was a place for travellers to rest. Recently, the term has come to mean a health-care facility for the dying. The hospice movement subsumes a variety of services given to the terminally ill, their families, and support persons. The movement sprang initially from dissatisfaction with the health-care community's preoccupation with technological care and insufficient emphasis on caring and psychological support. In the 1970s, the movement gained momentum. It derived impetus from new attitudes toward death and from the work of such people as Elisabeth Kübler-Ross, whose books challenged prevailing attitudes, and Cicely Saunders, founder of St. Christopher's Hospice in London, England. Saunders believed that the physical and social environments of dying people are as important as medical interventions on their behalf. The central concept of the hospice movement, as distinct from the acute-care model, is not saving life but improving or maintaining the quality of life until death. For additional information, see Chapter 48.

Crisis Centres

Crisis centres provide emergency services to clients experiencing life crises. These centres may operate out of a hospital or in the community, and most provide 24-hour telephone service. Some also provide direct counselling to people at the centre or in their homes. The primary purpose of a crisis centre is to help people cope with an immediate crisis and then provide guidance and support for long-term therapy.

Nurses working in crisis centres need well-developed communication and counselling skills. The nurse must immediately identify the person's problem, offer assistance to help the person cope, and perhaps later direct the person to resources for long-term support.

Telehealth

Telephone advice services are spreading across Canada. These services are generally available 24 hours a day, seven days a week. Nurses supply answers to health-related questions and advise callers about how to handle non-urgent situations (CIHI, 2001).

Mutual Support and Self-Help Groups

In North America today, there are more than 500 mutual support or self-help groups that focus on nearly every major health problem or life crisis people experience. Such groups arose largely because people felt their needs were not being met by the existing health-care system. Alcoholics Anonymous, which was formed in 1935, served as the model for many of these groups. Guidelines on how to start a self-help group are available from provincial mental health boards or similar agencies. The National Clearinghouse provides information on current support groups and guidelines about how to start a self-help group. The nurse's role in self-help groups is discussed in Chapter 26.

Providers of Health Care

The providers of health care, also referred to as the health-care team or health professionals, are health personnel from different disciplines who coordinate their skills to assist clients, families, groups, and communities. Their mutual goal is to restore a client's health and promote wellness. The choice of personnel for a particular client depends on the needs of the client. In the present system of health care, health teams commonly include the following personnel.

Nurse

The role of the nurse varies with the needs of the client (see Figure 15.1). As nursing roles have expanded, new dimensions for nursing practice have been established. See Chapter 1 for the roles of the nurse. Nurses can pursue a variety of practice specialties (e.g., critical care, community health, mental health, oncology). **A registered nurse (RN)** assesses a client's health status, identifies health problems, and develops and coordinates care. Also see Chapter 1 regarding nurse practitioner, clinical nurse specialist, and so on. A **licensed practical nurse (LPN),** also referred to as a registered practical nurse (RPN), is an autonomous practitioner who cares for clients with less complex needs and more predictable outcomes.

Figure 15.1 The role of the nurse varies with the needs of the client

Physician

The physician is responsible for medical diagnosis and for determining the therapy required by a person who has a disease or injury. The physician's traditional role is the treatment of disease and trauma (injury); however, many physicians are now including health promotion and disease prevention in their practice. Some physicians are specialists in surgery and are referred to as surgeons. An example is a neurosurgeon or an orthopedic surgeon. Others specialize in such areas as mental health (psychiatrist) or community health (medical officers).

Unlicensed Assistive Personnel

Unlicensed assistive personnel (UAPs) are health-care staff, such as nurse aides, hospital attendants, nurse technicians, and orderlies, who assume aspects of client care that do not require nursing judgement. These tasks include bathing, assisting with feeding, and collecting specimens under the direction of licensed staff, such as a registered nurse.

Dentist

Dentists diagnose and treat dental problems. Dentists are also actively involved in preventive measures to maintain healthy oral structures (e.g., teeth and gums). Some long-term care facilities have dentists on their staff. In acute-care facilities, trauma units may have dentists as part of the team.

Some dentists work with dental hygienists or dental assistants. Both categories of staff work under the direction of a dentist.

Pharmacist

A pharmacist prepares and dispenses pharmaceuticals in hospital and community settings. The role of the pharmacist in monitoring and evaluating the actions and effects of medications on clients is becoming increasingly prominent. A **clinical pharmacist** is a specialist who guides physicians in prescribing medications. A **pharmacy assistant** is also recognized in some provinces. This person administers medications to clients or works in the pharmacy under the direction of the pharmacist.

Dietitian or Nutritionist

When dietary and nutritional services are required, the dietitian or nutritionist may be a member of a health team. A **dietitian,** often a registered dietitian (RD), has special knowledge about the diets required to maintain health and to treat disease. Dietitians in hospitals generally are concerned with therapeutic diets, may design special diets to meet the nutritional needs of individual clients, and supervise the preparation of the meals to ensure that clients receive the proper diet.

A **nutritionist** is a person who has special knowledge about nutrition and food. The nutritionist in a community setting recommends healthy diets and gives broad advisory services about the purchase and preparation of foods. Community nutritionists often function at the preventive level. They promote health and prevent disease, for example, by advising families about balanced diets for growing children and pregnant women and assisting restaurants to develop heart-healthy menus.

Physiotherapist

The physiotherapist (PT), or physical therapist, assists clients with musculoskeletal problems. Physiotherapists treat the body by means of heat, water, exercise, massage, and electric current. They provide physical therapy in response to a physician's order. The physiotherapist's functions include assessing clients' mobility and strength, providing therapeutic measures (e.g., exercises and heat applications to improve mobility and strength), and teaching new skills (e.g., how to walk with an artificial leg). Some physiotherapists provide their services in hospitals; however, independent practitioners establish offices in communities and serve clients either at the office or in the home.

Respiratory Technologist

A respiratory technologist (RT) is skilled in therapeutic measures used in the care of clients with respiratory problems. These therapists are knowledgeable about oxygen therapy devices, intermittent positive pressure breathing respirators, artificial mechanical ventilators, and accessory devices used in inhalation therapy. Respiratory therapists administer many of the pulmonary function tests.

Occupational Therapist

An occupational therapist (OT) assists clients with an impaired function to gain the skills to perform activities of daily living. For example, an occupational therapist might teach a man with severe arthritis in his arms and hands how to adjust his kitchen utensils so that he can continue to cook. The therapist also teaches skills that are therapeutic and, at the same time, provide some satisfaction. For example, weaving is a recreational activity but also exercises the arthritic man's arm and hands.

Paramedical Technologists

Laboratory technologists, radiology technologists, and nuclear medicine technologists are just three kinds of paramedical technologists in the expanding field of medical technology. **Paramedical** means having some connection with medicine. Laboratory technologists examine such specimens as urine, feces, blood, and discharges from wounds to provide exact information that facilitates the medical diagnosis and the prescription of a therapeutic regimen. The radiology technologist assists with a wide variety of x-ray film procedures, from simple chest radiography to more complex fluoroscopy. The nuclear medicine technologist uses radioactive substances to provide diagnostic information, for example, about a client's liver, and can administer therapeutic doses of radioactive materials as part of a therapeutic regimen. These technologists have highly specialized skills and knowledge important to client care.

Social Worker

A social worker counsels clients and support persons about social problems, such as finances, marital difficulties, and adoption of children. It is not unusual for health problems to produce problems in day-to-day living and vice versa. For example, an elderly woman who lives alone and has a stroke resulting in impaired walking may find it impossible to continue to live in her third-floor apartment. Finding a more suitable living arrangement can be the responsibility of the social worker if the client has no support network in place. The current trend toward shorter acute-care hospitalizations has led to an increased need for rehabilitative services in skilled nursing facilities or in the home. Thus, social workers, who usually make the placement arrangements, are playing an increasingly important role on the health-care team.

Spiritual Support Person

Chaplains, pastors, rabbis, priests, and so on serve as part of the health-care team by attending to the spiritual needs of clients. In most facilities, local clergy volunteer their services on a regular or on-call basis. Hospitals affiliated with specific religions, as well as many large medical centres, have full-time chaplains on staff. They usually offer regularly scheduled religious services. The nurse is often instrumental in identifying the client's desire for spiritual support and notifying the appropriate person.

Case Managers

The case manager's role is to ensure fiscally sound, appropriate care in the best setting. This role is often filled by the member of the health-care team who is most involved in the client's care. Depending on the nature of the client's concerns, the case manager may be a nurse, a social worker, an occupational therapist, a physical therapist, or any other member of the health-care team.

Alternative Care Providers

Chiropractors, herbalists, acupuncturists, and other nontraditional health-care providers are playing increasingly important roles in the contemporary health-care system. These providers may practise alongside traditional health-care providers, or clients may use their services in conjunction with, or in lieu of, traditional therapies.

Factors Affecting Health-Care Delivery

Today's health-care consumers have greater knowledge about their health than in previous years, and they are increasingly influencing health-care delivery. Formerly, people expected a physician to make decisions about their care; today, however, consumers expect to be involved in making any decisions. Consumers have also become aware of how lifestyle affects health. As a result, they desire more information and services related to health promotion and illness prevention. A number of other factors affect the health-care delivery system.

Increasing Number of Older Adults

An increase in the number of older people is anticipated: from 3.9 million in the year 2000 to 4.9 million by 2011 (Statistics Canada, 1991). Chronic illnesses are prevalent in this group and frequently require special housing, treatment services, financial support, and social networks.

The frail elderly, considered to be people over age 85 years, are projected to be the fastest growing population in North America and will constitute 14 percent of the elderly population by 2030 (Lee & Estes, 1990).

Because only 5 percent of older people are institutionalized with health problems, substantial home management and nursing support services are required to assist those in their homes and communities.

Older people also need to feel they are part of a community even though they are approaching the end of their lives. The feeling of being a useful, wanted, and productive citizen is essential to every person's health. Special programs are being designed in communities so that the talents and skills of this group will be used and not lost to society. These programs—partial employment, for example—are designed especially for the older adult.

Advances in Technology

Scientific knowledge and technology related to health care are rapidly increasing. Improved diagnostic procedures and sophisticated equipment permit early recognition of diseases that might otherwise have remained undetected. New antibiotics and medications are continually being manufactured to treat infections and multiple drug-resistant organisms. Surgical procedures involving the heart, lungs, and liver that were nonexistent 20 years ago are common today. Laser and microscopic procedures streamline the treatment of diseases that required surgery in the past. Computers, bedside charting, and the ability to store and retrieve large volumes of information in databases are commonplace in health-care organizations.

These discoveries have changed the profile of the client. Clients are now more likely to be treated in the community, utilizing resources, technology, and treatments outside the hospital. For example, 30 years ago a person having cataract surgery had to remain in bed in the hospital for 10 days; today, most cataract removals are performed on an outpatient basis in outpatient surgical centres. All the technological advances and specialized treatments and procedures come, unfortunately, with a high price tag.

Economics

Paying for health-care services is becoming an issue. The health-care delivery system is very much affected by a country's total economic status. Inflation and the economic recession of the 1980s and early 1990s brought increasing concern about escalating health-care costs. Canada's medical care costs have increased more than 400 percent since 1965.

There are major reasons for this sizable increase in costs:

FOCUS ON CRITICAL THINKING

Rebecca Konapinksi is leaving the hospital after having major surgery. She is leaving the hospital with a drain that will stay in place for about ten days. It is obvious in talking to her that she is apprehensive and worried about who will change her dressing when she gets home. Her two small children are young and her husband travels a great deal.

1. What is meant by continuum of health-care service delivery?
2. How might Rebecca's family and friends provide health-care services to her?
3. How would the nurse provide health care to her?

See Appendix A for answers to these questions.

- Drug and pharmaceutical costs have been increasing.
- Existing equipment and facilities are continually becoming obsolete as research uncovers new and better methods in health care.
- Additional space, sophisticated equipment, and technology are required to provide new diagnostic and treatment methods.
- Inflation increases all costs.
- The total population has grown, and the demand for health-care services has increased.
- The number of people working within the health-care system has increased.

Women's Health

The women's movement has been instrumental in changing health-care practices. Examples are the provision of childbirth services in more relaxed settings, such as birthing centres, and the provision of overnight facilities for parents in children's hospitals. Traditionally, women's health issues have focused on the reproductive aspects of health, disregarding many health-care concerns that are unique to women.

Uneven Distribution of Services

Serious problems in the distribution of health services exist in Canada. Two facets of this problem are (1) uneven distribution, and (2) increased specialization. In some areas, particularly remote and rural locations, there are insufficient numbers of health-care professionals and services available to meet the health-care needs of individuals, families, and communities. Rural clients may often need to drive large distances to obtain the services they require.

Because of the highly specialized techniques and new knowledge that have emerged during the past 30 years of research, an increasing number of health-care personnel provide specialized services. They may be highly specialized technicians or technologists who have relatively narrow but exacting jobs, such as orthotic technologists, biomedical electronic technologists, and nuclear medicine technologists. Increased specialization is evident also among physicians. The largest physician specialties are general and family practice and internal medicine. This specialization leads to fragmentation of care and, often, increased cost of care. To clients, it may mean receiving care from 5 to 30 people during their hospital experience. This seemingly endless stream of personnel is often confusing and frightening.

Access to Health Care

Low income and rural residency have been associated with relatively higher rates of infectious diseases (e.g., tuberculosis, AIDS), problems with substance abuse, rape, violence, and chronic diseases (Aday, 1993). The use of health-care services is also affected by unemployment and poverty. Even though government assistance is available, eligibility for programs and benefits varies considerably from province to province and territory to territory.

Homeless Populations

The growing number of homeless individuals in towns and cities is an increasing health problem. The homeless differ from those who are poor. They are socially isolated, lack any type of permanent residence, and are disaffiliated from family and friends. Because of the conditions in which homeless people live (in shelters, on the streets, in parks, in tents, under temporary covers and dwellings, in transportation terminals, or in cars), their health problems are often exacerbated and sometimes become chronic.

Factors contributing to homelessness include the high cost of housing, alcohol and substance abuse, and changes from inpatient to outpatient services provided by mental health facilities. Homeless people have physical, mental, social, and emotional problems they must face (see box on the next page). Limited access to health-care services significantly contributes to the general poor health of the homeless.

Canadian Society Notes

Fact	Implications for Nursing Practice
The five principles of the Canada Health Act (CHA) are the cornerstone of the Canadian health-care system.	Nurses need to understand the principles of the Canada Health Act and the health-care system to deliver effective quality care within it.
The Canadian health-care system has evolved into its present form over four and a half decades. Saskatchewan, in 1947, was the first province to establish public, universal hospital insurance. Ten years later, the Canadian government passed legislation to permit the federal government to share in the cost of provincial hospital insurance plans. By 1961, all provinces and territories had public insurance plans that provided comprehensive coverage for in-hospital care.	Nurses' role as client advocate is important in today's health-care system to ensure that the health-care needs of all people are served.
Canada's health expenditures stand 5th of all industrialized nations and the highest of all publicly funded universal health-care systems world wide.	Nurses have a responsibility to be fiscally accountable.
Recent federal initiatives include the Commission on the Future of Health Care chaired by Roy Romanow and The Standing Senate Committee on Social Affairs, Science and Technology (the Health of Canadians — The Federal Role) chaired by The Honourable Michael Kirby.	Nurses need to understand government initiatives that will impact health care.

Factors Contributing to Health Problems of the Homeless

- Poor physical environment resulting in increased susceptibility to infections
- Inadequate rest and privacy
- Improper nutrition
- Poor access to facilities for personal hygiene
- Exposure to the elements
- Lack of social support
- Few personal resources
- Questionable personal safety (physical assault is a constant threat)
- Inadequate health care
- Mental illness
- Poor compliance with treatment plans
- Substance abuse

Demographic Changes

The characteristics of the Canadian family have changed considerably in the last few decades. The numbers of single-parent families and alternative family structures have increased markedly. Most of the single-parent families are headed by women, many of whom work and require assistance with child care or when a child is sick at home.

Recognition of the cultural and ethnic diversity of Canada is also increasing. The Canadian Nurses Association (1998) published "Cultural Diversity—Changes and Challenges," which acknowledges the increasingly diverse clients that nurses work with. Health-care professionals and agencies are aware of this diversity and are employing means to meet the challenges it presents. For example, more agencies are employing nurses who are bilingual and who can communicate with clients whose primary language is not English.

Contemporary Frameworks for Care

A number of approaches to client care support continuity of care and cost-effectiveness. They include managed care, case management, and patient-focused care.

Case Management

Case management describes a range of models for integrating health-care services for individuals or groups. Various case management models strive to provide cost-effective care and ensure quality outcomes. Generally, case

Key Responsibilities of Case Managers

- Assessing clients and their homes and communities
- Coordinating and planning client care
- Collaborating with other health professionals
- Monitoring clients' progress
- Evaluating client outcomes

management involves nurse-physician teams that assume collaborative responsibility for planning, assessing needs, and coordinating, implementing, and evaluating care for groups of clients from preadmission to discharge or transfer and recuperation. A case manager, however, may be a social worker or other appropriate professional.

Case managers generally coordinate care for a specific client population, such as clients with AIDS or chronic obstructive lung disease, in a particular setting. A critical component of their role is collaboration with other health-care professionals and the client to achieve established outcomes. Key responsibilities for case managers are shown in the box above.

Case managers usually have a minimum educational preparation of a baccalaureate degree.

Case management may be used as a cost-containment strategy in managed care. Both case management and managed care systems often use **critical pathways** to track the client's progress. A critical pathway is an interdisciplinary plan or tool for managed care of a client that specifies interdisciplinary assessments, interventions, treatments, and outcomes for specific health-related conditions across a time line. Critical pathways are also called critical paths, interdisciplinary plans, anticipated recovery plans, interdisciplinary care plans, and action plans. These plans can be developed for surgical procedures, medical diagnoses, emergency care, trauma care, and health-related interventions. They are usually used for high-volume case types or situations that have relatively predictable outcomes. The pathways are designed in collaboration with members of the health-care team who are involved in managing the case type and are considered best practices based on a body of evidence in that field. See Figure 15.2 for a sample critical pathway. Additional critical pathways are presented in later chapters.

Critical pathways establish the sequence and timing of interdisciplinary interventions and incorporate education, discharge planning, assessments, consultations, nutrition, medications, activities, diagnostic testing, therapeutic measures, and so on. They may be used in managed care settings, traditional delivery systems, or patient-focused care models. However, it is important to exercise clinical judgement when applying standard protocols and to refrain from using them as a "checklist" for all clients.

Patient-Focused Care

Patient-focused care is a delivery model that brings all services and care providers to the clients. The supposition is that if activities normally provided by auxiliary personnel (e.g., physical therapy, respiratory therapy, ECG testing, phlebotomy) are moved closer to the client, the number of personnel involved and the number of steps involved to get the work done are decreased. Proponents of this type of system believe that clients will perceive improved care and service and the agency will achieve cost savings. Patient-focused care units often have their own admitting, pharmacy, laboratory, and radiology areas, although variations exist among agencies. For instance, breast screening vans go out to rural areas, and some regional rehabilitation teams or programs make regular rounds to satellite centres.

Cross-training, development of multiskilled workers who can perform tasks or functions in more than one discipline, is an essential element of patient-focused care. For example, a health-care worker may be taught to obtain a 12-lead ECG and perform phlebotomy, or individuals who are already certified in one profession can take on a second certification, such as medical laboratory and x-ray technology, nursing and respiratory therapy, and physical and occupational therapy.

Because patient-focused care may result in the blurring of role boundaries, collaboration is vital during the design and implementation process. Efficiency, decreased costs, and the increased use of paraprofessionals may all be integral to the managed care system in the future. Many hospitals have adopted some components of patient-focused care in efforts to improve client and staff satisfaction and to reduce costs.

Models for the Delivery of Nursing

Contemporary configurations for the delivery of nursing include collaborative arrangements, such as managed care, case management, and patient-focused care discussed earlier. Other models specifically designed for the provision of nursing are the case method, the functional method, team nursing, primary nursing, differentiated practice, shared governance, and partners in practice. Frequently, delivery methods comprise components of more than one configuration.

Case Method

The case method, also referred to as total care, is one of the earliest nursing models developed. In this client-centred method, one nurse is assigned to and is responsible for the comprehensive care of a group of clients during an eight- or 12-hour shift. For each client, the nurse assesses needs, makes nursing plans, formulates nursing diagnoses, imple-

CRITICAL PATHWAY FOR CLIENT FOLLOWING LAPAROSCOPIC CHOLECYSTECTOMY

EXPECTED LENGTH OF STAY: Less than 24 hours

	Date ____________ Preoperative	Date ____________ 1st 24 hours following surgery
Daily outcomes	Client verbalizes understanding of preoperative teaching including turning, coughing, deep breathing, incentive spirometer, mobilization, and pain management. Client verbalizes ability to cope.	Client is afebrile. Client has a dry, clean wound with edges well approximated, healing by first intention. Client manages pain with non-pharmacological measures or oral medications. Client is independent in self-care. Client is fully ambulatory. Client has resumed preadmission urine and bowel elimination pattern. Client verbalizes home care instructions. Client tolerates usual diet. Client verbalizes ability to cope with ongoing stressors.
Tests and treatments	CBC Urinalysis Baseline physical assessment: with a focus on respiratory status and gastrointestinal function Anesthesia consult	Vital signs and O_2 saturation, neurovascular assessment, dressing and wound drainage assessment q15 min $\times$ 4; q30 min $\times$ 4; q1h $\times$ 4 and then q4h if stable Assess lung sounds and gastrointestinal function q4h and prn. Intake and output every shift. Assess voiding—if unable to void, try suggestive voiding techniques or catheterize q8h or prn if unable to void.
Knowledge deficit	Orient to room and surroundings. Provide simple, brief instructions. Review preoperative preparation including hospital and surgical routines. Reinforce preoperative teaching regarding specific postoperative care: turning, coughing, deep breathing, incentive spirometer, mobilization, and pain management.	Reorient to room and postoperative routine. Review plan of care and importance of early mobilization. Begin discharge teaching regarding wound care/dressing change.
Psychosocial	Assess anxiety related to pending surgery. Assess fears of the unknown and surgery. Encourage verbalization of concerns. Provide information regarding surgical experiences. Minimize external stimuli (e.g., noise, movement).	Assess level of anxiety. Encourage verbalization of concerns. Provide information and ongoing support and encouragement.
Diet	NPO Baseline nutritional assessment	Advance to clear liquids, if tolerated advance to full liquids/soft diet morning following surgery.
Activity	OOB ad lib until premedicated for surgery.	Provide safety precautions. Bathroom privileges with assistance evening after surgery and begin progressive ambulation to tolerance the morning following surgery until fully ambulatory.
Medications	NPO except ordered medications.	IM or PO analgesics Antibiotics if ordered IV fluids until adequate PO intake then intermittent IV device Discontinue prior to discharge.
Transfer/discharge plans	Assess discharge plans and support system.	Probable discharge within 24 hours of surgery. Complete discharge home care teaching when fully awake and oriented and before discharge. Provide a written copy of discharge instructions.

Figure 15.2 Example of a critical pathway for a client following a laparoscopic cholecystectomy

Source: Beyea, S. C. (1996). *Critical pathways for collaborative care.* Menlo Park, CA: Addison-Wesley Nursing, p. 111–112.

ments care, and evaluates the effectiveness of care. In this method, a client has consistent contact with one nurse during a shift but may have different nurses on other shifts. The case method, considered the precursor of primary nursing, continues to be used in a variety of practice settings, such as intensive-care nursing.

With the shortage of nursing personnel during World War II, the case method could no longer be the chief mode of care for clients. To meet staff shortages, managers hired personnel with less educational preparation than the professional nurse and developed on-the-job training programs for auxiliary helpers. The total care method became unfeasible in such situations, and the functional method was developed in response.

Functional Method

The functional nursing method focuses on the jobs to be completed (e.g., bedmaking, temperature measurement). In this task-oriented approach, personnel with less preparation than the professional nurse perform less complex care requirements. It is based on a production and efficiency model that gives authority and responsibility to the person assigning the work, for example, the nurse manager. Clearly defined job descriptions, procedures, policies, and lines of communication are required. The functional approach to nursing is economical and efficient and permits centralized direction and control. Its disadvantages are fragmentation of care and the possibility that nonquantifiable aspects of care, such as meeting the client's emotional needs, may be overlooked.

Team Nursing

In the early 1950s, Eleanor Lambertsen (1953) and her colleagues proposed a system of team nursing to overcome the fragmentation of care resulting from the task-oriented functional approach and to meet increasing demands for professional nurses created by advances in technological aspects of care. **Team nursing** is the delivery of individualized nursing care to clients by a nursing team led by a professional nurse. A nursing team consists of registered nurses, licensed (or registered) practical nurses, and assistive personnel. This team is responsible for providing coordinated nursing care to a group of clients during an eight- or 12-hour shift.

With the advent of managed care, team nursing is experiencing a resurgence. In this revisited form of team nursing, licensed nursing personnel (RNs and LPNs) are frequently paired with assistive personnel. The licensed nurse retains responsibility and authority for client care but delegates appropriate tasks to the assistive personnel. Contemporary proponents of this model believe the team approach increases the efficiency of the licensed nurse. Opponents state that inpatients' high acuity of illness leaves little to be delegated.

Primary Nursing

Primary nursing, a system in which one nurse is responsible for total care of a number of clients 24 hours a day, seven days a week, was introduced at the Loeb Center for Nursing and Rehabilitation, the Bronx, New York, in the early 1960s. It is a method of providing comprehensive, individualized, and consistent care.

Primary nursing uses the nurse's technical knowledge and management skills. The primary nurse assesses and prioritizes each client's needs, identifies nursing diagnoses, develops a plan of care with the client, and evaluates the effectiveness of care. Associates provide care, but the primary nurse coordinates it and communicates information about the client's health to other nurses and other health professionals. Primary nursing encompasses all aspects of the professional role, including teaching, advocacy, decision making, and continuity of care. The primary nurse is the first-line manager of the client's care with all its inherent accountabilities and responsibilities.

Differentiated Practice

As with managed care and case management, differentiated nursing practice seeks to provide quality care at an affordable cost. The model is developed within each health-care institution by the nurses employed there. The institution must first identify the nursing competencies required by the clients within the specific practice environment. This model further requires the delineation of roles among both licensed nursing personnel and nursing support personnel. This enables nurses to progress and assume roles and responsibilities appropriate to their level of experience, capability, and education.

Partners in Practice

Partners in practice is another system associated with managed care. The partners-in-practice system is a partnership established between an experienced senior registered nurse and an individual who supports the nurse as a technical assistant. The technical assistant is assigned to the nurse, not to a caseload of clients. By delegating tasks to the technical assistant, the registered nurse is, therefore, able to concentrate on providing professional client care.

The registered nurse is responsible for defining the role, standards, and nursing care activities. By providing direction and supervision, the registered nurse is also accountable for the overall care delivered in the partnership. An official contract is used to confirm the relationship, and both members are paired on the same time schedule.

Health-Care Economics

Although efforts have been made to control the costs of health care, these costs continue to increase. Employers, legislators, insurers, and health-care providers continue to collaborate in efforts to resolve the issues surrounding how to best finance health-care costs. Among these efforts, Canada has implemented some cost-containment strategies, including health-promotion and illness prevention activities, integrated systems, and supplementary insurance mechanisms.

Various commissions have been tasked to investigate and make recommendations for gaining control of health expenditures and reforming the system (e.g., National Forum on Health; Kirby Commission, Romanow Commission).

CHAPTER HIGHLIGHTS

- The health-care delivery system is a large, complex organization comprising a variety of agencies and many health-care professionals.
- Health-care delivery services can be categorized as primary, secondary, or tertiary, and generally, they can also be grouped by the type of service: (1) health promotion and illness prevention, (2) diagnosis and treatment, and (3) rehabilitation.
- Health care must be considered a right of all people.
- Hospitals provide a wide variety of services on an inpatient and outpatient basis. Hospitals can be categorized as acute care or long-term care. Many other settings, such as clinics, offices, and day-care centres, also provide care.
- Various providers of health care coordinate their skills to assist a client. Their mutual goal is to restore a client's health and promote wellness.
- The many factors affecting health-care delivery include health-care consumers, women's health, the increasing number of elderly people, advances in knowledge and technology, economic factors, fragmentation of care, increased costs, health care of the homeless, uneven distribution of health services, demographic changes, and access to health care.
- There are a number of frameworks for client health care, including managed care, case management, patient-focused care, and partners in practice.

READINGS AND REFERENCES

Suggested Readings

Akaho, E., Coffin, G. D., Kusano, T., Locke, L., & Okamoto, T. (1998). A proposed optimal health-care system based on a comparative study conducted between Canada and Japan. *Canadian Journal of Public Health, 89*, 301–307.

By comparing health-care systems in Canada and Japan, both of which have a universal health-care system for their citizens, the authors sought to describe an optimal health-care system. Data and information obtained were tabulated and compared from the standpoint of the effectiveness of the health insurance system and the feasibility of its application. Some of the recommendations made for an optimal health-care system include establishment of minimal user fees, centralized rational decision-making processes, private delivery system of health care, centralized computer-aided patient record system, insurance monitoring system, patient education, and physician guidelines.

Mildon, B. (1998). Hospital without walls. *Canadian Nurse, 94*(9), 31–34.

Mildon describes a new model of care delivery called the NCM (Nursing Care Manager) model that involves NCMs in group practice and puts the community nurse in charge. The model includes elements that incorporate control over practice (autonomy), accountability, continuity of care, collaborative practice, and continuing education.

Related Research

Clarke, H., & Beddome, G. (1993). Public health nurses' vision of their future reflects changing paradigms. *Image, 25*(4), 305–310.

Neidig, J., Megel, M., & Koehler, K. (1992). The critical path: An evaluation of the applicability of nursing case management in the NICU. *Neonatal Network, 11*, 45–52.

Selected References

Abrams, W., Beers, M., & Berkow, R. (Eds.). (1995). *The Merck manual of geriatrics* (2nd ed.). Whitehouse Station, NJ: Merck.

Aday, L. A. (1993). *At risk in America: The Health and Health Care Needs of Vulnerable Populations in the United States.* San Francisco: Jossey-Boss.

American Academy of Nursing Panel on Women's Health. (1997). Women's health and women's health care: Recommendations of the 1996 AAN expert panel on women's health. *Nursing Outlook, 45*(1), 7–15.

Canadian Institute for Health Information. (2001). *Health Care in Canada*. Ottawa, ON: Author.

Canadian Nurses Association. (2000, Feb). Cultural Diversity—Changes and Challenges. *Nursing Now, Issues and Trends in Canadian Nursing*, #7. Ottawa, ON: Author.

Cohen, E. L., & Cesta, T. G. (1993). *Nursing case management: From concepts to evaluation.* St. Louis, MO: Mosby-Year Book.

Consumers' Association of Canada. (1989). *Consumer Rights to Health Care*. Ottawa: Author.

Cowan, C., Braden, B., McDonnell, P., & Sivarajan, L. (1996). Business, households, and government: Health spending, 1994. *Health Care Financing Review, 17*(4), 157–161.

Deber, R., Hastings, J., & Thompson, G. (1991). Health care in Canada: Current trends and issues. *Journal of Public Health Policy, 12*, 72–82.

Etheredge, L., Jones, S., & Lewis, L. (1996). What is driving health system change? *Health Affairs, 15*(4), 93–101.

Hadley, E. (1996). Nursing in the political and economic marketplace: Challenges for the 21st century. *Nursing Outlook, 44*(1), 6–10.

Hansten, R., & Washburn, M. J. (1998). Professional practice: Facts and impact. *American Journal of Nursing, 98*, 42–45.

Health Canada. (1992). *Canada Health Act Annual Report*. Ottawa: Author.

Hudson, T. (1997). Senior surge: Are you ready? *Hospitals & Health Networks, 71*(7), 51–56.

Ignani, K. (1995). Navigating the health care marketplace. *Health Affairs, 14*(1), 221–225.

Jonas, S. (1992). *An introduction to the U.S. health care system*. (3rd ed.). New York: Springer.

Lairson, D., Schulmeier, G., Begley, C., Aday, L., Coyle, Y., & Slater, C. (1997). Managed care and community-oriented care: Conflict or complement? *Journal of Health Care for the Poor and Underserved, 8*(1), 36–55.

Lambertsen, E. C. *Nursing Team—Organization and Functioning.* Published for the Division of Nursing Education by the Bureau of Publications, Teachers College, Columbia University, 1953.

Lee, P., & Estes, C. L. (Eds.). (1990). *The nation's health.* Boston, MA: Jones & Bartlett.

Marelli, T. M. (1993). *The nurse manager's survival guide: Practical answers to everyday problems.* St. Louis, MO: Mosby-Year Book.

McGillis-Hall, L. (1997). Staff mix models: Complementary or substitution roles for nurses. *Nursing Administration Quarterly, 21*(2), 31–39.

McGivern, D. O. (1996). The evolution of primary care nursing. In M. D. Mozey & D. O. McGivern (Eds.), *Nurses, nurse practitioners.* Boston, MA: Little, Brown.

Smith, L. (1993). The coming health care shakeout. *Fortune, 127*(10), 70–75.

Statistics Canada. (1991). *Population projections for Canada, provinces, and territories: 1989–2011.* Catalogue 91-520. Ottawa: Statistics Canada.

Trossmen, S. (1998). Issues update: Quality managed care: A nursing perspective. *American Journal of Nursing, 98*, 56–58.

Tucker, S., Canobbio, M., Paquette, E., & Wells, M. (1996). *Patient care standards: Collaborative practice planning guides.* Philadelphia, PA: Mosby.

World Health Organization. (1981). *Global strategy for health for all by the year 2000.* Geneva: Author. Ser. No. 3, 32.

WEBLINKS

Health Canada
http://www.hc-sc.gc.ca/
A site of the federal government, which provides access to national legislation, policy statements, and related health-care information.

Canadian Public Health Association
http://www.cpha.ca
The CPHA advocates for improvements to personal and community health according to the public health principles of disease prevention, health promotion and protection, and healthy public policy.

Canadian Psychologist Association—Strengthening Health Care in Canada
http://www.cpa.ca/strengthening-1.html
The site provides access to a series of information briefs on health care in this country.

Commission on the Future of Health Care in Canada
http://www.healthcarecommission.ca/
Chaired by Roy Romanow, the mandate of the Commission on the Future of Health Care in Canada is "to ensure that our health system meets the challenges of the 21st century." The site provides access to the work of the Commission.

Canadian Healthcare Association
http://www.canadian-healthcare.org/
The Canadian Healthcare Association (CHA) is a federation of provincial and territorial hospital and health organizations across Canada. It represents a broad continuum of care, including acute care; home and community care; long-term care; public health; mental health; palliative care; addiction services; children, youth, and family services; housing services; and professional and licensing bodies.

Canadian Nurses Association
http://www.cna-nurses.ca
The site provides access to the position statements and "Trends and Issues" publications mentioned in this chapter.

Canadian Occupational Health Nurses Association
http://www.cohna-aciist.ca/english/
The site is sponsored by and speaks for Occupational Health Nurses in Canada.

CHAPTER 16

Community-Based Nursing

OBJECTIVES

After completing this chapter, you will be able to:

- Discuss factors influencing health-care reform.
- Identify essential aspects of the Canada Health Act, the *Alma-Ata Declaration,* and the *Report of the National Forum on Health* that address health promotion, illness prevention, and community-based nursing.
- Describe community-based health care.
- Analyze various community-based integrated health-care systems, community initiatives and conditions, and case management.
- List competencies community-based nurses need for practice.
- Explain essential aspects of collaborative health care: definitions, objectives, benefits, and the nurse's role.
- Delineate the role of the nurse in providing continuity of care.
- Differentiate community-based health care settings from traditional settings.
- Compare and contrast community-based nursing and traditional institutional-based nursing.

The health-care system is changing. Escalating health-care costs, expanding technology, changing patterns of demographics, shorter hospital stays, and diminishing access to health care are some of the factors motivating change. One of the greatest changes has been the shift of health-care delivery from institutions into the community and home environments (Coyte & McKeever, 2001). Health care, once considered safe only in hospital settings, is now provided in homes (see Chapter 17) and in ambulatory surgical, rehabilitation, and dialysis centres. Community-based care has been viewed as the solution to the troubles of the health-care system, and although hospitals and other health-care institutions will remain the main components of the health-care system of the future, they will likely have less prominence. Hunt (2001) suggested that by 2010, "70 percent of all nursing care will be provided in the home, with an adjunct increase in the availability of care in the community." Yet, as governments struggle to provide comprehensive health services to Canadians, irrespective of their geographical locations and economic status and at reasonable costs that can be accommodated by the populace, new issues arise. Unsustainable health care, inefficiencies, caregiver burden, and an inability to ensure equity of service across the country are but a few of the issues that remain to be addressed despite the move to community-based care over the past 10 years (Noseworthy, 2000). The trend remains toward an integrated health-care system—one which is community-based, multidisciplinary, and collaborative. The shift from institutional to community-based care also brings changes in the roles and responsibilities of health-care professionals.

Health-Care Reform

Consumers are more frequently concerned about accessing appropriate, cost-effective, and quality health care. While the Canadian health-care system has generally faired well in comparison with others internationally, few would argue that greater changes are necessary to meet growing public concerns, rising costs associated with universal access, and changes in the demographic profile (Attenborough, 1997). The Canadian Public Health Association (CPHA, 2000) has suggested eight building blocks for a reformed health-care system that could be addressed through legislative initiatives and restructuring responses suited to provincial systems. Whatever the approach, there is agreement that care needs to shift from a strict illness focus to the determinants of health and that care will feature service in a community-based environment.

The National Forum on Health (1997) suggests that medicare is sustainable but "requires reaffirmation of the fundamental importance of the single-payer, publicly financed model" (p. 141). It also stated that while health-care services are an important determinant of health, more recognition must go to the other determinants, such as socioeconomic status and education. The brief from the Canadian Nurses Association (CNA) to the Forum argued that a restructured health-care system based on the principles of primary health care is the best way to achieve health for all. Specifically, the CNA recommended that the government commit to a strong publicly funded health-care system with accessibility to essential health services; permit the public to play a greater role in health decisions; emphasize health promotion, health goals, and health research; and adopt a community health approach.

Nurses, too, are affecting health-care reform. Nurses provide a unique perspective on the health-care system because of their constant presence in a variety of settings and their contact both with consumers who receive the benefits of the system's most complex services and with those who have problems with the system's inefficiencies. The greater numbers of advanced practice nurses, including those identified as clinical nurse specialists and nurse practitioners, have resulted in the provision of primary care to many consumers who have previously been neglected—those living in rural areas, the poor, older adults, and women and children. It would appear, however, that the roles of nurses are expanding as they work at their full scope of practice. Through major nurses' organizations, nursing has presented a strong voice in describing what a new system should include and what nursing's contributions should be. Nurses will continue to play a critical role in shaping models of community-based care.

The forerunner for much of Canada's health-care reform was the 1978 World Health Organization (WHO) report *Primary Health Care*. The term *primary health care (PHC)* was coined in the World Health Assembly by the WHO and the United Nations International Children's Emergency Fund (UNICEF).

Over the past 25 years, Canadians have embraced the notions of PHC (1978) and the strategies for health promotion (Epp, 1986) that have arisen from them.

Primary health care is defined as

> *essential health care based on practical, scientifically sound, and socially acceptable methods and technology made universally accessible to individuals and families in the community through their full participation and at a cost that the community and country can afford to maintain at every stage of their development in the spirit of self-reliance and self-determinations.* (WHO, 1978)

PHC incorporates five principles:

1. Accessibility of services
2. A focus on health promotion and disease prevention
3. Public participation
4. An intersectoral approach
5. Use of appropriate technology

Three Strategic Areas for Health-Care Reform

- A publicly funded system best serves the health of Canadians. It offers clear advantages in terms of access to health services and cost containment for the system as a whole.
- The success of the health-care system is critically dependent on a vibrant nursing workforce. Targeted investments for recruitment and retention are recommended.
- A primary health-care approach provides the best framework for health-care reform in Canada. The five principles of primary health care, accessibility, public participation, prevention/health promotion, appropriate technology, and intersectoral co-operation, offer a framework for rebuilding the health-care system in Canada.

Source: Adapted from Canadian Nurses Association. (2000, June). *Framework for Canada's Health-Care System*. Ottawa, ON: Author. Available at www.cna-nurses.ca/pages/policies/pdfs/framework_for_canada_health_system.pdf

Deep concern about health care for the majority of the world's population, specifically low life expectancies, and high mortality rates among children led to the formation of a global health strategy called "primary health care." All members of the WHO were encouraged to take actions toward the attainment of health for all by the year 2000. This declaration, commonly referred to as the *Alma-Ata Declaration*, called for all countries to provide essential services to all people. These services included adequate food supply, safe water, adequate sanitation, maternal and child health care, immunization, the prevention and control of endemic diseases, provision of essential drugs, health education, and the treatment of common diseases and injuries.

The *Alma-Ata Declaration* emphasized health or well-being as a fundamental right and a world wide social goal. It attempted to address inequality in the health status of persons in all countries and to target government responsibility for policies that would promote *economic*, *social*, and *health* development. Both economic and social development were considered basic to the achievement of "health for all." PHC extends beyond the boundaries of traditional health-care services. It involves issues of the environment, agriculture, housing, and other social, economic, and political issues, such as poverty, transportation, unemployment, economic development to sustain the population, and so on. A major feature of PHC is that consumers, governments at all levels, and public institutions should be involved in the planning and delivery of health care.

Similarly, the roles of physicians and nurses change. For PHC to be realized and health-care reform to be successful, there is a need for health care to be organized in such a way that it spans geographical boundaries, bridges service sectors, and creates seamless linkages within and across disciplines serving the public. Additionally, it requires health-care providers, nurses included, to develop specialized skills in working with individuals, families, or communities that enable them to partner with, rather than merely provide care to, clients. Rachlis and Kushner (1994) have suggested that nurses are natural leaders in the move to what was expected to be less costly, community-based, and client-driven care.

PHC differs from primary care (PC) in that although primary care includes the need to practise in the context of family and community, the emphasis is on the delivery of personal health services by clinicians. PC addresses personal health services and not population-focused public health services.

Barnes and colleagues (1995) state that PHC is community driven and involves a "bottom-up" approach that requires active community involvement in making decisions to improve health. It is community based. PC, on the other hand, is expert driven and involves a "top-down" approach by health professionals who advise individuals and communities about what is best for their health. Other differences are shown in Table 16.1.

There are also similarities between PHC and PC. Both systems acknowledge the prevention and promotion components of health and well-being. Both systems strive for universal access to and affordability of health care, support empowerment of the client, and target those at risk for preventable health problems.

Consumers are also effecting major changes in health-care delivery systems as they increase their knowledge of health promotion, illness prevention, and treatment options. Consumers have had increasing influences on the health-care system, seeking information from nontraditional sources and expecting collaboration and a greater part of decision making about their own, their families, and, to some extent, their communities' health. These values and expectations are reflected in the *Consumer Rights to Health Care* and support the need for community-focused health-care services.

Health-care measures include those that promote wellness and prevent disease, as well as restoration and measures for illness intervention. As stated earlier, some nursing care is moving to the community environment, including both home and community settings for care. With this move has come a number of ways of thinking about community-based care. Some nurses view community care as the umbrella under which all services offered outside the hospital are included, while others think of it as one of the many distinct health-care services provided to clients. These differences in viewpoints attest to the importance of distinguishing community-based nursing and the competencies required for practice.

TABLE 16.1 Differences between Primary Care and Primary Health Care

Primary Care	Primary Health Care
■ Community participation is provider directed.	■ Community participation is client directed.
■ The professional's role is expert, provider, authority, team leader.	■ The professional's role is facilitator, consultant, resource.
■ Collaboration occurs among members of the health-care team.	■ Collaboration goes beyond the health-care sector.
■ The individual or family is the focus.	■ The community or some aggregate is the focus.
■ Access is limited.	■ Access is universal.
■ Health care is available within given health-care institutions.	■ Health care is available where people live and work.
■ Empowerment is a provider-assisted process.	■ Empowerment is a collaborative, enabling process.

Source: Adapted from D. Barnes, C. Eribes, T. Juarbe, M. Nelson, S. Proctor, L. Sawyer, M. Shaul, & A. I. Meleis. Primary health care and primary care: A confusion of philosophies. *Nursing Outlook, 43*(1), 7–16.

Community-Based Health Care

Community-based health care (CBHC) is a system that provides health-related services within the context of people's daily lives—that is, in places where people spend their time in the community, for example, in the home, in shelters, in long-term care residences, at work, in schools, in senior citizen centres, in ambulatory settings, and in hospitals. Care is provided to individuals who have common needs and live within a defined geographical region. The care is directed toward a specific *group* within the community. The group may be established by a geographical boundary, an employer, a school district, or a specific medical need or category. In contrast to the traditional health-care system that focused primarily on the ill and the injured, community-based care is holistic. It involves a broad range of services designed not only to restore health but also to promote health, prevent illness, and protect the public.

To be truly effective, a CBHC system needs to (1) provide easy access to the system, (2) be flexible in responding to the care needs that individuals, families, groups, and communities identify, (3) promote continuity of care between and among health-care agencies through improved communication mechanisms, and (4) provide appropriate support for family caregivers.

Although the course of change in health care is not entirely clear, the Pew Health Professions Commission has identified nine characteristics needed to build a new system. According to Romanow (2002), the future health care system will:

1. Establish a new Canadian health covenant as a tangible statement of Canadians' values and a guiding force for our publicly funded health-care system.
2. Create a Health Council of Canada to facilitate collaborative leadership in health.
3. Modernize the Canada Health Act by expanding coverage and renewing its principles.
4. Clarify coverage by distinguishing between direct and ancillary health services, and change practices contrary to the spirit of medicare.
5. Provide stable, predictable and long-term funding through a new dedicated cash-only transfer for medicare.
6. Address immediate issues through targeted funding.

These changes in the health-care system reflect the trends predicted in community health nursing practice and include further focus on acute and high needs populations, decreased services to well or low-risk families with corresponding limited case finding by nurses, a move to community development activities, further need for discharge planning, greater complexity and acuity of individuals cared for in the home environment, and a change in nursing working conditions, such as the use of extended hours, greater population specialization, increasing skill mix, and closer involvement with primary-care team members.

In Canada, health-care delivery is a provincial concern, and the manner in which health regions deliver community-based care differs widely across provinces. Indeed, even spending (Coyte & McKeever, 2001) varies dramatically. However, some features are common to all regions, including:

- A focus on health promotion and maintenance, education and management, and coordination and continuity of care within the community environment
- A focus on the health needs of individuals, families, and communities
- Integration of community-based care into larger health system offerings

Approaches

The health-care system as a whole is undergoing organizational and philosophical changes. Greater emphasis is being placed on the general health of the community as a whole, in contrast to the traditional system that focused on care of the ill and the injured. Various approaches are emerging to address this concept. Some of these are an integrated health-care system, community initiatives, community coalitions, managed care, case management, and outreach programs using lay health workers.

An *integrated health-care system* is one that makes all levels of care available in an integrated form—primary care (health promotion and disease prevention), secondary care, and tertiary care. Its goals are to facilitate continuity of care, recovery, positive health outcomes, and the long-term benefits of modifying harmful lifestyles through health promotion and disease prevention. In many parts of the country, hospitals are reflecting this concept by regional health authorities changing their names to "health-care organization" or "integrated health-care system." Movement of clients between settings is coordinated such that disruption in service is minimized. This type of system is sometimes referred to as "seamless care."

Community initiatives are being sponsored by some hospitals or local community agencies. These initiatives, called "healthy cities" and "healthier communities," involve members of the community to establish health priorities, set measurable goals, and determine actions to reach these goals. While health-care professionals and organizations may be involved in these activities, the goal is for the community to assume the direction, coordination, and implementation of health-care services in consultation with its resident members.

Community coalitions bring together individuals and groups for the shared purpose of improving the community's health (Butterfoss, Goodman, & Wandersman, 1994). Nurses are major participants and contributors in these coalitions and often assume leadership positions. Community coalitions may focus on a single or multifaceted problem and may be health promotive, illness and injury preventive, or restorative in service. Examples include establishment of an abuse program, a gang prevention program, an older adults assessment program, or an immunization program for a high-risk group.

In *managed care*, a popular model in health-care restructuring, health-care providers (hospitals, physicians, nurse practitioners, and so on) join together to meet health needs across the care continuum (see Chapter 15 for further details).

Case management is an integrative health-care model that tracks client care through a variety of care settings to ensure care continuity.

Weil and Karls (cited in McWilliam, 2000) addressed potential duplication and care fragmentation while ensuring clients receive "services in a supportive, effective, and cost-efficient manner" (p. 146). Three models of case management are used in Canada:

1. *The brokerage or service management model*, wherein health professionals are designated to assess client needs, implement service, and evaluate client progress while ensuring cost-effectiveness and, ideally, cost reduction
2. *Integrated team or provider-driven model*, wherein one professional provider is designated as primary caregiver to provide the leadership for care, while a team delivers services with the goal of achieving care continuity
3. *Self-managed care or client-centred model*, wherein clients assume, with caregiver support, personal control over care decisions

Outreach programs using lay health workers are a method of linking underserved or high-risk populations with the formal health-care system. They can minimize or reduce barriers to health care, increase access to services, and thus improve the health status of the community, especially with client groups with special needs, such as immigrant populations, single parents, and the homeless. They involve partnerships between nurses and members of the community. Interested and committed lay health workers who will assist their neighbours through outreach networks are identified. Nurses often provide training, consultation, and support to these individuals, who then assume responsibility for contact with these individuals and groups.

Community-Based Settings

Traditionally, community nursing services have been provided in regional and provincial/territorial health departments; in schools (school nursing); in workplaces (occupational nursing); and in homes (home health care and hospice nursing). Over the years, numerous other settings, many of which were discussed in Chapter 15, have been established. These include day-care centres, senior centres, storefront clinics, homeless shelters, mental health centres, crisis centres, drug rehabilitation programs, ambulatory care centres, and so on.

More recent settings for community-based nursing practice include *nurse-managed* community nursing centres, wellness programs, parish nursing, and telehealth projects.

Community Nursing Centres

Community nursing centres provide primary care to specific populations and are staffed by nurse practitioners and community health nurses. Although the nurses are the primary providers of care to clients visiting the centre, a physician's consultation is available as needed. Nursing centres may be located in schools, workplaces, or other sites in the community. However, as Murphy (1995) points out, nursing centres not only need to provide an actual site for care but must also support nurse-managed services across the health-care continuum, that is, services to clients in their home, community, hospital, or nursing home.

There are various categories of community nursing centres (Riesch, 1992):

- *Community outreach centres:* free-standing clinics are similar to the traditional community public health clinics
- *Institution-based centres:* associated with a large parent organization, such as a hospital, corporation, or university or college
- *Wellness centres:* provide such services as health promotion, health maintenance, education, counselling, and screening

Murphy (1995) suggests that nursing centres must be considered not only as a setting for care but also as a concept for the delivery of care which brings the nurse into direct contact with individuals, families, and the community in a way that maximizes the health of diverse populations and contributes to the notion of a health-care continuum. Hunt (2001) proposes a conceptualization of community-based care, which includes both acute care and community- or population-focused care as elements within its definition, while others place community-based care between acute care and population-focused care. It would be important for nurses to consider the perspective of care within the province/territory or health-care region with respect to community-based practice because the competencies for practice may differ. The following sections represent care exclusive of acute care or community/population-focused practice.

Wellness Programs

These programs, often staffed and managed by nurses, are located in the workplace, schools, or other community sites. Wellness programs are holistic in nature, focusing on the whole person, including relationships with the environment and other people.

Parish Nursing

"The parish nurse bridges spirituality and community health" (Barnum, 1996, p. 12). Parish nursing has become more common as faith communities seek to sustain and improve the health of their members. Krasnansky (1999) delineated parish practice as one which integrates client values, faith beliefs, and practices within a local community context. The International Parish Nurse Resource Centre describes the roles of the parish nurse as follows:

- *Personal health counsellor,* who discusses health issues and problems with individuals and makes home, hospital, and nursing home visits as needed
- *Health educator,* who educates and supports individuals through health education activities that promote an understanding of the relationship among values, attitudes, lifestyle, faith, and well-being
- *Referral source,* who acts as a liaison to other congregational and community resources
- *Facilitator,* who recruits and coordinates volunteers within the congregation and develops support groups
- *Integrator* of faith and health
- *Community assessor and evaluator,* who uses health promotion, illness prevention, treatment, and rehabilitative services to improve the health of parish members

Initially, parish nurses were volunteers as this service was becoming established, but now, some are employees paid by the congregation or an affiliated institution, such as a health system or community agency.

Ryan (1997, p. 4) stated that the "intent of parish nursing is to create the environment within which the parish nurse, patient, family, and congregation can interact, understand, and care for one another in light of their relationships to God, themselves, each other, the congregation, and the community around them.... [Further], parish nursing has organized and prepared nurses to perform the set of skills called for in the practice and self-management of health-related behaviours—the provider skills called for... in *Healthy People 2000.*"

Schools

School health services are performed at the individual, family, and community levels in order to provide comprehensive school health services. This includes activities both within the school and community environments that are directed to the health and well-being of children and youth, primarily through health promotion and illness prevention strategies. This activity is multisectoral in nature, drawing on the knowledge and skills of school personnel, community health nurses, families, and other community members. Normally, the acute-care needs of children are not addressed through school programs, except at a collective level for risk reduction and referral.

Occupational Health Settings

Large corporations often provide health services to employees in the workplace in an effort to maintain their health and safety. This is increasingly a multidisciplinary activity that includes physicians, occupational health nurses, human resource members, and specialized physical and occupational therapists. Nurses may be charged with the development of programs aimed at safety and accident prevention, the prevention and/or control of contagious diseases, lifestyle modification programs, and acute emergency care. Increasingly, health-care providers in the community have undertaken entrepreneurial activities to contract services for several small businesses or to offer specialized services in the community to which employees have access.

Home Care

Home care has been defined as "an array of services enabling Canadians, incapacitated in whole or in part, to live at home, often with the effect of preventing, delaying, or substitution for long-term care or acute care alternatives" (Health Canada Federal/Provincial/Territorial Working Group on Home Care cited in McWilliam, 2000, p. 143). Whether provided through the public system or private agency, home care has become a reality, rather than an option, for individuals and families. The home-care nurse provides treatment and rehabilitative services to individuals and families but increasingly looks at the collective needs of clients to assess the need for larger system responses to home- and chronic-care services within the community setting. For further information on this growing practice focus, see Chapter 17.

Telehealth Services

Telehealth projects use communication and information technology to provide health information and health-care services to people in rural, remote, or underserviced areas. Video conferences or "video clinics" enable health-care workers to provide distant consultation to assess and treat ambulatory clients who have a variety of health-care needs. These video conferences are similar to any outpatient clinic visit, except that the client and health-care specialist are kilometres apart. A related development to telehealth is *telenursing*, in which nurses provide client teaching and health promotion to distant clients. Clark (2000) suggested that nurses must learn to use technology in a manner that can enhance the quality of care but must also remember the essence of nursing care lies in the relationship established. In reference to technology, she included telecommunication strategies, access to knowledge and decision support, the Internet, and the roles that nurses play as both information brokers and information generators.

Community-Based Nursing

Community-based nursing (CBN) is nursing care directed toward a specific population or group within the community; care may be provided to individuals or groups, and it is designed to meet the needs of people as they move between and among care settings. Hunt (1998), however, suggested that community-based nursing is not defined by the setting but, instead, by "a philosophy of practice." Hunt (2001) placed clients in their natural environments, in the context of their families and communities. Practice is seen as autonomous, with decisions for care made in collaboration between the nurse and client and made congruent with personal and societal values and beliefs of both. Several components make up community-based care, including:

- Self-care, with the client and family assuming primary decision making for health care
- A focus on preventive care, whether at primary, secondary, or tertiary level
- A realization that care must be provided within the context of the community; that health and the social environment are interactive and must take into account the culture, values, and resources of the individual, family, and community
- The need for continuity of care to counteract the fragmentation of care currently existing in the health-care system
- Collaborative care among health-care providers and across sectors requiring shared responsibilities for communication to the end that the client's health can be optimized, regardless of the level of health currently in effect

The level of care provided may be primary, secondary, or tertiary. (See Table 15.2 on page 248, for descriptions of these levels.)

Community-based nursing is akin to primary health care and has been differentiated from community public health nursing. Community-based nursing care is not confined to one practice setting but extends beyond institutional boundaries and involves a network of nursing services, such as those that might be found in: nursing wellness centres, ambulatory care, acute care, long-term care, and home health and hospice services. For example, a nurse case manager may be involved in (1) visiting a newly admitted client in the hospital to take a detailed nursing history, confer with the primary nurse, and begin discharge planning; or (2) making several home visits to monitor a client recently transferred from a hospital to a long-term care

Figure 16.1 Community-based nursing meets the needs of people as they move between and among case settings

agency to discuss the client's progress with the nursing staff. In addition, this case manager may be involved in several consultative telephone calls to other health professionals (physicians, social workers, respiratory therapists, and so on) and other calls to clients who are managing self-care independently but who may need support. Similarly, nurses may work with groups to access services specific to their needs but not readily available in their community.

Competencies Required for Community-Based Care

The CNA in its document *Nursing with Communities—Making the Transition* suggested that the knowledge and skills required of community nurses has steadily grown since public health certificates were first offered in Canadian universities in 1920.

Nurses practising in community-based integrated health-care systems will need to have specific knowledge and skills. The Pew Health Professions Commission identified 17 competencies that future health professionals will require. Nursing skills in acute care and community-based settings are different, even though nurses in each setting use direct care and administrative, educative, and consultative skill sets in their practice. These competencies give direction to schools preparing future health professionals for practice. Nurses will need to know the following: (1) determinants of a healthy community, (2) primary and secondary preventive strategies for people of all ages, (3) health-promotion strategies for individuals, families, and communities, (4) collaborative and interdisciplinary teamwork, (5) determinants of an accessible, cost-effective, integrated health-care system, (6) decision-making processes that involve active participation by consumers and balance cost and quality care, (7) information management, and (8) differing cultural values. Community-based nurses will also require up-to-date clinical skills and knowledge of complex technology.

Barnes et al. (1995) point out that from a primary health-care perspective, nurses will need to be prepared for multiple levels of practice and will need increased clinical preparation in and with communities, as well as with the elderly and vulnerable populations within community settings. Nurses will also need education in public health policy and strategies to influence and effect change.

Collaborative Health Care

Collaboration among health-care professionals becomes increasingly important as the boundaries of each health-care profession change.

Labonte (1993) suggested that collaboration is a way of working together that addresses an interdependence, collective responsibility, and equality in the relationships directed to client needs (at individual, family, and community levels).

RESEARCH NOTE

What Are the Learning Needs of Nurses Preparing to Change from Acute to Community-Based Care?

With managed care and cost containment, nurses are moving from acute-care environments to community-based health-care settings. Although the acute-care nurses who are entering these new community-based environments are highly experienced, they may perceive that they lack community-based knowledge and nursing skills. On the basis of these perceptions, 879 nurses representing multiple nursing specialties and practice areas completed a 56-item survey to assess skills needed to function in acute care, home care, and community-based settings. Results indicated that for non-acute-care settings, the skills required to practise proficiently included wound care and dressing, knowledge of community resources, diabetes education, client and family advocacy, communication with third-party payers, and neonatal care.

Implications: Nurses leaving acute care to practise in community-based settings may require some retraining and extended orientations to enhance their proficiency in these environments. Schools of nursing should begin modifying their curricula to include increased emphasis on community-based nursing education and provide opportunities for students to practise in these settings. Nursing administrators should coordinate staff development efforts that meet the needs of staff who might be making the transition from acute to community-based settings.

Source: Bryan, Y., Bayley, E., Grindel, C., Kingston, M., Tuck, M., & Wood, L. (1997). Preparing to change from acute to community-based care: Learning needs of hospital-based nurses. *Journal of Nursing Administration, 27*(5), 35–44.

The Nurse as a Collaborator

Nurses collaborate with clients, peers, and other health-care professionals. They frequently collaborate about client care but may also be involved, for example, in collaborating on bioethical issues, legislation, health-related research, and with professional organizations. The box on page 273 outlines selected aspects of the nurse's role as a collaborator.

Prescott and coauthors (1987, 1991) view collaboration as important in the development of professional nursing practice and as a way to improve client outcomes. To fulfill a collaborative role, nurses need to assume accountability and increased authority in practice areas. Education is integral to ensuring that the members of each professional group understand the collaborative nature of their roles, specific contributions, and the importance of working together. Each professional needs to understand how an integrated delivery system centres on the client's health-care needs, rather than on the particular care given by one group.

Pew Commission Competencies for Future Practitioners

1. Care for the community's health
2. Expand access to effective care
3. Provide contemporary clinical care
4. Emphasize primary care
5. Participate in coordinated care
6. Ensure cost-effective and appropriate care
7. Practise prevention
8. Involve patients and families in decision-making processes
9. Promote healthy lifestyles
10. Access and use technology appropriately
11. Improve the health-care system
12. Manage information
13. Understand the role of the physical environment
14. Practise counselling on ethical issues
15. Accommodate expanded accountability
16. Participate in a racially and culturally diverse society
17. Continue to learn

Source: Adapted from deTornyay, R. (1992). Reconsidering nursing education: The report of the Pew Health Professions Commission. *Journal of Nursing Education, 31*, 296–301.

Competencies Basic to Collaboration

Key elements necessary for collaboration include effective communication skills, mutual respect, trust, and a decision-making process.

Communication Collaborating to solve complex problems requires effective communication skills.

Effective communication can occur only if the involved parties are committed to understanding each other's professional roles and appreciating each other as individuals. Additionally, they must be sensitive to differences among communication styles (Tannen, 1990). Instead of focusing on distinctions, a group of professionals needs to centre on their common ground—the client's needs.

Mutual Respect and Trust *Mutual respect* occurs when two or more people show or feel honour or esteem toward one another. *Trust* occurs when a person is confident in the actions of another person. Both mutual respect and trust imply a mutual process and outcome. They must be expressed both verbally and nonverbally.

Decision Making The decision-making process at the team level involves shared responsibility for the outcome. Obviously, to create a solution the team must follow each step of the decision-making process, beginning with a clear definition of the problem. Team decision making must be directed at the objectives of the specific effort. It requires full consideration and respect of diverse viewpoints. Members must be able to verbalize their perspectives in a nonthreatening environment.

An important aspect of decision making is the interdisciplinary team focusing on the client's priority needs and organizing interventions accordingly. The discipline best able to address the client's needs is given priority in planning and is responsible for providing its interventions in a timely manner. For example, a social worker may first direct attention to a client's social needs when these needs interfere with the client's ability to respond to therapy. Nurses, by the nature of their holistic practice, are often able to help the team identify priorities and areas requiring further attention.

Continuity of Care

A major responsibility of the nurse is to ensure continuity of care. **Continuity of care** is the coordination of health-care services by health-care providers for clients moving from one health-care setting to another and between and among health-care professionals. "It requires coordination and linkages across time, settings, providers, and consumers of health care" (Anderson & Helms cited in Sparbel & Anderson 2000). Continuity ensures uninterrupted health services as the client moves from one level of care to another, for example, from an acute-care hospital to home, or from home to a long-term care facility. This is of increasing importance as changes in the health-care system, nursing roles, and interprofessional relationships push for a "common understanding of continuity of care" (Sparbel & Anderson, 2000). In an integrated review of continuity of care, Sparbel and Anderson found that while the concept was not consistently nor well defined, it was "affected by a variety of communication and systems factors" (p. 22). To provide continuity of care, nurses need to:

- Involve the client and families or significant other in all phases (assessment, planning, implementing, and evaluating care) of entry and exit from one setting to another.
- Collaborate and communicate with other health-care professionals as needed.
- Ensure that required services for positive outcomes are both available and coordinated to provide seamless care (Sparbel & Anderson, 2000).

Discharge Planning

Discharge planning is frequently viewed as synonymous with continuity of care, although a broad range of evaluative methods used at individual, family, and community

The Nurse as a Collaborator

With Clients:

- Acknowledges, supports, and encourages clients' active involvement in health-care decisions
- Encourages a sense of client autonomy and an equal position with other members of the health-care team
- Helps clients set goals and objectives for health care that are mutually agreed upon
- Provides client consultation in a collaborative fashion

With Peers:

- Shares personal expertise with other nurses and elicits the expertise of others to ensure quality client care
- Develops a sense of trust and mutual respect with peers that recognizes their unique contributions

With Other Health-Care Professionals:

- Recognizes the contribution that individual members of the interdisciplinary team can make by virtue of their expertise and view of the situation
- Listens to each individual's views
- Shares health-care responsibilities in exploring options, setting goals, and making decisions with clients and families
- Participates in collaborative interdisciplinary research to increase knowledge of a clinical problem or situation

With Professional Nursing Organizations:

- Seeks out opportunities to collaborate with and within professional organizations
- Serves on committees in local, provincial/territorial, and national nursing organizations or specialty groups
- Supports professional organizations in political action to create solutions for professional and health-care concerns

With Legislators:

- Offers expert opinions on legislative initiatives related to health care
- Collaborates with other health-care providers and consumers on health-care legislation to best serve the needs of the public

levels are employed in the interest of quality improvement. Traditionally, discharge planning has been viewed as the process of preparing a client to leave one level of care for another within or outside the current health-care agency. It is focused at the individual client and family level. Within a facility, it can occur from one unit to another. For example, a client with a cerebral vascular accident may move from a medical unit to a rehabilitation unit, or a client with multiple trauma may move from emergency to an intensive care unit (ICU).

Traditional discharge planning has been considered as discharge from the hospital to home. However, discharges occur among many other settings. Clients may move from hospital to long-term care agencies, from rehabilitation centres to home, from home health-care settings to hospitals, and so on.

Each agency generally has its own policies and procedures related to discharge. Many agencies have *discharge planners*, a health or social services professional who coordinates the transition and acts as a link between the discharging agency and the receiving facility. Often, a nurse assumes this responsibility of providing continuity of care.

Discharge planning needs to begin when a client is admitted to an agency, especially in hospitals where length of stays are considerably shortened. Effective discharge planning involves (1) ongoing assessment to obtain comprehensive information about the client's ongoing needs, (2) statements of nursing diagnoses, and (3) plans to ensure the client's and caregivers' needs are met. In some situations, discharge planning necessitates health-team conferences and family conferences. At a health-team conference, health-team professionals focus on ways to individualize

FOCUS ON CRITICAL THINKING

Cathy is a registered nurse working in a public health clinic within a large urban centre. She works primarily with young adults and new mothers, both in the school system and within the clinic setting.

1. Review the principles and components of primary health care. What gaps do you identify?
2. What specific skills are required to intervene at the community level that might differ from those needed at the individual level?
3. What is the role of environmental factors in promoting the health of individuals?

See Appendix A for answers to these questions.

care for the client. At a family conference, both health professionals and the family discuss family issues related to the client. Both types of conferences give the client, family, and health-care professionals the opportunity to mutually plan care and set goals.

Nurses preparing to send clients home need to assess the following parameters:

- Client's personal and health data
- Client's knowledge of disease process(es), including signs and symptoms, treatment, and services
- Client's ability to perform the activities of daily living
- Any physical, cognitive, or other functional limitations the client may have
- Caregiver's responses and abilities
- Adequacy of the client's financial resources
- Community supports
- Hazards or barriers that the home environment presents
- Need for health-care assistance in the home

It is important that assessment focus equally on both strengths and deficits of the client's abilities, home, family, and community environments. Since all these factors play a part in the optimal care of the client, the nurse needs to build on strengths while attending to the deficits that currently hamper optimal health. Unless the goal of care is health and functioning, care provided will not be comprehensive.

The diagnoses and database establish nursing activities needed before the client is discharged. These activities most often include (1) teaching the client to cope with continuing self-care at home, and (2) a home-care referral.

Clients need help to understand their situation, to make health-care decisions, and to learn new health behaviours. Because of today's shortened hospital stays, it is often unrealistic to teach clients everything they need to know. Referral to a home health agency for follow-up teaching may be necessary. Details about effective teaching strategies are provided in Chapter 29.

Referrals

Regardless of the setting from and to which clients are moving, the referral process is a systematic problem-solving approach that helps clients to use resources that meet their health-care needs. The process involves knowledge of community resources and an ability to solve problems, set priorities, coordinate, and collaborate (McGuire, Gerber, & Clemen-Stone, 1996). McWilliams (2000, p. 146) noted that "accessing, coordinating and monitoring the multiple services and providers" involved in care, especially when the client moves to the community, is both complex and costly.

Referrals need to present as much information as possible about the client and the hospitalization. Most agencies in the current setting have well-established protocols and detailed referral forms. The assessment guide opposite can also be used as a guide, but increasingly, nurses must learn to both assess and clearly articulate those assessments to multiple audiences, including families and health-care providers. Beyond this, nurses are often called upon to examine client and family needs at a larger systems level to assist in the deliberations around the provision of health-care services in a community such that the full spectrum of client needs can be addressed and met in the spirit of primary health care. Education in public health policy and strategies to influence and effect change will also be essential.

Canadian Society Notes

Fact	Implications for Nursing Practice
VON's more than 50 different home nursing, health-promotion, support, and other services are delivered to a million Canadians and their families every year through 1,300 communities coast to coast.	Nurses need to be aware of resources that are available to clients under their care so that supplied services meet identified needs.
The Canadian government is strengthening the population health concept, recognizing that it is a major component of the new Health for All Policy for the 21st Century.	Nurses need to be aware that nursing the community is different from nursing *in* the community.The former focuses on population health and the latter on individuals.
A World Health Organization meeting in Canada in 1986 produced the Ottawa Charter for Health Promotion. The Charter highlighted the importance of strengthening community action, reorienting health services to place greater emphasis on health promotion, and the necessity for intersectoral action for health.	The nurse will need to involve individual and community-focused strategies in order to ensure health for all. An individual action may be referring a client to a weight loss program; while a community-focused strategy may be providing support to new mothers who wish to establish a cooperative baby sitting service.

Discharge Planning: Home Assessment Parameters

Personal and Health Database

Age; gender; height and weight; cultural data; a medical history; current health status; surgery

Abilities to Perform Activities of Daily Living (ADLs)

Abilities for dressing; eating; toileting; bathing (tub, shower, sponge); ambulating (with or without aids, such as a cane, crutches, walker, wheelchair); transferring (from bed to chair, in and out of bath, in and out of car); meal preparation; transportation; and shopping

Disabilities/Limitations

Sensory losses (auditory, visual); motor losses (paralysis, amputation); communication disorder; mental confusion or depression; incontinence; and so on

Caregivers' Responses/Abilities

Principal caregiver's relationship to client; thoughts and feelings about client's discharge; expectations for recovery; health and coping abilities; comfort with performing needed care

Financial Resources

Financial resources and needs (note equipment, supplies, medications, special foods required)

Community Supports

Family members, friends, neighbours, volunteers; resources, such as Victorian Order of Nurses; Meals on Wheels; nutrition services; health centres; community health nurses; day programs; legal assistance; home care; respite care

Home Hazard Appraisal

Safety precautions (stairs with or without handrails; lighting in rooms, hallways, stairways; night-lights in hallways or bathroom; grab bars near toilet and tub; firmly attached carpets and rugs); self-care barriers (lack of running water, lack of wheelchair access to bathroom or home, lack of space for required equipment, lack of elevator)
A detailed home hazard appraisal is provided in Chapter 33.

Need for Health-Care Assistance

Home-delivered meals; special dietary needs; volunteers for telephone reassurance, friendly visiting, transportation, shopping; assistance with bathing; assistance with housekeeping; assistance with wound care, ostomies, tubes, intravenous medications, and so on

CHAPTER HIGHLIGHTS

- Health-care costs, access to health care, and the quality of health care are major areas of concern about the current health-care system.
- The CNA position and the *Alma-Ata Declaration* by the WHO have set forth recommendations for health-care reform. All these focus on accessibility of health-care services, health promotion and disease prevention, and steps to consider how health-care costs can be reduced.
- Consumers are also supporting an increased emphasis on health-care measures that promote wellness and do so at individual, family, group, and community levels.
- Community-based health care (CBHC), similar to primary health care, provides health-related services in places where people spend their time—in homes, in shelters, in long-term care residences, at work, in schools, in senior citizen centres, and so on.
- CBHC is consumer driven and involves a broad range of services designed to promote health, prevent illness, restore health, and protect the public.
- Various approaches are emerging to address community-based care. These include an integrated health-care system, community initiatives, community coalitions, managed care, case management, and outreach programs using lay health workers.
- Numerous community-based settings have been established. More recent ones include nurse-managed community nursing centres, wellness programs, and parish nursing.
- Community-based nursing directs nursing care toward a specific population or group. It is not confined to one practice setting; it extends beyond institutional boundaries involving a network of nursing services: nursing wellness centres, ambulatory care, long-term care, home health, and hospice care.
- To practise in community-based health-care systems, nurses will need to learn new knowledge and competencies, such as determinants of a healthy community, primary and secondary preventive strategies, health-promotion strategies, collaborative and interdisciplinary

teamwork, information management, and so on. Education in public health policy and strategies to influence and effect change will also be essential.

- Intrasectoral and intersectoral collaboration are essential components of community-based care. Key elements of collaboration include effective communication skills, mutual respect, trust, a good decision-making process, and conflict management.
- It is predicted that nurses will emerge as community health-care leaders in the future. Because primary health care is directed toward the community and client, nurses' roles will change to those of facilitator, consultant, and resource, rather than those of expert provider and team leader.
- A major responsibility of the nurse is to ensure continuity of care as clients move from one level of care to another.
- Continuity of care extends beyond the individual and includes a series of actions both within and outside an individual agency, which involve (1) discharge planning that begins when clients are admitted to an agency, (2) collaboration with the client and support persons, and (3) interdisciplinary collaboration.

READINGS AND REFERENCES

Suggested Readings

Chalmers, K. I., Bramadat, I. J., & Andrusyszyn, M. (1998). The changing environment of community health practice and education: Perceptions of staff nurses, administrators and educators. *Journal of Nursing Education, 37*(3), 109–117.
Changes within the Canadian context of health necessitate changes in thinking about the preparation of nurses to undertake community practice. These authors present a study to explore the changing context of community practice in Canada.

Oberle, K., & Tenove, S. (2000). Ethical issues in public health nursing. *Nursing Ethics: An International Journal for Health Care Professionals*, 7, 425–438.

Shoultz, J., & Hatcher, P. A. (1997). Looking beyond primary care to primary health care: An approach to community-based action. *Nursing Outlook, 45*(1), 23–26.
Primary care and primary health care are clearly differentiated by these authors. They state that a clearer understanding of the definitions, goals, and principles of primary health care can make nurses more "street wise" and better prepared to advocate health for all with more confidence and direction.

Related Research

Chalmers, K., Bramadat, I. J, Cantin, B., Murnaghan, D., Shuttleworth, E., Scott-Findlay, S., & Tatarym, D. (2001). A smoking reduction and cessation program with registered nurses: Findings and implications for community health nursing. *Journal of Community Health Nursing, 18*, 115–134.

Zotti, M., Brown, P., & Stotts, R. (1996). Community-base nursing versus community health nursing: What does it all mean? *Nursing Outlook, 44*, 211–217.

Selected References

Alpert, H. B., Goldman, L. D., Kilroy, C. M., & Pike, A. W. (1992). 7 Gryzmish: Toward an understanding of collaboration. *Nursing Clinics of North America, 27*, 47–59.

American Nurses Association. (1992). *House of delegates report: 1992 convention, Las Vegas, Nev.* (pp. 104–120). Kansas City, MO: Author.

American Nurses Association. (1994). *Clinician's handbook of preventive services.* Waldorf, MD: American Nurses Publishing.

Angus, J. (2001). The material and social predicaments of home: Women's experiences after aortocoronary bypass surgery. *Canadian Journal of Nursing Research, 33*(2), 27–42.

Attenborough, R. (1997).The Canadian health care system: Development, reform and opportunities for nurses. *Journal of Obsetrics and Gynecology and Neonatal Nursing, 26*(20), 229.

Baggs, J. G., & Schmitt, M. H. (1988). Collaboration between nurses and physicians. *Image: The Journal of Nursing Scholarship, 20*, 145–149.

Baldwin, J. H., Conger, C. O., Abegglen, J. C., & Hill, E. M. (1998). Population-focused and community-based nursing. *Public Health Nursing, 15*, 12–18.

Barnes, D., Eribes, C., Juarbe, T., Nelson, M., Proctor, S., Sawyer, L., Shaul, M., & Meleis, A. I. (1995). Primary health care and primary care: A confusion of philosophies. *Nursing Outlook, 43*(1), 7–16.

Barnum, B. S. (1996). *Spirituality in nursing: From traditional to New Age.* New York: Springer Publishing Company.

Benson, L., & Ducanis, A. (1995). Nurses' perceptions of their role and role conflicts. *Rehabilitation Nursing, 20*, 204–211.

Butterfoss, F. D., Goodman, R. M., & Wandersman, A. (1993). Community coalitions for prevention and health promotion. *Health Education Research, 8*, 315–330.

Canadian Nurses Association. (1996). *Commitment required: making the right changes to improve the health of Canadians.* Ottawa, ON: Author.

Canadian Nurses Association. (1998); Nursing with communities — Making the transition. *Nursing now: issues and trends in Canadan nusing*, 5.

Canadian Public Health Association. (2000). *An ounce of prevention: Strengthening the balance of health care reform.* Board of Directors Issue paper, pp. viii. Ottawa: CPHA.

Chalmers, K. I., Bramadat, I. P., & Andrusyszyn, M. (1998). The changing environment of community health practice and education: Perceptions of staff nurses, administrators, and educators. *Journal of Nursing Education, 37*(3), 109–117.

Chez, N. (1998). Nursing in the field. *American Journal of Nursing, 98*(9), 68–70.

Clark, J. (2000). Old wine in new bottles: Delivering nursing in the 21st century. *Journal of Nursing Scholarship, 32*(1): 11–15.

Coeling, H. V., & Wilcox, J. R. (1994). Steps to collaboration. *Nursing Administration Quarterly, 18*, 44–55.

Coyte, P. C., & McKeever, P. (2001). Home care in Canada: Passing the buck. *Canadian Journal of Nursing Research, 33*(2), 11–25.

deTornyay, R. (1992). Reconsidering nursing education: The report of the Pew Health Professions Commission. *Journal of Nursing Education, 31*(7), 296–301.

Ellis, J. R., & Hartley, C. I. (1995). *Nursing in today's world: Challenges, issues, and trends* (5th ed.). Philadelphia, PA: Lippincott.

Epp, J. (1986). Achieving health for all: A framework for health promotion. Ottawa: Health and Welfare Canada.

Flarey, D. L. (1995). *Redesigning nursing care delivery: Transforming our future*. Philadelphia, PA: Lippincott.

Gruman, F. (1995). An expanded view of health: Implications for how healthcare works. *Healing, 3*(2), 23–26.

Grunfeld, E., Glossop, R., McDowell, I., & Danbrook, C. (1997). Caring for elderly people at home: The consequences to caregivers. *Canadian Medical Association Journal, 157*, 1101–1105.

Healthcare Forum. (1994). *What creates health?* San Francisco, CA: Author.

Henneman, E. A., Lee, J. L., & Cohen, J. I. (1995). Collaboration: A concept analysis. *Journal of Advanced Nursing, 21*, 103–109.

Hunt, R. (1998, October). Community-based nursing: Philosophy or setting? *American Journal of Nursing, 98*(10), 44–48.

Hunt, R. (2001). *Community-based nursing* (2nd ed.). Philadelphia, PA: Lippincott.

Institute of Medicine. (1994). *Defining primary care: An interim report*. Washington, D.C.: National Academy Press.

Krasnansky, S. (1999). Parish nursing—Who are parish nurses? APHA Section Newsletter, *Public Health Nurse*, Spring, 4.

Labonte, R. (1993). *Health promotion and empowerment: Practice frameworks. Issues in health promotion series #3*. Toronto: Centre for Health Promotion, University of Toronto, ParticipACTION.

Laffrey, S. (1994). Guest editorial: Primary care or primary health care: Which model will we choose for community health nursing? *Association of Community Health Nurse Educators Newsletter, 12*(11), 6.

Lamb, G., & Huggins, D. (1990). The professional nursing network. In G. M. Mayer, M. J. Madden, & E. Lowrenz (Eds.), *Patient care delivery models*. Rockville, MD: Aspen.

Marosy, J. P. (1994). Collaboration: A key to future success in long-term home care. *Journal of Home Health Care Practice, 6*, 42–48.

Matas, K. E., & Mermis, W. L. (1994). *Campus wellness project: Year 2*. Report submitted to the Department of Human Resources. Tempe, AZ: Arizona State University.

McEwen, M. (1994). Promoting interdisciplinary collaboration. *Nursing and Health Care, 15*, 304–307.

McFarlane, J., Kelly, E., Rodriguez, R., & Fehir, J. (1994). De madres a madres: Women building community coalitions for health. *Health Care for Women International, 15*, 465–476.

McGuire, S. L., Gerber, D. E., & Clemen-Stone, S. (1996). Meeting the diverse needs of clients in the community: Effective use of the referral process. *Nursing Outlook, 44*(5), 218–222.

McWilliam, C. L. (2000). Homecare: national perspectives and policies. In M. J. Stewart (Ed.), *Community nursing: Promotion Canadians' health* (2nd ed.). (pp. 143–155).

Merlis, M. (2000). Caring for the frail elderly: An international review. *Health Affairs, 19*, 141–149.

Molloy, S. P. (1994). Defining case management. *Home Healthcare Nurse, 12*, 51–54.

Murphy, B. (Ed.). (1995). *Nursing centers: The time is now*. New York: National League for Nursing Press.

Noseworthy, T. W. (2000). Continuing to build on our legacy: National Forum on Health, 1994-1997. In M. J. Stewart (Ed.), *Community Nursing: Promoting Canadians' Health* (2nd ed.). (pp. 128–142). Toronto: W. B. Saunders.

Paven-Nickoloff, A., & Sherrington, L. (1998). Link for kids. The telehealth project. *Canadian Nurse, 94*(8), 37–39.

Pew Health Professions Commission. (1991). *Healthy America: Practitioners for 2005*. Durham, NC: Author.

Prescott, P. A., Dennis, K. E., & Jacox, A. K. (1987). Clinical decision making of staff nurses. *Image: The Journal of Nursing Scholarship, 19*, 56–62.

Prescott, P. A., Phillips, C. Y., Ryan, J. W., & Thompson, K. O. (1991). Changing how nurses spend their time. *Image: The Journal of Nursing Scholarship, 23*, 23–28.

Rachlis, M., & Kushner, C. (1994). *Strong medicine*. Toronto: Harper Perennial.

Riesch, S. K. (1992). Nursing centers: An analysis of the anecdotal literature. *Journal of Professional Nursing, 8*(1), 16–25.

Romanow, R. J. (2002). Building on Values; Commission on the Future of Health Care in Canada. Ottawa, ON: Government of Canada.

Ryan, J. (1997). Assuring the future quality of parish nursing practice. *Perspectives in Parish Nursing Practice, 5*(3), 4.

Shoultz, J., & Hatcher, P. A. (1997). Looking beyond primary care to primary health care: An approach to community-based action. *Nursing Outlook, 45*(1), 23–26.

Sorrell, J. M., & Redmond, G. M. (2002). *Community-based nursing practice: Learning through students' stories*. Philadelphia, PA: F.A. Davis.

Sparbel, K. J. H., & Anderson, M. A. (2000). Integrated literature review of continuity of care: Part 1, Conceptual issues. *Image—Journal of Nursing Scholarship, 32*(1): 17–24.

Tannen, D. (1990). *You just don't understand*. New York: Ballantine Books.

Tellis-Nayak, M. (1998). The post-acute continuum of care: Understanding your patient's options. *American Journal of Nursing, 98*, 44–49.

Tsouros, A. O. (1990). *World Health Organization healthy cities project: A project becomes a movement*. Copenhagen, Denmark: FADL Publishers.

Velianoff, G. D., Neely, C., & Hall, S. (1993). Development levels of interdisciplinary collaborative practice committees. *Journal of Nursing Administration, 23*, 26–29.

Vollman, A., & Tenove, S. (2001). The Canadian health care delivery system. In J. C. Ross-Kerr & M. Wood (Eds.), *Canadian Fundamentals of Nursing* (2nd ed.). (pp. 22–47). Toronto: Mosby.

World Health Organization. (1978). *Primary health care: Report of the international conference on primary health care*. Geneva, Switzerland: Author.

World Health Organization. (1978). *Alma-Ata Declaration: Health for all by year 2000*. Geneva, Switzerland: WHO.

Zotti, M. E., Brown, P., & Stotts, R. C. (1996). Community-based nursing versus community health nursing: What does it all mean? *Nursing Outlook, 44*, 213–217.

WEBLINKS

Victorian Order of Nurses
http://www.von.ca/
The Victorian Order of Nurses for Canada (VON Canada) is a registered charity and national health-care organization that has been caring for Canadians in their homes and communities since 1897. The site provides information about the VON, the services offered, and how to access them.

National Forum on Health
http://wwwnfh.hc-sc.gc.ca/
The Forum has completed its work, presented its Report to the Prime Minister of Canada, and ended its operations on June 13, 1997. This Web site permits access to the Forum's publications and provides an overview of the discussion of the Forum members on the determinants of health.

Canada Health Act
http://laws.justice.gc.ca/en/C-6/index.html
A Department of Justice site that provides access to federal legislation including the Canada Health Act and regulations concerning billing.

Canadian Public Health Association
http://www.cpha.ca/
The Canadian Public Health Association (CPHA) is a national, independent, not-for-profit association representing public health interests in Canada.

CHAPTER 17

Home Care

OBJECTIVES

After completing this chapter, you will be able to:

- Define home health care.
- Compare the characteristics of home health nursing to those of institutionalized nursing care.
- Describe the types of home health agencies, including referral sources.
- Identify the roles of the home health nurse.
- Identify the essential aspects of the home visit.
- Discuss the safety and infection control dimensions applicable to the home care setting.
- Identify ways the nurse can recognize and minimize caregiver role strain.
- Apply the nursing process to care of the client in the home.
- Analyze factors influencing home care in Canada.

In the past decade, there has been an observable increase in the delivery of nursing services in home settings. A number of factors have contributed to this trend, among them rising health-care costs, an aging population, and a growing emphasis on managing chronic illness and stress, preventing illness, and enhancing the quality of life. In addition, home health care is surging to the forefront as a viable *entry* point in the health-care system. In the not-too-distant past, home health care occurred at the end of the client care continuum—that is, after discharge from an acute-care facility. Today, the trend is changing to use of home health-care services to avoid hospitalization.

Home health nursing practice differs from nursing in acute-care settings in many ways. For example, home health nurses assume a higher degree of autonomy and independence.

Because home health nurses must function independently in a variety of home settings and situations, employers generally prefer that the nurse be prepared at the baccalaureate level.

Home Health Nursing

Home nursing care is one of the fastest growing sectors of the health-care system. Several factors have contributed to the growth of home health care. These factors include (1) the increase in the older population, who are frequent recipients of home care; (2) the ability of agencies and institutions to successfully deliver high-technology services in the home; and (3) consumers who prefer to receive care in the home, rather than in an institution (Stulginsky, 1993a).

Clients who need home health care have a variety of physical, socioeconomic, and psychological needs. Some of these clients have medically unstable conditions and may have an acute problem, such as a wound infection, which requires dressing changes. Other clients may have a medically stable condition (e.g., insulin-dependent diabetes) but require long-term care to prevent exacerbation and subsequent hospitalization. The primary objectives of home care are service delivery and coordination, in addition to client and family education, and health promotion. Education focuses on independence for the client and family through the teaching of self-care. One of the benefits of home care is that problems related to lifestyle practices, environment, safety, and family dynamics can be assessed and interventions initiated by the nurse.

Palliative care nursing is often considered a subspecialty of home health nursing, as such services are frequently delivered to terminally ill clients in their residence. See Chapter 48 for further information on palliative care.

Definitions of Home Nursing

The delivery of nursing services in the home has been called a variety of terms, including home health nursing, home care nursing, and visiting nursing. Spradley and Allender (1996, p. 484) define home health care as "all the services and products provided to clients in their homes to maintain, restore, or promote their physical, mental, and emotional health." Home health nursing services might be provided in long-term care facilities, residential hospices, residential shelters for abused women and children and the homeless, or adult congregate living facilities.

The most commonly used definition of home care in Canada was developed in 1990 by the Federal/Provincial/Territorial Working Group on Home Care: "An array of services which enables clients incapacitated in whole or in part to live at home, often with the effect of delaying or substituting for long-term care or acute-care alternatives." Home care is a place for delivery of care, not a type of care. Home care may be delivered under a variety of organized structures and similarly numerous funding and client payment mechanisms. It may address needs specifically determined with a medical diagnosis or may compensate for functional deficits in the activities of daily living, for example, bathing and cleaning.

The focus of home health nursing is individuals and their families. This differs somewhat from the focus of community health nursing, which focuses on three general types of clients: individuals, families, and groups. Groups may be communities, at-risk aggregates, or persons with similar problems and needs.

Unique Aspects of Home Health Nursing

Home care nurses must function independently in a variety of unfamiliar home settings and situations. Because the home is the family's territory, power and control issues in delivering nursing care differ from those in the institution. For example, entry into a home is granted, not assumed; the nurse must, therefore, establish trust and rapport with the client and family. Health care that is provided is often given with other family members present. Families also may feel more free to question advice, to ignore directions, to do things differently, and to set their own priorities and schedules.

Home health nurses have identified significant advantages in caring for individuals and families in the home. The home setting is intimate; this intimacy fosters familiarity, sharing, connections, and caring between clients, families, and their nurse. Behaviours are more natural, cultural beliefs and practices are more visible, and multigenerational interactions tend to be displayed.

Home health nurses have also identified issues that negatively affect care in the home. More than any other care providers, these nurses have firsthand knowledge and experience about the burden of caregiving. In the interest of cutting health-care costs, policy makers, third-party payers, and medical providers are placing increasingly complex responsibilities on clients' families and significant other(s). Caregiving demands may go on for months or years, placing the caregivers themselves (many of whom are older adults) at risk for physiological and psychosocial problems. Additionally, nurses enter homes where the living conditions and support systems may be inadequate. When additional support or improved caregiving cannot be obtained for the client, home health nurses face difficult decisions (Stulginsky, 1993a).

The Home Health-Care System

Types of Home Health Agencies

Clients can receive home health-care services either through a home health agency or through a private duty nursing agency.

Current home-care services provided include nursing, home support, occupational therapy, physiotherapy, respiratory therapy, nutrition counselling, and social work. More complex services are emerging, such as home intravenous antibiotic therapy, life support/ventilator assistance systems, services for children with complex needs, enteral and parenteral nutrition, cancer therapy, and palliative care.

Home Health Agencies

Home health agencies offer skilled professional and paraprofessional services. Depending on the agency, professional providers may include registered nurses, licensed practical nurses, nurse practitioners, home health-care aides, physical therapists, occupational therapists, respiratory therapists, speech therapists, social workers, dietitians, and a pastoral care minister or chaplain. In addition, it is not unusual for home health agencies to offer the services of specialized nurses, such as enterostomal therapists or diabetes educators.

Home health agencies usually provide services once or twice a day, up to seven days a week. Because clients often require the services of several professionals simultaneously, case coordination (case management) is essential. This responsibility generally rests with the registered nurse.

There are several different types of home health agencies. These include the following:

- *Official or public agencies* are operated by provincial/territorial or local governments and financed primarily by public funds.
- *Voluntary or private not-for-profit agencies* are supported by donations, endowments, charities, such as the United Way, and third-party reimbursement. Because these are not-for-profit agencies, they are exempt from federal income tax.
- *Private, proprietary agencies* are for-profit organizations and are governed by either individual owners or national corporations. Some of these agencies participate in third-party reimbursement; others rely on "private-pay" sources.

Regardless of the type of agency, all home health agencies must meet specific standards for licensing, certification, and accreditation.

Private Duty Agencies

This type of agency provides professional nursing and home health aide care for up to 24 hours a day. Because private duty care is expensive, clients either have commercial insurance that provides reimbursement or can pay privately.

Medical Equipment Companies

Medical equipment companies provide health-care equipment for the client at home. The types of equipment can range from hospital beds and bedside commodes to ventilators and apnea monitors. Reimbursement for equipment is through government and private insurance. Nurses and therapists are often employed by these companies to provide client education and assist with sales and marketing activities. Referrals can be made to these companies by any health-care professional. To meet client needs for home care services and equipment and to ensure adequate reimbursement, nurses must understand the services available and the way clients are reimbursed.

Reimbursement

Home care is not included in the Canada Health Act; subsequently, its services are not insured in the same way as are physician services. Home care is delivered by public, private not-for-profit, and private for-profit agencies in Canada. The proportion of private versus public services varies by province. Home health-care services are reimbursed by three mechanisms: (1) provincial and municipal government funds, (2) private insurance, and (3) private payment by home care recipients. Within public home care agencies, professional services (e.g., nursing, therapies) are usually provided free of charge up to an identified figure per month, while user fees may apply to support services (personal care, house cleaning, transportation). User fees are generally allocated on a sliding scale based on income as determined by income tax returns. Clients may or may not be charged for supplies and equipment and may be responsible for the cost of their medications.

Generally speaking, Canadians who meet the eligibility criteria receive professional services at no charge, although there may be some resource limits that restrict them from receiving the level of service they have been assessed to need. In many cases, those who need support services, medical supplies, treatment equipment, or medications are required to pay user fees, based on an assessment of income. Health-care agencies need to adhere to established guidelines and provide care within the predetermined reimbursement levels.

RESEARCH NOTE

Who are Home Care Clients and What Is the Cost of Providing Care?

The goals of the Ontario-based study were to describe home care clients and their care providers; to determine the competencies required to provide their care; to determine the costs of the formal care providers; and to determine the burden of care for informal care providers. Structured interviews, documentation review, and a burden tool were used to collect the data from a variety of stakeholders. Of the clients who participated, almost half were over the age of 70 years, and slightly over half required acute care. The most common medical diagnoses related to cardiac function. Costs varied, depending upon the amount and type of care required and upon the coping ability of both the client and the family.

Implications: The study suggests the competencies required by registered nurses working with home care clients include pharmaceutical knowledge and strong assessment skills.

Source: Alcock, D., Danbrook, C., Walker, D., & Hunt, C. (1998). Home care clients, providers and costs. *Canadian Journal of Public Health, 89,* 297–300. Reproduced with permission of the Canadian Journal of Public Health.

Referral Process

Clients may be referred to home health-care providers by such sources as a physician, nurse, social worker, therapist (e.g., physical therapist), discharge planner, or family member. Families often initiate the process by approaching one of these referral sources or by directly contacting the home health agency to make inquiries.

A nursing assessment visit is scheduled to identify the client's needs. At this assessment, visit the nurse develops a plan of care that must be reviewed, approved, authorized, and signed by the attending physician before home health agency providers can continue with services.

Roles of the Home Health Nurse

Historically, nurses who provided direct services in the home were strong generalists who focused on long-term preventive, educational, remedial, and rehabilitative outcomes. Today, many home health nurses are generalists or specialists possessing high-technology skills that were formerly used only in acute-care settings. For example, nurses provide a variety of intravenous therapies in the home setting and monitor clients who are dependent on technologically complex medical equipment, such as ventilators and central lines. These nurses collaborate with physicians and other health-care professionals in providing care.

Major roles of the home health nurse are those of advocate, discharge planner, caregiver (provider of direct care), educator, and case manager or coordinator.

Advocate

Advocacy begins on the first visit. The nurse explores and supports the client's choices in health care; all viable options are considered. Advocacy includes discussion about the client's rights, advance directives, living wills, and substitute decision makers (proxy) for health care. It also usually involves assistance to access community resources, to make informed decisions, to recognize and cope with necessary changes in lifestyle, and to understand ways to effectively use the complex medical system. Advocacy can be a particular challenge when family members' or other caregivers' views differ from those of the client. In the event of conflict, the nurse, being the client's primary advocate, must ensure that the client's rights and desires are upheld.

Discharge Planner

Discharge planning is a major function of nurses working in home health-care agencies. Nurses attend discharge-planning rounds on the units and in associated clinics and consult with medical, nursing, and social work staff. They facilitate access to home health-care equipment and services during a client's discharge. By completing a detailed assessment before hospital discharge, a nurse can facilitate continuity of care.

Caregiver

The home health nurse's major role as caregiver is to assess and diagnose the client's actual and potential health problems, plan care, and evaluate the client's outcomes. Direct personal care activities, such as bathing, changing linens, feeding, and light housekeeping activities to maintain a clean and safe home environment, are usually provided by a family member or a home health aide arranged by the nurse. The home health nurse, however, will provide direct care for specific procedures and treatments, such as ostomy care, wound care, intravenous therapy, and so on, according to agency policies and practices. Much of the home health nurse's time is spent teaching others to provide required care.

Educator

The educative role of the home health nurse focuses on illness care, the prevention of problems, and the promotion of optimal wellness or well-being. Education is ongoing and can be considered the crux of home care practice; its goal is to help clients learn to manage as independently as possible. All home health nurses need to be skilled in teaching and learning principles and strategies that facilitate learning. (See Chapter 29 for detailed information.)

Case Manager or Coordinator

The home health nurse coordinates the activities of all other home health team members involved in the client's treatment plan. Coordination can occur individually, in person or by telephone, with a specific team member, such as the dietitian or respiratory therapist, or during a team conference where each team member provides information about the client's health status. The nurse is the main contact with the physician to report any changes in the client's condition and to bring about a revision in the plan of care as needed. Documentation of care coordination is a legal requirement and must be recorded on the client's medical record.

Perspectives of Home Care Clients

Home care clients include a diverse population that encompasses all ages, a variety of health problems, and families of different structures and cultural backgrounds.

Home care clients have a wide range of health problems that include disabilities, perinatal problems, mental illness, and acute and chronic illnesses. The majority of clients have medical-surgical problems that are similar to those seen in acute or extended-care facilities.

Although the person receiving care is considered the primary client in home care, the client's family can be considered secondary clients because often they are associated with caregiving and have a major impact on the client's wellness status. The home health nurse will encounter many different family structures, ranging from single families to extended families and dwellings that house multiple families. In the home setting, family members may include not only persons related by birth and marriage, but also friends, other significant individuals, and animals.

Various cultural influences also affect the client's health-care beliefs and practices. The home health nurse needs to be culturally sensitive, that is, to become aware of the client's culture and form a nursing care plan with the client that incorporates that person's culture. See Chapter 14 for detailed information about making cultural assessments and providing culturally competent care.

Selected Dimensions of Home Health Nursing

Selected dimensions of home health care include assessing the home for safety features, infection control, and caregiver support.

Client Safety

Hazards in the home are major causes of falls, fire, poisoning, and other accidents, such as those caused by improper use of household equipment (e.g., tools and cooking utensils). The appraisal of such hazards and suggestions for remedies is an essential nursing function. See the following box for a home hazard appraisal and Chapter 33 for potential hazards and preventive actions for individuals of all ages.

Obviously, home health nurses cannot expect to change a family's living space and lifestyle. However, they can express their concern and react appropriately when a situation suggests that an injury is imminent. Nurses must document information they provide and the family's response to instruction and make ongoing assessments about the family's use of safety precautions.

Other aspects of client safety relate to emergency situations. The home health nurse can assist the client and/or caregivers as follows:

- Post a list of all emergency telephone numbers (ambulance, fire, police, physician) at each telephone.
- Post a list of all the client's medications and potential side effects in a central location, such as on the refrigerator.
- Help the client and family apply for a medic-alert system, such as a bracelet or necklace. (Information on the Medic Alert System can be obtained by accessing the medic-alert Web site http://www.medicalert.ca/ or e-mail to medinfo@medicalert.ca.)
- Enroll the client in a Life Line (or similar program) that places all the client's vital medical information in one place for emergency personnel to have in the event of a life-threatening situation. The program can be obtained through a pharmacy, physician's office, the VON, or other community support groups.

Nurse Safety

Clients who live in less than desirable locations pose additional safety concerns for the nurse. Some home health agencies have contracts with security firms to escort nurses needing to see clients in potentially unsafe neighbourhoods. The nurse should discuss where the client lives with the security firm and determine the best mechanism to receive a security escort. The nurse should avoid taking any personal belongings during these visits and have a pre-established mechanism to signal for help.

Infection Control

The goal of infection control in the home is to protect clients, caregivers, and the general community from the transmission of disease. This is particularly important for clients who are immunocompromised, who have infectious or communicable diseases, and who have draining wounds, drainage tubes, or other invasive access devices. The nurse's major role in infection control is health teaching. Clients and caregivers need to learn about effective hand washing, use of gloves, handling of linens, disposal of

Home Hazard Appraisal for Adults

Assess the following:

- *Walkways and stairways (inside and outside).* Note uneven sidewalks or paths, broken or loose steps, absence of handrails or placement on only one side of stairways, insecure handrails, congested hallways or other traffic areas, and adequacy of lighting at night.
- *Floors.* Note uneven and highly polished or slippery floors and any unanchored rugs or mats.
- *Furniture.* Note hazardous placement of furniture with sharp corners. Note chairs or stools that are too low to get into and out of or that provide inadequate support.
- *Bathroom(s).* Note presence of grab bars around tubs and toilets, nonslip surfaces in tubs and shower stalls, handheld showerhead, adequacy of night lighting, need for raised toilet seat or bath chair in tub or shower, ease of access to shelves, and water temperature regulated at a maximum of 48°C.
- *Kitchen.* Note pilot lights (gas stove) in need of repair, inaccessible storage areas, and hazardous furniture.
- *Bedrooms.* Note adequacy of lighting, in particular the availability of night-lights and accessibility of light switches, ease of access to commode, urinal, or bedpan, and need for hospital bed and/or bed rails.
- *Electrical.* Note unanchored and/or frayed electrical cords and outlets that are overloaded or near water.
- *Fire protection.* Note presence or absence of smoke detectors, fire extinguisher, and fire escape plan, improper storage of combustibles (e.g., gasoline) or corrosives (e.g., rust remover [phosphoric acid]), and accessibility of emergency telephone numbers (fire, police).
- *Toxic substances.* Note improperly labelled cleaning solutions.
- *Communication devices.* Note presence of method to call for help such as a telephone or internal intercom in the bedroom and elsewhere (e.g., kitchen), and access to emergency telephone numbers.
- *Medications.* Note medications kept beyond date of expiry, adequacy of lighting for medication cabinet or storage, and method of disposal of sharp objects, such as needles used for injections.

wastes and soiled dressings, and the practice of universal precautions. Infection control can present a challenge to the home health nurse, especially if the home care facilities are not conducive to the most basic aseptic requirement, such as running water for hand washing.

An important aspect of infection control involves the home health nurse's equipment and supplies carried in a water-resistant bag. Supplies may include materials for hand washing; assessment equipment, such as stethoscope, blood pressure cuff and monitor, thermometer, tape measure, and wound diameter measuring tool; universal precautions items, such as goggles, masks, gloves, and spill kit; and antimicrobial cleaning agents. The aseptic practices associated with this equipment are often referred to as "bag technique." Nurses need to follow agency protocol in regard to bag technique. To keep the bag clean, nurses often hook the strap of the bag over the back of a chair or door knob in the client's home or place it directly on a clean surface (e.g., newspapers or a water-impermeable barrier contained within the bag). Used equipment is cleaned with antimicrobial soap before returning it to the bag. The hands are washed before entering the bag and after client care.

Caregiver Support

Caregiving may be directed to individuals of any age and varies from short-term to long-term according to the physical or mental disabilities of the care receivers. For example, some children who have permanent disabilities and adults who experience progressive deterioration, such as those with Alzheimer's disease or multiple sclerosis, require care on a permanent basis. Others who are recovering from a surgical procedure require care only on a temporary basis. Most caregivers stand in close relationships with the care receiver, that is, wife-husband, parent-child, friend-friend, or other significant relationships. Many caregiving relationships, therefore, are changes from the caring and caregiving intrinsic to all close relationships to an extraordinary and unequal burden for the caregiver. Caregivers, many of whom are older adults, may experience physical, emotional, social, and financial burdens that can seriously jeopardize their own health and well-being.

The home health nurse needs to recognize signs of caregiver role strain and suggest ways to minimize or alleviate this problem. Signs of caregiver overload include the following:

- Difficulty performing routine tasks for the client
- Reports of declining physical energy and insufficient time for caregiving
- Concern that caregiving responsibilities interfere with other roles, such as parent, spouse, colleague, friend
- Anxiety about ability to meet future care needs of client
- Feelings of anger and depression
- Dramatic change in the home environment's appearance

When caregiver role strain is identified, the nurse needs to encourage caregivers to express their feelings and, at the same time, convey understanding about the difficulties associated with caregiving and acknowledge the caregivers' competence. The nurse can obtain a realistic appraisal of the situation by asking a caregiver to describe a typical day and daily or weekly leisure and social activities. It is also helpful to identify activities for which assistance is desired. These activities may include client care needs, such as hygiene, mobility, feeding, or treatments; house cleaning; laundry; shopping; house repairs; yard work; transportation; doctor's or hairdresser's appointments; or respite.

When activities for which assistance is required are identified, the nurse and caregiver need to identify possible sources of help. Both volunteer and agency sources need to be explored. Volunteer sources of help may include family members (cousins, siblings), neighbours, friends, church associates, or caregiver support groups in the community. Other sources include, for example, a home health aide for light housekeeping and grocery shopping, Meals on Wheels, day care, transportation, and counselling and social services. Families with a chronically ill member may benefit from a weekend respite—a program some agencies provide, in which the client is admitted to a skilled unit for observation and care, enabling the caregiver a break from ongoing health-care needs.

Caregivers need to be reminded of the importance of caring for themselves by getting adequate rest, eating nutritious meals, asking for help, delegating household chores, and making time for leisure activities or simply some time alone. Family members other than the caregiver also may need help to learn ways to support the caregiver. The nurse may discuss with the caregiver the importance of regular phone calls, cards, letters, and visits; offer encouragement to take day trips or a vacation; listen without giving advice; acknowledge the burden of caregiving and the need to feel appreciated; and so on.

Applying the Nursing Process in the Home

The application of the nursing process is focused on the needs of individual clients and their caregivers.

Assessing

The home health nurse assesses not only the health-care demands of the client and family but also the home and community environment. Assessment actually begins when the nurse contacts the client for the initial home visit and reviews documents received from the referral agency. The goal of the initial visit is to obtain a comprehensive clinical picture of the client's needs.

Most agencies have an admissions packet that includes forms for consent to treatment; physical, psychosocial, and spiritual assessment; medications; pain assessment; family data; financial assessment, client's bill of rights; care plan; and daily visit notes. During the initial home visit, the home health nurse obtains a health history from the client, examines the client, observes the relationship of the client and caregiver, and assesses the home and community environment. Parameters of assessment of the home environment include client and caregiver mobility, client ability to perform self-care, the cleanliness of the environment, the availability of caregiver support, safety, food preparation, financial supports, and the emotional status of the client and caregiver.

Following assessment, the nurse determines whether further consults and support personnel are needed. For example, would the client benefit from a dietary consult or Meals on Wheels? Is a home health aide needed to assist with activities of daily living and homemaker tasks? Is a social worker needed to help with financial resources or future care needs, such as placement in a nursing home? What additional supplies does the client need?

Before terminating this initial assessment interview, the nurse also discusses what the client and family can expect from home care, what other health-care providers may be needed to help the client achieve independence, and the frequency of home visits.

Diagnosing

As in other care environments, the nurse identifies both actual and potential client problems (see Chapter 23 for detailed information about nursing diagnoses). Examples of common nursing diagnoses appropriate for home care include ***Knowledge Deficient,*** (specify), ***Home Maintenance Management, Impaired*** and ***Risk for Caregiver Role Strain*** (see following box). The deficit in knowledge may relate to lack of information about disease process, medications, self-care skills, and so on.

Planning and Implementing

During the planning phase, the nurse needs to encourage and permit clients to make their own health management decisions. Alternatives may need to be suggested for some decisions if the nurse identifies potential harm from a chosen course of action.

Strategies to meet goals generally include teaching the client and family techniques of care and identifying appropriate resources to assist the client and family in maintaining self-sufficiency.

To implement the plan, the home health nurse performs nursing interventions, including teaching; coordinates and uses referrals and resources; provides and monitors all levels of technical care collaborates with other disciplines and providers; identifies clinical problems and research knowledge; supervises ancillary personnel; and advocates for the client's right to self-determination. Technical skills commonly performed by home health nurses include blood

Nursing Diagnoses

Home Maintenance Management, Impaired

"The state in which an individual or family experiences or is at risk to experience a difficulty in maintaining a safe, hygienic, growth-producing home environment" (Carpenito, 2002, p. 203).

Related factors

- Impaired cognition
- Limitations in physical activity
- Fatigue
- Financial constraints
- Chronic debilitating disease
- Unavailable support system

Risk of Caregiver Role Strain

"A state in which an individual is at high risk to experience physical, emotional, social, and/or financial burdens in the process of giving care to another" (Carpenito, 2002, p. 46).

Related factors

- Insufficient respite
- Insufficient recreation
- Insufficient finances
- Lack of support
- Duration of caregiving required
- Unrealistic expectations for caregiver by others
- Unrealistic expectations of the caregiver

pressure measurement; body fluid collection (blood, urine, stool, sputum); wound care; respiratory care; all types of intravenous therapy; phototherapy; enteral nutrition; urinary catheterization; enterostomal care; and renal dialysis.

A large part of the nurse's implementing role involves teaching the client and caregiver the necessary skills for self-care—for example, administering injectable insulin, measuring blood glucose, and administering medications. Medication instruction about dosage, frequency of administration, and possible side effects is of particular concern for many clients. (See Chapter 28 for further information.) Clients who are receiving high-technology interventions are often anxious about their ability to manage such sophisticated equipment and to provide care that they believe only professional nurses or respiratory therapists, for example, are educated to perform. The home health nurse is challenged to allay the client's fears and to provide support through instruction, demonstration, and periodic evaluation of the client's and family's performance of such skills. Members of the home care team specially trained in the skill, such as intravenous nurses and respiratory therapists, generally make periodic visits to service the equipment as well as monitor the client's skills.

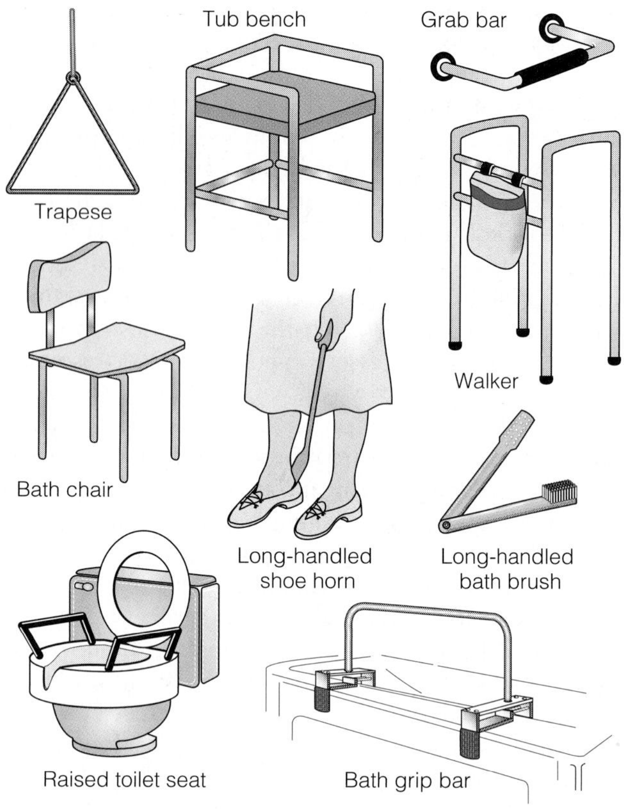

Figure 17.1 Home care assistive devices

Even though the client and family may become independent in self-care skills, the home health nurse still has the ultimate responsibility to ensure the client is receiving the prescribed therapy at the appropriate timed intervals. Ongoing communication with the physician about the client's progress is critical and the nurse must make ongoing assessments to ensure that all aspects of the care are being followed.

Evaluating and Documenting

Evaluation is carried out by the nurse on subsequent home visits by observing the same parameters assessed on the initial home visit. The nurse can also teach caregivers parameters of evaluation so that they can obtain professional intervention, if needed. Documentation of care given and the client's progress toward goal achievement at each visit is essential. Notes must also reflect plans for subsequent visits and when the client may be sufficiently prepared for self-care and discharge from the agency.

Trends Influencing Home Care

Provision of Services

Home care services through local, provincial, and territorial programs are generally available to residents of that district who, following an assessment, have been identified as meeting the criteria for receiving home care. Eligibility criteria vary from program to program. Although all provinces and territories have some form of government home care program, there is no one common approach to how services are funded and delivered. Services can differ within a province. Generally, within urban areas, a broader range of services is offered than in rural ones. For example, differences exist in referral sources, admission criteria, service limits, and length of stay on the program.

Veterans Affairs Canada offers home care services to clients with wartime or special-duty area service when the service is not available to them through provincial and territorial programs. The Department of Indian Affairs and Northern Development (DIAND) and Health Canada jointly offer a limited home care program, which has joint responsibility for on-reserve First Nations home care.

Depending on the province, territory and/or region, home care services may be delivered directly by home care program staff, by external agencies, or by a mix of both. There is a trend by publicly funded agencies toward contracting with private ones to deliver the service in an effort to decrease administrative costs.

In 1994, publicly funded home care programs provided 90 percent of home care services in Canada. It is estimated that this ratio has changed since then, as more private services are offered to help people who are not eligible for publicly funded home care and for those who wish to complement the public services they are receiving. The actual growth of privately purchased services paid for by clients, their families, or insurance companies is difficult to measure.

Changing Client Base

Clients requiring home care services are changing. Seniors constitute one of the fastest growing populations in Canada. In addition, a growth in seniors 75 years of age and over has resulted in increased service needs. Life expectancy has risen and has led to the survival of individuals with functional deficits. There is pressure from families, advocacy groups, and health-care systems to care for these individuals in the community.

Recent years have seen an increase in outpatient surgery, earlier hospital discharges, and a reduction in long-term and acute-care hospital beds. Improved technology has allowed for more delivery of services in the home; for example, home-based dialysis machines. For home care programs, these changes have meant more units of service per person served, the provision of care to more vulnerable, older, and frailer individuals, and more required complex home care services. Home health care has evolved into a challenging, rapidly growing field of nursing practice. Because of recent economic, governmental, social, and technological developments, nurses providing care in the home are caring for clients who are more acutely ill, go home from the hospital sooner, and who require more highly technical care and complex equipment than ever before. This is in addition to the increasing number of clients being maintained in their homes by long-term care services.

Consumers are becoming more informed and want to be involved in decisions regarding their health. They are seeking services that emphasize choice and quality of life, are as close to home as possible, and are delivered in the least intrusive manner possible.

Researching Home Care Service Delivery

Health-care costs to government for clients in home care are about one-half to three-quarters of the costs for clients in care facilities. This evidence suggests that enhancing home care services can contribute to savings for the Canadian health-care system. However, this evidence is far from conclusive. Little research has been done in the Canadian setting. Other areas of needed research include the lack of a national health-care system or consistent coverage of home care services from province to province, which represents a barrier to health-care delivery in Canada. How can the barriers be eliminated? Providing home care to clients in rural areas presents a challenge to a resource-strained health-care system. Informal care providers often play a major role in ensuring that individuals receive the care that they need at home. How do they respond when such care is required over a substantive period of time? All of these questions are appropriate to nurse researchers. For a detailed understanding of nursing research, see Chapter 3.

The Future of Home Health Care

What is the future for home health care? Experts in the home health-care industry have identified some trends:

1. Providing third-party reimbursement for community clinic nurse specialists and psychiatric nurse specialists. These advanced practice nurses can provide education, support, counselling, and therapy for clients and their families.
2. Utilizing nurse pain specialists to assess and manage pain in the home, thus avoiding costly hospitalizations and procedures.
3. Utilizing electronic home visits. A computerized phone system can obtain information, such as blood pressure readings, allowing case managers to review a client's progress.
4. Developing information systems, specific to home care's needs. These systems would support workload measurement, client outcome measurement, financial accountability, service utilization, and client satisfaction. These systems should link with other settings of care to provide better integration and easier movement for individuals through the care continuum.

FOCUS ON CRITICAL THINKING

Mr. Yao is a 67-year-old Chinese Canadian male with a 20-year history of hypertension and diabetes mellitus. He has recently undergone amputation of three toes due to poor circulation. Because he is progressing well and his diabetes is under control, he is being discharged from the acute-care setting to go home. He has been referred to home care, which will assign a nurse to change his foot dressings, administer intravenous antibiotics, and monitor his blood glucose levels.

1. How will the nurse's role differ when delivering care in the home environment as opposed to the acute-care environment?
2. What rights does the client have when being cared for at home that may not be afforded him while institutionalized?
3. What obligations to Mr. Yao does the nurse have when visiting him at home?
4. What factors could negatively impact the care of Mr. Yao in his own home?
5. Speculate about the financial savings derived from caring for a patient at home rather than in a hospital or other institution.

See Appendix A for answers to these questions.

Canadian Society Notes

Fact	Implications for Nursing Practice
Publicly funded home care programs exist in every province and territory. Home care is not included in the Canada Health Act; consequently, home care services are not insured in the same way as hospital and physician services.	Nurses are impacted and are advocates of the needs of their clients when home care costs are not covered by medicare.
In 1994, it was estimated that 90 percent of home care services in Canada were provided by publicly funded home care programs. It is estimated that this ratio has changed since then as more private services are offered to help people who are not eligible for publicly funded home care and for those who wish to complement the public services they are receiving.	Nurses must teach their clients/families to perform nursing activities when funding does not permit the nurse to be present in the home.
The Canadian Home Care Association (CHCA) (1998) argues that as home care programs take on clients whose needs are more complex, requiring technologically intensive services, the funds available in home care programs are being used more "quickly by a disproportionately small percentage of clients" (p. 10). Source: Canadian Home Care Association. *Investing in home care: A wise priority*. Briefing Paper, October 30, 1998.	Case management skills, such as coordination of services, financial accountability, and consultation help the nurse to provide care to such clients.
In 1997, the National Forum released its report, calling for increased integration of home care within the publicly funded health-care system.	Nurses need to be aware of the possible impact of such reports on their professional practice. For example, when acute care clients are discharged home, home care nurses need to be able to put the services in place that clients need.

CHAPTER HIGHLIGHTS

- Home health care has gained considerable recognition as an alternative to acute and subacute health-care facilities. The trend has changed from using home health care after hospitalization to using it to avoid hospitalization.
- Home health nursing is a rapidly growing industry providing a wide range of nursing services to clients in their places of residence. It may include the administration of physician-prescribed treatments, independent nursing interventions, and high-tech therapies, including chemotherapy and dialysis.
- Palliative care nursing, often considered a subspecialty of home nursing, supports the terminally ill client and the family during the last stages of life and during the family's bereavement.
- There are several types of home health agencies: official or public agencies, voluntary or private not-for-profit agencies, private proprietary agencies, and institution-based agencies. All home health agencies must meet specific standards for licensing, certification, and accreditation.
- Home health agencies offer skilled professional and paraprofessional services. Because clients often require the services of several professionals simultaneously, case coordination is essential.
- Private duty agencies provide professional nursing and home health aide care for up to 24 hours per day.
- Health-care agencies in Canada receive reimbursement for services they provide from various sources: provincial/territorial and municipal governments.
- Referrals for home health services may be made by the client's physician, a nurse, social worker, therapist, discharge planner, or family member.
- Major roles of the home health nurse are those of advocate, caregiver, educator, and case manager.
- The home health nurse assesses the care needs of clients in their home; plans, implements, and supervises that care; teaches clients and their families self-care; and mobilizes the resources of hospitals, physicians, and community agencies in meeting the needs of the clients and their families.
- Home care clients include a diverse population that encompasses all ages, a variety of health problems, and families of different structures and cultural backgrounds. The home health nurse needs to be culturally sensitive, that is, become aware of the client's culture and form a nursing care plan with the client that incorporates the client's culture.
- Important dimensions of home health nursing include the home visit, in which the nurse assesses the client and together they make plans for care; client and nurse safety; infection control; and caregiver support.

READINGS AND REFERENCES

Suggested Readings

Brendt, N. J. (1997). The home healthcare nurse and confidentiality and privacy. *Home Healthcare Nurse, 15*, 256–258.

This article defines privacy and confidentiality as two distinct legal concepts which the home health nurse must understand. Two distinct ways in which privacy is violated in health care are examined along with suggestions to ensure client confidentiality. Implications for the home health agency and nurse are identified with suggestions to maintain client privacy and confidentiality.

Murray, T. A. (1998, May/June). Using role theory concepts to understand transitions from hospital based nursing practice to home care nursing. *Journal of Continuing Nursing Education, 29*, 105–111.

Nurses changing from a hospital-based practice to a home health-care setting report feelings of anxiety, incompetency, and lack of the necessary skills to care for clients in the home. A model of the role transitions process is helpful in identifying the transition experienced by nurses new to the home health-care setting. Experiences during the initial transition period are critical in shaping the nurse's understanding of the role.

Ruppert, R. A. (1996). Caring for the lay caregiver. *American Journal of Nursing, 96*, 40–46.

The roles and responsibilities of lay caregivers are demanding when a patient requires long-term care at home. Caregivers are at risk for endangering their own physical and emotional health. The continuing education article describes how one program helped caregivers cope with their new role.

Spruhan, J. B. (1996). Beyond traditional nursing care: cultural awareness and successful home healthcare nursing. *Home Healthcare Nurse, 14*, 445–449.

This article reviews how an awareness of the client's culture affects the success of home health-care nursing. Four client cases are analyzed and cultural considerations are identified with implications for the home health nurse.

Related Research

Parisi, B., & Schneider, E. (1994). The role and theoretical model of the triage nurse in home health care practice. *Journal of Home Health Care Practice, 7*(1), 47–55.

Wendt, D. (1996). Building trust during the initial home visit. *Home Healthcare Nurse, 14*(2), 92–98.

Selected References

Ark, P. D., & Nies, M. (1996). Knowledge of skills of the home healthcare nurse. *Home Healthcare Nurse, 14*, 292–297.

Beckert, J. (1998). Hospital nurses in home care. *Case-Manager, 9*(4), 43–45.

Bohny, B. J. (1997). A time for self-care: Role of the home healthcare nurse. *Home Healthcare Nurse, 15*, 281–286.

Bonner, C., & Boyd, B. (1997). Managed care: Threat or opportunity for home health? *Online Journal of Issues in Nursing*. http://www.nursingworld.org/ojin/typ2/tpc2_5.htm 1/6/97.

Borneman, T. (1998). Caring for cancer patients at home: The effect on family caregivers. *Home Health Care Management and Practice, 10*(4), 25–33.

Canadian Home Care Association. (1998). *Portrait of Canada: An overview of public home care programs*. Ottawa: Author.

Carefoote, R. L. (1998). Health care issues: home care quality management—where are we now? Where do we go from here? *Canadian Journal of Nursing Administration, 11*(2), 78–92.

Carpenito, L. J. (2002). *Handbook of nursing diagnosis*. Philadelphia, PA: Lippincott.

Christopher, M. A., & Beck, T. L. (1997). Managed care: Its impact on visiting nurse associations. *Home Health Care Management & Practice, 9*(2), 43–49.

Ciliska, D., Hayward, S., Thomas, H., Mitchell, A., Dobbins, M., Underwood, J., Rafael, A., & Martin, E. (1996). A systematic overview of the effectiveness of home visiting as a delivery strategy for public health nursing interventions. *Canadian Journal of Public Health, 87*, 193–198.

Conradt, D. L. (1995). So you want to be in home care. *Journal of Home Health Care Practice, 7*(4), 53–63.

Coyte, P. C., & Young, W. (1997). Applied home care research. *International Journal of Health Care Quality Assurance, 10*, i–iv.

Ebersole, P. (1998). Home care and the elderly. *Home Care Provider, 3*(1), 7–8.

Federal/Provincial/Working Group on Home Care. (1990). *Report on Home Care*. Ottawa: Health Canada.

Free, K. W. (1996). Infection control and safety: Client education in the home. *Home Healthcare Nurse, 14*, 957–958.

Harris, M. D. (1997). Proposed revisions to Medicare conditions of participation. *Home Healthcare Nurse, 15*, 471–472.

Hawranik, P. (1998). The role of cognitive status in the use of inhome services: Implications for nursing assessment. *Canadian Journal of Nursing Research, 30*(2), 45–65.

Markle-Reid, M., Brown, G., & Roberts, J. (1998). Home care: Client characteristics and patterns of service utilization predictive of acute hospitalization. *Canadian Journal of Rehabilitation, 12*(1), 39–51.

National Advisory Council on Aging. (2000). *The NACA position on home care*. No. 20. Ottawa: Author.

National Health Forum. (1997). *The Public and Private Financing of Canada's Health System*. Ottawa, ON: Health Canada.

North American Nursing Diagnosis Association (NANDA). (2001). *Nursing diagnosis: Definitions and classification 2000–2001*. Philadelphia, PA: Author.

Pace, K. B. (1998). The information challenge in home health care. *Home Health Care Management and Practice, 10*(4), 39–44.

Reid, W. M., Pratt, J. R., & Webb, B. W. (1997). National committee for quality assurance standards: Critical to gaining a competitive advantage under managed care. *Home Health Care Management & Practice, 9*(2), 74–77.

Sorochan, M. W. (1997). Home care in Canada. *International Journal of Health Care Quality Assurance, 10*(4-5), v–x.

Spradley, B. W., & Allender, J. A. (1996). *Community health nursing: Concepts and practice*. (4th ed). Philadelphia, PA: Lippincott.

Spruhan, J. B. (1996). Beyond traditional nursing care: Cultural awareness and successful home healthcare nursing. *Home Healthcare Nurse, 14*, 445–449.

Stackhouse, J. C. (1998). *Into the community: Nursing in ambulatory and home care*. Philadelphia, PA: Lippincott-Raven.

Strang, V., Ogilvie, L., Andruski, L., Raiwet, C., Cullen, K., & Heinrich, M. (1999). Enhancing the quality of home health care. *Canadian Nurse, 95*(9), 28–32.

Stulginsky, M. M. (1993a). Nurses' home health experience. Part 1: The practice setting. *Nursing & Health Care, 14*, 402–407.

Stulginsky, M. M. (1993b). Nurses' home health experience. Part 2: The unique demands of home visits. *Nursing & Health Care, 14*, 476–485.

Temmink, D., Francke, A. L., Hutten, J. B. F., van der Zee, J., & Abu-Saad, H. H. (2000). Innovations in the nursing care of the chronically ill: A literature review from an international perspective. *Journal of Advanced Nursing, 31*, 1449–1458.

Wilkins, K., & Park, E. (1998). Home care in Canada. *Health Report, 19*(1), 29–37.

WEBLINKS

Caregiver Links
http://www.muskoka.com/caregiver/links.html
This link provides information and resources for both informal and formal care providers.

Canadian Home Care Association
http://www.cdnhomecare.on.ca/
Information on home care services and supports across the country is provided.

International Exchange on Home and Community Care (Health Canada)
http://www.homecareglobalexchange.com/
This is a discussion site operated by the federal government to promote dialogue on home care.

Victorian Order of Nurses
http://www.von.ca/
This is a national charitable organization that has provided health care services to Canadians in their homes and local communities since 1897.

CHAPTER 18

Rural Health Care

OBJECTIVES

After completing this chapter, you will be able to:

- Describe issues related to defining the terms "rural" and "remote."
- Discuss how the geographical and demographic diversity of rural communities contributes to differences in rural health-care issues.
- List health concerns of rural and remote residents.
- Identify factors related to rural health-care delivery.
- Analyze the broad scope of rural and remote nursing practice.
- Examine topics of concern to nurses in rural and remote practice.

Canada was originally a predominantly rural, agrarian-based nation and remained so until societal changes following World Wars I and II resulted in the growth of industry in urban centres. This growth led to the migration of rural residents to find employment in these industrial centres. However, almost one-quarter of Canadians continue to live in rural and remote regions of the country. There are multiple social, economic, cultural, and geographical factors related to the health care of this population and to health-care delivery. Correspondingly, nursing practice is affected by the diversity found within this huge geographical region of Canada. Health-care delivery is further complicated by incomplete and sometimes conflicting data on the health status of residents in these regions. There is a growing recognition that accurate statistics are essential to provide a comprehensive picture of the health-care needs and issues for rural residents.

Although there are many differences between Canada and the United States in how health care is provided, many similarities do exist among the factors related to rural health and health-care delivery (Bushy, 2000b). The settings in which persons live have an impact on the health of the population through environmental factors, occupational safety, the personal beliefs and health-care behaviours of the residents, demographics of the population, and access to health-care providers.

Definition of "Rural"

One obstacle identified by researchers is the lack of consensus regarding the definition of the term *rural* (Pong, 2000; Watanabe & Casebeer, 2000). The lack of a common definition leads to confusion regarding whether similar attributes and conditions are being discussed and studied within the context of the term "rural." A common definition would facilitate (1) the description of the health-care needs of rural and remote residents, and (2) the development of political coalitions to address common problems (Weinert & Boik, 1995). Regardless of the definition offered, it will usually include reference to three specific components: (1) the ecology, (2) occupations of residents, and (3) socio-cultural components (Hanson, 1999).

Statistics Canada is currently undertaking the formulation of a comprehensive definition of what constitutes "rural." Presently, Statistics Canada (1999) defines *rural* as communities of less than 1,000 persons and/or regions with a population density of less than 400 persons per square kilometre or communities outside metropolitan areas (with populations of 100,000 or more). Many persons consider that the remote and isolated northern communities are part of rural Canada. A specific definition of *remote* is not available within the literature, but geographical isolation, economic and labour force characteristics, access to goods and services, and availability of health care are elements that factor into whether an area is considered rural or remote.

The majority of Canadians of aboriginal descent continue to live in remote, northern, and rural areas of the country. Particular health issues related to this population have important implications when addressing the health-care needs of rural residents.

Factors in Rural Health Consideration

Geography

Although Canada is the second largest country in the world in size of landmass, it consists of a relatively small population. In addition, the majority of the 30 million Canadians live within 350 kilometres of the Canada-United States border (see Figure 18.1). Almost 80 percent of the population live in towns of over 1,000 persons or in large metropolitan areas. The percentage of Canadians living in rural regions of the country has decreased significantly over the past 70 years. In 1931, 45 percent of Canadians were rural based, with 31 percent of the population living on farms and 15 percent in small towns throughout the country. By 1996, the numbers had decreased to 3 percent of the population living on farms and 19 percent of the population considered rural, non-farm based (Statistics Canada, 2002). This decrease in population in the rural areas, coupled with the concentration of population in major centres along the border, contributes to issues for the delivery of health care to rural residents.

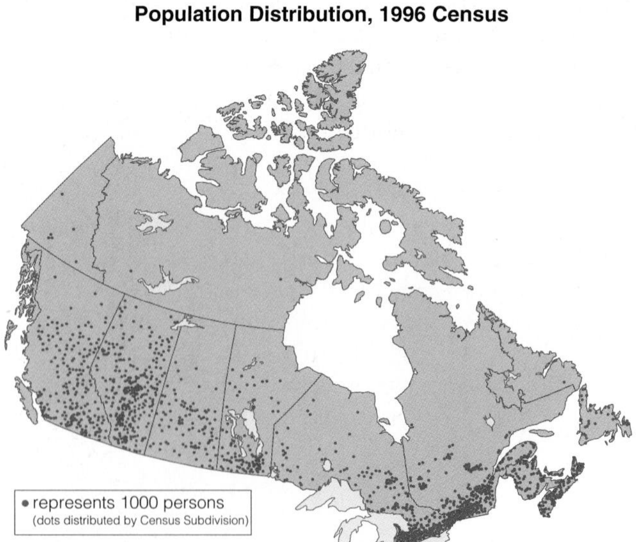

Figure 18.1 Map of Canada

Source: Map 'Population Distribution, 1996 Census', reproduced from the Statistics Canada. publication "A National Overview: Population and Dwelling Count", Catalogue 92–357, April 1997.

Figure 18.2 In northern Canada, travel is still often dependent on weather

It is just as difficult to specifically locate where the north begins on a map of the country. There would be general agreement that great distances and difficult terrain often separate the communities in northern Canada. With relatively few roads through a large geographical area, travel is still often dependent on weather (see Figure 18.2). For example, winter roads built on the ice and snow can only be built when the weather is cold enough to permit travel across the great frozen expanses of northern lakes and rivers. This, in turn, affects what goods may be transported into northern communities to be stored for use throughout the summer. These are factors that are not as important in the parts of Canada with an integrated highway system. In this chapter, health issues and health-care delivery for those in northern and remote areas will be discussed within the context of rural health. Issues of particular concern to northern residents will be highlighted.

There is enormous diversity within Canada between rural and northern communities. This becomes particularly evident when examining the vastly different geographical regions of the country—from the coastal towns and fishing villages in the maritime provinces, to rural farming and lumbering communities in Quebec, to the rolling prairie lands, to northern isolated communities set on the tundra, and the orchards and semi-arid farmlands and ranches of the interior of British Columbia. This lack of geographical homogeneity adds to the complexity of health-care issues and delivery systems across the country.

Demography

Similarly, great diversity exists between the residents in these communities. Many rural communities are experiencing an aging population, a trend that is expected to continue. The greatest decline in rural residents is occurring in the 20 to 24-year age range, as these individuals leave the rural regions for education and work. The declining economic conditions, particularly in the agricultural sector of the country, have also precipitated an even greater decrease in population. The resulting spiral eventuates in a decrease in resources available to a declining population, which, in turn, precipitates further migration from the area. One major impact of the migration of the rural youth to urban centres is the resultant increasing proportion of elderly who remain in rural communities (Bruce & Black, 2000). The elderly comprise a much larger percentage of the population in rural areas than in urban settings.

There has been a significant reduction in the number of family farms concomitant with a decrease in population (Troughton, 1999). The tendency toward the increased incorporation of mechanization in larger farms means that fewer people are needed to perform tasks previously requiring many persons, resulting in more people leaving the regions. The consequent decrease in population has a significant economic and socio-cultural impact on the residents and communities in rural areas.

A relatively new phenomenon is the emergence of the *rural/urban fringe zones* (Troughton, 1995). In the areas surrounding urban centres, the overflow of industrial and residential areas into the previously rural agricultural landscape has resulted in the conversion of this land from agricultural to residential areas, leading to an influx of residents who commute to urban areas for employment. This type of growth around all urban centres across the country has produced political, socioeconomic, and infrastructure changes that contrast with the previously stable rural countryside.

The percentage of rural residents with a university degree is half that of urban dwellers. Fertility rates in rural areas are higher than in urban centres, although both these rates have declined over the past 10 years. There is a greater percentage of children between the ages of 5 to 19 years in the rural areas than in urban settings (Fellegi, 1996).

Occupations in Rural Regions

Agriculture	Mining
Logging	Fishing
Oil and potash extraction	Tourism
Merchants	Service Sector

Occupations

Although the term *rural* is often equated with agriculture, other major industries in rural regions include mining, fishing, logging and forestry, and resource extraction, such as oil and potash. These industries have often existed as single major employers in communities, a factor that may have implications for community existence if the industry leaves the area. In addition, rural communities have a variety of merchants, service dealers and support services.

Persons employed in primary industries have a significantly higher rate of industrial accidents and injuries. Agriculture is one of the most dangerous occupations in Canada, with the fourth highest number of fatalities after mining, logging and forestry, and construction (Voaklander, Belton, Menon, Lim, & Schopflocher, 1999). For example, in 1999 there were 1,549 farm-related: injuries and 17 deaths in the province of Alberta. The leading cause of farm injury deaths were machinery related: being pinned or struck by machinery, tractor rollovers, and entanglements with power take-offs, grain augers, and other farm implements (Agriculture Alberta, 2001). Non-machinery-related injuries were caused in the handling and care of farm animals. Persons over 60 years of age were three times more likely to die from farm-related injuries. Distance and availability of resources affect health-care delivery to address this level of injuries and fatalities.

The economy of many rural and northern communities is based on a single resource that has implications in times of downturns in the economy or in times of growth and expansion. Unemployment rates are higher in rural areas, while average incomes are lower. The poverty rate is higher, and the annual salary that determines the poverty level is set lower for rural residents (Paquet, 2001). The 1999 before-tax low-income cutoffs for a single rural resident was set at $12,361, compared with $17,886 for an urban dweller in a city of 500,000 and over.

Health of Rural Residents

Health Issues

Although there is a perception that rural residents are healthier than their urban counterparts, statistics demonstrate that at least for the majority, this is not the case.

Canadian Society Notes

Fact	Implications for Nursing Practice
Almost nine million Canadians—about 30 percent of the population—live in rural and remote areas of the country.	Particular geographical factors influence the health and health-care programs of the local populations. For example, distance and lack of resources affect emergency care for persons involved in farming/ resource industry accidents.
In the 2001 Speech from the Throne, the government declared it was committed to rural Canada and rural Canadians to work with communities to develop successful solutions to the challenges they face.	Nurses working in rural areas need to participate in policy and program development initiatives of various governmental departments, recognizing how these actions impact health and health-care delivery within their communities.

Higher infant mortality, lower life expectancies, and a higher rate of injuries and death from accidents contribute to a more negative picture for rural residents (Bavington, 1994; Wilkins, 1992) who face multiple chemical, safety, and related health problems.

Respiratory Problems

Respiratory disease is a common health problem among agrarian rural dwellers. Exposure to grain dust, wood smoke, agricultural chemicals for crop production, and noxious gases emitted from silos or oil and gas wells have all been implicated as having immediate or long-term adverse effects on the health of this population. Depending upon the specific chemical and length of exposure, ill effects resulting from inhalation of toxic substances may result in systemic problems, such as headaches, blurred vision, or possibly convulsions. More localized effects on the respiratory system could include bronchitis, emphysema, or asthma (Last, Trouton, & Pengelly, 1998). Asthma is particularly prevalent in southern Alberta, an area noted for its wind and cattle feedlots.

Chemicals

Chemical contaminants can cause a variety of clinical manifestations, depending upon the agent, source, amount, and route of absorption. Skin disorders, such as dermatitis, are a common problem for those working with chemicals with-

Health Concerns for Rural Residents

- Respiratory problems
- Cancer
- Stress related to farm production and declining income
- Pesticide use
- Chemical contaminants
- Skin disease
- Zoonoses
- Mental health issues
- Water safety around dugouts and ponds
- Machinery injuries
- Injuries from livestock
- Safe play spaces for children
- Water supply safety
- Hearing protection
- Eyesight protection
- Suicide
- Motor vehicle collisions
- Substance abuse

out the use of personal protective equipment, such as gloves and coveralls. Canadian studies of pesticide use among farmers have found an increased risk of cancers among those exposed (Bushy, 2000b). Gastrointestinal problems from acute or insidious poisoning through ingestion of contaminated food or water supplies are also concerns encountered particularly after crop spraying. Food and water can quickly become contaminated if chemicals are applied to crops during windy weather (Geller & Ludtke, 1991).

Another concern for rural residents living close to gas wells is that sour gas emissions and toxins released during flaring are harming not only human health but also that of livestock. Anecdotal evidence related to an alleged increased incidence of birth defects among local sheep and cattle has been presented to the government and media by some residents of north central Alberta. The perception that oil and gas exploration and extraction are harmful to health is shared by many western rural dwellers even though, to date, no studies have substantiated this claim.

Cancer

With an increased societal emphasis on environmental issues has come the perception of an increased incidence of cancers among our rural population. Recently, many Canadians seem to have shifted their view of rural areas from a region that is natural, clean, and healthy to one that is polluted, hazardous, and possibly carcinogenic.

There is epidemiological evidence to support the fact that some cancers are more prevalent among rural populations. For example, skin cancer, especially of the lip, is linked to increased exposure to the sun and its ultraviolet (UV) radiation among farmers and others who work in the sun without adequate UVB protection. Cancers noted as being more prevalent among farmers are leukemia, non-Hodgkin's lymphoma, Hodgkin's disease, multiple myeloma, stomach cancer, skin cancers, including melanoma, and cancers of the prostate, brain, testis, and connective tissue (Blair & Zahm, 1991; Geller & Ludtke, 1991). One widely held hypothesis is that chronic exposure to agricultural chemicals over many years is the reason why farmers are at increased risk of developing certain cancers. However, due to the diverse nature of farm work, investigation of exposures to other agents, such as fuels, engine exhausts, paint and solvent fumes, grain dusts, viruses, and fungi, must also be evaluated in terms of their carcinogenic potential (Blair & Zahm, 1991).

Water Safety

Water safety is a two-fold concern; firstly, bodies of water, such as irrigation ditches or dugouts and northern lakes and rivers, are common sites of drowning; and secondly, contaminated wells and creeks that supply drinking water for rural residents also pose health risks. Children who drown are generally preschoolers who have fallen into the water, whereas adults generally drown when the vehicles they are riding in break through the ice (Kyeremanteng, 1999, 2000).

The leaching of agricultural chemicals from crops and nitrites from livestock manure into groundwater is a widespread concern for many farm families (Geller & Ludtke, 1991). Larger towns and cities tend to have rigorous testing of their water supplies, but since it is an expensive process, it is not routinely carried out by those living on farms and ranches who rely on shallow groundwater as their primary source of drinking water. Many remote and northern residents continue to obtain their drinking water from sources that are not treated to remove bacteria and parasites. This fact, coupled with inadequate sewage disposal, has resulted in outbreaks of infection that are most harmful to infants, children, the elderly, and persons who are immuno-compromised. According to the Second Report on the Health of Canadians, the lack of adequate water treatment has resulted in the incidence of water-borne infections in First Nations communities being two to three times higher than in the general population (Health Canada, 1999).

Zoonoses

Other risks for rural and remote residents are zoonoses. These are diseases that are communicated from animals to humans. One of the more common zoonoses is brucellosis that is contracted from cattle, swine, and goats. Humans acquire this disease, known as undulant fever, from ingestion of unpasteurized dairy products. Another zoonoses seen in rural and northern areas is rabies, which is often transmitted from foxes, raccoons, and skunks. Although tularemia is spread by insects in some locales in Canada, it can be transmitted from seals and may, therefore, be contracted by hunters in the northern and eastern coastal regions (Lochhaas, 1987).

In northern and arctic regions, trichinosis is another parasitic infection that is commonly found in wild game, such as bears, cougars, and walruses. From 1970 to 1997, Labrador, Quebec, the Northwest Territories, including present-day Nunavut, and the Yukon had the highest number of reported cases of trichinosis, numbering over 100 (Appleyard & Gajadhar, 2000). Hantavirus is a recent health concern which is prevalent in arid rural areas. This pathogen is spread through droppings from deer mice.

Agricultural Injuries

Out of approximately 440,300 Canadians employed in the agricultural industry, an average of 120 die each year as a result of agriculture-related injuries and an additional 1,200 are hospitalized (Statistics Canada, 2002; Hartling, Pickett, & Brison, 1998). Unlike fatality statistics, precise numbers of farm-related injuries are unknown. However, it is estimated that the number of injuries reported is certainly lower than that of actual occurrences. This is primarily due to the fact that (1) many rural residents who are injured doing farm work do not seek formal health-care services, and (2) not all hospitals report these injuries to the collaborators who, in turn, submit statistics to the Canadian Agricultural Injury Surveillance Program (CAISP).

The primary agents causing injury vary from one area of the country to another depending upon the type of farming that predominates. Of those injuries reported in Alberta, livestock, chiefly cattle, horses, and pigs, contributed to 46 percent of injuries, while another 25 percent were caused by farm machinery, such as tractors, combines, augers, and all-terrain vehicles. About 50 percent of the livestock injuries were the result of being kicked or hit by the animal, and 25 percent occurred while riding. The majority of injuries that involved machinery resulted when the operator was repairing or unclogging the machinery (Kyeremanteng, 2000). Persons at highest risk for injury are males between 18 and 34 years (Kyeremanteng, 1999). When injuries occur, farm income is jeopardized because operators of small family farms are not usually covered by Worker's Compensation.

Primary Industry Injuries

In 1998, there were approximately 279,200 people employed in Canada's primary industries, excluding agriculture. Primary industries include logging, fishing, mining, and other resource-extraction practices, such as trapping. Unlike agriculture, the majority of these industries are regulated by federal and provincial occupational health and safety legislation.

The number of time-loss injuries in 1996 included 6,255 in logging and forestry; 4,784 in mining, quarrying, and oil wells; and 642 in fishing and trapping. The overall incidence of injuries for these industries has decreased from 3.3 per 100 workers in 1993 to 2.7 per 100 workers in 1997. Although there has been a slight increase in the total number of fatalities during this period from 781 to 833, one must also take into account the fact that the total number of workers has also increased during this time (Human Resources Development Canada, 1999). The implementation of occupational health and safety programs is responsible for ensuring that appropriate safety equipment is available, properly maintained, and used correctly. Such programs have done much to reduce the incidence of occupational injuries and fatalities in these primary industries.

Employers are rewarded for keeping their workers healthy through the payment of lower insurance premiums, and by maintaining a safe work environment, the employer maintains a healthy reputation in the industry and in the community. If workers are injured on the job, they receive some remuneration during their recovery through provincial Worker's Compensation Boards, provided the worker followed proper procedures and used required safety equipment properly.

Safe Play Areas for Children

Designated safe play areas for small children living on farms are rare. As many parents are trying to manage farm work while providing care for small children, the preschool age group is especially at risk for injury. Once children reach school age, statistics show that there is a decrease in agriculture-related injuries and fatalities until children are 10 years of age or older. This may be because this is the age at which many farm children begin to help with work on the family farm. Schools not only provide farm children with an education but they also serve to protect them from farm hazards for several hours a day. Many of the farm injuries and deaths of pre-school children are due to drowning and being run over by vehicles carrying farm equipment.

From 1990 to 1996, 101 young persons, 19 years of age or under, died as a result of farm injuries in Canada. During this same period, an additional 611 children were hospitalized because of farm-related injuries. In response to concerns for child safety around the farm, the North American Guidelines for Children's Agricultural Tasks were developed (http://www.nagcat.com). With input from leading safety experts in Canada, the United States, and Mexico, this set of guidelines advises parents regarding appropriate chores that can be assigned to children ages seven to 16 years.

Motor Vehicle Collisions

When discussing motor vehicles, the most commonly considered are cars, trucks, and motorcycles. However, farm vehicles, such as tractors, all-terrain vehicles (ATVs), dirt bikes, and snowmobiles are also included in this category although they are primarily used for off-road activities. Injuries as a result of motor vehicle collisions are the leading cause of death for Canadians under 35 years of age (Emergency Nurses Association, 1995). In 1998, there were 2,927 deaths due to motor vehicle collisions across Canada (Transport Canada, 2000). The national death rate per 10,000 vehicles is 1.6, with the highest rate (6.3) in the Yukon. Of those drivers who were fatally injured, 46 percent had been drinking and driving and had an average blood alcohol level twice the legal limit.

Although the total number of collisions may be lower in rural Canada, the significance of these events in terms of loss of life are proportionately greater than those in urban areas. For example, the more sparsely populated northwestern region of Alberta had the highest mortality rate in the province, while Edmonton and Calgary, the largest urban centres, had the lowest average motor vehicle mortality (Alberta Centre for Injury Control and Research, 2000). Several conditions thought to affect the mortality rate of rural and northern regions are:

- Narrow gravel roads
- Higher traffic speeds
- Wildlife or livestock on the roads
- Lower rates of seat belt and child restraint use
- The practice of riding in the back of open pick-up trucks
- Limited emergency medical personnel
- Greater distances to emergency medical services

In addition to the majority of collisions that involve more than one vehicle, single vehicle rollovers are common. This may be the result of high speed and loose gravel on country back roads. ATV rollovers occur in the process of carrying out farm or ranch work. Numerous injuries are incurred when ATV, dirt bike, and snowmobile riders encounter barbed wire fences, especially while travelling at high speeds. In northern areas, snowmobile mishaps are the leading cause of injury and death. In much of the north, snowmobiles are more common than trucks and are largely used for recreational purposes. Faster and larger machines have contributed to an increased incidence of injury in recent years.

Another factor related to the increased mortality in motor vehicle collisions in rural areas is the geographical distance that must be travelled to get either the necessary resources to the person in need or the injured individual to the appropriate level of care. In trauma care, the first hour following a traumatic event is commonly referred to as the "golden hour," since the care delivered to the victim during this initial phase strongly influences patient outcome.

Accessing resources from great distances also markedly affects health-care costs. For example, approximately 13 percent of the health-care dollars in the Northwest Territories go toward medical transportation compared with the national average of less than 2 percent (CIHI, 2001). In the north, travel becomes particularly difficult in the spring and fall when roads are soft, ice bridges are melting or not yet solid, and fog, snow, and wind are prevalent.

The total number of deaths resulting from motor vehicle collisions has decreased markedly over recent years. In 1998, the fatalities had dropped to 2,927 from 4,154 10 years earlier (Transport Canada, 2000). This decrease may be attributed to a combination of factors: better engineering of vehicles and roads, advances in medical care, increased public awareness campaigns, and education regarding traffic safety through such initiatives as Mission Possible supported by the Canadian Automobile Association, the Heroes Program from the Canadian Injury Prevention Foundation, and the Prevent Alcohol and Risk-related Trauma in Youth (PARTY) in Alberta and Ontario.

Hearing Loss

Many rural residents are at increased risk for noise-induced hearing loss. Working with heavy equipment, such as grain dryers, tractors, combines, and augers, can lead to intense exposure to loud noises for various periods of time. Pig farmers are especially at risk during feeding time when they are exposed to high-pitched squeals. Another group at risk are farriers, who are exposed to high levels of noise while hammering metal horseshoes on the anvil (Crutchfield & Sparks, 1991).

In addition to these occupational risks for hearing loss, rural dwellers may also suffer from presbycusis, hearing loss that accompanies aging, and socioacusis, hearing loss that results from recreational activities, such as listening to loud music or gunshots during skeet shooting. Prevention of hearing loss and preservation of residual hearing may be accomplished through occupational health and safety education regarding:

- Reducing the length of exposure to harmful noise
- Surrounding the sound with a sound-dampening enclosure
- Isolating the sound by placing a barrier around the driver, such as a tightly enclosed tractor or heavy machinery cab
- Wearing proper hearing-protection equipment (Crutchfield & Sparks, 1991)

Loss of Eyesight

Loss of sight and eye injuries are health concerns for both rural and urban populations. However, because of the very nature of the work performed by rural residents, more eye injuries are seen in rural acute-care facilities. Farmers, ranchers, loggers, and sawmill workers are often plagued by foreign bodies, such as gravel and wood chips, lodged in their eyes. Farmers are at increased risk of getting chemical spray in their eyes when applying a variety of fertilizers, herbicides, and pesticides. Those who work in the oil industry on the rigs or as heavy-duty mechanics require medical attention regularly due to a variety of chemicals splashed into their eyes. For example, one particularly caustic substance known as "big orange" is a powerful engine degreaser that quickly causes sloughing of delicate ophthalmic tissues if it is not vigorously and immediately flushed.

Rural dwellers suffer a significant number of eye injuries from blunt trauma. These injuries occur as a result of a direct blow to the eye, such as when an animal pushes a person into a fence, throws a rider to the ground, or when a stone from a slingshot or a softball directly strikes the eye. Penetrating eye injuries are more likely to cause permanent loss of vision. When a projectile enters the eye, it may go right through or remain embedded within the globe. Examples of penetrating eye trauma include a pellet from a BB gun or a projectile, such as a solder pin, thrown off a running piece of machinery on the farm or in the oil and gas industry.

Flash burns are one of the more common injuries seen among welders. A similar type of burn also occurs when persons are in the sun for long periods without proper eye protection from UV rays. This injury may manifest as snow blindness in trappers or outfitters, especially in springtime, or in any other rural or remote-area resident who is not wearing protective eye lenses.

Mental Health Issues

Mental health issues are those that affect an individual's mood, behaviour, thinking, and perceptions. The problem may be the result of an organic process, such as Alzheimer's disease, or be of a functional nature, such as depression. The number of Canadians who seek care related to mental health issues is unknown (Canadian Institute for Health Information, 2001). However, in 1992, a national study by the Canadian Mental Health Association found that 47 percent of Canadians were feeling "very stressed" and approximately one-third of respondents said they were "really depressed" at least once a month. Mental illness affects more people than does breast cancer, Alzheimer's disease, or diabetes (Alberta Health & Wellness, 1999). Factors that may differentiate rural mental health issues and care from urban ones, and may affect whether or not residents seek care, are:

- The lack of infrastructure to support and mobilize resources
- Different situational variables precipitating a mental health event or crisis, such as drought conditions during which farmers are unable to produce crops
- The lack of anonymity in rural communities
- The stigma still associated with mental health problems
- Concern regarding confidentiality

Stress

"Farm stress" is a term which came into being in the 1980s and refers to various socioeconomic factors in the agricultural industry that cause a physical or emotional response in those who are directly or indirectly involved with farming or ranching (Bushy, 2000a). Farmers and their families face numerous stressors, such as dropping commodity prices as they compete in a global economy, increasing debt load, droughts, floods, and fear of losing not only their farm but also their family's homestead and traditional lifestyle. Many farmers hold jobs off the farms in order to make ends meet and then work long hours in the evenings and on weekends doing the work required to maintain their business. Agriculture-related injuries very often result in permanent disability or death, which, in turn, further increases the burden of stress on the farm family.

Another stressor facing farmers is the sense of loss of control over their livelihood and way of life. With the expansion of corporate factory farms has come the further decline of the family farm. Socialized to solve problems on their own, farmers are vulnerable to depression and other stress-related illness. The cumulative stress for many has become acute, and so many farmers are trying to sell their farms. In the meanwhile, substance abuse and suicide are becoming grave issues of concern.

Persons employed in other primary industries, such as fishing, logging, trapping, and mining, are facing similar stresses with the loss of their livelihood. Entire workforces become unemployed as mines are shut down, fishing is curtailed, as has occurred on the East Coast of Canada, and the logging industry faces restrictions on cutting timber with the tariffs that affect cross border trade.

Other members of the rural community are also affected by these stresses. If the economic base of the community is a primary industry, then the entire community relies on the collective health of the industry. For example, if farmers are facing bankruptcy, it is only a matter of time before local agri-businesses, grocery and clothing retailers, the service sector, and founding institutions, such as churches and schools, also become threatened.

The first step toward combating stress is initiating public awareness campaigns and educating rural and remote communities to recognize and act upon common signs and symptoms exhibited by family members and friends. Information sessions presented by health professionals to community organizations or within faith communities have been well received. This strategy makes use of the existing informal community networks and links them to formal health-care resources. One example is telephone farm stress hotlines that have been successful in offering farmers and their families confidential referrals related to emotional counselling, financial assistance, and crisis intervention.

Substance Abuse

The onset of substance abuse can be inadvertent and insidious. Commonly abused substances include tobacco, alcohol, narcotics, as well as a wide range of illicit drugs, such as cannabis and hallucinogens. In addition, the inhalation of various aerosol products and sniffing of glues and gasoline has become a growing problem among Canadian youth, especially in the more remote regions. One example that recently received much attention from the media was the problem of children of Davis Inlet in Labrador sniffing gasoline while many parents were abusing alcohol (http://www.cbc.ca/storyview/CBC/2002/01/09/innu020109).

Substance use may begin in response to curiosity, in an attempt to achieve peer approval, as is often the case with tobacco and alcohol use among youth, or as a means of achieving an altered mental state in an attempt to escape situations or events. Substance abuse refers to the inappropriate use of prescription drugs or the use of illicit drugs.

Alcohol continues to be the primary drug leading to health-related problems (Peterson, 1994). Alcohol abuse causes chronic disease, permanent disabilities, and fatalities that result from sensory and motor impairment. This, in turn, leads to a variety of traumatic injuries and deaths as a result of falls, drowning, and motor vehicle collisions. Multiple social and economic factors contribute to the fact that the Canadian aboriginal population is at increased risk of death due to alcohol and suicide (Rennie, Baird-Crooks, Remus, & Engels, 2000).

Suicide

The past decade has brought about an increased incidence of suicide among rural youth, with the highest rate occurring among the Canadian aboriginal population. This rate is six times that of the non-aboriginal population (Kalischuk, 1999). The national suicide rate in 1997 was 12 per 100,000. In Alberta, suicide is the leading cause of death for the 25- to 39-year age group and the second leading cause of death among those aged 10 to 24 years, accounting for over 400 deaths per year (Harrington, 2000).

Factors that are believed to contribute to a high incidence of suicide are depression and substance abuse; changing family, community, and economic dynamics; cultural changes that emphasize the valuing of increased personal freedom and heterogeneity; declining religious affiliations; and Western society's tendency to view suicide as a terminal means of problem solving. While these factors are also influential in urban settings, rural communities tend to be more isolated from formalized health and social services. The lack of anonymity within small communities and the fear of being stigmatized with a mental health problem pressure some rural and northern residents to keep their problems to themselves.

Special Concerns in First Nations Communities

The problems that exist for rural residents are magnified for those who live in First Nations communities (MacMillan, MacMillan, Offord, & Dingle, 1996). High infant morbidity and mortality and significantly higher accident and injury rates among all ages contribute to lowered life expectancies. Lack of clean water and sewage systems, inadequate housing, and high unemployment are contributing factors in this negative picture. The rate of diabetes among First Nations members is 6 percent of the population, compared with 2 percent in the general population. Non-insulin-dependent diabetes mellitus (NIDDM) is now being found in children as young as 10 to 12 years of age (Bobet, 1998).

The leading cause of mortality from injury among First Nations people is motor vehicle collisions, with rates that exceed 40 per 100,000 population. The suicide rate is two to three times higher in this population than among the general population. Males, particularly in the 15- to 29-year age group, are at the highest risk for suicide (Cooper, Corrado, Karlberg, & Adams, 1992; Gotowiec & Beiser, 1993–94). Social disruption, lack of hope for the future, substance abuse, and family violence have all been suggested as underlying or related factors for suicide. Efforts to combat these problems include community mobilization and awareness campaigns.

Health-Care Delivery

Health-Care Delivery Issues

There are many factors that contribute to making the delivery of appropriate and cost-effective health services to rural, remote, and northern populations a challenge. A major factor is the need to deliver a variety of health services to a population that is sparsely distributed over a large geographical area, with a limited number of health-care professionals. The inclusion of health issues of rural, remote, and northern residents within general statistics contributes to difficulties in being able to focus on specific concerns affecting these populations.

Additional dynamics affecting health-care delivery are:

- Communication issues
- Sparse resources

Nursing and Health-Care Delivery Issues

- Data gaps and inadequate information re health status of rural residents
- Distance
- Sparse population
- Limited infrastructure including transportation and communication
- Limited health-care resources and access to technology
- Educational preparation for generalist-specialist practice
- Recruitment and retention of professionals
- Ethical issues (lack of anonymity, confidentiality, resources)

- Difficulties in transportation
- Education, recruitment, and retention of health-care professionals
- Changing demographics and care requirements of the community

Health-care providers in rural, remote, and northern areas must possess a broad, generalized knowledge base to meet the diverse health-care needs of the residents.

Throughout the 1990s, the Canadian health-care system underwent sweeping changes. Two of the more significant changes affecting health-care delivery were drastic fiscal cutbacks and the regionalization of health-service administration and delivery. The intent of regionalization was to allow the board responsible for each regional health authority (RHA) the freedom to plan and implement the health-care services and programs they deemed most beneficial in meeting the needs of the residents within their jurisdiction. A major boon of regionalization has been that RHAs now have the autonomy to decide what constitutes appropriate care for their communities and how it is best offered within the budgets that are set by provincial governments. A significant price of this restructuring process, however, has been the closure of many rural hospitals, resulting in the need to travel even greater distances to receive care.

Rural, Remote, and Northern Nursing Practice

Nurses practise in multiple settings in rural, remote, and northern sites; they provide acute and extended care, community health, home care, occupational health, and mental health-care services and, in some provinces, are taking on expanded practice roles.

RESEARCH NOTE

"We're It": Issues and Realities in Rural Nursing Practice

A participatory action research study was conducted in northern British Columbia for the purpose of developing a deeper understanding of rural and remote nursing practice. Nurses working in three small acute-care hospitals, ranging in size from 12 to 16 beds, were observed during an entire shift and were later interviewed. Using interpretive phenomenology, the researcher developed the themes and patterns that emerged from the data regarding nursing practice. Findings included (1) the extensive responsibility that nurses carry for acute-care services, 24 hours a day, seven days a week; (2) the diversity of roles that nurses play; and (3) the difficulty and pleasure that nurses felt from caring for persons they knew. Recommendations arising from the study were the need to (1) value rural nursing practice, (2) critically examine health-care policies as they affect rural practice, (3) develop the infrastructure and systems locally to facilitate the delivery of care, and (4) improve the infrastructure for practice and education at the regional, provincial, and national levels.

Source: MacLeod, M. (1999). "We're It": Issues and realities in rural nursing practice. In W. Ramp, J. Kulig, I. Townshend, & V. McGowan (Eds.), Health in rural settings: Contexts for action (pp. 165–178). Lethbridge: University of Lethbridge Press.

Nursing Practice Issues

The majority of research regarding rural and remote nursing has come from Australia and the United States. Rural nursing in Canada lacks consistent definition and has not yet been formally recognized as a distinct specialized area of nursing practice (Rennie et al., 2000). While some claim that the only difference between rural and urban nursing is the environment in which nursing is practised, others disagree. Scharff (1998) claims that rural nursing is distinctive in terms of "its boundaries, intersections, dimensions, and even its very core" (p. 20). Describing the "core" of nursing as care and the unique relationship between the nurse and the patient, Scharff is adamant that "what happens at the core of rural nursing is something apart from what happens at the core of nursing anywhere else" (p. 20). This caring is based on interpersonal knowledge of the patients/clients, their families, and communities, as well as the relationship that exists between the nurses and their co-workers. In 2001, nursing researchers from across Canada, in collaboration with a geographer, began a major study on the nature of rural and remote nursing.

Bushy (2000) notes that rural nurses in Canada, the United States, and Australia share many common characteristics. Nurses are often described as highly visible members of the community—resourceful, flexible, autonomous, self-reliant, and effective team members (Hegney, 1997; Rosenthal, 1996). Above all else, rural nurses are described as *jack-of-all-trades*, *generalists*, and *specialist-generalists*. The need to maintain general practice skills covering all ages and all the conditions which clients/patients may present with is a major challenge for rural nurses. The introduction of Web-based programs offers the opportunity to provide education programs to nurses located in many communities where other types of education programming may not be feasible.

The high visibility of the nurse in the community (a key factor that affects nursing practice) and the resultant lack of anonymity mean that nurses may never be "off-duty" and may be consulted by friends and neighbours wherever they go. This lack of anonymity presents particular problems when these same friends and neighbours present with injuries and life-threatening illnesses. Other characteristics of rural practice are:

- Greater autonomy because there are fewer nurses and other health professionals
- Greater knowledge of the client's/patient's home and family conditions
- Closer interface with other health-care professionals
- Greater opportunity to affect health-care planning and policy at the local level because of the recognized role as a resource on health care and the prominence in the community

Education for Rural and Remote Practice

As early as 1975, a course in rural hospital nursing was offered at the Foothills Hospital School of Nursing in Calgary (Reimer & Mills, 1988). Across the country, some undergraduate nursing programs are beginning to include theory and clinical practice specific to rural nursing in their curricula. Other programs continue to use rural placements as practicum sites, with a lesser emphasis placed on the setting itself. It is essential that more nursing students be educated to practise in rural and remote acute-care and community settings.

Post-diploma education for northern, remote, and/or expanded practice nursing has a somewhat longer history. The Dalhousie Outpost Nursing (OPN) Program is perhaps one of the best known and longest running. It began in 1967 with a mandate to educate nurses for the roles and responsibilities inherent in nursing practice in northern and remote Canadian communities. The OPN Program closed in 1997 when federal funding that previously supported the program was withdrawn and re-allocated to regional initiatives (Martin-Misener, Vuckic, & May, 1999).

The recruitment and retention of nurses for practise in rural and remote/northern regions of Canada have been persistent problems. It is anticipated that with the projected national nursing shortage, there will be a need for an even greater emphasis on preparing and attracting nurses to practise in these areas. Nursing leaders and educators have a role in the education and psychological preparation of nurses to work in these diverse settings.

FOCUS ON CRITICAL THINKING

Mr. Donaldson is a 45-year-old farmer who presented to the Emergency Department with cellulitis in his right leg, secondary to a puncture wound from the tine of a pitchfork. He runs a family grain-and-cattle operation about 50 kilometres from town and the nearest hospital. He is given the choice of being admitted to hospital or returning to hospital every eight hours for a one-hour antibiotic treatment and for a daily dressing change. He is told he must limit his activity and keep his leg elevated as much as possible.

1. What issues should the nurse discuss with Mr. Donaldson to assist him in choosing his treatment options?
2. How might the patient's regime vary from that in an urban setting?
3. How might Mr. Donaldson's occupation influence his recovery?
4. What health-care delivery issues common to rural and remote residents affect Mr. Donaldson's treatment?

See Appendix A for answers to these questions.

CHAPTER HIGHLIGHTS

- Clear definitions for *rural*, *remote*, and *northern* areas are required to allow for data collection on health-care information of residents in these regions of the country. Currently, there is a lack of consensus regarding definitions of the terms *rural* and *remote*.
- Great diversity in the geography of Canada contributes to particular regional issues.
- The changing demographic profile of rural, remote, and northern residents presents challenges to residents, communities, and health-care professionals. There is a larger percentage of rural elderly within the population as a result of migration of young adults to urban centres.
- Rural and remote residents have higher infant mortality, lower life expectancy, and higher rates of injuries and death than urban residents.
- Common health concerns include respiratory illnesses, chemical exposures, cancer, hearing and sight problems, and zoonoses.
- Water safety includes two separate components: the contamination of drinking water supplies and drownings in ditches, dugouts, rivers, and lakes.
- Injuries and deaths within rural and remote primary industries are a significant factor in the health care of rural populations.
- Children are at particular risk for injury or death because of the lack of designated safe play areas for young children and because older children often work on family farms.
- Numerous factors contribute to high mortality rates from motor vehicle collisions.
- Stressors affecting rural and remote residents include droughts, floods, competition in a global economy, mine closures, logging restrictions, and fishing moratoriums.
- Social and economic factors contribute to increased mortality and morbidity within the aboriginal population in Canada.
- Challenges to health-service delivery are sparse population, distance, and difficulties in recruiting and retaining health-care professionals.
- A major challenge for rural nurses is to attain and maintain practice skills for providing care for all ages and health conditions.
- Key characteristics of rural and remote practice are lack of anonymity, greater autonomy, and broad generalist practice.

READINGS AND REFERENCES

Suggested Readings

Lee, H. (Ed.). (1998). *Conceptual basis for rural nursing*. New York: Springer Publishing.

This edited text presents a beginning conceptualization of rural nursing theory and practice. Key concepts for rural health and nursing from research in Montana are analyzed. Selected rural populations are highlighted. Rural clinical and professional issues are discussed.

Ramp, W., Kulig, J., Townsend, I., & McGowan, V. (Eds.). (1999). *Health in rural settings: Context for action*. Lethbridge, AB: University of Lethbridge Press.

This edited text, which contains papers by authors from multiple disciplines, offers a broad international perspective of rural health. Topics comprise rural geography, economic issues, community participation, cultural diversity, and impact of suicide.

Rennie, D., Baird-Crooks, K., Remus, G., & Engels, J. (2000). Rural nursing in Canada. In A. Bushy (Ed.), *Orientation to nursing in the rural community* (pp. 217–231). Thousand Oaks, CA: Sage.

This book chapter briefly describes the Canadian health-care system and examines the effect of nursing practice on the health of rural residents. Key factors relevant to nursing practice are discussed.

Selected References

Agriculture Alberta. (2001). *Growing safely: Injuries on the farm*. Retrieved May 8, 2001, from http:// www.agric.gov.ab.ca/ministry/agrinews/agrn0111.html.

Alberta Centre for Injury Control and Research (ACICR). (2000). *ACICR Motor Vehicle Injury FACTS*. Retrieved June 1, 2001, from http://www.med.ualberta.ca/acicr/pages/facts/carfact.html). Edmonton, AB:University of Alberta.

Alberta Health and Wellness. (1999). *Report on the health of Albertans: Looking through a wider lens*. Edmonton, AB: Government of Alberta, Alberta Health and Wellness.

Appleyard, G. D., & Gajadhar, A. A. (2000). A review of trichinellosis in people and wildlife in Canada. *Canadian Journal of Public Health, 91*, 293–297.

Bavington, B. (1994). Rural public health. *Canadian Journal of Public Health, 85*, 295–296.

Blair, A., & Zahm, S. H. (1991). Cancer among farmers. *Occupational Medicine: State of the Art Reviews, 6*, 335–353.

Bobet, E. (1998). *Diabetes Among first nations people*. Ottawa, ON: Health Canada.

Bruce, D., & Black, B. (2000). *Aging in community: The aging rural and small town population in Atlantic Canada*. Sackville, NB: Department of Geography, Mount Allison University.

Bushy, A. (2000a). Behavioral health care: Rural issues and strategies. In A. Bushy (Ed.),*Orientation to nursing in the rural community* (pp. 107–123). Thousand Oaks, CA: Sage Publications, Inc.

Bushy, A. (Ed.). (2000b). *Orientation to nursing in the rural community*. Thousand Oaks, CA: Sage Publications, Inc.

Canadian Institute for Health Information (CIHI). (2002). *Supply and distribution of registered nurses in rural and small town Canada, 2000.* (ISBN 1-894766-34-2).Ottawa, ON: Author.

Canadian Institute for Health Information (CIHI). (2001). *Health care in Canada*. (ISBN 1-896104-82-7). Ottawa, ON: Canadian Institute for Health Information and Statistics Canada.

Cooper, M., Corrado, R., Karlberg, A. M., & Adams, L. P. (1992). Aboriginal suicide in British Columbia: An overview. *Canada's Mental Health, 40*(3), 19–23.

Crutchfield, C. D., & Sparks, S. T. (1991). Effects of noise and vibration on farmworkers. *Occupational Medicine: State of the Art Review, 6*, 355–369.

Emergency Nurses Association. (1995). *Trauma Nursing Core Course Provider Manual*. Park Ridge, IL: Emergency Nurses Association.

Fellegi, I. (1996). *Understanding rural Canada: Structures and trends.* Available at http://www.statcan.ca:80/english/freepub/21F0016XIE/rural96/html/one_file/rural_e.htm. Ottawa, ON: Statistics Canada.

Geller, J. M., & Ludtke, R. L. (1991). Health risks in agriculture. In A. Bushy (Ed.), *Rural nursing* (Vol. 1). (pp. 334–347). Newbury Park, CA: Sage.

Gotowiec, A., & Beiser, M. (1993–94). Aboriginal children's mental health: Unique challenges. *Canada's Mental Health, 41*(4), 7–11.

Hanson, C. M. (1999). Care of clients in rural settings. In M. J. Clark (Ed.), *Nursing in the community: Dimensions of community health nursing* (3rd ed). (pp. 667–684). Stamford, CT: Appleton & Lange.

Harrington, G. (2000). Suicide awareness week in Alberta. *Injury Control Alberta, 2*(6), 2.

Hartling, L., Pickett, W., & Brison, R. J. (1998). Cross-country forum: The Canadian Agricultural Injury Surveillance Program: A new injury control initiative. *Chronic Diseases in Canada, 19*, 108–111.

Health Canada. (1999). *Toward a healthy future: Second report on the health of Canadians* (Cat. H39-468/1999E). Ottawa, ON: Minister of Public Works and Government Services Canada.

Hegney, D. (1997). Rural nursing practice. In L. Siegloff (Ed.), *Rural nursing in the Australian context* (Vol. 7). (pp. 43). Canberra, Australia: Royal College of Nursing.

Human Resources Development Canada. (1999). *Statistical Analysis Occupational Injuries and Fatalities Canada*. Retrieved June 18, 2001, from http://www.info.load-otea.hrdc.gc.ca/~oshwev/naoshstats. Ottawa, ON: Government of Canada.

Kalischuk, R. G. (1999). Healing within families following youth suicide: A rural health focus. In W. Ramp, J. Kulig, I. Townsend, & V. McGowan (Eds.), *Health in rural settings: Contexts for action* (pp. 107–132). Lethbridge, AB: University of Lethbridge Press.

Kyeremanteng, S. (1999). *Farm injury report.* Retrieved October 18, 1999, from http://www.agric.gov. ab.ca/ruraldev/safefarm/98farminjury.html. Edmonton, Alberta: Department of Agriculture.

Kyeremanteng, S. (2000). *Farm injury report.* Retrieved March 18, 2001, from http//www.agric.gov. ab.ca/ruraldev/safefarm/2000farminjury.html. Edmonton, Alberta: Department of Agriculture.

Last, J., Trouton, K., & Pengelly, D. (1998). *Taking our breath away: The health effects of air pollution and climate change.* Vancouver: David Suzuki Foundation. Retrieved May 2002, from http://www.davidsuzuki.org.

Lee, H. (Ed.). (1998). *Conceptual basis for rural nursing*. New York: Springer Publishing Co.

Lochhaas, T. (Ed.). (1987). *Mosby's Medical Dictionary* (2nd ed.). Toronto, ON: Mosby.

MacMillan, H. L., MacMillan, A. B., Offord, D. R., & Dingle, J. L. (1996). Aboriginal health. *Canadian Medical Association Journal, 155*, 1569–1578.

Martin-Misener, R., Vuckic, A., & May, R. (1999). Lessons learned from the Dalhousie Outpost Nursing Program. In W. Ramp, J. Kulig, I. Townsend, & V. McGowan (Eds.), *Health in rural settings: Contexts for action* (pp. 203–210). Lethbridge, AB: University of Lethbridge Press.

Paquet, B. (2001). *Low Income Cutoffs from 1990 to 1999 and Low Income Measure from 1989 to 1998* (Catalogue no. 75F0002MIE-00017). Ottawa, ON: Minister of Industry and Statistics Canada.

Peterson, L. E.(1994). Common mental health problems. In B. P. Yawn, A. Bushy, & R.A. Yawn (Eds.), *Exploring rural medicine: Current issues and concepts* (pp. 97–118). Thousand Oaks, CA: Sage Publications, Inc.

Pong, R. W. (2000). Rural health research in Canada: At the crossroads. *Australian Journal of Rural Health, 8*, 261–265.

Ramp, W., Kulig, J., Townsend, I., & McGowan, V. (Eds.). (1999). *Health in rural settings: Context for action.* Lethbridge, AB: University of Lethbridge Press.

Reimer, M., & Mills, C. (1988). Rural hospital nursing as an elective. *The Journal of Rural Health, 4*(2), 5–8.

Rennie, D., Baird-Crooks, K., Remus, G., & Engels, J. (2000). Rural nursing in Canada. In A. Bushy (Ed.), *Orientation to nursing in the rural community* (pp. 217–231).Thousand Oaks, CA: Sage.

Rosenthal, K. A. (1996). *Rural nursing: An exploratory narrative description.*Unpublished Dissertation. Denver, CO: University of Colorado.

Scharff, J. E. (1998). The distinctive nature and scope of rural nursing practice: Philosophical bases. In H. J. Lee (Ed.), *Conceptual basis of rural nursing* (pp. 19–38). New York: Springer Publishing Co.

Statistics Canada. (1999). *Profile of the census divisions and Subdivisions in Alberta.* Ottawa: Industry Canada.

Statistics Canada. (2002). *Canada at a Glance 2002* (catalogue 12-581-XPE). Ottawa: Minister Responsible for Statistics Canada.

Transport Canada. (2000). *Canadian motor vehicle traffic collision statistics.* Retrieved June 2, 2001, from http://www.tc.gc.ca/pol/en/t- facts_e/Highways_ Data_Menu.htm. Ottawa, ON: Transport Canada.

Troughton, M. J. (1995). Presidential address: Rural Canada and Canadian rural geography—an appraisal. *The Canadian Geographer*, *39*, 290–305.

Troughton, M. J. (1999). Defining "rural" for the 21st century. In W. Ramp, J. Kulig, I. Townshend, & V. McGowan (Eds.), *Health in rural settings: Contexts for action* (pp. 21–38). Lethbridge, AB: University of Lethbridge Printing Services.

Voaklander, D., Belton, K., Menon, M., Lim, G., & Schopflocher, D. (1999). *Agriculture-related injury in Alberta* (Vol. 2). (pp. 1).

Watanabe, M., & Casebeer, A. (2000). *Rural, remote, and northern health research: The quest for equitable health status for all Canadians. The Rural Health Research Summit.* Retrieved March 30, 2000, from http://www.unbc.ca/rural health/ Nation_Summit/.

Weinert, C., & Boik, R. J. (1995). MSU Rurality Index: Development and evaluation. *Research in Nursing & Health*, *18*, 453–464.

Wilkins, R. (1992). Health of the rural population: Selected indicators. In R. D. Bollman (Ed.), *Rural and small town Canada* (pp. 285–291). Toronto: Thompson Educational Publishing, Inc. in cooperation with Statistics Canada and the Canada Communications Group-Publishing, Supply and Services Canada.

WEBLINKS

Government of Canada—Canadian Rural Partnership
http://www.rural.gc.ca/home_e.phtml
This site provides access through a single window to knowledge, information, programs, and services for and about rural and remote Canada.

Health Canada—Rural Health
http://www.hc-sc.gc.ca/english/ruralhealth/index.html
This site describes the Office of Rural Health, which was established in Health Canada in 1998 in response to the federal government's commitment to applying a "rural lens" to its policies, programs, and services. Publications related to rural health are available on the site.

Society of Rural Physicians in Canada
http://www.srpc.ca/
The Society of Rural Physicians of Canada (SRPC) is the national voice of Canadian rural physicians. Founded in 1992, the SRPC's mission is to provide leadership for rural physicians and to promote sustainable conditions and equitable health care for rural communities. The site provides information about the society and its resources.

CBC

Canadian Case Study — Should Jacob Remain at Home?

Jacob was a 42-year-old father of two who had severe multiple sclerosis. He was first diagnosed at 31. He was confined to a wheelchair but demonstrated cognitive thinking. His speech was impacted because of the disease process. He was forced to retire from the workplace and apply for permanent disability in his late 30s because of changes in his health status. At his retirement, he and his wife decided to move from a small rural community into a large urban centre to provide them with greater access to health care resources such as occupational therapy and handibus services. They had found that these services were not available in their small community.

Six years ago, he was admitted to a long-term care facility because his wife could no longer provide the physical care that he required, even with the assistance of local Home Care staff who had funding limits. At that time, his wife was insistent that if resources were in place, she would very much prefer that Jacob return home. Because of Jacob's consistent requests to go home and the desire of his wife and family to have him there, Home Care decided to provide extra funding. With the assistance of the social worker, he was able to obtain government funds to ensure that his house was wheelchair accessible.

Jacob wished to stay in his own home and to continue using the services of Home Care staff. He was able to have nursing support seven days a week to help him with personal care. (Wilson, 2002). Part of the nursing role had been to help the family reduce both the strain and the stress which can aggravate the multiple sclerosis and precipitate a flair up of Jacob's symptoms. Other supportive measures implemented by the nurse included: initiating a regime of rest and exercise, instructing the family about a well-balanced diet, and encouraging self-catheterization. The latter was initiated as an attempt to reduce urinary retention as Jacob could no longer urinate.

Housekeeping support of about four hours a week was contracted to a private agency. His wife did some part-time work at the local library to provide extra income but also to give herself opportunities for social interaction and friendship. Their children, a boy and a girl, now 12 and 14 years old, are well aware of the changes occurring in their father's health.

The maximum funding for Home Care services was allocated at $2,200 per month. However, Jacob's care cost almost $10,000. The funding was constantly under review by Home Care because it was substantially over the base funding provided to other administrative needs to reduce costs and justify services because of funding restrictions imposed. Jacob's situation is perhaps fairly typical of Home Care services across the country. Wilson (2002) identified that several Canadian reports documented concern over the state of Home Care funding. A qualitative study by Aronson and Neysmith (1996) of visiting homemakers sought to explore the implications of financial cutbacks upon those receiving Home Care services. A sample of visiting homemakers working in Ontario participated in semi-structured interviews about their work experiences. Analysis of interview transcripts discovered potential exploitation and tensions introduced by funding limitations, and suggested that Home Care workers' ability to deliver high-quality, personalized care was compromised by organizational practices.

One advantage for Jacob and his wife, Marie, was that he was able to obtain most of this money directly from Home Care and they could manage the distribution of these funds. This helped him have some input into who would provide care for him. Jacob was aware that using a registered nurse was more expensive than hiring a less-qualified health-care professional. However, he feels that the nurse is better able to help him access services and to identify and evaluate his nursing needs.

QUESTIONS

1. Identify the variables in Jacob's situation that could give rise to ethical dilemmas.
2. What can you do to demonstrate advocacy for Jacob and his family?
3. Should there be a limit on the amount of health-care funding that is provided to an individual patient?
4. What process should be used to determine how health-care resources are allocated?

VIDEO RESOURCES

Series Title:	The National
Segment Title:	The Cost of Care
Telecast Date:	September 14, 1999
Running Time:	14.58

Sources: Aronson, J., Neysmith, S. M. (1996). The work of visiting homemakers in the context of cost cutting in long-term care. *Canadian Journal of Public Health, 87*(6), 422–5.

Sullivan, C. (2000). Canadian Study shows promising results on Home Care cost effectiveness. *Caring, 19*(6), 42–5.

Wilson, D. (2002). Commentary. Making a case for home care: There is a growing need for home care and additional research, yet funding remains a low priority in provincial/territorial budgets. *Canadian Nurse, 98*(1), 8–9.

SECTION 2

Human Functioning and Development

CHAPTER 19
Concepts of Growth and Development

CHAPTER 20
Development from Conception through Adolescence

CHAPTER 21
Development from Young through Older Adulthood

CHAPTER 19

Concepts of Growth and Development

OBJECTIVES

After completing this chapter, you will be able to:

- Describe essential facts related to growth and development.
- Differentiate growth from development.
- Discuss the stages of growth and development.
- Identify factors that influence growth and development.
- Explain the principles of growth and development.
- Identify developmental tasks associated with Havighurst's six age periods.
- Describe characteristics and implications of Freud's five stages of development.
- Identify Erikson's eight stages of development.
- Compare Peck's and Gould's stages of adult development.
- Explain Piaget's theory of cognitive development.
- Compare Kohlberg's and Gilligan's theories of moral development.
- Analyze Fowler's and Westerhoff's stages of spiritual development.

The terms *growth* and *development* both refer to dynamic processes. Often used interchangeably, these terms have different meanings. **Growth** is physical change and increase in size. It can be measured quantitatively. Indicators of growth include height, weight, bone size, and dentition. The pattern of physiological growth is similar for all people. However, growth rates vary during different stages of growth and development. For example, the growth rate is rapid during the prenatal, neonatal, infancy, and adolescent stages. The growth rate slows during childhood, and physical growth is minimal during adulthood.

Development is an increase in the complexity of function and skill progression. It is the capacity and skill of a person to adapt to the environment. Development is the behavioural aspect of growth; for example, a person develops the ability to walk, to talk, and to run.

Growth and development are independent but interrelated processes. For example, an infant's muscles, bones, and nervous system must grow to a certain point before the infant can sit up or walk. Growth generally takes place during the first 20 years of life; development continues after that. Principles of growth and development are shown in the accompanying box.

Factors Influencing Growth and Development

The factors that influence growth and development are genetic and environmental. The genetic inheritance of an individual is established at conception. It remains unchanged throughout life and determines such characteristics as gender, physical stature, and race. Environmental factors include family, religion, climate, culture, school, community, and nutrition. For example, poorly nourished children are more likely to have infections than are well-fed children and may not attain their full height potential.

Stages of Growth and Development

The rate of a person's growth and development is highly individual; however, the sequence of growth and development is predictable. Stages of growth usually correspond to certain developmental changes. See Table 19.1.

Growth and development are commonly thought of as having five major components: physiological, psychosocial, cognitive, moral, and spiritual. A discussion of some of the major theories relating to these components follows.

Principles of Growth and Development

- Growth and development are continuous, orderly, sequential processes influenced by maturational, environmental, and genetic factors.
- All humans follow the same pattern of growth and development.
- The sequence of each stage is predictable, although the time of onset, the length of the stage, and the effects of each stage vary with the person.
- Learning can either help or hinder the maturational process, depending on what is learned.
- Each developmental stage has its own characteristics. For example, Piaget suggests that in the sensorimotor stage (birth to two years), children learn to coordinate simple motor tasks.
- Growth and development occur in a *cephalocaudal* direction, that is, starting at the head and moving to the trunk, the legs, and the feet. This pattern is particularly obvious at birth, when the head of the infant is disproportionately large.
- Growth and development occur in a proximal to distal direction, that is, from the centre of the body outward. For example, infants can roll over before they can grasp an object with the thumb and second finger.
- Development proceeds from simple to complex, or from single acts to integrated acts. To accomplish the integrated act of drinking and swallowing a liquid from a cup, for example, the child must first learn a series of single acts: eye-hand coordination, grasping, hand-mouth coordination, controlled tipping of the cup, and then mouth, lip, and tongue movements to drink and swallow.
- Development becomes increasingly differentiated. *Differentiated development* begins with a generalized response and progresses to a skilled specific response. For example, an infant's initial response to a stimulus involves the total body; a five-year-old child can respond more specifically with laughter or fear.
- Certain stages of growth and development are more critical than others. It is known, for example, that the first 10 to 12 weeks after conception are critical. The incidence of congenital anomalies as a result of exposure to certain viruses, chemicals, or drugs is greater during this stage than others.
- The pace of growth and development is uneven. It is known that growth is greater during infancy than during childhood. Asynchronous development is demonstrated by rapid growth of the head during infancy and of the extremities at puberty.

TABLE 19.1 Stages of Growth and Development

Stage	Age	Significant Characteristics	Nursing Implications
Neonatal	Birth to 28 days	Behaviour is largely reflexive and develops to more purposeful behaviour.	Assist parents to identify and meet unmet needs.
Infancy	1 month to 1 year	Physical growth is rapid.	Control the infant's environment so that physical and psychological needs are met.
Toddlerhood	1 to 3 years	Motor development permits increased physical autonomy. Psychosocial skills increase.	Safety and risk-taking strategies must be balanced to permit growth.
Preschool	3 to 6 years	The preschooler's world is expanding. New experiences and the preschooler's social role are tried during play. Physical growth is slower.	Provide opportunities for play and social activity.
School age	6 to 12 years	Stage includes the pre-adolescent period (10 to 12 years). Peer group increasingly influences behaviour. Physical, cognitive, and social development increase, and communication skills improve.	Allow time and energy for the school-age child to pursue hobbies and school activities. Recognize and support child's achievements.
Adolescence	12 to 20 years	Self-concept changes with biological development. Values are tested. Physical growth accelerates. Stress increases, especially in face of conflicts.	Assist adolescents to develop coping behaviours. Help adolescents develop strategies for resolving conflicts.
Young adulthood	20 to 40 years	A personal lifestyle develops. Person establishes a relationship with a significant other and a commitment to something.	Accept adult's chosen lifestyle and assist with necessary adjustments relating to health. Recognize the person's commitments. Support change as necessary for health.
Middle adulthood	40 to 65 years	Lifestyle changes due to other changes; for example, children leave home, occupational goals change.	Assist clients to plan for anticipated changes in life, to recognize the risk factors related to health, and to focus on strengths rather than weaknesses.
Older adulthood			
Young-old	65 to 74 years	Adaptation to retirement and changing physical abilities is often necessary. Chronic illness may develop.	Assist clients to keep physically and socially active and to maintain peer group interactions.
Middle-old	75 to 84 years	Adaptation to decline in speed of movement, reaction time, and sensory abilities, and increasing dependence on others may be necessary.	Assist clients to cope with loss (e.g., hearing, eyesight, death of loved one). Provide necessary safety measures.
Old-old	85 and over	Increasing physical problems may develop.	Assist clients with self-care as required, and with maintaining as much independence as possible.

Growth and Development Theories

Developmental Task Theory (Havighurst)

Robert Havighurst believed that learning is basic to life and that people continue to learn throughout life. He described growth and development as occurring during six stages, each associated with six to 10 tasks to be learned. See Table 19.2. Havighurst believed that once a person learns to talk, it is mastered for life.

Havighurst promoted the concept of developmental tasks in the 1950s. A **developmental task** is "a task which arises at or about a certain period in the life of an individ-

TABLE 19.2 Havighurst's Age Periods and Developmental Tasks

Infancy and Early Childhood
1. Learning to walk
2. Learning to take solid foods
3. Learning to talk
4. Learning to control the elimination of body wastes
5. Learning sex differences and sexual modesty
6. Achieving psychological stability
7. Forming simple concepts of social and physical reality
8. Learning to relate emotionally to parents, siblings, and other people
9. Learning to distinguish right from wrong and developing a conscience

Middle Childhood
1. Learning physical skills necessary for ordinary games
2. Building wholesome attitudes toward oneself as a growing organism
3. Learning to get along with age-mates
4. Learning an appropriate masculine or feminine social role
5. Developing fundamental skills in reading, writing, and calculating
6. Developing concepts necessary for everyday living
7. Developing conscience, morality, and a scale of values
8. Achieving personal independence
9. Developing attitudes toward social groups and institutions

Adolescence
1. Achieving new and more mature relations with age-mates of both genders
2. Achieving a masculine or feminine social role
3. Accepting one's physique and using the body effectively
4. Achieving emotional independence from parents and other adults
5. Achieving assurance of economic independence
6. Selecting and preparing for an occupation
7. Preparing for marriage and family life
8. Developing intellectual skills and concepts necessary for civic competence
9. Desiring and achieving socially responsible behaviour
10. Acquiring a set of values and an ethical system as a guide to behaviour

Early Adulthood
1. Selecting a mate
2. Learning to live with a partner
3. Starting a family
4. Rearing children
5. Managing a home
6. Getting started in an occupation
7. Taking on civic responsibility
8. Finding a congenial social group

Middle Age
1. Achieving adult civic and social responsibility
2. Establishing and maintaining an economic standard of living
3. Assisting teenage children to become responsible and happy adults
4. Developing adult leisure-time activities
5. Relating oneself to one's spouse as a person
6. Accepting and adjusting to the physiological changes of middle age
7. Adjusting to aging parents

Later Maturity
1. Adjusting to decreasing physical strength and health
2. Adjusting to retirement and reduced income
3. Adjusting to death of spouse
4. Establishing an explicit affiliation with one's age group
5. Meeting social and civil obligations
6. Establishing satisfactory physical living arrangements

Source: Robert J. Havighurst. (1972). *Developmental tasks and education,* (3rd ed.). Copyright © 1972 by Longman Publishers, USA. Reprinted with permission.

ual, successful achievement of which leads to his happiness and to success with later tasks, while failure leads to unhappiness in the individual, disapproval by society, and difficulty with later tasks" (Havighurst, 1972, p. 2).

Havighurst's developmental tasks provide a framework that the nurse can use to evaluate a person's general accomplishments. However, some nurses find that the broad categories limit its usefulness as a tool in assessing specific accomplishments, particularly those of infancy and childhood.

Psychosocial Theories

Psychosocial development refers to the development of personality. **Personality** is a complex concept that is difficult to define. It can be considered as the outward (interpersonal) expression of the inner (intrapersonal) self. It encompasses a person's temperament, feelings, character traits, independence, self-esteem, self-concept, behaviour, ability to interact with others, and ability to adapt to life changes.

Many theorists attempt to account for psychosocial development in humans. Many of these theories explain the development of a person's personality and the causes of behaviour. The theorists discussed in this book are Freud, Erikson, Peck, and Gould.

Freud

Sigmund Freud (1923) introduced a number of concepts about development that are still used today. The concepts of the unconscious mind, defence mechanisms, and the id, ego, and superego are Freud's. The **unconscious mind** is the part of a person's mental life that the person is unaware of. This concept of the unconscious is one of Freud's major contributions to the field of psychiatry. **Defense mechanisms,** or **adaptive mechanisms** as they are more commonly called today, are the result of conflicts between inner impulses and the anxiety that attends these conflicts. The **id** is the source of instinctive and unconscious urges, which Freud considered chiefly sexual in nature. The id is also the source of all pleasure and gratification. The **ego** is formed by the person to make effective contact with social and physical needs. Through the ego, the id impulses are satisfied. The third aspect of the personality, according to Freud, is the **superego.** The superego is the source of feelings of guilt, shame, and inhibition. See Chapter 46 for additional information on adaptive processes and ego defence mechanisms. Freud proposed that the underlying motivation to human development is an energy form or life instinct, which he calls **libido.**

According to Freud's theory of psychosexual development, the personality develops in five overlapping stages from birth to adulthood. The libido changes its location of emphasis within the body from one stage to another. Therefore, a particular body area has special significance to a client at a particular stage. The first three stages (oral, anal, and phallic) are called *pregenital stages.* The culminating stage is the *genital stage.* Table 19.3 indicates characteristics for each stage.

If the individual does not achieve a satisfactory resolution at each stage, the personality becomes fixated at that stage. **Fixation** is immobilization or the inability of the personality to proceed to the next stage because of anxiety. For example, nurses can assist an infant's development by making feeding a pleasurable experience and by making toilet training a positive experience, thereby enhancing the child's feeling of self-control. Freud also emphasized the importance of infant-parent interaction. Therefore, the nurse as a caregiver should provide a warm, caring atmosphere for an infant and assist parents to do so when the infant returns to their care.

Erikson

Erik H. Erikson (1963, 1964) adapted and expanded Freud's theory of development to include the entire lifespan, believing that people continue to develop throughout life. He described eight stages of development. In contrast to Freud, Erikson believed the ego to be the conscious core of the personality. See Table 19.4.

Erikson envisioned life as a sequence of levels of achievement. Each stage signals a task that must be achieved. The resolution of the task can be complete, partial, or unsuccessful. Erikson believed that the greater the task achievement, the healthier is the personality of the person; failure to achieve a task influences the person's ability to achieve the next task. These developmental tasks can be viewed as a series of crises, and successful resolution of these crises is supportive to the person's ego. Failure to resolve the crises is damaging to the ego. After attaining one stage, the person may fall back and need to approach it again.

Erikson's eight stages reflect both positive and negative aspects of the critical life periods. The resolution of the conflicts at each stage enables the person to function effectively in society. Each phase has its developmental task, and the individual must find a balance between, for example, trust versus mistrust (stage 1) or generativity versus stagnation (stage 7).

When using Erikson's developmental framework, nurses should be aware of indicators of positive and negative resolution of each stage. It is also important to be aware that the environment is highly influential in development, according to Erikson. Nurses can enhance a client's development by being aware of the person's developmental stage and by helping the person develop coping skills relative to stressors experienced at that level. Nurses can enhance a client's positive resolution of a developmental task by providing the individual with appropriate opportunities and encouragement. For example, a 10-year-old child can be encouraged to be creative, to finish schoolwork, and to learn how to accomplish these tasks within the limitations imposed by health.

Erikson emphasized that people must change and adapt their behaviour to maintain control over their lives. In his view, no stage in personality development can be bypassed, but people can become fixated at one stage or regress to a previous stage. For example, a middle-aged woman who has never satisfactorily accomplished the task of resolving identity versus role confusion might regress to an earlier stage when stressed by an illness which she cannot cope with.

Peck

Theories and models about *adult* development are relatively recent compared with theories of infant and child development. Research into adult development has been stimulated by a number of factors, including increased longevity and healthier old age. In the past, development was viewed as complete by the time of physical maturity, and aging was considered a decline following maturity. The emphasis was on the decremental aspects, rather than the incremental aspects, of aging. However, Robert Peck believed that although physical capabilities and functions decrease with old age, mental and social capacities tend to increase in the latter part of life (Peck, 1968).

TABLE 19.3 Freud's Five Stages of Development

Stage	Age	Characteristics	Implications
Oral	Birth to 1 year	Mouth is the centre of pleasure. Feelings of dependence arise and can persist through life. An individual who is fixated at this stage may have difficulty in trusting others and may demonstrate nail biting, drug abuse, smoking, overeating, alcoholism, argumentiveness, and overdependence.	Feeding produces pleasure and a sense of comfort and safety. Feeding should be pleasurable and provided when required.
Anal	2 and 3 years	Anus and rectum are the centres of pleasure. This stage occurs during toilet training. Fixation at the anal stage can result in obsessive-compulsive personality traits, such as obstinacy, stinginess, cruelty, and temper tantrums.	Controlling and expelling feces provide pleasure and a sense of control. Toilet training should be a pleasurable experience, and appropriate praise can result in a personality that is creative and productive.
Phallic	4 and 5 years	The child's genitals are the centre of pleasure. Sexual and aggressive feelings associated with genitals come into focus. Masturbation offers pleasure, and the child experiences the Oedipus or Electra complex. The Oedipus complex refers to the male child's attraction for his mother and hostile attitudes toward his father. The Electra complex refers to the female's attraction for her father and hostile attitudes toward her mother. Fixation at this stage can result in difficulties with sexual identity and problems with authority.	The child identifies with the parent of the opposite sex and later takes on a love relationship outside the family. Encourage identity.
Latency	6 to 12 years	Energy is directed to physical and intellectual activities. Sexual impulses tend to be repressed. Unresolved conflicts at this stage can result in obsessiveness and lack of self-motivation.	Encourage child with physical and intellectual pursuits.
Genital	13 years and after	Energy is directed toward attaining a mature sexual relationship. This stage involves a reactivation of the pregenital impulses. These impulses are usually displaced, and the individual passes to the genital stage of maturity. An inability to resolve conflicts can result in sexual problems, such as frigidity, impotence, and the inability to have a satisfactory sexual relationship.	Encourage separation from parents, achievement of independence, and decision making.

Source: Adapted from Patricia H. Miller. (1993). *Theories of developmental psychology,* (3rd ed.). Copyright © 1983, 1989, 1993 by WH Freeman and Company. Used with permission.

Peck proposed three developmental tasks during old age, in contrast to Erikson's one (integrity versus despair):

1. *Ego differentiation versus work-role preoccupation.* An adult's identity and feelings of worth are highly dependent on that person's work role. On retirement, people may experience feelings of worthlessness unless they derive their sense of identity from a number of roles so that one such role can replace the work role or occupation as a source of self-esteem. For example, a man who likes to garden or golf can obtain ego rewards from those activities, replacing rewards formerly obtained from his occupation.
2. *Body transcendence versus body preoccupation.* This task calls for the individual to adjust to decreasing physical capacities and, at the same time, maintain feelings of well-being. Preoccupation with declining body functions reduces happiness and satisfaction with life.

TABLE 19.4 Erikson's Eight Stages of Development

Stage	Age	Central Task	Indicators of Positive Resolution	Indicators of Negative Resolution
Infancy	Birth to 18 months	Trust versus mistrust	Learning to trust others	Mistrust, withdrawal, estrangement
Early childhood	18 months to 3 years	Autonomy versus shame and doubt	Self-control without loss of self-esteem Ability to cooperate and to express oneself	Compulsive self-restraint or compliance Willfulness and defiance
Late childhood	3 to 5 years	Initiative versus guilt	Learning the degree to which assertiveness and purpose influence the environment Beginning ability to evaluate one's own behaviour	Lack of self-confidence Pessimism, fear of wrongdoing Overcontrol and overrestriction of own activity
School age	6 to 12 years	Industry versus inferiority	Beginning to create, develop, and manipulate Developing sense of competence and perseverance	Loss of hope, sense of being mediocre Withdrawal from school and peers
Adolescence	12 to 20 years	Identity versus role confusion	Coherent sense of self Plans to actualize one's abilities	Feelings of confusion, indecisiveness, and possible antisocial behaviour
Young adulthood	18 to 25 years	Intimacy versus isolation	Intimate relationship with another person Commitment to work and relationships	Impersonal relationships Avoidance of relationship, career, or lifestyle commitments
Adulthood	25 to 65 years	Generativity versus stagnation	Creativity, productivity, concern for others	Self-indulgence, self-concern, lack of interests and commitments
Maturity	65 years to death	Integrity versus despair	Acceptance of worth and uniqueness of one's own life Acceptance of death	Sense of loss, contempt for others

Source: Adapted from Erik H. Erikson. (1991). *Childhood and society*. Copyright 1950, © 1963 by W. W. Norton & Company, Inc., renewed © 1978, 1991 by Erik H. Erikson. Reprinted by permission of W. W. Norton & Company, Inc.

3. *Ego transcendence versus ego preoccupation.* Ego transcendence is the acceptance, without fear, of one's death as inevitable. This acceptance includes being actively involved in one's own future beyond death. Ego preoccupation, by contrast, results in holding onto life and a preoccupation with self-gratification.

Gould

Roger Gould is another theorist who has studied adult development. He believed that transformation is a central theme during adulthood: "Adults continue to change over the period of time considered to be adulthood and... developmental phases may be found during the adult span of life" (Gould, 1972, p. 33). According to Gould, the 20s are the time when a person assumes new roles; in the 30s, role confusion often occurs; in the 40s, the person becomes aware of time limitations in relation to accomplishing life's goals; and in the 50s, the acceptance of each stage as a natural progression of life marks the path to adult maturity. Gould's study of 524 men and women led him to describe seven stages of adult development:

- *Stage 1 (ages 16–18).* Individuals consider themselves part of the family, rather than individuals, and want to separate from their parents.
- *Stage 2 (ages 18–22).* Although the individuals have established autonomy, they feel it is in jeopardy; they feel they could be pulled back into their families.

- *Stage 3 (ages 22–28).* Individuals feel established as adults and autonomous from their families. They see themselves as well defined but still feel the need to prove themselves to their parents. They see this as the time for growing and building for the future.
- *Stage 4 (ages 29–34).* Marriage and careers are well established. Individuals question what life is all about and wish to be accepted as they are, no longer finding it necessary to prove themselves.
- *Stage 5 (ages 35–43).* This is a period of self-reflection. Individuals question values and life itself. They see time as finite, with little time left to shape the lives of adolescent children.
- *Stage 6 (ages 43–50).* Personalities are seen as set. Time is accepted as finite. Individuals are interested in social activities with friends and spouse and desire both sympathy and affection from spouse.
- *Stage 7 (ages 50–60).* This is a period of transformation, with a realization of mortality and a concern for health. There is an increase in warmth and a decrease in negativism. The spouse is seen as a valuable companion. (Gould, 1972)

Cognitive Theory (Piaget)

Cognitive development refers to the manner in which people learn to think, reason, and use language. It involves a person's intelligence, perceptual ability, and ability to process information. Cognitive development represents a progression of mental abilities from illogical to logical thinking, from simple to complex problem solving, and from understanding concrete ideas to understanding abstract concepts.

The most widely known cognitive theorist is Jean Piaget (1896–1980). His theory of cognitive development has contributed to other theories, such as Kohlberg's theory of moral development and Fowler's theory of the development of faith, both discussed in this chapter.

According to Piaget, cognitive development is an orderly, sequential process in which a variety of new experiences (stimuli) must exist before intellectual abilities can develop. Piaget's cognitive developmental process is divided into five major phases: the sensorimotor phase, the preconceptual phase, the intuitive thought phase, the concrete operations phase, and the formal operations phase. A person develops through each of these phases; each phase has its own unique characteristics. See Table 19.5.

In each phase, the person uses three primary abilities: assimilation, accommodation, and adaptation. **Assimilation** is the process through which humans encounter and react to new situations by using the mechanisms they already possess. In this way, people acquire knowledge and skills as well as insights into the world around them. **Accommodation** is a process of change whereby cognitive processes mature sufficiently to allow the person to solve problems that were unsolvable before. This adjustment is possible chiefly because new knowledge has been assimilated. **Adaptation**, or coping behaviour, is the ability to handle the demands made by the environment.

Nurses can employ Piaget's theory of cognitive development when developing teaching strategies. For example, a nurse can expect a toddler to be egocentric and literal; therefore, explanations to the toddler should focus on the needs of the toddler, rather than on the needs of others. A 13-year-old can be expected to use rational thinking and to reason; therefore, when explaining the need for a medication, a nurse can outline the consequences of taking and not taking the medication, enabling the adolescent to make a rational decision. Nurses must remember, however, that the range of normal cognitive development is broad, despite the ages arbitrarily associated with each level. When teaching adults, nurses may become aware that some adults are more comfortable with concrete thought and slower to acquire and apply new information than are other adults.

Moral Theories

Moral development, a complex process not fully understood, involves learning what ought to be and what ought not to be done. It is more than imprinting parents' rules and virtues or values upon children. The term **moral** means "relating to right and wrong." The terms *morality*, *moral behaviour*, and *moral development* need to be distinguished. **Morality** refers to the requirements necessary for people to live together in society; **moral behaviour** is the way a person perceives those requirements and responds to them; **moral development** is the pattern of change in moral behaviour with age. See Chapter 7.

Kohlberg

Lawrence Kohlberg's theory specifically addresses moral development in children and adults (Berkowitz & Oser, 1985). The morality of an individual's decision is not Kohlberg's concern; rather, he focuses on the reasons an individual makes a decision. According to Kohlberg, moral development progresses through three levels and six stages. Levels and stages are not always linked to a certain developmental stage because some people progress to a higher level of moral development than others.

At Kohlberg's first level, called the *premoral* or *preconventional level*, children are responsive to cultural rules and labels of good and bad, right and wrong. However, children interpret these in terms of the physical consequences of their actions, that is, punishment or reward. At the second level, the *conventional level*, the individual is concerned about maintaining the expectations of the family, group, or nation and sees this as right. The emphasis at this level is conformity and loyalty to one's own expectations as well as society's. Level three is called the *postconventional*, *autonomous*, or

TABLE 19.5 Piaget's Phases of Cognitive Development

Phases and Stages	Age	Significant Behaviour
Sensorimotor phase	Birth to 2 years	
Stage 1: Use of reflexes	Birth to 1 month	Most action is reflexive
Stage 2: Primary circular reaction	1 to 4 months	Perception of events is centred on the body Objects are extension of self
Stage 3: Secondary circular reaction	4 to 8 months	Acknowledges the external environment Actively makes changes in the environment
Stage 4: Coordination of secondary schemata	8 to 12 months	Can distinguish a goal from a means of attaining it
Stage 5: Tertiary circular reaction	12 to 18 months	Tries and discovers new goals and ways to attain goals Rituals are important
Stage 6: Inventions of new means	18 to 24 months	Interprets the environment by mental image Uses make-believe and pretend play
Preconceptual phase	2 to 4 years	Uses an egocentric approach to accommodate the demands of an environment Everything is significant and relates to "me" Explores the environment Language development is rapid Associates words with objects
Intuitive thought phase	4 to 7 years	Egocentric thinking diminishes Thinks of one idea at a time Includes others in the environment Words express thoughts
Concrete operations phase	7 to 11 years	Solves concrete problems Begins to understand relationships, such as size Understands right and left Cognizant of viewpoints
Formal operations phase	11 to 15 years	Uses rational thinking Reasoning is deductive and futuristic

Source: Adapted from J. Piaget. (1966). *The Origins of Intelligence in Children.* International Universities Press, Inc. Copyright © 1966. Used by permission.

principled level. At this level, people make an effort to define valid values and principles without regard to outside authority or to the expectations of others. For additional information about Kohlberg's levels, see Table 19.6.

Gilligan

After more than 10 years of research with female subjects, Carol Gilligan (1982) reported that women often consider the dilemmas Kohlberg used in his research to be irrelevant. Women scored consistently lower on his scale of moral development in spite of the fact that they approached moral dilemmas with considerable sophistication. Gilligan believes that most frameworks for research in moral development do not include the concepts of caring and responsibility.

Gilligan describes three stages in the process of developing an "ethic of care" (1982, p. 74). Each stage ends with a *transitional period*, a time when the individual recognizes a conflict or discomfort with some present behaviour and considers new approaches.

- *Stage 1, caring for oneself.* In this first stage of development, the person is concerned only with caring for the self. The individual feels isolated, alone, and unconnected to others. There is no concern or conflict with the needs of others because the self is the most important. The focus of this stage is survival. The end of this stage occurs when the individual begins to view this approach as selfish. At this time, the person also begins to see a need for relationships and connections with other people.

TABLE 19.6 Kohlberg's Stages of Moral Development

Level and Stage	Definition	Example
Level I Preconventional		
Stage 1: Punishment and obedience orientation	The activity is wrong if one is punished, and the activity is right if one is not punished.	A nurse follows a physician's order so as not to be disciplined.
Stage 2: Instrumental-relativist orientation	Action is taken to satisfy one's needs.	A client in hospital agrees to stay in bed if the nurse will buy the client a newspaper.
Level II Conventional		
Stage 3: Interpersonal concordance (good boy, nice girl)	Action is taken to please another and gain approval.	A nurse gives elderly clients in hospital sedatives at bedtime because the night nurse wants all clients to sleep at night.
Stage 4: Law and order orientation	Right behaviour is obeying the law and following the rules.	A nurse does not permit a worried client to phone home because hospital rules stipulate no phone calls after 9:00 p.m.
Level III Postconventional		
Stage 5: Social contract, legalistic orientation	Standard of behaviour is based on adhering to laws that protect the welfare and rights of others. Personal values and opinions are recognized, and violating the rights of others is avoided.	A nurse arranges for an East Indian client to have privacy for prayer each evening.
Stage 6: Universal-ethical principles	Universal moral principles are internalized. Person respects other humans and believes that relationships are based on mutual trust.	A nurse becomes an advocate for a hospitalized client by reporting to the nursing supervisor a conversation in which a physician threatened to withhold assistance unless the client agreed to surgery.

Source: Adapted from R. Duska and M. Whelan. (1975). *Moral development: A guide to Piaget and Kohlberg.* Copyright © 1975 by The Missionary Society of St. Paul the Apostle in the State of New York. Used by permission of Paulist Press.

- *Stage 2, caring for others.* During this stage, the individual recognizes the selfishness of earlier behaviour and begins to understand the need for caring relationships with others. Caring relationships bring with them responsibility. The definition of *responsibility* includes self-sacrifice, where "good" is considered to be "caring for others." The individual now approaches relationships with a focus of not hurting others. This approach causes the individual to be more responsive and submissive to others' needs, excluding any thoughts of meeting one's own. A transition occurs when the individual recognizes that this approach can cause difficulties with relationships because of the lack of balance between caring for oneself and caring for others.
- *Stage 3, caring for self and others.* During this last stage, a person sees the need for a balance between caring for others and caring for the self. The concept of responsibility now includes responsibility for the self and for other people. Care remains the focus on which decisions are made. However, the person recognizes the interconnections between the self and others and realizes that if one's own needs are not met, other people may also suffer.

Gilligan believes women often see morality in the integrity of relationships and caring so that the moral problems they encounter are different from those of men. Men tend to consider what is right to be what is just, whereas for women, what is right is taking responsibility for others as a self-chosen decision (Gilligan, 1982). The ethic of justice, or fairness, is based on the idea of equality: everyone should receive the same treatment. This is the developmental path usually followed by men and widely accepted by moral theorists. By contrast, the ethic of care is based on the premise of nonviolence: no one should be harmed. This is the path typically followed by women but given little attention in the literature of moral theory.

TABLE 19.7 Fowler's Stages of Spiritual Development

Stage	Age	Description
0. Undifferentiated	0 to 3 years	Infant unable to formulate concepts about self or the environment
1. Intuitive-projective	4 to 6 years	A combination of images and beliefs given by trusted others, mixed with the child's own experience and imagination
2. Mythic-literal	7 to 12 years	Private world of fantasy and wonder; symbols refer to something specific; dramatic stories and myths used to communicate spiritual meanings
3. Synthetic-conventional	Adolescent or adult	World and ultimate environment structured by the expectations and judgements of others; interpersonal focus
4. Individuating-reflective	After 18 years	Constructing one's own explicit system; high degree of self-consciousness
5. Paradoxical-consolidative	After 30 years	Awareness of truth from a variety of viewpoints
6. Universalizing	Maybe never	Becoming an incarnation of the principles of love and justice

Source: Adapted from J. Fowler and S. Keen. (1985). *Life maps: Conversations in the journey of faith.* Waco, TX: Word Books; and A. Hollander. (1980). *How to help your child have a spiritual life: A parents' guide to inner development.* New York: A and W Publishers. Used by permission.

In the development of maturity, according to Gilligan, both viewpoints blend "in the realization that just as inequality adversely affects both perspectives in an unequal relationship, so too violence is destructive for everyone involved" (Gilligan, 1982, p. 174). The blending of these two perspectives could give rise to a new view of human development and a better understanding of human relations.

Spiritual Theories

The spiritual component of growth and development refers to individuals' understanding of their relationship with the universe and their perceptions about the direction and meaning of life.

Fowler

James Fowler describes the development of faith as a force that gives meaning to a person's life. He uses the term *faith* as a form of knowing, a way of being in relation to "an ultimate environment." To Fowler, **faith** is a relational phenomenon; it is "an active 'mode-of-being-in-relation' to another or others in which we invest commitment, belief, love, risk and hope" (Fowler & Keen, 1985). Fowler's stages in the development of faith are given in Table 19.7.

Fowler's theory and developmental stages were influenced by the work of Piaget, Kohlberg, and Erikson. Fowler believes that the development of faith is an interactive process between the person and the environment. In each of Fowler's stages, new patterns of thought, values, and beliefs are added to those already held by the individual; therefore, the stages must follow in sequence. Faith stages, according to Fowler, are separate from the cognitive stages of Piaget—they evolve from a combination of knowledge and values.

Westerhoff

Westerhoff (Table 19.8) describes faith as a way of being and behaving that evolves from an experienced faith guided by parents and others during a person's infancy and childhood to an owned faith that is internalized in adulthood and serves as a directive for personal action. For the client who is ill, faith—whether in a higher authority (e.g., God, Allah, Jehovah), in the client's own self, in the health-care team, or in a combination of all—provides strength and trust.

Applying Growth and Development Concepts to Nursing Practice

Different theories explain one or more aspects of an individual's growth and development. Typically, theorists examine only one aspect of an individual's development, such as the cognitive, moral, or physical aspects. The area chosen for examination usually reflects the researcher's academic discipline and personal interest. The theorists may also limit the population that is studied to a particular part of the life span, such as infancy, childhood, or adulthood.

Although such theories can be useful, they have limitations. First, the theory chosen may explain only one aspect of the growth and development process. Yet, a person does

TABLE 19.8 Westerhoff's Four Stages of Faith

Stage	Age	Behaviour
Experience faith	Infancy/early adolescence	Experiences faith through interaction with others who are living a particular faith tradition
Affiliative faith	Late adolescence	Actively participates in activities that characterize a particular faith tradition; experiences awe and wonderment; feels a sense of belonging
Searching faith	Young adulthood	Through a process of questioning and doubting own faith, acquires a cognitive as well as an affective faith
Owned faith	Middle adulthood/old age	Puts faith into personal and social action and is willing to stand up for what the individual believes, even against the nurturing community

Source: Adapted from J. Westerhoff. (1976). *Will our children have faith?* (pp. 79–103). New York: Seabury Press.

not develop in fragmented sections but, rather, as a whole human being. Thus, the nurse may find it necessary to apply several theories for an adequate understanding of the growth and development of a client.

Another limitation of some theories is the suggestion that certain tasks are performed at a specific age. In most cases, the child or adult does accomplish the task at the time specified by the guidelines. In other cases, however, the nurse may find that an individual does not accomplish the task or meet the milestone at the exact time suggested by the theory. Such individual differences are not easily defined or categorized by a single theory. Human development is a complex synthesis of physiological, cognitive, psychological, moral, and spiritual development. Nurses should expect individual variations and take these into consideration when applying these theories about growth and development. In so doing, they will be better able to understand a client's development and plan effective nursing interventions.

Canadian Society Notes

Fact	Implications for Nursing Practice
Key Canadian Resources on Children's Health suggested by the Canadian Health Network: Best Start Resource Centre (maternal infant program of health promotion established by Ontario government in 1992); Caring for Kids (promoting healthy children, prepared by the Canadian Pediatric Society); Healthy Teeth (oral health for children in grades 3–6 by the Canadian Dental Association)	Nurses can assess and suggest these resources to parents, children, and teens, as appropriate to support health promotion practices.
Resources for Youth: Comprehensive School Health (healthy school environment, prepared by Canadian Health); Teen Net (interactive Web site prepared by University of Toronto at http://www.hc-sc.gc.ca/dca-dea/7-18yrs-ans/comphealth_e.html)	Nurses working within the school system need to understand concepts related to school health to promote wellness in this population.
The Office of Children's Environmental Health works with national and international partners to monitor and analyze scientific evidence on the impact of environmental threats on children's health; identify knowledge gaps and advocate for research activities to address them; coordinate development of policy and strategies to reduce environmental risks to children's health; and develop public education materials on strategies to reduce the risk of environmental threats to children.	Nurses, especially those in the community, need to promote the safety of children.

In nursing, developmental theories can be useful in guiding assessment, explaining behaviour, and providing a direction for nursing interventions. An understanding of a child's intellectual ability helps a nurse to anticipate and explain certain reactions, responses, and needs. Nurses can then encourage client behaviour that is appropriate for that particular developmental stage.

Theories are also useful in planning a nursing intervention. For instance, choosing the appropriate toy for a three-year-old boy requires some knowledge of the physical and cognitive development of the child, as well as a sensitivity for individual preferences.

In adult care, knowledge about the physical, cognitive, and psychological aspects of the aging process is a fundamental aspect of administering sensitive nursing care. For example, nurses can use their familiarity with the theories of development to help clients understand and anticipate the psychosocial changes that take place after retirement or the physical limitations that come with old age.

FOCUS ON CRITICAL THINKING

The client is a four-month-old child whose parents have recently immigrated from Ghana, Africa. They have been in Canada for about a year. Carol, the mother, attended prenatal classes and followed routine protocols to prepare for a vaginal delivery, which was uneventful. John weighed 2.5 kg at birth and now weighs about 7.3 kg. He is being seen at the well-baby clinic for a routine appointment. His mother comments that John recognizes her voice and is able to roll over, but he still needs two naps a day. She expresses concern that his movements appear clumsy.

1. What conclusions can you draw about the child's growth and development on the basis of the data provided?
2. What contextual factors might influence the client's future development?
3. What suggestions would you make to his mother to support John's growth and development?
4. What attitude and cognitive critical thinking skills did you use to answer the questions pertaining to this case?

See Appendix A for answers to these questions.

CHAPTER HIGHLIGHTS

- Growth and development are independent, interrelated processes.
- Growth is physical change and increase in size. The pattern of physiological growth is similar for all people.
- Development is an increase in the complexity of function and skill progression. It is the capacity and skill of the individual to adapt to the environment.
- There are several theories about the various stages and aspects of growth and development, particularly in regard to infant and child development. Theories and models about adult development are more recent.
- Each developmental stage has its own characteristics and unique challenges.
- A progression of sequential steps or tasks is proposed in most theories in which successful achievement of tasks is required in early stages before success can be achieved with later tasks.
- The rate of a person's growth and development is highly individual, but the sequence of growth and development is predictable.
- Heredity and environment are the primary factors influencing growth and development.
- Components of growth and development are generally categorized as physiological, psychosocial, cognitive, moral, and spiritual.
- The nurse's major role in relation to growth and development is to assess the client's growth and development using the standards proposed in these theories, to identify and report any problem areas, and to plan and implement nursing strategies that will maintain or promote the client's development.

READINGS AND REFERENCES

Suggested Readings

Kelleher, K. (1992, April/June). The afternoon of life: Jung's view of the tasks of the second half of life. *Perspectives in Psychiatric Care, 28,* 25–28.
Kelleher writes that Carl Jung believed middle age and old age have specific developmental tasks. For the mature individual, the goal is to consolidate a personality by integrating the conscious and unconscious parts of the self. The article reviews relevant literature and describes Jung's quest for self.

Maness, J. E. (1995). The impact of spinal cord injury on older adults' growth and development: A case study. *Nursing, 20,* 29–31.
In this case study, the author discusses how a spinal cord injury affected the achievement of developmental goals by a 73-year-old man for whom the usual coping mechanisms were not effective. Nurses on a neurosurgical unit learned how to incorporate psychological considerations of the injury into the older client's care plan. Strategies to intervene with growth and developmental concerns had a positive impact on the client's recovery.

Related Research

To, T., Cadarette, S. M., & Liu, Y. (2000). Child care arrangement and preschool development. *Canadian Journal of Public Health, 91,* 418–422.

Selected References

Berkowitz, M. W., & Oser, F. (Eds.). (1985). *Moral education: Theory and application.* Hillsdale, NJ: Lawrence Erlbaunt.

Erikson, E. H. (1963). *Childhood and society* (2nd ed.). New York: Norton. (Classic.)

Erikson, E. H. (1964). *Insight and responsibility: Lectures on the ethical implications of psychoanalytic insight.* New York: Norton. (Classic.)

Erikson, E. H. (1985). *The life cycle completed: A review.* New York: Norton.

Fowler, J. W. (1981). *Stages of faith: The psychology of human development and the quest for meaning.* New York: Harper & Row. (Classic.)

Fowler, J., & Keen, S. (1978 and 1985). *Life maps: Conversations in the journey of faith.* Waco, TX: Word Books.

Freud, S. (1923). *The ego and the id.* London: Hogarth Press.

Freud, S. (1961). *The ego and the id and other works* (Vol. 19). Strachey, J., translator. London: Hogarth Press and the Institute of Psychoanalysis. (Classic.)

Gilligan, C. (1982). *In a different voice: Psychological theory and women's development.* Cambridge, MA: Harvard University Press. (Classic.)

Gould, R. L. (1972). The phases of adult life: A study in developmental psychology. *American Journal of Psychiatry, 129,* 33–43. (Classic.)

Havighurst, R. J. (1972). *Developmental tasks and education* (3rd ed.). New York: Longman Publishers. (Classic.)

Health Canada, Children's Environmental Health. http://www.hc-sc.gc.ca/hecs-sesc/oceh/index.htm.

Kegan, R. (1982). *The evolving self: Problem and process in human development.* Cambridge, MA: Harvard University Press.

McShane, J. (1991). *Cognitive development: An information processing approach.* Oxford, U.K.: Basil Blackwell, Inc. (Classic.)

Munhall, P. L. (1982). Moral development: A prerequisite. *Journal of Nursing Education, 21,* 11–15.

Murray, T. R. (1999). *Human development theories: Windows on culture.* Thousand Oaks, CA: Sage.

Peck, R. (1968). Psychological developments in the second half of life. In B. L. Neugarten, (Ed.), *Middle age and aging.* Chicago: University of Chicago Press. (Classic.)

Piaget, J. (1966). *Origins of intelligence in children.* New York: Norton. (Classic.)

Westerhoff, J. (1976). *Will our children have faith?* New York: Seabury Press. (Classic.)

WEBLINKS

Canadian Health Network
http://www.canadian-health-network.ca/1children.html
This site provides accurate Canadian content that focuses on child health and wellness. It is funded by Health Canada and operated by the Canadian Child Care Federation. It is a public information site of value to parents and health-care providers.

Canadian Institute of Child Health
http://www.cich.ca/
The Canadian Institute of Child Health is a voice for children. Their role is working with governments to make sure the right kind of policies are developed; working with professionals and educators to equip them with the best in research and programs; and reaching out to families to help with the tasks of nurturing, protecting, educating, and empowering children.

Canadian Pediatric Society
http://www.caringforkids.cps.ca/index.htm
This site is provided by the Canadian Pediatric Society and offers advice from pediatricians.

Health Canada—Division of Childhood and Adolescence
http://www.hc-sc.gc.ca/pphb-dgspsp/ch-se_e.html
The Division of Childhood and Adolescence serves as a centre of expertise, leadership, and coordination within the federal government and Health Canada for issues, activities, and programs concerning children and youth.

CHAPTER 20

Development from Conception through Adolescence

OBJECTIVES

After completing this chapter, you will be able to:

- Identify tasks characteristic of different stages of development from infancy through adolescence.
- Describe usual physical development from infancy through adolescence.
- Trace psychosocial development according to Erikson from infancy through adolescence.
- Explain cognitive development according to Piaget from infancy through adolescence.
- Elucidate moral development according to Kohlberg from childhood through adolescence.
- Describe spiritual development according to Fowler throughout childhood and adolescence.
- Discuss assessment activities and expected characteristics from birth through late childhood.
- List essential activities of health promotion and protection to meet the needs of infants, toddlers, preschoolers, and school-age children.

Knowledge of human growth and development is essential for nurses if they are to identify developmental needs and problems. This chapter applies the concepts of growth and development, introduced in Chapter 19, to the prenatal period and to the neonate, infant, toddler, preschooler, school-age child, and adolescent. Each developmental stage includes physical, psychosocial, cognitive, moral, and spiritual aspects. Health assessment and promotion of health and wellness are emphasized.

Conception and Prenatal Development

Prenatal, or intrauterine, development lasts approximately nine calendar months (10 lunar months) or 38 to 40 weeks, depending on the method of calculation. (A lunar month is 28 days.) If the time is calculated from the day of conception, this stage of life is 38 weeks or 9 ½ lunar months. If the time is calculated from the first day of the last menstrual period, its average length is 10 lunar months or 40 weeks.

Traditionally, pregnancy has been divided into three periods called **trimesters,** each of which lasts about three months. Each trimester includes certain landmarks for developmental changes in the mother and the fetus. The two phases of intrauterine life can also be considered in trimestral terms. The embryonic phase is the first trimester, and the fetal phase includes the second and third trimesters.

The **embryonic phase** is the period during which the fertilized ovum develops into an organism with most of the human features. This period is considered to extend for either the first eight weeks or the first 12 weeks (first trimester) of pregnancy. Those authorities who consider the embryonic phase to be 12 weeks believe that some organs develop after eight weeks.

Within the first three weeks of life, tissues differentiate into three layers—the **ectoderm** (outer layer), **mesoderm** (middle layer), and **endoderm** or **entoderm** (inner layer). The ectoderm and endoderm are formed in the second week; the mesoderm forms in the third week. From these layers are formed all of the body's complex organs and systems as a series of outpouchings, inpouchings, foldings, and tubular formations.

Three other events occur concurrently during the first three weeks:

1. The embryo is implanted.
2. Placental function starts. The **placenta** is a flat, disc-shaped organ that is highly vascular. It normally forms in the upper segment of the endometrium of the uterus. Its functions are to exchange nutrients and gases between the embryo or fetus and the mother.
3. The fetal membranes differentiate.

The **fetal phase** of development is characterized by a period of rapid growth in the size of the fetus. Both genetic and environmental factors affect its growth.

At the end of the second trimester, or six lunar months, the fetus resembles a small baby. Because very little fat is present beneath the skin, the skin appears wrinkled, red, and transparent. The underlying vessels are visible. A protective covering, called **vernix caseosa,** begins to develop over the skin. This is a white cheese-like substance that adheres to the skin and can become 0.32 cm thick by birth. **Lanugo,** a fine downy hair, also covers the body. At about five months, the mother first perceives movement by the fetus, and the first fetal heartbeat may be heard.

At the end of the third trimester (9 ½ lunar months), the fetus has developed to approximately 50 cm and 3.2 to 3.4 kg. The lanugo has disappeared, and the skin has a more normal colour and appears less wrinkled. More subcutaneous fat makes the baby look more rotund; the last two months in utero are largely devoted to accumulating weight.

Health Promotion

During the intrauterine stage of development, the embryo or fetus relies on the maternal blood flow through the placenta to meet its basic survival needs. The health of the mother is essential for proper growth and development.

Oxygen To meet the fetal demands for oxygen, the pregnant mother gradually increases her normal blood flow by about one-third, peaking at about eight months; increases her respiratory rate by about 40 percent; and increases her cardiac output significantly. Initially, the heart of the embryo lies outside its body, but it is repositioned in the chest early in the second trimester. Fetal circulation travels from the placenta through two umbilical arteries, which carry blood depleted of oxygen away from the fetus. By 20 weeks, the fetal heartbeat is audible through a fetoscope; the heartbeat is audible as early as the 10th week if a Doppler stethoscope with ultrasound is used.

Nutrition and Fluids The fetus obtains nourishment from the placental circulation and by swallowing amniotic fluid. Nutritional needs are met when the mother eats a well-balanced diet containing sufficient calories to meet both her needs and those of the fetus.

Rest and Activity The fetus sleeps most of the time but does develop a pattern of sleep and wakefulness that can persist after birth. Fetal activity begins about the fourth lunar month of pregnancy.

Elimination Throughout pregnancy, fetal feces are formed from swallowed amniotic fluid, but normally no stool is passed until after birth. Inadequate oxygenation of the fetus during the third trimester can result in relaxation of the anal sphincter and passage of feces into the amniotic fluid. Urine normally is excreted into the amniotic fluid when the kidneys mature (16 to 20 weeks).

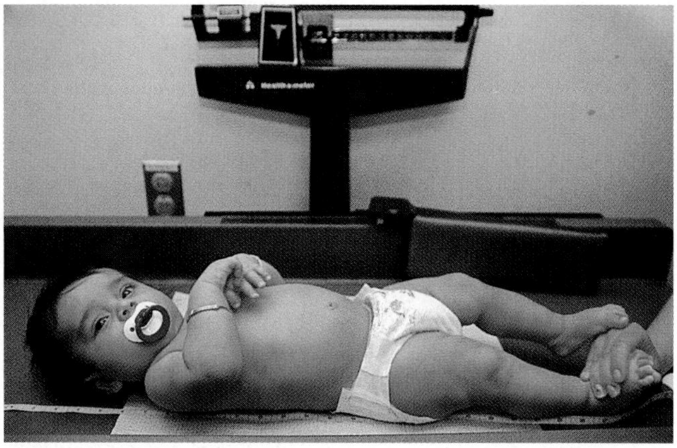

Figure 20.1 Measuring an infant head to heel, from the top of the head to the base of the heels

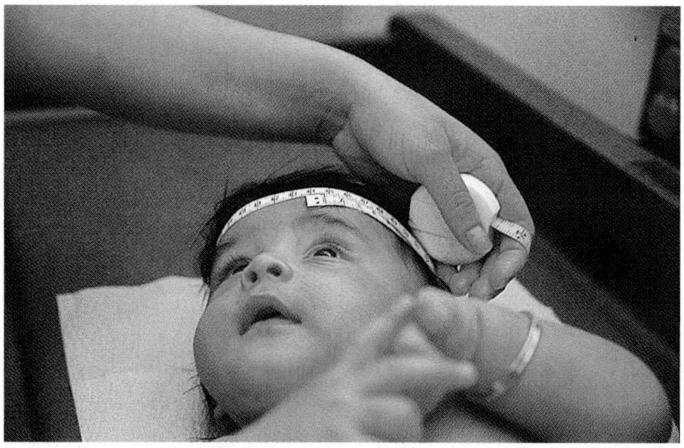

Figure 20.2 An infant's head circumference is measured around the skull, above the eyebrows

Temperature Maintenance Although amniotic fluid provides a constant temperature for the fetus, significant changes in maternal temperature can alter the temperature of the amniotic fluid and that of the fetus. Significant temperature rises due to illness, hot whirlpool baths, or saunas can result in birth defects.

Safety A safe environment for the fetus depends on the mother being free of illness and not ingesting alcohol, addictive drugs, or other medications not ordered by a health professional.

Neonates and Infants (Birth to 1 Year)

Babies are considered neonates from birth to the end of one month. Infants are babies from one month of age to one year.

Physical Development

An infant's basic task is survival, which requires breathing, sleeping, sucking, eating, swallowing, digesting, and eliminating. Because many of the infant's activities and pleasures are mouth centred, this stage in development is often referred to as Freud's *oral* stage (see Chapter 19). Infants undergo significant physiological change in these areas: weight, length, head growth, vision, and motor development.

Weight At birth, most babies weigh about 2.7 to 3.8 kg. Just after birth, most infants lose 5 to 10 percent of their birth weight because of fluid loss. This weight loss is normal, and infants usually regain that weight in about one week. After several days, babies usually gain weight at the rate of 150 to 210 g weekly for six months. By five months of age, infants usually reach twice their birth weight, and by age 12 months, three times their birth weight.

Length The average length of a Canadian newborn is about 50 cm. At birth, African-Canadian infants tend to be shorter. Female babies, on average, are smaller than male babies.

Two recumbent lengths are the crown-to-rump length (the sitting length) and the head-to-heel length (from the top of the head to the base of the heels). See Figure 20.1. Normally, the crown-to-rump length is approximately the same as the head circumference. By six months, infants gain another 13.75 cm of height. By 12 months, they add another 7.5 cm. The rate of increase in height is largely influenced by the baby's size at birth and by nutrition.

Head and Chest Circumference Assessment of head circumference is of particular importance in infants and children to determine the growth rate of the skull and the brain. An infant's head should be measured at every visit to the physician or nurse until the child is two years old (Figure 20.2). Normal head circumference (**normocephaly**) is often related to chest circumference. At birth, the average infant's head circumference is 35 cm and generally varies only 1 or 2 cm. The chest circumference of the newborn is usually less than the head circumference by about 2.5 cm. As the infant grows, the chest circumference becomes larger than the head circumference. At about nine or 10 months, the head and chest circumferences are about the same, and after one year of age, the chest circumference is larger.

Head Moulding The heads of most newborn babies are misshapen because of the moulding of the head that occurs during vaginal deliveries. Moulding of the head is made possible by **fontanelles** (unossified membranous gaps) in the bone structure of the skull and by overriding of the **sutures** (junction lines of the skull bones). Within a week, a newborn's head usually regains its symmetry, a fact that reassures parents. The larger anterior fontanelle (4 to 6 cm in diameter and diamond-shaped) can increase

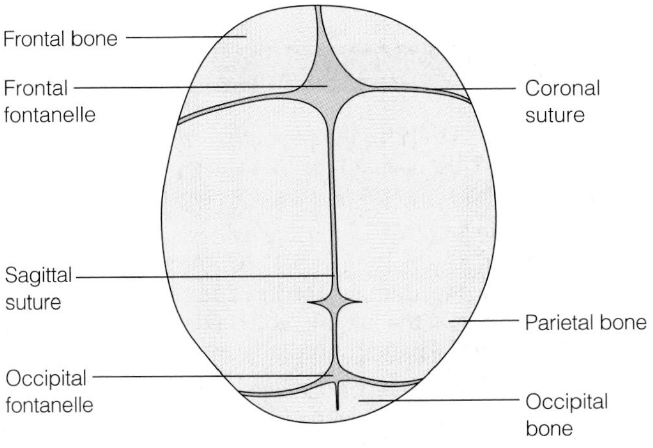

Figure 20.3 The bones of the skull, showing the fontanelles and the suture lines

in size for several months after birth. After six months, the size gradually decreases until closure occurs between nine and 18 months. The posterior fontanelle, between the parietal bones and the occipital bone, closes from four to eight weeks after birth (Figure 20.3).

Vision The newborn can follow large moving objects and blinks in response to bright light and sound. The pupils of the newborn respond slowly, and the eyes cannot focus on close objects. At four months, the infant can recognize familiar objects and follow moving ones. By six months, the infant can perceive colours. After nine months, most can recognize facial characteristics and often smile in response to a familiar face. By 12 months, depth perception has developed, and the infant will be able to recognize where a change in level occurs, such as at the edge of the bed.

Hearing Newborns with intact hearing will react with a startle to a loud noise, a reaction called the Moro reflex (see the discussion on reflexes that follows). Within a few days, they are able to distinguish different sounds. For example, the newborn can tell the difference between the mother's voice and that of another woman. At about five months of age, the infant will pause while sucking in order to listen to the mother's voice. A nine-month-old infant is able to locate the source of sounds and recognizes familiar ones. By one year, the infant listens to sounds, begins to distinguish words, and responds to simple instructions.

Smell and Taste The senses of smell and taste are functional shortly after birth. Newborns prefer sweet tastes and tend to decrease their sucking in response to liquids with a salty content. They are able to recognize the smell of their mother's milk and respond to this smell by turning toward the mother.

Touch The sense of touch is well developed at birth. Skin-to-skin touching is important for an infant's development. The infant responds positively to the warmth, love, and security that are perceived when touched, held, and cuddled. The newborn is also sensitive to temperature extremes and pain; however, babies react diffusely and cannot isolate the discomfort. The pain in the buttock caused by an open safety pin, for example, is not isolated in the buttock.

Reflexes The reflexes of the newborn are unconscious, involuntary responses. They are neither learned nor consciously carried out; rather, they are nervous system responses to a number of stimuli. Reflexes normally present at birth are the rooting, sucking, Moro, palmar grasp, plantar, tonic neck, stepping, and Babinski reflexes. See the accompanying box. Infant reflexes disappear during the first year of life. In addition, the abilities to yawn, stretch, sneeze, burp, and hiccup are all present at birth.

Motor Development Motor development is the development of the baby's abilities to move and to control the body. Initially, body movement is uncoordinated. At one month of age, the infant lifts the head momentarily when prone, turns the head when prone, and has a head lag when pulled to a sitting position. After six months, they can sit without support (Figure 20.4). At nine months, they can reach, grasp a rattle, and transfer it from hand to hand. At 12 months, they can turn the pages of a book, put objects into a container, walk with some assistance, and help to dress themselves.

Figure 20.4 An infant sits without support at 6 months of age

Infant Reflexes

- *Sucking reflex:* A feeding reflex that occurs when the infant's lips are touched. The reflex persists throughout infancy.
- *Rooting reflex:* A feeding reflex elicited by touching the baby's cheek, causing the baby's head to turn to the side that was touched. This reflex usually disappears after four months.
- *Moro reflex:* Often assessed to estimate the maturity of the central nervous system. A loud noise, a sudden change in position, or an abrupt jarring of the crib elicits this reflex. The infant reacts by extending both arms and legs outward with the fingers spread, then suddenly retracting the limbs. Often, the infant cries at the same time. This reflex disappears after four months.
- *Palmar grasp reflex:* Occurs when a small object is placed against the palm of the hand, causing the fingers to curl around it. This reflex disappears after three months.
- *Plantar reflex:* Similar to the palmar grasp reflex; an object placed just beneath the toes causes them to curl around it. This reflex disappears after eight months.
- *Tonic neck reflex (TNR) or fencing reflex:* A postural reflex. When a baby lying on its back turns its head to the right side, for example, the left side of the body shows a flexing of the left arm and the left leg. This reflex disappears after four months.
- *Stepping reflex (walking or dancing reflex):* Can be elicited by holding the baby upright so that the feet touch a flat surface. The legs then move up and down as if the baby were walking. This reflex usually disappears at about two months.
- *Babinski reflex:* When the sole of the foot is stroked, the big toe rises and the other toes fan out. A newborn baby has a positive Babinski. After age one year, the infant exhibits a negative Babinski; that is, the toes curl downward. A positive Babinski after age one year indicates brain damage.

Psychosocial Development

According to Erikson, the central crisis at this stage is *trust versus mistrust* (see Table 19.4 on page 314). Resolution of this stage determines how the person approaches subsequent developmental stages. During the first year of life, infants depend on the parents for all their physiological and psychological needs. Fulfillment of these needs is required for the infant to develop a basic sense of trust. Parents can enhance this sense of trust by (1) responding consistently to an infant's needs, (2) providing a predictable environment in which routines are established, and (3) being sensitive to the infant's needs and meeting these needs skillfully and promptly. Mothering behaviour, such as consistent care, handling, stroking, and cuddling, is essential for healthy psychosocial development. By eight months, most infants seem to be attached to their parents and may show displeasure when left with strangers.

Newborns react socially to caregivers by paying attention to the face or voice and by cuddling when held. They are able to interact with the environment by responding to various stimuli, such as touch and sound. See Table 20.1 for examples of motor and social development.

TABLE 20.1 Examples of Motor and Social Development in Infancy

Age	Motor Development	Social Development
Newborn	Turns head from side to side when in a prone position Grasps by reflex when object is placed in palm of hand	Displays displeasure by crying, and satisfaction by soft vocalizations Attends to adult face and voice by eye contact and quieting
6 months	Lifts chest and shoulders off table when prone, bearing weight on hands Manipulates small objects	Starts to imitate sounds Vocalizes one-syllable sounds: "ma-ma," "da-da"
9 months	Creeps and crawls Beginner pincer grasp with thumb and forefinger	Complies with simple verbal commands Displays fear of being left alone (e.g., going to bed) Waves "bye-bye"
12 months	Walks alone with help Uses spoon to feed self	Clings to mother in unfamiliar situations Demonstrates emotions, such as anger and affection

Infants have no understanding of waiting and no time frame by which to measure waiting. The initial reaction of an infant to stress is crying, and crying is the infant's way of communicating stress. Infants learn gradually to tolerate stress. According to Freud, infants have an oral focus, and they reduce tension by sucking and mouthing objects. Nurses and parents can also reduce the stress of an infant by maintaining the infant's routine as much as possible and limiting the number of strangers interacting with the infant.

Cognitive Development

According to Piaget, cognitive development is a result of interaction between an individual and the environment.

Piaget refers to the initial period of cognitive development as the *sensorimotor phase* (see Table 19.5 on page 316). This phase has six stages, three of which take place during the first year. From four to eight months, infants begin to have perceptual recognition. By six months, they respond to new stimuli, and they remember certain objects and look for them for a short time. By 12 months, infants have a concept of both space and time. They experiment to reach a goal, such as a toy on a chair.

An infant's cognitive development also proceeds from reflexive ability of the newborn to, by the age of one year, using one or two actions to attain a goal.

Moral Development

Infants associate right and wrong with pleasure and pain. What gives them pleasure is right, since they are too young to reason otherwise. When infants receive abundant positive responses from the parents, such as smiles, caresses, and voice tones of approval in these early months, they learn that certain behaviours are wrong or good and that pain or pleasure is the consequence. In later months and years, children can tell easily and quickly by changes in parental facial expressions and voice tones whether their behaviour is approved or disapproved.

Health Problems

A number of health problems of neonates and infants require interventions from health-care personnel. Safety concerns are of particular importance.

Failure-to-Thrive Syndrome Infants deprived of mothering, especially from three to 15 months, will not learn to form significant relationships or to trust others. Infants who fail to establish a loving, responsive relationship with a caregiver often fail to develop normally. The disturbed parent-child relationship can result in **failure-to-thrive syndrome**. Infants with this condition show delayed development without any physical cause. They are often malnourished and fail to gain weight and grow normally.

Infant Colic Colic is acute abdominal pain caused by periodic contractions of the intestines. It occurs during the first three months of life. Although the direct cause is not known, such factors as swallowing air, feeding too rapidly, allergies, taking excessive amounts of carbohydrates, infant emotional distress, and anxiety of the caregiver may be associated with colic.

To help relieve the colic, the nurse can assess the infant during feeding and suggest possible changes. Suggestions may include decreasing environmental stimuli during and after feeding, changing the formula or nipple, and increasing the burping frequency. Other suggestions include increasing the infant's water intake, cuddling the infant, and finding the position that provides the infant with the most comfort.

Crying Crying is often of great concern. When an infant's crying lasts up to 10 to 12 hours a day, it is described as colicky (see the preceding section). A crying or fussy period lasting one to two hours a day is usually considered normal for infants.

Child Abuse Reports of child abuse have increased in recent years. It can take various forms, including physical abuse, physical neglect, sexual abuse, and emotional abuse and neglect. Whiplash-shaking can lead to severe injury in infants. Cerebral damage, neurological defects, blindness, and mental retardation can result. These injuries often occur without external evidence of head injury. Nurses should suspect **shaken baby syndrome (SBS)** in infants less than one year old who have apnea, seizures, lethargy or drowsiness, bradycardia, respiratory difficulty, or coma or who die. Subdural and retinal hemorrhages accompanied by the absence of external signs of trauma are hallmarks of the syndrome.

Sudden Infant Death Syndrome The sudden and unexpected death of an infant may be a case of **sudden infant death syndrome (SIDS)**. A postmortem examination usually fails to reveal a cause. The highest incidence of SIDS occurs in the third and fourth months of life. Many factors are being investigated, including the position of the infant while sleeping (putting babies to sleep on their backs has reduced the incidence of SIDS), maternal smoking, nutrition, and crowded living conditions.

For problems related to safety, see Chapter 33.

Health Assessment and Promotion

Apgar Scoring Newborn babies can be assessed immediately by the **Apgar scoring system.** This provides a numeric indicator of the baby's physiological capacities to adapt to extrauterine life. Each of five signs is assigned a maximum score of 2, so that the total score achievable is 10. A score under 7 suggests that the baby is having difficulty, and a score under 4 indicates that the baby's condition is critical. Apgar

TABLE 20.2 Apgar Scoring System to Assess the Newborn

	Score		
Sign	**0**	**1**	**2**
1. Heart rate	Absent	Slow (below 100 per minute)	Above 100 per minute
2. Respirations	Absent	Slow, irregular	Regular rate, crying
3. Muscle tone	Flaccid	Some flexion of extremities	Active movements
4. Reflex irritability	None	Grimace	Cries
5. Colour	Body pale or cyanotic	Body pink, extremities blue	Body completely pink

scoring is usually carried out 60 seconds after birth and is repeated in five minutes. Those with very low scores require special resuscitative measures and care. See Table 20.2.

Developmental Screening Tests Development can be assessed by observing the infant's behaviour and by using standardized tests, such as the **Denver Developmental Screening Test (DDST)**. The DDST is used to screen children from birth to six years of age. The test is intended to estimate the abilities of a child compared with those of an average group of children of the same age and ethnic group. Four main areas of development are screened: (1) *personal-social*, (2) *fine motor adaptive*, (3) *language*, and (4) *gross motor*.

Ongoing Nursing Assessments During ongoing assessments, the nurse examines and observes the infant, taking into account variations that occur with developmental age and activity. For example, the pulse of the baby at birth is affected by the child's activity, rising up to 170 when the infant is crying and falling to as low as 70 during sleep.

In addition, the nurse actively listens to the caregiver for possible problems or areas of concern, and reviews with the parent the expected behaviour or characteristics for the particular age group. It is important for the caregiver to know that certain behaviours, responses, and activities of the infant are normal and expected. It is also important to discuss the many individual differences that can, quite normally, occur.

The assessment interview is also a time to be supportive of the parent's role, to assess the attachment of the mother to the infant, and to observe the interactions between the infant and parent. Assessment guidelines for growth and development of the infant are shown in the box below.

The first month of life is thought to be critical for physical adjustments to extrauterine life and for the psychosocial adjustment of the parents. From one month to one year, infants experience rapid change, with advances in physical growth and psychosocial development. For a summary of health and wellness promotion, see the box on the next page. For details of health and wellness promotion, see lifespan considerations in specific chapters later in this book.

DEVELOPMENTAL ASSESSMENT GUIDELINES

The Infant

In these five developmental areas, does the infant do the following?

1. **Physical Development**
   - Demonstrate physical growth (weight, length, head and chest circumference) within the normal range
   - Manifest appropriately sized fontanelles for age
   - Exhibit vital signs within normal range for age
2. **Motor Development**
   - Perform gross and fine motor milestones within the normal range for age
   - Exhibit reflexes appropriate for age
3. **Sensory Development**
   - Follow a moving object within normal range for age
   - Respond to sounds, such as talking or clapping hands
4. **Psychosocial Development**
   - Interact appropriately with parent through body movements and vocalizations
5. **Development in Activities of Daily Living**
   - Eat and drink appropriate amounts of breast milk, formula, and/or solid foods
   - Exhibit an elimination pattern within normal range for age
   - Exhibit rest and sleep patterns appropriate for age

Health Promotion Guidelines for Infants

Health Examinations

- At two weeks and at 2, 4, 6, and 12 months

Protective Measures

- Immunizations: diphtheria tetanus pertussis (acellular) vaccine (DTaP), inactivated poliovirus vaccine (IPV), measles-mumps-rubella vaccine (MMR), *Haemophilus influenzae* type B vaccine (Hib), hepatitis B vaccine (Hep B), varicella, pneumococcal conjugate vaccine, and meningococcal C conjugate vaccine; other vaccines as recommended
- Immunization schedules may vary from province to province
- Fluoride supplements, if there is inadequate water fluoridation (less than 0.7 part per million)
- Screening for tuberculosis
- Screening for phenylketonuria (PKU)
- Prompt attention for illnesses
- Appropriate skin hygiene and clothing
- Positional therapy

Infant Safety

- Importance of supervision
- Car seat, crib, playpen, bath, and home environment safety measures
- Feeding measures (e.g., avoid propping bottle)
- Providing toys with no small parts or sharp edges

Nutrition

- Breast-feeding and bottle-feeding techniques
- Formula preparation
- Feeding schedule
- Introduction of solid foods
- Need for iron supplements at four to six months

Elimination

- Characteristics and frequency of stool and urine elimination
- Diarrhea and its effects

Rest/Sleep

- Usual sleep and rest patterns

Sensory Stimulation

- Touch: holding, cuddling, rocking
- Vision: colourful, moving toys
- Hearing: soothing voice tones, music, singing
- Play: toys appropriate for development

Toddlers (1 to 3 Years)

Toddlers develop from having no voluntary control to being able to walk and speak. They also learn to control their bladder and bowels, and they acquire all kinds of information about their environment.

Physical Development

Two-year-old children lose the baby look. Toddlers are usually chubby, with relatively short legs and a large head (Figure 20.5). The face appears small when compared to the skull, but as the toddler grows, the face seems to grow from under the skull and appears better proportioned. Toddlers have a pronounced lumbar lordosis and a protruding abdomen. The abdominal muscles develop gradually with growth, and the abdomen flattens.

Weight Two-year-olds can be expected to weigh approximately four times their birth weight. The weight gain is about 2 kg between one year and two years and about 1 to 2 kg between two and three years. The three-year-old weighs about 13.6 kg.

Figure 20.5 The toddler appears chubby with relatively short legs and a large head

Height A toddler's height can be measured as height or length. Height is measured while the toddler stands, and length is measured while the toddler is in a recumbent position. Although the measurements differ slightly, to avoid confusion, nurses must specify which measurement is used. Between ages one and two years, the average growth in height is 10 to 12 cm, and between two and three years, it slows to 6 to 8 cm.

Head Circumference The head circumference of the toddler increases about 2.5 cm on average. By 24 months, the head is 80 percent of the average adult size and the brain is 70 percent of its adult size.

Sensory Abilities Visual acuity is fairly well established at one year; average estimates of acuity for the toddler are 20/70 at 18 months and 20/40 at two years of age. Accommodation to near and far objects is fairly well developed by 18 months and continues to mature with age. At three years of age, the toddler can look away from a toy prior to reaching out and picking it up. This ability requires the integration of visual and neuromuscular mechanisms.

The senses of hearing, taste, smell, and touch become increasingly developed and associated with each other. Hearing in the three-year-old is at adult levels. The taste buds of the toddler are sensitive to the natural flavours of food, and the three-year-old prefers familiar odours and tastes. Touch is a very important sense, and a distressed toddler is often soothed by tactile sensations.

Motor Abilities *Fine muscle coordination* and *gross motor skills* improve during toddlerhood. At the age of 18 months, babies can pick up small beads and place them in a receptacle. They can also hold a spoon and a cup and can walk upstairs with assistance. They will probably crawl down the stairs.

At two years, toddlers can hold a spoon and put it into their mouths correctly. They are able to run; their gait is steady; and they can balance on one foot and ride a tricycle. By three years, most children are toilet trained, although they still may have the occasional accident when playing or during the night.

Psychosocial Development

According to Freud, the ages of two and three years represent the *anal phase* of development, when the rectum and anus are the specially significant areas of the body (see Table 19.3 on page 313). Erikson sees the period from 18 months to three years as the time when the central developmental task is autonomy versus shame and doubt (see Table 19.4 on page 314).

Toddlers begin to develop their *sense of autonomy* by asserting themselves with the frequent use of the word "no." They are often frustrated by restraints to their behaviour and, between ages one and three years, may have temper tantrums. However, they slowly gain control over their emotions, usually with the guidance of their caregivers. Parents need to have a great deal of patience coupled with an understanding of the importance of this developmental milestone. To be effective, caregivers need to give the child some measure of control and, at the same time, be consistent in setting limits so that the child learns the results of misbehaviour. The nurse can also assist the parents and caregivers in promoting the toddler's development by suggesting the activities summarized in the box below.

Children learn to develop a sense of self through their immediate social environment, in which their parents play a significant role. If the children's social interactions with their parents are negative (e.g., constant disapproval regarding eating, toilet training, or other behaviour), the children may begin to see themselves as bad. This perception is the basis of a negative self-concept. Parents need to give toddlers positive input so that they can develop a positive and healthy self-concept (Sieving & Zirbel-Donisch, 1990). With a healthy sense of self-esteem and security, the toddler is able to deal with periodic failures later in life without damage to self-esteem.

Although toddlers like to explore the environment, they always need to have a significant person nearby. Parents need to know that young children experience acute **separation anxiety**—the fear and frustration that come with parental absences. Abandonment is their greatest fear. At this age, the child may have difficulty accepting a baby-sitter or strongly resist being left by the parents at a day-care centre. For example, toddlers may become highly anxious when separated from their parents and admitted to hospital. **Regression**, or reverting to an earlier development stage, may be indicated by bed wetting or using baby talk. Nurses can assist parents by helping them understand that this behaviour is normal and indicates that these toddlers are trying to establish their position in the family.

Fostering the Toddler's Psychosocial Development

- Provide toys suitable for the toddler, including some toys challenging enough to motivate but not so difficult that the toddler will fail. (Failure will intensify feelings of self-doubt and shame.)
- Make positive suggestions, rather than give commands. Avoid an emotional climate of negativism, blame, and punishment.
- Give the toddler choices, all of which are safe; however, limit number to two or three.
- When the toddler has a temper tantrum, make sure the child is safe, and then leave.
- Help the toddler to develop inner control by setting and enforcing consistent, reasonable limits.
- Praise the toddler's accomplishments.

Experience with separation helps the child cope with parental absences. Children need room for exploration and interaction with other children and adults. At the same time, they need to know that the parental bond of a loving and close relationship remains secure.

Toddlers assert their independence by saying "no" or by dawdling. During the toddler stage, receptive and expressive language skills are developing quickly. Children can understand words and follow directions long before they can actually form them into sentences. By one year of age, toddlers can recognize their own names.

Cognitive Development

According to Piaget, the toddler completes the fifth and sixth stages of the *sensorimotor phase* and starts the *preconceptual phase* at about two years of age (see Table 19.5 on page 316). In the fifth stage, the toddler solves problems by a trial-and-error process. By stage six, toddlers can solve problems mentally. For example, when given a new toy, the toddler will not immediately handle the toy to see how it works but will look at it carefully to think about how it works.

During Piaget's preconceptual phase, toddlers develop considerable cognitive and intellectual skills. They learn about the sequence of time. They have some symbolic thought; for example, a chair may represent a place of safety, and a blanket may symbolize comfort. Concepts start to form in late toddlerhood. A concept develops when the child learns words to represent classes of objects or thoughts. An example of a concrete concept is *table*, representing a number of articles of furniture that are all different, but all tables.

Moral Development

According to Kohlberg, the first level of moral development is the preconventional, when children respond to punishment and reward (see Table 19.6, page 317). During the second year of life, children begin to know that some activities elicit affection and approval. They also recognize that certain rituals, such as repeating phrases from prayers, also elicit approval. This provides children with feelings of security. By two years of age, toddlers are learning what attitudes their parents hold about moral matters.

Spiritual Development

According to Fowler, the toddler's stage of spiritual development is undifferentiated (see Table 19.7, page 318). Toddlers may be aware of some religious practices, but they are primarily involved in acquiring knowledge and learning emotional reactions, rather than establishing spiritual beliefs. A toddler may repeat short prayers at bedtime, conforming to a ritual, because praise and affection result. This parental or caregiver response enhances the toddler's sense of security.

Health Problems

Accidents Accidents are the leading cause of mortality of toddlers. They are curious and like to feel and taste everything. The most common causes of fatal injuries are automobile accidents, drowning, burns, poisoning, and falls. Parents or other caregivers need to take the appropriate preventive measures to guard against these health threats. (See Chapter 33.)

Visual Problems During this period, the toddler should be screened for amblyopia strabismus. The toddler may have **amblyopia** (reduced visual acuity in one eye) without obvious defect or change in the eye, while a toddler with **strabismus** (cross-eye) has unequally aligned eyes, and may experience reduced vision in one eye.

Dental Caries Dental caries occur frequently during the toddler period, often as a result of the excessive intake of sweets or a prolonged use of the bottle during naps and at bedtime.

Respiratory Tract and Ear Infections Respiratory and middle ear infections are common during toddlerhood.

Health Assessment and Promotion

Assessment activities for the toddler are similar to those for the infant in terms of measuring weight, length (height), and vital signs. Assessment guidelines for growth and development of the toddler are shown in the box on the next page.

Promoting health and wellness includes such areas as accident prevention, toilet training, and good dental hygiene. For a summary of health promotion for toddlers see the second box on the next page.

Preschoolers (4 and 5 Years)

During the preschool period, physical growth slows, but control of the body and coordination increase greatly. Preschoolers' worlds get larger as they meet relatives, friends, and neighbours.

Physical Development

By the time children are four or five years old, they appear taller and thinner than toddlers because children tend to grow more in height than in weight. The preschooler's brain reaches almost its adult size by five years. The extremities of the body grow more quickly than the body trunk, making the child's body appear somewhat out of proportion. The posture of preschoolers gradually changes as the pelvis is straightened and the abdominal muscles become stronger. Thus, the preschooler appears slender with erect posture.

DEVELOPMENTAL ASSESSMENT GUIDELINES

The Toddler

In these four developmental areas, does the toddler do the following?

1. **Physical Development**
   - Demonstrate physical growth (weight, height, and head circumference) within normal range
   - Manifest vital signs within normal range for age
   - Exhibit vision and hearing abilities within normal range

2. **Motor Development**
   - Perform gross and fine motor milestones within the normal range for age. For example, by three years of age, is the toddler able to do the following?
     - Walk up steps without assistance
     - Balance on one foot, jump, and walk on toes
     - Copy a circle
     - Build a bridge from blocks
     - Ride a tricycle

3. **Psychosocial Development**
   - Perform psychosocial developmental milestones for age. For example, by three years of age, is the toddler able to do the following?
     - Express likes and dislikes
     - Display curiosity and ask questions
     - Accept separation from mother for short periods of time
     - Begin to play and communicate with children and others outside the immediate family
     - Understand words such as "up," "down," "cold," and "hungry"
     - Speak in sentences of three to four words
     - Imitate religious rituals of the family

4. **Development of Activities of Daily Living**
   - Feed self
   - Eat and drink a variety of foods
   - Begin to develop bowel and bladder control
   - Exhibit a rest and sleep pattern appropriate for age
   - Dress self

Health Promotion Guidelines for Toddlers

Health Examinations

- At 15 and 18 months and then as recommended by the physician
- Dental visit starting at age three years
- Hearing tests by 18 months or earlier

Protective Measures

- Immunizations: continuing DTaP, IPV series, measles-mumps-rubella (MMR), *Haemophilus influenzae* type B (Hib), and hepatitis B vaccines as recommended
- Screenings for tuberculosis and lead poisoning
- Fluoride supplements, if there is inadequate water fluoridation (less than 0.7 part per million)

Toddler Safety

- Importance of supervision and teaching child to obey instructions
- Home environment safety measures (e.g., lock medicine cabinet)
- Outdoor safety measures (e.g., close supervision near water)
- Appropriate toys

Nutrition

- Importance of nutritious meals and snacks
- Teaching simple mealtime manners
- Dental care

Elimination

- Toilet training techniques

Rest/Sleep

- Dealing with sleep disturbances

Play

- Providing adequate space and a variety of activities
- Toys that allow "acting on" behaviours and provide motor and sensory stimulation

Weight Weight gain in preschool children is generally slow. By five years, they have added only another 3 to 5 kg to their three-year-old weight, increasing it to somewhere between 18 and 20 kg.

Height Preschool children grow about 5 to 6.25 cm each year. Thus, by five years of age, they double the birth length and measure 100 cm.

Vision Preschool children are generally **hyperopic** (farsighted), that is, unable to focus on near objects. As the eye grows in length, it becomes **emmetropic** (it refracts light normally). If the eyes become too long, the child becomes **myopic** (nearsighted), that is, unable to focus on objects that are far away. In severe cases of hyperopia or myopia, glasses may be prescribed. By the end of the preschool years, visual ability has improved; normal vision for the five-year-old is approximately 20/30. The Snellen E chart (see Chapter 27) can be used to assess the preschooler's vision.

Hearing and Taste The hearing of the preschool child has reached optimal levels, and the ability to listen (attending to and comprehending what is said) has matured since the toddler age. As for the sense of taste, preschoolers show their preferences by asking for something "yummy," and may refuse something they consider "yucky."

Motor Abilities By five years of age, children are able to wash their hands and face and brush their teeth by themselves. They are self-conscious about exposing their bodies and go to the bathroom without telling others. Typically, preschool children run with increasing skill each year. By five years of age, they run skillfully and can jump three steps. Preschoolers can balance on their toes and dress themselves without assistance.

Psychosocial Development

Erikson writes that the major developmental crisis of the preschooler is *initiative versus guilt* (see Table 19.4 on page 314). Preschoolers must solve problems in accordance with their consciences. Their personalities develop. Erikson views the crises at this time as important for the development of the individual's *self-concept*. According to Erikson, preschoolers must learn what they can do. As a result, preschoolers imitate behaviour, and their imaginations and creativity become lively.

Parents can enhance the self-concept of the preschooler by providing opportunities for new achievements where the child can learn, repeat, and master. For example, a child obtains a two-wheel bike with safety wheels and quickly learns coordination, balance, use of the brakes, and bicycle safety. Mastery of these tasks provides the child with a sense of accomplishment. The child is soon ready for the new challenge of mastering the two-wheeler.

Figure 20.6 Preschoolers often identify with the parent of the same sex and like to mimic behaviour

The self-concept of the preschooler is also based on gender identification. Preschoolers are aware of the two sexes. They often imitate sexual stereotypes and usually begin by identifying with the parent of the same sex. They may mimic the parent's behaviour, attitudes, and appearance (Figure 20.6). Parents need to be aware that preschoolers are curious about their own bodies and sexual functions, as well as those of others, and will often ask questions. Parents should not imply that a question is inappropriate or that a particular subject is bad.

Freud theorizes that the preschooler is in the *phallic stage* of development. The biological focus of the child during this stage is the genital area (see Table 19.3 on page 313).

The phase of close emotional relationships with both parents changes to the phase Freud referred to as the Electra or Oedipus complex (Engel, 1962). At this time, the child focuses feelings of love chiefly on the parent of the opposite sex, and the parent of the same sex may receive some hostile feelings. The child begins to develop sexual interests and becomes interested in clothes and hair styles.

During the preschool years, four *adaptive mechanisms* are learned: identification, introjection, imagination, and repression. **Identification** occurs when the child perceives the self as similar to another person and behaves like that person. For example, a boy may internalize the attitudes and gender behaviour of his father. **Introjection** is similar to identification. It is the assimilation of the attributes of others. When preschoolers observe their parents, they assimilate many of their values and attitudes. **Imagination** is an important part of preschoolers' lives. The preschooler has an active imagination and fantasizes in play; for example, a chair becomes a beautiful throne to a girl, and she is the ruler. **Repression** is removing experiences, thoughts, and impulses from awareness. The preschooler generally represses thoughts related to the Oedipus or Electra complex.

Preschool children gradually emerge as social beings. At the age of three or four, they learn to play with a small number of their peers. They gradually learn to play with more people as they grow older. Preschoolers participate more in the family than they did previously. In associations with neighbours, family guests, and baby-sitters, too, they learn about social relationships.

In their *speech*, children of four years are often dogmatic; they tend to believe that what they know is right. Four-year-olds love nonsense words such as "jump-jump" and can string them together much to an adult's exasperation. At four years, children are aggressive in their speech and capable of long conversations, often mixing fact and fiction. By five years of age, speaking skills are well developed. Children use words purposefully and ask questions to acquire information. They do not merely practise speaking as three- and four-year-olds do, but speak as a means of social interaction. Exaggeration is common among four- and five-year-olds.

Preschoolers also become increasingly aware of themselves. They play with their bodies largely out of curiosity. They know where the body begins and ends as well as the correct names for the different parts. By five years of age, they are able to draw a person, including all the features. Preschoolers also learn about their feelings; they know the words "cry," "sad," "laugh," and the feelings related to them. They also begin to learn how to control their feelings and behaviour. The preschooler uses the same types of *coping mechanisms* in response to stress as the toddler does, although protest behaviour (kicking, screaming) is less likely to occur in the older preschooler. Preschoolers usually have greater ability to verbalize stress.

Preschoolers need to feel that they are loved and that they are an important part of the family. The child who has to compete with siblings for parental attention will often display jealousy. Parents and caregivers should be aware that preschoolers need time to adjust to a new baby and may need additional attention or special activities to help them through this adjustment period. Preschoolers with older siblings may also experience sibling rivalry. Siblings may fight and argue and become aggressive because of their daily close proximity or competition for parental attention. Parents who can plan some special time or activity for each child will help that child to feel loved and may decrease the sibling rivalry.

Guidance and discipline are important parts of the parental role during the preschool years. As children seek independence from adults, they often test limits by refusing to cooperate and by repeatedly ignoring parental requests. These power struggles can sometimes be avoided by encouraging children to be responsible for their own behaviour as much as possible and by setting reasonable expectations and consistent limits. When conflict does occur, parents can employ mutual discussion and compromise.

Cognitive Development

The preschooler's cognitive development, according to Piaget, is the phase of *intuitive thought* (see Table 19.5 on page 316). Children are still egocentric, but egocentrism gradually subsides as they encounter wider experiences. Preschoolers learn through trial and error, and they think of only one idea at a time. They do not understand relationships, such as those between mother and father or sister and brother. Children start to form concepts in late toddlerhood or the early preschool years. Preschoolers become concerned about death as something inevitable, but they do not explain it. They also associate death with others rather than themselves.

Most children at the age of five years can count pennies; however, the opportunity to spend money usually does not occur until they attend school. Reading skills also start to develop at this age. Young children like fairy tales and books about animals and other children.

Moral Development

Preschoolers are capable of prosocial behaviour, that is, any action that a person takes to benefit someone else. The term *prosocial* is synonymous with *kind* and connotes sharing, helping, protecting, giving aid, befriending, showing affection, and giving encouragement.

At this stage of development, preschoolers do not have a fully formed conscience; however, they do develop some internal controls. Moral behaviour is largely learned by *modelling*, initially after parents and later, significant others. The preschooler usually behaves well in social settings.

Children who perceive their parents as strict may become resentful or overly obedient. Preschoolers usually control their behaviour because they want love and approval from their parents. Moral behaviour to a preschooler may mean taking turns at play or sharing. Nurses can assist parents by discussing moral development and encouraging parents to give preschoolers recognition for such actions as sharing. It is also important for parents to answer preschoolers' "why" questions and discuss values with them.

DEVELOPMENTAL ASSESSMENT GUIDELINES

The Preschooler

In these four developmental areas, does the preschooler do the following?

1. **Physical Development**
   - Demonstrate physical growth (weight, height) within normal range
   - Manifest vital signs within normal range for age
   - Exhibit vision and hearing abilities within normal range
2. **Motor Development**
   - Perform gross and fine motor milestones within the normal range for age. For example, by five years of age is the preschooler able to do the following?
     - Jump rope and skip
     - Climb playground equipment
     - Ride a bicycle with training wheels
     - Print letters and numbers
3. **Psychosocial Development**
   - Perform psychosocial developmental milestones for age. For example, by five years of age is the preschooler able to do the following?
     - Separate easily from parents
     - Display imagination and creativity
     - Enjoy playing with peers in cooperative activities
     - Understand right from wrong and respond to others' expectations of behaviour
     - Identify four colours
     - Exhibit increasing vocabulary using complete sentences and all parts of speech
     - Cooperate in doing simple chores (e.g., putting away toys)
     - Identify with individuals of own sex
4. **Development in Activities of Daily Living**
   - Demonstrate development of toilet training
   - Perform simple hygiene measures
   - Dress and undress self

Spiritual Development

Many preschoolers enroll in Sunday school or faith-oriented classes. The preschooler usually enjoys the social interaction of these classes. According to Fowler, children from the ages of four to six years are at the intuitive-projective stage of spiritual development (see Table 19.7 on page 318).

Faith, at this stage, is primarily a result of the teaching of significant others, such as parents and teachers. Children learn to imitate religious behaviour, for example, bowing the head in prayer, although they don't understand the meaning of the behaviour. Preschoolers require simple explanations, such as those in picture books, of spiritual matters. Children at this age use their imaginations to envision such ideas as angels or the devil.

Health Problems

Preschoolers often have health problems similar to those they had in toddlerhood. Respiratory tract problems and communicable diseases frequently occur as the preschooler interacts with other children at nursery school and day care. Accidents and dental caries continue to be problems during this age. Congenital abnormalities, such as cardiac disorders and hernias, are often corrected at this age.

Health Assessment and Promotion

During assessment, the preschooler can often participate in answering questions with assistance from parents or caregivers. For instance, children who attend preschool can describe the typical lunch and how much of it they usually eat. Preschoolers can also describe the types of activities they enjoy. Assessment guidelines for growth and development of the preschooler are shown in the box above.

Promoting health and wellness includes such areas as preventing accidents, dental health, good nutrition, cognitive stimulation, and sufficient sleep. For a summary of health promotion see the box on the next page. For additional information about wellness promotion, see life span considerations in later chapters.

School-Age Children (6 to 12 Years)

The school-age period starts when children are about six years of age, when the deciduous teeth are shed. This period includes the preadolescent (prepuberty) period. It ends at about 12 years, with the onset of puberty. Puberty is the age when the reproductive organs become functional and secondary sex characteristics develop. Because

Health Promotion Guidelines for Preschoolers

Health Examinations

- Every one to two years

Protective Measures

- Immunizations: continuing DTaP, IPV series, measles-mumps-rubella (MMR) vaccine; other immunizations as recommended
- Tuberculin skin test
- Vision and hearing screening
- Regular dental screenings and fluoride treatment

Preschooler Safety

- Educating child about simple safety rules (e.g., crossing the street)
- Teaching child to play safely (e.g., bicycle and playground safety)
- Educating to prevent poisoning

Nutrition

- Importance of nutritious meals and snacks

Elimination

- Teaching proper hygiene (e.g., washing hands after using bathroom)

Rest/Sleep

- Dealing with sleep disturbances (e.g., nightmares)

Play

- Providing times for group play activities
- Teaching child simple games that require cooperation and interaction
- Providing toys and dress-ups for role-playing

the average age of onset of puberty is 10 for girls and 12 for boys, some people define the school-age years as six to 10 for girls and six to 12 for boys. Skills learned during this stage are particularly important in relation to work later in life and willingness to try new tasks. In general, the period from six to 12 years is one of rapid and dramatic change.

Physical Development

The school-age child gains weight rapidly and thus appears less thin than previously. Individual differences due to both genetic and environmental factors are obvious at this time.

Weight At six years, boys tend to weigh about 21 kg, about 1 kg more than girls. The weight gain of school children from six to 12 years of age averages about 3.2 kg per year, but the major weight gains occur from age 10 to 12 for boys and from nine to 12 for girls. By 12 years of age, boys and girls weigh 40 to 42 kg on average; girls are usually heavier.

Height At six years, both boys and girls are about the same height, 115 cm. They are about 150 cm by 12 years. Before puberty, children of both sexes have a growth spurt—girls between 10 and 12 years and boys between 12 and 14 years. Thus, girls may well be taller than boys at 12 years, but boys are usually stronger.

The extremities tend to grow more quickly than the trunk; thus, school-age children's bodies appear somewhat ill-proportioned. By six years of age, the thoracic curvature starts to develop, and the lordosis disappears. Full adult posture is not assumed, however, until after the complete development of the skeletal musculature during the adolescent period.

Vision The depth and distance perception of children six to eight years of age is accurate. By age six years, children have full binocular vision. The eye muscles are well developed and coordinated, and both eyes can focus on one object at the same time. Because the shape of the eye changes during growth, the farsightedness of the preschool years gradually changes to 20/20 vision during the school-age years; 20/20 vision is usually well established between nine and 11 years of age.

Hearing and Touch Auditory perception is fully developed in school-age children, who are able to identify fine differences in voices, both in sound and in pitch. At this stage, children also have a well-developed sense of touch and are able to locate points of heat and cold on all body surfaces. They are also able to identify an unseen object, such as a pencil or a book, simply by touch. This ability is called **stereognosis.**

Prepubertal Changes Little change takes place in the reproductive and endocrine systems until the prepuberty period. During prepuberty, at about ages nine to 13 years, endocrine functions slowly increase. This change in endocrine function can result in increased perspiration and more active sebaceous glands.

Motor Abilities During the middle years (six to 10 years), children perfect their muscular skills and coordination. By nine years, most children are becoming skilled in games of interest, such as football or baseball. These skills are often associated with school, and many of them are learned there. By nine years, most children have sufficient fine motor control for such activities as building models or sewing.

Psychosocial Development

According to Erikson, the central task of school-age children is *industry versus inferiority*. At this time, children begin to create and develop a sense of competence and perseverance. School-age children are motivated by activities that provide a sense of worth. They concentrate on mastering skills that will help them function in the adult world. Although children of this age work hard to succeed, they are always faced with the possibility of failure, which can lead to a sense of inferiority. If children have been successful in previous stages, they are motivated to be industrious and to cooperate with others toward a common goal (see Table 19.4 on page 314).

Freud describes the period from six through 12 years of age as the latency stage. During this time, the focus is on physical and intellectual activities, while sexual tendencies seem to be repressed (see Table 19.3 on page 313).

In school, children have the restraints of the school system imposed on their behaviour, and they learn to develop controls. Children compare their skills with those of their peers in a number of areas, including motor development, social development, and language. This comparison assists in the development of self-concept.

As they grow older, schoolchildren learn to play with more children at one time. Usually the six- and seven-year-old is a member of a peer group. This group can be a greater influence than the family in teaching attitudes. During late childhood, children join with a small group of peers, which is formed by the children themselves. It is usually informal and transitory, and the leadership changes from time to time. During this period of socialization with others, children gradually become less self-centred and selfish and more cooperative and conscious of the group.

The schoolchild's self-concept continues to mature. Children recognize similarities and differences between themselves and others. School-age children compare themselves with others and obtain feedback from teachers and peers. Children who are successful and receive recognition for their efforts feel competent and in control of themselves and of the environment. Children who feel unaccepted by their peers, or who receive negative feedback and little recognition, can feel inferior and worthless.

Although the focus of interest for this age group has moved to school, peers, and other activities, the home remains the crucial place for the child's development of high self-esteem.

Figure 20.7 Expanding cognitive skills enable school-age children to interact cooperatively in activities of an increasingly complex nature, as shown by the children playing this board game

Cognitive Development

According to Piaget, the ages seven to 11 years mark the phase of *concrete operations* (see Table 19.5 on page 316). During this stage, the child changes from egocentric interactions to cooperative interactions (Figure 20.7). School-age children also develop an increased understanding of concepts that are associated with specific objects, for example, environmental conservation or wildlife preservation. Children at this time develop logical reasoning from intuitive reasoning. For example, they learn to add and subtract to obtain an answer to a problem. Children also learn about cause-and-effect relationships at this age; for example, they know that a stone will not float because it is heavier than water.

Money is a concept that gains meaning for children when they start school. By the time they are seven or eight years old, children usually know the value of most coins. The concept of time is also learned at this age. By six years of age, children enter school; the schedule in school helps them learn time periods. However, it is not until nine or 10 years of age that children are able to understand the long periods of time in the past. Knowing the time of day and the day of the week are relatively easy for children because they relate time to routine activities. For example, a child may go to school Monday through Friday, play on Saturday, go to Sunday school on Sunday morning, and go out with her father Sunday afternoon. Children are beginning to read the clock by the time they are six years old.

Reading skills are usually well developed later in childhood, and what a child reads is largely influenced by the family. By nine years of age, most children are self-motivated. They compete with themselves, and they like to plan in advance. By 12 years, they are motivated by inner drive, rather than by competition with peers. They like to talk, to discuss different subjects, and to debate.

Moral Development

Some school-age children are at Kohlberg's stage 1 of the *preconventional* level (punishment and obedience); that is, they act to avoid being punished. Some school-age children, however, are at stage 2 (*instrumental-relativist orientation*). These children do things to benefit themselves. Fairness, that is everyone getting a fair share or chance, becomes important. Later in childhood, most children progress to the *conventional* level. This level has two stages: Stage 3 is the *interpersonal concordance* ("good boy/nice girl") stage, and stage 4 is the *law and order orientation*. Children usually reach the conventional level between the ages of 10 and 13. The child shifts from the concrete interests of individuals to the interests of groups. The motivation for moral action at this stage is to live up to what significant others think of the child (see Table 19.6 on page 317).

Spiritual Development

According to Fowler, the school-age child is at stage 2 in spiritual development, the *mythic-literal* stage. Children learn to distinguish fantasy from fact. Spiritual facts are those beliefs that are accepted by a religious group, whereas fantasy is thoughts and images formed in the child's mind. Parents and the minister, rabbi, or priest help the child distinguish fact from fantasy. These people still influence the child more than peers in spiritual matters (see Table 19.7 on page 318).

When children do not understand such events as the creation of the world, they use fantasy to explain them. The school-age child needs to have such concepts as prayer presented in concrete terms. For example, the child thinks of a god as having human qualities, such as a kind old person or a person who punishes when behaviour does not meet his standards.

School-age children may ask many questions about religion and a higher power in these years and will generally believe that the higher power is good and always present to help. Just before puberty, children become aware that their prayers are not always answered and become disappointed. At this age, some children reject religion, whereas others continue to accept it. This decision is largely influenced by the parents. If a child continues religious training, the child is ready to apply reason, rather than blind belief, in most situations.

DEVELOPMENTAL ASSESSMENT GUIDELINES

The School-Age Child

In these four developmental areas, does the school-age child do the following?

1. **Physical Development**
   - Demonstrate physical growth (weight, height) within normal range
   - Manifest vital signs within normal range for age
   - Exhibit vision and hearing abilities within normal range
   - Demonstrate male or female prepubertal changes within normal range
2. **Motor Development**
   - Possess coordinated motor skills for age. For example, by 12 years of age, is the child able to do the following?
     - Do tricks on a bike, climb a tree
     - Throw and catch a small ball
     - Play a musical instrument
3. **Psychosocial Development**
   - Perform psychosocial developmental milestones for age. For example, by 12 years of age is the child able to do the following?
   - Make friends of the same sex and establish a peer group
   - Become less dependent on family and venture away from them
   - Interact well with parents
   - Control strong and impulsive feelings
   - Participate in organized competitions
   - Read, print, and manipulate numbers and letters easily
   - Exhibit a concept of money and make change for small amounts of money
   - Express self in a logical manner and talk through problems
   - Enjoy riddles and read and understand comics
   - Invest in a hobby or collection
   - Like to help others
   - Think of self as likable and healthy
4. **Development in Activities of Daily Living**
   - Demonstrate concern for personal cleanliness and appearance
   - Express need for privacy

Health Promotion Guidelines for School-Age Children

Health Examinations

- Annual physical examination or as recommended

Protective Measures

- Immunizations as recommended
- Tuberculin skin test
- Periodic vision, speech, and hearing screenings
- Regular dental screenings and fluoride treatment
- Providing accurate information about sexual issues (e.g., reproduction, AIDS)

School-Age Child Safety

- Using proper equipment when participating in sports and other physical activities (e.g., helmets, pads)
- Encouraging child to take responsibility for own safety (e.g., participating in bicycle and water safety courses)

Nutrition

- Importance of child eating a balanced diet and not skipping meals
- Experiences with food that may lead to obesity

Elimination

- Utilizing positive approaches for elimination problems (e.g., enuresis)

Play and Social Interactions

- Providing opportunities for a variety of organized group activities
- Accepting realistic expectations of child's abilities
- Acting as role models in acceptance of other persons who may be different
- Providing a home environment that limits television viewing and video games and encourages completion of homework

Health Problems

School-age children continue to have as many communicable diseases, dental caries, and accidents as preschoolers. However, at this age, homicide and violence can also be problems. Scabies, impetigo, and lice are also more prevalent at this age. In addition, alcohol abuse and drug abuse occur, although not as frequently as in adolescence.

Health Assessment and Promotion

During the assessment interview, the nurse responds to questions from the parent or other caregiver, gives appropriate feedback, and lends encouragement and support. The nurse also demonstrates interest in the child and enthusiasm for the child's strengths. Assessment guidelines for growth and development of the school-age child are shown in the box on the previous page.

Promoting health and wellness includes dental hygiene and regular dental examinations, safety measures to prevent accidents, promoting physical fitness, supporting autonomy and self-esteem, and hygiene measures to prevent infections. See the box above for health promotion guidelines. For additional information, see lifespan considerations in later chapters.

Adolescence (12 to 18 Years)

Adolescence is the period during which the person becomes physically and psychologically mature and acquires a personal identity. At the end of this critical period in development, the person is ready to enter adulthood and assume its responsibilities. The length of adolescence is culturally determined to some extent. In North America, adolescence is longer than in some cultures, extending to 18 or 20 years of age.

Puberty is the first stage of adolescence, in which sexual organs begin to grow and mature. **Menarche** (onset of menstruation) occurs in girls. **Ejaculation** (expulsion of semen) occurs in boys. For girls, puberty normally starts between 10 and 14 years; for boys, between 12 and 16 years. The adolescent period is often subdivided into three stages: early adolescence lasts from ages 12 to 13; middle adolescence extends from 14 to 16 years; and late adolescence extends from 17 to 18 or 20 years. Late adolescence is a more stable stage than the other two. In the late period, adolescents are involved mostly with planning their future and economic independence.

Physical Development

During puberty, growth is markedly accelerated compared with the slow, steady growth of the child. This period, marked by sudden and dramatic physical changes, is referred to as the *adolescent growth spurt.* In boys, the growth spurt usually begins between ages 12 and 16 years; in girls, it begins earlier, usually between ages 10 and 14 years. Because the growth spurt begins earlier in girls, many girls surpass boys in height at this time.

Physical Growth Physical growth continues throughout adolescence. Growth is fastest for boys at about 14 years, and the maximum height is often reached at about 18 or 19 years. Some men add another 1 or 2 cm to their height during their 20s as the vertebral column gradually continues to grow. During the period of 10 to 18 years of age, the average Canadian male doubles his weight, gaining about 32 kg, and grows about 41 cm. The fastest rate of growth in girls occurs at about age 12 years; they reach their maximum height at about 15 to 16 years. During ages 10 to 18 years, the average Canadian female gains about 25 kg and grows about 24 cm.

Physical growth during adolescence is greatly influenced by a number of factors, such as heredity, nutrition, medical care, illness, physical and emotional environment, family size, and culture. Generally, people in Canada have grown taller in recent years. This increase in average height is thought to be due to many of the preceding factors.

Growth is noted first in the musculoskeletal system. This growth follows a sequential pattern: the head, hands, and feet are the first to grow to adult status; next, the extremities reach their adult size. Because the extremities grow before the trunk, the adolescent looks leggy, awkward, and uncoordinated. After the trunk grows to full size, the shoulders, chest, and hips grow. Skull and facial bones also change proportions—the forehead becomes more prominent, and the jawbones develop.

Glandular Changes The eccrine and apocrine glands increase their secretions and become fully functional during puberty. The **eccrine glands,** found over most of the body, produce sweat. The **apocrine glands** develop in the axillae, anal and genital areas, external auditory canals, and around the umbilicus and areolae of the breasts. Apocrine sweat is released onto the skin in response to emotional stimuli only. **Sebaceous glands** also become active under the influence of androgens in both males and females. The sebaceous glands, which secrete **sebum,** become most active on the face, neck, shoulder, upper back, chest, and genitals.

Sexual Characteristics During puberty, both primary and secondary sex characteristics develop. **Primary sexual characteristics** relate to the organs necessary for reproduction, such as the testes, penis, vagina, and uterus. **Secondary sexual characteristics** differentiate the male from the female but do not relate directly to reproduction. Examples are pubic hair growth, breast development, and voice changes.

The first noticeable sign that puberty has begun in males is the appearance of pubic hair. The milestone of male puberty is considered to be the first ejaculation, which commonly occurs at about 14 years of age. Fertility follows several months later. Sexual maturity is achieved by age 18 years.

Often, the first noticeable sign of puberty in females is the appearance of the **breast bud,** although the appearance of hair along the labia may precede this. The milestone of female puberty is the menarche, which occurs about two years after the breast bud appears. At first, menstrual periods are scanty and irregular and may occur without ovulation. Ovulation is usually established one to two years after menarche. Female internal reproductive organs reach adult size about age 18 to 20 years.

Psychosocial Development

According to Erikson (1963, p. 261), the adolescent seeks answers to the questions "Who am I?" and "What am I to be?" The psychosocial task of the adolescent is the *establishment of identity.* The danger of this stage is role confusion (see Table 19.4 on page 314). The inability to settle on an occupational identity commonly disturbs the adolescent. Less commonly, doubts about sexual identity arise. Because of the adolescent's dramatic body changes, the development of a stable identity is difficult. Erikson says that adolescents help one another through this identity crisis by forming cliques and a separate youth culture. These cliques often exclude all those who are "different" in cultural background, aspects of dress, gestures, and tastes.

Adolescents are usually concerned about their body, their appearance, and their physical abilities. Hair styling, skin care, and clothes become very important. In-groupers of an adolescent clique can be excessively clannish and cruel in excluding out-groupers; this intolerance is a temporary defence against identity confusion (Erikson, 1963).

In their search for a new identity, adolescents have to refight the battles of many of the previous stages of development. The task of developing trust in self and others is again encountered when adolescents look for ideal persons whom they can trust and with whom they can prove trustworthy. Development of autonomy is restaged in their search for ways to express their right to choose freely. The search for an occupational role that allows expression of an autonomous, freely chosen direction is one example. Free choice and autonomy present conflicts to the adolescent. Conflict arises between behaving well in the eyes of the parents and behaving in a manner that may expose them to the ridicule of their peers. The sense of initiative is also restaged.

The adolescent has unlimited imagination and ambition and aspires to great accomplishments. The sense of industry is re-enacted when the adolescent chooses a career. The extent to which these tasks were achieved earlier influences the adolescent's ability to achieve a healthy self-concept and self-identity.

The adolescent needs to establish a **self-concept** that accepts both personal strengths and weaknesses. Faced with dramatic changes in body structure and function and greater expectations to assume responsibilities, many adolescents experience temporary difficulty in developing a positive self-image. Adolescents who are accepted, loved, and valued by family and peers generally tend to gain confidence and feel good about themselves. Adolescents who have difficulty forming relationships, or who are perceived by peers as too different and not included in adolescent cliques, may develop less favourable self-images and have low self-esteem. Adolescents need to learn to build on their strengths and not be preoccupied by such problems as acne.

Teenagers with physical challenges or illnesses are particularly vulnerable to peer rejection. Nurses and educators can promote peer understanding and acceptance. Adolescents gain self-concepts largely from the impressions that others have of them. If others accept individual differences—for example, a lost finger—teenagers accept those differences more readily. Establishing groups of peers who have similar problems can provide an opportunity for the individual to develop close relationships with others and feel valued and accepted.

Although **sexual identification** begins at about three or four years of age, it is a significant part of adolescence. Because sex roles are becoming less defined in Canadian society, adopting masculine and feminine roles is increasingly confusing to today's adolescent. Job and family roles are less traditional and gender specific. In forming a sexual identity, adolescents first fantasize the male or female role and then enact various aspects of that imagined role. In response to their own feelings and that of others, aspects of the role are either adopted or rejected. Later, adolescents begin to establish intimacy with a partner or partners. This intimacy lays the groundwork for the commitments of adulthood. Sexual experimentation is not part of true intimacy, but once intimacy is achieved, sexual activity is included.

Adolescents are sexually active and may engage in masturbation as well as heterosexual and homosexual activities. Homosexual activity during adolescence is not necessarily an indicator of sexual preference because both homosexual and heterosexual adolescents may experiment sexually with persons of the same and opposite sexes.

At about the age of 15 years, many adolescents gradually draw away from the family and gain independence. This *need for independence*, combined with the need for family support, sometimes creates conflict within the adolescent and between the adolescent and the family. The young person may appear hostile or depressed at times during this painful process. At this age, adolescents prefer to be with their peers rather than their parents and may seek advice from adults other than their parents. Parents sometimes are bewildered by this stage of development; instead of reducing controls, they increase them, causing the adolescent to rebel.

Adolescents also have to resolve their ambivalent feelings toward the parent of the opposite sex. As part of the resolution, adolescents may develop brief crushes on adults outside the family—teachers or neighbours, for example. Adolescents sometimes adopt some of the attributes of the adults with whom they are infatuated. This modelling can be helpful in the maturing process.

Some of the discord in the family at this time is due to the generation gap. The values of the adolescent may differ from those of the parents. This difference may be difficult for the parents to understand and to accept. Adolescents still need guidance from their parents, although they appear to neither want it nor need it. However, adolescents need to know that their parents care about them and that their parents still want to help them. Restrictions and guidance need to be presented in a manner that makes adolescents feel loved. They need consistency in guidance and fewer restrictions than previously. They should have the independence they can handle, yet know that their parents will assist them when they need help.

During adolescence, **peer groups** assume great importance (Figure 20.8). The peer group has a number of functions. It provides a sense of belonging, pride, social learning, and gender roles. Most peer groups have well-defined, gender-specific modes of acceptable behaviour. In adolescence, the peer groups change with age. They start as single-sex groups, evolve to mixed groups, and finally narrow to couples who share activities.

For homosexuals, adolescence is a difficult time. Because peer acceptance is crucial to self-acceptance, lesbian and gay adolescents usually conform to the heterosexual codes and behaviours of their peer groups, even though these do not feel natural or correct. Conforming may exact a great personal cost. Adolescents who choose to be openly gay or lesbian face not only the ostracism of their peers, but also the misunderstanding and hostility of parents, teachers, and other important adults.

Figure 20.8 Adolescent peer group relationships enhance a sense of belonging, self-esteem, and self-identity

Cognitive Development

Cognitive abilities mature during adolescence. Between the ages of 11 and 15 years, the adolescent begins Piaget's *formal operations phase* of cognitive development (see Table 19.5 on page 316). The main feature of this stage is that people can think beyond the present and beyond the world of reality. Adolescents are highly imaginative and idealistic. They consider things that do not exist but that might be and consider ways things could be or ought to be. This type of thinking requires logic, organization, and consistency.

The adolescent becomes more informed about the world and environment. Adolescents use new information to solve everyday problems and can communicate with adults on most subjects. The adolescent's capacity to absorb and use knowledge is great. Adolescents usually select their own areas for learning; they explore interests from which they may evolve a career plan. Study habits and learning skills developed in adolescence are used throughout life.

Moral Development

According to Kohlberg, the young adolescent is usually at the *conventional level* of moral development. Most still accept the Golden Rule and want to abide by social order and existing laws. Adolescents examine their values, standards, and morals. They may discard the values they have adopted from parents in favour of values they consider more suitable.

When adolescents move into the *postconventional* or *principled level*, they start to question the rules and laws of society. Right thinking and right action become a matter of personal values and opinions, which may conflict with societal laws. Adolescents consider the possibility of rationally changing the law and emphasize individual rights. Not all adolescents, or even adults, proceed to this postconventional level. See Kohlberg's stages of moral development in Table 19.6 on page 317.

Spiritual Development

According to Fowler, the adolescent or young adult reaches the *synthetic-conventional* stage of spiritual development (see Table 19.7 on page 318). As adolescents encounter different groups in society, they are exposed to a wide variety of opinions, beliefs, and behaviours regarding religious matters. The adolescent may reconcile the differences in one of the following ways:

- Deciding any differences are wrong
- Compartmentalizing the differences (For example, a friend may not be able to go to dances on Friday evenings because of religious observances, but the friend can share activities on other days.)
- Obtaining advice from a significant other, such as a parent or a minister

Often, the adolescent believes that various religious beliefs and practices have more similarities than differences. At this stage, the adolescent's focus is on interpersonal, rather than conceptual, matters.

Nursing activities relative to this stage of spiritual development include:

- Presenting an open, accepting attitude to adolescents' questions and statements regarding spiritual matters and their implications for health

Canadian Society Notes

Fact	Implications for Nursing Practice
Adolescent pregnancy continues to be at a high rate in Canada.	Nurses have a clinical, teaching, and consultant role to play in helping teenagers prevent unplanned pregnancies.
The Office of Children's Environmental Health works with national and international partners to monitor and analyze scientific evidence on the impact of environmental threats on children's health; identify knowledge gaps and advocate for research activities to address them; coordinate development of policy and strategies to reduce environmental risks to children's health; and develop public education materials on strategies to reduce the risk of environmental threats to children.	Nurses, especially those in the community, need to promote the safety of children and consistency with federal initiatives that will help program planning and resource allocation.
The Canada Prenatal Nutrition Program is a community-based program that supports pregnant women who face conditions of risk that threaten their health and the development of their babies. It is offered through Health Canada's regional offices.	Nurses need to be aware of this resource which provides information to promote health and healthy babies.

DEVELOPMENTAL ASSESSMENT GUIDELINES

The Adolescent

In these three developmental areas, does the adolescent do the following?

1. Physical Development

- Exhibit physical growth (weight, height) within normal range for age and gender
- Demonstrate male or female sexual development consistent with standards
- Manifest vital signs within normal range for age and gender
- Exhibit vision and hearing abilities within normal range

2. Psychosocial Development

- Interact well with parents, teachers, peers, siblings, and persons in authority
- Like self
- Think and plan for the future, such as university or a career
- Choose a lifestyle and interests that fit own identity
- Determine own beliefs and values
- Begin to establish a sense of identity in the family
- Seek help from appropriate persons about problems

3. Development in Activities of Daily Living

- Demonstrate knowledge of physical development, menstruation, reproduction, birth control, and methods for the prevention of sexually transmitted diseases
- Exhibit healthy lifestyle practices in nutrition, exercise, recreation, sleep patterns, and personal habits
- Demonstrate concern for personal cleanliness and appearance

- Arranging for adolescents to see a member of their religious faith, if so desired, or to talk with members of their church peer group for support
- Providing a comfortable environment in which adolescents can practise the rituals of their faith

Health Problems

The leading causes of death of adolescents are motor vehicle accidents, suicide, homicide, nonmotor accidents, and heart disease. Other health problems are depression, bereavement when it is excessive or deviates from normal expectations, tooth decay, gingivitis and malalignment of teeth, neglect, abuse, anorexia nervosa, bulimia, substance abuse, and sexually transmitted diseases.

Health Assessment and Promotion

Assessment guidelines for growth and development of the adolescent are shown in the box above. Adolescents are usually self-directed in meeting their health needs. Because of maturation changes, however, they need teaching and guidance in a number of health-care areas.

Promoting health and wellness includes screening for tobacco, alcohol, and drug use and for sexual practices, and checking blood pressure, height, and weight. For a summary of health promotion see the box on page 344. For additional information about wellness promotion, see lifespan considerations in later chapters.

FOCUS ON CRITICAL THINKING

Billy is a six-year-old boy entering grade 1. He is scared and hesitant to let go of his mother's hand. As the nursing student working in this setting, you have the opportunity of working with Billy and other young children as they start school.

1. How would you help Billy's mother reassure him?
2. On the basis of his age, what strategies might you use to teach Billy and his classmates about health promotion?

See Appendix A for answers to these questions.

Health Promotion Guidelines for Adolescents

Health Examinations

- As recommended by the physician

Protective Measures

- Immunizations as recommended, such as adult tetanus-diphtheria (Td) vaccine, hepatitis B vaccine, and meningococcal vaccine
- Screening for tuberculosis
- Periodic vision and hearing screenings
- Regular dental assessments
- Obtaining and providing accurate information about sexual issues

Adolescent Safety

- Adolescent's taking responsibility for using motor vehicles safely (e.g., completing a driver's education course, wearing seat belt and helmet)
- Making certain that proper precautions are taken during all athletic activities (e.g., medical supervision, proper equipment)
- Parents' keeping lines of communication open and being alert to signs of substance abuse and emotional disturbances in the adolescent

Nutrition and Exercise

- Importance of healthy snacks and appropriate patterns of food intake and exercise
- Factors that may lead to nutritional problems (e.g., obesity, anorexia nervosa, bulimia)
- Balancing sedentary activities with regular exercise

Social Interactions

- Encouraging adolescent to establish relationships that promote discussion of feelings, concerns, and fears
- Parents' encouraging adolescent peer group activities that promote appropriate moral and spiritual values
- Parents' acting as role models for appropriate social interactions
- Parents' providing a comfortable home environment for appropriate adolescent peer group activities

CHAPTER HIGHLIGHTS

- Intrauterine development lasts about nine months.
- Genetic and environmental factors affect the development of the fetus.
- A sense of trust and security in the newborn is essential for subsequent development; the infant derives this sense from parental love, warmth, and prompt attention to physical needs.
- Measurements of length, weight, head and chest circumferences, fontanelle size and status, reflex abilities, and motor development are important indicators of the newborn's growth and health.
- Infants from one month to one year reveal marked growth in size and stature with appropriate nutrition and care: birth weight doubles by five months and triples by 12 months.
- During infancy, motor development is notable: at three months, infants can raise their heads from the prone position; at six months, they can sit unsupported; and at 12 months, they can stand momentarily and walk with help.
- To develop cognitively, the infant needs a variety of sensory and motor stimuli.
- Early childhood spans the period from one to six years and is subdivided into two groups: the toddler group, age one to three years, and the preschool group, ages four and five years.
- During childhood, dramatic changes occur in physical, psychological, and cognitive development; the child moves from being a dependent person to becoming an independent person entering school.
- As the nervous system develops, body systems mature to the point where the child can control the body, achieve finer muscle control, and perform all the activities of daily living, such as washing and dressing.
- The child also develops a unique personality and way of behaving.
- Critical to psychosocial development during childhood is the development of a sense of autonomy and initiative.
- By the end of early childhood, the child has reached the phase of intuitive thought in cognitive development, has developed some internal moral controls, and is at the undifferentiated level of spiritual development.
- School-age children perfect their muscular skills and coordination and develop a sense of competence, perseverance, and self-worth.
- During emotional development, school-age children face Erikson's conflict of industry versus inferiority.

- School-age children begin to understand relationships and change from being egocentric to having cooperative interactions; according to Piaget, they are in the concrete operations phase of cognitive development.
- Most school-age children progress to the conventional level of moral development and to the mythic-literal stage of spiritual development.
- Rapid growth in height, development of secondary sexual characteristics, sexual maturity, and increasing independence from the family are major landmarks of adolescence.
- Peer groups assume great importance during adolescence; they provide a sense of belonging and self-esteem and facilitate the development of a positive self-concept.
- Adolescents are at Fowler's synthetic-conventional stage of spiritual development.
- Adolescents between the ages of 11 and 15 years begin the formal operations stage of cognitive development; they are able to think logically, rationally, and futuristically and can conceptualize things as they could be, rather than as they are.
- The adolescent is at Kohlberg's conventional level of moral development, and some proceed to the post-conventional or principled level.

READINGS AND REFERENCES

Suggested Readings

Chance, G. W. & Harmsen, E. (1998). Children are different: Environmental contaminants and children's health. *Canadian Journal of Public Health, 89*, Suppl 1, S9–13, S10–15.
Because of their rapid growth, and physiological and metabolic immaturity, the fetus and child are at increased risk from harm due to toxic substances in their environment. The authors provide an overview of the developmental physiological, anatomical, and behavioural features of the fetus, infant, and child that increase their vulnerability to environmental contaminants.

Gillis, A. (1996). Teens for healthy living. *The Canadian Nurse, 92*(6), 26–30.
The author describes a health-promotion program for teens in a rural area. The most significant areas of concern were establishing peer relationships, teen-parent relationships, sexuality issues, and self-esteem. The teens indicated they prefer one-to-one counselling with a peer, videos, and a drop-in school health centre as ways of meeting their needs. The formation of the program confirmed that it is best done in collaboration with teens.

Murray, R. B., & Zentner, J. P. (2000). *Health assessment and promotion strategies through the life span* (7th ed.). Upper Saddle River, NJ: Prentice Hall.
This book provides a comprehensive discussion of assessment and health promotion for the family and developing person from infancy through adolescence. It includes family development and relationships, physiological concepts, psychosocial concepts, and health-care and nursing applications.

Related Research

Glascoe, F. P. (1999). Using parents' concerns to detect and address developmental and behavioral problems. *Journal of the Society of Pediatric Nurses, 4(1)*, 24–35.

Reifsnider, E., Allan, J., & Percy, M. (2000). Low-income mothers' perceptions of health in their children with growth delay. *Journal of the Society of Pediatric Nurses, 5*, 122–130.

Wen, S. W., Liu, S., & Fowler, D. (1998). Trends and variations in neonatal length of in-hospital stay in Canada. *Canadian Journal of Public Health, 89*, 115–119.

Selected References

Berger, K. S. (2000). *The developing person through childhood and adolescence* (5th ed.). New York: Worth.

Edelman, K. L., & Mandle, C. L. (1998). *Health promotion throughout the lifespan* (4th ed.). St. Louis, MO: Mosby.

Engel, G. L. (1962). *Psychological development in health and disease.* Philadelphia, PA: Saunders. (Classic.)

Erikson, E. H. (1963). *Childhood and society* (2nd ed.). New York: Norton. (Classic.)

Fowler, J. W. (1981). *Stages of faith: The psychology of human development and the quest for meaning.* New York: Harper & Row.

Frankenburg, W., & Dobbs, J. B. (Eds.). (1992). *Denver II, 2nd.* Denver, CO: Denver Developmental Materials, Inc.

Freiberg, K. L. (1992, 1987). *Human development: A life-span approach.* Boston, MA: Jones & Bartlett.

Kohlberg, L. (1977). Recent research in moral development. New York: Holt, Rinehart, Winston. (Classic.)

Lee, P. (1998). Assessment of growth & development. *Paediatric Nursing, 10*(9), 21–23.

Murray, R. B., & Zentner, J. P. (2000). *Health assessment and promotion strategies through the life span* (7th ed.). Upper Saddle River, NJ: Prentice Hall.

National Advisory Committee on Immunization. (1998). *Canadian immunization guide.* Ottawa: Laboratory for Disease Control.

Piaget, J. (1966). *Origins of intelligence in children.* New York: Norton. (Classic.)

Pinyerd, E. J. (1992). Assessment of infant growth. *Journal of Pediatric Health Care, 6*, 302–308.

Roberts, J., Poffenroth, L., Roos, J., Bebchuk, J., & Carter, A. (1994). *Monitoring childhood immunizations: A Canadian approach, 84*, 1666–1668.

Sieving, R. E., & Zirbel-Donisch, S. T. (1990). Development and enhancement of self-esteem in children. *Journal of Pediatric Nursing, 4*, 290–296.

Wong, D. (1999). *Whaley and Wong's nursing care of infants and children* (6th ed.). St. Louis, MO: Mosby.

WEBLINKS

Canadian Institute of Child Health
http://www.cich.ca/
The role of the Canadian Institute of Child Health in child and family health involves working with governments to make sure the right kind of policies are developed; working with professionals and educators to equip them with the best in research and programs; and reaching out to families to help with the tasks of nurturing, protecting, educating, and empowering children.

Canadian Pediatric Society
http://www.caringforkids.cps.ca
This site provides information about children from Canadian pediatric experts.

Health Canada
http://www.hc-sc.gc.ca/english/index.html
This site provides a search engine to enable the user to access a range of Canadian child health resources.

Health Canada, the Canadian Paediatric Society, the Canadian Institute of Child Health, and the Canadian Foundation for the Study of Infant Deaths
http://www.hc-sc.gc.ca/hppb/childhood-youth/cyfh/sids/joint_statement.html
A joint position statement regarding reducing the risk of sudden infant death syndrome in Canada is available on this site.

CHAPTER 21

Development from Young through Older Adulthood

OBJECTIVES

After completing this chapter, you will be able to:

- Identify tasks characteristic of different stages of development during young, middle, and older adulthood.
- Describe usual physical development throughout young, middle, and older adulthood.
- Compare psychosocial development according to Erikson during young, middle, and older adulthood.
- Discuss changes in cognitive development according to Piaget throughout adulthood.
- Describe moral development according to Kohlberg throughout adulthood.
- Examine spiritual development according to Fowler throughout adulthood.
- Identify developmental assessment guidelines for young, middle-aged, and older adults.
- List examples of health-promotion topics for young, middle-aged, and older adults.
- Analyze selected health problems associated with young, middle-aged, and older adults.

The adult phase of development encompasses the years from the end of adolescence to death. Because the developmental tasks of young adults differ from those of older adults, adulthood is often divided into three phases: young adulthood, middle adulthood, and late adulthood. In this book, young adults are defined as people 20 to 40 years old; middle-aged adults as 40 to 65 years old; and older adults over 65 years old. In this chapter, we discuss the concepts of growth and development introduced in Chapter 19 applied to the young adult, the middle-aged adult, and the older adult. For each developmental stage, we apply psychosocial, cognitive, moral, and spiritual aspects. We address health assessment, promotion guidelines, and common health problems.

Young Adults (20 to 40 Years)

The age at which a person is considered an adult depends on how adulthood is described. Legally, a person in Canada can vote at 18 years. The legal age for alcohol consumption outside the home varies among the provinces and territories from 18 to 21 years. Another criterion of adulthood is financial independence, which is also highly variable. Some adolescents support themselves as early as 16 years of age, usually because of family circumstances. By contrast, some adults are financially dependent on their families for many years, for example, during prolonged education.

Adulthood may also be indicated by moving away from home and establishing one's own living arrangements. Yet, this independence also varies greatly. Some adolescents leave home because of family problems. In recent years, however, more young adults have been choosing to remain at home. In addition, many adults under 30 years have returned to their parents' homes to live. The factors contributing to this trend include high housing costs, high divorce rates, high unemployment rates, and the many problems resulting from substance abuse. Some young people who are employed full time receive only minimum wages and are unable to earn enough money to be totally self supporting.

Maturity is the state of maximal function and integration, or the state of being fully developed. Many other characteristics are generally recognized as representative of maturity. Mature individuals are guided by an underlying philosophy of life. They take many perspectives into account and are tolerant of the views of others. A comprehensive philosophy allows a person to make sense out of life and, thus, helps that person maintain a sense of purpose and hope in the face of human tragedies. Mature persons are open to new experiences and continued growth; they can tolerate ambiguity, are flexible, and can adapt to change. In addition, mature people have the quality of self-acceptance; they are able to be reflective and insightful about life and to see themselves as others see them.

Mature persons also assume responsibility for themselves and expect others to do the same. They confront the tasks of life in a realistic and mature manner, make decisions, and accept responsibility for those decisions.

Young adults are typically busy people who face many challenges. They are expected to assume new roles at work, in the home, and in the community, and to develop interests, values, and attitudes related to these roles.

Physical Development

People in their early 20s are in their prime years physically. The musculoskeletal system is well developed and coordinated. Young adulthood is the period when most athletic endeavours reach their peak. Indeed, at over 40 years, most athletes are considered old. All other systems of the body (e.g., cardiovascular, visual, auditory, and reproductive) are also functioning at peak efficiency during young adulthood.

Although physical changes are minimal during this stage, weight and muscle mass may change as a result of diet and exercise. In addition, extensive physical and psychosocial changes occur in pregnant and lactating women. These changes are discussed in maternal/child textbooks.

Psychosocial Development

In contrast to the minimal physical changes, psychosocial development of the young adult is great. The box below reviews this psychosocial development according to the theories of Freud, Erikson, and Havighurst.

Psychosocial Development: Young Adult

The young adult

- is in the *genital stage*, in which energy is directed toward attaining a mature sexual relationship, according to Freud's theory.
- is in the *intimacy versus isolation* phase of Erikson's stages of development.
- has the following developmental tasks, according to Havighurst:
  - Selecting a mate
  - Learning to live with a partner
  - Starting a family
  - Rearing children
  - Managing a home
  - Getting started in an occupation
  - Taking on civic responsibility
  - Finding a congenial social group

Figure 21.1 Many young women combine active careers with motherhood

Young adults face a number of new experiences and changes in lifestyle as they progress toward maturity. Choices must be made about education and employment, about whether to marry or remain single, about starting a home, and about rearing children. Social responsibilities include forming new friendships and assuming some community activities.

Occupational choice and education are largely inseparable. Education influences occupational opportunities; conversely, an occupation, once chosen, can determine the education needed and sought. Education enhances employment opportunities and usually ensures economic survival. As the role of women has changed, many women choose to assume active careers and civic roles in society, in addition to their roles as mother and/or wife (Figure 21.1).

Remaining single is becoming the lifestyle of more and more young adults. Many people choose to remain single, perhaps to pursue an education and then to have the freedom to pursue their chosen vocation. Some unmarried individuals choose to live with another person of the opposite or same sex and share living arrangements and certain expenses. Some are gay or lesbian and live with, or are involved with, a partner to whom they are committed.

Although alternative lifestyles are becoming more acceptable in society, traditional attitudes toward these various lifestyles can contribute social pressures that lead to stress responses. The multiple roles of adulthood (citizen, worker, taxpayer, homeowner, wife/husband, daughter/son, brother/sister, parent, friend, and so on) may also create stress as a result of role conflict.

Cognitive Development

Piaget believes that cognitive structures are complete during the *formal operations phase*, from roughly 11 to 15 years. See Table 19.5 on page 316. From that time, formal operations (for example, generating hypotheses) characterize thinking throughout adulthood and are applied to more areas. Egocentrism continues to decline. However, according to Piaget, these changes do not involve a change in the structure of thought, only a change in its content and stability.

Some researchers in the field of psychology have suggested that a sixth and qualitatively higher stage of cognitive development may follow formal operations. In addition to the adolescent ability to think in abstract terms, **postformal operations thinkers** possess an understanding of the temporary or relative nature of knowledge. They are able to comprehend the contradictions that exist in both personal and physical reality. For instance, in a personal realm, an individual may understand that feelings toward another are not simply love or hate but that these contrasting feelings may exist together in a relationship. Further research is needed to support the idea of a sixth stage of cognitive development.

Moral Development

Young adults who have mastered the previous stages of Kohlberg's theory of moral development now enter the *postconventional level.* See Table 19.6 on page 317. At this time, the person is able to separate self from the expectations and rules of others and to define morality in terms of personal principles. When individuals perceive a conflict with society's rules or laws, they judge according to their own principles. For example, a person may intentionally break the law and join a protest group, for example, to stop hunters from killing wild animals, believing that the principle of conservation of wildlife justifies the protest action. This type of reasoning is called principled reasoning. See also Gilligan's *ethic of care*, page 316. Gilligan argues that as individuals approach young adulthood, men and women tend to define moral problems somewhat differently. Men often use an "ethic of justice" and define moral problems in terms of rules and rights. Women, by contrast, often define moral problems in terms of obligations to care and to avoid hurt (Gilligan, 1982).

Spiritual Development

According to Fowler, the individual enters the *individuating-reflective* period sometime after 18 years of age. See Table 19.7 on page 318. During this period, the individual focuses on reality. A 27-year-old adult may ask philosophical questions regarding spirituality and may be self-conscious about spiritual matters. The religious teaching that the young adult had as a child may now be accepted or redefined.

Health Assessment and Promotion

Assessment guidelines for the growth and development of the young adult are shown in the next box.

DEVELOPMENTAL ASSESSMENT GUIDELINES

The Young Adult

In these three developmental areas, does the young adult do the following?

1. **Physical Development**
   - Exhibit weight within normal range for age and gender
   - Manifest vital signs (e.g., blood pressure) within normal range for age and gender
   - Demonstrate visual and hearing abilities within normal range
   - Exhibit appropriate knowledge (e.g., about sexually transmitted diseases) and attitudes about sexuality
2. **Psychosocial Development**
   - Feel independent from parents
   - Have a realistic self-concept
   - Like self and direction of life
   - Interact well with family
   - Cope with the stresses of change and growth
   - Have well-established bonds with significant others, such as marriage partner or close friends
   - Have a meaningful social life
   - Demonstrate emotional, social, and economic responsibility for own life
   - Have a set of values that guide behaviour
3. **Development in Activities of Daily Living**
   - Have a healthy lifestyle

Young adults are usually interested in meeting their health needs. However, because of the many stresses and changes that occur throughout this 20-year period, the nurse needs to offer teaching and guidance in several health-care areas. The nurse may wish to discuss some or all of the health promotion topics outlined in the following box. These topics are discussed in detail in subsequent chapters throughout the book.

Health Problems

Young adulthood is generally a healthy time of life. Health problems that are common in this age group include accidents, suicide, substance abuse, hypertension, sexually transmitted diseases (STDs), abuse of women, and certain malignancies. Some of these problems, such as accidents, substance abuse, and STDs, are related to lifestyle patterns and can, therefore, be prevented.

Accidents Among young adults, accidents are responsible for more deaths than all other causes combined. Motor vehicle accidents are, by far, the leading cause of mortality; other causes of accidental death for young adults include drowning, fires, burns, and firearms. Education about safety precautions and accident prevention is a major role of the nurse in promoting the health of young adults. For a further discussion of safety education for young adults, see Chapter 33.

Suicide Suicide is another leading cause of death in young adults. Many suicides may actually be mistaken for accidental deaths (automobile accidents, alcohol intoxication, and drug overdose). Suicide may result from problems in relationships with spouses or parents or from depression related to perceived occupational, academic, or financial failure. In general, suicide results from the young adult's inability to cope with the pressures, responsibilities, and expectations of adulthood.

The nurse's role in the prevention of suicide includes identifying factors that may indicate potential problems: depression; a variety of physical complaints, including weight loss, sleep disturbances, and digestive disorders; and decreased interest in social and work roles, along with an increase in isolation. A young adult identified as at risk for suicide should be referred to a mental health professional or a crisis centre. Nurses can also reduce the incidence of suicide by participating in educational programs that provide information about the early signs of suicide.

Substance Abuse Substance abuse is a major threat to the health of young adults. Alcohol, marijuana, amphetamines, and cocaine, for example, can bring about feelings of well-being that may be highly valued by people with adjustment problems. Prolonged use can lead to physical and psychological dependency and subsequent health problems. For example, drug abuse during pregnancy can lead to fetal damage. Prolonged use of alcohol can lead to such diseases as cirrhosis of the liver and cancer of the esophagus.

Nursing strategies related to substance abuse include teaching about the complications of their use, changing individual attitudes toward substance abuse, and counselling regarding problems that lead to substance abuse.

Smoking is another type of substance abuse that can lead to such diseases as lung cancer and cardiovascular disease. The nurse's role regarding smoking is to (1) serve as a role model by not smoking; (2) provide educational information regarding the dangers of smoking; (3) help make smoking socially unacceptable—for example, by posting "No Smoking" signs in client lounges and offices; and (4) suggest resources, such as hypnosis, lifestyle training, and behaviour modification, to clients who desire to stop smoking.

Sexually Transmitted Disease Sexually transmitted diseases (STDs), such as genital herpes, acquired immune deficiency syndrome (AIDS), syphilis, and gonorrhea, are common infections in young adults. Nursing functions

Health Promotion Guidelines for Young Adults

Health Tests and Screenings

- Routine physical examination (every 1–3 years for females; every 1–5 years for males)
- Immunizations as recommended, such as tetanus-diphtheria (Td) boosters, and mmr
- Regular dental assessments (e.g., every six months)
- Periodic vision and hearing screenings
- Breast self-examination monthly, 1 week after onset of period
- Professional breast examination every 1–3 years
- Papanicolaou smear annually
- Testicular self-examination every month
- Screening for cardiovascular disease (e.g., cholesterol test every 5 years, if results are normal; blood pressure to detect hypertension; baseline electrocardiogram at age 35 for males)
- Tuberculosis skin test for high-risk persons

Safety

- Motor vehicle safety reinforcement (e.g., using designated drivers when drinking, maintaining brakes and tires)
- Sun protection measures
- Workplace safety measures
- Water safety reinforcement (e.g., no diving in shallow water)

Nutrition and Exercise

- Importance of adequate iron intake in diet
- Nutritional and exercise factors that may lead to cardiovascular disease (e.g., obesity, cholesterol and fat intake, lack of vigorous exercise)

Social Interactions

- Encouraging personal relationships that promote discussion of feelings, concerns, and fears
- Setting short- and long-term goals for work and career choices

are largely educational. The use of condoms greatly reduces the transfer of infectious microorganisms from one partner to another. Knowledge about the symptoms of these diseases can help the client obtain early treatment. In dealing with a client with an STD, the nurse must be nonjudgmental and accepting of the client's lifestyle and treat any information obtained as confidential. See Table 12.6 for additional information.

Abuse of Women The problem of *battering*, or abuse of women, affects families at all socioeconomic levels. Stresses that predispose families to abuse may include financial problems, separation from family and community supports, and physical as well as social isolation. A nurse who works with women should (1) have open communication that will encourage them to share their problems; (2) help them develop self-esteem that will enable them to have the courage to leave the abusive situation; (3) provide information about resources, such as social services and shelters, that will allow them to start a new life; and (4) continue to support and educate the women so that they can understand the causes and results of abusive and violent behaviour.

Malignancies Testicular cancer is the most common neoplasm in men aged 20 to 34 years (Barkauskas et al., 1998). **Testicular self-examination,** a means of early identification of testicular cancer, should be conducted monthly. For additional information about self-examination of the testicles, see Chapters 12 and 27.

Of all cancers among women, cancer of the breast is a leading cause of death. Breast cancer is rare under the age of 30 years (Murray & Zentner, 1997). Young women need to form the habit of doing **breast self-examination** once a month. For detailed information, see Chapters 12 and 27. The earlier a breast lump is discovered, the greater is the effectiveness of treatment.

Young adult females should also be screened for cervical cancer by having a routine Papanicolaou (Pap) test. A **Pap test/smear** is done by obtaining and examining cells from the uterine cervical os. The cells are obtained during a pelvic examination. For more information on the vaginal exam, see Chapters 12 and 27. The nurse should also screen for high-risk factors for cervical cancer: sexual activity at an early age, multiple sexual partners, or a history of syphilis, herpes genitalis, or *Trichomonas* vaginitis. Many young adults are reluctant to have these examinations and screenings. Therefore, it is important for nurses to explain the purpose of the test and to encourage all young women to begin this preventive measure from age 20 years. See cancer screening guidelines in Chapter 12.

Middle-Aged Adults (40 to 65 Years)

The middle years, from 40 to 65 years, have been called the years of stability and consolidation. For most people, it is a time when children have grown up and moved away

Figure 21.2 Middle-aged adults have time to pursue interests that may have been put aside for child care

or are moving away from home. Thus, partners generally have more time for and with each other and time to pursue interests they may have deferred for years (Figure 21.2).

Physical Development

A number of changes take place during the middle years. At 40 years, most adults can function as effectively as they did in their 20s. However, during ages 40 to 65 years, many physical changes take place. See Table 21.1 for a summary of these changes.

Both men and women experience decreasing hormonal production during the middle years. The **menopause** refers to the so-called change of life in women, when menstruation ceases. It is said to have occurred when a woman has not had a menstrual period in one year. The menopause usually occurs anywhere between ages 40 and 55 years. The average is about 47 years. At this time, ovarian activity declines until ovulation ceases. Common symptoms are hot flashes, chilliness, a tendency of the breasts to become smaller and flabby, and a tendency to gain weight. Insomnia and headaches also occur with relative frequency. Psychologically, the menopause can be an anxiety-producing time, especially if the ability to bear children is an integral part of the woman's self-concept.

The **climacteric** (andropause) refers to the change of life in men, when sexual activity decreases. In men, there is no change comparable with the menopause in women. Androgen levels decrease very slowly; however, men can father children even in late life. The psychological problems that men experience are generally related to the fear of getting old and to retirement, boredom, and finances. See Chapters 12 and 27 for further details about sexual health.

Psychosocial Development

Before the mid-1900s, the developmental tasks of middle-aged adults received little attention. Havighurst (1972) outlines seven tasks for this age group (see box below). Erikson (1963) views the developmental choice of the middle-aged adult as *generativity versus stagnation.* **Generativity** is defined as the concern for establishing and guiding the next generation. In other words, the concern about providing for the welfare of humankind is as important as the concern of providing for self. People in their 20s and 30s tend to be self- and family-centred. In middle age, the self seems more altruistic, and concepts of service to others and love and compassion gain prominence. These concepts motivate charitable and altruistic actions, such as church work, social work, political work, community fund-raising drives, and cultural endeavours. Marriage partners have more time for companionship and recreation, and thus, marriage can be more satisfying in the middle years of life. Partners have time to work together in volunteer activities and time for one partner to go out for lunch and for the other to go fishing. Generative middle-aged persons are able to feel a sense of comfort in their lifestyle and receive gratification from charitable activities.

Psychosocial Development: Middle-Aged Adult

The middle-aged adult

- is in the *generativity versus stagnation* phase of Erikson's stages of development.
- has the following developmental tasks according to Havighurst:
  - Achieving adult civic and social responsibilities
  - Establishing and maintaining an economic standard of living
  - Assisting teenage children to become responsible and happy adults
  - Developing adult leisure-time activities
  - Relating oneself to one's spouse as a person
  - Accepting and adjusting to the physiological changes of middle age
  - Adjusting to aging parents

TABLE 21.1 Physical Changes of the Middle-Aged Adult

Category	Description
Appearance	Hair begins to thin, and grey hair appears. Skin turgor (fullness or elasticity) and moisture decrease, subcutaneous fat decreases, and wrinkling occurs. Fatty tissue is re-distributed, resulting in fat deposits in the abdominal area.
Musculoskeletal system	Skeletal muscle bulk decreases at about age 60 years. Thinning of the intervertebral discs causes a decrease in height of about 2 or 3 cm. Calcium loss from bone tissue is more common among postmenopausal women. Muscle growth continues in proportion to use.
Cardiovascular system	Blood vessels lose elasticity and become thicker.
Sensory perception	Visual acuity declines, often by the late 40s, especially for near vision (presbyopia). Auditory acuity for high-frequency sounds also decreases (presbycusis), particularly in men. Taste sensations also diminish.
Metabolism	Metabolism slows, resulting in weight gain.
Gastrointestinal system	Gradual decrease in tone of large intestine may predispose the individual to constipation.
Urinary system	Nephron units of the kidneys are lost during this time, and glomerular filtration rate decreases.
Sexuality	Hormonal changes take place in both men and women.

Erikson believes that people who are unable to expand their interests at this time, and who do not assume the responsibilities of middle age, suffer a sense of boredom and impoverishment, that is, stagnation. These people have difficulty accepting their aging bodies and become withdrawn and isolated. They are preoccupied with self and unable to give to others. Some may regress to younger patterns of behaviour, for example, adolescent behaviour.

Robert Peck (1968) believes that although physical capabilities and functions decrease with age, mental and social capacities tend to increase in the latter part of life. Peck recognizes four sets of developmental tasks that can be dealt with simultaneously during middle age. See the box on the following page.

The middle-aged person looks older and feels older. People usually accept the fact that they are aging; however, a few try to defy the years by the way they dress and even by their actions. Some men and women have extramarital affairs with and/or marry younger persons. A new freedom to be independent and follow one's individual interests arises. Prior to this period, the marriage partner or lover and other persons were crucial to a definition of self. Now, the middle-aged person does not make comparisons of self with others, no longer fears aging or death, relaxes the sense of competitiveness, and enjoys the independence and freedom of middle age. Other people's opinions become less important, and the earlier habit of trying to please everyone is overcome. The person establishes ethical and moral standards that are independent of the standards of others. The focus shifts from inner self and being to others and doing. Religious and philosophical concerns become important.

Gail Sheehy (1976) suggests that the transition into middle life is as critical as adolescence. She outlines characteristics of the **midlife crisis** and calls the decade between the ages of 35 and 45 years the "deadline decade." According to Sheehy, most women pass through the midlife crisis between 35 and 40 years and most men between 40 and 45 years. This crisis occurs when individuals recognize that they have reached the halfway mark of life. Although people of these ages are reaching their prime, they begin to recognize that time is at a premium and that life is finite. Youthfulness and physical strength can no longer be taken for granted.

Hultsch and Deutsch (1981) suggest that it is not the events themselves that make midlife a crisis, but an individual's response to these life events. How will an individual respond? According to Hultsch and Deutsch, the resources of the person, the ability to use effective coping strategies, and the life stage at which an event occurs will influence any changes in behaviour. Internal and external resources include physical health, family income, the social support system, intelligence, and personality. Thus, the crisis or transitions of midlife are not just within the individual but, rather, between the individual and the individual's world.

Cognitive Development

The middle-aged adult's cognitive and intellectual abilities change very little. Cognitive processes include reaction time, memory, perception, learning, problem solving, and creativity. Reaction time during the middle years stays much the same or diminishes during the later part of

Peck's Tasks of Middle Age

- *Valuing wisdom versus physical power and attractiveness.* As individuals approach middle age, physical strength and attractiveness decline. It then becomes necessary to gain satisfaction and ego strength through mental and intellectual abilities. Middle-aged persons must learn to rely more on their wisdom and accumulated experiences than on their physical powers.
- *Socializing versus sexualizing.* In middle age, people should begin to re-define their interpersonal relationships. It is no longer appropriate to relate to the opposite sex in terms of physical attractiveness; other criteria, such as friendship, warmth, and understanding, should be adopted.
- *Emotional flexibility versus emotional rigidity.* This task concerns the ability to become flexible, such as being able to shift emotional investment from one person to another and from one task to another. During this phase of life, the children often leave home, and parents may die. Middle-aged adults must be able to develop new roles, socially and emotionally, or they may find themselves isolated.
- *Mental flexibility versus mental rigidity.* Individuals often become set in their ways as they approach middle age. They may not seek new ideas or accept the novel solutions of others. To cope most effectively, however, middle-aged adults should strive to remain flexible in their thinking. The solutions of the past may not solve today's problems. New ideas and perspectives should be considered.

Source: Adapted from R. Peck. (1968). Psychological development in the second half of life. In B. L. Neugarten (Ed), *Middle age and aging* (p.89). Chicago: University of Chicago Press.

the middle years. Memory and problem solving are maintained through middle adulthood.

Learning continues and can be enhanced by increased motivation at this time in life.

Middle-aged adults are able to carry out all the strategies described in Piaget's phase of *formal operations.* See Table 19.5, page 316. Some may use *postformal operations* strategies to assist them in understanding the contradictions that exist in both the personal and physical aspects of reality (see the discussion on cognitive development of the young adult, page 349). The experiences of the professional, social, and personal life of middle-aged persons will be reflected in their cognitive performance. Thus, approaches to problem solving and task completion will vary considerably in a middle-aged group. The middle-aged adult can "reflect on the past and current experience and can imagine, anticipate, plan, and hope" (Murray & Zentner, 1997, p. 669).

Moral Development

According to Kohlberg, most adults move beyond the *conventional level* to the *postconventional level.* See Table 19.6 on page 317. Kohlberg believes that extensive experience of personal moral choice and responsibility is required before people can reach the postconventional level. Kohlberg found that few of his subjects achieved the third level of moral development. To move from stage 4, a *law and order orientation,* to stage 5, a *social contract orientation,* requires that the individual move to a stage in which rights of others take precedence. People in stage 5 take steps to support another's rights.

Spiritual Development

Not all adults progress through Fowler's stages to the fifth, called the *paradoxical-consolidative stage.* At this stage, the individual can view *truth* from a number of viewpoints. See Table 19.7 on page 318. Fowler's fifth stage corresponds to Kohlberg's fifth stage of moral development. Fowler believes that only some individuals after the age of 30 years reach this stage.

In middle age, people tend to be less dogmatic about religious beliefs, and religion often offers more comfort to the middle-aged person than it did previously. People in this age group often rely on spiritual beliefs to help them deal with illness, death, and tragedy.

Health Assessment and Promotion

Assessment guidelines for the growth and development of the middle-aged adult are shown in the following box.

Middle-aged adults usually take care of their health needs and are interested in maintaining health and preventing the acceleration of the aging process.

The nurse may choose to discuss some or all of the health promotion topics with the middle-aged adult client. (See the box on page 356.) These topics are discussed in detail in subsequent chapters throughout the book.

Health Problems

Many middle-aged adults remain healthy; however, the risk of developing a health problem is greater than that of the young adult. Leading causes of death in this age group

DEVELOPMENTAL ASSESSMENT GUIDELINES

The Middle-Aged Adult

In these three developmental areas, does the middle-aged adult do the following?

1. **Physical Development**
   - Exhibit weight within normal range for age and gender
   - Manifest vital signs (e.g., blood pressure) within normal range for age and gender
   - Manifest visual and hearing abilities within normal range
   - Exhibit appropriate knowledge and attitudes about sexuality (e.g., about menopause)
   - Verbalize any changes in eating, elimination, or exercise
2. **Psychosocial Development**
   - Accept aging body
   - Feel comfortable and respect self
   - Enjoy new freedom to be independent
   - Accept changes in family roles (e.g., having teenaged children and aging parents)
   - Interact well and share companionable activities with life partner
   - Expand and renew previous interests
   - Pursue charitable and altruistic activities
   - Have a meaningful philosophy of life
3. **Development in Activities of Daily Living**
   - Follow preventive health practice

include motor vehicle and occupational accidents and chronic diseases, such as cancer, and cardiovascular disease. Lifestyle patterns, in combination with aging, family history, developmental stressors (e.g., menopause, climacteric), and situational stressors (e.g., divorce), are often related to the health problems that do arise. For example, smoking and excessive alcohol consumption place an individual at greater risk of developing chronic respiratory problems, lung cancer, and liver disease. Overeating can result in obesity, diabetes mellitus, atherosclerosis, and its associated risk for hypertension and coronary artery disease. The nurse can play an important role in teaching middle-aged clients about preventive health care to avoid or minimize the risk of such health problems.

Accidents Changing physiological factors, as well as concern over personal and work-related responsibilities, may contribute to the accident rate of middle-aged people. Motor vehicle accidents are the most common cause of accidental death in this age group. Decreased reaction times and visual acuity may make the middle-aged adult prone to accidents. Other accidental causes of death for middle-aged adults include falls, fires, burns, poisonings, and drownings. Occupational accidents continue to be a significant safety hazard during the middle years.

Safety highlights for the middle-aged adult are presented in Chapter 33.

Cancer Cancer accounts for considerable mortality and morbidity in both men and women. It is the second leading cause of death among people between the ages of 25 and 64 years in Canada. The patterns of cancer types and incidences for men and women have changed over the past several decades. Men have a high incidence of cancer of the lung and bladder. In women, breast cancer is highest in incidence, followed by cancer of the colon and rectum, uterus, and lung. The incidence of lung cancer is increasing in women.

Female clients may need to be reminded to perform monthly breast self-examinations and male clients to perform monthly testicular self-examinations in order to detect growths. Postmenopausal women should report any vaginal bleeding.

Cardiovascular Disease Coronary artery disease (CAD) is a leading cause of death in Canada. Several factors contribute to the risk of CAD. These include smoking, obesity, hypertension, hyperlipidemia, diabetes mellitus, sedentary lifestyle, a family history of myocardial infarction or sudden death in a father younger than 55 years old or in a mother younger than 65 years old, and the individual's age. Men over 45 years of age and women over 55 years of age are at greater risk of developing CAD than are younger adults. Physical inactivity places individuals at greater risk of developing CAD than any other factor (Edelman & Mandle, 1998).

Obesity Middle-aged adults who gain weight may not be aware of some common facts about this age period. Decreased metabolic activity and decreased physical activity mean a decrease in caloric need. The nurse's role in nutritional health promotion is to counsel clients to prevent obesity by reducing caloric intake and engaging in regular exercise. Clients should also be warned that being overweight is a risk factor for many chronic diseases, such as diabetes and hypertension, and for problems of mobility, such as arthritis. Clients should seek medical advice before considering any major changes in their diets.

Alcoholism The excessive use of alcohol can result in unemployment, disrupted homes, accidents, and diseases. Nearly one in 10 Canadians report problems with their drinking of alcohol. Nurses can help clients by providing information about the dangers of excessive alcohol use, by helping the individual clarify values about health, and by referring the client to special groups, such as Alcoholics Anonymous.

Health Promotion Guidelines for Middle-Aged Adults

Health Tests and Screening

- Routine physical examination (annually for females; every 2–3 years or as directed by physician for males)
- Immunizations as recommended, such as a tetanus booster every 10 years and influenza and pneumococcal vaccinations
- Regular dental assessments (e.g., yearly)
- Tonometry for signs of glaucoma and other eye disease every 2–3 years or annually, if indicated
- Breast self-examination as for young adults, and then first day of every month after menopause
- Testicular self-examination monthly
- Screenings for cardiovascular disease (e.g., blood pressure measurement; electrocardiogram and cholesterol test as directed by the physician)
- Screenings for colorectal, breast, cervical, uterine, and prostate cancers (see Cancer Screening Guidelines in Chapter 12)
- Screening for tuberculosis every 2 years

Safety

- Motor vehicle safety reinforcement, especially when driving at night
- Workplace safety measures
- Home safety measures: keeping hallways and stairways lighted and uncluttered, using smoke and carbon monoxide detectors, using nonskid mats and hand rails in the bathrooms

Nutrition and Exercise

- Importance of adequate protein, calcium, and vitamin D in diet
- Nutritional and exercise factors that may lead to cardiovascular disease (e.g., obesity, cholesterol and fat intake, lack of vigorous exercise)
- An exercise program that emphasizes skill and coordination

Social Interactions

- The possibility of a midlife crisis: encourage discussion of feelings, concerns, and fears
- Providing time to expand and review previous interests
- Retirement planning (financial and possible diversional activities), with partner, if appropriate

Mental Health Changes Developmental stressors, such as the menopause, the climacteric, aging, and impending retirement, and situational stressors, such as divorce, unemployment, and death of a spouse, can precipitate increased anxiety and depression in middle-aged adults. The educated woman who is married, has children at home, and has not worked since her marriage is at greater risk for psychosocial disturbances (Edelman & Mandle, 1998). Clients may benefit from support groups or individual therapy to help them cope with specific crises.

Older Adults (Over 65 Years)

Seniors constitute one of the fastest growing groups in Canada. In 1998, there were an estimated 3.7 million Canadians 65 years of age and older, about 15 percent of the population. This is an increase of 57 percent from the 2.4 million in 1981; in contrast, the population in age ranges under the age of 65 years grew by less than 20 percent in the same period. The senior population is expected to grow even more rapidly during the next several decades, particularly once people born during the baby boom years, from 1946 to 1965, begin turning 65 early in the second decade of the new century. Statistics Canada has projected that by 2016, 16 percent of all Canadians will be 65 years or older (Statistics Canada, 1999).

The movement away from institutional care to community living, along with improved nutrition and health care, has led to an increased lifespan for individuals with disabilities. In Canada, those born before 1945 represent the first significantly large group of aging intellectually disabled adults.

Various systems are used to categorize the aging population (see the box below). Another term used to describe

Categorizing the Aging Population

55 to 64	—	the older population
65 to 74	—	the elderly
75 to 84	—	the aged
85 and older	—	the extreme aged
	or	
Age 60 to 74	—	the young-old
Age 75 to 84	—	the middle-old
Age 85 and older	—	the old-old

Source: G. Wold. (1993). *Basic geriatric nursing* (p. 5). St. Louis, MO: Mosby-Year Book.

> The National Advisory Council on Aging, on behalf of older Canadians, has requested that the term "older adults" or "seniors" be used instead of the word "elderly."

the *old-old*, or *extreme aged*, is *frail elderly*. The term **frail elderly,** however, is more likely to be used to describe the elderly individual who has significant physiological and functional impairment, whatever the age.

In the past, some scientists postulated theories of why people age. More recently, as both the absolute number and the population percentage of older people increase, there is renewed scientific interest in why people age, how people age, and what factors affect the physical, psychological, and functional status of older persons. Biological theories of aging are either intrinsic or extrinsic. *Intrinsic* theory addresses factors within the body; *extrinsic* theory encompasses factors in the environment. Table 21.2 describes the various biological theories of aging.

Physical Changes

As the person ages, a number of physical changes occur; some are visible, some are not. See Table 21.3 for a summary of the normal physical changes associated with aging.

TABLE 21.2 Common Biological Theories of Aging

Theory Type	Theory Name/Author (Date)	Hypotheses
Wear-and-tear theories	Wear-and-tear theory Pearl (1924)	Proposes that humans, like automobiles, have vital parts that run down with time, leading to aging and death.
	Rate of living theory Pearl (1928)	Proposes that the faster an organism lives, the quicker it dies.
	Stress theory Lamb (1977)	Proposes that cells wear out through exposure to internal and external stressors, including trauma, chemicals, and buildup of natural wastes.
Endocrine theory	Korenchevsky (1947)	Proposes that events occurring in the hypothalamus and pituitary are responsible for changes in hormone production and response that result in the organism's decline.
Free-radical theory	Harman (1955)	Proposes that unstable free radicals (groups of atoms) result from the oxidation of organic materials, such as carbohydrates and proteins. These radicals cause biochemical changes in the cells, and the cells cannot regenerate themselves.
Genetic theories	Programmed senescence theory Hayflick (1961)	Proposes that the organism is genetically programmed for a predetermined number of cell divisions, after which the cell/organism dies.
	Error catastrophe theory Orgel (1963)	Proposes that when damage to the protein synthesis occurs, faulty proteins will be synthesized and will gradually accumulate, causing a progressive decline in the organism.
Cross-linking theories	Collagen theory Vertzer (1957)	Proposes that the irreversible aging of proteins, such as collagen, is responsible for the ultimate failure of tissues and organs.
	Cross-linking theory Bjorkstein (1968)	Proposes that as cells age, chemical reactions create strong bonds, or cross-linkages, between proteins. These bonds cause loss of elasticity, stiffness, and eventual loss of function.
Immune theories	Immunological theory Walford (1969)	Proposes that the immune system becomes less effective with age, and viruses that have incubated in the body become able to damage body organs.
	Autoimmune theory Hallgren & Yunis (1977)	Proposes that a decrease in immune function may result in an increase in autoimmune responses, causing the body to produce antibodies that attack the body itself.

TABLE 21.3 Normal Physical Changes Associated with Aging

Physical Changes	Rationale
Integumentary	
Increased skin dryness	Decrease in sebaceous gland activity and tissue fluid
Increased skin pallor	Decreased vascularity
Increased skin fragility	Reduced thickness and vascularity of the dermis; loss of subcutaneous fat
Progressive wrinkling and sagging of the skin	Loss of skin elasticity, increased dryness, and decreased subcutaneous fat
Brown "age spots" (lentigo senilus) on exposed body parts (e.g., face, hands, arms)	Clustering of melanocytes (pigment-producing cells)
Decreased perspiration	Reduced number and function of sweat glands
Thinning and greying of scalp, pubic, and axillary hair	Progressive loss of pigment cells from the hair bulbs
Slower nail growth and increased thickening with ridges	Increased calcium deposition
Neuromusculoskeletal	
Decreased speed and power of skeletal muscle contractions	Decrease in muscle fibres
Slowed reaction time	Diminished conduction speed of nerve fibres and decreased muscle tone
Loss of height (stature)	Atrophy of intervertebral discs
Osteoporosis	Bone demineralization
Joint stiffness	Deterioration of joint cartilage
Impaired balance	Decreased muscle reaction time and coordination
Sensory/perceptual	
Loss of visual acuity	Degeneration leading to lens opacity (cataracts), thickening, and inelasticity (**presbyopia**)
Increased sensitivity to glare and decreased ability to adjust to darkness	Changes in the ciliary muscles; rigid pupil sphincter; decrease in pupil size
Partial or complete glossy white circle around the periphery of the cornea (**arcus senilis**)	Fatty deposits
Progressive loss of hearing (**presbycusis**)	Changes in the structures and nerve tissues in the inner ear; thickening of the eardrum
Decreased sense of taste, especially the sweet sensations at the tip of the tongue	Decreased number of taste buds in the tongue because of tongue atrophy
Decreased sense of smell	Atrophy of the olfactory bulb at the base of the brain (responsible for smell perception)
Increased threshold for sensations of pain, touch, and temperature	Possible nerve conduction and neuron changes

→

Integument

Obvious changes occur in the integumentary system (skin, hair, nails) with age. The skin becomes drier and more fragile, the hair loses colour, the fingernails and toenails become thickened and brittle, and in women over 60 years, facial hair increases.

Responses to these changes vary among individuals and cultures. For example, one person may feel distinguished with grey hair, whereas another may feel embarrassed or depressed, interpreting grey hair as a sign of losing one's youth.

These integumentary changes accompany progressive losses of subcutaneous fat and muscle tissue; muscle atrophy and loss of elastic fibre, resulting in a "double" chin; sagging of eyelids and earlobes; and wrinkling of skin, especially in areas exposed to the sun. Bony prominences become visible. In older women, the breasts become smaller and may sag; if large and pendulous, they may cause chafing where the skin surfaces touch. Loss of subcutaneous fat also decreases the older person's tolerance of the cold.

TABLE 21.3 Normal Physical Changes Associated with Aging *continued*

Physical Changes	Rationale
Pulmonary	
Decreased ability to expel foreign or accumulated matter	Decreased elasticity and ciliary activity
Decreased lung expansion; less effective exhalation; reduced vital capacity; and increased residual volume	Weakened thoracic muscles; calcification of costal cartilage, making the rib cage more rigid; dilation from inelasticity of alveoli
Difficult, short, heavy, rapid breathing (**dyspnea**) following exertion or intense exercise	Diminished delivery and diffusion of oxygen to the tissues to repay the normal oxygen debt because of changes in both respiratory and vascular tissues
Cardiovascular	
Reduced cardiac output and stroke volume, particularly during increased activity or unusual demands; may result in shortness of breath on exertion and pooling of blood in the extremities	Increased rigidity and thickness of heart valves (hence decreased filling/emptying abilities); decreased contractile strength
Reduced elasticity and increased rigidity of arteries	Increased calcium deposits in the muscular layer
Increase in diastolic and systolic blood pressure	Inelasticity of systemic arteries and increased peripheral resistance
Orthostatic hypertension	Reduced sensitivity of the blood pressure–regulating baroreceptors
Gastrointestinal	
Delayed swallowing time	Alterations in the swallowing mechanism
Increased tendency for indigestion	Gradual decrease in digestive enzymes, reduction in gastric pH, and slower absorption rate
Increased tendency for constipation	Decreased muscle tone of the intestines; decreased peristalsis
Urinary	
Reduced filtering ability of the kidney and impaired renal function	Decreased number of functioning nephrons (basic functional units of the kidney) and arteriosclerotic changes in blood flow
Less effective concentration of urine	Decreased tubular function
Urinary urgency and frequency	Enlarged prostate gland in men; weakened muscles supporting the bladder or weakness of the urinary sphincter in women
Tendency for **nocturnal frequency** and **retention** of residual urine	Decreased bladder capacity and tone
Genitals	
Prostate enlargement (benign) in men	Exact mechanism is unclear; possible endocrine changes
Multiple changes in women (shrinkage and atrophy of the vulva, cervix, uterus, fallopian tubes, and ovaries; reduction in secretions; and changes in vaginal flora)	Diminished secretion of female hormones and more alkaline vaginal pH

Neuromusculoskeletal

With aging comes gradual reduction in the speed and power of skeletal or voluntary muscle contractions and sustained muscular effort. Exercise can strengthen weakened muscles, and up to about age 50 years, the skeletal muscles can increase in bulk and density. After that time, there is a steady decrease in muscle fibres, ultimately leading to the typical wasted appearance of the very old person. Thus, older adults often complain about their lack of strength and how quickly they tire. Activities can still be carried out, but at a slower pace. Often, balance is impaired with age. Prolonged muscle efforts may be sustained by older people, provided they take judicious rest pauses and avoid capacity or peak performance.

The person's *reaction time* slows with age. Reaction time can be delayed further by decreased muscle tone as a

Figure 21.3 A regular program of exercise is important for maintenance of joint mobility and muscle tone and can promote socialization

result of diminished physical activity. Older people compensate for this reaction difference by being exceptionally cautious, for instance in their driving habits, which exasperates some impatient young drivers.

Slight loss in overall stature occurs with age. This can be exaggerated by muscular weakness resulting in a stooping posture and **kyphosis** (humpback of the upper spine). **Osteoporosis,** a decrease in bone density, along with increased brittleness of bone, make the elderly adult prone to serious fractures, some of which may be spontaneous and are called **pathologic fractures.** Osteoporosis occurs more frequently in people with insufficient intake of dietary calcium, in women after menopause, and in individuals who are immobilized or physically inactive.

Some degenerative joint changes occur, making movement stiffer and more restricted. Stiffness is aggravated by inactivity; for example, if a person sits too long, the joints become stiff, and the person has difficulty standing and walking. A continual program of physical activity and proper nutrition will slow bone density loss and decrease muscle atrophy and stiffness (Figure 21.3).

Sensory/Perceptual

Each of the five senses becomes less efficient in older adulthood. Changes in *vision* associated with aging include the obvious changes around the eye, such as the shrunken appearance of the eyes due to loss of orbital fat, the slowed blink reflex, and the looseness of the eyelids, particularly the lower lid, due to poorer muscle tone. Other changes result in loss of visual acuity, less power of adaptation to darkness and dim light, decrease in accommodation to near and far objects, loss of peripheral vision, and difficulty in discriminating similar colours, especially blues, greens, and purples.

By the age of 80 years, all older people have some lens opacity (**cataracts**) that reduces visual acuity and causes glare to be a problem. Surgical removal of cataracts is common at this age. Changes in the ciliary muscles, which control the shape of the lens, reduce the power of the lens to adjust to near and far vision. The diameter of the pupil is reduced, and the amount of light entering the eye is thereby restricted. This slows the reaction time to decreases in light or illumination, a problem compounded with driving at night. Diminished retinal function and reduced peripheral vision also occur.

The loss of *hearing* ability related to aging, called *presbycusis,* affects people over age 65 years. Gradual loss of hearing is more common among men than women, perhaps because men are more frequently in noisy work environments. Hearing loss is greater in the higher frequencies than the lower. Thus, older adults with hearing loss usually hear speakers with low, distinct voices best. Older adults may have more difficulty compensating for hearing loss than the young, who pay closer attention to the lip movements of the speaker.

Older people have a poorer sense of *taste* and *smell* and are less stimulated by food than the young. This change significantly affects appetite in the older adult, contributing to poor nutrition.

Loss of skin receptors takes place gradually, producing an increased threshold for *sensations of pain, touch,* and *temperature.* The older person may not be able to distinguish hot from cold or sense the intensity of heat. Stimuli causing severe pain in a younger person may cause only minor sensation or pressure in the elderly. This places the older adult at higher risk for burns and other injuries.

Pulmonary

Respiratory efficiency is reduced with age. The person inhales a smaller volume of air because of the musculoskeletal changes in the chest wall that reduce the size of the chest. A greater volume of residual air is left in the lungs after expiration, and the capacity to cough efficiently decreases because of weaker expiratory muscles.

Mucus secretions tend to collect more readily in the respiratory tree. Thus, susceptibility to respiratory infections increases in older adults. **Dyspnea** (difficult breathing) occurs frequently with increased activity, such as running for a bus or carrying heavy parcels upstairs.

Cardiovascular

The working capacity of the heart diminishes with age. This is particularly evident when increased demands are made on the heart muscles, such as during periods of exercise or emotional stress. The heart rate at normal rest does not change with age. However, the heart rate of the aged person is slow to respond to stress and slow to return to normal after periods of physical activity.

Changes in the arteries occur concurrently. Reduced arterial elasticity may result in diminished blood supply to, for instance, the legs and the brain, resulting in pain on exertion in the calf muscles and dizziness, respectively.

Blood pressure measurements often indicate a significant increase in systolic pressures and a slight increase in diastolic pressures. In addition, there may be a delay in the circulatory adjustments required when a person quickly stands up from a lying position. The delay results in an abrupt drop in systolic blood pressure known as **orthostatic hypotension.**

Gastrointestinal

The digestive system is also impaired by aging. Gradual decreases in digestive enzymes occur; examples are ptyalin in salivary secretions, which converts starch; pepsin and trypsin, which digest protein; and lipase, a fat-splitting enzyme.

There is also a decrease in the number of absorbing cells in the intestinal tract and a reduction in gastric pH. These factors lower the absorption rate, slowing the absorption of nutrients and drugs. The muscle tone of the intestines also decreases, causing a decrease in peristalsis and elimination. These changes in muscle tone, digestive juices, and intestinal activity may lead to **indigestion** and **constipation** in the older adult.

Urinary

The excretory function of the kidney diminishes with age, but usually not significantly below normal levels unless a disease process intervenes. The kidney's filtering abilities may also be impaired; thus, waste products may be filtered and excreted more slowly.

More noticeable changes are those related to the bladder. Complaints of **urinary urgency** and **urinary frequency** are common. The capacity of the bladder and its ability to completely empty diminish with age. Many older adults need to get up during the night to void (**nocturnal frequency**) and may experience **retention** of residual urine, predisposing the elderly adult to bladder infections.

Genitals

Degenerative changes in the gonads are gradual in men. Production of testosterone continues, and the testes can produce sperm well into old age, although there is a gradual decrease in the number of sperm produced. In women, the degenerative changes in the ovaries are noticed by the abrupt cessation of menses in middle age during the menopause.

Changes in the gonads of elderly women result from diminished secretion of the ovarian hormones. Some changes, such as the shrinking of the uterus and ovaries, go unnoticed. Other changes are obvious. The breasts atrophy, and lubricating vaginal secretions are reduced. Reduced natural lubrication is the cause of painful intercourse, which often necessitates the use of lubricating jellies.

Psychosocial Development

A number of theories explain psychosocial aging. According to **disengagement theory,** aging involves mutual withdrawal (disengagement) between the older person and others in that person's environment. This withdrawal relieves the older person of some of society's pressures and gradually reduces the number of people with whom the older person interacts. According to **activity theory,** the best way to age is to stay active physically and mentally, and according to **continuity theory,** people maintain their values, habits, and behaviours in old age. A person who is accustomed to having people around will continue to do so, and the person who prefers not to be involved with others will more likely disengage. This theory accounts for the great variety of behaviour seen in older people.

According to Erikson, the developmental task at this time is *integrity versus despair.* See Table 19.4 on page 314. People who attain ego integrity view life with a sense of wholeness and derive satisfaction from past accomplishments. They view death as an acceptable completion of life. According to Erikson, people who develop integrity accept "one's one and only life cycle" (Erikson, 1963, p. 263). By contrast, people who despair often believe they have made poor choices during life and wish they could live life over. Robert Butler sees integrity as bringing serenity and wisdom, and despair as resulting in the inability to accept one's fate. Despair gives rise to feelings of frustration, discouragement, and a sense that one's life has been worthless (Butler, 1963).

Acknowledging that the "young-old" and "old-old" differ not only in physical characteristics but also in psychosocial responses, many people have difficulty with Erikson's singular developmental task. Peck (1968) proposes the following three developmental tasks of the older adult in contrast to Erikson's task of ego integrity versus despair.

1. Ego differentiation versus work-role preoccupation.
2. Body transcendence versus body preoccupation.
3. Ego transcendence versus ego preoccupation.

For details about these tasks see Chapter 19. Havighurst (1972) and Duvall (1977) have further defined the developmental tasks of the older adult. See the box on the next page.

Retirement

Today, a majority of the people over 65 years are unemployed. However, many who are healthy continue to work on a full- or part-time basis. Work offers these people a better income, a sense of self-worth, and the chance to continue long-established routines. Some need to work for economic reasons.

Retirement can be a time when projects or recreational activities deferred for a long time can be pursued (Figure 21.4). Retired people are no longer governed by an alarm clock and can get up when they please. The enjoyment of staying up later is another luxury. Few older people, however, spend much time resting or sleeping. Being accustomed to activity most of their lives, most older adults find many outlets in travelling, jobs, community projects, volunteer services, intellectual or recreational pursuits, or hobbies, such as stamp collecting or fishing (Figure 21.5).

Developmental Tasks of the Older Adult

Havighurst (1972)

- Adjusting to decreasing physical strength and health
- Adjusting to retirement and reduced income
- Adjusting to the death of a spouse
- Establishing an explicit affiliation with one's age group
- Meeting social and civic obligations
- Establishing satisfactory living arrangements

Duvall (1977)

- Making satisfying living arrangements as aging progresses
- Adjusting to retirement income
- Establishing comfortable routines
- Safeguarding physical and mental health
- Maintaining love, sex, and marital relations
- Remaining in touch with other family members
- Keeping active and involved
- Finding meaning in life

Sources: Duvall, E. M. (1977). *Family development* (5th ed). (p. 390). Philadelphia, PA: Lippincott; Havighurst, R. J. (1972). *Developmental tasks and education* (3rd ed). New York: Longman. Reprinted with permission.

The lifestyle of later years is, to a large degree, formulated in youth. This fact was recognized by Robert Browning: "Grow old along with me! / The best is yet to be, / The last of life, for which the first was made." People who attempt suddenly to refocus and enrich their lives at retirement usually have difficulty. Those who learned early in life to live well-balanced and fulfilling lives are generally more successful in retirement. The person who has been concerned only with the accomplishments of the children, or who has been concerned only with the paycheque and job status, can be left with a feeling of emptiness when children leave and the job no longer exists. The later years can foster a sense of integrity and continuity, or they can be years of despair.

Economic Change

The financial needs of older people vary considerably. Though most need less money for clothing, entertainment, and work, and although some own their homes, costs continue to rise, making it difficult for some to manage. Food and medical costs alone are often a financial burden. Adequate financial resources enable the older person to remain independent.

Problems with income are often related to low retirement benefits, lack of pension plans for many workers, and the increased length of the retirement years. Older members of minority groups often have greater financial problems than older whites. Older women of all ages usually have lower incomes than men.

Nurses should be aware of the costs of health care. For example, while assisting a client to plan a diet, the nurse must consider which foods the client can afford to buy. The nurse or the client can request the physician to order lower-priced medications. In addition, the supplies used in a client's care should be as economical as possible.

Relocation

During late adulthood, many people experience relocation. A variety of factors may lead to this decision. The house or apartment may be too large or too expensive. The work involved in maintaining the house may become burdensome or impossible for the aged person or couple.

Figure 21.4 Many older adults find creative outlets during retirement

Figure 21.5 Retirement provides time for enjoying hobbies

Some older persons with decreased mobility want living arrangements that are all on one floor or need more accessible bathroom facilities.

Making the decision to move is often stressful. The older person may be moving to an apartment, which may mean leaving the comfort of the family home and the neighbours and friends of several decades. Some need to move nearer to their children for general support and supervision. For many, this decision is difficult and stressful. For others, relocation is voluntary. The person may be seeking a more moderate climate with better recreational facilities geared to a more leisurely lifestyle. Adjustment will be much easier for the older person making a voluntary move.

Some older people must relocate to long-term care facilities or nursing homes. The decision to enter a nursing home is frequently made when older people can no longer care for themselves, often because of problems of mobility and memory impairment. An increasing number of nursing home residents are in the very old age group (85 years and over), and most are women.

The facilities in nursing homes differ in many ways and offer varying degrees of independence to the residents. All provide meals but vary in giving other services, such as assistance with hygiene and dressing, physical therapy or exercise, recreational activities, transportation services, and medical and nursing supervision.

Nurses in hospitals should find out whether a client is being discharged to a nursing home or to a private home. All nursing homes provide nursing services to clients and require appropriate information to provide for continuity of care. Clients returning home, however, may require the assistance of a home care nurse or a personal support worker.

Maintaining Independence and Self-Esteem

Aging in place describes a process which enables older adults to age within the comfort and familiarity of their own homes. Most older people thrive on independence. It is important to them to be able to look after themselves even if they have to struggle to do so. Although it may be difficult for younger family members to watch an older person completing tasks in a slow, determined way, aging people need this sense of accomplishment. Offspring might notice that the aging father or mother with failing vision cannot keep the kitchen as clean as before. The aging parent may be slower and less meticulous in carpentry tasks or gardening. To maintain the older adult's sense of self-respect, nurses and family members need to encourage them to do as much as possible for themselves, provided that safety is maintained. Many young people err in thinking that they are helpful to older people when they take over for them and do the job much faster and more efficiently.

Aging people need to be recognized for their unique individual characteristics. It can be difficult to recognize these differences because older people have less energy than the young to show how they are different. Perhaps this is one reason older people tend to talk about past accomplishments, jobs, deeds, and experiences.

Nurses need to acknowledge the older client's ability to think, reason, and make decisions. The nurse can support a decision by an older client, even if eventually the decision is reversed because of failing health.

Older people appreciate thoughtfulness, consideration, and acceptance of their waning abilities. For example, having dinner out in a well-lit restaurant or not expecting grandmother to baby-sit for too many hours, if at all, are actions that recognize the diminished vision and energy of older people. The values and standards held by older people need to be accepted, whether they are related to ethical, religious, or household matters. For example, respect an older person's decision to hang the laundry outside, rather than to use a dryer, or to cook on a conventional stove, rather than in a microwave oven.

Facing Death and Grieving

Well-adjusted aging couples usually thrive on companionship. Many couples rely increasingly on their mates for this company and may have few outside friends. Great bonds of affection and closeness can develop during this period of aging together and nurturing each other. When a mate dies, the remaining partner inevitably experiences feelings of loss, emptiness, and loneliness. Many are capable and manage to live alone; however, reliance on younger family members increases with advancing age, and when ill health occurs. Some widows and widowers remarry, particularly the latter because most widowers are less inclined than widows to maintain a household.

More women than men face bereavement and solitude because women usually live longer. Older people are often reminded of their own mortality by the death of friends. It is a time when one's life is reviewed with happiness or regret. Feelings of serenity or guilt and inadequacy can arise. Independence established prior to loss of a mate makes this adjustment period easier. A person who has some meaningful friendships, economic security, ongoing interests in the community or private hobbies, and a peaceful philosophy of life copes more easily with bereavement. Successful relationships with children and grandchildren are also of inestimable value. See Chapter 48 for a discussion about facing death.

Nurses can sometimes help clients who are alone a great deal to adjust their living arrangements or lifestyle so that they have more companionship. Moving to a retirement home that has other people in similar circumstances and organized social activities is one example. Many communities provide social centres for the elderly, for example, drop-in centres or community centres that offer day trips for seniors. Nurses can refer clients to services and encourage them to obtain companionship.

Cognitive Development

Piaget's phases of cognitive development end with the formal operations phase. However, considerable research on cognitive abilities and aging is currently being conducted. We have already mentioned the concept of a sixth stage known as the postformal operations phase.

Intellectual capacity includes perception, cognitive agility, memory, and learning. **Perception,** or the ability to interpret the environment, depends on the acuteness of the senses. If the aging person's senses are impaired, the ability to perceive the environment and react appropriately is diminished. Changes in the nervous system may also affect perceptual capacity.

Changes in the cognitive structures occur as a person ages. It is believed that there is progressive loss of neurons. In addition, blood flow to the brain decreases, the meninges (i.e., the 3 membranes that envelop the brain and spinal cord) appear to thicken, and brain metabolism slows. As yet, little is known about the effects of these physical changes on the cognitive functioning of the older adult.

In older adults, changes in cognitive abilities are more often a difference in speed than in ability. Overall, the older adult maintains problem solving, judgement, creativity, and other well-practised cognitive skills. Intellectual loss generally reflects a disease process, such as atherosclerosis, which causes the blood vessels to narrow and diminishes perfusion of nutrients to the brain. Most older adults do not experience cognitive impairments.

Memory is also a component of intellectual capacity that involves the following steps:

1. Momentary perception of stimuli from the environment, referred to as **sensory memory**
2. Storage in **short-term memory** (information held in the brain for immediate use or what one has in mind at a given moment): an example of this type of memory is when you call information for a telephone number and remember the number only for the brief time needed to dial the number. Short-term memory also deals with activities or the recent past of minutes to a few hours that is often referred to as **recent memory.**
3. Encoding, by which information leaves short-term memory and enters **long-term memory,** the repository for information stored for periods longer than 72 hours and usually weeks and years: memories of childhood friends, teachers, and events are stored in long-term memory. Older people who remember the flowers in their wedding bouquet or the names of the boys on their dance card are drawing from long-term memory.

In older adults, retrieval of information from long-term memory can be slower, especially if the information is not frequently used. Most age-related differences occur in short-term memory. Older adults tend to forget the recent past. This forgetfulness can be improved by the use of memory aids, making notes or lists, and placing objects in consistent locations.

Older people need additional time for learning, largely because of the problem of retrieving information. Motivation is also important. Older adults have more difficulty than younger ones in learning information they do not consider meaningful. It is suggested that the older person remain mentally active to maintain cognitive ability at the highest possible level. Lifelong mental activity, particularly verbal activity, helps the older person retain a high level of cognitive function and may help maintain long-term memory. Cognitive impairment that interferes with normal life is not considered part of normal aging. A decline in intellectual abilities that interferes with social or occupational functions should always be regarded as abnormal. In such instances, family members should be advised to seek prompt medical evaluation.

Moral Development

According to Kohlberg, moral development is completed in the early adult years. Most old people stay at Kohlberg's conventional level of moral development (see Table 19.6 on page 317), and some are at the preconventional level. An older person at the preconventional level obeys rules to avoid pain and the displeasure of others. At stage 1, a person defines good and bad in relation to self, whereas older people at stage 2 may act to meet another's needs as well as their own. Older adults at the conventional level follow society's rules of conduct in response to the expectations of others.

The value and belief patterns that are important to older adults may have little or no significance to younger people because they developed during a time that was very different from today. In addition, a large number of today's elderly are either foreign-born or first-generation citizens. Cultural background, life experiences, gender, religion, and socioeconomic status all influence one's values. The nurse must identify and consider the specific values of the older client when nursing care is planned. (See Chapters 7 and 14.)

Spiritual Development

Older adults can contemplate new religious and philosophical views and try to understand ideas missed previously or interpreted differently. The older person also derives a sense of worth by sharing experiences or views. In contrast, the older adult who has not matured spiritually may feel impoverishment or despair as the drive for economic and professional success wanes.

Carson (1989, p. 44–45) states that religion "takes on new meaning for the elderly, who may find comfort, solace, and affirmation in religious activities." The older person's knowledge becomes wisdom, an inner resource for dealing with both positive and negative life experiences. Many older people have strong religious convictions and continue to attend religious meetings or services. Involvement in religion often helps the older adult to resolve issues related to the meaning of life, to adversity, or to good fortune. The "old-old" person who cannot attend formal services often continues religious participation in a more private manner. Many older adults watch television evangelists and some, being vulnerable to fund-raising ventures, send these organizations money that they can ill afford to spare.

According to Fowler and Keen (1985), some people enter the sixth stage of spiritual development, *universalizing*. See Table 19.7 on page 318. People whose spiritual development reaches this level think and act in a way that exemplifies love and justice.

Health Assessment and Promotion

Assessment guidelines for the development of the older adult are shown in the box on the next page. Assessment activities may include measurement of weight, height, and vital signs (see Chapter 27); observation of the skin for hydration status or presence of lesions; examination of visual acuity using the Snellen chart; examination of hearing acuity using the whisper, Weber, and Rinne tests (see Chapter 27); and questions about the following:

- Usual dietary pattern
- Any problems with bowel or urinary elimination
- Activity/exercise and sleep/rest patterns
- Family and social activities and interests
- Any problems with reading, writing, or problem solving
- Adjustment to retirement or loss of partner
- Economic situation

Canadian Society Notes

Fact	Implications for Nursing Practice
The Canadian Health Network is a Health Canada funded site which provides an extensive list of accurate and current resources for all Canadians. Visit http://www.canadian-health-network.ca.	These resources will provide a list of federal services available to older clients. Knowledge of this resource will assist the nurse to meet the needs of the older client.
Seniors constitute one of the fastest growing populations in Canada. In addition, a growth in the very old population (seniors over the age of 75 years of age) has resulted in increased costs for health care and social service programs.	Gerontological content is an integral element of life-long learning since the vast majority of nurses will care for older adults during their professional careers.
Almost all (96 percent in 1996) seniors speak one of the two official languages, but 4 percent of seniors cannot speak English or French; 12 percent speak a language other than English or French in their homes (Statistics Canada, 1999).	Obtaining an interpreter may be a necessary part of nursing care.

Older persons are usually concerned about their health and are interested in information and behavioural strategies directed toward improving it. Canada recognizes the health promotion model proposed by Epp (1986) as a framework for health promotion. The model suggests three mechanisms: self-care, mutual aid, and healthy environments. The nurse may wish to discuss some or all of the health promotion topics outlined in the box on page 367. These topics are discussed in detail in subsequent chapters throughout the book.

Health Problems

Health problems that older adults may experience include accidents, chronic disabling diseases, drug use and misuse, mental illness, abuse, and cancer. Leading causes of

DEVELOPMENTAL ASSESSMENT GUIDELINES

The Older Adult

In these three developmental areas, does the older adult do the following?

1. **Physical Development**
   - Adjust to physiological changes (e.g., appearance, sensory/perceptual, musculoskeletal, neurological, cardiovascular)
   - Adapt lifestyle to diminishing energy and ability
   - Maintain vital signs (especially blood pressure) within normal range for age and gender
2. **Psychosocial Development**
   - Manage retirement years in a satisfying manner
   - Participate in social and leisure activities
   - Have a social network of friends and support persons
   - View life as worthwhile
   - Have high self-esteem
   - Gain support from value system and/or spiritual philosophy
   - Accept and adjust to the death of significant others
3. **Development in Activities of Daily Living**
   - Exhibit healthy practices in nutrition, exercise, recreation, sleep patterns, and personal habits
   - Have the ability to care for self or to secure appropriate help with activities of daily living
   - Have satisfactory living arrangements and income to meet changing needs

death in people ages 65 years and over are heart disease, cerebrovascular disease (stroke), pneumonia/influenza, obstructive lung disease, cancer, and suicide.

Accidents

Accident prevention is a major concern for older people. Because vision is limited, reflexes are slowed, and bones are brittle, caution is required in climbing stairs, driving a car, and even walking. Driving, particularly night driving, requires caution because accommodation of the eye to light is impaired and peripheral vision is diminished. Older persons need to remember to turn the head before changing lanes, and they should not rely on side vision, for example, when crossing a street. Driving in foggy or other hazardous conditions should be avoided.

Fires are a hazard for the older adult with a failing memory. The older person may forget that the iron or stove is left on or may not extinguish a cigarette completely. Because of reduced sensitivity to pain and heat, care must be taken to prevent burns when the person has hot baths or uses heating devices.

Many older adults suffer and die each year from hypothermia. **Hypothermia** is a body temperature below normal. A lowered metabolism and loss of normal insulation from thinning subcutaneous tissue decrease the older client's ability to retain heat.

Because older clients who take analgesics or sedatives may become lethargic or confused, they should be monitored regularly and closely. Other measures to induce sleep should be used whenever possible. Nurses can help older clients make the home environment safe. Specific hazards can be identified and corrected; for example, hand rails can be installed on staircases. The nurse teaches the importance of taking only prescribed medications and contacting a health professional at the first indication of intolerance to them.

Guidelines for accident prevention for the older adult are detailed in Chapter 33.

Chronic Disabling Illness

Many older adults function well within the community without impairments; others are afflicted with one or more chronic illnesses that may seriously impair their functioning. Chronic conditions are more prevalent among older adults than among those in middle age. Examples of these are arthritis, rheumatism, osteoporosis, heart disease, stroke, obstructive lung disease, diabetes, hypertension, hearing and visual alterations, and cognitive dysfunctions. In addition, acute illnesses, such as pneumonia, fractures, trauma from falls, motor vehicle accidents, or other incidents, may create chronic health problems. There are regional variations in the presence of chronic conditions; for example, the prevalence of high blood pressure is higher in the Atlantic region than in the rest of Canada, as is the prevalence of arthritis in Ontario. Chronic illness brings about many changes to the client and to family members: the client, for example, may need increasing help with the activities of daily living, such as ambulation, feeding, hygiene, and so on; health-care expenses often escalate and may become an economic concern; family roles may need to be altered; and family members may need to change their lifestyle to meet caregiving needs.

Mental Illnesses

While, in general, older Canadians report a high level of life satisfaction, they face a number of threats to their emotional well-being. The *Canadian Family Physician* reported in 1999 that older adults are among the most undertreated population for mental health, estimating that mental health problems go undetected in more than one-third of those over the age of 65 years. Some older adults may begin to use alcohol to help them cope with the changes and problems of their older years. Mental illness

Health Promotion Guidelines for Older Adults

Health Tests and Screening

- As for middle-aged adults (see page 356)

Safety (see Chapter 33 for details)

- Home safety measures to prevent falls, fire, burns, scalds, and electrocution
- Motor vehicle safety reinforcement, especially when driving at night
- Precautions to prevent pedestrian accidents
- Education about medications

Nutrition and Exercise

- Importance of a well-balanced diet with fewer calories to accommodate lower metabolic rate and decreased physical activity
- Importance of sufficient amounts of vitamin D and calcium to prevent osteoporosis
- A regular program of moderate exercise to maintain joint mobility, muscle tone, and bone calcification

Elimination

- Importance of adequate roughage in the diet, adequate exercise, and at least 1500 mL of fluid daily to prevent constipation

Social Interactions

- Encouraging intellectual and recreational pursuits
- Encouraging personal relationships that promote discussion of feelings, concerns, and fears
- Availability of social community centres, programs, and support groups for seniors

may be a cause of suicide. In comparing the suicide rates among males, the rate for very old men (aged 80 to 84 years) was the highest in Canada in 1997.

Drug Use and Misuse

Older adults who frequently suffer from one or more chronic diseases often require medication. Episodes of acute illness may require additional medications. Clients may purchase over-the-counter (OTC) drugs to cope with common discomforts related to aging, such as constipation, sleep disturbance, and joint pain. The complexities involved in the self-administration of medication may lead to a variety of misuse situations, including taking too much or too little medication, combining alcohol and medication, combining prescribed medications with over-the-counter drugs, taking medications at the wrong time, taking someone else's medication, or noncompliance (i.e., failure to take a prescribed medication or to follow the instructions). Other potential misuse situations occur when more than one physician prescribes medications and the client fails to tell each doctor what has been previously prescribed.

Additionally, the pharmacodynamics of drugs are altered in older adults. The variations in absorption, distribution, metabolism, and excretion of drugs are related to physiological changes associated with aging. These variations are discussed in Chapter 28.

Dementia

Dementia is a general term for a permanent or progressive organic mental disorder that is characterized by personality changes, confusion, disorientation, deterioration of intellectual functioning, and impaired control of memory, judgement, and impulses (Wold, 1993). The most common type of dementia is Alzheimer's disease (AD). Its cause is unknown. Alzheimer's disease affects about 750,000 people in Canada (Canadian Study of Health & Aging

FOCUS ON CRITICAL THINKING

Mrs. Holly Drinkwater is a 78-year-old widow living in her own home in a rural part of the country. She has made one of her regular visits into the small local town to see her doctor about her diabetes. You have the opportunity of talking to her about her health status. She expresses concern about her failing vision and the opportunity to continue living in her own home.

See Appendix A for answers to these questions.

1. What is an adequate knowledge base for a nurse to make decisions about the care required by an older adult?
2. What assessment data would you deem important to collect regarding Mrs. Drinkwater's ability to remain within her own home?
3. Why is Mrs. Drinkwater's input and feedback important in nursing practice?

Working Group, 1994). The symptoms of AD have been grouped into three or four stages and may vary somewhat from client to client. The most prominent symptoms are cognitive dysfunctions, including decline in memory, learning, attention, judgement, orientation, and language skills. The symptoms are progressive, and all victims experience a steady decline in cognitive and physical abilities, lasting between seven and 15 years and ending in death. In the last stage, the client needs total assistance, is unable to communicate, is incontinent, and may be unable to walk.

There is no cure or specific treatment for AD. Several drugs have been developed, but none has been shown consistently to reverse the progression of the disease.

Many older adults with AD are cared for in the home. The burden of care is frequently on women—wives and daughters—who are themselves aging. AD is devastating for the families and caregivers of its victims. The caregivers often drive themselves to physical and emotional exhaustion while they render continuous care and experience the anguish of seeing a loved one turned into a person who no longer remembers who he or she is. The nurse's responsibility is to provide supportive nursing care, accurate information, and referral assistance.

Nurses need to be able to identify when delirium (a period of acute disorientation) is superimposed upon dementia—failure to do so has significant consequences for the older adult. The older adult may be misdiagnosed and receive treatment interventions more appropriate to dementia.

Aged Abuse

The rate of aged abuse is unknown. As the proportion of older adults in the population increases, it is possible that aged abuse will become an even greater problem. Aged abuse may affect either gender; however, the victims most often are women who are over 75 years of age, physically or mentally impaired, and dependent for care on the abuser. The abuse may involve physical, psychological, or emotional abuse; sexual abuse; financial abuse; violation of human or civil rights; and active or passive neglect.

When aged abuse involves physical neglect, victims may suffer from dehydration, malnutrition, and oversedation. The victim may be deprived of necessary articles, such as glasses, hearing aids, or walkers. Psychologically, the person may suffer verbal assaults, threats, humiliation, or harassment. Abuse may also include failure to provide appropriate medications or medical treatment, isolation, unreasonable confinement, lack of privacy, an unsafe environment, and involuntary servitude. Some victims are financially exploited by relatives who steal from them or misuse their property or funds. Others are beaten and even raped by family members. Most victims experience two or more forms of abuse.

Aged abuse or neglect may occur in private homes, senior citizens' homes, nursing homes, hospitals, and long-term care facilities. Many of the abusers are either sons or daughters and/or their spouses; others include spouses, relatives (grandchildren, siblings, nieces, and nephews), and, in some instances, health-care providers.

Older adults at home may fail to report abuse or neglect for many reasons. They may be ashamed to admit that their children have abused them. They may fear retaliation or being sent to an institution if they seek help. They frequently lack financial resources or lack the mental capacity to be aware of abuse or neglect and to report the situation. Examples of crimes are assault and financial abuse of an older person who is physically or mentally incompetent and has no trustworthy friend or relative to help. In some instances, nurses can intervene by educating responsible relatives about the needs and vulnerability of older adults and the resources available to provide increased home support. They should also report any abuse situation to the appropriate person in the health-care agency.

Nurses should be familiar with the laws of their particular jurisdiction regarding the reporting of suspected or known abuse. The legally competent adult cannot be forced, however, to leave the abusive situation and, in many cases, may decide to stay. If the client is not legally competent, court proceedings to attain guardianship can be initiated.

Cancer

Cancer is a significant health concern for older Canadians. Lung cancer is the second leading cause of death among older men, and the sixth leading cause among older women. Breast, prostate, and colorectal cancers are also leading causes of mortality. When assessing an older adult, the nurse should review the warning signs of cancer: change in bowel or bladder habits, sore that does not heal, unusual bleeding or discharge, thickening or lump in the breast or elsewhere, obvious change in a wart or mole, and nagging cough or hoarseness. Diagnosis is often complicated by the presence of co-existing chronic conditions and by common misperceptions about aging held by health-care professionals.

CHAPTER HIGHLIGHTS

- Adult development is often divided into three phases: young adults (20 to 40 years), middle-aged adults (40 to 65 years), and older adults (65 years onward). Late adulthood is usually classified into three periods: the young-old (60 to 74 years), the middle-old (75 to 84 years), and the old-old (85 and older).
- The young adult is essentially in a stable period physically, but psychological changes are great. Choices must be made about education, occupation, marriage, child rearing, a place to live, civic roles, and so on.
- The middle-aged adult needs to adjust to an aging body, the increasing dependence of parents, and the increasing independence of children; however, new independent interests can be pursued.
- Both middle-aged men and women enter a midlife crisis in which they need to re-examine their purpose and re-evaluate ways to use their energies and abilities.
- Older adults experience many physical changes associated with aging. All body systems undergo change: integumentary, neuromusculoskeletal, sensory/perceptual, pulmonary, cardiovascular, gastrointestinal, urinary, and genital.
- Several theories have been proposed to account for the biological aging process: wear-and-tear, rate of living, stress, endocrine, free-radical, programmed senescence, error catastrophe, collagen, cross-linking, immunological, and autoimmune theories.
- The older adult has to adjust to possible psychosocial changes, including retirement (which necessitates financial and social adjustments), relocation, increasing dependence on others, and coping with losses and death.
- Psychosocial theories about aging include the disengagement, activity, and continuity theories. Such theories reflect the controversial nature of our understanding of older adults.
- Cognitive development continues during young adulthood and the middle-aged years. Developments may extend beyond the formal operations phase of Piaget to one of postformal operations thinking. The intellectual abilities of the healthy older adult undergo minimal change. In older adults, retrieval of information from long-term memory can be slower. Most changes occur in short-term or recent memory.
- In the realm of moral development, most adults are in either Kohlberg's stage 4 (the law and order orientation) at the conventional level or in stage 5 (the social contract and legalistic orientation) at the postconventional level.
- Spiritual development of adults can continue into Fowler's *paradoxical-consolidative stage*. Some adults even enter the sixth stage of spiritual development, known as *universalizing*. Young adults often feel self-conscious about spiritual matters.
- Health-promotion information for all adults needs to include positive health practices that can promote health and wellness. These include (1) recommended physical, visual, hearing, and dental assessments; (2) screenings for cardiovascular disease and cancer; (3) breast and testicular self-examinations; (4) immunizations; (5) Papanicolaou smears for women; (6) safety precautions to prevent accidents; (7) the importance of appropriate nutrition and exercise; (8) for older adults, the importance of measures to prevent constipation; and (9) strong social interactions.
- Health problems of *young adults* include accidents, suicide, substance abuse, sexually transmitted diseases, abuse of women, and malignancies. Problems of *middle-aged* adults include accidents, cancer, cardiovascular disease, obesity, alcoholism, and mental health changes. Health problems of *older* adults include accidents, chronic disabling diseases, drug use and misuse, mental illness, aged abuse, and cancer.

READINGS AND REFERENCES

Suggested Readings

Maddox, M. (1999). Older women and the meaning of health. *Journal of Gerontological Nursing, 25*(12), 26–33.
Health promotion is an essential component of nursing care of older adults. In this article, Maddox explores, through a phenomenological study, what health means to older women. She identified five themes: (1) interactions with a being greater than themselves, (2) acceptance of self, (3) humour, (4) flexibility, and (5) being other-centred.

Murray, R. B., & Zentner, J. P. (2001). *Health assessment and promotion strategies through the life span* (7th ed.). Stamford, CT: Appleton & Lange.
Part IV of this book provides a comprehensive discussion of assessment and health promotion for the young, middle-aged, and older adults. It addresses family development and relationships, physiological concepts, psychosocial concepts, and health-care and nursing applications. For the older adult, additional sections include societal perspectives on aging, theories of aging, and socioeconomic concepts.

Selected References

Barkauskas, V., Bauman, L. C., Stoltenberg-Allen, K., & Darling-Fisher, C. (1998). *Barkauskas health and physical assessment* (2nd ed.). St. Louis, MO: Mosby.

Butler, R. (1963). The life review: An interpretation of reminiscence in the aged. *Psychiatry, 26,* 65.

Canadian Study of Health & Aging Working Group. (1994). Canadian study of health and aging: Study methods and prevalence of dementia. *Canadian Medical Association Journal, 150,* 899–912.

Carson, V. B. (1989). *Spiritual dimensions in nursing practice.* Philadelphia, PA: Saunders.

Ciocon, J., & Potter, J. (1988). Age related changes in human memory: Normal and abnormal. *Geriatrics, 43,* 43–48.

Conn, V. S., Taylor, S. G., & Kelley, S. (1991). Medication regimen complexity and adherence among older adults. *Image: Journal of Nursing Scholarship, 23,* 231–235.

Duvall, E. M. (1977). *Family development* (5th ed.). Philadelphia, PA: Lippincott. (Classic.)

Ebersole, P., & Hess, P. (1998). *Toward healthy aging: Human needs and nursing response* (5th ed.). St. Louis, MO: Mosby.

Edelman, C., & Mandle, C. L. (1998). *Health promotion throughout the life span* (4th ed.). St. Louis, MO: Mosby.

Eliopoulos, C. (1997). *Gerontological nursing* (4th ed.). Philadelphia, PA: Lippincott.

Epp, J. (1986). *Achieving health for all: A framework for health promotion.* Cat. No H39-1021 1986E. Ottawa: Minister of Supply and Services.

Erikson, E. H. (1963). *Childhood and society* (2nd ed.). New York: Norton. (Classic.)

Erikson, E. H. (1982). *The life cycle completed: A review.* New York: Norton. (Classic.)

Fowler, J. W. (1981). *Stages of faith: The psychology of human development and the quest for meaning.* New York: Harper & Row.

Fowler, J., & Keen, S. (1978, 1985). *Life maps: Conversations in the journey of faith.* Waco, TX: Word Books.

Freud, S. (1923). *The ego and the id.* London: Hogarth Press.

Freud, S. (1961). *The ego and the id and other works* (Vol. 19). J. Strachey, translator. London: Hogarth Press and the Institute of Psychoanalysis. (Classic.).

Gilligan, C. (1982). *In a Different Voice: Psychological Theory and Women's Development.* Cambridge, MA: Harvard University Press. (Classic).

Havighurst, R. J. (1972). *Developmental tasks and education* (3rd ed.). New York: Longman. (Classic.)

Hultsch, D. F., & Deutsch, F. (1981). *Adult development and aging.* New York: McGraw-Hill.

Keating, N. (1999). *Eldercare in Canada: Context, content and consequences.* Ottawa: Statistics Canada.

Kohlberg, L. (1971). *Recent research in moral development.* New York: Holt, Rinehart & Winston. (Classic.)

Kohlberg, L. (1981). *The psychology of moral development: Moral stages and the idea of justice.* San Francisco, CA: Harper & Row.

Mackenzie, C. S., Gekoski, W. L., & Knox, V. J. (1999). Do family physicians treat older patients with mental disorders differently from younger patients? *Canadian Family Physician, 45,* 1219–24.

McShane, J. (1991). *Cognitive development. An information processing approach.* Padstow, Cornwall: TJ Press Ltd.

Miller, P. H. (1993). *Theories of developmental psychology* (3rd ed.). New York: Freeman.

Murray, R. B., & Zentner, J. P. (1997). *Health assessment and promotion strategies through the life span* (6th ed.). Stamford, CT: Appleton & Lange.

National Advisory Council on Aging (NACA) (1999). *1999 and beyond: Challenges of an aging Canadian Society.* Ottawa: Author.

Novak, M. (1997). *Aging & society: A Canadian perspective* (3rd ed.). Toronto: Nelson.

Peck, R. (1955). Psychological developments in the second half of life. In J. Anderson, (Ed.), *Psychological aspects of aging.* Washington, DC: American Psychological Association. (Classic.)

Peck, R. (1968). Psychological development in the second half of life. In B. L. Neugarten, (Ed.), *Middle age and aging.* Chicago, IL: University of Chicago Press.

Sheehy, G. (1976). *Passages: Predictable crises of adult life.* New York: Dutton.

Sheehy, G. (1995). *New passages. Mapping your life across time.* New York: Ballantine Books.

Statistics Canada. (1999). "Mortality-Summary list of causes, 1997", catalogue No 84F209. Ottawa: Author.

Statistics Canada. (1999). *A portrait of seniors in Canada* (3rd ed.). Cat. No 89-519-XPE. Ottawa: Minister of Supply and Services.

Thomas, J. L. (1992). *Adulthood and aging.* Needham Heights, MA: Allyn & Bacon.

Ulijaszek, S. J., Johnston, R. E., & Preece, M. A. (1998). *The Cambridge encyclopedia of human growth and development.* New York: Cambridge University Press.

Wold, G. (1993). *Basic geriatric nursing.* St. Louis, MO: Mosby-Year Book.

WEBLINKS

Canadian Association on Gerontology
http://www.cagac.ca
The Canadian Association on Gerontology (CAG) is a national, multidisciplinary, scientific, and educational association established to provide leadership in matters related to the aging population. Their Web site identifies their mandate, publications, annual conference, and educational support to students.

Government of Canada—Seniors Canada On-line
http://www.seniors.gc.ca/index.jsp
Seniors Canada On-line is the Government's response to seniors' request for easy electronic access to seniors-related services.

Government of Canada
http://canada.gc.ca/cdns/indiv_e.html
This site provides access to government information related to Canadians of all ages.

Registered Nurses Association of Ontario—Best Practices Guidelines
http://www.rnao.org/bestpractices/index.asp
This site provides access to the best practice guidelines developed by the Registered Nurses Association of Ontario (RNAO), including their best practice guidelines for "Screening for Delirium, Dementia, and Depression in Older Adults" (November 2003).

SECTION 3

Nature of Nursing Practice

UNIT 1 Professional Practice Knowledge

CHAPTER 22
Critical Thinking

CHAPTER 23
The Nursing Process

CHAPTER 24
Documenting and Reporting

CHAPTER 25
Nursing Informatics

UNIT 2 Professional Practice Skills

CHAPTER 26
Nurse-Patient Relationship

CHAPTER 27
Health Assessment

CHAPTER 28
Medications

CHAPTER 29
Teaching

CHAPTER 30
Leading, Managing, and Influencing Change

CHAPTER 22

Critical Thinking

OBJECTIVES

After completing this chapter, you will be able to:

- Discuss characteristics, skills, and attitudes of critical thinking.
- Identify the elements of critical thinking according to Paul.
- Analyze the relationship among the nursing process, critical thinking, the problem-solving process, and the decision-making process.
- Examine ways of evaluating critical thinking.

Nurses must be **critical thinkers** because of the nature of the discipline and the complexity of their work.

- Nurses are expected to solve client problems by performing critical analysis of the factors associated with a variety of problems. This critical analysis, or *critical thinking*, allows the nurse to make better decisions.
- Creativity in thinking, problem solving, and decision making can enhance the effectiveness of the solutions or decisions made. Thus, critical thinking, problem solving, and decision making are interrelated processes, with creativity enhancing the result.
- Critical thinking is not limited to problem solving or decision making; professional nurses use critical thinking to make reliable observations, draw sound conclusions, create new information and ideas, evaluate lines of reasoning, question prevailing assumptions, and improve their self-knowledge.
- In a position statement on baccalaureate education, the Canadian Association of University Schools of Nursing (CAUSN) promotes and supports the use of critical thinking, thus acknowledging its importance and relevance to the discipline and practice of nursing (CAUSN, 1998).

Critical Thinking

The thinking process that guides nursing practice must be organized, purposeful, and disciplined, rather than random or undirected. Parse describes critical thinking as "carefully choosing a direction in light of personal tacit and explicit knowing" (1996, p. 139). Critical thinking involves calling into question the assumptions that underlie our usual ways of thinking and acting about situations and people and then being prepared to act differently on the basis of this critical questioning (Brookfield, 1987). "Assumptions are the seemingly self-evident rules about reality that we use to help us seek explanations, make judgements, or decide on various actions" (Brookfield, 1987, p. 44). In other words, our assumptions are those unquestioned givens that we take for granted as being self-evident truths. Paul (1988, p. 2–3) describes critical thinking as "the art of thinking about thinking." It is purposeful thinking in which the thinker systematically and habitually imposes criteria and intellectual standards on the thinking. The thinker is aware of and takes charge of the thinking process, guiding it according to the standards (Paul, 1995). "Critical," in this context, does not mean "eager to find fault" but instead "capable of judging carefully and accurately."

Critical thinking is essential to safe, competent, skillful nursing practice (Kataoka-Yahiro & Saylor, 1994). Because of the huge store of knowledge that nurses must use and the continuing rapid growth of this knowledge, nurses cannot be effective practitioners if they attempt to function with only the information acquired in school or outlined in books (Schank, 1990). Reilly and Oermann (1992, p. 217) state that "one cannot think critically about nursing without a basic knowledge of its concepts, theories, and content." As they plan and deliver care, nurses are expected to solve client problems by performing critical analysis of the factors associated with the problems. This critical analysis, or critical thinking, allows the nurse to make better decisions. Decisions that nurses must make about client care and about the distribution of limited resources force them to think and act in areas where there are neither clear answers nor standardized procedures, and where conflicting forces make decisions complex. Nurses, therefore, need to embrace the attitudes that promote critical thinking and master critical-thinking skills in order to process and evaluate both previously learned and new information.

Nurses use their critical-thinking skills in a variety of ways:

- *Nurses use knowledge from other subjects and fields.* Using insight from one subject to shed light on another subject requires critical-thinking skills. Because nurses deal holistically with human responses, they must draw meaningful information from other subject areas (i.e., make multi-disciplinary and interdisciplinary connections) in order to understand the meaning of the client data and plan effective interventions. Nursing students are required to take courses in the biological and social sciences and in the humanities so that they can acquire a strong foundation on which to build their knowledge and skill. For example, the nurse might use knowledge from nutrition, physiology, and physics to promote wound healing and prevent further injury to a client with a pressure ulcer.
- *Nurses deal with change in stressful environments.* Nurses work in rapidly changing situations. Treatments, medications, and technology change constantly, and a client's condition may change from minute to minute. Routine behaviours, therefore, may not be adequate to deal with the situation at hand. Familiarity with the routine for giving medications, for example, does not help the nurse deal with a client who is frightened of injections or with one who does not wish to take a medication. When unexpected situations arise, critical thinking enables the nurse to recognize important cues, respond quickly, and adapt interventions to meet specific client needs.
- *Nurses make important decisions.* During the course of a workday, nurses make vital decisions of many kinds. These decisions often determine the well-being of clients and even their very survival, so it is important that the decisions be sound. Nurses use critical-thinking skills to collect and interpret the information needed to make decisions. Nurses must, for example, use prudent judgement to decide which observations must be

TABLE 22.1 Characteristics of Critical Thinking

Characteristic	Explanation	Example
Rationality and reflection	Critical thinking is based on reasons and evidence, rather than on preference or self-interest. Critical thinkers do not "jump to conclusions." They take the time to collect data, weigh the facts, and think the matter through.	Sarah decided to become a nurse after watching a film in which nurses were shown as attractive and heroic. Michelle, who thinks more critically, asked a counsellor about the job opportunities available for nurses. She also talked to several nurses. After gathering and weighing her facts, Michelle decided to go to nursing school.
Healthy, constructive skepticism	Critical thinkers do not accept or reject ideas unless they understand them. They do not mindlessly follow rules but seek to understand the rationale behind them, following those that make sense and working to improve those that do not.	When a salesperson insisted that a new intravenous tubing was better than that being used on Nurse Mackey's unit, Nurse Mackey asked, "What do you mean by 'better'? What information do you have to show that this is so?"
Autonomy	Critical thinkers are not easily manipulated. They think for themselves, rather than being led by their peer group or passively accepting the beliefs of others.	No one in Lin's family had ever gone beyond high school. Although her sisters did not understand why she wanted to work hard, Lin said, "I've thought it out, and this is what I want to do. I believe it will be worth the effort."
Creative thinking	Critical thinkers create original ideas by finding connections among thoughts and concepts.	Nurse Wilson remembered a song his mother used to sing to him, and he sang it to help comfort a frightened child in the hospital.
Fair thinking	Critical thinking is not biased or one sided. Critical thinkers recognize the bias and prejudice of others' thinking and seek information from all points of view before taking a stand or action.	Nurse Maria Cardinal, the unit manager, needed to make the schedule for the Christmas and New Year's holidays. Before responding to a nurse's request to be off for Christmas, she asked all staff members to submit their preferences. Once she was able to determine that staffing was adequate for both holidays, she responded to the nurse's request.
Focus on what to believe and do	Critical thinking is used to decide on a course of action; make reliable observations; draw sound conclusions; solve problems; and evaluate policies, claims, and actions.	In the previous examples, Lin, Michelle, and Nurse Cardinal decided what to do. Nurse Wilson creatively solved a problem. Nurse Mackey evaluated the salesperson's claim to decide what to believe and, ultimately, what to do.

reported to the physician immediately and which can be noted in the client record for the physician to address later, during the routine visit with the client.

Table 22.1 describes the characteristics of critical thinking.

Creativity—original thinking—is a major component of critical thinking. When nurses incorporate creativity into their thinking, they are able to find unique solutions to unique problems. **Creative thinking** is thinking that results in the development of new ideas and products (Reilly & Oermann, 1992). Creativity in problem solving and decision making is the ability to develop and implement new and better solutions or ideas. "New ideas and creativity are important in nursing because they are at the root of individualized care" (Strader, 1992, p. 243).

Strader (1992) describes four stages in the creative process: preparation, incubation, insight, and verification. During the *preparation stage*, the creative thinker gathers information related to the problem or concern. During the *incubation stage*, the creative thinker unconsciously considers and consciously works on possible solutions or decisions. All possibilities, both old and new, are considered during this phase. Old possibilities may include a creative application of an effective solution used in a previous, similar situation. During the *insight stage*, appropriate solutions emerge and are developed, and the solution

Critical Thinking

Critical thinking may be described as "the art of thinking about thinking." (Paul, 1988, p. 2-3). In other words, the thinker is aware of and assumes charge of the thinking process. Also, it is the ability of individuals to call into question the assumptions that underlie their usual ways of thinking and acting about situations and people and then being prepared to act differently on the basis of this critical questioning (Brookfield, 1987). Critical, in this context, does not mean "eager to find fault" but rather "capable of judging carefully and accurately."

believed to be most appropriate is implemented. Finally, during the *verification stage*, the implemented solution is evaluated for its effectiveness.

During the first three stages, unconscious, intuitive, and creative thinking occur that can result in a unique solution to the problem at hand. Creative thinking is required when the nurse encounters a new situation or a client situation where traditional interventions are not effective. For example, Ned Wong, a pediatric home health nurse, is caring for nine-year-old Pauline, who has ineffective respirations following abdominal surgery. The physician has ordered incentive spirometry (a treatment device that promotes alveolar expansion). Pauline is frightened by the equipment and tires quickly during the treatments. Ned offers Pauline a bottle of blow bubbles and a blowing wand. Pauline is delighted with blowing bubbles. Ned knows that the respiratory effort in blowing bubbles will promote alveolar expansion and suggests that Pauline blow bubbles between incentive spirometry treatments.

Creative thinkers must possess knowledge of the problem. They must have assessed the present problem and be knowledgeable about the underlying facts and principles that apply. For example, in the previous situation, Ned knows the anatomy and physiology of respiratory function and is aware of the purpose of incentive spirometry. He also understands pediatric growth and development. In trying to assist Pauline, he builds on his knowledge and arrives at or derives a creative solution. Strader (1992) describes creative thinkers as:

- Able to generate ideas rapidly
- Flexible and spontaneous; that is, they are able to discard one viewpoint for another or change directions in thinking rapidly and easily
- Able to provide original solutions to problems
- Preferring complex thought processes to simple and easily understood ones
- Independent and self-confident, even when under pressure
- Exhibiting distinct individualism

Examples of Critical Thinking Cognitive Skills

- Critical analysis
- Reasoning inductively
- Reasoning deductively
- Making valid inferences
- Differentiating fact from opinion
- Evaluating the credibility of information sources
- Clarifying concepts
- Recognizing assumptions

Source: Adapted from R. Paul. (1993). *Critical thinking* (p. 129–130). Santa Rosa, CA: Foundation for Critical Thinking and Moral Critique, Sonoma State University.

Skills in Critical Thinking

Complex thinking processes, such as critical analysis, problem solving, and decision making, require the use of cognitive critical-thinking skills. For example, when nurses solve problems they make inferences, differentiate facts from opinions, evaluate the credibility of informational sources, and use a variety of other cognitive skills (see the box above).

Critical analysis involves the use of questions that one can apply to a particular situation or idea to determine essential information and ideas and discard superfluous information and ideas. The questions are *not* sequential steps; rather, they are a set of criteria for judging an idea. Not all questions will need to be applied to every situation, but one needs to be aware of all the questions in order to choose those questions appropriate to a given situation. Socrates (born about 470 B.C.) was a Greek philosopher who developed the Socratic method of question and answer. The box on the following page lists Socratic questions to use in critical analysis. **Socratic questioning** is a technique one can use to look beneath the surface, recognize and examine assumptions, search for inconsistencies, examine multiple points of view, and differentiate what one knows from what one believes. Nurses can employ Socratic questioning when listening to an end-of-shift report, reviewing a history or progress notes, planning care, or discussing a client's care with colleagues.

Two other skills used in complex thinking are inductive and deductive reasoning. In **inductive reasoning,** generalizations are formed from a set of facts or observations. When viewed together, certain bits of information suggest a particular interpretation proceeding from the specific to the general. For example, the nurse who observes that a client has dry skin, poor turgor, sunken eyes, and dark amber urine may make the generalization that the client is dehydrated. **Deductive reasoning,** by

Socratic Questions

Questions about the question (or problem)

- Is this question clear, understandable, and correctly identified?
- Is this question important?
- Could this question be broken down into smaller parts?
- How might ________ state this question?

Questions about assumptions

- You seem to be assuming ________; is that so?
- What could you assume instead? Why?
- Does this assumption always hold true?

Questions about point of view

- You seem to be using the perspective of ________. Why?
- What would someone who disagrees with your perspective say?
- Can you see this any other way?

Questions about evidence and reasons

- What evidence do you have for that?
- Is there any reason to doubt that evidence?
- How do you know?
- What would change your mind?

Questions about implications and consequences

- What effect would that have?
- What is the probability that will actually happen?
- What are the alternatives?
- What are the implications of that?

contrast, is reasoning from the general to the specific. The nurse starts with a conceptual framework—for example, Maslow's hierarchy of needs (see Chapter 5) or a self-care framework—and makes descriptive interpretations of the client's condition in relation to that framework. For example, the nurse who uses the needs framework might categorize data and define the client's problem in terms of elimination, nutrition, or protection needs.

In a more simplistic example, inductive reasoning is like looking at the pieces of a jigsaw puzzle and attempting to describe the whole (without seeing a picture of the completed puzzle). As the puzzler puts more and more pieces together, the whole picture becomes clearer. In deductive reasoning, the puzzler sees the whole picture (from the puzzle box cover) and puts the puzzle together by organizing the pieces into border pieces, or colours, or some other grouping.

By using critical thinking, the nurse also differentiates facts, inferences, judgements, and opinions (see Table 22.2).

Attitudes that Foster Critical Thinking

Certain attitudes are crucial to critical thinking. These *affective* dimensions are based on the assumption that a rational person is motivated to develop, learn, and grow. A critical thinker, according to Paul (1995), works to develop the following attitudes: independence of thought, fair-mindedness, insight into egocentricity and sociocentricity, intellectual humility and suspension of judgement, intellectual courage, integrity, perseverance, confidence in reason, interest in exploring both thoughts underlying feeling and feelings underlying thoughts, and curiosity.

TABLE 22.2 Differentiating Types of Statements

Statement	Description	Example
Facts	Can be corroborated through investigation	Blood pressure is affected by blood volume.
Inferences	Conclusions drawn from the facts, going beyond facts to make a statement about something not currently known	If blood volume is decreased (e.g., in hemorrhagic shock), the blood pressure will drop.
Judgements	Evaluation of facts or information that reflect values or other criteria; a type of opinion	It is harmful to the client's health if the blood pressure drops too low.
Opinions	Beliefs formed over time and include judgements that may fit facts or be in error	Nursing intervention can assist in maintaining the client's blood pressure within normal limits.

In addition to these attitudes, critical thinkers also reflect an attitude of contextual awareness, or the ability to take into account the specific circumstances or contexts of the different situations and people encountered.

Independence of Thought

Critical thinking requires that individuals think for themselves. People acquire many beliefs in their childhood, not necessarily based on reason but in order to have an explanation they can comprehend or because there are rational reasons for believing, but because there may have been rewards for believing or because they do not question authorities promoting the beliefs. As they mature and acquire knowledge and experience, critical thinkers examine their beliefs and assumptions in light of new evidence. Critical thinkers consider seriously a wide range of ideas, learn from them, and then make their own judgements about them.

Fair-Mindedness

Critical thinkers are fair minded, assessing all viewpoints with the same standards and not basing their judgements on personal or group bias or prejudice. Fair-mindedness helps one to consider opposing points of view and try to understand new ideas fully before rejecting or accepting them. Early educational reformer Carl Rogers (1969) proposed that one is not truly communicating with another person unless one allows the possibility that the other person may change one's own mind. The same applies to evidence: Critical thinkers strive to be open to the possibility that new evidence or information could change their minds.

Insight into Egocentricity and Sociocentricity

Critical thinkers are open to the possibility that their personal biases or social pressures and customs could unduly affect their thinking. They actively try to examine their own biases and bring them to awareness each time they think or make a decision. For example, a nurse spent extensive time trying to teach a client how to prevent a future recurrence of some problem but was mystified when the client appeared uninterested and did not follow the nurse's advice. The nurse's egocentric tendency to assume that all clients would be motivated and interested in preventive care (just because the nurse was) resulted in inaccurate assessment of the client's desire to learn; both the nurse's and the client's time was wasted. Had the nurse assessed the client's cultural background and beliefs about what caused the disease (that is, had the nurse collected sufficient evidence), the nurse might have identified a more relevant problem and developed a better care plan.

Intellectual Humility and Suspension of Judgement

Intellectual humility means having an awareness of the limits of one's own knowledge. Critical thinkers are willing to admit what they do not know; they are willing to seek new information and to rethink their conclusions in light of new knowledge. They never assume that what everybody knows to be right will always be right, because new evidence may emerge. This particularly applies to what appears to be confirmed "knowledge."

Intellectual Courage

With an attitude of courage, one is willing to consider and examine fairly one's own ideas or views, especially those to which one may have a strongly negative reaction. This type of courage comes from recognizing that beliefs or assumptions are sometimes false or misleading. Values, assumptions, and beliefs are not always acquired "rationally." (Values are discussed in Chapter 7.) Rational beliefs are those which have been examined and found to be supported by solid reasons and data. After such examination, it is inevitable that some ideas previously held to be true may be found to contain questionable elements and that some truth may emerge from ideas considered dangerous or false. Courage is needed to be true to new thinking in such cases, especially if social penalties for nonconformity are severe.

Integrity

Intellectual integrity requires that individuals apply the same rigorous standards of proof to their own knowledge and beliefs as they apply to the knowledge and beliefs of others. Critical thinkers question their own knowledge and beliefs or assumptions as quickly and thoroughly as they challenge those of another. They are readily able to admit and evaluate inconsistencies within their own beliefs and between their own beliefs and those of another.

Perseverance

Nurses who are critical thinkers show perseverance in seeking effective solutions to client and nursing problems. This determination enables them to clarify concepts and sort out related issues, in spite of difficulties and frustrations. Confusion and frustration are uncomfortable, but critical thinkers resist the temptation to find a quick and easy answer. Important questions tend to be complex and confusing and, therefore, often require a great deal of thought and research. An example is the temptation for a committee to come to a hasty conclusion on a complex issue.

Confidence in Reason

Critical thinkers believe that well-reasoned thinking will lead to trustworthy conclusions. Therefore, they cultivate an attitude of confidence in the reasoning process and examine emotion-laden arguments using the standards for evaluating thought, by asking questions such as, Is that argument fair? Is it based on sufficient evidence? and so on. The critical thinker develops skill in both inductive reasoning (forming generalizations from a set of facts or observations) and deductive reasoning (starting with a generalization and moving to specifics). As a critical thinker gains greater awareness of the thinking process and more experience in improving such thinking, confidence in the thinking process will grow. This confident thinker will not be afraid of disagreement and, indeed, will be concerned when all agree too quickly. Such an individual can serve as a role model to colleagues, inspiring and encouraging them to think critically as well.

Interest in Exploring Both Thoughts and Feelings

A critical thinker knows that emotions can influence thinking and that feelings often underlie thoughts. The rational, critical thinker adopts the attitude that feelings are real and need to be acknowledged. However, feelings need to be explored to determine whether they are based on reality or childhood interpretations, memories, or fears. Nurses need to identify, examine, and control or modify feelings that are interfering with clear critical thinking. To deal with strong negative emotion, the nurse can take these steps:

1. Limit action for a while to avoid hasty conclusions and impulsive decisions.
2. Discuss negative feelings with a confidant.
3. Expend some of the energy generated by the emotion by, for example, walking or exercising.
4. Reflect on the situation and determine whether the emotional response was appropriate. After the strong emotion has dissipated, the nurse can then objectively move toward needed conclusions or make required decisions.

Curiosity

The internal conversation going on within the mind of a critical thinker is filled with questions: Why do we believe this? What causes that? Does it have to be this way? Could something else work? What would happen if we did it another way? Who says that is so? The curious individual may value tradition but is not afraid to examine traditions to be sure they are still valid.

Contextual Awareness

While critical thinking is a rational process, it also entails a contextual dimension in which personal assumptions and actions are questioned within particular contexts. *Context* may be described as the unique experiences that individuals or clients bring with them to their specific situations or circumstances. Being conscious of context can be called *contextual awareness*. *Assumptions* are those unquestioned givens that we take for granted as being self-evident truths about others or situations that we encounter.

An important aspect of identifying and challenging assumptions is recognizing the significance of understanding the context within which assumptions and their subsequent actions result (Brookfield, 1987). Routinely, individuals encounter new or entirely different situations and/or people from themselves or their experiences, and the natural tendency is to rely on the values, beliefs, and assumptions derived from their own personal experiences. The ability to be able to deal rationally with such situations is, therefore, not always straightforward. In other words, if critical thinking is to be effective, it is also necessary to develop an awareness of the context or uniqueness of the people or situations encountered. Such awareness, for example, is apparent when individuals are able to acknowledge or recognize their own personal assumptions about another person or situation when dealing with that person in a particular context (Brookfield, 1987). For example, the client is not *only* a client but may also be a mother, a father, a sister, a brother, a secretary, a businessperson, a homemaker, and so on—someone who brings to the client role personal life stories and experiences that are frequently far removed from their current situation. The client's situation or circumstance could be one that is quite different from that of the nurse's own life experiences. Without contextual awareness, such a difference could be misunderstood and result in the creation of a barrier between the nurse and the client. In such a situation, for critical thinking to be effective, nurses need to be contextually aware and challenge their own assumptions and their taken-for-granted values, ideas, and stereotypical notions which cause them to respond or react in particular ways to clients and their unique situations. It is through such a process that nurses can provide individualized client care. See the box regarding Contextual Awareness for a clinical exemplar.

Elements and Standards of Critical Thinking

The critical thinker considers the elements of reasoning shown in Figure 22.1 (Paul, 1994b). These elements may be considered in any order and, therefore, are presented in a circular scheme. The relationship of Paul's elements of reasoning to the nursing process is shown in Table 22.3.

How can one know whether one's thinking is critical thinking? Paul (1995) proposes that thinkers can use universal standards, shown in the box on page 379, to assess

> **Contextual Awareness**
>
> Carmel is a 50-year-old Caucasian woman admitted to the nursing unit with a diagnosis of severe malnutrition and atopic dermatitis and is in acute alcohol withdrawal. Carmel's demeanour is combative, and at times, she is verbally abusive when she is responding to the nurse. Upon assessment, it becomes evident that Carmel is a drug addict as evidenced by the needle track marks on her arms, legs, abdomen, and neck. She has several open sores on her arms and legs that are draining with purulent exudate. Her clothes are dirty. She is missing most of her teeth, and she has body and head lice which the nurse must deal with immediately. In this particular situation or context, the nurse demonstrates contextual awareness by asking questions such as: What assumptions am I making about Carmel and her particular circumstances? What are my taken-for-granted beliefs about her as a person? Why do I think in this particular way? After all, I don't know Carmel. What is it that I would have to believe to allow me to make these assumptions about her? In other words, what is at the root of these assumptions that I instinctively make?

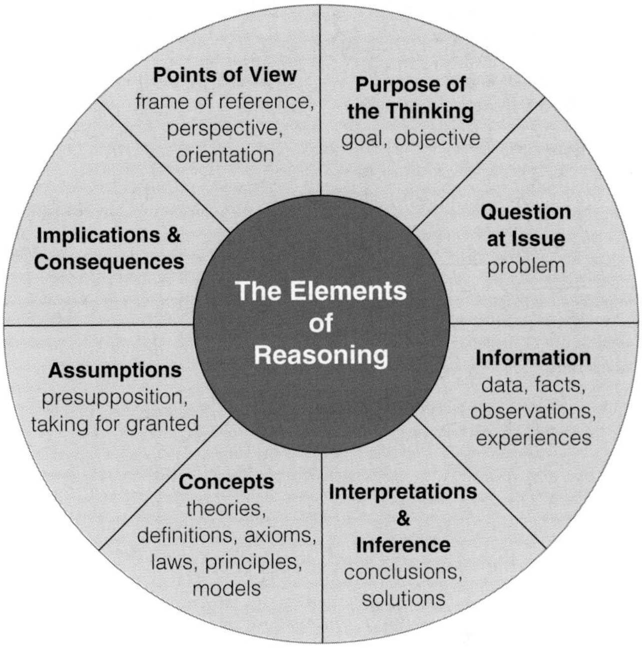

Figure 22.1 The elements of reasoning

Source: R. Paul. (1994). *Critical Thinking Workshops* (p. 111). Santa Rosa, CA: Foundation for Critical Thinking. Reprinted with permission.

reasoning. Explicitly stating the standards for critical thinking promotes the reliability and validity of the thinking and, thus, makes appropriate action more likely.

Applying Critical Thinking to Nursing Practice

Nurses function effectively some part of every day without thinking critically. Many small decisions are based primarily on habit with minimal thinking involved; examples include selecting what clothes to wear, choosing which route to take to work, and deciding what to eat for lunch. Psychomotor skills in nursing often involve minimal thinking, such as operating a familiar piece of equipment. But the higher-order skills of critical thinking are put into play as soon as a new idea or situation is encountered or a less-than-routine decision must be made. When setting priorities for the day, a nurse employs critical thinking. When assessing a client, identifying potential and actual problems, and moving through the nursing process, the nurse uses critical thinking at each stage of the process. When analyzing a situation and planning strategies for conflict resolution or change, the nurse manager needs critical-thinking attitudes and skills. The nurse clinician and nurse manager seek to be aware of their thinking while they are thinking, as they apply standards for thinking, and as their thinking progresses.

> **Standards for Critical Thinkers**
>
> - Explore thinking that underlies emotions and feelings.
> - Suspend judgement when there are insufficient data.
> - Develop criteria for evaluation and apply them fairly and accurately.
> - Evaluate the credibility of sources used to justify beliefs.
> - Make interdisciplinary connections and use insights from one subject or experience to illuminate and correct other subjects.
> - Differentiate facts from opinions.
> - Examine assumptions that underlie thoughts and behaviour.
> - Distinguish relevant from irrelevant data and important from trivial data.
> - Make plausible inferences and distinguish conclusions from the reasoning that supports them.
>
> **Source:** Adapted from R. Paul. (1988). "What, Then, Is Critical Thinking?" from the Eighth Annual and Sixth International Conference on Critical Thinking and Educational Reform. Rohnert Park, CA: Center for Critical Thinking and Moral Critique, Sonoma State University.

TABLE 22.3 Relationship of Paul's Elements of Reasoning to the Nursing Process

Paul's Element of Reasoning	Parallels to the Nursing Process	Clinical Application
Information	Assessing	*Data:* A 45-year-old man of First Nations' ancestry complains of severe headache; 9 kg overweight; blood pressure 180/96 mm Hg. States he has been taking high blood pressure pills only when he has a headache. Is employed as a maintenance worker; lives with wife, mother-in-law, and four children. Given these data, a critical thinker is aware that more data must be obtained about the client's cultural health values and reasons for stated behaviour. Failure to think critically and to obtain additional data leads to inaccurate goals, diagnosis, and interventions.
Purpose of thinking	Goal setting	*Goal:* To increase client's receptivity to taking medication in order to relieve headaches and prevent a cerebrovascular accident (CVA). Thinking critically, a nurse will, in addition, try to determine the client's goals and to agree to mutual goals.
Question at issue	Diagnosing	A critical thinker will defer identifying the client's diagnosis until more data are obtained and the client's priorities are known. This process will serve to prevent a premature diagnosis based on insufficient data.
Points of view		As a critical thinker, the nurse is aware that the client's point of view may differ from the nurse's. Although the nurse may support a certain medical belief system that puts high priority on preventing disease, the critical thinker is also aware that the client may hold other views of health and illness, therapy, and preventive measures.
Interpretation and inference (conclusions and recommendations)	Diagnosing	The critical thinker recognizes that the client's erratic use of the prescribed medication may have multiple causes (e.g., troublesome side effects, belief that illness is out of one's personal control, and preferred method of taking the medication may differ from the prescribed method) and will not infer a diagnosis with etiology until more data are obtained. Failure to think critically can lead to interpretations that are irrelevant, inadequate, and superficial (e.g., an erroneous interpretation that the client's problem is lack of sufficient knowledge).
Assumptions (presuppositions)		The critical thinker makes assumptions in accordance with a broad database and *mutually* set client goals. The critical thinker avoids making unverified assumptions, such as that an increase in knowledge will increase this client's compliance, or that this client is motivated to prevent a CVA.
Concepts (theories, laws, principles, models)	Diagnosing Planning	The critical thinker uses concepts about motivation, change theory, and multicultural nursing to understand the client's behaviour and motivation to change. Failure to think critically can lead to the exclusive reliance on a simplistic concept, such as "knowledge creates change."
Implications and consequences	Planning Implementing	The critical thinker considers the implications and consequences of selected nursing strategies before implementing plans of care. Plans of care, including goals and outcomes, are based on ongoing assessment of the client's cultural values, beliefs, and needs. Failure to think critically may lead to ineffective interventions, such as client teaching that focuses *only* on resolving a knowledge deficit about the prescribed medication. The critical thinker recognizes that a knowledge deficit may or may not be one of several problems.
Interpretation and inference	Evaluating	The critical thinker bases evaluation of client outcomes and the effectiveness of nursing interventions on well-developed criteria and considers whether outcomes have been validated. Failure to think critically may contribute to a lack of change in client behaviour and an inference that the client did not learn effectively and needs further instruction.

Problem Solving

Nurses use critical thinking to resolve problems related to direct client care. Nurse managers use critical thinking to resolve problems related to overall client care, unit administration, and staff interpersonal issues (see Chapter 28). Strader (1992, p. 228) defines **problem solving** as "the process used when a gap is perceived between an existing state (what *is* occurring) and a desired state (what *should be* occurring)." In problem solving, the nurse obtains information that clarifies the nature of the problem and suggests possible solutions. The nurse then carefully evaluates the possible solutions and chooses the best one to implement. The situation is carefully monitored over time to ensure its initial and continued effectiveness. The nurse does not discard the other solutions but holds them in reserve in the event that the first solution is not effective. The nurse may also encounter a similar problem in a different client situation where an alternative solution is determined to be the most effective. Therefore, problem solving for one situation contributes to the nurse's body of knowledge for problem solving in similar situations.

There are various approaches to problem solving. Five of the most commonly used are trial and error, intuition, the nursing process, the scientific method or research process, and the modified scientific method.

Trial and Error

One way to solve problems is through trial and error, in which a number of approaches are tried until a solution is found. Without considering alternatives systematically, however, one cannot know why the solution works. Trial-and-error methods in nursing care can be dangerous because the client might suffer harm if an approach is inappropriate.

Intuition

Intuition as a problem-solving method has not been considered either sound or legitimate. Rather, it has been viewed as a form of guessing and, as such, an inappropriate basis for nursing decisions. According to Benner and Tanner (1987), however, intuition is an essential and legitimate aspect of clinical judgement acquired through knowledge and experience. The nurse must first have the knowledge base necessary to practise in the clinical area and then use that knowledge in clinical practice. Clinical experience allows the nurse to recognize cues and patterns and begin to make correct decisions. In other words, nurses develop expertise in a specialty area, such as cardiovascular nursing, through continuous and meaningful exposure to clients who have experienced cardiovascular problems.

Experience is important in improving intuition because the rapidity of the judgement depends on the nurse having seen similar client situations many times before. Sometimes, nurses use the words "I had a feeling" to describe a leap (or a condensing) in the critical-thinking element of considering evidence. These nurses are able to judge quickly and decisively which evidence is most important and to act upon that limited evidence.

The reliability of intuitive decision making increases as the nurse gains experience in the clinical application of theory.

Nursing Process

The nursing process is the systematic method of assessing, planning, providing, and evaluating nursing care. Critical thinking is used throughout the nursing process. (See Chapter 23.)

Scientific Method and the Research Process

The research process, discussed in Chapter 3, is a formalized, logical, systematic approach to solving problems. The classic scientific method is most useful when the researcher is working in a controlled situation. Health professionals require a modified approach of the scientific method for solving problems, in both the nursing process and the medical process.

Table 22.4 compares the research process, or scientific method, with the modified scientific method. Critical thinking is important in all problem-solving processes as the nurse evaluates all potential solutions to a given problem and makes a decision to select the most appropriate solution for that situation.

TABLE 22.4 Comparison between the Research Process and the Modified Scientific Method

Research Process (Scientific Method)	Modified Scientific Method
State a research question or problem.	Define the problem.
Define the purpose of or the rationale for the study.	
Review related literature.	Gather information.
Formulate hypotheses and define variables.	Analyze the information.
Select a method to test hypotheses.	Develop solutions.
Select a population, sample, and setting.	
Conduct a pilot study.	Make a decision.
Collect the data.	Implement the decision.
Analyze the data.	Evaluate the decision.
Communicate conclusions and implications.	

Decision Making

Tschikota (1993, p. 389) states that "effective clinical decision making is critical to the future of professional nursing practice." Nurses make decisions in the course of solving problems, for example, in each step of the nursing process. Decision making, however, is also used in situations that do not involve problem solving. Nurses make value decisions (e.g., to keep client information confidential); time management decisions (e.g., taking clean linens to the client's room at the same time as the medication in order to save steps); scheduling decisions (e.g., to bathe the client before visiting hours); and priority decisions (e.g., which interventions are most urgent and which can be delegated).

Decision making is a critical-thinking process for choosing the best actions to meet a desired goal. **Decision making** is defined by Strader (1992, p. 233) as "the process of establishing criteria by which alternative courses of action are developed and selected." Decisions must be made whenever there are several mutually exclusive choices. For example, the individual who wishes to become a nurse in Canada can choose from many different university programs throughout the country. In order to make an appropriate decision, a prospective student must evaluate the different programs, as well as consider personal circumstances. Prospective students must make choices. Therefore, they must evaluate the different programs, as well as personal circumstances, to make a decision appropriate to their situation.

Nurses must make decisions and assist clients to make decisions. When faced with several clients' needs at the same time, the nurse must decide which client to assist first. When a client is trying to make a decision about what course of treatment to follow, the nurse may need to provide information or resources the client can use in making a decision. Nurses must make decisions in their own personal and professional lives. For example, the nurse must decide whether to work in a hospital or community setting.

Strader (1992) describes a seven-step decision-making process:

1. *Identify the purpose.* In this step, the nurse identifies why a decision is needed and what needs to be determined.
2. *Set the criteria.* When the nurse sets the criteria for decision making, three questions must be answered: what needs to be achieved, what needs to be preserved, and what needs to be avoided. For example, for a client with pain, the criteria would be as follows:
   a. What needs to be achieved? Relief of pain
   b. What needs to be preserved? Physical functioning, cognitive functioning, psychological functioning, client comfort
   c. What needs to be avoided? Central nervous system depression, respiratory depression, nausea
3. *Weight the criteria.* In this step, the decision maker sets priorities or ranks activities or services in order of importance from least important to most important as they relate to the specific situation. Because the weighting is specific to the situation, an activity may be ranked as most important in one situation and of less importance in another situation.
4. *Seek alternatives.* After establishing and weighting the criteria in the previous steps, the decision maker identifies all possible ways to meet the criteria. In clinical situations, the alternatives may be selected from a range of nursing interventions or client-care strategies.
5. *Test alternatives.* The nurse analyzes the alternatives to ensure that there is an objective rationale in relation to the established criteria for choosing one strategy over another.
6. *Troubleshoot.* In troubleshooting, the nurse tries to determine what might go wrong as a result of a decision and develops plans to prevent, minimize, or overcome any problems.
7. *Evaluate the action.* In evaluating the strategies used, the nurse determines how effective they were and whether they achieved the initial purpose.

The decision-making process and the nursing process share similarities. The nurse uses decision making in all steps of the nursing process. Table 22.5 compares the steps of these processes.

Developing Critical-Thinking Attitudes and Skills

After gaining an idea of what it means to think critically, solve problems, and make decisions, nurses need to become aware of their own thinking style and abilities. Acquiring critical-thinking skills and a critical attitude then becomes a matter of practice. Critical thinking is not an "either/or" phenomenon; people develop and use it more or less effectively along a continuum. Some people make better evaluations than others; some people believe information from nearly any source; and still others seldom believe anything without carefully evaluating the credibility of the information. Critical thinking is not easy. Solving problems and making decisions is risky. Sometimes, the outcome is not what was desired. With effort, however, everyone can achieve some level of critical thinking to become an effective problem solver and decision maker.

Self-Assessment

The nurse should reflect on some of the attitudes discussed earlier that facilitate critical thinking, attitudes such as curiosity, fair-mindedness, humility, courage, perseverance, and contextual awareness. A nurse might benefit from a rigorous personal assessment to determine which attitudes he or she already possesses and which need to be

RESEARCH NOTE

How Do Nurses Make Clinical Decisions?

Nurses use the clinical decision-making process to gather information, evaluate it, and make a judgement that results in the provision of client care. In one study, researchers sought to increase understanding of the clinical decision making of nurse practitioners. The sample consisted of 27 nurse practitioners, including six obstetric/gynecologic nurse practitioners and 11 inexperienced family nurse practitioners. All subjects cared for the same computer-simulated client whose case history, physical examination, and laboratory findings were based on an actual client with a vaginal discharge and genital rash. The computer ran interactively with videotape, making some client responses, physical examination findings, and laboratory findings visible. Because the simulation allowed for natural language entry, the nurse practitioners were able to interview the client by typing questions in their own words. Objective data were requested by the same process.

Findings indicated that all three groups used a process of clinical decision making in which diagnostic hypotheses helped them decide what data to collect. However, the nurse groups differed in their final diagnoses and in subsequent care decisions. The obstetric/gynecologic nurse practitioners tended to develop lists of diagnostic hypotheses reflecting the client's chief complaint. In contrast, the experienced and inexperienced family nurse practitioners tended to acquire subjective and objective data that did not appear to be hypothesis driven. The clinical decision-making process used by the obstetric/gynecologic nurse practitioners was more likely to result in correct diagnoses and more appropriate care decisions. The authors say these findings confirm the idea that the two processes—namely, deciding what information to acquire and then deciding on the intervention—probably rely on different bodies of knowledge. Data acquisition (the approach favoured by the family nurse practitioners) is process related, whereas diagnosis and management (the approach favoured by the obstetric/gynecologic nurse practitioners) are content related.

Implications: These findings suggest that expertise in an area chiefly reflects an understanding of the significance of the data acquired, which aids in making the correct diagnosis.

Source: J. E. White, D. G. Nativio, S. N. Kobert, & S. J. Engberg (1992, Summer). Content and process in clinical decision-Making by Nurse Practitioners. *Image: Journal of Nursing Scholarship, 24*(2), 153–158.

cultivated. This could also be done with a partner or as a group. The nurse first determines which attitudes are held strongly and form a base for thinking and which are held minimally or not at all. The nurse also needs to reflect on situations where he or she made decisions that were later regretted and to analyze thinking processes and attitudes, or ask a trusted colleague to assess them. Identifying weak or vulnerable skills and attitudes is also important.

TABLE 22.5 Comparison between the Nursing Process and the Decision-Making Process

Nursing Process	Decision-Making Process*
Assess	Identify the purpose
Diagnose	
Plan	Set the criteria
	Weight the criteria
	Seek alternatives
Implement	Test alternatives
	Troubleshoot
Evaluate	Evaluate the action

*The decision-making process parallels the nursing process but is also used during each step of the process.

Tolerating Dissonance and Ambiguity

The nurse needs to take deliberate efforts to cultivate critical-thinking attitudes. For example, to develop fair-mindedness, one could deliberately seek out information that is in opposition to one's own views; this provides practice in understanding and learning to be open to other viewpoints. It is a human tendency to seek out information that corresponds to one's previously held beliefs and to ignore evidence that may contradict cherished ideas. Nurses should increase their tolerance for ideas that contradict previously held beliefs, and they should practise suspending judgement.

Suspending judgement means tolerating ambiguity for a time. If an issue is complex, it may not be resolved quickly or neatly, and judgement should be postponed. For a while, the nurse will need to say, "I don't know" and be comfortable with that answer until more is known. Although postponing judgement may not be feasible in emergency situations, where fast action is required, it is usually feasible in other situations.

Canadian Society Notes

Fact	Implications for Nursing Practice
One of the defining characteristics of Canadian society is its focus on the notion of multiculturalism. A complex phenomenon, multiculturalism may be defined as "an official doctrine and corresponding set of policies and practices in which ethno-racial differences are formally promoted and incorporated as an integral component of the political, social, and symbolic order" (Fleras & Elliott, 1992, p. 22).	Critical thinking affords individuals the ability to be able to call into question the assumptions that underlie their usual ways of thinking and acting about real and perceived differences and then being prepared to act differently on the basis of this critical questioning (Brookfield, 1987).
In Canada, such a policy promotes a climate of tolerance and acceptance of individuals who are culturally and ethnically different.	Preceptors and/or clinical instructors enable nursing students to think critically through their role modelling, facilitating, guiding, and prioritizing behaviours (Myrick, 2002; Myrick & Yonge, 2002).

Seeking Situations Where Good Thinking Is Practised

Nurses will find it valuable to attend conferences in clinical or educational settings that support open examination of all sides of issues and respect opposing viewpoints. Cultivating a questioning attitude, using either Socratic questioning or another technique, is vital. Nurses need to review the standards for evaluating thinking and apply them to their own thinking. If nurses are aware of their own thinking and assumptions—while they are doing the thinking (metacognition)—they can detect thinking errors.

Creating Environments that Support Critical Thinking

A nurse cannot develop or maintain critical-thinking attitudes in a vacuum. Nurses in leadership positions must be particularly aware of the climate for thinking that they establish, and they must actively create a stimulating environment that encourages differences of opinion and fair examination of ideas and options. As leaders, nurses should encourage colleagues to examine evidence carefully before they come to conclusions, and to avoid "group think," the tendency to defer unthinkingly to the will of the group.

FOCUS ON CRITICAL THINKING

Critical thinking has many definitions. As both a student and a registered nurse, it is important to familiarize yourself with the characteristics of critical thinking and to develop critical thinking attitudes, knowledge, and skills. The implication is that you will be a more informed and safer practitioner.

1. Compare and contrast critical thinking in nursing with critical thinking in daily life situations.
2. How does your level of nursing knowledge and experience influence your ability to think critically in the clinical setting?

See Appendix A for answers to these questions.

CHAPTER HIGHLIGHTS

- Nurses need critical-thinking skills and attitudes to be safe, competent, skillful practitioners. Critical thinking is a purposeful mental activity in which ideas are produced and evaluated and judgements made.
- Critical thinking is reasonable, rational, reflective, autonomous, creative, and fair and inspires an attitude of inquiry that focuses on deciding what to believe or do.
- Critical thinkers have certain attitudes: independence of thought, humility, courage, integrity, perseverance, empathy, and fair-mindedness.
- Nurses use critical thinking as they apply knowledge from other subjects and fields to nursing practice, deal with change in stressful environments, and make important decisions related to client care. When nurses incorporate creativity into their thinking, they are able to find unique solutions to unique problems.
- Critical thinking consists of high-level cognitive processes that include problem solving and decision making. There are several problem-solving methods: trial and error, intuition, the nursing process, the scientific method, and the modified scientific method. Nurses use the scientific method or research process when they participate in nursing and health research.
- Elements of reasoning, according to Paul, include purpose of thinking, question at issue, information, interpretation and inference, concepts, assumptions, implications and consequences, and points of view. Critical thinkers consider these elements when solving problems and making decisions.
- If critical thinking is to be effective, it is also necessary to develop an awareness of one's own personal assumptions as well as the context of people or situations encountered. Such awareness is apparent when nurses recognize their own personal assumptions about a client or situation in a particular context (Brookfield, 1987). Nurses need to be contextually aware and challenge their own assumptions and their taken-for-granted values, ideas, and stereotypical notions which cause them to respond or react in particular ways to clients and their individual situations.
- The nursing process and critical thinking are interrelated and interdependent, but they are not identical. Both involve problem solving, decision making, and creativity.
- Decisions must be made whenever several mutually exclusive choices exist. Nurses must make decisions in both their personal and professional lives. The steps of the decision-making process include identifying the purpose of the decision, setting the criteria, weighting the criteria, seeking alternatives, testing alternatives, troubleshooting, and evaluating the action.
- Everyone has at least some level of critical-thinking skill, and that skill can be developed with practice. Some guidelines to enhance critical-thinking skills and attitudes include performing a self-assessment, tolerating dissonance and ambiguity, seeking situations where good thinking is productive, creating environments that support critical thinking, and practising and applying standards to one's thinking.

READINGS AND REFERENCES

Suggested Readings

Bandman, E. L., & Bandman, B. (1995). *Critical thinking in nursing* (2nd ed.). Norwalk, CT: Appleton & Lange.
This book addresses critical thinking and applies it to nursing. Three major sections address practical reasoning, deductive reasoning, and inductive reasoning in nursing.

Brookfield, S. D. (1987). *Developing critical thinking. Challenging adults to explore alternative ways of thinking and acting* (pp. 15–34). San Francisco, CA: Jossey-Bass.

Kennison, M., & Brace, J. (1997). Digging deeper for creative solutions. *Nursing 97, 27,* 52–54.
The authors point out that when a nurse analyzes a complex situation and makes an appropriate decision, the nurse uses critical thinking. They offer suggestions on how to improve critical-thinking skills. Several situations with clients are included together with critical-thinking analyses.

Kyzer, S. P. (1996, November/December). Professional development initiative. Sharpening your critical thinking skills. *Orthopaedic Nursing, 15*(6), 66–75.
Kyzer emphasizes the need for critical thinking in the current environment of constant and rapid change in health care. She presents two models: the Practitioner Model and the Organization Model. The Practitioner Model illustrates that one's ability to think critically is a combination of skills, thinking strategies, attitudes, and the person's foundations (experience and knowledge). The Organization Model illustrates that in addition to the practitioner's abilities, support or barriers may be provided to help or hinder the practitioner's development and use of critical thinking. Three tables provide examples of "Lack of Critical Thinking," "Barriers and Supports" [to critical thinking], and "Strategies for Improving Critical Thinking."

Related Research

Tschikota, S. (1993). The clinical decision making process of student nurses. *Journal of Nursing Education, 32*, 389–398.

Selected References

Bandman, E. L., & Bandman, B. (1995). *Critical thinking in nursing* (2nd ed.). Norwalk, CT: Appleton & Lange.

Benner, P., & Tanner, C. (1987, January). How expert nurses use intuition. *American Journal of Nursing, 87*, 23–31.

Brookfield, S. D. (1987). Developing critical thinking. *Challenging adults to explore alternative ways of thinking and acting* (pp. 15–34). San Francisco, CA: Jossey-Bass.

Canadian Association of University Schools of Nursing (CAUSN). (1998). *Position paper on baccalaureate education.* Ottawa: CAUSN.

Kataoka-Yahiro, M. K., & Saylor, C. (1994). A critical thinking model for nursing judgment. *Journal of Nursing Education, 33*(8), 351–355.

McAllister, M., & Ryan, M. (1995). Feminist pedagogy: Developing creative approaches for teaching students of nursing. *Journal of Nursing Education, 34*(5), 243–245.

Miller, M. A., & Babcock, D. E. (1996). *Critical thinking applied to nursing.* St. Louis, MO: Mosby.

Mitchell, G. J. (1995). Reflection: The key to breaking with tradition. *Nursing Science Quarterly, 8*, 2, 57.

Myrick, F. (2002). Preceptorship and critical thinking in nursing education. *The Journal of Nursing Education, 41*(4), 1–11.

Myrick, F., & Yonge, O. (2001). Creating a climate for critical thinking in the preceptorship experience. *Nurse Education Today, 21*, 461–467.

Myrick, F., & Yonge, O. (2002). Preceptor behaviors integral to the promotion of student critical thinking. *Journal of Nurses in Staff Development, 18*(3), 1–7.

National League for Nursing. (1992). *Criteria for the evaluation of baccalaureate and higher degree programs in nursing* (5th ed.). New York: Author.

Nicoteri, J. A. (1998). Critical thinking skills. *American Journal of Nursing, 98*(10), 62, 64.

Parse, R. R. (1996). Critical thinking: What is it? *Nursing Science Quarterly, 9*(4), 139.

Paul, R. W. (1985, May). Bloom's taxonomy and critical thinking instruction. *Educational Leadership*, 36–39.

Paul, R. W. (1988). What, then, is critical thinking? From the Eighth Annual and Sixth International Conference on Critical Thinking and Educational Reform. Rohnert Park, CA: Center for Critical Thinking and Moral Critique, Sonoma State University.

Paul, R. W. (1990). *Critical thinking.* Rohnert Park, CA: Sonoma State University.

Paul, R. W. (1994a). Overcoming the addiction to coverage. *Educational Visions, 2*(1), 11.

Paul, R. W. (1994b). *Critical thinking workshops* (manual). Rohnert Park, CA: Center for Critical Thinking and Moral Critique, Sonoma State University.

Paul, R. W. (1995). *Critical thinking: How to prepare students for a rapidly changing world.* Santa Rosa, CA: Foundation for Critical Thinking.

Reilly, D. E., & Oermann, M. H. (1992). Cognitive learning in the clinical setting. In *Clinical teaching in nursing education* (2nd ed.). (pp. 207–246). New York: National League for Nursing.

Rogers, C. R. (1969). *Freedom to learn.* Columbus, OH: Charles E. Merrill.

Rubenfeld, M. G., & Scheffer, B. K. (1995). *Critical thinking in nursing: An interactive approach.* Philadelphia, PA: Lippincott.

Schaefer, J. (1974, October). The interrelatedness of decision making and the nursing process. *American Journal of Nursing, 74*, 1852–1855.

Schank, M. J. (1990). Wanted: Nurses with critical thinking skills. *Journal of Continuing Education in Nursing, 21*(2), 86–89.

Sloane, P., & MacHale, D. (1995). *Improve your lateral thinking.* New York: Sterling.

Strader, M. (1992). Critical thinking. In E. J. Sullivan & P. J. Decker (Eds.), *Effective management in nursing* (3rd ed.). (pp. 225–248). Redwood City, CA: Addison-Wesley Nursing.

von Oech, R. (1990). *A whack on the side of the head: How you can be more creative.* New York: Warner.

West, T. G. (1979). *Plato's apology of Socrates: An interpretation, with a new translation.* Ithaca, NY: Cornell University Press.

WEBLINKS

Falcione, P. Critical Thinking: What It Is and Why It Counts
http://www.calpress.com/pdf_files/what&why.pdf
This article provides an excellent overview of critical thinking.

Critical Thinking Across the Continuum Project
http://www.kcmetro.cc.mo.us/longview/ctac/corenotes.htm
This site was established by Longview Community College in the United States. The authors discuss concepts critical to the process of critical thinking. This site also provides access to other resources on critical thinking.

Critical Thinking on the Web
http://www.philosophy.unimelb.edu.au/reason/critical/pages/nursing.html
This nursing specific site is one component of a large Web site of resources related to critical thinking, and includes such topics as how to read a paper.

CHAPTER 23

The Nursing Process

OBJECTIVES

After completing this chapter, you will be able to:

- Describe the components of the nursing process.
- Identify essential characteristics of the nursing process.
- Differentiate objective and subjective data and primary and secondary data.
- List three methods of data collection, and give examples of how each is useful.
- Compare directive and nondirective approaches to interviewing and closed and open-ended questions, providing examples, and listing advantages and disadvantages of each.
- Compare various frameworks used for nursing assessment.
- Differentiate various types of nursing diagnoses.
- Identify the components of a nursing diagnosis.
- Compare nursing diagnoses, medical diagnoses, and collaborative problems.
- Explain basic steps in the diagnostic process.
- Describe formats for writing nursing diagnoses.
- Discuss the characteristics of a nursing diagnosis.
- List guidelines in writing diagnostic statements.
- Enumerate advantages of a taxonomy of nursing diagnoses.
- Compare and contrast initial planning, ongoing planning, and discharge planning.
- Identify activities that occur in the planning process.
- Explain how standards of care and preprinted care plans can be individualized and used in creating a comprehensive nursing care plan.
- Outline essential guidelines for writing nursing care plans.
- Identify factors that the nurse must consider when setting priorities.
- State the purposes of establishing client goals/desired outcomes.
- Describe the relationship of goals/desired outcomes to the nursing diagnoses.
- Identify guidelines for writing goals/desired outcomes.
- Describe the process of generating and choosing nursing strategies.
- Discuss the five components of a nursing order.

A *process* is a series of planned actions or operations directed toward a particular result or goal. The **nursing process** is a systematic, rational method of planning and providing individualized nursing care. Its purpose is to identify a client's health status (actual or potential health-care problems or needs and strengths); to establish plans to meet the identified needs; and to deliver specific nursing interventions to meet those needs. The nursing process is cyclical; that is, the components of the nursing process follow a logical sequence, but more than one component may be involved at any one time (Figure 23.1).

The nursing process is described in the Canadian Definition and Standards for Nursing Practice as fundamental to the nurse's role in helping clients achieve optimal health (CNA, 1986). The second of the four standards opens with the statement, "Nursing practice requires the effective use of the nursing process" (p. 1).

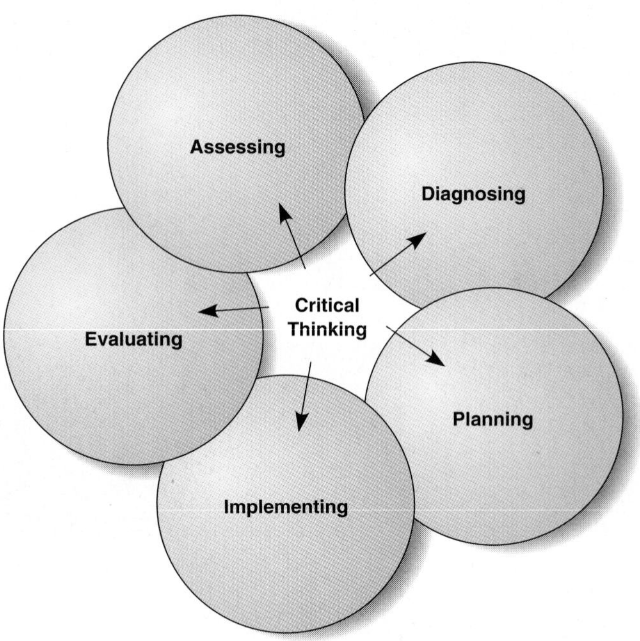

Figure 23.1 The five overlapping phases of the nursing process. Each phase depends upon the accuracy of the preceding phase. Each phase involves critical thinking.

Overview of the Nursing Process

Components of the Nursing Process

The nursing process consists of a series of five components or phases: assessing, diagnosing, planning, implementing, and evaluating. Although nursing theorists may use different terms to describe these phases, the activities of the nurse using the process are similar. To avoid misunderstanding, nurses should be familiar with alternative terms that describe the phases. For example, *nursing diagnosis* may be called *hypotheses*, and *implementation (implementing)* may be called *intervention* or *intervening*.

An overview of the five-phase nursing process is shown in Table 23.1. Each of the five components of the nursing process is discussed in depth in this chapter.

Canadian Society Notes

Fact	Implications for Nursing Practice
Assessment of the client must include the biological, psychological, social, cultural, and spiritual needs of the person. (CNA, 2002, *Code of Ethics)*	Nurses are expected to assess the whole person within the context of the situation, not just the physical symptoms or social situation.
Individual nurses have the primary responsibility for evaluating and promoting evidence in the context of their practice to ensure that nursing practice maximizes health and quality of life from the client's perspective. (CNA, 2000, *Evidence-based Decision-making and Nursing Practice*)	Nurses are expected to use research-based evidence to support their actions. For example, nurses should not continue to manage skin pressure areas with older clients in the same way they were initially taught without keeping up on the research literature to see if there is new evidence as to a better way.
In maintaining their professional standards of practice, nurses must consider safety, effectiveness, and cost when planning and providing client care. (CNA, 1996, *Policy Statement, Necessary Support for Safe Nursing Care*)	Nurses need to assess the environment in which care is delivered. Part of clinical decision making is to consider client safety (e.g., are the sidewalks too slippery for a client to safely walk to the clinic). Likewise, nurses share the responsibility to keep costs manageable for clients and for the larger health-care system (e.g., in considering which dressing supplies to use for wound care).

TABLE 23.1 Overview of the Nursing Process

Component and Description	Purpose	Activities
Assessing Collecting, organizing, validating, and documenting client data	■ To establish a database about the client's response to health concerns or illness and the ability to manage health-care needs	■ Establish a database: – Obtain a nursing health history. – Conduct a physical assessment. – Review client records. – Review relevant literature. – Consult support persons. – Consult health-care professionals. ■ Update data as needed. ■ Organize data. ■ Validate data. ■ Communicate/document data.
Diagnosing Analyzing and synthesizing data and generating hypotheses	■ To identify client strengths and health problems that can be prevented or resolved by collaborative and independent nursing interventions ■ To develop a list of nursing diagnoses and collaborative problems that will focus care	■ Interpret and analyze data: – Cluster or group data (generate tentative hypotheses). – Identify gaps and inconsistencies. ■ Determine client's strengths, risks, and problems. ■ Formulate nursing diagnoses and collaborative problem statements.
Planning Determining how to prevent, reduce, or resolve the identified client problems; how to support client strengths; and how to implement nursing interventions in an organized, individualized, and goal-directed manner	■ To develop an individualized care plan that specifies client goals/desired outcomes and related nursing interventions	■ Set priorities and goals/outcomes in collaboration with client. ■ Write goals/desired outcomes. ■ Select nursing strategies/interventions. ■ Consult other health-care professionals. ■ Write nursing orders and nursing care plan. ■ Communicate care plan to relevant health-care providers.
Implementing Carrying out the planned nursing interventions	■ To assist the client to meet desired goals/outcomes; promote wellness; prevent illness and disease; restore health; and facilitate coping with altered functioning	■ Reassess the client to update the database. ■ Determine need for nursing assistance. ■ Perform or delegate planned nursing interventions. ■ Communicate what nursing actions were implemented: – Document care and client responses to care. – Give verbal reports, as necessary.
Evaluating Measuring the degree to which goals/outcomes have been achieved and identifying factors that positively or negatively influence goal achievement	■ To determine whether to continue, modify, or terminate the plan of care	■ Collaborate with client and collect data related to desired outcomes. ■ Determine the extent to which goals/outcomes have been achieved. ■ Relate nursing actions to client outcomes. ■ Make decisions about problem status. ■ Review and modify the care plan as indicated or terminate nursing care.

TABLE 23.2 Examples of Critical Thinking in the Nursing Process

Nursing Process Activity	Critical-Thinking Skills
Assessing	Making reliable observations Distinguishing relevant from irrelevant data Distinguishing important from unimportant data Validating data Organizing data Categorizing data according to a framework Recognizing assumptions
Diagnosing	Finding patterns and relationships among cues Identifying gaps in the data Making inferences Suspending judgement when lacking data Making interdisciplinary connections Stating the problem Examining assumptions Comparing patterns with norms Identifying factors contributing to the problem
Planning	Involving the client Forming valid generalizations Transferring knowledge from one situation to another Choosing among potential interventions Developing evaluative criteria Making interdisciplinary connections Prioritizing client problems Generalizing principles from other sciences
Implementing	Applying knowledge to perform interventions Testing hypotheses
Evaluating	Deciding whether hypotheses are correct Making criterion-based evaluations

Source: Adapted from J. M. Wilkinson. (2000). *Nursing Process: A critical thinking approach.* Copyright © 2000 by Addison-Wesley Nursing, p. 37–39. Used with permission.

The five phases of the nursing process are not discrete entities but overlapping, continuing subprocesses. For example, assessing, the first phase of the nursing process, is often carried out during implementing and evaluating.

Each phase of the nursing process affects the others; they are closely interrelated. For example, if inadequate data are obtained during assessment, the nursing diagnoses or hypotheses will be incomplete or incorrect; this will be reflected in the planning, implementing, and evaluating phases.

Characteristics of the Nursing Process

The nursing process "provides the framework in which nurses use their knowledge and skills to express human caring" and to help clients meet their actual and potential health problems (Wilkinson, 2000, p. 4). The nursing process is *cyclic* and *dynamic* rather than static. It can be used as a framework for nursing care in all types of health-care settings, whether the client is an individual, a family, or a community.

The nursing process is also *client centred.* The nurse organizes the plan of care according to *client* problems rather than *nursing* goals. In the assessment phase, the nurse collects data to determine the client's habits, routines, and needs, enabling the nurse to incorporate client routines into the care plan as much as possible.

The nursing process is an adaptation of *problem-solving techniques* (see Chapter 27) and *systems theory* (see Chapter 6). It can be viewed as parallel to, but separate from, the medical process. Both processes (1) begin with data gathering and analysis; (2) base the action (intervention or treatment) on a problem statement (nursing diagnosis or medical diagnosis); and (3) include an evaluative component.

The medical process focuses on the disease process (treatment, cure); however, the nursing process is directed toward a client's *response* to disease and illness (care). Medicine, nursing, and other health disciplines collaborate in the management of many health problems.

Decision making is involved in every component of the nursing process. Nurses can be highly creative when using the nursing process. They are not bound by standard responses and may apply their repertoire of skills and knowledge to assist clients by using a variety of critical-thinking skills to carry out the nursing process. The nursing process, however, does not necessarily require the nurse to use all the possible critical-thinking skills (Table 23.2).

TABLE 23.3 Types of Assessment

Type	Time Performed	Purpose	Example
Initial assessment	Performed within specified time after admission to a health-care agency	To establish a complete database for problem identification, reference, and future comparison	Nursing admission assessment (see Figure 23.2)
Problem-focused assessment	Ongoing process integrated with nursing care	To determine the status of a specific problem	Hourly assessment of client's fluid intake and urinary output in an ICU
	Initial assessment when client presents for brief, episodic care	To identify new or evolving problems	Assessment of client's ability to perform self-care while assisting a client to bathe
Emergency assessment	During any physiological or psychological crisis	To identify life-threatening problems	Rapid assessment of a person's airway, breathing status, and circulation during a cardiac arrest
			Assessment of suicidal tendencies or potential for violence
Time-lapsed reassessment	Follow-up after initial assessment	To compare the client's current status to baseline data previously obtained	Reassessment of a client's functional health patterns in a home care or outpatient setting

Source: Adapted from M. Gordon. (1994). *Nursing diagnosis: Process and application* (3rd ed.). (p. 134). St. Louis, MO: Mosby.

Assessing

Assessing is the systematic and continuous collection, organization, validation, and documentation of data. In effect, assessing is a continuous process carried out during all phases of the nursing process. For example, in the evaluation phase, assessment is done to determine the outcomes of the nursing strategies and to evaluate goal achievement. All phases of the nursing process depend on the accurate and complete collection of data (information).

There are four different types of assessments: initial assessment, problem-focused assessment, emergency assessment, and time-lapsed reassessment (Table 23.3). These types vary according to their purpose, timing, time available, and client status.

The assessment process involves four closely related activities: collecting data, organizing data, validating data, and documenting data.

Collecting Data

Data collection is the process of gathering information about a client's health status. It must be both systematic and continuous to prevent the omission of significant data and reflect a client's changing health status.

A **database** (baseline data) is all the information about a client; it includes the nursing health history (see Components of a Nursing Health History in the box on the following page), physical assessment, the physician's history and physical examination, results of laboratory and diagnostic tests, and material contributed by other health-care personnel.

Client data should include past history as well as current problems. For example, a history of an allergic reaction to penicillin is a vital piece of historical data. Past surgical procedures, use of complementary therapies, and chronic diseases are also examples of historical data. Current data relate to onset of the current health concern, how it has been managed to date, impact on the individual (e.g., sleep, pain) and family, and so on.

Types of Data

Data can be subjective or objective. **Subjective data,** also referred to as **symptoms** or **covert data,** are apparent only to the person affected and can be described or verified only by that person. Itching, pain, and feelings of worry are examples of subjective data. Subjective data include

Components of a Nursing Health History

Biographical Data

Client's name, address, age, gender, marital status, occupation, religious preference, next of kin, and usual sources of health care

Chief Concern or Reason for Visit

The answer given to the question, "What is troubling you?" or, "What brought you to the hospital or clinic?" The chief concern should be recorded in the client's own words.

History of Present Illness or Health Concern

- Symptoms—description of each; steady, episodic, or worsening pattern
- Onset of symptoms sudden or gradual, how long ago, circumstances at time of onset
- How often the problem occurs
- Exact location of the distress
- Character of the complaint (e.g., intensity of pain or quality of sputum, emesis, or discharge)
- Other phenomena or symptoms associated with the chief concern
- Factors that aggravate or alleviate the problem

Past History

- *Medications:* all currently used prescription and over-the-counter medications, such as aspirin, nasal spray, vitamins, laxatives, birth control pills; or use of herbal remedies
- *Hospitalization for serious illnesses:* reasons for the hospitalization, dates, surgery performed, course of recovery, and any complications
- *Immunizations:* date of the last tetanus shot, flu shot
- *Accidents and injuries:* how, when, and where the incident occurred, type of injury, treatment received, and complications
- *Childhood illnesses:* such as chickenpox, mumps, measles, rubella (German measles), rubeola (red measles), streptococcal infections, scarlet fever, rheumatic fever, and other significant illnesses
- *Allergies:* drugs, animals, insects, or other environmental agents and the type of reaction that occurs
- *Infectious disease exposure*

Family History of Illness

To ascertain risk factors for certain diseases, the ages of siblings, parents, and grandparents and their current state of health or (if they are deceased) the cause of death are obtained. Particular attention should be given to such disorders as heart disease, cancer, diabetes, hypertension, obesity, allergies, arthritis, tuberculosis, bleeding, alcoholism, and mental health illnesses.

Lifestyle

- *Personal habits:* the amount, frequency, and duration of substance use (tobacco, alcohol, coffee, cola, tea, and illicit or recreational drugs)
- *Diet:* description of a typical diet on a normal day or any special diet, number of meals and snacks per day, who cooks and shops for food, ethnically distinct food patterns, and allergies

the client's sensations, feelings, values, beliefs, attitudes, and perception of personal health status and life situation. Information supplied by family members, significant others, or other health-care professionals is also considered subjective if it is based on perceptions.

Objective data, also referred to as **signs** or **overt data,** are detectable by an observer or can be tested against an accepted standard. They can be seen, heard, felt, or smelled, and they are obtained by observation or physical examination. For example, a discolouration of the skin or a blood pressure reading are objective data. During the physical examination, the nurse obtains the objective data needed to validate subjective data and to complete the assessment phase of the nursing process. A complete database of both subjective and objective data provides a baseline for determining the client's responses to nursing and medical interventions. Examples of subjective and objective data are shown in the box on page 394.

Sources of Data

Sources of data are *primary* or *secondary.* The client is the primary source of data. Family members or other support persons, other health professionals, records and reports, laboratory and diagnostic analyses, and relevant literature are secondary or indirect sources. In fact, all sources other than the client are considered secondary sources.

Client The best source of data is usually the client unless the client is too ill, young, or confused to communicate clearly. The client can usually provide subjective data that no one else can offer.

Support People Family members, friends, and caregivers who know the client well often can supplement or verify information provided by the client. They might convey information about the client's response to illness, the stresses

Components of a Nursing Health History *continued*

- *Sleep/rest patterns:* usual daily sleep/wake times, difficulties sleeping, remedies used for difficulties, napping
- *Activities of daily living (ADLs):* any difficulties experienced in the basic activities of eating, grooming, dressing, elimination, and mobility
- *Recreation/hobbies:* exercise activity and tolerance, hobbies and other interests

Social Data

- *Family relationships/friendships:* the client's support system in times of stress (who helps in time of need?); what effect the client's illness has on the family; and whether any family problems are affecting the client See also the discussion of family assessment in Chapter 6.
- *Ethnic affiliation:* health customs and beliefs; cultural practices that may affect health care and recovery See also detailed ethnic/cultural assessment guide in Chapter 14.
- *Educational history:* data about the client's highest level of education attained and any past difficulties with learning
- *Occupational history:* current employment status, the number of days missed from work because of illness, history of accidents on the job, occupational hazards with a potential for future disease or accident, the client's need to change jobs because of past illness, the employment status of both spouses or partners and the way child care is handled, and the client's overall satisfaction with the work
- *Economic status:* financial concerns
- *Home and neighbourhood conditions:* home safety measures and adjustments in physical facilities that may be required to help the client manage a physical disability, activity intolerance, and activities of daily living; the availability of neighbourhood and community services to meet the client's needs

Psychological Data

- *Major stressors* experienced in the past year and the client's perception of them
- *Usual coping pattern* with a serious problem or a high level of stress
- *Communication style:* ability to verbalize appropriate emotion; nonverbal communication—such as eye movements, gestures, use of touch, and posture; interactions with support persons; and the congruence of nonverbal behaviour and verbal expression

Patterns of Health Care

These are all health-care resources the client is currently using and has used in the past. These include: the family physician, specialists (e.g., ophthalmologist or gynecologist), dentist, alternative practitioners (e.g., herbalist or faith healers), health clinic, or health centre; whether the client considers the care being provided adequate; and whether access to health care is a problem.

the client was experiencing before the illness, family attitudes on illness and health, and the client's home environment.

Support people are an especially important source of data for a client who is very young, unconscious, or confused. In some cases—a client who is physically or emotionally abused, for example—the person giving information may wish to remain anonymous. Before eliciting data from support people, the nurse should ensure that the client, if mentally able, accepts such input. The nurse should also indicate on the nursing history what data was obtained from a support person.

Client Records Client records include information documented by various health-care professionals. Client records also contain data regarding the client's occupation, religion, and marital status. By reviewing such records before interviewing the client, the nurse can avoid asking questions for which answers have already been supplied. Repeated questioning can be stressful and annoying to clients and cause concern about the lack of communication among health-care professionals.

Medical records (e.g., medical history, physical examination, progress notes, and consultations) are often a source of a client's present and past health and illness patterns. These records can provide nurses with information about the client's coping behaviours, health practices, previous illnesses, and allergies.

Records of therapies by other health professionals, such as social workers, dietitians, or physiotherapists, help the nurse obtain relevant data not expressed by the client. For example, a social worker's report on a client's living conditions or a home care report on a client's coping at home can also be helpful to the nurse conducting an assessment.

Laboratory records also provide pertinent health information. For example, the determination of blood glucose level allows health professionals to monitor the effects of oral

Examples of Subjective and Objective Data

Subjective	Objective
"I feel weak all over when I exert myself."	Blood pressure 90/50 Apical pulse 104 Skin pale and diaphoretic
Client states he has a cramping pain in his abdomen. States, "I feel sick to my stomach."	Vomited 100 mL green-tinged fluid Abdomen firm and slightly distended Active bowel sounds auscultated in all 4 quadrants
"I'm short of breath."	Lung sounds clear bilaterally; diminished in right lower lobe
"He seems so sad today," wife states.	Cried during interview
"I would like to see the chaplain before surgery."	Holding open Bible Has small silver cross on bedside table

hypoglycemic medications. Any laboratory data about a client must be compared with established norms for that particular test and for the client's age, gender, and so on. Laboratory tests vary among agencies, and norms can, therefore, be different. Some laboratory tests, such as blood gases and pulmonary function tests, vary according to altitude above sea level. Therefore, a nurse relocating from Halifax to Calgary would need to attend to these differences.

The nurse must always consider the information in client records in light of the present situation. For example, if the most recent health record is five years old, it is likely that the client's health practices and coping behaviours have changed. Stressors in an individual's life often change, for example, when an alcoholic husband leaves home or a sick infant recovers.

Health-Care Professionals Because assessment is an ongoing process, verbal reports from other health-care professionals serve as other potential sources of information about a client's health. Nurses, social workers, physicians, and physiotherapists, for example, may have information from either previous or current contact with the client. Sharing of information among professionals is especially important to ensure continuity of care when clients are transferred to and from home and health-care agencies.

Literature The review of nursing and related literature, such as professional journals and reference texts, can provide additional information for the database. A literature review includes but is not limited to the following information:

- Standards or norms against which to compare findings (e.g., height and weight tables, normal developmental tasks for an age group)
- Cultural and social health practices
- Clinical practice guidelines
- Research evidence for nursing interventions and evaluation criteria relevant to a client's health problems
- Information about medical diagnoses, treatments, and prognoses

Data Collection Methods

The primary methods used to collect data are observing, interviewing, and examining. Observation occurs whenever the nurse is in contact with the client or support persons. Interviewing is used mainly while taking the nursing health history. Examining is the major method used in the physical health assessment.

In reality, the nurse uses all three methods simultaneously when assessing clients. For example, during the client interview, the nurse observes, listens, asks questions, and mentally retains information to explore in the physical examination.

Observing To *observe* is to gather data by using the five senses. Observation is a conscious, deliberate skill that is developed through effort and with an organized approach. Although nurses observe mainly through sight, most of the senses are engaged during careful observations. Examples of client data observed through four of the five senses are shown in Table 23.4.

TABLE 23.4 Observational Skills

Sense	Example of Client Data
Vision	Overall appearance (body size, general weight, posture, grooming); signs of distress or discomfort; facial and body gestures; skin colour and lesions; abnormalities of movement; nonverbal demeanour (e.g., signs of anger or anxiety); religious or cultural artifacts (e.g., books, icons, beads)
Smell	Body or breath odours
Hearing	Breath and heart sounds; bowel sounds; ability to communicate; language spoken; ability to initiate conversation; ability to respond when spoken to; orientation to time, person, and place; thoughts and feelings about self, others, and health status
Touch	Skin temperature and moisture; muscle strength (e.g., hand grip); pulse rate, rhythm, and volume; palpatory lesions (e.g., lumps, masses, nodules)

Observation has two aspects: (1) noticing the stimuli, and (2) selecting, organizing, and interpreting the data. A nurse who observes that a client's face is flushed must relate that observation to, for example, body temperature, activity, environmental temperature, and blood pressure. Errors can occur in selecting, organizing, and interpreting data. For example, a nurse might not notice certain signs, either because they are unexpected or because they do not conform to preconceptions about a client's illness. Nurses often need to focus on specific stimuli in order not to be overwhelmed by a multitude of stimuli. Observing, therefore, involves discriminating among stimuli, that is, distinguishing stimuli in a meaningful manner. For example, nurses caring for newborns learn to ignore the usual sounds of machines in the nursery but respond quickly to an infant's cry or movement.

The experienced nurse is often able to attend to an intervention (e.g., giving a bed bath or monitoring an intravenous infusion) and, at the same time, make important observations (e.g., noting a change in respiratory status or skin colour). The beginning student must learn to make observations and complete tasks simultaneously.

Nursing observations must be organized so that nothing significant is missed. Most nurses develop a particular sequence for observing events, usually focusing on the client first. For example, a nurse walks into a client's room and observes, in the following order:

- The client (e.g., response to greeting, verbalizations)
- Clinical signs of client distress (e.g., pallor or flushing, laboured breathing, and behaviour indicating pain or emotional distress)
- Threats to the client's safety, real or anticipated (e.g., a lowered side rail)
- The presence and functioning of associated equipment (e.g., intravenous equipment and oxygen)
- The immediate environment, including the people in it (e.g., appropriateness of lighting level, accessibility to personal items)

Interviewing An **interview** is a planned communication or a conversation with a purpose, for example, to get or give information, identify problems of mutual concern, evaluate change, teach, provide support, or provide counselling or therapy. Interviewing is a process that the nurse applies in most phases of the nursing process. During the assessment phase, the primary purpose of the interview is to gather data. One example of the interview is the nursing health history, which is a part of the nursing admission assessment.

There are two approaches to interviewing: directive and nondirective. The **directive interview** is highly structured and elicits specific information. The nurse establishes the purpose of the interview and guides the interview, at least at the outset, by asking closed questions (see the next section) that call for specific data. The client responds to questions but may have limited opportunity to ask questions or discuss concerns. Nurses frequently use directive interviews to gather and to give information when time is limited (e.g., in an emergency situation).

During a **nondirective interview,** or rapport-building interview, by contrast, the nurse facilitates the client's control of purpose, subject matter, and pacing. *Rapport* is an understanding between two or more people. The nurse encourages communication by asking open-ended questions (see the next section) and providing empathetic responses.

A combination of directive and nondirective approaches is usually appropriate during the information-gathering interview, the goals of which are to collect data and to begin to establish rapport. The nurse begins by asking open-ended questions to determine areas of concern for the client. If, for example, a client expresses worry about surgery, the nurse pauses to explore the client's worry and to provide support. Simply to note the worry, without dealing with it, can leave the impression that the nurse does not care about the client's concerns or dismisses them as unimportant. As the interview evolves, the nurse may use closed questions to obtain more specific data and to complete the nursing health history.

Kinds of Interview Questions Questions are often classified as closed or open-ended, and neutral or leading.

Closed questions, used in the directive interview, are restrictive and generally require only "yes" or "no" or short factual answers giving specific information. Examples of closed questions are: "What medication did you take?" "Are you having pain now? Show me where it is." "How old are you?" "When did you fall?" The highly stressed person and the person who has difficulty communicating will find closed questions easier to answer than open-ended questions.

Open-ended questions, associated with the nondirective interview, lead or invite clients to discover and explore (elaborate, clarify, or illustrate) their thoughts or feelings. An open-ended question specifies only the broad topic to be discussed and invites answers longer than one or two words. Such questions give clients the freedom to divulge only the information that they are ready to disclose. Responses may also convey clients' attitudes and beliefs. The open-ended question is useful at the beginning of an interview or to change topics and to elicit attitudes.

Examples of open-ended questions are: "How have you been feeling lately?" "What brought you to the hospital?" "How did you feel in that situation?" "Would you describe more about how you relate to your child?" "What would you like to talk about today?" These questions or statements require more than a yes or no or other short response. Open-ended questions usually begin with "what" or "how."

Selected Advantages and Disadvantages of Open-Ended and Closed Questions

Open-Ended Questions

Advantages

1. They let the interviewee do the talking.
2. The interviewer is able to listen and observe.
3. They are easy to answer and nonthreatening.
4. They reveal what the interviewee thinks is important.
5. They may reveal the interviewee's lack of information, misunderstanding of words, frame of reference, prejudices, or stereotypes.
6. They can provide information the interviewer may not ask for.
7. They can reveal the interviewee's degree of feeling about an issue.
8. They can convey interest and trust because of the freedom they provide.

Disadvantages

1. They take more time.
2. Only brief answers may be given.
3. Valuable information may be withheld.
4. They often elicit more information than necessary.
5. Responses are difficult to document and require skill in recording.
6. The interviewer requires skill in controlling an open-ended interview.
7. Responses require psychological insight and sensitivity from the interviewer.

Closed Questions

Advantages

1. Questions and answers can be controlled more effectively.
2. They require less effort from the interviewee.
3. They may be less threatening since they do not require explanations or justifications.
4. They take less time.
5. Information can be asked for sooner than it would be volunteered.
6. Responses are easily documented.
7. Questions are easy to use and can be handled by unskilled interviewers.

Disadvantages

1. They may provide too little information and require follow-up questions.
2. They may not reveal how the interviewee feels.
3. They do not allow the interviewee to volunteer possibly valuable information.
4. They may inhibit communication and convey lack of interest by the interviewer.
5. The interviewer may dominate the interview with questions.

Source: Table constructed, with permission, from material on p. 55–58 of Charles J. Stewart and William B. Cash, Jr., *Interviewing: Principles and practices*, 6th ed. © 1991 W.C. Brown, Dubuque, IA. All rights reserved.

The type of question a nurse chooses depends on the needs of the client at the time. For example, the nurse asks closed questions in an emergency or other acute situation when information must be obtained quickly. Nurses often find it necessary to use a combination of closed and open-ended questions throughout an interview to accomplish the goals of the interview and obtain needed information.

A **neutral question** is a question the client can answer without direction or pressure from the nurse. Examples are "How do you feel about that?" and "Why do you think you had the operation?" A **leading question,** by contrast, directs the client's answer. The phrasing of the question suggests what answer is expected. Examples are "You're stressed about surgery tomorrow, aren't you?" or "You will take your medicine, won't you?" The leading question gives the client less opportunity to decide whether the answer is true or not. Leading questions create problems if the client, in an effort to please the nurse, gives inaccurate responses. This can result in inaccurate data.

Planning the Interview and Setting Before beginning an interview, the nurse reviews available information, for example, the postoperative record, information about the current illness, or literature about the client's health problem. The nurse also reviews the data-collection form to make sure that the data to be collected are really needed and will serve some purpose related to the client's care. If a form is not available, most nurses prepare an interview guide to remember areas of information and determine what questions to ask.

Each interview is influenced by time, place, seating arrangement, and distance.

Time Nurses should try to schedule interviews with hospitalized clients for a time when the client is physically comfortable and free of pain, and when interruptions by friends, family, and other health professionals are minimal. Nurses should schedule interviews with clients in their homes at a time mutually selected with the client.

Place A well-lit, well-ventilated, moderate-sized room that is relatively free of noise, movements, and interruptions encourages communication. In addition, a place where others cannot overhear or see the client is desirable. Most people are inhibited when answering personal questions or expressing strong feelings in the sight or hearing of others.

Seating Arrangement A seating arrangement with the nurse behind a desk and the client seated across creates a formal setting that suggests a business meeting between a superior and a subordinate. In contrast, a seating arrangement in which the parties sit on two chairs placed at right angles to a desk or table or a few feet apart, with no table between, creates a less formal atmosphere, and the nurse and client tend to feel on equal terms. In groups, a horseshoe or circular chair arrangement can avoid a superior or head-of-the-table position.

When a client is in bed, the nurse can sit at a 45-degree angle to the bed. This position is less formal and intimidating than standing at the foot of the bed.

Distance People feel uncomfortable when talking to someone who is too close or too far away. Most people feel comfortable maintaining a distance of about a metre during an interview. Communication at a distance greater than this tends to be more impersonal and may suggest a lack of involvement on the part of the nurse. Some clients require more or less personal space depending on their cultural and personal needs.

Stages of an Interview An interview has three major stages: the opening or introduction, the body or development, and the closing.

The Opening The opening can be the most important part of the interview because what is said and done at that time sets the tone for the remainder of the interview. The purposes of the opening are to establish rapport and orient the interviewee. Either step can come first, depending on the situation, the relationship between the two parties, and the interviewer's choice. The rapport and orientation stages may occur at the same time and are often indistinguishable.

Establishing rapport is a process of creating goodwill and trust. It can begin with a greeting ("Good morning, Mr. Johnson") or a self-introduction ("Good morning. I'm Jennifer Thomas, a nursing student") accompanied by nonverbal gestures, such as a smile, a handshake, and a friendly manner. The nurse continues to develop rapport by asking questions about the person and may proceed with some small talk about the weather, sports, families, and the like. The nurse must be careful not to overdo this stage; too much superficial talk can arouse anxiety about what is to follow and may appear insincere.

In the orientation stage, the nurse explains the purpose and nature of the interview, for example, what information is needed, how long it will take, and what is expected of the client. The nurse usually states that the client has the right not to provide data and tells the client how the information will be used.

The following is an example of an interview introduction:

Step 1—Establish Rapport

Nurse: Hello, Ms. Goodwin, I'm Jim Fellows. I'm a nursing student, and I'll be assisting with your care here.
Client: Hi. Are you a student from the university?
Nurse: Yes, I'm in my final year. Are you familiar with the campus?
Client: Oh, yes! I'm an avid football fan. My nephew graduated in 2000, and I often attend football games with him.
Nurse: That's great! Sounds like fun.
Client: Yes, I enjoy it very much.

Step 2—Orientation

Nurse: May I sit down with you here for about 10 minutes to talk about how I can help you while you're here?
Client: All right. What do you want to know?
Nurse: Well, to plan your care after your operation, I'd like to get some information about your normal daily activities and what you expect here in the hospital. I'd like to make notes while we talk to get the important points and have them available to the other staff who will also look after you.
Client: OK. That's all right with me.
Nurse: If there is anything you don't want to talk about, please feel free to say so, and if there is anything you would rather I didn't write down, just tell me. Is this a good time for you?
Client: Sure, that will be fine.

The Body In the body of the interview, the client communicates what the client thinks, feels, knows, and perceives in response to questions from the nurse. The nurse can make the transition from the opening stage to this stage by asking an open-ended question that is related to the stated purpose, is easy to answer, and does not embarrass or place stress on the person. For example, "What brought you to the hospital today?"

CLINICAL GUIDELINES

Communication During an Interview

- Listen attentively, using all your senses, and speak slowly and clearly.
- Use language the client understands, and clarify points that are not understood.
- Plan questions to follow a logical sequence.
- Ask only one question at a time. Double questions limit the client to one choice and may confuse both the nurse and the client.
- Allow the client the opportunity to look at things the way they appear to the client and not the way they appear to the nurse or someone else.
- Do not impose your own values on the client.
- Avoid using personal examples, such as saying, "If I were you... "
- Nonverbally convey respect, concern, interest, and acceptance.
- Use and accept silence to help the client search for more thoughts or to organize them.
- Use eye contact unless culturally inappropriate.
- Be calm, unhurried, and sympathetic.

Effective development of the interview demands that the nurse use communication skills that make both parties feel comfortable and serve the purpose of the interview. See communication skills in Chapter 26. Brief guidelines for communicating during an interview are outlined in the box above.

The Closing The nurse usually terminates the interview when the needed information has been obtained. In some cases, however, a client terminates it, for example, when deciding not to give any more information or when unable to offer more information for some other reason—fatigue, for example. The closing is important in maintaining the rapport and trust and in facilitating future interactions. The following techniques are commonly used to close an interview (Stewart & Cash, 1994):

1. Signal that the interview is coming to an end by offering to answer questions: "Do you have any questions?" Be sure to allow time for the person to answer, or the offer will be regarded as insincere.
2. Declare completion of the purpose or task by saying, "Well, that's about all I need to know for now" or "Well, those are all the questions I have for now." Preceding a remark with the word "well" generally signals that the end of the interaction is near.
3. State appreciation or satisfaction about what was accomplished: "I really enjoyed meeting you, and I think we accomplished a great deal." "Those are all the questions I have. Thank you for your time and help." "The questions you have answered will be helpful in planning your nursing care."
4. Express concern for the person's welfare and future: "I'll see you on Thursday." "I hope all goes well for you. If you run into additional problems, be sure to get in touch with me."
5. Plan for the next meeting, if there is to be one. Include the day, time, place, topic, and purpose: "Let's get together again here on the 15th at 9:00 a.m. to see how you are managing then."
6. Reveal what will happen next. For example: "Ms. Goodwin, I will be responsible for giving you care three mornings per week while you are here. I will be in to see you each Monday, Tuesday, and Wednesday between eight o'clock and noon. At those times, we can adjust your care, if we need to."
7. Signal that the time is up if a time limit was agreed on or explain why the interview must close at that time: "Well, I see our time is up; did it ever go quickly today," or "I'm sorry, but we're going to have to end our discussion; I have another appointment in 10 minutes."
8. Provide a summary to verify accuracy and agreement. Summarizing serves several purposes: it helps to terminate the interview, it reassures the client that the nurse has listened, it checks the accuracy of the nurse's perceptions, it clears the way for new ideas, and it helps the client to note progress and forward direction (Brammer, 1993). Sometimes, clients may spontaneously offer a summary. At other times, the nurse must initiate it or ask the client to do so: "Let's look at what has happened in this interview. What do you think has been accomplished?" Summaries are particularly helpful for clients who are anxious or who have difficulty staying with the topic: "Well, it seems to me that you are especially worried about your hospitalization and chest pain because your father died of a heart attack five years ago, your wife has multiple sclerosis and depends on you for support and care, and you don't want to ask for too much help from your children. Is that correct? ... We'll do the best we can to help you with these concerns. I'll discuss this with you again tomorrow, and we'll decide what plans need to be made to help you."

Examining The *physical examination* or physical assessment is a systematic data collection method that uses observational skills (i.e., the senses of sight, hearing, smell, and touch) to detect health problems. To conduct the examination, the nurse uses techniques of inspection, auscultation, palpation, and percussion. These techniques are discussed in Chapter 27.

The physical assessment is carried out systematically. It may be organized according to the examiner's preference, in a head-to-toe approach, or a body systems approach. Usually, the nurse first records a general impression about the client's overall appearance and health status, for example, age, body size, mental and nutritional status, speech, and behaviour. Then, the nurse takes such measurements as vital signs, height, and weight. The **cephalocaudal** (head-to-toe) approach begins the assessment at the head, progresses to the neck, thorax, abdomen, and extremities, and ends at the toes. The nurse using a body systems approach investigates each system individually, that is, the respiratory system, the circulatory system, the nervous system, and so on. During the physical assessment, the nurse assesses all body parts and compares findings on each side of the body (e.g., lungs). These techniques are discussed in detail in Chapter 27.

Instead of giving a complete examination, the nurse may focus on a specific problem area noted from the nursing assessment, such as the client's inability to urinate. On occasion, the nurse may find it necessary to resolve a client complaint or problem (e.g., shortness of breath) prior to completing the examination. Alternatively, the nurse may perform a screening examination. A **screening examination,** also called a *review of systems*, is a brief review of essential functioning of various body parts or systems. An example of a screening examination is the nursing admission assessment form shown in Figure 23.2. Data obtained from this examination are measured against norms or standards, such as ideal height and weight standards or norms for body temperature or blood pressure levels.

Organizing Data

To obtain data systematically, the nurse uses an organized assessment framework, often referred to as a *nursing health history*, *nursing assessment*, or *nursing database*. Many frameworks are available for the systematic collection and documentation of assessment data. The framework may be modified according to the client's physical status.

Nursing Conceptual Models

Most schools of nursing and health-care agencies have developed their own structured assessment tools. Many of these are based on selected nursing theories (see Chapter 4). Two examples are Gordon's functional health pattern framework and Roy's adaptation model.

Gordon (1994) provides a framework of 11 functional health patterns. Gordon uses the word *pattern* to signify a sequence of recurring behaviour. The nurse collects data about dysfunctional as well as functional behaviour. Thus, by using Gordon's framework to organize data, nurses are able to discern emerging patterns.

Roy and Andrews (1999) outline the data to be collected according to the Roy adaptation model and classify observable behaviour into four categories: physiological, self-concept, role function, and interdependence.

Figure 23.2 is a concise data collection tool that is organized according to body systems and specific nursing concerns (e.g., screening for falls and allergies); it does not use one particular nursing model. In the box on page 402, the data from Amanda Aquilini is shown after being organized according to Gordon's 11 functional health patterns. Note how the categories in the box differ from those in Figure 23.2. As a rule, the nurse organizes the data using the same model on which the data collection tool is based. However, different models are provided here to demonstrate differences in organizing frameworks and to show that the nurse is not limited to the framework provided by the data collection tool.

Gordon's Typology of 11 Functional Health Patterns

- *Health-perception/health-management pattern:* Describes the client's perceived pattern of health and well-being and how health is managed
- *Nutritional/metabolic pattern:* Describes the client's pattern of food and fluid consumption relative to metabolic need and pattern indicators of local nutrient supply
- *Elimination pattern:* Describes the patterns of excretory function (bowel, bladder, and skin)
- *Activity/exercise pattern:* Describes the pattern of exercise, activity, leisure, and recreation
- *Sleep/rest pattern:* Describes patterns of sleep, rest, and relaxation
- *Cognitive/perceptual pattern:* Describes sensory-perceptual and cognitive patterns
- *Self-perception/self-concept pattern:* Describes the client's self-concept pattern and perceptions of self (e.g., self-conception/worth, comfort, body image, feeling state)
- *Role/relationship pattern:* Describes the client's pattern of role-participation and relationships
- *Sexuality/reproductive pattern:* Describes the client's patterns of satisfaction and dissatisfaction with sexuality pattern; describes reproductive patterns
- *Coping/stress-tolerance pattern:* Describes the client's general coping pattern and the effectiveness of the pattern in terms of stress tolerance
- *Value/belief pattern:* Describes the patterns of values, beliefs (including spiritual), and goals that guide the client's choices or decisions

Source: M. Gordon. (1994). *Nursing diagnosis: Process and application* (3rd ed.). (p. 70). St. Louis, MO: Mosby.

ADMISSION DATA

Date 4-16-03 Time 3:15p.m. Primary Language English

Arrived Via: ☐ Wheelchair ☐ Stretcher ☑ Ambulatory

From: ☐ Admitting ☐ ER ☑ Home ☐ Nursing Home ☐ Other

Admitting M.D. R. Katz Time Notified 5 p.m.

ORIENTATION TO UNIT

	YES	NO		YES	NO
Arm Band Correct	☒	☐	Visiting Hours	☒	☐
Allergy Band	☒	☐	Smoking Policy	☒	☐
Telephone	☒	☐	TV, Lights, Bed Controls,		
Electrical Policy	☒	☐	Call Lights, Side Rails	☒	☐
Educational Mat©l	☒	☐	Nurses Station	☒	☐
(TV Brochure)	☒	☐			

Family M.D. R. Katz

Weight 57 kg Height 158 cm BP:R — L 122/80

Temp. 39.4°C Pulse 92, weak Resp. 28, shallow

Source Providing Information ☑ Patient ☐ Other

Unable to Obtain History ☐

Reason for Admission (Onset, Duration, Pt.©s Perception)' "Chest cold" X2 weeks S.O.B on exertion. "Lung pain, fever," "Dr. says I have pneumonia."

ALLERGIES & REACTIONS

Drugs Penicillin

Food/Other

Signs & Symptoms rash, nausea

Blood Reaction ☐ Yes ☑ No Dyes/Shellfish ☐ Yes ☑ No

MEDICATIONS

Current Meds	Dose/Freq.	Last Dose
Synthroid	0.1 mg. daily	4-16, 8 a.m.

Disposition of Meds: ☒ Home ☐ Pharmacy ☐ Safe *At Bedside

MEDICAL HISTORY

☑ No Major Problems ☐ Gastro

☐ Cardiac ☐ Arthritis

☐ Hyper/Hypotension ☐ Stroke

☐ Diabetes ☐ Seizures

☐ Cancer ☐ Glaucoma

☐ Respiratory ☑ Other Childbirth-1998

Surgery/Procedures	Date
Appendectomy	1978
Partial thyroidectomy	1991

SPECIAL ASSISTIVE DEVICES

☐ Wheelchair ☐ Contacts ☐ Venous Access Device ☐ Dentures ☐ Partial ☐ Upper ☐ Lower

☐ Braces ☐ Hearing Aid

☐ Cane/Crutches ☐ Prosthesis

☐ Walker ☐ Glasses ☐ Epidural Catheter

☐ Other None

VALUABLES

Patient informed Hospital not responsible for personal belongings.

Valuables Disposition: ☐ Patient ☐ Safe ☐ Given to

Patient/SO Signature None

PSYCHOSOCIAL HISTORY

Recent Stress None

Coping Mechanism Not assessed because of fatigue

Support System Husband, coworkers, friends

Calm: ☑ Yes ☐ No

Anxious: ☐ Yes ☐ No Facial muscles tense; trembling

Religion Catholic, Would want Last Rites

Tobacco Use: ☐ Yes ☑ No

Alcohol Use: ☐ Yes ☑ No

Drug Use: ☐ Yes ☑ No

NEUROLOGICAL

Oriented: ☑ Person ☑ Place ☑ Time ☐ Confused ☐ Sedated ☐ Alert ☐ Restless ☑ Lethargic ☐ Comatose

Pupils: ☑ Equal ☐ Unequal ☑ Reactive ☐ Sluggish ☐ Other 3mm.

Extremity Strength: ☑ Equal ☐ Unequal

Speech: ☑ Clear ☐ Slurred ☐ Other

MUSCULO-SKELETAL

Normal ROM of Extremities ☑ Yes ☐ No

☑ Weakness ☐ Paralysis ☐ Contractures ☐ Joint Swelling ☑ Pain

☐ Other ↓ related to fatigue when coughing

RESPIRATORY

Pattern: ☐ Even ☐ Uneven ☑ Shallow ☑ Dyspnea ☑ Other diminished breath sounds

Breathing Sounds: ☐ Clear ☑ Other inspiratory crackles

Secretions: ☐ None ☑ Other pink, thick sputum

Cough: ☐ None ☑ Productive ☐ Nonproductive

CARDIOVASCULAR

Pulses: Apical Rate 92-W ☑ Reg. ☐ Irregular ☐ Pacemaker

S = Strong W = Weak A = Absent D = Doppler

Radial R 92 L — Pedal R — L —

Edema: ☑ Absent ☐ Present Site

Perfusion: ☐ Warm ☐ Dry ☑ Diaphoretic ☐ Cool (Hot)

GASTROINTESTINAL

Oral Mucosa ☐ Normal ☑ Other pale and dry

Bowel Sounds: ☑ Normal ☐ Other Abd. soft

Wt. Change: ☐ ☑ N/V Stool Frequency/Character 1/day;soft

Last B/M 4-15-03 ☐ Ostomy (type)

Equip.

GENITOURINARY

Urine: Last Voided This morning

☐ Normal ☐ Anuria ☐ Hematuria ☐ Dysuri ☐ Incontinent

☒ Other ↓ amount & frequency since ill

☐ Catheter (type) Other

LMP 4-1-03 ☐ Vaginal/Penile Discharge

Other

SELF CARE

Need Assist with: ☐ Ambulating ☐ Elimination ☐ Meals ☒ Hygiene ☐ Dressing

While fatigued

Amanda Aquilini [F. age 28]
#4637651

NORTH BROWARD HOSPITAL DISTRICT
NURSING ADMINISTRATION ASSESSMENT

Figure 23.2 Assessment for Amanda Aquilini. Nursing assessment tool. Courtesy of North Broward Hospital District, Broward County, Florida. Reprinted with permission.

NUTRITION

General Appearance: ☑ Well Nourished ☐ Emaciated ☐ Other ______

Appetite: ☐ Good ☐ Fair ☑ Poor -x2 days

Diet Liquid Meal Pattern 3/day

☐ Feeds Self ☐ Assist ☐ Total Feed

SKIN ASSESSMENT

Color: ☐ Normal ☐ Flushed ☑ Pale ☐ Dusky ☐ Cyanotic ☐ Jaundiced ☑ Other Cheeks flushed, hot

General Description Surgical scars: RLQ abdomen; anterior neck

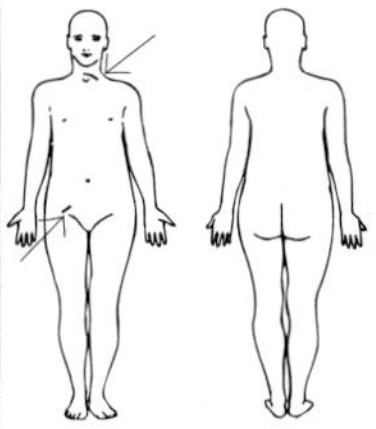

Note Cultures Obtained ______

PRESSURE SORE ™AT RISK∫ SCREENING CRITERIA

OVERALL SKIN CONDITION

Grade		
	0	Turgor (elasticity adequate, skin warm and moist)
√	1	Poor turgor, skin cold & dry
	2	Areas mottled, red or denuded
	3	Existing skin ulcer/lesions

BOWEL AND BLADDER CONTROL

Grade		
√	0	Always able to ask for bedpan
	1	Incontinence of urine
	2	Incontinence of feces
	3	Totally incontinent Confined to bed

REHABILITATIVE STATE

Grade		
	0	Fully ambulatory
√	1	Ambulated with assistance
	2	Chair to bed ambulation only
	3	Confined to bed
	4	Immobile in bed

NUTRITIONAL STATE

Grade		
	0	Eats all
√	1	Eats very little
	2	Refuses food often
	3	Tube feeding
	4	Intravenous feeding

MENTAL STATE

Grade		
√	0	Alert and clear
	1	Confused
	2	Disoriented/senile
	3	Stuporous
	4	Unconcious

CHRONIC DISEASE STATUS (i.e. COPD, ASCVD. Peripheral Vascular Disease, Diabetes, or Renal Disease, Cancer, Motor or Sensory Deficits, Elderly, Other)

Grade		
√	0	Absent
	1	One Present
	2	Two Present
	3	Three or more Present

TOTAL ______ Refer to Skin Care Protocol

FALLS SCREENING

If one or more of the following are checked institute fall precautions/plan of care

☐ History of Falls ☐ Unsteady Gait ☐ Confusion/Disorientation ☐ Dizziness

If two or more of the following are checked institute fall precautions/plan of care

☐ Age over 80 ☐ Utilizes cane, walker, w/c ☐ Sleeplessness

☐ Impaired vision ☐ Urgency/frequency in elimination

☐ Multiple Diagnoses ☐ Impaired hearing ☐ Medication/Sedative /Diuretic etc.

☐ Inability to understand or follow directions

NURSE SIGNATURE/TITLE	DATE	TIME
Mary Medina, RN	4-16-03	3:30pm
NURSE SIGNATURE/TITLE	DATE	TIME

EDUCATION/DISCHARGE PLANNING

1. What do you know about your present illness? "Dr. says I have pneumonia." "I will have an I.V."
2. What information do you want or need about your illness? ______
3. Would you like family/SO involved in your care? Husband, Michael
4. How long do you expect to be in the hospital? "1-2 days"
5. What concerns do you have about leaving the hospital? ______

CHECK APPROPRIATE BOX

Will patient need post discharge assistance with ADLs/physical functioning? ☐ Yes ☑ No ☐ Unknown

Does patient have family capable of and willing to provide assistance post discharge?

☑ Yes ☐ No ☐ Unknown ☐ No family

Is assistance needed beyond that which family can provide?

☐ Yes ☑ No ☐ Unknown

Previous admission in the last six months?

☐ Yes ☑ No ☐ Unknown

Patient lives with Husband and 1 child

Planned discharge to Home

Comments: Fatigue and anxiety may have interfered with learning. Re-teach anything covered at admission, later.

Social Services Notified ☐ Yes ☑ No

NARRATIVE NOTES

S--c/O sharp chest pain when coughing and dyspnea on exertion. States unable to carry out regular daily exercise for past week. Coughing relieved "if I sit up and sit still." Nausea associated with coughing. Having occasional "chills." Occasionally becomes frightened, stating, "I can't breathe." Well groomed but "too tired to put on make-up."

O--Chest expansion < 3cm, no nasal flaring or use of accessory muscles. Breath sounds and insp. crackles in Ⓡ upper and lower chest.

Assesses own supports as "good" (eg, relationship c̄ husband). Is "worried" about daughter. States husband will be out of town until tomorrow. Left 5-year-old daughter with neighbor. Concerned too about her work (is attorney). "I'll never get caught up." Had water at noon—no food today. Informed of need to save urine for 24 hr. specimen. IV D_5W LR 1000 mL started in Ⓡarm, 100 mL/hr. Slow capillary refill. Keeping head of bed↑ to facilitate breathing.

NORTH BROWARD HOSPITAL DISTRICT
NURSING ADMINISTRATION ASSESSMENT

Data for Amanda Aquilini, Organized According to Functional Health Patterns

Health Perception/Health Management
- Aware/understands medical diagnosis
- Gives thorough history of illnesses and surgeries
- Complies with Synthroid regimen
- Relates progression of illness in detail
- Expects to have antibiotic therapy and "go home in a day or two"
- States usual eating pattern "3 meals a day"

Nutritional/Metabolic
- 158 cm tall; weighs 57 kg
- Usual eating pattern "3 meals a day"
- "No appetite" since having "cold"
- Has not eaten today; last fluids at noon
- Nauseated
- Oral temp 39.4°C
- Decreased skin turgor

Elimination
- Usually no problem
- Decreased urinary frequency and amount × 2 days
- Last bowel movement yesterday, formed, "normal"

Activity/Exercise
- No musculoskeletal impairment
- Difficulty sleeping because of cough
- "Can't breathe lying down"
- States "I feel weak"
- Short of breath on exertion
- Exercises daily

Cognitive/Perceptual
- No sensory deficits
- Pupils 3 mm, equal, brisk reaction
- Oriented to time, place, and person
- Responsive, but fatigued
- Responds appropriately to verbal and physical stimuli
- Recent and remote memory intact
- States "short of breath" on exertion
- Reports "pain in lungs," especially when coughing
- Experiencing chills
- Reports nausea

Roy's Adaptation Model

Adaptive Modes

1. Physiological/Physical
   - Oxygenation
   - Nutrition
   - Elimination
   - Activity and rest
   - Protection
   - Senses
   - Fluid, electrolytes, and acid-base balance
   - Neurological function
   - Endocrine function
2. Self-concept/Group Identity
   - Physical self
   - Personal self
3. Role function
4. Interdependence

Source: C. Roy & H. A. Andrews. (1999). *The Roy adaptation model* (p. 102–114). Stamford, CT: Appleton & Lange.

Wellness Models

Nurses use wellness models to assist clients to identify health risks and to explore lifestyle habits and health behaviours, beliefs, values, and attitudes that influence levels of wellness. Such models generally include the following:

- Health history
- Physical fitness evaluation
- Nutritional assessment
- Sleep assessment
- Life-stress analysis
- Lifestyle and health habits
- Health beliefs
- Sexual health
- Spiritual health
- Relationships
- Health risk appraisal

Non-Nursing Models

Frameworks and models from other disciplines may also be helpful for organizing data. These frameworks are narrower than the model required in nursing; therefore, the

Data for Amanda Aquilini, Organized According to Functional Health Patterns *continued*

Self-Perception/Self-Concept
- Expresses "concern" and "worry" over leaving daughter with neighbours until husband returns
- Well-groomed, says, "Too tired to put on makeup"

Roles/Relationships
- Lives with husband and 5-year-old daughter
- Husband out of town; will be back tomorrow afternoon
- Child with neighbour until husband returns
- States "good" relationships with friends and co-workers
- Working mother, attorney

Coping/Stress
- Anxious: "I can't breathe"
- Facial muscles tense; trembling
- Expresses concerns about work: "I'll never get caught up"

Value/Belief
- Catholic
- No special practices desired, except anointing of the sick
- Middle-class, professional orientation
- No wish to see chaplain or priest at present

Medication/History
- Synthroid 0.1 mg per day
- Client has history of appendectomy, partial thyroidectomy

Nursing Physical Assessment
- 28 years old
- Height 158 cm; weight 57 kg
- TPR 39.4°C, 92, 28
- Radial pulses weak, regular
- Blood pressure 122/80 sitting
- Skin hot and pale, cheeks flushed
- Mucous membranes dry and pale
- Respirations shallow; chest expansion <3 cm
- Cough productive of small amounts of pale pink sputum
- Inspiratory crackles auscultated throughout right upper and lower chest
- Diminished breath sounds on right side
- Abdomen soft, not distended
- Old surgical scars: anterior neck, RLQ abdomen
- Diaphoretic

nurse usually needs to combine these with other approaches to obtain a complete history.

Body Systems Model The body systems model focuses on abnormalities of the following systems:

- Integumentary
- Respiratory
- Cardiovascular
- Nervous
- Musculoskeletal
- Gastrointestinal
- Genitourinary
- Reproductive

Maslow's Hierarchy of Needs Maslow's hierarchy of needs clusters data pertaining to the following:

- Physiological needs (survival needs)
- Safety and security needs
- Love and belonging needs
- Self-esteem needs
- Self-actualization needs

See Chapter 5 for detailed information.

Developmental Theories Several physical, psychosocial, cognitive, and moral developmental theories may be used by the nurse in specific situations. Examples include the following:

- Havighurst's age periods and developmental tasks
- Freud's five stages of development
- Erikson's eight stages of development
- Piaget's phases of cognitive development
- Kohlberg's stages of moral development

See Chapters 19, 20, and 21 for further information.

Validating Data

If the nursing process is to be an effective framework for nursing care, the information gathered during the assessment phase must be complete and accurate. **Validation** is the act of "double-checking" or verifying data (cues) to confirm that they are accurate and factual. Validating data helps the nurse:

- Ensure that assessment information is complete.
- Ensure that objective and related subjective data agree, or if they do not, to explore differences in perceptions.

TABLE 23.5 Validating Assessment Data

Guideline	Example
Compare subjective and objective data to verify the client's statements with your observations.	Client's perceptions of "feeling hot" need to be compared with measurement of the body temperature.
Clarify any ambiguous or vague statements.	*Client:* "I've felt sick on and off for 6 weeks." *Nurse:* "Describe what your sickness is like. Tell me what you mean by 'on and off'."
Be sure your data consist of cues and not inferences.	*Observation:* Dry skin and reduced tissue turgor *Inference:* Dehydration *Action:* Collect additional data that are needed to make the inference in the diagnosing phase. For example, determine the client's fluid intake, amount and appearance of urine, and blood pressure.
Double-check data that are extremely abnormal.	*Observation:* A resting pulse of 50 beats per minute or a blood pressure of 180/96 *Action:* Use another piece of equipment as needed to confirm abnormalities, or ask someone else to collect the same data.
Determine the presence of factors that may interfere with accurate measurement.	A crying infant will have an abnormal respiratory rate and will need quieting before accurate assessment can be made.
Use references (textbooks, journals, research reports) to explain phenomena.	A nurse considers tiny purple or bluish-black swollen areas under the tongue of an older client to be abnormal until reading about physical changes of aging. Such varicosities are not uncommon.

- Obtain additional information that may have been missed initially.
- Differentiate between cues and inferences. **Cues** are subjective or objective data that can be directly heard or observed by the nurse; that is, what the client says or what the nurse can see, hear, feel, smell, or measure. **Inferences** are the nurse's conclusions or interpretation of the cues (e.g., a nurse observes the cues that an incision is red, hot, and swollen; the nurse makes the inference that the incision is infected).
- Avoid jumping to conclusions and focusing too quickly on what seem like obvious problems.

Not all data require validation. For example, data such as height, weight, birth date, and most laboratory studies that can be measured with an accurate scale of measurement can be accepted as factual. As a rule, the nurse validates data when there are discrepancies between data obtained in the nursing interview (subjective data) and the physical examination (objective data), or when the client's statements differ at different times in the assessment. Guidelines for validating data are shown in Table 23.5.

To collect data accurately, nurses need to be aware of their own biases, values, and beliefs and to separate fact from inference, interpretation, and assumption. For example, a nurse seeing a man holding his arm to his chest might assume that he is experiencing chest pain, when, in fact, he has a painful hand.

The acceptance of assumptions as fact is called **premature closure.** To build an accurate database and avoid premature closure, nurses must validate assumptions regarding the client's physical or emotional behaviour. In the previous example, the nurse should ask the client why he is holding his arm to his chest. The client's response may validate the nurse's assumptions or prompt further questioning. Figure 23.2 on pages 400 and 401 shows that the nurse auscultated Amanda Aquilini's heart and lungs to validate her statement that she had "pain" in her "lungs" and "shortness of breath" on exertion. Failure to validate assumptions can lead to an inaccurate or incomplete nursing assessment.

Documenting Data

To complete the assessment phase, the nurse records client data. Accurate documentation is essential and should include all data collected about the client's health status. Data are recorded in a factual manner and not interpreted by the nurse. For example, the nurse records the client's breakfast intake (objective data) as "coffee 240 mL, juice 120 mL, 1 egg, and 1 slice of toast," rather than as "appetite good" (a judgement). A judgement or conclusion, such as "appetite good" or "normal appetite," may have different meanings for different people. To increase accuracy, the nurse records subjective data in the client's own words. Restating in other words what someone says increases the chance of changing the original meaning. Details of recording are discussed in Chapter 24.

Diagnosing

Diagnosing is the second phase of the nursing process. In this phase, nurses use critical-thinking skills to interpret assessment data and identify client strengths and problems. Diagnosing is a pivotal step in the nursing process. All activities preceding this phase are directed toward formulating the nursing diagnoses or hypotheses; all the care-planning activities following this phase are based on the nursing diagnoses.

The identification and development of nursing diagnoses began formally in 1973, when two faculty members of Saint Louis University, Kristine Gebbie and Mary Ann Lavin, perceived a need to identify nurses' roles in an ambulatory-care setting. The First National Conference to identify nursing diagnoses was sponsored by the Saint Louis University School of Nursing and Allied Health Professions in 1973. Subsequent national conferences have occurred in 1975, 1978, 1980, and every two years thereafter.

International recognition came with the First Canadian Conference in Toronto in 1977 and the International Nursing Conference in May 1987 in Calgary, Alberta, Canada (Hannah, Reimer, Mills, & Letourneau, 1987). In 1982, the conference group accepted the name North American Nursing Diagnosis Association (NANDA), recognizing the participation and contributions of nurses in the United States and Canada.

The purpose of NANDA is to define, refine, and promote a *taxonomy* (classification system) of nursing diagnostic terminology of general use to professional nurses. The members of NANDA include staff nurses, clinical specialists, faculty, directors of nursing, deans, theorists, and researchers. The group has currently approved more than 150 nursing diagnosis labels for clinical use and testing (NANDA, 2003).

NANDA Nursing Diagnoses

Definitions

For clarity, this chapter uses the terms adapted from Carpenito (2000). The term *diagnosis* refers to the diagnostic reasoning process; the standardized NANDA terms are called *diagnostic labels;* and the client's problem statement (diagnostic label plus etiology) is called a *nursing diagnosis.*

In 1990, NANDA adopted an official working definition of **nursing diagnosis,** shown in the box to the right, as well as a definition of **wellness diagnosis.** These definitions imply the following:

- *Professional nurses (registered nurses) are responsible for making nursing diagnoses*, even though other nursing personnel may contribute data to the process of diagnosing and may implement specified nursing care.
- *Nursing diagnoses describe a continuum of health states:* deviations from health, presence of risk factors, and areas of enriched personal growth. See "Types of Nursing Diagnoses" next.
- *The domain of nursing diagnosis includes only those health states that nurses are educated and licensed to treat.* For example, nurses are not educated to diagnose or treat such diseases as diabetes mellitus; this task is defined legally as within the practice of medicine. Yet, nurses can diagnose and treat ***Deficient Knowledge, Ineffective Coping,*** or ***Imbalanced Nutrition,*** all of which may accompany diabetes mellitus.
- *A nursing diagnosis is a judgement made only after thorough, systematic data collection.*

Types of Nursing Diagnoses

The major types of nursing diagnoses are actual, risk, possible, and wellness.

- An *actual diagnosis* is a client problem that is present at the time of the nursing assessment. An actual nursing diagnosis is based on the presence of associated signs and symptoms. Examples are ***Ineffective Breathing Pattern*** and ***Anxiety.***
- A *risk nursing diagnosis* is a clinical judgement that a problem does not exist, but the presence of **risk factors** indicates that a problem is likely to develop unless nurses intervene. For example, all people admitted to a hospital have some possibility of acquiring an infection; however, a client with diabetes or a compromised immune system is at higher risk than others.

1990 NANDA Definitions

Nursing Diagnosis

"Nursing diagnosis is a clinical judgment about individual, family, or community responses to actual and potential health problems/life processes. Nursing diagnoses provide the basis for selection of nursing interventions to achieve outcomes for which the nurse is accountable."

Wellness Diagnosis

"A wellness diagnosis is a clinical judgment about an individual, family, or community in transition from a specific level of wellness to a higher level of wellness."

Source: North American Nursing Diagnosis Association. *Taxonomy I, Revised–1990* (St. Louis: NANDA, 1990), p. 114, 117.

Therefore, the nurse would appropriately use the label ***Risk for Infection*** to describe the client's health status.

- A *possible diagnosis* is a clinical problem that may be present but more information is needed. An example is ***Possible Disturbance in Self-Concept.***
- A *wellness diagnosis* is one indicating a healthy response of a client who desires a higher level of wellness. An example of a wellness diagnosis would be ***Readiness for Enhanced Spiritual Well-Being.***

Components of a NANDA Nursing Diagnosis

A nursing diagnosis usually has three components: (1) the diagnostic label, (2) the defining characteristics, and (3) related factors. Risk diagnoses have (1) diagnostic label and (2) risk factors (NANDA, 2002).

Diagnostic Label (Problem) The problem statement, or diagnostic label, describes the client's health problem or response for which nursing therapy is given. It describes the client's health status clearly and concisely in a few words.

The purpose of the diagnostic label is to direct the formation of client goals and desired outcomes. It may also suggest some nursing interventions.

One of the major contributions of the NANDA taxonomy has been its utility as a standardized language for nursing in charting and referencing. NANDA introduced a new structure for its Taxonomy II, approved at the 14th biennial conference in April 2000 (NANDA, 2001). Overall, there are 13 domains (see box) further subdivided into 106 classes. For example, the diagnostic label, ***Impaired Gas Exchange,*** is classified under the domain Elimination, class Pulmonary System. In daily practice, the individual nurse uses only the diagnostic labels, but knowledge of the broad domains can be helpful as a framework for assessment.

Two objections are frequently raised about the use of the diagnostic labels. The first objection is that the term "label" suggests to many nurses a process of denying the individuality of the client, perhaps even of stereotyping people (Mitchell, 1991). One of the most frequently criticized nursing diagnoses is ***Noncompliance.*** As with many tools, this diagnostic label can be construed as something negative or positive. However, closer examination of the definition used in nursing clarifies that it is only an appropriate nursing diagnosis when the client has indicated that he or she has agreed to the therapeutic plan but then has difficulty following it. Specifically, **noncompliance** is defined as "behaviour of a person and/or caregiver that fails to coincide with a health-promoting or therapeutic plan agreed on by the person (and/or family and/or community) and health-care professional. In the presence of an agreed-on health-promoting or therapeutic plan, [the] person's or caregiver's behaviour is fully or partially nonadherent and may lead to clinically ineffective or partially ineffective outcomes" (NANDA, 2001, p. 122). For example, a client recovering from a myocardial infarction may recognize the need to exercise regularly but seeks the help of a nurse in cardiac rehabilitation because the client finds it difficult to follow a consistent activity program. For that client, the diagnosis would be accurate. However, another client who has chosen to not take prescribed medication for hypertension but, instead, is concentrating on balancing activity and rest and use of herbal remedies should not be identified as noncompliant. The second common objection has been cumbersome wording, a problem exacerbated when nurses added the domain and class name to the actual diagnosis. However, most diagnostic labels are only one to three words.

Under the Taxonomy II multiaxial system (much like the system used for medical diagnoses of psychiatric disorders), Axis 1 is the diagnostic label. Axes 2 to 7 are additional descriptors that may be used to make the diagnosis more specific (see Table 23.6).

Defining Characteristics **Defining characteristics** are the cluster of signs and symptoms that indicate the presence of a particular diagnostic label. For *actual* nursing diagnoses, the defining characteristics are in the client's signs and symptoms. For *risk* nursing diagnoses, there are no subjective and objective signs present. Thus, risk factors that cause the client to be more than "normally" vulnerable to the problem are identified instead.

Related Factors* and *Risk Factors The **related factors** component of a nursing diagnosis identifies one or more probable causes of the health problem, gives direction to the required nursing therapy, and enables the nurse to individualize the client's care. As shown in Table 23.7, the probable causes of ***Activity Intolerance*** include sedentary lifestyle, generalized weakness, and so on. Differentiating among possible causes in the nursing diagnosis is essential because each may require different nursing interventions. Refer to Table 23.8 for examples of diagnostic labels that have different related factors and, therefore, require different interventions.

NANDA Taxonomy II Domains

Health Promotion	Role Relationships
Nutrition	Sexuality
Elimination	Coping/Stress Tolerance
Activity/Rest	Life Principles
Perception/Cognition	Safety/Protection
Self-Perception	Comfort
Growth/Development	

Source: *NANDA Nursing diagnoses: Definitions and classification 2003–2004.* (2002). Philadelphia, PA: North American Nursing Diagnosis Association, p. 214–215.

TABLE 23.6 NANDA Taxonomy II Multiaxial System

Axis	Examples
Axis 1: Diagnostic Concept	Powerlessness Sleep pattern
Axis 2: Time	Acute: less than six months Intermittent: stopping or starting at intervals
Axis 3: Unit of Care	Family Community
Axis 4: Age	School-aged child Middle-aged adult
Axis 5: Health Status	Wellness Risk
Axis 6: Descriptor (a modifier that specifies)	Disturbed: agitated or interrupted Effective: producing the intended or expected effect
Axis 7: Topology (parts or regions of the body)	Mucous membranes Tactile

Source: NANDA International (2002). *NANDA Nursing Diagnoses: Definitions and Classification 2003–2004*. Philadelphia: NANDA.

Differentiating Nursing Diagnoses from Medical Diagnoses

Whereas a nursing diagnosis is a statement of nursing judgement and refers to a condition that nurses are licensed to treat, a medical diagnosis is made by a physician and refers to a condition that only a physician or nurse practitioner can treat. Medical diagnoses refer to disease processes—specific pathophysiological responses that are fairly uniform from one client to another. In contrast, nursing diagnoses describe a client's physical, sociocultural, psychological, and spiritual responses to an illness or a health problem. These responses vary among individuals. A client's medical diagnosis remains the same for as long as the disease process is present, but nursing diagnoses change as the client's responses change, as in the following example:

> Seventy-year-old Mary Cain and 20-year-old Kristi Vidan both have rheumatoid arthritis. Their disease processes are much the same. X-ray studies show that in both clients, the extent of inflammation and the number of joints involved are similar, and both clients experience almost constant pain. Ms. Cain views her condition as part of the aging process and is responding with acceptance. Ms. Vidan, however, is responding with anger and hostility because she views her disease as a threat to her personal identity, role performance, and self-esteem.

Nurses have responsibilities related to both medical and nursing diagnoses. Nursing diagnoses relate to the nurse's **independent functions,** that is, the areas of health care that are unique to nursing and separate and distinct from medical management. With regard to medical diagnoses, nurses work collaboratively in carrying out physician prescribed therapies.

Nurses may not prescribe *all* the care for a nursing diagnosis, but if the problem is a nursing diagnosis, the nurse can prescribe *most* of the interventions needed for prevention or resolution. For example, most clients with a nursing diagnosis of ***Pain*** have medical orders for analgesics, but many independent nursing interventions can also alleviate pain (e.g., guided imagery or teaching a client to "splint" an incision).

Differentiating Nursing Diagnoses from Collaborative Problems

A collaborative problem is a type of potential problem that nurses manage using both independent and physician

TABLE 23.7 Components of a Nursing Diagnosis

Diagnosis and Definition	Related Factors	Defining Characteristics
Activity Intolerance: Insufficient physiological or psychological energy to endure or complete required or desired daily activities	Bed rest or immobility Generalized weakness Imbalance between oxygen supply/demand Sedentary lifestyle	Verbal report of fatigue or weakness Abnormal heart rate or blood pressure response to activity Electrocardiographic changes reflecting arrhythmias or ischemia Exertional discomfort Pallor, cyanosis, vertigo, diaphoresis, confusion

Sources: NANDA International (2002). *NANDA Nursing Diagnoses: Definitions and Classification 2003–2004*. Philadelphia: NANDA.

TABLE 23.8 Examples of Nursing Interventions to Address Different Related Factors

Diagnostic Label (Problem)	Client	Related Factors	Example of Nursing Interventions
Colonic Constipation	Al Martinez	Long-term laxative use	Work with Mr. Martinez to develop a plan for gradual withdrawal from the laxatives; teach components of a high-fibre diet.
	Li Wong	Inactivity and insufficient fluid intake	Help Mr. Wong develop an exercise regimen that he can follow at home; obtain information about his daily schedule and types of fluids he likes; help Mr. Wong develop a plan for including sufficient amounts of fluids in his diet.
Ineffective Breast Feeding	Zoe James	Breast engorgement	Teach Ms. James to massage her breasts before feeding; use hot packs or hot shower before nursing infant.
	Jenny King	Inexperience and lack of knowledge	Teach Ms. King to feed infant on demand; show her how to be sure infant is sucking and swallowing; and demonstrate different holding positions for feedings.

prescribed interventions. Independent nursing interventions for a collaborative problem focus mainly on monitoring the client's condition and preventing development of the potential complication. Definitive treatment of the condition requires both medical and nursing interventions.

Collaborative problems tend to be present any time a particular disease or treatment is present; that is, each disease or treatment has specific complications that are always associated with it. For example, a statement of collaborative problems is "Potential complication of pneumonia: atelectasis, respiratory failure, pleural effusion, pericarditis, and meningitis."

Nursing diagnoses, by contrast, involve human responses, which vary greatly from one person to the next. Therefore, the same set of nursing diagnoses cannot be expected to occur with a particular disease or condition; moreover, a single nursing diagnosis may occur as a response to any number of diseases. For example, all postpartum clients have similar collaborative problems (potential complications), such as "Potential complication of childbearing: postpartum hemorrhage," but not all new mothers have the same nursing diagnoses. Some might experience ***Altered Parenting*** (delayed bonding), but most will not; some might have a ***Knowledge Deficit*** problem whereas others will not. See Table 23.9 for a comparison of nursing diagnoses, collaborative problems, and medical diagnoses.

The Diagnostic Process

The diagnostic process uses the critical-thinking skills of analysis and synthesis. *Critical thinking* is a cognitive process during which a person reviews data and considers explanations before forming an opinion. *Analysis* is the separation into components, that is, breaking down the whole into its parts. *Synthesis* is the opposite, that is, putting together the parts into the whole.

The diagnostic process is used continuously by most nurses. An experienced nurse may enter a client's room and immediately observe significant data and draw conclusions about the client. As a result of attaining knowledge, skill, and expertise in the practice setting, the expert nurse may seem to perform these mental processes automatically. Novice nurses, however, need guidelines to understand and formulate nursing diagnoses. The diagnostic process has three steps:

- Analyzing data
- Identifying health problems, risks, and strengths
- Formulating diagnostic statements

Analyzing Data

In the diagnostic process, analyzing involves the following steps:

1. Compare data against standards (identify significant cues).
2. Cluster cues (generate tentative hypotheses).
3. Identify gaps and inconsistencies.

For experienced nurses, these activities occur continuously rather than sequentially.

Comparing Data with Standards Nurses draw on knowledge and experience to compare client data to standards and norms and identify significant and relevant cues. A **standard** or **norm** is a generally accepted measure, rule, model, or pattern. The nurse uses a wide range of standards, such as growth and development patterns, normal vital signs, and

TABLE 23.9 Comparison of Nursing Diagnoses, Collaborative Problems, and Medical Diagnoses

Category	Nursing Diagnoses	Collaborative Problems	Medical Diagnoses
Example	***Activity Intolerance*** related to decreased cardiac output	Potential complication of myocardial infarction: congestive heart failure	Myocardial infarction
Description	Describe human responses to disease process or health problem; consist of a one-, two-, or three-part statement, usually including problem and related factors	Involve human responses—mainly physiological complications of disease, tests, or treatments; consist of a two-part statement of situation/pathophysiology and the potential complication	Describe disease and pathology; do not consider other human responses; usually consist of not more than three words
Orientation and responsibility for diagnosing	Oriented to the individual; nurses responsible for diagnosing	Oriented to pathophysiology; shared responsiblity for diagnosing	Oriented to pathology; physician responsible for diagnosing; diagnosis not within the scope of nursing practice
Treatment orders	Nurse orders most interventions to prevent and treat	Nurse collaborates with physician and other health-care professionals to prevent and treat; require medical orders for definitive treatment	Physician orders primary interventions to prevent and treat
Nursing focus	Treat and prevent	Prevent and monitor for onset or status of condition	Implement medical orders for treatment and monitor status of condition
Nursing actions	Independent	Some independent actions, but primarily for monitoring and preventing	Dependent (primarily)
Duration	Can change frequently	Present when disease or situation is present	Remains the same while disease is present
Classification system	Classification system is developed and being used but is not universally accepted	No universally accepted classification system	Well-developed classification system accepted by the medical profession

laboratory values. A **cue** is any piece of information or data that influences decisions. A cue is considered significant if it does any of the following (Gordon, 1994):

- *The cue points to change in a client's health status or pattern.* These may be positive or negative. For example, the client states: "I have recently experienced shortness of breath while climbing stairs," or "I have not smoked for three months."
- *The cue varies from norms of the client population.* The client's pattern may fit within cultural norms but vary from norms of the general society. The client may consider a pattern—for example, eating very small meals and having little appetite—to be normal. This pattern, however, may not be productive and may require further exploration.
- *The cue indicates a developmental delay.* To identify significant cues, the nurse must be aware of the normal patterns and changes that occur as the person grows and develops. For example, by age nine months, an infant is usually able to sit without support. The infant who has not accomplished this task needs further assessment for possible developmental delays.

Refer to Table 23.10 for specific examples of client cues and norms to which they may be compared. Significant cues and data clusters for Amanda Aquilini that were extracted from Figure 23.2 on pages 400–401 and the box on pages 402–403 are shown in Table 23.11.

Clustering Cues Clustering or grouping cues is a process of determining the relatedness of facts and determining

TABLE 23.10 Comparing Cues to Standards and Norms

Type of Cue	Client Cues	Standard/Norm
Deviation from population norms	Height is 158 cm tall. Woman with small frame Weight 109 kg	Height and weight tables indicate that the "ideal" weight for a woman 158 cm tall with a small frame is 49–53 kg.
Developmental delay	Child is 18 months old. Parents state child has not yet attempted to speak. Child laughs aloud and makes cooing sounds.	Children usually speak their first word by 10 to 12 months of age.
Changes in client's usual health status	Client states, "I'm just not hungry these days." Ate only 15% of food on breakfast tray Has lost 13 kg in past 3 months	Client usually eats three balanced meals per day. Adults typically maintain stable weight.
Dysfunctional behaviour	Tanya's mother reports that Tanya has not left her room for 2 days. Tanya is age 16. Tanya has stopped attending school and has withdrawn from social contact.	Adolescents usually like to be with their peers; social groups are very important. Functional behaviour includes school attendance.
Changes in client's usual behaviour	Mrs. Stuart reports that lately her husband gets angry easily. "Yesterday he even yelled at the dog." "He just seems so tense."	Mr. Stuart is usually relaxed and easygoing. He is friendly and kind to animals.

whether any patterns are present, whether the data represent isolated incidents, and whether the data are significant. This is the beginning of synthesis.

The nurse may cluster data *inductively* (as in Table 23.11) by combining data from different assessment areas to form a pattern, or the nurse may begin with a framework, such as Gordon's functional health patterns, and cluster the subjective and objective data into the appropriate categories (see the box on page 399). The latter is a *deductive* approach to data clustering, or pattern formation.

Experienced nurses may cluster data as they collect and interpret it, as evidenced in remarks or thoughts such as, "I'm getting a picture of...," or "This cue doesn't fit the picture." The novice nurse does not have the knowledge base or the clinical experience that aids in recognizing cues. Thus, the novice must take careful assessment notes, search data for abnormal cues, and use textbook resources for comparing the client's cues with the defining characteristics and etiological factors of the accepted nursing diagnoses.

Data clustering involves making inferences about the data. An **inference** is the nurse's judgement or interpretation of cues. The nurse interprets the possible meaning of the cues and labels the cue clusters with tentative diagnostic hypotheses. Data clustering or grouping for Amanda Aquilini is illustrated in Table 23.11, in which data are clustered according to standardized diagnosis labels.

Identifying Gaps and Inconsistencies in Data Skillful assessment minimizes gaps and inconsistencies in data. However, data analysis should include a final check to ensure that data are complete and correct.

Inconsistencies are conflicting data. Possible sources of conflicting data include measurement error, expectations, and conflicting or unreliable reports (Gordon, 1994). For example, a nurse may learn from the nursing history that the client reports not having seen a doctor in 15 years, yet during the physical health examination, he states, "My doctor takes my blood pressure every week." All inconsistencies must be clarified before a valid pattern can be established.

Identifying Health Problems, Risks, and Strengths

After data are analyzed, the nurse and client can together identify strengths and problems. This is primarily a decision-making process. See Chapter 22.

Determining Problems After grouping and clustering data, the nurse and client together identify tentative diagnoses. In addition, the nurse must determine whether the client's problem is a nursing diagnosis, medical diagnosis, or collaborative problem. See Figure 23.3 for a decision tree to aid in this decision. Also, refer to Table 23.9.

TABLE 23.11 Formulating Nursing Diagnoses for Amanda Aquilini

Functional Health Pattern	Client Cue Clusters	Inferences (Tentative Identification of Problems)	Formulating Diagnostic Statements
Health perception/ health management			No problem *Strength:* Shows healthy lifestyle, understanding of and compliance with treatment regimens
Nutritional/metabolic (includes hydration)	"No appetite" since having "cold" Has not eaten today; last fluids at noon today Nauseated ×2 days	***Altered Nutrition: Less than Body Requirements***	***Altered Nutrition: Less than Body Requirements*** related to decreased appetite and nausea and increased metabolism (secondary to disease process) *Strength:* Normal weight for height
	Last fluids at noon today Oral temp 39.4°C Skin hot and pale, cheeks flushed Mucous membranes dry Poor skin turgor *Cues from elimination pattern:* Decreased urinary frequency and amount ×2 days	***Fluid Volume Deficit***	***Fluid Volume Deficit*** related to intake insufficient to replace fluid loss secondary to fever and diaphoresis
Elimination	Decreased urinary frequency and amount ×2 days	Cues consist of elimination data but are actually symptoms of a fluid volume problem in the nutritional/metabolic functional health pattern	No elimination problem
Activity/exercise	States, "I feel weak standing at the sink and in the shower" Short of breath on exertion *Cues from cognitive/ perceptual pattern:* Responsive but fatigued "I can think OK, just weak" *Cues from cardiovascular pattern:* Radial pulses weak, regular Pulse rate 92	***Activity Intolerance*** ***Self-Care Deficit***	***Self-Care Deficit, Bathing/Hygiene*** related to activity intolerance secondary to ineffective airway clearance and sleep pattern disturbance *Strength:* No musculo-skeletal impairment, normal energy level is satisfactory, exercises regularly
Sleep/rest	Difficulty sleeping because of cough "Can't breathe lying down"	***Disturbed Sleep Pattern***	***Disturbed Sleep Pattern*** related to cough, pain, orthopnea, fever, and diaphoresis
Cognitive/perceptual	Reports pain in lungs, especially when coughing Responsive but fatigued "I can think OK, just weak"	***Pain*** These are cognitive/perceptual data, but they reflect symptoms of problems in the activity/ exercise pattern	***Pain (Chest), Acute*** related to cough secondary to pneumonia *Strength:* No cognitive or sensory deficits

→

TABLE 23.11 Formulating Nursing Diagnoses for Amanda Aquilini *continued*

Functional Health Pattern	Client Cue Clusters	Inferences (Tentative Identification of Problems)	Formulating Diagnostic Statements
Self-perception/ self-concept	Expresses "concern" and "worry" over leaving daughter with neighbours until husband returns	Cue is a symptom of a problem in the coping/ stress pattern	No self-perception/self-concept problem
Roles/relationships	Husband out of town; will be back tomorrow afternoon Child with neighbour until husband returns	***Altered Family Processes*** related to mother's illness and temporary unavailability of father to provide child care Cues also related to a problem in the coping/stress pattern	***Risk for Altered Family Processes*** related to mother's illness and temporary unavailability of father to provide child care *Strength:* Husband supportive; neighbours available and willing to help
Coping/stress	Anxious: "I can't breathe" Facial muscles tense; trembling Expresses concerns about work: "I'll never get caught up" *Cues from role/relationship pattern:* Husband out of town; will be back tomorrow afternoon Child with neighbour until husband returns *Cues from self-perception/ self-concept patterns:* Expresses "concern" and "worry" over leaving daughter with neighbours	***Anxiety*** related to difficulty breathing, inability to work, and child care	***Anxiety*** related to difficulty breathing and concerns over work and parenting roles
Medication/history	No significant cues	No problem	No problem
Physical assessment			
Cardiovascular	Radial pulses weak, regular Pulse rate 92	Cues are symptoms only; symptoms of exercise/rest and oxygenation problems	No cardiovascular problem
Oxygenation	Skin hot, pale, and moist Respirations shallow; chest expansion, 3 cm Cough productive of small amounts of pale pink sputum Inspiratory crackles auscultated throughout right upper and lower chest Diminished breath sounds on right side Mucous membranes pale	***Ineffective Airway Clearance*** related to disease process	***Ineffective Airway Clearance*** related to viscous secretions and shallow chest expansion secondary to pain, fluid volume deficit, and fatigue
Skin	Old surgical scars, anterior neck, RLQ abdomen	No problem now	Old problems; resolved

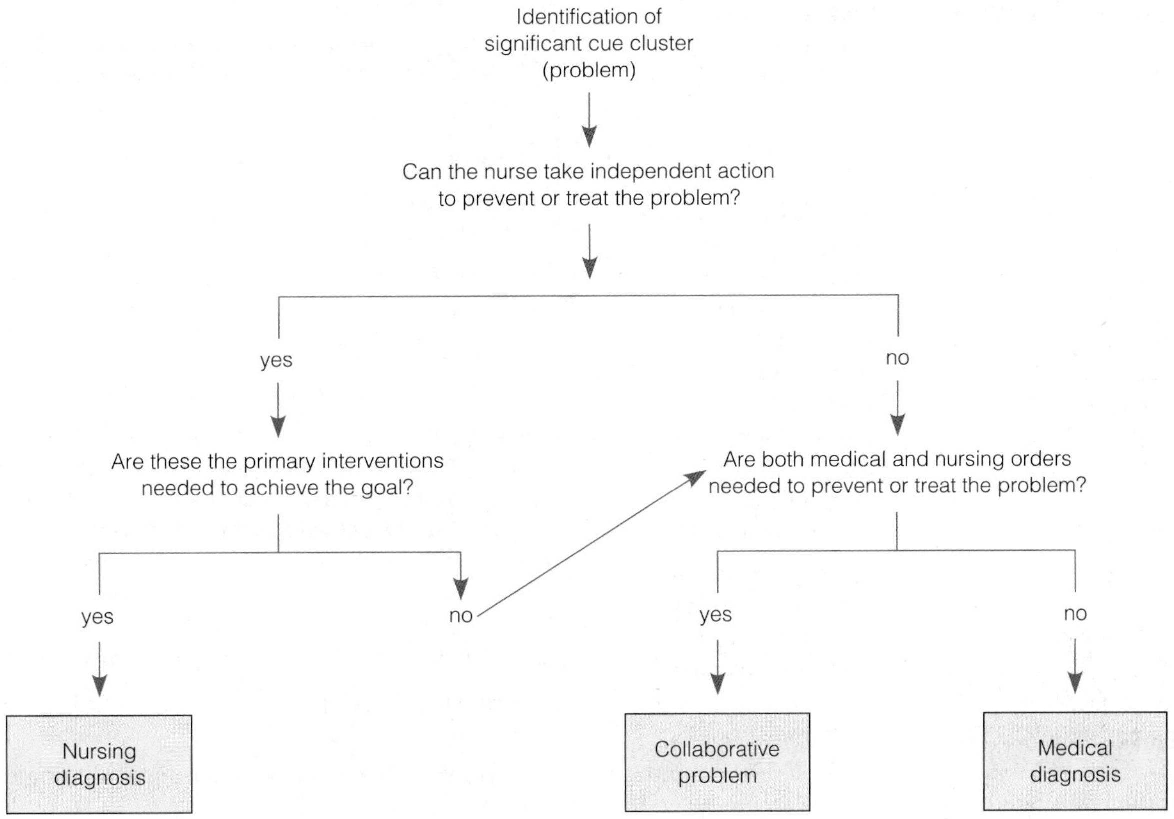

Figure 23.3 Decision tree for differentiating among nursing diagnoses, collaborative problems, and medical diagnoses

For examples, refer to the cue clusters and tentative identification of problems for Amanda Aquilini in Table 23.11. In this example, the nurse and client identified nine tentative problems: ***Altered Nutrition: Less than Body Requirements; Fluid Volume Deficit; Disturbed Sleep Pattern; Self-Care Deficit; Chest Pain; Altered Family Processes; Anxiety; Activity Intolerance; and Ineffective Airway Clearance.***

Determining Strengths At this stage, the nurse and client also establish the client's strengths, resources, and abilities to cope. Most people have a clearer perception of their problems or weaknesses than of their strengths and assets, which they often take for granted. By taking an inventory of strengths, the client can develop a more well-rounded self-concept and self-image. Strengths can be an aid to mobilizing health and regenerative processes.

A client's strength might be weight that is within the normal range for age and height, thus enabling the client to cope better with surgery. In another instance, a client's strengths might be absence of allergies and being a nonsmoker.

A client's strengths can be found in the nursing assessment record (health, home life, education, recreation, exercise, work, family and friends, religious beliefs, and sense of humour, for example), the health examination, and the client's records. See Table 23.11 for the five strengths identified for Amanda Aquilini.

Avoiding Errors in Diagnostic Reasoning

Some error is inherent in any human undertaking, and diagnosis is no exception. However, it is important that nurses make nursing diagnoses with a high level of accuracy. Nurses can avoid some common errors of reasoning by recognizing them and applying the appropriate critical-thinking skills. Error can occur at any point in the diagnostic process: data collection, data interpretation, and data clustering.

The following suggestions should help to minimize diagnostic error:

- *Verify.* Hypothesize possible explanations of the data, but realize that all diagnoses are only tentative until they are verified. Begin and end the diagnostic process by talking with the client and family. When collecting data, ask them what their health problems are and what they believe the causes to be. At the end of the process, ask them to verify your diagnoses.
- *Build a good knowledge base, and acquire clinical experience.* Nurses must apply knowledge from many different areas to recognize significant cues and patterns

and generate hypotheses about the data. To name only a few, principles from chemistry, anatomy, and pharmacology each help the nurse understand client data in a different way.

- *Have a working knowledge of what is normal.* Nurses need to know the population norms for vital signs, laboratory tests, speech development, breath sounds, and so on. In addition, nurses must determine what is normal for a particular person, taking into account age, physical makeup, lifestyle, culture, and the person's own perception of what is normal. For example, normal blood pressure for adults is in the range of 110/60 to 140/90 (Canadian Hypertension Recommendations Working Group, 2001). However, a nurse might obtain a reading of 90/50 that is normal for a particular client. The nurse should compare findings to the client's baseline when possible.
- *Consult resources.* Both novices and experienced nurses should consult appropriate resources whenever in doubt about a diagnosis. Professional literature, nursing colleagues, and other professionals are all appropriate resources.
- *Base diagnoses on patterns—that is, on behaviour over time—rather than on an isolated incident.* For example, even though Amanda Aquilini is concerned today about needing to leave her child with a neighbour, it is likely that this concern will be resolved without intervention by the next day. Therefore, the admitting nurse should not diagnose ***Altered Family Processes.***
- *Improve critical-thinking skills.* These skills help the nurse to be aware of and avoid errors in thinking, such as overgeneralizing, stereotyping, making unwarranted assumptions, and so on. See Chapter 22.

Formulating Diagnostic Statements

Most nursing diagnoses are written as two-part or three-part statements.

Basic Two-Part Statements

The basic two-part statement includes the following:

1. Diagnostic label (problem): statement of the client's response (NANDA label)
2. Related factors: factors contributing to or probable causes of the responses

Basic Two-Part Diagnostic Statement

Diagnostic label	*Related to*	*Related factors*
Constipation	related to	prolonged laxative use
Ineffective Breast-feeding	related to	breast engorgement

The two parts are joined by the words ***related to*** rather than *due to*. The phrase *due to* implies that one part causes or is responsible for the other part. By contrast, the phrase *related to* merely implies a relationship. Some examples of two-part nursing dignoses are shown in the box above.

Basic Three-Part Statements

The basic three-part nursing diagnosis statement includes:

1. Diagnostic label (problem): statement of the client's response (NANDA label)
2. Related factors and risk factors: contributing to or probable causes of the response
3. Defining characteristics manifested by the client: signs and symptoms

Actual nursing diagnoses can be documented by using the three-part statement (see the box below) because the signs and symptoms have been identified. This format cannot be used for risk diagnosis because the client does not have signs and symptoms of the diagnosis.

Collaborative Problems

Carpenito (1997) suggests that all collaborative problems begin with the diagnostic label "Potential Complication" (PC). Nurses should include in the diagnostic statement both the possible complication they are monitoring and the disease or treatment that is present to produce it. For example, if the client has a head injury and could develop increased intracranial pressure, the nurse should write the following:

Basic Three-Part Diagnostic Statement

Diagnostic label	*Related to*	*Related factor*	*As manifested by*	*Defining characteristics (signs and symptoms)*
Chronic low self-esteem	related to (r/t)	rejection by husband	as manifested by (a.m.b.)	hypersensitivity to criticism; states, "I don't know if I can manage by myself" and rejects positive feedback

RESEARCH NOTE

Are Hospital Nurses Expected to Use Nursing Diagnoses?

The purpose of this study was to identify (1) the number and type of institutions in the state of Illinois in which nursing diagnosis had been implemented, and (2) the current status of nursing diagnosis use (supports and barriers). Researchers surveyed 239 hospitals in Illinois during 1992. The people actually completing the surveys were primarily nurse administrators or educators. Of the 139 agencies (58 percent) responding, nursing diagnosis had been implemented in 109 (78 percent). Of the 109 agencies using nursing diagnosis, 95 percent used NANDA terminology. Most included nursing diagnosis in an orientation program; most had an individual responsible for continuing education related to nursing diagnosis; and 45 percent monitored the ongoing use of nursing diagnosis through quality improvement methods. When asked about barriers to use of nursing diagnoses, 26 percent of the surveyed hospitals named limited ongoing education, lack of motivation to learn, or nurses' difficulties in using the NANDA taxonomy.

Implications: The use of clinical terms to describe the health issues that nurses address is essential to the continuing development of the profession. This study identifies a higher rate of use of nursing diagnosis than did previous studies, perhaps indicating that even in these changing times of managed care, nursing diagnosis can be easily integrated into critical pathways and protocols by identifying those client responses most frequently encountered in daily practice. Results indicate that in-service education and further refinement of the NANDA taxonomy will support nurses in their use of nursing diagnoses.

Source: Whitley, G. G. Gulanick, M. (1996). Barriers to the use of nursing diagnosis language in clinical settings. *Nursing Diagnosis, 7*(1), 25–32.

Potential Complication of Head Injury: Increased intracranial pressure

When monitoring for a group of complications associated with a disease or pathology, the nurse states the disease and follows it with a list of the complications:

Potential Complication of Pregnancy-Induced Hypertension: Seizures, fetal distress, pulmonary edema, hepatic/renal failure, premature labour, CNS hemorrhage

Using Diagnostic Statements Effectively

Table 23.12 offers guidelines for learning to write useful diagnostic statements. Beginning nurses often prepare long lists but checking initial statements (hypotheses) with the client helps both nurse and client narrow down the list to those which are most important in the current clinical context.

Planning

Planning is a deliberative, systematic phase of the nursing process that involves decision making and problem solving. In planning, the nurse refers to the client's assessment data and diagnostic statements for direction in formulating client goals and designing the nursing interventions required to prevent, reduce, or eliminate the client's health problems. The product of the planning phase is a client care plan.

Although planning is basically the nurse's responsibility, input from the client and support persons is essential if a plan is to be effective. Nurses do not plan *for* the client but encourage the client to participate actively to the extent possible. In a home setting, the client's support people and/or caregivers are the ones who implement the plan of care; thus, its effectiveness depends largely on them.

Types of Planning

Planning begins with the first client contact and continues until the nurse-client relationship ends, usually when the client is discharged from the health-care agency.

Initial Planning

The nurse who performs the admission assessment usually develops the initial comprehensive plan of care. This nurse has the benefit of the client's body language as well as some intuitive kinds of information that are not available from the written database. Planning should be initiated as soon as possible after the initial assessment, especially because of the trend toward shorter hospital stays.

Collaborative Problems

Disease/Situation	*Complication*	*Related to*	*Etiology*
Potential complication of *childbirth:*	hemorrhage	related to	1. uterine atony 2. retained placental fragments 3. bladder distention
Potential complication of *diuretic therapy:*	arrhythmia	related to	low serum potassium

TABLE 23.12 Guidelines for Writing a Nursing Diagnostic Statement

Guideline	Correct Statement	Incorrect and/or Ambiguous Statement
1. State in terms of a problem, not a need.	***Fluid Volume Deficit*** (problem) related to fever	***Fluid replacement*** (need) related to fever
2. Word the statement so that it is legally advisable.	***Impaired Skin Integrity*** related to immobility (legally acceptable)	***Impaired Skin Integrity*** related to improper positioning (implies legal liability)
3. Use nonjudgmental statements.	***Spiritual Distress*** related to inability to attend church services secondary to immobility (nonjudgmental)	***Spiritual Distress*** related to strict rules necessitating church attendance (judgmental)
4. Make sure that both elements of the statement do *not* say the same thing.	***Risk for Impaired Skin Integrity*** related to immobility	***Impaired Skin Integrity*** related to ulceration of sacral area (response and probable cause are the same)
5. Be sure that cause and effect are correctly stated (i.e., the related factor causes the problem or puts the client at risk for the problem).	***Pain: Severe Headache*** related to fear of addiction to narcotics	***Pain*** related to severe headache
6. Word the diagnosis specifically and precisely to provide direction for planning nursing intervention.	***Altered Oral Mucous Membrane*** related to decreased salivation secondary to radiation of neck (specific)	***Altered Oral Mucous Membrane*** related to noxious agent (vague)
7. Use nursing terminology, rather than medical terminology, to describe the client's response.	***Risk for Ineffective Airway Clearance*** related to accumulation of secretions in lungs (nursing terminology)	***Risk for Pneumonia*** (medical terminology)
8. Use nursing terminology, rather than medical terminology, to describe the probable cause of the client's response.	***Risk for Ineffective Airway Clearance*** related to accumulation of secretions in lungs (nursing terminology)	***Risk for Ineffective Airway Clearance*** related to emphysema (medical terminology)

Ongoing Planning

Ongoing planning is done by all nurses who work with the client. As nurses obtain new information and evaluate the client's responses to care, they can individualize the initial care plan further. Ongoing planning also occurs at the beginning of a shift, home visit or clinic appointment. Using ongoing assessment data, the nurse carries out ongoing planning for the following purposes (Wilkinson, 2000):

1. To determine whether the client's health status has changed
2. To set the priorities for the client's care during the contact period (e.g., shift, home visit)
3. To decide which problems to focus on during the contact period
4. To coordinate the nurse's activities so that more than one problem can be addressed at each client contact

Discharge Planning

Discharge planning, the process of anticipating and planning for needs after discharge, is a crucial part of comprehensive health care and should be addressed in each client's care plan. Because the average stay of clients in acute-care hospitals has become shorter, people are often discharged still needing care. Although many clients are discharged to other agencies (e.g., nursing homes), such care is increasingly being delivered in the home. Effective discharge planning begins at first client contact and involves comprehensive and ongoing assessment to obtain information about the client's ongoing needs.

Developing Nursing Care Plans

The end product of the planning phase of the nursing process is a formal or informal plan of care. An **informal care plan** is a plan of action that exists in the nurse's mind. For example, the nurse may think, "Mrs. Phan is very tired. I will need to reinforce her teaching after she is rested." A **formal nursing care plan** is a written guide that organizes information about the client's care. The most obvious benefit of a formal written care plan is that it provides continuity of care. It is important that all caregivers use the same approach with a client. Nurses also use the written care plan for direction about what needs to be documented in client progress notes and as a guide for delegating and assigning staff to care for clients. When nurses use the client's nursing diagnoses to develop goals and nursing interventions, the result is a holistic, individualized plan of care that will best meet the client's unique needs.

Standardized care plans specify the nursing care for groups of clients with common needs (e.g., all clients with myocardial infarction). **Individualized care plans** are tailored to meet the unique needs of a specific client—needs that are not addressed by the standardized plans.

Care plans include the actions nurses must take to address the client's nursing diagnoses and produce the desired outcomes. The nurse begins the plan when the client is admitted to the agency and constantly updates it throughout the client's stay in response to changes in the client's condition and evaluations of goal achievement. During the planning phase, the nurse must:

1. Decide which of the client's problems need individualized plans and which problems can be addressed by standardized plans and routine care.
2. Choose and adapt standardized, pre-printed interventions and care plans, where appropriate.
3. Write individualized desired outcomes and nursing orders for client problems that require nursing attention beyond pre-planned, routine care.

The complete plan of care for a client may be made up of several different documents that (1) describe the routine care needed to meet basic needs (e.g., bathing, nutrition), (2) address the client's nursing diagnoses and collaborative problems, and (3) specify nursing responsibilities in carrying out the medical plan of care (e.g., keeping the client from eating or drinking before surgery; scheduling a laboratory test). A complete plan of care integrates dependent and independent nursing functions into a meaningful whole and provides a central source of client information.

Standardized Approaches to Care Planning

Most health-care agencies have devised a variety of pre-printed, standardized guides for providing essential nursing care to specified groups of clients who have certain needs in common (e.g., all clients with pneumonia). Standards of care, standardized care plans, protocols, policies, and procedures are developed and accepted by the nursing staff in order to (1) ensure that minimally acceptable standards of care are provided, and (2) promote efficient use of nurses' time by removing the need to handwrite common activities that are done over and over for many of the clients with common needs.

Unit standards of care are "detailed guidelines that represent the predicted care indicated in specific situations," such as a medical diagnosis, test, or treatment; a nursing diagnosis; or a collaborative problem (Carpenito, 1997, p. 77). Standards of care describe nursing care for groups of clients rather than individuals, and they describe achievable, rather than ideal, nursing care. They define the interventions for which nurses are held accountable; they do not contain medical orders. Standards of care are usually agency records and not part of the client's care plan, but they may be referred to in the plan (e.g., a nurse might write, "See standards of care for cardiac catheterization"). Standards of care may or may not be organized according to problems or nursing diagnoses.

Standardized care plans are also pre-planned, pre-printed guides for the nursing care of groups of clients with common needs (e.g., a specific nursing diagnosis, or all the nursing diagnoses associated with a particular medical condition). However, they should not be confused with *standards of care.* (See Figure 23.4 for ***Fluid Volume Deficit***.)

Like standards of care and standardized care plans, **protocols** are pre-printed and pre-planned to indicate the actions commonly required for a particular group of clients. For example, an agency may have a protocol for admitting a client to the intensive care unit, for administering magnesium sulfate to a client with pre-eclampsia, or for caring for a client receiving continuous epidural analgesia. Protocols may include both medical orders and nursing orders. Depending on the agency, protocols may or may not be included in the client's permanent record.

Policies and **procedures** are developed to govern the handling of frequently occurring situations. For example, a hospital may have a policy specifying the number of visitors a client may have. Some policies and procedures are similar to protocols and specify what is to be done, for example, in the case of cardiac arrest. If a policy covers a situation pertinent to client care, it is usually noted on the care plan (e.g., "Make social work referral according to Unit Policy Manual"). Policies are institution records and do not become a part of the care plan or permanent record.

A **standing order** is a written document about policies, rules, regulations, or orders regarding client care. Standing orders give nurses the authority to carry out specific actions under certain circumstances, often when a physician is not immediately available. In a hospital critical-care unit, a common example is the administration of emergency anti-arrhythmic medications when a client's cardiac monitoring pattern changes. In a home-care setting, a physician may write a standing order for the administration of epinephrine for a client who becomes excessively dyspneic.

Standardized Care Plan for Nursing Diagnosis of FLUID VOLUME DEFICIT

Related Factors	**Desired Outcomes**	**Nursing Order** (Identify Frequency)
✓Decreased oral intake	✓Urinary output > 30 mL/hr	✓Monitor intake and output q 1 h
✓Nausea	✓Urine specific gravity 1.005–1.025	✓Weigh daily
__Depression	✓Serum Na^+ normal	✓Monitor serum electrolyte levels X 1 or until normal
✓Fatigue, weakness	✓Mucous membranes moist	✓Check skin turgor and mucous membranes q 8 h
__Difficulty swallowing	✓Skin turgor good	✓Monitor temperature q 4 h
__Other:____	✓No weight loss	✓Administer prescribed IV therapy (Monitor according to protocol for "Intravenous Therapy") 1000 mL D_5 LR at 100 mL/hr
✓Excess fluid loss	✓8-hour intake = 400 mL oral	✓Offer oral liquids q 1 h Type clear, cold
✓Fever or increased metabolic rate	Other:	✓Instruct client regarding amount, type, and schedule of fluid intake
✓Diaphoresis		✓Assess understanding of type of fluid loss; teach accordingly
✓Vomiting		✓Mouth care prn with water
__Diarrhea		✓Institute measures to reduce fever (e.g., lower room temperature, remove bed covers, offer cold liquids)
__Burns		Other Nursing Orders:____ Monitor urine specific gravity q shift
__Other____		
Defining Characteristics		
✓Insufficient intake		
✓Negative balance of intake and output		
✓Dry mucous membranes		
✓Poor skin turgor		
__Concentrated urine		
__Hypernatremia		
✓Rapid, weak pulse		
__Falling B/P		
__Weight loss		

Plan Initiated by: M. Medina RN **Date** 4-15-03

Plan/outcomes evaluated____ **Date**____

Plan/outcomes evaluated____ **Date**____

Client: Amanda Aquilini

Figure 23.4 A standardized care plan for nursing diagnosis of ***Fluid Volume Deficit***

Regardless of whether care plans are handwritten, computerized, or standardized, nursing care must be individualized to fit the unique needs of each client. In practice, a care plan usually consists of both pre-printed and handwritten sections. The nurse uses standardized care plans for predictable, commonly occurring problems and handwrites an individual plan for unusual problems or problems needing special attention. For example, a standardized care plan for all "clients with a medical diagnosis of pneumonia" would probably include a nursing diagnosis of ***Fluid Volume Deficit*** and direct the nurse to assess the client's hydration status. On a respiratory or medical unit, this would be a common nursing diagnosis; therefore, Amanda Aquilini's nurse was able to obtain a standardized plan directing care commonly needed by clients with ***Fluid Volume Deficit.*** (See the Care Plan for Amanda Aquilini on pages 426–427 and Figure 23.4.) However, the nursing diagnosis ***Risk for Altered Family Processes*** would not be common to all clients with pneumonia; it is specific to Amanda. Therefore, the goals and nursing order for that diagnosis would need to be handwritten by the nurse.

Student Care Plans Because student care plans are a learning activity as well as a plan of care, they may be more lengthy and detailed than care plans used by nurses. To help students learn to write care plans, educators may suggest a five-column format: (1) nursing diagnosis or hypotheses; (2) goals/desired outcomes; (3) interventions; (4) rationale; and (5) evaluation. See the care plan on pages 426–427. A **rationale** is the scientific principle given as the reason for selecting a particular nursing intervention. Students may also be required to cite supporting literature for their stated rationale.

Computerized Care Plans Computers are increasingly being used to create and store nursing care plans. The computer can generate both standardized and individualized care plans. Nurses access the client's stored care plan from a centrally located terminal at the nurses' station or from terminals in client rooms. For an individualized plan, the nurse chooses the appropriate diagnoses from a menu suggested by the computer. The computer then lists possible goals and nursing interventions for those diagnoses; the nurse chooses those appropriate for the client and types in any additional goals and interventions or nursing actions not listed on the menu. The nurse can read the plan on the computer screen or print out an updated working copy each day.

Collaborative Care Plans: Clinical Guidelines and Critical Pathways Collaborative care planning is becoming increasingly important given the short hospital stays, subspecialization, and escalating health-care costs. Two types of multidisciplinary care plans are commonly used. Both types are standardized plans that outline the care required for clients with common, predictable—usually medical—conditions (e.g., pneumonia, hip replacement surgery). **Clinical guidelines** are systematically developed (regionally or nationally) statements of recommended methods of treatment for specific conditions under specific clinical circumstances based on the best research evidence currently available (Duff, Kitson, Seers, & Humphris, 1996). **Critical pathways,** also developed on the basis of research evidence, specify the sequence of care to be given on each day during a projected length of stay (or treatment regime) for the specific type of condition. In both cases, the intent is to standardize treatment based on best evidence to improve efficiency and effectiveness of health care. Interventions to be undertaken by nurses and other health-care providers and expected outcomes may be specified but are not provided in sufficient detail to guide all aspects of care. As with the use of standard nursing care plans, nurses need to individualize care according to client needs and responses.

Guidelines for Writing Nursing Care Plans

The nurse should use the following guidelines when writing nursing care plans:

1. *Date and sign the plan.* The date the plan is written is essential for evaluation, review, and future planning. The nurse's signature demonstrates accountability to the client and to the nursing profession since the effectiveness of nursing actions can be evaluated.
2. *Use category headings*, such as "Nursing Diagnoses," "Goals/Desired Outcomes," "Interventions," and "Evaluation." *Include a date for the evaluation of each goal.*
3. *Use accepted medical abbreviations and symbols and key words*, rather than complete sentences, to communicate your ideas. For example, write "Turn and reposition q2h," rather than "Turn and reposition the client every two hours." See Table 24.4 for a list of commonly used medical abbreviations and Table 24.5 for commonly used symbols.
4. *Refer to procedure books or other sources of information* rather than including all the steps on a written plan. For example, write: "See unit procedure book for tracheostomy care," or attach a standard nursing plan about such procedures as radiation-implantation care and preoperative or postoperative care.
5. *Tailor the plan to the unique characteristics of the client* by ensuring that the client's choices, such as preferences about the times of care and the methods used, are included. This reinforces the client's individuality and sense of control. For example, the written nursing order "Provide prune juice at breakfast, rather than regular juice" indicates that the client was given a choice of beverages.
6. *Ensure that the nursing plan incorporates preventive and health maintenance aspects as well as restorative ones.* For example, carrying out the order "Provide active-assistance ROM [range-of-motion] exercises to affected limbs q2h" prevents joint contractures and maintains muscle strength and joint mobility.

7. *Ensure that the plan contains orders for ongoing assessment* of the client (e.g., "Inspect incision q8h").
8. *Include collaborative and coordination activities in the plan.* For example, the nurse may write orders to ask a nutritionist or physical therapist about specific aspects of the client's care.
9. *Include plans for the client's discharge and home care needs.* It is often necessary to consult and make arrangements with the community health nurse, social worker, and specific agencies that supply client information and needed equipment. Add teaching and discharge plans as addenda if they are lengthy and complex.

The Planning Process

In the process of developing client care plans, the nurse engages in the following activities:

- Setting priorities
- Establishing client goals/desired outcomes
- Selecting nursing interventions
- Writing nursing orders

Setting Priorities

Priority setting is the process of establishing a preferential order for nursing diagnoses and interventions. The nurse and client begin planning by deciding which nursing diagnosis requires attention first, which second, and so on. Instead of rank-ordering diagnoses, nurses can group them as having high, medium, or low priority. Life-threatening problems, such as loss of respiratory or cardiac function, are designated as *high priority*. Health-threatening problems, such as acute illness and decreased coping ability, are assigned *medium priority* because they may result in delayed development or cause destructive physical or emotional changes. A *low-priority* problem is one that arises from normal developmental needs or that requires only minimal nursing support.

Although not a nursing framework, nurses frequently use Maslow's hierarchy of needs when setting priorities. In Maslow's hierarchy, physiological needs, such as air, food, and water, are basic to life and receive higher priority than the need for security or activity. Growth needs, such as self-esteem, are not perceived as "basic" in this framework. Thus, such nursing diagnoses as ***Ineffective Airway Clearance*** and ***Impaired Gas Exchange*** would take priority over such nursing diagnoses as ***Anxiety*** or ***Ineffective Coping***.

It is not necessary to resolve all high-priority diagnoses before addressing others. The nurse may partially address a high-priority diagnosis and then deal with a diagnosis of lesser priority. Furthermore, because clients usually have several problems, the nurse often deals with more than one diagnosis at a time. See Table 23.13 for priorities assigned to Amanda Aquilini's nursing diagnoses.

Priorities change as the client's responses, problems, and therapies change. The nurse must consider a variety of factors when assigning priorities. These include the following:

1. *Client's health values and beliefs:* Values concerning health may be more important to the nurse than to the client. For example, a client may believe being home for the children to be more urgent than a health problem. When there is such a difference of opinion, the client and nurse should discuss it openly to resolve any conflict. However, in a life-threatening situation, the nurse usually must take the initiative.
2. *Client's priorities:* Involving the client in prioritizing and care planning enhances cooperation. Sometimes, however, the client's perception of what is important conflicts with the nurse's knowledge of potential problems or complications. For example, the client may not regard turning and repositioning in bed as important, preferring to be undisturbed. The nurse, however, aware of the potential complications of prolonged bed rest (e.g., muscle weakness and decubitus ulcers), needs to inform the client and gain the client's agreement to carry out the necessary interventions.
3. *Resources available to the nurse and client:* If money, equipment, or personnel are scarce in a health-care agency, then a problem may be given a lower priority than usual. Nurses in a home setting, for example, do not have the resources of a hospital. If the necessary resources are not available, the solution of that problem might need to be postponed, or the client may need referral. Client resources, such as finances or coping ability, may also influence the setting of priorities. For example, a client who is unemployed may defer dental treatment; a client whose husband is terminally ill and dependent on her may feel unable to cope with nutritional guidance directed toward losing weight.
4. *Urgency of the health problem:* Regardless of the framework used, life-threatening situations require that the nurse assign them high priority. For example, in Table 23.13, although Amanda Aquilini is anxious about child care, her ***Ineffective Airway Clearance*** has higher priority. Situations that affect the integrity of the client, that is, those that could have a negative or destructive effect on the client, also have high priority. Such health problems as drug abuse and radical alteration of self-concept due to amputation can be destructive both to the individual and to the family.
5. *Medical treatment plan:* The priorities for treating health problems must be congruent with treatment by other health-care professionals. For example, a high priority for the client might be to become ambulatory; however, if the physician's therapeutic regimen calls for extended bed rest, then ambulation must assume a lower priority in the nursing care plan. The nurse can provide or teach exercises to facilitate ambulation later provided the client's health permits. The nursing diagnosis related to ambulation is not ignored; it is merely deferred.

TABLE 23.13 Assigning Priorities to Nursing Diagnoses for Amanda Aquilini

Nursing Diagnosis	Priority	Rationale
Ineffective Airway Clearance related to (1) viscous secretions secondary to fluid volume deficit, and (2) shallow chest expansion secondary to pain and fatigue	High priority	Loss of respiratory functioning is a life-threatening problem. The nurse's primary concern must be to promote Amanda's oxygenation by addressing the related factors.
Fluid Volume Deficit related to intake insufficient to replace fluid loss secondary to fever and diaphoresis	High priority	Severe ***Fluid Volume Deficit*** is life threatening. Although not that severe for Amanda, it is a high-priority problem because it is also a contributing factor for ***Ineffective Airway Clearance.*** Collaborative efforts to improve her hydration have already begun (intravenous fluids). The nurse must immediately and continuously assess and promote Amanda's hydration.
Anxiety related to (1) difficulty breathing, and (2) concerns over work and parenting roles	Medium priority	Although Amanda is concerned about work and parenting roles, these are not a threat to life. Also, treatment of her high-priority problem, ***Ineffective Airway Clearance,*** will relieve one of the related factors (dyspnea). Meanwhile, the nurse should provide symptomatic relief of Amanda's anxiety during periods of dyspnea because extreme anxiety could further compromise her oxygenation by causing her to breathe ineffectively and increasing the rate at which she uses oxygen.
Risk for Altered Family Processes related to mother's illness and temporary unavailability of father to provide child care	Low priority	Amanda's child is currently being cared for. If Amanda's husband returns as planned, this risk diagnosis will not develop into an actual diagnosis. No interventions are needed at present except for continued assessment and support.
Altered Nutrition: Less than Body Requirements related to decreased appetite, nausea, and increased metabolism secondary to disease process	Low priority	This problem is not currently health threatening, but it could be if it were to persist. It will almost certainly resolve in a day or two as the medical problem is treated. If the medical problem does not resolve quickly, this will change to a medium priority.
Self-Care Deficit, Bathing/Hygiene related to activity intolerance secondary to ineffective airway clearance and sleep pattern disturbance	Low priority	This problem is caused by other, higher priority problems; therefore, it will resolve as they resolve. Meanwhile, the nurse merely needs to assist Amanda with bathing and so on to support and conserve her energy until she is strong enough to resume her own care.
Disturbed Sleep Pattern related to cough, pain, orthopnea, fever, and diaphoresis	Low priority	Lack of sleep is health threatening. But for the moment, the nurse does not need to address this problem. ***Disturbed Sleep Pattern*** does contribute to Amanda's ***Ineffective Airway Clearance,*** but it is not the main cause. Therefore, measures to promote sleep will be low priority at least until evening. After the nurse has attended to Amanda's oxygenation and hydration needs, this problem priority will change.
Pain (Chest), Acute related to cough secondary to pneumonia	Not on care plan	The nurse did not write ***Pain*** as a problem on the care plan because ***Pain*** is to be addressed as the etiology of ***Disturbed Sleep Pattern*** and ***Ineffective Airway Clearance.*** The related factors to pain (cough and pneumonia) will be treated by medications (collaborative interventions). Independent nursing actions would address the problem rather than the related factors and would be the same as the nursing actions for ***Ineffective Airway Clearance.***

Establishing Client Goals/Desired Outcomes

After establishing priorities, the nurse and client set goals for each nursing diagnosis. On a care plan the **goals/desired outcomes** describe, in terms of observable client responses, what the nurse, through implementation of nursing orders, hopes the client will achieve. The terms *goal* and *desired outcome* are used interchangeably in this text except when discussing and using standardized language (see "The Nursing Outcomes Classification" that follows). Some references also use the terms *expected outcome, predicted outcome, outcome criterion,* and *objective.*

Some nursing literature differentiates the terms by defining *goals* as broad statements about the client's status and *desired outcomes* as the more specific, observable criteria used to evaluate whether the goals have been met. For example:

Goal (broad): Improve nutritional status
Desired outcome (specific): Gain 2.5 kg by April 25

When goals are stated broadly, as in this example, the care plan must include *both* goals and desired outcomes. They are sometimes combined into one statement linked by the words "as evidenced by," as follows:

Improved nutritional status as evidenced by weight gain of 2.5 kg by April 25

Writing the broad, general goal first may help students think of the specific outcomes that are needed, but the broad goal is just a starting point for planning. It is the specific, observable outcomes that *must* be written on the care plan and used to evaluate client progress. Table 23.14 shows both broad goals and desired outcomes.

TABLE 23.14 Deriving Desired Outcomes from Nursing Diagnoses

Nursing Diagnosis	Desired Outcomes
Walking, Impaired: inability to bear weight on left leg, related to inflammation of knee joint	Ambulate with crutches by end of the week Be able to stand without assistance by end of the month
Ineffective Airway Clearance related to poor cough effort, secondary to incision pain and fear of damaging sutures	Lungs will be clear to auscultation during entire postoperative period No skin pallor or cyanosis by 12 hours post operation Will demonstrate good cough effort within 24 hours after surgery

The Nursing Outcomes Classification Standardized nursing language is required if nursing data are to be included in computerized databases that are analyzed and used in nursing decisions. Working toward this end, researchers have developed a taxonomy, the **Nursing Outcomes Classification (NOC),** for describing client outcomes that respond to nursing interventions (Johnson & Maas, 1997). Each NOC outcome includes a definition, a measuring scale, and indicators. See Table 23.15 for a standardized client outcome associated with mobility level.

An NOC is similar to a *goal* in traditional language. It is "a measurable patient or family caregiver state, behaviour, or perception that is conceptualized as a variable and is largely influenced by and sensitive to nursing interventions" (Johnson & Maas, 1997, p. 22). The NOC is broadly stated. In order to be measured, an outcome must be made more specific by identifying the specific indicators that apply to a client. **Indicators** are similar to *desired outcomes* in traditional language. Indicators are also stated in neutral terms, but each outcome includes a five-point scale (a *measure*) that is used to rate the client's status on each indicator. When using the NOC taxonomy to write a *desired outcome* on a care plan, the nurse writes the label, the indicators that apply to the particular client, and the location on the measuring scale that is desired for each indicator. For example, using the NOC outcome in Table 23.15 for the client diagnosed in Table 23.14, the individualized desired outcomes would read as follows:

Mobility Level:
Transfer performance (5, completely independent)
Ambulation: walking (4, independent with assistive device)

Stated in *traditional* language, that goal would read: "Client will have improved mobility as evidenced by ability to transfer independently and walk with assistive device (walker)."

Purpose of Goals/Desired Outcomes Goals/desired outcomes serve the following purposes:

1. They provide direction for planning nursing interventions. Ideas for interventions come more easily if the desired outcomes state clearly and specifically what the nurse hopes the client will achieve.
2. They serve as criteria for evaluating client progress. Although developed in the planning step of the nursing process, desired outcomes serve as the criteria for judging nursing interventions and client progress in the evaluation step.
3. They enable the client and nurse to determine when the problem has been resolved.
4. They help motivate the client and nurse by providing a sense of achievement. As goals are met, both client and nurse can see that their efforts have been worthwhile. This provides motivation to continue following the plan, especially when difficult lifestyle changes need to be made.

TABLE 23.15 Example of a Standardized Client Outcome (NOC)

Mobility Level
Definition: Ability to move purposefully

Mobility level	Dependent, does not participate	Requires assistive person & device	Requires assistive person	Independent with assistive device	Completely independent
Indicators					
Balance performance	1	2	3	4	5
Body positioning performance	1	2	3	4	5
Muscle movement	1	2	3	4	5
Joint movement	1	2	3	4	5
Transfer performance	1	2	3	4	5
Ambulation: walking	1	2	3	4	5
Ambulation: wheelchair	1	2	3	4	5
Other: (specify)	1	2	3	4	5

Source: M. Johnson & M. Maas. (Eds.). (1997). *Nursing outcomes classification (NOC)* (p. 203). St. Louis, MO: Mosby. Used with permission.

Long-Term and Short-Term Goals Goals may be short term or long term. A short-term goal might be "Client will raise right arm to shoulder height by Friday." In the same context, a long-term goal might be "Client will regain full use of right arm in six weeks." Short-term goals are useful (1) for clients who require health care for a short time, and (2) for those who are frustrated by long-term goals that seem difficult to attain and who need the satisfaction of achieving a short-term goal.

In an acute-care setting, much of the nurse's time is spent on the client's immediate needs, so most goals are short term. However, clients in acute-care settings also need long-term goals to guide planning for their discharge to long-term agencies or home care, especially in a managed care environment. Long-term goals are often used for clients who live at home and have chronic health problems and for clients in nursing homes, extended-care facilities, and rehabilitation centres.

Relationship of Goals/Desired Outcomes to Nursing Diagnoses Goals are derived from and relate to the client's nursing diagnoses—primarily from the first clause (diagnostic label). The diagnostic label clause contains the unhealthy response; it states what should change. Therefore, the *essential* client goals are derived from the diagnostic label clause. For example, if the nursing diagnosis is ***Risk for Fluid Volume Deficit*** related to diarrhea and inadequate intake secondary to nausea, the *essential* goal statement might be:

> Maintain fluid balance as evidenced by urinary and stool output in balance with fluid intake, normal skin turgor, and moist mucous membranes.

For every nursing diagnosis, the nurse must write at least one desired outcome that, when achieved, directly demonstrates resolution of the diagnostic label clause.

Components of Goal/Desired Outcome Statements Goal/desired outcome statements should usually have the following four components:

1. ***Subject.*** The subject, a noun, is the client, any part of the client, or some attribute of the client, such as the client's pulse or urinary output. The subject is often omitted in goals; it is assumed that the subject is the client unless indicated otherwise.

2. ***Verb.*** The verb specifies an action the client is to perform, for example, what the client is to do, learn, or experience. Verbs that denote directly observable behaviours, such as *administer, demonstrate, show, walk,* must be used. See the accompanying box for some examples.

3. ***Conditions*** or ***modifiers.*** Conditions or modifiers may be added to the verb to explain the circumstances under which the behaviour is to be performed. They explain what, where, when, or how. For example:

   Walks with the help of a walker (how)

   Lists signs and symptoms of diabetes *after attending two group diabetes classes* (when)

   Weight will remain at existing level when at home (where)

   Discusses *Canada's Food Guide and recommended daily servings* (what)

Examples of Action Verbs

Apply	Explain	Share
Assemble	Help	Sit
Breathe	Identify	Sleep
Choose	Inject	State
Compare	List	Talk
Define	Move	Transfer
Demonstrate	Name	Turn
Describe	Prepare	Verbalize
Differentiate	Report	
Discuss	Select	

Conditions need not be included if the criterion of performance clearly indicates what is expected.

4. *Criterion of desired performance.* The criterion indicates the standard by which a performance is evaluated or the level at which the client will perform the specified behaviour. These criteria may specify time or speed, accuracy, distance, and quality. To establish a time-achievement criterion, the nurse needs to ask, "How long?" To establish an accuracy criterion, the nurse asks, "How well?" Similarly, the nurse asks, "How far?" and "What is the expected standard?" to establish distance and quality criteria, respectively. Examples are:

   Weighs 75 kg *by April* (time)

   Lists *five out of six* signs of diabetes (accuracy)

   Walks *one block per day* (time and distance)

   Administers insulin *using aseptic technique* (quality)

Table 23.16 illustrates the format that should be used to write outcomes.

Guidelines for Writing Goals/Desired Outcomes

The following guidelines can help nurses write useful goals and desired outcomes:

1. *Write goals and outcomes in terms of client responses, not nurse activities.* Beginning each goal statement with "the client will" may help focus it on client behaviours and responses. Avoid statements that start with *enable, facilitate, allow, let, permit,* or similar verbs followed by the word *client.* These verbs indicate what the nurse hopes to accomplish, not what the client will do.

   Correct: Client will drink 100 mL of water per hour (client behaviour)

   Incorrect: Maintain client hydration (nursing action)

2. *Be sure that desired outcomes are realistic for the client's capabilities, limitations, and designated timespan,* if it is indicated. *Limitations* refer to finances, equipment, family support, social services, physical and mental condition, and time. For example, the outcome "Measures insulin accurately" may be unrealistic for a client who has poor vision due to cataracts.
3. *Ensure that the goals and desired outcomes are compatible with the therapies of other professionals.* For example, the outcome "Will increase the time spent out of bed by 15 minutes each day" is not compatible with a physician's prescribed therapy of bed rest.
4. *Make sure that each goal is derived from only one nursing diagnosis.* For example, the goal "The client will increase the amount of nutrients ingested and show progress in the ability to feed self" is derived from two nursing diagnoses: ***Self-Care Deficit: Feeding*** and ***Imbalanced Nutrition: Less than Body Requirements.*** Keeping the goal statement related to only one diagnosis facilitates evaluation of care by ensuring that planned nursing interventions are clearly related to the diagnosis.

TABLE 23.16 Components of Goals/Desired Outcomes

Subject	Verb	Conditions/Modifiers	Criterion of Desired Performance
Client	drinks	2,500 mL of fluid	daily (time)
Client	administers	correct insulin dose	using aseptic technique (quality standard)
Client	lists	three hazards of smoking (after reading literature)	(accuracy indicated by "three hazards")
Client	recalls	five symptoms of diabetes before discharge	(accuracy indicated by "five symptoms")
Client	walks	the length of the hall without a walker	by date of discharge (time)
Client's ankle	measures	less than 25 cm in circumference	in 48 hours (time)
Client	carries out	leg ROM exercises as taught	every 8 hours (time)
Client	identifies	foods high in salt from a prepared list	before discharge (time)
Client	states	the purposes of prescribed medications	before discharge (time)

5. *Use observable, measurable terms for outcomes.* Avoid words that are vague and require interpretation or judgement by the observer. For example, such phrases as "increase daily exercise" and "improve knowledge of nutrition" can mean different things to different people. If used in outcomes, these phrases can lead to disagreements about whether the outcome was met. These phrases may be suitable for a broad client goal but are not sufficiently clear and specific to guide the nurse when evaluating client responses.

6. *Make sure the client considers the goals/desired outcomes important and values them.* Some outcomes, such as those for problems related to self-esteem, parenting, and communication, involve choices that are best made by the client or in collaboration with the client.

Some clients may know what they wish to accomplish with regard to their health problems; others may not know all the outcome possibilities. The nurse must actively listen to the client to determine personal values, goals, and desired outcomes in relation to current health concerns. Clients are usually motivated and expend the necessary energy to reach goals they consider important.

See the care plan for Amanda Aquilini on pages 426–427 for examples of desired outcomes for three of Amanda Aquilini's nursing diagnoses.

Selecting Nursing Interventions and Activities

Nursing interventions and activities are the actions that a nurse performs to achieve client goals. The specific strategies chosen should focus on eliminating or reducing the *related factors'* contributions to the nursing diagnosis, which is the second clause of the diagnostic statement.

When it is not possible to change the related factors, the nurse chooses interventions to treat the signs and symptoms. Examples of this situation would be ***Pain*** related to surgical incision and ***Anxiety*** related to unknown etiology.

Interventions for *risk* nursing diagnoses should focus on measures to reduce the client's risk factors.

Correct identification of the main related factors during the diagnosing phase provides the framework for choosing successful nursing interventions. For example, the diagnostic label ***Activity Intolerance*** may have several related factors—pain, weakness, sedentary lifestyle, anxiety, or cardiac arrhythmias. Interventions will vary according to the cause of the problem.

Types of Nursing Interventions Nursing interventions are identified and written during the planning step of the nursing process; however, they are actually performed during the implementing step. A **nursing intervention** is "any treatment, based upon clinical judgment and knowledge, that a nurse performs to enhance patient/client outcomes" (McCloskey & Bulechek, 1996, p. xvii). Nursing interventions include both direct and indirect care, as well as nurse-initiated, physician-initiated, and other provider-initiated treatments. *Direct care* is an intervention performed through interaction with the client. *Indirect care* is an intervention performed away from, but on behalf of, the client, such as interdisciplinary collaboration or management of the care environment.

Independent interventions are those activities that nurses are licensed to initiate on the basis of their knowledge and skills. They include physical care, ongoing assessment, emotional support and comfort, teaching, counselling, environmental management, and making referrals to other health-care professionals.

Physician-initiated treatments are activities carried out under the physician's orders or supervision, or according to specified routines (McCloskey & Bulechek, 1996). Medical orders commonly include orders for medications, intravenous therapy, diagnostic tests, treatments, diet, and activity. The nurse is responsible for explaining, assessing the need for, and administering the medical orders. Nursing orders may be written to individualize the medical order based on the client's status. For example, for a medical order of "Progressive ambulation, as tolerated," a nurse might write the following nursing orders:

1. Dangle for 5 min, 12 h postop.
2. Stand at bedside 24 h postop; observe for pallor, dizziness, and weakness.
3. Check pulse before and after ambulating. Do not progress if pulse >110.

Collaborative interventions are actions the nurse carries out in collaboration with other health-care team members, such as physical therapists, social workers, dietitians, and physicians. Collaborative nursing activities reflect the overlapping responsibilities of, and collegial relationships between, health personnel. For example, the physician might order physical therapy to teach the client crutch-walking. The nurse would be responsible for informing the physical therapy department and for coordinating the client's care to include the physical therapy sessions. When the client returns to the nursing unit, the nurse would assist with crutch-walking and collaborate with the physical therapist to evaluate the client's progress.

The amount of time the nurse spends in an independent versus collaborative role or on physician-initiated treatments varies according to the clinical area, type of institution, and specific position of the nurse.

Considering the Consequences of Each Strategy Usually, several possible interventions can be identified for each nursing diagnosis. The nurse's task is to choose those that are most likely to achieve the desired client outcomes. The nurse begins by considering the risks and benefits of each activity. An intervention may have more than one consequence. For example, the strategy "Provide accurate information" could result in the following client behaviours:

CARE PLAN FOR AMANDA AQUILINI

Nursing Diagnosis: *Ineffective Airway Clearance related to viscous secretions and shallow chest expansion*

Goals/Desired Outcomes	Nursing Orders	Rationale
Demonstrate adequate air exchange (goal), as evidenced by ■ Absence of pallor and cyanosis (skin and mucous membranes) ■ Using correct breathing/coughing technique after instruction ■ Productive cough ■ Symmetric chest expansion of at least 4 cm ■ Reports of chest pain <4 on a 1–10 scale within 30 min after receiving oral analgesics	Monitor respiratory status q4h: rate, depth, effort, skin colour, mucous membranes, amount and colour of sputum. Monitor results of blood gases, chest x-ray studies, and incentive spirometer volume, as available. Monitor level of consciousness. Auscultate lungs q4h.	To identify progress toward or deviations from goal. ***Ineffective Airway Clearance*** leads to poor oxygenation, evidenced by pallor, cyanosis, lethargy, and drowsiness.
	Take vital signs q4h (TPR, BP).	Inadequate oxygenation causes increased pulse rate. Respiratory rate may be decreased by narcotic analgesics. Shallow breathing further compromises oxygenation.
Within 48–72 hours ■ Lungs clear to auscultation ■ Respirations 12–22/min, pulse <100 beats/min ■ Inhaling normal volume of air on incentive spirometer	Instruct in breathing and coughing techniques. Remind to perform, and assist q3h.	To enable client to cough up secretions. May need encouragement and support because of fatigue and pain.
	Administer prescribed expectorant; schedule for maximum effectiveness.	Helps loosen secretions so they can be coughed up and expelled.
	Maintain Fowler's or semi-Fowler's position.	Gravity allows for fuller lung expansion by decreasing pressure of abdomen on diaphragm.
	Administer prescribed analgesics. Notify physician if pain not relieved.	Controls pleuritic pain by blocking pain pathways and altering perception of pain, enabling client to increase thoracic expansion. Unrelieved pain may signal impending complication.
	Administer oxygen by nasal cannula as prescribed. Provide portable oxygen if client goes off unit (e.g., for x-ray examination).	Supplemental oxygen makes more oxygen available to the cells even though less air is being moved by the client, thereby reducing the work of breathing.
	Assist with postural drainage daily at 0930.	Gravity facilitates movement of secretions upward through the respiratory passage.
	Administer prescribed antibiotic to maintain constant blood level. Observe for rash and GI or other side effects.	Resolves infection by bacteriostatic or bactericidal effect, depending on type of antibiotic used. Constant level required to prevent pathogens from multiplying. Allergies to antibiotics are common.

→

- Increased anxiety
- Decreased anxiety
- Wish to talk with the physician
- Desire to leave the hospital
- Relaxation

Determining the consequences of each strategy requires nursing knowledge and experience. For example, the nurse's experience may suggest that providing information the night before the client's surgery may increase the client's worry and tension, whereas maintaining the usual rituals before sleep is more effective. The nurse might then consider providing information several days before surgery.

Criteria for Choosing Nursing Strategies After considering the consequences of the alternative nursing strate-

CARE PLAN FOR AMANDA AQUILINI *continued*

Nursing Diagnosis: ***Fluid Volume Deficient related to intake insufficient to replace fluid loss***
(See standardized care plan for Fluid Volume Deficient, Figure 23.4, p. 418).

Nursing Diagnosis: Anxiety

Goals/Desired Outcomes	Nursing Orders	Rationale
Demonstrate decreased anxiety (goal), as evidenced by ■ Listening to and following instructions for correct breathing and coughing technique, even during periods of dyspnea	When client is dyspneic, stay with her; reassure her you will stay.	Presence of a competent caregiver reduces fear of being unable to breathe. Control of anxiety will help client to maintain effective breathing pattern.
■ Verbalizing understanding of condition, diagnostic tests, and treatments (by end of day)	Remain calm; appear confident. Encourage slow, deep breathing.	Reassures client the nurse can help her. Focusing on breathing may help client feel in control and decrease anxiety.
■ Decrease in reports of fear and anxiety; none within 12 hours ■ Voice steady, not shaky ■ Respiratory rate of 12–22/min	When client is dyspneic, give brief explanations of treatments and procedures. When acute episode is over, give detailed information about nature of condition, treatments, and tests.	Anxiety and pain interfere with learning. Knowing what to expect reduces anxiety.
■ Freely expressing concerns about work and parenting roles, but placing them in perspective in view of her illness	As client can tolerate, encourage to express and expand on her concerns about her child and her work. Explore alternatives as needed.	Awareness of source of anxiety enables client to gain control over it.
	Note whether husband returns as scheduled. If not, institute care plan for actual ***Altered Family Processes.***	Husband's continued absence would constitute a defining characteristic for this nursing diagnosis.

gies, the nurse chooses one or more that are likely to be most effective. Although the nurse bases this decision on knowledge and experience, the client's input is important.

The following criteria can help the nurse choose the best nursing strategy. The planned action must be:

- Safe and appropriate for the individual's age, health, and condition.
- Achievable with the resources available. For example, a home care nurse might wish to include a nursing order for an elderly client to "Check blood glucose daily"; but, in order for that to occur, either the client must have intact sight, cognition, and memory to carry this out independently, or daily visits from a home care nurse must be available and affordable.
- Congruent with the client's values, beliefs, and culture.
- Congruent with other therapies (e.g., if the client is not permitted food, the strategy of an evening snack must be deferred until health permits).
- Based on evidence from research, expert opinion, and experience.
- Within established standards of care as determined by government regulations and professional associations (Canadian Nurses Association, provincial or territorial professional associations, specialty organizations, such as the Canadian Association of Neuroscience Nurses) and the policies of the agency.

For examples of rationales, refer to the care plan for Amanda Aquilini above.

Writing Nursing Orders

After choosing the appropriate nursing interventions, the nurse writes them on the care plan as nursing orders. **Nursing orders** are instructions for the specific activities the nurse performs to help the client meet established health care goals. The term *order* connotes a sense of accountability for the nurse who gives the order and for the nurse who carries it out. See examples of nursing orders in the care plan for Amanda Aquilini above. The degree of detail included in the nursing orders depends to some degree on the health personnel who will carry out the order. For examples of the components of a nursing order, see Table 23.17.

TABLE 23.17 Components of Nursing Orders

Date	Action	Content Area	Time Element	Signature
4/14/03	Monitor	for verbalization of interest in group activities	with each client contact	J. Jonas RN
4/14/03	Instruct	(client) to avoid drinking liquids with meals if nausea occurs	evening shift, 4/14/03	J. Jonas RN
4/14/03	Pad	side rails	during periods of restlessness and confusion	C. Van RN
4/14/03	Discuss	(with family) their need for help with client's care at home	on Friday	L. Chung RN
4/14/03	Palpate	uterine fundus for firmness	hourly ×2, then q4h × 24h	C. Patti RN

Date Nursing orders are dated when they are written and reviewed regularly at intervals that depend on the individual's needs. In an intensive-care unit, for example, the plan of care will be continually monitored and revised. In a community clinic, weekly or biweekly reviews may be indicated.

Action Verb The verb starts the order and must be precise. For example, "Explain (to the client) the actions of insulin" is a more precise statement than "Teach (the client) about insulin." "Measure and record ankle circumference daily at 0900 h" is more precise than "Assess edema of left ankle daily." Sometimes, a modifier for the verb can make the nursing order more precise. For example, "Apply spiral bandage to left lower leg *firmly*" is more precise than "Apply spiral bandage to left leg."

Content Area The content is the where and the what of the order. In the preceding order, "spiral bandage" and "left lower leg" state the what and where of the order. The content area in this example would also clarify whether the foot or toes are to be left exposed.

Time Element The time element answers when, how long, or how often the nursing action is to occur. Examples are: "Assist client with tub bath *at 0700 daily*," or "Immerse client's left arm in sterile saline soak *for 1 h*."

Signature The signature of the nurse prescribing the order shows the nurse's accountability and has legal significance.

Relationship of Nursing Orders to Problem Status Depending on the type of client problem, the nurse writes orders for observation, prevention, treatment, and health promotion.

Observation orders include assessments made to determine whether a complication is developing, as well as observation of the client's responses to nursing and other therapies. The nurse should write observation orders for every problem type: actual, potential, possible, and collaborative. Some examples are "Auscultate lungs q8h," "Observe for redness over sacrum q2h," and "Record intake and output hourly."

Prevention orders prescribe the care needed to prevent complications or reduce risk factors. They are needed mainly for potential nursing diagnoses and collaborative problems. Examples of prevention orders are "Deep breathing and coughing exercises q2h" (prevents respiratory complications) and "If fundus is boggy, massage until firm" (prevents postpartum hemorrhage).

Treatment orders include teaching, referrals, physical care, and other care needed to treat an actual nursing diagnosis. Some orders may accomplish either prevention or treatment functions depending on the status of the problem. In the preceding examples, the order "Deep breathing and coughing exercises q2h" can also be intended to treat an existing respiratory problem and the order "If fundus is boggy, massage until firm" can also be intended to treat an actual postpartum hemorrhage.

Health promotion orders are appropriate when the client has no health problems or when the nurse makes a wellness nursing diagnosis. Such nursing interventions focus on helping the client identify areas for improvement that will lead to a higher level of wellness and actualize the client's overall health potential. Examples are "Discuss the importance of daily exercise" and "Explore infant-stimulation techniques" (Wilkinson, 1996, p. 195).

The Nursing Interventions Classification

A group of nurse researchers also recognized the need for a standardized language to describe the *interventions* that nurses perform. A taxonomy of nursing interventions referred to as the **Nursing Interventions Classification (NIC)** taxonomy has been developed by the Iowa Intervention Project (McCloskey & Bulechek, 1996). This taxonomy consists of three levels: (1) level 1: *domains*, (2) level 2: *classes*, and (3) level 3: *interventions*. Table 23.18 shows the six domains and 27 classes of interventions within the taxonomy.

TABLE 23.18 NIC Taxonomy

Level 1: Domains	Level 2: Classes (lettered for cross-referencing)
Domain 1 *Physiological: Basic* Care that supports physical functioning	A. Activity and Exercise Management: Interventions to organize or assist with physical activity and energy conservation and expenditure B. Elimination Management: Interventions to establish and maintain regular bowel and urinary elimination patterns and manage complications due to altered patterns C. Immobility Management: Interventions to manage restricted body movement and the sequelae D. Nutrition Support: Interventions to modify or maintain nutritional status E. Physical Comfort Promotion: Interventions to promote comfort using physical techniques F. Self-Care Facilitation: Interventions to provide or assist with routine activities of daily living
Domain 2 *Physiological: Complex* Care that supports homeostatic regulation	G. Electrolyte and Acid-Base Management: Interventions to regulate electrolyte/acid-base balance and prevent complications H. Drug Management: Interventions to facilitate desired effects of pharmacological agents I. Neurologic Management: Interventions to optimize neurological functions J. Perioperative Care: Interventions to provide care before, during, and immediately after surgery K. Respiratory Management: Interventions to promote airway patency and gas exchange L. Skin/Wound Management: Interventions to maintain or restore tissue integrity M. Thermoregulation: Interventions to maintain body temperature within a normal range N. Tissue Perfusion Management: Interventions to optimize circulation of blood and fluids to the tissue
Domain 3 *Behavioral* Care that supports psychosocial functioning and facilitates lifestyle changes	O. Behaviour Therapy: Interventions to reinforce or promote desirable behaviours or alter undesirable behaviours P. Cognitive Therapy: Interventions to reinforce or promote desirable cognitive functioning or alter undesirable cognitive functioning Q. Communication Enhancement: Interventions to facilitate delivering and receiving verbal and nonverbal messages R. Coping Assistance: Interventions to assist another to build on own strengths, to adapt to a change in function, or to achieve a higher level of function S. Patient Education: Interventions to facilitate learning T. Psychological Comfort: Interventions to promote comforts using psychological techniques
Domain 4 *Safety* Care that supports protection against harm	U. Crisis Management: Interventions to provide immediate short-term help in both psychological and physiological crises V. Risk Management: Interventions to initiate risk-reduction activities and continue monitoring risks over time
Domain 5 *Family* Care that supports the family unit	W. Childbearing Care: Interventions to assist in understanding and coping with the psychological and physiological changes during the childbearing period X. Lifespan Care: Interventions to facilitate family unit functioning and promote the health and welfare of family members throughout the lifespan
Domain 6 *Health System* Care that supports effective use of the health-care delivery system	Y. Health System Mediation: Interventions to facilitate the interface between patient/family and the health-care system a. Health System Management: Interventions to provide and enhance support services for the delivery of care b. Information Management: Interventions to facilitate communication among health-care providers

Source: J. C. McCloskey & G. M. Bulechek. (1996). *Nursing interventions classification (NIC)* (2nd ed.). (p. 56–57). Iowa Intervention Project. St. Louis, MO: Mosby-Year Book. Used with permission.

More than 400 interventions (level 3) have been developed. Similar to the NANDA diagnoses, each broadly stated intervention includes a label (name), a definition, and a list of *activities* that outline the key actions of nurses in carrying out the intervention (see the following box). The level 3 intervention *Touch* is one of several interventions developed within the *behavioural domain* and its *class* entitled *Coping Assistance*.

Example of an NIC Nursing Intervention Label

Intervention: Touch

DEFINITION: Providing comfort and communication through purposeful tactile contact

ACTIVITIES:

- Observe cultural taboos about touch.
- Give a reassuring hug, as appropriate.
- Put arm around patient's shoulders, as appropriate.
- Hold patient's hand to provide emotional support.
- Apply gentle pressure at wrist, hand, or shoulder of seriously ill patient.
- Rub back in synchrony with patient's breathing, as appropriate.
- Stroke body part in slow, rhythmical fashion, as appropriate.
- Massage around painful area, as appropriate.
- Elicit from parents common actions used to soothe and calm their child.
- Hold infant or child firmly and snugly.
- Encourage parents to touch newborn or ill child.
- Surround premature infant with blanket rolls (nesting).
- Swaddle infant snugly in a blanket to keep arms and legs close to the body.
- Place infant on mother's body immediately after birth.
- Encourage mother to hold, touch, and examine the infant while umbilical cord is being severed.
- Encourage parents to hold infant.
- Encourage parents to massage infant.
- Demonstrate quieting techniques for infants.
- Provide appropriate pacifier for non-nutritional sucking in newborns.
- Provide oral stimulation exercises before tube feedings in premature infants.

Source: J. C. McCloskey & G. M. Bulechek. (Eds). (1996). *Nursing interventions classification (NIC): Iowa Outcome Project* (2nd ed.). (p. 568). St. Louis, MO: Mosby-Year Book. Used with permission.

Examples of NIC Interventions Linked to the NANDA Nursing Diagnosis of *Disturbed Sleep Pattern*

Sleep Pattern, Disturbed

DEFINITION: Disruption of sleep time causes discomfort or interferes with desired lifestyle.

SUGGESTED NURSING INTERVENTIONS FOR PROBLEM RESOLUTION:
Dementia Management
Environmental Management
Environmental Management: Comfort
Medication Administration
Medication Management
Medication Prescribing
Security Enhancement
Simple Relaxation Therapy
Sleep Enhancement
Touch

ADDITIONAL OPTIONAL INTERVENTIONS:
Anxiety Reduction
Autogenic Training
Bathing
Calming Technique
Coping Enhancement
Energy Management
Exercise Promotion
Exercise Therapy: Ambulation
Kangaroo Care
Meditation
Music Therapy
Nutrition Management
Pain Management
Positioning
Progressive Muscle Relaxation
Self-Care Assistance: Toileting
Simple Massage
Urinary Incontinence Care: Enuresis

Source: J. C. McCloskey & G. M. Bulechek. (Eds). (1996). *Nursing interventions classification (NIC): Iowa Outcome Project* (2nd ed.). (p. 671). St. Louis, MO: Mosby-Year Book. Used with permission.

All NIC interventions have been linked to NANDA nursing diagnostic labels. The nurse can look up a client's nursing diagnosis to see which nursing interventions are suggested. However, each nursing diagnosis contains suggestions for several interventions, so nurses need to select the appropriate interventions based on their judgement and knowledge of the client. For example, the nursing diagnostic label ***Sleep Pattern Disturbed*** has 10 NIC interventions listed for problem resolution and 18 additional optional interventions. See the box above right.

When planning and documenting care in an agency that uses the NIC taxonomy, the nurse chooses from the computer (or writes if using a manual system) the broad intervention label (e.g., Touch). Not all the activities suggested for the intervention would be needed for every client, so the nurse chooses the activities appropriate for the client and individualizes them to fit the resources available in the agency.

When writing individualized nursing orders on a care plan, the nurse should record the activities rather than the broad intervention labels. The NIC taxonomy provides many

Benefits of the Nursing Interventions Classification (NIC)

- Helps demonstrate the impact that nurses have on the health-care delivery system
- Standardizes and defines the knowledge base for nursing curricula and practice
- Facilitates the appropriate selection of a nursing intervention
- Facilitates communication of nursing treatments to other nurses and other providers
- Enables researchers to examine the effectiveness and cost of nursing care
- Assists educators to develop curricula that better articulate with clinical practice
- Facilitates the teaching of clinical decision making to novice nurses
- Assists administrators in planning more effectively for staff and equipment needs
- Facilitates the development and use of nursing information systems
- Communicates the nature of nursing to the public

Source: J. C. McCloskey & G. M. Bulechek. (Eds). (1996). *Nursing interventions classification (NIC): Iowa Outcome Project* (2nd ed.). St. Louis, MO: Mosby-Year Book. Used with permission.

benefits to nurse practitioners, nurse educators, nurse administrators, and the nursing profession as a whole (see the box above).

Implementing

The nursing process is action oriented, client centred, and goal directed. After developing a plan of care based on the assessing and diagnosing phases, the nurse puts the plan into effect and evaluates the results. On the basis of this evaluation, the plan of care is either continued, modified, or terminated. As in all phases of the nursing process, clients and support persons are encouraged to participate as much as possible.

In the nursing process, implementing is the phase in which the nurse puts the nursing care plan into action. Broadly defined, implementing consists of doing, delegating, and recording. The nurse performs or delegates the nursing orders that were developed in the planning step and then concludes the implementing step by recording nursing activities and the resulting client responses.

Although the nurse may act on the client's behalf (e.g., referring the client to a community health nurse for home care), professional standards support client and family participation as in all phases of the nursing process. The degree of participation depends on the client's health status. For example, an unconscious man is unable to participate in his care and, therefore, needs to have care given to him. By contrast, an ambulatory client may require very little care from the nurse and carry out health-care activities independently.

Relationship of Implementing to Other Nursing Process Phases

The first three nursing process phases—assessing, diagnosing, and planning—provide the basis for the nursing actions performed during the implementing step. In turn, the implementing step provides the actual nursing activities and client responses that are evaluated in the final step (evaluating). Using data acquired during assessment, the nurse can individualize the care given in the implementing phase, tailoring the interventions to fit a specific client (e.g., Amanda Aquilini) rather than applying them routinely to categories of clients (e.g., all pneumonia clients).

Ongoing assessment occurs simultaneously with implementation. While implementing the nursing orders, the nurse continues to reassess the client at every contact, gathering data about the client's responses to the nursing actions and about any new problems that may develop.

For example:

Implementation	*Assessment*
While bathing an elderly client,	the nurse observes a reddened area on the client's sacrum.
When emptying a catheter bag,	the nurse measures 200 mL of strong-smelling, brown urine.

Finally, nurses implement nursing orders that specifically *direct* assessment. For example, a nursing order on the client's care plan might read, "Auscultate lungs q4h." When performing this activity, the nurse is both carrying out the nursing order (implementing) and performing an assessment. The following box summarizes categories of various nursing interventions.

Implementing Skills

To implement the care plan successfully, nurses need good cognitive, interpersonal, and technical skills. The skills are distinct from one another; in practice, however, nurses use them in various combinations and with different emphasis depending on the activity. For instance, when inserting a urinary catheter, the nurse needs cognitive knowledge of the principles and steps of the procedure, technical skill in draping the client and manipulating the equipment, and interpersonal skills to inform and reassure the client.

The **cognitive skills** (intellectual skills) include problem solving, decision making, critical thinking, and creative thinking (see Chapter 22). They are crucial to safe, intelligent nursing care.

Categories of Nursing Interventions

- Assessments to make a nursing diagnosis
- Assessments to gather information for a physician to make a medical diagnosis
- Nurse-initiated treatments in response to nursing diagnoses
- Physician-initiated treatments in response to medical diagnoses
- Activities performed to evaluate the effects of nursing or medical treatments; these are also assessments but for the purpose of evaluation, not diagnosis
- Administrative and indirect care behaviours that support interventions

Source: Adapted from J. C. McCloskey & G. M. Bulechek. (Eds.). (1996). *Nursing interventions classification (NIC)* (2nd ed.). St. Louis, MO: Mosby-Year Book. p. 18.

Interpersonal skills are necessary for all nursing activities: caring, comforting, referring, counselling, and supporting are just a few. They include conveying knowledge, attitudes, feelings, interest, and appreciation of the client's cultural values and lifestyle. Before nurses can be highly skilled in interpersonal relations, they must have self-awareness and sensitivity to others. See Chapter 26 for more detailed explanations of interpersonal skills.

Technical skills are "hands-on" skills such as manipulating equipment, giving injections, and bandaging, moving, lifting, and repositioning clients. These activities are also called procedures or psychomotor skills. The term *psychomotor* includes the interpersonal component, for example, the need to communicate with the client.

Technical skills require knowledge and, frequently, manual dexterity. The number of technical skills expected of a nurse has greatly increased in recent years because of the increased use of technology, especially in acute-care hospitals.

Process of Implementing

The process of implementing normally includes:

- Reassessing the client.
- Determining the nurse's need for assistance.
- Implementing the nursing orders (strategies).
- Delegating and supervising.
- Communicating the nursing actions.

Reassessing the Client Just before implementing an order, the nurse must reassess the client to make sure the intervention is still needed. Even though an order is written on the care plan, the client's condition may have changed. For example, Amanda Aquilini had a nursing diagnosis of ***Disturbed Sleep Pattern*** related to cough, pain, orthopnea, fever, and diaphoresis. During rounds, the nurse discovers that Amanda is sleeping and, therefore, defers the cooling back rub that had been planned as an intervention.

New data may indicate a need to change the priorities of care or the nursing strategies. For example, a nurse begins to teach Ms. Eves, who has diabetes, how to give herself insulin injections. Shortly after beginning the teaching, the nurse realizes that Ms. Eves is not concentrating on the lesson. Subsequent discussion reveals that she is worried about her eyesight and fears she is going blind. Realizing that the client's level of stress is interfering with her learning, the nurse ends the lesson and makes arrangements for the nurse practitioner from the diabetic clinic to meet with her. The nurse also provides supportive communication to help alleviate the client's stress.

Determining the Nurse's Need for Assistance When implementing some nursing strategies, the nurse may require assistance for one of the following reasons:

- The nurse is unable to safely implement the nursing strategies alone (e.g., turning an obese client in bed).
- Assistance would reduce stress on the client (e.g., turning a person who experiences acute pain when moved).
- The nurse lacks the knowledge or skills to implement a particular nursing activity (e.g., a nurse who is not familiar with a particular model of oxygen mask needs assistance the first time it is applied).

Implementing Nursing Orders (Interventions) It is important to explain to the client what will be done, what sensations to expect, and what the client is expected to do. For many nursing actions, it is also important to ensure the client's privacy, for example, by closing doors, pulling curtains, or draping the client. The number and kind of nursing activities is almost unlimited. Some examples are caring, communicating, helping, teaching, counselling, acting as a client advocate, leading, and managing. Nurses also coordinate client care. This activity involves scheduling client contacts with other health-care professionals (e.g., laboratory and x-ray technicians, physical and respiratory therapists), departments, or agencies and serving as a liaison among the members of the health-care team. Guidelines for implementing nursing interventions are shown in the box that follows.

Delegating and Supervising Delegating is another activity that occurs during the planning phase of the nursing process. While choosing nursing interventions and writing nursing orders on the client's care plan, the nurse must also determine who should actually perform the activity. The ability to delegate client care and assign tasks is a vital skill for registered nurses (RNs) because many health-care agencies have assistive personnel to perform

Guidelines for Implementing Nursing Interventions

- *Nursing actions should be based on scientific knowledge, nursing research, and professional standards of care.* The nurse must be aware of the scientific rationale for all interventions, as well as possible side effects or complications of the activities. When individualizing an action, the nurse takes care not to violate the scientific basis of the activity. For example, Ms. Li prefers to take an oral medication after meals; however, this medication is not absorbed well in the presence of food. Therefore, the nurse will need to explain to Ms. Li why this preference cannot be honoured.
- *Nurses should understand clearly the orders to be implemented and question any that are not understood.* The nurse is responsible for intelligent implementation of medical and nursing plans of care. This requires knowledge of each intervention, its purpose in the client's plan of care, any contraindications (e.g., allergies), and changes in the client's condition that may affect the order.
- *Nursing actions should be adapted to the individual client.* A client's beliefs, values, age, health status, and environment are factors that can affect the success of a nursing action. Although the nurse takes care not to violate the scientific basis of the activity, actions often need to be individualized. For example, Mr. Ault cannot swallow pills, so his nurse consults with the physician to change the order to a liquid form of the medication.
- *Nursing actions should always be safe.* For example, when changing a sterile dressing, the nurse practises sterile technique to prevent infection; when giving a medication, the nurse takes care to administer the correct dosage by the ordered route.
- *Nursing actions often require teaching, support, and comfort.* These independent nursing activities can enhance the effectiveness of nursing actions.
- *Nursing actions should be holistic.* The nurse must always view the client as a whole and consider the client's responses in that light.
- *Nursing actions should respect the dignity of the client and enhance the client's self-esteem.* Providing privacy and encouraging clients to make their own decisions are ways of respecting dignity and enhancing self-esteem.
- *Clients should be encouraged to participate actively in implementing the nursing actions.* Active participation enhances the client's sense of independence and control. However, clients vary in the degree of participation they desire. Some want total involvement in their care, whereas others prefer little involvement. The amount of desired involvement may be related to the severity of the illness; the number of stressors; or the client's energy, fear, understanding of the illness, and understanding of the intervention.

tasks previously done only by RNs. To delegate appropriately, the RN must match the needs of the client and family with the skills, knowledge, and scope of practice of the available caregivers. This requires knowing the background, experience, knowledge, skills, and strengths of each person and understanding which tasks are and are not within their legal scope of practice.

The RN has two responsibilities in making work assignments: (1) *appropriate delegation* of duties (that is, assigning people duties within their scope of practice); and (2) *adequate supervision* of personnel (Barter & Furmidge, 1994). The RN can assign certain tasks to an unlicensed person but cannot assign responsibility for total nursing care (CNA, 1995). The RN is responsible for seeing that delegated tasks are performed properly. Assistive personnel may perform such tasks as measuring intake and output, but the RN is still responsible for analyzing data, planning care, and evaluating outcomes. As stated in the Canadian Nurses Association Policy Statement on Unregulated Workers Supporting Nursing Care Delivery (1995), "if aspects of care are performed apart from the nursing process, inaccuracy in making critical observations may result, leading to unnecesary pain and suffering. Delays or errors in responding to the client's changing health-care needs increase both the potential for complications and the costs of treatment required to address complications" (p. 1). Thus, it is stressed that "assessment by a registered nurse is needed to detect potentially serious changes *when the client's condition is unstable or unpredictable*" [italics added] (p. 2). Because there are no universal standards for the training of unregulated workers, RNs often must assume responsibility for supplementing the training those staff members have received.

Documenting Nursing Actions After carrying out the nursing orders, the nurse completes the implementing phase by recording the interventions and client responses in the client record. For information on documenting and reporting, see Chapter 24.

Evaluating

To evaluate is to judge or to appraise. Evaluating is the fifth and last phase of the nursing process. In this context,

FOCUS ON CRITICAL THINKING

Mr. Frank Reynolds is an 85-year-old widower who lives by himself in a seniors' apartment, quite close to the home of his son, daughter-in-law, and three grandchildren (8, 13, 15 years of age). Eight years ago, he was diagnosed with Parkinson's disease. He had a fall about a month ago and was hospitalized overnight.

1. What is the role of the nursing process in providing care to Mr. Frank Reynolds?
2. What elements of Mr. Reynolds' life are important to include in your assessment?
3. What strategies might you use to gain Mr. Frank Reynolds' participation in a plan of care?

See Appendix A for answers to these questions.

evaluation is a planned, ongoing, purposeful activity in which clients and health-care professionals determine (1) the client's progress toward goal achievement, and (2) the effectiveness of the nursing care plan. Evaluation is an important aspect of the nursing process because conclusions drawn from the evaluation determine whether the nursing interventions should be terminated, continued, or changed.

Evaluation may be ongoing, intermittent, or terminal. **Ongoing evaluation** is done while or immediately after implementing a nursing order; it enables the nurse to make on-the-spot modifications in an intervention. **Intermittent evaluation,** performed at specified intervals (e.g., once a week), shows the extent of progress toward goal achievement and enables the nurse to correct any deficiencies and modify the care plan as needed. Evaluation continues (either ongoing or intermittently) until the client achieves the health goals and/or is discharged from nursing care. **Terminal evaluation** indicates the client's condition at the time of discharge. It includes the status of goal achievement and an evaluation of the client's self-care abilities with regard to follow-up care. Most agencies have a special discharge record for the terminal evaluation.

Through evaluating, nurses accept responsibility for their actions, indicate interest in the results of the nursing actions, and demonstrate a desire not to perpetuate ineffective actions but to adopt more effective ones.

Relationship of Evaluating to Other Nursing Process Phases

Evaluation depends on the effectiveness of the steps that precede it. Assessment data must be accurate and complete so that the nurse can formulate appropriate nursing diagnoses and desired outcomes. The desired outcomes must be stated concretely in behavioural terms if they are to be useful for evaluating client responses. And finally, without the implementing phase in which the plan is put into action, there would be nothing to evaluate.

The evaluating and assessing phases overlap. As previously stated, assessment (data collection) is ongoing and continuous at every client contact. However, data are collected for different purposes at different points in the nursing process. During the assessing phase, the nurse collects data for the purpose of making diagnoses. During the evaluating step, the nurse collects data for the purpose of comparing them to preselected goals and judging the effectiveness of the nursing care. The *act* of assessing (data collection) is the same; the differences lie in (1) when the data are collected, and (2) how the data are used.

Process of Evaluating Client Responses

The evaluation process has six components:

1. Identify the desired outcomes (indicators) that the nurse will use to measure client goal achievement. (This is done in the planning step.)
2. Collect data related to the desired outcomes (indicators).
3. Compare the data with the desired outcomes (indicators) and judge whether the desired outcomes have been achieved.
4. Relate nursing actions to client goals/desired outcomes.
5. Draw conclusions about problem status.
6. Continue to modify or terminate the client's care plan.

Identifying Desired Outcomes The desired outcomes formulated in the planning step are the criteria used to evaluate the client's response to nursing care. Desired outcomes serve two purposes: they (1) establish the kind of evaluative data that need to be collected, and (2) provide a standard against which the data are judged. For example, given the following expected outcomes, any nurse caring for the client would know what data to collect:

- Daily fluid intake will not be less than 2500 mL.
- Urinary output will balance with fluid intake.
- Residual urine will be less than 100 mL.

Collecting Data Using the clearly stated, precise, and measurable desired outcomes as a guide, the nurse collects data so that conclusions can be drawn about whether goals have been met. It is usually necessary to collect both objective and subjective data.

Some data may require interpretation. Examples of objective data requiring interpretation are the degree of tissue turgor of a dehydrated client or the degree of restlessness of a client with pain. When objective data need interpretation, the nurse may obtain the views of other nurses to substantiate whether change has occurred. Examples of subjective data needing interpretation include complaints of nausea or pain by the client. When interpreting subjective data, the nurse must rely upon either (1) the client's statements (e.g., "My pain is worse now than it was after breakfast"), or (2) objective indicators of the subjective data even though these indicators may require further interpretation (e.g., decreased restlessness, decreased pulse and respiratory rates, and relaxed facial muscles as indicators of pain relief). Data must be recorded concisely and accurately to facilitate the next part of the evaluating process.

Comparing Data with Outcomes If the first two parts of the evaluation process have been carried out effectively, it is relatively simple to determine whether a desired outcome has been met. Both the nurse and client play an active role in comparing the client's actual responses with the desired outcomes. Did the client drink 3 000 mL of fluid in 24 hours? Did the client walk unassisted the specified distance per day? When determining whether a goal has been achieved, the nurse can draw one of three possible conclusions:

1. The goal was met; that is, the client response is the same as the desired outcome.
2. The goal was partially met; that is, either a short-term goal was achieved but the long-term goal was not, or the desired outcome was only partially attained.
3. The goal was not met.

After determining whether a goal has been met, the nurse writes an evaluative statement (either on the care plan or in the nurse's notes). An **evaluation statement** consists of two parts: a conclusion and supporting data. The conclusion is a statement that the goal/desired outcome was met, partially met, or not met. The supporting data are the list of client responses that support the conclusion, for example:

> Goal met: Oral intake 300 mL more than output; skin turgor good; mucous membranes moist

See Table 23.19 for evaluation statements for Amanda Aquilini. Data in this table represent Ms. Aquilini's responses to care as observed by the night nurse on the morning after her admission to the unit. In practice, care plans usually do not have a column for evaluation statements; rather, evaluation statements are recorded in the nurses' notes.

Relating Nursing Actions to Client Goals/Outcomes The fourth aspect of the evaluating process is determining whether the nursing actions had any relation to the outcomes. It should never be assumed that a nursing action was the cause of or the only factor in meeting, partially meeting, or not meeting a goal.

For example, Mrs. Sophi Ringdale was obese and needed to lose 14 kg. When the nurse and client drew up a care plan, one goal was "Lose 1.4 kg by 4/7/03." A nursing strategy in the care plan was "Explain how to plan and prepare a 1000-calorie diet." On 4/7/03, the client weighed herself and had lost 1.8 kg. The goal had been met—in fact, exceeded. It is easy to assume that the nursing strategy was highly effective. However, it is important to collect more data before drawing that conclusion. On questioning the client, the nurse might find any of the following: (1) the client planned a 1000-calorie diet and prepared and ate the food; (2) the client planned a 1000-calorie diet but did not prepare the correct food; (3) the client did not understand how to plan a 1000-calorie diet, so she did not bother with it.

If the first possibility is found to be true, the nurse can safely judge that the nursing strategy "Explain how to plan and prepare a 1000-calorie diet" was effective in helping the client lose weight. However, if the nurse learns that either the second or third possibility actually happened, then it must be assumed that the nursing strategy did not affect the outcome. The next step for the nurse is to collect data about what the client actually did to lose weight. It is important to establish the relationship (or lack thereof) of the nursing actions to the client responses.

Drawing Conclusions about Problem Status The nurse uses the judgements about goal achievement to determine whether the care plan was effective in resolving, reducing, or preventing client problems. When goals have been met, the nurse can draw one of the following conclusions about the status of the client's problem:

- The risk problem stated in the nursing diagnosis has been resolved; or the risk nursing diagnosis is being prevented and the risk factors no longer exist. In these instances, the nurse documents that the goals have been met and discontinues the care for the problem.
- The potential problem stated in the nursing diagnosis is being prevented, but the risk factors are still present. In this case, the nurse keeps the problem on the care plan.
- The actual problem still exists even though some goals are being met. For example, a desired outcome on a client's care plan is "Will ingest 3 000 mL of fluid daily." Even though the data may show this outcome has been achieved, other data (dry oral mucous membranes) may indicate that there is a ***Fluid Volume Deficit.*** Therefore, the nursing interventions must be continued even though this one goal was met.

When goals have been partially met, or when goals have not been met, two conclusions may be drawn:

TABLE 23.19 Modified Care Plan for Amanda Aquilini (One problem only)*

Nursing Diagnosis: ***Anxiety*** related to difficulty breathing and concern about work and parenting roles.

Desired Outcomes	Evaluation Statements	Nursing Orders	Rationale
Demonstrates decreased anxiety, as evidenced by		a. When client is dyspneic, stay with her; reassure her you will stay.	a. Presence of a competent caregiver reduces fear of being unable to breathe. Control of anxiety will help client to maintain effective breathing pattern.
1. Listening to and following instructions for correct breathing and coughing technique, even during periods of dyspnea	1. Goal met. Performed coughing techniques as instructed during periods of dyspnea.	b. Remain calm, appear confident. c. Encourage slow, deep breathing.	b. Reassures client the nurse can help her. c. Focusing on breathing may help client feel in control and decrease anxiety.
2. Verbalizing understanding of condition, diagnostic tests, and treatments (by end of day 1)	2. Goal met. See nurse's notes for 3–11 shift. Stated, "I know I need to try to breathe deeply even when it hurts." Demonstrated correct use of incentive spirometer and stated understanding of the need to use it. Understands IV is for hydration and antibiotics. *(Evaluated 4/17/03, JW)*	d. When client is dyspneic, give brief explanations of treatments and procedures. e. ~~When acute episode is over, give detailed information about nature of condition, treatments, and tests.~~ *Reassess whether client needs any information on condition, treatments, or tests. (4/17/03, JW).*	d. Anxiety and pain interfere with learning. Knowing what to expect reduces anxiety. e. *Detailed information has been given. Because client shows understanding, there is no need to repeat information.*
3. Decrease in reports of fear and anxiety; none within 12 h	3. Goal met. States, "I know I can get enough air, but it still hurts to breathe."		
4. Voice steady, not shaky	4. Goal met. Speaks in steady voice.		
5. Respiratory rate of 12–22/min	5. Goal not met. Rate 26–36/min.		
6. Freely expressing concerns about work and parenting roles, but placing them in perspective in view of her illness	6. Goal partially met. Discussed only briefly on shift. Not done on night shift because of client's need to rest. *(Evaluated 4/17/03, JW)*	f. As client can tolerate, encourage to express and expand on her concerns about her child and her work. Explore alternatives as needed. *g. Note whether husband returns as scheduled. If he does not, institute care plan for actual **Altered Family Process.** (Do on 4/17, day shift) (4/17/03, JW)*	f. Awareness of source of anxiety enables client to gain control over it. g. Husband's continued absence would constitute defining characteristic for this nursing diagnosis. *It is important that this assessment be made right away, so child care can be arranged if needed.*

* In this care plan, a line has been drawn through portions the nurse wished to delete; additions to the care plan are shown in italics.

TABLE 23.20 Evaluation Checklist

Assessing	Diagnosing	Planning	Implementing
_____ Are data complete, accurate, and validated?	_____ Are nursing diagnoses relevant and accurate?	***Desired outcomes***	_____ Was client input obtained at each step of the nursing process?
_____ Do new data require changes in the care plan?	_____ Are nursing diagnoses supported by the data?	_____ Do new nursing diagnoses require new goals?	_____ Were goals and nursing interventions acceptable to the client?
	_____ Has problem status changed (i.e., potential, actual, possible)?	_____ Are goals realistic?	_____ Did the caregivers have the knowledge and skill to perform the interventions correctly?
	_____ Are the diagnoses stated clearly and in correct format?	_____ Was enough time allowed for goal achievement?	_____ Were explanations given to the client prior to implementing?
	_____ Have any nursing diagnoses been resolved?	_____ Do the goals address all aspects of the problem?	
		_____ Does the client still concur with the goals?	
		_____ Have client priorities changed?	
		Nursing orders	
		_____ Do nursing orders need to be written for new nursing diagnoses or new goals?	
		_____ Are the nursing orders related to the stated goals?	
		_____ Is there a rationale to justify each nursing order?	
		_____ Are the nursing orders clear, specific, and detailed?	
		_____ Are new resources available?	
		_____ Do the nursing orders address all aspects of the client's goals?	
		_____ Were all nursing orders clearly effective?	

1. The care plan may need to be revised since the problem is only partially resolved. The revisions may need to occur during assessing, diagnosing, or planning phases, as well as implementing.
2. The care plan does not need revision because the client merely needs more time to achieve the previously established goal(s). In order to make this decision, the nurse must assess why the goals are being only partially achieved, including whether the evaluation was conducted too soon.

Reviewing and Modifying the Nursing Care Plan After drawing conclusions about the status of the client's problems, the nurse modifies the care plan as indicated. Depending on the agency, modifications may be made by drawing a single line through portions of the care plan, or marking portions using a highlighting pen, or writing "Discontinued" (dc'd) and the date.

Whether or not goals were met, there are a number of decisions to make about continuing, modifying, or terminating nursing care for each problem. Before making individual modifications, the nurse must first determine why the plan as a whole was not completely effective. This requires a review of the entire care plan and a critique of the nursing process steps involved in its development. See Table 23.20 for a checklist to use when reviewing a care plan.

Assessing An incomplete or incorrect database influences all subsequent steps of the nursing process and care plan. If data are incomplete, the nurse needs to reassess the client and record the new data. In some instances, new data may indicate the need for new nursing diagnoses, new goals, and new nursing orders.

Diagnosing If the database is incomplete, new diagnostic statements may be required. If the database is complete, the nurse needs to analyze whether the problems were identified correctly and whether the nursing diagnoses are relevant to that database. After making judgements about problem status, the nurse revises or adds new diagnoses as needed to reflect the most recent client data.

Planning: Desired Outcomes If a nursing diagnosis is inaccurate, obviously the goal statement will need revision. If the nursing diagnosis is appropriate, the nurse then checks that the goals are realistic and attainable. Unrealistic goals require correction. The nurse should also determine whether priorities have changed and whether the client still agrees with the priorities. Goals must also be written for any new nursing diagnoses.

Planning: Nursing Orders The nurse investigates whether the nursing strategies were related to goal achievement and whether the best nursing strategies were selected. Even when diagnoses and goals are appropriate, the nursing strategies selected may not have been the best ones to achieve the goal. New nursing orders may reflect changes in the amount of nursing care the client needs, scheduling changes, or rearrangement of nursing activities to group similar activities or to permit longer rest or activity periods for the client. If new nursing diagnoses have been written, then new nursing orders will also be necessary.

Implementing Even if all sections of the care plan appear to be satisfactory, the manner in which the plan was implemented may have interfered with goal achievement. Before selecting new interventions, the nurse should check whether the nursing orders were carried out. Other personnel may not have carried them out, either because the orders were unclear or because they were unreasonable in terms of external constraints, such as resources.

After making the necessary modifications to the care plan, the nurse implements the modified plan and begins the nursing process cycle again. Refer to Table 23.19 to see how the plan for Amanda Aquilini was modified after evaluation of goal achievement and review of the nursing process. A line has been drawn through portions the nurse wished to delete; additions to the care plan are shown in italics.

Evaluating the Quality of Nursing Care

In addition to evaluating goal achievement for individual clients, nurses are also involved in evaluating and modifying the overall quality of care given to groups of clients. This is an essential part of professional accountability.

Quality Assurance A **quality-assurance (QA) program** is an ongoing, systematic process designed to evaluate and promote excellence in the health care provided to clients. Quality assurance frequently refers to evaluation of the level of care provided in a health-care agency, but it may be limited to the evaluation of the performance of one nurse or more broadly involve the evaluation of the quality of the care in an agency, or even in a province or territory.

Quality assurance requires evaluation of three components of care: structure, process, and outcome. Each type of evaluation requires different criteria and methods, and each has a different focus.

Structure evaluation focuses on the setting in which care is given. It answers the question, What effect does the setting have on the quality of care? Structural standards describe desirable environmental and organizational characteristics that influence care, such as equipment and staffing.

Process evaluation focuses on how the care was given. It answers such questions as these: Is the care relevant to the client's needs? Is the care appropriate, complete, and timely? Process standards focus on the manner in which the nurse uses the nursing process. Some examples of process criteria are "Checks client's identification band before giving medication" and "Performs and records chest assessment, including auscultation, once per shift."

Outcome evaluation focuses on demonstrable changes in the clients' health status as a result of nursing care. Outcome criteria are written in terms of client responses or health states, just as they are for evaluation within the nursing process. For example, "How many clients undergoing hip repairs develop pneumonia?" or "How many clients who have a colostomy experience an infection that delays discharge?"

Quality Improvement Quality improvement (QI) is also known as continuous quality improvement (CQI), total quality management (TQM), or persistent quality improvement (PQI). According to Schroeder (1994, p. 3), QI is

> *the commitment and approach used to continuously improve every process in every part of an organization, with the intent of meeting and exceeding customer expectations and outcomes.*

Unlike quality assurance, QI follows client care rather than organizational structure, focuses on process rather than individuals, and uses a systematic approach with the intention of *improving* the quality of care rather than *ensuring* the quality of care. QI studies often focus on identifying and correcting a system's problems, such as duplication of services in a hospital or improving services.

Nursing Audit An *audit* means the examination or review of records. A *retrospective audit* is the evaluation of a client's record after discharge from an agency. *Retrospective* means "relating to past events." A *concurrent audit* is the evaluation of a client's health care while the client is still receiving care from the agency. These evaluations use interviewing, direct observation of nursing care, and review of clinical records to determine whether specific evaluative criteria have been met.

Nursing Process Summarized

The nursing process is foundational to nursing practice. Its basic structure can be modified for the split-second decision making sometimes necessary in critical care environments or the complex, long-range planning and evaluation necessary for community health promotion programs. It is characterized by being:

- Open and flexible to meet the unique needs of clients, families, communities, and whole populations.
- Cyclic and dynamic with a built-in plan for evaluation, reassessment, and modification.
- Client centred and individualized.
- Interpersonal and collaborative as a process and as a means of communication.
- Planned and goal directed.
- Creative.
- Universally applicable.

CHAPTER HIGHLIGHTS

- The nursing process is a systematic, rational method of planning and providing individualized nursing care for individuals, families, groups, and communities.
- The goals of the nursing process are to identify a client's actual or potential health-care needs and strengths, to establish plans to meet the identified needs, and to deliver and evaluate specific nursing interventions to meet those needs.
- The nursing process can be used in all health-care settings; it is cyclic and dynamic, client centred, interpersonal and collaborative, and universally applicable. It provides a framework for nurses' accountability and responsibility.
- The nursing process is organized into five interrelated, interdependent phases: assessing, diagnosing, planning, implementing, and evaluating.
- Assessing involves collecting, organizing, validating, and recording data.
- Diagnosing is the process of making a clinical judgement (nursing diagnosis or hypothesis) about a client's potential or actual health problems.
- Planning involves setting priorities, writing goals/desired outcomes, and establishing a written plan for nursing interventions.
- Implementing is carrying out or delegating the nursing interventions. It incorporates all the activities performed to promote health, prevent complications, treat present problems, and facilitate the client's coping with chronic alterations in health status.
- Evaluating is the process of comparing client responses to preselected outcomes to determine whether goals have been met. It includes review and modification of the care plan.
- Assessment involves active participation by the client and nurse in obtaining subjective and objective data about the client's health status.
- The client is the primary source of data. Secondary sources are family, friends, health team members, the health record, and pertinent literature.
- Subjective data are the client's personal perceptions, often gathered during the nursing health history.
- Objective data (e.g., data observed and collected during the physical examination) are detectable by an observer.
- Some data must be validated. Subjective data can be used to validate objective data, and vice versa. Primary and secondary data can also be used to validate each other.
- Skills required for data collection are communicating, interviewing, observing, and examining.
- Observation is a conscious, deliberate skill involving use of the senses.
- The nurse uses a combination of directive and nondirective interviewing (including closed and open-ended questions) to obtain the nursing health history.
- Nursing models provide frameworks for collecting and organizing client data.
- Data must be recorded in a factual manner, separating interpretation or inferences.
- A nursing diagnosis is a clinical judgement about the client's responses to actual and potential health problems or life processes.
- A nursing diagnosis provides the basis for selecting independent nursing interventions to achieve outcomes for which the nurse is accountable.
- A wellness diagnosis is a clinical judgement about a client in transition from a specific level of wellness to a higher level of wellness.

- Nursing diagnoses differ from medical diagnoses and collaborative problems in orientation, duration, and nursing focus.
- The critical-thinking skills used in diagnosing include analysis, synthesis, inductive reasoning, and decision making.
- The three phases of the diagnostic process are: data analysis; identification of the client's health problems, health risks, and strengths; and formulation of diagnostic statements.
- In data analysis and processing, the nurse compares data against standards to identify significant cues, clusters the data, and identifies gaps and inconsistencies.
- Significant cues are those that (1) point to change in a client's health status or pattern, (2) vary from norms of the client population, or (3) indicate a developmental delay.
- It is important to identify client strengths as well as problems.
- A nursing diagnosis should be clear, concise, client centred, related to only one problem, and based on reliable and relevant assessment data.
- Planning involves the nurse, support persons, and other caregivers.
- The planning process includes setting diagnostic priorities, establishing client goals/desired outcomes, selecting nursing interventions, writing nursing orders, and developing a nursing care plan.
- Nursing diagnoses are assigned high, medium, and low priorities in consultation with the client, if possible.
- Desired outcomes describe specific and measurable client responses and help the nurse evaluate the effectiveness of the nursing interventions.
- Goal statements and desired outcomes are written in terms of the client's behaviour.
- The nursing care plan provides direction for individualized care of the patient.
- Standardized care plans should be adapted to meet individual client needs.
- Nursing interventions and activities are developed from the client's diagnostic statements and goals/desired outcomes.
- Nursing activities are the specific actions taken by the nurse to help the client meet goals and desired outcomes.
- Independent nursing interventions are those the nurse is licensed to prescribe or delegate.

READINGS AND REFERENCES

Suggested Readings

Andresen, G. P. (1998). Assessing the older patient. *RN, 61*(3), 45–56.

This CEU article addresses the normal physiological changes that occur with aging, enabling the nurse to differentiate signs and symptoms of disease from age-related changes and recognize nursing interventions that can maintain or strengthen older adults' health. A comprehensive table indicates age-related changes and the clinical significance of 14 laboratory values in older adults. A second table offers a systems approach to indicate assessment findings, physiological causes, and nursing implications.

Bowles, K. J., & Naylor, M. D. (1996). Nursing interventions classification systems. *Image: Journal of Nursing Scholarship, 28*(4), 303–308.

This provides an overview of work that has been done to create a standardized language for nursing interventions. It compares three systems for classifying nursing interventions: the Iowa Nursing Intervention Classification (NIC), the Omaha System, and the Home Health Care Classification.

Brown, S. J. (1995). An interviewing style for nursing assessment. *Journal of Advanced Nursing, 21*(2), 340–343.

Brown reviews the literature on health-care interviewing styles and critiques the traditional "provider question-client answer" style. She suggests an alternative style, the conversational interview, which is described as more client focused and less interpersonally controlling and is believed to produce an accurate shared understanding of the client's health status.

Burgess, C., & Casault, C. A. (1998). Does nursing care make a difference? *Axon, 20*(1),14–15.

A Canadian nurse educator and nurse manager report on the outcomes of nursing care in an acute stroke unit based on identification of common nursing diagnoses, nursing interventions, and outcome measures. The article includes a useful chart showing these nursing process components and the results that they achieved.

Greenwood, D. (1996). Nursing care plans: Issues and solutions. *Nursing Management, 27*(3), 37–40.

This explains why nursing care plans are not well utilized in some institutions. It describes a care plan that addresses some of those issues.

Pesut, D. J., & Herman, J. (1998). OPT: Transformation of nursing process for contemporary practice. *Nursing Outlook, 46*(1), 29–36.

Contemporary trends and forces suggest that transformation of the nursing process is needed. The outcome-present state-test (OPT) reasoning model emphasizes reflection, outcome specification, and testing within the context of clinical narratives. This transitional reasoning model builds on the heritage of the nursing process and is more responsive and relevant to current nursing practice needs than previous nursing process models.

Sparks, S. M. (1997, April/June). Noun phrases for nursing diagnoses. *Nursing Diagnoses: The Journal of Nursing Language and Classification, 8*(2), 49–54.
Sparks proposes a list of qualifiers to replace the current list and recommends a revised list of nursing diagnoses using noun phrases to improve their clinical usefulness, allow for alphabetization, and enhance clarity. Examples include *Grieving Dysfunction*, rather than *Dysfunctional Grieving* and *Mobility Impairment*, rather than *Impaired Physical Mobility*.

Wright, L. M., & Leahey, M. (2000). *Nurses and families: A guide to family assessment and intervention* (3rd ed.). Philadelphia, PA: F. A. Davis.
These well-known Canadian authors use a modified version of the nursing process with emphasis on the assessment and intervention stages in working with families experiencing health problems. This text includes the Calgary Family Assessment Model and the Calgary Family Intervention Model as well as useful chapters on preparing for, conducting, and recording family interviews. Of practical interest to even the beginning nurse is a chapter on "How to do a 15-minute (or shorter) family interview," p. 273–288.

You make the diagnosis: Case studies. January/March 1993 through October/December 1997 (all issues). *Nursing Diagnosis.*
This series of case studies prepared by various authors provides clinical examples of situations for which the reader is asked to make nursing diagnoses based on the data presented. The authors who submitted the case studies provide an analysis of diagnoses they would select. The author's analysis is followed by a commentary by another nurse author. *Nursing Diagnosis* grants permission for users to copy the case studies and analyses for educational purposes.

Related Research

Anonymous. (2001). Determining cost of nursing inttervention. *Nursing Economics, 19*, 146–60.

Coenen, A., Ryan, P., Sutton, J., Devine, E. C., Werley, H. H., & Kelber, S. (1995). Use of the Nursing Minimum Data Set to describe nursing interventions for select nursing diagnoses and related factors in an acute care setting. *Nursing Diagnosis, 6*, 108–114.

Heaven, C. M., & Maguire, P. (1996). Training hospice nurses to elicit patient concerns. *Journal of Advanced Nursing, 23*, 280–286.

Henry, S. B., Holzemer, W. L., Randell, C., Hsieh, S.-F., & Miller, T. J. (1997, Second Quarter). Comparison of Nursing Interventions Classification and Current Procedural Terminology codes for categorizing nursing activities. *Image: Journal of Nursing Scholarship, 29*, 133–138.

Maas, M. L., Johnson, M., & Moorhead, S. (1996). Classifying nursing-sensitive patient outcomes. *Image: Journal of Nursing Scholarship, 28*, 295–301.

O'Connor, N. A. Kershaw, T. & Hameister A. D. (2001). Documenting patterns of nursing interventions using cluster analysis. *Journal of Nursing Measurement, 9*, 73–90.

Roberts, B. L., Madigan, E. A., Anthony, M. K., & Pabst, S. L. (1996). The congruence of nursing diagnoses and supporting clinical evidence. *Nursing Diagnosis, 7*, 108–115.

Sisson, J., Furner, J., & Ransome, C. (1996, August 21). Staff nurses' ability to assess community patients: A study. *Nursing Standard, 10*, 34–37.

Whitley, G. G., & Tousman, S. A. (1996). A multivariate approach for validation of anxiety and fear. *Nursing Diagnosis*, 7(3), 116–123.

Selected References

Alfaro-LeFevre. (1998). *Applying the nursing process. A step-by-step guide* (4th ed.). Philadelphia/New York: Lippincott.

American Nurses Association. (1995). *Nursing's social policy statement.* Philadelphia, PA: Lippincott.

American Nurses Association. (1998). *Standards of clinical nursing practice* (2nd ed.). Kansas City, MO: Author.

Anderson, B., & Hannah, K. J. (1993). A Canadian nursing data set: A major priority. *Canadian Journal of Nursing Administration, 6*(2), 7–13.

Bandman, E. L., & Bandman, B. (1995). *Critical thinking in nursing* (2nd ed.). Norwalk, CT: Appleton & Lange.

Barter M., & Furmidge, M. L. (1994). Unlicensed assistive personnel; issues relating to delegation and supervision. *Journal of Nursing Administration, 24*(4), 36–40.

Brammer, L. M. (1993). *The helping relationship* (5th ed.). San Francisco, CA: Jossey-Bass.

Brooten, D., & Naylor, M. D. (1995, Summer). Nurses' effect on changing patient outcomes. *Image: Journal of Nursing Scholarship, 27*(2), 95–99.

Burgess, C., & Casault, C. A. (1998). Does nursing care make a difference? *Axon, 20*(1),14–15.

Canadian Hypertension Recommendations Working Group. (2001). The 2000 Canadian hypertension recommendations: A summary. *Canadian Journal of Cardiovascular Nursing, 11*(4), 4–6.

Canadian Nurses Association. (1986). *Definition of nursing practice, standards of nursing practice.* Ottawa: Author.

Canadian Nurses Association. (1995). *Unregulated health care workers supporting nursing care delivery.* Ottawa: Author.

Canadian Nurses Association. (1996). *Necessary Support for Safe Nursing Care.* Ottawa: Author.

Canadian Nurses Association. (2002). *Code of Ethics for Registered Nurses.* Ottawa: Author.

Canadian Nurses Association. (2002). *Evidence-based decision-making nursing practice.* Ottawa: Author.

Carnevali, D. L., & Thomas, M. D. (1993). *Diagnostic reasoning and treatment decision making in nursing.* Philadelphia, PA: Lippincott.

Carpenito, L. J. (1997). *Handbook of nursing diagnosis* (7th ed.). Philadelphia, PA: Lippincott.

Carpenito, L. J. (1999). *Handbook of nursing diagnosis* (8th ed.). Philadelphia, PA: Lippincott.

Carpenito, L. J. (2000). *Nursing diagnosis: Application to clinical practice* (8th ed.). Philadelphia, PA: Lippincott.

Coenen, A., & Wake, M. (1996). Developing a database for an International Classification for Nursing Practice (ICNP). *International Nursing Review, 43*, 183–187.

Doenges, & M., Moorhouse, M. E. (2003). Application of nursing process and nursing diagnosis: *An interactive text for diagnostic reasoning.* (4th ed.). Philadelphia: F. A. Davis.

Duff, L. A., Kitson, A. L., Seers, K., & Humphris, D. (1996). Clinical guidelines: An introduction to their development and implementation. *Journal of Advanced Nursing, 23*, 887–895.

Frauman, A. C., & Skelly, A. H. (1999). Evolution of the nursing process. *Clinical Excellence for Nurse Practitioners, 3*, 238–244.

Gadow, S. (1995). Clinical epistemology: A dialectic of nursing assessment. *Canadian Journal of Nursing Research, 27*(2), 25–34.

Gordon, M. (1994). *Nursing diagnosis: Process and application* (3rd ed.). Hightown, NJ: McGraw-Hill.

Hall, L. (1955, June). Quality of nursing care. *Public Health News.* Newark, NJ: State Department of Health.

Hannah, K. J., Reimer, M., Mills, W. C., & Letourneau, S. (1987). *Clinical judgement and decision making: The future with nursing diagnosis.* Toronto: John Wiley & Sons.

Harris, M. R., & Warren, J. J. (1995). Patient outcomes: Assessment issues for the CNS. *Clinical Nurse Specialist, 9*(2), 82–86.

Higuchi, K. A., Dulberg, C., & Duff, V. (1999). Factors associated with nursing diagnosis utilization in Canada. *Nursing Diagnosis, 10*, 137–147.

Holt, P. (1995). Role of questioning skills in patient assessment. *British Journal of Nursing, 4*(19), 1145–1146.

Iowa Intervention Project. (1995, Spring). Validation and coding of the NIC taxonomy structure. *Image: Journal of Nursing Scholarship, 27*(1), 43–49.

Johnson, M., & Maas, M. (Eds.). (1997). *Nursing outcomes classification (NOC).* St. Louis, MO: Mosby-Year Book.

Joint Commission on Accreditation of Healthcare Organizations. (1996). *1997 accreditation manual of hospitals.* Oakbrook Terrace, IL: Author.

Joint Commission on Accreditation of Healthcare Organizations. (1997). *Accreditation manual for hospitals.* Chicago, IL: Joint Commission on Accreditation of Healthcare Organizations, Nursing Services.

Lutzen, K., & Tishelman, C. (1996). Nursing diagnosis: A critical analysis of underlying assumptions. *International Journal of Nursing Studies, 33*(2), 190–200.

Mark, B. A. (1995). The black box of patient outcomes research. *Image: Journal of Nursing Scholarship, 27*(1), 42.

McCloskey, J. C., & Bulechek, G. M. (Eds.). (1996). *Nursing interventions classification (NIC)* (2nd ed.). St. Louis, MO: Mosby-Year Book.

McKenzie, P. (1995). Looking beyond the tears... assessment skills. *Professional Leader, 2*(2), 20, 23.

Mitchell, G. J. (1991). Nursing diagnosis: An ethical analysis. *Image: Journal of Nursing Scholarship, 23*(2),99–103.

North American Nursing Diagnosis Association. (1990). *Taxonomy I, revised—1990.* St. Louis, MO: Author.

North American Nursing Diagnosis Assoication. (2001). *Nursing diagnoses: Definitions and classification, (2001–2002).* Philadelphia: Author.

North American Nursing Diagnosis Association. (2003). *Nursing diagnoses: Definitions & classification, 2003–2004.* Philadelphia, PA: Author.

North, S., & Serkes, P. (1996). Improving documentation of initial nursing assessment. *Nursing Management, 27*(4), 30, 33.

Popkess-Vawter, S. (1991). Wellness nursing diagnosis: To be or not to be? *Nursing Diagnosis, 2*(1), 19–25.

Roy, C., & Andrews, H. A. (1999). *The Roy adaptation model* (2nd ed.). Stamford, CT: Appleton & Lange.

Schroeder, P. S. (Ed.). (1994). Improving quality and performance: concepts, programs, and techniques. St. Louis: Mosby.

Sieh, A., & Brentin, L. (1997). *The nurse communicates.* Philadelphia, PA: Saunders.

Skinn, B., & Stacey, D. (1994). Establishing an integrated framework for documentation: Use of a self-reporting health history and outpatient oncology record. *Oncology Nursing Forum, 21*, 1557–1566.

Stewart, C. J., & Cash, W. B. (1994). *Interviewing: Principles and practices* (7th ed.). Dubuque, IA: Brown & Benchmark.

Tucker, S. M., Paquette, E. V., Canobbio, M. M., & Wells, M. F. (1996). *Patient care standards: Collaborative practice planning guide.* St. Louis, MO: Mosby.

Vessey, J. A., & Richardson, B. L. (1993). A holistic approach to symptom assessment and intervention. *Holistic Nursing Practice,* 7(2), 13–21.

Ward, A. K. (1998). Organizational and professional factors and the use of nursing diagnosis in Canada. In P. Lemone & M. J. Rantz (Eds.), *Classification of nursing diagnoses: Proceedings of the 12th Conference* (pp. 381). Glendale, CA: CINAHL Information Systems.

Whitley, G. G. (1996). Barriers to the use of nursing diagnosis language in clinical settings. *Nursing Diagnosis,* 7(1), 25–32.

Wilkinson, J. M. (2001). *Nursing process and critical thinking.* Upper Saddle River, NJ: Prentice Hall.

Wilkinson, J. M. (2000). *Nursing diagnosis handbook with NIC interventions and NOC outcomes* (7th ed.). Upper Saddle River, NJ: Prentice Hall Health.

Windle, P. E. (1994). Critical pathways: An integrated documentation tool. *Nursing Management, 25*(9), 80F.

Wright, L. M., & Leahey, M. (2000). *Nurses and families: A guide to family assessment and intervention* (3rd ed.). Philadelphia, PA: F. A. Davis.

WEBLINKS

North American Nursing Diagnosis Association
http://www.nanda.org
This site provides information on publications and conferences related to the use of nursing diagnosis.

CHAPTER 24

Documenting and Reporting

OBJECTIVES

After completing this chapter, you will be able to:

- Discuss reasons for keeping client records.
- Explain how various forms in the client record (e.g., flowsheets, progress notes, care plans, critical pathways, Kardexes®, discharge/transfer forms) are used to document steps of the nursing process (assessment, diagnosis, planning, implementation, and evaluation).
- Describe different documentation methods: source-oriented, problem-oriented, PIE, Focus Charting®, charting by exception, FACT, CORE, computerized records, and the case management model.
- Compare the documentation needed for clients in acute-care, home health care, and long-term care settings.
- Identify and discuss guidelines for effective recording that meet legal and ethical standards.
- List abbreviations and symbols commonly used for charting.
- Enumerate the measures used to maintain the confidentiality of client records.
- Describe the nurse's role in reporting, conferring, and making referrals.
- Identify essential guidelines for reporting client data.

Effective communication among health-care professionals is vital to the quality of client care. Generally, health-care personnel communicate through discussion, reports, and records. A **discussion** is an informal oral consideration of a subject by two or more health-care personnel to identify a problem or establish strategies to resolve a problem. A **report** is oral, written, or computer-based communication intended to convey information to others. For instance, nurses always report on clients at the end of a hospital work shift. A **record** is written or computer based. The process of making an entry on a client record is called **recording, charting,** or **documenting.**

A clinical record, also called a **chart** or client record, is a formal, legal document that provides evidence of a client's care. Although health-care organizations use different systems and forms for documentation, all client records have similar information.

Each health-care organization has policies about recording and reporting client data, and each nurse is accountable for practising according to these standards. In addition, the Canadian Council of Health Services Accreditation (CCHSA) has specific guidelines for documentation, and each province has a regulatory body. For example, in Alberta, nurses are accountable to the standards of their professional organization. The Alberta Association of Registered Nurses (1999) states, "The registered nurse documents timely, accurate reports of data collection, interpretation, planning, implementing, and evaluating care" (p. 5).

Ethical and Legal Considerations

The client's record is the cornerstone of communication between several disciplines involved in the care of clients. The coordination of this information is vital so that all individuals involved understand and use the information to benefit the patient. Without it, effective, safe, and proper care would be impossible.

Documentation is a vital aspect of nursing practice. As professionals, nurses are responsible and accountable for their own actions. The client's record is considered a legal document; thus, nurses need to be aware of the legal and ethical standards of documentation.

Legally, the nurse's documentation needs to be clear, concise, and accurate. Opinions must be avoided unless related to nursing or medical diagnosis. Statements that are made by clients or family members must be quoted with accuracy. Detailed descriptions of what was observed need to be recorded and changes from previous assessment highlighted.

Charting should occur so that if the nurse is called to testify several years later, the record will allow recollection of what occurred and give credible evidence of the care provided. It is possible that as many as five years could pass before the case comes to court. As the nurse's memory may have faded, the record may provide the only accurate evidence of events. With a well-constructed record, the nurses and other caregivers who made the notes will be able to impart their testimony more forcefully, according the testimony with greater weight. The court will be interested in looking at all aspects of the record, including flowsheets, graphic records, and progress and nurses' notes. Together, all this information will provide a complete picture of events.

As a legal record, the chart is the property of the agency (Rozovsky, 1994) or the medical professional responsible for the client's care. Legally, clients do not own their records to "take away" with them, but they do have the legal right to access their records. There are, however, exceptions to access within mental health legislation. It is thought that, in certain circumstances, this access would be detrimental to the client (Rozovsky, 1994).

Ensuring Confidentiality of Electronic Health Records

Because of the increased use of client information stored electronically, health-care agencies have developed policies and procedures to ensure the privacy and confidentiality of client information stored in computers. The following are some suggestions for ensuring the confidentiality of computerized records:

1. A personal password is needed to enter and sign off computer files. Do not share this password with anyone, including other health-care team members.
2. After logging on, never leave a computer terminal unattended.
3. Do not leave client information displayed on the monitor where others may see it.
4. Follow agency procedures for documenting sensitive material, such as a diagnosis of acquired immune deficiency syndrome (AIDS).

Purposes of Client Records

Client records are used by a multidisciplinary health-care team for a number of purposes, such as facilitating communication, planning client care, auditing for quality assurance, legal documentation, and as sources for research and education.

Communication

The client record is the primary communication source for all members of the multidisciplinary health-care team. Each health-care professional contributes to the care of the client in various ways and uses the client record to access and document information.

Planning and Continuity of Client Care

Each health-care professional uses data from the client's record to plan and maintain continuity of care for that client. A physician, for example, may order a specific antibiotic after establishing that the client's temperature is steadily rising and that laboratory tests reveal the presence of a certain microorganism. Nurses use baseline and ongoing assessment data to evaluate the effectiveness of the nursing care plan.

Auditing for Quality Assurance

An audit is a review of records. Client records are regularly audited for quality assurance to evaluate the care provided by all health-care professionals. For information about quality assurance, see Chapter 23. Accrediting agencies, such as the CCHSA, may review client records to determine if a particular health agency is meeting its stated standards.

Research

Nurses can use data from the client record for various research studies to assist with identifying nursing care problems. The treatment plans for a number of clients with the same health problems can yield information helpful in treating a particular client. Also, information from records may assist health-care planners to identify agency needs, such as overutilized and underutilized hospital services.

Education

Students in nursing and other health-care disciplines often use client records as educational tools. A client record provides a comprehensive overview of the client concerning the medical and nursing diagnosis, signs and symptoms of the condition, diagnostic findings, behaviours, effective treatment strategies, and factors that affect the outcome of the condition. The student can use the information found in the client record to assist with understanding the patterns to look for in various client conditions.

TABLE 24.1 Components of the Source-Oriented Record

Form	Information
Admission (face) sheet	Legal name, birth date, age
	Address
	Marital status; closest relatives or person to notify in case of emergency
	Date, time, and admitting diagnosis
	Food or drug allergies
	Name of admitting (attending) physician
Initial nursing assessment	Findings from the initial nursing history and physical health assessment
Graphic record (see Figure 24.6, page 454)	Body temperature, pulse rate, respiratory rate, blood pressure, daily weight, and bowel movements
Daily care record (see Figure 24.7, pages 456–458)	Activity, diet, bathing, and elimination records; may also include restraints, isolation precautions, treatments
Special flowsheets	Examples: 24-hour fluid balance record
Medication record (see Chapter 28)	Name, dosage, route, time, date, site of administered medications
	Name or initials of person administering the medication
Interdisciplinary notes (Figure 24.1, page 446)	Pertinent assessment of client from various disciplines (physicians, physical/respiratory therapists, etc.)
	Specific nursing care including teaching and client's responses
	Client's complaints and how client is coping
Medical history and physical examination	Past and family medical history, present medical problems, differential or current diagnoses, findings of physical examination by the physician
Physician's order sheet	Medical orders for medications, treatments, and so on
Consultation records	Reports by medical and clinical specialists
Diagnostic reports	Examples: laboratory reports, x-ray reports, CT scan reports
Client discharge plan and referral summary	Started on admission and completed upon discharge; includes nursing problems, general information, and referral data

Documentation Systems

A number of documentation systems are in current use: source-oriented record, problem-oriented record, PIE, Focus Charting®, charting by exception, FACT, CORE, outcome documentation, computerized documentation, and case management.

Source-Oriented Record

The traditional client record is **source oriented.** Each person or department makes notations in a separate section or sections of the client's chart. For example, the admission department has an admission sheet; the physician has a physician's order sheet and a physician's history sheet; all disciplines record on interdisciplinary notes; and other departments or personnel have their own records. In this type of record, information about a particular problem is distributed throughout the record. For example, if a client had left hemiplegia (paralysis of the left side of the body), data about this problem might be found in the physician's history sheet, on the physician's order sheet, and in the interdisciplinary notes. See Table 24.1 for the components of a source-oriented record.

Narrative charting is a traditional part of the source-oriented record. It consists of written notes that include routine care, normal findings, and client problems. There is no right or wrong order to the information, although a chronological order is frequently used. Currently, narrative recording is being replaced by other systems, such as PIE and Focus. Narrative charting is expedient in emergency situations (Figure 24.1).

Source-oriented records are convenient because care providers from each discipline can easily locate the forms on which to record data, and it is easy to trace the information specific to one's discipline. The disadvantage is that information about a particular client problem is scattered throughout the chart, so it is difficult to find chronological information on a client's problems and progress.

Problem-Oriented Medical Record

In the **problem-oriented medical record (POMR),** or **problem-oriented record (POR),** established by Lawrence Weed in the 1960s, the data are arranged according to the problems the client has rather than according to the source of the information. Members of the health-care team contribute to the problem list, plan of care, and progress notes. Plans for each active or potential problem are drawn up, and progress notes are recorded for each problem.

The POR has the advantages that (1) it encourages collaboration, and (2) the problem list in the front of the

INTERDISCIPLINARY NOTES

Date	Time		Disc
2/13/03	1400	Passive ROM exercises provided for R arm and leg. ———	
		Active assistive exercises to L arm and leg. Has scratch ———	
		marks on L and R forearms. States, "My skin on my back ———	
		and arms has been itchy for a week." Rash not evident. ———	
		No previous history of pruritus. Is allergic to elastoplast	
		but has not been in contact. Dr. J. Wong notified. ———	
		——— Tom Ritchie RN	
	1430	Applied calamine lotion to back and arms. Incontinent	
		of urine. Is restless. ——— Tom Ritchie RN	

Figure 24.1 An example of interdisciplinary notes

chart alerts caregivers to the client's needs and makes it easier to track the status of each problem. Its disadvantages are that (1) caregivers differ in their ability to use the required charting format, (2) it takes constant vigilance to maintain an up-to-date problem list, and (3) it is somewhat inefficient because assessments and interventions that apply to more than one problem must be repeated.

The POR has four basic components:

1. Database
2. Problem list
3. Plan of care
4. Progress notes

In addition, flowsheets and discharge notes are added to the record as needed.

Database

The database consists of all information known about the client when the client first enters the health-care agency. It includes the nursing assessment, the physician's history, social and family data, and the results of the physical examination and baseline diagnostic tests. Data are constantly updated as the client's health status changes.

Problem List

The problem list (Figure 24.2) is derived from the database. It is usually kept at the front of the chart and serves as an index to the numbered entries in the progress notes. Problems are listed in the order in which they are identified, and the list is continually updated as new problems are identified and others resolved. All caregivers may contribute to the problem list, which includes the client's

No.	Date Entered	Date Inactive	Client Problem
#1	3/9/03		CVA resulting in Rt hemiplegia and left-sided weakness
#1A	3/9/03		Self-care deficit (hygiene, toileting, grooming, feeding)
#1B	3/9/03		Impaired physical mobility (unable to turn and position self) Redefined 2/7/03
#1C	3/9/03		Total urinary incontinence Redefined 2/15/03
#1D	3/9/03		Progressive dysphasia
#2	3/9/03		Constipation r/t immobility Redefined 6/10/03
#3	3/9/03		History of depression
#4	3/9/03		Essential hypertension
#2	*6/10/03*		*Risk for constipation r/t insufficient fiber intake*
#1C	1/17/03		Nocturnal urinary incontinence
#1B	2/7/03		Impaired physical mobility (needs major assistance to transfer and walk)

Figure 24.2 A client's problem list in the POR system. Note that problems 1B, 1C, and 2 were redefined on the dates indicated and listed subsequently.

physiological, psychological, social, cultural, spiritual, developmental, and environmental needs. Physicians write problems as medical diagnoses, surgical procedures, or symptoms; nurses write problems as nursing diagnoses.

As the client's condition changes or more data are obtained, it may be necessary to "redefine" problems. Figure 24.2 illustrates how this has been done for problems 1B, 1C, and 2.

Plan of Care

The initial list of orders or plan of care is made with reference to the active problems. Care plans are generated by the person who lists the problems. Physicians write physician's orders or medical care plans; nurses write nursing care plans. The written plan in the record is listed under each problem in the progress notes (discussed next) and is not isolated as a separate list of orders.

Progress Notes

Progress notes in the POR are made by all health-care professionals involved in a client's care; they all use the same type of sheet for notes. Progress notes are numbered to correspond to the problems on the problem list and may be lettered for the type of data. For example, **SOAP** is an acronym for subjective data, objective data, assessment, and planning.

S—*Subjective Data* are information obtained from what the client says. They describe the client's perceptions and experience of the problem. When possible, the nurse quotes the client's words; otherwise, they are summarized. Subjective data is included only when it is important and relevant to the problem.

O—*Objective Data* consist of information that is measured or observed by use of the senses (e.g., vital signs, laboratory and x-ray results). Examples of subjective and objective data are provided in Chapter 23.

A—*Assessment* is the interpretation or conclusions drawn about the subjective and objective data. During the initial assessment, the problem list is created from the database; so, the "A" entry should be a statement of the problem. In all subsequent SOAP notes for that problem, the "A" should describe the client's condition and level of progress rather than merely restating the diagnosis or problem.

P—*Planning* is the plan of care designed to resolve the stated problem. The initial plan is written by the person who enters the problem into the record. All subsequent plans, including revisions, are entered into the progress notes.

Over the years, the SOAP format has been modified. The acronyms SOAPIE and SOAPIER refer to formats that add interventions, evaluation, and revision.

I—*Interventions* refer to the specific interventions that have actually been performed by the caregiver.

E—*Evaluation* includes client responses to nursing interventions and medical treatments. This is primarily reassessment data.

R—*Revision* reflects care plan modifications suggested by the evaluation. Changes may be made in desired outcomes, interventions, or target dates.

See Figure 24.3 for an example of progress notes using the SOAP, SOAPIER, and PIE formats.

PIE

The **PIE** charting model originated from the nursing process and is similar to the SOAP charting. PIE is an acronym for problems, interventions, and evaluation of nursing care. This system consists of a client care assessment flowsheet and progress notes. The flowsheet covers a 24-hour period and uses specific assessment criteria in a particular format, such as human needs or functional health patterns. After the assessment, the nurse establishes and records specific problems on the progress notes. The *problem statement* is labelled "P" and referred to by number (e.g., P #5). The *interventions* employed to manage the problem are labelled "I" and numbered according to the problem (e.g., I #5). The *evaluation* of the effectiveness of the interventions is also labelled and numbered according to the problem (e.g., E #5).

The PIE system eliminates the traditional care plan and incorporates an ongoing care plan into the progress notes. Therefore, the nurse does not have to create and update a separate plan. A disadvantage is that the nurse must review all the nursing notes before giving care to determine which problems are current and which interventions were effective.

Focus Charting®

Focus Charting® is intended to make the client and client concerns and strengths the focus of care. Three columns for recording are usually used: date and time, focus, and progress notes (see the example at the end of this section). The *focus* may be a condition, a nursing diagnosis, a behaviour, a sign or symptom, an acute change in the client's condition, or a client strength. The progress notes are organized into data (D), action (A), and response (R), referred to as DAR or DARP, where (P) stands for future actions or future interventions. The *data category* consists of observations of client status and behaviours, including data from flowsheets (e.g., vital signs, pupil reactivity). The nurse records both subjective and objective data in this section.

The *action category* includes immediate and future nursing actions. It may also include any changes to the plan of care. The *response category* describes the client's response to any nursing and medical care. (See the example on the next page.)

The Focus Charting® system provides a holistic perspective of the client and the client's needs. It also provides a framework for the progress notes (DAR). The three components do not need to be recorded in order, and each note does not need to have all three categories.

SOAP Format

6/6/03 #5 Generalized pruritus

1400 S—"My skin is itchy on my back and arms, and it's been like this for a week."

O—Skin appears clear—no rash or irritations noted. Marks where client has scratched noted on left and right forearms. Allergic to elastoplast but has not been in contact.

No previous history of pruritus.

A—Skin integrity impaired: cause unknown.

P—Instructed to not scratch skin.

—Applied calamine lotion to back and arms at 1430 h.

—Cut fingernails.

—Assess further to determine whether recurrence associated with specific drugs or foods.

—Refer to physician and pharmacist for assessment.

Tom Ritchie, RN

SOAPIER Format

6/6/03 #5 Generalized pruritus

1400 S—"My skin is itchy on my back and arms, and it's been like this for a week."

O—Skin appears clear—no rash or irritation noted. Marks where client has scratched noted on left and right forearms. Allergic to elastoplast but has not been in contact.

No previous history of pruritus.

A—Skin integrity impaired.

P—Instruct to not scratch skin.

—Apply calamine lotion as necessary.

—Cut nails to avoid scratches.

—Assess further to determine whether recurrence associated with specific drugs or foods.

—Refer to physician and pharmacist for assessment.

I —Instructed not to scratch skin. Applied calamine lotion to back and arms at 1430 h. Assisted to cut fingernails. Notified physician and pharmacist of problem.

1600 E—States, "I'm still itchy. That lotion didn't help."

R—Remove calamine lotion and apply hydrocortisone ungt. as ordered.

Tom Ritchie, RN

PIE Format

6/6/03 #5 Generalized pruritus r/t unknown cause

1400 P—States, "My skin is itchy on my back and arms, and it's been like this for a week." Skin appears clear. No rash or irritations noted. Marks where client has scratched noted on left and right forearms. Allergic to elastoplast but has not been in contact. No previous history of pruritus.

I —Instructed not to scratch skin. Applied calamine lotion to back and arms at 1430 h. Assisted to cut fingernails. Notified physician and pharmacist of problem.

E—States, "I'm still itchy. That lotion didn't help."

Tom Ritchie, RN

Figure 24.3 Examples of nursing progress notes using SOAP, SOAPIER, and PIE formats

Flowsheets are frequently used in the client's chart to augment recording data.

Date/Hour	*Focus*	*Progress Notes*
2/11/03 0900	Neuro status	***D:*** Unresponsive to verbal stimuli; responsive to painful stimuli. Pupils pinpoint and equal. Dr. Ward visited. ***A:*** Neuro assessment and vital signs q15 min. ***R:*** See flowsheets. ***P:*** Continue with vital signs q15 min.

Charting by Exception

Charting by exception (CBE) is a documentation system in which only significant findings or exceptions to norms are recorded. CBE incorporates three key components (Murphy & Burke, 1990):

1. *Unique flowsheets that highlight significant findings and define assessment parameters and findings.* The flowsheets include a sheet for the nursing and physician orders to perform assessments or interventions, the graphic record (see Figure 24.6, p. 454), the client teaching record, and the client discharge note.
2. *Documentation by reference to the agency's printed standards of nursing practice* eliminates much of the repetitive charting of routine care. An agency using CBE must develop its own specific standards of nursing practice that identify the minimum criteria for client care, regardless of clinical area. Some units may also have unit-specific standards unique to their type of client. For example, "The nurse must ensure that the unconscious client has oral care at least q2h." Documentation of care according to these specified standards involves only a check mark in the routine standards box on the graphic record. If all the standards are not

implemented, an asterisk on the flowsheet is made with reference to the nurses' notes. All exceptions to the standards are fully described in narrative form on the nurses' notes.

3. *Bedside accessibility of documentation forms.* In the CBE system, all flowsheets are kept at the client's bedside to allow immediate recording and to eliminate the need to transcribe data from the nurse's worksheet to the permanent record.

FACT

The FACT system of documentation is named for its elements. It has many similarities to CBE and is designed to eliminate redundant and irrelevant data and inconsistencies in recording. The four main elements are:

F Flowsheets that are individualized

A Assessment sheet that is standardized with baseline parameters

C Concise integrated progress notes and flowsheets that are used to document the client's condition and response

T Timely entries that are recorded after care is given

RESEARCH NOTE

Can "Charting by Exception" Save Nurses' Time?

One medical centre kept track of all the time nurses spend writing in the client's chart, writing notes to transfer to the chart at a later time, documenting administration of analgesics, and giving the shift report. Nurses spent an average of 27 percent, or 2.5 hours per shift, on documentation. Among other findings, the researchers noted that trends in client status, such as postoperative urinary retention, were not obvious in the charting. After charting by exception was integrated with a critical pathway, a pilot project was conducted with 50 clients on an orthopedic/neurological unit. Charting time dropped to 0.82 hour per shift—a 67 percent reduction in documentation time. In addition, trends in client status were obvious, overtime decreased 37 percent on the pilot unit, and shift report time was shorter.

Implications: Many nurses worry about the quality of client care they can achieve on short-staffed units. Because it is efficient, charting by exception may help reduce stress by allowing nurses to use more of their time for client care. Used properly, this method can clearly record the nurse's advocacy role for the client as well.

Source: Short, M. S. (1997). Charting by exception on a clinical pathway. *Nursing Management, 28*(8), 45–46.

To use FACT documentation, the nurse must start with a complete database on each client. Only significant information and exceptions to the normal are recorded. The assessment is recorded on an assessment action flowsheet. An assessment flowsheet is used for frequent assessments, such as blood pressure or neurological assessments. Progress notes are written in narrative style to document a client's clinical progress and any significant changes in health status.

This system of documentation is computer ready, and it eliminates duplication and supports consistent language.

CORE

The CORE documentation system focuses on the nursing process. It consists of a database, plans of care, flowsheets, progress notes, and discharge summary. CORE documentation calls for assessing the client's functional and cognitive status within eight hours of admission (Springhouse, 1995).

The progress notes use a DAE format:

D Data

A Action

E Evaluation

This system has been found to be most useful in acute-care and long-term care facilities.

Outcome Documentation

This system of documentation focuses on a client's behaviour. It presents the client's condition in relation to predetermined outcomes; for example, "The client's blood pressure will be 120/80 while sitting by the time of discharge."

The standards that are used to evaluate outcomes are specific client behaviours, a specific standard, the conditions under which the behaviours occur, and a target date or time by which the behaviours occur.

Computerized Documentation

Computerized clinical record systems are being developed as a way to manage the huge volume of information required in contemporary health care. Nurses use computers to store the client's database, add new data, create and revise care plans, and document client progress. See Figure 24.4. Some institutions have a computer terminal at each client's bedside, or nurses carry a small handheld terminal, enabling the nurse to document care immediately after it is given.

Multiple flowsheets are not needed in computerized record systems because information can be easily retrieved in a variety of formats. For example, the nurse can obtain results of a client's blood test, a schedule of all clients on the unit who are to have surgery during the day, a suggested list of interventions for a nursing diagnosis, a graphic chart of a client's vital signs, or a printout of all the progress

Figure 24.4 A bedside computer

Selected Pros and Cons of Computer Documentation

Pros

- Nurses can use their time efficiently.
- The system links various sources of client information.
- Client information, requests, and results are sent and received quickly.
- Bedside terminals can synthesize information from monitoring equipment.
- Computer records can facilitate a focus on client outcomes.
- Information is legible.
- The system incorporates and reinforces standards of care.
- Standard terminology improves communication.
- Bedside terminals eliminate need to take notes on a worksheet before recording.
- Bedside terminals permit the nurse to check an order immediately before administering a treatment or medication.
- Links to monitors improve accuracy of documentation.

Cons

- Client's privacy may be infringed upon if security measures are not used.
- Breakdowns make information temporarily unavailable.
- System is expensive.
- Extended training periods may be required when a new or updated system is installed.

notes for a client. Many systems can generate a work list for the shift with a list of all the treatments, procedures, and medications needed by the client.

Computers make care planning and documentation relatively easy. To record nursing actions and client responses, the nurse either chooses from standardized lists of terms or types narrative information into the computer. Automated speech-recognition technology now allows nurses to enter data by voice for conversion to written documentation.

The computerization of clinical records has made it possible to transmit information from one care setting to another. Selected pros and cons of computer documentation are shown in the box on the left. See Chapter 25 for additional information.

Case Management

The case management model emphasizes quality, cost-effective care delivered within an established length of stay (LOS). This model uses a multidisciplinary approach to planning and documenting client care using *critical pathways.* These forms identify the outcomes that certain groups of clients are expected to achieve on each day of care, along with the interventions necessary for each day. See Figure 24.5 for more information about critical pathways.

Along with critical pathways, the case management model incorporates graphics and flowsheets. Progress notes typically use some type of charting by exception. For example, if goals are met, no further charting is required. Goals that are not met are called **variances.** They are deviations to what is planned on the critical pathway—unexpected occurrences that affect the planned care or the client's responses to care. When a variance occurs, the nurse writes a note documenting the unexpected event, the cause, and actions taken to correct the situation or justify the actions taken. See Table 24.2 for an example of how a variance might be documented.

The case management model promotes collaboration and teamwork among caregivers, helps decrease length of stay, and makes efficient use of time. Because care is goal focused, the quality may improve. However, critical pathways work best for clients with one or two diagnoses and few individualized needs. Data from clients with multiple diagnoses (e.g., a client with a hip fracture, pneumonia, diabetes, and pressure sore) or those with an unpredictable course of symptoms (e.g., a neurological client with seizures) are difficult to document on a critical path.

Documenting Nursing Activities

The client record should describe the client's ongoing status and reflect the full range of the nursing process. Regardless of the records system used in an agency, nurses document evidence of the nursing process on a variety of forms throughout the clinical record (Table 24.3).

	OUTCOME INTERVENTION	T	I	T	EXCEPTIONS/*	OUTCOME STATUS:
Pain Mgmt.	**Patient will verbalize/indicate comfort or tolerance of pain.** *Location & pain rating (0-10 pain scale) q 4 hrs. **PCA/CEA/IM analgesics.** Comfort measures Back rub	 1700	 LJ	1600 1800	C/O pain of "10" in R knee cea at 6 mL/hr. ↑ to 8mL/hr c̄ no relief. Dr. Green notified. Percocet tablet given p.o. Still c/o pain at "8" on scale.	1800 LJ M/(N) 0600____M/N
Endocrine	**Patient will have no s/s of hypo/ hyperglycemia.**					1800 LJ (M)/N 0600____M/N

Signature	Initials	Signature	Initials	Signature	Initials
Laura Jiminez RN	LJ				

Date @ 0700: 2/1/03 To Date @ 0700: 2/2/03

Figure 24.5 Excerpt from a critical pathway documentation form. Note: (T) = time; (I) = initials; (M/N) = met/not met

Source: Courtesy of Shawnee Mission Medical Center, Merriam, KS.

TABLE 24.2 Example of Variance Documentation (Critical Pathway)

An elderly client has had a below-the-knee amputation. On the third postoperative day, he has a temperature of 38.8°C. Lung sounds are clear, and he is not coughing. The nurse notices redness and skin breakdown over the client's sacrum. The critical pathway outcomes specified for day 3 are "Oral temperature 37.7°C" and "Skin intact over bony prominences." The nurse should chart the following variances:

Date/Time	Variation	Cause	Action Taken/Plans
4/16/03 0900	Elevated temperature	Possible sepsis	4/16-Blood cultures 33 per order. Monitor temp. q1h. Monitor I&O, hydration, and mental status.
4/16/03 1130	Impaired skin integrity: pressure sore on sacrum	Client does not move about in bed unless reminded	4/16-Positioned on L side. Turn side-to-side q2h while awake. On every client contact, remind client to move about in bed. Apply Duoderm daily after bath.

Table 24.3 Documentation for the Nursing Process

Step*	Documentation Forms
Assessment	Initial assessment form, various flowsheets
Nursing diagnosis	Nursing care plan, Kardex®, critical path, interdisciplinary notes, problem list
Planning	Nursing care plan, critical path
Intervention	Interdisciplinary notes, flowsheets
Evaluation	Interdisciplinary notes

*All steps are recorded on discharge/referral summaries.

Nursing Care Plans

There are two types of nursing care plans: traditional and standardized. The *traditional care plan* is written for each client. The form varies from agency to agency according to the needs of the client and the department. Most forms have three columns: one for nursing diagnoses, a second for expected outcomes, and a third for nursing interventions. See Chapter 23 for additional information.

Standardized care plans have been developed to save documentation time. These plans may be based on an institution's standards of practice, thereby helping provide a high quality of nursing care. Standardized plans must be individualized by the nurse in order to adequately address individual client needs.

Kardexes®

The **Kardex®** is a widely used, concise method of organizing and recording data about a client, making information quickly accessible to all health-care professionals. The system consists of a series of cards kept in a portable index file or on computer-generated forms. The card for a particular client can be quickly turned up to reveal specific data. The Kardex® may or may not become a part of the client's permanent record. In some organizations, it is a temporary worksheet written in pencil for ease in recording frequent changes in details of a client's care. The information on Kardexes® may be organized into sections, for example:

- Pertinent information about the client, such as name, room number, age, religion, marital status, admission date, physician's name, diagnosis, type of surgery and date, occupation, and next of kin
- List of medications, with the date of order and the times of administration for each
- List of intravenous fluids, with dates of infusions
- List of daily treatments and procedures, such as irrigations, dressing changes, postural drainage, or measurement of vital signs
- List of diagnostic procedures ordered, such as roentgenography or laboratory tests
- Allergies
- Specific data on how the client's physical needs are to be met, such as type of diet, assistance needed with feeding, elimination devices, activity, hygienic needs, and safety precautions (e.g., use of side rails)
- A problem list, stated goals, and a list of nursing approaches to meet the goals and relieve the problems

Although much of the information on the Kardex® may be recorded by the nurse in charge or a delegate (e.g., the ward clerk), any nurse who cares for the client plays a key role in initiating the record and keeping the data current.

Flowsheets

Flowsheets, also called abbreviated progress notes, enable nurses to record nursing data quickly and concisely and provide an easy-to-read record of the client's condition over time.

The time parameters for flowsheets can vary from minutes to months. In a hospital intensive care unit, a client's blood pressure may be monitored by the minute, whereas in an ambulatory clinic, a client's blood glucose level may be recorded once a month.

Flowsheets commonly used are the graphic (clinical) record, the fluid intake and output record, the medication record, and daily nursing care records.

Graphic (Clinical) Record

This record (see Figure 24.6) indicates body temperature, pulse, respiratory rate, blood pressure, weight, oxygen saturation level, and, in some agencies, other significant clinical data, such as admission or postoperative day, bowel movements, appetite, and activity.

24-Hour Fluid Balance Record

All routes of fluid intake and all routes of fluid loss or output are measured and recorded on this form. Information about ways to measure and record specific amounts of fluid intake and output are described in Chapter 40.

Medication Record

Medication flowsheets usually include designated areas for the date of the medication order, the expiration date, the medication name and dose, the frequency of administration and route, and the nurse's signature. Some records also include a place to document the client's allergies. A sample medication record is shown in Chapter 28.

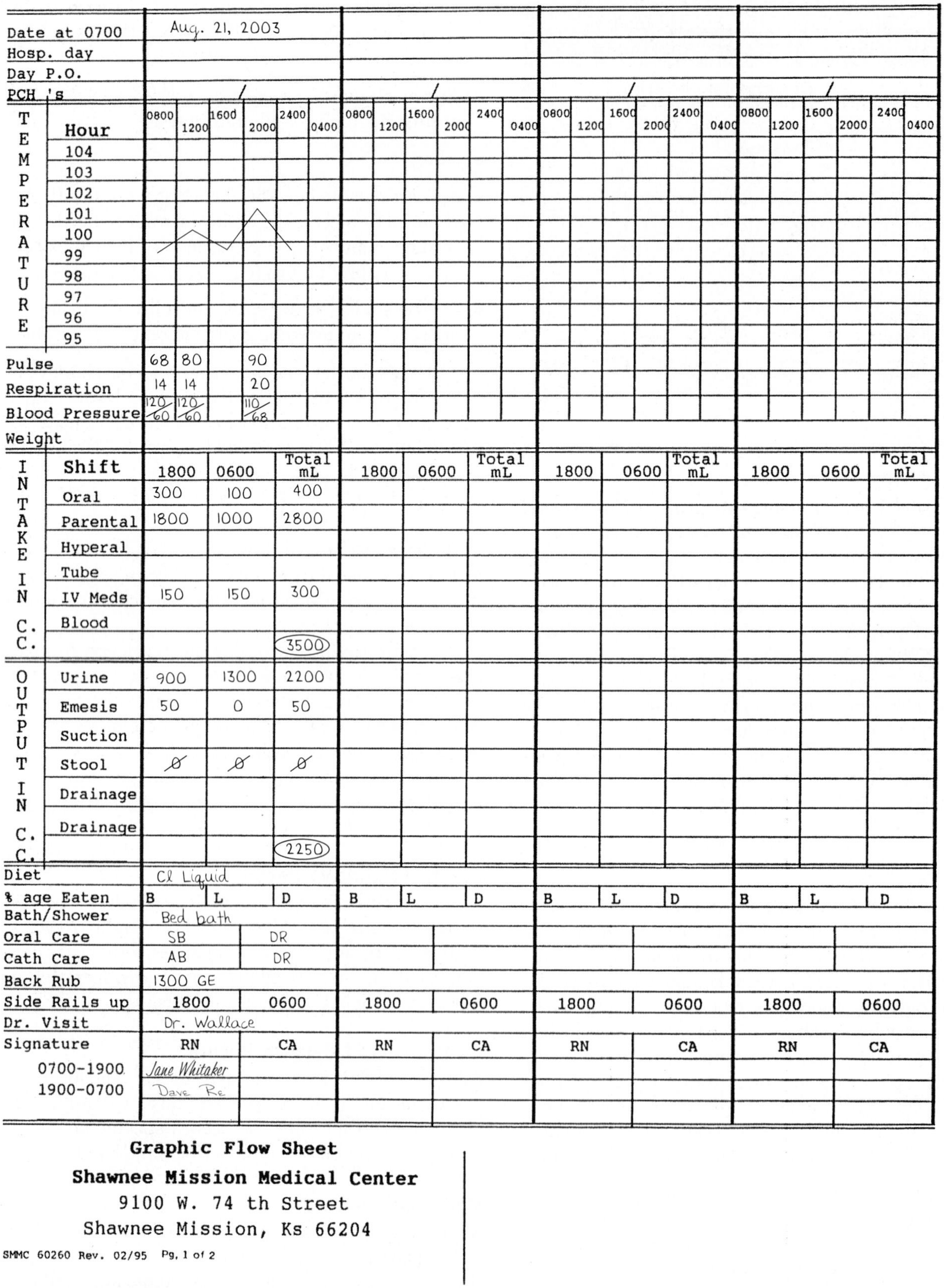

	Day 1	Day 2	Day 3	Day 4
Date at 0700	Aug. 21, 2003			
Hosp. day				
Day P.O.				
PCH 's	/	/	/	/

TEMPERATURE Hour	0800	1200	1600	2000	2400	0400	0800	1200	1600	2000	2400	0400	0800	1200	1600	2000	2400	0400	0800	1200	1600	2000	2400	0400
104																								
103																								
102																								
101																								
100																								
99																								
98																								
97																								
96																								
95																								
Pulse	68	80		90																				
Respiration	14	14		20																				
Blood Pressure	120/60	120/60		110/68																				
Weight																								

INTAKE IN C.C. Shift	1800	0600	Total mL	1800	0600	Total mL	1800	0600	Total mL	1800	0600	Total mL
Oral	300	100	400									
Parental	1800	1000	2800									
Hyperal												
Tube												
IV Meds	150	150	300									
Blood												
			(3500)									
OUTPUT IN C.C.												
Urine	900	1300	2200									
Emesis	50	0	50									
Suction												
Stool	Ø	Ø	Ø									
Drainage												
Drainage												
			(2250)									

	Day 1			Day 2			Day 3			Day 4		
Diet	Cl Liquid											
% age Eaten	B	L	D	B	L	D	B	L	D	B	L	D
Bath/Shower	Bed bath											
Oral Care	SB	DR										
Cath Care	AB	DR										
Back Rub	1300 GE											
Side Rails up	1800	0600		1800	0600		1800	0600		1800	0600	
Dr. Visit	Dr. Wallace											
Signature	RN	CA		RN	CA		RN	CA		RN	CA	
0700-1900	Jane Whitaker											
1900-0700	Dave Re											

Graphic Flow Sheet
Shawnee Mission Medical Center
9100 W. 74 th Street
Shawnee Mission, Ks 66204

SMMC 60260 Rev. 02/95 Pg. 1 of 2

Figure 24.6 A clinical graph record

Source: Courtesy of Shawnee Mission Medical Center, Merriam, KS.

Daily Nursing Care Record

The daily nursing care is often recorded on a flowsheet (Figure 24.7). These records may include categories related to diet, hygiene, activity, elimination, treatments, protective precautions, diagnostic studies, and so on.

Progress Notes

Progress notes made by nurses provide information about the progress a client is making toward achieving desired outcomes. Therefore, in addition to assessment and reassessment data, progress notes include information about client problems and nursing interventions. The format used depends on the documentation system in place in the institution. Various kinds of nursing progress notes are discussed in "Documentation Systems," earlier in this chapter. These include narrative nursing notes, SOAP and PIE notes, charting by exception, and Focus Charting®.

Nursing Discharge/Referral Summaries

A discharge note and referral summary are completed when the client is being discharged and transferred to another institution or to a home setting where a visit by a community health nurse is required. See the discussion of discharge planning in Chapter 23, and the assessment parameters suggested when preparing clients to go home. Many institutions provide forms for these summaries. Some records combine the discharge plan, including instructions for care, follow-up appointments, and the final progress note. Many are designed with checklists to facilitate data recording.

If the client is being transferred to another institution or to a home setting where a visit by a home health nurse is required, the discharge note takes the form of a referral summary. Regardless of format, discharge and referral summaries usually include some or all of the following:

- Description of client's physical, mental, and emotional status at discharge or transfer
- Resolved health problems
- Unresolved continuing health problems and continuing care needs; may include a review-of-systems checklist that considers integumentary, respiratory, cardiovascular, neurological, musculoskeletal, gastrointestinal, elimination, and reproductive problems
- Treatments that are to be continued (e.g., wound care, oxygen therapy)
- Current medications
- Restrictions that relate to (1) activity, such as lifting, stair climbing, walking, driving, work, (2) diet, and (3) bathing, such as sponge bath, tub, or shower
- Functional/self-care abilities in terms of vision, hearing, speech, mobility with or without aids, meal preparation and eating, preparing and administering medications, and so on
- Comfort level
- Support networks including family, significant others, religious adviser, community self-help groups, home care and other community agencies available, and so on
- Client education provided in relation to disease process, activities and exercise, special diet, medications, specialized care or treatments, follow-up appointments, and so on
- Discharge destination (e.g., home, nursing home) and mode of discharge (e.g., walking, wheelchair, ambulance)
- Referral services (e.g., social worker, home health nurse)

Long-Term Care Documentation

Nurses need to familiarize themselves with regulations influencing the kind and frequency of documentation required in long-term care facilities. Usually, the nurse completes a nursing care summary at least once a week for clients requiring skilled care and every two weeks to a month for those requiring intermediate care. Summaries should address the following (see Figure 24.7):

- Specific problems noted in the care plan
- Mental status
- Activities of daily living (ADLs)
- Hydration and nutrition status
- Safety measures needed (e.g., bed rails)
- Medications
- Treatments
- Preventive measures

Guidelines for documentation in long-term care facilities are shown in the box below.

Long-Term Care Documentation Guidelines

- Complete the assessment and screening forms and plan of care within the time period specified by agency policy.
- Document and report any change in the client's condition to the physician and the client's family within 24 hours.
- Document all measures implemented in response to a change in the client's condition.
- Keep a record of any visits and of phone calls from family, friends, and others regarding the client.
- Write nursing summaries and progress notes that comply with the frequency and standards required by agency policy.
- Make sure that progress notes address the client's progress in relation to the goals or outcomes defined in the plan of care.
- Review and revise the plan of care according to agency policies or whenever the client's health status changes.

RESIDENT CARE PLAN PART I **CENTRAL PARK LODGES**

SAFETY & RISK FACTORS

Allergies
Drugs ☐ Yes ☐ No (See Health Record)
Foods/Environment ☐ Yes ☐ No ______

	Yes	No
Able to use Call Bell	☐	☐
Risk for Falls	☐	☐
Elopement Risk	☐	☐
Choking Risk	☐	☐
Suicide Risk	☐	☐
Seizures	☐	☐

Oxygen Therapy Flow Rate ______

	Yes	No	Date
Social Alcohol	☐	☐	______
Passes Accompanied	☐	☐	______
Unaccompanied	☐	☐	______

DATS# ______
Smoking ☐ Yes ☐ No ☐ Supervision ☐ Apron
Cigarettes/Matches Kept with ☐ Resident ☐ Staff

MOBILITY

☐ Independent ______
☐ Supervision ______
☐ Assistance ______
☐ Dependent ______

Aides: ☐ Cane
☐ Walker
☐ Wheelchair - Serial # ______
☐ Gerichair
☐ Other ______

DEVICES

	Yes	No	Specify
Wanderguard	☐	☐	______
Side Rails	☐	☐	______
Reverse Seat Belt	☐	☐	______
Lap Tray	☐	☐	______
Bed/Chair Check	☐	☐	______
Other Alarm Type			______

SPIRITUAL SUPPORT

Religious Affiliation ______
Congregation/Parish ______ Phone ______
Attends Services ☐ Onsite ☐ Offsite
Date Sacrament of the Sick Received ______
Funeral Arrangements ______

COMMUNICATION/ORIENTATION

Language(s) Spoken/Understood ______
Communication Aides ______

ORIENTATION:	**YES**	**OCC'L**	**NO**
Family	☐	☐	☐
Staff	☐	☐	☐
Self	☐	☐	☐
Room/Unit	☐	☐	☐
Facility	☐	☐	☐
Time Day/Month/Year	☐	☐	☐

MMSE Score Date ______

THERAPEUTIC INTERVENTIONS

Social Interaction Skills

	Active	Passive
1:1	☐	☐
Small Group	☐	☐
Large Group	☐	☐

SOCIAL SERVICES INTERVENTION

Guardian ☐
Trustee ☐
EPOA ☐
Personal Directive ☐
Comments ______

COMPANION INVOLVEMENT

Companion ☐ Yes ☐ No
Comments ______

BIRTHDAY: YR ____ MO ____ DAY ____ SEX ____
ROOM ______ NAME ______ ______ PHYSICIAN: ______

Figure 24.7 A daily care record

Source: Used with permission. Bow-Crest Care Centre, Calgary, Alberta.

RESIDENT CARE PLAN PART II **CENTRAL PARK LODGES**

EATING

☐ Independent
☐ Swallowing Difficulty

Equipment Required ____________

Assistance Required
☐ Set Up Tray/Open Cartons
☐ Intermittent Encouragement
☐ Constant Encouragement
☐ Complete Feed

Location/Setting of Meal ____________

TOILETING

☐ Independent
☐ Remind/Bring Equipment
☐ Intermittent Supervision/Assistance
☐ 1 Person Constant Supervision
☐ 1 Person Transfer on/off Toilet
☐ 2 Person Transfer on/off Toilet
☐ Toilet on Supp. Days only
☐ Not Toileted
☐ Pericare/Personal Hygiene

Equipment Required
☐ Bedpan ☐ Commode
☐ Urinal ☐ Toilet

DRESSING

☐ Independent

Assistance Required
☐ Assemble Clothes or Equipment
☐ Intermittent Supervision/Assistance
☐ Constant Supervision to Dress Self
☐ Total Assist
☐ Bedridden (gowns or pajamas)

Assist With
☐ Undergarments ☐ Socks/Stockings
☐ Shirt/Blouse ☐ Pants
☐ Buttons/Zippers ☐ Shoes
☐ Pajamas
☐ Pressure Stockings

TRANSFERING

	D	E	N
Independent	☐	☐	☐
Position Equipment (Walker, W/C, etc.)	☐	☐	☐
1 Person verbal cueing, guidance, stand by assistance	☐	☐	☐
1 Person Supervision	☐	☐	☐
1 Person Physical Ass.	☐	☐	☐
2 Person Physical Ass.	☐	☐	☐
2 Person Lift	☐	☐	☐

Mechanical Lift -Type ____________

NUTRITIONAL NEEDS

Diet Type ____________

Diet Consistency ____________

Tube Feeding
Formula ____________
Volume/24hr. ____________
Rate of Flow ____________
Vol. H_2O/24hr. ____________
Adm. Time ____________
Tube Type ____________
Date Changed ____________

ELIMINATION

Bladder
☐ Continent
☐ Incontinent
☐ Dribbles
☐ Stress Incontinence
☐ Catheter/Condom

Type ____________
Size ____________
Date Change ____________

Bowel
☐ Continent
☐ Incontinent
☐ Oozes
☐ Smears
☐ Incontinent Following Suppository

Management Procedure
Toilet Times ____________

Incontinent Product Used:
Days ____________
Evenings ____________
Nights ____________
Requires Assistance ☐ Yes ☐ No

Ostomy Product Type ____________
Self Care ☐ Total Care ☐

SLEEP/REST PERIODS

Rest Time: ____________
Bed Time: ____________

DAILY HYGIENE

☐ Independent ☐ Supervise
☐ Remind/Set Up ☐ Total Assist
☐ Bed Bath ☐ At Sink

Assistance Required
☐ Upper Extremities
☐ Lower Extremities
☐ Perineum
☐ Dentures
☐ Own Teeth
☐ Mouth Care

BATH

☐ Tub ☐ Shower ☐ Sponge
☐ Self ☐ Assist ☐ Dependent

Bath Day: ____________ ☐ AM ☐ PM
Hairdresser Day: ____________

Laundry ☐ Facility ☐ Family

SENSORY DEFICITS/AIDES

Vision
Functional ☐
Impaired ☐
Glasses ☐
Labelled ☐

Hearing
Functional ☐
Impaired ☐
Aides
R Serial # ____________
L Serial # ____________

Dentures
Upper ☐
Lower ☐
Partial ☐
Labelled ☐

Prosthesis
____

SKIN INTEGRITY

Braden Scale Score ____________ Date ____________
☐ Risk for Skin Breakdown
☐ Wounds
Location ____________

Reposition q ____________

☐ Professional Footcare

RESIDENT CARE PLAN PART III — **CENTRAL PARK LODGES**

BEHAVIOURS OF DAILY LIVING			POTENTIAL FOR INJURY
☐ Wandering ☐ Hoarding/Rummaging ☐ Aggressive/Angry Behaviour ☐ Agitated/Anxious ☐ Suspicious Behaviour ☐ Sad or Depressed	☐ Demands Attention ☐ Suicidal Behaviour ☐ Resists Treatment or Refuses Care	☐ Ingestion of Foreign Substance ☐ Inappropriate Sexual Behaviour ☐ Inappropriate Smoking ☐ Other ____________ ____________	☐ Falls ☐ Choking ☐ Impaired Judgement ☐ Restraints ☐ Risk of Seizures ☐ Elopement ☐ Strikes Out ☐ Unable to use call bell ☐ Other ____________

DATE	PROBLEM	FREQUENCY	ACTION/INTERVENTION	TIME FRAMES

> **Home Care Documentation**
>
> - Complete a comprehensive nursing assessment and develop a plan of care.
> - Write a progress note at each client visit, noting any changes in the client condition; nursing interventions performed (including education and instructional brochures and materials provided to the client and home caregiver); client responses to nursing care; and vital signs as indicated.
> - Keep a copy of the care plan in the client's home and update it as the client's condition changes.
> - Report changes in the plan of care to the physician and document that these were reported.
> - Encourage the client or home caregiver to record data when appropriate.
> - Write a discharge summary, including the client's health status at discharge, outcomes achieved, and recommendations for further care.

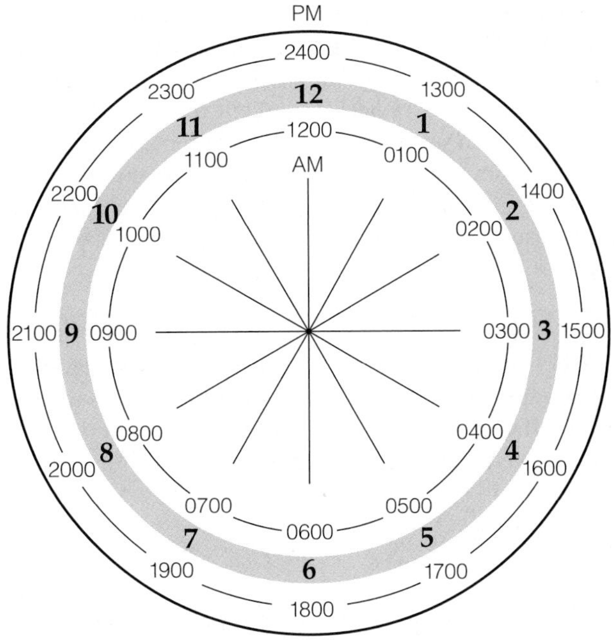

Figure 24.8 The 24-hour clock

Home Care Documentation

Home care is one of the fastest growing areas in health care in Canada due to an increasing older population and shorter hospitalizations. Documentation of home care provided will follow professional, regulatory, and accreditation standards as outlined by the respective agencies and may vary by province or territory (Iyer & Camp, 1999).

Some home care agencies use print-based documentation. Others use lap tops and wireless technology.

Guidelines for Recording

Because the client's record is a legal document and may be used to provide evidence in court, many factors are considered in recording. Health-care personnel must not only maintain the confidentiality of the client's record but also meet legal standards in the process of recording.

Date and Time

Document the date and time of each recording. This is essential not only for legal reasons but also for client safety. Record the time according to the 24-hour clock (military clock), which avoids confusion about whether a time was a.m. or p.m. (Figure 24.8).

Timing

Follow the agency's policy about the frequency of documenting and adjust the frequency as a client's condition indicates; for example, a client whose blood pressure is changing requires more frequent documentation than a client whose blood pressure is constant. As a rule, documenting should be done as soon as possible after an assessment or intervention. No recording should be done *before* providing nursing care.

Legibility

All entries must be legible and easy to read to prevent interpretation errors. Hand printing or easily understood handwriting is usually permissible. Follow the agency's policies about handwritten recording.

Permanence

All entries on the client's record are made in dark ink so that the record is permanent and changes can be identified. Dark ink reproduces well on microfilm and in duplication processes. Follow the agency's policies about the type of pen and ink used for recording.

Accepted Terminology and Abbreviations

Use only commonly accepted *abbreviations*, *symbols*, and *terms* that are specified by the agency. Many abbreviations are standard and used universally; others are used only in certain geographical areas. Some agencies supply a list of the abbreviations they accept. When in doubt about whether to use an abbreviation, write the term out in full until certain about the abbreviation. Abbreviations that are not official can lead to misunderstandings. For example, "D/c" may mean "discharge" or "discontinue"; "od" could mean "once a day" or "right eye." Table 24.4 lists some common abbreviations (except those used for medications, which are described in Chapter 28). Table 24.5 indicates commonly accepted symbols. The metric system (Systeme Internationale d'unites) is used when documenting measurements (e.g., height, weight, volume).

Correct Spelling

Correct spelling is essential for accuracy in recording. If you are unsure how to spell a word, look it up in a dictionary or other resource books. Two decidedly different medications may have almost similar spellings; for example, digitoxin and digoxin.

Signature

Each recording on the nursing notes is signed by the nurse making it. The signature includes the *name* and *title;* for example, "Susan J. Green, RN."

Some agencies permit initials rather than first name (e.g., SJ Green). The following title abbreviations are often used, but nurses need to follow agency policy about how to sign their names.

RN	registered nurse
LPN	licensed practical nurse
NA	nursing assistant
NS	nursing student
RA	resident attendant
SN	student nurse

Accuracy

The client's name and identifying information should be stamped or written on each page of the clinical record. Before making any entry, check that it is the correct chart. Do not identify charts by room number only; check the client's name. Special care is needed when caring for clients with the same last name.

Notations on records must be accurate and correct. Accurate notations consist of facts or observations rather than opinions or interpretations. It is more accurate, for example, to write that the client "refused medication" (fact) than to write that the client "was uncooperative" (opinion); or to write that a client "was crying" (observation) is preferable to noting that the client "was depressed" (interpretation). Similarly, when a client expresses worry about the diagnosis or problem, this should be quoted directly on the record: "Stated: 'I'm worried about my leg.'" When describing something, avoid general words, such as *large, good,* or *normal,* which can be interpreted differently. For example, chart specific data such as "2 cm × 3 cm bruise," rather than "large bruise."

When a *recording error* is made, draw a line through it and write the word *error* above it with your initials or name (depending on agency policy). Do not erase, blot out, or use correction fluid. The original entry must remain visible.

Sample Recording

Date: Dec 10/03 Time: 0100

error AJR
Pulse ~~180 beats/min~~ 108 beats/min ____
________________ Abby J. Roberts NS

Write on every line but never between lines. If a *blank* appears in a notation, draw a line through the blank space so that no additional information can be recorded at any other time or by any other person, and sign the notation.

Sample Recording

Date: Nov 7/03 Time: 0730

Urine cloudy, light brown with dark flecks.
No odour. ________________ Lin I. Ma NS
C/o burning pain in pubic region prior to
voiding. ________________ Lin I. Ma NS

Sequence

Document events in the order in which they occur; for example, record assessments, then the nursing interventions, and then the client's responses. Update or delete problems as needed. Events documented out of sequence must be clearly identified as a late entry, according to agency policy.

Appropriateness

Record only information that is significant to the client's health problems and care. Any other personal information that the client conveys is inappropriate for the record. Recording irrelevant information may be considered an invasion of the client's privacy and/or libellous. A client's disclosure that she was addicted to heroin 20 years ago, for example, *would not* be recorded on the client's medical record unless it had a direct bearing on the client's health.

Completeness

The information that is recorded needs to be complete and helpful to the client and health-care professionals.

Nurses' notes need to reflect the nursing process. Record all assessments, dependent and independent nursing interventions, client problems, client comments and responses to interventions and tests, progress toward goals, and communication with other disciplines.

TABLE 24.4 Commonly Used Abbreviations

Abbreviation	Term
abd	abdomen
ABO	the main blood group system
ac	before meals (*ante cibum*)
ADL	activities of daily living
ad lib	as desired (*ad libitum*)
adm	admitted or admission
am	morning (*ante meridiem*)
amb	ambulatory
amt	amount
approx	approximately (about)
bid	twice daily (*bis in die*)
BM (bm)	bowel movement
BP	blood pressure
BR	bed rest
BRP	bathroom privileges
c̄	with
C	Celsius (centigrade)
CBC	complete blood count
CBR	complete bed rest
CDA	Canadian Diabetic Association
Cl	client
cm	centimetre
c/o	complains of
DAT	diet as tolerated
D/C	discontinue
drsg	dressing
Dx	diagnosis
ECG (EKG)	electrocardiogram
fld	fluid
g	gram
GI	gastrointestinal
GP	general practitioner
gtt	drops (*guttae*)
h	hour (*hora*)
H_2O	water
hs	at bedtime (*hora somni*)
I&O	intake and output
j	joule
IV	intravenous
kg	kilogram
kJ	kilojoule
L	litre
Lab	laboratory
liq	liquid
LMP	last menstrual period
lt (L)	left
m	metre
meds	medications
mg	milligram
mL	millilitre
mod	moderate
neg	negative
nil (ō) or ∅	none
no. (#)	number
NPO	nothing by mouth (*per ora*)
NS	normal saline
O_2	oxygen
od	daily (*omni die*)
OD	right eye (*oculus dexter*); overdose
OOB	out of bed
os	mouth or opening
OS	left eye (*oculus sinister*)
pc	after meals (*post cibum*)
PE (PX)	physical examination
per	by or through
pm	afternoon (*post meridiem*)
PO	by mouth (*per os*)
postop	postoperative(ly)
preop	preoperative(ly)
prep	preparation
prn	when necessary (*pro re nata*)
pt	patient
q	every (*quaque*)
qd	every day (*quaque die*)
qh (q1h)	every hour (*quaque hora*)
q2h, q3h, and so on	every 2 hours, 3 hours, and so on
qhs	every night at bedtime (*quaque hora somni*)
qid	four times a day (*quater in die*)
req	requisition
Rt (rt, R)	right
S (s̄)	without (*sine*)
SI	Systeme Internationale d'unites (metric system)
spec	specimen
STAT	at once, immediately (*statim*)
tid	three times a day (*ter in die*)
TL	team leader
TLC	tender loving care
TPR	temperature, pulse, respirations
VO	verbal order
VS	vital signs
WNL	within normal limits
wt	weight

TABLE 24.5 Commonly Used Symbols

Symbol	Term	Symbol	Number
>	greater than	$\bar{o}$	0
<	less than	$\overline{ss}$	1/2
=	equal to	$\bar{i}$	1
↑	increased	$\overline{ii}$	2
↓	decreased	$\overline{iii}$	3
♀	female	$\overline{iv}$	4
♂	male	$\bar{v}$	5
°	degree	$\overline{vi}$	6
#	number; fracture	$\overline{vii}$	7
×	times	$\bar{x}$	10
@	at		

Canadian Society Notes

Fact	Implications for Nursing Practice
In 1970, nurses' notes were declared admissible as evidence by the Supreme Court of Canada.	This attests to the importance of nurses' records of the care provided to and the progress made by clients and means that nurses' notes can serve to support cases for or against nurses, physicians, or hospitals.
There are agency and government regulations that govern how records ought to be made and organized: • The Canadian Council on Hospital Accreditation (CCHA) • Professional nursing organizations • Health-care agencies in which nurses work.	Nurses need to be familiar with general standards of documentation and have access to specific standards of the area or specialty in which they work.

Care that is *omitted* because of the client's condition or refusal of treatment must also be recorded. Document what was omitted, why it was omitted, and who was notified.

Conciseness

Recordings need to be brief, as well as complete, to save time in communication. The client's name and the word *client* are omitted. For example, write "Perspiring profusely. Respirations shallow, wet, 28/min." End each thought or sentence with a period.

Legal Prudence

Accurate, complete documentation should give legal protection to the nurse, the client's other caregivers, the health-care facility, and the client. Admissible in court as a legal document, the clinical record provides proof of the quality of care given to a client.

The nurse's charting should present an accurate, complete representation of quality care. Documentation may be critical in determining whether a standard of care was met. In most instances, failure to completely document the course of a patient's treatment regime may mean that the court will assume the act was not done (Keatings & Smith, 2000). Incompleteness seriously undermines the "strength" of the evidence, that is, how probative it is (how much the testimony proves, or how convincing it is that the act was actually done). If the record is incomplete, it may not be accorded much weight.

For the best legal protection, the nurse should not only adhere to professional standards of nursing care but also follow agency policy and procedures for intervention and documentation in all situations—especially high-risk situations. For example:

> 1100 hours-Complained of feeling dizzy. Raised side rails and instructed to stay in bed and ring call bell if requiring assistance. 1130 hours—found beside bed on floor. Said, "I climbed over these rails all by myself." When asked about pain, replied, "I feel fine but a little dizzy." Helped into bed. BP 100/60 P90 R24 Dr. RJ Naden notified. ________________ RS Woo RN

Reporting

Reports can be either oral or written. The purpose of reporting is to communicate specific information to a person or group of people. A report should be concise, including only pertinent information and no extraneous detail.

Change-of-Shift Reports

A **change-of-shift report** is a report usually given to nurses starting the next shift. Its purpose is to provide continuity of care for clients by providing the new caregivers a quick summary of client needs and details of care to be given.

Change-of-shift reports may be written or given orally, either in a face-to-face exchange or by audiotape

Key Elements of a Change-of-Shift Report

- Follow a particular order (e.g., follow room numbers in a hospital).
- Provide basic identifying information for each client (e.g., name, room number, bed designation).
- For new clients, provide the reason for admission or medical diagnosis (or diagnoses), surgery (date), diagnostic tests, and therapies in past 24 hours.
- Include significant changes in client's condition and present information in order (i.e., assessment, nursing diagnoses, interventions, outcomes, and evaluation). For example, "Mr. Ronald Oakes said he had an aching pain in his left calf at 1400 hours. Inspection revealed no other signs. Calf pain is related to altered blood circulation. Rest and elevation of his legs on a footstool for 30 minutes provided relief."
- Provide exact information, such as "Ms. Jessie Jones received Demerol 100 mg intramuscularly at 2000 hours," *not* "Ms. Jessie Jones received some Demerol during the evening."
- Report client's need for special emotional support. For example, a client who has just learned that his biopsy results revealed malignancy and who is now scheduled for a laryngectomy needs time to discuss his feelings before preoperative teaching is begun.
- Include current nurse-prescribed and physician-prescribed orders.
- Provide a summary of newly admitted clients, including diagnosis, age, general condition, plan of therapy, and significant information about the client's support people.
- Report clients that have been transferred or discharged from the unit.
- Clearly state priorities of care and care that is due after the shift begins. For example, in a 7 a.m. report, the nurse might say, "Mr. Li's vital signs are due at 0730, and his IV bag will need to be replaced by 0800." Give this information at the end of that client's report, as memory is best for the first and last information given.
- Be concise. Don't elaborate on background data or routine care (e.g., do not report "Vital signs at 0800 and 1200" when that is the unit standard). Do not report coming and going of visitors unless there is a problem or concern or if the visitors are involved in teaching and care. Social support and visits are the norm.

recording. The face-to-face report permits the listener to ask questions during the report; written and tape-recorded reports are often briefer and less time consuming. Reports are sometimes given at the bedside, and clients as well as nurses may participate in the exchange of information. See the box above for key elements of a change-of-shift report.

Telephone Reports

Health-care professionals frequently report about a client by telephone. Nurses inform physicians about a change in a client's condition; a radiologist reports the results of an x-ray study; a nurse may confer with a nurse on another unit about a transferred client.

The nurse receiving a telephone report should document the date and time, the name of the person giving the information, and what information was received and should sign the notation. For example:

> June 6/03 10:35 am GL Messina, laboratory technician, reported by telephone that Mrs. Sara Ames's hematocrit was 39/100 mL. _____ Barbara Ireland RN

If there is any doubt about the information given over the telephone, the person receiving the information should repeat it back to the sender to ensure accuracy.

When giving a telephone report to a physician, it is important that the nurse be concise and accurate. Begin with your name and relationship to the client (e.g., "This is Jana Gomez; I'm calling about your patient, Dorothy Mendes. I'm her registered nurse on the 7 p.m. to 7 a.m. shift.").

Telephone reports usually include the client's name and medical diagnosis, changes in nursing assessment, vital signs related to baseline vital signs, significant laboratory data, and related nursing interventions. The nurse should have the client's chart ready to give the physician any further information.

After reporting, the nurse should document the date, time, and content of the call. For example:

> Dorothy Mendes admitted 1200; burning abdominal pain upper right quadrant (URQ) BP 120/80, P100, R20 on admission. Demerol 100 mg IM on admission. At 1515 pm BP 100/40, P120, R30. Pain unchanged. Colour pale and perspiring. Reported by telephone to Dr. Burns at 1535 pm. ___________ RS Woo RN

Telephone Orders

Physicians often order a therapy (e.g., a medication) for a client by telephone. Most agencies have specific policies about telephone orders.

Guidelines for Telephone Orders

1. Do not accept an order from a prescriber you do not know.
2. Ask the prescriber to speak slowly and clearly.
3. Ask the prescriber to spell out the medication if you are not familiar with it.
4. Question the drug, dosage, or changes if they seem inappropriate for this client.
5. Read the order back to the prescriber at the end. Use words for abbreviations (e.g., three times a day for tid).
6. When writing a dosage, always put a number before a decimal (e.g., 0.3 mL) but never after a decimal (e.g., 6 mg).
7. Write out units (e.g., 20 units of insulin, *not* 20 u of insulin).
8. Follow agency protocol about the prescriber's protocol for signing telephone orders (e.g., within 24 hours).

Source: Adapted from Cirone, N. (1998). Taking orders by phone. *Nursing 98, 28*(8), 56.

While the physician gives the order, write it down and repeat it back to the physician to ensure accuracy. Question the physician about any order that is ambiguous, unusual (e.g., an abnormally high dosage of a medication), or contraindicated by the client's condition. Then, transcribe the order onto the physician's order sheet, indicating it as a verbal order (VO) or telephone order (TO). See the box above for selected guidelines.

Once the order is transcribed on the physician's order sheet, the order must be countersigned by the physician within a time period described by agency policy. Many acute-care hospitals require that this be done within 24 hours.

Conferring

To **confer** is to consult another person or persons for advice, information, ideas, or instructions. Nurses confer with colleagues and other health-care professionals about some aspect of client care or to elicit or validate data needed to plan nursing care. Two ways nurses share information are through the nursing care conference and nursing rounds.

Nursing Care Conference

A nursing care conference is a meeting of a group of nurses to discuss possible solutions to certain problems of a client, such as inability to cope with an event or lack of progress toward goal attainment. The nursing care conference allows each nurse an opportunity to offer an opinion about possible solutions to the problem. Other health-care professionals may be invited to attend the conference to offer their expertise; for example, a social worker may discuss the family problems of a severely burned child, or a dietitian may discuss the dietary problems of a client who has diabetes.

Nursing conferences are most effective when there is a climate of respect—that is, nonjudgmental acceptance of others even though their values, opinions, and beliefs may seem different. Nurses need to accept and respect each person's contributions, listening with an open mind to what others are saying even when there is disagreement.

Nursing Rounds

Nursing rounds are procedures in which a group of nurses visits selected clients at each client's bedside to:

- Obtain information that will help plan nursing care.
- Provide clients the opportunity to discuss their care.
- Evaluate the nursing care the client has received.

FOCUS ON CRITICAL THINKING

Mrs. Chase was admitted to the unit following a vaginal hysterectomy. Upon her return to the unit, your initial observations were that she was drowsy but responded to verbal stimuli. Her vital signs in the recovery room were BP 102/50, P 98, Resps 20/min, O_2 sat 92% on 3 L /min O_2 per nasal prongs. Her abdominal dressing was intact, with some drainage noted, and her JP drain was patent with sanguineous fluid present in the drain. You also noticed that her vaginal flow appeared to be more than what was reported to you by the recovery room nurse.

Upon checking the pad, Mrs. Chase grasped her abdomen tightly and showed facial grimacing.

1. Using DARP charting, what would your documentation focus on postoperatively?
2. Which flowsheets would you use?
3. Legally, what would be most pertinent for you to consider in this situation?

See Appendix A for answers to these questions.

During rounds, the nurse assigned to the client provides a brief summary of the client's nursing needs and the interventions being implemented. Nursing rounds offer advantages to both clients and nurses: clients can participate in the discussions, and nurses can see the client and the equipment being used. To facilitate client participation in nursing rounds, nurses need to use terms that the client can understand. Medical terminology excludes the client from discussion.

CHAPTER HIGHLIGHTS

- Nurses must accurately document each step of the nursing process on a client record.
- Client records are legal documents and are admissible as evidence in a court of law.
- In source-oriented clinical records, recording is organized around the source of the information.
- In problem-oriented clinical records, recording is organized around client problems.
- Eight documentation systems include PIE, Focus Charting®, charting by exception, FACT, CORE, outcome documentation, computer documentation, and case management.
- Computer records have simplified nursing documentation. The use of computer terminals at the bedside allows immediate documentation of nursing actions.
- The case management model focuses on standardized interventions given within a defined time frame.
- The case management record for a client incorporates graphics and flowsheets along with critical pathways that serve as both an abbreviated care plan and a documentation form.
- The Kardex® record is used for quick access to current data about clients.
- The content of progress notes should be accurate, sequential, appropriate, complete, concise, legally prudent, and ethical.
- Principles of documentation for long-term care are the same as for acute care; however, documentation in long-term care is (1) less frequent, and (2) focuses more on daily functioning, preventive measures, and restorative care.
- In home health care, documentation needs to follow professional, regulatory, and accreditation standards.
- Correctly formatted charting should be legible, use correct terminology and spelling, and include date, time, and appropriate signature.
- Record entries are made *after* nursing assessments, interventions, and evaluations.
- The nurse has a duty to protect the confidentiality of the client's record; this includes special measures to protect information stored in computers.
- Common methods of communication by nurses are reporting and conferring.

READINGS AND REFERENCES

Suggested Readings

Eggland, E. T. (1995). Charting smarter: Using new mechanisms to organize your paperwork. *Nursing 95, 25*(9), 34–42.
This explains how to document the nursing process, even within the framework of multidisciplinary forms and critical pathways. It includes a helpful list of "Do's and Dont's" of daily charting.

Mosher, C., & Bontomasi, R. (1996). How to improve your shift report. *American Journal of Nursing, 96*(8), 32–34.
This describes how one hospital improved the efficiency and effectiveness of nurses' shift reports and, at the same time, moved from a task orientation to a client-problem focus. Using a "by exception" approach, reports now address each problem identified on the plan of care but note only significant interventions for those problems. They also communicate client progress toward identified outcomes on the plan of care. A patient profile card was created for routine information, and nurses use a change-of-shift report sheet on which problems are reported.

Mosher, C., Rademacher, K., Day, G., & Fanelli, D. (1996). Documenting for patient-focused care. *Nursing Economics, 14*(4), 218–223.
This describes how one hospital implemented multidisciplinary documentation that uses charting by exception. It argues that the idea of "nursing" documentation is no longer feasible in today's managed-care environment.

Related Research

Boldreghini, S., & Larrabee, J. H. (1998). Difference in nursing documentation before and after computerization. *Online Journal of Nursing Informatics, 2*(1) no pagination.

Davis, B. D., Billings, J. R., & Ryland, R. K. (1994). Evaluation of nursing process documentation. *Journal of Advanced Nursing, 19*, 960–968.

Pabst, M. K., Scherubel, J. C., & Minnick, A. B. (1996). The impact of computerized documentation on nurses' use of time. *Computers in Nursing, 14*(1), 25–30.

Selected References

Alberta Association of Registered Nurses. (1999). *Nursing practice standards*. Calgary, AB: Author.

Barbera, M. L. (1994). Giving report. How to sidestep common pitfalls. *Nursing, 24*(9), 41.

Blachly, B., & Young, H. M. (1998). Reducing the burden of paperwork: Modified charting by exception for medications. *Journal of Gerontological Nursing, 24*(6), 16–20.

Briggs, S., & Pate, E. W., Jr. (1996). Successful implementation of computerized documentation in home health care. *Home Health Care Management and Practice, 8*(3), 36–44.

Burke, L. J., & Murphy, J. (1988). *Charting by exception: A cost-effective quality approach*. New York: John Wiley.

Burke, L. J., & Murphy, J. (1995). *Charting by exception applications: Making it work in clinical settings*. Albany, NY: Delmar.

Calfee, B. (1994). 7 things you should never chart. *Nursing, 24*(3), 43.

Chase, S. K. (1997). Charting critical thinking: Nursing judgments and patient outcomes. *Dimensions of Critical Care Nursing, 16*(2), 102–111.

Cirone, N. (1998). Taking orders by phone? *Nursing 98, 28*(8), 56–57.

Cox, S. S. (1994). Taping report: Tips to record by. *Nursing, 24*(3), 64.

Eggland, E. T., & Heinemann, D. S. (1994). *Nursing documentation: Charting, recording, and reporting*. Philadelphia, PA: Lippincott.

Heartfield, M. (1996). Nursing documentation and nursing practice: A discourse analysis. *Journal of Advanced Nursing, 24*(1), 98–103.

Iyer, P. W. (1991a, June). Thirteen charting rules. *Nursing 91, 21*, 40-44.

Iyer, P. W. (1991b, July). Six more charting rules to keep you legally safe. *Nursing 91, 21*, 34–39.

Iyer, P. W., & Camp, N. H. (1999). *Nursing documentation: A nursing process approach* (3rd ed.). St. Louis: Mosby.

Keatings, M., & Smith, O. B. (2000). *Ethical and legal issues in Canadian nursing* (2nd ed.). Toronto: W. B. Saunders.

Lampe, S. (1994). *Focus charting: Documentation for patient-centered nursing care*. Minneapolis, MI: Creative Nursing Management.

Mandell, M. (1994). Not documented, not done. *Nursing, 24*(8), 62–63.

Marrelli, T. M., & Harper, D. S. (2000). *Nursing documentation handbook* (3rd ed.). St. Louis, MO: Mosby.

Meintz, S. L., & Shaha, S. H. (1992, January). Our hand-held computer beats them all. *RN, 55*, 52–55, 57.

Merkouris, A. V. (1995). Computer-based documentation and bedside terminals. *Journal of Nursing Management, 3*(2), 81–85.

Milholland, K., & Heller, B. (1992). Computer-based patient record: From pipe dream to reality. *Computers in Nursing*, 191.

Mosher, C., & Bontomasi, R. (1996). How to improve your shift report. *American Journal of Nursing, 96*(8), 32–34.

Murphy, J., & Burke, L. J. (1990). Charting by exception: A more efficient way to document. *Nursing 90, 20*, 65, 68-69.

Penner, M. (1996). The computerization of an emergency department: One hospital's experience. *Topics in Emergency Medicine, 18*(1), 48–62.

Rasmussen, N. (1994). Clinical pathways of care: The route to better communication. *Nursing, 24*(2), 47–49.

Rozovsky, L. (1994). *The Canadian patient's book of rights. A consumer's guide to Canadian health law*. Toronto: Doubleday.

Scharf, L. (1997). Revising nursing documentation to meet patient outcomes. *Nursing Management, 28*(4), 38–39.

Scoates, G. H., Fishman, M., & McAdam, B. (1996). Health care focus documentation—more efficient charting. *Nursing Management, 27*(8), 30–32.

Simpson, R. L. (1994). Ensuring patient data privacy, confidentiality, and security. *Nursing Management, 25*(7), 18–20.

Springhouse. (1995). *Mastering documentation*. Springhouse, PA: Springhouse.

WEBLINKS

Canadian Council of Health Services Accreditation
http://www.cchsa.ca/english/indexeng_n.html
Canadian Council of Health Services Accreditation is an organization to help health services organizations achieve greater degrees of excellence for the benefit of all Canadians. The process of accreditation assists health services organizations to identify their strengths and weaknesses and better understand the objectives and intricacies of their organization.The CCHSA can give the organization ideas about improving documentation systems and ways to become more consistent in standardizing charting across regions.

CHAPTER 25

Nursing Informatics

OBJECTIVES

After completing this chapter, you will be able to:

- Define nursing informatics.
- Differentiate among data, information, and knowledge.
- Identify nursing informatics applications used in direct client care.
- Discuss the advantages of and concerns about electronic health records.
- Describe the concepts of privacy, confidentiality, data integrity, and security related to the electronic health record (EHR).
- List the uses of nursing informatic applications.
- Identify ways nursing informatic applications may be used by nurse administrators in the areas of personnel, facilities management, finance, and quality assurance.
- Examine the role of nursing informatics in each step of the research process.

Nurses constantly use data and information to make decisions and to deliver quality care to their patients. Nurses are bombarded with information in their work environment. They gather patient assessment data, integrate the data and information to develop care plans, communicate patient information to both patients and other health-care team members, and manage budget and staffing data.

Advances in information technology, both computer hardware and software, have led to increased opportunities for nurses to use these technologies to better manage their work. Faster computers and improved software process data rapidly into useful information. The convergence of information technology and communications technology allows for rapid and secure transmission of information among health-care professionals through such venues as the Internet. These advances have made information and communications technology commonplace. It is imperative that nurses understand the opportunities available to enhance their practice and be able to integrate these in ways that lead to better patient care.

Nursing informatics is a term that is used to describe the integration of information technologies with nursing, not just the use of computers. Staggers and Thompson (2002) developed a comprehensive definition of nursing informatics:

> *Nursing informatics is a specialty that integrates nursing science, computer science, and information science to manage and communicate data, information, and knowledge in nursing practice. Nursing informatics facilitates the integration of data, information, and knowledge to support patients, nurses, and other providers in their decision-making in all roles and settings. This support is accomplished through the use of information structures, information processes, and information technology.*
>
> *Beyond the definition, the goal of nursing informatics is to improve the health of populations, communities, families, and individuals by optimizing information management and communication. This includes the use of information and technology in direct provision of care, in establishing effective administrative systems, in managing and delivering educational experiences, in supporting lifelong learning and in supporting nursing research (p. 260).*

This chapter is structured to describe the impact of nursing informatics and its applications on the four nursing domains of (1) care provision, (2) education, (3) administration, and (4) research.

Before nursing informatics can be understood, there must be an explanation of the inter-relationships of data, information, and knowledge. Data are raw, individual observations that have not been interpreted. Examples of data are age, weight, blood pressure, number of admissions, and number of workload units. Information results when data are interpreted, organized, or structured in a meaningful way. For example, such data as age, disease, blood pressure, and score on a mental status exam can be integrated to provide information about fall risk. Knowledge is the further synthesis of information to identify relationships that provide fuller understanding of an issue or subject area. Once raw data are integrated to provide information about fall risk, the nurse's knowledge about care maps or fall reduction programs, derived from both practice and the nursing literature, allows for evidence-based decisions to be made to provide the most effective care to the patient.

All three concepts—data, information, and knowledge—are influenced by nursing informatics applications. Raw data can be collected and stored by computer systems. Electronic monitoring of vital signs and ECG in intensive care units includes recording on the electronic patient record. The integration of data to provide useful information is demonstrated when statistics are available on the prevalence of immunizations for a specific disease in various communities. Knowledge is enhanced through the integration of care maps or decision-support systems, which analyze raw data and nursing assessments and suggest nursing diagnoses with recommended interventions. Although the examples given all relate to clinical nursing practice, nursing informatics applications also support data, information, and knowledge integration in education, administration, and research.

Nursing Informatics Applications in Clinical Nursing Practice

Many activities of the registered nurse involve collecting, recording, and using data. Nursing informatics applications are well suited to assist the nurse in these functions. Specifically, the nurse records client information in electronic records that replace or supplement the written medical record, accesses other departments' information on the client from centralized computers, perhaps using the Internet to manage client scheduling, and uses programs for unique applications such as home health nursing and case management.

Figure 25.1 Nursing informatics applications are well suited to assist the nurse in collecting, recording, and using data

Assessment

In the typical shift of a nurse providing direct client care, as much as one-third of the time may be spent recording in the client's record. Additional time is spent trying to access data about the client that may be somewhere in the medical record or elsewhere in the health-care agency. Nurses need access to standardized forms, policies, and procedures. Also, nurses need to be able to gather broader client information, such as length of stay, for specific diagnoses. Computers can assist with each of these.

Bedside Data Entry and Client Monitoring

Several different types of computers and systems are designated as bedside data entry or bedside terminals. These allow recording of client assessments, medication administration, and progress notes, care plan updating, determining patient acuity, and accrued charges. The terminal can be fixed or handheld, hardwired to the central system, or it can be cordless with the ability to transmit the data to distant sites, such as from the client's home to the agency office.

Nursing has benefited greatly from the myriad of client monitors. Examples in everyday practice are the digital or tympanic thermometers, digital scales, pulse oximetry, electrocardiography (ECG)/telemetry/hemodynamic monitoring, apnea monitors, fetal heart monitors, blood glucose analyzers, ventilators, and intravenous (IV) pumps. These instruments can be used in any care setting, from intensive care to the home. Most keep a record of the most recent values. Some can transmit their data to a more sophisticated computer or print out a paper record. Some have digital displays that "talk" to the user, giving instructions or results. Most also have error detection or alarms that indicate either that the instrument is malfunctioning or that the assessed value is outside predetermined parameters. These devices, with their minute but powerful computer chips, make it possible to extend the nurse's observations and provide valid and reliable data.

In various specialty areas of health care, clients undergo diagnostic procedures in which computers play a major role. Computed tomography (CT) scans and magnetic resonance imaging (MRI) use computers extensively to perform tests and analyze the findings. Blood gas analyzers, pulmonary function test machines, and intracranial pressure monitors all use computer processing. Heart-lung bypass machines are controlled by digital circuits. There are many more examples of ways that computers assist us in monitoring and diagnosing client conditions.

Electronic Health Records

The ability to retrieve client data electronically from a variety of sources over time provides many benefits to nurses and patients. Several terms, such as computer-based patient record (CPR), electronic health record (EHR), or personal health record, have been used interchangeably to denote the electronic record. In Canada, there are several terms, with discrete definitions, that are used. An *electronic health record* has been defined by the Federal Provincial/Territorial Advisory Committee on Health Infostructure (2001) as follows:

> *A longitudinal collection of personal health information of a single individual, entered or accepted by health care providers, and stored electronically. The record may be made available at any time to providers, who have been authorized by the individual, as a tool in the provision of health care services. The individual has access to the record and can request changes to its content. The transmission and storage of the record is under strict authority (p. 17).*

A *patient record*, or *computerized patient record (CPR)*, is generally taken to mean a record of a patient's demographic data, such as name and date of birth, the patient's diagnosis, and details about assessments and interventions provided by health professionals during an episode of care from *one* health organization. A consumer's copy of the health data, whether paper or electronic, is called a *personal health record.*

The use of electronic health records across Canada is still in the developmental phase in many areas. The move to the use of electronic patient records requires a significant investment for the Canadian health-care system; however, the benefits far outweigh the costs. The Canadian Nurses Association (CNA), in *Nursing Now: Issues and Trends in Canadian Nursing, vol. 13* (2002) identifies seven benefits accrued to patients and nurses from the implementation of the electronic health record:

1. Availability of comprehensive information on the care of clients/patients covering the continuum of health service delivery, across health professionals and time
2. Convenience and ease of access, transfer and retrieval of information, for example, workload and intervention data can be easily retrieved and aggregated for administrative purposes
3. Ability to dynamically view or display data from different views to support clinical, administrative, and research functions; for example, nurses can easily request data on all of the patient's current medications or all of the patient's test results over a period of time across health organizations; nurses can request necessary data to support the clinical audit and measurement of patient outcomes
4. Provision of a dynamic approach to nursing research and to the development of new nursing knowledge, for example, the outcome of nursing interventions: what works and what does not work under what circumstances
5. Improved data quality and standardization of clinical documentation; data are automatically verified as they are entered to ensure accuracy; data from feeder systems (e.g., admission, discharge, transfer, pharmacy, clinical laboratory, and physicians' offices) can be entered

directly, eliminating data entry errors; information is structured and standardized, facilitating more effective analysis and communications between health service providers and organizations

6. Improved continuity of client/patient care through the sharing of information between health organizations and health professionals
7. Direct access to knowledge bases and decision-support software tools to support improved decision making and better client/patient outcomes

Data Protection

Although there are many benefits associated with the use of electronic health records, there are also several areas of concern. Data protection is of vital concern to both patients and nurses. Data protection is an umbrella term that includes the concepts of privacy, confidentiality, integrity, and security. *Privacy* is defined as the right of an individual to control the circulation of personal information and to freedom from unreasonable interference in the individual's private life (Working Group 3, 1997). The right to privacy is determined by legislation. In Canada, the Privacy Act governs the personal information practices of federal government institutions, and the Personal Information Protection and Electronic Documents Act governs the private sector. A number of provinces have enacted specific health information protection legislation governing the collection, use, and dissemination of personal health information. Examples of this legislation include the Personal Health Information Act in Manitoba and the Health Information Act in Alberta.

Confidentiality is defined as a third party's obligation to protect the personal information entrusted to it (Working Group 3, 1997). *Data integrity* involves the collection, storage, and transmission of data in a manner that preserves the integrity or accuracy and completeness of the data (Hannah, Ball, & Edwards, 1999). Because privacy legislation and the accompanying guiding principles are very broad, guidelines have been developed to assist organizations in developing policies and practices that will protect the confidentiality and integrity of health information entrusted to them. The Canadian Organization for the Advancement of Computers in Health (COACH) has developed a widely used set of guidelines outlined in *Guidelines for the Protection of Health Information* (2001).

Security refers to the procedures and technologies required to restrict access to and maintain the integrity of health information. Procedures and technologies are required to address hardware, software, and organizational aspects of security. Hardware and software are maintained through a combination of user identification, user authorization, and review of users' interactions with the system (Hannah et al., 1999). The Canadian Standards Association oversees technical standards for security technologies.

Nurses, more than any other health professional, use, collect, and record health information constantly in the provision of nursing services. It is vital for the individual nurse to be aware of the legislation, guidelines, and institutional policies designed to protect patients' health information so that the nurse can act in a manner consistent with these requirements.

Data Standardization and Classifications

In order to fully develop the potential of electronic health records, it must be possible to share data across institutions and along the care continuum. Historically, each institution, home care agency, continuing care facility, laboratory, physician's office, or pharmacy has developed a way of collecting and storing patient data electronically. However, the problem arises when this information is to be shared with another health-care professional or organization because there is no standardized method of storing data. For example, in recording a person's birth date, the elements of year, month, and day are configured in many different ways. When various information systems try to look at date of birth, unless the pattern conforms to that organization's way of coding, the data cannot be shared. One of the mandates of the Canadian Institute for Health Information (CIHI) is to coordinate and promote the development and maintenance of national health information standards. For example, this would include agreeing, at the national level, on a standard for the order in which to collect and store date of birth. This is a simplistic example of health data and standards to describe all types of health data are required to realize the full benefits of an electronic health record that can be used across Canada by all health facilities and providers.

Not only are standards required for specifying how to code such specific data elements as the example of date of birth, but classification systems are also necessary to consistently describe common concepts within nursing and across disciplines. At the international level, the International Council of Nurses (ICN) has developed a universal system for defining and describing nursing practice called the International Classification of Nursing Practice (ICNP®). ICNP® provides a common framework that facilitates the integration of other nursing vocabularies and classification systems to allow for the comparison of nursing data across organizations, health sectors, and countries. The CNA has endorsed the use of ICNP®.

The Canadian Institute for Health Information (CIHI) has developed the Canadian Classification of Health Interventions (CCI). The CCI was developed to allow for the standardized collection of health interventions, regardless of service provider or service setting. For example, the same coding would be used for "exercise" whether a nurse, a physiotherapist, or a recreational therapist performed the intervention. The CCI was also developed to be consistent with the concepts and terminology of the ICNP®. Becoming familiar with the concepts and language of the ICNP® and CCI will allow the nurse to structure data collection and recording in ways that facilitate sharing of nursing information.

Tracking Client Status

Once an EHR has been established, the nurse can retrieve and display a client's physiological parameters across time. In addition to the rather straightforward viewing of trends in vital signs, for example, the nurse can also track more global client progress. Standardized nursing care plans, care maps, critical pathways, or other prewritten treatment protocols can be stored in the computer and easily placed in the EHR electronically. Then, the nurse and other health-care personnel can examine progression and variance from the expected plan directly on the computer.

Electronic Access to Client Data

Besides information systems designed for record keeping, other computers are used extensively in health care to assess and monitor clients' conditions. The data accumulated from various electronic devices can be part of the EHR and also stored for research purposes. Electronic records take up much less space than paper records and may be stored more securely. Copies can be made easily onto different electronic media (e.g., magnetic tape, microfiche) that tend to be more compact and durable than paper. Data can also be transmitted to a consulting specialist in another location over a secure network.

Intervention

Nursing informatics applications are not only useful in managing the assessment of patients, but also in providing and coordinating care. From care planning through patient education and practice management, nursing practice benefits from the application of nursing informatics.

Consumer Informatics

Increasingly, patients are accessing information about their condition and care from the Internet and gaining assistance from both lay and professionally led online support groups. Nurses need to use this source of information to promote the health of their patients and guide them to reliable health information on the Internet. The Health Summit Working Group, Mitretek Systems' Health Information Technology Institute, that included health-care providers, medical librarians, information resource experts, and consumers, developed a comprehensive set of evaluation criteria. Table 25.1 displays the criteria (Health Summit Working Group, 1998).

The Health on the Net (HON) Foundation has developed a Code of Conduct to help standardize the reliability of health information available on the Internet. The HON code defines a set of principles that hold Web site developers to basic ethical standards in the presentation of health information. Sites displaying the HON code seal have been reviewed and conform to this code. Consumers can be confident of the information found on a site displaying the HON seal (www.hon.ch). Nurses who are informed about evaluation criteria, such as those outlined above, and those of the HON code seal, can more effectively guide patients' acquisition of reliable knowledge, information, and support from the Internet.

TABLE 25.1 Criteria for Evaluating Health Information on the Internet Developed by the Health Summit Working Group

Credibility	includes the source, currency, relevance/utility, and editorial review process for the information.
Content	must be accurate and complete, and an appropriate disclaimer provided.
Disclosure	includes informing the user of the purpose of the site, as well as any profiling or collection of information associated with using the site.
Links	are evaluated according to selection, architecture, content, and back linkages.
Design	encompasses accessibility, logical organization (navigability), and internal search capability.
Interactivity	includes feedback mechanisms and means for exchange of information among users.
Caveats	include clarification of whether site function is to market products and services or is a primary information content provider.

Source: Mitretek Systems, Health Summit Working Group, 1998. *Criteria for evaluating health information on the Internet.* http://www.hitiweb.mitretek.org.docs/policy.html

Telehealth

The greatest gains in applying nursing informatics concepts in the community setting have come from the convergence of information technology and telecommunications applications. Telehealth has been defined by the Industry Canada Advisory Council on Health Infostructure as "the use of communications and information technology to deliver health and healthcare services and information over large and small distances" (Picot and Cradduck, 2000). A national working group, chaired by the CNA, has further defined nursing telepractice as "client-centred forms of nursing practice which occur through, or are facilitated by, the use of telecommunications or electronic means. Nursing telepractice uses the nursing process, which encompasses client assessment, planning, and implementation through the provision of information, referral, education and support, evaluation, and documentation" (*Nursing Now #9*, 2002, p. 1). Major changes in the telehealth industry in Canada and elsewhere are affecting the technologies and applications previously considered under the umbrella of telehealth. The new "buzz-word" is no longer *videoconferencing*, or even *telehealth* or *telemedicine* but, rather, *e-health*. This term is being used to describe a collection of electronic health-care activities.

Benefits of Telehealth

Continuity of client care
Removes geographical barriers to care
Centralized health records
Collaboration among health-care team
Involvement of client in care
Continuing education tool

Continuing advances in information and telecommunications technology drive novel approaches to delivering patient care services. Such products as cardiac monitoring and hemodialysis systems, complete with telephone coupling mechanisms, allow for in-home monitoring of clients without the need for a nursing visit. The use of videophones allows for home care video visits, particularly popular for monitoring elderly clients. Picot (1997) identified the following home care services that can be tele-assisted: wound management; oncology patient management via home infusion; blood glucose meters with telecommunications capabilities; telemonitoring of hemodialysis; and emergency or alert systems linking homes to clinics or hospitals. Telecounselling using videoconferencing or videophones continues to increase as the majority of mental health professionals are located in urban areas. The option of telecounselling reduces travel costs for both the client and professional, and research reports high satisfaction with the service (Elford and House, 1996). Call centres, accessed by toll-free numbers, are used in many jurisdictions to provide health information or first-level triage over the telephone or the Internet. Nurses are frequently the front-line providers of telephone triage.

Nursing telepractice has been determined to be within the scope of nursing practice in all Canadian nursing jurisdictions. The CNA policy statement, *The Role of the Nurse in Telepractice* (2001), can be found on the association's Web site. Concerns regarding nursing telepractice relate to legal and ethical issues. Although telepractice is within the scope of practice, it has yet to be determined to which jurisdiction's standards the nurse will be held when the nurse and client are physically in different jurisdictions and the interaction occurs on the Internet. Each jurisdiction using nursing telepractice is also charged with the responsibility of developing policies and procedures to protect the client's privacy. As these issues are being resolved, telehealth applications hold great potential for extending the ability of nursing to reach individuals and communities and provide better access to health-care services.

Evidence-Based Decision Making

The CNA's *Policy Statement on Evidence-based Decision-making and Nursing Practice* (1998) states that "the utilization of evidence-based decision making by registered nurses is an important element of quality nursing practice" (p.1). In order to apply evidence to decision making, the nurse must first access the evidence. Access to full-text articles through online databases, such as Proquest or OVID, and online journals provides the nurse with the opportunity to use current, readily accessible evidence on which to base nursing decisions. Nurses must become familiar with the available online professional resources and search programs and strategies to be able to accomplish this task. Literature searching has traditionally been related to formal research but must be incorporated into basic evidence-based practice. The box below identifies the names and locations of several online journals of interest to nurses, while the box on the following page identifies the addresses for searchable health-related literature databases.

Practice Management

Beyond direct client care, computers also assist nurses in many ways in the management of their work. In hospitals, data terminals are commonly used to order supplies, tests, meals, and services from other departments. Tracking of these orders allows the nursing service to determine the most frequent or most costly items used by a particular nursing unit. This information may lead to decisions to modify a budget, provide different staffing, move supplies to a different location, or make other changes for more efficient and higher quality care.

Computers and handheld devices, such as personal digital assistants (PDAs), are used extensively for scheduling. Client appointments can be easily entered or changed. Special notes or tags can be applied to the appointment as a reminder to the provider to perform particular services.

Online Full-Text Journals

Bandolier: Evidence-based health care
http://www.jr2.ox.ac.uk/Bandolier/

IMIA Newsletters
http://www.imia.org/

Internet Journal of Advanced Nursing Practice
http://www.ispub.com/journals/ijanp.html

Internet Journal of Health Promotion
http://www.ijhp.org/index.html

Western Journal of Nursing Research
http://www.sagepub.co.uk/journals/details/j0044.html
(by subscription only)

Nursing Standard Online
http://www.nursing-standard.co.uk/

Nursing Trends and Issues
http://www.nursingworld.org/readroom/nti/

Online Journal of Issues in Nursing
http://www.nursingworld.org/ojin/

Online Journal of Nursing Informatics
http://cac.psu.edu/~dxm12/OJNI.html

> **Searchable Health-Related Literature Database**
>
> Cinahl Direct
> Cumulative Index to Nursing and Allied Health Literature. Paid membership required.
> **http://www.cinahl.com/**
>
> Medline
> National Library of Medicine offers PubMed and Internet Grateful Med, two free systems to search MEDLINE.
> **http://www.nlm.nih.gov/databases/freemedl.html**
>
> Springhouse Reference Library
> References over 100 nursing journals. Output includes bibliographic data and abstracts. No membership required.
> **http://www.springnet.com/journals.html**

The schedule for a single day can be printed so that all personnel have a copy. Staffing patterns can also be coordinated. Special requests for days off or continuing education classes can be entered and the schedule can be viewed for a day, week, month, or year.

In community settings, case managers must also be able to track a group of clients—the caseload. Software programs allow the case manager to enter client data and integrate this with predesigned care tracking templates.

Literature Access and Retrieval

In our information age, it is a challenge to keep abreast of the information on any subject. Computers have significantly improved our abilities in this area by presenting catalogues of materials in a way that can be searched systematically. Previously, users needed to leaf through multiple collections of printed indexes one keyword or topic at a time. Now, continuously updated cumulative indexes of related materials can be searched electronically in a fraction of the time. These bibliographic retrieval systems may be stored on CD-ROM or on a mainframe computer that can be accessed online. The searcher can specify the date, language, document type, and other characteristics of the citation for desired materials. Once a list of search matches is displayed on the computer screen, users can select all or certain citations and either print them or store them on their own local disk. Search results can include journals and other magazines, books, videotapes, computer programs, dissertations, or other documents. The previous box lists commonly used bibliographic systems and databases.

In addition to searching lists of documents, actual complete publications and materials may also be available in computerized and online formats. These include medical textbooks, the full text of journals, drug references, digitized x-rays or scans, and graphics, including clip art. Through the Internet, both classic and the most current information can be found on any topic. Users can access statistics from the Centers for Disease Control and Prevention, census data, and the National Library of Medicine. See the box on the previous page for selected journals available online.

Nursing Informatics Applications in Nursing Education

Nursing students and graduates alike can benefit from the application of nursing informatics to education. Because of the exponential growth of knowledge both in nursing and related fields, the student and the graduate must be continually learning in order to provide quality nursing service to individuals, families, and communities.

Just as computers have become standard instructional tools in the primary and secondary school systems, they are used extensively in all aspects of nursing education. Nursing programs require computerized libraries, faculty members use technological teaching strategies in the classroom and for outside assignments, and academic record keeping is facilitated by database programs.

Teaching and Learning

Computers enhance academics for both students and faculty in at least four ways. These include (1) access to literature, (2) computer-assisted instruction (CAI), (3) strategies for learning at a distance, and (4) data management.

Literature Access

Nurses, both students and graduates, must be adept at searching and retrieving evidence from the literature to support the provision of quality service to the public. Searchable databases and online full-text journals have been previously discussed.

Computer-Assisted and Web-Based Instruction

Computer-assisted instruction software is available on a variety of nursing topics. At some schools, faculty members author their own programs to meet the unique needs of their students. Course syllabi that contain worksheets or activities that students can complete on the computer may be distributed in electronic format or online through the institution network. Commercial CAI programs are available for individual student purchase.

Nursing has enjoyed the computer revolution in the form of CAI—dozens of software programs that help nursing students and nurses learn and demonstrate learning. There are programs that cover topics from drug dosage calculations to ethical decision making. Programs are classified according to format: tutorial, drill-and-practice, simulation, or testing. CAI can contain diagrams, graphics, limited motion, and audio. A variation of CAI is interactive videodisc, which combines full motion and sound video with text on a laser videodisc controlled by the user through the computer. CAI programs on CD-ROM incorporate digitized video. All forms of CAI allow almost instant access to any section of the program and can be designed to branch to different sections depending on the user's responses.

The Internet offers many sites with multimedia learning opportunities on a variety of nursing and health-related topics. Graduates often choose to complete this type of instruction as part of their demonstration of continued competence. Nursing portals, such as www.nursingnet.org or www.nurseceu.com, list a large array of continuing education opportunities available online. Nursing students will also be able to find online tutorials at these sites.

Distance Delivery

The integration of information technology and communications technology, particularly the Internet, allows people to communicate effectively over large distances and various time zones. In one model of distance delivery, students receive course materials either in class or through the mail and then communicate with the instructor and each other through e-mail or in online forums or chat rooms. Discussions can be either synchronous, when all students participate at the same "real" time, or asynchronous, when students participate at different times but contribute to the same discussion. Videoconferencing, enabled by information technology and telecommunications applications, is also used to allow students at various sites to participate in class discussions. Completely online programs exist for post-R.N. baccalaureate degrees and master's degrees (www.athabascau.ca and www.ucalgary.ca).

Data Management

Computers are also very useful for maintaining results of students' grades or attendance using spreadsheets. Often, faculty are able to scan student exam answer sheets directly into a gradebook on the computer. The program can then calculate percentages, sort student scores in order, and print results for both students and faculty. Grades from multiple exams plus scores on essays or other projects are calculated into final grades.

The computer is ideal for conducting certain types of learning evaluations. Large banks of potential test items can be written and the computer can generate different exams for each student depending on the selection criteria designated by the faculty. In addition, the students' answers can be scored electronically and the overall exam results analyzed quickly.

Nursing Informatics Applications in Nursing Administration

As indicated earlier in a section of this chapter, the volume of data that nurses need to have available and the additional volume of data generated by nurses can, and must be, managed electronically. Nursing administrators require this data in order to develop strategic plans for the organization. Management Information Systems and Hospital Information Systems are tools used by nurse administrators.

Management Information Systems

A **management information system (MIS)** is designed to facilitate the organization and application of data used to manage an organization or department. The system provides analyses used for planning, decision making, and evaluation of management activities. All levels of management benefit from the ability to access the data.

Hospital Information Systems

A **hospital information system (HIS)** is like an MIS except that it focuses on the types of data needed in managing client care activities and health-care organizations. As with any system, the goal is to provide people with the data they need to determine appropriate actions and have control over them. Typically, an HIS will have subsystems in the areas of admissions, medical records, clinical laboratory, pharmacy, and finance. The personnel in these areas enter the data needed to allow management of billing, quality assurance, scheduling, and inventory, both within their own areas and across the institution as a whole. Increasingly, accrediting organizations mandate the use of an HIS and require that reports be submitted using computerized formats. Eventually, integrated HISs will form the centre of all record keeping and analysis for interdisciplinary health care.

Human Resources

All employers must maintain a database, computerized or not, on each employee. In addition to the usual demographic and salary data, the database for licensed or certified health-care personnel has unique fields for such areas as life support certification, health requirements (e.g., tuberculosis testing, hepatitis immunization, rubella titres), and performance appraisals. Administrators can use this human resources database to communicate with employees, examine staffing patterns, and create budget projections.

Medical Records Management

Costs are inherent in, and reflected by, medical records. It is expensive to keep records, but it is even more expensive not to be able to access what is in them. Therefore, nurses require computerized information systems that allow client records to be searched for trends, such as the most common presenting diagnoses, number of cases by diagnosis-related groups, most expensive cases, length-of-stay or days case is open, and client outcomes. Nurse informaticists can assist administrators in the design and implementation of systems that allow for such searches to be generated, analyzed, printed, and distributed.

Facilities Management

Many aspects of managing buildings and non-nursing services can be facilitated by computer. Heating, air conditioning, and ventilation systems are computer controlled. Security devices, such as identification cards, bar codes, or magnetic strip readers, permit only authorized personnel to enter client or private areas. Computers also manage and report inventory, tracking everything from pillowcases to syringes.

Budget and Finance

The budget itself is generally a spreadsheet program. This software allows tracking as well as forecasting and planning. In uncertain times, the ability to perform "what if" calculations is especially valuable. Computers can effect cost savings by reducing the clerical time needed for accounts payable and receivable. In cases where nursing can directly bill and be reimbursed by payers, the same benefits of computerized accounting apply.

Quality Assurance and Utilization Reviews

Both internal and external stakeholders in health-care organizations need to know that the services and activities of the organization have positive results. Once standards, pathways, key indicators, and other vital data have been identified and described, computers can facilitate the analysis of the data. Quality is considered a process and not an end point. Applying this perspective, computerized systems are ideal for taking a snapshot view of the institution's quality indices at any time.

Utilization review consists of examining trends and proposing advantageous disposition of resources (specifically, length of stay). For example, might clients who have had a fractured hip repaired have equivalent outcomes at lesser cost if transferred sooner from the hospital to a skilled nursing facility? Studies can be conducted with computer analyses to answer such questions.

Nursing Informatics Applications in Nursing Research

Computers are invaluable assistants in the conduct of both quantitative and qualitative nursing research. In each step of the research process, computers facilitate generation, refinement, analysis, and output. Computer resources are an important component of the planning phase of any research project. The size of the computer and its storage capacity must be adequate for the amount of data that will be collected, and the proper software programs must be in place to manage and analyze the data. Computerized word processing is also an integral component in the publication and dissemination of research.

Problem Identification

The first step of the research process is to identify and describe the problem of interest. The computer can be useful in locating current literature about the problem and related concepts. Perhaps, unknown to the researcher, a solution to the problem has already been found and reported. A search of existing documents and e-mails to colleagues may help define the problem.

Literature Review

An exhaustive review of the literature can be time consuming. Without computer access to online or CD-ROM bibliographic databases, the researcher must wade through huge volumes of printed material. The software programs that facilitate searches contain thesauruses so that the most appropriate terms can be selected. If the researcher determines that little has been published on the topic of interest, closely related terms and topics must also be searched. It is not unusual for a researcher to collect more than 100 pertinent articles or books during the literature review.

Electronic citation management software is available to assist in cataloguing all references in a personal "library" database that can be searched and sorted along key words to produce reference lists related to a particular topic. The references selected can then be automatically formatted according to the requirements of the institution or journal.

Research Design

The design of a research study, including the choice of specific research method, is always driven by the research question. At the design stage, the investigator determines whether the study will use a qualitative or quantitative approach, what instruments will be used to collect data, and the types of analyses that will be carried out on the data to answer the research questions. Computers may be used during this step to search the literature for instruments that have already been established or to design and test instruments that need to be developed for the particular study. In addition, the investigator would not likely select an instrument or design that requires extensive computer or mathematical analysis if such resources are not available.

Data Collection and Analysis

Once the types of data to be collected have been determined, the investigator can create computer forms for collecting the data. These may include the informed consent document, a tool to collect demographic data, or recording forms for research variables.

Increasingly, study participants are completing quantitative data collection instruments online with the data input automatically into a database. Computer-assisted interviewing also allows for online capture of qualitative data. This eliminates the errors that may occur when research assistants enter data into a computer manually. The electronically captured data can then be exported into various statistical analysis and qualitative analysis programs.

When the variables have been coded, other programs can be used to calculate descriptive and analytic statistics. Calculations that formerly were extremely time consuming and complex can now be done by computer programs quickly and accurately. Commonly used software programs for quantitative data analysis include SPSS (Statistical Package for the Social Sciences), SAS (Statistical Analysis System), SysSTAT, and MYSTAT. These programs perform analyses and display output in tables, charts, lists, and other easily read formats.

Software programs can assist with the analysis and coding of qualitative data. Such programs as Nudist, Ethnograph, and QUALPRO assist the researcher in finding and coding sections of text and organizing coded material.

Research Dissemination

Research is of limited value if the findings are not widely dispersed to the practitioners who can use the findings to improve their practice. Computer word processing programs are used to author the final reports of research and to send the reports to various readerships. Many journals now require that manuscripts submitted for publication include both hard copy and electronic versions. As noted earlier in this chapter, there are an increasing number of electronic journals. Authors can also send an article or data to interested persons instantaneously via e-mail.

Computers are frequently used to present research at meetings. Using computer projectors to display screens of data and findings also allows the researcher to highlight, modify, and manipulate content in an instant. Internet capabilities allow researchers to collaborate on a study from distant locations and to examine and analyze the data simultaneously onscreen.

Research Grants

Funds are available from a variety of resources to support the conduct of nursing research. The budget in a grant application may include a request to purchase computers or software needed to carry out the proposed study. Funds may also be requested to pay people to enter data into the computer and to run the statistical analyses.

Information about available grant funding is most easily found online. Forms to be completed are computer generated and often must be submitted to the funding agency in electronic format.

Conclusion

The field of nursing informatics will continue to evolve as advances are made in the underlying disciplines of nursing science, computer science, information science, and telecommunications. Nurses are encouraged to keep abreast of these developments through involvement in professional organizations, such as the Canadian Nursing Informatics Association. Nurses must understand the underpinnings of nursing informatics and be able to take advantage of the opportunities provided by nursing informatics applications to advance the practice of nursing and to provide quality service to the public.

Canadian Society Notes

Fact	Implications for Nursing Practice
The Canadian Nurses Association has worked with the Canadian Institute for Health Information (CIHI) to develop the Canadian Classification of Health Interventions to allow for the standardized collection of health intervention by all health professionals and cross-mapping to ICNP®.	Nurses must become familiar with nursing practice classification systems so they can collect and record data in formats that can be shared nationally and internationally to advance the quality of nursing practice.
Federal/Provincial/Territorial Advisory Committee on Health Infostructure is developing a national plan for a national health infostructure.	Nurses will be able to access and use e-health data and resources to provide services to individuals and communities. This will require that nurses keep up with emerging e-health technology and resources.
Info-Santé CLSC, a teletriage service in the Province of Quebec, responds to 2.5 million calls per year, increasing citizens' capacity for self-care and contributing to more appropriate use of health services. Similar initiatives can be found across Canada.	Nurses require nursing telepractice skills to provide increased access to health-care services for Canadians.

FOCUS ON CRITICAL THINKING

At lunch break, one of your nursing co-workers tells you and the others at the table that your assigned patient is her sister's boyfriend. She also tells you that someone left a document open on the computer screen at the unit desk showing a lab report about your patient indicating that he had tested positive for HIV. Your co-worker says that she is trying to decide what to tell her sister. When you get back to the unit, you log in to the computer and locate the lab report that was seen by your co-worker. However, you notice that there is an appended note indicating that further testing revealed that the first result was a false positive.

1. Discuss the privacy, confidentiality, data integrity, and security implications of this situation from the viewpoints of you the nurse, the patient, and the co-worker.

See Appendix A for answers to this question.

RESEARCH NOTES

Does an Automated Documentation System in a Hospital Save Nurses' Time?

These authors conducted a study comparing how nursing time was spent on a regular surgical unit and a surgical unit with computerized data entry systems. Nurses' activities were sampled both before and after the automated system was installed in the test unit. A total of more than 14,000 observations were made of over 70 nursing activities in six categories: patient care, unit care, personnel education, personal time, standby time, and research/student supervision.

On the test unit, computer terminals were installed at every bedside, at the central nurses' station, and at the ends of the hallways. Findings indicated that the amount of time the nurses spent on documentation was reduced from 13.7 percent to 10.8 percent after three months of having the computers. When care plans and nurses' progress notes were added to the computers, documentation took even less of the nurses' time (9.1 percent). In spite of the computer capabilities, 60 percent of the documentation was still done by hand. It is not known how much the documentation time could be reduced if all these tasks were also on the automated system.

The nurses liked many aspects of the computer system—especially the legibility and completeness. Forty percent of the entries were made at the systems located at the central nurses' station. There were two primary areas of nurses' dissatisfaction with the system: because only the nurses contributed to the computerized progress notes, there was no longer a chronological flow of their notes with those of other disciplines; and because the system could not produce flowsheets, a nurse had to look other places to get a complete idea of the client's condition.

Implications: Although there were some major advantages to the automated charting system, the time savings did not translate into increased productivity as measured in this study. The advantages also must be balanced against the disadvantages. There are many factors affecting whether such systems should be implemented.

Source: Pabst, M. K., Scherubel, J. C., & Minnick, A. F. 1996. The impact of computerized documentation on nurses' use of time. *Computers in Nursing. 14,* 25–30.

CHAPTER HIGHLIGHTS

- Bedside entry of nursing data is becoming more prevalent.
- Electronic health records (EHRs) enable longitudinal data to be collected on a client and be made available to all health-care providers who require it.
- Concerns regarding privacy and confidentiality, data integrity, and security of health records have arisen as electronic databases and communications have proliferated.
- Hospital information systems (HISs) organize data from various areas in the hospital such as admissions, medical records, clinical laboratory, pharmacy, and finance.
- Telehealth and nursing telepractice, the conduct of the health-care profession using electronic means of communication, are growing areas that generate both excitement and concerns.
- Computer monitoring and diagnosing of client conditions are widespread. Examples include digital or tympanic thermometers, digital scales, pulse oximetry, ECG/telemetry/hemodynamic monitoring, apnea monitors, fetal heart monitors, blood glucose analyzers, ventilators, IV pumps, CT, and MRI.
- Data terminals in health-care settings allow placing of order requests and retrieval of client data. Appointments can be scheduled electronically.

- Computers are used by home health nurses to record client data and to communicate with the central office. Clients can also have devices in the home that allow them to monitor their health status.
- Computers are used extensively to locate and access data through online databases and Internet searching. Many full text nursing journals are available online.
- Computer-assisted instruction programs include tutorials, drill-and-practice, and simulations.
- In distance learning, the faculty and student may be located far apart and communicate via the Internet, phone, fax, and video technologies.
- Nursing informatics applications are used in nursing administration to manage personnel, human resources, facilities, budgets, quality assurance, utilization review, and staffing and scheduling.
- Each step of the nursing research process makes use of informatics technology. In particular, computer systems and applications are used to access literature, analyze data, and report findings.

READINGS AND REFERENCES

Suggested Readings

Andrew, W. F., & Dick, R. S. (1995, July/August). Applied information technology: A clinical perspective—Feature Focus: The computer-based patient record (Part 3). *Computers in Nursing, 13*, 176–181.
This is the third and last article in a series describing the computer-based patient record (CPR). The article describes the 12 attributes of CPRs as delineated by the Institute of Medicine. It also presents five additional trends in the needs of a comprehensive CPR: a clinical data dictionary, a clinical data repository, flexible input capabilities, ergonomically designed data presentation, and automated support. The authors believe that a few effective CPR systems will emerge from the many that have been tried and come into widespread use.

Bowles, K. H. (1997, July). The barriers and benefits of nursing information systems. *Computers in Nursing, 15*(4), 191–196.
This article describes the evolution of nursing information systems and the design goals for current systems. The lack of a unified nursing language and individual and organizational factors, such as characteristics of the nurse, the unit, the administrative philosophy, and workload issues, are discussed as barriers to NIS development. Increased nurse involvement, education, research, and recognition of the benefits of computerization are suggested to overcome the barriers. A review of the literature provides the reader with evidence of improved efficiency, patient safety and satisfaction, and ability to measure quality as benefits of NIS. Areas for further research are identified.

Nagelkerk, J., Ritola, P. M., & Vandort, P. J. (1998, January/February). Nursing informatics: The trend of the future. *Journal of Continuing Education in Nursing, 29*(1), 17–21.
Nursing informatics is a combination of computer information and nursing sciences. The authors state it is essential to prepare nurses for computerized technology to use the most cost-effective methods. Six essential factors for preparing nurses for computerization are strong leadership, effective communication, organized training sessions, established time frames, planned change, and tailored software.

Sibbald, B. (1998). Nursing informatics for beginners. *Canadian Nurse, 94*(4), 22–30.
Sibbald discusses the significance of nursing informatics for nurses. She emphasizes that through informatics, nurses can make decisions based on the latest research, up-to-the-minute patient data, and on-site consultations with experts worldwide. Informatics can not only help nurses improve quality care, it allows them to document their worth for the first time.

Selected References

Ball, M. J., Hannah, K. J., Newbold, S. K., & Douglas, J. V. (Eds). (2000). *Nursing Informatics: Where caring and technology meet.* (3rd ed.). New York: Springer-Verlag.

Brennan, P. F., Schneider, S. J., & Tornquist, E. M. (1996). *Information networks for community health.* New York: Springer.

Canadian Nurses Association. (2000). Telehealth: Great potential or risky terrain? *Nursing now: Issues and trends in Canadian nursing, 9*, 1–4.

Canadian Nurses Association. (2001). What is nursing informatics, and why is it so important? *Nursing Now: Issues and trends in Canadian nursing, 11*, 1–4.

Canadian Nurses Association. (April, 2002). Demystifying the electronic health record. In *Nursing Now Issues and Trends in Canadian Nursing*, 13. Ottawa: Author.

Carty, B. (2000). *Nursing informatics: Education for practice.* New York: Springer.

Computer-Based Patient Record Institute. (1992). *Newsletters and membership brochures.* Chicago, IL: Author.

CNA (1998). *Policy Statement: Evidence-based Decision-making and Nursing Practice.* Ottawa: Canadian Nurses Association.

CNA (2001). *Policy Statement: The role of nurse in telepractice.* Ottawa: Canadian Nurses Association.

Degoulet, P. (1996). *Introduction to medical informatics.* New York: Springer.

Degoulet, P., & Fieschi, M. (1997). *Computers in health care: Introduction to clinical informatics.* New York: Springer.

Dennis, K. E. (1996). The value of bedside computer systems in restructuring nursing care. In M. E. Mills, C. A. Romano, & B. R. Heller (Eds.), *Information management in nursing and health care* (pp. 222–229). Springhouse, PA: Springhouse.

Digmen, L., & McCarten, J. (2002). Informatics: Point of care documentation. *Canadian Nurse, 98*(4), 26–29.

Edwards, M. J. A. (2002). *The internet for nurses and allied health professionals* (3rd ed.). New York: Springer-Verlag.

Elford, D. R., & House, A. M. (1996). Telemedicine experience in Canada: 1956-1996. Paper presented at the Medicine 2001 Conference, Montreal.

Federal/Provincial/Territorial Advisory Committee on Health Infostructure. (2001). *Tactical plan for a pan-Canadian Health Infostructure.* Health Canada. Available at: www.hc-sc.gc.ca/ohih-bsi/pubs/2001_plan/plan_e.html

Gordon, C., & Christensen, J. P. (1995). *Health telematics for clinical guidelines and protocols.* Amsterdam, The Netherlands: IOS Press.

Hannah, K. J., & Edwards, M. J. A. (1998). Nursing informatics. *Canadian Journal of Nursing Research, 30*(1), 61–70.

Hannah, K. J., Ball, M. J., & Edwards, M. J. (1995). *Introduction to nursing informatics.* New York: Springer.

Hannah, K. J., Ball, M.J., & Edwards, M. J. A. (1999). *Introduction to Nursing Informatics* (2nd ed.). New York: Springer-Verlag.

Health Information Technology Institute of Mitretek System Health Summit Working Group. (1999). *Criteria for assessing the quality of health information on the Internet: Policy paper.* http://www.hitiweb.mitritek.org/docs/policy.html.

Hebda, T. L., Czar, P., & Mascara, C. (1998). *Handbook of nursing informatics.* Menlo Park, CA: Addison Wesley Longman.

Hebert, M. (2000). A national strategy to develop nursing informatics competencies. *Canadian Journal of Nursing Leadership, 13*(2), 11–14.

Johnston, B., Heeler, J., Dueser, K., & Sousa, K. (2000). Outcomes of the Kaiser Permante tele-home health research project. *The Archives of Family Medicine, 9,* 40–45.

Kjervik, D. K. (1997, March/April). Telenursing—Licensure and communication challenges. *Journal of Professional Nursing, 13,* 65.

Kreider, N. A. (1997). *The systems challenge: Getting the clinical information support you need to improve patient care.* Chicago, IL: American Hospital Publishing.

Mattingly, R. (1996). *Management of health information: Functions and applications.* Clifton Park, NY: Delmar.

McDaniel, A. M. (1997, May/June). Developing and testing a prototype patient care database. *Computers in Nursing, 15,* 129–136.

Mills, E. C., Romano, C. A., & Heller, B. R. (1996). *Information management in nursing and health care.* Springhouse, PA: Springhouse.

Nagelkirk, J., Ritola, P. M., & Vandort, P. J. (1998). Nursing informatics: The trend of the future. *Journal of Continuing Education in Nursing, 29*(1), 17–21.

Nicoll, L. H. (1998). *Computers in nursing's guide to the Internet* (2nd ed.). Philadelphia, PA: Lippincott-Raven.

Nicoll, L. H., & Ouellette, T. H. (1997). *Nurses' guide to the Internet.* Philadelphia, PA: Lippincott.

Osheroff, J. A. (1995). *Computers in clinical practice: Managing patients, information and communication.* Philadelphia, PA: American College of Physicians.

Picot, J. (1997). *The telehealth industry in Canada.* Ottawa: Health Canada.

Picot, J., & Cradduck, T. (2000). *The telehealth industry in Canada: Industry profile and capability analysis.* Ottawa: Industry Canada.

Rosen, E. L., & Routon, C. M. (1998). American Nursing Informatics role survey. *Computers in Nursing, 16*(3), 171–175.

Russo, H. (2001). Window of opportunity for home care nurses: Telehealth technologies. *Online Journal of Issues in Nursing, 6,* 3.

Saba, V. K., & McCormick, K. A. (1996). *Essentials of computers for nurses* (2nd ed.). New York: McGraw-Hill.

Simpson, R. L. (1995, December). Technology: Nursing the system. Nursing informatics certification. *Nursing Management, 26,* 49–50.

Staggers, N. T., & Thompson, C. B. (2002). The evolution of definitions for nursing informatics: A critical analysis and revised definition. *Journal of the American Medical Informatics Association, 9*(3), 255–261.

Tapp, A. (2002). Legal Matters: Cyberlaw. *Canadian Nurse, 98*(4), 30–31.

Turley, J. P. (1996, Winter). Toward a model for nursing information. *Image: Journal of Nursing Scholarship, 28*(4), 309–313.

Weghorst, S. J., Siegburg, H. B., & Morgan, K. S. (Eds.). (1996). *Medicine meets virtual reality: Health care in the information age.* Amsterdam, The Netherlands: IOS Press.

Working Group 3, Partnership for Health Informatics/Telematics. (1997). *Working Group 3: Privacy, confidentiality, data integrity, and security: Background document (Revised).* EHTO Journal 4, http://www.ehto.org/hps/issue4/canada2.html

WEBLINKS

Canadian Institute for Health Information
www.cihi.ca
The Canadian Institute for Health Information (CIHI) is an independent, national, not-for-profit organization working to improve the health of Canadians and the health-care system by providing through its site quality, reliable, and timely health information.

Canadian Nurses Association (CNA)
www.can-nurses.ca
The Canadian Nurses Association's mission is to advance the quality of nursing in the interest of the public.

Canadian Organization for the Advancement of Computers in Health (COACH)
www.coachorg.com
The Canadian Organization for the Advancement of Computers in Health is an organization of more than 750 health executives, physicians, nurses, allied health professionals, researchers, educators, information technology managers, and vendors. Information about the association, its publications, and resources are available through this site.

HEAL*Net*/*RE*LAIS: Putting Health Research to Work
http://hiru.mcmaster.ca/nce/default.htm
The site is that of a national group of researchers who focus on enhancing the use and utility of information in health-care decision making at all levels.

Health Canada
www.hc-sc.gc.ca
The federal government site that links directly to Health Canada.

Health on the Net
www.hon.ch
Created in 1995, Health on the Net is a not-for-profit international Swiss organization. Its mission is to guide lay persons or nonmedical users and medical practitioners to useful and reliable online medical and health information.

National Nursing Informatics Project
http://206.191.29.104/pages/resources/nni/nnicausn.htm
The site provides an overview of the project, which is designed to identify the competencies and educational requirements of nurses related to information technology.

CHAPTER 26

Nurse-Patient Relationship

OBJECTIVES

After completing this chapter, you will be able to:

- Discuss various descriptions, actions, and outcomes associated with "caring."
- Describe essential aspects of the comforting process.
- List essential aspects of communication and the communication process.
- Analyze factors influencing the communication process.
- Differentiate verbal and nonverbal communication.
- Describe four phases of the helping relationship.
- Identify features of effective groups.

Communication is a critical skill for nursing. It is the process by which humans meet their survival needs, build relationships, and experience joy. In nursing, communication is used to gather information, to teach and persuade, and to express caring and comfort. Comforting is the process by which nurses assist clients and significant others to face the distresses and discomforts they may encounter. In nursing, communication is an integral part of the helping relationship.

Caring

Caring is considered by many nurses to be an essential aspect of nursing. Madeleine Leininger (1984) states that *care* is the essence of nursing and the dominant, distinctive, and unifying feature of nursing. She says that there can be no cure without caring but that there may be caring without curing. She emphasizes that human caring, although a universal phenomenon, varies among cultures in its expressions, processes, and patterns; it is largely culturally divided.

Leininger (1984) identifies many caring constructs (see the box below). She believes that health-care personnel should work toward an understanding of care and the values, health beliefs, and lifestyles of different cultures, which will form the basis for providing culture-specific care.

Jean Watson (1985), who also believes the practice of caring is central to nursing, describes caring as grounded in a set of universal human values (kindness, concern, and love of self and others). Caring is described as the moral ideal of nursing; it involves the will to care, the intent to care, and caring actions. Caring actions include communication, positive regard, support, or physical interventions by the nurse (Watson, 1985). Gadow (1985) offers that caring is not just an interpersonal technique to which one becomes "expert." Caring involves a commitment to protect and enhance dignity in any relationship. In other words "caring as the moral ideal of nursing is concern, above all, for the dignity of patients" (Gadow, 1985, p. 32).

Miller (1995, p. 32) defines caring as "intentional action that conveys physical and emotional security and genuine connectedness with another person or group of people. Caring validates the humanness of both the care giver and the cared for."

According to Gadow (1984) and Noddings (1984), caring may or may not involve action or verbal communication. The most caring act may be nonaction as desired by the client.

Leininger's Descriptions of Care and Caring

- Caring includes assistive, supportive, and facilitative acts toward or for another individual or group with evident or anticipated needs.
- Caring serves to ameliorate or to improve human conditions or life ways. It emphasizes healthful, enabling activities of individuals and groups that are based on culturally defined, ascribed, or sanctioned helping modes.
- Caring is essential to human development, growth, and survival.
- Caring behaviours include comfort, compassion, concern, coping behaviour, empathy, enabling, facilitating, interest, involvement, health consultative acts, health instruction acts, health maintenance acts, helping behaviours, love, nurturance, presence, protective behaviours, restorative behaviours, sharing, stimulating behaviours, stress alleviation, succor, support, surveillance, tenderness, touching, and trust.

RESEARCH NOTE

How Can Nurses Show Caring While They Are Implementing Care?

The purpose of this study was to determine client and staff perceptions of the frequency and importance of "caring behaviours" by nurses. Questionnaires were administered to psychiatric, medical, and surgical clients and staff. To measure importance, researchers used an existing instrument that included 50 caring behaviours. To measure frequency of occurrence, they used an instrument with the same 50 caring behaviours and asked how often the behaviours occurred.

Clients and staff agreed fairly well about the frequency with which certain behaviours occurred. For example, they agreed that "explains and facilitates" occurred rarely, and that "monitors and follows through" occurred often. However, there was disagreement about the importance of behaviours. Psychiatric clients thought "explains and facilitates" most important; and staff in all areas thought "comfort" was most important. Both clients and staff perceived that the behaviours thought to be most important were not the ones that occurred most often (e.g., "explains and facilitates" was important but occurred rarely).

Implications: This study suggests that clients will feel cared for, and nursing care can be implemented more successfully, if nurses find out what is important to each client and use those priorities during the implementing phase of the nursing process. This means individualized care—even within the framework of standardized, multidisciplinary care plans and critical pathways.

Source: von Essen, L., & Sjoden, P. (1995). Perceived occurrence and importance of caring behaviours among patients and staff in psychiatric, medical and surgical care. *Journal of Advanced Nursing, 21*, 266–276.

The outcomes of caring are varied. Caring can promote self-actualization, promote individual growth, preserve human dignity and worth, augment self-healing, and relieve distress. Conversely, "caring" may not evoke a tangible outcome. It may not be a means to an end; it may be regarded as an end in itself. The goodness of caring is often found in the process itself—that of engagement and connection.

Comforting

Comforting is a characteristic unique to nursing and an essential aspect of caring. "Making the patient as comfortable as possible" has been a frequent nursing action since the days of Nightingale. Even though, as Donahue says (1989), nurses have always provided comfort measures that provide strength, solace, support, encouragement, hope, and assistance, the concepts of comfort and comforting have not been developed or structured for nursing science. Specifically what is involved in comforting and how comfort is provided have become the focus of research in the past decade.

The Comforting Process

Comforting is a complex process that "includes discrete, transitory actions, such as touching, or broad, longer lasting interventions, such as listening" (Morse, 1996, p. 6). The comforting process is *client led* because it occurs in response to cues presented by the client. The comforting measures provided, however, are generally *nurse controlled* in that nurses select the appropriate comfort measures and adjust them according to the needs of the client. Comfort is not merely a passive process on the part of the client, however. Clients are often actively engaged in increasing their personal comfort. In these instances, nurses support the clients' own attempts to achieve comfort. Thus, the comfort process, whenever possible, involves cooperative actions of both clients and nurses.

Comfort

The desired outcome or product of comforting is *comfort*. The origin of the word *comfort* is the Latin word *confortare*, meaning "to strengthen greatly." Comfort implies a renewal, an amplification of power or sense of control, an invigorating influence, a positive mind-set, and a readiness for action. It enables the client to perform the usual activities of daily life.

Comfort Needs

Kolcaba identifies comfort needs within four contexts: physical, psychospiritual, social, and environmental (Kolcaba, 1991, 1995a).

- *Physical comfort needs* relate to bodily sensations and the physiological problems associated with the medical diagnosis.
- *Psychospiritual comfort needs* relate to the internal awareness of self, including esteem, concept, sexuality, and meaning in one's life. They can also include the person's relationship to a higher order or being.
- *Social comfort needs* relate to interpersonal, family, and social relationships.
- *Environmental comfort needs* relate to the external background of human experience and can include light, noise, ambience, colour, temperature, and natural versus synthetic elements.

Intensity (Type) of Comfort

Three types of comfort described by Kolcaba are relief, ease, and transcendence. *Relief* from discomfort is the experience of having a specific need met. Relief may be incomplete, partial, or temporary, lasting only a short time until discomfort arises again. It enables the client to return to former functions or a peaceful death. *Ease* refers to a state of calm or peaceful contentment. This state of comfort can exist without a prior state of discomfort or may indicate complete relief from discomforts that are lasting, rather than temporary relief from severe discomforts. This state of comfort enables the client to perform activities efficiently. *Transcendence* refers to the state in which the client rises above problems or pain. This state of comfort differs from the other two states in that the client is invigorated or inspired for extraordinary performance as an end state, rather than ordinary performance, which is the end state for relief and ease. Extraordinary performance requires unusual effort to shed one's preoccupation with pain, disability, or other difficulties. For example, transcendence may be necessary when illness and injury cause a permanent change in the body, such as with clients who have debilitating arthritis and pain or a spinal cord injury.

Comfort Measures

Comfort measures may be provided both directly to the client and indirectly through other personnel, family, or environment. Examples of indirect actions include maintaining a quiet environment, coordinating the activities of other health-care personnel, and supporting the client's family members or significant others. Comfort measures are initiated when the nurse perceives client distress or discomfort or the client indicates a specific need for comforting. Because there are such diverse states of discomfort, nurses need to be creative and innovative in providing specific, individualized care. Comfort care may require simple physical actions, such as providing a warm blanket, offering a cup of tea, or applying lotion to dry skin. However, it also requires nursing knowledge and skills specific to the client's medical and nursing problems. Examples include interventions for skin breakdown, pain, infection, airway clearance, confusion, and so on. Comfort measures also encompass the client's psychospiritual,

TABLE 26.1 Communication Strategies for Providing Comfort

Characteristic	Description	Examples of the Nurse's Verbal Response
Pity	An expression of regret or sorrow *for* a client who is suffering, distressed, or unhappy; confirms the sufferer's state; facilitates acceptance of reality	"This must be really awful for you." "This is the worst kind of grief—losing a baby."
Sympathy	An expression of the nurse's *own* sorrow for the client's condition or situation; has an "I am sorry" focus; shows acceptance of the client's state, thereby providing comfort	"I feel sad for you." "I'm so sorry about the results of the biopsy."
Compassion	Expresses a strong emotional response to the client's distress; leads to sharing of the suffering; shows acceptance of the client's problem; strengthens and comforts; nurse experiences the client's pain	"It could have happened to any of us; it's nothing you did." "If you want to talk, I'm here to listen."
Consolation	Involves soothing and encouraging to ease discomfort and pain; may offer support and hope; expresses feelings of concern in nurse; can alter focus to the positive without negating crisis	***To a family member:*** "She's holding her own; she's still very sick but she's stable; this has been difficult for her." ***To a client:*** "You've done very well so far."
Commiseration	Used commonly in support groups or when the nurse has experienced the client's problem in some form; nurse and client have mutual response to a common experience; the nurse sincerely communicates agreement and understanding	"I can truly understand some of what you're going through. I had a mastectomy two years ago." "I was really scared, too, the first time I saw a baby on a respirator; I was afraid to touch anything."
Reflexive reassurance	Spontaneous reaction by the nurse to try to calm the client who feels anxiety and distress over some circumstance; the nurse's response is intended to balance the client's feelings	"You're going to be fine" (when you know the client will be). "No, I don't think you're being silly, but you know they will make sure the spinal is working before they begin the surgery."

Source: Adapted from Morse, J. M.; Bottorff, J.; Anderson, G.; O'Brien, B. & Solberg, S; 1992 Beyond empathy: Expanding expressions of caring. *Journal of Advanced Nursing, 17,* 809–821.

social, and environmental realms. Examples of psychospiritual comfort measures are talking in soothing tones, acknowledging and accepting feelings, offering presence, and encouraging decision making. Social measures may include supporting family and friends and encouraging visits by family and friends. Environmental comfort measures may involve merely opening a window or removing clutter. Table 26.1 provides examples of specific communication strategies that provide comfort.

Because the goal of any comforting measure is enhanced comfort, success in comfort care is evaluated by comparing comfort levels before and after intervention. Absolute or total comfort in a hospital setting is often not possible. Nurses are, therefore, challenged to encourage and inspire clients to rise above adversities.

Communicating

The term *communication* has various meanings depending on the context in which it is used. To some, communication is the interchange of information between two or more people; in other words, the exchange of ideas or thoughts. This kind of communication uses such methods as talking and listening or writing and reading. However, painting, dancing, and storytelling are also methods of communication. In addition, thoughts are conveyed to others not only by spoken or written words but also by gestures or body actions.

Communication may have a more personal connotation than the interchange of ideas or thoughts. It can be a transmission of feelings or a more personal and social interaction between people. In this context, communica-

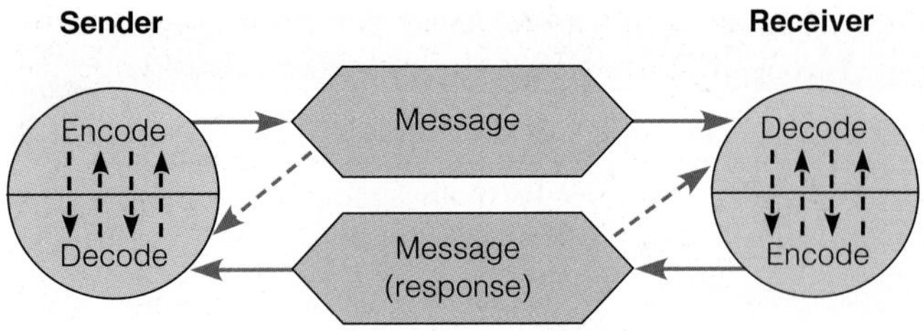

Figure 26.1 The communication process. The dashed arrows indicate intrapersonal communication (self-talk). The solid lines indicate interpersonal communication.

tion is often synonymous with relating. Frequently, one member of a couple comments that the other is not communicating. Some teenagers complain about a generation gap—being unable to communicate with understanding or feeling to a parent or authority figure. Sometimes, a nurse is said to be efficient but lacking in something called *bedside manner*. For the purpose of this text, **communication** is any means of exchanging information or feelings between two or more people. It is a basic component of human relationships, including nursing.

The intent of any communication is to elicit a response. Thus, communication is a process. It has two main purposes: (1) to influence others and (2) to obtain information. Communication can be described as helpful or unhelpful. The former encourages a sharing of information, thoughts, or feelings between two or more people. The latter hinders or blocks the transfer of information and feelings.

Nurses who communicate effectively are better able to initiate change that promotes health, establish a trusting relationship with a client and support persons, and prevent legal problems associated with nursing practice. Effective communication is essential for the establishment of a nurse-client relationship.

Communication can occur on an intrapersonal level within a single individual as well as on interpersonal and group levels. Intrapersonal communication is the communication that you have with yourself; another name is *self-talk*. Both the sender and the receiver of a message usually engage in this type of communication. It involves thinking about the message before it is sent, while it is being sent, and after it is sent, and it occurs constantly. Consequently, intrapersonal communication can interfere with a person's ability to hear a message as the sender intended.

The Communication Process

Face-to-face communication involves a sender, a message, a receiver, and a response, or feedback (Figure 26.1). Communication is a reciprocal process that involves the sending and receiving of messages between more than one individual (Balzer Riley, 2000).

In its simplest form, communication is a two-way process involving the sending and the receiving of a message. Because the intent of communication is to elicit a response, the process is ongoing; the receiver of the message then becomes the sender of a response, and the original sender then becomes the receiver.

Sender

The *sender*, a person or group who wishes to convey a message to another, can be considered the *source-encoder*. This term suggests that the person or group sending the message must have an idea or reason for communicating (source) and must put the idea or feeling into a form that can be transmitted. **Encoding** involves the selection of specific signs or symbols (codes) to transmit the message, such as which language and words to use, how to arrange the words, and what tone of voice and gestures to use. For example, if the receiver speaks English, the sender usually selects English words. If the message is "Mr. Johnson, smoking is not permitted in patient rooms in this hospital," the tone of voice selected will be one of firmness, and a shake of the head or a pointing index finger can reinforce it. The nurse must not only deal with dialects and foreign languages but also must cope with two language levels—the layperson's and the health professional's.

Message

The second component of the communication process is the *message* itself—what is actually said or written, the body language that accompanies the words, and how the message is transmitted. The medium used to convey the message is the channel, and it can target any of the receiver's senses. It is important for the channel to be appropriate for the message, and it should help make the intent of the message more clear.

Talking face-to-face with a person may be more effective in some instances than telephoning or writing a message. Recording messages on tape or communicating by radio or television may be more appropriate for larger audiences. Written communication is often appropriate for long explanations or for a communication that needs to be preserved. The nonverbal channel of touch is often highly effective (Figure 26.2).

Receiver

The *receiver*, the third component of the communication process, is the listener, who must listen, observe, and attend. This person is the *decoder*, who must perceive what the sender intended (interpretation). Perception uses all the senses to receive verbal and nonverbal messages. To **decode** means to relate the message perceived to the receiver's storehouse of knowledge and experience and to sort out the meaning of the message. Whether the message is decoded accurately by the receiver, according to the sender's intent, depends largely on their similarities in knowledge and experience and sociocultural background. If the meaning of the decoded message matches the intent

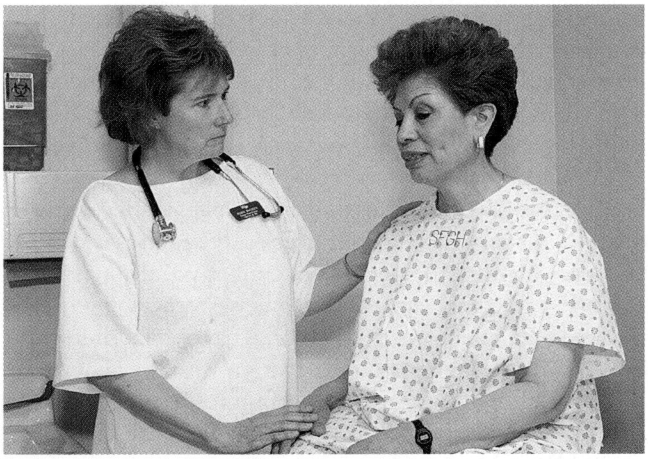

Figure 26.2 Appropriate forms of touch can communicate caring

of the sender, then the communication has been effective. Ineffective communication occurs when the message sent is misinterpreted by the receiver. For example, Mr. Johnson may perceive the message accurately—"No smoking is allowed in my room." However, if experience has taught him that he can smoke in his room if a certain nurse is on duty, he will interpret the intent of the message differently.

Response

The fourth component of the communication process, the response, is the message that the receiver returns to the sender. It is also called **feedback**. Feedback can be either verbal, nonverbal, or both. Nonverbal examples are a nod of the head or a yawn. Either way, feedback allows the sender to correct or reword a message. In the case of Mr. Johnson, the receiver may appear irritated or say, "Well, the nurse on evening shift lets me smoke." The sender then knows the message was interpreted accurately. However, now the original sender becomes the receiver, who is required to decode and respond.

Modes of Communication

Communication is generally carried out in two different modes: verbal and nonverbal. **Verbal communication** uses the spoken or written word; **nonverbal communication** uses other forms, such as gestures or facial expressions and touch. Although both kinds of communication occur concurrently, the majority of communication (some say 80 to 90 percent) is nonverbal. Learning about nonverbal communication is thus important for nurses in developing effective communication patterns and relationships with clients.

Verbal Communication

Verbal communication is largely conscious because people choose the words they use. The words used vary among individuals according to culture, socioeconomic background, age, and education. As a result, countless possibilities exist for the ways ideas are exchanged. An abundance of words can be used to form messages. In addition, a wide variety of feelings can be conveyed when people talk.

When choosing words to say or write, nurses need to consider (1) pace and intonation, (2) simplicity, (3) clarity and brevity, (4) timing and relevance, (5) adaptability, (6) credibility, and (7) humour.

Pace and Intonation The manner of speech, as in the pace or rhythm and intonation, will modify the feeling and impact of the message. The intonation can express enthusiasm, sadness, anger, or amusement. The pace of speech may indicate interest, anxiety, boredom, or fear.

Simplicity Simplicity includes the use of commonly understood words, brevity, and completeness. Many complex technical terms become natural to nurses. However, laypersons often misunderstand these terms. Words such as *vasoconstriction* or *cholecystectomy* are meaningful to the nurse and easy to use but are ill advised when communicating with clients. Nurses need to learn to select appropriate understandable terms based on the age, knowledge, culture, and education of the client. For example, instead of saying to a client, "The nurses will be catheterizing you tomorrow for a urinalysis," it may be more appropriate and understandable to say, "Tomorrow we need to get a sample of your urine, so we will collect it by putting a small tube into your bladder." The latter statement is more likely to elicit a response from the client as to why it is needed and whether it will be uncomfortable because the client understands the message being conveyed by the nurse.

Clarity and Brevity A message that is direct and simple will be more effective. Clarity is saying precisely what is meant and brevity is using the fewest words necessary. The result is a message that is simple and clear. An aspect of this is congruence, or consistency, in which the nurse's behaviour or nonverbal communication matches the words spoken. When the nurse tells the client, "I am interested in hearing what you have to say," the nonverbal behaviour would include the nurse facing the client, making eye contact, and leaning forward. The goal is to communicate clearly so that all aspects of a situation or circumstance are understood. To ensure clarity in communication, nurses also need to speak slowly and enunciate carefully.

Timing and Relevance No matter how clearly or simply words are stated or written, the timing needs to be appropriate to ensure that words are heard. Moreover, the messages need to relate to the person or to the person's interests and concerns.

Nurses need to be aware of both relevance and timing when communicating with clients. This involves sensitivity to the client's needs and concerns. For example, a client who is enmeshed in fear of cancer may not hear the nurse's explanations about the expected procedures before and after gallbladder surgery. In this situation, it is better for the nurse first to encourage the client to express concerns, and then to deal with those concerns. The necessary explanations can be provided at another time when the client is able to listen.

Another problem in timing is asking several questions at once. For example, a nurse enters a client's room and says in one breath, "Good morning, Mrs. Brody. How are you this morning? Did you sleep well last night? Your husband is coming to see you before your surgery, isn't he?" The client no doubt wonders which question to answer first, if any. A related pattern of poor timing is to ask a question and then not wait for an answer before making another comment.

Adaptability Spoken messages need to be altered in accordance with behavioural cues from the client. This adjustment is referred to as *adaptability.* What the nurse says and how it is said must be individualized and carefully considered. This requires astute assessment and sensitivity on the part of the nurse. For example, a nurse who usually smiles, appears cheerful, and greets the client every afternoon with an enthusiastic "Hi, Mrs. Brown!" notices that she is not smiling and appears distressed. It is important for the nurse to modify tone of speech and express concern in facial expression while moving toward her.

Credibility *Credibility* means "worthiness of belief, trustworthiness, reliability." Credibility may be the most important criterion of effective communication. Nurses foster credibility by being consistent, dependable, and honest. The nurse needs to be knowledgeable about what is being discussed and to have accurate information. Nurses should convey confidence and certainty in what they are saying while being able to acknowledge their limitations. "I don't know the answer to that, but I will find someone who does."

Humour The use of humour can be a positive and powerful tool in the nurse-client relationship, but it must be used with care. Humour can be used to help clients adjust to difficult and painful situations. The physical act of laughter can be both an emotional and physical release, reducing tension by providing a different perspective and promoting a sense of well-being.

Nonverbal Communication

Nonverbal communication is sometimes called *body language.* It includes gestures, body movements, use of touch, and physical appearance, including adornment. Nonverbal communication often tells others more about what a person is *feeling* than what is actually said does because nonverbal behaviour is controlled less consciously than verbal behaviour. Nonverbal communication either reinforces or contradicts what is said verbally. For example, if a nurse says to a client, "I'd be happy to sit here and talk to you for a while" and yet glances nervously at a watch every few seconds, the actions contradict the verbal message. The client is more likely to believe the nonverbal behaviour which conveys "I am very busy and need to leave."

Observing and interpreting the client's nonverbal behaviour is an essential skill for nurses to develop. To observe nonverbal behaviour efficiently requires a systematic assessment of the person's overall physical appearance, posture, gait, facial expressions, and gestures. Whatever is observed, the nurse needs to exercise caution in interpretation, always clarifying any observation with the client.

Transculturally, nonverbal communication varies widely. Even in such behaviours as smiling and handshaking, cultures differ. For example, to many Hispanics, smiling and handshaking are an integral part of an interaction and essential to establishing trust. The same behaviour might be perceived by a Russian as insolent and frivolous.

The nurse cannot always be sure of the correct interpretation of the feelings expressed nonverbally. The same feeling can be expressed nonverbally in more than one way, even within the same cultural group. For example, anger may be communicated by aggressive or excessive body motion, or it may be communicated by frozen stillness. In some cultures, a smile may be used to conceal anger. Therefore, the interpretation of such observations requires validation with the client. For example, the nurse might say, "You look like you have been crying. Is something upsetting you?"

Personal Appearance Clothing and adornments can be rich sources of information about a person. Although choice of apparel is highly personal, it may convey social and financial status, culture, religion, group association, and self-concept. Charms and amulets may be worn for decorative or for health protection purposes. When the symbolic meaning of an object is unfamiliar, the nurse can inquire about its significance, which may foster rapport with the client.

How a person dresses is often an indicator of how the person feels. Someone who is tired or ill may not have the energy or the desire to maintain normal grooming. When a person known for immaculate grooming becomes lax about appearance, the nurse may suspect a loss of self-esteem or a physical illness. The nurse must validate these observed nonverbal data by asking the client. For acutely ill clients in hospital or home care settings, a change in grooming habits may signal that the client is feeling better. A man may request a shave or a woman may request a shampoo and some makeup.

Posture and Gait The ways people walk and carry themselves are often reliable indicators of self-concept, current mood, and health. Erect posture and an active, purposeful stride suggest a feeling of well-being. Slouched posture and a slow, shuffling gait suggest depression or physical discomfort. Tense posture and a rapid, determined gait suggest anxiety or anger. The posture of people when they are sitting or lying can also indicate feelings or mood. Again, the nurse clarifies the meaning of the observed behaviour by describing to the client what the nurse sees and then asking what it means or whether the nurse's interpretation is correct. For example, "You look like it really hurts you to move. I'm wondering how your pain is and if you might need something to make you more comfortable?"

Facial Expression No part of the body is as expressive as the face (Figure 26.3). Feelings of surprise, fear, anger, disgust, happiness, and sadness can be conveyed by facial expressions. Although the face may express the person's genuine emotions, it is also possible to control these muscles so the emotion expressed does not reflect what the person is feeling. When the message is not clear, it is important to get feedback to be sure of the intent of the expression. Many facial expressions convey a universal meaning. The smile expresses happiness. Contempt is conveyed by the mouth turned down, the head tilted back, and the eyes directed down the nose. No single expression can be interpreted accurately, however, without considering other reinforcing physical cues, the setting in which it occurs, the expression of others in the same setting, and the cultural background of the client.

Nurses need to be aware of their own expressions and what they are communicating to others. Clients are quick to notice the nurse's facial expression, particularly when the client feels unsure or uncomfortable. The client who questions the nurse about a feared diagnostic result will watch whether the nurse maintains eye contact or looks away when answering. The client who has had disfiguring surgery will examine the nurse's face for signs of disgust. It is impossible to control all facial expression, but the nurse must learn to control expressions of feelings like fear or disgust in some circumstances.

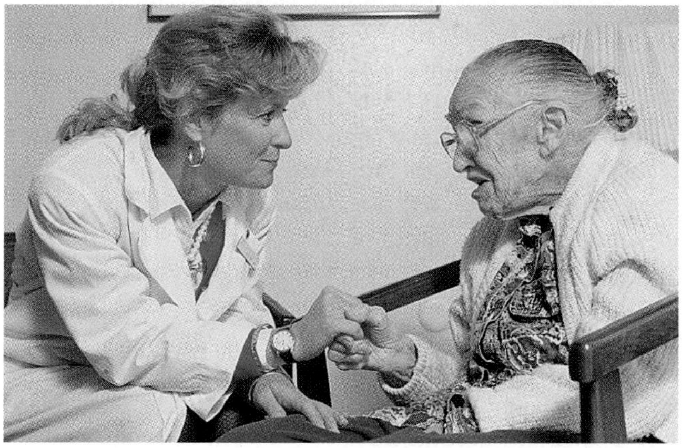

Figure 26.3 The nurse's facial expression communicates warmth and caring

Eye contact is another essential element of facial communication. In many cultures, mutual eye contact acknowledges recognition of the other person and a willingness to maintain communication. Often, a person initiates contact with another person with a glance, capturing the person's attention prior to communicating. A person who feels weak or defenceless often averts the eyes or avoids eye contact; the communication received may be too embarrassing or too dominating. See Chapter 14 for ethnic and cultural information regarding facial expression and eye contact.

Gestures Hand and body gestures may emphasize and clarify the spoken word, or they may occur without words to indicate a particular feeling or to give a sign. A parent awaiting information about his child in surgery may wring his hands or pick his nails. A gesture may more clearly indicate the size or shape of an object. A wave good-bye or the motioning of a visitor toward a chair are gestures that have relatively universal meanings. Some gestures, however, are culture specific. The Anglo-American gesture meaning "shoo" or "go away" means "come here" or "come back" in some Asian cultures. In the Hmong culture, it is considered rude to point at something with your toe.

For people with special communication problems, such as the deaf, the hands are invaluable in communication. Many deaf people learn sign language. Ill persons who are unable to reply verbally can similarly devise a communication system using the hands. The client may be able to raise an index finger once for "yes" and twice for "no." Other signals can often be devised by the client and the nurse to denote other meanings.

Factors Influencing the Communication Process

Many factors influence the communication process. Some of these are development, gender, values and perceptions, personal space, territoriality, roles and relationships, time, environment, congruence, and attitudes.

Development

Language, psychosocial, and intellectual development moves through stages across the life span. Knowledge of a client's developmental stage will allow the nurse to modify the message accordingly. The use of dolls and games with simple language may help explain a procedure to an eight-year-old. With adolescents who have developed more abstract thinking skills, a more detailed explanation can be given, whereas a well-educated, middle-aged business executive may wish to have detailed technical information provided. Older clients are apt to have had a wider range of experiences with the health-care system, which may influence their response or understanding. With aging also come changes in vision and hearing acuity that can affect nurse-client interactions.

Gender

From an early age, females and males communicate differently. Girls tend to use language to seek confirmation, minimize differences, and establish intimacy. Boys use language to establish independence and negotiate status within a group. These differences can continue into adulthood so that the same communication may be interpreted differently by a man and a woman.

Values and Perceptions

Values are the standards that influence behaviour, and perceptions are the personal view of an event. Because each person has unique personality traits, values, and life experiences, each will perceive and interpret messages and experiences differently. For example, if the nurse draws the curtains around a crying woman and leaves her alone, the woman may interpret this as "The nurse thinks that I will upset others and that I shouldn't cry" or "The nurse respects my need to be alone." It is important for the nurse to be aware of a client's values and to validate or correct perceptions to avoid creating barriers in the nurse-client relationship.

Personal Space

Personal space is the distance people prefer in interactions with others. *Proxemics* is the study of distance between people in their interactions. Middle-class North Americans use definite distances in various interpersonal relationships, along with specific voice tones and body language. Communication, thus, alters in accordance with four distances, each with a close and a far phase, that have been described by Hall (1969):

1. Intimate: Physical contact to 0.45 m
2. Personal: 0.45–1.22 m
3. Social: 1.22–3.66 m
4. Public: 3.6 m and beyond

Intimate distance communication is characterized by body contact, heightened sensations of body heat and smell, and vocalizations that are low. Vision is intense, restricted to a small body part, and may be distorted. Intimate distance is frequently used by nurses. Examples include cuddling a baby, touching the sightless client, positioning clients, observing an incision, and restraining a toddler for an injection. It is a natural protective instinct for people to maintain a certain amount of space immediately around them, and the amount varies with individuals and cultures. When someone who wants to communicate steps too close, the receiver automatically steps back a pace or two. In their therapeutic roles, nurses often are required to violate this personal space. However, it is important for them to be aware when this will occur and to forewarn the client. In many instances, the nurse can respect (not come as close as) a person's intimate distance. In other instances, the nurse may come within intimate distance to communicate warmth and caring.

Personal distance is less overwhelming than intimate distance. Voice tones are moderate, and body heat and smell are noticed less. Physical contact, such as a handshake or touching a shoulder, is possible. More of the person is perceived at a personal distance so that nonverbal behaviours, such as body stance or full facial expressions, are seen with less distortion. Much communication between nurses and clients occurs at this distance. Examples occur when nurses are sitting with a client, giving medications, or establishing an intravenous infusion. Communication at a close personal distance can convey involvement by facilitating the sharing of thoughts and feelings. At the outer extreme of 1.22 m, however, less involvement is conveyed. Bantering and some social conversations are usually at this distance.

Social distance is characterized by a clear visual perception of the whole person. Body heat and odour are imperceptible, eye contact is increased, and vocalizations are loud enough to be overheard by others. Communication is, therefore, more formal and is limited to seeing and hearing. The person is protected and out of reach for touch or personal sharing of thoughts or feelings. Social distance allows more activity and movement back and forth. It is expedient in communicating with several people at the same time or within a short time. Examples occur when nurses make rounds or wave a greeting to someone. Social distance is important in accomplishing the business of the day. However, it is frequently misused. For example, the nurse who stands in the doorway and asks a client, "How are you today?" will receive a more noncommittal reply than the nurse who moves to a personal distance to inquire.

Public distance requires loud, clear vocalizations with careful enunciation. Although the faces and forms of people are seen at public distance, individuality is lost. Instead, the perception is of the group of people or the community.

Territoriality

Territoriality is a concept of the space and things that an individual considers as belonging to the self. Territories marked off by people may be visible to others. For example, clients in a hospital often consider their territory as bounded by the curtains around the bed unit or by the walls of a private room. This human tendency to claim territory must be recognized by all health-care workers. Clients often feel the need to defend their territory when it is invaded by others; for example, when a visitor or nurse removes a chair to use at another bed, the visitor has inadvertently violated the territoriality of the client whose chair was removed. Nurses need to obtain permission from clients to remove, rearrange, or borrow objects in their hospital area.

Roles and Relationships

The roles and the relationship between sender and receiver affect the communication process. Such roles as nursing student and instructor, client and physician, or parent and child affect the content and responses in the communication process. Choice of words, sentence structure, and tone of voice vary considerably from role to role. In addition, the specific relationship between the communicators is significant. The nurse who meets with a client for the first time communicates differently from the nurse who has previously developed a relationship with that client.

Environment

People usually communicate most effectively in a comfortable environment. Temperature extremes, excessive noise, and a poorly ventilated environment can all interfere with communication. Also, lack of privacy may interfere with a client's communication about matters the client considers private. For example, a client who is worried about the ability of his wife to care for him after discharge from hospital may not wish to discuss this concern with a nurse within hearing of other clients in the room. Environmental distraction can impair and distort communication.

Congruence

In **congruent** communication, the verbal and nonverbal aspects of the message match. Clients more readily trust the nurse when they perceive the nurse's communication as congruent. This will also help to prevent miscommunication. When teaching a client how to care for a colostomy, the nurse might say, "You won't have any problem with this." If the nurse looks worried or disgusted while saying this, the client is less likely to trust the words.

Interpersonal Attitudes

Attitudes convey beliefs, thoughts, and feelings about people and events. Attitudes are communicated convincingly and rapidly to others. Such attitudes as caring, warmth, respect, and acceptance facilitate communication, whereas condescension, lack of interest, and coldness inhibit communication.

Caring and *warmth* convey a feeling of emotional closeness, in contrast to an impersonal approach. Caring is more enduring and intense than warmth. It conveys deep and genuine concern for the person, whereas warmth conveys friendliness and consideration, shown by acts of smiling and attention to physical comforts (Brammer, 1988). Caring involves giving feelings, thoughts, skill, and knowledge. It requires psychological energy and poses the risk of gaining little in return, yet by caring, people usually reap the benefits of greater communication and understanding.

Respect is an attitude that emphasizes the other person's worth and individuality. It conveys that the person's hopes and feelings are special and unique, even though similar to others in many ways. People have a need to be different from—and, at the same time, similar to—others. Being too

Canadian Society Notes

Fact	Implications for Nursing Practice
Health is an experience constructed through relationships with others and a shared repertoire of intersubjective meanings (Labonte, 1993).	Our expanded understandings of health and the importance of relationships suggest the need for research of our relational practices.
Hartrick (2002) notes the following assumptions that hinder individuals to move beyond disease care relationships: • Practitioners engage in relationships as a "means to an end." • Relationships are helpful but not absolutely essential to the health-care process. • Communication skills are the foundation for relational practice.	To promote relationships that foster a valuing of health promotion relationships, nurses must believe that: • Relating is no longer the property of the expert practitioner. • Nurses, in assuming that relational practice is dispensable, ignore the influence that relationship is having on health and health promotion. • The attributes of human relating extend far deeper into human experience than behavioural skills and require an appreciation of people's connectedness, relational awareness, and an interest in the movement of relationship.
Nurse-patient interactions involve negotiation and engagement in order to determine agendas and boundaries needed for therapeutic relationships (May & Purkis, 1995).	Nurse-patient relationships are discovered, defined, and negotiated. Each relationship is unique and, therefore, is an open forum for discovery and change. By embracing negotiation as a necessary condition of therapeutic relationships, both novices and advanced nurses will enhance their nursing practice.

different can be isolating and threatening. A nurse conveys respect by listening open-mindedly to what the other person is saying, even if the nurse disagrees. Nurses can learn new ways of approaching situations when they conscientiously listen to another person's perspective.

Acceptance emphasizes neither approval nor disapproval. The nurse willingly receives the client's honest feelings and actions without judgement. An accepting attitude allows clients to express personal feelings freely and to be themselves. The nurse may need to restrict acceptance in situations where clients' actions are harmful to themselves or to others.

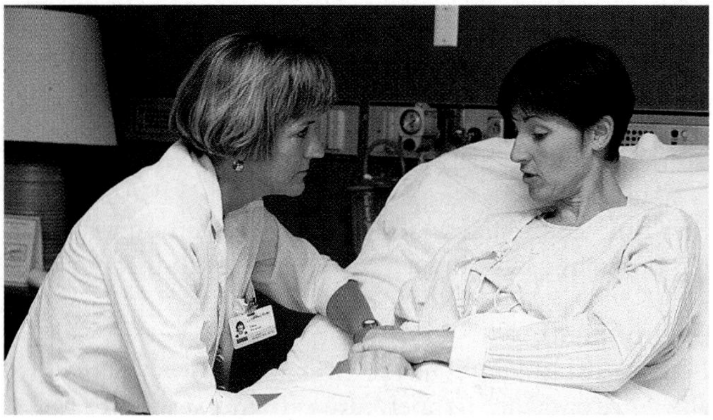

Figure 26.4 The nurse conveys attentive listening and actions of physical attending

Therapeutic Communication

Therapeutic communication promotes understanding and can help establish a constructive relationship between the nurse and the client. Unlike the social relationship, where there may not be a specific purpose or direction, the therapeutic helping relationship is client and goal directed.

Nurses need to respond not only to the content of a client's verbal message but also to the feelings expressed. It is important to understand how the client views the situation and feels about it before responding. The content of the client's communication is the words or thoughts, as distinct from the feelings. Sometimes, people can convey a thought in words while their emotions contradict the words; that is, words and feelings are incongruent. For example, a client says, "I am glad my spouse has left me; my spouse was very cruel." However, the nurse observes that the client is in tears as this is said. To respond to the client's *words*, the nurse might simply rephrase, saying "You are pleased that your spouse has left you." To respond to the client's *feelings*, the nurse would need to acknowledge the tears in the client's eyes, saying, for example, "You seem saddened by all this." Such a response helps the client to focus on feelings. In some instances, the nurse may need to know more about the client and resources for coping with these feelings.

Sometimes, clients need time to deal with their feelings. Strong emotions are often draining. People usually need to deal with feelings before they can cope with other matters, such as learning new skills or planning for the future. This is most evident in hospitals when clients learn that they have a terminal illness. Some require hours, days, or even weeks before they are ready to start other tasks. Some need only time to themselves, others need someone to listen, others need assistance identifying and verbalizing feelings, and others need assistance making decisions about future courses of action.

Attentive Listening

Attentive listening is listening actively using all the senses, as opposed to listening passively with just the ear. It is probably the most important technique in nursing and is basic to all other techniques. Attentive listening is an active process that requires energy and concentration. It involves paying attention to the total message, both verbal and nonverbal, and noting whether these communications are congruent. Attentive listening means absorbing both the content and the feeling the person is conveying without selectivity. The listener does not select or listen solely to what the listener wants to hear; the nurse focuses not on the nurse's own needs but, rather, on the client's needs. Attentive listening conveys an attitude of caring and interest, thereby encouraging the client to talk.

Attentive listening also involves listening for key themes in the communication. The nurse must be careful not to react quickly to the message. The speaker should not be interrupted and the nurse (the responder) should take time to think about the message before responding. As a listener, the nurse also should ask questions either to obtain additional information or to clarify.

Nurses need to be aware of their own biases. A message that reflects different values or beliefs should not be discredited for that reason. Rondeau (1992) suggests that the message sender (i.e., the client) should decide when to close a conversation. When the nurse closes the conversation, the client may assume that the nurse considers the message unimportant.

In summary, attentive listening is a highly developed skill, but, fortunately, it can be learned with practice. A nurse can convey attentiveness in listening to clients in various ways. Common responses are nodding the head, uttering "uh huh" or "mmm," repeating the words that the client has used, or saying "I see what you mean." Each nurse has characteristic ways of responding, and the nurse must take care not to sound insincere or phony.

Physical Attending

Egan (2002) has outlined five specific ways to convey physical attending, which he defines as the manner of being present to another or being with another. Listening, in

Actions of Physical Attending

- *Face the other person squarely.* This position says, "I am available to you." Moving to the side lessens the degree of involvement.
- *Adopt an open posture.* The nondefensive position is one in which neither arms nor legs are crossed. It conveys that the person wishes to encourage the passage of communication, as the open door of a home or an office does.
- *Lean toward the person.* People move naturally toward one another when they want to say or hear something—by moving to the front of a class, by moving a chair nearer a friend, or by leaning across a table with arms propped in front. The nurse conveys involvement by leaning forward, closer to the client.
- *Maintain good eye contact.* Mutual eye contact, preferably at the same level, recognizes the other person and denotes willingness to maintain communication. Eye contact neither glares at nor stares down another but is natural.
- *Try to be relatively relaxed.* Total relaxation is not feasible when the nurse is listening with intensity, but the nurse can show relaxation by taking time in responding, allowing pauses as needed, balancing periods of tension with relaxation, and using gestures that are natural.

These five attending postures need to be adapted to the specific needs of clients in a given situation. For example, leaning forward may not be appropriate at the beginning of an interview. It may be reserved until a closer relationship develops between the nurse and the client. The same applies to eye contact, which is generally uninterrupted when the communicators are very involved in the interaction.

his frame of reference, is what a person does while attending. The five actions of physical attending, which convey a "posture of involvement," are described in the box above.

Therapeutic communication techniques facilitate communication and focus on the client's concerns (Table 26.2). Techniques that specifically focus on comforting a client are shown in Table 26.1 on page 483.

Barriers to Communication

Nurses need to recognize barriers or nontherapeutic responses to effective communication. See Table 26.3. Failure to listen, improperly decoding the client's intended message, and placing the nurse's needs above the client's needs are major barriers to communication.

The Helping Relationship

Nurse-client relationships are referred to by some as *interpersonal relationships*, by others as *therapeutic relationships*, and by still others as *helping relationships*. Helping is a growth facilitating process that strives to achieve two basic goals (Egan, 1998):

1. Help clients manage their problems in living more effectively and develop unused or underused opportunities more fully.
2. Help clients become better at helping themselves in their everyday lives.

A helping relationship may develop over weeks of working with a client, or over minutes. The keys to the helping relationship are (1) the development of trust and acceptance between the nurse and the client, and (2) an underlying belief that the nurse cares about and wants to help the client.

The helping relationship is influenced by the personal and professional characteristics of the nurse and the client. Age, gender, appearance, diagnosis, education, values, ethnic and cultural background, personality, expectations, and setting can all affect the development of the nurse-client relationship. Consideration of all these factors, combined with good communication skills and sincere interest in the client's welfare, will enable the nurse to create a helping relationship.

Characteristics of helping relationships are named in the box below.

Characteristics of a Helping Relationship

A helping relationship:

- Is an intellectual and emotional bond between the nurse and the client and is focused on the client.
- Respects the client as an individual, including
  a. Maximizing the client's abilities to participate in decision making and treatments
  b. Considering ethnic and cultural aspects
  c. Considering family relationships and values.
- Respects client confidentiality.
- Focuses on the client's well-being.
- Is based on mutual trust, respect, and acceptance.

TABLE 26.2 Therapeutic Communication Techniques

Technique	Description	Examples
Using silence	Accepting pauses or silences that may extend for several seconds or minutes without interjecting any verbal response.	Sitting quietly (or walking with the client) and waiting attentively until the client is able to put thoughts and feelings into words.
Providing general leads	Using statements or questions that (1) encourage the client to verbalize; (2) choose a topic of conversation; and (3) facilitate continued verbalization.	"Perhaps you would like to talk about…" "Would it help to discuss your feelings?" "Where would you like to begin?" "And then what?" "Tell me more...."
Being specific and tentative	Making statements that are specific, rather than general, and tentative, rather than absolute.	"You scratched my arm." (specific statement) NOT: "You are as clumsy as an ox." (general statement) "You seem unconcerned about Mary." (tentative statement) NOT: "You don't care about her and you never will." (absolute statement)
Using open-ended questions	Asking broad questions that lead or invite the client to explore (elaborate, clarify, describe, compare, or illustrate) thoughts or feelings. Open-ended questions specify only the topic to be discussed and invite answers that are longer than one or two words.	"I'd like to hear more about that." "Tell me about …." "How have you been feeling lately?" "What brought you to the hospital?" "What is your opinion?" "You said you were frightened yesterday. How do you feel now?"
Using touch	Providing appropriate forms of touch to reinforce caring feelings. Because tactile contacts vary considerably among individuals, families, and cultures, the nurse must be sensitive to the differences in attitudes and practices of clients and self.	Putting an arm over the client's shoulder, with permission. Placing your hand over the client's hand, with permission.
Restating or paraphrasing	Actively listening for the client's basic message and then repeating those thoughts and/or feelings in similar words. This conveys that the nurse has listened and understood the client's basic message and also offers clients a clearer idea of what they have said.	*Client*: "I couldn't manage to eat any dinner last night—not even the dessert." *Nurse*: "You had difficulty eating yesterday." *Client*: "Yes, I was very upset after my family left." *Client*: "I have trouble talking to strangers." *Nurse*: "You find it difficult talking to people you do not know?"
Seeking clarification	A method of making the client's *broad overall* meaning of the message more understandable. It is used when paraphrasing is difficult or when the communication is rambling or garbled. To clarify the message, the nurse can restate the basic message or confess confusion and ask the client to repeat or restate the message.	"I'm puzzled." "I'm not sure I understand that." "Would you please say that again?" "Would you tell me more?"
	Nurses can also clarify their own message with statements.	"I meant this rather than that." "I guess I didn't make that clear—I'll go over it again."

TABLE 26.2 Therapeutic Communication Techniques *continued*

Technique	Description	Examples
Perception checking or seeking consensual validation	A method similar to clarifying that verifies the meaning of *specific words,* rather than the overall meaning of a message.	*Client*: "My husband *never* gives me any presents." *Nurse*: "You mean he has *never* given you a present for your birthday or Christmas?" *Client*: "Well—not *never.* He does get me something for my birthday and Christmas, but he never thinks of giving me anything at any other time."
Offering self	Suggesting one's presence, interest, or wish to understand the client without making any demands or attaching conditions that the client must comply with to receive the nurse's attention.	"I'll stay with you until your daughter arrives." "We can sit here quietly for a while; we don't need to talk unless you would like to." "I'll help you to dress to go home."
Giving information	Providing, in a simple and direct manner, specific factual information the client may or may not request. When information is not known, the nurse states this and indicates who has it or when the nurse will obtain it.	"Your surgery is scheduled for 11 a.m. tomorrow." "You will feel a pulling sensation when the tube is removed from your abdomen." "I do not know the answer to that, but I will find out from Mrs. King, the nurse in charge."
Acknowledging	Giving recognition, in a nonjudgmental way, of a change in behaviour, an effort the client has made, or a contribution to a communication. Acknowledgment may be with or without understanding, verbal or nonverbal.	"You trimmed your beard and mustache and washed your hair." "I notice you keep squinting your eyes. Are you having difficulty seeing?" "You walked twice as far today with your walker."
Clarifying time or sequence	Helping the client clarify an event, situation, or happening in relationship to time.	*Client*: "I vomited this morning." *Nurse*: "Was that after breakfast?" *Client*: "I feel that I have been asleep for weeks." *Nurse*: "You had your operation Monday, and today is Tuesday."
Presenting reality	Helping the client to differentiate the real from the unreal.	"That telephone ring came from the program on television." "That's not a dead mouse in the corner; it is a discarded washcloth." "Your magazine is here in the drawer. It has not been stolen."
Focusing	Helping the client expand on and develop a topic of importance. It is important for the nurse to wait until the client finishes stating the main concerns before attempting to focus. The focus may be an idea or a feeling; however, the nurse often emphasizes a feeling to help the client recognize an emotion disguised behind words.	*Client*: "My wife says she will look after me, but I don't think she can, what with the children to take care of, and they're always after her about something—clothes, homework, what's for dinner that night." *Nurse:* "You are worried about how well she can manage."
Reflecting	Directing ideas, feelings, questions, or content back to clients to enable them to explore their own ideas and feelings about a situation.	*Client*: "What can I do?" *Nurse*: "What do you think would be helpful?" *Client*: "Do you think I should tell my husband?" *Nurse*: "You seem unsure about telling your husband."

→

TABLE 26.2 Therapeutic Communication Techniques *continued*

Technique	Description	Examples
Summarizing and planning	Stating the main points of a discussion to clarify the relevant points discussed. This technique is useful at the end of an interview or to review a health teaching session. It often acts as an introduction to future care planning.	"During the past half hour we have talked about..." "Tomorrow afternoon we may explore this further." "In a few days I'll review what you have learned about the actions and effects of your insulin."

Phases of the Helping Relationship

The helping relationship process can be described in terms of four sequential phases, each characterized by identifiable tasks and skills. The relationship must progress through the stages in succession because each builds on the one before. Nurses can identify the progress of a relationship by understanding these phases: preinteraction phase, introductory phase, working (maintaining) phase, and termination phase. Table 26.4 on page 497 summarizes the tasks and skills required.

Preinteraction Phase

The preinteraction phase is similar to the planning stage before an interview. In most situations, the nurse has information about the client before the first face-to-face meeting. Such information may include the client's name, address, age, medical history, and/or social history. Planning for the initial visit may generate some anxious feelings in the nurse. If the nurse recognizes these feelings and identifies specific information to be discussed, positive outcomes can evolve.

Introductory Phase

The introductory phase, also referred to as the *orientation phase* or the *prehelping phase*, is important because it sets the tone for the rest of the relationship. During this initial encounter, the client and the nurse closely observe each other and form judgements about the other's behaviour. The three stages of this introductory phase are opening the relationship, clarifying the problem, and structuring and formulating the contract (Brammer, 1988). Other important tasks of the introductory phase include getting to know each other and developing a degree of trust.

After introductions, the nurse may initially engage in some social interaction to put the client at ease. For example, the nurse and client may talk about what a nice day it is and what they would like to do if at home.

During the initial parts of the introductory phase, the client may display some resistive behaviours. *Resistive behaviours* are those that inhibit involvement, cooperation, or change. They may be due to difficulty in acknowledging the need for help and, thus, a dependent role, fear of exposing and facing feelings, anxiety about the discomfort involved in changing problem-causing behaviour patterns, and fear or anxiety in response to the nurse's approach, which may, in the client's opinion, be inappropriate.

Resistive behaviours can be overcome by conveying a caring attitude, genuine interest in the client, and competence. These behaviours of the nurse also foster the development of trust in the relationship. *Trust* can be described as a reliance on someone without doubt or question, or the belief that the other person is capable of assisting in times of distress and, in all likelihood, will do so. To trust another person involves risk; clients become vulnerable when they share thoughts, feelings, and attitudes with the nurse. Trust, however, enables the client to express thoughts and feelings openly.

By the end of the introductory phase, clients should begin to:

- Develop trust in the nurse.
- View the nurse as a competent professional capable of helping.
- View the nurse as honest, open, and concerned about their welfare.
- Believe the nurse will try to understand and respect their cultural values and beliefs.
- Believe the nurse will respect client confidentiality.
- Feel comfortable talking with the nurse about feelings and other sensitive issues.
- Understand the purpose of the relationship and the roles.
- Feel that they are active participants in developing a mutually agreeable plan of care.

Working Phase

During the working phase of a helping relationship, the nurse and the client begin to view each other as unique individuals. They begin to appreciate this uniqueness and care about each other. *Caring* is sharing deep and genuine concern about the welfare of another person. Once caring develops, the potential for empathy increases.

TABLE 26.3 Barriers to Communication

Barrier	Description	Examples
Stereotyping	Offering generalized and oversimplified beliefs about groups of people that are based on experiences too limited to be valid. These responses categorize clients and negate their uniqueness as individuals.	"Two-year-olds are brats." "Women are complainers." "Men don't cry." "Most people don't have any pain after this type of surgery."
Agreeing and disagreeing	Akin to judgmental responses, agreeing and disagreeing imply that the client is either right or wrong and that the nurse is in a position to judge this. These responses deter clients from thinking through their position and may cause a client to become defensive.	*Client*: "I don't think Dr. Broad is a very good doctor. He doesn't seem interested in his patients." *Nurse*: "Dr. Broad is head of the Department of Surgery and is an excellent surgeon."
Being defensive	Attempting to protect a person or health-care services from negative comments. These responses prevent the client from expressing true concerns. The nurse is saying, "You have no right to complain." Defensive responses protect the nurse from admitting weaknesses in the health-care services, including personal weaknesses.	*Client*: "Those night nurses must just sit around and talk all night. They didn't answer my light for over an hour." *Nurse*: "I'll have you know we literally run around on nights. You're not the only client, you know."
Challenging	Giving a response that makes clients prove their statement or point of view. These responses indicate that the nurse is failing to consider the client's feelings, making the client feel it necessary to defend a position.	*Client*: "I felt nauseated after that red pill." *Nurse*: "Surely you don't think I gave you the wrong pill?" *Client*: "I feel as if I am dying." *Nurse*: "How can you feel that way when your pulse is 60?" *Client*: "I believe my husband doesn't love me." *Nurse*: "You can't say that; why, he visits you every day."
Probing	Asking for information chiefly out of curiosity, rather than with the intent to assist the client. These responses are considered prying and violate the client's privacy. Asking "why" is often probing and places the client in a defensive position.	*Client*: "I was speeding along the street and didn't see the stop sign." *Nurse*: "Why were you speeding?" *Client*: "I didn't ask the doctor when he was here." *Nurse*: "Why didn't you?"
Testing	Asking questions that make the client admit to something. These responses permit the client only limited answers and often meet the nurse's need, rather than the client's.	"Who do you think you are?" (forces people to admit their status is only that of client) "Do you think I am not busy?" (forces the client to admit that the nurse really *is* busy)
Rejecting	Refusing to discuss certain topics with the client. These responses often make clients feel that the nurse is rejecting not only their communication but also the clients themselves.	"I don't want to discuss that. Let's talk about..." "Let's discuss other areas of interest to you rather than the two problems you keep mentioning." "I can't talk now. I'm on my way for coffee break."

→

TABLE 26.3 Barriers to Communication *continued*

Barrier	Description	Examples
Changing topics and subjects	Directing the communication into areas of self-interest, rather than considering the client's concerns, is often a self-protective response to a topic that causes anxiety. These responses imply that what the nurse considers important will be discussed and that clients should not discuss certain topics.	*Client*: "I'm separated from my wife. Do you think I should have sexual relations with another woman?" *Nurse*: "You like gardening. This sunshine is good for my roses. I have a beautiful rose garden."
Unwarranted reassurance	Using clichés or comforting statements of advice as a means to reassure the client. These responses block the fears, feelings, and other thoughts of the client.	"You'll feel better soon." "I'm sure everything will turn out all right." "Don't worry."
Passing judgement	Giving opinions and approving or disapproving responses, moralizing, or implying one's own values. These responses imply that the client *must* think as the nurse thinks, fostering client dependence.	"That's good (bad)." "You shouldn't do that." "That's not good enough." "What you did was wrong (right)."
Giving common advice	Telling the client what to do. These responses deny the client's right to be an equal partner. Note that giving *expert*, rather than common, advice is therapeutic.	*Client*: "Should I move from my home to a nursing home?" *Nurse*: "If I were you, I'd go to a nursing home where you'll get your meals cooked for you."

The working phase has two major stages: *exploring and understanding thoughts and feelings*, and *facilitating and taking action*. The nurse helps the client to explore thoughts, feelings, and actions and helps the client plan a program of action to meet pre-established goals.

Exploring and Understanding Thoughts and Feelings

The nurse requires the following skills for this phase of the helping relationship.

- *Empathetic listening and responding*. Nurses must listen attentively and communicate (respond) in ways that indicate they have listened to what was said and understand how the client feels. The nurse responds to content or feelings, or both, as appropriate. The nurse's nonverbal behaviours are also important. Nonverbal behaviours indicating empathy include moderate head nodding, a steady gaze, moderate gesturing, and little activity or body movement. According to Egan (1998, p. 73), **empathy** "can be seen as an *intellectual* process that involves understanding correctly another person's emotional state and point of view" and also as an emotional response experienced by the helper. Empathetic listening focuses on a kind of "being with" clients to develop an understanding of them and their world. This understanding, however, must also be communicated effectively to the client—an empathetic response. The end result of empathy is comforting and caring for the client and a helping, healing relationship.
- *Respect*. The nurse must show respect for the client's willingness to be available, as well as a desire to work with the client, and a manner that conveys the idea of taking the client's point of view seriously.
- *Genuineness*. Personal statements can be helpful in solidifying the rapport between the nurse and the client. The nurse might offer such comments as "I recall when I was in (a similar situation), and I felt angry about being put down." Egan (1998) outlines five behaviours that are components of genuineness. See the box on page 498. Nurses need to exercise caution when making references about themselves. These statements must be used with discretion. The extreme of matching each of the client's problems with a better story of the nurse's own is of little value to the client.
- *Concreteness*. The nurse must assist the client to be concrete and specific, rather than to speak in generalities. When the client says, "I'm stupid and clumsy," the nurse narrows the topic to the specific by pointing out, "You tripped on the scatter rug."
- *Confrontation*. The nurse points out discrepancies between thoughts, feelings, and actions that inhibit the client's self-understanding or exploration of specific areas. This is done empathetically, not judgmentally.

TABLE 26.4 Tasks and Skills for Each Phase of the Helping Relationship

Phase	Tasks	Skills
Preinteraction phase	The nurse reviews pertinent knowledge, considers potential areas of concern, and develops plans for interaction.	Recognizing limitations and seeking assistance, as required.
Introductory phase		
1. Opening the relationship	Both client and nurse identify each other by name. When the nurse initiates the relationship, it is important to explain the nurse's role to give the client an idea of what to expect. When the client initiates the relationship, the nurse needs to help the client express concerns and reasons for seeking help. Vague, open-ended questions, such as "What's on your mind today?" are helpful at this stage.	A relaxed, attending attitude to put the client at ease. It is not easy for all clients to receive help.
2. Clarifying the problem	Because the client initially may not see the problem clearly, the nurse's major task is to help clarify the problem.	Attentive listening, paraphrasing, clarifying, and other effective communication techniques discussed in this chapter. A common error at this stage is to ask too many questions of the client.
3. Structuring and formulating the contract (obligations to be met by both the nurse and client)	Nurse and client develop a degree of trust and verbally agree about (1) location, frequency, and length of meetings, (2) overall purpose of the relationship, (3) how confidential material will be handled, (4) tasks to be accomplished, and (5) duration and indications for termination of the relationship.	Communication skills listed above and ability to overcome resistive behaviours if they occur.
Working phase	Nurse and client accomplish the tasks outlined in the introductory phase, enhance trust and rapport, and develop caring.	
1. Exploring and understanding thoughts and feelings	The nurse assists the client to explore thoughts and feelings and acquires an understanding of the client. The client explores thoughts and feelings associated with problems, develops the skill of listening, and gains insight into personal behaviour.	Listening and attending skills, empathy, respect, genuineness, concreteness, self-disclosure, and confrontation. Skills acquired by the client are nondefensive listening and self-understanding.
2. Facilitating and taking action	The nurse plans programs within the client's capabilities and considers long- and short-term goals. The client needs to learn to take risks (i.e., accept that either failure or success may be the outcome). The nurse needs to reinforce successes and help the client recognize failures realistically.	Decision-making and goal-setting skills. Also, for the nurse: reinforcement skills; for the client: risk-taking.
Termination phase	Nurse and client accept feelings of loss. The client accepts the end of the relationship without feelings of anxiety or dependence.	For the nurse: summarizing skills. For the client: abilities to handle problems independently.

Components of Genuineness

- The genuine helper does not take refuge in or overemphasize the role of counsellor.
- The genuine person is spontaneous.
- The genuine person is nondefensive.
- The genuine person displays few discrepancies—that is, the person is consistent and does not think or feel one thing but say another.
- The genuine person is capable of deep self-disclosure (self-sharing) when it is appropriate.

During this first stage of the working phase, the intensity of interaction increases, and such feelings as anger, shame, or self-consciousness may be expressed. If the nurse is skilled in this stage, and if the client is willing to pursue self-exploration, the outcome is a beginning of understanding on the part of the client about behaviour and feelings.

Facilitating and Taking Action Ultimately, the client must make decisions and take action to become more effective. The responsibility for action belongs to the client. The nurse, however, collaborates in these decisions, provides support, and may offer options or information.

Termination Phase

The termination phase of the relationship is often expected to be difficult and filled with ambivalence. However, if the previous phases have evolved effectively, the client generally has a positive outlook and feels able to handle problems independently. On the other hand, because caring attitudes have developed, it is natural to expect some feelings of loss, and each person needs to develop a way of saying good-bye.

Many methods can be used to terminate relationships. Summarizing or reviewing the process can produce a sense of accomplishment. This may include sharing reminiscences of how things were at the beginning of the relationship and comparing them with how they are now. It is also helpful for both the nurse and the client to express their feelings about termination openly and honestly. Thus termination discussions need to start in advance of the termination interview. This allows time for the client to adjust to independence. In some situations, referrals are necessary, or it may be appropriate to offer an occasional standby meeting to give support as needed. Follow-up phone calls are another intervention that eases the client's transition to independence.

Developing Helping Relationships

Whatever the practice setting, the nurse establishes some type of helping relationship in which mutual goals (outcomes) are set with the client or, if the client is unable to participate, with support persons. Although special training in counselling techniques is advantageous, there are many ways of helping clients that do not require special training.

- *Listen actively.* (See the discussion of attentive listening earlier in this chapter.)
- *Help to identify what the person is feeling.* Often, clients who are troubled are unable to identify or to label their feelings and consequently have difficulty working them out or talking about them. Such responses as "You seem angry about taking orders from your boss" or "You sound as if you've been lonely since your wife died" can help clients recognize what they are feeling and talk about it.
- *Put yourself in the other person's shoes (i.e., empathize).* Communicate to the client in a way that shows an understanding of the client's *feelings* and the behaviour and *experience* underlying these feelings.
- *Be honest.* In effective relationships, nurses honestly recognize any lack of knowledge by saying, "I don't know the answer to that right now"; openly discuss their own discomfort by saying, for example, "I feel uncomfortable about this discussion"; and admit tactfully that problems do exist, for instance, when a client says, "I'm a mess, aren't I?"
- *Be genuine.* Clients will sense whether or not the nurse is truly concerned.
- *Use your ingenuity.* There are always many courses of action to consider in handling problems. Whatever course is chosen needs to further the achievement of the client's goals (outcomes), be compatible with the client's value system, and offer the probability of success.
- *Be aware of cultural differences* that may affect meaning and understanding. See Chapter 14. To facilitate nurse-client interaction, recognize the language(s) and/or dialect(s) the client uses. Provide a bilingual interpreter as needed for clients limited in the use of the English language.
- *Maintain client confidentiality.* To maintain the client's right to privacy, share information only with other health-care professionals as needed for effective care and treatment.
- *Know your role and your limitations.* Every person has unique strengths and problems. When you feel unable to handle some problems, the client should be informed and referred to the appropriate health-care professional. Clarify functions and roles, specifically what is expected of the client, the nurse, and the physician.

Group Communication

People are born into a group (i.e., a family) and interact with others at all stages of life in various groups: peer groups, work groups, recreational groups, religious groups, and so on. A **group** is two or more people who have shared needs and goals, who take each other into account in their actions and who, thus, are held together and set apart from others by virtue of their interactions. Groups exist to help people achieve goals (outcomes) that would be unattainable by individual effort alone. For example, groups can often solve problems more effectively than one person by pooling the ideas and expertise of several individuals; in addition, information can be disseminated to groups more quickly than to individuals.

Group Dynamics

The communication that takes place between members of any group is known as **group dynamics.** The manner of this communication will be determined by a number of interrelated factors and variables. Members of the group will have an effect on the group dynamics on the basis of their motivation for participating and their similarity to other group members and the goal of that group.

The unique dynamics of each group will influence its maturation or group process, as well as the effectiveness of the group. Three main functions are required for any group to be effective. It must maintain a degree of group unity or cohesion. It needs to develop and modify its structure to improve its effectiveness. And, it must accomplish its goals. The characteristics of an effectively functioning group are shown in Table 26.5.

Types of Health-Care Groups

Much of a nurse's professional life is spent in a wide variety of groups, ranging from *dyads* (two-person groups) to large professional organizations. As a participant in a group, the nurse may be required to fulfill different roles: member or leader, teacher or learner, adviser or advisee, and so on.

Common types of health-care groups include task groups, teaching/learning groups, self-help groups, self-awareness/growth groups, therapy groups, and work-related social support groups. There are similarities and differences among the characteristics of these various types of groups and the nurse's role.

Task Groups

The task group is one of the most common types of work-related groups to which nurses belong. Examples are health-care planning committees, nursing service committees, nursing team meetings, nursing care conference groups, and hospital staff meetings. The focus of such groups is the completion of a specific task, and the format is defined at the outset by the leader and/or members. The methods vary according to the task to be performed.

The leader of a task group, usually called the *chairperson,* must be accepted by the members as an appropriate leader and, therefore, should be an expert in the area of task emphasis. The chairperson's role is to identify the specific task, clarify communication, and assist in expressing opinions and offering solutions. *Committee members* are generally selected in terms of their individual functional role and employment status rather than in terms of their personal characteristics. Member participation is determined by the task. A target date for termination of the group is usually set in advance.

Teaching/Learning Groups

The major purpose of teaching/learning groups is to impart information to the participants. Examples of teaching groups include continuing education and client health-care groups. Numerous subjects are often handled via the group teaching format: childbirth techniques, birth control methods, effective parenting, nutrition, management of chronic illness, such as diabetes, exercise for middle-aged and older adults, and instructions to family members about follow-up care for discharged clients. A nurse who leads a group in which the primary purpose is to teach or learn must be skilled in the teaching-learning process discussed in Chapter 29.

Self-Help Groups

A self-help group is a small, voluntary organization composed of individuals who share a similar health, social, or daily living problem. These groups are based on the helper-therapy principle: Those who help are helped most. One of the central beliefs of the self-help movement is that people who experience a particular social or health problem have an understanding of that condition which those without it do not.

Self-help groups are available for a range of problems (e.g., stillbirth, parenting, pregnant adolescents, divorce, drug abuse, cancer, menopause, mental illness, diabetes, acquired immune deficiency syndrome [AIDS], women's health, caregivers of elderly people, and grief). Alcoholics' Anonymous was the first self-help group. Positive aspects of self-help groups are outlined in the box on page 501.

The major functions of the nurse's role in self-help groups include the following:

- Helping clients form such groups by identifying key people who can act as facilitators

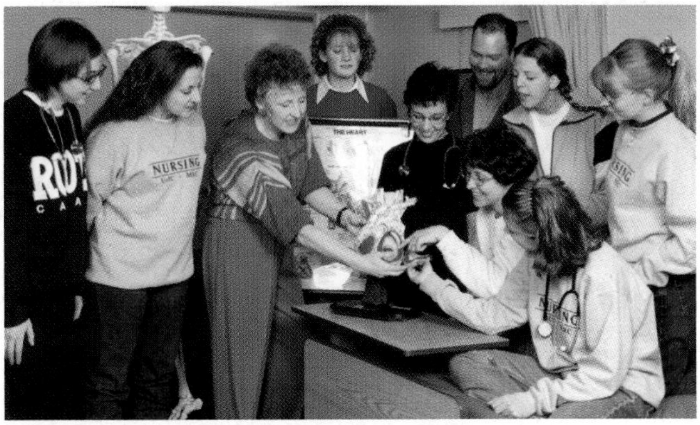

Figure 26.5 Teaching can occur within groups

TABLE 26.5 Comparative Features of Effective and Ineffective Groups

Factor	Effective Groups	Ineffective Groups
Atmosphere	Informal, comfortable, and relaxed. It is a working atmosphere in which people demonstrate their interest and involvement.	Obviously tense. Signs of boredom may appear.
Goal setting	Goals, tasks, and objectives are clarified, understood, and modified so that members of the group can commit themselves to goals structured through cooperation.	Unclear, misunderstood, or imposed goals may be accepted by members. The goals are structured through competition.
Leadership and member participation	Shift from time to time, depending on the circumstances. Different members assume leadership at various times because of their knowledge or experience.	Delegated and based on authority. The chairperson may dominate the group, or the members may defer unduly. Member participation is unequal, with high-authority members dominating.
Communication	Open and two-way. Ideas and feelings are encouraged, both about the problem and about the group's operation.	Closed or one-way. Only idea production is encouraged. Feelings are ignored or taboo. Members may be tentative or reluctant to be open and may have "hidden agendas" (personal goals at cross-purposes with group goals).
Decision making	By consensus, although various decision-making procedures appropriate to the situation may be instituted.	By the highest authority in the group, with minimal involvement by members; or an inflexible style is imposed.
Cohesion	Facilitated through high levels of inclusion, trust, liking, and support.	Either ignored or used as a means of controlling members, thus promoting rigid conformity.
Conflict tolerance	The reasons for disagreements or conflicts are carefully examined, and the group seeks to resolve them. The group accepts unresolvable basic disagreements and lives with them.	Attempts may be made to ignore, deny, avoid, suppress, or override controversy by premature group action.
Power	Determined by the members' abilities and the information they possess. Power is shared. The issue is how to get the job done.	Determined by position in the group. Obedience to authority is strong. The issue is who controls.
Problem solving	High. Constructive criticism is frequent, frank, relatively comfortable, and oriented toward removing an obstacle to problem solving.	Low. Criticism may be destructive, taking the form of either overt or covert personal attacks. It prevents the group from getting the job done.
Self-evaluation as a group	Frequent. All members participate in evaluation and decisions about how to improve the group's functioning.	Minimal. What little evaluation there is may be done by the highest authority in the group rather than by the membership as a whole.
Creativity	Encouraged. There is room within the group for members to become self-actualized and interpersonally effective.	Discouraged. People are afraid of appearing foolish if they put forth a creative thought.

Source: Wilson, H. S. & Kneisl C. R. (1996). *Psychiatric nursing* (5th ed.) (p. 736). Redwood City, CA: Addison Wesley Nursing. Used by permission.

Positive Aspects of Self-Help Groups

- Members can experience almost instant kinship because the essence of the group is the idea that "you are not alone."
- Members can talk about their feelings and listen to the concerns of others, knowing they all share this experience.
- The group atmosphere is generally one of acceptance, support, encouragement, and caring.
- Many members act as role models for newer members and can inspire them to attempt tasks they might consider impossible.
- The group provides the opportunity for people to help as well as to *be* helped—a critical component in restoring self-esteem.

- Sharing expertise with clients and helping them gain appropriate knowledge and skills
- Informing clients and support persons about existing self-help groups available to them
- Participating as a member of a self-help group when this is appropriate. The nurse's role is that of a resource person, that is, being "on tap, but not on top."
- Helping out in times of crisis

Self-Awareness/Growth Groups

The purpose of self-awareness/growth groups is to develop or use interpersonal strengths. The overall aim is to improve the person's functioning in the group to which they return, whether job, family, or community. From the beginning, broad goals are usually apparent, for example, to study communication patterns, group process, or problem solving. Because the focus of these groups is interpersonal concerns around current situations, the work of the group is oriented to reality testing with a here-and-now emphasis. Members are responsible for correcting inefficient patterns of relating and communicating with each other. They learn group process through participation and involvement and guided exercises.

Therapy Groups

Therapy groups work toward self-understanding, more satisfactory ways of relating or handling stress, and changing patterns of behaviour toward health.

Members of the therapy group are referred to as clients or, in some settings, as patients. They are selected by health-care professionals after extensive selection interviews that consider the pattern of personalities, behaviours, needs, and identification of group therapy as the treatment of choice. Duration of therapy groups is not usually set. A termination date is usually mutually determined by the therapist and members.

Work-Related Social Support Groups

Many nurses experience high levels of vocational stress, for example, hospice, emergency, and acute-care nurses. Various types of group support can buffer such stress. Group members who know about the work of others can encourage and challenge members to be more creative and enthusiastic about their work and to achieve more. For example, a nurse may help another team member consider alternative strategies for intervention. Members also can share the joys of success and the frustration of failure through active listening without giving advice or making judgements.

Communication and the Nursing Process

Communication is an integral part of the nursing process. Nurses use communication skills in each phase of the nursing process. Communication is also important when caring for clients who have communication problems.

Assessing Communication

To assess the client's communication, the nurse determines communication impairments or barriers and communication style. Remember that culture may influence when and how a client speaks. Obviously, language varies according to age and development. With children, the nurse observes sounds, gestures, and vocabulary.

Impairments to Communication

Various barriers may alter a client's ability to send, receive, or comprehend messages. These include language deficits, sensory deficits, cognitive impairments, structural deficits, and paralysis. The nurse must assess each to determine their presence.

Language Deficits Determine the client's primary language for communicating and whether a fluent interpreter is required. Some clients who use English as a second language may have language skills that are inadequate to meet their needs.

Sensory Deficits The ability to hear, see, feel, and smell are important adjuncts to communication. Deafness can significantly alter the message the client receives; impaired vision alters the ability to observe nonverbal behaviour, such as a smile or a gesture; inability to feel and smell can impair the client's capabilities to report injuries or detect the smoke from a fire. For clients with severe hearing impairments, follow these steps:

- Look for a Medic-Alert bracelet (or necklace or tag) indicating hearing loss.
- Determine whether the client wears a hearing aid and whether it is functioning.

- Observe whether the client is attempting to see your face to read lips.
- Observe whether the client is attempting to use hands to communicate with sign language.

Cognitive Impairments Any disorder that impairs cognitive functioning (e.g., cerebrovascular disease, Alzheimer's disease, and brain tumours or injuries) may affect a client's ability to use and understand language. These clients may develop total loss of speech, impaired articulation, or the inability to find or name words. Certain medications, such as sedatives, antidepressants, and neuroleptics, may also impair speech, causing the client to use incomplete sentences or to slur words.

The nurse assesses whether these clients respond when asked a question and, if so, assesses the following: Is the client's speech fluent or hesitant? Does the client use words correctly? Can the client comprehend instructions as evidenced by following directions? Can the client repeat words or phrases? In addition, the nurse assesses the client's ability to understand written words: Can the client follow written directions? Can the client respond correctly by pointing to a written word? Can the client read aloud? Can the client recognize words or letters if unable to read whole sentences? The nurse uses large, clearly written words when trying to establish abilities in this area.

When the client is unconscious, the nurse looks for any indication that suggests comprehension of what is communicated (e.g., tries to arouse the client verbally and through touch). Ask a closed question, such as "Can you hear me?" and watch for a nonverbal response, such as a nod of the head for yes or a shake for no; or ask for a hand squeeze or blink of the eye once for yes or twice for no.

Structural Deficits Structural deficits of the oral and nasal cavities and respiratory system can alter a person's ability to speak clearly and spontaneously. Examples include cleft palate, artificial airways, such as an endotracheal tube or tracheostomy, and laryngectomy (removal of the larynx). Extreme dyspnea (shortness of breath) can also impair speech patterns.

Paralysis If verbal impairment is combined with paralysis of the upper extremities that impairs the client's ability to write, the nurse should determine whether the client can point, nod, shrug, blink, or squeeze a hand. Any of these could be used to devise a communication system.

Style of Communication

In assessing communication style, the nurse considers both verbal and nonverbal communication. In addition to physical barriers, some psychological illnesses (e.g., depression or psychosis) influence the ability to communicate. The client may demonstrate constant verbalization of the same words or phrases, a loose association of ideas, or flight of ideas.

Verbal Communication When assessing verbal communication, the nurse focuses on three areas: the content of the message, the themes, and verbalized emotions. In addition, the nurse considers the following:

- Whether the communication pattern is slow, rapid, quiet, spontaneous, hesitant, evasive, and so on
- The vocabulary of the individual, particularly any changes from the vocabulary normally used. For example, a person who normally never swears may indicate increased stress or illness by an uncharacteristic use of profanity.
- The presence of hostility, aggression, assertiveness, reticence, hesitance, anxiety, or loquaciousness (incessant verbalization) in communication
- Difficulties with verbal communication, such as slurring, stuttering, inability to pronounce a particular sound, lack of clarity in enunciation, inability to speak in sentences, loose association of ideas, flight of ideas, or the inability to find or name words or identify objects
- Refusal or inability to speak

Nonverbal Communication Consider nonverbal communication in relation to the client's culture. Pay particular attention to facial expression, gestures, body movements, affect, tone of voice, posture, and eye contact.

Diagnosing Communication Problems

Impaired communication may be used as a nursing diagnosis when "an individual experiences, or could experience, a decreased ability to send or receive messages (i.e., has difficulty exchanging thoughts, ideas, or desires)" (Carpenito, 2000). The NANDA diagnosis of ***Impaired Verbal Communication*** indicates more specifically that there is or may be a decreased ability or inability to speak, although others can be understood. ***Impaired Verbal Communication*** is also used when the client is not fluent in communicating through the dominant language.

Carpenito (2000) points out that this diagnosis may not be useful when an individual's communication problems are a manifestation of a psychiatric illness or a coping problem. In those instances, the diagnoses of ***Acute*** or ***Chronic Confusion, Ineffective Coping, Anxiety,*** or ***Fear*** may be appropriate. Other nursing diagnoses used for clients experiencing communication problems that involve impaired verbal communication as the etiology could include the following:

- ***Anxiety*** related to impaired verbal communication
- ***Powerlessness*** related to impaired verbal communication
- ***Self Esteem, Chronic Low*** related to impaired verbal communication
- ***Social Isolation*** related to impaired verbal communication

Planning for Effective Communication

When a nursing diagnosis related to impaired communication has been made, the nurse and client determine goals/ outcomes and begin planning ways to promote effective communication. The overall client goal for persons with ***Impaired Verbal Communication*** is to reduce or resolve the factors impairing the communication. Specific nursing interventions will be planned from the stated etiology. Examples of outcome criteria to evaluate the effectiveness of nursing interventions and achievement of client goals follow.

The client:

- Communicates that needs are being met.
- Begins to establish a method of communication:
  a. Signals yes/no to direct questions using vocalization or agreed-upon physical cue (e.g., eye blink, hand squeeze)
  b. Uses verbal or nonverbal techniques to indicate needs
- Perceives the message accurately, as evidenced by appropriate verbal and/or nonverbal responses
- Communicates effectively:
  a. Using dominant language
  b. Using translator/interpreter
  c. Using sign language
  d. Using word board or picture board
  e. Using a computer
- Regains maximum communication abilities
- Expresses minimum fear, anxiety, frustration, and depression
- Uses resources appropriately

Implementing

When nurses interact with clients who have problems with speech or language, Boss (1991) suggests four categories of nursing interventions to facilitate communication.

Manipulate the Environment

A quiet environment with limited distractions will make the most of the communication efforts of both the client and the nurse and increase the possibility of effective communication. Sufficient light will help in conveying nonverbal messages, which is especially important if visual or auditory acuity is impaired. Initially, the nurse needs to provide a calm, relaxed environment that will help reduce any anxiety the client may have. It should be remembered that any factor that affects communication can create feelings of frustration, anxiety, depression, or hostility in the client. Communication normally contributes to clients' sense of security and feelings that they are not alone, so communication problems may cause some clients to feel isolated and confused. To further reduce these emotions, the nurse should acknowledge and praise the client's attempts at communication.

Provide Support

The nurse should convey encouragement to the client and provide nonverbal reassurance, perhaps by touch, if appropriate. If the nurse does not understand, it is critical to let the client know so that the nurse can provide clarification with other words or through some other means of communication. When speaking with a client who will have difficulty understanding, the nurse should check frequently to determine what the client has heard and understood. Using open-ended questions will help obtain accurate information about the effectiveness of communication. For example, Maria Perez, who has limited English skills, is being taught about diet related to her Crohn's disease. If the nurse asks, "Do you understand what to eat?" Maria may nod her head yes. However, this does not give her nurse confirmation that the message given has been received. Rather, the nurse needs to say, "What do you think will be good for you to eat when you go home?" The nurse's body language (e.g., gestures, posture, facial expression, and eye contact) should convey acceptance and approval.

Employ Measures to Enhance Communication

First, determine how the client can best receive messages: by listening, by looking, through touch, or through an interpreter. Ways to help communication include keeping words simple and concrete and discussing topics of interest to the client. It is often helpful to use alternative communication strategies, such as word boards, pictures, or paper and pencil.

Often, interpreters can assist a client and nurse to communicate when the client lacks fluency in the dominant language. Some hospitals have a list of interpreters for various languages who can assist at the bedside. If the client's support person offers to interpret, it is important to ask the client's permission for the sake of confidentiality. Then, instruct the person to interpret as precisely as possible, without interpretation.

Educate the Client and Support Persons

Sometimes, clients and support people can be prepared in advance for communication problems, for example, before an intubation or throat surgery. By explaining anticipated problems, the client is often less anxious when problems arise.

Evaluating Communication

Evaluation is useful for both client and nurse communication.

Client Communication

To establish whether client goals have been met in relation to communication, the nurse must listen actively, observe

FOCUS ON CRITICAL THINKING

You are the nursing student assigned to care for Mr. Manasovitz, a 45-year-old man, who will be returning from the recovery room after undergoing the removal of a mass from his abdomen. While you are preparing his room for his return, the nurse and physician arrive to talk with Mrs. Manasovitz about her husband's surgery. The physician explains that the mass was malignant and invasive. Mr. Manasovitz is a candidate for chemotherapy, but his prognosis is guarded because of the extent of the tumour growth. Mrs. Manasovitz looks away, closes her eyes, and only nods her head "yes." As the physician leaves, the nurse approaches Mrs. Manasovitz, sits next to her, and puts her arm around Mrs. Manasovitz, who begins to cry. The nurse uses a soothing voice to tell Mrs. Manasovitz that it is okay to cry and provides assurance by remaining with her. The two of them sit in silence until Mrs. Manasovitz is able to express her feelings. The nurse listens attentively. Later, the nurse offers to get a cup of coffee for Mrs. Manasovitz and offers to assist her at this difficult time.

1. Interpret Mrs. Manasovitz's nonverbal behaviour in response to the news about her husband's surgery.
2. Evaluate the nurse's response toward Mrs. Manasovitz on the basis of the concepts of caring and comforting.
3. Why is it important for the nurse to effectively communicate with Mrs. Manasovitz at this time?
4. The nurse was described as listening attentively to Mrs. Manasovitz. Cite actions that portray attentive listening.
5. Think about your past experiences when you or a family member has been ill. What relationship characteristics did you most value on the part of the nurse caring for you?

See Appendix A for answers to these questions.

nonverbal cues, and use therapeutic communication skills to determine that communication was effective. Examples of evaluative statements indicating goal achievement could be "Using picture board effectively to indicate needs" or "The client stated, 'I listened more closely to my daughter yesterday and found out how she feels about our divorce.'"

Nurse Communication

For nurses to evaluate the effectiveness of their own communication with clients, process recordings are frequently used. A **process recording** is a verbatim (word-for-word) account of a conversation. It can be taped or written and includes all verbal and nonverbal interactions of both the client and nurse.

TABLE 26.6 Sample Process Recording

Mary Jane Adams, a nursing aide, reports to Irene Olsen, the staff nurse, that Sandra Barrett, the client in room 815, had finished only her orange juice when Ms. Adams collected the breakfast trays. Mrs. Barrett had been admitted two days earlier for diagnostic studies. Concerned about the client, Ms. Olsen walks down the corridor to room 815, knocks, and enters. Mrs. Barrett turns away from the window, tears in her eyes, as Ms. Olsen enters.

Nurse/Client Dialogue	Communication Skill
NURSE: Good morning, Mrs. Barrett. CLIENT: Hello.	Acknowledging
NURSE: I understand you didn't eat your breakfast. CLIENT: I wasn't hungry.	Making a specific statement, but ignoring the nonverbal
NURSE: Is something wrong? CLIENT: No. (Eyes fill with tears.)	Asking a closed question that fails to facilitate exploration
NURSE: You look sad, as if you're about to cry. CLIENT: (Cries)	Giving feedback
NURSE: I'll sit here a while with you. (Sits down.) CLIENT: (Continues to cry.)	Offering self

TABLE 26.6 Sample Process Recording *continued*

Nurse/Client Dialogue	Communication Skill
NURSE: (After a 30-second pause) Sometimes it's hard to share the things you're concerned about with someone you don't know well. I'd like to be able to help.	Using silence, Empathizing, Supporting, Offering self
CLIENT: (Angrily) You can help me by telling me the truth.	
NURSE: (Leans forward and maintains eye contact.)	Actively listening and demonstrating interest
CLIENT: Everyone beats around the bush when I ask them what's wrong with me. The head nurse said, "What do *you* think is wrong?" That kind of put-off drives me up the wall!	
NURSE: You're angry because you're not getting any answers. It seems as if the staff knows something about your condition and they're keeping it from you.	Paraphrasing
CLIENT: They all seem to be in cahoots. Nobody tells me anything. (Pause) (Softly) If the news was good, they wouldn't beat around the bush.	
NURSE: I'm wondering if you're worried that because people haven't answered your question it means that you have a serious illness?	Paraphrasing
CLIENT: Good news is always easy to give.	
NURSE: Yes, people do seem to be able to deliver good news easier and faster. I also know that we don't have any news—good or bad—to give you because none of the laboratory or x-ray results are back yet. I know that doesn't help answer your questions, but I hope it relieves you a bit from worrying that there is some bad news that's being withheld.	Giving information Supporting
CLIENT: Well, when my father-in-law had surgery for a bleeding ulcer, the x-ray and laboratory results were available immediately.	
NURSE: When there's a question of emergency surgery being needed, then test results are asked for immediately. Usually, though, it's preferable to wait for an accurate reading and a thorough written report.	Giving information
CLIENT: Are you absolutely sure?	
NURSE: You don't sound convinced.	Acknowledging the implied
CLIENT: Listen, I don't mean to give you a hard time. It's just that ... it may not seem like an emergency to my doctor or the lab people, but it sure is to me. I can't stand not knowing. I don't know the results of the tests I had yesterday. I don't know how many more tests I have to have. Will I have to have surgery? When can I go home?	
NURSE: The problem you need help with now is finding out the answers to four questions: What are the results of yesterday's tests? Is your doctor considering any other tests for you, and if so, what are they? Is surgery being planned? And when can you go home? Let's try to figure out how you can get the answers to these questions.	Summarizing Encouraging problem solving
CLIENT: Well, I can't call my doctor on the phone. All his receptionist will do is take the message. And, anyway, I'm afraid that he'll be offended if he thinks I'm complaining about him. You won't tell him, will you?	
NURSE: No, not unless you and I decide together that it would be the best solution.	Encouraging collaboration
CLIENT: I suppose I could try to forget about it and be patient, just like everyone tells me to.	
NURSE: You've tried that, but you're still worried, fearful, and angry. Let's think of some other possibilities.	Encouraging further exploration
CLIENT: Maybe you could call his office for me! Since you're a nurse, they'll probably put your call right through.	

TABLE 26.6 Sample Process Recording *continued*

Nurse/Client Dialogue	Communication Skill
NURSE: So far, there are three possible solutions—calling his office yourself, waiting until he comes to visit you later this afternoon, or having me call his office. Are there any other possible solutions that we haven't considered?	Focusing on solutions
CLIENT: I can't think of any other.	
NURSE: Okay, then, which do you think would be best?	Demonstrating respect for the client
CLIENT: I guess I'd feel better if you called his office. I just don't want him to think that I'm criticizing him.	
NURSE: You're concerned about what he might think of you because of this phone call. Let's discuss how I should handle the call and what I should say.	Paraphrasing Encouraging collaboration and problem solving

After a few minutes, they develop a plan for calling Mrs. Barrett's physician, and Ms. Olsen makes the call. The physician has decided to call both the laboratory and the x-ray department for the results of Mrs. Barrett's tests and promises to phone her as soon as he learns the results. They will discuss further possible tests and treatment plans that afternoon when he makes his hospital rounds. Mrs. Barrett asks Ms. Olsen to stay with her while she receives the physician's telephone call about the tests.

Source: Adapted from material by Carol Ren Kneisl, President and Educational Director, Nursing Transitions, Williamsville, New York.

One method of writing a process recording is to make two columns on a page. The first column lists what the nurse and the client said along with the associated nonverbal behaviour. The second column contains interpretive comments about the nurse's responses. An example of a process recording is found in Table 26.6.

Once a process recording has been completed, it should be analyzed in terms of the content and meaning of the interaction based on communication theory. Each of the nurse's statements is interpreted in terms of the communication skill used, with the rationale for and effectiveness of its use. Any barriers to effective communication can be identified with a possible alternative response noted. The outcome for nurses should be increased awareness and insight regarding their communication strengths, as well as identification of areas for future skills development.

CHAPTER HIGHLIGHTS

- Communication is a critical nursing skill used to gather information, to teach and persuade, and to express caring and comfort.
- Caring is said to be the essence of nursing. It includes assistive, supportive, and facilitative acts for individuals or groups.
- Caring acts promote individual growth, preserve human dignity and worth, augment self-healing, and relieve distress.
- Comforting is a complex process that is undergoing research. Enhanced comfort is the desired outcome or product of comforting in which the client experiences relief of discomfort, ease, or transcendence.
- Comfort needs can be viewed in a framework of physical, psychospiritual, social, and environmental needs. Nurses need to be knowledgeable, skilled, and innovative to individualize comforting strategies.
- Communication is a two-way interpersonal process involving the sender of the message and the receiver of the message. It also involves intrapersonal messages, or self-talk, which can affect the message, the interpretation of the message, and the response.
- Because the sender must encode the message and determine the appropriate channels for conveying it, and because the receiver must perceive the message, decode it, and then respond, the communication process includes four elements: sender, message, receiver, and feedback.
- Verbal communication is effective when the criteria of pace and intonation, simplicity, clarity and brevity, timing, relevance, adaptability, and credibility are met.
- Nonverbal communication often reveals more about a person's thoughts and feelings than verbal communication; it includes personal appearance, posture and gait, facial expressions, and gestures.

- When assessing verbal and nonverbal behaviours, the nurse needs to consider cultural influences and be aware that a single nonverbal expression can indicate any of a variety of feelings and that words can have various meanings.
- When communication is effective, verbal and nonverbal expressions are congruent.
- Many factors influence the communication process: development, gender, values and perceptions, personal space (intimate, personal, social, and public distance), territoriality, roles and relationships, time and environment, congruence, and attitudes.
- Many techniques facilitate therapeutic communication: attentive listening; paraphrasing; clarifying; using open questions and statements; focusing; being specific; using touch and silence; clarifying reality, time, or sequence; providing general leads; and summarizing.
- Communication techniques specifically used to provide comfort to a distressed client include honest and sincere expression of pity, sympathy, compassion, commiseration, consolation, and reflexive assurance.
- Techniques that inhibit communication include offering unvalidated reassurance, stating approval or disapproval, giving common (not expert) advice, stereotyping, and being defensive.
- The effective nurse-client relationship is a helping relationship that facilitates growth and provides support, comfort, and hope.
- Four phases of the helping relationship include the preinteraction phase, the introductory phase, the working phase, and the termination phase; each has a specific purpose or goal and requires specific skills of the nurse.
- To help clients with communication problems, the nurse manipulates the environment, provides support, employs measures to enhance communication, and educates the client and support persons.
- Process recordings are frequently made by nurses to evaluate their own communication. With them, nurses can analyze both the process and the content of the communication.
- Nurses interact with groups of clients and colleagues in a wide variety of settings. To use groups rationally and effectively, nurses must understand the features of effective groups.
- Effective groups produce outstanding results, succeed in spite of difficulties, and have members who feel responsible for the output of the group. They accomplish their goals (outcomes), maintain cohesion, and develop and modify their structure in ways that improve effectiveness.

READINGS AND REFERENCES

Suggested Readings

Peplau, H. E. (1960). Talking with patients. *American Journal of Nursing, 60,* 964–966.
This classic article explains how nursing communication with a client differs from communication between laypeople. It offers a beginning nursing student helpful suggestions for meaningful communication with clients.

Sullivan, G. H., & Wolfe, S. (1996). When communication breaks down. *RN, 59,* 61–65.
The authors look at the consequences in sample cases when nurses fail to communicate clearly and effectively with clients, other nurses, and physicians. Suggestions are included for how to prevent this miscommunication.

Related Research

Halldórsdóttir, S., & Hamrin, E. (1997). Caring and uncaring encounters within nursing and health care from the cancer patient's perspective. *Cancer Nursing, 20*(2), 120–128.

Jenny, J., & Logan, J. (1996). Caring and comfort metaphors used by patients in critical care. *Image: Journal of Nursing Scholarship, 28*(4), 349–352.

Kotechi, C. N. (2002). Baccalaureate nursing students communication process in the clinical setting. *Journal of Nursing Education. 41*(2). 61–68.

Olson, J. K. (1995). Relationships between nurse-expressed empathy, patient-perceived empathy and patient distress. *Image: Journal of Nursing Scholarship, 27*(4), 317–322.

Smith, M. K., & Sullivan, J. M. (1997, March/April). Nurses' and patients' perceptions of most important caring behaviours in a long-term care setting. *Geriatric Nursing, 18*(2), 70–73.

Wolfe, Z. R., Giardino, E. R., Osborne, P. A., & Ambrose, M. S. (1994, Summer). Dimensions of nurse caring. *Image: Journal of Nursing Scholarship, 26*(2), 107–111.

Selected References

Baillie, L. (1996). A phenomenological study of the nature of empathy. *Journal of Advanced Nursing, 24,* 1300–1308.

Balzer R. J. (2000). *Communication in nursing.* St. Louis, MO: Mosby.

Boss, B. J. (1991). Managing communication disorders in stroke. *Nursing Clinics of North America, 26,* 985–996.

Boykin, A., & Schoenhoffer, S. (1993). *Nursing is caring: A model for transforming practice.* New York: National League of Nursing Press. Pub. No. 15-2549.

Brammer, L. M. (1988). *The helping relationship: Process and skills* (4th ed.). Englewood Cliffs, NJ: Prentice Hall.

Carpenito, L. J. (2000). *Nursing diagnosis: Application to clinical practice* (8th ed.). Philadelphia, PA: Lippincott.

Chinn, P. L. (Ed.). (1991). *Anthology on caring.* New York: National League for Nursing Press. Pub. No. 15-2392.

Deering, C. G. (1999). To speak or not to speak? Self-disclosure with patients. *American Journal of Nursing, 99*(1), 34–39.

Donahue, P. (1989). *Nursing: The finest art.* St. Louis, MO: Mosby.

Egan, G. (1990). *The skilled helper: A systematic approach to effective helping* (4th ed.). Pacific Grove, CA: Brooks/Cole.

Egan, G. (2002). *The skilled helper: A problem-management approach to helping* (7th ed.). Pacific Grove, CA: Brooks/Cole.

Farley, M. J. (1992). Thought and talk: The intrapersonal component of human communication. *AORN Journal, 56,* 481–484.

Gadow, S. (1984). Touch and technology: Two paradigms of patient care. *Journal of Religion and Health, 23*(1), 63–69.

Gadow, S. A. (1985). Nurse and patient: The caring relationship. In A. H. Bishop & J. R. Scudder (Eds.), *Caring, curing, coping* (pp. 31–43). Tuscaloosa, Al: University of Alabama Press.

Hall, E. T. (1969). *The hidden dimension.* Garden City, NJ: Doubleday. (Classic.)

Hartrick, G. (2002). Beyond interpersonal communication: The significance of relationship in health promoting practice. In L. Young & C. Hayes (Eds.), *Transforming health promotion practice: Concepts, Issues, and Applications.* Philadelphia, PA: F. A. Davis Co.

Hawthorne, D., & Yurkovich, N. (1994, November/December). Caring: The raison d'être of the professional nurse. *CJONA,* 7(4), 35–55.

Kolcaba, K. Y. (1991). A taxonomic structure for the concept of comfort. *Image: Journal of Nursing Scholarship, 23*(4), 237–240.

Kolcaba, K. Y. (1992). Holistic comfort: Operationalizing the construct as a nurse-sensitive outcome. *Advances in Nursing Science, 15*(1), 1–10.

Kolcaba, K. Y. (1994). A theory of holistic comfort for nursing. *Journal of Advanced Nursing, 19,* 1178–1184.

Kolcaba, K. Y. (1995a, June). Comfort as process and product merged in holistic nursing art. *Journal of Holistic Nursing, 13*(2), 117–131.

Kolcaba, K. Y. (1995b, Winter). The art of comfort care. *Image: Journal of Nursing Scholarship,* 27(4), 287–289.

Kolcaba, K. Y., & Kolcaba, R. J. (1991). An analysis of the concept of comfort. *Journal of Advanced Nursing, 16,* 1301–1310.

Labonte, R. (1993). *Health promotion and empowerment: Practice frameworks.* Toronto: Centre for Health Promotion.

Leininger, M. M. (1984). *Care: The essence of nursing and health.* Thorofare, NJ: Charles B. Slack.

May, C. R., & Purkis, M. E. (1995). The configuration of nurse-patient relationships: A critical view. *Scholarly Inquiry for Nursing Practice: An International Journal, 9,* 283–295.

Mayeroff, M. (1971). *On caring.* New York: Harper and Row.

Miller, K. L. (1995). Keeping the care in nursing care. Our biggest challenge. *JONA, 25*(11), 29–32.

Milstead, J. A. (1996). Basic tools for the orthopaedic staff nurse: Assertiveness. *Orthopaedic Nursing, 15,* 23–29.

Morse, J. (1996). The science of comforting. *Reflections, 22*(4), 6–7.

Morse, J. M., Bottorff, J., Anderson, G., O'Brien, B., & Solberg, S. (1992). Beyond empathy: Expanding expressions of caring. *Journal of Advanced Nursing, 17*(7), 809–821.

Morse, J. M., Bottorff, J. I., & Hutchinson, S. (1994). The phenomenology of comfort. *Journal of Advanced Nursing, 20*(1), 189–195.

Noddings, N. (1984). *Caring: A feminine approach to ethics and moral education.* Berkeley: University of California Press.

Pabst, M. K., Scherubel, J. C., & Minnick, A. E. (1996). The impact of computerized documentation on nurses' use of time. *Computers in Nursing, 14,* 25–30.

Purtilo, R., & Haddad, A. (1996). *Health professional and patient interaction* (5th ed.). Philadelphia, PA: Saunders.

Rondeau, K. V. (1992). Effective communication means really listening. *Canadian Journal of Medical Technology, 52*(2), 78–80.

Sieh, A., & Brentin, L. K. (1997). *The nurse communicates.* Philadelphia, PA: Saunders.

Smith, M. K., & Sullivan, J. M. (1997, March/April). Nurses' and patients' perceptions of most important caring behaviours in a long-term care setting. *Geriatric Nursing, 18*(2), 70–73.

Sundeen, S. J., Stuart, G.W., Rankin, E. A. D., & Cohen, S. A. (1998). *Nurse-client interaction* (6th ed.). St. Louis, MO: Mosby.

Watson, J. (1985). *Nursing: Human science and human care.* Norwalk, CT: Appleton-Century-Crofts.

Watson, J. (1988). New dimensions of human caring theory. *Nursing Science Quarterly, 1*(4), 175–181.

Watson, J. (1997). The theory of human caring: Retrospective and prospective. *Nursing Science Quarterly, 10,* 49–52.

Watson, J. (2002). *Assessing and measuring caring in nursing and health science.* New York: Springer.

Wurzbach, M. E. (1996). Comfort and nurses' moral choices. *Journal of Advanced Nursing, 24,* 260–264.

WEBLINKS

Alberta Association of Registered Nurses
http://www.nurses.ab.ca/ARNDocs/boundary.htm
This Web site includes the following documents about enacting the practice of nurse-patient relationship: "Professional Boundaries for Registered Nurses: Guidelines for the Nurse-Client Relationship" "Professional Boundaries for Registered Nurses: The Nurse-Client Relationship" "Professional Boundaries: A Discussion Paper on Expectations for Nurse-Client Relationships"

Registered Nurses Association of Manitoba
http://www.crnm.mb.ca/
"Professional Boundaries for Therapeutic Relationships"—This document provides an interpretation of the expectations of registered nurses in establishing therapeutic relationships and maintaining appropriate boundaries with clients and their significant others.

CHAPTER 27

Health Assessment

OBJECTIVES

After completing this chapter, you will be able to:

- Identify the purposes of the physical health examination.
- List expected outcomes of health assessment.
- Discuss the various steps in selected assessment procedures.
- Describe suggested sequencing to conduct a physical health assessment in an orderly manner.
- Examine variations in assessment techniques appropriate for clients of different ages.
- Explain the four methods of examining.
- Analyze the significance of selected physical findings.

Assessing a client's health status is a major component of nursing care and has two aspects: (1) the nursing health history discussed in Chapter 23, and (2) the physical assessment discussed in this chapter. It is becoming increasingly more common for registered nurses to conduct complete physical health assessments in community agencies and hospitals as part of their expanding roles as clinical nurse specialists and nurse practitioners.

Physical Health Assessment

A complete health assessment may be conducted starting at the head and proceeding in a systematic manner downward to the toes (head-to-toe assessment). However, the procedure can vary according to the age of the individual, the severity of the illness, the preferences of the nurse, and the location of the examination. Whatever order a nurse chooses to perform an assessment, it is important to be consistent each time it is done. A consistent approach that is routinely practised reduces the likelihood of forgetting or omitting certain parts of the assessment. In addition, consistency in examination facilitates systematic documentation of the findings. The order of head-to-toe assessment is given in the accompanying box. Regardless of what procedure is used, the client's energy and time need to be considered. The health assessment is, therefore, conducted in a systematic and efficient manner that requires the fewest position changes for the client.

The sequence of the assessment differs with children and adults. With children, always proceed from the least invasive or uncomfortable to the more invasive. Examination of the head and neck, heart and lungs, and range of motion can be done early in the process, while the ears, mouth, abdomen, and genitals should be left for the end of the exam.

Frequently, nurses assess a specific body area instead of the entire body. These specific assessments are made in relation to client complaints, the nurse's own observation of problems, the client's presenting problem, nursing interventions provided, and medical therapies. Examples of these situations and assessments are provided in Table 27.1.

Some of the reasons for a physical health examination include:

- Obtaining baseline data about the client's functional abilities
- Supplementing, confirming, or refuting data obtained in the nursing history
- Obtaining data that will help the nurse establish nursing diagnoses and plan the client's care
- Evaluating the physiological outcomes of health care and, thus, the progress of a client's health problem
- Making clinical judgements on a client's health status

Some organizations have developed screening tools and guidelines that can assist nurses in certain aspects of their physical assessment. For example, nurses should be aware of the Canadian Cancer Society guidelines for screening asymptomatic clients (see the box on page 512).

Head-to-Toe Framework

- General survey
- Vital signs
- Head
  - Hair, scalp, cranium, face
  - Eyes and vision
  - Ears and hearing
  - Nose and sinuses
  - Mouth and oropharynx
  - Cranial nerves
- Neck
  - Muscles
  - Lymph nodes
  - Trachea
  - Thyroid gland
  - Carotid arteries
  - Neck veins
- Upper extremities
  - Skin and nails
  - Muscle strength and tone
  - Joint range of motion
  - Brachial and radial pulses
  - Biceps tendon reflexes
  - Tendon reflexes
  - Sensation
- Chest and back
  - Skin
  - Breasts and axillae
  - Chest shape and size
  - Lungs
  - Heart
  - Spinal column
- Abdomen
  - Skin
  - Abdominal sounds
  - Specific organs (e.g., liver, bladder)
- Genitals
  - Testicles
  - Vagina
  - Urethra
- Anus and rectum
- Lower extremities
  - Skin and toenails
  - Gait and balance
  - Joint range of motion
  - Femoral, popliteal, posterior tibial, and pedal pulses
  - Tendon and plantar reflexes
  - Sensation

TABLE 27.1 Nursing Assessments Addressing Specific Client Situations

Situation	Physical Assessment
Client complains of abdominal pain.	Inspect, auscultate, and palpate the abdomen; assess vital signs.
Client is admitted with a head injury.	Assess level of consciousness using Glasgow Coma Scale (see Table 27.12); assess pupils for reaction to light and accommodation; assess vital signs.
The nurse prepares to administer a cardiotonic drug to a client.	Assess apical pulse and compare with baseline data.
The nurse administers postural drainage.	Auscultate lungs before and after the procedure.
The client has just had a cast applied to the lower leg.	Assess peripheral perfusion of toes, capillary blanch test, pedal pulse, if able, and vital signs.
The client's fluid intake is minimal.	Assess tissue turgor, fluid intake and output, and vital signs.

Preparing the Client

Prior to the assessment, the nurse should explain when and where it will take place, why it is important, and what will happen during the assessment. Health assessments are usually painless; however, it is important to determine in advance any positions that are contraindicated for a particular client. The nurse assists the client, as needed, to undress and put on a gown.

Clients should empty their bladders before the examination. Doing so helps them feel more relaxed and makes palpation of the abdomen and the pubic area more comfortable. If a urinalysis is required, the urine should be collected at the time the client empties his or her bladder. Since an empty rectum facilitates rectal examination, the client should be encouraged to defecate before a complete examination.

Health Assessment of the Older Adult

- Be aware of normal physiological changes that occur with age.
- Expose only areas of the body to be examined in order to avoid chilling.
- Permit ample time for the client to answer your questions and assume the required positions.
- Be aware of cultural differences. The client may want a family member present during disrobing.
- Arrange for an interpreter (e.g., family member) if the client's language differs from that of the nurse.
- Ask clients how they wish to be addressed, such as Mrs., Miss, or Mr.
- Adapt assessment techniques to any sensory impairment; for example, make sure the clients have their eyeglasses or hearing aids.

If clients are elderly or frail, it is wise to plan several assessment times in order to not overtire them. Often, clients are anxious about what the nurse will find. They can be reassured during the assessment by explanations at each step.

When assessing older adults, it is important to recognize that people of the same age may differ markedly. The previous box provides special considerations for assessing the older adult.

Preparing the Environment

It is important to prepare the environment before starting the assessment. The time for the physical assessment should be convenient to both the client and the nurse. The environment should be well lit and the equipment should be systematically arranged for the examination. A disorganized environment does not convey professional competence to the client.

It is important to provide the client with privacy. Most people are embarrassed if their bodies are exposed or if others can overhear or view them during the assessment. Family and friends should not be present unless the client specifically asks for someone to be present in the room.

A client who is physically relaxed will usually experience little discomfort. The room should be warm and comfortable for the client.

Positioning

Several positions are frequently required during the physical assessment. It is important to consider the client's ability to assume a position. The client's physical condition, energy level, and age should also be taken into consideration. Some positions are embarrassing and uncomfortable and, therefore, should not be maintained for long. The assessment is organized so that several body areas can be assessed in one position, thus minimizing the number of position changes needed (see Table 27.2).

Canadian Cancer Society Information and Guidelines

Colorectal Cancer

*Warning signs:

- Change in bowel habits (e.g., diarrhea, constipation, or both lasting more than two weeks)
- Frequent or constant cramps lasting more than two weeks
- Blood in or on the stool, stools that are narrower than normal
- General stomach discomfort, frequent gas pains
- A strong need to move your bowels but with little stool (tenesmus)
- A feeling that the bowel does not completely empty
- Unexplained weight loss, constant tiredness

One or more of the following tests may be performed:

- Digital rectal exam, fecal occult blood, sigmoidoscopy, colonoscopy, biopsy, barium enema

Breast Cancer

- Eight out of 10 women with breast cancer have no family history
- Every woman from age 20 years should do a breast self-exam (BSE) monthly
- Menstruating women should do the BSE between the seventh and 14th day after the start of the period
- Women who do not have a regular cycle or who are not menstruating should do a BSE at the same time each month (e.g., the last or first day of the month)
- All women between 50 and 69 years should have a mammogram every two years in combination with physical examination of the breasts by a trained health professional
- Mammography screening guidelines for women under 50 and over 70 vary by province and territory
- All women, regardless of their age, should discuss the benefits and risks of BSE and mammography with their physician/health-care provider

Incidence of breast cancer increases with:

- Age
- If a woman has had her mother, sister, or daughter diagnosed with breast cancer
- If a woman has never had a child or had her first child after age 30 years

Cervical Cancer

- Many women who develop cervical cancer have no known risk factors (apart from having had sexual intercourse)
- The use of condoms may reduce the risk of cervical cancer
- All women who are sexually active (or who have been sexually active) should have a Pap test screen every 1 to 3 years until aged 70 years and then once every five years thereafter

Incidence of cervical cancer increases with the:

  - More sexual partners a woman has
  - Younger a woman is when she begins sexual activity

Uterine Cancer

- High-calorie, high-fat diet is associated with endometrial cancer
- Only 50 percent of women who develop the disease have risk factors
- Cancer of the uterus is the most common cancer of the female reproductive tract
- A woman should see a doctor if she has any of the following symptoms:
  Unusual vaginal bleeding or discharge
  Difficult or painful urination
  Pain during intercourse
  Pain in the pelvic area
- Pelvic exam, biopsy, and dilation and curretage (D & C) are effective in detecting the disease

Risk of uterine cancer increases with:

- Age: Women between 50 and 74 years who are obese and have hypertension
- Women who have abnormal vaginal bleeding after menopause
- Women who continue to have periods after they are 50 years
- Women who have never had children or who receive hormone therapy

Prostate Cancer

- Prostate is the second leading cause of death among men in Canada
- It is recommended that all men over the age of 50 years talk to their family doctors about the benefits and risks of digital rectal examination and the Prostate Specific Antigen (PSA) test
- Men in high risk groups include African-Canadians and those with a family history of prostate cancer
- Symptoms include:
  Frequency, urgency, hesitancy, and painful urination
  Blood in the urine
  Pain in the lower back, pelvic area, upper thighs, and painful ejaculation
- Men in high risk groups should discuss screening tests with their family physician at age 40 years

*The Canadian Cancer Society is developing guidelines for mass colorectal screening.

Source: Canadian Cancer Society, 2003.www.cancer.ca

TABLE 27.2 Client Positions and Body Areas Assessed

Position	Description	Areas Assessed	Cautions
Dorsal recumbent 	Back-lying position with knees flexed and hips externally rotated; small pillow under the head; soles of feet on the surface	Head and neck, axillae, anterior thorax, lungs, breasts, heart, extremities, peripheral pulses, vital signs, and vagina	May be contraindicated for clients who have cardiopulmonary problems; Not used for abdominal assessment because of the increased tension of abdominal muscles
Supine (horizontal recumbent) 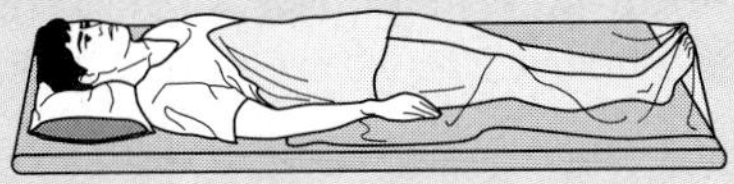	Back-lying position with legs extended; with or without pillow under the head	Head, neck, axillae, anterior thorax, lungs, breasts, heart, abdomen, extremities, peripheral pulses	Tolerated poorly by clients with cardiovascular and respiratory problems
Sitting 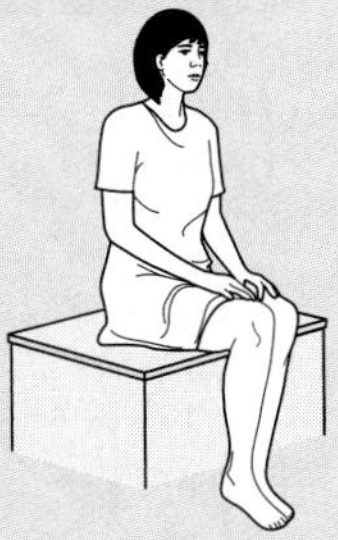	A seated position, back unsupported and legs hanging freely	Head, neck, posterior and anterior thorax, lungs, breasts, axillae, heart, vital signs, upper and lower extremities, reflexes	Aged and weak clients may require support
Lithotomy 	Back-lying position with feet supported in stirrups; the hips should be in line with the edge of the table	Female genitals, rectum, and female reproductive tract	May be uncomfortable and tiring for aged people and often embarrassing
Genupectoral (knee-chest) 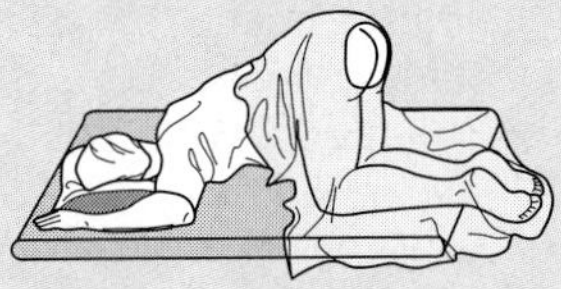	Kneeling position with torso at a 90° angle to hips	Rectum	Uncomfortable position, tolerated poorly by clients who have respiratory problems; tiring and embarrassing
Sims' 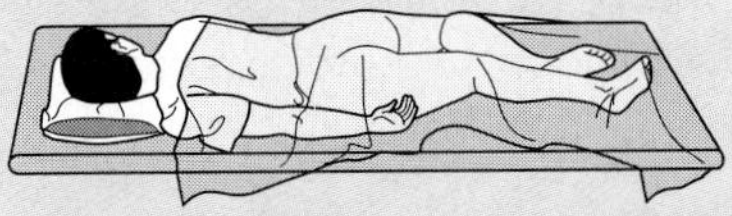	Side-lying position with lowermost arm behind the body, uppermost leg flexed at hip and knee, upper arm flexed at shoulder and elbow	Rectum, vagina	Difficult for the aged and people with limited joint movement
Prone 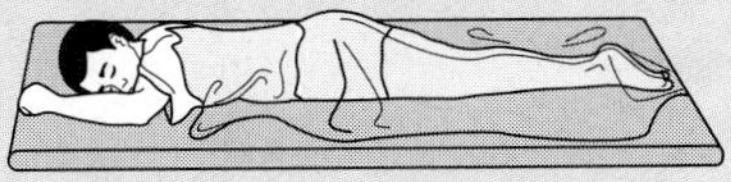	Lies on abdomen with head turned to the side, with or without a small pillow	Posterior thorax, hip joint movement	Often not tolerated by the aged and people with cardiovascular and respiratory problems

Draping

Drapes should be arranged so that the area to be assessed is exposed and other body areas are covered. Exposure of the body is frequently embarrassing to clients. Drapes provide not only a degree of privacy but also warmth. Drapes are made of paper, cloth, or bed linen.

Instrumentation

All equipment required for the health assessment should be clean, in good working order, and readily accessible. Equipment is frequently set up on trays, ready for use.

Photographs of various instruments are shown in Table 27.3 below.

Methods of Examining

Four primary techniques are used in the physical examination: inspection, palpation, percussion, and auscultation. These techniques are discussed throughout this chapter as they apply to each body system.

Inspection

Inspection is the visual examination, that is, assessing by observing with the eyes. It should be deliberate, purposeful, and systematic. The nurse inspects with the naked eye and with a lighted instrument, such as an otoscope (used to view the ear). In addition to visual observations, olfactory (smell) and auditory (hearing) cues are noted. Nurses

TABLE 27.3 Equipment and Supplies Used for a Health Examination

Instruments and Supplies		Purpose
Flashlight or penlight	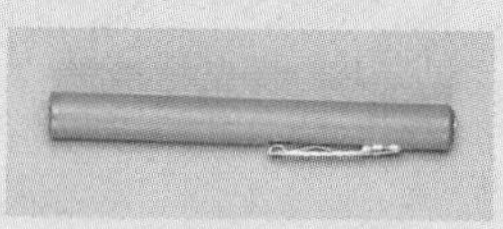	To assist viewing of the pharynx and cervix or to determine the reactions of the pupils of the eye
Laryngeal or dental mirror	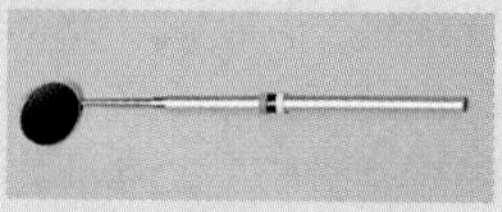	To observe the pharynx and oral cavity
Nasal speculum		To permit visualization of the lower and middle turbinates; usually a penlight is used for illumination
Ophthalmoscope	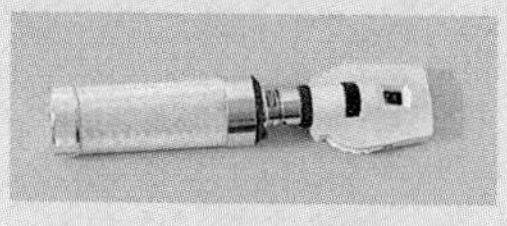	A lighted instrument to visualize the interior of the eye
Otoscope	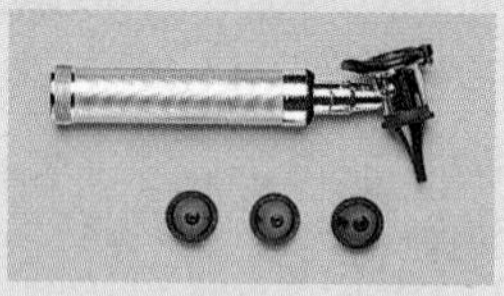	A lighted instrument to visualize the eardrum and external auditory canal (a nasal speculum may be attached to the otoscope to inspect the nasal cavities)
Percussion (reflex) hammer	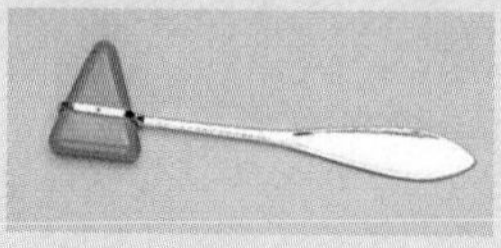	An instrument with a rubber head to test reflexes
Sphygmomanometer and cuff (see Figure 31.21, p. 734)		To measure the blood pressure
Stethoscope (see Figure 31.17, p. 725)		To auscultate body sounds (e.g., blood pressure, chest, bowel sounds)
Thermometer (see Figures 31.4, 31.5, 31.6 on p. 715)		To measure body temperature

TABLE 27.3 Equipment and Supplies Used for a Health Examination *continued*

Instruments and Supplies		Purpose
Tuning fork	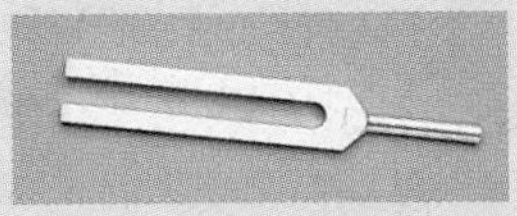	A two-pronged metal instrument used to test hearing acuity and vibratory sense
Vaginal speculum (various sizes) (see Figure 27.82)		To assess the cervix and the vagina
Assorted containers and slides		For specimens
Cotton applicators		To obtain specimens; to test sensory function
Disposable pads		To absorb liquid
Drapes		To cover the client
Gloves (sterile and unsterile)	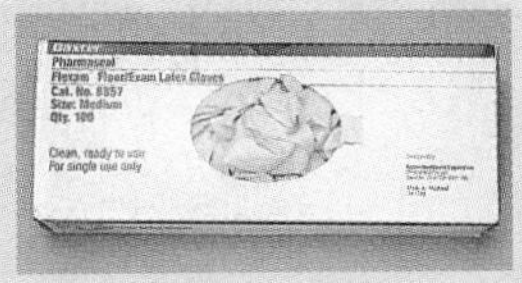	To protect the nurse and client
Lubricant		To ease insertion of instruments (e.g., vaginal speculum)
Tongue blades (depressors)		To depress the tongue during assessment of the mouth and pharynx

frequently use visual inspection to assess moisture, colour, and texture of body surfaces, as well as shape, position, size, colour, and symmetry of the body. Lighting must be sufficient for the nurse to see clearly; either natural or artificial light can be used. When using the auditory senses, it is important to have a quiet environment for accurate hearing. Observation can be combined with the other assessment techniques.

Palpation

Palpation is the examination of the body using the sense of touch. The pads of the fingers are used because their concentration of nerve endings makes them highly sensitive to tactile discrimination. Palpation is used to determine (1) texture (e.g., of the hair); (2) temperature (e.g., of a skin area); (3) vibration (e.g., of a joint); (4) position, size, consistency, and mobility of organs or masses; (5) distention (e.g., of the urinary bladder); (6) pulsation; and (7) the presence of pain upon pressure.

There are two types of palpation: light and deep. *Light* (superficial) *palpation* should always precede *deep palpation* because heavy pressure on the fingertips can dull the sense of touch. For light palpation, the nurse extends the fingers of the dominant hand parallel to the skin surface and presses gently while moving the hand in a circle

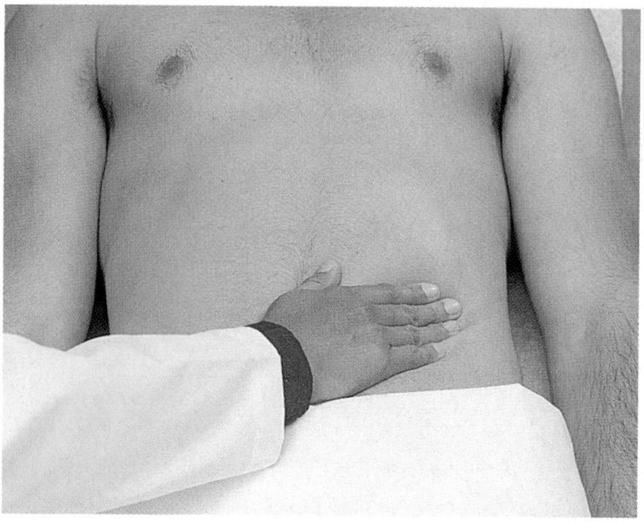

Figure 27.1 The position of the hand for light palpation

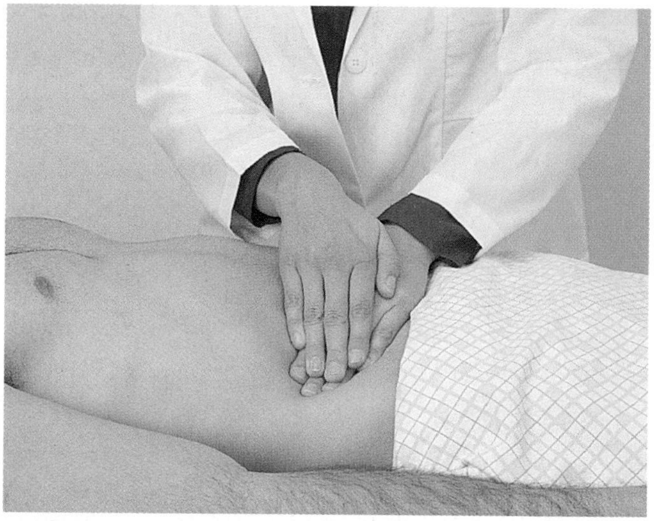

Figure 27.2 The position of the hands for deep bimanual palpation

(Figure 27.1). The skin is slightly depressed in light palpation. If it is necessary to determine the details of a mass, the nurse presses lightly several times, rather than holding the pressure constant. See the box below for the characteristics of masses.

Deep palpation is done with two hands (bimanually) or one hand. In deep bimanual palpation, the nurse extends the dominant hand as for light palpation, then places the fingerpads of the nondominant hand on the dorsal surface of the distal interphalangeal joint of the middle three fingers of the dominant hand (Figure 27.2). The top hand applies pressure while the lower hand remains relaxed to perceive the tactile sensations. For deep palpation using one hand, the fingerpads of the dominant hand press over the area to be palpated. Often, the other hand is used to support a mass or organ from below (Figure 27.3). *Deep palpation is done only with extreme caution and with a qualified instructor because pressure can damage internal organs. It is not indicated in clients who have acute abdominal pain or pain that is not yet diagnosed.*

To test skin temperature, it is best to use the dorsum or back of the hand and fingers where the skin is thinnest.

Characteristics of Masses

Location
Size—Measure in centimetres
Shape—Oval, round, elongated, irregular
Consistency—Soft, firm, hard
Surface—Smooth, nodular
Mobility—Fixed, mobile
Pulsatility—Present or absent
Tenderness—Degree of tenderness to palpation

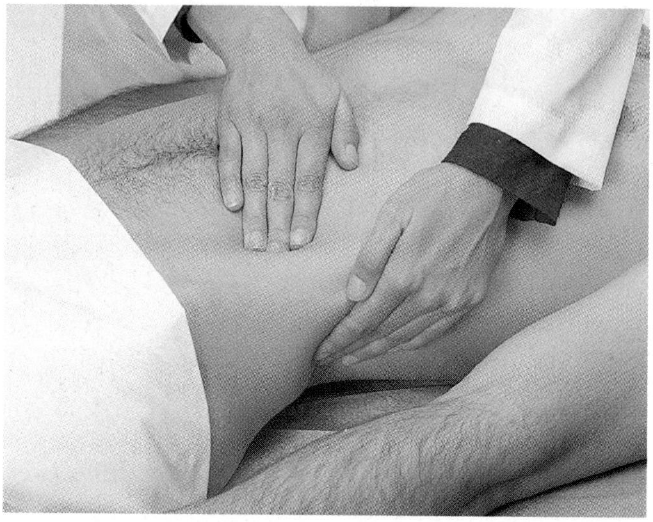

Figure 27.3 Deep palpation using the lower hand to support the body while the upper hand palpates the organ

To test for vibration, the nurse should use the palmar surface of the hand. General guidelines for palpation include the following:

- The nurse's hands should be clean and warm, and the fingernails short.
- Areas of tenderness should be palpated last.
- Deep palpation, if indicated, should be done after superficial palpation.

The effectiveness of palpation depends largely on the client's level of relaxation. Nurses can assist a client to relax by (1) gowning and/or draping the client appropriately; (2) positioning the client comfortably; (3) ensuring that their own hands are warm before beginning; and (4)

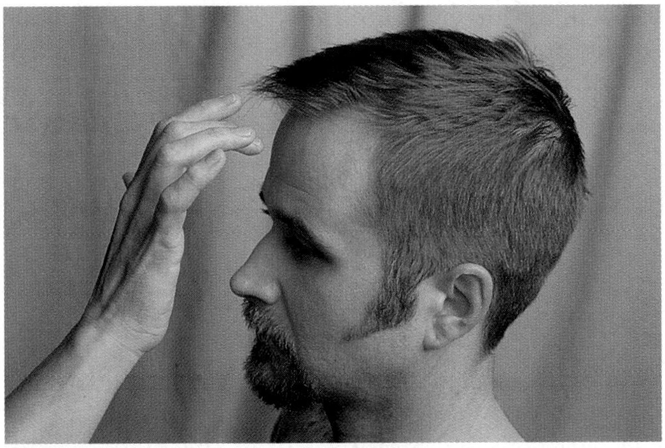

Figure 27.4 **Direct percussion:** Using one hand to strike the surface of the body

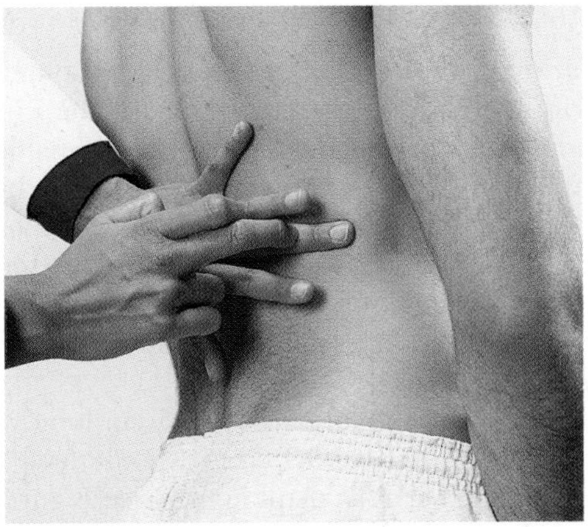

Figure 27.5 **Indirect percussion:** Using the finger of one hand to tap the finger of the other hand

communicating with the client during the exam. During palpation, the nurse should be sensitive to the client's verbal and facial expressions indicating discomfort.

Percussion

Percussion is the act of striking the body surface to elicit sounds that can be heard or vibrations that can be felt. There are two types of percussion: direct and indirect. In *direct percussion,* the nurse strikes the area to be percussed directly with the pads of two, three, or four fingers or with the pad of the middle finger. The strikes are rapid, and the movement is from the wrist. See Figure 27.4. This technique is not generally used to percuss the thorax but is useful in percussing an adult's sinuses.

The second type, *indirect percussion,* is the striking of an object (e.g., a finger) held against the body area to be examined. In this technique, the middle finger of the nondominant hand, referred to as the **pleximeter,** is placed firmly on the client's skin. Only the distal phalanx and joint of this finger should be in contact with the skin. The nurse strikes the pleximeter at the distal interphalangeal joint with the tip of the flexed middle finger of the other hand. The tip of the middle finger that strikes the pleximeter is known as the **plexor** (Figure 27.5). Some nurses may find a point between the distal and proximal joints to be a more comfortable pleximeter point. The motion comes from the wrist; the forearm remains stationary. The angle between the plexor and the pleximeter should be 90 degrees, and the blows must be firm, rapid, and short to obtain a clear sound.

Percussion is used to determine the size and shape of internal organs by establishing their borders. It indicates whether tissue is fluid filled, air filled, or solid. Percussion elicits five types of sound: flatness, dullness, resonance, hyperresonance, and tympany. **Flatness** is an extremely dull sound produced by very dense tissue, such as muscle or bone. **Dullness** is a thud-like sound produced by dense tissue, such as the liver, spleen, or heart. **Resonance** is a hollow sound such as that produced by lungs filled with air. **Hyperresonance** is not present in a healthy individual. It is described as booming and can be heard over a diseased lung (e.g., in the client with emphysema). **Tympany** is a musical or drum-like sound produced from an air-filled stomach. On a continuum, flatness reflects the most dense tissue (the least amount of air) and tympany the least dense tissue (the greatest amount of air). A percussion sound is described according to its intensity, pitch, duration, and quality. See Table 27.4.

TABLE 27.4 Percussion Sounds and Tones

Sound	Intensity	Pitch	Duration	Quality	Example of Location
Flatness	Soft	High	Short	Extremely dull	Muscle, bone
Dullness	Medium	Medium	Moderate	Thud-like	Liver, heart
Resonance	Loud	Low	Long	Hollow	Normal lung
Hyperresonance	Very loud	Very low	Very long	Booming	Emphysematous lung
Tympany	Loud	High (distinguished mainly by musical timbre)	Moderate	Musical	Stomach filled with gas (air)

Auscultation

Auscultation is the process of listening to sounds produced within the body. Auscultation may be direct or indirect. *Direct auscultation* is the use of the unaided ear, for example, to listen to a respiration wheeze or the grating of a moving joint. *Indirect auscultation* is the use of a stethoscope to listen to sounds from within the body, such as bowel sounds or valve sounds of the heart. A stethoscope amplifies the sounds and conveys them to the nurse's ears.

The stethoscope should be 30 to 35 cm long with an internal diameter of about 0.3 cm. It should have both a flat-disc and a bell-shaped diaphragm. (See Figure 31.17 on page 725.) The flat-disc diaphragm is best for transmitting high-pitched sounds (e.g., bronchial sounds), and the bell-shaped diaphragm is best for transmitting low-pitched sounds, such as heart sounds. The earpieces of the stethoscope should fit comfortably into the nurse's ears with the earpieces facing forward. The diaphragm of the stethoscope is placed firmly but lightly against the client's skin. If a client is very hairy, it may be necessary to dampen the hairs with a moist cloth so that they will lie flat against the skin and not cause scratching sounds.

Auscultated sounds are described according to their pitch, intensity, duration, and quality. The **pitch** is the frequency of the vibrations (the number of vibrations per second). Low-pitched sounds, such as some heart sounds, have fewer vibrations per second than high-pitched sounds, such as bronchial sounds. The **intensity** (amplitude) refers to the loudness or softness of a sound. Some body sounds are loud, for example, bronchial sounds heard from the trachea; others are soft, for example, normal breath sounds heard in the lungs. The **duration** of a sound is its length (long or short). The **quality** of a sound is a subjective description, for example, whistling, gurgling, or snapping.

General Survey

Physical assessment begins with a general survey that involves observation of the client's general appearance and behaviour and measurement of vital signs, height, and weight.

Many components of the general survey are assessed while taking the client's health history, such as the client's body build, posture, hygiene, and mental status.

Appearance and Behaviour

The general appearance and behaviour of an individual must be assessed in relationship to current circumstances. For example, an individual who has recently experienced a personal loss may appropriately appear depressed. Also, the client's age, gender, and race are useful factors in interpreting findings that suggest increased risk for known conditions. Procedure 27.1 describes how to assess general appearance and mental status.

PROCEDURE 27.1 Assessing General Appearance and Mental Status

NURSING HISTORY FOCUS

Chronological age, race, cultural background, and general health status; achievement of developmental tasks; body image concerns; self-esteem; educational level, thought processes; general health history; stressors (past and present); changes in personality, behaviour, or memory; lifelong problems (e.g., poor job history, alcoholism, drug abuse, disciplinary problems)

ASSESSMENT	NORMAL FINDINGS	DEVIATIONS FROM NORMAL
General Appearance		
Observe body build, height, and weight in relation to the client's age, lifestyle, and health.	Varies with lifestyle	Thin or obese
Observe the client's posture and gait, standing, sitting, and walking.	Relaxed, erect posture; coordinated movement	Tense, slouched, bent posture; uncoordinated movement; tremors
Observe the client's overall hygiene and grooming. Relate these to the person's activities prior to the assessment.	Clean, neat	Unclean, unkempt

PROCEDURE 27.1 Assessing General Appearance and Mental Status *continued*

ASSESSMENT	NORMAL FINDINGS	DEVIATIONS FROM NORMAL
Note body and breath odour in relation to activity level.	No body odour or minor body odour relative to work or exercise; no breath odour	Foul body odour; ammonia odour; acetone breath odour; foul breath
Observe for signs of distress in posture (e.g., bending over because of abdominal pain) or **facial expression** (e.g., wincing or laboured breathing).	No signs of distress	Signs of distress
Note obvious signs of health or illness (e.g., in skin colour or breathing).	Healthy appearance	Pallor; weakness; obvious illness
Behaviour		
Assess the client's attitude.	Cooperative	Negative, hostile, withdrawn
Note the client's affect/mood; assess the appropriateness of the client's response and level of orientation to time, place, and persons, and situation.	Appropriate to situation Orientated	Inappropriate to situation Not orientated
Listen for quantity of speech (amount and pace), **quality** (loudness, clarity, inflection), **and organization** (coherence of thought, overgeneralization, vagueness).	Understandable, moderate pace Exhibits thought association	Rapid or slow pace Uses generalizations; lacks association
Listen for relevance and organization of thoughts.	Logical sequence Makes sense; has sense of reality	Illogical sequence Flight of ideas; confusion

Lifespan Considerations

Children

- Measure length of children up to age 2 years in the recumbent position. Make sure the knees are fully extended.
- Weigh infants without any clothing. Older children should be weighed with only their underwear.
- Head circumference should be measured at each visit until age 2 years.

Vital Signs

Vital signs are measured (1) to establish baseline data against which to compare future measurements, and (2) to detect actual and potential health problems. See Chapter 31 for measurements of temperature, pulse, respirations, and blood pressure.

Height and Weight

In adults, the ratio of weight to height provides a general measure of health. By asking clients about their height and weight before actually measuring them, the nurse obtains some idea of the person's self-image. Excessive discrepancies between the client's responses and the measurements may provide clues to actual or potential problems in self-concept. It is also important that the nurse and client be aware of any significant unintentional weight gain or loss.

The nurse measures height with a measuring stick attached to weight scales or to a wall. The client removes the shoes and stands erect, with heels together, buttocks and back of the head against the measuring stick, and eyes looking straight ahead. The nurse raises the L-shaped sliding arm on the weight scale until it rests on top of the client's head or places a small flat object such as a ruler or book on the client's head. The edge of the flat object should abut the measuring guide.

Weight is usually measured when a client is admitted to a health agency and often regularly, for example, each morning before breakfast. The nurse should use the same scale each time (because there may be some variation among scales), take the measurements at the same time each day, and make sure the client wears the same kind of clothing and no shoes. The client stands on a platform, and the weight is read from a digital display panel or a balancing arm. Clients who cannot stand are weighed on bed or chair scales. The bed scales have canvas straps or a stretcherlike apparatus. A machine lifts the client above the bed, and the weight is reflected either on a digital display panel or on a balance arm like that of a standing scale.

Standardized charts have the average heights and weights of children and adults. It is important to remember that these averages provide only general guidelines for assessing growth, development, and nutritional status.

An example of a standardized height and weight chart is the body mass index (BMI). The BMI is a useful indicator of a person's overall health status. It is useful in providing guidelines in adults aged 20 to 65 years. BMI does not apply to infants, children, adolescents, pregnant and breast-feeding women, and adults over the age of 65 years. BMI is calculated by taking the weight of the individual in kilograms and dividing it by the height in metres squared. The formula is as follows:

$$\text{BMI} = \text{weight (kg)/height (m}^2\text{)}$$

For example, an individual weighing 75 kg and measuring 150 cm tall would have a BMI of 33.3, which, as may be seen from the table below, would put them at an increased risk.

The Integument

The integument includes the skin, hair, and nails. The examination begins with a generalized inspection in a well-lit environment.

BMI Health Effects

< 18.5	May be associated with health problems for some people
18.5 – 24.5	Good weight for most people
25.0 – 29.9	May lead to health problems in some people
>30	Increased risk of developing health problems

Source: Health Canada (2003). http://www.hc-sc.gc.ca/hpfb-dgpsa/onpp-bppn/bmi_chart_java_e.html © Reproduced with the permission of the Minister of Public Works and Government Services Canada, 2003.

Skin

Assessment of the skin involves inspection and palpation. In some instances, the nurse may also need to use the olfactory sense to detect unusual skin odours; these are usually most evident in the skinfolds or in the axillae. Pungent body odour is frequently related to poor hygiene, **hyperhidrosis** (excessive perspiration), or **bromhidrosis** (foul-smelling perspiration). The entire skin surface may be assessed at one time or as each aspect of the body is assessed.

Pallor is the result of inadequate circulating blood or hemoglobin and subsequent reduction in tissue oxygenation. It may be difficult to determine in clients with dark skin. It is usually characterized by the absence of underlying red tones in the skin and may be most readily seen in the buccal mucosa. In brown-skinned clients, pallor may appear as a yellowish-brown tinge; in black-skinned clients, the skin may appear ashen gray. Pallor in all people is usually most evident in areas with the least pigmentation, such as the conjunctiva, oral mucous membranes, nail beds, palms of the hand, and soles of the feet.

Cyanosis (a bluish tinge) is most evident in the nail beds, lips, and buccal mucosa. In dark-skinned clients, close inspection of the palpebral conjunctiva (the lining of the eyelids) and palms and soles may also show evidence of cyanosis. **Jaundice** (a yellowish tinge) may first be evident in the sclera of the eyes and then in the mucous membranes and the skin. Nurses should take care not to confuse jaundice with the normal yellow pigmentation in the sclera of a dark-skinned or black client. If jaundice is suspected, the posterior part of the hard palate should also be inspected for a yellowish colour tone. **Erythema** is a redness associated with a variety of skin disorders.

Dark-skinned clients have areas of lighter pigmentation, such as the palms, lips, and nail beds. Localized areas of hyperpigmentation (increased pigmentation) and hypopigmentation (decreased pigmentation) may also occur as a result of changes in the distribution of **melanin** (the dark pigment) or in the function of the melanocytes in the epidermis. An example of hyperpigmentation in a defined area is a birthmark; an example of hypopigmentation is vitiligo. **Vitiligo,** seen as patches of hypopigmented skin, is caused by the destruction of melanocytes in the area. **Albinism** is the complete or partial lack of melanin in the skin, hair, and eyes. Other localized colour changes may indicate a problem, such as edema or a localized infection. **Edema** is the presence of excess interstitial fluid. When edema is present, the tissues appear swollen and the skin is shiny, taut, and blanched. If the edema is accompanied by inflammation, the skin will appear reddened (erythematous). Generalized edema is most often an indication of impaired venous circulation and, in some cases, reflects cardiac dysfunction or vein abnormalities.

A skin lesion is an alteration in a client's normal skin appearance. **Primary skin lesions** are those that appear initially in response to some change in the external or internal environment of the skin (see the box below). **Secondary skin lesions** are those that do not appear initially but result from changes to the primary lesion, such as those caused by trauma or infection of the primary lesion. For example, a vesicle or blister (primary lesion) may rupture and cause an erosion (secondary lesion). Table 27.5 describes secondary lesions. Nurses are responsible for describing skin lesions accurately in terms of location (e.g., face), distribution (i.e., body regions involved), and configuration (the arrangement or position of several lesions), as well as colour, shape, size, firmness, texture, and characteristics of individual lesions.

Primary Skin Lesions

Macule, Patch Flat, unelevated change in colour. *Macules* are 1 mm to 1 cm in size and circumscribed. Examples: freckles, measles, petechiae, flat moles. *Patches* are larger than 1 cm and may have an irregular shape. Examples: port wine birthmark, vitiligo (white patches), rubella.

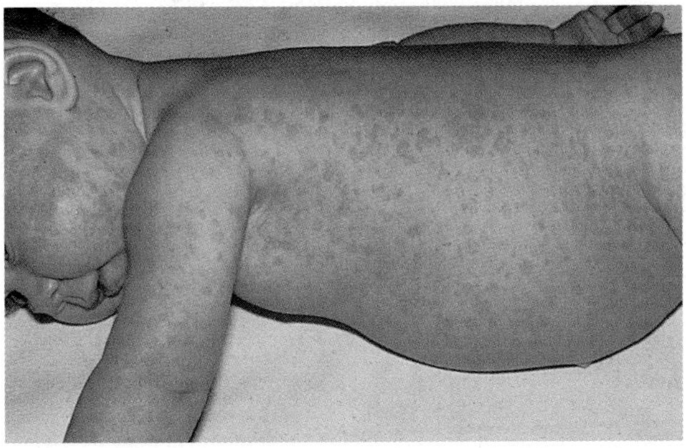

Diffuse, discrete erythematous macules (rubella)

Papule, Plaque Circumscribed, solid elevation of skin. *Papules* are less than 1 cm. Examples: warts, acne, pimples, elevated moles. *Plaques* are larger than 1 cm. Examples: psoriasis, rubeola.

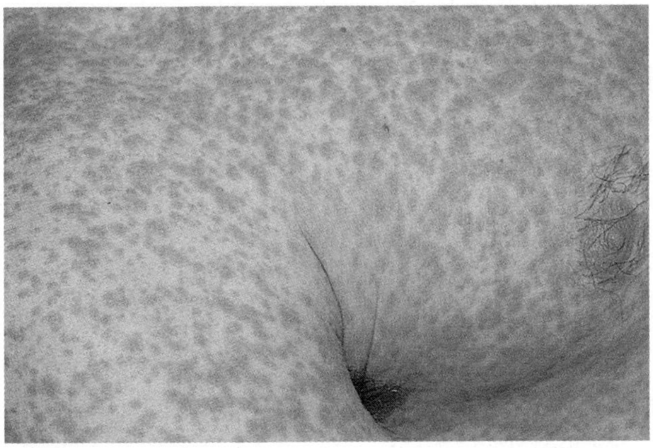

Diffuse, varying-sized, confluent maculo-papular lesions (rubeola)

Nodule, Tumour Elevated, solid, hard mass that extends deeper into the dermis than a papule. *Nodules* have a circumscribed border and are 0.5 to 2 cm. Examples: squamous cell carcinoma, fibroma. *Tumours* are larger than 2 cm and may have an irregular border. Examples: malignant melanoma, hemangioma.

Solitary, shiny brown, 1.25-cm nodule (squamous cell carcinoma)

Cyst A 1-cm or larger, elevated, encapsulated, fluid-filled or semisolid mass arising from the subcutaneous tissue or dermis. Examples: sebaceous and epidermoid cysts, chalazion of the eyelid.

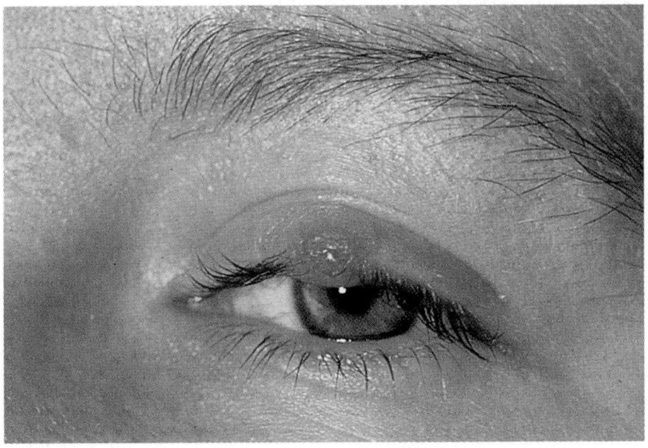

Reddened, circumscribed swelling on upper eyelid (chalazion)

Primary Skin Lesions *continued*

Pustule Vesicle or bulla filled with pus. Examples: acne vulgaris, impetigo.

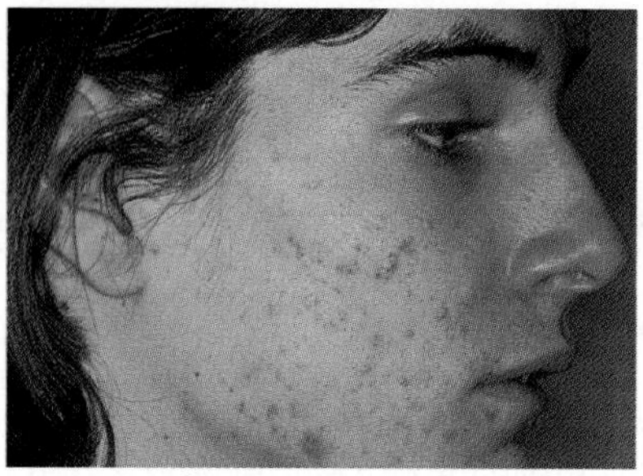

Diffuse, varying-sized, erythematous pustules on the cheeks (acne vulgaris)

Vesicle, Bulla A circumscribed, round or oval, thin, translucent mass filled with serous fluid or blood. Vesicles are less than 0.5 cm. Examples: herpes simplex, early chicken pox, small burn blister. *Bullae* are larger than 0.5 cm. Examples: large blister, second-degree burn, herpes simplex.

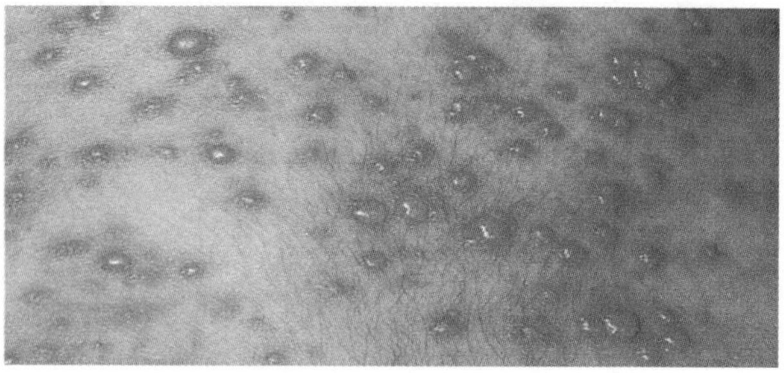

Clustered vesicles on an erythematous base (chicken pox)

Wheal A reddened, localized collection of edema fluid; irregular in shape. Size varies. Examples: hives, mosquito bites.

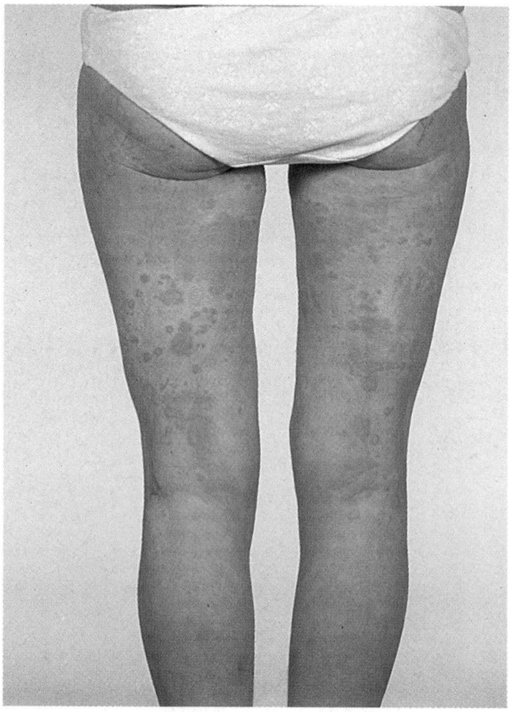

Diffuse, elevated, reddened lesions of varying size on backs of legs (hives)

Procedure 27.2 describes how to assess the skin.

PROCEDURE 27.2 Assessing the Skin

NURSING HISTORY FOCUS

Pain or itching; presence and spread of any lesions, bruises, abrasions, pigmented spots; previous experience with skin problems; associated clinical signs; family history; presence of problems in other family members; related systemic conditions; use of medications, lotions, home remedies; excessively dry or moist feel to the skin; tendency to bruise easily; any association of the problem to season of year, stress, occupation, medications, recent travel, housing, personal contact, and so on; any recent contact with allergens (e.g., metal, paint)

ASSESSMENT	NORMAL FINDINGS	DEVIATIONS FROM NORMAL
Inspect skin colour (best assessed under natural light and on areas not exposed to the sun).	Varies from light to deep brown; from ruddy pink to light pink; from yellow overtones to olive	Pallor, cyanosis, jaundice, erythema

TABLE 27.5 Secondary Skin Lesions

Type of Lesion	Description	Examples
Scale	White, grey, or silver flakes of greasy keratinized skin tissue	Dandruff, psoriasis, and eczema
Crust	Dried serum or pus on the skin surface after vesicles or pustules burst	Scab on abrasion, impetigo, herpes, eczema
Fissure	A linear crack that extends into the dermis	Athlete's foot, or cracks at the corner of the mouth
Erosion	A moist, shallow depression caused by wearing away of the epidermis	Areas following rupture of chicken pox and smallpox vesicles
Excoriation	Linear or hollowed-out crusted area exposing dermis	Abrasion, scratch
Ulcer	Deep, irregularly shaped area of skin loss that extends into the dermis or below	Chancres, stasis ulcers, decubitus ulcers (pressure sores)
Lichenification	Hard, rough, thickened area of epidermis following chronic irritation	Chronic dermatitis
Scar	Flat area of red, silver, or white connective tissue after a skin lesion has healed	Healed surgical wound or other lesion, such as acne
Atrophy	Dry translucent, paperlike skin surface from thinning or wasting of the skin	Aged skin, striae

PROCEDURE 27.2 Assessing the Skin *continued*

ASSESSMENT	NORMAL FINDINGS	DEVIATIONS FROM NORMAL
Inspect uniformity of skin colour.	Generally uniform except in areas exposed to the sun; areas of lighter pigmentation (palms, lips, nail beds) in dark-skinned people	Areas of either hyperpigmentation or hypopigmentation (e.g., vitiligo, albinism, edema)
Assess edema, if present (i.e., location, colour, temperature, and the degree to which the skin remains indented or pitted when pressed by a finger).		**Scale for Describing Edema** 1+ Barely detectable 2+ Indentation of less than 5 mm 3+ Indentation of 5 to 10 mm 4+ Indentation of more than 10 mm
Inspect, palpate, and describe skin lesions (see Table 27.5 and the box on Primary Skin Lesions). Palpate lesions to determine shape and texture. Describe lesions according to colour, distribution, and configuration.	Freckles, some birthmarks, some flat and raised nevi (moles); no abrasions or other lesions	Various interruptions in skin integrity
Observe and palpate skin moisture.	Moisture in skinfolds and the axillae (varies with environmental temperature and humidity, body temperature, and activity)	Excessive moisture (e.g., in hyperthermia); excessive dryness (e.g., in dehydration)

PROCEDURE 27.2 Assessing the Skin *continued*

DESCRIBING SKIN LESIONS

- *Size, shape, and texture.* Note size in millimetres and whether the lesion is circumscribed or irregular; round or oval shaped; flat, elevated, or depressed; solid, soft, or hard; rough or thickened; fluid filled or has flakes. Measure the size.
- *Colour.* There may be no discolouration, one discrete colour (e.g., red, brown, or black), or several colours, as with *ecchymosis* (a bruise), in which an initial dark red or blue colour fades to a yellow colour. When colour changes are limited to the edges of a lesion, they are described as *circumscribed;* when spread over a large area, they are described as *diffuse.*
- *Distribution.* Distribution is described according to the location of the lesions on the body and symmetry or asymmetry of findings in comparable body areas.
- *Configuration.* Configuration refers to the arrangement of lesions in relation to each other. Configurations of lesions may be annular (arranged in a circle); clustered together or grouped; linear (arranged in a line); arc or bow shaped; merged together or indiscrete; follow the course of cutaneous nerves; or meshed in the form of a network.

ASSESSMENT	NORMAL FINDINGS	DEVIATIONS FROM NORMAL
Palpate skin temperature. Compare the two feet and the two hands using the backs of your fingers.	Uniform; within normal range	Generalized hyperthermia (e.g., in fever); generalized hypothermia (e.g., in shock); localized hyperthermia (e.g., in infection); localized hypothermia (e.g., in arteriosclerosis)
Note skin turgor (fullness or elasticity) by lifting and pulling the skin on an extremity into a tent position.	When tented, skin springs back to previous state	Skin stays tented or moves back slowly (e.g., in dehydration)

Lifespan Considerations

Children

- Newborns may have jaundiced skin for several weeks after birth.
- In dark-skinned races, areas of increased pigmentation may be found in the sacral area of infants and young children.
- Newborns may have milia (whiteheads), small, white nodules usually found over the nose and face, and vernix caseosa (white, cheesy, greasy, protective material on the skin).

Older Adults

- The skin loses its elasticity and wrinkles. Wrinkles first appear on the skin of the face and neck.
- The skin appears thin and translucent because of loss of dermis and subcutaneous fat.
- The skin is dry and flaky because sebaceous and sweat glands are less active.
- The skin takes longer to return to its natural shape after being tented between the thumb and finger.
- Flat, tan to brown coloured macules, referred to as *senile lentigines* or *melanotic freckles,* are normally apparent on the back of the hand and other skin areas that are exposed to the sun. These macules may be as large as 1 to 2 cm.
- Warty lesions *(seborrheic keratosis)* with irregularly shaped borders and a scaly surface often occur on the face, shoulders, and trunk. These benign lesions begin as yellowish to tan and progress to a dark brown or black.
- Vitiligo tends to increase with age and is thought to result from an autoimmune response.
- Cutaneous tags *(acrochordons)* are most commonly seen in the neck and axillary regions. These skin lesions vary in size and are soft, often flesh coloured, and pedicled.

Lifespan Considerations *continued*

- Visible, bright red, fine, dilated blood vessels *(telangiectasias)* commonly occur as a result of the thinning of the dermis and the loss of support for the blood vessel walls.
- Pink to slightly red lesions with indistinct borders *(actinic keratoses)* may appear at about age 50 years, often on the face, ears, backs of the hands, and arms. They often become malignant.

Hair

Assessing a client's hair includes inspecting the hair, considering developmental changes, and determining the individual's hair care practices and the factors influencing them. Much of the information about hair can be obtained by questioning the client.

Normal hair is resilient and evenly distributed. In people with severe protein deficiency (kwashiorkor), the hair colour is faded and appears reddish or bleached, and the texture is coarse and dry. Some therapies cause **alopecia** (hair loss), and some disease conditions affect the coarseness of hair. For example, hypothyroidism can cause very thin and brittle hair.

Procedure 27.3 describes how to assess the hair.

PROCEDURE 27.3 Assessing the Hair

NURSING HISTORY FOCUS

Recent use of hair dyes, rinses, or curling or straightening preparations; recent chemotherapy (if alopecia is present); presence of disease, such as hypothyroidism, which can be associated with dry, brittle hair

ASSESSMENT	NORMAL FINDINGS	DEVIATIONS FROM NORMAL
Inspect the evenness of growth over the scalp.	Evenly distributed hair	Patches of hair loss (i.e., alopecia)
Inspect hair thickness or thinness.	Thick hair	Very thin hair
Inspect hair texture and oiliness.	Silky, resilient hair	Brittle hair; excessively oily or dry hair
Note presence of infections or infestations by parting the hair in several areas.	No infection or infestation	Flaking, sores, lice, nits (louse eggs), and ringworm
Inspect amount of body hair.	Variable Bilateral evenness	**Hirsutism** (excessive hairiness) in women and children Uneven distribution

Lifespan Considerations

Older Adults

- The age at which the scalp hair greys is influenced largely by genetic factors.
- In older age, there is loss of scalp, pubic, and axillary hair.
- In older women, some facial hair becomes coarse.
- Hairs of the eyebrows, ears, and nostrils become bristlelike and coarse in older adults.

Nails

Nails are inspected for nail plate shape, angle between the nail and the nail bed, nail texture, nail bed colour, and the intactness of the tissues around the nails. Parts of the nail are shown in Figure 27.6.

The nail plate is normally colourless and a convex curve. The angle between the nail and the nail bed is normally 160 degrees (Figure 27.7, *A*). One nail abnormality is the spoon shape, in which the nail curves upward from the nail bed (Figure 27.7, *B*). This condition, called **koilonychia,** may be seen in clients with iron deficiency anemia. **Clubbing** is a condition in which the angle between the nail and the nail bed is 180 degrees or greater (Figure 27.7, *C* and *D*). Clubbing may be caused by a long-term lack of oxygen and may be seen in clients with cardiac conditions.

Nail texture is normally smooth. Excessively thick nails can appear in the elderly, in the presence of poor circulation, or in relation to a chronic fungal infection. Excessively thin nails or the presence of grooves or furrows can reflect prolonged iron deficiency anemia. *Beau's lines* are horizontal depressions in the nail that can result from injury or severe illness (Figure 27.7, *E*).

The nail bed is highly vascular, a characteristic that accounts for its pink colour in Caucasian people. A bluish or purplish tint to the nail bed may reflect cyanosis, and pallor may reflect poor arterial circulation.

The tissue surrounding the nails is normally intact epidermis. **Paronychia** is an inflammation of the tissues surrounding a nail. The tissues appear inflamed and swollen and tenderness is usually present. A **blanch test** can be carried out to test the capillary refill. Normal nail bed capillaries blanch when pressed but quickly turn pink or their usual colour when pressure is released. A slow rate of capillary refill may indicate circulatory problems.

Procedure 27.4 describes how to assess the nails.

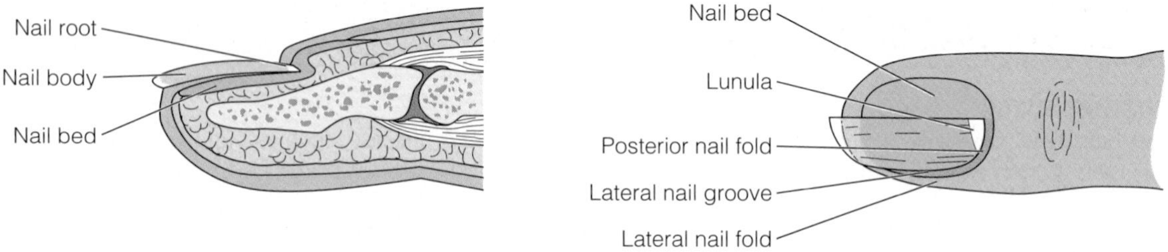

Figure 27.6 The parts of a nail

PROCEDURE 27.4 Assessing the Nails

NURSING HISTORY FOCUS

Presence of diabetes mellitus, peripheral circulatory disease, previous injury, or severe illness

ASSESSMENT	NORMAL FINDINGS	DEVIATIONS FROM NORMAL
Inspect nail plate shape to determine its curvature and angle.	Convex curvature; angle between nail and nail bed of about 160° (Figure 27.7, *A*)	Spoon nail (Figure 27.7, *B*); clubbing (180° or greater) (Figure 27.7, *C* and *D*)
Inspect nail texture.	Smooth texture	Excessive thickness (e.g., result of poor circulation, iron deficiency anemia); excessive thinness or presence of grooves or furrows (e.g., in iron deficiency anemia); Beau's lines (transverse white lines or grooves (Figure 27.7, *E*)
Inspect nail bed colour.	Highly vascular and pink; dark-skinned clients may have brown or black pigmentation in longitudinal streaks	Bluish or purplish tint (may reflect cyanosis); pallor (may reflect poor arterial circulation)

PROCEDURE 27.4 Assessing the Nails *continued*

ASSESSMENT	NORMAL FINDINGS	DEVIATIONS FROM NORMAL
Inspect tissues surrounding nails.	Intact epidermis	Hangnails; paronychia (inflammation)
Perform blanch test to test capillary refill. Press two or more nails between your thumb and index finger; look for blanching and return of usual colour to nail bed.	Prompt return of pink or usual colour	Delayed return of pink or usual colour (may indicate circulatory impairment)

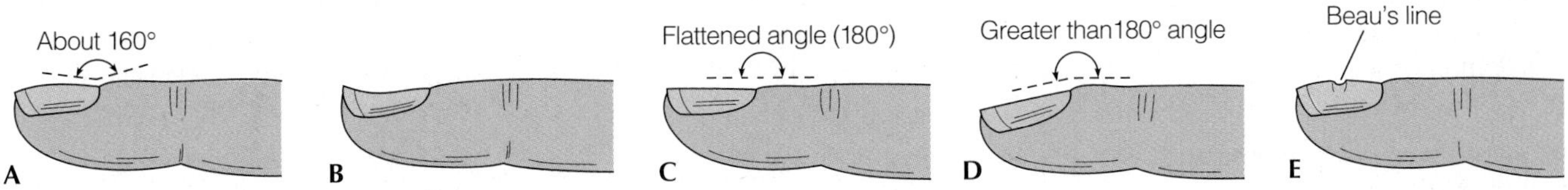

Figure 27.7 *A,* A normal nail, showing the convex shape and the nail plate angle of about 160 degrees; *B,* a spoon-shaped nail, which may be seen in clients with iron deficiency anemia; *C,* early clubbing; *D,* late clubbing (may be caused by long-term lack of oxygen); *E,* Beau's line on nail (may result from severe injury or illness)

Lifespan Considerations

Older Adults

- The nails grow more slowly and thicken.
- Longitudinal bands commonly develop in older adults, and the nails tend to split.
- Bands across the nails may indicate protein deficiency; white spots, zinc deficiency; and spoon-shaped nails, iron deficiency.

Head

Assessment of the head includes inspection, palpation, and percussion. The nurse examines the skull, face, eyes, ears, nose, sinuses, mouth, and pharynx.

Skull and Face

There is a range of normal shapes of skulls. A normal head size is referred to as **normocephalic.**

Procedure 27.5 describes how to assess the skull and face.

PROCEDURE 27.5 Assessing the Skull and Face

NURSING HISTORY FOCUS

Any past problems with lumps or bumps, itching, scaling, or dandruff; any history of loss of consciousness, dizziness, seizures, headache, facial pain, or injury; when and how any lumps occurred; length of time any other problem existed; any known cause of problem; associated symptoms, treatment, and recurrences

ASSESSMENT	NORMAL FINDINGS	DEVIATIONS FROM NORMAL
Inspect the skull for size, shape, and symmetry. If skull is of abnormal size, measure its circumference just above the eyebrows.	Rounded (normocephalic and symmetric, with frontal, parietal, and occipital prominences); smooth skull contour	Lack of symmetry; increased skull size with more prominent nose and forehead; longer mandible (may indicate excessive growth hormone or increased bone thickness)

→

PROCEDURE 27.5 Assessing the Skull and Face *continued*

ASSESSMENT	NORMAL FINDINGS	DEVIATIONS FROM NORMAL
Palpate the skull for nodules or masses and depressions. Use a gentle rotating motion with the fingertips. Begin at the front and palpate down the midline, then palpate each side of the head.	Smooth, uniform consistency; absence of nodules or masses	Sebaceous cysts; local deformities from trauma
Inspect the facial features (e.g., symmetry of structures and of the distribution of hair).	Symmetric or slightly asymmetric facial features; palpebral fissures equal in size; symmetric nasolabial folds Even distribution of hair	Increased and/or uneven distribution of facial hair; thinning of eyebrows; asymmetric features; exophthalmus; myxedema facies; moon face
Inspect the eyes for edema and hollowness.	No edema/ hollowness	Periorbital edema; sunken eyes
Note symmetry of facial movements. Ask the client to elevate the eyebrows, frown, or lower the eyebrows, close the eyes tightly, puff the cheeks, and smile and show the teeth. See Table 27.13, Cranial Nerve VII, on page 588.	Symmetric facial movements	Asymmetric facial movements (e.g., eye on affected side cannot close completely); drooping of lower eyelid and mouth; involuntary facial movements (i.e., tics or tremors)

Lifespan Considerations

Infants

- Most newborns' heads are shaped according to the method of delivery for about one week.
- The posterior fontanel (soft spot) generally closes by eight weeks, but the anterior fontanelle may persist for up to 18 months.
- Voluntary head control should be present after six months of age.
- Occipital flattening of positional origin results when an infant spends prolonged periods with the head in the same position against a flat surface. Flattening may occur before birth from wedging against a maternal pelvic bone, or it may occur postnatally.

Eyes and Vision

Many people consider vision the most important sense because it allows them to interact freely with their environment and enjoy the beauty of life around them. To maintain optimum vision, people need to have their eyes examined regularly throughout life. It is recommended that people have their eyes tested yearly or more frequently if there is a family history of diabetes, hypertension, blood dyscrasia, or eye disease (e.g., glaucoma).

An eye assessment should be carried out as part of the client's initial physical examination; periodic reassessments need to be made for clients in long-term care. Examination of the eyes includes assessment of **visual acuity** (the degree of detail the eye can discern in an image), ocular movement, **visual fields** (the area an individual can see when looking straight ahead), and external structures. If the client wears contact lenses or has an artificial eye, consideration should be given to individual hygiene practices. For the anatomic structures of the eye, see Figures 27.8 and 27.9.

Many people wear eyeglasses or contact lenses to correct common refractive errors of the lens of the eye. These errors include **myopia** (nearsightedness), **hyperopia** (farsightedness), and **presbyopia** (loss of elasticity of the lens and, thus, loss of ability to see close objects). Presbyopia begins at about 45 years of age. People with presbyopia notice that they have difficulty reading newsprint. Often, two corrective lenses (bifocals) are required—one for near vision or reading, the other for far vision. **Astigmatism,** an uneven curvature of the cornea that prevents horizontal and vertical rays from focusing on the retina, is a common problem that may occur in conjunction with myopia and hyperopia.

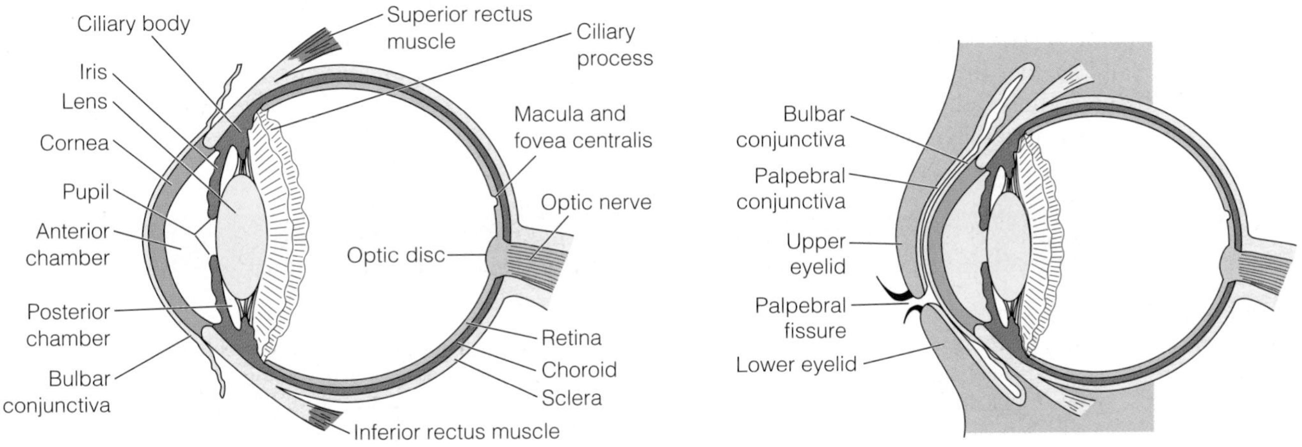

Figure 27.8 Anatomic structures of the right eye, lateral view

Three types of eye charts are available to test visual acuity (Figure 27.10). The child acquires normal 20/20 vision by six years of age. Visual acuity can be tested on a standard Snellen chart. Visual acuity is documented as two numbers (e.g., 20/20). The first number indicates the distance of the client from the chart (i.e., 20 feet), and the second number indicates the distance at which a normal eye can read the chart. For example, a test result of 20/200 means that at 20 feet, the client can read the chart that a person with normal vision could read at 200 feet. In other words, the larger the second number, or denominator, the worse the visual acuity. People with denominators of 40 or more on the Snellen chart, with or without corrective lenses, need to be referred to an ophthalmologist.

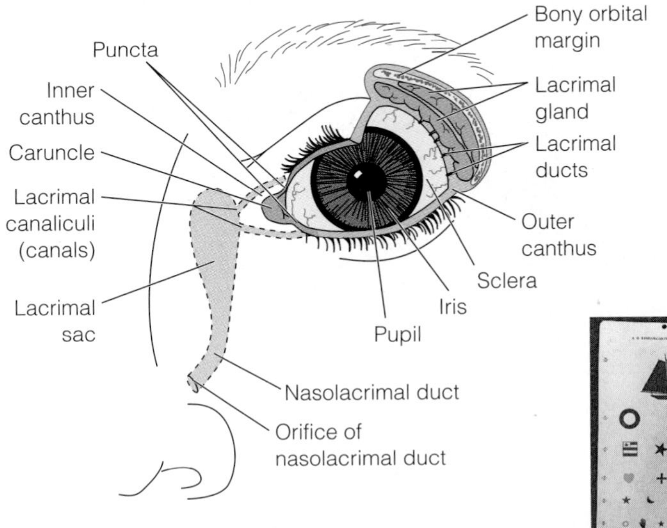

Figure 27.9 The external structures and lacrimal apparatus of the left eye

Cataracts are an opacity of the lens of the eye. Most cataracts tend to occur in individuals over the age of 65 years. However, cataracts also occur in infants due to a malformation of the lens, for example, if a mother contracts rubella in the first trimester of pregnancy. A common treatment is removal of the lens and replacement of the lens with an implant. **Glaucoma** is a disruption in the circulation of the aqueous fluid which causes an increase in intraocular pressure and a reduced blood supply to the optic disc. Glaucoma is the most common cause of blindness in people over 40 years. It can be managed if diagnosed early. Danger signs of glaucoma include blurred or foggy vision, loss of peripheral vision, difficulty focusing on close objects, difficulty adjusting to dark rooms, and seeing rainbow-coloured rings around lights.

Pupils are black, are equal in size (about 3 to 7 mm in diameter), and have round, smooth borders. Enlarged pupils **(mydriasis)** may indicate injury or glaucoma or result from certain drugs (e.g., atropine). Constricted pupils **(miosis)**

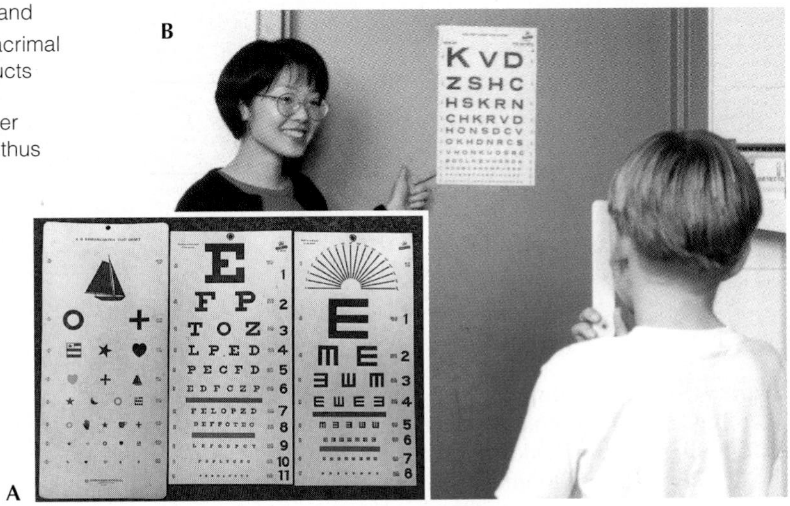

Figure 27.10 *A*, Three types of eye charts; the preschool children's chart (left), Snellen standard chart (centre), and the Snellen E chart for clients unable to read (right); *B*, Nurse examining for vision using Snellen chart

may indicate an inflammation of the iris or result from such drugs as morphine or pilocarpine. Pupils may become slightly irregular and smaller in older adults, making it more difficult to examine the eyes. Unequal pupils **(anisocoria)** may result from a central nervous system disorder; however, slight variations may be normal. The iris is normally flat and round. A bulging toward the cornea can indicate increased intraocular pressure.

Procedure 27.6 describes how to assess a client's eye structures and visual acuity.

PROCEDURE 27.6 Assessing the Eye Structures and Visual Acuity

NURSING HISTORY FOCUS

Family history of diabetes, hypertension, blood dyscrasia, or eye disease, injury, or surgery; client's last visit to an ophthalmologist; current use of eye medications; use of contact lenses or eyeglasses; hygienic practices for corrective lenses; current symptoms of eye problems (e.g., changes in visual acuity, blurring of vision, tearing, spots, photophobia, itching, or pain)

ASSESSMENT	NORMAL FINDINGS	DEVIATIONS FROM NORMAL
External Eye Structures		
Inspect the eyebrows for hair distribution and alignment and skin quality and movement. (Ask client to raise and lower the eyebrows.)	Hair evenly distributed; skin intact	Loss of hair; scaling and flakiness of skin
	Eyebrows symmetrically aligned; equal movement	Unequal alignment and movement of eyebrows
Inspect the eyelashes for evenness of distribution and direction of curl.	Equally distributed; curled slightly outward	Turned inward
Inspect the eyelids for surface characteristics (e.g., skin quality and texture), **position in relation to the cornea, ability to blink, and frequency of blinking.** For proper visual examination of the upper eyelids, elevate the eyebrows with your thumb and index fingers, and have the client close the eyes (Figure 27.11). Inspect the lower eyelids while the client's eyes are closed.	Skin intact; no discharge; no discolouration	Redness, swelling, flaking, crusting, plaques, discharge, nodules, lesions
	Lids close symmetrically	Lids close asymmetrically, incompletely, or painfully
	Approximately 15 to 20 involuntary blinks per minute; bilateral blinking	Rapid, monocular, absent, or infrequent blinking
	When lids open, no visible sclera above corneas, and upper and lower borders of cornea are slightly covered	Ptosis, ectropion, or entropion; rim of sclera visible between lid and iris (possible hyperthyroidism)

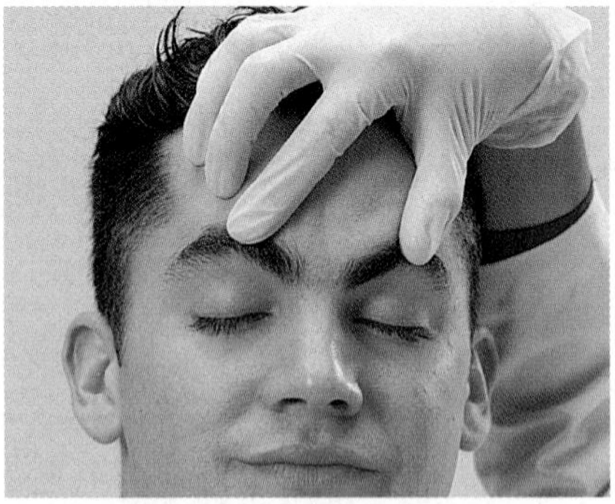

Figure 27.11 Inspecting the upper eyelids

ASSESSMENT	NORMAL FINDINGS	DEVIATIONS FROM NORMAL
Inspect the bulbar conjunctiva (lying over the sclera) **for colour, texture, and the presence of lesions.** Retract the eyelids with your thumb and index finger, exerting pressure over the upper and lower bony orbits and ask the client to look up, down, and from side to side.	Transparent; capillaries sometimes evident; sclera appears white (yellowish in dark-skinned clients)	Jaundiced sclera (e.g., in liver disease); excessively pale sclera (e.g., in anemia); reddened sclera; lesions or nodules (may indicate damage by mechanical, chemical, allergenic, or bacterial agents)

PROCEDURE 27.6 Assessing the Eye Structures and Visual Acuity *continued*

ASSESSMENT	NORMAL FINDINGS	DEVIATIONS FROM NORMAL
Inspect the palpebral conjunctiva (lining of the eyelids) **by everting the lids. Note colour, texture, and the presence of lesions.** Evert both lower lids and ask the client to look up. Then gently retract the lower lids with the index fingers. **Evert the upper lids if a problem** (e.g., a foreign body) **is suspected.** See the accompanying box.	Shiny, smooth, and pink or red	Extremely pale (possible anemia); extremely red (inflammation); nodules or other lesions

EVERTING THE UPPER EYELID

- Ask the client to look down while keeping the eyes slightly open. *Closing the eyelids contracts the orbicular muscle, which prevents lid eversion.*
- Gently grasp the client's eyelashes with the thumb and index finger. Pull the lashes gently downward. *Upward or outward pulling on the eyelashes causes muscle contraction.*
- Place a cotton-tipped applicator stick about 1 cm above the lid margin, and push it gently downward while holding the eyelashes (Figure 27.12). These actions evert the lid, that is, flip the lower part of the lid over on top of itself.
- Hold the margin of the everted lid or the eyelashes against the ridge of the upper bony orbit with the applicator stick or the thumb (Figure 27.13).
- Inspect the conjunctiva for colour, texture, lesions, and foreign bodies.
- To return the lid to its normal position, gently pull the lashes forward, and ask the client to look up and blink.

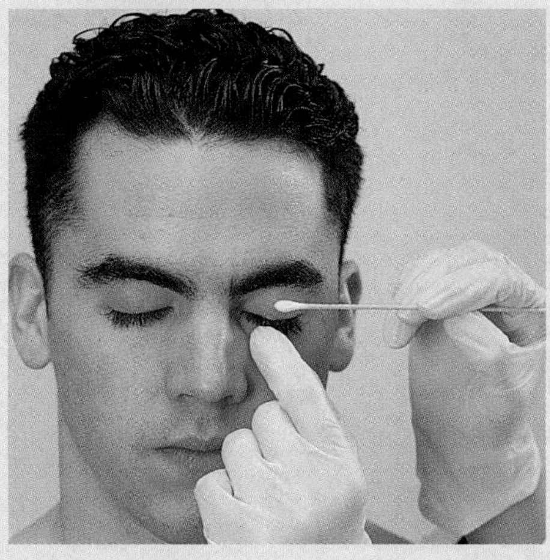

Figure 27.12 Everting the upper eyelid

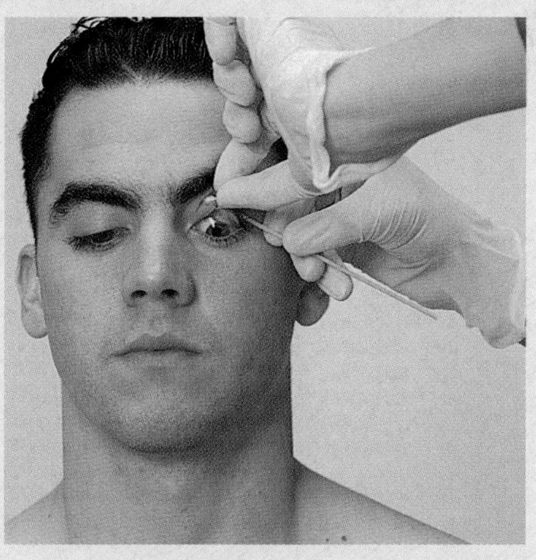

Figure 27.13 Holding the margin of the everted upper eyelid

ASSESSMENT	NORMAL FINDINGS	DEVIATIONS FROM NORMAL
Inspect and palpate the lacrimal gland. See the box on page 532.	No edema or tenderness over lacrimal gland	Swelling or tenderness over lacrimal gland
Inspect and palpate the lacrimal sac and nasolacrimal duct.	No edema or tearing	Evidence of increased tearing; regurgitation of fluid on palpation of lacrimal sac

PROCEDURE 27.6 Assessing the Eye Structures and Visual Acuity *continued*

ASSESSMENT	NORMAL FINDINGS	DEVIATIONS FROM NORMAL
Inspect the cornea for clarity and texture. Ask the client to look straight ahead. Hold a penlight at an oblique angle to the eye, and move the light slowly across the corneal surface. Tangential lighting best shows corneal regularity.	Transparent, shiny and smooth; details of the iris are visible In older people, a thin, grayish white ring around the margin, called arcus senilis, may be evident	Opaque; surface not smooth (may be the result of trauma or abrasion) Arcus senilis in clients under age 40 years is abnormal
Perform the corneal sensitivity (reflex) test to determine the function of the fifth (trigeminal) cranial nerve. Ask the client to keep both eyes open and look straight ahead. With a wisp of cotton, approach from behind and beside the client, and lightly touch the cornea with the cotton wisp. This test is not done on clients wearing contact lenses.	Client blinks when the cornea is touched, indicating that the trigeminal nerve is intact	One or both eyelids fail to respond

PALPATING THE LACRIMAL GLAND, LACRIMAL SAC, AND NASOLACRIMAL DUCT

- Using the tip of your index finger, palpate the lacrimal gland (Figure 27.14).
- Observe for edema between the lower lid and the nose.
- Observe for evidence of increased tearing.
- Using the tip of your index finger, palpate inside the lower orbital rim near the inner canthus (Figure 27.15).

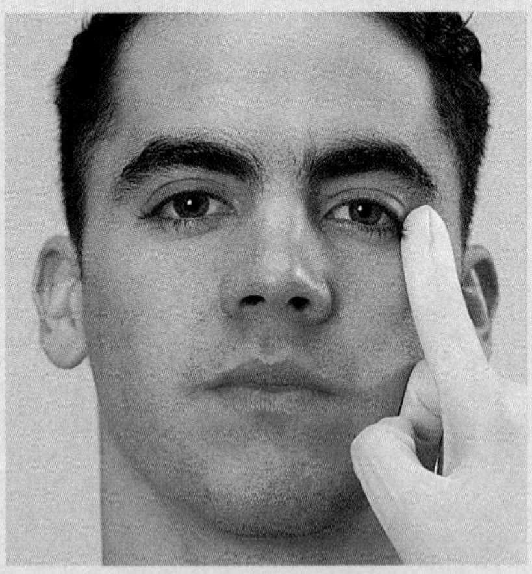

Figure 27.14 Palpating the lacrimal gland

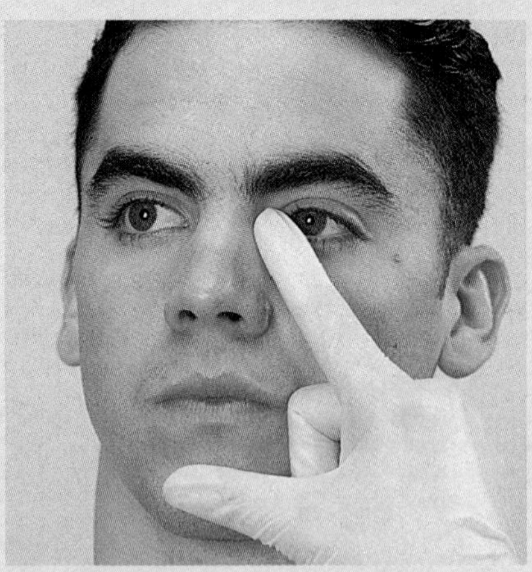

Figure 27.15 Palpating the lacrimal sac and the nasolacrimal duct

ASSESSMENT	NORMAL FINDINGS	DEVIATIONS FROM NORMAL
Inspect the anterior chamber for transparency and depth. Use the same oblique lighting as used to test the cornea.	Transparent No shadows of light on iris	Cloudy Crescent-shaped shadows on far side of iris

PROCEDURE 27.6 Assessing the Eye Structures and Visual Acuity *continued*

ASSESSMENT	NORMAL FINDINGS	DEVIATIONS FROM NORMAL
Inspect the pupils for colour, shape, and symmetry of size. Pupil charts are available in some agencies. See Figure 27.16 for variations in pupil diameters.	About 3 mm in diameter Black in colour; equal in size; normally 3–7 mm in diameter; round, smooth border, iris flat and round	Shallow chamber (possible glaucoma) Cloudiness, mydriasis, miosis, anisocoria; bulging of iris toward cornea

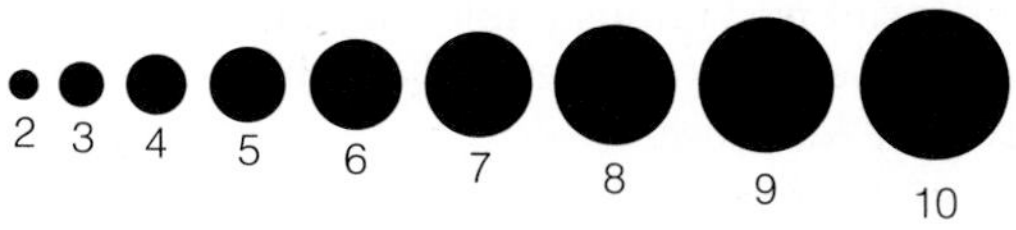

Figure 27.16 Variations in pupil diameters in millimetres

ASSESSMENT	NORMAL FINDINGS	DEVIATIONS FROM NORMAL
Assess each pupil's direct and consensual reaction to light. The muscle fibers of the iris are controlled by the autonomic nervous system. See the box below.	Illuminated pupil constricts (direct response) Nonilluminated pupil constricts (consensual response)	Neither pupil constricts Unequal responses Absent responses
Assess each pupil's reaction to accommodation.	Pupils constrict when looking at near object; pupils dilate when looking at far object; pupils converge when near object is moved toward nose	One or both pupils fail to constrict, dilate, or converge

ASSESSING PUPIL REACTIONS

Direct and Consensual Reaction to Light

- Partially darken the room.
- Ask the client to look straight ahead.
- Using a penlight or flashlight and approaching from the side, shine a light on the pupil.
- Observe the response of the illuminated pupil. It should constrict (direct response).
- Shine the light on the pupil again, and observe the response of the other pupil. It should also constrict (consensual response).

Reaction to Accommodation

- Hold an object (a penlight or pencil) about 10 cm from the bridge of the client's nose.
- Ask the client to look first at the top of the object and then at a distant object (e.g., the far wall) behind the penlight. Alternate the gaze from the near to the far object.
- Observe the pupil response. The pupils should constrict when looking at the near object and dilate when looking at the far object.
- Next, move the penlight or pencil toward the client's nose. The pupils should converge.

To record normal assessment of the pupils, use the abbreviation PERRLA (pupils equally round and react to light and accommodation).

Visual Fields

ASSESSMENT	NORMAL FINDINGS	DEVIATIONS FROM NORMAL
Assess peripheral visual fields to determine function of the retina and neuronal visual pathways to the brain and second (optic) cranial nerve. See the box on page 534.	When looking straight ahead, client can see objects in the periphery	Visual field smaller than normal (possible glaucoma); one-half vision in one or both eyes (indicates nerve damage)

PROCEDURE 27.6 Assessing the Eye Structures and Visual Acuity *continued*

ASSESSMENT	NORMAL FINDINGS	DEVIATIONS FROM NORMAL
Extraocular Muscle Tests		
Assess six ocular movements to determine eye alignment and coordination. These can be performed on clients over 6 months of age. See the box on page 535.	Both eyes coordinated; move in unison, with parallel alignment	Eye movements not coordinated or parallel; one or both eyes fail to follow a penlight in specific directions, such as **strabismus** (cross-eye or squint)
	End-point **nystagmus** (rapid involuntary movement of the eyeball on the extreme lateral gaze)	Nystagmus other than end-point (may indicate neurological impairment)

ASSESSING PERIPHERAL VISUAL FIELDS

- Have the client sit directly facing you at a distance of 60 to 90 cm.
- Ask the client to cover the right eye with a card and look directly at your nose.
- Cover or close your eye directly opposite the client's covered eye (i.e., your left eye), and look directly at the client's nose.
- Hold an object (e.g., a penlight or pencil) in your fingers, extend your arm, and move the object into the visual field from various points in the periphery (Figure 27.17). The object should be at an equal distance from the client and yourself. Ask the client to tell you when the moving object is first spotted.
  a. To test the *temporal field* of the left eye, extend and move your right arm in from the client's right periphery. Temporally, peripheral objects can be seen at right angles (90 degrees) to the central point of vision.
  b. To test the *upward (superior) field* of the left eye, extend and move the right arm down from the upward periphery. The upward field of vision is normally 50 degrees because the orbital ridge is in the way.
  c. To test the *downward (inferior) field* of the left eye, extend and move the right arm up from the lower periphery. The downward field of vision is normally 70 degrees because the cheekbone is in the way.
  d. To test the *nasal field* of the left eye, extend and move your left arm in from the periphery. The nasal field of vision is normally 50 degrees away from the central point of vision because the nose is in the way.
- Repeat the above steps for the right eye, reversing the process.

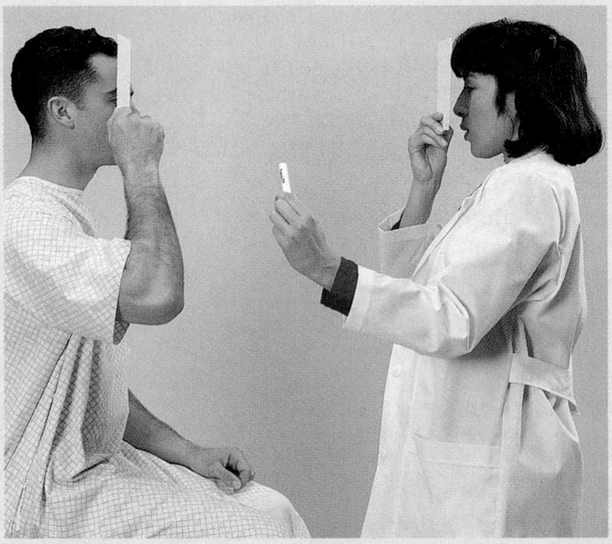

Figure 27.17 Assessing the client's left peripheral visual field

ASSESSMENT	NORMAL FINDINGS	DEVIATIONS FROM NORMAL
Visual Acuity		
Assess near vision by providing adequate lighting and asking the client to read from a magazine or newspaper held at a distance of 36 cm. If the client normally wears glasses or corrective lenses, the glasses or lenses should be worn during the test.	Able to read newsprint	Difficulty reading newsprint, unless due to aging process

PROCEDURE 27.6 Assessing the Eye Structures and Visual Acuity *continued*

ASSESSMENT	NORMAL FINDINGS	DEVIATIONS FROM NORMAL
Assess distance vision by asking the client to wear corrective lenses, unless they are used for reading only, that is, for distances of only 36 cm.	20/20 vision on Snellen chart from age six years onward	Denominator of 40 or more on Snellen chart with corrective lenses

ASSESSING THE SIX OCULAR MOVEMENTS

- Stand directly in front of the client and hold the penlight at a comfortable distance, such as 30 cm in front of the client's eyes.
- Ask the client to hold the head in a fixed position facing you and to follow the movements of the penlight with the eyes *only*.
- Move the penlight in a slow, orderly manner through the six cardinal fields of gaze, that is, from the centre of the eye along the lines of the arrows in Figure 27.18 and back to the centre.
- Stop the movement of the penlight periodically so that nystagmus can be detected.
- These six positions are used because six muscles guide the movements of each eye. Four *rectus* muscles (superior, inferior, lateral, and medial) move the eye in the direction indicated. Two *oblique* muscles (superior and inferior) rotate the eyeball on its axis. Cranial nerves III (oculomotor), IV (trochlear), and VI (abducens) innervate these muscles. Moving the object through the six positions can identify a nonfunctioning muscle or associated cranial nerve.

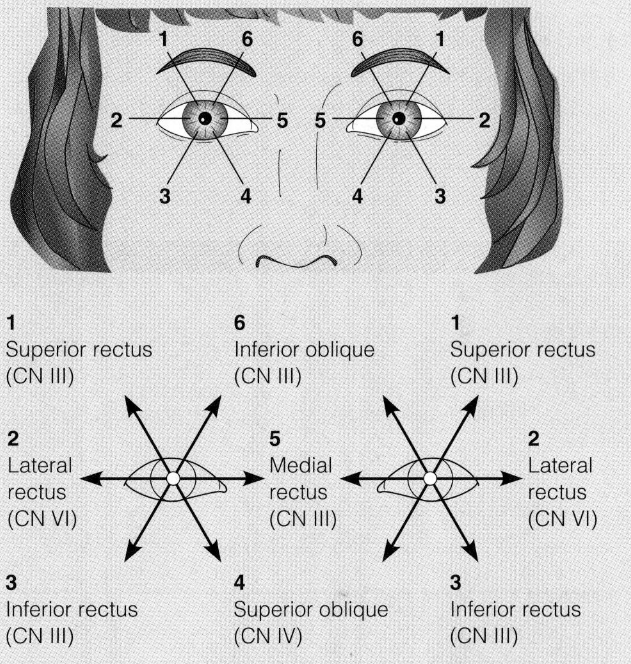

Figure 27.18 The six muscles that govern eye movement

ASSESSING DISTANCE VISION

- Ask the client to stand or sit 6 m (20 ft) from a Snellen chart, cover the eye not being tested, and identify the letters on the Snellen chart.
- Take three readings: right eye, left eye, both eyes.
- Record the readings of each eye and both eyes, that is, the smallest line from which the person is able to read one-half or more of the letters.
- At the end of each line of the Snellen chart are standardized numbers. The top line is 20/200. The numerator (top number) is always 20, the distance (in feet) the person stands from the chart.

The denominator (bottom number) is the distance from which the normal eye can read the chart. Therefore, a person who has 20/40 vision can see at 20 feet from the chart what a normal-sighted person can see at 40 feet from the chart. Visual acuity is recorded as "$\bar{s}$c" (without correction), or "$\bar{c}$c" (with correction). Also indicate how many letters were misread in the line, for example, "visual acuity 20/40—2$\bar{c}$c" indicates that two letters were misread in the 20/40 line by a client wearing corrective lenses.

ASSESSMENT	NORMAL FINDINGS	DEVIATIONS FROM NORMAL
Perform functional vision tests if the client is unable to see the top line (20/200) of the Snellen chart. See the box on page 536.		Functional vision only (e.g., light perception, hand movements, counting fingers at 30 cm)

PROCEDURE 27.6 Assessing the Eye Structures and Visual Acuity *continued*

PERFORMING FUNCTIONAL VISION TESTS

Light Perception

Shine a penlight into the client's eye from a lateral position, and then turn the light off. Ask the client to tell you when the light is on or off. If the client knows when the light is on or off, the client has light perception, and the vision is recorded as "LP."

Hand Movements (H/M)

Hold your hand 30 cm from the client's face and move it slowly back and forth, stopping it periodically. Ask the client to tell you when your hand stops moving. If the client knows when your hand stops moving, record the vision as "H/M 30 cm."

Counting Fingers (C/F)

Hold up some of your fingers 30 cm from the client's face, and ask the client to count your fingers. If the client can do so, note on the vision record "C/F 30 cm."

Lifespan Considerations

Children

VISUAL ACUITY

- Infants four weeks of age should gaze at and follow bright objects.
- Ability to focus with both eyes should be present by six months of age.
- Preschool children can be tested with picture cards.

EXTERNAL EYE STRUCTURES

- Children with epicanthal folds may appear to have misaligned eyes.
- Dark-skinned children may have darker or gray-blue sclerae with or without small brown macules.

Older Adults

VISUAL ACUITY

- Visual acuity decreases as the lens ages and becomes more opaque and loses elasticity (presbyopia).
- The ability of the iris to accommodate to darkness and dim light diminishes.
- Peripheral vision diminishes.
- The adaptation to light (glare) and dark decreases.
- Accommodation to far objects often improves, but accommodation to near objects decreases.
- Colour vision declines; older people are less able to perceive purple colours and to discriminate pastel colours.
- Many older people wear corrective lenses; they are most likely to have hyperopia. Visual changes are due to loss of elasticity (presbyopia) and transparency of the lens.
- The number of vitreous floaters increases with age.

EXTERNAL EYE STRUCTURES

- The skin around the orbit of the eye may darken.
- The eyes may appear dry and lustreless because of the decrease in tear production from the lacrimal glands.
- The eyeball may appear sunken because of the decrease in orbital fat.
- Skinfolds of the upper lids may seem more prominent, and the lower lids may sag.
- A thin, grayish white arc or ring *(arcus senilis)* appears around part or all of the cornea. It results from an accumulation of a lipid substance on the cornea. The cornea tends to cloud with age.
- The iris may appear pale with brown discolourations as a result of pigment degeneration.
- The conjunctiva of the eye may appear paler than that of younger adults and may take on a slightly yellow appearance because of the deposition of fat.
- Pupil reaction to light and accommodation is normally symmetrically equal but may be less brisk.
- The pupils can appear smaller in size, unequal, and irregular in shape because of sclerotic changes in the iris.

Ears and Hearing

Assessment of the ear includes direct inspection and palpation of the external ear, inspection of the remaining parts of the ear by an **otoscope,** and determination of auditory acuity. The ear is usually assessed during an initial physical examination; periodic reassessments may be necessary for long-term clients or those with hearing problems.

The ear is divided into three parts: external ear, middle ear, and inner ear. Most of the structures mentioned next are illustrated in Figure 27.19. The external ear includes the **auricle** or **pinna,** the external auditory canal, and the **tympanic membrane,** or eardrum. Landmarks of the auricle include the **lobule** (earlobe), **helix** (the posterior curve of the auricle's upper aspect), **antihelix** (the anterior curve of the auricle's upper aspect), **tragus** (the cartilaginous protrusion at the entrance to the ear canal), **triangular fossa** (a depression of the antihelix), and **external auditory meatus** (the entrance to the ear canal). Although not part of the ear, the **mastoid,** a bony prominence behind the ear, is another important landmark. The external ear canal is curved, is about 2.5 cm long in the adult, and ends at the tympanic membrane. The tympanic membrane separates the external ear from the middle ear. It is covered with skin that has many fine hairs, glands, and nerve endings. The glands secrete **cerumen** (earwax), which lubricates and protects the canal.

The middle ear is an air-filled cavity that starts at the tympanic membrane and contains three **ossicles** (bones of sound transmission): the **malleus** (hammer), which is the most easily seen, the **incus** (anvil), and the **stapes** (stirrups) (see Figure 27.19). The **eustachian tube,** another part of the middle ear, connects the middle ear to the nasopharynx. The tube stabilizes the air pressure between the external atmosphere and the middle ear, thus preventing rupture of the tympanic membrane and discomfort produced by marked pressure differences.

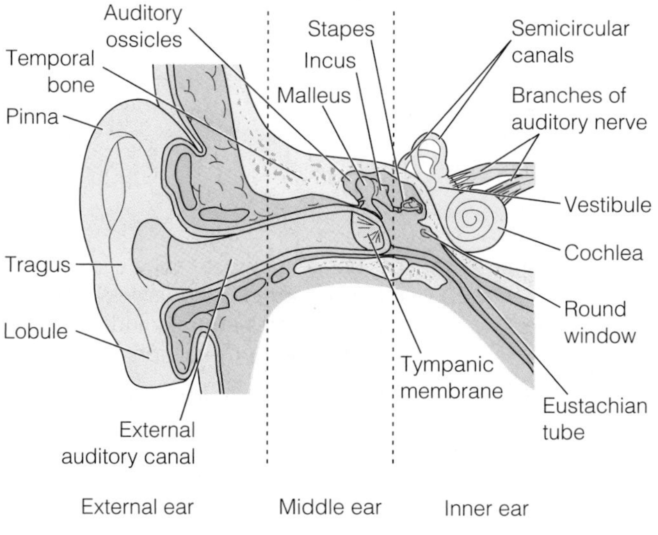

Figure 27.19 Anatomic structures of the external, middle, and inner ear

The inner ear contains the **cochlea,** a seashell-shaped structure essential for sound transmission and hearing, and the **vestibule** and **semicircular canals,** which contain the organs of equilibrium.

Sound transmission and hearing are complex processes. In brief, sound can be transmitted by air conduction or bone conduction. Air-conducted transmission occurs by this process:

1. A sound stimulus enters the external canal and reaches the tympanic membrane.
2. The sound waves cross the tympanic membrane and reach the ossicles.
3. The sound waves travel along the vibrating ossicles to the opening in the inner ear (oval window). The ossicles vibrate.
4. The cochlea receives the sound vibrations.
5. The stimulus travels to the auditory nerve (the eighth cranial nerve) and the cerebral cortex.
6. The electrical impulses from the auditory nerve are intepreted as sound in the cerebral cortex.

Bone-conducted sound transmission occurs when skull bones transport the sound directly to the auditory nerve.

The curvature of the external ear canal differs with age. In the infant and toddler, the canal has an upward curvature. By age three years, the ear canal assumes the more downward curvature of adulthood.

Audiometric evaluations, which measure hearing at various decibels, are recommended for elderly people. A common hearing deficit with age is loss of ability to hear high-frequency sounds, such as *f, s, sh,* and *ph.* This neurosensory hearing deficit does not respond well to the use of a hearing aid.

Conduction hearing loss is the result of interrupted transmission of sound waves through the outer and middle ear structures. Possible causes are a tear in the tympanic membrane or an obstruction, due to swelling or other causes, in the auditory canal. **Sensorineural hearing loss** is the result of damage to the inner ear, the auditory nerve, or the hearing centre in the brain. **Mixed hearing loss** is a combination of conduction and sensorineural loss. Procedure 27.7 describes how to assess the ears and hearing.

PROCEDURE 27.7 Assessing the Ears and Hearing

NURSING HISTORY FOCUS

Family history of hearing problems or loss; presence of any ear problems; medication history, especially if there are complaints of ringing in ears; any hearing difficulty: its onset, factors contributing to it, and how it interferes with activities of daily living; use of a corrective hearing device: when and from whom it was obtained

ASSESSMENT	NORMAL FINDINGS	DEVIATIONS FROM NORMAL
Auricles		
Inspect the auricles for colour, symmetry of size, and position. To inspect position, note the level at which the superior aspect of the auricle attaches to the head in relation to the eye. See Figure 27.20.	Colour same as facial skin	Bluish colour of earlobes (e.g., cyanosis); pallor (e.g., frostbite); excessive redness (inflammation or fever)
	Symmetric position; line drawn from lateral angle of eye to point where top part of auricle joins head is horizontal; an imaginary line drawn from the top to the bottom of the ear should vary no more than 10 degrees from the vertical	Low-set ears (associated with a congenital abnormality, such as Down syndrome)

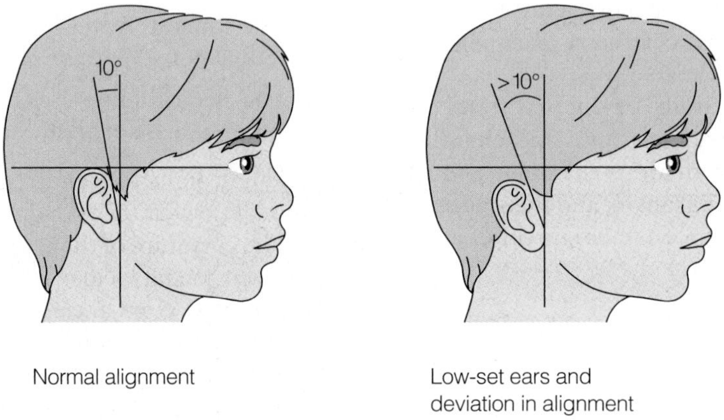

Figure 27.20 Normal alignment of a child's ears

ASSESSMENT	NORMAL FINDINGS	DEVIATIONS FROM NORMAL
Palpate the auricles for texture, elasticity, and areas of tenderness. ▪ Pull the auricle upward, downward, and backward. ▪ Fold the pinna forward (it should recoil). ▪ Push in on the tragus. ▪ Apply pressure to the mastoid process.	Mobile, firm, and not tender; pinna recoils after it is folded	Lesions (e.g., cysts); flaky, scaly skin (e.g., seborrhea); tenderness when moved or pressed (may indicate inflammation or infection of external ear)

PROCEDURE 27.7 Assessing the Ears and Hearing *continued*

ASSESSMENT	NORMAL FINDINGS	DEVIATIONS FROM NORMAL
External Ear Canal and Tympanic Membrane		
Using an otoscope, inspect the external ear canal for cerumen, skin lesions, pus, and blood.	Distal third contains hair follicles and glands Dry cerumen, greyish tan colour; or sticky, wet cerumen in various shades of brown	Redness and discharge Scaling Excessive cerumen obstructing canal

INSPECTING THE EXTERNAL EAR CANAL WITH AN OTOSCOPE

- Prior to inserting the otoscope, inspect the ear canal for the presence of foreign objects or tumours.
- Attach a speculum to the otoscope. Use the largest diameter that will fit the ear canal without causing discomfort. *This achieves maximum vision of the entire ear canal and tympanic membrane.*
- Tip the client's head slightly away from you. For an adult, straighten the ear canal by pulling the pinna up and back (Figure 27.21). *Straightening the ear canal facilitates vision of the ear canal and the tympanic membrane.*
- Hold the otoscope either (1) right side up, with your fingers between the otoscope handle and the client's head, or (2) upside down, with your fingers and the ulnar surface of your hand against the client's head (Figure 27.22). *This stabilizes the head and protects the eardrum and canal from injury if a quick head movement occurs.*
- Gently insert the tip of the otoscope into the ear canal, avoiding pressure by the speculum against either side of the ear canal. *The inner two-thirds of the ear canal is bony; if the speculum is pressed against either side, the client will experience discomfort.*

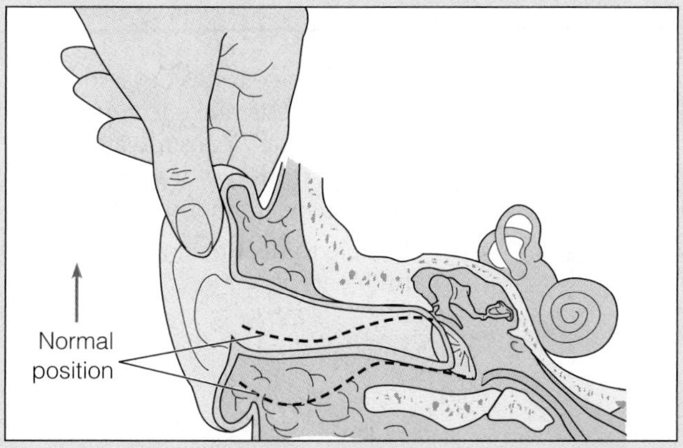

Figure 27.21 Straightening the ear canal of an adult by pulling the pinna up and back

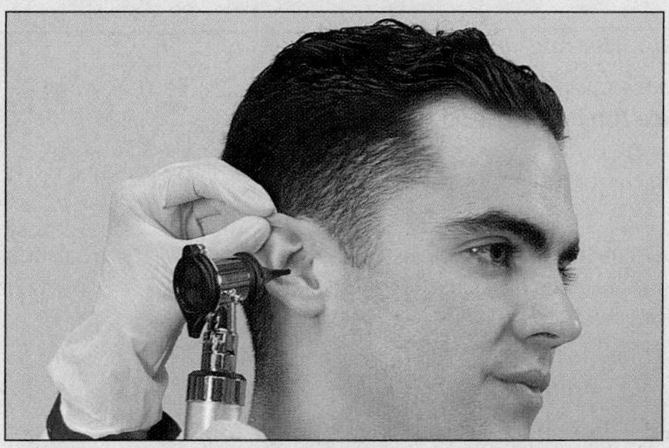

Figure 27.22 Inserting an otoscope

PROCEDURE 27.7 Assessing the Ears and Hearing *continued*

ASSESSMENT	NORMAL FINDINGS	DEVIATIONS FROM NORMAL
Inspect the tympanic membrane for colour and gloss. See Figure 27.23.	Pearly grey colour; semi-transparent Light reflex at 5 o'clock in right ear and 7 o'clock in left ear	Pink to red; some opacity, yellow-amber, white, blue, or deep red, dull surface

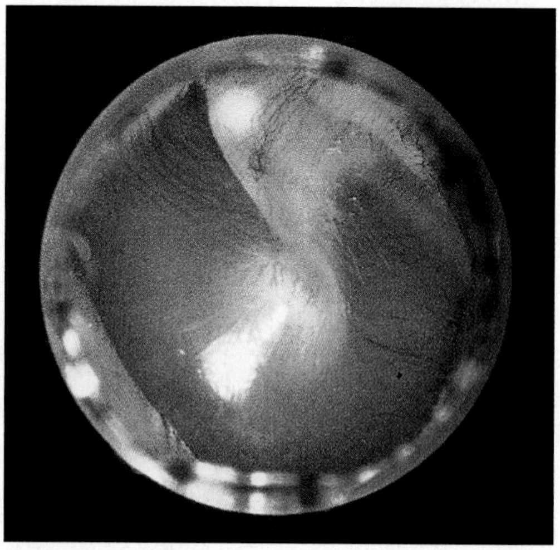

Figure 27.23 Normal tympanic membrane with light reflex at 7 o'clock (left ear)

ASSESSMENT	NORMAL FINDINGS	DEVIATIONS FROM NORMAL
Gross Hearing Acuity Tests		
Assess client's response to normal voice tones. If client has difficulty hearing normal voice, proceed with the following tests.	Normal voice tones audible	Normal voice tones not audible (e.g., requests nurse to repeat words or statements, leans toward the speaker, turns the head, cups the ears, or speaks in loud tone of voice)
Perform the watch tick test. The ticking of a watch has a higher pitch than the human voice. ■ Have the client occlude one ear. Out of the client's sight, place a ticking watch 2 to 3 cm from the unoccluded ear. ■ Ask what the client can hear. Repeat with the other ear.	Able to hear ticking in both ears	Unable to hear ticking in one or both ears

PROCEDURE 27.7 Assessing the Ears and Hearing *continued*

ASSESSMENT	NORMAL FINDINGS	DEVIATIONS FROM NORMAL
Tuning Fork Tests		
Perform Weber's test to assess bone conduction.	Sound is heard in both ears or is localized at the centre of the head (Weber negative)	Sound is heard better in impaired ear, indicating a bone-conductive hearing loss (e.g., due to obstruction of ossicles), *or* sound is heard better in ear without a problem, indicating a sensorineural disturbance (nerve or inner ear damage)
Conduct the Rinne test to compare air conduction to bone conduction.	Air-conducted (AC) hearing is greater than bone-conducted (BC) hearing, that is, AC > BC (positive Rinne)	Bone conduction time is equal to or longer than the air conduction time, that is, BC > AC or BC = AC (negative Rinne; indicates a conductive hearing loss)

PERFORMING TUNING FORK TESTS

Weber's Test

This test assesses bone conduction by testing the lateralization (sideward transmission) of sounds.

- Hold the tuning fork at its base. Activate it by tapping the fork gently against the back of your hand near the knuckles or by stroking the fork between your thumb and index fingers. It should be made to ring softly.
- Place the base of the vibrating fork on top of the client's head (Figure 27.24) and ask where the client hears the noise.

Rinne Test

This test compares air conduction to bone conduction.

- Ask the client to block the hearing in one ear intermittently by moving a fingertip in and out of the ear canal.
- Hold the handle of the activated tuning fork on the mastoid process of one ear (Figure 27.25) until the client states that the vibration can no longer be heard.
- Immediately hold the still-vibrating fork prongs in front of the client's ear canal (Figure 27.26). Push aside the client's hair if necessary. Ask whether the client now hears the sound. Sound conducted by air is heard more readily than sound conducted by bone. The tuning fork vibrations conducted by air are normally heard longer.

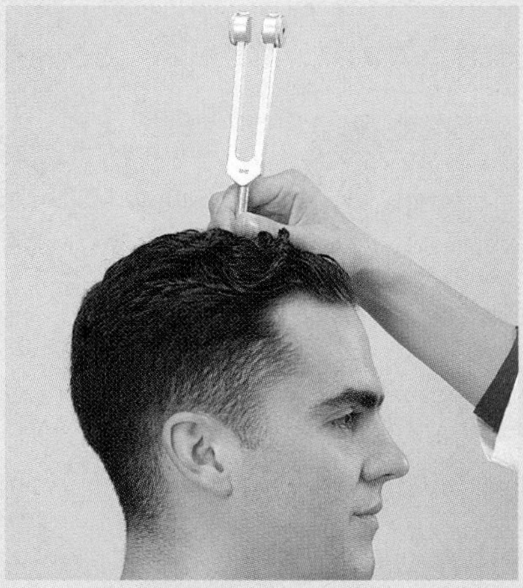

Figure 27.24 Placing the base of a tuning fork on the client's skull (Weber's test)

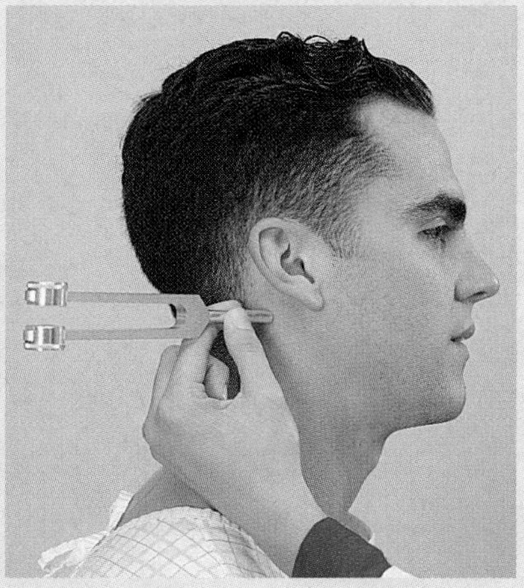

Figure 27.25 Placing the base of the tuning fork on the mastoid process (Rinne test)

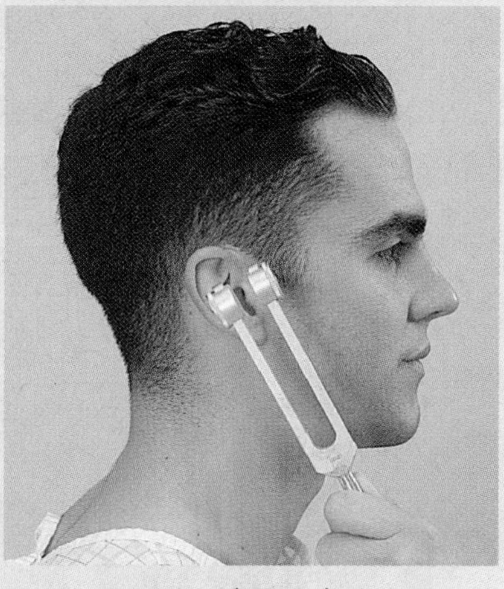

Figure 27.26 Placing the tuning fork prongs in front of the client's ear (Rinne test)

PROCEDURE 27.7 Assessing the Ears and Hearing *continued*

Lifespan Considerations

Children

- A horizontal line at the level of the eye should be even with the top of the ear. The auricle should angle no more than 10 degrees from vertical. Variation from these findings may indicate mental retardation or renal abnormalities (Ashwill & Droske, 1997).
- To assess gross hearing, ring a bell from behind the infant or have the parent call the child's name to check for a response. Infants may blink at a sharp sound. At three to four months, the infant will turn head and eyes toward the sound.
- To inspect the external canal and tympanic membrane, pull the pinna downward and back in children less than three years old. Insert the speculum approximately 1 cm.

Older Adults

- The skin of the ear may appear dry and be less resilient because of the loss of connective tissue.
- Increased coarse and wirelike hair growth occurs along the pinna, antihelix, and tragus.
- The tympanic membrane is more translucent and less flexible.
- Earwax is drier.
- The pinna increases in both width and length, and the earlobe elongates.
- Sensorineural hearing loss occurs.
- Generalized hearing loss *(presbycusis)* occurs in all frequencies, although the first symptom is the loss of high-frequency sounds: the *f, s, sh,* and *ph* sounds. To such persons, conversation can be distorted and result in what appears to be inappropriate or confused behaviour.

Nose and Sinuses

The nasal passages can be inspected very simply with a flashlight. However, a nasal *speculum* and a penlight or an otoscope with a nasal attachment facilitates examination of the nasal attachment.

Assessment of the nose includes inspection and palpation of the external nose (the upper third of the nose is bone; the remainder is cartilage); patency of the nasal cavities; and inspection of the nasal cavities.

If the client reports difficulty or abnormality in smell, the nurse may test the client's olfactory sense by asking the client to identify common odours, such as coffee or mint. This is done by asking the client to close the eyes and placing vials containing the scent under the client's nose.

The nurse inspects, palpates, and percusses the facial sinuses (Figure 27.27). Procedure 27.8 describes how to assess the nose and sinuses.

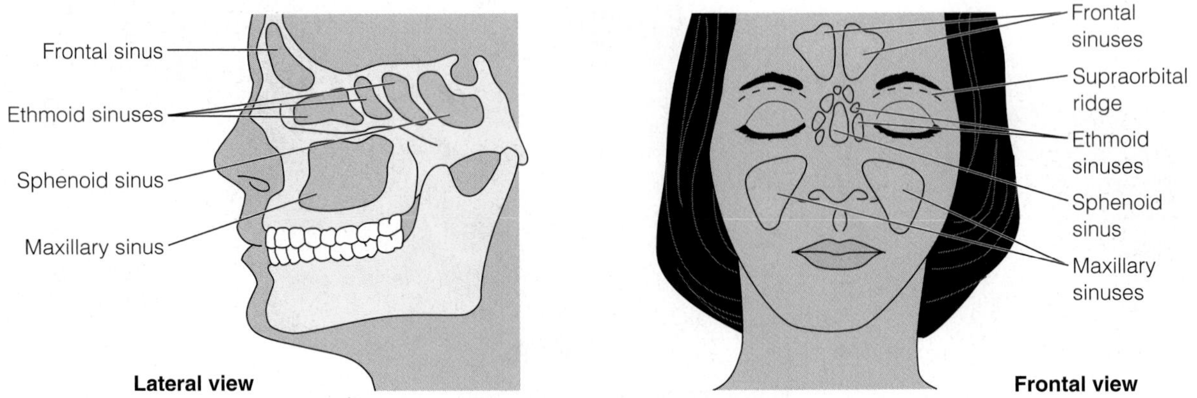

Figure 27.27 The facial sinuses

PROCEDURE 27.8 Assessing the Nose and Sinuses

NURSING HISTORY FOCUS

History of allergies, difficulty breathing through the nose, sinus infections, injuries to nose or face, nosebleeds; any medications taken; any changes in sense of smell; any facial or nasal surgery

ASSESSMENT	NORMAL FINDINGS	DEVIATIONS FROM NORMAL
Nose		
Inspect the external nose for any deviations in shape, size, or colour and flaring or discharge from the nares.	Symmetric and straight No discharge or flaring Uniform colour	Asymmetric Discharge from nares Localized areas of redness or presence of skin lesions
Lightly palpate the external nose to determine any areas of tenderness, masses, and displacements of bone and cartilage.	Not tender; no lesions	Tenderness on palpation; presence of lesions
Determine patency of both nasal cavities. Ask the client to close the mouth, exert pressure on one naris, and breathe through the opposite naris. Repeat the procedure to assess patency of the opposite naris.	Air moves freely as the client breathes through the nares	Air movement is restricted in one or both nares
Inspect the nasal cavities using a flashlight and/or a nasal speculum. See the accompanying box for nasal speculum insertion and use.	Mucosa pink Clear, watery discharge No lesions Nasal septum intact and in midline	Mucosa red or pale, edematous Abnormal discharge (e.g., purulent) Presence of lesions (e.g., polyps) Septum deviated

USING A NASAL SPECULUM

- Hold the speculum in your left hand for the client's right nostril and your right hand for the left nostril.
- Facing the client, insert the tip of the *closed* speculum (with the blades horizontal) about 1 cm or up to the point at which the blade widens. Care must be taken to avoid pressure on the nasal septum, which is sensitive.
- Stabilize the speculum with your index finger against the side of the nose (Figure 27.28). Use the other hand to hold the penlight and to position the head.
- With the client's head erect, open the speculum as much as possible and inspect the floor of the nose (vestibule) and the anterior portion of the septum.

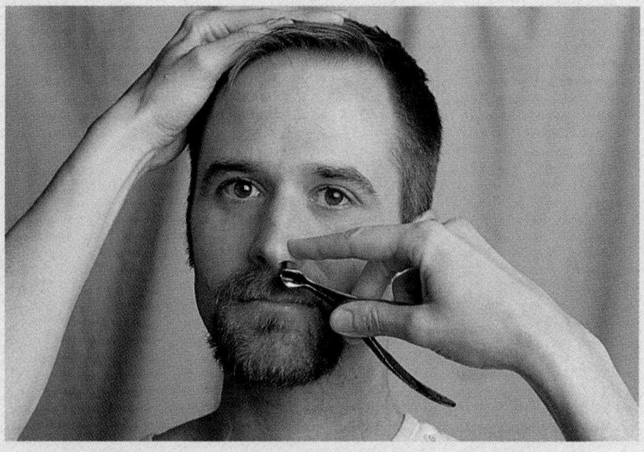

Figure 27.28 Using a nasal speculum to inspect the nasal passages

PROCEDURE 27.8 Assessing the Nose and Sinuses *continued*

USING A NASAL SPECULUM *continued*

To facilitate inspection of the middle meatus and middle turbinates, ask the client to tilt the head back. The posterior turbinate is rarely seen because of its position (Figure 27.29).

- Inspect the lining of the nares (mucosa). Observe for the presence of redness, swelling, growths, and discharge. Inspect the position of the nasal septum between the nasal chambers, noting in particular any deviation to right or left.

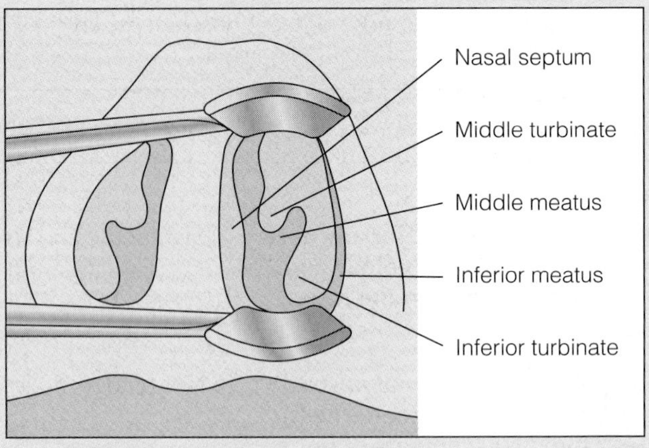

Figure 27.29 The inferior and middle turbinates of the nasal passage

ASSESSMENT	NORMAL FINDINGS	DEVIATIONS FROM NORMAL
Facial Sinuses		
Palpate the maxillary and frontal sinuses for tenderness.	Not tender	Tenderness in one or more sinuses

Lifespan Considerations

Children

- A speculum is usually not necessary to examine the septum, turbinates, and vestibule; it might cause a child to be apprehensive. Instead, push the tip of the nose upward with the thumb and shine a light into the naris.

Older Adults

- In older adults, the sense of smell diminishes markedly because of a decrease in the number of olfactory nerve fibres and atrophy of the remaining fibres. Older persons are less able to identify and discriminate odours.
- Nosebleeds may result from hypertensive disease or other arterial vessel changes in older adults.

Mouth and Oropharynx

The mouth and pharynx are composed of a number of structures: lips, inner and buccal mucosa, the tongue, floor of the mouth, teeth and gums, hard and soft palates, uvula, salivary glands, tonsillar pillars, and tonsils. Anatomic structures of the mouth are shown in Figure 27.30.

By age 25 years, most people have all their permanent teeth. For information about structures of the teeth, see Chapter 34.

Normally, three pairs of salivary glands empty into the oral cavity: the parotid, submandibular, and sublingual glands (see Figure 27.30). The *parotid gland* is the largest and empties through the Stensen's duct opposite the second molar. The *submandibular gland* empties through Wharton's duct, which is situated at the side of the frenulum on the floor of the mouth. The *sublingual salivary gland* lies in the floor of the mouth and has numerous openings.

Dental **caries** (cavities) and **periodontal disease (pyorrhea)** are the two problems that most frequently affect the teeth. Both problems are commonly associated with plaque and tartar deposits. **Plaque** is an *invisible* soft film that adheres to the enamel surface of teeth; it consists of bacteria, molecules of saliva, and remnants of epithelial cells and leukocytes. When plaque accumulates on the teeth, tartar (dental calculus) forms. **Tartar** is a visible, hard deposit of plaque and dead bacteria that forms at the gum lines. Tartar buildup can alter the fibres that attach the teeth to the gum and eventually disrupt bone tissue. Periodontal disease is characterized by **gingivitis** (inflamed gums), bleeding, receding gum lines, and the formation of pockets between the teeth and gums. In advanced periodontal disease, the teeth are loose, and pus is evident when the gums are pressed.

Other problems nurses may see are **glossitis** (inflammation of the tongue), **stomatitis** (inflammation of the oral mucosa), and **parotitis** (inflammation of the parotid salivary gland). The accumulation of foul matter (food, microorganisms, and epithelial elements) on the teeth and gums is referred to as **sordes.**

Physical examination of the mouth includes inspection and palpation techniques. It is recommended that the nurse wear gloves when in contact with the buccal mucosa. Equipment needed for assessment of the mouth and pharynx includes tongue blade, gauze squares (2 × 2), a penlight or flashlight, and disposable gloves. See Procedure 27.9.

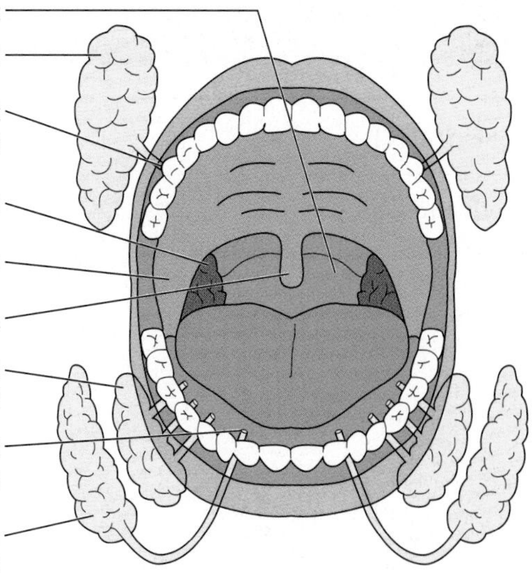

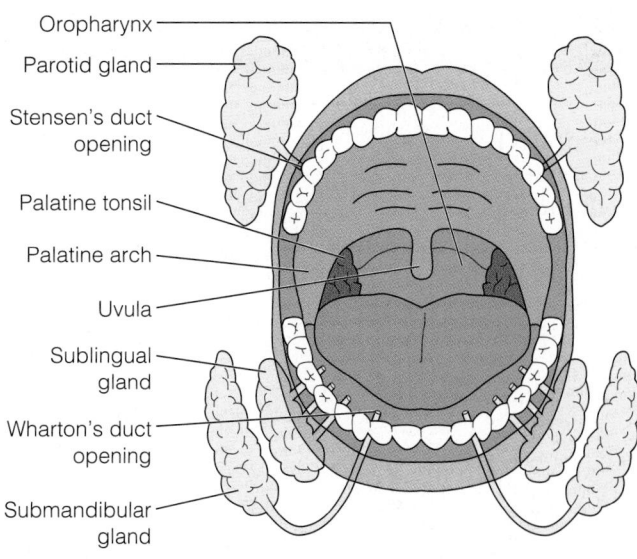

Figure 27.30 Anatomic structures of the mouth

PROCEDURE 27.9 Assessing the Mouth and Oropharynx

NURSING HISTORY FOCUS

Routine pattern of dental care, last visit to dentist; length of time ulcers or other lesions have been present; any denture discomfort; any medications client is receiving

ASSESSMENT	NORMAL FINDINGS	DEVIATIONS FROM NORMAL
Lips and Buccal Mucosa		
Inspect the outer lips for symmetry of contour, colour, and texture. Ask the client to purse the lips as if to whistle.	Uniform pink colour (darker, e.g., bluish hue, in dark-skinned clients)	Pallor; cyanosis
	Soft, moist, smooth texture	Blisters; generalized or localized swelling; fissures, crusts, or scales (may result from excessive moisture, nutritional deficiency, or fluid deficit)
	Symmetry of contour	
	Ability to purse lips	Inability to purse lips (indicative of facial nerve damage)
Inspect and palpate the inner lips and buccal mucosa for colour, moisture, texture, and the presence of lesions. See the box on the next page.	Uniform pink colour (freckled brown pigmentation in dark-skinned clients)	Pallor; white patches (leukoplakia)
		Excessive dryness
	Moist, smooth, soft, glistening, and elastic texture (drier oral mucosa in elderly due to decreased salivation)	Mucosal cysts; irritations from dentures; abrasions, ulcerations; nodules

→

PROCEDURE 27.9 Assessing the Mouth and Oropharynx *continued*

ASSESSMENT	NORMAL FINDINGS	DEVIATIONS FROM NORMAL
Teeth and Gums		
Inspect the teeth and gums while examining the inner lips and buccal mucosa.	32 adult teeth	Missing or broken teeth Ill-fitting dentures
	Smooth, white, shiny tooth enamel	Brown or black discolouration of the enamel (may indicate staining or the presence of caries)
	Pink gums (bluish or dark patches in dark-skinned clients)	Excessively red gums
	Moist, firm texture to gums	Spongy texture; bleeding; tenderness (may indicate periodontal disease)
	No retraction of gums (pulling away from the crown of the tooth)	Receding, atrophied gums; swelling that partially covers the teeth

INSPECTING AND PALPATING THE INNER LIP, BUCCAL MUCOSA, TEETH, AND GUMS

Inner Lip and Front Teeth

- Ask the client to relax the mouth, and for better visualization, pull the lip outward away from the teeth.
- Grasp the lip on each side between the thumb and index finger (Figure 27.31).
- Palpate any lesions for size, tenderness, and consistency.
- Inspect the front teeth and gums.

Buccal Mucosa and Back Teeth

- Ask the client to open the mouth. Using a tongue blade, retract the cheek (Figure 27.32).
- View the surface buccal mucosa from top to bottom and back to front. A flashlight or penlight will help illuminate the surface. Repeat the procedure for the other side.
- Ask the client to open the mouth again. Using gloves and a penlight, move a finger along the inside cheek.
- Another finger may be moved outside the cheek.
- Examine the back teeth. For proper vision of the molars, use the index fingers of both hands to retract the cheek (Figure 27.33). Ask the client to relax the lips and first close, then open, the jaw. Closing the jaw assists in observation of tooth alignment and loss of teeth; opening the jaw assists in observation of dental fillings and caries. Observe the number of teeth, tooth colour, the state of fillings, dental caries, and tartar along the base of the teeth. Note the presence and fit of partial or complete dentures.

Gums

- Inspect the gums around the molars. Observe for bleeding, colour, retraction (pulling away from the teeth), edema, and lesions.
- Assess the texture of the gums by gently pressing the gum tissue with a tongue blade.

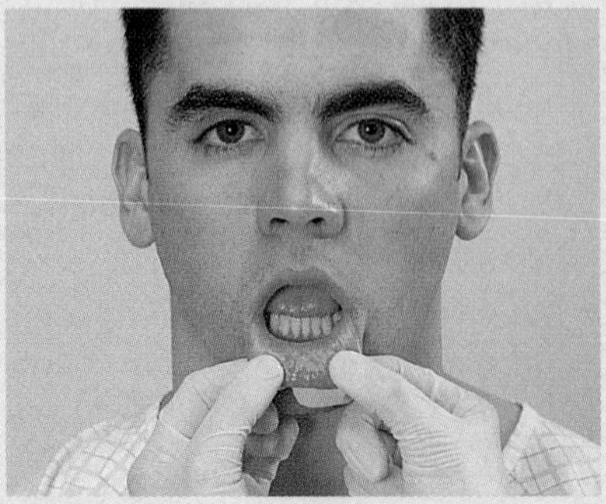

Figure 27.31 Inspecting the mucosa of the lower lip

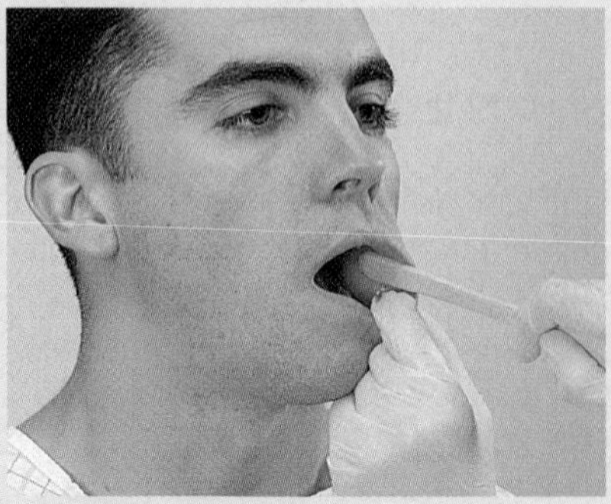

Figure 27.32 Inspecting the buccal mucosa using a tongue blade

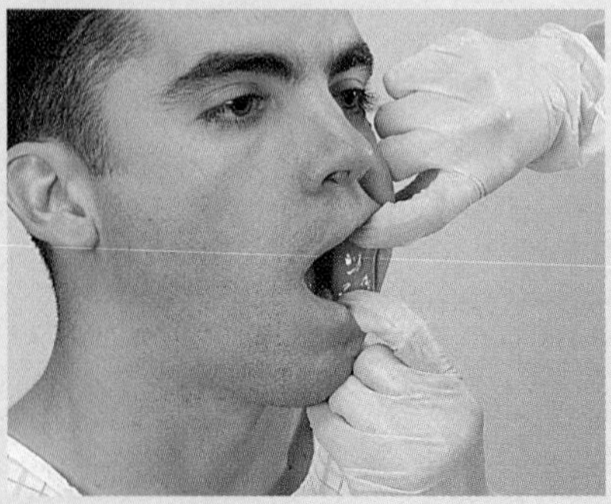

Figure 27.33 Inspecting the back teeth

PROCEDURE 27.9 Assessing the Mouth and Oropharynx *continued*

ASSESSMENT	NORMAL FINDINGS	DEVIATIONS FROM NORMAL
Inspect the dentures. Ask the client to remove complete or partial dentures. Inspect their condition, noting, in particular, broken or worn areas.	Smooth, intact dentures	Ill-fitting dentures; irritated and excoriated area under dentures
Tongue/Floor of the Mouth		
Inspect the surface of the tongue for position, colour, and texture. Ask the client to protrude the tongue.	Central position	Deviated from centre (may indicate damage to hypoglossal [twelfth cranial] nerve)
	Pink colour (some brown pigmentation on tongue borders in dark-skinned clients); moist; slightly rough; thin, whitish coating	Smooth red tongue (may indicate iron, vitamin B_{12}, or B_3 deficiency); black tongue (may indicate immuno-suppression or a fungal infection) Dry, furry tongue (associated with fluid deficit)
	Smooth, lateral margins; no lesions	Nodes, ulcerations, discolourations (white or red areas); areas of tenderness
Inspect tongue movement. Ask the client to roll the tongue upward and move it from side to side.	Moves freely; no tenderness	Restricted mobility
Inspect the base of the tongue, the mouth floor, and the frenulum. Ask the client to place the tip of the tongue against the roof of the mouth.	Smooth tongue base with prominent veins Varicosities (tiny bluish-black or purple swollen areas) in elderly people	Swelling; ulceration
Palpate the tongue and floor of the mouth for any nodules, lumps, or excoriated areas. To palpate the tongue, use a piece of gauze to grasp its tip (stabilizes it), and with the index finger of your other hand, palpate the anterior two-thirds of the tongue, its borders, and its base (Figure 27.34). To assess function of the glosso-pharyngeal and hypoglossal nerves, see the neurological assessment later in this chapter.	Smooth with no palpable nodules	Swelling; nodules

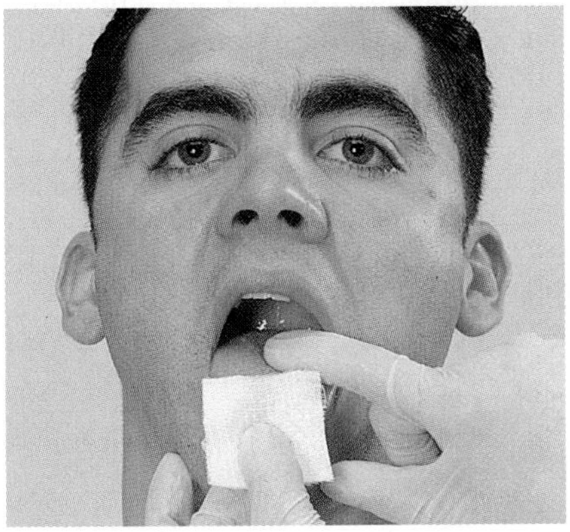

Figure 27.34 Palpating the tongue

PROCEDURE 27.9 Assessing the Mouth and Oropharynx *continued*

ASSESSMENT	NORMAL FINDINGS	DEVIATIONS FROM NORMAL
Salivary Glands		
Inspect salivary duct openings for any swelling or redness. See the discussion of salivary glands, page 544.	Same as colour of buccal mucosa and floor of mouth	Inflammation (redness and swelling)
Palates and Uvula		
Inspect the hard and soft palate for colour, shape, texture, and the presence of bony prominences. Ask the client to open the mouth wide and tilt the head backward. Then depress tongue with a tongue blade, as necessary, and use a penlight for appropriate visualization.	Light pink and smooth soft palate Lighter pink hard palate, more irregular texture	Discolouration (e.g., jaundice or pallor) Palates the same colour Irritations Bony growths (exostoses) growing from the hard palate
Inspect the uvula for position and mobility while examining the palates. To observe the uvula, ask the client to say "ah" so that the soft palate rises.	Positioned in midline of soft palate	Deviation to one side from tumour or trauma; immobility (may indicate damage to trigeminal (fifth cranial) nerve or vagus (tenth cranial) nerve
Oropharynx and Tonsils		
Inspect the oropharynx for colour and texture. Inspect one side at a time to avoid eliciting the gag reflex. To expose one side of the oropharynx, press a tongue blade against the tongue on the same side about halfway back while the client tilts the head back and opens the mouth wide. Use a penlight for illumination, if needed.	Pink and smooth posterior wall	Reddened or edematous; presence of lesions, plaques, or exudate
Inspect the tonsils (behind the fauces) **for colour, discharge, and size.**	Pink and smooth No discharge Of normal size (see the accompanying box for a grading system to describe the size of tonsils)	Inflamed Presence of discharge Swollen

GRADING SYSTEM TO DESCRIBE SIZE OF TONSILS

- Grade 1 (normal): The tonsils are behind the tonsillar pillars (the soft structures supporting the soft palate).
- Grade 2: The tonsils are between the pillars and the uvula.
- Grade 3: The tonsils touch the uvula.
- Grade 4: One or both tonsils extend to the midline of the oropharynx.

PROCEDURE 27.9 Assessing the Mouth and Oropharynx *continued*

Lifespan Considerations

Children

- Tooth development should be appropriate for age. See Chapter 34. Permanent teeth are darker than deciduous teeth.
- White spots on teeth may indicate excessive fluoride ingestion.
- Drooling is normal up to two years of age.
- The tonsils are normally larger in children than in adults and usually extend beyond the palatine arch until the age of 11 or 12 years.
- Inspect the palate for a cleft.

Older Adults

- The oral mucosa may be drier than that of younger persons because of decreased salivary gland activity. Decreased salivation occurs in elderly people taking prescribed medications, such as antidepressants, antihistamines, decongestants, diuretics, antihypertensives, tranquilizers, antispasmodics, and antineoplastics. Extreme dryness is associated with dehydration.
- Some receding of the gums occurs, giving an appearance of increased toothiness.
- There may be a brownish pigmentation to the gums, especially in black persons.
- Taste sensations diminish. Diminished taste sensation is due to atrophy of the taste buds and a decreased sense of smell. It indicates diminished function of the fifth and seventh cranial nerves.
- Tiny purple or bluish-black swollen areas (varicosities) under the tongue, known as *caviar* spots, are not uncommon.
- The teeth may show signs of staining, erosion, chipping, and abrasions due to loss of dentin. Tooth loss occurs as a result of gum disease but is preventable with good dental hygiene.

Neck

Examination of the neck includes the muscles, lymph nodes, trachea, thyroid gland, carotid arteries, and jugular veins. Areas of the neck are defined by the sternocleidomastoid muscles, which divide each side of the neck into two triangles: the anterior and posterior (Figure 27.35). The trachea, thyroid gland, anterior cervical nodes, and carotid artery lie within the anterior triangle (Figure 27.36); the carotid artery runs parallel and anterior to the sternocleidomastoid muscle. The posterior lymph nodes lie within the posterior triangle (Figure 27.37).

Each sternocleidomastoid muscle extends from the upper sternum and the medial third of the clavicle to the mastoid process of the temporal bone behind the ear (see Figure 27.35). These muscles turn and laterally flex the head. Each trapezius muscle extends from the occipital bone of the skull to the lateral third of the clavicle. These muscles draw the head to the side and back, elevate the chin, and elevate the shoulders to shrug them.

Lymph nodes in the neck that collect lymph from the head and neck structures are grouped serially and referred to as *chains*. See Figure 27.37 and Table 27.6, both on page 550. The deep cervical chain is not shown in Figure 27.37 because it lies beneath the sternocleidomastoid muscle.

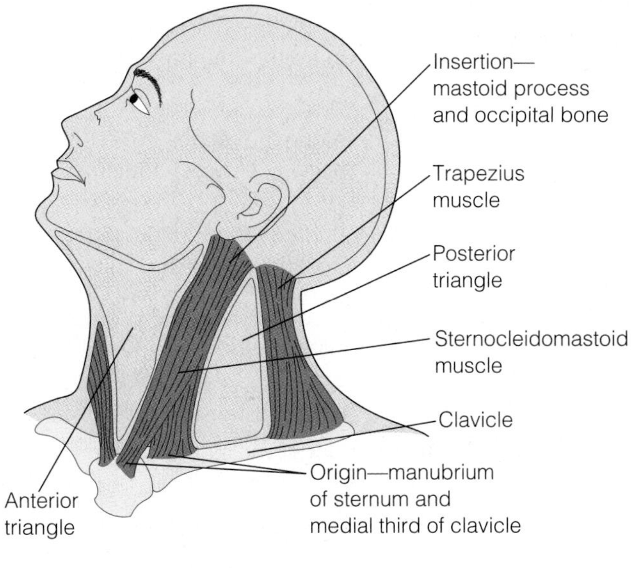

Figure 27.35 Major muscles of the neck

Procedure 27.10 describes how to assess the neck.

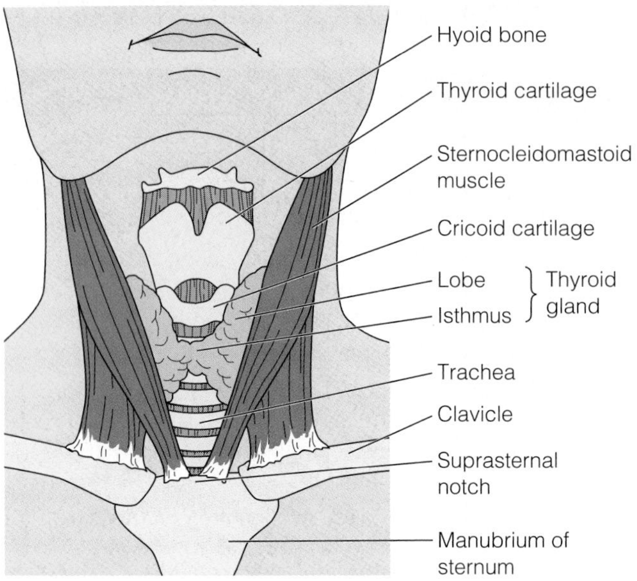

Figure 27.36 Structures of the neck

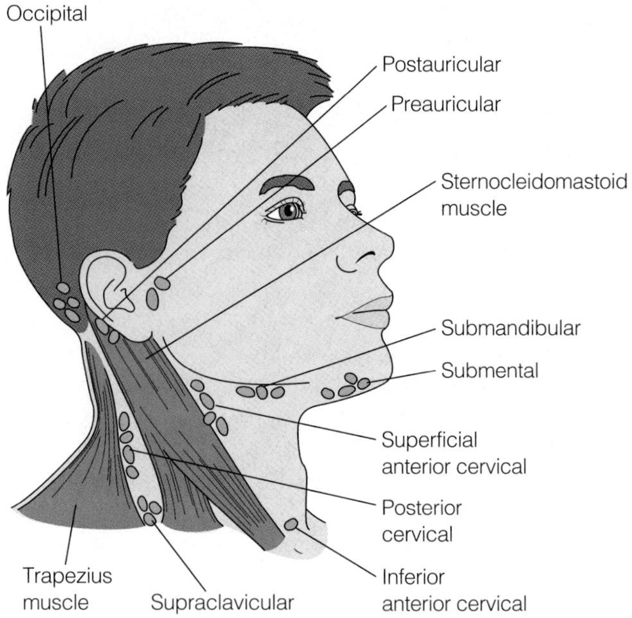

Figure 27.37 Lymph nodes of the neck

TABLE 27.6 Lymph Nodes of the Head and Neck

Node Centre	Location	Area Drained
Head		
Occipital	At the posterior base of the skull	The occipital region of the scalp and the deep structures of the back of the neck
Postauricular (mastoid)	Behind the auricle of the ear or in front of the mastoid process	The parietal region of the head and part of the ear
Preauricular	In front of the tragus of the ear	The forehead and upper face
Floor of Mouth		
Submandibular (submaxillary)	Along the medial border of the lower jaw, halfway between the angle of the jaw and the chin	The chin, upper lip, cheek, nose, teeth, eyelids, part of the tongue, and part of the floor of the mouth
Submental	Behind the tip of the mandible, in the midline, under the chin	The anterior third of the tongue, gums, and floor of the mouth
Neck		
Superficial (anterior) cervical chain	Along the anterior to the sternocleidomastoid muscle	The skin and neck
Posterior cervical chain	Along the anterior aspect of the trapezius muscle	The posterior and lateral regions of the neck, occiput, and mastoid
Deep cervical chain	Under the sternocleidomastoid muscle	The larynx, thyroid gland, trachea, and upper part of the esophagus
Supraclavicular	Above the clavicle, in the angle between the clavicle and the sternocleidomastoid muscle	The lateral regions of the neck and lungs

PROCEDURE 27.10 Assessing the Neck

NURSING HISTORY FOCUS

Any problems with neck lumps; neck pain or stiffness; when and how any lumps occurred; any previous diagnoses of thyroid problems; medications and any other treatments provided (e.g., surgery, radiation)

ASSESSMENT	NORMAL FINDINGS	DEVIATIONS FROM NORMAL
Neck Muscles		
Inspect the neck muscles (sternocleidomastoid and trapezius) for abnormal swellings or masses. Ask the client to hold the head erect.	Muscles equal in size; head centred	Unilateral neck swelling; head tilted to one side
Observe head movement. Ask client to:	Coordinated, smooth movements with no discomfort	Muscle tremor, spasm, or stiffness
■ Move the chin to the chest (determines function of the sternocleidomastoid muscle).	Head flexes 45°	Limited range of motion; painful movements; involuntary movements (e.g., up-and-down nodding movements associated with Parkinson's disease)
■ Move the head back so that the chin points upward (determines function of the trapezius muscle).	Head hyperextends 60°	Head hyperextends less than 60°
■ Move the head so that the ear is moved toward the shoulder on each side (determines function of the sternocleidomastoid muscle).	Head laterally flexes 40°	Head laterally flexes less than 40°
■ Turn the head to the right and to the left (determines function of the sternocleidomastoid muscle).	Head laterally rotates 70°	Head laterally rotates less than 70°
Test the cranial accessory nerve (CN XI). Ask the client to shrug the shoulders and move the head from side to side.	Able to shrug the shoulders and move head to sides	Unable to shrug the shoulders or move the head to either side
Lymph Nodes		
Palpate the entire neck for enlarged nymph nodes, using the guidelines in the box on the following page.	Not palpable	Enlarged, palpable, possibly tender
Trachea		
Palpate the trachea for lateral deviation. Place your fingertip or thumb on the trachea in the suprasternal notch (see Figure 27.36), and then move your finger laterally to the left and the right in spaces bordered by the clavicle, the anterior aspect of the sternocleidomastoid muscle, and the trachea.	Central placement in midline of neck; spaces are equal on both sides	Deviation to one side; thyroid enlargement; enlarged lymph nodes

→

PROCEDURE 27.10 Assessing the Neck *continued*

PALPATING NECK LYMPH NODES

- Face the client, and bend the client's head forward slightly or toward the side being examined to relax the soft tissue and muscles.
- Palpate the nodes using the pads of the fingers. Move the fingertips in a gentle rotating motion.
- When examining the *submental* and *submandibular nodes,* place the fingertips under the mandible on the side nearest the palpating hand, and pull the skin and subcutaneous tissue laterally over the mandibular surface so that the tissue rolls over the nodes.
- When palpating the *supraclavicular nodes,* have the client bend the head forward to relax the tissues of the anterior neck and to relax the shoulders so that the clavicles drop. Use your hand nearest the side to be examined when facing the client (i.e., use your left hand to palpate the client's right nodes). Use your free hand to flex the client's head forward, if necessary. Hook your index and third fingers over the clavicle lateral to the sternocleidomastoid muscle (Figure 27.38).
- When palpating the *anterior cervical nodes* and *posterior cervical nodes,* move your fingertips slowly in a forward circular motion against the sternocleidomastoid and trapezius muscles, respectively.

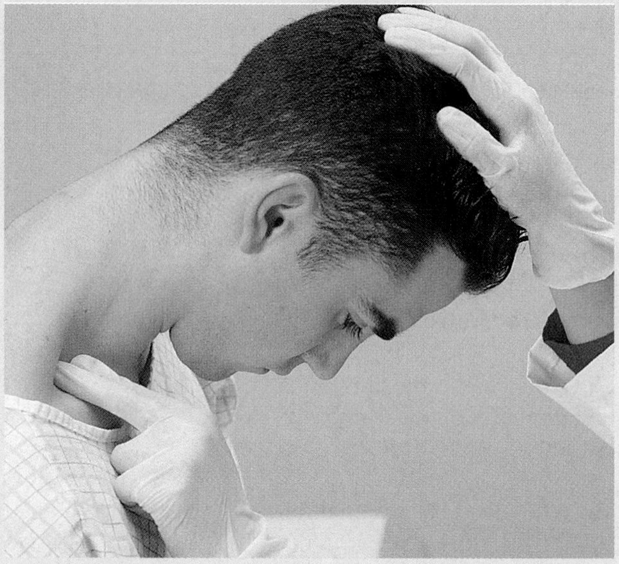

Figure 27.38 Palpating the supraclavicular lymph nodes

- To palpate the *deep cervical nodes,* bend or hook your fingers around the sternocleidomastoid muscle.

ASSESSMENT	NORMAL FINDINGS	DEVIATIONS FROM NORMAL
Thyroid Gland		
Inspect the thyroid gland.		
■ Stand in front of the client.		
■ Observe the lower half of the neck overlying the thyroid gland for symmetry and visible masses.	Not visible on inspection	Visible diffuseness or local enlargement
■ Ask the client to hyperextend the head and swallow. If necessary, offer a glass of water to make it easier for the client to swallow. This action determines how the thyroid and cricoid cartilages move and whether swallowing causes a bulging of the gland.	Gland ascends during swallowing but is not visible	Gland is not fully movable with swallowing
Palpate the thyroid gland for smoothness. Note any areas of enlargement, masses, or nodules. See the accompanying box for palpation methods.	Lobes may not be palpated If palpated, lobes are small, smooth, centrally located, painless, and rise freely with swallowing	Solitary nodules

PROCEDURE 27.10 Assessing the Neck *continued*

PALPATING THE THYROID GLAND

Stand in front of or behind the client, and ask the client to lower the chin slightly. *Lowering the chin relaxes the neck muscles, facilitating palpation.*

Posterior Approach

- Place your hands around the client's neck, with your fingertips on the lower half of the neck over the trachea (Figure 27.39).
- Ask the client to swallow (taking a sip of water, if necessary), and feel for any enlargement of the *thyroid isthmus* as it rises. The isthmus lies across the trachea, below the cricoid cartilage. See Figure 27.36.
- To examine the right thyroid lobe, have the client lower the chin slightly and turn the head slightly to the right (the side being examined). With your left fingers, displace the trachea slightly to the right. With your right fingers, palpate the right thyroid lobe. Have the client swallow while you are palpating.
- Repeat the last step in reverse to examine the left thyroid lobe.

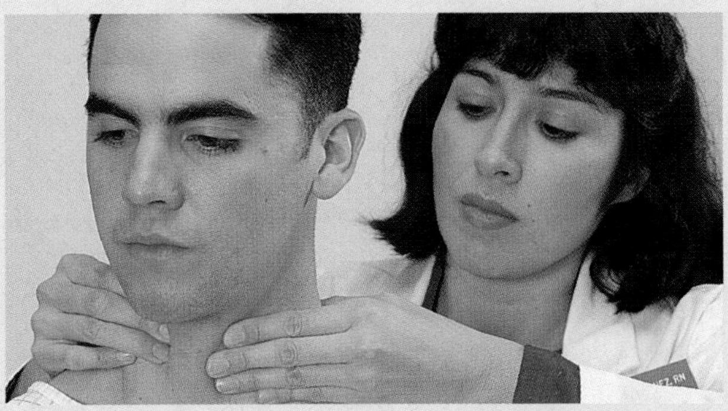

Figure 27.39 Placement of the fingertips over the trachea to begin palpation of the thyroid gland (posterior approach)

Anterior Approach

- Place the tips of your index and middle fingers over the trachea, and palpate the thyroid isthmus as the client swallows.
- To examine the right thyroid lobe, have the client lower the chin slightly and turn the head slightly to the right. With your right fingers, displace the trachea slightly to the client's right (your left). With your left fingers, palpate the right thyroid lobe.
- To examine the left thyroid lobe, repeat the last step in reverse.

ASSESSMENT	NORMAL FINDINGS	DEVIATIONS FROM NORMAL
If enlargement of the gland is suspected, auscultate over the thyroid area for a bruit (a soft rushing sound created by turbulent bloodflow). Use the bell-shaped diaphragm of the stethoscope.	Absence of bruit	Presence of bruit

Lifespan Considerations

Child

- Examine the neck while the child is lying flat on the back. Neck mobility is determined by lifting the head and turning it from side to side.
- An infant's neck is normally short. The neck lengthens at about three or four years of age.

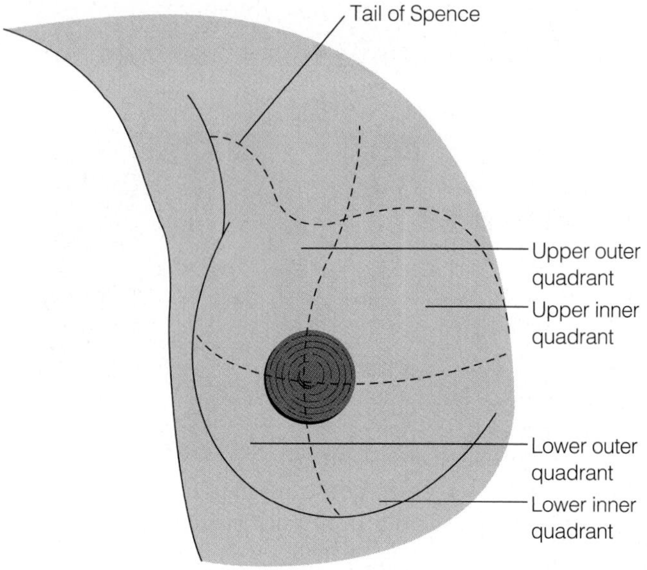

Figure 27.40 Four breast quadrants and the axillary tail of Spence

Breast Health Guidelines

All women age 20 years and older

- Monthly breast self-exam and notify your doctor of any abnormal or unusual changes

Women age 40–69 years

- Monthly breast self-exam
- Clinical breast exam by a trained health professional at least every two years for women over 40
- Screening mammography every two years for women over 50
- Note: Women under age 50 years or over 69 years who are at a higher risk for cancer should consult their doctor/health-care professional about mammography
- Mammography screening guidelines for under 50 or over 69 years vary by province and territory

Source: Canadian Cancer Society. www.cancer.ca

Breasts and Axillae

The breasts of men and women need to be inspected and palpated. Men have some glandular tissue beneath each nipple, a potential site for malignancy, whereas mature women have glandular tissue throughout the breast. In females, the largest portion of glandular breast tissue is located in the upper outer quadrant of each breast. From this quadrant, there is a projection of breast tissue into the axilla, called the **axillary tail of Spence** (Figure 27.40). The majority of breast tumours are located in this upper outer breast quadrant and in the tail of Spence. During assessment, the nurse can localize specific findings by using this division of the breast into quadrants and the axillary tail.

Clients need to be instructed to do a **breast self-examination (BSE)** once a month. Teaching for self examination of the breasts is outlined in Chapter 12. Clients also need to be informed about breast health guidelines. See the accompanying box.

Procedure 27.11 describes a nursing assessment of the breasts and axillae.

PROCEDURE 27.11 Assessing the Breasts and Axillae

NURSING HISTORY FOCUS

History of breast self-examination; technique used and when performed in relation to the menstrual cycle; history of breast masses and what was done about them; any pain or tenderness in the breasts and relation to menstrual cycle; any discharge from the nipple; medication history (some medications, like oral contraceptives, steroids, digitalis, and diuretics, may cause nipple discharge and exogenous estrogens may be associated with developing cysts or cancer); risk factors for breast cancer, such as a family history of breast cancer, alcohol consumption, high-fat diet, obesity, use of oral contraceptives, menarche before age 12 years, menopause after age 55 years, age 30 years or more at first pregnancy.

ASSESSMENT	NORMAL FINDINGS	DEVIATIONS FROM NORMAL
Inspect the breasts for symmetry and contour or shape while the client is in a sitting position.	*Females:* Rounded shape; slightly unequal in size; generally symmetric *Males:* Breasts even with the chest wall; if obese, may be similar in shape to female breasts	Recent change in breast size; swellings; marked asymmetry

PROCEDURE 27.11 Assessing the Breast and Axillae *continued*

ASSESSMENT	NORMAL FINDINGS	DEVIATIONS FROM NORMAL
Inspect the skin of the breast for localized discolourations or hyperpigmentation, retraction or dimpling, localized hypervascular areas, swelling or edema (Figure 27.41). 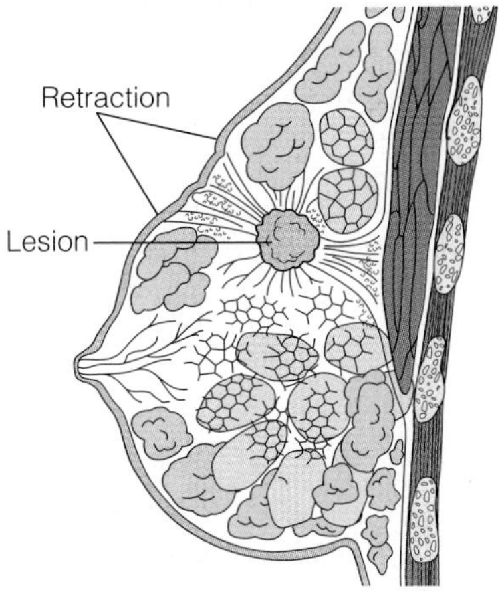 **Figure 27.41** A lesion causing retraction of the skin	Skin uniform in colour (same in appearance as skin of abdomen or back) Skin smooth and intact Diffuse symmetric horizontal or vertical vascular pattern in light-skinned people **Striae** (stretch marks); moles and nevi	Localized discolourations or hyperpigmentation Retraction or dimpling Unilateral, localized hypervascular areas Swelling or edema appearing as pig skin or orange peel due to exaggeration of the pores
Accentuate any retraction by having the client: ■ Raise the arms above the head. ■ Push the hands together, with elbows flexed (Figure 27.42). ■ Press the hands down on the hips (Figure 27.43).	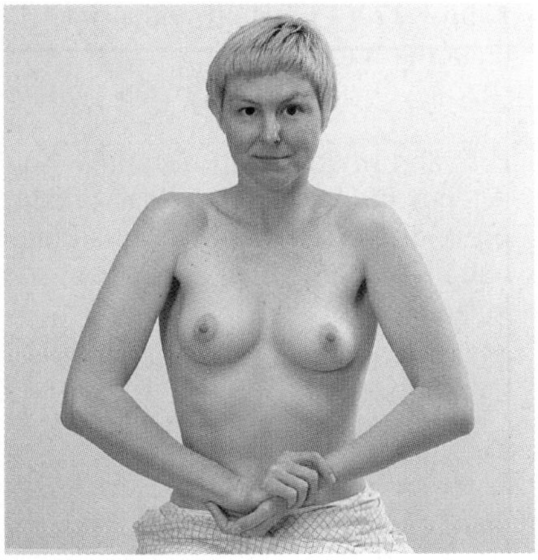 **Figure 27.42** Pushing the hands together to accentuate retraction of breast tissues	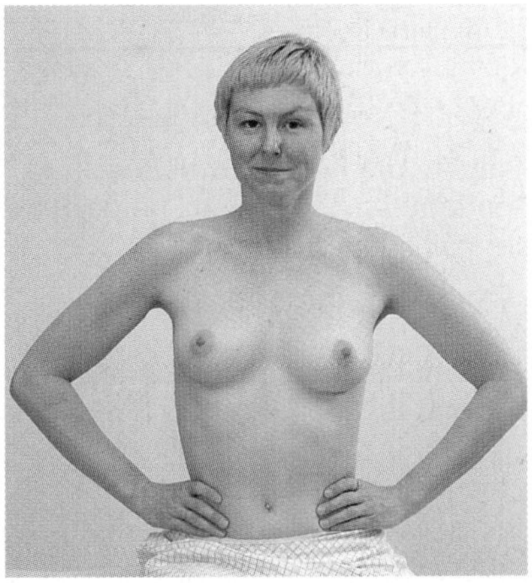 **Figure 27.43** Pressing the hands down on the hips to accentuate retraction of breast tissue
Inspect the areola area for size, shape, symmetry, colour, surface characteristics, and any masses or lesions.	Round or oval and bilaterally the same Colour varies widely, from light pink to dark brown Irregular placement of sebaceous glands on the surface of the areola (Montgomery's tubercles)	Any asymmetry, mass, or lesion

PROCEDURE 27.11 Assessing the Breast and Axillae *continued*

ASSESSMENT	NORMAL FINDINGS	DEVIATIONS FROM NORMAL
Inspect the nipples for size, shape, position, colour, discharge, lesions.	Round, everted, and equal in size; similar in colour; soft and smooth; both nipples point in same direction	Asymmetrical size and colour
	No discharge, except for colostrum in pregnant females	Presence of discharge, crusts, or cracks
	Inversion of one or both nipples that is present from puberty	Recent inversion of one or both nipples
Palpate the axillary, subclavicular (infraclavicular), and supraclavicular lymph nodes (Figure 27.44) while the client sits with the arms abducted and supported on the nurse's forearm. Use the palmar surfaces of the fingertips to palpate the four areas of the axilla: ■ The edge of the greater pectoral muscle (musculus pectoralis major) along the anterior axillary line ■ The thoracic wall in the midaxillary area ■ The upper part of the humerus ■ The anterior edge of the latissimus dorsi muscle along the posterior axillary line	No tenderness, masses, or nodules 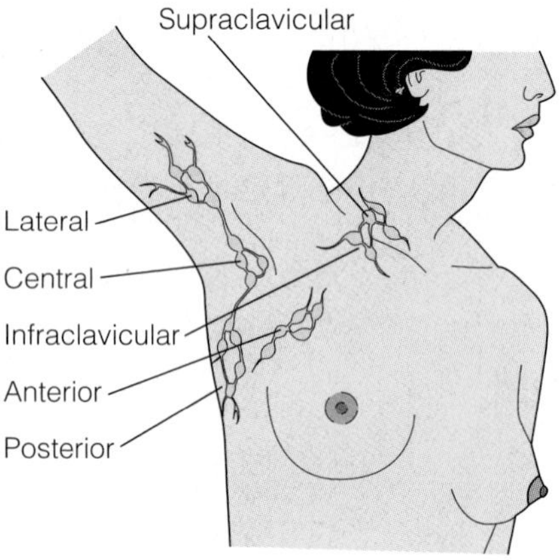 **Figure 27.44** Lymph nodes that drain the breast tissues	Tenderness, masses, or nodules
Palpate the breast for masses and tenderness. See the box on page 557 for palpation methods.	Firm and smooth with a granular consistency; firm transverse ridge of compressed tissue in the lower quadrant (inframammary ridge) especially noted in large breasts	Heat, redness, swelling, tenderness, masses, or nodules
Palpate the areola and the nipples for masses. Compress each nipple to determine the presence of any discharge. If discharge is present, milk the breast along its radii to identify the lobe producing discharge. Assess any discharge for amount, colour, consistency, and odour. Note also any tenderness on palpation.	No tenderness, masses, nodules, or nipple discharge	Tenderness, masses, nodules, or nipple discharge
Palpate the male breasts and the axillary lymph nodes when the client is supine.	Flat disc of undeveloped breast tissue beneath the nipple	As above for female client

PROCEDURE 27.11 Assessing the Breast and Axillae *continued*

PALPATING A CLIENT'S BREAST

Palpation of the breast is generally performed while the client is supine. In the supine position, the breasts flatten evenly against the chest wall, facilitating palpation. For clients who have a past history of breast masses, who are at high risk for breast cancer, or who have pendulous breasts, examination in both a supine and a sitting position is recommended.

- If the client reports a breast lump, start with the "normal" breast to obtain baseline data that will serve as a comparison to the reportedly involved breast.
- To enhance flattening of the breast, instruct the client to abduct the arm and place her hand behind her head. Then place a small pillow or rolled towel under the client's shoulder.
- For palpation, use the palmar surface of the middle three fingertips (held together) and make a gentle rotary motion on the breast.
- Choose one of two patterns for palpation:
  a. Hands-of-the-clock or spokes-on-a-wheel (Figure 27.45)
  b. Concentric circles (Figure 27.46)
- Choose any starting point for palpation, but start and end at a fixed point to ensure that all breast surfaces are assessed.
- Pay particular attention to the upper outer quadrant area and the tail of Spence where the majority of breast cancers develop.
- If you detect a mass, record the following data:
  a. *Location:* the exact location relative to the quadrants and axillary tail or the clock (as in Figure 27.45) and the distance from the nipple, in centimetres
  b. *Size:* the length, width, and thickness of the mass in centimetres; if you are able to determine the discrete edges, record this fact
  c. *Shape:* whether the mass is round, oval, lobulated, indistinct, or irregular
  d. *Consistency:* whether the mass is hard or soft
  e. *Mobility:* whether the mass is movable or fixed

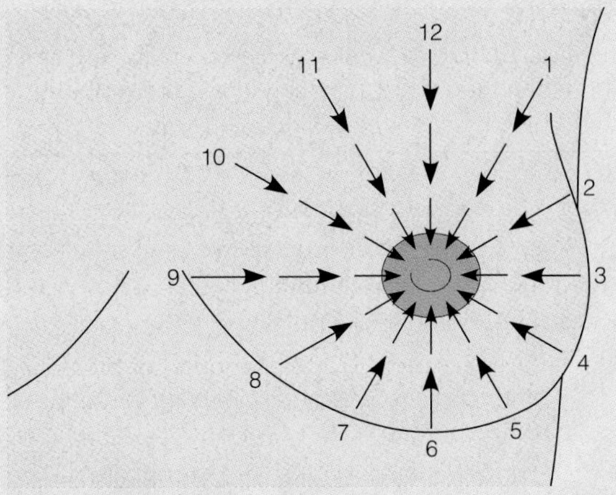

Figure 27.45 Hands-of-the-clock or spokes-on-a-wheel pattern of breast palpation

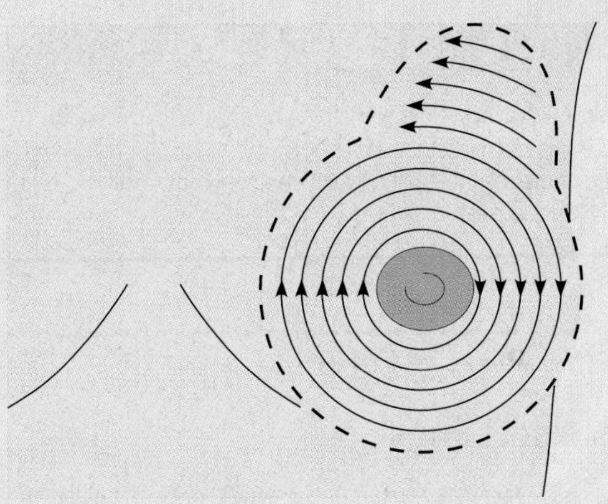

Figure 27.46 Concentric circles pattern for breast palpation

  f. *Skin over the lump:* whether it is reddened, dimpled, or retracted
  g. *Nipple:* whether it is displaced or retracted
  h. *Tenderness:* whether palpation is painful

PROCEDURE 27.11 Assessing the Breast and Axillae *continued*

Lifespan Considerations

Children

- Newborns up to two weeks of age may have breast enlargement and white discharge from the nipples (witch's milk).

Adolescents

- Female breast development begins between 12 and 13 years of age and occurs in five stages. Development may be asymmetrical.
  - Stage 1 Elevation of the nipple
  - Stage 2 Development of a small mound of breast and nipple (breast bud stage) and widening of the areola
  - Stage 3 Further enlargement of breast and areola; nipple flush with the breast surface
  - Stage 4 Projection of the areola and nipple forming a secondary mound over the breast
  - Stage 5 Recession of areola in most women by about age 14 or 15 years, leaving only the nipple projecting
- Male breast development reaches only the second stage. *Gynecomastia,* enlargement of breast tissue, occurs normally during puberty and may affect only one breast.

Pregnant Females

- Breast, areola, and nipple size increase.
- The areolae and nipples darken; nipples may become more erect; areolae contain small, scattered, elevated Montgomery's glands.
- Superficial veins become more prominent and jagged linear stretch marks may develop.
- A thick yellow fluid (colostrum) may be expressed from the nipples after the first trimester.

Older Adults

- In the postmenopausal female, breasts change in shape and often appear pendulous or flaccid; they lack the firmness they had in younger years.
- The presence of breast lesions may be detected more readily because of the decrease in connective tissue.
- General breast size remains the same. Although glandular tissue atrophies, the amount of fat in breasts (predominantly in the lower quadrants) increases in most women.

Thorax and Lungs

Assessing the thorax and lungs is important in assessing the client's aeration status. Changes in the respiratory system can occur slowly or quickly. In clients with asthma or chronic obstructive pulmonary disease (COPD), such as chronic bronchitis and emphysema, changes are frequently gradual.The client's posture is important to note. Some people with chronic respiratory problems tend to bend forward or even prop their arms on a support to elevate their clavicles. This posture is an attempt to expand the chest fully and, thus, breathe with less effort.

Chest Landmarks

Before beginning the assessment, the nurse must be familiar with a series of imaginary lines on the chest wall and be able to locate the position of each rib and some spinous processes. These landmarks help the nurse to identify the position of underlying organs (e.g., lobes of the lung) and to record abnormal assessment findings.

Figure 27.47 shows the anterior, lateral, and posterior series of lines. The *midsternal line* is a vertical line running through the centre of the sternum. The *midclavicular lines* (right and left) are vertical lines from the midpoints of the clavicles. The *anterior axillary lines* (right and left) are vertical lines from the anterior axillary folds (Figure 27.47, *A*). Figure 27.47, *B*, shows the three imaginary lines of the lateral chest. The *posterior axillary line* is a vertical line from the posterior axillary fold. The *midaxillary line* is a vertical line from the apex of the axilla. The anterior axillary line is as described for part *A*. Figure 27.47, *C*, shows the posterior chest landmarks. The *vertebral line* is a vertical line along the spinous processes. The *scapular lines* (right and left) are vertical lines from the inferior angles of the scapulae.

Locating the position of each rib and certain spinous processes is essential for identifying underlying lobes of the lung. Figure 27.48, *A*, shows an anterior view of the chest and underlying lungs; Figure 27.48, *B*, a posterior view; and Figure 27.48, *C*, right and left lateral views. Each lung is first divided into the upper and lower lobes by an oblique fissure that runs from the level of the spinous

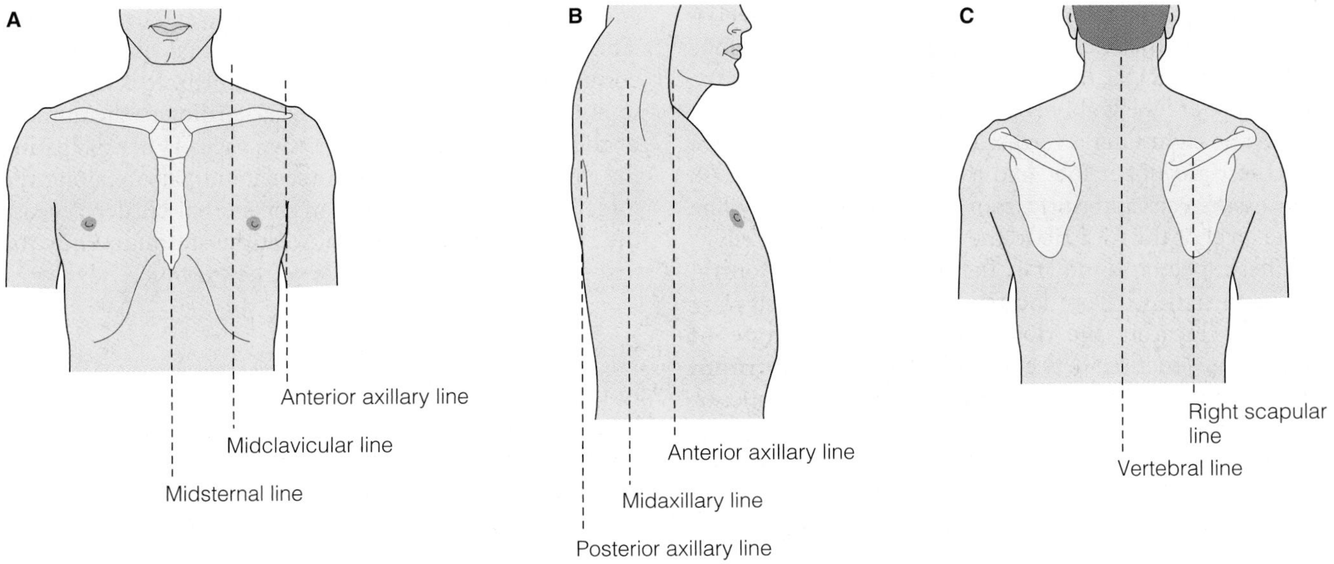

Figure 27.47 Chest wall landmarks: *A,* anterior chest; *B,* lateral chest; *C,* posterior chest

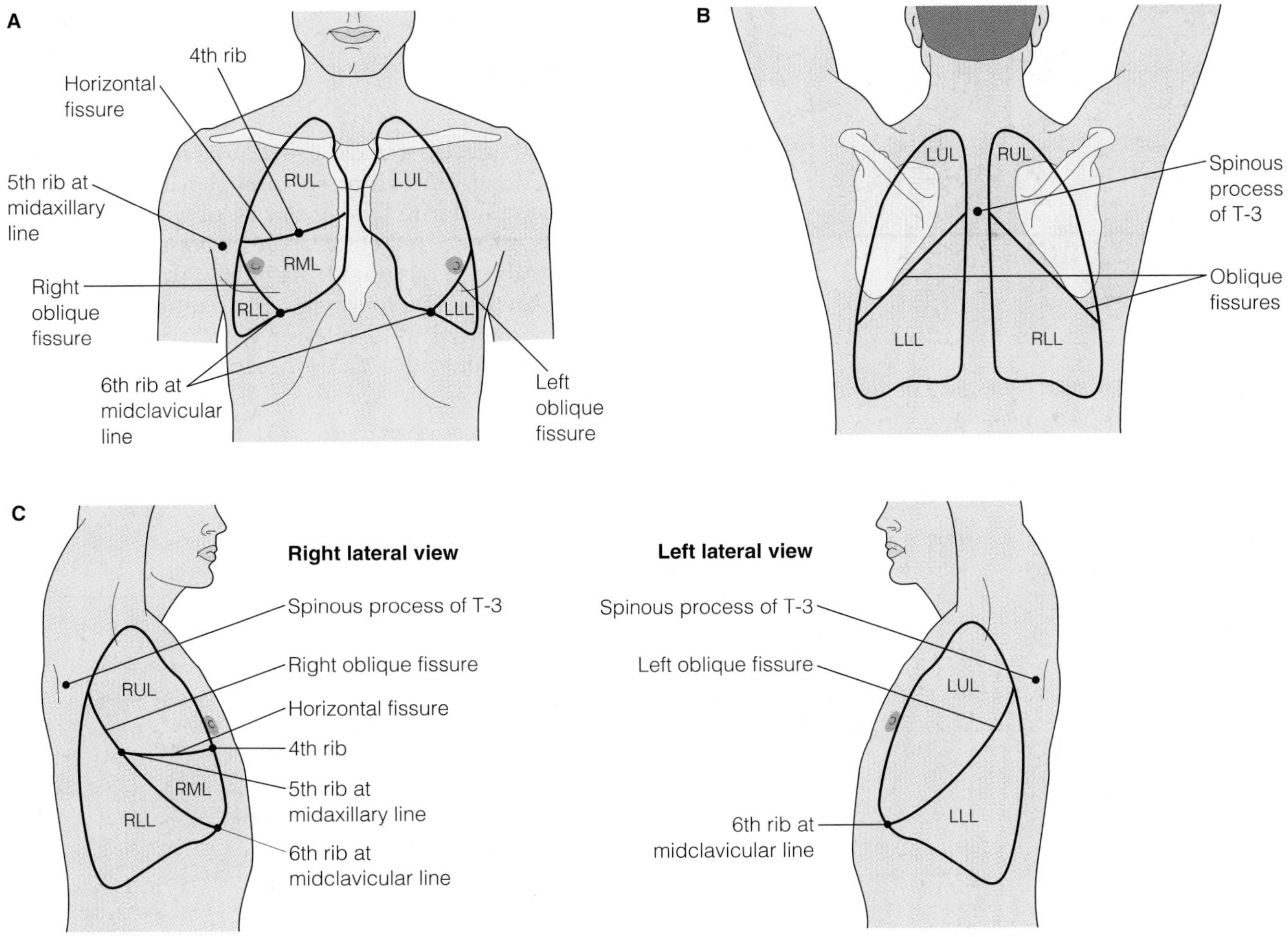

Figure 27.48 Chest landmarks: *A,* anterior chest landmarks and underlying lungs; *B,* posterior chest landmarks and underlying lungs; *C,* lateral chest landmarks and underlying lungs

process of the third thoracic vertebra (T-3) to the level of the sixth rib at the midclavicular line. The right upper lobe is abbreviated RUL; the right lower lobe, RLL. Similarly, the left upper lobe is abbreviated LUL; the left lower lobe, LLL. The right lung is further divided by a minor fissure into the right upper lobe and right middle lobe (RML). This fissure runs anteriorly from the right midaxillary line at the level of the fifth rib to the level of the fourth rib.

These specific landmarks, that is, T-3 and the fourth, fifth, and sixth ribs, are located as follows. The starting point for locating the ribs anteriorly is the **angle of Louis,** the junction between the body of the **sternum** (breastbone) and the **manubrium** (the handle-like superior part of the sternum that joins with the clavicles). The superior border of the second rib attaches to the sternum at this manubriosternal junction (Figure 27.49). The nurse can identify the manubrium by first palpating the clavicle and following its course to its attachment at the manubrium. The nurse then palpates and counts distal ribs and intercostal spaces (ICSs) from the second rib. It is important to note that an ICS is numbered according to the number of the rib immediately *above* the space. When palpating for rib identification, the nurse should palpate along the midclavicular line rather than the sternal border because the rib cartilages are very close at the sternum. Only the first seven ribs attach directly to the sternum.

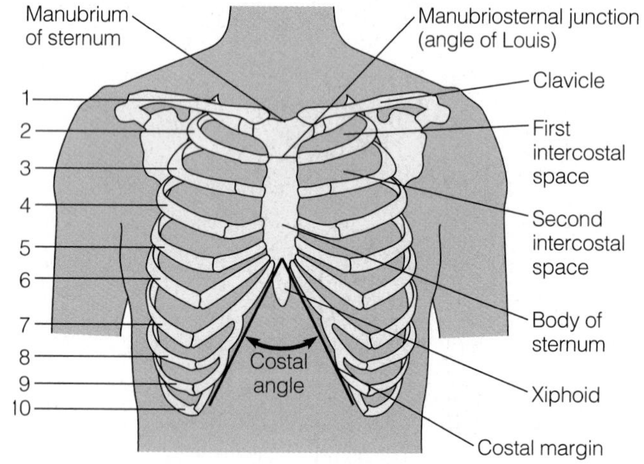

Figure 27.49 Location of the anterior ribs in relation to the angle of Louis and the sternum

Chest Shape and Size

In the infant, the thorax is rounded; that is, the diameter from the front to the back (anteroposterior) is equal to the transverse diameter. It is also cylindrical, having a nearly equal diameter at the top and the base. When a child reaches six years, the anteroposterior diameter has decreased in proportion to the transverse one. In adults, the thorax is oval. Its anteroposterior diameter is two times smaller than its transverse diameter (Figure 27.50). The overall shape of the thorax is elliptical; that is, its diameter is smaller at the top than at the base. In elderly people, kyphosis and osteoporosis alter the size of the chest cavity as the ribs move downward and forward.

Breath Sounds

Abnormal breath sounds, called **adventitious breath sounds,** occur when air passes through narrowed airways or airways filled with fluid or mucus, or when pleural linings are inflamed. Table 27.7 describes normal breath sounds. Adventitious sounds are often superimposed over normal sounds. The four types of adventitious sounds—crackles (referred to as rales or **crepitations),** gurgles, pleural friction rubs, and wheezes—are described in

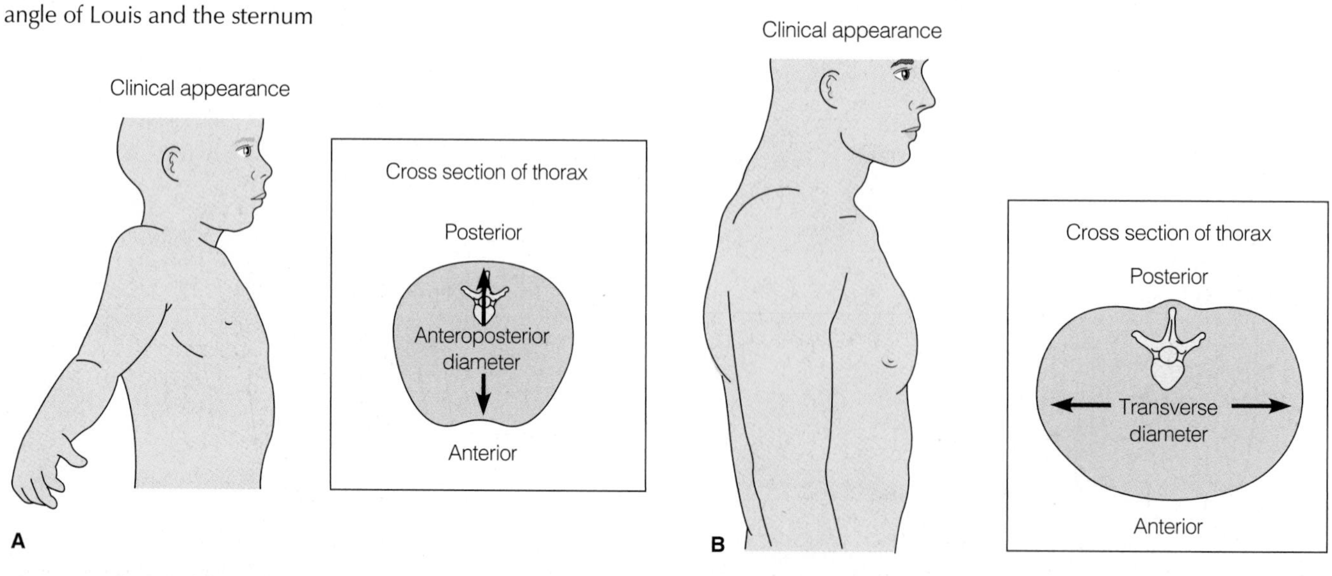

Figure 27.50 Configurations of the thorax showing anteroposterior diameter and transverse diameter: *A,* infant; *B,* adult

TABLE 27.7 Normal Breath Sounds

Type	Description	Location	Characteristics
Vesicular	Soft-intensity, low-pitched, "gentle sighing" sounds created by air moving through smaller airways (bronchioles and alveoli)	Over peripheral lung; best heard at base of lungs	Best heard on inspiration, which is about 2.5 times longer than the expiratory phase (5:2 ratio)
Bronchovesicular	Moderate-intensity and moderate-pitched "blowing" sounds created by air moving through larger airways (bronchi)	Between the scapulae and lateral to the sternum at the first and second intercostal spaces	Equal inspiratory and expiratory phases (1:1 ratio)
Bronchial (tubular)	High-pitched, loud, "harsh" sounds created by air moving through the trachea	Anteriorly over the trachea; not normally heard over lung tissue	Louder than vesicular sounds; have a short inspiratory phase and long expiratory phase (1:2 ratio)

TABLE 27.8 Adventitious Breath Sounds

Name	Description	Cause	Location
Crackles (rales)	Fine, short, interrupted crackling sounds; alveolar rales are high pitched. Sound can be simulated by rolling a lock of hair near the ear. Best heard on inspiration but can be heard on both inspiration and expiration. May not be cleared by coughing.	Air passing through fluid or mucus in any air passage	Most commonly heard in the bases of the lower lung lobes
Gurgles (rhonchi)	Continuous, low-pitched, coarse, gurgling, harsh, louder sounds with a moaning or snoring quality. Best heard on expiration but can be heard on both inspiration and expiration. May be altered by coughing.	Air passing through narrowed air passages as a result of secretions, swelling, tumours	Loud sounds can be heard over most lung areas but predominate over the trachea and bronchi
Friction rub	Superficial grating or creaking sounds heard during inspiration and expiration. Not relieved by coughing.	Rubbing together of inflamed pleural surfaces	Heard most often in areas of greatest thoracic expansion (e.g., lower anterior and lateral chest)
Wheeze	Continuous, high-pitched, squeaky musical sounds. Best heard on expiration. Not usually altered by coughing.	Air passing through a constricted bronchi as a result of secretions, swelling, tumours	Heard over all lung fields
Stridor	Predominantly an inspiratory wheeze	Partial obstruction of larynx or trachea	Louder in neck than over chest wall

Table 27.8. Absence of breath sounds over some lung areas is also a significant finding that is associated with collapsed and surgically removed lobes.

Assessment of the lungs and thorax includes all methods of examination: inspection, palpation, percussion, and auscultation. The following are needed for the examination:

(1) stethoscope, (2) a marking pencil, and (3) a centimetre ruler. The nurse usually examines the posterior chest first, then the anterior chest. For posterior and lateral chest examinations, the client is uncovered to the waist and in a sitting position. A sitting or lying position may be used for anterior chest examination. The sitting position is preferred because it maximizes chest expansion. Good lighting is essential, especially for chest inspection.

Procedure 27.12 describes how to assess the thorax and lungs.

PROCEDURE 27.12 Assessing the Thorax and Lungs

NURSING HISTORY FOCUS

Family history of illness (e.g., cancer, allergies, tuberculosis); lifestyle (e.g., smoking and occupational hazards like inhaling fumes); any medications being taken; current problems (e.g., swellings, coughs, wheezing, pain)

ASSESSMENT	NORMAL FINDINGS	DEVIATIONS FROM NORMAL
Posterior Thorax		
Inspect the shape and symmetry of the thorax from posterior and lateral views. Compare the anteroposterior diameter to the lateral diameter.	Anteroposterior to transverse diameter in ratio of 1:2 Chest symmetric	Barrel chest; increased anteroposterior to lateral diameter Chest asymmetric
Inspect the spinal alignment for deformities. Have the client stand. From a lateral position, observe the three normal curvatures: cervical, thoracic, and lumbar.	Spine vertically aligned	Exaggerated spinal curvatures (kyphosis, lordosis); lateral deviation of spine (scoliosis)
Palpate the posterior thorax.		
■ For clients who have no respiratory complaints, rapidly assess the temperature and integrity of all chest skin.	Skin intact; uniform temperature	Skin lesions; areas of hyperthermia
■ For clients who do have respiratory complaints, palpate all chest areas for bulges, tenderness, or abnormal movements. Avoid deep palpation for painful areas, especially if a fractured rib is suspected. *In such a case, deep palpation could lead to displacement of the bone fragment against the lungs.*	Chest wall intact; no tenderness; no masses	Lumps, bulges; depressions; areas of tenderness; movable structures (e.g., rib)
Palpate the posterior chest for respiratory excursion (thoracic expansion). Place the palms of both your hands over the lower thorax with your thumbs adjacent to the spine and your fingers stretched laterally (Figure 27.51). Ask the client to take a deep breath while you observe the movement of your hands and any lag in movement.	Full and symmetric chest expansion (i.e., when the client takes a deep breath, your thumbs should move apart an equal distance and at the same time; normally the thumbs separate 3–5 cm during deep inspiration)	Asymmetric and/or decreased chest expansion

PROCEDURE 27.12 Assessing the Thorax and Lungs *continued*

ASSESSMENT	NORMAL FINDINGS	DEVIATIONS FROM NORMAL

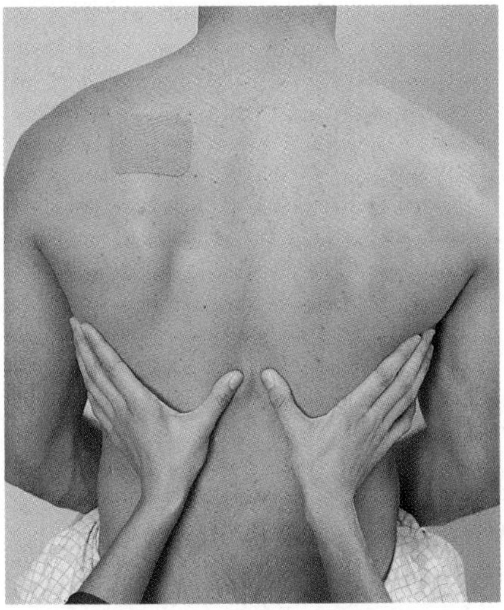

Figure 27.51 Position of the nurse's hands when assessing respiratory excursion on the posterior thorax

Palpate the chest for vocal (tactile) fremitus, the faintly perceptible vibration felt through the chest wall when the client speaks.

- Place the palmar surfaces of your fingertips or the ulnar aspect of your hand or closed fist on the posterior chest, starting near the apex of the lungs (Figure 27.52, position A).
- Ask the client to repeat such words as "blue moon" or "one, two, three."
- Repeat the two steps, moving your hands sequentially to the base of the lungs, through positions B through E in Figure 27.52.
- Compare the fremitus on both lungs and between the apex and the base of each lung, using either one hand and moving it from one side of the client to the corresponding area on the other side *or* using two hands that are placed simultaneously on the corresponding areas of each side of the chest.

Normal findings: Bilateral symmetry of vocal fremitus; fremitus is heard most clearly at the apex of the lungs

Low-pitched voices of males are more readily palpated than higher-pitched voices of females

Deviations from normal: Decreased or absent fremitus (associated with pneumothorax)

Increased fremitus (associated with consolidated lung tissue, as in pneumonia)

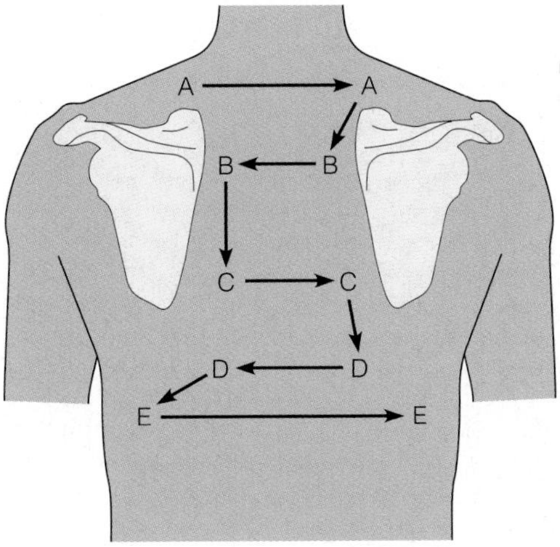

Figure 27.52 Areas and sequence for palpating tactile fremitus on the posterior chest

PROCEDURE 27.12 Assessing the Thorax and Lungs *continued*

ASSESSMENT	NORMAL FINDINGS	DEVIATIONS FROM NORMAL
Percuss the thorax. *Note:* Percussion on a rib normally elicits dullness.	Percussion notes resonate, except over scapula Lowest point of resonance is at the diaphragm (i.e., at the level of the eighth to tenth rib posteriorly)	Asymmetry in percussion sounds Areas of dullness or flatness over lung tissue (associated with consolidation of lung tissue or a mass)
Percuss for diaphragmatic excursion (movement of the diaphragm during maximal inspiration and expiration).	Excursion is 3–5 cm bilaterally in females and 5–6 cm in males Diaphragm is usually slightly higher on the right side	Restricted excursion (associated with lung disorder)

PERCUSSING THE THORAX

Percussing for Normal Thorax Sounds

Percussion of the thorax is performed to determine whether underlying lung tissue is filled with air, liquid, or solid material and to determine the positions and boundaries of certain organs. Because percussion penetrates to a depth of 5 to 7 cm, it detects superficial, rather than deep, lesions. Percussion sounds and tones are described in Table 27.4, page 517.

- Ask the client to bend the head and fold the arms forward across the chest. *This separates the scapula and exposes more lung tissue to percussion.*
- Percuss in the intercostal spaces at about 5-cm intervals in a systematic sequence (Figure 27.53). Figure 27.54 shows normal percussion sounds in the posterior chest.
- Compare one side of the lung with the other.
- Percuss the lateral thorax every few centimetres, starting at the axilla and working down to the eighth rib.

Percussing for Diaphragmatic Excursion

- Ask the client to take a deep breath and hold it while you percuss downward along the scapular line until dullness is produced at the level of the diaphragm. Mark this point with a marking pencil, and repeat the procedure on the other side of the chest.
- Ask the client to take a few normal breaths and then expel the last breath completely and hold it. Meanwhile, percuss upward from the marked point to assess and mark the diaphragmatic excursion during deep expiration on each side.

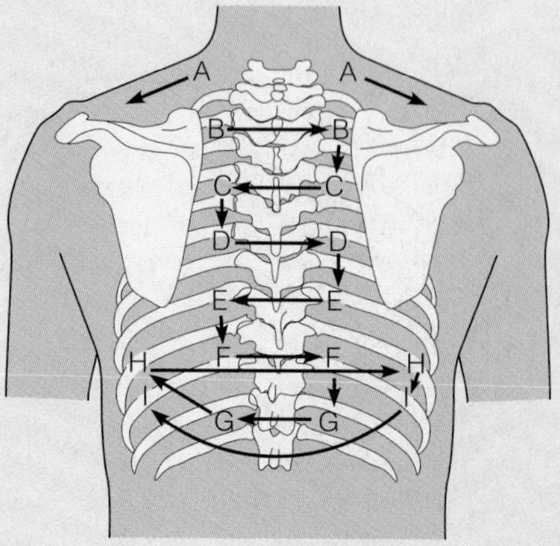

Figure 27.53 Sequence for posterior chest percussion

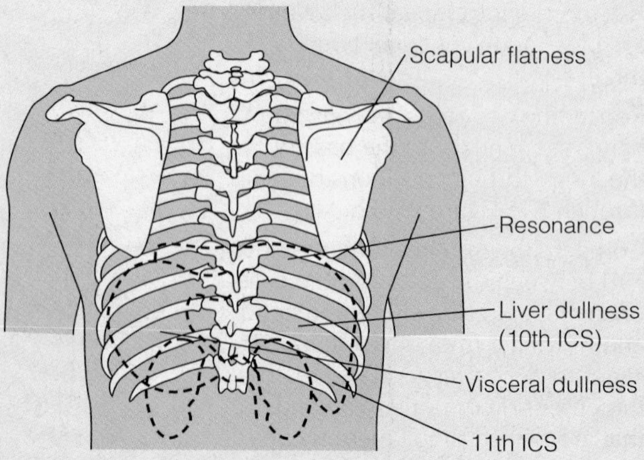

Figure 27.54 Normal percussion sounds on the posterior chest

PROCEDURE 27.12 Assessing the Thorax and Lungs *continued*

ASSESSMENT	NORMAL FINDINGS	DEVIATIONS FROM NORMAL
Auscultate the chest using the flat-disc diaphragm of the stethoscope (best for transmitting the high-pitched breath sounds). ■ Use the systematic zigzag procedure used in percussion (see Figure 27.53). ■ Ask the client to take slow, deep breaths through the mouth. Listen at each point to the breath sounds during a complete inspiration and expiration. ■ Compare findings at each point with the corresponding point on the opposite side of the chest.	Vesicular and bronchovesicular breath sounds (see Table 27.7, p. 561)	Adventitious breath sounds (e.g., crackles, rhonchi, wheeze, friction rub; see Table 27.8, p. 561) Absence of breath sounds (associated with collapsed and surgically removed lung lobes)
Anterior Thorax		
Inspect breathing patterns (e.g., respiratory rate and rhythm).	Quiet, rhythmic, and effortless respirations	See Chapter 31 and Chapter 39 for abnormal breathing patterns and sounds
Inspect the costal angle (angle formed by the intersection of the costal margins) **and the angle at which the ribs enter the spine.**	Costal angle is less than 90°, and the ribs insert into the spine at approximately a 45° angle (Figure 27.49, p. 560)	Costal angle is widened (associated with chronic obstructive pulmonary disease)
Palpate the anterior chest (see posterior chest palpation).		
Palpate the anterior chest for respiratory excursion. ■ Place the palms of both hands on the lower thorax, with fingers laterally along the lower rib cage and thumbs along the costal margins (Figure 27.55). ■ Ask the client to take a deep breath while you observe the movement of your hands.	Full symmetric excursion; thumbs normally separate 3–5 cm	Asymmetric and/or decreased respiratory excursion

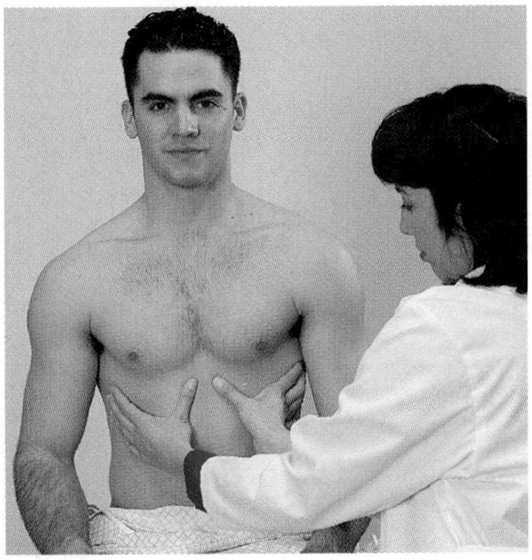

Figure 27.55 Position of nurse's hands when assessing respiratory excursion on the anterior thorax

PROCEDURE 27.12 Assessing the Thorax and Lungs *continued*

ASSESSMENT	NORMAL FINDINGS	DEVIATIONS FROM NORMAL
Palpate tactile fremitus in the same manner as for the posterior chest and using the sequence shown in Figure 27.56. If the breasts are large and cannot be held back adequately for palpation, this part of the examination is usually omitted.	Same as posterior tactile fremitus Fremitus is normally decreased over heart and breast tissue	Same as posterior fremitus
Percuss the anterior chest systematically. ■ Begin above the clavicles in the supraclavicular space, and proceed downward to the diaphragm (Figure 27.57). ■ Compare one side of the lung to the other. ■ Ask the female client to hold her own breasts back.	Percussion notes resonate down to the sixth rib at the level of the diaphragm but are flat over areas of heavy muscle and bone, dull on areas over the heart and the liver, and tympanic over the stomach (Figure 27.58)	Asymmetry in percussion notes Areas of dullness or flatness over lung tissue

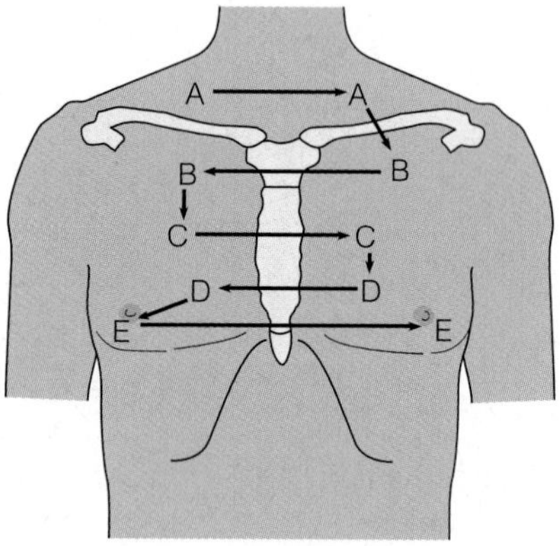

Figure 27.56 Areas and sequence for palpating tactile fremitus on the anterior chest

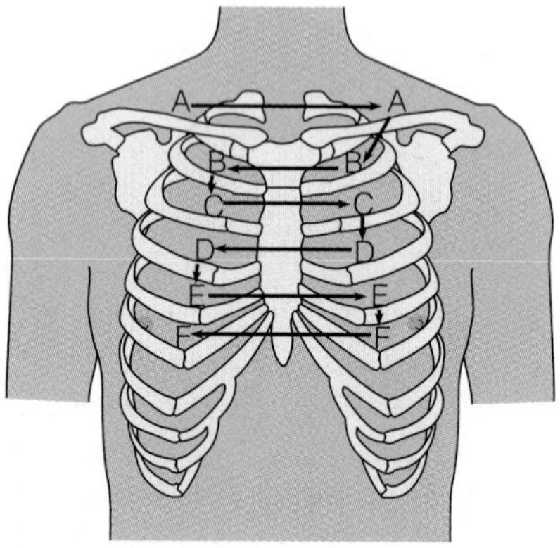

Figure 27.57 Sequence for percussing the anterior chest

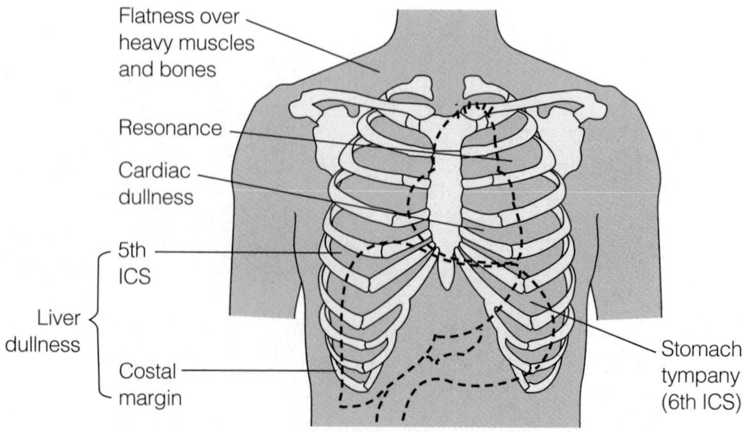

Figure 27.58 Normal percussion sounds on the anterior chest

PROCEDURE 27.12 Assessing the Thorax and Lungs *continued*

ASSESSMENT	NORMAL FINDINGS	DEVIATIONS FROM NORMAL
Auscultate the trachea.	Bronchial (tubular) breath sounds (see Table 27.7, p. 561)	Adventitious breath sounds (see Table 27.8, p. 561)
Auscultate the anterior chest. Use the sequence used in percussion (Figure 27.57), beginning over the bronchi between the sternum and the clavicles.	Bronchovesicular and vesicular breath sounds (see Table 27.7, p. 561)	Adventitious breath sounds (see Table 27.8, p. 561)

Lifespan Considerations

Children

- To assess tactile fremitus in infants, place the hand over the crying infant's chest.
- Auscultated sounds will be louder and harsher in infants.
- Infants and children up to age six years tend to breathe more abdominally than thoracically.
- Chest circumference is measured at delivery and in early infancy (e.g., up to nine months) to rule out birth injuries, congenital anomalies, or other dysfunction.

Older Adults

- The thoracic curvature may be accentuated (kyphosis) because of osteoporosis and changes in cartilage resulting in collapse of the vertebrae.
- The anteroposterior diameter of the chest deepens, giving the person a barrel-chested appearance. This is due to loss of skeletal muscle strength in the thorax and diaphragm and constant lung inflation from excessive expiratory pressure on the alveoli.
- Breathing rate and rhythm are unchanged at rest; the rate normally increases with activity but may take longer to return to the resting rate.
- Inspiratory muscles become less powerful, and the inspiration reserve volume decreases (see Table 39.1). A decrease in depth of respiration is therefore apparent.
- Expiration may require the use of accessory muscles. The expiratory reserve volume (see Table 39.1) significantly increases because of the increased amount of air remaining in the lungs at the end of a normal breath.
- Small airways lose their cartilaginous support and elastic recoil; as a result, they tend to close, particularly in basal or dependent portions of the lung.
- Alveolar tissue loses its elasticity and changes to fibrous tissue. This thicker alveolar membrane decreases the pulmonary diffusion capacity. As a result, arterial oxyhemoglobin saturation and PaO_2 are slightly lower than those of young adults. Exertional capacity also decreases.
- Cilia in the airways decrease in number and are less effective in removing mucus; elderly clients are therefore at greater risk for pulmonary infections.

Cardiovascular and Peripheral Vascular Systems

Heart

Nurses assess the cardiovascular system through observations (inspection), palpation, and auscultation. The examination includes palpation of upper and lower extremity pulses; inspection of jugular venous distention; measurement of blood pressure bilaterally and while standing versus lying flat or sitting; and inspection, palpation, and auscultation of the heart. It is important to follow a systematic assessment of the cardiovascular system starting with inspection and moving through to auscultation. Although heart examinations are initially performed while the client is in a semireclined position, other positions, such as left lateral recumbent, leaning forward, and standing, may also be used.

To assess the client's heart, the nurse must first determine its exact location. In the average adult, most of the heart lies behind and to the left of the sternum. A small portion (the right atrium) extends to the right of the sternum. The upper portion of the heart (both atria), referred to as its **base,** lies toward the back. The lower portion (the

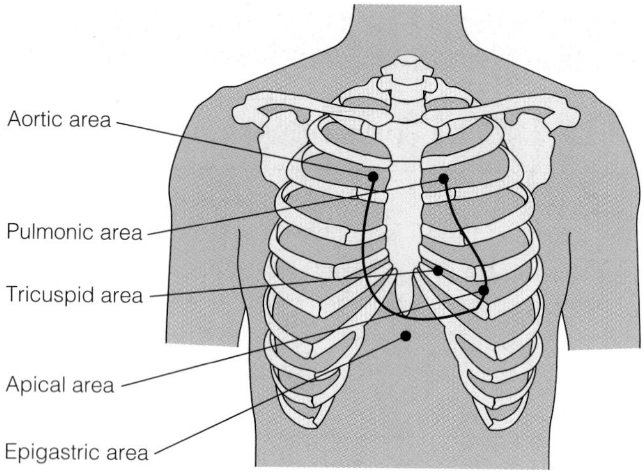

Figure 27.59 Anatomic sites of the precordium

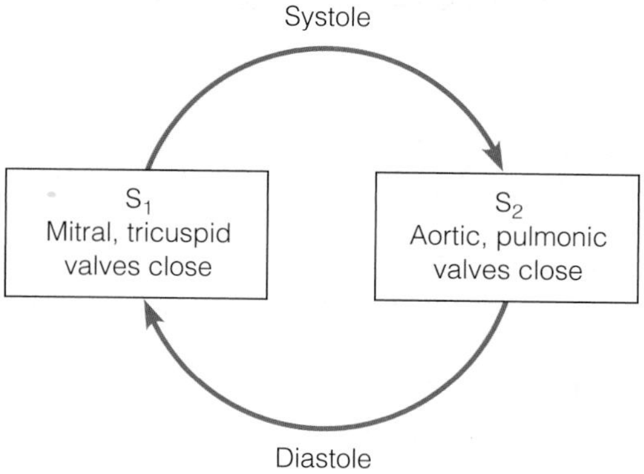

Figure 27.60 Relationship of heart sounds to systole and diastole

ventricles), referred to as its **apex,** points forward. The apex of the left ventricle actually touches the anterior chest wall at or medial to the left midclavicular line (LMCL) and at or near the fifth left intercostal space (LICS), which is slightly below the left nipple. See Figure 31.14 on page 720. This point where the apex touches the anterior chest wall is known as the **point of maximal impulse (PMI).** The point of maximal impulse refers to the point where the apical impulse is most readily seen or felt.

The **precordium,** the area of the chest overlying the heart, is inspected and palpated simultaneously for the presence of abnormal pulsations or lifts or heaves. The terms **lift** and **heave,** often used interchangeably, refer to a rising along the sternal border with each heartbeat. A lift occurs when cardiac action is very forceful. It should be confirmed by palpation with the palm of the hand. Enlargement or overactivity of the left ventricle produces a heave lateral to the apex, whereas enlargement of the right ventricle produces a heave at or near the sternum.

Several heart sounds can be heard by auscultation. The normal first two heart sounds are produced by closure of the valves of the heart. The first heart sound, $\mathbf{S_1}$, occurs when the atrioventricular (A-V) valves close and is best heard at the apex. These valves close when the ventricles have been sufficiently filled. Although the right and left A-V valves do not close simultaneously, the closures occur closely enough to be heard as one sound (S_1), a dull, low-pitched sound described as "lub." After the ventricles empty their blood into the aorta and pulmonary arteries, the semilunar valves close, producing the second heart sound, $\mathbf{S_2}$, described as "dub." S_2 has a higher pitch than S_1 and is also shorter. The S_2 is best heard in the aortic and pulmonic areas. These two sounds, S_1 and S_2 ("lub-dub"), occur within one second or less, depending on the heart rate.

Heart sounds are audible anywhere on the precordial area, but they are best heard over the aortic, pulmonic, tricuspid, and apical areas (Figure 27.59). Each area is associated with the closure of heart valves: the aortic area with the aortic valve (inside the aorta as it arises from the left ventricle); the pulmonic area with the pulmonic valve (inside the pulmonary artery as it arises from the right ventricle); the tricuspid area with the tricuspid valve (between the right atrium and ventricle); and the apical (mitral) area with the mitral valve (between the left atrium and ventricle).

Associated with these sounds are systole and diastole. **Systole** is the period in which the ventricles contract. It begins with the first heart sound and ends at the second heart sound. Systole is normally shorter than diastole. **Diastole** is the period in which the ventricles relax. It starts with the second sound and ends at the subsequent first sound. Normally, no sounds are audible during these periods (Figure 27.60). The experienced nurse, however, may auscultate extra heart sounds (S_3 and S_4) during diastole. Both sounds are low in pitch and heard best at the apex, with the bell of the stethoscope, and with the client either supine or lying on the left side. S_3 (often referred to as a gallop rhythm) occurs early in diastole right after S_2 and sounds like "lub-dub-*ee*" (S_1, S_2, S_3) or "Kentuc-*ky*." It often disappears when the client sits up. S_3 is normal in children and young adults. In older adults, it may indicate heart failure. S_4 is rarely heard in healthy young adults. It occurs near the very end of diastole just before S_1 and creates the sound of "*dee*-lub-dub" (S_4, S_1, S_2) or "*Ten*-nessee." S_4 may be heard in many elderly clients and can be a sign of hypertension. An S_4 may be heard following acute myocardial infarction or in elderly patients with cardiovascular disease. The presence of an S_4 indicates an increased resistance to ventricular filling, which occurs because of a loss of compliance in the ventricular walls (e.g., hypertensive disease, coronary heart disease).

Normal heart sounds are summarized in Table 27.9.

TABLE 27.9 Normal Heart Sounds

		Area			
Sound or Phase	**Description**	**Aortic**	**Pulmonic**	**Tricuspid**	**Apical**
S_1	Dull, low-pitched, and longer than S_2; sounds like "lub"	Less intensity than S_2	Less intensity than S_2	Louder than or equal to S_2	Louder than or equal to S_2
Systole	Normally silent interval between S_1 and S_2				
S_2		Louder than S_1	Louder than S_1; abnormal if louder than the aortic S_2 in adults over 40 years of age	Less intensity than or equal to S_1	Less intensity than or equal to S_1
Diastole	Normally silent interval between S_2 and next S_1				

Central Vessels

The *carotid arteries* supply oxygenated blood to the head and neck (Figure 27.61). Because they are the only source of blood to the brain, prolonged occlusion of one of these arteries can result in serious brain damage. The carotid pulses correlate with central aortic pressure, thus reflecting cardiac function better than the peripheral pulses. When cardiac output is diminished, the peripheral pulses may be difficult or impossible to feel, but the carotid pulse should be felt easily.

The carotid is also auscultated for a bruit, and if a bruit is found, the carotid artery is then palpated for a thrill. A **bruit** (a blowing or swishing sound), best heard with the diaphragm of the stethoscope, is created by turbulence of bloodflow due either to a narrowed arterial lumen (a common development in older people) or to a condition, such as anemia or hyperthyroidism, that elevates cardiac output. A **thrill,** which frequently accompanies a bruit, is a vibrating sensation, like the purring of a cat or water running through a hose. It, too, indicates turbulent bloodflow due to arterial obstruction.

The *jugular veins* drain blood from the head and neck directly into the superior vena cava and right side of the heart (see Figure 27.61). The external jugular veins are superficial and may be visible above the clavicle. The internal jugular veins lie deeper along the carotid artery and may transmit pulsations onto the skin of the neck. Normally, external neck veins are distended and visible when a person lies down; they are flat and not as visible when a person stands up because gravity encourages venous drainage. By inspecting the jugular veins for pulsations and distention, the nurse can assess the adequacy of function of the right side of the heart and venous pressure. Bilateral jugular vein distention (JVD) may indicate right-sided heart failure.

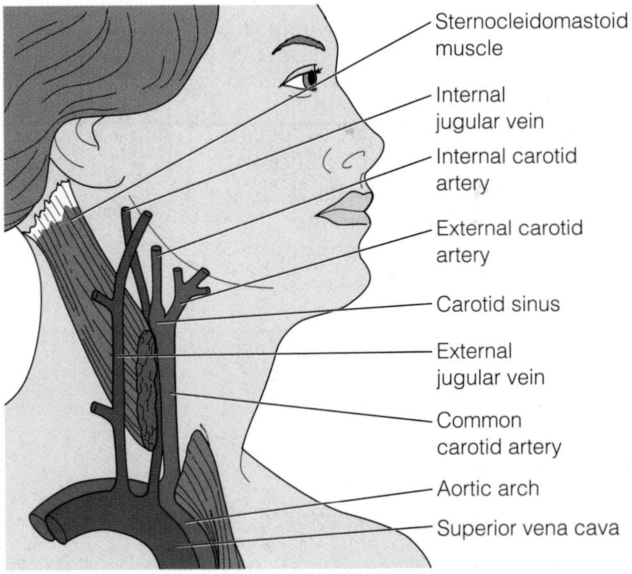

Figure 27.61 Arteries and veins of the right side of the neck

Procedure 27.13 describes how to assess the heart and central vessels.

PROCEDURE 27.13 Assessing the Heart and Central Vessels

NURSING HISTORY FOCUS

Family history of incidence and age of heart disease, high cholesterol levels, high blood pressure, stroke, obesity, congenital heart disease, and rheumatic fever; client's past history of rheumatic fever, heart murmur, heart attack, or heart failure; present symptoms indicative of heart disease (e.g., fatigue, dyspnea, orthopnea, edema, cough, chest pain, palpitations, syncope, hypertension, wheezing, hemoptysis); presence of diseases that affect heart (e.g., obesity, diabetes, lung disease, endocrine disorders); lifestyle habits that are risk factors for cardiac disease (e.g., smoking, alcohol intake, eating and exercise patterns, areas and degree of perceived stress)

ASSESSMENT	NORMAL FINDINGS	DEVIATIONS FROM NORMAL
Simultaneously inspect and palpate the precordium for the presence of abnormal pulsations, lifts, or heaves. To locate the valve areas of the heart, see the box below.	No pulsations, although some people have aortic pulsations	Pulsations
■ Inspect and palpate the aortic and pulmonic areas, observing them at an angle and to the side, to note the presence or absence of pulsations. Oblique artificial lighting is helpful. *Observing these areas at an angle increases the likelihood of seeing pulsations.*		
■ Inspect and palpate the tricuspid area for pulsations and heaves or lifts.	No pulsations No lift or heave	Pulsations Diffuse lift or heave, indicating enlarged or overactive right ventricle
■ Inspect and palpate the apical area for pulsation, noting its specific location (it may be displaced laterally or lower) and diameter. If displaced laterally, record the distance between the apex and the MCL in centimetres.	Pulsations are usually visible only in slim adults and palpable in most adults PMI in fifth LICS at or medial to MCL Diameter of 1 to 2 cm No lift or heave	PMI displaced laterally or lower (indicates enlarged heart) Diameter over 2 cm (indicates enlarged heart or aneurysm) Diffuse lift or heave lateral to apex (indicates enlargement or overactivity of left ventricle)
■ Inspect and palpate the epigastric area at the base of the sternum for abdominal aortic pulsations.	Aortic pulsations	Bounding abdominal pulsations (e.g., aortic aneurysm)

LOCATING THE AORTIC, PULMONIC, TRICUSPID, AND APICAL AREAS OF THE PRECORDIUM

- Locate the angle of Louis (the point of attachment). It is felt as a prominence on the sternum.
- Move your fingertips down each side of the angle until you can feel the second intercostal spaces. The client's right second intercostal space is the *aortic area,* and the left second intercostal space is the *pulmonic area.*
- At the third intercostal space, left sternal border is Erbs point. Murmurs are best heard with the bell of the stethoscope at this area.
- From the pulmonic area, move your fingertips down three left intercostal spaces along the side of the sternum. The left fifth intercostal space close to the sternum is the *tricuspid* or *right ventricular area.*
- From the tricuspid area, move your fingertips laterally 5 to 7 cm to the left midclavicular line (LMCL). This is the *apical* or *mitral area,* or point of maximal impulse (PMI). If you have difficulty locating the PMI, have the client roll onto the left side to move the apex closer to the chest wall.

PROCEDURE 27.13 Assessing the Heart and Central Vessels *continued*

ASSESSMENT	NORMAL FINDINGS	DEVIATIONS FROM NORMAL
Auscultate the heart in all four anatomic sites: aortic, pulmonic, tricuspid, and apical (mitral). Auscultation need not be limited to these areas; however, the nurse may need to move the stethoscope to find the most audible sounds for each client.	S_1: Usually heard at all sites; Usually louder at the apical and tricuspid areas	Increased or decreased intensity Varying intensity with different beats
	S_2: Usually heard at all sites; Usually louder at base of heart and aortic and pulmonic areas	Increased intensity at aortic area Increased intensity at pulmonic area
	Systole: Silent interval; Slightly shorter duration than diastole at normal heart rate (60–90 beats/min)	
	Diastole: Silent interval; Slightly longer duration than systole at normal heart rates	Sharp-sounding ejection clicks
	S_3 in children and young adults	S_3 in older adults
	S_4 in many older adults	S_4 may be a sign of hypertension, coronary disease

AUSCULTATING THE HEART

- Eliminate all sources of room noise. *Heart sounds are of low intensity, and other noise hinders the nurse's ability to hear them.*
- Keep the client in a supine position with head elevated 30 to 45 degrees.
- Use both the flat-disc diaphragm and the bell-shaped diaphragm to listen to all areas.
- In every area of auscultation, distinguish both S_1 and S_2 sounds.
- When auscultating, concentrate on one particular sound at a time in each area: the first heart sound, followed by systole, then the second heart sound, then diastole. Systole and diastole are normally silent intervals.
- Later, re-examine the heart while the client is in the upright sitting position. *Certain sounds are more audible in certain positions.*

ASSESSMENT	NORMAL FINDINGS	DEVIATIONS FROM NORMAL
Carotid Arteries		
Palpate the carotid artery, using extreme caution. See the box on the next page.	Symmetric pulse volumes	Asymmetric volumes (possible stenosis or thrombosis)
	Full pulsations, thrusting quality	Decreased pulsations (may indicate impaired left cardiac output)
Alert: Avoid carotid massage, which can cause stimulation of the carotid sinus and a reflex drop in the apical pulse rate.	Quality remains same when client breathes, turns head, and changes from sitting to supine position	Increased pulsations
	Elastic arterial wall	Thickening, hard, rigid, beaded, inelastic walls (indicate arteriosclerosis)
Auscultate the carotid artery to determine the presence of a bruit. See the box on the next page.	No sound heard on auscultation	Presence of a bruit in one or both arteries (suggests occlusive artery disease)

PROCEDURE 27.13 Assessing the Heart and Central Vessels *continued*

PALPATING AND AUSCULTATING THE CAROTID ARTERY

Palpation

- Palpate only one carotid artery at a time. *This ensures adequate cerebral bloodflow through the other and, thus, prevents possible ischemia. Ischemia* is a deficiency of blood in a body part due to constriction or obstruction of a blood vessel.
- Palpate at the halfway point to avoid the carotid sinus.
- If possible, place client at a 30° angle. Avoid exerting too much pressure and massaging the area. *Pressure can occlude the artery, and carotid sinus massage can precipitate bradycardia.* The *carotid sinus* is a small dilation at the beginning of the internal carotid artery just above the bifurcation of the common carotid artery, in the upper third of the neck.
- Ask the client to turn the head slightly toward the side being examined. *This makes the carotid artery more accessible.*

Auscultation

- Turn the client's head slightly away from the side being examined. *This facilitates the placement of the stethoscope.*
- Auscultate the carotid artery on one side and then the other.
- Listen for the presence of a bruit.
- If you hear a bruit, gently palpate the artery to determine the presence of a thrill.

ASSESSMENT	NORMAL FINDINGS	DEVIATIONS FROM NORMAL
Jugular Veins		
Inspect the jugular veins for distention while the client is placed in a semi-Fowler's position (30–45° angle), with the head supported on a small pillow.	Veins not visible (indicating right side of heart is functioning normally)	Veins visibly distended (indicating advanced cardiopulmonary disease) Bilateral measurements above 3 cm are considered elevated (may indicate right-sided heart failure) Unilateral distention (may be caused by local obstruction)
If jugular distention is present, assess the jugular venous pressure (JVP). ■ Locate the highest visible point of distention of the internal jugular vein. Although either the internal or the external jugular vein can be used, the internal jugular vein is more reliable. *The external jugular vein is more easily affected by obstruction or kinking at the base of the neck.* ■ Measure the vertical height of this point in centimetres from the sternal angle (the point at which the clavicles meet; Figure 27.62). ■ Repeat the two preceding steps on the other side. ■ Pressures causing distention more than 3 or 4 cm above the sternal angle are usually considered elevated.		

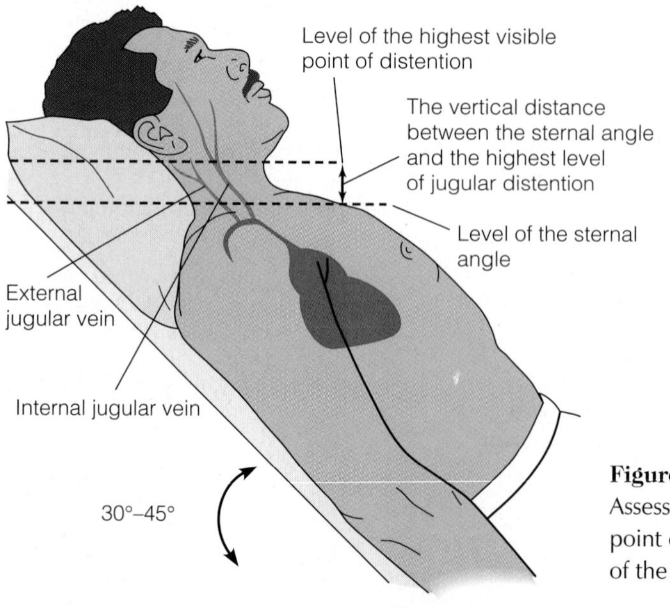

Figure 27.62 Assessing the highest point of distention of the jugular vein

PROCEDURE 27.13 Assessing the Heart and Central Vessels *continued*

Lifespan Considerations

Children

- Heart sounds are louder because of the thinner chest wall.
- A third heart sound, best heard at the apex, is present in about one-third of all children.
- The PMI is higher and more medial in children under eight years old.

Older Adults

- If no disease is present, heart size remains the same throughout life.
- Cardiac output and strength of contraction decrease, thus lessening the older person's activity tolerance.
- The heart rate returns to its resting rate more slowly after exertion than it did when the individual was younger.
- S_4 heart sound is considered normal in older adults.
- Extra systoles commonly occur. Ten or more extra systoles per minute are considered abnormal.
- Sudden emotional and physical stresses may result in cardiac arryhthmias and heart failure.

Peripheral Vascular System

Assessing the peripheral vascular system includes measuring the blood pressure; palpating peripheral pulses; inspecting, palpating, and auscultating the carotid pulse; inspecting the jugular and peripheral veins; and inspecting the skin and tissues to determine **perfusion** (blood supply to an area) to the extremities. Certain aspects of peripheral vascular assessment are often incorporated into other parts of the assessment procedure. For example, blood pressure is usually measured at the beginning of the physical examination (see the section on assessing blood pressure in Chapter 31). Pulse sites and pulse assessments are described in Chapter 31.

Procedure 27.14 describes how to assess the peripheral vascular system.

PROCEDURE 27.14 Assessing the Peripheral Vascular System

NURSING HISTORY FOCUS

Past history of heart disorders, varicosities, arterial disease, and hypertension; lifestyle, specifically exercise patterns, activity patterns and tolerance, smoking habits, and use of alcohol

ASSESSMENT	NORMAL FINDINGS	DEVIATIONS FROM NORMAL
Peripheral Pulses		
Palpate the peripheral pulses (except the carotid pulse) **on both sides of the client's body simultaneously and systematically to determine the symmetry of pulse volume.**	Symmetric pulse volumes Full pulsations	Asymmetric volumes (indicate impaired circulation) Absence of pulsation (indicates arterial spasm or occlusion) Decreased, weak, thready pulsations (indicate impaired cardiac output or arterial insufficiency or occlusion) Increased pulse volume (may indicate hypertension, high cardiac output, or circulatory overload)

PROCEDURE 27.14 Assessing the Peripheral Vascular System *continued*

ASSESSMENT	NORMAL FINDINGS	DEVIATIONS FROM NORMAL
Peripheral Veins		
Inspect the peripheral veins in the arms and legs for the presence and/or appearance of superficial veins when limbs are dependent and when limbs are elevated.	In dependent position, distention and nodular bulges at calves are present When limbs are elevated, veins collapse (veins may appear tortuous or distended in older people)	Distended veins in the anteromedial part of thigh and/or lower leg or on posterolateral part of calf from knee to ankle
Assess the peripheral leg veins for signs of phlebitis. Compare one limb with the other.	Limbs not tender Symmetric in size	Tenderness on palpation Pain in calf muscles with passive dorsiflexion of the foot **(Homans' sign)** (It should be noted from the research literature that a positive Homans' sign is a poor clinical test for the detection of a deep vein thrombosis [DVT] [see for example, Cranley, Canos, & Sull, 1976; Delis, Hunt, Strachan, & Nicolaides, 2001; Sternbach, 1989].) Warmth and redness over vein Swelling of one calf or leg
Peripheral Perfusion		
Inspect the skin of the hands and feet for colour, temperature, edema, and skin changes.	Natural skin colour Skin temperature not excessively warm or cold No edema Skin texture resilient and moist	Cyanosis, pallor, erythema Skin cool or hot to touch Marked edema Skin thin and shiny or thick, waxy, shiny, and fragile; reduced hair; ulceration
Assess the adequacy of arterial flow if arterial insufficiency is suspected.	*Buerger's test:* Original colour returns in 10 seconds; veins in feet or hands fill in about 15 seconds	Delayed colour return or mottled appearance; delayed venous filling; marked redness of arms or legs (indicates arterial insufficiency)
	Capillary refill test: Immediate return of colour	Delayed return of colour (arterial insufficiency)

ASSESSING THE ADEQUACY OF ARTERIAL BLOOD FLOW

Buerger's Test (Arterial Adequacy Test)

- Assist the client to a supine position. Ask the client to raise one leg or one arm about 30 cm above heart level, move the foot or hand briskly up and down for about one minute, and then sit up and dangle the leg or arm.
- Observe the time elapsed until return of original colour and vein filling. Original colour normally returns in 10 seconds; veins fill in about 15 seconds.

Capillary Refill Test

- Squeeze the client's fingernail and toenail between your fingers sufficiently to cause blanching.
- Release the pressure, and observe how quickly normal colour returns. Colour normally returns immediately.

Other Assessments

- Inspect the fingernails for changes indicative of circulatory impairment. See the section on assessment of nails earlier in this chapter.
- See also peripheral pulse assessment in Procedure 31.2.

PROCEDURE 27.14 Assessing the Peripheral Vascular System *continued*

Lifespan Considerations

Children

- Palpation of pulses in the lower extremities (particularly the femoral pulses) is essential to screen for coarctation of the aorta.

Older Adults

- The overall effectiveness of blood vessels decreases as smooth muscle cells are replaced by connective tissue. The lower extremities are more likely to show signs of arterial and venous impairment because of the more distal and dependent position.
- Proximal arteries become thinner and dilate.
- Peripheral arteries become thicker and dilate less effectively because of arteriosclerotic changes in the vessel walls.
- Blood vessels lengthen and become more tortuous and prominent. Varicosities occur more frequently.
- In some instances, arteries may be palpated more easily because of the loss of supportive surrounding tissues. Often, however, the most distal pulses of the lower extremities are more difficult to palpate because of decreased arterial perfusion.
- Systolic and diastolic blood pressures may increase. See Chapter 31, page 733 for Canadian guidelines for measurement of blood pressure, follow-up, and lifestyle counselling.
- Peripheral edema is frequently observed and is most commonly the result of chronic venous insufficiency or low protein levels in the blood (hypoproteinemia).
- Carotid artery assessment is an essential aspect of peripheral vascular examination in the older adult.

Abdomen

The nurse locates and describes abdominal findings in a client by using two common methods of subdividing the abdomen: quadrants and regions. To divide the abdomen into quadrants, the nurse imagines two lines: a vertical line from the xiphoid process to the pubic symphysis, and a horizontal line across the umbilicus (Figure 27.63). These quadrants are labeled right upper quadrant *(1)*, left upper quadrant *(2)*, right lower quadrant *(3)*, and left lower quadrant *(4)*. Using the second method, division into nine regions, the nurse imagines two vertical lines that extend superiorly from the midpoints of the inguinal ligaments, and two horizontal lines, one at the level of the edge of the lower ribs and the other at the level of the iliac crests (Figure 27.64). Specific organs or parts of organs lie in each abdominal region. See Tables 27.10 and 27.11.

In addition, practitioners often use certain landmarks to locate abdominal signs and symptoms. These are the xiphoid process of the sternum, the costal margins, the midline (a line drawn from the tip of the sternum through the umbilicus to the pubic symphysis), the anterosuperior iliac spine, the inguinal ligaments (Poupart's ligaments), and the superior margin of the pubic symphysis (Figure 27.65).

Assessment of the abdomen involves all four methods of examination (inspection, auscultation, palpation, and percussion). When assessing the abdomen, the nurse performs inspection first, followed by auscultation, percussion, and/or palpation. *Auscultation is done before these techniques because palpation and percussion cause movement or stimulation of the bowel, which can increase bowel motility and, thus, heighten bowel sounds, creating false results.*

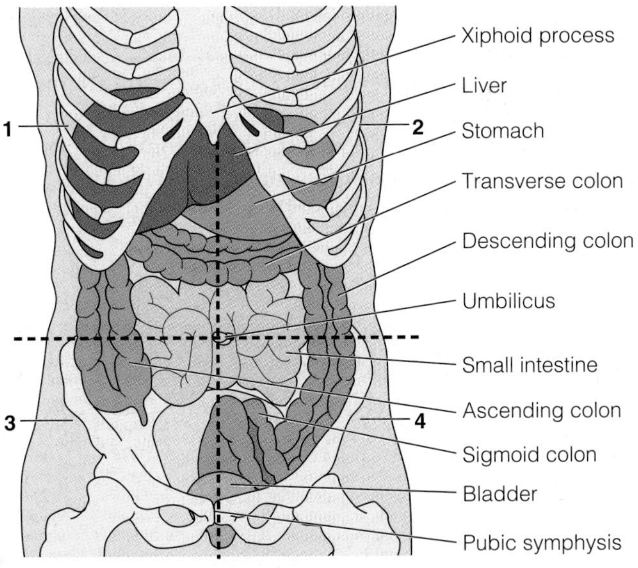

Figure 27.63 The four abdominal quadrants and the underlying organs: *1,* right upper quadrant; *2,* left upper quadrant; *3,* right lower quadrant; *4,* left lower quadrant

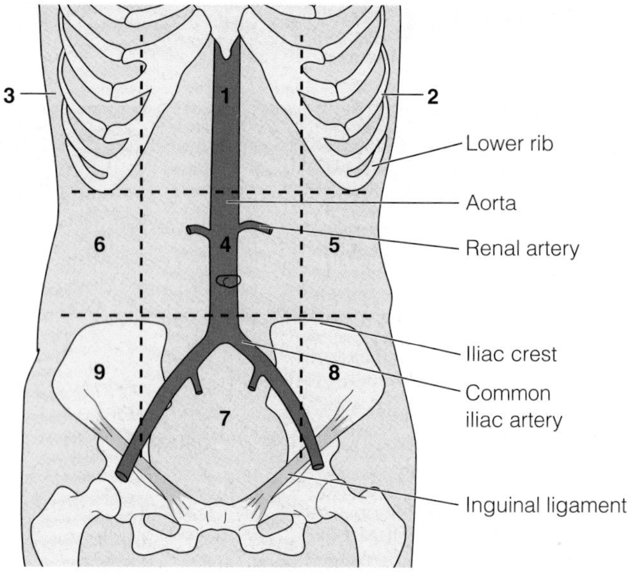

Figure 27.64 The nine abdominal regions: *1,* epigastric; *2, 3,* left and right hypochondriac; *4,* umbilical; *5, 6,* left and right lumbar; *7,* suprapubic and hypogastric; *8, 9,* left and right inguinal or iliac

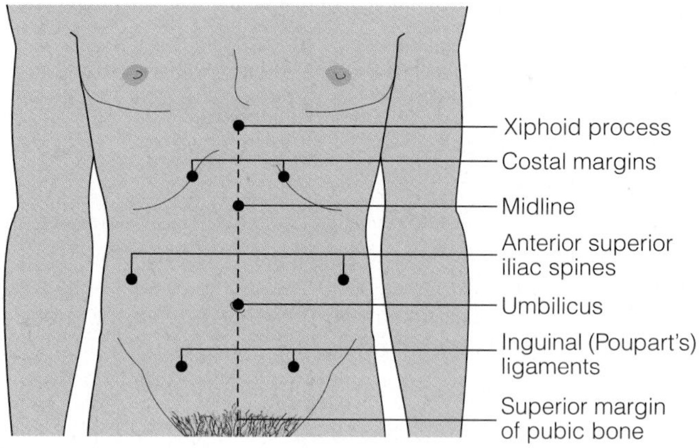

Figure 27.65 Landmarks commonly used to identify abdominal areas

To facilitate validity of observations and enhance client comfort, the nurse asks the client to urinate before beginning the assessment and assists the client to a supine position with the arms placed comfortably at the sides. The nurse also places small pillows beneath the knees and the head. This position and an empty bladder prevent tension in the abdominal muscles. By contrast, the abdominal muscles tense when the client is sitting or supine with knees and arms extended and with hands clasped behind the head.

The nurse should ensure that the room is warm and expose only the client's abdomen from chest line to the pubic area to avoid chilling and shivering, which can tense the abdominal muscles. An examining light, a tape measure (metal or unstretchable cloth), a water-soluble skin-marking pencil, and a stethoscope are necessary for the examination.

Procedure 27.15 describes how to assess the abdomen.

TABLE 27.10 Organs in the Four Abdominal Quadrants

Right Upper Quadrant	Left Upper Quadrant	Left Lower Quadrant	Right Lower Quadrant
Liver	Left lobe of liver	Lower lobe of left kidney	Lower lobe of right kidney
Gallbladder	Stomach	Sigmoid colon	Cecum
Duodenum	Spleen	Section of descending colon	Appendix
Head of pancreas	Upper lobe of left kidney	Left ovary	Section of ascending colon
Right adrenal gland	Pancreas	Left fallopian tube	Right ovary
Upper lobe of right kidney	Left adrenal gland	Left ureter	Right fallopian tube
Hepatic flexure of colon	Splenic flexure of colon	Left spermatic cord	Right ureter
Section of ascending colon	Section of transverse colon	Part of uterus	Right spermatic cord
Section of transverse colon	Section of descending colon		Part of uterus

TABLE 27.11 Organs in the Nine Abdominal Regions

Right Hypochondriac	Right Inguinal	Umbilical	Left Lumbar
Right lobe of liver Gallbladder Part of duodenum Hepatic flexure of colon Upper half of right kidney Suprarenal gland	Cecum Appendix Lower end of ileum Right ureter Right spermatic cord Right ovary	Omentum Mesentery Lower part of duodenum Part of jejunum and ileum	Descending colon Lower half of left kidney Part of jejunum and ileum
Right Lumbar	**Epigastric**	**Hypogastric (Pubic)**	**Left Inguinal**
Ascending colon Lower half of right kidney Part of duodenum and jejunum	Aorta Pyloric end of stomach Part of duodenum Pancreas Part of liver	Ileum Bladder Uterus	Sigmoid colon Left ureter Left spermatic cord Left ovary
		Left Hypochondriac	
		Stomach Spleen Tail of pancreas Splenic flexure of colon Upper half of left kidney Suprarenal gland	

PROCEDURE 27.15 Assessing the Abdomen

NURSING HISTORY FOCUS

Incidence of abdominal pain: its location, onset, sequence, and chronology; its quality (description); its frequency; associated symptoms (e.g., nausea, vomiting, diarrhea); bowel habits; incidence of constipation or diarrhea (have client describe what client means by these terms); change in appetite, food intolerances, and foods ingested in last 24 hours; specific signs and symptoms (e.g., heartburn, flatulence and/or belching, difficulty swallowing, hematemesis, blood or mucus in stools, and aggravating and alleviating factors); previous problems and treatment (e.g., stomach ulcer, gallbladder surgery, history of jaundice)

ASSESSMENT	NORMAL FINDINGS	DEVIATIONS FROM NORMAL
Inspection of the Abdomen		
Inspect the abdomen for skin integrity (refer to the discussion of skin assessment earlier in this chapter).	Unblemished skin Uniform colour	Presence of rash or other lesions Tense, glistening skin (may indicate ascites, edema)
	Silver-white striae or surgical scars	Purple striae (associated with Cushing's disease)
Inspect the abdomen for contour and symmetry.		
■ Observe the abdominal contour (profile line from the rib margin to the pubic bone) while standing at the client's side when the client is supine.	Flat, rounded (convex), or scaphoid (concave)	Generalized distention (associated with gas retention, obesity, ascites, or tumours) Lower abdominal distention (may indicate bladder distention, pregnancy, or ovarian mass) Markedly scaphoid abdomen (associated with malnutrition)

→

PROCEDURE 27.15 Assessing the Abdomen *continued*

ASSESSMENT	NORMAL FINDINGS	DEVIATIONS FROM NORMAL
■ Ask the client to take a deep breath and to hold it (makes any abnormality, such as an enlarged liver or spleen more obvious).	No evidence of enlargement of liver or spleen	Evidence of enlargement of liver or spleen
■ Assess the symmetry of contour while standing at the foot of the bed. ■ If distention is present, measure the abdominal girth by placing a tape around the abdomen at the level of the umbilicus (Figure 27.66).	Symmetric contour 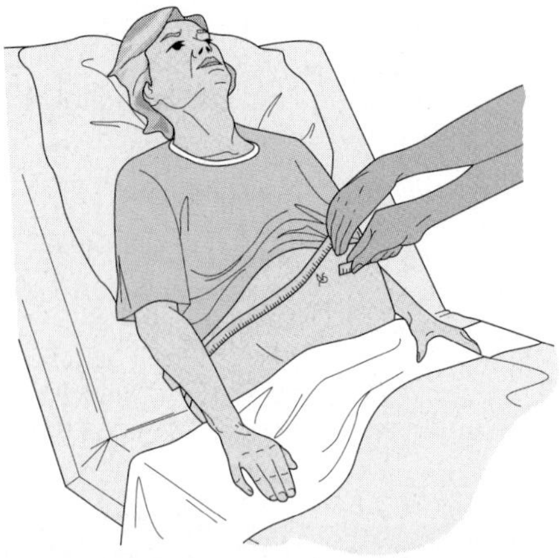 **Figure 27.66** Measuring the abdominal girth at the level of the umbilicus	Asymmetric contour, such as localized protrusions around umbilicus, inguinal ligaments, or scars (possible hernia or tumour)
Observe abdominal movements associated with respiration, peristalsis, or aortic pulsations.	Symmetric movements caused by respiration Visible peristalsis in very lean people Aortic pulsations in thin persons at epigastric area	Limited movement due to pain or disease process Visible peristalsis in clients who are not lean (with bowel obstruction) Marked aortic pulsations
Observe the vascular pattern.	No visible vascular pattern	Visible venous pattern (dilated veins) is associated with liver disease, ascites, and venocaval obstruction
Auscultation of the Abdomen		
Auscultate the abdomen for bowel sounds and vascular sounds. Auscultation should be done in all four quadrants of the abdomen.	Audible bowel sounds Absence of arterial bruits	Absent, hypoactive, or hyperactive bowel sounds Loud bruit over aortic area (possible aneurysm) Bruit over renal, iliac, or femoral arteries

PROCEDURE 27.15 Assessing the Abdomen *continued*

AUSCULTATING THE ABDOMEN

Warm the hands and the stethoscope diaphragms. *Cold hands and a cold stethoscope may cause the client to contract the abdominal muscles, and these contractions may be heard during auscultation.*

For Bowel Sounds

- Use the flat-disc diaphragm. *Intestinal sounds are relatively high-pitched and best accentuated by the flat-disc diaphragm.* Light pressure with the stethoscope is adequate to detect sounds.
- Ask when the client last ate. *The frequency of sounds relates to the state of digestion or the presence of food in the gastrointestinal tract. Shortly after or long after eating, bowel sounds may normally increase. They are loudest when a meal is long overdue. Four to seven hours after a meal, bowel sounds in the RLQ may be heard continuously over the ileocecal valve area while the digestive contents from the small intestine empty through the valve into the large intestine.*
- Place the flat-disc diaphragm of the stethoscope in each of the four quadrants of the abdomen (Figure 27.67). Many nurses begin in the lower right quadrant in the area of the cecum.

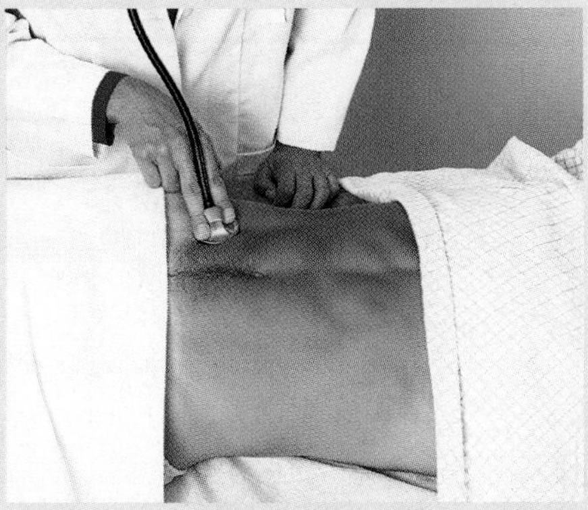

Figure 27.67 Auscultating the abdomen for bowel sounds

- Listen for active bowel sounds—irregular gurgling noises occurring about every five to 20 seconds. The duration of a single sound may range from less than a second to more than several seconds.
- Normal bowel sounds are described as *audible.* Alterations in sounds are described as *absent* or *hypoactive,* that is, extremely soft and infrequent (e.g., one per minute), and *hyperactive* or *increased,* that is, high-pitched, loud, rushing sounds that occur frequently (e.g., every 3 seconds), also known as *borborygmi.* Absence of sounds indicates a cessation of intestinal motility. Hypoactive sounds indicate decreased motility and are usually associated with manipulation of the bowel during surgery, inflammation, paralytic ileus, or late bowel obstruction. Hyperactive sounds indicate increased intestinal motility and are usually associated with diarrhea, an early bowel obstruction, or the use of laxatives.
- If bowel sounds appear to be absent, listen for 3–5 minutes before concluding that they are absent. *Because bowel sounds are so irregular, a longer time and more sites are used to confirm absence of sounds.*

For Vascular Sounds

- Use the bell of the stethoscope over the aorta, renal arteries, iliac arteries, and femoral arteries (Figure 27.68).
- Listen for bruits (blowing sound due to restricted blood flow through narrowed vessels).

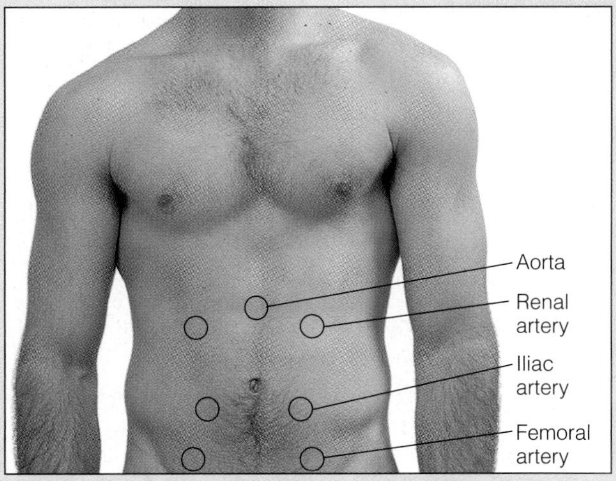

Figure 27.68 Auscultatory areas for vascular sounds

PROCEDURE 27.15 Assessing the Abdomen *continued*

ASSESSMENT	NORMAL FINDINGS	DEVIATIONS FROM NORMAL
Percussion of the Abdomen **Percuss several areas in each of the four quadrants** to determine the amount of *tympany* (gas in stomach and intestines) and *dullness* (a decrease, absence, or flatness of resonance heard over solid masses or fluid). Use a systematic pattern: begin in the lower left quadrant, then proceed to the lower right quadrant, the upper right quadrant, and the upper left quadrant (Figure 27.69).	Tympany over the stomach and gas-filled bowels; dullness, especially over the liver and spleen or a full bladder	Large dull areas (associated with presence of fluid or a tumour)
Percussion of the Liver **Percuss the liver** to determine its size (see the box below).	6–12 cm in the midclavicular line; 4–8 cm at the midsternal line	Enlarged size (associated with liver disease)

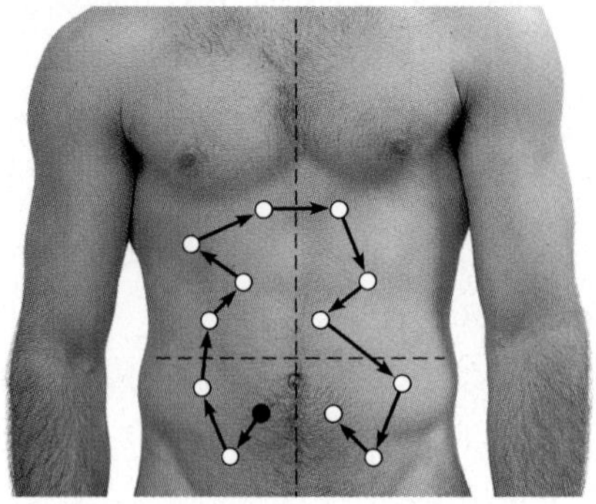

Figure 27.69 Systematic percussion sites for all four quadrants

PERCUSSING THE LIVER

Percussion to determine liver size begins in the right midclavicular line below the level of the umbilicus and proceeds as follows:

1. Percuss upward over tympanic areas until a dull percussion sound indicates the lower liver border. Mark the site with a skin-marking pencil. See Figure 27.70.
2. Then, percuss downward at the right midclavicular line, beginning from an area of lung resonance and progressing downward until a dull percussion sound indicates the upper liver border (usually at the fifth to seventh interspace). Mark this site.
3. Measure the distance between the two marks (upper and lower liver border) in centimetres to establish the liver span or size.
4. Repeat steps 1 to 3 at the midsternal line.

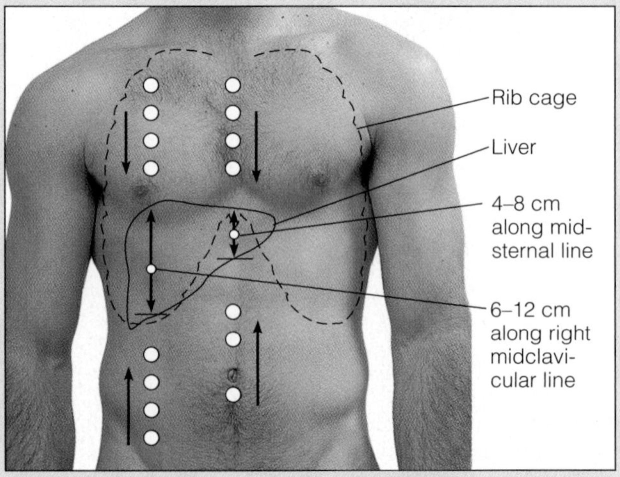

Figure 27.70 Percussion pattern to determine liver size

PROCEDURE 27.15 Assessing the Abdomen *continued*

ASSESSMENT	NORMAL FINDINGS	DEVIATIONS FROM NORMAL
Palpation of the Abdomen		
Perform light palpation first to detect areas of tenderness and/or muscle guarding. Systematically explore all four quadrants.	No tenderness; relaxed soft abdomen with smooth, consistent tension; pain free	Tenderness and hypersensitivity Superficial masses Localized areas of increased tension
Perform deep palpation over all four quadrants with extreme caution.	As for light palpation	Generalized or localized areas of tenderness Mobile or fixed masses Muscle tightness, guarding, and pain

PALPATING THE ABDOMEN

Palpation is used to detect tenderness, the presence of masses or distention, and the outline and position of abdominal organs (e.g., the liver, spleen, and kidneys). Two types of palpation are used: light and deep. *In some practice settings, palpation is limited to light abdominal palpation to assess tenderness and bladder palpation to assess for distention.* Before palpation, (1) ensure that the client's position is appropriate for relaxation of the abdominal muscles, and (2) warm the hands. *Cold hands can elicit muscle tension and thus impede palpatory evaluation.*

Light Palpation

- Hold the palm of your hand slightly above the client's abdomen with your fingers parallel to the abdomen.
- Depress the abdominal wall lightly, about 1 cm or to the depth of the subcutaneous tissue, with the pads of your fingers (Figure 27.71).
- Move the finger pads in a slight circular motion.
- Note areas of slight tenderness or superficial pain, large masses, and muscle guarding. To determine areas of tenderness, ask the client to tell you about them, watch for changes in the client's facial expressions, and note areas of muscle guarding.

Deep Palpation

- Palpate sensitive areas last.
- Press the distal half of the palmar surface of the fingers of one hand into the abdominal wall *or* use the bimanual method of palpation discussed earlier in this chapter, page 517.
- Depress the abdominal wall about 4–5 cm (Figure 27.72).
- Note masses and the structure of underlying contents. If a mass is present, determine its size, location, mobility, contour, consistency, and tenderness. Normal abdominal structures that may be mistaken for masses include the lateral borders of the rectus abdominis muscles; the feces-filled colon; the aorta; and the uterus.

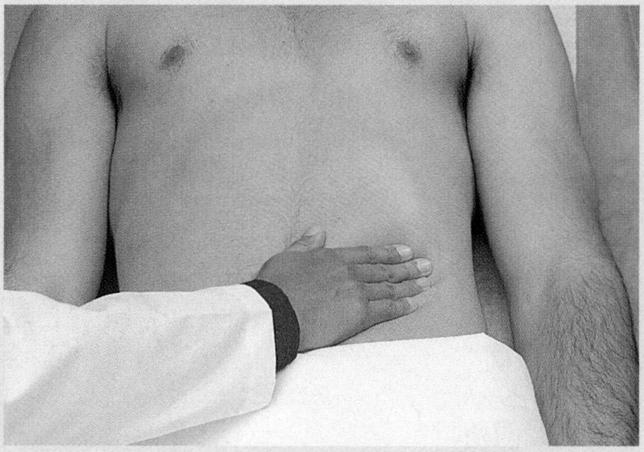

Figure 27.71 Light palpation of the abdomen

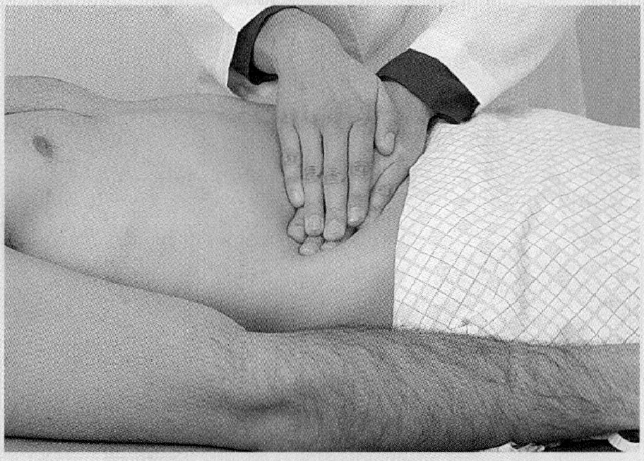

Figure 27.72 Deep palpation of the abdomen

PROCEDURE 27.15 Assessing the Abdomen *continued*

ASSESSMENT	NORMAL FINDINGS	DEVIATIONS FROM NORMAL
Palpation of the Liver		
Palpate the liver with extreme caution to detect enlargement and tenderness.	May not be palpable	Enlarged (abnormal finding, even if liver is smooth and not tender)
	Border feels smooth	Smooth but tender; nodular or hard

PALPATING THE LIVER

Two bimanual approaches are used in palpation of the liver. In using the *first* method, place one hand along the anterior rib cage and the other hand on the posterior rib cage.

- Stand on the client's right side.
- Place your left hand on the posterior thorax at about the 11th or 12th rib. This hand is used to push upward and provide support of underlying structures for the subsequent anterior palpation.
- Place your right hand along the rib cage at about a 45° angle to the right of the rectus abdominis muscle or parallel to the rectus muscle with the fingers pointing toward the rib cage (Figure 27.73).
- While the client exhales, exert a gradual and gentle downward and forward pressure beneath the costal margin until you reach a depth of 4 to 5 cm. *During expiration, the abdominal wall relaxes, facilitating deep palpation.*
- Maintain your hand position, and ask the client to inhale deeply. *This makes the liver border descend and moves the liver into a palpable position.*
- While the client inhales, feel the liver border move against your hand. It should feel firm and have a regular contour. If you do not palpate the liver initially, ask the client to take two or three more deep breaths while you maintain or apply slightly more palpation pressure. Livers are harder to palpate in obese, tense, or very physically fit people.
- If the liver is enlarged (i.e., palpable below the costal margin), measure the number of centimetres it extends below the costal region.

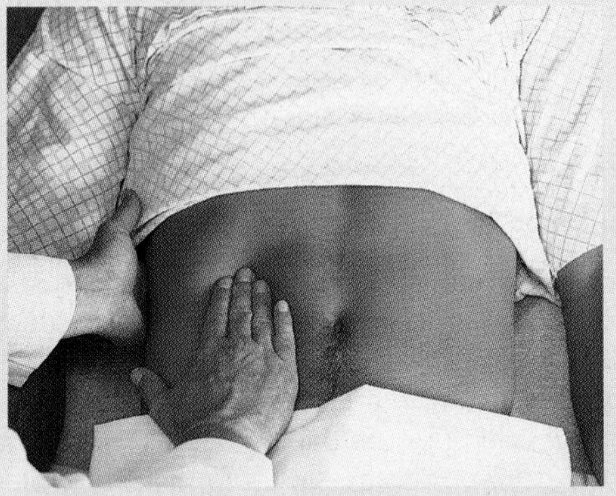

Figure 27.73 Palpating the liver

A *second* method is the bimanual palpation method discussed on page 516, in which one hand is superimposed on the other (Figure 27.2, earlier). The techniques and principles used for palpating the liver with one hand apply to the two-hand method as well.

ASSESSMENT	NORMAL FINDINGS	DEVIATIONS FROM NORMAL
Palpation of the Bladder		
Palpate the area above the pubic symphysis if the client's history indicates possible urinary retention (Figure 27.74).	Not palpable	Distended and palpable as smooth, round, tense mass (indicates urinary retention)

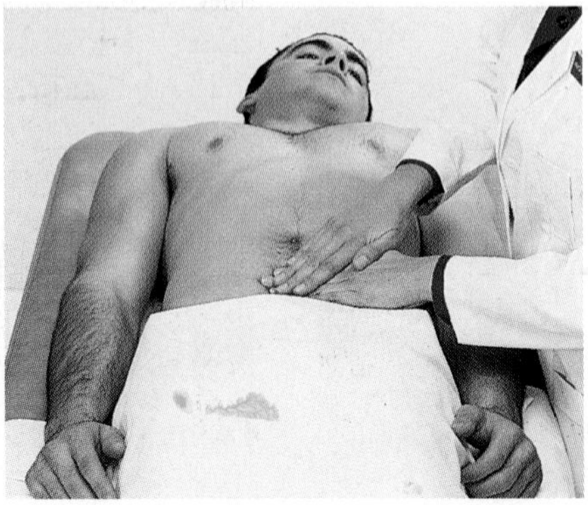

Figure 27.74 Palpating the bladder

PROCEDURE 27.15 Assessing the Abdomen *continued*

Lifespan Considerations

Children

- The abdomen of the newborn and infant is round. Toddlers have a characteristic "pot belly" appearance, which persists until about the fifth year.
- Peristaltic waves are usually more visible than in adults.
- Children may not be able to pinpoint areas of tenderness; by observing facial expressions the examiner can determine areas of maximum tenderness.
- The liver is relatively larger than in adults. It can be palpated 1 to 2 cm below the right costal margin.

Older Adults

- The rounded abdomens of many older persons are due to an increase in adipose tissue and a decrease in muscle tone.
- The abdominal wall is slacker and thinner, making palpation easier and more accurate than in younger clients. Muscle wasting and loss of fibroconnective tissue occur.
- The side effects of drugs are often manifested in the gastrointestinal tract (e.g., nausea, vomiting, and diarrhea).
- The pain threshold in the elderly is often higher; major abdominal problems, such as appendicitis or other acute emergencies, may, therefore, go undetected.
- It is important to differentiate between gastrointestinal and cardiac pain. Gastrointestinal pain may be located in the chest or abdomen, and, classically, cardiac pain is located in the chest. However, it is important to note that clients may present with atypical symptoms (e.g., abdominal pain, nausea and vomiting, back pain, and shortness of breath) from cardiac disease, such as acute myocardial infarction (Then, Rankin, & Fofonoff, 2001), which may lead to a misdiagnosis. Factors aggravating gastrointestinal pain are usually related to either ingestion or lack of food intake; gastrointestinal pain is usually relieved by antacids, food, or assuming an upright position. Common factors that can aggravate cardiac pain are activity or anxiety; cardiac pain is relieved by rest or nitroglycerin.
- Emptying time of the stomach is slower because gastric acid secretion is decreased, resulting in indigestion and intolerance of certain foods. Decreases in the production of pancreatic enzymes also contribute to complaints of indigestion and anorexia.
- Stool passes through the intestines at a slower rate in elderly clients, and the perception of stimuli that produce the urge to defecate often diminishes.
- Fecal incontinence may occur in confused or neurologically impaired older adults.
- Many older persons erroneously believe that the absence of a daily bowel movement signifies constipation. When assessing for constipation, the nurse must consider the client's diet, activity, medications, and characteristics and ease of passage of feces as well as the frequency of bowel movements.
- The incidence of colon cancer is higher among older adults than younger adults. Symptoms include a change in bowel function, rectal bleeding, and weight loss. Changes in bowel function, however, are associated with many factors, such as diet, exercise, and medications.
- Decreased absorption of oral medications often occurs with aging.
- In the liver, impaired metabolism of some drugs may occur with aging.

Musculoskeletal System

The musculoskeletal system encompasses the muscles, bones, and joints. The completeness of an assessment of this system depends largely on the needs and problems of the individual client. The nurse usually assesses the musculoskeletal system for muscle strength, tone, size, and symmetry of muscle development, fasciculations, and tremors. A **fasciculation** is an abnormal contraction (shortening) of a bundle of muscle fibres. A **tremor** is an involuntary trembling of a limb or body part. Tremors may involve large groups of muscle fibres or small bundles of muscle fibres. An **intention tremor** becomes more apparent when an individual attempts a voluntary movement, such as holding a cup of coffee. A **resting tremor** is more apparent when the client is at rest and it diminishes with activity.

Joints are assessed for tenderness, swelling, thickening, crepitation (the sound of bone grating on bone), presence of nodules, and range of motion. The amount of joint movement can be measured by a goniometer, a device that measures the angle of the joint in degrees (Figure 27.75). Body posture is assessed for normal standing and sitting positions. For information about body posture, see Chapter 43.

Procedure 27.16 describes how to assess the musculoskeletal system.

PROCEDURE 27.16 Assessing the Musculoskeletal System

NURSING HISTORY FOCUS

History or presence of muscle pain: onset, location, character, associated phenomena (e.g., redness and swelling of joints), and aggravating and alleviating factors; any limitations to movement or inability to perform activities of daily living; previous sports injuries; any loss of function without pain

ASSESSMENT	NORMAL FINDINGS	DEVIATIONS FROM NORMAL
Muscles		
Inspect the muscles for size. Compare the muscles on one side of the body (e.g., of the arm, thigh, and calf) to the same muscle on the other side. For any discrepancies, measure the muscles with a tape.	Equal size on both sides of the body	**Atrophy** (a decrease in size) or **hypertrophy** (an increase in size)
Inspect the muscles and tendons for contractures (shortening).	No contractures	Malposition of body part (e.g., a foot fixed in dorsiflexion)
Inspect the muscles for fasciculations and tremors. Inspect any tremors of the hands and arms by having the client hold the arms out in front of the body.	No fasciculations or tremors	Presence of fasciculation or tremor
Palpate muscles at rest to determine muscle tonicity (the normal condition of tension, or tone, of a muscle at rest)	Normally firm	Atonic (lacking tone)
Palpate muscles for flaccidity, spasticity, and smoothness of movement while the client is active and passive.	Smooth coordinated movements	**Flaccidity** (weakness or laxness) or **spasticity** (sudden involuntary muscle contraction)
Test muscle strength. See tests in the accompanying box. Compare the right side with the left side.	Equal strength on each body side	25% or less of normal strength
Bones		
Inspect the skeleton for normal structure and deformities.	No deformities	Bones misaligned
Examine for scoliosis in persons over age 12 years. Client stands facing away from the nurse and bends over to touch the toes.	Straight spine	A hump in the thoracic spine, indicating a lateral curve
Palpate the bones to locate any areas of edema or tenderness.	No tenderness or swelling	Presence of tenderness or swelling (may indicate fractures, neoplasms, or osteoporosis)
Joints		
Inspect the joints for swelling.	No swelling	One or more swollen joints
Palpate each joint for tenderness, smoothness of movement, swelling, crepitation, presence of nodules.	No tenderness, swelling, crepitation, or nodules Joints move smoothly	Presence of tenderness, swelling, crepitation, or nodules
Assess joint range of motion. Table 43.1 lists the types of joint movements.	Varies to some degree in accordance with person's genetic makeup and degree of physical activity	Limited range of motion in one or more joints

PROCEDURE 27.16 Assessing the Musculoskeletal System *continued*

TESTING AND GRADING MUSCLE STRENGTH

Muscle Activity

Sternocleidomastoid: Client turns the head to one side against the resistance of your hand. Repeat with the other side.

Trapezius: Client shrugs the shoulders against the resistance of your hands.

Deltoid: Client holds arm up and resists while you try to push it down.

Biceps: Client fully extends each arm and tries to flex it while you attempt to hold arm in extension.

Triceps: Client flexes each arm and then tries to extend it against your attempt to keep arm in flexion.

Wrist and finger muscles: Client spreads the fingers and resists as you attempt to push the fingers together.

Grip strength: Client grasps your index and middle fingers while you try to pull the fingers out.

Hip muscles: Client is supine, both legs extended; client raises one leg at a time while you attempt to hold it down.

Hip abduction: Client is supine, both legs extended. Place your hands on the lateral surface of each knee; client spreads the legs apart against your resistance.

Hip adduction: Client is in same position as for hip abduction. Place your hands between the knees; client brings the legs together against your resistance.

Hamstrings: Client is supine, both knees bent. Client resists while you attempt to straighten the legs.

Quadriceps: Client is supine, knee partially extended; client resists while you attempt to flex the knee.

Muscles of the ankles and feet: Client resists while you attempt to dorsiflex the foot and again resists while you attempt to plantar flex the foot.

Grading Muscle Strength

0: 0% of normal strength; complete paralysis

1: 10% of normal strength; no movement, contraction of muscle is palpable or visible

2: 25% of normal strength; full muscle movement against gravity, with support

3: 50% of normal strength; normal movement against gravity

4: 75% of normal strength; normal full movement against gravity and against minimal resistance

5: 100% of normal strength; normal full movement against gravity and against full resistance

ASSESSMENT	NORMAL FINDINGS	DEVIATIONS FROM NORMAL
■ Ask the client to move selected body parts. Measure the amount of movement using a goniometer, as indicated.		

Lifespan Considerations

Children

- Lordosis (swayback) can be seen in young children.
- Pronation of the feet is common in children between 12 and 30 months of age.
- Genu varum (bowleg) is normal in children for 1 year after beginning to walk.
- Check infants for developmental dysplasia of the hip (congenital dislocation) by examining for asymmetric gluteal folds, asymmetric abduction of the legs, or apparent shortening of the femur.

Older Adults

- Muscle mass decreases progressively with age, but there are wide variations among different individuals.
- The decrease in speed, strength, resistance to fatigue, reaction time, and coordination in the older person is due to a decrease in nerve conduction and muscle tone.
- The bones become more fragile, and osteoporosis leads to a loss of total bone mass. As a result, elderly people are predisposed to fractures and compressed vertebrae.
- In most elderly people, osteoarthritic changes in the joints can be observed.

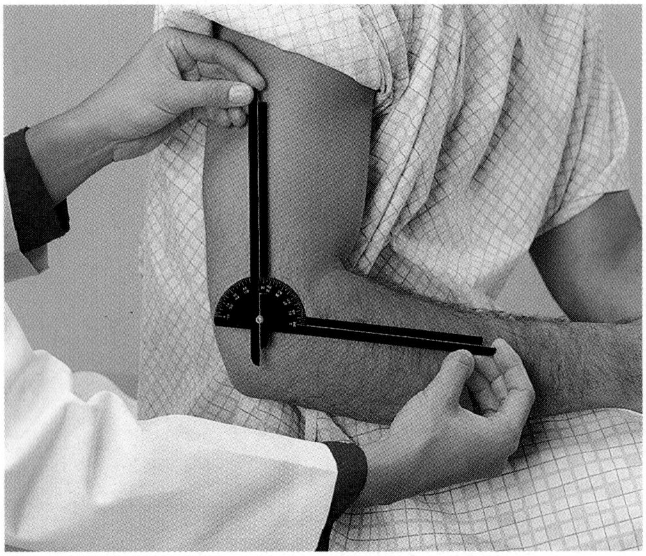

Figure 27.75 A goniometer is used to measure joint range of motion

Neurological System

Three major considerations determine the extent of a neurological exam: (1) the client's chief complaints, (2) the client's physical condition (i.e., level of consciousness and ability to ambulate), because many parts of the examination require movement and coordination of the extremities, and (3) the client's willingness to participate and co-operate. A thorough neurological examination may take one to three hours. If the results of these tests raise questions, more extensive evaluations are made.

Examination of the neurological system includes assessment of (1) mental status, including level of consciousness, (2) the cranial nerves, (3) reflexes, (4) motor function, and (5) sensory function. Parts of the neurological assessment are performed throughout the health examination. For example, the nurse performs a large part of the mental status assessment during the taking of the history and when observing the client's general appearance. Also, the nurse assesses the function of many cranial nerves. Cranial nerves II, III, IV, V, and VI (ophthalmic branch), are assessed with the eyes and vision, and cranial nerve VIII (cochlear branch) is assessed with the ears and hearing.

Nursing History Focus

The client is assessed for presence of pain in the head, back, or extremities; onset and aggravating and alleviating factors; disorientation to time, place, or person; speech disorder; and any history of loss of consciousness, fainting, convulsions, trauma, tingling or numbness, tremors or tics, limping, paralysis, uncontrolled muscle movements, loss of memory, mood swings, or problems with smell, vision, taste, touch, or hearing.

Mental Status

Assessment of mental status reveals the client's general cerebral function. These functions include intellectual (cognitive) as well as emotional (affective) functions.

If problems with use of language, memory, concentration, or thought processes are noted during the nursing history, a more extensive examination is required during neurological assessment. Major areas of mental status assessment include language, orientation, memory, attention span, and calculation.

Language

Any defects in or loss of the power to express oneself by speech, writing, or sign language, or to comprehend spoken or written language due to disease or injury of the cerebral cortex, is called **aphasia.** Aphasias can be categorized as sensory or receptive aphasia and motor or expressive aphasia.

Sensory or *receptive aphasia* is the loss of the ability to comprehend written or spoken words. Two types of sensory aphasia are auditory (or acoustic) aphasia and visual aphasia. Clients with *auditory aphasia* have lost the ability to understand the symbolic content associated with sounds. Clients with *visual aphasia* have lost the ability to understand printed or written figures.

Motor or *expressive aphasia* involves loss of the power to express oneself by writing, making signs, or speaking. Clients may find that even though they can recall words, they have lost the ability to combine speech sounds into words.

If there is evidence of language deficit related to aphasia, assessment is as follows:

1. Point to common objects, and ask the client to name them.
2. Ask the client to read some words and to match the printed words with pictures.
3. Ask the client to respond to simple verbal and written commands, such as "point to your toes" or "raise your left arm."

Orientation

The nurse determines the client's orientation to *time, place,* and *person* by tactful questioning. Orientation is easily assessed by asking the client the city and province of residence, year, time of day, date, day of the week, duration of illness, and names of family members. More direct questioning may be necessary for some people, for example, "Where are you now?" or "What day is it today?"

Memory

The nurse listens for lapses in memory, first asking the client about difficulty with memory. If problems are apparent, three categories of memory are tested: immediate recall, recent memory, and remote memory.

To assess *immediate recall:*

- Ask the client to repeat a series of three digits (e.g., 7-4-3) spoken slowly.
- Gradually increase the number of digits (e.g., 7-4-3-5, 7-4-3-5-6, and 7-4-3-5-6-7-2) until the client fails to repeat the series correctly.
- Start again with a series of three digits, but, this time, ask the client to repeat them backward. The average person can repeat a series of five to eight digits in sequence and four to six digits in reverse order.

To assess *recent memory:*

- Ask the client to recall the recent events of the day, such as how the client got to the clinic. This information must be validated, however.
- Ask the client to recall information given early in the interview, such as the name of a doctor.
- Provide the client with three facts to recall (e.g., a colour, an object, an address) or a three-digit number, and ask the client to repeat all three. Later in the interview, ask the client to recall all three items.

To assess *remote memory*, the nurse asks the client to describe a previous illness or surgery (e.g., one experienced five years ago) or a birthday or anniversary.

Attention Span and Calculation

The nurse tests the client's ability to concentrate, or attention span, by asking the client to recite the alphabet or to count backward from 100. To test the client's ability to calculate, the nurse asks the client to subtract 7 or 3 progressively from 100; that is, 100, 93, 86, 79, or 100, 97, 94, 91. This standard test is often referred to as the *serial sevens* or *serial threes test.* Normally, an adult can complete the serial sevens test in about 90 seconds with three or fewer errors. Because educational level and language or cultural differences affect calculating ability, this test may be inappropriate for some people.

Changes in the mental function of some older people are shown in the accompanying box.

Level of Consciousness

Level of consciousness (LOC) can lie anywhere along a continuum from a state of alertness to coma. A fully alert client responds to questions spontaneously; a comatose client may not respond to verbal stimuli. The Glasgow Coma Scale was originally developed to predict recovery from a head injury; however, it is used by many professionals to assess LOC. It tests three major areas: eye response, motor response, and verbal response. An assessment totaling 15 points indicates the client is alert and completely oriented. A comatose client scores 7 or less. See Table 27.12.

Older Adults: Changes in Mental Function

- Changes in mental status are the result of physical or psychological disorders (e.g., fever, fluid and electrolyte imbalances).
- Short-term memory is often less efficient.
- Because old age is often associated with loss of support persons, depression is a common disorder. It may be manifested by mood changes, weight loss, anorexia, constipation, and early morning awakening.
- The stress of being in unfamiliar situations can cause confusion in the elderly person.

Cranial Nerves

For the specific functions of and assessment methods for each cranial nerve, see Table 27.13. The nurse needs to be aware of nerve functions to detect abnormalities.

Reflexes

A **reflex** is an automatic response of the body to a stimulus. It is not voluntarily learned or conscious. The deep tendon reflex (DTR) is activated when a tendon is stimulated (tapped) and its associated muscle contracts. The quality of

TABLE 27.12 Levels of Consciousness: Glasgow Coma Scale

Faculty Measured	Response	Score
Eye opening	Spontaneous	4
	To verbal command	3
	To pain	2
	No response	1
Motor response	To verbal command	6
	To localized pain	5
	Flexes and withdraws	4
	Flexes abnormally	3
	Extends abnormally	2
	No response	1
Verbal response	Oriented, converses	5
	Disoriented, converses	4
	Uses inappropriate words	3
	Makes incomprehensible sounds	2
	No response	1

TABLE 27.13 Cranial Nerve Functions and Assessment Methods

Cranial Nerve	Name	Type	Function	Assessment Method
I	Olfactory	Sensory	Smell	Ask client to close eyes and identify different mild aromas, such as coffee, vanilla, peanut butter, orange, lemon, lime, chocolate.
II	Optic	Sensory	Vision and visual fields	Ask client to read Snellen chart; check visual fields by confrontation; and conduct an ophthalmoscopic examination.
III	Oculomotor	Motor	Extraocular eye movement (EOM); movement of sphincter of pupil; movement of ciliary muscles of lens; opening of upper eyelid	Assess six ocular movements and pupil reaction.
IV	Trochlear	Motor	EOM; specifically moves eyeball downward and laterally	Assess six ocular movements.
V	Trigeminal			
	Ophthalmic branch	Sensory	Sensation of cornea, skin of face, and nasal mucosa	While client looks upward, lightly touch lateral sclera of eye to elicit blink reflex. To test light sensation, have client close eyes, wipe a wisp of cotton over client's forehead and paranasal sinuses. To test deep sensation, use alternating blunt and sharp ends of a safety pin over same areas.
	Maxillary branch	Sensory	Sensation of skin of face and anterior oral cavity (tongue and teeth)	Assess skin sensation as for ophthalmic branch above.
	Mandibular branch	Motor and sensory	Muscles of mastication; sensation of skin of face	Ask client to clench teeth.
VI	Abducens	Motor	EOM; moves eyeball laterally	Assess directions of gaze.
VII	Facial	Motor and sensory	Facial expression; taste (anterior two-thirds of tongue); closing of eyelid	Ask client to smile, raise the eyebrows, frown, puff out cheeks, close eyes tightly. Ask client to identify various tastes placed on tip and sides of tongue: sugar (sweet), salt, lemon juice (sour), and quinine (bitter); identify areas of taste.
VIII	Auditory			
	Vestibular branch	Sensory	Equilibrium	Assessment methods are discussed with cerebellar functions (in next section).
	Cochlear branch	Sensory	Hearing	Assess client's ability to hear spoken word and vibrations of tuning fork.
IX	Glosso-pharyngeal	Motor and sensory	Swallowing ability; tongue movement; taste (posterior tongue)	Apply tastes on posterior tongue for identification. Ask client to move tongue from side to side and up and down.
X	Vagus	Motor and sensory	Sensation of pharynx and larynx; swallowing; vocal cord movement	Assessed with cranial nerve IX; assess client's speech for hoarseness.
XI	Accessory	Motor	Head movement; shrugging of shoulders	Ask client to shrug shoulders against resistance from your hands and turn head to side against resistance from your hand (repeat for other side).
XII	Hypoglossal	Motor	Protrusion of tongue; moves tongue up and down and side to side	Ask client to protrude tongue at midline, then move it side to side.

Scale for Grading Reflex Responses

0	No reflex response
+1	Minimal activity (hypoactive)
+2	Normal response
+3	More active than normal
+4	Maximal activity (hyperactive)

a reflex response varies among individuals and by age. As a person ages, reflex responses may become less intense.

Reflexes are tested using a percussion hammer. The response is described on a scale of 0 to +4. See the accompanying box for a scale describing reflex responses. Experience is necessary to determine appropriate scoring for an individual. When assessing reflexes, it is important for the nurse to compare one side of the body with the other to evaluate the symmetry of response.

Several reflexes are normally tested during the physical examination: (1) the biceps reflex, (2) the triceps reflex, (3) the brachioradialis reflex, (4) the patellar reflex, (5) the Achilles reflex, and (6) the plantar (Babinski) reflex.

Biceps Reflex

This reflex tests the spinal cord level C-5, C-6.

1. Partially flex the client's arm at the elbow and rest the forearm over the thighs, placing the palm of the hand up.
2. Place the thumb of your nondominant hand horizontally over the biceps tendon.
3. With your other hand, hold the percussion hammer between thumb and index finger.
4. Deliver a blow (slight downward thrust) with the percussion hammer to your thumb.
5. Observe the normal slight flexion of the elbow, and feel the bicep's contraction through your thumb (Figure 27.76, *A*).

Triceps Reflex

This reflex tests the spinal cord level C-7, C-8.

1. Flex the client's arm at the elbow, and support it in the palm of your nondominant hand.
2. Palpate the triceps tendon about 2 to 5 cm above the elbow.
3. Deliver a blow with the percussion hammer directly to the tendon (Figure 27.76, *B*).
4. Observe the normal slight extension of the elbow.

Brachioradialis Reflex

This reflex tests the spinal cord level C-3, C-6.

1. Rest the client's arm in a relaxed position on your forearm or on the client's own leg.
2. Deliver a blow with the percussion hammer directly on the radius 2 to 5 cm above the wrist or the styloid process, the bony prominence on the thumb side of the wrist (Figure 27.76, *C*).
3. Observe the normal flexion and supination of the forearm. The fingers of the hand may also extend slightly.

Patellar Reflex

This reflex tests the spinal cord level L-2, L-3, L-4.

1. Ask the client to sit on the edge of the examining table so that the legs hang freely.
2. Locate the patellar tendon directly below the patella (kneecap).
3. Deliver a blow with the percussion hammer directly to the tendon (Figure 27.76, *D*).
4. Observe the normal extension or kicking out of the leg as the quadriceps muscle contracts.
5. If no response occurs, and you suspect the client is not relaxed, ask the client to interlock the fingers and pull. This action often enhances relaxation so that a more accurate response is obtained.

Achilles Reflex

This reflex tests the spinal cord level S-1, S-2.

1. With the client in the same position as for the patellar reflex, slightly dorsiflex the client's ankle by supporting the foot lightly in your hand.
2. Deliver a blow with the percussion hammer directly to the Achilles tendon just above the heel (Figure 27.76, *E*).
3. Observe and feel the normal plantar flexion (downward jerk) of the foot.

Plantar (Babinski) Reflex

This plantar, or Babinski, reflex is superficial. It may be absent in adults without pathology or overridden by voluntary control.

1. Use a moderately sharp object, such as the handle of the percussion hammer, a key, or the dull end of a pin or applicator stick.
2. Stroke the lateral border of the sole of the client's foot, starting at the heel, continuing to the ball of the foot, and then proceeding across the ball of the foot toward the big toe (Figure 27.76, *F*).
3. Observe the response. Normally, all five toes bend downward; this reaction is negative Babinski. In a positive (abnormal) Babinski response, the toes spread outward and the big toe moves upward. A positive Babinski is normal until a child ambulates.

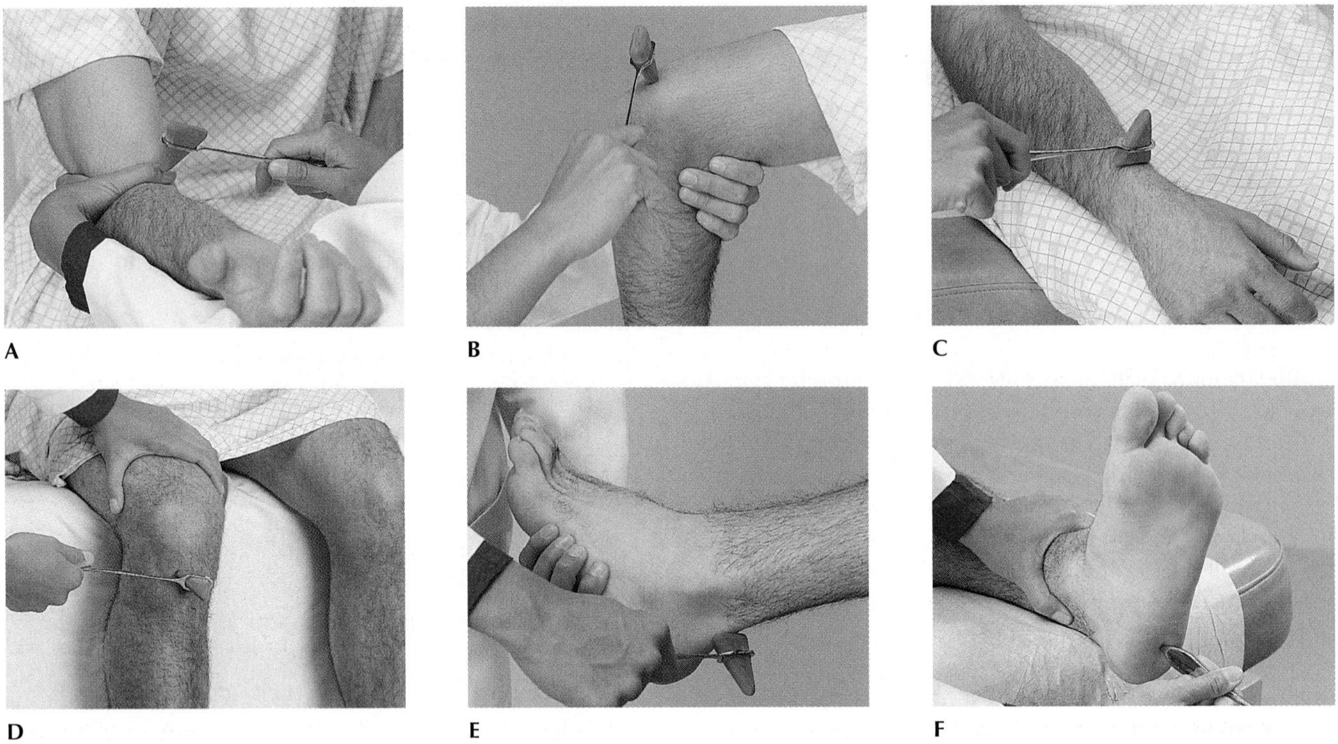

Figure 27.76 Testing reflexes: *A,* the biceps reflex; *B,* the triceps reflex; *C,* the brachioradialis reflex; *D,* the patellar reflex; *E,* the Achilles reflex; *F,* the plantar (Babinski) reflex

Motor Function

Neurological assessment of the motor system evaluates proprioception and cerebellar function. Structures involved in proprioception are the proprioceptors, the posterior columns of the spinal cord, the cerebellum, and the vestibular apparatus (which is innervated by cranial nerve VIII) in the labyrinth of the internal ear.

Proprioceptors are sensory nerve terminals, occurring chiefly in the muscles, tendons, joints, and the internal ear, that give information about movements and the position of the body. Stimuli from the proprioceptors travel through the posterior columns of the spinal cord. Deficits of function of the posterior columns of the spinal cord result in impairment of muscle and position sense. Clients with such an impairment often must watch their own arm and leg movements to ascertain the position of the limbs.

The cerebellum (1) helps to control posture; (2) acts with the cerebral cortex to make body movements smooth and coordinated; and (3) controls skeletal muscles to maintain equilibrium. Procedure 27.17 describes how to assess motor function.

Sensory Function

Sensory functions include touch, pain, temperature, position, and tactile discrimination. The first three are routinely tested. The spinothalamic tract conducts sensations of superficial pain and temperature to the sensory cortex. The posterior column conducts the sensation of position. Generally, the face, arms, legs, hands, and feet are tested for touch and pain, although all parts of the body can be tested. If the client complains of numbness, peculiar sensations, or paralysis, the practitioner should check sensation more carefully over flexor and extensor surfaces of limbs, mapping out clearly any abnormality of touch or pain by examining responses in the area about every 2.5 cm. This is a lengthy procedure. Abnormal responses to touch stimuli include loss of sensation **(anesthesia)**; more than normal sensation **(hyperesthesia)**; less than normal sensation **(hypoesthesia)**; or an abnormal sensation such as numbness and prickling as "pins and needles" **(paresthesia).**

A more detailed neurological examination includes position sense, temperature sense, and tactile discrimination.

Three types of tactile discrimination are generally tested: **one-** and **two-point discrimination,** the ability to sense whether one or two areas of the skin are being stimulated by pressure; **stereognosis,** the act of recognizing objects by touching and manipulating them; and **extinction,** the failure to perceive touch on one side of the body when two symmetric areas of the body are touched simultaneously. To assess sensory function, the nurse needs the following equipment:

- Wisps of cotton to assess light touch sensation
- Tongue blade to assess pain sensation
- Test tubes of hot and cold water for skin temperature assessment (optional)

Procedure 27.18 describes how to assess sensory function.

PROCEDURE 27.17 Assessing Motor Function

ASSESSMENT	NORMAL FINDINGS	DEVIATIONS FROM NORMAL
Gross Motor and Balance Tests There are several gross motor function and balance tests. Generally, the Romberg test and one other are used.		
Walking Gait **Ask the client to walk across the room and back** with eyesight focused ahead, and assess the client's gait.	Has upright posture and steady gait with opposing arm swing; walks unaided, maintaining balance	Has poor posture and unsteady, irregular, staggering gait with wide stance; bends legs only from hips; has rigid or no arm movements
Romberg Test **Ask the client to stand with feet together and arms resting at the sides,** first with eyes open, then closed. Stand close during this test to prevent the client from falling.	**Negative Romberg's:** May sway slightly but is able to maintain upright posture and foot stance	**Romberg's sign:** Cannot maintain foot stance; moves the feet apart to maintain stance
Standing on One Foot with Eyes Closed **Ask the client to close the eyes and stand on one foot and then the other.** Stand close to the client during this test.	Maintains stance for at least five seconds	Cannot maintain stance for five seconds
Heel-Toe Walking **Ask the client to walk a straight line, placing the heel of one foot directly in front of the toes of the other foot.**	Maintains heel-toe walking along a straight line	Assumes a wider foot gait to stay upright
Toe or Heel Walking **Ask the client to walk several steps on the toes and then on the heels.**	Able to walk several steps on toes or heels	Cannot maintain balance on toes or heels
Fine Motor Tests for the Upper Extremities		
Finger-to-Nose Test **Ask the client to abduct and extend the arms at shoulder height and rapidly touch the nose alternately with one index finger and then the other.** The client repeats the test with the eyes closed if the test is performed easily.	Repeatedly and rhythmically touches the nose	Misses the nose or cannot do it rapidly
Alternating Supination and Pronation of Hands on Knees **Ask the client to pat both knees with the palms of both hands and then with the backs of the hands alternately at an ever-increasing rate.**	Can alternately supinate and pronate hands at rapid pace	Performs with slow, clumsy movements and irregular timing; has difficulty alternating from supination to pronation
Finger to Nose and to the Nurse's Finger **Ask the client to touch the nose and then your index finger,** held at a distance of about 45 cm, **at a rapid and increasing rate.**	Performs with coordination and rapidity	Misses the finger and moves slowly

→

PROCEDURE 27.17 Assessing Motor Function *continued*

ASSESSMENT	NORMAL FINDINGS	DEVIATIONS FROM NORMAL
Fine Motor Tests for the Upper Extremities continued		
Fingers to Fingers **Ask the client to spread the arms broadly at shoulder height and then bring the fingers together at the midline, first with the eyes open and then closed, first slowly and then rapidly.**	Performs with coordination and rapidity	Moves slowly and is unable to touch fingers consistently
Fingers to Thumb (Same Hand) **Ask the client to touch each finger of one hand to the thumb of the same hand as rapidly as possible.**	Rapidly touches each finger to thumb with each hand	Cannot coordinate this fine discrete movement with one or both hands
Fine Motor Test for the Lower Extremities Ask the client to lie supine to perform this test.		
Heel Down Opposite Shin **Ask the client to place the heel of one foot just below the opposite knee and run the heel down the shin to the foot.** Repeat with the other foot. The client may also use a sitting position for this test.	Demonstrates bilateral equal coordination	Has tremors or is awkward; heel moves off shin

PROCEDURE 27.18 Assessing Sensory Function

ASSESSMENT	NORMAL FINDINGS	DEVIATIONS FROM NORMAL
Light Touch Sensation **Compare the light touch sensation of symmetric areas of the body.** *Sensitivity to touch varies among different skin areas.* ■ Ask the client to close the eyes and to respond by saying "yes" or "now" whenever the client feels the cotton wisp touching the skin. ■ With a wisp of cotton, lightly touch one specific spot and then the same spot on the other side of the body (Figure 27.77).	Light tickling or touch sensation	Anesthesia, hyperesthesia, hypoesthesia, and paresthesia

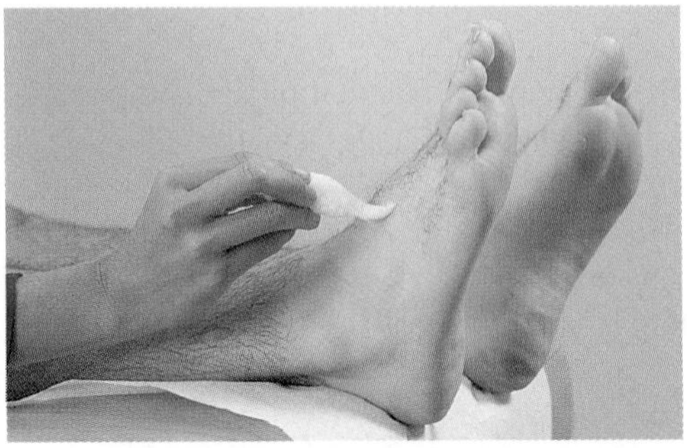

Figure 27.77 Assessing light touch sensation

PROCEDURE 27.18 Assessing Sensory Function *continued*

ASSESSMENT	NORMAL FINDINGS	DEVIATIONS FROM NORMAL
Light Touch Sensation continued		
■ Test areas on the forehead, cheek, hand, lower arm, abdomen, foot, and lower leg. Check the distal area of the limb first (i.e., the hand before the arm, and the foot before the leg), because the sensory nerve may be assumed to be intact if sensation is felt at its most peripheral part.		
■ Ask the client to point to the spot where the touch was felt. *This demonstrates whether the client is able to determine tactile location (point localization),* that is, able to accurately perceive where the client was touched.		
■ If areas of sensory dysfunction are found, determine the boundaries of sensation by testing responses about every 2.5 cm in the area. Make a sketch of the sensory loss area for recording purposes.		
Pain Sensation		
Assess pain sensation.		
■ Ask the client to close the eyes and to say "sharp," "dull," or "don't know" when the sharp or dull end of the tongue blade is felt.	Able to discriminate "sharp" and "dull" sensations	Areas of reduced, heightened, or absent sensation (map them out for recording purposes)
■ Alternately use the sharp and dull end of the tongue blade to lightly prick designated anatomic areas at random, such as the hand, foot, lower leg, abdomen (Figure 27.78). The face is not tested in this manner. *Alternating the sharp and dull ends of the instrument more accurately evaluates the client's response.*		
■ Allow at least two seconds between each test to prevent summation effects of stimuli (i.e., several successive stimuli perceived as one stimulus).		

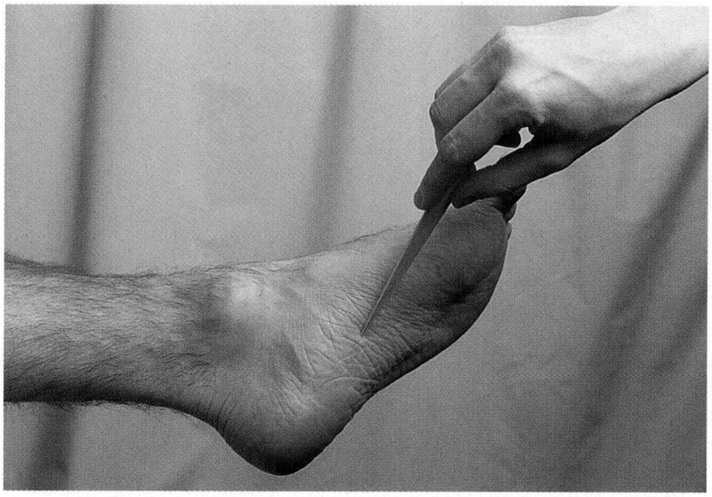

Figure 27.78 Assessing pain sensation using a broken tongue blade

PROCEDURE 27.18 Assessing Sensory Function *continued*

ASSESSMENT	NORMAL FINDINGS	DEVIATIONS FROM NORMAL
Temperature Sensation Temperature sensation is not routinely tested if pain sensation is found to be within normal limits. If pain sensation is not normal or is absent, testing sensitivity to temperature may prove more reliable. ■ Touch skin areas with test tubes filled with hot or cold water. ■ Have client respond by saying "hot," "cold," or "don't know."	Able to discriminate between "hot" and "cold" sensations	Areas of dulled or lost sensation (when sensations of pain are dulled, temperature sense is usually also impaired because distribution of these nerves over the body is similar)
Position or Kinesthetic Sensation Commonly, the middle fingers and the large toes are tested for the *kinesthetic sensation* (sense of position). ■ To test the fingers, support the client's arm with one hand and hold the client's palm in the other; to test the toes, place the client's heels on the examining table. ■ Ask the client to close the eyes. ■ Grasp a middle finger or a big toe firmly between your thumb and index finger, and exert the same pressure on both sides of the finger or toe while moving it. ■ Move the finger or toe until it is up, down, or straight out, and ask the client to identify the position. ■ Use a series of brisk up-and-down movements before bringing the finger or toe suddenly to rest in one of the three positions.	Can readily determine the position of fingers and toes	Unable to determine the position of one or more fingers or toes
Tactile Discrimination For all tests, the client's eyes need to be closed.		
One- and Two-Point Discrimination Alternately stimulate the skin with two pins simultaneously and then with one pin. Ask whether the client feels one or two pinpricks.	Perception varies widely in adults over different parts of the body. Normally, a person can distinguish a one-point stimulus from a two-point stimulus within the following minimum distances: Fingertips, 2.8 mm Palms of hands, 8–12 mm Chest, forearm, 40 mm Back, 50–70 mm Upper arm, thigh, 75 mm Toes, 3–8 mm	Unable to sense whether one or two areas of the skin are being stimulated by pressure

PROCEDURE 27.18 Assessing Sensory Function *continued*

ASSESSMENT	NORMAL FINDINGS	DEVIATIONS FROM NORMAL
Tactile Discrimination continued		
Stereognosis Place familiar objects, such as a key, paper clip, or coin, in the client's hand, and ask the client to identify them.	Able to recognize specific objects (stereognosis)	Unable to recognize specific objects (astereognosis)
If the client has a motor impairment of the hand and is unable to manipulate an object, write a number or letter on the client's palm using a blunt instrument, and ask the client to identify it.	Able to identify numbers or letters written on palm	Unable to identify numbers or letters written on palm (graphesthesia)
Extinction Phenomenon Simultaneously stimulate two symmetric areas of the body, such as the thighs, the cheeks, or the hands.	Both points of stimulus are felt	Failure to perceive touch on one side of the body when two symmetric areas of the body are touched simultaneously

Lifespan Considerations

Children

- For children under age five years, the Denver Developmental Screening Test II provides a comprehensive neurological evaluation—particularly for motor function.
- Reflexes commonly tested in newborns include the **rooting reflex**—when the baby's cheek is touched, the head turns toward that side; **palmar grasp**—baby's fingers curl around an object; **tonic neck reflex**—when the baby is supine and the head is turned to one side, the arm and leg on that side extend while those on the opposite side flex (fencing position). Most of these disappear by six months of age. **Babinski's reflex,** normally present in the newborn, disappears by the age of 12 to 24 months.

Older Adults

- Because older clients tire more easily than younger clients, a total neurological assessment is often done at a different time from the other parts of the physical assessment.
- Although there is a progressive decrease in the number of functioning neurons in the central nervous system and in the sense organs, the older client usually functions well because of the abundant reserves in the number of brain cells.
- Impulse transmission and reaction to stimuli are slower.
- Many older clients have some impairment of hearing, vision, smell, temperature and pain sensation, memory, and mental endurance.
- Coordination changes, including a reduced speed of fine finger movements. Standing balance remains intact, and Romberg's test remains negative.
- Reflex responses may slightly increase or decrease. Many show loss of Achilles reflex, and the plantar reflex may be difficult to elicit.
- When testing sensory function, give the older client time to respond. Older clients normally have decreased perception of deep pain and of temperature stimuli. Many also reveal a decrease or absence of position sense in the large toes.

Female Genitals and Inguinal Lymph Nodes

The examination of the genitals and reproductive tract of women includes assessment of the inguinal lymph nodes and inspection and palpation of the external genitals.

Completeness of the assessment of the genitals and reproductive tract depends on the needs and problems of the individual client. In most practice settings, generalist nurses perform only inspection of the external genitals and palpation of the inguinal lymph nodes.

Assessment of adolescent girls is limited to an inspection of the external genitals. The following box shows the five stages of pubic hair development during puberty. For all sexually active adolescents and all adult females, an annual Papanicolaou test (Pap test) is advised for detecting

Five Stages of Pubic Hair Development in Females

Stage 1 Preadolescence. No pubic hair except for fine body hair.

Stage 2 Usually occurs at ages 11 and 12 years. Sparse, long, slightly pigmented curly hair develops along the labia.

Stage 3 Usually occurs at ages 12 and 13 years. Hair becomes darker in colour and curlier and develops over the pubic symphysis.

Stage 4 Usually occurs between ages 13 and 14 years. Hair assumes the texture and curl of the adult but is not as thick and does not appear on the thighs.

Stage 5 Sexual maturity. Hair assumes adult appearance and appears on the inner aspect of the upper thighs.

cancer of the cervix and uterus. If there is an increased or abnormal vaginal discharge, specimens should be taken to check for sexually transmitted disease.

Examination of the genitals usually creates uncertainty and apprehension in females, and the lithotomy position required can cause embarrassment. The nurse must explain each part of the examination in advance and perform the examination in an objective and efficient manner. Appropriate draping is essential to prevent undue exposure of the client, and good lighting is required for the nurse to ensure accuracy of inspection. The nurse wears disposable gloves for this genital examination to prevent the transfer of microorganisms from the client to the nurse and from the nurse to other clients.

Procedure 27.19 describes how to assess the female genitals and inguinal lymph nodes.

PROCEDURE 27.19 Assessing the Female Genitals and Inguinal Lymph Nodes

NURSING HISTORY FOCUS

Age of onset of menstruation, last menstrual period (LMP), regularity of cycle, duration, amount of daily flow, and whether menstruation is painful; incidence of pain during intercourse; vaginal discharge; number of pregnancies, number of live births, labour or delivery complications; urgency and frequency of urination at night; blood in urine, painful urination, incontinence; history of sexually transmitted disease, past and present

ASSESSMENT	NORMAL FINDINGS	DEVIATIONS FROM NORMAL
Inspect the distribution, amount, and characteristics of pubic hair.	There are wide variations; generally kinky in the menstruating adult, thinner and straighter after menopause Distributed in the shape of an inverse triangle	Scant pubic hair (may indicate hormonal problem) Hair growth should not extend over the abdomen
Inspect the skin of the pubic area for parasites (e.g., lice), **inflammation, swelling, and lesions** (e.g., fissures, excoriations, scars, varicosities, leukoplakia). To assess pubic skin adequately, separate the labia majora and labia minora.	Pubic skin intact, no lesions Skin of vulva area slightly darker than rest of the body Labia round, full, and relatively symmetric in adult females	Lice, lesions, scars, fissures, swelling, erythema, or leukoplakia
Inspect the clitoris, urethral orifice, and vaginal orifice when separating the labia minora.	Clitoris does not exceed 1 cm in width and 2 cm in length Urethral orifice appears as a small slit and is the same colour as surrounding tissues No inflammation, swelling, or discharge	Presence of lesions (the clitoris is a common site for syphilitic chancres in younger females and cancerous lesions in older females) Presence of inflammation, swelling, or discharge

PROCEDURE 27.19 Assessing the Female Genitals and Inguinal Lymph Nodes *continued*

ASSESSMENT	NORMAL FINDINGS	DEVIATIONS FROM NORMAL
Palpate the inguinal lymph nodes (Figure 27.79). Use the pads of the fingers in a rotary motion, noting any enlargement or tenderness.	No enlargement or tenderness	Enlargement and tenderness

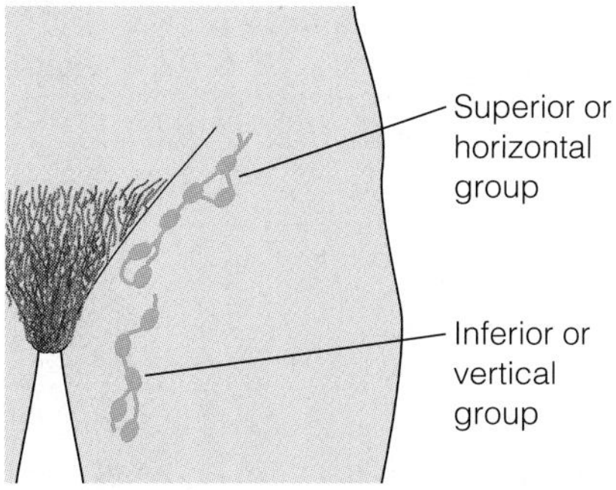

Figure 27.79 Lymph nodes of the groin area

Lifespan Considerations

Children

- Infants can be held in a supine position on the mother's lap with the knees supported in a flexed position and separated.
- The labia and clitoris in newborns may be edematous and appear enlarged in response to maternal estrogen.
- Tell the child what you are going to do and ensure that you also have the parent or guardian's approval to perform the examination.

Older Adults

- Loss of pubic hair and a flattening of the labia occur.
- The vulva atrophies as a result of a reduction in vascularity, elasticity, adipose tissue, and estrogen levels. Because the vulva is more fragile, it is more easily irritated.
- The vaginal environment becomes drier and more alkaline, resulting in an alteration of the type of flora present and a predisposition to vaginitis. Dyspareunia (difficult or painful coitus) is also a common occurrence.
- The cervix and uterus decrease in size.
- The fallopian tubes and ovaries atrophy.
- Ovulation and estrogen production cease.
- Vaginal bleeding unrelated to estrogen therapy is abnormal in older women.
- Prolapse of the uterus occurs in older females, especially those who have had multiple pregnancies.
- Older females may be arthritic and find the lithotomy position uncomfortable. A semilithotomy position may be necessary.

Examination of the Internal Genitals

In many agencies, only midwives, labour and delivery nurses, and nurse practitioners examine the internal genitals. However, generalist nurses often assist with this examination and need to be familiar with the procedure. Examination of the internal genitals involves (1) palpating Skene's and Bartholin's glands; (2) assessing the pelvic musculature; (3) inserting a vaginal speculum to inspect the cervix and vagina; and (4) obtaining a Papanicolaou smear.

Palpation of Skene's (paraurethral) glands (Figure 27.80) is performed by inserting a gloved index finger palm upward into the vagina about 2.5 cm and milking the glands by pressing gently upward and outward. Discharge and tenderness are abnormal. If discharge is present, specimens are taken and gloves are changed before proceeding with further examination.

Bartholin's glands are located on the posterior aspect of the vaginal orifice. These are palpated as shown in Figure 27.81. Normally Bartholin's glands are not tender or palpable.

To assess the *pelvic musculature*, the examiner (1) places two gloved fingers (index and middle finger) into the vagina; (2) asks the client to constrict her vaginal orifice; (3) asks the client to bear down while the fingers spread

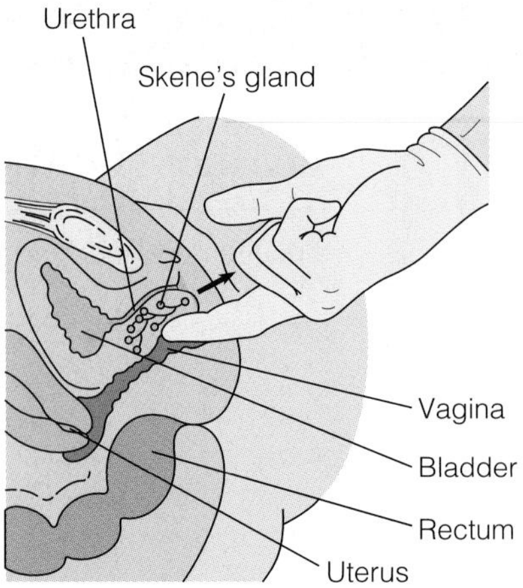

Figure 27.80 Palpating Skene's glands

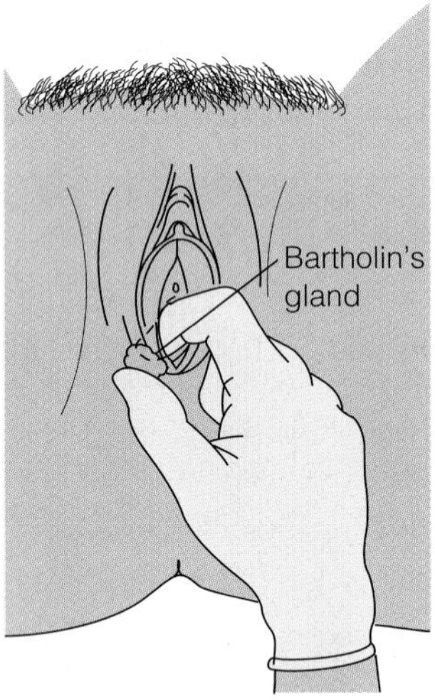

Figure 27.81 Palpating Bartholin's gland

the vaginal wall laterally; and (4) observes the vaginal wall for bulges. Normally, a **nulliparous** woman (one who has never had a child) will have a high degree of muscle tone, whereas a **multiparous** woman (one who has had two or more pregnancies resulting in viable offspring) will have less tone. The walls should be intact with no bulges. Deviations from normal include a **cystocele** (bulging of the anterior wall and the bladder) and a **rectocele** (bulging of the posterior wall as a result of a prolapse of the posterior wall and the rectum).

The *speculum examination* of the vagina involves the insertion of a plastic or metal speculum that consists of two blades and an adjustable thumb screw (Figure 27.82). Various sizes are available (small, medium, and large); the appropriate size needs to be selected for each client. A virgin or a sexually inactive older woman will probably require a small speculum; otherwise, the size of the speculum depends on the individual's sexual and obstetric history. The speculum may be lubricated with water-soluble lubricant if specimens are *not* being collected. Most examiners lubricate the speculum with warm water. After visualizing the cervix, the examiner takes Papanicolaou smear specimens from one or more of the sites shown in Figure 27.83. The vagina is observed as the speculum is withdrawn. Following the speculum examination, the examiner may insert gloved fingers into the vagina to palpate the uterus and ovaries for any abnormalities.

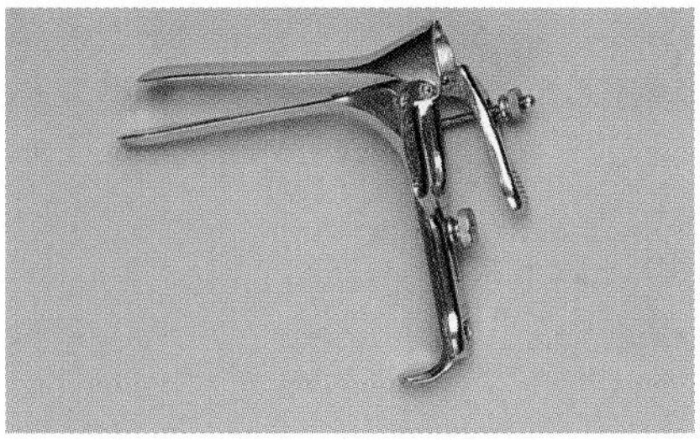

Figure 27.82 A vaginal speculum

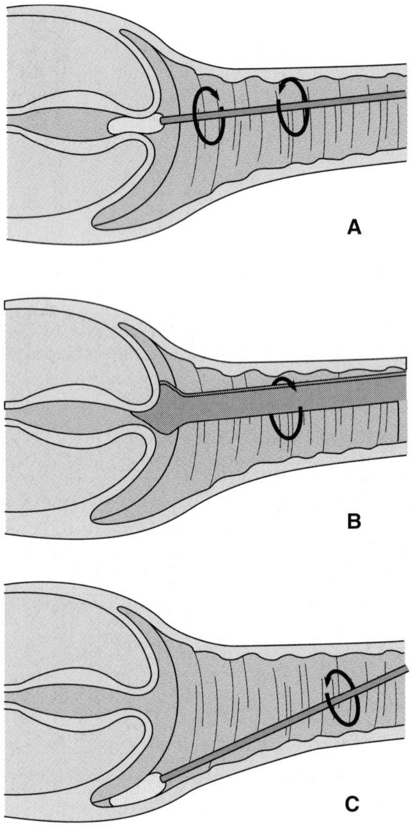

Figure 27.83 Methods of obtaining Pap smears:
A, Endocervical. A cotton swab is inserted into the cervical os and rotated clockwise and counterclockwise in the os.
B, Cervical scrape. An Ayre spatula with the longer end inserted into the cervical os is rotated to scrape cells from the outer surface. *C,* Vaginal smear or pool. A cotton-tipped applicator or elongated spatula is inserted along the vaginal floor.

TABLE 27.14 Five Stages of Development of Pubic Hair, Penis, and Testes/Scrotum (12 to 16 Years)

Stage	Pubic Hair	Penis	Testes/Scrotum
1 (preadolescent)	None, except for body hair like that on the abdomen	Size is relative to body size, as in childhood	Size is relative to body size, as in childhood
2	Scant, long, slightly pigmented at base of penis	Slight enlargement occurs	Becomes reddened in colour and enlarged
3	Darker, begins to curl and becomes more coarse; extends over pubic symphysis	Elongation occurs	Continuing enlargement
4	Continues to darken and thicken; extends on the sides, above and below	Increase in both breadth and length; glans develops	Continuing enlargement; colour darkens
5	Adult distribution that extends to inner thighs, umbilicus, and anus	Adult appearance	Adult appearance

The nurse's responsibilities when assisting with an examination of the internal female genitals include the following:

1. *Assembling equipment.* These include drapes, gloves, vaginal speculum of correct size, warm water or lubricant, and supplies for cytology studies (cotton applicators, normal saline solution, Ayre spatula for a cervical scrape, slides, and fixative spray or solution for the specimen).
2. *Preparing the client.* Advise the client not to douche prior to the procedure. Explain the procedure. It should take only five minutes and is normally not painful. Assist the client to a lithotomy position as needed, and drape her appropriately.
3. *Supporting the client during the procedure.* This involves explaining the procedure as needed, and encouraging the client to take deep breaths that will help the pelvic muscles relax.

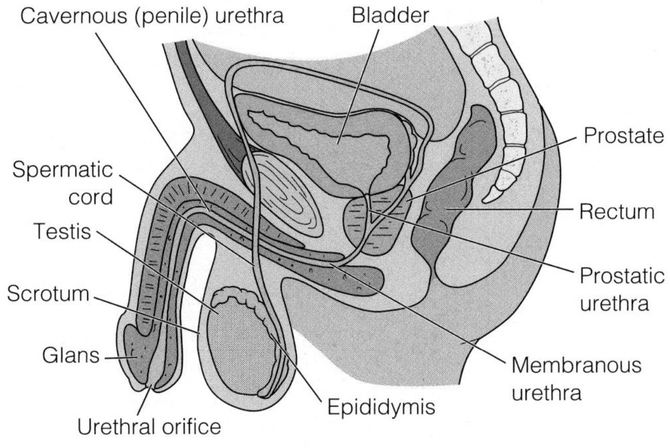

Figure 27.84 The male urogenital tract

4. *Monitoring and assisting the client after the procedure.* Assist the client from the lithotomy position and with perineal care as needed. Observe any discharge from the vagina. Normally, characteristics of cervical mucus vary throughout the menstrual cycle from clear to white and from thin to thick, even stringy. Three common types of vaginal infections produce characteristic discharge: monilial or yeast infections produce a thick, white, curdy, patchy discharge; trichomonal infections produce a profuse, watery, grey or green, frothy, odourous discharge; bacterial infections produce an odourous discharge.
5. *Documenting the procedure.* Include the date and time it was performed, the name of the physician, and any nursing assessments and interventions.

Male Genitals and Inguinal Area

In adult men, complete examination should include assessment of the external genitals, the presence of any hernias, and the prostate gland. The male reproductive and urinary systems (Figure 27.84) share the urethra, which is the passageway for both urine and semen. Therefore, in physical assessment of the male, these two systems are frequently assessed together.

The techniques of inspection and palpation are used to examine the male genitals. Equipment needed includes gloves and a penlight to transilluminate any mass. The client may be in a lying or sitting position.

Development of secondary sex characteristics is assessed in relationship to the client's age. See Table 27.14 for the five stages of the development of pubic hair, the penis, testes, and scrotum during puberty.

All male clients should be screened for the presence of inguinal or femoral hernias. A **hernia** is a protrusion of the intestine through the inguinal canal. The loop of bowel may extend down to the scrotum. Structures of the inguinal area are shown in Figure 27.85. An *indirect inguinal hernia* is a loop of bowel that enters the internal inguinal ring. It may stay in the canal, exit through the external ring, or pass into the scrotum. A *direct inguinal hernia* enters the inguinal canal directly through a weakness in the abdominal wall just behind the external inguinal ring. It does not pass through the inguinal canal. A *femoral hernia* is lower and more lateral than an inguinal hernia and may look like an enlarged lymph node.

Cancer of the prostate gland is the most common cancer in adult men and occurs primarily in men over age 50 years.

Examination of the prostate gland is performed with the examination of the rectum and anus (see Procedure 27.21).

Testicular cancer is much rarer than prostate cancer and occurs primarily in young men aged 15 to 35 years. Testicular cancer is most commonly found on the anterior and lateral surfaces of the testes. **Testicular self-examination** should be conducted monthly. See Chapter 12.

Procedure 27.20 describes how the nurse can conduct an assessment of the male genitals and inguinal area.

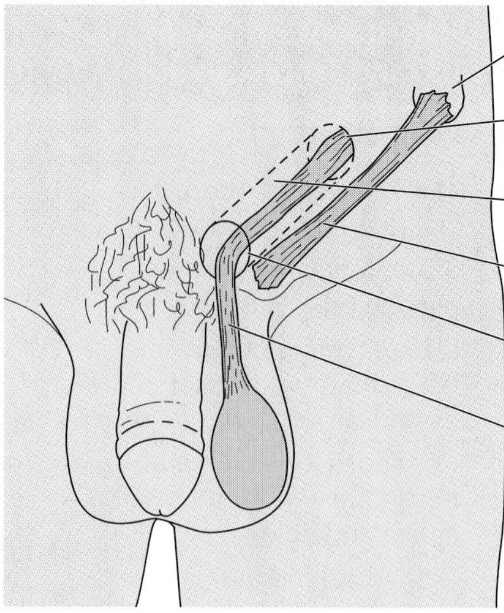

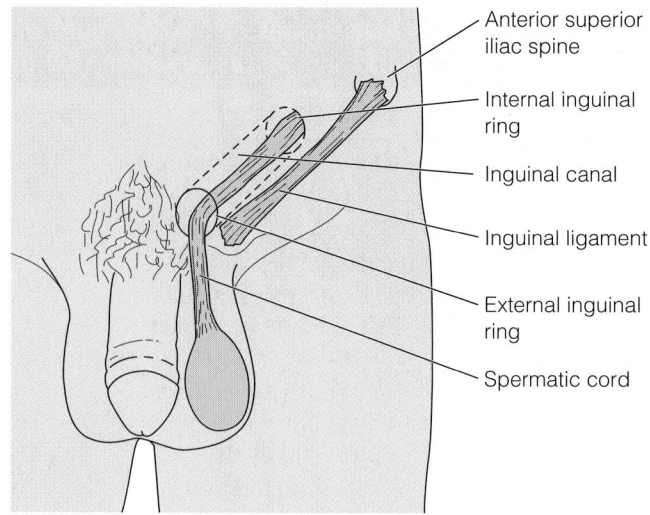

Figure 27.85 Structures of the inguinal area

PROCEDURE 27.20 Assessing the Male Genitals and Inguinal Area

NURSING HISTORY FOCUS

Usual voiding patterns and any changes, bladder control, urinary incontinence, frequency, urgency, abdominal pain; any symptoms of sexually transmitted disease; any swellings that could indicate presence of hernia; family history of nephritis, malignancy of the prostate, or malignancy of the kidney

ASSESSMENT	NORMAL FINDINGS	DEVIATIONS FROM NORMAL
Pubic Hair		
Inspect the distribution, amount, and characteristics of pubic hair.	Triangular distribution, often spreading up the abdomen	Scant amount or absence of hair
Penis		
Inspect the penile shaft and glans penis for lesions, nodules, swellings, and inflammation.	Penile skin intact Appears slightly wrinkled and varies in colour as widely as other body skin In uncircumcised males: Foreskin is easily retractable from the glans penis Small amount of thick white smegma between the glans and foreskin	Presence of lesions, nodules, swellings, or inflammation

PROCEDURE 27.20 Assessing the Male Genitals and Inguinal Area *continued*

ASSESSMENT	NORMAL FINDINGS	DEVIATIONS FROM NORMAL
Inspect the urethral meatus for swelling, inflammation, and discharge. ■ Compress or ask the client to compress the glans slightly to open the urethral meatus to inspect it for discharge. ■ If the client has reported a discharge, instruct the client to strip the penis from the base to the urethra (i.e., grasp the base of the penis, with the thumb at the front and finger behind, and while applying moderate pressure, move the thumb and fingers slowly down the shaft of the penis). Collect a specimen for culture.	Pink and slitlike appearance Positioned at the tip of the penis	Inflammation; discharge Variation in meatal locations (e.g., *hypospadias,* on the underside of the penile shaft, and *epispadias,* on the upper side of the penile shaft)
Palpate the penis for tenderness, thickening, and nodules. Use your thumb and first two fingers.	Smooth and semifirm Is slightly movable over the underlying structures	Presence of tenderness, thickening, or nodules Immobility
Scrotum		
Inspect the scrotum for appearance, general size, and symmetry. ■ To facilitate inspection of the scrotum during a physical examination, ask the client to hold the penis out of the way. ■ Inspect all skin surfaces by spreading the rugated surface skin and lifting the scrotum, as needed, to observe posterior surfaces.	Scrotal skin is darker in colour than that of the rest of the body and is loose Size varies with temperature changes (the dartos muscles contract when the area is cold and relax when the area is warm) Scrotum appears asymmetric (left testis is usually lower than right testis)	Discolourations; any tightening of skin (may indicate edema or mass) Marked asymmetry in size
Palpate the scrotum to assess status of underlying testes, epididymis, and spermatic cord. Palpate both testes simultaneously for comparative purposes. The palpation procedure is outlined in the next box.	Testicles are rubbery, smooth, and free of nodules and masses Testis is about 2 × 4 cm Epididymis is resilient, normally tender, and softer than the spermatic cord Spermatic cord is firm	Testicles are enlarged, with uneven surface (possible tumour) Testis has swelling that transilluminates (possible hydrocele) Epididymis is nonresilient and painful

PROCEDURE 27.20 Assessing the Male Genitals and Inguinal Area *continued*

PALPATING THE SCROTUM

- Using your first two fingers and thumb, palpate each testis for size, consistency, shape, smoothness, and presence of masses. During assessment of male adolescents, establish the descent of the testicles into the scrotum; note undescended testes.
- Palpate the epididymis between your thumb and index finger. It is located at the top of the testis and extends behind it.
- Palpate the spermatic cord between thumb and index finger. It is usually found at the top lateral portion of the scrotum and feels firm.
- If swelling, irregularities, or nodules are detected during the scrotal examination, attempt to transilluminate the lesion. This is done by darkening the room and shining a flashlight behind the scrotum through the mass. Serous fluid causes the light to show with a red glow; tissue or blood does not transilluminate.
- Describe all scrotal masses in terms of their size, shape, placement, consistency, tenderness, and presence of transillumination.

ASSESSMENT	NORMAL FINDINGS	DEVIATIONS FROM NORMAL
Inguinal Area		
Inspect both inguinal areas for bulges while the client is standing, if possible. ■ First, have the client remain at rest. ■ Next, have the client hold the breath and strain or bear down as though having a bowel movement. *Bearing down may make the hernia more visible.*	No swelling or bulges	Swelling or bulge (possible inguinal or femoral hernia)
Palpate for hernias.	No palpable bulge	Palpable bulge in the area

PALPATING A HERNIA

Direct Hernia

- Using your right hand for the client's right side or left hand for the client's left side, advance your index finger into the loose scrotal skin and over the external inguinal ring.
- Instruct the client to bear down.
- If a hernia is present, a palpable bulge will appear in the area.

Indirect Hernia

- Attempt to move the index or little finger into the path of the inguinal canal (see Figure 27.85, earlier) while the client flexes the knee on the same side.
- When your finger has moved as far as possible, ask the client to bear down.
- If a hernia is present, it will be felt as a mass of tissue touching the finger and withdrawing from it.

Femoral Hernia

- Palpate the inguinal area directly again, first while the client is at rest and then while the client bears down.
- If a hernia is present, a bulge will be felt most prominently when the client bears down.

PROCEDURE 27.20 Assessing the Male Genitals and Inguinal Area *continued*

Lifespan Considerations

Children

- The foreskin of the uncircumcised infant is normally tight the first two or three months of life and is not readily retractable.
- The scrotum is usually palpated to determine whether testes are descended.
- Tell the boy what you are going to do and ensure that you also have the parent or guardian's approval to perform the examination.
- In young boys, the cremasteric reflex can cause the testes to ascend into the inguinal canal. If possible, have the boy sit cross-legged, which stretches the muscle and decreases the reflex (Ashwill & Droske, 1997).

Older Adults

- The penis decreases in size with age; the size and firmness of the testes decrease.
- Testosterone is produced in smaller amounts.
- More time and direct physical stimulation are required for an older man to achieve an erection, but the patient can maintain the erection for a longer period before ejaculation than he could at a younger age.
- Seminal fluid is reduced in amount and viscosity.
- Urinary frequency, nocturia, dribbling, and problems with beginning and ending the stream are usually the result of prostatic enlargement.

Rectum, Anus, and Prostate

Rectal examination, an essential part of every *comprehensive* physical examination, involves inspection and palpation (digital examination). The extent of the assessment of the rectum and anus depends on the rectal problems stated by the client in the nursing history. An interior view of the rectum and anal canal is shown in Figure 35.4.

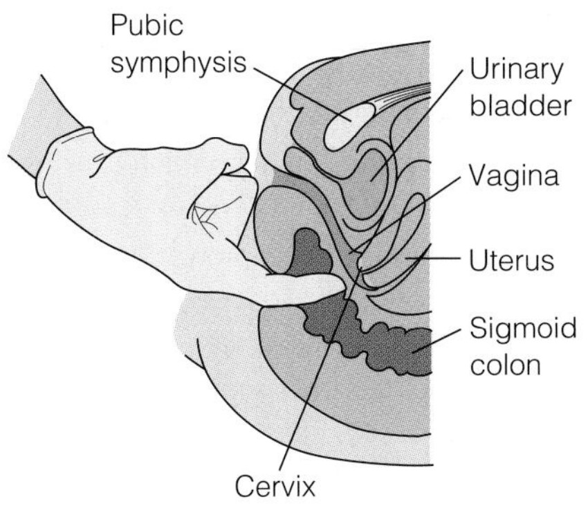

Figure 27.86 Palpating the cervix through the anterior rectal wall

In adults, a left lateral or Sims' position with the upper leg acutely flexed is required for the examination. For females, a dorsal recumbent position with hips externally rotated and knees flexed or a lithotomy position may also be used. For males, a standing position while the client bends over the examining table may also be used. This position is commonly used to examine the prostate gland. For all rectal examinations, the nurse should wear gloves.

In women, the cervix can be palpated through the anterior rectal wall (Figure 27.86). It is felt as a small (2 to 3 cm), round, firm but movable mass that should not be confused with a tumour.

Because digital examination can cause apprehension and embarrassment in the client, it is important that the nurse (1) drape the client appropriately to prevent undue exposure of body parts,(2) proceed with the examination in a competent and gentle way, (3) help the client relax by encouraging the client to take slow, deep breaths (tension can cause spasms of the anal sphincters, making the examination uncomfortable), (4) inform the client about potential sensations, such as feelings of defecation or passing gas, and (5) assure the client that accidental defecation is unlikely. Procedure 27.21 describes how to assess the rectum and anus.

PROCEDURE 27.21 Assessing the Rectum and the Anus

NURSING HISTORY FOCUS

History of bright blood in stools, tarry black stools, diarrhea, constipation, abdominal pain, excessive gas, hemorrhoids, or rectal pain; family history of colorectal cancer; when last stool specimen for occult blood was performed and the results; and if not obtained during the genitourinary examination, any signs or symptoms of prostate enlargement (e.g., slow urinary stream, hesitance, frequency, dribbling, and nocturia)

ASSESSMENT	NORMAL FINDINGS	DEVIATIONS FROM NORMAL
Inspect the anus and surrounding tissue for colour, integrity, and skin lesions. Then, ask the client to bear down as though defecating. *Bearing down creates slight pressure on the skin that may accentuate rectal fissures, rectal prolapse, polyps, or internal hemorrhoids.* Describe the location of all abnormal findings in terms of a clock, with the 12 o'clock position toward the pubic symphysis.	Intact perianal skin; usually slightly more pigmented than the skin of the buttocks Anal skin is normally more pigmented, coarser, and moister than perianal skin and is usually hairless	Presence of fissures (cracks), ulcers, excoriations, inflammations, abscesses, protruding **hemorrhoids** (dilated veins seen as reddened protrusions of the skin), lumps or tumours, fistula openings, or **rectal prolapse** (varying degrees of protrusion of the rectal mucous membrane through the anus)
Palpate the rectum for anal sphincter tonicity, nodules, masses, and tenderness.	Anal sphincter has good tone	Hypertonicity of the anal sphincter (may occur in the presence of an anal fissure or other lesion that causes contraction) Hypotonicity of anal sphincter (may occur after rectal surgery or result from a neurological deficiency)
	Rectal wall is smooth and not tender	Rectal wall is tender and nodular

PALPATING THE RECTUM

- Lubricate your gloved index finger, and instruct the client to bear downward as though having a bowel movement. *This relaxes the anal sphincter.*
- Slowly insert your finger into the anus and into the rectum in the direction of the umbilicus. The anal canal (distance from the anal opening to the anorectal junction) is short (less than 3 cm). The posterior wall of the rectum follows the curve of the coccyx and sacrum. The nurse's finger is usually able to palpate a distance of 6 to 10 cm.
- Never force digital insertion. If lesions are painful or bleeding occurs, discontinue the examination.
- Ask the client to tighten the anal sphincter around your finger, and note the tone of the anal sphincter.
- Rotate the pad of the index finger along the anal and the rectal walls, feeling for nodules, masses, and tenderness.
- Note the location of any abnormalities of the rectum (e.g., "anterior wall, 2 cm proximal to the internal anal sphincter").

On withdrawing the finger from the rectum and anus, observe it for feces. A specimen may be used to test for occult blood.	Brown colour	Presence of mucus, blood, or black tarry stool

PROCEDURE 27.21 Assessing the Rectum and Anus *continued*

ASSESSMENT	NORMAL FINDINGS	DEVIATIONS FROM NORMAL
Palpate the prostate gland (if the client is male) through the anterior wall of the rectum (Figure 27.87). You should be able to feel the median sulcus, which divides the gland into two lobes.	No tenderness Edges are discrete Gland is about 4 cm in diameter, firm, rubbery, smooth, and mobile	Enlarged; not movable Nodular surface; tenderness

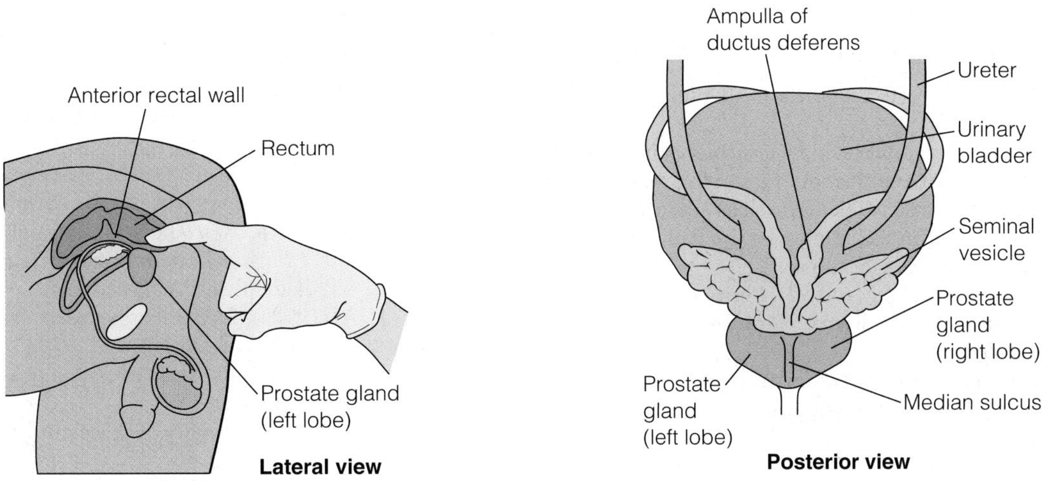

Figure 27.87 Palpating the prostate gland through the anterior wall of the rectum

FOCUS ON CRITICAL THINKING

Not all patients are comfortable with physical examination. Patients from different cultures with different health practices may feel particularly anxious about undergoing a physical assessment. Mrs. J., a 32-year-old Asian individual, came to the clinic because she felt a lump in her breast. Upon doing the breast examination, the patient shrieks and asks, "What do you think you are doing?"

1. How would you respond to this patient?
2. How would you develop nursing interventions to help put patients at ease for an invasive procedure that has a vital role in physical assessment?
3. How will you address patients in a manner likely to gain their trust and cooperation?

See Appendix A for answers to these questions.

CHAPTER HIGHLIGHTS

- The health examination is conducted to assess the function and integrity of the client's body parts.
- The health examination may entail a complete head-to-toe assessment or individual assessment of a body system or body part.
- The health assessment is conducted in a systematic manner that requires the fewest position changes for the client.
- Aspects of the physical assessment procedures should be incorporated in the assessment, intervention, and evaluation phases of the nursing process.
- Data obtained in the physical health examination supplement, confirm, or refute data obtained during the nursing history.
- Nursing history data help the nurse focus on specific aspects of the physical health examination.

- Data obtained in the physical health examination help the nurse establish nursing diagnoses, plan the client's care, and evaluate the outcomes of nursing care.
- Initial assessment findings provide baseline data about the client's functional abilities against which subsequent assessment findings are compared.
- Skills in inspection, palpation, percussion, and auscultation are required for the physical health examination; these skills are used in that order throughout the examination except during abdominal assessment, when auscultation follows inspection and precedes percussion and palpation.
- Knowledge of the normal structure and function of body parts and systems is an essential are prerequisite to conducting physical assessment.

READINGS AND REFERENCES

Suggested Readings

Holmgren, C. (1992). Perfecting the art: Abdominal assessment. *RN, 55*, 28–34.
The author demonstrates taking a gastrointestinal-specific history and physical examination. Observing the abdominal contours and skin are included as well as auscultation, percussion, and palpation techniques. At the end of the article are 20 multiple-choice questions.

Kuhn, J. K., & McGovern, M. (1992). Peripheral vascular assessment of the elderly client. *Journal of Gerontological Nursing, 19*, 35–38.
The atherosclerotic process often takes its toll on the blood vessels of elderly clients, causing disabling and painful problems. These authors state that a thorough assessment of an elderly person's peripheral vascular system, combined with appropriate health teaching, can prevent or delay such problems as ischemic pain, skin ulcerations, gangrene, or amputation. The assessment includes the client interview, inspection, palpation, auscultation, and special techniques to employ if arterial or venous insufficiency is suspected.

Related Research

Misener, T. R., & Fuller, S. G. (1995). Testicular versus breast and colorectal cancer screening: Early detection practices of primary care physicians. *Cancer Practice, 3*, 310–316.

Selected References

Ashwill, J. W., & Droske, S. C. (1997). *Nursing care of children: Principles and practice.* Philadelphia, PA: Saunders.

Barkauskas, V., Baumann, L. C., & Darling-Fisher, C. (1998). *Barkauskas' health and physical assessment* (3rd ed.). St. Louis, MO: Mosby.

Bates, B. (2003). *A guide to physical examination and history taking* (8th ed.). Philadelphia, PA: Lippincott.

Carpenito, L. (2000). *Nursing diagnosis: Application to Clinical practice*. (8th ed). Philadelphia, PA: Lippincott.

Cranley, J. J., Canos, A. J., & Sull, W. J. (1976). The diagnosis of deep venous thrombosis: Fallibility of clinical symptoms and signs. *Archives of Surgery, 111*(1), 34–36.

Delis, K. T., Hunt, N., Strachan, R. K., & Nicolaides, A. N. (2001). Incidence, natural history and risk factors of deep vein thrombosis in elective knee arthroscopy. *Thrombosis & Haemostasis, 86*(3), 817–821.

Health and Welfare Canada. (1988). Promoting healthy weights: A discussion paper. Ottawa: Minister of Supply and Services. http://www.hc-sc.gc.ca/hppb/nutrition/bmi/

Jarvis, C. (2003). *Physical examination and health assessment* (4th ed.). Philadelphia, PA: Saunders.

Kirton, C. A. (1996a). Physical assessment: Assessing for a carotid bruit. *Nursing, 26*(10), 55.

Kirton, C. A. (1996b). Physical assessment: Assessing for ascites. *Nursing, 26*(4), 53.

Kirton, C. A. (1996c). Physical assessment: Assessing breath sounds. *Nursing, 26*(6), 50–51.

Kirton, C. A. (1996d). Physical assessment: Assessing normal heart sounds. *Nursing, 26*(2), 56–57.

Memmler, R. L., Cohen, B. J., & Wood, D. L. (1996). *Structure and function of the human body* (6th ed.). Philadelphia, PA: Lippincott-Raven.

O'Hanlon-Nichols, T. (1998). Basic assessment series. Gastrointestinal system. *American Journal of Nursing, 98*, 48–53.

O'Hanlon-Nichols, T. (1998). Basic assessment series. A review of the adult musculoskeletal system: A guide to a key aspect of patient care. *American Journal of Nursing, 98*, 48–52.

Owen, A. (1998). Respiratory assessment revisited: Refresh your technique for spotting pulmonary problems. *Nursing 98, 28*(4), 48–49.

Sternbach, G. (1989). John Homans: The dorsiflexion sign. *Journal of Emergency Medicine*, 7(3), 287–290.

Then, K. L., Rankin, J. A., & Fofonoff, D. A. (2001). Atypical presentation of acute myocardial infarction in 3 age groups. *Heart and Lung, 30*, 285–293.

Thomas, D. O. (1996, April). Assessing children—it's different. *RN, 59*, 45, 53.

Thompson, J. M., & Wilson, S. F. (1996). *Health assessment for nursing practice.* St. Louis, MO: Mosby-Year Book.

WEBLINKS

Canadian Cancer Society
http://www.cancer.ca/english/index.asp
This site provides educational resources related to cancer, including risk reduction.

Calgary Health Region
http://www.calgaryhealthregion.ca/hlthconn/topics/mens.htm
This site provides information to the public on a range of topics, including prostate cancer.

CHAPTER 28

Medications

OBJECTIVES

After completing this chapter, you will be able to:

- Define selected terms related to the administration of medications.
- Describe legal aspects of administering drugs.
- Identify physiological factors and individual variables affecting medication action.
- List various routes of medication administration.
- Discuss essential parts of a medication prescription.
- Recognize common abbreviations used in prescriptions.
- List the essential steps to follow when administering medication.
- Describe physiological changes in older adults that alter administration and effectiveness of medication.
- Outline steps required to administer oral medications safely.
- Outline steps required for nasogastric and gastrostomy tube medication administration.
- Identify equipment required for parenteral medications.
- Describe how to mix drugs from vials and ampules.
- List sites used for subcutaneous, intramuscular, and intradermal injections.

Strictly speaking, a drug is any chemical substance that can have an effect on living organisms, especially if it is used in the treatment, diagnosis, or prevention of a condition or disease. In the health-care context, the words *medication* and *drug* are used interchangeably. Unfortunately, the term "drug" has connotations of illegally obtained substances, such as crack cocaine (coke), amphetamines (speed), ecstasy, cannabis (marijuana), or heroin, that are taken for nontherapeutic use. There is increased interest in researching the use of certain illegal substances as therapeutic agents. For example, in Canada, the Federal government has approved the growing, preparation, and use of marijuana for limited therapeutic purposes.

Such drugs as opium, castor oil, and vinegar were used in ancient times. Over the centuries, the number of drugs available has dramatically increased, and knowledge about these drugs has become more comprehensive.

In Canada, medications are usually dispensed on the order of physicians, dentists, and nurse practitioners. The written direction for the preparation and administration of a drug is called a **prescription**. One drug can have as many as four kinds of names: its generic name, official

TABLE 28.1 Types of Drug Preparations

Type	Description
Aerosol spray or foam	A liquid, powder, or foam deposited in a thin layer on the skin by air pressure
Aqueous solution	One or more drugs dissolved in water
Aqueous suspension	One or more drugs dispersed in a liquid, such as water
Caplet	A solid form, shaped like a capsule, coated and easily swallowed
Capsule	A gelatinous container to hold a drug in powder, liquid, or oil form
Cream	A nongreasy, semisolid preparation used on the skin
Elixir	A sweetened and aromatic solution of alcohol used as a vehicle for medicinal agents
Extract	A concentrated form of a drug made from vegetables or animals
Gel or jelly	A clear or translucent semisolid that liquefies when applied to the skin
Inhalation	A solution of a drug, or a combination of drugs, administered as a nebulized mist
Liniment	A medication mixed with alcohol, oil, or soapy emollient and applied to the skin
Lotion	A medication in a liquid suspension applied to the skin
Lozenge (troche)	A flat, round, or oval preparation that dissolves and releases a drug when held in the mouth
Ointment (salve, unction)	A semisolid preparation of one or more drugs used for application to the skin and mucous membrane
Paste	A preparation like an ointment, but thicker and stiff, that penetrates the skin less than an ointment
Pessary	A type of medicated suppository that is normally inserted into the vagina
Pill	One or more drugs mixed with a cohesive material, in oval, round, or flattened shapes
Powder	A finely ground drug or drugs; some are used internally, others externally
Suppository	One or several drugs mixed with a firm base such as gelatin and shaped for insertion into the body (e.g., the rectum); the base dissolves gradually at body temperature, releasing the drug
Syrup	An aqueous solution of sugar often used to disguise unpleasant-tasting drugs
Tablet	A powdered drug compressed into a hard small disc; some are readily broken along a scored line; others are enteric coated to prevent them from dissolving in the stomach
Tincture	An alcoholic or water-and-alcohol solution prepared from drugs derived from plants
Transdermal patch	A semipermeable membrane shaped in the form of a disc or patch that contains a drug to be absorbed through the skin over a long period of time

name, chemical name, and trademark or brand name. The **generic name** is given before a drug becomes official. The **official name** is the name under which it is listed in one of the official publications (e.g., the *Compendium of Pharmaceuticals and Specialties [CPS]*, the *Canadian Formulary [CF]*, the *United States Pharmacopeia*). The **chemical name** is the name by which a chemist knows it; this name describes the constituents of the drug precisely. The **trademark,** or **brand name,** is the name given by the drug manufacturer. Because one drug may be manufactured by several companies, it can have several trade names. For example, the drug aspirin (official name) is known by the trade names Bayer and Entrophen. Medications are available in a variety of forms. See Table 28.1.

Pharmacology is the science concerned with drugs and their actions on living organisms. **Pharmacy** is the practice of preparing, compounding, and dispensing drugs. The word also refers to the place where drugs are prepared and dispensed. Drugs are prepared by a **pharmacist,** a person licensed to prepare and dispense drugs and to make up prescriptions. A **clinical pharmacist** is a specialist who often guides the physician in prescribing drugs.

Drug Standards

Drugs may have natural (e.g., plant, mineral, and animal) sources, or they may be synthesized in the laboratory. For example, digitalis and opium are plant derived, iron and sodium chloride are minerals, insulin and vaccines may have animal or human sources, and the sulfonamides and propoxyphene hydrochloride (the analgesic Darvon) are the products of laboratory synthesis. Early drugs were derived from the three natural sources only. During the past 45 years, however, more and more drugs have been produced synthetically.

Drugs vary in strength and activity. Drugs derived from plants, for example, vary in strength according to the age of the plant, the variety, the place in which it is grown, and the method by which it is preserved. Drugs must be pure and of uniform strength if drug dosages are to be predictable in their effect. Drug standards have therefore been developed to ensure uniform quality. In North America, official drugs are designated by the Canadian and American Federal Food, Drug and Cosmetic Acts. In Canada, drugs are listed in the *British Pharmacopoeia*. Drugs on the list are described according to a variety of properties including their specific chemical and physical properties where and how they are produced, identity and purity, method of storage, category and normal dosages. In the United States, the *United States Pharmacopoeia (USP)* is used to identify the drugs.

A **pharmacopoeia** (also spelled *pharmacopeia*) is a book containing a list of products used in medicine, with descriptions of the product, chemical tests for determining identity and purity, and formulas and prescriptions. The *Canadian Formulary* lists drugs used extensively in Canada but not necessarily listed in the *British Pharmacopoeia*. The United States' *National Formulary* lists drugs and their therapeutic value and can include drugs that may still be used but not listed in the *USP*.

Pharmacopoeias and formularies are invaluable reference sources for nurses and nursing students. Nurses not only administer thousands of medications but also are responsible for assessing their effectiveness and recognizing unfavourable reactions to drugs. Since it is impossible to commit to memory all pertinent information about a very large number of drugs, nurses must have a reliable reference readily available.

Legal Aspects of Drug Administration

The administration of drugs in Canada is controlled by law. Canadians proposed legislation concerning the sale of drugs, cosmetics, and medical devices quite some time before these concerns became evident in the United States. For example, in 1875, the Parliament of Canada passed an act to prevent the sale of contaminated food, alcohol, and drugs (both controlled and restricted). By the early part of the 20th century, a legal framework was established in Canada for drug control. By 1908, all medicines, as well as tobacco and alcohol, had some regulations.

Until 1996, the Canadian Food and Drugs Act (FDA, 1953) was the major piece of legislation that was responsible for the regulation of drugs in Canada. The Food and Drug Regulations prescribe:

- The standards of composition
- Strength
- Potency
- Purity
- Quality or other property of the article of food or drug to which they refer

(Department of Justice)

The second purpose of the Canadian Food and Drugs Act is to address the purchasing and advertising of drugs, cosmetics, foods, and medical devices, and enforce regulations. For example, no individuals shall be allowed to "manufacture, prepare, preserve, package, or store for sale any drug under unsanitary conditions" (Department of Justice, Oct 25, 2000, p. 2).

Canadian Narcotic Control Act and The Controlled Drugs and Substances Act

The Canadian Narcotic Control Act was first passed in 1961 when it replaced the Canadian Opium and Narcotic Act of 1952. Regulations regarding possession, sale, manufacture, production, and distribution of narcotics are all covered in the Canadian Narcotic Control Act. The National Health and Welfare department is responsible for the administration of policies, while the Royal Canadian Mounted Police are responsible for the enforcement of the act.

More recently, the Canadian Narcotic Control Act has been subsumed under the Controlled Drugs and Substances Act developed, outlined, and accepted on June 20th, 1996.

In 2000, the Federal Government of Canada permitted the legal growing of marijuana in order that it may be tested for its medicinal properties. Marijuana has been found to be effective in relieving nausea in chemotherapy, controlling epileptic seizures, treating glaucoma, and easing the pain of acquired immune deficiency syndrome (AIDS) sufferers. Interestingly, in 2000, the Provincial Court of Appeal in Ontario struck down prohibitions on marijuana use in the Controlled Drugs and Substances Act. The provincial court's ruling in effect served a warning to the federal government to amend the Act or simple possession of marijuana will become legal. See Table 28.2 for a summary of American drug legislation. Table 28.3 provides a summary of Canadian drug legislation.

Nurses need to:

- know how nursing practice acts in their jurisdictions define and limit their functions; and
- be able to recognize the limits of their own knowledge and skill.

To function beyond the limits of nursing practice acts or beyond one's ability is to endanger clients' lives and leave oneself open to malpractice suits. Under the law, nurses are responsible for their own actions, regardless of whether there is a written order. If a physician writes an incorrect order (e.g., Demerol 500 mg, instead of Demerol 50 mg), a nurse who administers the written incorrect dosage is responsible for the error. Therefore, nurses should question any order that appears unreasonable and refuse to give the medication until the order is clarified.

TABLE 28.2 United States Drug Legislation

Legislation	Content
Food, Drug, and Cosmetic Act (1938)	Implemented by Food and Drug Administration (FDA); requires that labels be accurate and that all drugs be tested for harmful effects.
Durkham-Humphrey Amendment (1952)	Clearly differentiates drugs that can be sold only with a prescription, those that can be sold without a prescription, and those that should not be refilled without a new prescription.
Kefauver-Harris Amendment (1962)	Requires proof of safety and efficacy of a drug for approval.
Comprehensive Drug Abuse Prevention and Control Act (1970) (Controlled Substances Act)	Categorizes controlled substances and limits how often a prescription can be filled; established government-funded programs to prevent and treat drug dependence.

TABLE 28.3 Canadian Drug Legislation

Legislation	Content
Proprietary or Patent Medicine Act (1908)	Protects the public against unsafe and ineffective over-the-counter drugs.
Canada Food and Drugs Act (1953)	Prohibits advertising any food, drug, cosmetic, or device as a cure for certain specified diseases. Sets standards for manufacture, distribution, and sale of all drugs, with the exception of narcotics.
Canadian Narcotic Control Act (1961)	Allows only authorized people to possess narcotics. Specifies records about narcotics that must be kept.
Controlled Drugs and Substances Act (1996)	Canadian Narcotic Control Act is subsumed under this act.

Another aspect of nursing practice governed by law is the use of controlled substances. In hospitals, controlled substances are kept in a locked drawer, cupboard, medication cart, or computer-controlled dispensing system.

Agencies have special forms for recording the use of controlled substances (for example, "Restricted Drug Administration" form). The information required usually includes the name of the client, the date and time of administration, the name of the drug, the dosage, and the signature of the person who prepared and gave the drug. The name of the physician who ordered the drug may also be part of the record. Included on the record are details of the controlled substances wasted during the drug preparation.

In most agencies, counts of controlled substances are taken at the end of each shift. The count total should tally with the total at the end of the last shift minus the number used. If the totals do not tally, the discrepancy must be reported immediately. In facilities that use a computerized dispensing system, manual counts are not required because the dispensing system runs a continuous count; however, discrepancies must be accounted for.

Effects of Drugs

The **therapeutic effect** of a drug relates to the reason the drug is prescribed. The therapeutic effect is also known

TABLE 28.4 Therapeutic Actions of Drugs

Drug Type	Description	Examples
Palliative	Relieves the symptoms of a disease but does not affect the disease itself	Morphine sulfate, acetominophen for pain
Curative	Cures a disease or condition	Penicillin for infection
Supportive	Supports body function until other treatments or the body's response can take over	Norepinephrine bitartrate for low blood pressure; acetominophen for high body temperature
Substitutive	Replaces body fluids or substances	Thyroxine for hypothyroidism, insulin for diabetes mellitus
Chemotherapeutic	Destroys malignant cells	Methotrexate for leukemia
Restorative	Returns the body to health	Vitamin, mineral supplements

as the *desired effect* or the *primary effect*. For example, the therapeutic effect of morphine sulfate is analgesia, and the therapeutic effect of diazepam is relief of anxiety. See Table 28.4 for kinds of therapeutic actions.

A **side effect,** or secondary effect, of a drug is one that is unintended. Side effects are usually predictable and may be either harmless or potentially harmful. For example, digitalis (digoxin) increases the strength of myocardial contractions (desired effect), but it can have the side effect of decreasing the heart rate too much (bradycardia). Some side effects are tolerated for the drug's therapeutic effect; more severe side effects, also called *adverse effects,* may justify the discontinuation of a drug.

Drug toxicity (deleterious effects of a drug on an organism or tissue) results from overdosage, ingestion of a drug intended for external use, and buildup of the drug in the blood because of impaired metabolism or excretion (cumulative effect). Some toxic effects are apparent immediately; some are not apparent for weeks or months. Fortunately, most drug toxicity can be avoided if careful attention is paid to dosage and by monitoring for toxicity. An example of a toxic effect is liver failure due to the cumulative effect of methotrexate (antimetabolite that is used to treat rheumatoid arthritis and certain types of cancer).

A **drug allergy** is an immunological reaction to a drug. When a client is first exposed to a foreign substance (antigen), the body may react by producing antibodies. A drug can be antigenic and induce an allergic reaction.

Allergic reactions can be either mild or severe. A mild reaction has a variety of symptoms, from skin rashes to diarrhea. See Table 28.5. An allergic reaction can occur anytime from a few minutes to two weeks after the administration of the drug.

A severe allergic reaction usually occurs immediately after the administration of the drug; it is called an **anaphylactic reaction.**

Common symptoms of an anaphylactic reaction (also known as anaphylactic shock) include bronchospasm, laryngeal edema, acute hypotension, and tachycardia. This response can be fatal if the symptoms are not noticed immediately and treatment is not obtained promptly.

Drug tolerance exists in a person who has unusually low physiological activity in response to a drug and who requires increases in the dosage to maintain a given therapeutic effect. Drugs that commonly produce tolerance are opiates, barbiturates, ethyl alcohol, and tobacco. A **cumulative effect** is the increasing response to repeated doses of a drug that occurs when the rate of administration exceeds the rate of metabolism or excretion. As a

TABLE 28.5 Common Mild Allergic Responses

Symptom	Description/Rationale
Skin rash	Either an intraepidermal vesicle rash or a rash typified by an urticarial wheal or macular eruption; rash is usually generalized over the body
Pruritus	Itching of the skin with or without a rash
Angioedema	Edema due to increased permeability of the blood capillaries
Rhinitis	Excessive watery discharge from the nose
Lacrimal tearing	Excessive tearing
Nausea, vomiting	Stimulation of these centres in the brain
Wheezing and dyspnea	Shortness of breath and wheezing upon inhalation and exhalation due to accumulated fluids and swelling of the respiratory tissues
Diarrhea	Irritation of the mucosa of the large intestine

result, the amount of the drug builds up in the client's body unless the dosage is adjusted. Toxic symptoms may occur. An **idiosyncratic effect** occurs when an individual's response to a drug is extreme sensitivity in low dosage, extreme sensitivity in high dosage, or a response that is quite different from the usual response expected.

A **drug interaction** occurs when the administration of one drug before, at the same time as, or after another drug alters the effect of one or both drugs. The effect of one or both drugs may be either increased *(potentiating* or *synergistic effect)* or decreased *(inhibiting effect)*. Drug interactions may be beneficial or harmful. For example, probenecid, which blocks the excretion of penicillin, can be given with penicillin to increase blood levels of the penicillin for longer periods (potentiating effect). Two analgesics, such as acetominophen and codeine, are often given together because together they provide greater pain relief (additive effect). In addition, certain foods may adversely interact with a medication and potentiate or inhibit its effect. For example, large amounts of leafy, green vegetables may inhibit the anticoagulant effect of Coumadin (warfarin).

Certain conditions may be unintentionally caused by therapy. This is referred to as **iatrogenic disease**. Some examples of iatrogenic disease as a result of drug therapy are liver damage, renal failure, and fetal abnormalities.

Drug Misuse

Drug misuse is the improper use of common medications in ways that lead to acute and chronic toxicity. Both over-the-counter drugs and prescription drugs may be misused. Laxatives, antacids, vitamins, headache remedies, and cough and cold medications are often self-prescribed and overused. Most people suffer no harmful effects from these drugs.

Drug abuse is inappropriate intake of a substance, either continually or periodically. By definition, drug use is abusive when society considers it abusive. For example, the intake of alcohol at work may be considered alcohol abuse, but intake at a social gathering may not. **Drug dependence** is a person's reliance on or need to take a drug or substance. There are two types of drug dependence: psychological and physical. **Psychological dependence** refers to an individual's need to use a drug on a regular or sporadic basis to obtain a particular outcome. For example, a drug may be used to reduce anxiety or make the individual feel happy. Psychological dependence may also be accompanied by feelings of need or cravings of the drug.

Physical dependence is associated with an altered physiological state in which there may be biochemical changes in body tissues, especially the nervous system. A person who is dependent on a drug and who stops using the medication will experience withdrawal symptoms.

Illicit drugs, also called *street drugs*, are those sold illegally. Illicit drugs are of two types: (1) drugs unavailable for purchase under any circumstances, such as heroin (in North America), and (2) drugs normally available with a prescription that are being obtained through illegal channels (for example, Ritalin). Illicit drugs often are taken because of their mood-altering effect; that is, they make the person feel happy or relaxed.

Actions of Drugs on the Body

The action of a drug in the body can be described in terms of its **half-life**, the time interval required for the body's elimination processes to reduce the concentration of the drug in the body by one-half. For example, if a drug's half-life is eight hours, then the amount of drug in the body is as follows:

Initially: 100%

After 8 hours: 50%

After 16 hours: 25%

After 24 hours: 12.5%

After 32 hours: 6.25%

Because the purpose of most drug therapy is to maintain a constant drug level in the body, repeated doses are required to maintain that level. When an orally administered drug is absorbed from the gastrointestinal tract into the blood plasma, its concentration in the plasma increases until the elimination rate equals the rate of absorption. This point is known as the **peak plasma level** (Figure 28.1). Unless the client receives another dose of the drug, the concentration steadily decreases. Key terms related to drug actions are listed and described in the next box.

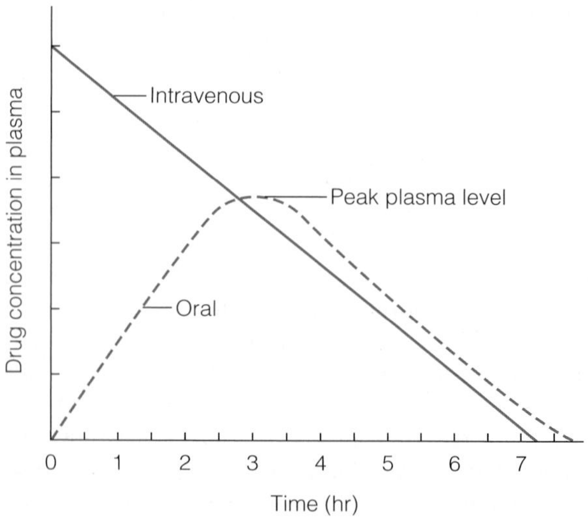

Figure 28.1 A graphic plot of drug concentration in the blood plasma following a single dose

Key Terms Related to Drug Action

- *Onset of action:* The time after administration until the body initially responds to the drug
- *Peak plasma level:* The highest plasma level achieved by a single dose, when the elimination rate of a drug equals the absorption rate
- *Drug half-life (elimination half-life):* The time required for the elimination process to reduce the concentration of the drug to one-half what it was at initial administration
- *Plateau:* A maintained concentration of a drug in the plasma during a series of scheduled doses

Pharmacodynamics

Pharmacodynamics is the process by which a drug alters cell physiology. Drugs act on cellular structures known as receptors. Any drug that has a direct action on a receptor and alters its functional properties is known as an **agonist.** A drug that interacts with a cell receptor without stimulating it and blocks the action of the agonist is known as an **antagonist.** Drugs that have a synergistic effect produce a response by stimulating enzyme activity or hormone production.

Pharmacokinetics

Pharmacokinetics is the study of the absorption, distribution, biotransformation, and excretion of drugs.

Absorption

Absorption is the process by which a drug passes into the bloodstream. Unless the drug is administered directly into the bloodstream, absorption is the first step in the movement of the drug through the body. For absorption to occur, the correct form of the drug must be given by the route intended. Drugs may be absorbed into the body by various routes, such as:

- skin
- mucous membranes
- inhalation
- injection
- oral ingestion

The rate of absorption can also be decreased by administering a vasoconstrictor, such as epinephrine.

The rate of absorption of a drug in the stomach is variable. Food, for example, can delay the dissolution and absorption of some drugs as well as their passage into the small intestine where most drug absorption occurs. Food can also combine with molecules of certain drugs, thereby changing their molecular structure and subsequently inhibiting or preventing their absorption. Another factor that affects the absorption of some drugs is the acid medium in the stomach. Acidity can vary according to the time of day, foods ingested, and the age of the client. Some drugs do not dissolve or have limited ability to dissolve in the gastrointestinal fluids, decreasing their absorption into the bloodstream. Some drugs are absorbed by tissues before they reach the stomach. For example, nitroglycerin is administered under the tongue where it is absorbed into the blood vessels that carry it directly to the heart, the intended site of action. If swallowed, this drug will be absorbed into the bloodstream and carried to the liver where it will be destroyed.

A drug administered directly into the bloodstream (i.e, intravenously) is immediately absorbed in the vascular system. This is the route of choice for rapid action. Because subcutaneous tissue has a poorer blood supply than muscle tissue, absorption from subcutaneous tissue is slower. The rate of absorption of a drug can be accelerated by the application of heat. Heat increases blood flow to the area. Conversely, cold decreases blood flow to the area and decreases the rate of absorption. Some drugs intended to be absorbed slowly are suspended in a low-solubility medium, such as oil. The absorption of drugs from the rectum into the bloodstream tends to be unpredictable. Therefore, this route is normally used when other routes are unavailable or when the intended action is localized to the rectum or sigmoid colon.

Distribution

Distribution is the transportation of a drug from its site of absorption to its site of action. When a drug enters the bloodstream, it is carried to the most vascular organs—that is, liver, kidneys, and brain. Body areas with lower blood supply—that is, skin and muscles—receive the drug later. The chemical and physical properties of a drug largely determine the area of the body to which the drug will be attracted. For example, fat-soluble drugs will accumulate in fatty tissue, whereas other drugs may bind with plasma proteins.

Biotransformation

Biotransformation, also called **detoxification** or **metabolism,** is a process by which a drug is converted to a less active form. Most biotransformation takes place in the liver where many drug-metabolizing enzymes in the cells detoxify the drugs. The products of this process are called **metabolites.** There are two types of metabolites: active and inactive. An *active metabolite* has a pharmacological action itself, whereas an *inactive metabolite* does not.

The biotransformation may be impaired if a person has an unhealthy liver. Nurses must be alert to the accumulation of the active drug in these clients and to subsequent toxicity.

Excretion

Excretion is the process by which metabolites and drugs are eliminated from the body. Most metabolites are eliminated by the kidneys in the urine; however, some are excreted in the feces, the breath, perspiration, saliva, and breast milk. Certain drugs, such as general anesthetic agents, are excreted in an unchanged form via the respiratory tract. The efficiency with which the kidneys excrete drugs and metabolites diminishes with age. Older people may require smaller doses of a drug because the drug and its metabolites may accumulate in the body.

Factors Affecting Medication Action

Other factors may also affect the action of a drug. A person may not respond in the same manner to successive doses of a drug. In addition, the identical drug and dosage may affect individuals differently.

Developmental Factors

During pregnancy, women must be very careful about taking medications. Most drugs are contraindicated because of the possible adverse effects on the fetus.

Infants usually require smaller dosages because of their body size and the immaturity of their organs, especially the liver and kidneys. They often do not have all the enzymes required for drug metabolism and, therefore, may require different medications from those for adults. In adolescence or adulthood, allergic reactions may occur to drugs formerly tolerated.

Older adults have different responses to medications due to physiological changes that accompany aging. These changes include decreased liver and kidney function, which can result in the accumulation of the drug in the body. In addition, the older person may be on multiple drugs, and incompatibilities may occur.

Older adults often experience decreased gastric mobility, gastric acid production, and blood flow, all of which can impair drug absorption. Increased adipose tissue and decreased total body fluid proportionate to the body mass can increase the possibility of drug toxicity. Older adults may have a decreased number of protein-binding sites and changes in the blood-brain barrier. The latter permits fat-soluble drugs to move readily to the brain, often resulting in dizziness and confusion.

Gender

Differences in the way men and women respond to drugs are chiefly related to the distribution of body fat and fluid and hormonal differences. Historically, most drug research was conducted on men. More recently, drug researchers have included both women and men in their studies when appropriate.

Cultural, Ethnic, and Genetic Factors

Recent research has indicated ethnicity and culture may contribute to differences in responses to medications. This has given rise to a new field of study called **pharmacoanthropology** (Kudzma, 1992). It is thought that a toxic reaction may be due to a genetic effect that results in being unable to eliminate a drug or in metabolizing a drug too quickly. It is also known that a drug that is normal for a Caucasian may cause diverse effects in an Asian (Kudzma, 1992). Cultural practices can also affect a drug's action. Clients who take herbal remedies may counteract prescribed medications. The accompanying box provides guidelines for nurses who care for clients from other cultures.

Diet

Foods can affect the action of a medication. For example, certain foods that are capable of acidifying the urine (e.g., cheeses, eggs, cranberries, plums, poultry) can potentiate the effects of aspirin (acetylsalicylic acid).

Environment

The client's environment can affect the action of drugs, particularly those used to alter behaviour and mood. Therefore, nurses assessing the effects of a drug need to consider the drug in the context of the client's personality.

Environmental temperature may also affect drug activity. When environmental temperature is high, the peripheral blood vessels dilate, which can intensify the action of vasodilators. In contrast, a cold environment and consequent vasoconstriction may inhibit the action of vasodilators but enhance the action of vasoconstrictors. A client who takes a sedative or analgesic in a busy, noisy environment may have less benefits than if the environment is quiet and peaceful.

Medications for Clients from Other Cultures

- Ask about health beliefs and practices.
- Observe for unusual medication responses.
- Ask about folk or home medications prescribed by a nontraditional healer.
- Remember that there is considerable diversity within cultural groups.
- Include culturally sensitive information in health teaching.
- Use printed and visual materials that are in the language of the client.
- Encourage clients to voice their concerns and questions about medications.

Source: Adapted from National Council on Patient Information and Education. (1994). *Talk about presumptions,* p. 8.

Psychological Factors

A client's expectations of the effects of a drug can impact the response to the drug. For example, a client who believes that codeine is ineffective as an analgesic may experience no relief from pain after it is given.

Illness and Disease

Illness and disease can also affect the action of drugs. For example, acetominophen can reduce the body temperature of a feverish client but has no effect on the body temperature of a client without fever. Drug action is altered in clients with circulatory, liver, or kidney dysfunction.

Time of Administration

The time of administration of oral medications affects the relative speed with which they act. Orally administered medications are absorbed more quickly if the stomach is empty. Thus, oral medications taken two hours before meals act faster than those taken after meals. However, some medications, for example, iron preparations, irritate the gastrointestinal tract and need to be given after a meal when they will be better tolerated. Circadian rhythms will cause variations in urinary output and blood circulation which may affect the action and response to a drug.

Routes of Administration

The route of drug administration is associated with the extent of the therapeutic response that occurs, as well as the specific rate of the action. Therefore, the route chosen also needs to be determined on the basis of the individual patient. For example, a client who is vomiting will not have good absorption of the drug from the gastrointestinal system when the drug is administered orally. The client may not be able to retain the drug in the stomach for a sufficient period of time in order for the drug to take effect. See Table 28.6. The route of administration should be indicated when the drug is ordered.

Oral

Oral administration is the most common, least expensive, and most convenient route for most clients. In oral administration, the drug is swallowed. Oral administration is considered to be the safest method of medication administration.

The major disadvantages of oral administration are possibly unpleasant taste of the drugs, irritation of the gastric mucosa, irregular absorption from the gastrointestinal tract, slow absorption, and in some cases, harm to the client's teeth. For example, ferrous sulphate can stain the teeth.

Sublingual

In sublingual administration, a drug is placed under the tongue where it dissolves (Figure 28.2). In a relatively short time, the drug is largely absorbed into the blood vessels on the underside of the tongue in the salivary secretions. The medication should not be swallowed. The medication, once absorbed in the mucosal membranes, enters the systemic circulation without first passing through the liver. Nitroglycerin is one example of a drug commonly given in this manner.

Buccal

Buccal means "pertaining to the cheek." In buccal administration, a medication (e.g., a tablet) is held in the mouth between the teeth and against the mucous membrane of the cheek until the drug dissolves (Figure 28.3). The drug may act locally on the mucous membranes of the mouth or systemically when it is swallowed in the saliva.

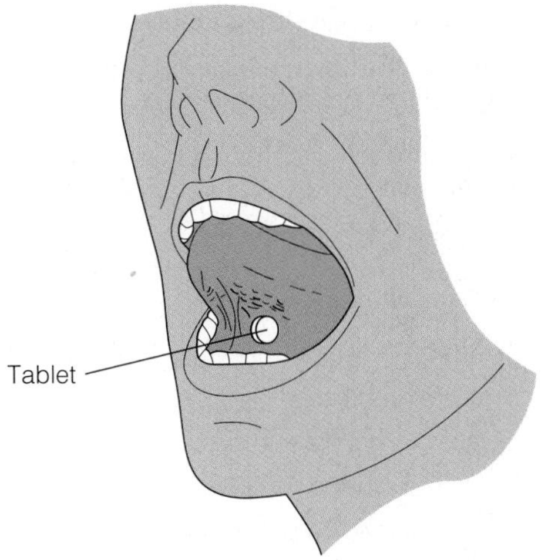

Figure 28.2 Sublingual administration of a tablet

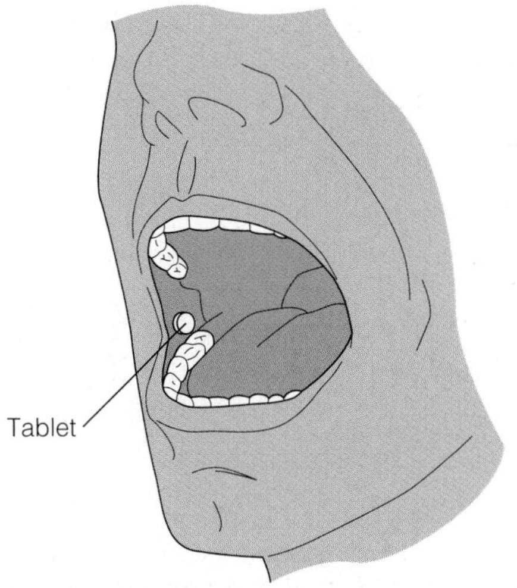

Figure 28.3 Buccal administration of a tablet

TABLE 28.6 Routes of Administration

Route	Advantages	Disadvantages
Oral	Most convenient Usually least expensive Safe, does not break skin barrier Administration usually does not cause stress	Inappropriate for clients with nausea or vomiting Drug may have unpleasant taste or odour Inappropriate when gastrointestinal tract has reduced motility Inappropriate if client cannot swallow or is unconscious Cannot be used before certain diagnostic tests or surgical procedures Drug may discolour teeth, harm tooth enamel Drug may irritate gastric mucosa Drug can be aspirated by seriously ill clients
Sublingual	Same as for oral, *plus* Drug can be administered for local effect Drug is rapidly absorbed into the bloodstream More potent than oral route because drug directly enters the blood and bypasses the liver	If swallowed, drug may be inactivated by gastric juice Drug must remain under tongue until dissolved and absorbed
Buccal	Drug must remain against the cheek until dissolved and absorbed	Drug must remain against the cheek until dissolved and absorbed
Rectal	Can be used when drug has objectionable taste or odour Drug released at slow, steady rate	Dose absorbed is unpredictable
Vaginal	Provides local therapeutic effect	Limited use
Topical	Provides a local effect Few side effects	May be messy and may soil clothes Drug can enter body through abrasions and cause systemic effects
Transdermal	Prolonged systemic effect Few side effects Avoids gastrointestinal absorption problems	Leaves residue on the skin that may soil clothes
Subcutaneous	Onset of drug action faster than oral	Must involve sterile technique because it breaks skin barrier More expensive than oral Can administer only small volume Slower absorption than intramuscular administration Some drugs can irritate tissues and cause pain Can be anxiety producing
Intramuscular	Pain from irritating drugs is minimized Can administer larger volume than subcutaneous Drug is rapidly absorbed	Breaks skin barrier Can be anxiety producing
Intradermal	Absorption is slow (this is an advantage in testing for allergies)	Amount of drug administered must be small Breaks skin barrier
Intravenous	Rapid effect	Limited to highly soluble drugs Drug distribution inhibited by poor circulation
Inhalation	Introduces drug throughout respiratory tract Rapid localized relief Drug can be administered to unconscious client	Drug intended for localized effect can have systemic effect Of use only for the respiratory system

Parenteral

Parenteral administration is administration of drugs by injection. Parenteral administration is the most rapid form of systemic therapy. The following are some of the more common routes for parenteral administration:

- *Subcutaneous (hypodermic)*—into the subcutaneous (connective) tissue, just below the skin
  - rate of absorption is slow
- *Intramuscular*—into a muscle
  - rate of absorption is more rapid than subcutaneous because of increased blood flow of the tissue
- *Intradermal*—under the epidermis (into the dermis)
  - rate of absorption is slow
- *Intravenous*—into a vein
  - rate of absorption is rapid and immediate

Some of the less commonly used routes for parenteral administration are **intra-arterial** (into an artery), **intracardiac** (into the heart muscle), **intraosseous** (into a bone), **intrathecal** or **intraspinal** (into the spinal canal), **intrapleural** (into the pleural space), **epidural** (into the epidural space), and **intra-articular** (into a joint). Sterile equipment and sterile drug solution are essential for all parenteral therapy. The main advantage of parenteral administration is fast absorption.

Topical

Topical applications are those applied to a circumscribed surface area of the body. They affect only the area to which they are applied. Topical applications include the following:

- *Dermatological preparations*—applied to the skin
- *Instillations and irrigations*—applied into body cavities or orifices, such as the urinary bladder, eyes, ears, nose, rectum, or vagina
- *Inhalations*—administered into the respiratory tract by a nebulizer or positive pressure breathing apparatus. Air, oxygen, and vapour are generally used to carry the drug into the lungs. See Chapter 39 for some specifics.

Medication Prescription

A physician usually determines the client's medication needs and prescribes medications, although in some settings, nurse practitioners prescribe drugs. Each health agency will have its own policies. Medication orders may be written, verbal, or telephoned. Nurses need to know the agency policies about medication prescriptions. (For example, who is permitted to accept telephone and verbal orders.)

Policies about physicians' prescriptions vary considerably from agency to agency. For example, a client's medications are frequently automatically cancelled after surgery or an examination involving an anesthetic agent. A new prescription following the procedure or surgery must then be written. Most agencies also have lists of abbreviations officially accepted for use in the agency. Both nurses and physicians may need to refer to these lists. These abbreviations can be used on legal documents, such as clients' charts. See Table 28.7 for a list of some accepted abbreviations.

Types of Medication Prescriptions

Common medication prescriptions include the stat order, the single order, the standing order, the prn order, and the protocol order.

1. The **standing order** (routine order) is the most common type of order that indicates a drug is to be given regularly for a set period of time or until a specified termination date is reached. A standing order may be carried out indefinitely (e.g., multiple vitamins daily) until an order is written to cancel it, or it may be carried out for a specified number of days (e.g., Demerol 100 mg IM q4h ×3 days). In some agencies, standing orders are automatically cancelled after a specified number of days and must be then reordered.
2. The **single order** or "one-time order" is for medication to be given once at a specified time (e.g., Seconal 100 mg po hs before surgery).
3. A **stat order** is a single order of medication that is to be administered immediately (e.g., Demerol 100 mg IM stat).
4. A **prn order,** "as needed order," permits the nurse to give a medication when, in the nurse's judgement, the client requires it (e.g., Tylenol #3 2 tabs po q4h prn). The nurse must use good judgement about when the medication is needed and when it can be safely administered.
5. A **protocol order** is a set of criteria and orders under which a medication is to be administered. For example, heparin protocols are often used for a variety of clients and conditions.

Essential Parts of a Drug Order

The drug order has seven essential parts as listed in the box on page 619. In addition, unless it is a standing order, it should state the number of doses or the number of days the drug is to be administered.

Client

The *client's full name,* that is, the first and last names and middle initials or names, should always be used to avoid confusion between two clients who have the same last name. In health-care agencies, an identifying armband must be on all clients that is used to compare information that accompanies each dose of medication. In some agencies,

TABLE 28.7 Common Abbreviations Used in Medication Orders

Abbreviation	Explanation	Example of Administration Time
ac	before meals	0700, 1100, and 1700 hours
ad lib	freely, as desired	
aq	water	
bid	twice a day	1000 and 2200 hours
c̄	with	
cap	capsule	
dil	dissolve, dilute	
elix	elixir	
g	gram	
gr	grain	
gtt	drop	
h	an hour	
hs	at bedtime (hour of sleep)	
ID	intradermal	
IM	intramuscular	
IV	intravenous	
kg	kilogram	
L	litre	
mcg or μg	microgram	
mg	milligram	
no.	number	
OD	right eye	
OS	left eye	
OU	both eyes	

Abbreviation	Explanation	Example of Administration Time
pc	after meals	0900, 1300, and 1900 hours
po or PO	by mouth	
prn	when needed	
q	every	
qAM (om)	every morning	1000 hours
qh (q1h)	every hour	
q2h	every 2 hours	0800, 1000, 1200 hours, and so on
q3h	every 3 hours	0900, 1200, 1500 hours, and so on
q4h	every 4 hours	1000, 1400, 1800 hours, and so on
q6h	every 6 hours	0600, 1200, 1800, 2400 hours
qid	four times a day	1000, 1400, 1800, 2200 hours
qod	every other day	0900 hours on odd dates
qs	sufficient quantity	
Rx	take	
s̄	without	
sc or Sc or sq	subcutaneous	
Sig or S	label	
sos	if it is needed	
ss or ss̄	one half	
stat	at once	
sup or supp	suppository	
susp	suspension	
tab	tablet	
tid	three times a day	1000, 1400, and 1800 hours

the client's identification number and physician's name are put on the order as further identification. Some hospitals imprint the client's name, identification number, and room number on all forms.

Date

In addition to *the day, the month, and the year* the order was written, some agencies also require that the *time of day* be written. Writing the time of day on the order can eliminate errors when the nursing shifts change and makes clear when certain orders automatically terminate. For example, in some settings, narcotics can be ordered only for 48 hours after surgery. Therefore, a drug that is ordered at 1600 hours November 1, 2003, is automatically cancelled at 1600 November 3, 2003. Many health agencies use the 24-hour clock, which eliminates confusion between morning and afternoon times. Time with the 24-hour clock starts at midnight, which is 0000 hours (see Chapter 24).

Medication

The *name of the drug to be administered* must be clearly written—in either generic or trade name form.

Dosage and Frequency

The *dosage of the drug* includes the amount, the times or frequency of administration, and, in many instances, the strength; for example, tetracycline *250 mg* (amount) *four times a day* (frequency); hydrochloric acid *10%* (strength) *5 mL* (amount) *three times a day with meals* (time and frequency). Dosages should be written in the metric system.

Essential Parts of a Drug Order

- Full name of the client
- Date and time the order is written
- Name of the drug to be administered
- Dosage of the drug
- Route of administration
- Frequency of administration
- Signature of the person writing the order

Route

Also included in the order is the *route of administration* of the drug. This part of the order, like other parts, is frequently abbreviated. See Table 28.7 for abbreviations of routes of administration. It is not unusual for a drug to have several possible routes of administration; therefore, it is essential that the route be included in the order.

The *signature* of the ordering physician or nurse makes the drug order a legal request. An unsigned order has no validity, and the ordering physician or nurse needs to be notified if the order is unsigned.

When a physician writes a prescription for a client, the prescription also includes information for the pharmacist. Therefore, a prescription's content differs from that of a medication order in a hospital. Compare the parts of a prescription listed in the following box with those shown in Figure 28.4.

Communicating a Medication Order

A drug order is written on the client's chart by a physician or by a registered nurse receiving a telephone or verbal order from a physician. Most agencies have a specified time frame (e.g., 24 or 48 hours) in which the physician issuing the telephone or verbal order must cosign the order written by the nurse. The medication order is then copied by a nurse or clerk to a Kardex or medication administration record (MAR). Increasingly, nurses are being provided with computer printouts of a client's medications instead of copying the physician's order. This method avoids errors of copying and saves nursing time.

Medication administration records (Figure 28.5) vary in form, but all include the client's name, room, and bed number; drug name and dose; and times and method of administration. In some agencies, the date the order was prescribed and the date the order expires are also included.

The nurse should always question the physician about any order that is ambiguous, unusual (e.g., an abnormally high dosage of a medication), or contraindicated. When the nurse believes that a medication prescription is inappropriate, the following actions are required:

Parts of a Prescription

- Descriptive information about the client: name, address, and sometimes age, health insurance number (or identification number)
- Date on which the prescription was written
- The Rx symbol, meaning "take thou"
- Medication name, dosage, and strength
- Route of administration
- Dispensing instructions for the pharmacist, for example, "Dispense 30 capsules"
- Directions for administration to be given to the client, for example, "Sig. Tab 1 i with meals"
- Refill and/or special labelling, for example, "Refill × 1"
- Prescriber's signature

Name Jane Cleary Age 36

Address 3376 W. 141st St., Regina SK Date Nov 1, 2003

This prescription will be filled generically unless physician signs on line stating "Dispense as written."

℞

Tetracycline 250 mgm po

Disp. #30

Sig. 1 qid take on an empty stomach

Dispense as Written ______ F. March Substitution Permissible

Frances March, M.D. 120 Madison Road Regina, SK

Ph. No. 685-9533

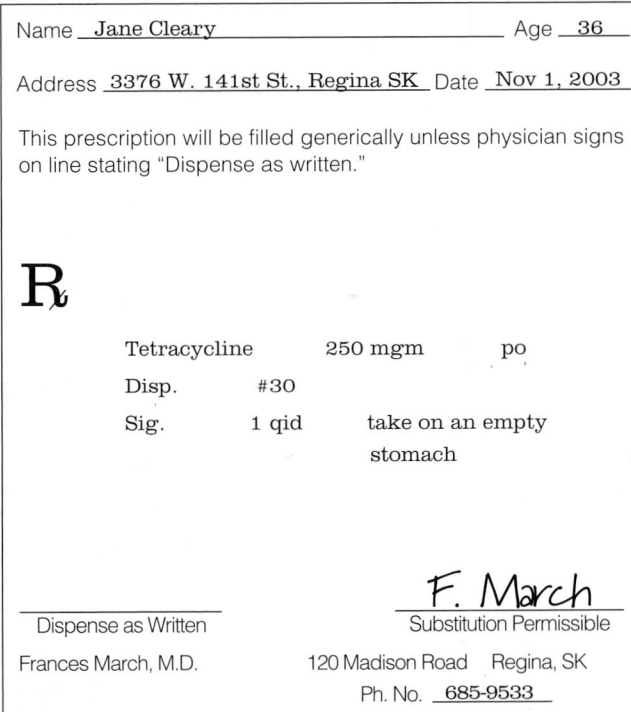

Figure 28.4 A prescription filled out by a physician

- Contact the physician and discuss the rationale for believing the medication or dosage to be inappropriate.
- Document in notes the following: when the physician was notified, what was conveyed to the physician, and how the physician responded.
- If the physician cannot be reached, document all attempts to contact the physician and the reason for withholding the medication.

Medication Administration Record

Time and Date: 24h from 08:00 21 May 03 through 07:00 22 May 03

Name: Waters, Jane **Location:** 236B

Patient ID: 817643 **Physican:** James Aspen, MD

08 09 10 11 12 13 14 15 16 17 18 19 20 21 22 23 24 01 02 03 04 05 06 07

Solutions

08 09 10 11 12 13 14 15 16 17 18 19 20 21 22 23 24 01 02 03 04 05 06 07

Order #1 Flagyl l gm
q.8.h. iv.minibag

14 22 06

Medications

Order #2 Digoxin tab 0.125 mg *lst*
(1 tab) PO daily

08 Ventolin 1.2 puffs 9.4 h during day

PRN Medications

Order #3 Tylenol #3 1-2 tabs q4h prn

Allergies: Cortisone **Checked by:** S.S. Rollers

Figure 28.5 Medication administration record

- If someone else gives the medication, document data about the client's condition before and after the medication.
- If an incident report (see Chapter 24) is indicated, clearly document factual information.

Systems of Measurement

Three systems of measurement are used in Canada: the metric system, the apothecaries' system, and the household system, which is similar to the apothecaries' system.

Metric System

The metric system, devised by the French in the latter part of the 18th century, is the standard system of measurement in Canada and most European countries. In the metric system, the basic unit of length is the metre, the basic unit of mass is the gram, and the basic unit of volume is the litre.

Prefixes derived from Latin designate subdivisions of the basic unit: *deci* (1/10 or 0.1), *centi* (1/100 or 0.01), and *milli* (1/1,000 or 0.001). Multiples of the basic unit are designated by prefixes derived from Greek: *deca* (10), *hecto* (100), and *kilo* (1,000). Only the measurements of volume (the litre) and of weight (the gram) are discussed in this chapter. These are the measures used in medication administration (Figure 28.6). The kilogram (kg) is a multiple of the gram, and the milligram (mg) and microgram (mcg or μg) are subdivisions. Fractional parts of the litre are usually expressed in millilitres (mL), for example, one-half of a litre is 500 mL; multiples of the litre are usually expressed as litres or millilitres, for example, 2.5 litres or 2,500 mL.

Household System

Many people are more familiar with household measures. Household measures may be used when more accurate systems of measure are not required. Included in household measures are drops, teaspoons, tablespoons, cups, and glasses. Equivalent units of the household system are listed in Table 28.8.

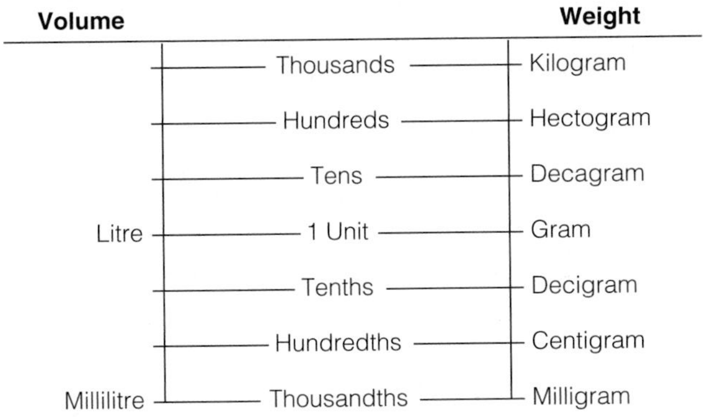

Figure 28.6 Basic metric measurements of volume and weight

Apothecaries' System

A system that is much older than the metric system, known as the **Apothecaries' System,** was brought to North America from Britain during the Colonial period. Some of the units of mass used in the apothecaries' system include the scruple, the dram, the ounce, and the pound. Units of volume are the fluid dram, the fluid ounce, the pint, the quart, and the gallon.

It is important to emphasize that although the pound and the fluid ounce may be seen in clinical practice, the standard units of measurement used should be the metric system.

Converting Units of Weights and Measure

Converting Weights within the Metric System

It is relatively simple to arrive at equivalent units of weight within the metric system because the system is based on units of 10. Only three metric units of weight are used for drug dosages—the gram (g), milligram (mg), and microgram (mcg or μg); 1,000 mg or 1,000,000 mcg equals 1 g. Equivalents are computed by dividing or multiplying; for example, to change milligrams to grams, the nurse divides the number of milligrams by 1,000. The simplest way to divide by 1,000 is to move the decimal point three places to the left:

500 mg = ? g
Move the decimal point three places to the *left:*
Answer = 0.5 g

Conversely, to convert grams to milligrams, multiply the number of grams by 1,000, or move the decimal point three places to the right:

0.006 g = ? mg
Move the decimal point three places to the *right:*
Answer = 6 mg

TABLE 28.8 Approximate Volume Equivalents: Metric, Apothecaries', and Household Systems

Metric		Apothecaries'		Household
1 mL	=	15 minims (min or m)	=	15 drops (gtt)
5 mL	=	12 fluid drams	=	1 teaspoon (tsp)
15 mL	=	4 fluid drams ʒ	=	1 tablespoon (Tbsp)
30 mL	=	1 fluid ounce ℥	=	30 mL
500 mL	=	1 pint (pt)	=	500 mL
1,000 mL (1 L)	=	1 quart (qt)	=	1,000 mL
4,000 mL	=	1 gallon (gal)	=	4,000 mL

Converting Weights and Measures between Systems

When preparing client medications, a nurse may need to convert weights or volumes from one system to another. For example, a client may know his weight in pounds, yet the amount of drug to be given is based on mg/kg of body weight (1 kg = 2.2 lb). To prepare the correct dose, the nurse must convert from the apothecaries' (pounds) to the metric system (kilograms).

$$2.2 \text{ lb} = 1 \text{ kg}$$
$$110 \text{ lb} = x \text{ kg}$$
$$x = \frac{110 \times 1}{2.2}$$
$$= 50 \text{ kg}$$

- Millilitres are commonly used in prescribing liquid medications, such as cough syrups, laxatives, antacids, and antibiotics for children.
- Litres and millilitres are the volumes commonly used in preparing solutions for enemas, irrigating solutions for douches, bladder irrigations, and solutions for cleaning open wounds.

The conversion of milligrams to grams was previously discussed. The decimal point is moved three spaces to the left:

$$3{,}000 \text{ mg} = 3 \text{ g}$$

Calculating Dosages

Several formulas can be used to calculate drug dosages. One formula uses ratios:

$$\frac{\text{dose on hand}}{\text{quantity on hand}} = \frac{\text{desired dose}}{\text{quantity desired } (x)}$$

For example, erythromycin 500 mg is ordered. It is supplied in a liquid form containing 250 mg in 5 mL. To calculate the dosage, the nurse uses the formula:

$$\frac{\text{dose on hand (250 mg)}}{\text{quantity on hand (5 mL)}} = \frac{\text{desired dose (500 mg)}}{\text{quantity desired } (x)}$$

Then, the nurse cross-multiplies:

$$250\,x = 5 \text{ mL} \times 500 \text{ mg}$$
$$x = \frac{5 \text{ mL} \times 500 \text{ mg}}{250 \text{ mg}}$$
$$x = 10 \text{ mL}$$

Therefore, the dose ordered is 10 mL. The nurse can also use this formula to calculate dosages:

$$\text{Amount to administer } (x) = \frac{\text{desired dose}}{\text{dose on hand}} \times \text{quantity on hand}$$

TABLE 28.9 Approximate Weight Equivalents: Metric and Apothecaries' Systems

Metric	Apothecaries'
30 g	= 1 ounce
500 g	= 1.1 pound (lb)
1,000 g (1 kg)	= 2.2 lb

For example, heparin is often distributed in large vials in prepared dilutions of 10,000 units per mL. If the order calls for 5,000 units, the nurse can use the preceding formula to calculate:

$$x = \frac{5{,}000 \text{ units}}{10{,}000 \text{ units}} \times 1 \text{ mL}$$
$$x = .05 \text{ mL}$$

Therefore, the nurse injects 0.5 mL for a 5000-unit dose.

Dosages for Children

Although dosage is stated in the medication order, nurses must understand something about the safe dosage for children. Unlike adult dosages, children's dosages are not always standard. Body size significantly affects dosage.

Body Surface Area

Body surface area is determined by using a nomogram and the child's height and weight. This is considered to be the most accurate method of calculating a child's dose. Standard nomograms give a child's body surface area according to weight and height (Figure 28.7). The formula is the ratio of the child's body surface area to the surface area of an average adult (1.7 square metres, or 1.7 m^2), multiplied by the normal adult dose of the drug:

$$\text{Child's dose} = \frac{\text{surface area of child } (m^2)}{1.7 \text{ m}^2} \times \text{normal adult dose}$$

For example, a child who weighs 10 kg and is 50 cm tall has a body surface area of 0.4 m^2. Therefore, the child's dose of tetracycline, corresponding to an adult dose of 250 mg, would be as follows:

$$\text{Child's dose} = \frac{0.4 \text{ m}^2}{1.7 \text{ m}^2} \times 250 \text{ mg}$$
$$= 0.23 \times 250 = 58.82 \text{ mg}$$

Administering Medications Safely

The nurse should always assess a client's health status and obtain a medication history prior to giving *any* medication. In general, the nurse assesses the client *prior* to administering any medication to obtain baseline data by which to evaluate the effectiveness of the medication. The extent of the assessment depends on the client's illness or current condition. For example, the nurse assesses a dyspneic client's respirations carefully before administering any medication that might affect breathing. It is important to determine whether the route of administration is suitable. For example, a client who is nauseated may not be able retain in the stomach a drug taken orally.

The **medication history** includes information about the drugs the client is taking currently or has taken recently. This includes prescription drugs; over-the-counter drugs, such as antacids, alcohol, and tobacco; vitamins and herbal remedies; and illegal drugs, such as heroin. Sometimes, an incompatibility with one or more of these drugs affects the choice of a new medication.

An important part of the history is clients' knowledge of their drug allergies. Drug allergies must be carefully elicited from the client and documented. Some clients may have had a coincidental event when they took a drug for the first time. Such clients may associate that event as an allergy when, in fact, what they experienced was *not* a true allergic reaction (e.g., nausea caused by morphine administration).

Information also needs to be gathered regarding the dose, frequency, and length of time the client has been on a medication. Medications that are used on a prn basis can at times be underutilized, therefore not achieving the effect, or they can be overutilized, leading to toxic effects and, possibly, drug dependence.

History of the client's normal eating habits is also important to note since, in assessing the client, it is also necessary to gather information regarding other conditions or risk factors as they may influence the administration of medications. Sometimes, the medication schedule needs to be coordinated with mealtimes or the ingestion of foods. When a medication must be taken with food on a specified schedule, clients can often adjust their mealtime or have a snack (e.g., with a bedtime medication). In addition, certain foods are incompatible with certain medications, for example, milk is incompatible with tetracycline.

It is essential that the effect/response of the client to the drug be documented. Positive, negative, and neutral effects need to be noted as these may impact the need for dosage change, maintenance, or change in medication. A client with poor eyesight, for example, may require special labels for the medication container; older clients with unsteady hands may not be able to hold a syringe or to inject themselves or another person. The key clinical guidelines for administering medications are listed in the next box.

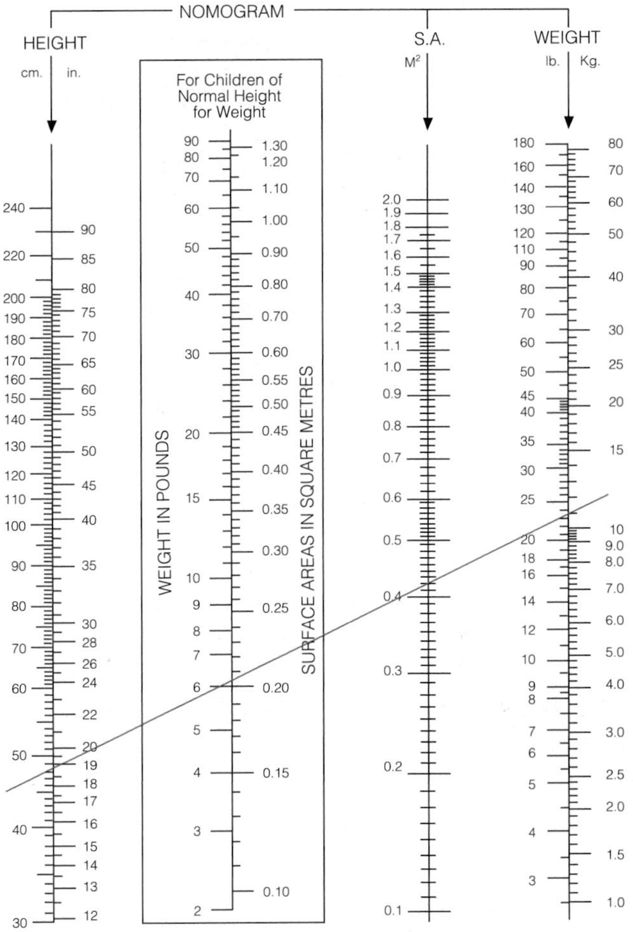

Figure 28.7 Nomogram with estimated body surface area. A straight line is drawn between the child's height (on the left) and the child's weight (on the right). The point at which the line intersects the surface area column is the estimated body surface area.

Process of Administering Medications

The five "rights" of drug administration include: right drug, right dose, right time, right route, and right client.

When administering any drug, regardless of the route of administration, the nurse must do the following:

1. *Identify the client.* Errors can and do occur, often because one client gets a drug intended for another. In hospitals, most clients wear some sort of identification, such as a wristband with name and hospital identification number. Before giving the client any drug, check the identification band with the medication administration record (MAR). As a double-check, if unsure or if the client has no wristband, ask the client's name, have the family identify the client, or ask another nurse to identify the client before administering any medication.

Clinical Guidelines for Administering Medications

- Nurses are responsible for the medications they administer. Nurses should question orders that they consider are incorrect or incomplete.
- Be knowledgeable about medications you administer.
- Federal laws govern the uses of narcotics and controlled drugs. Keep these medications in a locked place.
- Use only medications that are in a clearly labelled container.
- Do not use liquid medications that are cloudy or have changed colour.
- Before administering a medication, identify the client correctly (i.e., checking the identification bracelet *and* asking clients to state their name).
- Do not leave medications at the bedside (e.g., nitroglycerin or cough syrup, except for those medications where policy permits).
- If a client vomits after taking an oral medication, determine if client has vomited up medication and report this to the nurse in charge or the physician, or both.
- Double check when administering certain medications. For example, have another nurse check the dosages of anticoagulants, insulin, and certain IV preparations.
- Most hospital policies require new orders from the physician for the client's postsurgery care.
- Document when and why a medication is omitted.
- When a medication error is made, report it immediately to the nurse in charge or the physician, or both, and complete an incident form.

2. *Client assessment.* Prior to administration of any medication, ensure that the appropriate assessment relevant for each drug is done. For example, prior to the administration of an antihypertensive (medication for high blood pressure), the blood pressure must be checked.
3. *Inform the client.* If the client is unfamiliar with the medication, the nurse should explain the intended action as well as any side effects or adverse effects that might occur.
4. *Administer the drug.* Read medication orders and records carefully and check against the name on the medication container or on the drawer in which the client's container is kept if a medication cart is used. Then, administer the correct medication in the prescribed dosage, by the route ordered, at the correct time.
5. *Provide adjunctive interventions as indicated.* Clients may need help when receiving medications. They may require physical assistance, for instance, in assuming positions for intramuscular injections, or they may need guidance about measures, such as drinking fluids, to enhance drug effectiveness and prevent complications. Nurses must anticipate questions, comments, and fears from clients about their medications. The nurse can allay fears by listening carefully to clients' concerns and giving correct information. Ongoing support and surveillance of clients will also help decrease anxiety regarding medication.
6. *Record the drug administered.* The facts recorded in the chart, in ink or by computer printout, are name of the drug, dosage, method of administration, specific relevant data, such as pulse rate (taken in most settings prior to the administration of digitalis), and any other pertinent information. The record should also include the exact time of administration and the signature of the nurse providing the medication. Many medication records are designed so that the nurse signs his or her full name and designation once on the page and initials each medication administered. Often, medications that are given regularly are recorded on a special flow record or on computer, and prn or stat medications are recorded separately.
7. *Evaluate the client's response to the drug.* It is essential that the effect/response of the client to the drug be documented. Positive, negative, and neutral effects need to be noted as these may impact the need for dosage change and maintenance or change in medication. The anxious client may show the desired effects of a tranquilizer by behaviour that reflects a lowered stress level (e.g., slower speech or fewer random movements). The effectiveness of a sedative can often be measured by how well a client slept; the effectiveness of an antispasmodic, by how much pain the client feels. In all nursing activities, nurses need to be aware of the medications that a client is taking and record their effectiveness as assessed by the client and the nurse on the client's chart as well as report the client's response to other members of the health-care team as appropriate.

See the following box for the five "rights" to accurate drug administration.

Developmental Considerations

Infants and Children

Knowledge of growth and development is essential for the nurse administering medications to children. Oral medications for children are usually prepared in sweetened liquid form to make them more palatable. The parents may provide suggestions about what method is best for their child. Necessary foods, such as milk or orange juice, should not be used to mask the taste of medications because the child may develop unpleasant associations and refuse that food in the future.

Children tend to fear any procedure in which a needle is used because they anticipate pain or because the procedure is unfamiliar and threatening. The nurse needs to acknowledge that the child will feel some pain, since denying this fact only deepens the child's distrust. After the injection, the nurse (or the parent) can cuddle and speak softly to the infant and give the child a toy to dispel the child's association of the nurse only with pain.

Five "Rights" of Drug Administration

- Right drug
- Right dose
- Right time
- Right route
- Right client

DDTRC

RESEARCH NOTE

What Kind of Discharge Medication Instructions Provide a Higher Level of Medication Knowledge?

Adherence to a medication regimen by older adults who are discharged from the emergency department (ED) is an essential part of effective treatment. Researchers have demonstrated that delivery of well-structured instructions increases clients' knowledge of discharge regimens and increases adherence among ED populations. This study compared the level of medication knowledge of elderly ED clients receiving instruction by one of two teaching methods: (1) the usual preprinted discharge instructions with hand-written medication information, and (2) individualized computer-generated discharge instructions designed within a geragogy framework. *Geragogy* refers to the art and science of helping older adults learn.

The geragogy intervention included large-print, easily readable, specific information ordered within the elderly memory schema. This schema consists of purpose, administration, and emergency information, in that order. The Knowledge of Medication Subtest by Horn and Swain (1977) was administered by telephone 48 to 72 hours after discharge. Sixty patients (38 women, 22 men) with a mean age of 76 years were randomly assigned to groups and completed the study at three rural ED sites. Findings revealed that subjects in the geragogy-based intervention group demonstrated significantly more knowledge of medications than did subjects experiencing the usual discharge teaching method.

Implications: These findings suggest that a medication teaching intervention geared to the special needs of the elderly can be effective in increasing medication knowledge.

Source: Hayes, K. S. (1998). Randomized trial of geragogy-based medication instruction in the emergency department. *Nursing Research, 47*(4), 211–218.

Older Adults

An older person can present special problems, most of which are related to physiological changes, to past experiences, and to established attitudes toward medications. Altered pharmacokinetics in the elderly include changes in absorption, distribution, metabolism, and excretion. The physiological changes in elderly persons that may affect the administration and effectiveness of medications are included in the box below.

Some pharmacokinetic changes enhance the possibility of cumulative drug effects and toxicity. For example, impaired circulation delays the action of medications given intramuscularly or subcutaneously. Digitalis, which is frequently taken by older people, can accumulate to toxic levels and be lethal due to altered blood flow and kidney function.

It is not uncommon for older clients to take several different medications daily. The possibility of error increases with the number of medications taken, whether self-administered at home or administered in a hospital. The greater number of medications also compounds the problem of drug interactions. Careful routine review of client medications, potential effects and adverse side effects, drug and food interactions, and client's response to the drug is imperative.

Physiological Changes Associated with Aging that Influence Medication Administration and Effectiveness

- Altered memory
- ↓ acute vision
- ↓ in renal function, resulting in slower elimination of drugs and higher drug concentrations in the bloodstream for longer periods
- ↓ slower absorption from the gastrointestinal tract
- ↑ proportion of body fat to lean body mass, which facilitates retention of fat-soluble drugs and ↑ potential for toxicity
- ↓ liver function, which hinders biotransformation of drugs
- ↓ gastric emptying time and an ↑ in the pH of gastric fluids can ↑ stomach irritation (e.g., aspirin)
- Altered quality of organ responsiveness, resulting in adverse effects becoming pronounced before therapeutic effects are achieved

Older adults usually require smaller dosages of drugs, especially sedatives and other central nervous system depressants. Reactions of older clients to medications, particularly sedatives, are unpredictable and often bizarre. It is not uncommon to see irritability, confusion, disorientation, restlessness, and incontinence as a result of sedatives. Nurses, therefore, need to observe clients carefully for untoward reactions.

Attitudes of older people toward medical care and medications vary. Older people tend to believe in the wisdom of the physician more readily than younger people. Some older people are bewildered by the prescription of several medications and may passively accept their medications from nurses but not swallow them and then spit them out after the nurse leaves the room. For this reason, the nurse is advised to stay with clients until they have swallowed the medications. Other clients may be suspicious of medications and actively refuse them.

Older people are mature adults capable of reasoning. Therefore, the nurse needs to explain the reasons for and the effects of medications. This education can prevent clients from continuing to take a medication long after there is a need for it or from discontinuing a drug too quickly. For example, clients should know that diuretics will cause them to urinate more frequently and may reduce ankle edema. Instructions about medications need to be given to all clients. These instructions should include when to take the drug, what effects to expect, and when to consult a health-care professional.

Remembering to take drugs can be difficult for most people, including older adults. Because some older clients are required to take several medications daily, and because visual acuity and memory may be impaired, the nurse needs to develop simple, realistic plans for clients to follow at home. If medications are scheduled to be taken with meals or at bedtime, clients are not as likely to forget. Some clients may take their medications and then an hour later not remember whether they took them. One solution to forgetfulness is to use a special container or glass strictly for medications. An empty glass or container indicates that the person took the pills. Loss of visual acuity presents problems that can be overcome by writing out the plan in block letters large enough to be read. In some situations, the help of a spouse, son, daughter, or home care provider can be enlisted.

Oral Medications

The oral route is the most common route by which medications are given. This is the most common route of choice as long as a client can swallow and retain the drug in the stomach. See Procedure 28.1. Oral medications are contraindicated when a client is vomiting, has continuous gastric or intestinal suction, or is unconscious and unable to swallow. Generally these clients have the order "nothing by mouth" (NPO).

PROCEDURE 28.1 Administering Oral Medications

PURPOSE

- To provide a medication that has systemic effects or local effects on the gastrointestinal tract or both (see specific drug action)

Assessment Focus
Allergies to medication(s); client's ability to swallow the medication; presence of vomiting or diarrhea that would interfere with the ability to absorb the medication; specific drug action; side effects, interactions, and adverse reactions; client's knowledge of and learning needs about the medication

Equipment

- ❑ Medication tray or cart
- ❑ Disposable medication cups: small paper or plastic cups for tablets and capsules, waxed or plastic calibrated medication cups for liquids
- ❑ Medication administration record (MAR) or computer printout
- ❑ Pill crusher
  or
  Syringe of appropriate size for child's mouth and medication amount
- ❑ Straws to administer medications that may discolour the teeth or to facilitate the ingestion of liquid medication for certain clients
- ❑ Drinking glass and water or juice

PROCEDURE 28.1 Administering Oral Medications *continued*

INTERVENTION

1. **Organize the supplies.**

- Assemble the medication tray and cups in the medicine room, or place the medication cart outside the client's room.
- Assemble the medication cards or records for each client together so that medications can be prepared for one client at a time. *Organization of supplies saves time and reduces the chance of error.*

2. **Verify the client's ability to take medication orally.**

- Determine whether the client can swallow, is on NPO, is nauseated or vomiting, has gastric suction, or has diminished or absent bowel sounds.

3. **Verify the order for accuracy.**

- Check the accuracy of the MAR or of the printout with the physician's written order. It should contain the following information:
  a. client's name
  b. drug name and dosage
  c. frequency and time for administration
  d. route of administration
- Check the expiration date.
- Report any discrepancies in the order to the nurse in charge or the physician, as agency policy dictates.
- Check the last time the medication was administered and compare to the drug order.

4. **Obtain appropriate medication.**

- Read the MAR and take the appropriate medication from the shelf, drawer, or refrigerator. The medication may be dispensed in a bottle, box, or unit-dose package.
- Compare the label of the medication container or unit-dose package against the order on the MAR. If these are not identical, recheck the client's chart. If there is still a discrepancy, check with the nurse in charge or the pharmacist.

5. **Prepare the medication.**

- Calculate and prepare correct drug dose.
- While preparing the medication, recheck the prepared drug and container with the MAR. *This second check reduces the chance of error.*

TABLETS OR CAPSULES

- Pour the required number into the bottle cap, and then transfer the medication to the disposable cup without touching the tablets (Figure 28.8). All tablets or capsules to be given to the client may be placed in the same cup.
- Do not touch medication with fingers.

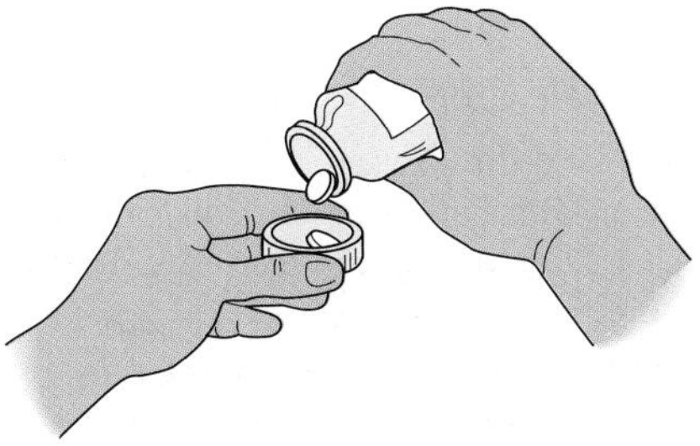

Figure 28.8 Pouring a tablet into the container

- Keep narcotics and medications that require specific assessments, such as pulse measurements, respiratory rate or depth, or blood pressure, separate from the others. *This enables the nurse to withhold the medication if indicated.*
- Break only scored tablets, if necessary, to obtain the correct dosage. Use a file or cutting device, if needed (Figure 28.9). Discard unused portions of divided tablets according to agency policy.

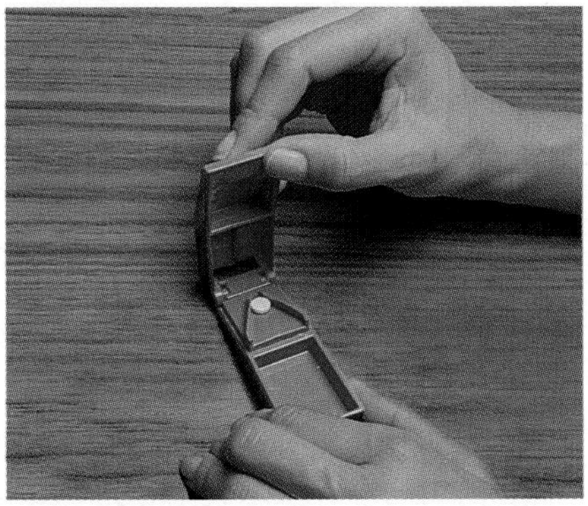

Figure 28.9 A cutting device can be used to divide tablets

- If the client has difficulty swallowing, crush the tablets to a fine powder with a pill crusher or between two medication cups or spoons. Then mix the powder with a small amount of soft food (e.g., custard, applesauce). *Note:* Check with pharmacy before crushing tablets. Sustained-action, enteric-coated, buccal, or sublingual tablets should not be crushed.
- Place packaged unit-dose capsules or tablets (Figure 28.10, *A*) directly into the medicine cup. Do not remove the wrapper until at the bedside. *The wrapper keeps the medication clean and facilitates identification.*

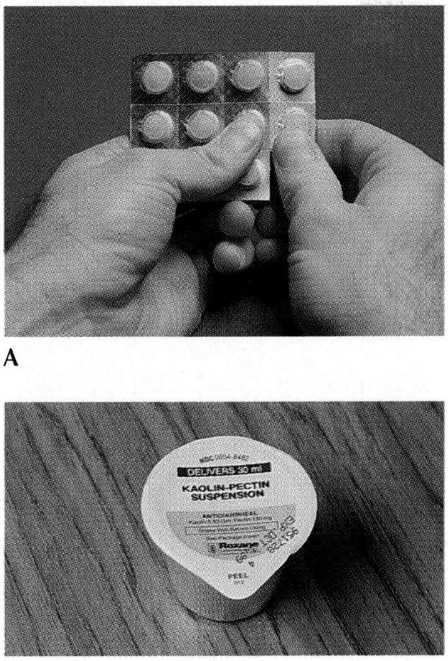

A

B

Figure 28.10 Unit-dose packages: *A*, tablets; *B*, liquid medications

LIQUID MEDICATION

- Thoroughly mix the medication before pouring. Discard any medication that has changed colour or turned cloudy.
- Remove the cap and place it upside down on the countertop to avoid contaminating its inside.

PROCEDURE 28.1 Administering Oral Medications *continued*

- Hold the bottle so the label is next to your palm, and pour the medication away from the label (Figure 28.11). *This prevents the label from becoming soiled and unreadable as a result of spilled liquids.*

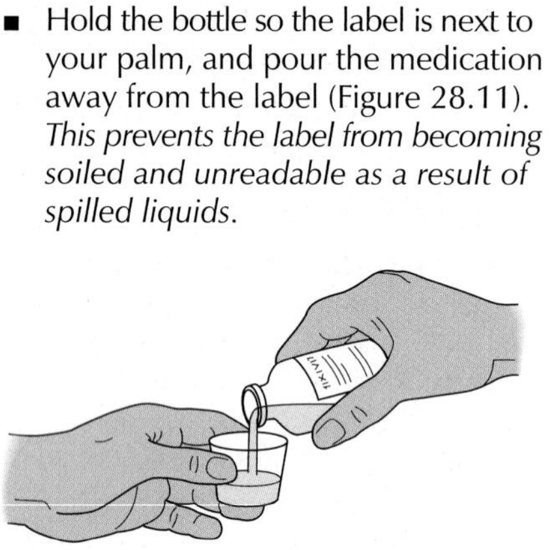

Figure 28.11 Pouring a liquid medication from a bottle

- Hold the medication cup at eye level and fill it to the desired level using the bottom of the **meniscus** (crescent-shaped upper surface of a column of liquid) to align with container scale (Figure 28.12). *This method ensures accuracy of measurement.*

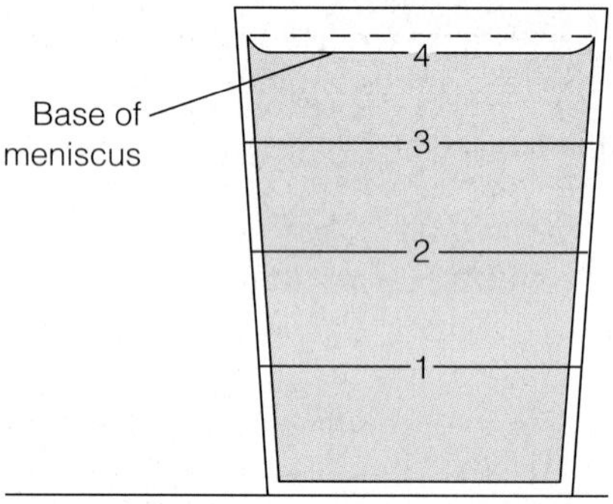

Figure 28.12 The bottom of the meniscus is the measuring guide

- Before capping the bottle, wipe the lip with a paper towel. *This prevents the cap from sticking.*
- When giving small amounts of liquids (e.g., less than 5 mL), prepare the medication in a sterile syringe *without* the needle.
- Keep *unit-dose* liquids in their package and open them at the bedside.

ORAL NARCOTICS AND CONTROLLED DRUGS

- If an agency uses a manual recording system for controlled substances, check the narcotic record for the previous drug count and compare it with the supply available. Some medications, including narcotics, are kept in plastic containers that are sectioned and numbered.
- Remove the next available tablet and drop it in the medicine cup.
- After removing a tablet, record the necessary information on the appropriate narcotic control record and sign it.

Note: Computer-controlled dispensing systems allow access only to the selected drug and automatically record its use.

ALL MEDICATIONS

- Place the prepared medication and MAR together on the tray or cart.
- Return the bottle, box, or envelope to its storage place and recheck the label on the container. *This third check further reduces the risk of error.*
- Avoid leaving prepared medications unattended. *This precaution prevents potential mishandling errors.*

6. Administer the medication at the correct time.

- Identify the client by comparing the name on the MAR with the name on the client's identification bracelet and by asking the client's name. *Accurate identification is essential to prevent error.*
- Explain the purpose of the medication and how it will help using language that the client can understand. Include relevant information about effects; for example, tell the client receiving a diuretic to expect an increase in urine. *Information facilitates acceptance of and compliance with the therapy.*
- Assist the client to a sitting position or, if not possible, to a side-lying position. *These positions facilitate swallowing and prevent aspiration.*
- Take the required assessment measures, such as pulse, respiratory rates, or blood pressure. Take the apical pulse rate before administering digitalis preparations. Take blood pressure before giving antihypertensive drugs. Take the respiratory rate prior to administering narcotics. *Narcotics depress the respiratory centre.* If any of the findings are above or below the predetermined parameters, consult the physician before administering the medication.
- Give the client sufficient water or preferred juice to swallow the medication. Before using juice, check for any food and medication incompatibilities. *Fluids ease swallowing and facilitate absorption from the gastrointestinal tract.* Liquid medications other than antacids or cough preparations are generally diluted with 15 mL of water to facilitate absorption.
- If the client is unable to hold the pill cup, use the pill cup to introduce the medication into the client's mouth, and give only one tablet or capsule at a time. *Putting the cup to the client's mouth maintains the cleanliness of the nurse's hands and the medication. Giving one medication at a time eases swallowing.*
- If an older child or adult has difficulty swallowing, ask the client to place the medication on the back of the tongue before taking the water. *Stimulation of the back of the tongue produces the swallowing reflex.*
- If the medication has an objectionable taste, ask the client to suck a few ice chips beforehand, or give the medication with juice, applesauce, or bread if there are no contraindications. *The cold will desensitize the taste buds, and juices or bread can mask the taste of the medication.*
- If the client says that the medication you are about to give is different from what the client has been receiving, do not give the medication without checking the original order. Most clients are familiar with the appearance of medications

PROCEDURE 28.1 Administering Oral Medications *continued*

taken previously. *Unfamiliar medications may signal a possible error or a change from one company brand to another.*

- Stay with the client until all medications have been swallowed. *The nurse must see the client swallow the medication before the drug administration can be recorded.* A physician's order or agency policy is required for medications left at the bedside.

7. **Document each medication given.**

- Record the medication given, dosage, time, route, any complaints or assessments of the client, and your signature.
- If medication was refused or omitted, record this fact on the appropriate record; document the reason, when possible, and the nurse's actions according to agency policy.

8. **Dispose of all supplies appropriately.**

- Return the medication records to the appropriate file for the next administration time.
- Replenish stock (e.g., medication cups) and return cart to medicine room.
- Discard used disposable supplies.

9. **Evaluate the effects of the medication.**

- Return to the client when the medication is expected to take effect (usually 30 minutes) to evaluate the effects of the medication on the client.
- Monitor client for side effects, especially following an initial dose.

Variation: Giving Oral Medications to Infants and Children

- Select an appropriate vehicle to measure and administer the medication, for example, plastic disposable cup, plastic syringe without needle, or tuberculin syringe (see page 631). For young infants, a plastic syringe is usually used. For older infants who can drink from a cup, a medicine cup can be used. Whenever possible, give children a choice about use of a spoon, dropper, or syringe.
- Dilute the oral medication, if indicated, with a small amount of water. *Many oral medications are readily swallowed if they are diluted with a small amount of water. If large quantities of water are used, the child may refuse to drink the entire amount and receive only a portion of the medication.*
- Crush medications that are not supplied in liquid form and mix them with substances available on most pediatric units, such as flavoured syrup, jam, or a fruit puree. *Note*: When selecting a substance to mix with a medication, *avoid essential food items,* such as milk, cereal, and orange juice. *If essential food items are used, the child may become intolerant of them and refuse these foods in the diet.*
- *Note*: Do not crush enteric-coated medications as you will be destroying the benefit provided by the enteric coating.
- Disguise disagreeable-tasting medications with sweet-tasting substances mentioned previously. However, present any altered medication to the child honestly and not as a food or treat.
- To prevent aspiration and choking, position infants in a semi-reclining position, and administer the medication slowly in divided doses by spoon or a plastic syringe.
- If using a spoon, retrieve and refeed medication that is thrust outward by the infant's tongue.
- If using a syringe, place it along the side of the infant's tongue. *This position prevents gagging and expulsion of the medication.*
- A child's parents or guardians may be able to provide valuable information on how best to give medications to their children. However, a nurse may need to partially restrain a child who refuses to cooperate or consistently resists despite explanation, encouragement, and attempts to determine the reason for the behaviour. To restrain the child:
  a. Place the child in your lap with the right arm behind you.
  b. Grasp the child's left hand firmly by your left hand.
  c. Secure the head between your arm and body.
- Follow all medication with a drink of water, juice, a Popsicle, or frozen juice bar. *This removes any unpleasant aftertaste.*
- For children who take sweetened medications on a long-term basis, follow the medication administration with oral hygiene. *These children are at high risk for dental caries.*

Evaluation Focus
Desired effect (e.g., relief of pain or decrease in body temperature); any adverse effects or side effects (e.g., nausea, vomiting, skin rash, change in vital signs)

PROCEDURE 28.1 Administering Oral Medications *continued*

Home Care Considerations

Instruct the client to

- Learn the names of the medications, their actions, and possible adverse effects.
- Keep all medications out of reach of children and pets.
- Set up a medication schedule. Weekly pill containers (available at the pharmacy) or a written plan may be helpful.
- If using a syringe to administer the medication to an infant or child, remove and dispose of the plastic cap that fits on the end of the syringe. Infants and small children have been known to choke on these caps.
- Always check the medication label to make sure the correct medication is being taken.
- Request labels printed with larger type on medication containers if there is difficulty reading the label.
- Check the expiration date and discard outdated medications.
- Do not crush or cut a tablet or capsule without first checking with the physician or pharmacist. Doing so may affect the medication's absorption.
- Take the medications only as prescribed. Immediately consult the nurse, pharmacist, or physician about any problems with the medication.
- Ask the pharmacist to substitute child-proof caps with ones that are more easily opened, as necessary.
- If a dose or more is missed, do not take two or more doses; ask the pharmacist or physician for directions.
- Never stop taking the medication without the physician's permission.
- Always check with the pharmacist before taking any nonprescription medications. Some over-the-counter medications can interact with the prescribed medication.

Nasogastric and Gastrostomy Medications

For clients who cannot take anything by mouth (NPO) and have **nasogastric tubes** or a **gastrostomy tube** in place, an alternative route for administering medications is through the nasogastric or gastrostomy tube. A nasogastric (NG) tube is inserted by way of the nasopharynx and is placed into the client's stomach for the purpose of feeding the client or to remove gastric secretions. A gastrostomy tube is surgically placed directly into the client's stomach and provides another route for administering nutrition and medications. See Chapter 38 for further discussion of nasogastric and gastrostomy tubes. Guidelines for administering medications by nasogastric tubes and gastrostomy tubes are shown in the following box.

Parenteral Medications

Nurses give **parenteral** medications intradermally (ID), subcutaneously (SC or SQ), intramuscularly (IM), or intravenously (IV). Because these medications are absorbed more quickly than oral medications and are irretrievable once injected, the nurse must prepare and administer them carefully and accurately. Administering parenteral drugs requires the same nursing knowledge as for oral and topical drugs; however, because injections are invasive procedures, aseptic technique must be used to minimize the risk of infection.

Equipment

Syringes

To administer parenteral medications, nurses use injectable equipment (i.e., syringes, needles, vials, and ampules). Syringes have three parts: the tip, which connects with the needle; the barrel, or outside part, on which the scales are printed; and the plunger, which fits inside the barrel (Figure 28.13). When handling a syringe, the nurse may touch the outside of the barrel and the handle of the plunger; however, the nurse must avoid letting any unsterile object contact the tip or inside of the barrel, the shaft of the plunger, or the shaft or tip of the needle.

There are several kinds of syringes, differing in size, shape, and material. The three most commonly used types are the standard hypodermic syringe, the insulin syringe, and the tuberculin syringe (Figure 28.14). *Hypodermic syringes* come in 2-, 2.5-, and 3-mL sizes. They usually have two scales marked on them: the minim and the millilitre. The millilitre scale is the one normally used; the minim scale is used for very small dosages.

Insulin syringes are similar to hypodermic syringes, but they have a scale specially designed for insulin: a 100-unit

CLINICAL GUIDELINES

Administering Medications by Nasogastric or Gastrostomy Tube

- Follow five rights of medication administration.
- Always check with the pharmacist to see if the client's medications come in a liquid form because these are less likely to cause tube obstruction.
- If medications do not come in liquid form, check to see if they may be crushed (enteric-coated, sustained-action, buccal, and sublingual medications should never be crushed).
- Dissolve crushed tablets in warm water. Cold liquids may cause client discomfort and may not dissolve medication.
- Read medication labels carefully before opening a capsule.
- Open capsules and mix the contents with water only with the pharmacist's advice.
- Do not administer whole or undissolved medications.
- If the tube is connected to suction, disconnect the suction and keep the tube clamped for 20–30 minutes after giving the medication to enhance absorption.
- Always check and confirm NG placement before administering medications (this may be done by checking gastric pH or by auscultating air).
- Flush the tube with at least 15 to 30 mL (5 to 10 mL for children) of water before administering medications if not contraindicated.
- If you are giving several medications, administer each one separately and flush with at least 5 mL (3 mL for children) of water between each if not contraindicated.
- When you have finished administering all medications, flush with another 15 to 30 mL of water to clear the tube if not contraindicated.

Source: Lehmann, S., & Barber, J. (1991). Giving medications by feeding tube: How to avoid problems. *Nursing 91,* p. 61; and Petrosino, B. M., Christian, B. J., Wolfe, J., et al. (1989). Implications of selected problems with nasoenteral tube feedings. *Critical Care Quarterly, 12,* p. 1.

calibrated scale intended for use with U-100 insulin. Several low-dose insulin syringes are also available and frequently have a nonremovable needle. All insulin syringes are calibrated on the 100-unit scale in North America. The correct choice of syringe is based on the amount of insulin required.

The *tuberculin syringe* was originally designed to administer tuberculin. It is a narrow syringe calibrated in tenths and hundredths of a millilitre (up to 1 mL) on one scale and in sixteenths of a minim (up to 1 minim) on the other scale. This type of syringe can also be useful in administering other drugs, particularly when small or precise measurement is indicated (e.g., pediatric dosages). Syringes are made in other sizes as well (e.g., 5, 10, 20, and 50 mL). These are not generally used to administer drugs directly but can be useful for adding medications to intravenous solutions or for irrigating wounds.

Most syringes used today are made of plastic and are individually packaged for sterility in a paper wrapper or a rigid plastic container (Figure 28.15). The syringe and needle may be packaged together or separately.

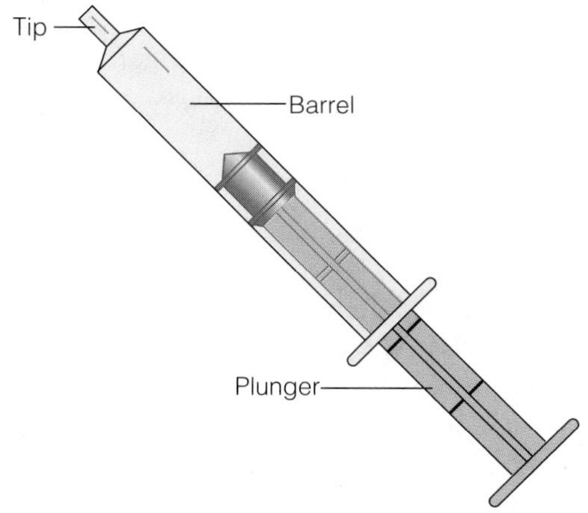

Figure 28.13 The three parts of a syringe

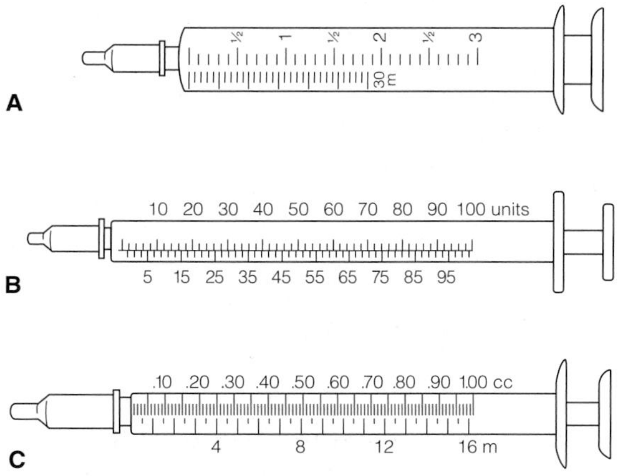

Figure 28.14 Three kinds of syringes: *A,* hypodermic syringe marked in tenths (0.1) of millilitres and in minims; *B,* insulin syringe marked in 100 units; *C,* tuberculin syringe marked in tenths and hundredths (0.01) of cubic millimetres and in minims.

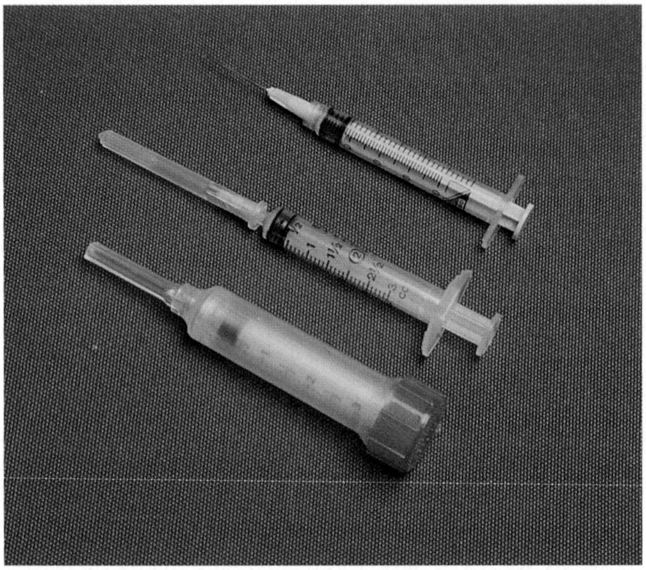

Figure 28.15 Disposable plastic syringes and needles: *top,* with syringe and needle exposed; *middle,* with plastic cap over the needle; *bottom,* with plastic case over the needle and syringe

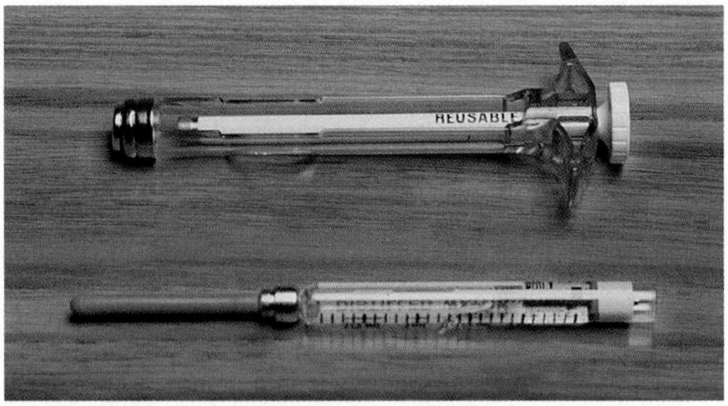

A

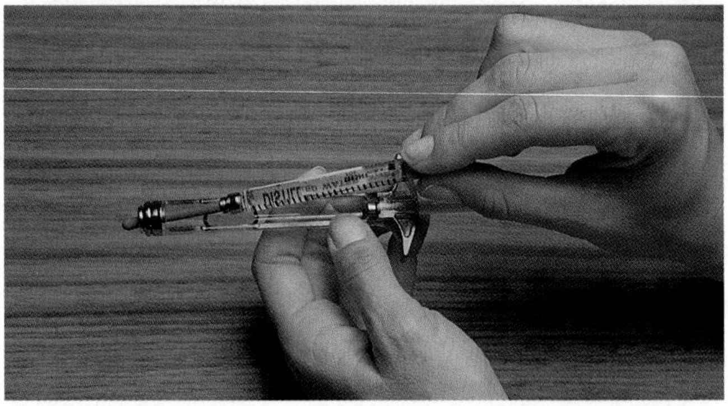

B

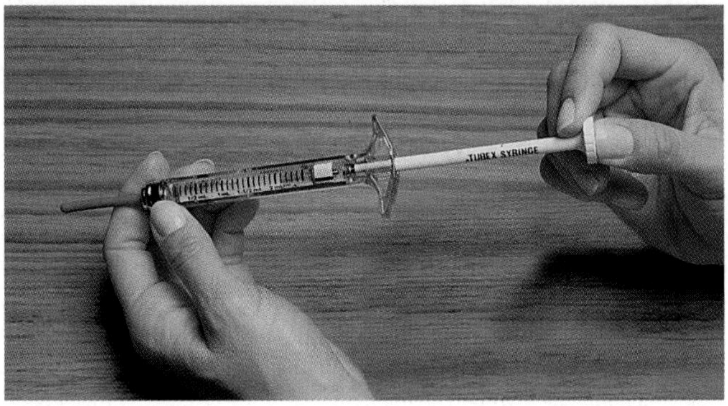

C

Figure 28.16 *A,* syringe and prefilled sterile cartridge with needle; *B,* assembling the device; *C,* the cartridge slides into the syringe barrel, turns, and locks at the needle end. The plunger then screws into the cartridge end.

Injectable medications are frequently supplied in disposable *prefilled unit-dose systems.* These are available as (1) prefilled syringes ready for use, or (2) prefilled sterile cartridges and needles that require the attachment of a reusable holder (injection system) before use (Figure 28.16). Examples of the latter system are the Tubex and Carpuject injection systems. The manufacturers provide specific directions for use. Because most prefilled cartridges are overfilled, excess medication must be ejected before the injection to ensure the right dosage.

Needles

Needles are made of stainless steel, and most are disposable. Reusable needles (e.g., for special procedures) need to be sharpened periodically before resterilization because the points become dull with use and are occasionally damaged or acquire burrs on the tips. A dull or damaged needle should *never* be used.

A needle has three discernible parts: the hub, which fits onto the syringe; the cannula, or shaft, which is attached to the hub; and the bevel, which is the slanted part at the tip of the needle (Figure 28.17). A disposable needle has a plastic hub. Needles used for injections have three variable characteristics:

1. *Slant or length of the bevel.* The bevel of the needle may be short or long. Longer bevels provide the sharpest needles and cause less discomfort and are commonly used for subcutaneous and intramuscular injections. Short bevels are used for intradermal and intravenous injections because a long bevel can become occluded if it rests against the side of a blood vessel.
2. *Length of the shaft.* The shaft length of commonly used needles varies from 1/2 to 2 inches. The appropriate needle length is chosen according to the client's muscle development, the client's weight, and the type of injection.
3. *Gauge (or diameter) of the shaft.* The gauge varies from #18 to #28. The larger the gauge number, the smaller the diameter of the shaft. Smaller gauges produce less tissue trauma, but larger gauges are necessary for viscous medications, such as penicillin.

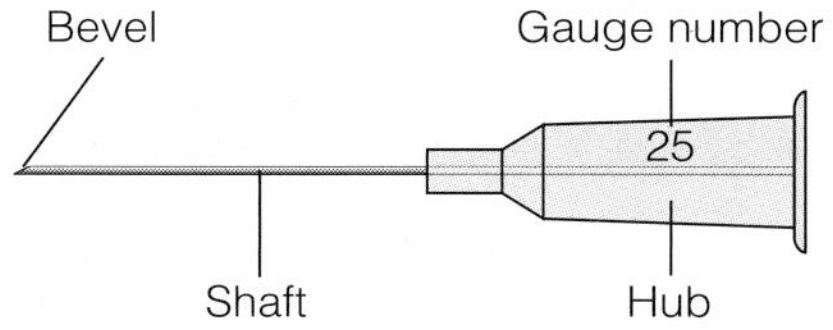

Figure 28.17 The parts of a needle

For an adult requiring a subcutaneous injection, it is usual to use a needle of #24 to #26 gauge and 3/8 to 5/8 inch long. Obese clients may require a 1-inch needle. For intramuscular injections, a longer needle (e.g., 1 to 1½ inches) with a larger gauge (e.g., #20 to #22 gauge) is used. Slender adults and children usually require a shorter needle. The nurse must assess the client to determine the appropriate needle length.

Preventing Needle-Stick Injuries

One of the most potentially hazardous procedures that health-care personnel face is using and disposing of needles and sharps. Needle-stick injuries present a major risk for infection with hepatitis B virus, human immunodeficiency virus (HIV), and many other pathogens. Standards have been set by the Canadian Centre for Occupational Health and Safety (http://www.ccohs.ca/oshanswers/diseases/needlestick_injuries.html#_1_5) to prevent such injuries. Some of these are summarized in the box on page 634. If an accidental needle-stick injury occurs, the nurse needs to follow specific steps outlined by the agency.

Safety syringes have been designed in recent years to protect health-care workers. Some systems have syringes with retractable needles that lock and seal inside the syringe barrel. Others have needles that can be sheathed in a plastic guard once the needle is withdrawn from the skin. A more recent needleless syringe (Biojector 2000) uses high-pressure carbon dioxide to penetrate the client's skin with medication, dispersing it in an area larger than a needle stick. Different syringe sizes can be used to control the depth of penetration so that either subcutaneous or intramuscular injections can be administered. For more information, see Martin, 1998. Needleless IV systems have also been developed. See "Intravenous Medications" later in this chapter.

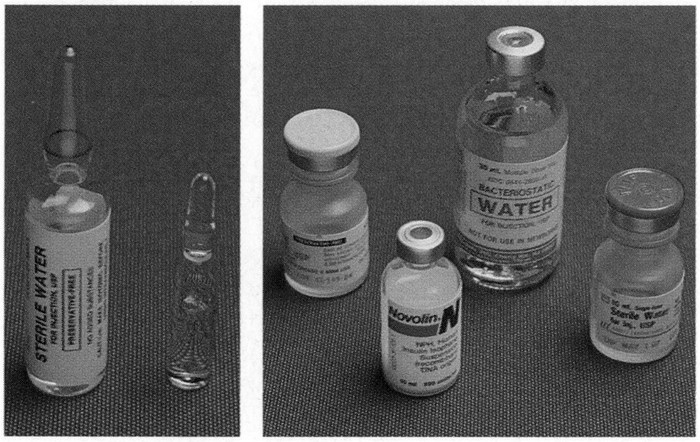

A **B**

Figure 28.18 *A,* ampules; *B,* vials

Preparing Injectable Medications

Injectable medications can be prepared by withdrawing the medication from an ampule or vial into a sterile syringe, by using prefilled syringes, or more recently by using needleless injection systems.

Ampules and Vials

Ampules and *vials* (Figure 28.18) are frequently used to package sterile parenteral medications. An **ampule** is a glass container usually designed to hold a single dose of a drug. It is made of clear glass and has a distinctive shape with a constricted neck. Ampules vary in size ranging from 1.0 mL to 10 mL or more. Most ampule necks have coloured marks around them, indicating where they are prescored for easy opening.

To access the medication in an ampule, the ampule must be broken at its constricted neck. Traditionally, files have been used to score the ampule. Today, *ampule openers* are available that prevent injury from broken glass. The device consists of a plastic cap that fits over the top of an ampule and a cutter within the cap that scores the neck of the ampule when rotated. The head of the ampule, when broken, remains inside the cap, so it can then be ejected into a sharps container. If an ampule opener is not available, the neck should be filed with a small file, then broken off at that point. Once the ampule is broken, the fluid is aspirated into a syringe.

A **vial** is a small glass bottle with a sealed rubber cap. Vials come in different sizes, from single to multidose vials. They usually have a metal or plastic cap that protects the rubber seal.

To access the medication in a vial, the vial must be pierced with a needle. In addition, air must be injected into a vial before the medication can be withdrawn. Failure to inject air before withdrawing the medication leaves a vacuum within the vial that makes withdrawal difficult.

Several drugs (e.g., penicillin) are dispensed as powders in vials. A liquid (solvent or diluent) must be added to a powdered medication before it can be injected. The technique of adding a solvent to a powdered drug to prepare it for administration is called **reconstitution.** Powdered drugs usually have printed instructions (enclosed with each packaged vial) that describe the amount and kind of solvent to be added. Commonly used solvents are sterile water or sterile normal saline. Some preparations are supplied in individual-dose vials; others come in multidose vials. The following are two examples of the preparation of powdered drugs:

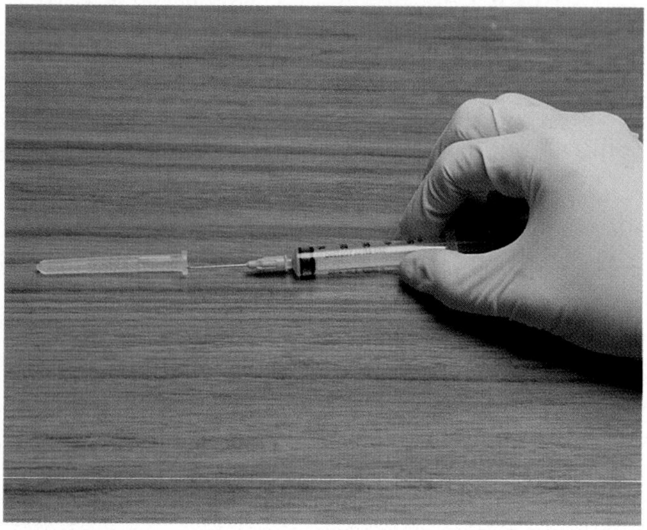

Figure 28.20 Recapping a used needle using the scoop method

- *Single-dose vial:* Instructions for preparing a single-dose vial instruct that 1.5 mL of sterile water be added to the sterile dry powder, thus providing a single dose of 2 mL. The volume of the drug powder was 0.5 mL. Therefore, the 1.5 mL of water plus the 0.5 mL of powder results in 2 mL of solution. In other instances, the addition of a solution does *not* increase the volume. Therefore, it is important to follow the manufacturer's directions.
- *Multidose vial:* A dose of 750 mg of a certain drug is ordered for a client. On hand is a 10-g multidose vial. The directions for preparation read: "Add 8.5 mL of sterile water, and each millilitre will contain 1.0 g or 1,000 mg." To determine the amount to inject, the nurse calculates as follows:

  amount to administer (x):

$$\frac{\text{desired dose}}{\text{dose on hand}} \times \text{quantity on hand}$$

$$x = \frac{750\text{ mg}}{1000\text{ mg}} \times 1\text{ mL}$$

$$= 0.75\text{ mL}$$

The nurse will give 0.75 mL of the medication.

Some researchers recommend that the nurse always use a **filter needle** when withdrawing medications from ampules and vials to prevent withdrawing glass and rubber particles (Beyea & Nicoll, 1995; Hahn, 1990; Keen, 1986; and McConnell, 1982). Glass and rubber particulate have been found in medications withdrawn with a regular needle. After drawing the medication into the syringe, the filter needle is replaced with the regular needle for injection. This prevents tracking of the medication through the client's tissues during the insertion of the needle, which, in turn, minimizes discomfort (Beyea & Nicoll, 1995).

Avoiding Puncture Injuries

- Use appropriate puncture-proof disposal containers to dispose of *uncapped* needles and sharps. These are provided in all client areas (Figure 28.19). Never throw sharps in wastebaskets. Sharps include any items that can cut or puncture skin, such as:
  - Needles
  - Surgical blades
  - Lancets
  - Razors
  - Broken glass
  - Broken capillary pipettes
  - Exposed dental wires
  - Reusable items (e.g., large-bore needles, hooks, rasps, drill points)
  - ANY SHARP INSTRUMENT!
- Never bend or break needles before disposal.
- Never recap used needles except under specified circumstances (e.g., when transporting a syringe to the laboratory for an arterial blood gas or blood culture).
- When recapping a needle:

  Use a safety mechanical device that firmly grips the needle cap and holds it in place until it is ready to recap.

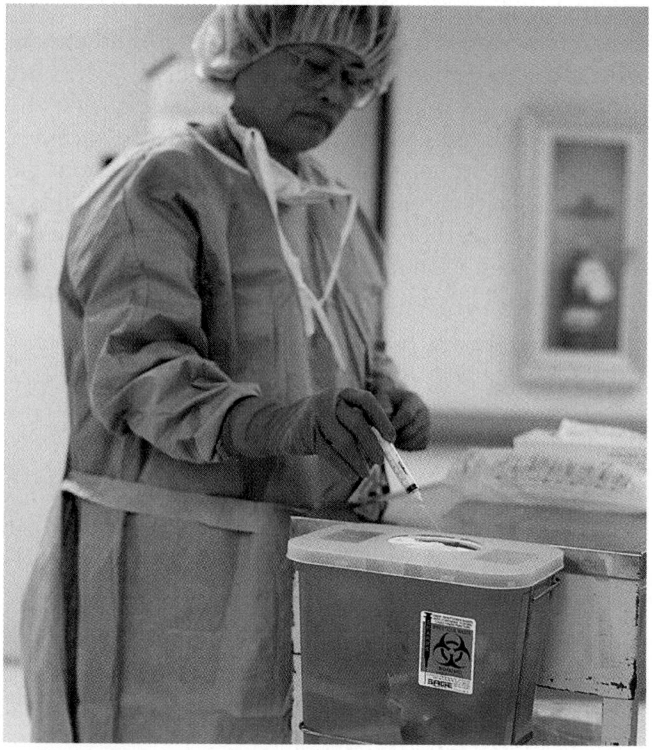

Figure 28.19 A disposal container for contaminated needles and other sharps

Precautions must also be taken with clients who have latex allergies. Multidose vials with rubber stoppers may contain latex; therefore, strict policies and procedures are in place to prevent cross-contamination and an allergic reaction in the client. Many agencies require the removal of the rubber stopper prior to drawing up of medications. Individual hospital policies must be adhered to.

Procedures 28.2 and 28.3 describe how to prepare medications from ampules and vials.

PROCEDURE 28.2 Preparing Medications from Ampules

Equipment

- ❑ MAR or computer printout
- ❑ Ampule of sterile medication
- ❑ File (if ampule is not scored) and small gauze square, or ampule opener
- ❑ Alcohol swabs
- ❑ Needle and syringe
- ❑ Filter needle (optional)

INTERVENTION

1. **Check the medication order, including drug administration, to ensure accuracy.**

- Check client allergies.
- Follow five rights of medication administration.
- Check the label on the ampule carefully against the MAR or client's chart to make sure that the correct medication is being prepared.
- Follow the three checks for administering medications. Read the label on the medication
  - a. before it is taken off the shelf,
  - b. before withdrawing the medication, and
  - c. after placing it back on the shelf.

2. **Prepare the medication ampule for drug withdrawal.**

- Flick the upper stem of the ampule several times with a fingernail or, holding the upper stem of the ampule, make a large circle with the arm extended. *This will bring all the medication down to the main portion of the ampule.*
- Partially file the neck of the ampule, if necessary, to start a clean break.
- Place a piece of sterile gauze between your thumb and the ampule neck or around the ampule neck, and break off the top by bending it toward you (Figure 28.21). *The sterile gauze protects the fingers from the broken glass and any glass fragments will spray away from the nurse.*

or

Place the antiseptic wipe packet over the top of the ampule before breaking off the top. *This method ensures that all the glass fragments fall into the packet and reduces the risk of cuts.*

- Dispose of the top of the ampule in the sharps container.

3. **Withdraw the medication.**

- Place the ampule on a flat surface.
- If using a filter needle to withdraw the medication, disconnect the regular needle, leaving its cap on, and attach the filter needle to the syringe. *The filter needle prevents glass particles from being withdrawn with the medication.*
- Remove the cap from the filter needle and insert the needle into the centre of the ampule. Do not touch the rim of the ampule with the needle tip or shaft. *This will keep the needle sterile.* Withdraw the amount of drug required for the dosage.
- With a single-dose ampule, hold the ampule slightly on its side, if necessary, to obtain all the medication. (Figure 28.22).
- If a filter needle was used to withdraw the medication, replace it with a regular needle and tighten the cap at the hub of the needle before injecting the client.
- If a filter needle was not used, recap the needle.

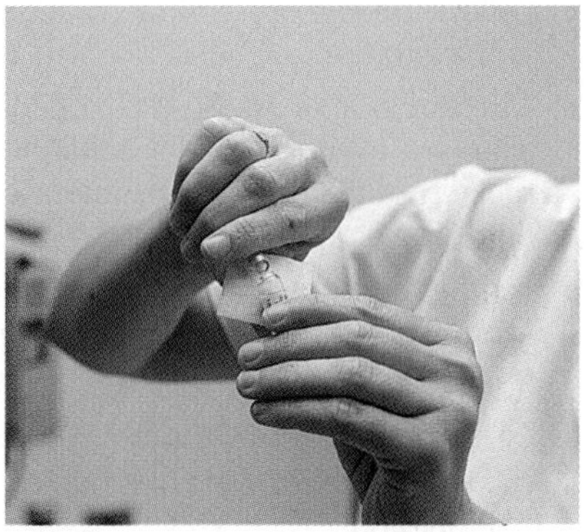

Figure 28.21 Breaking the neck of an ampule

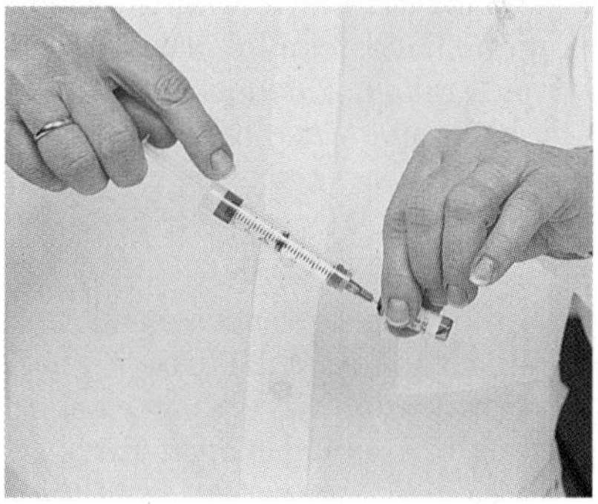

Figure 28.22 Withdrawing a medication from an ampule

PROCEDURE 28.3 Preparing Medications from Vials

Equipment

- ❑ MAR or computer printout
- ❑ Vial of sterile medication
- ❑ Alcohol swabs
- ❑ Needle and syringe
- ❑ Filter needle (optional)
- ❑ Sterile water or normal saline, if drug is in powdered form

INTERVENTION

1. Check the medication order, including drug administration, to ensure accuracy.

- Check client allegies.
- Follow the five rights of medication administration.
- Check the label on the vial carefully against the MAR or client's chart to make sure that the correct medication is being prepared.
- Follow the three checks for administering medications. Read the label on the medication
  - a. before it is taken off the shelf,
  - b. before withdrawing the medication, and
  - c. after placing it back on the shelf.

2. Prepare the medication vial for drug withdrawal.

- Mix the solution, if necessary, by rotating the vial between the palms of the hands, not by shaking. *Some vials contain aqueous suspensions which settle when they stand. In some instances, shaking is contraindicated because it may cause the mixture to foam.*
- Remove the protective metal cap, and clean the rubber cap of a previously opened vial with an alcohol swab by rubbing in a circular motion. *The antiseptic cleans the cap of dust or grease and reduces the number of microorganisms.*

3. Withdraw the medication.

- Attach a filter needle as agency practice dictates to draw up premixed liquid medications from multidose vials. *The filter prevents any solid particles from being drawn up through the needle.*
- Ensure that the needle is firmly attached to the syringe.
- Remove the cap from the needle; then draw up into the syringe the amount of air equal to the volume of the medication to be withdrawn.
- Carefully insert the needle into the upright vial through the centre of the rubber cap, maintaining the sterility of the needle.
- Inject the air into the vial, keeping the bevel of the needle above the surface of the medication (Figure 28.23). *The air will allow the medication to be drawn out easily because negative pressure will not be created inside the vial. The bevel is kept above the medication to avoid creating bubbles in the medication.*

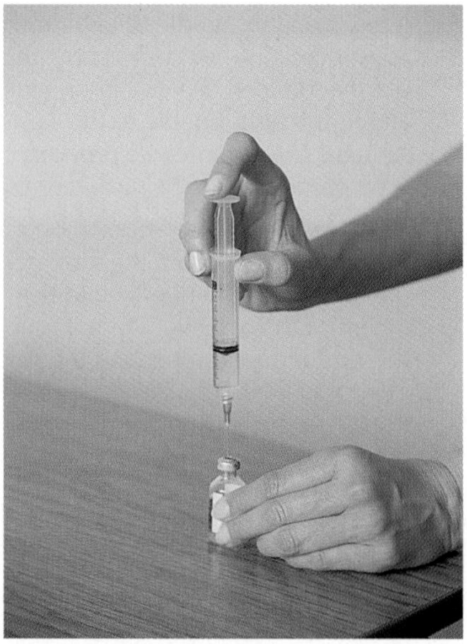

Figure 28.23 Injecting air into a vial

- Withdraw the prescribed amount of medication using *either* of the following methods:
  - a. Hold the vial down (i.e., with the base lower than the top); move the needle tip so that it is below the fluid level; and withdraw the medication (Figure 28.24). Avoid drawing up the last drops of the vial. *Proponents of this method say that keeping the vial in the upright position while withdrawing the medication allows particulate matter to precipitate out of the solution. Leaving the last few drops reduces the chance of withdrawing foreign particles* (Beyea & Nicoll, 1995).

    or
  - b. Invert the vial; ensure the needle tip is below the fluid level; and gradually withdraw the medication (Figure 28.25). *Keeping the tip of the needle below the fluid level prevents air from being drawn into the syringe.*
- Hold the syringe and vial at eye level to *determine that the correct dosage of drug is drawn into the syringe.* Eject air remaining at the top of the syringe into the vial.
- When the correct volume of medication is obtained, withdraw the needle from the vial, and replace the cap over the needle, thus maintaining its sterility.
- If necessary, tap the syringe barrel to dislodge any air bubbles present in the syringe. *The tapping motion will cause the air bubbles to rise to the top of the syringe where they can be ejected out of the syringe.*
- Replace the filter needle, if used, with a regular needle of the correct gauge and length before injecting the client.

PROCEDURE 28.3 Preparing Medications from Vials *continued*

Variation: Preparing and Using Multidose Vials

- Read the manufacturer's directions.
- Withdraw an equivalent amount of air from the vial before adding the solvent, unless otherwise indicated by the directions.
- Add the amount of sterile water or saline indicated in the directions.
- If a multidose vial is reconstituted, label the vial with the date and time it was prepared, type and amount of solvent added, the amount of drug contained in each millilitre of solution, and your initials. *Time is an important factor to consider in the expiration of these medications.*
- Once the medication is reconstituted, store it in a refrigerator or as recommended by the manufacturer.

Changing the Needle

It may be necessary to change the needle once the medication has been drawn from the vial so as not to deposit the medication at the injection site. This may be indicated by agency policy or by type of medication being administered. This prevents tracking of the medication through the client's tissues during insertion of the needle.

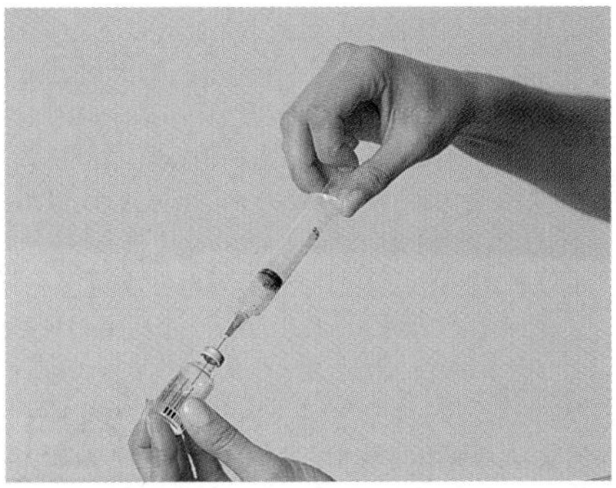

Figure 28.24 Withdrawing a medication from a vial that is held with the base down

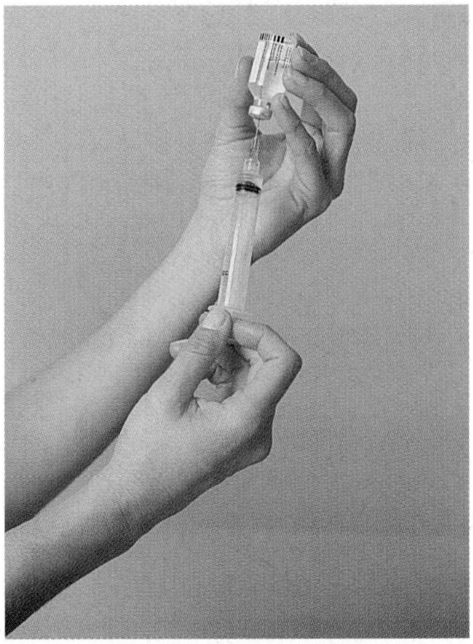

Figure 28.25 Withdrawing a medication from an inverted vial

Mixing Medications in One Syringe

Frequently, clients need more than one drug injected at the same time. To spare the client the experience of being injected twice, two drugs (if compatible) are often mixed together in one syringe and given as one injection. It is common, for instance, to combine two types of insulin in this manner or to combine injectable preoperative medications, such as morphine or meperidine (Demerol) with atropine or scopolamine. Drugs can also be mixed in intravenous solutions. The nurse should consult a pharmacist or check a compatibility chart before mixing the drugs.

The nurse should check agency policy regarding mixing of insulins in the same syringe.

Procedure 28.4 describes how to mix medications in one syringe.

PROCEDURE 28.4 Mixing Medications Using One Syringe

Equipment

- ❑ MAR or computer printout
- ❑ Two vials of medication, or one vial and one ampule, or two ampules, or one vial or ampule and one cartridge
- ❑ Alcohol swabs
- ❑ Sterile hypodermic or insulin syringe and needle (if insulin is being given, use a small-gauge hypodermic needle, e.g., #26 gauge)
- ❑ Additional sterile subcutaneous or intramuscular needle (optional)

PROCEDURE 28.4 Mixing Medications Using One Syringe *continued*

INTERVENTION

1. Check the medication.

- Follow the five rights of medication administration.
- Confirm the compatibility of the drugs being mixed. Consult a pharmacist if required.
- Check client allergies.
- Check the label on the ampule or vial carefully against the MAR or client's chart to make sure that the correct medication is being prepared.
- Follow the three checks for administering medications. Read the label on the medication (1) when you first pick up the medication, (2) before withdrawing the medication, and (3) when replacing it.
- Before preparing and combining the medications, ensure that the total volume of the injection is appropriate for the injection route site.

2. Prepare the medication ampule or vial for drug withdrawal.

- See Procedure 28.2, step 2, for an ampule.
- Inspect the appearance of the medication for clarity. Some medications are always cloudy. *Preparations that have changed in appearance should be discarded.*
- If using insulin, thoroughly mix the solution in each vial prior to administration. Rotate the vials between the palms of the hands and invert the vials. *Mixing ensures an adequate concentration and thus an accurate dose. Shaking insulin vials can make the medication frothy, making precise measurement difficult.*
- Clean the tops of the vials with alcohol swabs.

3. Withdraw the medications.

MIXING MEDICATIONS FROM TWO VIALS

- Withdraw a volume of air equal to the volume of medication to be withdrawn from vial A. Inject this into vial A. Withdraw the needle.
- Withdraw a volume of air equal to the volume of medication to be withdrawn from volume B. Inject this into vial B.
- Withdraw the required amount of medication from vial B. *The same needle is used to inject air into and withdraw medication from the second vial. It must not be contaminated with the medication in vial A.*
- Using a newly attached sterile needle, withdraw the required amount of medication from vial A. If using a syringe with a fused needle, withdraw the medication from vial A. The syringe now contains a mixture of medications from vials A and B. *With this method, neither vial is contaminated by microorganisms or by medication from the other vial.*

MIXING MEDICATIONS FROM ONE VIAL AND ONE AMPULE

- First prepare and withdraw the medication from the vial. *Ampules do not require the addition of air prior to withdrawal of the drug.*
- Then withdraw the required amount of medication from the ampule.

MIXING MEDICATIONS FROM ONE CARTRIDGE AND ONE VIAL OR AMPULE

- First ensure that the correct dose of the medication is in the cartridge. Discard any excess medication and air.
- Draw up the required medication from a vial or ampule into the cartridge. Note that when withdrawing medication from a vial, an equal amount of air must first be injected into the vial.
- If the total volume to be injected exceeds the capacity of the cartridge, use a syringe with sufficient capacity to withdraw the desired amount of medication from the vial or ampule, and transfer the required amount from the cartridge to the syringe.

Mixing Insulins

Figure 28.26 is an example of mixing regular insulin, which is clear, with NPH (neutral protamine Hagedorn) insulin, which is cloudy. You should always withdraw the regular insulin first to prevent contamination by the NPH insulin. The nurse should check agency policy regarding mixing of insulins in the same syringe.

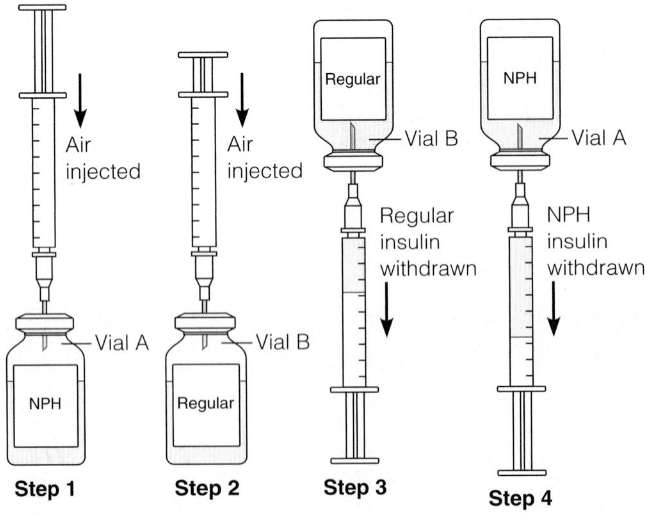

Figure 28.26 Mixing intermediate- and short-acting insulin together

Intradermal Injections

An **intradermal** injection is the administration of a drug into the dermal layer of the skin just beneath the epidermis. Usually, only a small amount of drug is injected (e.g., 0.1 mL). This method of administration is frequently indicated for allergy and tuberculin tests and for vaccinations. Common sites for intradermal injections are the flexor aspect of the forearm, the upper chest, and the back beneath the scapulae (Figure 28.27).

The equipment normally used is a 1-mL syringe calibrated into hundredths of a millilitre. The needle is short ($^1/_2$ to $^5/_8$ inch long) and frequently a #25, #26, or #27 gauge is used. After the site is cleaned, the skin is held taut, and the syringe is held at about a 15-degree angle to the skin with the bevel of the needle upward. The needle is then inserted through the epidermis into the dermis, and the fluid is injected. The drug produces a small bleb just under the skin (Figure 28.28). The needle is then withdrawn quickly, and the site is lightly wiped with an alcohol swab. The area is not massaged because the medication may disperse into the tissue or out through the needle insertion site. Intradermal injections are absorbed slowly through blood capillaries in the area.

Subcutaneous Injections

Vaccines, preoperative medications, narcotics, insulin, and heparin are examples of drugs administered **subcutaneously** (just beneath the skin). Common sites for subcutaneous (SC) injections are the outer aspect of the upper arms and the anterior aspect of the thighs. These areas are convenient and normally have good blood circulation. Other areas that can be used are the abdomen, the scapular areas of the upper back, and the upper ventrogluteal and dorsogluteal areas (Figure 28.29). Only small doses (0.5 to 1 mL) of medication are usually injected via the subcutaneous route.

The type of syringe for subcutaneous injections depends on the medication to be given. Generally a 2-mL syringe is used for most SC injections. However, if insulin is being

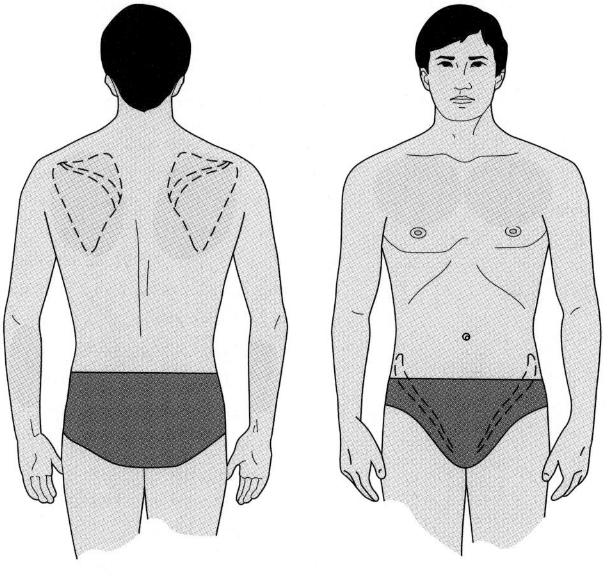

Figure 28.27 Body sites commonly used for intradermal injections

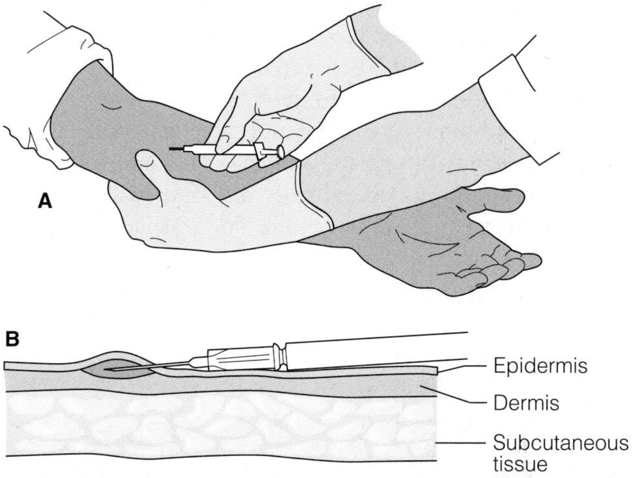

Figure 28.28 For an intradermal injection: *A,* the needle enters the skin at a 15-degree angle; and *B,* the medication forms a bleb under the epidermis

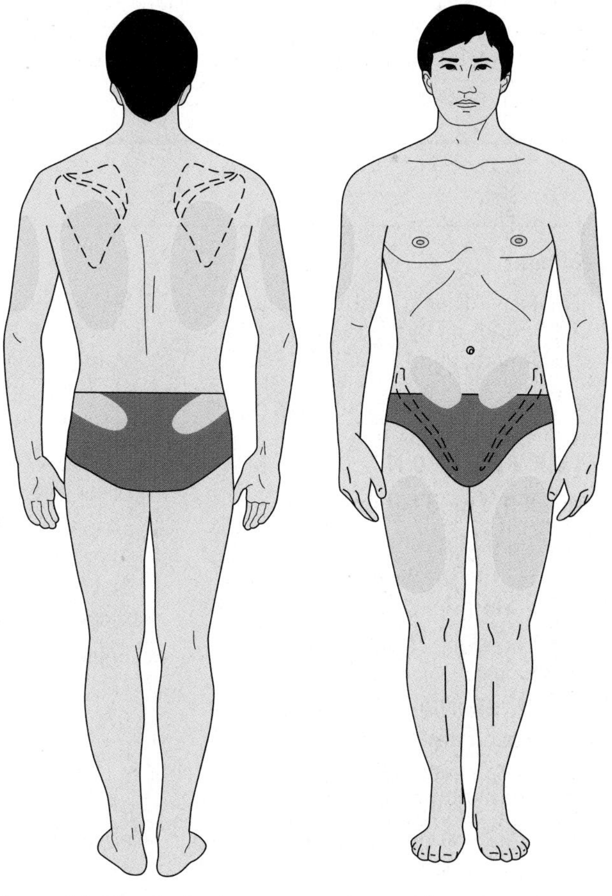

Figure 28.29 Body sites commonly used for subcutaneous injections

administered, an insulin syringe is used; and if heparin is being administered, a tuberculin syringe or prefilled cartridge may be used.

Needle sizes and lengths are selected based on the client's body mass, the intended angle of insertion, and the planned site. Generally, a #25-gauge, $^5/_8$-inch needle is used for adults of normal weight and the needle is inserted at a 45-degree angle; a $^3/_8$-inch needle is used at a 90-degree angle. A child may need a $^1/_2$-inch needle inserted at a 45-degree angle.

One method nurses use to determine length of needle is to pinch the tissue at the site and select a needle length that is half the width of the skinfold. To determine the angle of insertion, a general rule to follow relates to the amount of tissue that can be bunched or grasped at the site. A 45-degree angle is used when 2.5 cm of tissue can be grasped at the site; a 90-degree angle is used when 5 cm of tissue can be grasped.

For administering insulin to adults, the Canadian Diabetes Association recommends that a small-gauge needle is used (e.g., #28) to minimize tissue injury and subcutaneous leakage. Unless otherwise indicated, the insulin should be injected at a 90-degree angle.

Subcutaneous injection sites need to be systematically rotated to minimize tissue damage, aid absorption, and avoid discomfort. This is especially important for insulin-dependent diabetics who must receive repeated injections. Insulin can be absorbed at different rates depending on the injection site chosen. The blood glucose level of the client with diabetes may fluctuate slightly depending on the injection site.

It is recommended that different sites be used for self-injection of insulin (e.g., lateral aspect of upper arm, anterior and lateral thighs, and abdomen).

The steps for administering a subcutaneous injection are described in Procedure 28.5.

PROCEDURE 28.5 Administering a Subcutaneous Injection

PURPOSES

- To provide a medication the client requires (see specific drug action)
- To allow slower absorption of a medication compared with either the intramuscular or intravenous route

Assessment Focus
Allergies to medication; specific drug action; side effects and adverse reactions; client's knowledge and learning needs about the medication; status and appearance of subcutaneous site for lesions, erythema, swelling, ecchymosis, inflammation, and tissue damage from previous injections; ability to cooperate during the injection; and previous injection sites used

Equipment

- ❑ Client's MAR or computer printout
- ❑ Vial or ampule of the correct sterile medication
- ❑ Syringe and needle (e.g., 2-mL syringe, #25-gauge needle, $^3/_8$ or $^5/_8$ inch long)
- ❑ Alcohol swabs
- ❑ Dry sterile gauze for opening an ampule (optional)
- ❑ Disposable gloves

INTERVENTION

1. Check the medication order.

- See Procedure 28.2, step 1.

2. Prepare the medication from the vial or ampule.

- See Procedure 28.2 (ampule) or 28.3 (vial).

3. Identify the client, and assist the client to a comfortable position.

- Check the client's identification band and ask the client's name.
- Depending on the site to be used, assist the client to a position in which the arm, leg, or abdomen can be relaxed. *A relaxed position of the site minimizes discomfort.*
- Obtain assistance in holding an uncooperative client or small child. *This prevents injury due to sudden movement after needle insertion.*

4. Select and clean the site.

- Select a site that has not been used frequently and is free of tenderness, hardness, swelling, scarring, itching, burning, or localized inflammation. *These conditions could hinder the absorption of the medication and also increase the likelihood of injury and discomfort at the injection site.*
- Clean the site with an alcohol swab. Clean the site according to agency policy (e.g., insulin sites). Start at the centre of the site and clean in a widening circle to about 5 cm. Allow the area to dry thoroughly. *The mechanical action of swabbing removes skin secretions, which contain microorganisms.*
- Place and hold a clean swab between the third and fourth fingers of the nondominant hand, or position the swab on the client's skin above the intended site. *Doing so keeps the swab readily accessible when the needle is withdrawn.*

PROCEDURE 28.5 Administering a Subcutaneous Injection *continued*

5. Prepare the syringe for injection.

- Remove the needle cap while waiting for the alcohol to dry. Pull the cap straight off to avoid contaminating the needle by the outside edge of the cap. *The needle will become contaminated if it touches anything but the inside of the sterile cap.*
- Confirm that the medication and the dosage are both correct.
- Don gloves if agency policy requires.

6. Inject the medication.

- Grasp the syringe in your dominant hand by holding it between your thumb and fingers. Prepare to inject at a 90-degree angle (Figure 28.30).

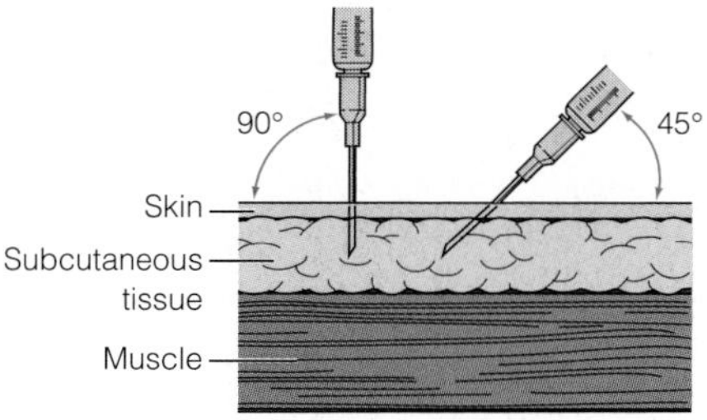

Figure 28.30 Inserting a needle into the subcutaneous tissue at a 90-degree angle

- Insert the needle with the dominant hand and use a firm steady push (Figure 28.31). The nondominant hand can be used to immobilize the extremity of an infant or a young child as the needle is inserted. Recommendations vary about whether to pinch or spread the skin and at what angle to administer subcutaneous injections. The most important consideration is the depth of the subcutaneous tissue in the area to be injected. If the client has more than $1/2$ inch of adipose tissue in the injection site, it would be safe to administer the injection at a 90-degree angle with the skin spread. If the client is thin and lacks adipose tissue, the subcutaneous injection should be given with the skin pinched and at a 45- to 60-degree angle (Thow & Holme, 1990).
- When the needle is inserted, move your nondominant hand to the end of the plunger. Some nurses find it easier to move the nondominant hand to the barrel of the syringe and the dominant hand to the end of the plunger. If the nondominant hand is holding the extremity of an infant or small child, use the dominant hand to aspirate and inject the medication.

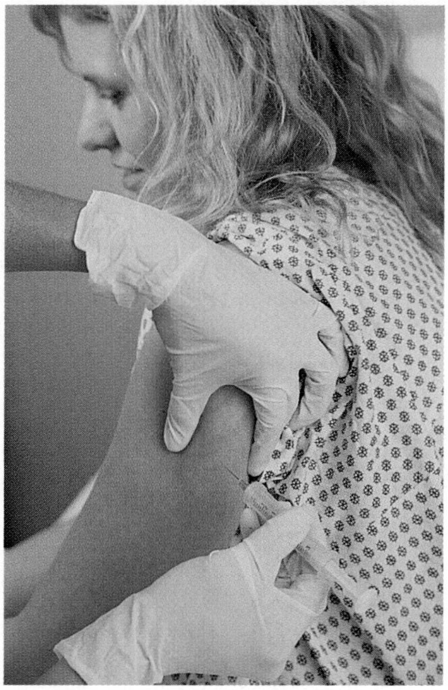

Figure 28.31 Administering a subcutaneous injection

- Aspirate by pulling back on the plunger. If blood appears in the syringe, withdraw the needle, discard the syringe, and prepare a new injection. The appearance of blood indicates that the needle is in a blood vessel. If blood does not appear, continue to administer the medication. *Subcutaneous medications may be dangerous if injected directly into the bloodstream; they are intended for the subcutaneous tissues where the absorption time is greater.* See variation for administering a heparin injection.
- Inject the medication by holding the syringe steady and depressing the plunger with a slow, even pressure. *Holding the syringe steady and injecting the medication at an even pressure minimizes discomfort for the client.*

7. Remove the needle.

- Remove the needle slowly and smoothly, pulling along the line of insertion while depressing the skin with your nondominant hand. *Depressing the skin places countertraction on it and minimizes the client's discomfort when the needle is withdrawn.*
- If bleeding occurs, apply pressure to the site with dry sterile gauze until it stops. Bleeding rarely occurs after subcutaneous injection.

8. Dispose of supplies appropriately.

- Discard the uncapped needle and attached syringe into designated receptacles. *Proper disposal protects the nurse and others from injury and contamination. The Centers for Disease Control (in the United States) recommend not capping the needle before disposal to reduce the risk of needle-stick injuries.*
- Remove gloves. Wash hands.

9. Document all relevant information.

- Document the medication given, dosage, time, route, any assessments, and add your signature.
- Many agencies prefer that medication administration be recorded on the medication record. The nurse's notes are used when prn medications are given or when there is a problem.

10. Assess the effectiveness of the medication at the time it is expected to act.

Variation: Administering a Heparin Injection

The subcutaneous administration of heparin requires special precautions because of the drug's anticoagulant properties.

- Select a site on the abdomen away from the umbilicus and above the level of the iliac crests and below the lower rib cage. Some agencies support the practice of subcutaneous injection of heparin in the thighs or arms as alternate sites to the abdomen.

PROCEDURE 28.5 Administering a Subcutaneous Injection *continued*

- Use a $^3/_8$-inch, #25- or #26-gauge needle, and insert it at a 90-degree angle. If a client is very lean or wasted, use a needle longer than $^3/_8$ inch, and insert it at a 45-degree angle. The arms or thighs may be used as alternate sites.
- Do not aspirate when giving heparin by subcutaneous injection. *Aspiration can possibly damage the surrounding tissue and cause bleeding as well as bruising.*
- Do not massage the site after the injection. *Massaging could cause bleeding and ecchymoses and hasten drug absorption.*
- Alternate the sites of subsequent injections.

Evaluation Focus
Desired effect (e.g., relief of pain, sedation, lowered blood sugar or decreased urine glucose, a prothrombin time within pre-established limits); any adverse effects (e.g., nausea, vomiting, skin rash); clinical signs of side effects

Home Care Considerations

- If the client has impaired vision, consider prefilling syringes and storing them in an appropriate environment (e.g., the refrigerator).
- For frequent injections, develop a plan with the client for site rotation.
- Advise clients to avoid using dull or damaged needles.
- For insulin-dependent clients, ensure that at least one knowledgeable support person can correctly inject insulin in an emergency situation and recognize and treat hypoglycemia.

Intramuscular Injections

Injections into muscle tissue (**intramuscular** injections) are absorbed more quickly than subcutaneous injections because muscles have a more extensive blood supply. Muscles can also take a larger volume of fluid without discomfort than subcutaneous tissues can, although the amount varies among individuals, chiefly with muscle size and condition and with the site used. An adult with well-developed muscles can usually safely tolerate up to 3 mL of medication in the gluteus medius, gluteus maximus, and ventrogluteal muscles (Figure 28.32). A volume of 1 to 2 mL is usually recommended for adults with less developed muscles. Volumes of 0.5 to 1 mL are recommended for the deltoid muscle (Beyea & Nicoll, 1995).

Depending on the amount of medication to be administered, usually 2- or 3-mL syringes are used for an intramuscular injection. The standard prepackaged intramuscular needle is 1 inch and #21 or #22 gauge. Several factors indicate the size and length of the needle to be used: the muscle, the type of solution, the amount of adipose tissue covering the muscle, and the age of the client. For example, a smaller needle, such as a #23- to #25- gauge needle, 1 inch long is commonly used for the deltoid muscle. More viscous solutions require a larger gauge (e.g., #20 gauge). Very obese clients may require a needle longer than $1^1/_2$ inches (e.g., 2 inches), and emaciated clients may require a shorter needle (e.g., $^5/_8$ inch). Infants and young children usually require smaller, shorter needles (#22 to #25 gauge, $^5/_8$ to 1 inch long).

A major consideration in the administration of intramuscular injections is the selection of a safe site located away from large blood vessels, nerves, and bone.

Several body sites can be used for intramuscular injections. The preferred site is the *ventrogluteal site*, but this site cannot be used for children under seven months of age. The *vastus lateralis site* is the preferred site for children under seven months. When these sites are contraindicated, alternative sites, such as the *dorsogluteal*, *deltoid*, and *rectus femoris*, may be used. These sites are discussed in detail below. Contraindications for using a specific site include tissue injury, and presence of nodules, lumps, abscesses, tenderness, or other pathology.

Ventrogluteal Site

The ventrogluteal site, also known as von Hochsteter's site, is in the gluteus medius muscle, which lies over the gluteus minimus (see Figure 28.32). The ventrogluteal site is the *preferred* site for intramuscular injections because the area (1) contains no large nerves or blood vessels; (2) provides the greatest thickness of gluteal muscle consisting of both the gluteus medius and gluteus minimus; (3) is sealed off by bone; and (4) contains consistently less fat

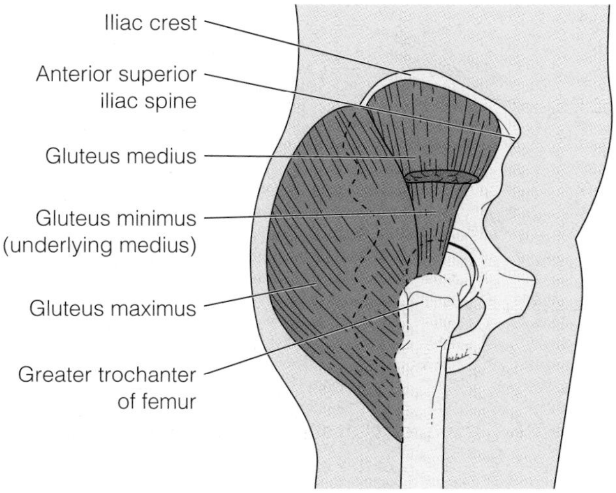

Figure 28.32 Lateral view of the right buttock showing the three gluteal muscles used for intramuscular injections

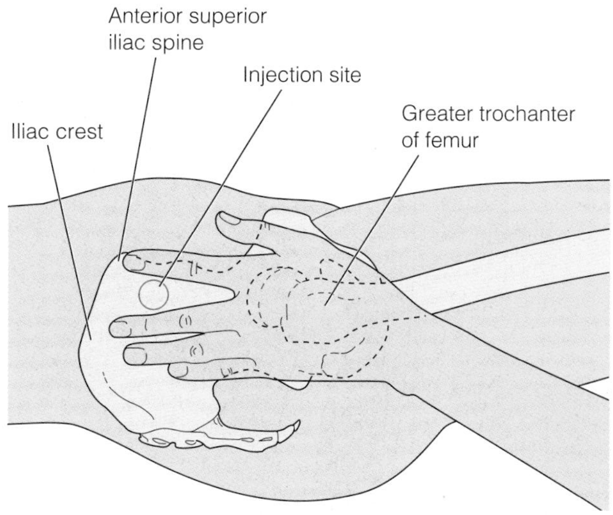

Figure 28.33 The ventrogluteal site for an intramuscular injection

than the buttock area, thus eliminating the need to determine the depth of subcutaneous fat.

The ventrogluteal site is suitable for children over seven months (Beyea & Nicoll, 1996). The client position for the injection can be a supine, prone, or side-lying position. To establish the exact site, the nurse places the heel of the hand on the client's greater trochanter, with the fingers pointing toward the client's head. The right hand is used for the left hip, and the left hand for the right hip. With the index finger on the client's anterior superior iliac spine, the nurse stretches the middle finger dorsally (pointing to the client's head), palpating the iliac crest and then pressing below it. The triangle formed by the index finger, the middle finger, and the iliac crest demarcates the injection site (Figure 28.33).

Vastus Lateralis Site

The vastus lateralis muscle is usually thick and well developed in both adults and children. It is recommended as the site of choice for intramuscular injections for infants seven months and younger by the American Academy of Pediatrics (1986). Because there are no major blood vessels or nerves in the area, it is desirable for infants whose gluteal muscles are poorly developed. It is situated on the anterior lateral aspect of the thigh (Figure 28.34). The middle third of the muscle is suggested as the site. It is established by dividing the area between the greater trochanter of the femur and the lateral femoral condyle into thirds and selecting the middle third (Figure 28.35). The client can assume a supine or a sitting position for an injection into this site.

Dorsogluteal Site

The dorsogluteal site is composed of the thick gluteal muscles of the buttocks (see Figure 28.32). The dorsogluteal site can be used for adults and for children with well-developed gluteal muscles. Because these muscles are developed by walking, this site should not be used for children under three years unless the child has been walking for at least one year. The nurse must choose the injection site carefully to avoid striking the sciatic nerve, major blood vessels, or bone. This site is recommended only when all other IM sites are contraindicated.

The nurse palpates the posterior superior iliac spine, then draws an imaginary line to the greater trochanter of the femur. This line is lateral to and parallel to the sciatic nerve. The injection site is, then, lateral and superior to this line (Figure 28.36). Palpating the ilium and the trochanter is important; visual calculations alone can result in an injection that is placed too low and injures other structures.

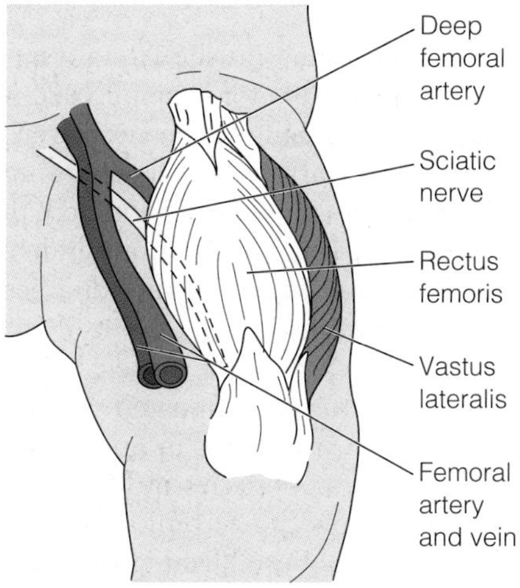

Figure 28.34 The vastus lateralis muscle of the upper thigh, used for intramuscular injections

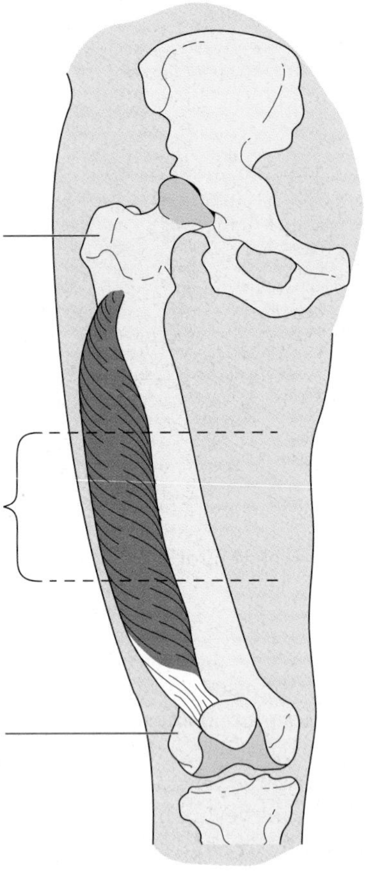

Figure 28.35 The vastus lateralis site of the right thigh, used for an intramuscular injection

The client needs to assume a prone position with the toes pointed inward, or a side-lying position with the upper knee flexed and in front of the lower leg. These positions promote muscle relaxation and, therefore, minimize discomfort from the injection.

Deltoid Site

The deltoid muscle is found on the lateral aspect of the upper arm. It is not used often for intramuscular injections because it is a relatively small muscle and is very close to the radial nerve and radial artery. It is sometimes considered for use in adults because of rapid absorption from the deltoid area, but no more than 1 mL of solution can be administered. This site is recommended for the administration of hepatitis B vaccine in adults.

To locate the densest part of the muscle, the nurse palpates the lower edge of the acromion and the midpoint on the lateral aspect of the arm that is in line with the axilla. A triangle within these boundaries indicates the deltoid muscle about 5 cm below the acromion process (Figure 28.37). Another method of establishing the deltoid site is to place four fingers across the deltoid muscle, with the first finger on the acromion process; the site is three finger breadths below the acromion process (Figure 28.38).

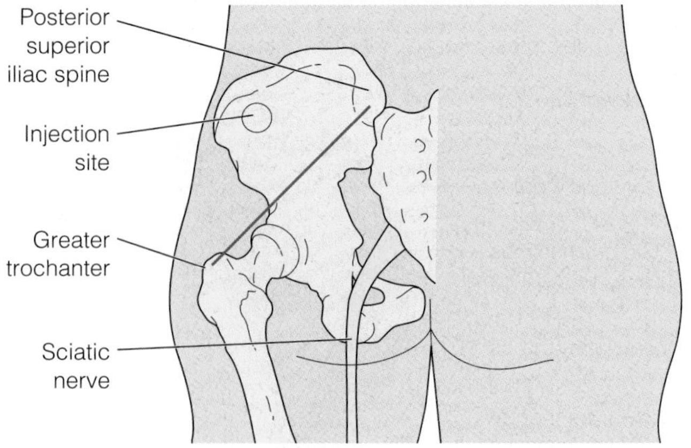

Figure 28.36 The dorsogluteal site for an intramuscular injection

Rectus Femoris Site

The rectus femoris muscle, which belongs to the quadriceps muscle group, is used only occasionally for intramuscular injections. It is situated on the anterior aspect of the thigh (Figure 28.39). Its chief advantage is that clients who administer their own injections can reach this site easily. Its main disadvantage is that an injection here may cause considerable discomfort for some people.

IM Injection Technique

Procedure 28.6 describes how to administer an intramuscular injection using the Z-track technique, which is recommended for some intramuscular injections (Beyea & Nicoll, 1995).

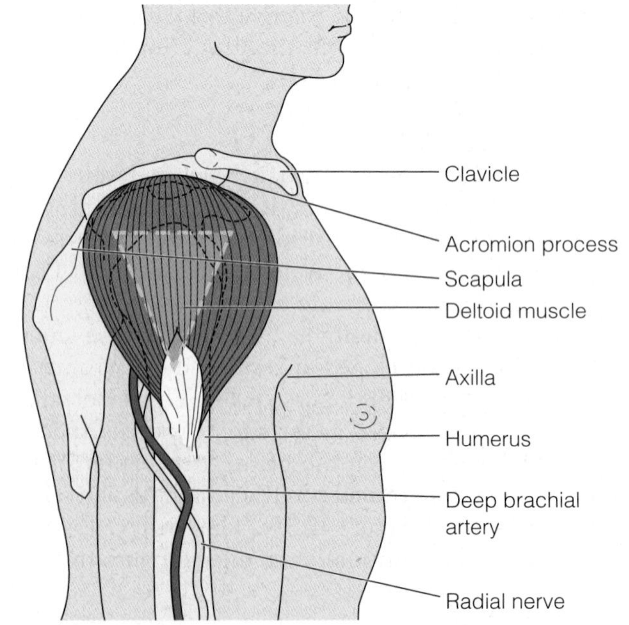

Figure 28.37 The deltoid muscle of the upper arm, used for intramuscular injections

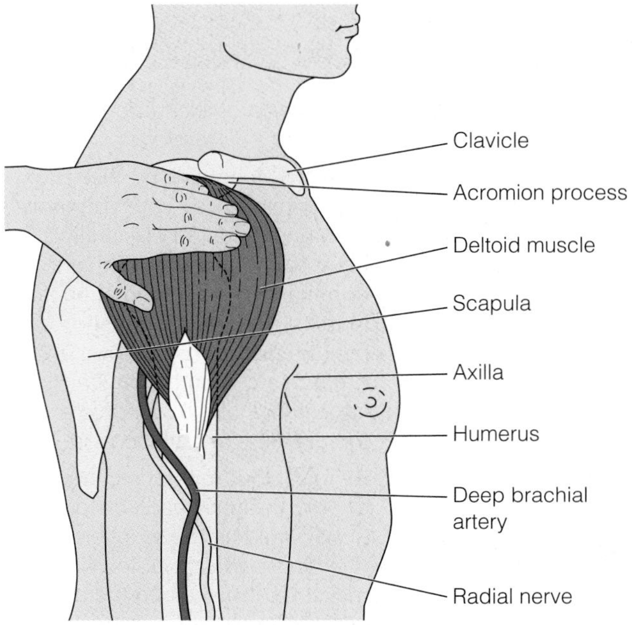

Figure 28.38 A method of establishing the deltoid muscle site for an intramuscular injection

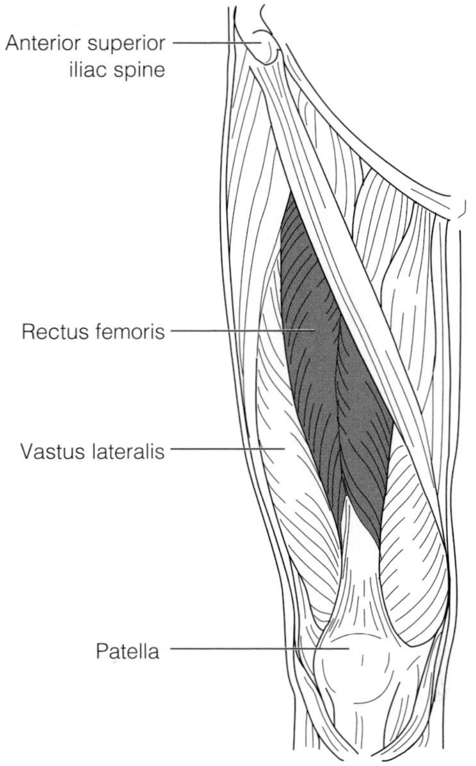

Figure 28.39 The rectus femoris muscle of the upper right thigh, used for intramuscular injections

PROCEDURE 28.6 Administering an Intramuscular Injection

PURPOSE

- To provide a medication the client requires (see specific drug action)

Assessment Focus
Allergies to medication(s); specific drug action, side effects, and adverse reactions; client's knowledge of and learning needs about the medication; tissue integrity of the selected site; client's age and weight to determine site and needle size; client's ability or willingness to cooperate

Equipment

- ❑ MAR or computer printout
- ❑ Sterile medication (usually provided in an ampule or vial)
- ❑ Syringe and needle of a size appropriate for the amount of solution to be administered
- ❑ Alcohol swabs
- ❑ Disposable gloves

INTERVENTION

1. Check the medication order for accuracy.

- See Procedure 28.2, step 1.

2. Prepare the medication from the vial or ampule.

- See Procedure 28.2 (ampule) or 28.3 (vial).
- Whenever feasible, change the needle on the syringe before the injection. Note that the needle must be changed for certain medications. *Because the outside of a new needle is free of medication, it does not irritate subcutaneous tissues as it passes into the muscle.*
- Invert the syringe needle and expel all excess air.

→

PROCEDURE 28.6 Administering an Intramuscular Injection *continued*

3. Identify the client, and assist the client to a comfortable position.

- Check the client's arm band, and ask the client's name.
- Assist the client to a supine, lateral, prone, or sitting position, depending on the chosen site. If the target muscle is the gluteus medius (ventrogluteal site), have the client in the supine position flex the knee(s); in the lateral position, flex the upper leg; and in the prone position, "toe in." *Appropriate positioning promotes relaxation of the target muscle.*
- Obtain assistance to immobilize an infant or young child. The parent may hold the infant or young child. *This prevents accidental injury during the procedure.*

4. Select, locate, and clean the site.

- Wash hands.
- Select a site free of skin lesions, tenderness, swelling, hardness, or localized inflammation and one that has not been used frequently.
- If injections are to be frequent, alternate sites. If necessary, discuss with the prescribing physician an alternative method of providing the medication. Check agency policy about rotating sites.
- Determine whether the size of the muscle is appropriate to the amount of medication to be injected. An average adult's deltoid muscle can usually absorb 0.5 mL of medication, although some authorities believe 1 mL can be absorbed by a well-developed deltoid muscle. The gluteus medius muscle can often absorb 1 to 3 mL, although 3 mL may be very painful.
- Locate the exact site for the injection. See the discussion of sites earlier in this chapter.
- Don gloves if agency policy requires.
- Clean the site with an alcohol swab. Using a circular motion, start at the centre and move outward about 5 cm.
- Hold a clean swab between the third and fourth fingers of your nondominant hand in readiness for needle withdrawal, or position the swab on the client's skin above the intended site. Allow skin to dry prior to injecting medication.

5. Prepare the syringe for injection.

- Remove the needle cover without contaminating the needle.
- Confirm that the medication, the dose, time, and route are correct.
- If using a prefilled unit-dose medication, take caution to avoid dripping medication on the needle prior to injection. If this does occur, change needles if possible. *Medication left on the needle can cause pain when it is tracked through the subcutaneous tissue.*

6. Inject the medication using the Z-track technique.

- Use the nondominant hand to pull the skin laterally and downward approximately 2.5 cm (1 inch) at the site (Figure 28.40). Under some circumstances, such as for an emaciated client or an infant, the muscle may be pinched. *Pulling the skin and subcutaneous tissue or pinching the muscle makes it firmer and facilitates needle insertion.*
- Holding the syringe between the thumb and forefinger (as if holding a pencil), pierce the skin quickly at a 90-degree angle (Figure 28.41), and insert the needle into the muscle. *Using a quick motion lessens the client's discomfort.*
- Aspirate by holding the barrel of the syringe steady with your nondominant hand and by pulling back on the plunger with your dominant hand. If blood appears in the syringe, withdraw the needle, discard the syringe, and prepare a new injection. *The appearance of blood indicates the needle is in a blood vessel.*
- If blood does not appear, inject the medication steadily and slowly, holding the syringe steady. Injecting medication slowly permits it to disperse into the muscle tissue, thus decreasing the client's discomfort. *Holding the syringe steady minimizes discomfort.*
- Wait 10 seconds.

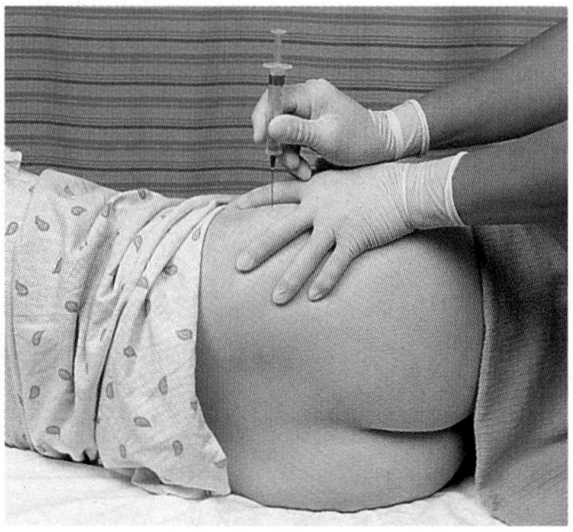

Figure 28.41 Administering an intramuscular injection into the ventrogluteal site

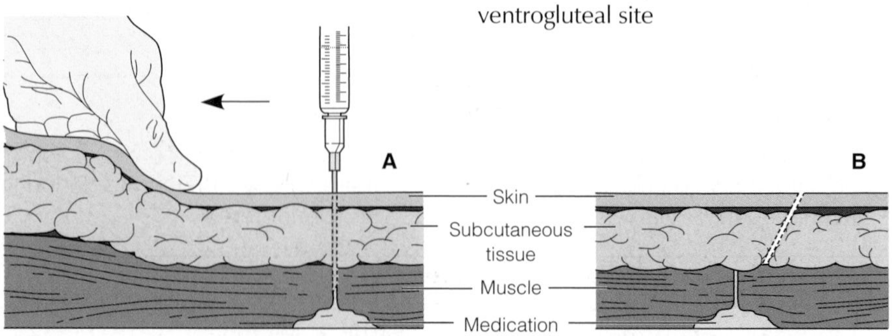

Figure 28.40 Inserting an intramuscular needle at a 90-degree angle using the Z-track method: *A*, skin pulled to the side; *B*, skin released. *Note*: When the skin returns to its normal position after the needle is withdrawn, a seal is formed over the intramuscular site. This prevents seepage of the medication into the subcutaneous tissues and subsequent discomfort.

PROCEDURE 28.6 Administering an Intramuscular Injection *continued*

7. Withdraw the needle.

- Withdraw the needle slowly and steadily. *This minimizes tissue injury.*
- Release the lateral pull of skin (Z track).
- Apply gentle pressure at the site with a clean swab. Do *not* massage the site. *Massaging the site can result in tissue irritation.*
- If bleeding occurs, apply pressure with a dry sterile gauze until it stops.

8. Discard the uncapped needle and attached syringe into the proper receptacle.

- Remove gloves. Wash hands.

9. Document all relevant information.

- Include the time of administration, drug name, dose, route, and the client's reactions.

10. Assess effectiveness of the medication at the time it is expected to act.

Evaluation Focus

Desired effect (e.g., relief of pain or vomiting, reduction in body temperature); local skin or tissue reactions at injection site; any adverse reactions or side effects

Intravenous Medications

Medications administered intravenously (IV) enter the bloodstream directly through a vein. The IV route is appropriate when medications are too irritating to tissues to be given by other routes, or when a rapid effect is required. When an intravenous line is already established, this route is desirable because it avoids the discomfort of other parenteral routes. Medications are administered intravenously by the following methods:

- Large volume infusion of intravenous fluid
- Intermittent intravenous infusion (Piggyback or Tandem setups)
- Volume-controlled infusion (often used for children)
- Intravenous push (IVP) or bolus
- Intermittent injection ports (device)

In all these methods, the client has an existing intravenous line or an IV access site, such as a saline/heparin lock.

Most agencies have procedures and policies about who may administer an IV medication. Chapter 40 describes the technique for performing a venipuncture and establishing an IV line. There are potential hazards in administering intravenous medications that include rapid, severe reactions to the medication, infection, and fluid volume overload.

With all IV medication administration, it is very important to observe clients closely for signs of adverse reactions. The drug enters the bloodstream directly and acts immediately, and there is no way it can be withdrawn or its action terminated. Therefore, the nurse must take special care to avoid any errors in the preparation of the drug and the calculation of the dosage. When the drug being administered is particularly potent, an antidote to the drug should be available. In addition, the vital signs are assessed before, during, and after infusion of the drug.

Before adding any medications to an existing intravenous infusion, the nurse must do the following:

- Inspect and palpate the intravenous insertion site for signs of infection, infiltration, or a dislocated catheter.
- Inspect the surrounding skin for redness, pallor, or swelling.
- Palpate the surrounding tissues for coldness and the presence of edema, which could indicate leakage of the IV fluid into the tissues (extravasation).

Large Volume Infusions

Mixing a medication into a large-volume IV container is the safest and easiest way to administer a drug intravenously. The drugs are diluted in volumes of 50 mL, 100 mL, 200 mL, 500 mL, or 1,000 mL of compatible fluids. It may be necessary to consult a pharmacist to confirm compatibility. Such fluids as IV normal saline or Ringer's lactate are frequently used. Commonly added drugs are potassium chloride and vitamins. It may also be necessary to ensure the compatibility of some drugs with the plastic IV bag and tubing.

The main danger of infusing a large volume of fluid is circulatory overload (hypervolemia). See Chapter 40.

The medication is usually added to a fluid container before it is hung. In some hospitals, the pharmacist adds the medication to the container, or premixed fluid containers are used (for example, potassium chloride in 1000 mL D_5W). See Procedure 28.7.

PROCEDURE 28.7 Adding Medications to Intravenous Fluid Containers

PURPOSES

- To provide and maintain a constant level of a medication in the blood
- To administer well-diluted medications at a continuous and slow rate

Assessment Focus
Signs of infiltration, infection, or a dislodged needle at the infusion site: redness, pallor, swelling, coldness or edema of the surrounding tissues; vital signs for baseline data; allergies to medications; compatibility of medication(s) and IV fluid

Equipment

- ❑ MAR or computer printout
- ❑ Correct sterile medication
- ❑ Diluent for medication in powdered form (see manufacturer's instructions)
- ❑ Correct fluid container
- ❑ Alcohol swabs
- ❑ Sterile syringe of appropriate size (e.g., 5 or 10 mL) and a 1- to $1\frac{1}{2}$-inch, #20- or #21-gauge sterile needle or equivalent from needleless system
- ❑ IV additive label

INTERVENTION

1. **Check the medication order for accuracy, and confirm the compatibility of the drugs and solutions being mixed.**

- Check the physician's orders carefully for the medication, dosage, route, and frequency. Verify which infusion solution is to be used with the medication.
- Consult a pharmacist, if required, to confirm compatibility of the drugs and solutions being mixed.

2. **Prepare the medication from a vial or ampule.**

- See Procedure 28.2 (ampule) or 28.3 (vial).
- Check the agency's practice for using a filter needle or a needleless system to withdraw premixed liquid medications from multidose vials or ampules.

3. **Add the medication.**

- Check the client's identification band and ask the client's name.
- Locate the injection port of the fluid container and carefully remove its cover. Wipe the port with the antiseptic or alcohol swab. *This reduces the risk of introducing microorganisms into the container when the needle is inserted.*
- Remove the needle cap from the syringe, insert the needle through the centre of the injection port, and inject the medication into the bag or bottle (Figure 28.42).
- Mix the medication and solution by gently rotating the bag or bottle (Figure 28.43). *This should disperse the medication throughout the solution.*
- Complete the IV additive label with name and dose of medication, date, time, and nurse's initials. Attach it to the bag or bottle (Figure 28.44). *This documents that medication has been added to the solution.*
- Spike the bag or bottle with IV tubing. Clamp the tubing and hang the IV. *Clamping prevents rapid infusion of the solution.*
- Regulate infusion rate as ordered.

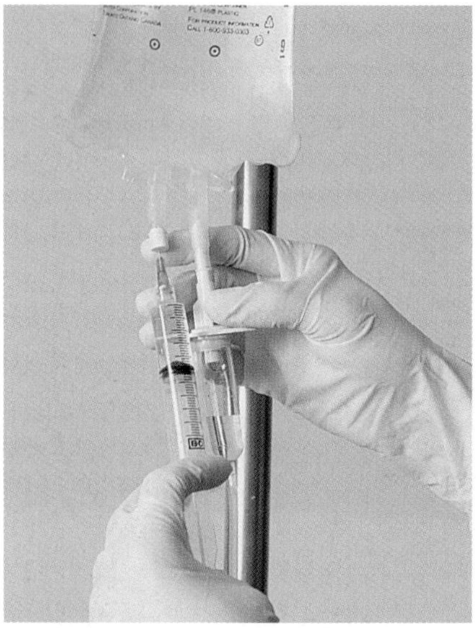

Figure 28.42 Inserting a medication through the injection port of a fluid container

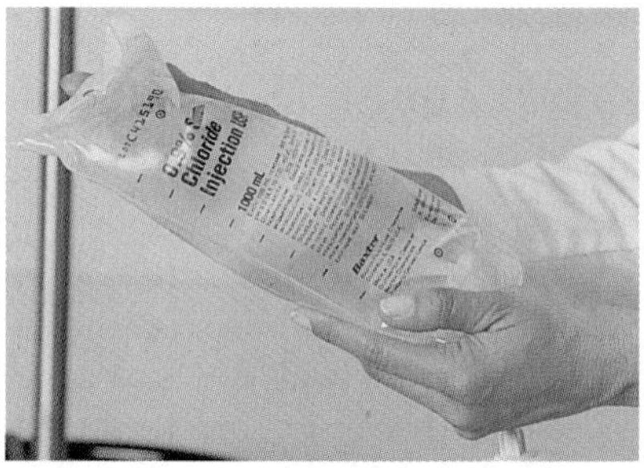

Figure 28.43 Rotating an intravenous bag to distribute a medication

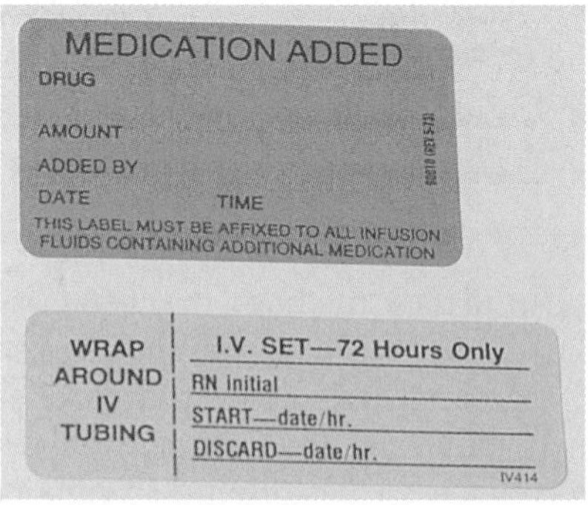

Figure 28.44 *Top*, label indicating a medication added to an IV infusion; *Bottom*, label indicating time of an IV set change

PROCEDURE 28.7 Adding Medications to Intravenous Fluid Containers *continued*

Adding To an Existing Infusion

- Determine that the IV solution in the container is sufficient for adding the medication. *Sufficient volume is necessary to dilute the medication adequately.*
- Confirm the desired dilution of the medication, that is, the amount of medication per millilitre of solution.
- Close the infusion clamp. *This prevents the medication from infusing directly into the client as it is injected into the bag.*
- Wipe the medication port with the alcohol swab. *This reduces the risk of introducing microorganisms into the container when the needle is inserted.*
- Remove the needle cover from the medication syringe.
- While supporting and stabilizing the bag with your thumb and forefinger, carefully insert the syringe needle through the port and inject the medication. *The bag is supported during the injection of the medication to avoid punctures.* If the bag or bottle is too high to reach easily, lower it from the IV pole.
- Remove the bag from the pole and gently rotate it. *This will mix the medication and solution.*
- Rehang the container and regulate the flow rate. *This establishes the correct flow rate.*
- Complete the medication label and apply.

5. **Dispose of the equipment and supplies according to agency practice.** *This prevents inadvertent injury to others and the spread of microorganisms.*

Intermittent Intravenous Infusions

An intermittent infusion is a method of administering a medication mixed in a small amount of IV solution, such as 50 or 100 mL. The drug is administered over a short period of time (15–60 minutes) at regular intervals (e.g., every eight hours). Two commonly used additive setups are the *tandem* and the *piggyback.*

In a tandem setup, a second container is attached to the line of the first container at the lower, secondary port (Figure 28.45, *A*). It permits medications to be administered intermittently or simultaneously with the first solution.

In the piggyback alignment, a second set connects the second container to the tubing of the first container at the upper port (Figure 28.45, *B*). This setup is used solely for intermittent drug administration. Various manufacturers describe these sets differently, so the nurse must check the manufacturer's labelling and directions carefully.

The tubing of additive sets is attached to ports of the primary infusion tubing using a needleless system. These systems use threaded-lock or lever-lock cannulae to connect the additive set to the ports of the primary infusion (Figure 28.46). Because the systems are needleless, accidental needle-stick injuries are prevented. The design also prevents touch contamination at the IV connection site.

Volume-Control Infusions

Intermittent medications may also be administered by **volume-control** sets, such as Buretrol, Soluset, Volutrol, and Pediatrol (Figure 28.47). They are small fluid containers (100 to 150 mL in size) attached below the primary infusion container so that the medication is administered through the client's IV line. Volume-control sets are frequently used to infuse solutions into children and

Adding a Medication to a Volume-Control Infusion

- It is important to note that the compatibility of the medication, the intravenous solution, and any pre-existing additives (e.g., KCL) must be determined before mixing the solutions together.
- Withdraw the required dose of the medication into a syringe.
- Ensure that there is sufficient fluid in the volume-control fluid chamber to dilute the medication. Generally, at least 50 mL of fluid is used. Check the directions from the drug manufacturer or consult the pharmacist.
- Close the inflow to the fluid chamber by adjusting the upper roller or slide clamp above the fluid chamber; also ensure that the clamp on the air vent of the chamber is open.
- Clean the medication port on the volume-control fluid chamber with an alcohol swab.
- Inject the medication into the port of the partially filled volume control set.
- Gently rotate the fluid chamber until the fluid is well mixed.
- Open the line's upper clamp, and regulate the flow by adjusting the lower roller or slide clamp below the fluid chamber.
- Attach a medication label to the volume-control fluid chamber.
- Document relevant data, and monitor the client and the infusion.
- Flush tubing following administration of medication to prevent subsequent mixing of medications being administered by the volume control set.

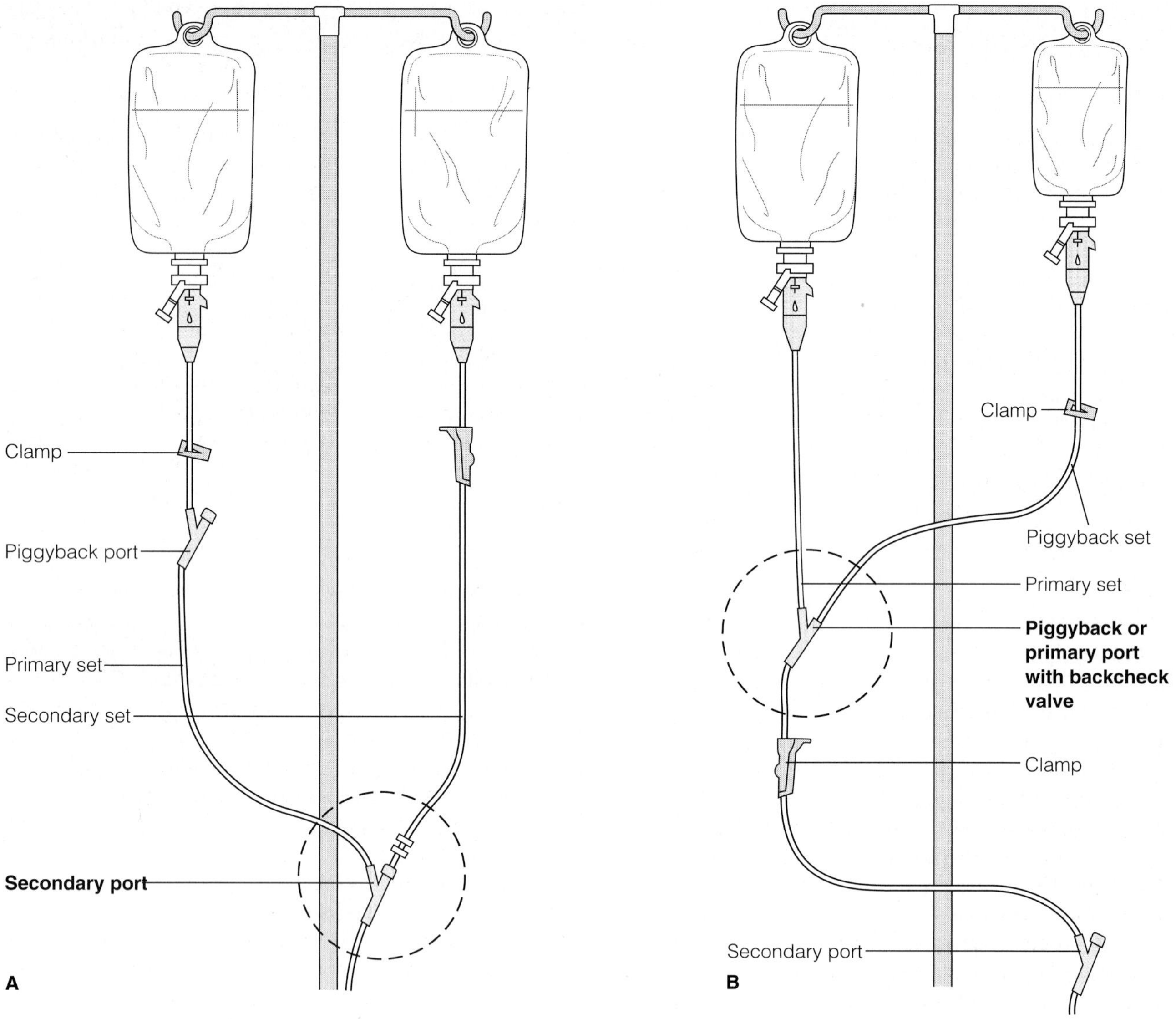

Figure 28.45 Secondary intravenous lines: *A,* a tandem intravenous alignment; *B,* an intravenous piggyback (IVPB) alignment

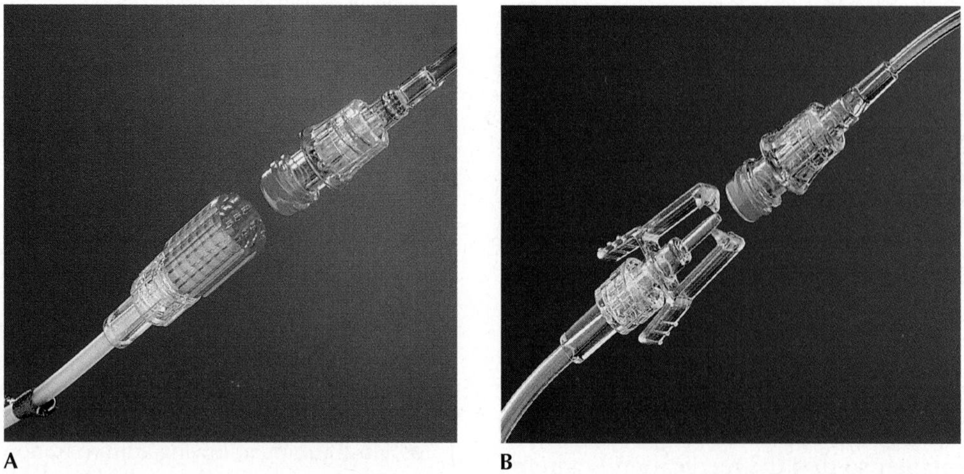

Figure 28.46 Cannulae used to connect the tubing of additive sets to primary infusions: *A*, threaded-lock cannula; *B*, lever-lock cannula

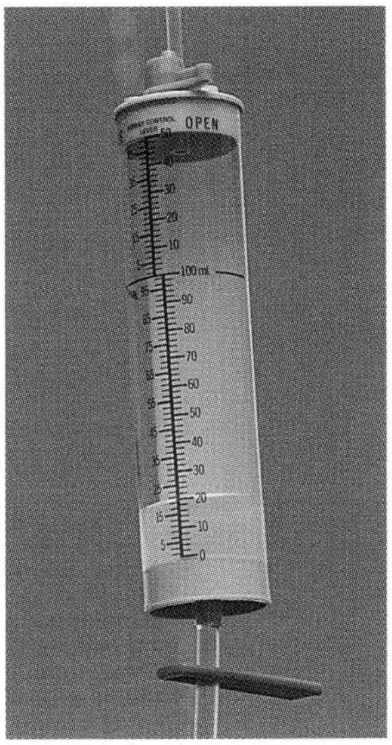

Figure 28.47 A volume-control set above the drip chamber of an intravenous infusion

older clients when the volume administered is critical and must be carefully monitored. See the box on page 649 for additional information.

Intravenous Push (IVP)

Intravenous push (bolus) is the intravenous administration of an undiluted drug directly into the systemic circulation. It is used when a medication cannot be diluted or in an emergency. An IV bolus can be introduced directly into a vein by venipuncture, into an existing IV line through an injection port, or through an IV lock. Administration of intravenous push drips is considered a transfer of medical function. The nurse should check the agency policy (certification may be required).

There are two major disadvantages to this method of drug administration: any error in administration cannot be corrected after the drug has entered the client, and the drug may be irritating to the lining of the blood vessels. Before administering a bolus, the nurse should look up the maximum concentration recommended for the particular drug and the rate of administration. The rate of injection is dependent on the medication that is being administered. See Procedure 28.8.

Intermittent Injection Ports

Intermittent injection ports, also called *PRN adapters* or *injection caps*, may be attached to an intravenous catheter or needle to allow medications to be administered intravenously without requiring repeated needle sticks or a continuous intravenous infusion. Intermittent injection ports have either a resealable latex injection site for needle access or a port that allows a syringe or a needleless adapter to be connected for administering medications. Needleless systems are preferred; they significantly reduce the risk of needle-stick injuries among health-care professionals. Procedure 28.8 describes how to convert an intravenous infusion to an intermittent injection port. With the needleless system, the injection adapter may be affixed at the time of intravenous catheter placement, allowing a closed system to be maintained.

Intermittent injection ports may be flushed with sterile saline prior to medication administration and with saline or heparinized saline afterward. Flushing the port maintains patency of the intravenous catheter and port and reduces the risks of mixing incompatible medications within the system. See Procedure 28.8.

Clients who require long-term venous access for administering medications (e.g., people receiving chemotherapy for cancer treatment) may have a specialized catheter or port to allow central venous access. The catheter may be tunneled subcutaneously and accessed through an intermittent injection port attached to the distal end of the venous catheter. Other devices have an *implantable port* or *vascular access port* surgically inserted under the skin so that no portion of the device exits the body. To administer

PROCEDURE 28.8 Administering Intravenous Medications Using IV Push

PURPOSE

- To achieve immediate and maximum effects of a medication

Assessment Focus
Signs of infiltration or infection at the infusion site or saline/heparin lock insertion site: redness, pallor, or swelling of the surrounding skin, coldness and edema of the surrounding tissues; vital signs for baseline data; allergies to medications; compatibility of medication(s) and IV fluid; specific drug action; side effects; normal dosage; recommended administration time; time of peak of action; patency of IV line by assessing flow rate

PROCEDURE 28.8 Administering Intravenous Medications Using IV Push *continued*

Equipment

- ❑ Physician's order for medications, dosage, route, and rate of administration

IV PUSH FOR AN EXISTING LINE

- ❑ Medication in a vial or ampule
- ❑ Sterile syringe (3 to 5 mL) to prepare the medication
- ❑ Sterile needles #21 to #25 gauge, 1 inch, or equivalent from a needleless system
- ❑ Alcohol swabs
- ❑ Watch with a digital readout or second hand

IV PUSH FOR A HEPARIN/SALINE LOCK

- ❑ Medication in a vial or ampule
- ❑ Sterile syringe (3 to 5 mL) to prepare the medication
- ❑ Sterile syringe (3 mL) for the saline or heparin flush
- ❑ Vial of normal saline to flush the IV catheter. *This maintains the patency of the heparin/saline lock. Saline is frequently used for peripheral locks.*
- ❑ Sterile needles (#21 gauge) or equivalent from a needleless system
- ❑ Alcohol swabs
- ❑ Watch with a digital readout or second hand
- ❑ Disposable gloves

INTERVENTION

1. Prepare the medication.

EXISTING LINE

- Prepare the medication according to the manufacturer's direction. *It is important to have the correct dose and the correct dilution.*

HEPARIN/SALINE LOCK

a. Flushing with saline

- Prepare two syringes, each with 1 mL of sterile normal saline.

b. Flushing with heparin

- Prepare one syringe with 1 mL of heparin flush solution if indicated by agency policy.
- Prepare two syringes with 1 mL each of sterile, normal saline.
- Draw up the medication into a syringe.

2. Wash hands and don gloves if agency policy requires. *This reduces the transmission of microorganisms and reduces the likelihood of the nurse's hands contacting the client's blood.*

3. Confirm the client's identity.

4. Administer the medication by IV push.

HEPARIN/SALINE LOCK WITH NEEDLE

- Clean the diaphragm with the alcohol swab. *This prevents microorganisms from entering the circulatory system during the needle insertion.*
- Insert the needle of the syringe containing normal saline through the centre of the diaphragm and aspirate for blood if indicated by agency policy (Figure 28.48). *The presence of blood confirms that the catheter or needle is in the vein. In some situations, blood will not return even though the lock is patent.*
- Flush the lock by injecting 1 mL of stenle saline slowly. *This removes blood from the needle and the lock.*
- Remove the needle and syringe.
- Clean the lock's diaphragm with an alcohol swab. *This prevents the transfer of microorganisms.*
- Insert the needle of the syringe containing the prepared medication through the centre of the diaphragm.
- Inject the medication slowly at the recommended rate of infusion. Use a watch or digital readout to time the injection. Observe the client closely for adverse reactions. Remove the needle and syringe when all medication is administered. *A too rapid injection of the drug can have a serious untoward reaction.*
- Withdraw the needle and syringe.
- Clean the diaphragm of the lock.
- Attach the second sterile saline syringe, and inject 1 mL of saline. *The saline injection flushes the medication through the catheter and prepares the lock for heparin if this medication is used. Heparin is incompatible with many medications.*

HEPARIN/SALINE LOCK WITH NEEDLELESS SYSTEM

- Remove the protective cap from the needleless port.
- Insert syringe containing normal saline into the valve.
- Flush the lock with 1 mL sterile saline. *This clears the lock of blood.*
- Remove the syringe.
- Insert the syringe containing the medication into the valve (Figure 28.49).

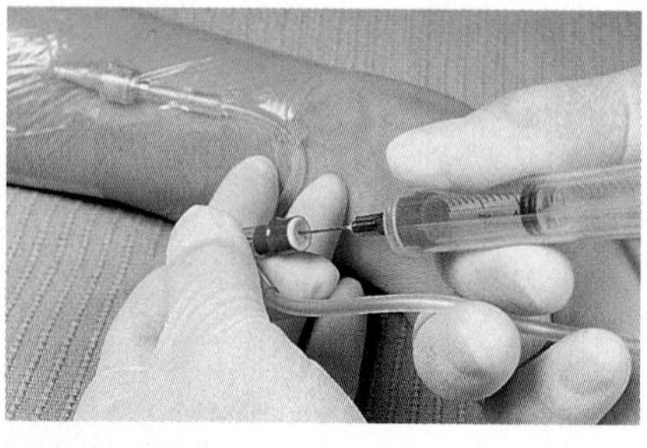

Figure 28.48 Inserting a needle through the diaphragm of an IV lock

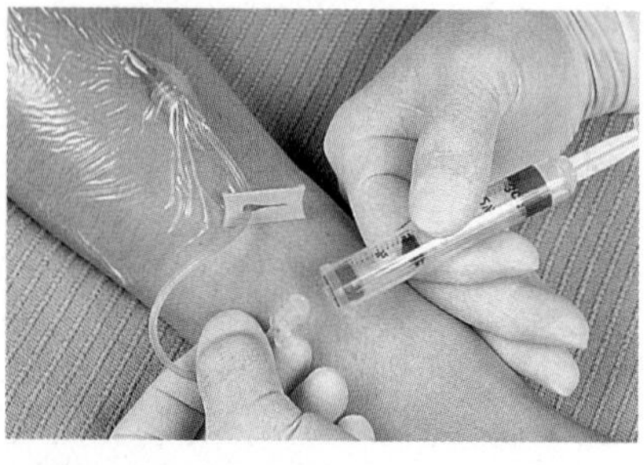

Figure 28.49 Using a needleless system to inject a medication into the valve of an IV lock

PROCEDURE 28.8 Administering Intravenous Medications Using IV Push *continued*

- Inject the medication following the precautions described previously.
- Withdraw the syringe.
- Repeat injection of 1 mL of sterile saline.
- Place a new sterile cap over the valve.

EXISTING LINE

- Identify the injection port closest to the client. Some ports have a circle indicating the site for the needle insertion. *An injection port must be used because it is self sealing. Any puncture to the plastic tubing will leak.*
- Clean the port with an alcohol swab.
- Stop the IV flow by closing the clamp or pinching the tubing above the injection port (Figure 28.50).
- Connect the syringe to the IV system through the injection port.
  a. Needle system
  - Hold the port steady.
  - Insert the needle of the syringe that contains the medication through the centre of the port (see Figure 28.50). *This prevents damage to the IV line and to the diaphragm of the port.*

  b. Needleless system
  - Remove the cap from the needleless injection port. Connect the tip of the syringe directly to the port.

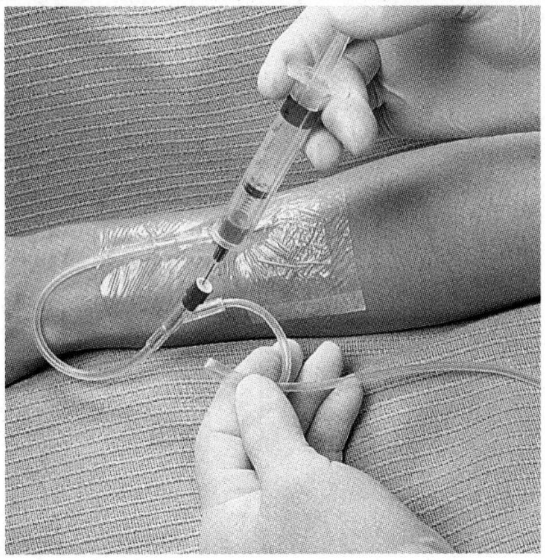

Figure 28.50 Injecting a medication by IV bolus to an existing IV

- Pull back on the plunger of the syringe in order to aspirate a small amount of blood if indicated by agency policy. *This confirms that the port is patent and that the medication will enter the bloodstream.*
- After observing the blood, continue to keep the clamp closed and inject the medication at the ordered rate. Use the watch or digital readout to time the medication administration. *This ensures safe drug administration because a too rapid injection could be dangerous.*
- Release the clamp or tubing.
- After injecting the medication, withdraw the needle, or, for a needleless system, detach the syringe, and attach a new sterile cap to the port.

5. **Dispose of equipment according to agency practice.** *This reduces needle-stick injuries and spread of microorganisms.*
6. **Remove and dispose of gloves. Wash hands.**
7. **Observe the client closely for adverse reactions.**
8. **Determine agency practice about recommended times for changing the heparin/saline lock.** *Some agencies advocate a change every 48 to 72 hours for peripheral IV devices.*
9. **Document all relevant information.**

- Record the date, time, drug, dose, and route; client response; and assessment of infusion or heparin lock site if appropriate.

Evaluation Focus
Desired effect of medication; any adverse reactions or side effects; change in vital signs; status of heparin/saline lock site; patency of IV infusion, if running

medications, the port is accessed using a specialized needle through the skin. See Chapter 40 for more information about central venous lines.

Topical Medications

Topical medications are those that are applied locally to the skin or to mucous membranes in such areas as the eye, external ear canal, nose, vagina, and rectum. Traditionally, topical application to the skin was limited to medications intended to produce a local effect at the administration site. However, several medications (e.g., nitroglycerin and estrogen) have been "packaged" in special **transdermal** delivery systems that gradually release a predictable amount of active substance into the bloodstream for as long as a week.

Most topical applications used therapeutically are not absorbed well, completely, or predictably when applied to intact skin because the skin's thick outer layer serves as a natural barrier to drug diffusion. This route of absorption through the skin, called **percutaneous,** can be increased if the skin is altered by a laceration, burn, or some other problem. However, if high concentrations or large amounts of a topical medication are applied to the skin, especially if it is done repeatedly, sufficient amounts of the drug can enter the bloodstream to cause systemic effects.

Percutaneous absorption of petroleum products, oils, and organic solvents, as well as drugs dissolved in them (such as insecticides), is often rapid and complete. It is an important cause of industrial and environmental poisoning.

CLINICAL GUIDELINES

Applying Skin Preparations

Powder

Make sure the skin surface is dry. Spread apart any skin folds, and sprinkle the site until the area is covered with a fine *thin* layer. Cover the site with a dressing if ordered.

Suspension-Based Lotion

Shake the container before use to distribute suspended particles. Put a little lotion on a small gauze dressing or pad, and apply the lotion to the skin by stroking it evenly in the direction of the hair growth.

Creams, Ointments, Pastes, and Oil-Based Lotions

Warm and soften the preparation in the gloved hands to make it easier to apply and to prevent chilling (if a large area is to be treated). Smear it evenly over the skin using long strokes that follow the direction of the hair growth. Explain that the skin may feel somewhat greasy after application. Apply a sterile dressing if necessary.

Aerosol Spray

Shake the container well to mix the contents. Hold the spray container at the recommended distance from the area (usually about 15 to 30 cm, but check the label). Cover the client's face with a towel if the upper chest or neck is to be sprayed. Have client wear goggles if indicated. Spray the medication over the specified area.

Transdermal Patches

Select a clean, dry area that is free of hair and matches the manufacturer's recommendations. Remove the patch from its protective covering, holding it without touching the adhesive edges, and apply it by pressing firmly with the palm of the hand for about 10 seconds. Advise the client to avoid using a heating pad over the area to prevent an increase in circulation and the rate of absorption. Remove the patch at the appropriate time, folding it so that the medicated side is covered.

Skin Applications

Topical skin or *dermatologic* preparations include ointments, pastes, creams, lotions, powders, sprays, and patches. See Table 28.1 earlier in this chapter. General guidelines for applying topical medications are shown in the box above. Before applying a dermatological preparation, thoroughly clean the area with soap and water and pat it dry. Skin encrustations harbor microorganisms and these, as well as previously applied applications, can prevent the medication from coming in contact with the area to be treated. Nurses should wear gloves when administering skin applications and always use surgical asepsis when an open wound is present.

Ophthalmic Instillations

Medications for the eyes, called **ophthalmic** medications, are instilled in the form of liquids or ointments. Eye drops are packaged in monodrip plastic containers that are used to administer the preparation. Ointments are usually supplied in small tubes. All containers must state that the medication is for ophthalmic use. Sterile preparations and sterile technique are indicated. Prescribed liquids are usually dilute, for example, less than 1 percent strength.

Procedure 28.9 illustrates how to administer ophthalmic instillations.

PROCEDURE 28.9 Administering Ophthalmic Instillations

PURPOSE

- To provide an eye medication the client requires (e.g., an antibiotic) to treat an infection or for other reasons (see specific drug action)

Assessment Focus

Allergy to medication; appearance of eye and surrounding structures for lesions, exudate, erythema, or swelling; the location and nature of any discharge, lacrimation, and swelling of the eyelids or of the lacrimal gland; client complaints (e.g., itching, burning, pain, blurred vision, and photophobia); client behaviour (e.g., squinting, blinking excessively, frowning, or rubbing the eyes); client's level of consciousness and ability or willingness to cooperate (e.g., restlessness, disorientation); specific drug action and side effects; client's knowledge about the medication

PROCEDURE 28.9 Administering Ophthalmic Instillations *continued*

Equipment

- ❑ Sterile absorbent sponges soaked in sterile normal saline
- ❑ Disposable gloves
- ❑ Medication
- ❑ Dry sterile absorbent sponges
- ❑ Sterile eye dressing (pad) as needed and paper eye tape to secure it

INTERVENTION

1. Check the medication order and the medication.

- Check the physician's order for the preparation, strength, and number of drops. Also, confirm the prescribed frequency of the instillation and which eye is to be treated. Abbreviations are frequently used to identify the eye: OD (right eye), OS (left eye), OU (both eyes).
- Check the expiration date and ensure that the medication is clearly labelled.

2. Prepare the client.

- Check the client's identification band, and ask the client's name.
- Explain the technique to the client or to the parents of a child. The administration of an ophthalmic medication is not usually painful. Ointments are often soothing to the eye, but some liquid preparations may sting initially.
- For a young child, use a doll to demonstrate the procedure. *This facilitates cooperation and decreases anxiety.*
- Assist the client to a comfortable position, either sitting or lying.
- For a young child, enlist assistance to immobilize the arms and head. The parent may hold the child. *This prevents accidental injury during medication administration.*

3. Clean the eyelid and the eyelashes.

- Don gloves if agency policy requires.
- Use sterile cotton balls moistened with sterile irrigating solution or sterile normal saline, and wipe from the inner canthus to the outer canthus. *If not removed, material on the eyelid and lashes can be washed into the eye. Cleaning toward the outer canthus prevents contamination of the other eye and the lacrimal duct.*

4. Administer the eye medication.

- Check the ophthalmic preparation for the name, strength, and number of drops if a liquid is used. Draw the correct number of drops into the shaft of the dropper if a dropper is used. If ointment is used, discard the first bead. *Checking medication data is essential to prevent a medication error. The first bead of ointment from a tube is considered to be contaminated.*
- Instruct the client to look up to the ceiling. Give the client a dry sterile absorbent sponge. *The person is less likely to blink if looking up. While the client looks up, the cornea is partially protected by the top eyelid. A sponge is needed to press on the nasolacrimal duct after a liquid instillation or to wipe excess ointment from the eyelashes after an ointment is instilled.*
- Expose the lower conjunctival sac by placing the thumb or fingers of your nondominant hand on the client's cheekbone just below the eye and gently drawing down the skin on the cheek. If the tissues are edematous, handle the tissues carefully to avoid damaging them. *Placing the fingers on the cheekbone minimizes the possibility of touching the cornea, avoids putting any pressure on the eyeball, and prevents the person from blinking or squinting.*
- Approach the eye from the side and instill the correct number of drops onto the outer third of the lower conjunctival sac. Hold the dropper 1 to 2 cm above the sac (Figure 28.51). *The client is less likely to blink if a side approach is used. When instilled into the conjunctival sac, drops will not harm the cornea as they might if dropped directly on it. The dropper must not touch the sac or the cornea.*

or

- Holding the tube above the lower conjunctival sac, squeeze 2 cm of ointment from the tube into the lower conjunctival sac from the inner canthus outward (Figure 28.52).

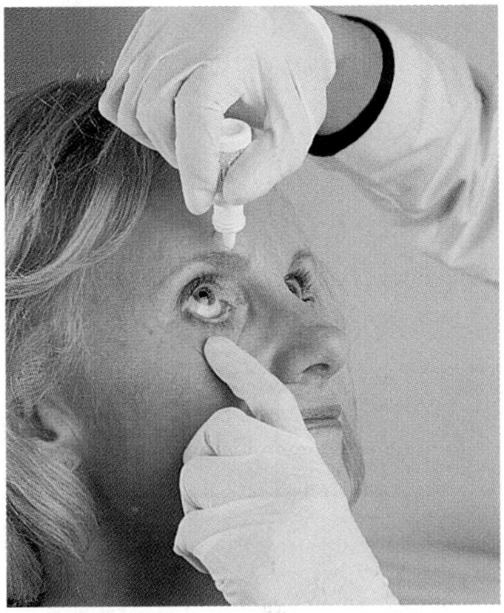

Figure 28.51 Instilling an eye drop into the lower conjunctival sac

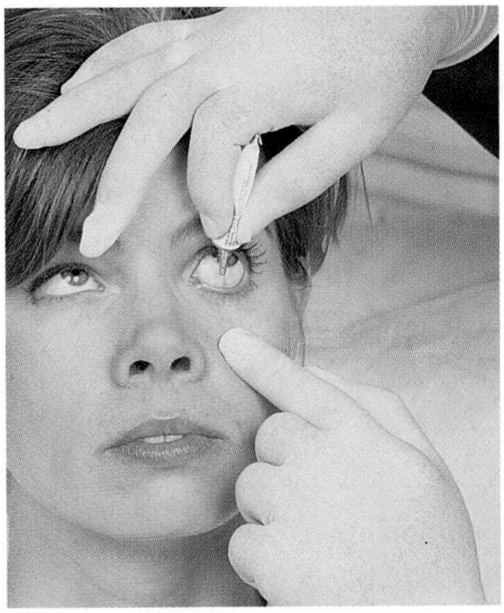

Figure 28.52 Instilling an eye ointment into the lower conjunctival sac

PROCEDURE 28.9 Administering Ophthalmic Instillations *continued*

- Instruct the client to close the eyelids but not to squeeze them shut. *Closing the eye spreads the medication over the eyeball. Squeezing can injure the eye and push out the medication.*
- For liquid medications, press firmly or have the client press firmly on the nasolacrimal duct for at least 30 seconds (Figure 28.53). Check agency practice. *Pressing on the nasolacrimal duct prevents the medication from running out of the eye and down the duct.*

5. Clean the eyelids as needed.

- *Wipe the eyelids gently from the inner to the outer canthus to collect excess medication.*
- Remove gloves.

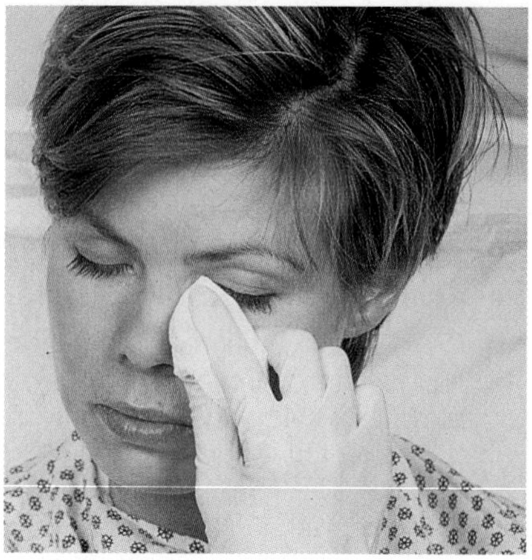

Figure 28.53 Pressing on the nasolacrimal duct

6. Apply an eye pad if needed, and secure it with tape.

7. Assess the client's response.

- Assess responses immediately after the instillation and again when the medication is expected to act.

8. Document all relevant information.

- Record nursing assessments and interventions. Include the name of the drug, the strength, the number of drops if a liquid, the time, and the response of the client.

Evaluation Focus
Relief of complaints; change in appearance of eye in accordance with drug action; amount and character of exudate; adverse reactions or side effects of medication

Otic Instillations

Medical aseptic technique is used to instill medications to the ear, called **otic** medications, unless the tympanic membrane is damaged, in which case sterile technique is used. The position of the external auditory canal varies with age. In the child under three years of age, it is directed upward. In the adult, the external auditory canal is an S-shaped structure about 2.5 cm long. Procedure 28.10 explains how to administer otic instillations.

PROCEDURE 28.10 Administering Otic Instillations

PURPOSES

- To soften earwax so that it can be readily removed at a later time
- To provide local therapy to reduce inflammation, destroy infective organisms in the external ear canal, or both
- To relieve pain

Assessment Focus
Allergy to medication; the pinna of the ear and meatus for signs of redness and abrasions; the type and amount of any discharge; complaints of discomfort; ability to cooperate during the procedure; specific drug action and side effects; client's knowledge about the medication to be used

Equipment

- ❑ Cotton-tipped applicator
- ❑ Correct medication bottle with a dropper
- ❑ Flexible rubber tip (optional) for the end of the dropper, which prevents injury from sudden motion, for example, by a child or disoriented client
- ❑ Cotton fluff
- ❑ Gloves as necessary

PROCEDURE 28.10 Administering Otic Instillations *continued*

INTERVENTION

1. **Check the medication order.**
- Check the physician's order for the kind of medication; the time, amount, and dosage; and which ear is to be treated.

2. **Prepare the client.**
- Check the client's identification band, and ask the client's name.
- Obtain assistance to immobilize a young child. *This prevents accidental injury due to sudden movement during the procedure.*
- Assist the client to a side-lying position with the ear being treated facing up.

3. **Clean the pinna of the ear and the meatus of the ear canal.**
- Don gloves if contact with body fluid is possible.
- Use cotton-tipped applicators and solution to wipe the pinna and external auditory meatus. *Remove any discharge before the instillation so that it won't be washed into the ear canal.*

4. **Administer the ear medication.**
- Warm the medication container in your hand, or place it in warm water for a short time. *This promotes client comfort.*
- Partially fill the ear dropper with medication.
- Straighten the auditory canal. For an infant, gently pull the pinna down and back (Figure 28.54). For an adult or a child older than three years of age, pull the pinna upward and backward. See Figure 27.21, page 539. *The auditory canal is straightened so that the solution can flow the entire length of the canal.*
- Instill the correct number of drops along the side of the ear canal (Figure 28.55).
- Press gently but firmly a few times on the tragus of the ear. *Pressing on the tragus assists the flow of medication into the ear canal.*

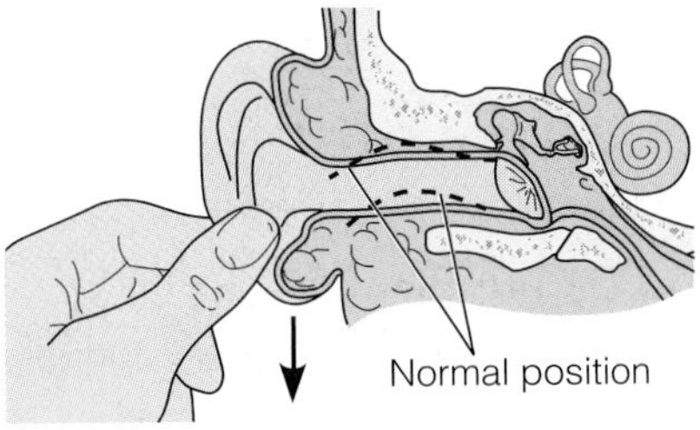

Figure 28.54 Straightening the ear canal of a child by pulling the pinna down and back

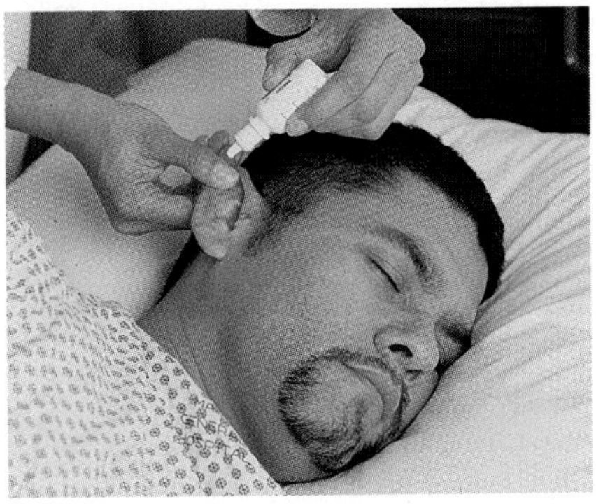

Figure 28.55 Instilling ear drops

- Ask the client to remain in the side-lying position for about five minutes. *This prevents the drops from escaping and allows the medication to reach all sides of the canal cavity.*
- Insert a small piece of cotton fluff loosely at the meatus of the auditory canal for 15 to 20 minutes. Do not press it into the canal. *The cotton helps retain the medication when the client is up. If pressed tightly into the canal, the cotton would interfere with the action of the drug and the outward movement of normal secretions.*

5. **Assess the client's response.**
- Assess the character and amount of discharge, appearance of the canal, discomfort, and so on, immediately after the instillation and again when the medication is expected to act. Inspect the cotton ball for any drainage.

6. **Document all relevant information.**
- Document all nursing assessments and interventions relative to the procedure.
- Include the time, medication, the dose, and any complaints of pain. Many agencies use flowsheets; others may require that a notation be made on the nurse's notes.

Evaluation Focus
Relief of complaints; change in appearance of ear in accordance with drug action; amount and character of discharge; adverse reactions or side effects of medication

Nasal Instillations

Nasal instillations (nose drops and sprays) usually are instilled for their astringent effect (to shrink swollen mucous membranes), to loosen secretions and facilitate drainage, or to treat infections of the nasal cavity or sinuses. Nasal decongestants are the most common nasal instillations. Many of these products are available without a prescription. Clients need to be taught to use these agents with caution. Chronic use of nasal decongestants may lead to a rebound effect, that is, an increase in nasal congestion. If excess decongestant solution is swallowed, serious systemic effects may also develop, especially in children. Saline drops are safer as a decongestant for children.

Usually, clients self-administer nasal sprays. In the supine position with the head tilted back, the client holds the tip of the container just inside the nares and inhales as the spray enters the nasal passages. For clients who use nasal sprays repeatedly, the nares need to be assessed for irritation. In children, nasal sprays are given with the head in an upright position to prevent excess spray from being swallowed.

Nasal drops are used to treat sinus infections. Clients need to learn ways to position themselves to effectively treat the affected sinus:

- To treat the *ethmoid* and *sphenoid* sinuses, instruct the client to lie back with the head over the edge of the bed or a pillow under the shoulders so that the head is tipped backward (Figure 28.56).
- To treat the *maxillary* and *frontal* sinuses, instruct the client to assume the same back-lying position, with the head turned toward the side to be treated (Figure 28.57).

The client should also be instructed to (1) breathe through the mouth to prevent aspiration of medication into the trachea and bronchi, (2) remain in a back-lying position for at least one minute so that the solution will come into contact with all of the nasal surface, and (3) avoid blowing the nose for several minutes.

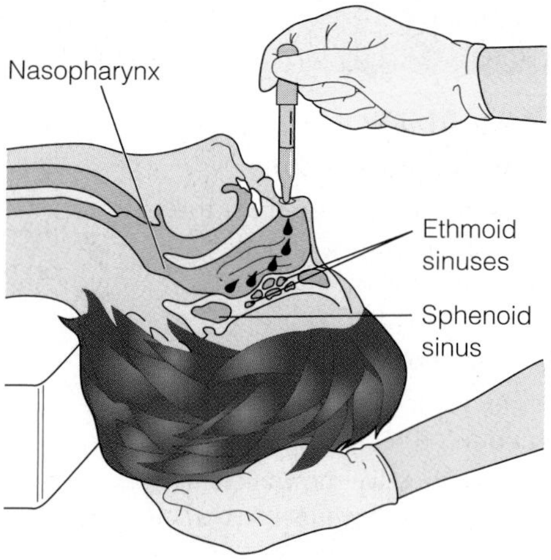

Figure 28.56 Position of the head to instill drops into the ethmoid and sphenoid sinuses

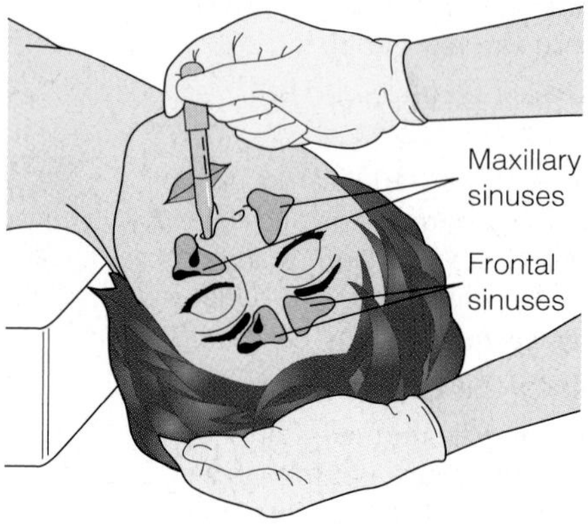

Figure 28.57 Position of the head to instill drops into the maxillary and frontal sinuses

Vaginal Instillations

Vaginal medications, or instillations, are inserted as creams, jellies, foams, or suppositories to treat infection or to relieve vaginal discomfort, for example, itching or pain. Medical aseptic technique is usually used. Vaginal creams, jellies, and foams are applied by using a tubular applicator with a plunger. Suppositories are inserted with the index finger of a gloved hand. Suppositories are designed to melt at body temperature, so they are generally stored in the refrigerator to keep them firm for insertion. See Procedure 28.11 for administering vaginal instillations.

PROCEDURE 28.11 Administering Vaginal Instillations

PURPOSES

- To treat or prevent infection
- To reduce inflammation
- To relieve vaginal discomfort

Assessment Focus
Allergy to medications; vaginal orifice for inflammation; amount, character, and odour of vaginal discharge; complaints of vaginal discomfort (e.g., burning or itching)

Equipment

- ❑ Drape
- ❑ Correct vaginal suppository or cream
- ❑ Applicator for vaginal cream
- ❑ Disposable gloves
- ❑ Lubricant for a suppository
- ❑ Disposable towel
- ❑ Clean perineal pad

PROCEDURE 28.11 Administering Vaginal Instillations *continued*

INTERVENTION

1. **Check the medication order and identify the client.**

- Carefully check the physician's order for the specific medication ordered, its dosage, and the time of administration.
- Check the client's identification band, and ask the client's name.

2. **Prepare the client.**

- Explain to the client that a vaginal instillation is normally a painless procedure and, in fact, may bring relief from itching and burning if an infection is present. Many people feel embarrassed about this procedure, and some may prefer to perform the procedure themselves if instruction is provided.
- Provide privacy, and ask the client to void. *If the bladder is empty, the client will have less discomfort during the treatment, and the possibility of injuring the vaginal lining is decreased.*

3. **Position and drape the client appropriately.**

- Assist the client to a back-lying position with the knees flexed and the hips rotated laterally.
- Drape the client appropriately so that only the perineal area is exposed.

4. **Prepare the equipment.**

- Unwrap the suppository, and put it on the opened wrapper.

  or

- Fill the applicator with the prescribed cream, jelly, or foam. Directions are provided with the manufacturer's applicator.

5. **Assess and clean the perineal area.**

- Put gloves on. *Gloves prevent contamination of the nurse's hands from vaginal and perineal microorganisms.*
- Inspect the vaginal orifice, note any odour or discharge from the vagina, and ask about any vaginal discomfort. (See Assessment Focus, earlier.)
- Provide perineal care to remove microorganisms. *This decreases the chance of moving microorganisms into the vagina.*

6. **Administer the vaginal suppository, cream, foam, or jelly.**

SUPPOSITORY

- Lubricate the rounded (smooth) end of the suppository which is inserted first. *Lubrication facilitates insertion.*
- Lubricate your gloved index finger.
- Expose the vaginal orifice by separating the labia with your nondominant hand.
- Insert the suppository about 8 to 10 cm along the posterior wall of the vagina, or less if resistance is met (Figure 28.58). The posterior wall of the vagina is about 2.5 cm longer than the anterior wall because the cervix protrudes into the uppermost portion of the anterior wall. The anterior wall is usually about 6 to 7.5 cm.

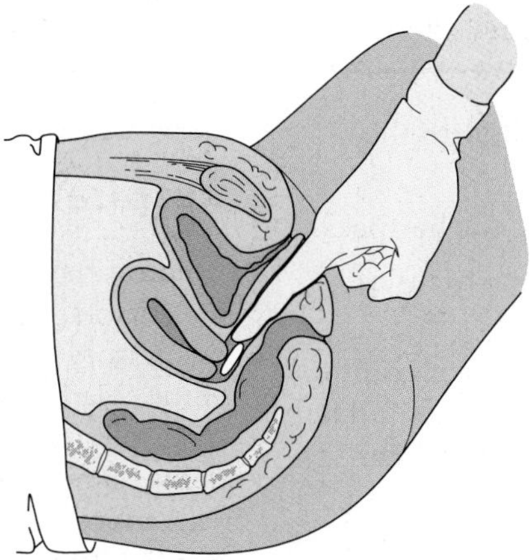

Figure 28.58 Instilling a vaginal suppository

- Withdraw the finger, and remove the gloves, turning them inside out. Discard appropriately. *Turning the gloves inside out prevents the spread of microorganisms.*
- Ask the client to remain lying in the supine position for 5 to 10 minutes following insertion. The hips may also be elevated on a pillow. *This position allows the medication to flow into the posterior fornix after it has melted.*

VAGINAL CREAM, JELLY, OR FOAM

- Gently insert the applicator about 5 cm.
- Slowly push the plunger until the applicator is empty (Figure 28.59).

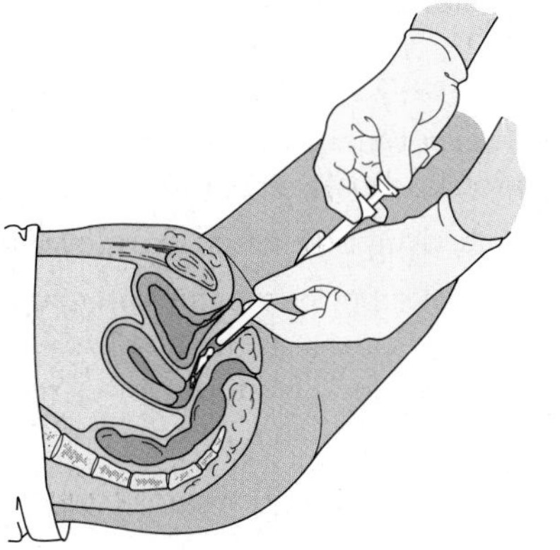

Figure 28.59 Using an applicator to instill a vaginal cream

- Remove the applicator and place it on the towel. *The applicator is put on the towel to prevent the spread of microorganisms.*
- Discard the applicator if disposable or clean it according to the manufacturer's directions.
- Remove the gloves, turning them inside out. Discard appropriately.
- Ask the client to remain lying in the supine position for 5 to 10 minutes following the insertion.

7. **Ensure client comfort.**

- Dry the perineum with tissues as required.
- Apply a clean perineal pad and a T-binder if there is excessive drainage.

PROCEDURE 28.11 Administering Vaginal Instillations *continued*

8. Document all relevant information.

- Record the instillation and assessments as for other medications and instillations.

9. Assess the client's response.

Evaluation Focus
Relief of complaints; amount, character, and odour of discharge; appearance of vaginal orifice to compare with baseline data; adverse reactions or side effects of medication

Rectal Instillations

Insertion of medications into the rectum in the form of suppositories is a frequent practice. Rectal administration is a convenient and safe method of giving certain medications. Advantages include the following:

- It avoids irritation of the upper gastrointestinal tract in clients who encounter this problem.
- It is advantageous when the medication has an objectionable taste or odour.
- The drug is released at a slow but steady rate.
- Rectal suppositories are thought to provide higher levels of medication in the bloodstream (titres) because the venous blood from the lower rectum is not transported through the liver.

To insert a rectal suppository:

- Check the medication order with the medication.
- Identify the client.
- Assist the client to a left lateral position, with the upper leg flexed.
- Fold back the top bedclothes to expose the buttocks.
- Put a glove on the hand that will be used to insert the suppository.
- Unwrap the suppository and lubricate the smooth rounded end, or see manufacturer's instructions. The rounded end is usually inserted first and lubricant reduces irritation of the mucosa.
- Lubricate the gloved index finger.
- Encourage the client to relax by breathing through the mouth.
- Insert the suppository gently into the anal canal, rounded end first (or according to manufacturer's instructions), along the rectal wall using the gloved index finger (Figure 28.60). For an adult, insert the suppository beyond the internal sphincter (i.e., 10 cm); for a child or infant, insert it 5 cm or less.
- Avoid embedding the suppository in feces.
- Press the client's buttocks together for a few minutes.
- Ask the client to remain in the left lateral or supine position for at least five minutes to help retain the suppository. The suppository should be retained for at least 30 to 40 minutes or according to manufacturer's instructions.

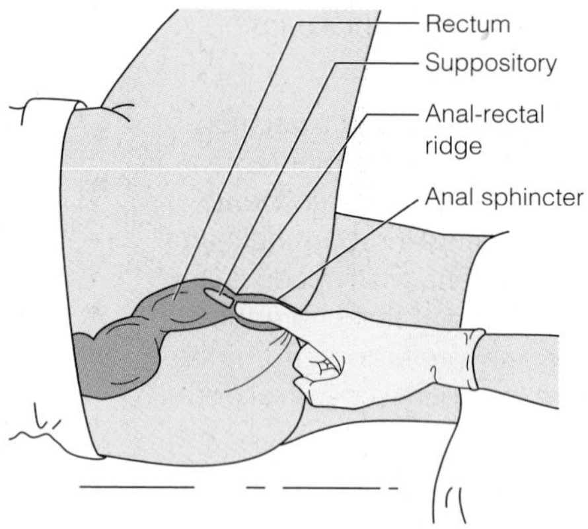

Figure 28.60 Inserting a rectal suppository beyond the internal sphincter and along the rectal wall

Respiratory Inhalation

Medications administered by inhalation, such as bronchodilators, are frequently given to clients who have chronic respiratory disease, such as asthma, emphysema, or bronchitis. Medications for inhalation are often administered by respiratory technologists with the use of *nebulizers* that deliver a fine spray or mist of medication to the client.

A **metered-dose inhaler** (MDI) is a *handheld nebulizer* (HHN) that can be used by clients to self-administer measured doses of an aerosol medication. To ensure correct delivery of the prescribed medication by MDIs, nurses need to instruct clients to use aerosol inhalers correctly. The client compresses the medication canister by hand to release medication through a mouthpiece. An extender or spacer may be attached to the mouthpiece to facilitate medication absorption for better results. Spacers are holding chambers into which the medication is fired and from which the client inhales so that the dose is not lost by exhalation (Woodcock, 1997). The box opposite provides instructions for clients on using an MDI. *Breath-activated MDIs* are being produced in which inhalation triggers the release of a premeasured dose of medication.

CLIENT TEACHING

Using a Metered-Dose Inhaler

- Make sure the canister is firmly and fully inserted into the inhaler.
- Remove the mouthpiece cap and, holding the inhaler upright, shake the inhaler for three to five seconds to mix the medication evenly.
- Tilt the head back slightly.
- Goggles may be required.
- Hold the canister upside down.
  a. Hold the MDI 1 to 2 cm from the open mouth (Figure 28.61).

  or

  b. Put the mouthpiece far enough into the mouth so that the mouthpiece extends beyond the teeth. Close the lips tightly around the mouthpiece. An MDI with a spacer or extender is always placed in the mouth (Figure 28.62).

Administering the Medication

- Inhale and exhale for several breaths, inhaling slowly and deeply through the nose.
- Then, inhale slowly and deeply through the mouth while at the same time pressing down *once* on the medication canister. Continue to inhale for two to three seconds.
- Hold your breath for five to 10 seconds or longer, if possible.
- Remove the inhaler from or away from the mouth.
- Exhale slowly through *pursed* lips.
- If another puff is prescribed, wait for one to three minutes before the next inhalation. Remember to reshake the inhaler.
- After the inhalation is completed, rinse mouth with tap water and blow the nose to remove any remaining medication and reduce irritation and risk of infection.
- Clean the MDI mouthpiece after each use. Use mild soap and water, rinse it, and let it air dry before replacing it on the device.
- Disinfect the mouthpiece weekly by soaking it for 20 minutes in 500 mL of water and 60 mL of vinegar.
- Store the canister at room temperature. Avoid extremes of temperature.
- Follow the physician's orders about frequency of use.
- Report adverse reactions, such as restlessness, palpitations, nervousness, or rash, to your physician.

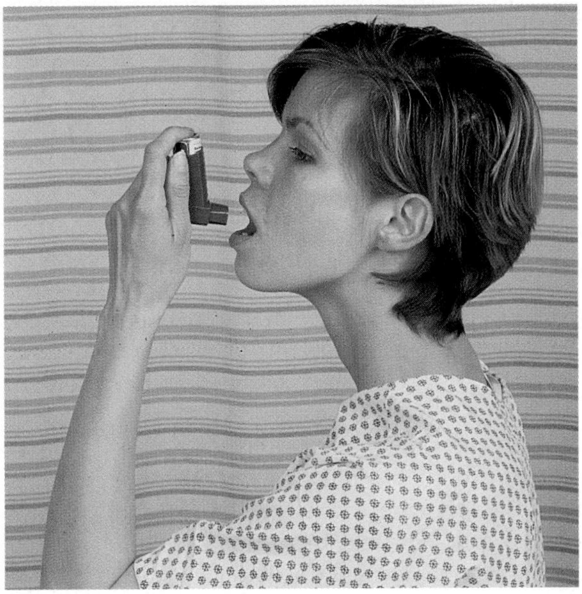

Figure 28.61 Inhaler positioned away from the open mouth

Figure 28.62 An extender spacer attached to a mouthpiece placed in the mouth

Source: Weixler, D. (1994). Correcting metered-dose inhaler misuse. *Nursing 94,* (24), 62–64; and Borkgren, M., & Gronkiewicz, C. (1995). Update your asthma care from hospital to home. *American Journal of Nursing, 95*(1), 28.

Irrigations

An **irrigation (lavage)** is the washing out of a body cavity by a stream of water or other fluid which may or may not be medicated. Irrigation is performed for one or more of the following reasons:

- To clean the area, that is, to remove a foreign object or excessive secretions or discharge
- To apply heat or cold
- To apply a medication, such as an antiseptic
- To reduce inflammation
- To relieve discomfort

Surgical asepsis is required when there is a break in the skin (e.g., in a wound irrigation) or whenever a sterile body cavity (e.g., the bladder) is entered. Some irrigations (e.g., a vaginal, rectal, or gastric irrigation) are often safely conducted using medical asepsis.

Different kinds of syringes are used for irrigations. The most common are the Asepto and the rubber bulb (Figure 28.63). The syringes are often calibrated, permitting the nurse to determine the amount of irrigant being delivered at any given time.

The *Asepto syringe* is a plastic (or glass) syringe with a rubber bulb. Squeezing the air out of the bulb produces negative pressure, and fluid can be sucked into the syringe. When the bulb is squeezed again, the fluid is ejected from the syringe. Asepto syringes come in several sizes ranging from 30 mL to 120 mL.

The *rubber bulb syringe* is often used for irrigating the ears. Like the Asepto syringe, the rubber bulb syringe comes in a range of sizes.

Other syringes that can be used are the *piston syringe*, which has a tip to which a catheter can be attached, and the Pomeroy syringe. Catheters may be used for deep-wound irrigations and for some types of bladder irrigations. The *Pomeroy syringe* is a metal syringe commonly used for ear irrigations. A shield near the tip prevents the solution from spraying outward. Plastic squeezable bottles are also available for irrigations. These are commonly used for perineal irrigations and some wound irrigations.

The type, amount, temperature, and strength of the solution and the frequency of the irrigation are ordered by the physician. Generally, normal saline at body temperature (37°C) is used unless specified otherwise. The amount of solution used varies with the site and purpose of the irrigation. Guidelines for administering eye and ear irrigations are shown in the box opposite.

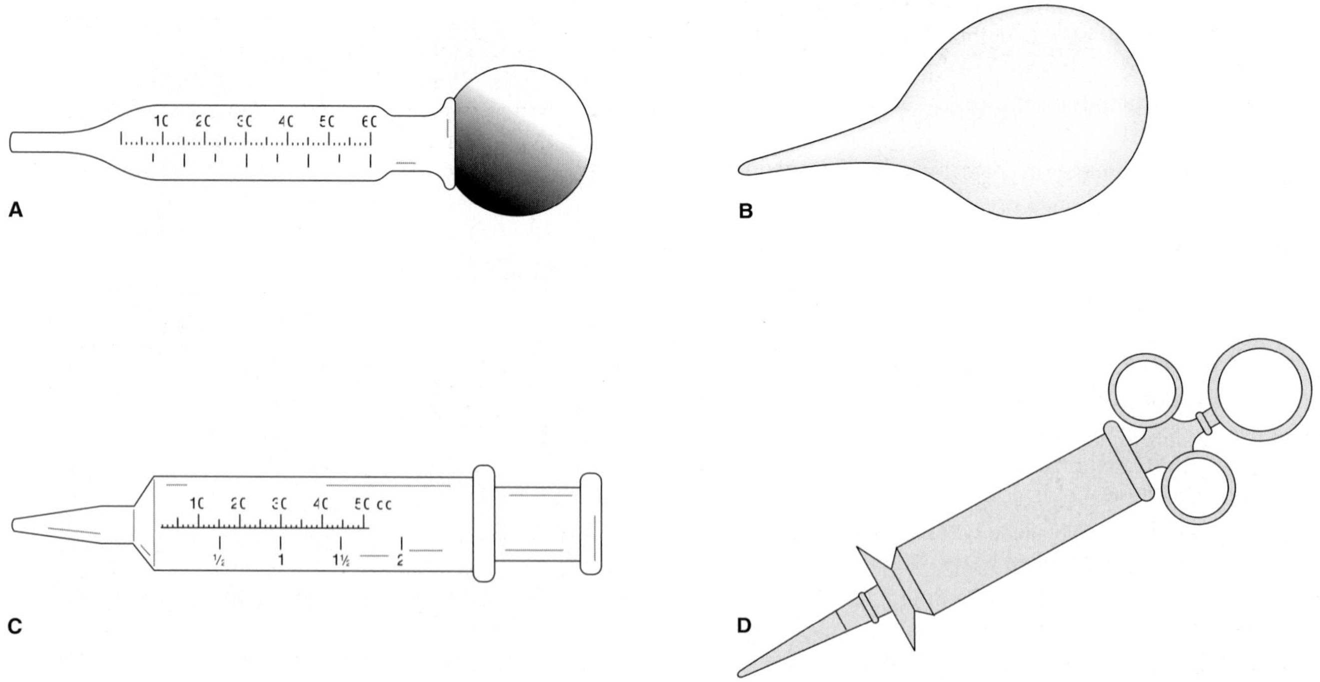

Figure 28.63 Four types of syringes commonly used for irrigations: *A*, Asepto; *B*, rubber bulb; *C*, piston syringe; *D*, Pomeroy

CLINICAL GUIDELINES

Guidelines for Administering an Eye and Ear Irrigation

- Assess the site and surrounding structures for exudate, erythema, swelling, discharge, or other lesions before the irrigation. Determine the client's chief complaints (burning, pain, itching, and so on).
- Assemble required equipment: irrigating solution; appropriate irrigating syringe; receptacle to receive irrigation returns (e.g., K-shaped basin); moistureproof drape; disposable gloves; and cotton swabs, as needed.
- Position the client appropriately in a sitting or lying position with the head tilted toward the affected eye or ear.
- Place the fluid-receiving receptacle below the affected area and a moisture-resistant pad beneath the receptacle.
- Put on disposable gloves.
- Clean the eyelids or ear meatus before the irrigation, as necessary, using moistened cotton swabs.

Administering the Irrigation

Eye Irrigation

- Expose the lower conjunctival sac by separating the lids with the thumb and forefinger to prevent reflex blinking. *Or,* to irrigate in stages, first hold the lower lid down, then hold the upper lid up. Exert pressure on the bony prominences of the cheekbone and beneath the eyebrow when holding the eyelids to minimize the possibility of pressing the eyeball and causing discomfort.
- Fill and hold the eye irrigator about 2.5 cm above the eye to ensure an even, safe pressure of the solution.
- Irrigate the eye, directing the solution on the lower conjunctival sac and from the inner canthus to the outer canthus. Directing the solution in this way prevents possible injury to the cornea and prevents fluid and contaminants from flowing down the nasolacrimal duct.
- Irrigate until the solution leaving the eye is clear (no discharge is present) or until all the solution has been used.
- Dry around the eye with cotton balls.

Ear Irrigation

- Straighten the ear canal.
- Insert a rubber-tipped syringe into the external auditory meatus, and direct the solution gently upward against the top of the canal. The solution is instilled gently because strong pressure from the fluid can cause discomfort and damage the tympanic membrane.
- Dry the outside of the ear with absorbent cotton balls. Place a cotton fluff in the auditory meatus to absorb the excess fluid.
- Assist the client to a side-lying position on the affected side. Lying with the affected side down helps drain the excess fluid by gravity.

For All Irrigations

- Assess the client for any discomfort and the appearance and odour of the fluid returns.
- Document all relevant information, including all nursing assessments and interventions relative to the procedure; the type, concentration, amount, and temperature of the solution used; the appearance of the returns; and the presence of any discomfort.

FOCUS ON CRITICAL THINKING

Mr. Ketron is a 20-year-old client who just returned to the nursing unit from surgery after undergoing an emergency appendectomy. He is awake and complaining of mild incisional pain. His dressing is dry and intact, and he has an intravenous infusion of lactated Ringer's solution running at 125 mL/hr. He is to receive Kefzol (a cefazolin, cephalosporin antibiotic) 1 g intravenously every four hours until he is able to tolerate fluids, at which time he will be placed on oral Suprax (cefixime) 200 mg twice daily until discharged and for one week after returning home. He also has an order for morphine sulfate 10 mg to be given every four hours intramuscularly, as necessary, for pain.

1. It is always possible that a person receiving antibiotic drugs may experience side effects or an allergic reaction to the drug. How does an allergic reaction differ from a drug side effect?
2. Predict the possible consequences of not obtaining a medication history from Mr. Ketron despite the fact that he will be receiving antibiotics and pain medication.
3. Mr. Ketron is complaining of pain and you have prepared his intramuscular injection of morphine. How will you select the best site to give the morphine injection?
4. What precautions should you take prior to administering Mr. Ketron's intravenous antibiotic medication?
5. Mr. Ketron will be placed on the oral antibiotic when he can tolerate food and oral fluids. What difference does it make if this drug is given before or after meals?

See Appendix A for answers to these questions.

CHAPTER HIGHLIGHTS

- Federal drug legislation in Canada regulates the production, prescription, distribution, and administration of drugs.
- Nursing practice acts define limits on the nurse's responsibilities regarding medications.
- Medications have several names. Nurses need to know the *generic* and *trade* names of a medication and be aware of both its therapeutic and side effects.
- Adverse effects of medications include drug toxicity, drug allergy, drug tolerance, idiosyncratic effect, and drug interactions.
- Several factors can affect the action of dosage. These include pregnancy; age; gender; cultural, ethnic, and genetic factors; diet; client environment; psychological factors; illness and disease; and time of administration.
- Various routes are used to administer medications: oral, sublingual, buccal, parenteral, topical, or via a nasogastric or gastrostomy tube. When administering a medication, the nurse must ensure that it is appropriate for the route specified.
- Medication orders must include the client name, date and time the order is written, name of the medication, dosage, route, frequency of administration, and signature of the person writing the order. Nurses must question any unclear orders before implementing the order.
- Telephone or verbal orders must be cosigned by the physician within a time specified by agency policy (usually 24 to 48 hours).
- Several formulas can be used to calculate dosages. Pediatric dosages are calculated by incorporating the child's weight or body surface area.
- Nurses must always assess a client's physical status before giving any medication and obtain a medication history.
- When administering medications, the nurse observes the *five rights* to ensure accurate administration. When preparing medications, the nurse checks the medication container label against the medication card form or printout *three* times.
- The nurse who prepares the medication administers it and must never leave a prepared medication unattended.
- The nurse *always* identifies the client appropriately before administering a medication and stays with the client until the medication is taken.
- Medications, once given, are documented as soon as possible after administration.
- Medications given parenterally act more quickly than those given orally or topically and must be prepared using aseptic technique.
- When preparing two insulins to be mixed in the same syringe, a vial of unmodified insulin should never be contaminated with modified insulin.
- Proper site selection is essential for an intramuscular injection to prevent tissue, blood vessel, bone, and nerve damage. The nurse should always palpate anatomic landmarks when selecting a site.
- The Z-track method for intramuscular injection is recommended to prevent discomfort caused by seepage of the medication into subcutaneous tissues.
- Clients receiving a series of injections should have the injection sites rotated.
- After use, needles should not be recapped but must be placed in puncture-resistant disposal containers.
- Intravenous medications can be administered by various methods: in a large volume infusion of intravenous fluid; by intermittent intravenous infusion; by volume-controlled infusion; by intravenous push (IVP) or bolus; or by intermittent venous access. In all these methods, the client has an existing intravenous line or an IV access site, such as a saline/heparin lock.
- Topical medications are applied to the skin and mucous membranes primarily for their local effects, although some systemic effects may occur.
- A *metered-dose inhaler* (MDI) is a *handheld nebulizer* (HHN) that can be used by clients to self-administer measured doses of an aerosol medication. To ensure correct delivery of the prescribed medication by MDIs, nurses need to instruct clients to use aerosol inhalers correctly.
- Irrigations of body cavities may be performed (1) to remove a foreign object or excessive secretions or discharge, (2) to apply heat or cold, (3) to apply a medication, such as an antiseptic, (4) to reduce inflammation, or (5) to relieve discomfort.
- Surgical asepsis for an irrigation is required when there is a break in the skin (e.g., in a wound irrigation) or whenever a sterile body cavity (e.g., the bladder) is entered.

READINGS AND REFERENCES

Suggested Readings

Covington, T. P., & Trattler, M. R. (1997, January). Bull's eye! Finding the right target for I.M. injections. *Nursing 97*, 27(1), 62–63.

This article with four descriptive illustrations explains how to give an intramuscular injection into the ventrogluteal site of an adult. It shows how to locate the site and how to give the medication.

Martin, D. (1998, July). Sharpen your technique for needle-free injection. *Nursing 98, 28*(7), 52–53.

This illustrated article describes a method of administering medications without a needle. This system uses high-pressure carbon dioxide to pierce the skin with the medication.

Whitman, M. (1995, August). Push is on: Delivering medications safely by IV bolus. *Nursing 95, 25*(8), 52–54.

The author describes some of the dangers associated with IV push, i.e., speed shock, extravasation, and pain. Also included is a table describing five differing lines and the IV push method for each.

Related Research

Walters, J. (1992). Nurses' perceptions of reportable medication errors and factors that contribute to their occurrence. *Applied Nursing Research, 92*, 86–88.

Selected References

American Diabetes Association. (1991). *Clinical practice recommendations.* American Diabetes Association 1990–1991. *Diabetes Care, 14*(Suppl. 2), 1–81.

Ascione, F. (1996). Medication compliance in the elderly. *Generations, 18*(2), 28–33.

Beyea, S. C., & Nicoll, L. H. (1995, February). Administration of medications via the intramuscular route: An integrative review of the literature and research-based protocol for the procedure. *Applied Nursing Research, 8*(1), 23–33.

Beyea, S., & Nicoll, L. (1996, January). Back to basics: Administering IM injections the right way. *American Journal of Nursing, 96*(1), 34–35.

Cohen, M., & Cohen, H. (1996, November). Medication errors: Following a game plan. *Nursing 96, 26*(11), 34–37.

Davis, N., Leape, L., Nightingale, S., Weate, W., & Galper, C. (1997, April). Medication errors: Rx for disaster. *Patient Care, 31*(8), 30–34, 36–39, 44–46.

Department of Justice Canada. (2000). Food and drugs act: Food and drug regulations. http://laws.justice.gc.ca/en/F-27/C.R.C.-c.870/115860.html

Fleming, D. F. (2000). Mightier than the syringe. *American Journal of Nursing, 100(11)*, 44–48.

Gilbar, P. J. (1999). A guide to enteral drug administration in palliative care. *Journal of Pain & Symptom Management*, 17(3), 197–207.

Goode, C., Titler, M., Rakel, B., Ones, D., Kleiber, C., Small, S., & Triolo, P. (1991, November/December). A meta-analysis of effects of heparin flush and saline flush: Quality and cost implication. *Nursing Research, 40*(6), 324–329.

Hayes, C. (1998). Injection technique: Intramuscular - 2 (Practical procedures for nurses, part 18.4). *Nursing Times, 94*(44), Nov.

Hayes, K. S. (1998, July/August). Randomized trial of geragogy-based medication instruction in the emergency department. *Nursing Research, 47*(4), 211–218.

Horn, B., & Swain, M. (1977). *Development of criterion measures of nursing care*. Ann Arbor, MI: University of Michigan.

Keen, M. F. (1986). Comparison of intramuscular injection techniques to reduce site discomfort and lesions. *Nursing Research, 35*(4), 207–210.

Konick-McMahan, J. (1996). Full speed ahead: Pushing intravenous medications. *Nursing 96, 26*, 26–31.

Kudzma, E. C. (1992, December). Drug response: All bodies are not created equal. *American Journal of Nursing, 92*, 48–50.

Lehmann, S., & Barber, J. (1991). Giving medications by feeding tube: How to avoid problems. *Nursing 91, 21*(11), 58–61.

Logue, R. M. (2003). Self-medication and the elderly, flow technology can help. *American Journal of Nursing, 102*(7), 51–55.

Malacharia, B., & Feloney, C. D. H. (2003). Going with the flow of anticoagulant therapy. *Nursing 2003, 33*(3), 36–42.

Mallet, J., & Bailey, C. (Eds.). (1996). The Royal Marsden NHS Trust Manual of Clinical Nursing Procedures (4th ed.). London: Blackwell Science Ltd. chapter 15, Guidelines – administration of injections – intramuscular injection. *Action B*, pp. 241–242.

Martin, D. (1998, July). Sharpen your technique for needle-free injection. *Nursing 98, 28*(7), 52–53.

McCaffery, M., & Pasero, C. (2000). How to choose the best route for an opiod. *Nursing 2000, 30*(12), 34–39.

McConnell, E. A. (1998). Clinical do's & don'ts. Giving medications through an enteral feeding tube. *Nursing 98, 28*(3), 66.

McConnell, E. A. (1999, January). Clinical do's and don'ts. *Nursing 99, 29*(1), 26.

Miller, D., & Miller, H. (2000). To crush or not to crush. *Nursing 2000, 30*(2), 50–52.

Murphy, J. (1991, July/August). Reducing the pain of intramuscular (IM) injections. *Advancing Clinical Care, 6*, 35.

Nath, C., & Donte, C. (2000). Lessons learned about insulin therapy. *Nursing 2000, 30*(1), 40–45.

Nicoll, L. H., & Beyea, S. C. (1996, March 8). Subcutaneous administration of insulin in adults: An integrative review of research. *The Online Journal of Knowledge Synthesis for Nursing, 3*. Document Number 4.

Olohan, K., & Zappitelli, D. (2003). The insulin pump, making life with diabetes easier. *American Journal of Nursing, 103*(4), 48–56.

Peloso, P. M. (2000). NSAIDs: A Faustain bargain. *American Journal of Nursing, 100*(6), 30–50.

Rankin, J. A., & Then, K. L. (2001). The international normalized ratio (INR): A review for orthopaedic nurses. *Journal of Orthopaedic Nursing, 5*(2), 89–92.

Then, K. L., & Rankin, J. A. (1999). The international normalized ratio (INR): A review. *Canadian Journal of Cardiovascular Nursing, 10*(1-2), 40–42.

Riley, D. (1998). Drugs and drug policy in Canada: A brief review and commentary. Canadian Foundation for Drug Policy & International Harm Reduction Association. http://www.parl.gc.ca/36/2/parlbus/commbus/senate/com-elille-e/rep-e/rep-nov98-e.htm

Rodger, M. A., & King, L. (2000). Drawing up and administering intramuscular injections: A review of the literature. *Journal of Advanced Nursing, 31*(3), 574–582.

Shuster, J. (1997). Adverse drug reactions. *Nursing 97, 27*(11), 35–39.

Weixler, D. (1994). Correcting metered-dose inhaler misuse. *Nursing 94, 24*(7), 62–64.

Woodcock, A. (1997). Use of spacers with metered dose inhalers. *Lancet, 349*(9050), 446.

WEBLINKS

Canadian Centre on Substance Abuse
http://www.ccsa.ca/
A nonprofit organization working to reduce the harm associated with the use of alcohol, tobacco, and other drugs.

The Centre for Addiction and Mental Health (CAMH)
http://www.camh.net/
The centre is a public hospital providing direct patient care for people with mental health and addiction problems, a research facility, an education and training institute, and a community-based organization providing health promotion services across the province of Ontario.

Canadian Pharmacists Association
http://www.cdnpharm.ca/index.cfm
The association is the national organization for pharmacists. Their Web site provides a source for drug information, pharmacy practices, and patient information.

Health Canada—Drug Strategy
http://www.hc-sc.gc.ca/hppb/cds-sca/cds/index.html
The site provides an overview of Canada's drug strategy.

Canadian Diabetes Association
http://www.diabetes.ca
The Canadian Diabetes Association's Web site is an online resource for people with, and affected by, diabetes and for health-care professionals treating those affected by the disease. The site provides access to a range of educational and support resources.

CHAPTER 29

Teaching

OBJECTIVES

After completing this chapter, you will be able to:

- Discuss the three main constructs of learning theory.
- Describe the three domains of learning.
- Analyze factors that facilitate learning throughout the life span.
- Identify factors that interfere with learning.
- Contrast the nursing process and the teaching process.
- Assess learning needs of learners and the learning environment.
- Identify nursing diagnoses that reflect the learning needs of clients.
- Describe the essential aspects of a teaching plan.
- Outline guidelines for effective teaching.
- Discuss advantages and disadvantages of selected teaching strategies.
- List the challenges of teaching clients of different cultures.
- Identify methods to evaluate learning.
- Demonstrate effective documentation of teaching-learning activities.

Client education is a major aspect of nursing practice and an important independent nursing function. Legislation related to nursing frequently has included client teaching as a function of nursing, thereby making teaching a legal and professional responsibility.

Client education is multifaceted, involving promoting, protecting, and maintaining health. It involves teaching about reducing health risk factors, increasing a person's level of wellness, and taking specific protective health measures. See the box below for specific areas of health teaching.

Learning

Like all people, clients have a variety of learning needs. A **learning need** is a desire or a requirement to know something that is presently unknown by the learner. Learning needs include new intellectual knowledge but can also include a new or different skill or physical ability, a new behaviour, or changing an old behaviour. **Learning** is a change in human disposition or capability that persists and that cannot be solely accounted for by growth.

Learning is represented by a change in behaviour. See the box at the right for attributes of learning.

Attributes of Learning

Learning is:

- An experience that occurs inside the learner
- The discovery of the personal meaning and relevance of ideas
- A consequence of experience
- A collaborative and cooperative process
- An evolutionary process
- A process that is both intellectual and emotional

An important aspect of learning is the individual's desire to learn and to act on the learning, referred to as **compliance.** In the health-care context, compliance is the extent to which a person's behaviour coincides with medical or health advice. Compliance is best illustrated when the person recognizes and accepts the need to learn and then follows through with the appropriate behaviours that reflect the learning. For example, a person diagnosed as having diabetes willingly learns about the special diet needed and then plans and follows the learned diet.

Areas for Client Health Teaching

Promotion of Health

- Increasing a person's level of wellness
- Growth and development topics
- Fertility control
- Hygiene
- Nutrition
- Exercise
- Stress management
- Lifestyle modification
- Resources within the community

Prevention of Illness/Injury

- Health screening (e.g., blood glucose levels, blood pressure, blood cholesterol, Pap test, mammograms, vision, hearing, routine physical examinations)
- Reducing health risk factors (e.g., lowering cholesterol level)
- Specific protective health measures (e.g., immunizations, use of condoms, use of sunscreen, use of medication, umbilical cord care)
- First aid
- Safety (e.g., using seat belts, helmets, walkers)

Restoration of Health

- Information about tests, diagnosis, treatment, medications
- Self-care skills or skills needed to care for family member
- Resources within health-care setting and community

Adapting to Altered Health and Function

- Adaptations in lifestyle
- Problem-solving skills
- Adaptation to changing health status
- Strategies to deal with current problems (e.g., home IV skills, medications, diet, activity limits, prostheses)
- Strategies to deal with future problems (e.g., fear of pain in terminal cancer, future surgeries or treatments)
- Information about treatments and likely outcomes
- Referrals to other health-care facilities or services
- Facilitation of positive self-image
- Grief and bereavement counselling

Canadian Society Notes

Fact	Implications for Nursing Practice
The Canadian Nurses Association Web site suggests that nurses can influence programs and policies that address the health-care needs of clients through learning and teaching cost-effective approaches and techniques.	Nurses have a responsibility to teach others about cost-effective health-care practices.
The Valuing Literacy in Canada program will contribute $2.5 million over five years to stimulate applied research aimed at providing policy makers and practitioners with leading-edge knowledge on literacy. (Social Sciences and Humanities Research Council of Canada)	Nurses need to be aware of the literacy level of their clients and to incorporate this knowledge into their teaching plans.
The Victorian Order of Nurses (VON) Canada is employing point-of-care technology that gives the nurse access to complete and current patient data.	Nurses need current information upon which to base their teaching of clients.

Andragogy is the art and science of teaching adults, in contrast to **pedagogy,** the discipline concerned with helping children learn. Nurses can use the following andragogic concepts about learners as a guide for client teaching (Knowles, 1984):

- As people mature, they move from dependence to independence.
- An adult's previous experiences can be used as a resource for learning.
- An adult's readiness to learn is often related to a developmental task or social role.
- An adult is more oriented to learning when the material is useful immediately, not sometime in the future.

Learning Theories

Theories about how and why people learn can be traced to the 17th century. Three main theoretical constructs are behaviourism, cognitivism, and humanism.

Behaviourism

Behaviourism was originally advanced by Edward Thorndike, whose major contribution applicable to teaching is that learning should be based on the learner's behaviour. In addition to Thorndike, major behaviourist theorists include I. Pavlov, B. F. Skinner, and A. Bandura.

Behaviourists believe that the environment influences behaviour and how a person controls it; moreover, they maintain that it is the essential factor determining human action. In the behaviourist school of thought, an act is called a *response* when it can be traced to the effects of a stimulus.

Skinner's and Pavlov's work focused on **conditioning** behavioural responses to a stimulus that causes the response or behaviour. Skinner also introduced the importance of *positive reinforcement* in fostering repetition of an action. Bandura (1971) introduced a modelling theory. He claims that most learning comes from observational learning and instruction rather than from overt trial-and-error behaviour. Bandura's research focuses on **imitation,** the process by which individuals copy or reproduce what they have observed, and **modelling,** the process by which a person learns by observing the behaviour of others.

Cognitivism

Cognitivism depicts learning as a complex cognitive activity. In other words, learning is largely a mental or intellectual or thinking process. The learner structures and processes information. Perceptions are selectively chosen by the individual, and personal characteristics have an impact on how a cue is perceived. Cognitivists also emphasize the importance of social, emotional, and physical contexts in which learning occurs, such as the teacher-learner relationship and environment. Developmental readiness and individual readiness (expressed as motivation) are other key factors associated with cognitive approaches.

Major cognitive theorists include J. Piaget, K. Lewin, and B. Bloom. Piaget's five major phases of cognitive development are discussed in Chapter 19. Lewin (1951) says that learning involves four different types of change: change in cognitive structure, change in motivation, change in one's sense of belonging to the group, and gain in voluntary muscle control. His widely known theory of change has three basic stages: unfreezing, moving, and refreezing. These stages are discussed in detail in Chapter 30.

Bloom (1956) has identified three domains or areas of learning: cognitive, affective, and psychomotor. The *cognitive domain* includes six intellectual skills from the simple to the complex, beginning with knowing, comprehending, and applying. The *affective domain* includes feelings, emotions, interests, attitudes, and appreciations. It involves five major learning categories. The *psychomotor domain* includes motor skills, such as giving an injection. It includes seven categories from perception (lowest level) to origination (highest level). Nurses should include each of these three domains in client teaching plans. For example, teaching a client how to irrigate a colostomy is in the psychomotor domain. But an important part of a teaching plan for a client with a colostomy is to teach why a specific amount of fluid is used and when the irrigation should be carried out; this is in the cognitive domain. Helping the client accept the colostomy and maintain self-esteem is in the affective domain.

Humanism

Humanistic learning theory focuses on both cognitive and affective qualities of the learner. Prominent members of this school of thought include Abraham Maslow and Carl Rogers. According to humanistic theory, learning is believed to be self-motivated, self-initiated, and self-evaluated. Each individual is viewed as a unique composite of biological, psychological, social, cultural, and spiritual factors. Learning focuses on self-development and achieving full potential; it is best when it is relevant to the learner. Autonomy and self-determination are important; the learner identifies the learning needs and takes the initiative to meet these needs. The learner is thus an active participant and takes responsibility for meeting individual learning needs.

Using Learning Theories

The major attributes of *behaviourist* theories include the careful identification of what is to be taught and the immediate identification of and reward for correct responses. However, the theory is not easily applied to complex learning situations and is limiting in terms of the learner's role in the teaching process. Nurses applying behaviouristic theory will:

- Provide sufficient practice time and both immediate and repeat testing and re-demonstration.
- Provide opportunities for learners to solve problems by trial and error.
- Select teaching strategies that avoid distracting information and that evoke the desired response.
- Praise the learner for correct behaviour, and provide positive feedback at intervals throughout the learning experience.
- Provide role models of the desired behaviour.

The major attributes of *cognitive* theory are its recognition of developmental levels of learners and acknowledgement of the learner's motivation and environment. However, some or many of the motivational and environmental factors may be beyond the teacher's control. Nurses applying cognitive theory will:

- Provide a social, emotional, and physical environment conducive to learning.
- Encourage a positive teacher-learner relationship.
- Select multisensory teaching strategies since perception is influenced by the senses.
- Recognize that personal characteristics have an impact on how cues are perceived, and develop appropriate teaching approaches to target different learning styles.
- Assess a person's developmental and individual readiness to learn, and adapt teaching strategies to the learner's developmental level.
- Select behavioural objectives and teaching strategies that encompass the cognitive, affective, and psychomotor domains of learning.

The major attributes of *humanism* are its focuses on the feelings and attitudes of learners, on the importance of the individual in identifying learning needs and in taking responsibility for them, and on the self-motivation of the learners to work toward self-reliance and independence. Nurses applying humanistic theory will:

- Encourage the learners to establish goals, and promote self-directed learning.
- Encourage active learning by serving as a facilitator, mentor, or resource for the learner.
- Expose the learner to new relevant information, and ask appropriate questions to encourage the learner to seek answers.

Factors Facilitating Learning

Motivation

Motivation to learn is the desire to learn. It greatly influences how quickly and how much a person learns. Motivation is generally greatest when a person recognizes a need and believes the need will be met through learning. It is not enough for the need to be identified and verbalized by the nurse; it must be experienced by the client. Often, the nurse's task is to help the client personally work through the problem and identify the need. Sometimes, clients or support people need help identifying relevant situational elements before they can see a need. For instance, clients with heart disease may need to know the effects of smoking before they recognize the need to stop smoking. Or, adolescents may need to know the consequences of an untreated sexually transmitted disease before they see the need for treatment.

Readiness

Readiness to learn is the demonstration of behaviours or cues that reflect the learner's motivation to learn at a specific time. Readiness reflects not only the desire or willingness to learn but also the ability to learn at a specific time. For example, a client may want to learn self-care during a dressing change, but, if he will experience pain or discomfort, he may not be able to learn. The nurse can provide pain medication to make the client more comfortable so that he is more able to learn. The nurse's role is often to encourage the development of readiness.

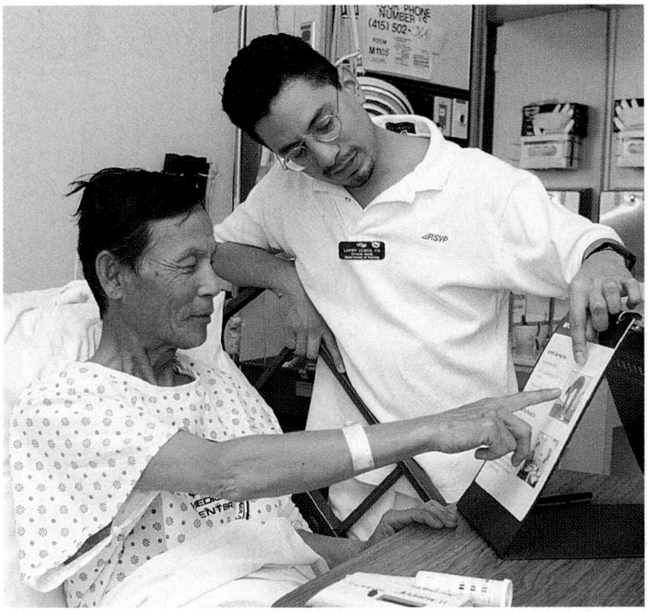

Figure 29.1 Learning is facilitated when the client is interested and actively involved

Active Involvement

When the learner is actively involved in the process of learning, learning becomes more meaningful. If the learner actively participates in planning and discussion, learning is faster and retention is better (Figure 29.1). Active learning promotes critical thinking, enabling learners to problem solve more effectively. Clients who are actively involved in learning about their health care may be more able to apply the learning to their own situation. For example, clients who are actively involved in learning about their therapeutic diets may be more able to apply the principles being taught to their cultural food preferences and their usual eating habits. Passive learning, such as listening to a lecture or watching a film, does not foster optimal learning.

Relevance

The knowledge or skill to be learned must be personally relevant to the learner. The client can learn more easily if he can connect the new knowledge to that which she already knows or has experienced. For example, if a client is diagnosed with hypertension and is overweight and has symptoms of headaches and fatigue, she is more likely to understand the need to lose weight if she remembers having more energy when she weighed less. The nurse needs to validate the relevance of learning with the client throughout the learning process.

Feedback

Feedback is information relating a person's performance to a desired goal. It has to be meaningful to the learner. Feedback that accompanies the practice of psychomotor skills helps the person learn those skills. Support of desired behaviour through praise, positively worded corrections, and suggestions of alternative methods are ways of providing positive feedback. Negative feedback, such as ridicule, anger, or sarcasm, can lead people to withdraw from learning. Such feedback, viewed as a type of punishment, may cause the client to avoid the teacher in order to avoid punishment.

Nonjudgmental Support

People learn best when they believe they are accepted and will not be judged. The person who expects to be judged as a "poor" or "good" client will not learn as well as the person who feels no such threat. Once learners have succeeded in accomplishing a task or understanding a concept, they gain self-confidence in their ability to learn. This reduces their anxiety about failure and can motivate greater learning. Successful learners have increased confidence with which to accept failure.

Simple to Complex

Learning is facilitated by material that is logically organized and proceeds from the *simple to the complex.* Such organization enables the learner to comprehend new information, assimilate it with previous learning, and form new understandings. Of course, simple and complex are relative terms depending on the level at which the person is learning. What is simple for one person may be complex for another.

Repetition

Repetition of key concepts and facts facilitates retention of newly learned material. Practice of psychomotor skills, particularly with feedback from the nurse, improves performance of those skills and facilitates their transfer to another setting.

Timing

People retain information and psychomotor skills best when the time between learning and active use of the learning is short; the longer the time interval, the more learning is forgotten. For example, a person who is only shown literature and videotapes about administering insulin and is not permitted to administer the insulin until discharge from the hospital is unlikely to remember what was learned. However, if the person is allowed to give the injections while in the hospital, the person's learning will be enhanced.

Environment

An *optimal learning environment* facilitates learning by reducing distraction and providing physical and psychological comfort. It has adequate lighting that is free from glare, a comfortable room temperature, and good ventilation. Most students know what it is like to try to learn in a hot, stuffy room; the consequent drowsiness interferes with concentration. Noise can also distract the student and

TABLE 29.1 Barriers to Learning

Barrier	Explanation	Nursing Implications
Acute illness	Client requires all resources and energy to cope with illness.	Defer teaching until client is less ill.
Pain	Pain decreases ability to concentrate.	Deal with pain before teaching.
Prognosis	Client can be preoccupied with illness and unable to concentrate on new information.	Defer teaching to a better time.
Biorhythms	Mental and physical performances have a circadian rhythm.	Adapt time of teaching to suit client.
Emotion (e.g., anxiety, denial, depression, grief)	Emotions require energy and distract from learning.	Deal with emotions and possible misinformation first.
Language	Client may not be fluent in the nurse's language.	Obtain services of an interpreter or nurse with appropriate language skills.
Age		
Older adults	Vision, hearing, and motor control can be impaired in older adults.	Consider sensory and motor deficits in teaching plan.
Children	Children have a shorter attention span.	Plan shorter and more active learning episodes.
Culture/Religion	There may be cultural or religious restrictions on certain types of knowledge, for example, birth control information.	Assess the client's cultural/religious needs when planning learning activities.
Physical disability	Visual, hearing, sensory, or motor impairments may interfere with a client's ability to learn.	Plan teaching activities appropriate to learner's physical abilities. For example, provide audio learning tools for the client who is blind, or large-print materials for the client whose vision is impaired.
Mental disability	Impaired cognitive ability may affect the client's capacity for learning.	Assess client's capacity for learning and plan teaching activities to complement the client's ability while planning more complex learning for the client's caregivers.

interfere with listening and thinking. To facilitate learning in a hospital setting, nurses should choose a time when no visitors are present and interruptions are unlikely.

Privacy is essential for some learning. For example, when a client is learning to irrigate a colostomy, the presence of others can be embarrassing and, thus, interfere with learning. However, when a client is particularly anxious, having a support person present may give the client confidence.

Factors Inhibiting Learning

Many factors inhibit learning. Some of the most common are described next and in Table 29.1.

Emotions

Emotions, such as fear, anger, and depression, can impede learning. A high level of anxiety resulting in agitation and the inability to focus or concentrate can also inhibit learning. Clients or families who are experiencing extreme emotional states may not hear spoken words or may retain only part of the communication. Emotional responses, such as fear and anxiety, may be relieved by information that relieves uncertainty. Medications may be prescribed for extremely distraught clients or families to reduce their anxiety and put them in an emotional state where understanding or learning can occur. By contrast, clients who appear disinterested and unconcerned may need to be cautioned about potential problems in order to increase their motivation to learn.

Physiological Events

Learning can be inhibited by *physiologial events,* such as a critical illness, pain, or sensory deficits. Because the client cannot concentrate and apply energy to learning, the learning itself is impaired. The nurse should try to reduce the physiological barriers to learning as much as possible before teaching. Providing analgesics and rest before teaching is often helpful.

Cultural Barriers

There are also *cultural barriers* to learning, such as language or values. Obviously, the client who does not understand the nurse's language will learn little. Western medicine may conflict with cultural healing beliefs and practices. To be effective, nurses must deal directly with this conflict; otherwise, the client may be partially or totally noncompliant with recommended treatments. Another impediment to learning is *differing values* held by the client and the health team. For example, a client who comes from a culture that does not value slimness may have difficulty learning about a reducing diet.

Psychomotor Ability

It is important that the nurse be aware of a client's psychomotor skills when planning teaching. Psychomotor skills can be affected by health. For example, an elderly client who has severe osteoarthritis of the hands may not be able to tie a bandage. The following physical abilities are important for learning psychomotor skills:

1. *Muscle strength.* For example, an older client who cannot rise from a chair because of insufficient leg and muscle strength cannot be expected to learn to lift herself out of a bathtub without assistance.
2. *Motor coordination.* Gross motor coordination is required for such movements as walking, and fine motor coordination is needed when using utensils, such as a fork for eating. For example, a client who has advanced amyotrophic lateral sclerosis (ALS) involving the lower limbs will probably be unable to use a walker.
3. *Energy.* Energy is required for most psychomotor skills, and learning these skills uses more energy. People who are ill or elderly often have limited energy resources; learning and carrying out these skills must be timed for when the client's energy sources are not depleted.
4. *Sensory acuity.* Sight is used for most learning (e.g., walking with crutches, changing a dressing, drawing a medication into a syringe). Clients who are visually impaired often need the assistance of a support person to carry out such tasks.

Teaching

Teaching is a system of activities intended to produce learning. The teaching process is intentionally designed to produce specific learning.

The teaching-learning process involves dynamic interaction between teacher and learner. Each participant in the process communicates information, emotions, perceptions, and attitudes to the other. The teaching process and the nursing process are much alike. See Table 29.2.

TABLE 29.2 Comparison of the Teaching Process and the Nursing Process

Step	Teaching Process	Nursing Process
1	Collect data; analyze client's learning strengths and deficits.	Collect data; analyze client's strengths and deficits.
2	Make educational diagnoses.	Make nursing diagnoses.
3	Prepare teaching plan: ■ Write learning objectives. ■ Select content and time frame. ■ Select teaching strategies.	Plan nursing goals/ desired outcomes, and select interventions.
4	Implement teaching plan.	Implement nursing strategies.
5	Evaluate client learning based on achievement of learning objectives.	Evaluate client outcomes based on achievement of goal criteria.

Nurses teach a variety of learners in various settings. They teach clients and their families or significant others in the hospital, the home, or in assisted living and long-term care facilities. Nurses teach professional colleagues and subordinate health-care personnel in academic institutions, such as vocational schools, colleges, and universities, and in health-care facilities, such as hospitals or nursing homes. Nurses also teach large and small groups of learners in community health education programs.

Teaching Clients and Their Families

Nurses may teach individual clients in one-to-one teaching episodes. For example, the nurse may teach about wound care while changing a client's dressing or may teach about diet, exercise, and other lifestyle behaviours that minimize the risk of a heart attack for a client who has a cardiac problem. The nurse may also be involved in teaching family members or other support people who are caring for the client. Nurses working in obstetric and pediatric areas teach parents and sometimes grandparents how to care for children.

Because of decreased length of hospital stays, time constraints on client education may occur. Nurses need to provide client education that will ensure the client's safe transition from one level of care to another and make appropriate plans for follow-up education in the client's home. Discharge plans must include both information about what the client has been taught before transfer or discharge and what remains for the client to learn to perform self-care in the home or other residence.

Teaching in the Community

Nurses are often involved in community health education programs. Such teaching activities may be voluntary as part of the nurse's involvement in an organization, such as the Red Cross or Planned Parenthood, or they may be compensated as part of the nurse's work role. Community teaching activities may be to large groups of people who have an interest in some aspect of health, such as nutrition classes, cardiopulmonary resuscitation (CPR), cardiac risk factor reduction classes, and bicycle or swimming safety programs. Community education programs can also be for small groups or individual learners, such as childbirth classes or family planning information.

Teaching Health Personnel

Nurses are also involved in the instruction of professional colleagues. Nurses in nursing practice settings are often involved in the clinical instruction of nursing students. Experienced nurses may function as preceptors for students, new graduate nurses or for newly employed nurses. Nurses with specialized knowledge and experience may share that knowledge and experience with nurses who are new to that practice area. Such specialized courses include acute care nursing, perioperative nursing, and quality improvement/quality assurance.

Nurses may also be involved in teaching other health-care professionals. Nurses may participate in the education of medical students or allied health students. In this capacity, the nurse educator is often clarifying for other health-care professionals what the role of the nurse is or how the nurse can assist them in their care of the client. The nurse may also teach health-care colleagues knowledge or skills that are considered the domain of nursing, such as nonpharmaceutical comfort measures.

Teaching Guidelines

The following guidelines for effective learning and teaching may be helpful to nurses:

- Teaching activities should help a learner meet individual learning objectives. These objectives should be determined by the client (learner) and the nurse (teacher). If certain activities do not assist the learner, these need to be reassessed; perhaps other activities can replace them. For example, explanation alone may not be able to teach a client to handle a syringe. Actually handling the syringe may be more effective (Figure 29.2).
- Rapport between teacher and learner is essential. A relationship that is both accepting and constructive will best assist learning. The nurse should take time to establish rapport before teaching.
- The teacher who uses the client's previous learning in the present situation encourages the client and facilitates learning of new skills. For example, a person who already knows how to cook can use this knowledge when learning to prepare food for a special diet.
- The nurse-teacher must be able to communicate clearly and concisely. The words used need to have the same meaning to the learner as to the teacher. For example, a client who is taught not to put water on an area of skin may think a wet washcloth is permissible for washing the area. In effect, the nurse needs to explain that no water or moisture should touch the area.
- Knowledge of the learners and the factors that affect their learning should be established before planning the teaching.
- When the learner is involved in planning, learning is often enhanced.
- Teaching that involves a number of the learner's senses often enhances learning. For example, when teaching about changing a surgical dressing, the nurse can tell the client about the procedure (hearing), show how to change the dressing (sight), and show how to manipulate the equipment (touch).
- The anticipated behavioural changes that indicate that learning has taken place must always be within the context of the client's lifestyle and resources. For example, it would probably not be reasonable to expect a woman to soak in a tub of hot water four times a day if she did not have a bathtub and had to heat water on a stove.

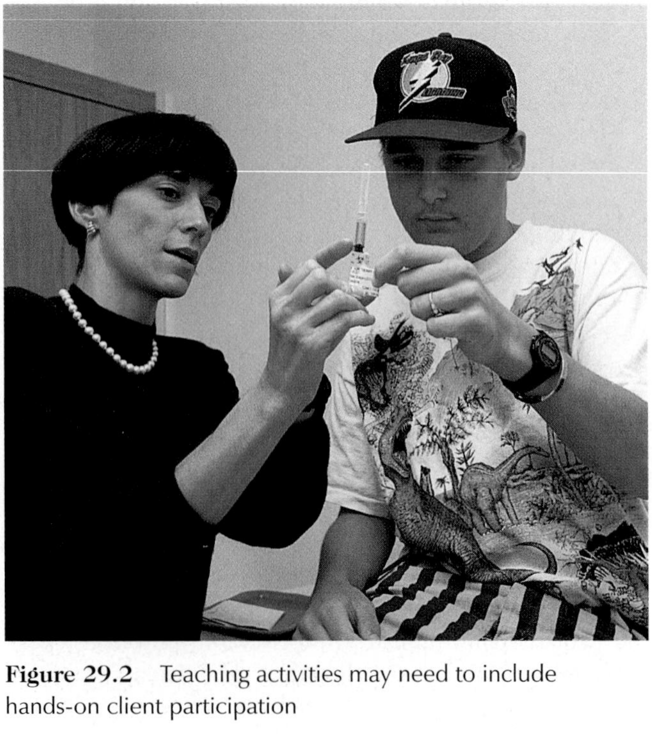

Figure 29.2 Teaching activities may need to include hands-on client participation

There are certain factors within the external environment that can optimize teaching; these include the setting, noise, temperature, lighting, furniture, and teaching resources. An environment that supports patient and family education will facilitate health. The nurse needs to both identify obstacles within the environment that challenge patient education and to remove them. For example, if the patient's roommate will not turn down the television, is there another place where teaching can be conducted? Some changes to improve the teaching environment can be done independently, and others require a team effort.

Assessing

A comprehensive assessment of learning needs incorporates data from the nursing history and physical assessment and addresses the client's support system. It also considers client characteristics that may influence the learning process: for example, readiness to learn, motivation to learn, and reading and comprehension level.

The nurse's own knowledge of common learning needs required by clients experiencing similar health problems is another source of information. Learning needs change as the client's health status changes, so nurses must constantly reassess them.

Nursing History

Several elements in the nursing history provide clues to learning needs. These elements include (1) age, (2) the client's understanding and perceptions of the health problem, (3) health beliefs and practices, (4) cultural factors, (5) economic factors, (6) learning style, and (7) client's support systems. Examples of interview questions to elicit this information are shown in the accompanying box.

ASSESSMENT INTERVIEW

Learning Needs and Characteristics

Primary Health Problem

- Tell me what you know about your current health problem. What do you think caused it?
- What concerns do you have about it?
- How has the problem affected what you can or cannot do during your usual activities (e.g., work, recreation, shopping, housework)?
- What do you or did you do at home to relieve the problem? How helpful was it?
- How have the treatments you have started helped your problem?
- What, if any, difficulties have the treatments caused you (e.g., inconvenience, cost, discomfort)?
- Tell me about the tests (surgery, treatments) you are going to have.

Health Beliefs

- How would you describe your health generally?
- What things do you usually do to keep healthy?
- What health problems do you think you may be at risk for because of family history, age, diet, occupation, inadequate exercise, or other habits, such as smoking?
- What changes would you be willing to make to decrease your risk for these problems or to improve your health?

Cultural Factors

- What language do you use most often when speaking and writing?
- Do you seek the advice of another health practitioner?
- Do you use herbs or other medications or treatments commonly used in your cultural group?
- Does your current doctor know about these?
- What advice or treatments given previously by your doctor conflicted with values or beliefs you consider important?
- When a conflict arose, what did you do?

Learning Style

- Note the client's age and developmental level.
- What level of education have you received?
- Do you like to read?
- Where do you obtain health information (e.g., physician, nurse, magazines, books, pharmacist, and so on)?
- How do you best learn new things?
  a. By reading about them
  b. By talking about them
  c. By watching a movie or demonstration
  d. By computer
  e. By listening to the teacher
  f. By first being shown how something works and then doing it
  g. On your own or in a group

Client Support System

- Would you like a family member or friend to help you learn about things you need to do to take care of yourself?
- Who do you think would be interested in learning with you?

Age

Age provides information on the person's developmental status that may indicate distinctive health teaching content and teaching approaches. Simple questions to school-age children and adolescents will elicit information on what they know. Observing children in play provides information about their motor and intellectual development as well as relationships with other children. For older people, conversation and questioning may reveal slow recall or limited psychomotor skills, sensory deficits, and learning difficulties.

Client's Understanding of Health Problem

Clients' perceptions of their current health problems and concerns may indicate knowledge deficits or misinformation. In addition, the effects of the problem on the client's usual activities can alert the nurse to other areas requiring instruction. For example, people who cannot manage self-care at home often need information about community resources and services.

Health Beliefs and Practices

A client's health beliefs and practices are important to consider in any teaching plan. The health belief model described in Figure 9.6 on page 138 provides a predictor of preventive health behaviour. However, even if a nurse is convinced that a particular client's health beliefs should be changed, doing so may not be possible because so many factors are involved in a person's health beliefs.

Cultural Factors

Many cultural groups have their own beliefs and practices, a number of them related to diet, health, illness, and lifestyle. It is therefore important to know how the practices and values held by clients affect their learning needs.

Folk beliefs of certain groups may also affect learning. Although the client may readily understand the health-care information being taught, this learning may not be implemented in the home where folk health practices prevail. For additional information, see Chapter 14 and the section on transcultural teaching later in this chapter.

Economic Factors

Economic factors can also affect a client's learning. For example, a client who cannot afford to obtain a new sterile syringe for each injection of insulin may find it difficult to learn to administer the insulin when the nurse teaches that a new syringe should be used each time.

Learning Style

Considerable research has been done on people's learning styles. The best way to learn varies with the individual. Some people are visual learners and learn best by watching. Other people do not visualize an activity well; they learn best by actually manipulating equipment and discovering how it works. Other people can learn well from reading things presented in an orderly fashion. Still other people learn best in groups where they can relate to other people. For some, stressing the thinking part of a skill and its logic will promote learning. For other people, stressing the feeling part or interpersonal aspect motivates and promotes learning.

Sometimes, the nurse does not have the time to assess each learner, identify the person's particular learning style, and then adapt teaching accordingly; what the nurse can do, however, is to ask clients how they have learned things best in the past or how they like to learn. Many people know what helps them learn, and the nurse can use this information in planning the teaching. Using a variety of teaching techniques and varying activities during teaching are good ways to match learners with learning styles. One technique will be effective for some clients, whereas other techniques will be suited to clients with different learning styles.

Client Support System

The nurse explores the client's support system to determine the extent to which others may enhance learning and offer support. Family members or a close friend may help the client perform required skills at home and maintain required lifestyle changes.

Physical Examination

The general survey part of the physical examination provides useful clues to the client's learning needs, such as mental status, energy level, and nutritional status. Other parts of the physical examination reveal data about the client's physical capacity to learn and to perform self-care activities. For example, visual ability, hearing ability, and muscle coordination affect the selection of content and approaches to teaching.

Readiness to Learn

Clients who are ready to learn often behave differently from those who are not. A client who is ready may search out information, for instance, by asking questions, reading books or articles, talking to others, and generally showing interest. The person who is not ready to learn is more likely to avoid the subject or situation. In addition, the unready client may change the subject when it is brought up by the nurse. For example, the nurse might say, "I was wondering about a good time to show you how to change your dressing," and the client responds, "Oh, my wife will take care of everything."

The nurse assesses for:

- *Physical readiness.* Is the client able to focus on things other than physical status, or are pain, fatigue, and immobility using up all of the client's time and energy?
- *Emotional readiness.* Is the client emotionally ready to learn self-care activities? Clients who are extremely anxious, depressed, or grieving over their health status are not ready.

- *Cognitive readiness.* Can the client think clearly at this point? Are the effects of anesthesia and analgesia altering the client's level of consciousness?

Nurses can promote readiness to learn by providing physical and emotional support during the critical stage of recovery. As the client stabilizes physically and emotionally, the nurse can provide opportunities to learn.

The time when readiness to learn is at its peak is called the teachable moment. This can happen anywhere at any time. Nurses need to take advantage of such times in addition to scheduled teaching activities.

Motivation

As discussed earlier, motivation relates to whether the client wants to learn and is usually greatest when the client is ready, the learning need is recognized, and the information being offered is meaningful to the client.

Nurses can increase a client's motivation in several ways:

- By relating the learning to something the client values, and helping the client see the relevance of the learning
- By helping the client make the learning situation pleasant and nonthreatening
- By encouraging self-direction and independence
- By demonstrating a positive attitude about the client's ability to learn
- By offering continuing support and encouragement as the client attempts to learn (i.e., positive reinforcement)
- By creating a learning situation where the client is likely to succeed (succeeding in small tasks motivates the client to continue learning)

Reading Level

The nurse should not assume that a client's reading level is equal to the highest grade or level of formal education the client has completed. Dowe, Lawrence, Carlson, and Keyserling (1997) recommend that clients should be asked the level of education they have attained and their preference for health teaching materials. They also state that health teaching materials for clients with low literacy levels should be written at a low readability level (eighth grade or lower). See the accompanying research box. Many readability formulas are available to assess reading levels of client educational material. The SMOG index is shown in the box on page 678. Several computer programs, such as RIGHTwriter and Grammatique, also rate the reading levels of written material. It should be noted that assessed reading levels may vary between the different formulas or computer programs. Readability formulas mainly focus on the length of sentences and the number of syllables in each word. Doak, Doak, and Root (1996) advise that several other factors affect readability:

- Print size and type style
- Colour contrast between the ink and the paper
- Whether it looks hard to read
- The number of components and facts in each paragraph
- The use of familiar words in an unfamiliar context

Readability formulas are also available in at least 12 languages other than English (Doak, Doak, & Root, 1996).

Diagnosing

Nursing diagnoses for clients with learning needs can be designated in two ways: as the client's primary concern or problem, or as the etiology of a nursing diagnosis associated with the client's response to health alterations or dysfunction. Clinical applications of the following diagnoses are shown in Table 29.3.

Learning Need as the Diagnostic Label

The North American Nursing Diagnosis Association (NANDA) includes the following diagnostic labels appropriate to a client's learning needs when the learning need is the primary concern:

- ***Knowledge Deficient:*** the state in which an individual or group experiences a deficiency in cognitive knowledge or psychomotor skills concerning the condition

RESEARCH NOTE

Clients' Use of Health Teaching Materials at Three Readability Levels

The study examined how much clients use and learn from literature about medications that is written at three different readability levels. Level 1 literature had a SMOG readability of grade 6; Level 2 readability was grade 9; and Level 3 readability was grade 12. Results showed an interaction effect on knowledge score between the readability level of the medication literature and the amount of schooling the participants reported. People with higher education learned most from the hardest (Level 3) literature and persons with the least schooling learned the most from the easiest (Level 1) literature.

Implications: Nurses should provide clients with various options of health education literature and ask clients their preference for level of literature. Educators should prepare health education literature at various levels to meet clients' various learning needs.

Source: Dowe, M. C., Lawrence, P. A., Carlson, J., & Keyserling, T .C. (1997). Patients' use of health-teaching materials at three readability levels. *Applied Nursing Research, 10*(2), 86–93.

Determining Readability Level of Written Materials Using the SMOG Index

To determine the reading level of learning materials for clients, choose 30 sentences in the reading. Pick 10 from the beginning, 10 from the middle, and 10 from the end of the reading. Count all the words with three or more syllables; total these. Obtain the nearest square root of this number of three or more syllabic words. Add three to the square root. This gives you the SMOG grades. Find the number in the list below, and read across to find the reading grade level.

Number of Words with Three or More Syllables	*Reading Grade Level*
0–2	4
3–6	5
7–12	6
13–20	7
21–30	8
31–42	9
43–56	10
57–72	11
73–90	12

To decrease the reading level and simplify the client educational material:

- Use smaller words.
- Avoid words with several syllables.
- Write shorter sentences.
- Explain terms that must be used.
- Use easy, common words.

Source: Adapted from S.T. Stephens. (1992). Patient educational materials: Are they readable? *Oncology Nursing Forum, 19,* 84; and M. Wong. (1992). Self-care instructions: Do patients understand educational materials? *Focus on critical care, 19,* 47–49.

or treatment plan (Carpenito, 1999). Conley (1998) proposes ***Information-Seeking Behaviours*** as an alternative diagnosis to ***Knowledge Deficient.***

Whenever the diagnostic label ***Knowledge Deficient*** is used, either the client is seeking health information or the nurse has identified a learning need. The area of deficiency should always be included in the diagnosis. Following are examples using the NANDA label ***Knowledge Deficient*** as the primary concern (problem):

- ***Knowledge Deficient: low-calorie diet*** related to inexperience with newly ordered therapy
- ***Knowledge Deficient: home safety hazards*** related to denial of declining health and lack of interest in learning

A second nursing diagnostic label where a learning need may be the primary concern (problem) is:

- ***Health-Seeking Behaviours:*** active seeking (by a person in stable health) of ways to alter personal health habits and/or the environment in order to move toward a higher level of health (NANDA, 2003).

When this diagnostic label is used, the client is seeking health information; the client does not have an altered response or dysfunction at the time but may be seeking information to improve health or prevent illness. This diagnosis is especially appropriate for clients attending community health education programs. Following are examples using the NANDA label ***Health-Seeking Behaviour*** as the primary concern (problem):

- ***Health-Seeking Behaviour: exercise and activity*** related to desire to improve health behaviours and decrease risk of heart disease. This diagnosis may be appropriate for the client who has identified a personal health risk for a cardiac condition and wants to minimize that risk through exercise.
- ***Health-Seeking Behaviour: home safety hazards*** related to desire to minimize risk of injury. This diagnosis may be appropriate for parents of a toddler who are seeking information to ensure that their home is safe for their child. The diagnosis might also be used when an older adult seeks information to ensure that the home is free of risk factors for falls or other injuries common to the older adult.

A third nursing diagnostic label where a learning need may be the primary concern is:

- ***Noncompliance (Adherence, Ineffective):*** the state in which an individual or group desires to comply but factors are present that deter adherence to health-related advice given by health professionals.

The diagnostic label ***Noncompliance*** should be used with caution. The nurse must recognize that compliance and noncompliance are not always matters of choice. In general, the diagnosis ***Noncompliance*** is associated with the desire to comply but the inability to do so because of intervening factors (NANDA, 2003). Factors that influence a client's compliance with health teaching include understanding or comprehension of the teaching, sensory or motor deficits that may have interfered with learning (such as vision or hearing deficits), the experienced negative side effects of the treatment, financial inability to carry out the treatment plan, language barriers, or ineffective teaching on the part of the health-care team.

Knowledge Deficit as the Etiology

Another way to deal with identified learning needs of clients is to write the knowledge deficit as the etiology, or second part, of the diagnosis statement. Such nursing diagnoses are written in the following format:

TABLE 29.3 Clinical Application: Assessment Data Clusters and Related Nursing Diagnoses

Data Cluster	Nursing Diagnosis
The nurse brings Mr. Wong the first dose of a medication ordered by his physician. The nurse asks whether anyone has explained what this medication is and why he is taking it. He says no.	***Knowledge Deficient: medication information*** related to lack of exposure to information regarding newly prescribed medication
Mildred Cumming is a 74-year-old widow with a history of hypertension. Her blood pressure is 150/96. She is on daily antihypertensive therapy. When asked if she is taking her medication as prescribed, she tells the nurse that she is taking her medication every other day because it is expensive and she cannot afford to take it every day.	***Noncompliance with medication plan*** related to insufficient finances
George Evans is a 45-year-old man who has come to the clinic for his annual physical examination. He expresses concern about his family history of heart disease and requests information about activities to decrease his risk of heart disease.	***Health-Seeking Behaviour: nutrition information*** to reduce risk of heart disease related to desire to decrease risk of heart disease ***Health-Seeking Behaviour: activity and exercise information*** to reduce risk of heart disease related to desire to decrease risk of heart disease

- ***Risk for*** (specify) related to knowledge deficit (or lack of skill).

Examples include the following:

- ***Risk for Parenting, Impaired*** related to knowledge deficit: skills in infant care and feeding
- ***Risk for Infection*** related to knowledge deficit: sexually transmitted diseases and their prevention

Other nursing diagnoses in which a knowledge deficit can be the etiology include:

- ***Risk for Injury***
- ***Ineffective Breast-feeding***
- ***Impaired Adjustment***
- ***Ineffective Coping***
- ***Ineffective Health Maintenance***

It must also be noted that most NANDA-approved nursing diagnoses imply a teaching-learning need. For example, the nursing diagnosis ***Constipation*** suggests the need for a review of bowel hygiene practices, including diet, hydration, and exercise/activity.

Planning

Developing a teaching plan (see the following sample teaching plan for wound care) is accomplished in a series of steps. Involving the client at this time promotes the formation of a meaningful plan and stimulates client motivation. The client who helps formulate the teaching plan is more likely to achieve the desired outcomes.

Determining Teaching Priorities

The client's learning needs must be ranked according to priority. The client and the nurse should do this together, with the client's priorities always being considered. Once a client's priorities have been addressed, the client is generally more motivated to concentrate on other identified learning needs. For example, a man who wants to know all about coronary artery disease may not be ready to learn how to change his lifestyle until he meets his own need to learn more about the disease. Nurses can also use theoretical frameworks, such as Maslow's hierarchy of needs, to establish priorities. See Chapter 5.

Setting Learning Objectives

Learning objectives can be considered the same as *desired outcomes for other nursing diagnoses.* They are written in the same way. Like client outcomes, learning objectives:

- State the client (learner) behaviour or performance, not nurse behaviour. For example, "Will identify personal risk factors for heart disease" (client behaviour), not "To teach the client about cardiac risk factors" (nurse behaviour).
- Reflect an observable, measurable activity. The performance may be visible (e.g., walking) or invisible (e.g., adding a column of figures). However, it is necessary to be able to deduce whether an unobservable activity has been mastered from some performance that represents the activity. Therefore, the performance of an objective might be written: "Selects low-fat foods from a menu" (observable), not "understands

Sample Teaching Plan: Wound Care

Assessment of Learner: A 24-year-old male college student suffered a 7-cm laceration on the lower anterior part of the left leg during a hockey game. The laceration was cleaned, sutured, and bandaged. The client was given an appointment to return to the health clinic in 10 days for suture removal. Client states that he lives in the college dormitory and is able to care for wound if given instructions. Client is able to understand and read English.

Nursing Diagnosis: ***Knowledge Deficient*** related to care of sutured wound.

Long-Term Goals: Client's wound will heal completely without infection or other complications.

Intermediate Goal: At clinic appointment, client's wound will be healing without signs of infection, loss of function, or other complication.

Short-Term Goals: Client will respond to questions regarding wound care. Client will perform return demonstration of wound cleansing and bandaging.

Behavioural Objectives	Content Outline	Teaching Methods
Upon completion of the instructional session, the client will:		
1. Describe normal wound healing.	I. Normal wound healing	Describe normal wound healing with the use of audiovisuals.
2. Describe signs and symptoms of wound infection.	II. Infection Signs and symptoms include wound warm to touch, malalignment of wound edges, and purulent wound drainage. Signs of systemic infection include fever and malaise.	Discuss the mechanism of wound infection. Use audiovisuals to demonstrate infected wound appearance. Provide handout describing signs and symptoms of wound infection.
3. Identify equipment needed for wound care.	III. Wound care equipment a. Cleansing solution as prescribed by physician (e.g., clear water, mild soap and water, or antimicrobial solution) b. Bandaging material: Telfa, gauze wrap, adhesive tape	Demonstrate equipment needed for cleansing and bandaging wound. Provide handout listing equipment needed.
4. Demonstrate wound cleansing and bandaging.	IV. Demonstration of wound cleansing and bandaging on the client's wound or a mannequin	Demonstrate wound cleansing and bandaging on the client's wound or a mannequin. Provide handout describing procedure for cleansing and bandaging wound.
5. Describe appropriate action if questions or complications arise.	V. Resources available for client's questions include health clinic, emergency department.	Discuss available resources. Provide handout listing available resources and follow-up treatment plan.
6. Identify date, time, and location of follow-up appointment for suture removal.	VI. Follow-up treatment plan; where and when	Provide written instructions.

Evaluation: The client will:

1. Respond to questions regarding self-care of wound.
2. Return demonstration of wound cleansing and bandaging.
3. State contact person and telephone number to obtain assistance.
4. State date, time, and location of follow-up appointment.

Selected Verbs for Learning Objectives

Cognitive Domain	Affective Domain	Psychomotor Domain
compares	alters	adapts
contrasts	answers	arranges
defines	attends	assembles
describes	chooses	begins
differentiates	complies	calculates
draws	conforms	calibrates
explains	completes	changes
identifies	defends	constructs
labels	differentiates	creates
lists	discusses	demonstrates
matches	displays	dismantles
names	follows	manipulates
plans	helps	measures
prepares	initiates	moves
recites	joins	organizes
restates	justifies	proceeds
selects	modifies	reacts
solves	participates	rearranges
sorts	responds	shows
states	revises	starts
summarizes	shares	works
underlines	uses	
writes	verifies	

Source: Adapted from N. E. Gronlund. (1985). *Stating objectives for classroom instruction* (3rd ed.) (p. 37–40). Toronto: Collier Macmillan.

low-fat diet" (unobservable). Selected measurable verbs used for learning objectives are shown in the box above. Avoid using such words as *knows, understands, believes,* and *appreciates;* they are neither observable nor measurable.

- May add conditions or modifiers as required to clarify what, where, when, or how the behaviour will be performed. Examples are: "Demonstrates four-point crutch gait *correctly*" (condition), "Irrigates his colostomy *independently* (condition) as taught," or "States *three* (condition) factors that affect blood sugar level."
- Include criteria specifying the time by which learning should have occurred. For example, "The client will state three things that affect blood sugar level *by end of second diabetic class.*"

Learning objectives can reflect the learner's command of simple to complex concepts. For example, the learning objective "The client will list cardiac risk factors" is a low-level knowledge objective that simply requires the learner to identify all cardiac risk factors; it does not suggest application of the knowledge to the learner's own behaviours. The learning objective "The client will list *personal* cardiac risk factors" requires that the learner not only know cardiac risk factors in general but also know personal behaviours that increase risk for cardiac disease.

In writing learning objectives, the nurse must be specific about what behaviours and knowledge (cognitive, psychomotor, and affective) the learner must have to be able to positively influence one's health state. In most cases, the learning needs are more complex than simple acquisition of knowledge and include the application of that knowledge to oneself.

Choosing Content

The content, or what is to be taught, is determined by learning objectives. For instance, "Identify appropriate sites for insulin injection" means the nurse must include content about the body sites suitable for insulin injections. Nurses can select among many sources of information, including books, nursing journals, and other nurses and health-care professionals. Whatever sources the nurse chooses, content should be:

- Accurate
- Current
- Based on learning objectives
- Adjusted for the learner's age, developmental stage, culture, and ability
- Consistent with information the nurse is teaching
- Selected with consideration of how much time and what resources are available for teaching

Selecting Teaching Strategies

The method of teaching that the nurse chooses should be suited to the individual, to the material to be learned, and to the teacher (Figure 29.3). For example, the person who cannot read needs material presented in other ways; a discussion

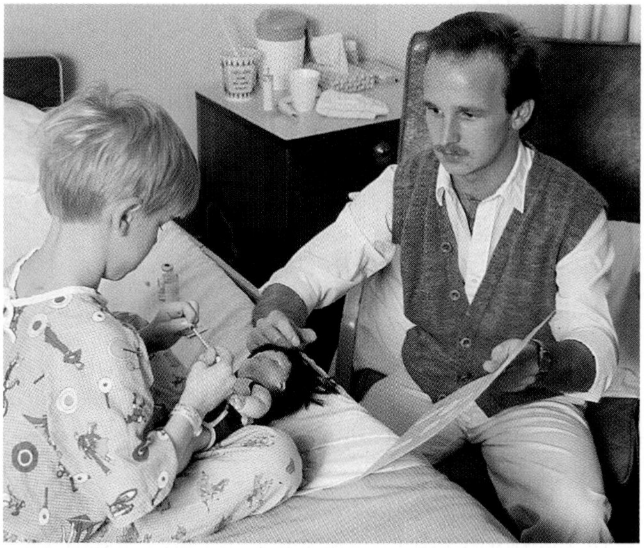

Figure 29.3 Teaching materials and strategies should be suited to the client's age and learning abilities

is usually not the best strategy for teaching how to give an injection; and a teacher using group discussion for teaching should be a competent group leader. As stated earlier, some people are visually oriented and learn best through seeing; others learn best through hearing and having the skill explained. See Table 29.4 for selected teaching strategies.

Teaching Tools

Having the right tools facilitates teaching. They may include handouts, medical equipment and supplies, photo albums, overhead transparencies, flip charts, bulletin boards, models of the human body, audio and videotapes, closed circuit television, and computer programs. Tools will need to be carefully selected for the individual patient on the basis of the nurse's assessment.

Ordering Learning Experiences

To save nurses time in constructing their own teaching guides, some health agencies have developed teaching guides for teaching sessions that nurses commonly give. These guides standardize content and teaching methods and make it easier for the nurse to plan and implement client teaching. Standardized teaching plans also ensure consistency of content for the learner, thereby decreasing the risk of confusion if different practices are taught. For example, when teaching infant bathing, the nurse on the unit should be consistent about which soaps are appropriate for the infant's bath and which are not. Whether the nurse is implementing a plan devised by another or developing an individualized teaching plan, some guidelines can help the nurse order the learning experience.

- Start with something the learner is concerned about; for example, before learning how to self-administer insulin, an adolescent wants to know how to adjust lifestyle and still play football.
- Review what the learner knows, and then proceed to the unknown. This gives the learner confidence. Sometimes, you will not know the client's knowledge or skill base and will need to elicit this information, either by asking questions or by having the client fill out a form, such as a pretest.
- Address early on any area that is causing the client anxiety. A high level of anxiety can impair concentration in other areas. For example, a woman highly anxious about turning her husband in bed might not be able to learn about bathing him until she has successfully learned to turn him.
- Teach the basics before proceeding to the variations or adjustments. It is confusing to learners to have to consider possible adjustments and variations before they master the basic concepts. For example, when teaching a female client how to insert a retention catheter, it is best to teach the basic procedure before teaching any adjustments that might be needed if the catheter stops draining after insertion.
- Schedule time for review of content and to answer questions the learner(s) may have in order to clarify information.

Implementing

The nurse needs to be flexible in implementing any teaching plan because the plan may need revising. The client may tire sooner than anticipated or be faced with too much information too quickly; the client's needs may change; or external factors may intervene. For instance, the nurse and the client, Mr. Brown, have planned to irrigate his colostomy at 10 a.m., but when the time comes, Mr. Brown wants additional information before actually doing it himself.

In this case, the nurse alters the teaching plan and discusses the desired information, provides written information, and defers teaching the psychomotor skill until the next day. It is also important for nurses to use teaching techniques that enhance learning and reduce or eliminate any barrier to learning, such as pain or fatigue. See Table 29.1 earlier in the chapter for barriers to learning.

Guidelines for Teaching

When implementing a teaching plan, the nurse may find the following eight guidelines helpful.

1. The optimal time for each session depends largely on the learner. Whenever possible, ask the client for help to choose the best time, for example, when they feel most rested or when no other activities are scheduled.
2. The pace of each teaching session also affects learning. Nurses should be sensitive to any signs that the pace is too fast or too slow. A client who appears confused or does not comprehend material when questioned may be finding the pace too fast. When the client appears bored and loses interest, the pace may be too slow, the learning period may be too long, or the client may be tired.
3. An environment can detract from or assist learning; for example, noise or interruptions usually interfere with concentration, whereas a comfortable environment promotes learning. If possible, the client should be out of bed for learning activities. Most people associate their bed with rest and sleep, not with learning. Changing the position of the client to a position and place associated with activity or learning may influence the amount of learning that takes place. For example, a client who is shown a videotape while in bed may be more likely to become drowsy during instruction than a client who is sitting in a bedside chair.

TABLE 29.4 Selected Teaching Strategies

Strategy	Major Type of Learning	Characteristics
Explanation or description (e.g., lecture)	Cognitive	Teacher controls content and pace. Learner is passive and, therefore, retains less information than when actively participating. Feedback is determined by teacher. May be given to individual or group.
One-to-one discussion	Affective, cognitive	Encourages participation by learner. Permits reinforcement and repetition at learner's level. Permits introduction of sensitive subjects.
Answering questions	Cognitive	Teacher controls most of content and pace. Teacher must understand question and what it means to learner. Learner may need to overcome cultural perception that asking questions is impolite and may embarrass the teacher. Can be used with individuals and groups. Teacher sometimes needs to confirm whether question has been answered by asking learner, for example, "Does that answer your question?"
Demonstration	Psychomotor	Often used with explanation. Can be used with individuals, small or large groups. Does not permit use of equipment by learners; learner is passive.
Discovery	Cognitive, affective	Teacher guides problem-solving situation. Learner is active participant; therefore, retention of information is high.
Group discussions	Affective, cognitive	Learner can obtain assistance from supportive group. Group members learn from one another. Teacher needs to keep the discussion focused and prevent monopolization by one or two learners.
Practice	Psychomotor	Allows repetition and immediate feedback. Permits hands-on experience.
Printed and audiovisual materials	Cognitive	Forms include books, pamphlets, films, programmed instruction, and computer learning. Learners can proceed at their own speed. Nurse can act as resource person, need not be present during learning. Potentially ineffective if reading level is too high. Teacher needs to select language that meets learner's needs if English is a second language.
Role-playing	Affective, cognitive	Permits expression of attitudes, values, and emotions. Can assist in development of communication skills. Involves active participation by learner. Teacher must create supportive, safe environment for learners to minimize anxiety.
Modelling	Affective, psychomotor	Nurse sets example by attitude, psychomotor skill.
Computer-assisted learning programs	All types of learning	Learner is active. Learner controls pace. Provides immediate reinforcement and review. Use with individuals or groups.

4. Teaching aids can foster learning and help focus a learner's attention. To ensure the transfer of learning, the nurse should use the type of supplies or equipment the client will eventually use. Before the teaching session, the nurse needs to assemble all equipment and visual aids and ensure that all audiovisual equipment is functioning effectively. See the accompanying box for teaching tools for children.
5. Learning is more effective when the learners discover the content for themselves. Ways to increase learning include stimulating motivation and stimulating self-direction, for example, (1) by providing specific, realistic, achievable objectives; (2) by giving feedback; and (3) by helping the learner derive satisfaction from learning. The nurse may also encourage self-directed independent learning by encouraging the client to explore sources of information required.
6. Repetition reinforces learning. Summarizing content, rephrasing (using other words), and approaching the material from another point of view are ways of repeating and clarifying content. For instance, after discussing the kinds of foods that can be included in a diet, the nurse describes the foods again, but in the context of the three meals eaten during one day.

Teaching Tools for Children

- *Visits.* Visiting the hospital and treatment rooms; seeing people dressed in uniforms, scrub suits, protective gear
- *Dress-up.* Touching and dressing up in the clothing they will see and wear
- *Colouring books.* Using colouring books to prepare for treatments, surgery, or hospitalization; shows what rooms, people, and equipment will look like
- *Story books.* Story books describe how the child will feel, what will be done, and what the place will look like. Parents can read these stories to children several times before the experience. Younger children like this repetition.
- *Dolls.* Practising procedures that they will later experience on dolls or teddy bears gives a sense of mastery of the situation. Custom dolls are often available for inserting tubes and giving injections, for example.
- *Puppet play.* Puppets can be used in role-play situations to provide information and show the child what the experience will be like; they help the child express emotions.
- *Health fairs.* Health fairs can educate children about their bodies and ways to stay healthy. Fairs can focus on high-risk problems that children face, such as accidents and poisoning, and on other topics identified in the community as a concern.

7. It is helpful to employ "organizers" to introduce material to be learned. Advanced organizers provide a means of connecting unknown material to known material and generating logical relationships. For example: "You understand how urine flows down a catheter from the bladder. Now I will show you how to inject fluid so that it flows up the catheter into the bladder." The details that follow are then seen within a framework that adds meaning.
8. Using a layperson's vocabulary enhances communication. Often, nurses use terms and abbreviations that have meaning to other health-care professionals but make little sense to clients. Even such words as *urine* or *feces* may be unfamiliar to clients, and abbreviations, such as RR (recovery room) or PAR (postanesthesia room), are often misunderstood.

Teaching Strategies

Nurses can choose from a number of special teaching strategies: client contracting, group teaching, computer-assisted instruction, discovery/problem solving, and behaviour modification. Any strategy the nurse selects must be appropriate for the learner and the learning objectives.

Client Contracting

Client contracting involves establishing a learning contract with a client that specifies certain objectives and when they are to be met. Here is an example of a self-contract:

> I, Amy Martin, will exercise strenuously for 20 minutes three times per week for a period of two weeks and will then buy myself six yellow roses.
>
> Amy Martin
> July 30, 2003

The contract, drawn up and signed by the client and the nurse, may specify the learning objectives, the responsibilities of the client and the nurse, and the methods of follow-up and evaluation. The contract can be changed in two ways: (1) if the client meets the contract objectives and wants to negotiate new learning objectives, and (2) if the client decides that it is not possible to meet the existing learning objectives and wants to revise them (Rankin & Stallings, 1996). The learning contract allows for freedom, mutual respect, and mutual responsibility.

Group Teaching

Group instruction is economical, and it provides members with an opportunity to share with and learn from others. A small group allows for discussion in which everyone can participate. A large group often necessitates a lecture technique or use of films, videos, slides, or role-playing by teachers.

It is important that all members involved in group instruction have a need in common (e.g., prenatal health or preoperative instruction). It is also important that sociocultural factors be considered in the formation of a group.

Computer-Assisted Instruction (CAI)

Computer-assisted instruction (CAI) can be used to teach the following:

- Complex problem-solving skills
- Application of information
- Psychomotor skills

Programs can be used for:

- Individual health-care professionals or clients using one computer.
- Families or small groups of three to five clients gathered around one computer taking turns running the program and answering questions together.
- Large groups with the computer screen projected onto an overhead screen and a teacher or one learner using the keyboard and/or mouse.
- Individuals or small groups at computers using programs through shared network platforms or through Internet sites. Internet computer sources for health education are numerous.

Individuals using a computer are able to set the pace that meets their learning needs. Small groups are less able to do this, and large groups progress through the program at a pace that may be too slow for some learners and too fast for others. It is, therefore, helpful to group together learners of similar needs and abilities. Whether using the computer alone or in large groups, learners read and view informational material, answer questions, and receive immediate feedback. Some computer programs feature simulated situations that allow learners to manipulate objects on the screen to learn psychomotor skills. When used to teach such skills, CAI must be followed up with practice on actual equipment supervised by the teacher.

The nurse's role in assisting the client to learn using computer-assisted instruction and/or the Internet will vary according to individual client needs (for example, computer literacy). See Chapter 25, "Nursing Informatics."

Discovery/Problem Solving

In using the discovery/problem-solving technique, the nurse presents some initial information and then asks the learners a question or presents a situation related to the information. The learner applies the new information to the situation and decides what to do. Learners can work alone or in groups. This technique is well suited to family learning. The teacher guides the learners through the thinking process necessary to reach the best solution to the question or the best action to take in the situation. This may also be referred to as anticipatory problem solving. For example, the nurse educator might present information on diabetes and glucose management. Then, the nurse might ask the learners how they think their insulin and/or diet should be adjusted if their morning glucose was too low. In this way, clients learn what critical components they need to consider to reach the best solution to the problem.

Behaviour Modification

The behaviour modification system for changing behaviour has as its basic assumptions (1) that human behaviours are learned and can be selectively strengthened, weakened, eliminated, or replaced, and (2) that a person's behaviour is under conscious control. Under this system, desirable behaviour is regarded, and undesirable behaviour is ignored. The client's response is the key to behaviour change. For example, clients trying to quit smoking are not criticized when they smoke, but they are praised or rewarded when they go without a cigarette for a certain period of time. For some people, a learning contract is combined with behaviour modification and includes the following pertinent features:

- Positive reinforcement (e.g., praise) is used.
- The client participates in the development of the learning plan.
- Undesirable behaviour is ignored, not criticized.
- The expectation of the client and the nurse is that the task will be mastered (i.e., the behaviour will change).
- Success is maximized through positive reinforcement; failure and the threat of failure are minimized.

Transcultural Teaching

The nurse and clients of different cultural and ethnic backgrounds have additional barriers to overcome in the teaching-learning process. These barriers include language and communication problems, differing concepts of time, conflicting cultural healing practices, beliefs that may positively or negatively influence compliance with health teaching, and unique high-risk or high-frequency health problems that can be addressed with health-promotion instruction. See Chapter 14 for detailed information. Nurses should consider the following guidelines when teaching clients from various ethnic backgrounds.

- *Obtain teaching materials, pamphlets, and instructions in languages used by clients.* Nurses who are unable to read the foreign language material for themselves can have the interpreter read the material to them. The nurse can then evaluate the quality of the information and update it with the interpreter's help as needed.
- *Use visual aids, such as pictures, charts, or diagrams, to communicate meaning.* Audiovisual material may be

helpful if English is spoken clearly and slowly. Even if understanding the verbal message is a problem for the client, seeing a skill or procedure may be helpful. In some instances, an interpreter can be asked to clarify the visual aid. Alternatively, the video may be available in several languages.

- *Use concrete, rather than abstract, words.* Use simple language (short sentences, short words), and present only one idea at a time.
- *Allow time for questions.* This helps the client mentally separate one idea or skill from another.
- *Avoid the use of medical terminology or health-care language,* such as "taking your vital signs" or "apical pulse." Rather, nurses should say they are going to take a blood pressure reading or listen to the client's heart.
- *If understanding another's pronunciation is a problem, validate brief information in writing.* For example, during assessments, write down numbers, words, or phrases and have the client read them to verify accuracy.
- *Use humour very cautiously.* Meaning can change in the translation process.
- *Do not use slang words or colloquialisms.* These may be interpreted literally.
- *Do not assume that a client who nods, uses eye contact, or smiles is indicating an understanding of what is being taught.* These responses may simply be the client's way of indicating respect. The client may feel that asking the nurse questions or stating a lack of understanding is inappropriate because it might embarrass the nurse or cause the nurse to "lose face."
- *Invite and encourage questions during teaching.* Let clients know they are urged to ask questions and be involved in making information more clear. When asking questions to evaluate client understanding, avoid asking negative questions. These can be interpreted differently by people for whom English is a second language. "How far can you bend your hip after surgery?" is better than the negative question "You don't understand how far you can bend your hip after surgery, do you?" With particularly difficult information or skills teaching, the nurse might say, "Most people have some trouble with this. May I please help you go through this one more time?" In some cultures, expressing a need is not appropriate, and expressing confusion or asking to be shown something again is considered rude.
- *When explaining procedures or functioning related to personal areas of the body, it may be appropriate to have a nurse of the same sex do the teaching.* Because of modesty concerns in many cultures and beliefs about what is considered appropriate and inappropriate male-female interaction, it is wise to have a female nurse teach a female client about personal care, birth control, sexually transmitted diseases, and other potentially sensitive topics. If an interpreter is needed during explanation of procedures or teaching, the interpreter should also be female.
- *Include the family in planning and teaching.* This promotes trust and mutual respect. Identify the authoritative family member and incorporate that person into the planning and teaching to promote compliance and support of health teaching. In some cultures, the male head of household is the critical family member to include in health teaching; in other cultures, it is the eldest female member.
- *Consider the client's time orientation.* The client may be oriented to the past, present, future, or a combination of these. The client may be more oriented to the present than the nurse is. Cultures with a predominant orientation to the present include the Mexican American, Navajo Native American, Appalachian, Inuit, and Filipino American cultures. Preventing future problems may be less significant for these clients than for others, so teaching prevention may be more difficult. For example, teaching a client why and when to take medications may be more difficult if the client is oriented to the present. In such instances, the nurse can emphasize preventing short-term problems, rather than long-term problems. Failure to keep clinic appointments or to arrive on time is common in clients who have a present-time orientation. The nurse can help by arranging transportation and by accommodating these clients when they do come, rather than rescheduling an appointment that they probably will not keep.

  Schedules may be very flexible in present-oriented societies, with sleeping and eating patterns varying greatly. Teaching clients to take medications at bedtime or with a meal does not necessarily mean that these activities will occur at the same time each day. For this reason, the nurse should assess the client's daily routine before teaching the client to pair a treatment or medication with an event the nurse assumes occurs at the same time every day. When teaching a client when to take medication, the nurse should determine whether a clock or watch is available to the client and whether the client can tell time.
- *Identify cultural health practices and beliefs.* Noncompliance with health teaching may be related to conflict with folk medicine beliefs. Noncompliance may also be related to lack of understanding or to fatalism, which is a belief system in which life events are held to be predestined or fixed in advance and the individual is powerless to change them. To encourage compliance, the nurse may need to involve the client in learning about the causes and preventability of certain health problems.

The nurse should treat the client's cultural healing beliefs with respect and try to identify whether any are in agreement or in conflict with what is being taught. The nurse can then focus on the ones in agreement to promote the integration of new learning with familiar health practices. The client will need an explanation of why certain folk healing practices are harmful and how the recommended health practices will improve health.

Evaluating

Evaluating Learning

Evaluating is both an ongoing and a final process in which the client, the nurse, and often the support people determine what has been learned. This process is the same as evaluating client achievement of desired outcomes for other nursing diagnoses. Learning is measured against the predetermined learning objectives selected in the planning phase of the teaching process. Thus, the objectives serve not only to direct the teaching plan but also to provide outcome criteria for evaluation. For example, the objective "Selects foods that are low in carbohydrates" can be evaluated by asking the client to name such foods or to select low-carbohydrate foods from a list.

The best method for evaluating depends on the type of learning. In *cognitive learning*, the client demonstrates acquisition of knowledge. Examples of the evaluation tools for cognitive learning include the following:

- Direct observation of behaviour (e.g., observing the client selecting the solution to a problem using the new knowledge)
- Written measurements (e.g., tests)
- Oral questioning (e.g., asking the client to restate information or correct verbal responses to questions)
- Self-reports and self-monitoring. These can be useful during follow-up phone calls and home visits. Evaluating individual self-paced learning, as might occur with computer-assisted instruction, often incorporates self-monitoring.

The acquisition of *psychomotor skills* is best evaluated by observing how well the client carries out a procedure, such as changing a dressing or carrying out a urinary self-catheterization.

Affective learning is more difficult to evaluate. Whether attitudes or values have been learned may be inferred by listening to the client's responses to questions, noting how the client speaks about relevant subjects, and by observing the client's behaviour that expresses feelings and values. For example, do clients who state that they value health actually use condoms every time they have sex with a new partner?

Following evaluation, the nurse may find it necessary to modify or repeat the teaching plan if the objectives have not been met or have been met only partially. For the hospitalized client, follow-up teaching in the home or by phone may be needed.

Behaviour change does not always take place immediately after learning. Often, individuals accept change intellectually first and then change their behaviour only periodically (for example, Mrs. Green, who knows that she must lose weight, diets and exercises off and on). If the new behaviour is to replace the old behaviour, it must emerge

FOCUS ON CRITICAL THINKING

Mrs. Marcos is a 59-year-old bank vice-president who is heavily relied upon by her boss and co-workers. She moved to Canada from the Philippines five years ago. Three days ago, she was admitted to the hospital with complaints of shortness of breath and mild chest pain. A diagnostic evaluation indicates that she has significant coronary artery disease but has not yet suffered a heart attack. Her physician has indicated that Mrs. Marcos will need to make significant lifestyle changes to reduce her heart attack risk. As her nurse, you recognize Mrs. Marcos' need to learn about her disease process, diet, exercise, and stress reduction. As you begin teaching Mrs. Marcos, you note that she is very pleasant and frequently nods her head, but she also seems preoccupied and is readily distracted.

1. How would you evaluate Mrs. Marcos' readiness to learn?
2. Of what benefit would a learning needs assessment be inasmuch as Mrs. Marcos is obviously a well-educated client?
3. You recognize that you have a great deal of information to teach Mrs. Marcos and you are concerned that you will not be able to teach it all. What can you do to help Mrs. Marcos and still feel that you have accomplished your teaching goals?
4. How will you know if your teaching is effective?
5. How might your teaching differ if you were teaching Mrs. Marcos at home, rather than in a hospital or acute-care setting?

See Appendix A for answers to these questions.

gradually; otherwise, the old behaviour may prevail. The nurse can assist clients with behaviour change by allowing for client vacillation and by providing encouragement.

Evaluating Teaching

It is important for nurses to evaluate their own teaching and the content of the teaching program, just as they evaluate the effectiveness of nursing interventions for other nursing diagnoses. Evaluation should include a consideration of all factors—the timing, the teaching strategies, the amount of information, whether the teaching was helpful, and so on. The nurse may find, for example, that the client was overwhelmed with too much information, was bored, or was motivated to learn more.

Both the client and the nurse should evaluate the learning experience. The client may tell the nurse what was helpful, interesting, and so on. Feedback questionnaires and videotapes of the learning sessions can also be helpful.

The nurse should not feel ineffective as a teacher if the client forgets some of what is taught. Forgetting is normal and should be anticipated. Having the client write down information, repeating it during teaching, giving handouts on the information, and having the client be active in the learning process all promote retention.

Documenting

Documentation of the teaching process is essential because it provides a legal record that the teaching took place and communicates the teaching to other health-care professionals. If teaching is not documented, legally it did not occur.

It is also important to document the responses of the client and support people to teaching activities. What did the client or support person say or do to indicate that learning occurred? Has the client demonstrated mastery of a skill or the acquisition of knowledge? The nurse records this in the client's chart as evidence of learning. Many agencies have multiple-copy client teaching forms that include the medical and nursing diagnoses, the treatment plan, and the client education. After the teaching session is completed, the client and the nurse sign the form and a copy of the form is given to the client as a record of teaching and as reinforcement of the content taught. A second copy of the completed and signed form is placed in the client's chart. The parts of the teaching process that should be documented in the client's chart include the following:

- Diagnosed learning needs
- Learning objectives
- Topics taught
- Client outcomes
- Need for additional teaching
- Resources provided

The written teaching plan that the nurse uses as a resource to guide future teaching sessions might also include these elements:

- Actual information and skills taught
- Teaching strategies used
- Time framework and content for each class
- Teaching outcomes and methods of evaluation

CHAPTER HIGHLIGHTS

- Teaching clients and families about their health needs is a major role of the nurse. Nurses also teach colleagues, other health-care professionals, subordinates, nursing and other health-care students, and groups in community education programs.
- Learning is represented by a change in behaviour.
- Three main theories of learning are behaviourism, cognitivism, and humanism.
- Bloom has identified three learning domains: cognitive, affective, and psychomotor.
- A number of factors facilitate learning, including motivation, readiness, active involvement, relevance, feedback, nonjudgmental support, repetition, timing, environment, and progressing from simple to complex concepts.
- Such factors as emotions, certain physiological events, psychomotor deficits, and cultural barriers may impede learning.
- Teaching, like the nursing process, consists of six activities: assessing the learner, diagnosing learning needs, developing a teaching plan, implementing the plan, evaluating learning outcomes and teaching effectiveness, and documenting instructional activities.
- Learning objectives guide the content of the teaching plan and are written in terms of client or learner behaviour.
- Teaching strategies should be suited to the client, the material to be learned, and the teacher. They should be adjusted to the client's developmental level and health status.
- A teaching plan is a written plan consisting of learning objectives, content to teach, a time frame for teaching, and strategies to use in teaching the content. The plan must be revised when the client's needs change or the teaching strategies prove ineffective.

- Adaptations in teaching will facilitate learning for clients who are illiterate, older, or from different cultural backgrounds.
- Evaluation of the teaching-learning process is both an ongoing and a final process.
- Documentation of client teaching is essential to communicate the teaching to other health-care professionals and to provide a record for legal and accreditation purposes.

READINGS AND REFERENCES

Suggested Readings

Jasovsky, D. A. (1998, April). Patient education: Where are your patient education resources? *American Journal of Nursing, 98*(4), 16AAAA–16BBBB. (Continuing Care Extra).

The author describes a project that organizes and centralizes client education resources throughout a community hospital. A committee of professionals representing different departments (e.g., nursing, cardiology, dietary, respiratory, rehab, discharge planning, and social services) conducted a survey to discover the kind of education programs being offered and education material being distributed by various departments. From this survey, a client education resources manual was developed to enable nurses to plan for and meet the needs of clients and families along the continuum of care.

Paterson, B., Kieloch, B., & Gmiterek, J. (2001). "They never told us anything": Postdischarge instruction for families of persons with brain disabilities. *Rehabilitation Nursing, 26*(2), 48–53.

Findings are presented of a research study involving interviews with families of survivors of traumatic brain injury and focus groups with health-care professionals and third-party insurance adjusters involved in the caring for the injured individual. Most family members did not recall any teaching to them of what they might expect when their family member came home. This was in contrast to the views of the professionals and adjusters who identified that extensive teaching had been done. The implications of such findings suggest the need for printed material, follow-up, and on-going teaching with families.

Related Research

Albright, J., de Guzman, C., Acebo, P., Paiva, D., Faulkner, M., & Swanson, J. (1996). Readability of patient education materials: Implications for clinical practice. *Applied Nursing Research, 9*(3), 139–143.

Baker, D. A., Blais, D., Reed, L., Vaillancourt, C., Gervais, S., & Beaulieu, P. (1999). Descriptive study to compare patient recall of information: Nurse-taught versus video supplement. *Canadian Onology Nursing Journal 9*(3) 115–120.

Robinson, A., & Miller, M. (1996). Making information accessible: Developing plain English discharge instructions. *Journal of Advanced Nursing, 24*(3), 528–535.

Selected References

Bandura, A. (1971). Analysis of modeling processes. In A. Bandura (Ed.), *Psychological modeling.* Chicago, IL: Aldine.

Bloom, B. S. (Ed.). (1956). *Taxonomy of education objectives. Book 1, Cognitive domain.* New York: Longman.

Carpenito, L. J. (1999). *Nursing diagnosis: Application to clinical practice* (8th ed.). Philadelphia, PA: Lippincott.

Chally, P. S. (1992, March). Empowerment through teaching. *Journal of Nursing Education, 31*(3), 117–120.

Chu Lai, S., & Cohen, M. N. (1999). Promoting lifestyle changes. *American Journal of Nursing, 99*(4), 63–67.

Conley, V. M. (1998, October/December). Beyond knowledge deficit to a proposal for information-seeking behaviours. *Nursing Diagnosis, 9*(4), 129–135.

Doak, C. C., Doak, L. G., & Root, J. H. (1996). *Teaching patients with low literacy skills* (2nd ed.). Philadelphia, PA: Lippincott.

Dowe, M. C., Lawrence, P. A., Carlson, J., & Keyserling, T. C. (1997). Patient's use of health-teaching materials at three readability levels. *Applied Nursing Research, 10*(2), 86–93.

Gronlund, N. E. (1985). *Stating objectives for classroom instruction* (3rd ed.). New York: Macmillan.

Knowles, M. S. (1984). *Andragogy in action.* San Francisco, CA: Jossey-Bass.

Lewin, D. (1948). *Resolving social conflicts.* G. W. Lewin (Ed.). New York: Harper and Brothers. (Classic.)

Lewin, K. (1951). *Field theory in social science.* New York: Harper and Row. (Classic.)

Logan, J., & Boss, M. (1993, March). Nurses' learning patterns. *Canadian Nurse, 89*(3), 18–22.

Lowry, M., & Johnson, M. (1999). Network. Computer assisted learning: The potential for teaching and assessing in nursing. *Nurse Education Today, 19*(7), 521–526.

Maslow, A. H. (1970). *Motivation and personality.* New York: Harper and Row. (Classic.)

North American Nursing Diagnosis Association. (2003). NANDA Nursing Diagnosis: Definitions and classification 2003–2004. Philadelphia, PA: Author.

Pavlov, I. P. (1927). *Conditioned reflexes* (trans. G.V. Anrep). London, UK: Oxford University Press. (Classic.)

Piaget, J. (1966). *Origins of intelligence in children.* New York: Norton. (Classic.)

Rankin, S. H., & Stallings, K. D. (1996). *Patient education: Issues, principles, practices* (3rd ed.). Philadelphia, PA: Lippincott.

Redman, B. K. (2001). *The practice of patient education* (8th ed.). St. Louis, MO: Mosby.

Rutledge, D. N., & Donaldson, N. E. (1998, June). Improving readability of print materials in patient care and health services. *Online-Journal-of-Clinical-Innovations, 1*(3), 1–27.

Skinner, B. F. (1953). *Science and human behaviour.* New York: Macmillan. (Classic.)

Stephens, S. T. (1992, January/February). Patient educational materials: Are they readable? *Oncology Nursing Forum, 19*(1), 84.

WEBLINKS

ABC Canada Literacy Foundation
http://www.abc-canada.org/
The Foundation is a Canada wide educational organization that focuses on literacy skills. This site identifies literacy statistics, an overview of related workplace issues, and publications.

Canadian Association for the Study of Adult Education
http://www.oise.utoronto.ca/CASAE/maineng.html
The site provides a variety of resources, including abstracts, conference proceedings, and related Weblinks that focus on the education of adult learners.

Canadian Nurses Association
http://www.cna-nurses.ca
Through this site, the user has access to resources of the Canadian Nurses Association in which the role of the nurse as client-teacher is identified.

Diabetes Nurses Interest Group of the RNAO
http://users.gtn.net/dnig/
The site provides networking opportunities with nurses who are involved in diabetes education and care.

CHAPTER 30

Leading, Managing, and Influencing Change

OBJECTIVES

After completing this chapter, you will be able to:

- Compare and contrast leadership and management.
- Describe the four functions of management.
- Discuss the roles and functions of nurse managers.
- Identify the skills and competencies needed by a nurse manager.
- Describe the stages of change.
- Analyze strategies for dealing with resistance to change.
- Compare and contrast the levels of management.
- Differentiate formal from informal leaders.
- Distinguish between different leadership styles.
- List the characteristics of an effective leader.

The professional nurse frequently assumes the roles of leader and manager. These two roles are linked; that is, managers must have leadership abilities, and leaders often manage, but the two roles differ.

A **leader** influences others to work together to accomplish a specific goal. Leaders are often visionary; they are informed, articulate, confident, and self-aware. Leaders also usually have excellent interpersonal skills and are excellent listeners and communicators. They have initiative and the ability and confidence to innovate change, motivate, facilitate, and mentor others (Kent & Hunter, 1997).

A **manager** is an employee of an organization who is given authority, power, and responsibility for planning, organizing, coordinating, and directing the work of others, and for establishing and evaluating standards. Managers understand organizational structure and culture. They control human, financial, and material resources. Managers set goals, make decisions, and solve problems. They initiate and implement change (Kent & Hunter, 1997).

The Nurse as Leader and Manager

As *leaders*, nurses influence clients and their family members, students, physicians, other health-care professionals, and members of the community, including politicians and legislators. Because of their skills, knowledge, and competence, nurses play an important role in health promotion, disease prevention, and health-care delivery.

Nurse leaders can be instrumental in establishing policies and procedures and in initiating change, both within and outside of health-care organizations. Additionally, nurse leaders promote the concept of caring in society by advocating for changes that promote physical, psychosocial, and social wellness in the society as a whole. Leaders may focus on the task at hand, relationships with people, or both (Tappen, 2001). Leaders focused on the task concentrate on activities to increase productivity, while leaders focused on relationships address the needs of persons with whom they are working. The purposes of nursing leadership vary according to the level of application and include (1) improving the health status of individuals or families, (2) increasing the effectiveness and level of satisfaction among professional colleagues, and (3) improving the attitudes of citizens and legislators toward the nursing profession and their expectations of it (Leddy & Pepper, 1993).

As *managers*, nurses are responsible for managing their personal lives and client care; some nurses assume a management position within the organization as nurse managers, supervisors, or executives. As a manager, the nurse is responsible for (1) efficiently accomplishing the goals of the organization, (2) efficiently using the organization's resources, (3) ensuring effective client care, and (4) ensuring compliance with institutional, professional, regulatory, and governmental standards of care. Managers are also responsible for planning for the use of any assistive personnel, and for delegation to and supervision of assistive workers in the work setting (Canadian Nurses Association [CNA], 1995).

Table 30.1 further compares the leader and manager roles. Figure 30.1 illustrates some of the leading and managing roles.

Leadership

Leadership may be formal or informal. The **formal leader**, or appointed leader, is selected by an organization and given official authority to make decisions and act. An **informal leader** is not officially appointed to direct activities of others

TABLE 30.1 Comparison of Leader and Manager Roles

Leaders	Managers
May or may not have official appointment to the position	Are appointed officially to the position
Have power and authority to enforce decisions only so long as followers are willing to be led	Have power and authority to enforce decisions
Influence others toward goal setting, either formally or informally	Carry out predetermined policies, rules, and regulations
Interested in risk taking and exploring new ideas	Maintain an orderly, controlled, rational, and equitable structure
Relate to people personally in an intuitive and empathetic manner	Relate to people according to their roles
Feel rewarded by personal achievements	Feel rewarded when fulfilling organizational mission or goals
May or may not be successful as managers	Are managers as long as the appointment holds

Source: Douglass, L. M. (1992). *The effective nurse: Leader and manager* (4th ed.) (p. 6). St. Louis, MO: Mosby-Year Book. Used with permission.

A

B

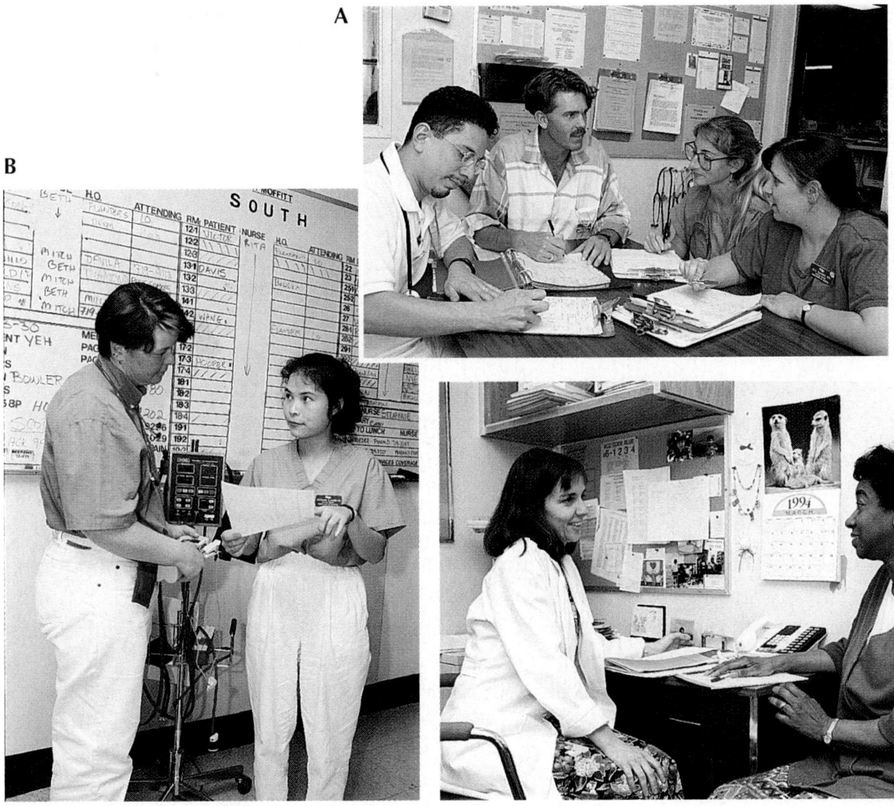

C

Figure 30.1 Nurses as leaders and managers. *A*, The nurse manager discusses work assignments during change-of-shift report. *B*, The nurse delegates basic client care activities to the assistive personnel. *C*, The nurse consults the social worker during discharge planning.

but is selected by the group as its leader because of seniority, age, special abilities, or a charismatic personality and plays an important role in influencing colleagues, co-workers, or other group members to achieve the group's goals.

Leadership Theory

Early leadership theories focused on what leaders are (trait theories), what leaders do (behavioural theories), and how leaders adapt their leadership style according to the situation (contingency theories). Current leadership theories address how leaders combine traits, behaviours, and contingencies to effectively lead.

Classical Leadership Theories

The *trait theorists* found that leaders often possess specific traits and abilities, including good judgement, decisiveness, knowledge, adaptability, integrity, tact, popularity, nonconformity, and cooperativeness (Bass, 1990). The *behaviourists* believed that through education, training, and life experiences, effective leaders develop a particular *style of leadership*. These styles have been characterized as autocratic, democratic, laissez-faire, and bureaucratic.

Autocratic (*authoritarian, directive*) leaders make decisions for the group. The leader believes individuals are externally motivated and incapable of independent decision making. Likened to a dictator, the autocratic leader determines policies, giving orders and directions to the group. Under this type of leadership, the group may feel secure because procedures are well defined and activities are predictable. Productivity may also be high. However, the group's needs for creativity, autonomy, and self-motivation are not met, and the degree of openness and trust between the leader and the group members is minimal or absent (Tappen, 2001). Members are often dissatisfied with this type of leadership; however, at times an autocratic style is the most effective. When urgent decisions are necessary (e.g., a cardiac arrest, a unit fire, or a mass casualty event), one person must assume the responsibility to make decisions without being challenged by other team members. When group members are unable or do not wish to participate in making a decision, the authoritarian style solves the problem and enables the individual or group to move on. This style can also be effective when a project must be completed quickly and efficiently.

Democratic (*participative, consultative*) leaders encourage group discussion and decision making. This type of leader assumes individuals are internally motivated, capable of making decisions, and value independence. Group productivity and satisfaction are high as group members contribute to the work effort. The democratic leader acts as a catalyst or facilitator, actively guiding the group toward achieving the group's goals. Providing constructive criticism, offering information, making suggestions, and asking questions become the focus of the participative leader. This type of leadership demands that the leader have faith in the group members to accomplish the goals. Although democratic leadership has been shown to be less efficient and

TABLE 30.2 Comparison of Authoritarian, Democratic, and Laissez-Faire Leadership Styles

	Authoritarian	Democratic	Laissez-Faire
Degree of freedom	Little freedom	Moderate freedom	Much freedom
Degree of control	High control	Moderate control	No control
Leader activity level	High	High	Minimal
Assumption of responsibility	Primarily the leader	Shared	Abdicated
Output of the group	High quantity, good quality	Creative, high quality	Variable, may be of poor quality
Efficiency	Very efficient	Less efficient than authoritarian	Inefficient

Source: Tappen, R. M. (1995). *Nursing leadership and management: Concepts and practice* (3rd ed.). (p. 82). Philadelphia, PA: F. A. Davis. Reprinted with permission.

more cumbersome than authoritarian leadership, it allows more self-motivation and more creativity among group members. It also calls for a great deal of cooperation and coordination among group members. This style of leadership can be extremely effective in the health-care setting (Tappen, 2001).

The **laissez-faire** (*nondirective, permissive, ultraliberal*) leader presupposes the group is internally motivated and recognizes the group's need for autonomy and self-regulation. The leader assumes a "hands-off" approach. However, group members may act independently and at cross purposes because of a lack of cooperation and coordination. A laissez-faire style is most effective for groups whose members have both personal and professional maturity so that once the group has made a decision, the members become committed to it and have the required expertise to implement it. Individual group members then perform tasks in their area of expertise, while the leader acts as resource person. Table 30.2 compares the authoritarian, democratic, and laissez-faire leadership styles.

The **bureaucratic** leader presumes the group is externally motivated. However, the bureaucrat does not trust self or others to make decisions. Instead, the bureaucrat relies on the organization's rules, policies, and procedures to direct the group's work efforts. Group members are usually dissatisfied with the leader's inflexibility and impersonal relations with them.

According to *contingency theorists*, effective leaders adapt their style of leadership to the situation. A popular contingency theory is **situational leadership.** Important aspects of situational leadership are (1) the task behaviours and relationship behaviours of the leader, (2) consideration of the staff members' abilities, (3) the nature of the task to be done, and (4) the context or environment in which the task takes place. The *task-oriented* style of leadership is concerned with getting the work done and, therefore, focuses on activities that encourage group productivity. The *relationship-oriented* style of leadership is concerned with interpersonal relationships and, therefore, focuses on activities that meet group members' needs. Unlike the singular style of authoritarian, democratic, and laissez-faire leadership styles, situational leaders adapt their style of leadership to the readiness and willingness of the individual or group to perform the assigned task.

When employees are insecure or unable or unwilling to perform the task, the leader uses a *telling* high-task/low-relationship style of leadership in which specific directions are provided. If the group is motivated and willing but unable to perform the task, the leader again uses a highly directive *selling* high-task/high-relationship style of leadership, but in this case, the leader explains decisions and provides the opportunity for clarification. When the group is able but unwilling or lacking in confidence, a *participative* high-relationship/low-task style of leadership is used. With this style, the leader shares ideas and facilitates decision making. The final style, *delegating*, a low-task/low-relationship style, is used for a group that is willing, able, and confident to perform the task. A delegating leader turns responsibility for decision making and implementation over to the group (Hersey & Blanchard, 1988).

Contemporary Leadership Theories

Contemporary theorists have described charismatic leaders, transactional leaders, transformational leaders, connective leaders, and shared leadership.

Charismatic leadership is rare and is characterized by an emotional relationship between the leader and the group members. The charming personality of the leader evokes strong feelings of commitment to both the leader and the leader's cause and beliefs. The followers of a charismatic leader often overcome extreme hardship to achieve the group's goals because of faith in the leader.

Transactional leadership represents the traditional manager focused on the day-to-day tasks of achieving organizational goals. The transactional leader understands and meets the needs of the group. Relationships with followers are based on an exchange for some resource valued by the follower. These incentives are used to promote loyalty and performance. For example, in order to ensure adequate staffing on the night shift, the nurse manager entices a staff nurse to work the night shift in exchange for a weekend shift off.

In contrast, **transformational leadership** fosters creativity, risk taking, commitment, and collaboration by empowering the group to share in the organization's vision. The leader inspires others with a clear, attractive, and attainable goal and enlists them to participate in attaining the goal. Through shared values, honesty, trust, and continual learning, the leader empowers the group. Independence, individual growth, and change are facilitated. Cottingham (1988) suggests that through transformational leadership, "followers are converted into leaders, and leaders are converted into change agents" (p. 26). According to Grohar-Murray and DiCroce (2003), the transformational leader grows and develops along with the followers.

Connective leadership also promotes collaboration and teamwork, not only within the organization, but between organizations. Connective leaders use their interpersonal skills to connect professionals, organizations, and communities to combine efforts toward a shared vision (Klakovich, 1994). As health care moves to provide a continuum of care, the network developed through connective leadership will be invaluable.

Shared leadership recognizes that a professional work force is made up of many leaders. No one person is considered to have knowledge or ability beyond that of other members of the work group. Appropriate leadership is thought to emerge in relation to the challenges that confront the work group. Examples of shared leadership in nursing are self-directed work teams, shared governance, and co-leadership.

Canadian Society Notes

Fact	Implications for Nursing Practice
Influential reports written by Dr. Helen Mussallem, who was the Executive Director of the Canadian Nurses Association (CNA) from 1963 to 1981, examined nursing education in Canada and the changing role of the nurse.	Nursing education and the role and influence of nurses in Canada has dramatically changed over the past five decades.
In 1999, the Minister of Health appointed Dr. Judith Shamian as the Executive Director, Nursing Policy Health Canada.	The appointment of a nursing leader to a key role in Health Canada increases the visibility and opportunity to affect health policy and effect change.
Mr. R. Calnan, who was elected President of the CNA in 2002, advocates for nurses to be active in communicating with health policy makers and the public on the vital role nurses can play in sustaining and improving the health-care system in Canada.	Nursing leaders at all levels within organizations can encourage and speak out for nurses and the profession.

Effective Leadership

Much has been written about effective leadership and style; some descriptive statements about effective leaders are listed in the box on the next page. Leadership is a learned process. To be an effective leader requires an understanding of such factors as needs, goals, and rewards that motivate people; knowledge of leadership skills and of the group's activities; and possession of the interpersonal skills to influence others. Principles of effective leadership include vision, influence, and power.

Bennis (1989) suggests *vision* is the first basic ingredient of leadership. Terry (1993) describes vision as the "heart of leadership." **Vision** is a mental image of a possible and desirable future state. Leaders transform visions into realistic goals and communicate their visions to others who accept them as their own.

Influence is an informal strategy used to gain the cooperation of others without exercising formal authority. Influence is exercised through persuasion and excellent communication skills; it is based on a trusting relationship with the followers (Manfredi, 1996).

Power is a force that can shape how people function (Grohar-Murray & DiCroce, 2003). Power can be negative, exploiting others and preventing actions, or it can be positive, taking into account and energizing others. French and Raven (1959) have described five types of power: reward, coercive, legitimate, expert, and referent. **Reward power** is based on the incentives the leader can offer the followers for their cooperation. **Coercive power** is based on the fear of retribution or withholding of rewards. **Legitimate power** is related to the authority associated with a specific position or role. **Expert power** pertains to the respect others have for one's personal abilities, knowledge, or skills. **Referent power** is associated with the admiration and respect for the leader because of the leader's charisma and success.

Glennon (1992, p. 41) encourages humanistic leadership as a means of creating an environment "that is stimulating, motivating, and empowering to the professional nurse." Strategies for humanistic leadership are identified in the box on the next page.

Characteristics of Effective Leaders

- Use a leadership style that is natural to them
- Use a leadership style appropriate to the task and the members
- Assess the effects of their behaviour on others and the effects of others' behaviour on themselves
- Are sensitive to forces acting for and against change
- Express an optimistic view about human nature
- Are energetic
- Are open and encourage openness so that real issues are confronted
- Facilitate personal relationships
- Plan and organize activities of the group
- Are consistent in behaviour toward group members
- Delegate tasks and responsibilities to develop members' abilities, not merely to get tasks performed
- Involve members in all decisions
- Value and use group members' contributions
- Encourage creativity
- Encourage feedback about their leadership style

Strategies for Putting Humanistic Leadership into Action

- Praise or positively recognize staff and colleagues.
- Always think good thoughts about yourself and others.
- Always give before you get—give colleagues and staff a reason for doing whatever it is that you are asking of them.
- Smile often—it generates enthusiasm and goodwill.
- Remember the names of the people with whom you work.
- Think, act, and look successful.
- Always greet others with a positive, affirmative statement.
- Write informal appreciation notes; this shows appreciation and reinforces positive performance.
- Get out of the office; make a point of circulating among those who work in your circle of influence.
- Talk less and listen more; encourage communication and the sharing of ideas and information.
- Don't condemn, criticize, or complain; instead, work on ways to improve the situation or solve the problem.

Source: Adapted from Glennon, T. K. (1992, Spring). Empowering nurses through enlightened leadership. *Revolution: The Journal of Nurse Empowerment, 2*, 40–44.

Management

The manager's job is to accomplish the work of the organization. To this end, managers perform a number of roles and functions that vary with the type of organization and the level of management.

Levels of Management

Although not officially a manager within the organization, the staff nurse performs a number of supervisory functions in the course of client care delivery for which management skills are essential. These skills include communication, delegation, and motivation. Staff nurses in organizations that have implemented shared governance are even more involved in management functions traditionally performed by managers, including planning, allocation of resources, establishing standards, and so on.

Traditional management is divided into three levels of responsibility.

First-level managers are responsible for managing the work of nonmanagerial personnel and the day-to-day activities of a specific work group or groups. Their primary responsibility is for motivating staff to achieve the organization's goals. This level of manager represents staff in reports to upper administration and vice versa.

Middle-level managers supervise a number of first-level managers and are responsible for the activities in the departments they supervise. Middle-level managers serve as liaisons between first-level managers and upper-level managers.

Upper-level managers are organizational executives who are primarily responsible for establishing goals and developing strategic plans. According to the CNA (1993), the chief executive nurse is responsible for nursing services, ensures that nursing standards are met, and promotes collaborative practices to provide effective client care.

Management Functions

Four management functions have been described: planning, organizing, directing, and controlling. These four functions help to achieve the broad goal of quality client care.

Planning

Planning is an ongoing process that involves (1) assessing a situation, (2) establishing goals and objectives based on assessment of a situation or future trends, and (3) developing a plan of action that identifies priorities, delineates who is responsible, determines deadlines, and describes how the intended outcome is to be achieved and evaluated.

In short, it involves deciding what to do, when, where, and how to do it, and by whom, and with what resources. Distribution of money, personnel, equipment, and physical space are included in resource allocation. An upper-level manager, such as a nurse executive, spends considerable time planning the department's goals and services and determining numbers and types of nurses and other personnel needed to provide these services. On the other hand, a first-level manager, such as a staff nurse, spends less time planning but manages each client by assessing the client; sets goals, needs, and priorities; and develops an individualized plan of care.

Organizing

Organizing is also an ongoing process. After identifying the work and evaluating human and material resources, the manager arranges the work into smaller units. Organizing involves determining responsibilities, communicating expectations, and establishing the chain of command for authority and communication. Although upper-level managers delegate much of the work and the responsibility and accountability for the work to others, they need to ensure that department objectives, priorities, job descriptions, lines of communication, nursing standards, procedures, and policies clearly describe the expectations.

Directing

Directing is the process of getting the organization's work accomplished. Directing involves assigning and communicating expectations about the task to be completed; providing instruction and guidance; and ongoing decision making. Upper-level managers devote less time to directing than to planning, organizing, and controlling. Directing at this level of management generally involves supervision of the next level of managers, such as those in middle management (e.g., supervisors, assistant or associate directors, or assistant administrators). Unit managers (charge nurses) and staff nurses devote more time to the directing function. For example, charge nurses direct shift work by assigning clients and scheduling meal and break times. Staff nurses direct the care of clients by ordering nursing care, communicating care in written care plans and shift reports, and supervising care that is given by others.

Controlling

Controlling is the process of ensuring that plans are carried out and evaluating outcomes. It includes evaluating staff. The manager measures results or actions against standards or desired outcomes and then reinforces effective actions or changes ineffective ones. For example, an upper-level manager evaluates the effectiveness of recruitment, staff turnover, and budget performance. The charge nurse appraises staff performance. The staff nurse determines whether nursing interventions have helped the client achieve desired outcomes.

Principles of Management

The primary difference between a leader and a manager is that the manager has authority, accountability, and responsibility.

Authority is defined as the "official power to act. It is the power given by the organization to direct the work of others" (Marquis & Huston, 2000, p. 147). It is an integral component of managing. Authority is conveyed through leadership actions; it is determined largely by the situation, and it is always associated with responsibility and accountability. According to Redfern and Hull (1996), authority needs to be sanctioned not only by others but also from within. That is, the manager must feel worthy of the authority granted; authority can be undermined by self-doubt.

Accountability is the ability and willingness to assume responsibility for one's actions and to accept the consequences of one's behaviour. Accountability can be viewed as hierarchic, starting at the individual level, then the institutional or professional level, and then the societal level. At the individual or client level, accountability is reflected in the nurse's ethical integrity. At the institutional level, it is reflected in the statement of philosophy and objectives of the nursing department and nursing policies. At the professional level, it is reflected in standards of practice developed by national or provincial/territorial nursing associations. At the societal level, it is reflected in legislated nurse practice acts.

Responsibility is an obligation to complete a task. Managers are responsible for utilization of resources, communication to subordinates, and implementation of organizational goals and objectives.

Skills and Competencies of Nurse Managers

To be effective managers, nurses need to be able to think critically, communicate well, manage resources effectively and efficiently, enhance employee performance, build and manage teams, manage conflict, manage time effectively, delegate effectively, and initiate and manage change.

Critical Thinking

Critical thinking is a creative cognitive process that includes creativity, problem solving, and decision making (Sullivan & Decker, 2001). See Chapter 22.

Communicating

Managers report spending 80 to 90 percent of their day communicating (Bass, 1990). Good communication is essential to other critical interpersonal skills and often determines the manager's success as a leader. Managers use both verbal and written communication to develop relationships, gather information, encourage and support staff, coach, discipline, negotiate, deal with conflict, and recognize the efforts of others (Smith, 1999). Effective managers communicate assertively, expressing their ideas clearly, accurately, and honestly. An important adjunct to communication is information systems. Communication systems provide a means for rapid transmittal of information both within and outside of the organization.

One effect of information systems is to facilitate **networking,** a process whereby professional links are established through which people can share ideas, knowledge, and information, offer support and direction to each other, and facilitate accomplishment of professional goals.

Managing Resources

One of the greatest responsibilities of managers is their accountability for human, fiscal, and material resources. Budgeting and determining variances between the actual and budgeted expenses are crucial skills for any manager.

Enhancing Employee Performance

There are several ways of enhancing employee performance. The manager may provide day-to-day coaching or serve as a mentor or preceptor. The term **mentor** is defined by Wood and Ross-Kerr (2003) as "a senior individual in the profession or organization to the mentee who facilitates the novice's entry into the system by explaining the expectations of the role and the intricacies of the culture. The mentor is a role model, as well as a counsellor, modelling successful behaviours for the role to which the novice aspires" (p. 389).

In the clinical area, the term **preceptor** is used to describe mentoring relationships in which the experienced nurse assists the "new" nurse in improving clinical nursing skill and judgement. The preceptor also instills understanding of the routines, policies, and procedures of the institution and the unit.

Mentors provide support. Often, the mentor-protégé relationship is that of teacher-learner: the mentor instructs the protégé in the expected role, introduces the protégé to those who are important to the achievement of goals, listens to and helps the protégé evaluate ideas in light of institutional policy, and challenges the protégé to advance in professional practice.

Building and Managing Teams

In addition to personnel development, the manager is responsible for building and managing the work team. Familiarity with group processes and the roles that group members play facilitates the manager's ability to lead the group and enhances development of the group into a work team. Groups develop in stages during which roles and relationships are established. Detailed information about group stages and roles is discussed in Chapter 26.

Evaluating the group's work is another responsibility of the manager. Effectiveness, efficiency, and productivity are three outcome measures that are frequently used. In health care, **effectiveness** is a measure of the quality or quantity of services provided. **Efficiency** is a measure of the resources used in the provision of nursing services. In nursing, **productivity** is a performance measure of both the effectiveness and efficiency of nursing care. Productivity is frequently measured in the amount of nursing resources used per client or in terms of required versus actual hours of care provided.

RESEARCH NOTE

Organizational Trust and Empowerment: Effects on Staff Nurse Commitment

It had been suggested that nurses feel empowered when they have access to information, receive support, have the resources required for their work, and have opportunities for education. Affective commitment to an organization has been related to a sense of empowerment. In this study, the authors tested a model that linked empowerment, commitment, and the trust nurses had in their work organization. They used a non-experimental survey design with a sample of 300 female and 300 male nurses in urban tertiary care centres in Ontario. The research found that trust of management was closely linked to the information and support nurses believed they received.

Implications: Nurse managers can create high-trust work environments by empowering nurses through providing information, support and guidance, educational opportunities, and resources.

Source: Laschinger, H. K. S., Finnegan, J., Shamian, J., & Casier, S. (2000). Organizational trust and empowerment in restructured healthcare settings. Effects on staff nurse commitment. *Journal of Nursing Administration, 30*(9), 413–425.

Delegating

Delegation is the transference of responsibility and authority for the performance of an activity to a competent individual. The delegator retains accountability for the outcome. Delegation is a tool that allows the manager to devote more time to tasks that cannot be delegated. It also enhances the skills and abilities of the delegatee, which builds self-esteem, promotes morale, and enhances teamwork and attainment of the organization's goals. Delegation involves defining the task, determining who can perform the task, describing the expectation, seeking agreement, meeting time lines, monitoring performance, and providing feedback to the delegatee regarding performance (Sullivan & Decker, 2001).

Registered nurses (RNs) increasingly delegate components of nursing care to other health-care workers, especially with the increased use of unlicensed assistive personnel (UAPs), personal care aides, and home support workers. An RN who delegates a task to another health-care worker is accountable for selecting an appropriately skilled caregiver and for continued evaluation of the client's care. The delegatee assumes responsibility for the actual performance of the task or procedure. Guidelines for delegating nursing tasks and procedures appear in the next box.

Guidelines for Delegating Tasks and Procedures

- Know your legislated and professional responsibilities for delegating.
- Learn your employing agency's procedures and policies about delegation.
- Know the legal definition and the customary knowledge, skills, and job description for each health-care discipline represented on your team.
- Be aware of individual variations in work abilities. Along with different categories of caregivers are individual variations. Each individual has different experiences and may not be capable of performing every task cited in the job description.
- Follow the "Four Rights" of delegation (Hansten & Washburn, 1992):
  a. The *right task* (one that can be delegated, rather than falling within the nurse's scope of practice alone)
  b. The *right person* (one qualified and competent to do the job)
  c. The *right communication* (a clear, concise description of the task, the objective, and your expectations)
  d. The *right feedback* (timely evaluation of the worker's performance while doing the task and after completing it)
- When unsure about an assistant's abilities to perform a task, observe while the person performs it, or demonstrate it to the person and get a return demonstration before allowing the person to perform it independently.
- Clarify reporting expectations to ensure the task is accomplished.
- Ensure client safety. Consider the stability of the client's condition, the desired response of the client to the procedure, and the degree of monitoring, supervision, or support needed and available to the delegatee.
- Create an atmosphere that fosters communication, teaching, and learning. For example, encourage staff to ask questions, listen carefully to their concerns, and make use of every opportunity to teach.

Change

Change is the process of making something different from what it was (Sullivan & Decker, 2001). Change can involve gaining new knowledge or adapting what is currently known in the light of new information. It can also involve obtaining new skills. Change can involve individual clients, families, communities, organizations, nursing as a profession, and the entire health-care delivery system. Change is an integral aspect of nursing, and nurses are often **change agents,** that is, individuals who initiate, motivate, and implement change. Characteristics of effective change agents are listed in the box below.

Types of Change

Unplanned change is usually haphazard, and the results can be unpredictable. *Drift* is a type of unplanned change in which change occurs without effort on anyone's part. *Situational,* or *natural, change* also may be considered unplanned and occurs without any control by a person or group. An example is the change that occurs as a result of a war or a natural disaster. However, not all situational changes are negative; for example, Nurse Smith may be unexpectedly offered a position that was considered a future goal but had not been applied for at present.

According to Lippitt (1973), **planned change** is an intended, purposive attempt by an individual, group, organization, or larger social system to influence its own status quo or that of another organism or a situation. Problem-solving skills, decision-making skills, and interpersonal skills are important factors in planned change.

Change may also be considered covert or overt. A *covert change* is hidden or occurs without the individual's awareness. For example, a person can become increasingly deaf without being aware of this fact. *Overt change* is change of which a person is aware, for example, the development of abdominal pain or shortness of breath while walking up stairs. People who experience overt change may also experience anxiety. Overt change often necessitates

Characteristics of Effective Change Agents

- Have excellent communication and interpersonal skills with individuals, groups, administration, and all levels of the organization involved in change
- Project expertise
- Have knowledge of available resources and how to use them: people, time, money, facilities, information
- Are skilled in problem solving
- Are skilled in teaching
- Are respected by those involved in the change
- Have ability to encourage and nurture those going through change
- Are self-confident, are able to take risks, and can inspire trust in themselves and others
- Are able to make decisions
- Have a broad base of knowledge
- Have a good sense of timing

behavioural changes that are at variance with the person's needs or goals. An example is a diagnosis of cancer and the subsequent need for therapy even though it interferes with the person's work and family life.

Another type of change is *developmental change*, which refers to the physio-psycho-social changes that occur during the life cycle (see Chapters 19, 20, and 21). This type of change is normally gradual and often not consciously planned. An example is the decreasing physical capability of an elderly person. This kind of change is slow and generally permits the individual time to adapt. The individual does not plan the physical changes of aging; they just happen. However, the individual may make plans for dealing with the physical changes (e.g., moving to a smaller, one-floor residence that is easier to care for and in which it is easier to move around).

Models of Change

According to Lewin (1948), change involves three stages: unfreezing, moving, and refreezing. During the *unfreezing* stage, the need for change is recognized, driving and restraining forces are identified, alternative solutions are generated, and participants are motivated to change. In the second stage, *moving*, participants agree the status quo is undesirable and the actual change is planned in detail and implemented. In the final stage, *refreezing*, the change is integrated and stabilized. Table 30.3 compares Lewin's theory of change with those of Lippitt, Havelock, and Rogers.

An important aspect of planning change is establishing the likelihood of the acceptance of the change and then determining the criteria by which that acceptance can be identified. Accepting change often takes time, particularly when it does not fit into a person's attitudinal framework. See the box opposite for stages in the acceptance of change.

To facilitate acceptance of the change, the change agent also needs to identify common driving and restraining forces (see the box opposite on that topic).

Guidelines for dealing with resistance are found in the third box opposite.

Examples of Change

It is exciting to realize how effective nurses can be when they determine the need for change and then plan strategies to bring it about. The following examples outline changes initiated by nurses who have identified a need to "do something" in each of two spheres of influence: the workplace and the community.

TABLE 30.3 Theories of Change

Lewin (1948)	Lippitt (1958)	Havelock (1973)	Rogers (1983)
1. Unfreezing	1. Diagnosing the problem	1. Building a relationship	1. *Knowledge.* The individual, called the decision-making unit, is introduced to change and begins to comprehend it.
2. Moving	2. Assessing the motivation and the capacity for change	2. Diagnosing the problem	2. *Permission.* The individual develops an attitude toward the change that may be favourable or unfavourable.
3. Refreezing	3. Assessing the change agent's motivation and resources	3. Acquiring relevant resources	3. *Decision.* The person makes a choice to adopt or not to adopt the change.
	4. Selecting progressive change objectives	4. Choosing the solution	4. *Implementation.* The person acts on the choice. At this time, alterations may take place.
	5. Choosing an appropriate role for the change agent	5. Gaining acceptance	5. *Confirmation.* The individual looks for confirmation that the choice was right. If the person encounters mixed messages, the choice may be changed.
	6. Maintaining the change once it has been initiated	6. Stabilization and generating self-renewal	

Sources: Lewin, K., *Field theory in social science* (New York: Harper and Row, 1951); Lippitt, R., Watson, J. & Westley, B. *The Dynamics of Planned Change* (New York: Harcourt Brace, 1958); R. Havelock, *The Change agent's guide to innovations in education* (Englewood Cliffs, NJ: Educational Technology Publications, 1973); E. Rogers, *Diffusion of Innovations,* 3rd ed. (New York: Free Press, 1983).

Stages in the Acceptance of Change

The individual

1. Becomes aware of the new idea, system, or practice.
2. Seeks more information about the change.
3. Evaluates the information and relates it to the present situation.
4. Mentally tries out the proposed change.
5. Actually tries out the change, on a small scale, if possible.
6. Adopts and integrates the change into the present system.

When introducing a change, the nearer the people involved in the change are to the process, the easier the implementation of the change. These stages of acceptance can then naturally evolve.

Source: Stevens, B. (1975). Effecting change. *Journal of Nursing Administration, 5*, 25. Used with permission.

Common Driving and Restraining Forces

Motivating Forces

- Perception that the change is challenging
- Economic gain
- Perception that the change will improve the situation
- Visualization of the future impact of change
- Potential for self-growth, recognition, achievement, and improved relationships

Restraining Forces

- Fear that something of personal value will be lost (e.g., threat to job security or self-esteem)
- Misunderstanding of the change and its implications
- Low tolerance for change related to intellectual or emotional insecurity
- Perception that the change will not achieve goals; failure to see the big picture
- Lack of time or energy
- Perceived loss of freedom to engage in particular behaviours

Guidelines for Dealing with Resistance

1. Communicate with those who oppose the change. Get to the root of their reasons for opposition.
2. Clarify information and provide accurate information.
3. Be open to revisions but clear about what must remain.
4. Present the negative consequences of resistance (threats to organizational survival, compromised client care, and so on).
5. Emphasize the positive consequences of the change and how the individual or group will benefit. However, do not spend too much energy on rational analysis of why the change is good and why the arguments against it do not hold up. People's resistance frequently flows from feelings that are not rational.
6. Keep resisters involved in face-to-face contact with supporters. Encourage proponents to empathize with opponents, recognize valid objections, and relieve unnecessary fears.
7. Maintain a climate of trust, support, and confidence.
8. Divert attention by creating a different "disturbance." Energy can shift to a "more important" problem inside the system, thereby redirecting resistance. Alternatively, attention can be brought to an external threat to create a "bully phenomenon." When members perceive a greater environmental threat (such as competition or restrictive governmental policies), they tend to unify internally.
9. Follow the "politics of change." (a) Analyze the organizational chart; know the formal lines of authority. Identify informal lines as well. (b) Identify key persons who will be affected by the change. Pay attention to those immediately above and below the point of change. (c) Find out as much as possible about these key people. What interests them, gets them excited, turns them off? What is on their personal and organizational agendas? Who typically aligns with whom on important decisions? (d) Begin to build a coalition of support before you start the change process. Identify the key people who will most likely support your idea and those who are most likely to be persuaded easily. Talk informally with them to flush out possible objections to your idea and potential opponents. What will the costs and benefits be to them—especially in political terms? Can your idea be modified in ways that retain your objectives but appeal to more key people?

Source: Sullivan, E. J. & Decker, P. J. (1997). *Effective leadership and management in nursing* (4th ed.). Copyright © 1997 by Benjamin Cummings Publishing Company. Reprinted with permission.

Workplace

At each of three shift meetings, Nurse Hawkins, unit manager, listened to nurses complain about problems with getting clients' laboratory work done and reported to the unit in a timely manner. She conferred with other head nurses and other health-care professionals on the unit. It appeared that similar complaints were widespread.

At the next meeting of nurse managers, Nurse Hawkins described the problem. The group appointed a task force, with Nurse Hawkins as chair, and asked it to present a plan to solve the problem at the next meeting. After gathering more data, the task force invited representatives from the other health-care professionals staff and the laboratory director to meet with them to review the data, consider alternative solutions, and select a plan to solve the problem.

By the next meeting of nurse managers, a preliminary plan to alter the system of laboratory reporting had been devised, and all concerned were working cooperatively to implement the plan.

Community

Every nurse plays several roles besides that of registered nurse. Each resides in a community, and many are parents. Some serve on school boards and some belong to or participate in religious, club, or scouting activities. There are numerous opportunities for nurses to contribute to the health and welfare of the communities in which they live.

Consider one example of a group of nursing students who recognized a health problem within their community and developed a plan to intervene. Many of the students were parents of children in local elementary schools where a high percentage of children were being sent home daily with head lice. Because of previously enacted budget cuts, the district's school nurses were each responsible for between three and five schools. The students volunteered to work with the district nurses to provide screening and health teaching at each of the elementary schools, thereby helping resolve the community's problems.

All nurses are affected by change; nobody can avoid it. Knowledgeable nurses make rational plans to deal with both opportunities to initiate and guide needed change as well as to respond to change that affects them in the workplace, government, organizations, and the community. To recognize these opportunities for change and respond to the factors that influence nursing from without, it is helpful to consider the history of nursing, current trends in nursing, and present political, social, technological, and economic issues.

FOCUS ON CRITICAL THINKING

You have just interviewed for two nursing positions and are trying to decide which job to pursue. During your first interview for a team member position, the nurse manager, Mr. Caruso, was cheerful, spoke highly of his current staff, complimented them for their ability to set goals and participate in decision making, listened to your ideas, and explored ways that you could contribute to this team's effectiveness. The second nurse manager, Mrs. Turner, was also cheerful and talkative. She provided you with a job description as a primary nurse caregiver, explained her expectations of you as a new employee, and spoke of new programs she was attempting to implement. Both nurse managers talked about changes taking place in their facilities and the need for employees to remain flexible.

1. On the basis of the brief data provided, speculate about the leadership style of each of these nurse managers.
2. Think about managers (or leaders) you have known and admired. What characteristics did they have that you would like to integrate into your own management style?
3. Both nurse managers spoke of changes that were taking place in their facility. As a nurse, how can you assist your peers who are unhappy and seem to resist change even when it is positive?
4. What factors should you consider before making a decision about accepting a position in a "team nursing" environment as opposed to a "primary nursing" environment?

See Appendix A for answers to these quetions.

Cultural Considerations for Management

1. Significant changes have occurred in the ethnic composition of Canada with increased migration from Eastern and Southeast Asian countries, as well as from other non-European countries (Statistics Canada, 2001).
2. Impact on nursing management is two-fold: (1) the provision of care to this diverse population, and (2) the employment of persons with varied backgrounds and languages.
3. To successfully manage these changes, guidelines for nurse leaders include:
   a. Developing a clear vision of the diversity of the population to be served.
   b. Exploring the current corporate culture regarding diversity.
   c. Modifying assumptions and practices to address the population needs.
   d. Providing opportunities for, and encouraging, current employees to learn about and engage in awareness regarding cultural diversity.
   e. Assisting in the design of culturally sensitive programs to help eliminate stereotypes, prevent misunderstandings, and provide quality care.
   f. Examining the workforce in the community and the hiring, mentoring, and promotion practices of the organization.
   g. Adjusting practice to include the cultural diversity that exists within the client population and the workforce.

CHAPTER HIGHLIGHTS

- The professional nurse frequently assumes the roles of leader and manager. Leaders influence others to accomplish a specific goal, whereas managers are employees of an organization with responsibility and accountability for accomplishing the tasks of the organization.
- Several leadership styles have been described, including autocratic, democratic, laissez-faire, and bureaucratic. These styles are often blended to fit the situation. Nurses need to know which style is most consistent with their behaviour and learn to incorporate aspects of other styles into their practice.
- Descriptions of leadership, including charismatic, transactional, transformational, connective, and shared, address the traits, behaviours, and relationships between leaders and followers.
- Managers plan, organize, direct, and control in order to accomplish the work of the organization.
- Nurse managers work in the organizational framework of the employing agency. Principles of management include authority, accountability, and responsibility.
- Networking is the establishment of professional linkages to obtain information, share ideas, and facilitate the accomplishment of professional goals. Nurses can develop professional networks throughout their careers in a variety of settings, including school, work, professional organizations, and social groups.
- Delegation is a management tool that a manager can use to improve productivity. The manager transfers responsibility and authority to another but retains accountability for the task.
- Nurses frequently act as change agents in relation to clients, families, work settings, and communities. Change is stressful and may be resisted. Planned change requires problem-solving skills, decision-making skills, and interpersonal competence.

READINGS AND REFERENCES

Suggested Readings

Laschinger, H. K. S., Finegan, J., Shamian, J., & Casier, S. (2000). Organizational trust and empowerment in restructured healthcare settings. Effects on staff nurse commitment. *Journal of Nursing Administration, 30*(9), 413–425.
The authors describe a study they had conducted to examine the empowerment, commitment, and trust that nurses had in the organizations in which they worked. Findings demonstrated that nurse managers can create high-trust work environments by empowering nurses through providing information, support and guidance, educational opportunities, and resources for nurses.

Parkman, C. A. (1996). Delegation. Are you doing it right? *American Journal of Nursing, 96*, 43–48.
This article outlines ways nurses can protect their clients and themselves by learning how to delegate safely. Questions nurses need to ask and the steps to take to ensure safe delegation are included. A helpful box outlines essential skills for unlicensed assistive personnel (UAPs) in terms of basic care, communication, decision making, and critical thinking.

Related Research

Hansen, J. E. O, Woods, C. Q., Boyle, D. K., Bott, M. I., & Taunton, R. I. (1995). Nurse manager personal traits and leadership characteristics. *Nursing Administration Quarterly, 19*(4), 23–35.

King, T. (2000). Paradigms of Canadian nurse managers: Lens for viewing leadership and management. *Canadian Journal of Nursing Leadership, 13*(1), 15–20.

Manfredi, C. M. (1996). A descriptive study of nurse managers and leadership. *Western Journal of Nursing Research, 18*(3), 314–329.

Selected References

American Organization of Nurse Executives. (1992). The role and functions of the hospital nurse manager. *Nursing Management, 23*(9), 36–38.

Bass, B. (1990). *Bass and Stodgill's handbook of leadership: Theory, research and managerial applications* (3rd ed.). New York, NY: Free Press.

Bennis, W. G. (1989). *On becoming a leader.* Reading, MA: Addison-Wesley.

Buresh, B., & Gordon S. (2000). *From silence to voice: What nurses know and must communicate to the public.* Ottawa: Canadian Nurses Association.

Canadian Nurses Association. (1993). *Chief executive nurse.* Ottawa, ON: Author. Retrieved May 11, 2001 from http://www.cna-nurses.ca/pages/policies/chiefnurse.html.

Canadian Nurses Association. (1995). *Unregulated health care workers supporting nursing care delivery.* Ottawa, ON: Author. Retrieved May 11, 2001 from http://www.cna-nurses.ca/pages/policies/ unreg_health_work.html

Cottingham, C. (1988). Transformation leadership: A strategy for nursing. *Today's OR Nurse, 10,* 24–27.

Dienemann, J., & Shaffer, C. (1992). Manager responsibilities in community agencies and hospitals. *Journal of Nursing Administration, 22*(5), 40–45.

Douglas, L. M. (1992). *The effective nurse: Leader and manager.* St. Louis, MO: Mosby-Year Book.

French, J. R. P., & Raven, B. (1959). The bases of social power. In C. Cartwright & A. Zander (Eds.), *Studies of social power.* Ann Arbor, MI: Institute for Social Research. (Classic.)

Glennon, T. K. (1992, Spring). Empowering nurses through enlightened leadership. *Revolution: The Journal of Nurse Empowerment, 2,* 40–44.

Greenleaf, R. K. (1991). *The servant as leader.* Indianapolis, IN: The Robert K. Greenleaf Center.

Grohar-Murray, M. E., & DiCroce, H. R. (2003). *Leadership and management in nursing* (3rd ed.). Upper Saddle River, NJ: Prentice Hall.

Hansten, R. I., & Washburn, M. (1992). Delegation: How to deliver care through others. *American Journal of Nursing, 92*(3), 87–90.

Havelock, R. (1973). *The change agent's guide to innovations in education.* Englewood Cliffs, NJ: Educational Technology Publications. (Classic.)

Hersey, P., & Blanchard, K. (1988). *Management of organizational behavior* (5th ed.). Englewood Cliffs, NJ: Prentice-Hall.

Kent, C., & Hunter, D. (1997). Management material. *Nursing Times, 93*(5), 36–37.

Klakovich, M. D. (1994). Connective leadership for the 21st century: A historical perspective and future directions. *Advances in Nursing Science, 16*(4), 42–54.

Leddy, S., & Pepper, J. M. (1998). *Conceptual bases of professional nursing* (4th ed.). Philadelphia, PA: Lippincott.

Lewin, K. (1948). *Resolving social conflicts.* New York, NY: Harper and Brothers. (Classic.)

Lippitt, G. L. (1973). *Visualizing change: model building and the change process.* La Jolla, CA: University Associates. (Classic.)

Marquis, B. L., & Huston, C. J. (2000). *Management decision making for nurses* (3rd ed.). Philadelphia, PA: Lippincott.

McIntyre, M., & Thomlinson, E. (2003). *Realities of Canadian Nursing: Professional, Practice and Power Issues.* Philadelphia: Lippincott, Williams & Wilkins.

O'Leary, J. G., Wendelgass, S. T., & Zimmerman, H. E. (1986). *Winning strategies for nursing managers.* Philadelphia, PA: Lippincott.

Redfern, L., & Hull, C. (1996). Power and authority: Is there a difference? *Nursing Times, 92*(37), 36–37.

Shortell, S. M., & Kaluzny, A. D. (1994). *Health care management.* Albany, NY: Delmar.

Smith, D. L. (1999). Issues in managerial communication. In J. M. Hibberd & D. L. Smith (Eds.), *Nursing management in Canada* (pp. 535–553). Toronto: W.B. Saunders Canada (a division of Harcourt Brace & Company, Canada).

Statistics Canada. (2001). Ethnocultural portrait of Canada. http://www.12statcan.ca/english/census01.

Sullivan, E. J., & Decker, P. J. (2001). *Effective leadership and management in nursing* (5th ed.). Upper Saddle River, NJ: Prentice-Hall.

Tappen, R. M. (1995). *Nursing leadership and management: Concepts and practice* (3rd ed.). Philadelphia, PA: F. A. Davis.

Tappen, R. M. (1998). *Essentials of nursing leadership and management.* Philadelphia, PA: F. A. Davis.

Tappen, R. M. (2001). *Nursing leadership and management: Concepts and practice.* (4th ed.). Philadelphia, PA: F. A. Davis Company.

Terry, R. W. (1993). *Authentic leadership.* San Francisco, CA: Jossey-Bass.

Wood, M. & Ross-Kerr, J. (2003). Career development in nursing. In J. Ross-Kerr & M. Wood (Eds.), *Canadian Nursing Issues and Perspectives* (4th ed.). Toronto: Mosby.

WEBLINKS

Canadian Nurses Association
www.cna-nurses.ca
This Web site provides information regarding the Canadian Nurses Association, its policies and guidelines, current news, and links to provincial sites.

International Council of Nurses
www.icn.ch
The Web site of the International Council of Nurses includes guidelines for improving health-care practices related to multiple issues, links to national and international organizations, and current news and updates.

CBC

Canadian Case Study — How Do We Get to Know Mrs. M.?

Mrs. M. is an 81-year-old widow who lives by herself in her own home in the downtown core of a large city in eastern Canada. Her two-storey home is about 45 years old with a large front veranda and a series of several steps down to the sidewalk. Like many of her generation, she lives in a house that is too big for her needs, but it is her home. There is a well-lit street light quite near the front gate, and the bus stop is two houses down. When her husband was alive, he took pride in the outside appearance of the house and spent a great deal of time working in the garden. Mrs M. has been unable to maintain the garden or address the ongoing maintenance needs of the house since his death about six years ago. The kitchen has a gas stove with a pilot light that sometimes has to be relit. There are no smoke detectors in the house. Mrs. M. spends most of her days on the downstairs level but her bedroom is upstairs, as is the main bathroom. Her son built her a small toilet and sink in the closet under the stairs.

Like many older adults, she does experience some health problems. Five years ago, she was diagnosed with osteoarthritis. She has had several falls recently and was hospitalized for a brief period. During her hospitalization, Mrs. M. was prescribed an anti-inflammatory medication and was also placed on medication to lower blood pressure. She told the nurse that she was discouraged because she was unable to do everything for herself that she wished because of chronic fatigue, pain, reduced manual dexterity from decreasing joint function, and diminished mobility related to joint stiffness. The family informed one of the nurses that they had noticed that Mrs. M.'s appearance had deteriorated. Upon admission, her hair was in need of washing and the three buttons on the back of her dress were undone. Staff knew that discharge planning was a process that should begin with an assessment made upon the patient's admission (Daly, Sawchuck, & Wertenberger, 2000), and they had already initiated it.

Part of the initial assessment of Mrs. M. while she was in hospital was assessment and intervention related to her complaints of pain. Huber, Feser, and Hughes' (1999) retrospective chart audit indicated that documentation regarding pain assessment by nurses was both inconsistent and incomplete. However, inservice education for nurses, which focused on problems in pain assessment, use of standardized forms, and an explanation of various interventions resulted in both improved documentation and pain management outcomes.

Mrs. M. has experienced a gradual decrease in visual acuity over the past few years because of her diabetes. The condition was diagnosed when she was in her early seventies. She has been controlled by oral hypoglycemia agents for about the past decade and by diet. During her gradual loss of vision, Mrs. M. organized some assistance for herself. A young granddaughter helped her with some of the interior housework and did her shopping. Mrs. M. used to be heavily involved in her church, doing volunteer work and teaching Sunday school. She enjoyed the time that she spent with the young children. Although she now stays close to home, she is anxious to keep her independence and to care for herself. She is not anxious about her blindness or her diabetes, which occasionally gets out of control. She feels that she is still competent and able to maintain her independence. However, she worries about imposing on her family, especially her grandchildren. She feels that they have their own lives to live.

With her recent falls, the family has asked for agency assistance during the day, while several grandchildren take turns staying with her during the night. Because of these additional activities, she is complaining of disrupted sleep. Her daughter recommended an over-the-counter remedy to help her sleep at night. This often leaves her feeling confused and she is wondering if she should continue to take it.

QUESTIONS

1. Explore the role of the nursing process in structuring a plan of care for Mrs. M.
2. What theories or models could you use to guide your assessment, diagnosis, and formulation of goals for this client?
3. What strategies might you use to gain Mrs. M.'s participation in a plan of care?
4. Mrs. M. is taking several medications. What are the implications for Mrs M.'s health?

VIDEO RESOURCES

Series Title:	Health Show
Segment Title:	Prescribing Cascasde
Show Number:	#166
Telecast Date:	January 27, 1998
Running Time	5:52

Sources: Carson, M. M., & Ross, M. M. (2000). Getting the elderly back home. *The Canadian Nurse*, *96*(2), 31–35. Daly, S., Sawchuk, P. J. & Wertenberger, D. H. (2000). Sending the elderly home: Assessing the risk. *The Canadian Nurse*, *96*(2), 27–30. Huber, S., Feser, L., & Hughes, D. (1999). A collaborative approach to pain assessment. *The Canadian Nurse*, *95*(8), 22–30. McNamara, C., & Vandewater, D. (1999). The expanded role of nurse in geriatrics. *The Canadian Nurse*, *95*(5), 34–36.

SECTION 4

Nursing Therapeutics

CHAPTER 31
Vital Signs

CHAPTER 32
Asepsis

CHAPTER 33
Safety

CHAPTER 34
Hygiene

CHAPTER 35
Fecal Elimination

CHAPTER 36
Urinary Elimination

CHAPTER 37
Skin Integrity and Wound Care

CHAPTER 38
Nutrition

CHAPTER 39
Oxygenation

CHAPTER 40
Fluid, Electrolyte, and Acid-Base Balance

CHAPTER 41
Sensory Perception

CHAPTER 42
Rest and Sleep

CHAPTER 43
Activity and Exercise

CHAPTER 44
Clients Having Surgery: Promoting Healthy Recovery

CHAPTER 45
Pain Management

CHAPTER 46
Self-Concept

CHAPTER 47
Stress and Coping

CHAPTER 48
Loss, Grieving, and Death

CHAPTER 31

Vital Signs

OBJECTIVES

After completing this chapter, you will be able to:

- Describe factors that affect the vital signs and accurate measurement of them.
- Identify the normal range variations in body temperature, pulse, respirations, and blood pressure that occur from infancy to old age.
- Identify factors influencing the body's heat production.
- Outline ways in which the body loses heat.
- Explain the body's system of thermoregulation.
- Compare oral, tympanic, rectal, and axillary methods of measuring body temperature.
- List advantages and disadvantages of each body temperature site.
- Describe appropriate nursing care for alterations in body temperature.
- Identify sites commonly used to assess the pulse and state the reasons for use of each.
- Analyze the characteristics that should be included when assessing pulses.
- Explain how to measure the apical pulse and apical-radial pulse.
- Describe the mechanics of breathing and the mechanisms that control respirations.
- Identify the characteristics that should be included in a respiratory assessment.
- Differentiate between systolic and diastolic blood pressure.
- Describe five phases of Korotkoff's sounds.
- Identify various methods and sites used to measure blood pressure.
- Perform accurate assessment, recording, and reporting of vital signs.

The **vital** or **cardinal signs** are body temperature, pulse, respirations, and blood pressure. These signs, which should be looked at in total, are checked to monitor the functions of the body. Vital signs reflect changes in function that otherwise might not be observed. Monitoring a client's vital signs should not be an automatic or routine procedure; it should be a thoughtful, scientific assessment. Vital signs, which should be evaluated with reference to the client's present and prior health status, are compared with accepted normal standards. See Table 31.1.

When and how often to assess a specific client's vital signs are chiefly nursing judgements, depending on the client's health status. Some agencies have policies about taking clients' vital signs, and physicians may specify frequency (e.g., "Blood pressure q2h"). Ordered assessments, however, should be considered the minimum; a nurse should measure vital signs more often if the client's health status requires it. Examples of times to assess vital signs are listed in the accompanying box.

Body Temperature

Body temperature, measured in heat units called degrees, reflects the balance between heat produced and heat lost from the body. There are two kinds of body temperature: core temperature and surface temperature. **Core temperature** is the temperature of the deep tissues of the body, such as the cranium, thorax, abdominal cavity, and pelvic cavity. It remains relatively constant. The **surface temperature** is the temperature of the skin, subcutaneous tissue, and fat. It, by contrast, fluctuates in response to the environment.

The normal core body temperature is a range of temperatures. When measured orally, the average body temperature of an adult is between 36.7° and 37°C.

The body continually produces heat as a byproduct of metabolism. When the amount of heat produced by the body exactly equals the amount of heat lost, the person is in **heat balance** (Figure 31.1).

A number of factors affect the body's heat production. The most important are these five:

1. *Basal metabolic rate.* The **basal metabolic rate (BMR)** is the rate of energy utilization in the body required to maintain essential activities, such as breathing. Metabolic rates decrease with age. In general, the younger the person, the higher is the BMR (Marieb, 1998).

Times to Assess Vital Signs

- On admission to a health-care agency to obtain baseline data
- When a client has a change in health status or reports symptoms, such as chest pain or feeling hot or faint
- Before and after surgery or an invasive procedure
- Before and/or after the administration of a medication that could affect the respiratory or cardiovascular systems, (e.g., before giving a digitalis preparation)
- Before and after any nursing intervention that could affect the vital signs (e.g., ambulating a client who has been on bed rest)

TABLE 31.1 Variations in Normal Vital Signs by Age

Age	Temperature in Degrees Celsius	Pulse (Average and Ranges)	Respirations (Average and Ranges)	Blood Pressure (mm Hg)
Newborns	36.8 (axillary)	130 (80–180)	35 (30–80)	73/55
Infants 1–12 months	37.5–37.7			
1–3 years	37.7 (rectal)	120 (80–140)	30 (20–40)	90/55
6–9 years	37 (oral)	100 (75–120)	20 (15–25)	95/57
10 years	37 (oral)	70 (50–90)	19 (15–25)	102/62
Teen years	37 (oral)	70 (50–90)	18 (15–20)	120/80
Adult	37 (oral)	80 (60–100)	16 (12–20)	120/80
Older Adult (>70 years)	36 (oral)	80 (60–100)	16 (15–20)	150/78

Note:
- Diastolic blood pressures plateau before age 60 years and drop thereafter.
- Systolic blood pressures rise with age.

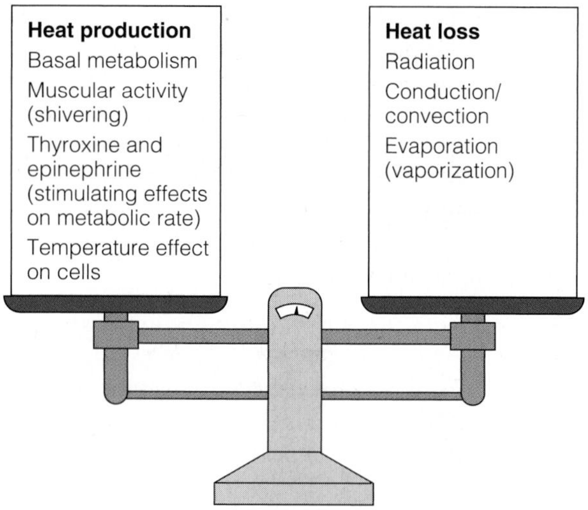

Figure 31.1 As long as heat production and heat loss are properly balanced, body temperature remains constant. Factors contributing to heat production (and temperature rise) are shown on the left side of the scale; those contributing to heat loss (and temperature drop) are shown on the right side of the scale.

Source: Adapted from Marieb, E. N. (1998). *Human anatomy and physiology* (4th ed.). (p. 953). Menlo Park, CA: Benjamin/Cummings. Adapted with permission.

2. *Muscle activity.* Muscle activity, including shivering, increases the BMR.
3. *Thyroxine output.* Increased thyroxine output increases the rate of cellular metabolism throughout the body. This effect is called **chemical thermogenesis,** the stimulation of heat production in the body through increased cellular metabolism.
4. *Epinephrine, norepinephrine, and sympathetic stimulation.* These hormones immediately increase the rate of cellular metabolism in many body tissues. Epinephrine and norepinephrine directly affect liver and muscle cells, thereby increasing cellular metabolism.
5. *Fever.* Fever increases the cellular metabolic rate and thus further increases the body's temperature.

Heat is lost from the body through radiation, conduction, convection, and vaporization. **Radiation** is the transfer of heat from the surface of one object to the surface of another without contact between the two objects, mostly in the form of infrared rays. For example, radiation accounts for 60 percent of the heat lost by a nude person standing in a room at normal room temperature (Guyton and Hall, 2000).

Conduction is the transfer of heat from one molecule to a molecule of lower temperature. Conductive transfer cannot take place without contact between the molecules and normally accounts for minimal heat loss, except, for example, when a body is immersed in cold water. The amount of heat transferred depends on the temperature difference and the amount and duration of the contact.

Convection is the dispersion of heat by air currents. The body usually has a small amount of warm air adjacent to it. This warm air rises and is replaced by cooler air, and so people always lose a small amount of heat through convection.

Vaporization (evaporation) is continuous evaporation of moisture from the respiratory tract, from the mucosa of the mouth, and from the skin. This continuous and unnoticed water loss is called insensible water loss, and the accompanying heat loss is called **insensible heat loss.** Insensible heat loss accounts for about 10 percent of basal heat loss. When the body temperature increases, vaporization accounts for greater heat loss.

Regulation of Body Temperature

The system that regulates body temperature has three main parts: (1) sensors in the shell and in the core, (2) an integrator in the hypothalamus, and (3) an effector system that adjusts the production and loss of heat. Most *sensors* or *sensory receptors* are in the skin. The skin has more receptors for cold than warmth. Therefore, skin sensors detect cold more efficiently than warmth.

When the skin becomes chilled over the entire body, three physiological processes take place to increase the body temperature:

1. Shivering increases heat production.
2. Sweating is inhibited to decrease heat loss.
3. Vasoconstriction decreases heat loss.

The **hypothalamic integrator,** the centre that controls the core temperature, is located in the preoptic area of the hypothalamus. When the sensors in the hypothalamus detect heat, they send out signals intended to reduce the temperature, that is, to decrease heat production and increase heat loss. When the cold sensors are stimulated, signals are sent out to increase heat production and decrease heat loss.

The signals from the cold-sensitive receptors of the hypothalamus initiate *effectors,* such as vasoconstriction, shivering, and the release of epinephrine, which increases cellular metabolism and, hence, heat production. When the warmth-sensitive receptors in the hypothalamus are stimulated, the effector system sends out signals that initiate sweating and peripheral vasodilation. Also, when this system is stimulated, the person consciously makes appropriate adjustments, such as putting on additional clothing in response to cold or turning on a fan in response to heat.

Factors Affecting Body Temperature

Nurses should be aware of the factors that can affect a client's body temperature in order to recognize normal temperature variations and understand the significance of body temperature measurements that deviate from normal. Among the factors that affect body temperature are the following:

1. *Age.* The infant is greatly influenced by the temperature of the environment and must be protected from extreme changes. Until puberty, children's temperatures continue to be more labile than those of adults. Many older people, particularly those over 75 years, are at risk of hypothermia (temperatures below 36°C) for a variety of reasons, such as inadequate diet, loss of subcutaneous fat, lack of activity, and reduced thermoregulatory efficiency. Older people are also particularly sensitive to extremes in the environmental temperature due to decreased thermoregulatory controls. See Table 31.1 for a summary of the variations in body temperature by age.
2. *Diurnal variations (circadian rhythms).* Body temperatures normally change throughout the day, varying as much as 1°C between the early morning and the late afternoon. The point of highest body temperature is usually reached between 2000 and 2400 hours (8:00 p.m. and midnight), and the lowest point is reached during sleep between 0400 and 0600 hours (4:00 and 6:00 a.m.). See Figure 31.2.
3. *Exercise.* Hard work or strenuous exercise can increase body temperature to as high as 38.3°C to 40°C when measured rectally.
4. *Hormones.* Women usually experience more hormone fluctuations than men do. In women, progesterone secretion at the time of ovulation raises body temperature by about 0.3° to 0.6°C above basal temperature (Ladewig et al., 1998).
5. *Stress.* Stimulation of the sympathetic nervous system can increase the production of epinephrine and norepinephrine, thereby increasing metabolic activity and heat production. Nurses may anticipate that a highly stressed or anxious client could have an elevated body temperature for that reason.
6. *Environment.* Extremes in environmental temperatures can affect a person's temperature regulatory systems. If the temperature is assessed in a very warm room and the body temperature cannot be modified by convection, conduction, or radiation, the temperature will be elevated. Similarly, if the client has been outside in extremely cold weather without suitable clothing, the body temperature may be low.

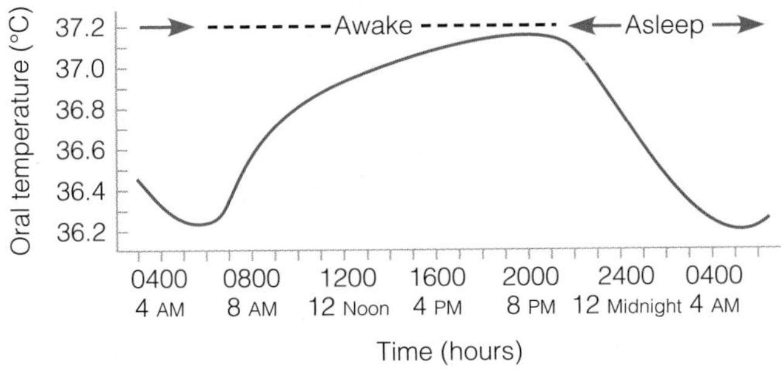

Figure 31.2 Range of oral temperatures during 24 hours for a healthy young adult

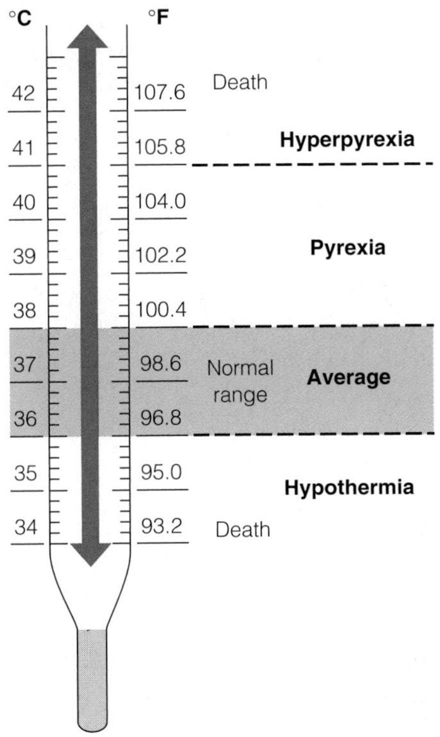

Figure 31.3 Terms used to describe alterations in body temperature (oral measurements) and ranges in Celsius (Centigrade) and Fahrenheit scales

Alterations in Body Temperature

Pyrexia

A body temperature above the usual range is called **pyrexia, hyperthermia,** or (in lay terms) **fever.** A very high fever, such as 41°C, is called **hyperpyrexia** (Figure 31.3). The client who has a fever is referred to as **febrile;** the one who does not have fever is **afebrile.**

Fevers may be described as intermittent, remittent, relapsing, and constant. During an **intermittent fever,** the body temperature alternates at regular intervals between periods of fever and periods of normal or subnormal temperatures. During a **remittent fever,** a wide range of temperature fluctuations (more than 2°C) occurs over a 24-hour period, all of which are *above* normal. In a **relapsing fever,** short febrile periods of a few days are interspersed with periods of one or two days of normal temperature. During a **constant fever,** the body temperature fluctuates minimally but always remains above normal.

The clinical signs of fever vary with the onset, course, and abatement stages of the fever (see the box on the next page).

Clinical Signs of Fever

Onset (cold or chill stage)

- Increased heart rate
- Increased respiratory rate and depth
- Shivering
- Pallid, cold skin
- Complaints of feeling cold
- Cyanotic nail beds
- "Gooseflesh" appearance of the skin
- Cessation of sweating

Course

- Absence of chills
- Skin that feels warm
- Photosensitivity
- Increased pulse and respiratory rates
- Increased thirst
- Mild to severe dehydration
- Drowsiness, restlessness, delirium, or convulsions
- Herpetic lesions of the mouth
- Loss of appetite (if the fever is prolonged)
- Malaise, weakness, and aching muscles

Defervescence (fever abatement)

- Skin that appears flushed and feels warm
- Sweating
- Decreased shivering
- Possible dehydration

These signs occur as a result of changes in the *set point* of the temperature control mechanism regulated by the hypothalamus. Under normal conditions, whenever the core temperature rises above 37°C, the rate of heat loss becomes greater than heat production, resulting in a fall in temperature toward the set point level. Conversely, when the core temperature falls below 37°C, the rate of heat production becomes greater than heat loss, resulting in a rise in temperature toward the set point.

In a fever, however, the set point of the hypothalamic thermostat changes suddenly from the normal level to a higher than normal value (e.g., 39.5°C) as a result of the effects of tissue destruction, pyrogenic substances, or dehydration on the hypothalamus. Although the set point changes rapidly, the core body temperature (i.e., the blood temperature) reaches this new set point only after several hours. During this interval, the usual heat production responses that cause elevation of the body temperature occur: chills, feeling of coldness, cold skin due to vasoconstriction, and shivering.

When the core temperature reaches the new set point, the person feels neither cold nor hot and no longer experiences chills. Depending on the degree of temperature elevation, various other signs (shown in the box above) may occur at this stage. Very high temperatures, such as 41° to 42°C, damage the parenchyma of cells throughout the body, particularly in the brain, where destruction of neuronal cells is irreversible. Damage to the liver, kidneys, and other body organs can also be great enough to disrupt functioning and eventually cause death.

When the cause of the high temperature is suddenly removed, the set point of the hypothalamic thermostat is suddenly reduced to a lower value, perhaps even back to the original normal level. In this instance, the hypothalamus now attempts to lower the temperature to 37°C, and the usual heat loss responses causing a reduction of the body temperature occur: excessive sweating and a hot, flushed skin due to sudden vasodilation. This sudden change of events is known as the *crisis*, the *flush*, or the *defervescent stage* of a pyrexic condition. A more gradual return of the body temperature to normal is referred to as a resolution of pyrexia by *lysis*.

Nursing interventions for a client who has a fever are designed to support the body's normal physiological processes, provide comfort, and prevent complications. During the course of the fever, the nurse must closely monitor the client's vital signs.

Nursing measures during the chill phase are designed to help the client decrease heat loss. At this time, the body's physiological processes are attempting to raise the core temperature to the new set point temperature. During the flush or crisis phase, the body processes are attempting to lower the core temperature to the reduced or normal set point temperature. At this time, the nurse takes measures to increase heat loss and decrease heat production. Nursing interventions for a client with fever are shown in the box on the next page.

Hypothermia

Hypothermia is a core body temperature below the lower limit of normal. The three physiological mechanisms of hypothermia are (1) excessive heat loss; (2) inadequate heat production to counteract the heat loss; and (3) impaired hypothalamic thermoregulation. The clinical signs of hypothermia are given in the second box on the next page.

Nursing Interventions for Clients with Fever

- Monitor vital signs.
- Assess skin colour and temperature.
- Monitor white blood cell count, hematocrit value, and other pertinent laboratory reports for indications of infection or dehydration.
- Remove excess blankets when the client feels warm, but provide extra warmth when the client feels chilled.
- Provide adequate nutrition and fluids (e.g., 2,500–3,000 mL per day if not contraindicated) to meet the increased metabolic demands and prevent dehydration. Clients who sweat profusely can become dehydrated.
- Measure intake and output.
- Reduce physical activity to limit heat production, especially during the flush stage.
- Administer antipyretics (drugs that reduce the level of fever), as ordered.
- Provide oral hygiene to keep the mucous membranes moist. They can become dry and cracked as a result of excessive fluid loss.
- Provide a tepid sponge bath to increase heat loss through conduction.
- Provide dry clothing and bed linens.

Hypothermia may be accidental or induced. *Accidental hypothermia* can occur as a result of (1) exposure to a cold environment (i.e., below 16°C), (2) immersion in cold water, and (3) lack of adequate clothing, shelter, or heat. In older people, the problem can be compounded by a decreased metabolic rate and the use of sedatives, which depress the metabolic rate.

Managing hypothermia involves removing the client from the cold and rewarming the client's body. For the client with mild hypothermia, the body is rewarmed by applying blankets; for the client with severe hypothermia, a hyperthermia blanket (an electrically controlled blanket that provides a specified temperature) is applied, and warm intravenous fluids are given. Wet clothing, which increases heat loss because of the high conductivity of water, should be replaced with dry clothing. See the accompanying box for nursing interventions for clients who have hypothermia.

Induced hypothermia is the deliberate lowering of the body temperature to decrease the need for oxygen by the body tissues. Induced hypothermia can involve the whole body or a body part. It may be indicated for certain surgical cases (e.g., cardiac and brain surgery) but remains controversial.

Clinical Signs of Hypothermia

- Decreased body temperature, pulse, and respirations
- Severe shivering (initially)
- Feelings of cold and chills
- Pale, cool, waxy skin
- Hypotension
- Decreased urinary output
- Lack of muscle coordination
- Disorientation
- Drowsiness progressing to coma

Assessing Body Temperature

The four most common sites for measuring body temperature are oral, rectal, axillary, and the tympanic membrane. Each of the sites has advantages and disadvantages (Table 31.2).

The body temperature is frequently measured *orally*. This method reflects changing body temperature more quickly than does the rectal method. If a client has injested cold or hot food or fluids or has been smoking, the nurse should wait 30 minutes before taking the temperature orally to ensure that the temperature of the mouth has not been affected by the temperature of the food, fluid, or warm smoke.

Rectal temperature readings are considered to be the most accurate. In some agencies, taking temperatures rectally is contraindicated for clients with myocardial infarction. It is believed that inserting a rectal thermometer can produce vagal stimulation, which can cause bradycardia. Rectal temperatures are usually contraindicated in clients who are undergoing rectal surgery or have diarrhea or diseases of the rectum.

The axilla is the preferred site for measuring temperature in newborns because it is accessible and offers no possibility of rectal perforation. However, research indicates that the axillary method is inaccurate when assessing a fever

Nursing Interventions for Clients with Hypothermia

- Provide a warm environment (room temperature).
- Provide dry clothing.
- Apply warm blankets.
- Keep limbs close to body.
- Cover the client's scalp with a cap or turban.
- Supply warm oral or intravenous fluids.
- Apply warming pads.

TABLE 31.2 Advantages and Disadvantages of Four Sites for Body Temperature Measurement

Site	Advantages	Disadvantages
Oral	Most accessible and convenient	Mercury-in-glass thermometers can break if bitten; therefore, they are contraindicated for children under six years and clients who are confused or who have convulsive disorders.
		Inaccurate if client is a mouth breather, has just ingested hot or cold food or fluid, or has smoked.
		Could injure the mouth following oral surgery.
Rectal	Most reliable measurement	Inconvenient and more unpleasant for clients; difficult for client who cannot turn to the side.
		Could injure the rectum following rectal surgery.
		Placement of the thermometer at different sites within the rectum yields different temperatures, yet placement at the same site each time is difficult.
		A rectal glass thermometer does not respond to changes in arterial temperatures as quickly as an oral thermometer; misleading information may be acquired.
		Presence of stool may interfere with thermometer placement. If the stool is soft, the thermometer may be embedded in stool, rather than against the mucosal wall of the rectum. If the stool is impacted, the depth of the thermometer insertion may be insufficient.
		In newborns and infants, insertion of the rectal thermometer has resulted in ulcerations and rectal perforations. *Many agencies advise against using rectal thermometers on neonates.*
Axillary	Noninvasive	The thermometer must be left in place for a long time to obtain an accurate measurement.
Tympanic membrane	Readily accessible; reflects the core temperature; very fast	Can be uncomfortable and involves risk of injuring the membrane if the probe is inserted too far. Repeated measurements may vary. Right and left measurements can differ. Presence of cerumen can affect the reading.

and that rectal perforation using a well-lubricated thermometer during temperature measurement is relatively rare (Bickley & Szilagyi, 2003). Nurses should check agency protocol when taking the temperature of newborns, infants, toddlers, and children. The axillary method of temperature assessment is appropriate for adult clients with oral inflammation or wired jaws, for clients recovering from oral surgery, clients who are breathing through their mouths (e.g., following nasal surgery), irrational clients, and clients for whom other temperature sites are contraindicated.

The tympanic membrane temperature measures core body temperature. Taking the tympanic membrane temperature is a common practice and if performed properly, is quick, safe, and reliable. Like the sublingual oral site, the tympanic membrane has an abundant arterial blood supply, primarily from branches of the external carotid artery. Because temperature sensors applied directly to the tympanic membrane can be uncomfortable and involve risk of membrane injury or perforation, noninvasive *infrared thermometers* are used.

In addition to the four common sites for measuring temperature, a chemical thermometer may be applied to the *forehead.* See Types of Thermometers next. Forehead temperature measurements are most useful for infants and children on occasions when a more invasive measurement is not necessary. If the forehead indicates a temperature elevation, a glass or electronic thermometer should be used to obtain a more accurate measurement.

Types of Thermometers

Traditionally, body temperatures have been measured using *mercury-in-glass thermometers.* Oral thermometers may have long, slender tips or short, rounded tips (Figure 31.4). The rounded thermometer can be used at the rectal as well as other sites. In some agencies, thermometers may be colour coded; for example, blue or red thermometers may be used for rectal temperatures and silver ones for oral and axillary temperatures. In view of technological advances in temperature assessment equipment, the risk of glass breakage, and the potential mercury hazard, this type is used infrequently.

Electronic thermometers offer another method of assessing body temperatures. They provide a reading in only two to 60 seconds, depending on the model. The equipment consists of a battery-operated portable electronic unit, a probe that the nurse attaches to the unit, and a probe cover, which

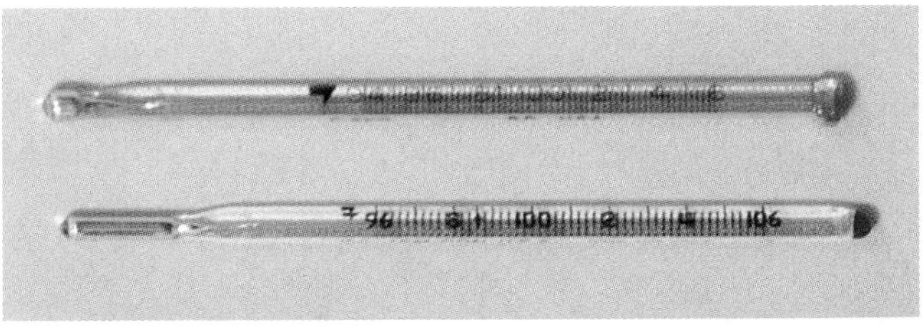

Figure 31.4 Two types of thermometer tips

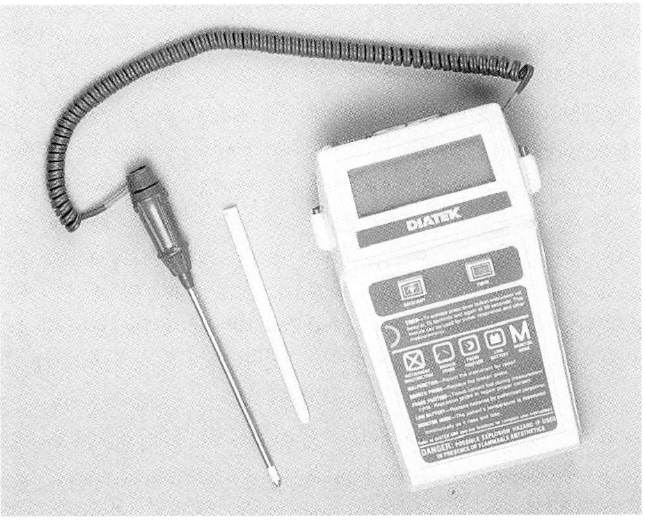

Figure 31.5 An electronic thermometer. Note the probe and probe cover.

is usually disposable (Figure 31.5). Some models have a different circuit and probe for each method of measurement.

Chemical disposable thermometers are also used to measure body temperatures. Chemical thermometers using liquid crystal dots or bars, heat-sensitive tape, or patches applied to the forehead change colour to indicate temperature. Some of these are single use and others may be reused. One type that has small chemical dots at one end is shown in Figure 31.6. To read the temperature, the nurse notes the highest reading among the dots that have changed colour.

Temperature-sensitive tape may also be used to obtain a general indication of body surface temperature. It does not indicate the core temperature. The tape contains liquid crystals that change colour according to temperature. When applied to the skin, usually on the forehead or abdomen, the temperature digits on the tape respond by changing colour (Figure 31.7). The skin area should be dry. After the length of time specified by the manufacturer (e.g., 15 seconds), a colour appears on the tape. The tape is removed and discarded after the colour has been compared with the scale provided by the manufacturer. This method is particularly useful at home and for infants whose temperatures are to be monitored for any reason.

Infrared thermometers sense body heat in the form of infrared energy given off by a heat source, which, in the ear canal, is primarily the tympanic membrane. See Figure 31.8. The infrared thermometer makes no contact with the tympanic membrane.

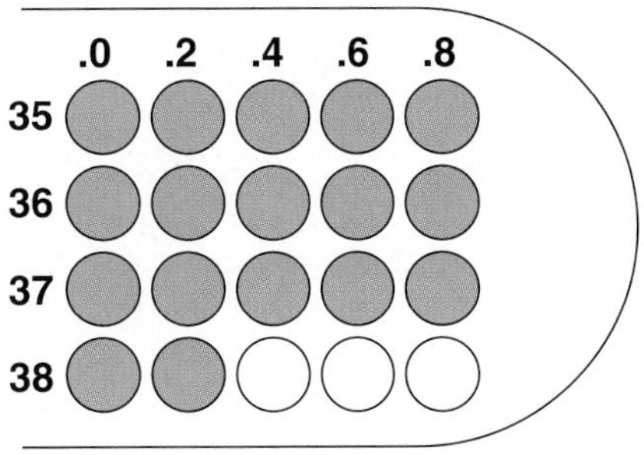

Figure 31.6 A chemical thermometer showing a reading of 38.2°C

Temperature Scales

The body temperature is measured in degrees on the Celsius (centigrade) scale in keeping with Canada's adoption of the International System of Units as the national standard of measurement in 1971, (Metric Commission Canada,

RESEARCH NOTE

How Do Different Sites and Methods of Temperature Measurement Differ in Clients with Fevers?

In this study, the researchers compared temperature readings in febrile clients using an electronic thermometer placed in the oral and axillary sites, a rectal probe thermometer, an infrared tympanic thermometer, and a pulmonary artery catheter. The pulmonary artery site most closely resembles a "core" temperature. Clients in an intensive care unit were evaluated every hour during the day and every four hours at night at all five sites. A total of 13 people who had a temperature of at least 37.8°C according to their pulmonary artery temperature were assessed.

The results showed that the temperatures measured by the rectal probe were closest to those of the pulmonary artery. In order, the next closest were oral, tympanic, and axillary. For pulmonary artery fevers over 38.3°C, the tympanic and rectal sites had the fewest false-negative readings.

Implications: Most people with fevers do not have a pulmonary artery catheter in place. The rectal temperature is the closest to measuring core temperature, but both oral and tympanic sites can be used if using the rectal site is not possible.

Source: Schmitz, T., Blair, N., Falk, M., & Levine, C. (1995). A comparison of five methods of temperature measurement in febrile intensive care patients. *American Journal of Critical Care, 4,* 286–292.

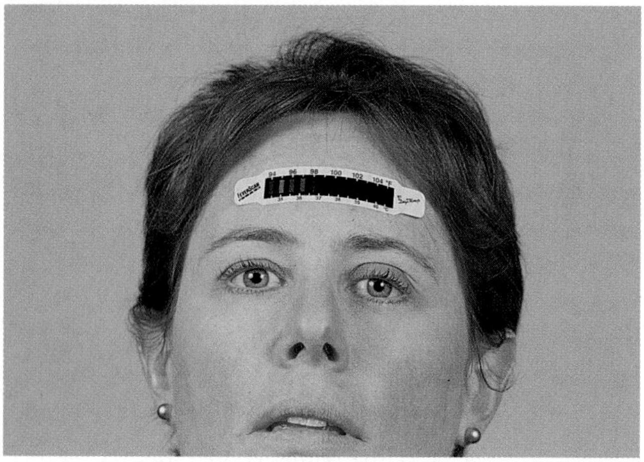

Figure 31.7 A temperature-sensitive skin tape

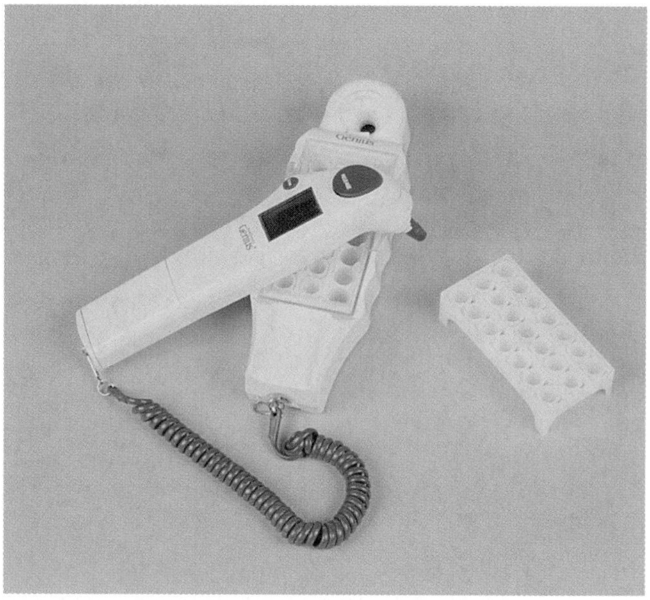

Figure 31.8 An infrared (tympanic) thermometer used to measure the tympanic membrane temperature

1982). On a glass thermometer, the Celsius scale normally extends from 34° to 42°C. Body temperatures rarely extend beyond these scales. See Figure 31.3 earlier.
Procedure 31.1 explains how to measure body temperature.

PROCEDURE 31.1 Assessing Body Temperature

PURPOSES

- To establish baseline data for subsequent evaluation
- To identify if the core temperature is within normal range
- To determine changes in the core temperature in response to specific therapies (e.g., antipyretic medication, immunosuppressive therapy, invasive procedure)
- To monitor clients at risk for alterations in temperature (e.g., clients at risk for infection or diagnosis of infection; those who have been exposed to temperature extremes; those with a leukocyte count below 5,000 or above 12,000)

Assessment Focus
Clinical signs of fever (see p. 712); clinical signs of hypothermia (see p. 713); site most appropriate for measurement (see p. 714); factors that may alter core body temperature (see p. 711)

Equipment

- ❑ Oral, rectal, axillary, or tympanic thermometer
- ❑ Towel, if the axillary site is used
- ❑ Water-soluble lubricant and tissue, if the rectal site is used
- ❑ Disposable gloves, if the rectal site is used
- ❑ Disposable probe cover if an electronic thermometer is used
- ❑ Disposable sheath if tympanic thermometer is used

INTERVENTION

Using a Tympanic Thermometer

- Apply a disposable sheath to the probe. Different sheaths fit adults and infants. They should be applied without being touched.
- Select the ear opposite the side on which the client may have been lying. *The ear against a surface can build up heat.*
- Use your right hand to hold the thermometer when using the client's right ear, left hand for the left ear. *This helps achieve the proper angle for a good seal.*

PROCEDURE 31.1 Assessing Body Temperature *continued*

- Gently pull the pinna upward and back for children over age three years and adults (Figure 31.9), straight back for children under age three years. *This straightens the ear canal.*
- Place the probe tip into the outer position of the ear canal just at the opening. The probe tip seals the opening of the canal.
- Press the button on the electronic thermometer. Do not wait too long to do this. The presence of the probe can "draw down" the temperature reading.
- Remove the thermometer when alerted to do so. Read the temperature on the screen.
- Remove and discard the probe cover. Covers can be ejected without being touched.
- Return the unit to the charging base.

USING AN ELECTRONIC THERMOMETER

- Remove the electronic unit from the battery charging base.
- Remove the temperature probe. If the probe is not attached, attach it to the appropriate circuit (oral, rectal, or axillary) in models that have separate circuits.
- Place a disposable cover securely on the probe.

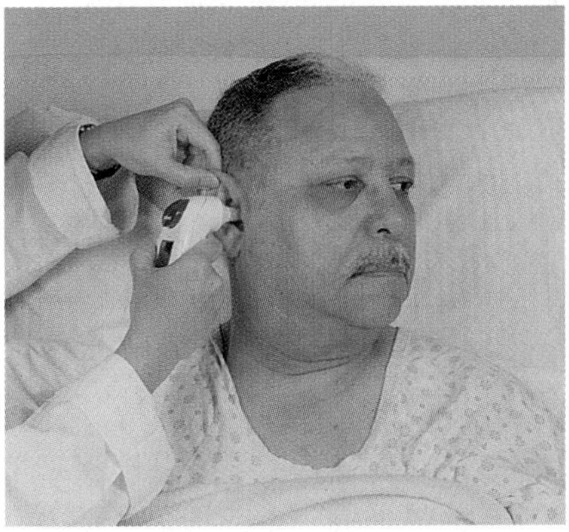

Figure 31.9 Pull the pinna of the ear up and back while inserting the tympanic thermometer

- Switch the machine on if attachment of the probe does not automatically prepare the machine for functioning.
- Insert the thermometer probe as indicated in "Using a Glass Thermometer."
- Listen for a sound indicating that the maximum measurement has been reached, and read the temperature on the dial or readout.
- Remove the thermometer.
- Record the temperature.
- Remove and discard the probe cover.
- Return the unit to the charging base.

USING A GLASS THERMOMETER (MERCURY)

1. Prepare the client.

- Ascertain which method of taking the temperature is appropriate for the client.

For an Oral Temperature

- Determine the time the client last ingested hot or cold food or fluids or had smoked. *To obtain an accurate oral temperature reading, allow 15 to 30 minutes to elapse between a client's oral intake or smoking and the measurement.*

For a Rectal Temperature

- Provide privacy before folding the bedclothes back to expose the buttocks. *Privacy is essential because exposure of the buttocks embarrasses most people.*
- Assist the client to assume a lateral position.

For an Axillary Temperature

- Expose the client's axilla. If the axilla is moist, dry it with the towel using a patting motion. *Friction created by rubbing can raise the temperature of the axilla.*

2. Prepare the equipment.

- Remove the thermometer from its package, and check the temperature reading on the thermometer.
- Shake down the mercury (if necessary) by holding the thermometer between the thumb and forefinger at the end farthest from the bulb. Snap the wrist downward. Repeat until the mercury is below 35°C.
- Place the thermometer in a plastic sheath according to agency policy.

3. Take the temperature.

For an Oral Temperature

- Place the thermometer or probe at the base of the tongue to the right or left of the frenulum in the posterior sublingual pocket (Figure 31.10). *The thermometer needs to reflect the core temperature of the blood in the larger blood vessels of the posterior pocket.*
- Ask the client to close the lips, not the teeth, around the thermometer. *A client who bites the thermometer can break it and injure the mouth.*
- Leave the thermometer in place a sufficient time for the temperature to register or for the length of time recommended by the agency.

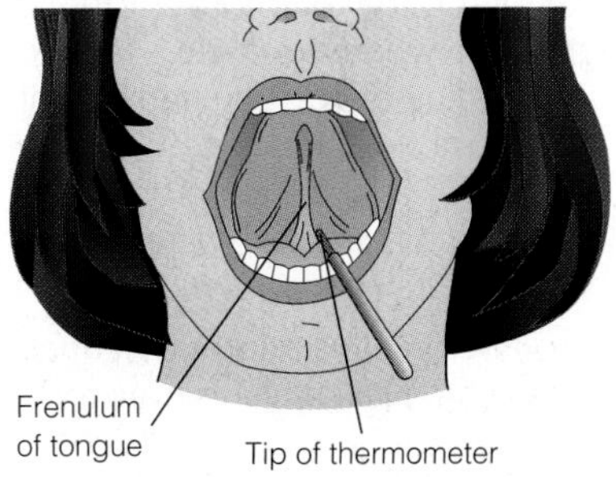

Figure 31.10 The tip of the oral thermometer is placed beside the frenulum below the tongue

PROCEDURE 31.1 Assessing Body Temperature *continued*

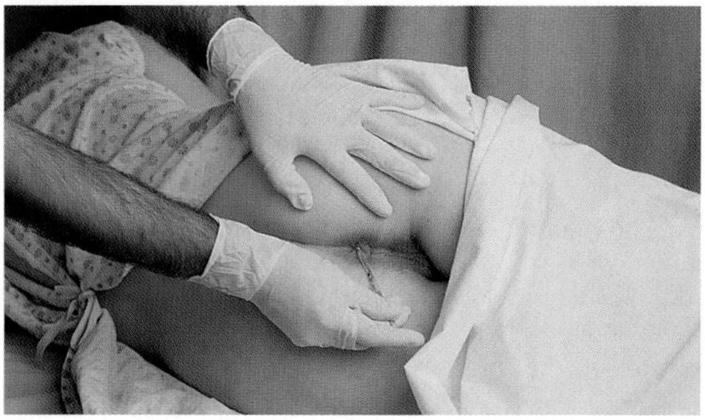

Figure 31.11 Inserting a rectal thermometer

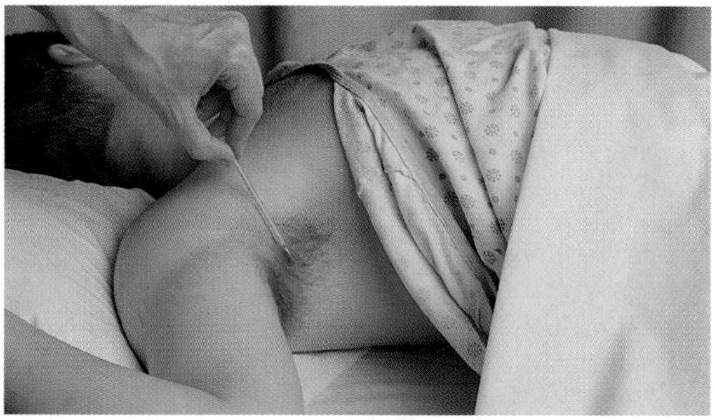

Figure 31.12 Placing the bulb of the thermometer in the centre of the axilla

For a Rectal Temperature

- Place some water-soluble lubricant on a piece of tissue. Then apply lubricant to the thermometer. *The lubricant facilitates insertion of the thermometer without irritating the mucous membrane.*
- Don disposable gloves. With the nondominant hand, raise the client's upper buttock to expose the anus.
- Ask the client to take a deep breath, and insert the thermometer into the anus anywhere from 2.5 to 4 cm, depending on the age and size of the client (for example, 3.7 cm for an adult). *Taking a deep breath often relaxes the external sphincter muscle, thus easing insertion.*
- Do not *force* insertion of the thermometer. *Difficulty inserting the thermometer could indicate the rectum is obstructed.*
- Hold the thermometer in place for three minutes or for the length of time recommended by the agency (Figure 31.11). *The thermometer may become displaced inside or outside the anus if not held in place.*

For an Axillary Temperature

- Place the thermometer in the centre of the client's axilla (Figure 31.12).
- Assist the client to place the arm tightly across the chest to keep the thermometer in place.
- Leave the thermometer in place for nine minutes or according to agency protocol. For infants and children, leave the thermometer in place five minutes.
- Remain with the client, and hold the thermometer in place if the client is irrational or very young.

4. **Remove the thermometer.**

- Wipe the thermometer with a tissue. Wipe in a rotating manner toward the bulb. *The thermometer is wiped from the area of least contamination to that of greatest contamination.*
- Discard the tissue or sheath in a receptacle used for contaminated items.

5. **Read the temperature.**

- Hold the thermometer at eye level and rotate it until the mercury column is clearly visible. The upper end of the mercury column registers the client's body temperature. (See Figure 31.4.)

6. **Clean and shake down the thermometer.**

- Wash the thermometer in tepid, soapy water. Organic material, such as mucus, must be removed. *Organic materials on the thermometer can harbour microorganisms.*
- Rinse the thermometer in *cold* water, dry it, and store it dry. *Hot water expands the mercury and may break the thermometer.*
- Shake down the thermometer and return it to its container or discard it. Some agencies have equipment designed for spinning down the mercury levels.
- If the thermometer is to be disinfected before storage, follow agency policy.

7. **Document the temperature.**

- Record the temperature to the nearest indicated tenth (for example, 37.1°C) on a designated flowsheet. *Recording the temperature immediately ensures it is not forgotten.*

Evaluation Focus
The temperature measurement in relation to baseline data or normal range for age of client; time of day and any other influencing factors; relationship to other vital signs

PROCEDURE 31.1 Assessing Body Temperature *continued*

Home Care Considerations

- Teach the client correct use and accurate reading of the type of thermometer to be used. Reinforce the importance of reporting the site and type of thermometer used and the value of using one consistently. Provide a recording chart or table if indicated.
- Discuss means of keeping the thermometer clean and avoiding cross-contamination.
- Ensure water-soluble lubricant is available if using a rectal thermometer.
- Have the client or family member demonstrate use of the thermometer so that correct technique can be reinforced.
- Ensure the client or family member knows what temperature readings should be reported and to whom.

Safety Precautions

The nurse is responsible for assessing the client accurately and safely. Safety is a major consideration when assessing temperature due to the disadvantages of the various sites and equipment. Never apply force to insert a thermometer. If it does not enter easily, reassess the site and consider using a different location or type of thermometer.

Although the oral site is the most common, it should not be used if the client cannot cooperate or there is a risk that they may bite the thermometer. The rectal thermometer should always be held in place and never left unattended. Severe injury could occur if the client rolled onto the thermometer.

If a glass thermometer does not shake down easily or has any signs of cracks, dispose of it according to institutional policy. Mercury is a dangerous substance, and its disposal is controlled.

Pulse

The **pulse** is a wave of blood created by contraction of the left ventricle of the heart. The heart is a pulsating pump, and blood enters the arteries with each contraction, causing pressure pulses or pulse waves. Generally, the pulse wave represents the stroke volume output and the amount of blood that enters the arteries with each ventricular contraction. **Compliance** of the arteries is their ability to contract and expand. When a person's arteries lose their distensibility, as can happen in old age, greater pressure is required to pump the blood into the arteries.

When an adult is resting, the heart pumps about 5 L of blood each minute. This volume is called the **cardiac output.** The cardiac output (CO) is the result of the stroke volume (SV) times the heart rate (HR) per minute:

$$CO = SV \times HR$$

In a healthy person, the pulse reflects the heartbeat; that is, the pulse rate is the same as the rate of the ventricular contractions of the heart. However, in some types of cardiovascular disease, the heartbeat and pulse rates can differ. For example, a client's heart may produce very weak or small pulse waves that are not detectable in a peripheral pulse distal to the heart. In these instances, the nurse should assess the heartbeat *and* the peripheral pulse. See the section on assessing the apical pulse later in this chapter. A **peripheral pulse** is located in the periphery of the body, for example, in the foot, hand, or neck. The **apical pulse,** in contrast, is a central pulse; that is, it is located at the apex of the heart.

Factors Affecting Pulse Rate

The rate of the pulse is expressed in beats per minute (BPM). A pulse rate varies according to a number of factors. The nurse should consider each of the following factors when assessing a client's pulse:

- *Age.* As age increases, the pulse rate gradually decreases. See Table 31.1 for specific variations in pulse rates from birth to adulthood.
- *Gender.* After puberty, the average male's pulse rate is slightly lower than the female's.
- *Exercise.* The pulse rate normally increases with activity. The rate of increase in the professional athlete is often less than in the average person because of greater cardiac size, strength, and efficiency.
- *Fever.* The pulse rate increases (1) in response to the lowered blood pressure that results from peripheral vasodilation associated with elevated body temperature, and (2) with an increased metabolic rate.
- *Medications.* Some medications decrease the pulse rate, and others increase it. For example, cardiotonics (e.g., digitalis preparations) decrease the heart rate, whereas epinephrine increases it.
- *Hemorrhage.* Loss of blood from the vascular system (hemorrhage) normally increases pulse rate. In adults,

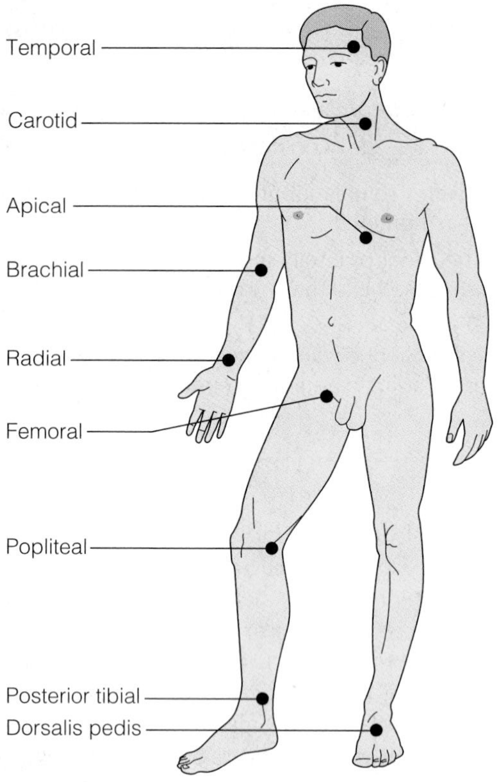

Figure 31.13 Nine sites commonly used for assessing a pulse (See Figure 31.16 also.)

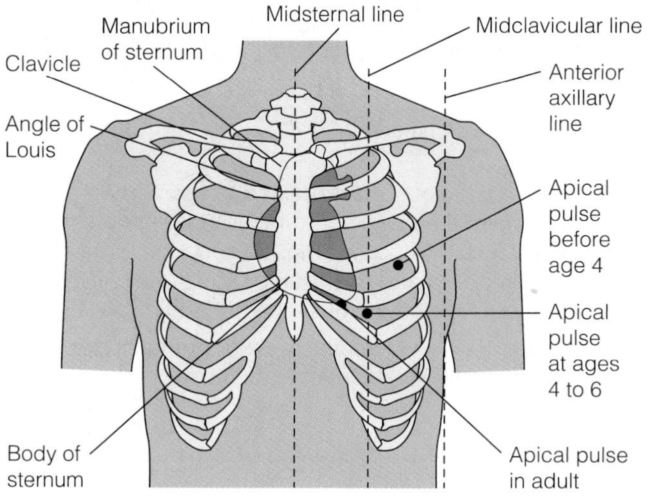

Figure 31.14 Location of the apical pulse for a child under four years, a child four to six years, and an adult

the loss of a small amount of blood (e.g., 500 mL, the amount lost after a blood donation) results in a temporary adjustment of the heart rate as the body compensates for the lost blood volume. An adult has about 5 L of blood in the system and can usually lose up to 10 percent without adverse effects.

- *Stress.* In response to stress, sympathetic nervous stimulation increases the overall activity of the heart. Stress increases the rate as well as the force of the heartbeat. Fear and anxiety, as well as the perception of severe pain, stimulate the sympathetic system.
- *Position changes.* When a person assumes a sitting or standing position, blood usually pools in dependent vessels of the venous system. Pooling results in a transient decrease in the venous blood return to the heart and a subsequent reduction in blood pressure and increase in heart rate.

Pulse Sites

Nine of the sites where a pulse is commonly taken (Figure 31.13) are the following:

1. *Temporal,* where the temporal artery passes over the temporal bone of the head. The site is superior (above) and lateral to (away from the midline of) the eye.
2. *Carotid,* at the side of the neck where the carotid artery runs between the trachea and the sternocleidomastoid muscle. Never press both carotids at the same time as this can cause a reflex drop in blood pressure or pulse rate.
3. *Apical,* at the apex of the heart. In an adult, this is located on the left side of the chest, no more than 8 cm to the left of the sternum (breastbone) and at the fourth, fifth, or sixth intercostal space (area between the ribs). For a child seven to nine years of age, the apical pulse is located at the fourth or fifth intercostal spaces. Before four years of age, it is left of the midclavicular line (MCL); between four and six years, it is at the MCL. See Figure 31.14.
4. *Brachial,* at the inner aspect of the biceps muscle of the arm (especially in infants) or medially in the antecubital space (elbow crease).
5. *Radial,* where the radial artery runs along the radial bone, on the thumb side of the inner aspect of the wrist.
6. *Femoral,* where the femoral artery passes alongside the inguinal ligament.
7. *Popliteal,* where the popliteal artery passes behind the knee. This point may be difficult to locate, but it can be palpated if the client flexes the knee slightly.
8. *Posterior tibial,* on the medial surface of the ankle, where the posterior tibial artery passes behind the medial malleolus.
9. *Pedal (dorsalis pedis),* where the dorsalis pedis artery passes over the bones of the foot. This artery can be palpated by feeling the dorsum (upper surface) of the foot on an imaginary line drawn from the middle of the ankle to the space between the big and second toes.

TABLE 31.3 Reasons for Using Specific Pulse Site

Pulse Site	Reasons for Use
Radial	Readily accessible
Temporal	Used when radial pulse is not accessible
Carotid	Used in infants
	Used in cases of cardiac arrest
	Used to determine circulation to the brain
Apical	Routinely used in infants and children up to three years of age
	Used to determine discrepancies with radial pulse
	Used to monitor some medication effects
Brachial	Used to measure blood pressure
	Used during cardiac arrest in infants
Femoral	Used in cases of cardiac arrest
	Used in infants and children
	Used to determine circulation to the leg
Popliteal	Used to determine circulation to the lower leg
Posterior tibial	Used to determine circulation to the foot
Pedal	Used to determine circulation to the foot

The radial site is most commonly used. It is easily detected in most people and readily accessible. The reasons for use of each site are given in Table 31.3.

Assessing the Pulse

A pulse is commonly assessed by palpation (feeling) or auscultation (hearing). The middle three fingertips are used for palpating all pulse sites except the apex of the heart. A stethoscope is used for assessing apical pulses and fetal heart tones. A Doppler ultrasound stethoscope (DUS; see Figure 31.15) is used for pulses that are difficult to assess. The DUS headset has earpieces similar to standard stethoscope earpieces, but it has a long cord attached to a volume-controlled audio unit and an ultrasound transducer. The DUS detects movement of blood through a blood vessel, magnifying the sound. In contrast to the conventional stethoscope, it excludes environmental sounds. It cannot detect bloodflow in deep vessels or in blood vessels underlying bone, such as the vessels in the abdomen, thorax, or skull.

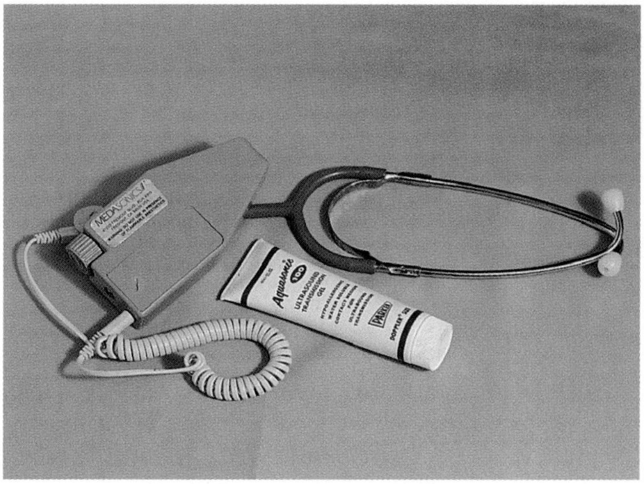

Figure 31.15 An ultrasound (Doppler) stethoscope

A pulse is normally palpated by applying moderate pressure with the three middle fingers of the hand. The pads on the most distal aspects of the finger are the most sensitive areas for detecting a pulse. With excessive pressure, one can obliterate a pulse, whereas with too little pressure, one may not be able to detect it. Before the nurse assesses the *resting* pulse, the client should assume a comfortable position. The nurse should also be aware of:

- Any medication that could affect the heart rate.
- Whether the client has been physically active. If so, wait 10 to 15 minutes until the client has rested and the pulse has returned to its usual rate.
- Any baseline data about the normal heart rate for the client. For example, a physically fit athlete may have a heart rate below 60 beats per minute.
- Whether the client should assume a particular position (e.g., sitting). In some clients, the rate changes with the position because of changes in bloodflow volume and autonomic nervous system activity.

When assessing the pulse, the nurse collects the following data: the rate, rhythm, volume, arterial wall elasticity, and presence or absence of bilateral equality. The *normal pulse rates* are shown in Table 31.1. An excessively fast heart rate (e.g., over 100 beats per minute in an adult) is referred to as **tachycardia.** A heart rate in an adult of 60 beats per minute or less is called **bradycardia.** If a client has tachycardia or bradycardia, the apical pulse should be assessed.

The **pulse rhythm** is the pattern of the beats and the intervals between the beats. Equal time elapses between beats of a normal pulse. A pulse with an irregular rhythm is referred to as a **dysrhythmia** or **arrhythmia.** It may consist of random, irregular beats or a predictable pattern of irregular beats. When a dysrhythmia is detected, the apical pulse should be assessed. An electrocardiogram (ECG or EKG) is necessary to further define the dysrhythmia.

TABLE 31.4 Scale for Measuring Pulse Volume

Scale	Description of Pulse
0	Absent, not discernible
1	Thready or weak, difficult to feel
2	Normal, detected readily, obliterated by strong pressure
3	Bounding, difficult to obliterate

Pulse volume, also called the pulse strength or amplitude, refers to the force of blood with each beat. Usually, the pulse volume is the same with each beat. It can range from absent to bounding. A normal pulse can be felt with moderate pressure of the fingers and can be obliterated with greater pressure. A forceful or full blood volume that is obliterated only with difficulty is called a *full* or *bounding* pulse. A pulse that is readily obliterated with pressure from the fingers is referred to as *weak*, *feeble*, or *thready*. A pulse volume is usually measured on a scale of 0 to 3 (Table 31.4).

The **elasticity of the arterial wall** reflects its expansibility or its deformities. A healthy, normal artery feels straight, smooth, soft, and pliable. Older people often have inelastic arteries that feel twisted (tortuous) and irregular upon palpation.

When assessing a peripheral pulse to determine the adequacy of blood flow to a particular area of the body, the nurse should also assess the corresponding pulse on the other side of the body. The second assessment gives the nurse data to compare the pulses. For example, when assessing the blood flow to the right foot, the nurse assesses the right dorsalis pedis pulse and then the left dorsalis pedis pulse. If the client's right and left pulses are the same, the client's dorsalis pedis pulses are *bilaterally equal.*

Peripheral Pulse Assessment

A peripheral pulse, usually the radial pulse, is assessed by palpation in most individuals. Exceptions include:

- Newborns and children up to two or three years. Apical pulses are assessed in these clients.
- Very obese or elderly clients, whose radial pulse may be difficult to palpate. Doppler equipment may be used for these clients, or the apical pulse is assessed.
- Individuals with heart disease, who would require both apical and radial pulse assessment.
- Individuals for whom circulation to a specific body part must be assessed; for example, following leg surgery, the pedal (dorsalis pedis) as well as radial pulse are assessed.

Procedure 31.2 provides guidelines for assessing a peripheral pulse.

PROCEDURE 31.2 Assessing a Peripheral Pulse

PURPOSES

- To establish baseline data for subsequent evaluation
- To identify if the pulse rate is within normal range
- To determine if the pulse rhythm is regular and the pulse volume is appropriate
- To compare the equality of corresponding peripheral pulses bilaterally
- To monitor and assess changes in the client's health status
- To monitor clients at risk for pulse alterations (e.g., those with a history of heart disease or experiencing cardiac arrhythmias, hemorrhage, acute pain, infusion of large volumes of fluids, fever)

Assessment Focus
Clinical signs of cardiovascular alterations, other than pulse rate, rhythm, or volume (e.g., dyspnea [difficult breathing], fatigue, pallor, cyanosis [bluish discolouration of skin and mucous membranes], palpitations, syncope [fainting], impaired peripheral tissue perfusion as evidenced by skin discolouration and cool temperature); factors that may alter pulse rate (e.g., emotional status and activity level); site most appropriate for assessment

Equipment

- ❑ Watch with a second hand or indicator
- ❑ If using Doppler ultrasound stethoscope, the transducer in the DUS probe, a stethoscope headset, and transmission gel

PROCEDURE 31.2 Assessing a Peripheral Pulse *continued*

INTERVENTION

1. Prepare the client.

- Select the pulse site. Normally, the radial pulse is taken unless otherwise warranted.
- Assist the client to a comfortable resting position. When the radial pulse is assessed, the client's arm can rest alongside the body, the palm facing downward. Alternatively, the forearm can rest at a 90-degree angle across the chest with the palm downward. For the client who can sit, the forearm can rest across the thigh, with the palm of the hand facing downward or inward. Position a child comfortably in the parent's arms, or have the parent remain close by. *Having the parent close or holding the child may decrease anxiety and yield more accurate results.*

2. Palpate and count the pulse.

- Place three middle fingertips lightly and squarely over the pulse point (Figure 31.16). *Using the thumb is contraindicated because the thumb has a pulse that the nurse could mistake for the client's pulse.*
- If the pulse is regular, count for 30 seconds and multiply by 2. If it is irregular, count for one minute. When taking a client's pulse for the first time or obtaining baseline data, count the pulse for a full minute. *An irregular pulse requires a full minute's count for a correct assessment and indicates the need to take the apical pulse.*

3. Assess the pulse rhythm and volume.

- Assess the pulse rhythm by noting the pattern of the intervals between the beats. A normal pulse has equal time periods between beats. *If this is an initial assessment, assess for one minute.*
- Assess the pulse volume. A normal pulse can be felt with moderate pressure, and the pressure is equal with each beat. A forceful pulse volume is full; an easily obliterated pulse is weak.

4. Document and report pertinent assessment data.

- Record the pulse site, rate, rhythm, and volume on the appropriate records. Compare to previous recordings if available.
- Report to the nurse in charge pertinent data such as (a) pale skin colour and cool skin temperature, (b) a pulse rate faster or slower than normal for the client, (c) a full, bounding, or weak pulse volume, and (d) an irregular pulse rhythm.

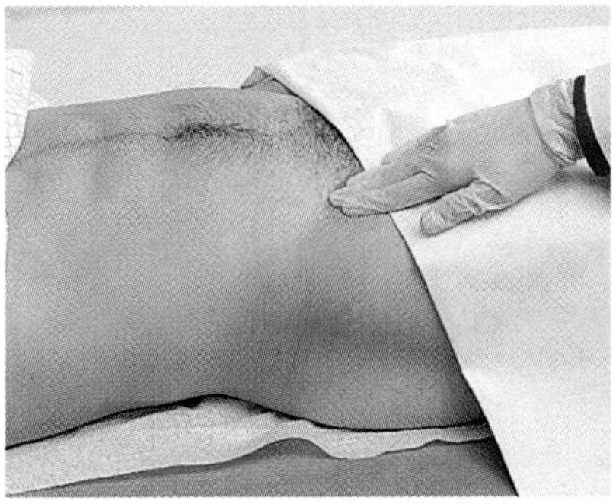

D

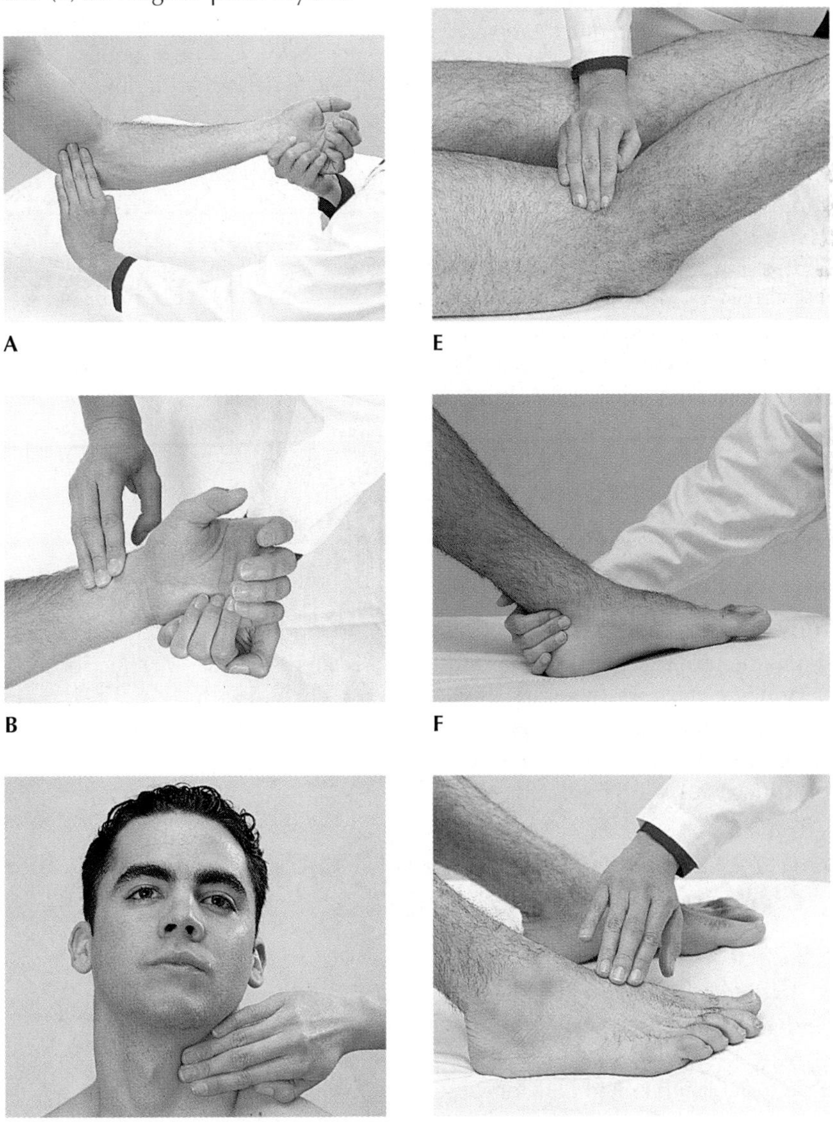

A E B F C G

Figure 31.16 Assessing the pulses: *A,* brachial; *B,* radial; *C,* carotid; *D,* femoral; *E,* popliteal; *F,* posterior tibial; and *G,* pedal (dorsalis pedis)

PROCEDURE 31.2 Assessing a Peripheral Pulse *continued*

Variation: Using a DUS

- Apply transmission gel to the probe at the narrow end of the plastic case housing the transducer or to the client's skin. *Ultrasound beams do not travel well through air. The gel makes an airtight seal, which then promotes optimal ultrasound wave transmission.*
- Press the "on" button.
- Hold the probe against the skin over the pulse site. Use a light pressure, and keep the probe in contact with the skin. *Too much pressure can stop the blood flow and obliterate the signal.*
- Distinguish arterial sounds from venous sounds. The arterial sound is distinctively pulsating and has a pumping quality. The venous sound is intermittent and varies with respirations. *Both arterial and venous sounds are heard simultaneously through the DUS because major arteries and veins are situated close together throughout the body.*
- If arterial sounds cannot be easily heard, reposition the probe.
- After assessing the pulse, remove all the gel from the probe to prevent damage to its surface. Clean the transducer with aqueous solutions. *Alcohol or other disinfectants may damage the face of the transducer.* Remove all gel from the client's skin.

Evaluation Focus

The pulse rate in relation to baseline data or normal range for age of client; relationship of pulse rate and volume to other vital signs; pulse rhythm and volume in relationship to baseline data and health status; if assessing peripheral pulses, equality, rate, and volume in corresponding extremities

Home Care Considerations

- If appropriate, teach the client or family member to take a pulse. Ensure correct technique by having them demonstrate.
- Assist in obtaining and using an electronic pulse device if indicated.
- Ensure that the client or family member is aware of what pulse findings should be reported and to whom. Provide a recording document.

Apical Pulse Assessment

Assessment of the apical pulse is indicated for clients whose peripheral pulse is irregular as well as for clients with known cardiovascular, pulmonary, and renal diseases. It is commonly assessed prior to administering medications that affect heart rate. The apical site is also used to assess the pulse for newborns, infants, and children up to two to three years old. Procedure 31.3 presents guidelines for assessing the apical pulse.

PROCEDURE 31.3 Assessing an Apical Pulse

PURPOSES

- To obtain the heart rate of newborns, infants, and children two to three years old or of an adult with an irregular peripheral pulse
- To establish baseline data for subsequent evaluation
- To determine whether the cardiac rate is within normal range and the rhythm is regular
- To monitor clients with cardiac disease and those receiving medications to improve heart action

Assessment Focus

Clinical signs of cardiovascular alterations, other than pulse rate, rhythm, or volume (e.g., dyspnea, fatigue, pallor, cyanosis, syncope); factors that may alter pulse rate (e.g., emotional status, activity level, and medications that affect heart rate, such as digoxin, beta blockers, or calcium channel blockers)

PROCEDURE 31.3 Assessing an Apical Pulse *continued*

Equipment

- ❑ Watch with a second hand or indicator
- ❑ Stethoscope with a bell-shaped or flat-disc diaphragm
- ❑ Antiseptic wipes
- ❑ If using ultrasound, a stethoscope headset as indicated, a DUS, diaphragm probe (transducer), and transmission gel

INTERVENTION

1. Position the client appropriately; ensure privacy.

- Assist an adult or young child to a comfortable supine position or to a sitting position.
- Place a baby in a supine position, and offer a pacifier if the baby is crying or restless. *Crying and physical activity will increase the pulse rate.* For this reason, take the apical pulse rate of infants and small children before assessing body temperatures.
- Demonstrate the procedure to the child using a stuffed animal or doll, and allow the child to handle the stethoscope before beginning the procedure. *This will decrease anxiety and promote cooperation.*
- Expose the area of the chest over the apex of the heart.

2. Locate the apical impulse.

- This is the point over the apex of the heart where the apical pulse can be heard most clearly.
- Palpate the angle of Louis (the angle between the manubrium, the top of the sternum, and the body of the sternum). It is palpated just below the suprasternal notch and is felt as a prominence (Figure 31.14, earlier).
- Slide your index finger just to the left of the client's sternum, and palpate the second intercostal space. Place your middle or next finger in the third intercostal space, and continue palpating downward until you palpate the fifth intercostal space.
- If the client is an adult, move your index finger laterally along the fifth intercostal space to the midclavicular line (MCL). Normally, the apical impulse is palpable at or just medial to the MCL. For a child under age seven years, move your finger along the fourth intercostal space to a position between the MCL and the anterior axillary line (Figure 31.14, earlier).

3. Auscultate and count heartbeats.

- Use antiseptic wipes to clean the earpieces and diaphragm of the stethoscope (Figure 31.17). *The diaphragm needs to be cleaned and disinfected if soiled with body substances.*
- Warm the diaphragm of the stethoscope by holding it in the palm of the hand for a moment. *The metal of the diaphragm is usually cold and can startle the client when placed immediately on the chest.*
- Insert the earpieces of the stethoscope into your ears in the direction of the ear canals, or slightly forward, to facilitate hearing.

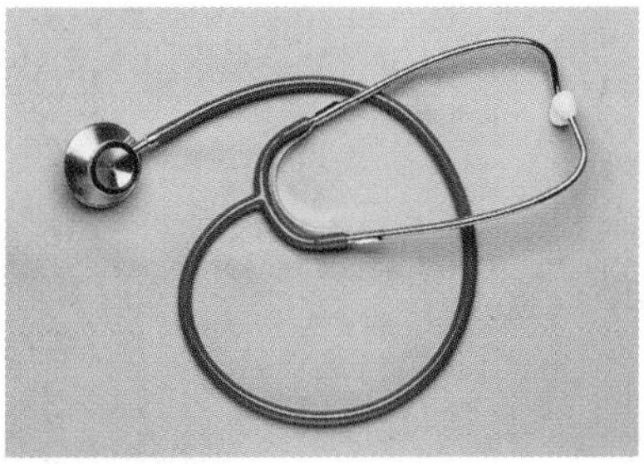

A

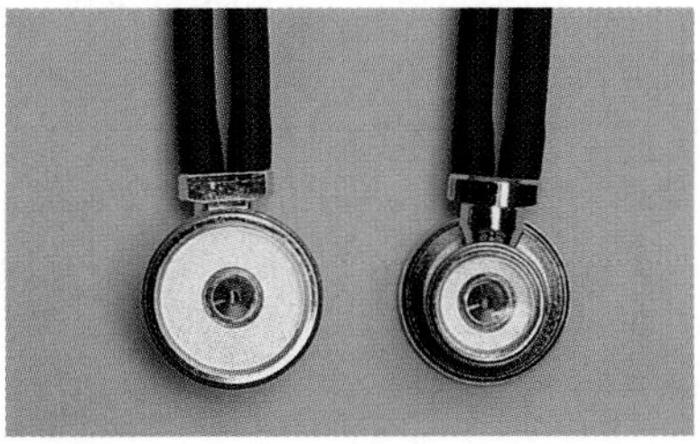

B

Figure 31.17 *A,* Stethoscope with both a bell-shaped and flat-disc amplifier; *B;* Close-up of a flat-disc amplifier (left) and a bell amplifier (right)

- Tap your finger lightly on the diaphragm to be sure it is the active side of the head. If necessary, rotate the head to select the diaphragm side.
- Place the diaphragm of the stethoscope over the apical impulse (Figure 31.18) and listen for the normal S_1 and S_2 heart sounds, which are heard as "lub-dub." Each lub-dub is counted as one heartbeat. *The heartbeat is normally loudest over the apex of the heart. The two heart sounds are produced by closure of the valves of the heart.* The S_1 heart sound (lub) occurs when the atrioventricular valves close after the ventricles have been sufficiently filled. The S_2 heart sound (dub) occurs when the semilunar valves close after the ventricles empty.
- If the rhythm is regular, count the heartbeats for 30 seconds and multiply by 2. If the rhythm is irregular or if the apical pulse is being taken on an infant or child, count the beats for 60 seconds. *A 60-second count provides a more accurate assessment of an irregular pulse than a 30-second count.*

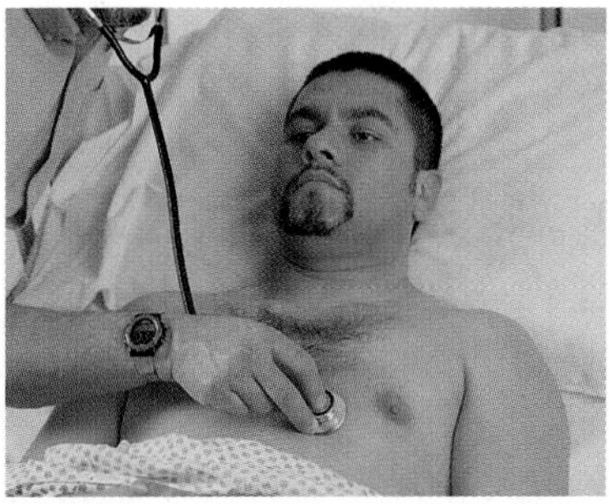

Figure 31.18 Taking an apical pulse using the flat disc of the stethoscope. Note how the amplifier is held against the chest.

PROCEDURE 31.3 Assessing an Apical Pulse *continued*

4. Assess the rhythm and the strength of the heartbeat.

- Assess the rhythm of the heartbeat by noting the pattern of intervals between the beats. A normal pulse has equal time periods between beats.
- Assess the strength (volume) of the heartbeat. Normally, the heartbeats are equal in strength and can be described as strong or weak.

5. Document and report pertinent assessment data.

- Record the pulse site and rate, rhythm, and volume on the appropriate records.
- Report to the nurse in charge any pertinent data such as pallor, cyanosis, dyspnea, tachycardia, bradycardia, irregular rhythm, and reduced strength of the heartbeat.

Evaluation Focus
The apical rate in relation to baseline data or normal range for the age of the client; relationship to other vital signs; apical pulse rhythm and volume in relationship to baseline data and health status

Home Care Considerations

- Teach the client to monitor the pulse prior to taking medications that affect the heart rate.
- Instruct the client which notable changes in heart rate or rhythm (regularity) are to be reported to the health-care provider.

Apical-Radial Pulse Assessment

An **apical-radial pulse** may need to be assessed for clients with certain cardiovascular disorders. Normally, the apical and radial rates are identical. An apical pulse rate greater than a radial pulse rate can indicate that the thrust of the blood from the heart is too weak for the wave to be felt at the peripheral pulse site, or it can indicate that vascular disease is preventing impulses from being transmitted.

Any discrepancy between the two pulse rates (called a **pulse deficit**) needs to be reported promptly. In no instance is the radial pulse greater than the apical pulse.

An apical-radial pulse can be taken by two nurses or one nurse, although the two-nurse technique is more accurate. Procedure 31.4 outlines the steps for assessing an apical-radial pulse.

PROCEDURE 31.4 Assessing an Apical-Radial Pulse

PURPOSE

- To determine adequacy of peripheral circulation or presence of pulse deficit

Assessment Focus
Clinical signs of hypovolemic shock (hypotension, pallor, cyanosis, and cold, clammy skin)

Equipment

- ❑ Watch with a second hand or indicator
- ❑ Stethoscope
- ❑ Antiseptic wipes

INTERVENTION

1. Position the client appropriately.

- Assist the client to assume the position described for taking the apical pulse. See Procedure 31.3, step 1.
- If previous measurements were taken, determine what position the client assumed and use the same position. *This ensures an accurate comparative measurement.*

PROCEDURE 31.4 Assessing an Apical-Radial Pulse *continued*

2. **Locate the apical and radial pulse sites.**
   - In the two-nurse technique, one nurse locates the apical impulse by palpation or with the stethoscope while the other nurse palpates the radial pulse site. See Procedures 31.2 and 31.3.
3. **Count the apical and radial pulse rates.**

Two-Nurse Technique

- Place the watch where both nurses can see it.
- Decide on a time to begin counting. A time when the second hand is on 12, 3, 6, or 9 is usually selected. The nurse taking the radial pulse says "Start" at the designated time. *This ensures that simultaneous counts are taken.*
- Each nurse counts the pulse rate for 60 seconds. Both nurses end the count when the nurse taking the radial pulse says "Stop." *A full 60-second count is necessary for accurate assessment of any discrepancies between the two pulse sites.*
- The nurse who assesses the apical rate also assesses the apical pulse rhythm and volume (i.e., whether the heartbeat is strong or weak). If the pulse is irregular, note whether the irregular beats come at random or at predictable times.
- The nurse assessing the radial pulse rate also assesses the radial pulse rhythm and volume.

One-Nurse Technique

- Assess the apical pulse for 60 seconds.
- Assess the radial pulse for 60 seconds.

4. **Document and report pertinent assessment data.**
   - Promptly report any notable changes from previous measurements or any discrepancy between the two pulses.
   - Document the apical and radial (AR) pulse rates, rhythm, volume, and any pulse deficit.
   - Record any other pertinent observations, such as pallor, cyanosis, or dyspnea.
   - Check the physician's orders for any directions related to a discrepancy in the AR pulse rates.

Evaluation Focus
Equality of apical and radial pulse rates; relationship to other vital signs, in particular respiratory rate and blood pressure; skin colour and temperature

Respirations

Respiration is the act of breathing. **External respiration** refers to the interchange of oxygen and carbon dioxide between the alveoli of the lungs and the pulmonary blood. **Internal respiration,** by contrast, takes place throughout the body; it is the interchange of these same gases between the circulating blood and the cells of the body tissues.

Inhalation or **inspiration** refers to the intake of air into the lungs. **Exhalation** or **expiration** refers to breathing out or the movement of gases from the lungs to the atmosphere. **Ventilation** is also used to refer to the movement of air in and out of the lungs. **Hyperventilation** refers to very deep, rapid respirations; **hypoventilation** refers to very shallow slow respirations.

There are basically two types of breathing: **costal (thoracic) breathing** and **diaphragmatic (abdominal) breathing.** Costal breathing involves the external intercostal muscles and other accessory muscles, such as the sternocleidomastoid muscles. It can be observed by the movement of the chest upward and outward. By contrast, diaphragmatic breathing involves the contraction and relaxation of the diaphragm, and it is observed by the movement of the abdomen, which occurs as a result of the diaphragm's contraction and downward movement.

Mechanics and Regulation of Breathing

During *inhalation*, the following processes normally occur (Figure 31.19): the diaphragm contracts (flattens), the ribs move upward and outward, and the sternum moves outward, thus enlarging the thorax and permitting the lungs to expand. During *exhalation* (Figure 31.20), the diaphragm relaxes, the ribs move downward and inward, and the sternum moves inward, thus decreasing the size of the thorax as the lungs are compressed. Normally, breathing is carried out automatically and effortlessly. An inspiration lasts one to 1.5 seconds, and an expiration lasts two to three seconds.

Respiration is controlled by (1) respiratory centres in the medulla oblongata and the pons of the brain, and (2) by chemoreceptors located centrally in the medulla and peripherally in the carotid and aortic bodies. These centres and receptors respond to changes in the concentrations of oxygen (O_2), carbon dioxide (CO_2), and hydrogen (H^+) in the arterial blood. See Chapter 39 for details.

Assessing Respirations

Respirations should be assessed when the client is relaxed because exercise affects respirations, increasing their rate and depth. Anxiety is likely to affect respiratory rate and depth as well. Respirations may also need to be assessed after exercise to identify the client's tolerance to activity. Before assessing a client's respirations, a nurse should be aware of:

- The client's normal breathing pattern
- The influence of the client's health problems on respirations
- Any medications or therapies that might affect respirations
- The relationship of the client's respirations to cardiovascular function

The rate, depth, rhythm, and special characteristics of respirations should be assessed.

The *respiratory rate* is normally described in breaths per minute. Breathing that is normal in rate and depth is called **eupnea.** Abnormally slow respirations are referred to as **bradypnea,** and abnormally fast respirations are called **tachypnea** or **polypnea. Apnea** is the absence of breathing. For the respiratory rates for different age groups, see Table 31.1. Several factors influence respiratory rate; some are listed in Table 31.5.

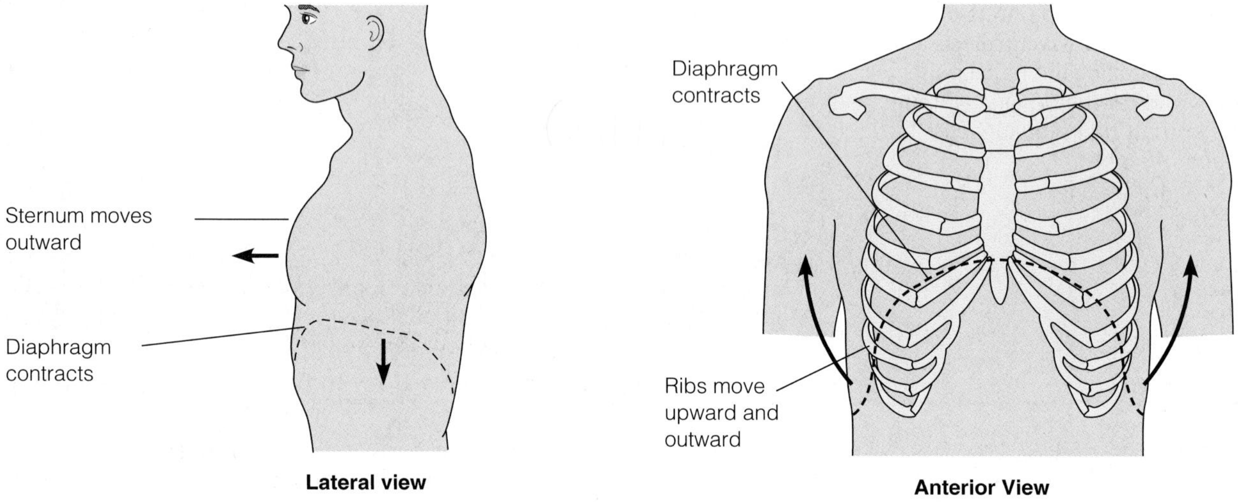

Figure 31.19 Respiratory inhalation: *Left,* lateral view; *Right,* anterior view

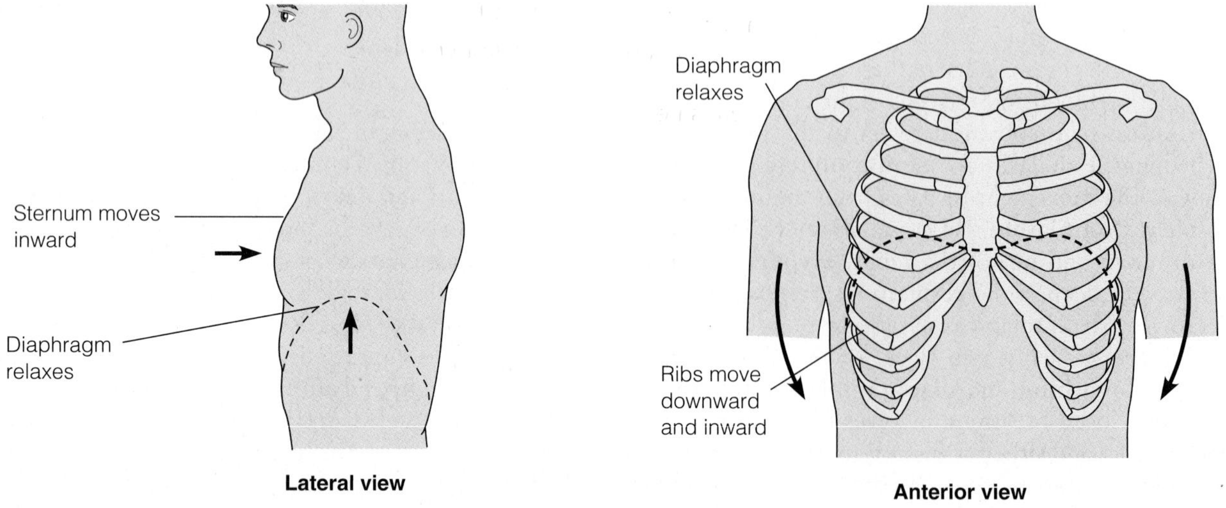

Figure 31.20 Respiratory exhalation: *Left,* lateral view; *Right,* anterior view

TABLE 31.5 Major Factors Influencing Respiratory Rate

Factor	Influence
Exercise: increases metabolism	Increase
Stress: readies the body for "fight or flight"	Increase
Environment: increased temperature	Increase
Environment: decreased temperature	Decrease
Increased altitude: lower oxygen concentration	Increase
Certain medications (e.g., narcotic, analgesic)	Decrease
Increased intracranial pressure	Decrease

The *depth* of a person's respirations can be established by watching the movement of the chest. Respiratory depth is generally described as normal, deep, or shallow. *Deep respirations* are those in which a large volume of air is inhaled and exhaled, inflating most of the lungs. *Shallow respirations* involve the exchange of a small volume of air and often the minimal use of lung tissue. During a normal inspiration and expiration, an adult takes in about 500 mL of air. This volume is called the **tidal volume.** For further information about pulmonary volumes and pulmonary capacities, see Chapter 39.

Body position also affects the amount of air that can be inhaled. People in a supine position experience two physiological processes that suppress respiration: an increase in the volume of blood inside the thoracic cavity and compression of the chest. Consequently, clients lying on their back have poorer lung aeration which predisposes them to the stasis of fluids and subsequent infection.

Altered Breathing Patterns and Sounds

Breathing Patterns

Rate

- *Tachypnea*—rapid respiration marked by quick, shallow breaths
- *Bradypnea*—abnormally slow breathing
- *Apnea*—cessation of breathing

Volume

- *Hyperventilation*—an increase in the amount of air in the lungs characterized by increased rate and depth of breaths; may be associated with anxiety
- *Hypoventilation*—a reduction in the amount of air in the lungs, characterized by shallow respirations

Rhythm

- *Cheyne-Stokes breathing*—rhythmic waxing and waning of respirations, from very deep to very shallow breathing and temporary apnea; often associated with cardiac failure, increased intracranial pressure, or brain damage

Ease or Effort

- *Dyspnea*—difficult and laboured breathing during which the individual has a persistent, unsatisfied need for air and feels distressed
- *Orthopnea*—ability to breathe only in upright sitting or standing positions

Breath Sounds

Audible without Amplification

- *Stridor*—a shrill, harsh sound heard during inspiration with laryngeal obstruction
- *Stertor*—snoring or sonorous respiration, usually due to a partial obstruction of the upper airway
- *Wheeze*—continuous, high-pitched musical squeak or whistling sound occurring on expiration and sometimes on inspiration when air moves through a narrowed or partially obstructed airway
- *Bubbling*—gurgling sounds heard as air passes through moist secretions in the respiratory tract
- *Kussmaul breathing*—abnormally deep, very rapid sighing respirations characteristic of diabetic ketoacidosis

Chest Movements

- *Intercostal retraction*—indrawing between the ribs
- *Substernal retraction*—indrawing beneath the breastbone
- *Suprasternal retraction*—indrawing above the clavicles
- *Flail chest*—the ballooning out of the chest wall through injured rib spaces; results in *paradoxical breathing,* during which the chest wall balloons on expiration but is depressed or sucked inward on inspiration
- *Tracheal tugging*—downward tugging of the trachea with each heart contraction as an effect of an aortic aneurysm

Secretions and Coughing

- *Hemoptysis*—the presence of blood in the sputum
- *Productive cough*—a cough accompanied by expectorated secretions
- *Nonproductive cough*—a dry, harsh cough without secretions

Certain medications also affect the respiratory depth. For example, barbiturates, such as secobarbital sodium, when taken in large doses depress the respiratory centres in the brain thereby depressing the respiratory rate and depth.

Respiratory rhythm or **pattern** refers to the regularity of the expirations and the inspirations. Normally, respirations are evenly spaced. Respiratory rhythm can be described as *regular* or *irregular*. An infant's respiratory rhythm may be less regular than an adult's. See Chapter 39 for details about abnormal respiratory rhythms.

Respiratory quality or **character** refers to those aspects of breathing that are different from normal, effortless breathing. Two of these are the amount of effort a client must exert to breathe and the sound of breathing. Usually, breathing does not require noticeable effort; some clients, however, breathe only with decided effort, referred to as *laboured breathing*.

The *sound* of breathing is also significant. Normal breathing is silent, but a number of abnormal sounds, such as a wheeze, are obvious to the nurse's ear. Many sounds occur as a result of the presence of fluid in the lungs and are most clearly heard with a stethoscope. See Chapter 27 for methods used to assess lung sounds. For details about altered breathing patterns and terms used to describe various patterns and sounds, see the previous box. Procedure 31.5 provides guidelines for assessing respirations.

PROCEDURE 31.5 Assessing Respirations

PURPOSES

- To acquire baseline data against which future measurements can be compared
- To monitor abnormal respirations and respiratory patterns and identify changes
- To assess respirations before the administration of a medication, such as morphine (an abnormally slow respiratory rate may warrant withholding the medication)
- To monitor respirations following the administration of a general anesthetic or any medication that influences respirations
- To monitor clients at risk for respiratory alterations (e.g., those with fever, pain, acute anxiety, chronic obstructive pulmonary disease, respiratory infection, pulmonary edema or emboli, chest trauma or constriction, brain stem injury)

Assessment Focus
Skin and mucous membrane colour (e.g., cyanosis or pallor); position assumed for breathing (e.g., use of orthopneic position); signs of cerebral anoxia (e.g., irritability, restlessness, drowsiness, or loss of consciousness); chest movements (e.g., retractions between the ribs or above or below the sternum); activity tolerance; chest pain; dyspnea; medications affecting respiratory rate

Equipment

- ❑ Watch with a second hand or indicator

INTERVENTION

1. Determine the client's activity schedule.

- Choose a suitable time to monitor the respirations. *A client who has been exercising will need to rest for a few minutes to permit the accelerated respiratory rate to return to normal. An infant or child who is crying will have an abnormal respiratory rate and will need quieting before respirations can be accurately assessed.*

2. Observe or palpate and count the respiratory rate.

- Place a hand against the client's chest to feel the client's chest movements, or place the client's arm across the chest and observe the chest movements while appearing to take the radial pulse. Because young children are diaphragmatic breathers, observe the rise and fall of the abdomen. *Awareness of respiratory rate assessment could cause the client to voluntarily alter the respiratory pattern.*
- Count the respiratory rate for 30 seconds if the respirations are regular. Count for 60 seconds if they are irregular. An inhalation and an exhalation count as one respiration.

PROCEDURE 31.5 Assessing Respirations *continued*

3. **Observe the depth, rhythm, and character of respirations.**
   - Observe the respirations for depth by watching the movement of the chest. During deep respirations, a large volume of air is exchanged; during shallow respirations, a small volume is exchanged.
   - Observe the respirations for regular or irregular rhythm. Normally, respirations are evenly spaced.
   - Observe the character of respirations—the sound they produce and the effort they require. Normally, respirations are silent and effortless.
4. **Document and report pertinent assessment data.**
   - Document the respiratory rate, depth, rhythm, and character on the appropriate records.
   - Report:
     a. Respiratory rate significantly above or below the normal range and any notable change in respirations from previous assessments
     b. Irregular respiratory rhythm
     c. Inadequate respiratory depth
     d. Abnormal character of breathing—orthopnea, wheezing, stridor, or bubbling
     e. Any complaints of dyspnea

Evaluation Focus
The respiratory rate in relation to baseline data or normal range for age; relationship to other vital signs; respiratory depth, rhythm, and character in relation to baseline data and health status

Home Care Considerations

- Monitor respiratory rate following the administration of respiratory depressants, such as morphine.
- Always monitor respirations for at least 30 seconds.

The effectiveness of respirations is measured, in part, by the uptake of oxygen from the air into the blood and the release of carbon dioxide from the blood into expired air. The amount of hemoglobin in arterial blood that is saturated with oxygen can be measured indirectly through pulse oximetry. Using a pulse oximeter monitor applied to the client's finger, toe, or other site provides a digital readout of both the client's pulse rate and the oxygen saturation (see Chapter 39 for further information regarding pulse oximetry).

Blood Pressure

Arterial blood pressure is a measurement of the pressure exerted by the blood on the vessel walls as it flows through the arteries. Because the blood moves in waves, there are two blood pressure measures: the **systolic pressure,** which is the pressure of the blood exerted on the artery wall as a result of contraction of the maximum left ventricle, that is, the pressure of the height of the blood wave; and the **diastolic pressure,** which is the pressure when the ventricles are at rest. Diastolic pressure, then, is the lower pressure present at all times within the arteries. The difference between the systolic and the diastolic pressures is called the **pulse pressure.**

Blood pressure is measured in millimetres of mercury (mm Hg) and recorded as a fraction. The systolic pressure is written over the diastolic pressure. The average blood pressure of a healthy adult is 120/80 mm Hg (see Table 31.1 for age variations). A number of health conditions may be reflected by changes observed in blood pressure recordings among individuals. It is important for the nurse to know a specific client's baseline blood pressure as blood pressure can vary considerably. For example, if a client's usual blood pressure is 120/80 mm Hg, and it is assessed following surgery to be 80/20 mm Hg, the physician needs to be informed. The trend or pattern of BP readings is usually of greater significance than a single result.

Determinants of Blood Pressure

Arterial blood pressure is the result of several factors: the pumping action of the heart, the peripheral vascular resistance (the resistance supplied by the blood vessels through which the blood flows), elasticity of vessel walls, and blood volume and viscosity.

Pumping Action of the Heart

Cardiac output is the volume of blood pumped into the arteries by the heart. When the pumping action of the heart is weak, less blood is pumped into arteries, and the blood pressure decreases. When the heart's pumping action is strong and the volume of blood pumped into the circulation increases, the blood pressure increases.

Peripheral Vascular Resistance

Peripheral resistance can increase blood pressure. The diastolic pressure is especially affected. Some factors that create resistance in the arterial system are the size of the arterioles and capillaries, compliance of the arteries, and the viscosity of the blood.

The *size* of the arterioles and the capillaries determines the extent of the peripheral resistance to the blood in the body. A *lumen* is a channel within a tube; the smaller the lumen of a vessel, the greater the resistance. Normally, the arterioles are in a state of partial constriction. Increased vasoconstriction raises the blood pressure, whereas vasodilation lowers the blood pressure.

Elasticity

The arteries contain smooth muscles that permit them to contract, thus decreasing their compliance (distensibility, elasticity). The arteries account for most of the peripheral resistance. A major factor reducing arterial compliance is a pathological change affecting the arterial walls. Elastic and muscular tissues of the arteries are replaced with fibrous tissue; thus, the arteries lose much of their compliance. This condition, most common in middle-aged and elderly adults, is known as **arteriosclerosis.**

Blood Volume

When the blood volume decreases (for example, as a result of a hemorrhage or dehydration), the blood pressure decreases because of decreased fluid in the arteries. Conversely, when the volume increases (for example, as a result of an intravenous infusion), the blood pressure increases because of the greater fluid volume within the circulatory system.

Blood Viscosity

Viscosity is a physical property that results from friction of molecules in a fluid. In a viscous (or "thick") fluid, there is a great deal of friction among the molecules as they slide by each other. The blood pressure is higher when the blood is highly viscous, that is, when the proportion of red blood cells to the blood plasma is high. This proportion is referred to as the **hematocrit.** The viscosity increases markedly when the hematocrit is more than 60 to 65 percent.

Factors Affecting Blood Pressure

Age, exercise, stress, race, obesity, gender, medications, diurnal variations, and disease processes are factors influencing blood pressure.

- *Age.* Newborns have a mean systolic pressure of about 73 mm Hg. The pressure rises with age, reaching a peak at the onset of puberty. One quick way to determine the normal systolic blood pressure of a child is to use the following formula:

  Normal systolic BP = 80 + (2 × child's age in years)
- *Exercise.* Physical activity increases the cardiac output and hence the blood pressure; thus, 20 to 30 minutes of rest following exercise is indicated before the resting blood pressure can be reliably assessed.
- *Stress emotions.* Stimulation of the sympathetic nervous system increases cardiac output and vasoconstriction of the arterioles, thus increasing the blood pressure reading. Severe pain, however, can decrease blood pressure greatly and cause shock by inhibiting the vasomotor centre and producing vasodilation.
- *Race.* Males of African origin over 35 years usually exhibit higher blood pressures than Caucasian males of the same age.
- *Obesity.* Generally, overweight and obese people have higher blood pressure than people of normal weight.
- *Gender.* After puberty, females usually have lower blood pressures than males of the same age; this difference is thought to be due to hormonal variations. Women generally have higher blood pressure following menopause.
- *Medications.* Many medications may increase or decrease the blood pressure; nurses should be aware of specific medications a client is receiving and consider their possible impact when interpreting blood pressure readings.
- *Diurnal variations.* Blood pressure is usually lowest early in the morning when the metabolic rate is lowest, then rises throughout the day and peaks in the late afternoon or early evening.
- *Disease process.* Any condition affecting the cardiac output, blood volume, blood viscosity, and/or compliance of the arteries has a direct effect on the blood pressure.

Hypertension

Hypertension is a condition in which blood pressure is persistently greater than 140 mm Hg systolically or greater than 90 mm diastolically. Usually asymptomatic, it is often a contributing factor to myocardial infarctions (heart attacks), heart failure, stroke, peripheral vascular disease, and blindness. An elevated blood pressure of unknown cause is called primary hypertension. An elevated blood pressure of known cause is called secondary hypertension. Hypertension is a widespread health problem. The diagnosis is made when the average of multiple systolic blood pressure readings is higher than 140 mm Hg, or two or more diastolic readings on two visits subsequent to the initial assessment are 90 mm Hg or higher. Criteria for follow-up have been developed and are described in Table 31.6. Factors associated with hypertension include thickening of the arterial walls, which reduces the size of the arterial lumen, loss of elasticity of the arteries, as well as lifestyle factors, such as cigarette smoking, obesity, heavy alcohol consumption, caffeine consumption, lack of physical exercise, high blood cholesterol levels, and continued exposure to stress. Follow-up care should include counselling for lifestyle changes as well as monitoring the blood pressure itself.

TABLE 31.6 Criteria for Follow-Up Based on Initial Blood Pressure Measurement (for Adults Age 18 Years and Older)

For individuals with no previous history of high blood pressure

Initial BP Level (mm Hg)*

Systolic	Diastolic	Recommended Action**
<130	<85	Recheck in 2 years.
130–139	85–89	Reassess within 1 year.[a]
140–159	90–99	Confirm elevation by rechecking BP at least three times within a six-month period.[a,b]
160–179	100–109	Ensure follow-up care within 1 month.[a,b]
180–199	110–119	Ensure follow-up care within 1 week.[a,b]
≥200	≥120	Ensure immediate care.[b]

For individuals who have been diagnosed and/or are being treated for high blood pressure

Initial BP Level (mm Hg)*

Systolic	Diastolic	Recommended Action**
<140	<90	Ensure follow-up care in 3–6 months.
140–159	90–99	Assess compliance with therapy; recheck BP within one month.[b]
160–199	110–119	Assess compliance with therapy; recheck BP within one to two weeks. [a,b]
≥200	≥120	Ensure immediate care.[b]

If systolic and diastolic categories are different from above criteria, follow recommendations for shorter time follow-up; e.g., 160/90 (treated) should be evaluated within 1 month.

[a] Provide (or reinforce) lifestyle counselling.

[b] Refer to Canadian Hypertension Society guidelines for appropriate assessment and management of high blood pressure.

* Based on the average of at least two blood pressure measurements.

** Clinical judgement is required when interpreting blood pressure readings; clinicians should consider level of blood pressure, signs and symptoms suggestive of target organ damage, and presence of other cardiovascular risk factors when scheduling follow-up.

Source: Abbott, D., Campbell, N., Carruthers-Czyewski, P., et al. (1994). Guidelines for measurement of blood pressure, follow-up, and lifestyle counselling. *Canadian Journal of Public Health, 85*(Supplement 2), S29–S35.

Hypotension

Hypotension is a blood pressure that is below normal, that is, a systolic reading consistently between 85 and 110 mm Hg in an adult. **Orthostatic hypotension** is a blood pressure that falls when the client sits or stands. It is usually the result of peripheral vasodilation in which the blood leaves the central body organs, especially the brain, and moves to the periphery, often causing the person to feel faint. Hypotension can also be caused by analgesics, such as meperidine hydrochloride (Demerol), bleeding, severe burns, and prolonged diarrhea and vomiting. It is important to monitor hypotensive clients carefully to prevent falls. When measuring the blood pressure of a client who has orthostatic hypotension, do the following:

- Place the client in a supine position for two to three minutes. This allows the blood pressure and pulse to stabilize in this position.
- Record the client's pulse and blood pressure.
- Assist the client to slowly sit or stand. Support the client in case of faintness.
- After one minute in the upright position, recheck the pulse and blood pressure in the same sites as previously.
- Record the results.

Assessing Blood Pressure

Equipment

Blood pressure is measured with a *blood pressure cuff*, a *sphygmomanometer*, and a *stethoscope*. The blood pressure cuff consists of a rubber bladder that can be inflated with air (Figure 31.21). The bladder is covered with cloth and has two tubes attached to it. One tube connects to a bulb that inflates the bladder. A small valve on the side of this bulb releases the air from the bladder. When the valve is closed, air pumped into the bladder remains there. The other tube is attached to a sphygmomanometer.

The sphygmomanometer indicates the pressure of the air within the bladder. There are two types of sphygmomanometers: *aneroid* and *mercury* (Figure 31.22). The aneroid sphygmomanometer is a calibrated dial with a needle that points to markings that correlate with BP values.

The mercury sphygmomanometer is a calibrated cylinder filled with mercury and is the preferred method, or "gold standard." The pressure is indicated at the point to which the rounded curve (the base) of the meniscus rises (Figure 31.23). The blood pressure reading should be determined when the nurse's eye is at the level of the rounded curve in order to be accurate. If the nurse's eye is looking up or down, a distortion in the reading can occur. A distortion that occurs as a result of the angle of view is called **parallax.**

Some agencies use electronic sphygmomanometers (Figure 31.24) which eliminate the need to listen to the sounds of the client's systolic and diastolic blood pressures through a stethoscope. Electronic blood pressure devices should be calibrated against an aneriod sphygmomanometer to check accuracy.

Doppler ultrasound stethoscopes (DUSs) are also used to assess blood pressure. See Figure 31.15 earlier in the chapter. These are of particular value when blood pressure sounds are difficult to hear, such as in infants, obese clients, and clients in shock. A systolic blood pressure assessed with a DUS is recorded with a large D, for example, 85D. Systolic pressure may be the only blood pressure obtainable with some ultrasound models.

Blood pressure cuffs come in various sizes; the bladder must be the correct width and length for the client's arm (Figure 31.25). If the bladder is too narrow, the blood pressure reading will be erroneously elevated; if it is too wide, the reading will be underestimated. The arm circumference, not the age of the client, should be used to determine bladder size. See accompanying box for appropriate cuff size in relation to arm circumference. The calcuation is : (bladder width × 2.5) ± 4 cm = the arm circumference (Campbell et al., 1995).

The length of the bladder also affects the accuracy of measurement. The bladder should be sufficiently long to cover 80 percent of the limb's circumference.

Blood pressure cuffs are made of nondistensible material so that an even pressure is exerted around the limb. Most cuffs are held in place by hooks, snaps, or Velcro. Others have a cloth bandage that is long enough to encircle the limb several times; this type is closed by tucking the end of the bandage into one of the bandage folds.

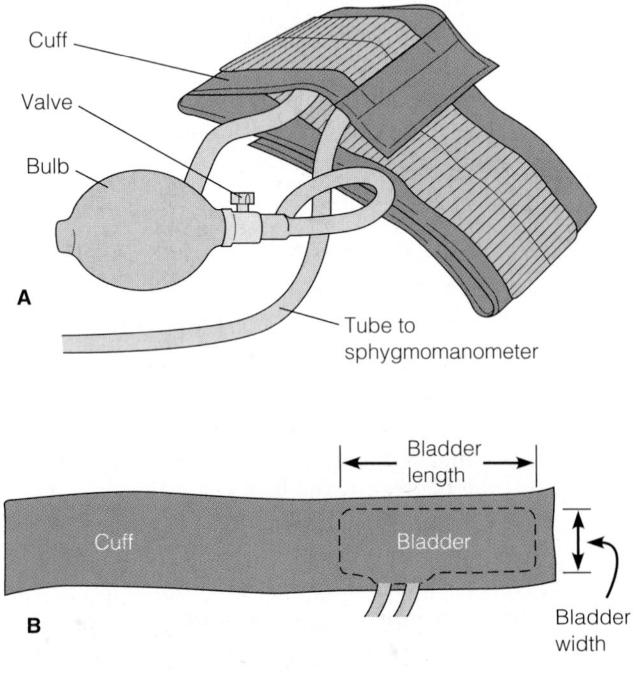

Figure 31.21 *A,* A blood pressure cuff and bulb; *B,* the bladder inside the cuff

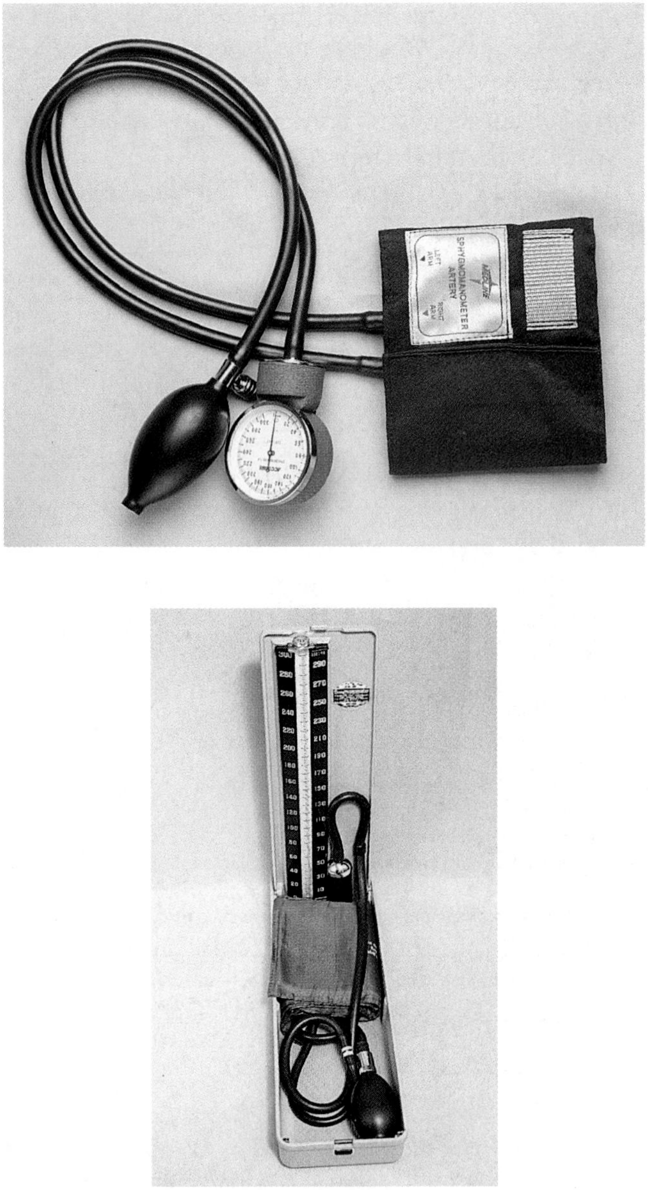

Figure 31.22 Blood pressure equipment: *A,* an aneroid manometer and cuff; *B,* a mercury manometer and cuff

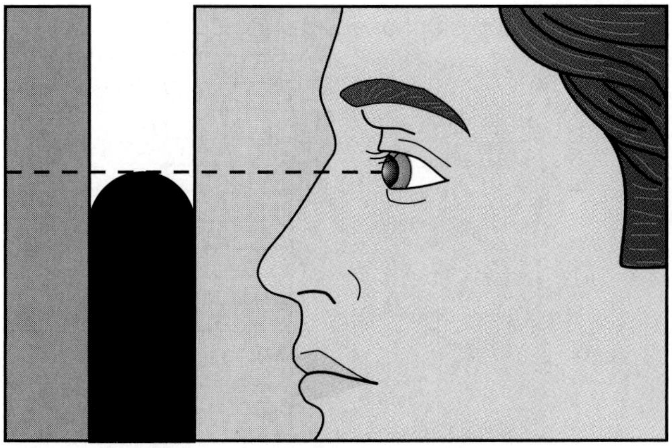

Figure 31.23 In order to obtain an accurate reading from a mercury manometer, position the meniscus at eye level

Sites

Blood pressure is usually assessed in the client's arm using the brachial artery and a standard stethoscope. If the arm is very large or grossly misshapen and the conventional cuff cannot be properly applied, leg or forearm measurements can be taken. To obtain a *thigh blood pressure*, apply an appropriate-sized cuff to the thigh, and auscultate the pulsations of the blood over the popliteal artery.

Assessing the blood pressure on a client's thigh is usually indicated in these situations:

- The blood pressure cannot be measured on either arm (e.g., because of burns or other trauma).
- The blood pressure in one thigh is to be compared with the blood pressure in the other thigh.

Blood pressure is *not* measured on a client's arm or thigh in the following situations:

- The shoulder, arm, or hand (or the hip, knee, or ankle) is injured or diseased.
- A cast or bulky bandage is on any part of the limb.
- The client has had removal of axilla or inquinal lymph nodes on that side.

Correct Adult Cuff Bladder Sizes

Mid-arm circumference (cm)	Cuff bladder size* (cm)
>18–26	9 × 18 (small cuff)
>26–33	12 × 23 (regular cuff)
>33–41	15 × 33 (large cuff)
>41	18 × 36 (thigh cuff)

*Manufacturers may use the same nomenclature but have different cuff dimensions.

Source: Reproduced with permission of *Can J Cardiol*; 11(Suppl H): 7H.

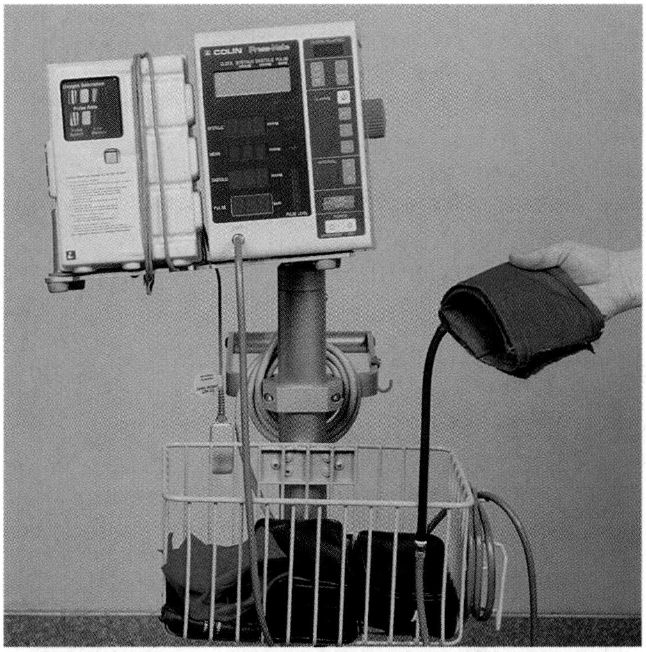

Figure 31.24 Automatic blood pressure monitors register systolic, diastolic, and mean blood pressures

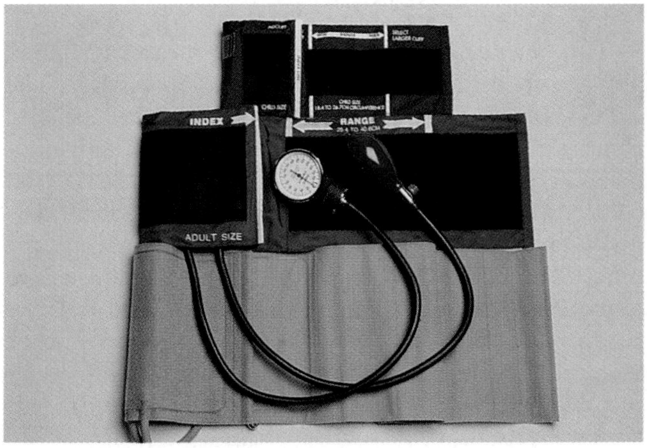

Figure 31.25 Three standard cuff sizes: a small cuff for an infant, small child, or frail adult; a normal adult-size cuff; and a large cuff for measuring the blood pressure on the leg or on the arm of an obese adult

- The client has an intravenous infusion in that limb.
- The client has an arteriovenous fistula (e.g., for renal dialysis) in that limb.

Methods

Blood pressure can be assessed directly or indirectly. *Direct (invasive monitoring) measurement* involves the insertion of a catheter into the brachial, radial, or femoral artery. Arterial pressure is represented as wave-like forms displayed on an oscilloscope. With correct placement, this pressure reading is highly accurate.

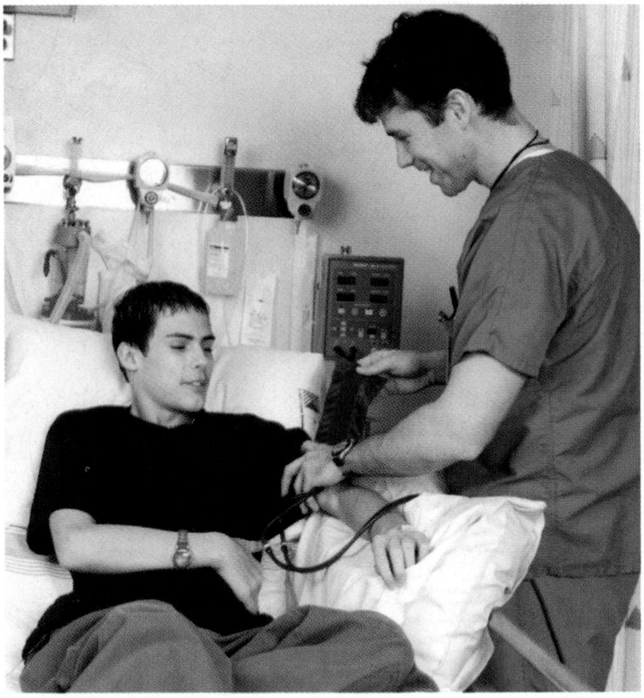

Figure 31.26 Applying a blood pressure cuff

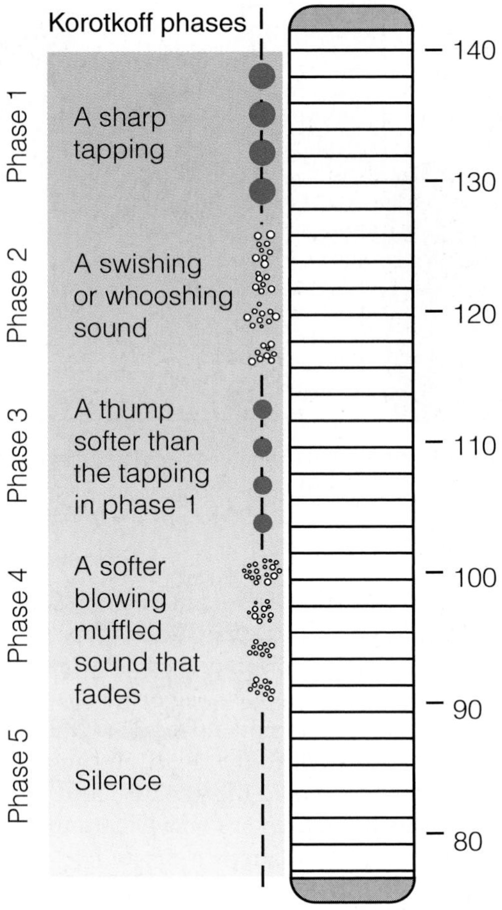

Figure 31.27 Korotkoff's sounds can be differentiated into five phases. In the illustration, the blood pressure is 138/90 or 138/102/90.

Two *noninvasive indirect methods* of measuring blood pressure are the auscultatory and palpatory methods. The *auscultatory method* is most commonly used in hospitals, clinics, and homes. Required equipment is a sphygmomanometer, a cuff, and a stethoscope. When carried out correctly, the auscultatory method is relatively accurate.

When taking a blood pressure using a stethoscope, the nurse identifies five phases in the series of sounds called **Korotkoff's sounds** (Figure 31.27). Standard practice requires the initial determination of the palpatory systolic pressure. The cuff is then pumped to 30 mm Hg above the palpatory systolic pressure. Pressure is released slowly (2 mm Hg/beat), while sounds heard through the stethoscope are related to the manometer readings. Five phases occur (see the box opposite).

The *palpatory method* is sometimes used when Korotkoff's sounds cannot be heard and electronic equipment to amplify the sounds is not available, or when an auscultatory gap occurs. An **auscultatory gap,** which occurs particularly in hypertensive clients, is the temporary disappearance of sounds normally heard over the brachial artery when the cuff pressure is high, followed by the reappearance of the sounds at a lower level. This temporary disappearance of sounds occurs in the latter part of phase 1 and phase 2 and may cover a range of 40 mm Hg. Instead of listening for the blood flow sounds, the nurse palpates the pulsations of the artery as the pressure in the cuff is released. The systolic pressure is read from the sphygmomanometer when the first pulsation is felt. A single whip-like vibration, felt in addition to the pulsations, identifies the point at which the pressure in the cuff nears the diastolic pressure. This vibration is no longer felt when the cuff pressure is below the diastolic pressure. To palpate the diastolic pressure, the nurse applies light to moderate pressure over the pulse point.

Common Errors in Assessing Blood Pressure

The importance of the accuracy of blood pressure assessments cannot be overemphasized. Many judgements about a client's health are made on the basis of blood pressure. It is an important indicator of the client's condition and is used extensively as a basis for nursing interventions. Two possible reasons for blood pressure errors are haste on the part of the nurse and subconscious bias. For example, a nurse may be influenced by the client's previous blood pressure measurements or diagnosis and "hear" a value consistent with the practitioner's expectations. Some reasons for erroneous blood pressure readings are given in Table 31.7. Procedure 31.6 gives guidelines for assessing blood pressure.

Korotkoff's Sounds

Phase 1 The pressure level at which the first faint, clear tapping or thumping sounds are heard. These sounds gradually become more intense. To ensure that they are not extraneous sounds, the nurse should identify at least two consecutive tapping sounds. The first tapping sound heard during deflation of the cuff is called the systolic blood pressure.

Phase 2 The period during deflation when the sounds have a muffled, whooshing, or swishing quality.

Phase 3 The period during which the blood flows freely through an increasingly open artery and the sounds become crisper and more intense and again assume a thumping quality but softer than in phase 1.

Phase 4 The time when the sounds become muffled and have a soft, blowing quality.

Phase 5 The pressure level when the last sound is heard. This is followed by a period of silence. The pressure at which the last sound is heard is known as the diastolic blood pressure in adults.*

*For children under 13 years, the American Heart Association (AHA) (1987) recommends that the onset of phase 4, where the sounds become muffled, be considered the diastolic pressure. The technique for measuring adult blood pressure should be used for children 13 years and older.

TABLE 31.7 Selected Sources of Error in Blood Pressure Assessment

Error	Effect
Bladder cuff too narrow	Erroneously high
Bladder cuff too wide	Erroneously low
Arm unsupported	Erroneously high
Insufficient rest before the assessment	Erroneously high
Repeating assessment too quickly	Erroneously high systolic or low diastolic readings
Cuff wrapped too loosely or unevenly	Erroneously high
Deflating cuff too quickly	Erroneously low systolic and high diastolic readings
Deflating cuff too slowly	Erroneously high diastolic reading
Failure to use the same arm consistently	Inconsistent measurements
Arm above level of the heart	Erroneously low
Assessing immediately after a client eats a meal, smokes a cigarette, consumes alcohol, or is having pain	Erroneously high
Failure to identify auscultatory gap	Erroneously low systolic pressure and erroneously low diastolic pressure

PROCEDURE 31.6 Assessing Blood Pressure

PURPOSES

- To obtain a baseline measure of arterial blood pressure for subsequent evaluation
- To determine the client's hemodynamic status (e.g., stroke volume of the heart and blood vessel resistance)
- To identify and monitor changes in blood pressure resulting from a disease process and medical therapy (e.g., presence or history of cardiovascular disease, renal disease, circulatory shock, or acute pain; rapid infusion of fluids or blood products)

Assessment Focus
Signs and symptoms of hypertension (e.g., headache, ringing in the ears, flushing of face, nosebleeds, fatigue); signs and symptoms of hypotension (e.g., tachycardia, dizziness, mental confusion, restlessness, cool and clammy skin, pale or cyanotic skin); factors affecting blood pressure (e.g., activity, emotional stress, pain, time the client last smoked, ingested caffeine, alcohol or food, full bowel or bladder)

Equipment

- ❑ Stethoscope or DUS
- ❑ Blood pressure cuff of the appropriate size (newborn, infant, child, small adult, adult, large adult, thigh)
- ❑ Sphygmomanometer

→

PROCEDURE 31.6 Assessing Blood Pressure *continued*

INTERVENTION

Steps:

1. Explain the procedure to the patient/client and request that he or she not talk during the procedure. *This encourages cooperation and reduces anxiety; talking can increase blood pressure.*
2. Have the individual seated with back support in a quiet, comfortable environment with legs uncrossed. Allow a five-minute rest period. *Physical exertion and environmental factors can increase blood pressure.*
3. Support the patient's arm so that it is at heart level. *Blood pressure changes 8 to 10 mm Hg for every 10 cm the antecubital fossa is above or below heart level.*
4. Remove any restrictive clothing from the arm and expose the area of the brachial artery. *Clothing over the artery interferes with ability to hear sounds. Tight clothing may cause venous congestion and inaccurate readings.*
5. Choose an appropriate cuff size. *A cuff too large or too small will cause an inaccurate reading.*
6. Ensure that the sphygmomanometer is at eye level. *Gradations on the device are more accurately read at eye level.*
7. Palpate the brachial artery and centre the bladder over the brachial artery. Wrap cuff snugly around the arm so that the edge of the cuff is 3 cm above the crease of the elbow (Figure 31.28). *A loosely wrapped cuff gives falsely high blood pressure readings. Placement of cuff above antecubital space provides room for stethoscope placement.*
8. Determine the level for maximum inflation by palpating the radial (or brachial) artery and rapidly inflating the cuff until the pulse is no longer palpable. Note this pressure on the sphygmomanometer and add 30 mm Hg. This number is the maximal inflation level. *Failure to recognize the auscultory gaps can lead to errors of up to 55/80 mm Hg in blood pressure.*
9. Rapidly deflate the cuff. Wait 30 to 60 seconds before re-inflating. *Venous congestion can occur during inflation and deflation of the blood pressure cuff and can lead to errors in blood pressure reading.*
10. Place the stethoscope gently over the brachial artery. (The ear tips should be directed down and forward.) *Heavy pressure distorts the shape of the artery and the sound. Placing the stethoscope directly over the artery makes more accurate readings possible.*

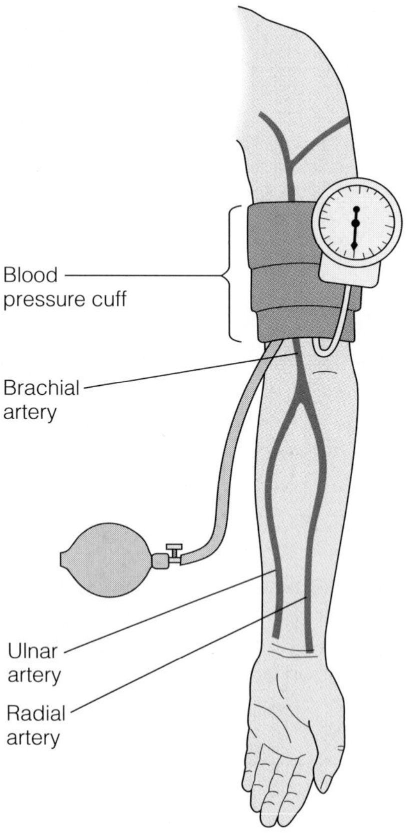

Figure 31.28 Location of the brachial artery and application of the cuff

11. Rapidly and steadily inflate the cuff to the maximal inflation level, as per step 8. *Rapid cuff inflation helps to prevent venous congestion.*
12. Release the air in the cuff so that the pressure falls at a steady rate of 2 mm Hg per beat. *Deflation which is too fast or too slow can cause an inaccurate reading.*
13. Do not re-inflate the cuff once the air is being released to recheck either systolic or diastolic pressure. *Re-inflating the cuff while measuring blood pressure is uncomfortable for the patient and can cause an inaccurate reading.*
14. Note the systolic pressure at the onset of two consecutive beats and diastolic pressure at the point at which sounds disappear. Read the pressure to the closest 2 mm Hg mark on the manometer. *The point at which the first sounds appear is the systolic pressure (phase I – Korotkoff's sounds); the disappearance of sounds is the better estimate of diastolic pressure (phase V – Korotkoff's sounds).*
15. Listen for at least 10 to 20 mm Hg below the last sound to confirm the disappearance, then deflate rapidly. *Although uncommon, Korotkoff's sounds may reappear after the initial disappearance of sound and can lead to overestimation of the diastolic pressure of up to 80 mm Hg.* If sounds persist to zero, or close to zero, use the muffling of sounds (phase 4) to indicate diastolic pressure. *The use of phase 4 in these instances is a more reliable estimate of blood pressure than phase 5.*
16. Record systolic/diastolic pressure as well as patient's position, cuff size, and arm used for measurement. Note also any auscultory gap or irregular pulse. If sounds are heard close to zero, record both phases 4 and 5.

PROCEDURE 31.6 Assessing Blood Pressure *continued*

Conditions for measuring blood pressure should be consistent for future comparisons.

17. If sounds are difficult to hear, reposition the arm and relocate brachial artery by palpation. Wait a minimum of one minute before repeating steps 10 to 15. *These measures provide a consistent approach in controlling for factors which can interfere with obtaining an accurate blood pressure measurement. The waiting period avoids venous congestion.*
18. Remove the cuff. Wipe the cuff with an approved disinfectant. *Cuffs can become significantly contaminated.*
19. If this is the client's initial examination, repeat the procedure on the client's other arm. There should be a difference of no more than 5 to 10 mm Hg between arms. The arm found to have the higher pressure should be used for subsequent readings. *These measures provide for consistent future comparisons.*

Variation: Taking a Thigh Blood Pressure

- Help the client to assume a prone position. If the client cannot assume this position, measure the blood pressure while the client is in a supine position with the knee slightly flexed. *Slight flexing of the knee will facilitate placing the stethoscope on the popliteal pulse.*
- Expose the thigh, taking care not to expose the client unduly.
- Locate the popliteal artery (Figure 31.29).
- Wrap the cuff evenly around the midthigh with the compression bladder over the posterior aspect of the thigh and the bottom edge above the knee. *The bladder must be directly over the posterior popliteal artery if the reading is to be accurate.*

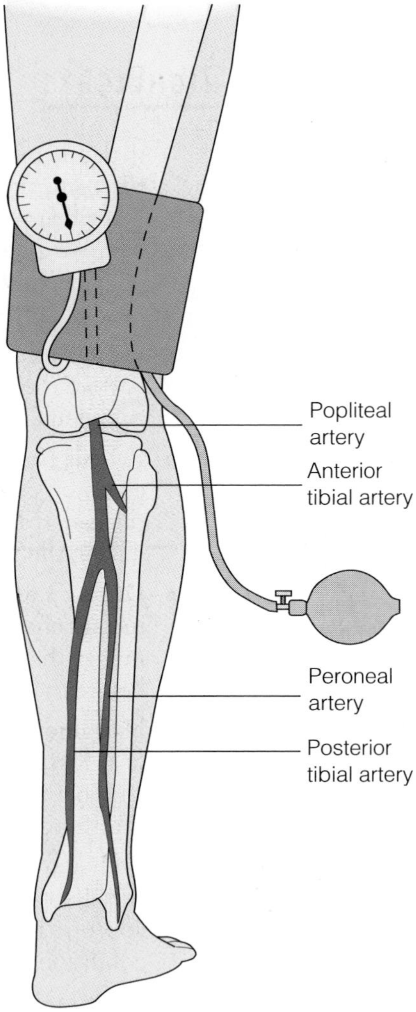

Figure 31.29 Location of the popliteal artery and application of the cuff

- Perform a preliminary palpatory determination of systolic pressure by palpating the popliteal artery (Figure 31.16, *E*). The systolic pressure in the popliteal artery is usually 20 to 30 mm Hg higher than that in the brachial artery because of the use of a larger bladder; the diastolic pressure is usually the same.
- Auscultate the pressure in the same manner as for the arm.

Variation: Using an Electronic Indirect Blood Pressure Monitoring Device

- Unplug the electronic unit from the electrical outlet.
- Place the blood pressure cuff on the extremity according to the manufacturer's guidelines.
- Turn on the blood pressure switch.
- When the device has determined the blood pressure reading, note the digital results.
- Record the blood pressure according to agency policy.

Source: Modified from Abbott, D., Campbell, N., Carruthers-Czyewski, P., et al. (1994). Guidelines for measurement of blood pressure, follow-up and lifestyle counselling. *Canadian Journal of Public Health, 85*(Supplement 2), S29–S35.

Evaluation Focus
The blood pressure in relation to baseline data, normal range for age, and health status; relationship to pulse and respirations

FOCUS ON CRITICAL THINKING

Mrs. Burne, 75 years old, has just been transferred to her own bed from the Recovery Room stretcher following a total hip replacement for osteoarthritis. After verbal report from the registered nurse, you assess her vital signs and record the following: BP 140/92, right arm, supine; temperature (tympanic) 35.8°C; pulse (radial) 98, occasional irregular beat; respirations 28, shallow.

1. How might you interpret these values?
2. What variables might have influenced this assessment data?
3. How would you proceed?

See Appendix A for answers to these questions.

CHAPTER HIGHLIGHTS

- Vital signs reflect changes in body function that otherwise might not be observed.
- Various sites and methods can be used to assess vital signs. The nurse selects the site and method that are safe for the client and will provide the most accurate measurement possible.
- The most accurate values are obtained when the client is at rest and comfortable.
- Changes in one vital sign can trigger changes in other vital signs.
- Vital signs are assessed when a client is admitted to a health-care agency to establish baseline data and when there is a change or possibility of a change in the client's condition.
- Data obtained from measurement of vital signs are used to plan and implement appropriate nursing interventions.
- Vital signs are also used to evaluate a client's response to nursing interventions or prescribed medical therapy.
- Knowledge of the normal ranges of vital signs and of the factors that regulate and influence vital signs helps the nurse interpret measurements that deviate from normal.
- Body temperature is the balance between heat produced by the body and heat lost from the body.
- Heat is produced by the body's metabolic processes which can be accelerated by muscle activity, thyroxine output, stimulation of the sympathetic nervous system, and fever.
- Knowledge of factors affecting heat production and heat loss helps the nurse implement appropriate interventions when the client has a fever or hypothermia.
- The system that regulates body temperature has three parts: sensory receptors, primarily in the skin; the hypothalamic integrator, which controls the core temperature; and an effector system, which initiates responses that either prevent heat loss and increase heat production (e.g., peripheral vasoconstriction, shivering, and release of epinephrine, which increases metabolism) or increase heat loss through sweating and peripheral vasodilation.
- Factors affecting body temperature include age, diurnal variations, exercise, hormones, stress, and environmental temperatures.
- Pyrexia (fever) is a common sign of disease. Four common types of fever are intermittent, remittent, relapsing, and constant. Clinical signs of fever vary during the onset, course, and abatement stages.
- During a fever, the set point of the hypothalamic thermostat changes suddenly from the normal level to a higher than normal level, but several hours elapse before the core temperature reaches the new set point.
- Hypothermia involves three mechanisms: excessive heat loss, inadequate heat production by body cells, and increasing impairment of hypothalamic thermoregulation.
- Body temperature can be measured by oral, tympanic, rectal, or axillary routes. The nurse selects the most appropriate site according to the client's age and condition.
- Pulse rate and volume reflect the stroke volume output, the compliance of the client's arteries, and the adequacy of blood flow.
- Normally, a peripheral pulse reflects the client's heartbeat, but it may differ from the heartbeat in clients with certain cardiovascular diseases; in these instances, the nurse takes an apical pulse and compares it with the peripheral pulse.
- Many factors affect a person's pulse rate: age, gender, exercise, presence of fever, certain medications, hemorrhage, stress, and (in some situations) position changes.

- Although the radial pulse is the site most commonly used, eight other sites may be used in certain situations.
- Respirations are normally quiet, effortless, and automatic and are assessed by observing respiratory rate, depth, rhythm, and sound.
- Blood pressure reflects cardiac output, peripheral vascular resistance, blood volume, and blood viscosity. Peripheral vascular resistance varies according to the size of the arterioles and capillaries and the compliance of the arteries.

READINGS AND REFERENCES

Suggested Readings

Erickson, R. S., Meyer, L. T., & Woo, T. M. (1996). Accuracy of chemical dot thermometers in critically ill adults and young children. *Image, 28*, 23–28.
Chemical dot thermometers are widely used in outpatient and ambulatory settings. It is important to know their accuracy and how they compare with other temperature measurements. In this article, the results of a study comparing chemical dot and electronic measures orally and in the axilla are reported. The researchers conclude that chemical dot thermometers are compact, portable, and acceptable indicators of general temperature.

McKenzie, N. E. (1998). Upping the body's thermostat: Learning how to maneuver the peaks and valleys of body temperature. *Nursing 98, 28*(10), 41–45, N228.
McKenzie discusses the physiology of the body's thermostat and mechanisms of fever, and explores the variables involved in differentiating normal from abnormal temperature among individuals. Clients who have certain conditions and who need immediate evaluation are emphasized.

Selected References

Abbott, D., Campbell, N., Carruthers-Czyewski, P., et al. (1994). Guidelines for measurement of blood pressure, follow-up, and lifestyle counselling. *Canadian Journal of Public Health, 85*(Supplement 2), S29–S35.

Alpert, B. (2000). Cuff width and accuracy of measurement of blood pressure. *Blood Pressure Monitoring, 5*(3), 151–152.

American Heart Association. (1987). *Recommendations for human blood pressure determination by sphygmomanometers.* Pub no. 701005. Author.

Base-Smith, V. (1996). Nondisposable sphygmomanometer cuffs harbor frequent bacterial colonization and significant contamination by organic and inorganic matter. *American Association of Nurse Anesthetists Journal, 64*, 141–145.

Bayne, C. G. (1997). Technology assessment: Vital signs: Are we monitoring the right parameters? *Nursing Management, 28*, 74–76.

Beevers, G., & Lip, G. (2001). ABC of hypertension: Blood pressure measurement Part I – Sphygmomanometry: Factors common to all techniques. *British Medical Journal, 322*, 981–985.

Beevers, G., Lip, G., & O'Brien, E. (2001). ABC of hypertension: Blood pressure measurement: Part II—Conventional sphygmomanometry: Technique of auscultory blood pressure measurement. *British Medical Journal, 322*, 1043–1048.

Bernardo, L. M., Clemence, B., Henker, R., Hogue, B., Schenkel, K., & Walters, P. (1996). A comparison of aural and rectal temperature measurements in children with moderate and severe injuries. *Journal of Emergency Nursing, 22*, 403–408.

Bickley, L. S., & Szilagyi, P. (2003). *Bates' guide to physical examination and history taking* (7th ed.). Philadelphia, PA: Lippincott.

Braun, S. K., Preston, P., & Smith, R. N. (1998). Getting a better read on thermometry. *RN, 61*, 57–60.

Bushey, P., Chulay, M., & Holland, S. (1997). Correlation of indirect blood pressure measurements and systemic blood pressure. *Critical Care Nurse, 17*, 12.

Campbell, N., McKay, D., Chockalingam, A., & Fodor, J. G. (1994). Errors in Assessment of blood pressure. 1. Patient Factors 2. Sphygmomanometers and blood pressure cuffs 3. Blood pressure measuring techniques. *Canadian Journal of Public Health, 85*, (Supplement 2).

Campbell, N., Myers, M. G., & McKay, D. W. (1999). Is usual measurement of blood pressure meaningful? *Blood Pressure Monitoring, 4*(2), 71–76.

Campbell, N. R. C., et al. (1995). Self measurement of blood pressure: Recommendations of the Canadian Coalition for High Blood Pressure Prevention and Control. *Canadian Journal of Cardiology, 11*(Supplement 11), 17H.

Canadian Association of Cardiology. (1995). Measurement of blood pressure: A satellite symposium of the world conference on hypertension control. *Canadian Journal of Cardiology, 11*(Supplement H).

Canadian Hypertension Recommendations Working Group. (2002). 2001 Canadian hypertension recommendations. *Canadian Nurse, 98*, 17–21.

Carpenito, L. J. (1999). *Nursing diagnosis: Application to clinical practice* (8th ed.). Philadelphia, PA: Lippincott.

Cowan, T. (1997). Product review: Ambulatory blood pressure monitors. *Professional Nurse, 12*, 373–376.

Evans, D., Hodgkinson, B., & Berry, J. (2001). Vital signs in hospital patients: A systematic review. *International Journal of Nursing Studies, 38*, 643–650.

Flo, G., & Brown, M. (1995). Comparing three methods of temperature taking: Oral mercury-in-glass, oral Diatek, and tympanic First Temp. *Nursing Research, 44*, 120–122.

Gilbert, M., Barton, A., & Counsell, C. M. (2002). Comparison of oral and tympanic temperatures in adult surgical patients. *Applied Nursing Research, 15*, 42–47.

Grant, L. P., Binder, S. K., & Campbell, N. R. C. (1999). The effect of crossing legs on blood pressure: A randomized single-blind cross-over study. *Blood Pressure Monitoring, 4*, 97–101.

Guyton, A. C., & Hall, J. F. (2000). *Textbook of medical physiology* (10th ed.). Philadelphia, PA: Saunders.

Hasel, K. L., & Erickson, R. S. (1995). Effect of cerumen on infrared ear temperature measurement. *Journal of Gerontological Nursing, 21*, 6–14.

Irnin, S. M. (1999). Comparison of the oral thermometer versus the tympanic thermometer. *American Journal of Nursing, 13*, 85.

Ladewig, P., London, M., & Olds, S. (1998). *Maternal-Newborn Nursing Core: The nurse, the family and the community* (4th ed.). Menlo Park, CA: Addison-Wesley.

Lanham, D. M. (1999). Accuracy of tympanic temperature readings in children under 6 years of age. *Pediatric Nursing, 25*, 39–42.

Marieb, E. N. (1998). *Human anatomy and physiology* (4th ed.). Menlo Park, CA: Benjamin/Cummings.

Marks, L. A., & Groch, A. (2000). Optimizing cuff width for noninvasive measurement of blood pressure. *Blood Pressure Monitoring, 5*(3), 153–158.

McConnell, E. A. (1998). Automated vital signs monitoring devices. *Nursing Management, 29*, 49–51.

Metric Commission Canada Sector 9.10 Health and Welfare. (1982). The SI manual in health care (2nd ed.). Toronto: Government of Ontario.

Morley, C. (1992, February). Measuring infants' temperatures. *Midwives Chronicle, 105*(1249), 26–29.

Netea, R.T., Lenders, J. W. M., Smits, P., & Thien, T. (1999). Arm position is important for blood pressure measurement. *Journal of Human Hypertension, 13*, 105–109.

Nicholls, P. H. (1997). Consult stat. Wrist and finger BP monitors offer accurate alternatives. *RN, 60*, 64.

Olds, S. B., London, M. L., & Ladewig, P. A. W. (2000). *Maternal newborn nursing: A family and community-based approach.* Upper Saddle River, NJ: Prentice Hall Health.

Rice, K. L. (1998). Sounding out blood flow with a Doppler device. *Nursing 98, 28*, 56–57.

Schmitz, T., Blair, N., Falk, M., & Levine, C. (1995, April). A comparison of five methods of temperature measurement in febrile intensive care patients. *American Journal of Critical Care, 4*, 286–292.

Thomas, D. O. (1996, April). Assessing children—it's different. *RN, 59*, 38–45, 53.

Winslow, E. H., Jacobson, E. F., & Beazlie, M. A. (1997). Research for practice: Tympanic thermometers: Accuracy is questionable. *American Journal of Nursing, 95*, 71.

Youde, J. H., Manktelow, B., Ward-Close, S., & Potter, J. F. (1999). Measuring postural changes in blood pressure in the healthy elderly. *Blood Pressure Monitoring, 4*, 1–5.

Zarnke, K., Levine, M., McAlister, F., Campbell, N., Myers, M., McKay, D., et al. (2001). The 2000 Canadian recommendations for the management of hypertension: Part two—Diagnosis and assessment of people with high blood pressure. *Canadian Journal of Cardiology, 17*, 1249–1263.

WEBLINKS

Canadian Heart and Stroke Foundation
http://www2.heartandstroke.ca/
This site, maintained by the Heart and Stroke Foundation of Canada, serves as a reliable source of information on heart disease and stroke. The Foundation's mission is to improve the health of Canadians by preventing and reducing disability and death from heart disease and stroke through research, health promotion, and advocacy.

Canadian Council of Cardiovascular Nurses
www.cardiovascularnurse.com
The Canadian Council of Cardiovascular Nurses maintains this site for its members and others interested in the speciality. Their mission is to advance the profession and cardiovascular health of Canadians through education, standards, research, and health promotion. Information includes future conferences, news, journals, standards, national and provincial/territorial committee links, and employment opportunities.

Canadian Coalition for High Blood Pressure Prevention and Control
http://www.canadianbpcoalition.org/
The group seeks to increase public knowledge of cardiovascular diseases and high blood pressure. The site provides a variety of educational resources, including an emphasis on teaching correct blood pressure measurement by health-care professionals.

CHAPTER 32

Asepsis

OBJECTIVES

After completing this chapter, you will be able to:

- Differentiate between the concepts of medical and surgical asepsis.
- Identify risks for nosocomial infections.
- Describe signs and symptoms of localized and systemic infections.
- List six links in the chain of infection.
- Analyze factors influencing a microorganism's capability to produce an infectious process.
- Describe the difference between specific and nonspecific defences of the body.
- Identify anatomical and physiological barriers that defend the body against microorganisms.
- Differentiate active from passive immunity.
- Identify people at risk for acquiring an infection.
- Outline relevant nursing diagnoses and contributing factors for clients at risk for infection and those who have an infection.
- Describe interventions to reduce risks for infections.
- Discuss measures that break each link in the chain of infection.
- Compare and contrast category-specific, disease-specific, universal, body substance, standard, routine practices, and transmission-based isolation precaution systems.
- Explain the measures to take in the event of a blood-borne pathogen exposure.
- Correctly perform aseptic practices, including hand washing, donning and removing a face mask, gowning, donning and removing disposable gloves (clean versus sterile), bagging articles, and managing equipment used for isolation clients.
- Determine when specific aseptic practices should be implemented.

Nurses are directly involved in providing a biologically safe environment. Microorganisms exist everywhere in the environment: in air, in water, in soil, and on body surfaces, such as the skin, intestinal tract, and other areas open to the outside (e.g., mouth, upper respiratory tract, vagina, and lower urinary tract). Most microorganisms are harmless, and some are even beneficial in that they perform essential functions in the body. Some microorganisms found in the intestines (e.g., enterobacteria) produce substances called **bacteriocins,** which are lethal to related strains of bacteria. Others produce antibiotic-like substances and toxic metabolites that repress the growth of other microorganisms. Some microorganisms are normal **resident flora** (the collective bacteria in a given area) in one part of the body and produce infection in another. For example, *Escherichia coli* is a normal inhabitant of the large intestine but a common cause of infection of the urinary tract. See Table 32.1 for common resident organisms.

An **infection** is an invasion of body tissue by microorganisms and their subsequent proliferation there. Such a microorganism is called an infectious agent. If the microorganism produces no clinical evidence of disease, the infection is called *asymptomatic* or *subclinical.* Some subclinical infections can cause significant damage, for example, cytomegalovirus (CMV) infection in a pregnant woman can lead to significant disease in the unborn child. A detectable alteration in normal tissue function, however, is called **disease.** Microorganisms vary in their **virulence** (i.e., their ability to produce disease).

Microorganisms also vary in the severity of the diseases they produce and their degree of communicability. For example, the common cold virus is more readily transmitted than the bacillus that causes leprosy (*Mycobacterium leprae*). If the infectious agent can be transmitted to an individual by direct or indirect contact, through a vector or vehicle, or as an air-borne infection, the resulting condition is called a **communicable disease.**

Pathogenicity is the ability to produce disease; thus, a pathogen is a microorganism that causes disease. Many microorganisms that are normally harmless can cause disease under certain circumstances. A "true" pathogen causes disease or infection in a healthy individual. An **opportunistic pathogen** causes disease only in a susceptible individual.

Infectious diseases are a major cause of death worldwide and a leading cause of illness in Canada. The control of the spread of microorganisms and the protection of people from communicable diseases and infections are carried out on international, national, provincial, community, and individual levels. The World Health Organization (WHO) is the major regulatory agency at the international level. In Canada, the Laboratory Centre for Disease Control (LCDC) is the principal public health agency at the national level concerned with disease prevention and control. At the provincial/territorial level, health departments track epidemics and illnesses as reports are made throughout a particular area.

Asepsis is the freedom from disease-causing microorganisms. In order to decrease the possibility of transferring microorganisms from one place to another, aseptic technique is used. There are two basic types of asepsis: medical and surgical. **Medical asepsis** includes all practices intended to confine a specific microorganism to a specific area, limiting the number, growth, and transmission of microorganisms.

In medical asepsis, objects are referred to as clean or dirty. **Clean** denotes the absence of almost all microorganisms. **Dirty** (soiled, contaminated) denotes the likely

TABLE 32.1 Examples of Common Resident Organisms

Body Area	Organisms
Skin	*Staphylococcus epidermidis*
	Propionibacterium acnes
	Staphylococcus aureus
	Corynebacterium xerosis
	Pityrosporum oxale (yeast)
Nasal passages	*Staphylococcus aureus*
	Staphylococcus epidermidis
Oropharynx	*Streptococcus pneumoniae*
Bronchi, lungs	None
Mouth	*Streptococcus mutans*
	Lactobacillus
	Bacteroides
	Actinomyces
Stomach	None
Esophagus	None
Intestine	*Bacteroides*
	Fusobacterium
	Eubacterium
	Lactobacillus
	Streptococcus
	Enterobacteriaceae
	Shigella
	Escherichia coli
Urethral orifice	*Staphylococcus epidermidis*
Urethra (lower)	*Proteus*
Bladder, ureters, kidneys	None
Vagina	*Lactobacillus*
	Bacteroides
	Clostridium
	Candida albicans
Blood, lymph system	None

presence of microorganisms, some of which may be capable of causing infection. Aseptic measures are protective as they are designed to reduce the number of potentially infective agents.

Surgical asepsis, or *sterile technique*, refers to those practices that keep an area or object free of all microorganisms; it includes practices that destroy all microorganisms and spores. Surgical asepsis is used for all procedures involving the sterile areas of the body.

The opposite of asepsis is **sepsis.** Sepsis is the state of infection and can take many forms, including septic shock.

Types of Organisms Causing Infections

Four major categories of microorganisms cause infection in humans: bacteria, viruses, fungi, and parasites. **Bacteria** are by far the most common infection-causing microorganisms. Several hundred species can cause disease in humans and can live and be transported through air, water, food, soil, body tissues and fluids, and inanimate objects. Most of the organisms in Table 32.1 are bacteria.**Viruses** consist primarily of nucleic acid and, therefore, must enter living cells in order to reproduce. Common viruses include the rhinovirus (causes the common cold), hepatitis, herpes, and human immunodeficiency virus (HIV) families. **Fungi** include yeasts and moulds. *Candida albicans* is a yeast considered to be normal flora in the human vagina. **Parasites** live on other living organisms. They include protozoa, such as the one that causes malaria, helminths (worms), and arthropods (mites, fleas, ticks).

Types of Infections

Colonization is the process by which strains of microorganisms become resident flora. In this state, the microorganisms may grow and multiply but do not cause disease. Infection occurs when newly introduced or resident microorganisms succeed in invading a part of the body where the host's defence mechanisms are ineffective and the pathogen causes tissue damage. The infection becomes a disease when the signs and symptoms of the infection are unique and can be differentiated from other conditions.

Infections can be local or systemic. A **local infection** is limited to the specific part of the body where the microorganisms remain. If the microorganisms spread and damage different parts of the body, the infection is **systemic.** When a culture of the person's blood reveals microorganisms, the condition is called **bacteremia.** When bacteremia results in systemic infection, it is referred to as **septicemia.**

Infections are also acute or chronic. **Acute** infections generally appear suddenly or last a short time. A **chronic** infection may occur slowly, over a very long period, and may last months or years.

Nosocomial Infections

Nosocomial infections are classified as infections that are associated with the delivery of health-care services in a health-care facility. Nosocomial infections can either develop during a client's stay in a facility or manifest after discharge. Nosocomial organisms may also be acquired by health personnel working in the facility (e.g., hepatitis B infection and HIV infection) and can cause significant illness and time lost from work.

Nosocomial infections have received increasing attention in recent years. The most common settings where nosocomial infections develop are surgical or medical intensive-care units in hospitals. A report from the U.S. National Nosocomial Infection Surveillance (NNIS) System (1996) revealed that the urinary tract was the most common nosocomial infection site.

The microorganisms that cause nosocomial infections can originate from the clients themselves (an **endogenous** source) or from the hospital environment and hospital personnel (**exogenous** sources). Most nosocomial infections appear to have endogenous sources. The NNIS reports that between 1990 and 1996, *Escherichia coli*, *Staphylococcus aureus*, and enterococci were the most common infecting organisms.

A number of factors contribute to nosocomial infections. **Iatrogenic** infections (those that are due to any aspect of medical therapy) are the direct result of diagnostic or therapeutic procedures. One example of an iatrogenic infection is bacteremia that results from an intravascular line. Not all nosocomial infections are iatrogenic, nor are all nosocomial infections preventable.

Another factor contributing to the development of nosocomial infections is the *presence of compromised hosts*, that is, clients whose normal defences have been lowered by surgery or illness.

The hands of personnel are a common vehicle for the spread of microorganisms. *Insufficient hand washing* is, thus, an important factor contributing to the spread of nosocomial organisms.

The cost of nosocomial infections to the client, the facility, and funding sources (e.g., insurance companies and federal, provincial/territorial, or local governments) is great. Nosocomial infections extend hospitalization time, increase clients' time away from work, cause disability and discomfort, and even result in loss of life. See Table 32.2.

Chain of Infection

Six links make up the chain of infection (Figure 32.1): the etiologic agent, or microorganism; the place where the organism naturally resides (reservoir); a portal of exit from the reservoir; a method (mode) of transmission; a portal of entry into a host; and the susceptibility of the host.

TABLE 32.2 Nosocomial Infections

Most Common Organisms	Causes
Urinary Tract	
Escherichia coli	Catheterization technique
Enterococcus species	Contamination of closed drainage system
Pseudomonas aeruginosa	Inadequate hand washing
Surgical Sites	
Staphylococcus aureus	Inadequate hand washing
Enterococcus species	Improper dressing change technique
Pseudomonas aeruginosa	
Bloodstream	
Coagulase-negative staphylococci	Inadequate hand washing
Staphylococcus aureus	Improper intravenous fluid, tubing, and site care technique
Enterococcus species	
Pneumonia	
Staphylococcus aureus	Inadequate hand washing
Pseudomonas aeruginosa	Improper suctioning technique
Enterobacter species	

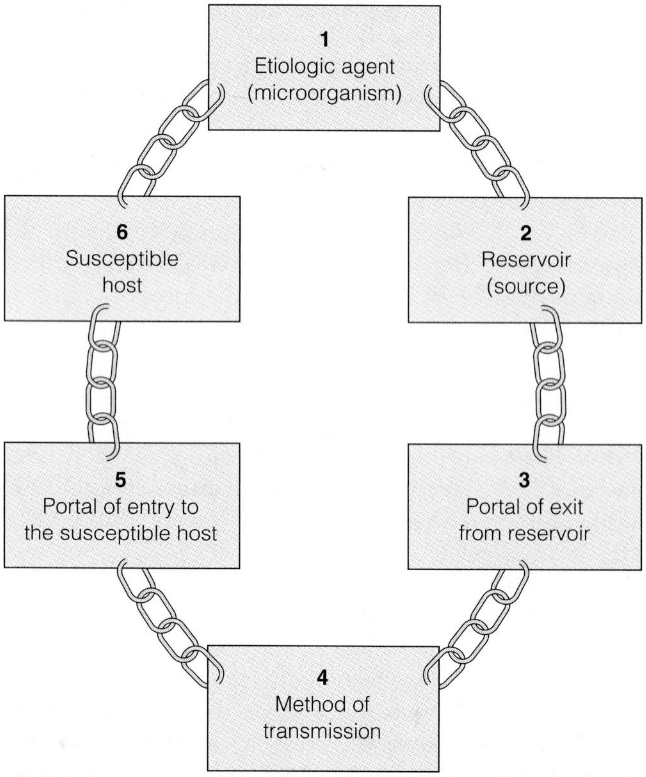

Figure 32.1 The chain of infection

Etiologic Agent

The extent to which any microorganism is capable of producing an infectious process depends on the number of organisms present, the virulence and potency of the organisms (pathogenicity), the ability of the organisms to enter the body, the susceptibility of the host, and the ability of the organisms to live in the host's body.

Some microorganisms, such as the smallpox virus, have the ability to infect almost all susceptible people after exposure. By contrast, microorganisms, such as the tuberculosis bacillus, infect a relatively small number of the population who are susceptible and exposed, usually people who are poorly nourished and living in crowded conditions.

A **carrier** is a person or animal that harbours a specific infectious agent and serves as a potential source of infection yet does not manifest any clinical signs of disease. The carrier state may also exist in the incubation period, convalescence, and postconvalescence of an individual with a clinically recognizable disease. This type of carrier is referred to as an *incubatory* or *convalescent carrier.* Under either circumstance, the carrier state may be of short duration (*temporary* or *transient carrier*) or long duration (*chronic carrier*).

Reservoir

There are many **reservoirs,** or sources of microorganisms. Common sources are other humans, the client's own microorganisms, plants, animals, or the general environment. People are the most common source of infection for others and for themselves (Table 32.3). The person with, for example, an influenza virus frequently spreads it to others. When resistance is lowered by fatigue and other factors, an infection may develop.

Insects, birds, and other animals are common reservoirs of infection. The *Anopheles* mosquito carries the malaria parasite. Food, water, milk, and feces also can be reservoirs.

Portal of Exit from Reservoir

Before an infection can establish itself in a host, the microorganisms must leave the reservoir. Common human reservoirs and their associated portals of exit are summarized in Table 32.3.

Method of Transmission

After a microorganism leaves its source or reservoir, it requires a means of transmission to reach another person or host through a *receptive portal of entry.* There are three mechanisms:

1. *Direct transmission.* Direct transmission involves immediate and direct transfer of microorganisms from person to person through touching, biting, kissing, or sexual intercourse. Droplet spread is also a form of direct contact but can occur only if the source and the host are

TABLE 32.3 Human Reservoirs, Common Infectious Microorganisms, and Portals of Exit

Body Area (Source)	Common Infectious Organisms	Portals of Exit
Respiratory tract	Parainfluenza virus *Mycobacterium tuberculosis* *Staphylococcus aureus*	Nose or mouth through sneezing, coughing, breathing, or talking; endotracheal tubes or tracheostomies
Gastrointestinal tract	Hepatitis A virus *Salmonella* species	Mouth: saliva, vomitus; anus: feces; ostomies; drainage tubes (e.g., nasogastric or T-tubes)
Urinary tract	*Escherichia coli* enterococci *Pseudomonas aeruginosa*	Urethral meatus and urinary diversion ostomies
Reproductive tract (including genitals)	*Neisseria gonorrhoeae* *Treponema pallidum* Herpes simplex virus (HSV) type 2 Hepatitis B virus (HBV)	Vagina: vaginal discharge; urinary meatus: semen, urine
Blood	Hepatitis B virus Human immunodeficiency virus (HIV) *Staphylococcus aureus* *Staphylococcus epidermidis*	Open wound, needle puncture site, any disruption of intact skin or mucous membrane surfaces
Tissue	*Staphylococcus aureus* *Escherichia coli* *Proteus* species Streptococcus beta-hemolytic A or B	Drainage from cut or wound

within one metre of each other. Sneezing, coughing, spitting, singing, or talking can project droplet spray into the conjunctiva or onto the mucous membranes of the eye, nose, or mouth of another person.

2. *Indirect transmission.* Indirect transmission may be either vehicle borne or vector borne.
   a. **Vehicle-borne transmission.** A *vehicle* is any substance that serves as an intermediate means to transport and introduce an infectious agent into a susceptible host through a suitable portal of entry. *Fomites* (inanimate materials or objects), such as handkerchiefs, toys, soiled clothes, cooking or eating utensils, and surgical instruments or dressings, can act as vehicles. Water, food, milk, blood, serum, and plasma are other vehicles. For example, food or water may become contaminated by a food handler who transports the hepatitis A virus. The food is then ingested by a susceptible host.
   b. **Vector-borne transmission.** A *vector* is an animal or insect that serves as an intermediate means of transporting the infectious agent. Transmission may occur by injecting salivary fluid during biting or by depositing feces or other materials on the skin through the bite wound or a traumatized skin area.
3. *Air-borne transmission.* **Air-borne transmission** may involve droplets or dust. **Droplet nuclei,** the residue of evaporated droplets emitted by an infected host, such as someone with tuberculosis, can remain in the air for long periods. Dust particles containing the infectious agent (e.g., *Clostridium difficile* spores from the soil) can also become air-borne. The material is transmitted by air currents to a suitable portal of entry, usually the respiratory tract, of another person.

Portal of Entry to the Susceptible Host

Before a person can become infected, microorganisms must enter the body. The skin is a barrier to infectious agents; however, any break in the skin can readily serve as a portal of entry. Microorganisms can enter the body through the same routes they use to leave the body. Often, microorganisms enter the body of the host by the same route they used to leave the source.

Susceptible Host

A **susceptible host** is any person who is at risk for infection. **Compromised hosts** are persons "at increased risk," individuals who, for one or more reasons, are more likely than others to acquire an infection. Impairment of the body's natural defences and a number of other factors can affect susceptibility to infection.

Body Defences against Infection

Individuals normally have defences that protect the body from infection. These defences can be categorized as nonspecific and specific. **Nonspecific defences** protect the person against all microorganisms, regardless of prior exposure. **Specific (immune) defences,** by contrast, are directed against identifiable bacteria, viruses, fungi, or other infectious agents.

Nonspecific Defences

Nonspecific body defences include anatomical and physiological barriers and the inflammatory response.

Anatomical and Physiological Barriers

Intact skin and mucous membranes are the body's first line of defence against microorganisms. Unless the skin and mucosa become cracked and broken, they are an effective barrier against bacteria. Fungi can live on the skin, but they cannot penetrate it. The dryness of the skin also acts as a deterrent to bacteria, which are most plentiful in moist areas of the body, such as the perineum and axillae. Resident bacteria of the skin also prevent other bacteria from multiplying. They use up the available nourishment, and the end products of their metabolism inhibit other bacteria. Normal secretions make the skin slightly acidic; acidity also inhibits bacterial growth.

The *nasal passages* have a defensive function. As entering air follows the tortuous route of the passage, it comes in contact with moist mucous membranes and *cilia.* These trap microorganisms, dust, and foreign materials. The *lungs* have alveolar **macrophages** (large phagocytes). **Phagocytes** are cells that ingest microorganisms, other cells, and foreign particles.

Each body orifice also has protective mechanisms. The *oral cavity* regularly sheds mucosal epithelium to rid the mouth of colonizers. The flow of saliva and its partial buffering action help prevent infections. Saliva contains microbial inhibitors, such as lactoferrin, lysozyme, and secretory IgA.

The *eye* is protected from infection by tears, which continually wash microorganisms away and contain inhibiting lysozyme. The *gastrointestinal tract* also has defences against infection. The high acidity of the stomach normally prevents microbial growth. The resident flora of the large intestine help prevent the establishment of disease-producing microorganisms. Peristalsis also tends to move microbes out of the body.

The *vagina* also has natural defences against infection. When a girl reaches puberty, lactobacilli ferment sugars in the vaginal secretions, creating a vaginal pH of 3.5 to 4.5. This low pH inhibits the growth of many disease-producing microorganisms. The *entrance to the urethra* normally harbours many microorganisms. These include *Staphylococcus epidermidis* coagulase (from the skin) and *Escherichia coli* (from feces). It is believed that the urine flow has a flushing and bacteriostatic action that keeps the bacteria from ascending the urethra. An intact mucosal surface also acts as a barrier.

Inflammatory Response

Inflammation is a local and nonspecific defensive response of the tissues to injury or infection. It is an adaptive mechanism that destroys or dilutes the injurious agent, prevents further spread of the injury, and promotes the repair of damaged tissue. It is characterized by five signs: (1) pain, (2) swelling, (3) redness, (4) heat, and (5) impaired function of the body part, if the injury is severe. Commonly, words with the suffix *-itis* describe an inflammatory process. For example, *appendicitis* means inflammation of the appendix; *gastritis* means inflammation of the stomach.

Injurious stressors (inflammatory agents) to body tissues can be categorized as physical agents, chemical agents, and microorganisms. *Physical agents* include mechanical objects causing trauma to tissues, excessive heat or cold, and radiation. *Chemical agents* include external irritants (e.g., strong acids, alkalis, poisons, and irritating gases) and internal irritants (substances manufactured within the body, such as excessive hydrochloric acid in the stomach). *Microorganisms* include the broad groups of bacteria, viruses, fungi, and parasites.

The inflammatory response involves a series of dynamic events commonly referred to as the three stages of the inflammatory response:

First stage: Vascular and cellular responses

Second stage: Exudate production

Third stage: Reparative phase

Vascular and Cellular Responses At the start of the first stage of inflammation, constriction of the blood vessels occurs at the site of injury, lasting only a few moments. This initial constriction is rapidly followed by dilation of small blood vessels (occurring as a result of histamine released by the injured tissues). Thus, more blood flows to the injured area. This marked increase in blood supply is referred to as **hyperemia** and is responsible for the characteristic signs of redness and heat.

Vascular permeability increases at the injured site with the dilation of the vessels in response to tissue necrosis, the release of chemical mediators (e.g., bradykinin, serotonin, and prostaglandin), and the release of histamine. The result of this altered permeability is an outpouring of fluid, proteins, and leukocytes into the interstitial spaces, clinically manifested by the characteristic inflammatory signs of swelling (edema) and pain. The pain is caused by the pressure of accumulating fluid on local nerve endings and the chemical mediators that are thought to irritate the nerve endings. Too much fluid pouring into such areas as the pleural or pericardial cavity can seriously affect organ function. In other areas, such as joints, mobility is impaired.

Blood flow slows in the dilated vessels. This altered rate of flow helps in moving more **leukocytes** (white blood cells) to the injured tissues. Normally, blood cells flow along the centre of a blood vessel while plasma without cells streams around them against the walls of the blood vessel. When the blood flow slows, leukocytes aggregate or line up along this inner surface of the blood vessels. This process is known as **margination.** Leukocytes then move through the blood vessel wall into the affected tissue spaces, a process called **emigration.**

The actual passage of blood corpuscles through the blood vessel wall is referred to as **diapedesis.** Leukocytes are attracted to injured cells by **chemotaxis.**

In response to the exit of leukocytes from the blood vessels, the bone marrow produces large numbers of leukocytes and releases them into the bloodstream **(leukocytosis).** The exact mechanism stimulating this increase is unknown, but it is another sign associated with inflammation. A normal leukocyte count of 4,500 to 11,000 per cubic millimetre of blood can rise to 20,000 or more when inflammation occurs.

Exudate Production In the second stage of inflammation, the inflammatory **exudate** is produced, consisting of fluid that escaped from the blood vessels, dead phagocytic cells, and dead tissue cells and products that they release. A plasma protein called **fibrinogen** (which is converted to fibrin when it is released into the tissues), thromboplastin (a product released by injured tissue cells), and platelets together form an interlacing network to make a barrier, wall off the area, and prevent spread of the injurious agent. During the second stage, the injurious agent is overcome, and the exudate is cleared away by lymphatic drainage.

The nature and amount of exudate vary according to the tissue involved and the intensity and duration of the inflammation. The major types of exudate are *serous, purulent,* and *hemorrhagic* (sanguineous).

Reparative Phase The third stage of the inflammatory response involves the repair of injured tissues by regeneration or replacement with fibrous tissue (scar) formation. **Regeneration** is the replacement of destroyed tissue cells by cells that are identical or similar in structure and function. It involves not only replacement of damaged cells one by one but also organization of these cells so that the architectural pattern and function of the tissue are restored. The ability to reproduce cells varies considerably from one type of tissue to another. For example, epithelial tissues of the skin and of the digestive and respiratory tracts have a good regenerative capacity provided that their underlying support structures are intact. The same holds true for osseous, lymphoid, and bone marrow tissues. Tissues that have little regenerative capacity include nervous, muscular, and elastic tissues.

When regeneration is not possible, repair occurs by *fibrous tissue formation.* **Fibrous (scar) tissue** has the capacity to proliferate under the unusual conditions of ischemia and altered pH. The inflammatory exudate with its interlacing network of fibrin provides the framework for this tissue to develop. Damaged tissues are replaced with the connective tissue elements of collagen, blood capillaries, lymphatics, and other tissue-bound substances. In the early stages of this process, the tissue is called **granulation tissue.** It is a fragile, gelatinous tissue, appearing pink or red because of the many newly formed capillaries. Later in the process, the tissue shrinks (the capillaries are constricted, even obliterated) and the collagen fibres contract, so that a firmer fibrous tissue remains. This is called **cicatrix,** or scar.

Specific Defences

Specific defences of the body involve the immune system, which responds to foreign protein in the body (e.g., bacteria or transplanted tissues). In some cases, the immune system even responds to the body's own proteins. Foreign proteins in the body are called **antigens** and are considered invaders. If the proteins originate in a person's own body, the antigen is called an **autoantigen. Immunity** is the specific resistance of the body to infection (pathogens or their toxins). There are two major types of immunity: active and passive. See Table 32.4. In **active immunity,** the host produces its own antibodies in response to natural antigens (e.g., infection) or artificial antigens (e.g., vaccines). With **passive immunity,** the host receives natural (e.g., from a nursing mother) or artificial (e.g., from an injection of immune serum) antibodies produced by another source.

Antibody-Mediated Defences

Another name for the *antibody-mediated defences* is **humoral (circulating) immunity** because these defences reside ultimately in the B lymphocytes and are mediated by antibodies produced by B cells. **Antibodies,** also called **immunoglobulins,** are part of the body's plasma proteins. The antibody-mediated responses defend primarily against the extracellular phases of bacterial and viral infections.

B cells are activated when they recognize a foreign invader, an antigen. They then differentiate into plasma cells, which secrete antibodies (and serum proteins) that bind specifically to the foreign substance and initiate a variety of elimination responses. The B cell response to an antigen may produce antibody molecules of five classes of immunoglobulins (Ig) designated by the letters M, G, A, D, and E, usually written as follows: IgM, IgG, IgA, IgD, and IgE. The presence of IgM in a laboratory

TABLE 32.4 Types of Acquired Immunity

Type	Antigen or Antibody Source	Duration
1. Active	Antibodies are produced by the body in response to an antigen.	Long
a. Natural	Antibodies are formed in the presence of active infection in the body.	Lifelong
b. Artificial	Antigens (vaccines or toxoids) are administered to stimulate antibody production.	Many years: the immunity must be reinforced by booster inoculations
2. Passive	Antibodies are produced by another source, animal or human.	Short
a. Natural	Antibodies are transferred naturally from an immune mother to her baby through the placenta or in colostrum.	Six months to one year
b. Artificial	Immune serum (antibody) from an animal or another human is injected.	Two to three weeks

analysis shows current infection. Before an antibody response, the phagocytic cells of the blood bind and ingest foreign substances. The rate of binding and phagocytosis increases if IgG antibodies (which indicate past infection and subsequent immunity) are present.

Cell-Mediated Defences

The **cell-mediated defences,** or **cellular immunity,** occur through the T-cell system. On exposure to an antigen, the lymphoid tissues release large numbers of activated T cells into the lymph system. These T cells pass into the general circulation. There are three main groups of T cells: (1) helper T cells, which help in the functions of the immune system; (2) cytotoxic T cells, which attack and kill microorganisms and sometimes the body's own cells; and (3) suppressor T cells, which can suppress the functions of the helper T cells and the cytotoxic T cells. When cell-mediated immunity is lost, as occurs with HIV infection, an individual is "defenceless" against most viral, bacterial, and fungal infections.

Factors Increasing Susceptibility to Infection

Whether a microorganism causes an infection depends on a number of factors previously mentioned. One of the most important factors is host susceptibility, which is affected by age, heredity, level of stress, nutritional status, immunization status, current medical therapy, pre-existing disease processes, and some past or recent surgical interventions.

Age influences the risk of infection. Newborns and elderly people have reduced defences against infection. Infections are a major cause of death among newborns, who have immature immune systems and are protected only for the first two or three months by immunoglobulins passively received from the mother. Between one and three months of age, infants begin to synthesize their own immunoglobulins. Immunizations against diphtheria, tetanus, and pertussis are usually started at two months, when the infant's immune system can respond.

With advancing age, the immune responses again become weak. Although there is still much to learn about aging, it is known that immunity to infection decreases with advancing age. Because of the prevalence of influenza and pneumonia and their potential for causing death, the LCDC recommends annual immunization against influenza for the elderly and for persons with chronic cardiac, respiratory, metabolic, and renal diseases.

Heredity influences the development of infection in that some people have a genetic susceptibility to certain infections. For example, some may be deficient in serum immunoglobulins, which play a significant role in the internal defence mechanism of the body.

The nature, number, and duration of physical and emotional *stressors* can influence susceptibility to infection. Stressors elevate blood cortisone. Prolonged elevation of blood cortisone decreases anti-inflammatory responses, depletes energy stores, leads to a state of exhaustion, and decreases resistance to infection. For example, a person recovering from a major operation or injury is more likely to develop an infection than a healthy person.

Resistance to infection depends on adequate *nutritional status.* Because antibodies are proteins, the ability to synthesize antibodies may be impaired by inadequate nutrition, especially when protein reserves are depleted (e.g., as a result of injury, surgery, or debilitating diseases, such as cancer).

Some *medical therapies* predispose a person to infection. Radiation treatments for cancer destroy not only cancerous cells but also some normal cells, thereby rendering the person more vulnerable to infection. Some *diagnostic procedures* may also predispose the client to an infection, especially when the skin is broken or sterile body cavities are penetrated during the procedure.

Certain *medications* also increase susceptibility to infection. Antineoplastic (anticancer) medications may depress bone marrow function, resulting in inadequate production of white blood cells necessary to combat infections. Anti-inflammatory medications, such as adrenal corticosteroids, inhibit the inflammatory response that is an essential defence against infection. Even some antibiotics that are used to treat infections can have adverse effects. Antibiotics may kill resident flora, allowing the proliferation of strains that would not grow and multiply in the body under normal conditions. Certain antibiotics can also induce resistance in some strains of organisms.

Any *disease* that lessens the body's defences against infection places the client at risk. Examples are chronic pulmonary disease, which impairs ciliary action and weakens the mucous barrier; peripheral vascular disease, which restricts blood flow; burns, which impair skin integrity; chronic or debilitating diseases, which deplete protein reserves; and such immune system diseases as leukemia and aplastic anemia, which alter the production of white blood cells. Diabetes mellitus is a major underlying disease predisposing clients to infection because compromised peripheral vascular status and increased serum glucose levels increase susceptibility.

Assessing

Nursing History

During the nursing history, the nurse assesses (1) the degree to which a client is at risk for developing an infection, and (2) any client complaints suggesting the presence of an infection. To identify clients at risk, the nurse reviews the client's chart and structures the nursing interview to collect data regarding the factors influencing the development of infection, especially existing disease process, history of recurrent infections, current medications and therapeutic measures, current emotional stressors, nutritional status, and history of immunizations. See the accompanying box for a sample assessment interview.

To obtain subjective data that may indicate the presence of an infection, the nurse asks whether the client has experienced loss of energy, loss of appetite, nausea, headache, or other signs associated with specific body systems (e.g., difficulty urinating, urinary frequency, or a sore throat).

ASSESSMENT INTERVIEW

Clients at Risk for Infections

- When were you last immunized for diphtheria, tetanus, poliomyelitis, rubella, measles, influenza, hepatitis, and pneumococcal pneumonia?
- When did you last have a tuberculin skin test?
- What infections have you had in the past, and how were these treated?
- Have any of these infections recurred?
- Are you taking any antineoplastic, anti-inflammatory, or antibiotic medications?
- Have you had any recent diagnostic procedure or therapy that penetrated your skin or a body cavity?
- What past surgeries have you had?
- How would you describe your nutritional status in terms of a well-balanced diet?
- On a scale of 1 to 10, how would you rate the stress you have experienced in the last six months?

Physical Assessment

Signs and symptoms of an infection vary according to the body area involved. For example, sneezing, watery or mucoid discharge from the nose, and nasal stuffiness commonly occur with an infection of the nose and sinuses; urinary frequency and possible cloudy or discoloured urine often occur with a urinary infection. Signs and symptoms of localized infection include:

- Localized swelling
- Localized redness
- Pain or tenderness with palpation or movement
- Palpable heat at the infected area
- Loss of function of the body part affected, depending on the site and extent of involvement

In addition, open wounds may exude drainage of various colours.

Signs and symptoms of *systemic infection* include:

- Fever
- Increased pulse and respiratory rate, if the fever is high
- Lassitude, malaise, and loss of energy
- Anorexia and, in some situations, nausea and vomiting
- Enlargement and tenderness of lymph nodes that drain the area of infection

Laboratory Data

Laboratory data that indicate the presence of an infection include the following:

- Elevated leukocyte (white blood cell or WBC) count (5,000 to 10,000/mm^3)
- Increases in specific types of leukocytes as revealed in the differential white blood cell count. Specific types

of white blood cells are increased or decreased in certain infections.

- Elevated *erythrocyte sedimentation rate (ESR)*. Sedimentation normally takes place slowly, but the rate increases in the presence of an inflammatory process.
- Urine, blood, sputum, or other drainage *cultures* (laboratory cultivations of microorganisms in a special growth medium) that indicate the presence of pathogenic microorganisms. See also Procedure 37.1, "Obtaining a Specimen of Wound Drainage" on pages 946–947.

Diagnosing

The NANDA (1999–2002) nursing diagnostic label for problems associated with the transmission of microorganisms is ***Risk for Infection:*** the state in which an individual is at risk to be invaded by an opportunistic or pathogenic microorganism from endogenous or exogenous sources.

When using this label, the nurse should identify the specific focus (risk factors):

1. *Inadequate primary defences*, such as broken skin, traumatized tissue, decreased ciliary action, stasis of body fluids, change in pH of secretions, or altered peristalsis
2. *Inadequate secondary defences*, such as leukopenia, immunosuppression, decreased hemoglobin, or suppressed inflammatory response (Carpenito, 1999)

Clients who have, or are at risk for, an infection are prime candidates for other physical and psychological problems. Examples of nursing diagnoses or collaborative problems that may arise from the actual presence of an infection include:

- ***Hypothermia*** related to physiological effects of infection
- ***Activity Intolerance*** if the client is fatigued, connected to infusion devices, or in discomfort
- ***Nutrition: Imbalanced, Less Than Body Requirements*** if the client is too ill to eat adequately
- ***Pain, Acute*** if the client is experiencing tissue damage and discomfort
- ***Impaired Social Interaction*** or ***Social Isolation*** if the client is required to be separated from others during a contagious episode
- ***Self-Esteem, Situational Low*** if the client is experiencing negative feelings about self related to the infection process
- ***Anxiety*** if the client is apprehensive regarding changes in life activities resulting from the infection or its treatment, such as absence from work or inability to perform usual functions

Clinical examples of assessment data clusters and related nursing diagnoses are shown in Table 32.5.

TABLE 32.5 Clinical Application: Examples of Assessment Data Clusters and Related Nursing Diagnoses

Data Cluster	Nursing Diagnosis
Kim Bradley, a 40-year-old shipyard worker, is admitted to emergency with a puncture wound in his foot. He reports stepping on a rusty nail that penetrated his shoe. Wound is 6 mm in diameter, unclean, and inflamed with slight serosanguineous discharge. He reports no immunization since childhood.	***Risk for infection*** related to compromised host defence related to lack of immunization (tetanus) and site for organism invasion secondary to trauma
Kuniko Tanaka, 12 years old, has had a diagnosis of chickenpox confirmed and must stay home from school until her lesions are dry. She anticipates "feelings of boredom," missing her friends and school, and in particular, missing her art classes.	***Diversional activity deficient*** related to confinement for communicable disease

Planning

The major goals for clients susceptible to infection are to:

- Maintain or restore defences
- Avoid the spread of infectious organisms
- Reduce or alleviate problems associated with the infection

Desired outcomes depend on the individual client's condition. Examples of desired outcomes, although established in the planning phase, are provided in Table 32.10 in the "Evaluating" section later in this chapter.

Nursing strategies to meet the three broad goals stated above generally include using meticulous medical and surgical aseptic techniques to prevent the spread of potentially infectious microorganisms, implementing measures to support the defences of a susceptible host, and teaching clients about protective measures to prevent infections and the spread of infectious agents when an infection is present.

The Nursing Interventions Classification (NIC) system can be used as a resource to plan nursing interventions (McCloskey & Bulechek, 2000). Examples of NIC interventions related to clients at risk for infection include:

- Environmental management
- Infection control
- Infection protection
- Risk identification
- Teaching: Individual
- Wound care

Specific nursing activities associated with each of these interventions can be selected to meet the individual needs of the client.

Planning for Home Care

Clients being discharged following hospital care for an infection often require continued care to completely eliminate the infection or to adapt to a chronic state. In addition, such clients may be at increased risk for reinfection or development of an opportunistic infection following therapy for existing pathogens.

In preparation for discharge, the nurse needs to know the client's and family's risks, needs, strengths, and resources. The accompanying box describes the specific assessment data required prior to establishing a discharge plan. Using the data gathered about the home situation, the nurse tailors the teaching plan for the client and family. See the accompanying Home Care Teaching Guide below and the Wellness Teaching box that follows.

Implementing

Whenever possible, the nurse invokes strategies to prevent infection. If infection cannot be prevented, the nurse works to prevent the spread of the infection within and between persons and to treat the existing infection. In the sections that follow, specific nursing activities are described that interfere with the chain of infection to prevent and control transmission of infectious organisms and that promote care of the infected client. These activities are summarized in Table 32.6.

Preventing Nosocomial Infections

Meticulous use of medical and surgical asepsis is necessary to prevent transport of potentially infectious microorganisms. As discussed previously in this chapter, nosocomial infections are those acquired in relation to health-care services. Many nosocomial infections can be prevented through the use of proper hand washing, environmental controls, sterile technique when warranted, and identification and management of clients at risk for infections.

Hand Washing

The importance of hand washing in every setting, including hospitals, cannot be overemphasized. It is considered the single most effective infection control measure. Any person may harbour microorganisms that are currently

---

CLIENT TEACHING

Home Care Teaching Guide

Environmental Management

- Discuss injury-proofing the home to prevent the possibility of further tissue injury (e.g., use of padding, handrails, removal of hazards).
- Explore ways to control the environmental temperature and airflow (especially if client has an air-borne pathogen).
- Determine the advisability of visitors and family members in close proximity to the client.
- Describe ways to manipulate the bed, the room, and other household facilities.

Infection Control

- Teach proper hand washing and related hygienic measures to all family members.
- Discuss antimicrobial soaps and effective disinfectants.
- Ensure access to and proper use of gloves and other barriers as indicated by the type of infection or risk.
- Discuss the relationship between hygiene, rest, activity, and nutrition in the chain of infection.
- Instruct about proper administration of medication.

Infection Protection

- Teach the client and family members the signs and symptoms of infection, and when to contact a health-care provider.
- Teach the client and family members how to avoid infections.
- Suggest techniques for safe food preservation and preparation.
- Emphasize the need for current immunizations of all family members.

Wound Care

- Teach the client and family the signs of wound healing and of wound infection.
- Explain the proper technique for changing the dressing and disposing of the soiled one.
- Delineate the factors that promote wound healing.

Referrals

- Provide appropriate information regarding how to access community resources, home care agencies, sources of supplies, and community or public health departments for immunizations.

WELLNESS TEACHING

Preventing Infections in the Home

- Wash your hands before handling foods, before eating, after using the toilet, before and after any required home care treatment, and after touching any body substances (e.g., wound drainage).
- Keep your fingernails short, clean, and well-manicured to eliminate rough edges or hangnails, which can harbour microorganisms.
- Do not share personal care items: toothbrush, wash-cloths, and towels.
- Wash raw fruits and vegetables before eating them.
- Refrigerate all opened and nonpackaged foods.
- Clean used equipment (e.g., emesis basin) with soap and water, and disinfect it with a chlorine bleach solution.
- Place contaminated dressings and other disposable items containing body fluids in moistureproof plastic bags.
- Put used needles in a puncture-resistant container with a screw-top lid. Label so as not to discard in the garbage.
- Clean obviously soiled linen separately from other laundry. Rinse in cold water, wash in hot water, if possible, and add a cup of bleach to the wash.
- Avoid coughing, sneezing, or breathing directly on others. Cover the mouth and nose to prevent the transmission of air-borne microorganisms.
- Be aware of any signs or symptoms of an infection, and report these immediately to your health-care contact person.
- Maintain a sufficient fluid intake to promote urine production and output.

TABLE 32.6 Nursing Interventions That Break the Chain of Infection

Link	Interventions	Rationale
Etiologic agent (microorganism)	Ensure that articles are correctly cleaned and disinfected or sterilized before use.	Correct cleaning, disinfecting, and sterilizing reduce or eliminate microorganisms.
	Educate clients and support persons about appropriate methods to clean, disinfect, and sterilize articles.	Knowledge of ways to reduce or eliminate microorganisms is a step in the direction of gaining compliance with aseptic practices.
Reservoir (source)	Change dressings and bandages when they are soiled or wet.	Moist dressings are ideal environments for microorganisms to grow and multiply.
	Assist clients to carry out appropriate skin and oral hygiene.	Hygienic measures reduce the numbers of resident and transient microorganisms and the likelihood of infection.
	Dispose of damp, soiled linens appropriately.	Damp, soiled linens provide an environment for microorganism growth.
	Dispose of feces and urine in appropriate receptacles.	Urine and feces contain many microorganisms. Feces may also be the source of certain microorganisms, such as the hepatitis A virus, in asymptomatic carriers.
	Ensure that all fluid containers, such as bedside water jugs and suction and drainage bottles, are covered or capped.	Prolonged exposure increases the risk of contamination by air-borne pathogens.
	Empty suction and drainage bottles at the end of each shift or before they become full, or according to agency policy.	Drainage harbours microorganisms that, if left for long periods, proliferate and are at risk of transmission to others.
Portal of exit from the reservoir	Avoid talking, coughing, or sneezing over open wounds or sterile fields, and cover the mouth and nose when coughing and sneezing.	These measures limit the number of microorganisms that escape from the respiratory tract.

TABLE 32.6 Nursing Interventions That Break the Chain of Infection *continued*

Link	Interventions	Rationale
Method of transmission	Wash hands between client contacts; after touching blood, any body fluids, nonintact skin, and mucous membranes; and before performing invasive procedures or touching open wounds. Instruct clients and support persons to wash hands before handling food or eating, after eliminating, and after touching infectious material.	Hand washing is an important means of controlling and preventing the transmission of microorganisms.
	Place discarded soiled materials in moistureproof refuse bags.	Moistureproof bags prevent the spread of microorganisms by capillary action.
	Steadily hold used bedpans away from clothing to prevent spillage, and dispose of urine and feces in appropriate receptacles.	Feces in particular contain many microorganisms.
	Initiate standard practice for ALL clients at ALL times, regardless of their diagnosis or presumed infection status.	All clients may harbour potentially infectious microorganisms that can be transmitted to others.
	Wear masks and eye protection when in close contact with clients who have infections transmitted by droplets from the respiratory tract.	Masks and eyewear reduce the spread of droplet-transmitted microorganisms.
	Wear gloves when handling secretions and excretions. Wear gowns if there is danger of soiling clothing with blood, any body fluids, nonintact skin, and mucous membranes.	Gloves and gowns prevent soiling of the hands and clothing.
	Wear masks and eye protection when sprays of body fluid are possible (e.g., during irrigation procedures).	Masks and eye protection provide protection from microorganisms in clients' blood, body fluids, nonintact skin, and mucous membranes.
Portal of entry to the susceptible host	Use sterile technique (see p. 768) for invasive procedures (e.g., injections, catheterizations).	Invasive procedures penetrate the body's natural protective barriers to microorganisms.
	Use sterile technique when exposing open wounds or handling dressings.	Open wounds are vulnerable to microbial infection.
	Place used disposable needles and syringes in puncture-resistant containers for disposal.	Injuries from needles contaminated by blood or body fluids from an infected client or carrier are a primary cause of hepatitis B virus (HBV) and HIV transmission to health-care workers.
	Provide all clients with their own personal care items.	People have less resistance to another person's microorganisms than to their own.
Susceptible host	Maintain the integrity of the client's skin and mucous membranes.	Intact skin and mucous membranes protect against invasion by microorganisms.
	Ensure that the client receives a balanced diet.	A balanced diet supplies proteins and vitamins necessary to build or maintain body tissues.
	Educate the public about the importance of immunizations.	Immunizations protect people against some infectious diseases.

harmless yet potentially harmful to self or to others *if they find a portal of entry*. As a health-care worker's hands are in continuous contact with patients and their environments, those hands are most at risk for contamination with organisms. Subsequent transfer of the organisms to other patients and health-care personnel, to the environment, or to the health-care worker involved might then occur. It is critical that hands be washed frequently and correctly. An adequate amount of soap, rubbing the hands together to create friction, and ensuring that rinsing occurs under running water are essential components of a hand washing procedure. Procedure 32.1 describes correct hand washing techniques.

Plain soap will successfully remove most transient microbial flora, whereas antimicrobial (antiseptic) soap is

PROCEDURE 32.1 Hand Washing

PURPOSES

- To reduce the number of microorganisms on the hands
- To reduce the risk of transmission of microorganisms to clients
- To reduce the risk of cross-contamination among clients
- To reduce the risk of transmission of infectious organisms to oneself

Equipment

- ❑ Soap
- ❑ Warm running water
- ❑ Hand brush if necessary
- ❑ Disposable towels

INTERVENTION

1. Prepare and assess the hands.

- File the nails short. *Short nails are less likely to harbour microorganisms, scratch a client, or puncture gloves.*
- Remove all jewellery. Some nurses prefer to slide their watches up above their elbows. Others pin the watch to the uniform. *Microorganisms can lodge in the settings of jewellery and under rings on fingers. Removal facilitates proper cleaning of the hands and arms.*
- Check hands for breaks in the skin, such as hangnails or cuts. Use lotions to prevent hangnails and cracked, dry skin. A nurse who has broken skin areas may have to change work assignments or wear gloves for protection.
- Do not apply fingernail polish or artificial nails. Both may harbour microorganisms.

2. Turn on the water, and adjust the flow.

- There are five common types of faucet controls:
  - **a.** Hand-operated handles
  - **b.** Knee levers. Move these with the knee to regulate flow and temperature (Figure 32.2).
  - **c.** Foot pedals. Press these with the foot to regulate flow and temperature (Figure 32.3).
  - **d.** Elbow controls. Move these with the elbows instead of the hands.
  - **e.** Infrared controls. The water runs when motion is detected at a preset distance.
- Adjust the flow so that the water is warm. *Warm water removes less of the protective oil of the skin than does hot water.*

3. Wet the hands thoroughly by holding them under the running water, and apply soap to the hands.

- Hold the hands lower than the elbows so that the water flows from the arms to the fingertips. *The water should flow from the least contaminated to the most contaminated area; the hands are generally considered more contaminated than the lower arms.*

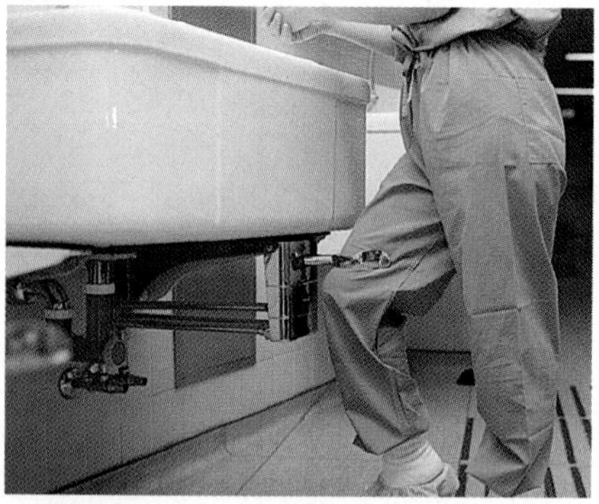

Figure 32.2 A knee-lever faucet control

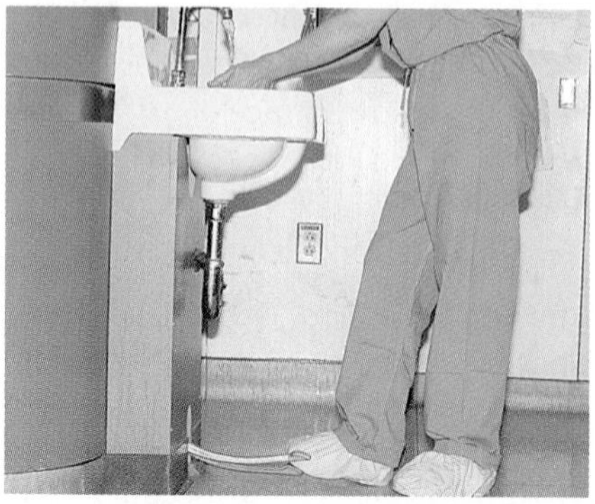

Figure 32.3 A foot-pedal faucet control

- If the soap is liquid, apply 2 to 4 mL (1 tsp). If it is bar soap, rub it firmly between the hands.

4. Thoroughly wash and rinse the hands.

- Using constant friction with brisk rubbing and circular movements, wash the palm, back, and wrist of each hand. Interlace the fingers and thumbs and move the hands back and forth (Figure 32.4), continuing the motion for 15 seconds minimum. *Friction and brisk action helps remove microorganisms mechanically. Interlacing the fingers and thumbs cleans the interdigital spaces.*
- Rinse the hands.
- Wash hands for a minimum of 15 seconds. For a more thorough washing, extend the time for wetting, washing, and rinsing.

Figure 32.4 Interlacing the fingers during hand washing

PROCEDURE 32.1 Hand Washing *continued*

5. **Thoroughly dry the hands and arms.**

- Dry hands and arms thoroughly from fingertips to wrist using a separate paper towel for each arm. *Moist skin becomes chapped readily; chapping produces lesions. Following hand washing, fingertips would be considered cleaner than forearms.*
- Discard each paper towel in the appropriate container.

6. **Turn off the water.**

- Use a dry, clean paper towel to grasp a hand-operated control (Figure 32.5). *This prevents the nurse from picking up microorganisms from the faucet handles.*

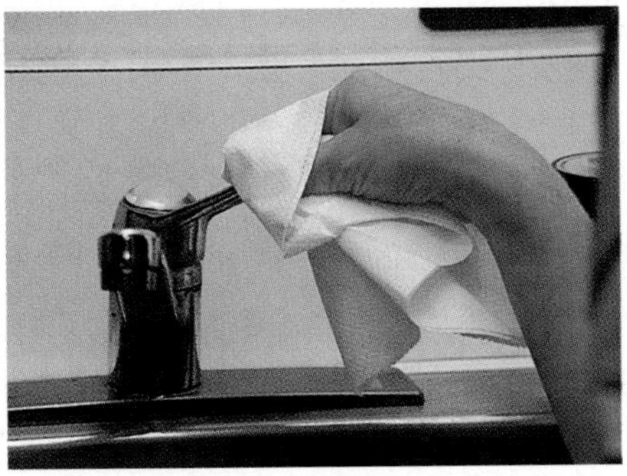

Figure 32.5 Using a paper towel to grasp the handle of a hand-operated faucet

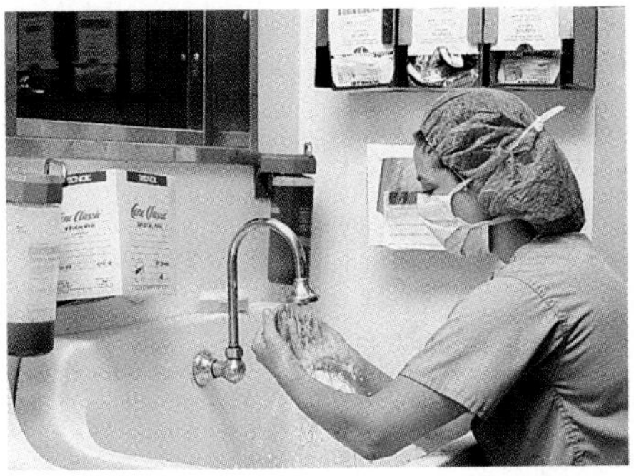

Figure 32.6 The hands are held higher than the elbows during a hand wash before sterile technique

Variation: Hand Washing before Sterile Techniques

- Apply the soap and wash as described in steps 3 and 4, but hold the hands higher than the elbows during this hand wash. Wet the hands and forearms under the running water, letting it run from the fingertips to the elbows so that the hands become cleaner than the elbows. (Figure 32.6). Larson (1996) recommends that at least two minutes of friction be used for surgical hand washing. *In this way, the water runs from the area with the fewest microorganisms to areas with a relatively greater number.*
- After washing and rinsing, use a towel to dry one hand thoroughly in an encircling motion from the fingers to the elbow. Use a clean towel to dry the other hand and arm. *A clean towel prevents the transfer of microorganisms from one elbow (least clean area) to the other hand (cleanest area).*

Home Care Considerations

- Keep fingernails clean, short, and well trimmed.
- Remove all rings from your fingers and your wristwatch. You may leave a plain wedding band in place.
- Wash hands carefully before and after any hands-on care.
- If there is no running water, use commercially available hand washing agents that require no water.
- Use bactericidal soap and paper towels when washing hands.
- Always turn the water off with a dry paper towel.

Children

- Teach young children hand washing as soon as they can actively participate.

designed for use under conditions of heavy microbial soiling or if antimicrobial-resistant organisms are a factor or a possibility. Waterless hand scrub products are available and, in some studies, have demonstrated superior efficacy of performance when compared with plain or antiseptic soaps. The decision as to what product, the amount of soap to use, the frequency of performing hand washing, as well as the actual technique implemented remains with the health-care worker; it is a decision that must be made with an unrelenting conscientious attitude. Clinical guidelines addressing frequency of hand washing are shown in the next box.

CLINICAL GUIDELINES

Recommendations on Hand Washing (LCDC, 1998, revised 1999)

Indications for frequency depend on:

- type, intensity, duration, and sequence of activity
- degree of contamination associated with the contact
- susceptibility to infection of the health-care recipient

Hands must be washed:

- between direct contact with individual patients/residents/clients
- before performing invasive procedures
- before caring for patients in intensive-care units and immunocompromised patients
- after contact with items known or considered likely to be contaminated with blood, body fluids, secretions, or excretions
- between certain procedures on the same patient where soiling of hands is likely, to avoid cross-contamination of body sites
- after situations or procedures in which microbial or blood contamination of hands is likely
- immediately before and after removing gloves
- before preparing, handling, serving or eating food, and before feeding a patient when hands are visibly soiled after personal body functions, e.g., toilet use, blowing one's nose
- whenever the health-care provider is in doubt about the necessity for doing so
- prior to entering the unit/agency at the beginning of a work period and when leaving at the end of a work period

Source: Reproduced from *Canada Communicable Disease Report, 24: Suppl. S8: 1–55*, Health Canada, (1998) © Minister of Public Works and Government Services Canada, 2002.

RESEARCH NOTE

How Do Nurses Determine the Effectiveness of Infection Control Practices?

In this study, the researchers studied the use of a bacteriostatic soap to reduce the nosocomial transmission of methicillin-resistant *Staphylococcus aureus* (MRSA). A neonate was discharged from a hospital nursery after a case of bullous impetigo caused by MRSA. In the next seven weeks, 18 more cases of MRSA were diagnosed in that nursery. The staff implemented a variety of infection control measures to stop the transmission of the organism. These measures included changing the way umbilical cord care and circumcision care were done; and modifying, surveying, and monitoring hand washing, diaper care, use of gloves, use of gowns and linens, and disinfection procedures. In spite of all the measures taken, the infections did not stop.

Finally, a 0.3 percent triclosan soap was tried, to be used in all hand washing and bathing. No further cases of MRSA occurred, and this achievement lasted the subsequent 3½ years leading to publication of the article.

Implications: The use of antimicrobial agents in hand washing and bathing can be effective in eliminating the microorganisms that cause nosocomial infections when other infection control practices have not been successful.

Source: Zafar, A. B., Butler, R. C., Reese, D. J., Gaydos, L. A., & Mennonna, P. A. (June, 1995). Use of 0.3% triclosan (Bacti-Stat) to eradicate an outbreak of methicillin-resistant *Staphylococcus* aureus in a neonatal nursery. *American Journal of Infection Control, 23*, 200–208.

Supporting Defences of a Susceptible Host

People are constantly in contact with microorganisms in the environment. Normally, a person's natural defences ward off the development of an infection. *Susceptibility* is the degree to which an individual can be affected, that is, the likelihood of an organism causing an infection in that person. The following factors affect a person's susceptibility.

Hygiene

Maintaining the intactness of the skin and mucous membranes retains a barrier against microorganisms entering the body. In addition, oral care, including flossing the teeth, reduces the likelihood of an oral infection. Regular and thorough bathing and shampooing remove microorganisms and dirt that can cause an infection.

Nutrition

A balanced diet enhances the health of all body tissues, helps keep the skin intact, and promotes the skin's ability to repel microorganisms. Adequate nutrition enables tissues to maintain and rebuild themselves and helps keep the immune system functioning well.

Fluid

An adequate fluid intake permits a fluid output that flushes out the bladder and urethra, removing microorganisms that could cause an infection.

Rest and Sleep

Adequate rest and sleep are essential to health and to renewing energy. See Chapter 42.

Stress

Excessive stress predisposes people to infections. Nurses can assist clients to learn stress-reducing techniques. See Chapter 47.

Immunizations

Immunizations have dramatically decreased the incidence of infectious diseases. It is recommended that immuniza-

TABLE 32.7 Routine Immunization Schedules for Infants and Children—Canada

Age at Vaccination	DTaP[1]	IPV	Hib[2]	MMR	Td[3] or dTap[10]	Hep B[4] (3 doses)	V	PC	MC
Birth									
2 months	x	x	x					x[8]	x[9]
4 months	x	x	x			infancy		x	x
6 months	x	(x)[5]	x			or		x	x
12 months				x		preadolescence	x[7]	x	
18 months	x	x	x	(x)[6] or		(9–13 years)			or
4–6 years	x	x		(x)[6]					
14–16 years					x[10]				x[9]

DTaP	Diphtheria, tetanus, pertussis (acellular) vaccine
IPV	Inactivated poliovirus vaccine
Hib	*Haemophilus influenzae* type b conjugate vaccine
MMR	Measles, mumps, and rubella vaccine
Td	Tetanus and diphtheria toxoid, adult type with reduced diphtheria toxoid
dTap	Tetanus and diptheria toxoid, acellular pertussis, adolescent/adult type with reduced diptheria and pertussis components
Hep B	Hepatitis B vaccine
V	Varicella
PC	Pneumococcal conjugate vaccine
MC	Meningococcal C conjugate vaccine

Notes:

1. DTaP (diptheria, tetanus, acellular or component pertussis) vaccine is the perferred vaccine for all doses in the vaccination series, including completion of the series in children who have received ≥1 dose of DPT (whole cell) vaccine.
2. Hib schedule shown is for PRP-T or HbOC vaccine. If using PRP-OMP, give at 2, 4, and 12 months of age.
3. Td (tetanus and diphtheria toxoid), a combined absorbed "adult type" preparation for use in people ≥7 years of age, contains less diphtheria toxoid than preparations given to younger children and is less likely to cause reactions in older people.
4. Hepatitis B vaccine can be routinely given to infants or preadolescents, depending on the provincial/territorial policy; three doses at 0-, 1-, and 6-month intervals are preferred. The second dose should be administered at least 1 month after the first dose, and the third at least 2 months after the second dose. A two-dose schedule for adolescents is also possible.
5. This dose is not needed routinely, but can be included for convenience.
6. A second dose of MMR is recommended, at least 1 month after the first dose, for the purpose of better measles protection. For convenience, options include giving it with the next scheduled vaccination at 18 months of age, or with school entry (4–6 years) vaccinations (depending on the provincial/territorial policy), or at any intervening age that is practicable. The need for a second dose of mumps and rubella vaccine is not established but may benefit (given for convenience as MMR). The second dose of MMR should be given at the same visit as DTaP IPV (± HIB) to ensure high uptake rates.
7. Children aged 12 months to 12 years should receive one dose of varicella vaccine. Individuals ≥ 13 years of age should receive two doses at leasts 28 days apart.
8. Recommended schedule, number of doses, and subsequent use of 23 valent polysaccharide pneumococcal vaccine depend on the age of the child when vaccination is begun for specific recommendations).
9. Recommended schedule and number of doses of meningococcal vaccine depends on the age of the child for specific recommendations).
10. dTap adult formulation with reduced diptheria toxoid and pertussis component.

Source: *Canadian Immunization Guide* (6th ed., 2002). © Minister of Public Works and Government Services Canada, 2002.

Note: There are provincial and territorial variations to this immunization schedule.

tions begin shortly after birth and be completed in early childhood, except for boosters. See Tables 32.7 and 32.8 for recommended immunizations. Immunizations may be given by injection, inhalation, oral solutions, or nasal sprays. They are frequently given in combination to minimize multiple injections. Because there are frequent changes to immunization schedules, it is advisable to update immunization schedules yearly. The information can be obtained in Canada from the Health Canada National Advisory Committee on Immunization. Similar committees exist in other countries, including the United States, Australia, and the United Kingdom, and as part of the World Health Organization.

There are also immunization programs for high-risk groups, such as health-care personnel, older adults who are chronically ill, and people travelling, each requiring individual assessment. In view of the increased risk of exposure to communicable diseases, the following vaccines are recommended for all health-care workers and others providing personal care: diphtheria, tetanus toxoid, measles, polio, rubella, hepatitis B, influenza, and, in specific risk situations, hepatitis A and the Bacillus of Calmette and Guerin (BCG).

TABLE 32.8 Routine Immunization for Adults—Canada

Vaccine or Toxoid	Indication	Further Doses
Diphtheria (adult preparation)	All adults	Every 10 years, preferably given with tetanus toxoid (Td)
Tetanus	All adults	Every 10 years, preferably given as Td
Influenza	Adults ≥65 years; adults <65 years at high risk of influenza-related complications	Every year using current vaccine formulation
Pneumococcal	Adults ≥65 years; conditions with increased risk of pneumococcal diseases	None usually
Measles	All adults born in 1970 or later who are susceptible to measles	Preferably given as MMR
Rubella	Susceptible women of childbearing age and health-care workers	May be given as MMR
Mumps	Adults born in 1970 or later with no history of mumps	May be given as MMR

Source: *Canadian Immunization Guide* (6th ed., 2002). © Minister Public Works and Government Services Canada, 2002.

Cleaning, Disinfecting, and Sterilizing

The first links in the chain, the etiologic agent and the reservoir, are interrupted by the use of **antiseptics** (antimicrobial agent that removes both transient and resident flora on living tissue, e.g., skin), **disinfectants** (agents that destroy pathogens other than spores), and by sterilization.

Cleaning

Cleanliness inhibits the growth of microorganisms. When cleaning visibly soiled objects, nurses must always wear gloves to avoid direct contact with infectious microorganisms. Most objects used in the care of clients, whether forceps or drawsheets, can be cleaned by rinsing them in cold water to remove any organic material, washing them with hot soapy water, then rinsing them again to remove the soap. The following steps should be followed when cleaning objects in a hospital or in a home:

1. Rinse the article with cold water to remove organic material. Hot water coagulates the protein of organic material and tends to make it adhere. Examples of organic material are blood and pus.
2. Wash the article in hot water and soap. The emulsifying action of soap reduces surface tension and facilitates the removal of dirt. Washing dislodges the emulsified dirt.
3. Use an abrasive, such as a stiff-bristled brush, to clean equipment with grooves and corners. Friction helps dislodge foreign material.
4. Rinse the article well with warm to hot water.
5. Dry the article. It is now considered clean.
6. Clean the brush and sink. These are considered soiled until they are cleaned appropriately, usually with a disinfectant.

Disinfecting

A disinfectant is a chemical preparation, such as phenol or iodine compounds, used on inanimate objects. Disinfectants are frequently caustic and toxic to tissues. An antiseptic is a chemical preparation used on skin or tissue. Disinfectants and antiseptics often have similar chemical components, but the disinfectant is a more concentrated solution.

Both antiseptics and disinfectants are said to have bactericidal or bacteriostatic properties. A *bactericidal* preparation destroys bacteria, whereas a *bacteriostatic* preparation prevents the growth and reproduction of some bacteria.

When disinfecting articles, nurses need to follow agency protocol, manufacturer recommendations, and also consider the following:

1. The type and number of infectious organisms. Some microorganisms are readily destroyed, whereas others require longer contact with the disinfectant.
2. The recommended concentration of the disinfectant and the duration of contact.
3. The temperature of the environment. Most disinfectants are intended for use at room temperature.
4. The presence of soap. Some disinfectants are ineffective in the presence of soap or detergent.
5. The presence of organic materials. The presence of saliva, blood, pus, or excretions can readily inactivate many disinfectants.
6. The surface areas to be treated. The disinfecting agent must come into contact with all surfaces and areas.

Sterilizing

Sterilization is a process that destroys *all* microorganisms, including spores and viruses.

Four commonly used methods of sterilization are moist heat, gas, boiling water, and radiation.

Moist Heat For sterilizing, moist heat (steam) can be employed in two ways: as steam under pressure or as free steam. Steam under pressure attains temperatures higher than the boiling point. Autoclaves supply steam under pressures of 6.8 to 7.7 kg and temperatures of 121° to 123°C.

Free steam, 100°C, is used to sterilize objects that would be destroyed at the higher temperature and pressure of the autoclave. Usually, it is necessary to steam the article for 30 minutes on three consecutive days. The intervals are required so that unkilled spores will return to their vegetative state and again become vulnerable to the heat.

Gas Ethylene oxide gas destroys microorganisms by interfering with their metabolic processes. It is also effective against spores. Its advantages are good penetration and effectiveness for heat-sensitive items. Its major disadvantage is its toxicity to humans.

Boiling Water This is the most practical and inexpensive method for sterilizing in the home. The main disadvantage is that spores and some viruses are not killed by this method. The water temperature rises no higher than 100°C. Boiling a minimum of 15 minutes is advised for disinfection of articles in the home.

Radiation Both ionizing and nonionizing radiation can be used for disinfection and sterilization. Ultraviolet light, a type of nonionizing radiation, can be used for disinfection. Its main drawback is that the ultraviolet rays do not penetrate deeply. Ionizing radiation is used effectively in industry to sterilize foods, drugs, and other items that are sensitive to heat. Its main advantage is that it is effective for items difficult to sterilize; its chief disadvantage is that the equipment is very expensive.

Nurses should be familiar with the cleaning, disinfecting, and sterilizing protocols of the agency in which they practice.

Isolation Precautions

The history of Canada's isolation guidelines, under the guidance of the Laboratory Centre for Disease Control (LCDC), parallels that of the United States' Centers for Disease Control and Prevention (CDC).

Isolation refers to measures designed to prevent the spread of infections or potentially infectious microorganisms to health personnel, clients, and visitors. A variety of infection control measures are used to decrease the risk of transmission of microorganisms in hospitals.

In the early 1990s, isolation guidelines were established that allowed health facilities to choose between two systems: category-specific or disease-specific isolation.

Category-specific isolation precautions were based on the presumed major mechanism of transmission and included seven categories: (1) strict isolation, (2) contact isolation, (3) respiratory isolation, (4) tuberculosis isolation, (5) enteric precautions, (6) drainage/secretions precautions, and (7) blood/body fluid precautions.

Disease-specific isolation precautions provided precautions for specific diseases. These precautions delineated use of private rooms with special ventilation, having the client share a room with other clients infected with the same organism, and gowning to prevent gross soilage of clothes for specific infectious diseases.

In 1987, the CDC and LCDC presented recommendations (revised in 1988) for *universal precautions (UP)* on *all clients* to decrease the risk of transmitting unidentified pathogens. Universal precautions apply to those body fluids associated with *blood-borne pathogens*, namely, hepatitis B virus, hepatitis C virus, and HIV. This includes blood and other body fluids containing visible blood. The recommendation did not imply that universal precautions replace disease-specific or category-specific precautions but that they be used in conjunction with them.

The *body substance isolation* (BSI) system, introduced in the early 1990s, employs generic infection control precautions for *all* clients, except those with the few diseases transmitted through the air. The body substance isolation system, conceptualized in 1984 (Jackson & Lynch, 1984), is a system based on three premises:

1. All people have an increased risk for infection from microorganisms placed on their mucous membranes and nonintact skin.
2. All people are likely to have potentially infectious microorganisms in all of their moist body sites and substances.
3. An unknown portion of clients and health-care workers will always be colonized or infected with potentially infectious microorganisms in their blood and other moist body sites and substances.

The term *body substance* includes not only blood and some body fluids but also urine, feces, wound drainage, oral secretions, and any other body substance. Barrier precautions address the activity performed as opposed to the diagnosis.

A two-tiered system evolved in the mid-1990s that selected the best recommendations from all previous work into Standard Precautions (SP) and three categories of Transmission-Based Precautions. This framework is directed at acute-care facilities and does not address specific needs of long-term care, ambulatory care, and home care agencies. To this end, LCDC advocates the term "Routine Practices" in place of "Standard Precautions" to emphasize the need to apply precautions to all patients, no matter the venue of health care. Their 1999 guidelines provide recommendations that include these settings, as well as address prevention of transmission of tuberculosis, blood-borne pathogens, hemorrhagic fevers, and vancomycin-resistant enterococci (VRE).

In addition to precautions discussed in this chapter, significant emphasis is placed on avoiding injury due to sharp instruments, measures to be taken in case of exposure to blood-borne pathogens, and communication of biohazards to employees. Health Canada requires that Workplace Hazardous Materials Information System (WHMIS) labels be affixed to containers of regulated waste and to refrigerators and freezers containing blood or other potentially infectious materials. The labels required are fluorescent orange or orange-red and feature the biohazard symbol shown in Figure 32.7.

LCDC Isolation Precautions (1999)

The LCDC presented new guidelines for isolation precautions in hospitals in 1999. These guidelines designate two tiers of precautions:

Tier 1: Standard Precautions

Tier 2: Transmission-Based Precautions

Standard Precautions (Routine Practices)

These precautions are used in the care of all hospitalized persons regardless of their diagnosis or possible infection status. They apply to blood, all body fluids, secretions, and excretions (*except sweat*), nonintact skin, and mucous membranes whether or not blood is present or visible.

Thus, they combine the major features of UP (universal precautions) and BSI (body substance isolation). Recommended practices for Standard Precautions are shown in the box opposite.

Transmission-Based Precautions

These precautions are used in addition to Standard Precautions for clients with *known* or *suspected* infections that are spread in one of three ways: by air-borne transmission, droplet transmission, or by contact. The three types of transmission-based precautions may be used alone or in combination but always *in addition* to Standard Precautions. They encompass all the conditions or diseases previously listed in the category-specific or disease-specific classifications. Recommended practices for Transmission-Based Precautions are shown in the following box.

Air-Borne Precautions are used for clients known or suspected to have serious illnesses transmitted by air-borne droplet nuclei smaller than 5 microns. Examples of such illnesses include measles (rubeola); varicella (including disseminated zoster); and tuberculosis.

Droplet Precautions are used for clients known or suspected to have serious illnesses transmitted by particle droplets larger than 5 microns. Examples of such illnesses are diphtheria (pharyngeal); pertussis; mumps; rubella; influenza, pneumonia, or scarlet fever in infants and young children; and pneumonic plague.

Contact Precautions are used for clients known or suspected to have serious illnesses easily transmitted by direct client contact or by contact with items in the client's environment. Such illnesses include gastrointestinal, respiratory, skin, or wound infections or colonization with multidrug-resistant bacteria; specific enteric infections, such as *Clostridium difficile*, and enterohemorrhagic *Escherichia coli*, *Shigella*, and hepatitis A in diapered or incontinent clients; respiratory syncytial virus, parainfluenza virus, or enteroviral infections in infants and young children; and highly contagious skin infections, such as herpes simplex virus, impetigo, pediculosis, and scabies.

In addition to the preceding precautions, additional measures may be used for specific communicable diseases such as vancomycin-resistant entercocci (VRE) and Sudden Acute Respiratory Syndrome (SARS).

Figure 32.7 Biohazard infectious materials

Source: Health Canada. Workplace Hazardous Materials Information System. http://www.hc-sc.gc.ca/hecs-sesc/whmis/whmis_symbols.htm

Compromised Clients

Compromised clients (those highly susceptible to infection) are often infected by their own microorganisms, by microorganisms on the inadequately washed hands of health-care personnel, and by nonsterile items (food, water, air, and client-care equipment). Clients who are severely compromised include those who:

- Have diseases, such as leukemia, that depress the client's resistance to infectious organisms.
- Have extensive skin impairments, such as severe dermatitis or major burns that cannot be effectively covered with dressings.

Guidelines for severely compromised (immunocompromised) clients include the use of Standard Precautions as described earlier.

Isolation Practices

Initiation of practices to prevent the transmission of microorganisms is generally a nursing responsibility and is based on a comprehensive assessment of the client.

Recommended Isolation Precautions in Hospitals (LCDC, 1999)

Standard Precautions "Routine Practices" (Tier One)

- Designed for *all* clients in hospital.
- These precautions apply to blood; all body fluids, excretions, and secretions except sweat; nonintact (broken) skin; and mucous membranes.
- Designed to reduce risk of transmission of microorganisms from recognized and unrecognized sources.

1. Wash hands after contact with blood, body fluids, secretions, excretions, nonintact skin, mucous membranes, and contaminated objects whether or not gloves are worn. Hands are washed between client contacts.
   a. Wash hands immediately after removing gloves.
   b. Use a plain soap for routine hand washing.
   c. Use an antimicrobial agent or an antiseptic agent for the control of specific outbreaks of infection.
2. Wear clean gloves when touching blood, body fluids, secretions, excretions, nonintact skin and mucous membranes, and contaminated items (e.g., soiled gowns).
   a. Clean gloves can be unsterile unless their use is intended to prevent the entrance of microorganisms into the body. See the discussion of sterile gloves in this chapter.
   b. Remove gloves before touching noncontaminated items and surfaces.
   c. Wash hands immediately after removing gloves.
3. Wear a mask, eye protection, or a face shield if splashes or sprays of blood, body fluids, secretions, or excretions can be expected.
4. Wear a clean, nonsterile gown if client care is likely to result in splashes or sprays of blood, body fluids, secretions, or excretions. The gown is intended to protect clothing.
   a. Remove a soiled gown carefully to avoid the transfer of microorganisms to others (i.e., clients or other health-care workers, or self).
   b. Wash hands after removing gown.
5. Handle client care equipment that is soiled with blood, body fluids, secretions, or excretions carefully to prevent the transfer of microorganisms to others and to the environment.
   a. Make sure reusable equipment is cleaned and reprocessed correctly.
   b. Dispose of single-use equipment correctly.
6. Handle, transport, and process linen that is soiled with blood, body fluids, secretions, or excretions in a manner to prevent contamination of clothing and the transfer of microorganisms to others and to the environment.
7. Prevent injuries from used scalpels, needles, or other equipment, and place in puncture-resistant containers.

Transmission-Based Precautions (Tier Two)

Air-borne Precautions

Use the Standard Precautions as well as the following:

1. Place client in a private room that has negative air pressure, six to nine air changes per hour, and either discharge of air to the outside or a filtration system for the room air. Keep doors closed.
2. If a private room is not available, place client with another client who is infected with the same microorganism.
3. Wear a respiratory device (N95 respirator) when entering the room of a client who is known or suspected of having primary tuberculosis.
4. Susceptible people should not enter the room of a client who has rubella (measles) or varicella (chickenpox). If they must enter, they should wear a respirator.
5. Limit movement of client outside the room to essential purposes. Place a surgical mask on the client during transport.
6. Wash hands after removing respiratory device.

Droplet Precautions

Use the Standard Precautions as well as the following:

1. Place client in private room.
2. If a private room is not available, place client with another client who is infected with the same microorganism.
3. Wear a mask if working within 1 metre of the client.
4. Limit movement of client outside the room to essential purposes. Place a surgical mask on the client during transport.
5. Wash hands after removing mask.

Contact Precautions

Use the Standard Precautions as well as the following:

1. Place client in private room.
2. If a private room is not available, place client with another client who is infected with the same microorganism.

Recommended Isolation Precautions in Hospitals (LCDC, 1999) *continued*

3. Wear gloves on entering patient's room.
   a. Change gloves after contact with infectious material.
   b. Remove gloves before leaving client's room.
   c. Use an antimicrobial agent to wash hands immediately after removing gloves.
   d. After hand washing, do not touch possibly contaminated surfaces or items in the room.
4. Wear a gown (see Standard Precautions) when entering a room if there is a possibility of contact with infected surfaces or items, or if the client is incontinent, has diarrhea, a colostomy, or wound drainage not contained by a dressing.
   a. Remove gown in the client's room.
   b. Make sure uniform does not contact possible contaminated surfaces.
5. Limit movement of client outside the room.
6. Dedicate the use of noncritical client care equipment to a single client or to clients with the same infecting microorganisms.

Source: Reproduced from *Canada Communicable Disease Report, 25: Suppl. S4: 1–55*, Health Canada, (1999) © Minister of Public Works and Government Services Canada, 2002.

This assessment takes into account the status of the client's normal defence mechanisms, the client's ability to implement necessary precautions, and the source and mode of transmission of the infectious agent. The nurse then decides whether to wear gloves, gowns, masks, or protective eyewear. In all client situations, nurses must *wash their hands before and after giving care.*

In addition to the precautions cited within this chapter, the nurse implements aseptic precautions when performing many specific therapies discussed throughout this book. The following are some examples:

- Use strict aseptic technique when performing any invasive procedure (e.g., inserting an intravenous needle or catheter, suctioning an airway, and inserting a urinary catheter) and when changing surgical dressings.
- Handle needles and syringes carefully to avoid needlestick injuries. See Chapter 28.
- Change intravenous tubing and solution containers according to agency policy (e.g., every 48 to 72 hours). See Chapter 40.
- Check all sterile supplies for expiry date and intact packaging.
- Prevent urinary infections by maintaining a closed urinary drainage system with a downward flow of urine. Do not irrigate a catheter unless ordered to do so. Provide regular catheter and perineal care. Keep the drainage bag and spout off the floor. See Chapter 36.
- Implement measures to prevent impaired skin integrity (see Chapter 37) and to prevent accumulation of secretions in the lungs (for example, encourage the client to move, breathe deeply, and cough at least every two hours).

Personal Protective Equipment

Gloves

Gloves are worn for three reasons. First, they protect the hands when the nurse is likely to handle any body substances, for example, blood, urine, feces, sputum, mucous membranes, and nonintact skin. Second, gloves reduce the likelihood of nurses' transmitting their own endogenous microorganisms to individuals receiving care. Nurses who have open sores or cuts on the hands must wear gloves for protection. Third, gloves reduce the chance that the nurse's hands will transmit microorganisms from one client or a fomite to another client. In all situations, gloves are changed between client contacts. The hands are washed each time gloves are removed for two primary reasons: (1) the gloves may have imperfections or be damaged during wearing so that they could allow microorganism entry, and (2) the hands may become contaminated during glove removal. For most activities, disposable *clean* gloves are used. No special technique is required to don clean disposable gloves.

If a gown is worn, the nurse pulls the gloves up to cover the cuffs of the gown. If a gown is not worn, the nurse pulls up the cuffs to cover the wrists. Sterile gloves are used when the hand will come in contact with an open wound or when the hands might introduce microorganisms into a body orifice which is normally considered sterile (see Procedure 32.3 on p. 774–775).

To remove the gloves, the nurse follows the steps in the box on the next page.

Many of the gloves used in infection control are made of latex rubber, as are various other items used in health care (catheters, blood pressure cuffs, rubber sheets, intravenous tubing, stockings and binders, adhesive bandages, and dental dams). As a result of the frequent use of gloves, health-care workers and clients with chronic illnesses have increasingly reported allergic reactions to latex. In addition, latex gloves lubricated by powder or cornstarch are particularly allergenic because the latex allergen adheres to the powder, which is aerosolized during glove use and inhaled by the user. Latex gloves that are labelled "hypoallergenic" still contain measurable latex and should not be used by or on persons with known latex sensitivity. The people at greatest risk for

CLINICAL GUIDELINES

Removing Disposable Gloves

- Remove the first glove by grasping it on its palmar surface well below the cuff, taking care to touch only glove to glove (Figure 32.8). This keeps the soiled parts of the used gloves from touching the skin of the wrist or hand. ("glove to glove")
- Pull the first glove completely off by inverting or rolling the glove inside out.
- Continue to hold the inverted removed glove by the fingers of the remaining gloved hand. Place the first two fingers of the bare hand inside the cuff of the second glove (Figure 32.9). Touching the outside of the second soiled glove with the bare hand is avoided. ("skin to skin")
- Pull the second glove off to the fingers by turning it inside out. This pulls the first glove inside the second glove. The soiled part of the glove is folded to the inside to reduce the chance of transferring any microorganisms by direct contact.
- Using the bare hand, continue to remove the second glove, which is now inside out, and dispose of the gloves in the refuse container (Figure 32.10).
- Wash hands.

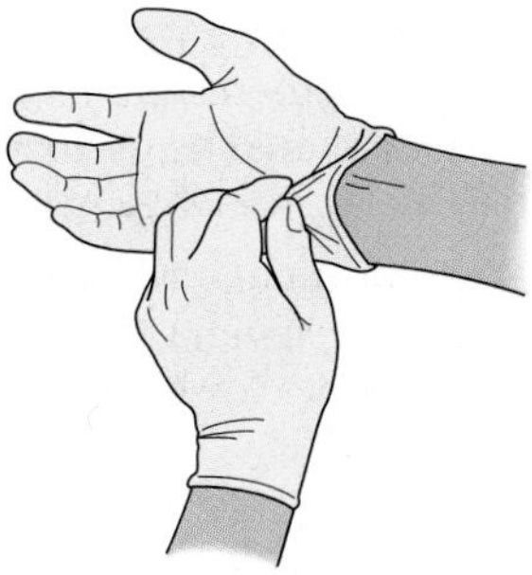

Figure 32.8 Plucking the palmar surface below the cuff of a contaminated glove

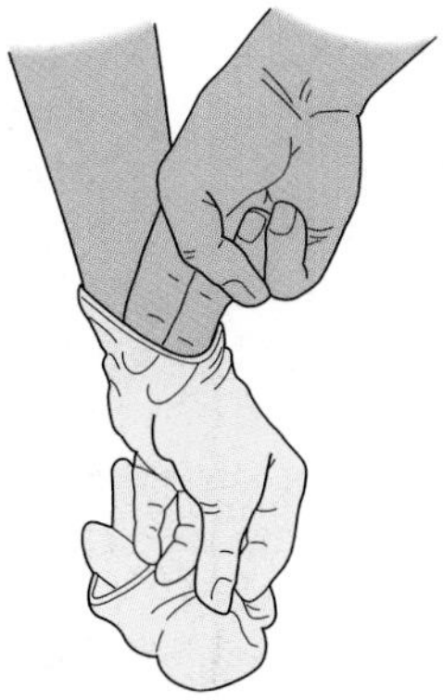

Figure 32.9 Inserting fingers to remove the second contaminated glove

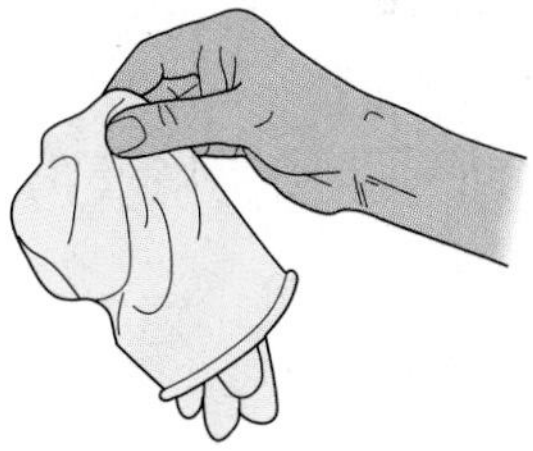

Figure 32.10 Holding contaminated gloves, which are inside out

developing latex allergies are those with other allergic conditions and those who have had frequent or long-term exposure to latex.

Latex allergies can be either local or systemic and may take the form of dermatitis, urticaria (hives), bronchospasm, or anaphylaxis. Clients and health-care workers should be assessed for possible allergies through thorough history taking. Ask clients if they have had any adverse reactions to such items as balloons, condoms, and dishwashing or utility gloves. Strategies to avoid sensitization or exposure to latex include use of nonlatex products, nonlatex barriers between latex products and the skin, and gloves that are unpowdered. People with significant allergies should have no contact with latex products. Health-care agencies are striving to provide alternatives to latex equipment and supplies.

Gowns

Clean or disposable impervious (water-resistant) gowns or plastic aprons are worn during procedures when the nurse's uniform is likely to become soiled. *Single-use gown technique* (using a gown only once before it is discarded or laundered) is the usual practice in health-care agencies. After the gown is worn, the nurse discards it (if it is paper) or places it in a laundry hamper. Before leaving the client's room, the nurse makes sure that hands are washed.

Sterile gowns may be indicated when the nurse changes the dressings of a client with extensive wounds (e.g., burns).

Always assume a gown worn for protection is contaminated. Guidelines for donning and removal of gowns are shown in the next box.

Face Masks

Masks are worn to reduce the risk for transmission of organisms by droplet contact and airborne routes and by splatters of body substances. The CDC recommends that masks be worn under the following conditions:

- Only by those close to the client if the infection (e.g., measles, mumps, or acute respiratory diseases in children) is transmitted by large-particle aerosols (droplets). Large-particle aerosols are transmitted by close contact and generally travel short distances (about 1 m).

CLINICAL GUIDELINES

Gowning

Donning a Clean Gown

- Pick up a clean gown, and allow it to unfold in front of you without allowing the inside of the gown to touch any area visibly soiled with body substances.
- Fasten the ties at the neck to keep the gown in place.
- Overlap the gown at the back as much as possible, and fasten the waist ties or belt (Figure 32.11). Overlapping securely covers the uniform at the back. Waist ties keep the gown from falling away from the body and prevent inadvertent soiling of the uniform.

Removing a Gown after Use

- Remove gloves, wash hands.
- Avoid touching soiled parts on the outside of the gown, if possible. The top part of the gown may be soiled, for example, if you have been holding an infant with a respiratory infection.
- Roll up the gown with the soiled part inside, and discard it in the appropriate container.

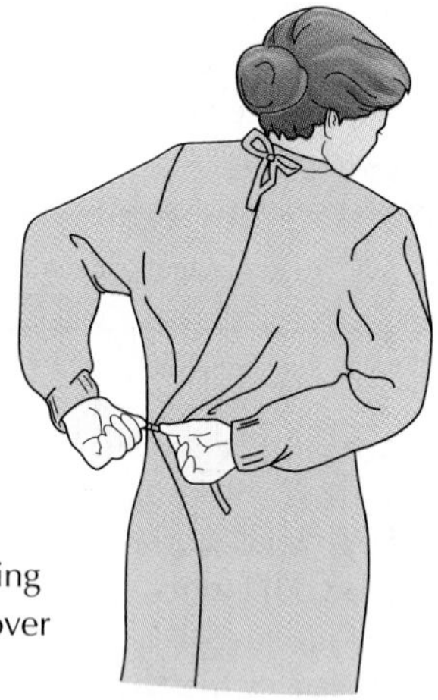

Figure 32.11 Overlapping the gown at the back to cover the nurse's uniform

CLINICAL GUIDELINES

Using Disposable Masks

- Apply the mask, touching only the strings.
- Ensure that the mask covers the mouth and the nose because air moves into and out of both.
- If the mask has a metal strip, adjust this firmly over the bridge of the nose. A secure fit prevents both the escape and the inhalation of microorganisms around the edges of the mask and the fogging of eyeglasses.
- If glasses are worn, fit the upper edge of the mask under the glasses. Keeping the edge of the mask under the glasses helps prevent them from clouding.
- Avoid unnecessary talking and, if possible, sneezing or coughing when caring for an at-risk client (e.g., when exposing an open wound).
- Wear the mask only once, and do not wear any mask longer than the manufacturer recommends or once it becomes wet. A mask should be used only once because it becomes ineffective when moist.
- When removing a mask with strings, first untie the *lower* strings of the mask. This prevents the top part of the mask from falling onto the chest. Do not undo one set of strings and leave the mask hanging around the neck.
- Discard a disposable mask in the waste container touching only the strings.
- Wash hands.

- By all persons entering the room if the infection (e.g., pulmonary tuberculosis) is transmitted by small-particle aerosols (droplet nuclei). Small-particle aerosols remain suspended in the air and, thus, travel greater distances by air. Special masks that provide a tighter face seal and better filtration may be used for these infections.

Various types of masks differ in their filtration effectiveness and fit. Single-use disposable surgical masks are effective for use while the nurse provides care to most clients but should be changed if they become wet or soiled. These masks are discarded in the waste container after use. Disposable particulate respirators of different types *may* be effective for droplet transmission, splatters, and air-borne microorganisms. Some respirators now available are effective in preventing inhalation of tuberculin organisms.

During certain techniques requiring surgical asepsis (sterile technique), masks are worn (1) to prevent droplet contact transmission of exhaled microorganisms to the sterile field or to a client's open wound, and (2) to protect the nurse from splashes of body substances from the client.

Because the effectiveness of disposable masks and respirators against air-borne microorganisms is questionable, *susceptible* caregivers are usually not assigned to clients with the specific air-borne disease in question. However, caregivers who are immune to specific diseases (e.g., chickenpox, tuberculosis, measles, mumps, and rubella) can provide care to clients with these diseases. Guidelines for donning and removing face masks are shown in the box above.

Eyewear

Protective eyewear (goggles, glasses, or face shields) and masks may be indicated in situations where body substances may splatter the face. Figure 32.12 shows an eye shield and mask.

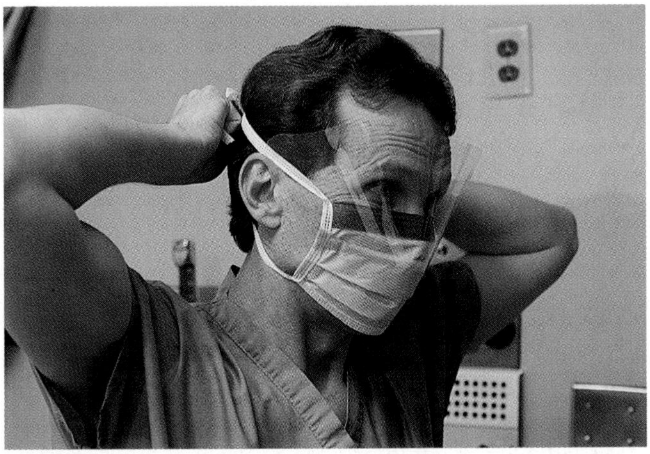

Figure 32.12 A face mask and eye protection covering the nose, mouth, and eyes

Disposal of Soiled Equipment and Supplies

Many pieces of equipment are supplied for single use only and are disposed of after use. Some items, however, are reusable. Agencies have specific policies and procedures for handling soiled equipment (e.g., disposal, cleaning, disinfecting, and sterilizing); the nurse needs to be familiar with these practices. Appropriate handling of soiled equipment and supplies is essential for these reasons:

- To prevent inadvertent exposure of health-care workers to articles contaminated with body substances
- To prevent contamination of the environment

See the box below for removing soiled personal protective equipment. For information about cleaning, disinfecting, and sterilizing, see pages 760–761 earlier in this chapter.

Bagging Most articles do not need to be placed in bags unless they are contaminated, or likely to have been contaminated, with infective material, such as pus, blood, body fluids, feces, or respiratory secretions. Contaminated articles need to be enclosed in a sturdy bag impervious to microorganisms before removal from the client's room. Some agencies use labels or bags of a particular colour that designate them as infective wastes.

LCDC guidelines recommend the following methods:

- A single bag, if it is sturdy and impervious to microorganisms, and if the contaminated articles can be placed in the bag without soiling or contaminating its outside
- Double-bagging if the above conditions are not met

Follow agency protocol, or use the following LCDC guidelines to handle and bag soiled items:

- Place garbage and soiled *disposable* equipment, including dressings and tissues, in the plastic bag that lines the waste container. Some agencies separate dry and wet waste material and incinerate dry items, such as paper towels and disposable items. No special precautions are required for disposable equipment that is not contaminated.
- Place *nondisposable* or *reusable* equipment that is visibly soiled in a labelled bag before removing it from the client's room or cubicle, and send it to a central processing area for decontamination. Some agencies may require that glass and metal items be placed in separate bags from rubber and plastic items. Glass and metal can be sterilized in an autoclave, but rubber and plastic are damaged by this process and must be cleaned by other methods, such as gas sterilization.
- Disassemble *special procedure trays* into component parts. Some components are disposable; others need to be sent to the laundry or central services for cleaning and decontaminating.
- Bag soiled *clothing* before sending it home or to the agency laundry.

Linens Handle soiled linen as little as possible and with minimal manipulation before placing it in the laundry hamper. This prevents gross microbial contamination of the air and persons handling the linen. Close the bag before sending it to the laundry in accordance with agency protocol.

Laboratory Specimens Laboratory specimens, if placed in a leakproof container with a secure lid, need no special precautions. Use care when collecting specimens to avoid contaminating the outside of the container. Containers that are visibly contaminated on the outside should be placed inside a sealable plastic bag before sending them to the laboratory. This prevents personnel from having hand contact with potentially infective material.

Dishes Dishes require no special precautions. Soiling of dishes can largely be prevented by encouraging clients to

---

CLINICAL GUIDELINES

Removing Soiled Personal Protective Equipment

- Remove gloves first, as they are the most soiled. If wearing a gown that is tied at the waist in front, undo the ties before removing gloves.
- Wash hands.
- Remove the eyewear.
- Holding it by the strings, remove the mask.
- Remove the gown.
- Use gown, gloves, and masks only once; discard in appropriate receptacle immediately upon removal.

wash their hands before eating. Some agencies use paper dishes for convenience, which are disposed of in the refuse container.

Blood Pressure Equipment Blood pressure equipment needs no special precautions unless it becomes contaminated with infective material. If it does become contaminated, follow agency practice. Cleaning procedures vary according to whether it is a wall or portable unit.

Thermometers Nondisposable used thermometers are generally disinfected after use. Check agency practice.

Disposable Needles, Syringes, and Sharps Place needles, syringes, and "sharps" (e.g., lancets, scalpels, and broken glass) into a puncture-resistant container. To avoid puncture wounds, do not detach needles from the syringe or recap the needle before disposal. See Chapter 28, page 634, for preventing needle-stick injuries.

Toys Personal toys that are visibly contaminated are bagged and sent home. Agency toys, if visibly soiled, may require cleaning. Check agency practice. Depending on the type of microorganism and its transmission and the child's hygiene behaviours, special precautions may be required. For example, a child who has an enteric infection that may be spread by contact transmission or by fomites may not be allowed to share toys with others.

Transporting Clients with Infections

Transporting clients with infections outside their own rooms is avoided unless absolutely necessary. If a client must be moved, the nurse implements appropriate measures to prevent soilage of the environment. For example, the nurse ensures that any draining wound is securely covered or places a surgical mask on the client who has an airborne infection. In addition, the nurse notifies personnel at the receiving area of any infection risk so that they can maintain necessary precautions. Follow agency protocol.

Psychosocial Needs of Isolation Clients

Clients requiring isolation precautions can develop several problems as a result of the separation from others and of the special precautions taken in their care. Two of the most common are sensory deprivation and decreased self-esteem related to feelings of inferiority. *Sensory deprivation* occurs when the environment lacks normal stimuli for the client, for example, communication with others. Nurses should, therefore, be alert to common clinical signs of sensory deprivation: boredom, inactivity, slowness of thought, daydreaming, increased sleeping, thought disorganization, anxiety, hallucinations, and panic.

Chapter 46 provides information on the development of self-esteem and self-esteem disturbances. A client's *feeling of inferiority* can be due to the perception of the infection itself or to the required precautions. In North America, many people place a high value on cleanliness, and the idea of being "soiled," "contaminated," or "dirty" can give clients the feeling that they are at fault and substandard. Although this is inaccurate, the infected persons may feel "not as good" as others and blame themselves.

Nurses need to provide care that prevents these two problems or that deals with them positively. Nursing interventions include the following:

- Assess the individual's need for stimulation.
- Initiate measures to help meet the need, including regular communication with the client and diversionary activities, such as toys for a child and books, television, or radio for an adult; provide a variety of foods to stimulate the client's sense of taste; stimulate the client's visual sense by providing a view or an activity to watch.
- Explain the infection and the associated procedures to help clients and their significant others understand the situation.
- Demonstrate warm, accepting behaviour. Avoid conveying to the client any sense of annoyance about the precautions or any feelings of revulsion about the infection.
- Do not use stricter precautions than are indicated by the diagnosis or the client's condition.

Sterile Technique

An object is sterile only when it is free of all microorganisms. It is well known that sterile technique is practised in operating rooms, labour and delivery rooms, and special diagnostic areas. Sterile technique is also employed for many procedures in general care areas (such as administering injections, changing wound dressings, performing urinary catheterizations, and administering intravenous therapy). In these situations, all the principles of surgical asepsis are applied as in the operating or delivery room; however, the details of implementation vary. For example, before an operating room procedure, the "scrub" nurse generally puts on a mask and cap, performs a surgical hand scrub, and then dons a sterile gown and gloves. In a general care area, the nurse may only perform a hand wash and don sterile gloves. The basic principles of surgical asepsis and examples from nursing practice that relate to each principle appear in Table 32.9.

Sterile Field

A **sterile field** is a microorganism-free area. Nurses often establish a sterile field by using the innermost side of a sterile wrapper or by using a sterile drape. When the field is established, sterile supplies and sterile solutions can be placed on it. Sterile forceps are used in many instances to handle and transfer the sterile supplies.

TABLE 32.9 Principles and Practices of Surgical Asepsis

Principle	Practices
All objects used in a sterile field must be sterile.	All articles are sterilized appropriately by dry or moist heat, chemicals, or radiation before use.
	Sterile articles can be stored for only a prescribed time; after that, they are considered unsterile.
	Always check a package containing a sterile object for intactness, dryness, and expiration date. Any package that appears open, torn, punctured, or wet is considered unsterile. Never assume an item is sterile; if in doubt, consider the item unsterile.
	Storage areas should be clean, dry, off the floor, and away from sinks.
	Always check chemical indicators of sterilization before using a package. The indicator is often a tape used to fasten the package or contained inside the package. The indicator changes colour during sterilization, indicating that the contents have undergone a sterilization procedure. If the colour change is not evident, the package is considered unsterile. Commercially prepared sterile packages may not have indicators but are marked with the word *sterile*.
Sterile objects become unsterile when touched by unsterile objects.	Handle sterile objects that will touch open wounds or enter body cavities only with sterile forceps or sterile gloved hands.
	Discard or resterilize objects that come into contact with unsterile objects.
	Whenever the sterility of an object is questionable, assume the article is unsterile.
Sterile items that are out of vision or below the waist level of the nurse are considered unsterile.	Once left unattended, a sterile field is considered unsterile.
	Sterile objects are always kept in view. Nurses should not turn their backs on a sterile field.
	Only the front part of a sterile gown (from the waist to the shoulder) and 5 cm above the elbows to the cuff of the sleeves are considered sterile.
	Always keep sterile gloved hands in sight and above waist level; touch only objects that are sterile.
	Sterile draped tables are considered sterile only at surface level.
	Once a sterile field becomes unsterile, it must be set up again before proceeding.
Sterile objects can become unsterile by prolonged exposure to air-borne microorganisms.	Keep doors closed and traffic to a minimum in areas where a sterile procedure is being performed; moving air can carry dust and microorganisms.
	Keep areas in which sterile procedures are carried out as clean as possible by frequent damp cleaning with detergent germicides to minimize contaminants in the area.
	Keep hair clean and short, tied back, or enclosed in a net to prevent hair from falling on sterile objects. Microorganisms on the hair can make a sterile field unsterile.
	Wear surgical caps in operating rooms, delivery rooms, and burn units.
	Refrain from sneezing or coughing over a sterile field. This can render the field unsterile because of the spray of droplets containing microorganisms from the respiratory tract. Some nurses recommend that masks covering the mouth and the nose be worn when working over a sterile field or an open wound.
	Nurses with mild upper respiratory tract infections refrain from carrying out sterile procedures, or wear masks.
	When working over a sterile field, talking should be kept to a minimum. Turn the head from the field if talking is necessary.
	To prevent microorganisms from falling over a sterile field, refrain from reaching over a sterile field, unless sterile gloves are worn, and refrain from moving unsterile objects over a sterile field.
Fluids flow in the direction of gravity.	Hold instruments with the tips below the handles. When the tips are held higher than the handles, fluid can flow onto the handle and become contaminated by the hands. When the forceps are again pointed downward, the fluid flows back down and contaminates the tips.
	During a surgical hand wash, hold the hands higher than the elbows to prevent contaminants from the forearms from reaching the hands.

TABLE 32.9 Principles and Practices of Surgical Asepsis *continued*

Principle	Practices
Moisture that passes through a sterile object draws microorganisms from unsterile surfaces above or below to the sterile surface by capillary action.	Sterile moistureproof barriers are used beneath sterile objects. Liquids (sterile saline or antiseptics) are frequently poured into containers on a sterile field. If they are spilled onto the sterile field, the barrier keeps the liquid from seeping beneath it. Keep the sterile covers on sterile equipment dry. Damp surfaces can attract microorganisms in the air. Replace sterile drapes that do not have a sterile barrier underneath when they become moist.
The edges of a sterile field are considered unsterile.	A 2.5-cm margin at each edge of an opened drape is considered unsterile because the edges are in contact with unsterile surfaces. Place all sterile objects more than 2.5 cm inside the edges of a sterile field. Any article that falls outside the edges of a sterile field is considered unsterile.
The skin is unsterile and cannot be sterilized.	Use sterile gloves or sterile forceps to handle sterile items. Prior to a surgical aseptic procedure, wash the hands to reduce the number of microorganisms on them.
Conscientiousness, alertness, and honesty are essential qualities in maintaining surgical asepsis.	When a sterile object becomes unsterile, it does not necessarily change in appearance. The person who sees a sterile object become contaminated must correct or report the situation. Do not set up a sterile field ahead of time for future use.

So that their sterility can be maintained, supplies may be wrapped in a variety of materials. Commercially prepared items are frequently wrapped in plastic, paper, or glass. In the past, it was not unusual for sterile liquids (e.g., sterile water for irrigations) to be supplied in large containers and used many times. This practice is considered undesirable today because once a container has been opened, there can be no guarantee that it is sterile. Liquids are preferably packaged in amounts adequate for single use only; leftover liquid is discarded.

Procedure 32.2 describes how to establish and maintain a sterile field.

Sterile Gloves

Sterile gloves may be donned by the open or the closed method. The open method is most frequently used outside the operating room because the closed method requires that the nurse wear a sterile gown. Gloves are worn during many procedures to maintain the sterility of equipment and protect the client.

Sterile gloves are packaged with a cuff of about 5 cm and with the palms facing upward when the package is opened. The package usually indicates the size of the glove (e.g., size 6 or 7½).

Latex and vinyl sterile gloves are available to protect the nurse from contact with blood and body fluids. *Latex* is more flexible than vinyl, moulds to the wearer's hands, allows freedom of movement, and has the added feature of resealing tiny punctures automatically. Therefore, wear latex gloves, if possible, when performing tasks (1) that demand flexibility; (2) that place stress on the material (e.g., turning stopcocks, handling sharp instruments or tape); and (3) that involve a high risk of exposure to pathogens. *Vinyl* gloves should be chosen for persons with latex allergies or for tasks unlikely to stress the glove material, requiring minimal precision, or with minimal risk of exposure to pathogens.

Procedure 32.3 describes how to don and remove sterile gloves using the open method.

Sterile Gowns

Sterile gowning and closed gloving are chiefly carried out in operating or delivery rooms. The closed method of gloving can be used only when a sterile gown is worn because the gloves are handled through the sleeves of the gown. Prior to these procedures, the nurse dons a hair cover and a mask, and performs a surgical hand wash.

Procedure 32.4 describes the steps in donning a sterile gown and sterile gloves by the closed method.

Infection Control for Health-Care Workers

The LCDC provides guidelines to protect health-care workers from occupational exposure to blood-borne pathogens in the workplace. *Occupational exposure* is defined as reasonably anticipated skin, eye, mucous membrane, or

PROCEDURE 32.2 Establishing and Maintaining a Sterile Field

PURPOSE

- To maintain the sterility of supplies and equipment

Equipment

- ❑ Package containing a sterile drape
- ❑ Sterile equipment as needed (e.g., packaged gauze, wrapped sterile bowl, antiseptic solution, sterile forceps)

INTERVENTION

1. Confirm the sterility of the package.

- Ensure that the package is clean and dry; if moist, it is considered contaminated and must be discarded.
- Check the sterilization expiration dates on the package, and look for any indications that it has been previously opened or punctured.

2. Open the package.

To Open a Wrapped Package on a Clean Surface

- Place the package in the centre of the work area so that the top flap of the wrapper opens away from you. *This position prevents the nurse from reaching directly over the exposed sterile contents, which could contaminate them.*
- Reaching from the side of the package (not over it), pinch the first flap on the outside of the wrapper between the thumb and index finger (Figure 32.13). *Touching only the outside of the wrapper maintains the sterility of the inside of the wrapper.* Pull the flap open, laying it flat on the far surface.
- Repeat for the side flaps, opening the top one first. Use the right hand for the right flap, and the left hand for the left flap (Figure 32.14). *By using both hands, the nurse avoids reaching over the sterile contents.*
- Pull the fourth flap toward you by grasping the corner that is turned down (Figure 32.15). Make sure that the flap does not touch any object. *If the inner surface touches any unsterile article, it is contaminated.*

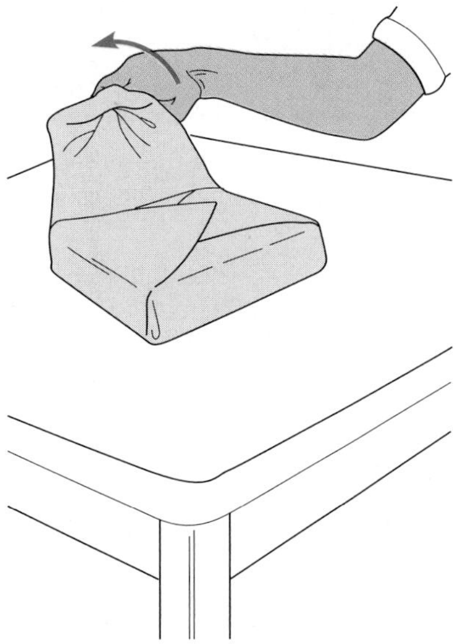

Figure 32.13 Opening the first flap of a sterile wrapped package

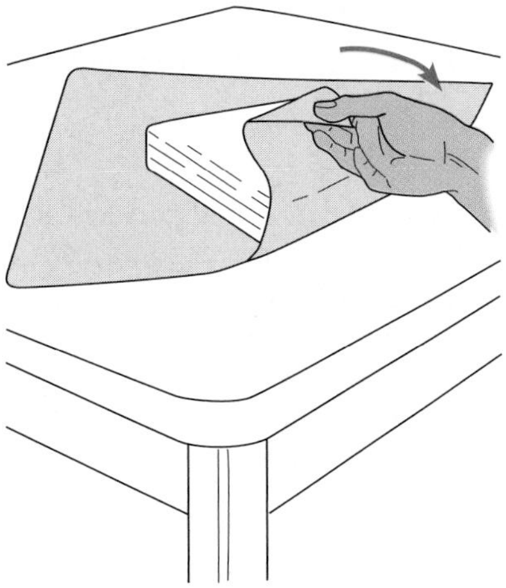

Figure 32.15 Pulling the last flap toward oneself by grasping the corner

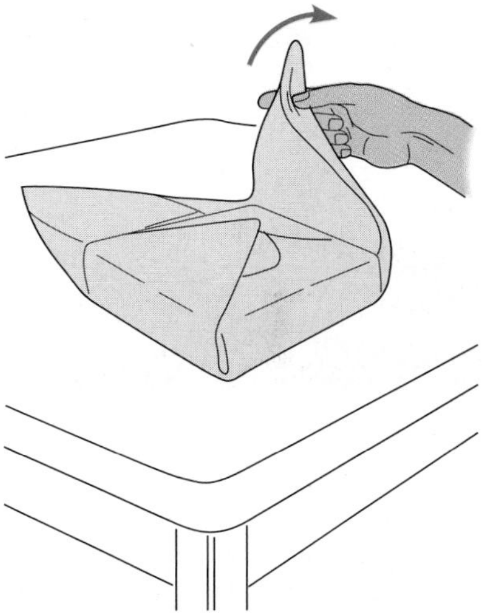

Figure 32.14 Opening the second flap to the side

To Open a Wrapped Package while Holding It

- Hold the package in one hand with the top flap opening away from you.
- Using the other hand, open the package as described above, pulling the corners of the flaps well back and not reaching across the contents of the package (Figure 32.16). *The hands are considered contaminated, and at no time should they touch the contents of the package.*

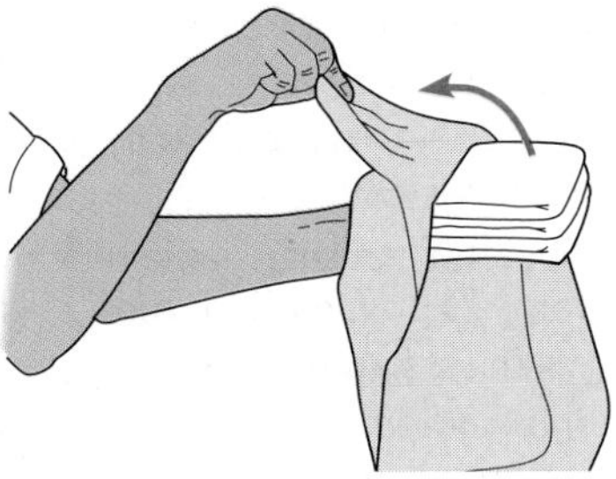

Figure 32.16 Opening a wrapped package while holding it

PROCEDURE 32.2 Establishing and Maintaining a Sterile Field *continued*

To Open Commercially Prepared Packages

Commercially prepared sterile packages and containers usually have manufacturer's directions for opening.

- If the flap of the package has a peel back corner, hold the container in one hand and pull back on the flap with the other hand (Figure 32.17).

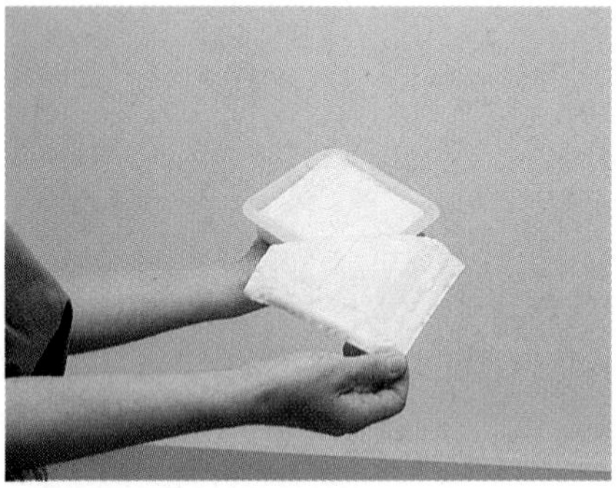

Figure 32.17 Opening a sterile package that has a peel back corner

- If the package has a peel back edge, grasp both sides of the edge, one with each hand, and pull apart gently (Figure 32.18).

Figure 32.18 Opening a sterile package that has a partially sealed edge

3. Establish a sterile field by using a sterile drape.

- Open the package containing the drape as described in step 2.
- With one hand, pluck the corner of the drape that is folded back on the top.

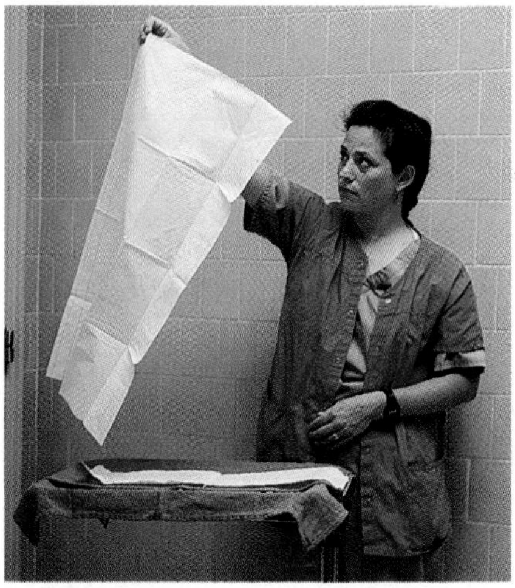

Figure 32.19 Allowing a drape to open freely without touching any objects

- Lift the drape out of the cover and allow it to open freely without touching any objects (Figure 32.19). *If the drape touches the outside of the package or any unsterile surface or object, it is considered contaminated.*
- Discard the cover.
- With the other hand, carefully pick up another corner of the drape, holding it well away from yourself.
- Lay the drape on a clean and dry surface, placing the bottom (i.e., the freely hanging side) farthest from you (Figure 32.20). *By placing the lowermost side farthest away, the nurse avoids leaning over the sterile field and contaminating it.*

4. Add necessary sterile supplies.

To Add Wrapped Supplies to a Sterile Field

- Open each wrapped package as described in the preceding steps.
- With the free hand, grasp the corners of the wrapper and hold them against the wrist of the other hand (Figure 32.21). *The unsterile hand is now covered by the sterile wrapper.*

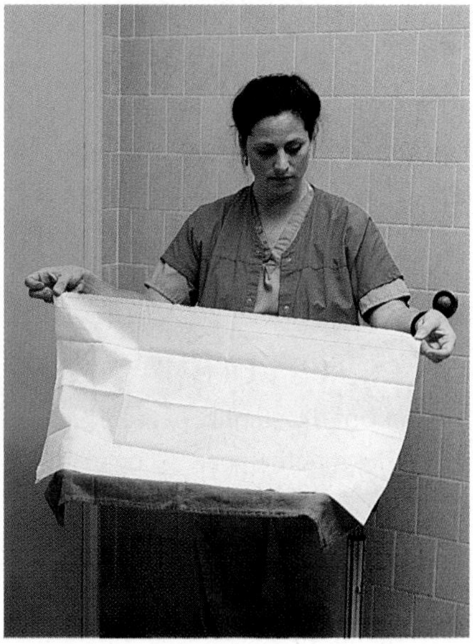

Figure 32.20 Placing a drape on a surface

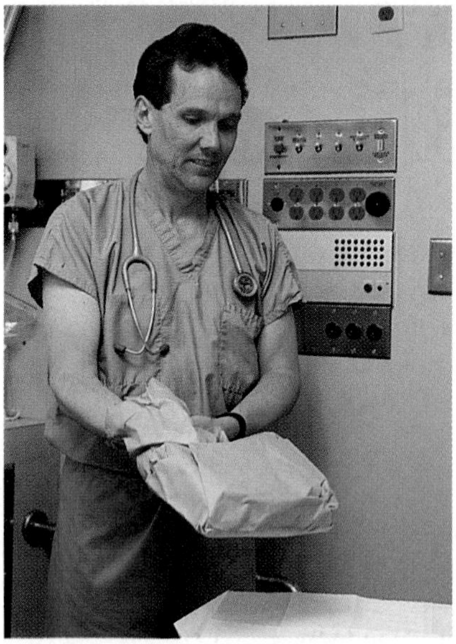

Figure 32.21 Adding wrapped sterile supplies to a sterile field

- Place the sterile item on the sterile field by approaching from an angle, rather than holding the arm over the field.
- Discard the wrapper.

PROCEDURE 32.2 Establishing and Maintaining a Sterile Field *continued*

TO ADD COMMERCIALLY PACKAGED SUPPLIES TO A STERILE FIELD

- Open each package as previously described.
- Standing slightly back from the sterile field, grasp both peel back edges in the nondominant hand. Use a sterile forcep or sterile-gloved hand to remove the item and place it onto the sterile field. *These actions minimize the likelihood of air-borne transmission of microorganisms.*

  Alternatively, ensure both peel back edges are pulled well into the dominant hand. Holding the package securely, approach the sterile field with the forearm at a horizontal angle, at a height of approximately 10 to 15 cm. Lay the contents on the sterile field and lighten grip on the package to release sterile contents. *Care must be taken to prevent contamination of the sterile items by the package edges.*

TO ADD STERILE SOLUTION TO A STERILE CONTAINER

Sterile liquids (e.g., normal saline) frequently need to be poured into containers within a sterile field. Unwrapped bottles or flasks that contain sterile solution are considered sterile on the inside and contaminated on the outside because the bottle has been handled.

- Before pouring any liquid, read the label three times to ensure you have the correct solution and concentration (strength).
- Obtain the exact amount of solution, if possible. *Once a sterile container has been opened, its sterility cannot be ensured for future use unless it is used again immediately.*
- Remove the lid or cap from the bottle and invert the lid before placing it on a surface that is not sterile. *Inverting the lid maintains the sterility of the inside surface because it is not allowed to touch an unsterile surface.*
- Hold the bottle at a slight angle so that the label is uppermost. *Any solution that flows down the outside of the bottle during pouring will not damage or obliterate the label.*
- Hold the bottle of fluid at a height of 10 to 15 cm over the container and to the side of the sterile field so that as little of the bottle as possible is over the field. *At this height, there is less likelihood of contaminating the sterile field by touching the field or by reaching an arm over it.*
- Pour the solution gently to avoid splashing the liquid. *If the sterile drape is on an unsterile surface, any moisture will contaminate the field by facilitating the movement of microorganisms through the sterile drape.*
- Replace the lid securely on the bottle if you plan to use it again, and provide the date and time of opening according to agency policy. *Replacing the lid immediately maintains the sterility of the inner aspect of the lid and the solution.* In many agencies, a sterile container of solution that is opened is used only once and then discarded.
- If bottle of solution is used again, the lip of the container should be cleansed by pouring a small amount of solution (then discarding) prior to pouring solution into the sterile container.

5. Use sterile forceps to handle certain sterile supplies.

Forceps are commonly used for such techniques as changing a sterile dressing and shortening a drain. Transfer forceps are used to move a sterile article from one place to another, for example, transferring sterile gauze from its package to a sterile dressing tray. Forceps may be discarded or re-sterilized after use. Commonly used forceps include hemostats, or artery forceps (Figure 32.22), and tissue forceps (Figure 32.23).

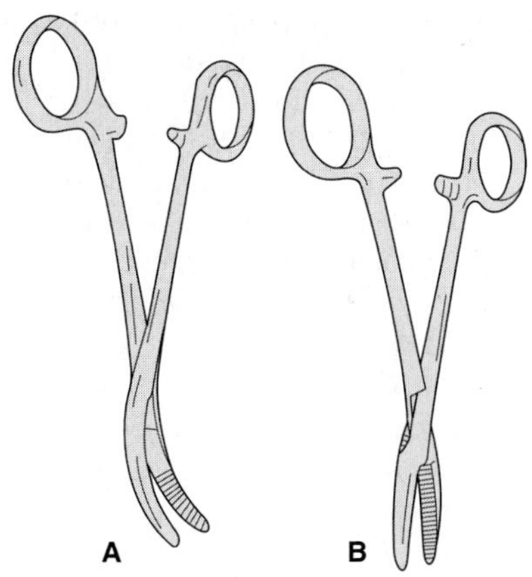

Figure 32.22 Hemostats: *A*, curved; *B*, straight

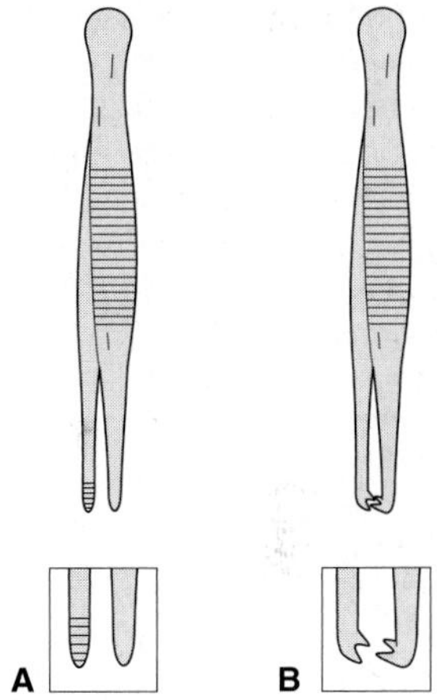

Figure 32.23 Tissue forceps: *A*, plain; *B*, toothed

PROCEDURE 32.2 Establishing and Maintaining a Sterile Field *continued*

- Keep the tips of wet forceps lower than the wrist at all times unless you are wearing sterile gloves (Figure 32.24). *Gravity prevents liquids on the tips of the forceps from flowing to the handles and later back to the tips, thus making the forceps unsterile. The handles are unsterile once they are held by the bare hand.*
- Hold sterile forceps above waist level. *Items held below waist level are considered contaminated.*
- Hold sterile forceps within your visual field. *When out of sight, forceps may, unknown to the user, become contaminated. Any forceps that go out of sight should be considered unsterile.*
- When using forceps to lift sterile supplies out of a commercially prepared package, be sure that the forceps do not touch the edges or outside of the wrapper. *The edges and outside of the package are exposed to the air and handled and are, thus, unsterile.*

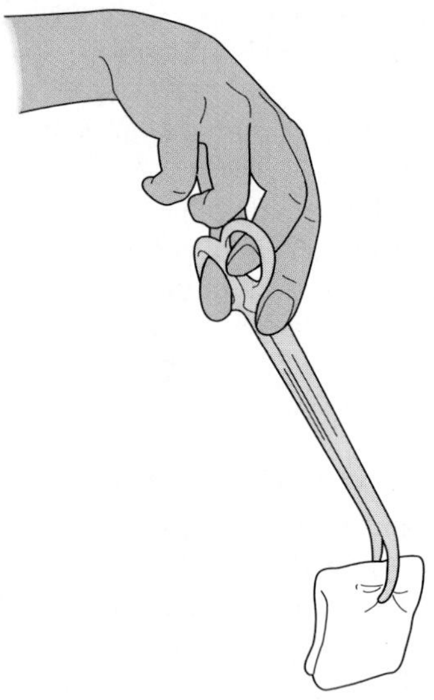

Figure 32.24 Holding forceps with an ungloved hand, keeping the tips pointing downward

- When placing forceps whose handles were in contact with the bare hand, position the handles outside the sterile area. *The handles of these forceps harbour microorganisms from the bare hand.*
- Deposit a sterile item on a sterile field without permitting moist forceps to touch the sterile field when the surface under the sterile field is unsterile and a barrier drape is not used. A *barrier drape* is resistant to moisture and should be used whenever a procedure involves moisture. *Made of chemically treated cotton or synthetic materials, barrier drapes prevent a sterile field from becoming contaminated when the drape becomes wet. It is known that a sterile cloth becomes unsterile when dampened (even with sterile water) if it is on an unsterile surface or has contact with any unsterile object. Microorganisms can move through a damp sterile cloth from an unsterile surface by capillary action.*

Home Care Considerations

- Clean and wipe dry a flat surface for the sterile field.
- Keep pets out of the area when setting up for and performing sterile procedures.
- Dispose of all soiled materials in a waterproof bag. Check with the home care nurse as to how to dispose of medical refuse.

PROCEDURE 32.3 Donning and Removing Sterile Gloves (Open Method)

PURPOSES

- To enable the nurse to handle sterile objects freely
- To prevent clients at risk (e.g., those with open wounds) from becoming infected by microorganisms on the nurse's hands

Equipment

- ❑ Package of sterile gloves

PROCEDURE 32.3 Donning and Removing Sterile Gloves (Open Method) *continued*

INTERVENTION

1. **Open the package of sterile gloves.**
   - Place the package of gloves on a clean dry surface. *Any moisture on the surface could contaminate the gloves.*
   - Some gloves are packed in an inner as well as an outer package. Open the outer package without contaminating the gloves or the inner package. See Procedure 32.2.
   - Remove the inner package from the outer package.
   - Open the inner package as in step 2 of Procedure 32.2 or according to the manufacturer's directions. Some manufacturers provide a numbered sequence for opening the flaps and folded tabs to grasp for opening the flaps. If no tabs are provided, pluck the flap so that the fingers do not touch the inner surfaces. *The inner surfaces, which are next to the sterile gloves, will remain sterile.*
2. **Put the first glove on the dominant hand.**
   - If the gloves are packaged so that they lie side by side, grasp the glove for the dominant hand by its cuff (on the palmar side) with the thumb and first finger of the nondominant hand. Touch only the inside of the cuff (Figure 32.25). *The hands are not sterile. By touching only the inside of the glove, the nurse avoids contaminating the surface to remain sterile.*

     or
   - If the gloves are packaged one on top of the other, grasp the cuff of the top glove as above, using the opposite hand.
   - Insert the dominant hand into the glove and pull the glove on. Keep the thumb of the inserted hand against the palm of the hand during insertion (Figure 32.26). *If the thumb is kept against the palm, it is less likely to contaminate the outside of the glove.*

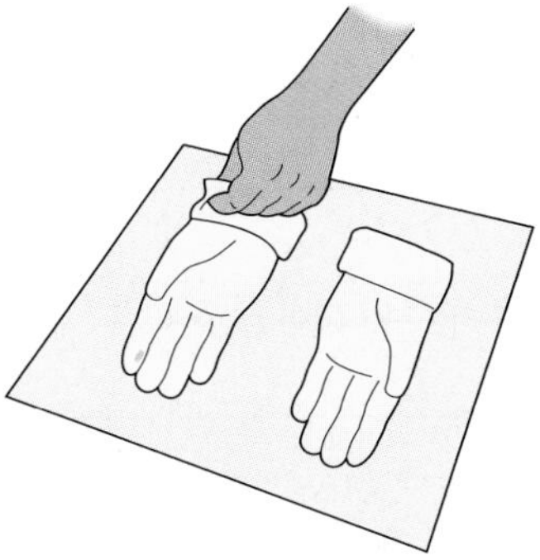

Figure 32.25 Picking up the first sterile glove

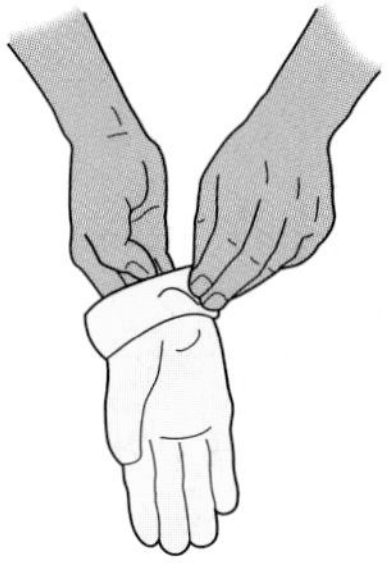

Figure 32.26 Putting on the first sterile glove

Figure 32.27 Picking up the second sterile glove

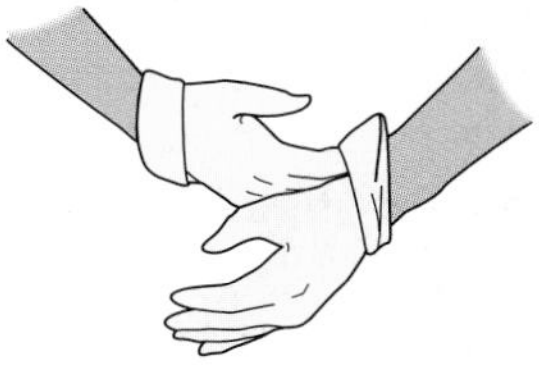

Figure 32.28 Putting on the second sterile glove

   - Leave the cuff turned down.
3. **Put the second glove on the nondominant hand.**
   - Pick up the other glove with the sterile gloved hand, inserting the gloved fingers under the cuff and holding the gloved thumb close to the gloved palm (Figure 32.27). *This helps prevent accidental contamination of the glove by the bare hand.*
   - Pull on the second glove carefully. Hold the thumb of the gloved first hand as far as possible from the palm (Figure 32.28). *In this position, the thumb is less likely to touch the arm and become contaminated.*
   - Adjust each glove so that it fits smoothly, and carefully pull the cuffs up by sliding the fingers under the cuffs.
4. **Remove and dispose of used gloves.**
   - Remove them by turning them inside out. See removal of disposable gloves on page 765.

PROCEDURE 32.4 Donning a Sterile Gown and Sterile Gloves (Closed Method)

PURPOSES

- To enable the nurse to work closely to a sterile field and handle sterile objects freely
- To protect clients from becoming contaminated with microorganisms on the nurse's hands, arms, and clothing

Equipment

- ❑ A sterile pack containing a sterile gown
- ❑ A package of sterile gloves

INTERVENTION

Donning a Sterile Gown

1. Open the package of sterile gloves.

- Remove the outer wrap from the sterile gloves and leave the gloves in their inner sterile wrap on the sterile field. *If the inner wrapper is not touched, it will remain sterile.* See Procedure 32.2, step 2.

2. Unwrap the sterile gown pack.

3. Wash and dry hands carefully. (See "Variation" at the end of Procedure 32.1 and review agency practice.)

4. Put on the sterile gown.

- Grasp the sterile gown at the neck, hold it away from you, and permit it to unfold freely without touching anything, including the uniform. *The gown will be unsterile if its outer surface touches any unsterile objects.*
- Put the hands inside the shoulders of the gown, and work the arms partway into the sleeves without touching the outside of the gown (Figure 32.29).
- If donning sterile gloves by using the *closed* method (see below), work the hands down the sleeves only to the proximal edge of the cuffs.

  or
- If donning sterile gloves by using the *open* method, work the hands down the sleeves and through the cuffs.
- Have a co-worker wearing a hair cover and mask grasp the neck ties without touching the outside of the gown and pull the gown upward to cover the neckline of your uniform in front and back. The co-worker ties the neck ties. Gowning continues at step 8.

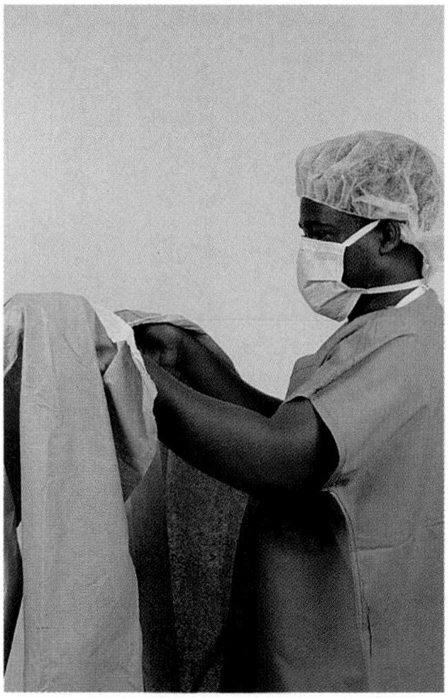

Figure 32.29 Putting on a sterile gown

Donning Sterile Gloves (Closed Method)

5. Open the sterile wrapper containing the sterile gloves.

- Open the sterile glove wrapper while the hands are still covered by the sleeves (Figure 32.30).

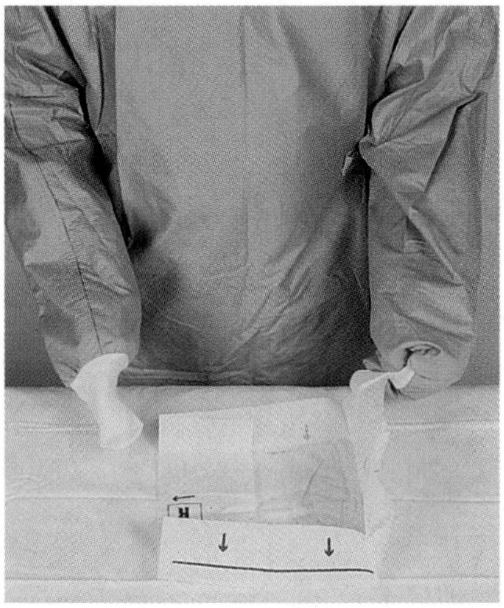

Figure 32.30 Opening the sterile glove wrapper

6. Put the glove on the nondominant hand. Figures 32.31 through 32.33 show a right-handed person.

- With the *dominant* hand, pick up the *opposite* glove with the thumb and index finger, handling it through the sleeve.
- Lay the glove on the opposite gown cuff, thumb side down, with the glove opening pointed toward the fingers (see Figure 32.31). Position the dominant hand palm upward inside the sleeve.
- Use the nondominant hand to grasp the cuff of the glove through the gown cuff, and firmly anchor it.
- With the dominant hand working through its sleeve, grasp the upper side of the glove's cuff, and stretch it over the cuff of the gown.
- Pull the sleeve up to draw the cuff over the wrist as you extend the fingers of the nondominant hand into the glove's fingers (see Figure 32.32).

7. Put the glove on the dominant hand.

- Place the fingers of the gloved hand under the cuff of the remaining glove.
- Place the glove over the cuff of the second sleeve.
- Extend the fingers into the glove as you pull the glove up over the gown cuff (see Figure 32.33).

PROCEDURE 32.4 Donning a Sterile Gown and Sterile Gloves (Closed Method) *continued*

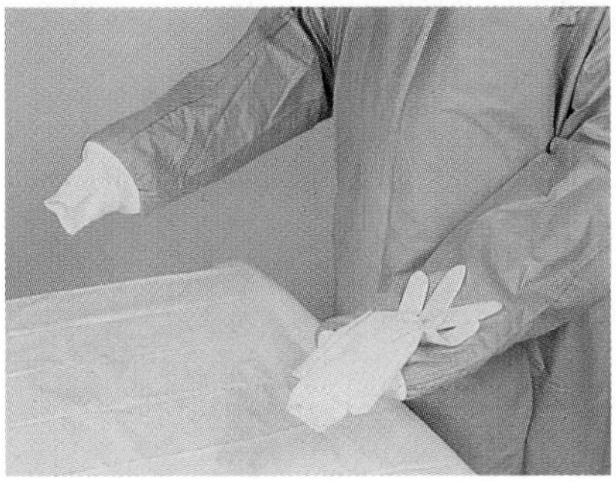

Figure 32.31 Positioning the first sterile glove for the nondominant hand

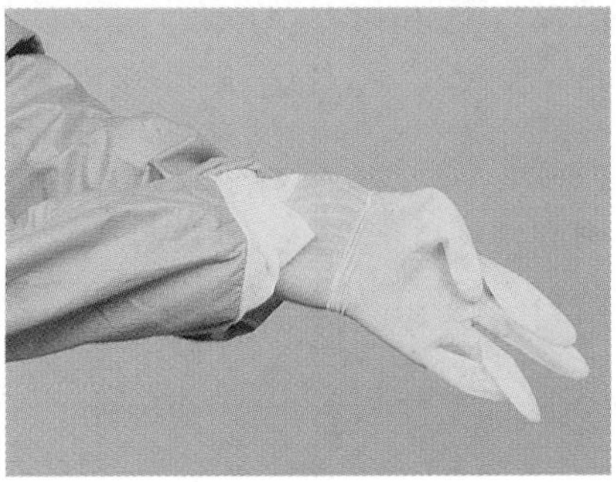

Figure 32.32 Pulling on the first sterile glove

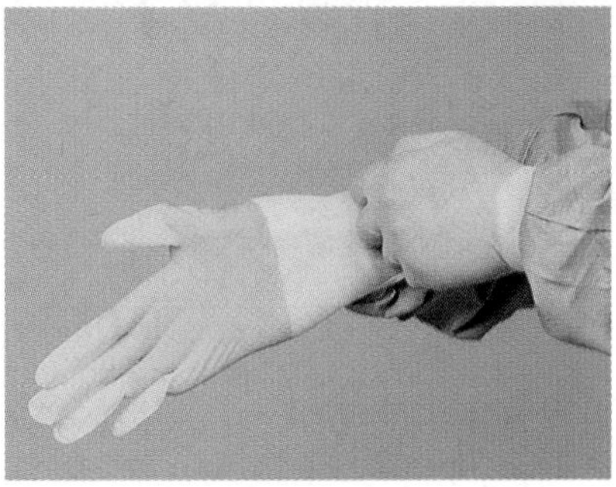

Figure 32.33 Extending the fingers into the second glove of the dominant hand

COMPLETION OF GOWNING

8. Complete gowning as follows:

- Have a co-worker wearing a hair cover and mask hold the waist tie of your gown using sterile gloves or a sterile forcep or drape. *This approach keeps the ties sterile.*
- Make a three-quarter turn, then take the tie from the co-worker and secure it in front of the gown.

or

- Have a co-worker wearing sterile gloves take the two ties at each side of the gown and tie them at the back of the gown, making sure that your uniform is completely covered. *Both methods ensure that the back of the gown remains sterile.*
- When worn, sterile gowns should be considered *sterile* only in front from the waist to the shoulder. The sleeves should be considered sterile from the cuff to 5 cm above the elbow, since the arms of a scrubbed person must move across a sterile field. Moisture collection and friction areas, such as the neckline, shoulders, underarms and back, should be considered unsterile.

parenteral contact with blood or other potentially infectious materials that may result from the performance of an employee's duties.

There are three major modes of transmission of infectious fluids in the clinical setting:

1. *Puncture wounds* from contaminated needles or other sharps
2. *Skin contact*, which allows infectious fluids to enter through wounds and broken or damaged skin
3. *Mucous membrane* contact, which allows infectious fluids to enter through mucous membranes of the eyes, mouth, and nose

Conscientious use of routine precautions, appropriately using personal protective equipment (gloves, masks, gowns, goggles, face shields, shoe covers, special resuscitative equipment), and avoiding carelessness in the clinical area will reduce the risk of injury to the caregiver. Measures to be taken in case of possible exposure to hepatitis B and HIV are outlined in the next box.

The Canadian Immunization Guide (1998) recommends that health-care employers make the hepatitis B vaccine and vaccination series available to all employees. Other vaccinations may also be made available (e.g., nurses working in an obstetric area should be vaccinated against rubella to protect pregnant clients and their fetuses).

Role of the Infection Control Nurse

All health-care organizations must have interdisciplinary infection control committees. Representatives from the clinical laboratory, housekeeping, maintenance, dietary, and client care areas are included. An important member of this committee is the infection control nurse. This nurse's role has a focus on the latest research and practices in preventing, detecting, and treating infections. All infections are reported to the nurse in a manner that allows for recording and analyzing statistics that can assist in improving infection control practices. In addition, the infection control nurse may be involved in employee education and implementation of the blood-borne pathogen exposure control plan mandated by occupational health and safety regulatory bodies.

CLINICAL GUIDELINES

Steps to Follow after Exposure to Blood-Borne Pathogens

- Report the incident immediately to appropriate personnel within the agency.
- Complete an injury report.
- Seek appropriate evaluation and follow-up. This includes the following:
  - Identification and documentation of the source individual when feasible and legal
  - Testing of the source individual's blood when feasible and consent is given
  - Making results of the test available to the source individual's health-care provider
  - Testing of blood of exposed health-care provider (with consent)
  - Postexposure prophylaxis if medically indicated (e.g., hepatitis B vaccine for HBV, or recommended agents for HIV)
  - Medical counselling regarding personal risk of infection or risk of infecting others
- For a puncture or laceration:
  - Encourage bleeding.
  - Clean the area with soap and water.
  - Initiate first aid and seek treatment, if indicated.
  - For a mucous membrane exposure (eyes, nose, mouth), flush with saline solution or water for five to 10 minutes.

HIV Postexposure Protocol

- For "high-risk" exposure (high blood volume *and* source with a high HIV titre), three-drug treatment is encouraged. It must be started within one to two hours.
- For "low-risk" exposure (neither high blood volume nor source with a high HIV titre), two-drug treatment is encouraged. It must be started within one to two hours.
- Drug prophylaxis is for four weeks.
- Drug regimens vary. Drugs commonly used are zidovudine, lamivudine, and indinavir.
- HIV antibody tests are done shortly after exposure (baseline), and six weeks, three months, and six months thereafter.

Evaluating

Using data collected during care—vital signs, breath sounds, skin status, characteristics of urine or other drainage, laboratory blood values, and so on—the nurse judges whether client outcomes have been achieved. Examples of client goals and related outcomes are shown in Table 32.10.

If outcomes are not achieved, the nurse may need to consider questions such as the following:

- Were appropriate measures implemented to prevent skin breakdown and lung infection?
- Was strict aseptic technique implemented for invasive procedures?
- Are prescribed medications affecting the immune system?
- Is client placement appropriate to reduce the risk of transmission of microorganisms?
- Did the client and family misunderstand or fail to comply with necessary instructions?

TABLE 32.10 Evaluation Goals and Outcomes: Risk for Infection

Goal	Examples of Desired Outcomes
Maintain body defences	Skin integrity intact
	Mucous membranes intact
	WBC values within normal range
	T cell levels within normal range
	Respiratory assessment findings within normal range (e.g., respiratory rate, rhythm, depth, and breath sounds)
	Urinary tract assessment findings within normal range (e.g., urine colour, clarity, odour, and consistency)
	Gastrointestinal tract assessment findings within normal range (e.g., stool colour, odour, and consistency, and emesis is absent)
	Immunizations recommended for age are current
Avoid spread of microorganisms	Describes mode of transmission of microorganism
	Demonstrates infection control practices that reduce transmission
	Follows prescribed treatment for diagnosed infection

FOCUS ON CRITICAL THINKING

Mrs. Cortez is a 76-year-old woman who is independent, lives alone, and prefers not to rely on others unless absolutely necessary. She was active and healthy until about six months ago, at which time she developed a persistent upper respiratory infection. Because she was unable to obtain or prepare food, she lost weight and became very weak. She finally sought medical attention, but she has not yet fully recovered. Her primary-care provider has admitted Mrs. Cortez to the acute-care facility for shortness of breath, productive cough, dehydration, and nutritional deficiency.

1. Mrs. Cortez's primary-care provider suspects that Mrs. Cortez has pneumonia, a serious respiratory infection. What data support Mrs. Cortez's increased risk for such an infection?
2. What other information or assessment data would be helpful to you when planning care for Mrs. Cortez?
3. You recognize that standard precautions (routine practices) are instituted for all hospitalized clients. Explain why the use of such precautions may not be sufficient to prevent the spread of Mrs. Cortez's respiratory infection to others.
4. What can you do to prevent the spread of Mrs. Cortez's infection to other hospitalized clients and at the same time prevent Mrs. Cortez from getting infections from other clients?
5. You note that the housekeeping aide is leaving Mrs. Cortez's room. The aide stops to wash her hands, soaping them and rubbing them together under running water for about five seconds. She then turns off the water and proceeds with drying her hands. Should you intervene, and if so, what should you do?

See Appendix A for answers to these questions.

CHAPTER HIGHLIGHTS

- Microorganisms are everywhere. Most are harmless and some are beneficial; however, many can cause infection in susceptible persons.
- Effective control of infectious disease is an international, national, community, and individual responsibility.
- Asepsis is the freedom from infection or infectious material.
- Medical aseptic practices limit the number, growth, and transmission of microorganisms.
- Surgical aseptic practices keep an area or objects free of all microorganisms.
- The incidence of nosocomial infections is significant. Major sites for these infections are the respiratory and urinary tracts, the bloodstream, and surgical or open wounds.
- Factors that contribute to nosocomial infection risks are invasive procedures, medical therapies, the existence of susceptible persons, inappropriate use of antibiotics, and insufficient hand washing after client contact and after contact with body substances.
- An infection can develop if the six links in the chain of infection—infectious agent, reservoir, portal of exit, mode of transmission, portal of entry, and susceptible host—are not interrupted.
- Aseptic practices can be used to break most of the six links in the chain of infection.
- Humans have both specific and nonspecific defences that combat infectious agents.
- Intact skin and mucous membranes are the body's first line of defence against microorganisms.
- Some normal body flora release bacteriocins and antibiotic-like substances that inhibit microbial growth and destroy foreign bacteria.
- Some body secretions (e.g., saliva and tears) contain enzymes that act as antibacterial agents.
- The inflammatory response limits physical, chemical, and microbial injury and promotes repair of injured tissue.
- Immunity is the specific resistance of the body to infectious agents.
- Acquired immunity is active or passive and, in either case, may be naturally or artificially induced.
- Especially at risk of acquiring an infection are the very young or old; those with poor nutritional status, a deficiency of serum immunoglobulins, multiple stressors, insufficient immunizations, or an existing disease process; and those receiving certain medical therapies.
- Preventing infections in healthy or ill persons and preventing the transmission of microorganisms from infected clients to others are major nursing functions.
- The nurse must be knowledgeable about sources and modes of transmission of microorganisms.
- Microorganisms are invisible, and nurses have an ethical obligation to ensure that appropriate aseptic measures are taken to protect clients, support people, and health personnel, including themselves.

READINGS AND REFERENCES

Suggested Readings

Doody, L., & Crnkovic, A. (2001). Blood exposure: Remember the emotional side. *Journal of Emergency Nursing, 27*(5), 450–453.
The authors present first-hand experience of sustaining a needle-stick injury from an HIV-infected patient.

Milam, M.W., Hall, H., Pringle, T., Buchanan, K. (2001). Bacterial contamination of fabric stethoscope covers: The velveteen rabbit of healthcare. *Infection Control and Hospital Epidemiology, 22*(10), 653–655.
The research results of this study present the need to question the adornment of the health-care worker's attire.

Selected References

Association for Professionals in Infection Control and Epidemiology, Inc. (2000). *APIC text of infection control and epidemiology*. Washington, DC: Author.

Boyce, J. M., & Pittet, D. (2002, Oct). Guideline for hand hygiene in health care settings. http://www.cdc.gov/mmwr/preview/mmwrhtml/rr5111bal.htm

British Columbia Ministry of Health. (2000, Feb). Vancomycin-resistant enterococci: From the Health files #74. Author. Retrieved June 13, 2002 from http://www.hlth.gov.bc.ca/hlthfile74.html

Broadhead, J. M., Parra, D. S., & Skeleton, P. A. (2001). Emerging multiresistant organisms in the ICU: Epidemiology, risk factors, surveillance, and prevention. *Critical Care Nursing Quarterly, 24*(2), 20–29.

Canadian Nurses Association. (1993). Position statement: Blood-borne pathogens. Ottawa: Author.

Carpenito, L. J. (2002). *Handbook of nursing diagnosis* (9th ed.). Philadelphia, PA: Lippincott.

Centers for Disease Control. (1996a). Guideline for isolation precautions in hospitals, Part I: Evolution of isolation practices. *American Journal of Infection Control, 24*(1), 24–31.

Chan, R., Molassiotis, A., Chan, E., Ho, B., Lai, C., Lam, P., Shit, F., & Yiu, I. (2002). Nurses' knowledge of and compliance with universal precautions in an acute care hospital. *International Journal of Nursing Studies, 39*, 157–163.

Cookson, B. D. (2000). Methicillin-resistant *Staphylococcus aureus* in the community: New battlefronts or are the battles lost? *Infection Control and Hospital Epidemiology, 21*, 398–403.

Dyck, R. J. (2000). Historical development of latex allergy. *AORN Journal*, 72, 27–29, 32–33, 35–40.

Hargreaves, J., Larry, S., Hansen, S., Bren, V., Fillipi, G., Lacher, C., Esslinger, V., & Watne, T. (2001). Bacterial contamination associated with electronic faucets: A new risk for healthcare facilities. *Infection Control and Hospital Epidemiology, 22*, 202–205.

Health Canada: Laboratory Centre for Disease Control. (1999). Routine practices and additional precautions for preventing the transmission of infection in health care; Revision of isolation and precaution techniques. *Canada Communicable Disease Report, 25*(Suppl. S4). http://www.hc-sc.gc.ca/hpb/lcdc/publicat/ccdr/99vol25/25s4/index.html

Health Canada: Laboratory Centre for Disease Control. (2002). *Canadian immunization guide* (6th ed.). Ottawa: Canadian Medical Association. http://www.hc-sc.gc.ca/pphb.dgspsp/publicat/cig-gci/index.html

Health Canada: Laboratory Centre for Disease Control. (1997). Canadian contingency plan for viral hemorrhagic fevers and other related diseases. *Canadian Communicable Disease Report, 23*(Supplement S1). http://www.hc-sc.gc.ca/hpb/lcdc/ publicat/ccdr/98vol23/23s1/index.html

Health Canada: Laboratory Centre for Disease Control. (1997). Infection control guidelines: Preventing the spread of vancomycin-resistant enterococci (VRE) in Canada. *Canadian Communicable Disease Report, 23*(Supplement S8). http://www.hc-sc.gc.ca/hpb/lcdc/publicat/ccdr/98vol23/23s8/index.html

Health Canada: Laboratory Centre for Disease Control. (1997). Infection control guidelines: Preventing the transmission of bloodborne pathogens health care and public service. *Canadian Communicable Disease Report, 23*(Suppl. S3). http://www.hc-sc.gc.ca/hpb/lcdc/publicat/ccdr/98vol23/23s3/index.html

Health Canada: Laboratory Centre for Disease Control. (1996). Guidelines for preventing the transmission of tuberculosis in Canadian health care facilities and other institutional settings. *Canadian Communicable Disease Report, 22*(Supplement S1). http://www.hc-sc.gc.ca/hpb/lcdc/publicat/ccdr/ 98vol22/22s1/index.html

Health Canada: Workplace Hazardous Materials Information System. http://www.hc-sc.gc.ca/hecs-sejc/whmis/whmis_symbols.htm

Heseltine, P. (2001). Why don't doctors and nurses wash their hands? *Infection Control and Hospital Epidemiology, 22*, 199–200.

Jackson, M., & Lynch, P. (1984). Infection control: Too much or too little?. . . undiagnosed cases. *American Journal of Nursing, 87*, 208–210.

Kim, T., Oh, P. I., & Simor, A. E. ((2001). The economic impact of methicillin-resistant *Staphylococcus aureus* in Canadian hospitals. *Infection Control and Hospital Epidemiology, 22*, 99–104.

Larson, E. (1996). AIPC guideline for hand antisepsis in health-care settings. In *AIPC infection control and applied epidemiology: Principles and practice*. St. Louis: Mosby.

Lenehan, G. P. (2002). Hand creams and medical gloves. *Journal of Emergency Nursing, 28*, 106.

Lenehan, G. P. (2002). Latex allergy: Separating fact from fiction. *Nursing, 32*, 58–64.

Lenehan, G. P. (2001). If infection control practitioners could say one thing to emergency nurses, what would it be? *Journal of Emergency Nursing, 27*, 415–416.

MacMillan, S. (1997). Continuous quality improvement tools for busy practitioners. *The Canadian Journal of Infection Control, 12*, 7–8.

Maryland Department of Health and Mental Hygiene. (2002). Guidelines for the prevention and control of vancomycin-resistant enterococci (VRE) in long term care facilities. Maryland: Author. Retrieved June 13, 2002 from http://edcp.org/guidelines/vre96.html.

McCloskey, J. C., & Bulechek, G. M. (Eds.). (2000). *Nursing Interventions Classification (NIC)* (3rd ed.). St. Louis, MO: Mosby.

North American Nursing Diagnosis Association. (2003). *NANDA Nursing diagnoses: Definitions and classification 2003–2004.* Philadelphia, PA: Author.

Mitchell, A., Cummins, T., Spearing, N., Adama, J., & Gilroy, L. (2002). Nurses' experience with vancomycin-resistant enterococci (VRE). *Journal of Clinical Nursing, 11*, 126–133.

Papia, G., Louie, M., Tralla, A., Johnson, C., Collins, V., & Simor, A. E. (1999). Screening high-risk patients for methicillin-resistant *Staphylococcus aureus* on admission to the hospital: Is it cost effective? *Infection Control and Hospital Epidemiology, 20*, 473–477.

Springhouse Corporation. (1998). *Healthcare professional guides: Safety and infection control.* Springhouse, PA: Springhouse.

U.S. Department of Health and Human Services, National Nosocomial Infections Surveillance (NNIS) System, Hospital Infections Program, National Center for Infectious Diseases, Centers for Disease Control and Prevention, Public Health Service. (1996, May). National Nosocomial Infections Surveillance Semi-Annual Report. Atlanta, GA.

Zafar, A. B., Butler, R. C., Reese, D. J., Gaydos, L. A., & Mennonna, P. A. (1995). Use of 0.3% triclosan (Bacti-Stat) to eradicate an outbreak of methicillin-resistant staphylococcus aureus in a neonatal nursery. *American Journal of Infection Control, 23*, 200–208.

WEBLINKS

Health Canada: Laboratory Centre for Disease Control
http://www.hc-sc.gc.ca/hpb/lcdc/publicat/ccdr/99vol25/25s4/index.html
This federal government site provides information on practices related to the prevention of transmission of infections in health care.

Canadian Communicable Disease Report
http://www.hc-sc.gc.ca/pphb-dgspsp/publicat/ccdr-rmtc/02vol28/index.html
The Web site contains this publication of the Public Health Branch of Health Canada.

CHAPTER 33

Safety

OBJECTIVES

After completing this chapter, you will be able to:

- Discuss factors that affect people's ability to protect themselves from injury.
- Carry out a focused safety assessment interview.
- Identify common potential hazards in the home.
- Give examples of NANDA nursing diagnostic labels for clients at risk for unintentional injury.
- Plan strategies to maintain safety in the health-care setting, home, and community, including prevention strategies across the life span for thermal injury, falls, poisoning, suffocation or choking, and motor vehicle accidents.
- Describe the use and legal implications of restraints.
- List desired outcomes to use in evaluating the selected strategies for injury prevention.

A healthy environment is fundamental to life, and attention to the effect of the environment on human health is imperative if we are to attain the goal of health for all. To achieve concrete results, environmental responsibility must be practised at the individual level, in the workplace, and in the home.

As decision makers, caregivers, and role models for healthy behaviour, nurses and physicians should encourage and implement measures to achieve environmental responsibility in the settings where they practice and the health-care system in general (CNA, 1996).

A fundamental concern of nurses is prevention of accidents and injury, as well as assisting the injured. Motor vehicle accidents, falls, drowning, fire and burns, poisoning, inhalation and ingestion of foreign objects, and firearm use are major causes of unintentional injury and death.

Nurses need to be aware of what constitutes a safe environment for a particular person or for a group of people in home and community settings. Unintentional injuries are often caused by human conduct and can, therefore, be prevented.

Canadian Society Notes

Fact	Implications for Nursing Practice
Assessment of the client must include the biological, psychological, social, cultural, and spiritual needs of the person. Source: CNA. (2002). Code of Ethics.	The registered nurse is expected to comply with the Code.
Individual nurses have the primary responsibility for evaluating and promoting evidence in the context of their practice to ensure that nursing practice maximizes health and quality of life from the client's perspective. Source: CNA. (2002). Evidence-based Decision-making and Nursing Practice.	Nurses are expected to use research-based evidence to support their actions.
In maintaining their professional standards of practice, nurses must consider safety, effectiveness, and cost when planning and providing client care. Source: CNA. (2001). Policy Statement, "Necessary Support for Safe Nursing Care."	Nurses need to assess the environment in which care is delivered.

Factors Affecting Safety

Canada is the eighth highest among 18 industrialized countries in the occurrence of accidental deaths. Injuries are the leading cause of death in Canadians in the first two decades of life (Statistics Canada, 1991a). Health Canada has recognized injuries as a major health concern. (Injury Awareness and Prevention Centre, 1991).

The ability of people to protect themselves from injury is affected by such factors as age and development, lifestyle, mobility and health status, sensory-perceptual alterations, cognitive awareness, psychosocial state, ability to communicate, safety awareness, and environmental factors. Nurses need to be aware of things in the environment that are potentially harmful to health, to understand the illness and injury process sufficiently to be able to predict the probable outcome of certain events, and to learn to use available data to avoid undesirable outcomes (Statistics Canada, 1991b).

Age and Development

Through knowledge and accurate assessment of the environment, people learn to protect themselves from many injuries. Children walking to school learn to stop before crossing the street and wait for oncoming traffic. They also learn not to touch a hot stove. For the very young, learning about the environment is essential. Only through knowledge and experience do children learn what is potentially harmful.

Elderly people can have difficulty with movement and diminished sensual acuity which contribute to the likelihood of injury. Specific age-related potential hazards and preventive measures are discussed later in this chapter. The next box summarizes selected hazards for each age group.

Lifestyle

Lifestyle factors that place people at risk include unsafe work environments; residence in neighbourhoods with high crime rates; access to guns and ammunition; insufficient income to buy safety equipment or make necessary repairs; and access to illicit drugs, which may also be contaminated by harmful additives. Risk-taking behaviour is a factor in some accidents.

Selected Safety Hazards throughout the Life Span*

- *Developing fetus:* Exposure to maternal smoking, alcohol consumption, addictive drugs, x-rays (first trimester), certain pesticides
- *Newborns and infants:* Falling, suffocation in crib, choking from aspirated milk or ingested objects, burns from both water or spilled hot liquids, automobile accidents, crib or playpen injuries, electric shock, poisoning
- *Toddlers:* Physical trauma from falling, banging into objects, or getting cut by sharp objects, automobile accidents, burns, poisoning, drowning, and electric shock
- *Preschoolers:* Injury from traffic, playground equipment, and other objects; choking, suffocation, and obstruction of airway and ear canal by foreign objects; poisoning; drowning; fire and burns; harm from other people or animals
- *Adolescents:* Vehicle (automobile, bicycle) accidents, recreational accidents, firearms, substance abuse
- *Older adults:* Falling, burns, and pedestrian and automobile accidents

*Preventive measures are discussed later in this chapter.

Mobility and Health Status

People who have impaired mobility due to paralysis, muscle weakness, and poor balance or coordination are obviously prone to injury. Clients with spinal cord injury and paralysis of both legs may be unable to move even when they perceive discomfort. Hemiplegic clients or those with leg casts often have poor balance and fall easily. Clients weakened by illness or surgery are not always fully aware of their condition.

Sensory-Perceptual Alterations

Accurate sensory perception of environmental stimuli is vital to safety. People with impaired touch perception, hearing, taste, smell, and vision are highly susceptible to injury. A person who does not see well may trip over a toy or not see an electrical cord. Deaf people do not hear a siren in traffic, and people with impaired olfactory sense may not smell burning food or escaping gas.

Cognitive Awareness

Awareness is the ability to perceive environmental stimuli and body reactions and to respond appropriately through thought and action. Clients with impaired awareness include people who are sleep deprived, unconscious or semiconscious persons, disoriented people (e.g., those who may not understand where they are or what to do to help themselves), people who perceive stimuli that do not exist, and people whose judgement is altered by disease or medications, such as narcotics, tranquilizers, hypnotics, and sedatives. Mildly confused clients may momentarily forget where they are, wander from their rooms, misplace personal belongings, and so forth.

Emotional State

Extreme emotional states can alter the ability to perceive environmental hazards. Stressful situations can reduce a person's level of concentration, cause errors of judgement, and decrease awareness of external stimuli. Depressed people may think and react to environmental stimuli more slowly than normal.

Ability to Communicate

People with diminished ability to receive and convey information are also at risk for injury. Aphasic clients, people with language barriers, and those unable to read are among them. For example, the person unable to interpret the sign "No smoking—oxygen in use" may cause a fire.

Safety Awareness

Information is crucial to safety. Clients in unfamiliar environments frequently need specific safety information. Lack of knowledge about unfamiliar equipment, such as oxygen tanks, intravenous tubing, and hot packs, is a potential hazard. Healthy clients need knowledge about water safety, car safety, fire prevention, ways to prevent the ingestion of harmful substances, and many preventive measures related to specific age-related hazards.

Environmental Factors

A safe home requires well-maintained flooring and carpets, a nonskid bathtub or shower surface, functioning smoke alarms that are strategically placed, and knowledge of fire escape routes. Outdoor areas, such as swimming pools, need to be safely secured and maintained. Adequate lighting, both inside and out, will minimize the potential for accidents.

In the workplace, machinery, industrial belts and pulleys, and chemicals may create danger. Worker fatigue, noise and air pollution, or working at great heights or in subterranean areas may also create occupational hazards. The work environment of the nurse may also be unsafe. The health-care worker needs to maintain an awareness of potential risk.

Adequate street lighting, safe water and sewage treatment, and regulation of sanitation in food buying and handling all contribute to a healthy, hazard-free community. A safe and secure community strives to be free of excess noise, crime, traffic congestion, dilapidated housing, or unprotected creeks and landfills.

Assessing

Assessing clients at risk for accidents and injury involves (1) noting pertinent indicators in the nursing history and physical examination; (2) using specifically developed risk assessment tools; and (3) evaluating the client's home environment.

Nursing History and Physical Examination

The nursing history and physical examination can reveal considerable data about the client's safety practices and risks for injury. Data include age and developmental level; general health status; mobility status; presence or absence of physiological or perceptual deficits, such as olfactory, visual, tactile, taste, or other sensory impairments; altered thought processes or other impaired cognitive or emotional capabilities; substance abuse; any indications of abuse or neglect; and an accident and injury history. A safety history also needs to include the client's awareness of hazards, knowledge of safety precautions both at home and work, and any perceived threats to safety.

Risk Assessment Tools

Risk assessment tools are available to determine clients at risk both for specific kinds of injury, such as falls, or for the general assessment necessary to keep clients safe in their homes and in health-care settings. In general, these tools direct the nurse to appraise the factors affecting safety as they have been outlined earlier. The tools summarize specific data contained in the client's nursing history and physical examination. Client risk factors and environmental hazards for falls are discussed later in this chapter (see "Falls").

Home Hazard Appraisal

Hazards in the home are major causes of falls, fire, poisoning, suffocation, and other accidents, such as those caused by improper use of household equipment, tools, and cooking utensils. See Chapter 17 for a summary of specific data necessary for a home hazard appraisal.

Diagnosing

NANDA offers several diagnostic labels related to safety issues, including:

- ***Risk for Injury:*** A state in which the individual is at risk for injury as a result of environmental conditions interacting with the individual's adaptive and defence resources
- ***Risk for Poisoning:*** Accentuated risk for accidental exposure to, or ingestion of, drugs or dangerous products in doses sufficient to cause poisoning
- ***Risk for Suffocation:*** Accentuated risk for inadequate air available for inhalation
- ***Risk for Trauma:*** Accentuated risk of accidental tissue injury, such as a wound, burn, or fracture
- ***Risk for Aspiration:*** Accentuated risk for the entry of gastrointestinal secretions, oropharyngeal secretions, solids, or fluids into tracheo-bronchial passages
- ***Disuse Syndrome, Risk for:*** Deterioration of body systems as the result of prescribed or unavoidable musculoskeletal inactivity
- ***Knowledge Deficient* (accident prevention):** Inability to state or explain information or demonstrate a required skill related to safety of self and others (Carpenito, 2000)

Planning

When planning care to prevent accidents and injury, the nurse considers all factors affecting the client's safety, specifies desired outcomes, and selects nursing activities to meet these outcomes. The major goal for clients with safety risks is to prevent accidents and injury. To meet this goal, clients often need to change their health behaviour and may need to modify the environment.

Desired outcomes associated with preventing injury depend on the individual client.

Nursing interventions to meet desired outcomes are largely directed toward helping the client and family to:

- Identify environmental hazards in home and community.
- Demonstrate safety practices appropriate to the home, health-care agency, community, and workplace.
- Experience a decrease in the frequency or severity of injury.
- Demonstrate safe childrearing practices or lifestyle practices.

Implementing

Promoting Safety across the Lifespan

Hazards to safety occur at all ages and vary according to the age and developmental level of the individual. Measures to ensure the safety of people of all ages focus on (1) observation or prediction of potentially harmful situations so that harm can be avoided; and (2) client education that empowers clients to safeguard themselves and their families from injury.

Newborns and Infants

Injuries are the leading cause of death among Canadian children (Health Canada, 1996). Many of these deaths are preventable. Safe Kids Canada (Sidsky, 1996) is a national program focused on increasing public awareness of unintentional injuries. Infants who are completely dependent on others for care are oblivious to such dangers as falling

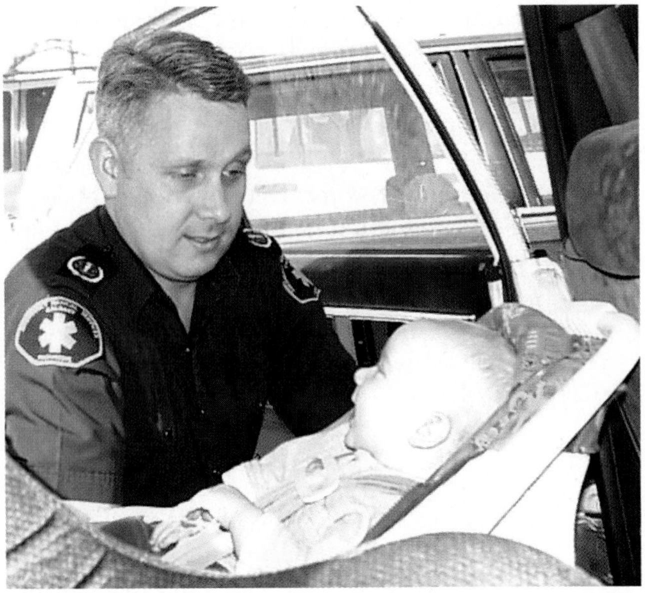

Figure 33.1 Infant car seat—for up to 9 kg

Figure 33.2 Toddler car seat—for toddlers between 9 kg and 18 kg. *Transport Safety for Infants and Toddlers*. Canadian Motor Vehicle Safety Standards.

or ingesting harmful substances. Parents may need to learn about the amount of observation necessary to maintain infant safety. They also need help to identify and remove common hazards in and around the home as well as first-aid information that includes cardiopulmonary resuscitation (CPR) and interventions for airway obstruction. Common accidents during infancy include burns, suffocation or choking, automobile accidents, falls, and poisoning. In 1990, suffocation accounted for 42 percent of all injury-related deaths of children under the age of one year (Health Canada, 1996). Education, such as the correct use of approved car seats for infants, and support of parents can make them more knowledgeable and better prepared to protect their children from accidents and injuries (see Figure 33.1). Safety measures for newborns and infants are listed in the box opposite.

Toddlers

Toddlers are curious and like to feel and taste everything. They are fascinated by things that pose potential dangers, such as garden pools and busy streets, so they need constant supervision and protection. Parents can prevent many accidents by "toddler-proofing" the home or other settings where the child will be. This includes the use of federally approved car restraints (see Figure 33.2) and removing or securing all items that can pose a safety hazard to the child in any setting. It may be necessary to inspect for and remove sources of lead from the environment. Lead poisoning (plumbism) is a risk for children exposed to lead paint chips, fumes from leaded gasoline, or any "leaded" substances. The ingestion of lead-based paint chips is the most common cause of lead poisoning in children. Safety measures for toddlers are listed in the box opposite.

Preschoolers

Children of preschool age are active and often very clumsy, making them susceptible to injury. Control of the environment must continue, keeping such hazards as matches, medicines, and other potential poisons out of reach. Safety education for the child must begin at this stage. Education of the preschooler involves learning how to cross streets, what traffic signals mean, and how to ride bicycles and other wheeled toys safely. Children must be cautioned to avoid hazards, such as busy streets, swimming pools, and other potentially dangerous areas. Parents must maintain careful surveillance; the developmental level of the preschooler does not allow for self-reliance in matters of safety. Parents must also keep in mind that their child's cognitive and motor skills increase quickly; hence, safety measures must keep up with the acquisition of new skills. Safety measures for preschoolers are listed in the box opposite.

School-Age Children

By the time children attend school, they are learning to think before they act. They often prefer adult equipment to toys. They want to be active with other children in such pursuits as bicycling, hiking, swimming, and boating. Although sensitive to peer pressure, the school-age child responds to rules. Children of this age engage in fantasy and colourful imagination. They often imitate actions of parents and superheroes who they identify with.

Injuries are the leading cause of death among Canadians throughout childhood. In 1990, unintentional injuries (such as automobile crashes, poisoning, and falls) accounted for 70 percent of injury-related deaths (Health Canada, 1996). School-age children are also involved in many minor

Safety Measures throughout the Lifespan

Newborns and Infants

- Use a federally approved car seat at all times (including coming home from hospital). Never transport unless the infant is buckled into a rear facing seat in the back seat of the car. Do not place the infant seat in the passenger side if the car has an air bag. (The seat itself is fastened by the car seat belt according to the manufacturer's directions.)
- Never leave the infant unattended on a raised surface.
- Check the temperature of the infant's bath water and formula prior to using.
- Hold the infant upright during feeding. Do not prop the bottle. Cut food in small pieces, and do not feed the infant peanuts or popcorn.
- Investigate the infant's crib for compliance with federal safety regulations: slats no more than 6 cm apart, lead-free paint, height of crib sides, tight fit of mattress to crib.
- Use a playpen with sides made of small-sized netting. Never leave playpen sides down.
- Provide large soft toys with no small detachable or sharp-edged parts.
- Use guardgates on stairs and screens on windows. Supervise the infant in the walker, swing, and highchair.
- Cover electrical outlets. Coil cords out of reach.
- Place plants, household cleaners, and wastebaskets out of reach. Lock away potential poisons, such as medicines, paint, and gasoline.

Toddlers

- Continue to use federally approved car seat or seat belts at all times. These seats face forward, in the back seat of the car at all times. The seat itself is fastened by the car seat belt according to the manufacturer's directions. The seat should never be placed in a vehicle seat equipped with an air bag.
- Teach children not to put objects in the mouth, including pills (unless given by parent).
- Keep objects with sharp edges (such as furniture and knives) out of children's reach.
- Place hot pots on back burners with handles turned inward.
- Keep cleaning solutions, insecticides, and medicines in locked cupboards.
- Keep windows and balconies screened.
- Never leave a child alone in the bathroom, tub, or near any water source (for example, a pool). Teach children to swim. Fence in pools, and supervise at all times. Do not overfill bathtub. Do not let toddlers play near ditches or wells, or fluid gallon pails.
- Teach children not to run or ride a tricycle into the street.
- Obtain a low bed when the child begins to climb.
- Cover outlets with safety covers or plugs.

Preschoolers

- Do not allow children to run with candy or other objects in the mouth.
- Teach children not to put small objects in the mouth, nose, and ears.
- Remove doors from unused equipment, such as refrigerators.
- Teach preschoolers to cross streets safely and obey traffic signals.
- Check Halloween treats before allowing children to eat them. Discard loose or open candy.
- Teach children to play in "safe" areas, not on streets and railroad tracks.
- Teach preschoolers the dangers of playing with matches and playing near charcoal, fire, and heating appliances.
- Teach children to avoid strangers and to keep parents informed of their whereabouts.
- Teach preschoolers not to walk in front of swings and not to push others off playground equipment.
- Teach farm safety.

School-Age Children

- Teach children safety rules for recreational and sports activities: never swim alone; always wear a life jacket when in a boat; and wear a protective helmet and knee and elbow pads when needed.
- Supervise contact sports and activities in which children aim at a target.
- Teach children to obey all traffic and safety rules for bicycling, skateboarding, and roller skating.
- Teach children to use light or reflective clothing when walking or cycling at night.
- Teach children safe ways to use the stove, garden tools, and other equipment.
- Supervise children when they use saws, electric appliances, tools, and other potentially dangerous equipment.
- Teach children not to play with fireworks, gunpowder, or firearms. Keep firearms unloaded, locked up, and out of reach.
- Teach children to avoid excavations, quarries, vacant buildings, and playing around heavy machinery.
- Teach children the effects of drugs and alcohol on judgement and coordination.
- Teach farm safety.

Safety Measures throughout the Lifespan *continued*

Adolescents

- Have adolescents complete a driver's education course, and take practice drives with them in various kinds of weather.
- Set firm limits on automobile use, namely, never to drive after drinking or using drugs and never to ride with a driver who has done so. Encourage adolescents to call home for a ride if they have been drinking, assuring them they can do so without a reprimand.
- Teach adolescents to wear a safety helmet when riding motorcycles, scooters, and other sports vehicles. Teach safety rules for water sports.
- Encourage adolescents to use proper equipment when participating in sports. Schedule a physical examination before participation, and be certain there is medical supervision for all athletic activities.
- Encourage adolescents to swim, jog, and go boating in groups so they can obtain help in case of an accident.
- Teach rules for hunting and the proper care and use of firearms.
- Inform the adolescent of the dangers of drugs, alcohol, and unprotected sex. Be alert to changes in the adolescent's mood and behaviour. Listen to and maintain open communication with the adolescent. Open communication is a powerful preventive measure.
- Teach about occupational health and safety regulations in relation to employment. Teach about rights and responsibilities of the employer and employee.
- Set a good example of behaviour that the adolescents can follow.

Young Adults

- Reinforce motor vehicle safety: drive defensively, use "designated drivers" if alcohol is consumed, routinely check brakes and tires, and use seat and shoulder belts or car seats for all passengers.
- Remind the young adult to repair potential fire hazards, such as electrical wiring.
- Reinforce water safety: know the depth of a pool before diving; supervise backyard pools and other water activities.
- Discuss evaluating the potential for workplace injuries or death when making decisions about a career or occupation. Encourage the young adult to participate actively in programs that reduce occupational hazards.
- Discuss avoiding excessive sun radiation by limiting exposure, using sun-blocking agents, and wearing protective clothing. Explain the skin changes that may indicate a cancerous condition.
- Encourage young adults who are unable to cope with the pressures, responsibilities, and expectations of adulthood to seek counselling.

Middle-Aged Adults

- Reinforce motor vehicle safety: use seat belts and drive within the speed limit, especially at night. Test visual acuity periodically.
- Make certain stairways are well lighted and uncluttered.
- Equip bathrooms with hand grasps and nonskid bath mats.
- Test smoke detectors and fire alarms regularly.
- Keep all machines and tools in good working condition at work and at home. Follow safety precautions when using machinery.

Older Adults

- Encourage the client to have regular vision and hearing tests.
- Assist the client to have a home hazard appraisal.
- Encourage the client to keep as active as possible.

accidents, frequently resulting from outdoor activities and recreational equipment, such as swings, bicycles, skateboards, and swimming pools. Safety measures for school-age children are listed in the box on the previous page.

Adolescents

Obtaining a driver's licence is an important event in the life of an adolescent in North America, but the privilege is not always wisely handled. Teenagers may use driving as an outlet for stress, as a way to assert independence, or as a way to impress peers. When setting limits on automobile use, parents need to assess the teenager's level of responsibility, common sense, and ability to resist peer pressure. The age of the teenager alone does not determine readiness to handle this responsibility.

Adolescents are at risk for sports injuries because their coordination skills are not fully developed. However, sports activities are important to the adolescent's self-esteem and overall development. In addition to providing beneficial exercise, sports activities enhance social and personal development. They help the adolescent experience competition, teamwork, and conflict resolution.

Suicide and homicide account for 21.2 percent of injury deaths among teenagers (Health Canada, 1996). Adolescent males commit suicide at a higher rate than do adolescent females, and African-Canadians commit homicide at a higher rate than European Canadians. Suicides by firearms, drugs, and automobile exhaust are the most common. The suicide rate is highest among 15- to 19-year-olds (Health Canada, 1996). Factors influencing the high suicide and homicide rates include economic deprivation, family breakup, and the availability of firearms, which are the most frequently used weapons. Cutting or stabbing tools are the next most frequently used weapons. Safety measures for adolescents are listed in the box opposite.

Young Adults

Motor vehicle accidents are by far the leading cause of mortality in this group; other causes of unintentional death among young adults include drowning, fires, burns, and firearms.

One safety hazard for many young adults is exposure to natural radiation from sunbathing or outdoor activities. Prolonged and intense exposure to the sun is directly related to skin cancer.

Suicide is another leading cause of death in young adults. Many suicides may actually be mistaken for accidental deaths (automobile accidents, alcohol poisoning, and drug overdose). In general, suicide results from the young adult's inability to cope with the pressures, responsibilities, and expectations of adulthood.

The nurse's role in the prevention of suicide includes identifying behaviours that may indicate potential problems, such as depression; a variety of physical complaints, including weight loss, sleep disturbances, and digestive disorders; and decreased interest in social and work roles along with an increase in isolation. A young adult identified as at risk for suicide should be referred to a mental health professional or a crisis centre. Nurses can also reduce the incidence of suicide by participating in educational programs that provide information about the early signs of suicide. Safety measures for young adults are listed in the box opposite.

Middle-Aged Adults

Changing physiological factors, as well as concern over personal and work-related responsibilities, may contribute to the accident rate of middle-aged persons. Stress renders an individual at any age more vulnerable to injury. Tension during middle age related to financial, marital, health, and alcohol or drug problems increases the risk of injury. Motor vehicle accidents are the most common cause of accidental death in this age group. Decreased reaction times and visual acuity may make the middle-aged adult prone to accidents. Other accidental causes of death among middle-aged adults include falls, fires, burns, poisonings, and drownings. Occupational accidents continue to be a significant safety hazard during the middle years. Safety meaures for middle-aged adults are listed in the box opposite.

Older Adults

Injury leading to death or hospitalization is higher for seniors than any other age group in Canada (Health Canada, 1996). Because vision is impaired, reflexes are slowed, and bones are brittle, climbing stairs, driving a car, and even walking require caution. Driving, particularly night driving, requires caution because accommodation of the eye to light is impaired and peripheral vision is diminished. Older persons need to learn to turn the head before changing lanes and should not rely on side vision, for example, when crossing a street. Driving in a fog or other hazardous conditions should be avoided.

Fires are a hazard for the elderly person with a failing memory. The older person may forget that the iron or stove is left on or may not extinguish a cigarette completely. Because of reduced sensitivity to pain and heat, care must be taken to prevent burns when the person bathes or uses heating devices.

Older people at risk of wandering off due to organic brain syndromes need to wear identification devices. They can also be registered with the local Alzheimer's Association Safe Return Program.

Because older clients who take analgesics or sedatives may become lethargic or confused, they should be monitored regularly and closely. Other measures to induce sleep should be used whenever possible. Nurses can help elderly clients make the home environment safe. Specific hazards can be identified and corrected; for example, handrails can be installed on staircases. The nurse teaches the importance of taking only prescribed medications and contacting a health-care professional at the first indication of intolerance to the medications. Safety measures for older adults are listed in the box opposite.

Preventing Specific Hazards

Implementing measures to prevent specific hazards or accidents, such as burns, fire, falls, poisoning, suffocation, electrocution, and so on, is a critical aspect of nursing care. Teaching clients about safety is another important aspect. Nurses usually have opportunities to teach while providing care.

Scalds and Burns

A **scald** is a burn from a hot liquid or vapour, such as steam. A **burn** results from excessive exposure to thermal, chemical, electrical, or radioactive agents.

Common home hazards causing scalds include the following:

- Pot handles that protrude over the edge of a stove
- Electrical appliances used to heat liquids or oils, especially those with dangling cords that are within reach of crawling infants and young children
- Excessively hot bath water

In health-care agencies, the risk of scalds and burns is greater for clients whose skin sensitivity to temperature is impaired. Scalds can occur from overly hot bath water, and burns from therapeutic applications of heat (see Chapter 37). It is important for the nurse to assess how well clients can protect themselves and what special precautions, if any, need to be taken.

Fires

Fires continue to be a constant risk in health-care settings as well as in homes. Agency fires usually result from malfunctioning electrical equipment or combustion of anesthetic gas. Home fires most frequently result from careless disposal of burning cigarettes or matches, from burning grease, or from faulty electrical wiring.

Agency Fires In health-care agencies, fire is particularly hazardous when people are incapacitated and unable to leave the building without assistance. This makes it extremely important for nurses to be aware of the fire safety regulations and fire prevention practices of the agency in which they work. When a fire occurs, the nurse follows four sequential priorities:

1. Protect and evacuate clients who are in immediate danger.
2. Report the fire.
3. Contain the fire.
4. Extinguish the fire.

Extinguishing the fire requires knowledge of three categories of fire, classified according to the type of material that is burning:

Class A: Paper, wood, upholstery, rags, ordinary rubbish

Class B: Flammable liquids and gases

Class C: Electrical

The right type of extinguisher must be used to fight the fire. Extinguishers have picture symbols showing the type of fire for which they are to be used. Directions for use are also attached to the extinguisher.

Home Fires Nursing interventions for home fires focus on teaching fire safety. Preventive measures include the following:

- Keep emergency numbers near the telephone or stored for speed dialing.
- Be sure the smoke alarms are in operation and appropriately located.
- Have a family "fire drill" plan. Every member needs to know the plan for the nearest exit from different locations of the home.
- Keep fire extinguishers available and in working order.
- Close windows and doors, if possible; cover the mouth and nose with a damp cloth when exiting through a smoke-filled area; and avoid heavy smoke by assuming a bent position with the head as close to the floor as possible.

Falls

People of any age can fall, but infants and older adults are particularly prone to falling and incurring serious injury. Falls are leading causes of acute and chronic morbidity, premature institutionalization, and mortality among seniors (Alexander, Rivara, & Wolf, 1992; Riley, 1992; Scott & Gallager, 1997). One in three older persons falls each year (Graafmans et al., 1996). In Canada, falls are the sixth leading cause of death (Raina & Torrance, 1995). In people 75 years and older, falls are the major cause of fatal injuries and account for twice as many deaths as motor vehicle accidents (O'Loughlin et al., 1991; Raina & Torrence, 1995). Most falls occur in the home and are a major threat to the independence of older adults. Fear of falling is common in older adults, even in those who have not experienced a fall. This fear is of particular concern for those who live alone and who anticipate being helpless and unable to summon help after a fall. In the case of these individuals, the nurse should encourage daily or more frequent contact with a friend or family member, installation of a personal emergency response system, and measures to maintain a physical environment that prevents falls. Risk factors and associated preventive measures are shown in Table 33.1.

Prevention of falls in health-care agencies is an ongoing concern. Health-care environments are designed with many safety features to reduce the risk of falls, such as railings along corridors; a nurse call system at each bedside; safety bars in toilet areas; locks on beds, wheelchairs, and stretchers; side rails on beds; night-lights; and so on. In addition, nurses can implement measures to decrease the incidence of falls. See the box opposite.

Patient safety is a concern with any hospital bed. For the patient, safety may mean the difference between a quick recovery and possible complications. Patient health and safety are the primary focus in care provided. The Advanta Bed (Figure 33.3) is designed to reduce the risk of patient injury throughout the patient care process, including bed articulation, patient transfer, and patient egress. (See box opposite).

A caregiver is typically responsible for several patients at once. In order to improve patient care and caregiver peace of mind, the optional Patient Position Monitor automatically sounds an alarm to alert the caregiver of any position change, attempted patient egress, or a patient who is out of bed. The new system is designed to work with a variety of mattresses.

TABLE 33.1 Risk Factors for Falls and Preventive Measures

Risk Factor	Preventive Measures
Poor vision	Ensure eyeglasses are functional. Ensure appropriate lighting. Mark doorways and edges of steps, as needed. Keep the environment tidy.
Cognitive dysfunction (confusion, disorientation, impaired memory or judgement)	Set safe limits to activities. Remove unsafe objects.
Impaired gait or balance and difficulty walking because of lower extremity dysfunction (e.g., arthritis)	Wear shoes or well-fitted slippers with nonskid soles. Use ambulatory devices as necessary (cane, crutches, walker, braces, wheelchair). Provide assistance with ambulation, as needed. Monitor gait and balance. Adapt living arrangements to one floor, if necessary. Encourage exercise and activity, as tolerated, to maintain muscle strength, joint flexibility, and balance. Ensure uncluttered environment with securely fastened rugs.
Difficulty getting in and out of chair or in and out of bed	Encourage client to request assistance. Keep the bed in the low position. Install grab bars in bathroom. Provide raised toilet seat.
Orthostatic hypotension	Instruct client to rise slowly from a lying to sitting to standing position, and to stand in place for several seconds before walking.
Urinary frequency or receiving diuretics	Provide a bedside commode. Assist with voiding on a frequent and scheduled basis.
Weakness from disease process or therapy	Encourage client to summon help. Monitor activity tolerance.
Current medication regimen that includes sedatives, hypnotics, tranquilizers, narcotic analgesics, diuretics	Attach side rails to the bed. Keep the rails in place and the bed in the lowest position. Monitor orientation and alertness status. Encourage annual or more frequent review of all medications prescribed.

CLINICAL GUIDELINES

Preventing Falls in Health-Care Agencies

- Orient clients, on admission, to their surroundings, and explain the call system.
- Carefully assess the client's risk for falling.
- Alert all personnel to the client's risk for falling.
- Assign clients at risk for falls to rooms near the nursing station where they can be more closely supervised.
- Encourage the client and family to use the nurse call system to request assistance; ensure that the bell is within easy reach.
- Answer patient calls promptly.
- Place bedside tables and overbed tables near the bed or chair so that clients do not overreach and consequently lose their balance.
- Always keep hospital beds in the low position when not providing care so that clients can move in or out of bed easily.
- Keep side rails up and the bed in the low position for sedated and unconscious clients when they are unattended.
- Lock wheels on beds, wheelchairs, and stretchers.
- Ensure that the client wears nonskid footwear.
- Use bed or chair safety monitoring devices as needed.

RESEARCH NOTE

Does a Fall Prevention Program Help Older Women Decrease Their Incidence of Falls, and Is a Group Teaching or One-to-One Strategy More Effective?

Ryan and Spellbring initially presented a 27-item inventory rated on a scale of always, sometimes, and never to 45 women aged 65 years and older. Examples of the items: (1) Do you walk in your stocking feet? (2) Do you keep a flashlight in good working order in your home? (3) Do you sit a moment before getting up to get your balance before you walk? (4) Are bath mats in place in your tub or shower? In addition, several physical measures commonly associated with falls were obtained, including visual acuity, sitting and standing blood pressures, the Romberg test for balance, and a functional gait assessment. The women were selected on the basis of the following criteria: they had to be ambulatory with or without assistive devices, and they had to live alone in their own residences so that any home or personal modifications to prevent falls would be under their sole control.

The subjects were randomly assigned to one of three groups (two treatment and one control), with 15 women per group. A *standardized* fall prevention program was given to the two treatment groups. Group A received the program in a *small group format* of seven to eight women. Group B received the educational program in *one-to-one sessions* with the nurse. The control group received a presentation on health promotion, with no fall prevention information presented.

Post-intervention data collected at three months and six months revealed that the women in this study made a number of fall prevention changes following the educational program offered. The greatest number of changes was made by the group format subjects. Changes included avoiding the use of bath oils while bathing; purchasing night-lights, flashlights, nonskid bath mats, and slippers; eliminating scatter rugs and clutter; and rearranging furniture.

Implications: Nurses can be instrumental in teaching older adults about fall prevention and facilitating a change in behaviour. A small-group educational session seems to be most effective.

Source: Ryan, J. W., & Spellbring, A. M. (1996). Implementing strategies to decrease risk of falls in older women. *Journal of Gerontological Nursing, 22*(12), 25–31.

Safety monitoring devices are also available to prevent falls. Some monitoring systems use a chair or bed sensor (Figure 33.4); others use a leg band. These devices trigger an alarm when the client attempts to get out of bed or a chair unassisted. Procedure 33.1 describes how to use these devices.

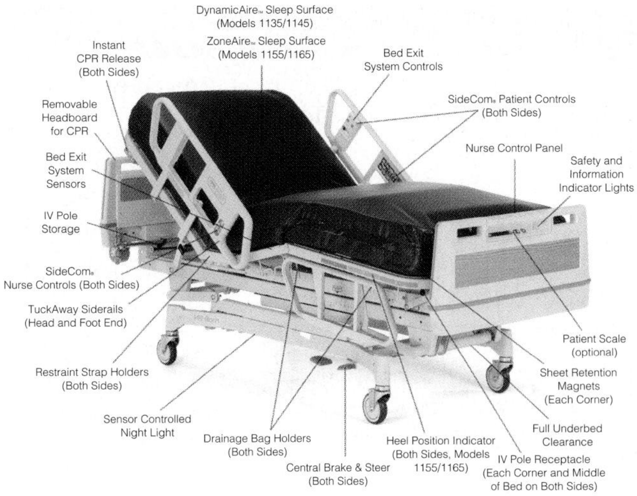

Figure 33.3 The **Advanta Bed** is designed for ***Improved Patient Safety*** © 2002 Hill-Rom Services, Inc. Reprinted with permission. ALL RIGHTS RESERVED.

Additional Patient Safety Features

- Low height of 38.7 cm
- Raised head and foot boards
- Retractability
- Instant CPR (a manual override that provides instant, uninterrupted lowerage of the head to a full flat position without the caregiver having to bear the weight of the patient)
- Automatic night light
- Easy-grip side rails
- Smaller openings in side rails
- COMposer® Communication System interface, *optional*

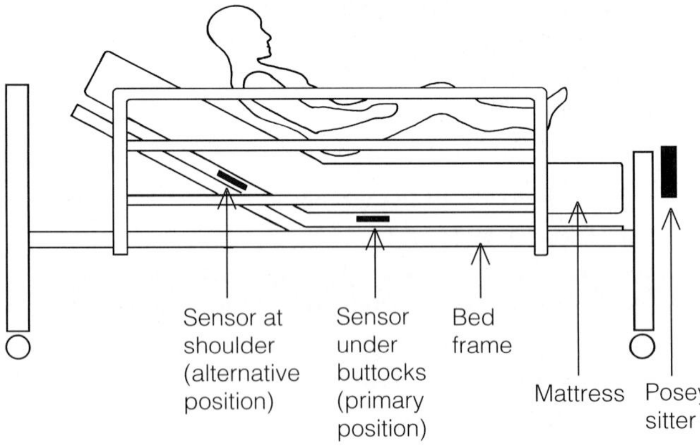

Figure 33.4 Bed exit monitoring device

Poisoning

The major reasons for poisoning in children are inadequate supervision and improper storage of many household toxic substances. Implementing poison prevention for children is focused on teaching parents to "childproof" the environment, including disposing of unused medications properly by returning them to a pharmacy. Adolescent and adult poisonings are usually caused by insect or snake bites and drugs used for recreation or in suicide attempts. Implementing poison prevention in these age groups focuses on dissemination of information and counselling. Poisoning in older adults usually results from accidental ingestion of a toxic substance (e.g., due to failing eyesight) or an overdose of a prescribed medication (e.g., due to impaired memory). Implementing poison prevention with older adults focuses on safeguarding the environment and monitoring the underlying problems.

PROCEDURE 33.1 Using a Bed or Chair Exit Safety Monitoring Device

A bed or chair safety monitor (see Figure 33.4) is an electronic device with a position-sensitive switch that triggers an audio alarm when the client attempts to get out of the bed or chair unassisted. When activated, the alarm alerts the nurse and provides an opportunity for the nurse to intervene.

Assessment Focus
Mobility status; judgement about ability to get out of bed safely; proximity of client's room or chair to nurses' station; position of side rails and functioning status of call light

PURPOSES

- To alert the nurse that the client is attempting to get out of bed
- To help decrease the risk of client falls

Equipment

- ❑ Alarm and control device
- ❑ Connection to nurse call system (optional)
- ❑ Sensor device

INTERVENTION

1. **Explain to the client and support people the purpose and procedure for using safety monitoring.**
- Explain that the device does not limit mobility in any manner; rather, it alerts the staff when the client is about to get out of bed or a chair.
- Explain that the nurse must be called when the client needs to get out of bed.
2. **Obtain the appropriate sensor device and control unit.**
3. **Test the battery device and alarm sound.** *This ensures that the device is functioning properly prior to use.*
4. **Apply the sensor pad or leg band.**
- Place the leg band according to the manufacturer's recommendations. The usual position for a bed or chair sensor is under the mattress or chair cushion directly beneath the client's buttocks. For clients at high risk of falling, the sensor may be placed under the shoulders.
- For a bed or chair device, set the time delay for determining the client's movement patterns from one to 12 seconds.
- Connect the sensor pad to the control unit and the nurse call system. *The alarm device is position sensitive. For example, when a leg band approaches a near vertical position (such as in walking, crawling, or kneeling as the client attempts to get out of bed), the audio alarm is triggered, causing a sharp, shrill sound.*
5. **Instruct the client to call the nurse when the client wants or needs to get up, and assist as required.**
- When assisting the client to rise, deactivate the alarm by unsnapping the alarm device from the elastic band.
- Assist the client back to bed, and reattach the alarm device to the sensor.
6. **Ensure client safety with additional safety precautions.**
- Place call button within client reach, lift all side rails, and lower the bed to its lowest position. *The alarm device is not a substitute for other precautionary measures.*
- Place monitoring device stickers on the client's door, chart, and Kardex®.
7. **Document relevant data.**
- Record that monitoring device is intact when applied.
- Record all assessments.
- Record all safety precautions and interventions discussed and employed.

Evaluation Focus
Status of the monitoring device; effectiveness of safety precautions

Home Care Considerations

Instruct caregivers to

- Test the monitoring device every 12 to 24 hours to ensure that it is working.
- Check the volume of the alarm to ascertain if they can hear it.

CLIENT TEACHING

Preventing Poisoning

- Lock potentially toxic agents, including drugs and cleaning agents, in a cupboard, or attach special plastic hooks to the inside of cabinet doors to keep them securely closed. Unlatching these hooks requires firmer thumb pressure than small children can usually exert.
- Avoid storing toxic liquids or solids in food containers, such as soft drink bottles, peanut butter jars, or milk cartons.
- Do not remove container labels or reuse empty containers to store different substances.
- Do not rely on cooking to destroy toxic chemicals in plants. Never use anything prepared from nature as a medicine or "tea."
- Teach children never to eat any part of an unknown plant or mushroom and not to put leaves, stems, bark, seeds, nuts, or berries from any plant into their mouths.
- Place poison warning stickers (designed for children) on containers of bleach, lye, kerosene, solvent, and other toxic substances.
- Do not refer to medicine as candy or pretend false enjoyment when taking medications in front of children; allow them to see the necessity of the medicine without glamourizing it.
- Read and follow label directions on all products before using them.
- Keep syrup of ipecac on hand at all times. Syrup of ipecac is a nonprescription emetic available in single-dose 15-mL vials in all drugstores. Use it only after advice from the local poison control centre or the family physician.
- Display the phone number of the poison control centre near or on all telephones in the home so that it is available to babysitters, family, and friends.

In response to the ever increasing number of poison hazards, many countries have established poison control centres that provide accurate, up-to-date information about potential hazards and recommend treatment as needed. For certain poisons, specific antidotes or treatments are available; for many, there is no specific therapy.

Nurses intervene in community settings by educating the public about what to do in the event of poisoning. Identify the specific poison by searching for an opened container, empty bottle, or other evidence. Contact the poison control centre, indicate the exact quantity of poison the person ingested, and state the person's age and apparent symptoms. Keep the person as quiet as possible and lying on the side or sitting with head placed between the legs to prevent aspiration of vomitus. The box above provides additional guidelines for teaching clients to prevent poisoning.

Carbon Monoxide Poisoning

Carbon monoxide (CO) is an odourless, colourless, tasteless gas that is very toxic. Exposure to CO can cause symptoms including headaches, dizziness, weakness, nausea, vomiting, or loss of muscle control. Prolonged exposure to CO can lead to unconsciousness, brain damage, or death. Learning the steps to prevent CO danger is particularly important because all gasoline-powered vehicles, lawn mowers, kerosene stoves, barbecues, and burning wood emit CO. Incomplete or faulty combustion of any fuel, including natural gas used in furnaces, can produce CO. Carbon monoxide detectors for homes are commercially available.

Suffocation or Choking

Choking and suffocation are common accidents that occur among infants and small children. In 1990, suffocation accounted for 42 percent of all injury-related deaths of children under one year of age (Health Canada, 1996).

Suffocation, or asphyxiation, is lack of oxygen due to interrupted breathing. Suffocation occurs when the air source is cut off for any reason. One common reason for choking is food or a foreign object becoming lodged in the throat. The universal sign of distress in this case is observation of the victim grasping and pointing to the neck and throat area without speaking. The emergency response is the **Heimlich maneuver,** or abdominal thrust, which can dislodge the foreign object and re-establish an airway. See Figure 33.5.

Other causes of suffocation are drowning, gas or smoke inhalation, accidental coverage of the nose and mouth by a piece of plastic, accidental strangulation by the shoulder harness of a seat belt, and being trapped in a confined space (e.g., a discarded refrigerator). If a person does not receive immediate relief from suffocation, the interrupted breathing leads to respiratory and cardiac arrest and death. Any obstruction to the air passages must be immediately removed and life support measures instituted when an arrest occurs.

Bike or Sport Injuries

Bicycle related injuries are a major source of death and disability among children, accounting for greater than

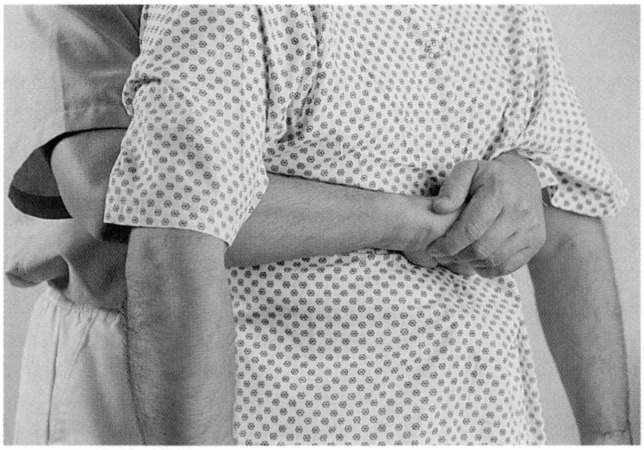

Figure 33.5 Performing the Heimlich maneuver

600 deaths and numerous visits to emergency every year (Canadian Hospitals Injury Reporting and Prevention Programs, 1998). Among the children who die from bike accidents, 85 percent die from head injuries that could have been prevented by wearing a helmet. Children and adults should be encouraged to wear bike helmets for cycling, in-line skating, and skiing. In Alberta, injuries related to snowmobiles are also on the rise. Between 1995 and 1999, the number of trauma cases has more than doubled, and 90 percent of the cases were males. Only 56 percent of snowmobilers were wearing a helmet at the time of the accident (Injury Control Alberta, 2000). As a result, prevention/safety education—the Sled Smart program—began during the winter of 2000–2001 by visiting northern Alberta schools.

Safety Concerns for Health-Care Workers

Factors Affecting Workplace Health

There are many issues that exist today in the health-care environment that place health-care workers at risk. A recent survey done for the Canadian Labour Force by Judith Shamian (executive director of Nursing Policy for Health Canada) indicates that nurses are more likely than any other occupation to suffer from illness and disability (Shamian, 1999). On average, nurses lost 6.3 percent of the work week due to illness.

Several factors account for the absence level in various groups of health-care workers. The factors determined by Health Canada (1998) include the physical health of the workers, (frequently related to age), work environment, degree of job stress, employer/employee relations, and workplace violence.

It is not surprising that nurses as employees in today's health-care system experience high levels of stress. Shamian (1999) quotes Sullivan, who found that nurses, when compared with workers from nonhealth-care fields, reported higher levels of psychological demand, lower levels of decision authority, higher levels of physical

The Occupational Health and Safety Team

Nurses who work in hospitals and in community and other health-care settings must be aware of and adhere to provincial/territorial regulations of occupational health and safety. The work of the occupational health and safety team strives to reduce the number of occupational accidents, occupational disease, or the transmission of contagious disease to other workers. The implementation of WHMIS (Workplace Hazardous Materials Information System) is a key component of workplace safety guidelines, which all workers must be aware of. WHMIS is a system designed to communicate information about hazardous materials in the workplace. Legislation to implement WHMIS has been enacted at the federal, provincial, and territorial levels.

Each province and territory uses a common system of labelling for containers of controlled products. WHMIS also requires education programs so that employees will understand these labels.

The law requires that the Canadian supplier of a WHMIS-controlled product intended for use in a workplace in Canada transmit an MSDS (Materials Safety Data Sheet) disclosing prescribed information as a condition of sale. Also, a Canadian importer of a controlled product must obtain or prepare an MSDS as a condition of importation.

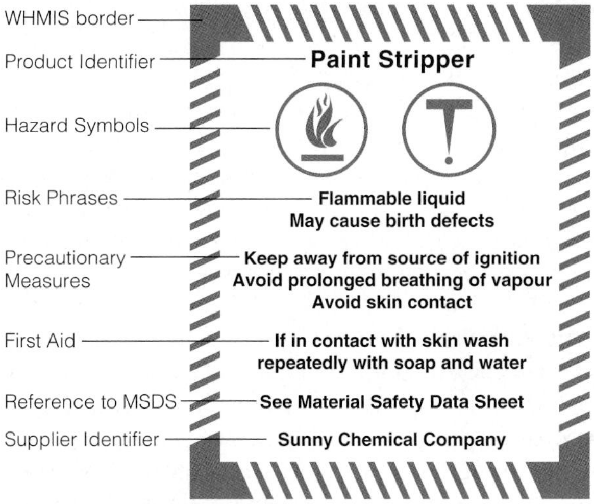

WHMIS System of Labelling

Source: Adapted from Workplace Hazardous Materials Information System, URL: http://www.hc-sc.gc.ca/hecs-sesc/whmis/labels.htm, 2002 © Adapted and Reproduced with the permission of the Minister of Public Works and Government Services Canada.

demand, heavier work, and lower levels of job satisfaction. These factors contribute to the finding that nurses face the highest level of stress across the groups in health care. Health agencies are recognizing that stress is an occupational hazard and are working on providing the necessary support services for employees. Most often, services include employee assistance programs through which staff can gain access to professional counselling and stress management programs. Another avenue for reaching employees with respect to their health is through a health promotion/wellness program. This program is designed to create a culture that supports healthy activities and behaviours in both personal and organizational health.

Violence in the Workplace

Research shows that a "trend toward increasing violence is found in all health-care settings, rural as well as inner city and urban areas" (ICN, 1999, p. 5). In the past decade, the Canadian Nurses Association and most provincial/territorial nursing associations have become increasingly concerned with the number of members contacting them about experiences involving violence in the workplace. Nurses work in a variety of settings and care for different kinds of individuals, which puts them at risk. These individuals may be mentally or chemically impaired or may be experiencing extreme stress from disease or other stresses, such as family difficulties, unemployment, or poverty.

Research shows that the majority of nurses encounter some form of violence in their workplace and that, most often, experiences are reported to a colleague rather than to supervisors (B.C. Nurses Union Survey, 1991; Fédération Des Infirmières Du Québec, 1995). "Nurses are at particularly high risk of verbal and emotional abuse, physical violence, and sexual harassment" during their working lives (CNA, 2002, p. 1). These findings are a cause for concern for the health and safety of all nurses. The CNA suggests that nurses must assertively refuse to tolerate violence and harassment, and provide support to those who have been abused by taking individual and collective action within the workplace and through nursing organizations (2002). (See Table 33.2 for responsibilities in ensuring a safe working environment). The CNA also proposes that "it is the responsibility of all employees to ensure a safe and secure working environment of open communication, with policies and protocols to support employees reporting violence in the workplace" (p. 1).

Restraining Clients

Restraints are protective devices used to limit the physical activity of the client or a part of the body. They can be classified as physical or chemical. *Physical restraints* are any manual method or physical or mechanical device, material, or equipment attached to the client's body; they cannot

TABLE 33.2 Ensuring a Safe Workplace

The responsibility to ensure a safe workplace is shared by:

Individual Nurses	To increase their knowledge and skills regarding the issue of violence, and take a proactive stance in refusing to tolerate violence and harassment. Skills should include assessment of potentially violent situations. As members of an interdisciplinary team, nurses provide health promotion strategies to provide and support nonviolent interactions in families, and provide treatment for victims and survivors of violence.
Employers	To provide administrative support and structure to promote the safety of all employees, including nurses. Policies and procedures are the first step in ensuring a safe workplace. Security equipment and personnel should be provided as well as education in preventing and responding to violence. Facilities should be planned or modified to discourage aggressive behaviour. Clear documentation processes and follow-up mechanisms that support the nurse should be in place.
Governments	To provide the legislative mechanisms and adequate resources to ensure a safe workplace.
Nursing Organizations	To provide advocacy and information. This emphasizes the principle that nurses have the right to safe workplaces to provide client care. These organizations also protect the public.
Nurses at all levels of the organization	Have a role to play in promoting changes in societal attitudes regarding violence. Health care and the delivery of nursing services are best carried out in a climate of mutual respect. Every health-care employee is entitled to be treated with dignity and respect.
Public	To report violence of clients by nurses and nurses by clients to provincial/territorial nursing regulatory bodies.

Source: Canadian Nurses Association. (March 2002). *Position statement on violence.* Ottawa: Author; Canadian Nurses Association. (November 2001). *Position statement on quality practice environments for registered nurses.* Ottawa: Author.

Alternatives to Restraints

- Assign nurses in pairs to act as "buddies" so that one nurse can observe the client when the other leaves the unit.
- Place unstable clients in an area that is constantly or closely supervised.
- Prepare clients before a move to limit relocation shock and resultant confusion.
- Stay with a client using a bedside commode or bathroom if the client is confused or sedated or has a gait disturbance or a high-risk score for falling.
- Monitor all the client's medications, and if possible, attempt to lower or eliminate dosages of sedatives or psychotropics.
- Position beds at their lowest level from the floor to facilitate getting in and out of bed.
- Replace full-length side rails with half- or three-quarter-length rails to prevent confused clients from climbing over rails or falling from the end of the bed.
- Use rocking chairs to help confused clients expend some of their energy so that they will be less inclined to wander.
- Wedge pillows or pads against the sides of wheelchairs to keep clients well positioned.
- Place a removable lap tray on a wheelchair to provide support and help keep the client in place.
- To quiet agitated clients, try a warm beverage, soft lights, a back rub, or a walk.
- Use "environmental restraints," such as pieces of furniture or large plants as visual barriers, to discourage clients from wandering beyond appropriate areas.
- Place a picture or any other personal item on the door to clients' rooms to help them identify their room.
- Try to determine the causes of the client's *sundowner's syndrome* (nocturnal wandering and disorientation as darkness falls, associated with dementia). Possible causes include poor hearing, poor eyesight, or pain.
- Establish ongoing assessment to monitor changes in physical and cognitive functional abilities and risk factors.
- Where the technology has been implemented, have the client wear a special bracelet that will trigger a building alarm system when the client leaves a secure area.

be removed easily and they restrict the client's movement. *Chemical restraints* are medications, such as neuroleptics, anxiolytics, sedatives, and psychotropic agents, used to control socially disruptive behaviour.

The purpose of restraints is to ensure the physical safety of the person being restrained or of other persons who may otherwise be harmed by the unrestrained person. Nurses are encouraged to reduce the use of restraints and use safe alternatives whenever possible. The Alberta Association of Registered Nurses (AARN) follows the "Least Restraint Practice," which means "the nurse will exhaust all possible alternative interventions before deciding to use a restraint" (2003, p. 1). Alternatives to restraints include redirection, limits, using time outs, the use of medications, psychosocial interventions, and safe, physical escort techniques (De Prospero, Rogers, & Bocchino, 1999; Kozub & Skidmore, 2001). Alternatives to restraints are shown in the box left.

The safety of individuals must be considered before applying a restraint. Many harmful physical effects, such as skin breakdown, immobilization, urinary incontinence, increased agitation, physical and mental deterioration, and even death have been noted in the literature. Ethical issues of autonomy and individual's rights to respect and dignity must be considered in using restraints (AARN, 1999; CNA, 2002). The use of restraints brings up many legal issues as well.

Legal Implications of Restraints

Because restraints restrict a person's ability to move freely, their use has legal implications. Legal issues arise from concern related to the informed consent of clients, families, and/or guardians, the safety of patients, and the authorization of restraints. There are situations where the use of restraints may be appropriate. Examples would include self-injurious behaviour of the individual or a threat to the personal safety of the staff, patients, or others in the practice setting (AARN, 2003). To protect clients and to avoid legal problems, the nurse should follow these guidelines:

- Know the agency's restraint policies. Policies should cover all types of physical and chemical restraints and specify how and when to apply them and what procedures to follow.
- When determining the need for a restraint, always assess the underlying reason for a client's restlessness, agitation, or confusion.
- Apply restraints only when necessary for the client's health and safety, not for convenience or to cope with understaffing.
- Avoid being influenced by a family member's advice not to restrain the client, even when the person offers to sit with the client.
- Obtain a physician's order before applying a restraint. If the client needs to be restrained immediately, apply the restraint and then notify the physician as soon as possible. In many agencies, standing orders allow the use of restraints under certain circumstances provided that a written order is obtained from the physician within 24 hours.

- Recognize the competent adult's right to make decisions regarding personal care and treatment, and obtain appropriate consent. Check agency policies if necessary restraint is refused. An agency may require the client to sign a release of liability should injury result; otherwise, the agency has the option of refusing to continue care. For clients who are declared legally incompetent, obtain consent from proxy or alternate decision maker as permitted under law.
- Keep in mind the *principle of least restraint;* that is, restrain the client only to the extent necessary to accomplish the restraint's purpose.
- Make sure that a physical restraint fits properly.
- When a restraint is applied, document:
  a. The exact times the restraint was applied and removed
  b. The client's behaviour while the restraint was applied
  c. The assessment and care provided while the restraint was applied and removed (e.g., assessment of circulation and range-of-motion exercises)
  d. Notification of the physician
- Periodically re-evaluate the need for the restraint.

Selecting a Restraint

Before selecting a restraint, nurses need to clearly understand its purpose and measure it against the following five criteria:

1. *It restricts the client's movement as little as possible.* If a client needs to have one arm restrained, do not restrain the entire body.
2. *It does not interfere with the client's treatment or health problem.* If a client has poor blood circulation to the hands, apply a restraint that will not aggravate that circulatory problem.
3. *It is readily changeable.* Restraints need to be changed frequently, especially if they become soiled. Keeping other guidelines in mind, choose a restraint that can be changed with minimal disturbance to the client.
4. *It is safe for the particular client.* Choose a restraint with which the client cannot self-inflict injury. For example, a physically active child could incur injury trying to climb out of a crib if one wrist is tied to the side of the crib. A jacket restraint would restrain the child more safely.

Kinds of Restraints

There are several kinds of restraints. Among the most common are the jacket restraint, the belt restraint, the mitt or hand restraint, limb restraints, elbow restraints, mummy restraints, and crib nets. Geri chairs and wheelchairs used to confine client activity can also be considered restraints. In long-term care, the use of vest restraints has decreased as compared with the use of belt restraints. A newer model of vest restraint is the Segufix restraint, which uses magnetic locks to secure the vest in place. These body restraints are used to ensure the safety of confused or sedated clients in beds or wheelchairs.

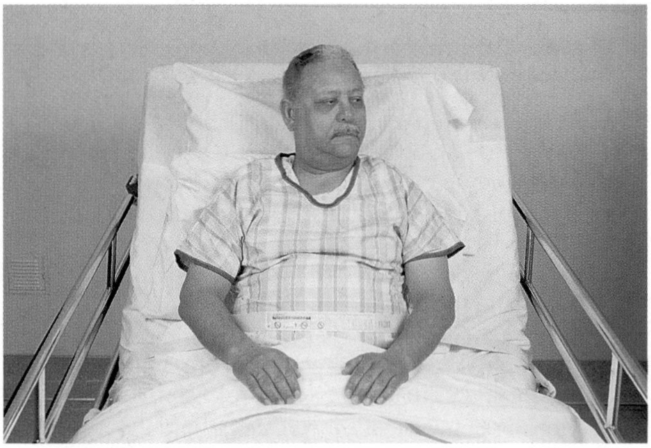

Figure 33.6 A poncho-type vest restraint

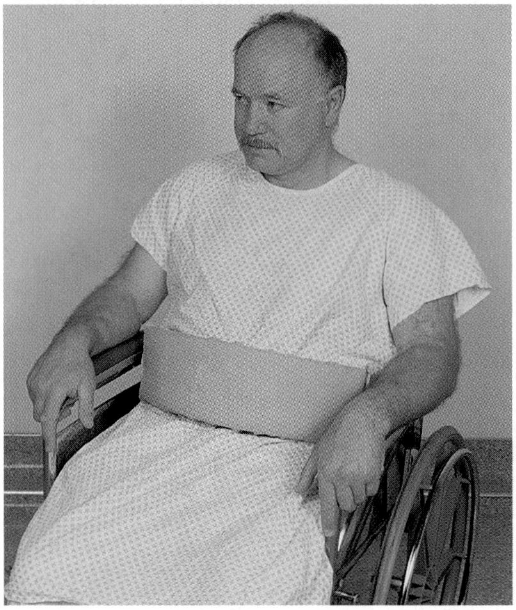

Figure 33.7 A belt restraint

Belt or safety strap body restraints (Figure 33.7) are used to ensure the safety of all clients who are being moved on stretchers or in wheelchairs. Some wheelchairs have a soft padded safety bar that attaches to side brackets that are installed under the arm rests. To prevent the person from slumping forward, the nurse then attaches a shoulder "Y" strap to the bar and over the client's shoulders to the rear handles. Other safety belt models have a three-loop design. One loop surrounds the person's waist and attaches to the rear handles. If such restraints are unavailable, the nurse can place a folded towel or small sheet around the client's waist and fasten it at the back of the wheelchair. Belt restraints may also be used for certain clients confined to beds or to chairs.

A *mitt or hand restraint* (Figure 33.8) is used to prevent confused clients from using their hands or fingers to scratch and injure themselves. For example, a confused client may need to be prevented from pulling at intravenous tubing or a head bandage following brain surgery. Hand or mitt restraints allow the client to be ambulatory and/or to move the arm freely rather than be confined to a bed or a chair. Mittens need to be removed at least every two hours to permit the client to wash and exercise the hands. The nurse also needs to take off the mitten regularly to check the circulation to the hand.

Limb restraints (Figure 33.9), which are generally made of cloth, may be used to immobilize a limb, primarily for therapeutic reasons (e.g., to maintain an intravenous infusion).

Elbow restraints (Figure 33.10) are used to prevent infants or small children from flexing their elbows to touch or scratch a skin lesion or to reach the head when a scalp vein infusion is in place. This restraint consists of a piece of material with pockets into which plastic or wooden tongue depressors are inserted to provide rigidity.

The *mummy restraint* is a special folding of a blanket or sheet around the child to prevent movement during a procedure, such as gastric washing, eye irrigation, or collection of a blood specimen.

When using restraints, the nurse may find the guidelines in the box on page 802 helpful. See Procedure 33.2 for applying restraints.

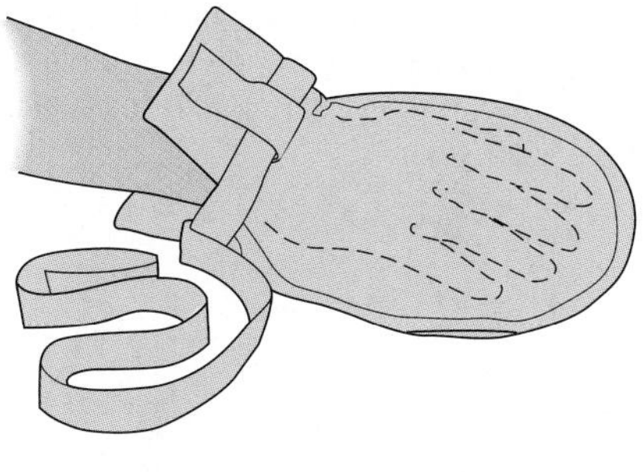

Figure 33.8 A mitt restraint

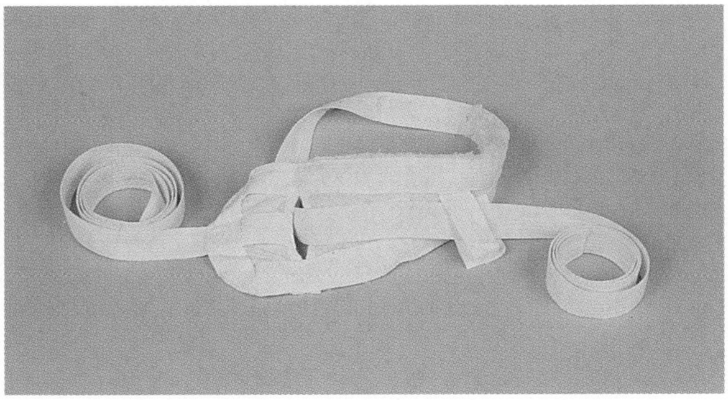

Figure 33.9 A limb restraint

Figure 33.10 An elbow restraint

Evaluating

To prevent client injury, the nurse's role is largely educative, and desired outcomes reflect the client's acquisition of knowledge of hazards, behaviours that incorporate safety practices, and skills to perform in the event of certain emergencies. Examples of desired outcomes follow. The nurse needs to individualize these for clients. The client:

- Describes methods to prevent specific hazards (e.g., falls, suffocation, choking, fires, drowning, electric shock).
- Reports use of home safety measures (e.g., fire safety measures, smoke detector maintenance, fall prevention strategies, burn prevention measures, poison prevention measures, safe storage of hazardous materials, firearm safety precautions, electrocution prevention, water safety precautions, bicycle safety, motor vehicle safety).
- Alters home physical environment to reduce the risk of injury.
- Describes emergency procedures for poisoning and fire.
- Describes age-specific risks or work safety risks or community safety risks.
- Demonstrates correct use of child safety seats.
- Demonstrates correct administration of cardiopulmonary resuscitation.

PROCEDURE 33.2 Applying Restraints

PURPOSE

- To enable the client to receive treatment and to allow the treatment to proceed without client interference (e.g., to prevent movements that would disrupt therapy to a limb connected to tubes or appliance)

Assessment Focus
Behaviour indicating the possible need for a restraint; underlying cause for assessed behaviour (to ascertain what other protective measures may be implemented before applying a restraint); status of skin to which restraint is to be applied; circulatory status distal to restraints and of extremities; effectiveness of other available safety precautions

Equipment

Select the kind and size of restraint required by the client. See "Selecting a Restraint" earlier in this chapter.

INTERVENTION

1. Explain to client and support people the purpose and procedure for using the restraint.

2. Apply the selected restraint.

Belt Restraint (Safety Belt)

- Determine that the safety belt is in good order. If a Velcro safety belt is to be used, make sure that both pieces of Velcro are intact.
- If the belt has a long portion and a shorter portion, place the long portion of the belt behind (under) the bedridden client and secure it to the movable part of the bed frame. *The long attached portion will then move up when the head of the bed is elevated and will not tighten around the client.* Place the shorter portion of the belt around the client's waist, over the gown. There should be a finger width between the belt and the client.

  or
- Attach the belt around the client's waist and fasten it at the back of the chair.

  or
- If the belt is attached to a stretcher, secure the belt firmly over the client's hips or abdomen. Belt restraints need to be applied to all clients on stretchers even when the side rails are up.

Vest Restraint

- Ensure that vest is the correct size and check the fit periodically.
- Place vest on client, with opening at the front or the back, according to manufacturer's recommendations.
- Pull the tie on the end of the vest flap across the chest, and place it through the slit on the opposite side of the chest.
- Repeat for the other tie.
- Use a half-bow knot (quick-release knot) to secure each tie around the movable bed frame or behind the chair to a chair leg (Figure 33.11). *A half-bow knot does not tighten or slip when the attached end is pulled but unties easily when the loose end is pulled.* Do not tie the vest to the head of the bed. *This prevents compression of the brachial plexus in the axilla.*

  or
- Fasten the ties together behind the chair using a square (reef) knot (Figure 33.12). *This knot does not tighten with pulling and does not slip when pressure is released.*
- Ensure that the client is positioned appropriately to enable maximum chest expansion for breathing.

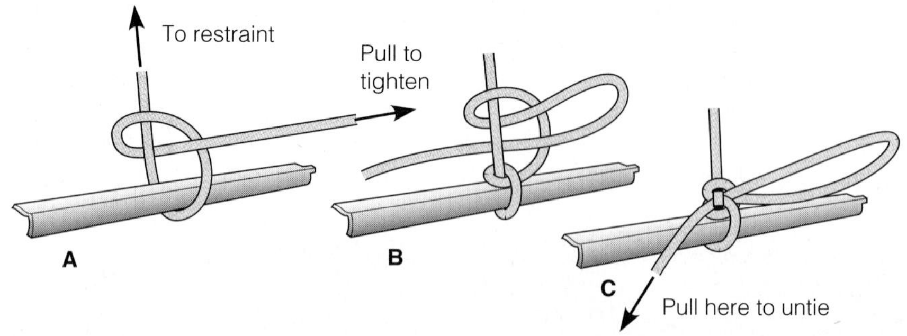

Figure 33.11 To make a half-bow knot (quick-release knot), first place the restraint tie under the side frame of the bed (or around a chair leg). *A,* Bring the free end up, around, under, and over the attached end of the tie and pull it tight. *B,* Again, take the free end over and under the attached end of the tie, but this time make a half-bow loop. *C,* tighten the free end of the tie and the bow until the knot is secure. To untie the knot, pull the end of the tie and then loosen the first cross over the tie.

PROCEDURE 33.2 Applying Restraints *continued*

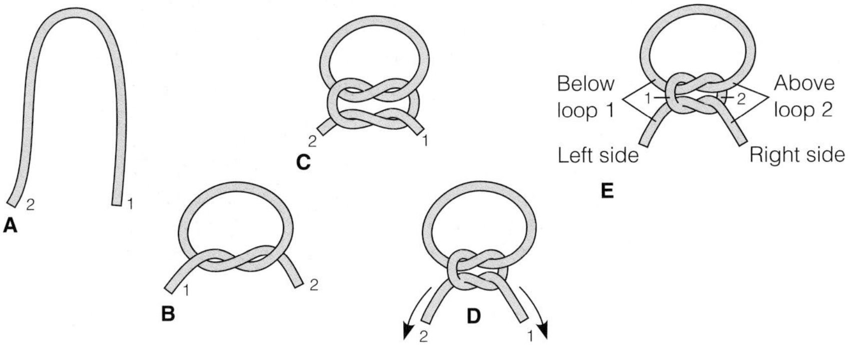

Figure 33.12 To make a square (reef) knot: *A,* Form a "U" loop. *B,* Pass one end (1) over and under the other. *C,* Take the same end (1), and pass it over, under, and over the other. *D,* Pull knot tight. *E,* When the knot is tied correctly, the ties on each side are both either above or below the loop.

Mitt Restraint

- Apply the commercial thumbless mitt (Figure 33.8, earlier) to the hand to be restrained. Make sure the fingers can be slightly flexed and are not caught under the hand.
- Follow the manufacturer's directions for securing the mitt.
- If a mitt is to be worn for several days, remove it at least every two to four hours. Wash and exercise the client's hand, then re-apply a clean mitt as indicated. Check agency practices about recommended intervals for removal.
- Assess the client's circulation to the hands shortly after the mitt is applied and at regular intervals. *Feelings of numbness or discomfort or inability to move the fingers could indicate impaired circulation to the hand.*

Wrist or Ankle Restraint

- Pad bony prominences on the wrist or ankle, if needed, to *prevent skin breakdown.*
- Apply the padded portion of a commercially prepared restraint around the ankle or wrist (Figure 33.13).
- Pull the tie of the commercially made restraint through the slit in the wrist portion or through the buckle.
- Using a half-bow knot (quick-release knot) or a square knot, as appropriate, attach the other end of the commercial restraint to the movable portion of the bed frame, never to the side rails or to the non-moving bed frame. *If the ties are attached to the movable portion, the wrist or ankle will not be pulled when the bed position is changed.*

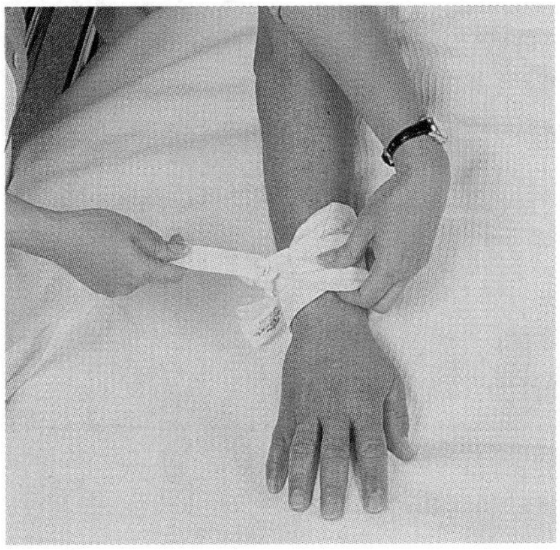

Figure 33.13 Make sure that two fingers can be inserted between the restraint and the wrist or ankle

Elbow Restraint

- Examine the restraint to make sure that the tongue depressors are intact, that is, all in place and not broken.
- Place the child's elbow in the centre of the restraint. Make sure that the ends of the tongue depressors are covered by the padded material. *This prevents them from irritating the skin.*
- Wrap the restraint smoothly around the arm.
- Secure the restraint, using safety pins, ties, or tape. Ensure that it is not so tight that it obstructs blood circulation.
- (Optional) After the restraint is applied, pin it to the child's shirt. *This prevents it from sliding down the arm.*

Mummy Restraint

- Obtain a blanket or sheet large enough so that the distance between opposite corners is about twice the length of the infant's body. Lay the blanket or sheet on a flat dry surface.
- Fold down one corner, and place the baby on it in the supine position.
- Fold the right side of the blanket over the infant's body, leaving the left arm free (Figure 33.14, *A*). The right arm is in a natural position at the side.
- Fold the excess blanket at the bottom, up under the infant (Figure 33.14, *B*[2]).
- With the infant's left arm in a natural position beside the body, fold the left side of the blanket over the infant, including the arm, and tuck the blanket under the body (Figure 33.14, *B*[3]).
- Remain with the infant who is in a mummy restraint until the specific procedure is completed.

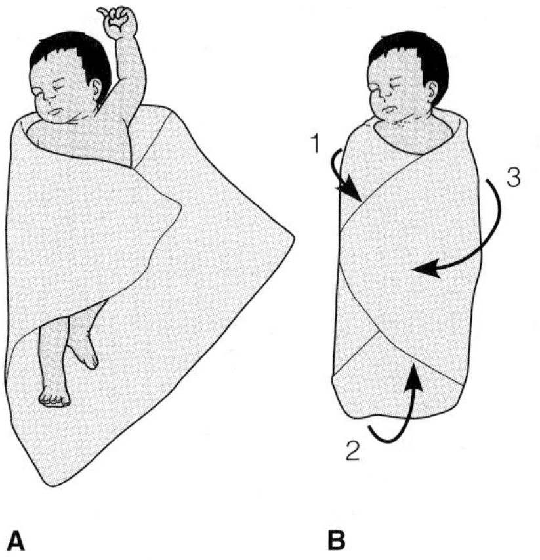

Figure 33.14 Making a mummy restraint

PROCEDURE 33.2 Applying Restraints *continued*

3. Document relevant information for all types of restraints.

- Record on the client's chart the time the physician was notified, the type of restraint applied, the time it was applied, the reason for its application, the client's response to the restraint, and the times that the restraints are removed and skin care given.
- Record any other interventions, assessments, and explanations to client and significant others.
- Adjust the nursing care plan as required, for example, to include releasing the restraint q2h, assessing circulation, sensation, and motion of restrained extremities; providing skin care; and providing range-of-motion exercises.

Evaluation Focus
Client's response to restraint; circulatory status of restrained limbs; skin status beneath restraints

CLINICAL GUIDELINES

Applying Restraints

- Obtain consent from the client or guardian.
- Ensure that a physician's order has been provided, or in an emergency, obtain one within 24 hours after applying the restraint according to agency policy.
- Assure the client and the client's support people that the restraint is temporary and protective. A restraint must never be applied as punishment for any behaviour or merely for the nurse's convenience.
- Apply the restraint in such a way that the client can move as freely as possible without defeating the purpose of the restraint.
- Ensure that limb restraints are applied securely but not so tightly that they impede blood circulation to any body area or extremity.
- Pad bony prominences (e.g., wrists and ankles) before applying a restraint over them. The movement of a restraint without padding over such prominences can quickly abrade the skin.
- Always tie a limb restraint with a knot that will not tighten when pulled.
- Tie the ends of a body restraint to the part of the bed that moves to elevate the head. Never tie the ends to a side rail or to the fixed frame of the bed if the bed position is to be changed.
- Assess the restraint every 30 minutes. Some facilities have specific forms to be used to record ongoing assessment.
- Release all restraints at least every two to four hours, and provide range-of-motion (ROM) exercises (see Chapter 43) and skin care (see Chapter 37).
- Reassess the continued need for the restraint at least every eight hours. Include an assessment of the underlying cause of the behaviour necessitating use of the restraint.
- When a restraint is temporarily removed, do not leave the client unattended.
- Immediately report to the nurse in charge and record on the client's chart any persistent reddened or broken skin areas under the restraint.
- At the first indication of cyanosis or pallor, coldness of a skin area, or a client's complaint of a tingling sensation, pain, or numbness, loosen the restraint and exercise the limb.
- Apply a restraint so that it can be released quickly in case of an emergency and with the body part in a normal anatomical position.
- Provide emotional support verbally and through touch.

FOCUS ON CRITICAL THINKING

Mr. Moore is a 72-year-old widower who is recovering from a fall in which he fractured his hip and underwent surgical repair one week ago. He will be staying with his son for two weeks after he is discharged from the hospital, but he is eager to return to his own home. Once he is home, his son will visit nightly after work, he will receive Meals on Wheels once a day, and a home care attendant will visit weekly to assist him with hygienic care until he is more independent. Mr. Moore's wife died three years ago, but he has remained independent and continued his social functions. He lives in a small three-bedroom house with his dog and cat, and he enjoys gardening. Prior to fracturing his hip he walked his dog daily. You will be his home care nurse.

1. While hospitalized, Mr. Moore experienced some mild confusion during the night, but his nurses decided not to restrain him. What are the best reasons for avoiding the use of restraints for some clients, such as Mr. Moore?
2. What are some of the factors that may affect Mr. Moore's safety after he returns home?
3. What do you need to assess in regard to Mr. Moore's safety, and what suggestions can you make for enhancing his safety?
4. What strengths do you note about Mr. Moore that may protect him from injury when he returns home?

See Appendix A for answers to these questions.

CHAPTER HIGHLIGHTS

- Education is a major health protection strategy in preventing accidents.
- When planning to meet safety needs of clients, nurses need to consider physical factors in the environment and the psychological and physiological state of the individual.
- Accidents are a major cause of death among individuals of all ages in Canada.
- Nurses need awareness of what constitutes a safe environment for specific individuals and for groups of people in the home, community, and workplace.
- Hazards to safety occur at all ages and vary according to the age and development of the individual.
- Measures to ensure the safety of people of all ages focus on (1) observation or prediction of situations that are potentially harmful, and (2) client education that empowers clients to safeguard themselves and their families from injury. Modification of the environment is often necessary to make it safe.
- Nursing assessment of safety includes assessment of age, lifestyle, mobility, sensory alterations, level of awareness, emotional state, and environmental factors.
- Nursing diagnoses for clients at risk for unintentional injury can be categorized as ***Risk for Injury***, with these subcategories: ***Risk for Trauma, Risk for Poisoning, Risk for Suffocation***, and ***Risk for Aspiration, Risk for Disuse Syndrome***, and ***Knowledge Deficient.***
- Nurses must be familiar with the fire procedures in the health-care agency where they practise. In the event of a fire, the nurse must (1) protect clients from injury, (2) report, (3) contain, and (4) extinguish.
- Falls are a common cause of injury among the very young, the elderly, and the ill or injured.
- To prevent falls, the nurse must provide constant surveillance for infants and young children and carefully assess older clients' safety needs.
- Major reasons for poisoning in children are inadequate supervision and improper storage of household toxic substances.
- Suffocation can occur when foreign objects are swallowed or inhaled, cutting off the person's oxygen supply.
- Side rails and handrails protect hospitalized clients from falls; restraints keep clients from falling and from inflicting injuries on themselves and others.
- Because restraints restrict a client's basic freedom to move, careful assessment and accurate, complete documentation are important when restraints are used.
- Various alternatives to restraints must be considered before a restraint is applied.

READINGS AND REFERENCES

Suggested Readings

Gielen, A. C., & Collins, B. (1993). Community based interventions for injury prevention. *Family & Community Health, 15*(4), 1–11.

This article validates the magnitude and severity of the safety problem in the United States, citing injuries as the third leading cause of death overall. The authors suggest a multidisciplinary, systems approach to injury prevention, bringing to bear technological, legislative, and behavioural interventions. They consider community-based action as critical to such an approach and outline possible applications of community-based preventions and what the results could be.

Tideiksaar, R. (1996). Preventing falls: How to identify risk factors, reduce complications. *Geriatrics, 51*(2), 43–46, 49–50, 53–55.

Preventing falls requires a systematic, diagnostic approach focused on identifying and reducing risk factors. Specific preventive strategies include treating underlying medical conditions, prescribing an exercise program to improve mobility, removing fall hazards in the home, and taking steps to minimize the fear of falling.

Related Research

Bryant, H., & Fernald, L. (1997). Nursing knowledge and use of restraint alternatives: Acute and chronic care. *Geriatric Nursing, 18*(2), 57–60.

Cruz, V., Abdul-Hamid, M., & Heater, B. (1997). Research-based practice: Reducing restraints in an acute care setting—phase 1. *Journal of Gerontological Nursing, 23*(2), 33–40, 54–55.

Graafmans, W. C., Ooms, M. E., Hofster, M. A., Bezemer, P. D., Bouter, L. M., & Lips, P. (1996). Falls in the elderly: A prospective study of risk factors and risk profiles. *American Journal of Epidemiology, 143*, 1129–1136.

Terpstra, T. L., & Van Doren, E. (1998). Reducing restraints: Where to start. *Journal of Continuing Education in Nursing, 29*(1), 10–16.

Selected References

Alberta Association of Registered Nurses. (2003). Position statement on the use of restraints in client care settings. Edmonton: Author.

Alexander, B. H., Rivara, F. P., & Wolf, M. E. (1992). The cost and frequency of hospitalization for fall related injuries in older adults. *American Journal of Public Health, 82*(7), 1020–1023.

British Columbia Nurses Union Survey. (1991, February). Violence. Vancouver: Author.

Canadian hospitals injury reporting and prevention programs. (1998). Summary statistics CHIRPP database: for the year 1998. http://www.hc-sc.gc.ca/pphb-dgspsp/injury-bles/sscd98-spds98/98stats_e.pdf.

Canadian Nurses Association. (2002). *Evidence-based decision making and nursing practice*. Ottawa: Author.

Canadian Nurses Association. (2001). *Quality professional practice environments for registered nurses*. Ottawa: Author.

Canadian Nurses Association. (2002). *Code of ethics for registered nurses*. Ottawa: Author.

Canadian Nurses Association. (1996). *Joint CNA/CMA position statement on environmentally responsible activity in the health sector*. Ottawa: Author.

Canadian Nurses Association. (2001). *Position statement on quality professional practice environments for registered nurses*. Ottawa: Author.

Canadian Nurses Association. (2002). *Position statement on violence*. Ottawa: Author.

Carpenito, L. J. (2000). *Nursing diagnosis: Applications to clinical practice* (7th ed.). Philadelphia, PA: Lippincott.

Carroll, V. (1996). Violence in the workplace: We are the missing link. *American Journal of Nursing, 96*(12), 80.

Chalifour, R. (1997). Focus on quality. Implementing a non-restraint environment. *Canadian Nurse, 93*(6), 47–48.

DeProspero Rogers, P., & Bocchino, N. (1999). Restraint-free care: Is it possible: Can we make physical restraint a last resort in acute care? *American Journal of Nursing, 99*(10), 26–34.

Doenges, M. E., Moorhouse, M. F., & Burley, J. (2003). *Application of nursing process and nursing diagnoses: An interactive text for diagnostic reasoning* (4th ed.). Philadelphia, PA: F. A. Davis.

Fédération Des Infirmières Du Québec. (1995). *Violence against nurses at work*. Quebec: Author.

Health Canada, Laboratory Centre for Disease Control. (1998). *Canadian Hospitals Injury Reporting and Prevention Program (CHIRP)*. Ottawa: Author.

Health Canada. (1998). *Influencing employee health: Workplace health system*. Ottawa: Canadian Fitness and Lifestyle Research Institute.

Health Canada. (1996). *Fact sheets: All injuries*. Available at http:www.hc-sc.gc.ca/hppb/cny/factsheets/all_injuries/allinj.htm.

Health and Welfare Canada. (1996). *Personal injury*. Ottawa: Queens Printer.

Hospital Focus. (1997). Patient care: An inside look at using restraint with restraints. *RN, 60*(10), 20E, 20G.

Injury Awareness & Prevention Centre. (1991). *A safer Canada: Year 2000 injury control objectives for Canada*. Proceedings of a symposium held in Edmonton, May 21–22, 1991. Edmonton: Author.

Injury Control Alberta. (2000). *Quick facts: snowmobiling. Alberta Centre for Injury Control and Research, 2*(6), 4.

International Council of Nurses. (1999). *Guidelines on coping with violence in the workplace*. Geneva: Author.

Kobs, A. (1998). Questions and answers from the JCAHO. Restraints revisited. *Nursing Management, 29*(1), 17–18.

Kozub, M., & Skidmore, R. (2001). Least to most restrictive interventions: A continuum for mental health care facilities. *Journal of Psychosocial Nursing, 39*(3), 32–38.

Lusk, S. L. (1997). Noise exposures: Effects on hearing and prevention of noise induced hearing loss. *AAOHN, J,45*(8), 397–405, 409–410.

McCloskey, J. C., & Bulechek, G. M. (2000). *Iowa intervention project: Nursing interventions classifications (NIC)* (3rd ed.). St. Louis, MO: Mosby.

McConnell, E. (1996). Applying wrist restraints. *Nursing, 26*(1), 28.

Murray, R. B., & Zentner, J. P. (1997). *Health assessment and promotion strategies through the lifespan* (6th ed.). Stamford, CT: Appleton & Lange.

North American Nursing Diagnosis Association. (2003). *NANDA Nursing diagnoses: Definitions and classification 2003–2004.* Philadelphia, PA: Author.

Northridge, M., Nevitt, M., Kelsey, J., & Link, B. (1995). Home hazards and falls in the elderly: The role of health and functional status. *American Journal of Public Health, 85*(4), 509–515.

O'Loughlin, J., Robitaille, Y., Boivin, J. F., & Suissa, S. (1991). Incidence and risk factors for falls and injurious falls among the community living elderly. *American Journal of Epidemiology, 137*, 342–354.

Raina, P., & Torrance, V. (1995). *Injury Mortality and Morbidity in Canadian Seniors* 1979–1991. Unpublished report, division of Aging-Related Diseases, LCDC, Bureau of Cancer. Ottawa: Health Canada.

Riley, R. (1992). Accidental falls and injuries among seniors. *Health Reports (Statistics Canada), 4*(4), 341–354.

Rubenstein, L. Z., Josephson, K. R., & Osterweil, D. (1996). Falls and fall prevention in the nursing home. *Clinics in Geriatric Medicine, 12*, 881–902.

Ryan, J. W., & Spellbring, A. M. (1996). Implementing strategies to decrease risk of falls in older women. *Journal of Gerontological Nursing, 22*(12), 25–31.

Scott, V., & Gallager, E. (1997). The epidemiology of fall-related injuries among older persons in British Columbia: Implications for prevention. *B.C. Health and Disease Surveillance, 6*(8/9), 94–106.

Shamian, J. (1999). *Illness and disability of nurses.* Ottawa: Author.

Sidsky, M. (1996). Safe Kids Canada. *Injury Prevention, 2*(1), 70–72.

Statistics Canada. (1991a). Mortality: Summary list of causes. *Health Reports 1989, 3*(1), (suppl. 12). Ottawa: Queens Printer.

Statistics Canada. (1991b). *Mortality and hospitalization.* Ottawa: Queens Printer.

Tideiksaar, R. (1996). Preventing falls: How to identify risk factors, reduce complications. *Geriatrics, 51*(2), 43–46, 49–50, 53–55.

Todd, J. F. (1997, October). Device errors. Heating devices: how to avoid burns. *Nursing, 27*(10), 83.

Weber, J., Kehoe, T., Bakoss, M., Kiley, M., & Dzigiel, J. M. (1996, June). Prevention update. Safety at home: A practical home-injury control program for independent seniors. *Caring, 15*(6), 62–66.

Workers Compensation Board of British Columbia (WBC of BC) (1998b). *What's WHMIS?* Richmond: Author.

WEBLINKS

Health in Action
http://www.health-in-action.org
This is an interactive Web site designed for injury prevention and health promotion practitioners in Alberta to share their programs, research, and resources.

Statistics Canada
http://www.statcan.ca
Statistics Canada contains statistical information and many reports including the statistical report prepared by the federal, provincial, and territorial advisory committee on population health entitled *The Health of Canadians.*

Health Canada
http:www.hc-sc.gc.ca/hppb/cny/factsheets/all_injuries/allinj.htm
Health Canada fact sheets provide up-to-date information on injuries in all stages of life.

Alberta Centre for Injury Control and Research
http://www.med.ualberta.ca/acicr
The Alberta Centre for Injury Control and Research (ACICR) strengthens and helps coordinate injury control in Alberta. This Centre provides support for agencies, practitioners, and other key stakeholders who do work related to injury prevention, emergency medical services, acute care, and rehabilitation. ACICR is a part of an expanding network of injury control expertise that reaches not only across Alberta but throughout Canada and around the world.

Health Canada: Personal Injury
http://www.hc-sc.gc.ca/englins/injury.htm
This Web site is a link under Health Canada's online information about Healthy Living. It provides Canadians with facts on unintentional injuries and how they can be prevented.

WHMIS: Workplace Hazardous Materials Information System
http://www.hc-sc.gc.ca/hecs-sesc/whmis/index.htm
The Workplace Hazardous Materials Information System (WHMIS) is Canada's hazard communication standard. The key elements of the system are cautionary labelling of containers of WHMIS "controlled products," the provision of material safety data sheets (MSDSs), and worker education programs.

CHAPTER 34

Hygiene

OBJECTIVES

After completing this chapter, you will be able to:

- Describe kinds of hygienic care nurses provide to clients.
- List factors influencing personal hygiene.
- Identify normal and abnormal findings obtained during inspection and palpation of the skin, feet, nails, mouth, hair, eyes, ears, and nose.
- Discuss common problems of the skin, feet, nails, mouth, hair, eyes, ears, and nose and formulate related nursing diagnoses.
- Outline guidelines for planning and implementing nursing interventions for the skin, feet, nails, mouth, hair, eyes, ears, and nose.
- List outcome criteria to evaluate goal achievement.
- Identify the purposes of bathing.
- Describe various types of baths.
- Enumerate steps in perineal and genital care.
- Explain specific ways in which nurses help hospitalized clients with oral hygiene.
- List steps in removing contact lenses and inserting and removing artificial eyes.
- Describe steps for inserting and removing hearing appliances.
- Identify safety and comfort measures underlying bed-making procedures.

Hygiene is the science of health and its maintenance. Personal hygiene is the self-care by which people attend to such functions as bathing, toileting, general body hygiene, and grooming. Hygiene is a highly personal matter determined by individual values and practices. It involves care of the skin, hair, nails, teeth, oral and nasal cavities, eyes, ears, and perineal and genital areas.

It is important for nurses to know exactly how much assistance a client needs for hygienic care. Clients may require help after urinating or defecating, after vomiting, and whenever they become soiled, for example, from wound drainage or from profuse perspiration. See Table 34.1 for factors influencing hygiene practices.

Nurses commonly use the following terms to describe kinds of hygienic care. *Early morning care* is provided to clients as they awaken in the morning. This care consists of providing a urinal or bedpan to the client confined to bed, washing the face and hands, and giving oral care. *Morning care* is provided after clients have breakfast. It usually includes the provision of a urinal or bedpan (to clients who are not ambulatory), a bath or shower, perineal care, back massages, and oral, nail, and hair care. Making the client's bed is part of morning care. *Afternoon care* often includes providing a bedpan or urinal, washing the hands and face, and assisting with oral care to refresh clients. *Hour of sleep (HS) care* or *evening care* is provided to clients before they retire for the night. It usually involves providing for elimination needs, washing face and hands, giving oral care, and giving a back massage. *As-needed (prn) care* is provided as required by the client. For example, a client who is *diaphoretic* (sweating profusely) may need bathing and changes of clothes and linen frequently.

TABLE 34.1 Factors Influencing Individual Hygienic Practices

Factor	Variables
Culture	North American culture places a high value on cleanliness. Many North Americans bathe or shower once or twice a day, whereas people from some other cultures bathe once a week. Some cultures consider privacy essential for bathing, whereas others practise communal bathing. Body odour is offensive in some cultures and accepted as normal in others.
Religion	Ceremonial washings are practised by some religions.
Environment	Finances may affect the availability of facilities for bathing. For example, homeless people may not have warm water available; soap, shampoo, shaving lotion, and deodorants may be too expensive for people who have limited resources.
Developmental level	Children learn hygiene in the home. Practices vary according to the individual's age; for example, preschoolers can carry out most tasks independently with encouragement.
Health and energy	Ill people may not have the motivation or energy to attend to hygiene. Some clients who have neuromuscular impairments may be unable to perform hygienic care.
Personal preferences	Some people prefer a shower to a tub bath.

Skin

The skin is the largest organ of the body. It serves five major functions:

1. It protects underlying tissues from injury by preventing the passage of microorganisms. The skin and mucous membranes are considered the body's first line of defence.
2. It regulates the body temperature. Cooling the body occurs through the heat loss processes of evaporation of perspiration, and by radiation and conduction of heat from the body when the blood vessels of the skin are vasodilated. Body heat is conserved through lack of perspiration and vasoconstriction of the blood vessels. See Chapter 31 for a detailed discussion of body heat losses and gains.
3. It secretes **sebum,** an oily substance that softens and lubricates the hair and skin, prevents the hair from becoming brittle, and decreases water loss from the skin when the external humidity is low. Because fat is a poor conductor of heat, sebum lessens the amount of heat lost from the skin. Sebum also has a **bactericidal** (bacteria-killing) action.
4. It transmits sensations through nerve receptors, which are sensitive to pain, temperature, touch, and pressure.
5. It produces and absorbs vitamin D in conjunction with ultraviolet rays from the sun, which activate a vitamin D precursor present in the skin.

The normal skin of a healthy person has transient and resident microorganisms that are not usually harmful. See Table 32.1 on page 744.

TABLE 34.2 Focus on Aging Skin

As one ages, marked changes occur with one's skin. Changes occur due to intrinsic (natural aging) and extrinsic (environmental factors) processes.

Skin Alterations Due to Aging	Implications for the Older Adult
Subcutaneous and dermal tissue become thin	Increases risk of skin tears, less capacity to insulate
Decreased sebaceous and sweat gland activity	Perspiration is decreased, skin becomes dryer, and pruritus (itching) may occur
Vascularity to the skin decreases	Skin temperature is cooler, and pallor may be apparent
Loss of subcutaneous tissue	Wrinkling, sagging, and senile purpura are common
Nail growth rate declines	Nails become softer and tear easily
Melanocytes (cells that make the pigment that colours hair and skin) reduce in number	Hair greys, increase in pigmented spots that are blotchy in appearance

Source: Adapted from Sims, L., D'Amico, D., Stiesmeyer, J., & Webster, J. (1995). *Health assessment in nursing* (pp. 145, 147, 149, 150). Redwood City, CA: Addison Wesley Nursing. © Adapted by permission of Pearson Education Inc., Upper Saddle River, N.J.

Sudoriferous (sweat) glands are on all body surfaces except the lips and parts of the genitals. The body has from two to five million, which are all present at birth. They are most numerous on the palms of the hands and the soles of the feet. Sweat glands are classified as apocrine and eccrine. The **apocrine glands,** located largely in the axillae and anogenital areas, begin to function at puberty under the influence of androgens. Although their secretion is produced almost constantly, apocrine glands are of little use in thermoregulation. The secretion of these glands is odourless, but when decomposed or acted upon by bacteria on the skin, it takes on a musky, unpleasant odour. The **eccrine glands** are important physiologically. They are more numerous than the apocrine glands and are found chiefly on the palms of the hands, the soles of the feet, and forehead. The sweat they produce cools the body through evaporation. Sweat is made up of water, sodium, potassium, chloride, glucose, urea, and lactate.

Assessing

Assessment of the client's skin and hygienic practices includes (1) a nursing history to determine the client's skin care practices, self-care abilities, and past or current skin problems; (2) physical assessment of the skin; and (3) identification of clients at risk for developing skin impairments.

Nursing History

Data about the client's *skin care practices* enable the nurse to incorporate the client's needs and preferences as much as possible in the plan of care and to determine necessary learning needs. Assessment of the client's *self-care abilities* determines the amount of nursing assistance and the kind of bath (bed, tub, or shower) the client requires. Important considerations include the client's balance (for tub and shower), ability to sit unsupported (in the tub or bed), activity tolerance, coordination, adequate muscle strength, appropriate joint range of motion, and vision. Cognition and motivation are also essential. Clients whose cognitive function is impaired or whose illness alters energy levels and motivation will also need assistance. It is important for the nurse to determine the client's functional level to maintain and promote as much client independence as possible.

The *presence of past or current skin problems* alerts the nurse to specific nursing interventions or referrals the client may require. The client may provide descriptions of these problems during the nursing history, or the nurse may observe some during the physical examination that follows. Common skin problems and implications for nursing interventions are shown in Table 34.3. Types and descriptions of skin lesions are shown in Chapter 27. Questions to elicit data about the client's skin care practices, self-care abilities, and skin problems are shown in the box on page 810.

Physical Assessment

Physical assessment of the skin, which involves inspection and palpation, is described in Chapter 27. A systematic head-to-toe assessment facilitates collection of data about skin colour, uniformity of colour, texture, turgor, temperature, intactness, and lesions.

Diagnosing

Self-Care Deficit diagnoses are used for clients who have problems performing hygiene care. Three of NANDA's four self-care deficit diagnoses, specified as ***Self-Care Deficit: Bathing/Hygiene, Self-Care Deficit: Dressing/Grooming,*** and ***Self-Care Deficit: Toileting,*** are discussed in this chapter. The fourth diagnosis, ***Self-Care Deficit: Feeding,*** is discussed in Chapter 38.

TABLE 34.3 Common Skin Problems

Problem and Appearance	Nursing Implications
Abrasion Superficial layers of the skin are scraped or rubbed away. Area is reddened and may have localized bleeding or serous weeping.	1. Prone to infection; therefore, wound should be kept clean and dry. 2. Do not wear rings or jewellery when providing care to avoid causing abrasions to clients. 3. Lift, do not pull, a client across a bed. See Chapter 43.
Excessive Dryness Skin can appear flaky and rough.	1. Prone to infection if the skin cracks; therefore, provide alcohol-free lotions to moisturize the skin and prevent cracking. 2. Bathe client less frequently; use no soap, or limit use of nonirritating soap. Rinse skin thoroughly because soap can be irritating and drying. 3. Encourage increased fluid intake, if health permits, to prevent dehydration.
Ammonia Dermatitis (Diaper Rash) Caused by skin bacteria reacting with urea in the urine. The skin becomes reddened and is sore.	1. Keep skin dry and clean by applying protective ointments containing zinc oxide to areas at risk (e.g., buttocks and perineum). 2. Boil an infant's diapers or wash them with an antibacterial detergent to prevent infection. Rinse diapers well because detergent is irritating to an infant's skin.
Acne Inflammatory condition with papules and pustules.	1. Keep the skin clean to prevent secondary infection. 2. Treatment varies widely.
Erythema Redness associated with a variety of conditions, such as rashes, exposure to sun, elevated body temperature.	1. Wash area carefully to remove excess microorganisms. 2. Apply antiseptic spray or lotion to prevent itching, promote healing, and prevent skin breakdown.
Hirsutism Excessive hair on a person's body and face, particularly in women.	1. Remove unwanted hair by using depilatories, shaving, electrolysis, or tweezing. 2. Enhance client's self-concept. See Chapter 46.

Difficulties encountered by the client in performing bathing activities include the inability to wash the body or body parts, to obtain or get to a water source, and to regulate water temperature or flow. Difficulties in dressing and grooming include inability to obtain, put on, take off, fasten, or replace articles of clothing; and to maintain appearance at a satisfactory level. Toileting problems may involve difficulties getting to the toilet or commode or sitting on and rising from it. In addition, the client may experience problems manipulating clothing for toileting, carrying out proper toilet hygiene, or flushing the toilet or emptying the commode. The reasons (etiologies or related factors) for these problems are varied. See the boxes on pages 807 and 810.

Clinical examples of assessment data clusters and related nursing diagnoses are shown in Table 34.4.

Associated diagnoses include the following:

- ***Knowledge Deficient*** related to
  a. Lack of experience with skin condition (acne) and need to prevent secondary infection
  b. New therapeutic regimen to manage skin problems
  c. Lack of experience in providing hygiene care to dependent person
  d. Unfamiliarity with devices available to facilitate sitting on or rising from toilet
- ***Self-Esteem, Situational Low*** related to
  a. Visible skin problem (e.g., acne or alopecia)
  b. Body odour

The diagnoses ***Risk for Impaired Skin Integrity*** and ***Impaired Skin Integrity*** are discussed in Chapter 37.

ASSESSMENT INTERVIEW

Skin Hygiene

Skin Care Practices

- What are your usual showering or bathing times?
- What hygienic products do you routinely use (e.g., bath oils, powder, facial cleansing creams, body lotions or creams, deodorants, antiperspirants)?
- What facial cosmetic products do you use?
- How and when do you clean make-up applicators and puffs? (Applicators should be kept clean, and products used around the eyes in particular should be discarded after four months to prevent bacterial and fungal infections.)
- What hygienic or cosmetic products do you not use because of the skin problems they create (e.g., skin dryness or allergic reactions)?

Self-Care Abilities

- Do you have any problems managing your hygienic practices (e.g., baths and facial care)? If so, what are these?
- How can the nurses best help you?

Skin Problems

- Do you have any tendency toward skin dryness, itchiness, rashes, bruising, excessive perspiration, or lack of perspiration? Have you had skin or scalp lesions in the past?
- Do you have any allergic tendencies? If so, what?

Positive responses to any of these require further exploration in terms of duration (when did it start?); frequency (how often have you had this?); description of lesion or rash; any associated signs, such as fever or nausea; aggravating factors (e.g., season of the year, stress, occupation, medication, recent travel, housing, personal contact); alleviating factors (e.g., medications, lotions, home remedies); and any family history of the problem.

TABLE 34.4 Clinical Application: Assessment Data Clusters and Related Nursing Diagnoses for Clients with Skin Problems

Data Cluster	Nursing Diagnosis
Stan Bailey, 75 years old, suffered a "stroke" two weeks ago that resulted in paralysis of his left side. He states, "I don't want a bath. I can wash myself. I just want to be left alone." He is withdrawn and uncommunicative.	***Self-Care Deficit: Bathing/Hygiene*** related to paralyzed left upper and lower limbs and lack of motivation
Mark Drake, a 15-year-old, has facial pustules and papules. Facial skin is inflamed. He states, "I hate going to school or anywhere looking like this. I don't think any girl wants to go out with me. Can you do something to get rid of this?"	***Self-Esteem Disturbance*** related to facial pustules and/or papules

Etiologies of Self-Care Deficits

Visual impairment
Activity intolerance or weakness
Pain or discomfort
Mental impairment
Neuromuscular or skeletal impairment
Psychological or motivational impairment
Medically prescribed restriction
Therapeutic procedure restraining mobility (e.g., intravenous infusion, cast)
Environmental barriers

Planning

In planning care, the nurse identifies nursing interventions that will assist the client to achieve these goals:

- Maintain or improve skin cleanliness
- Maintain circulation to the skin
- Improve or maintain a sense of well-being

Nursing activities may include assisting dependent clients with bathing, skin care, and perineal care, providing back massages to promote circulation, and instructing clients about appropriate hygienic practices and therapies to prevent skin lesions. Although the nursing interventions discussed in this chapter focus on hygienic measures, the etiology of the nursing diagnoses established may point to other interventions that promote circulation, promote self-esteem, restore nutritional status, correct fluid deficits or excesses, or prevent problems associated with immobility. Nursing strategies to deal with these etiologies are provided in other chapters.

Planning to assist a client with personal hygiene includes consideration of the client's personal preferences, health, and limitations; the best time to give the care; and the equipment, facilities, and personnel available. A client's

HOME CARE ASSESSMENT

Hygiene

Client and Environment

- *Self-care abilities for hygiene:* Assess the client's ability to bathe, to regulate water taps, to dress and undress, to groom, and to use the toilet.
- *Self-care aids required:* Determine if there is a need for a tub/shower seat (Figure 34.1), a hand shower, a nonskid surface or mat in the tub or shower, hand bars on the sides of the tub (Figure 34.2), or a raised toilet seat.
- *Facilities:* Check for the presence of laundry facilities and running water.
- *Mechanical barriers:* Note furniture obstructing access to the bathroom and toilet, or a doorway too narrow for a wheelchair.

Family

- *Caregiver availability, skills, and responses:* Determine whether individuals are available and able to assist with bathing, dressing, toileting, nail care, hair shampoo, shopping for hygienic or grooming aids, and so on.
- *Education needs:* Assess whether the caregiver needs instruction in how to assist the client in and out of the tub, on and off the toilet, and so on.
- *Family role changes and coping:* Assess effects of client's illness on financial status, parenting, spousal roles, sexuality, and social roles.

Community

- Explore resources that will provide assistance with bathing, laundry, and foot care (e.g., home health aid, podiatrist).
- Consult a social worker as needed to coordinate placement of a client unable to remain in the home or to identify community resources that will help the client stay in the home.
- Consider a consult with (1) a physical therapist to assess, develop, and improve the client's motor function, (2) a home care nurse to provide follow-up for care, teaching, and support, and (3) an occupational therapist to assess and develop abilities to perform activities of daily living.

personal preferences—about when and how to bathe, for example—should be followed as long as they are compatible with the client's health and the equipment available. Nurses need to provide whatever assistance the client requires, either directly or by delegating this task to other nursing personnel. Examples of desired outcomes developed in the planning phase are shown in the "Evaluating" section, Table 34.6, on page 820.

Planning for Home Care

To provide for continuity of care, the nurse must assess the client's and family's abilities for care, and the need for referrals and home health services. See the box above. In addition, the nurse needs to determine the client's learning needs. See the Client Teaching boxes throughout this chapter.

Implementing

General Principles of Skin Care

1. *An intact, healthy skin is the body's first line of defence.* Nurses need to ensure that all skin care measures prevent injury and irritation. Scratching the skin with jewellery or long, sharp fingernails must be avoided. Harsh rubbing or use of rough towels and washcloths can cause tissue damage, particularly when the skin is irritated or when circulation or sensation is diminished. Bottom bedsheets are kept taut and free from wrinkles to reduce friction and abrasion to the skin. Top bed linens are arranged to prevent undue pressure on the toes. When necessary, bed cradles on footboards are used to keep bedclothes off the feet.
2. *The degree to which the skin protects the underlying tissues from injury depends on the general health of the cells, the amount of subcutaneous tissue, and the dryness of the skin.* Skin that is poorly nourished and dry is less easily protected and more vulnerable to injury. When the skin is dry, lotions or creams with lanolin can be applied, and bathing is limited to once or twice a week.
3. *Moisture in contact with the skin for more than a short time can result in increased bacterial growth and irritation.* After a bath, the client's skin is dried carefully. Particular attention is paid to such areas as the axillae, the groin, beneath the breasts, and between the toes, where the potential for irritation is greatest. A nonirritating dusting powder, such as cornstarch, tends to reduce moisture and can be applied to these areas after they are dried. Clients who are incontinent of urine or feces or who perspire excessively are provided with immediate skin care to prevent skin irritation.
4. *Body odours are caused by resident skin bacteria acting on body secretions.* Cleanliness is the best deodorant. Commercial deodorants and antiperspirants can be

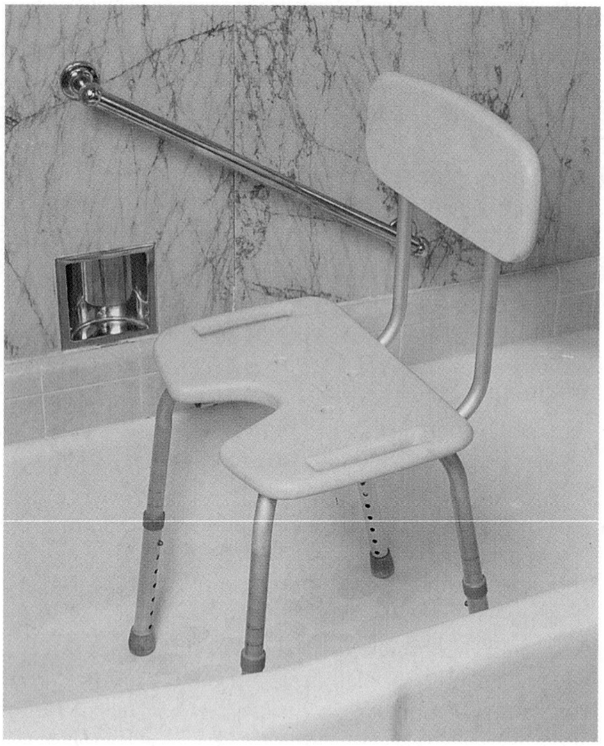

Figure 34.1 Tub/shower seat in the home

Figure 34.2 Hand bars on the sides of the bathtub

applied only after the skin is cleaned. Deodorants diminish odours, whereas antiperspirants reduce the amount of perspiration. Neither is applied immediately after shaving because of the possibility of skin irritation, nor are they used on skin that is already irritated.

5. *Skin sensitivity to irritation and injury varies among individuals and in accordance with their health.* Generally speaking, skin sensitivity is greater in infants, very young children, and older people. A person's nutritional status also affects sensitivity. Emaciated or obese persons tend to experience more skin irritation and injury. The same tendency is seen in individuals with poor dietary habits and insufficient fluid intake. Even in healthy persons, skin sensitivity is highly variable. Some people's skin is sensitive to the chemicals in skin care agents and cosmetics. Hypoallergenic cosmetics and soaps or soap substitutes are available for these people. The nurse needs to ascertain whether the client has any sensitivities and what agents are appropriate to use.
6. *Agents used for skin care have selective actions and purposes.* Commonly used agents are described in Table 34.5.

Bathing

Sponge baths are suggested for the newborn because daily tub baths are not considered necessary. After the bath, the infant should be immediately dried and wrapped. Parents need to be advised that the infant's ability to regulate body temperature has not yet fully developed. Infants perspire minimally, and shivering starts at a lower temperature than it does in adults; therefore, infants lose more heat before shivering begins. In addition, because the infant's body surface area is very large in relation to body mass, the body loses heat readily.

Bathing removes accumulated oil, perspiration, dead skin cells, and some bacteria. The nurse can appreciate the quantity of oil and dead skin cells produced when observing a person after the removal of a cast that has been on for six weeks. The skin is crusty, flaky, and dry underneath the cast. Applications of oil over several days are usually necessary to remove the debris.

Excessive bathing, however, can interfere with the intended lubricating effect of the sebum, causing dryness of the skin. This is an important consideration, especially for older adults, who produce less sebum.

In addition to cleaning the skin, bathing also stimulates circulation. A warm or hot bath dilates superficial arterioles, bringing more blood and nourishment to the skin. Vigorous rubbing has the same effect. Rubbing with long smooth strokes from the distal to proximal parts of extremities (from the point farthest from the body to the point closest) is particularly effective in facilitating venous blood flow.

Bathing also produces a sense of well-being. It is refreshing and relaxing and frequently improves morale, appearance, and self-respect. Some people take a morning shower for its refreshing, stimulating effect. Others prefer an evening bath because it is relaxing. These effects are more evident when a person is ill. For example, it is not uncommon for clients who have had a restless or sleepless night to feel relaxed, comfortable, and sleepy after a morning bath.

Bathing offers an excellent opportunity for the nurse to assess ill clients. The nurse can observe the condition of the client's skin and physical conditions, such as sacral

TABLE 34.5 Agents Commonly Used on the Skin

Type	Description
Soap	Lowers surface tension and, thus, helps in cleaning. Some soaps contain antibacterial agents that can change the natural flora of the skin.
Detergent	Used instead of soap for cleaning. Some people who are allergic to soaps may not be allergic to detergents and vice versa.
Bath oil	Used in bathwater; provides an oily film on the skin that softens and prevents chapping. Oils can make the tub surface slippery, and clients should be instructed about safety measures (e.g., using nonskid tub surface or mat).
Skin cream, lotion	Provides a film on the skin that prevents evaporation and, therefore, chapping.
Powder	Can be used to absorb water and prevent friction. For example, powder under the breasts can prevent skin irritation. Some powders are antibacterial.
Deodorant	Masks or diminishes body odours.
Antiperspirant	Reduces the amount of perspiration.

Changing a Hospital Gown for a Client with an Intravenous Infusion without a Pump

- Slip the gown completely off the arm without the infusion and onto the tubing connected to the arm with the infusion.
- Holding the container above the client's arm, slide the sleeve up over the container to remove the used gown.
- Place the clean gown sleeve for the arm with the infusion over the container as if it were an extension of the client's arm, from the inside of the gown to the sleeve cuff.
- Rehang the container. Slide the gown carefully over the tubing toward the client's hand.
- Guide the client's arm and tubing into the sleeve, taking care not to pull on the tubing or IV site.
- Assist the client to put the other arm into the second sleeve of the gown, and fasten as usual.
- Count the rate of flow of the infusion to make sure it is correct before leaving the bedside.

edema or rashes. While assisting a client with a bath, the nurse can also assess the client's psychosocial needs, such as orientation to time and ability to cope with the illness. Learning needs, such as a diabetic client's need to learn foot care, can also be assessed.

Caution is needed when bathing clients who are receiving intravenous therapy. Easy-to-remove gowns that have Velcro or snap fasteners along the sleeves may be used. If a special gown is not available, the nurse needs to pay special attention when changing the client's gown after the bath (or whenever the gown becomes soiled). General guidelines are provided in the box below left. These guidelines do not apply if the client has an IV pump or controller. In this situation, use a special gown or do not put the sleeve of a gown over the client's involved arm.

Two categories of baths are given to clients: cleaning and therapeutic. *Cleaning baths* are given chiefly for hygiene purposes and include these types:

- *Complete bed bath.* The nurse washes the entire body of an individual who needs total assistance in bed.
- *Self-help bed bath.* Clients confined to bed are able to bathe themselves with assistance from the nurse for washing the back and perhaps the feet.
- *Partial bath (abbreviated bath).* Only the parts of the client's body that might cause discomfort or odour, if neglected, are washed: the face, hands, axillae, perineal area, and back. Omitted are the arms, chest, abdomen, legs, and feet. The nurse provides this care for individuals who need total assistance and assists self-sufficient clients confined to bed by washing their backs. Some ambulatory clients prefer to take a partial bath at the sink. The nurse can assist them by washing their backs.
- *Towel bath.* The towel bath is an in-bed bath that uses a quick-drying solution containing a disinfectant, a cleaning agent, and a softening agent mixed with water. This commercially prepared solution is used at a temperature of 43.3° to 46°C. The solution dries in a few seconds, avoiding the need to dry the client and thereby speeding the bathing process. The following procedure is suggested:
  - Fold a large terry cloth towel in a plastic bag and saturate it with the solution provided.
  - Wring out the towel, then unroll it over the client, at the same time moving the top bed linen off the client.
  - Fold excess towel under the client's chin for subsequent use.
  - Use a gentle massaging motion to clean the body, starting at the feet and working toward the head.
  - Fold the towel upward after the massage and replace with a clean sheet.
  - Use the part of the towel folded under the chin to clean the client's face, neck, and ears.

- Remove the towel, then roll the client to one side and apply the clean side of the towel to the back of the neck, the back, and the buttocks.
- Remove the towel.
- Place clean linen on the bed, dress the client, and position the client appropriately.

- *Bag bath.* The "bag bath" was developed to satisfy the cultural requirement of daily bathing without the harmful side effects of traditional bathing. The equipment needed is a plastic bag, 10 to 12 washcloths, and a nonrinsable cleaner and water mixture. The solution and washcloths are warmed in a microwave. The warming time is about one minute, but the nurse needs to determine how long it takes to attain a desirable temperature. Each area of the body is cleaned with a different cloth and then air dried. Because the body is not rubbed dry, the emollient in the solution remains on the skin, leaving it clean and soft. Staff value the time savings and find it easy to perform.
- *Tub bath.* Tub baths are preferred to bed baths because it is easier to wash and rinse in a tub. Tubs are also used for therapeutic baths. The amount of assistance the nurse offers depends on the abilities of the client. There are specially designed tubs for clients needing total assistance. These tubs greatly reduce the work of the nurse in lifting clients in and out of the tub and offer greater benefits than a sponge bath in bed.
- *Shower.* Many ambulatory clients are able to use shower facilities and require only minimal assistance from the nurse.

The water for a bath should feel comfortably warm to the client. People vary in their sensitivity to heat; generally, the temperature should be 43° to 46°C. Most clients will verify a suitable temperature. The water for a bed bath should be changed when cleansing from a dirtier to a cleaner area, or when bath water becomes dirty or cool.

Therapeutic baths are given for physical effects, such as to soothe irritated skin or to treat an area (e.g., the perineum). Medications may be placed in the water. A therapeutic bath is generally taken in a tub one-third or one-half full. The client remains in the bath for a designated time, often 20 to 30 minutes. If the client's back, chest, and arms are to be treated, these areas need to be immersed in the solution. The bath temperature is generally included in the order; 37.7° to 46°C may be ordered for adults and 40.5°C is usually ordered for infants. Procedure 34.1 provides guidelines for bathing clients.

PROCEDURE 34.1 Bathing an Adult or Pediatric Client

Before bathing a client, determine (1) the type of bath the client needs and what assistance the client requires; (2) other care the client is receiving, such as roentgenography or physiotherapy, so that the bath can be coordinated with those activities to prevent undue fatigue; and (3) the bed linen required.

The caregiver should wear gloves when in the presence of body fluids or open lesions.

PURPOSES

- To remove transient microorganisms, body secretions and excretions, and dead skin cells
- To stimulate circulation to the skin
- To produce a sense of well-being
- To promote relaxation and comfort
- To prevent or eliminate unpleasant body odours

Assessment Focus
Condition of the skin (colour, texture and turgor, presence of pigmented spots, temperature, lesions, excoriations, and abrasions); fatigue; presence of pain and need for adjunctive measures (e.g., an analgesic) before the bath; range of motion of the joints and any other aspects of health that affect the bathing process

Equipment

- ❑ Bedpan or urinal
- ❑ Changing table
- ❑ Bath blanket
- ❑ Gloves as indicated or if giving perineal care
- ❑ Washcloths
- ❑ Soap
- ❑ Basin
- ❑ Water between 43° and 46°C for adults, 38° and 40°C for children
- ❑ Two bath towels
- ❑ Additional bed linen and towels, if required
- ❑ Hygiene supplies, such as lotion, powder, and deodorant
- ❑ Clean gown or pajamas as needed

PROCEDURE 34.1 Bathing an Adult or Pediatric Client *continued*

INTERVENTION

1. **Prepare the client and the environment.**

- Invite a parent or family member to participate, if desired.
- Close the windows and doors to make sure that the room is free from drafts. *Air currents increase loss of heat from the body by convection.*
- Provide privacy by drawing the curtains or closing the door. *Hygiene is a personal matter.* Some agencies provide signs indicating the need for privacy.
- Offer the client a bedpan or urinal or ask whether the client wishes to use the toilet or commode. *The client will be more comfortable after voiding, and voiding before cleaning the perineum is advisable.*
- During the bath, assess each area of the skin carefully.

FOR A BED BATH

2. **Prepare the bed, and position the client appropriately.**

- Place the bed in the high position. Place an infant or small child on a changing table or elevated crib. *This avoids undue strain on the nurse's back.*
- Remove the top bed linen and replace it with the bath blanket. If the bed linen is to be reused, place it over the bedside chair. If it is to be changed, place it in the linen hamper.
- Assist the client to move near you. *This facilitates access without undue reaching and straining.*
- Remove the client's gown.

3. **Make a bath mitt with the washcloth (Figure 34.3).** *A bath mitt retains water and heat better than a cloth loosely held.*

- Triangular method: (1) Lay your hand on the washcloth; (2) fold the top corner over your hand; (3,4) fold the side corners over your hand; and (5) tuck the second corner under the cloth on the palmar side to secure the mitt.

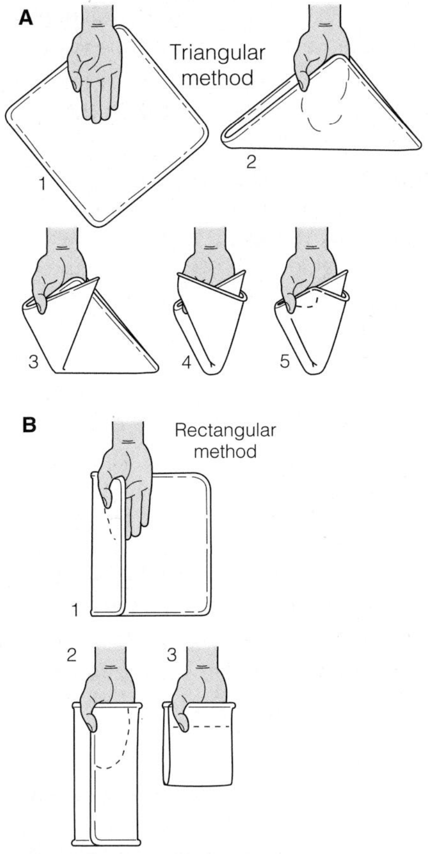

Figure 34.3 Making a bath mitt: *A*, triangular method; *B*, rectangular method

- Rectangular method: (1) Lay your hand on the washcloth and fold one side over your hand; (2) fold the second side over your hand; (3) fold the top of the cloth down; and (4) tuck it under the folded side against your palm to secure the mitt.

4. **Wash the face.**

- Place one towel across the client's chest.
- Wash the client's eyes with water only and dry them well. Use a separate corner of the washcloth for each eye. *Using separate corners prevents transmitting microorganisms from one eye to the other.* Wipe from the inner to the outer canthus. *Cleaning from the inner to the outer canthus prevents secretions from entering the nasolacrimal ducts.*
- Ask whether the client wants soap used on the face. *Soap has a drying effect, and the face, which is exposed to the air more than other body parts, tends to be drier.*
- Wash, rinse, and dry the client's face, neck, and ears.

5. **Wash the arms and hands.** (Omit the arms for a partial bath.)

- Place the bath towel lengthwise under the arm. *It protects the bed from becoming wet.*
- Wash, rinse, and dry the arm, using long, firm strokes from distal to proximal areas (from the point farthest from the body to the point closest). *Firm strokes from distal to proximal areas increase venous blood return.*
- Wash the axilla well. Repeat for the other arm. Exercise caution if an intravenous infusion is present, and check its flow after moving the arm.
- Place a towel directly on the bed and put the basin on it. Place the client's hands in the basin. *Many clients enjoy immersing their hands in the basin and washing themselves.* Assist the client, as needed, to wash, rinse, and dry the hands, paying particular attention to the spaces between the fingers.

6. **Wash the chest and abdomen.** (Omit the chest and abdomen for a partial bath. However, the areas under a woman's breasts may require bathing if these areas are irritated.)

- Fold the bath blanket down to the client's pubic area, and place the towel over the chest and abdomen.
- Wash, rinse, and dry the chest and abdomen, giving special attention to the skinfold under the breasts. Keep the chest and abdomen covered with the towel between the wash and the rinse.
- Replace the bath blanket when the areas have been dried. Avoid undue exposure when washing

PROCEDURE 34.1 Bathing an Adult or Pediatric Client *continued*

the chest and abdomen. For some clients, it may be preferable to wash the chest and the abdomen separately. In that case, place the bath towel horizontally across the abdomen first and then across the chest.

7. **Wash the legs and feet.** (Omit legs and feet for a partial bath.)
- Wrap one of the client's legs and feet with the bath blanket, ensuring that the pubic area is well covered.
- Place the bath towel lengthwise under the other leg, and wash that leg. Use long, smooth, firm strokes, washing from the ankle to the knee to the thigh. *Washing from distal to proximal areas stimulates venous blood flow.*
- Rinse and dry that leg, reverse the coverings, and repeat for the other leg.
- Wash the feet by placing them in the basin of water (Figure 34.4).

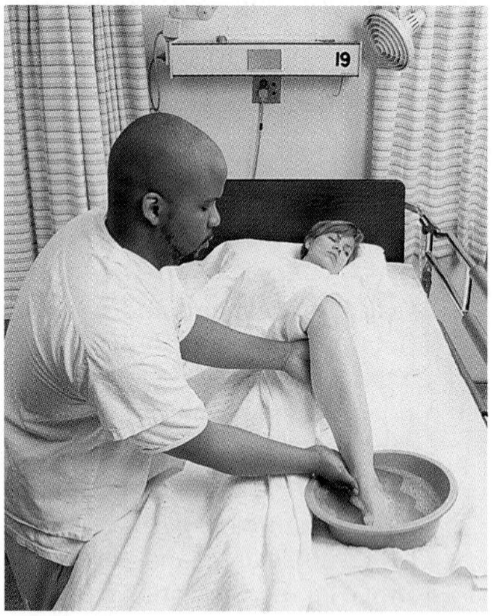

Figure 34.4 Soaking a foot in a basin

- Dry each foot. Pay particular attention to the spaces between the toes. If you prefer, wash one foot after that leg, before washing the other leg.
- Obtain fresh, warm bathwater now or when necessary. *Water may become dirty or cold.* Because surface skin cells are removed with washing, the bathwater from dark-skinned clients may be dark; however, this does not mean the client is dirty.

8. **Wash the back and then the perineum.**
- Assist the client to turn to a prone position or side-lying position facing away from you, and place the bath towel lengthwise alongside the back and buttocks.
- Wash and dry the back, buttocks, and upper thighs, paying particular attention to the gluteal folds. Avoid undue exposure of the client.
- Assist the client to the supine position, and determine whether the client can wash the perineal-genital area independently. If the client cannot do so, drape the client as shown in Figure 34.5 and wash the area. See Procedure 34.2.

9. **Assist the client with grooming aids, such as powder, lotion, or deodorant.**
- Use powder sparingly. Release as little as possible into the atmosphere. *This will avoid irritation of the respiratory tract by powder inhalation.*
- Help the client to put on a clean gown or pajamas.
- Assist the client to care for hair, mouth, and nails. Some people prefer or need mouth care prior to the bath.

10. **Document pertinent data.**
- Record assessments, such as excoriation in the folds beneath the breasts or reddened areas over bony prominences.
- Record the type of bath given (i.e., complete, partial, or self-help). This is usually recorded on a flowsheet.

For a Tub Bath or Shower

11. **Prepare the client and the tub.**
- Fill the tub about one-third to one-half full of water at 43° to 46°C. *Sufficient water is needed to cover the perineal area.*
- Cover all intravenous catheters or wound dressings with plastic coverings, and instruct client to prevent wetting these areas, if possible.
- Obtain assistance with holding a pediatric client as indicated. *Holding minimizes contamination of open skin areas.*
- Apply a rubber bath mat or towel to the floor of the tub if safety strips are not on tub floor. *These prevent slippage of the client during the bath or shower.*
- Use a small basin or large sink for a small child. *Smaller containers decrease the danger of slippage of an active child and possible drowning.*

12. **Assist the client into the shower or tub.**
- Assist the client taking a standing shower with the initial adjustment of the water temperature and water flow pressure, as needed. Some clients need a chair to sit in the shower because of weakness. Elderly people often feel faint under hot water.
- Explain how the client can signal for help, leave the client for two to five minutes, and place an "occupied" sign on the door. Follow agency policy regarding supervision of a client during a tub bath (for example, leaving client unattended).
- Never leave an infant or small pediatric client unattended in a tub. *Slippage and drowning can occur in a matter of seconds and in very little water.*

13. **Assist the client with washing and getting out of the tub.**
- Wash the client's back, lower legs, and feet, if necessary.
- Assist the client out of the tub. Place a bath towel over the client's shoulders and drain the tub of water before the client attempts to get out of it. *Draining the water first lessens the likelihood of a fall. The towel prevents chilling.*

14. **Dry the client, and assist with follow-up care.**
- Follow step 9.

PROCEDURE 34.1 Bathing an Adult or Pediatric Client *continued*

- Assist the client back to the room.
- Clean the tub or shower in accordance with agency practice, discard used linen in the laundry hamper, and place the "unoccupied" sign on the door.

15. Document pertinent data.

- Follow step 10.

Evaluation Focus
Client tolerance of procedure (note respiratory rate and effort, and pulse rate); status of skin (dryness, turgor, lesions, and so on); client strength and percentage of bath done without assistance

Home Care Considerations

Suggest that the client or family do the following:

- Consider purchasing a bath seat that fits in the tub or shower.
- Install a hand shower for use with a bath seat and shampooing.
- Use a nonskid surface on the tub or shower.
- Install hand bars on both sides of the tub or shower to facilitate transfers in and out of the tub or shower.
- Carefully monitor the temperature of the bathwater.
- Apply lotion and oil *after* a bath because these solutions can make a tub surface slippery.

Lifespan Considerations

- Encourage a child's participation appropriate for developmental level.
- Closely supervise children in the bathtub. Do not leave them unattended.
- Assist adolescents, as needed, to choose deodorants and antiperspirants. Secretions from newly active sweat glands react with bacteria on the skin, causing a pungent odour.
- To minimize skin dryness in older adults, avoid excessive use of soap and use lotions and bath oils.
- Protect children and older adults from injury related to hot water burns.

Perineal-Genital Care

Perineal-genital care is also referred to as *perineal care* or *peri-care.* Perineal care as part of the bed bath is embarrassing for many clients. Nurses also may find it embarrassing initially, particularly with clients of the opposite sex. Most clients who require a bed bath from the nurse are able to clean their own genital areas with minimal assistance. The nurse may need to hand a moistened washcloth and soap to the client, rinse the washcloth, and provide a towel.

Because some clients are unfamiliar with terminology for the genitals and perineum, it may be difficult for nurses to explain what is expected. Most clients, however, understand what is meant if the nurse simply says, "I'll give you a washcloth to finish your bath." Older clients may be familiar with the term *private parts.* Whatever expression the nurse uses, it needs to be one that the client understands and one that is comfortable for the nurse to use.

The nurse needs to provide perineal care efficiently and matter-of-factly. Nurses should wear gloves while providing this care for the comfort of the client and to protect themselves from infection. Procedure 34.2 explains how to provide perineal-genital care.

Client Teaching

Clients often need information about dry skin, skin rashes, diaper rash, and acne. The box on page 820 provides some guidelines for these problems.

Evaluating

Using data collected during care, the nurse judges whether desired outcomes have been achieved. Examples of client goals and related outcomes are shown in Table 34.6.

If the outcomes are not achieved, the nurse explores reasons why. For example:

- Did the nurse overestimate the client's functional abilities (physical, mental, emotional) for self-care?
- Were provided instructions not clear?
- Were appropriate assistive devices or supplies not available to the client?
- Did the client's condition change?
- Were required analgesics provided before hygienic care?
- What currently prescribed medications and therapies could affect the client's abilities or tissue integrity?

PROCEDURE 34.2 Providing Perineal-Genital Care

PURPOSES

- To remove normal perineal secretions and odours
- To promote client comfort

Assessment Focus
Presence of irritation, excoriation, inflammation, swelling; excessive discharge; odour; pain or discomfort; presence of urinary or fecal incontinence; recent rectal or perineal surgery; presence of indwelling catheter; perineal-genital hygiene practices; self-care abilities

Equipment

Perineal-genital care provided in conjunction with the bed bath

- ❑ Bath towel
- ❑ Bath blanket
- ❑ Disposable gloves
- ❑ Bath basin with water at 43° to 46°C
- ❑ Soap
- ❑ Washcloth

Special perineal-genital care

- ❑ Bath towel
- ❑ Bath blanket
- ❑ Disposable gloves
- ❑ Cotton balls or swabs
- ❑ Solution bottle, pitcher, or container filled with warm water or a prescribed solution
- ❑ Bedpan to receive rinse water
- ❑ Moisture-resistant bag or receptacle for used cotton swabs
- ❑ Perineal pad

INTERVENTION

1. Prepare the client.

- Offer the client an appropriate explanation, being particularly sensitive to any embarrassment felt by the client.
- Determine whether the client is experiencing any discomfort in the perineal-genital area.
- Place a bath towel under the client's hips. *The bath towel prevents the bed from becoming soiled.*

2. Position and drape the client, and clean the upper inner thighs.

FOR FEMALES

- Position the female in a back-lying position, with the knees flexed and spread well apart (abducted).
- Cover her body and legs with the bath blanket. Fold the top bed linen to the foot of the bed, maintaining client privacy. Drape the legs by tucking the bottom corners of the bath blanket under the inner sides of the legs (see Figure 34.5). *Minimum exposure lessens embarrassment and helps provide* warmth. Bring the middle portion of the base of the blanket up over the pubic area.
- Don gloves, and wash and dry the upper inner thighs.

Figure 34.5 Draping the client for perineal-genital care

FOR MALES

- Cover with a bath blanket (over top linen). Fold the top linen to the foot of the bed, taking care to maintain client privacy.
- Position the male client in a supine position with knees slightly flexed and hips slightly externally rotated.
- Don gloves, and wash and dry the upper inner thighs.

3. Inspect the perineal area.

- Note particular areas of inflammation, excoriation, or swelling, especially between the labia in females and the scrotal folds in males.
- Also note excessive discharge or secretions from the orifices and the presence of odours.

4. Wash and dry the perineal-genital area.

FOR FEMALES

- Clean the labia majora. Then, spread the labia to wash the folds between the labia majora and the labia minora (Figure 34.6). *Secretions that tend to collect around the labia minora facilitate bacterial growth.*

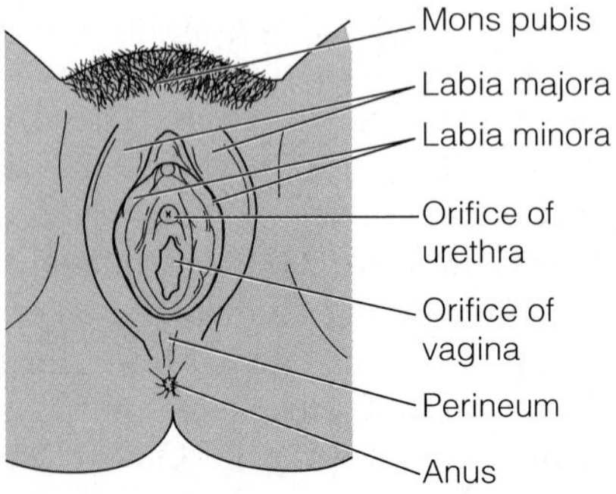

Figure 34.6 Female genitals

- Use separate quarters of the washcloth for each stroke, and wipe from the pubis to the rectum. For menstruating women and clients with indwelling catheters,

PROCEDURE 34.2 Providing Perineal-Genital Care *continued*

use disposable wipes, cotton balls, or gauze. Take a clean ball for each stroke. *Using separate quarters of the washcloth or new cotton balls or gauze prevents the transmission of microorganisms from one area to the other. Wipe from the area of least contamination (the pubis) to that of greatest (the rectum).* For those individuals with catheters, wash not only around the catheter but 7.5–10 cm down the catheter as well.

- Rinse the area well. You may place the client on a bedpan and use a periwash or solution bottle to pour warm water over the area. Dry the perineum thoroughly, paying particular attention to the folds between the labia. *Moisture supports the growth of many microorganisms.*

FOR MALES

- Wash the penis, cleansing the urethra and then the shaft, washing away from the urethra. Cleansing away from the urethra prevents the introduction of microorganisms.
- Wash and dry the penis using firm strokes. *Handling the penis firmly may prevent an erection.*
- If the client is uncircumcised, retract the prepuce (foreskin) to expose the glans penis (the tip of the penis) for cleaning. Replace the foreskin after cleaning the glans penis (Figure 34.7). *Retracting the foreskin is necessary to remove the smegma that collects under the foreskin and facilitates bacterial growth.*

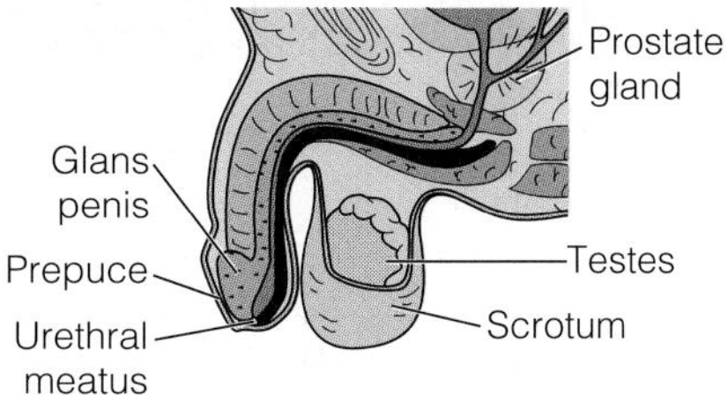

Figure 34.7 Male genitals

- If the client has a urinary catheter, cleanse 7.5–10 cm down the catheter away from the urethra with a clean area of the washcloth.
- Wash and dry the scrotum. The posterior folds of the scrotum may need to be cleaned in step 6 with the buttocks. *The scrotum tends to be more soiled than the penis because of its proximity to the rectum; thus, it is usually cleaned after the penis.*

5. **Inspect perineal orifices for intactness.**

- Inspect particularly around the urethra in clients with indwelling catheters. *A catheter may cause excoriation around the urethra.*

6. **Clean between the buttocks.**

- Assist the client to turn onto the side facing away from you.
- Pay particular attention to the anal area and posterior folds of the scrotum in males. Clean the anus with toilet tissue before washing it, if necessary.
- Dry the area well.
- For postdelivery or menstruating females, apply a perineal pad, as needed, from front to back. *This prevents contamination of the vagina and urethra from the anal area.*

7. **Document any assessments (redness, swelling, discharge).**

Evaluation Focus
Perineal-genital skin integrity; presence of inflammation, excoriation, swelling, discharge; localized areas of tenderness

- Is the client's fluid and food intake adequate or appropriate to maintain skin and mucous membrane moisture and integrity?

Feet

Proper assessment and care of feet is important at any age. This care becomes even more important with aging and when such conditions as circulatory disturbances or diabetes mellitus are present. Refer to the guidelines (Procedure 34.3) for providing foot care.

Developmental Variations

At birth, a baby's foot is relatively unformed. The arches are supported by fatty pads and do not take their full shape until five to six years of age. During childhood, the bones and small muscles of the feet are easily damaged by tight, binding stockings and ill-fitting shoes. For normal development, it is important that the arches be supported and that the bony structures and the feet grow with no external restrictions. Feet are not fully grown until about age 20 years. Healthy feet remain relatively unchanged during life. However, the elderly often require special attention for their feet. For example, reduced blood supply and accompanying arteriosclerosis can make a foot prone to infection following trauma.

Assessing

Nursing History

The nurse determines the client's history of (1) normal nail and foot care practices; (2) type of footwear worn; (3) self-care abilities; (4) presence of factors that place the client at risk for foot problems; (5) any foot discomfort; and (6) any perceived problems with foot mobility. To elicit such data, the nurse asks the client the questions in the box on page 822.

CLIENT TEACHING

Skin Problems and Care

Dry Skin

- Use cleansing creams to clean the skin, rather than soap or detergent, which cause drying and, in some cases, allergic reactions.
- Use bath oils, but take precautions to prevent falls caused by slippery tub surfaces.
- Thoroughly rinse soap or detergent, if used, from the skin.
- Bathe less frequently when environmental temperature and humidity are low.
- Increase fluid intake.
- Humidify the air with a humidifier or by keeping a tub or sink full of water.
- Use moisturizing or emollient creams that contain lanolin, petroleum jelly, or cocoa butter to retain skin moisture.

Skin Rashes

- Keep the area clean by washing it with a mild soap. Rinse the skin well, and pat it dry.
- To relieve itching, try a tepid bath or soak. Some over-the-counter preparations, such as Caladryl lotion, may help but should be used with full knowledge of the product.
- Avoid scratching the rash to prevent inflammation, infection, and further skin lesions.
- Choose clothing carefully. Too much clothing can cause perspiration and aggravate a rash.

Acne

- Wash the face frequently with soap or detergent and hot water to remove oil and dirt.
- Avoid using oily creams, which aggravate the condition.
- Avoid using cosmetics that block the ducts of the sebaceous glands and the hair follicles.
- Never squeeze or pick at the lesions. This increases the potential for infection and scarring.

TABLE 34.6 Evaluation Goals and Outcomes: Self-Care, Bathing, Dressing, Grooming

Goal	Examples of Desired Outcomes
Maintains skin cleanliness	Obtains bath supplies
	Regulates water flow and temperature
	Bathes in tub twice weekly with assistance
	Washes and dries body with direction
	Gets in and out of tub with assistance
Maintains clean-clothed appearance	Chooses and obtains clean clothing from closet and drawers
	Puts on and removes clothing
	Fastens clothing with assistance
	Ties shoes with assistance
Maintains well-groomed appearance	Applies make-up
	Shaves self
	Cares for nails
	Combs or brushes hair
	Uses caregiver help for shampoo
Maintains sense of well-being	Reports satisfaction with appearance
	Reports satisfaction with level of dependence

Physical Assessment

Each foot and toe is inspected for shape, size, and presence of lesions and is palpated to assess areas of tenderness, edema, and circulatory status. Normally, the toes are straight and flat. See Table 34.7 for physical assessment methods for the feet. Common foot problems include calluses, corns, unpleasant odours, plantar warts, fissures between the toes, and fungal infections such as athlete's foot.

A **callus** is a thickened portion of epidermis, a mass of keratotic material. Most calluses are painless and flat and are found on the bottom or side of the foot over a bony prominence. Calluses are usually caused by pressure from shoes. They can be softened by soaking the foot in warm water with Epsom salts. Creams with lanolin help to keep the skin soft and prevent the formation of calluses.

A **corn** is a keratosis caused by friction and pressure from a shoe. It commonly occurs on the fourth or fifth toe, usually on a bony prominence, such as a joint. Corns are usually conical (circular and raised). The base is the surface of the corn and the apex is in deeper tissues, sometimes even attached to bone. Corns are generally removed surgically. They are prevented from reforming by relieving the pressure on the area (i.e., wearing comfortable shoes) and massaging the tissue to promote circulation. The use of oval corn pads should be avoided because they increase pressure and decrease circulation.

PROCEDURE 34.3 Providing Foot Care

PURPOSES

- To maintain the skin integrity of the feet
- To prevent foot infections
- To prevent foot odours
- To assess or monitor foot problems

Assessment Focus
Skin integrity; presence of edema or tenderness; circulatory status; usual foot care practices; self-care abilities

Equipment

- ❑ Washbasin containing warm water
- ❑ Pillow
- ❑ Moisture-resistant disposable pad
- ❑ Towels
- ❑ Soap
- ❑ Washcloth
- ❑ Toenail cleaning and trimming equipment
- ❑ Lotion or foot powder

INTERVENTION

1. Prepare the equipment and the client.

- Fill the washbasin with warm water at about 40° to 43°C. *Warm water promotes circulation and comforts and refreshes the feet.*
- Assist the ambulatory client to a sitting position in a chair, or the bed client to a supine or semi-Fowler's position.
- Place a pillow under the bed client's knees. *This provides support and prevents muscle fatigue.*
- Place the washbasin on the moisture-resistant pad at the foot of the bed for a bed client or on the floor in front of the chair for an ambulatory client.
- For a bed client, pad the rim of the washbasin with a towel. *The towel prevents undue pressure on the skin.*

2. Wash the foot and soak it as required.

- Place one of the client's feet in the basin, and wash it with soap, paying particular attention to the interdigital areas. Prolonged soaking is generally not recommended for diabetic clients or individuals with peripheral vascular disease. *Prolonged soaking may remove natural skin oils, thus drying the skin and making it more susceptible to cracking and injury.*
- Rinse the foot well to remove soap. Soap irritates the skin if not properly removed.
- Rub callused areas of the foot with the washcloth. *This helps remove dead skin layers.*
- If the nails are brittle or thick and require trimming, replace the water and allow the foot to soak for 10 to 20 minutes. *Soaking softens the nails and loosens debris under them.*
- Clean the nails as required with an orange stick. *This removes excess debris that harbours microorganisms.*
- Remove the foot from the basin and place it on the towel.

3. Dry the foot thoroughly and apply lotion or foot powder.

- Blot the foot gently with the towel to dry it thoroughly, particularly between the toes. *Harsh rubbing can damage the skin. Thorough drying reduces the risk of infection.*
- Apply lotion or lanolin cream. *This lubricates dry skin.*

  or
- Apply a foot powder containing a nonirritating deodorant if the feet tend to perspire excessively. *Foot powders have greater absorbent properties than regular bath powders; some also contain menthol, which makes the feet feel cool.*

4. If agency policy permits, trim the nails of the first foot while the second foot is soaking.

- See the discussion on nails for the appropriate method to trim nails. Note that in many agencies, toenail trimming requires a physician's order or is contraindicated for clients with diabetes mellitus, toe infections, and peripheral vascular disease unless performed by a podiatrist or general practice physician.

5. Document any pertinent data.

- Record any signs of inflammation, infection, breaks in the skin, corns, troublesome calluses, bunions, and pressure areas. This is of particular importance for clients with peripheral vascular disease and diabetes.

Evaluation Focus
Skin colour and temperature; skin integrity; presence of foot odour; discomfort; tenderness; peripheral circulation

ASSESSMENT INTERVIEW

Foot Hygiene

Foot Care Practices

- How often do you wash your feet and cut your toenails?
- What hygiene products do you usually use on your feet (e.g., soap, foot powder or deodorant, lotion, or cream)?
- What type of shoes and socks do you wear?
- How often do you change your socks or put on clean socks?
- Do you ever go barefoot? If so, when, where, and how often?

Self-Care Abilities

- Do you have any problems managing your foot care? If so, what are these?
- How can the nurses best help you?

Foot Problems and Risk Factors

- Do you have any problems with foot odour?
- Do you have any foot discomfort? If so, where? When does this occur? What do you do to relieve the discomfort? Does this discomfort affect how you walk?
- Have you noticed any problems with foot mobility (e.g., joint stiffness)?
- Do you have diabetes, any circulatory problems with your feet (e.g., swelling, changes in skin colour, arthritis), or any instances of prolonged exposure to chemicals or water?

Unpleasant odours occur as a result of perspiration and its interaction with microorganisms. Regular and frequent washing of the feet and wearing clean hosiery help minimize odour. Foot powders and deodorants also help prevent this problem.

Plantar warts appear on the sole of the foot. These warts are caused by the virus *Papovavirus hominis*. They are moderately contagious. The warts are frequently painful and often make walking difficult. The physician may curettage the warts, freeze them with solid carbon dioxide several times, or apply salicylic acid.

Fissures, or deep grooves, frequently occur between the toes as a result of dryness and cracking of the skin. The treatment of choice is good foot hygiene and application of an antiseptic to prevent infection. Often, a small piece of gauze is inserted between the toes in applying the antiseptic and is left in place to assist healing by allowing air to reach the area.

Athlete's foot, or **tinea pedis** (ringworm of the foot), is caused by a fungus. The symptoms are scaling and cracking of the skin, particularly between the toes. Sometimes, small blisters form, containing a thin fluid. In severe cases, the lesions may also appear on other parts of the body, particularly the hands. Treatments usually involve the application of commercial antifungal ointments or powders. Prevention is important. Common preventive measures are keeping the feet well ventilated, drying the feet well after bathing, wearing clean socks or stockings, and not going barefoot in public showers.

An **ingrown nail,** the growing inward of the nail into the soft tissues around it, most often results from improper nail trimming. Pressure applied to the area causes localized pain. Treatment involves frequent, hot antiseptic soaks and surgical removal of the portion of nail embedded in the skin. Preventing recurrence involves appropriate instruction and adherence to proper nail-trimming techniques.

TABLE 34.7 Assessment of the Feet

Method	Normal Findings	Deviations from Normal
Inspect all skin surfaces, particulary between the toes, for cleanliness, odour, dryness, inflammation, swelling, abrasions, or other lesions.	Intact skin Absence of swelling or inflammation	Excessive dryness Areas of inflammation or swelling (e.g., corns, calluses) Fissures Scaling and cracking of skin (e.g., athlete's foot) Plantar warts
Palpate anterior and posterior surfaces of ankles and feet for edema.	No swelling	Swelling or pitting edema See Chapter 27.
Palpate dorsalis pedis pulse on dorsal surface of foot and posterior tibial pulse behind the medial malledus.	Strong, regular pulses in both feet	Weak or absent pulses in one foot or both feet
Compare skin temperatures of the two feet.	Warm skin temperature	Cool skin temperature in one or both feet
Assess sensation of touch.	Sensation of touch	Absence of sensation
Assess movement.	Movement of feet or toes	Decreased movement of feet or toes

Diagnosing

A number of nursing diagnoses may apply to clients with foot or foot care problems. The most common diagnostic labels, along with possible contributing factors, are as follows:

- ***Self-Care Deficit*** (foot care) related to
  a. Visual impairment
  b. Impaired hand coordination
  c. Other contributing factors (see the box "Etiologies of Self-Care Deficits" on page 810).
- ***Risk for Impaired Skin Integrity*** related to
  a. Altered tissue perfusion: peripheral (associated with edema, inadequate arterial circulation)
  b. Poorly fitting shoes
- ***Risk for Infection*** related to
  a. Impaired skin integrity (ingrown toenail, corn, trauma)
  b. Deficient nail or foot care
- ***Knowledge Deficient*** (diabetic foot care) related to
  a. Lack of exposure to information
  b. Newly established medical diagnosis (diabetes) and necessary foot hygiene practices

Examples of assessment data clusters and related nursing diagnoses are shown in Table 34.8.

TABLE 34.8 Clinical Application: Assessment Data Clusters and Related Nursing Diagnoses for Clients with Foot Problems

Data Cluster	Nursing Diagnosis
Sally Brown, an 83-year-old widow, lives alone. She has homemaker services twice a week and Meals on Wheels service daily. She manages to shower once a week with daughter's help. She has pronounced hand tremors and obvious cataracts. She states, "I can't see well enough to cut my nails, and even if I could see, my hands shake so badly."	***Self-Care Deficit:*** (foot care) ***Hygiene*** related to impaired hand coordination and visual impairment
Kyle Stevens, 14 years old, lives with his mother and eight sisters and brothers in a three-room walk-up. The bathroom down the hall is shared with other tenants in the building. His shoes are ragged and fit poorly. He states, "I can't get new ones."	***Risk for Impaired Skin Integrity*** related to poorly fitting shoes and limited access to bathing facilities
Jim Wakefield, 64 years old, was recently diagnosed with diabetes mellitus. He states he has heard of "diabetes" and is worried because a friend of his father's had diabetes and, after cutting his foot, had his leg amputated.	***Knowledge Deficient*** (diabetic foot care) related to misinterpretation of information

Planning

Planning involves (1) identifying nursing interventions that will help the client maintain or restore healthy foot care practices, and (2) establishing desired outcomes for each client. Interventions may include teaching the client about correct nail and foot care, proper footwear, and ways to prevent potential foot problems (e.g., infection, injury, and decreased circulation). For clients with self-care difficulties, the nurse plans a schedule for soaking the client's feet and assisting with regular cleaning and trimming of nails (if not contraindicated). Foot and nail care is often provided during the client's bath but may be provided at any time in the day to accommodate the client's preference or schedule. The frequency of foot care is determined by the nurse and client and is based on objective assessment data and the client's specific problems. For some clients, the feet need to be bathed daily; for those whose feet perspire excessively, bathing more than once a day may be necessary. Examples of desired outcomes to evaluate the achievement of goals and effectiveness of nursing interventions follow. The client does the following:

- Participates in self-care (foot hygiene) to optimal level of capacity (specify)
- Describes hygienic and other interventions (e.g., proper footwear) to maintain skin integrity, prevent infection, and maintain peripheral tissue perfusion
- Demonstrates optimal hygiene, as evidenced by
  a. Intact, pink, smooth, soft, hydrated, and warm skin
  b. Intact cuticles and skin surrounding nails
  c. Correct foot care and nail care practices

Implementing

Procedure 34.3 describes how to provide foot care. See also the discussion of nails. During these procedures, the nurse has the opportunity to teach the client appropriate methods for foot care, that is, methods designed to prevent tissue injury and infection. Because of reduced peripheral circulation to the feet, clients with diabetes or peripheral vascular disease are particularly prone to infection if skin breakage occurs. Many foot problems can be prevented by teaching the client simple foot care guidelines. See the box on the next page.

CLIENT TEACHING

Foot Care

- Wash the feet daily, and dry them well, especially between the toes.
- When washing, inspect the skin of the feet for breaks or red or swollen areas. Use a mirror, if needed, to visualize all areas.
- To prevent burns, check the water temperature before immersing the feet.
- Use creams or lotions to moisten the skin, or soak the feet in warm water with Epsom salts to avoid excessive drying of the skin of the feet. Lotion will also soften calluses. A lotion that reduces dryness effectively is a mixture of lanolin and mineral oil.
- To prevent or control an unpleasant odour due to excessive foot perspiration, wash the feet frequently and change socks and shoes at least daily. Special deodorant sprays or absorbent foot powders are also helpful.
- File the toenails, rather than cutting them, to avoid skin injury. File the nails straight across the ends of the toes. If the nails are too thick or misshapen to file, consult a podiatrist.
- Wear clean stockings or socks daily. Avoid socks with holes or darns that can cause pressure areas.
- Wear correctly fitting shoes that neither restrict the foot nor rub on any area; rubbing can cause corns and calluses. Check worn shoes for rough spots in the lining. Break in new shoes gradually by increasing the wearing time 30 to 60 minutes each day.
- Avoid walking barefoot because injury and infection may result. Wear footwear (for example, shower sandals) in public showers and in change areas to avoid contracting athlete's foot or other infections.
- Several times each day, exercise the feet to promote circulation. Point the feet upward, point them downward, and move them in circles.
- Avoid wearing constricting garments, such as knee-high elastic stockings, and avoid sitting with the legs crossed at the knees or ankles, which may decrease circulation.
- When the feet are cold, use extra blankets and wear warm socks rather than using heating pads or hot water bottles, which may cause burns. Test bathwater before stepping into it.
- Wash any cut on the foot thoroughly, apply a mild antiseptic, and notify the physician if indicated.
- Avoid self-treatment for corns or calluses. Pumice stones and some callus and corn applications are injurious to the skin. Consult a podiatrist or physician first.
- Notify the physician if you notice abnormal sores or drainage, pain, or changes in temperature, colour, and sensation of the foot.

Evaluating

See examples of desired outcomes earlier in the "Planning" section.

Nails

Nails are normally present at birth. They continue to grow throughout life and change very little until people are elderly. At that time, the nails tend to be tougher, more brittle, and, in some cases, thicker. The nails of an older person normally grow less quickly than those of a younger person and may be ridged and grooved.

Assessing

During the nursing history, the nurse explores the client's usual nail care practices, self-care abilities, and any problems associated with them. See the assessment box opposite. Physical assessment involves inspection of the nails (see also Chapter 27).

Diagnosing

Nursing diagnoses related to nail care and nail problems include ***Self-Care Deficit*** and ***Risk for Infection.*** Examples of these nursing diagnoses and contributing factors follow:

- ***Self-Care Deficit: Grooming*** related to
  a. Impaired vision
  b. Impaired hand coordination
- ***Risk for Infection*** around the nail bed related to
  a. Impaired skin integrity of cuticles
  b. Altered peripheral circulation

Planning

The nurse identifies measures that will assist the client to develop or maintain healthy nail care practices. A schedule of nail care needs to be established. Examples of desired outcomes used to evaluate the effectiveness of nursing interventions follow.

ASSESSMENT INTERVIEW

Nail Hygiene

- What are your usual nail care practices?
- Do you have any problems managing your nail care? If so, what are these?
- Have you had any problems associated with your nails (e.g., inflammation of the tissue surrounding the nail, injury, prolonged exposure to water or chemicals, circulatory problems)?

The client does the following:

- Demonstrates healthy nail care practices, as shown by
  a. Clean, short nails with smooth edges
  b. Intact cuticles and hydrated surrounding skin
- Describes factors contributing to the nail problem
- Describes preventive interventions for the specific nail problem
- Demonstrates nail care as instructed
- Has pink nail beds and quick return of nail bed colour after blanch test

Implementing

To provide nail care, the nurse needs a nail cutter or sharp scissors, a nail file, an orange stick to push back the cuticle, hand lotion or mineral oil to lubricate any dry tissue around the nails, and a basin of water to soak the nails if they are particularly thick or hard.

Hands or feet are soaked, if needed, and dried; then the nail is cut or filed straight across beyond the end of the finger or toe. See Figure 34.8. Avoid trimming or digging into nails at the lateral corners. This predisposes the client to ingrown toenails. Clients who have diabetes or circulatory problems should have their nails filed, rather than cut; inadvertent injury to tissues can occur if scissors are used. After the initial cut or filing, the nail is filed to round the corners, and the nurse cleans under the nail. The nurse then gently pushes back the cuticle, taking care not to injure it. The next finger or toe is cared for in the same manner. Any abnormalities, such as an infected cuticle or inflammation of the tissue around the nail, are recorded and reported.

Evaluating

See examples of desired outcomes earlier in the "Planning" section.

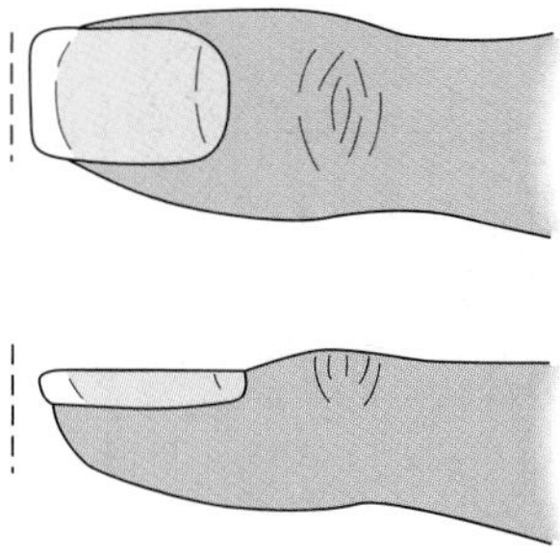

Figure 34.8 Fingernails are trimmed straight across

Mouth

Developmental Variations

Teeth usually appear five to eight months after birth. Each tooth has three parts: the crown, the root, and the pulp cavity (Figure 34.9). The **crown** is the exposed part of the tooth that is outside the gum. It is covered with a hard substance called **enamel.** The ivory-coloured internal part of the crown below the enamel is the **dentin.** The root of a tooth is embedded in the jaw and covered by a bony tissue called **cementum.** The **pulp cavity** in the centre of the tooth contains the blood vessels and nerves.

By the time children are two years old, they usually have all 20 of their temporary teeth (Figure 34.10). At about age six or seven years, children start losing their deciduous teeth, and these are gradually replaced by the 32 permanent teeth (Figure 34.11). By age 25 years, most people have all their permanent teeth.

The incidence of periodontal disease increases during pregnancy because the rise in female hormones affects gingival tissue and increases its reaction to bacterial plaque. Many pregnant women experience more bleeding from the gingival sulcus during brushing and increased redness and swelling of the **gingiva** (the gum).

Some older adults may have few permanent teeth left, and some have **dentures.** Older individuals may lose teeth

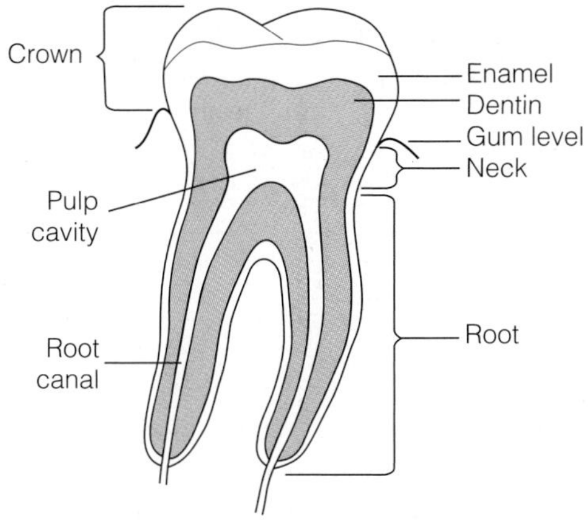

Figure 34.9 The anatomical parts of a tooth

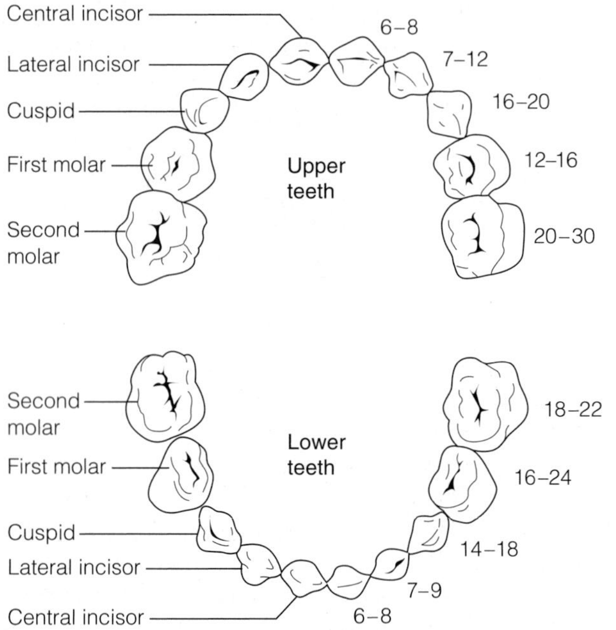

Figure 34.10 Temporary teeth and their times of eruption (stated in months)

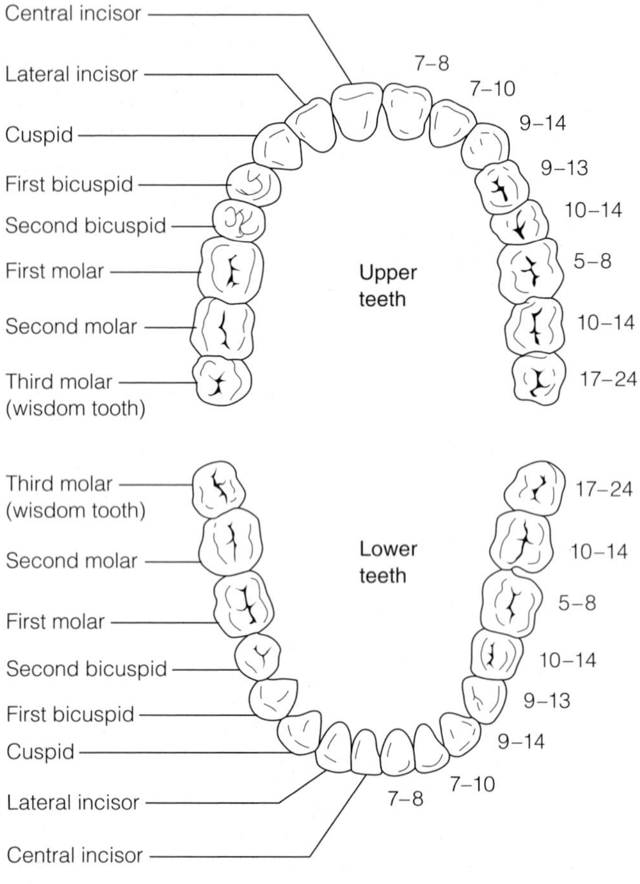

Figure 34.11 Permanent teeth and their times of eruption (stated in years)

mainly because of **periodontal disease** (gum disease), rather than **dental caries** (cavities); however, caries can also be the cause of lost teeth in middle-aged adults.

Some receding of the gums and a brownish pigmentation of the gums occur with age. Because saliva production decreases with age, dryness of the oral mucosa is a common finding in older people.

Assessing

Assessment of the client's mouth and hygiene practices includes (1) a nursing history, (2) physical assessment of the mouth, and (3) identification of clients at risk for developing oral problems.

Nursing History

During the nursing history, the nurse obtains data about the client's oral hygiene practices, including dental visits, self-care abilities, and past or current mouth problems. Data about the client's oral hygiene help the nurse determine learning needs and incorporate the client's needs and preferences in the plan of care. Assessment of the client's *self-care abilities* determines the amount and type of nursing assistance to provide. See the box opposite for definitions and descriptions of functional level. Clients whose hand coordination is impaired, whose cognitive function is impaired, whose illness alters energy levels and motivation, or whose therapy imposes restrictions on activities will need assistance from the nurse. Information about *past or current problems* alerts the nurse to specific interventions required or referrals that may be necessary. Questions to elicit this information are shown in the box opposite.

Physical Assessment

For information about mouth assessment, see Chapter 27. Dental caries (cavities) and periodontal disease are the two problems that most frequently affect the teeth. Both problems are commonly associated with plaque and tartar deposits. **Plaque** is an *invisible* soft film that adheres to the enamel surface of teeth; it consists of bacteria, molecules of saliva, and remnants of epithelial cells and leukocytes. When plaque is unchecked, tartar (dental calculus) is formed. **Tartar** is a visible, hard deposit of plaque and dead bacteria that forms at the gum lines. Tartar buildup can alter the fibres that attach the teeth to the gum and eventually disrupt bone tissue. Periodontal disease is characterized by **gingivitis** (red, swollen gingiva), bleeding, receding gum lines, and the formation of pockets between the teeth and gums. In advanced periodontal disease (**pyorrhea**), the teeth are loose and pus is evident when the gums are pressed. See Table 34.9 for additional problems of the mouth.

Identifying Clients at Risk

Certain clients are prone to oral problems because of lack of knowledge or the inability to maintain oral hygiene. Among

Definitions and Descriptions for Functional Level (Oral Hygiene)

- *Totally dependent:* Nurse completes the entire procedure.
- *Moderately dependent:* Nurse prepares brush; rinses client's mouth; positions client.
- *Semidependent:* Nurse provides equipment; client performs the task.

Source: Wilkinson, J. M. (1997). *Nursing Diagnosis & Intervention Pocket Guide* (6th ed.). (p. 234). Redwood City, CA: Addison-Wesley Nursing.

ASSESSMENT INTERVIEW

Oral Hygiene

Oral Hygiene Practices

- What are your usual mouth care and/or denture care practices?
- What oral hygiene products do you routinely use (e.g., mouthwash, type of toothpaste, dental floss, denture cleaner)?
- When was your last dental examination, and how often do you see your dentist?

Self-Care Abilities

- Do you have any problems managing your mouth care?

Past or Current Mouth Problems

- Have you had or do you have any problems, such as bleeding, swollen or reddened gums, ulcerations, lumps, or tooth pain?

these are seriously ill, confused, comatose, depressed, and dehydrated clients. In addition, people with nasogastric tubes or those receiving oxygen are likely to develop dry oral mucous membranes, especially if they breathe through their mouths. Clients who have had oral or jaw surgery must have meticulous oral hygiene care to prevent the development of infections.

Healthy-appearing individuals, too, may be at risk. High-risk variables, such as inadequate nutrition, excessive intake of refined sugars, and family history of periodontal disease, also need to be identified. Some older people may also be at risk, for example, those who choose salty or enamel-eroding sugary foods because of a decline in their number of taste buds. The decreased saliva production in older adults, which produces a dry mouth and thinning of the oral mucosa, is another factor.

A dry mouth can be aggravated by poor fluid intake, heavy smoking, alcohol use, high salt intake, anxiety, and many medications. Medications that can cause dryness of the mouth include diuretics; laxatives, if used excessively; and tranquilizers, such as chlorpromazine (Thorazine) and diazepam (Valium). Some chemotherapeutic agents used to treat cancer also cause oral dryness and lesions.

Diagnosing

Three nursing diagnoses related to problems with oral hygiene and the oral cavity are ***Self-Care Deficit, Altered Oral Mucous Membrane,*** and ***Knowledge Deficit.*** Note that NANDA includes oral hygiene in the diagnostic label ***Self-Care Deficient: Bathing/Hygiene.*** In this book, the diagnosis ***Self-Care Deficit: Oral Hygiene*** will be used for clients unable to perform oral care independently. This includes the inability to brush or floss teeth or clean dentures. Related factors are shown in the box on page 810, "Etiologies of Self-Care Deficits."

The diagnosis ***Altered Oral Mucous Membrane*** refers to the state in which an individual experiences disruptions in the tissue layers of the oral cavity. Manifestations include a coated tongue; dry mouth; dental caries; halitosis; gingivitis; oral plaque, pain, discomfort, erythema, lesions or ulcers; and lack of or decreased salivation. These may be the result of inadequate oral hygiene; physical injury or drying effect (e.g., mouth breathing, oxygen therapy, decreased salivation, temperature extreme, NPO); mechanical trauma (e.g., surgery, injury from oral tube, broken teeth or ill-fitting dentures); chemical trauma (e.g., side-effects of medications); or radiation injury.

Clinical examples of assessment data clusters and related nursing diagnoses are shown in Table 34.10.

Planning

The goals for clients with oral hygiene or oral problems are:

- To maintain or improve oral hygiene practices
- To maintain or restore the integrity of the oral tissues
- To prevent associated risks such as dental caries and inflammation or injury of the gums, tongue, or oral mucosa

Implementing

Good oral hygiene includes daily stimulation of the gums, mechanical brushing and flossing of the teeth, and flushing of the mouth. The nurse is often in a position to help people maintain oral hygiene by helping or teaching them to clean the teeth and oral cavity, by inspecting whether clients (especially children) have done so, or by actually providing mouth care to clients who are ill or incapaci-

TABLE 34.9 Common Problems of the Mouth

Problem	Description	Nursing Implications
Halitosis	Bad breath	Teach or provide regular oral hygiene.
Glossitis	Inflammation of the tongue	As above
Gingivitis	Inflammation of the gums	As above
Periodontal disease	Gums appear spongy and bleeding	As above
Reddened or excoriated mucosa		Check for ill-fitting dentures.
Excessive dryness of the buccal mucosa		Advise increased fluid intake, as client's health permits.
Cheilosis	Cracking of lips	Advise client to lubricate lips; use antimicrobial ointment to prevent infection.
Dental caries	Teeth have darkened areas, may be painful	Advise client to see a dentist.
Sordes	Accumulation of foul matter (food, microorganisms, and epithelial elements) in the mouth	Teach or provide regular cleaning.
Stomatitis	Inflammation of the oral mucosa	Teach or provide regular cleaning.
Parotitis	Inflammation of the parotid salivary glands	Teach or provide regular oral hygiene.

tated. The nurse can also be instrumental in identifying problems that require the intervention of a dentist or oral surgeon and arranging a referral.

Promoting Oral Health through the Life Span

A major role of the nurse in promoting oral health is to teach clients about specific oral hygienic measures.

Infants and Toddlers

Most dentists recommend that dental hygiene should begin when the first tooth erupts and be practised after each feeding. Cleaning can be accomplished by using a wet washcloth or a cotton ball or small gauze moistened with water.

Dental caries occur frequently during the toddler period, often as a result of the excessive intake of sweets or a prolonged use of the bottle during naps and at bedtime. The nurse should give parents the following instructions to promote and maintain dental health:

- Beginning at about 18 months of age, brush the child's teeth with a soft toothbrush. Use only a toothbrush moistened with water. Introduce toothpaste later; use one that contains fluoride.
- Give a fluoride supplement daily or as recommended by the physician or dentist, unless the drinking water is fluoridated.
- Schedule an initial dental visit for the child at about two or three years of age, as soon as all 20 primary teeth have erupted.

TABLE 34.10 Clinical Application: Assessment Data Clusters and Related Nursing Diagnoses for Clients with Oral Cavity Problems

Data Cluster	Nursing Diagnosis
Mary Brown, 77 years old, suffered a cerebrovascular accident. She is unconscious and breathing through the mouth via O_2 face mask. 2,500 mL of intravenous fluid ordered daily.	***Self-Care Deficit: Oral Hygiene*** related to cognitive inability (unconsciousness)
Joe Kwan, 46 years old, was admitted with a fractured femur. His teeth are stained from heavy smoking. One large cavity is evident in second lower left molar. He has tartar buildup along gum margins and pronounced halitosis. Gums are reddened in some areas and bleed when flossed. He states, "I can't remember when I last saw a dentist."	***Altered Oral Mucous Membrane*** related to ineffective oral hygiene

- Some dentists recommend an inspection type of visit when the child is about 18 months old to provide an early pleasant introduction to the dental examination.

- Seek professional dental attention for any problems, such as discolouring of the teeth, chipping, or signs of infection, such as redness and swelling.

Preschoolers and School-Age Children

Because deciduous teeth guide the entrance of permanent teeth, dental care is essential to keep these teeth in good repair. Abnormally placed or lost deciduous teeth can cause misalignment of permanent teeth. Fluoride remains important at this stage to prevent dental caries. Preschoolers need to be taught to brush their teeth after eating and to limit their intake of refined sugars. Parental supervision may be needed to ensure the completion of these self-care activities. Regular dental checkups are required during these years when permanent teeth appear.

Adolescents and Adults

Proper diet and tooth and mouth care should be taught to adolescents and adults. Specific measures to prevent tooth decay and periodontal disease are shown in the box below.

Examples of desired outcomes, although developed in the planning phase, are provided in Table 34.11 in the "Evaluating" part of this section of the chapter.

During the planning phase, the nurse also identifies interventions that will help the client achieve these goals. Nursing interventions may include:

- Teaching clients about good oral hygiene practices and other measures to prevent tooth decay
- Assisting dependent clients with oral care
- Providing special oral hygiene for clients who are debilitated, unconscious, or have lesions of the mucous membranes or other oral tissues

WELLNESS TEACHING

Measures to Prevent Tooth Decay

- Brush the teeth thoroughly after meals and at bedtime. Assist children or inspect their mouths to be sure the teeth are clean. If the teeth cannot be brushed after meals, vigorous rinsing of the mouth with water is recommended.
- Floss the teeth daily.
- Ensure an adequate intake of nutrients, particularly calcium, phosphorus, vitamins A, C, and D, and fluoride.
- Avoid sweet foods and drinks between meals. Take them in moderation at meals.
- Eat coarse, fibrous foods (cleansing foods), such as fresh fruits and raw vegetables.
- Have topical fluoride applications as prescribed by the dentist.
- Have a checkup by a dentist every six months.

Care of Teeth

Brushing and Flossing the Teeth

Thorough brushing of the teeth is important in preventing tooth decay. The mechanical action of brushing removes food particles that can harbour and incubate bacteria. It also stimulates circulation in the gums, thus maintaining their healthy firmness. One of the techniques recommended for brushing teeth is called the **sulcular technique,** which removes plaque and cleans under the gingival margins. Many toothpastes are marketed. Fluoride toothpaste is often recommended because of its antibacterial protection. An effective dentifrice can also be made using baking soda.

Caring for Artificial Dentures

Some people have artificial teeth in the form of a plate—a complete set of teeth for one jaw. A person may have a lower plate or an upper plate or both. When only a few artificial teeth are needed, the individual may have a bridge rather than a plate. A bridge may be fixed or removable. Artificial teeth are fitted to the individual and usually will not fit another person. People who wear dentures or other types of oral prostheses should be encouraged to use them. Those who do not wear their prostheses are prone to shrinkage of the gums, which results in further tooth loss.

Like natural teeth, artificial dentures collect microorganisms and food. They need to be cleaned regularly, at least once a day. They can be removed from the mouth, scrubbed with a toothbrush, rinsed, and reinserted. Some people use a dentifrice for cleaning teeth, and others use commercial cleaning compounds for plates.

Assisting Clients with Oral Care

When providing mouth care for partially or totally dependent clients, the nurse should wear gloves to guard against infections. Other required equipment includes a curved basin that fits snugly under the client's chin (e.g., a kidney basin) to receive the rinse water and a towel to protect the client and the bedclothes. See Procedure 34.4.

Foam swabs are often used in health-care agencies to clean the mouths of dependent clients. These swabs are convenient and effective in removing excess debris from the teeth and mouth but should be used infrequently and for short periods (i.e., less than three days). Pearson (1996) reports that foam swabs are not as effective as a toothbrush in removing plaque from "sheltered" areas of the teeth and gingival crevices.

PROCEDURE 34.4 Brushing and Flossing the Teeth

PURPOSES

- To remove food particles from around and between the teeth
- To remove dental plaque
- To enhance the client's feeling of well-being
- To prevent sordes and infection of the oral tissues

Assessment Focus
Self-care abilities; presence of tooth caries; gum inflammation; halitosis; status of oral mucosa and lips; usual mouth care practices

Equipment

- ❑ Towel
- ❑ Disposable gloves
- ❑ Curved basin (emesis basin)
- ❑ Toothbrush
- ❑ Cup of tepid water
- ❑ Dentifrice
- ❑ Mouthwash
- ❑ Dental floss, at least two pieces 20 cm in length
- ❑ Floss holder (optional)

INTERVENTION

1. Prepare the client.

- Explain the procedure.
- Assist the client to a sitting position in bed if the client's health permits. If not, assist the client to a side-lying position with the head on a pillow so that the client can spit out the rinse water.

2. Prepare the equipment.

- Place the towel under the client's chin.
- Don gloves. *Wearing gloves while providing mouth care prevents the nurse from acquiring infections. Gloves also prevent transmission of microorganisms to the client.*
- Moisten the bristles of the toothbrush with tepid water, and apply the dentifrice to the toothbrush.
- Use a soft toothbrush (a small one for a child) and the client's choice of dentifrice. For the person who does not have dentifrice, use baking soda or water only.
- For the client who must remain in bed, place or hold the curved basin under the client's chin, fitting the small curve around the chin or neck.
- Inspect the mouth and teeth.

3. Brush the teeth.

- Hand the toothbrush to the client, or brush the client's teeth as follows:

  a. Hold the brush against the teeth with the bristles at a 45-degree angle (Figure 34.12).

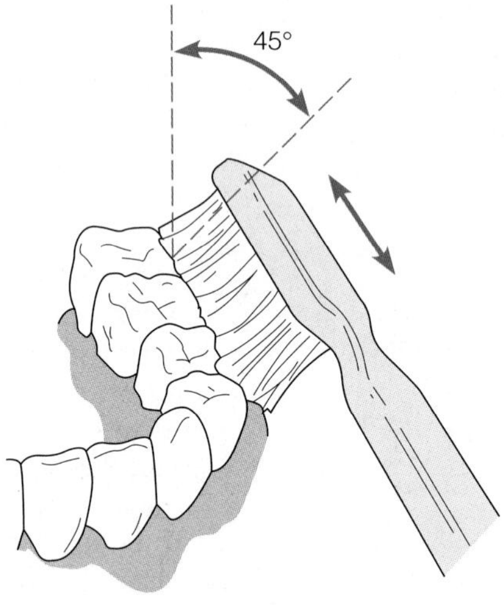

Figure 34.12 The sulcular technique: placing the bristles at a 45-degree angle against the teeth

The tips of the outer bristles should rest against and penetrate under the gingival sulcus (Figure 34.13). The brush will clean under the sulcus of two or three teeth at one time. *This sulcular technique removes plaque and cleans under the gingival margins.*

  b. Move the bristles back and forth using a vibrating or jiggling motion, from the sulcus to the crowns of the teeth.

  c. Repeat until all outer and inner surfaces of the teeth and sulci of the gums are cleaned.

Figure 34.13 Directing the tips of the outer bristles under the gingival margins

  d. Clean the biting surfaces by moving the brush back and forth over them in short strokes (Figure 34.14).

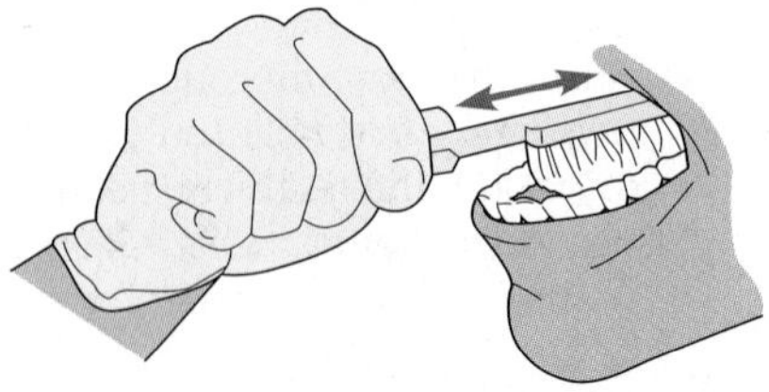

Figure 34.14 Brushing the biting surfaces

  e. If the tongue is coated, brush it gently with the toothbrush. *Brushing removes accumulated materials and coatings. A coated tongue may be caused by poor oral hygiene and low fluid intake. Brushing gently and carefully helps prevent gagging or vomiting.*

PROCEDURE 34.4 Brushing and Flossing the Teeth *continued*

- Hand the client the water cup or mouthwash to rinse the mouth vigorously. Then, ask the client to spit the water and excess dentifrice into the basin. Some agencies supply a standard mouthwash. Alternatively, a mouth rinse of normal saline can be an effective cleaner and moisturizer. This may require a physician's order. *Vigorous rinsing loosens food particles and washes out already loosened particles.*
- Repeat the preceding steps until the mouth is free of dentifrice and food particles.
- Remove the curved basin, and help the client wipe the mouth.

4. Floss the teeth.

- Assist the client to floss independently, or floss the teeth as follows. Waxed floss is less likely to fray than unwaxed floss; particles between the teeth attach more readily to unwaxed floss than to waxed floss. Some believe that waxed floss leaves a residue on the teeth and that plaque then adheres to the wax.

  a. Wrap one end of the floss around the third finger of each hand (Figure 34.15).

  b. To floss the upper teeth, use your thumb and index finger to stretch the floss (Figure 34.16). Move the floss up and down between the teeth from the tops of the crowns to the gum and along the gum lines as far as possible. Make a "C" with the floss around the tooth edge being flossed. Start at the back on the right side and work around to the back of the left side, or work from the centre teeth to the back of the jaw on either side.

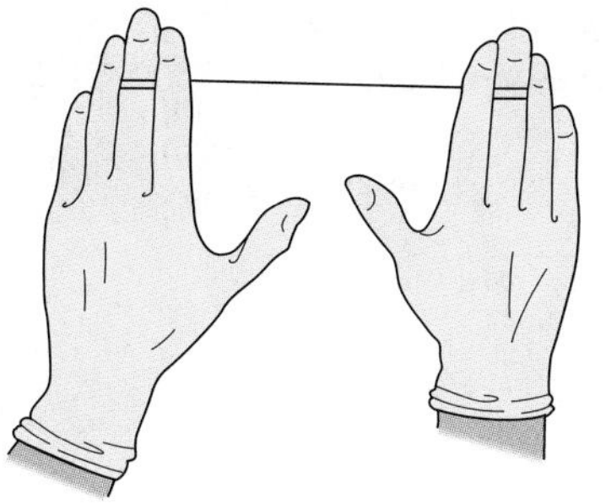

Figure 34.15 Stretching the floss between the third finger of each hand

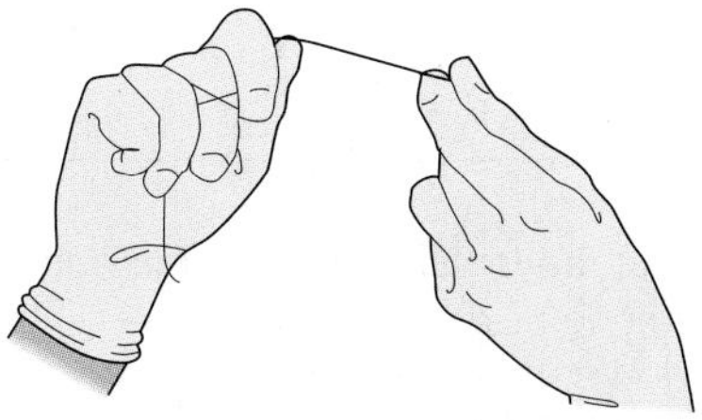

Figure 34.16 Flossing the upper teeth by using the thumbs and index fingers to stretch the floss

  c. To floss the lower teeth, use your index fingers to stretch the floss (Figure 34.17).

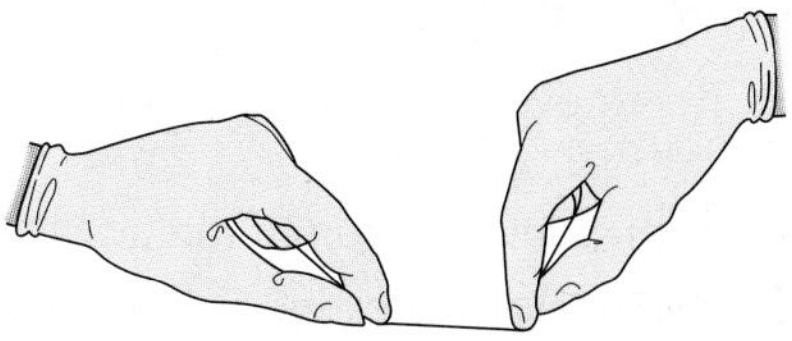

Figure 34.17 Flossing the lower teeth by using the index fingers to stretch the floss

- Give the client tepid water or mouthwash to rinse the mouth and a curved basin in which to spit the water.
- Assist the client in wiping the mouth.

5. Remove and dispose of equipment appropriately.

- Remove and clean the curved basin.
- Remove and discard the gloves.

6. Document oral hygienic care and assessment of the teeth, tongue, gums, and oral mucosa. Include any problems, such as sores or inflammation and swelling of the gums.

Evaluation Focus
Condition of the oral mucosa, gums, tongue, and lips; condition of the dentures

Most people prefer privacy when they take their artificial teeth out to clean them. Many do not like to be seen without their teeth; one of the first requests of many postoperative clients is "May I have my teeth in, please?" Procedure 34.5 describes how to clean artificial dentures.

Special Oral Hygiene

For the client who is debilitated or unconscious or who has excessive dryness, sores, or irritations of the mouth, it may be necessary to clean the oral mucosa and tongue in addition to the teeth. Agency practices differ in regard to special mouth care and the frequency with which it is provided. Depending on the health of the client's mouth, special care may be needed every two to eight hours.

Mouth care for unconscious or debilitated people is important because their mouths tend to become dry and consequently predisposed to infections. Dryness occurs because the client cannot take fluids by mouth, is often breathing through the mouth, or may be receiving oxygen, which tends to dry the mucous membranes.

The nurse can use commercially prepared mouthwashes, tepid water, or normal saline (according to agency policy) for oral hygiene. Long-term use of commercially prepared mouthwashes can lead to further dryness of the mucosa and

PROCEDURE 34.5 Cleaning Artificial Dentures

Before commencing to clean artificial dentures, determine (1) areas in the mouth that require ongoing assessment, and (2) whether the client has upper and lower dentures.

Assessment Focus
Health status of gums, oral mucosa, and tongue; condition of dentures; fit and comfort of dentures

PURPOSES

- To remove food particles and microorganisms from artificial teeth
- To prevent infection of the oral tissues
- To enhance the client's feeling of well-being

Equipment

- ❑ Disposable gloves
- ❑ Tissue or piece of gauze
- ❑ Denture container
- ❑ Clean washcloth
- ❑ Toothbrush or stiff-bristled brush
- ❑ Dentifrice or denture cleaner
- ❑ Tepid water
- ❑ Container of mouthwash
- ❑ Curved basin (emesis basin)
- ❑ Towel

INTERVENTION

1. Prepare the client.

- Assist the client to a sitting or side-lying position.

2. Remove the dentures.

- Don gloves. *Wearing gloves protects the nurse and client from infection.*
- If the client cannot remove the dentures, take the tissue or gauze, grasp the upper plate at the front teeth with your thumb and second finger, and move the denture up and down slightly (Figure 34.18). *The slight movement breaks the suction that holds the plate on the roof of the mouth.*

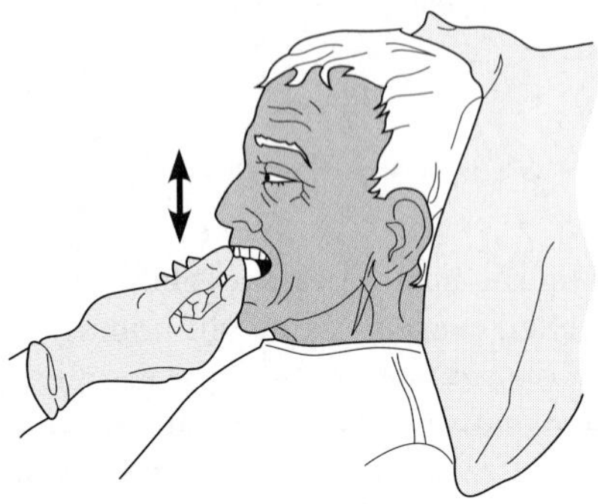

Figure 34.18 Removing the top dentures by first breaking the suction

- Lower the upper plate, move it out of the mouth, and place it in the denture container.
- Lift the lower plate, turning it so that the left side, for example, is slightly lower than the right, to remove the plate from the mouth without stretching the lips. Place the lower plate in the denture container.
- Remove a partial denture by exerting equal pressure on the border of each side of the denture, not on the clasps, which can bend or break.

3. Clean the dentures.

- Take the denture container to a sink. Take care not to drop the dentures. *They may break.* Place a washcloth in the bowl of the sink or fill the sink with water. *A washcloth or sink filled with water prevents damage if the dentures are dropped.*
- Using a toothbrush or special stiff-bristled brush, scrub the dentures with the cleaning agent and tepid water. *Hot water is not used because heat will change the shape of some dentures.*
- Rinse the dentures with tepid running water. *Rinsing removes the cleaning agent and food particles.*
- If the dentures are stained, soak them in a commercial cleaner. Be sure to follow the manufacturer's directions. To prevent corrosion, dentures with metal parts should not be soaked overnight. The following mixtures are substitutes for commercial cleaner:

  a. 5 to 10 mL white vinegar and 240 mL warm water

  or

  b. 5 mL chlorine bleach, 10 mL water softener, and 240 mL warm water. It is essential to mix the water softener with the bleach to prevent denture corrosion and to rinse well before replacing in the mouth.

4. Inspect the dentures and the mouth.

- Observe the dentures for any rough, sharp, or worn areas that could irritate the tongue or mucous membranes of the mouth, lips, and gums.
- Inspect the mouth for any redness, irritated areas, or indications of infection.
- Assess the fit of the dentures. People who have them should see a dentist at least once a year to check the fit and the presence of any irritation to the soft tissues of the mouth.

5. Return the dentures to the mouth.

- Assist to clean the oral mucosa with dampened gauze or foam brush. Have client rinse mouth with water. If the client cannot insert the dentures independently, insert the plates one at a time. Hold each plate at a slight angle while inserting it, to avoid injuring the lips (Figure 34.19).

PROCEDURE 34.5 Cleaning Artificial Dentures *continued*

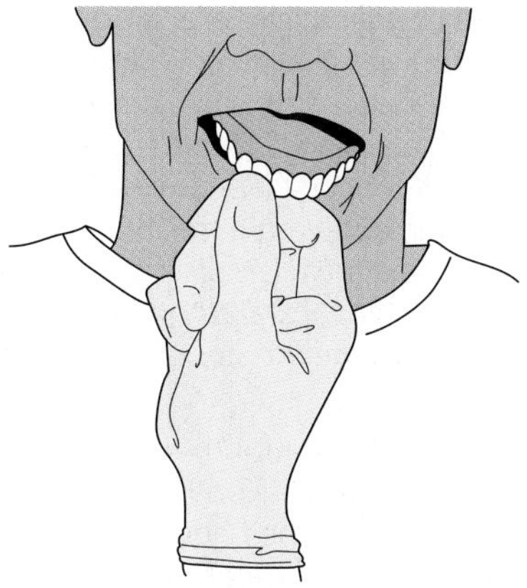

Figure 34.19 Inserting the dentures at a slight angle

6. **Assist the client as needed.**
   - Wipe the client's hands and mouth with the towel.
   - If the client does not want to or cannot wear the dentures, store them in a denture container with water. Label the cup with the client's name and identification number.
7. **Remove and discard gloves.**
8. **Document all relevant information.**
   - Document all assessments, and include any problems, such as an irritated area on the mucous membrane.

Evaluation Focus
Condition of the oral mucosa, gums, tongue, and lips; condition of the dentures

changes in tooth enamel. Applicator swabs may also be used. Mineral oil is contraindicated because aspiration of it can initiate an infection (lipid pneumonia). Hydrogen peroxide is *not* recommended for use in oral care because it irritates healthy oral mucosa and may alter the microflora of the mouth (Tombes & Gallucci, 1993). Normal saline solution is recommended for oral hygiene for the dependent client. (A physician's order may be required.)

Procedure 34.6 focuses on oral care for the unconscious person but may be adapted for conscious persons who are seriously ill or have mouth problems.

Evaluating

Using data collected during care—status of oral mucosa, lips, tongue, teeth, and so on—the nurse judges whether desired outcomes have been achieved. Examples of client goals and related outcomes are shown in Table 34.11.

If outcomes are *not* achieved, the nurse and client need to explore the reasons before modifying the care plan. Examples of factors to consider are similar to those shown for ***Self-Care Deficit*** on page 810.

PROCEDURE 34.6 Providing Special Oral Care

PURPOSES

- To maintain the integrity of the lips, tongue, and mucous membranes of the mouth
- To prevent oral infections
- To clean and moisten the membranes of the mouth and lips

Assessment Focus
Status of the oral mucosa, lips, tongue, and teeth; presence of halitosis

Equipment

- ❑ Towel
- ❑ Curved basin (emesis basin)
- ❑ Disposable gloves
- ❑ Bite-block to hold the mouth open and teeth apart (optional)
- ❑ Toothbrush
- ❑ Cup of tepid water
- ❑ Dentifrice or denture cleaner
- ❑ Tissue or piece of gauze to remove dentures (optional)
- ❑ Denture container, as needed
- ❑ Mouthwash
- ❑ Rubber-tipped bulb syringe
- ❑ Suction catheter with suction apparatus (optional)
- ❑ Applicators and cleaning solution for cleaning the mucous membranes
- ❑ Petroleum jelly (Vaseline)

PROCEDURE 34.6 Providing Special Oral Care *continued*

INTERVENTION

1. Prepare the client.

- Position the unconscious client in a side-lying position with the head of the bed lowered. *In this position, the saliva automatically runs out by gravity rather than being aspirated into the lungs.* This position is the one of choice for the unconscious client receiving mouth care. If the client's head cannot be lowered, turn it to one side. *The fluid will readily run out of the mouth or pool in the side of the mouth, where it can be suctioned.*
- Place the towel under the client's chin.
- Place the curved basin against the client's chin and lower cheek to receive the fluid from the mouth (Figure 34.20).
- Don gloves.

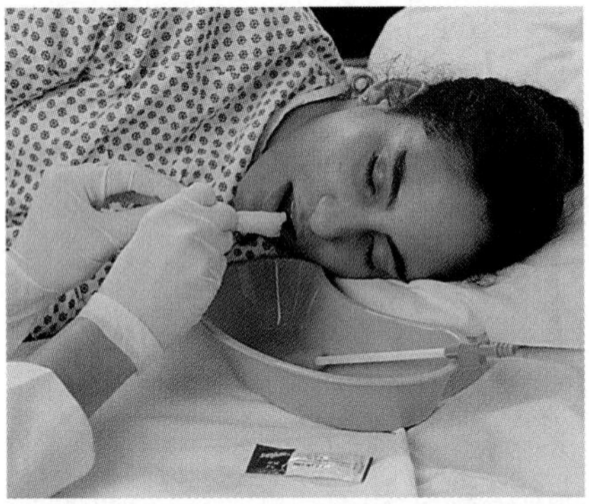

Figure 34.20 Position of client and placement of curved basin when providing special mouth care

2. Clean the teeth and rinse the mouth.

- If the person has natural teeth, brush the teeth as described in Procedure 34.4. Brush gently and carefully to avoid injuring the gums. If the client has artificial teeth, clean them as described in Procedure 34.5.
- Rinse the client's mouth by drawing about 10 mL of water or mouthwash into the syringe and injecting it gently into each side of the mouth. *If the solution is injected with force, some of it may flow down the client's throat and be aspirated into the lungs.*
- Rinse toothbrush with water and continue to brush.
- Repeat rinsing until the mouth is free of dentifrice, if used.
- Watch carefully to make sure that all the rinsing solution has run out of the mouth into the basin. If not, suction the fluid from the mouth. See the section on oropharyngeal suctioning in Chapter 39. *Fluid remaining in the mouth may be aspirated into the lungs.*

3. Inspect and clean the oral tissues.

- If the tissues appear dry or unclean, clean them with the applicators or gauze and water following agency policy.
- Picking up one applicator, wipe the mucous membrane of one cheek. If no commercially prepared applicators are available, wrap a small gauze square around a tongue blade and moisten it. Discard the applicator or tongue blade in a waste container, and with a fresh one, clean the next area. *Using separate applicators for each area of the mouth prevents the transfer of microorganisms from one area to another.*
- Clean all the mouth tissues in an orderly progression using separate applicators: the cheeks, roof of the mouth, base of the mouth, and tongue.
- Observe the tissues closely for inflammation and dryness.
- Suction the fluid from the mouth if necessary.
- Remove and discard gloves.

4. Ensure client comfort.

- Remove the basin, and dry around the client's mouth with the towel. Replace artificial dentures, if indicated.
- Lubricate the client's lips with petroleum jelly. *Lubrication prevents cracking and subsequent infection.*

5. Document pertinent data.

- Record special oral hygiene and pertinent observations.
- Report pertinent assessment data to the nurse in charge.

Evaluation Focus
Status of oral tissues, lips, and tongue; any irritation, dryness, or lesions

Consider...

What actions you would take if the client did *not* meet the following outcomes:

- "Breath is free of halitosis." (Data reveal marked halitosis.)
- "Gums are firm, well hydrated, not bleeding, and of uniform colour." (Data reveal spongy gums and bleeding during flossing.)

Hair

The appearance of the hair often reflects a person's feelings of well-being. A person who feels ill may not groom hair as before. The hair may also reflect state of health (e.g., excessive coarseness and dryness may be associated with endocrine disorders, such as hypothyroidism).

Each person has particular ways of caring for hair. Many dark-skinned people need to oil their hair daily

TABLE 34.11 Evaluation Goals and Outcomes: Oral Hygiene and Health

Goal	Desired Outcomes
Improves oral hygiene practices	Mucosa, tongue, and lips are pink, moist, and intact
	Dental surfaces are free of debris and plaque
	Breath is free of halitosis
	Brushes teeth after meals and at bedtime
	Flosses teeth daily
	Obtains regular dental care
	Uses fluoridation or fluoride supplements, as recommended
Maintains integrity of oral tissues	Mucosa is intact, smooth, well hydrated, and uniform in colour
	Gums are firm, well hydrated, not bleeding, and of uniform colour
	Tongue is well hydrated
	Lips are smooth and well hydrated
	Oral tissues are free of inflammation and pain

RESEARCH NOTE

What Are the Effects of Hydrogen Peroxide Rinses on the Normal Oral Mucosa?

Oral mucosal effects of hydrogen peroxide mouth rinses were investigated in normal volunteers. Following a two-week control period, 35 subjects were randomly assigned to rinse with either normal saline, one-quarter-strength hydrogen peroxide (0.75 percent), or one-half-strength hydrogen peroxide (1.5 percent) four times daily for two weeks. Mucosal status, buccal microbial adherence, salivary flow rate (SFR), and subjective reactions were assessed weekly. In the normal saline group, no significant changes were noted in any of the observed parameters and subjective reports were unremarkable. In both hydrogen peroxide groups, significant mucosal abnormalities were observed and subjective complaints were numerous (e.g., burning, stinging, tingling sensations; unpleasant aftertaste; "furry" or "numb" tongue; dry mouth; increased expectoration and thirst; chapped lips; increased roughness of the mucosa; and so on). Bacterial adherence was significantly reduced in the quarter-strength hydrogen peroxide group but not in the half-strength hydrogen peroxide group. Despite reports of dry mouth, SFRs were not altered significantly.

Implications: Because hydrogen peroxide rinses are associated with mucosal abnormalities and elicit overwhelmingly negative subjective reactions in normal individuals, they are not recommended for oral care.

Source: Tombes, M. B., & Gallucci, B. (1993). The effects of hydrogen peroxide rinses on the normal oral mucosa. *Nursing Research, 42,* 334–337.

because it tends to be dry. Oil prevents the hair from breaking and the scalp from drying. A wide-toothed comb is usually used because finer combs pull and break the hair. Some people brush their hair vigorously before retiring at night, others comb their hair frequently.

Developmental Variations

Newborns may have **lanugo** (the fine hair on the body of the fetus, also referred to as *down* or *woolly hair*) over their shoulders, back, and sacrum. This generally disappears, and the hair distribution on the eyebrows, head, and, eyelashes of young children subsequently becomes noticeable. Some newborns have hair on their scalps; others are free of hair at birth but grow hair over the scalp during the first year of life.

Pubic hair usually appears in early puberty followed, in about six months, by the growth of axillary hair. Boys develop facial hair in later puberty.

In adolescence, the sebaceous glands increase in activity as a result of increased hormone levels. As a result, hair follicle openings enlarge to accommodate the increased amount of sebum, which can make the adolescent's hair more oily.

In older adults, the hair is generally thinner, grows more slowly, and loses its colour as a result of aging tissues and diminishing circulation. Men often lose their scalp hair and may become completely bald. This phenomenon may occur even when a man is relatively young. The older person's hair also tends to be drier than normal. With age, axillary and pubic hair becomes finer and scanter, in contrast to the eyebrows, which become bristly and coarse. Many women develop hair on their faces, which may be a concern to them.

Assessing

Nursing History

During the nursing history, the nurse elicits data about usual hair care, self-care abilities, history of hair or scalp problems, and conditions known to affect the hair. Chemotherapeutic agents and radiation of the head may cause **alopecia** (hair loss). Hypothyroidism may cause the hair to be thin, dry, and/or brittle. Use of some hair dyes and curling or straightening preparations can cause the hair to become dry and brittle. Questions to elicit these data are shown in the Assessment Interview box below.

Physical Assessment

Physical assessment of the hair is discussed in Chapter 27. Problems include dandruff, hair loss, ticks, pediculosis, scabies, and hirsutism.

Dandruff Often accompanied by itching, **dandruff** appears as a diffuse scaling of the scalp. In severe cases, it involves the auditory canals and the eyebrows. Dandruff can usually be treated effectively with a commercial shampoo. In severe or persistent cases, the client may need the advice of a physician.

Hair Loss Hair loss and growth are continual processes. Some permanent thinning of hair normally occurs with aging. Baldness, common in men, is thought to be a hereditary problem for which there is no known remedy other than the wearing of a hairpiece or a costly surgical hair transplantation in which hair is taken from the back or the sides of the scalp and surgically moved to the hairless area. Although some medications are being developed, their long-term outcomes are unknown.

Ticks Small grey-brown parasites that bite into tissue and suck blood, **ticks** transmit several diseases to people, in particular Rocky Mountain spotted fever, Lyme disease, and tularemia. Ticks should never be forcibly pulled from the skin because the sucking apparatus remains and may become infected. To ease removal, cover the tick with mineral oil or a lubricating jelly, such as petroleum jelly. This deprives the tick of oxygen, causing suffocation.

ASSESSMENT INTERVIEW

Hair Care

Hair Care Practices

- What are your usual hair care practices?
- What hair care products do you routinely use (e.g., hair spray, lubricant, shampoo, conditioners, hair dye, curling or straightening preparations)?

Self-Care Abilities

- Do you have any problems managing your hair?

Past or Current Hair Problems

- Have you had any of the following conditions or therapies: recent chemotherapy, hypothyroidism, radiation of the head, unexplained loss of hair, growth of excessive body hair?

Pediculosis (Lice) Lice are parasitic insects that infest mammals. Infestation with lice is called **pediculosis.** Hundreds of varieties of lice infest humans. Three common kinds are *Pediculus capitis* (the head louse), *Pediculus corporis* (the body louse), and *Pediculus pubis* (the crab louse).

Pediculus capitis is found on the scalp and tends to stay hidden in the hairs; similarly, *Pediculus pubis* stays in pubic hair. *Pediculus corporis* tends to cling to clothing so that when a client undresses, the lice may not be evident on the body; these lice suck blood from the person and lay their eggs on the clothing. The nurse can suspect their presence in the clothing if (1) the person habitually scratches, (2) there are scratches on the skin, and (3) there are hemorrhagic spots on the skin where the lice have sucked blood.

Head and pubic lice lay their eggs on the hairs; the eggs look like oval particles, similar to dandruff, clinging to the hair. Bites and pustular eruptions may also be noticed at the hair lines and behind the ears.

Lice are very small, greyish white, and difficult to see. The crab louse in the pubic area has red legs. Lice may be contracted from infested clothes and direct contact with an infested person.

The treatment widely used is gamma benzene hexachloride (Kwell), available as a cream, a lotion, and a shampoo. If the client has head lice, the hair is washed with the shampoo and the bed linens are changed. This treatment is repeated seven days later, if needed. A client with pubic or body lice takes a bath or shower, dries, and applies the lotion or cream—to the entire body surface for body lice, and to the pubic area and adjacent areas for pubic lice. After 8 to 12 hours the lotion is washed off, and clean clothing and linens are supplied. Treatment should be repeated in seven days only if live lice are noted. The nurse should wear gloves during application to avoid prolonged contact with the medicated lotion/shampoo.

Scabies Scabies is a contagious skin infestation by the itch mite. The characteristic lesion is the burrow produced by the female mite as it penetrates into the upper layers of the skin. Burrows are short, wavy, brown or black threadlike lesions most commonly observed between the webs of the fingers and the folds of the wrists and elbows. The mites cause intense itching that is more pronounced at night because the increased warmth of the skin has a stimulating effect on the parasites. Secondary lesions caused by scratching include vesicles, papules, pustules, excoriations, and crusts. Treatment involves thorough cleansing of the body with soap and water to remove scales and debris from crusts, and then an application of a scabicide lotion. All bed linens and clothing should be washed in very hot or boiling water.

Hirsutism The growth of excessive body hair is called **hirsutism.** The acceptance of body hair in the axillae and on the legs is largely dictated by culture. In North America, the well-groomed woman, as depicted in magazines, has no hair on her legs or under her axillae (although this idea is changing). In many European cultures, it is not customary for well-groomed women to remove this hair.

Excessive facial hair on a woman is thought unattractive in most Western and Asian cultures. For example, some Japanese brides follow the custom of shaving their faces the day before the wedding.

The cause of excessive body hair is not always known. Older women may have some on their faces, and women in menopause may also experience the growth of facial hair. These conditions may be due to the action of the endocrine system. It is also thought that heredity influences both the pattern of hair distribution and the production of androgens by the adrenal glands.

Diagnosing

Nursing diagnoses related to hair hygiene and hair and scalp problems include ***Self-Care Deficit: Grooming, Impaired Skin Integrity, Risk for Infection,*** and ***Body Image, Disturbed.*** Examples of these nursing diagnoses with contributing factors follow:

- ***Self-Care Deficit: Grooming*** related to
  a. Activity intolerance
  b. Imposed immobility (bed rest)
  c. Pain in upper extremities
  d. Altered level of consciousness
  e. Lack of motivation associated with depression
- ***Impaired Skin Integrity*** related to
  a. Scalp laceration
  b. Insect bite
- ***Risk for Infection*** related to
  a. Scalp laceration
  b. Insect bite
- ***Body Image, Disturbed*** related to
  a. alopecia
  b. hirsutism

Planning

In planning care, the nurse identifies nursing activities that will assist the client to achieve these goals:

- Maintain or improve hair care
- Maintain or improve a sense of well-being
- Prevent specific hair and scalp problems

Examples of desired outcomes to evaluate the effectiveness of nursing interventions follow. The client does the following:

- Performs hair grooming with assistance (specify)
- Has clean, well-groomed, resilient hair with a healthy sheen
- Has reduced or absent scalp lesions or infestations
- Describes contributing factors, interventions, and preventive measures for specific hair problem (e.g., dandruff)

Plans for assisting the client should take into account the client's personal preferences, health, and energy resources as well as the time, equipment, and personnel available. Often, clients like to receive hair care after a bath, before receiving visitors, and before retiring. At some agencies, shampoos can be given to clients only after a physician's order.

Implementing

Brushing and Combing Hair

To be healthy, hair needs to be brushed daily. Brushing has three major functions: it stimulates the circulation of blood in the scalp, it distributes the oil along the hair shaft, and it helps arrange the hair.

Long hair may present a problem for clients confined to bed as it may become matted. It should be combed and brushed at least once a day to prevent this. A brush with stiff bristles provides the best stimulation to blood circulation in the scalp. The bristles should not be so sharp that they injure the client's scalp, however. A comb with dull, even teeth is advisable. A comb with sharp teeth might injure the scalp; combs that are too fine can pull and break the hair. Some clients are pleased to have their hair tied neatly in the back or braided until other assistance is available or until they feel better and can look after it themselves.

Dark-skinned people often have thicker, drier, curlier hair than light-skinned people. Spiralled or very curly hair may stand out from the scalp. Although the shafts of spiraled hair look strong and wiry, they have less strength than straight hair shafts and can break easily.

Some African-Canadians have their spiraled hair straightened. Even if straightened, the hair tends to tangle and mat easily, especially at the back and the sides if the client is confined to bed. Other African-Canadians style their hair in small braids (Figure 34.21). These braids do

Figure 34.21 An African-Canadian's hair styled with braids

not have to be unbraided for shampooing and washing. The nurse should obtain the client's permission before any such unbraiding. Some African-Canadian clients need to oil their hair daily because it tends to be dry. Oil also prevents the hair strands from breaking and the scalp from becoming too dry.

Procedure 34.7 describes how to provide hair care for African-Canadian clients.

PROCEDURE 34.7 Providing Hair Care for African-Canadian Clients

PURPOSES

- To stimulate the blood circulation to the scalp
- To distribute hair oils and provide a healthy sheen
- To increase the client's sense of well-being
- To assess or monitor hair or scalp problems (e.g., matted hair or dandruff)

Assessment Focus
Usual hair care practices; routinely used hair care products; self-care abilities; any scalp problems

Equipment

- ❑ Large, open-toothed or long-toothed comb (a pick)
- ❑ Towel
- ❑ Lubricant (optional)

INTERVENTION

1. Position and prepare the client appropriately.

- Assist the client who can sit to move to a chair. *Hair is more easily brushed and combed when the client is in a sitting position.* If the client's health permits, assist a client confined to bed to a sitting position by raising the head of the bed. Otherwise, assist the client to alternate side-lying positions, and do one side of the head at a time.
- If the client remains in bed, place a clean towel over the pillow and the client's shoulders. Place it over the sitting client's shoulders. *The towel collects any removed hair, dirt, and scaly material.*
- Remove any pins or ribbons in the hair.

2. Comb the hair.

- Apply a lubricant as the client indicates or as needed.
- Using a large and open-toothed comb, start at the neckline and lift and fluff the hair outward, moving upward toward the forehead (Figure 34.22).

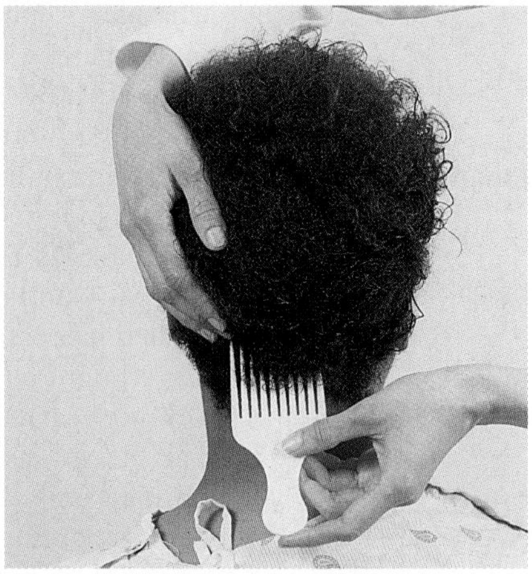

Figure 34.22 Using a large open-toothed comb to comb an African-Canadian client's hair from the neckline upward toward the forehead

- Continue fluffing the hair outward and upward until all of the hair is combed on one half of the head. Repeat the procedure for the other half.

3. Remove tangles gradually.

- After the hair has been lubricated, weave and lift your opened fingers through the hair to ease the tangles free.

or

- Support the hair securely at the base of the scalp, if possible, to prevent pulling and discomfort. Insert a long-toothed comb into the ends of the hair and carefully comb out the ends of the tangles (Figure 34.23).

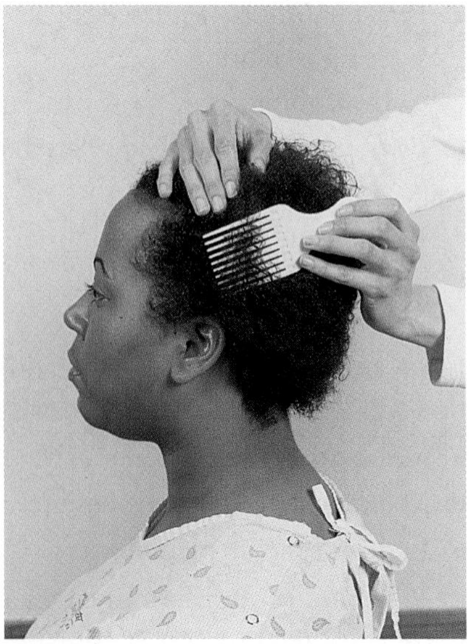

Figure 34.23 Removing tangles with a long-toothed comb

PROCEDURE 34.7 Providing Hair Care for African-Canadian Clients *continued*

- Repeat this step, each time working the comb farther up the hair shaft toward the scalp, until the hair is untangled.

4. Document assessments and nursing interventions.

- Record problems such as excessive dandruff, very dry or very oily hair, or the presence of lice.

Evaluation Focus
Such problems as dandruff, alopecia, pediculosis, scalp lesions, or excessive dryness or mats

Shampooing the Hair

Hair should be washed as often as needed to keep it clean. There are several ways to shampoo clients' hair depending on their health, strength, and age. The client who is well enough to take a shower can shampoo while in the shower. The client who is unable to shower may be given a shampoo while sitting on a chair in front of a sink. The back-lying client who can move to a stretcher can be given a shampoo on a stretcher wheeled to a sink. The client who must remain in bed can be given a shampoo with water brought to the bedside. Volunteer beauticians with portable shampoo chairs may be available to assist with hair care.

Shampoo basins to catch the water and direct it to the washbasin or other receptacle are usually made of plastic or metal. A pail or large washbasin can be used as a receptacle for the shampoo water. If possible, the receptacle should be large enough to hold all the shampoo water so that it does not have to be emptied during the shampoo.

Water used for the shampoo should be 40.5°C for an adult or child to be comfortable and not injure the scalp. Usually, the client will supply a liquid or cream shampoo. If the shampoo is being given to destroy lice, a medicated shampoo may be used as ordered by the physician. Dry shampoos are also available. They will remove some of the dirt, odour, and oil. Their main disadvantage is that they dry the hair and scalp.

How often a person needs a shampoo is highly individual, depending largely on the person's activities and the amount of sebum secreted by the scalp. Oily hair tends to look stringy and dirty, and it feels unclean to the person.

Procedure 34.8 below explains how to provide a shampoo for a client confined to bed.

PROCEDURE 34.8 Shampooing the Hair of a Client Confined to Bed

PURPOSES

- To stimulate the blood circulation to the scalp through massage
- To clean the hair and increase the client's sense of well-being

Assessment Focus
Routinely used shampoo products; any scalp problems; activity tolerance of the client

Equipment

- ❑ Comb and brush
- ❑ Plastic sheet or pad
- ❑ Two bath towels
- ❑ Shampoo basin
- ❑ Washcloth or pad
- ❑ Bath blanket
- ❑ Receptacle for the shampoo water
- ❑ Cotton balls (optional)
- ❑ Pitcher of water
- ❑ Bath thermometer
- ❑ Liquid or cream shampoo
- ❑ Hair dryer

PROCEDURE 34.8 Shampooing the Hair of a Client Confined to Bed *continued*

INTERVENTION

1. Verify agency policy and the physician's order.

- Determine whether a physician's order is needed before a shampoo can be given. *Some agencies require an order.*
- Determine the type of shampoo to be used (e.g., medicated shampoo).

2. Prepare the client.

- Determine the best time of day for the shampoo. Discuss this with the client. A person who must remain in bed may find the shampoo tiring. Choose a time when the client is rested and can rest after the procedure.
- Assist the client to the side of the bed from which you will work.
- Remove pins and ribbons from the hair, and brush and comb it to remove any tangles.

3. Arrange the equipment.

- Put the plastic sheet or pad on the bed under the head. *The plastic keeps the bedding dry.*
- Remove the pillow from under the client's head, and place it under the shoulders. *This hyperextends the neck.*
- Tuck a bath towel around the client's shoulders. *This keeps the shoulders dry.*
- Place the shampoo basin under the head (Figure 34.24), putting a folded washcloth or pad where the client's neck rests on the edge of the basin. If the client is on a stretcher, the neck can rest on the edge of the sink with the washcloth as padding. *Padding supports the muscles of the neck and prevents undue strain and discomfort.*
- Fanfold the top bedding down to the waist, and cover the upper part of the client with the bath blanket. *The folded bedding will stay dry, and the bath blanket, which can be discarded after the shampoo, will keep the client warm.*

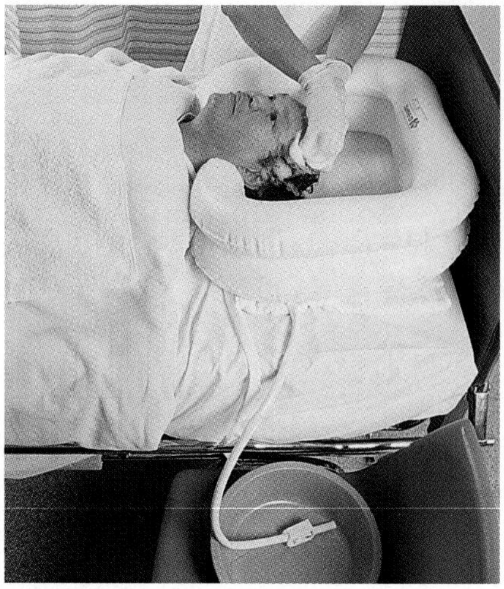

Figure 34.24 Shampooing the hair of a client confined to bed. Note the shampoo basin and the receptacle below.

- Place the receiving receptacle on a table or chair at the bedside. Put the spout of the shampoo basin over the receptacle.

4. Protect the client's eyes and ears.

- Place a damp washcloth over the client's eyes. The washcloth protects the eyes from soapy water. A damp washcloth will not slip.
- Place cotton balls in the client's ears if indicated. *These keep water from collecting in the ear canals.*

5. Shampoo the hair.

- Wet the hair thoroughly with the water.
- Apply shampoo to the scalp. Make a good lather with the shampoo while massaging the scalp with the pads of your fingertips. Massage all areas of the scalp systematically, for example, starting at the front and working toward the back of the head. *Massaging stimulates the blood circulation in the scalp. The pads of the fingers are used so that the fingernails will not scratch the scalp.*
- Rinse the hair briefly, and apply shampoo again.
- Make a good lather and massage the scalp as before.
- Rinse the hair thoroughly this time to remove all the shampoo. *Shampoo remaining in the hair may dry and irritate the hair and scalp.*
- Squeeze as much water as possible out of the hair with your hands.

6. Dry the hair thoroughly.

- Rub the client's hair with a heavy towel.
- Dry the hair with the dryer. Set the temperature at "warm."
- Continually move the dryer to prevent burning the client's scalp.

7. Ensure client comfort.

- Assist the person confined to bed to a comfortable position.
- Arrange the hair using a clean brush and comb.

8. Document the shampoo and any assessments.

- Report any problems noted to the nurse in charge.

Evaluation Focus
Any scalp problems or intolerance to procedure

Lifespan Considerations

- Shampoo an infant's hair daily to prevent seborrhea.
- Monitor school-age children for nits (pediculosis).
- Ensure adequate warmth for older adults, who are susceptible to chilling.

Beard and Mustache Care

Beards and mustaches also require daily care. The most important aspect of the care is to keep them clean. Food particles tend to collect in beards and mustaches, and they need washing and combing periodically. Clients may also wish a beard or mustache trim to maintain a well-groomed appearance. A beard or mustache should not be shaved off without the client's consent.

Male clients often shave or are shaved after a bath. Frequently clients supply their own electric or safety razors. See the box below for the steps involved in shaving facial hair with a safety razor.

Evaluating

See examples of desired outcomes in the earlier "Planning" section.

Eyes

Normally, eyes require no special hygiene because lacrimal fluid continually washes the eyes, and the eyelids and lashes prevent the entrance of foreign particles. Special interventions are needed, however, for unconscious clients and for clients recovering from eye surgery or those with eye injuries, irritations, infections, or systemic diseases affecting the eyes. In unconscious clients, the blink reflex may be absent, and excessive drainage may accumulate along eyelid margins. In clients with eye trauma or eye infections, excessive discharge or drainage is common.

Using a Safety Razor to Shave Facial Hair

- When possible, it is preferable to shave a client using an electric razor.
- Don gloves in case there are facial nicks and contact with blood.
- Apply shaving cream or soap and water to soften the bristles and make the skin more pliable.
- Hold the skin taut, particularly around creases, to prevent cutting the skin.
- Hold the razor so that the blade is at a 45-degree angle to the skin, and shave in short, firm strokes in the direction of hair growth, being careful not to cut or nick the skin.
- After shaving the entire area, wipe the client's face with a wet washcloth to remove any remaining shaving cream and hair.
- Dry the face well, then apply aftershave lotion or powder as the client prefers.
- To prevent irritating the skin, pat on the lotion with the fingers and avoid rubbing the face.

Excessive secretions on the lashes need to be removed before they dry on the lashes as crusts. Clients who wear eyeglasses, contact lenses, or an artificial eye also may require instruction from and care by the nurse.

Assessing

Nursing History

During the nursing history, the nurse obtains data about the client's eyeglasses or contact lenses, recent examination by an ophthalmologist, and any history of eye problems and related treatments. Questions to elicit these data are shown in the box on the next page.

Physical Assessment

In physical assessment, all external eye structures are inspected for signs of inflammation, excessive drainage, encrustations, or other obvious abnormalities. Inspection of the external eye structures is discussed in Chapter 27.

Diagnosing

Nursing diagnoses related to eye problems may include ***Self-Care Deficit, Risk for Infection,*** and ***Risk for Injury.*** Examples of these diagnoses and possible contributing factors follow:

- ***Self-Care Deficit*** (contact lens insertion, removal, and cleaning) related to
  - a. Knowledge deficit
  - b. Impaired vision associated with cataracts
- ***Risk for Infection*** related to
  - a. Improper contact lens hygiene
  - b. Accumulation of secretions on eyelids
- ***Risk for Injury*** related to
  - a. Prolonged wearing of contact lenses
  - b. Absence of blink reflex associated with unconsciousness
  - c. Falls, especially in elderly

Planning

In planning care, the nurse identifies nursing activities that will assist the client to maintain the integrity of the eye structures or a prosthesis and to prevent eye injury and infection. Nursing activities may include teaching clients about how to insert, clean, and remove contact lenses or a prosthesis and ways to protect the eyes from injury and strain. Examples of desired outcomes to evaluate the effectiveness of nursing interventions follow.

- Conjunctiva and sclera free of inflammation
- Eyelids free of secretions
- No tearing
- No eye discomfort

ASSESSMENT INTERVIEW

Eyes

For Clients Who Wear Eyeglasses

- When do you use your glasses?
- What is your vision like with and without the glasses?

For Clients Who Wear Contact Lenses

- How often do you wear lenses? Daily? On special occasions?
- How long do you wear your lenses in a given day, including sleep time?
- Do you have any problems with the lenses (e.g., cleaning, insertion, removal, damage)?
- Do you carry an emergency identification label to alert others to remove the lenses and ensure appropriate care in an emergency? (If not, advise the client to acquire one.)
- What are your insertion and removal procedures?
- What are your cleaning and storage procedures?
- Have you had any problems with either or both eyes or eyelids, such as excessive tearing, burning, redness, sensitivity to light, swelling, or feelings of dryness? Describe them.
- Are you using any eyedrops or ointments? (These medications can combine chemically with *soft* lenses and cause lens damage and eye irritation.)

For Clients Who Have a Prosthesis

- How long have you worn a prosthesis?
- How do you care for your prosthesis?
- Do you have any discharge or redness around the orbital cavity?
- Do you have any periorbital pain or swelling?

For All Clients

- When did you last have your eyesight tested?
- Are you currently taking any eye medication? If so, provide name, dosage, and frequency.
- Do you have any of the following eye problems: difficulty reading or seeing objects, blurring of vision, tearing, spots or floaters, photophobia (sensitivity to light), burning, itching, dryness, pain, double vision, flashing lights, or halos around lights?

- Demonstrates appropriate methods of caring for contact lenses
- Describes interventions to prevent eye injury and infection

Implementing

Eye Care

Dried secretions that have accumulated on the lashes need to be softened and wiped away. Soften dried secretions by placing a sterile cotton ball moistened with sterile water or normal saline over the lid margins. Wipe the loosened secretions from the inner canthus of the eye to the outer canthus to prevent the particles and fluid from draining into the lacrimal sac and nasolacrimal duct.

If the client is unconscious and lacks a blink reflex or cannot close the eyelids completely, drying and irritation of the cornea must be prevented. Lubricating eye drops may be ordered. See the box for providing eye care for the comatose client.

Eye Safety

Eye safety is also an important consideration of eye care. The body's natural eye defences can be augmented by instructing the client to wear safety lenses, goggles, or shields for high-risk activities.

Eyeglass Care

It is essential that the nurse exercise caution when cleaning eyeglasses to prevent breaking or scratching the lenses.

Eye Care for the Comatose Client

When a comatose client's corneal reflex is impaired, eye care is essential to keep moist the areas of the cornea that are exposed to air.

- Administer moist compresses to cover the eyes every two to four hours.
- Clean the eyes with saline solution and cotton balls. Wipe from the inner to outer canthus. This prevents debris from being washed into the nasolacrimal duct.
- Use a new cotton ball for each wipe. This prevents extending infection in one eye or to the other eye.
- Instill ophthalmic ointment or artificial tears into the lower lids as ordered. This keeps the eyes moist.
- If the client's corneal reflex is absent, keep the eyes moist with artificial tears and protect the eye with a protective shield. These should be ordered by a physician.
- Monitor the eyes for redness, exudate, or ulceration.

Glass lenses can be cleaned with warm water and dried with a soft cloth that will not scratch the lenses. Plastic lenses are easily scratched and may require special cleaning solutions and drying cloths. When not being worn, all glasses should be placed in a case labelled appropriately, and stored in the client's bedside table drawer.

Contact Lens Care

Contact lenses, thin curved discs of hard or soft plastic, fit on the cornea of the eye directly over the pupil. They float on the tear layer of the eye. For some people, contact lenses offer several advantages over eyeglasses: (1) they cannot be seen and, thus, have cosmetic value; (2) they are highly effective in correcting some astigmatisms; (3) they are safer than glasses for some physical activities; (4) they do not fog, as eyeglasses do; and (5) they provide better vision in many cases.

Contact lenses may be either hard or soft or a compromise between the two types—gas-permeable lenses. *Hard contact lenses* are made of a rigid, unwettable, airtight plastic that does not absorb water or saline solutions. They usually cannot be worn for more than 12 to 14 hours and are rarely recommended for first-time wearers.

Soft contact lenses cover the entire cornea. Being more pliable and soft, they mold to the eye for a firmer fit. The duration of extended wear varies by brand from one to 30 days or more. Eye specialists recommend that long-wear brands be removed and cleaned at least once a week. These lenses require scrupulous care and handling.

Gas-permeable lenses are rigid enough to provide clear vision but are more flexible than the traditional hard lens. They permit oxygen to reach the cornea, thus providing greater comfort, and will not cause serious damage to the eye if left in place for several days.

Most clients normally care for their own contact lenses. In general, each lens manufacturer provides detailed cleaning instructions. Depending on the type of lens and cleaning method used, warm tap water, normal saline, or special rinsing or soaking solutions may be used.

All users should have a special container for their lenses. Some contain a solution so that the lenses are stored wet; in others, the lenses are dry. Each lens container has a label indicating whether it is for the right or left lens. It is essential that the correct lens be stored in the appropriate cup so that it can be worn in the correct eye. Clean gloves should be worn when removing or inserting contact lenses.

Removing Contact Lenses *Hard* contact lenses must be positioned directly over the cornea for proper removal. If the lens is displaced, the nurse asks the client to look straight ahead, and gently exerts pressure on the upper and lower lids to move the lens back onto the cornea. Figure 34.25 shows the steps needed to remove a hard lens. To avoid lens mix-ups, the nurse places the first lens in its designated cup in the storage base before removing the second lens.

Removal of *soft* lenses varies in two ways. First, after separating the eyelids with the nondominant hand, move the lens down to the inferior part of the sclera using the pad of the dominant index finger (Figure 34.26). This reduces the risk of damage to the cornea. Second, remove the lens by gently pinching the lens between the pads of the thumb and index finger of your dominant hand (Figure 34.27). Pinching causes the lens to double up so that air enters underneath the lens, overcoming the suction and allowing removal. Use the pads of the fingers to prevent scratching the eye or the lens with the fingernails.

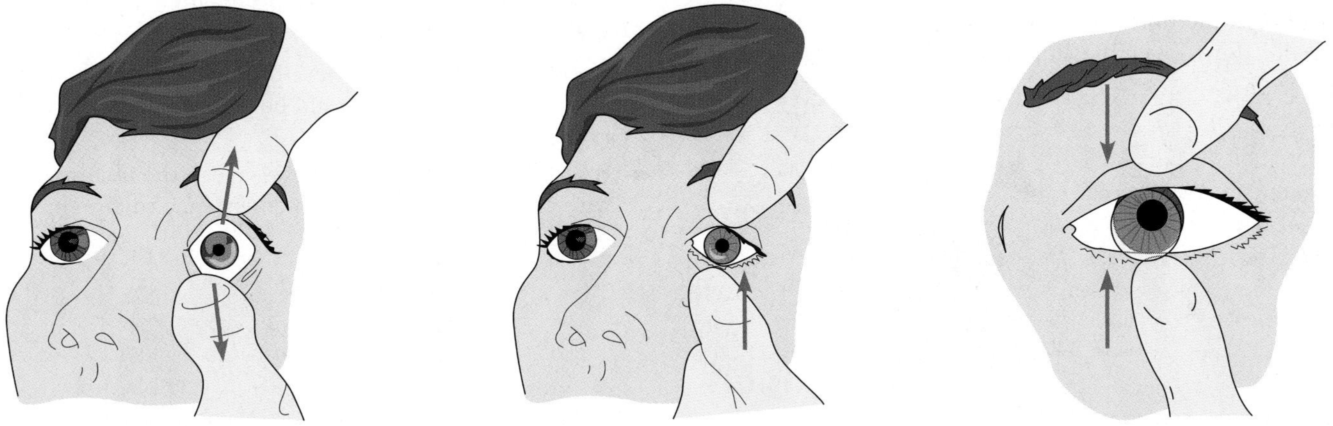

A B C

Figure 34.25 Removing hard contact lenses: *A,* Separate the eyelids until they are beyond the edges of the lens; *B;* Hold the top eyelid stationary at the edge of the lens, and lift the bottom edge of the contact lens by pressing the lower lid at its margin; *C,* After the lens is slightly tipped, slide the lens out of the eye by moving both eyelids toward each other

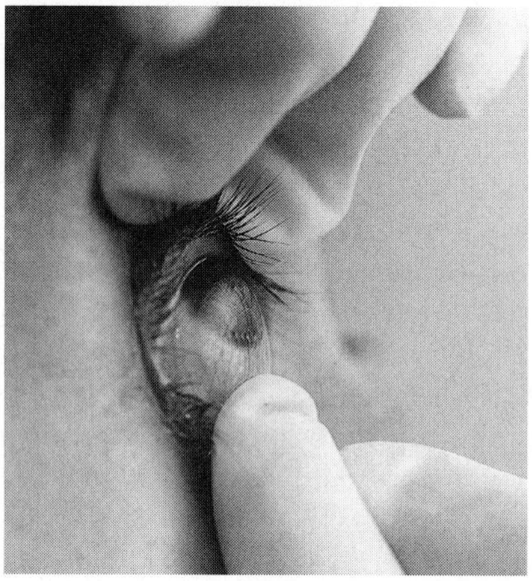

Figure 34.26 Moving a soft lens down to the inferior part of the sclera

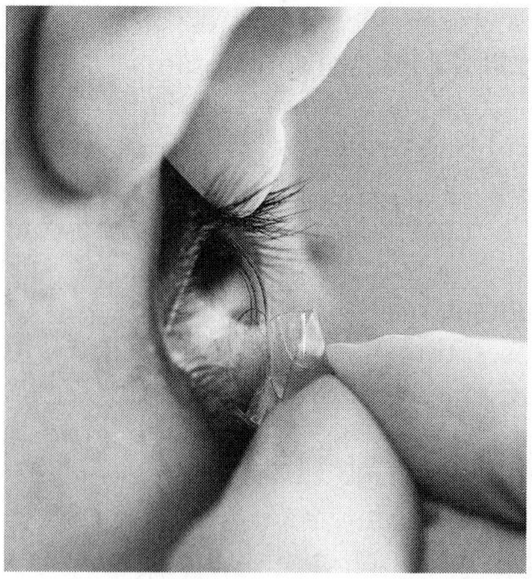

Figure 34.27 Removing a soft lens by pinching it between the pads of the thumb and index finger

Inserting Contact Lenses Seriously ill clients whose contact lenses have been removed will not need them re-inserted until they become more active in their care and require the lenses to see properly. Contact lenses need to be lubricated in a sterile, nonirritating wetting solution (usually a saline solution) before they are inserted. The wetting solution helps the lens glide over the cornea, thus reducing the risk of injury. Most clients, when well, will re-insert the lenses independently.

Artificial Eyes (Prosthesis)

Artificial eyes are usually made of plastic instead of glass. Some are permanently implanted; others are removed regularly for cleaning as required. Most clients who wear a removable artificial eye follow their own care regimen. Even for an unconscious client, daily removal and cleaning may not be necessary.

To remove an artificial eye, the nurse dons clean gloves and uses the dominant thumb to pull the client's lower eyelid down over the infraorbital bone, exerting slight pressure below the eyelid to overcome the suction (Figure 34.28). An alternative method is to compress a small rubber bulb and apply the tip directly to the eye. As the nurse gradually releases the finger pressure on the bulb, the suction of the bulb counteracts the suction holding the eye in the socket and draws the eye out of the socket.

The artificial eye is cleaned with warm normal saline and placed in a container filled with water or saline solution. The socket and tissues around the eye are usually cleaned with cotton wipes and normal saline. To re-insert the eye, the nurse uses the thumb and index finger of one hand to retract the eyelids, exerting pressure on the supraorbital and infraorbital bones. Holding the eye between the thumb and index finger of the other hand, the nurse slips the eye gently into the socket (Figure 34.29).

General Eye Care

Many clients may need to learn specific information about care of the eyes. Some examples follow:

- Avoid home remedies for eye problems. Eye irritations or injuries at any age should be treated medically and immediately.
- If dirt or dust gets into the eyes, clean them copiously with clean, tepid water as an emergency treatment.

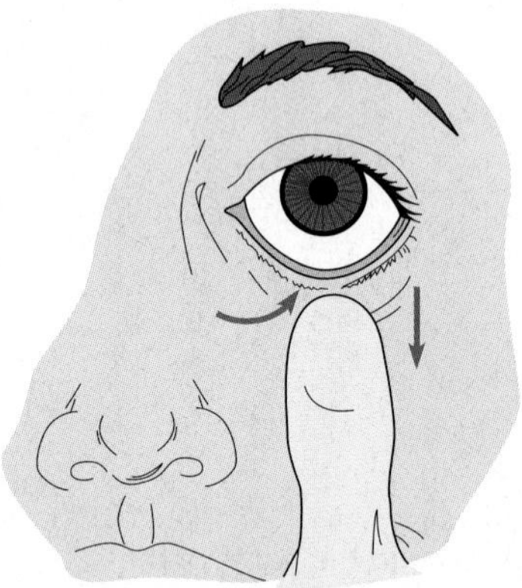

Figure 34.28 Removing an artificial eye by retracting the lower eyelid and exerting slight pressure below the eyelid

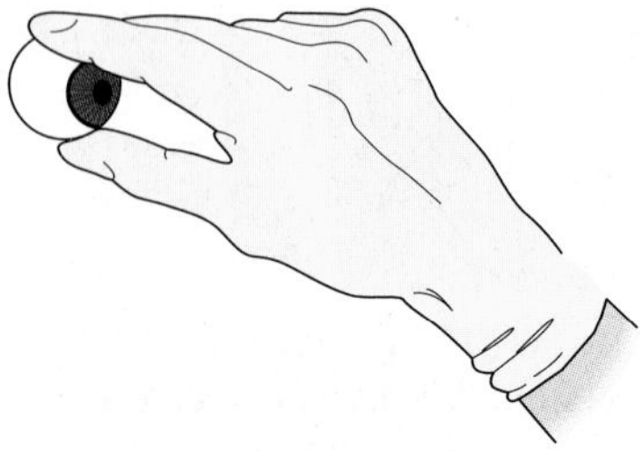

Figure 34.29 Holding an artificial eye between the thumb and index finger for insertion

- Take measures to guard against eyestrain and to protect vision, such as maintaining adequate lighting for reading and wearing protective eye goggles/glasses.
- Schedule regular eye examinations, particularly after age 40 years, to detect such problems as cataracts and glaucoma.

Evaluating

See examples of desired outcomes provided earlier in the "Planning" section.

Ears

Normal ears require minimal hygiene. Clients who have excessive **cerumen** (earwax) and dependent clients who have hearing appliances may require assistance from the nurse. Hearing appliances are usually removed before surgery.

Cleaning the Ears

The auricles of the ears are cleaned during the bed bath. The nurse or client must remove excessive cerumen that is visible or that causes discomfort or hearing difficulty. Visible cerumen may be loosened and removed by retracting the auricle downward. If this measure is ineffective, irrigation is necessary (see the section on otic irrigation in Chapter 28). Clients need to be advised never to use bobby pins, toothpicks, or cotton-tipped applicators to remove cerumen. Bobby pins and toothpicks can injure the ear canal and rupture the tympanic membrane; use of cotton-tipped swabs is discouraged because they may impact the cerumen.

Care of Hearing Appliances

A hearing appliance is a battery-powered, sound-amplifying device used by hearing-impaired persons. It consists of a microphone that picks up sound and converts it to electric energy, an amplifier that magnifies the electric energy electronically, a receiver that converts the amplified energy back to sound energy, and an earmould that directs the sound into the ear. There are several types of hearing appliances:

- *Behind-the-ear (BTE, or postaural) aid.* This is the most widely used type because it fits snugly behind the ear. The hearing appliance case, which holds the microphone, amplifier, and receiver, is attached to the earmould by a plastic tube (Figure 34.30).
- *In-the-ear appliance (ITE, or intra-aural).* This one-piece aid has all its components housed in the earmould (Figure 34.31).
- *In-the-canal (ITC) appliance.* This is the most compact and least visible aid, fitting completely inside the ear canal. In addition to having cosmetic appeal, the ITC does not interfere with telephone use or the wearing of eyeglasses. However, it is not suitable for clients with progressive hearing loss; it requires adequate ear canal diameter and length for a good fit; and it tends to plug with cerumen more than other aids.
- *Eyeglasses appliance.* This is similar to the behind-the-ear aid, but the components are housed in the temple of the eyeglasses. A hearing appliance can be in one or both temples of the glasses.
- *Body hearing appliance.* This pocket-sized aid, used for more severe hearing losses, clips onto an undergarment, shirt pocket, or harness carrier supplied by the manufacturer. The case, containing the microphone and amplifier, is connected by a cord to the receiver, which snaps into the earpiece.

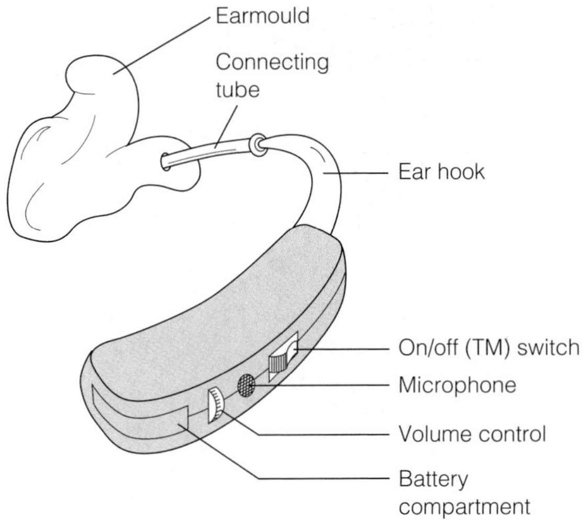

Figure 34.30 A behind-the-ear hearing appliance

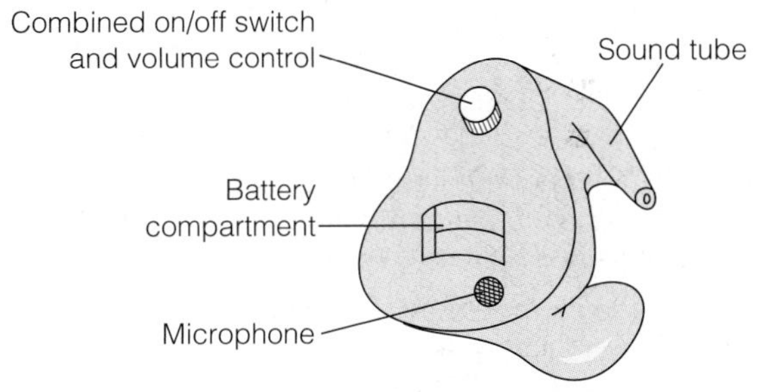

Figure 34.31 An in-the-ear hearing appliance

For correct functioning, hearing appliances require appropriate handling during insertion and removal, regular cleaning of the earmould, and replacement of dead batteries. With proper care, hearing appliances generally last five to 10 years. Earmoulds generally need readjustment every two to three years.

Procedure 34.9 describes how to remove, clean, and insert a hearing appliance.

PROCEDURE 34.9 Removing, Cleaning, and Inserting a Hearing Appliance

PURPOSE

- To maintain proper hearing appliance function

Assessment Focus
Any problems with the hearing appliance; hearing appliance care practices; presence of inflammation, excessive wax or drainage, or discomfort in the external ear canal; any change in hearing acuity

Equipment

- ❑ Client's hearing appliance
- ❑ Soap, water, and towels or a damp cloth
- ❑ Pipe cleaner or toothpick (optional)
- ❑ New battery (if needed)

INTERVENTION

1. Remove the hearing appliance.

- Turn the hearing appliance off and lower the volume. The on/off switch may be labelled "O" (off), "M" (microphone), "T" (telephone), or "TM" (telephone/microphone). *The batteries continue to run if the aid is not turned off.*
- Remove the earmould by rotating it slightly forward and pulling it outward.
- If the aid is not to be used for several days, remove the battery. *Removal prevents corrosion of the aid from battery leakage.*
- Store the hearing appliance in a safe place. Avoid exposure to heat and moisture. *Proper storage prevents loss or damage.*

2. Clean the earmould.

- Detach the earmould, *if possible.* Disconnect the earmould from the receiver of a body hearing appliance or from the hearing appliance case of behind-the-ear and eyeglass aids where the tubing meets the hook of the case. Do not remove the earmould if it is glued or secured by a small metal ring. *Removal facilitates cleaning and prevents inadvertent damage to the other parts.*
- If the earmould is *detachable,* soak it in a mild soapy solution. Rinse and dry it well. Do not use isopropyl alcohol. *Alcohol can damage the hearing appliance.*
- If the earmould is *not detachable* or is for an in-the-ear aid, wipe the earmould with a damp cloth.
- Check that the earmould opening is patent. Remove any excess moisture through the opening or remove debris (e.g., earwax) with a pipe cleaner or toothpick.
- Reattach the earmould if it was detached from the rest of the hearing appliance.

3. Insert the hearing appliance.

- Determine from the client if the earmould is for the left or the right ear.
- Check that the battery is inserted in the hearing appliance. Turn off the hearing appliance, and make sure the volume is turned all the way down. *A volume that is too loud is distressing.*
- Inspect the earmould to identify the ear canal portion. Some earmoulds are fitted for only the ear canal and concha; others are fitted for all the contours of the ear. The canal portion, common to all, can be used as a guide for correct insertion.
- Line up the parts of the earmould with the corresponding parts of the client's ear.
- Rotate the earmould slightly forward, and insert the ear canal portion.
- Gently press the earmould into the ear while rotating it backward.
- Check that the earmould fits snugly by asking the client if it feels secure and comfortable.
- Adjust the other components of a behind-the-ear or body hearing appliance.
- Turn the hearing appliance on, and adjust the volume according to the client's needs.

4. Correct problems associated with improper functioning.

- If the sound is weak or there is no sound:
  - **a.** Ensure that the volume is turned high enough.
  - **b.** Ensure that the earmould opening is not clogged.
  - **c.** Check the battery by turning the aid on, turning up the volume, cupping your hand over the earmould, and listening. A constant whistling sound indicates the battery is functioning. If necessary, replace the battery. Be sure that the negative (–) and positive (+) signs on the battery match those on the aid.
  - **d.** Ensure that the ear canal is not blocked with wax, which can obstruct sound waves.
- If the client reports a whistling sound or squeal after insertion:
  - **a.** Turn the volume down.
  - **b.** Ensure that the earmould is properly attached to the receiver.
  - **c.** Re-insert the earmould.

PROCEDURE 34.9 Removing, Cleaning, and Inserting a Hearing Appliance *continued*

5. Document pertinent data.

- Report and record any problems the client has with the hearing appliance.

Evaluation Focus
Absence of inflammation; wax buildup or discomfort in external ear canal; adequacy of hearing acuity with aid inserted; comfort of aid when inserted

Nose

Nurses usually need not provide special care for the nose because clients can ordinarily clear nasal secretions by blowing gently into a soft tissue. When the external nares are encrusted with dried secretions, they should be cleaned with a cotton-tipped applicator or moistened with saline or water. The applicator should not be inserted beyond the length of the cotton tip; inserting it further may cause injury to the mucosa.

Supporting a Hygienic Environment

Because people are usually confined to bed when ill, often for long periods, the bed becomes an important element in the client's life. A place that is clean, safe, and comfortable contributes to the client's ability to rest and sleep and to a sense of well-being. Basic furniture in a health-care facility includes the bed, bedside table, overbed table, one or more chairs, and a storage space for clothing. Most bed units also have a nurse call system, light fixtures, electric outlets, and hygienic equipment in the bedside table. Four types of equipment often installed in an acute-care facility are a *suction outlet* for several kinds of suction, an *oxygen outlet* for most oxygen equipment, an air outlet for nebulizers and humidifiers, and a *sphygmomanometer* to measure the client's blood pressure. Some long-term care agencies also permit clients to have *personal furniture*, such as a television, a chair, and lamps, at the bedside. In the home, a client often has personal and medical equipment.

Environment

When providing a comfortable environment, it is important to consider the client's age, severity of illness, and level of activity. See the Research Note for promoting comfort in an older adult with Alzheimer's disease.

Temperature

The very young, the very old, and the acutely ill frequently need a room temperature higher than normal. A room temperature between 20 and 23°C is comfortable for most clients.

Ventilation

Good ventilation is important to remove unpleasant odours and stale air. Odours caused by urine, draining wounds, or vomitus, for example, can be offensive to people. Room deodorizers can help eliminate odours. However, good hygienic practices are the best way to prevent offensive body and breath odours. Hospitals are required to monitor smoking. Hospitals frequently no longer have smoking areas and prohibit smoking in client rooms.

Noise

Ill persons are usually sensitive to noise, such as clanging of metal equipment, loud talking, and laughter. Nurses should try to control noise in health-care settings.

Hospital Beds

The frame of a hospital bed is divided into three sections. This permits the head and the foot to be elevated separately. Most hospital beds have electric motors to operate

RESEARCH NOTE

Using Massage to Reduce Agitation

Researchers in a study queried whether episodes of agitated behaviour, common in individuals with Alzheimer's disease, would benefit from massage. Effectiveness of slow-stroke massage administered by caregivers in a home setting was measured. These family caregivers were given instruction on techniques of slow-stroke massage, which they administered over a 10-day period for a maximum of seven-minute sessions. The massage was given before activities that were known to cause agitation. Results showed that physical expressions of agitation (pacing, wandering, resisting) were reduced; however, massage was less effective against verbal displays of agitation.

This technique has the potential to calm agitated individuals, possibly increasing the length of time they are able to remain at home in a familiar environment.

Source: Rowe, M., & Alfred, D. (1999). The effectiveness of slow-stroke massage in diffusing agitated behaviors in individuals with Alzheimer's disease. *Journal of Gerontological Nursing, 25*(6), 22–34.

the movable joints. The motor is activated by pressing a button or moving a small lever, located either at the side of the bed or on a small panel separate from the bed but attached to it by a cable, which the client can readily use.

Hospital beds are usually 66 cm high and 0.9 m wide, narrower than the usual bed so that the nurse can reach the client from either side of the bed without undue stretching. The length is usually 1.9 m. Bariatric beds are available to accommodate clients who are obese. Some beds can be extended in length to accommodate very tall clients. Long-term care facilities for ambulatory clients usually have low beds to facilitate movement in and out of bed. Most hospital beds have "high" and "low" positions that can be adjusted either mechanically or electrically by a button or lever. The high position permits the nurse to reach the client without undue stretching or stooping. The low position allows the client to step easily to the floor.

Mattresses

Mattresses are usually covered with a water-repellent material that resists soiling and can be cleaned easily. Most mattresses have handles on the sides called lugs by which the mattress can be moved.

Many special mattresses are also used in hospitals to relieve pressure on the body's bony prominences, such as the heels. They are particularly helpful for clients confined to bed for a long time. For additional information about mattresses, see Chapter 37.

Side Rails

Side rails, or safety sides, are used on both hospital beds and stretchers. They are of various shapes and sizes and are usually made of metal. Devices to raise and lower them differ. Often, one or two knobs are pulled to release the side and permit it to be moved. When side rails are being used, it is important that the nurse *never* leave the bedside while the rail is lowered. Some side rails have two positions: up and down. Others have three: high, intermediate, and low. The down and low positions are employed when a side rail is not needed. With some models, the bed foundation (the mattress and frame supporting it) must be raised before the side rail can be put in the low position; otherwise the side rail might hit the floor and be damaged. The intermediate position is used when the bed is in the low position and the nurse is present. The up or high side rail position is used when a client is in bed and requires protection from falling. Some agencies have a release form that the client can sign if the use of side rails is refused.

Footboard or Footboot

These are used to support the immobilized client's foot in a normal right angle to the legs to prevent plantar flexion contractures. See Chapter 43.

Bed Cradles

A bed cradle, sometimes called an *Anderson frame*, is a device designed to keep the top bedclothes off the feet, legs, and even abdomen of a client. The bedclothes are arranged over the device and may be pinned in place. There are several types of bed cradles. One of the most common is a curved metal rod that fits over the bed. Part of the cradle fits under the mattress, and small metal brackets press down on each side of the mattress to keep the cradle in place. The frame of some cradles extends over half of the width of the bed, above one leg.

Intravenous Rods

Intravenous rods (poles, stands, standards), usually made of metal, support intravenous (IV) infusion containers while fluid is being administered to a client. These rods were traditionally freestanding on the floor beside the bed. Intravenous rods are often attached to the hospital beds. Some hospital units have overhead hanging rods on a track for IVs.

Making Beds

Nurses need to be able to prepare hospital beds in different ways for specific purposes. In most instances, beds are made after the client receives certain care and when beds are unoccupied. At times, however, nurses need to make an occupied bed or prepare a bed for a client who is having surgery (an anesthetic, postoperative, or surgical bed).

Regardless of what type of bed equipment is available, whether the bed is occupied or unoccupied, or the purpose for which the bed is being prepared, certain guidelines pertain to all bed-making. These are summarized in the box below.

CLINICAL GUIDELINES

Bed-Making

- Wash hands thoroughly after handling a client's bed linen. Linens and equipment that have been soiled with secretions and excretions harbour microorganisms that can be transmitted to others directly or by the nurse's hands or uniform.
- Hold soiled linen away from uniform.
- Linen for one client is *never* (even momentarily) placed on another client's bed or furniture.
- Place soiled linen directly in a portable linen hamper or tucked into a pillow case at the end of the bed before it is gathered up for disposal.
- Do not shake soiled linen in the air because shaking can disseminate secretions and excretions and the microorganisms they contain.
- When stripping and making a bed, conserve time and energy by stripping and making up one side as much as possible before working on the other side.
- To avoid unnecessary trips to the linen supply area, gather all linen before starting to strip a bed.

An *unoccupied bed* can be either closed or open. Generally, the top covers of an open bed are folded back (thus the term *open bed*) to make it easier for a client to get in. Open and closed beds are made the same way, except that the top sheet, blanket, and bedspread of a *closed bed* are drawn up to the top of the bed and under the pillows.

Beds are often changed after bed baths. The linen can be collected before the bath. The linen is not usually changed unless it is soiled. Check the policy at each clinical agency. Unfitted sheets, blankets, and bedspreads are mitred at the corners of the bed. The purpose of mitring is to secure the bedclothes while the bed is occupied. Figure 34.32 shows how to mitre the corner of a bed.

Procedure 34.10 explains how to change an unoccupied bed.

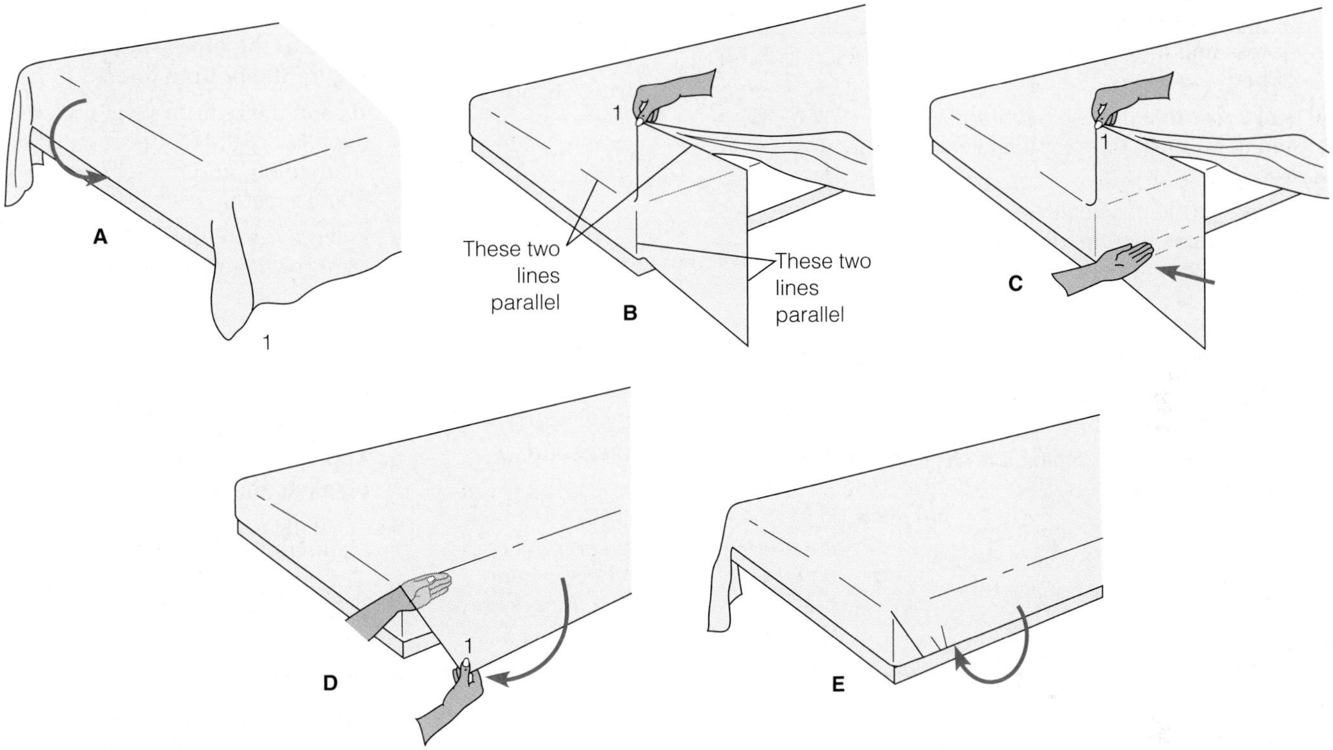

Figure 34.32 Mitring the corner of a bed: *A,* Tuck in the bedcover (sheet, blanket, and/or spread) firmly under the mattress at the bottom or top of the bed; *B,* Lift the bedcover at point 1 so that it forms a triangle with the side edge of the bed and the edge of the bedcover is parallel to the end of the bed; *C,* Tuck the part of the cover that hangs below the mattress under the mattress while holding the cover at point 1 against the mattress; *D,* Bring point 1 down toward the floor while the other hand holds the fold of the cover against the side of the mattress; *E,* Remove the hand and tuck the remainder of the cover under the mattress, if appropriate. The sides of the top sheet, blanket, and bedspread may be left hanging freely rather than tucked in. The bedspread is mitred separately and left hanging freely if the top sheet and blanket are tucked in.

PROCEDURE 34.10 Changing an Unoccupied Bed

PURPOSES

- To promote the client's comfort
- To provide a clean, neat environment for the client
- To provide a smooth, wrinkle-free bed foundation, thus minimizing sources of skin irritation

Equipment

- ❑ Two large sheets
- ❑ Cloth drawsheet (optional)
- ❑ One blanket
- ❑ One bedspread
- ❑ Waterproof drawsheet or waterproof pads (optional)
- ❑ Pillowcase(s) for the head pillow(s)
- ❑ Portable linen hamper, if available

→

PROCEDURE 34.10 Changing an Unoccupied Bed *continued*

INTERVENTION

1. **Place the fresh linen on the client's chair or overbed table; do not use another client's bed or furniture.** This prevents cross-contamination (the movement of microorganisms from one client to another) via linen.
2. **Assess and assist the client out of bed.**
   - Make sure that this is an appropriate and convenient time for the client to be out of bed.
   - Assess the client's health status to determine that the person can safely get out of bed. In some hospitals, it is necessary to have a written order if the client has been in bed continuously.
   - Assess the client's pulse and respirations if indicated.
   - Assist the client to a comfortable chair.
3. **Strip the bed.**
   - Check bed linens for any items belonging to the client, and detach the call bell or any drainage tubes from the bed linen.
   - Loosen all bedding systematically, starting at the head of the bed on the far side and moving around the bed up to the head of the bed on the near side. *Moving around the bed systematically prevents stretching and reaching and possible muscle strain.*
   - Remove the pillowcases, if soiled, and place the pillows on the bedside chair near the foot of the bed.
   - Fold reusable linens, such as the bedspread and top sheet on the bed, into fourths. First, fold the linen in half by bringing the top edge even with the bottom edge, and then grasp it at the centre of the middle fold and bottom edges (Figure 34.33). *Folding linens saves time and energy when reapplying the linens on the bed.*
   - Remove the waterproof pad and discard it if soiled.
   - Roll all soiled linen inside the bottom sheet, hold it away from your uniform, and place it directly in the linen hamper. *These actions are essential to prevent the transmission of microorganisms to the nurse and others.*

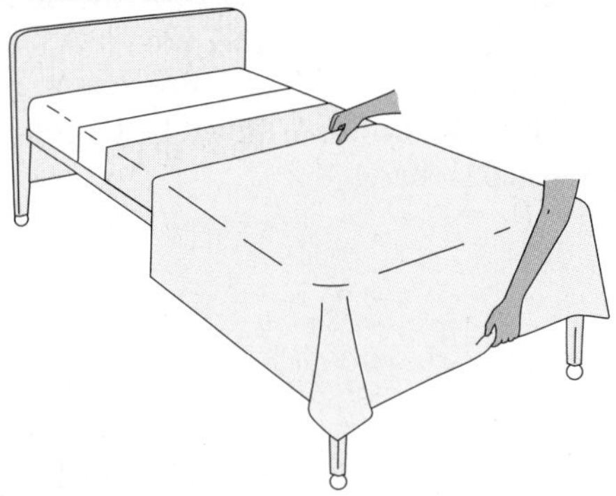

Figure 34.33 Folding reusable linens into fourths when removing them from the bed

   - Grasp the mattress securely, using the lugs if present, and move the mattress up to the head of the bed.
4. **Apply the bottom sheet and drawsheet.**
   - Place the folded bottom sheet with its centre fold on the centre of the bed. Make sure the sheet is hemside down for a smooth foundation. Spread the sheet out over the mattress, and allow a sufficient amount of sheet at the top to tuck under the mattress. *The top of the sheet needs to be well tucked under to remain securely in place, especially when the head of the bed is elevated.* Place the sheet along the edge of the mattress at the foot of the bed and do not tuck it in (unless it is a contour sheet).
   - Mitre the sheet at the top corner on the near side (Figure 34.32, earlier) and tuck the sheet under the mattress, working from the head of the bed to the foot.
   - If a waterproof drawsheet is used, place it over the bottom sheet so that the centre fold is at the centre line of the bed and the top and bottom edges will extend from the middle of the client's back to the area of the midthigh or knee. Fanfold the uppermost half of the folded drawsheet at the centre or far edge of the bed and tuck in the near edge.
   - Lay the cloth drawsheet over the waterproof sheet in the same manner.
   - *Optional:* Before moving to the other side of the bed, place the top linens on the bed hemside up, unfold them, tuck them in, and mitre the bottom corners. *Completing the entire side of the bed saves time and energy.*
5. **Move to the other side and secure the bottom linens.**
   - Tuck in the bottom sheet under the head of the mattress, pull the sheet firmly, and mitre the corner of the sheet.
   - Pull the remainder of the sheet firmly so that there are no wrinkles. *Wrinkles can cause discomfort for the client.* Tuck the sheet in at the side.
   - Complete this same process for the drawsheet(s).
6. **Apply or complete the top sheet, blanket, and spread.**
   - Place the top sheet, hemside up, on the bed so that its centre fold is at the centre of the bed and the top edge is even with the top edge of the mattress.
   - Unfold the sheet over the bed.
   - *Optional:* Make a vertical or a horizontal toe pleat in the sheet to provide additional room for the client's feet.
     a. *Vertical toe pleat:* Make a fold in the sheet 5 to 10 cm perpendicular to the foot of the bed (Figure 34.34).

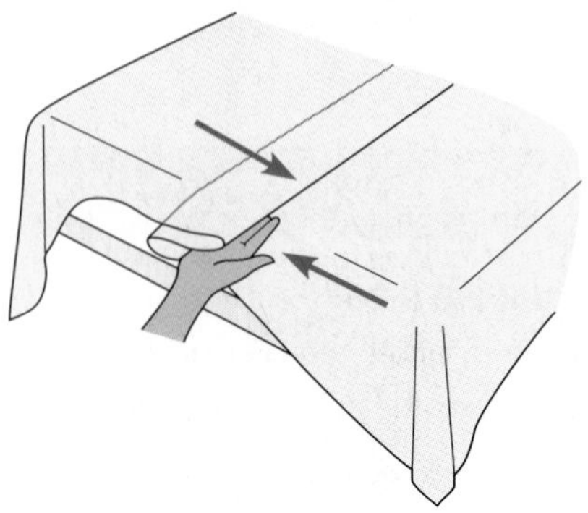

Figure 34.34 A vertical toe pleat

PROCEDURE 34.10 Changing an Unoccupied Bed *continued*

b. *Horizontal toe pleat:* Make a fold in the sheet 5 to 10 cm across the bed near the foot (Figure 34.35).

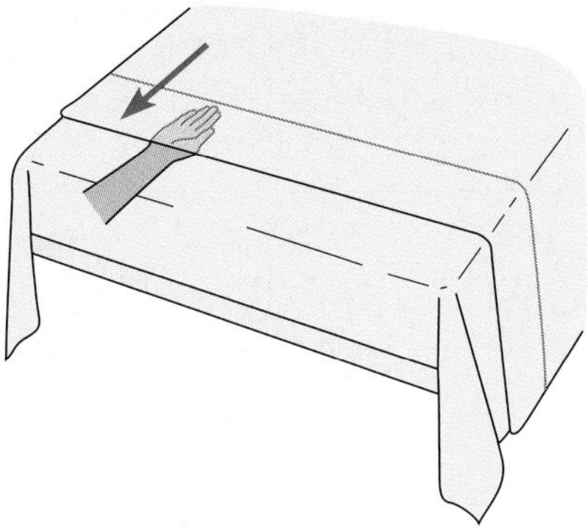

Figure 34.35 A horizontal toe pleat

- Loosening the top covers around the feet after the client is in bed is another way to provide additional space.
- Follow the same procedure for the blanket and the spread, but place the top edges about 15 cm from the head of the bed to allow a cuff of sheet to be folded over them.
- Tuck in the sheet, blanket, and spread at the foot of the bed, and mitre the corner using all three layers of linen. Leave the sides of the top sheet, blanket, and spread hanging freely unless toe pleats were provided.
- Fold the top of the top sheet down over the spread, providing a cuff. *The cuff of sheet makes it easier for the client to pull the covers up.*
- Move to the other side of the bed and secure the top bedding in the same manner.

7. **Put clean pillowcases on the pillows as required.**

- Grasp the closed end of the pillowcase at the centre with one hand.
- Gather up the sides of the pillowcase and place them over the hand grasping the case. Then grasp the centre of one short side of the pillow through the pillowcase (Figure 34.36).

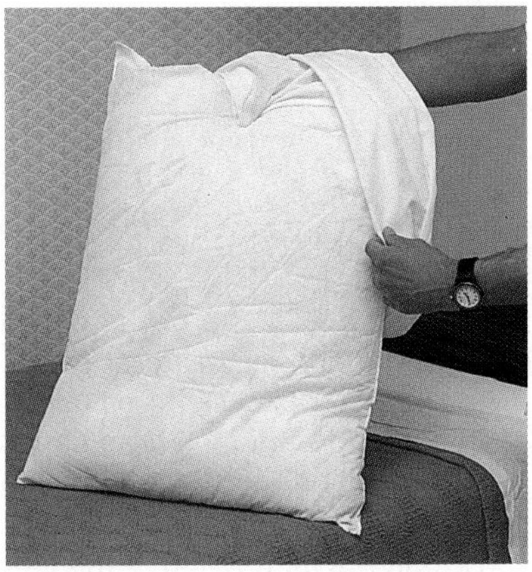

Figure 34.36 Method for putting a clean pillowcase on a pillow

- With the free hand, pull the pillowcase over the pillow.
- Adjust the pillowcase so that the pillow fits into the corners of the case and the seams are straight. *A smoothly fitting pillowcase is more comfortable than a wrinkled one.*
- Place the pillows appropriately at the head of the bed.

8. **Provide for client comfort and safety.**

- Attach the signal cord so that the client can conveniently use it. Some cords have clamps that attach to the sheet or pillowcase. Others are attached by a safety pin.
- If the bed is currently being used by a client, either fold back the top covers at one side or fanfold them down to the centre of the bed. *This makes it easier for the client to get into the bed.*
- Place the bedside table and the overbed table so that they are available to the client.
- Ensure the bed brakes are locked.
- Leave the bed in the high position if the client is returning by stretcher, or place in the low position if the client is returning to bed after being up.

9. **Document and report pertinent data.**

- Bed making is not normally recorded.
- Record any nursing assessments, such as the client's physical status and pulse and respiratory rates before and after being out of bed, as indicated.
- Record any observations of drainage noted on bed linen.

Changing an Occupied Bed

Some clients may be too weak to get out of bed. Either the nature of their illness may contraindicate their sitting out of bed, or they may be restricted in bed by the presence of traction or other therapies. When changing an *occupied bed*, the nurse works quickly and disturbs the client as little as possible to conserve the client's energy, using the following guidelines:

- Maintain the client in good body alignment. Never move or position a client in a manner that is contraindicated by the client's health. Obtain help, if necessary, to ensure the client's safety.
- Move the client gently and smoothly. Rough handling can cause the client discomfort and abrade the skin.
- Explain to the client what you plan to do throughout the procedure before you do it. Use terms that the client can understand.
- Use the bed-making time, like the bed bath time, to assess and meet the client's needs.

Procedure 34.11 describes how to change an occupied bed.

PROCEDURE 34.11 Changing an Occupied Bed

PURPOSES

- To conserve the client's energy and maintain current health status
- To promote client comfort
- To provide a clean, neat environment for the client
- To provide a smooth, wrinkle-free bed foundation, thus minimizing sources of skin irritation

Assessment Focus
Specific orders or precautions for moving and positioning the client; presence of incontinence or excessive drainage from other sources indicating the need for protective waterproof pads; skin condition and need for special mattress (e.g., egg crate), footboard, or heel protectors

Equipment

- ❑ Two large sheets
- ❑ Cloth drawsheet (optional)
- ❑ One blanket
- ❑ One bedspread
- ❑ Waterproof drawsheet or waterproof pads (optional)
- ❑ Pillowcase(s) for the head pillow(s)
- ❑ Portable linen hamper, if available

INTERVENTION

1. Remove the top bedding.

- Remove any equipment attached to the bed linen, such as a signal light.
- Loosen all the top linen at the foot of the bed, and remove the spread and the blanket.
- Leave the top sheet over the client (the top sheet can remain over the client if it is being changed and if it will provide sufficient warmth), *or* replace it with a bath blanket as follows:
  - **a.** Spread the bath blanket over the top sheet.
  - **b.** Ask the client to hold the top edge of the blanket.
  - **c.** Reaching under the blanket from the side, grasp the top edge of the sheet and draw it down to the foot of the bed, leaving the blanket in place.
  - **d.** Remove the sheet from the bed and place it in the soiled linen hamper.

2. Move the mattress up on the bed.

- Place the bed in the flat position if the client's health permits.
- With the assistance of another health-care provider, grasp the mattress lugs and, using good body mechanics, move the mattress up to the head of the bed.

3. Change the bottom sheet and drawsheet.

- Assist the client to turn on the side facing away from the side where the clean linen is.
- Raise the side rail nearest the client. *This protects the client from falling.* If there is no side rail, have another nurse support the client at the edge of the bed.
- Loosen the foundation of the linen on the side of the bed near the linen supply.
- Fanfold the drawsheet and the bottom sheet at the centre of the bed (Figure 34.37) as close to the client as possible. Doing this leaves the near half of the bed free to be changed.

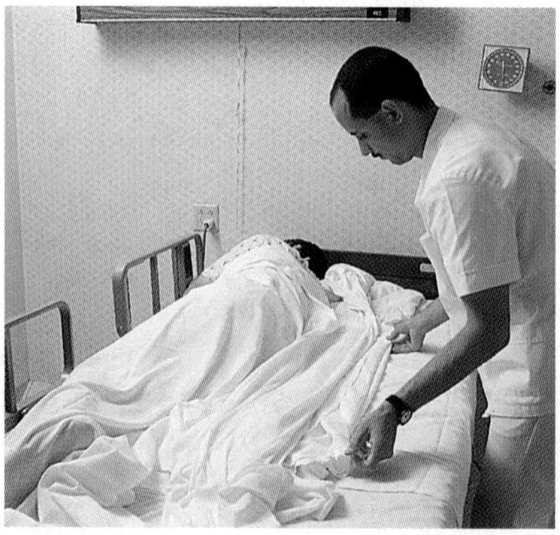

Figure 34.37 Fanfolding soiled linen as close to the client as possible

- Place the new bottom sheet on the bed, and vertically fanfold the half to be used on the far side of the bed as close to the client as possible. Tuck the sheet under the near half of the bed and mitre the corner if a contour sheet is not being used.
- Place the clean drawsheet on the bed with the centre fold at the centre of the bed. Fanfold the uppermost half vertically at the centre of the bed and tuck the near side edge under the side of the mattress.
- Assist the client to roll over toward you onto the clean side of the bed. The client rolls over the fanfolded linen at the centre of the bed.
- Move the pillows to the clean side for the client's use. Raise the side rail before leaving the side of the bed.
- Move to the other side of the bed and lower the side rail. Remove the used linen and place it in the portable hamper.
- Unfold the fanfolded bottom sheet from the centre of the bed.
- Facing the side of the bed, use both hands to pull the bottom sheet so that it is smooth and tuck the excess under the side of the mattress.
- Unfold the drawsheet fanfolded at the centre of the bed and pull it tightly with both hands. Pull the sheet in three sections: (a) face

PROCEDURE 34.11 Changing an Occupied Bed *continued*

the side of the bed to pull the middle section; (b) face the far top corner to pull the bottom section; and (c) face the far bottom corner to pull the top section.

- Tuck the excess drawsheet under the side of the mattress.

4. Reposition the client in the centre of the bed.

- Reposition the pillows at the centre of the bed.
- Assist the client to the centre of the bed. Determine what position the client requires or prefers and assist the client to that position.

5. Apply or complete the top bedding.

- Spread the top sheet over the client and either ask the client to hold the top edge of the sheet or tuck it under the shoulders. The sheet should remain over the client when the bath blanket or used sheet is removed.
- Complete the top of the bed.

6. Ensure continued safety of the client.

- Raise the side rails. Place the bed in the low position before leaving the bedside.
- Ensure bed brakes are locked.
- Attach the signal cord to the bed linen within the client's reach.
- Put items used by the client within easy reach.

Evaluation Focus
Client comfort and safety; patency of all drainage tubes; client's ability to summon help when needed

FOCUS ON CRITICAL THINKING

It is the fourth day following Mrs. Baptista's abdominal surgery. She is progressing well, is ambulating several times each day, has been providing for her own hygienic needs, and is planning on going home tomorrow. During your early morning assessment, you note that Mrs. Baptista's hair is oily and matted and she has an unpleasant body odour. Her dentures in a container at the bedside are in need of cleaning. You check her abdominal incision and verify that there is no drainage, redness, or signs of infection. You inquire about her ability to take care of her own bath and personal needs, and offer to assist her with her bath. She replies that she had a bath yesterday, doesn't feel that she needs another one today, and requests to omit her personal care for the day.

1. Support or contradict the use of the nursing diagnosis ***Self-Care Deficit: Bathing/Hygiene*** as an appropriate nursing diagnosis for Mrs. Baptista.
2. Explain why it would be in Mrs. Baptista's best interests for you to assist her with hygienic care, even though she doesn't feel she needs a bath.
3. What factors should you consider before you attempt to encourage Mrs. Baptista to attend to her personal care?
4. What approaches might you use if you feel that Mrs. Baptista does need her hair shampooed and needs to have her personal care attended to?
5. What advantages does performing baths and personal hygiene for clients offer the nurse?

See Appendix A for answers to these questions.

CHAPTER HIGHLIGHTS

- Clients' hygienic practices are influenced, to a large degree, by their sociocultural background.
- When clients cannot meet their own hygiene needs, the nurse assists them.
- The major functions of the skin are to help regulate body temperature, to protect underlying tissues, to secrete sebum, and to contain nerve receptors that act in sensory perception.
- When planning hygiene care, the nurse must take the client's preferences into consideration.
- Nurses provide perineal-genital care for clients who are unable to do so for themselves.
- Nurses can often teach clients how to prevent foot problems.
- Oral hygiene should include daily dental flossing and mechanical brushing of the teeth.

- Regular dental checkups and fluoride supplements are recommended to maintain healthy teeth.
- Nurses provide special oral care to clients who are helpless (e.g., unconscious) and who have oral problems.
- Hair care includes daily combing and brushing and regular shampooing.
- African-Canadian clients' hair may require special care.
- Nurses may need to assist clients with their artificial eyes, eyeglasses, and contact lenses.
- Clients with a hearing appliance may require nursing assistance with the device.
- Changing bed linens is a part of maintaining hygiene.
- It is important to keep beds clean and comfortable for clients.

READINGS AND REFERENCES

Suggested Readings

Beuscher, T. L. (1998). Community outreach foot care for the elderly: A winning proposition. *Home Healthcare Nurse, 16*(1), 37–44.

Beuscher describes one home health agency's development of a foot care program for the elderly. Monthly foot care clinics were begun in six community senior centres and staffed by home care nurses. A modest fee was charged to cover costs. The nurses learned new skills, clients received care they were unable to perform, and senior centres were able to offer a new program to their members.

Kelechi, T. (1996). Foot care in the home: Nursing and agency responsibilities. *Home Healthcare Nurse, 14*(9), 721–731.

Foot care is an integral component of overall client care provided in the home. This article categorizes three levels of foot care that can be provided and gives nurses and agencies guidelines for developing policies and procedures that direct this type of care.

Related Research

Astrom, A. N. (1996). Dimensionality of dental-health behavior. *American Journal of Health Behavior, 20*(3), 67–76.

Pearson, L. S. (1996). A comparison of the ability of foam swabs and toothbrushes to remove dental plaque: Implications for nursing practice. *Journal of Advanced Nursing, 23*(1), 62–69.

Sheppard, C. M., & Brenner, P. S. (2000). The effects of bathing and skin care practices on skin quality and satisfaction with an innovative product. *Journal of Gerontological Nursing, 26*(10), 36–45, 55–56.

Wallace, K. G., Koeppel, K., Senko, A., et al. (1997). Effect of attitudes and subjective norms on intention to provide oral care to patients receiving antineoplastic chemotherapy. *Cancer Nursing, 20*(1), 34–41.

Selected References

American Society of Ophthalmic Registered Nurses. (1996). *Ophthalmic procedures: A nursing perspective* (Vol. 1). San Francisco, CA: Author.

Barnett, J. (1991, September). A reassessment of oral healthcare. *Professional Nurse, 6*, 703–704, 706–708.

Beuscher, T. L. (1998, January). Community outreach: Foot care for the elderly: A winning proposition. *Home Healthcare Nurse, 16*(1), 37–44.

Carpenito, L. J. (2002). *Handbook of nursing diagnosis* (9th ed.). Philadelphia, PA: Lippincott.

Carruth, A. K., Ricks, D., & Pullen, P. (1995, September). Bag baths: An alternative to the bed bath. *Nursing Management, 26*(9), 75–78.

Claphan, L. (1997). Preventing foot problems in patients with diabetes. *Professional Nurse, 12*(12), 851–853.

Engberg, I. B., Lindell, M., & Nyren-Nolberger, U. (1998). Prevalence of skin and genital mucous membrane irritations in patients confined to bed. *International Journal of Nursing Studies, 32*(3), 315–324.

Fishman, T. D., Freedline, A. D., & Kahn, D. (1996). Putting the best foot forward. *Nursing 96, 26*(1), 58–60.

Freeman, E. (1997). International perspectives on bathing. *Journal of Gerontological Nursing, 23*(5), 40–44.

Goldblum, K. (Ed.). (1997). *Core curriculum for ophthalmic nursing*. Dubuque, IA: Kendall/Hunt.

Gooch, J. (1989, October). Skin hygiene. *Professional Nurse, 5*(1), 13, 16, 18.

Hauk, L. (1986, September/October). Enabling clients to manage dentures. *Geriatric Nursing, 7*, 254–255.

Hektor, L., & Touhy, T. (1997, May). The history of the bath: From art to task. *Journal of Gerontological Nursing, 23*(5), 7–15.

Holmes, S. (1996). Nursing management of oral care in older patients. *Nursing Times, 92*(9), 37–39.

Johnson, M., & Maas, M. (Eds.). (2000). *Nursing outcomes classification (NOC)*. St. Louis, MO: Mosby.

Kayser-Jones, J., Bird, W. F., Paul, S. M., et al. (1995, December). An instrument to assess the oral health status of nursing home residents. *Gerontologist, 35*, 814–824.

Kelechi, T. (1996). Foot care in the home: Nursing and agency responsibilities. *Home Healthcare Nurse, 14*(9), 721–731.

Kelechi, T., & Lukacs, K. (1991, September). Nursing foot care for the aged. *Journal of Gerontological Nursing, 17*, 40–43.

Marieb, E. N. (1998). *Human anatomy and physiology* (4th ed.). Menlo Park, CA: Addison Wesley Longman.

Mauizio, S. J., & Rogers, J. L. (1997, March). Prevention update: Oral hygiene to the home care patient. *Caring, 16*(3), 54–55.

McConnell, E. (1998). Communicating with a hearing-impaired patient. *Nursing, 28*(1), 32.

Ney, D. F. (1993, March/April). Cerumen impaction, ear hygiene practices, and hearing acuity. *Geriatric Nursing, 14*(2), 70–73.

North American Nursing Diagnosis Association. (2003). *NANDA nursing diagnoses: Definitions and classification 2003–2004*. Philadelphia, PA: Author.

Pearson, L. S. (1996). A comparison of the ability of foam swabs and toothbrushes to remove dental plaque: Implications for nursing practice. *Journal of Advanced Nursing, 23*(1), 62–69.

Rogers, R. (1996). Hear my plea ... ear care ... continuing education. *Nursing Times, 92*, 36–37.

Rowe, M., & Alfred, D. (1999). The effectiveness of slow-stroke massage in diffusing agitated behaviors in individuals with Alzheimer's disease. *Journal of Gerontological Nursing, 25*(6), 22–34.

Skewes (1994). No more bed baths ... bag bath ... the technique that lessens the risk of skin impairment. *RN, 57*(1), 34–35.

Stone, C. (1999). Preventing cerumen impaction in nursing facility residents. *Journal of Gerontological Nursing, 25*(5), 43–45.

Tombes, M. B., & Galluci, B. (1993, November/December). The effects of hydrogen peroxide rinses on the normal oral mucosa. *Nursing Research, 42*(6), 334–337.

Winslow, E. G. (1994). Don't use H_2O_2 for oral care. *American Journal of Nursing, 94*(3), Nurse Pract. Extra Ed., 19.

WEBLINKS

Health Canada Promotion Branch
http://www.hc-sc.gc.ca/hppb/
Health Promotion Online (HPO), Health Canada, is Health Canada's health promotion branch on the Internet. HPO gives health promoters the resources they need in an easy-to-use, bilingual Web site.

Health Canada
http://www.hc-sc.gc.ca/english/iyh/index.html
Health Canada online provides a resource called *It's Your Health* that provides information on prevention and information of disease, the environment, food (storage and safety), lifestyle choices, medical treatment (devices and drugs), and consumer products and hobbies.

CHAPTER 35

Fecal Elimination

OBJECTIVES

After completing this chapter, you will be able to:

- Describe the functions of the lower intestinal tract.
- Identify factors that influence fecal elimination and patterns of defecation.
- Distinguish normal from abnormal characteristics and constituents of feces.
- Outline methods used to assess the intestinal tract.
- Differentiate five common fecal elimination problems.
- Identify common causes and effects of selected fecal elimination problems.
- List examples of nursing diagnoses for clients with elimination problems.
- Discuss measures that maintain normal fecal elimination patterns.
- Relate common interventions to specific fecal elimination problems.
- Describe essentials of stoma care for clients with ostomies.
- State desired outcomes essential for evaluating the client's progress.

The elimination of feces is a prominent public topic in North America. Laxative advertisements describing such feelings as tiredness due to irregularity keep the subject in the public consciousness. Some older adults are preoccupied with their bowels. People who have had a bowel movement once a day for 75 years can view missing one day as a serious problem, even though they may not have eaten anything for two days and, thus, have little fecal matter to eliminate.

Nurses frequently are consulted or involved in assisting clients with elimination problems. These problems can be embarrassing to clients and can cause considerable discomfort.

Physiology of Defecation

Elimination of the waste products of digestion from the body is essential to health. The excreted waste products are referred to as **feces** or **stool.**

Large Intestine

The large intestine extends from the ileocecal (ileocolic) valve, which lies between the small and large intestines, to the anus. The colon (large intestine) in the adult is generally about 125 to 150 cm long. It has seven parts: the cecum; ascending, transverse, and descending colons; sigmoid colon; rectum; and anus or external orifice (Figure 35.1).

The large intestine is a muscular tube lined with mucous membrane (Figure 35.2). The muscle fibres are both circular and longitudinal, permitting the intestine to enlarge and contract in both width and length. The longitudinal muscles are shorter than the colon and, therefore, cause the large intestine to form pouches, or **haustra.**

The colon's main functions are the absorption of water and nutrients, the mucal protection of the intestinal wall, and fecal elimination. The contents of the colon normally represent foods ingested over the previous four days, although most of the waste products are excreted within 48 hours of **ingestion** (the act of taking food). The digestion products leaving the stomach through the small intestine and then passing through the ileocecal valve are called **chyme.** The colon absorbs water and significant amounts of sodium and chloride as food passes along it. As much as 1,500 mL of chyme passes into the large intestine daily, and all but about 100 mL is absorbed in the proximal half of the colon. The 100 mL of fluid is excreted in the feces (Guyton & Hall, 2000).

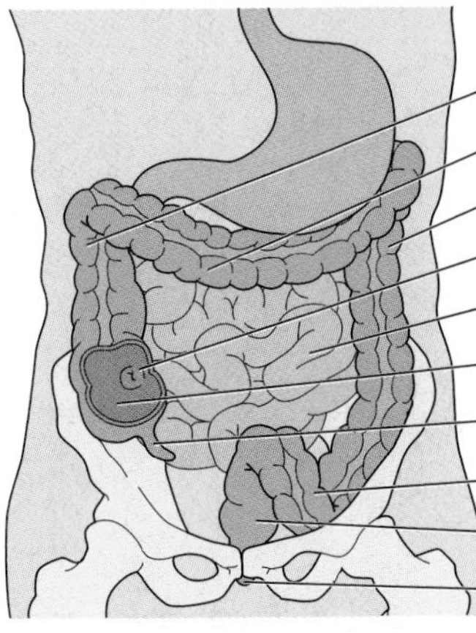

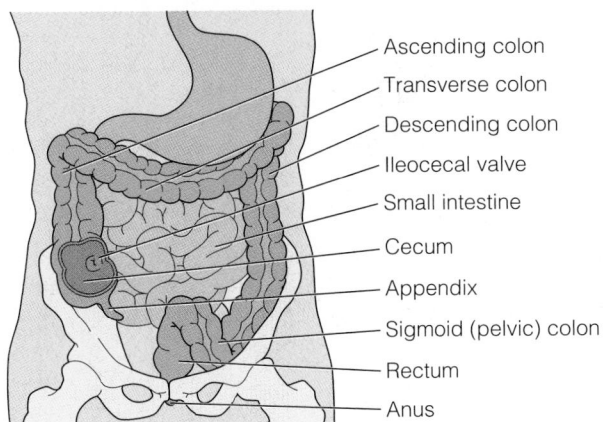

Figure 35.1 The large intestine and rectum

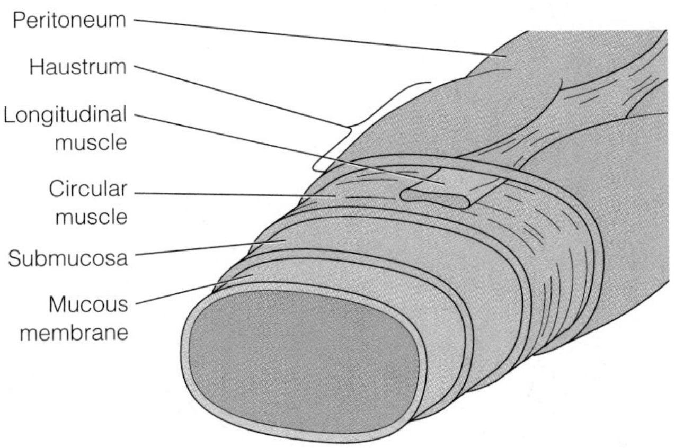

Figure 35.2 The layers of the wall of the large intestine

The colon also serves a protective function in that it secretes mucus. This mucus contains large amounts of bicarbonate ions. The mucus secretion is stimulated by excitation of parasympathetic nerves. During extreme stimulation—for example, as a result of emotions—large amounts of mucus are secreted, resulting in the passage of stringy mucus with little or no feces. Mucus serves to protect the wall of the large intestine from trauma by the acids formed in the feces, and it serves as an adherent for holding the fecal material together. Mucus also protects the intestinal wall from bacterial activity.

The colon acts to transport along its lumen the products of digestion, which are eventually eliminated through the anal canal. These products are flatus and feces. Flatus is largely air and the byproducts of the digestion of carbohydrates. Three types of movement occur in the large intestine: haustral churning, colon peristalsis, and mass peristalsis (Figure 35.3). **Haustral churning** or **shuffling** involves movement of the chyme back and forth within the haustra. In addition to mixing the contents, this action aids in the absorption of water and moves the contents forward to the next haustra. **Peristalsis** is wavelike movement produced by the circular and longitudinal muscle fibres of the intestinal walls; it propels the intestinal contents forward. Colon peristalsis is very sluggish and is thought to move the chyme very little along the large intestine. **Mass peristalsis,** the third type of colonic movement, involves a wave of powerful muscular contraction that moves over large areas of the colon. Usually,

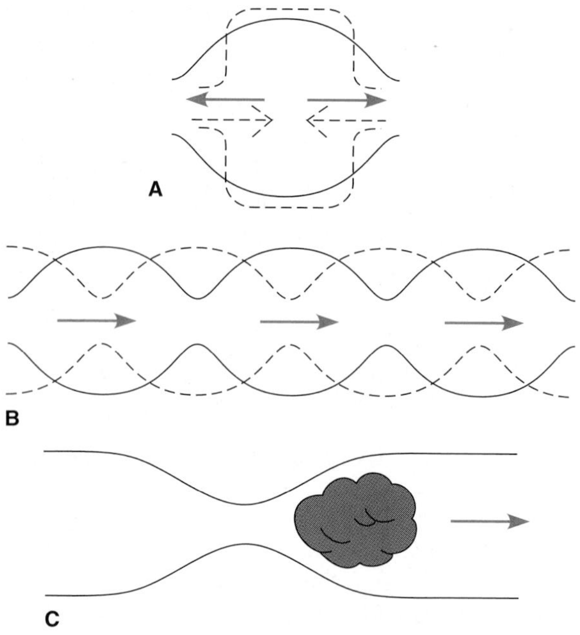

Figure 35.3 Three types of intestinal movements: *A*, haustral churning; *B*, peristalsis; *C*, mass peristalsis

mass peristalsis occurs after eating, stimulated by the presence of food in the stomach and small intestine. In adults, mass peristaltic waves occur only a few times a day.

Rectum and Anal Canal

The rectum in the adult is usually 10 to 15 cm long; the most distal portion, 2.5 to 5 cm long, is the anal canal. In the rectum are three folds of tissue that extend across the rectum and several folds that extend vertically. Each of the vertical folds contains a vein and an artery. It is believed that these folds help retain feces within the rectum. When the veins become distended, as can occur with repeated pressure, a condition known as **hemorrhoids** occurs.

The anal canal is bounded by an internal and an external sphincter muscle (Figure 35.4). The *internal sphincter* is under involuntary control, and the *external sphincter* normally is voluntarily controlled. The external sphincter's action is augmented by the levator ani muscles of the pelvic floor. The internal sphincter muscle is innervated by the autonomic nervous system; the external sphincter is innervated by the somatic nervous system.

Defecation

Defecation is the expulsion of feces from the anus and rectum. It is also called a *bowel movement.* The frequency of defecation is highly individual, varying from several times per day to two or three times per week. The amount defecated also varies from person to person. When peristaltic waves move the feces into the sigmoid colon and the rectum, the sensory nerves in the rectum are stimulated and the individual becomes aware of the need to defecate.

When the *internal* anal sphincter relaxes, feces move into the anal canal. After the individual is seated on a toilet or bedpan, the *external* anal sphincter is relaxed voluntarily. Expulsion of the feces is assisted by contraction of the abdominal muscles and the diaphragm, which increases abdominal pressure, and by contraction of the levator ani muscles of the pelvic floor, which moves the feces through the anal canal. Normal defecation is facilitated by (1) thigh flexion, which increases the pressure within the abdomen, and (2) a sitting position, which increases the downward pressure on the rectum.

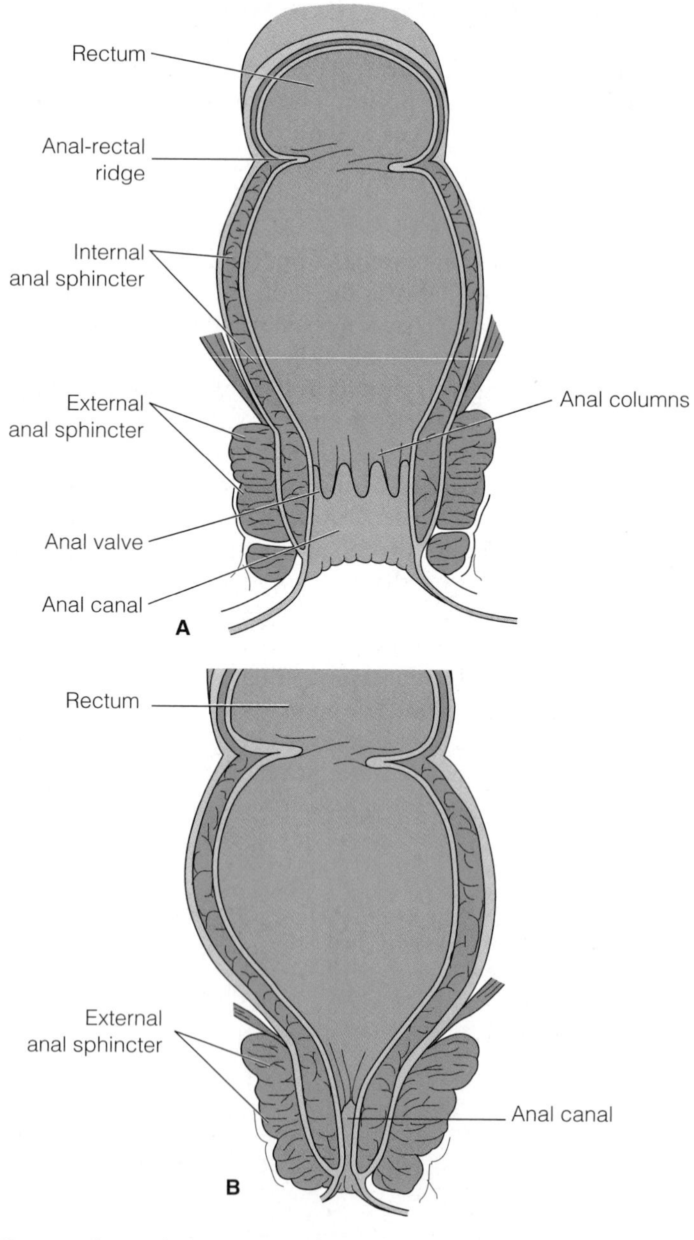

Figure 35.4 The rectum, anal canal, and anal sphincters: *A*, open; *B*, closed

If the defecation reflex is ignored, or if defecation is consciously inhibited by contracting the external sphincter muscle, the urge to defecate normally disappears for a few hours before occurring again. Repeated inhibition of the urge to defecate can result in expansion of the rectum to accommodate accumulated feces and eventual loss of sensitivity to the need to defecate. Constipation can be the ultimate result.

Feces

Normal feces are made of about 75 percent water and 25 percent solid materials. They are soft but formed. If the feces are propelled very quickly along the large intestine, there is not time for most of the water in the chyme to be absorbed and the feces will be more fluid, containing perhaps 95 percent water. Normal feces require a normal fluid intake; feces that contain less water may be hard and difficult to expel.

Feces are normally brown, chiefly due to the presence of stercobilin and urobilin, which are derived from **bilirubin** (a red pigment in bile). Another factor that affects fecal colour is the action of bacteria, such as *Escherichia coli* or staphylococci, which are normally present in the large intestine. The action of microorganisms on the chyme is also responsible for the odour of feces. See Table 35.1 for characteristics of normal and abnormal feces.

TABLE 35.1 Characteristics of Normal and Abnormal Feces

Characteristic	Normal	Abnormal	Possible Cause
Colour	Adult: brown Infant: yellow	Clay or white	Absence of bile pigment (bile obstruction); diagnostic study using barium
		Black or tarry	Drug (e.g., iron); bleeding from upper gastrointestinal tract (e.g., stomach, small intestine); diet high in red meat and dark green vegetables (e.g., spinach)
		Red	Bleeding from lower gastrointestinal tract (e.g., rectum); some foods (e.g., beets)
		Pale	Malabsorption of fats; diet high in milk and milk products and low in meat
		Orange or green	Intestinal infection
Consistency	Formed, soft, semisolid, moist	Hard, dry	Dehydration; decreased intestinal motility resulting from lack of fibre in diet, lack of exercise, emotional upset, laxative abuse
		Diarrhea	Increased intestinal motility (e.g., due to irritation of the colon by bacteria)
Shape	Cylindrical (contour of rectum), about 2.5 cm in diameter in adults	Narrow, pencil-shaped, or stringlike stool	Obstructive condition of the rectum
Amount	Varies with diet (about 100–400 g per day)		
Odour	Aromatic: affected by ingested food and person's own bacterial flora	Pungent	Infection, blood
Constituents	Small amounts of undigested roughage, sloughed dead bacteria and epithelial cells, fat, protein, dried constituents of digestive juices (e.g., bile pigments), inorganic matter (calcium, phosphates)	Pus	Bacterial infection
		Mucus	Inflammatory condition
		Parasites	
		Blood	Gastrointestinal bleeding
		Large quantities of fat	Malabsorption
		Foreign objects	Accidental ingestion

An adult usually forms 7 to 10 L of flatus (gas) in the large intestine every 24 hours. The gases include carbon dioxide, methane, hydrogen, oxygen, and nitrogen. Some are swallowed with food and fluids taken by mouth; others are formed through the action of bacteria on the chyme in the large intestine; and other gas diffuses from the blood into the gastrointestinal tract.

Factors That Affect Defecation

Defecation patterns vary at different stages of life. Circumstances of diet, fluid intake and output, activity, psychological factors, lifestyle, medications and medical procedures, and disease also affect defecation.

Development

Newborns and Infants

Meconium is the first fecal material passed by the newborn, normally up to 24 hours after birth. It is black, tarry, odourless, and sticky. Transitional stools, which follow for about a week, are generally greenish yellow; they contain mucus and are loose.

Infants pass stool frequently, often after each feeding. Because the intestine is immature, water is not well absorbed and the stool is soft, liquid, and frequent. When the intestine matures, bacterial flora increase. After solid foods are introduced, the stool becomes less frequent and firmer.

Infants who are breast fed have bright yellow to golden feces, and infants who are taking formula will have dark yellow or tan stool that is more formed.

Toddlers

Some control of defecation starts at 1½ to 2 years of age. By this time, children have learned to walk, and the nervous and muscular systems are sufficiently well developed to permit bowel control. A desire to control daytime bowel movements and to use the toilet generally starts when the child becomes aware of (1) the discomfort caused by a soiled diaper, and (2) the sensation that indicates the need for a bowel movement. Daytime control is normally attained by age 2½ after a process of toilet training.

School-Age Children and Adolescents

School-age children and adolescents have similar bowel habits to adults. Patterns of defecation vary in frequency, quantity, and consistency. Some school-age children may delay defecation because of an activity, such as play.

Older Adults

Constipation is a common problem in the older adult population. Many older people believe that "regularity" means a bowel movement every day. Those who do not meet this criterion often seek over-the-counter preparations to relieve what they believe to be constipation. Older clients should be advised that normal patterns of bowel elimination vary considerably. For some, a normal pattern may be every other day; for others, twice a day. Adequate roughage in the diet, adequate exercise, and six to eight glasses of fluid daily are essential preventive measures of constipation. A cup of hot water or tea at a regular time in the morning is helpful for some. Responding to the **gastrocolic reflex** (increased peristalsis of the colon after food has entered the stomach) is also an important consideration.

The older adult should be warned that consistent use of laxatives inhibits natural defecation reflexes and is thought to cause, rather than cure, constipation. The habitual user of laxatives eventually requires larger or stronger doses because the effect is progressively reduced with continual use. Laxatives may also interfere with the body's electrolyte balance and decrease the absorption of certain vitamins. The reasons for constipation can range from lifestyle habits (e.g., lack of exercise) to serious malignant disorders. The nurse should evaluate any complaints of constipation carefully for each individual. A change in bowel habits over several weeks with or without weight loss, pain, or fever should be referred to a physician for a complete medical evaluation.

Diet

Sufficient bulk (cellulose, fibre) in the diet is necessary to provide fecal volume. Bland diets and low-fibre diets are lacking in bulk and, therefore, create insufficient residue of waste products to stimulate the reflex for defecation. Low-residue foods, such as rice, eggs, and lean meats, move more slowly through the intestinal tract. Increasing fluid intake with such foods increases their rate of movement.

Certain foods are difficult or impossible for some people to digest. This inability results in digestive upsets and, in some instances, the passage of watery stools. Irregular eating can also impair regular defecation. Individuals who eat at the same times every day usually have a regularly timed, physiological response to the food intake and a regular pattern of peristaltic activity in the colon.

Spicy foods can produce diarrhea and flatus in some individuals. Excessive sugar can also cause diarrhea. Other foods that may influence bowel elimination include the following:

- Gas-producing foods, such as cabbage, onions, cauliflower, bananas, and apples
- Laxative-producing foods, such as bran, prunes, figs, chocolate, and alcohol
- Constipation-producing foods, such as cheese, pasta, eggs, and lean meat

Fluid

When fluid intake is inadequate or output (urine or vomitus, for example) is excessive for some reason, the body continues to absorb fluid from the chyme as it passes along the colon. As a result, the chyme becomes drier than normal, resulting in hard feces. In addition, reduced fluid intake slows the chyme's passage along the intestines, further increasing the reabsorption of fluid from the chyme. Healthy fecal elimination usually requires a daily fluid intake of 2,000 to 3,000 mL. If chyme moves abnormally quickly through the large intestine, however, there is less time for fluid to be absorbed into the blood; as a result, the feces are soft or even watery.

Activity

Activity stimulates peristalsis, thus facilitating the movement of chyme along the colon. Weak abdominal and pelvic muscles are often ineffective in increasing the intra-abdominal pressure during defecation or in controlling defecation. Weak muscles can result from lack of exercise, immobility, or impaired neurological functioning. Clients confined to bed are often constipated.

Psychological Factors

Some people who are anxious or angry experience increased peristaltic activity and subsequent diarrhea. In contrast, people who are depressed may experience slower intestinal motility, resulting in constipation.

Defecation Habits

Early bowel training may establish the habit of defecating at a regular time. Many people defecate after breakfast, when the gastrocolic reflex causes mass peristaltic waves in the large intestine. If a person ignores this urge to defecate, water continues to be absorbed, making the feces hard and difficult to expel. When the normal defecation reflexes are inhibited or ignored, these conditioned reflexes tend to be progressively weakened. When habitually ignored, the urge to defecate is ultimately lost. Adults may ignore these reflexes because of the pressures of time or work. Hospitalized clients may suppress the urge because of embarrassment about using a bedpan or lack of privacy or because defecation is too uncomfortable.

Medications

Some drugs have side effects that can interfere with normal elimination. Some cause diarrhea; others, such as large doses of certain tranquilizers and repeated administration of morphine and codeine, cause constipation because they decrease gastrointestinal activity through their action on the central nervous system. Iron tablets, which have an astringent effect, act more locally on the bowel mucosa to cause constipation.

Some medications directly affect elimination. **Laxatives** are medications that stimulate bowel activity and so assist fecal elimination. Other medications soften stool, facilitating defecation. Certain medications, such as dicyclomine hydrochloride (Bentyl), suppress peristaltic activity and sometimes are used to treat diarrhea.

Some medications affect the appearance of the feces. Any drug that causes gastrointestinal bleeding (e.g., aspirin products) can cause the stool to be red or black. Iron salts may cause the stool to be black because of the oxidation of the iron; antibiotics may cause a grey-green discolouration because of effects on digestion; and antacids may cause a whitish discolouration or white specks in the stool.

Diagnostic Procedures

Before certain diagnostic procedures, such as visualization of the sigmoid colon (sigmoidoscopy), the client is often restricted from ingesting food or fluid preceding the examination. The client may also be given a cleansing enema prior to the examination. In these instances, the client usually will not defecate normally until eating has been resumed.

Anesthesia and Surgery

General anesthetics cause the normal colonic movements to cease or slow down by blocking parasympathetic stimulation to the muscles of the colon. Clients who have regional or spinal anesthesia are less likely to experience this problem.

Surgery that involves direct handling of the intestines can cause temporary cessation of intestinal movement. This condition, called *paralytic ileus,* usually lasts 24 to 48 hours. Listening for bowel sounds that reflect intestinal motility is an important nursing assessment following surgery. See Chapter 27 for assessment of bowel sounds.

Pathological Conditions

Spinal cord injuries and head injuries can decrease the sensory stimulation for defecation. Impaired mobility may limit the client's ability to respond to the urge to defecate when the client is unable to reach a toilet or summon assistance. As a result, the client may experience constipation. Or, a client may experience fecal incontinence because of poorly functioning anal sphincters (see page 863).

Pain

Clients who experience discomfort when defecating (e.g., following hemorrhoid surgery) often suppress the urge to defecate to avoid the pain. Such clients can experience constipation as a result.

Common Fecal Elimination Problems

Five common problems are related to fecal elimination: constipation, fecal impaction, diarrhea, bowel incontinence, and flatulence.

Constipation

Constipation is defined as fewer than three bowel movements per week (Vickery, 1997). This infers the passage of small, dry, hard stool or the passage of no stool for a period of time. It occurs when the movement of feces through the large intestine is slow, thus allowing time for additional absorption of fluid from the large intestine. Associated with constipation are difficult evacuation of stool and increased effort or straining of the voluntary muscles of defecation. The person may also have a feeling of incomplete stool evacuation after defecation. It is important to define constipation in relation to the person's regular elimination pattern. Some people normally defecate only a few times a week; other people defecate more than once a day. Careful assessment of the person's habits is necessary before a diagnosis of constipation is made. See the box below for frequent defining characteristics of constipation.

Many causes and factors contribute to constipation. Among them are the following:

- Insufficient fibre intake
- Insufficient fluid intake
- Insufficient activity or immobility
- Irregular defecation habits
- Change in daily routine
- Lack of privacy
- Chronic use of laxatives or enemas
- Emotional disturbances, such as depression or mental confusion
- Medications, such as opiates or iron salts

Constipation can be hazardous to some clients. Straining associated with constipation often is accompanied by holding the breath. This Valsalva maneuver can present serious problems to people with heart disease, brain injuries, or respiratory disease. Holding the breath increases the intrathoracic and the intracranial pressures. To some degree, this pressure can be reduced if the person exhales through the mouth while straining. However, avoiding straining altogether is the best precaution.

Defining Characteristics for Constipation

- Decreased frequency of defecation
- Hard, dry, formed stools
- Straining at stool; painful defecation
- Reports of rectal fullness or pressure or incomplete bowel evacuation
- Abdominal pain, cramps, or distention
- Use of laxatives
- Decreased appetite
- Headache

Fecal Impaction

Fecal impaction is a mass or collection of hardened, putty-like feces in the folds of the rectum. Impaction results from prolonged retention and accumulation of fecal material. In severe impactions, the feces accumulate and extend well up into the sigmoid colon and beyond. Fecal impaction is recognized by the passage of liquid fecal seepage (diarrhea) and no normal stool. The liquid portion of the feces seeps out around the impacted mass (Figure 35.5). Impaction can also be assessed by digital examination of the rectum, during which the hardened mass can often be palpated.

Along with fecal seepage and constipation, symptoms include frequent but nonproductive desire to defecate and rectal pain. A generalized feeling of illness results; the client becomes anorexic, the abdomen becomes distended, and nausea and vomiting may occur.

The causes of fecal impaction are usually poor defecation habits and constipation. Certain medications (see previous page) also contribute to impactions. The barium used in radiological examinations of the upper and lower gastrointestinal tracts can be a causative factor. Therefore, after these examinations, measures are usually taken to ensure removal of the barium.

An impaction can sometimes be palpated through the client's abdomen. Digital examination of the impaction through the rectum should be done gently and carefully

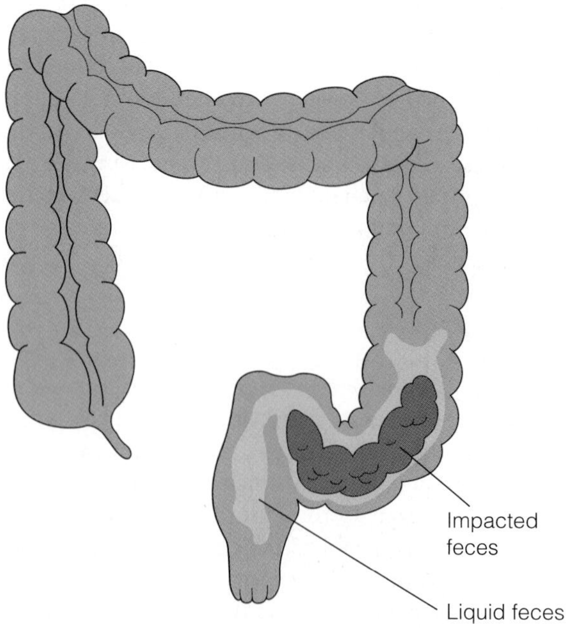

Figure 35.5 A fecal impaction with liquid feces passing around the impaction

because stimulation of the vagus nerve in the rectal wall can slow the client's heart. Some nurses advise against digital rectal examination without a physician's order.

Although fecal impaction can generally be prevented, digital removal of impacted feces is sometimes necessary. When fecal impaction is suspected, the client, as ordered by a physician, is often given an oil retention enema, a cleansing enema two to four hours later, and daily additional cleansing enemas, suppositories, or stool softeners. If these measures fail, manual removal is often necessary.

Diarrhea

Diarrhea refers to the passage of liquid feces and an increased frequency of defecation. It is the opposite of constipation and results from rapid movement of fecal contents through the large intestine. Rapid passage of chyme reduces the time available for the large intestine to absorb water and electrolytes. Some people pass stool with increased frequency, but diarrhea is not present unless the stool is relatively unformed and excessively liquid. The person with diarrhea finds it difficult or impossible to control the urge to defecate for very long. Diarrhea and the threat of incontinence are sources of concern and embarrassment. Often, spasmodic cramps are associated with diarrhea. Bowel sounds are increased (see Chapter 27). Sometimes the client passes blood and excessive mucus; nausea and vomiting may also occur. With persistent diarrhea, irritation of the anal region extending to the perineum and buttocks generally results. Fatigue, weakness, malaise, and emaciation are the results of prolonged diarrhea.

When the cause of diarrhea is irritants in the intestinal tract, diarrhea is thought to be a protective flushing mechanism. It can create serious fluid and electrolyte losses in the body, however, that can develop within frighteningly short periods of time, particularly in infants and small children. Table 35.2 lists some of the major causes of diarrhea and the physiological responses of the body.

TABLE 35.2 Major Causes of Diarrhea

Cause	Physiological Effect
Psychological stress (e.g., anxiety)	Increased intestinal motility and mucus secretion
Medications	
Antibiotics	Inflammation and infection of mucosa due to overgrowth of pathogenic intestinal microorganisms
Iron	Irritation of intestinal mucosa
Cathartics	Irritation of intestinal mucosa
Allergy to food, fluid, drugs	Incomplete digestion of food or fluid
Intolerance of food or fluid	Increased intestinal motility and mucus secretion
Diseases of the colon, e.g.,	
Malabsorption syndrome	Reduced absorption of fluids
Crohn's disease	Inflammation of the mucosa often leading to ulcer formation
Others	
Surgical operations	Variable

Bowel Incontinence

Bowel incontinence, also called **fecal incontinence,** refers to the loss of voluntary ability to control fecal and gaseous discharges through the anal sphincter. The incontinence may occur at specific times, such as after meals, or it may occur irregularly. Two types of bowel incontinence are described: partial and major. *Partial incontinence* is the inability to control flatus or to prevent minor soiling. *Major incontinence* is the inability to control feces of normal consistency.

Fecal incontinence is generally associated with impaired functioning of the anal sphincter or its nerve supply, such as in some neuromuscular diseases, spinal cord trauma, and tumours of the external anal sphincter muscle.

Fecal incontinence is an emotionally distressing problem that can ultimately lead to social isolation. Afflicted persons withdraw into their homes or, if in the hospital, the confines of their room to minimize the embarrassment associated with soiling. Such people may come to prefer easily washable night garments to street clothes. Incontinent feces are acidic and contain digestive enzymes that are highly irritating to skin. Therefore, the area around the anal region should be kept clean and dry and be protected with zinc oxide or other ointment. In addition, a rectal pouch can be used. See page 882 for details. Several surgical procedures are also used for the treatment of fecal incontinence. These include repair of the sphincter and fecal diversion or colostomy.

Flatulence

Air or gas in the gastrointestinal tract is called **flatus.** There are three primary causes of flatus: (1) action of bacteria on the chyme in the large intestine, (2) swallowed air, and (3) gas that diffuses from the bloodstream into the intestine.

Flatulence is the presence of *excessive* flatus in the intestines and leads to stretching and inflation of the intestines *(intestinal distention).* This condition is also referred to as *abdominal distention.* Large amounts of air and other gases can accumulate in the stomach, resulting in gastric distention.

Most gases that are swallowed are expelled through the mouth by **eructation** (belching). The gases formed in the large intestine are chiefly absorbed through the intestinal capillaries into the circulation. Flatulence can occur in the colon, however, from a variety of causes, such as foods (e.g., cabbage, onions), abdominal surgery, or narcotics. If the gas is propelled by increased colon activity before it can be absorbed, it may be expelled through the anus. If excessive gas cannot be expelled through the anus, it may be necessary to insert a rectal tube or provide a return flow enema to remove it.

Bowel Diversion Ostomies

An **ostomy** is an opening on the abdominal wall for the elimination of feces or urine. There are many types of ostomies. A **gastrostomy** is an opening through the abdominal wall into the stomach. A **jejunostomy** is an opening through the abdominal wall into the jejunum. An **ileostomy** is an opening into the ileum (small bowel). A **colostomy** is an opening into the colon (large bowel). A **ureterostomy** is an opening into the ureter. Gastrostomies and jejunostomies are generally performed to provide an alternative feeding route. The purpose of bowel and urinary ostomies is to divert and drain fecal or urinary material. Urinary diversion ostomies are discussed in Chapter 36. Bowel diversion ostomies are often classified according to (1) their status as permanent or temporary, (2) their anatomic location, and (3) the construction of the **stoma,** the opening created in the abdominal wall by the ostomy.

Permanence

Colostomies can be either temporary or permanent. Temporary colostomies are generally performed for traumatic injuries or inflammatory conditions of the bowel. They allow the distal diseased portion of the bowel to rest and heal. Permanent colostomies are performed to provide a means of elimination when the rectum or anus is nonfunctional as a result of a birth defect or a disease, such as cancer of the bowel. The diseased portion may or may not be removed.

Anatomic Location

An ileostomy generally empties from the distal end of the small intestine. A cecostomy empties from the cecum (the first part of the ascending colon). An ascending colostomy empties from the ascending colon. A transverse colostomy empties from the transverse colon. A descending colostomy empties from the descending colon. A sigmoidostomy empties from the sigmoid colon (Figure 35.6).

The location of the ostomy influences the character and management of the fecal drainage. The farther along the bowel, the more formed is the stool because the large bowel absorbs water from the fecal mass. In addition, more control over the frequency of stomal discharge can be established. For example:

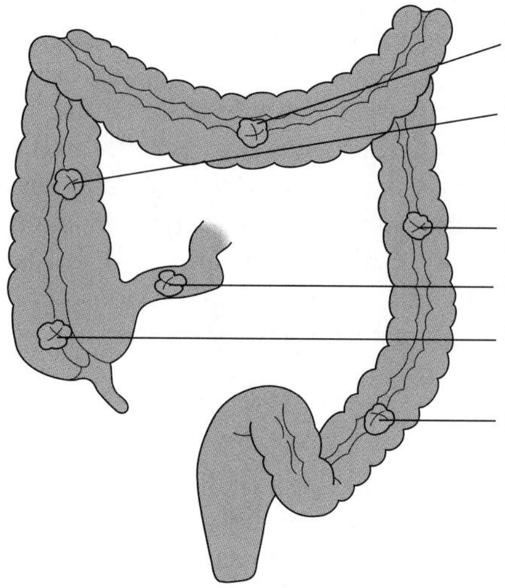

Figure 35.6 The locations of bowel diversion ostomies

- An ileostomy produces liquid fecal drainage. Drainage is constant and cannot be regulated. Ileostomy drainage contains some digestive enzymes, which are damaging to the skin. For this reason, ileostomy clients must wear an appliance continuously and take special precautions to prevent skin breakdown. Compared with colostomies, however, odour is minimal because fewer bacteria are present.
- An ascending colostomy is similar to an ileostomy in that the drainage is liquid and cannot be regulated, and digestive enzymes are present. Odour, however, is a problem requiring control (e.g., a deodorant inside the appliance).
- A transverse colostomy produces a malodorous, mushy drainage because some of the liquid has been absorbed. There is usually no control.
- A descending colostomy produces increasingly solid fecal drainage. Stools from a sigmoidostomy are of normal or formed consistency, and the frequency of discharge can be regulated. People with a sigmoidostomy may not have to wear an appliance at all times, and odours can usually be controlled.

The length of time that an ostomy is in place also helps determine the consistency of the stool, particularly with transverse and descending colostomies. Over time, the stool becomes more formed because the remaining functioning portions of the colon tend to compensate by increasing water absorption.

Construction of the Stoma

Stoma constructions are described as single, loop, divided, or double-barrelled colostomies. The *single* stoma is created when one end of bowel is brought out through an opening onto the anterior abdominal wall. This is referred to as an *end* or *terminal* colostomy; the stoma is permanent (Figure 35.7).

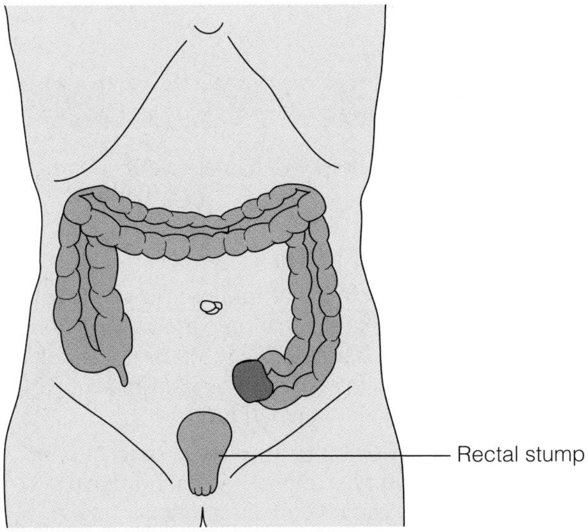

Figure 35.7 End colostomy: the diseased portion of bowel is removed and a rectal pouch remains

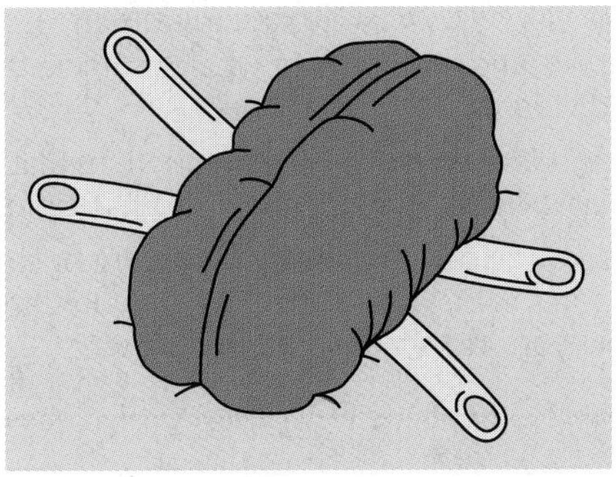

Figure 35.8 Loop colostomy with support device placed to maintain position of the bowel on the abdomen

In the *loop colostomy*, a loop of bowel is brought out onto the abdominal wall and supported by a plastic bridge, a glass rod, or a piece of rubber tubing (Figure 35.8). A loop stoma has two openings: (1) the proximal or afferent end, which is active, and (2) the distal or efferent end, which is inactive. The loop colostomy is usually performed in an emergency procedure and is often situated on the right transverse colon. It is a bulky stoma that is more difficult to manage than a single stoma.

The *divided colostomy* consists of two edges of bowel brought out onto the abdomen but separated from each other (Figure 35.9). The opening from the digestive or proximal end is the colostomy. The distal end in this situation is often referred to as a mucous fistula, since this section of bowel continues to secrete mucus. The divided colostomy is often used in situations where spillage of feces into the distal end of the bowel needs to be avoided.

The *double-barrelled colostomy* resembles a double-barrelled shotgun (Figure 35.10). In this type of colostomy, the proximal and distal loops of bowel are sutured together for about 10 cm and both ends are brought up onto the abdominal wall.

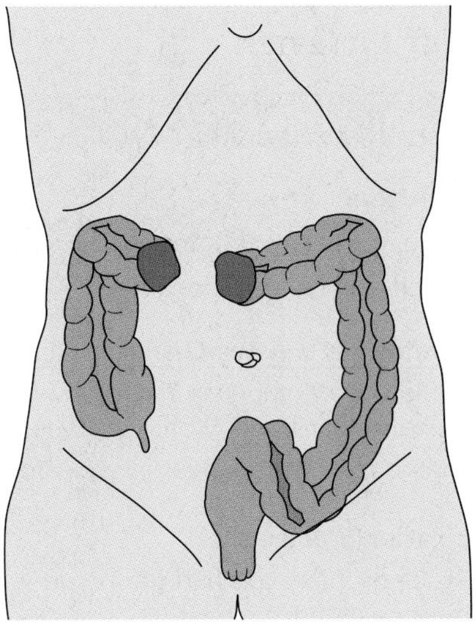

Figure 35.9 Divided colostomy with two separated stomas

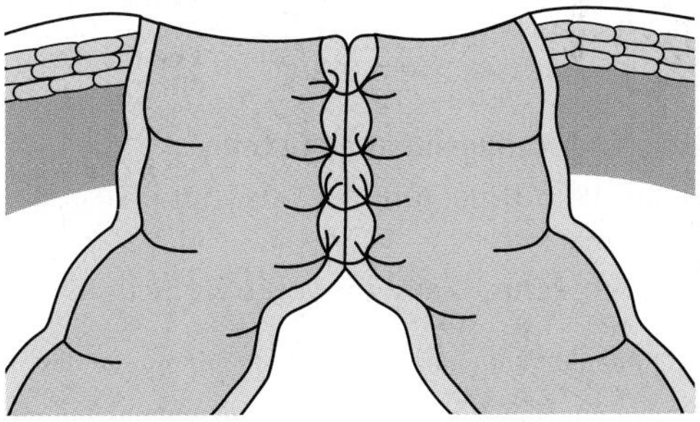

Figure 35.10 Double-barrelled colostomy

Assessing

Assessment of fecal elimination includes taking a nursing history; performing a physical examination of the abdomen, rectum, and anus; and inspecting the feces. The nurse also should review any data obtained from relevant diagnostic tests.

Nursing History

A nursing history for fecal elimination helps the nurse ascertain the client's normal pattern. The nurse elicits a description of usual feces and any recent changes and collects information about any past or current problems with elimination, the presence of an ostomy, and factors influencing the elimination pattern.

Examples of interview questions to elicit this information are shown in the next box. The number of questions to ask is adapted to the individual client according to the client's responses in the first three categories. For example, questions about factors influencing elimination might be addressed only to clients who are experiencing problems.

ASSESSMENT INTERVIEW

Fecal Elimination

Defecation Pattern

- What is the frequency and time of day of defecation?
- Has this pattern changed recently?

Description of Feces and Any Changes

- How would you describe your stool in terms of colour, texture (hard, soft, watery), shape, odour?
- Have you noticed any changes in your stool recently?

Fecal Elimination Problems

- What problems have you had or do you now have with your bowel movements? (constipation, diarrhea, excessive flatulence, seepage or incontinence)
- When and how often does it occur?
- What causes it? (food, fluids, exercise, emotions, medications, disease, surgery)
- What methods have you used to remedy the problem, and how effective were they?

Presence and Management of Ostomy

- What is your usual routine with your colostomy/ileostomy?
- What problems, if any, do you have with it?
- How can the nurses help you manage your colostomy/ileostomy?

Factors Influencing Elimination

- *Use of elimination aids.* What routines do you follow to maintain your usual defecation pattern? Do you use natural aids, such as specific foods or fluids (e.g., a glass of hot lemon juice before breakfast), laxatives, or enemas to maintain elimination?
- *Diet.* What foods do you believe affect defecation? What foods do you typically eat? What foods do you always avoid? Do you take meals at regular times?
- *Fluid.* What amount and kind of fluid do you take each day (e.g., six glasses of water, five cups of coffee)?
- *Exercise.* What is your usual daily exercise pattern? (Obtain specifics about exercise, rather than asking whether it is sufficient; ideas of what is sufficient vary among individuals.)
- *Medications.* Have you taken any medications that could affect the gastrointestinal tract (e.g., iron, antibiotics)?
- *Stress.* Are you experiencing any long-term or short-term stressors? If so, what are these? Do you think these affect your defecation pattern? How?

When eliciting data about the client's defecation pattern, the nurse needs to understand that the time of defecation and the amount of feces expelled are as individual as the frequency of defecation. Often, the patterns individuals follow depend largely on early training and on convenience. Most people develop the habit of defecating after breakfast, when the gastrocolic reflex causes mass movements in the large intestine.

Physical Examination

Physical examination of the abdomen, rectum, and anus is discussed in Chapter 27. Physical examination of the abdomen in relation to fecal elimination problems includes inspection, auscultation, percussion, and palpation with specific reference to the intestinal tract. Auscultation precedes palpation because palpation can alter peristalsis. Examination of the rectum and anus includes inspection and palpation.

Inspecting the Feces

The client's stool is inspected for colour, consistency, shape, amount, odour, and the presence of abnormal constituents. See Table 35.1 earlier for a summary of normal and abnormal characteristics of stool and possible causes.

Diagnostic Studies

Diagnostic studies of the gastrointestinal tract include direct visualization techniques, indirect visualization techniques, and laboratory tests for abnormal constituents.

Visualization Techniques

Direct visualization techniques include **anoscopy,** the viewing of the anal canal; **proctoscopy,** the viewing of the rectum; **proctosigmoidoscopy,** the viewing of the rectum and sigmoid colon; and **colonoscopy,** the viewing of the large intestine. *Indirect visualization* of the gastrointestinal tract is achieved by roentgenography. Radiographs of the gastrointestinal tract can detect strictures, obstructions, tumours, ulcers, inflammatory disease, or other structural changes, such as hiatal hernias. Visualization of the tract is enhanced by the introduction of a radiopaque substance, such as barium. For examination of the upper gastrointestinal tract or small bowel, the client drinks the barium sulfate. This examination is often referred to as a "barium swallow." For examination of the lower gastrointestinal tract, the client is given an enema containing barium. This examination is commonly referred to as a "barium enema." These radiographs usually include *fluoroscopic examination;* that is, projection of the x-ray films onto a screen that permits continuous observation of the flow of barium.

Laboratory Tests

Collecting Stool Specimens The nurse is responsible for collecting stool specimens ordered for laboratory analysis. Before obtaining a specimen, the nurse needs to determine the reason for collecting the stool specimen and the correct method of obtaining and handling it (i.e., how much stool to obtain, whether a preservative needs to be added to the stool, and whether it needs to be sent immediately to the laboratory). It may be necessary to confirm this information by checking with the agency laboratory. In many situations, only a single specimen is required; in others, timed specimens are necessary, and every stool passed is collected within a designated time period.

Nurses need to give clients the following instructions:

- Defecate in a clean bedpan or bedside commode.
- Do not contaminate the specimen, if possible, by urine or menstrual discharge. Void before the specimen collection.
- Do not place toilet tissue in the bedpan after defecation. Contents of the paper can affect the laboratory analysis.
- Notify the nurse as soon as possible after defecation, particularly for specimens that need to be sent to the laboratory immediately.

To secure a stool specimen from a baby or young child who is not toilet trained, the nurse obtains newly passed feces from the diaper.

When obtaining stool samples, that is, when handling the client's bedpan, when transferring the stool sample to a specimen container, and when disposing of the bedpan contents, the nurse follows medical aseptic technique meticulously. Wear disposable gloves to prevent hand contamination, and take care not to contaminate the outside of the specimen container. Use one or two clean tongue blades to transfer the specimen to the container and then wrap them in a paper towel before disposing of them in the waste container. This practice lessens the chance of contact with other articles and the spread of microorganisms. The amount of stool to be sent depends on the purpose for which the specimen is collected. Usually about 2.5 cm of formed stool or 15 to 30 mL of liquid stool is adequate. For some timed specimens, however, the entire passed stool may need to be sent. Visible pus, mucus, or blood should be included in sample specimens. For a stool culture, the nurse dips a sterile swab into the specimen, preferably where purulent fecal matter is present, and using sterile technique, places the swab in a sterile test tube.

Because fresh specimens provide the most accurate results, the nurse sends the specimen to the laboratory immediately. If this is not possible, the nurse follows the directions on the specimen container. In some instances, refrigeration is indicated because bacteriological changes take place in stool specimens left at room temperature.

Testing Feces for Occult Blood Stool is tested for **occult** (hidden) **blood** to detect gastrointestinal bleeding not visible to the eye. Bleeding can occur as a result of ulcers, inflammatory disease, or tumours. The test for occult blood, often referred to as the **guaiac test,** can be readily performed by the nurse in the clinical area or by the client at home. Guaiac paper used in the test is sensitive to fecal blood content.

A commonly used test product to measure occult blood is the *Hemoccult test,* which uses a chemical reagent to detect the presence of the enzyme peroxidase in the hemoglobin molecule. To perform the test, the nurse or client uses a

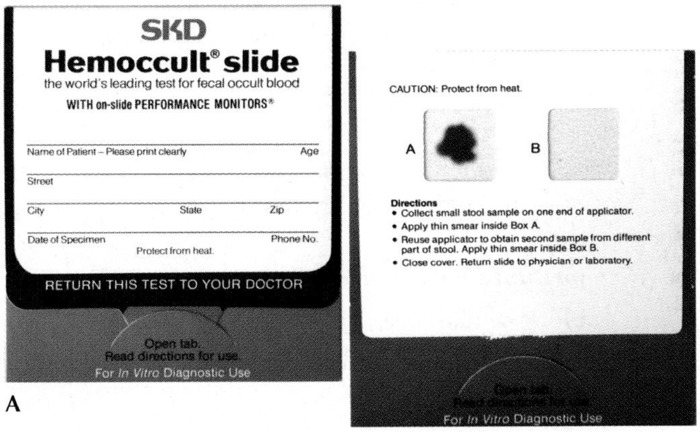

A

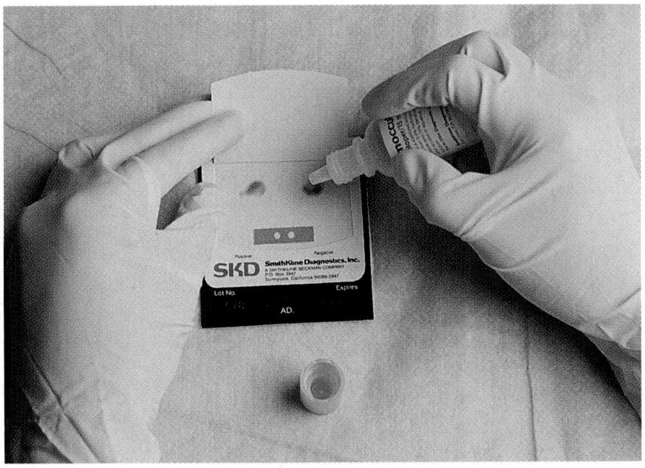

B

Figure 35.11 *A,* The front cover of a Hemoccult slide. A thin smear of feces on the slide; *B,* Opening the flap on the back of the slide and applying two drops of developing fluid over each smear

CLIENT TEACHING

Assessing Stool for Occult Blood

- Avoid restricted foods, medications, and vitamin C for the period recommended by the manufacturer and during the test. Usually, specified foods and vitamin C are restricted for three days before the test and specified medications for seven days before the test, as recommended by the physician.
- Use a ballpoint pen to label the specimens with your name, address, age, and date of specimen. Usually, three specimens are collected from consecutive and different bowel movements. Each specimen must be dated accurately.
- Avoid collecting specimens during your menstrual period and for three days afterward and while you have bleeding hemorrhoids or blood in your urine.
- Remove toilet bowl cleaners from the toilet bowl. Flush the toilet twice before proceeding with the test.
- Avoid contaminating the specimen with urine or toilet tissue. Empty your bladder before the test. To facilitate specimen collection, transfer the stool to a clean, dry container. Wear disposable gloves.
- Use the tongue blade provided to transfer the specimen to the test folder or tape. Only a small amount of stool is required. Take the sample from the centre of a formed stool to ensure a uniform sample.
- Wrap the tongue blade in a paper towel and dispose of it in the waste receptacle. Do not flush the stick.
- Follow the manufacturer's directions explicitly for the test product being used. Test products vary. For example, for the *Hemoccult test,* a thin layer of feces is smeared over the boxes inside the envelope, and a drop of developing solution is applied on the opposite side of the specimen paper. For the *Hematest,* a thin layer of feces is smeared onto guaiac filter paper, a tablet is placed in the middle of the specimen, and two or three drops of water are added to the tablet.
- Consult your health-care provider if there is any problem understanding the instructions.
- Return completed specimens to your physician or laboratory as instructed.

tongue blade to place a small amount of stool on a slide or card, places a few drops of the reagent onto the smear, and then observes for a colour change (Figure 35.11). A blue colour indicates a guaiac-positive result; that is, the presence of occult blood. No colour change or any colour other than blue is a negative finding, indicating the absence of blood in the stool.

Certain foods, medications, and vitamin C can produce inaccurate test results. *False-positive results* can occur if the client has recently ingested (1) red meat (beef, lamb, liver, and processed meats); (2) *raw* vegetables or fruits, particularly radishes, turnips, horseradish, and melons; or (3) certain medications that irritate the gastric mucosa and cause bleeding, such as aspirin or other nonsteroidal anti-inflammatory drugs, steroids, iron preparations, and anticoagulants. *False-negative results* can occur if the client has taken more than 250 mg per day of vitamin C from all sources (dietary and supplemental) up to three days before the test—even if bleeding is present. Guidelines for instructing clients to assess their stool for occult blood are shown in the box above.

Diagnosing

NANDA includes the following diagnostic labels for fecal elimination problems (Carpenito, 2002):

- ***Bowel Incontinence:*** A change in usual bowel habits characterized by involuntary passage of stool
- ***Constipation:*** A change in usual bowel habits characterized by a decrease in frequency and/or passage of hard, dry stools
- ***Risk for Constipation:*** Risk for a decrease in a person's normal frequency of defecation accompanied by difficult or incomplete passage of stool and/or passage of excessively hard, dry stool
- ***Perceived Constipation:*** A self-diagnosis of constipation; a daily bowel movement is ensured through abuse of laxatives, enemas, or suppositories
- ***Diarrhea:*** Passage of loose, unformed stools

Defining characteristics and etiologies of these diagnostic labels are discussed earlier (see "Common Fecal Elimination Problems"). Clinical application of these diagnoses are shown in Table 35.3.

Fecal elimination problems may affect many other areas of human functioning. Examples of possible nursing diagnoses include:

- ***Risk for Fluid Volume Deficient*** related to
  a. Prolonged diarrhea
  b. Abnormal fluid loss through ostomy
- ***Risk for Impaired Skin Integrity*** related to
  a. Prolonged diarrhea
  b. Bowel incontinence
  c. Bowel diversion ostomy

HOME CARE ASSESSMENT

Fecal Elimination

Client and Environment

- *Self-care abilities for toileting:* Ability to get to the toilet, to manipulate clothing for toileting, to perform toilet hygiene, and to flush the toilet
- *Mechanical aids required:* Walker, cane, wheelchair, raised toilet seat, grab bars, bedpan, commode
- *Mechanical barriers that limit access to the toilet or are unsafe:* Poor lighting, cluttered pathway to bathroom, narrow doorway for wheelchair, and so on
- *Bowel elimination problem:* Alterations in characteristics of feces, diarrhea, constipation, incontinence, presence of ostomy, and methods of handling these
- *Level of knowledge:* Planned bowel management or training program; prescribed medications; ostomy care; dietary alterations; and fluid and exercise requirements or restrictions
- *Facilities:* Adequacy of bathroom facilities to facilitate toilet hygiene and ostomy care, and to contain potentially infectious fecal effluent or stool

Family

- *Caregiver availability and skills:* People able to assist with toileting, medications, ostomy care, or other prescribed therapeutic measures
- *Family role changes and coping:* Effect on financial status, parenting and spousal roles, sexuality, social roles
- *Alternative potential primary or respite caregivers:* For example, other family members, volunteers, church members, paid caregivers or housekeeping services; available community respite care (adult day care, senior centres)

Community

- *Availability of and familiarity with possible sources of assistance:* Equipment and supply companies, financial assistance, home health-care agencies

TABLE 35.3 Clinical Application: Assessment Data Clusters and Related Nursing Diagnoses

Data Cluster	Nursing Diagnosis
Mrs. Amy Ballaster states she feels fullness in her rectum and wants to move her bowels but cannot, even with straining. Her last bowel movement was three days ago. She lives alone and tends to eat only tea, toast, and noodle soup. Because of arthritis, her activities (gardening and walking) have decreased. Bowel sounds are decreased.	***Constipation*** related to inadequate physical activity and insufficient fibre in diet
Marvin Lombardi reports having loose, liquid, light brown stools for two days. Passage of stools is associated with cramping abdominal pain. Bowel sounds are increased. Temperature is 38°C. He has not taken any medications but reports a feeling of general malaise. He states he "ate at a fast-food restaurant two nights ago."	***Diarrhea*** of unknown etiology, possibly related to spoiled food
Mary Kuoko has had involuntary leakage of stool. She states her clothing is soiled several times a day. She says she is too embarrassed to go out with her friends because of the fecal odour. Last bowel movement was more than three days ago. Digital examination reveals impaction.	***Bowel Incontinence*** related to fecal impaction
Mr. Dan Deer had a bowel diversion ostomy two days ago. Effluent is continuous and liquid. Peristomal skin is intact. Disposable colostomy device was applied.	***Risk for Impaired Skin Integrity*** related to discharge from bowel diversion ostomy

- ***Self-Esteem, Situational Low*** related to
  a. Ostomy
  b. Fecal incontinence
  c. Need for assistance with toileting
- ***Knowledge Deficient*** (bowel training, ostomy management) related to lack of previous experience
- ***Anxiety*** related to
  a. Lack of control of fecal elimination secondary to ostomy
  b. Response of others to ostomy

Based upon the assessment, a nurse may formulate other diagnoses independent of NANDA.

Planning

The major goals for clients with fecal elimination problems are to:

- Maintain or restore normal bowel elimination pattern.
- Maintain or regain normal stool consistency.
- Prevent associated risks, such as fluid and electrolyte imbalance, skin breakdown, abdominal distention, and pain.

Examples of desired outcomes related to each of these goals, although established in the planning phase, are provided in Table 35.6 in the "Evaluating" section of this chapter.

Appropriate nursing interventions that relate to these broad goals must be identified. Preventive and corrective interventions need to be included. The Iowa Intervention Project's Nursing Interventions Classification can be used to plan nursing interventions (McCloskey & Bulechek, 2000). Examples of NIC interventions to maintain or enhance fecal elimination include:

- Constipation/impaction management
- Bowel incontinence care
- Bowel management
- Bowel training
- Diarrhea management
- Coping enhancement
- Ostomy care

Specific nursing activities associated with each of these interventions can be selected to meet the client's individual needs. A sample care plan using NIC interventions and selected activities is provided on pages 873–874.

Planning for Home Care

Clients who have bowel diversion ostomies, require fecal incontinence pouches, or have other ongoing elimination problems will need continuing care in the home setting. In preparation for discharge, the nurse needs to assess the client's and family's abilities to meet specific care needs. The box on page 869 outlines the specific assessment data required before developing a home care plan. Using the assessment data, the nurse designs a teaching plan for the client and family (see the Home Care Teaching Guide box on the opposite page).

Implementing

Promoting Regular Defecation

The nurse can help clients achieve regular defecation by attending to (1) the provision of privacy, (2) timing, (3) nutrition and fluids, (4) exercise, and (5) positioning. See the box on page 871 for wellness teaching related to bowel elimination.

Privacy

Privacy during defecation is extremely important to many people. The nurse should, therefore, provide as much privacy as possible to clients but may need to stay with clients who are too weak to be left alone. Some clients also prefer to wipe, wash, and dry themselves after defecating. A nurse may need to provide water and a washcloth and towel for this purpose. Clients should be assisted with handwashing following defecation.

Timing

A client should be encouraged to defecate when the urge to defecate is recognized. To establish regular bowel elimination, the client and nurse can discuss when mass peristalsis normally occurs and provide time for defecation. Many people have well-established times and routines for defecation that should be part of the client's schedule. Other activities, such as bathing and ambulating, should not interfere with the defecation time. Also, clients should not be hurried but given adequate time to defecate.

Nutrition and Fluids

The diet a client needs for regular normal elimination varies, depending on the kind of feces the client currently has, the frequency of defecation, and the types of foods that the client finds assist normal defecation.

For Constipation Increase daily fluid intake, and instruct the client to drink hot liquids and fruit juices, especially prune juice. Include fibre in the diet, that is, foods such as prunes, raw fruit, bran products, and whole-grain cereals and bread.

For Diarrhea Encourage oral intake of fluids and bland food. Eating small amounts of bland foods can be helpful because they are more easily absorbed. Diarrhea can lead to potassium losses. See the discussion of hypokalemia in Chapter 40. Excessively hot or cold fluids should be avoided because they stimulate peristalsis. In addition, highly spiced

HOME CARE TEACHING GUIDE

Fecal Elimination

Maintaining Fecal Elimination

- See "Wellness Teaching" below.

Facilitating Toileting

- Ensure safe and easy access to the toilet. Make sure lighting is appropriate, scatter rugs are removed or securely fastened, and so on.
- Facilitate instruction, as needed, about transfer techniques. Contact a physical therapist or other appropriate health-care professional.
- Suggest ways that garments can be adjusted to make disrobing easier for toileting (e.g., Velcro closing on clothing).

Monitoring Bowel Elimination Pattern

- If appropriate, instruct the client to keep a record of time and frequency of stool passage, any associated pain, and colour and consistency of the stool.

Dietary Alterations

- Provide information about required food and fluid alterations to promote defecation (box on Wellness Teaching) or to manage diarrhea (see p. 872).

Medications

- Discuss problems associated with overuse of laxatives, if appropriate, and the use of alternatives to laxatives, suppositories, and enemas (e.g., Metamucil).
- If the client is taking a constipating medication (e.g., narcotic analgesic), discuss the addition of a fibre supplement once a day.

Measures Specific to Elimination Problem

- Provide instructions associated with specific elimination problems and treatment, such as:
  a. Constipation (see box below)
  b. Diarrhea (see p. 872)
  c. Ostomy care (see p. 882–886)
- See also Bowel Training Programs (p. 881).

Referrals

- Make appropriate referrals to home care or community care social worker for assistance with resources such as installation of grab bars and raised toilet seats, structural alterations for wheelchair access, homemaker or home health-care aide services to assist with ADLs, and enterostomal therapy nurse for assistance with stoma care and selection of ostomy appliances.

Community Agencies and Other Sources of Help

- Provide information about companies where durable medical equipment (e.g., raised toilet seats, commodes, bedpans, urinals) can be purchased, rented, or obtained free of charge, and where medical supplies, such as incontinence pads or ostomy irrigating supplies and appliances, can be obtained.
- Suggest additional sources of information and help such as ostomy self-help and support groups or clubs.

WELLNESS TEACHING

Healthy Defecation

- Establish a regular exercise regimen.
- Include high-fibre foods, such as vegetables, fruits, and whole grains, in the diet.
- Maintain fluid intake of 2,000 to 3,000 mL a day.
- Do not ignore the urge to defecate.
- Allow time to defecate, preferably at the same time each day.
- Avoid over-the-counter medications to treat constipation and diarrhea.

foods and high-fibre foods can aggravate diarrhea. See the box on page 872 for details about managing diarrhea.

For Flatulence Limit carbonated beverages, the use of drinking straws, and chewing gum—all of which increase the ingestion of air. Gas-forming foods, such as cabbage, beans, onions, and cauliflower, should also be avoided.

Exercise

Regular exercise helps clients develop a regular defecation pattern. A client with weak abdominal and pelvic muscles (which impede normal defecation) may be able to strengthen them with the following isometric exercises.

- In a supine position, the client tightens the abdominal muscles as though pulling them inward, holding them for about 10 seconds, and then relaxing them. This should be repeated five to 10 times, four times a day, depending on the client's health.
- Again in a supine position, the client can contract the thigh muscles and hold them contracted for about 10

seconds, repeating the exercise five to 10 times, four times a day. This helps the client confined to bed gain strength in the thigh muscles, thereby making it easier to use a bedpan.

Positioning

Although the squatting position best facilitates defecation, on a toilet seat, the best position for most people seems to be leaning forward.

For clients who have difficulty moving themselves to and from the toilet, an elevated toilet seat can be attached to a regular toilet. Clients then do not have to lower themselves far down onto the seat and do not have to lift as far off the seat. Elevated toilet seats can be purchased for use in the home.

A bedside **commode,** a portable chair with a toilet seat and a receptacle beneath that can be emptied, is often used for the adult client who can get out of bed but is unable to walk to the bathroom. Some commodes can slide over the base of a regular toilet when the waste receptacle is removed, thus providing clients the privacy of a bathroom. Some commodes have a seat and can be used as a chair (Figure 35.12). Potty chairs are available for children.

CLIENT TEACHING

Managing Diarrhea

- Drink at least eight glasses of water per day to prevent dehydration.
- Avoid alcohol, beverages with caffeine, and excessively cold fluids, which aggravate the problem.
- Ingest foods with sodium and potassium. Most foods contain sodium. Potassium is found in dairy products, meats, and many vegetables and fruits, especially tomatoes, potatoes, bananas, peaches, and apricots.
- Limit foods containing insoluble fibre, such as whole-wheat and whole-grain breads and cereals, and raw fruits and vegetables.
- Increase foods containing soluble fibre, such as oatmeal and skinless fruits and potatoes.
- Limit fatty foods (e.g., dairy products and packaged processed meats).
- Thoroughly clean and dry the perianal area after passing stool to prevent skin irritation and breakdown. Use soft toilet tissue to clean and dry the area. Apply a moisture-barrier cream or ointment, such as zinc oxide or petrolatum, as needed.
- Discontinue medications, as recommended by the physician, or foods that cause diarrhea.
- When diarrhea has stopped, re-establish normal bowel flora by taking fermented dairy products, such as yogurt or buttermilk.

Clients restricted to bed may need to use a **urinal,** a receptacle for urine only (Figure 35.13), or a **bedpan,** a receptacle for urine and feces. Female clients use a bedpan for both urine and feces; male clients use a bedpan for feces and a urinal for urine.

Most male clients are able to use a urinal independently either in bed or when standing at the bedside. The nurse must remain with clients who need support to stand at the bedside. For clients who cannot stand at the bedside, place the urinal between the client's legs with the handle uppermost so that urine will flow into the urinal.

There are two main types of bedpans, the regular high-back pan and the slipper, or fracture, pan (see Figure 35.13). The slipper pan has a low back and is used for clients unable to raise their buttocks because of physical problems or therapy that contraindicates such movement. Many older adults benefit from the use of a slipper pan. Clinical guidelines for giving and removing a bedpan are shown in the box on page 875.

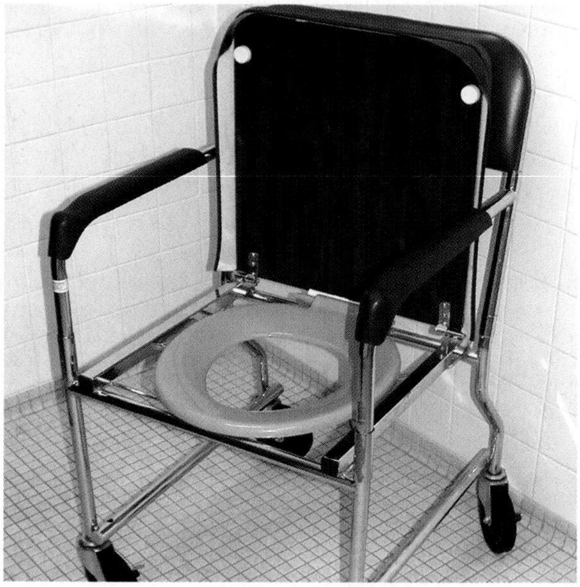

Figure 35.12 A commode with overlying seat

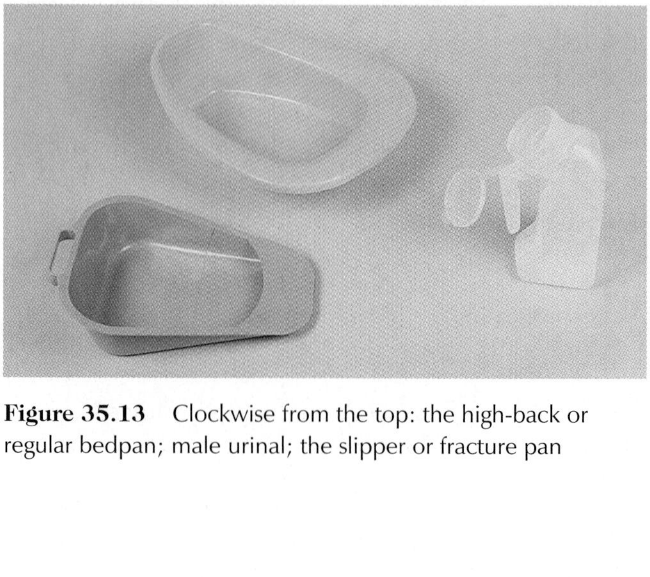

Figure 35.13 Clockwise from the top: the high-back or regular bedpan; male urinal; the slipper or fracture pan

SAMPLE CARE PLAN FOR ALTERED BOWEL ELIMINATION

ASSESSMENT DATA

Nursing Assessment

Mrs. Emma Brown is a 78-year-old widow of nine months. She lives alone in a low-income housing complex for older people. Her two children live with their families in a city approximately 240 km away. She has always enjoyed cooking for her family; however, now that she is alone, she does not cook for herself. As a result, she has developed irregular eating patterns and tends to prepare soup-and-toast meals. She gets little exercise and has bouts of insomnia since her husband's death. For the past month, Mrs. Brown has been having a problem with constipation. She states she has a bowel movement about every three to four days and her stools are hard and painful to excrete. Mrs. Brown decides to attend the health fair sponsored by the housing complex and seeks assistance from Laura Anderson, the public health nurse.

Physical Examination

Height: 162 cm
Weight: 65 kg
Temperature: 36.2°C
Pulse: 82 BPM
Respirations: 20/minute
Blood pressure: 128/74 mm Hg
Active bowel sounds, abdomen slightly distended

Diagnostic Data

CBC: Hgb 10.8
Urinalysis negative

Nursing Diagnosis

Constipation related to low-fibre diet and inactivity (as evidenced by infrequent, hard stools; painful defecation; abdominal distention)

Client Goal(s):

Mrs. Brown will (1) establish a regular pattern of bowel elimination; (2) develop and maintain an exercise program; and (3) initiate nutritional alterations that will enhance regular bowel elimination.

Desired Outcomes

1. Increases daily fluid intake to 2,000 mL unless contraindicated
2. Includes fibre in at least one meal per day
3. Walks for 20 minutes at least three times per week
4. Verbalizes relief of constipation by the second week

---

*Nursing Interventions and Selected Activities with Rationale *[in italics]*

Constipation/Impaction Management

■ Identify factors (e.g., medications, bed rest, diet) that may cause or contribute to constipation.	*Assessing causative factors is an essential first step in teaching and planning for improved bowel elimination.*
■ Encourage increased fluid intake, unless contraindicated.	*Sufficient fluid intake is necessary for the bowel to absorb sufficient amounts of liquid to promote proper stool consistency.*
■ Evaluate medication profile for gastrointestinal side effects.	*Constipation is a common side effect of many drugs, including narcotics and antacids.*
■ Teach Mrs. Brown how to keep a food diary.	*An appraisal of food intake will help identify if Mrs. Brown is eating a well-balanced diet and consuming adequate amounts of fluid and fibre. Excessive meat or refined food intake will produce small, hard stools.*
■ Instruct Mrs. Brown on a high-fibre diet, as appropriate.	*Fibre absorbs water, which adds bulk and softness to the stool and speeds up passage through the intestines.*
■ Instruct her on the relationship of diet, exercise, and fluid intake to constipation and impaction.	*Fibre without adequate fluid can aggravate, not facilitate, bowel function.*

Exercise Promotion

■ Encourage verbalization of feelings about exercise or need for exercise.	*Perceptions of the need for exercise may be influenced by misconceptions, cultural and social beliefs, fears, or age.*
■ Assist in identifying a positive role model for maintaining the exercise program.	*Individuals who have been successful in an exercise program can assist Mrs. Brown by providing incentive and enhancing motivation. For example, a walking partner may be beneficial.*
■ Inform Mrs. Brown about the health benefits and physiological effects of exercise.	*Activity influences bowel elimination by improving muscle tone and stimulating peristalsis.*

→

SAMPLE CARE PLAN FOR ALTERED BOWEL ELIMINATION *continued*

■ Instruct her about appropriate types of exercise for her level of health, in collaboration with a physician.	*Any individual beginning an exercise program should consult a physician primarily for a cardiac evaluation. Mrs. Brown's age and lack of activity should be considered in planning the level of activity.*
■ Assist Mrs. Brown to set short-term and long-term goals for the exercise program.	*Realistic goal-setting provides direction and motivation.*

Evaluation

Goals not met. Mrs. Brown has kept a food diary and is able to identify the need for more fluid and fibre but has not consistently included fibre in her diet. She has started a walking program with a neighbour but is only able to walk for 10 minutes at a time twice a week. She states her last bowel movement was three days ago.

*Interventions and activities selected are only a sample of those suggested in the *Nursing Interventions Classification (NIC)* and should be individualized for each client.

Source: McCloskey, J. C., & Bulechek, G. M. (2000). *Iowa intervention project: Nursing interventions classification (NIC)* (3rd ed.). St. Louis, MO: Mosby.

Teaching about Medications

Cathartics and Laxatives

Cathartics are drugs that induce defecation. They can have a strong, purgative effect. A laxative is mild in comparison to a cathartic, and it produces frequent soft or liquid stools that are sometimes accompanied by abdominal cramps. Examples of cathartics are castor oil, cascara, phenolphthalein, and bisacodyl (Dulcolax). Table 35.4 on page 876 describes the different types of laxatives.

Laxative abuse is believed to be a common problem. Older adults, in particular, often use laxatives improperly. Persistent self-administration of laxatives, however, can result in chronic constipation. There is a trend toward the "natural laxative" approach; that is, the use of increased dietary fibre, such as that found in fruits and vegetables, to obtain a laxative effect.

Laxatives are contraindicated in the client who has nausea, cramps, colic, vomiting, or undiagnosed abdominal pain. Clients need to be informed about the dangers of laxative use. Continual use of laxatives to encourage bowel evacuation weakens the bowel's natural responses to fecal distention, resulting in chronic constipation. To eliminate chronic laxative use, it is usually necessary to teach the client about dietary fibre, regular exercise, taking sufficient fluids, and establishing regular defecation habits. In addition, any medication regimen should be examined to see whether it could cause constipation.

Some laxatives are given in the form of **suppositories.** These act in various ways: by softening the feces; by releasing gases, such as carbon dioxide, to distend the rectum; or by stimulating the nerve endings in the rectal mucosa. The best results can be obtained by inserting the suppository 30 minutes before the client's usual defecation time or when the peristaltic action is greatest, such as after breakfast.

Antidiarrheal Medications

These medications are usually reserved for treatment of chronic diarrhea (more than three to four weeks). They slow down the motility of the intestine or absorb excess fluid in the intestine. Guidelines for using antidiarrheals are shown in the box on page 876.

Antiflatulent Medications

Antiflatulent agents, such as simethicone, do not decrease the formation of flatus but they do coalesce the gas bubbles and facilitate their passage by belching through the mouth or expulsion through the anus. These agents are frequently combined with an antacid. Suppositories can also be given to relieve flatus by increasing intestinal motility.

Administering Enemas

An **enema** is a solution introduced into the rectum and large intestine. The action of an enema is to distend the intestine and sometimes to irritate the intestinal mucosa, thereby increasing peristalsis and the excretion of feces and flatus.

Types of Enemas

Enemas are classified into four groups: cleansing, carminative, retention, and return-flow.

CLINICAL GUIDELINES

Giving and Removing a Bedpan

- Provide privacy.
- Wear disposable gloves.
- If the bedpan is metal, warm it by rinsing it with warm water.
- Adjust the bed to a height appropriate to prevent back strain.
- Elevate the side rail on the opposite side to prevent the client from falling out of bed.
- Ask the client to assist by flexing the knees, resting the weight on the back and heels, and raising the buttocks, *or* by using a trapeze bar, if present.
- Help lift the client as needed by placing one hand under the lower back, resting your elbow on the mattress, and using your forearm as a lever.
- Place a regular bedpan so that the client's buttocks rest on the smooth, rounded rim. Place a slipper pan with the flat, low end under the client's buttocks (Figure 35.14).

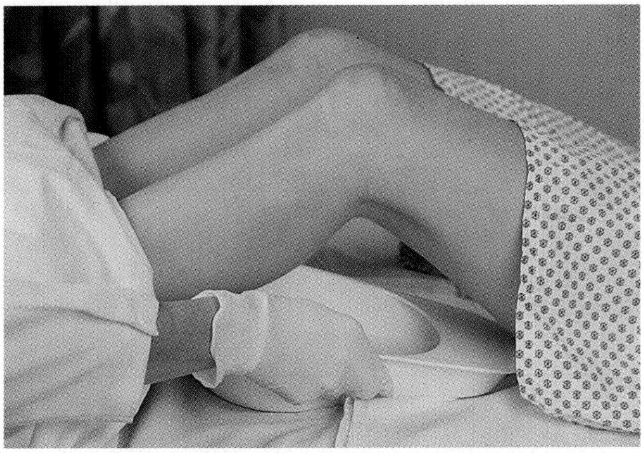

Figure 35.14 Placing a slipper pan under the buttocks

- For the client who cannot assist, obtain the assistance of another nurse to help place the client onto the bedpan. Turn the client on his or her side, place the bedpan against the buttocks, and roll the client back onto the bedpan.
- To provide a more normal position for the client's lower back, elevate the client's bed to a semi-Fowler's position, if permitted. If elevation is contraindicated, support the client's back with pillows as needed to prevent hyperextension of the back.
- Cover the client with bed linen to maintain comfort and self-dignity.
- Provide toilet tissue, place the call light within reach, lower the bed to the low position, elevate the side rails, and leave the client alone, if not contraindicted.
- Answer the call bell promptly.
- Don gloves when removing the bedpan, return the bed to the position used when giving the bedpan, hold the bedpan steady to prevent spillage of its contents, cover the bedpan, and place it on the adjacent chair.
- If the client needs assistance, wipe the client's perineal area with several layers of toilet tissue. If a specimen is to be collected, discard the soiled tissue into a moistureproof receptacle other than the bedpan. For female clients, clean from the urethra toward the anus to prevent transferring rectal microorganisms into the urinary meatus.
- Wash the perineal area of dependent clients with soap and water as indicated and thoroughly dry the area.
- For all clients, offer warm water, soap, a washcloth, and a towel to wash the hands.
- Assist the client to a comfortable position, empty and clean the bedpan, and return it to the bedside.
- Remove and discard your gloves and wash your hands.
- Spray the room with air freshener, as needed, to control odour, unless contraindicated because of respiratory problems or allergies.
- Document colour, odour, amount, and consistency of urine and feces, and the condition of the perineal area.

Cleansing Enemas Cleansing enemas are intended to remove feces. They are given chiefly to

- Prevent the escape of feces during surgery.
- Prepare the intestine for certain diagnostic tests such as radiography or visualization tests (e.g., colonoscopy).
- Remove feces in instances of constipation or impaction.
- Establish regular bowel function as part of a bowel training program.

Cleansing enemas use a variety of solutions. See Table 35.5 for commonly used solutions.

TABLE 35.4 Types of Laxatives

Type	Action	Examples	Pertinent Teaching Information
Bulk-forming	Increases the fluid, gaseous, or solid bulk in the intestines	Psyllium hydrophilic mucilloid (Metamucil)	May take 12 or more hours to act. Sufficient fluid must be taken.
Emollient/stool softener	Softens and delays the drying of the feces; permits fat and water to penetrate feces	Docusate sodium (Colace)	Refrigerated oil has less odour. Mixing with fruit juice decreases unpleasant taste.
Wetting agents	Lowers the surface tension of the feces, thus helping water to penetrate the feces	Docusate sodium (Colace)	Slow-acting; may take several days.
Stimulant/irritant	Irritates the intestinal mucosa or stimulates nerve endings in the wall of the intestine, causing rapid propulsion of the contents	Bisacodyl (Dulcolax)	Acts more quickly than bulk-forming agents. Fluid is passed with the feces. May cause cramps. Prolonged use may cause fluid and electrolyte imbalance.
Lubricant	Lubricates the feces in the colon	Mineral oil (Haley's M-O)	Prolonged use inhibits the absorption of some fat-soluble vitamins.
Saline/osmotic	Draws water into the intestine by osmosis, distends bowel, and stimulates peristalsis	Epsom salts, magnesium hydroxide (milk of magnesia), magnesium citrate, sodium phosphate (Fleet enema)	May be rapid acting. Can cause fluid and electrolyte imbalance, particularly in elderly people and children with cardiac and renal diseases. Should not be used by elderly clients. Prolonged use inhibits the absorption of some fat-soluble vitamins.

Hypertonic solutions (e.g., sodium phosphate) exert osmotic pressure, which draws fluid from the interstitial space into the colon. The increased volume in the colon stimulates peristalsis and hence defecation. A commonly used hypertonic enema is the commercially prepared Fleet Enema. *Hypotonic solutions* (e.g., tap water) exert a lower osmotic pressure than the surrounding interstitial fluid, causing water to move from the colon into the interstitial space. Before the water moves from the colon, it stimulates peristalsis and defecation. Because the water moves out of the colon, the tap water enema should not be repeated because of danger of circulatory overload when the water moves from the interstitial space into the circulatory system.

Isotonic solutions (i.e., physiological [normal] saline) are considered the safest enema solutions to use. They exert the same osmotic pressure as the interstitial fluid surrounding the colon. Therefore, there is no fluid movement into or out of the colon. The instilled volume of saline in the colon stimulates peristalsis.

Guidelines for Using Antidiarrheal Medications

- If the diarrhea persists for more than three or four days, determine the underlying cause. Using a medication, such as an opiate, when the cause is an infection, toxin, or poison may prolong diarrhea.
- Long-term use of over-the-counter medications (e.g., loperamide hydrochloride [Imodium]) can produce dependence.
- Some antidiarrheal agents can cause drowsiness (e.g., diphenoxylate hydrochloride [Lomotil]) and should not be used when driving an automobile or running machinery.
- Opiate dosage requirements are usually smaller than for analgesia.
- Kaolin-pectin preparations (e.g., Kaopectate) may absorb nutrients.

RESEARCH NOTE

Is Power Pudding an Effective Natural Laxative Therapy?

Constipation is a common problem among the older adult population, particularly those who are sedentary. A large home care agency in northern Virginia launched a study to determine whether a natural laxative therapy in the form of a good-tasting pudding called "Power Pudding" could relieve and prevent episodes of constipation and eliminate the need for stool softeners, cathartics, or laxatives.

"Power Pudding" consists of equal portions of applesauce, wheat bran flakes, whipped topping (Cool Whip), and canned, stewed prunes. Some prune juice may be added to facilitate blending.

Sixteen older adults between the ages of 65 and 93 years participated in the study. With their physician's approval, they were instructed to discontinue all laxatives, stool softeners, and cathartics and to eat a quarter cup of the pudding with breakfast. Pudding amounts were increased slightly if the subject did not have a soft bowel movement within three days and decreased if the subject had loose stools.

Findings revealed that these individuals developed an acceptable stool consistency and elimination pattern. One week of daily quarter-cup servings of the pudding yielded results of three to six bowel movements per week; portions of a half cup had the same results; and one-cup portions resulted in four bowel movements per week.

Implications: Nurses working in the community need to consider this nonpharmacological nursing intervention when constipation is reported by the older person. Before implementing this remedy, however, the nurse should obtain a physician's order and take a bowel history.

Source: Neal, L. (1995). Power puddings: Natural laxative therapy for the elderly who are homebound. *Home Healthcare Nurse, 13*(3), 66–71.

Soapsuds enemas stimulate peristalsis by increasing the volume in the colon and irritating the mucosa. Only pure soap (i.e., castile soap) should be used in order to minimize mucosal irritation.

Some enemas are *large volume* (i.e., 500 to 1,000 mL) for an adult and others are *small volume*, including hypertonic solutions. The latter, available commercially, act by drawing water into the colon, thus stimulating defecation. The amount of solution administered for a high-volume enema will depend on the age of the individual. See the box in Procedure 35.1 for approximate volumes of solutions.

Cleansing enemas may also be described as *high* or *low*. A *high enema* is given to cleanse as much of the colon as possible. The client changes from the left lateral position to the dorsal recumbent position and then to the right lateral position during administration so that the solution can follow the large intestine. See Figure 35.1 earlier. The low enema is used to clean the rectum and sigmoid colon only. The client maintains a left lateral position during administration. A physician's order should specify when a high-enema technique is to be used.

The force of flow of the solution is governed by (1) the height of the solution container, (2) size of the tubing, (3) viscosity of the fluid, and (4) resistance of the rectum. The higher the solution container is held above the rectum, the faster is the flow and the greater is the force (pressure) in the rectum. During most adult enemas, the solution container should be no higher than 30 cm above the rectum. During a high cleansing enema, the solution container is usually held 30 to 45 cm above the rectum because the fluid is instilled farther to clean the entire bowel. For an infant, the solution container is held no more than 7.5 cm above the rectum.

Carminative Enema A *carminative enema* is given primarily to expel flatus. The solution instilled into the rectum releases gas, which, in turn, distends the rectum and the colon, thus stimulating peristalsis. For an adult, 60 to 80 mL of fluid is instilled.

Oil Retention Enema An *oil retention enema* introduces oil into the rectum and sigmoid colon. The oil is retained for a relatively long period (e.g., one to three hours). It acts to soften the feces and to lubricate the rectum and anal canal, thus facilitating passage of the feces.

Return-Flow Enema A *return-flow enema* is used occasionally to expel flatus. Alternating flow of 100 to 200 mL of fluid into and out of the rectum and sigmoid colon stimulates peristalsis. This process is repeated five or six times until the flatus is expelled and abdominal distention is relieved.

There are also other types of enemas; for example, medicated enemas such as *antibiotic* enemas used to treat infections locally, *antihelmintic* enemas used to kill helminths, such as worms and intestinal parasites, and *nutritive* enemas used to administer fluids and nutrients to the rectum.

Equipment

Commercially prepared, low-volume, disposable enema kits are commonly used today. The kit includes a flexible bottle of solution with a prelubricated, firm tip.

Equipment for a large-volume enema is listed in Procedure 35.1. A caregiver should wear disposable gloves during administration of an enema to prevent contact with body fluids, blood, and microorganisms.

Procedure 35.1 describes how to administer an enema.

TABLE 35.5 Commonly Used Enema Solutions

Solution	Constituents	Action	Time to Take Effect	Adverse Effects
Hypertonic	90–120 mL of solution (e.g., sodium phosphate)	Draws water into the colon	5–10 min	Retention of sodium
Hypotonic	500–1,000 mL of tap water	Distends colon, stimulates peristalsis, and softens feces	15–20 min	Fluid and electrolyte imbalance; water intoxication
Isotonic	500–1,000 mL of normal saline (9 mL NaCl to 1,000 mL water)	Distends colon, stimulates peristalsis, and softens feces	15–20 min	Possible sodium retention
Soapsuds	500–1,000 mL (3–5 mL soap to 1,000 mL water)	Irritates mucosa, distends colon	10–15 min	Irritates and may damage mucosa
Oil (mineral, olive, cottonseed)	90–120 mL	Lubricates the feces and the colonic mucosa	1–3 hours	

PROCEDURE 35.1 Administering an Enema

Before administering an enema, determine whether a physician's order is required. At some agencies, a physician must order the kind of enema and the time to give it, for example, the morning of the examination. When the client has rectal disease, the physician may also specify the size of the rectal tube to use. At other agencies, enemas are given at the nurse's discretion (i.e., as necessary on a prn order). In addition, determine the presence of kidney or cardiac disease that contraindicates the use of a hypotonic solution.

Assessment Focus
When the client last had a bowel movement and the amount, colour, and consistency of the feces; presence of abdominal distention (the distended abdomen appears swollen and feels firm, rather than soft, when palpated); whether the client has sphincter control; whether the client can use a toilet or commode or must remain in bed and use a bedpan; presence of bowel sounds

Equipment

- ❑ Disposable underpad
- ❑ Bath blanket
- ❑ Bedpan or commode
- ❑ Disposable gloves
- ❑ Water-soluble lubricant, if tubing is not prelubricated

Large-Volume Enema

- ❑ Solution container with tubing of correct size and tubing clamp
- ❑ Correct solution, amount, and temperature (see the accompanying box)

Small-Volume Enema

- ❑ Prepackaged container of enema solution with lubricated tip

INTERVENTION

1. Prepare the client.

- Explain the procedure to the client. Indicate that the client may experience a feeling of fullness while the solution is being administered. Careful explanation is especially important for the preschool child. *An enema is an intrusive procedure and, therefore, threatening.*
- Assist the adult client to a left lateral position, with the right leg as acutely flexed as possible (Figure 35.15). *This position facilitates the flow of solution by gravity into the sigmoid and descending colon, which are on the left side. Having the right leg acutely flexed provides for adequate exposure of the anus.*
- For infants and small children, the dorsal recumbent position is frequently used. Position them on a small padded bedpan with support for the back and head. Secure the legs by placing a diaper under the bedpan and then over and around the thighs.
- Place the underpad under the client's buttocks to protect the bed linen, and drape the client with the bath blanket.

2. Prepare the equipment

- Lubricate about 5 cm of the rectal tube (some commercially prepared enema sets already have lubricated nozzles). *Lubrication facilitates insertion through the sphincters and minimizes trauma.*

PROCEDURE 35.1 Administering an Enema *continued*

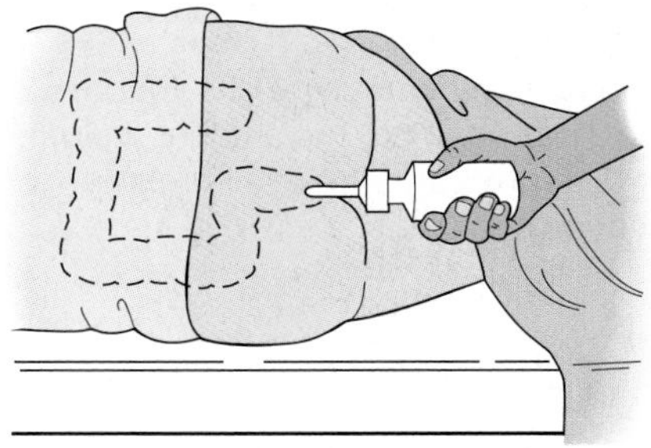

Figure 35.15 Assuming a left lateral position for an enema. Note the commercially prepared enema.

- Run some solution through the connecting tubing of a large volume enema set and the rectal tube to expel any air in the tubing; then close the clamp. *Air instilled into the rectum, although not harmful, causes unnecessary distention.*

3. **Don gloves, and insert the rectal tube.**

- For clients in the left lateral position, lift the upper buttock to ensure good visualization of the anus.
- Insert the tube smoothly and slowly into the rectum, directing it toward the umbilicus (Figure 35.16). *The angle follows the normal contour of the rectum. Slow insertion prevents spasm of the sphincter.*

LARGE-VOLUME ENEMAS

Age	Volume
18 months	50–200 mL
18 months–5 years	200–300 mL
5–12 years	300–500 mL
12 years and older	500–1,000 mL

Temperature
For adult 37.7–40°C
For children 37.7°C

- Insert the tube 7.5 to 10 cm in an adult. *Because the anal canal is about 2.5 to 5 cm long in the adult, insertion to this point places the tip of the tube beyond the anal sphincter into the rectum.* Insert the tube 5 to 7.5 cm in the child and only 2.5 to 3.75 cm in the infant.

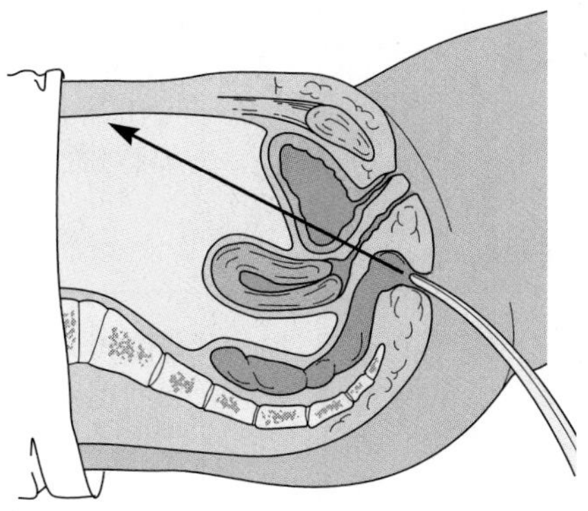

Figure 35.16 Inserting the rectal tube following the direction of the rectum

- If resistance is encountered at the internal sphincter, ask the client to take a deep breath, then run a small amount of solution through the tube to relax the internal anal sphincter.
- Never force tube entry. If resistance persists, withdraw the tube, and report the resistance to the nurse in charge.

4. **Slowly administer the enema solution.**

Raise the solution container, and open the clamp to allow fluid flow.

or

Compress a pliable container by hand.

- During most adult low enemas, hold the solution container no higher than 30 cm above the rectum. *The higher the solution container is held above the rectum, the faster will be the flow and the greater the force (pressure) in the rectum.* During a high enema (if ordered), hold the solution container a little higher (e.g., 45 cm). *The fluid must be instilled farther to clean the entire bowel.* For children, lower the height of the solution container appropriately for the age of the child. See agency protocol.
- Administer the fluid slowly. If the client complains of fullness or cramps, use the clamp to stop the flow for 30 seconds, or until fullness or cramps subside, and then restart the flow at a slower rate. *Administering the enema slowly and stopping the flow momentarily decrease the likelihood of intestinal spasm and premature expulsion of the solution.*
- If you are using a plastic commercial container, roll it up as the fluid is instilled. *This prevents subsequent suctioning of the solution.* See Figure 35.17.
- After all the solution has been instilled or when the client cannot hold any more and wants to defecate (the urge to defecate usually indicates that sufficient fluid has been administered), close the clamp, and remove the rectal tube from the anus.
- Place the rectal tube in a disposable towel as you withdraw it.

5. **Encourage the client to retain the enema.**

- Ask the client to remain lying down. *It is easier for the client to retain the enema when lying down than when sitting or standing because gravity promotes drainage and peristalsis.*
- To assist a small child in retaining the solution, apply firm pressure over the anus with tissue wipes, or firmly press the buttocks together.
- Ensure that the client retains the solution for the appropriate amount of time, for example, five to 10 minutes for a cleansing enema or at least 30 minutes for a retention enema.

6. **Assist the client to defecate.**

- Assist the client to a sitting position on the bedpan, commode, or toilet. *A sitting position facilitates the act of defecation.*
- Ask the client who is using the toilet not to flush it. *The nurse needs to observe the feces.*
- If a specimen of feces is required, ask the client to use a bedpan or commode.

PROCEDURE 35.1 Administering an Enema *continued*

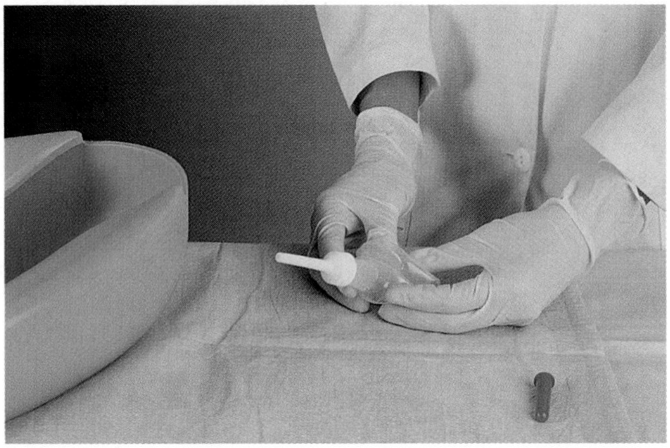

Figure 35.17 Rolling up a commercial enema container

7. **Record and report relevant data.**

- Record administration of the enema; type of solution; length of time solution was retained; the amount, colour, and consistency of the returns; and the relief of flatus and abdominal distention.

Evaluation Focus
Amount, colour, and consistency of returns; relief of flatus or abdominal distention; any problems encountered (e.g., resistance at the external or internal sphincter when inserting the rectal tube)

Home Care Considerations

Teach the caregiver or client the following:

- To make saline solution, mix one teaspoon of table salt to 500 mL of tap water.
- Use enemas only as directed. Do not rely on them for regular bowel evacuation.
- Prior to administration, make sure a bedpan, commode, or toilet is nearby.

Lifespan Considerations

- Provide a careful explanation to the parents and child prior to the procedure.
- Use an isotonic solution for children to avoid fluid and electrolyte shifts.
- Hold the buttocks together, if necessary, to assist the child to retain fluids.
- Refer to agency guidelines or the health-care provider's orders to determine the amount of solution and the distance to insert the rectal tube.
- For older clients, monitor the client's tolerance throughout the procedure and during evacuation, watching for vagal episodes, dysrhythmias, and fluid and electrolyte disturbances.
- Avoid overexertion or fatigue for older clients.
- Protect older adults' skin from prolonged exposure to moisture.
- Assist older clients with perineal care.

Digital Removal of a Fecal Impaction

Digital removal involves breaking up the fecal mass digitally and removing it in portions. Because the bowel mucosa can be injured during this procedure, some agencies restrict and specify the personnel permitted to conduct digital disimpactions. Rectal stimulation is also contraindicated for some people because it may cause an excessive vagal response resulting in cardiac arrhythmia. Before disimpaction, it may be suggested that an oil retention enema be given and held for 30 minutes. (Check agency policy and physician's order.) After a disimpaction, the nurse can use various interventions to remove remaining feces, such as a cleansing enema or the insertion of a suppository as ordered by the physician.

For digital removal of a fecal impaction:

1. Obtain assistance from a second person who can comfort the client during the procedure.
2. Ask the client to assume a left side-lying position, with the knees flexed and the back toward the nurse.
3. Place a bedpad under the client's buttocks and a bedpan nearby to receive stool.
4. Drape the client for comfort and to avoid unnecessary exposure of the body.

5. Put on a pair of clean gloves, and liberally lubricate the index finger to be inserted.
6. Gently insert the index finger into the rectum, and move the finger toward the client's umbilicus along the length of the rectum.
7. Loosen and dislodge stool by gently massaging around it. Break up stool by working the finger into the hardened mass, taking care to avoid injury to the mucosa of the rectum (Figure 35.18).
8. Carefully work stool downward to the end of the rectum and remove it in small pieces. Continue to remove as much fecal material as possible. Periodically assess the client for signs of fatigue, such as facial pallor, diaphoresis, or change in pulse rate.
9. Following disimpaction, assist the client to clean the anal area and buttocks. Then, assist the client onto a bedpan or commode for a short time because digital stimulation of the rectum often induces the urge to defecate.
10. A cleansing enema may be ordered after the oil retention enema or after the disimpaction.

Decreasing Flatulence

There are a number of ways to reduce or prevent flatus, which include exercise, moving in bed, ambulation, and avoiding gas-producing foods. Movement stimulates peristalsis and the escape of flatus and reabsorption of gases into the intestinal capillaries. One method of treating flatulence involves the insertion of a rectal tube:

1. Use a rectal tube 22 to 30 French for adults and a smaller size for children.
2. Have the client assume a side-lying position.
3. Lubricate the rectal tube to reduce mucous membrane irritation.
4. Expose the anus and insert the rectal tube into the rectum 7.5 to 10 cm. The rectal tube will stimulate peristalsis. Do not force the tube in if it does not insert easily. Secure the tube in place.
5. Wrap an abdominal or incontinence pad around the end of the rectal tube to catch any liquid that may be expelled. Some nurses suggest inserting the rectal tube and then placing the end into a receptacle filled with water. The passage of flatus will be seen as bubbles are produced.
6. Leave the tube in no longer than 30 minutes to avoid irritation of the rectal mucosa. If abdominal distention is not relieved, the tube may be inserted every two to three hours.
7. Encourage the client to assume various positions in bed.

If a rectal tube does not relieve flatus, consult with the physician about a suppository, enema, or medication.

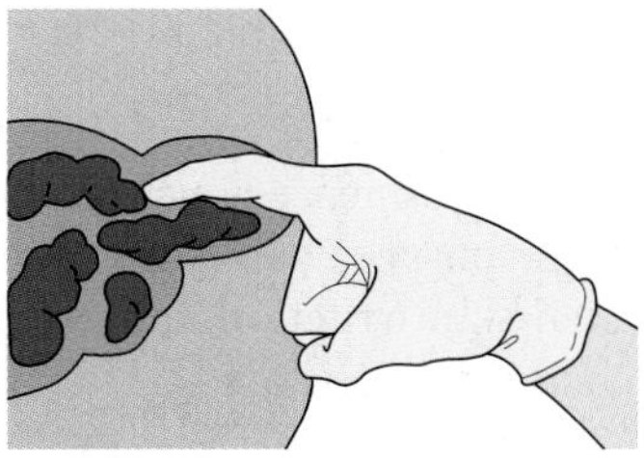

Figure 35.18 Digital removal of fecal impaction

Bowel Training Programs

For clients who have chronic constipation, frequent impactions, or fecal incontinence, *bowel training programs* may be helpful. The program is based on factors within the client's control and is designed to help the client establish normal defecation. Such matters as food and fluid intake, exercise, and defecation habits are all considered. Before beginning such a program, clients must understand it and want to be involved. The major phases of the program are as follows:

- Determine the client's usual bowel habits and factors that help and hinder normal defecation.
- Design a plan with the client that includes the following:
  a. Fluid intake of about 2,500 to 3,000 mL per day, unless contraindicted
  b. Increase in fibre in the diet
  c. Intake of hot drinks, especially just before the usual defecation time
  d. Increase in exercise
- Maintain the following daily routine for two to three weeks:
  a. Administer a cathartic suppository (e.g., Dulcolax) 30 minutes before the client's defecation time to stimulate peristalsis.
  b. When the client experiences the urge to defecate, assist the client to the toilet or commode or onto a bedpan. Note the length of time between the insertion of the suppository and the urge to defecate.
  c. Provide the client with privacy for defecation and a time limit; 30 to 40 minutes is usually sufficient.
  d. Teach the client to lean forward at the hips, to apply pressure on the abdomen with the hands, and to bear down for defecation. These measures increase pressure on the colon. Straining should be avoided because it can cause hemorrhoids.
- Provide positive feedback when the client successfully defecates. Refrain from negative feedback if the client fails to defecate.
- Offer encouragement to the client, and convey that patience is often required. Many clients require weeks or months of training to achieve success.

Fecal Incontinence Pouch

To collect and contain large volumes of feces, the nurse may place a fecal incontinence pouch (rectal pouch) around the anal area. The purpose of the pouch is to prevent progressive perianal skin irritation and breakdown and frequent linen changes necessitated by incontinence.

Ostomy Management

Clients with fecal diversions need considerable psychological support, instruction, and physical care. This section is limited to the nurse's physical interventions of stoma assessment, application of an appliance to collect feces, and promotion of predictable evacuation with colostomy irrigation. Many agencies have enterostomal therapy nurses to assist these clients.

Stoma and Skin Care

Care of the stoma and skin is important for all clients who have ostomies. The fecal material from a colostomy or ileostomy is irritating to the peristomal skin. This is particularly true of ileal effluent, which contains digestive enzymes. It is important to assess the peristomal skin for irritation each time the appliance is changed. See the box opposite for assessing a stoma. Any irritation or skin breakdown needs to be treated immediately. The skin is kept clean by washing off any excretion and drying thoroughly. A barrier, such as karaya gum, is applied over the skin around the stoma to prevent contact with any excretion. An appliance (bag) is then fitted to the stoma so that there is no leakage around it. It is exceedingly important to dry the skin before attaching the appliance. The pouch will not adhere to moist skin, causing effluent to leak onto the skin. Numerous pouch systems are commercially available. All appliances have three features in common: (1) a pouch to collect the effluent, (2) an outlet at the bottom for easy emptying, and (3) a faceplate. Temporary, disposable pouches are made of transparent plastic and have a peel-off adhesive square into which a hole the size of the stoma is cut. Permanent pouches may be clear or opaque, rubber or vinyl, and have a solid ring faceplate that fits around the stoma (Figure 35.19).

Odour control is essential to clients' self-esteem. As soon as clients are ambulatory, they can learn to work with the ostomy in the bathroom to avoid odours at the bedside. Selecting the appropriate kind of appliance promotes odour control. An intact appliance contains odours. The appliance should be rinsed thoroughly when it is emptied. Deodorizers can be placed in the pouch of the appliance, or pouches with charcoal filter discs are available. In limited circumstances, a physician may order preparations for oral intake to control odour.

Disposable ostomy appliances can be applied for up to seven days. They need to be changed whenever the effluent leaks onto the peristomal skin or when it cannot be rinsed completely away. Many people prefer to change them daily or whenever they become soiled, but this practice can be detrimental to the integrity of the peristomal skin and is expensive. Check agency practice in this regard. Some people recommend removing the pouch and skin barrier twice a week to clean and inspect the peristomal skin. If the skin is erythematous, eroded, denuded, or ulcerated, the ostomy appliance should be changed every 24 to 48 hours to allow appropriate treatment of the skin. More frequent changes are recommended if the client complains of pain or discomfort. Procedure 35.2 explains how to change a bowel diversion ostomy appliance.

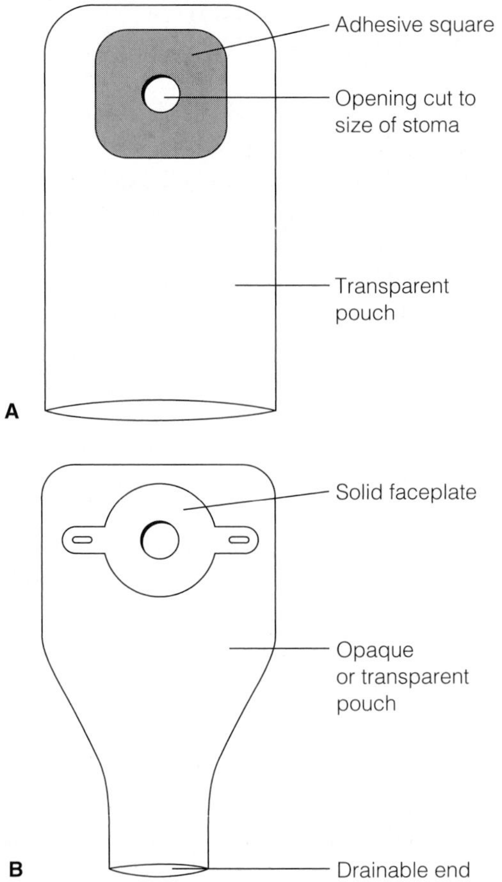

Figure 35.19 Ostomy appliances: *A*, temporary, disposable; *B*, permanent, reusable

Colostomy Irrigation

A colostomy irrigation, similar to an enema, is a form of stoma management used only for clients who have a sigmoid or descending colostomy. It is not done for ileostomies because the feces are usually liquid. The purpose of irrigation is to distend the bowel sufficiently to stimulate peristalsis, which stimulates evacuation. When a regular evacuation pattern is achieved, the wearing of a colostomy pouch is unnecessary.

Assessing a Stoma

- *Stoma colour.* The stoma should appear red, similar in colour to the mucosal lining of the inner cheek. Very pale or darker-coloured stomas with a bluish or purplish hue indicate impaired blood circulation to the area.
- *Stoma size and shape.* Most stomas protrude slightly from the abdomen. New stomas normally appear swollen, but swelling generally decreases over two or three weeks or for as long as six weeks. Failure of swelling to recede may indicate a problem, such as blockage.
- *Stomal bleeding.* Slight bleeding initially when the stoma is touched is normal, but other bleeding should be reported.
- *Status of peristomal skin.* Any redness and irritation of the peristomal skin—the 5 to 12.5 cm of skin surrounding the stoma—should be noted. Transient redness after removal of adhesive is normal.
- *Amount and type of feces.* For ileal effluent and feces (colostomy effluent), assess the amount, colour, odour, and consistency. Inspect for abnormalities, such as pus or blood. For a urinary diversion ostomy, assess the amount, colour, clarity, and odour of the urine.
- *Symptoms.* Statements of burning sensation under the faceplate may indicate skin breakdown. The presence of abdominal discomfort or distention also needs to be determined, in addition to presence of bowel sounds.

PROCEDURE 35.2 Changing a One-Piece, Drainable Bowel Diversion Ostomy Appliance

Before changing a bowel diversion ostomy appliance, determine the kind of ostomy and its placement on the abdomen. It is important to confirm which is the functioning stoma and any orders about the care of the stomas.

PURPOSES

- To assess and care for the peristomal skin
- To collect effluent for assessment of the amount and type of output
- To minimize odours for the client's comfort and self-esteem

Assessment Focus
Stoma size and shape; colour of stoma; presence of swelling; status of peristomal skin; amount and type of effluent; allergy to tape; type and size of appliance currently used; complaints of discomfort; client and support people's learning needs; client's emotional status

Equipment

- ❑ Disposable gloves
- ❑ Electric or safety razor
- ❑ Bedpan
- ❑ Solvent (presaturated sponges or liquid)
- ❑ Moistureproof bag (for disposable pouches)
- ❑ Cleaning materials, including tissues, warm water, mild soap (optional), washcloth or cotton balls, towel
- ❑ Tissue or gauze pad
- ❑ Skin barrier (paste, powder, water, or liquid skin sealant)
- ❑ Stoma measuring guide
- ❑ Pen or pencil and scissors
- ❑ Clean ostomy appliance, with optional belt
- ❑ Tail closure clamp
- ❑ Special adhesive, if needed
- ❑ Stoma guidestrip, if needed
- ❑ Deodorant (liquid or tablet) for a nonodourproof colostomy bag

INTERVENTION

1. Determine the need for an appliance change.

- Assess the used appliance for leakage of effluent. *Effluent can irritate the peristomal skin.*
- Ask the client about any discomfort at or around the stoma. *A burning sensation may indicate breakdown beneath the faceplate of the pouch.*
- Assess the fullness of the pouch. Pouches need to be emptied when they are one-third to one-half full. *The weight of an overly full bag may loosen the faceplate and separate it from the skin, causing the effluent to leak and irritate the peristomal skin.*
- If there is pouch leakage or discomfort at or around the stoma, change the appliance.

2. Select an appropriate time.

- Avoid times close to meal or visiting hours. *Ostomy odour and effluent may reduce appetite or embarrass the client.*
- Avoid times immediately after the administration of any medications that may stimulate bowel evacuation. *It is best to change the pouch when drainage is least likely to occur.*

PROCEDURE 35.2 Changing a One-Piece, Drainable Bowel Diversion Ostomy Appliance *continued*

3. **Prepare the client and the support people.**
- Explain the procedure to the client and the support people. Changing an ostomy appliance should not cause discomfort, but it may be distasteful to the client. *Support persons are often more supportive if properly informed.*
- Communicate acceptance and support to the client. It is important to change the appliance competently and quickly.
- Provide privacy, preferably in the bathroom, where clients can learn to deal with the ostomy as they would at home.
- Assist the client to a comfortable sitting or lying position in bed or preferably a sitting or standing position in the bathroom. *Lying or standing positions may facilitate smoother pouch application, that is, avoid wrinkles.*
- Don gloves, and unfasten the belt if the client is wearing one.

4. **Shave the peristomal skin of well-established ostomies, as needed.**
- Use an electric or safety razor on a regular basis to remove excessive hair. *Hair follicles can become irritated or infected by repeated pulling out of hairs during removal of the appliance and skin barrier.*

5. **Empty and remove the ostomy appliance.**
- Empty the contents of the pouch through the bottom opening into a bedpan. *Emptying before removing the pouch prevents spillage of effluent onto the client's skin.*
- Assess the consistency and the amount of effluent.
- Peel the bag off slowly while holding the client's skin taut. *Holding the skin taut minimizes client discomfort and prevents abrasion of the skin.*
- If the appliance is disposable, discard it in a moistureproof bag.

6. **Clean and dry the peristomal skin and stoma.**
- Use toilet tissue to remove excess stool.
- Use warm water, mild soap (optional), and cotton balls or a washcloth and towel to clean the skin and stoma. Check agency practice on the use of soap. *Soap is sometimes not advised because it can be irritating to the skin.*
- Use a special skin cleanser to remove dried, hard stool. *This emulsifies the stool, making removal less damaging to the skin.*
- Dry the area thoroughly by patting with a towel or cotton balls. *Excess rubbing can abrade the skin.*

7. **Assess the stoma and peristomal skin.**
- Inspect the stoma for colour, size, shape, and bleeding.
- Inspect the peristomal skin for any redness, ulceration, or irritation. Transient redness *after the removal of adhesive* is normal.
- Place a piece of tissue or gauze pad over the stoma, and change it as needed. *This absorbs any seepage from the stoma.*

8. **Apply paste-type skin barrier if needed.**
- Fill in abdominal creases or dimples with paste. *This establishes a smooth surface for application of the skin barrier and pouch.*
- Allow the paste to dry for one to two minutes or as recommended by the manufacturer.

9. **Prepare and apply the skin barrier (peristomal seal).**

FOR A SOLID WAFER OR DISC SKIN BARRIER
- Use the guide (Figure 35.20) to measure the size of the stoma.
- On the backing of the skin barrier, trace a circle the same size as the stomal opening.
- Cut out the traced stoma pattern to make an opening in the skin barrier. Make the opening no more than 0.3 to 0.4 cm larger than the stoma. *This minimizes the risk of effluent contacting peristomal skin.*
- Remove the backing to expose the sticky adhesive side.

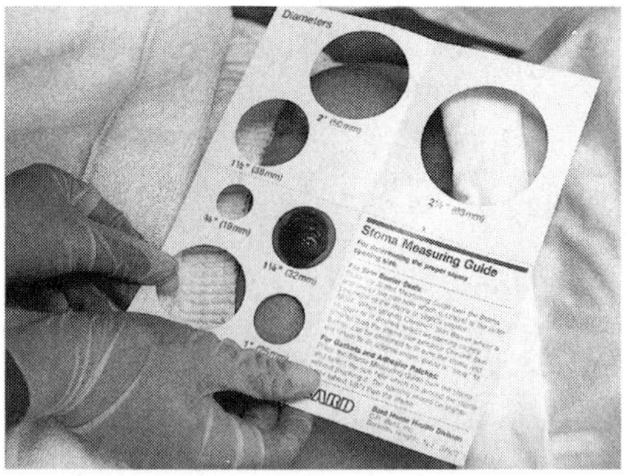

Figure 35.20 A guide for measuring the stoma

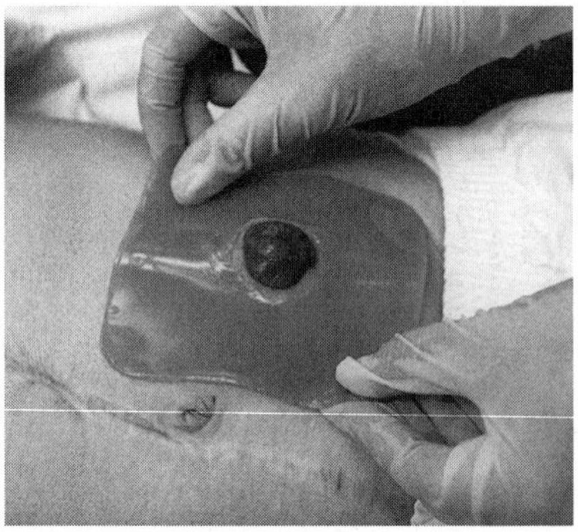

Figure 35.21 Centring the skin barrier over the stoma

- Centre the skin barrier over the stoma, and gently press it onto the client's skin, smoothing out any wrinkles or bubbles (Figure 35.21).

FOR LIQUID SKIN SEALANT
- Cover the stoma with a gauze pad. *This prevents contact with the skin sealant.*
- Either wipe or apply the product evenly around the peristomal skin to form a thin layer of the liquid plastic coating to the area.
- Allow the skin barrier to dry until it no longer feels tacky.

10. **Fill in any exposed skin around an irregularly shaped stoma.**
- Apply paste to any exposed skin areas. Use a nonalcohol-based product if the skin is excoriated. *Alcohol may cause stinging and burning.*

or

PROCEDURE 35.2 Changing a One-Piece, Drainable Bowel Diversion Ostomy Appliance *continued*

- Sprinkle peristomal powder on the skin, wipe off the excess, and dab the powder with a slightly moist gauze or an applicator moistened with a liquid skin barrier. *This creates a barrier or seal.*

11. Prepare and apply the clean appliance.

- Remove the tissue over the stoma before applying the pouch.

FOR A DISPOSABLE POUCH WITH ADHESIVE SQUARE

- If the appliance does not have a precut opening, trace a circle 0.3 to 0.4 cm larger than the stoma size on the appliance's adhesive square. *The opening is made slightly larger than the stoma to prevent rubbing, cutting, or trauma to the stoma.*
- Cut out the circle in the adhesive. Take care not to cut any portion of the pouch.
- Peel off the backing from the adhesive seal.
- Centre the opening of the pouch over the client's stoma, and apply it directly onto the skin barrier (Figure 35.22).
- Gently press the adhesive backing onto the skin and smooth out any wrinkles, working from the stoma outward. *Wrinkles allow seepage of effluent, which can irritate the skin or soil clothing.*
- Remove the air from the pouch. *Removing the air helps the pouch lie flat against the abdomen.*

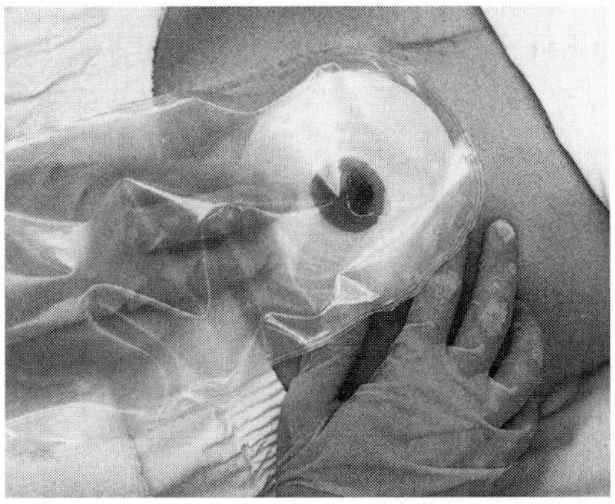

Figure 35.22 Applying the disposable pouch

- Place a deodorant in the pouch (optional).
- Close the pouch by turning up the bottom a few times, fanfolding its end lengthwise, and securing it with a tail closure clamp.

FOR A REUSABLE POUCH WITH FACEPLATE ATTACHED

- Apply either adhesive cement or a double-faced adhesive disc to the faceplate of the appliance depending on the type of appliance being used. Follow the manufacturer's directions.
- Insert a coiled paper guidestrip (15-cm strip of 1.3-cm wide paper) into the faceplate opening (Figure 35.23). The strip should protrude slightly from the opening and expand to fit it. *The guidestrip helps the nurse centre the appliance over the stoma and prevents pressure or irritation to the stoma due to an ill-fitting appliance.*
- Using the guidestrip, centre the faceplate over the stoma.
- Firmly press the adhesive seal to the peristomal skin. The guidestrip will fall into the pouch; commercially prepared guidestrips will dissolve in the pouch.
- Place a deodorant in the bag if the bag is not odourproof. Most pouches are odourproof.
- Close the end of the pouch with the designated clamp.

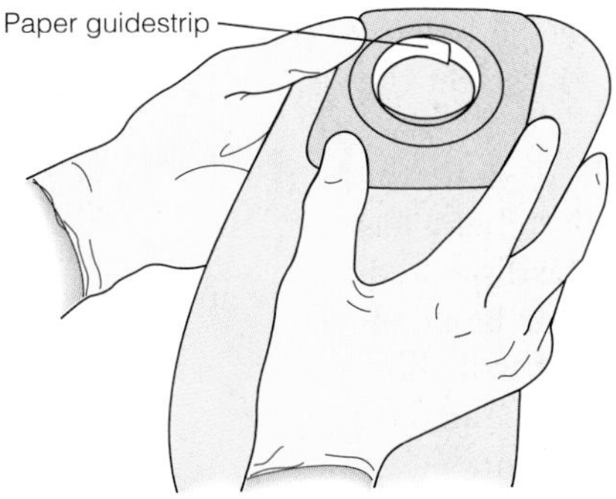

Figure 35.23 The coiled paper guidestrip in the faceplate opening

- Attach the pouch belt, and fasten it around the client's waist (optional).

12. Dispose of equipment, or clean reusable equipment.

- Discard a disposable appliance in a plastic bag before placing in the waste container.
- If feces are liquid, measure the volume. Note the character, consistency, and colour before emptying the feces into a toilet or hopper.
- Wash reusable bags with cool water and mild soap, rinse, and dry.
- Wash a soiled belt with warm water and mild soap, rinse, and dry.
- Remove and discard gloves.

13. Report and record pertinent assessments and interventions.

- Report any increase in stoma size, change in colour indicative of circulatory impairment, and presence of skin irritation or erosion.
- Record on the client's chart discolouration of the stoma; the appearance of the peristomal skin; the amount and type of drainage; the client's fatigue, discomfort, and significant behaviour about the ostomy; and skills learned by the client.
- Adjust the teaching plan and nursing care plan as needed. Include on the teaching plan the equipment and procedure used. *Client learning is facilitated by consistent nursing interventions.*

Variation: Applying the Skin Barrier and Appliance as One Unit

If a disc- or wafer-type skin barrier is used, the skin barrier and appliance can be applied as one unit. Applying the skin barrier and the appliance together not only is quicker but also is thought to reduce the chance of wrinkles. It also is easier for the client to apply without help.

- Prepare the skin barrier by measuring the size of the stoma, tracing a circle on the backing of the skin barrier, and cutting out the traced stoma pattern to make an opening in the skin barrier.

PROCEDURE 35.2 Changing a One-Piece, Drainable Bowel Diversion Ostomy Appliance *continued*

- Prepare the appliance by cutting an opening 0.3 to 0.4 cm larger than the stoma size (if not already present) and peeling off the backing from the adhesive seal.
- Centre the opening of the pouch over the skin barrier.
- Remove the skin barrier backing to expose the sticky adhesive side.
- Centre the skin barrier and appliance over the stoma, and press it onto the client's skin.

Evaluation Focus
Colour and size of stoma; amount, colour, and consistency of feces; status of peristomal skin; client responses and learning needs

Home Care Considerations

- Provide the client with the names and phone numbers of an enterostomal therapist and supply vendor.
- Suggest additional sources of information such as the Crohn's and Colitis Foundation of Canada and Canadian Association of Gastroenterology.
- Inform the client of signs to report to a health-care provider (e.g., peristomal redness, skin breakdown, and changes in stomal colour).

Routine daily irrigations for control of the time of elimination ultimately become the client's decision. Some clients prefer to control the time of elimination through rigid dietary regulation and not be bothered with irrigations, which can take up to an hour to complete. When regulation by irrigation is chosen, it should be done at the same time each day. Control by irrigations also necessitates some control of the diet. For example, laxative foods that might cause an unexpected evacuation need to be avoided.

For most clients, a relatively small amount of fluid (300 to 500 mL) stimulates evacuation. For others, up to 1,000 mL may be needed because a colostomy has no sphincter and the fluid tends to return as it is instilled. This problem is reduced by the use of a cone on the irrigating catheter. The cone helps hold the fluid within the bowel during the irrigation.

Before starting an irrigation, assess the client's readiness to select and use the equipment. Because many types of irrigation sets are available, clients should begin with a "starter set" until they are familiar with the colostomy and the problems of irrigating it. Later, with the help of an enterostomal therapy nurse, the client can select the set most appropriate for the client's needs.

If the client has had a colostomy for a long time, the irrigation needs to be given at the time the client has established, or the pattern of regularity will be disrupted. For a newly established colostomy, select a time based on the client's previous bowel habits and one that will allow the client to participate in usual daily activities. Encourage the client to select the time and to maintain it.

Evaluating

The goals established during the planning phase are evaluated according to specific desired outcomes also established in that phase. Examples of these are shown in Table 35.6.

If outcomes are not achieved, the nurse should explore the reasons. The nurse might consider some or all of the following questions:

- Were the client's fluid intake and diet appropriate?
- Was the client's activity level appropriate?
- Are prescribed medications or other factors affecting the gastrointestinal function?
- Do the client and family understand the provided instructions well enough to comply with the required therapy?
- Were sufficient physical and emotional support provided?

Consider...

What actions you would take if the client did *not* meet the following outcome:

- "Decreased frequency of bowel evacuation" *or* "No more than two bowel movements per day" (Data reveal continuing episodic abdominal cramping and four to five episodes of diarrhea daily.)

TABLE 35.6 Evaluation Goals and Outcomes: Fecal Elimination

Goal	Examples of Desired Outcomes
Constipation	
Maintain or restore usual bowel elimination pattern and regain normal stool consistency	Identifies usual pattern of bowel elimination Identifies factors that alter bowel function Ingests adequate fluids (e.g., eight glasses of water daily) Ingests adequate amount of fibre (e.g., eats two high-fibre vegetables or fruits and at least one bran muffin or high-fibre bread or cereal daily) Walks for at least 20 minutes daily Reports: (1) bowel movement at least every three days, (2) regular time for defecation, (3) easy passage of stool Stool amount, colour, and consistency within normal limits Absence of distention, discomfort, and feeling of incomplete bowel evacuation
Perceived Constipation	
Restore normal bowel elimination pattern	Verbalizes understanding of need to decrease use of laxatives, enemas, and suppositories Accepts as normal an interval of two to three days between bowel movements Alters diet and exercise pattern to include adequate daily amounts of fibre, fluids, and exercise (see ***Constipation***) Reports decreased use of laxative or suppository (e.g., only once per week)
Diarrhea	
Restore normal bowel elimination pattern	Reports stools of normal consistency and colour Reports decreased frequency of bowel evacuation (e.g., no more than two bowel movements per day) Absence of abdominal pain
Prevent potential problems associated with diarrhea	Maintains fluid and electrolyte balance, as evidenced by: a. Serum electrolyte values of: 135–145 mmol/L Potassium 3.5–5.0 mmol/L Chloride 95–105 mmol/L Bicarbonate 21–28 mmol/L b. Normal or baseline body weight or (specify weight gain) c. Normal skin turgor Maintains perianal skin integrity, as evidenced by absence of redness or breakdown
Bowel Incontinence	
Restore usual bowel elimination pattern	Identifies factors causing incontinence Keeps a daily bowel evacuation diary that includes time, amount, and stool consistency Reports fewer episodes of incontinence and soiling
Prevent potential problems associated with incontinence	Uses appropriate measures to maintain perianal skin integrity (e.g., hygienic measures and protective skin barriers) Demonstrates effective coping skills, as evidenced by: a. Ability to meet self-care needs b. Reports of participation in social activities once or twice per week

FOCUS ON CRITICAL THINKING

Mr. Jakes is a 62-year-old man who suffered a cerebrovascular accident (stroke) about three months ago. He underwent aggressive medical management and extensive physical therapy which has had a beneficial effect on his overall functioning. Currently, Mr. Jakes is able to provide much of his own care but must rely on an assistive device for safe ambulation. He is being followed on an outpatient basis by home health-care services. During your visit with Mr. Jakes at his home, you learn that he has been experiencing abdominal discomfort, increased flatulence, and intermittent diarrhea for the past several days. He states that he usually has a bowel movement every one to two days, and his last normal bowel movement was about six or seven days ago. His wife says that he is not eating or drinking well because he feels bloated and uncomfortable much of the time.

1. What conclusions, if any, can be drawn about Mr. Jakes' abdominal distress, diarrhea, and flatulence?
2. You learn that Mr. Jakes' stools have been liquid, in very small amounts, and at infrequent intervals, generally occurring when he feels the urge to defecate. What additional data are important to obtain from him?
3. What nursing intervention is most appropriate prior to making suggestions to correct the problem he is experiencing?
4. What suggestions can you give him about maintaining a regular bowel pattern?
5. Explain why cathartics and laxatives are generally contraindicated for people in Mr. Jakes' situation.

See Appendix A for answers to these questions.

CHAPTER HIGHLIGHTS

- Primary functions of the large bowel are the excretion of digestive waste products and the maintenance of fluid balance.
- Patterns of fecal elimination vary greatly among people, but a regular pattern of fecal elimination with formed, soft stools is essential to health and a sense of well-being.
- A variety of factors affect defecation: developmental level, diet, fluid intake, activity and exercise, psychological factors, regular defecation, medications, diagnostic procedures, anesthesia, and pathological conditions.
- Common fecal elimination problems include constipation, fecal impaction, diarrhea, bowel incontinence, and flatulence. Each has specific defining characteristics and contributing causes that often relate to or are identical to the factors that affect defecation.
- Assessment relative to fecal elimination includes a nursing history; physical examination of the abdomen, rectum, and anus; and in some situations, visualization studies and inspection and analysis of stool for abnormal constituents, such as blood.
- A nursing history includes data about the client's defecation pattern, description of feces and any changes or problems associated with elimination, and data about possible factors altering bowel elimination.
- Physical examination of the abdomen includes methods of inspection, auscultation, percussion, and palpation. Physical examination of the rectum and anus includes inspection and palpation.
- When inspecting the client's stool, the nurse must observe its colour, consistency, shape, amount, odour, and the presence of abnormal constituents.
- A function of the nurse is to assist clients with endoscopic and radiographic studies of the large intestine. Client assistance for visualization involves diet and bowel preparation before the study and appropriate follow-up care after the study.
- Clients also often need assistance to obtain stool specimens for laboratory analysis. In many agencies, nurses test the stool for occult blood.
- Lack of exercise, irregular defecation habits, stress, bland diets, and overuse of laxatives are all thought to contribute to constipation. Sufficient fluid and fibre intake are required to keep feces soft.
- An adverse effect of constipation is straining during defecation, during which the Valsalva maneuver may be used. Cardiac problems may ensue.
- An adverse effect of prolonged diarrhea is fluid and electrolyte imbalance.
- Digital removal of an impaction should be carried out gently because of vagal nerve stimulation and subsequent depressed cardiac rate. An order is often necessary.
- Normal defecation is often facilitated in both well and ill clients by providing privacy, teaching clients to attend to defecation urges promptly, assisting clients to normal sitting positions whenever possible, encouraging appropriate food and fluid intake, and scheduling regular exercise.

- Additional nursing strategies include administering cathartics and antidiarrheals; administering cleansing, carminative, or retention enemas; removing an impaction digitally; inserting rectal tubes to decrease flatulence; applying protective skin agents; monitoring fluid and electrolyte balance; and instructing clients in ways to promote normal defecation.
- Clients who have bowel diversion ostomies require special care, with attention to psychological adjustment, diet, and stoma and skin care. A variety of stomal management methods are available to these clients depending on the type and position of the ostomy.

READINGS AND REFERENCES

Suggested Readings

Benton, J. M., O'Hara, P. A., Chen, H., Harper, D. W., & Johnston, S. F. (1997, January/February). Changing bowel hygiene practice successfully: A program to reduce laxative use in a chronic care hospital. *Geriatric Nursing, 18*(1), 12–17.
The authors discuss how laxative use was reduced in a long-term care facility from 91.2 percent to less than 40 percent. They include details about key factors underlying the implementation of the standards of care for the bowel hygiene program in relation to hydration, dietary fibre, regular and consistent toileting, and desired outcome standards.

Chelvanayagam, S., & Norton, C. (1999, Dec.-Jan.). Focus on continence: Causes and assessment of faecal incontinence. *British Journal of Community Nursing, 4*(1), 32–35.
Fecal incontinence remains an unmentionable subject and clients frequently conceal their symptoms because of embarrassment. These authors describe the structure and function of the anal sphincters in maintaining continence. They discuss the causes and assessment of fecal incontinence. Questions are suggested which will help to identify both problems and appropriate nursing intervention.

Related Research

Bliss, D. Z., Johnson, S., Savik, K., Clabots, C. R., & Gerding, D. N. (2000, March-April). Fecal incontinence in hospitalized patients who are acutely ill. *Nursing Research, 49*, 101–108.

Brocklehurst, J., Dickinson, E., & Windsor, J. (1999, Sept.). Focus on continence. Laxatives and faecal incontinence in long-term care. *Nursing Standard, 13*(52), 32–36.

Gibson, C., Opalka, P., Moore, C., Brady, R., & Mion, L. (1995, October). Effectiveness of bran supplement on the bowel management of elderly rehabilitation patients. *Journal of Gerontological Nursing, 21*(10), 21–30, 54–55.

Hinrichs, M. D., & Huseboe, J. (2001). Research based protocol: Management of constipation. *Journal of Gerontological Nursing, 27*(2), 17–28.

Selected References

Anastasi, J. K., & Sun, V. (1996). Controlling diarrhea in the HIV patient. *American Journal of Nursing, 96*(8), 35–42.

Benton, J. M., O'Hara, P. A., Chen, H., Harper, D. W., & Johnston, S. F. (1997). Changing bowel hygiene practice successfully: A program to reduce laxative use in a chronic care hospital. *Geriatric Nursing, 18*(1), 12–17.

Bentsen, D., & Braun, J. W. (1996, July). Controlling fecal incontinence with sensory retraining managed by advanced practice nurses. *Clinical Nurse Specialist, 10*(4), 171–176.

Borwell, B. (1996, November). Colostomies and their management. *Nursing Standard, 11*(8), 49–55.

Bryant, G. A. (2000, Feb.). When spinal cord injury affects the bowel. *RN, 63*(2), 26–30.

Butler, M. (1998, January). Laxatives and rectal preparations. *Nursing Times, 94*(3), 56–58.

Carpenito, L. J. (2002). *Handbook of nursing diagnosis* (9th ed.). Philadelphia, PA: Lippincott.

Dammel, T. (1997, July). Fecal occult-blood testing. *Nursing 97, 27*(7), 44–45.

Demata, E. U. (2000, April–June). Faecal incontinence: Nursing management. *World Council of Enterostomal Therapists Journal, 20*(2), 12–16.

Emly, M. (1993, January). Abdominal massage. *Nursing Times, 89*, 34–36.

Guyton, A. C., & Hall, J. E. (2000). *Textbook of medical physiology* (10th ed.). Philadelphia, PA: Saunders.

Hinrichs, M., Huseboe, J., Tang, J. H. C., & Titler, M. G. (2001, Feb.). Research-based protocol: Management of constipation. *Journal of Gerontological Nursing, 27*(2), 17–29.

Jensen, L. L. (1997, September). Fecal incontinence: Evaluation and treatment. *Journal of Wound, Ostomy, and Continence Nurses, 24*(5), 277–282.

Johnson, M., & Maas, M. (Eds.). (2000). *Iowa outcomes project: Nursing outcomes classification (NOC)*. St. Louis, MO: Mosby.

Lambright Eckler, J. A. (1996, March). Combating infection: Defending against diarrhea. *Nursing 96, 26*(3), 22–23.

Lucas, M., Emery, S., & Beynon, J. (Eds.). (1999). *Incontinence*. Malden, MA: Blackwell Science.

Maestri-Banks, A., & Burns, D. (1996, May). Assessing constipation. *Nursing Times, 92*(21), 28–30.

McCloskey, J. C., & Bulechek, G. M. (Eds.). (2000). *Iowa intervention project: Nursing interventions classification (NIC)* (3rd ed.). St. Louis, MO: Mosby.

North American Nursing Diagnosis Association. (2000). *NANDA nursing diagnoses: Definitions and classification 2000–2001*. Philadelphia, PA: Author.

Petticrew, M. (1997). Treatment of constipation in older people. *Nursing Times, 93*(48), 55–56.

Powell, M., & Rigby, D. (2000). Management of bowel dysfunction: Evacuation difficulties. *Nursing Standard, 14*(47), 47–51, 53–54.

Roberts, D. J. (1997). The pursuit of colostomy continence. *Journal of Wound, Ostomy, and Continence Nurses, 24*(2), 92–97.

Salter, M. (1996, November). Advances in ileostomy care. *Nursing Standard, 11*(9), 49–53.

Stewart, E., Innes, J., Mackenzie, J., Gordon, R., & Downie, G. (1997, January). A strategy to reduce laxative use among older people. *Nursing Times, 93*(4), 35–36.

Soffer, E. E., & Hull, T. (2000, Aug.). Fecal incontinence: A practical approach to evaluation and treatment. *American Journal of Gastroenterology, 95*, 1873–1880.

Vickery, G. (1997, July/August). Basics of constipation. *Gastroenterology Nursing, 20*(4), 125–128.

Wald, A. (1997, July). Fecal incontinence: Three steps to successful management. *Geriatrics, 52*(7), 44–52.

WEBLINKS

Crohn's and Colitis Foundation of Canada (CCFC)
http://www.ccfc.ca/
The Crohn's and Colitis Foundation of Canada is a national not-for-profit voluntary medical research foundation. The site describes the association and provides access to their resources.

Irritable Bowel Syndrome (IBS) Self Help and Support Group
http://www.ibsgroup.org/
The Irritable Bowel Syndrome (IBS) Self Help Group was formed in 1987 to provide support to those who suffer from IBS, those who are looking for support for someone who has IBS, and medical professionals who want to learn more about IBS.

Canadian Association of Gastroenterology
http://www.cag-acg.org/
The association was founded in 1962 to promote the study of the digestive tract in health and disease. Its members are drawn from numerous health-care disciplines. The Web site provides information useful for all its members.

CHAPTER 36

Urinary Elimination

OBJECTIVES

After completing this chapter, you will be able to:

- Describe the process of urination, from urine formation through micturition.
- Identify factors that influence urinary elimination.
- Discuss common alterations in urine production and elimination.
- List common causes of selected urinary problems.
- Describe nursing assessment of urinary function, including subjective and objective data.
- Outline normal and abnormal characteristics and constituents of urine.
- Explain how to collect urine specimens and conduct selected tests.
- Describe diagnostic measures to assess kidney function and urinary tract abnormalities.
- Develop nursing diagnoses related to urinary elimination.
- List goals and desired outcomes for clients with nursing diagnoses related to urinary elimination.
- Discuss interventions to maintain normal urinary elimination and to assist clients with altered urinary elimination.
- Enumerate ways to prevent urinary infection.
- Identify interventions for clients with retention catheters or urinary diversions.

Elimination from the urinary tract is usually taken for granted. Only when a problem arises do most people become aware of their urinary habits and any associated symptoms.

A person's urinary habits depend on both social culture and personal habit. In Canada, most people are accustomed to privacy and clean (even decorative) surroundings while they urinate. The lack of privacy that is normal in many European and Asian countries surprises and frequently disturbs Canadians travelling there.

Personal habits regarding urination are affected by the social propriety of leaving to urinate, the availability of a private clean facility, and initial bladder training. Urinary elimination is essential to health, and voiding can be postponed for only so long before the urge normally becomes too great to control.

Physiology of Urinary Elimination

Urinary elimination depends on effective functioning of four urinary tract organs: kidneys, ureters, bladder, and urethra (Figure 36.1).

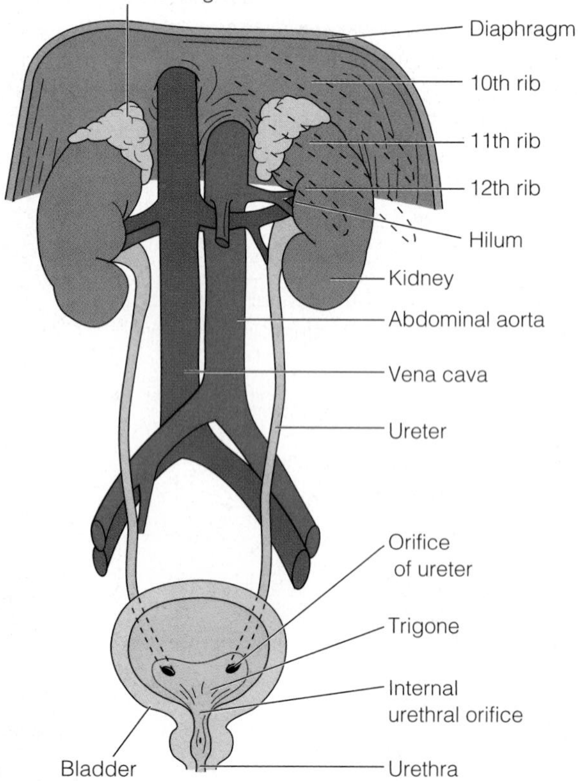

Figure 36.1 Anatomical structures of the urinary tract

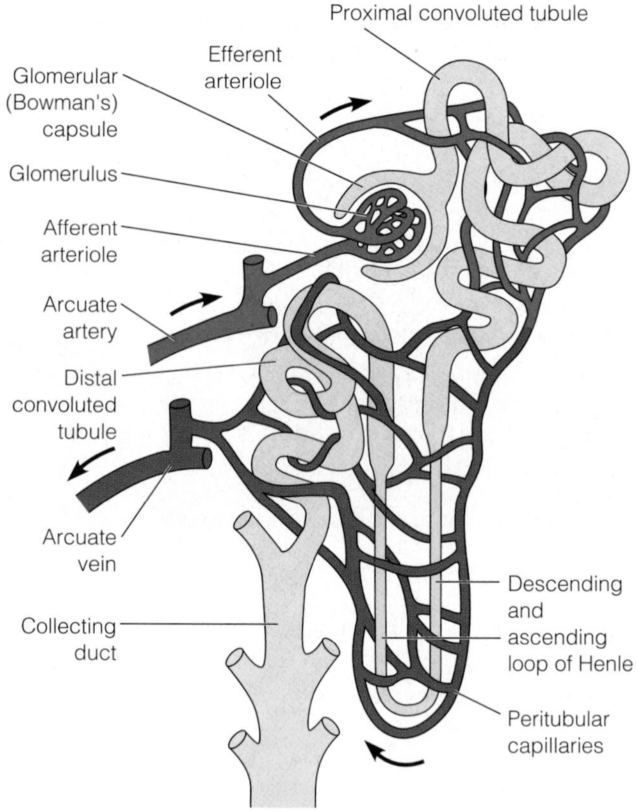

Figure 36.2 The nephrons of the kidney are composed of six parts: the glomerulus, Bowman's capsule, proximal convoluted tubule, loop of Henle, distal convoluted tubule, and collecting duct

Kidneys

The paired kidneys are situated on either side of the spinal column behind the peritoneal cavity. They are the primary regulators of fluid and acid-base balance in the body. The functional units of the kidneys, the nephrons, filter the blood and remove metabolic wastes. In the average adult, 1,200 mL of blood, or about 21 percent of the cardiac output, passes through the kidneys every minute. Each kidney contains approximately one million nephrons. Each nephron has a **glomerulus,** a tuft of capillaries surrounded by **Bowman's capsule** (Figure 36.2). The endothelium of glomerular capillaries is porous, allowing fluid and solutes to readily move across this membrane into the capsule. Plasma proteins and blood cells, however, are too large to cross the membrane normally. Glomerular filtrate is similar in composition to plasma, made up of water, electrolytes, glucose, amino acids, and metabolic wastes.

From Bowman's capsule, the filtrate moves into the tubule of the nephron. In the proximal convoluted tubule, most of the water and electrolytes are reabsorbed. Solutes, such as glucose, are reabsorbed in the loop of Henle, but in the same area, other substances are secreted into the filtrate, concentrating the urine. In the distal convoluted tubule, additional water and sodium are reabsorbed under the control of hormones, such as antidiuretic hormone (ADH) and aldosterone. This controlled reabsorption allows fine regulation of fluid and electrolyte balance in the body. When fluid intake is low or the concentration of solutes in the blood is high, ADH is released from the anterior pituitary, more water is reabsorbed in the distal tubule, and less urine is excreted. By contrast, when fluid intake is high or the blood solute concentration is low, ADH is suppressed. Without ADH, the distal tubule becomes impermeable to water, and more urine is excreted. Aldosterone also affects the tubule. When aldosterone is released from the adrenal cortex, sodium and water are reabsorbed in greater quantities, increasing the blood volume and decreasing urinary output.

Ureters

Once the urine is formed in the kidneys, it moves through the collecting ducts into the calyces of the renal pelvis and from there into the ureters. The ureters are from 25 to 30 cm long in the adult and about 1.25 cm in diameter. The upper end of each ureter is funnel-shaped as it enters the kidney. The lower ends of the ureters enter the bladder at the posterior corners of the floor of the bladder (see Figure 36.1). At the junction between the ureter and the bladder, a flaplike fold of mucous membrane acts as a valve to prevent **reflux** (backflow) of urine up the ureters.

Bladder

The urinary bladder is a hollow, muscular organ that serves as a reservoir for urine and as the organ of excretion. When empty, it lies behind the symphysis pubis. In the male, the bladder lies in front of the rectum and above the prostate gland (Figure 36.3); in the female, it lies in front of the uterus and vagina (Figure 36.4). The wall of the bladder is made up of four layers: (1) an inner mucous layer, (2) a connective tissue layer, (3) three layers of smooth muscle fibres, some of which extend lengthwise, some obliquely, and some more or less circularly, and (4) an outer serous layer. The smooth muscle layers are collectively called the **detrusor muscle.** The **trigone** at the base of the bladder is a triangular area marked by the ureter openings at the posterior corners and the opening of the urethra at the anterior inferior corner. Urine exits the bladder through the urethra.

The bladder is capable of considerable distention because of *rugae* (folds) in the mucous membrane lining and because of the elasticity of its walls. When full, the dome of the bladder may extend above the symphysis pubis; in extreme situations, it may extend as high as the umbilicus.

Urethra

The urethra extends from the bladder to the urinary **meatus** (opening). In the adult female, the urethra lies directly behind the symphysis pubis, anterior to the vagina, and is about 4.0 cm long (see Figure 36.4). The urethra serves only as a passageway for the elimination of urine. The urinary meatus is located between the labia minora, in front of the vagina and below the clitoris. The male urethra is about 20 cm long and serves as a passageway for semen as well as urine (see Figure 36.3). The meatus is located at the distal end of the penis.

The internal sphincter muscle situated at the base of the urinary bladder is under involuntary control. The external sphincter muscle is under voluntary control, allowing the individual to choose when urine is eliminated.

In both males and females, the urethra has a mucous membrane lining that is continuous with the bladder and the ureters. Thus, an infection of the urethra can extend

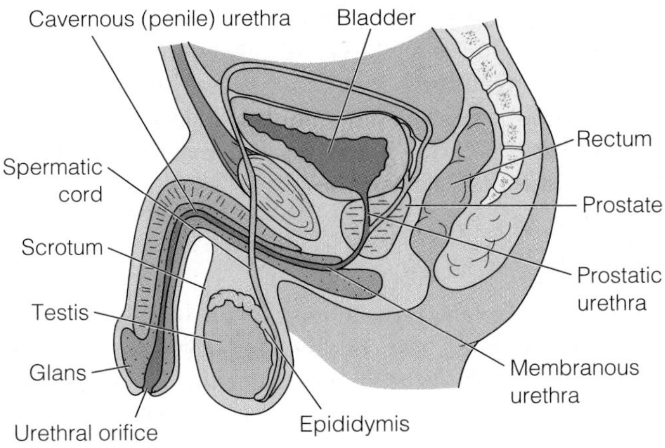

Figure 36.3 The male urogenital system

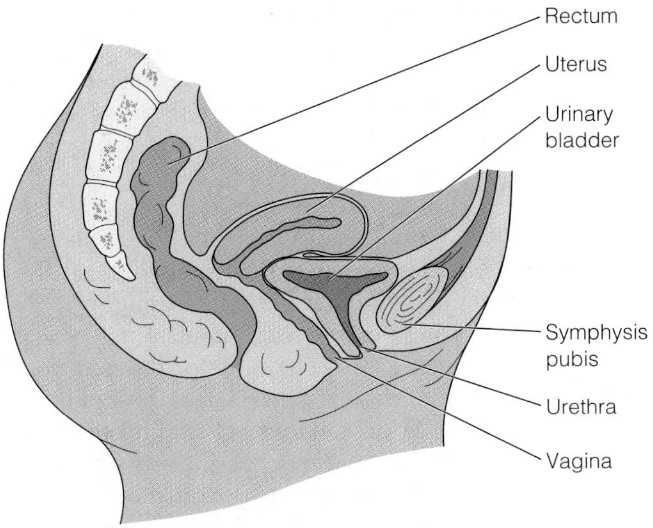

Figure 36.4 The female urogenital system

through the urinary tract to the kidneys. Women are particularly prone to urinary tract infections because of their short urethra and the proximity of the urinary meatus to the vagina and anus.

Urination

Micturition, voiding, and **urination** all refer to the process of emptying the urinary bladder. Urine collects in the bladder until pressure stimulates special sensory nerve endings in the bladder wall called *stretch receptors.* This occurs when the adult bladder contains between 250 and 450 mL of urine. In children, a considerably smaller volume, 50 to 200 mL, stimulates these nerves.

The stretch receptors transmit impulses to the spinal cord, specifically to the voiding reflex centre located at the level of the second to fourth sacral vertebrae, causing the internal sphincter to relax and stimulating the urge to void. If the time and place are appropriate for urination, the conscious portion of the brain relaxes the external urethral sphincter muscle and urination takes place. If the time and place are inappropriate, the micturition reflex usually subsides until the bladder becomes more filled and the reflex is stimulated again.

Voluntary control of urination is possible only if the nerves supplying the bladder and urethra, the neural tracts of the spinal cord and brain, and the motor area of the cerebrum are all intact. The individual must be able to sense that the bladder is full. Injury to any of these parts of the nervous system—for example, by a cerebral hemorrhage or spinal cord injury above the level of the sacral region—results in intermittent involuntary emptying of the bladder. Older people whose cognition is impaired may not be aware of the need to urinate or be able to respond to this urge by seeking toilet facilities.

Factors Affecting Voiding

Numerous factors affect the volume and characteristics of the urine produced and the manner in which it is excreted.

Developmental Factors

Infants

Urine output varies according to fluid intake but usually is about 15 to 60 mL a day after birth, increasing to 250 to 500 mL a day during the first year. An infant may urinate as often as 20 times a day. The urine of the neonate is colourless and odourless and has a specific gravity of 1.008. Because newborns and infants have immature kidneys, they are unable to concentrate urine very effectively.

Infants are born without urinary control. Most will develop this between the ages of two and five years. Control during the daytime normally precedes nighttime control.

Preschoolers

The preschooler is able to take responsibility for independent toileting. Parents need to realize that accidents do occur, and the child should never be punished or chastised for this. Children often forget to wash their hands or flush the toilet and need instruction in wiping themselves. Girls should be taught to wipe from front to back to prevent contamination of the urinary tract by feces.

School-Age Children

The school-age child's elimination system reaches maturity during this period. The kidneys double in size between ages five and 10 years. During this period, the child urinates six to eight times a day and averages one to two bowel movements per day. **Enuresis,** which is defined as the involuntary passing of urine when control should be established, can be a problem for some school-age children. About 10 percent of all six-year-olds experience difficulty controlling the bladder. **Nocturnal enuresis,** or bed wetting, is the involuntary passing of urine during sleep. Bed wetting should not be considered a problem until after the age of six years. The incidence of nocturnal enuresis declines as the child matures. About 75 percent of children with bed wetting experience this problem because of a small bladder capacity.

Older Adults

The excretory function of the kidney diminishes with age, but usually not significantly below normal levels unless a disease process intervenes. Blood flow can be reduced by arteriosclerosis, impairing renal function. With age, the number of functioning nephrons (the basic functional units of the kidney) decreases to some degree, impairing the kidney's filtering abilities.

The more noticeable changes with age are those related to the bladder. Complaints of urinary urgency and urinary frequency are common. In men, these changes are often due to an enlarged prostate gland and in women, to weakened muscles supporting the bladder or weakness of the urethral sphincter. The capacity of the bladder and its ability to completely empty diminish with age. This explains the need for older adults to arise during the night to void (**nocturnal frequency**) and the **retention** of residual urine, predisposing the older adult to bladder infections.

See Table 36.1 for a summary of the developmental changes affecting urinary output.

Psychosocial Factors

For many people, a set of conditions helps stimulate the micturition reflex. These conditions include privacy, normal position, sufficient time, and occasionally, running water. Circumstances that counter the client's accustomed conditions may produce anxiety and muscle tension. As a result, the person is unable to relax the abdominal and perineal

TABLE 36.1 Changes in Urinary Elimination through the Life Span

Stage	Variations
Fetus	The fetal kidney begins to excrete urine between the 11th and 12th weeks of development.
Infant	Ability to concentrate urine is minimal; therefore, urine appears light yellow.
	Because of neuromuscular immaturity, voluntary urinary control is absent.
Child	Kidney function reaches maturity between the first and second years of life; urine is concentrated effectively and appears a normal amber colour.
	Between 18 and 24 months of age, the child starts to recognize bladder fullness and is able to hold urine beyond the urge to void.
	At approximately $2\frac{1}{2}$ to three years of age, the child can perceive bladder fullness, hold urine after the urge to void, and communicate the need to urinate.
	Full urinary control usually occurs at age four or five years; daytime control is usually achieved by age three years.
	The kidneys grow in proportion to overall body growth.
Adult	The kidneys reach maximum size between 35 and 40 years of age.
	After 50 years, the kidneys begin to diminish in size and function. Most shrinkage occurs in the cortex of the kidney as individual nephrons are lost.
Older adult	An estimated 30 percent of nephrons are lost by age 80 years.
	Renal blood flow decreases because of vascular changes and a decrease in cardiac output.
	The ability to concentrate urine declines.
	Bladder muscle tone diminishes, causing increased frequency of urination and nocturia (awakening to urinate at night).
	Diminished bladder muscle tone and contractibility may lead to residual urine in the bladder after voiding, increasing the risk of bacterial growth and infection.
	Urinary incontinence may occur due to mobility problems or neurological impairments.

muscles and the external urethral sphincter, and voiding is inhibited. People may also voluntarily suppress urination (*voluntary urinary retention*) because of perceived time pressures; for example, nurses often ignore the urge to void until they are able to take a break. This behaviour can increase the risk of urinary tract infections.

Fluid and Food Intake

The healthy body maintains a balance between the amount of fluid ingested and the amount of fluid eliminated. Therefore, when the amount of fluid intake increases, the output normally increases. Certain fluids, such as alcohol, increase fluid output by inhibiting the production of antidiuretic hormone. Fluids that contain caffeine (e.g., coffee, tea, and cola drinks) also increase urine production. By contrast, food and fluids high in sodium can cause fluid retention as water is retained to maintain the normal concentration of electrolytes.

Some foods and fluids can change the colour of urine. For example, beets and blackberries can cause urine to appear red; foods containing carotene can cause the urine to appear yellower than usual.

Medications

Many medications, particularly those affecting the autonomic nervous system, interfere with the normal urination process and may cause retention. See the following box.

Diuretics (e.g., chlorothiazide, furosemide, and ethacrynic acid) increase urine formation by preventing the reabsorption of water and electrolytes from the tubules of the kidney into the bloodstream. Diuretics are commonly prescribed for hypertension and cardiac disease.

Muscle Tone and Activity

Regular exercise increases muscle tone and the metabolic rate. Good muscle tone is important to maintain the stretch and contractility of the detrusor muscle so the bladder can fill adequately and empty completely. Clients who require a retention catheter for a long period may have poor bladder muscle tone because continuous drainage of urine prevents the bladder from filling and emptying normally. Abdominal and pelvic muscle tone also contribute: abdominal muscle contraction assists in bladder emptying; pelvic muscle tone is a factor in being able to retain urine voluntarily once the urge to urinate is perceived.

Medications That May Cause Urinary Retention

- Anticholinergic and antispasmodic medications, such as atropine, belladonna, Donnatal (containing atropine), and papaverine
- Antidepressant and antipsychotic agents, such as MAO inhibitors and phenothiazines
- Antiparkinsonism drugs, such as levodopa, trihexyphenidyl (Artane), and benztropine mesylate (Cogentin)
- Antihistamine preparations, such as Actifed and Sudafed
- Beta-adrenergic blockers, such as propranolol (Inderal)
- Antihypertensives, such as hydralazine (Apresoline) and methyldopate (Aldomet)

Pathological Conditions

Some diseases and pathologies can affect the formation and excretion of urine. Diseases of the kidneys may affect the ability of the nephrons to produce urine. Abnormal amounts of protein or blood cells may be present in the urine, or the kidneys may virtually stop producing urine altogether, a condition known as renal failure. Heart and circulatory disorders, such as heart failure, shock, or hypertension, can affect blood flow to the kidneys, interfering with urine production. If abnormal amounts of fluid are lost through another route (e.g., vomiting or high fever), water is retained by the kidneys and urinary output falls.

Processes that interfere with the flow of urine from the kidneys to the urethra affect urinary excretion. A urinary stone (calculus) may obstruct a ureter, blocking urine flow from the kidney to the bladder. Hypertrophy of the prostate gland, a common condition affecting older men, may partially obstruct the urethra, impairing urination and bladder emptying.

Surgical and Diagnostic Procedures

Some surgical and diagnostic procedures can affect the passage of urine and the urine itself. The urethra may swell following a cystoscopy, and surgical procedures on any part of the urinary tract may result in some postoperative bleeding; as a result, the urine may be red- or pink-tinged for a time.

Spinal anesthetics can affect the passage of urine because they decrease the client's awareness of the need to void. Surgery on structures adjacent to the urinary tract (e.g., the uterus) can also affect voiding because of swelling in the lower abdomen.

Altered Urine Production

Although people's patterns of urination are highly individual, most people void about five to seven times a day. People usually void when they first awaken in the morning, before they go to bed, and around mealtimes. Table 36.2 shows the average urinary output per day at different ages.

Polyuria

Polyuria refers to the production of abnormally large amounts of urine by the kidneys, often several litres more than the client's usual daily output. Polyuria can follow excessive fluid intake, a condition known as **polydipsia,** or may be associated with such diseases as diabetes mellitus, diabetes insipidus, or chronic nephritis. **Diuresis** is another term for the production and excretion of large amounts of urine. This term is often used when medications are given to promote urine output (diuretics) or to describe the effect of ingested substances, such as caffeine or alcohol, on urine production. Polyuria or diuresis can cause excessive fluid loss, leading to intense thirst, dehydration, and weight loss.

Oliguria and Anuria

The terms *oliguria* and *anuria* are used to describe decreased urinary output. **Oliguria** is low urine output, usually less than 500 mL a day or 30 mL an hour. **Anuria** refers to a lack of urine production, with no effective urinary output. Although oliguria may occur as a result of abnormal fluid losses or a lack of fluid intake, it often indicates impaired blood flow to the kidneys or impending renal failure and should be promptly reported to the physician. Restoring renal blood flow and urinary output promptly can prevent renal failure and its complications.

TABLE 36.2 Average Daily Urine Output by Age

Age	Amount (mL)
1 to 2 days	15–60
3 to 10 days	100–300
10 days to 2 months	250–450
2 months to 1 year	400–500
1 to 3 years	500–600
3 to 5 years	600–700
5 to 8 years	700–1,000
8 to 14 years	800–1,400
14 years through adulthood	1,500
Older adulthood	1,500 or less

Altered Urinary Elimination

Despite normal urine production, a number of factors or conditions can affect urinary elimination. Frequency, urgency, dysuria, and nocturia often are manifestations of underlying conditions, such as a urinary tract infection. Enuresis, incontinence, and retention, on the other hand, may be either a manifestation or the primary problem affecting urinary elimination. Selected factors associated with altered patterns of urine elimination are identified in Table 36.3.

Frequency and Nocturia

Urinary frequency is voiding at frequent intervals, that is, more often than usual. An increased intake of fluid causes some increase in the frequency of voiding. Such conditions as urinary tract infection, stress, and pregnancy can cause frequent voiding of small quantities (50 to 100 mL) of urine. Total fluid intake and output may be normal.

Nocturia is voiding two or more times at night. Like frequency, it is usually expressed in terms of the number of times the person gets out of bed to void, for example, "nocturia × 4."

Urgency

Urgency is the feeling that the person *must* void. There may or may not be a great deal of urine in the bladder, but the person feels a need to void immediately. Urgency accompanies psychological stress and irritation of the trigone and urethra. It is also common in young children who have poor external sphincter control.

TABLE 36.3 Selected Factors Associated with Altered Urinary Elimination

Pattern	Selected Associated Factors
Polyuria	Ingestion of fluids containing caffeine or alcohol Prescribed diuretic Presence of thirst, dehydration, and weight loss History of diabetes mellitus, diabetes insipidus, or kidney disease
Oliguria, anuria	Decrease in fluid intake Signs of dehydration (see Chapter 40) Presence of hypotension, shock, or heart failure History of kidney disease Signs of renal failure, such as elevated blood urea nitrogen (BUN) and serum creatinine, edema, hypertension
Frequency or nocturia	Pregnancy Increase in fluid intake Urinary tract infection Any known contributing or initiating causes, such as stress
Urgency	Presence of psychological stress Urinary tract infection
Dysuria	Urinary tract inflammation, infection, or injury Presence of other signs that may accompany dysuria, such as hesitancy, hematuria, pyuria (pus in the urine) and frequency
Enuresis	Family history of enuresis Difficult access to toilet facilities Home stresses
Incontinence	Bladder inflammation or other disease Difficulties in independent toileting (mobility impairment) Leakage when coughing, laughing, sneezing Cognitive impairment
Retention	Distended bladder on palpation and percussion Associated signs, such as pubic discomfort, restlessness, frequency, and small urine volume Recent anesthesia Recent perineal surgery Presence of perineal swelling Medications prescribed Lack of privacy or other factors inhibiting micturition

Dysuria

Dysuria means voiding that is either painful or difficult. It can accompany a stricture (decrease in calibre) of the urethra, urinary infections, and injury to the bladder and urethra. Often, clients will say they have to push to void or that burning accompanies or follows voiding. The burning may be described as severe, like a hot poker, or more subdued, like a sunburn. Often, **urinary hesitancy** (a delay and difficulty in initiating voiding) is associated with dysuria.

Enuresis

Enuresis is defined as involuntary urination in children beyond the age when voluntary bladder control is normally acquired, usually four or five years of age. **Nocturnal** (nighttime) enuresis often is irregular in occurrence and affects boys more often than girls. **Diurnal** (daytime) enuresis may be persistent and pathological in origin. It affects women and girls more frequently.

Urinary Incontinence

Urinary incontinence (UI), or involuntary urination, is a symptom, not a disease. It can have a significant impact on the client's life, creating physical problems, such as skin breakdown, and possibly leading to psychosocial problems, such as embarrassment, isolation, and social withdrawal. Although incontinence is common in older adults, it is not a normal consequence of aging and can often be treated.

Urinary Retention

When the emptying of the bladder is impaired, urine accumulates and the bladder becomes overdistended, a condition known as **urinary retention (UR).** Overdistention of the bladder causes poor contractility of the detrusor muscle, further impairing urination. Common causes of urinary retention include prostatic hypertrophy (enlargement), surgery, and some medications (see the box on page 896).

Clients with urinary retention may experience overflow voiding or incontinence, eliminating 25 to 50 mL of urine at frequent intervals. The bladder is firm and distended on palpation and may be displaced to one side of midline.

Neurogenic Bladder

Impaired neurological function can interfere with the normal mechanisms of urine elimination, resulting in a **neurogenic bladder.** The client with a neurogenic bladder does not perceive bladder fullness and is unable to control the urinary sphincters. The bladder may become flaccid and distended or spastic, with frequent involuntary urination.

Assessing

A complete assessment of a client's urinary function includes the following:

- Nursing history
- Physical assessment of the genitourinary system, hydration status, and examination of the urine
- Relating the data obtained to the results of any diagnostic tests and procedures

Nursing History

The nurse determines the client's normal voiding pattern and frequency, appearance of the urine and any recent changes, any past or current problems with urination, the presence of an ostomy, and factors influencing the elimination pattern.

Examples of interview questions to elicit this information are shown in the box opposite. The number of questions asked depends on the individual and the responses to the first three categories.

Physical Assessment

Complete physical assessment of the urinary tract usually includes percussion of the kidneys to detect areas of tenderness. Palpation and percussion of the bladder are also performed. See Chapter 27. If the client's history or current problems indicate a need for it, the urethral meatus of both male and female clients is inspected for swelling, discharge, and inflammation.

Because problems with urination can affect the elimination of wastes from the body, it is important that the nurse assess the skin for colour, texture, and tissue turgor as well as the presence of edema. If incontinence, dribbling, or dysuria is noted in the history, the skin of the perineum should be inspected for irritation because contact with urine can excoriate the skin.

Assessing Urine

Normal urine consists of 96 percent water and 4 percent solutes. Organic solutes include urea, ammonia, creatinine, and uric acid. Urea is the chief organic solute. Inorganic solutes include sodium, chloride, potassium, sulfate, magnesium, and phosphorus. Sodium chloride is the most abundant inorganic salt. Characteristics of normal and abnormal urine are shown in Table 36.4.

Measuring Urinary Output

Normally, the kidneys produce urine at a rate of approximately 60 mL per hour or about 1,500 mL per day. Urine output is affected by many factors, including fluid intake, body fluid losses through other routes, such as perspiration and breathing, and the cardiovascular and renal status of the individual.

ASSESSMENT INTERVIEW

Urinary Elimination

Voiding Pattern

- How many times do you void during a 24-hour period?
- Has this pattern changed recently?
- Do you need to get out of bed to void at night? How often?

Description of Urine and Any Changes

- How would you describe your urine in terms of colour, clarity (clear, transparent, or cloudy), and odour (faint or strong)?

Urinary Elimination Problems

What problems have you had or now have with passing your urine?

- Passage of small amounts of urine?
- Voiding at more frequent intervals?
- Trouble getting to the bathroom in time or feeling an urgent need to void?
- Painful voiding?
- Difficulty starting urine stream?
- Frequent dribbling of urine or feeling of bladder fullness associated with voiding small amounts of urine?
- Reduced force of stream?
- Accidental leakage of urine? If so, when does this occur (e.g., when coughing, laughing, or sneezing; at night; during the day)?
- Past urinary tract illness, such as infection of the kidney, bladder, or urethra; urinary calculi; surgery of kidney, ureters, or bladder?

Presence and Management of Urinary Diversion Ostomy

1. What is your usual routine with your ostomy?
2. What problems, if any, do you have with it?
3. How can the nurse help you manage it?

Factors Influencing Urinary Elimination

- *Medications.* Do you take any medications that could increase urinary output (e.g., diuretic) or cause retention of urine (e.g., anticholinergic-antispasmodic, antidepressant-antipsychotic, antiparkinsonism, antihistamines, antihypertensives)? Note specific medication, dosage, and frequency.
- *Fluid intake.* What amount and kind of fluid do you take each day (e.g., six glasses of water, five cups of coffee, three cola drinks with or without caffeine)?
- *Environmental factors.* Do you have any problems with toileting (mobility, removing clothing, toilet seat too low, facility without grab bar)?
- *Presence of long-term catheter.* How do you care for your catheter? Do you have any discomfort with it or other problems? How can the nurse help you manage it?
- *Stress.* Are you experiencing any long-term or short-term stress? If so, what are the stressors? Do you think these affect your urinary pattern?
- *Disease.* Have you had or do you have any illnesses that may affect urinary function, such as hypertension, heart disease, neurological disease (e.g., multiple sclerosis), cancer, prostatic enlargement, diabetes mellitus, or diabetes insipidus?
- *Diagnostic procedures.* Have you recently had a cystoscopy or spinal anesthetic?

Urine outputs below 30 mL per hour may indicate low blood volume or kidney malfunction and must be reported. In children, normal urine volume is 300 to 1,500 mL per day (see Table 36.2).

To measure fluid output, the nurse follows these steps:

- Wear clean gloves to prevent contact with microorganisms or blood in the urine.
- Ask the client to void in a clean urinal, bedpan, commode, or toilet collection device ("hat").
- Instruct the client to keep urine separate from feces and to avoid putting toilet paper in the urine collection container.
- Pour the voided urine into a calibrated container.
- Holding the container at eye level, read the amount in the container. Containers usually have a measuring scale on the inside.
- If a clean specimen is required, pour some urine into the specimen container and discard the remainder, unless all urine is to be saved.
- Record the amount on the fluid intake and output sheet, which may be at the bedside or in the bathroom.
- Rinse the urine collection and measuring containers with cool water and store appropriately.
- Remove gloves and wash hands.
- Calculate and document the total output on the client's chart at the end of each shift and at the end of 24 hours.

Many clients can measure and record their own urine output when the procedure is explained to them.

When measuring urine from a client who has an indwelling catheter, the nurse follows these steps:

- Don clean gloves.
- Take the clean calibrated container to the bedside.

TABLE 36.4 Characteristics of Normal and Abnormal Urine

Characteristic	Normal	Abnormal	Nursing Considerations
Amount in 24 hours (adult)	1,200–1,500 mL	Under 1,200 mL Over 1,500 mL	Urinary output normally is approximately equal to fluid intake. Output of less than 30 mL/hr may indicate decreased blood flow to the kidneys and should be immediately reported.
Colour, clarity	Straw, amber Transparent	Dark amber Cloudy Dark orange Red or dark brown Mucus plugs, viscid, thick	Concentrated urine is darker in colour. Dilute urine may appear almost clear or very pale yellow. Some foods and drugs may colour urine (e.g., beets, phenazopyridine, phenytoin). Red blood cells in the urine (hematuria) may be evident as pink, bright red, or rusty brown urine. Menstrual bleeding can also colour urine but should not be confused with hematuria. White blood cells, bacteria, pus, or contaminants, such as prostatic fluid, sperm, or vaginal drainage, may cause cloudy urine.
Odour	Faint aromatic	Offensive	Some foods (e.g., asparagus) cause a musty odour; infected urine can have a fetid odour; urine high in glucose has a sweet odour.
Sterility	No microorganisms present	Microorganisms present	Urine specimens may be contaminated by bacteria from the perineum during collection.
pH	4.5–8	Under 4.5 Over 8	Freshly voided urine is normally somewhat acidic. More acidic urine (low pH) is found in acidosis, starvation, diarrhea, or with a diet high in protein foods or cranberries. Alkaline urine may indicate a state of alkalosis, urinary tract infection, or a diet high in fruits and vegetables.
Specific gravity	1.010–1.025	Under 1.010 Over 1.025	Diluted urine has a lower specific gravity; concentrated urine has a higher specific gravity.
Glucose	Not present	Present	Glucose in the urine indicates high blood glucose levels and may be indicative of undiagnosed or uncontrolled diabetes mellitus.
Ketone bodies (acetone)	Not present	Present	Ketones, the end product of the breakdown of fatty acids, are not normally present in the urine. They may be present in the urine of clients who have uncontrolled diabetes mellitus, are in a state of starvation, or who have ingested excessive amounts of aspirin.
Blood	Not present	Occult (microscopic) Bright red	Blood may be present in the urine of clients who have urinary tract infection, kidney disease, or bleeding from the urinary tract.

- Place the container under the urine collection bag so that the spout of the bag is above the container but not touching it. The calibrated container is not sterile, but the inside of the collection bag is sterile.
- Open the spout and permit the urine to flow into the container.
- Close the spout, then proceed as described in the previous list.

Measuring Residual Urine

Residual urine (urine remaining in the bladder following the voiding) is normally not present or consists of only a few millilitres. However, a bladder outlet obstruction (e.g., enlargement of the prostate gland) or loss of bladder muscle tone may interfere with complete emptying of the bladder during urination. Manifestations of urine retention may include frequent voiding of small amounts (e.g., less than 100 mL in an adult). Urinary stasis and urinary tract infection are possible consequences of incomplete bladder emptying. Residual urine is measured to assess the amount of retained urine after voiding and determine the need for interventions (e.g., medications to promote detrusor muscle contraction).

To measure residual urine, the nurse catheterizes the client immediately after the client has voided. The amount of urine voided and the amount obtained by catheterization are measured and recorded. An indwelling catheter may be inserted if the residual urine exceeds a specified amount.

Collecting Urine Specimens

The nurse is responsible for collecting urine specimens for a number of tests: clean voided specimens for routine urinalysis, *clean-catch* or *midstream urine specimens* for urine culture, and timed urine specimens for a variety of tests depending on the client's specific health problem.

Clean Voided Specimen

Many clients are able to collect a clean voided specimen and provide the specimen independently with minimal instructions. Male clients generally are able to void directly into the specimen container, and female clients usually sit or squat over the toilet, holding the container between their legs during voiding. About 120 mL of urine is generally required. Clients who are seriously ill, physically incapacitated, or disoriented may need to use a bedpan or urinal in bed; others may require supervision or assistance in the bathroom. Whatever the situation, explicit directions are required:

- The specimen must be free of fecal contamination, so urine must be kept separate from feces.
- Female clients should discard the toilet tissue in the toilet or in a waste bag, rather than in the bedpan, because tissue in the specimen makes laboratory analysis more difficult.
- Put the lid tightly on the container to prevent spillage of the urine and contamination of other objects.

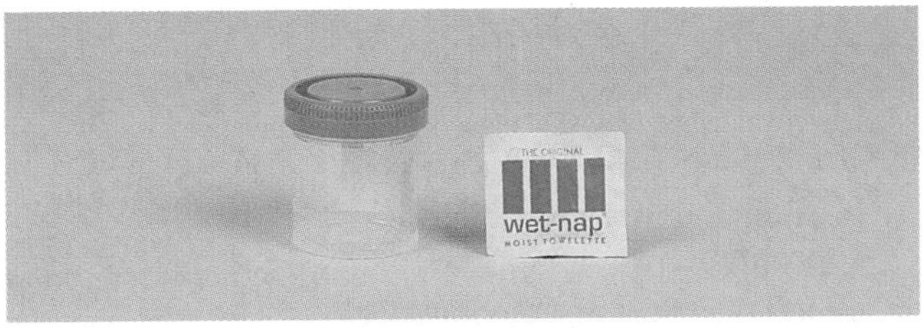

Figure 36.5 Disposable clean-catch specimen equipment

- If the outside of the container has been contaminated by urine, clean it with a disinfectant and place in a clean plastic bag.

The nurse must (1) make sure that the specimen label and the laboratory requisition carry the correct information, and (2) attach them securely to the specimen. Inappropriate identification of the specimen can lead to errors of diagnosis or therapy for the client.

Clean-Catch or Midstream Specimen

Clean-catch or midstream voided specimens are collected when urine culture is ordered to identify microorganisms causing urinary tract infection. Although some contamination by skin bacteria may occur with a clean-catch specimen, the risk of introducing microorganisms into the urinary tract through catheterization is more significant. Care is taken to ensure that the specimen is as free as possible from contamination by microorganisms around the urinary meatus. Clean-catch specimens are collected into a sterile specimen container with a lid. Disposable clean-catch kits are available (Figure 36.5). Procedure 36.1 explains how to collect a clean-catch urine specimen.

PROCEDURE 36.1 Collecting a Urine Specimen for Culture and Sensitivity by Clean Catch

PURPOSE

- To determine the presence of microorganisms, the type of organism(s), and the antibiotics to which the organisms are sensitive

Assessment Focus
Ability of the client to provide the specimen; colour, odour, and consistency of the urine; presence of clinical signs of urinary tract infection (e.g., frequency, urgency, dysuria, hematuria, flank pain, cloudy urine with foul odour)

Equipment

- ❑ Disposable or sterile gloves
- ❑ Antiseptic towelette, such as povidone-iodine
- ❑ Sterile cotton balls or 2 × 2 gauze pads
- ❑ Sterile specimen container
- ❑ Specimen identification label
- ❑ Completed laboratory requisition form
- ❑ Urine receptacle, if the client is not ambulatory
- ❑ Basin of warm water, soap, washcloth, and towel for the nonambulatory client
- ❑ Some agencies may use prepared disposable clean-catch kits

PROCEDURE 36.1 Collecting a Urine Specimen for Culture and Sensitivity by Clean Catch *continued*

INTERVENTION

1. Instruct and assist the client appropriately.

- Inform the client that a urine specimen is required; give the reason, and explain the method to be used to collect it.

2. For an ambulatory client who is able to follow directions, instruct the client how to collect the specimen.

- Direct or assist the client to the bathroom.
- Ask the client to wash hands.
- Ask the client to wash and dry the genital and perineal area with soap and water. *Washing the perineal area reduces the number of skin and transient bacteria, decreasing the risk of contaminating the urine specimen.*
- Instruct the client how to clean the urinary meatus with antiseptic towelettes. *The antiseptic further reduces bacterial contamination of the urinary meatus and the risk of contaminating the specimen.*

For Female Clients

- Use each towelette only once. Clean the perineal area from front to back, and discard the towelette. Use all towelettes provided (usually two or three). *Cleaning from front to back cleans the area of least contamination to the area of greatest contamination.*

For Male Clients

- If uncircumcised, retract the foreskin slightly to expose the urinary meatus.
- Using a circular motion, clean the urinary meatus and the distal portion of the penis. Use each towelette only once, then discard.
- Clean several centimetres down the shaft of the penis. *This cleans from the area of least contamination to the area of greatest contamination.*

3. For a client who requires assistance, prepare the client and equipment.

- Don gloves.
- Wash the perineal area with soap and water; rinse and dry.
- Assist the client onto a clean commode or bedpan. If using a bedpan or urinal, position the client as upright as allowed or tolerated. *Assuming a normal anatomical position for voiding facilitates urination.*
- Clean the urinary meatus and perineal area as described in step 2.

4. Collect the specimen from a nonambulatory client or instruct an ambulatory client how to collect it.

- Open the sterile specimen container, taking care not to contaminate the inside of the specimen container or lid. *It is important to maintain sterility of the specimen container to prevent contamination of the specimen.*
- Instruct the client to start voiding. *Bacteria in the distal urethra and at the urinary meatus are cleared by the first few millilitres of urine expelled.*
- Place the specimen container into the stream of urine and collect the specimen, taking care not to touch the container to the perineum or penis. *It is important to avoid contaminating the interior of the specimen container and the specimen itself.*
- Collect 30 to 60 mL of urine in the container.
- Cap the container tightly, touching only the outside of the container and the cap. *This prevents contamination or spilling of the specimen.*
- If necessary, clean the outside of the specimen container with disinfectant and place in a clean plastic bag. *This prevents transfer of microorganisms to others.*
- Remove gloves if handling another person's urine. Wash hands.

5. Label the specimen, and transport it to the laboratory.

- Ensure that the specimen label and the laboratory requisition carry the correct information. Attach them securely to the specimen. *Inaccurate identification or information on the specimen container can lead to errors of diagnosis or therapy.*
- Arrange for the specimen to be sent to the laboratory immediately. *Bacterial cultures must be started immediately, before any contaminating organisms can grow, multiply, and produce false results.*

6. Document pertinent data.

- Record collection of the specimen, any pertinent observations of the urine in terms of colour, odour, or consistency, and any difficulty in voiding that the client experienced.

Evaluation Focus
Appearance and odour of urine; amount voided, if output is being assessed

Home Care Considerations

Instruct the client and support person to

- Wash hands well with warm, soapy water before and after collecting urine samples.
- Wear gloves if handling another person's urine.
- If carrying the specimen to a laboratory, place the urine container in a clean, clear plastic bag.
- Label the container with the person's name and date of birth.

Timed Urine Specimen

Some urine examinations require collection of all urine produced and voided over a specific period of time, ranging from one to two hours to 24 hours. Timed specimens generally either are refrigerated or contain a preservative to prevent bacterial growth or decomposition of urine components. To collect a timed urine specimen, follow these steps:

- Obtain a specimen container with preservative (if indicated) from the laboratory. Label the container with identifying information for the client, the test to be performed, time started, and time of completion.
- Provide a clean receptacle to collect urine (bedpan, commode, or toilet collection device).
- Post signs in the client's chart, Kardex®, room, and bathroom alerting personnel to save all urine during the specified time.
- At the start of the collection period, have the client void and discard this urine.
- Save all urine produced during the timed collection period in the container, refrigerating or placing the container on ice as indicated. Avoid contaminating the urine with toilet paper or feces.
- At the end of the collection period, instruct the client to completely empty the bladder and save this voiding as part of the specimen. Take the entire amount of urine collected to the laboratory with the completed requisition.
- Record collection of the specimen, time started and completed, and any pertinent observations of the urine on appropriate records.

Indwelling Catheter Specimen

Sterile urine specimens can be obtained from closed drainage systems by inserting a sterile needle attached to a syringe through a drainage port in the tubing. Aspiration of urine from catheters can be done only with self-sealing rubber catheters—not plastic, silicone, or Silastic catheters. When self-sealing rubber catheters are used, the needle is inserted just above the place where the catheter is attached to the drainage tubing. The area from which to obtain urine may be marked by a patch on the catheter. For further information about urinary catheters, see Urinary Catheterization later in the chapter.

To collect a specimen from a Foley (retention) catheter or a drainage tube, follow these steps:

- Don disposable gloves.
- If there is no urine in the catheter, clamp the drainage tubing for about 15 to 20 minutes. This allows fresh urine to collect in the catheter.
- Wipe the area where the needle will be inserted with a disinfectant swab. The site should be distal to the tube leading to the balloon to avoid puncturing this tube. Disinfecting the needle insertion site removes any microorganisms on the surface of the catheter, thereby avoiding contamination of the needle and the entrance of microorganisms into the catheter.
- Insert the needle at a 30- to 45-degree angle (Figure 36.6). This angle of entrance facilitates self-sealing of the rubber.
- Withdraw the required amount of urine, for example, 3 mL for a urine culture or 30 mL for a routine urinalysis.
- Transfer the urine to the specimen container. Make sure the needle does not touch the outside of the container if a sterile culture tube is used.
- Without recapping the needle, discard the syringe and needle in an appropriate sharps container.
- Cap the container.
- Unclamp the drainage tubing.
- Remove gloves and discard appropriately.
- Label the container, and send the urine to the laboratory immediately for analysis or refrigeration.
- Record collection of the specimen and any pertinent observations of the urine on the appropriate records.

Urine Testing

Several simple urine tests are often done by nurses on the nursing units. These include tests for specific gravity, pH, and the presence of abnormal constituents, such as glucose, ketones, protein, and occult blood.

Specific Gravity

The **specific gravity** of urine is a measure of its concentration, or the amount of solutes (metabolic wastes and electrolytes) present in the urine. A *urinometer* or *hydrometer* in a cylinder of urine or a *spectrometer* or *refractometer*

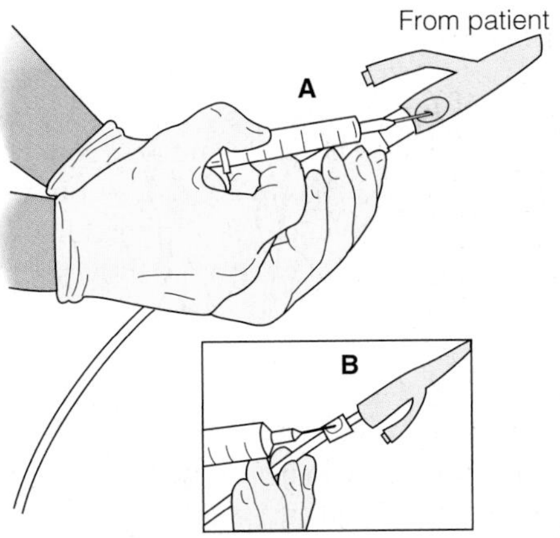

Figure 36.6 Obtaining a urine specimen from a retention catheter: *A,* from a specific area near the end of the catheter; *B,* from an access port in the tubing

is used to measure the specific gravity. The specific gravity of distilled water is 1.00; the specific gravity of urine normally ranges from 1.010 to 1.025. As urine becomes more concentrated, its specific gravity increases. Excess fluid intake or diseases affecting the ability of the kidneys to concentrate urine can result in low specific gravity readings. A high specific gravity may indicate fluid deficit or dehydration, or excess solutes, such as glucose, in the urine.

Urinary pH

Urinary pH is measured to determine the relative acidity or alkalinity of urine and assess the client's acid-base status. Quantitative measurements of urine pH can be performed in the laboratory, but dip sticks or litmus paper often are used on nursing units or in clinics to obtain less precise pH measurements. Urine normally is slightly acidic, with an average pH of 6 (7 is neutral, less than 7 is acidic, greater than 7 is alkaline).

Many commercially prepared kits available to test abnormal constituents in the urine can be used by nurses in a health-care facility or by clients in the home setting. These kits contain the required equipment and an appropriate *reagent* (substance used in a chemical reaction to detect a specific substance). Reagents may be in the form of a tablet, fluid, or paper strips or dipsticks. When the urine contacts the reagent, a chemical reaction occurs, causing a colour change that is then compared with a chart to interpret the significance of the colour. Specific directions for the amount of urine needed, the time required for the chemical reaction, and the meaning of the colours produced vary among manufacturers. Thus, it is essential that nurses and clients read and follow directions supplied by each manufacturer. In addition, testing materials need to be checked to ascertain that they are not outdated.

Clients need to be instructed to wash their hands well with warm, soapy water before and after collecting and testing urine samples and to wear gloves if handling another person's urine.

Glucose

Urine is tested for glucose to screen clients for diabetes mellitus and to assess clients during pregnancy for abnormal glucose tolerance. Normally, the amount of glucose in the urine is negligible, although individuals who have ingested large amounts of sugar may show small amounts of glucose in their urine.

Ketones

Ketone bodies, a product of the breakdown of fatty acids, normally are not present in the urine. They may, however, be found in the urine of clients with poorly controlled diabetes. Urine ketone testing with reagent tablets or a dipstick also is used to evaluate ketoacidosis in clients who are alcoholic, fasting, starving, or consuming high-protein diets.

Protein

Protein molecules normally are too large to escape from glomerular capillaries into the filtrate. If the glomerular membrane has been damaged, however (e.g., because of an inflammatory process, such as glomerulonephritis), it can become "leaky," allowing proteins to escape. Urine testing for the presence of protein generally is done with a reagent strip (dipstick).

Occult Blood

Normal urine is free from blood. When blood is present, it may be clearly visible or not visible (**occult**). Commercial reagent strips are used to test for occult blood in the urine.

Diagnostic Tests

Blood levels of two metabolically produced substances, urea and creatinine, are routinely used to evaluate renal function. Both are normally eliminated by the kidneys through filtration and tubular secretion. Urea, the end product of protein metabolism, is measured as **blood urea nitrogen (BUN). Creatinine** is produced in relatively constant quantities by the muscles. The **creatinine clearance** test uses 24-hour urine and serum creatinine levels to determine the glomerular filtration rate, a sensitive indicator of renal function.

Visualization procedures also may be used to evaluate urinary function. The KUB is a radiograph of the kidneys, ureters, and bladder. **Intravenous pyelography (IVP)** and **retrograde pyelography** also are radiographic studies used to evaluate the urinary tract. In an intravenous pyelogram, contrast medium is injected intravenously; during retrograde pyelography, the contrast medium is instilled directly into the renal pelvis via the urethra, bladder, and ureters. Following injection or instillation of the contrast medium, radiographs are taken to evaluate urinary tract structures. **Computed tomography (CT)** is a painless, noninvasive radiographic procedure that has the unique capability of distinguishing minor differences in the density of tissues. **Renal ultrasonography** is a noninvasive test that uses reflected sound waves to visualize the kidneys. During a **cystoscopy,** the bladder, ureteral orifices, and urethra can be directly visualized using a **cystoscope,** a lighted instrument inserted through the urethra.

Nurses are responsible for preparing clients before these studies and for follow-up care.

Diagnosing

The North American Nursing Diagnosis Association (NANDA) includes one general diagnostic label for urinary elimination problems and several labels that are more specific (Carpenito, 2002):

- ***Urinary Elimination, Impaired:*** The state in which a person experiences a disturbance in urine elimination.

Other NANDA nursing diagnoses related to urinary elimination include the following.

- ***Urinary Incontinence, Stress:*** The state in which one experiences a loss of urine of less than 50 mL occurring with increased abdominal pressure (e.g., sneezing, coughing, laughing, lifting).
- ***Urinary Incontinence, Reflex:*** The state in which one experiences an involuntary loss of urine, occurring at somewhat predictable intervals when a specific bladder volume is reached.
- ***Urinary Incontinence, Urge:*** The state in which an individual experiences involuntary passage of urine occurring soon after a strong sense of urgency to void.
- ***Urinary Incontinence, Functional:*** The state in which one experiences an involuntary, unpredictable passage of urine.
- ***Urinary Incontinence, Total:*** The state in which one experiences a continuous and unpredictable loss of urine.
- ***Urinary Retention (Acute/Chronic):*** The state in which one experiences incomplete emptying of the bladder.

Clinical examples of assessment data clusters and related nursing diagnoses are shown in Table 36.5.

Problems of urinary elimination also may become the etiology for other problems experienced by the client. Examples include:

- ***Risk for Infection*** if the client has urinary retention or undergoes an invasive procedure, such as catheterization or cystoscopic examination.
- ***Self-Esteem, Situational Low*** if the client is incontinent. Incontinence can be physically and emotionally distressing to clients because it is considered socially unacceptable. Often, the client is embarrassed about dribbling or having an accident and may restrict normal activities for this reason.
- ***Risk for Impaired Skin Integrity*** if the client is incontinent. Bed linens and clothes saturated with urine irritate and excoriate the skin. Prolonged skin dampness leads to dermatitis (inflammation of the skin) and subsequent formation of decubitus ulcers.
- ***Social Isolation*** if the client is incontinent (see also ***Self-Esteem Disturbance***).
- ***Self-Care Deficit: Toileting*** if the client has functional incontinence.
- ***Risk for Fluid Volume Deficient*** or ***Fluid Volume Excess*** if the client has impaired urinary function associated with a disease process.
- ***Body Image, Disturbed*** if the client has a urinary diversion ostomy.
- ***Knowledge Deficient*** if the client requires self-care skills to manage (e.g., a new urinary diversion ostomy).
- ***Risk for Caregiver Role Strain*** if the client is incontinent and being cared for by a family member for extended periods.

TABLE 36.5 Comparison Application: Assessment Data Clusters and Related Nursing Diagnoses

Data Cluster	Nursing Diagnosis
Mrs. Amy Brown, 75 years old, reports accidental loss of urine before she is able to reach the toilet. She is aware of the urge to void but states, "Because of my stroke, I sometimes can't get there soon enough."	***Urinary Incontinence, Functional*** related to mobility deficit
Anthony Cherry, a teenager with a spinal cord injury, has no awareness of bladder filling, the urge to void, or feelings of bladder fullness. He reports loss of urine at fairly regular intervals.	***Urinary Incontinence, Reflex*** related to neurological impairment (spinal cord lesion)
Tammy Tyndale reports dribbling whenever she laughs, coughs, or sneezes. She is eight months pregnant.	***Urinary Incontinence, Stress*** related to high intra-abdominal pressure associated with pregnancy
Mr. Gino Mingo is wheelchair bound from the effects of multiple sclerosis. He has a constant flow of urine at unpredictable times, including nocturia. He is unaware of bladder filling and of incontinence.	***Urinary Incontinence, Total*** related to neurological impairment
Mrs. Gail Brady reports urinary urgency, difficulty in getting to the bathroom in time, frequency (more often than every two hours), and leakage of urine when unable to reach the toilet in time.	***Urinary Incontinence, Urge*** related to unknown etiology

Planning

The goals established will vary according to the diagnosis and defining characteristics. Examples of overall goals for clients with urinary elimination problems may include:

- Maintain or restore a normal voiding pattern
- Regain normal urine output
- Prevent associated risks, such as infection, skin breakdown, fluid and electrolyte imbalance, and lowered self-esteem
- Perform toilet activities independently with or without assistive devices

Examples of desired outcomes for each of these goals are provided in Table 36.6 in the "Evaluating" section.

Selected nursing strategies to achieve the goals for problems of altered urinary elimination are discussed in the "Implementing" section. For example, for *urinary incontinence*, the following strategies may be considered: keeping a voiding record or diary; scheduled toileting; prompted voiding; Kegel (pelvic muscle) exercises; dietary and fluid intake alterations; assistive devices, such as a bedside commode, mobility aids, or a raised toilet seat; and incontinence aids, such as a condom drainage device for males, absorbent pads, and protective clothing.

For *urinary retention*, the nurse may consider such strategies as bladder training, positioning and relaxation techniques, Credé's maneuver, intermittent self-catheterization, and parasympathomimetic medications as indicated and prescribed.

The Iowa Intervention Project's Nursing Interventions Classification (NIC) system can also be used to plan nursing interventions (McCloskey & Bulechek, 2000). Examples of NIC interventions to manage urinary elimination problems include:

- Urinary elimination management
- Urinary incontinence care
- Urinary habit training
- Urinary bladder training
- Urinary retention care
- Pelvic muscle exercise

Specific nursing activities associated with each of these interventions can be selected to meet the individual needs of the client. A sample nursing care plan using NIC nursing interventions and activities is provided opposite.

Planning for Home Care

To provide for continuity of care, the nurse needs to consider the client's needs for teaching and assistance with care in the home. Discharge planning includes assessment of the client's and family's resources and abilities for self-care, available financial resources, and the need for referrals and home care services. The box on page 908 outlines an assessment of home care capabilities related to urinary elimination problems and needs. The Home Care Teaching Guide box on pages 909–910 addresses the learning needs of the client and family.

Implementing

Maintaining Normal Urinary Elimination

Most interventions to maintain normal urinary elimination are independent nursing functions. These include promoting adequate fluid intake, maintaining normal voiding habits, and assisting with toileting.

Promoting Fluid Intake

Increasing fluid intake increases urine production, which, in turn, stimulates the micturition reflex. A normal daily intake averaging 1,500 mL of measurable fluids is adequate for most adult clients.

Many clients have increased fluid requirements, necessitating a higher daily fluid intake. For example, clients who are perspiring excessively (have diaphoresis) or who are experiencing abnormal fluid losses through vomiting, gastric suction, diarrhea, or wound drainage require fluid to replace these losses in addition to their normal daily intake requirements.

Clients who are at risk for urinary tract infection or urinary calculi (stones) should consume 2,000 to 3,000 mL of fluid daily. Dilute urine and frequent urination reduce the risk of urinary tract infection as well as stone formation.

Increased fluid intake may be contraindicated for some clients, such as those with kidney failure or heart failure. For these clients, a fluid restriction may be necessary to prevent fluid overload and edema.

Maintaining Normal Voiding Habits

Prescribed medical therapies often interfere with a client's normal voiding habits. When a client's urinary elimination pattern is adequate, the nurse helps the client adhere to normal voiding habits as much as possible. Clinical guidelines are in the box on page 911.

Assisting with Toileting

Clients who are weakened by a disease process or impaired physically require assistance to toilet. The nurse should assist these clients to the bathroom and remain with them if the client is at risk for falling. The bathroom should contain an easily accessible call signal to summon help if needed. Clients also need to be encouraged to use handrails placed near the toilet.

For clients unable to use bathroom facilities, the nurse provides urinary equipment close to the bedside (e.g., urinal, bedpan, commode) and provides the necessary assistance to use them.

Assisting clients to use bedpans and urinals is discussed in Chapter 35. Effective methods to transfer a client from bed to commode (or wheelchair) are also discussed in Chapter 43.

Preventing Urinary Tract Infections

The rate of urinary tract infection (UTI) in women is about 20 percent yearly compared with a rate of 0.1 percent in men, and it accounts for 40 percent of all nosocomial infections (Marchiondo, 1998). Most UTIs are caused by bacteria common to the intestinal environment (e.g., *Escherichia coli*). These gastrointestinal bacteria can colonize the perineal area and move into the urethra, especially when there is urethral trauma, irritation, or manipulation. Women are particularly at risk because of the short urethra and its proximity to the anal and vaginal areas.

SAMPLE CARE PLAN FOR URINARY ELIMINATION

ASSESSMENT DATA

Nursing Assessment

Mr. John Baker is a 68-year-old shopkeeper who was admitted to the hospital with urinary retention, hematuria, and fever. The admitting nurse gathers the following information when taking a nursing history. Mr. Baker states he has noticed urinary frequency during the day for the past two weeks and that he does not feel he has emptied his bladder after urinating. He also has to get up two or three times during the night to urinate. Over the past few days, he has had difficulty starting urination, and urine dribbles afterward. He verbalizes the embarrassment his urinary problems cause in his dealings with the public. Mr. Baker is concerned about the cause of this urinary problem. He is diagnosed with benign prostatic hypertrophy and referred to a urologist who suggests a transurethral resection of the prostate (TURP) in several months. He is placed on antibiotic therapy.

Physical Examination

Height: 185.4 cm
Weight: 85.7 kg
Temperature: 38.1°C
Pulse: 88 BPM
Respirations: 20/minute
Blood pressure: 146/86 mm Hg
Catherization for urinary retention yielded 300 mL amber urine. Foley left in place for two days.

Diagnostic Data

CBC normal; urinalysis: amber, clear, pH 6.5, specific gravity 1.025, negative for glucose, protein, ketone, RBCs, and bacteria; IVP: evidence of enlarged prostate gland

Nursing Diagnosis

Urinary retention, acute related to bladder neck obstruction by enlarged prostate gland (as evidenced by dysuria, frequency, nocturia, dribbling, hesitancy, and bladder distention).

Client Goal(s):

The client will demonstrate an understanding of prostatic hypertrophy and its treatment, and improve urinary elimination patterns.

Desired Outcomes

1. Reports reduction of incontinent episodes
2. Monitors urinary output, recognizing that fluid intake should equal output
3. Verbalizes a state of dryness that is personally satisfactory
4. Describes how an enlarged prostate gland interferes with urination
5. Describes one or two aspects of treatment

---

*Nursing Interventions and Selected Activities with Rationale *[in italics]*

Urinary Incontinence Care

■ Monitor urinary elimination, including consistency, odour, volume, and colour.	*These parameters help determine adequacy of urinary tract function.*
■ Help the client select appropriate incontinence garment or pad for short-term management while more definitive treatment is designed.	*Appropriate undergarments can help diminish the embarrassing aspects of urinary incontinence.*
■ Instruct Mr. Baker to limit fluids for two to three hours before bedtime.	*Decreased fluid intake several hours before bedtime will decrease the incidence of urinary retention and overflow incontinence and promote rest.*
■ Instruct him to drink a minimum of 1,500 mL per day.	*Increased fluids during the day will increase urinary output and discourage bacterial growth.*
■ Limit ingestion of bladder irritants (e.g., colas, coffee, tea, and chocolate).	*Alcohol, coffee, and tea have a natural diuretic effect and are bladder irritants.*

Urinary Retention Care

■ Instruct Mr. Baker or a family member to record urinary output.	*This serves as an indicator of urinary tract and renal function and of fluid balance.*
■ Catheterize for residual urine, as ordered.	*An enlarged prostate compresses the urethra so that urine is retained. Checking for residual urine provides information about bladder emptying.*
■ Implement intermittent catheterization, as ordered.	*This helps maintain tonicity of the bladder muscle by preventing overdistention and providing for complete emptying.*
■ Provide enough time for bladder emptying (10 minutes).	*In addition to the effect of an enlarged prostate on the bladder, stress or anxiety can inhibit relaxation of the urinary sphincter. Sufficient time should be allowed for micturition.*

→

SAMPLE CARE PLAN FOR URINARY ELIMINATION *continued*

■ Instruct the client in ways to avoid constipation or stool impaction.	*Impacted stool may place pressure on the bladder outlet, causing urinary retention.*
Teaching: Disease Process	
■ Appraise Mr. Baker's current level of knowledge about benign prostatic hypertrophy.	*Assessing the client's knowledge will provide a foundation for building a teaching plan based on his present understanding of his condition.*
■ Explain the pathophysiology of the disease and how it relates to urinary anatomy and function.	*In this case, urinary retention and overflow incontinence are caused by obstruction of the bladder neck by an enlarged prostate gland.*
■ Describe the rationale behind management, therapy, and treatment recommendations (e.g., TURP).	*Adequate information about treatment options is important to diminish anxiety, promote compliance, and enhance decision making.*
■ Instruct Mr. Baker on which signs and symptoms to report to the health-care provider (e.g., burning on urination, hematuria, oliguria).	*In the individual with prostatic hypertrophy, urinary retention and an overdistended bladder reduce blood flow to the bladder wall, making it more susceptible to infection from bacterial growth. Monitoring for these manifestations of urinary tract infection is essential to prevent urosepsis.*

Evaluation

Goal not met. Following removal of the Foley catheter, Mr. Baker reported continued difficulty initiating a urinary stream but experienced less dribbling of urine. He and his wife selected an undergarment that was acceptable to Mr. Baker, and he reports that he feels more confident. Intake is approximately 200 mL in excess of output. He is able to discuss the correlation between his enlarged prostate and urinary difficulties. A transurethral resection of the prostate is scheduled in two weeks.

*Interventions and activities selected are only a sample of those suggested in the *Nursing interventions classification (NIC),* and should be individualized for each client.

Source: McCloskey, J. C., & Bulechek, G. M. (2000). *Iowa intervention project: Nursing interventions classification (NIC)* (3rd ed.). St. Louis, MO: Mosby.

HOME CARE ASSESSMENT

Urinary Elimination

Client and Environment

- *Self-care abilities:* Ability to consume adequate fluids, to perceive bladder fullness, to ambulate and get to the toilet, to manipulate clothing for toileting, and to perform hygiene measures after toileting
- *Assistive devices required:* Ambulatory aids, such as walker, cane, or wheelchair; safety devices, such as grab bars; toileting aids, such as raised toilet seat, urinal, commode, or bedpan; presence of a urinary catheter
- *Home environment for factors that interfere with toileting:* Distance to the bathroom from living areas or bedrooms; barriers, such as stairways, scatter rugs, clutter, or narrow doorways that interfere with bathroom access; lighting (including night lighting that allows gradual transition from dark bedroom to light bathroom)
- *Urinary elimination problems:* Type of incontinence and precipitating factors; manifestations of urinary tract infection, such as dysuria, frequency, urgency; evidence of prostatic hypertrophy and effect on urination; ability to perform self-catheterization and care for other urinary elimination devices, such as indwelling catheter, urinary diversion ostomy, or condom drainage
- *Current level of knowledge:* Fluid and dietary intake modifications to promote normal patterns of urinary elimination; bladder training methods and specific techniques to promote voiding; care for indwelling catheter or ostomy (if appropriate)

HOME CARE ASSESSMENT

Urinary Elimination *continued*

Family

- *Caregiver availability, skills, and responses:* Ability and willingness to assume responsibilities for care, including assisting with toileting, intermittent catheterization, indwelling catheter care, urinary drainage devices or ostomy care; ready access to laundry facilities; access to and willingness to use respite or relief caregivers
- *Family role changes and coping:* Effect on spousal and family roles, sleep-rest patterns, sexuality, and social interactions
- *Financial resources:* Ability to purchase protective pads and garments, supplies for catheterization or ostomy care

Community

- *Environment:* Access to public restrooms and sanitary facilities
- *Current knowledge of and experience with community resources:* Medical and assistive equipment, home care agencies, local pharmacies, available financial assistance, support and educational organizations

HOME CARE TEACHING GUIDE

Urinary Elimination

Facilitating Urinary Elimination Self-Care

- Teach the client and family to maintain easy access to toilet facilities, including removing scatter rugs and ensuring that halls and doorways are free of clutter.
- Suggest graduated lighting for nighttime voiding: a dim night-light in the bedroom and low-wattage hallway lighting.
- Advise the client and family to install grab bars and elevated toilet seats, as needed.
- Provide for instruction in safe transfer techniques. Contact physical therapy to provide training, as needed.
- Suggest clothing that is easily removed for toileting, such as elastic waist pants or Velcro closures.

Promoting Urinary Elimination

- Instruct the client to respond to the urge to void as soon as possible; avoid voluntary urinary retention.
- Teach the client to empty the bladder completely at each voiding.
- Emphasize the importance of drinking eight to 10 eight-ounce glasses of water daily.
- Teach female clients about Kegel exercises to strengthen perineal muscles (see page 913).
- Inform the client about the relationship between tobacco use and bladder cancer and provide information about smoking cessation programs, as indicated.
- Teach the client to promptly report any of the following to the primary-care provider: pain or burning on urination, changes in urine colour or clarity (e.g., bright red, rusty, or cloudy urine), malodorous urine, or changes in voiding patterns (e.g., nocturia, frequency, dribbling).

Asepsis

- Teach the client to maintain perineal-genital cleanliness, washing with soap and water daily and cleansing the anal and perineal area after defecating.
- Instruct female clients to wipe from front to back (from the urinary meatus toward the anus) after voiding, and to discard toilet paper after each swipe.
- Provide information about products to protect the skin, clothing, and assistive devices for clients who are incontinent. Emphasize the importance of cleaning and drying the perineal area after incontinence episodes. Instruct in the use of protective skin barrier products, as needed.
- Teach clients with an indwelling catheter and their family about care measures, such as cleaning the urinary meatus, managing and emptying the collection device, maintaining a closed system, and bladder irrigation or flushing, if ordered.
- For clients with a urinary diversion, teach about care of the stoma, drainage devices, and surrounding skin. For continent diversions, teach the client how to catheterize the stoma to drain urine.
- For clients with an indwelling catheter or urinary diversion, emphasize the importance of maintaining a generous fluid intake (1,500 mL), and of promptly reporting changes in urinary output, signs of urinary retention, such as abdominal pain and a palpable bladder, and manifestations of urinary tract infection, such as malodorous urine, abdominal discomfort, fever, or confusion.

HOME CARE TEACHING GUIDE

Urinary Elimination *continued*

Medications

- Emphasize the importance of taking medications as prescribed. Instruct the client to take the full course of antibiotics ordered to treat a urinary tract infection, even though symptoms are relieved.
- Inform the client and family about any expected changes in urine colour or odour associated with prescribed medications.
- For clients with urinary retention, emphasize the need to contact the primary-care provider before taking any medication (even over-the-counter medications, such as antihistamines) that may exacerbate symptoms (see the box on page 896).
- For clients taking medications that may damage the kidneys (e.g., aminoglycoside antibiotics), stress the importance of maintaining a generous fluid intake while taking the medication.
- Suggest measures to reduce anticipated side effects of prescribed medications, such as increasing intake of potassium-rich foods when taking a potassium-depleting diuretic, such as furosemide.

Dietary Alterations

- Teach the client about dietary changes to promote urinary function, such as consuming cranberry juice and foods that acidify the urine to reduce the risk of repeated urinary tract infections or forming calcium-based urinary stones.
- Instruct clients with stress or urge incontinence to limit their intake of caffeine, alcohol, citrus juices, and artificial sweeteners as these are bladder irritants that may increase incontinence. Also teach clients to limit their evening fluid intake to reduce the risk of nighttime incontinence episodes.

Measures Specific to Urinary Problems

- Provide instructions for clients with specific urinary problems or treatments, such as
  a. Timed urine specimens (page 903)
  b. Urinary incontinence (page 911)
  c. Urinary retention (page 915)
  d. Retention catheters (page 916)

Referrals

- Make appropriate referrals to home care agencies, community agencies, or social services for assistance with resources, such as grab bars and raised toilet seats; providing wheelchair access to bathrooms; obtaining toileting aids, such as commodes, urinals, or bedpans; and services such as home care aides for assistance with activities of daily living.

Community Agencies and Other Resources

- Provide information about resources for durable medical equipment, such as commodes or raised toilet seats; possible financial assistance; and medical supplies, such as drainage bags, incontinence briefs, or protective pads.
- Suggest additional sources of information and help, such as the United Ostomy Association of Canada, Canadian Continence Foundation, or Kidney Foundation of Canada.

For women who have experienced a UTI, nurses need to provide instructions about ways to prevent a recurrence. Marchiondo (1998) provides the following guidelines that are useful for anyone:

- Drink eight 250 mL glasses of water per day to flush bacteria out of the urinary system.
- Practice frequent voiding (every two to four hours) to flush bacteria out of the urethra and prevent organisms from ascending into the bladder.
- Avoid use of harsh soaps, bubble bath, powder, or sprays in the perineal area. These substances can be irritating to the urethra and encourage inflammation and bacterial infection.
- Avoid tight-fitting pants or other clothing that creates irritation to the urethra and prevents ventilation of the perineal area.
- Wear cotton, rather than nylon, underclothes. Accumulation of perineal moisture facilitates bacterial growth and cotton enhances ventilation of the perineal area.
- Girls and women should always wipe the perineal area from front to back following urination or defecation in order to prevent introduction of gastrointestinal bacteria into the urethra.
- If recurrent urinary infections are a problem, take showers, rather than baths. Bacteria present in bathwater can readily enter the urethra.
- Increase the acidity of urine through regular intake of vitamin C and drinking two to three glasses of cranberry juice daily or take cranberry tablets.
- Postmenopausal women who experience recurrent UTIs may benefit from regular use of an estradiol vaginal cream, as ordered by a physician.
- Void after sexual intercourse.

CLINICAL GUIDELINES

Maintaining Normal Voiding Habits

Positioning

- Assist the client to a normal position for voiding: standing for males; for females, squatting or leaning slightly forward when sitting. These positions enhance movement of urine through the tract by gravity.
- If the client is unable to ambulate to the lavatory, use a bedside commode for females and a urinal for males standing at the bedside if possible.
- If necessary, encourage the client to push over the pubic area with the hands or to lean forward to increase intra-abdominal pressure and external pressure on the bladder.

Relaxation

- Provide privacy for the client. Many people cannot void in the presence of another person.
- Allow the client sufficient time to void.
- Suggest that the client read or listen to music.
- Provide sensory stimuli that may help the client relax. Pour warm water over the perineum of a female or have the client sit in a warm bath to promote muscle relaxation. Applying warmed blankets or towels to the lower abdomen of both men and women may also foster muscle relaxation.
- Turn on running water within hearing distance of the client to stimulate the voiding reflex and to mask the sound of voiding for people who find this embarrassing.
- Provide ordered analgesics and emotional support to relieve physical and emotional discomfort to decrease muscle tension.

Timing

- Assist clients who have the urge to void immediately. Delays only increase the difficulty in starting to void, and the desire to void may pass.
- Offer toileting assistance to the client at usual times of voiding, for example, on awakening, before or after meals, and at bedtime.

For Bed-Confined Clients

- Warm the bedpan. A cold bedpan may prompt contraction of the perineal muscles and inhibit voiding.
- Elevate the head of the client's bed to Fowler's position, place a small pillow or rolled towel at the small of the back to increase physical support and comfort, and have the client flex the hips and knees. This position simulates the normal voiding position as closely as possible.

Managing Urinary Incontinence

It is important to remember that urinary incontinence is not a normal part of aging and often is treatable. Independent nursing interventions for clients with urinary incontinence (UI) include: (1) a behaviour-oriented continence training program that may consist of bladder training, habit training, prompted voiding, pelvic muscle exercises, and positive reinforcement; (2) meticulous skin care; and (3) for males, application of an external drainage device (condom).

Continence (Bladder) Training

A continence training program requires the involvement of the nurse, the client, and support people. Clients must be alert and physically able to follow a program. The goal of training is to decrease the frequency of UI. A bladder training program may include the following:

- Education of the client and support people.
- **Bladder training,** which requires that the client postpone voiding, resist or inhibit the sensation of urgency, and void according to a timetable rather than according to the urge to void. The goals are to gradually lengthen the intervals between urination to correct the client's habit of frequent urination, to stabilize the bladder, and to diminish urgency. This form of training may be used for clients who have bladder instability and urge incontinence. Delayed voiding provides larger voided volumes and longer intervals between voiding. Initially, voiding may be encouraged every two to three hours except during sleep and then every four to six hours. A vital component of bladder training is inhibiting the urge-to-void sensation. To do this, the nurse instructs the client to practice deep, slow breathing until the urge diminishes or disappears. This is performed every time the client has a premature urge to void. See the following box.
- **Habit training,** also referred to as timed voiding or scheduled toileting, attempts to keep clients dry by having them void at *regular* intervals. With habit training, there is no attempt to motivate the client to delay voiding if the urge occurs.
- **Prompted voiding** supplements habit training by encouraging the client to try to use the toilet (prompting) and reminding the client when to void.

RESEARCH NOTE

Is Bladder Training Effective to Treat Urinary Incontinence?

This study looked at the effectiveness of bladder training to reduce episodes of urinary incontinence in functionally independent community-dwelling women. Nineteen subjects whose age ranged between 64 and 88 years were enrolled in the study. During an initial in-home visit, participants were asked about urinary incontinence; all considered urinary incontinence to be a problem and reported involuntary loss of urine at least weekly.

Participants completed a voiding diary during the first week. On the basis of this diary, a voiding schedule was prescribed for each subject, and instructions to maintain a voiding record were given. The voiding schedule was adjusted weekly, with gradually increasing intervals for those who experienced two or fewer episodes of incontinence the previous week. Positive reinforcement of efforts and successes was provided throughout the study.

At the conclusion of the study, the researchers found that the mean reduction in the number of incontinent episodes was 87.3 percent. Eleven of the 16 participants (69 percent) completing the study were completely continent.

Implications: Urinary incontinence is a distressing problem that commonly affects older women and may result in embarrassment and social isolation. Nurses are in an ideal position to teach clients skills that can significantly reduce this problem. Bladder training, which involves voiding on a schedule at gradually increasing intervals, is one method that has been found effective in reducing episodes of incontinence. When bladder training is combined with pelvic muscle exercises and minor dietary modifications, many clients become completely continent.

Source: Publicover, C., & Bear, M. (1997). The effect of bladder training on urinary incontinence in community-dwelling older women. *Journal of Wound, Ostomy and Continence Nurses Society, 24,* 319–324.

CLINICAL GUIDELINES

Bladder Training

- Determine the client's voiding pattern and encourage voiding at those times, or establish a regular voiding schedule and help the client to maintain it whether the client feels the urge or not (e.g., on awakening, every one or two hours during the day and evening, before retiring at night, every four hours at night). The stretching-relaxing sequence of such a schedule tends to increase bladder muscle tone and promote more voluntary control. Encourage the client to inhibit the urge-to-void sensation when a premature urge to void is experienced. Instruct the client to practise slow, deep breathing until the urge diminishes or disappears.
- When the client finds that voiding can be controlled, the intervals between voiding can be lengthened slightly without loss of continence.
- Regulate fluid intake, particularly during evening hours, to help reduce the need to void during the night.
- Encourage fluids about half an hour before the voiding time between the hours of 0600 and 1800.
- Avoid excessive consumption of citrus juices, carbonated beverages (especially those containing artificial sweeteners), alcohol, and drinks containing caffeine as these irritate the bladder and tend to cause detrusor instability, increasing the risk of incontinence.
- Schedule diuretics early in the morning.
- Explain to clients that adequate fluid intake is required to ensure adequate urine production to stimulate the micturition reflex.
- Apply protector pads to keep the bed linen dry, and provide specially made waterproof underwear to contain the urine and decrease the client's embarrassment. Avoid using diapers, which are demeaning and also suggest that incontinence is permissible.
- Assist the client with an exercise program to increase the tone of abdominal and pelvic muscles.
- Provide positive reinforcements to encourage continence. Praise clients for attempting to go to the toilet and for maintaining continence.

Pelvic Muscle Exercises

Pelvic muscle exercises, referred to as *Kegel exercises,* strengthen pelvic floor muscles in women and can reduce episodes of incontinence. The client can identify perineal muscles by stopping urination midstream or by tightening the anal sphincter as if to hold a bowel movement.

The following technique is sometimes used to teach Kegel exercises. Ask the client to think of her perineal muscles as an elevator. When the client relaxes, the elevator is on the first floor. To perform the exercise, contract the perineal muscles, bringing the elevator to the second, third, and fourth floors. Keep the elevator on the fourth floor for a few seconds, and then gradually relax the area. When the exercise is properly performed, contraction of the muscles of the buttocks and thighs is avoided.

Kegel exercises can be performed anytime, anywhere, sitting or standing. Specific client instructions for performing Kegel exercises are summarized in the next box.

Maintaining Skin Integrity

Skin that is continually moist becomes macerated. Urine that accumulates on the skin is converted to ammonia,

CLIENT TEACHING

Kegel Exercises

- First, sit or stand with the legs apart.
- Pull your rectum, urethra, and vagina up inside, and hold for a count of three to five seconds. The pull should be felt at the cleft of your buttocks.
- Initially perform each contraction 10 times, five times daily.
- Develop a schedule that will help remind you to do these exercises, for example, while driving to work, when working at the kitchen sink, or at scheduled times (e.g., 0700, 1000, 1300, 1600, and 1900 hours).
- Try to start and stop your stream of urine.
- To control episodes of stress incontinence, brace the muscles and use the Kegel maneuver when doing any activity that increases intra-abdominal pressure, such as coughing, laughing, sneezing, or lifting.

which is very irritating to the skin. Because both skin irritation and maceration predispose the client to skin breakdown and ulceration, the incontinent person requires meticulous skin care. To maintain skin integrity, the nurse washes the client's perineal area with soap and water after episodes of incontinence, rinses it thoroughly, dries it thoroughly, and provides clean, dry clothing or bed linen. If the skin is irritated, the nurse applies barrier creams, such as zinc oxide ointment, to protect it from contact with urine. If it is necessary to pad the client's clothes for protection, the nurse should use products that absorb wetness and leave a dry surface in contact with the skin.

Specially designed *incontinence drawsheets* may be used that provide significant advantages over standard drawsheets for incontinent clients confined to bed. These sheets are like a drawsheet but are double layered, with a quilted upper nylon or polyester surface and an absorbent viscose rayon layer below. The rayon soaker layer generally has a waterproof backing on its underside. Fluid (i.e., urine) passes through the upper quilted layer and is absorbed and dispersed by the viscose rayon, leaving the quilted surface dry to the touch. This absorbent sheet helps maintain skin integrity; it does not stick to the skin when wet, decreases the risk of bedsores, and reduces odour.

Applying External Urinary Drainage Devices

The application of a condom or external catheter connected to a urinary drainage system is commonly prescribed for incontinent males. Use of a condom appliance is preferable to insertion of a retention catheter because the risk of urinary tract infection is minimal.

Methods of applying condoms vary according to how long the condom is to be worn. Condoms that are to be worn for a short period are generally applied with elastic tape only; if the condom is to be worn for a longer period (e.g., a few days), additional measures are required to protect the foreskin and to ensure secure attachment. The nurse needs to follow the manufacturer's instructions when applying a condom. First, the nurse determines when the client experiences incontinence. Some clients may require a condom appliance at night only, others continuously. Procedure 36.2 describes how to apply and remove a drainage condom.

PROCEDURE 36.2 Applying a Condom Catheter

PURPOSES

- To collect urine and control urinary incontinence
- To permit the client physical activity without fear of embarrassment because of leaking urine
- To prevent skin irritation as a result of urine incontinence

Assessment Focus
Times of urinary incontinence; amount of urine passed (e.g., large, dribble); skin irritation, excoriation, swelling, and discolouration of penis

Equipment

- ❑ Leg drainage bag with tubing or urinary drainage bag with tubing
- ❑ Condom sheath
- ❑ Bath blanket
- ❑ Disposable gloves
- ❑ Basin of warm water and soap
- ❑ Washcloth and towel
- ❑ Elastic tape or Velcro strap

PROCEDURE 36.2 Applying a Condom Catheter *continued*

INTERVENTION

1. Prepare the equipment.

- Assemble the leg drainage bag or urinary drainage bag for attachment to the condom sheath.
- Roll the condom outward onto itself to facilitate easier application. On some models, an inner flap will be exposed. *This flap is applied around the urinary meatus to prevent the reflux of urine* (Figure 36.7).

2. Position and drape the client.

- Position the client in either a supine or a bed-sitting position.
- Drape the client appropriately with the bath blanket, exposing only the penis.

3. Inspect and clean the penis.

- Don gloves.
- Inspect the penis for skin irritation (contact dermatitis), excoriation, swelling, or discolouration. *The nurse needs to obtain baseline data.*
- Clean the genital area, and dry it thoroughly. *This minimizes skin irritation and excoriation after the condom is applied.*

4. Apply and secure the condom.

- Roll the condom smoothly over the penis, leaving 2.5 cm between the end of the penis and the rubber or plastic connecting tube (Figure 36.8). *This space prevents irritation of the tip of the penis and provides for full drainage of urine.*
- Secure the condom firmly, but not too tightly, to the penis by wrapping a strip of elastic tape or Velcro around the base of the penis over the condom (follow manufacturer's instructions). The elastic tape or Velcro strip should not come in contact with the skin and should hold the condom in place without impeding blood circulation to the penis. *Ordinary tape is contraindicated because it is not flexible and can stop blood flow.*

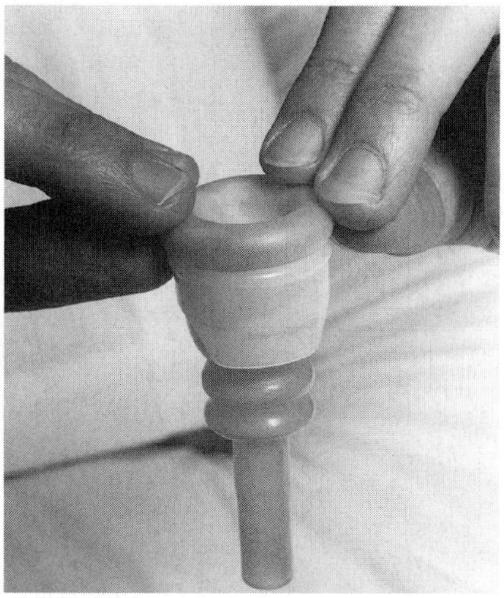

Figure 36.7 Before application, roll the condom outward onto itself

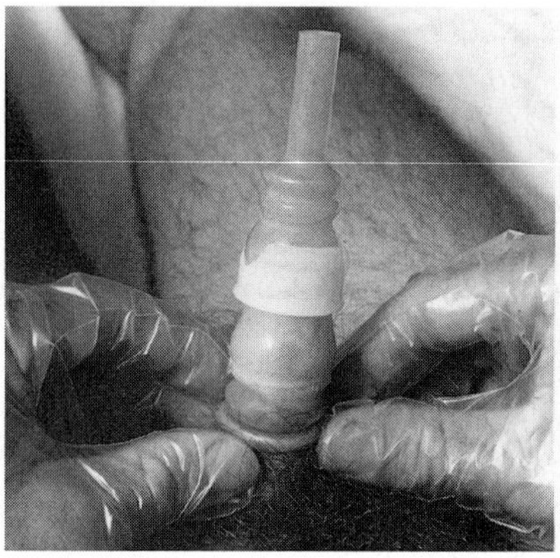

Figure 36.8 Rolling the condom over the penis

5. Securely attach the urinary drainage system.

- Make sure that the tip of the penis is not touching the condom and that the condom is not twisted. *A twisted condom could obstruct the flow of urine and decrease circulation to the tip of the penis.*
- Attach the urinary drainage system to the condom.
- Remove gloves.
- If the client is to remain in bed, attach the urinary drainage bag to the bed frame.

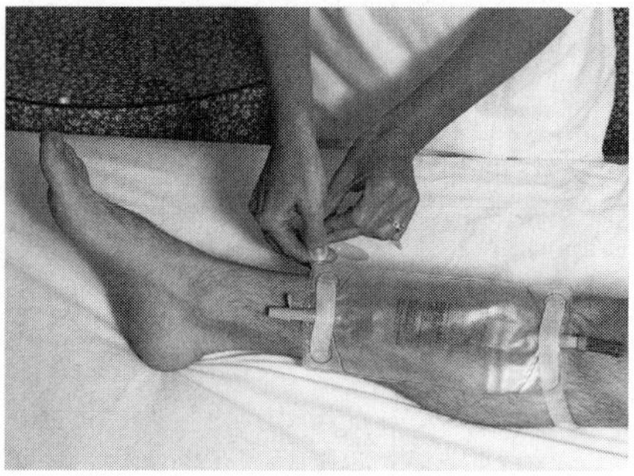

Figure 36.9 Attaching the urinary drainage bag to the leg

- If the client is ambulatory, attach the bag to the client's leg (Figure 36.9). *Attaching the drainage bag to the leg helps control the movement of the tubing and prevents twisting of the thin material of the condom appliance at the tip of the penis.*

6. Teach the client about the drainage system.

- Instruct the client to keep the drainage bag below the level of the condom and to avoid loops or kinks in the tubing.

7. Document pertinent data.

- Record the application of the condom, the time, and pertinent observations, such as irritated areas on the penis.

8. Inspect the penis 15 to 30 minutes following the condom application, and check urine flow.

- Assess the penis for swelling and discolouration, which indicates that the condom is too tight.

9. Change the condom daily, and provide skin care.

- Remove the elastic tape or Velcro strip and roll off the condom.
- Wash the penis with soapy water, rinse, and dry it thoroughly.
- Assess the foreskin for signs of irritation, swelling, and discolouration.

Evaluation Focus
Penis swelling and discolouration; urine flow; skin irritation

Managing Urinary Retention

Interventions that assist the client to maintain a normal voiding pattern, discussed earlier, also apply when dealing with urinary retention. If these actions are unsuccessful, the physician may order a cholinergic drug, such as bethanechol chloride (Urecholine) to stimulate bladder contraction and facilitate voiding. Clients who have a **flaccid** bladder (weak, soft, and lax bladder muscles) may use manual pressure on the bladder to promote bladder emptying. This is known as **Credé's maneuver** or *Credé's method.* It is not advised without a physician's order and is used only for clients who have lost and are not expected to regain voluntary bladder control. When all measures fail to initiate voiding, urinary catheterization may be necessary to empty the bladder completely. An indwelling Foley catheter may be inserted until the underlying cause is treated; alternatively, intermittent straight catheterization (every three to four hours) may be performed because the risk of urinary tract infection is believed by some to be less than with an indwelling catheter.

Urinary Catheterization

Urinary catheterization is the introduction of a catheter through the urethra into the urinary bladder. This is usually performed only when absolutely necessary because the procedure incurs certain hazards. Because the urinary structures are normally sterile, except at the end of the urethra, the danger exists of introducing microorganisms into the bladder. Clients who have lowered immune resistance are at the greatest risk. Once an infection is introduced into the bladder, it can ascend the ureters and eventually involve the kidneys. The hazard of infection remains after the catheter is in place because normal defence mechanisms, such as intermittent flushing of microorganisms from the urethra through voiding, are bypassed. Thus, strict sterile technique is used for catheterization.

Another hazard is trauma, particularly in the male client, whose urethra is longer and more tortuous. It is important to insert a catheter along the normal contour of the urethra. Damage to the urethra can occur if the catheter is forced through strictures or at an incorrect angle. In males, the urethra is normally curved (see Figure 36.3, earlier), but it can be straightened by elevating the penis to a position perpendicular to the body.

Catheters are commonly made of rubber or plastics although they may be made from latex, silicone, or polyvinylchloride (PVC). They are sized by the diameter of the lumen using the French (Fr) scale: the larger the number, the larger is the lumen. Either *straight catheters,* inserted to drain the bladder and then immediately removed, or *retention catheters,* which remain in the bladder to drain urine, may be used.

The straight catheter is a single-lumen tube with a small eye or opening about 1.25 cm from the insertion tip (Figure 36.10, *A*). The *coudé catheter* is a variation of the straight catheter. It is more rigid than other straight catheters and has a tapered, curved tip (see Figure 36.10, *B*). This catheter may be used for men with prostatic hypertrophy as it is more easily controlled and less traumatic on insertion.

The *retention,* or *Foley, catheter* is a double-lumen catheter. The larger lumen drains urine from the bladder. A second, smaller lumen is used to inflate a balloon near the tip of the catheter to hold the catheter in place within the bladder (Figure 36.11). Clients who require continuous or intermittent bladder irrigation may have a *three-way Foley catheter* (Figure 36.12). The three-way catheter has a third lumen through which sterile irrigating fluid can flow into the bladder. The fluid then exits the bladder through the drainage lumen along with the urine.

The balloons of retention catheters are sized by the volume of fluid used to inflate them. The three commonly used sizes are 5-mL, 10-mL, and 30-mL balloons. The size of the balloon is indicated on the catheter along with the diameter, for example, "18 Fr—5 mL." The following box provides guidelines for catheter selection.

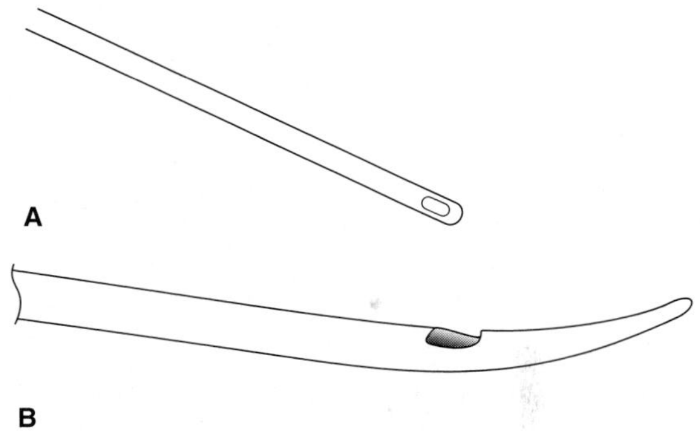

Figure 36.10 Two types of straight catheters: *A,* a red-rubber or Robinson catheter; *B,* a coudé catheter

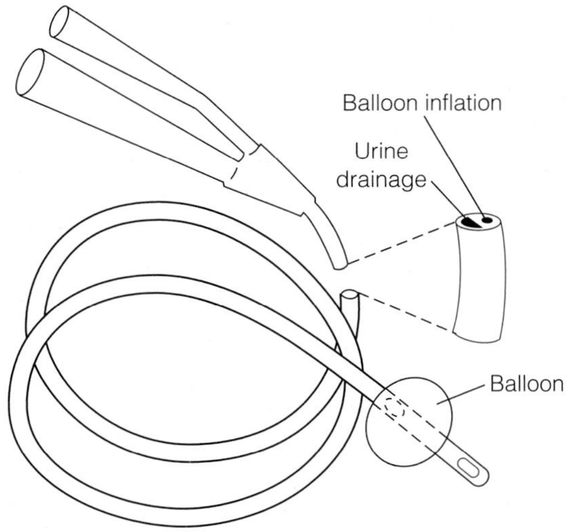

Figure 36.11 A retention (Foley) catheter with the balloon inflated

Selecting an Appropriate Catheter

- Select the type of material in accordance with the estimated length of the catheterization period and client's allergies.
  a. Use *plastic* catheters for short periods only (e.g., one week or less) because they are inflexible.
  b. Use a *latex* or *rubber* catheter for periods of two or three weeks.
  c. Use *silicone* catheters for long-term use (e.g., two to three months) because they create less encrustation at the urethral meatus. However, they are expensive.
  d. Use *PVC* catheters for four- to six-week periods. They soften at body temperature and conform to the urethra.
- Determine appropriate catheter length by the client's gender. For adult females, use a 22-cm catheter; for adult males, a 40-cm catheter.
- Determine appropriate catheter size by the size of the urethral canal. Use sizes 8 Fr or 10 Fr for children and 14 Fr or 16 Fr for adults. Men frequently require a larger size than women do, for example, 18 Fr.
- Select the appropriate balloon size. For adults, use a 5-mL balloon to facilitate optimal urine drainage. The smaller balloons allow more complete bladder emptying because the catheter tip is closer to the urethral opening in the bladder. However, a 30-mL balloon or larger is commonly used to achieve hemostasis of the prostatic area following a prostatectomy. Use 3-mL balloons for children.

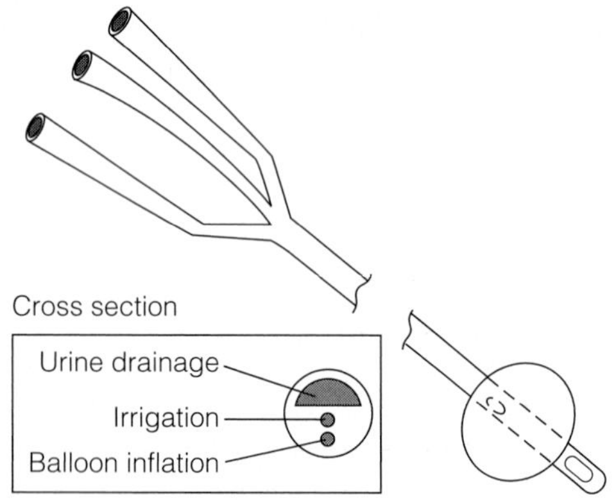

Figure 36.12 A three-way Foley catheter

Retention catheters usually are connected to a *closed gravity drainage system.* This system consists of the catheter, drainage tubing, and a collecting bag for the urine. A closed system should not be opened anywhere along the system from catheter to collecting bag. Closed systems reduce the risk of microorganisms entering the system and infecting the urinary tract. Urinary drainage systems typically depend on the force of gravity to drain urine from the bladder to the collecting bag.

Catheterization of females and males using straight catheters is described in Procedures 36.3 and 36.4, respectively. Procedure 36.5 outlines how to insert a retention catheter.

Nursing Interventions for Clients with Retention Catheters

Nursing care of the client with an indwelling catheter and continuous drainage is largely directed toward preventing infection of the urinary tract and encouraging urinary flow through the drainage system. It includes encouraging adequate amounts of fluid intake, accurately recording the fluid intake and output, changing the retention catheter and tubing, maintaining the patency of the drainage system, preventing contamination of the drainage system, and teaching these measures to the client.

Fluids

The client with a retention catheter should drink up to 3,000 mL per day, if permitted. Increased fluid intake ensures an increased urine output, which keeps the bladder flushed out and decreases the likelihood of urinary stasis and subsequent infection. Increased volumes of urine also minimize the risk of sediment or other particles obstructing the drainage tubing. Accurate recording of fluid intake and output is discussed in Chapter 40.

Dietary Measures

Acidifying the urine of clients with a retention catheter may reduce the risk of urinary tract infection and calculus formation. Such foods as eggs, cheese, meat and poultry, whole grains, cranberries, plums and prunes, and tomatoes tend to increase the acidity of urine. Conversely, most fruits and vegetables, legumes, and milk and milk products result in alkaline urine.

Perineal Care

The retention catheter should be cleaned by swabbing down the tubing away from the meatus. Agency practices regarding catheter care vary considerably. The nurse should check agency practice in this regard.

Changing the Catheter and Tubing

Indwelling catheters are used only when absolutely necessary and removed as soon as possible. However, some clients require long-term catheterization. Whenever possible, the closed catheter drainage system should be maintained, and the tubing not disconnected from the catheter for any reason.

PROCEDURE 36.3 Female Urinary Catheterization Using a Straight Catheter

Before inserting a urinary catheter, check (1) the order authorizing the catheterization, (2) whether the order or policy specifies a maximum amount of urine to be removed during the catheterization (if the client is retaining urine), and (3) the client's chart for any direction about the type or size of catheter to use.

PURPOSES

- To relieve discomfort due to bladder distention or to provide gradual decompression of a distended bladder
- To assess the amount of residual urine if the bladder empties incompletely
- To obtain a urine specimen
- To empty the bladder completely prior to surgery

Assessment Focus
When the client last voided and amount; presence of urinary retention; symptoms of urinary infection; voiding pattern; ability to maintain position during catheterization; allergies (latex, antiseptic solution)

Equipment

- ❑ Flashlight or lamp
- ❑ Mask, if required by agency policy
- ❑ Bath blanket or drape
- ❑ Soap, a basin of warm water, a washcloth, and a towel
- ❑ Disposable gloves
- ❑ A sterile catheterization kit containing
  - ❑ Water-soluble lubricant
  - ❑ Sterile gloves
- ❑ Sterile drapes, fenestrated drape (optional) to place over the perineum
- ❑ Antiseptic solution
- ❑ Cotton balls or gauze squares
- ❑ Forceps
- ❑ Basin for urine (base of kit can be used)
- ❑ Sterile catheter of appropriate size (e.g., for an adult 14 Fr or 16 Fr is often used)
- ❑ Specimen container, as required
- ❑ Bag or receptacle for disposal of the cotton balls

INTERVENTION

1. Assess for urinary retention.

- Percuss and palpate the bladder.
- To percuss the bladder, place the middle finger of one hand against the skin, and strike it sharply with the middle finger of the other hand. When the bladder is full, the resulting sound will be duller than normal.
- To palpate the bladder, indent the skin more than 1.3 cm just above the pubic symphysis by pressing the fingers of one hand on the fingers of the other. *This increases the pressure for palpation.*

  or

- Use a portable bladder or ultrasound device to assess bladder fullness.
- Place the handheld scanner over the bladder.
- Interpret the printout according to the manufacturer's recommendations.

2. Prepare the client.

- Explain the catheterization to the client, and provide privacy. *Exposure of the genitals is embarrassing to most clients.* Some people fear that the procedure will be painful; explain that normally a catheterization is painless and that there may be a sensation of pressure. *Relieving the client's tension can facilitate insertion of the catheter because the urinary sphincters are more likely to be relaxed.*
- Assist the client to a supine position, with knees flexed and thighs externally rotated. Pillows can be used to support the knees and to elevate the buttocks, unless contraindicated. *Raising the client's pelvis gives the nurse a better view of the urinary meatus and reduces the risk of contaminating the catheter.*
- Drape the client. *This maintains comfort and prevents unnecessary exposure.* Cover the client's chest and abdomen with a bath blanket. Pull the client's gown up over her hips. Cover her legs and feet as for perineal care. See Figure 34.5 on page 818.
- Don disposable gloves.
- Wash the perineal-genital area with warm water and soap. *Cleaning reduces the number of microorganisms around the urinary meatus and the possibility of introducing microorganisms with the catheter.*
- Rinse and dry the area well. *Rinsing removes soap that could inhibit the action of the antiseptic, if used later.*
- Remove disposable gloves.
- Obtain assistance if the client requires help in maintaining the required position. *The client must remain still throughout the procedure to maintain a clear view of the urinary meatus and prevent contamination of the sterile field.*

3. Prepare the equipment.

- Adjust the light to view the urinary meatus. It may be necessary to use a flashlight or to place a gooseneck lamp at the foot of the bed so that it focuses on the perineal area.
- Put on a mask, gown, and cap, if required by agency policy.

4. Create a sterile field.

- At the client's bedside, open a sterile kit and the catheter, if it is packaged separately, and put on the sterile gloves (see Procedure 32.3, p. 774).

→

PROCEDURE 36.3 Female Urinary Catheterization Using a Straight Catheter *continued*

- Drape the client with the sterile drape, being careful to protect its sterility and the sterility of your gloves. Place the drape under the buttocks while keeping the edges cuffed over your gloves. *This prevents contamination of the gloves against the client's buttocks.* If a fenestrated drape is provided, place it over the perineal area, exposing only the labia.
- Place the sterile kit on the drape between the client's thighs. *This facilitates access to supplies.*
- Pour the antiseptic solution over the cotton balls if they are not already prepared and if meatal cleansing with an antiseptic is agency practice (see step 5).
- Lubricate the insertion tip of the catheter liberally, and place it in the sterile container ready for use. *Water-soluble lubricant facilitates insertion of the catheter by reducing friction. Lubrication is done at this point because the nurse will subsequently have only one sterile hand available.*
- Open the urine specimen container, and keep the top sterile. *This prepares the container for specimen collection.*

5. **Clean the meatus with antiseptic (if recommended by agency).**

- Check agency protocol about cleaning the meatus. *There is controversy regarding the value of meatal cleaning using antiseptics before catheterization.*
- Using the nondominant hand, separate the labia minora with your thumb and one finger or another two fingers.
- Expose the urinary meatus adequately by retracting the tissue of the labia minora in an upward (anterior) direction (Figure 36.13). Clean first from the meatus downward and then on either side using a new swab for each stroke (Figure 36.14). Once the meatus is cleaned, do not allow the labia to close over it. *Keeping the labia apart prevents the risk of contaminating the urinary meatus. Note:* Your hand that touches the client becomes unsterile. It remains in position exposing the urinary meatus while your other hand remains sterile holding the sterile forceps.

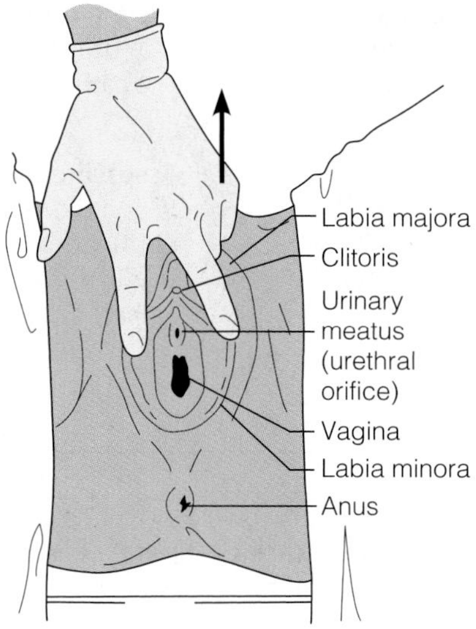

Figure 36.13 To expose the urinary meatus, separate the labia minora and retract the tissue upward

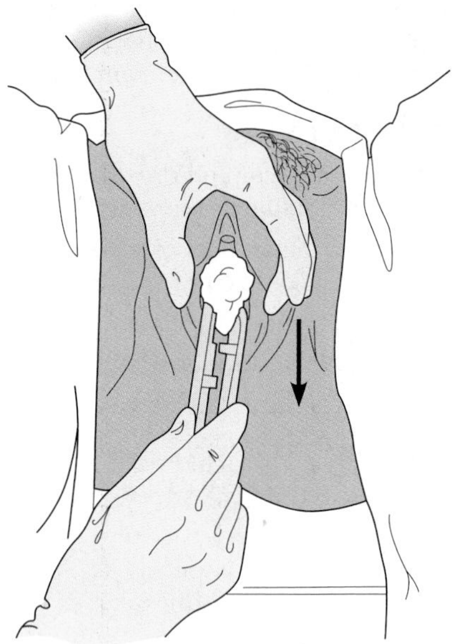

Figure 36.14 When cleaning the urinary meatus, move the swab downward

6. **Inspect the meatus.**

- With the urinary meatus exposed (see Figure 36.13), assess any signs, such as excoriation of the tissues surrounding the urinary meatus, swelling of the urinary meatus, or the presence of discharge around the urinary meatus. *This assessment provides baseline data.* If any discharge is present, obtain a culture swab.

7. **Insert the catheter until urine flows.**

- Place the drainage end of the catheter in the urine receptacle. Pick up the insertion end of the catheter with your uncontaminated, sterile, gloved hand, holding it about 5 cm from the insertion tip. *Because the adult female urethra is approximately 4 cm long, the catheter is held far enough from the end to allow full insertion into the bladder and to maintain control of the tip of the catheter so it will not accidentally become contaminated.*
- Gently insert the catheter into the urinary meatus until urine flows. Insert the catheter in the direction of the urethra. If the catheter meets resistance during insertion, do not force it. *Forceful pressure against the urethra can produce trauma.* Ask the client to take deep breaths. *This helps relax the external sphincter.* If this does not relieve the resistance, discontinue the procedure and report the problem to the nurse in charge. Exercise caution to prevent the catheter tip from becoming contaminated. If it becomes contaminated, discard it.
- When the urine flows, transfer your hand from the labia to the catheter to hold it in place. *This prevents its expulsion by a possible bladder contraction.*

8. **Collect a urine specimen (if required).**

- Pinch the catheter, and transfer the drainage end of it into the sterile specimen bottle. Usually 30 mL of urine is sufficient for a specimen. Securely place the top on the specimen container, and set it aside for labelling later.

9. **Empty or partially drain the bladder, and then remove the catheter.**

- For adults experiencing urinary retention, some orders limit the amount of urine drained to 1,000 mL. Limiting the amount of urine drained has

PROCEDURE 36.3 Female Urinary Catheterization Using a Straight Catheter *continued*

been a controversial issue. *Rapid removal of large amounts of urine was once thought to induce engorgement of the pelvic blood vessels and hypovolemic shock. However, retained urine may serve as a reservoir for microorganisms to multiply.* Usually, agency policy or the physician indicates the amount to be removed and times at which the remaining urine is to be withdrawn. Research findings support the premise that *complete* drainage of a distended bladder is likely to be more comfortable and certainly seems as safe as threshold clamping (Sueppel, 1995).

- Pinch the catheter. *This prevents leakage of urine.* Remove the catheter slowly.

10. Promote client comfort.

- Dry the client's perineum with a towel or drape. *Excess lubricant and solution in the area can irritate the skin.*

11. Assess the urine.

- Inspect the urine for colour, clarity, odour, and the presence of any abnormal constituents, such as blood.
- Measure the amount of urine.
- Remove gloves.

12. Document the catheterization.

- Include assessments before and after the procedure; type and size of catheter inserted; time; characteristics and amount of urine obtained; whether a specimen was sent to the laboratory; and client response to the procedure.

Evaluation Focus
Signs of urinary infection; discomfort; bladder distention; amount, colour, and clarity of urine

Home Care Considerations

For intermittent catheterization, instruct the client to

- Follow instructions for sterile technique.
- Wash hands well with warm water and soap prior to handling equipment or performing catheterization.
- Monitor for signs and symptoms of urinary tract infection, including burning, urgency, abdominal pain, cloudy urine; in older adults, confusion may be an early sign.
- Ensure adequate oral intake of fluids.
- After each catheterization, assess the urine for colour, odour, clarity, and the presence of blood.

Life Span Considerations

- Adapt the size of the catheter for pediatric clients.
- Older clients may need help to maintain the required position or a different position for this procedure. Obtain the assistance of another nurse to flex and hold client's knees and hips, as necessary.

or

- Place the client in a modified Sims' position.

PROCEDURE 36.4 Male Urinary Catheterization Using a Straight Catheter

PURPOSES

- See Procedure 36.3, page 917.

Assessment Focus
See Procedure 36.3, page 917.

Equipment

See Procedure 36.3. A 16 Fr or 18 Fr catheter is often used for an adult male.

INTERVENTION

1. Assess for urinary retention.

- Percuss and palpate the bladder or use a portable bladder ultrasound device as in Procedure 36.3, step 1, page 917.

PROCEDURE 36.4 Male Urinary Catheterization Using a Straight Catheter *continued*

2. **Prepare the client.**
- Explain the catheterization as in Procedure 36.3.
- Assist the client to a supine position, with the knees slightly flexed and the thighs slightly apart. *This allows greater relaxation of the abdominal and perineal muscles and permits easier insertion of the catheter.*
- Drape the client by folding the top bedclothes down so that the penis is exposed and the thighs are covered. Use a bath blanket to cover the client's chest and abdomen.
- Don disposable gloves.
- Wash the penis and dry it well, cleansing the urethra first, then down the shaft of the penis away from the urethra.
- Remove disposable gloves.

3. **Create a sterile field.**
- Open the sterile tray, and don the sterile gloves (see Procedure 32.3, on page 774).
- Place a drape under the penis and a second drape above the penis over the pubic area. If a fenestrated drape is available, place it over the penis and pubic area, exposing only the penis.
- Place the sterile kit on the sterile drape over the client's thighs or next to the thigh.
- Pour the antiseptic solution over the cotton balls if they are not already prepared.
- Lubricate the insertion tip of the catheter liberally for about 5 to 15 cm. Place it in the sterile container ready for insertion. *Water-soluble lubricant facilitates insertion of the catheter by reducing friction. This step is done before cleaning because the nurse will subsequently have only one sterile hand available.*

4. **Clean the urinary meatus with antiseptic (if recommended by the agency).**
- Grasp the penis firmly behind the glans with the nondominant hand, and spread the meatus between the thumb and forefinger. Retract the foreskin of an uncircumcised male. The hand holding the penis is now considered contaminated. *Grasp the penis firmly to avoid stimulating an erection.*
- With the dominant hand, use sterile forceps to pick up a swab. Clean the meatus first, and then wipe the tissue surrounding the meatus in a circular motion. Discard each swab after only one wipe. *Using forceps maintains the sterility of your gloves.*

5. **Insert the catheter.**
- Place the drainage end of the catheter in the urine receptacle. Then, pick up the insertion end of the catheter with your uncontaminated, sterile, gloved hand, holding it about 8 to 10 cm from the insertion tip for an adult or about 2.5 cm for a baby or small boy. In some agencies, the catheter is picked up with forceps. *The male urethra is approximately 20 cm long. Holding the catheter far enough from the end to maintain control of the tip of the catheter avoids accidental contamination.*
- Lift the penis to a position perpendicular to the body (90-degree angle), and exert slight traction (pulling or tension upward). Insert the catheter steadily about 20 cm or until urine begins to flow. *Lifting the penis so that it is perpendicular to the body straightens the downward curvature of the urethra.*
- To bypass slight resistance at the sphincters, twist the catheter slightly, or wait until the sphincter relaxes. Ask the client to take deep breaths or try to void. If difficult resistance is met, discontinue the procedure, and report the problem. *Slight resistance is normally encountered at the external and internal urethral sphincters. Deep breathing can help relax the external sphincter. Forceful pressure exerted against a major resistance can traumatize the urethra.*
- While the urine flows, lower the penis, and transfer your hand to hold the catheter in place at the meatus.

6. **Drain the urine from the bladder.**
- Collect a urine specimen (if required) after the urine has flowed for a few seconds. Pinch the catheter, and transfer the drainage end of the catheter into the sterile specimen bottle taking care not to contaminate the specimen container. Usually 30 mL of urine is sufficient for a specimen.
- Empty the bladder, or drain the amount of urine specified in the order. See Procedure 36.3, step 9.

7. **Make the client comfortable.**
- Dry the penis with a towel or drape.
- Replace the foreskin. *This prevents a mechanical phimosis (constriction), which may compromise circulation to the glans.*
- Remove gloves.

8. **Assess the client and the urine as in Procedure 36.3, and document the procedure and the assessments.**

Evaluation Focus
See Procedure 36.3, page 919.

PROCEDURE 36.5 Inserting a Retention (Indwelling) Catheter

PURPOSES

- To facilitate accurate measurement of urinary output for critically ill clients whose output needs to be monitored hourly
- To provide for intermittent or continuous bladder drainage and irrigation
- To prevent urine from contacting an incision after perineal surgery
- To manage incontinence when other measures have failed

Assessment Focus
Distention of urinary bladder; signs of urinary infection; voiding pattern; ability to maintain position during catheterization; allergies

Equipment

In addition to the equipment used for a straight catheterization, the following equipment is needed:

- ❑ Sterile retention catheter (14 Fr or 16 Fr for adults, 8 Fr or 10 Fr for children are often used)
- ❑ Prefilled syringe (sterile water is often used)
- ❑ Nonallergenic tape or a catheter stabilizing or strapping device (e.g., urological cath-strap)
- ❑ Safety pin or clip
- ❑ Urine collection bag and tubing (the tubing may be attached to the retention catheter if a closed drainage system is used)

INTERVENTION

1. **Prepare the client and the equipment.**

- Explain to the client why the retention catheter is to be inserted, how long it will be in place, and how the urinary drainage equipment needs to be handled to maintain and facilitate the drainage of urine. Reassure the client that the procedure is painless. Some clients fear spillage of urine when they experience the urge to void during insertion of the catheter and for a short time after the catheter is in place. Reassure these clients that the catheter drains the urine and that the urge to void will disappear.
- Follow the procedure for straight catheterization up to and including creating a sterile field.

2. **Test the catheter balloon.**

- Attach the prefilled syringe to the balloon valve, and inject the fluid. *Sterile water, rather than sterile saline, should be used because the saline can crystallize and prevent complete deflation of the balloon.* The balloon should inflate appropriately and not leak. Withdraw the fluid, and set aside the catheter with the syringe attached for later use. If the balloon leaks or does not inflate adequately, replace the catheter. In such a case, withdraw the fluid, and detach the syringe for later use. Ask another nurse to obtain a second catheter and open the package for you, then test the new balloon, *or* remove the equipment and obtain another catheter; then start again with the new sterile equipment.

3. **Follow steps as for straight catheterization.**

- Lubricate the insertion tip of the catheter.
- Remove the sterile cap from the specimen container.
- Expose and clean the urinary meatus and surrounding tissues with antiseptic, if recommended.
- Insert the catheter and inflate the balloon.
- Collect a urine specimen as required.

4. **Move the catheter farther into the bladder, and inflate the balloon.**

- Insert the catheter an additional 2.5 to 5 cm beyond the point at which urine began to flow. The balloon of the catheter is located behind the opening at the insertion tip, and sufficient space needs to be provided to inflate the balloon. *This ensures that the balloon is inflated inside the bladder and not in the urethra, where it could produce trauma.*
- Inflate the balloon by injecting the contents of the prefilled syringe into the valve of the catheter (Figure 36.15, *A*). Placement of the catheter and balloon in a male client is shown in Figure 36.15, *B*. If the client complains of discomfort or pain during the balloon inflation, withdraw the fluid, insert the catheter a little farther, and inflate the balloon again. Insert no more fluid than the balloon size indicates (e.g., 5 mL, 10 mL, or 30 mL), and remove the syringe. A special valve prevents backflow of the fluid out of the catheter.
- Follow agency policy when using a 30-mL balloon. Some agency policies state that only 15 mL of fluid is injected for inflation.

5. **Ensure effective balloon inflation.**

- When the balloon is safely inflated, apply slight tension on the catheter until you feel resistance. *Resistance indicates that the catheter balloon is inflated appropriately and that the catheter is well anchored in the bladder.*

→

PROCEDURE 36.5 Inserting a Retention (Indwelling) Catheter *continued*

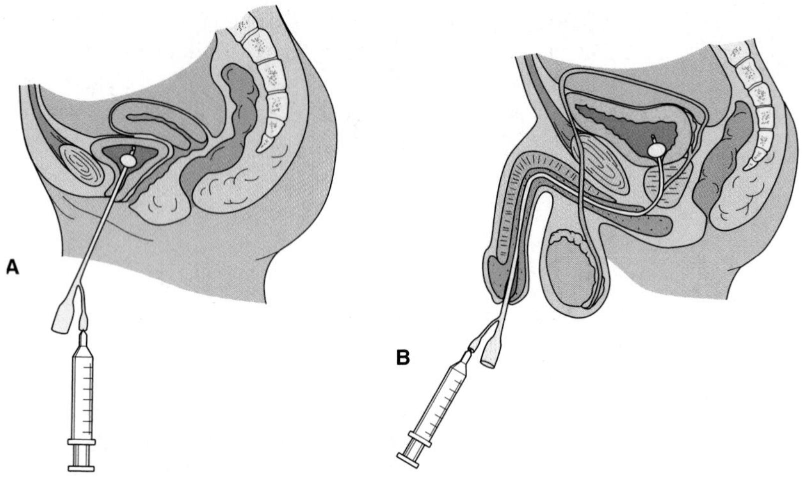

Figure 36.15 Placement of retention catheter and inflated balloon in *A*, female client; and *B*, male client

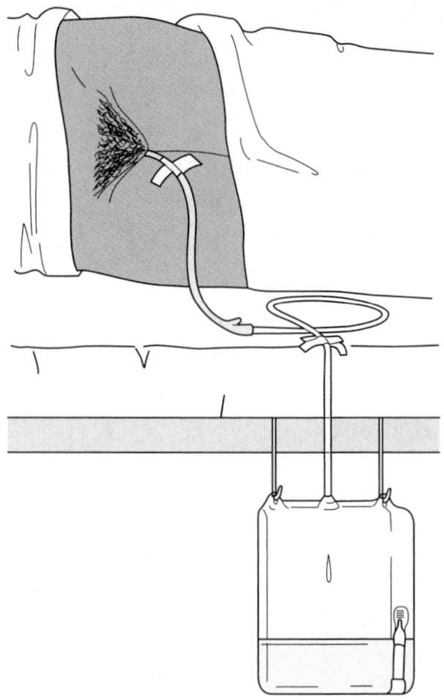

Figure 36.16 Tape the catheter to the inside of a female's thigh

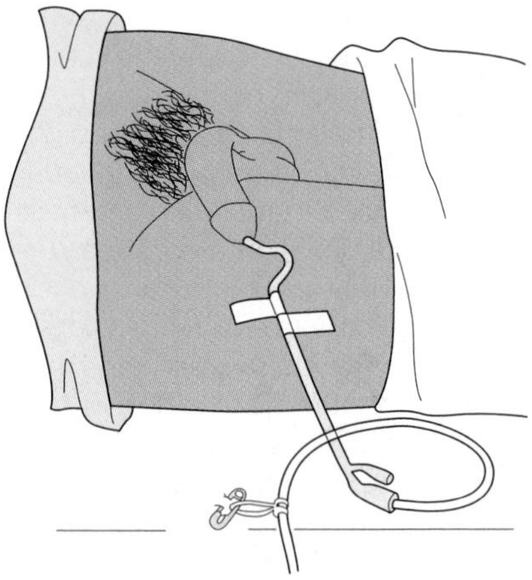

Figure 36.17 Tape the catheter to the thigh or abdomen of a male client

6. **Anchor the catheter.**
   - Tape the catheter with nonallergenic tape to the inside of a female's thigh or to the thigh or abdomen of a male client (Figures 36.16 and 36.17). Some nurses prefer taping the male catheter to the abdomen whenever there is increased risk of excoriation at the penile-scrotal junction. *Taping restricts the movement of the catheter, thus reducing friction and irritation in the urethra when the client moves. It also prevents skin excoriation at the penile-scrotal junction in the male.*
7. **Establish effective drainage.**
   - Ensure that the emptying base of the drainage bag is closed.
   - Secure the drainage bag to the bed frame using the hook or strap provided. Suspend the bag off the floor, but keep it below the level of the client's bladder (see Figure 36.16). *Urine flows by gravity from the bladder to the drainage bag. The bag should be off the floor so that the emptying spout does not become grossly contaminated.*
   - Coil the drainage tubing loosely beside the client so that the remaining tubing runs in a straight line down to the drainage bag. Fasten the vertical tubing to the bedclothes with tape, a tubing clamp, or a safety pin and elastic band (see Figures 36.16 and 36.18). *The drainage tubing should not loop below its entry into the drainage bag, which would impede the flow of urine by gravity.*
8. **Document pertinent data.**
   - Record the time and date of the catheterization; the type and size of catheter; the reason for catheterization; how much fluid was used to inflate the balloon; assessments before and after the procedure, including amount, colour, and clarity of urine obtained; whether a specimen was taken and sent to the laboratory; whether all urine was emptied from the bladder; and the client's response.

Evaluation Focus
Amount, colour, and clarity of urine; any discomfort; fluid intake, palpable bladder

PROCEDURE 36.5 Inserting a Retention (Indwelling) Catheter *continued*

Home Care Considerations

Instruct the client to

- Never pull on the catheter.
- Ensure that there are no kinks or twists in the tubing.
- Keep the urine drainage bag below the level of the bladder.
- Empty the drainage bag regularly.
- Take a shower, rather than a tub bath; sitting in a tub allows bacteria easier access into the urinary tract.

Routine changing of catheter and tubing is not recommended. Collection of sediment in the catheter or tubing or impaired urine drainage are indicators for changing the catheter and drainage system. When this occurs, the catheter and drainage system are removed and discarded, and a new sterile catheter with a closed drainage system is inserted.

Guidelines to prevent catheter-associated urinary tract infections are given in the box below. Ongoing assessment of clients with retention catheters is a high priority. The box that follows provides guidelines.

Client Teaching

Usually, nurses need to teach the client some principles about the gravity drainage system and the importance of maintaining a closed system. The client has to understand that the drainage tubing and drainage bag need to be kept lower than the bladder at all times. The client also needs to know how to prevent tension on the catheter tubing, to prevent loops or kinks in the drainage tubing, and to avoid lying on the tubing. Understanding how to manipulate the system when ambulating can give the client a sense of independence. Some clients also benefit from instruction about fluid intake measurement and perineal care. Clients who wish to be involved in recording fluid intake measurements need information about how to compute these values and which foods are considered fluids.

CLINICAL GUIDELINES

Preventing Catheter-Associated Urinary Infections

- Have an established infection control program.
- Catheterize clients only when necessary, by using aseptic technique, sterile equipment, and trained personnel.
- Maintain a sterile closed-drainage system.
- Do not disconnect the catheter and drainage tubing unless absolutely necessary.
- Remove the catheter as soon as possible.
- Follow and reinforce good hand washing technique.
- Provide routine perineal hygiene, including cleansing with soap and water after defecation. Prevent contamination of the catheter with feces in the incontinent client.

Removing Retention Catheters

Retention catheters are removed after their purpose has been achieved, usually on the order of the physician. If the catheter has been in place for a short time (e.g., a few days), the client usually has little difficulty regaining normal urinary elimination patterns. Swelling of the urethra, however, may initially interfere with voiding, so the nurse should regularly assess the client for urinary retention until voiding is re-established.

Clients who have had a retention catheter for a prolonged period may require bladder retraining to regain bladder muscle tone. With an indwelling catheter in place, the bladder muscle does not stretch and contract regularly as it does when the bladder fills and empties by voiding. A few days prior to removal, the catheter may be clamped for specified periods of time (e.g., two to four hours), then released to allow the bladder to empty. This allows the bladder to distend and stimulates its musculature. A physician's order may be required.

To remove a retention catheter, the nurse follows these steps:

- Obtain a receptacle for the catheter (e.g., a disposable basin); a clean towel; disposable gloves; and a sterile syringe to deflate the balloon. The syringe should be large enough to withdraw *all* the solution in the catheter balloon. The size of the balloon is indicated on the label at the end of the catheter.
- Ask the client to assume a supine position as for a catheterization.

CLINICAL ASSESSMENT

Ongoing Assessment of Clients with Retention Catheters

- Ensure that there are no obstructions in the drainage tubing. Check that there are no kinks in the tubing, the client is not lying on the tubing, and the tubing is not clogged with mucus or blood.
- Check that there is no tension on the catheter or tubing, that the catheter is securely taped to the thigh or abdomen, and that the tubing is fastened appropriately to the bedclothes.
- Ensure that gravity drainage is maintained. Make sure there are no loops in the tubing below its entry to the drainage receptacle and that the drainage receptacle is below the level of the client's bladder.
- Ensure that the drainage system is well sealed or closed. Check that there are no leaks at the connection sites in open systems. Apply waterproof tape around the connection site of the catheter and tubing.
- Observe the flow of the urine every two or three hours, and note colour, odour, and any abnormal constituents. If blood clots are present, check the catheter more frequently to assess patency.

- Optional: Obtain a sterile specimen before removing the catheter. Check agency protocol.
- Remove the tape attaching the catheter to the client, don gloves, and then place the towel between the legs of the female client or over the thighs of the male.
- Insert the syringe into the injection port of the catheter, and withdraw the fluid from the balloon. If all the fluid cannot be removed, report this fact to the nurse in charge before proceeding.
- Do *not* pull the catheter while the balloon is inflated; doing so may injure the urethra.
- After all the fluid is withdrawn from the balloon, gently withdraw the catheter, and place it in the waste receptacle.
- Dry the perineal area with a towel.
- Remove gloves.
- Measure the urine in the drainage bag, and record the removal of the catheter. Include in the recording (1) the time the catheter was removed; (2) the amount, colour, and clarity of the urine, (3) the intactness of the catheter; and (4) instructions given to the client.
- Following removal of the catheter, determine the time of the first voiding and the amount voided during the first 24 hours. Compare this output to the client's intake.

Intermittent Self-Catheterization

Intermittent self-catheterization is performed by many clients who have some form of neurogenic bladder dysfunction, such as that caused by spinal cord injury. Medical aseptic technique is used. Intermittent self-catheterization:

- Enables the client to retain independence and gain control of the bladder.
- Reduces incidence of urinary tract infection.
- Protects the upper urinary tract from reflux.
- Allows normal sexual relations without incontinence.
- Reduces the use of aids and appliances.
- Frees the client from embarrassing dribbling.
- Enables some clients to return to work.

The procedure for self-catheterization is similar to that used by the nurse to catheterize a client. Essential steps are outlined in the box opposite. Because the procedure requires great motivation and physical and mental preparation, client assessment is important. The client should have:

- Sufficient manual dexterity to manipulate a catheter.
- Sufficient mental ability.
- Motivation and acceptance of the procedure.
- For females, reasonable agility to access the urethra.
- Bladder capacity not less than 100 mL.

Before teaching intermittent self-catheterization, the nurse should establish the client's voiding patterns, the volume voided, fluid intake, and residual amounts. Self-catheterization is easier to learn for males because of the visibility of the urinary meatus. Females need to learn initially with the aid of a mirror but eventually should perform the procedure by using only the sense of touch (as described in the Client Teaching box).

Urinary Irrigations

An **irrigation** is a flushing or washing out with a specified solution. A *bladder irrigation* is carried out on a physician's order, usually to wash out the bladder and sometimes to apply a medication to the bladder lining. *Catheter irrigations* may be performed to maintain or restore the patency of a catheter, for example, to remove pus or blood clots blocking the catheter.

The *closed method* is the preferred technique for catheter or bladder irrigation because it is associated with a lower risk of urinary tract infection. Closed catheter irrigations may be either continuous or intermittent. A three-way, or triple lumen, catheter (see Figure 36.12 on p. 916) generally is used for closed irrigations. The irrigating solution flows into the bladder through the irrigation port of the catheter and out through the urinary drainage lumen of the catheter (Figure 36.18).

CLIENT TEACHING

Intermittent Self-Catheterization

- Catheterize as often as needed to maintain an acceptable residual urine volume. At first, catheterization may be necessary every two to three hours, increasing to four to six hours.
- Attempt to void before catheterization; insert the catheter to remove residual urine if unable to void or if amount voided is insufficient (e.g., less than 100 mL).
- Assemble all needed supplies ahead of time. Good lighting is essential, especially for women.
- If female, remove a tampon before carrying out intermittent self-catheterization. A tampon can inhibit catheterization.
- Wash your hands.
- Clean the urinary meatus with either a towelette or soapy washcloth, then rinse with a wet washcloth. If female, clean the area from front to back.
- Assume a position that is comfortable and that facilitates passage of the catheter, such as a semireclining position in bed or sitting on a chair or the toilet. Men may prefer to stand over the toilet; women may prefer to stand with one foot on the side of the bathtub.
- Apply lubricant to the catheter tip (2.5 cm for women; 5 to 12.5 cm for men).
- Insert the catheter until urine flows through.
  a. If *female,* locate the meatus using a mirror or other aid, or use the "touch" technique as follows:
     - Place the index finger of your nondominant hand on your clitoris.
     - Place the third and fourth fingers at the vagina.
     - Locate the meatus between the index and third fingers.
     - Separate the labia with your dominant hand.
     - Direct the catheter through the meatus and then upward and forward toward the umbilicus.

  b. If *male,* hold the penis with a slight upward tension at a 60- to 90-degree angle to insert the catheter. Return the penis to its natural position after catheter insertion when urine starts to flow.
     - Hold the catheter in place until all urine is drained.
     - Withdraw the catheter slowly to ensure complete drainage of urine.
     - Contact your care provider if your urine appears cloudy or contains sediment; if you have bleeding, difficulty, or pain when passing the catheter; or if you have a fever.
     - Drink at least 1,500 mL of fluid a day, unless contraindicated, to ensure adequate bladder filling and flushing. To keep your urine acidic and reduce the risk of bladder infections, drink cranberry and prune juices.

Techniques for setting up and maintaining a continuous or intermittent closed catheter irrigation are outlined in Procedure 36.6 on the following page.

Occasionally, an *open irrigation* may be necessary to restore catheter patency. The risk of injecting microorganisms into the urinary tract is greater with open irrigations as the connection between the indwelling catheter and the drainage tubing is broken. Strict precautions to maintain the sterility of the drainage tubing connector and interior of the indwelling catheter must be taken to minimize this risk.

The open method of catheter or bladder irrigation is performed with double-lumen indwelling catheters; it may be necessary for clients who develop blood clots and mucus fragments that occlude the catheter and when it is undesirable to change the catheter. The steps involved in performing an open method of irrigation are shown in the box on page 926.

Urinary Diversions

A urinary diversion is the surgical rerouting of urine from the kidneys to a site other than the bladder. Urinary diversions are usually created when the bladder must be removed, for example, because of cancer or trauma. The ureters may be brought directly to the surface of the skin to form small stomas *(cutaneous ureterostomy).* This procedure, however, has some disadvantages in that the stomas provide direct access for microorganisms from the skin to the kidneys, the small stomas are difficult to fit with an appliance to collect the urine, and they may stenose, impairing urine drainage.

The most common urinary diversion is the *ileal conduit* or *ileal loop* (Figure 36.19). In this procedure, a segment of the ileum is removed and the intestinal ends are reattached. One end of the portion removed is closed with sutures to create a pouch, and the other end is brought out through the abdominal wall to create a stoma.

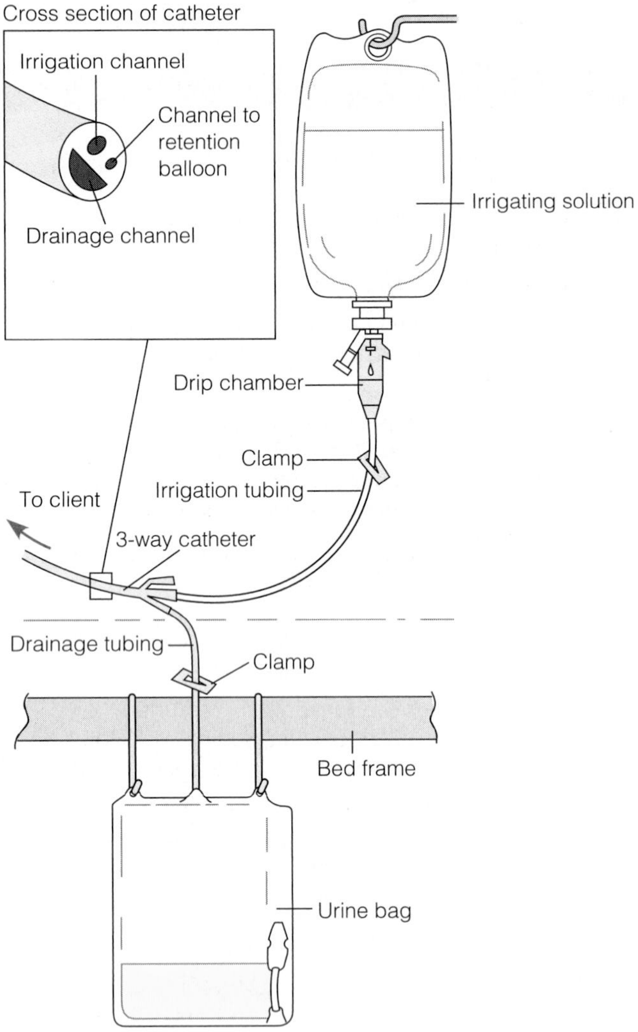

Figure 36.18 A closed catheter or bladder irrigation system

Open Method of Catheter Irrigation

- Obtain a sterile Asepto or piston syringe (see Figure 28.63, p. 662); sterile basin and sterile irrigating solution at room temperature; sterile collection basin; sterile protective tubing cap; sterile waterproof drape; sterile gloves; and antiseptic swabs.
- Establish a sterile field close to the client's thigh. Place the sterile waterproof drape under the catheter and apply sterile gloves.
- Clean the junction between the catheter and the drainage tubing with antiseptic swabs.
- Disconnect the catheter and drainage tubing. Hold the catheter and tubing about 2.5 cm from their ends and place them on a sterile surface to avoid contaminating them.
- Cover the open end of the drainage tubing with the sterile protection cap.
- Draw irrigation fluid into the syringe and instill it slowly into the catheter.
- Remove the syringe and allow the irrigating solution to drain by gravity from the catheter into the collection basin.
- Repeat irrigations depending on the amount of solution to be instilled or until urine runs freely through the catheter and drainage is clear.
- Cleanse the ends of the catheter and drainage tubing with antiseptic swabs and reconnect the catheter and drainage tubing, maintaining the sterility of the ends of the tubing and the inside of the catheter.
- Remove gloves.
- Assess and document the irrigation returns.

PROCEDURE 36.6 Irrigating a Catheter or Bladder (Closed System)

Before irrigating a catheter or bladder, check (1) the reason for the irrigation; (2) the order authorizing the continuous or intermittent irrigation (in most agencies, a physician's order is required); (3) the type of sterile solution, the amount, and strength to be used, and the rate (if continuous); and (4) the type of catheter in place. If these are not specified on the client's chart, check agency protocol.

PURPOSES

- To maintain the patency of a urinary catheter and tubing (continuous irrigation)
- To free a blockage in a urinary catheter or tubing (intermittent irrigation)

Assessment Focus
Amount, clarity, and colour of urine; comparison of fluid intake to output; presence of bladder distention; level of discomfort

PROCEDURE 36.6 Irrigating a Catheter or Bladder (Closed System) *continued*

Equipment

- ❑ Disposable gloves
- ❑ Disposable water-resistant sterile towel
- ❑ Three-way retention catheter in place
- ❑ Sterile drainage tubing and bag (if not in place)
- ❑ Sterile antiseptic swabs
- ❑ Sterile receptacle
- ❑ Sterile irrigating solution warmed or at room temperature
- ❑ Infusion tubing
- ❑ IV pole

INTERVENTION

1. Prepare the client.

- Explain the procedure and its purpose to the client. The irrigation should not be painful or uncomfortable. *Clear explanations reduce the client's anxiety.*
- Provide for privacy and drape the client as needed to allow access to the retention catheter.
- Don gloves.
- Empty, measure, and record the amount and appearance of urine present in the drainage bag. Discard urine and gloves. *Emptying the drainage bag allows more accurate measurement of urinary output after the irrigation is in place or completed. Assessing the character of the urine provides baseline data for later comparison.*

2. Prepare the equipment.

- Wash hands.
- Connect the irrigation infusion tubing to the irrigating solution and flush the tubing with solution. *Flushing the tubing removes air and prevents it from being instilled into the bladder.*
- Connect the irrigation tubing to the input port of the three-way catheter. Connect the drainage bag and tubing to the urinary drainage port if not already in place.

3. Irrigate the bladder.

a. For **continuous irrigation,** open the flow clamp on the urinary drainage tubing (if present). *This allows the irrigating solution to flow out of the bladder continuously.*
   - Open the regulating clamp on the irrigating tubing and adjust the flow rate as prescribed by the physician or according to agency policy, if not specified.
   - Assess the drainage for amount, colour, and clarity. The amount of drainage should equal the amount of irrigant entering the bladder plus expected urine output.

b. For **intermittent irrigation,** determine whether the solution is to remain in the bladder for a specified time.
   - If the solution is to remain in the bladder (a bladder irrigation or instillation), close the flow clamp on the urinary drainage tubing. *Closing the flow clamp allows the solution to be retained in the bladder and in contact with bladder walls.*
   - If the solution is being instilled to irrigate the catheter, open the flow clamp on the urinary drainage tubing. *Irrigating solution will flow through the urinary drainage port and tubing, removing mucus shreds or clots.*
   - Open the flow clamp on the irrigating tubing, allowing the specified amount of solution to infuse. Clamp the tubing.
   - After the specified period the solution is to be retained, open the drainage tubing flow clamp and allow the bladder to empty.

4. Assess the client and the urinary output.

- Assess the client's comfort.
- Assess the amount, colour, and clarity of drainage; note any abnormal constituents, such as blood clots, pus, or mucus shreds.
- To document urine output, empty the drainage bag and measure the contents. Subtract the amount of irrigant instilled from the total volume of drainage to obtain urine output.

5. Document the irrigation.

- Include all assessments obtained before and after performing the irrigation.

Variation: Closed Irrigation Using a Two-Way Indwelling Catheter

1. Assemble the equipment, including:

- Clean disposable gloves
- Disposable water-resistant towel
- Sterile irrigating solution
- Sterile basin
- Sterile 30- to 50-mL syringe with a #18- or #19-gauge needle
- Sterile antiseptic swabs

2. Prepare the client (see step 1 of main procedure for catheter irrigation).

3. Prepare the equipment.

- Wash hands and don gloves.
- Place the disposable water-resistant towel under the catheter.
- For a bladder irrigation or instillation, clamp the drainage tubing distal to the injection port on the tubing or catheter. *Clamping prevents the urine and solution from draining into the drainage bag.* For a catheter irrigation, leave the tubing unclamped.
- Using aseptic technique, open supplies and pour the irrigating solution into the sterile basin or receptacle. *Aseptic technique is vital to reduce the risk of instilling microorganisms into the urinary tract during the irrigation.*
- Remove the cap from the needle and draw the prescribed amount of irrigating solution into the syringe, maintaining the sterility of the syringe and solution.
- Using the antiseptic swab, clean the port on the catheter or drainage tubing through which the solution will be instilled.

→

PROCEDURE 36.6 Irrigating a Catheter or Bladder (Closed System) *continued*

4. **Irrigate the bladder.**
   - Insert the needle into the port.
   - Gently inject the solution into the catheter. In adults, about 30 to 40 mL generally is instilled for catheter irrigations; 100 to 200 mL may be instilled for bladder irrigation or instillation. Smaller amounts are used for children. *Gentle instillation reduces the risks of injury to bladder mucosa and of bladder spasms.*
   - When the total amount to be instilled has been injected (or for catheter irrigation, when urine is flowing freely), remove the needle from the port and discard the syringe and uncapped needle in an appropriate receptacle (sharps container). *Safe disposal of the syringe and needle is important to minimize the risk of needle-stick injury.*
   - After the prescribed dwelling time for a bladder irrigation, remove the clamp from the drainage tubing and allow the urine and irrigating solution to drain into the drainage bag.
   - Assess the drainage for amount, colour, and clarity. The amount of drainage should equal the amount of irrigant entering the bladder plus expected urine output.
5. **Assess the client and the urinary output and document the procedure as previously noted.**

Evaluation Focus
Catheter patency; amount, colour, odour, and clarity of drainage; client comfort

The ureters are implanted into the ileal pouch. The ileal stoma is more readily fitted with an appliance than ureterostomies because of its larger size. The mucous membrane lining of the ileum also provides some protection from ascending infection. Urine drains continuously from the ileal pouch.

Highly motivated clients may be candidates for a continent urinary diversion. The *Kock pouch*, or continent *ileal bladder conduit*, also uses a portion of the ileum to form a reservoir for urine. In this procedure, nipple valves are formed by doubling the tissue backward into the reservoir where the pouch connects to the skin and the ureters connect to the pouch. These valves close as the pouch fills with urine, preventing leakage and reflux of urine back toward the kidneys. The client empties the pouch by inserting a clean catheter approximately every four hours. Between catheterizations, a small dressing is worn to protect the stoma and clothing.

A *continent vesicostomy* (sometimes also known as a Kock pouch) may be formed when the bladder is left intact but voiding through the urethra is not possible (e.g., due to an obstruction or a neurogenic bladder). The ureters remain connected to the bladder, and the bladder wall is sutured to the abdominal wall, forming a stoma (Figure 36.20).

When caring for clients with a urinary diversion, the nurse must accurately assess intake and output, note any changes in urine colour, odour, or clarity (mucus shreds are commonly seen in the urine of clients with an ileal diversion), and frequently assess the condition of the stoma and surrounding skin. Clients who must wear a urine collection appliance are at risk for impaired skin integrity because of irritation by urine. Well-fitting appliances are vital. The nurse should consult with an enterostomal therapist to identify the most appropriate appliance for the client's needs.

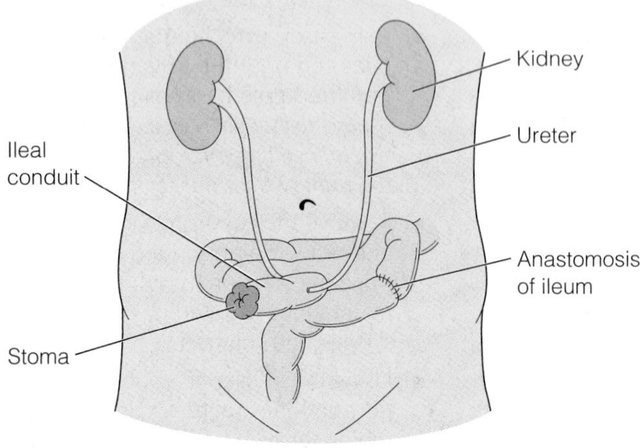

Figure 36.19 An ileal conduit

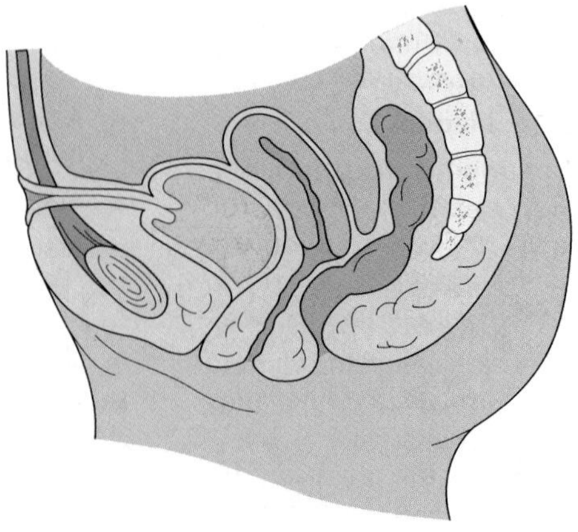

Figure 36.20 A continent vesicostomy (Kock pouch)

Clients with urinary diversions may experience problems with their body image and sexuality and may require assistance in coping with these changes and managing the stoma. Most clients are able to resume their normal activities and lifestyle.

Suprapubic Catheter Care

A **suprapubic** catheter is inserted through the abdominal wall above the symphysis pubis into the urinary bladder (Figure 36.21). The physician inserts the catheter using local anesthesia or during bladder or vaginal surgery. The catheter may be secured in place with sutures, with a body seal, or with both sutures and a body seal. The catheter is then attached to a closed drainage system.

Care of clients with a suprapubic catheter includes regular assessments of the client's urine, fluid intake, and comfort; maintenance of a patent drainage system; skin care around the insertion site; periodic clamping of the catheter preparatory to removing it; and measurement of residual urine. Orders generally include leaving the catheter open to drainage for 48 to 72 hours, then clamping the catheter for three- to four-hour periods during the day until the client can void satisfactory amounts. Satisfactory voiding is determined by measuring the client's residual urine after voiding.

Evaluating

Using the overall goals and desired outcomes identified in the planning stage, the nurse collects data to evaluate the effectiveness of nursing activities. Examples of desired outcomes for the identified goals are listed in Table 36.6.

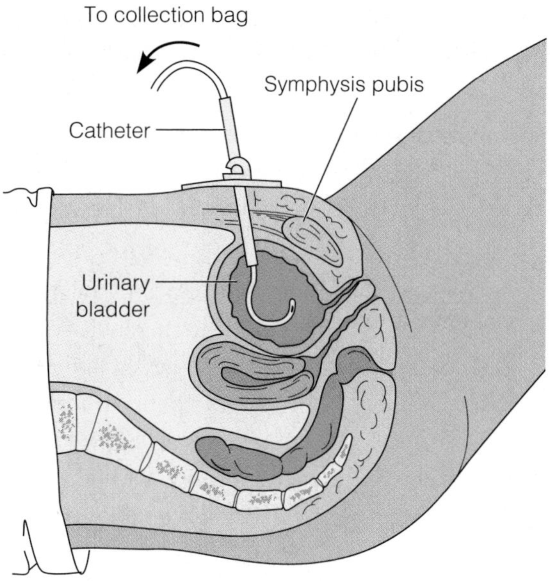

Figure 36.21 A suprapubic catheter in place

Care of the catheter insertion site involves sterile technique. Dressings around the suprapubic catheter are changed whenever they are soiled with drainage to prevent bacterial growth around the insertion site and reduce the potential for infection. Procedures for cleaning wounds and changing dressings are discussed in Chapter 37. Any redness and discharge at the skin around the insertion site must be reported.

If the desired outcomes are *not* achieved, the nurse, client, and support people, if appropriate, need to explore the reasons before modifying the care plan. For example, if the outcome "Remains dry between voidings and at

FOCUS ON CRITICAL THINKING

Mrs. Kennedy, 48 years old, is recovering from an automobile accident in which she sustained blunt trauma to her abdomen which necessitated the removal of her spleen. Additionally, she has a fractured femur and a mild concussion. She has an indwelling urinary catheter in place. Upon entering Mrs. Kennedy's room to collect a urine specimen ordered for culture and sensitivity, you note that Mrs. Kennedy is restless and moaning. Her abdominal dressing is dry and intact and her urinary bag contains about 200 mL of golden-coloured urine. Her abdomen is tender and distended. When questioned, Mrs. Kennedy is able to communicate that she is in pain but is unable to communicate the specifics of her pain.

1. Is it correct to assume that Mrs. Kennedy is experiencing incisional pain? Why, or why not?
2. What actions should be taken prior to administering pain medication to Mrs. Kennedy?
3. What precautions should be taken when collecting a urine sample from a person with an indwelling urinary catheter, and why?
4. What measures can be taken to prevent Mrs. Kennedy from developing a urinary tract infection if it is not already present?
5. What interventions may be useful in helping Mrs. Kennedy establish a normal urinary pattern following the removal of her catheter?

See Appendix A for answers to these questions.

TABLE 36.6 Evaluation Goals and Outcomes: Urinary Elimination

Goal	Examples of Desired Outcomes
Restore normal voiding pattern	Absence of pain, burning, hesitancy, or urgency with urination Voids at three- to four-hour intervals with no more than one voiding during the night Remains dry between voidings and at night Performs pelvic floor muscle exercises correctly at specified frequency
Perform toilet activities independently with or without assistive devices	Able to access toilet facilities or appropriate receptacle (urinal, commode) for voiding Able to manipulate clothing for voiding Able to get on and off toilet unassisted Cleans perineal area with tissue (and as necessary with soap and water) appropriately after voiding and defecating
Regain normal urine output	Quantity of urine at each voiding is within expected range (e.g., greater than 150 mL) Bladder empties completely with each voiding (e.g., bladder is nonpalpable and postvoid residual is less than 100 mL) Urine colour, clarity, and odour are within normal limits Urinalysis values are within expected ranges (specific gravity, pH, protein, glucose, and ketones)
Avoid complications associated with altered urinary elimination (urinary tract infection, skin breakdown, fluid and electrolyte imbalance, body image disturbance, social isolation)	Absence of manifestations of UTI, such as dysuria, frequency, urgency, hematuria, or pyuria Identifies symptoms of and measures to prevent UTI Drinks at least 1,500 mL of fluid daily Fluid intake and output are balanced Serum electrolytes remain within expected values Skin of perineal area and over bony prominences (sacrum, hips), or around urinary stoma if client has one, remains intact Cares for urinary stoma and drainage collection devices as instructed Demonstrates appropriate technique in performing intermittent self-catheterization States or demonstrates acceptance of urinary diversion and ability to adjust to change in lifestyle Maintains or returns to previous social involvement

night" is *not* met, examples of questions that need to be considered include:

- What is the client's perception of the problem?
- Does the client understand and comply with the health-care instructions provided?
- Is access to toilet facilities a problem?
- Can the client manipulate clothing for toileting? Are there adjustments that can be made to allow easier disrobing?
- Are scheduled toileting times appropriate?
- Is there adequate transition lighting for nighttime toileting?
- Are mobility aids, such as a walker, elevated toilet seat, or grab bar, needed? If currently used, are they appropriate or adequate?
- Is the client performing pelvic floor muscle exercises appropriately as scheduled?
- Is the client's fluid intake adequate? Does the timing of fluid intake need to be adjusted (e.g., restricted after dinner)?
- Is the client restricting caffeine, citrus juice, carbonated beverages, and artificial sweetener intake?
- Is the client taking a diuretic? If so, when is the medication taken? Do the times need to be adjusted (e.g., taking second dose no later than 4 p.m.)?
- Should continence aids, such as a condom catheter or absorbent pads, be considered or used?

Consider...

What actions would you take if the client did *not* meet the following outcome criteria?

- "Quantity of urine at each voiding is within expected range." (Data reveal that no more than 90 mL is eliminated at each voiding.)
- "Urine colour, clarity, and odour are within normal limits." (Data reveal that urine is cloudy, rusty in colour, and has a strong unpleasant odour; client complains of burning on urination.)
- "Drinks at least 1,500 to 2,000 mL of fluid daily." (Data reveal that the client is drinking an average of about 1,100 mL daily.)

CHAPTER HIGHLIGHTS

- Urinary elimination depends on normal functioning of the urinary, cardiovascular, and nervous systems.
- Urine is formed in the nephron, the functional unit of the kidney, through a process of filtration, reabsorption, and secretion. Hormones, such as antidiuretic hormone (ADH) and aldosterone, affect the reabsorption of sodium and water, thus affecting the amount of urine formed.
- The normal process of urination is stimulated when sufficient urine collects in the bladder to stimulate stretch receptors. Impulses from stretch receptors are transmitted to the spinal cord and the brain, causing relaxation of the internal sphincter (unconscious control), and, if appropriate, relaxation of the external sphincter (conscious control).
- In the adult, urination generally occurs after 250 to 450 mL of urine has collected in the bladder.
- Many factors influence a person's urinary elimination, including growth and development, fluid intake, stress, activity, medications, and various diseases.
- Alterations in urine production and elimination include polyuria, oliguria, anuria, frequency, nocturia, urgency, dysuria, enuresis, hematuria, incontinence, and retention. Each may have various influencing and associated factors that need to be identified.
- Assessment of a client's urinary function includes: (1) nursing history that identifies normal voiding patterns, usual urine and recent changes, past and current problems with urination, and factors influencing the elimination pattern; (2) a physical assessment of the genitourinary system; (3) inspection of the urine for amount, colour, clarity, and odour, and if indicated, (4) testing of urine for specific gravity, pH, and the presence of glucose, ketone bodies, protein, and occult blood.
- Incontinence can be physically and emotionally distressing to clients because it is considered socially unacceptable.
- Bladder training can often reduce episodes of incontinence.
- Clients with urinary retention not only experience discomfort but also are at risk of urinary tract infection.
- The most common cause of urinary tract infection is invasive procedures, such as catheterization and cystoscopic examination. Females, in particular, are prone to ascending urinary tract infections because of their short urethras.
- Goals for the client with problems with urinary elimination include maintaining or restoring normal elimination patterns and preventing associated risks, such as skin breakdown.
- In planning for home care, the nurse considers the client's needs for teaching and assistance or assistive devices in the home.
- Nursing interventions related to urinary elimination are generally directed toward facilitating the normal functioning of the urinary system or toward assisting the client with particular problems.
- Interventions include (1) assisting the client to maintain an appropriate fluid intake, (2) assisting the client to maintain normal voiding patterns, (3) monitoring the client's daily fluid intake and output, and (4) maintaining cleanliness of the genital area.
- Urinary catheterization is frequently required for clients with urinary retention but is only performed when all other measures to facilitate voiding fail. Sterile technique is essential to prevent ascending urinary infections.
- Care of clients with indwelling catheters is directed toward preventing infection of the urinary tract and encouraging urinary flow through the drainage system.
- Clients with urinary retention may be taught to perform intermittent self-catheterization to enhance their independence, reduce the risk of infection, and eliminate incontinence.
- Bladder or catheter irrigations may be used to apply medication to bladder walls or maintain catheter patency.
- When the urinary bladder is removed, a urinary diversion is formed to allow urine to be eliminated from the body. The ileal conduit or ileal loop is the most common diversion and requires that the client wear a urine collection device continually over the stoma.

READINGS AND REFERENCES

Suggested Readings

Hiser, V. (1999). Nursing interventions for urinary incontinence in home health. *Journal of Wound, Ostomy and Continence Nurses, 26*(3), 1423–1460.

Urinary incontinence (UI) is a significant health-care concern for many clients and often for their families. The author reviews the epidemiology, causes, assessment, and management of UI in the home care setting. Emphasis is placed on the role of the nurse as coordinator of an interdisciplinary team providing care for the client with UI residing in the home.

Milne, J. (2000). The impact of information on health behaviours of older adults with urinary incontinence. *Clinical Nursing Research, 9*(2), 161–176.

The purpose of this quantitative study was to explore the impact of education about urinary incontinence on the help-seeking behaviours of older adults. The author describes the purpose of the study, research question, method, findings, and implications for nursing practice. Results emphasized the importance of registered nurses providing information to clients.

Scura, K. W., & Whipple, B. (1997, April). How to provide better care for the postmenopausal woman. *American Journal of Nursing, 97*(4), 36–44.

These authors address the nurse's role in recognizing and meeting common health-care needs in older women. Urinary incontinence is one of three commonly unrecognized and undertreated problems affecting older women, along with osteoporosis and breast cancer. The types of urinary incontinence are defined and measures to address each are presented, with the focus on teaching and maintaining the client's independence and self-esteem.

Related Research

Chiverton, P. A., Wells, T. J., Brink, C. A., & Mayer, R. (1996, September). Psychological factors associated with urinary incontinence. *Clinical Nurse Specialist, 10*(5), 229–233.

Koch, T., & Kelly, S. (1999). Identifying strategies for managing urinary incontinence with women who have multiple sclerosis. *Journal of Clinical Nursing, 8*(5), 550–559.

Roberts, R. O., Jacobsen, S. J., Rhodes, T., Reilly, W. T., Girman, C. J., Talley, N. J., & Lieber, M. M. (1998). Urinary incontinence in a community-based cohort: Prevalence and healthcare-seeking. *Journal of the American Geriatrics Society, 46*(4), 467–472.

Robinson, J. P. (2000). Managing urinary incontinence in the nursing home: Residents' perspectives. *Journal of Advanced Nursing, 31*(1), 68–77.

Selected References

Asci, J. A., & Beyea, S. C. (1996, February). Urologic update. Indwelling urinary catheters: An integrative review of the research. *Online Journal of Knowledge Synthesis for Nursing, 3*(Doc 2, Online #26), 1–7.

Bardsley, A. (1999). Continence. A sense of control... assessment and treatment of bladder dysfunction. *Nursing Times, 95*(31), 66, 69.

Booth, F. (1999). Adopting a positive approach to urinary continence. *British Journal of Community Nursing, 4*(4), 161–162, 164–166.

Bradley, M., & Pupiales, M. (1997, July). Essential elements of ostomy care. *American Journal of Nursing, 97*(7), 38–46.

Brazier, A. M., & Palmer, M. H. (1995, September/October). Collecting clean-catch urine in the nursing home: Obtaining the uncontaminated specimen. *Geriatric Nursing: American Journal of Care for the Aging, 16*(5), 217–224.

Carpenito, L. J. (2002). *Handbook of nursing diagnosis* (9th ed.). Philadelphia, PA: Lippincott, Williams and Wilkins.

Chiverton, P. A., Wells, T. J., Brink, C. A., & Mayer, R. (1996, September). Psychological factors associated with urinary incontinence. *Clinical Nurse Specialist, 10*(5), 229–233.

Colley, W. (1997, March). Know how: Male catheterization. *Nursing Times, 93*(11), 32–33.

Connor, P. A., & Kooker, B. M. (1996, April). Nurses' knowledge, attitudes, and practices in managing urinary incontinence in the acute care setting. *MEDSURG Nursing, 5*(2), 87–92.

Dolman, M. (1998, Sept.). Practice update. Strategies to promote continence in the community. *British Journal of Community Nursing, 3*(8), 385–386, 388–392.

Dorey, G. (1997, February). Post-prostatectomy incontinence. *Physiotherapy, 83*(2), 68–72.

Duffield, P. (1997, April). Urinary tract infections in the elderly: A common complication of aging. *ADVANCE for Nurse Practitioners, 5*(4), 30–32.

Gallo, M. L., Fallon, P. J., & Staskin, D. R. (1997, February). Urinary incontinence: Steps to evaluation, diagnosis, and treatment. *Nurse Practitioner: American Journal of Primary Health Care, 22*(2), 21–22, 24, 26.

Gallo, M., & Sasso, K. C. (1997, March). Key components of patient education for pelvic floor stimulation in the treatment of urinary incontinence. *Urologic Nursing, 17*(1), 10–16.

Getliffe, K. A. (1996, March). Bladder instillations and bladder washouts in the management of catheterized patients. *Journal of Advanced Nursing, 23*(3), 548–554.

Goshorn, J. (1996, September). Clinical snapshot. Kidney stones: Strategies for managing this common, excruciating condition. *American Journal of Nursing, 96*(9), 40–41.

Hancock, R., Bender, P., Dayhoff, N., & Nyhuis, A. (1996, September). Factors associated with nursing interventions to reduce incontinence in hospitalized older adults. *Urologic Nursing, 16*(3), 79–85.

Johnson, M., & Maas, M. (Eds.). (2000). *Iowa outcomes project: Nursing outcomes classification (NOC)*. St. Louis, MO: Mosby.

Johnson, S. T. (2000). From incontinence to confidence. *American Journal of Nursing, 100*(2), 69–70, 72–74, 76.

Krichbaum, K. E., Pearson, V., & Hanscom, J. (2000, January). Better care in nursing homes: Advanced practice nurses' strategies for improving staff use of protocols. *Clinical Nurse Specialist, 14*(1), 40–46.

Kurtz, M. J., Van Zandt, D. K., & Sapp, L. R. (1996, November/December). A new technique in independent intermittent catheterization: The Mitrofanoff catheterizable channel. *Rehabilitation Nursing, 21*(6), 311–314.

Mahony, C. (1997, December). The impact of incontinence problems on self-esteem. *Nursing Times, 93*(52), 58, 60.

Malone-Lee, J. (1999). Know how: Managing incontinence. *Nursing Times, 95*(18), 74–75.

Marchiondo, K. (1998, March). A new look at urinary tract infection. *American Journal of Nursing, 98*(3), 34–39.

McCloskey, J. C., & Bulechek, G. M. (Eds.). (2000). *Iowa intervention project: Nursing interventions classification (NIC)* (3rd ed.). St. Louis, MO: Mosby.

McConnell, E. A. (1995, December). Clinical do's and don'ts. Inflating an indwelling urinary catheter balloon. *Nursing, 25*(12), 13.

McKinney, B. (1995, November). Cut your patients' risk for nosocomial UTI. *RN, 58*(11), 20–24.

McLoughlin, A., & Sciuto, D. (1996, September/October). GN management. Catheter patrols: A unique way to reduce the use of convenience urinary catheters. *Geriatric Nursing, 17*(5), 240–244.

Miller, J. B. (2000). Urinary incontinence: A classification system and treatment protocols for the primary care provider. *Journal of the American Academy of Nurse Practitioners, 12*(9), 374–378.

Moore, K. N. (1995, October). Intermittent self-catheterisation: Research-based practice. *British Journal of Nursing, 4*(18), 1057–1058, 1060, 1062–1063.

Newman, D. K. (1994, August). Strategies for managing urinary incontinence in homebound patients. *ADVANCE for Nurse Practitioners, 2*(8), 11–14.

North American Nursing Diagnosis Association. (2003). *NANDA nursing diagnoses: Definitions and classification 2003–2004.* Philadelphia, PA: Author.

O'Brien, J. (1996, February). Evaluating primary care interventions for incontinence. *Nursing Standard, 10*(23), 40–43.

Palmer, M. H. (1996, December). A new framework for urinary continence outcomes in long-term care. *Urologic Nursing, 16*(4), 136–151.

Pearson, B. D., & Kelber, S. (1996). Urinary incontinence: Treatments, interventions, and outcomes. *Clinical Nurse Specialist, 10*(4), 177–183.

Peters, S. (1997, May). Don't ask, don't tell: Breaking the silence surrounding female urinary incontinence. *ADVANCE for Nurse Practitioners, 5*(5), 41–44.

Promfret, I. (2000). Know how: Penile sheaths. *Community Nurse, 6*(8), 28–29.

Robinson, J. P. (2000). Managing urinary incontinence following radical prostatectomy. *Journal of Wound, Ostomy and Continence Nurses, 27*(3), 138–145.

Sasso, K. C., & Gallo, M. (1996, December). Patient selection criteria for treatment of urinary incontinence with pelvic floor stimulation. *Urologic Nursing, 16*(4), 135–139.

Schakenbach, L. (1997, July). Consult stat. The proper way to manage a distended bladder. *RN, 60*(7), 63.

Schultz, A., Dickey, G., & Skoner, M. (1997, March). Self-report of incontinence in acute care. *Urologic Nursing, 17*(1), 23–28.

Sueppel, C. (1995, June). Rapid or slow bladder decompression? *Urologic Nursing, 15*(2), 64–66.

Upson, C., & Kirby, K. A. (1995, June). Catheter clamping after catheterization and rapid urine loss. *Urologic Nursing, 15*(2), 63–64.

Williams, K. S., Crichton, N. J., & Roe, B. (1997, April). Disseminating research evidence: A controlled trial in continence care. *Journal of Advanced Nursing, 25*(4), 691–698.

Willis, J. (1997, January/February). Continence: Padded sell … continence services … continence pads. *Nursing Times, 93*(5), 86, 89.

Winn, C. (1996, January). Basing catheter care on research principles. *Nursing Standard, 10*(18), 38–40.

WEBLINKS

The Canadian Continence Foundation
http://www.continence-fdn.ca/
A nonprofit organization that has as its focus the support of individuals with continence problems.
The site provides a description of the association and the support that it provides.

Promoting Continence in Canada—VON
http://www.continence.von.ca/
Educational material published by the Victorian Order of Nurses.

Kidney Foundation of Canada
http://www.kidney.ca/index-eng.html
The Kidney Foundation of Canada is a volunteer association that provides support to individuals with kidney disease.

CHAPTER 37

Skin Integrity and Wound Care

OBJECTIVES

After completing this chapter, you will be able to:

- Discuss factors affecting skin integrity.
- Describe how wounds are classified.
- Distinguish the differences between acute and chronic wounds.
- Identify clients at risk for pressure ulcer formation.
- Describe the four stages of pressure ulcer development.
- Differentiate wound healing by primary and secondary intention.
- Explain the three phases of wound healing.
- List the main complications of wound healing.
- Describe factors that affect wound healing.
- Identify key assessment data pertinent to the integument.
- Outline nursing diagnoses associated with impaired skin integrity.
- Develop essential planning goals to maintain skin integrity and promote wound healing.
- Outline health promotive strategies to maintain skin integrity.
- List essential steps of obtaining wound specimens, applying transparent and hydrocolloid dressings, and irrigating a wound.
- Discuss purposes of commonly used dressing materials and supportive/immobilizing devices.
- Explain physiological responses to heat and cold and purposes of thermal applications.
- Describe methods of applying dry and moist heat and cold.

The skin, or integument, is the largest organ in the body and serves a variety of important functions in maintaining health and protecting the individual from harm. While impaired skin integrity is not common in most healthy individuals, it may pose a threat to vulnerable populations (e.g., elderly) as well as those experiencing a health crisis or an invasive procedure.

The prevention of breakdown should be the essential goal of any skin care program (Ferreira & Thorpe Critten, 1998) and nurses routinely encourage health-promotive practices to maintain their clients' skin integrity. However, when disruptions occur, effective wound management requires a comprehensive knowledge of the wound healing process, sensitivity to the experience of the client, and care based on the most recent and valid research literature.

Skin Function and Integrity

Intact skin refers to surface skin and skin layers that are free of disruption or alteration. See Chapter 27 for details regarding physical examination of the integument. The skin provides a protective interface between the environment and the internal organs of the body. It also plays a major role in thermoregulation, vitamin D synthesis, immune function, and the transmission of the sensory impulses of touch, pain, pressure, vibration, and temperature. As an organ of communication, the appearance of the skin is closely linked with self-perception. When the integrity of the skin is damaged or scarred, changes may occur in self-esteem, body image, and social interactions (Wysocki, 1999).

Skin integrity is influenced by factors intrinsic to the individual, such as age, genetics, and general health, as well as extrinsic factors, such as trauma and exercise. For example, the skin of the very young and of the older adult is more fragile and the risk for injury is greater. Sensory or cognitive impairments, poor nutrition, obesity, infection, medications (e.g., corticosteroids), and many chronic illnesses can also interfere with the appearance and function of the integument.

Classification of Wounds

Wounds are frequently described according to how they are acquired, the intactness of the skin or mucous membrane, and the degree of wound contamination. See Table 37.1.

- *Clean wounds* are uninfected wounds in which minimal inflammation is encountered and the respiratory, alimentary, genital, and urinary tracts are not entered. Clean wounds may be closed surgical wounds created under sterile conditions.
- *Clean-contaminated wounds* are surgical wounds in which the respiratory, alimentary, genital, or urinary tract has been entered. Such wounds show no evidence of infection.

TABLE 37.1 Types of Wounds

Type	Cause	Description and Characteristics
Incision	Sharp instrument (e.g., knife or scalpel), usually intentional	Open wound; painful; deep or shallow
Contusion	Blow from a blunt instrument	Closed wound, skin appears ecchymotic (bruised) because of damaged blood vessels
Abrasion	Surface scrape, either unintentional (e.g., scraped knee from a fall) or intentional (e.g., dermal abrasion to remove pockmarks)	Open wound involving the skin; painful
Puncture	Penetration of the skin and often the underlying tissues by a sharp instrument, either intentional or unintentional	Open wound
Laceration	Tissues torn apart, often from accidents (e.g., with machinery)	Open wound; edges are often jagged
Penetrating wound	Penetration of the skin and the underlying tissues, usually unintentional (e.g., from a bullet or metal fragments)	Open wound

- *Contaminated wounds* include open, fresh, accidental wounds and surgical wounds involving a major break in sterile technique or a large amount of spillage from the gastrointestinal tract. Contaminated wounds show evidence of inflammation.
- *Dirty* or *infected wounds* include old, accidental wounds containing dead tissue and wounds with evidence of a clinical infection, such as purulent drainage.

Wounds are also classified by depth, that is, the tissue layers involved in the wound. Partial-thickness wounds are confined to the dermis and epidermis and heal by regeneration. Full-thickness wounds involve the dermis, epidermis, subcutaneous tissue and, possibly, muscle and bone. They generally require connective tissue repair.

Wounds are considered to be *acute* or *chronic*, depending on the healing process as well as the inflammatory "response" to trauma. An acute wound is one that heals within an expected time frame, while a chronic wound does not heal in a timely fashion and the skin fails to return to its previous anatomical appearance and/or function.

Pressure Ulcers

Pressure ulcers are one type of skin breakdown usually considered to be chronic.

Pressure ulcers are also called **decubitus ulcers,** *pressure sores, bedsores,* or *distortion sores.* A pressure ulcer is any lesion caused by unrelieved *pressure* (a compressing downward force on a body area) that results in damage to underlying tissue, and their severity ranges from reddening of the skin to severe deep craters that have formed down to muscle and bone, as defined by the U.S. Department of Health and Human Services Public Health Service's Panel for the Prediction and Prevention of Pressure Ulcers in Adults (PPPPUA, 1992).

Pressure ulcers are a problem in both acute-care settings and long-term-care settings, including homes. In developing the clinical practice guideline *Pressure Ulcers in Adults: Prediction and Prevention,* the PPPPUA reported that "prevalence [of clients with pressure ulcers] in skilled care and nursing home facilities is approximately 23 percent. In the most extensive study of acute care facilities, there was a prevalence of 9.2 percent. Special high-risk populations include quadriplegic patients (60 percent prevalence in one study) and elderly patients admitted for femoral fracture (66 percent incidence)" (PPPPUA, 1994). In 1992, a Canadian task force determined the prevalence of pressure ulcers in institutions within the provinces of Ontario and Quebec. This study included 2,384 patients; 20 percent medical, 17 percent surgical, and 32 percent extended care. It was determined that 25.7 percent had at least one pressure ulcer (57.2 percent had stage I, 42.8 percent had stages II-IV) (Foster, Frisch, Denis, Forler, & Jago, 1992).

This chapter uses pressure ulcers to identify healing strategies for chronic wounds; however, chronic ulcers may be caused by many factors. For more information on other types of chronic ulcers, the Canadian Association of Wound Care has published "Best Practice Recommendations" for wound bed preparation, venous leg ulcers, diabetic foot ulcers, as well as pressure ulcers. (See accompanying box.)

RESEARCH NOTE

Best Practices

The Canadian Association of Wound Care (CAWC) is a nonprofit organization of health-care professionals from each region across Canada dedicated to collaborative, interdisciplinary wound care. The CAWC focuses on five key areas of practice: (1) public policy, (2) clinical practice, (3) education, (4) research, and (5) linkages to the international community in wound care. Annual regional and national conferences encourage the sharing of knowledge and foster networking of practitioners in the field of wound care. In November 2000 and February 2001, the CAWC scientific board members (including nurses, physicians, physical therapists, and podiatrists) published four articles in the peer-reviewed journal *Ostomy/ Wound Management* that challenged health-care professionals to practise wound care on the basis of best practice initiatives. The articles provided recommendations for wound bed preparation as well as pressure, venous, and diabetic ulcer management.
The CAWC Web site is: **www.cawc.net**.

Etiology of Pressure Ulcers

Pressure ulcers are due to localized **ischemia,** a deficiency in the blood supply to the tissue. The tissue is caught between two hard surfaces, usually the surface of the bed and the bony skeleton. When blood cannot reach the tissue, the cells are deprived of oxygen and nutrients, the waste products of metabolism accumulate in the cells, and the tissue consequently dies. Prolonged, unrelieved pressure also damages the small blood vessels.

Pressure ulcers usually occur over bony prominences. After the skin has been compressed, blood flow is interrupted, and the skin becomes pale. When pressure is relieved, the skin takes on a bright red flush called **reactive hyperemia,** which is the body's mechanism for preventing pressure ulcers. The flush is due to vasodilation; extra blood floods to the area to compensate for the preceding period of impeded blood flow. Reactive hyperemia usually lasts one-half to three-quarters as long as the duration of impeded blood flow to the area (PPPPUA, 1992). If the redness disappears in that time, no tissue damage can be anticipated. If, however, the redness does not disappear, then tissue damage (abnormal reactive hyperemia) has occurred.

Two other factors frequently act in conjunction with pressure to produce pressure ulcers: *friction* and *shearing force*. **Friction** is a force acting parallel to the skin surface. For example, sheets rubbing against skin create friction. Friction can abrade the skin, that is, remove the superficial layers, making it more prone to breakdown.

Shearing force is a combination of friction and pressure. It occurs commonly when a client assumes a Fowler's position in bed. In this position, the body tends to slide downward toward the foot of the bed. This downward movement is transmitted to the sacral bone and the deep tissues. At the same time, the skin over the sacrum tends not to move because of the adherence between the skin and the bedsheets. The skin and superficial tissues are, thus, relatively unmoving in relation to the bed surface, whereas the deeper tissues are firmly attached to the skeleton and move downward. This causes a shearing force in the area where the deeper tissues and the superficial tissues meet. The force damages the blood vessels and tissues in this area.

Risk Factors

Several factors contribute to the formation of pressure ulcers: immobility and inactivity, inadequate nutrition, fecal and urinary incontinence, decreased mental status, diminished sensation, excessive body heat, and advanced age.

Immobility

Although pressure is the major cause of pressure ulcers, immobility and inactivity are also important risk factors. **Immobility** refers to a reduction in the amount and control of movement a person has. Normally, people move when they experience discomfort due to pressure on an area of the body. Healthy people rarely exceed their tolerance to pressure. However, paralysis, extreme weakness, immobility, or any cause of decreased activity can hinder a person's ability to change positions independently and relieve the pressure, even if the person can perceive the pressure.

Inadequate Nutrition

Nutritional factors are crucial in the development of pressure ulcers. Generally, prolonged inadequate nutrition causes weight loss, muscle atrophy, and the loss of subcutaneous tissue. These three reduce the amount of padding between the skin and the bones, thus increasing the risk of pressure sore development. More specifically, inadequate intakes of protein, carbohydrates, fluids, and vitamin C contribute to pressure ulcer formation.

Hypoproteinemia (abnormally low protein content in the blood), due either to inadequate intake or abnormal loss, predisposes the client to dependent edema. **Edema** (the presence of excess fluid in the tissues) makes skin more prone to injury by decreasing its elasticity, resilience, and vitality. Edema increases the distance between the capillaries and the cells, thereby slowing the diffusion of oxygen to the tissue cells and of metabolites away from the cells.

Fecal and Urinary Incontinence

Moisture from incontinence promotes skin **maceration** (tissue softened by prolonged wetting or soaking) and makes the epidermis more easily eroded and susceptible to injury. Digestive enzymes in feces also contribute to skin excoriation. Any accumulation of secretions or excretions is irritating to the skin, harbours microorganisms, and makes an individual prone to skin breakdown and infection.

Decreased Mental Status

Individuals with a reduced level of awareness, for example, those who are unconscious or heavily sedated, are at risk for pressure ulcers because they are less able to recognize and respond to pain associated with prolonged pressure.

Diminished Sensation

Paralysis or other neurological disease may cause loss of sensation in a body area. Loss of sensation reduces a person's ability to respond to injurious heat and cold and to feel the tingling ("pins and needles") that signals loss of circulation.

Excessive Body Heat

Body heat is another factor in the development of pressure sores. An elevated body temperature increases the body's metabolic rate, thus increasing the need of the cells for oxygen. This increased need is particularly severe in the cells of an area under pressure, which are already oxygen deficient. Therefore, severe infections with accompanying elevated body temperatures may affect the body's ability to deal with the effects of tissue compression.

Advanced Age

The aging process brings about several changes in the skin and its supporting structures, making the older person more prone to impaired skin integrity and altered wound healing. These changes are outlined in Table 37.2.

Other Factors

Other factors contributing to the formation of pressure sores are poor lifting techniques, incorrect positioning, repeated injections in the same area, hard support surfaces, and incorrect application of pressure-relieving devices.

Stages of Pressure Ulcers

Presssure ulcers can be classified either by stages or by colour, even though pressure ulcers do not actually progress in stages. Therefore it would be wrong to apply the sequence of stage numbers in reverse to describe the healing of an ulcer. There are four recognized stages in pressure ulcer formation related to observable tissue damage (PPPPUA, 1992). See Figures 37.1 and 37.2.

Stage I: Nonblanchable erythema of intact skin (in lightly pigmented skin); this is the heralding lesion of skin ulceration. In darker skin, a purple-blue discolouration is noted.

Stage II: Partial-thickness skin loss involving epidermis, dermis, or both. The ulcer is superficial and presents clinically as an abrasion, blister, or shallow crater.

Stage III: Full-thickness skin loss involving damage or necrosis of subcutaneous tissue that may extend down to, but not through, underlying fascia. The ulcer presents clinically as a deep crater with or without undermining of adjacent tissue.

Stage IV: Full-thickness skin loss with extensive destruction, tissue necrosis, or damage to muscle, bone, or supporting structures, such as a tendon or joint capsule. Undermining and sinus tracts may also be associated with stage IV pressure ulcers.

Risk Assessment Tools

Although clients may be at risk for developing a number of different alterations in skin integrity, the most common and most preventable are pressure ulcers. Several risk assessment tools are available that provide the nurse with systematic means of identifying clients at high risk for pressure ulcer development. The PPPPUA recommends that the tool include data collection in the areas of immobility, incontinence, nutrition, and level of consciousness.

TABLE 37.2 The Implications of Aging Skin

Change	Implication
Thinning and flattening of the epidermis	■ Increased vulnerability to trauma ■ Increased skin susceptibility to shearing stress, thereby promoting blister formation and skin tears ■ Decreased tissue barrier properties ■ Impairment of the skin's barrier functions, allowing certain drugs and irritants to be more easily absorbed
Decreased epidermal proliferation	■ Slow-down in production of new skin cells, resulting in an inability of the epidermis to replace itself as quickly
Cells in the horny layer lose elastin fibres	■ Decreased wound contraction ■ Delayed cellular migration and proliferation ■ Skin becomes like a worn rubber band—it does not snap back fast or have much elasticity ■ Underlying tissue more vulnerable to injury ■ Increased rate of wound dehiscence ■ Decreased wound contraction
Atrophy of the dermis	■ Skin easily bruised and susceptible to injury ■ Decreased skin temperature
Decreased vascularity of the dermis	■ Increased vulnerability to trauma ■ Decreased wound capillary growth ■ Increased rate of wound dehiscence ■ Underlying tissue more vulnerable to injury ■ Decreased tensile strength ■ Delayed collagen remodelling
Changes to and loss of collagen and elastic fibres	■ Skin not as moist or as well lubricated ■ Increased loss of moisture resulting in dehydration
Decrease in number of oil and sweat glands	■ Impaired cutaneous immune and inflammatory responses ■ Reduced ability to clear foreign materials and fluids
Vascular response is compromised	■ Decreased wound capillary growth ■ Altered metabolic response
Nerve endings become abnormal	■ Decreased production of cytokines ■ Altered or reduced sensation
Fragility	■ Skin tears and bruises easily ■ Loss of cushion effect ■ Skin no longer as thick

Source: Mulder, G. D., Haberer, P. A., & Jeter, K. F. (Eds.). (1999). *Clinicians' pocket guide to chronic wound repair* (4th ed.). Springhouse, PA: Springhouse Corporation.

The two validated assessment tools supported by the PPPPUA are the Braden scale and the Norton scale.

In 1987, Bergstrom, Braden, Laguzza, and Holman published the Braden Scale for Predicting Pressure Sore Risk. Their scale consists of six subscales: sensory perception, moisture, activity, mobility, nutrition, and friction and shear (Figure 37.3). A total of 23 points is possible. The creators state that an adult who scores 16 or below is considered at risk; an older person may be at risk with a score of 17 or 18. Other researchers have found that the Braden scale predicted clients who would develop ulcers but did not (VandenBosch et al., 1996) or that a score of 19 had the best predictive value (Harrison et al., 1996). For best results, nurses should become familiar with the proper use of the scale.

Norton's Pressure Area Risk Assessment Form Scale (Table 37.3) includes the categories of general physical

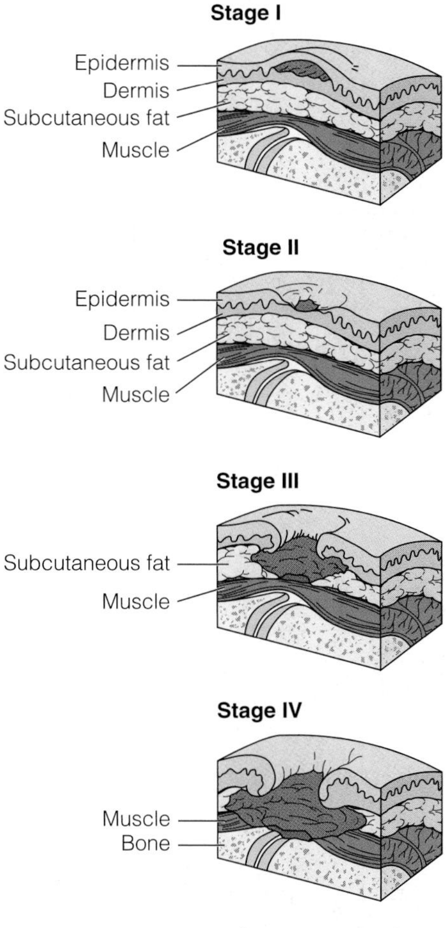

Figure 37.1 Four stages of pressure ulcers

Source: US Department of Health and Human Services. (1992). PPPPUA, Clinical practice guideline, *Pressure ulcers in adults: Prediction and prevention,* Pub. no. 92-0047. (p. 8). Rockville, MD: Public Health Service.

condition, mental state, activity, mobility, and incontinence. A category of medications was added in 1987, making a possible score of 24. The author states that scores of 15 or 16 should be viewed as indicators, not predictors, of risk (Anthony, 1987). The Braden and Norton tools should be used when the client first enters the health-care agency and whenever the client's condition changes.

Wound Healing

Healing is a quality of living tissue; it is also referred to as **regeneration** (renewal) of tissues. Healing can be considered in terms of *types of healing,* having to do with the decision to allow the wound to heal itself or to purposefully close the wound, and *phases of healing,* which refer to the steps in the body's natural processes of tissue repair. The phases are the same for all wounds, but the rate of healing depends on such factors as the type of healing, the location and size of the wound, and the health of the client.

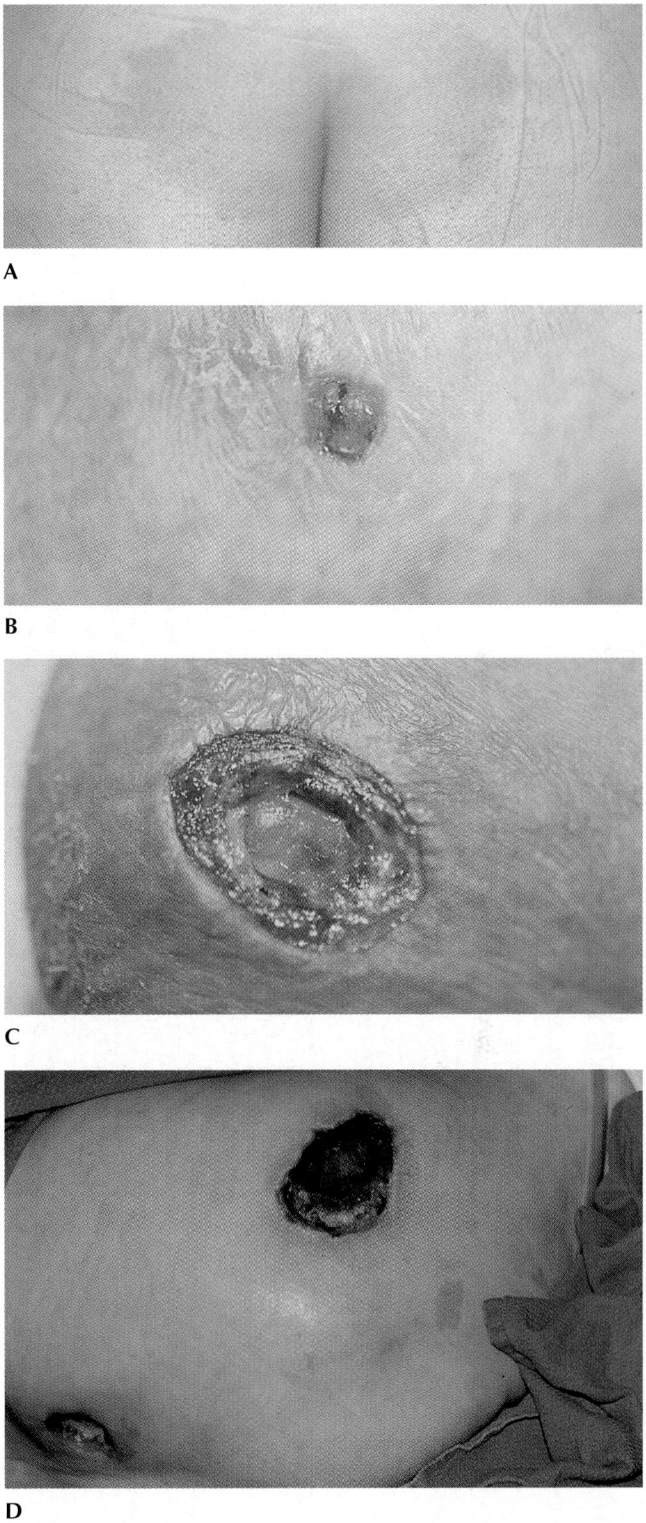

Figure 37.2 The four stages of a decubitus ulcer: *A, Stage I:* Nonblanchable erythema signalling potential ulceration; *B, Stage II:* Abrasion, blister, or shallow crater involving the epidermis and, possibly, the dermis; *C, Stage III:* Deep ulcer exhibiting necrotic tissue and extending through the subcutaneous layer; *D, Stage IV:* Tissue necrosis and damage involving muscle, bone, or supporting structures

BRADEN SCALE FOR PREDICTING PRESSURE SORE RISK

Patient's Name ________________ Evaluator's Name ________________ Date of Assessment

					Date of Assessment			
SENSORY PERCEPTION Ability to respond meaningfully to pressure-related discomfort	**1. Completely Limited:** Unresponsive (does not moan, flinch, or grasp) to painful stimuli, due to diminished level of consciousness or sedation, OR limited ability to feel pain over most of body surface.	**2. Very Limited:** Responds only to painful stimuli. Cannot communicate discomfort except by moaning or restlessness, OR has a sensory impairment which limits the ability to feel pain or discomfort over 1/2 of body.	**3. Slightly Limited:** Responds to verbal commands but cannot always communicate discomfort or need to be turned, OR has some sensory impairment which limits ability to feel pain or discomfort in 1 or 2 extremities.	**4. No Impairment:** Responds to verbal commands. Has no sensory deficit which would limit ability to feel or voice pain or discomfort.				
MOISTURE Degree to which skin is exposed to moisture	**1. Constantly Moist:** Skin is kept moist almost constantly by perspiration, urine, etc. Dampness is detected every time patient is moved or turned.	**2. Moist:** Skin is often but not always moist. Linen must be changed at least once a shift.	**3. Occasionally Moist:** Skin is occasionally moist, requiring an extra linen change approximately once a day.	**4. Rarely Moist:** Skin is usually dry; linen requires changing only at routine intervals.				
ACTIVITY Degree of physical activity	**1. Bedfast:** Confined to bed.	**2. Chairfast:** Ability to walk severely limited or nonexistent. Cannot bear own weight and/or must be assisted into chair or wheelchair.	**3. Walks Occasionally:** Walks occasionally during day but for very short distances, with or without assistance. Spends majority of each shift in bed or chair.	**4. Walks Frequently:** Walks outside the room at least twice a day and inside room at least once every 2 hours during waking hours.				
MOBILITY Ability to change and control body position	**1. Completely Immobile:** Does not make even slight changes in body or extremity position without assistance.	**2. Very Limited:** Makes occasional slight changes in body or extremity position but unable to make frequent or significant changes independently.	**3. Slightly Limited:** Makes frequent though slight changes in body or extremity position independently.	**4. No Limitations:** Makes major and frequent changes in position without assistance.				
NUTRITION Usual food intake pattern	**1. Very Poor:** Never eats a complete meal. Rarely eats more than 1/3 of any food offered. Eats 2 servings or less of protein (meat or dairy products) per day. Takes fluids poorly. Does not take a liquid dietary supplement, OR is NPO and/or maintained on clear liquids or IV's for more than 5 days.	**2. Probably Inadequate:** Rarely eats a complete meal and generally eats only about 1/2 of any food offered. Protein intake includes only 3 servings of meat or dairy products per day. Occasionally will take a dietary supplement, OR receives less than optimum amount of liquid diet or tube feeding.	**3. Adequate:** Eats over half of most meals. Eats a total of 4 servings of protein (meat, dairy products) each day. Occasionally will refuse a meal, but will usually take a supplement if offered, OR is on a tube feeding or TPN regimen, which probably meets most of nutritional needs.	**4. Excellent:** Eats most of every meal. Never refuses a meal. Usually eats a total of 4 or more servings of meat and dairy products. Occasionally eats between meals. Does not require supplementation.				
FRICTION AND SHEAR	**1. Problem:** Requires moderate to maximum assistance in moving. Complete lifting without sliding against sheets is impossible. Frequently slides down in bed or chair, requiring frequent repositioning with maximum assistance. Spasticity, contractures, or agitation leads to almost constant friction.	**2. Potential Problem:** Moves feebly or requires minimum assistance. During a move skin probably slides to some extent against sheets, chair, restraints, or other devices. Maintains relatively good position in chair or bed most of the time but occasionally slides down.	**3. No Apparent Problem:** Moves in bed and in chair independently and has sufficient muscle strength to lift up completely during move. Maintains good position in bed or chair at all times.					
				Total Score				

Figure 37.3 Braden Scale for Predicting Pressure Sore Risk

Source: US Department of Health and Human Services. (1992). Clinical practice guideline, *Pressure ulcers in adults: Prediction and prevention,* Pub. no. 92-0047. (p. 16-17) Rockville, MD: Public Health Service. Copyright © Barbara Braden and Nancy Bergstrom, 1988. Reprinted with permission.

TABLE 37.3 Norton's Pressure Area Risk Assessment Form (Scoring System)

A General Physical Condition		B Mental State		C Activity		D Mobility		E Incontinence	
Good	4	Alert	4	Ambulatory	4	Full	4	Absent	4
Fair	3	Apathetic	3	Walks with help	3	Slightly limited	3	Occasional	3
Poor	2	Confused	2	Chairbound	2	Very limited	2	Usually urinary	2
Very bad	1	Stuporous	1	Bedfast	1	Immobile	1	Double	1

Source: D. Norton, R. McLaren, and A.N. Exton-Smith. (1962). *An investigation of geriatric nursing problems in hospital.* Edinburgh: Churchill Livingstone. Reissued, 1975. Used by permission.

Types of Wound Healing

There are two types of healing, distinguished by the amount of tissue loss. **Primary intention healing** occurs where the tissue surfaces have been **approximated** (closed) and there is minimal or no tissue loss; it is characterized by the formation of minimal granulation tissue and scarring. It is also called *primary union* or *first intention healing*. An example of wound healing by primary intention is a closed surgical incision.

A wound that is extensive and involves considerable tissue loss, and in which the edges cannot or should not be approximated, heals by **secondary intention healing.** An example of wound healing by secondary intention is a pressure ulcer. Secondary intention healing differs from primary intention healing in three ways: (1) the repair time is longer; (2) the scarring is greater; and (3) the susceptibility to infection is greater.

Delayed closure is defined as an anatomically precise closure that is delayed for a few days but undertaken before granulation tissue becomes visible. Delayed closure is most often used in the presence of an abscess (Leaper & Gottrup, 1998).

Phases of Wound Healing

Wound healing involves three overlapping but distinct phases: inflammatory, proliferative, and maturation.

Inflammatory Phase

The *inflammatory phase* is initiated immediately after injury and lasts three to six days. Two major processes occur during this phase: hemostasis and phagocytosis.

Hemostasis (the cessation of bleeding) results from vasoconstriction of the larger blood vessels in the affected area, retraction (drawing back) of injured blood vessels, the deposition of **fibrin** (connective tissue), and the formation of blood clots in the area. The blood clots, formed from blood platelets, provide a matrix of fibrin that becomes the framework for cell repair. A scab also forms on the surface of the wound. Consisting of clots and dead and dying tissue, this scab serves to aid hemostasis and inhibit contamination of the wound by microorganisms. Below the scab, epithelial cells migrate into the wound from the edges. The epithelial cells serve as a barrier between the body and the environment, preventing the entry of microorganisms.

The inflammatory phase also involves vascular and cellular responses intended to remove any foreign substances and dead and dying tissues. The blood supply to the wound increases, bringing with it substances and nutrients needed in the healing process. The area appears reddened and edematous as a result.

During cell migration, leukocytes (specifically, neutrophils) move into the interstitial space. These are replaced about 24 hours after injury by macrophages, which arise from the blood monocytes. These macrophages engulf microorganisms and cellular debris by a process known as **phagocytosis.** The macrophages also secrete an angiogenesis factor (AGF), which stimulates the formation of epithelial buds at the end of injured blood vessels. The microcirculatory network that results sustains the healing process and the wound during its life. This inflammatory response is essential to healing, and measures that impair inflammation, such as steroid medications, can place the healing process at risk.

Proliferative Phase

The *proliferative phase*, the second phase in healing, extends from day 3 or 4 to about day 21 post injury. Fibroblasts (connective tissue cells), which migrate into the wound starting about 24 hours after injury, begin to synthesize collagen and a substance called proteoglycan about day 5 post injury. **Collagen** is a whitish protein substance that adds tensile strength to the wound. As the amount of collagen increases, so does the strength of the wound; thus, the chance that the wound will open progressively decreases. If the wound is sutured, a raised "healing ridge" appears under the intact suture line. In a wound that is not sutured, the new collagen is often visible.

Capillaries grow across the wound, increasing the blood supply, which brings with it oxygen and nutrients needed for healing. Fibroblasts move from the bloodstream into the wound, depositing fibrin. As the capillary network develops, the tissue becomes a translucent red colour. This tissue, called **granulation tissue,** is fragile and bleeds easily.

When the skin edges of a wound are not sutured, the area must be filled in with granulation tissue. When the granulation tissue matures, marginal epithelial cells migrate to it, proliferating over this connective tissue base to fill the wound. If the wound does not close by epithelialization, the area becomes covered with dried plasma proteins and dead cells. This is called **eschar.** Initially, wounds healing by secondary intention ooze blood-tinged (serosanguineous) drainage. Later, if they are not covered by epithelial cells, they become covered with thick, grey, fibrinous tissue that is eventually converted into dense scar tissue.

Maturation Phase

The *maturation phase* begins about day 21 and healing can extend one or two years after the injury. Fibroblasts continue to synthesize collagen. The collagen fibres themselves, which were initially laid in a haphazard fashion, reorganize into a more orderly structure. During maturation, the wound is remodelled and contracted. The scar becomes stronger but the repaired area is never as strong as the original tissue. In some individuals, particularly dark-skinned persons, an abnormal amount of collagen is laid down. This can result in a hypertrophic scar, or **keloid.**

Kinds of Wound Drainage

Exudate is material, such as fluid and cells, that has escaped from blood vessels during the inflammatory process and is deposited in tissue or on tissue surfaces. The nature and amount of exudate vary according to the tissue involved, the intensity and duration of the inflammation, and the presence of microorganisms.

There are three major types of exudate: serous, purulent, and sanguineous (hemorrhagic). A **serous exudate** consists chiefly of serum (the clear portion of the blood) derived from blood and the serous membranes of the body, such as the peritoneum. It looks watery and has few cells. An example is the fluid in a blister from a burn.

A **purulent exudate** is thicker than serous exudate because of the presence of **pus,** which consists of leukocytes, liquefied dead tissue debris, and dead and living bacteria. The process of pus formation is referred to as **suppuration,** and the bacteria that produce pus are called **pyogenic bacteria.** Not all microorganisms are pyogenic. Purulent exudates vary in colour, some acquiring tinges of blue, green, or yellow. The colour may depend on the causative organism.

A **sanguineous (hemorrhagic) exudate** consists of large amounts of red blood cells, indicating damage to capillaries that is severe enough to allow the escape of red blood cells from plasma. This type of exudate is frequently seen in open wounds. Nurses often need to distinguish whether the sanguineous exudate is dark or bright. A bright sanguineous exudate indicates fresh bleeding, whereas dark sanguineous exudate denotes older bleeding.

Mixed types of exudates are often observed. A serosanguineous (consisting of clear and blood-tinged drainage) exudate is commonly seen in surgical incisions. A purosanguineous discharge (consisting of pus and blood) is often seen in a new wound that is infected.

Complications of Wound Healing

Hemorrhage

Some escape of blood from a wound is normal. **Hemorrhage** (persistent bleeding), however, is abnormal. It may be caused by a dislodged clot, a slipped ligature, or erosion of a blood vessel, for example.

Internal hemorrhage may often be detected by swelling or distention in the area of the wound and, possibly, sanguineous drainage from a surgical drain. Some clients will have a **hematoma,** a localized collection of blood underneath the skin that may appear as a reddish blue swelling. A large hematoma may be dangerous in that it places pressure on blood vessels and can, thus, obstruct blood flow.

External hemorrhage is often easily identified from the blood that either appears under a dressing or escapes from the dressing and pools under the client. The risk of hemorrhage is greatest during the first 48 hours after surgery. Hemorrhage is an emergency; the nurse should apply extra sterile pressure dressings to the area and monitor the client's vital signs. In many instances, the client must be taken to the operating room for surgical intervention.

Infection

A wound can be infected with microorganisms at the time of injury, during surgery, or postoperatively, that is, during open wound healing. Surgical wounds can be classified as clean, clean-contaminated, contaminated, or dirty or infected wounds. Wounds that occur as a result of injury (e.g., bullet and knife wounds) are most likely to be contaminated at the time of injury. Surgery involving the intestines can also result in infection from the microorganisms inside the intestine. Surgical site infections (SSIs) are most likely to become apparent two to 11 days postoperatively, but with early discharge, it is estimated that between 12 percent and 84 percent of SSIs are detected after patients are discharged from the hospital (Mangram, Horan Silver, & Jarvis, 1999).

Dehiscence with Possible Evisceration

Dehiscence is the partial or total rupturing of a sutured wound. Dehiscence usually involves an abdominal wound in which the layers below the skin also separate. **Evisceration** is the protrusion of the internal viscera through an incision. A number of factors, including obesity, smoking, poor nutrition, multiple trauma, failure of suturing, excessive coughing, vomiting, and dehydration, heighten a client's risk of wound dehiscence. Wound dehiscence is more likely to occur four to five days postoperatively before extensive collagen is deposited in the wound. Clients at risk for dehiscence may be prescribed an abdominal binder for support.

An increase in the flow of serosanguineous drainage into the wound dressing can indicate an impending dehiscence. Dehiscence may also be preceded by sudden straining, and it is not unusual for a client to feel that "something has given way." When dehiscence or evisceration occurs, the wound should be quickly supported by large sterile dressings soaked in sterile normal saline. The client is placed in bed with knees bent to decrease pull on the incision and emotional support is provided. The surgeon should be notified, as immediate surgical repair of the area may be necessary.

Factors Affecting Wound Healing

Developmental Considerations

Skin disruptions may occur at any time during the life cycle; however, older persons are more likely to experience structural and functional skin changes that adversely affect skin integrity and wound healing. (See Table 37.2.)

Nutrition

Wound healing places additional demands on the body. Clients require a diet rich in protein, carbohydrates, lipids, vitamins A and C, and minerals, such as iron, zinc, and copper. Malnourished clients may require time to improve their nutritional status before surgery, if this is possible. Obese clients are at increased risk of wound infection and slower healing because adipose tissue usually has a minimal blood supply.

Lifestyle

People who exercise regularly tend to have a good circulation and because blood brings oxygen and nourishment to the wound, they are more likely to heal quickly. Smoking reduces the amount of functional hemoglobin in the blood, thus limiting the oxygen-carrying capacity of the blood.

Medications

Anti-inflammatory drugs (e.g., steroids and aspirin), heparin, and antineoplastic agents interfere with healing. Prolonged use of antibiotics may make a person susceptible to wound infection by resistant organisms.

Contamination and Infection

Contamination of a wound surface with microorganisms (colonization) is an inevitable result. Because the colonizing organisms compete with new cells for oxygen and nutrition, and their byproducts can interfere with a healthy surface condition, the presence of contamination can impair wound healing and lead to infection. When the microorganisms colonizing the wound multiply excessively or invade tissues, infection occurs. Signs and symptoms of infection include redness, induration, swelling, pain, change in exudate (amount or character), and potential loss of function. Friable granulation tissue, nonstable epithelial bridges, or a failure to respond to therapy are "subtle" signs of infection (Dolynachuk, Campbell, Houghton, Orsted, Sibbald, & Atkinson, 2000). Clients who are immunosuppressed, such as those with human immunodeficiency virus (HIV) infection or receiving myelosuppressive treatment for cancer, are especially susceptible to wound infections.

Assessing

Assessment of Skin Integrity

Nursing History and Physical Examination

Collection of data about the health of the integument is an essential aspect of any comprehensive assessment framework. During the review of systems as part of the nursing history, information is collected regarding skin diseases, previous bruising, general skin condition, skin lesions, and usual healing of sores. Inspection and palpation of the skin focus on determination of skin colour, temperature, texture, turgor, presence of edema, vascularity, and characteristics of any lesions that are present. Particular attention is paid to skin condition in areas most likely to break down: in skinfolds, such as under the breasts; in areas that are frequently moist, such as the perineum; and in areas that receive extensive pressure, such as the coccyx and trochanters (Figure 37.4). The following box describes guidelines for assessing the common pressure sites.

Assessment of Wounds

Initial Assessment of Acute Wounds

Acute wounds usually are seen shortly after an injury (e.g., at the scene of an accident or in an emergency centre). Guidelines for initial assessment and care of these wounds are shown in the box on page 945.

Sutured Wounds

Sutured wounds are regularly assessed to determine the progress of healing. Assessment of a sutured wound involves observation of its size and location; the approximation of wound edges; the condition of the wound closure devices (e.g., sutures, staples), as well as the presence of any odour, swelling, redness, bruising, or pain. The status of any drains and the type and amount of drainage are also important to note.

If the wound itself cannot be directly inspected, the dressing is inspected and other data regarding the wound (e.g., the presence of pain) are assessed. Many treated wounds are covered with a transparent occlusive dressing that permits observation of the wound without exposure to the air.

CLINICAL GUIDELINES

Assessing Common Pressure Sites

- Be sure there is good lighting, preferably natural or fluorescent, because incandescent lights can create a transilluminating effect.
- Regulate the environment before beginning the assessment so that the room is neither too hot nor too cold. Heat can cause the skin to flush; cold can cause the skin to blanch or become cyanotic.
- Inspect pressure areas (see Figure 37.4) for blanching, whitish or reddened spots; discolouration can be caused by impaired blood circulation to the area.
- Inspect pressure areas for abrasions and excoriations. An **abrasion** (wearing away of the skin) can occur when skin rubs against a sheet (e.g., when the client is pulled). **Excoriations** (loss of superficial layers of the skin) can occur when the skin has prolonged contact with body secretions or excretions or with dampness in skinfolds.
- Palpate the surface temperature of the skin over the pressure areas (warm your hands first). Normally, the temperature is the same as that of the surrounding skin. Increased temperature is abnormal and may be due to inflammation or blood trapped in the area.
- Palpate over bony prominences and dependent body areas for the presence of edema, which feels spongy.

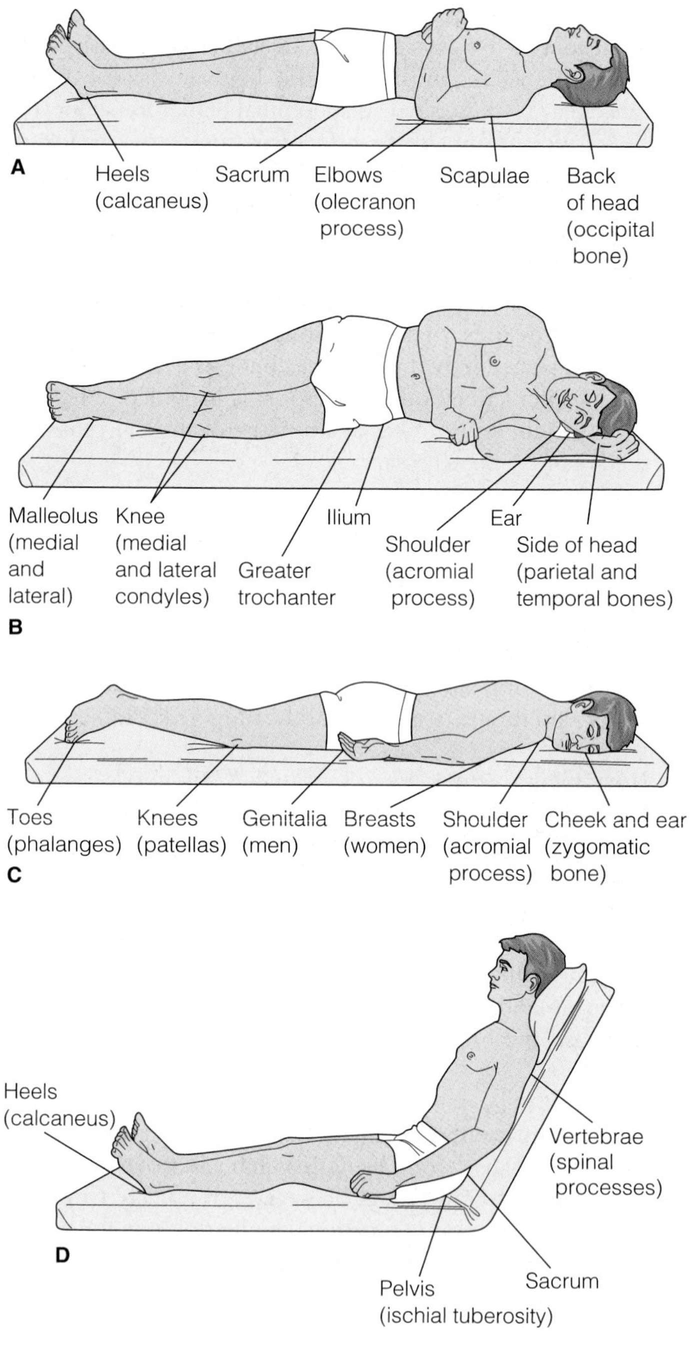

Figure 37.4 Body pressure areas in *A,* supine position; *B,* lateral position; *C,* prone position; *D,* Fowler's position

Chronic Wounds

A pressure ulcer is an example of a chronic wound. When a pressure ulcer (or any chronic ulcer) is present, the nurse needs to use a tool that will accurately and consistently assess the wound and surrounding skin. The quantifiable tool should compare two or more measurements over time, be able to detect small changes in the wound, and be reproducible in a clinical setting. This assessment will provide baseline data to evaluate the repair process and be used to drive treatment decisions. Two examples are the Pressure Sore Status Tool (PSST) and the PUSH Tool (Woodbury, Houghton, Campbell, & Keast, 1999).

When a pressure ulcer is present, the nurse notes the following:

- Location of the lesion
- Size of lesion in centimetres (Measure length, width, and depth, beginning with length [head to toe] and then width [side to side]. To measure depth, insert a sterile gloved finger at the deepest part of the wound, and then measure the finger against a measuring guide.)
- Stage of the ulcer (see Figure 37.1)
- Colour of the wound bed and location of necrosis or eschar
- Condition of the wound margins
- Integrity of surrounding skin
- Clinical signs of infection, such as redness, warmth, swelling, pain, odour, exudate (note colour of exudate), and blanching

CLINICAL GUIDELINES

Acute Wounds

Initial Assessment

- Assess the size and severity of the wound. If it is severe, have someone call an ambulance or, if in an emergency centre, inform the physician.
- Inspect the wound for bleeding. The amount of bleeding varies according to the type of wound and location. Penetrating wounds may cause internal bleeding.
- Inspect the wound for foreign bodies (soil, broken glass, shreds of cloth, or other foreign substances).
- Assess associated injuries, such as fractures, internal bleeding, spinal cord injuries, or head trauma.
- If the wound is contaminated with foreign material, determine when the client last had a tetanus toxoid injection. A tetanus immunization or booster may be necessary.

Initial Care Response

- Control severe bleeding by (1) applying direct pressure over the wound, and (2) elevating the involved extremity.
- Prevent infection by (1) cleaning or flushing abrasions or lacerations with water and (2) covering the wound with a clean dressing, if possible (a sterile dressing is preferred). When applying a dressing, wrap the wound tightly enough to apply pressure and approximate the wound edges, if possible. If the first layer of dressing becomes saturated with blood, apply a second layer. Do so without removing the first layer of dressing because blood clots might be disturbed, resulting in more bleeding.
- Control swelling and pain by applying ice over the wound and surrounding tissues.
- If bleeding is severe or if internal bleeding is suspected, and if emergency equipment is available, assess the client for signs of shock (rapid thready pulse, cold clammy skin, pallor, lowered blood pressure).

Laboratory Data

Laboratory data can often support the nurse's clinical assessment of the wound's progress in healing. A *decreased leukocyte count* can delay healing and increase the possibility of infection. *Blood coagulation studies* are also significant. Prolonged coagulation times can result in excessive blood loss and prolonged clot absorption. Hypercoagulability can lead to intravascular clotting. Intra-arterial clotting can result in a deficient blood supply to the wound area. *Serum protein analysis* provides an indication of the body's nutritional reserves for rebuilding cells. *Wound cultures* can either confirm or rule out the presence of infection. Sensitivity studies are helpful in the selection of appropriate antibiotic therapy. The nurse obtains a wound culture whenever an infection is suspected.

Procedure 37.1 provides guidelines to obtain a specimen of wound drainage.

Diagnosing

The NANDA nursing diagnoses (2001) that relate to clients who have skin wounds or who are at risk for skin breakdown are:

- ***Risk for Impaired Skin Integrity:*** the state in which an individual's skin is at risk for being adversely altered.
- ***Impaired Skin Integrity:*** the state in which an individual experiences damage to the epidermal and/or dermal tissue.
- ***Impaired Tissue Integrity:*** the state in which an individual experiences damage to the integumentary, corneal, mucous membrane, or subcutaneous tissues of the body.

Impaired Skin Integrity commonly applies to stage I and II (partial-thickness skin loss) pressure ulcers and to superficial wounds extending through the epidermis and/or the dermis. ***Impaired Tissue Integrity*** applies to stage III and IV (full-thickness skin loss) pressure ulcers and to wounds extending into subcutaneous tissue, muscle, or bone.

Additional nursing diagnoses may be appropriate for clients with existing impaired skin or tissue integrity. Examples of these diagnoses include:

- ***Risk for Infection*** if the skin impairment is severe, the client is immunosuppressed, or the wound is caused by trauma
- ***Pain*** related to nerve involvement within the tissue impairment or as a consequence of procedures used to treat the wound
- ***Body Image, Disturbed*** if the wound or dressing cause the client significant negative feelings about his or her appearance
- ***Anxiety*** if the client experiences apprehension related to care of the wound or the eventual outcome of the healing process

See Table 37.4.

Planning

The major goals for clients at ***Risk for Impaired Skin Integrity*** (e.g., pressure sore development) are to maintain skin integrity and to avoid potential associated risks. Clients with ***Impaired Skin Integrity*** need to demonstrate progressive wound healing and regain intact skin. In the event that the client is unable to heal, the goal may be to palliate the wound.

PROCEDURE 37.1 Obtaining a Specimen of Wound Drainage

PURPOSES

- To identify the microorganisms potentially causing an infection and the antibiotics to which they are sensitive
- To evaluate the effectiveness of antibiotic therapy

Assessment Focus
Pain at the wound site; systemic signs of infection (e.g., fever, chills); appearance of the wound and the character and amount of wound drainage

Equipment

- ❑ Disposable gloves
- ❑ Sterile gloves
- ❑ Moisture-resistant bag
- ❑ Sterile dressing set
- ❑ Normal saline and irrigating syringe
- ❑ Culture tube with swab and culture medium (aerobic and anaerobic tubes are available) and/or sterile syringe with needle for anaerobic culture
- ❑ Completed labels for each container
- ❑ Completed requisition to accompany the specimens to the laboratory

INTERVENTION

1. **Remove any dressings that cover the wound.**

- Put on disposable gloves.
- Remove the dressing and observe the drainage present.
- Hold the dressing so that the client does not see the drainage. *The appearance of the drainage could upset the client.*
- Determine the amount of the drainage, for example, one 5 cm × 5 cm (2 × 2) gauze saturated with pale yellow drainage.
- Discard the dressing in the moisture-resistant bag. Handle it carefully so that the dressing does not touch the outside of the bag. *Touching the outside of the bag will contaminate it.*
- Remove gloves and dispose of them properly.

2. **Open the sterile dressing set using sterile technique.**
3. **Assess the wound.**

- Put on sterile gloves.
- Assess the appearance of the tissues in and around the wound and the drainage. Infection can cause reddened tissues with a thick discharge, which may be foul-smelling, whitish, or coloured.

4. **Clean the wound.**

- Irrigate the wound with normal saline until all visible exudate has been washed away. See Procedure 37.2 on page 956.
- After irrigating, apply a sterile gauze pad to the wound. *This absorbs excess saline.*
- If a topical antimicrobial ointment or cream is being used to treat the wound, use a swab to remove it. *Residual antiseptic must be removed prior to culture.*
- Remove and discard sterile gloves.

5. **Obtain the culture.**

- Open a specimen tube and place the cap upside down on a firm, dry surface so that the inside will not become contaminated, *or* if the swab is attached to the lid, twist the cap to loosen the swab. Hold the tube in one hand, and take out the swab in the other (Figure 37.5).
- Rotate the swab back and forth over clean areas of granulation tissue from the sides or base of the wound. *Microorganisms most likely to be responsible for a wound infection reside in viable tissue.*

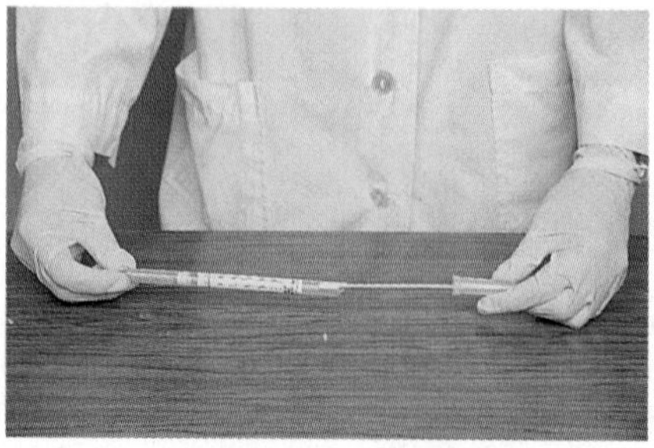

Figure 37.5 A culture tube for a wound specimen

- Do *not* use pus or pooled exudate to culture. *These secretions contain a mixture of contaminants that are not the same as those causing the infection.*
- Avoid touching the swab to intact skin at the wound edges. *This prevents the introduction of superficial skin organisms into the culture.*
- Return the swab to the culture tube, taking care not to touch the top or the outside of the tube. *The outside of the container must remain free of pathogenic microorganisms to prevent their spread to others.*
- If required, crush the inner ampule containing the medium for organism growth at the bottom of the tube. *This ensures that the swab with the specimen is surrounded by culture medium.*
- Twist the cap to secure it.
- If a specimen is required from another site, repeat the preceding steps. Specify the exact site (e.g., inferior drain site or lower aspect of incision) on the label of each container. Be sure to put each swab in the appropriately labelled tube.

6. **Dress the wound.**

- Apply any ordered medication to the wound.
- Cover the wound with a sterile wound dressing, as ordered.

7. **Arrange for the specimen to be transported to the laboratory immediately.** Be sure to include the completed requisition.

PROCEDURE 37.1 Obtaining a Specimen of Wound Drainage *continued*

8. Document all relevant information.

- Record on the client's chart the taking of the specimen and source.
- Include the date and time; the examination requested; the appearance of the wound; the colour, consistency, amount, and odour of any drainage; and any discomfort experienced by the client.

Variation: Obtaining a Specimen for Anaerobic Culture Using a Sterile Syringe and Needle

- Insert a sterile 10-mL syringe (without needle) into the wound, and aspirate 1 to 5 mL of drainage into the syringe.
- Attach the #21-gauge needle to the syringe, and expel all air from the syringe and needle.
- Immediately inject the drainage into the anaerobic culture tube.
- Label the tube or syringe appropriately.
- Send the syringe of drainage to the laboratory immediately.

Evaluation Focus
The character of the drainage (amount, colour, consistency, and odour); any client discomfort; appearance of the wound

Examples of specific desired outcomes related to these goals, although established in the planning phase, are provided in Table 37.10 in the "Evaluating" section of this chapter. Nursing orders aimed at maintaining intact skin and promoting wound healing are included in Table 37.5 on page 949.

TABLE 37.4 Clinical Application: Assessment Data Clusters and Related Nursing Diagnoses for Clients at Risk for or Impaired with *Impaired Skin Integrity*

Data Cluster	Nursing Diagnosis
Judith Yellowchild, an 85-year-old, is pale, emaciated, and listless. Weight is 41 kg. She is incontinent of urine, has no bowel control, and is bedridden.	***Risk for Impaired Skin Integrity*** related to incontinence and immobility
Matthew Brown, an obese 70-year-old hemiplegic, complains of discomfort in his left heel after attempting to move in bed. Superficial skin abrasion 1.2 cm in diameter is present at base of left heel.	***Impaired Skin Integrity*** (stage II pressure ulcer) related to friction

Planning for Home Care

Increasingly, wound care is provided in the home rather than in health-care facilities. The client and family assume much of the responsibility for assessing and treating existing wounds and for helping to prevent pressure ulcers. The accompanying box outlines a home care assessment appropriate for clients who have wounds or pressure ulcers or who are at risk for developing alterations in skin integrity. In planning for client discharge, nurses are accountable for teaching the client and family wound preventive and care measures. See the "Home Care Teaching Guide" box that follows for a model. A critical pathway (described in Chapter 17) may also be useful for planning client care at home.

Implementing

Nursing interventions are focused in two main areas. The first is preventative measures directed toward maintaining skin integrity. Secondly, when an actual skin disruption or trauma becomes apparent, the nursing care approach further extends to treating the wound and supporting wound healing (see Table 37.5). With the increasingly rapid transition of the client from the hospital to home, clients at risk for skin disruptions, as well as their support people, need to be educated about measures to prevent and treat skin breakdown. (See the following Home Care Teaching Guide.)

HOME CARE ASSESSMENT

Wound Prevention and Care

Client and Environment

- *Current level of knowledge:* Understanding of the cause of the wound or risk for developing a pressure ulcer; prevention or treatment strategies
- *Self-care abilities for mobility:* Physical ability to change position, ambulate, and transfer, including the use of assistive devices
- *Self-care abilities for wound care:* Manual dexterity and visual acuity necessary to perform skin assessments and wound treatments
- *Facilities:* Presence of running water, garbage, bathroom needed to perform wound care and contain potentially infectious materials
- *Current level of nutrition:* Eating habits and preferences, laboratory values indicating need for teaching or other intervention

Family

- *Caregiver availability, skills, and responses:* Willingness to assist with wound care and actions to prevent pressure ulcers
- *Family role changes and coping:* Effect on financial status, parenting and spousal roles, sexuality, social roles
- *Alternative potential primary or respite caregivers:* For example, other family members, volunteers, church members, paid care givers or housekeeping services, available community respite care (adult day care, senior centres, and so on)

Community

- *Resources:* Availability and familiarity with possible sources of assistance, such as equipment and supply companies, organizations that offer medical supplies or financial assistance, home care agencies

CLIENT TEACHING

Home Care Teaching Guide

Maintaining Intact Skin

- Discuss relationship between adequate nutrition (especially fluids, protein, vitamins B and C, iron, and calories) and healthy skin.
- Demonstrate appropriate positions for pressure relief.
- Establish a turning or repositioning schedule.
- Demonstrate application of appropriate skin protection agents and devices.
- Instruct to report persistent reddened areas.
- Identify potential sources of skin trauma and means of avoidance.

Promoting Wound Healing

- Discuss importance of adequate nutrition (especially fluids, protein, vitamins B and C, iron, and calories).
- Instruct in wound assessment and provide mechanism for documenting.
- Emphasize principles of asepsis, especially hand washing and proper methods of handling used dressings.
- Provide information about signs of wound infection and other complications to report.
- Reinforce appropriate aspects of pressure ulcer prevention.
- Demonstrate wound care techniques, such as wound cleansing and dressing change.
- Discuss pain control measures, if needed.

Prevention Strategies

Many interventions exist to help preserve a client's skin and underlying tissues. An initial step involves identifying clients at risk for breakdown since risk factors provide the basis for prophylaxis (Maklebust & Sieggreen, 2000). Refer to the Braden and Norton risk assessment tools outlined on pages 938–941.

Providing Skin Care

The client's skin should be kept clean and dry and free of irritation and maceration by urine, feces, sweat, incomplete drying after a bath, soap, or alcohol. When bathing the client, the nurse should minimize the force and friction applied to the skin, using mild cleansing agents that minimize irritation and dryness and that do not disrupt the

TABLE 37.5 Nursing Orders and Rationales for Selected Nursing Interventions: Potential or Actual Impaired Skin Integrity

Nursing Intervention	Nursing Orders	Rationale
Inspect skin at regular intervals.	■ Obtain baseline data using an established tool. ■ Reassess client at risk at least daily in the hospital and at least weekly in the home.	Although the frequency of assessment depends on client condition, regular assessment and documentation is essential to an effective plan.
Keep skin clean, dry, and moisturized.	■ Apply moisturizer to skin. Avoid harsh soaps, alcohol, and hot water.	These can dry skin excessively.
	■ Apply skin protection around perineal area as indicated.	Contact between skin and urine, feces, or wound drainage causes irritation.
Provide appropriate pressure-relieving devices and measures.	■ Implement a turn schedule, avoiding the 90-degree lateral position. ■ Provide support mattresses or pads to prevent breakdown of bony prominences.	Length of time in each position is determined by condition of the skin when pressure is removed. 90-degree position causes excessive pressure on trochanter. Use special pads to relieve pressure points.
	■ Do not massage bony prominences or use doughnut-shaped devices.	These have been shown to cause tissue damage.
Advocate for adequate nutrition.	■ Monitor body weight and serum albumin.	Helps indicate nutritional need.
	■ Provide sufficient fluid and caloric intake. ■ Supplement vitamins and protein, if indicated.	Protein, calories, vitamins, and hydration are required for healthy skin and wound healing.
Document wound assessment at regular intervals and systematically.	■ Cleanse wound prior to assessment.	Loose debris, drainage, and dressing particles interfere with accurate assessment.
	■ Measure wound depth, or if covered with eschar, state "unable to determine." Include presence of tunnels or tracks and undermining.	Assessment helps determine healing.
	■ Measure wound size using a ruler, tracing, or calibrated photograph. ■ Determine condition of the wound bed: percent of wound that is granulation tissue, epithelium, necrotic tissue, fibrin slough, eschar.	Decrease in wound size helps determine effectiveness of treatment and predicts time to complete healing.
	■ Evaluate wound edges and skin.	Thick edges indicate chronic wound, red skin may indicate inflammation or infection, inadequate pressure relief, or irritation from the dressing.
	■ Evaluate any exudate or odour. Be sure to smell the wound and not the old dressing.	Necrotic or infected wounds have more noxious odours than clean wounds.
Apply appropriate wound treatments and dressings.	■ Select dressings based on current wound assessment and adjust dressing type as wound condition changes.	Dressings may be used to protect, absorb, cleanse, humidify, or debride a wound. A correct match with wound needs is essential.

skin's "natural barriers." Also, the nurse should avoid hot water, which increases skin dryness and irritation..Nurses can minimize dryness by avoiding exposure to cold and low humidity. Dry skin is best treated with moisturizing lotions.

In addition, massage over bony prominences should be avoided. Traditionally, nurses have used massage to stimulate blood circulation, with the intention of preventing pressure sores. However, scientific evidence does not support this belief; in fact, massage may lead to deep tissue trauma (PPPPUA, 1994).

Managing Nutrition

Since a compromised nutritional status is a major risk factor for pressure ulcer development, focused efforts must

TABLE 37.6 Role of Selected Nutrients in Wound Healing

Nutrient	Role	Recommendation for Adults
Calories	■ Fuel for cell energy	■ 30 to 35 kcal/kg/day or enough to maintain positive nitrogen balance
Protein	■ "Protein protection"	■ 1.25 to 1.50 g/kg/day or enough to maintain positive nitrogen balance
Vitamin C (Ascorbic acid)	■ Building block for cells and tissues ■ Hydroxylation of proline and lysine in collagen synthesis ■ Enhances epithelialization, collagen synthesis, and cross-linking	■ RDA = 60 mg supplement ■ If deficient, 500 mg b.i.d. ■ Need long time to develop clinical scurvy from vitamin C deficiency ■ Low toxicity
Vitamin A	■ Can reverse steriod effects on skin and delayed healing	■ RDA = 4,000 IU supplement ■ If deficient, 20,000 IU × 10 days ■ None
Vitamin E	■ No known role in wound healing	■ RDA 12 to 15 mg ■ Correct deficiencies
Zinc	■ Cell mitosis and cell proliferation	■ No improvement in wound healing with supplementation, unless zinc deficient ■ *Use with caution!* Large doses can be toxic and may inhibit copper metabolism and impair immune function
Fluid	■ Essential fluid environment for all cell function	■ 30 to 35 mL/kg/day ■ Increase by another 10 to 15 mL/kg if patient is on an air-fluidized bed ■ Use noncaffeine, nonalcoholic fluids without sugar ■ Water is best (2,500 mL/day)

Source: Adapted with permission from (1999). Nutritional aspects of wound healing. *Home Healthcare Nurse, 17*(11), 719–730. Taken from Maklebust, J. & Sieggreen, M. (2000). *Pressure Ulcers*. USA: Springhouse, p. 91.

be directed toward ensuring a diet adequate in calories, nutrients, and protein for the client. It is recommended that the diet meet the client's metabolic needs and be similar to that which supports wound healing as described in Table 37.6. Unless contraindicated, a fluid intake of at least 2,500 mL/day should be promoted. Although there is no evidence to support that excessive doses of vitamins or minerals enhance wound healing, adequate amounts are extremely important. Nutritional management of any client at risk for skin disruptions may best be achieved in consultation with a registered dietician or nutritionist.

Positioning

To prevent skin breakdown, clients must be positioned to minimize pressure on tissues overlying body prominences. See Figure 37.4. Changes of position and transfers must be accomplished at regular intervals without shear or friction damage (see Chapter 43).

In addition to proper positioning, the client should be assisted to be as mobile as possible because activity enhances circulation. If the client cannot move independently, range-of-motion exercises are implemented.

Any at-risk client confined to bed—even when a special support mattress is used—should be repositioned at least every two hours, depending on the client's need, to allow another body surface to bear the weight. Six body positions can usually be used: prone, supine, right and left lateral (side-lying), and right and left Sims' positions. When a lateral position is used, the nurse should avoid positioning the client directly on the trochanter and, instead, position the client off the trochanter on a 30-degree angle. A written schedule should be established for turning and repositioning.

Avoiding Skin Trauma

Providing the client with a smooth, firm, and wrinkle-free foundation on which to sit or lie helps prevent skin trauma. To prevent injury due to friction and shearing forces, clients must be positioned, transferred, and turned correctly (see Chapter 43). For bedridden clients, shearing force can be

RESEARCH NOTE

Does the Degree of Lateral Positioning Make a Difference in Oxygenation of Tissues?

It is commonly accepted that positioning clients on their sides reduces pressure to the sacral and coccyx areas and, thus, reduces pressure ulcer formation. However, such positioning does increase pressure to the area of the trochanter and puts that area at risk for a pressure ulcer. In this study, researchers gathered data on the transcutaneous oxygen and carbon dioxide pressures in the trochanteric and retro-trochanteric areas of healthy participants.

Volunteers with a mean age of 52 years were placed on a foam mattress. Electrodes and probes were placed on the left trochanteric and retro-trochanteric areas. After determining resting pressures while the participant was in a 90-degree *right* lateral position, the volunteer was turned onto the *left* side and readings were recorded every minute for 20 minutes in both a 90-degree left lateral position and a 30-degree left lateral position.

Findings indicated that in the 90-degree left lateral position, mean transcutaneous oxygen pressures dropped from 69.4 mm Hg to 7.4 mm Hg and the transcutaneous carbon dioxide pressures rose from 36.3 mm Hg to 85.5 mm Hg. In contrast, in the 30-degree lateral position, pressure changes from the resting values were not statistically significant.

Implications: Although both the 90-degree and 30-degree lateral positions are effective in relieving pressure from the sacrum and coccyx, the findings from this study are consistent with previous research indicating that the 90-degree position results in almost complete obliteration of oxygen in the skin over the trochanter. Thus, this position, if used repeatedly, could readily result in pressure ulcer damage to the trochanter. Further study is needed, but extreme caution should be used in placing clients in the 90-degree lateral position, as opposed to the 30-degree position.

Source: Colin, D., Abraham, P., Preault, L., Bregeon, C., & Saumet, J. L. (1996, May/June). Comparison of 90° and 30° laterally inclined positions in the prevention of pressure ulcers using transcutaneous oxygen and carbon dioxide pressures. *Advances in Wound Care, 9*(3), 35–38.

reduced by elevating the head of the bed to no more than 30 degrees if this position is not contraindicated by the client's condition (for example, clients with respiratory disorders may find it easier to breathe in Fowler's position). When the head of the bed is raised, the skin and superficial fascia stick to the bed linen while the deep fascia and skeleton slide down toward the bottom of the bed. As a result, blood vessels in the sacral area become twisted, and the tissues in the area can become ischemic and necrotic. Frequent shifts in position, even if only slight, effectively change pressure points. The client should shift weight every 15 to 30 minutes and, whenever possible, exercise or ambulate to stimulate blood circulation.

When assisting a client to change position, nurses should use a lifting device such as a drawsheet rather than dragging the client across or up in bed. The friction that results from dragging the skin against a sheet can cause blisters and abrasions, which may contribute to more extensive tissue damage.

Providing Supportive Devices

For clients confined to bed, special support surfaces and positioning devices can be used to protect bony prominences. Three types of support surfaces can be used to relieve pressure. The *overlay mattress* is applied on top of the standard bed mattress. A *replacement mattress* is a mattress that replaces the standard mattress; most are made of foam and gel combinations. *Specialty beds* replace hospital beds. They provide pressure relief, eliminate shearing and friction, and decrease moisture. Examples are high-air-loss (HAL) beds, low-air-loss (LAL) beds, and beds that provide kinetic therapy. Kinetic beds (e.g., RotoRest) provide continuous passive motion or oscillation therapy, which is intended to counteract the effects of a client's immobility. See Table 37.7 for selected mechanical devices for reducing pressure on body parts.

When a client is confined to bed or to a chair, pressure-reducing devices, such as pillows made of foam, gel, air, or a combination of these, can be used. When the client is sitting, weight should be distributed over the entire seating surface so that pressure does not centre on just one area. To protect a client's heels in bed, supports, such as wedges or pillows, can be used to raise the heels completely off the bed. Doughnut-type devices should not be used (PPPPUA, 1994).

Wound Management

Nursing interventions for the client with a skin disruption or trauma are aimed at maximizing wound healing and preventing or treating infection. The preventive caring practices listed in the previous section continue to be integral to the client with a wound; however, further treatment may involve wound cleansing, the application of dressings, and pain control. Essential for any practitioner engaging in wound care activities is the strict adherence to aseptic techniques for controlling transmission of pathogenic microorganisms and preventing infection. See accompanying guidelines.

Clients with wounds may also experience self-esteem and body-image disturbances and social isolation. The nurse's approach, therefore, should be focused not only on achieving a healed wound but also on attending to the potential psychosocial suffering of the client (Dolynchuk et al., 2000).

TABLE 37.7 Mechanical Devices for Reducing Pressure on Body Parts

Device	Description/Comments
Gel flotation pads	Polyvinyl, silicone, or Silastic pads filled with a gelatinous substance similar to fat
Pillows and wedges (foam, gel and air, foam and fluid)	Can raise a body part (e.g., heels) off the bed surface
Heel protectors, padded splints, foam wedges	Limit pressure on heels when the client is in bed
Foam mattress	Foam moulds to the body
Alternating pressure mattress	Composed of a number of cells in which the pressure alternately increases and decreases; uses a pump
Water bed	Special mattress filled with water; controls temperature of water
Air-fluidized (AF) bed (static high-air-loss [HAL] bed)	Forced temperature-controlled air is circulated around millions of tiny silicone-coated beads, producing a fluidlike movement. Provides uniform support to body contours. Decreases skin maceration by its drying effect. Moisture from the client penetrates the bedsheet and soaks the beads. Airflow forces the beads away from the client and rapidly dries the sheet. A major disadvantage is that the head of the bed cannot be elevated.
Static low-air-loss (LAL) bed	Mattress consists of many air-filled cushions divided into four or five sections. Separate controls permit each section to be inflated to a different level of firmness; thus, pressure can be reduced on bony prominences but increased under other body areas for support.
Active or second-generation low-air-loss (LAL) bed	Like the static LAL, but in addition, it greatly pulsates or rotates from side to side, thus stimulating capillary blood flow and facilitating movement of pulmonary secretions.

Guidelines for Preventing Infection and the Transmission of Bloodborne Pathogens

Standard Precautions

- Wear gloves when touching blood and body fluids, mucous membranes, or nonintact skin of all clients, and when handling items or surfaces soiled with blood or body fluids.
- Wash hands thoroughly after removing gloves and if contaminated with blood or body fluids.
- Wear gowns if necessary. Refer to Chapter 32 on asepsis for standard precautions.

Wound Care

- Wash hands before and after caring for wounds.
- Wear gloves, surgical masks, and protective eyewear as appropriate if procedures commonly cause droplets or splashing of blood or body fluids (e.g., wound irrigation).
- Touch an open or fresh surgical wound only when wearing sterile gloves or using sterile forceps.
- Remove, change, or reinforce dressings over closed wounds when they become wet.

Sources: Adapted from Maklebust, J. A. (1996). Using wound care products to promote a healing environment. *Critical Care Nursing Clinics of North America, 8*, 141–158; and Van Rijswijk, L. (1996). The fundamentals of wound assessment. *Ostomy/Wound Management, 42*(7), 40–42, 44, 461.

Treating Pressure Ulcers

Pressure sores are a challenge for nurses because of the number of variables involved (e.g., risk factors, types of ulcers, and degrees of impairment) and the numerous treatment measures advocated. Existing and potential infections are the most serious complications of pressure sores. In treating pressure sores, nurses should follow the agency skin/wound management protocols. Prompt treatment can prevent further tissue damage and pain and facilitate wound healing. See the accompanying box for clinical guidelines regarding treating pressure ulcers and Table 37.8 for dressings for pressure ulcers.

The RYB Colour Code

To guide wound care, the nurse can use the RYB colour code of wounds developed by Marion Laboratories (Stotts, 1990). This concept is based on the colour of an open wound—red, yellow, or black (RYB)—rather than the depth or size of a wound. On this scheme, the goals of wound care are to *protect* (cover) red, *cleanse* yellow, and *debride* black.

Wounds that are *red* are usually in the late regeneration phase of tissue repair (i.e., developing granulation tissue). They need to be protected to avoid disturbance to regenerating tissue. The nurse protects red wounds by (1) gentle cleansing, (2) avoiding the use of dry gauze or wet-to-dry dressings,

CLINICAL GUIDELINES

Treating Pressure Ulcers

- Minimize direct pressure on the ulcer. Reposition the client at least every two hours. Make a schedule, and record position changes on the client's chart.
- Clean and dress the ulcer using principles of asepsis. Refrain from using antiseptics that may interfere with healing.
- If the pressure ulcer is *infected,* obtain a sample of the drainage for culture and sensitivity to antibiotic agents (see Procedure 37.1).
- If the client cannot keep weight off the pressure ulcer, use a pressure-relieving device.
- Teach the client to move, if only slightly, to relieve pressure.
- Provide range-of-motion (ROM) exercises as the client's condition permits.

(3) applying a transparent film or hydrocolloid dressing, and (4) changing the dressing as infrequently as possible.

Yellow wounds are characterized primarily by liquid to semiliquid "slough" that is often accompanied by purulent drainage. The nurse *cleanses* yellow wounds to remove nonviable tissue. Methods used may include applying wet-to-damp dressings; irrigating the wound; using absorbent dressing materials such as impregnated nonadherent, hydrogel dressings or other exudate absorbers; and consulting with the physician about the need for a topical antimicrobial to minimize bacterial growth.

Black wounds are covered with thick necrotic tissue, or eschar. Black wounds require **debridement** (removal of the necrotic material). Removal of nonviable tissue from a wound must occur before the wound can heal. Debridement may be achieved in four different ways: sharp, mechanical, chemical, and autolytic. In sharp debridement, a scalpel or scissors is used to separate and remove dead tissue. In many settings, specially trained nurses and physical therapists are permitted to perform sharp debridement. Mechanical debridement is accomplished through scrubbing force or wet-to-damp dressings. Chemical debridement is more selective than sharp or mechanical techniques. Collagenase enzyme agents are currently most recommended for this use. In autolytic debridement, dressings that contain wound moisture facilitate the body's own enzymatic breakdown of necrotic tissue. Although this method takes longer than the other three, it is the most selective and, therefore, causes the least damage to healthy surrounding and healing tissues. When the eschar is removed, the wound is treated as yellow, then red. When more than one colour is present, the nurse treats the most serious colour first, that is, black, then yellow, then red. Agency policy and requirement for a physician's order must be checked prior to any type of debridement.

CLINICAL GUIDELINES

Cleaning Wounds

- Use physiological solutions, such as isotonic saline or lactated Ringer's solution, to clean or irrigate wounds. If antimicrobial solutions are used, make sure they are well diluted.
- When possible, warm the solution to body temperature before use. This prevents lowering of the wound temperature, which slows the healing process.
- If a wound is grossly contaminated by foreign material, bacteria, slough, or necrotic tissue, clean the wound at every dressing change. Foreign bodies and devitalized tissue act as a focus for infection and can delay healing.
- If a wound is clean, has little exudate, and reveals healthy granulation tissue, avoid repeated cleaning. Unnecessary cleaning can delay wound healing by traumatizing newly produced, delicate tissues, reducing the surface temperature of the wound, and removing exudate which itself may have bactericidal properties.
- Use gauze squares. Avoid using cotton balls and other products that shed fibres onto the wound surface. The fibres become embedded in granulation tissue and can act as foci for infection. They may also stimulate "foreign body" reactions, prolonging the inflammatory phase of healing and delaying the healing process.
- Clean superficial noninfected wounds by irrigating them with normal saline, as ordered by a physician. The hydraulic pressure of an irrigating stream of fluid dislodges contaminating debris and reduces bacterial colonization.
- To retain wound moisture, avoid drying a wound after cleaning it.

Cleaning Wounds

Wound cleansing involves the removal of debris (e.g., foreign material, excess slough, necrotic tissue, bacteria, and other contaminants). In the past, antimicrobial agents, such as providone-iodine (Betadine), hydrogen peroxide, alcohol, and Dakin's solution were commonly used. However, current clinical research has established that these agents can be cytotoxic. The choices of cleansing solution and method depend largely on the nature of the wound and agency protocol. Recommended guidelines for cleaning wounds are shown in the box above.

The major principle of wound cleansing is moving from an area of "least contamination" to an area of "most contamination" ("clean to dirty"). Depending on the wound, these areas are sometimes difficult to distinguish. Commonly used methods to clean a surgical wound and drain site are outlined in Chapter 44.

TABLE 37.8 Selected Types of Wound Dressings

Dressing	Description	Purpose	Examples
Transparent adhesive films	Adhesive semipermeable polyurethane or other synthetic films are *nonabsorbent* dressings that allow exchange of oxygen and moisture vapour between the atmosphere and wound bed. They are impermeable to bacteria and water.	To provide protection against contamination and friction; to maintain a clean moist surface that facilitates cellular migration; to provide insulation by preventing fluid evaporation; and to facilitate wound assessment	Op-Site, Tegaderm, Biocclusive, ACU-derm
Impregnated low adherent dressings	Woven or nonwoven cotton or synthetic materials that are impregnated with medicated or unmedicated ointments. Require secondary dressings to secure them in place.	Designed to provide a contact dressing of low adherence and support the delivery of topical antibacterials and antibiotics	Vaseline gauze, Carragauze, Dermagran Wet Dressing, Xeroform, Adaptic, Jelonet, Bactigras, Sofratulle
Hydrocolloids	Waterproof adhesive wafers, pastes, or powders. Wafers, designed to be worn for up to seven days, consist of two layers. The inner adhesive layer has particles that absorb exudate and form a hydrated gel over the wound; the outer film provides a seal.	To absorb light to moderate exudate; to produce a moist environment that facilitates debridement and healing but does not cause maceration of surrounding skin; to protect the wound from bacterial contamination, foreign debris, and urine or feces	DuoDERM, Comfeel, Tegasorb, Restore,
Hydrogels	*Hydrophilic polymers* prepared in sheets or gels. May require secondary dressing.	Assist with the liquefication of necrotic tissue or slough; rehydrate the wound bed; and fill in dead space	Aquasorb, ClearSite, IntraSite, Vigilon, Normlgel, Hypergel, Duoderm hydroactive gel, Tegagel
Polyurethane foams	Sheet dressings of mainly polyurethane foams. Prime function is absorbency.	To absorb moderate amounts of exudate	Lyofoam, Allevyn, Biatain, Mepilex, Hydrasorb
Exudate absorbers/ alginates	Nonadherent dressings of powder, beads or granules, or paste that conform to the wound surface and absorb up to 20 times their weight in exudate; require a secondary dressing.	To provide a moist wound surface by interacting with exudate; to form a gelatinous mass; to absorb exudate; to eliminate dead space or pack wounds; and to support debridement	Debrisan, Sorbsan, Aquacel, Algisite, Kaltostat, Tegagen, Combiderm
Antimicrobials	Topical antimicrobial agents	To decrease surface bacteria without excessive toxicity to the cells in the wound base	Cadexomer iodine, Nanocystalline, silver dressings
Debriding agents	Enzyme	To support and assist the enzymatic debridement of necrotic tissue in the wound	Collagenase Santyl
Biologic devices	Skin equivalent/skin substitute	Assists in the healing of "difficult to treat" wounds	Dermagraft, Apligraf ™
Devices	Negative pressure therapy	Assists with the management of high exudating wounds	Vacuum-Assisted Closure (VAC Therapy)

Wound Irrigation and Packing

An **irrigation (lavage)** is the washing or flushing out of an area. Sterile technique is required for a wound irrigation because there is a break in the skin integrity.

Using piston syringes instead of bulb syringes to irrigate a wound reduces the risk of aspirating drainage and provides safe, effective pressure. For deep wounds with small openings, a sterile straight catheter may also be necessary. Frequently used irrigation solutions are sterile normal saline, lactated Ringer's solution, and antibiotic solutions. See Procedure 37.2 for the steps involved in irrigating a wound.

Following wound irrigation, gauze **packing** is often placed in a wound to facilitate the formation of granulation tissue and healing by secondary intention. Generally, the *wet-to-damp* technique is used, whereby moistened non-cotton-filled gauzes are packed in the wound to absorb exudates, but they are not allowed to dry before removal. Gauzes with cotton fibers are contraindicated because they can pull loose and remain in the wound, encouraging bacterial growth and contamination.

Dressing Wounds

Dressings are applied for the following purposes:

- To protect the wound from mechanical injury
- To protect the wound from microbial contamination
- To provide or maintain humidity of the wound
- To provide thermal insulation
- To absorb drainage or debride a wound, or both
- To prevent hemorrhage (when applied as a pressure dressing or with elastic bandages)

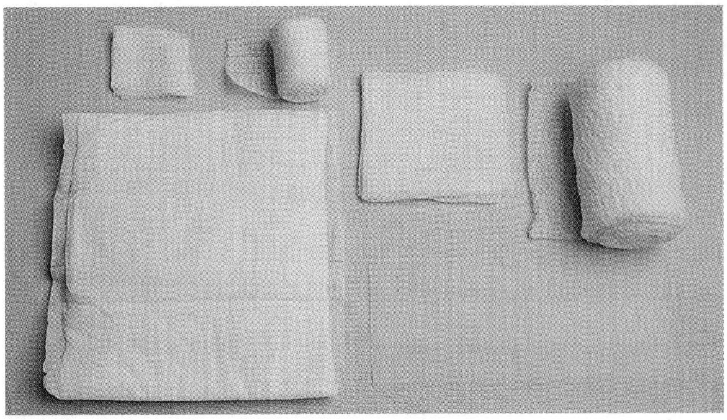

Figure 37.6 Some frequently used dressing materials (clockwise from bottom left): surgipad or abdominal pad, 2 × 2 gauze, 2-inch roller gauze, 4 × 4 gauze, 4-inch roller gauze, and nonadherent absorbent dressing

- To splint or immobilize the wound site and thereby facilitate healing and prevent injury
- To provide psychological (aesthetic) comfort

Types of Dressing

Various dressing materials are available to cover wounds. The type of dressing used depends on (1) the location, size, and type of the wound; (2) the amount of exudate; (3) whether the wound requires debridement, is infected, or has sinus tracts; and (4) such considerations as frequency of dressing change, ease or difficulty of dressing application, and cost. Table 37.8 describes these materials.

Common gauze dressings (Figure 37.6) may be applied in several ways to achieve different goals (see Table 37.9). Other dressing materials are used for specific types and conditions of wounds.

TABLE 37.9 Modes of Applying Gauze Dressings

Dressing	Description	Purpose
Dry-to-dry	A layer of wide-mesh cotton gauze lies next to the wound surface. A second layer of dry absorbent cotton or Dacron is on top.	Protect the wound. If the wound is open or draining, necrotic debris and exudate are trapped in the interstices of the gauze layer and are removed when the dressing is removed.
Wet-to-dry	Next to the wound surface is a layer of wide-mesh cotton gauze saturated with saline or an antimicrobial solution. This layer is covered by a moist absorbent material that is moistened with the same solution.	Debride the wound. Necrotic debris is softened by the solution and then adheres to the mesh gauze as it dries. It is removed when the dressing is removed. Also, moisture helps dilute viscous exudate.
Wet-to-damp	A variation of the wet-to-dry dressing, this dressing is removed before it has completely dried (see box on page 957).	The wound is debrided when the gauze is removed.
Wet-to-wet	A layer of wide-mesh gauze saturated with saline lies next to the wound surface. Above is a second layer of absorbent material saturated with the same solution. The entire dressing is kept moist with a wetting agent.	The wound surface is continually bathed. Moisture dilutes viscous exudate.

PROCEDURE 37.2 Irrigating a Wound

Before irrigating a wound, determine (1) the type of irrigating solution to be used, (2) the frequency of irrigations, and (3) the temperature of the solution.

PURPOSES

- To clean the area
- To apply heat and hasten the healing process
- To apply an antimicrobial solution

Assessment Focus
Appearance and size of the wound; the character of the exudate; presence of pain and the time of the last pain medication; clinical signs of systemic infection; allergies to the wound irrigation agent, tape, or latex

Equipment

- ❑ Sterile dressing equipment and dressing materials
- ❑ Sterile irrigating syringes (e.g., a 30- to 50-mL piston syringe) with a catheter of an appropriate size (e.g., #18 or #19) attached or a 250-mL squeezable bottle with irrigating tip
- ❑ Sterile basin for the irrigating solution
- ❑ Moistureproof bag
- ❑ Sterile basin to receive the irrigation returns
- ❑ Irrigating solution, usually 200 mL of solution warmed to body temperature, according to the agency's or physician's choice
- ❑ Clean disposable gloves
- ❑ Sterile gloves
- ❑ Moistureproof sterile drape
- ❑ Sterile straight catheter or irrigating tip, if needed

INTERVENTION

1. Verify the physician's order.

- Confirm the type and strength of the solution.

2. Prepare the client.

- Assist the client to a position in which the irrigating solution will flow by gravity from the upper end of the wound to the lower end and then into the basin.
- Place the waterproof drape over the client and the bed.
- Put on disposable gloves and remove and discard the old dressing.
- Remove gloves and don new ones.
- With forceps, clean from the centre of the wound outward using circular strokes.
- Use a separate swab for each stroke, and discard each swab after use. *This prevents the introduction of microorganisms to other wound areas.*
- Assess the wound and drainage.
- Remove and discard disposable gloves.

3. Prepare the equipment.

- Open the sterile dressing set and supplies.
- Pour the ordered solution into the solution container.
- Put on sterile gloves.
- Position the sterile basin below the wound to receive the irrigating fluid.

4. Irrigate the wound.

- Instill a steady stream of irrigating solution into the wound. Make sure all areas of the wound are irrigated.
- Use either a syringe with a catheter attached or a 250-mL squeezable bottle with irrigating tip to flush the wound. *Effective irrigation requires 4 to 15 pounds per square inch of pressure. These devices provide this pressure; bulb syringes do not* (Maklebust, 1996).
- If you are using a catheter, insert the catheter into the wound until resistance is met. Do not force the catheter. *Forcing the catheter can cause tissue damage.*
- Continue irrigating until the solution becomes clear (no exudate is present). *The irrigation washes away tissue debris and drainage so that later returns are clearer.*
- Dry the area around the wound. *Moisture left on the skin promotes the growth of microorganisms and can cause skin irritation and breakdown.*

5. Assess and dress the wound.

- Assess the appearance of the wound, noting in particular the type and amount of exudate and the presence and extent of granulation tissue.
- Pack the wound if ordered.
- Apply a sterile dressing to the wound as ordered (e.g., moist transparent wound barrier dressing).

6. Document all relevant information.

- Document the irrigation, the solution used, the appearance of the irrigation returns, and nursing assessments. Note the presence of any exudate and sloughing tissue.

Evaluation Focus
Character of irrigation returns; the extent of wound healing (i.e., the amount of granulation tissue); discomfort associated with wound irrigation; colour and amount of exudates

CLINICAL GUIDELINES

Applying Wet-to-Damp Dressings

- Open the packages of the sterile dressing set, fine-mesh gauze, and sterile solution container.
- Pour the ordered solution into the solution container.
- Put on sterile gloves.
- Place the fine-mesh gauze dressings into the solution container, and thoroughly saturate them with solution. The entire gauze must be moistened to enhance its absorptive abilities.
- If agency protocol indicates, clean the wound.
- Wring out the packing material so that it is *slightly* moist. Avoid packing that is too wet. An excessively wet wound bed increases the risk for bacterial growth and may macerate surrounding skin.
- Pack the moistened dressings into all depressions and grooves of the wound, ensuring that all *exposed surfaces* are covered. If necessary, use forceps to feed the gauze gradually into deep depressed areas. Necrotic tissue is usually more prevalent in depressed wound areas and needs to be covered with gauze.
- Avoid applying packing too tightly. A tight application inhibits wound edges from contracting and compresses capillaries.
- To prevent maceration of the surrounding skin, pack only to the edge of the wound without overlapping the skin.
- If necessary, protect surrounding skin with a skin barrier (e.g., skin sealant or hydrocolloid dressing).
- Apply a damp secondary dressing (e.g., 4 × 4 gauze) over the wet dressings to absorb excess exudate.
- Cover all the dressings with a surgipad or abdominal pad. The pad protects the wound from external contaminants.
- Remove gloves inside out and discard them.

To remove the dressings, wear disposable gloves. If packing material adheres to any tissue during removal, soak it with normal saline. This facilitates removal and preserves new granulation tissue.

Transparent Wound Barriers Transparent wound barriers are often applied to wounds, including ulcerated or burned skin areas (Figure 37.7). These dressings offer several advantages:

- They are nonporous, self-adhesive dressings that do not require changing as other dressings do. They are often left in place until healing has occurred or as long as they remain intact.
- Because they are transparent, the wound can be assessed through them.
- Because they are occlusive, the wound remains moist and retains the serous exudate, which promotes epithelial growth, hastens healing, and reduces the risk of infection.
- Because they are elastic, they can be placed over a joint without disrupting the client's mobility.
- They adhere only to the skin area around the wound and not to the wound itself because they keep the wound moist.
- They allow the client to shower or bathe without removing the dressing.
- They can be removed without damaging wound tissues.

Procedure 37.3 describes how to apply a moist transparent wound barrier.

Hydrocolloid Dressings Hydrocolloid dressings (see Table 37.8) are frequently used over venous stasis leg ulcers and pressure ulcers. These dressings offer several advantages:

- They reduce the frequency of dressing changes.
- They do not need a "cover" dressing and are water resistant, so the client can shower or bathe.
- They can be moulded to uneven body surfaces.
- They provide an effective bacterial barrier.
- They decrease pain and, thus, reduce the need for analgesics.
- They absorb *some* drainage and, therefore, can be used on draining wounds.

These dressings have certain limitations, however:

- They are opaque and obscure wound visibility.
- They have a limited absorption capacity.

Figure 37.7 A transparent wound dressing

PROCEDURE 37.3 Applying a Moist Transparent Wound Barrier Dressing

Before applying or changing a moist transparent wound barrier, determine agency protocol about solutions used to clean the wound and whether clean or sterile technique is to be used. Many agencies recommend clean rather than sterile technique for chronic wounds, such as a decubitus ulcer.

PURPOSES

- To provide a moist wound environment and promote wound healing
- To protect the wound from trauma and infectious agents
- To facilitate assessment of wound healing

Assessment Focus
Appearance and size of the wound; the amount and character of exudate; complaints of discomfort; signs of systemic infection (e.g., elevated body temperature, diaphoresis, malaise; leukocytosis)

Equipment

- ❑ Disposable gloves
- ❑ Hair scissors or clippers
- ❑ Alcohol or acetone
- ❑ Moistureproof bag
- ❑ Sterile gloves (optional)
- ❑ Sterile gauze and the wound-cleaning agents specified by the physician or agency (e.g., sterile saline)
- ❑ Wound barrier dressing
- ❑ Scissors
- ❑ Paper tape

INTERVENTION

1. Verify physician's order and check allergies.

2. Obtain assistance as needed.

- If the size of the wound necessitates it, acquire the assistance of a co-worker to help apply the dressing.

3. Thoroughly clean the skin area around the wound.

- Put on disposable gloves.
- Clean the skin around the wound well with normal saline or a non-irritating wound cleansing agent. Always rinse the adjacent skin well prior to applying a dressing.
- Clip the hair about 5 cm around the wound area, if indicated.
- If adherence of the dressing is a concern, clean the area adjacent to the wound with alcohol or acetone, and allow it to dry. Alcohol or acetone defats the skin. Defatted, clean, dry skin ensures better adhesion of the dressing.
- Remove gloves, and dispose of them in the moistureproof bag.

4. Clean the wound, if indicated.

- Put on clean disposable or sterile gloves in accordance with agency practice.
- Clean the wound with the prescribed solution. Either (a) pour the sterile solution directly on the wound and collect drainage with an emesis basin, or (b) with forceps, use a moist sterile gauze to clean the wound.
- Dry the surrounding skin with a dry gauze.

5. Assess the wound.

- See "Assessment Focus" earlier in the procedure.

6. Apply the wound barrier.

- Remove part of the paper backing on the dressing. If you have an assistant, remove all of the paper backing; the two of you should hold the coloured tabs attached to the dressing.
- Apply the dressing at one edge of the wound site, allowing at least 2.5-cm coverage of the skin surrounding the wound.
- Gently lay or press the barrier over the wound. Keep it free of wrinkles, but avoid stretching it too tightly. *A stretched dressing restricts mobility.*
- Cut off the coloured tabs after the wound is completely covered.
- Remove and dispose of gloves appropriately.

7. Reinforce the dressing only if absolutely needed.

- Apply paper or other porous tape to the edges of the dressing.

8. Assess the wound area at least daily.

- Determine the extent of serous fluid accumulation under the dressing, wound healing, and the need to repair the dressing.
- If excessive serum has accumulated, consider replacing the transparent wound barrier with a more absorbent type of dressing, such as hydrocolloid.
- If the dressing is leaking, remove it and apply another dressing.

9. Document the procedure and all nursing assessments.

Evaluation Focus
Amount of granulation tissue or degree of healing; amount of serous fluid under dressing (see step 8); discomfort associated with wound care

- They can soften and wrinkle at the edges with wear and movement.
- They can be difficult to remove and may leave a residue on the skin.

Because of these limitations, hydrocolloid dressings should not be used for infected wounds or those with deep tracts or fistulas (abnormal passage that develops between a hollow organ and the skin or between two hollow organs).

Procedure 37.4 describes how to apply hydrocolloid dressings.

PROCEDURE 37.4 Applying a Hydrocolloid Dressing

A hydrocolloid dressing should be changed whenever it becomes dislodged, leaks, or develops an odour. If the wound has substantial drainage or yellow slough, the dressing may need to be changed every 24 to 72 hours. When drainage subsides, the dressing may be left in place for three to seven days. The procedure may be clean or sterile depending on agency policy.

Assessment Focus
See Procedure 37.3.

PURPOSES

- To maintain a moist wound surface and promote healing
- To prevent the entrance of microorganisms into the wound
- To minimize wound discomfort
- To promote autolysis of necrotic material by white blood cells
- To decrease the frequency of dressing changes

Equipment

- ❑ Clean disposable gloves
- ❑ Moistureproof bag
- ❑ Dressing set
- ❑ Sterile normal saline or other cleaning agent used by the agency
- ❑ Sterile gloves (optional)
- ❑ Hydrocolloid dressing at least 3–4 cm larger than wound on all four sides
- ❑ Paper tape

INTERVENTION

1. Verify physician's orders and check allergies.

2. Remove the old dressing.

- Put on disposable gloves.
- Pull the dressing off gradually in the direction of hair growth. *This minimizes skin irritation.*
- Dispose of the soiled dressing in the moistureproof bag.

3. Clean the skin area around the wound.

- Gently wash the skin surrounding the wound with a mild cleansing agent or with normal saline, and dry it thoroughly with gauze squares.
- Leave the residue that is difficult to remove on the skin. It will wear off in time. *Attempts to remove residue can irritate the surrounding skin.*
- Remove gloves and dispose of them in the moistureproof bag.

4. Clean the wound, if indicated.

- Open the sterile dressing supplies.
- Pour saline or other cleaning agent into the sterile container.
- Put on disposable or sterile gloves in accordance with agency protocol.
- With forceps, clean the wound with the prescribed solution.

5. Assess the wound.

- Observe the appearance and the size of the wound and the amount and character of exudate.
- Determine presence of pain.

6. Apply the dressing.

- Follow the manufacturer's instructions.
- Remove and dispose of the gloves.
- Optional: Tape all four sides of the dressing as required or according to agency protocol. *Taping prevents the dressing from sticking to bed linens and the edges from lifting.*

7. Assess and change the dressing, as indicated.

- Inspect the dressing at least daily for leakage, dislodgement, odour, and wrinkling.
- Change the dressing if any of these signs are present.

8. Document the technique and all nursing assessments.

Evaluation Focus
Amount of granulation tissue or degree of healing; amount and character of any drainage; any discomfort associated with wound care

Securing Dressings

The nurse tapes the dressing over the wound, ensuring that it covers the entire wound and does not become dislodged. The correct type of tape should be selected and, ideally, the ends of the tape should be folded over slightly in advance of securing to aid ease of removal. Elastic tape can provide pressure; nonallergenic tape is used when a client is allergic to other tape. The nurse follows these steps:

1. Place the tape so that the dressing cannot be folded back to expose the wound. Place strips at the ends of the dressing, and space tapes evenly in the middle (Figure 37.8, *A*).
2. Ensure that the tape is long and wide enough to adhere to several centimetres of skin on each side of the dressing, but not so long or wide that the tape loosens with activity (Figure 37.8, *B*).
3. Place the tape in the opposite direction from the body action, for example, across a body joint or crease, not lengthwise (Figure 37.9).

Montgomery straps (tie tapes) are commonly used for wounds requiring frequent dressing changes (Figure 37.10). These straps prevent skin irritation and discomfort caused by removing the adhesive each time the dressing is changed. Nonallergenic tie tapes are available for people with sensitive skin. If these are not available, the nurse can protect the skin by applying tincture of benzoin to the site where the adhesive is to be placed.

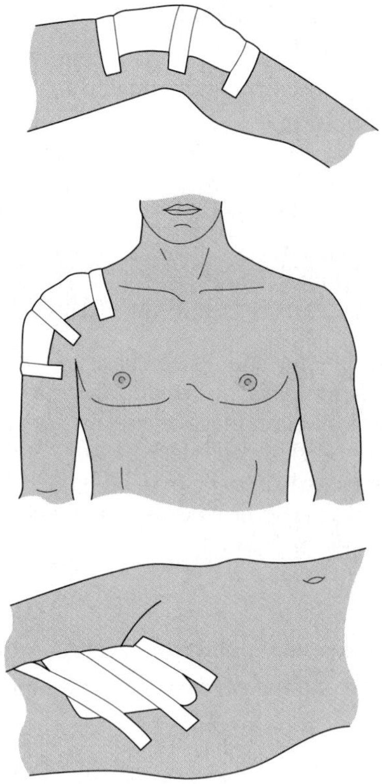

Figure 37.9 Dressings over moving parts must remain secure in spite of the movement. Place the tape over a joint at a right angle to the direction the joint moves.

Supporting and Immobilizing Wounds

Bandages and binders serve various purposes:

- Supporting a wound (e.g., a fractured bone)
- Immobilizing a wound (e.g., a strained shoulder)
- Applying pressure (e.g., elastic bandages on the lower extremities to improve venous blood flow)
- Securing a dressing (e.g., for an extensive abdominal surgical wound)
- Retaining warmth (e.g., a flannel bandage on a rheumatoid joint)

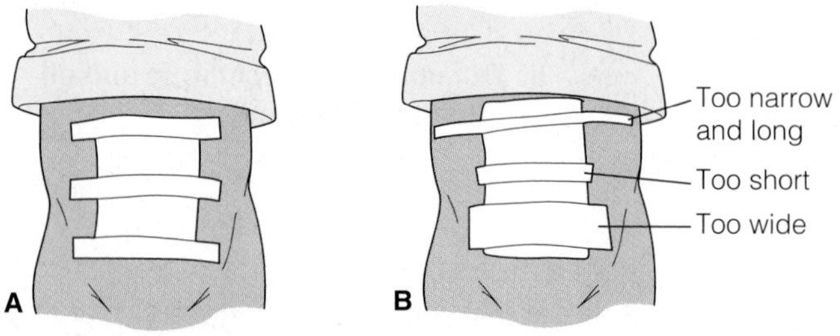

Figure 37.8 The strips of tape should be placed at the ends of the dressing and must be sufficiently long and wide to secure the dressing. The tape should adhere to intact skin.

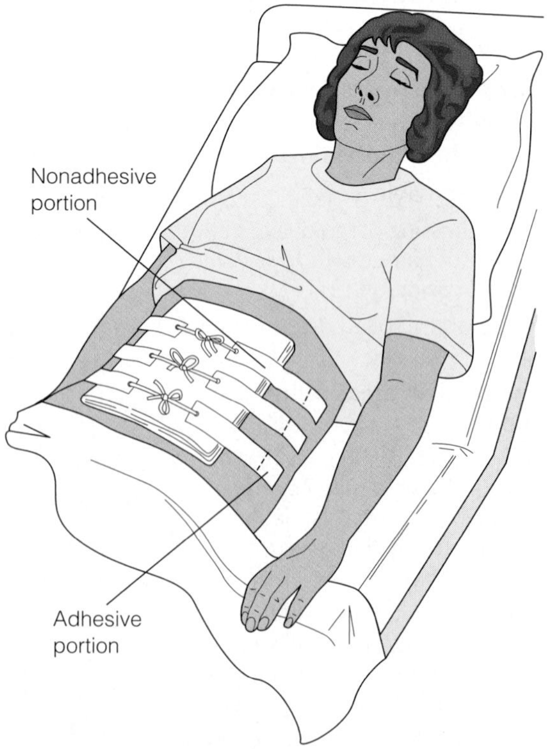

Figure 37.10 Montgomery straps, or tie tapes, are used to secure large dressings that require frequent changing.

CLINICAL GUIDELINES

Bandaging

- Whenever possible, bandage the part in its normal position, with the joint slightly flexed to avoid putting strain on the ligaments and the muscles of the joint.
- Pad between skin surfaces and over bony prominences to prevent friction from the bandage and consequent abrasion of the skin.
- Always bandage body parts by working from the distal to the proximal end to aid the return flow of venous blood.
- Bandage with even pressure to prevent interference with blood circulation.
- Whenever possible, leave the end of the body part (e.g., the toes) exposed so that you will be able to determine the adequacy of the blood circulation to the extremity.
- Cover dressings with bandages at least 5 cm beyond the edges of the dressing to prevent the dressing and wound from becoming contaminated.
- Face the client when applying a bandage to maintain uniform tension and the appropriate direction of the bandage.

CLINICAL GUIDELINES

Assessing Before Applying Bandages or Binders

- Inspect and palpate the area for swelling.
- Inspect for the presence of and status of wounds (open wounds will require a dressing before a bandage or binder is applied).
- Note the presence of drainage (amount, colour, odour, viscosity).
- Inspect and palpate for adequacy of circulation: skin temperature, blanching (capillary refill), peripheral pulses, colour, and sensation. Pale or cyanotic skin, cool temperature, tingling, and numbness can indicate impaired circulation.
- Ask the client about any pain experienced (location, intensity, onset, quality).
- Assess the ability of the client to reapply the bandage or binder, when needed (home care).
- Assess the capabilities of the client regarding activities of daily living (e.g., to eat, dress, comb hair, bathe), and assess the assistance required during the convalescence period.

There are several types of bandages and binders and several ways in which they are applied. When correctly applied, they promote healing, provide comfort, and can prevent injury. Clinical guidelines for bandaging are provided in the box above.

Bandages

A bandage is a strip of cloth used to wrap some part of the body. Bandages are available in various widths, most commonly 1.5 to 7.5 cm, and are usually supplied in rolls for easy application to a body part.

Many types of materials are used for bandages. Gauze is one of the most commonly used; it is light and porous and readily moulds to the body. It is also relatively inexpensive, so it is generally discarded when soiled. Gauze is frequently used to retain dressings on wounds and to bandage the fingers, hands, toes, and feet. It supports dressings and, at the same time, permits air to circulate; it can also be impregnated with gels or other medications for application to wounds.

Many kinds of elasticized bandages are applied to provide pressure to an area. They are commonly used as tensor bandages or as partial stockings to provide support and improve the venous circulation in the legs.

The width of the bandage used depends on the size of the body part to be bandaged. For example, a 2.5-cm bandage is used for a finger, a 5-cm bandage for an arm, and a 7.5-cm or 10-cm bandage for a leg. The larger the circumference of a part, the wider the bandage. Padding (e.g., abdominal pads and gauze squares) is frequently used to cover bony prominences (e.g., the elbow) or to separate skin surfaces (e.g., the fingers).

Before applying a bandage, the nurse needs to know its purpose and to assess the area requiring support. See the box above for assessment guidelines. When bandages are used to secure dressings, the nurse wears gloves to prevent contact with body fluids.

Basic Turns for Roller Bandages

Circular Turn *Circular turns* are used chiefly to anchor bandages or to bandage certain areas, such as the proximal aspect of a finger or a wrist. Instructions for circular turns are as follows:

- Apply the end of the bandage to the part of the body to be bandaged.
- Encircle the body part a few times or as often as needed, each turn directly covering the previous turn (Figure 37.11). This provides even support to the area.
- Secure the end of the bandage with tape. Clips and pins should not be used as they can be uncomfortable when situated over an injured area and cause pressure areas.

Spiral Turn *Spiral turns* are used to bandage cylindrical body parts, such as wrists, upper arms, or lower legs.

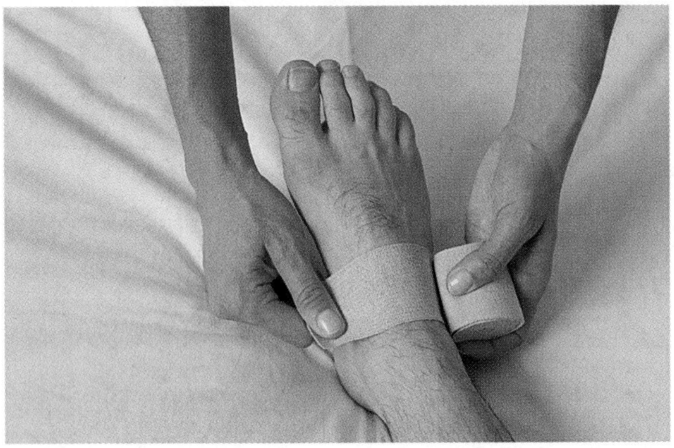

Figure 37.11 Starting a bandage with two circular turns

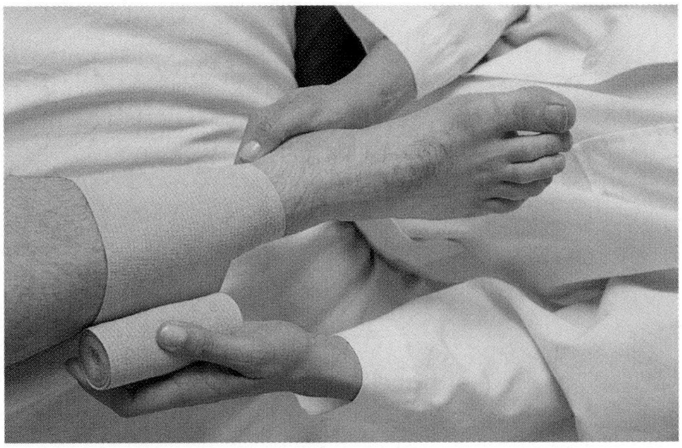

Figure 37.12 Applying spiral turns

- Make two circular turns to anchor the bandage.
- Continue spiral turns at about a 30-degree angle, each turn overlapping the preceding one by one-half to two-thirds the width of the bandage (Figure 37.12).
- Terminate the bandage with two circular turns, and secure the end as described for circular turns.

Spiral Reverse Turn *Spiral reverse turns* are used to bandage cone-shaped body parts, such as the lower leg or forearm.

- Anchor the bandage with two circular turns, and bring the bandage upward at about a 30-degree angle.
- Place the thumb of the free hand on the upper edge of the bandage (Figure 37.13, *A*). The thumb will hold the bandage while it is folded on itself.
- Unroll the bandage about 15 cm, then turn the hand so that the bandage falls over itself (Figure 37.13, *B*).
- Continue the bandage around the limb, overlapping each previous turn by one-half to two-thirds the width of the bandage. Make each bandage turn at the same position on the limb so that the turns of the bandage will be aligned (Figure 37.13, *C*).
- Terminate the bandage with two circular turns, and secure the end as described for circular turns.

Figure-Eight Turn A *figure-eight turn* is used to bandage an elbow, knee, or ankle joint because it permits some movement after application.

- Anchor the bandage with two circular turns.
- Carry the bandage above the joint, around it, and then below it, making a figure eight (Figure 37.14).
- Continue above and below the joint, overlapping the previous turn by one-half to two-thirds the width of the bandage.
- Terminate the bandage above the joint with two circular turns, and secure the end appropriately.

Binders

A *binder* is a type of bandage designed for a specific body part; for example, the triangular binder (sling) fits the arm. Binders are used to support large areas of the body, such as the abdomen, arm, or chest.

Triangular Arm Binder (Sling) A *triangular arm binder* or *sling* is usually applied as a full triangle to support the arm, elbow, and forearm of the client or to reduce or prevent swelling of a hand. Most agencies use commercial strap slings. To apply a large arm sling:

- Place one end of the unfolded triangular binder over the shoulder of the uninjured side so that the binder

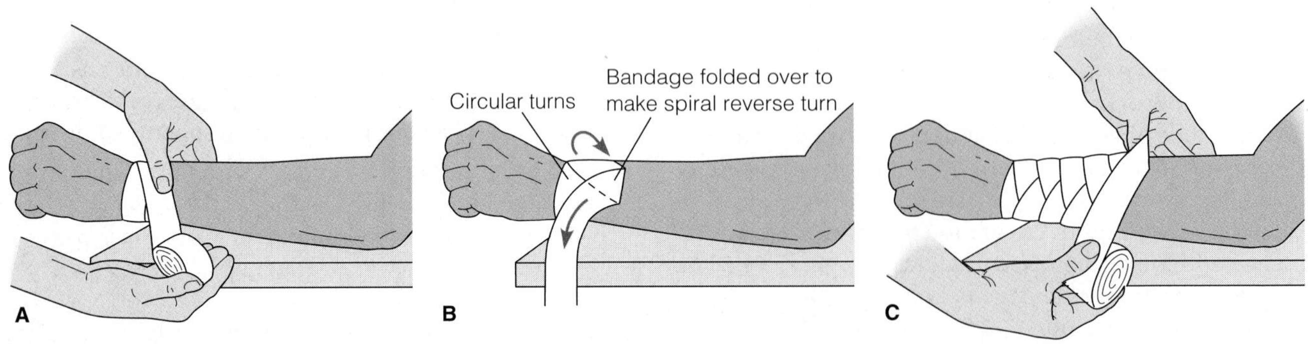

Figure 37.13 Applying spiral reverse turns

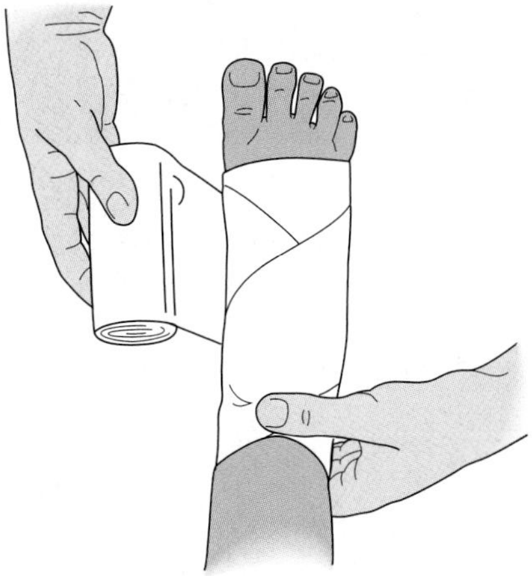

Figure 37.14 Applying a figure-eight bandage

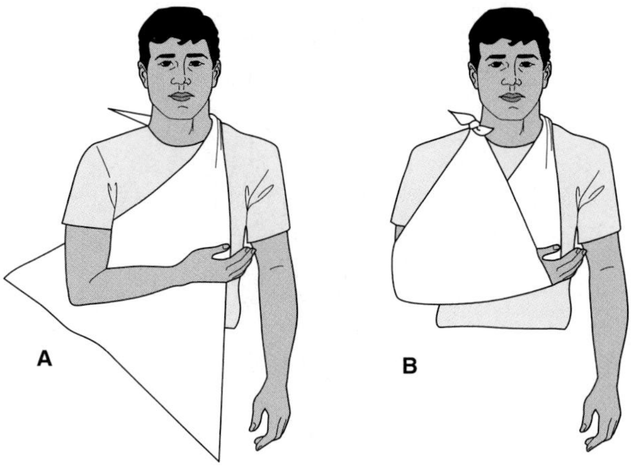

Figure 37.15 Large arm sling

falls down the front of the chest of the client with the point of the triangle (apex) under the elbow of the injured side.

- Take the upper corner, and carry it around the neck until it hangs over the shoulder on the injured side (Figure 37.15, *A*).
- Bring the lower corner of the binder up over the arm to the shoulder of the injured side. Using a square knot, secure this corner to the upper corner at the side of the neck on the involved side.
- Fold the sling neatly at the elbow, and secure it with safety pins or tape. It may be folded and fastened at the front (Figure 37.15, *B*).

T-Binder (Single or Double) *T-binders* are used to retain pads, dressings, or packs in the perineal area. Single T-binders are often used for females, and double T-binders for males to prevent undue pressure on the penis. The double T-binder can also provide greater support for large dressings on both males and females. To apply a T-binder:

- Bring the waist tails around the client, overlap them, and secure them with a pin placed horizontally. The pins placed horizontally allow comfort when bending at the waist and moving.
- Bring the centre tail up between the legs (Figure 37.16). The two tails of the double T-binder are brought up on either side of the penis and scrotum.
- Fasten the ties at the waist with a safety pin placed horizontally.

Straight Abdominal or Scultetus (Many-Tailed) Binders Straight abdominal and Scultetus binders are used to support the abdomen. A straight binder is also used to support the chest. Chest binders often have shoulder straps. To apply these binders, follow these steps:

- With the client in a supine position, place the abdominal binder smoothly under the client, with the upper border of the binder at the waist and the lower border at the level of the gluteal fold. A binder placed above the waist can interfere with respiration; one placed too low can interfere with elimination and walking.
- Apply padding over the iliac crests if the client is thin.
- For a straight abdominal binder, bring the ends around the client, overlap them, and secure them with pins or Velcro (Figure 37.17).
- For a Scultetus binder, bring the tails over to the centre from alternate sides (Figure 37.18). The last tail is secured with a safety pin or Velcro. Each tail should overlap the preceding one by about half the width of the tail for maximum support. In thin people, the tails may extend beyond the other side and require folding back.
  a. For clients who have had abdominal surgery, lace the tails from the bottom up. This provides maximum upward support.

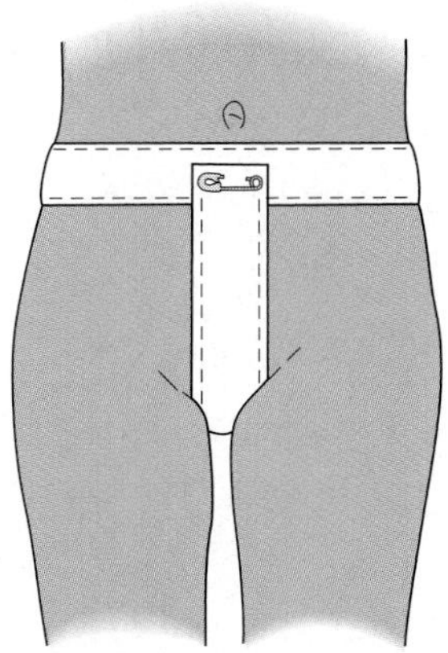

Figure 37.16 Single-tail T-binder

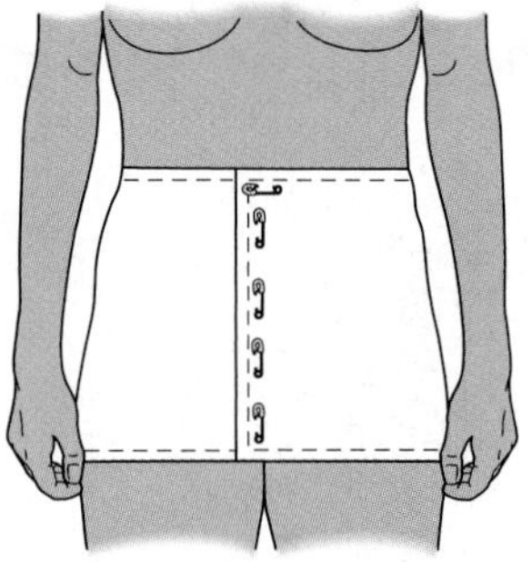

Figure 37.17 A straight abdominal binder

b. For the postpartum client, lace the tails from the top down. This provides downward pressure on the uterus.

Evaluating

The goals established during the planning phase are evaluated according to specific desired outcomes also established in that phase. Examples of these are shown in Table 37.10.

To judge whether client outcomes have been achieved, the nurse uses data collected during care, such as skin status over bony prominences and perineal area, nutritional and fluid intake, mental status, signs of healing if an ulcer is present, and so on. If outcomes are *not* achieved, the nurse should explore the reasons why:

- Has the client's physical condition changed?
- Were risk factors correctly identified?
- Were appropriate lifting devices and techniques used?
- Did the client fail to comply with instructions about moving and turning? Why?
- Were appropriate pressure-relieving devices used, and were they applied correctly?
- Was the repositioning schedule adhered to?
- Are the client's nutritional and fluid intake adequate?
- Were appropriate measures used to control incontinence and protect the client's skin?

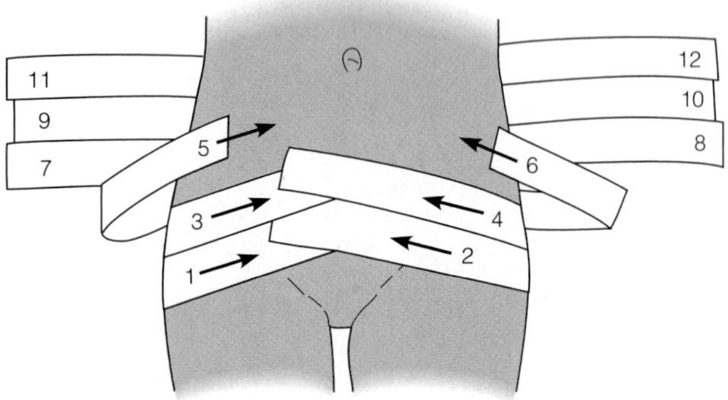

Figure 37.18 Scultetus (many-tailed) binder

TABLE 37.10 Evaluation Goals and Outcomes: Skin Integrity and Wound Healing

Goal	Examples of Desired Outcomes
Maintain skin integrity	Skin intact over bony prominences
	Skin is supple without signs of edema or dehydration
	Skin colour in expected range (e.g., no redness, or redness that blanches and returns to normal within a few minutes)
	Skin temperature within normal range
Promote primary intention wound healing	Wound edges are approximated
	Decrease (or absence) of serosanguineous drainage
	Decrease in surrounding skin inflammation
	Absence of purulent drainage
	Absence of wound odour
Promote secondary intention wound healing	Decrease in length, width, and depth of wound
	Presence of and increase in granulation tissue
	Intact skin surrounding wound
	Decrease (or absence) of drainage
Support the nonhealing wound (palliation)	Pain control
	Infection control
	Odour control
	Absence of further breakdown

- Was the wound supported and immobilized effectively?
- Were stringent aseptic practices implemented when cleaning and changing dressings to prevent infection?
- Was the client receiving anti-inflammatory medications that interfere with healing?
- Was the appropriate dressing applied to keep the wound moist or absorb exudate, or both as needed?

Consider...

What actions you would take if the client did *not* meet the following outcome criteria?

- "Wound edges are approximated" and "Absence of purulent drainage" (Data reveal a 2.5-cm dehiscence at base of wound containing thick yellow discharge.)
- "Skin intact over bony prominences" (Data reveal a stage I decubitus ulcer on the coccyx.)

FOCUS ON CRITICAL THINKING

You have been assigned to care for Mr. Johns, a 74-year-old client being treated for a urinary tract disorder. Mr. Johns suffered a cerebrovascular accident (stroke) six months ago and has had difficulty ambulating and attending to his own needs because of right-sided weakness. While assessing Mr. Johns, you note that he is thin for his height, incontinent of foul-smelling urine, and has deeply reddened areas on his right hip, coccyx, and entire peritoneal area. Mr. Johns is alert and oriented to person, place, and time, but he has decreased sensation on his entire right side. He spends most of his time in bed or sitting at his bedside in a chair due to his difficulty with ambulation.

1. What data suggest that Mr. Johns is particularly vulnerable to pressure sore development?
2. What additional information do you need in order to use the Braden scale to determine Mr. Johns' potential for pressure sore development?
3. What independent measures can you take to protect Mr. Johns' skin from further breakdown?
4. Considering that Mr. Johns does have impaired skin integrity, why is it important to institute treatment for pressure sores at this time?

See Appendix A for answers to these questions.

Heat and Cold

Heat and cold are applied to the body for local and systemic effects. See Table 37.11 for the effects of heat and cold.

Physiological Responses

Local Effects of Heat

Heat is an old remedy for aches and pains; people often equate heat with comfort and relief. Heat causes **vasodilation** and increases blood flow to the affected area, bringing oxygen, nutrients, antibodies, and leukocytes.

Application of heat promotes soft tissue healing and increases suppuration. The increase in blood flow also dissipates the heat, that is, draws it away from the affected area. A possible disadvantage of heat is that it increases capillary permeability, which allows extracellular fluid and such substances as plasma proteins to pass through the capillary walls and may result in edema or an increase in pre-existing edema. Heat is often used for clients with musculoskeletal problems, such as joint stiffness from arthritis, contractures, and low back pain.

Local Effects of Cold

Generally, the physiological effects of cold are opposite to the effects of heat. Cold lowers the temperature of the skin and underlying tissues and causes **vasoconstriction.**

Vasoconstriction reduces blood flow to the affected area and, thus, reduces the supply of oxygen and metabolites, decreases the removal of wastes, and produces skin pallor and coolness. Prolonged exposure to cold results in impaired circulation, cell deprivation, and subsequent damage to the tissues from lack of oxygen and nourishment. The signs of tissue damage due to cold are a bluish purple mottled appearance of the skin, numbness, and sometimes blisters and pain. Cold is most often used for sports injuries (e.g., sprains, strains, fractures) to limit post-injury swelling and bleeding.

Systemic Effects of Heat and Cold

Heat applied to a localized body area, particularly a large body area, may cause excessive peripheral vasodilation, which produces a drop in blood pressure. A significant drop in blood pressure can cause fainting. Clients who have heart or pulmonary disease and who have circulatory disturbances,

TABLE 37.11 Physiological Effects of Heat and Cold

Heat	Cold
Vasodilation	Vasoconstriction
Increases capillary permeability	Decreases capillary permeability
Increases cellular metabolism	Decreases cellular metabolism
Relaxes muscles	Relaxes muscles
Increases inflammation; increases blood flow to an area	Slows bacterial growth; decreases inflammation
Decreases pain by relaxing muscles	Decreases pain by numbing the area, slowing the flow of pain impulses, and by increasing the pain threshold
Sedative effect	Local anesthetic effect
Reduces joint stiffness by decreasing viscosity of synovial fluids	Decreases bleeding

Variables Affecting Physiological Tolerance to Heat and Cold

- *Body part.* The back of the hand and foot are not very temperature sensitive. In contrast, the inner aspect of the wrist and forearm, the neck, and the perineal area are temperature sensitive.
- *Size of the exposed body part.* The larger the area exposed to heat and cold, the lower the tolerance.
- *Individual tolerance.* The very young and the very old generally have the lowest tolerance. Persons who have neurosensory impairments may have a high tolerance, but the risk of injury is greater.
- *Length of exposure.* People feel hot and cold applications most while the temperature is changing. After a period of time, tolerance increases.
- *Intactness of skin.* Injured skin areas are more sensitive to temperature variations.

such as arteriosclerosis, are more prone to this effect than healthy people. With extensive cold applications and vasoconstriction, a client's blood pressure can increase because blood is shunted from the cutaneous circulation to the internal blood vessels. Shivering, a generalized effect of prolonged cold, is a normal response as the body attempts to warm itself.

Thermal Tolerance

Various parts of the body differ in tolerance to heat and cold. The physiological tolerance of individuals also varies. See the box above. Specific conditions necessitate precautions in the use of hot or cold applications:

- *Neurosensory impairment.* People with sensory impairments are unable to perceive that heat is damaging the tissues and are at risk for burns or are unable to perceive discomfort from cold and prevent tissue injury.
- *Impaired mental status.* People who are confused or have an altered level of consciousness need monitoring during applications to ensure safe therapy.
- *Impaired circulation.* People with peripheral vascular disease, diabetes, or congestive heart failure lack the normal ability to dissipate heat via the blood circulation, which puts them at risk for tissue damage with heat and cold applications.
- *Immediately after injury or surgery.* Heat increases bleeding and swelling.
- *Open wounds.* Cold can decrease blood flow to the wound, thereby inhibiting healing.

Adaptation of Thermal Receptors

Heat and cold receptors adapt to temperature changes. When they are subjected to an abrupt change in temperature, the receptors are strongly stimulated initially. This strong stimulation declines rapidly during the first few seconds and then more slowly during the next half hour or more as the receptors adapt to the new temperature (Guyton & Hall, 2000).

Nurses and clients need to understand this adaptive response when applying heat and cold. Clients may be tempted to change the temperature of a thermal application because of the change in thermal sensation following adaptation. Increasing the temperature of a hot application after adaptation can result in serious burns. Decreasing the temperature of a cold application can result in pain and serious impairment of circulation to the body part. See Table 37.12 for temperatures of hot and cold applications.

TABLE 37.12 Temperatures for Hot and Cold Applications

Description	Temperature	Application
Cold	15–18°C	Cold pack
Cool	18–27°C	Cool compresses
Tepid	32–38°C	Sponge bath
Warm	37–40°C	Warm bath, aquathermia pads
Hot	40–43°C	Hot soak, irrigations, hot compresses

Rebound Phenomenon

The rebound phenomenon occurs at the time the maximum therapeutic effect of the hot or cold application is achieved and the opposite effect begins. For example, heat produces maximum vasodilation in 20 to 30 minutes; continuation of the application beyond 30 to 45 minutes brings tissue congestion, and the blood vessels then *constrict* for reasons unknown. If the heat application is continued, the client is at risk for burns because the constricted blood vessels are unable to dissipate the heat adequately via the blood circulation.

With cold applications, maximum vasoconstriction occurs when the involved skin reaches a temperature of 15°C. Below 15°C, vasodilation begins. This mechanism is protective: it helps prevent freezing of body tissues normally exposed to cold, such as the nose and ears. It also explains the ruddiness of the skin of a person who has been walking in cold weather.

An understanding of the rebound phenomenon is essential for the nurse and client. Thermal applications must be halted *before* the rebound phenomenon begins.

Applying Heat and Cold

The application of heat and cold therapies may occur in both dry and moist forms. The choice of a particular modality

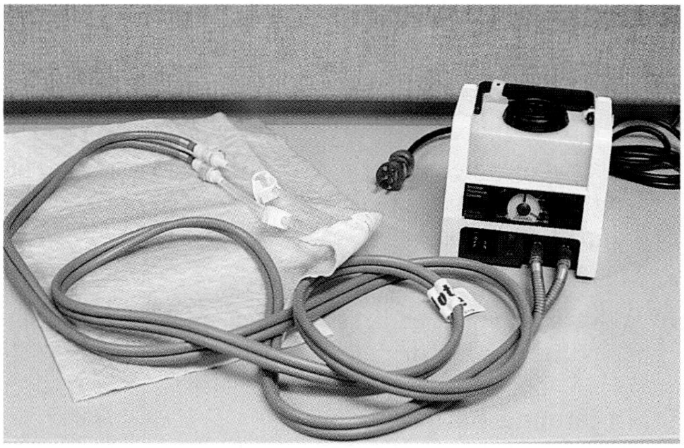

Figure 37.19 An aquathermia heating unit

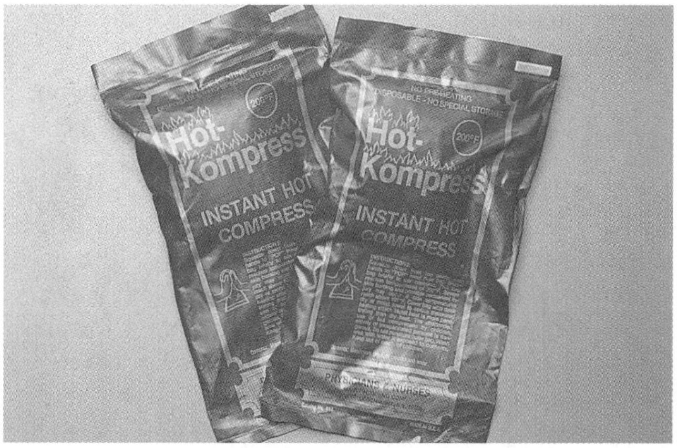

Figure 37.20 Commercially prepared disposable hot packs

is based on its therapeutic effect and the desired response of the client. Since moisture conducts heat more readily, moist heat applications penetrate more deeply into the tissues. Clients receiving moist heat applications, however, are more at risk for burns and skin maceration and, thus, require careful monitoring.

For all local applications of heat or cold, the nurse should follow these guidelines:

- Obtain physician's order if required.
- Consult institutional policies and procedures in relation to heat and cold therapy.
- Identify at-risk individuals or those with conditions that might contraindicate treatment (e.g., altered mental status, bleeding).
- Establish the client's temperature tolerance.
- Explain the application to the client and measures taken to prevent injury.
- Discuss with the client the expected sensations to be felt.
- Thoroughly inspect the area to be treated.
- Check that all equipment is properly functioning (e.g., no damaged cords, intact heating elements).
- Enlist the client's participation in the treatment (e.g., timing of application) and report any discomfort.
- Whenever possible, apply the heat or cold measure in a manner whereby the client can withdraw from it if necessary.
- After initiating the application, place the call system within reach and return 5 to 10 minutes later to observe for any untoward signs. Cease treatment if problems arise (e.g., cold—shivering).
- Evaluate the client's response to the application and document accordingly.

Aquathermia Pad

The *aquathermia* or *aquamatic pad* (also referred to as a *K-pad*) is a pad constructed with tubes containing water. The pad is attached by tubing to an electrically powered control unit that has an opening for water and a temperature gauge (Figure 37.19). Some aquathermia pads have an absorbent surface through which moist heat can be applied. The other surface of the pad is waterproof. These pads are disposable.

To apply an aquathermia pad, the nurse carries out the following steps:

- Fill the reservoir of the unit two-thirds full of *distilled* water.
- Set the desired temperature. Check the manufacturer's instructions. Most units are set at 40.5°C for adults.
- Cover the pad and plug in the unit. Some manufacturers suggest warming the pad before applying it.
- Apply the pad to the body part. The treatment is usually continued for 10 to 15 minutes. Check orders and agency protocol.

Hot and Cold Packs

Commercially prepared *hot* and *cold packs* (Figure 37.20) provide heat or cold for a designated time. Directions on the package tell how to initiate the heating or cooling process, for example, by striking, squeezing, or kneading the pack.

Electric Pads

Electric pads provide a constant, even heat, are lightweight, and can be moulded to a body part. Electric pads, however, can burn. Nurses should advise clients to avoid using the high setting and never to lie on the pad. Some models have waterproof covers for use when the pad is placed over a moist dressing.

In applying electric pads, the nurse follows these guidelines:

- Do not insert sharp objects (e.g., pins) into the pad. The pin could damage a wire and cause an electric shock.
- Ensure that the body area is dry unless there is a waterproof cover on the pad. Electricity in the presence of water can cause a shock.

- Use pads with a preset heating switch so a client cannot increase the heat.
- Do not place the pad under the client. Heat will not dissipate, and the client may be burned.

Ice Bag, Ice Glove, Ice Collar

Ice bags, ice gloves, and ice collars are filled either with ice chips or with an alcohol-based solution. They are applied to the body to provide cold to a localized area (e.g., a collar is often applied to the throat following a tonsillectomy). Always wrap the container in a towel or cover.

Compresses

Compresses can be either warm or cold. A *compress* is a moist gauze dressing applied to a wound. When hot compresses are ordered, the solution is heated to the temperature indicated by the order or according to agency protocol, for example, 40.5°C. When there is a break in the skin or when the body part (e.g., an eye) is vulnerable to microbial invasion, sterile technique is necessary; therefore, sterile gloves are needed to apply the compress, and all materials must be sterile.

Soak

A *soak* refers to immersing a body part (e.g., an arm) in a solution or to wrapping a part in gauze dressings and then saturating the dressing with a solution. Sterile technique is generally indicated for open wounds, such as a burn or an unhealed surgical incision. Determine agency protocol regarding the temperature of the solution. Hot soaks are frequently done to soften and remove encrusted secretions and dead tissue.

Sitz Bath

A *sitz bath*, or hip bath, is used to soak a client's pelvic area. The client sits in a special tub or chair and is usually immersed from the midthighs to the iliac crests or umbilicus. Special tubs or chairs are preferred because when the legs are also immersed, as in a regular bathtub, blood circulation to the perineum or pelvic area is decreased. Disposable sitz baths are also available.

The temperature of the water should be from 40° to 43°C unless the client is unable to tolerate the heat. Determine agency protocol. Some sitz tubs have temperature indicators attached to the water taps. The duration of the bath is generally 15 to 20 minutes depending on the client's health. To provide a sitz bath:

- Verify physician's orders.
- Assist the client into the tub. Provide support for the client's feet; a footstool can prevent pressure on the backs of the thighs.
- Pad edges of sitz bath chair with towels or bath blanket to reduce pressure areas.
- Provide a bath blanket for the client's shoulders, and eliminate drafts to prevent chilling.
- Observe the client closely during the bath for signs of faintness, dizziness, weakness, accelerated pulse rate, and pallor.
- Maintain the water temperature.
- Following the sitz bath, assist the client out of the tub. Help the client to dry.

Tepid Sponge Bath

The purpose of a cooling sponge bath is to reduce a client's fever by promoting heat loss through conduction and vapourization. A *tepid* sponge bath generally refers to one in which the water temperature is 32°C–38°C throughout the bath. A tepid bath may be given with gradual cooling of the water.

The decision to give a tepid sponge bath is generally made only when a marked temperature increase is noted and when the client is not in the chilling (shivering) phase of a fever. Some agencies require a physician's order; others permit a decision by a nurse.

To provide a cooling sponge bath, the nurse should:

- Determine the client's vital signs.
- Protect the client's bed with moistureproof material.
- Sponge the face, arms, legs, back, and buttocks. The chest and abdomen are not usually sponged. Each area is sponged slowly and gently. Rubbing may increase heat production.
- Sponge one body part and then another. The sponge bath should take about 30 minutes. A bath given more quickly tends to increase the body's heat production by causing shivering.
- Discontinue the bath if the client becomes pale or cyanotic, shivers, or if the pulse becomes rapid or irregular.
- Pat each area dry.
- Reassess the vital signs at 15 minutes and after completing the sponge bath.

Hyperthermia and Hypothermia Blankets

Hyperthermia and *hypothermia blankets* are used to increase or decrease a client's body temperature. The blanket has an associated control panel on which the desired temperature is set and the client's core temperature registers. Manufacturer's instructions should be followed closely.

CHAPTER HIGHLIGHTS

- Maintaining skin integrity is an important independent function of nursing.
- Wounds are described as acute or chronic; closed or open; and clean, clean-contaminated, contaminated, or dirty (infected). Wounds are also classified by depth as partial thickness or full thickness. In addition, wounds are classified according to how they are acquired, as incisions, contusions, abrasions, punctures, lacerations, and penetrating wounds.
- A pressure ulcer is any lesion caused by unrelieved pressure that results in damage to underlying tissues. Pressure ulcers usually occur over bony prominences.
- Two other factors that act in conjunction with pressure to produce a pressure ulcer are friction and shearing forces.
- Several factors increase the risk for the development of pressure ulcers: immobility and inactivity, inadequate nutrition, fecal and urinary incontinence, decreased mental status, diminished sensation, excessive body heat, and advanced age.
- There are four stages of pressure ulcer development which vary according to the degree of tissue damage.
- There are two types of wound healing that are distinguished by the amount of tissue loss: primary intention healing and secondary intention healing.
- The wound-healing process has three phases: inflammatory, proliferative, and maturation.
- Major types of wound exudate are serous, purulent, and sanguineous (hemorrhagic). Exudate can be a combination of two or three (e.g., serosanguineous). The process of pus formation is referred to as suppuration.
- The main complications of wound healing are hemorrhage, infection, dehiscence, and evisceration, each of which is identifiable by specific clinical signs and symptoms.
- Factors affecting wound healing include developmental stage, nutritional status, lifestyle, medications, and the presence of infection.
- Several risk assessment tools are available to identify clients at risk for pressure ulcer development. They include scoring systems to evaluate a person's degree of risk.
- Meticulous skin examination of common pressure ulcer sites by the nurse is an important ongoing assessment activity for clients at risk.
- When a pressure ulcer is present, the nurse describes the ulcer in terms of location, size, depth, stage, colour, status of wound margins and surrounding skin, and specific signs of infection, if present.
- Wound assessment is an ongoing process to evaluate healing; the nurse assesses wounds by visual inspection, palpation, and the sense of smell. Essential data for wounds include wound appearance, size, drainage, swelling, pain, and the presence of tubes and drains.
- Laboratory data that may be used to assess the progress of wound healing include leukocyte count, blood coagulation studies, serum protein analysis, and wound cultures. Nurses are usually responsible for obtaining specimens of wound drainage for culture.
- The NANDA nursing diagnoses ***Risk for Impaired Skin Integrity, Impaired Skin Integrity,*** and ***Impaired Tissue Integrity*** apply to clients who have skin wounds or who are at risk for skin breakdown.
- Nursing diagnoses related to clients with existing impaired skin or tissue integrity may include ***Risk for Infection, Pain, Anxiety,*** and ***Body Image, Disturbed.***
- Major goals for clients at risk for skin impairments are to maintain skin integrity and avoid potential associated risks.
- Nursing interventions aimed at preventing skin disruptions include conducting ongoing assessment of risk factors and skin status; providing skin care to maintain skin integrity; ensuring adequate nutrition; implementing measures to avoid skin trauma; providing supportive devices; and client teaching.
- Treatment for pressure ulcers varies according to the stage of the ulcer and agency protocol.
- Major nursing responsibilities related to wound care include preventing infection, preventing further tissue damage, preventing hemorrhage, promoting healing, and preventing skin excoriation around draining wounds.
- Wound care may involve cleaning wounds, changing dressings, maintaining drains, irrigating, inserting packing, and applying bandages and binders.
- The RYB colour code of wounds can assist nurses to provide appropriate nursing interventions for wounds that heal by secondary intention. In this scheme, the nurse protects *red*, cleanses *yellow*, and debrides *black* according to agency policy and physician's orders.
- Various dressing materials are available to protect wounds and to keep the wound bed moist, thus facilitating healing.
- Several synthetic dressings have been developed for use with specific types of wounds. These include transparent adhesive films, impregnated nonadherent dressings, hydrocolloids, hydrogels, polyurethane foams, and exudate absorbers. The nurse must be aware of the specific purposes of each and their indications for use.
- The type of dressing used depends on (1) location, size, and type of the wound; (2) amount of exudate;

(3) whether or not the wound requires debridement, is infected, or has sinus tracts; and (4) such considerations as frequency of dressing change, ease or difficulty of dressing applications, and cost.

- Heat and cold produce specific local physiological and systemic responses that account for their therapeutic effects.
- Various parts of the body differ in tolerance to heat and cold. The physiological tolerance of individuals also varies. Specific conditions, such as neurosensory and circulatory impairments, necessitate precautions when applying heat or cold.
- When applying heat and cold, clients and nurses need to be aware of the effects of thermal receptor adaptation and the rebound phenomenon.

READINGS AND REFERENCES

Suggested Readings

Beaumont, E., & Anderson-Dam, M. (1998, December). Technology scorecard–Wound care science at the crossroads: A guide for selecting from the latest wound care products. *American Journal of Nursing, 98*(12), 16–21.

This article offers basic principles of wound care and nine guidelines for wound management. It also describes three new biological-biosynthetic wound care products introduced in 1998 (Apligraf, Inerpan, and Regranex), odour-control products, such as CarboFlex Odor Control Dressing (ConvaTec), Nexcare Waterproof Bandage with tattoo designs, new easy-to-use wound measuring tools, and latex-free products (dressings, elastic bandages and wraps, gloves, adhesive tape, and liquid adhesive skin protective and adhesive remover).

Related Research

Colin, D., Abraham, P., Preault, L., Bregeon, C., & Saumet, L. J. (1996, May/June). Comparison of 90° and 30° laterally inclined positions in the prevention of pressure ulcers using transcutaneous oxygen and carbon dioxide pressures. *Advances in Wound Care, 9*(3), 35–38.

Pieper, B., Sugrue, M., Weiland, M., Sprague, K., & Heiman, C. (1998, January). Risk factors, prevention methods, and wound care for patients with pressure ulcers. *Clinical Nurse Specialist, 12*(1), 7–14.

Sterling, C. (1996, November). Methods of wound assessment documentation: A study. *Nursing Standard, 11*(10), 38–41.

Selected References

Anthony, D. (1987, August). Norton revises risk scores. *Nursing Times, 83*, 6.

Bergstrom, N., Braden, J. B., Laguzza, A., & Holman, V. (1987, July/August). The Braden Scale for predicting pressure sore risk. *Nursing Research, 36*, 205–210.

Capobianco, M. L., & McDonald, D. D. (1996, November/December). Factors affecting the predictive validity of the Braden Scale. *Advances in Wound Care: The Journal for Prevention and Healing, 9*, 32–36.

Carpenito, L. J. (2002). *Handbook of nursing diagnosis* (9th ed). Philadelphia, PA: Lippincott.

Chang, H., Wind, S., & Kerstein, M. D. (1996, June). Moist wound healing. *Dermatology Nursing, 8*, 174–176, 204.

Dolynchuk, K., & Hull, P. (1999). The role of Apligraf™ in the treatment of venous leg ulcers. *Ostomy/Wound Management, 45*(1), 34–43.

Dolynachuk K., Keast, D., Campbell, K., Houghton, P., Orsted, H., Sibbald, G., & Atkinson, A. (2000, November). Best practices for the prevention and treatment of pressure ulcers. *Ostomy Wound Management, 46*(11), 38–52.

Ferreira, T. B., & Thorpe-Critten, L. (1998, May). Skin wounds: Assessment and care. *The Canadian Nurse, 4*(5), 31–35.

Foster C., Frisch S. R., Denis N., Forler Y., & Jago, M. (1992). Prevalence of pressure ulcers in Canadian institutions. CAST *Journal, II* (2), 23–31.

Gordon, B. (1996, May/June). Conservative sharp wound debridement: State Boards of Nursing positions. *Journal of Wound, Ostomy, and Continence Nursing, 23*, 137–143.

Guyton, A. C., & Hall, J. (2000). *Textbook of medical physiology* (10th ed). Philadelphia, PA: Saunders.

Harrison, M. B., Wells, G., Fisher, A., & Prince, M. (1996, February). Practice guidelines for the prediction and prevention of pressure ulcers: Evaluating the evidence. *Applied Nursing Research, 9*, 9–17.

Hess, C. T. (1998, July). Wound care: Preventing skin breakdown. *Nursing 98*, 7, 28–29.

International Committee on Wound Management. (1996). ICWM World Council consensus statement on cost effective wound care. Evaluating your supply use to prepare for managed care. *Ostomy/Wound Management, 42*(2), 72, 74–76.

Krasner, D., Rodeheaver, G., & Jibbald, G. (2001). *Chronic wound care: A Clinical source book for healthcare professionals* (3rd ed.). Wayne, PA: HMP Publications.

Leaper, D. J., & Gottrup, F. (1998). Surgical Wounds. In D. J. Leaper & K. G. Harding (Eds.), *Wounds: biology and management* (pp. 23–40). London, UK: Oxford University Press.

Maklebust, J. (1987, June). Pressure ulcers: Etiology and prevention. *Nursing Clinics of North America, 22*, 359–377.

Maklebust, J. (1991, December). Pressure ulcer update. *RN, 54*, 56–63.

Maklebust, J. (1996, June). Using wound care products to promote a healing environment. *Critical Care Nursing Clinics of North America, 8*(2), 141–158.

Maklebust, J. (1999). An update on horizontal patient support surfaces: AHCPR Guidelines Revisited. *Ostomoy/Wound Management, 45*(1A Suppl), 70S–77S.

Maklebust, J., & Sieggreen, M. (2000). *Pressure ulcers* (3rd ed.). Springhouse, PA: Springhouse.

Mangram, A. J., Horan, T. C., Pearson, M. L., Silver, L. C., & Jarvis, W. R. The Hospital Infection Control Practices Advisory Committee. (1999). Guidelines for prevention of surgical site infection. *Infection Control and Hospital Epidemiology, 20*, 247–278.

McConnell, E. A. (1997, May). Clinical do's and don'ts: Using dry heat to promote healing. *Nursing, 27*(5), 22.

McConnell, E. A. (1998, June). Clinical do's and don'ts: Applying cold treatment. *Nursing 98, 28*(6), 26.

Motta, G. J. (1993, December). How moisture-retentive dressings promote healing. *Nursing 93, 23*, 26–34.

Mulder, G. D., Haberer, P. A., & Jeter, K. F. (Eds.). (1999). Clinicians' pocket guide to chronic wound repair (4th ed.). Springhouse, PA: Springhouse Corporation.

North American Nursing Diagnosis Association. (2001). *NANDA nursing diagnoses: Definitions and classification 2000–2001*. Philadelphia, PA: Author.

Norton, D. (1975, February). Research and the problem of pressure sores. *Nursing Mirror, 140*, 65–67.

Norton, D., McLaren, R., & Exton-Smith, A. N. (1962, 1975). An investigation of geriatric nursing problems in hospital. Edinburgh, UK: Churchill Livingstone. (Classic).

Ovington, L. G. (1999). Dressing and adjunctive therapies: AHCPR guidelines revisited. *Ostomy/Wound Management, 45*(lA Suppl), 94S–106S.

Panel for the Prediction and Prevention of Pressure Ulcers in Adults. (1992). *Pressure ulcers in adults: Prediction and prevention. Quick reference guide for clinicians.* AHCPR Publication No. 92-0050. Rockville, MD: Agency for Health Care Policy and Research, Public Health Service, U.S. Department of Health and Human Services.

Panel for the Prediction and Prevention of Pressure Ulcers in Adults. (1994). *Pressure ulcers in adults: Prediction and prevention. Clinical practice guideline.* AHCPR Publication No. 95-0653. Rockville, MD: Agency for Health Care Policy and Research, Public Health Service, U.S. Department of Health and Human Services.

Schaffer, D. B. (1997, November). Closed suction wound drainage. *Nursing, 27*(11), 62–64.

Stotts, N. A. (1990, February). Seeing red, yellow, and black. The three-color concept of wound care. *Nursing 90, 20*, 59–61.

Sundberg, J., & Meller, R. (1997). A retrospective review of the use of cadexomer iodine in the treatment of chronic wounds. *Wounds, 9*(3), 68–86.

U.S. Department of Health and Human Services. (1992). Clinical practice guideline. *Pressure ulcers in adults: Prediction and prevention.* Pub no. 9-0047. Rockville, MD: Public Health Service.

VandenBosch, T., Montoye, C., Satwicz, M., Durkee-Leonard, K., & Boylan-Lewis, B. (1996, May). Predictive value of the Braden Scale and nurse perception in identifying pressure ulcer risk. *Applied Nursing Research, 9*, 80–86.

Van Rijswijk, L. (1996, August). The fundamentals of wound assessment. *Ostomy/Wound Management, 42*(7), 40–42, 44, 46, 48–50.

Van Rijswijk, L., & Cuzzell, J. Z. (1991, June). Managing full-thickness wounds. *American Journal of Nursing, 91*, 18, 22.

Van Rijswijk L., & Braden, B. J. (1999). Pressure ulcer patient and wound assessment: AHCPR Guidelines Revisited. *Ostomy/Wound Management, 45*(lA Suppl), 56S–67S.

Woodbury, M. G., Houghton, P. E., Campbell, K. E., & Keast, D. H. (1999). Pressure ulcer assessment instruments: A critical appraisal. *Ostomy/Wound Management, 45*(5), 42–55.

Wysocki, A. B. (1999, Dec.). Skin anatomy, physiology and pathophysiology. *Nursing Clinics of North America, 34*(4), 777–797.

WEBLINKS

National Pressure Ulcer Advisory Panel
www.npuap.org
This U.S. organization developed The Pressure Ulcer Scale for Healing (PUSH Tool) to provide a quick reliable tool to monitor the change in pressure ulcer status over time.

European Pressure Ucler Advisory Panel
www.epuap
The mission of this European organization is to provide the relief to persons suffering from or at risk of pressure ulcers, in particular through research and the education of the public.

Canadian Association of Wound Care
www.cawc.net
Canada's only interdisciplinary organization dedicated to the advancement of wound care practice. Web site provides information on the importance of wound bed preparation and the causes of ulcers.

Association for the Advancement of Wound Care
www.aawc1.com
The Association for the Advancement of Wound Care is a nonprofit organization. It was formed to promote and achieve excellence in education, clinical practice, public policy, and research regarding wound care.

Wound Healing Society
www.woundheal.org
The society is a nonprofit, international organization that provides a forum for discussions among scientists, physicians, licensed practitioners, industrial representatives, and others with interest in the field of wound healing.

University of Toronto, Faculty of Medicine, Continuing Education
www.twhc.ca
The University of Toronto, Faculty of Medicine, Continuing Education offers the International Interdisciplinary Wound Care Course (IIWCC). This course is a one year distance learning program available to all health care disciplines.

Canadian Association of Enterostomal Therapy
www.caet.ca
The CAET is a nursing organization that focuses on the nursing specialty of enterostomal therapy, which explores ostomy, wound, and continence issues. The CAET offers a certificate of Enterostomal Therapy through a distance learning program.

Wound, Ostomy, Continence Nurses Society
www.wocn.org
A United States based international society of nurses who are experts in the care of patients with wound, ostomy, and continence problems.

CHAPTER 38

Nutrition

OBJECTIVES

After completing this chapter, you will be able to:

- Identify essential nutrients and dietary sources of each.
- Describe normal digestion, absorption, and metabolism of carbohydrates, proteins, and fats.
- Explain essential aspects of energy balance.
- Discuss body weight and body mass standards.
- List factors influencing nutrition.
- Outline developmental nutritional considerations.
- Evaluate a diet using Canada's Food Guide for Healthy Eating.
- Discuss essential components and purposes of nutritional screening and nutritional assessment.
- Identify risk factors for and clinical signs of malnutrition.
- Describe nursing interventions to promote optimal nutrition.
- Discuss nursing responsibilities for interventions provided to treat clients with nutritional problems.
- Plan, implement, and evaluate nursing care related to nutritional problems.

Nutrition is the sum of all the interactions between an organism and the food it consumes. In other words, nutrition is what a person eats and how the body uses it. **Nutrients** are organic, inorganic, and energy-producing substances found in foods and required for body functioning. People require the essential nutrients in food for the growth and maintenance of all body tissues and the normal functioning of all body processes.

An adequate food intake consists of a balance of essential nutrients: water, carbohydrates, proteins, fats, vitamins, and minerals. Foods differ greatly in their **nutritive value** (the nutrient content of a specified amount of food), and no one food provides all essential nutrients. In addition, the way in which foods are processed and/or cooked can make a difference in their nutritional value. Nutrients have three major functions: (1) providing energy for body processes and movement, (2) providing structural material for body tissues, and (3) regulating body processes.

In order to understand how the body uses the nutrients that are ingested, one must understand what the terms *metabolism*, *anabolism*, and *catabolism* mean. **Metabolism** refers to the chemical reactions that occur in the body cells. Energy metabolism refers to how the ingested nutrients are transformed into sources that can be used by the body as fuel. This is a continuous process that includes energy-using reactions that build (**anabolism**) and energy-producing reactions that break down (**catabolism**).

As a nurse, being well informed about the ever-changing topic of nutrition is a critical component of health promotion. It is essential that your nutrition knowledge is based on reliable science so that you can be a critical consumer of available information.

Essential Nutrients

The body's most basic nutrient need is water. (Body fluids are discussed in Chapter 40.) Because every cell requires a continuous supply of fuel, the most urgent nutritional need after water is for nutrients that provide fuel, or energy. The energy-providing nutrients are carbohydrates, proteins, and fats. These are called **macronutrients.** Hunger impels people to eat enough energy-providing nutrients to satisfy their energy needs, but no clear-cut body signals lead a person to ingest certain vitamins or minerals, both of which are often referred to as **micronutrients.**

Macronutrients

Carbohydrates

Carbohydrates are composed of the elements carbon (C), hydrogen (H), and oxygen (O) and are of two basic kinds: (1) simple carbohydrates (sugars), and (2) complex carbohydrates (starches and fibre).

Types of Carbohydrates

Sugars Sugars, the simplest of all carbohydrates, are water soluble and are produced naturally by both plants and animals. Sugars may be **monosaccharides** (single molecules) or **disaccharides** (double molecules). Of the three monosaccharides (glucose, fructose, and galactose), glucose is, by far, the most abundant.

Most sugars are produced naturally by plants, especially fruits, sugar cane, and sugar beet. However, lactose, a combination of glucose and galactose, is found in milk. Processed or refined sugars (e.g., table sugar, molasses, and corn syrup) are those that have been extracted and concentrated from natural sources. Processed sugars are added to such foods as soft drinks, cookies, candy, ice cream, and some cereals.

Starches Starches are the insoluble, nonsweet forms of carbohydrate. They are **polysaccharides;** that is, they are composed of branched chains of dozens, sometimes hundreds, of glucose molecules. Like sugars, nearly all starches exist naturally in plants, such as grains, legumes, and potatoes. Starches are processed in various ways, for example, in making such foods as cereals, breads, flour, and puddings.

Fibre Fibre, another type of polysaccharide, is a complex carbohydrate derived from plants that cannot be digested by humans but supplies roughage or bulk to the diet. This bulk satisfies the appetite and also helps the digestive tract to function effectively and to eliminate wastes.

Digestion

Carbohydrates can only be absorbed if they are in the form of a monosaccharide. Through the digestive process, carbohydrates are broken down into absorbable molecules. Most carbohydrate digestion occurs in the small intestine. Fibres are not digested but influence the speed of digestion. Hence, the consumption of fibre contributes to a feeling of satiety because it delays gastric emptying.

Carbohydrate Metabolism

Monosaccharides, in the form of glucose, fructose, and galactose, arrive at the liver where fructose and galactose are converted into glucose. The liver releases the glucose into the blood where the glucose levels are kept fairly constant by various hormones. After the ingestion of foods, the glucose levels are increased. This causes the pancreas to release insulin. The insulin helps move the glucose out of the bloodstream into cells for storage, thus returning the blood glucose levels to normal. Muscle and liver cells can store the excess glucose as glycogen. When blood glucose levels fall below normal, the pancreas is stimulated to release glucagons, and this causes the liver to release glycogen. This returns the blood glucose levels to normal. This simplified overview of carbohydrate metabolism describes how it occurs in healthy individuals. However, this process becomes much more complicated when abnormal nutritional states exist or when an underlying pathological condition is present.

Proteins

Proteins are organic substances composed of amino acids. Like carbohydrates, proteins contain carbon, hydrogen, and oxygen, but proteins also contain nitrogen. Every cell in the body contains some protein, and about three-quarters of body solids are proteins.

Amino acids are categorized as essential or nonessential. **Essential amino acids** are those that cannot be manufactured in the body and must be supplied as part of the protein ingested in the diet. Essential amino acids, threonine, leucine, isoleucine, valine, lysine, methionine, phenylalanine, tryptophan, and histidine, are necessary for tissue growth and maintenance. Arginine appears to have a role in the immune system.

Nonessential amino acids are those that the body can manufacture. The body takes apart amino acids derived from the diet and reconstructs new ones from their basic elements (carbohydrates and nitrogen). Nonessential amino acids include glycine, alanine, aspartic acid, glutamic acid, proline, hydroxyproline, cystine, tyrosine, and serine.

Proteins may be complete or incomplete. **Complete proteins** contain all the essential amino acids plus many nonessential ones. Most animal proteins, including meats, poultry, fish, dairy products, and eggs, are complete proteins. Some animal proteins, however, contain less than the required amount of one or more essential amino acids and, therefore, cannot alone support continued growth. These proteins are sometimes referred to as **partially complete proteins.** Examples are some fish, which have small amounts of methionine, and the milk protein casein, which has little arginine.

Incomplete proteins lack one or more essential amino acids (most commonly lysine, methionine, or tryptophan) and are usually derived from vegetables. If, however, an appropriate mixture of plant proteins is provided in the diet, a balanced ration of essential amino acids can be achieved. For example, a combination of corn (low in tryptophan and lysine) and beans (low in methionine) is a complete protein. Such combinations of two or more vegetables are called **complementary proteins.** Another way to take full advantage of vegetable proteins is to eat them with a small amount of animal protein. Examples are spaghetti with cheese, rice with pork, noodles with tuna, and cereal with milk. See also the discussion of vegetarian diets later in this chapter.

Digestion

Digestion of protein foods begins in the stomach. However, most protein is digested in the small intestine where enzymes break it down into successively smaller molecules and finally into amino acids, the end products of protein digestion. The pancreas secretes the proteolytic enzymes trypsin, chymotrypsin, and carboxypeptidase; glands in the intestinal wall secrete aminopeptidase and dipeptidase.

Protein Metabolism

The liver coordinates the metabolism of amino acids. Protein synthesis is a complicated process that assembles amino acids that can be used to create proteins used by the body. Unlike glucose and fat, amino acids cannot be stored as such. Amino acids can be stripped of their nitrogen and metabolized as an energy source. A person's state of nitrogen balance is an important indicator of what is going on in the body. Normally, a person is in a neutral nitrogen balance state, meaning the amount of nitrogen being made is equal to that being lost. If the protein synthesis exceeds the protein breakdown, as in pregnancy, growth, and recovery from injury, then a positive nitrogen state exists. However, a negative nitrogen state occurs when the protein synthesis is less than the protein breakdown. This negative state could occur during starvation or malnutrition or in the catabolic phase of recovery.

Lipids

Lipids are organic substances that are greasy and insoluble in water but soluble in alcohol or ether. Lipids include triglycerides (fats and oils), phospholipids (lecithin), and sterols (cholesterols). Lipids have the same elements (carbon, hydrogen, and oxygen) as carbohydrates. Triglycerides have proportionally less oxygen and so provide more than double the amount of calories for an equivalent amount of carbohydrate.

Triglycerides

Triglycerides account for about 95 percent of the fats found in foods. They are composed of a glycerol molecule (with a chain of three carbon atoms) with three fatty acids attached. It is important to understand the degree of saturation of the carbon atoms in order to understand how these fatty acids function in the body. Fatty acids are described as saturated or unsaturated according to the relative number of hydrogen atoms they contain. **Saturated fatty acids** are those in which all carbon atoms are filled to capacity (i.e. saturated) with hydrogen; an example is butyric acid found in butter. An **unsaturated fatty acid** is one that could accommodate more hydrogen atoms than it currently does. Omega-3 fatty acids are polyunsaturated fats that have been shown to lower serum triglyceride levels, reduce blood pressure, and decrease factors involved with blood clotting and strokes. Omega-3 fatty acid is found primarily in cold water fish (e.g., albacore, tuna, sardines, lake trout). Alpha-linolenic acid, found in green leafy vegetables, hazelnuts, flax oil, canola oil, soybean products, and walnuts, can, to a limited extent, be converted by the human body into omega-3 fatty acid.

Lipids that are essential for maintaining healthy skin and growth in children are linoleic acid and alpha-linolenic acid. These two components are termed **essential fatty acids** because they cannot be synthesized in the body like all other fatty acids. Essential fatty acids also play a critical role in inflammation and the clotting mechanism.

Saturated fats are generally solid at room temperature. The exceptions being coconut and palm oils. Unsaturated fats have been hydrogenated by adding hydrogen to some of the double bonds to improve the stability and increase the function of the fat or oil. A consequence of hydrogenation is the alteration of the double hydrogen bonds resulting in a shift from the *cis* position to the *trans* position. The result is trans-fats, which are not normally found in nature. The impact of trans-fat on the population is that 2 percent to 4 percent of total caloric intake comes from these fats in the typical North American diet. The negative side is that trans-fats are reported to raise the "bad" cholesterol (LDL) levels.

Phospholipids

Phospholipids contain a glycerol molecule and two fatty acids. They occur naturally in almost all foods. Rich sources include liver, eggs, wheat germ, and peanuts. They work as emulsifiers to keep fats suspended in the blood and other body fluids. They provide structure to the cell membrane and help in the transport of fat-soluble substances across that membrane. Lecithin is the best known phospholipid.

Sterols

Sterols contain carbon, hydrogen, and oxygen arranged in rings. Cholesterol, bile acids, sex hormones, adrenocortical hormones, and vitamin D are sterols. Cholesterol is found in all cell membranes. The cholesterol found in food is just cholestrol—it is neither "good" nor "bad." The terms good and bad cholesterol are related to the **lipoprotein** (a group of compounds made by the body to move water-insoluable lipids) packages that transport the cholesterol through the blood. There are two lipoproteins that play a role in cholesterol levels: low-density lipoproteins (LDLs) and high-density lipoproteins (HDLs). These endogenous lipoproteins carry fat and cholesterol to the tissues for use in energy production and for exchange with other products in cell metabolism. They are classified according to their ratio of fat to protein, and as their concentration of protein increases, their density increases. Because the LDLs carry cholesterol to the cells and deposit it there, they are considered to be the so-called "bad" cholesterol. The HDLs carry cholesterol from the tissues to the liver for catabolism and excretion and so are considered the "good" cholesterol.

Digestion

Although the chemical digestion of fats begins in the stomach, fats are primarily digested in the small intestine. The end products of fat digestion are glycerol and fatty acids. Some fat is excreted in the feces.

Fat Metabolism

Fatty acids and glycerol enter cells where they can be catabolized for energy or rebuilt and stored as triglycerides. Fat metabolism is regulated by hormones. Fat catabolism is regulated by adrenocorticotropin (ACTH), epinephrine, glucagons, and glucocorticoids, whereas the anabolic process is stimulated by insulin.

Micronutrients

A **vitamin** is an organic compound that cannot be manufactured by the body and is needed in small quantities to catalyze metabolic processes. Thus, when vitamins are lacking in the diet, metabolic deficits result. Vitamins are generally classified as fat-soluble or water-soluble. **Water-soluble vitamins** include C and the B-complex vitamins: B_1 (thiamine), B_2 (riboflavin), B_3 (niacin or nicotinic acid), B_6 (pyridoxine), B_9 (folic acid), B_{12} (cobalamin), pantothenic acid, and biotin. The body cannot store water-soluble vitamins; thus, people must get a daily supply in the diet. Water-soluble vitamins can be affected by food processing, storage, and preparation.

Fat-soluble vitamins include vitamins A, D, E, and K. The body can store these vitamins, although there is a limit to the amounts of vitamins E and K the body can store. Therefore, a daily supply of fat-soluble vitamins is not absolutely necessary. Vitamin content is highest in fresh foods that are consumed as soon as possible after harvest.

Minerals are found in organic compounds, as inorganic compounds, and as free ions. Upon oxidation, minerals leave an ash, which can be acidic or alkaline. Calcium and phosphorus make up 80 percent of all the mineral elements in the body. There are two categories of minerals: macrominerals and microminerals. **Macrominerals** are those that people require in daily amounts over 100 mg. They include calcium, phosphorus, sodium, potassium, magnesium, chloride, and sulfur. **Microminerals** are those that people require in daily amounts less than 100 mg. They include iron, zinc, manganese, iodine, fluoride, copper, cobalt, chromium, and selenium.

Common problems associated with the lack of mineral nutrients are iron deficiency resulting in anemia and osteoporosis resulting from loss of bone calcium. Additional information about major minerals associated with the body's fluid and electrolyte balance is given in Chapter 40.

Energy Balance

Energy balance is the relationship between the energy derived from food and the energy used by the body. The body uses energy for voluntary activities, such as walking and talking, and for involuntary activities, such as breathing and secreting enzymes. In theory, one should be able to determine a person's energy balance by comparing their energy intake with their energy output. It is, however, more complex because each person metabolizes and stores nutrients in an unique way although the process is the same.

Traditionally, we have determined one's energy balance by considering the caloric value of the nutrients ingested. Recently, the calorie theory has come into question because it does not fully explain the difficulty that exists with regard to maintaining a normal weight for some individuals with an obesity problem. An alternative approach to energy balance that has been proposed by Montignac (1999) is related to the glycemic potential of nutrients ingested. Both approaches to energy balance will be presented for your consideration.

The Caloric Theory Approach

The amount of energy that nutrients or foods supply to the body is their **caloric value.** A **calorie** is a unit of heat energy. A **small calorie** is the amount of heat required to raise the temperature of 1 gram of water 1°C. This unit of measure is used only in chemistry and physics. A **large calorie (Calorie, kilocalorie [kcal])** is the amount of heat required to raise the temperature of 1 gram of water from 15° to 16°C and is the unit used in nutrition. It was recommended in 1970 that the unit **kilojoule (kJ)**, a metric measurement, replace the kilocalorie. A kilojoule is the amount of energy required when a force of 1 newton (N) moves 1 kilogram of weight to a distance of 1 metre.

One calorie (kcal) equals 4.18 kJ. The energy liberated from the metabolism of food has been determined to be:

- 4 calories/gram (about 16 kJ) of carbohydrates
- 4 calories/gram (about 16 kJ) of protein
- 9 calories/gram (about 37 kJ) of fat

Metabolism refers to all biochemical and physiological processes by which the body grows and maintains itself. Metabolic rate is normally expressed in terms of the rate of heat liberated during these chemical reactions. The **basal metabolic rate (BMR)** is the baseline number of calories required to support involuntary body functions at rest after a 12-hour fast. The **resting energy expenditure (REE)** is similar to the BMR, but with no 12-hour fasting period. The two terms are often used interchangeably. Refer to Table 38.1 (see page 180, Table 7.3 in Dudek, 2001) for the equations to calculate the REE from body weight.

It is estimated that about 10 percent of the caloric intake in a normal mixed diet will be used to digest, absorb, transport, metabolize, and store the nutrients. This is known as the **thermic effect of food.** The remaining percentage of calories consumed is either used to support physical activity or stored as reserve in the form of glycerides or glycogen. The number of calories burned depends on the length and intensity of the physical activity. Also, heavier people will expend more calories than lighter people to perform the same activity.

There are multiple factors that influence a person's BMR. Lean body mass (muscle) requires more calories for maintenance than does adipose (fat) tissue. Thus, men and active children, who have a greater proportion of muscle mass, will have a higher BMR than have women, who have a greater proportion of adipose tissue. Also, this helps explain why our BMR decreases as we lose muscle mass through the aging process, especially if the aging person is sedentary. The thyroid hormones (thyroxine, or T_4 and tri-iodothyrine, or T_3) regulate the BMR. Any abnormalities in these hormone levels will influence the BMR by increasing (hyperthyroidism) or decreasing (hypothroidism) it. Fever and disease states will increase the BMR. Every 0.83°C (1°F) rise in body temperature will increase the BMR by about 7 percent. Increased cell activity associated with pathological conditions, such as cancer, head injury, or trauma, will increase the metabolic demand on the body. Pregnancy and lactation increase the metabolic needs of the body. Living in a very hot or very cold environment will increase the metabolic rate because the body uses more energy to regulate its temperature. During a stressful event, the release of stress hormones will raise the BMR. Ingestion of certain drugs can either increase (e.g., amphetamines) or decrease (e.g., narcotics, muscle relaxants) the BMR.

The Glycemic Index Approach

A food's **glycemic index (GI)** is determined by how quickly blood glucose levels rise after the food, a carbohydrate, is ingested. To understand the tenets of this approach to energy balance, one must understand the metabolic process and the roles of glucagon and insulin. The primary function of carbohydrates is to provide fuel for energy production. After carbohydrates are ingested, they are broken down into glucose. If the glucose is not used immediately, it can be stored by the liver as glycogen. **Glycemic** level refers to the amount of glucose present in the blood. The glycemic peak, or maximum absorption level, occurs about 30 minutes after ingestion of the food. If the glycemic level becomes low, meaning the body is in need of fuel or glucose, the pancreas secretes the hormone glucagon, which re-establishes the glycemic level. If the glycemic levels become high, following a glycemic peak, then the pancreas secretes another hormone, insulin. The role of insulin is to eliminate the excess glucose from the blood and facilitate its storage in the liver or muscles or as glycerides in the adipocytes (fat cells). If a carbohydrate has a high GI, then its ingestion will lead to high levels of glucose in the blood—a condition referred to as **hyperglycemia.** The GI of a food can be altered by the way it is processed or prepared. For example, instant potatoes have a GI of 95; baked potatoes have a GI of 90; potatoes boiled without skin have a GI of 70; and potatoes boiled with skin have a GI of 65 (Table 38.2). (Refer to Table 2.2, p. 43, Dudek, 2001 for a list of glycemic indices for selected foods.)

For some people, maintaining a balance between the blood glucose level and the insulin level is problematic. The result can be a state of hyperinsulinemia, meaning there is excess insulin present in the blood. If the state of hyperinsulinemia persists, glucose is stored in the adipocytes. In addition, this phenomenon is worsened by the development of **insulin resistance,** in which the sensitivity to insulin by the receptors on the cells is diminished. These two problems become classic hallmarks for the development of type 2 diabetes and syndrome X.

For people prone to weight gain, watching their caloric intake may not be sufficient. They may need to pay closer attention to the glycemic index of the carbohydrate than to its caloric value.

Factors Affecting Nutrition

Although the nutritional content of food is important to consider in determining an eating plan, other major factors influence the selection and ingestion of food. Patterns of eating are influenced by stage of development, gender, ethnicity and culture, beliefs about food, personal preferences, religious practices, lifestyle, medications or therapy, state of health, alcohol abuse, advertising, and psychological factors.

Stage of Development

People in rapid periods of growth (i.e., infancy and adolescence) have increased needs for nutrients. Older people, on the other hand, need fewer calories and may need dietary changes in view of the risk of coronary heart disease, osteoporosis, and hypertension. See the section "Nutritional Variations throughout the Life Cycle."

Gender

Nutrient requirements are different for men and women because of body composition and reproductive functions. The larger muscle mass of men means a greater need for calories and proteins. Because of menstruation, women require more iron than men do.

Ethnicity and Culture

The environment in which an individual is raised plays a major role in that person's food preferences and dietary habits. These dietary traditions have been passed on for generations. Dietary practices can include the way in which foods are prepared, what to eat or not to eat when a person is ill or pregnant, foods associated with rites of passage, and the variety of foods that are routinely included in the diet.

When a person is unwell or pregnant, it is important that the nurse understands the ramifications that person's culture will have on his or her overall nutritional state. For example, when giving information to a pregnant woman about her need for increased nutritients, the nurse must know if the information is congruent with the client's ethnic background. If the information is incongruent, then equivalent food sources must be substituted. Teaching this client may also include discussing cultural myths about certain foods.

Nurses should not use a "good food, bad food" approach but, rather, should realize that variations of intake are acceptable under different circumstances. The only "universally" accepted guidelines are (1) to eat a wide variety of foods to provide adequate nutrients, and (2) to eat moderately to maintain correct body weight (Herron, 1991). Food preference probably differs as much among individuals of the same cultural background as it does generally between cultures. Not all Italians like pepperoni, for example, and many undoubtedly eat tacos.

TABLE 38.1 Equations for Predicting Resting Energy Expenditure From Body Weight*

Gender and Age Range (y)	Equation to Derive REE in kcal/day	Gender and Age Range (y)	Equation to Derive REE in kcal/day
Men		Women	
0–3	(60.9 × wt) − 54	0–3	(61.0 × wt) − 51
3–10	(22.7 × wt) + 495	3–10	(22.5 × wt) + 499
10–18	(17.5 × wt) + 651	10–18	(12.2 × wt) + 746
18–30	(15.3 × wt) + 679	18–30	(14.7 × wt) + 496
30–60	(11.6 × wt) + 879	30–60	(8.7 × wt) + 829
>60	(13.5 × wt) + 487	>60	(10.5 × wt) + 596

*According to the World Health Organization (1985). These equations are derived from data on basal metabolism rate (wt = weight in kilograms).
From National Research Council. (1989). *Recommended Dietary Allowances* (10th ed.). Washington, DC: National Academy of Science.

Source: Dudek, S. (2001). *Nutrition essentials for nursing practice* (4th ed.). Philadelphia, PA: Lippincott.

TABLE 38.2 Glycemic Indices of Selected Foods

High (>60)	Moderate (40–60)	Low (<40)
Glucose	Bran muffin	Apple
Gatorade	Bran Chex	Pear
Potato, baked	Orange juice	PowerBar
Cornflakes	Boiled potato	Chocolate milk
Rice cakes	Rice, white	Fruit yogurt, low-fat
Potato, microwaved	Rice, brown	Chickpeas
Jelly beans	Popcorn	P R Bar
Vanilla wafers	Corn	Lima beans
Cheerios	Sweet potato	Split peas, yellow
Cream of wheat, instant	Pound cake	Skim milk
Graham cracker	Banana, overripe	Apricots, dried
Honey	Peas, green	Green beans
Watermelon	Bulgur	Banana, underripe
Bagel	Bake beans	Lentils
Bread, white	Rice, white parboiled	Kidney beans
Bread, whole wheat	Lentil soup	Barley
Shredded wheat	Orange	Grapefruit
Soft drink	All-Bran cereal	Fructose
Mars bar	Pumpernickel bread	
Grape-Nuts cereal	Spaghetti (no sauce)	
Stoned Wheat Thins	Apple juice	
Cream of wheat, regular		
Table sugar		
Raisins		
Oatmeal		
Ice cream		

Source: Dudek, S. (2001). *Nutrition essentials for nursing practice* (4th ed.). Philadelphia: Lippincott.

Beliefs about Food

Beliefs about effects of foods on health and well-being can affect food choices. Many people acquire their beliefs about food from television, magazines, and other media.

Food fads that involve nontraditional food practices are relatively common. A **fad** is a widespread but short-lived interest or practice followed with considerable zeal. It may be based either on the belief that certain foods have special powers or on the notion that certain foods are harmful. Examples of some food fads are given in the next box. Food fads typically appeal to the individual seeking a miracle cure for a disease or the person who desires superior health and wants to delay aging. Some fad diets are harmless, but others are potentially dangerous. Determining the needs that a fad diet fills for the client enables the nurse both to support these needs and to suggest a more nutritious diet.

Personal Preferences

People develop likes and dislikes based on associations with a typical food. Parents are key role models in their child's taste preferences. So, if Mom or Dad like or dislike certain foods, the child will probably have similar preferences. Also, the parents' eating patterns will be mimicked by the child. These preferences and habits are then carried into adulthood.

Individual likes and dislikes can also be related to familiarity. Children often say they dislike a food before they sample it. Some adults are very adventuresome and eager to try new foods. Others prefer to eat the same foods over and over again. Preferences in the tastes, smells, flavours (blends of taste and smell), temperatures, colours, shapes, and sizes of food influence a person's food choices. For example, some people may prefer sweet and sour tastes to

Examples of Food Fads and Myths

- Eating large amounts of yogurt and vitamin E retards aging.
- Honey is healthier than sugar, more readily digested, and a cure for the common cold.
- Cabbage and onions "turn" breast milk.
- Raw eggs, rare lean beef, and oysters increase sexual potency or fertility.
- Yogurt is more nutritious than milk.

bitter or salty tastes. Textures play a great role in food preferences. Some people prefer crisp food to limp food, firm to soft, tender to tough, smooth to lumpy, or dry to soggy.

Religious Practices

Religious practice can influence the food selection and preparation. Some Protestant faiths prohibit consumption of meat, caffeine, or alcohol. Both Orthodox Judaism and Islam prohibit the consumption of pork or pork products. Some religions have strict guidelines for the preparation of foods or the combinations of foods that cannot be ingested at the same time. The nurse must be sensitive to the client's religious beliefs when issues surrounding nutrition become paramount.

Lifestyle

A person's lifestyle is linked to his or her eating patterns. For some individuals, meal preparation is not important. These people rely on restaurants and convenience foods to meet their nutritional needs. Others may place a great deal of importance on what they ingest and how that food is produced and prepared. Whatever a person's lifestyle, the important consideration is to eat nourishing and well-balanced meals. So, it is important that people are well informed about what they are eating.

Eating nourishing, well-balanced meals is not possible for some people. A person's socioeconomic status can play a major role in one's state of nutrition. Some people cannot afford to purchase meat and fresh vegetables. Others may not have access to foods because of their physical state (e.g., cannot walk or drive to buy food). Some people live in institutions where they are totally dependent on caregivers to feed and nourish them.

A person's level of activity also is a factor to consider in determining one's nutritional status. A less active person requires fewer nutrients than does a person who is engaged in heavy physical activity on a regular basis.

Medications and Therapy

The relationship between drugs and nutrition is a critical component for nurses to consider. Some drugs can alter appetite, disturb taste perception, or interfere with nutrient absorption or excretion. Clients should be encouraged to ask their pharmacist if there are known interactions between drugs and foods. For example, consumption of cheese, red wine, or chicken liver can have a very negative reaction in those who take monoamine oxidase inhibitors (MAOIs) for clinical depression. Selected drug and nutrient interactions are shown in Table 38.3. It is important for the client to know if the medications should be taken with food or on an empty stomach. Also, it is important for the clients to tell their pharmacist, physician, and nurse if they are taking any herbal remedies or over-the-counter medications. These nonprescription remedies and drugs can have a negative interaction with prescribed drugs or with foods they are eating. The nurse plays an important role in determining if the client is knowledgeable about taking medications and in reinforcing correct information.

Therapies (e.g., chemotherapy and radiation) prescribed for certain diseases may also adversely affect eating patterns and nutrition. Normal cells of the bone marrow and the gastrointestinal mucosa are naturally very active and particularly susceptible to antineoplastic agents. Oral ulcers, intestinal bleeding, or diarrhea resulting from the toxicity of antineoplastics can seriously diminish a person's nutritional status.

The effects of radiotherapy depend on the area that is treated. For example, radiotherapy of the head and neck may cause decreased salivation, taste distortions, and swallowing difficulties; radiotherapy of the abdomen and pelvis may cause malabsorption, nausea, vomiting, and diarrhea. Many clients feel profound fatigue and anorexia.

Health

An individual's health status greatly affects eating habits and nutritional status. The lack of teeth, ill-fitting teeth, or a sore mouth makes chewing food difficult. Difficulty swallowing (dysphagia) due to a painfully inflamed throat or a stricture of the esophagus can prevent a person from obtaining adequate nourishment. Disease processes and surgery of the gastrointestinal tract can affect digestion, absorption, metabolism, and excretion of essential nutrients. Gastrointestinal and other diseases also create anorexia, nausea, vomiting, and diarrhea, all of which can adversely affect a person's appetite and nutritional status. Gallstones, which can block the flow of bile, are a common cause of impaired lipid digestion. Metabolic processes can be impaired by diseases of the liver. Diseases of the pancreas can affect glucose metabolism or fat digestion. Allergies to foods are a critical factor to consider.

TABLE 38.3 Selected Drug-Nutrient Interactions

Drug	Effect on Nutrition
Acetylsalicylic acid (aspirin)	Decreases serum folate and folacin nutrition
	Increases excretion of vitamin C, thiamine, potassium, amino acids, and glucose
	May cause nausea and gastritis
Antacids containing aluminum or magnesium hydroxide (Maalox)	Decrease absorption of phosphate and vitamin A
	Inactivate thiamine
	May cause deficiency of calcium and vitamin D
Thiazide diuretics (Diuril, HydroDIURIL)	Increase excretion of sodium, potassium, chloride, calcium, magnesium, zinc, and riboflavin
	May cause anorexia, nausea, vomiting, diarrhea, or constipation
Potassium chloride (Kaochlor, K-Lor, Slow-K)	Decreases absorption of vitamin B_{12}
	May cause diarrhea, nausea, or vomiting
	Increases excretion of potassium, magnesium, and calcium
	May cause anorexia, nausea, or vomiting
	Is incompatible with protein hydrolysates
Laxatives	May cause calcium and potassium depletion
	Mineral oil and phenolphthalein (Ex-Lax) decrease absorption of vitamins A, D, E, and K
Antihypertensives	Hydralazine (Apresoline) may cause anorexia, vomiting, nausea, and constipation
	Methyldopa (Aldomet) increases need for vitamin B_{12} and folate
	May cause dry mouth, nausea, vomiting, diarrhea, constipation
Anti-inflammatory agents	Colchicine decreases absorption of vitamin B_{12}, carotene, fat, lactose, sodium, potassium, protein, and cholesterol
	Prednisone decreases absorption of calcium and phosphorus
Antidepressants	Amitriptyline (Elavil) increases food intake (large amounts may suppress intake)
Antineoplastics	Can cause nausea, vomiting, malabsorption, diarrhea

Alcohol Abuse

Excessive alcohol use contributes to nutritional deficiencies in a number of ways. Alcohol may replace food in a person's diet, and it can also depress the appetite. Excessive alcohol can have a toxic effect on the intestinal mucosa, thereby decreasing the absorption of nutrients. The need for vitamin B increases because it is used in alcohol metabolism. Alcohol can impair the storage of nutrients and increase nutrient catabolism and excretion. Alcohol abuse is also associated with liver disease.

Advertising

Food producers try to persuade people to change from the product they currently use to the brand of the producer. Often, popular celebrities are used to influence television viewers' or radio listeners' choices. Advertising is thought to influence people's, particularly children's, food choices and eating patterns. It is interesting to note how foods are laid out in a grocery store and what types of food are close at hand at the checkout counter. Of note is that products such as alcoholic beverages, cakes and other dessert mixes, soups, tea, coffee, frozen dinners, and soft drinks are more heavily advertised than products such as milk, canned seafood, bread, cheese, poultry, vegetables, and fruits (Christian & Greger, 1994).

Psychological Factors

A person's emotional state is a major factor in his or her eating pattern. The role of various neurotransmitters, such as serotonin, is important to consider in relation to mood and food ingestion. For example, through a complex process, the ingestion of carbohydrates boosts the release of serotonin in the brain. The release of serotonin leads to relaxation and a reduction in anxiety. For some people, being upset or distressed will cause them to eat very little. This reduction of food ingestion could be related to the release of increased amounts of epinephrine, which is a component of the stress-response syndrome.

Nutritional Variations throughout the Life Cycle

Neonate to 1 Year

The neonate's fluid and nutritional needs are met by breast milk or formula. Fluid needs of infants are proportionately greater than those of adults because of a higher metabolic rate, immature kidneys, and greater water losses through the skin and the lungs. The latter is largely due to rapid respirations. Therefore, fluid balance is a critical factor. Under normal environmental conditions, infants do not need additional water; however, neonates in very warm environments may require additional fluids. In these cases, water may be prescribed.

The total daily nutritional requirement of the newborn is about 80 to 100 mL of breast milk or formula per kilogram of body weight. The newborn infant's stomach capacity is about 90 mL, and feedings are required every two and a half to four hours.

The newborn infant is usually fed "on demand." **Demand feeding** usually means that the child is fed when hungry. This method tends to decrease the problem of overfeeding or underfeeding the infant. The newborn who is hungry usually cries and exhibits tension in the entire body. During feeding, the infant sucks readily and needs burping after each 30 mL of formula or after five minutes of breast feeding. Burping is done by holding the infant in an upright position while gently patting the back. *Parents should be warned that infant bottles should never be propped up for feeding.* There is a real danger that aspiration or choking could result.

Infants demonstrate satisfaction by slowing their sucking activity or by falling asleep. Once satisfaction has been demonstrated, infants should not be coaxed into finishing the feeding. This could lead to discomfort or overfeeding. When feeding is completed, healthy infants can be placed in a lateral or supine position for sleep during the first six months of life to reduce the risk of sudden infant death syndrome, or SIDS.

Regurgitation, or spitting up, of predigested milk during or after a feeding is a common occurrence during the first year. Although this may be of concern to parents, it does not usually result in nutritional deficiency. Demonstration of adequate weight gain should reassure parents that the infant is receiving adequate nutrition.

The addition of solid food to the diet usually takes place between four and six months of age. Six-month-old infants can consume solid food more readily because they can sit up and have a decreased sucking reflex. Solid foods (strained or pureed) are generally introduced in the following order: cereals (rice), fruits, vegetables (yellow before green), and strained meats. Foods are introduced one at a time, usually with only one new food introduced every five days. With the eruption of teeth at about seven to nine months, the infant is ready to chew and can begin to experience different textures of food. At this time, the infant enjoys finger foods, such as pieces of skinless fruit, dry cereal, or toast.

At about six months of age, infants require iron supplementation to prevent iron deficiency anemia. **Iron deficiency anemia** is a form of anemia caused by inadequate supply of iron for synthesis of hemoglobin. Iron-fortified cereals are usually recommended by six months of age and are continued until the child reaches 18 months.

Weaning from the breast or bottle to the cup takes place gradually and is usually achieved by age one year. Some infants have difficulty giving up the bottle, particularly at nap time or bedtime. Parents should be warned that having the bottle in bed can lead to **bottle mouth syndrome.** The term describes decay of the teeth caused by constant contact with sweet liquid from the bottle. Some dentists advocate brushing or cleaning the infant's teeth to prevent bottle mouth syndrome, especially for the infant who requires a bottle only at nap or bedtime. Weaning from the bottle can be facilitated by increasingly diluting the formula with water until the infant is drinking plain water; most infants do not like to drink plain water. By the age of one year, most infants can be completely fed on table food, and milk intake is about 600 mL per day.

Toddler

Because of a maturing gastrointestinal tract, toddlers can eat most foods and adjust to three meals each day. In addition, by age three years when most of the deciduous teeth have emerged, the toddler is able to bite and chew adult table food. Toddlers' manipulative skills are sufficiently well developed for them to learn how to feed themselves. Before the age of 20 months, most toddlers require help with glasses and cups because their wrist control is limited.

Developing independence may be exhibited through the toddler's refusal of certain foods. Meals should be short because of the toddler's brief attention span and environmental distractions. Often, toddlers display their liking of rituals by eating foods in a certain order, cutting foods a specific way, or accompanying certain foods with a particular drink.

The toddler is less likely to have fluid imbalances than the infant. The toddler's gastrointestinal function is more mature, and the percentage of fluid body weight is lower. A healthy toddler weighing 15 kg needs about 1,250 mL of fluid per 24 hours.

During the toddler stage, the caloric requirement decreases to 1,200 to 1,800 kcal per day because of a decrease in the rate of growth. From one to two years of age, the toddler may be eating a combination of prepared toddler foods and some table foods. Parents should be instructed to read labels carefully and be aware that the table foods offer more variety and are less expensive and more nutritious than prepared toddler foods. Deficiencies of iron, calcium, and vitamins C and A, which are common toddler deficiencies, should also be discussed.

Three-year-olds often use mealtime to control the family conversation and gain attention by their constant chatter and disruption. Parents may need to anticipate the child's needs, make adjustments in their food preparation, and determine the acceptable level of table manners for the child's developmental level. The following suggestions may help parents meet the child's nutritional needs and promote effective parent-child interactions: (1) make mealtime a pleasant time by avoiding tensions at the table and discussions of bad behaviour; (2) offer a variety of simple, attractive foods in small portions, and avoid meals that combine foods into one dish, such as a stew; (3) do not use food as a reward or punish a child who does not eat; (4) schedule meals, sleep, and snack times that will allow for optimum appetite and behaviour; and (5) avoid the routine use of sweet desserts.

Preschooler

The preschooler eats adult foods and should have the required amounts from the four food groups. The preschooler requires 1,600 kcal per day. Parents should become informed about the diet of their child in day-care or preschool settings so that they can be sure of meeting the child's total nutritional needs. Children at this age are very active and may rush through the meal to return to playing. The four-year-old still requires parents' help in cutting meat and may spill milk when pouring from a large container. Parents also need to teach the preschooler how to use utensils and should provide them with the opportunity to practise (e.g., buttering bread). However, four- and five-year-olds often use their fingers to pick food up. Table manners are marginal at best. Active children often require snacks between meals. Cheese, fruits, yogurt, raw vegetables, and milk are good choices. Children at this age may enjoy helping in the kitchen, and both girls and boys should be encouraged to do so.

The preschooler is even less susceptible than the toddler to fluid imbalances. The average five-year-old weighing 20 kg requires at least 75 mL of liquid per kilogram of body weight per day, or 1,500 mL every 24 hours.

School-Age

Nutrition continues to be a high priority for growing children. School-age children require a balanced diet, including 2,400 kcal per day. School-age children eat three meals a day and one or two nutritious snacks. Children need a protein-rich food at breakfast to sustain the prolonged physical and mental effort required at school. Studies have shown that children who skip breakfast become inattentive and restless by late morning and have decreased problem-solving ability. Undernourished children become fatigued easily and face a greater risk of infection, resulting in frequent absences from school.

The average healthy eight-year-old weighing 30 kg requires about 1,750 mL of fluid per day. Many school-age children have only one meal a day with their family, at dinner. Mealtime should be a social time enjoyed by all, and parents should refrain from discussing a child's poor eating habits at this time. Parents should be aware that children learn many of their food habits by observing their parents. Eating a balanced diet should be the norm for both parents and children.

The school-age child generally eats lunch at school. The child may bring lunch from home or buy lunch at the school cafeteria. Many dietary problems stem from this independence in food choices. The children may trade their food, not eat lunch at all, or buy sweets or junk food with their lunch money. Parents should discuss with the child the foods that they should eat and continue to provide a balanced diet in the home setting.

Poor eating habits may result in obesity. Obesity in school-age children tends to result in decreased activity as well as psychosocial problems. Obese children may be ridiculed by their peers and discriminated against by peers and adults. Such behaviour reinforces an already low self-esteem. Counselling should include the following:

- Reviewing the child's eating habits, including snacks
- Altering meal content
- Using rewards other than food
- Regular exercise

Adolescents

The adolescent's need for nutrients and calories increases, particularly during the growth spurt. In particular, the need for protein, calcium, vitamin D, iron, and B vitamins increases during adolescence. An adequate diet for an adolescent is three to four servings of milk products daily as well as appropriate amounts of meat, vegetables, fruits, breads, and cereals.

Many parents may observe that teenagers, particularly boys, seem to be eating all the time. Teenagers have active lifestyles and irregular eating patterns. They tend to diet or snack frequently, often eating high-calorie foods, such as doughnuts, soft drinks, ice cream, and fast foods. Parents and nurses can promote better lifelong eating habits by encouraging teenagers to eat healthy snacks. Parents can provide healthy snacks, such as fruits and cheese, and, at the same time, limit the amount of "junk food" available in the home. The teenager's food choices relate to physical, social, and emotional factors and impulses and may not be influenced by teaching. Nurses need to advise parents that adolescents must take responsibility for their decisions in many areas of life, and parents should avoid conflicts that relate to food.

Common problems related to nutrition and self-esteem among adolescents include obesity, anorexia nervosa, and bulimia. **Obesity** is a common problem of the preadolescent period and continues to be a problem in the adolescent period. It is estimated that 10 to 16 percent of people between the ages of 10 and 19 years are obese. Obese adolescents are frequently rejected by their peers, badgered by their parents, and ridiculed on television and in the movies. Many feel ugly and socially unacceptable. Depression is not unusual among obese adolescents. Treatment of obesity in this age group includes education on nutrition as well as assessment of psychosocial problems that may produce overeating.

Under social pressure to be slim, some adolescents severely limit their food intake to a level significantly below that required to meet the demands of normal growth. In some instances, the adolescent may develop an eating disorder, such as anorexia or bulimia. Anorexia nervosa and bulimia are severe psychophysiological conditions usually seen in adolescent girls and young women. **Anorexia nervosa** is characterized by a prolonged inability or refusal to eat, rapid weight loss, and emaciation in persons who continue to believe they are fat. People with anorexia may also induce vomiting and use laxatives and diuretics to remain thin. **Bulimia** is an uncontrollable compulsion to consume enormous amounts of food and then expel it by self-induced vomiting or by taking laxatives. These illnesses are most effectively treated in the early stages by psychotherapy. Hospitalization may be necessary when the effects of malnutrition become life threatening.

Young Adult

The nutritional habits established during young adulthood often lay the foundation for the patterns maintained throughout a person's life. Many young adults are aware of the four food groups but may not be knowledgeable about how many servings of each group they need or how much constitutes a serving. The nurse should provide the young adult client with such resources as a chart or list that contains the foods and the amounts needed in each category.

Young adult females are at risk for developing iron deficiency anemia because of blood loss during their menstrual cycle. Therefore, they need to ensure that they are consuming adequate amounts of iron. Iron-rich foods include red meats, organ meats (liver and kidney), eggs, lentils, sole, cashews, molasses, broccoli, spinach, cooked oatmeal, raisins, and prune juice.

The problems of obesity and hypertension may begin during young adulthood. Obesity may occur during the young adult years as the active teen becomes the sedentary adult but does not decrease caloric intake. The overweight or obese young adult is at risk for hypertension, a major health problem for this age group.

Middle-Aged Adult

Middle-aged adults should follow a meal plan that is congruent with their activity levels and state of health. This means that there may need to be a reduction in the amount of food that is eaten on a regular basis. Also, persons in this group need to be aware of their triglyceride levels and cholesterol (LDLs, HDLs, and total cholesterol) and plan their nutritional intake accordingly. Individuals need to be cognizant of the type of fats they are consuming. In the case of some individuals, it is necessary to monitor the type of carbohydrate and its GI. There is no evidence that vitamins or other supplements are needed unless they are specifically prescribed by a physician because of signs of nutritional deficiency or because of an insufficient diet. Two thousand to 3,000 mL of fluid should be included in the daily diet. Postmenopausal women need to ingest sufficient calcium and vitamin D to prevent **osteoporosis** (a decrease in bone density).

Middle-aged adults who gain weight may not be aware of some common facts about this age period. Decreased metabolic activity and decreased physical activity mean a decrease in caloric need. The nurse's role in nutritional health promotion is to counsel clients to prevent obesity by reducing caloric intake and participating in regular exercise. Clients should also be warned that being overweight is a risk factor for many chronic diseases, such as type 2 diabetes and hypertension, and for problems of mobility, such as osteoarthritis.

For the client who requires additional management resources, a variety of programs are frequently available. Most programs use behaviour modification techniques and group support to assist clients in reaching their goals. Clients should seek medical advice before considering any major changes in their eating patterns.

Older Adults

Older adults should follow a meal plan congruent with their state of health, which may be deteriorating or may include one or more chronic conditions. Portion sizes may need to be reduced if the person is sedentary. Some older adults may need more carbohydrates for fibre and bulk, but most nutrient requirements remain relatively unchanged. Such physical changes, such as tooth loss and impaired sense of taste and smell, may also affect eating habits. Decreased saliva and gastric juice secretion may also affect a person's nutrition.

Psychosocial factors may also contribute to nutritional problems. Some older people who live alone do not want to cook for themselves or eat alone. As a result, they may adopt poor dietary habits. Death of the spouse, anxiety, depression, dependence on others, and lowered income all affect eating habits. See Table 38.4. Guidelines for the inclusion of high-nutrient foods that are compatible with the nutritional needs of older adults are summarized in the box on page 985.

TABLE 38.4 Problems Associated with Nutrition in Older Adults

Problem	Nursing Interventions
Difficulty chewing (may lead to a deficiency in vitamins A and C, minerals, and fibre)	Encourage regular visits to the dentist to have teeth and dentures repaired, refitted, or replaced.
	Chop fruits and vegetables finely; shred green, leafy vegetables; select ground meat, poultry, or fish.
Lowered glucose tolerance	Eat more carbohydrates (e.g., whole-wheat breads, cereals, brown rice, pasta, potatoes, and legumes) rather than sugar-rich foods.
Decreased social interaction, loneliness	Promote appropriate social interaction at meals, when possible.
	Encourage the client and spouse to take an interest in food preparation and serving, perhaps as an activity they can do together.
	If food preparation is not possible, suggest community resources, such as Meals-on Wheels.
	Suggest picnics in the yard or inviting friends over for meals.
Loss of appetite and senses of smell and taste	Eat essential, nutrient-dense foods first; follow with desserts and low-nutrient-density foods.
	Review dietary restrictions, and find ways to make meals appealing within these guidelines.
	Eat small meals frequently instead of three large meals a day.
Limited income	Suggest using generic brands and coupons.
	Substitute milk, dairy products, and beans for meat.
	Avoid convenience foods, if able to cook. Buy foods that are on sale and freeze for future use.
	Suggest community resources and nutrition programs.
Difficulty sleeping at night	Have the major meal at noon and a lighter meal in the evening.
	Avoid tea, coffee, or other stimulants in the late afternoon or evening.

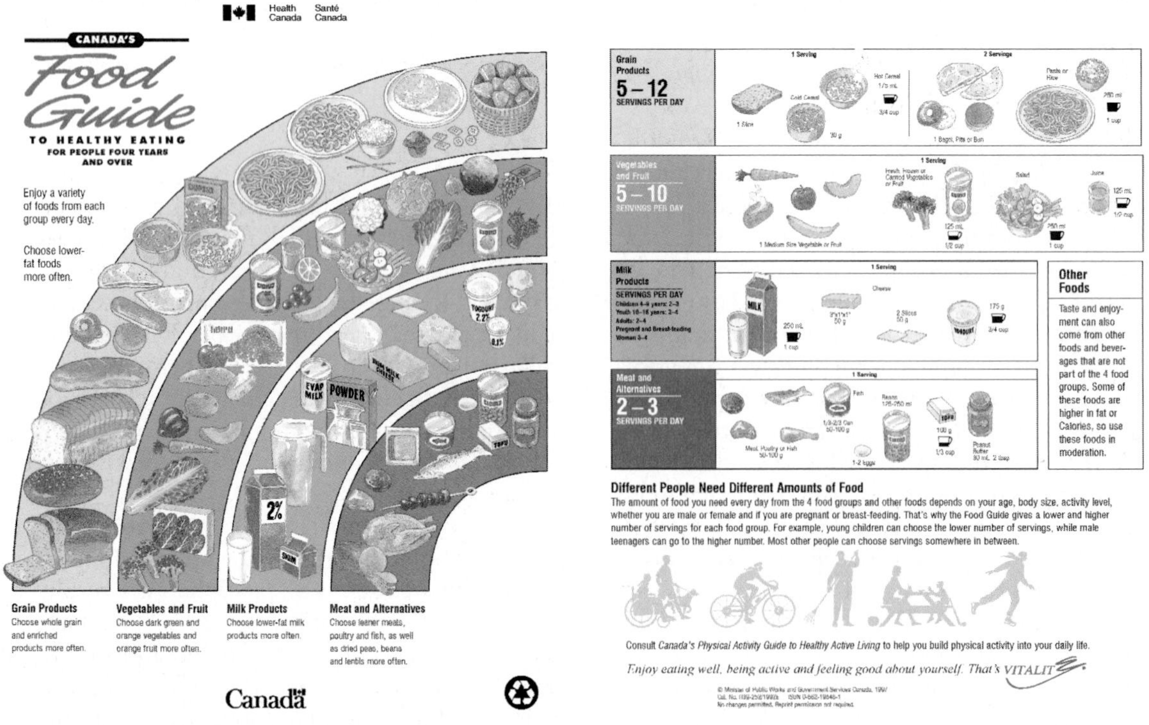

Figure 38.1 Canada's Food Guide to Healthy Eating

Source: Reproduced with permission from *Canada's Food Guide to Healthy Eating, Health Canada, 1992* © Minister of Public Words and Government Services Canada, 2002.

WELLNESS TEACHING

Nutrition for Older Adults

- *Include at least the minimal number of servings from each of the following groups:*

Grain products	5–12 servings
Vegetables and fruits	5–10 servings
Milk products	2–4 servings
Meat and alternatives	2–3 servings

- *Reduce caloric intake.* Caloric needs generally decrease in older people often because of decreased activity. Older adults need to consume nutrient-dense foods and avoid foods that are high in calories but have few nutrients ("empty-calorie" foods).
- *Reduce fat consumption.* Use leaner cuts of meat, and limit portions to 100 to 150 g per day. (But be sure intake of meat group is sufficient, because older people often consume inadequate amounts of these foods.) Broil, boil, or bake foods instead of frying them. Use low-fat milk and cheese; limit intake of butter, margarine, and salad dressings.
- *Reduce consumption of empty calories.* Substitute fruit or puddings made with low-fat milk in place of pastry, cookies, and rich desserts.
- *Reduce sodium consumption for clients who have hypertension or other cardiac problems.* Avoid canned soups, ketchup, mustard. Avoid salted, smoked, cured, and pickled meats (e.g., ham and bacon), poultry, and fish. Do not add salt when cooking foods or at the table.
- *Ensure adequate calcium intake (at least 800 mg) to prevent bone loss.* Milk, cheese, yogurt, cream soups, puddings, and frozen milk products are good sources.
- *Ensure adequate vitamin D intake.* Vitamin D is essential to maintain calcium homeostasis. Include milk because other dairy products are not usually fortified with vitamin D. If milk cannot be tolerated because of a lactose deficiency, provide vitamin supplements.
- *Consume fibre-rich foods to prevent constipation and minimize use of laxatives.* Because fibre-rich foods provide bulk and a feeling of fullness, they help people control their appetites and lose weight.
- *Ensure adequate fluid intake.*

WELLNESS TEACHING

Reducing Dietary Fat

- Cook meat by grilling, baking, broiling, or microwaving rather than frying.
- Substitute air-popped popcorn or pretzels for such snacks as potato chips, cheese puffs, corn chips, and nuts.
- Read labels. Some crackers, for example, are high in fat; others are not.
- Limit desserts high in fat, such as candy, ice cream, cake, and cookies.
- Substitute hard candies for chocolate bars.
- Use skim or reduced-fat milk instead of whole milk for drinking as well as in recipes.
- Use less butter or margarine on breads.
- Remove fat from meat and skin from chicken before cooking.
- Choose leaner meats, poultry, and fish.
- Use less dressing or low-fat dressings on salads.
- Eat plant sources of protein (e.g., kidney, lima, and navy beans).

Standards for a Healthy Diet

Various daily food guides have been developed to help healthy people meet the daily requirements of essential nutrients and to facilitate meal planning. Food group plans emphasize the general types or groups of foods, rather than the specific foods, because related foods are similar in composition and often have similar nutrient values. For example, all grains, whether wheat or oats, are significant sources of carbohydrate, iron, and the B vitamin thiamine. Daily food guides that are currently used include *Canada's Food Guide to Healthy Eating.*

Canada's Food Guide to Healthy Eating

Canada's Food Guide to Healthy Eating includes dietary guidelines for Canadians four years old and over. The food guide depicts a rainbow comprising four arcs. The smallest arc represents meat and alternative protein sources because this category of foods should comprise the smallest portion (two to three servings) of daily nutrients. Milk products forms a larger arc and more servings per day depending on the person's age. Vegetables and fruits are represented (five to 10 servings) in the next larger arc. The largest arch represents grain products because this is the category that most of food intake (five to 12 servings) should come from. The guidelines stress that one should choose a variety of foods from within each of the four groups.

Foods selected according to the guide supply 1,000 to 1,400 kcal. Those who need more calories or nutrients should increase the number and size of servings from the various groups and/or add other foods. Recommendations also include a decrease in fat consumption and limited use of salt, alcohol, and caffeine. See Nutrition Recommendations for Canadians in the box right.

Food Labels

To be knowledgeable about the food that one is ingesting, it is helpful to read the food labels on packaged food stuffs. Each label will contain the ingredients in order of proportion. Also, the number of calories supplied for each serving is indicated. The caloric content is further subdivided into proteins, carbohydrates, and fats. Fats are categorized further into saturated, monosaturated, or unsaturated. Some packages may list the sodium or potassium content as well.

Vegetarian Diets

People may become vegetarians for economic, health, religious, ethical, or ecological reasons. There are two basic vegetarian diets: those that use only plant foods and those that include milk, eggs, and dairy products. Some people eat fish and poultry but not beef, lamb, or pork; others eat only fresh fruit, juices, and nuts; and still others eat plant foods and dairy products but not eggs. See the Types of Vegetarians box below.

Nutrition Recommendations for Canadians

- The Canadian diet should provide energy consistent with the maintenance of body weight within the recommended range.
- The Canadian diet should include essential nutrients in amounts recommended.
- The Canadian diet should include no more than 30 percent of energy as fat (33 g/1,000 kcal) and no more than 10 percent as saturated fat (11 g/100 kcal).
- The Canadian diet should provide 55 percent of energy as carbohydrate (138 g/1,000 kcal) from a variety of sources.
- The sodium content of the Canadian diet should be reduced.
- The Canadian diet should include no more than 5 percent of total energy as alcohol, or two drinks daily, whichever is less.
- The Canadian diet should contain no more caffeine than the equivalent of four regular cups of coffee per day.
- Community water supplies containing fluoride less than 1 mg/L should be fluoridated to that level.

Source: Health Canada *Nutrition Recommendations 1990.* Ottawa, 1996, Health Canada. Reproduced with the permission of the Minister of Supply and Services Canada, 1996.

Types of Vegetarians

Type	Description
Vegans	Strict vegetarians; avoid all foods of animal origin
Lacto-ovo-vegetarians	Use dairy products and eggs but avoid eating flesh
Lacto-vegetarians	Use dairy products but avoid eating flesh and eggs
Ovo-vegetarians	Use eggs but avoid dairy products and flesh
Pesco-vegetarians	Use dairy products, eggs, and fish but avoid all meat products
Partial vegetarians (semi-vegetarians)	Avoid selected meats (e.g., red meat)
Fruitarians	Use only fresh (raw) fruits, juices, nuts, honey, and/or olive oil
Macrobiotic vegetarians	Progress through 10 dietary stages from a widely inclusive selection to a restrictive selection

Combinations of Plant Proteins That Provide Complete Proteins

Grains plus legumes = complete protein
Legumes plus nuts or seeds = complete protein
Grains, legumes, nuts, or seeds plus milk or milk products (e.g., cheese) = complete protein

Grains	Legumes	Nuts and Seeds
brown rice	black beans	almonds
barley	kidney beans	Brazil nuts
corn meal	lima beans	cashews
millet	soybeans	pecans
oats/oatmeal	lentils	walnuts
rye	tofu	pumpkin seeds
whole wheat	black-eyed peas	sesame seeds
	split peas	sunflower seeds

Examples: black-eyed peas and rice
lentil soup and whole wheat bread
beans and tortillas
lima beans and sesame seeds

or

cereal with milk
macaroni with cheese

Vegetarian diets can be nutritionally sound if they include a wide variety of foods and if proper protein complementation and vitamin and mineral supplementation are provided. Because the proteins found in plant foods are incomplete proteins, vegetarians must eat complementary protein foods to obtain all the essential amino acids. A plant protein can be *complemented* by combining it with a different plant protein. The combination produces a complete protein. See the box opposite. Obtaining complete proteins is especially important for growing children and pregnant and lactating women, whose protein needs are high. Generally, legumes (starchy beans, peas, lentils) have complementary relationships with grains, nuts, and seeds. Complementary foods must be eaten in the same meal. Such diets as the fruitarian diet do not provide sufficient amounts of essential nutrients and are not recommended for long-term use.

Foods of animal origin are the best source of vitamin B_{12}. Therefore, vegans (strict vegetarians) need to obtain this vitamin from other sources: brewer's yeast, foods fortified with vitamin B_{12}, or a vitamin supplement. Because iron from plant sources is not absorbed as efficiently as iron from meat, vegans should eat iron-rich foods (e.g., green leafy vegetables, whole grains, raisins, and molasses) and iron-enriched foods. They should eat a food rich in vitamin C at each meal to enhance iron absorption. Calcium deficiency is a concern only for strict vegetarians. It can be prevented by including in the diet soybean milk and tofu (soybean curd) fortified with calcium and leafy green vegetables.

Altered Nutrition

Malnutrition occurs when the nutritional reserves are depleted and the nutrients being ingested are insufficient to meet day-to-day demands or the demands placed on the body by added metabolic stress. Malnutrition can occur even though the person is ingesting a large number of calories. For example, a person who primarily eats processed foods high in fats and carbohydrates may have a major deficiency of protein. Improper digestion and absorption of food may lead to malnutrition. An inadequate food intake may be caused by the inability to acquire and prepare food, inadequate knowledge about essential nutritients and a balanced diet, discomfort during or after eating, **dysphagia** (difficulty swallowing), **anorexia** (loss of appetite), or nausea or vomiting. Improper digestion and absorption of nutrients may be caused by an inadequate production of hormones or enzymes or by underlying pathological conditions resulting in inflammation or obstruction of the gastrointestinal tract.

A malnourished person may have greater than or less than **ideal body weight** (IBW). Ideal body weight is the weight recommended for optimal health. To determine an individual's IBW, the nurse can consult a standardized table, such as the Metropolitan Life Insurance Company Height and Weight Table, or can quickly calculate an approximate body weight by using the Rule of 5 for women and the Rule of 6 for men. See the box below. These approximate weights can be increased or decreased by 10 percent depending on the person's body frame.

Inadequate nutrition may be associated with weight loss, but not always. It is, however, associated with generalized weakness, altered functional ability, delayed wound healing, increased susceptibility to infection, decreased immunocompetence, and impaired pulmonary function. In the case of the hospitalized patient, malnutrition may prolong the length of time spent in the hospital. When a person is experiencing malnutrition, the stored glycogen is mobilized from the muscle and liver stores. These sources can only last for about 24 hours, and then the body fat stores are mobilized in the form of ketones, an alternative fuel to glucose.

Protein-calorie malnutrition (PCM), once associated with starvation in the developing countries, is now recognized as a significant problem for clients with long-term deficiencies in caloric intake (e.g., elderly, fad dieters, those with chronic diseases or who live in institutions). Characteristics of PCM are weakness, apathy, increased risk of infection, poor drug tolerance, and poor wound healing.

To calculate an individual's percent of ideal body weight use this formula:

$$\% \text{ IBW} = \frac{\text{Actual body weight (ABW)}}{\text{Ideal body weight (IBW)}} \times 100$$

Approximating Ideal Body Weight

Rule of 5 for females:	Rule of 6 for males:
45 kg for 1.5 metres of height	48 kg for 1.5 metres of height
+ 2.3 kg for each 2.5 cm over 1.5 metres	+ 2.8 kg for each 2.5 cm over 1.5 metres
± 10% for body-frame size	± 10% for body-frame size

Calculating and Interpreting Percentage of Ideal Body Weight (IBW)

>120% of IBW	Obese
110–120% of IBW	Overweight
90–110% of IBW	IBW
80–90% of IBW	Mildly underweight
70–80% of IBW	Moderately underweight
<70% of IBW	Severely underweight

Generally accepted standards for interpreting percent of IBW are shown in the previous box.

Excess body weight places people at risk for multiple health problems. Adipose tissue located in the visceral area of the abdomen is the most significant to the development of disease conditions. People with visceral fat are more prone to developing a metabolic disorder known as syndrome X. This syndrome includes cardiovascular disease, type 2 diabetes, and hypertension. In addition, fat located in the abdominal area is highly correlated with obstructive sleep apnea. Men are more likely to develop deposits of visceral fat, especially in midlife. Post-menopausal women also increase the likelihood of developing abdominal obesity.

Adipose tissue located in the peripheral areas of the body does not place the individual at such a high risk for developing other health problems as does abdominal obesity, but it can lead to problems related to mobility, the development of varicose veins, and it increases the risk of developing osteoarthritis in weight-bearing joints. Peripheral obesity can also contribute to psychological problems associated with a person's attempts to achieve a more perfect body shape because it seems that reducing the size of one's thighs, upper arms, or hips can be difficult.

The Nursing Care Process

It is important in the care of all individuals that nurses consider the nutritional status of their patients or clients. Nutritional states are often overlooked until a major health problem is presented. Nutrition is one area that the nurse can focus on in the promotion of a healthy lifestyle and illness prevention. In order to assist a patient or client to improve an existing health problem or to achieve an optimal nutritional state, the nurse needs to conduct an assessment of the patient, develop and implement appropriate nursing interventions, and then evaluate the effectiveness of the intervention.

Nutritional Assessment

The purpose of a nutritional assessment is to gather and interpret data to determine the client's nutritional status and to identify problems. A nutritional assessment is a collaborative endeavour. The nurse can conduct the initial nutritional assessment, and if deemed necessary, additional in-depth screening may be performed by a nutritionist or dietician and the physician. Table 38.5 provides an overview of data that should be included in a nutritional assessment.

TABLE 38.5 Components of a Nutritional Assessment

Dietary Data	■ Diet history ■ 24-hour food recall ■ Food diary ■ Mood and food ingestion ■ Usual eating pattern ■ Food preferences ■ Food allergies/intolerances ■ Ability to prepare food ■ Eating companions	**Anthropometric Data**	■ Height ■ Weight ■ Weight change ■ Usual/ideal weight ■ BMI ■ Waist circumference ■ WHR ■ Skinfold thickness (optional)
Health Data	■ Detailed history of current/past health states ■ Family history ■ Physical activity level ■ Physical ability ■ Use of tobacco ■ Alcohol consumption ■ Drugs—prescribed and over-the-counter/herbal remedies/recreational drugs	**Physical Examination**	■ Manifestations of malnutrition ■ Presence of edema
		Laboratory Data	■ Hemoglobin ■ Hematocrit ■ Serum albumin ■ Serum transferrin ■ Urinary urea nitrogen (UUN) ■ Urinary creatinine excretion ■ Total lymphocyte count (TLC) ■ Total serum cholesterol ■ LDL ■ HDL ■ Fasting blood glucose level ■ TSH ■ Blood urea nitrogen (UN) ■ Serum creatinine

Summary of Risk Factors for Nutritional Problems

Diet History

- Chewing or swallowing difficulties (including ill-fitting dentures, dental caries, and missing teeth)
- Inadequate food intake
- Restricted or fad diets
- No nutrient intake for 10 or more days
- Intravenous fluids (other than total parenteral nutrition for 10 or more days)
- Inadequate food budget
- Inadequate food preparation facilities
- Inadequate food storage facilities
- Physical disabilities
- Living and eating alone

Medical History

- Unintentional weight loss or gain of 10 percent within six months
- Fluid and electrolyte imbalance
- Oral and gastrointestinal surgery
- Dental problems: difficulty chewing, ill-fitting dentures
- Gastrointestinal problems: anorexia, dysphagia, nausea, vomiting, diarrhea, constipation
- Chronic illness: end-stage renal disease, liver disease, human immunodeficiency virus (HIV) infection, chronic obstructive pulmonary disease (COPD), cancer
- Alcohol or substance abuse
- Neurological or cognitive impairment
- Catabolic or hypermetabolic condition: burns, trauma
- Adolescent pregnancy or closely spaced pregnancies

Medication History*

- Aspirin
- Antacid
- Antidepressants
- Antihypertensives
- Anti-inflammatory agents
- Antineoplastic agents
- Digitalis
- Laxatives
- Diuretics (thiazides)
- Potassium chloride

*The potential effects of some medications on nutrition are shown in Table 38.3 on page 980.

Nutritional Screening

The nurse may use a screening tool, such as the Subjective Global Assessment (SGA), to determine the nutritional status of a client. The data collected on the SGA can then be incorporated into the nursing history. Clients who are found to be at moderate or high risk are followed up with a comprehensive assessment by the dietician. See Summary of Risk Factors in the box left.

The Subjective Global Assessment (SGA), reported by Baker and colleagues (1982) and Detsky and colleagues (1987), is a method of subjectively classifying clients as either well nourished, moderately malnourished, or severely malnourished on the basis of a dietary history and physical examination. The SGA dietary history consists of five key components:

1. History of weight loss over the preceding six months and two weeks
2. Current pattern of dietary intake in comparison with the usual pattern
3. Presence of gastrointestinal symptoms that may reduce food intake
4. Functional capacity, which ranges from bedridden to fully ambulatory
5. Primary medical diagnosis and metabolic demands created by the underlying disease

The SGA physical examination emphasizes three features:

1. Loss of subcutaneous fat
2. Muscle wasting
3. Presence of edema and ascites

These physical features are scored as normal (0), mild (1), moderate (2), and severe (3).

The authors of the SGA report that they were able to provide approximately 80 percent positive identification of malnutrition when comparing the SGA with traditional assessment methods that included anthropometrics and laboratory tests. Because the SGA is a subjective assessment, the effectiveness of the tool depends largely on the experience of the health-care professional collecting and interpreting the data.

Physical Examination

Physical examination reveals nutritional deficiencies and excesses in addition to obvious weight changes. Assessment focuses on rapidly proliferating tissues, such as skin, hair, nails, eyes, and mucosa, but also includes a systematic review comparable with any routine physical examination. Clinical signs associated with malnutrition are provided in Table 38.6. These signs of malnutrition must be viewed as *suggestive* of malnutrition because the signs are nonspecific. For example, a red conjunctiva may indicate an infection, rather than a nutritional deficit, and

TABLE 38.6 Clinical Signs of Malnutrition

Area of Examination	Signs Associated with Malnutrition
General appearance and vitality	Apathetic, listless, looks tired, easily fatigued
Weight	Overweight or underweight
Skin	Dry, flaky, or scaly; pale or pigmented; presence of petechiae or bruises; lack of subcutaneous fat
Nails	Brittle, pale, ridged, or spoon-shaped
Hair	Dry, dull, sparse, loss of colour, brittle
Eyes	Pale or red conjunctiva, dryness (xerophthalmia), soft cornea (keratomalacia), dull cornea
Lips	Swollen, red cracks at side of mouth (angular stomatitis), vertical fissures (cheilosis)
Tongue	Swollen; beefy red or magenta coloured; smooth appearance; decrease or increase in size
Gums	Spongy, swollen, inflamed; bleed easily
Muscles	Underdeveloped, flaccid, wasted, soft
Gastrointestinal system	Anorexia, indigestion, diarrhea, constipation, enlarged liver
Nervous system	Decreased reflexes, sensory loss, burning and tingling of hands and feet (paresthesias), mental confusion or irritability

dry, dull hair may be related to excessive exposure to the sun rather than kwashiorkor (severe protein depletion). To confirm malnutrition, clinical findings need to be substantiated with laboratory tests and dietary data.

Dietary Data

A dietary history includes data about the client's usual eating patterns and habits; allergies and food intolerances; frequency, types, and quantities of foods consumed; and social, economic, ethnic, or religious factors influencing nutrition. Specific factors to consider include, but are not limited to, living and eating alone, ability to purchase foods and prepare a meal, and the availability of refrigeration and cooking facilities.

Other information that is important addresses the client's appetite and hunger. These are two different aspects of eating and should not be considered the same. A client may claim to have a "good" appetite and yet ingest very little food. Others may say they are never hungry, and yet they are observed to be eating frequently. Sometimes, this is why keeping a food diary with associated mood states may help the person realize how much, in fact, is being consumed and why. It is important to know if the client has eating binges. Does the client eat frequently in restaurants? What does the client know and understand about healthy nutrition and *Canada's Food Guide to Healthy Eating*?

Four possible methods for collecting dietary data are a 24-hour food recall, a food-frequency record, a food diary, and a diet history.

For a **24-hour food recall,** the nurse asks the client to recall all the food and beverages the client consumes during a typical 24-hour period. The data obtained is then generally evaluated according to *Canada's Food Guide to Healthy Eating* to judge overall adequacy.

A **food-frequency record** is a checklist that indicates how often general food groups or specific foods are eaten. Frequency may be categorized as times/day, times/week, times/month, or frequently, seldom, never. This record, like the 24-hour food recall, provides information about the types of foods eaten but not the quantities. When specific foods or nutrients are suspected of being deficient or excessive, the health-care professional may use a selective food frequency that focuses, for example, on fat, fruit, vegetable, and fibre intake.

A **food diary** is a detailed record of measured amounts (portion sizes) of all food and fluids a client consumes during a specified period of time, usually three to seven days.

A **diet history** is a comprehensive, time-consuming assessment of a client's food intake that involves an extensive interview by a nutritionist or dietitian. It includes characteristics of foods usually eaten, as well as the frequency and amount of food consumed. Thus, it may include a 24-hour recall, a food-frequency record, and a food diary. Medical and psychosocial factors are also assessed to evaluate their impact on nutritional requirements, food habits, and choices. Data obtained are analyzed by computer and translated into caloric and nutrient intake. Results are compared with the recommended dietary allowances that are appropriate for the client's age, gender, and condition.

Health History

Information about the client's current health status and past health status needs to be obtained. This information should include medications, both prescribed and over-the-counter drugs (e.g., vitamins, herbal preparations) that the client is taking. The use and frequency of use of recreational drugs also need to be addressed. This may be the opportune time to ascertain what the client knows about the interactions between food and the drugs being taken. Information about the client's family history needs to be collected. Is there a history of heart disease, obesity, eating disorders, diabetes, and so on? Does the client exercise on a regular basis? Does the client use tobacco? If so, how much, how often, and for how long? Does the client consume alcohol? If so, how much, and how often? Does the client have any disabilities that may limit the ability to prepare food or eat? For example, if a person has advancing multiple sclerosis, there may be an intention tremor that causes the hands to shake so much that it is difficult to cook or use a regular fork or spoon. Does the client have difficulty swallowing? Is there a problem with choking or aspiration of food when eating?

Some of the health history information may have to be obtained from family members if the client has a cognitive impairment or speech disability. Also, some of this information may be obtained from other health professionals' histories if the nurse has access to such documentation.

Anthropometric Measurements

Anthropometric measurements are noninvasive techniques that aim to quantify changes in body composition. The client's **height** and **weight** should be obtained. Self-reported data are often inaccurate, so accurate equipment and standardized procedures must be used to ensure accurate and precise readings. A beam-balance scale can be used to obtain weight and to measure the person's height. The person should not be wearing shoes and should have on only light clothing when stepping onto the scale. The client should be able to stand on the scale without any support, and should have voided prior to being weighed. If the client is bedridden or unable to stand independently, a metabolic scale can be used, if available. A person should be weighed at the same time each day if repeated weight recordings are required. Bathroom scales are not always accurate, so they should only be used to obtain an approximation of the person's weight.

The weight obtained should be compared to the client's **usual and ideal body weights** to determine **weight change.** Refer to the box below and Table 38.7.

Calculating and Interpreting the Percent of Deviation from Usual Body Weight and the Percent of Weight Loss

Calculating Percent of Usual Body Weight

$$\% \text{ usual body weight} = \frac{\text{Current weight}}{\text{Usual body weight}} \times 100$$

Mild malnutrition	85–90%
Moderate malnutrition	75–84%
Severe malnutrition	less than 74%

Calculating Percent of Weight Loss

$$\% \text{ weight loss} = \frac{\text{Usual weight} - \text{current weight}}{\text{Usual weight}} \times 100$$

Significant weight loss	Severe weight loss
5% over 1 mo	>5% over 1 mo
7.5% over 3 mo	>7.5% over 3 mo
10% over 6 mo	>10% over 6 mo

Source: Wilson, J. M. (1996, November/December). Nutritional assessment and its application. *Journal of Intravenous Nursing, 19*(16), 307–314.

Calculating Percentage of Weight Loss

Accurate assessment of the client's height, current body weight (CBW), and usual body weight (UBW) is essential. Although the client's current body weight can be compared with an ideal body weight discussed earlier, the IBW is based on healthy people and does not account for changes in the client's body composition that accompany illness or reflect any changes in weight. The client's usual body weight better reflects weight change and the possibility of malnutrition (Evans-Stoner, 1997b). Calculation and interpretation of the percent of deviation from UBW and the percent of weight loss are shown in the box below. An important aspect of weight assessment, obtained in the nursing history, is a description of weight change. The nurse should describe any weight loss or gain, the duration of the change, and whether the weight change was intentional or unintentional.

An adult's **Body Mass Index (BMI)** can be calculated from the height and weight measurements. The BMI is an indicator of overall adiposity or obesity and can be used to determine if an individual is at risk for developing serious health problems. A BMI, however, must be used with caution for certain individuals—for example, those who have a large lean body mass or who have ascites—because their weight may not be attributable to adipose tissue. To calculate BMI, refer to the following steps or to the nomogram on the next page.

1. Measure the person's height in metres (e.g., 1.5 m).
2. Measure the weight in kilograms (e.g., 60 kg).
3. Calculate the BMI using the following formula:

$$\text{BMI} = \frac{\text{Weight in kilograms}}{(\text{Height in metres})^2}$$

or

$$\frac{60 \text{ kilograms}}{1.5 \times 1.5 \text{ metres}^2} = 26.6 \text{ kg/m}^2$$

TABLE 38.7 Body Mass Index (BMI) Nomogram

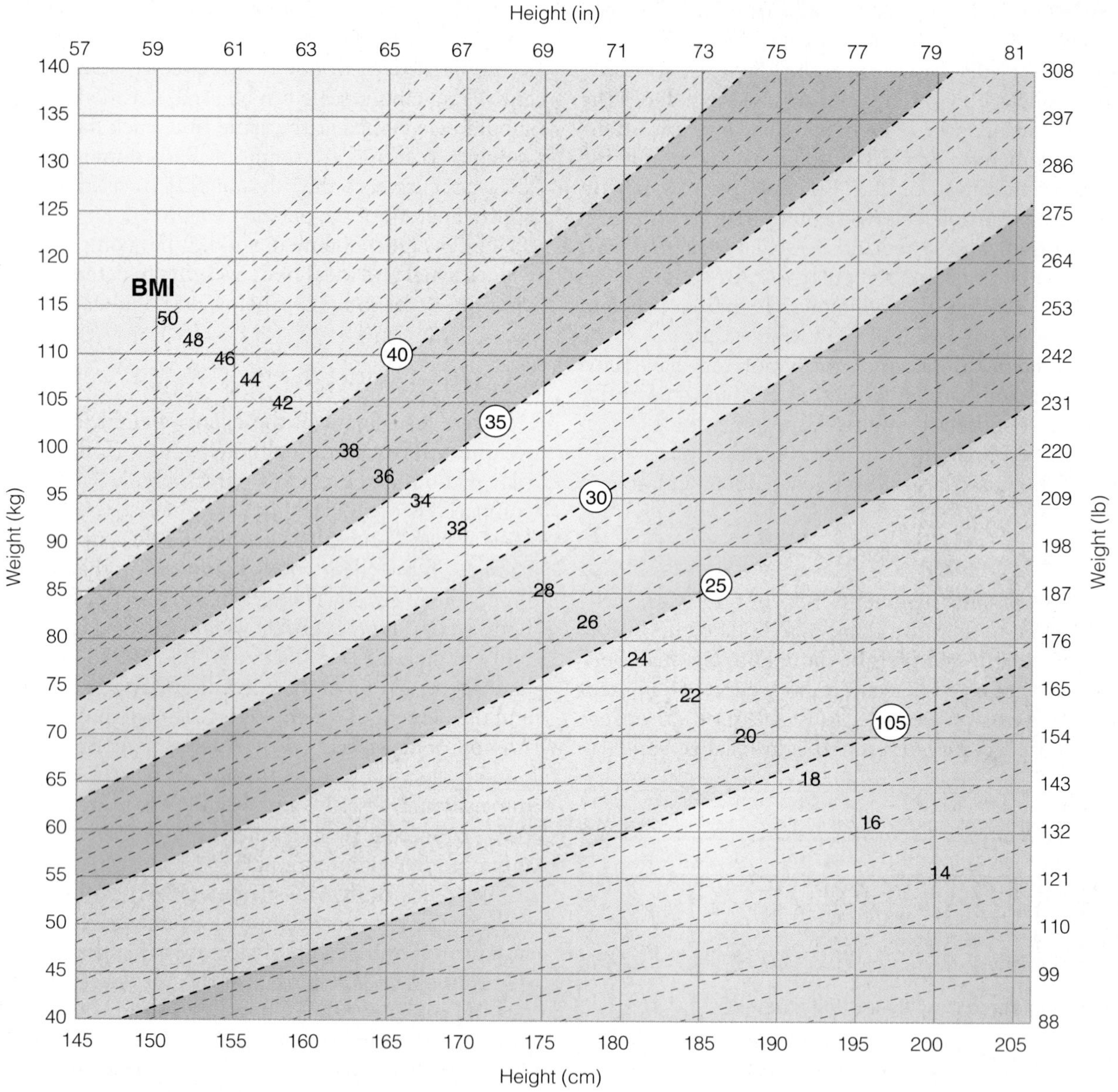

Body Mass Index Chart

Source: www.hc-sc.gc.ca/hpfb-dy[sa/onpp-bppn/bmi_chart_java_e.html, Health Canada, 2003.

Classification of weight based on BMI is as follows:

Underweight	<18.49
Normal	18.5–24.9
Overweight	25.0–29.9
Obesity class 1	30.0–34.9
Obesity class 2	35.0–39.9
Extreme obesity	>40.0

Other important measures to obtain when determining degree of adiposity and location of adipose tissue are the **waist circumference (WC)** and the hip circumference. The ratio of the waist circumference to the hip circumference is called the **Waist Hip Ratio (WHR)**. These two measures can be used to ascertain where the adipose tissue is located. As discussed earlier in this chapter, adipose tissue located in the visceral area of the abdomen places the individual at risk for the development of syndrome X and its comorbidities. To obtain a WC, have clients remove belts or tight-fitting clothing around the midsection of the body. Have them stand erect and breathe normally. Place the tape measure around the largest circumference of the waist area over the umbilicus. An accurate assessment of this circumference can be a challenge when determining the WC in an individual with a very large abdominal panus (skin fat fold).

To obtain the hip circumference, have the person stand erect. The person should be wearing very lightweight clothing that is not bulky around the hip area. The hip circumference is taken around the largest part of the buttocks. If you have the client place the thumb on the top of the iliac crest and extend the hand open so that the small finger is reaching toward the hip joint, the tip of the small finger can be used to determine where to place the measuring tape. The gender-specific cutoffs can be used to identify relative risk for the development of diseases associated with obesity. For men, a WC greater than 102 cm places them at high risk. For women, a WC greater than 88 cm places them at high risk. The WHR can be used to determine body fat distribution. A WHR greater than 1 is indicative that a man has visceral fat accumulations. For a woman, a WHR greater than 0.8 is indicative of the presence of visceral fat deposits.

When interpreting the results of the BMI, WC, and WHR, one must consider the relationship of these measures to each other. For example, a male client may have a BMI of 26, a WC of 103 cm, and a WHR of 1.2. The BMI would indicate that he is only slightly overweight, but his WC and WHR indicate that his fat is located in the visceral region, which places him at risk for developing comorbidities associated with obesity. Then, if he smokes, is sedentary, and has high levels of LDL cholesterol and low levels of HDL, his risk factors are increased.

Skinfold thicknesses can be obtained to determine fat stores. The fold of skin measured includes subcutaneous tissue but not the underlying muscle. It is measured in millimetres using special calipers (Figure 38.2).

Changes in anthropometric measurements often occur slowly and reflect chronic, rather than acute, changes in nutritional status. They are, therefore, used to monitor the client's progress over months to years, rather than days to weeks. Ideally, initial and subsequent measurements need to be taken by the same clinician. In addition, measurements obtained need to be interpreted with caution. Fluctuations in hydration status that often occur during illness can influence the accuracy of results. In addition, normal standards often do not account for normal changes in body composition, such as those that occur with aging (Evans-Stoner, 1997b).

Laboratory Data

Biochemical data measure what is happening internally when an altered nutrition state exists. These tests are invasive and are usually ordered by the client's physician. These tests are important to aid in the diagnosis and treatment of the client. The nurse needs to know why the tests are ordered and what the results mean. Not all the tests described may need to be conducted.

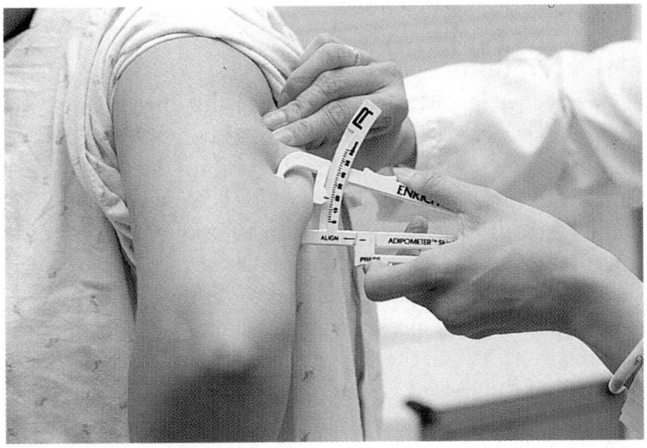

Figure 38.2 Measuring the triceps skinfold

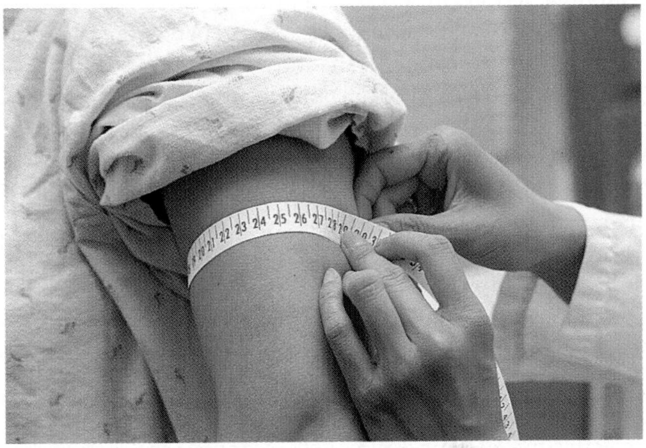

Figure 38.3 Measuring the mid-upper-arm circumference

Laboratory Tests

Laboratory tests provide objective data to the nutritional assessments, but because many factors can influence these tests, no single test specifically predicts nutritional risk or measures the presence or degree of a nutritional problem. The tests most commonly used are serum proteins (serum albumin, prealbumin, transferring, retinal-binding protein, and C-reactive protein), urinary urea nitrogen and creatinine, total lymphocyte count, hemoglobin, hematocrit, total serum cholesterol, LDL, HDL, fasting blood gluose, and TSH.

Blood Tests

Serum Proteins

Serum protein levels, as mentioned earlier, provide an estimate of visceral protein stores. Tests commonly include hemoglobin, albumin, transferrin, and total iron-binding capacity. A low *hemoglobin* level may be evidence of iron deficiency anemia. However, abnormal blood loss or a pathological process, such as gastrointestinal cancer, must be ruled out before iron deficiency related to diet is confirmed.

Edema may be present if the client is experiencing malnutrition. When the serum protein is low, edema results because of the loss of colloidal osmotic pressure required to maintain the normal shift of fluid between the capillaries and the surrounding interstitial spaces. The edema may be present around the ankles or hands because of gravitational forces on the extremities, or it may affect the heart and lung actions in severe conditions.

Albumin, which accounts for over 50 percent of the total serum proteins, is one of the most common visceral proteins evaluated as part of the nutritional assessment. Because there is so much albumin in the body and because it is not broken down very quickly (i.e., it has a long half-life [18–20 days]), albumin concentrations change slowly. Thus, a low serum albumin level is a useful indicator of prolonged protein depletion rather than acute or short-term changes in nutritional status. However, many conditions besides malnutrition can depress albumin concentration, such as altered liver function, hydration status, and losses from open wounds and burns.

Transferrin is a protein that binds and carries iron from the intestine through the serum. Because it has a shorter half-life than albumin (8–9 days), transferrin is likely to respond more quickly to protein depletion than albumin. Serum transferrin can be measured directly or by a *total iron-binding capacity (TIBC) test*, which indicates the amount of iron in the blood to which transferrin can bind. Conversion of the TIBC reading to a transferrin measurement is calculated by a standard mathematical formula. Transferrin levels below normal indicate protein loss, iron deficiency anemia, pregnancy, hepatitis, and liver dysfunction. An increase in total iron-binding capacity can indicate iron deficiency; a decrease, anemia.

Prealbumin (PAB), also referred to as thyroxine-binding albumin and transthyretin, has the shortest half-life and smallest body pool, and is, therefore, the serum protein most responsive to rapid changes in nutritional status but unfortunately is expensive. It may, however, be performed when initiating total parenteral nutrition for clients in their homes.

Total Lymphocyte Count

Certain nutrient deficiencies and forms of protein-calorie malnutrition (PCM) can depress the immune system. The total number of lymphocytes decreases as protein depletion occurs.

Cholesterol Tests

Total serum cholesterol is a measure of all cholesterol (HDL, LDL, very-low density liproprotein). It does not separate out the HDL and the LDL, so they must be measured separately. High levels of total cholesterol are indicative of being at risk for cardiovascular disease. The levels of LDL and HDL more accurately reflect the risk factor for cardiovascular disease.

Glucose Tests

Fasting blood glucose level is conducted to assess for type 2 diabetes and for hyperglycemic hyperosmolar nonketonic syndrome (HHNS), a condition that develops mostly in older adults and people receiving total parenteral nutrition or peritoneal dialysis. An elevated blood glucose level is an indicator of excess glucose in the blood.

Thyroid Function

Assessing the function of a client's thyroid is important to determining if their BMR is being regulated normally. If a client's thyroid stimulating hormone (TSH) levels are elevated, it is indicative that the thyroid is not producing adequate amounts of thyroxine (T_4) and tri-iodothyronine (T_3), and hence the rate of metabolism may be slowed.

Urinary Tests

Urinary urea nitrogen and *urinary creatinine* are measures of protein catabolism and the state of nitrogen balance. **Urea,** the chief end product of amino acid metabolism, is formed from ammonia detoxified by the liver, circulated in the blood, and transported to the kidneys for excretion. Urea concentrations in the blood (BUN or blood urea nitrogen) and urine (UUG or urinary urea nitrogen), therefore, directly reflect the intake and breakdown of dietary protein, the rate of urea production in the liver, and the rate of urea removal by the kidneys.

The state of nitrogen balance is determined by comparing the nitrogen intake (grams of protein) to the nitrogen output over a 24-hour period. A positive nitrogen balance exists when intake exceeds nitrogen output; a negative nitrogen balance occurs when output exceeds nitrogen intake. Protein intake must be accurately recorded and kidney function must be normal to ensure the validity of a UUN.

Urinary creatinine reflects a person's total muscle mass because creatinine is the chief end product of the creatine produced when energy is released during skeletal muscle metabolism. The rate of creatinine formation is directly proportional to the total muscle mass. Creatinine is removed from the bloodstream by the kidneys and excreted in the urine at a rate that closely parallels its formation. The greater the muscle mass, the greater is the excretion of creatinine. As skeletal muscle atrophies during malnutrition, creatinine excretion decreases. Standards for creatinine excretion are developed on the basis of gender and height. Urinary creatinine is also influenced by protein intake, exercise, age, renal function, and thyroid function.

Planning

Major goals for clients with or at risk for nutritional problems include:

- Maintain or restore optimal nutritional status
- Promote healthy nutritional practices
- Prevent complications associated with malnutrition
- Decrease weight
- Regain specified weight

Examples of desired outcomes related to some of these goals, although established in the planning phase, are provided in the Evaluating section of this chapter.

Examples of Nursing Intervention Classifications (NIC) interventions to enhance an individual's nutrition include (McCloskey & Bulechek, 2000):

- Nutritional counselling
- Nutrition management
- Nutritional monitoring
- Nutrition therapy
- Weight management
- Weight reduction assistance
- Weight gain assistance
- Energy management
- Exercise promotion
- Behaviour modification
- Enteral tube feeding
- Total parenteral nutrition (TPN) administration

Specific nursing activities associated with each of these interventions can be selected to meet the individual needs of the client. A sample nursing care plan using NIC interventions and selected activities is provided on pages 996–997.

Planning for Home Care

To provide for continuity of care, the nurse must consider the client's need for assistance with nutrition. Some clients will need help with feeding, purchasing food, and preparing meals; others will need instructions about enteral and total parenteral nutrition therapy.

Home care planning incorporates an assessment of the client's and family's abilities for self-care, financial resources, and the need for referrals and home health services. The box on page 998 outlines a home care assessment in regard to nutritional problems and needs. A major aspect of discharge planning involves instructional needs of the client and family. See the Home Care Teaching Guide in the box on page 999.

Implementing

Nursing interventions to promote optimal nutrition for hospitalized clients are often provided in collaboration with the physician who writes the diet orders and the dietitian who informs clients about special diets. The nurse reinforces this instruction and, in addition, creates an atmosphere that encourages eating, provides assistance with eating, monitors the client's appetite and food intake, administers enteral and parenteral feedings, and consults with the physician and dietitian about nutritional problems that arise.

In the community setting, the nurse's role is largely educational. For example, nurses promote optimal nutrition at health fairs, in schools, at prenatal classes, and with well or ill clients and support people in their homes. In the home setting, nurses also initiate nutritional screens, refer clients at risk to appropriate resources, instruct clients about enteral and parenteral feedings, and offer nutrition counselling as needed. Nutrition counselling involves more than simply providing information. The nurse must help clients integrate diet changes into their lifestyles and provide strategies to motivate them to change their eating habits.

Assisting with Special Diets

Alterations in the client's diet are often needed to treat a disease process, such as diabetes mellitus, to prepare for a special examination or surgery, to increase or decrease weight, to restore nutritional deficits, or to allow an organ to rest and promote healing. Diets are modified in one or more of the following aspects: texture, kilocalories, specific nutrients, seasonings, or consistency.

Clients who do not have special needs eat the *regular* (standard or house) *diet*, a balanced diet that supplies the metabolic requirements of a sedentary person (about 2,000 kcal). Most agencies offer clients a daily menu from which to select their meals for the next day; others provide standard meals to each client on the general diet. Certain foods (e.g., cabbage, which tends to produce flatus, and highly seasoned and fried foods, which are difficult for some people to digest) are usually omitted from the regular diet.

A variation of the regular diet is the *light diet*, designed for postoperative and other clients who are not ready for the regular diet. Foods in the *light diet* are plainly cooked and fat is usually omitted, as are bran and foods containing a great deal of fibre. Not all agencies provide a light diet.

SAMPLE CARE PLAN FOR NUTRITION

ASSESSMENT DATA

Nursing Assessment

Mrs. Rose Santini, a 59-year-old homemaker, attends a community hospital-sponsored health fair. She approaches the nutrition information booth, and the clinical specialist in nutritional support gathers a nutritional history. Mrs. Santini is very upset about her 9 kg weight gain. She relates to the nurse clinician that since the death of her husband one month ago, she has lost interest in many of her usual physical and social activities. She no longer attends YMCA exercise and swimming sessions and has lost contact with her couples bridge group. Mrs. Santini states she is bored, depressed, and very unhappy about her appearance. She has a small frame and has always prided herself on her petite figure. She says her eating habits have changed considerably. She snacks while watching TV and rarely prepares a complete meal.

Physical Examination

Height: 162.6 cm
Weight: 63.6 kg
Temperature: 37°C
Pulse: 76 BPM
Respirations: 16/minute
Blood pressure: 144/84 mm Hg

Diagnostic Data

CBC normal, urinalysis negative, chest x-ray negative, thyroid profile within normal limits

Client Goal(s):

The client will (1) change undesirable behaviours that contribute to weight gain; and (2) reach her ideal body weight for height and frame.

Desired Outcomes

1. Plans three menus each day that result in a 500-calorie reduction in intake
2. Develops a physical exercise plan that engages her in 15–20 minutes of exercise by day 5
3. Identifies eating habits that contribute to weight gain by day 2

---

*Nursing Interventions and Selected Activities with Rationale *[in italics]*

Weight Reduction Assistance

- Determine current eating patterns by having Mrs. Santini keep a diary of what, when, and where she eats.
  Increases awareness of activities and foods that contribute to excessive intake.
- Set a weekly goal for weight loss.
  The desirable weight loss rate is 0.5–0.9 kg per week.
- Encourage use of internal reward systems when goals are accomplished.
  Goal setting provides motivation which is essential for a successful weight-loss program.
- Set a realistic plan with Mrs. Santini to include reduced food intake and increased energy expenditure.
  A combined plan of calorie reduction and exercise can enhance weight loss since exercise increases caloric utilization.
- Assist client to identify motivation for eating and internal and external cues associated with eating.
  Awareness of factors that contribute to overeating will assist the individual in planning behaviour modification techniques to avoid situations that prompt excess food consumption.
- Develop a daily meal plan with a well-balanced diet, reduced calories, and reduced fat.
  Overweight people are often nutritionally deprived. Intake must be reduced by 500 calories per day to obtain a 0.5-kg per-week weight loss.
- Encourage attendance at support groups for weight loss and/or refer to a community weight control program.
  Support groups can provide companionship, increase motivation, and offer practical solutions to problems associated with dieting.

Nutritional Counselling

- Facilitate identification of eating behaviours to be changed.
  Increases individual's awareness of those actions that contribute to excessive intake.
- Use accepted nutritional standards to assist Mrs. Santini in evaluating adequacy of dietary intake.
  Comparing the individual's dietary history with nutritional standards will facilitate identification of nutritional deficiencies and/or excesses.
- Help Mrs. Santini to consider factors of age, past eating experiences, culture, and finances in planning ways to meet nutritional requirements.
  Social, economic, physical, and psychological factors play a role in nutrition and/or malnutrition.
- Discuss Mrs. Santini's knowledge of the basic four food groups, as well as perceptions of the needed diet modification.
  Helps determine the patient's knowledge base and identify misconceptions and/or gaps in understanding.

SAMPLE CARE PLAN FOR NUTRITION *continued*

■ Discuss food likes and dislikes.	*Incorporating Mrs. Santini's food preferences into the dietary plan will promote adherence to the weight-loss program.*
■ Assist Mrs. Santini in stating her feelings and concerns about goal achievement.	*Fear of success, failure, or other concerns may block goal achievement.*
Behaviour Modification	
■ Assist Mrs. Santini to identify strengths, and reinforce these.	*Reinforcing strengths enhances self-esteem and encourages the individual to draw upon these assets during the weight-loss program.*
■ Encourage her to examine her own behaviour.	*Involving Mrs. Santini in self-appraisal will promote identification of behaviours that may be contributing to excessive caloric intake.*
■ Identify the behaviour to be changed in specific, concrete terms (e.g., stop snacking in front of the TV).	*Identification of specific behaviours is essential for planning behaviour modification.*
■ Consider that it is easier to increase a behaviour than to decrease a behaviour (e.g., increase activities or hobbies that involve the hands, such as sewing, versus decreasing TV snacking).	*Habitual behaviours are difficult to change. Breaking old habits may be easier if viewed from the standpoint of increasing an enjoyable, healthy activity.*
■ Choose reinforcers that are meaningful to Mrs. Santini.	*Positive reinforcement is not likely to be an effective part of behaviour modification if the reinforcer is meaningless to the individual.*

Evaluation

Goal met. Mrs. Santini kept a dietary log for five days and has planned balanced meals each day, resulting in a daily deficit of 400–500 calories. She is aware that she eats excessively because she is bored and depressed. She has re-established her former social contacts, including her church bridge club. Mrs. Santini has purchased a stationary bicycle and exercises 20 minutes daily. She enrolled in a knitting class that meets two nights per week. She has lost 0.7 kg in the past week. As a reward, Mrs. Santini renewed her membership to the YMCA.

*Interventions and activities selected are only a sample of those suggested in the *Nursing Interventions Classification (NIC)* and should be individualized for each client.

Source: McCloskey, J. C., & Bulechek, G. M. (2000). *Iowa interventions project: Nursing Interventions Classification (NIC)* (3rd ed.). St. Louis, MO: Mosby.

Temporary Consistency Modifications

Diets that are modified in consistency are often given to clients before and after surgery or to promote healing in clients with gastrointestinal distress. These diets include nothing by mouth or per ora (NPO), clear liquid, full liquid, soft, and diet as tolerated.

Nothing per Ora In this diet, food and fluid are prohibited, for example, before an anesthesia to prevent aspiration of stomach contents or after surgery until bowel sounds return. Most well-nourished clients can accommodate NPO for several days without problems; however, some clients may require nutrition and fluids intravenously.

Clear Liquid Diet This diet is limited to water, tea, coffee, clear broths, ginger ale or other carbonated beverages, strained and clear juices, and plain gelatin. This diet provides the client with fluid and carbohydrate (in the form of sugar) but does not supply adequate protein, fat, vitamins, minerals, or calories (no more than 600 kcal/day). It is a short-term diet (24–36 hours) provided for clients after certain surgery or in the acute stages of infection, particularly of the gastrointestinal tract. The major objectives of this diet are to relieve thirst, prevent dehydration, and minimize stimulation of the gastrointestinal tract. Examples of foods allowed in clear liquid, full liquid, and soft diets are shown in the box on page 1000.

Full Liquid Diet This diet contains only liquids or foods that turn to liquid at body temperature, such as ice cream. Full liquid diets are often eaten by clients who have gastrointestinal disturbances or are otherwise unable to tolerate solid or semisolid foods. This diet is not recommended for long-term use because it is low in iron, protein, and calories. In addition, its cholesterol content is high because of the amount of milk offered. Clients who must receive only liquids for long

HOME CARE ASSESSMENT

Nutrition

Client/Environment

- *Self-care abilities:* Assess ability to feed self, to purchase food, and to prepare meals.
- *Adaptive feeding aids required:* Determine need for special drinking cups, plates, or feeding utensils (see feeding aids on pages 1001–1002).
- *Instructional needs:* Consider nutritional requirements (e.g., *Canada's Food Guide to Healthy Eating*, dietary guidelines, special diet); adaptive aids available; recommended lifestyle variations; management of enteral/parenteral nutrition.
- *Physical environment:* Assess adequacy of water, electricity, refrigeration and telephone facilities; and presence of clean, secure area to store and set up enteral/parenteral equipment, as needed.
- *Abilities to manage enteral/parenteral nutrition* (discussed on pages 1002–1012): Assess cognitive abilities to manage procedures and follow prescribed schedule; adequacy of manual dexterity to open sterile packages and handle equipment; adequacy of visual acuity to read numbers on syringes and pumps; ability to prepare formulas; ability to evaluate status of enteral/parenteral access device and report problems.

Family

- *Caregiver availability, skills, and willingness:* Primary and secondary persons able to assist with food purchase, meal preparation, and feeding and able to comprehend and administer special diets or enteral/parenteral nutrition required.
- *Family role changes and coping:* Effect on parenting and spousal roles, financial resources, and social roles.
- *Alternative potential primary or respite caregivers:* For example, other family members, volunteers, church members, paid caregivers, or housekeeping services; available community respite care (adult day care, senior centres) and so on.

Community

- *Current knowledge, use, and experience with community resources:* Nutritional counselling services; home health agencies for enteral/parenteral nutrition support; dietitian or nutritionist for planning appropriate meals for prescribed diet, ways to include ethnic food preferences into the diet, and providing written meal plans; medical equipment and supply sources; financial assistance services; support and educational services such as:
  - Weight management programs (e.g., Weight Watchers)
  - National Centre for Nutrition and Dietetics for information on all nutrition topics
  - National Eating Disorder Information Centre
  - Meals-on-Wheels

periods are usually given a nutritionally balanced oral supplement, such as Sustacal. The full liquid diet is monotonous and difficult for clients to accept. Planning six or more feedings per day may encourage a more adequate intake.

Soft Diet The soft diet is easily chewed and digested. It is often ordered for clients who have difficulty chewing and swallowing. It is a low-residue (low-fibre) diet containing very few uncooked foods; however, restrictions vary among agencies and according to individual tolerance. Examples of foods that can be included in a soft or semisoft diet are shown in the box on page 1000. The **pureed diet** is a modification of the soft diet. Liquid may be added to the food, which is then blended to a semisolid consistency.

Diet as Tolerated Diet as tolerated is ordered when the client's appetite, ability to eat, and tolerance for certain foods may change. For example, on the first postoperative day, a client may be given a clear liquid diet. If no nausea occurs, normal intestinal motility has returned, and the client feels like eating, the diet may be advanced to a full liquid, light, or regular diet.

Modification for Disease

Many special diets may be prescribed to meet requirements for disease process or altered metabolism. For example, a client with diabetes mellitus may need a diabetic diet recommended by the Canadian Diabetes Association (CDA), an obese client may need a calorie-restricted diet, a cardiac client may need sodium and cholesterol restrictions, and a client with allergies will need a nonallergenic diet.

Some clients must follow certain diets (e.g., the diabetic diet) for a lifetime. If the diet is long term, the client must not only understand the diet but also develop a healthy, positive attitude toward it. Assisting clients and support persons with special diets is a function shared by the dietitian

HOME CARE TEACHING GUIDE

Healthy Nutrition

- Instruct clients about the content of a healthy diet based on *Canada's Food Guide to Healthy Eating*.
- Encourage clients, particularly older clients, to reduce dietary fat (see Wellness Teaching: Reducing Dietary Fat, page 985).
- Instruct strict vegetarians, as needed, about proper protein complementation and additional vitamin and mineral supplementation.
- Discuss foods high in specific required nutrients, such as protein, iron, calcium, vitamin C, fibre, and so on.
- Discuss importance of properly fitted dentures and dental care.
- Discuss safe food preparation and preservation techniques as appropriate.

Dietary Alterations

- Explain the purpose of the diet.
- Discuss allowed and prohibited foods.
- Explain the importance of reading food labels when selecting foods.
- Include family or significant others as appropriate.
- Reinforce information provided by the dietitian or nutritionist as appropriate.
- Discuss substitutes for sugar and herbs and spices as alternatives to salt.

For Overweight Clients

- Discuss physiological, psychological, and lifestyle factors that predispose to weight gain.
- Provide information about normal weight range and recommended calorie intake.
- Discuss principles of a well-balanced diet (see *Canada's Food Guide to Healthy Eating* or other food guidelines) and high- and low-calorie foods.
- Encourage intake of low-calorie, caffeine-free beverages and plenty of water.
- Discuss ways to adapt eating practices by using smaller plates, smaller servings, chewing each bit a specified number of times, and putting fork down between bites.
- Discuss ways to control the desire to eat by taking a walk, drinking a glass of water, or doing slow, deep-breathing exercises.
- Discuss the importance of exercise and help the client plan an exercise program.
- Discuss stress-reduction techniques (see Chapters 11 and 47).
- Provide information about available community resources (e.g., weight-loss groups, dietary counselling, exercise programs, self-help groups).

For Underweight Clients

- Discuss factors contributing to inadequate nutrition and weight loss.
- Discuss recommended calorie intake and normal weight range.
- Provide information about the content of a balanced diet based on the *Canada's Food Guide to Healthy Eating*.
- Provide information about ways to increase calorie intake (e.g., high-protein or high-calorie foods and supplements).
- Discuss ways to manage, minimize, or alter the factors contributing to malnourishment.
- If appropriate, discuss ways to purchase low-cost nutritious foods.
- Provide information about community agencies that can assist in providing food (e.g., Meals-On-Wheels).

For Clients Requiring Enteral/Parenteral Nutrition

See Client Teaching for Home Nutrition Therapy later in this chapter.

or nutritionist and the nurse. The dietitian informs the client and support persons about the specific foods allowed and not allowed and assists the client with meal planning. The nurse reinforces this instruction, assists the client to make changes, and evaluates the client's responses.

All dietary instructions must be individually designed to meet the client's intellectual ability, motivation level, lifestyle, culture, and economic status. Both nutritionists and dietitians can often help adapt a diet to suit the client. Simple verbal instructions need to be given and reinforced with written material. Family and support people must be included in the dietary instruction.

Stimulating the Appetite

Physical illness, unfamiliar or unpalatable food, environmental and psychological factors, medications or therapies, and physical discomfort or pain may depress the appetites of many clients. A short-term decrease in food intake usually is not a problem for adults; over time, however, it leads to weight loss, decreased strength and stamina, and other nutritional problems. A decreased food intake is often accompanied by a decrease in fluid intake, which may cause fluid and electrolyte problems. See Chapter 40 for further information. Stimulating a person's appetite requires the nurse

Examples of Foods for Clear Liquid, Full Liquid, and Soft Diets

Clear Liquid	Full Liquid	Soft
Coffee, regular and decaffeinated Tea Carbonated beverages Bouillon, fat-free broth Clear fruit juices (apple, cranberry, grape) Other fruit juices, strained Popsicles Gelatin Sugar, honey Hard candy	All foods on clear liquid diet, plus: Milk and milk drinks Puddings, custards Ice cream, sherbet Vegetable juices Refined or strained cereals (e.g., cream of rice) Cream, butter, margarine Eggs (in custard and pudding) Yogurt	All foods on full and clear liquid diets, plus: *Meat:* All lean, tender meat, fish, or poultry (chopped, shredded); spaghetti sauce with ground meat, over pasta *Meat alternatives:* Scrambled eggs, omelette, poached eggs; cottage cheese and other mild cheese *Vegetables:* Mashed potatoes, sweet potatoes, or squash; vegetables in cream or cheese sauce; other cooked vegetables as tolerated (e.g., spinach, cauliflower, asparagus tips), chopped and mashed, as needed; avocado *Fruits:* Cooked or canned fruits; bananas, grapefruit and orange sections without membranes, applesauce *Breads and cereals:* Enriched rice, barley, pasta; all breads; cooked cereals (e.g., oatmeal) *Desserts:* Soft cake, bread pudding

to determine the reason for the lack of appetite and then to deal with the problem. Some interventions for improving the client's appetite are summarized in the box right.

Assisting Clients with Meals

Because clients in health-care agencies are frequently confined to their beds, meals are often brought to the client. The client receives a tray that has been assembled in a central kitchen. Nursing personnel may be responsible for giving out and collecting the trays; however, in most settings, this is done by special dietary personnel. Long-term care facilities and some hospitals serve meals to ambulatory clients in a special dining area. Other agencies have a coffee shop for food or machines from which clients can obtain sandwiches and beverages. Guidelines for providing meals to clients are summarized in the box on page 1001.

People who frequently require help with their meals are older adults who are weakened, clients who are blind, those who must remain in a back-lying position, and those who cannot use their hands. The client's nursing care plan will indicate that assistance is required with meals.

The nurse must be sensitive to clients' feelings of embarrassment, resentment, and loss of autonomy. Whenever possible, the nurse should help incapacitated clients feed themselves, rather than feed them. Some clients become depressed because they require help and because they believe they are burdensome to busy nursing personnel. Although feeding a client is time consuming, nurses should try to appear unhurried and convey that they have ample time. Sitting at the bedside is one way to convey this impression.

When feeding a client, ask in which order the client would like to eat the food. If the client cannot see, tell the

Improving Appetite

- Relieve illness symptoms that depress appetite prior to mealtime; for example, give an analgesic for pain, an antipyretic for fever, or allow rest for fatigue.
- Provide familiar food that the person likes. Often, the relatives of clients are pleased to bring food from home but may need some guidance about special diet requirements.
- Select small portions so as not to discourage the anorexic client.
- Avoid unpleasant or uncomfortable treatments immediately before or after a meal.
- Provide a tidy, clean environment that is free of unpleasant sights and odours. A soiled dressing, a used bedpan, an uncovered irrigation set, or even used dishes can negatively affect the appetite.
- Encourage or provide oral hygiene before mealtime. This improves the client's ability to taste.
- Reduce psychological stress. A lack of understanding of therapy, the anticipation of an operation, and fear of the unknown can cause anorexia. Often, the nurse can help by discussing feelings with the client, giving information and assistance, and allaying fears.
- Stimulate the client's appetite by having the client remember favourite foods and to think about those foods and their tastes. If possible, have family members supply these foods.

client which food is being given. Always allow ample time for the client to chew and swallow the food before offering more. Also, provide fluids as requested, or if the client is unable to communicate, offer fluids after every three or four mouthfuls of solid food. It is important to make the time a pleasant one, choosing topics of conversation that are of interest to clients who want to talk.

Although normal utensils should be used whenever possible, special utensils may be needed to assist a client to eat. For clients who have difficulty drinking from a cup or glass, a straw often permits them to obtain liquids with less effort and less spillage. Special drinking cups are also available. One model has a spout; another is specially designed to permit drinking with less tipping of the cup than is normally required.

Many adaptive feeding aids are available to help clients maintain independence. A standard eating utensil with a built-up or widened handle helps clients who cannot grasp objects easily. Utensils with wide handles can be purchased, or a regular eating utensil can be modified by taping foam around the handle. The foam increases friction and, thus, steadies the client's grasp. Handles may be bent or angled to compensate for limited motion. Collars or bands that prevent the utensil from being dropped can be attached to the end of the handle and fit over the client's hand.

Plates with rims and plastic or metal plate guards enable the client to pick up the food by first pushing it against this raised edge. A suction cup or damp sponge or cloth may be placed under the dish to keep it from moving while the client is eating. No-spill mugs and two-handled drinking cups are especially useful for persons with impaired hand coordination. Stretch terry cloth and knitted or crocheted glass covers enable the client to keep a secure grasp on a glass. Lidded tip-proof glasses are also available. Figures 38.5 and 38.6 show some of these aids.

Special Community Nutritional Services

In many places, community programs have been developed to help special groups of the population meet their nutritional needs. For older people who cannot prepare meals or leave their homes, ready-to-eat meals or frozen dinners are delivered to the home by local organizations. Meals-on-Wheels is one such well-known organization. For people who can prepare meals but are physically handicapped and unable to shop for groceries, some organizations provide grocery delivery services.

Providing Client Meals

- Offer the client assistance with hand washing and oral hygiene prior to a meal.
- Most people sit during a meal; if it is permitted, assist the client to a comfortable position in bed or in a chair, whichever is appropriate.
- Clear the overbed table so that there is space for the tray. If the client must remain in a lying position in bed, arrange the overbed table close to the bedside so that the client can see and reach the food.
- Check each tray for the client's name, the type of diet, and completeness. Do *not* leave an incorrect diet for a client to eat.
- Assist the client as required to remove the food covers, butter the bread, pour the tea, and cut the meat.
- For a blind person, identify the placement of the food as you would describe the time on a clock (Figure 38.4). For instance, the nurse may say, "The potatoes are at eight o'clock, the chicken at 12 o'clock, and the green beans at 4 o'clock."
- After the client has completed the meal, observe how much and what the client has eaten and the amount of fluid taken. Record fluid intake and calorie count, as required.
- If the client is on a special diet or is having problems eating, record the amount of food eaten and any pain, fatigue, or nausea experienced.

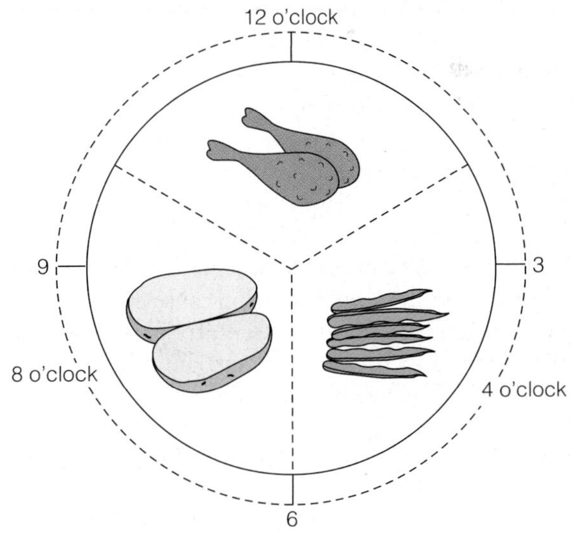

Figure 38.4 For a client who is blind, the nurse can use the clock system to describe the location of food on the plate

- If the client is not eating, document this so that changes can be made, such as rescheduling the meals, providing smaller, more frequent meals, or obtaining special self-feeding aids.

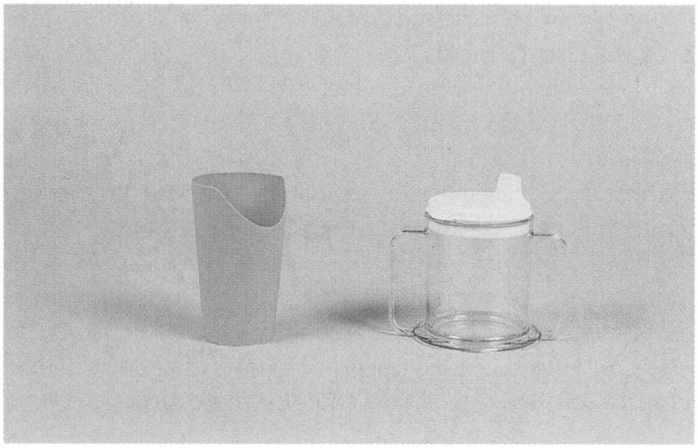

Figure 38.5 Left to right: cup with hole for nose, two-handled cup with spout

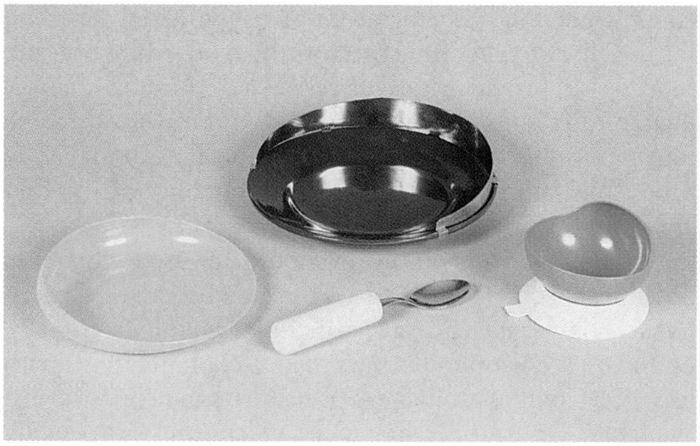

Figure 38.6 Clockwise from top: dinner plate with guard attached; bowl with stable base and lip; wide-handled spoon; lipped plate

Enteral Nutrition

Alternative feeding methods to ensure adequate nutrition include both **enteral** (through the gastrointestinal system) and **parenteral** (intravenous) methods. *Enteral nutrition* (EN), also referred to as *total enteral nutrition* (TEN), is provided when the client is unable to ingest foods or the upper gastrointestinal tract is impaired and the transport of food to the small intestine is interrupted. Enteral feedings are administered through nasogastric and small-bore feeding tubes or through gastrostomy or jejunostomy tubes.

Parenteral nutrition is discussed later in this chapter.

Enteral Access Devices

Enteral access is achieved by means of nasogastric or nasointestinal tubes, or gastrostomy or jejunostomy tubes.

A **nasogastric tube** is inserted through one of the nostrils, down the nasopharynx, and into the alimentary tract. In some instances, the tube is passed through the mouth and pharynx, although this route may be more uncomfortable for the adult client and cause gagging. This approach is often used for infants who are obligatory nose breathers (who must breathe through the nose) and premature infants who have no gag reflex.

Traditional firm, *large-bore* nasogastric tubes (i.e., those larger than 12 Fr in diameter) are placed in the stomach. Examples are the *Levin tube*, a flexible rubber or plastic, single-lumen tube with holes near the tip, and the *Salem sump tube*, with a double lumen. The larger tube of the Salem sump tube drains gastric contents; the smaller tube allows for an inflow of atmospheric air, which prevents a vacuum if the gastric tube adheres to the wall of the stomach. Irritation of the gastric mucosa is thereby avoided. Softer, more flexible, and less irritating *small-bore* tubes (smaller than 12 Fr in diameter) are frequently used.

Nasogastric tubes are used for clients who have intact gag and cough reflexes, who have adequate gastric emptying, and who require short-term feedings. Procedure 38.1 provides guidelines for inserting a nasogastric tube. Procedure 38.2 outlines the steps for removing a nasogastric tube.

Although the focus of this chapter is nutrition, *nasogastric tubes* may be inserted for reasons other than providing a route for feeding the client. These include:

- To prevent nausea, vomiting, and gastric distention following surgery. In this case, the tube is attached to a suction source.
- To remove stomach contents for laboratory analysis.
- To lavage (wash) the stomach in cases of poisoning or overdose of medications.

A **nasoenteric tube,** a longer tube than the nasogastric tube (at least 16 cm for an adult) is inserted through one nostril down into the upper small intestine. Some agencies may require specially trained nurses or physicians for this procedure. Nasoenteric tubes are used for clients who are at risk for aspiration. Clients at risk for aspiration are those that manifest the following (Metheny et al., 1998):

- Decreased level of consciousness
- Poor or absent cough or gag reflexes
- Endotracheal intubation
- Recent extubation
- Inability to cooperate with the procedure
- Restlessness or agitation

Gastrostomy and **jejunostomy** devices are used for long-term nutritional support, generally more than six to eight weeks. Conventional tubes are placed surgically or by laparoscopy through the abdominal wall into the stomach (gastrostomy) or into the jejunum (jejunostomy).

PROCEDURE 38.1 Inserting a Nasogastric Tube

Before inserting a nasogastric tube, determine the size of tube to be inserted and whether or not the tube is to be attached to a suction, and verify the physician's order.

PURPOSES

- To administer tube feedings and medications to clients unable to eat by mouth or swallow a sufficient diet without aspirating food or fluids into the lungs
- To establish a means for suctioning stomach contents to prevent gastric distention, nausea, and vomiting
- To remove stomach contents for laboratory analysis
- To lavage (wash) the stomach in case of poisoning or overdose of medications

Assessment Focus
Patency of nares and intactness of nasal tissues (note especially history of nasal surgery or deviated septum); presence of gag reflex; mental status or ability to cooperate with procedure

Equipment

- ❑ Large- or small-bore tube
- ❑ Guidewire or stylet for small-bore tube
- ❑ Solution basin filled with warm water (if a plastic tube is being used) or ice (if a rubber tube is being used)
- ❑ Nonallergenic adhesive tape, 2.5 cm wide
- ❑ Disposable gloves
- ❑ Water-soluble lubricant
- ❑ Facial tissues
- ❑ Glass of water and drinking straw
- ❑ 20- to 50-mL syringe with an adapter
- ❑ Basin
- ❑ pH test strip or meter
- ❑ Stethoscope
- ❑ Disposable pad or towel
- ❑ Clamp or plug (optional)
- ❑ Suction apparatus, if required
- ❑ Gauze square or plastic specimen bag and elastic band
- ❑ Safety pin and elastic band

INTERVENTION

1. **Verify the physician's order, and check agency policy.**
2. **Prepare the client.**
   - Explain to the client what you plan to do. The passage of a gastric tube is not painful, but it is unpleasant because the gag reflex is activated during insertion.
   - Assist the client to a high-Fowler's position if health condition permits, and support the head on a pillow. *It is often easier to swallow in this position, and gravity helps the passage of the tube.*
   - Place a towel or disposable pad across the chest.
3. **Assess the client's nares.**
   - Ask the client to hyperextend the head, and, using a flashlight, observe the intactness of the tissues of the nostrils, including any irritations or abrasions.
   - Examine the nares for any obstructions or deformities by asking the client to breathe through one nostril while occluding the other.
   - Select the nostril that has the greater airflow.
4. **Prepare the tube.**
   - If a rubber tube is being used, place it on ice for 5 to 10 minutes. *This stiffens the tube, facilitating insertion.* If a plastic tube is being used, place it in warm water until the tube is softer and more flexible. *This facilitates insertion.*
5. **Determine how far to insert the tube.**
   - Use the tube to mark off the distance from the tip of the client's nose to the tip of the earlobe and then from the tip of the earlobe to the tip of the sternum (Figure 38.7). *This length approximates the distance from the nares to the stomach. This distance varies among individuals.*
   - Mark this length with adhesive tape if the tube does not have markings.
6. **Insert the tube.**
   - Don gloves.
   - Lubricate the tip of the tube well with water-soluble lubricant or water to ease insertion. *A water-soluble lubricant dissolves if the tube accidentally enters the lungs. An oil-based lubricant, such as petroleum jelly, will not dissolve and could cause respiratory complications if it enters the lungs.*
   - Insert the tube, with its natural curve toward the client, into the selected nostril. Ask the client to hyperextend the neck, and gently advance the tube toward the nasopharynx. *Hyperextension of the neck reduces the curvature of the nasopharyngeal junction.*
   - Direct the tube along the floor of the nostril and toward the ear on that side. *Directing the tube along the floor avoids the projections (turbinates) along the lateral wall.*
   - Slight pressure is sometimes required to pass the tube into the nasopharynx, and some clients' eyes may water at this point. Tears are a natural body response. Provide the client with tissues, as needed.
   - If the tube meets resistance, withdraw it, relubricate it, and insert it

PROCEDURE 38.1 Inserting a Nasogastric Tube *continued*

in the other nostril. *The tube should never be forced against resistance because of the danger of injury.*

- Once the tube reaches the oropharynx (throat), the client will feel the tube in the throat and may gag. Ask the client to tilt the head forward, and encourage the client to drink, if permitted, and swallow or to dry swallow. *Tilting the head forward facilitates passage of the tube into the posterior pharynx and esophagus, rather than into the larynx; swallowing moves the epiglottis over the opening to the larynx* (Figure 38.8).
- If the client gags, stop passing the tube momentarily. Have the client rest, take a few breaths, and take sips of water, if permitted, to calm the gag reflex.
- In cooperation with the client, pass the tube 5 to 10 cm with each swallow, until the indicated length is inserted.
- If the client continues to gag and the tube does not advance with each swallow, withdraw it slightly, and inspect the throat by looking through the mouth. *The tube may be coiled in the throat.* If so, withdraw it until it is straight, and try again to insert it. Remove the tube immediately if the client becomes cyanotic and/or SOB.

7. Ascertain correct placement of the tube.

- Aspirate stomach contents, and check their pH.
- Auscultate air insufflation (ausculate epigastrium, LUQ).
- If the signs do not indicate placement in the stomach, advance the tube 5 cm, and repeat the tests.

8. Secure the tube by taping it to the bridge of the client's nose.

- If the client has oily skin, wipe the nose first with alcohol.
- Cut 7.5 cm of tape, and split it lengthwise at one end, leaving a 2.5-cm tab at the end.
- Place the tape over the bridge of the client's nose, and bring the split ends either under and around the tubing or, under the tubing and back up over the nose (Figure 38.9). *Taping in this manner prevents the tube from pressing against and irritating the edge of the nostril.*

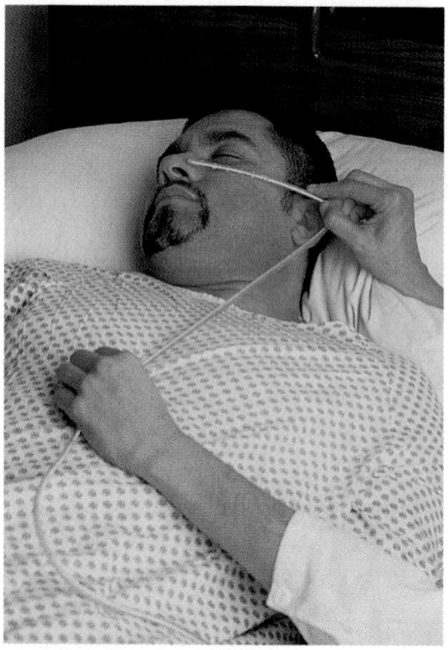

Figure 38.7 Measuring the appropriate length to insert a nasogastric tube

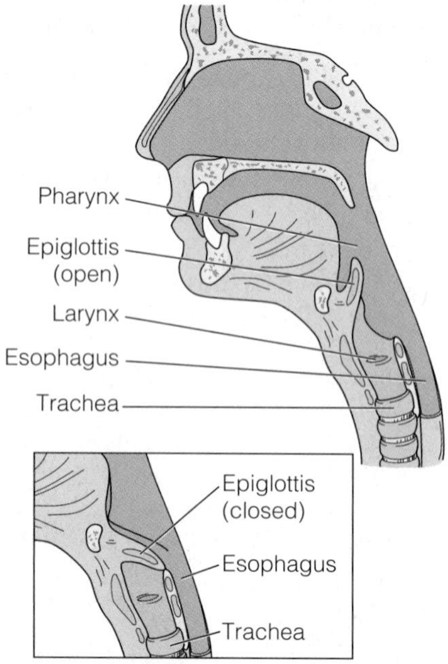

Figure 38.8 Swallowing closes the epiglottis

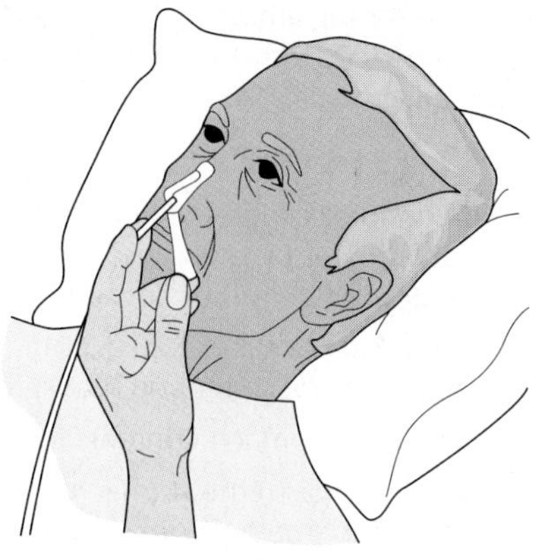

Figure 38.9 Taping a nasogastric tube to the bridge of the nose

9. Attach the tube to a suction source or feeding apparatus as ordered, or clamp the end of the tubing. Send gastric contents for lab analysis as ordered.

- The tube, if inserted preoperatively, is usually clamped or plugged; or it may be covered with a gauze square or plastic specimen bag and an elastic band.

10. Secure the tube to the client's gown.

- Loop an elastic band around the end of the tubing, and attach the elastic band to the gown with a safety pin.

or

- Attach a piece of adhesive tape to the tube, and pin the tape to the gown. *The tube is attached to prevent it from dangling and pulling.*

11. Establish a plan for providing nasogastric tube care.

- Inspect the nostril for discharge and irritation.
- Clean the nostril and tube with moistened, cotton-tipped applicators.
- Apply water-soluble lubricant to the nostril if it appears dry or encrusted.
- Change the adhesive tape, as required.
- Give frequent mouth care. *The client may breathe through the mouth and may be NPO.*

PROCEDURE 38.1 Inserting a Nasogastric Tube *continued*

12. If suspension is applied, ensure that the patency of both the nasogastric and suction tubes is maintained.

- Irrigations of the tube with 30 mL of normal saline may be required at regular intervals. In some agencies, irrigations must be ordered by the physician. Managing gastrointestinal suction and irrigating a nasogastric tube are discussed in Procedure 44.3, page 1253.
- Keep accurate records of the client's fluid intake and output, and record the amount and characteristics of the drainage.

13. Document all relevant information.

- Document the type of tube inserted, date and time of tube insertion, type of suction used, colour and amount of gastric contents, and the client's tolerance of the procedure.

Evaluation Focus
Degree of client comfort; client tolerance of tube; correct placement of nasogastric tube in stomach; client understanding of restrictions; colour and amount of gastric contents if attached to suction or contents aspirated

Pediatric Considerations

- For infants and young children, restraints may be necessary during tube insertion and throughout therapy. *Restraints will prevent accidental dislodging of the tube.*
- Place the infant in an infant seat, or position the infant with a rolled towel or pillow under the head and shoulders.
- When assessing the nares, obstruct one of the infant's nares, and feel for air passage from the other. If the nasal passageway is very small or is obstructed, an orogastric tube may be more appropriate.
- For infants and young children, measure appropriate nasogastric tube length from the nose to the tip of the earlobe and then to the point midway between the umbilicus and the xiphoid process.
- If an orogastric tube is used, measure from the tip of the earlobe to the corner of the mouth to the xiphoid process.
- Do not hyperextend or hyperflex an infant's neck. *Hyperextension or hyperflexion of the neck could occlude the airway.*
- For infants or small children, tape the tube to the area between the end of the nares and the upper lip, as well as to the cheek.

The surgical opening is sutured tightly around the tube or catheter to prevent leakage. Care of this opening before it heals requires surgical asepsis. When the incision heals (10 to 14 days), the tube or catheter may be removed and reinserted for each feeding. Between feedings, a prosthesis may be used to close the ostomy opening. It consists of a shaft 3 to 5 cm long with internal and external flanges and a screw cap. Physician's orders are needed.

Percutaneous endoscopic gastrostomy (PEG) and **percutaneous endoscopic jejunostomy (PEJ)** are being used. These procedures do not require general anesthesia or the use of an operating room. PEG Tubes have separate feeding and medication ports and can be interconnected with traditional feeding tubing sets. For the special care requirements of PEG Tubes, please see Procedure 38.3, p. 1011. PEG or PEJ is usually performed in the endoscopy suite but may also be done in the client's room. Using an endoscope to visualize the inside of the stomach, the physician makes a puncture through the skin and subcutaneous tissues of the abdomen into the stomach and inserts the PEG or PEJ catheter through the puncture. The catheter has internal and external bumpers and an inflatable retention balloon to maintain placement. Once the opening has healed, replacement tubes can be inserted without the use of endoscopy.

Testing Feeding Tube Placement

Before feedings are introduced, tube placement is confirmed by radiography, particularly when a small-bore tube has been inserted or when the client is at risk for aspiration. After placement is confirmed, the nurse marks the tube with indelible ink or tape at its exit point from the nose and documents the length of visible tubing for baseline data. The nurse is responsible, however, for verifying tube placement (i.e., gastrointestinal placement versus respiratory placement) before each intermittent feeding and at regular intervals (e.g., at least once per shift) when continuous feedings are being administered.

A method to check tube placement follows:

Measure the pH of aspirated fluid. This is the recommended method to determine tube placement. Testing the pH of aspirates can help distinguish gastric from respiratory and intestinal placement (Metheny et al., 1998):

- Gastric aspirates tend to be acidic and have a pH of 1 to 4 but may be as high as 6 if the client is receiving medications that control gastric acid.

PROCEDURE 38.2 Removing a Nasogastric Tube

Assessment Focus
Presence of bowel sounds; absence of nausea or vomiting when tube is clamped

Equipment

- ❑ Disposable pad
- ❑ Tissues
- ❑ Disposable gloves
- ❑ 50-mL syringe (optional)
- ❑ Plastic disposable bag

INTERVENTION

1. **Confirm the physician's order to remove the tube.**
2. **Prepare the client.**
   - Explain that the procedure will cause no discomfort.
   - Assist the client to a sitting position, if the client's health permits.
   - Place the disposable pad across the client's chest to collect any spillage of mucous and gastric secretions from the tube.
   - Provide tissues to the client to wipe the nose and mouth after tube removal.
3. **Detach the tube.**
   - Disconnect the nasogastric tube from the suction apparatus, if present.
   - Unpin the tube from the client's gown.
   - Remove the adhesive tape securing the tube to the nose.
4. **Remove the tube.**
   - Put on disposable gloves.
   - (Optional) Instill 50 mL of air into the tube if not contraindicated. *This clears the tube of any contents, such as feeding or gastric drainage.*
   - Ask the client to take a deep breath and to hold it. *This closes the glottis, thereby preventing accidental aspiration of any gastric contents.*
   - Pinch the tube with the gloved hand. *Pinching the tube prevents any contents inside the tube from draining into the client's throat.*
   - Quickly and smoothly withdraw the tube.
   - Place the tube in the plastic bag. *Placing the tube immediately into the bag prevents the transference of microorganisms from the tube to other articles or people.*
   - Observe the intactness of the tube.
5. **Ensure client comfort.**
   - Provide mouth care, if desired.
   - Assist the client as required to blow the nose. *Excessive secretions may have accumulated in the nasal passages.*
6. **Dispose of the equipment appropriately.**
   - Place the pad, bag with tube, and gloves in the receptacle designated by the agency. *Correct disposal prevents the transmission of microorganisms.*
7. **Assess the nasogastric drainage if suction was used.**
   - Measure the amount of gastric drainage, and record it on the client's fluid output record.
   - Inspect the drainage for appearance and consistency.
8. **Document all relevant information.**
   - Record the removal of the tube, the amount and appearance of any drainage if connected to suction, and any relevant assessments of the client.

Evaluation Focus
Presence of bowel sounds; absence of nausea or vomiting when tube is removed; intactness of tissues of the nares

- Small intestinal aspirates generally have a pH equal to or higher than 6.
- Respiratory secretions are more alkaline with values of 7 or higher. However, there is a slight possibility of respiratory placement when the pH reading is as low as 6.

Therefore, when pH readings are 6 or higher, radiographic confirmation of tube location needs to be considered, especially in clients with diminished cough and gag reflexes (Metheny et al., 1998).

Ausculate the epigastrium while injecting 5 to 20 mL of air if not contraindicated. Air injected into the stomach produces whooshing, gurgling, or bubbling sounds over the epigastrium and the upper left quadrant. Accuracy of this method in predicting placement is less reliable than pH testing (Metheny et al., 1998).

Currently, the most effective method appears to be radiographic verification of tube placement. Repeated x-ray studies, however, are not feasible in terms of cost and radiation risk. More research is required to devise effective alternatives, especially for placement of small-bore tubes. In the meantime, nurses should (1) ensure initial radiographic verification of small-bore tubes, (2) aspirate contents when possible and check their acidity, (3) closely observe the client for signs of obvious respiratory distress, and (4) suspect tube dislodgement after episodes of coughing, sneezing, gagging, and vomiting.

Enteral Feedings

The frequency of feedings and amounts to be administered are ordered by the physician. Liquid feeding mixtures are available commercially or may be prepared by the dietary department in accordance with the physician's orders. A standard formula provides 1 kcal/mL of solution with protein, fat, carbohydrate, minerals, and vitamins in specified proportions.

Enteral feedings can be given intermittently or continuously. *Intermittent feedings* are the administration of 300 to 500 mL of enteral formula several times per day. The stomach is the preferred site for these feedings which are usually administered over at least 30 minutes.

Continuous feedings are generally administered over a 24-hour period using an infusion pump that guarantees a constant flow rate (Figure 38.10). Continuous feedings are essential when feedings are administered in the small bowel. They are also used when smaller-bore gastric tubes are in place or when gravity flow is insufficient to instill the feeding.

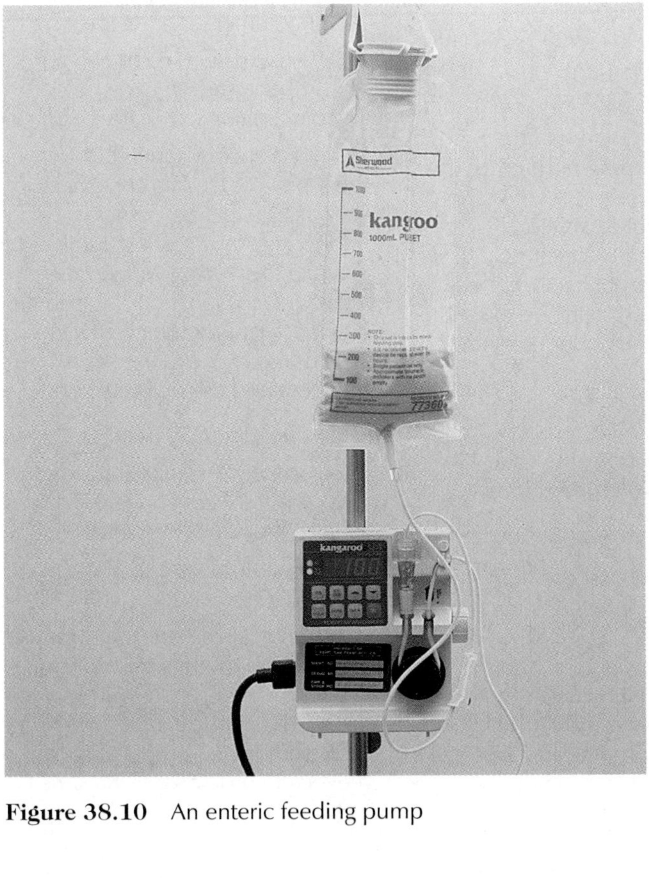

Figure 38.10 An enteric feeding pump

Cyclic feedings are continuous feedings that are administered in less than 24 hours (e.g., 12 to 16 hours). These feedings, often administered at night and referred to as nocturnal feedings, allow the client to attempt to eat regular meals through the day. Because nocturnal feedings may use higher nutrient densities and higher infusion rates than the standard continuous feeding, particular attention needs to be given to monitoring fluid status and circulating volume overload.

Enteral feedings are administered to clients through open or closed systems. *Open systems* use an open-top container or a syringe (without plunge) for administration. Enteral feedings for use with open systems are provided in flip-top cans or powdered formulas that are reconstituted with sterile water. Sterile water, rather than tap water, is used to reduce the risk of microbial contamination. *Closed systems* consist of a prefilled container that is spiked with enteral tubing and attached to the enteral access device. Prefilled containers generally have one litre of formula and can hang safely for 24 to 36 hours if sterile technique is used (Lord et al., 1996).

Procedure 38.3 provides the essential steps involved in administering a tube feeding, and Procedure 38.4 indicates the steps involved in administering a gastrostomy or jejunostomy tube feeding.

Before administering a tube feeding, the nurse must determine any food allergies of the client and assess tolerance to previous feedings. See Table 38.8 for essential assessments to conduct before administering tube feedings. The nurse must also check the expiration date on a commercially prepared formula or the preparation date and time of agency-prepared solution, discarding any formula that has passed the expiration date or solution more than 24 hours old.

Feedings are usually administered at room temperature unless the order specifies otherwise. The nurse warms the specified amount of solution in a basin of warm water or leaves it to stand for a while until it reaches room temperature. Because a formula that is warmed can grow microorganisms, it should not hang longer than the manufacturer recommends. If it will hang longer, it should be kept cool with ice chips. Continuous feeding should be kept cold; excessive heat coagulates feedings of milk and egg, and hot liquids can irritate the mucous membranes. However, excessively cold feedings can reduce the flow of digestive juices by causing vasoconstriction and may cause cramps.

PROCEDURE 38.3 Administering a Tube Feeding

Before commencing a nasogastric or orogastric feeding, determine the type, amount, and frequency of feedings and tolerance of previous feedings.

PURPOSES

- To restore or maintain nutritional status
- To administer medications

Assessment Focus

Clinical signs of malnutrition or dehydration (see Table 40.5); allergies to any food in the feeding; presence of bowel sounds; any problems that suggest lack of tolerance of previous feedings (e.g., delayed gastric emptying, abdominal distention, dumping syndrome, constipation, or dehydration)

Equipment

- ❑ Correct amount of feeding solution
- ❑ 20- to 50-mL syringe with an adapter
- ❑ Emesis basin
- ❑ Large syringe without plunger or large bulb syringe
  or
  Calibrated plastic feeding bag with tubing that can be attached to the feeding tube
  or
  Prefilled bottle with a drip chamber, tubing, and a flow-regulator clamp
- ❑ pH test strip or meter
- ❑ Measuring container from which to pour the feeding (if using open system)
- ❑ Water (60 mL, unless otherwise specified) at room temperature
- ❑ Feeding pump as required

INTERVENTION

1. **Verify physicians's order, and check agency policy.**
2. **Prepare the client and the feeding.**

- Explain to the client that the feeding should not cause any discomfort but may cause a feeling of fullness. For an adult, the usual intermittent feeding will take about 30 minutes; the exact length of time depends largely on the volume of the feeding.
- Provide privacy for this procedure if the client desires it. *Nasogastric feedings are embarrassing to some people.*
- Assist the client to a Fowler's position in bed or a sitting position in a chair, the normal position for eating. If a sitting position is contraindicated, a slightly elevated right side-lying position is acceptable. *These positions enhance the gravitational flow of the solution and prevent aspiration of fluid into the lungs.*

3. **Assess tube placement.**

- Attach the syringe to the open end of the tube, aspirate alimentary secretions. Check the pH. McConnell (1997) advises (a) allowing one hour to elapse before testing the pH if the client has received a medication, and (2) using a pH meter, rather than pH paper if the client is receiving a continuous feeding or if food colouring has been added to the formula.

4. **Assess residual feeding contents.**

- Aspirate all the stomach contents, and measure the amount prior to administering the feeding. *This is done to evaluate absorption of the last feeding, that is, whether undigested formula from a previous feeding remains.*
- If 100 mL (or more than half the last feeding) is withdrawn, refer to agency policy before proceeding. The precise amount is usually determined by the physician's order or by agency policy. *At some agencies, a feeding is withheld when the specified amount or more of formula remains in the stomach. In other agencies, the amount withdrawn (the undigested portion) is subtracted from the total feeding and that volume is administered slowly.*
  or
  Re-instill the gastric contents into the stomach if this is the agency policy or physician's order. Remove the syringe bulb or plunger, and pour the gastric contents via the syringe into the nasogastric tube. *Removal of the contents could disturb the client's electrolyte balance.*
- If the client is on a continuous feeding, check the gastric residual every four to six hours or according to agency protocol.

5. **Administer the feeding.**

- Before administering feeding:
  a. Check the expiration date of the feeding.
  b. Warm the feeding to room temperature. *An excessively cold feeding may cause cramps.*
- When an open system is used, clean the top of the feeding container with alcohol before opening it. *This minimizes the risk of contaminants entering the feeding syringe or feeding bag. Place label on the feeding bag that includes the client's name, type of feeding, the time commenced, and the finishing time.*

Feeding Bag (Open System)

- Hang the bag from an infusion pole about 30 cm above the tube's point of insertion into the client.
- Clamp the tubing, and add the formula to the bag.
- Open the clamp, run the formula through the tubing, and reclamp the tube. *The formula will displace the air in the tubing, thus preventing the instillation of excess air into the client's stomach or intestine.*

PROCEDURE 38.3 Administering a Tube Feeding *continued*

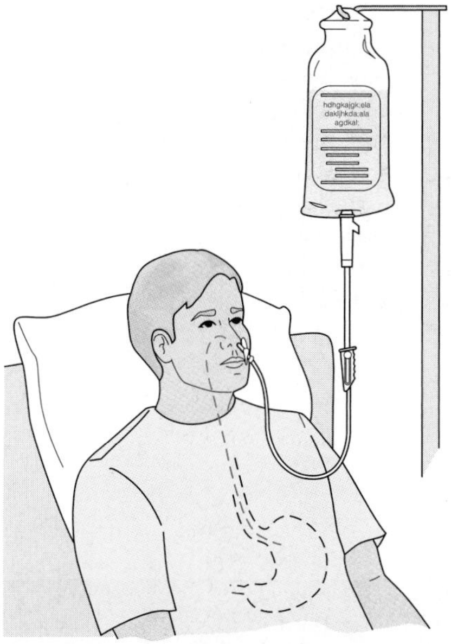

Figure 38.11 Using a calibrated plastic bag to administer a tube feeding

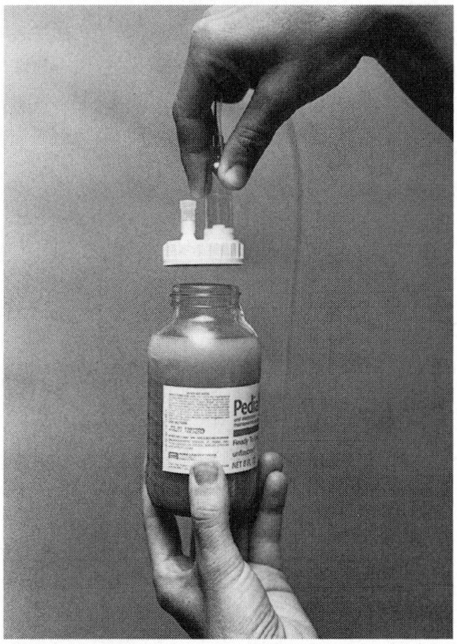

Figure 38.12 A prefilled bottle with drip chamber

- Attach the bag to the nasogastric tube (Figure 38.11), and regulate the drip by adjusting the clamp to the drop factor on bag (e.g., 20 drops/mL).

Prefilled Bottle with Drip Chamber (Closed System)

- Remove the screw-on cap from the container, and attach the administration set with the drip chamber and tubing (Figure 38.12).
- Close the clamp on the tubing.
- Hang the container on an intravenous pole about 30 cm above the tube's insertion point into the client. *At this height, the formula should run at a safe rate into the stomach or intestine.*
- Squeeze the drip chamber to fill it to one-third to one-half of its capacity.
- Open the tubing clamp, run the formula through the tubing, and reclamp the tube. *The formula will displace the air in the tubing, thus preventing the instillation of excess air.*
- Attach the feeding set tubing to the feeding tube, and regulate the drip rate to deliver the feeding over the desired length of time. Prefilled tube-feeding sets can be attached to a feeding pump to regulate the flow.

6. **Rinse the feeding tube immediately before all of the formula has run through the tubing.**

- Instill 50 to 100 mL of water through the feeding tube according to agency policy and physician's orders. *Water flushes the lumen of the tube, preventing future blockage by sticky formula.*
- Be sure to add the water before the feeding solution has drained from the neck of a syringe or from the tubing of an administration set. Before adding water to a feeding bag or prefilled tubing set, first clamp and disconnect both feeding and administration tubes. *Adding the water before the syringe or tubing is empty prevents the instillation of air into the stomach or intestine and, thus, prevents unnecessary distention.*

7. **Clamp and cover the feeding tube.**

- Clamp the feeding tube before all of the water is instilled. *Clamping prevents leakage and air from entering the tube if done before water is instilled.*
- Cover the end of the feeding tube with gauze held by an elastic band. *Covering the tube end prevents leakage from it.*

8. **Ensure client comfort and safety.**

- Pin the tubing to the client's gown. *This minimizes pulling of the tube, thus preventing discomfort and dislodgement.*
- Ask the client to remain sitting upright in Fowler's position or in a slightly elevated right lateral position for at least 30 minutes. *These positions facilitate digestion and movement of the feeding from the stomach along the alimentary tract, and prevent potential aspiration of the feeding into the lungs.*
- Check the agency's policy on the frequency of changing the nasogastric tube and the use of smaller-lumen tubes if a large-bore tube is in place. *These measures prevent irritation and erosion of the pharyngeal and esophageal mucous membranes.*

9. **Dispose of equipment appropriately.**

- If the equipment is to be reused, wash it thoroughly with soap and water so that it is ready for reuse.
- Change the equipment every 24 hours or according to agency policy.

10. **Document all relevant information. Document verification of tube placement prior to tube feeding.**

- Document the feeding, including amount and kind of solution taken, duration of the feeding, and assessments of the client.
- Record the volume of the feeding and water administered on the client's intake and output record.

11. **Monitor the client for possible problems.**

- Carefully assess clients receiving tube feedings for problems such as nausea, diarrhea, cramps, and/or regurgitation.
- To prevent dehydration, give the client supplemental water in addition to the prescribed tube feeding, as ordered.

PROCEDURE 38.3 Administering a Tube Feeding *continued*

Variation: Continuous-Drip Feeding

- If the feeding is a continuous-drip tube feeding, place a label on the container.
- Clamp the tubing at least every four to six hours or as indicated by agency protocol or the manufacturer, and aspirate and measure the gastric contents. Then, flush the tubing with 30 to 50 mL of water as ordered or according to agency policy. *This determines adequate absorption and verifies correct placement of the tube. If placement of a small-bore tube is questionable, a repeat x-ray should be done.*
- Determine agency protocol regarding withholding a feeding. Many agencies withhold the feeding if more than 75 to 100 mL of feeding is aspirated.
- To prevent spoilage or bacterial contamination, do not allow the feeding solution to hang longer than four to eight hours. *Check agency policy or manufacturer's recommendations regarding time limits.*
- Follow agency policy regarding how frequently to change the feeding bag and tubing. *Changing the feeding bag and tubing every 24 hours reduces the risk of contamination.*

Evaluation Focus
Tolerance of feeding; regurgitation and feelings of fullness after feedings; weight gain or loss; fecal elimination pattern (e.g., diarrhea, flatulence, constipation); skin turgor; urine output; glucose and acetone in urine

Pediatric Considerations

- Feeding tubes may be reinserted at each feeding to prevent irritation of the mucous membrane, nasal airway obstruction, and stomach perforation that may occur it the tube is left in place continuously. Check agency practice.
- Position a small child or infant in your lap, provide a pacifier, and hold and cuddle the child during feedings. This promotes comfort, supports the normal sucking instinct of the infant, and facilitates digestion.
- Check agency policy or physician's orders about the acceptable amounts of stomach aspirates and re-instillation of residual feedings.

PROCEDURE 38.4 Administering a Gastrostomy or Jejunostomy Feeding

Before commencing a gastrostomy or jejunostomy feeding, determine the type and amount of feeding to be instilled, frequency of feedings, and any pertinent information about previous feedings (e.g., the position in which the client best tolerates the feeding).

Assessment Focus
See Procedure 38.3 on page 1008.

PURPOSES

- To improve or maintain nutritional status
- To administer medications

Equipment

- ❑ Correct amount of feeding solution
- ❑ Graduated container to hold the feeding
- ❑ Large bulb syringe
- ❑ Graduated container with 60 mL of water to flush the tubing
- ❑ Graduated container to measure residual formula

For a Tube Sutured in Place

- ❑ 4 × 4 gauze squares to cover the end of the tube
- ❑ Elastic band

For Tube Insertion

- ❑ Clean disposable gloves
- ❑ Moistureproof bag
- ❑ Water-soluble lubricant
- ❑ #18 Fr whistle-tip catheter or other feeding tube
- ❑ Tubing clamp

For Cleaning the Peristomal Skin and Dressing the Stoma

- ❑ Mild soap and water
- ❑ Petrolatum, zinc oxide ointment, or other skin protectant
- ❑ Precut 4 × 4 gauze squares
- ❑ Uncut 4 × 4 gauze squares
- ❑ Abdominal pads
- ❑ Abdominal binder or Montgomery straps, if required

PROCEDURE 38.4 Administering a Gastrostomy or Jejunostomy Feeding *continued*

INTERVENTION

1. Assess and prepare the client.

- See Procedure 38.3 on page 1008.

2. Insert a feeding tube if one is not already in place.

- Wearing gloves, remove the ostomy dressing. Then discard the dressing and gloves in the moistureproof bag.
- Lubricate the end of the tube, and insert it into the ostomy opening 10 to 15 cm.

3. Check the patency of a tube that is sutured or secured in place.

- Determine correct placement of the tube by aspirating secretions and checking the pH.
- Pour 15 to 30 mL of water into the syringe, remove the tube clamp, and allow the water to flow into the tube. *This determines the patency of the tube. If water flows freely, the tube is patent.*
- If the water does not flow freely, notify the nurse in charge and/ or physician.

4. Check for residual formula.

- Attach the bulb to the syringe, and compress the bulb. *Compressing the bulb before the syringe is attached to the feeding tube prevents the instillation of air into the stomach or jejunum.*
- Attach the syringe to the end of the feeding tube, and withdraw and measure the stomach or jejunal contents.
- Follow agency practice if there is no more than 50 mL of undigested formula. Hold the feeding if there is more than 100 mL or more than half of the last feeding remaining, and recheck in 3 to 4 hours or according to agency policy. Notify the physician of residual amount stated in orders or agency policy.
- For continuous feedings, check the residual every 4 to 6 hours, and hold feedings according to agency policy. The physician should be notified of residual amount stated in orders or agency policy.

5. Administer the feeding.

- Hold the syringe 7 to 15 cm above the ostomy opening.
- Slowly pour the solution into the syringe, and allow it to flow through the tube by gravity.
- Just before all the formula has run through and the syringe is empty, add 30 mL of water. *Water flushes the tube and preserves its patency.*
- If the tube is sutured in place, hold it upright, remove the syringe, and then clamp or plug the tube to prevent leakage. Cover the end of the tube with a 4 × 4 gauze, and secure the gauze with a rubber band.
- If a catheter was inserted for the feeding, remove it as ordered by the physician.

6. Ensure client comfort and safety.

- After the feeding, ask the client to remain in the sitting position or a slightly elevated right lateral position for at least 30 minutes. *This minimizes the risk of aspiration.*
- Assess status of peristomal skin. *Gastric or jejunal drainage contains digestive enzymes that can irritate the skin.* Document any redness and broken skin areas.
- Check orders about cleaning the peristomal skin, applying a skin protectant, and applying appropriate dressings. Generally, the peristomal skin is washed with mild soap and water or with normal saline at least once daily. Petrolatum, zinc oxide ointment, or other skin protectant may be applied around the stoma, and precut 4 × 4 gauze squares may be placed around the tube. The precut squares are then covered with regular 4 × 4 gauze squares, and the tube is coiled over them. The coiled tube is covered with abdominal pads and secured with either an abdominal binder, Montgomery straps, or tape.
- Observe for common complications of enteral feedings: aspiration, hyperglycemia, abdominal distention, diarrhea, and fecal impaction. Report findings to physician. Often, a change in formula or rate of administration can correct problems.
- When appropriate, teach the client how to administer feedings and when to notify the health-care provider concerning problems. Gastrostomy, jejunostomy, and PEG tube feedings may also be continuous (administered via enteral pump).

Variation: Percutaneous Endoscopic Gastrostomy (PEG)

- A percutaneous endoscopic gastrostomy (PEG) is kept in place with a short cross-piece or bolster near the skin level at the stoma.
- Clean the stoma daily with soap and water or saline using a cotton swab or small piece of gauze in a circular motion.
- Rotate the bolster and clean the skin under it.
- Rotate the tube daily in a full circle between the thumb and forefinger according to physician's orders and agency policy.
- After cleaning, allow the skin to air dry.
- Report any signs of redness, pain, soreness, swelling, or drainage to the health-care provider.
- Do not apply a dressing over the PEG. *A dressing and tape may result in skin excoriation and breakdown.*

7. Document all assessments and interventions.

Evaluation Focus
See Procedure 38.3, page 1010.

TABLE 38.8 Assessing Clients Receiving Tube Feedings

Assessment	Rationale
Allergies to any food in the feeding	Common allergenic foods include milk, eggs, and vegetable oil.
Bowel sounds prior to each feeding or, for continuous feedings, every four to eight hours	To determine intestinal activity (peristalsis).
Abdominal distention, at least daily, measure abdominal girth at the umbilicus	Abdominal distention may indicate intolerance to a previous feeding.
Correct placement of tube, before feedings	To prevent aspiration of feedings.
Presence of regurgitation and feelings of fullness after feedings	May indicate delayed gastric emptying, need to decrease quantity or rate of the feeding, or high fat content of the formula.
Dumping syndrome: nausea, vomiting, diarrhea, cramps, pallor, sweating, heart palpitations, increased pulse rate, and fainting after a feeding	Jejunostomy clients may experience these symptoms, which result when hypertonic foods and liquids suddenly distend the jejunum. To make the intestinal contents isotonic, body fluids shift rapidly from the client's vascular system.
Diarrhea, constipation, or flatulence	The lack of bulk in liquid feedings may cause constipation. The presence of hypertonic or concentrated ingredients may cause diarrhea and flatulence.
Urine for sugar and acetone	Hyperglycemia may occur if the sugar content is too high.
Hematocrit and urine specific gravity	Both increase as a result of dehydration.
Serum BUN and sodium levels	Feeding formula may have a high protein content. If a high protein intake is combined with an inadequate fluid intake, the kidneys may not be able to excrete nitrogenous wastes adequately.

Parenteral Nutrition

Parenteral nutrition (PN), also referred to as *total parenteral nutrition* (TPN) or *intravenous hyperalimentation* (IVH), is provided when the gastrointestinal tract is nonfunctional because of an interruption in its continuity or because its absorptive capacity is impaired. Parenteral nutrition (PN) is administered intravenously through a central venous catheter into the superior vena cava. (See Figure 40.13.)

Parenteral feedings are solutions of dextrose, water, fat, proteins, electrolytes, vitamins, and trace elements; it is the provision of all needed calories. Because TPN solutions are *hypertonic* (highly concentrated in comparison to the solute concentration of blood), they are injected only into high-flow central veins where they are diluted by the client's blood.

TPN is a means of achieving an anabolic state in clients who are unable to maintain a normal nitrogen balance. Such clients may include those with severe malnutrition, severe burns, bowel disease disorders (e.g., ulcerative colitis or enteric fistula), acute renal failure, hepatic failure, metastatic cancer, or major surgeries where nothing may be taken by mouth for more than five days.

Infection control is of utmost importance during TPN therapy. The nurse must always observe surgical aseptic technique when changing solutions, tubing, dressings, and filters.

TPN solutions are a mixture of 10 to 50 percent dextrose in water, amino acids, and special additives such as vitamins (e.g., B complex, C, D, K), minerals (e.g., potassium, sodium, chloride, calcium, phosphate, magnesium), and trace elements (e.g., cobalt, zinc, manganese). Additives are adapted to each client's nutritional needs. Fat emulsions may be given to provide essential fatty acids to correct and/or prevent essential fatty acid deficiency or to supplement the calories for clients who, for example, have high calorie needs or cannot tolerate glucose as the only calorie source.

Because TPN solutions are high in glucose, infusions are started gradually to prevent hyperglycemia. The client needs to adapt to TPN therapy by increasing insulin output from the pancreas. For example, an adult client may be given 1 litre (40 mL/h) of TPN solution the first day; if the infusion is tolerated, the amount may be increased to 2 litres (80 mL/h) for 24 to 48 hours, and then to 3 litres (120 mL/h) within three to five days. Glucose levels are monitored during the infusion.

When TPN therapy is to be discontinued, the TPN infusion rates are decreased slowly to prevent hyperinsulinemia and hypoglycemia. Weaning a client from TPN may take up to 48 hours but can occur in six hours as long as the client receives adequate carbohydrates either orally or intravenously.

Evaluating

The goals established in the planning phase are evaluated according to specific desired outcomes also established in that phase. Examples of these are shown in Table 38.9.

CLIENT TEACHING

Home Nutrition Therapy

Enteral feedings may be continued beyond hospital care in the client's home or may be initiated in the home. Clients and caregivers need the following instructions to manage these feedings:

- *Preparation of the formula.* Include name of the formula and how much and how often it is to be given; the need to inspect the formula for expiration date and leaks and cracks in bags or cans; how to mix or prepare the formula, if needed; and aseptic techniques, such as swabbing the container's top with alcohol before opening it, and changing the syringe administration set and reservoir every 24 hours.
- *Proper storage of the formula.* Include the need to refrigerate diluted or reconstituted formula and formula that contains additives.
- *Administration of the feeding.* Include proper handwashing technique; how to fill and hang the feeding bag; operation of an infusion pump, if indicated; the feeding rate; and client positioning during and after the feeding.
- *Management of the enteral access device.* Include site care, aseptic precautions, dressing change, as indicated, how the site should look normally, and flushing protocols (e.g., type of irrigant and schedule).
- *Daily monitoring needs.* Include temperature, weight, and intake and output.
- *Signs and symptoms of complications to report.* Include fever, increased respiratory rate, decrease in urine output, increased stool frequency, and altered level of consciousness.
- *Who to contact regarding questions or problems.* Include emergency telephone numbers of home care agency, nursing clinician and/or physician, or other 24-hour on-call emergency number.

TABLE 38.9 Evaluation Goals and Outcomes

Goal	Examples of Desired Outcomes
Maintain or improve nutritional status	■ Weight within range for height and body frame ■ Body mass index within expected range ■ Ingests recommended servings from *Canada's Food Guide to Healthy Eating* ■ Uses fats sparingly ■ Uses salt, sodium, sugars, and alcohol in moderation
Decrease weight	■ Identifies factors contributing to excess weight (or risk of excess weight) ■ Monitors eating habits for specified period (e.g., one week) and identifies behaviours that need to be modified to lose weight (or prevent weight gain) ■ Chooses and ingests a diet that reduces daily caloric intake (e.g., reduces calories by 500 per day for each 0.5 kg of weight loss desired per week) ■ Establishes a physical activity program of 20 to 30 minutes duration at least three times per week ■ Loses prescribed amount of weight (specify) ■ Verbalizes improvement in feelings about self and satisfaction with support provided
Regain specified weight	■ Identifies factors contributing to inadequate nutritional intake ■ Identifies necessary dietary alterations and foods high in needed nutrients (e.g., calcium, iron, protein, total calories) ■ Consumes a well-balanced diet to restore deficient nutrients ■ Demonstrates decrease (or absence) of signs of malnutrition, as evidenced by: a. Weight gain of specified kilograms per week b. Skinfold measurements or 80 percent of the standard measurement c. Reports of increased energy (specify) d. Hemoglobin, serum albumin or prealbumin, serum transferrin, and lymphocyte counts within normal ranges

If the outcomes are *not* achieved, the nurse should explore the reasons. The nurse might consider the following questions:

- Was the cause of the problem correctly identified?
- Was the family included in the teaching plan? Are they supportive?
- Is the client experiencing symptoms that cause loss of appetite (e.g., pain, nausea, fatigue)?
- Were the outcomes unrealistic for this person?
- Were the client's food preferences considered?
- Is anything interfering with digestion or absorption of nutrients (e.g., diarrhea)?

FOCUS ON CRITICAL THINKING

Mrs. Lee is a 75-year-old woman who has recently been diagnosed with chronic lung disease, which has left her very susceptible to pneumonia. As a result, her physician has ordered three different oral medications that have resulted in her losing her appetite and suffering a 10-kilogram weight loss. Once overweight, Mrs. Lee is now within weight standards for her age and height. Mrs. Lee tells her visiting nurse, "Nothing sounds good and nothing tastes good. Meat is particularly distasteful to me right now." Mrs. Lee lives alone and is responsible for her own meal preparation.

1. How does Mrs. Lee's age and health status impact her nutritional needs?
2. What further information do you need regarding Mrs. Lee's present diet?
3. What alternatives can you offer while Mrs. Lee is unable to tolerate meat?
4. Offer suggestions for ways to enhance Mrs. Lee's intake during this period of decreased appetite.
5. Do you think that Mrs. Lee is a good candidate for a feeding tube? Why, or why not?

See Appendix A for answers to these questions.

CHAPTER HIGHLIGHTS

- Although people are continually bombarded with information about what to eat and what not to eat, each person is responsible for selecting foods that provide essential nutrients. Nurses can assist people to evaluate the information they receive about nutrients.
- Essential nutrients are grouped into six categories: water, carbohydrates, fats, proteins, vitamins, and minerals.
- Nutrients serve three basic purposes: forming body structures (such as bones and blood), providing energy, and helping to regulate the body's biochemical reactions.
- Energy balance is the relationship between the energy derived from food and the energy used by the body.
- The amount of energy that nutrients or foods supply to the body is their *caloric value*. The amount of energy required to maintain basic body functions is referred to as the resting energy expenditure (REE). The *basal metabolic rate* (BMR) is the rate at which the body metabolizes food to maintain the energy and requirements of a person who is awake and at rest.
- A person's state of energy balance can be determined by comparing caloric intake with caloric expenditure.
- Ideal body weight (IBW) is the weight recommended for optimal health.
- Body mass index (BMI) is one indicator of changes in body fat stores, whether a person's weight is appropriate for height, and may provide a useful estimate of nutrition.
- Factors influencing a person's nutrition include development, gender, ethnicity and culture, beliefs about foods, personal preferences, religious practices, lifestyle, medications and medical therapy, health status, alcohol abuse, advertising, and psychological factors, such as stress, isolation, and depression.
- Nutritional needs vary considerably according to age, growth, and energy requirements. Adolescents have high energy requirements due to their rapid growth; a diet plentiful in milk, meats, green and yellow vegetables, and fresh fruits is required. Older adults often need to reduce their caloric intake because of decreases in metabolic rate and activity levels. Fats, sugary foods, and sodium must often be limited.
- Various daily food guides have been developed to help healthy people meet the daily requirements of essential nutrients and to facilitate meal planning. This includes *Canada's Food Guide to Healthy Eating*.

- Both inadequate and excessive intakes of nutrients result in malnutrition. The effects of malnutrition can be general or specific, depending on which nutrients and what level of deficiency or excess are involved.
- Some of the long-range effects of certain nutrient excesses are among the many factors involved in certain diseases, such as coronary artery disease and cancer.
- Assessment of nutritional status may involve all or some of the following: nursing history data, nutritional screening, physical examination, calculation of the percentage of weight loss, a dietary history, anthropometric measurements, and laboratory data.
- Major goals for clients with or at risk for nutritional problems include the following: maintain or restore optimal nutritional status, decrease or regain specified weight, promote healthy nutritional practices, and prevent complications associated with malnutrition.
- Assisting clients and support persons with therapeutic diets is a function shared by the nurse and the dietitian. The nurse reinforces the dietitian's instructions, assists the client to make beneficial changes, and evaluates the client's response to planned changes.
- Because many hospitalized clients have poor appetites, a major responsibility of the nurse is to provide nursing interventions that stimulate their appetites.
- Whenever possible, the nurse should help incapacitated clients to feed themselves; a number of self-feeding aids help clients who have difficulty handling regular utensils.
- The nurse can refer clients to various community programs that help meet nutritional needs.
- Enteral feedings, administered through nasogastric, nasointestinal, gastrostomy, or jejunostomy tubes, are provided when the client is unable to ingest foods or the upper gastrointestinal tract is impaired.
- A nasogastric or nasointestinal tube is used to provide enteral nutrition for short-term use (less than six weeks), while a gastrostomy or jejunostomy tube can be used to supply nutrients via the enteral route for long-term use.
- Total parenteral nutrition (TPN), provided when the gastrointestinal tract is nonfunctional (e.g., absorptive capacity impaired), is given intravenously into a large central vein (e.g., the superior vena cava).

READINGS AND REFERENCES

Suggested Readings

Gant, R. (1997, December). Detection and correction of underweight problems in nursing home residents. *Journal of Gerontological Nursing, 23*(12), 26–31.

Gant reports a study to identify the underweight people living in a retirement facility at different functional levels and to plan and carry out nursing interventions in cooperation with the rest of the multidisciplinary team to increase their weight to within normal limits. Of the 205 residents who live in the home, 48 (23.4 percent) were found to be under the lower limit of ideal weight tables. With the aid of individual care plans and calorie-rich, low-volume diets, they succeeded in increasing the weight of 29 residents to within the normal range within 2 to 12 months. Seven residents died during the experimental period, and three continued to lose weight. The rest of the residents remained stable at their original low weight.

Loan, T., Magnuson, B., & Williams, S. (1998, August). Debunking six myths about enteral feeding. *Nursing 98, 28*(8), 43–48.

This continuing education article, with tests included, outlines six misconceptions about enteral feeding that could be doing clients a disservice. They include myths about bowel sounds, feeding tube locations, aspiration of feedings, stopping feedings, and so on.

Morris, V. M., & Rorie, J. L. (1997, December). Nutritional concerns in women's primary care. *Journal of Nurse-Midwifery, 42*(6), 509–520.

Health-care professionals need to be aware of current guidelines for nutritional monitoring, including those in *Healthy People 2000*, to provide primary care screening for nutritional factors that affect the health status of women. This article reviews the relationship between dietary habits and specific health concerns, including cardiovascular disease, obesity, osteoporosis, cancer, and diabetes; special attention is paid to high-risk groups. It also examines the relationship between improved nutrition status and the reduction of the major causes of morbidity in women.

Morrison, S. G. (1997, December). Feeding the elderly population. *Nursing Clinics of North America, 32*(4), 791–812.

Because nurses are often the health-care providers who are present in all health-care delivery sites, including the physician's office, the clinic, congregate sites, health fairs, or within the homes of older adults, they need to incorporate routine nutrition screening and intervention activities into their practice. This article describes (1) a nutrition assessment of older adults, (2) nutritional guidelines for the elderly population, (3) factors that affect oral intake in older adults, and (d) interventions to meet their nutritional needs.

Related Research

Blaum, C. S., O'Neill, E. F., Clements, K. M., et al. (1999, October). Validity of the Minimum Data Set for assessing nutritional status in nursing home residents. *American Journal of Clinical Nutrition, 66*(4), 787–794.

David, J. H. (1996, November/December). Total parenteral nutrition (TPN) at home: Prototype high tech home care nursing. *Gastroenterology Nursing, 19*(6), 207–209.

Ritchie, C. S., Burgio, K. L., Locher, J. L., et al. (1997, October). Nutritional status of urban homebound older adults. *American Journal of Clinical Nutrition, 66*(4), 815–818.

Selected References

Bond, S. (1998, September 2). Why eating matters. *Nursing Standard, 12*(50), 26–27.

Bowers, S. (1996, October). Tubes: A nurse's guide to enteral feeding devices. *MedSurg Nursing, 5*(5), 313–326.

Canada's Food Guide to Healthy Eating. Catalog No. 1139–252/1992E. Ottawa: Health and Welfare Canada.

Cason, K. L. (1998, September). Maintaining nutrition during drug therapy. *Nursing 98, 28*(9), 54–55.

Cerrato, P. (1997, November). Vitamins and minerals. *RN, 60*(11), 52–56.

Christian, J. L., & Greger, J. L. (1994). *Nutrition for Living* (4th ed.). Redwood City, CA: Benjamin/Cummings.

Dudek, S. G. (2001). *Nutrition essentials for nursing practice* (4th ed.). Philadelphia, PA: Lippincott.

Evans-Stoner, N. (1997a, December). Guidelines for care of the patient on home nutrition support. *Nursing Clinics of North America, 32*(4), 769–775.

Evans-Stoner, N. (1997b, December). Nutrition assessment: A practical approach. *Nursing Clinics of North America, 32*(4), 637–650.

Galica, L. A. (1997, December). Parenteral nutrition. *Nursing Clinics of North America, 32*(4), 705–717.

Gants, R. (1997, December). Detection and correction of underweight problems in nursing home residents. *Journal of Gerontological Nursing, 23*(12), 26–31.

Goff, K. (1997, December). Metabolic monitoring in nutrition support. *Nursing Clinics of North America, 32*(4), 741–753.

Guenter, P., Jones, S., & Erickson, M. (1997, December). Enteral nutrition therapy. *Nursing Clinics of North America, 32*(4), 651–667.

Hammond, K. (1997, December). Physical assessment: A nutritional perspective. *Nursing Clinics of North America, 32*(4), 779–790.

Herron, D. G. (1991, December). Strategies for promoting a healthy dietary intake. *Nursing Clinics of North America, 26*, 875–884.

Holmes, S. (1998, August 5). Food for thought. *Nursing Standard, 12*(46), 23–26.

Jeffery, R. W., & French, S. A. (1998, February). Epidemic obesity in the United States: Are fast foods and television viewing contributing? *American Journal of Public Health, 88*(2), 277–280.

Johnson, M., & Maas, M. (Eds.). (2000). *Iowa outcomes project: Nursing Outcomes Classification (NOC)*. St. Louis, MO: Mosby.

Jones, S. A., & Guenter, P. (1997, February). Automatic flush feeding pumps: A move forward in enteral nutrition. *Nursing 97, 27*(2), 56–58.

Krupp, K. B., & Heximer, B. (1998, April). Going with the flow: How to prevent feeding tubes from clogging. *Nursing 98, 28*(4), 54–55.

Kurz, J. M. (1997, March). How safe is home TPN? *American Journal of Nursing, 97*(3), 16L.

Loan, T., Magnuson, B., & Williams, S. (1998, August). Debunking six myths about enteral feeding. *Nursing 98, 28*(8), 43–47.

Lord, L. M. (1997, December). Enteral access devices. *Nursing Clinics of North America, 32*(4), 685–704.

Lord, L. M., Lipp, J., & Stull, S. (1996, December). Adult tube feeding formulas. *MedSurg Nursing, 5*(6), 407–421.

Lyman, B., & Marquardt, P. (1997, December). Nutrition screening tool. *Home Healthcare Nurse, 15*(12), 835–842.

Mahan, K. L., & Escott-Stump, S. (2000). *Krause's Food, Nutrition & Diet Therapy*. Philadelphia: W. B. Saunders Company.

McCloskey, J. C., & Bulechek, G. M. (Eds.). (2000). *Iowa intervention project: Nursing Interventions Classification (NIC)* (3rd ed.). St. Louis, MO: Mosby.

McConnell, E. A. (1997, January). Clinical do's and don'ts. Inserting a nasogastric tube. *Nursing 97, 27*(1), 72.

McConnell, E. A. (1997, August). Clinical do's and don'ts. How to determine gastric pH. *Nursing 97, 27*(8), 26.

McConnell, E. A. (1997, July). Clinical do's and don'ts. Administering parenteral nutrition. *Nursing 98, 28*(7), 18.

McLaren, S., & Green, S. (1998, August 19). Nutritional screening and assessment. *Nursing Standard, 12*(48), 28–29.

Metheny, N., Reed, L., Worseck, M., & Clark, J. (1993a, May). How to aspirate fluid from small-bore feeding tubes. *American Journal of Nursing, 93*(5), 86–88.

Metheny, N., Reed, L., Wiersema, L., McSweeney, M., Wehrle, J. C., & Clark, J. (1993b, November/December). Effectiveness of pH measurements in predicting feeding tube placement: An update. *Nursing Research, 42*(6), 324.

Metheny, N., Wehrle, M. A., Wiersema, L., & Clark, J. (1998, May). Testing feeding tube placement: Auscultation vs. pH method. *American Journal of Nursing, 98*(5), Nursing Practice Extra Edition, 37–43.

Miller, A. (1997, August 20). Know how: Vitamins and minerals. Key micronutrient requirements during adolescence 11–18 years. *Nursing Times, 93*(34), 72–73.

Miller, A. (1997, September 24). Know how: Vitamins and minerals. Key micronutrient requirements during adulthood 19–40 years. *Nursing Times, 93*(39), 34–35.

Montignac, M., Dumesnil, J. G., & Rogers, J. (translator). (1999). *Eat yourself slim*. Michel Ange Network Inc. North America.

Moore, J. (1998, May). Vitamins and health: The role of a balanced diet. *Community Nurse, 4*(4), 15–17.

Morris, V. M., & Rorie, J. L. (1997, November/December). Nutritional concerns in women: Primary care. *Journal of Nurse-Midwifery, 42*(6), 509–520.

Morrison, S. G. (1997, December). Feeding the elderly population. *Nursing Clinics of North America, 32*(4), 791–812.

National Institutes of Health, National Heart, Lung and Blood Institute. Washington, DC: Author. *Clinical Guidelines on the Identification, Evaluation, and Treatment of Overweight and Obesity in Adults*. NIH Publication No. 98–4083. Sept. 1998.

National Institutes of Health Web site: http://www.nih.gov/guidelines/obesity/bmi_tbl.htm

Oberc, M. C. (1991). Inserting and maintaining a gastric or jejunal tube. In D. A., Smith (Ed.), *Comprehensive child and family nursing skills* (pp. 418–428). St. Louis, MO: Mosby.

Osak, M. P. (1993, Spring). Nutrition and wound healing. *Plastic Surgery Nursing, 13*, 29–36.

Osato, E. E., Stone, J. T., Phillips, S. L., & Winnie, D. M. (1993, August). Clinical manifestations: Failure to thrive in the elderly. *Journal of Gerontological Nursing, 19*, 28–34.

Pratt, J. C., & Tolbert, C. G. (1996, May). Tube feeding aspiration. *American Journal of Nursing, 96*(5), 37.

Reid, M. (1998, June). Device errors: Enteral feeding tubes. *Nursing 98, 28*(6), 25.

Report of a joint consultation undertaken by the World Health Organization and the Food and Agricultural Organization. (1998, July 22). Carbohydrate and nutrition. *Nursing Standard, 12*(44), 32–33.

Rhodes, V. A. (1990, December). Nausea, vomiting, and retching. *Nursing Clinics of North America, 25*, 885–900.

Salom, I. L. (1997, January). Weight control and nutrition: Knowing when to intervene. *Geriatrics, 52*(1), 33–34, 39–42.

Scott, A., & Hamilton, K. (1998, August 19). Nutritional screening: An audit. *Nursing Standard, 12*(48), 46–47.

Taylor, L. J., & Faria, S. H. (1997, October). Practice teaching: Caring for the patient with a gastrostomy/jejunostomy tube. *Home Care Provider, 2*(5), 221–224.

US Department of Health and Human Services, Public Health Service. (1990). *Healthy People 2000: National health promotion and disease prevention objectives.* DHHS Pub no. (PHS) 91–50212. Washington, D.C.: US Government Printing Office.

Walters, E. (1998, February 25). Know how: Nutritional assessment. *Nursing Times, 94*(8), 68–69.

Watson, L. A. (1991). "Patterns of Hunger in Healthy Adults." Unpublished dissertation, University of Arizona.

Weinstein, D. S., & Furman, J. (1997, December). Enteral formulas. *Nursing Clinics of North America, 32*(4), 669–683.

White, S. (1998, April 1). Percutaneous endoscopic gastrostomy (PEG). *Nursing Standard, 12*(28), 41–47.

Wilson, J. M. (1998, November/December). Nutritional assessment and its application. *Journal of Intravenous Nursing, 19*(6), 307–314.

Wood, P., & Vogen, B. D. (1998, July/August). Feeding the anorectic client: Comfort foods and happy hour. *Geriatric Nursing, 19*(4), 192–194.

Yen, P. K. (1994, July/August). Focus on women's nutrition. *Geriatric Nursing, 15*(4), 225–226.

Yen, P. K. (1998, May/June). Adding calories to medications. *Geriatric Nursing, 19*(3), 168–169.

WEBLINKS

American Dietetic Association
www.eatright.org
This site introduces the American Dietetic Association and the services that it provides to its members and the public.

Health Canada
http://www.hc-sc.gc.ca/english/lifestyles/food_nutr.html
This site is sponsored by Health Canada and provides an introduction to public information on food and nutrition. The site also has a search tool and permits access to Canadian legislative policy, allergy alerts, and other federal resources.

USDA Human Nutrition Center on Research on Aging at Taft University
http://healthletter.taft.edu/
This site provides access to the nutrition newsletter of the USDA Human Nutrition Center on Research on Aging at Taft University.

Office of Nutrition Policy and Promotion (ONPP)
http://www.hc-sc.gc.ca/hpfb-dgpsa/onpp-bppn/index_e.html
This specific site is operated by Health Canada. The ONPP promotes the nutritional health and well-being of Canadians by acting as a central hub for current, reliable nutrition information available through the Web.

CHAPTER 39

Oxygenation

OBJECTIVES

After completing this chapter, you will be able to:

- Outline the structure and function of the respiratory system.
- Describe the processes of breathing (ventilation) and gas exchange (respiration).
- Explain the role and function of the cardiovascular system in transporting oxygen and carbon dioxide to and from body tissues.
- Identify factors influencing respiration and circulatory function.
- List common manifestations of impaired respiratory function.
- Discuss the manifestations of cardiovascular disorders.
- Outline the signs of an obstructed airway.
- Identify common responses to alterations in respiratory and circulatory status.
- Describe the nurse's role in caring for clients undergoing diagnostic procedures related to cardio-respiratory function.
- Identify and describe nursing measures to promote cardio-respiratory function and oxygenation.
- Explain the use of therapeutic measures, such as artificial airways, medications, oxygen therapy, inhalation therapy, pharyngeal suction, and chest drainage to promote cardio-respiratory function.
- Describe the critical nature of cardiopulmonary resuscitation.
- State outcome criteria for evaluating client responses to measure and promote adequate oxygenation.

Oxygen is a clear, odourless gas that constitutes approximately 21 percent of the air we breathe. Oxygen is necessary for all living cells and the absence of oxygen can lead to death. Oxygen transport to body tissues and the removal of carbon dioxide and other byproducts is a complex process. The major systems involved in this process include the lungs, heart, and blood. Although all systems in the body are indirectly involved in the oxygenation process, the lungs (respiratory system) and the heart (cardiovascular system) are directly and interdependently involved. Impaired function of either system can negatively affect the other system. This impairment can cause significant changes in the ability to breathe, transport gases, eliminate wastes, and can result in respiratory failure, cardiac dysfunction, and general inability to participate in activities of daily living.

Respiration is the process of gas exchange between the individual and the environment. The process of respiration (gas transport, delivery of oxygen to the cells) involves several components:

1. Pulmonary ventilation or breathing; the movement of air between the atmosphere and the alveoli of the lungs
2. Diffusion of oxygen and carbon dioxide between the alveoli and pulmonary capillaries
3. Transport of oxygen and carbon dioxide to and from tissues via the blood
4. Diffusion and perfusion of oxygen and carbon dioxide between the capillaries and the cells of body tissues

The respiratory system has a major role in the first two components of respiration, while the cardiovascular system has a major role in the last two components. The steps involved in transport of carbon dioxide occur in the reverse order of oxygen delivery.

Any impairment in gas transport caused by either a respiratory or cardiovascular disease will lead to compromised gas exchange at the cellular level.

Physiology of the Respiratory System

The primary function of the respiratory system is gas exchange. Oxygen from inspired air diffuses from alveoli in the lungs into the blood in the pulmonary capillaries. Carbon dioxide, a waste product produced during cell metabolism, diffuses from the blood into the alveoli and is exhaled. Exchange of oxygen and carbon dioxide occurs at the alveolar-capillary membrane. The organs of the respiratory system facilitate this gas exchange and protect the body from foreign matter, such as particulates and pathogens.

Structure of the Respiratory System

The respiratory system (Figure 39.1) is divided structurally into the *upper airway* and the *lower airway*. The mouth, nose, and pharynx compose the upper airway. The larynx connects the upper and the lower airways. The lower airway, often referred to as the tracheo-bronchial tree, includes the trachea, right and left mainstream bronchi, bronchioles, alveoli, pulmonary capillary network, and pleural membranes.

Air enters through the nose, where it is warmed, humidified, and filtered. Large particles in the air are trapped by the hairs at the entrance of the nares, and smaller particles are filtered and trapped as air changes direction on contact with the nasal turbinates and septum. The *sneeze reflex* is initiated by irritants in nasal passages which causes stimulation of the respiratory centre in the medulla by the trigeminal nerve (cranial nerve V). A large volume of air rapidly exits through the nose and mouth during a sneeze, helping clear nasal passages of foreign matter.

Inspired air passes from the nose through the pharynx, commonly known as the throat. The pharynx is a shared pathway for air and food. It includes both the nasopharynx and the oropharynx, which are richly supplied with lymphoid tissue that traps and destroys pathogens entering with the air.

The larynx is a cartilaginous structure that can be identified externally as the Adam's apple. In addition to its role in providing for speech, the larynx is important for maintaining airway patency and protecting the lower airways from swallowed food and fluids. During swallowing, the inlet to the larynx (the epiglottis) closes, routing food to the esophagus. The epiglottis is open during breathing, allowing air to move freely into the lower airways.

Below the larynx, the trachea leads to the right and left main bronchi (primary bronchi) and the conducting airways of the lungs. Within the lungs, the primary bronchi divide repeatedly into smaller and smaller bronchi, ending with the terminal bronchioles. Together, these airways are known as the *bronchial tree*. The trachea and bronchi are lined with mucosal epithelium. These cells produce a thin layer of mucus, the "mucus blanket," that traps pathogens and microscopic particulate matter. These foreign particles are then swept upward toward the larynx, throat, and nasopharynx by cilia (tiny hairlike projections on the epithelial cells) where they are either swallowed or expectorated. The *cough reflex* is triggered by irritants in the larynx, trachea, or bronchi. It is described in the next box.

Until air passes through the terminal bronchioles and enters the respiratory bronchioles and alveoli, no gas exchange occurs. The respiratory zone of the lungs includes the respiratory bronchioles (which have scattered air sacs in their walls), the alveolar ducts, and the alveoli (see Figure 39.1). Alveoli have very thin walls composed of a single layer of epithelial cells covered by a thick mesh of pulmonary capillaries. The alveolar and capillary walls form the **alveolar-capillary membrane,** where gas exchange occurs between the air on the alveolar side and the blood on the capillary side. The airways move air to and from the alveoli; the right ventricle and

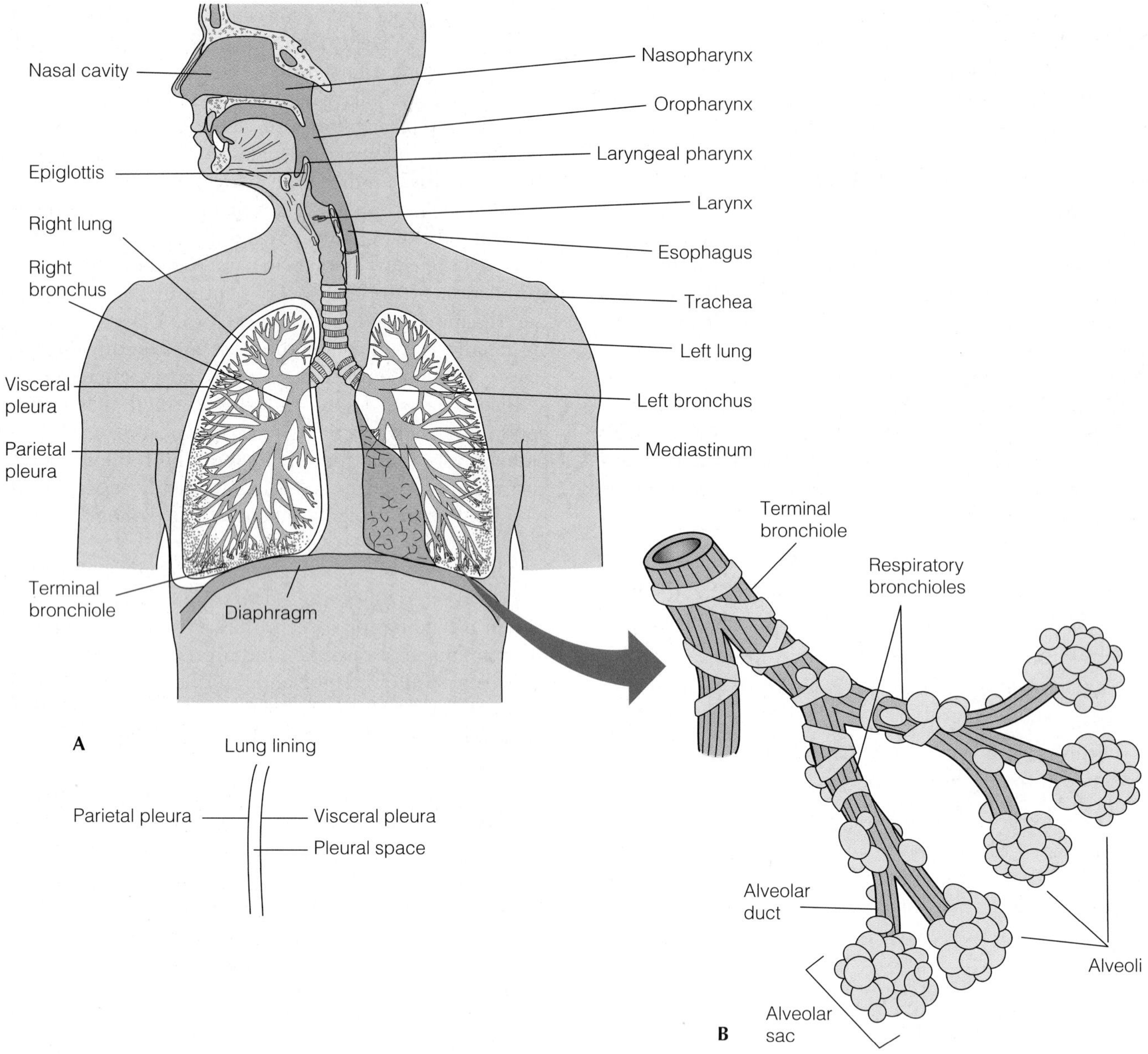

Figure 39.1 *A,* Organs of the respiratory tract; *B,* Respiratory bronchioles, alveolar ducts, and alveoli

The Cough Reflex

- Nerve impulses are sent through the vagus nerve to the medulla.
- A large inspiration of approximately 2.5 L occurs.
- The epiglottis and glottis (vocal cords) close.
- A strong contraction of abdominal and internal intercostal muscles dramatically raises the pressure in the lungs.
- The epiglottis and glottis open suddenly.
- Air rushes outward with great velocity.
- Mucus and any foreign particles are dislodged from the lower respiratory tract and are propelled up and out.

the pulmonary vascular system transport blood to the capillary side of the membrane. (See the section later in this chapter on the structure of the cardiovascular system.)

The outer surface of the lungs is covered by a thin, double layer of tissue known as the pleura. The parietal pleura lines the thorax and surface of the diaphragm. It doubles back to form the visceral pleura, covering the external surface of the lungs. Between these pleural layers is a potential space referred to as the **pleural space,** which contains a small amount of pleural fluid, a serous lubricating solution. This fluid prevents friction during the movements of breathing and allows the two layers to slide over each other without separating. The pressure in the pleural space is usually negative.

Pulmonary Ventilation

Ventilation of the lungs is accomplished through the act of breathing: **inspiration** (*inhalation*) when air flows into the lungs, and **expiration** (*exhalation*) as air moves out of the lungs. The forces that are involved with ventilation include: elastic recoil properties, airway resistance, and inspiratory muscle efforts. The diaphragm and the external intercostal muscles (muscles that are between the ribs) are the major muscles of inspiration. Adequate ventilation depends on several factors:

- Clear airways
- An intact central nervous system and respiratory centre
- An intact thoracic cavity capable of expanding and contracting
- Adequate pulmonary compliance and recoil

As noted previously, a number of mechanisms, including ciliary action and the cough reflex, work to keep airways open and clear. In some cases, however, these defences may be overwhelmed. The inflammation, edema, and excess mucus production that occur with some types of pneumonia may clog small airways, impairing ventilation of the distal alveoli.

The respiratory centres of the medulla and pons in the brain stem control breathing. Severe head injury or drugs that depress the central nervous system (e.g., opiates, anesthetics, or barbiturates) can affect the respiratory centres, impairing the drive to breathe.

Expansion and recoil of the lungs occurs passively in response to changes in pressures within the thoracic cavity and the lungs themselves. The **intrapleural pressure** (pressure in the pleural cavity surrounding the lungs) is always slightly negative in relation to atmospheric pressure (-4 to -10 mm Hg). This negative or sub-atmospheric pressure is essential because it creates suction that holds the visceral pleura and the parietal pleura together as the chest cage expands and contracts. The recoil tendency of the lungs is a major factor in creating this negative pressure. The intrapleural fluid also contributes by causing the pleura to adhere together, much like a film of water can cause two glass slides to adhere together.

The **intrapulmonary pressure** (pressure within the lungs) always equalizes with atmospheric pressure. Inspiration occurs when the diaphragm and intercostal muscles contract, increasing the size of the thoracic cavity. The volume of the lungs increases, decreasing intrapulmonary pressure. Air then rushes into the lungs to equalize this pressure with atmospheric pressure. Conversely, when the diaphragm and intercostal muscles relax, the volume of the lungs decreases, intrapulmonary pressure rises, and air is expelled.

The degree of chest expansion during normal breathing is minimal, requiring little energy expenditure. In adults, approximately 500 mL of air is inspired and expired with each breath. This is known as **tidal volume.** Breathing during strenuous exercise or some types of heart disease requires greater chest expansion and effort. At this time, more than 1,500 mL of air may be moved with each breath. *Accessory muscles of inspiration,* including the anterior neck muscles, sternocleidomastoid muscles, scalene muscles, intercostal muscles, and muscles of the abdomen, are employed. Active use of accessory muscles and noticeable increase in breathing effort are seen in clients with obstructive pulmonary disease.

Diseases, such as polio, or trauma, such as spinal cord injury, can affect the muscles of respiration, impairing the ability of the thoracic cavity to expand and contract. A gunshot wound or other trauma to the chest wall may allow intrapleural pressure to equalize with the atmosphere, causing the lung to collapse.

Lung compliance, the expansibility or stretchability of lung tissue, plays a significant role in the ease of ventilation. At birth, the fluid-filled lungs are stiff and resistant to expansion, similar to that of a new balloon that is difficult to inflate. With each subsequent breath, the alveoli become more compliant and easier to inflate, just as a balloon becomes easier to inflate after several tries. Lung compliance tends to decrease with aging, making it more difficult to expand the alveoli and increasing the risk of **atelectasis,** or collapse of a portion of the lung. The decreased compliance in the elderly may be the result of chest wall rigidity from calcification of intercostal cartilage, decreased mobility of the ribs, or loss of elastic fibres in the lungs.

In contrast to lung compliance is **elastic recoil (elasticity),** the continual tendency of the lungs to collapse and return to the resting state. Just as lung compliance is necessary for normal inspiration, lung recoil is necessary for normal expiration. Although elastic fibres in lung tissue contribute to lung recoil, the *surface tension* of fluid lining the alveoli has the greatest effect on recoil. Fluid molecules tend to draw together, reducing the size of the alveoli. **Surfactant,** a lipoprotein produced by specialized alveolar cells, acts like a detergent, reducing the surface tension of alveolar fluid. Without surfactant, lung expansion is exceedingly difficult and the lungs collapse. Premature infants whose lungs are not yet capable of producing adequate surfactant develop *respiratory distress syndrome (RDS)*; adults can develop *adult respiratory distress syndrome (ARDS)*, which may develop as a complication of serious illness or trauma.

Alveolar Gas Exchange

After the alveoli are ventilated, the second phase of the respiratory process—*the diffusion of oxygen from the alveoli and into the pulmonary blood vessels*—begins. **Diffusion** is the movement of gases or other particles from an area of greater pressure or concentration to an area of lower pressure or concentration.

Pressure differences in the gases on each side of the respiratory membrane obviously affect diffusion. When the pressure of oxygen is greater in the alveoli than in the blood, oxygen diffuses into the blood. The **partial pressure** (the pressure exerted by each individual gas in a mixture according to its concentration in the mixture) of oxygen (PO_2) in the alveoli is about 100 mm Hg, whereas the PO_2 in the venous blood of the pulmonary arteries is about 60 mm Hg. These pressures rapidly equalize, however, so that the arterial oxygen pressure also reaches about 100 mm Hg. By contrast, carbon dioxide in the venous blood entering the pulmonary capillaries has a partial pressure of about 45 mm Hg (PCO_2), whereas that in the alveoli has a partial pressure of about 40 mm Hg. Therefore, carbon dioxide diffuses from the blood into the alveoli where it can be eliminated with expired air. When referring to the pressure of gas in the arterial blood, the abbreviation is PaO_2. When referring to partial pressure in venous blood, there is no "a," therefore the abbreviation is PO_2.

Transport of Oxygen and Carbon Dioxide

The third part of the respiratory process involves the transport of respiratory gases. Oxygen needs to be transported from the lungs to the tissues, and carbon dioxide must be transported from the tissues back to the lungs. Normally, most of the oxygen (97 percent) combines loosely with **hemoglobin** (oxygen-carrying red pigment) in the red blood cells and is carried to the tissues as **oxyhemoglobin** (the compound of oxygen and hemoglobin). The remaining oxygen is dissolved and transported in the fluid of the plasma and cells.

Several factors affect the rate of oxygen transport from the lungs to the tissues:

1. Cardiac output
2. Number of erythrocytes and blood hematocrit
3. Exercise

Normal **cardiac output** (amount of blood pumped by the heart) is approximately 5 L per minute. Any pathological condition that decreases cardiac output (e.g., damage to the heart muscle, blood loss, or pooling of blood in the peripheral blood vessels) diminishes the amount of oxygen delivered to the tissues. The heart attempts to compensate for inadequate output by increasing its pumping rate (heart rate), but with severe damage or blood loss, this compensatory mechanism may not restore adequate blood flow and oxygen to the tissues.

The second factor influencing oxygen transport is the number of **erythrocytes** (red blood cells, or RBCs) and the hematocrit. The **hematocrit** is the percentage of the blood that is made up of erythrocytes. In men, the number of circulating erythrocytes normally averages about five million per cubic millilitre of blood, and in women, about $4\frac{1}{2}$ million per cubic millilitre. Normally, the hematocrit is about 40 to 54 percent in men and 37 to 47 percent in women. Increasing the red blood cells (RBCs) or decreasing the plasma component of the blood will result in an increased hematocrit (blood will be more viscous). An increased hematocrit results in more resistance and a slower blood flow, reducing the cardiac output and, therefore, reducing oxygen transport (e.g., dehydration—plasma content decreased; polycythemia—number of RBCs is increased).

Exercise also has a direct influence on oxygen transport. In well-trained athletes, oxygen transport can be increased up to 20 times the normal rate, due, in part, to an increased cardiac output and to increased use of oxygen by the cells (utilization coefficient).

Carbon dioxide, continually produced in the processes of cell metabolism, is transported from the cells to the lungs in three ways. (1) The majority (about 65 percent) is carried inside the red blood cells as bicarbonate (HCO_3^-) and is an important component of the bicarbonate buffer system (see Chapter 40). (2) A moderate amount of carbon dioxide (30 percent) combines with hemoglobin as *carbaminohemoglobin* for transport. (3) Smaller amounts (5 percent) are transported in solution in the plasma and as *carbonic acid* (the compound formed when carbon dioxide combines with water).

Respiratory Regulation

Respiratory regulation includes both neural and chemical controls to maintain the correct concentrations of oxygen, carbon dioxide, and hydrogen ions in body fluids. The nervous system of the body adjusts the rate of alveolar ventilations to meet the needs of the body so that PO_2 and PCO_2 remain relatively constant. The body's "respiratory centre" consists of two groups of neurons located in the medulla oblongata and pons of the brain (dorsal respiratory group, pneumotaxic centre of upper and lower pons).

A **chemosensitive** centre in the medulla oblongata is highly responsive to increases in blood CO_2 or hydrogen ion concentration. By influencing other respiratory centres, this centre can increase the activity of the inspiratory centre and the rate and depth of respirations.

In addition to this direct chemical stimulation of the respiratory centre in the brain, special neural receptors sensitive to decreases in O_2 concentration are located outside the central nervous system in the carotid bodies (just above the bifurcation of the common carotid arteries) and aortic bodies. Decreases in arterial oxygen concentrations stimulate these *chemoreceptors*, and they, in turn, stimulate the respiratory centre to increase ventilation. Of the three blood gases (hydrogen, oxygen, and carbon dioxide) that can trigger chemoreceptors, increased carbon dioxide concentration is the strongest stimulator of respiration.

However, in clients with certain lung ailments, such as **emphysema,** oxygen concentrations, *not carbon dioxide concentrations*, play a major role in regulating respiration. For such clients, decreased oxygen concentrations are the main stimuli for respiration. This is sometimes called the *hypoxic drive.* Increasing the concentration of oxygen can depress the respiratory rate, and therefore, it is important that only low concentrations of supplemental oxygen be administered to these clients.

Physiology of the Cardiovascular System

The respiratory and cardiovascular systems are closely linked and dependent upon one another to deliver oxygen to the tissues of the body. Alterations in function of either system can affect the other and lead to tissue **hypoxia,** or lack of oxygen.

The heart and the blood vessels make up the cardiovascular system. Together with blood, the cardiovascular system is the major transport system of the body, bringing oxygen and nutrients to the cells and removing wastes for disposal. The heart serves as the system pump, moving blood through the vessels to the tissues and then back to the heart.

The Heart

The heart is a hollow, cone-shaped organ about the size of a fist. It is located in the mediastinum, between the lungs and underlying the sternum. It is enclosed by a double layer of fibroserous membrane known as the *pericardium.* The parietal, or outermost, pericardium serves to protect the heart and anchor it to surrounding structures. The visceral pericardium adheres to the surface of the heart, forming the heart's outermost layer, the epicardium. A thin layer of serous fluid separates the parietal pericardium from the visceral pericardium. This arrangement prevents any friction rub between the two layers when the heart beats in the chest. The heart wall contains two additional layers: the *myocardium*, cardiac muscle cells that form the bulk of the heart and contract with each beat; and the *endocardium* lining the inside of the heart's chambers and great vessels.

Four hollow chambers within the heart, two upper *atria* and two lower *ventricles*, are separated longitudinally by the *interventricular septum*, forming two parallel pumps (Figure 39.2). The atria and ventricles are separated from one another by the *atrioventricular valves*, the *tricuspid valve* on the right and the *bicuspid* or *mitral valve* on the left. The ventricles, in turn, are separated from the great vessels (the pulmonary arteries and aorta) by the *semilunar valves:* the *pulmonic valve* on the right and the *aortic valve* on the left. The valves serve to direct the flow of blood, allowing it to move from the atria to the ventricles and from the ventricles to the great vessels, but preventing backflow.

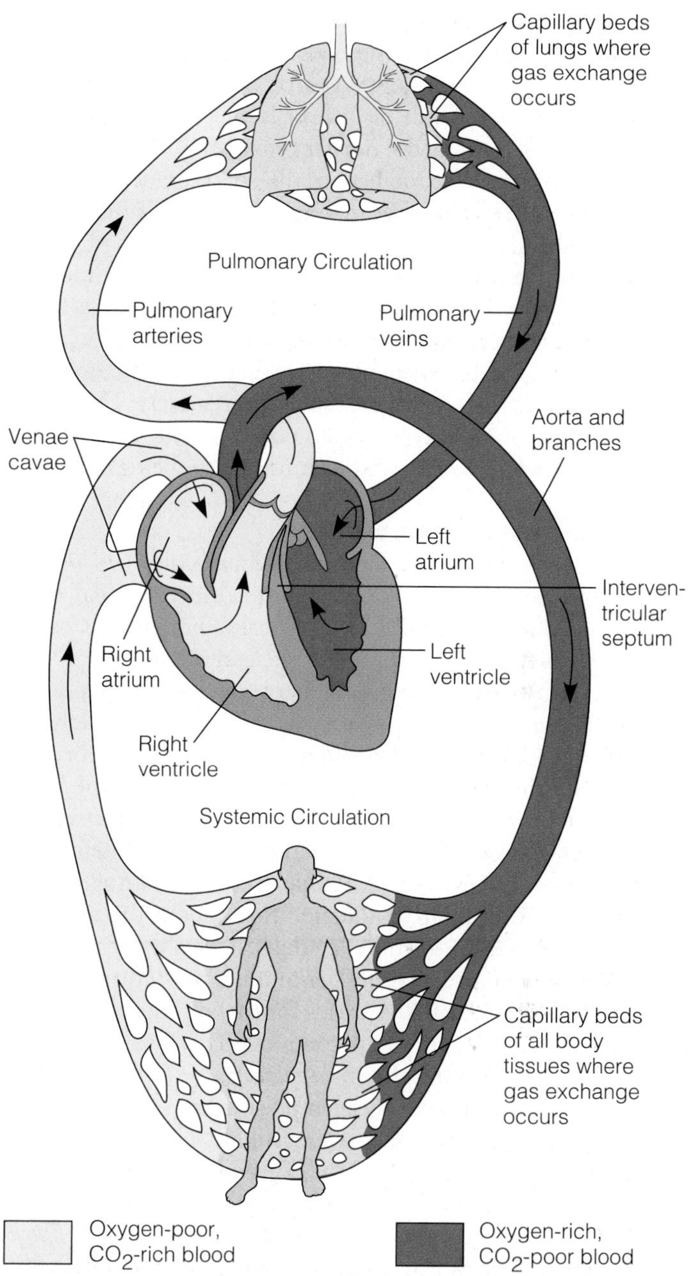

Figure 39.2 The heart and blood vessels. The left side of the heart pumps oxygenated blood into the arteries. Deoxygenated blood returns via the venous system into the right side of the heart.

Deoxygenated blood from the veins enters the right side of the heart through the superior (blood from head) and inferior (blood from body) venae cavae. Blood then flows into the right ventricle, which pumps it through the pulmonary artery into the lungs for gas exchange. Freshly oxygenated blood returns to the left atrium via the pulmonary veins. From the left atrium, the blood enters the left ventricle to be pumped out to the systemic circulation through the aorta.

Coronary Circulation

The heart muscle moves blood to the lungs and peripheral tissues but receives no oxygen or nourishment from the blood within its chambers. Instead, it is supplied by a network of vessels known as the *coronary circulation.* The coronary arteries originate at the base of the aorta, branching out to encircle and penetrate the myocardium. The coronary arteries fill during ventricular relaxation, bringing oxygen-rich blood to the myocardium. If these arteries become clogged with atherosclerotic plaque or are obstructed by a blood clot, the myocardium area that is being supplied is deprived of oxygen, and the client may develop chest pain (angina) or experience a myocardial infarction (heart attack). The *cardiac veins* drain the deoxygenated blood from the myocardium into the *coronary sinus,* which empties into the right atrium.

Cardiac Conduction System

With each heartbeat, the myocardium contracts *(systole)* and relaxes *(diastole).* Contraction is a mechanical event that occurs in response to electrical stimulation. Cardiac muscle is unique in that, unlike skeletal muscle, it can generate an electrical impulse and contraction independently of the nervous system. A network of specialized cells and pathways known as the *cardiac conduction system* normally controls the electrical activity and contraction of the heart.

The primary pacemaker of the heart is the *sinoatrial* (*SA* or *sinus*) *node* located at the junction of the right atrium and superior vena cava. The SA node normally initiates electrical impulses that are conducted throughout the atria and result in atrial contraction. In adults, it usually fires at a regular rate of 60 to 100 times per minute, the "normal" heart rate. The impulse then spreads throughout the atria via the *interatrial pathways.* These conduction pathways converge and narrow through the *atrioventricular (AV) node,* slightly delaying transmission of the impulse to the ventricles. This delay allows the atria to contract slightly before ventricular contraction occurs. From the AV node, the impulse then spreads through the ventricular conduction pathways: the *bundle of His,* the right and left *bundle branches,* and the *Purkinje fibres.* The Purkinje fibres are the terminal branches of both the right and left bundle branches through which ventricular muscles of the heart are stimulated to contract.

Cardiac Output

As the ventricles contract during systole, blood flows out of the ventricles into the great vessels and circulation. The heart muscle then relaxes, a phase known as diastole, allowing the ventricles to refill and the cardiac muscle to be perfused. This contraction and relaxation of the heart is known as the *cardiac cycle* or the heartbeat. The SA node stimulates the cardiac cycle to repeat between 60 and 100 times a minute in an adult.

With each contraction, a certain amount of blood, known as the **stroke volume** (SV), is ejected from the ventricles into the circulation. In adults, the average stroke volume is about 70 mL per beat. **Cardiac output** (CO) is the amount of blood pumped by the ventricles in one minute. Cardiac output is calculated by multiplying the stroke volume times the heart rate ($SV \times HR = CO$). The cardiac output is an important indicator of how well the heart is functioning as a pump. If the cardiac output is poor, tissue perfusion is decreased, and as a result, there is less oxygen and nutrients that reach the cells.

Cardiac output is affected by several factors:

- *Heart rate.* Heart rate is influenced by the autonomic nervous system, blood pressure, hormones, such as thyroid hormone, and some medications. An increased heart rate increases cardiac output even if the stroke volume does not change. However, heart rates that are very high or are sustained for any period of time may cause the cardiac output to drop. Conversely, cardiac output decreases when the heart rate falls, if the stroke volume remains constant. Very rapid heart rates, for example, more than 150 beats per minute, may not allow adequate time for the ventricles to fill, causing cardiac output to fall.
- *Preload.* Preload is the degree to which muscle fibres in the ventricle are stretched at the end of the relaxation period (diastole). Preload largely depends on the amount of blood returning to the heart from the venous circulation. Increased volume causes increased stretch, leading to more forceful contraction of cardiac muscle fibres. For example, exercise increases venous return and the amount of blood in the ventricle prior to contraction; therefore, the heart contracts more forcefully, and stroke volume and cardiac output increase during exercise.
- *Contractility.* This is the inherent ability of cardiac muscle fibres to shorten, or contract. Stroke volume decreases if contractility is poor, reducing cardiac output. Contractility of the heart muscle depends on the available ATP and calcium ions, the degree of sympathetic and autonomic nervous system stimulation, the amount of contractile proteins available in the muscle cells, and stimulation by any pharmacological agents.
- *Afterload.* Blood flows from an area of higher pressure to an area of lower pressure. In order to move blood into the circulatory system, the ventricles must generate sufficient pressure to overcome vascular resistance or the pressure within the arteries, known as afterload. The right ventricle pumps blood into the low-pressure, low-resistance pulmonary vascular system; therefore, the pressures generated by the right ventricle are fairly low. The left ventricle, by contrast, pumps blood into the higher-pressure systemic arterial system, generating much higher pressures and requiring more work. Systemic vasoconstriction increases the arterial blood pressure and afterload, increasing the cardiac workload; vasodilation, on the other hand, reduces arterial pressure and the workload of the heart.

The Blood Vessels

With each cardiac contraction, blood is ejected into a closed system of blood vessels that transports blood to the tissues and returns it to the heart. The heart supports two circulatory systems: (1) the low-pressure pulmonary system, and (2) the higher-pressure systemic circulatory system.

Deoxygenated blood from the right ventricle enters the *pulmonary vascular system* through the *pulmonary arteries.* The pulmonary arteries subdivide into lobar arteries. These lobar arteries follow the main bronchi into the lungs then branch out to form arterioles and the dense capillary networks that encompass the alveoli. Oxygen diffuses into the blood from the alveoli, and carbon dioxide diffuses into the alveoli from the blood. The blood then returns to the left side of the heart via the venules and the *pulmonary veins.* Note that the pulmonary vascular system is the only part of the circulatory system in which *arteries* (which transport blood away from the heart) carry deoxygenated blood and *veins* (which transport blood toward the heart) contain oxygenated blood.

The muscular left ventricle of the heart pumps oxygenated blood into the *aorta.* The blood then moves into major arteries that branch from the aorta into successively smaller arteries, *arterioles,* and, finally, the thin-walled *capillary beds* of organs and tissues. It is in the capillary beds that oxygen and nutrients are exchanged for metabolic waste products. The deoxygenated blood then returns to the heart through a series of *venules* and veins that become progressively larger until they empty into the right atrium via the superior and inferior venae cavae.

With the exception of capillaries, blood vessel walls have three distinct layers, or *tunics.* (1) The innermost layer, the *tunica intima,* is smooth endothelium that facilitates blood flow. As individuals age, the intimal wall lining becomes less elastic and thicker and begins to degenerate and calcify. This does not allow adequate perfusion of nutrients into the cell, causing further degeneration. (2) The *tunica media* is made up of elastic fibres and smooth muscle cells innervated by the autonomic nervous system. This allows vessels to constrict or dilate depending on the needs of the body. The tunica media is thicker and more muscular than in veins, a feature that helps maintain blood pressure and continuous circulation to the tissues. (3) The outermost layer of blood vessels is the *tunica adventitia,* a layer of connective tissue that supports, protects, and anchors the vessel to surrounding tissues. Capillaries contain only one thin layer of tunica intima, allowing gases and molecules to diffuse between the blood and the tissues.

Arterial Circulation

The arterial circulation moves blood pumped by the heart to the tissues by maintaining a constant flow to the capillary beds.

Blood flow—the volume of blood flowing through a given vessel, organ, or the entire circulation over a specific period of time—is determined by *pressure differences* and *resistance.* Blood always moves from an area of higher pressure to an area of lower pressure. The greater the difference between pressures, the greater the blood flow. The **blood pressure** is the force exerted on arterial walls by the blood flowing within the vessel (see Chapter 31 for a further explanation of blood pressure). The *mean arterial pressure (MAP)* is the pressure that maintains bloodflow to the tissues throughout the cardiac cycle. It is a product of the cardiac output times the peripheral vascular resistance (CO × PVR = MAP).

Resistance is the opposition to blood flow. There is an inverse relationship between the movement of blood through the vascular system and resistance (e.g., as bloodflow decreases, resistance increases). **Peripheral vascular resistance (PVR)** impedes or opposes blood flow to the tissues and is determined by:

- The viscosity, or thickness, of the blood
- Blood vessel length
- Blood vessel diameter

Venous Return

In contrast to the high-pressure arterial system, venous pressure is too low to adequately return blood from peripheral tissues to the heart without assistance. The fall in intrathoracic pressure that occurs with breathing draws blood upward toward the heart is an adaptation known as the *respiratory pump.* Skeletal muscle activity contributes to the *muscular pump,* as muscle contractions "milk" blood toward the heart. Venous valves are vital in making these pumps work; once blood passes a valve, it cannot flow backward away from the heart.

Blood

Blood serves as the transport medium within the cardiovascular system, bringing oxygen and nutrients from the environment (via the lungs and gastrointestinal system) to the cells. Blood is a complex mixture of living formed elements (the blood cells) and proteins suspended in fluid (the plasma). Its primary functions are as follows:

- Transporting oxygen, nutrients, and hormones needed for cell metabolism to the cells, and metabolic wastes from the tissues for elimination
- Regulating acid-base balance, body temperature, pH, and fluid volume
- Preventing infection and blood loss

As previously noted, most oxygen is transported bound to hemoglobin. **Hemoglobin** is a major component of red blood cells (erythrocytes), whose predominant responsibility is tissue oxygenation. Hemoglobin binds easily with oxygen, releasing it in the body tissues. When all four heme groups of the hemoglobin molecule are bound to oxygen, it is said to be *fully saturated.* Oxygen binding is affected by several factors, including the PO_2, temperature, pH, and PCO_2. Up to a certain point (about 70 mm Hg), the higher the PO_2, the greater the affinity of hemoglobin for oxygen and the more saturated the hemoglobin molecules. The relationship to temperature, pH, and PCO_2 are the opposite: at higher temperatures, greater hydrogen ion concentrations (lower pH), and higher PCO_2 levels, the affinity for oxygen decreases, and hemoglobin releases its oxygen molecules. *Anemia* (too few RBCs that contain too little or abnormal hemoglobin) interferes with oxygen delivery to the tissues, which often leads to fatigue and activity intolerance.

Life Span Considerations

At birth, profound changes occur in the respiratory and cardiovascular systems. The fluid-filled lungs drain, the PCO_2 rises, and the neonate takes the first breath. The lungs gradually expand with each subsequent breath, reaching full inflation by two weeks of age. As the lungs expand, pressures in the pulmonary vascular system fall, changing pressure relationships within the heart. The *foramen ovale* between the atria closes as pressures on the right side of the heart fall and pressures on the left side increase. Arterial PO_2 rises and arterial PCO_2 falls, prompting closure of the *ductus arteriosus* between the pulmonary artery and aorta.

Respiratory and pulse rates are highest and most variable in newborns. The respiratory rate of a neonate is 40 to 80 breaths per minute; in infancy, it averages about 30 per minute. The rate gradually decreases, averaging around 25 per minute in the preschooler and reaching the adult rate of 12 to 18 per minute by late adolescence. Because of rib cage structure, infants rely almost exclusively on diaphragmatic movement for breathing. An infant's breathing pattern is primarily **abdominal breathing,** with the abdomen rising and falling with each breath.

The resting heart rate for a neonate ranges from 80 to 200 beats per minute, decreasing to 80 to 150 in infancy and early childhood, and reaching the adult rate of 60 to 100 by about age 10 years. Irregular heart rates are common in infants and young children, often increasing and decreasing with each breath. This pattern of irregularity is known as *sinus arrhythmia,* a normal variation of the heart rate.

As the conversion from fetal circulation takes place and pressures in the left side of the heart rise, the arterial blood pressure increases. Immediately after birth (one to three days of age) the blood pressure averages about 65/40. By one month, the arterial pressure is about 90/55. It rises gradually to the adult "norm" of 120/80. With aging, blood pressure may again rise as arteriosclerosis affects the blood vessels, narrowing their lumen and decreasing their compliance (ability to distend). During middle adulthood, however, the incidence of *hypertension,* or an elevated blood pressure, increases significantly. Hypertension, known as the silent killer because of its lack of symptoms, is a major risk factor for cardiovascular disease.

During infancy and childhood, upper respiratory infections are common and, fortunately, usually not serious. Infants and preschoolers also are at risk for airway obstruction by foreign objects, such as coins, peanuts, and small toys. *Cystic fibrosis* is a congenital disorder that affects the lungs, causing them to become congested with thick, tenacious (sticky) mucus. *Asthma* is another chronic disease often identified in childhood. The airways of the asthmatic child respond to such stimuli as allergens, exercise, or cold air by constricting, becoming edematous, and producing excessive mucus. Airflow is impaired, and the child may wheeze as air moves through narrowed air passages.

As individuals age, the chest wall becomes more rigid and the lungs less elastic. More air is retained in the lungs at the end of each breath, and the **vital capacity,** or maximum amount of air that can be exchanged with each breath, decreases. The client with severe issues in elasticity may have a *barrel chest,* with an anterior-posterior (AP) diameter approximately equal to the lateral diameter (normally, the AP diameter is about half the lateral diameter in adults). The older client is at increased risk for acute respiratory diseases, such as pneumonia, and chronic diseases, such as emphysema and chronic bronchitis. *Chronic obstructive pulmonary disease (COPD)* is seen more frequently in older adults, particularly after years of exposure to cigarette smoke or industrial pollutants.

Congenital heart defects may affect infants and children; however, acquired heart diseases are rare in childhood. *Rheumatic fever* is an inflammatory disorder that may occur following streptococcal infection (e.g., strep throat). For most people, the heart continues to function effectively well into older adulthood unless the blood supply to the heart muscle is impaired by blood vessel disease. *Cardiovascular disease (CVD)* is the leading cause of death in Canada, the United States, and the world. *Atherosclerosis,* the buildup of fatty plaque within the arteries, is the major contributor.

Although children are rarely affected by diseases of the blood vessels, both children and adults can have disorders of coagulation and platelets. Some disorders of coagulation are inherited (e.g., hemophilia), and in others, the etiology is not known.

Factors Affecting Respiratory and Cardiovascular Function

Factors that influence oxygenation affect the cardiovascular system as well as the respiratory system. These factors include environment, lifestyle, health status, pharmacological agents, stress and coping, and gender.

Environment

Altitude, heat, cold, and air pollution affect oxygenation. The higher the *altitude*, the lower the partial pressure of the oxygen (PO_2) an individual breathes. As a result, the person at high altitudes has increased respiratory and cardiac rates and increased respiratory depth, which usually become most apparent when the individual exercises.

The peripheral blood vessels dilate in response to *heat*, consequently, blood flows to the skin, increasing the amount of heat lost from the body surface. With vasodilation, the lumens of blood vessels enlarge, thus decreasing the resistance to the blood flow. In response, the heart rate and cardiac output increase to maintain blood pressure. The increased cardiac output requires additional oxygen, which causes increased rate and depth of breathing. In contrast, in a *cold* environment, the peripheral blood vessels constrict, raising the blood pressure, which, in turn, decreases cardiac action, thereby reducing the need for oxygen.

Healthy people exposed to *air pollution*, such as smog, often experience stinging of the eyes, headache, dizziness, coughing, and choking. People who have a history of existing lung conditions or disease and altered respiratory function experience varying degrees of respiratory difficulty in a polluted environment. Some individuals are unable to maintain activities of daily living in such an environment and require health-care assistance.

Lifestyle

Physical exercise or activity increases the rate and depth of respirations and the heart rate and hence the supply of oxygen in the body. With regular vigorous exercise, the heart muscle becomes more powerful and efficient. Aerobic exercise reduces the risk of cardiovascular disease by slowing the atherosclerotic process. Sedentary people, by contrast, have a higher risk of cardiovascular disease. They also lack the alveolar expansion and deep breathing patterns of people who participate in regular activity and they are less able to respond effectively to respiratory stressors.

Certain occupations predispose an individual to lung disease. For example, silicosis is seen more often in sandstone blasters and potters than in the rest of the population; asbestosis in asbestos workers; anthracosis in coal miners; and organic dust disease in farmers and agricultural employees who work with mouldy hay.

The cardiovascular and respiratory systems are affected by cigarette smoking. Nicotine increases the heart rate, blood pressure, and peripheral vascular resistance, increasing the heart's workload. Smoking causes vasoconstriction of vessels, increased viscosity of the blood, and platelet adherence. Smoking can also potentiate further damage to the intimal wall lining of vessels, particularly if those vessels are already affected by atheleroslcerosis, causing impairment of tissue oxygenation.

Diet and other lifestyle factors also affect both cardiac and respiratory functions. A healthy diet with adequate calories, protein, and other nutrients is important to maintain good immune function and increase resistance to disease. Along with certain vitamins and minerals, dietary protein is important to prevent anemia. In Canada, over 40 percent of men and women have elevated total plasma cholesterol levels. The Heart and Stroke Foundation of Canada recommends that less than 30 percent of total calories come from fats.

Recent studies suggest that moderate alcohol use (about 30 mL of alcohol per day) may actually reduce the risk of heart disease; however, excessive alcohol intake negatively affects the body in several other ways. Alcohol is a respiratory depressant, slowing respirations. Alcohol abusers often are malnourished, thereby increasing their risk of anemia and infections. Excess alcohol intake also increases the risk of hypertension, liver disease, and coagulation problems.

Health Status

In the healthy person, the cardiovascular and respiratory systems can provide sufficient oxygen to meet the body's needs. Diseases of the cardiovascular system often affect the delivery of oxygen to the cells of the body, while diseases of the respiratory system can adversely affect the oxygenation of the blood.

There are numerous respiratory and cardiovascular diseases that affect oxygenation. One cardiovascular condition that is often overlooked that affects oxygenation is **anemia.** Anemia is described in the section "Blood Alterations" later in this chapter.

Pharmacological Agents

Narcotics, such as morphine and meperidine hydrochloride (Demerol), in high doses can decrease the rate and depth of respirations by depressing the respiratory centre of the medulla. Other pharmacological agents that can affect respiratory and cardiac function include bronchodilators and beta blockers. Bronchodilators, although given to improve oxygenation by dilating the bronchial tree, can also cause increased cardiac workload by increasing heart rate and blood pressure. Caution must also be used when giving beta blockers to individuals with respiratory conditions because these medications can cause an increase in bronchoconstriction, thereby further compromising respiratory status. When administering bronchodilators, beta blockers, and narcotic analgesics, the nurse must monitor ongoing respiratory status.

Stress and Coping

When stress and stressors are encountered, both psychological and physiological responses can affect oxygenation. Some people may **hyperventilate** in response to stress.

When this occurs, arterial PaO_2 rises and $PaCO_2$ falls. The person may experience light-headedness and numbness and tingling of the fingers, toes, and around the mouth as a result.

Physiologically, when an individual experiences stress, the sympathetic nervous system is stimulated and epinephrine and norepinephrine are released. Epinephrine causes the heart to contract more forcefully and the bronchioles to dilate, increasing blood flow and oxygen delivery to active muscles. Norepinephrine increases the blood pressure by causing vasoconstriction. Although these responses are adaptive in the short term, when stress continues they can be destructive, increasing the risk of cardiovascular disease by increasing heart rate and blood pressure. See Chapter 47 for further discussion of stress and coping.

Other emotions, such as anger, may also be connected to heart disease. Recent studies indicate that people who repress their anger or become hostile appear to have a higher incidence of heart disease.

Gender

Through middle adulthood (until menopause), estrogen has a protective effect in women, slowing the progress of atherosclerosis and reducing the risk of cardiovascular disease. This effect is lost at menopause, but hormone replacement therapy may be beneficial in reducing this risk later in life. Among people in their 40s and 50s, men also have a higher incidence of hypertension than women.

Alterations in Function

Respiratory Alterations

Respiratory function can be altered by conditions that affect the following:

- The movement of air into or out of the lungs
- The diffusion of oxygen and carbon dioxide between the alveoli and the pulmonary capillaries
- The transport of oxygen and carbon dioxide via the blood to and from the tissue's cells

Three major alterations in respiration are hypoxia, altered breathing patterns, and obstructed or partially obstructed airway.

Hypoxia

Hypoxia is a condition of insufficient tissue oxygenation. Hypoxia can be further defined into four categories: anemic hypoxia, hypoxic hypoxia, circulatory hypoxia, and histotoxic hypoxia. Anemic hypoxia occurs when individuals have a low hemoglobin and, therefore, have a decrease in the oxygen-carrying capacity of the cells. Hypoxic hypoxia results when oxygen levels remain low despite the body's ability to carry oxygen (e.g., occurs with high altitude, hypoventilation). Circulatory hypoxia refers to states in which cardiac output is decreased and, therefore, the oxygen-carrying ability is normal but the blood flow is decreased. Histotoxic hypoxia occurs as a result of the body's inability to adequately utilize available oxygen (e.g., cyanide poisoning).

Hypoventilation is reduced rate and depth of respiration that usually results in an increase in carbon dioxide levels in the blood (referred to as **hypercarbia** or **hypercapnia**). Hypoventilation may occur because of diseases of the respiratory muscles, drugs, or anesthesia.

Hypoxia can also develop when the diffusion of oxygen from alveoli into the arterial blood decreases (e.g., pulmonary edema), or it can result from problems in the delivery of oxygen to the tissues (e.g., anemia, heart failure, and embolism). The term **hypoxemia** refers to reduced oxygen in the blood and is characterized by a low partial pressure of oxygen (PaO_2) in arterial blood or a low hemoglobin saturation. See the box below for the signs of hypoxia.

Cyanosis is a bluish discolouration of the skin, nailbeds, and mucous membranes due to reduced hemoglobin-oxygen saturation. Cyanosis is said to occur when the blood contains about 5 g or more of unoxygenated hemoglobin per 100 mL of blood, or from arterial oxygenation saturations of less than 85 percent. Factors that can mask the signs of hypoxemia include anemia or the administration of epinephrine.

Adequate oxygenation is essential for cerebral functioning. The cerebral cortex can tolerate hypoxia for only three to five minutes before permanent damage occurs. The face of the acutely hypoxic person usually appears anxious, tired, and drawn. The person usually assumes a sitting position, often leaning forward slightly to permit greater expansion of the thoracic cavity.

With *chronic* hypoxia, the client often appears fatigued and is lethargic. The client's fingers and toes may be clubbed as a result of long-term lack of oxygen in the arterial blood supply. With clubbing, the base of the nail becomes swollen and the ends of the fingers and toes increase in size. The angle between the nail and the base of the nail increases to more than 180 degrees.

Signs of Hypoxia

- Rapid pulse
- Rapid, shallow respirations and dyspnea
- Increased restlessness or light-headedness
- Flaring of the nares
- Substernal or intercostal retractions/indrawing
- Cyanosis

Altered Breathing Patterns

Breathing patterns refer to the rate, volume, rhythm, and relative ease or effort of respiration. Normal respiration **(eupnea)** is quiet, rhythmic, and effortless. **Tachypnea** (rapid respiratory rate) is seen with fevers, metabolic acidosis, pain, and with hypercapnia (elevated blood CO_2) or hypoxemia. **Bradypnea** is an abnormally slow respiratory rate, which may be seen in clients who have been given anesthetic gases (a respiratory depressant), who have metabolic alkalosis, or who have increased intracranial pressure (e.g., from brain injuries). **Apnea** is the cessation of breathing. For further information, see Chapter 27.

Hyperventilation, often called alveolar hyperventilation, is an increased movement of air into and out of the lungs. During hyperventilation, the rate and depth of respirations increase, and more CO_2 is eliminated than is produced. One particular type of hyperventilation that accompanies metabolic acidosis is **Kussmaul's breathing,** by which the body attempts to compensate (give off excess body acids) by blowing off the carbon dioxide through deep and rapid breathing. Hyperventilation can also occur in response to stress, as mentioned earlier.

Hypoventilation is inadequate alveolar ventilation, that is, ventilation that does not meet the body's requirements. As a result, carbon dioxide is retained in the bloodstream. Hypoventilation can occur as a result of collapse of the alveoli, leaving too few functioning alveoli to meet the body's ventilation needs; or it may result from airway obstruction or the side effects of some drugs.

Abnormal respiratory *rhythms* create an irregular breathing pattern. Three abnormal respiratory rhythms are described in the box below.

Normal breathing is effortless, and respirations are evenly spaced and vary little in depth. The subjective sensation of difficult or laboured breathing is called **dyspnea**. The dyspneic person often appears anxious and may experience *shortness of breath* (SOB), a feeling of being unable to get enough air. Often, the nostrils are flared because of the increased effort of inspiration. The skin and mucous membranes may appear dusky and the heart rate is usually increased. **Orthopnea** is the inability to breathe except in an upright or standing position.

Abnormal Breathing Patterns

- *Cheyne-Stokes respirations.* Marked rhythmic waxing and waning of respirations from very deep to very shallow breathing and temporary apnea; common causes include congestive heart failure, increased intracranial pressure, and drug overdose
- *Apneusis.* Prolonged gasping inspiration followed by a very short, usually inefficient expiration; associated with central nervous system disorders
- *Biot's (cluster) respirations.* Shallow breaths interrupted by apnea; may be seen in clients with central nervous system disorders

Obstructed Airway

A completely or partially obstructed airway can occur anywhere along the upper or lower respiratory passageways. An upper airway obstruction—that is, in the nose, pharynx, or larynx—can arise because of a foreign object, such as food; because the tongue falls back into the oropharynx when a person is unconscious; or when secretions collect in the passageways. In the latter instance, the respirations will sound gurgly or bubbly as the air attempts to pass through the secretions. Lower airway obstruction involves partial or complete occlusion of the passageways in the bronchi and lungs.

Maintaining an open (patent) airway is a nursing responsibility, one that often requires immediate action. Partial obstruction of the upper airway passages is indicated by a low-pitched snoring sound during inhalation. Complete obstruction is indicated by extreme inspiratory effort that produces no chest movement. Such a client, in an effort to obtain air, may also exhibit marked sternal and intercostal retractions. Lower airway obstruction is not always as easy to observe. **Stridor,** a harsh, high-pitched sound, may be heard during inspiration. The client may have altered arterial blood gas levels, restlessness, anxiety, dyspnea, and **adventitious breath sounds** (abnormal breath sounds). See Table 27.8.

Cardiovascular Alterations

Cardiovascular function can be altered by conditions that affect the following:

1. The function of the heart as a pump
2. Blood flow to organs and peripheral tissues
3. The composition of the blood and its ability to transport oxygen and carbon dioxide

Three major alterations in cardiovascular function are (1) decreased cardiac output, (2) impaired tissue perfusion, and (3) disorders that affect the composition or amount of blood available for transport of gases.

Decreased Cardiac Output

Although the heart normally is able to increase its rate and force of contraction to increase cardiac output during exercise, fever, or other times of need, some conditions interfere with these mechanisms.

The vessels that supply blood to the heart muscle may become occluded by atherosclerosis or a blood clot, shutting off the blood supply to a portion of the myocardium. When this happens, the tissue becomes *necrotic* and dies, a condition known as a **myocardial infarction (MI)** or heart attack. If a large portion of the heart muscle is affected, particularly in the left ventricle, cardiac output falls because the affected muscle no longer contracts.

Heart failure may develop if the heart is not able to keep up with the body's need for oxygen and nutrients to the tissues. Heart failure can occur as a result of myocardial infarction, cardiomyopathy, and chronic overwork of the heart, such as in clients with uncontrolled hypertension or extensive arteriosclerosis. In *congestive heart failure* (CHF), the vessels of the pulmonary system become congested or engorged with blood. This may cause fluid to escape into the alveoli and interfere with gas exchange, a condition known as *pulmonary edema*. Other diseases, such as myocarditis and cardiomyopathy, also can affect the heart muscle, impairing its ability to contract and pump.

Very irregular or excessively rapid or slow heart rates can decrease the cardiac output. With irregular or very rapid heart rates, the ventricles may not fill adequately between beats, so the stroke volume (amount pumped with each beat) falls. If the heart rate is too slow, the heart may not be able to increase its stroke volume enough to maintain the cardiac output. Abnormalities of the heart rate and rhythm are known as *dysrhythmias* and can be identified on the electrocardiogram (ECG).

Alterations in the structure of the heart can affect cardiac output. Congenital heart defects result in abnormal blood flow and may even allow venous and arterial blood to mix. The oxygen supply to the tissues is affected in this case. Acquired heart diseases, such as bacterial endocarditis and rheumatic fever, may damage the heart valves, affecting the flow of blood within the heart and to the great vessels. For example, if the mitral (bicuspid) valve becomes scarred and *stenotic* (constricted), it may not open fully, impairing filling of the left ventricle. Or, if the mitral valve does not fully close *(mitral insufficiency)*, blood may escape back or *regurgitate* into the left atrium instead of entering the aorta each time the ventricle contracts.

Impaired Tissue Perfusion

Atherosclerosis is, by far, the most common cause of impaired blood flow to organs and tissues. As vessels narrow and become obstructed, distal tissues receive less blood, oxygen, and nutrients. **Ischemia** is a lack of blood supply due to obstructed circulation. Any artery in the body may be affected by atherosclerosis, although the effects are often related to coronary arteries, vessels supplying blood to the brain, and arteries in peripheral tissues. Obstruction of the coronary arteries causes myocardial ischemia, often resulting in *angina pectoris*. If the cerebral vessels are affected, the result may be a *transient ischemic attack (TIA)* or a *stroke*. Peripheral vascular disease leads to ischemia of distal tissues, such as the legs and feet, resulting in coagulation problems, gangrene, and amputation.

The major risk factors for atherosclerosis include cigarette smoking, high fat intake, obesity, and a sedentary lifestyle. Hypertension and diabetes also increase the risk for atherosclerosis, particularly if the blood pressure or blood glucose levels are not maintained at near-normal levels. Other nonmodifiable risk factors include gender, age, race, and family history.

Although much less common, other disorders, such as vessel inflammation, arterial spasm, and blood clots, also can occlude blood vessels, leading to ischemia. Tissue edema can impair flow through vessels and increases the distance oxygen and nutrients must diffuse across to reach cells.

On the venous side, incompetent valves may allow blood to pool in the veins, causing edema and decreasing venous return to the heart. Veins also can become inflamed, reducing blood flow and increasing the risk of thrombus (clot) formation. Thrombi may then break loose, becoming emboli. These emboli tend to travel as far as the pulmonary circulation, where they become trapped in pulmonary vessels *(pulmonary emboli)*, occluding blood supply to the capillary side of the alveolar-capillary membrane. Although alveolar ventilation to the affected area often remains adequate if the clots are relatively small, no gas exchange occurs because of impaired blood flow.

Blood Alterations

Because most oxygen is transported to the tissues in combination with hemoglobin, the problems of inadequate red blood cells (RBCs), low hemoglobin levels, or abnormal hemoglobin structure can affect tissue oxygenation. Anemia has several different causes: RBCs are lost along with other components because of acute or chronic bleeding; if the diet is deficient in iron or folic acid, hemoglobin and RBCs are not formed adequately; and some disorders cause RBCs to break down excessively. People with sickle-cell disease produce an abnormal form of hemoglobin and may experience tissue ischemia during exacerbations of the disease.

Blood volume also affects tissue oxygenation. If the blood volume is inadequate, as in hemorrhage or severe dehydration, the blood pressure and cardiac output fall, and tissues may become ischemic. Conversely, clients with *hypervolemia* (excess blood volume), which can result from fluid retention or kidney failure, may develop heart failure and peripheral edema, leading to tissue ischemia.

Assessing

Nursing assessment of oxygenation status includes a history, physical examination, pulse oximetry, cardiac monitoring, and review of relevant diagnostic data.

Nursing History

A comprehensive nursing history relevant to oxygenation status should include data about current and past respiratory and cardiovascular problems; lifestyle; presence of cough, sputum, pain; medications for heart, blood pressure, or breathing; and presence of risk factors for impaired oxygenation status. Examples of interview questions to elicit this information are shown in the box on the following page.

ASSESSMENT INTERVIEW

Oxygenation

Current Respiratory Problems

- Have you noticed any changes in your breathing pattern (e.g., shortness of breath, difficulty breathing, need to be in upright position to breathe, or rapid and shallow breathing)? (See below for cough, sputum, and pain.)
- If so, which of your activities might cause these symptom(s) to occur?
- How many pillows do you use to sleep at night?

History of Respiratory Disease

- Have you had colds, the flu, allergies, croup, asthma, tuberculosis, bronchitis, pneumonia, or emphysema?
- How frequently have these occurred? How long did they last? And how were they treated?
- Have you been exposed to any pollutants?
- Have you had a fever?

Current or Past Cardiovascular Problems

- Do you have high blood pressure?
- Do you have any history of heart disease, such as angina, heart attack, or heart failure? Have you ever had a cardiac catheterization, angiography, or angioplasty? Have you ever been diagnosed with rheumatic fever, endocarditis, pericarditis, or other diseases of the heart? If so, when?
- Have you ever been told that you have peripheral vascular disease? Do you ever develop pain in the calves of your legs when walking? How far can you walk before it occurs? What do you do to relieve it?
- Do you have pain in your lower limbs when resting? Does changing your position make the symptoms better or worse? Do you have pain, redness, or swelling in your calves?
- Do your feet and ankles ever swell or feel very cold, numb, or tingling?
- Do you become extremely fatigued with activity? Have you ever been told that you are anemic?

Lifestyle

- Do you smoke? If so, how much? If not, did you smoke previously, and when did you stop?
- Does any member of your family smoke?
- Is there cigarette smoke or other pollutants (e.g., fumes, dust, coal, asbestos) in your workplace?
- Do you use alcohol? If so, how many drinks (mixed drinks, glasses of wine, or beers) do you usually have per day or per week?
- Describe your exercise patterns. What exercise (types) do you participate in? How often do you exercise, and for how long?

Presence of Cough

- How often and how much do you cough?
- Is it *productive,* that is, accompanied by sputum, or *nonproductive,* that is, dry?
- Does the cough occur during certain activities or at certain times of the day?

Description of Sputum

- When is the sputum produced?
- What is the amount, colour, thickness, odour?
- Is it ever tinged with blood?

Presence of Chest Pain

- Do you experience any pain with breathing or activity?
- Where is the pain located?
- Describe the pain. How does it feel?
- Does it occur when you breathe in or out?
- How long does it last, and how does it affect your breathing?
- Do you experience any other symptoms when the pain occurs (e.g., nausea, shortness of breath or difficulty breathing, light-headedness, palpitations)?
- What activities precede your pain?
- What do you do to relieve the pain?

Presence of Risk Factors

- Do you have a family history of lung cancer, asthma, other respiratory diseases, cardiovascular disease (including strokes), or tuberculosis?
- The nurse should also note the client's height, weight, activity pattern, and dietary assessment. In addition to smoking, risk factors include obesity, sedentary lifestyle, and diet high in saturated fats.

Medication History

- Have you taken or do you take any over-the-counter or prescription medications for heart, blood pressure, or breathing (e.g., bronchodilator, inhalant, narcotic)?
- If so, which ones? And what are the dosages, times taken, and results, including side effects?
- Do you use any herbal supplements? If so, which?

Physical Examination

In assessing a client's oxygenation status, the nurse uses all four physical examination techniques: inspection, palpation, percussion, and auscultation. The nurse first observes the rate, depth, rhythm, and quality of respirations, noting the position the client assumes for breathing. Some clients with chronic respiratory problems prefer to bend forward at the waist to ease breathing or to sit leaning over a table because these positions permit greater lung expansion. Lying on the back or on either side restricts expansion of part of the thorax (the underlying portion). This relatively small increase in expansion may be important to a dyspneic client. Chapter 27 provides additional information on assessing respirations.

Variations in the shape of the thorax may indicate adaptation to chronic respiratory conditions. For example, clients with emphysema frequently develop a *barrel chest,* in which the ratio of the anteroposterior to lateral diameter is 1 to 1. Normally, the anteroposterior diameter of the adult thorax is one half the transverse diameter.

To examine the cardiovascular system, the nurse first evaluates the blood pressure in both arms (the results should be within 10 mm Hg of each other) and palpates peripheral pulses for their strength and equality. See Procedure 27.14 in Chapter 27, "Assessing a Peripheral Pulse." Auscultation is done to determine the apical pulse rate, rhythm, and the quality of heart sounds, and carotid arteries are auscultated for bruits. Information about the cardiovascular system is obtained by assessing the skin for colour, temperature, hair distribution, lesions, and peripheral edema. Clients with extensive peripheral vascular disease may have cool feet with weak pulses and shiny, nearly hairless shins. Pitting edema of the feet and ankles may be noted in clients with heart failure. See Chapter 27 for specific techniques for assessing the respiratory and cardiovascular systems.

Pulse Oximetry

A **pulse oximeter** is a noninvasive device that measures oxygen saturation (SaO_2, or O_2 Sat), the amount of oxygenated hemoglobin in arterial blood. The pulse oximeter is connected to a sensor attached to the client's finger (Figure 39.3), toe, nose, earlobe, or forehead (or around the hand or foot of a neonate). It can detect hypoxemia before clinical signs and symptoms, such as dusky skin colour and dusky nailbeds, develop.

The pulse oximeter uses infrared light and a process known as **spectrophotometry** to measure the amount of oxygenated hemoglobin in arterial blood. Normal SaO_2 is 95 to 100 percent. An SaO_2 below 70 percent is life threatening.

Because pulse oximetry measures only the amount of hemoglobin that is bound with oxygen, it can create misleading results if the client's hemoglobin is bound to another substance, such as carbon monoxide, or if the patient is hypothermic (decreased body temperature causes severe peripheral vasoconstriction making pulse oximetry highly inaccurate).

The *oximeter unit* display indicates (1) the oxygen saturation (expressed as a percentage), and (2) the pulse rate. A preset alarm system signals high and low SaO_2 measurements and a high and low pulse rate. The high and low SaO_2 levels for adults are generally preset at 100 percent and 85 percent, respectively (95 percent and 80 percent for neonates). The high and low pulse rates for adults are usually preset at 140 and 50 beats per minute (200 and 100 for neonates). These alarm limits can, however, be changed according to the manufacturer's directions.

Procedure 39.1 explains how to set up and use a pulse oximeter.

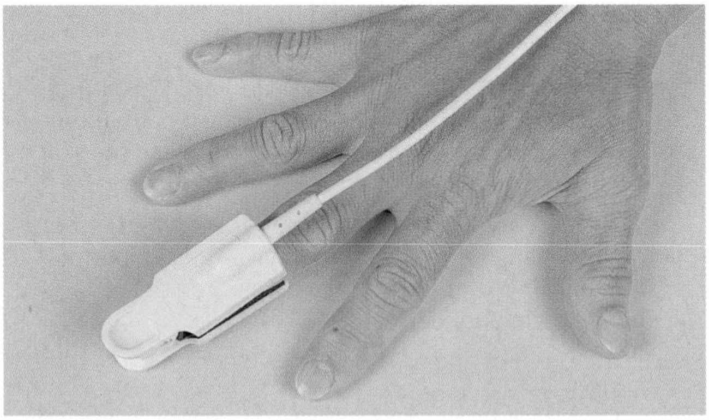

Figure 39.3 A finger clip sensor for a pulse oximeter

PROCEDURE 39.1 Using a Pulse Oximeter

PURPOSES

- To measure the arterial blood oxygen saturation (SaO_2)
- To detect the presence of hypoxemia before visible signs develop
- To monitor for changes in oxygen saturation during and following pharmacological interventions

Assessment Focus
Risk factors for development of hypoxemia (e.g., respiratory or cardiac disease); vital signs and skin and nailbed colour as baseline data; allergy to adhesive; tissue perfusion of extremities; hemoglobin level

PROCEDURE 39.1 Using a Pulse Oximeter *continued*

Equipment

- ❑ Pulse oximeter
- ❑ Nail polish remover, as needed
- ❑ Sheet or towel

INTERVENTION

1. Select an appropriate sensor.

- Choose a sensor appropriate for the client's weight and size. Because weight limits of infant, pediatric, and adult sensors overlap, a neonatal sensor could be used for an infant or a pediatric sensor for a small adult. See the manufacturer's directions for weight limits.
- If the client is allergic to adhesive, use a clip or reflectance sensor without adhesive.

2. Select an appropriate site.

- Use a location appropriate for the type of sensor.
- If using an extremity, assess the proximal pulse and capillary refill at the point closest to the site. *Decreased circulation can alter the SaO_2 measurements.*
- If the client has low tissue perfusion due to peripheral vascular disease or therapy using vasoconstrictive medications, use a nasal sensor or a reflectance sensor on the forehead.
- Avoid using lower extremities that have a compromised circulation and extremities that are used for infusions or other invasive monitoring.

3. Prepare the site.

- Remove client's nail polish or acrylic nails. *These items can interfere with accurate measurements.*

4. Apply the sensor, and connect it to the pulse oximeter.

- Make sure the LED and photodetector are accurately aligned, that is, opposite each other on either side of the finger, toe, nose, or earlobe. Many sensors have markings to facilitate correct alignment of the LED and photodetector. *Correct alignment is essential for accurate SaO_2 measurement.*
- Attach the sensor cable to the connection outlet on the oximeter. Appropriate connection will be confirmed by an audible beep indicating each arterial pulsation. Turn on the machine according to the manufacturer's directions. *Some devices have a wheel that can be turned clockwise to increase the signal volume and counterclockwise to decrease it.*
- Ensure that the bar of light or waveform on the face of the oximeter fluctuates with each pulsation and reflects the pulse volume or strength. *A signal that is too weak will not produce an accurate SaO_2 measurement.*

5. Set and turn on the alarm.

- Check the preset alarm limits for high and low oxygen saturation and high and low pulse rates.
- Change these alarm limits according to the manufacturer's directions, as indicated.
- Ensure that the audio and visual alarms are on before you leave the client. A tone will be heard and a number will blink on the faceplate.

6. Ensure client safety.

- Inspect the location of an adhesive toe or finger sensor every four hours and a spring-tension sensor every hour. Move it slightly or change the location as needed. *Movement prevents tissue necrosis due to prolonged pressure.*
- Inspect the sensor site tissues for irritation from adhesive sensors.

7. Ensure the accuracy of measurement.

- Minimize motion artifacts by using an adhesive sensor, or immobilize the client's monitoring site. *Movement of the client's finger or toe may be misinterpreted by the oximeter as arterial pulsations.*
- Cover a sensor with a sheet or towel to block large amounts of light from external sources (e.g., sunlight, procedure lamps, or bilirubin lights in the nursery). *Large amounts of outside light may be sensed by the photodetector and alter the SaO_2 value.*
- Verify that the client's hemoglobin level is normal. *An SaO_2 measurement may register normal when the client's hemoglobin is low because the available hemoglobin to carry oxygen is fully saturated. Even with a normal SaO_2, the client may by hypoxemic.*

8. Document all relevant information.

- Record the application of the pulse oximeter, its type and size, and all nursing assessments.

Evaluation Focus
Oxygen saturation level; pulse rate and other vital signs; tissue response to the sensor

Cardiac Monitoring

Cardiac monitoring allows continuous observation of the client's cardiac rhythm. It is used in many instances: for clients who have known or suspected cardiovascular disease; during and after surgery; to monitor responses to drug therapy; and to monitor clients at risk for serious complications, such as shock. Electrodes placed on the client's chest may be attached to a bedside monitor. The monitor is equipped with alarms used to warn of potential problems, such as very fast or very slow heart rates and lethal arrhythmias. The alarm limits are set for 20 beats higher and lower than the client's baseline rate, often at 100 to 110 and 50 to 55, respectively, for adults. For ambulatory clients (in the hospital or at home), the electrodes connect to a transmitter unit. This unit electronically sends the signal to a central monitor for display or may store the information to be retrieved later in the physician's office.

Diagnostic Studies

The physician may order various diagnostic tests to assess respiratory and cardiovascular status, function, and oxygenation. Included are sputum specimens, throat cultures, skin testing for allergies, venous and arterial blood specimens, pulmonary and cardiac function tests, and visualization procedures. Often, it is the nurse who collects specimens to be sent to the laboratory for analysis.

Specimens

Sputum is the mucous secretion from the lungs, bronchi, and trachea. It is important to differentiate it from *saliva*, the clear liquid secreted by the salivary glands in the mouth, sometimes referred to as "spit." Healthy individuals do not produce sputum. Clients need to cough to bring sputum up from the lungs, bronchi, and trachea into the mouth in order to expectorate it into a collecting container. Sputum specimens are usually collected for one or more of the following reasons:

- For *culture and sensitivity*, to identify a specific microorganism and its drug sensitivities.
- For *cytology*, to identify the origin, structure, function, and pathology of cells. Specimens for cytology often require serial collection of three early-morning specimens and are tested to identify cancer in the lung and its specific cell type.
- For *acid-fast bacillus* (AFB), which also requires serial collection, often for three consecutive days, to identify the presence of tuberculosis (TB). Some agencies use a special glass container when the presence of AFB is suspected.
- To assess the *effectiveness of therapy*.

Sputum specimens are often collected in the morning. Upon awakening, the client can cough up the secretions that have accumulated during the night. Sometimes, specimens are collected during postural drainage, when the client can more readily produce sputum. When a client cannot cough, the nurse must sometimes use pharyngeal suctioning to obtain a specimen.

To collect a sputum specimen, the nurse follows these steps:

- Offer mouth care so that the specimen will not be contaminated with microorganisms from the mouth. Do not use mouthwash.
- Ask the client to breathe deeply and then cough up 15 to 30 mL of sputum.
- Wear gloves to avoid direct contact with the sputum. Follow special precautions if tuberculosis is suspected, obtaining the specimen in a room equipped with a special airflow system or ultraviolet light. If these options are not available, wear a mask capable of filtering droplet nuclei.
- Ask the client to **expectorate** (spit out) the sputum into the specimen container. Make sure the sputum does not contact the outside of the container (Figure 39.4). If the outside of the container does become contaminated, wash it with a disinfectant. Place in a plastic bag for transport to the lab.
- Following sputum collection, offer mouthwash to remove any unpleasant taste.
- Document the amount of sputum collected, colour, odour, consistency (thick, tenacious, watery), and presence of hemoptysis.

A **throat culture** sample is collected from the mucosa of the oropharynx and tonsillar regions using a culture swab. The sample is then cultured and examined for the presence of disease-producing microorganisms. To obtain a throat culture specimen, the nurse inserts the swab into the oropharynx and runs the swab along the tonsils and areas on the pharynx that are reddened or contain exudate. The gag reflex, active in some clients, may be decreased by having the client sit upright if health permits, open the mouth, extend the tongue, and say "ah," and by taking the specimen quickly. The sitting position and extension of the tongue help expose the pharynx; saying "ah" relaxes the throat muscles and helps minimize contraction of the constrictor muscle of the pharynx (the gag reflex). If the posterior pharynx cannot be seen, use a light and depress the tongue with a tongue blade (Figure 39.5).

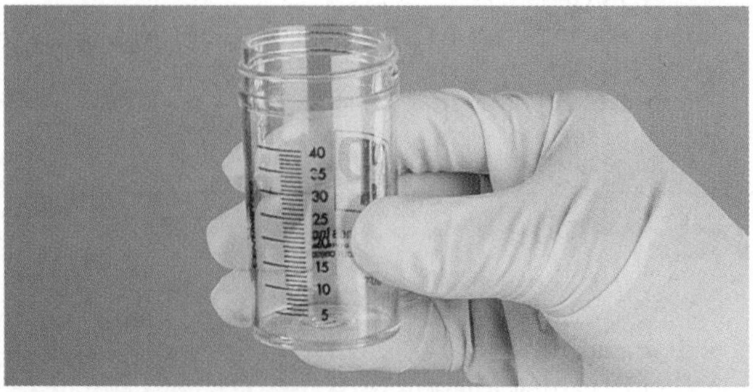

Figure 39.4 Sputum specimen container

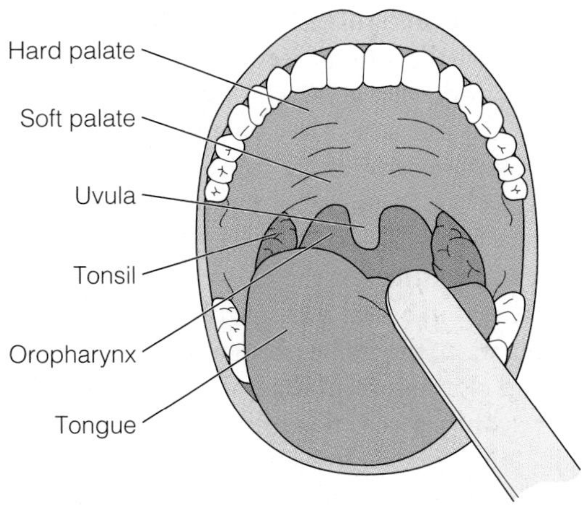

Figure 39.5 Depressing the tongue to view the pharynx

Blood Tests

Specimens of venous blood are taken for a *complete blood count* (CBC), which includes hemoglobin and hematocrit measurements, erythrocyte (RBC) count, leukocyte (WBC) count, RBC indices, and a differential white cell count.

The *hemoglobin* is a measure of the total amount of hemoglobin in the blood. The *hematocrit* measures the percentage of red blood cells in the total blood volume. Normal values for both hemoglobin and hematocrit vary, with males having higher levels than females. Hemoglobin and hematocrit increase with dehydration as the blood becomes more concentrated, and decrease with hypervolemia and resulting hemodilution. Both the hemoglobin and hematocrit are related to the RBC count, the number of RBCs in whole blood. The normal reference range for RBCs is 4.5 to 6.0×10^{12}/L. It also varies by gender and age. Low RBC counts are indicative of anemia; clients with chronic hypoxia may develop higher than normal counts, a condition known as *polycythemia. RBC indices* may be performed as part of the CBC to evaluate the size, weight, and hemoglobin concentration of RBCs.

The *leukocyte* or *white blood cell* count determines the number of circulating WBCs in whole blood. The normal reference range for WBCs is 4.0 to 11.0×10^{9}/L. High WBC counts are often seen in the presence of a bacterial infection; by contrast, WBC counts may be low if a viral infection is present. In the WBC differential, leukocytes are identified by type, and the percentage of each type is determined. This information is useful in diagnosing certain disorders that have characteristic patterns of distribution.

A number of other tests may be performed on blood serum (the liquid portion of the blood). These often are referred to as *blood chemistries.* Common chemistry examinations include determining serum electrolytes (sodium, potassium, chloride, calcium, and bicarbonate); certain enzymes that may be present (including lactic dehydrogenase [LDH], creatine kinase [CK], creative kinase myocardial band [CKMB], aspartate aminotransferase [AST], and alanine aminotransferase [ALT]); serum glucose; hormones, such as thyroid hormone; metabolic waste products, such as creatinine and blood urea nitrogen (BUN); and other substances, such as cholesterol and triglycerides. These tests provide valuable diagnostic cues. For example, the enzymes LDH, CK, and CKMB are released into the blood during a myocardial infarction. Elevated levels of these enzymes can help differentiate between an MI and chest pain from a different cause, such as angina or pleuritic pain.

Measurement of *arterial blood gases* is another important diagnostic procedure (see Chapter 40). Specimens of arterial blood are normally taken by respiratory or specialty nurses or medical technicians. Blood for these tests is taken from the radial, brachial, or femoral arteries. Because of the relatively great pressure of the blood in these arteries, it is important to prevent hemorrhaging by applying pressure to the puncture side for at least five minutes after removing the needle.

Electrocardiography

Electrocardiography provides a graphic recording of the heart's electrical activity. Electrodes placed on the skin transmit the electrical impulses to an oscilloscope or graphic recorder. The wave forms recorded, the *electrocardiogram* or *ECG*, can then be examined to detect dysrhythmias and alterations in conduction indicative of myocardial ischemia or damage, enlargement of the heart, or drug effects.

Stress electrocardiography uses ECGs to assess the client's response to an increased cardiac workload during exercise. As the body's demand for oxygen increases with exercise, the cardiac workload increases, as does the oxygen demand of the heart muscle itself. Clients with coronary artery disease may develop chest pain and characteristic ECG changes during exercise.

Pulmonary Function Tests

Pulmonary function tests measure lung volume and capacity. Clients undergoing pulmonary function tests, which are usually carried out by a respiratory therapist, do not require an anesthetic. The tests are painless, but the client's cooperation is essential. Clients breathe into a machine and forcefully exhale all their breath and then inhale again. Pulmonary readings are recorded throughout the procedure and compared with any previous readings and with the baseline normals according to age, gender, height, and weight. Nurses need to explain the tests to people beforehand and help clients get rest afterward because the tests are often tiring. See Table 39.1 for a description of the measurements taken and Figure 39.6 for their relationships and normal adult values.

TABLE 39.1 Pulmonary Volumes and Capacities

Measurement	Description
Tidal volume (V_T)	Volume inhaled and exhaled during normal quiet breathing
Inspiratory reserve volume (IRV)	Maximum amount of air that can be inhaled over and above a normal breath
Expiratory reserve volume (ERV)	Maximum amount of air that can be exhaled following a normal exhalation
Residual volume (RV)	The amount of air remaining in the lungs after maximal exhalation
Total lung capacity (TLC)	The total volume of the lungs at maximum inflation; calculated by adding the V_T, IRV, ERV, and RV
Vital capacity (VC)	Total amount of air that can be exhaled after a maximal inspiration; calculated by adding the V_T, IRV, and ERV
Inspiratory capacity (IC)	Total amount of air that can be inhaled following normal quiet exhalation; calculated by adding the V_T and IRV
Functional residual capacity (FRC)	The volume left in the lungs after normal exhalation; calculated by adding the ERV and RV
Minute volume (MV)	The total volume or amount of air breathed in one minute

Visualization Procedures

A number of visualization procedures can be done to examine the respiratory tract and cardiovascular system. As these procedures are invasive, they require written informed consent. Roentgenography (x-ray), lung scan, endoscopy (bronchoscopy and laryngoscopy), angiography, and echocardiography are a few.

X-ray examination of the chest is done both to diagnose disease and to assess the progress of a disease. For an x-ray examination, the nurse needs to inform the client that jewellery and clothing from the waist up must be removed.

A **lung scan** records the emissions from radioisotope-tagged albumin injected intravenously as it circulates through the lung. A lung scan usually involves perfusion and ventilation scans. The *perfusion scan* (Q scan) is used to assess blood flow through the pulmonary vascular system. The *ventilation scan* (V scan), performed after the perfusion scan, detects ventilation abnormalities, particularly in clients with emphysema. For this scan, the client inhales a radioactive gas through a mask and then exhales it into room air. Radiation precautions are necessary only for mothers who are breast-feeding as the amount of radioactivity is very small. The scan may take 20 to 40 minutes.

Angiography is also an invasive procedure requiring informed consent of the client. A radiopaque dye is injected into the vessels to be examined. Using fluoroscopy and x-rays, the flow through the vessels is assessed and areas of narrowing or blockage can be observed. *Coronary angiography* is performed to evaluate the extent of coronary artery disease; *pulmonary angiography* may be performed to assess the pulmonary vascular system, particularly if pulmonary emboli are suspected. Other vessels that may be studied include the carotid and cerebral arteries, the renal arteries, and the vessels of the lower extremities.

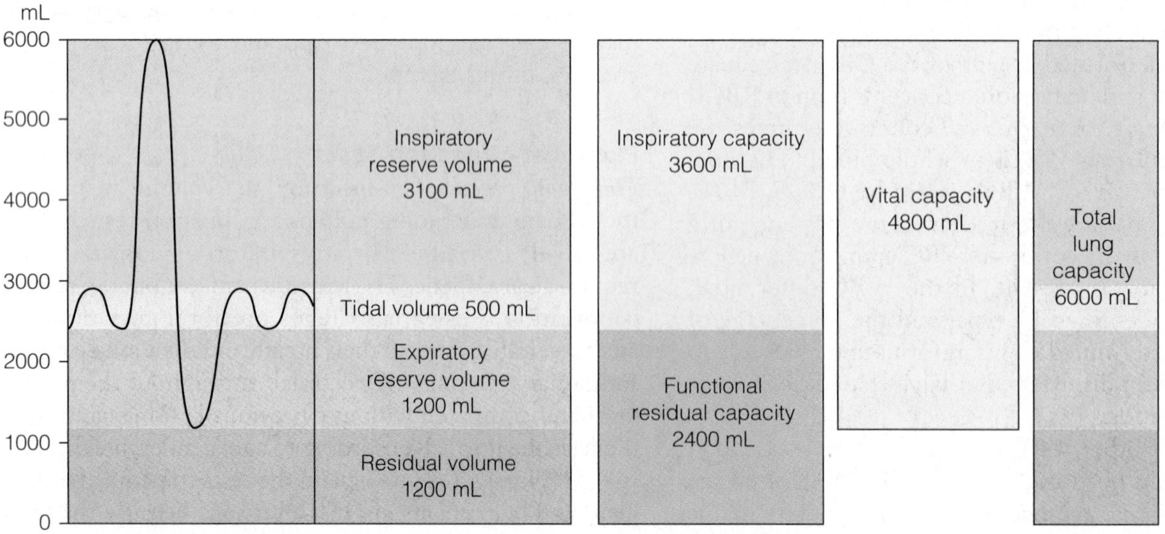

Figure 39.6 The relationship of lung volumes and capacities. Volumes (mL) shown are for an average adult male; female volumes are 20 to 25 percent smaller.

Echocardiography is a noninvasive test that uses ultrasound to visualize structures of the heart and evaluate left ventricular function. Images are produced as ultrasound waves reflect back to a transducer after striking cardiac structures. The client needs to be informed that this test causes no discomfort, although the conductive gel used may be cold.

Laryngoscopy and **bronchoscopy** are sterile procedures using a laryngoscope and bronchoscope, respectively. During the procedure, tissue samples may also be taken for biopsy. A local anesthetic and muscle relaxant (e.g., Versed) are usually given before the examination. A local anesthetic is sprayed on the client's pharynx to prevent gagging; alternatively, the client gargles with an anesthetic to anesthetize the throat. The bronchoscope is then inserted to visualize the larynx or bronchi. Informed consent is required for these procedures. Food and fluids are withheld after the procedure until the gag reflex returns.

Hemodynamic Studies

Hemodynamics is the study of the forces or pressures involved in blood circulation. Hemodynamic studies or monitoring procedures may be performed to evaluate fluid status and cardiovascular function. Parameters evaluated in hemodynamic studies include heart rate, arterial blood pressure, central venous pressure, pressures in the pulmonary vascular system, and cardiac output. Some of these parameters—for example, heart rate, arterial blood pressure, and venous pressure—are measured directly using an arterial, central venous, or pulmonary artery catheter; others, such as the stroke volume and cardiac output, are calculated. Hemodynamic studies are performed in a diagnostic cardiac laboratory and require written informed consent. Clients in intensive and cardiac care units may undergo continuous hemodynamic monitoring to evaluate cardiovascular status and the effect of interventions. Nurses in these units are responsible for ongoing hemodynamic monitoring.

Diagnosing

The North American Nursing Diagnosis Association (NANDA) includes the following diagnostic labels for clients with oxygenation problems (Carpenito, 2002):

- ***Ineffective Airway Clearance:*** A state in which one is unable to clear secretions or obstructions from the respiratory tract to maintain a clear airway.
- ***Ineffective Breathing Pattern:*** Inspiration and/or expiration that does not provide adequate ventilation.
- ***Impaired Gas Exchange:*** A state in which one experiences an excess or deficit in oxygenation or carbon dioxide elimination or both at the alveolar-capillary membrane.
- ***Ineffective Tissue Perfusion:*** The state in which one experiences a failure to nourish the tissues at the capillary level.
- ***Decreased Cardiac Output:*** A state in which the amount of blood pumped by the heart is inadequate to meet the metabolic needs of the body.
- ***Activity Intolerance:*** A state in which one has insufficient energy (physiological or psychological) to complete required or desired daily activities.

Clinical applications of these diagnoses are shown in Table 39.2.

The preceding nursing diagnoses may also be the etiology of several other nursing diagnoses. Examples follow:

- ***Anxiety*** related to ineffective airway clearance and feeling of suffocation
- ***Fatigue*** related to ineffective breathing pattern
- ***Fear*** related to chronic disabling respiratory illness
- ***Powerlessness*** related to inability to maintain independence in self-care activities because of altered cardiac tissue perfusion
- ***Sleep Pattern, Disturbed*** related to orthopnea and required O_2 therapy
- ***Social Isolation*** related to activity intolerance and inability to travel to usual social activities

Planning

The overall goals for a client with oxygenation problems are to:

- Maintain a patent airway.
- Improve comfort and ease of breathing.
- Maintain or improve pulmonary ventilation and oxygenation.
- Maintain or improve tissue perfusion.
- Maintain or restore an adequate cardiac output.
- Improve ability to participate in physical activities.
- Prevent risks associated with oxygenation problems, such as skin and tissue breakdown, syncope, acid-base imbalances, and feelings of hopelessness and social isolation.

Examples of specific outcomes are provided in Table 39.3 in the "Evaluating" section.

Nursing strategies to achieve the goals for problems of oxygenation are discussed in the next section. Examples of nursing interventions to *facilitate pulmonary ventilation* may include ensuring a patent airway, positioning, encouraging deep breathing and coughing, and ensuring adequate hydration. Other nursing interventions helpful to ventilation are suctioning, lung inflation techniques, administration of analgesics before deep breathing and coughing, postural drainage, and percussion and vibration. Nursing strategies to *facilitate the diffusion of gases* through the alveolar membrane include encouraging coughing, deep breathing, and suitable activity. To *promote the transport of oxygen and carbon dioxide*, the nurse can optimize cardiac

TABLE 39.2 Clinical Application: Assessment Data Clusters and Related Nursing Diagnoses

Data Cluster	Nursing Diagnosis
Barry Galloway reports recent flu with malaise, diaphoresis, headache, nausea, and vomiting. He now has fever and chills, chest pain, and painful nonproductive cough. Rhonchi (gurgles) auscultated anteriorly over bronchi.	***Ineffective Airway Clearance*** related to inflammatory process and dehydration
Mr. Michael Parry has shortness of breath, moist cough, and fatigue. His lips and nailbeds are cyanotic. Respirations are 32 and shallow. He uses pursed-lip breathing and accessory muscles (intercostal and supraclavicular) to exhale. Blood gases indicate elevated $PaCO_2$. He has a history of COPD and is most comfortable sitting in an orthopneic position.	***Impaired Gas Exchange*** related to alveolar-capillary membrane changes
Gloria Way, 32, reports severe upper abdominal pain and abdominal distention on her first postoperative day following cholecystectomy. She is reluctant to perform deep breathing and coughing exercises. Respirations are 18 but shallow.	***Ineffective Breathing Pattern*** related to upper abdominal incisional pain
Don Sburunnry Bear, 78, experienced a massive MI four years ago that damaged 35 percent of his left ventricle. He now experiences dyspnea with minimal activity. His respiratory rate is 28, and he has crackles in both lung bases. He has 3+ pitting edema to the ankles of both feet. His pulse is 110, weak, and irregular. His blood pressure is 90/60 on both arms.	***Decreased Cardiac Output*** related to left ventricular damage
Mrs. Gloria Papadopolis reports that she is having increasing difficulty travelling because she experiences severe pain in her calf muscle after walking for more than a city block. The pain subsides if she rests for a few minutes but returns with activity. Her feet are cool and pale; pedal and posterior tibial pulses are not palpable.	***Ineffective Tissue Perfusion (peripheral)*** related to impaired lower extremity circulation—venous insufficiency
Meiying Ho reports that she just does not seem to have enough energy to keep up with her nine-month-old daughter. Even though the baby is sleeping through the night and Meiying naps with her in the afternoon, she is always tired. Her skin colour is pale, and CBC shows a low hemoglobin and hematocrit.	***Activity Intolerance (Level 2)*** related to anemia and potential tissue hypoxia

output by reducing stress, planning appropriate activities, and positioning the client for improved vascular blood flow. A client's nursing care plan should also include appropriate collaborative nursing interventions, such as oxygen therapy, tracheostomy care, and maintenance of a chest tube.

Examples of NIC interventions to support or improve oxygenation include (McCloskey & Bulechek, 2000):

- Acid-base management
- Activity therapy
- Airway management
- Airway suctioning
- Anxiety reduction
- Cardiac care
- Chest physiotherapy
- Circulatory care
- Cough enhancement
- Energy management
- Hemodynamic regulation
- Oxygen therapy
- Positioning
- Respiratory monitoring

Specific nursing activities associated with each of these interventions can be selected to meet the individual needs of the client. The interventions selected must be appropriate for the client's nursing diagnosis and desired outcomes. A sample nursing care plan using NIC interventions and selected activities is provided opposite.

Examples of NOC outcome classifications are (Johnson & Maas, 2000):

- Circulation status
- Energy conservation
- Respiratory status: gas exchange
- Respiratory status: ventilation
- Tissue perfusion: cardiac
- Tissue perfusion: peripheral
- Vital signs status

Specific *indicators* for each outcome group can be selected for the individual.

Planning for Home Care

To provide for continuity of care, the nurse needs to consider the client's learning needs and needs for assistance with care in the home. Planning incorporates an assessment of

SAMPLE CARE PLAN FOR INEFFECTIVE AIRWAY CLEARANCE

ASSESSMENT DATA

Nursing Assessment

Johti Singh is a 39-year-old secretary who was admitted to the hospital with an elevated temperature; fatigue; rapid, laboured respirations; and mild dehydration. The nursing history reveals that Ms. Singh has had a "bad cold" for several weeks that just would not go away. She has been dieting for several months and skipping meals. Ms. Singh mentions that in addition to her full-time job as a secretary, she is attending college classes two evenings a week. She has smoked one package of cigarettes per day since she was 18 years old. Chest x-ray confirms pneumonia.

Physical Examination

Height: 167.6 cm
Weight: 54.4 kg
Temperature: 39.4°C
Pulse: 116 BPM
Respirations: 24/minute
Blood pressure: 118/70 mm Hg
Skin pale; cheeks flushed; chills; nasal flaring; use of accessory muscles; inspiratory crackles with diminished breath sounds right base; thick, yellow sputum

Diagnostic Data

Chest x-ray: right lobar infiltration
WBC: 14.0×10^9/L
pH: 7.49 (normal 7.35–7.45)
$PaCO_2$: 33 mm Hg (normal 35–45 mm Hg)
HCO_3: 20 mmol/L (normal 21–28 mmol/L)
PaO_2: 80 mm Hg (normal 80–100 mm Hg)

Nursing Diagnosis

Ineffective Airway Clearance related to thick sputum, secondary to pneumonia, and fatigue (as evidenced by rapid respirations, nasal flaring, and adventitious breath sounds)

Client Goal(s):

The client will demonstrate effective coughing and increased air exchange.

Desired Outcomes

1. Coughs and deep breathes q1h within first 24 hr
2. Expectorates secretions from airway whenever necessary
3. Increases fluid intake to 3000 mL by day 2
4. Exhibits normal breath sounds throughout all lung fields

---

*Nursing Interventions and Selected Activities with Rationale *[in italics]*

Cough Enhancement

- Assist Ms. Singh to a sitting position with head slightly flexed, shoulders relaxed, and knees flexed. — *Lying flat causes the abdominal organs to shift toward the chest, crowding the lungs and making it more difficult to breathe.*
- Encourage her to take several deep breaths. — *Deep breathing promotes oxygenation prior to controlled coughing.*
- Encourage her to take a deep breath, hold for two seconds, and cough two or three times in succession. — *Controlled coughing is accomplished by closure of the glottis and the explosive expulsion of air from the lungs by the work of abdominal and chest muscles.*
- Encourage use of incentive spirometry, as appropriate. — *Breathing exercises help maximize ventilation.*
- Promote systemic fluid hydration, as appropriate. — *Adequate fluid intake enhances liquefaction of pulmonary secretions and facilitates expectoration of mucus.*

Respiratory Monitoring

- Monitor rate, rhythm, depth, and effort of respirations. — *Provides a basis for evaluating adequacy of ventilation.*
- Note chest movement, watching for symmetry, use of accessory muscles, and supraclavicular and intercostal muscle retractions. — *Presence of nasal flaring and use of accessory muscles of respiration may occur in response to ineffective ventilation.*
- Auscultate breath sounds, noting areas of decreased or absent ventilation and presence of adventitious sounds. — *As fluid and mucus accumulate, abnormal breath sounds can be heard, including crackles and diminished breath sounds, owing to fluid-filled air spaces and diminished lung volume.*
- Auscultate lung sounds after treatments to note results. — *Assists in evaluating prescribed treatments and client outcomes.*
- Monitor client's ability to cough effectively. — *Respiratory tract infections alter the amount and character of secretions. An ineffective cough compromises airway clearance and prevents mucus from being expelled.*
- Monitor client's respiratory secretions. — *People with pneumonia commonly produce rust-coloured, purulent sputum.*

→

SAMPLE CARE PLAN FOR INEFFECTIVE AIRWAY CLEARANCE *continued*

■ Institute respiratory therapy treatments (e.g., nebulizer), as needed.	*A variety of respiratory therapy treatments may be used to open constricted airways and liquefy secretions.*
■ Monitor for increased restlessness, anxiety, and air hunger.	*These clinical manifestations would be indicators of hypoxia.*
■ Note changes in SaO_2, tidal CO_2, and changes in arterial blood gas values, as appropriate.	*Evaluates the status of oxygenation, ventilation, and acid-base balance.*

Oxygen Therapy

■ Instruct Ms. Singh about importance of leaving oxygen delivery device on.	*Oxygen demand is greater during febrile illness and physical stress. At low PaO_2 levels in the atmosphere, oxygen saturation falls rapidly; therefore, oxygen should be maintained, especially during activity.*
■ Periodically check oxygen delivery device to ensure that the prescribed concentration is being delivered.	*Too much or too little oxygen can be detrimental, especially in the client with a history of smoking.*
■ Observe for signs of oxygen-induced hypoventilation.	*In individuals with chronic lung disease, the stimulus for breathing is low oxygen levels rather than elevated carbon dioxide. This client is at risk for COPD because of smoking. Administration of high level of oxygen could lead to hypoventilation.*

Evaluation

Goal partially met. Ms. Singh coughs and deep breathes purposefully q1–2h during the day. Her fluid intake is approximately 1,500 mL each day. Cough continues to be productive of moderately thick, rust-coloured sputum. Inspiratory crackles continue to be present in right lower lobe. Her PaO_2 is 85 mm Hg on room air.

*Interventions and activities selected are only a sample of those suggested in the *Iowa intervention project: Nursing Interventions Classification (NIC),* and should be individualized for each client.

Source: McCloskey, J. C., & Bulechek, G. M. (2000). *Iowa intervention project: Nursing interventions classification (NIC)* (3rd ed.). St. Louis, MO: Mosby.

the client's and family's knowledge and abilities for self-care, financial resources, and evaluation of the need for referrals and for home health services. The box opposite outlines a home care assessment related to the client's oxygenation problems and needs. The Home Care Teaching Guide box that follows addresses the learning needs of the client and family.

Implementing

Promoting Oxygenation

Most people in good health give little thought to their respiratory and cardiovascular function. Changing position frequently, ambulating, and exercising usually maintain adequate ventilation, gas exchange, and cardiovascular function. The boxes on page 1043 list other ways to promote healthy breathing and maintain a healthy heart.

When people become ill, their respiratory and cardiovascular functions may be inhibited for such reasons as pain and immobility. Shallow respirations inhibit both diaphragmatic excursion and lung distensibility. The result of inadequate chest expansion is stasis and pooling of respiratory secretions, which ultimately harbour microorganisms and promote infection.

Interventions by the nurse to maintain the normal respirations of clients include:

- Positioning the client to allow for maximum chest expansion
- Encouraging or providing frequent changes in position
- Encouraging ambulation
- Implementing measures that promote comfort, such as giving pain medications
- Fluids/humidification
- Deep breathing and coughing

The semi-Fowler's or high-Fowler's position allows maximum chest expansion in bed-confined clients, particularly dyspneic clients. The nurse also encourages clients to turn from side to side frequently so that alternate sides of the chest are permitted maximum expansion. Dyspneic clients often sit in bed and lean over their overbed tables

HOME CARE ASSESSMENT

Oxygenation

Client

- *Self-care abilities:* Ability to ambulate and perform ADLs independently
- *Exercise and activity pattern:* Type and regularity of usual exercise; perceived and actual energy for desired and required leisure activities
- *Assistive devices required:* Supplemental oxygen, humidifier, nebulizer treatments or inhalers; walker, cane, or wheelchair; grab bars, shower chair, and other devices to promote safety and minimize energy expenditure; scale to monitor weight on a regular basis
- *Home environment for factors that impair airway clearance, gas exchange, or activity tolerance:* Indoor pollutants, such as cigarette smoke, dust, and allergens, such as pet dander; lack of humidity in the air; and barriers, such as stairs
- *Current level of knowledge:* Importance of avoiding smoking and other pollutants; dietary salt and other restrictions (if appropriate); recommended activities; medications; need to limit exposure to respiratory infections; foot care (for clients with impaired tissue perfusion); use of prescribed nebulizer or inhalers, home oxygen; activity level

Family

- *Caregiver availability, skills, and responses:* Ability and willingness to provide care as needed (help with ADLs, providing meals, assisting with transportation and shopping, caring for dependents; performing treatments, such as percussion and postural drainage)
- *Family role changes and coping:* Effect on financial status, parenting and spousal roles, sexuality, social roles
- *Alternative potential primary or respite caregivers:* For example, other family members, volunteers, church members, paid caregivers or housekeeping services; available community respite care (e.g., adult day care, senior centres)
- *Financial resources*

Community

- *Environment:* Usual temperature and humidity, presence of air pollutants, such as automobile exhaust, industrial smoke and pollutants, smoke from field burning
- *Current knowledge of and experience with community resources:* Medical and assistive equipment and supply companies, respiratory and physical therapy services, home care agencies, local pharmacies, available financial assistance, support and educational organizations, such as the local heart association, COPD support groups, cardiac rehabilitation services

HOME CARE TEACHING GUIDE

Oxygenation

Tissue Perfusion

- The length of anti-embolic stockings should be based on the individual patient condition (e.g., if a client has history of popliteal clots, thigh-high or full stockings would be recommended to facilitate venous return throughout the leg). Clients may need to have stockings of varying degrees of leg compression depending on the day-to-day physical condition. Stockings may produce varying degrees of leg compression, and client's ability to tolerate the stockings may be an issue.
- Individuals with latex allergies may not be able to wear anti-embolic stockings because of the amount of latex material in the majority of stockings. Other patients, such as the elderly, experience difficulty with anti-embolic stockings because of the energy and strength required to pull the stockings on. Appropriate assistance and/or home care may have to be arranged once patients go home.
- Emphasize to the client and family the importance of not smoking. Refer them to smoking cessation programs as needed. For family members resistant to not smoking, emphasize the need to avoid smoking inside the home.
- Instruct the client in effective coughing techniques, such as controlled coughing or "huff" coughing (see "Deep Breathing and Coughing" in the next section).

→

HOME CARE TEACHING GUIDE

Oxygenation *continued*

- Discuss the significance of changes in sputum, including the amount and characteristics such as colour, viscosity, and odour. Instruct the client when to contact a health-care provider.
- Teach the client to maintain a fluid intake of 2,500 mL to 3,000 mL per day if not contraindicated.
- Instruct the client how to use nebulizers or inhalers if prescribed.
- Teach the client and family how to use home oxygen delivery systems.

Promoting Effective Breathing

- See "Promoting Oxygenation" page 1040.
- Teach relaxation techniques, such as progressive muscle relaxation, meditation, and visualization. Use pre-recorded tapes, as needed.
- Help the client identify specific factors that affect breathing, such as stress, exposure to allergens or air pollution, and exposure to cold. Assist with identifying possible interventions and measures to avoid these factors.

Maintaining Cardiac Output and Tissue Perfusion

- Teach the symptoms of heart failure to the client and family and emphasize when to contact the care provider.
- Teach the client about the importance of maintaining regular physical activity to promote circulation and vascular health. Emphasize the need to increase activity levels gradually with the goal of exercising (walking, swimming, weight training, or aerobic exercise as recommended by the physician) for at least 20 minutes four to five times per week.
- Instruct the client to avoid exposure to extremes of temperature (heat and cold).

Dietary Alterations

- Instruct the client and family about prescribed dietary restrictions, such as a low-sodium diet. Refer to a dietitian, as needed, for further instruction.
- Discuss dietary measures to reduce the risk of atherosclerosis, including reducing total and saturated fats in the diet, reducing weight, if overweight, and increasing the intake of dietary fibre.

Medications

- Teach the client about prescribed medications, including the dose, the desired effects and possible adverse effects, and any precautions about using a medication with food, beverages, or other medications.

Specific Measures for Oxygenation Problems

- Provide instructions for specific procedures and problems, such as:
  a. Suctioning oropharyngeal and nasopharyngeal cavities (see page 1058)
  b. Caring for a temporary or permanent tracheostomy (see pages 1055)
  c. Preventing the spread of tuberculosis and other respiratory infections to family members and others
- Teach cardiopulmonary resuscitation, or refer for instruction.

Referrals

- Make appropriate referrals to home care agencies or community social services for assistance in obtaining medical and assistive equipment, such as grab bars, respiratory and physical therapy services, and home care or housekeeping services to assist with ADLs.

Community Agencies and Other Sources of Help

- Provide information about where durable medical equipment can be purchased, rented, or obtained free of charge; how to access home oxygen equipment and support services; physical and occupational therapy services; and where to obtain supplies, such as anti-embolism stockings, tracheostomy supplies, or nutritional supplements.
- Suggest additional sources of information, such as Canadian Lung Association, Heart and Stroke Foundation of Canada, and the Asthma and Allergy Foundation.

(which are raised to a suitable height), usually with a pillow for support. This *orthopneic position* is an adaptation of the high-Fowler's position. It has a further advantage in that, unlike in high-Fowler's, the abdominal organs are not pressing on the diaphragm. Also, a client in the orthopneic position can press the lower part of the chest against the table to facilitate exhaling.

Immobility is detrimental to cardiovascular function. Without exercise of the calf and leg muscles, blood pools in the veins of the lower extremities. This stagnant blood

WELLNESS TEACHING

Promoting Healthy Breathing

- Sit straight and stand erect to permit full lung expansion.
- Exercise regularly.
- Breathe through the nose.
- Breathe in so as to expand the chest fully.
- Do not smoke cigarettes, cigars, or pipes or use chewing tobacco.
- Eliminate or reduce the use of household pesticides and irritating chemical substances.
- Do not incinerate garbage.
- Avoid exposure to second-hand smoke.
- Use building materials that do not emit vapours.
- Make sure furnaces, ovens, wood stoves, and fireplaces are correctly ventilated.
- Support a pollution-free environment.

flow may allow clots to develop *(venous thrombosis)*. With time, these clots can break loose and become emboli, eventually lodging in the small vessels of the pulmonary vascular system. Blood flow and gas exchange in the lungs are then impaired.

Interventions by the nurse to maintain cardiovascular function in clients include:

- Positioning with the legs elevated to promote venous return to the heart
- Avoiding pillows under the knees or more than 15 degrees of knee flexion to improve blood flow to the lower extremities and reduce venous stagnation
- Avoid crossing legs, ankles
- Encouraging leg exercises (such as flexion and extension of the feet, active contraction and relaxation of calf muscles) for a client on bed rest, and promoting ambulation as soon as possible
- Encouraging or providing frequent position changes

Deep Breathing and Coughing

The nurse can facilitate respiratory functioning by encouraging deep breathing exercises and coughing to remove secretions. Breathing exercises are frequently indicated for clients with restricted chest expansion, such as those with chronic obstructive pulmonary disease (COPD) or clients recovering from thoracic surgery and pneumonia.

A commonly employed breathing exercise is abdominal (diaphragmatic) and pursed-lip breathing. *Abdominal (diaphragmatic) breathing* permits deep full breaths with little

WELLNESS TEACHING

Promoting a Healthy Heart

- Exercise regularly, participating in at least 20 minutes (40 minutes is preferrable) of vigorous exercise four to five times a week.
- Do not smoke.
- Maintain your ideal weight.
- Eat a diet low in total fat, saturated fats, and cholesterol and high in fibre.
- Drink alcohol in moderation, if at all, consuming no more than 30 mL of alcohol a day (one cocktail, one to one and a half glasses of wine or beer).
- Reduce stress, and manage anger.
- Effectively manage diabetes and hypertension, maintaining blood glucose and blood pressure levels within normal limits.
- If female, consider hormone replacement therapy after menopause (or after a total hysterectomy). Females should consult their physicians regarding hormone replacement therapy.
- Consult your health-care provider about the advisability of low-dose aspirin therapy to further reduce the risk of cardiovascular disease.

effort. *Pursed-lip breathing* helps the client develop control over breathing. The pursed lips create a resistance to the air flowing out of the lungs, thereby prolonging exhalation and preventing airway collapse by maintaining positive airway pressure. The client purses the lips as if about to whistle and breathes out slowly and gently, tightening the abdominal muscles to exhale more effectively. The client usually inhales to a count of three and exhales to a count of seven. The following box provides instructions to perform abdominal (diaphragmatic) and pursed-lip breathing.

Forceful coughing often is less effective than using controlled or huff coughing techniques. Instructions for these coughing techniques are provided in the box on the next page.

Hydration

Adequate hydration maintains the moisture of the respiratory mucous membranes. Normally, respiratory tract secretions are thin and, therefore, are moved readily by ciliary action. However, when the client is dehydrated or when the environment has a low humidity, the respiratory secretions can become thick and tenacious. Fluid intake should be individually determined on the basis of respiratory and cardiovascular status. See Chapter 40 for normal daily fluid intake.

Humidifiers are devices that add water vapour to inspired air. Room humidifiers provide cool mist to room air. Nebulizers are used to deliver humidity and medications.

CLIENT TEACHING

Abdominal (Diaphragmatic) and Pursed-Lip Breathing

- Assume a comfortable semi-sitting position in bed or a chair *or* a lying position in bed with one pillow.
- Flex your knees to relax the muscles of the abdomen.
- Place one or both hands on your abdomen, just below the ribs.
- Concentrate on feeling your abdomen rise as far as possible; stay relaxed, and avoid arching your back. If you have difficulty raising your abdomen, take a quick, forceful breath through the nose.
- Then, purse your lips as if about to whistle, and breathe out slowly and gently, making a slow "whooshing" sound without puffing out the cheeks. This *pursed-lip breathing* creates a resistance to air flowing out of the lungs, increases pressure within the bronchi (main air passages), and minimizes collapse of smaller airways, a common problem for people with chronic obstructive pulmonary disease.
- Concentrate on feeling the abdomen fall or sink, and tighten (contract) the abdominal muscles while breathing out to enhance effective exhalation. Count to seven during exhalation.
- Use this exercise every two hours and whenever feeling short of breath, and increase gradually to five to 10 minutes four times a day. Regular practice will help you do this type of breathing without conscious effort. The exercise, once learned, can be performed when sitting upright, standing, and walking.

They also are used with oxygen delivery systems to provide moistened air directly to the client. Their purposes are to prevent mucous membranes from drying and becoming irritated and to loosen secretions for easier expectoration. It is important to follow the manufacturer's directions for cleaning and maintenance of humidifiers to reduce potential sources of bacterial growth.

Medications

A number of types of medications may be used for clients with oxygenation problems. Bronchodilators, expectorants, and cough suppressants are some medications that may be used to treat respiratory problems. *Bronchodilators*, including sympathomimetic drugs and xanthines, reduce bronchospasm, opening tight or congested airways and facilitating ventilation. These drugs may be administered orally or intravenously, but the preferred route is by inhalation to prevent many systemic side effects. *Expectorants* help "break up" mucus, making it more liquid and easier to expectorate. Guaifenesin is a common expectorant found in many prescription and nonprescription cough syrups. When frequent or prolonged coughing interrupts sleep, a *cough suppressant*, such as codeine, may be prescribed. See the box below for client teaching about cough medications.

Other medications may be used to improve oxygenation by improving cardiovascular function. The *digitalis glycosides* act directly on the heart to improve the strength of contraction and slow the heart rate. *Beta-adrenergic blocking agents*, such as propranolol, affect the sympathetic nervous system to reduce the workload of the heart. These drugs, however, can negatively affect people with asthma or COPD as they may constrict airways. Other drugs, such as *nitrates*, *calcium channel blockers*, and *angiotensin-converting enzyme (ACE) inhibitors*, reduce the workload of the heart

CLIENT TEACHING

Controlled and Huff Coughing

- Inhale deeply, and hold your breath for a few seconds.
- Cough twice: the first cough loosens the mucus; the second expels secretions.
- For huff coughing, lean forward and exhale sharply with a "huff" sound. This technique helps keep your airways open while moving secretions up and out of the lungs.
- Rest.
- Try to avoid prolonged episodes of coughing as these may cause fatigue and hypoxia.

CLIENT TEACHING

Using Cough Medications

- Do not take cough medications in excessive amounts because of adverse side effects. Consult your nurse, pharmacist, or physician, as needed.
- If you have diabetes mellitus, avoid cough syrups that contain sugar or alcohol; these can disturb glucose metabolism.
- Be aware of side effects (e.g., drowsiness) that can make the operation of machinery dangerous.
- Be aware of interactions of cough medications with prescription and other nonprescription medications.

and prevent vasoconstriction. In addition, various drugs are used to treat cardiac dysrhythmias. *Direct vasodilators* may be used for clients with peripheral vascular disease.

Incentive Spirometry

Incentive spirometers, also referred to as *sustained maximal inspiration devices* (SMIs), may be used for the following:

- Maintain or improve pulmonary ventilation
- Counteract the effects of anesthesia or hypoventilation
- Loosen respiratory secretions
- Facilitate respiratory gaseous exchange
- Expand collapsed alveoli

Incentive spirometers measure the flow of air inhaled through the mouthpiece. Therefore, they offer an incentive to improve *inhalation* (Figure 39.7).

The client should be assisted into position, preferably an upright sitting position in bed or a chair. This position facilitates maximum ventilation. The box right lists instructions for clients in the use of incentive spirometers.

Percussion, Vibration, and Postural Drainage

Percussion, vibration, and postural drainage (PVD) are dependent nursing functions performed according to a physician's order and agency policy. These procedures may be contraindicated for some conditions (for example, rib fractures and bleeding disorders). **Percussion,** sometimes called *clapping,* is forceful striking of the skin with cupped hands. Mechanical percussion cups and vibrators are also available. When the hands are used, the fingers and

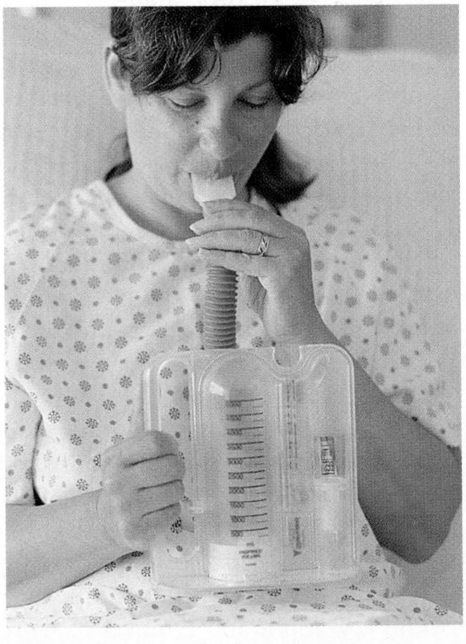

Figure 39.7 Plastic disposable volume-oriented incentive spirometer, or SMI

CLIENT TEACHING

Using an Incentive Spirometer

- Hold or place the spirometer in an upright position. A tilted *flow-oriented* device requires less effort to raise the balls or discs; a volume-oriented device will not function correctly unless upright.
- Exhale normally.
- Seal the lips tightly around the mouthpiece.
- Take in a *slow, deep breath* to elevate the balls or cylinder, and then hold the breath for two seconds initially, increasing to six seconds (optimum), to keep the balls or cylinder elevated, if possible.
- For a flow-oriented device, avoid brisk, low-volume breaths that snap the balls to the top of the chamber. Greater lung expansion is achieved with a very slow inspiration than with a brisk, shallow breath, even though it may not elevate the balls or keep them elevated while you hold your breath. Sustained elevation of the balls or cylinder ensures adequate ventilation of the alveoli (lung air sacs).
- If you have difficulty breathing only through the mouth, a nose clip can be used.
- Remove the mouthpiece, and exhale normally.
- Cough after the incentive effort. Deep ventilation may loosen secretions, and coughing can facilitate their removal.
- Relax, and take several normal breaths before using the spirometer again.
- Repeat the procedure several times and then four or five times hourly. Practice increases inspiratory volume, maintains alveolar ventilation, and prevents atelectasis (collapse of the air sacs).
- Clean the mouthpiece with water and shake it dry. Change disposable mouthpieces every 24 hours.

thumb are held together and flexed slightly to form a cup, as one would to scoop up water. Percussion over congested lung areas can mechanically dislodge tenacious secretions from the bronchial walls.

Cupped hands trap the air against the chest. The trapped air sets up vibrations through the chest wall to the secretions.

To percuss a client's chest, the nurse follows these steps:

- Position client (lateral recommended if tolerated by client).
- Cover the area with a towel or gown to reduce discomfort.
- Ask the client to breathe slowly and deeply to promote relaxation.
- Alternately flex and extend the wrists rapidly to strike the chest (Figure 39.8).
- Percuss each lung segment as indicated by the physician, physiotherapist, or agency policy.

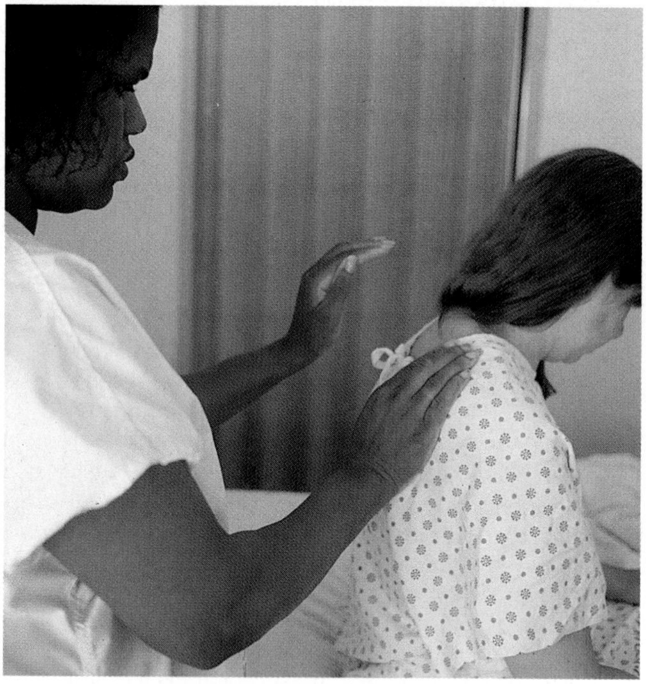

Figure 39.8 Percussing the upper posterior chest

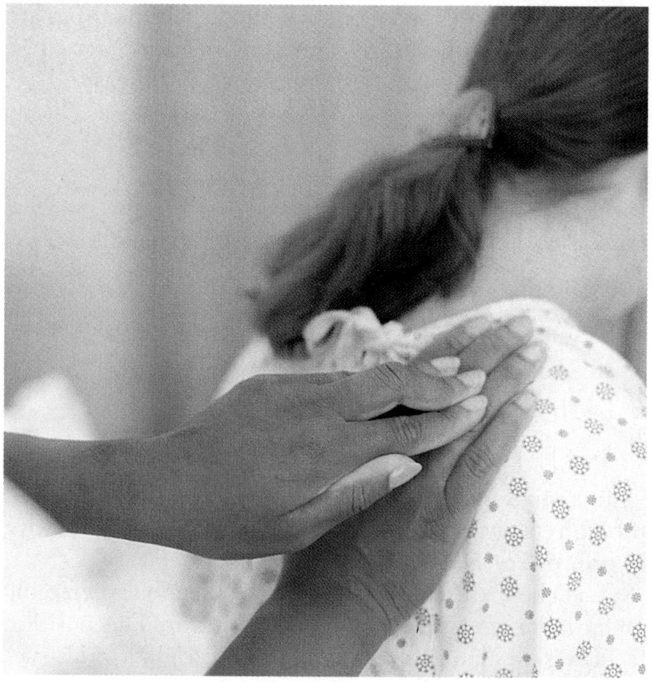

Figure 39.9 Vibrating the upper posterior chest

When done correctly, the percussion action should produce a hollow, popping sound. Percussion is avoided over certain easily injured structures, such as the breasts, sternum, spinal column, and kidneys.

Vibration is a series of vigorous quiverings produced by hands that are placed flat against the client's chest wall. Vibration is used after percussion to increase the turbulence of the exhaled air and, thus, loosen thick secretions. It is often done alternately with percussion.

To vibrate the client's chest, the nurse follows these steps:

- Place hands, palms down, on the chest area to be drained, one hand over the other with the fingers together and extended (Figure 39.9). Alternatively, the hands may be placed side by side.
- Ask the client to inhale deeply and exhale slowly through the nose or pursed lips.
- During the exhalation, tense all the hand and arm muscles, and using mostly the heel of the hand, vibrate (shake) the hands. Stop the vibrating when the client inhales.
- Vibrate during five exhalations over each affected lung segment.
- After each vibration, encourage the client to cough and expectorate secretions into the sputum container.

Postural drainage is the drainage by gravity of secretions from various lung segments. Secretions that remain in the lungs or respiratory airways promote bacterial growth and subsequent infection. They also can obstruct the smaller airways and cause atelectasis. Secretions in the major airways, such as the trachea and the right and left main bronchi, are usually coughed into the pharynx where they can be expectorated, swallowed, or effectively removed by suctioning.

A wide variety of positions is necessary to drain all segments of the lungs, but not all positions are required for every client. Only those positions that drain specific affected areas are used. The lower lobes require drainage most frequently because the upper lobes drain during normal daily activities. Prior to postural drainage, the client may be given a bronchodilator medication or nebulization therapy to loosen secretions as ordered by a physician. Frequently, postural drainage treatments are scheduled two or three times daily, as ordered by a physician depending on the degree of lung congestion. Be aware of the client's exercise tolerance as postural drainage can be tiring. Postural drainage should also be avoided after meals as it puts the client at risk for vomiting and aspiration.

The nurse needs to evaluate the client's tolerance of postural drainage by assessing the stability of the client's vital signs, particularly the pulse and respiratory rates, and by noting signs of intolerance, such as pallor, diaphoresis, dyspnea, and fatigue. Some clients do not react well to certain drainage positions, and the nurse must make appropriate adjustments. For example, some become dyspneic in the Trendelenburg's position and require only a moderate tilt or a shorter time in that position.

The sequence for PVD is usually as follows: positioning, percussion, vibration, and removal of secretions by coughing or suction. Each position is usually assumed for 10 to 15 minutes, although beginning treatments may start with shorter times which are gradually increased. Usually, the entire treatment, including preparatory nebulization and deep breathing as well as all postures, takes 30 minutes.

Before and immediately after PVD, the nurse should auscultate the client's lungs and compare the findings with baseline data. Following PVD, document the amount, colour, and character of expectorated secretions, and note how well the client tolerated the procedure.

Oxygen Therapy

Clients who have difficulty ventilating all areas of their lungs, those whose gas exchange is impaired, or people with heart failure may require oxygen therapy to prevent hypoxia. The concentration, method of delivery, and number of litres per minute of oxygen should be prescribed by a physician or nurse practitioner. In certain circumstances (e.g., sudden onset of chest pain or shortness of breath), registered nurses may initiate oxygen therapy according to agency policy.

Safety precautions are essential during oxygen therapy (see the box on safety precautions below). Although oxygen by itself will not burn or explode, it does facilitate combustion. For example, a bedsheet ordinarily burns slowly when ignited in the atmosphere; however, if saturated with free-flowing oxygen and ignited by a spark, it will burn rapidly and explosively. The greater the concentration of the oxygen, the more rapidly fires start and burn, and such fires are difficult to extinguish. Because oxygen is colourless, odourless, and tasteless, people are often unaware of its presence.

Oxygen Therapy Safety Precautions

- Place cautionary signs reading "No Smoking: Oxygen in Use" on the client's door, at the foot or head of the bed, and on the oxygen equipment.
- Instruct the client and visitors about the hazard of smoking with oxygen in use.
- For home oxygen use or when the facility permits smoking, teach family members and roommates to smoke only outside or in provided smoking rooms away from the client.
- Make sure that electric devices (such as razors, hearing aids, radios, televisions, and heating pads) are in good working order to prevent the occurrence of short-circuit sparks.
- Avoid materials that generate static electricity, such as woolen blankets and synthetic fabrics. Cotton blankets should be used, and clients and caregivers are advised to wear cotton fabrics.
- Avoid the use of volatile, flammable materials, such as oils, greases, alcohol, ether, and acetone (e.g., nail polish remover) near clients receiving oxygen.
- Ground electric monitoring equipment, suction machines, and portable diagnostic machines.
- Make known the location of fire extinguishers, and make sure personnel are trained in their use and in protocols associated with fire safety.

Oxygen Therapy for Clients with COPD

Low-flow oxygen systems are essential for clients with COPD. A high carbon dioxide level in the blood is the normal stimulus to breathe. However, people with COPD may chronically have a high carbon dioxide level, and their stimulus to breathe is hypoxemia (low blood oxygen level). High flows of oxygen can potentially relieve this hypoxemia, removing the stimulus to breathe; low flows, by contrast, maintain a slightly hypoxemic state, maintaining the respiratory drive. Clients who have COPD and are receiving oxygen therapy should be observed carefully (especially when therapy is first initiated) for respiratory depression or arrest.

Oxygen is supplied in several different ways. In hospitals and long-term care facilities, it is usually piped into wall outlets at the client's bedside, making it readily available for use at all times. Tanks or cylinders of oxygen under pressure are also frequently available for use when wall oxygen either is unavailable or impractical (e.g., for transporting oxygen-dependent clients between treatment areas).

Clients who require oxygen therapy in the home may use small cylinders of oxygen, oxygen in liquid form, or an oxygen concentrator. Portable oxygen delivery systems are available to increase the client's independence. Home oxygen therapy services are readily available in most communities. These services generally supply the oxygen and delivery devices, training for the client and family, equipment maintenance, and emergency services should a problem occur.

Oxygen administered from a cylinder or wall-outlet system is dry. Dry gases dehydrate the respiratory mucous membranes. Humidifying devices that add water vapour to inspired air are, thus, an essential adjunct of oxygen therapy, particularly for litre flows over 2 L per minute. These devices provide 20 to 40 percent humidity. The oxygen passes through sterile distilled water or tap water and then along a line to the device through which the moistened oxygen is inhaled (e.g., a cannula, nasal catheter, or oxygen mask).

Humidifiers prevent mucous membranes from drying and becoming irritated and loosen secretions for easier expectoration. Oxygen passing through water picks up water vapour before it reaches the client. The more bubbles created during this process, the more water vapour is produced. Very low litre flows (e.g., 1 to 2 L per minute by nasal cannula) do not require humidification.

Oxygen cylinders need to be handled and stored with caution and strapped securely in wheeled transport devices or stands to prevent possible falls and outlet breakages. They should be placed away from traffic areas and heaters.

To use an oxygen wall outlet, the nurse carries out these steps:

- Attach the flow meter (Figure 39.10) to the wall outlet, exerting firm pressure. The flow meter should be in the off position.
- Fill the humidifier bottle with sterile distilled water in accordance with agency protocol. (This can be done before coming to the bedside.) The sterile distilled water should be changed every 24 hours or according to agency policy.
- Attach the humidifier bottle to the base of the flow meter.
- Attach the prescribed oxygen tubing and delivery device to the humidifier.
- Regulate the flow meter to the prescribed level.

Oxygen Delivery Systems

A number of systems are available to deliver oxygen to the client. The choice of system depends on the client's oxygen needs, comfort, and developmental considerations, agency policy, and physician's orders. With many systems, the oxygen delivered mixes with room air before being inspired. The amount of oxygen delivered is determined by regulating its flow rate (e.g., 2 to 6 L per minute). Precise regulation of the percentage of inspired oxygen, or fraction of inspired oxygen (FiO_2), is not possible. When it is important to regulate the percentage of oxygen received by the client more precisely, a device such as a Venturi mask may be used.

Cannula

The nasal cannula (nasal prongs) is the most common and inexpensive device used to administer oxygen. See Figure 39.11. The nasal cannula is easy to apply and does not interfere with the client's ability to eat or talk. It is relatively comfortable, permits some freedom of movement, and is usually well tolerated by the client. It delivers a relatively low concentration of oxygen (24 to 45 percent) at flow rates of 2 to 6 L per minute. Above 6 L per minute, the client tends to swallow air, and the FiO_2 is *not* increased.

Administering oxygen by cannula is detailed in Procedure 39.2.

Face Mask

Face masks that cover the client's nose and mouth may be used for oxygen inhalation. Exhalation ports on the sides of the mask allow exhaled carbon dioxide to escape. A variety of oxygen masks are marketed. Four of these are:

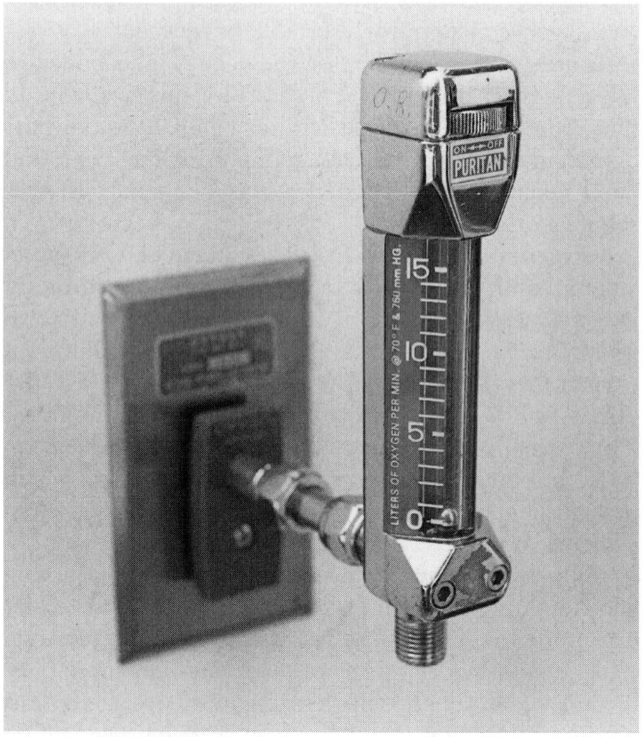

Figure 39.10 An oxygen flow meter attached to a wall outlet

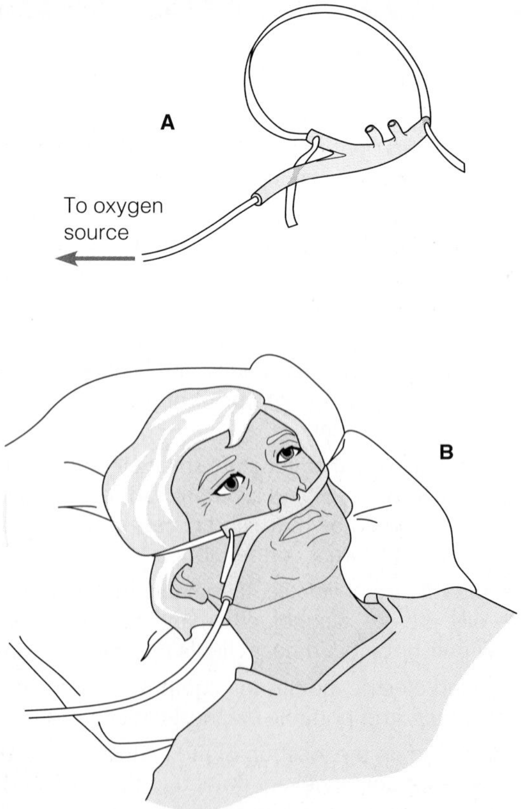

Figure 39.11 *A,* Nasal cannula; *B,* the cannula in place

PROCEDURE 39.2 Administering Oxygen by Cannula, Face Mask, or Face Tent

Before administering oxygen, check (1) the prescription for oxygen, including the administering device and the litre flow rate (L/min) or the percentage of oxygen; (2) the levels of oxygen (PO_2) and carbon dioxide ($PaCO_2$) in the client's arterial blood (PaO_2 is normally 80 to 100 mm Hg; $PaCO_2$ is normally 35 to 45 mm Hg); (3) whether the client has COPD, (4) the SaO_2, and (5) the hemoglobin.

PURPOSES

Cannula

- To deliver a relatively low concentration of oxygen when only minimal O_2 support is required
- To allow uninterrupted delivery of oxygen while the client ingests food or fluids

Face Mask

- To provide moderate O_2 support and a higher concentration of oxygen and/or humidity than is provided by cannula

Face Tent

- To provide high humidity
- To provide oxygen when a mask is poorly tolerated
- To provide a high flow of O_2 when attached to a Venturi system

Assessment Focus
Vital signs; arterial blood gas levels; oxygen saturation levels; signs of hypoxia (e.g., tachycardia, tachypnea, dyspnea); signs of hypercarbia (e.g., restlessness, hypertension, headache); lung sounds; patency of nares (if nasal cannula is to be used); mental status; signs of oxygen toxicity (e.g., tracheal irritation, cough, decreased pulmonary ventilation); mouth breathing

Equipment

Cannula

- ❑ Oxygen supply with a flow meter
- ❑ Nasal cannula and tubing
- ❑ Gauze pads, tape, and safety pin, as needed

Face Mask

- ❑ Oxygen supply with a flow meter
- ❑ Humidifier with sterile distilled or tap water according to agency policy
- ❑ Prescribed face mask of the appropriate size
- ❑ Padding for the elastic band

Face Tent

- ❑ Oxygen supply with a flow meter
- ❑ Humidifier with sterile distilled or tap water according to agency policy
- ❑ Face tent of the appropriate size
- ❑ Gauze pads, tape, and safety pin, as needed

INTERVENTION

1. Determine the need for oxygen therapy, and verify the prescription for the therapy.

- In an emergency situation, provide the client with oxygen first prior to commencing a complete respiratory assessment.
- Perform a respiratory assessment to determine the need for O_2 therapy and to develop baseline data if not already available.

2. Prepare the client and the support people.

- Assist the client to a semi-Fowler's position, if possible. *This position permits easier chest expansion and, hence, easier breathing.*
- Explain that oxygen is not dangerous when safety precautions are observed and that it will ease the discomfort of dyspnea. Inform the client and support people about the safety precautions connected with oxygen use.

3. Set up the oxygen equipment and the humidifier.

4. Turn on the oxygen at the prescribed rate, and ensure proper functioning of the equipment.

- Check that the oxygen is flowing freely through the tubing. There should be no kinks in the tubing, and the connections should be airtight. There should be bubbles in the humidifier as the oxygen flows through the water. You should feel the oxygen at the outlets of the cannula, mask, or tent. At low levels, flow of oxygen can be determined by placing O_2 tubing/cannula in water to assess bubbling (flow of oxygen).
- Set the oxygen at the flow rate ordered, for example, 2 to 6 L/min.

5. Apply the appropriate oxygen delivery device.

CANNULA

- Put the cannula over the client's face, with the outlet prongs fitting into the nares and the elastic band around the head (Figure 39.11, opposite). Some models have a strap to adjust under the chin.
- Pad the tubing and band over the ears and cheekbones, as needed.

FACE MASK

- Guide the mask toward the client's face, and apply it from the nose downward.
- Fit the mask to the contours of the client's face (see Figure 39.12, p. 1051). *The mask should mould to the face so that very little oxygen escapes into the eyes or around the cheeks and chin.*

→

PROCEDURE 39.2 Administering Oxygen by Cannula, Face Mask, or Face Tent *continued*

- Secure the elastic band around the client's head so that the mask is snug but comfortable.
- Pad the band behind the ears and over bony prominences. *Padding will prevent irritation from the mask.*

FACE TENT

- Place the tent over the client's face, and secure the ties around the head (see Figure 39.16, p. 1052).

6. Assess the client regularly.

- Secure the oxygen tubing to the client's gown or clothing with a safety pin (to prevent causing skin breakdown from friction of tube pulling).
- Assess the client's level of anxiety, colour, and ease of respirations, and provide support while the client adjusts to the device.
- Assess the client in 15 to 30 minutes depending on the client's condition, and regularly thereafter. Assess vital signs, colour, breathing patterns, chest movements, and oxygen saturation levels.
- Assess the client regularly for clinical signs of hypoxia, tachycardia, confusion, dyspnea, restlessness, and cyanosis. Obtain arterial blood gas results if they are available.

NASAL CANNULA

- Assess the client's nares for encrustations and irritation. Apply a water-soluble lubricant, as required, to soothe the mucous membranes.

FACE MASK OR TENT

- Inspect the facial skin frequently for dampness or chafing, and dry and treat it as needed.

7. Inspect the equipment on a regular basis.

- Check the litre flow and the level of water in the humidifier in 30 minutes and whenever providing care to the client.
- Maintain the level of water in the humidifier.
- Make sure that safety precautions are being followed.

8. Document relevant data.

- Record the initiation of the therapy and all nursing assessments.

Evaluation Focus
Vital signs; signs of hypoxia, hypercarbia; bilateral lung sounds; blood gas levels; colour of skin, nails, lips, earlobes, and mucous membranes of the nose, mouth, and pharynx; activity tolerance; level of anxiety

- The *simple face mask* delivers oxygen concentrations from 40 to 60 percent at litre flows of 5 to 8 L per minute, respectively (Figure 39.12).
- The *partial rebreather mask* delivers oxygen concentrations of 60 to 90 percent at litre flows of 6 to 10 L per minute, respectively, depending on client respiratory rate and depth. The oxygen reservoir bag that is attached allows the client to rebreathe about the first third of the exhaled air in conjunction with oxygen (Figure 39.13). Thus, it increases the FiO_2 by recycling expired oxygen. The partial rebreather bag must not totally deflate during inspiration to avoid carbon dioxide buildup. If this problem occurs, the nurse increases the litre flow of oxygen.
- The *nonrebreather mask* delivers the highest oxygen concentration possible—that is, 95 to 100 percent—by means other than intubation or mechanical ventide depending on client respiratory rate and depth. One-way valves on the mask and between the reservoir bag and the mask prevent the room air and the client's exhaled air from entering the bag so that only the oxygen in the bag is inspired (Figure 39.15). To prevent carbon dioxide buildup, the nonrebreather bag must not totally deflate during inspiration. If it does, the nurse can correct this problem by increasing the litre flow of oxygen.
- The *Venturi mask* delivers oxygen concentrations varying from 24 to 50 percent at litre flows of 4 to 10 L per minute (Figure 39.14). The Venturi mask has wide-bore tubing and colour-coded jet adapters that correspond to a precise oxygen concentration and litre flow. For example, one colour-coded adapter delivers a 24 percent concentration of oxygen at 4 L per minute, and another colour-coded adapter delivers a 35 percent concentration of oxygen at 8 L per minute. The Venturi mask can either be humidified through room air, or additional humidification may be necessary. Follow manufacturer's directions and agency policy for use of the Venturi mask.

Initiating oxygen by mask is much the same as initiating oxygen by cannula except that the nurse must find a mask of appropriate size. Smaller sizes are available for children. Administering oxygen by mask or face tent is detailed in Procedure 39.2.

Face Tent

Face tents (Figure 39.16) can replace oxygen masks when masks are poorly tolerated by clients. Face tents provide varying concentrations of oxygen, for example, 30 to 50 percent concentration of oxygen at 4 to 8 L per minute. Frequently inspect the client's facial skin for dampness or chafing, and dry and treat, as needed. As with face masks, the client's facial skin must be kept dry.

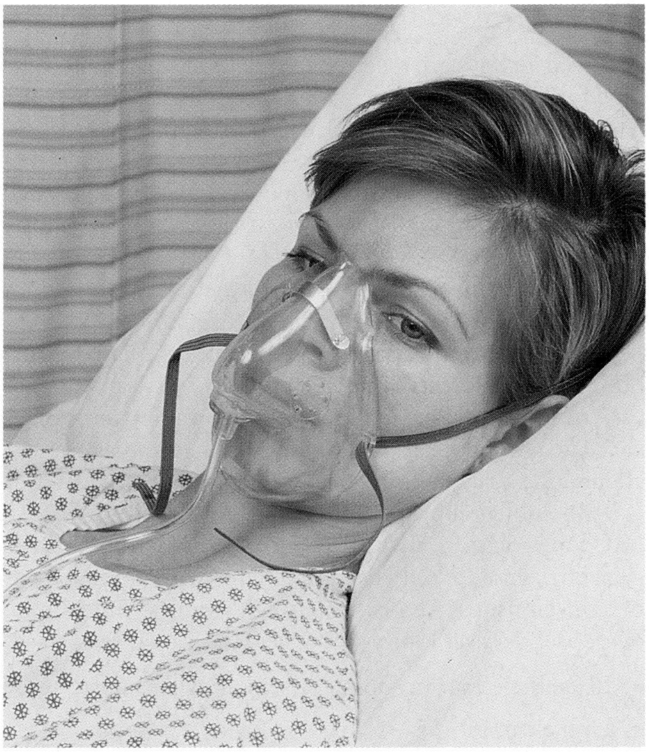

Figure 39.12 A simple face mask

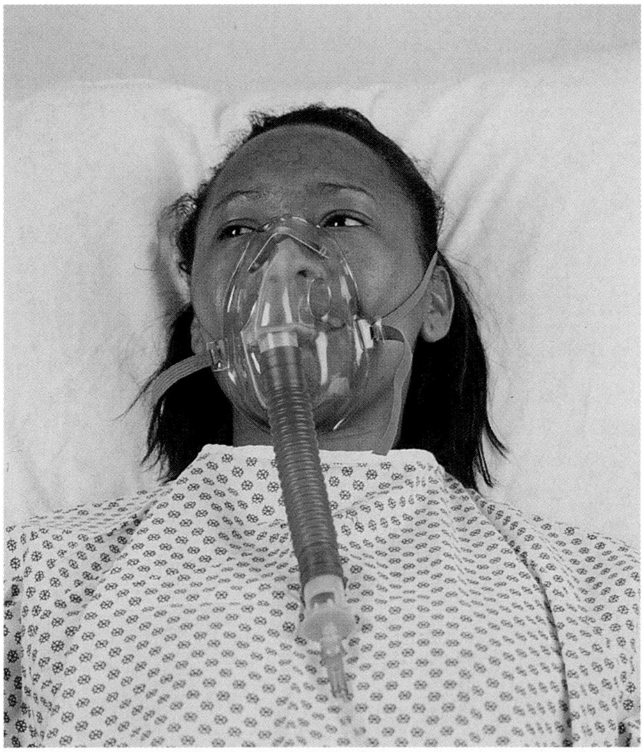

Figure 39.14 Venturi mask

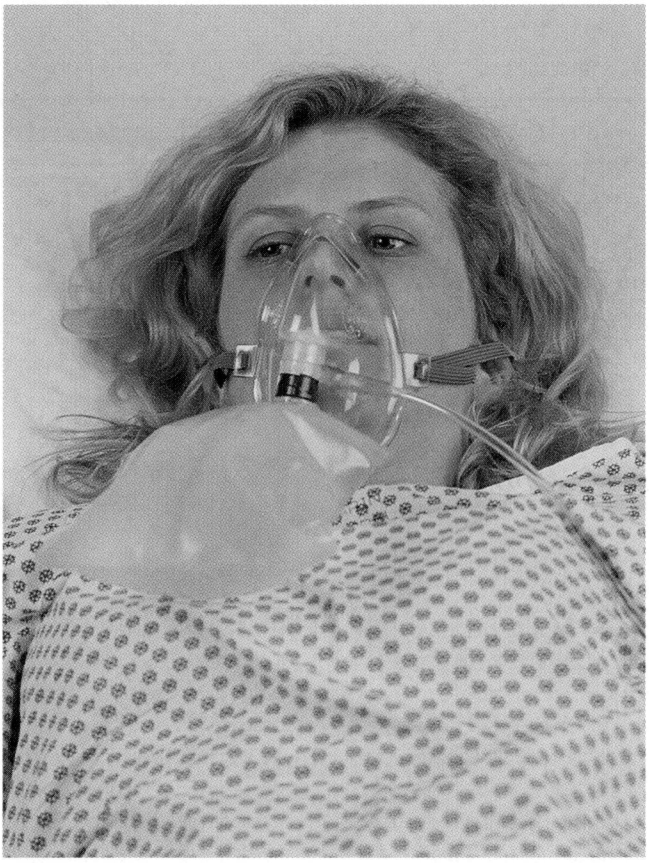

Figure 39.13 A partial rebreather mask

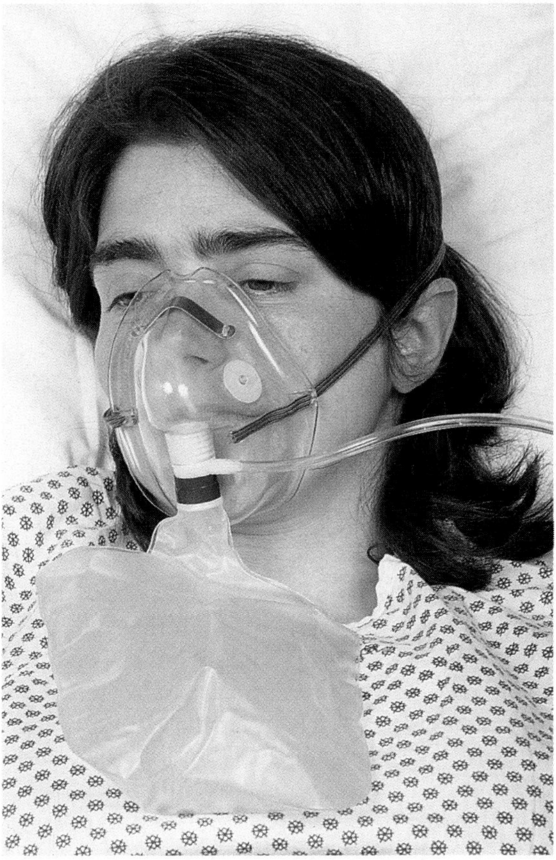

Figure 39.15 A nonrebreather mask

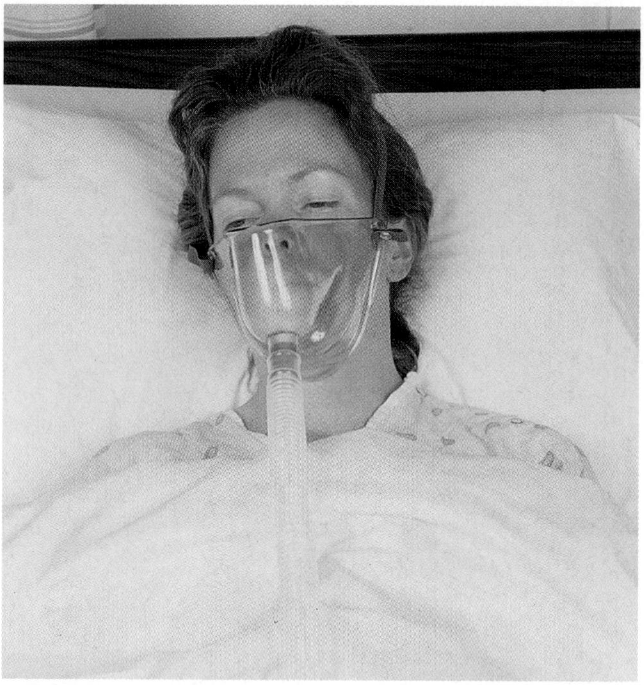

Figure 39.16 An oxygen face tent

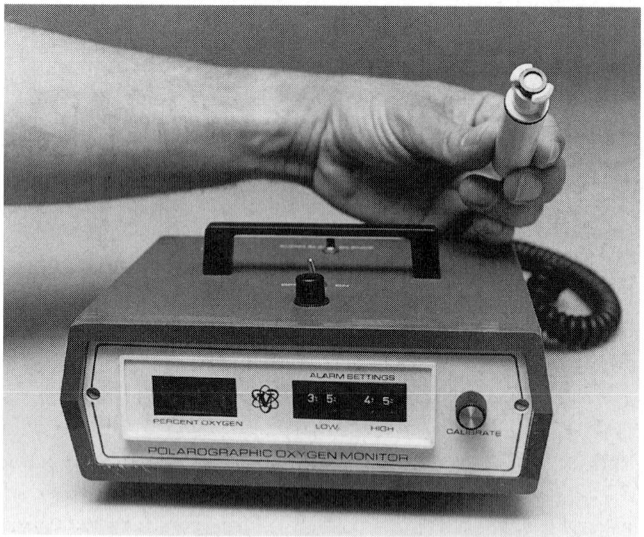

Figure 39.17 An oxygen analyzer

Oxygen Analyzer

Oxygen analyzers (Figure 39.17) measure the concentration of oxygen being received by the client. The analyzer is first used to measure the concentration of oxygen in the room. It should register 0.21 (21 percent). If it does not, the nurse adjusts the dial to this calibration. The nurse then places the sample tube next to the client's nose, monitors the reading on the analyzer, and adjusts the oxygen flow rate to obtain the desired fraction of inspired oxygen (FiO_2).

Artificial Airways

Artificial airways are inserted to maintain a patent air passage for clients whose airway has become or may become obstructed. A patent airway is necessary so that air can flow to and from the lungs. Four of the more common types of airways are oropharyngeal, nasopharyngeal, endotracheal, and tracheostomy.

Oropharyngeal and Nasopharyngeal Airways

Oropharyngeal and nasopharyngeal airways are used to keep the upper air passages open when they may become obstructed by secretions or the tongue. These airways are easy to insert and have a low risk of complications. Sizes vary and should be appropriate to the size and age of the client. The airway should be well lubricated with water or water-soluble gel prior to inserting.

Oropharyngeal airways (Figure 39.18) stimulate the gag reflex and are only used for clients with altered levels of consciousness (e.g., because of general anesthesia, overdose, or head injury). To insert the airway:

- Place the client in supine or semi-Fowler's position.
- Don clean gloves.
- Hold the lubricated airway by the outer flange, with the distal end pointing up.
- Open the client's mouth and insert the airway along the top of the tongue.
- When the distal end of the airway reaches the soft palate at the back of the mouth, rotate the airway 180 degrees downward, and slip it past the uvula into the oral pharynx.
- If not contraindicated, place the client in a side-lying position to allow secretions to drain out of the mouth.
- The oropharynx may be suctioned as needed by inserting the suction catheter alongside the airway.
- Do not tape the airway in place; remove it when the client begins to cough or gag.
- Provide mouth care at least every two hours, keeping suction available at the bedside.
- Oxygen therapy via face mask may be required or ordered.
- Humidification may be required.

Nasopharyngeal airways are tolerated better by alert clients. They are inserted through the nares, terminating in the oropharynx (Figure 39.19). When caring for a client with a nasopharyngeal airway, provide frequent oral and nares care, repositioning the airway in the other naris every eight hours or as ordered to prevent necrosis of the mucosa. Oxygen therapy may be required or ordered. Humidification may be required.

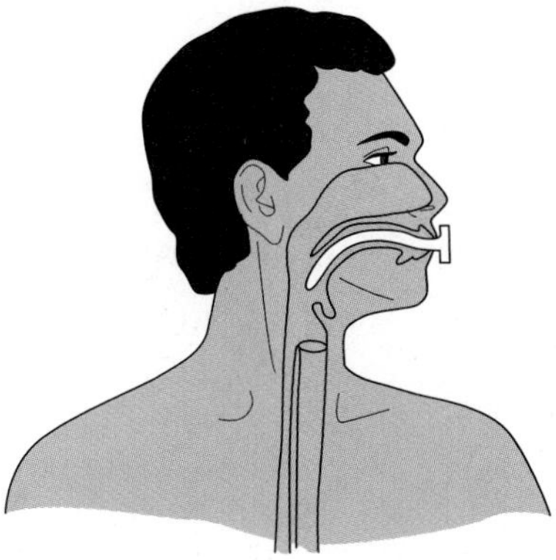

Figure 39.18 An oropharyngeal airway in place

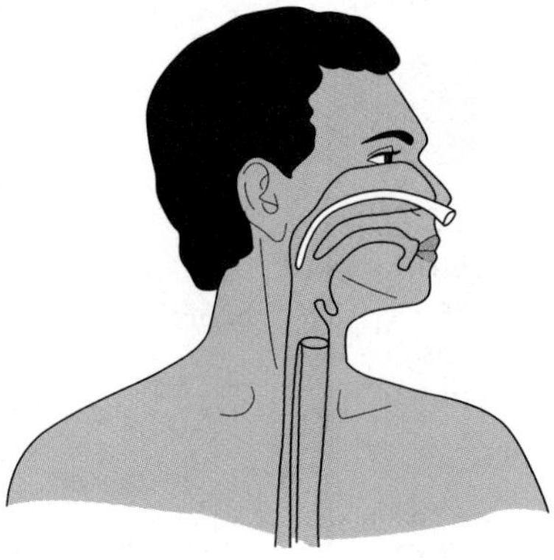

Figure 39.19 A nasopharyngeal airway in place

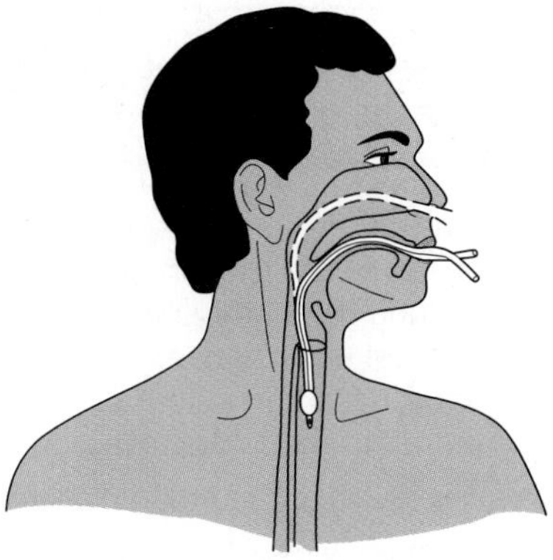

Figure 39.20 An endotracheal tube in place

Endotracheal Tubes

Endotracheal tubes are most commonly inserted for clients who have had general anesthetics or for those in emergency situations where mechanical ventilation is required. An endotracheal tube is inserted through either the mouth or the nose and into the trachea with the guide of a laryngoscope (Figure 39.20) by the physician or nurse with specialized education. The tube terminates just superior to the bifurcation of the trachea into the bronchi. The tube may have an air-filled cuff to prevent air leakage around it. Because an endotracheal tube passes through the epiglottis and glottis, the client is unable to speak while it is in place. Nursing interventions for clients with endotracheal tubes are shown in the next box.

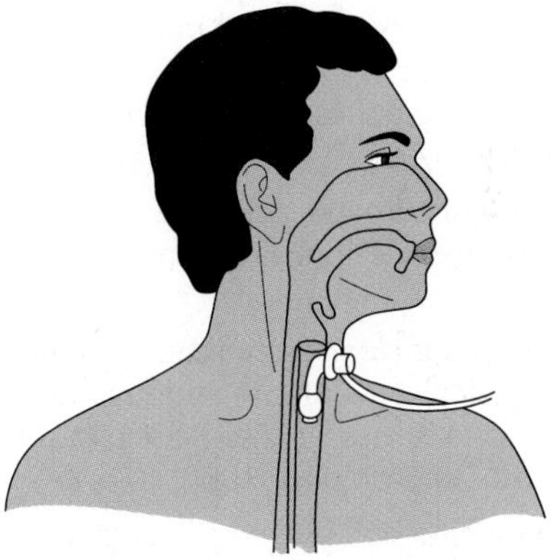

Figure 39.21 A tracheostomy tube in place

Tracheotomy/Tracheostomy

Clients who need long-term airway support may have a **tracheotomy,** a surgical incision in the trachea just below the larynx. A tracheostomy is the opening made for the tube itself. A curved tracheostomy tube is inserted to extend through the stoma into the trachea (Figure 39.21). Tracheostomy tubes may be either plastic or metal and are available in different sizes.

Tracheostomy tubes (Figure 39.22) have an outer cannula that is inserted into the trachea and a flange that rests against the neck and allows the tube to be secured in place with tape or ties. All tubes also have an obturator, used to insert the outer cannula and then removed. The obturator is kept at the client's bedside in case the tube becomes dislodged and needs to be re-inserted. Some tracheostomy tubes have an inner cannula that may be removed for periodic cleaning.

Cuffed tracheostomy tubes (Figure 39.23) are surrounded by an inflatable cuff that produces an airtight seal between the tube and the trachea. This seal prevents aspiration of oropharyngeal secretions and air leakage between the tube and the trachea. Cuffed tubes are often used immediately after a tracheostomy and are essential when ventilating a tracheostomy client with a mechanical ventilator. Children do not require cuffed tubes because their tracheas are small enough to seal the air space around the tube.

Low-pressure cuffs are commonly used to distribute a low, even pressure against the trachea, thus decreasing the risk of tracheal tissue necrosis. Deflation of the cuff should be according to manufacturer's recommendations and agency policy. The foam cuff does not require injected air; instead, when the port is opened, ambient air enters the balloon, which then conforms to the client's trachea. Air is removed from the cuff prior to insertion or removal of the tube.

The nurse provides tracheostomy care for the client with a new or recent tracheostomy to maintain patency of the tube and reduce the risk of infection. Initially, a tracheostomy may need to be suctioned (see the section on suctioning that follows) and cleaned as often as every one to two hours. After the initial inflammatory response subsides, tracheostomy care may only need to be done once or twice a day depending on the client. Procedure 39.3 describes tracheostomy care.

Nursing Interventions for Clients with Endotracheal Tubes

- Assess the client's respiratory status at least every one to two hours, or more frequently if indicated. Include respiratory rate, rhythm, depth, equality of chest excursion, and lung sounds; level of consciousness; and colour of skin and mucous membranes in the assessment.
- Assess oxygen saturation levels.
- Frequently assess nasal and oral mucosa for redness and irritation. Report any abnormal findings to the physician.
- Secure the endotracheal tube with tape to prevent accidental movement of the tube further into or out of the trachea. Assess the position of the tube frequently. Notify the physician immediately if the tube is dislodged out of the airway. If the tube advances into a main bronchus, it may need to be slightly withdrawn to ensure ventilation of both lungs.
- Unless contraindicated, place the client in a side-lying or semiprone position, as tolerated, to prevent aspiration of oral secretions.
- Using sterile or clean technique (depending on agency policy), suction the endotracheal tube as needed to remove excessive secretions. See Procedure 39.5 on page 1060.
- Closely monitor cuff pressure, maintaining a pressure of 20 to 25 mm Hg (or as recommended by the tube manufacturer) to minimize the risk of tracheal tissue necrosis. Depending on the manufacturer's specifications and agency policy, the cuff may be deflated and re-inflated periodically.
- Provide oral and nasal care every two to four hours. Use an oropharyngeal airway to prevent the client from biting down on an oral endotracheal tube. Move oral endotracheal tubes to the opposite side of the mouth every eight hours or per agency protocol, taking care to maintain the position of the tube in the trachea.
- Provide humidified air or oxygen because the upper airways, which normally moisten the air, are bypassed by the endotracheal tube.
- If the client is on mechanical ventilation, ensure that all alarms are enabled at all times as the client cannot call for help should an emergency occur.
- Communicate frequently with the client, providing a note pad or picture board for the client to use for communicating.

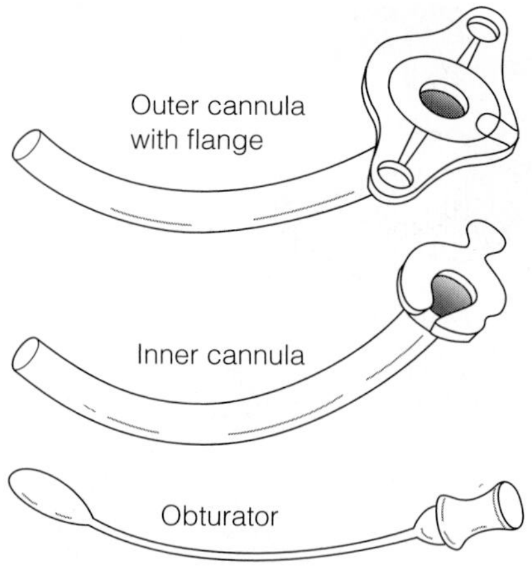

Figure 39.22 Components of a tracheostomy tube

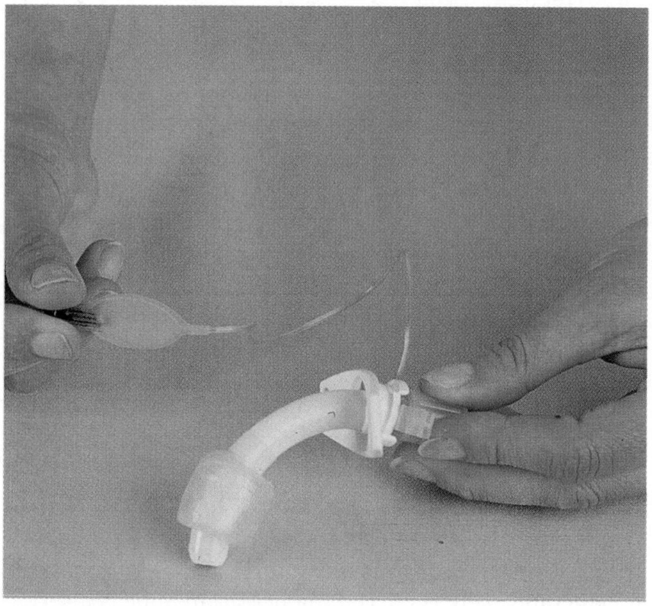

Figure 39.23 A tracheostomy tube with a low-pressure cuff

When the client breathes through a tracheostomy, air is no longer filtered and humidified as it is when passing through the upper airways; therefore, special precautions are necessary. Humidity may be provided with a mist collar. Clients with long-term tracheostomies require a 4 × 4 gauze held in place with a cotton tie over the stoma to filter air as it enters the tracheostomy. Tracheostomy filters are also commercially available.

PROCEDURE 39.3 Providing Tracheostomy Care

PURPOSES

- To maintain airway patency
- To maintain cleanliness and prevent infection at the tracheostomy site
- To facilitate healing and prevent skin excoriation around the tracheostomy incision
- To promote comfort

Assessment Focus
Respiratory status, including ease of breathing, rate, rhythm, depth, and lung sounds; pulse rate; oxygen saturation levels; character and amount of secretions from tracheostomy site; presence of drainage on tracheostomy dressing or ties; appearance of incision (note any redness, swelling, purulent discharge, or odour); twill tapes secured to outer cannula flange

Equipment

- ❑ Sterile disposable tracheostomy cleaning kit or supplies, including sterile containers, sterile nylon brush and/or pipe cleaners, sterile applicators, gauze squares
- ❑ Towel or drape to protect bed linens
- ❑ Sterile suction catheter kit (suction catheter and sterile container for solution)
- ❑ Sterile normal saline
- ❑ Sterile gloves (two pairs)
- ❑ Mask and goggles if required
- ❑ Recommended cleaning solution for cannula
- ❑ Clean gloves
- ❑ Moistureproof bag
- ❑ Commercially prepared sterile tracheostomy dressing or sterile 4 × 4 gauze dressing
- ❑ Cotton twill ties
- ❑ Clean scissors

INTERVENTION

1. Verify physician's orders and agency policy.

2. Prepare the client and the equipment.

- Assist the client to a semi-Fowler's or Fowler's position to promote lung expansion.
- Explain the procedure to the client and provide for a means of communication, such as eye blinking or raising a finger to indicate pain or distress.
- Open the tracheostomy kit or sterile basins. Pour the recommended cleaning solution into containers.
- Establish a sterile field.
- Open other sterile supplies, as needed, including sterile applicators, suction kit, and tracheostomy dressing.

3. Suction the tracheostomy tube.

- Don sterile gloves and mask, goggles, and gown if required.
- Suction the full length of the tracheostomy tube to remove secretions and ensure a patent airway (see Procedure 39.5).
- Rinse the suction catheter, and discard inside the glove of one hand.
- Using the gloved hand, unlock the inner cannula (if present) and remove it by gently pulling it out toward you in line with its curvature. Place the inner cannula in the solution. *This moistens and loosens dried secretions.*
- Remove the soiled tracheostomy dressing, and discard the glove and the dressing.
- Remove used gloves and don sterile gloves.

4. Clean the incision site and tube flange.

- Using sterile applicators or gauze dressings moistened with a cleaning solution, clean the incision site (Figure 39.24). Use each applicator or gauze dressing only once, then discard. *This avoids contaminating a clean area with a soiled gauze dressing or applicator.*

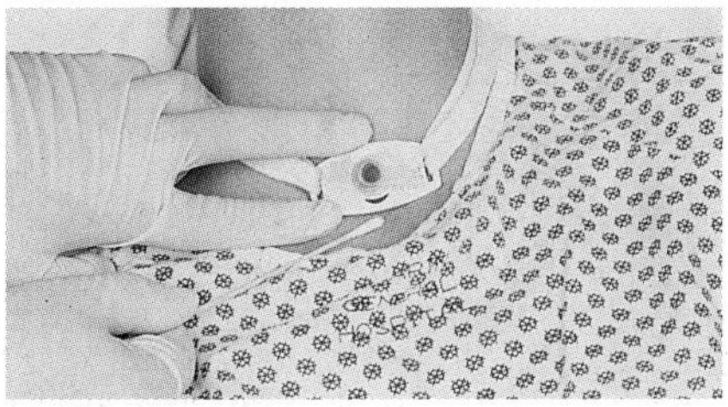

Figure 39.24 Using an applicator stick to clean the tracheostomy site

- Cleaning solutions, such as sterile normal saline, may be used to remove encrustations. It is important to check the policy of the institution for the specific solution used in tracheostomy care. Thoroughly rinse the cleaned area using gauze squares moistened with sterile normal saline.
- Clean the flange of the tube in the same manner.
- Thoroughly dry the client's skin and tube flanges with dry gauze squares.

5. Clean the inner cannula.

- Remove the inner cannula from the soaking solution.
- Clean the lumen and entire inner cannula thoroughly using the brush or pipe cleaners moistened with sterile normal saline (Figure 39.25). Inspect the cannula for cleanliness by holding it at eye level and looking through it into the light.
- Rinse the inner cannula thoroughly in sterile normal saline. *Thorough rinsing is important to remove the soaking/cleaning solution from the inner cannula.*
- After rinsing, gently tap the cannula against the inside edge of the sterile saline container. Use a pipe cleaner folded in half to dry only the inside of the cannula; do not dry the outside. *This removes excess liquid from the cannula and prevents*

PROCEDURE 39.3 Providing Tracheostomy Care *continued*

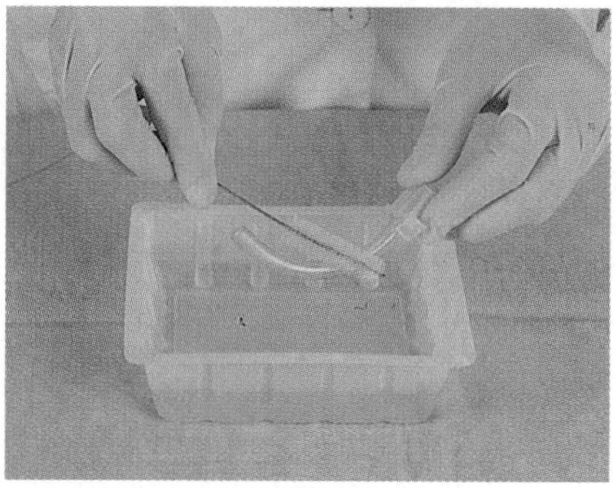

Figure 39.25 Cleaning the inner cannula with a brush

possible aspiration by the client while leaving a film of moisture on the outer surface to lubricate the cannula for re-insertion.

- Using sterile technique, suction the outer cannula. *Suctioning removes secretions from the outer cannula.*

6. Replace the inner cannula, securing it in place.

- Insert the inner cannula by grasping the outer flange and inserting the cannula in the direction of its curvature.
- Lock the cannula in place by turning the lock (if present) into position to secure the flange of the inner cannula to the outer cannula.

7. Apply a sterile dressing.

- Use a commercially prepared tracheostomy dressing of nonraveling material, or open and refold a 4 × 4 gauze dressing into a V shape as shown in Figure 39.26, *A* to *D*. Avoid using cotton-filled gauze squares or cutting the 4 × 4 gauze. *Cotton lint or gauze fibres can be aspirated by the client, potentially creating a tracheal abscess.*
- Place the dressing under the flange of the tracheostomy tube as shown in Figure 39.26, *E*.
- While applying the dressing, ensure that the tracheostomy tube is securely supported. *Excessive movement of the tracheostomy tube irritates the trachea.*

8. Change the tracheostomy ties.

TWO-STRIP METHOD

- Cut two unequal strips of twill tape, one approximately 25 cm long and the other about 50 cm long. *Cutting one tape longer than the other allows them to be fastened at the side of the neck for easy access and to avoid the pressure of a knot on the skin at the back of the neck.*

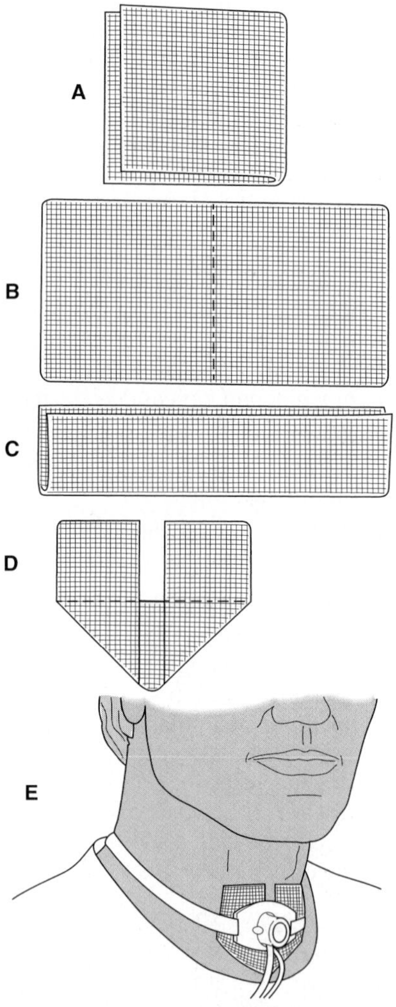

Figure 39.26 Folding a 4 × 4 gauze to make a tracheostomy dressing

- Cut a 1-cm lengthwise slit approximately 2.5 cm from one end of each strip. To do this, fold the end of the tape back onto itself about 2.5 cm, then cut a slit in the middle of the tape from its folded edge.
- Leaving the old ties in place, thread the slit end of one clean tape through the eye of the tracheostomy flange from the bottom side; then thread the long end of the tape through the slit, pulling it taut until it is securely fastened to the flange. *Leaving the old ties in place while securing the clean ties prevents inadvertent dislodging of the tracheostomy tube. Securing tapes in this manner avoids the use of knots, which can come untied or cause pressure and irritation.*
- If old ties are very soiled or it is difficult to thread new ties onto the tracheostomy flange with old ties in place, have an assistant don a sterile glove and hold the tracheostomy in place while you replace the ties.
- Repeat the process for the second tie.
- Ask the client to flex the neck. Slip the longer tape under the client's neck, place a finger between the tape and the client's neck (Figure 39.27), and tie the tapes together at the side of the neck. *Flexing the neck increases its circumference the way coughing does. Placing a finger under the ties prevents making the ties too tight, which could interfere with coughing or place pressure on the jugular veins.*

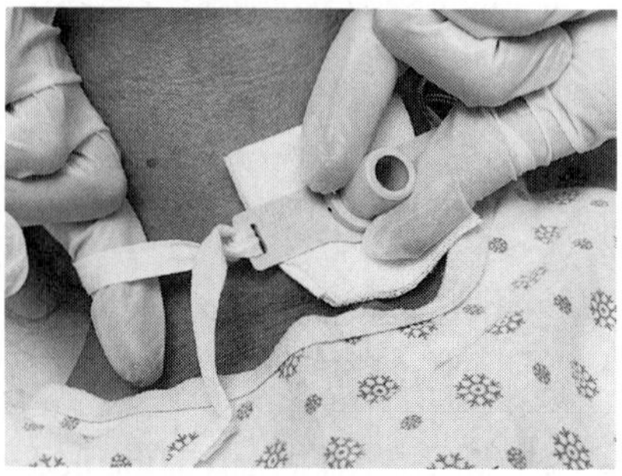

Figure 39.27 Placing a finger underneath the tie tape before tying it

- Tie the ends of the tapes using square knots. Cut off any long ends, leaving approximately 1 to 2 cm.

PROCEDURE 39.3 Providing Tracheostomy Care *continued*

Square knots prevent slippage and loosening. Adequate ends beyond the knot prevent the knot from inadvertently untying.

- Once the clean ties are secured, remove the soiled ties and discard.

ONE-STRIP METHOD

- Cut a length of twill tape 2.5 times the length needed to go around the client's neck from one tube flange to the other.
- Thread one end of the tape into the slot on one side of the flange.
- Bring both ends of the tape together, and take them around the client's neck, keeping them flat and untwisted.
- Thread the end of the tape next to the client's neck through the other flange slot from the back to the front.
- Have the client flex the neck. Tie the loose ends with a square knot at the side of the client's neck, allowing for slack by placing a finger under the ties as with the two-strip method. Cut off long ends.

9. **Tape and pad the tie knot.**
   - Place a folded 4 × 4 gauze square under the tie knot, and apply tape over the knot. *This reduces skin irritation from the knot and prevents confusing the knot with the client's gown ties.*
10. **Check the tightness of the ties.**
    - Frequently check the tightness of the tracheostomy ties and position of the tracheostomy tube. *Swelling of the neck may cause the ties to become too taut, interfering with coughing and circulation. Ties can loosen in restless clients, allowing the tracheostomy tube to extrude from the stoma.*
11. **Document all relevant information.**
    - Record suctioning, tracheostomy care, and the dressing change, noting your assessments.

Evaluation Focus
Character and amount of secretions; drainage from the tracheostomy; appearance of the tracheostomy incision; pulse rate and respiratory status compared with baseline data; complaints of pain or discomfort at the tracheostomy site

Suctioning

When clients have difficulty handling their secretions or an airway is in place, suctioning may be necessary to clear air passages. **Suctioning** refers to the aspiration of secretions through a catheter connected to a suction machine or wall suction outlet. Even though the upper airways (the oropharynx and nasopharynx) are not sterile, sterile technique is recommended for all suctioning to avoid introducing pathogens into the airways.

Suction catheters may be either open-tipped or whistle-tipped (Figure 39.28). The whistle-tipped catheter is less irritating to respiratory tissues, although the open-tipped catheter may be more effective for removing thick mucus plugs. Most suction catheters have a thumb port on the side to control the suction. The catheter is connected to suction tubing, which, in turn, is connected to a collection chamber and suction control gauge (Figure 39.29).

Oropharyngeal or *nasopharyngeal suctioning* remove secretions from the upper respiratory tract. *Endotracheal suctioning* is used to remove secretions from the trachea and bronchi. The nurse decides when suctioning is needed by assessing the client for signs of respiratory distress or evidence that the client is unable to cough up and expectorate secretions. Dyspnea, bubbling or rattling breath sounds, poor skin colour (cyanosis), decreased SaO_2 levels (also called O_2 sats), or a change in vital signs may indicate the need for suctioning. Good nursing judgement is necessary, as suctioning irritates mucous membranes and can increase secretions if performed too frequently. Procedure 39.4 outlines oropharyngeal and nasopharyngeal suctioning.

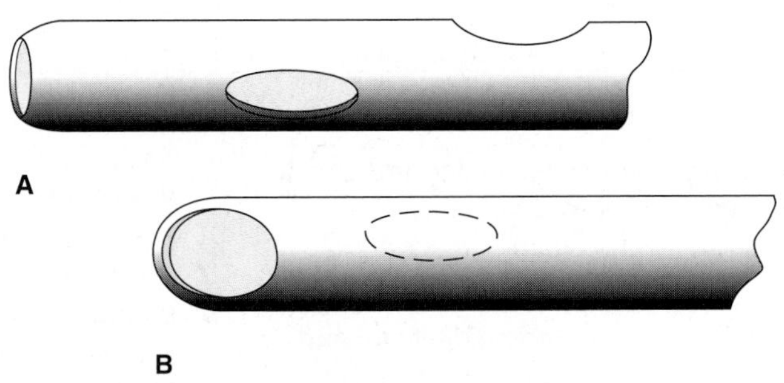

Figure 39.28 Types of suction catheters. *A*, open-tipped; *B*, whistle-tipped

Figure 39.29 A wall suction unit

Following endotracheal intubation or a tracheotomy, the trachea and surrounding respiratory tissues are irritated and react by producing excessive secretions. Suctioning is necessary to remove these secretions and maintain a patent airway. The frequency of suctioning depends on the client's assessment data and how recently the intubation was done.

Suctioning is associated with several complications: hypoxemia, trauma to the airway, nosocomial infection, and cardiac dysrhythmias, which are related to the hypoxemia. Techniques to minimize or decrease these complications include the following (according to agency policy and physician's orders):

- *Hyperinflation.* This involves giving the client breaths that are one to $1\frac{1}{2}$ times the tidal volume set on the ventilator through the ventilator circuit or via a manual resuscitation bag. Three to five breaths are delivered before and after each pass of the suction catheter.
- *Hyperoxygenation.* This can be done with a manual resuscitation bag or through the ventilator and is performed by increasing the oxygen flow (usually to 100 percent) before suctioning and between suction attempts.

PROCEDURE 39.4 Suctioning Oropharyngeal and Nasopharyngeal Cavities

PURPOSES

- To remove secretions that obstruct the airway
- To facilitate ventilation
- To obtain secretions for diagnostic purposes
- To prevent infection that may result from accumulated secretions

Assessment Focus
Clinical signs indicating the need for suctioning: restlessness; gurgling sounds during respiration; adventitious breath sounds when the chest is auscultated; change in mental status; colour of skin and mucous membranes; rate and pattern of respirations; pulse rate and rhythm, oxygen saturation level

Equipment

- ❑ Towel or moisture-resistant pad
- ❑ Portable or wall suction machine with tubing and collection receptacle
- ❑ Sterile disposable container for fluids
- ❑ Sterile normal saline or water
- ❑ Sterile gloves, goggles, mask, and gown if necessary
- ❑ Sterile suction catheter kit (#12 to #18 Fr for adults; #8 to #10 Fr for children; and #5 to #8 Fr for infants); if both the oropharynx and the nasopharynx are to be suctioned, one sterile catheter is required for each
- ❑ Water-soluble lubricant (for nasopharyngeal suctioning)
- ❑ Y-connector (if catheter doesn't have suction control part)
- ❑ Sterile gauzes
- ❑ Moisture-resistant disposal bag
- ❑ Sputum trap, if specimen is to be collected

INTERVENTION

1. Verify physician's order and check agency policy.

2. Prepare the client.

- Explain to the client that suctioning will relieve breathing difficulty and that the procedure is painless but may be uncomfortable and stimulate the cough, gag, or sneeze reflex. *Knowing that the procedure will relieve breathing problems is often reassuring and enlists the client's cooperation.*
- Position a *conscious* person who has a functional gag reflex in the semi-Fowler's position with the head turned to one side for oral suctioning or with the neck hyperextended for nasal suctioning. *These positions facilitate the insertion of the catheter and help prevent aspiration of secretions.*
- Position an *unconscious* client in the lateral position, facing you. *This position allows the tongue to fall forward so that it will not obstruct*

PROCEDURE 39.4 Suctioning Oropharyngeal and Nasopharyngeal Cavities *continued*

the catheter on insertion. Lateral position also facilitates drainage of secretions from the pharynx and prevents the possibility of aspiration.

- Place the towel or moisture-resistant pad over the pillow or under the chin.

3. **Prepare the equipment.**

- Set the pressure on the suction gauge, and turn on the suction. Follow agency policy and manufacturer's recommendations regarding appropriate pressure ranges to use.

PORTABLE UNIT

- A variety of portable and hand-held suction units are available. It is advised to check with the manufacturer's specifications for the calibrated pressure rating prior to using these units.
- Open the lubricant if performing nasopharyngeal suctioning.
- Open the sterile suction package.
  - **a.** Set up the cup or container, touching only its outside.
  - **b.** Pour sterile water or saline into the container.
  - **c.** Don the sterile gloves (and wear mask and goggles if required). *The sterile gloved hands maintain the sterility of the suction catheter and prevent the transmission of microorganisms to the nurse.*
- With your sterile gloved hand, pick up the catheter, and attach it to the suction unit (Figure 39.30).

4. **Make an approximate measure of the depth for the insertion of the catheter and test the equipment.**

- Measure the distance between the tip of the client's nose and the earlobe, or about 13 cm for an adult.
- Mark the position on the tube with the fingers of the sterile gloved hand.
- Test the pressure of the suction and the patency of the catheter by applying your sterile gloved finger or thumb to the port or open branch of the Y-connector (the suction control) to create suction.

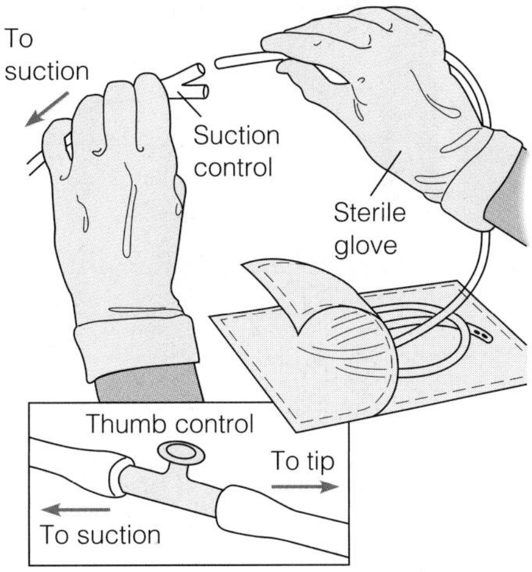

Figure 39.30 Attaching the catheter to the suction unit

5. **Lubricate and introduce the catheter.**

- Preoxygenate the client based on client's condition.
- For nasopharyngeal suction, lubricate the catheter tip with sterile water, saline, or water-soluble lubricant; for oropharyngeal suction, moisten the tip with sterile water or saline. *This reduces friction and eases insertion.*

FOR AN OROPHARYNGEAL SUCTION

- Pull the tongue forward, if necessary, using gauze.
- Do not apply suction (that is, leave your finger off the port) during insertion. *Applying suction during insertion causes trauma to the mucous membrane.*
- Advance the catheter about 13 cm or the premeasured distance along one side of the mouth into the oropharynx. *Directing the catheter along the side prevents gagging.*

FOR A NASOPHARYNGEAL SUCTION

- Without applying suction, insert the catheter the premeasured or recommended distance into either naris, and advance it along the floor of the nasal cavity. *This avoids the nasal turbinates.*
- Never force the catheter against an obstruction. If one nostril is obstructed, try the other.

6. **Perform suctioning.**

- Apply your finger to the suction control port to start suction, and gently rotate the catheter. *Gentle rotation of the catheter ensures that all surfaces are reached and prevents trauma to any one area of the respiratory mucosa due to prolonged suction.*
- Apply intermittent suction for five to 10 seconds while slowly withdrawing the catheter, then remove your finger from the control, and remove the catheter.
- A suction attempt should last only 10 to 15 seconds. During this time, the catheter is inserted, the suction applied and discontinued, and the catheter removed.
- It may be necessary during oropharyngeal suctioning to apply suction to secretions that collect in the vestibule of the mouth and beneath the tongue.

7. **Clean the catheter, and repeat suctioning as above.**

- Wipe off the catheter with sterile gauze if it is thickly coated with secretions. Dispose of the used gauze in a moisture-resistant bag.
- Flush the catheter with sterile water or saline.
- Relubricate the catheter, and repeat suctioning until the air passage is clear.
- Allow 30-second to 1-minute intervals between each suction, and limit suction attempts to two or three times. Assess cardiopulmonary status between each suctioning attempt. *Applying suction for too long may cause secretion to increase or may decrease the client's oxygen supply.*
- Alternate nares for repeat suctionings.

8. **Encourage the client to breathe deeply and to cough between suctions.** *Coughing and deep breathing help carry secretions from the trachea and bronchi into the pharynx where they can be reached with the suction catheter.*

PROCEDURE 39.4 Suctioning Oropharyngeal and Nasopharyngeal Cavities *continued*

9. Obtain a specimen if required.

Use a sputum trap (Figure 39.31) as follows:

- Attach the suction catheter to the rubber tubing of the sputum trap.
- Attach the suction tubing to the sputum trap air vent.
- Suction the client's nasopharynx or oropharynx. The sputum trap will collect the mucus during suctioning.
- Remove the catheter from the client. Disconnect the sputum trap rubber tubing from the suction catheter. Remove the suction tubing from the trap air vent.
- Connect the rubber tubing of the sputum trap to the air vent. *This retains any microorganisms in the sputum trap.*
- Connect the suction catheter to the tubing.
- Flush the catheter to remove secretions from the tubing.

10. Promote client comfort.

- Provide oral or nasal hygiene.
- Assist the client to a position that facilitates breathing.

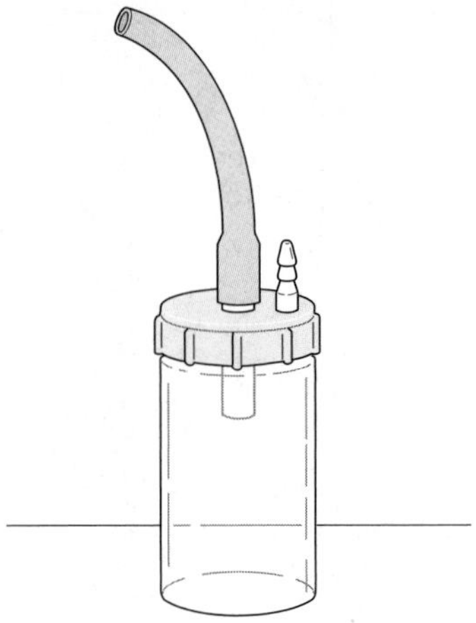

Figure 39.31 A sputum collection trap

11. Dispose of equipment and ensure availability for the next suction.

- Dispose of the catheter, gloves, water, and waste container. Wrap the catheter around your sterile gloved hand, holding it as the glove is removed over it for disposal.
- Rinse the suction tubing, as needed, by inserting the end of the tubing into the water container. Empty and rinse the suction collection container as needed or indicated by protocol. Change the suction tubing and container at least daily.
- Ensure that supplies are available for the next suctioning (suction kit, gloves, water or normal saline).

12. Assess the effectiveness of suctioning.

- Auscultate the client's breath sounds to ensure they are clear of secretions. Observe client's colour of skin and mucous membranes, dyspnea, level of anxiety, vital signs, and oxygen saturation level.

13. Document relevant data.

- Record the procedure: the amount, consistency, colour, and odour of sputum (e.g., foamy, white mucus; thick, green-tinged mucus; or blood-flecked mucus), the number of suctioning attempts, and the client's breathing status before, during, and after the procedure.

Evaluation Focus
Appearance of secretions suctioned; breath sounds; respiratory rate, rhythm, and depth; pulse rate and rhythm; skin colour; oxygen saturation level

For tracheostomy and endotracheal suctioning, the diameter of the suction catheter should be about half the inside diameter of the tracheostomy or endotracheal tube so that hypoxia can be prevented. The nurse uses sterile techniques to prevent infection of the respiratory tract. See Procedure 39.5.

PROCEDURE 39.5 Suctioning a Tracheostomy or Endotracheal Tube

PURPOSES

- To maintain a patent airway and prevent airway obstructions
- To promote respiratory function (optimal exchange of oxygen and carbon dioxide into and out of the lungs)
- To prevent pneumonia that may result from accumulated secretions

Assessment Focus
Presence of congestion on auscultation of the thorax; client's inability to remove the secretions through coughing

PROCEDURE 39.5 Suctioning a Tracheostomy or Endotracheal Tube *continued*

Equipment

- ❑ Resuscitation bag (Ambu bag) connected to 100 percent oxygen
- ❑ Sterile towel
- ❑ Equipment for suctioning the oropharyngeal cavity (see Procedure 39.4)
- ❑ Goggles and mask, if necessary
- ❑ Gown, if necessary
- ❑ Sterile gloves
- ❑ Moisture-resistant bag

INTERVENTION

1. Verify the physician's orders and check agency policy.

2. Prepare the client.

- Inform the client that suctioning usually causes some intermittent coughing and that this assists in removing the secretions.
- If not contraindicated due to the client's health, place the client in semi-Fowler's position to promote deep breathing, maximum lung expansion, and productive coughing. *Deep breathing oxygenates the lungs, counteracts the hypoxic effects of suctioning, and may induce coughing. Coughing helps loosen and move secretions.*
- If necessary, provide analgesia as ordered by the physician prior to suctioning. *Endotracheal suctioning stimulates the cough reflex, which can cause pain in clients who have had thoracic or abdominal surgery or who have experienced traumatic injury. Premedication can increase the client's comfort during the suctioning procedure.*

3. Prepare the equipment.

- Attach the resuscitation apparatus to the oxygen source (Figure 39.32).

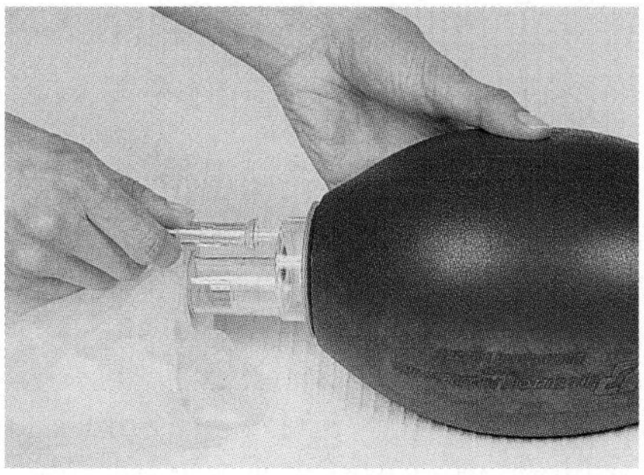

Figure 39.32 Attaching the resuscitation apparatus to the oxygen source

Adjust the oxygen flow to "100% flush."

- Open the sterile supplies in readiness for use.
- Place the sterile towel, if used, across the client's chest below the tracheostomy.
- Turn on the suction, and set the pressure in accordance with agency policy and manufacturer's recommendations.
- Put on goggles, mask, and gown, if necessary.
- Put on sterile gloves.
- Holding the catheter in the dominant hand and the connector in the nondominant hand, attach the suction catheter to the suction tubing (see Figure 39.30, p. 1059).

4. Flush and lubricate the catheter.

- Using the dominant hand, place the catheter tip in the sterile saline solution.
- Using the thumb of the nondominant hand, occlude the thumb control, and suction a small amount of the sterile solution through the catheter. *This determines that the suction equipment is working properly and lubricates the outside and the lumen of the catheter. Lubrication eases insertion and reduces tissue trauma during insertion. Lubricating the lumen also helps prevent secretions from sticking to the inside of the catheter.*

5. If the client does *not* have copious secretions, hyperventilate the lungs with a resuscitation bag before suctioning as ordered by a physician and according to agency policy.

- Summon an assistant, if one is available, for this step.
- Using your nondominant hand, turn on the oxygen to 12 to 15 L/min.
- If the client is receiving oxygen, disconnect the oxygen source from the tracheostomy tube using your nondominant hand.
- Attach the resuscitator to the tracheostomy or endotracheal tube (Figure 39.33).

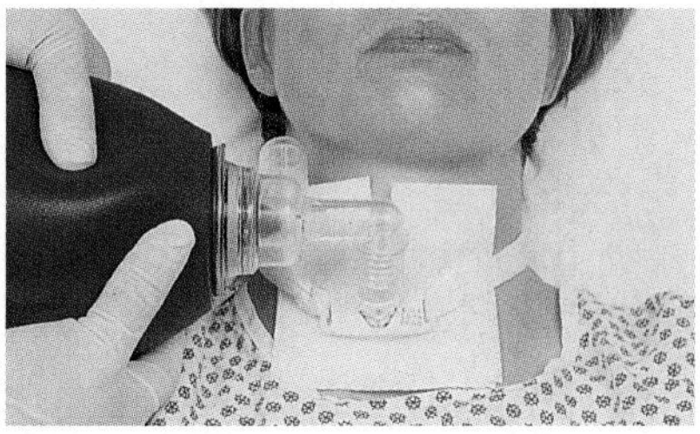

Figure 39.33 Attaching the resuscitator to the tracheostomy

- Compress the Ambu bag three to five times as the client *inhales.* This is best done by a second person who can use both hands to compress the bag, providing a greater inflation volume.
- Observe the rise and fall of the client's chest to assess the adequacy of each ventilation.
- Remove the resuscitation device, and place it on the bed or the client's chest with the connector facing up.

6. If the client has copious secretions, do *not* hyperventilate with a resuscitator. Instead:

- Keep the regular oxygen delivery device on, and increase the litre flow or adjust the FiO_2 to 100 percent for several breaths before suctioning according to agency policy. *Hyperventilating a client who has copious secretions can force the secretions deeper into the respiratory tract.*

PROCEDURE 39.5 Suctioning a Tracheostomy or Endotracheal Tube *continued*

7. **Quickly but gently insert the catheter without applying any suction.**

- With your nondominant thumb off the suction port, quickly but gently insert the catheter into the trachea through the tracheostomy tube (Figure 39.34). *To prevent tissue trauma and oxygen loss, suction is not applied during insertion of the catheter.*

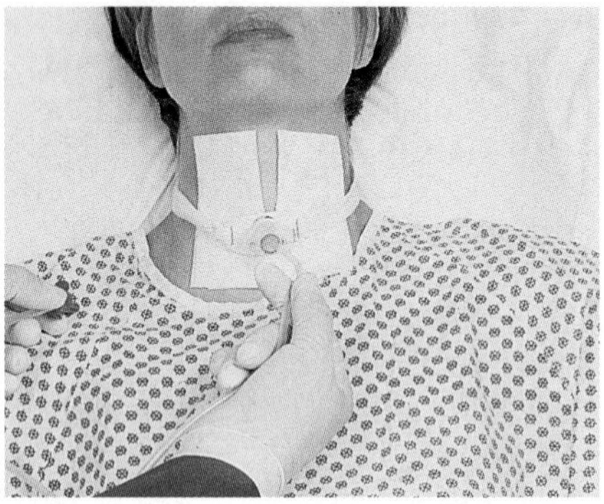

Figure 39.34 Inserting the catheter into the trachea through the tracheostomy tube

- Insert the catheter about 12.5 cm for adults, less for children, or less if the client coughs or you feel resistance. Resistance usually means that the catheter tip has reached the bifurcation of the trachea. To prevent damaging the mucous membranes at the bifurcation, withdraw the catheter about 1 to 2 cm before applying suction.

8. **Perform suctioning.**

- Apply intermittent suction for 5 to 10 seconds by placing and removing the nondominant thumb over the thumb port. *Suction time is restricted to 10 seconds or less to minimize oxygen loss.*
- Rotate the catheter by rolling it between your thumb and forefinger while slowly withdrawing it. *This prevents tissue trauma by minimizing the suction time against any one part of the trachea.*
- Withdraw the catheter completely, and release the suction.
- Hyperventilate the client.
- Then suction again.

9. **Reassess the client's oxygenation status, and repeat suctioning.**

- Observe the client's respirations and skin colour. Check the client's pulse, if necessary, using your nondominant hand.
- Encourage the client to breathe deeply and to cough between suctions.
- Allow two to three minutes between suctions, when possible. *This provides an opportunity for reoxygenation of the lungs.*
- Flush the catheter, and repeat suctioning two or three times until the air passage is clear and the breathing is relatively effortless and quiet.
- After each suction, pick up the resuscitation bag with your nondominant hand and ventilate the client with five breaths.

10. **Dispose of equipment and ensure availability for the next suction.**

- Flush the catheter and suction tubing.
- Turn off the suction, and disconnect the catheter from the suction tubing.
- Wrap the catheter around your sterile hand, and peel the glove off so that it turns inside out over the catheter.
- Discard the glove and the catheter in the moisture-resistant bag.
- Replenish the sterile fluid and supplies so that the suction is ready to be used again. *Clients who require suctioning often require it quickly, so it is essential to leave the equipment at the bedside ready for use.*

11. **Provide for client comfort and safety.**

- Assist the client to a comfortable, safe position that aids breathing. If the person is conscious, a semi-Fowler's position is frequently indicated. If the person is unconscious, Sims' position aids in the drainage of secretions from the mouth.

12. **Document relevant data.**

- Record the suctioning procedure, including the amount and description of suction returns, cardiopulmonary assessment before and after suctioning, and client response.

Evaluation Focus
Respiratory rate, depth, and character after suctioning; tracheal breath sounds; colour of skin and nailbeds; character and amount of secretions suctioned; changes in vital signs; oxygen saturation level

Chest Tubes and Drainage Systems

If the thin, double-layered pleural membrane is disrupted by lung disease, surgery, or trauma, the negative pressure between the pleural layers may be lost. The lung then collapses because it is no longer drawn outward as the diaphragm and intercostal muscles contract during inhalation. When air collects in the pleural space, it is known as a **pneumothorax.** Blood or fluid in the pleural space, a **hemothorax,** places pressure on lung tissue and also interferes with lung expansion. Chest tubes may be inserted into the pleural cavity to restore negative pressure and drain collected fluid or blood. Because air rises, chest tubes for pneumothorax often are placed in the upper anterior thorax, whereas chest tubes used to drain fluid are generally placed in the lower lateral chest wall.

When chest tubes are inserted, they must be connected to a sealed drainage system or a one-way valve that allows air and fluid to be removed from the chest cavity but prevents air from entering from the outside. Water-seal drainage systems are used to prevent outside air from entering the chest tube. Sterile disposable systems commonly are used. These systems typically have a closed collection chamber for drainage that is connected to the water-seal chamber (Figure 39.35). When the client inhales, the water prevents air from entering the system from the atmosphere. During exhalation, however, air can exit the chest cavity, bubbling up through the water. Suction can be added to the system to facilitate removing air and secretions from the chest cavity. The drainage system should always be kept below the level of the client's chest to prevent fluid and drainage from being drawn back into the chest cavity.

A Heimlich valve or comparable system may be used for ambulatory clients who have a pneumothorax. These valves allow air to escape from the chest cavity, but they close during inhalation to prevent air from entering.

Nursing responsibilities regarding drainage systems include the following:

- Assist with the insertion and removal of the tube.
- Maintain the water seal and patency of the drainage system.
- Assess the client's vital signs, cardiovascular status, and respiratory status.

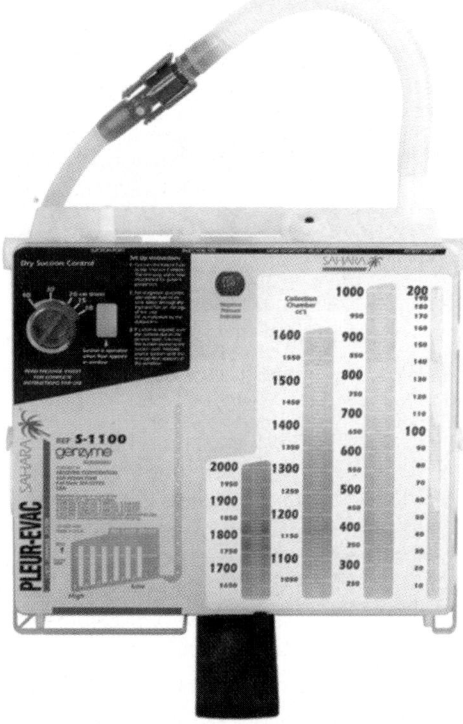

Figure 39.35 A disposable chest drainage system. Fluid and blood collect in the white calibrated chambers. The red chamber provides the water seal, and the blue chamber is a suction-control chamber.

- Monitor the patency and integrity of the drainage system.
- Provide nursing measures to promote optimal respiratory functioning (e.g., fluids, positioning).
- Keep rubber-tipped clamps and a sterile occlusive dressing near the client. The chest tube will need to be clamped quickly, close to the insertion site, if connections are broken or an air leak develops in the drainage system. A physician's order is required to clamp a chest tube. Clamping a chest tube is a controversial practice. It is recommended that the nurse inquire about the reason for clamping the tube prior to carrying out the order. Some policies allow the nurse to clamp a chest tube in any of the following critical circumstances: a) When disconnecting the chest drainage system to change the collection unit; b) When the chest drainage system breaks or the integrity is disrupted for any reason; c) When removing the chest tube. (Note that removing the chest tube is an advanced competency and the nurse must be certified to do this procedure). In these circumstances, double clamp using non-toothed or rubber tipped clamps The chest clamp must be unclamped as soon as possible.

Preventing Venous Stasis

When clients have limited mobility or are confined to bed, venous return to the heart is impaired and the risk of venous stasis increases. Immobility is a problem not only for ill or debilitated clients but also for some travellers who sit with legs dependent for long periods in a motor vehicle or an airplane. Venous stasis can lead to thrombus formation and edema of the extremities.

Preventing venous stasis is an important nursing intervention to reduce the risk of complications following surgery, trauma, or major medical problems. Positioning and leg exercises are discussed in Chapter 44. Anti-embolism stockings and sequential compression devices are additional measures to help prevent venous stasis.

Anti-Embolic Stockings

Anti-embolic stockings are firm elastic hosiery that provide varying degrees of leg compression. They are frequently used in clients with limited mobility, either because of restricted activities or because of prolonged standing (e.g., supermarket checkers, surgeons, and surgery technicians). Knee-high, thigh, and full stockings are available. Presized stockings are commonly used; some clients may require custom-made stockings. The length of the anti-embolic stockings should be based on the individual patient condition (e.g., if a client has a history of popliteal clots, thigh-high or full stockings would be recommended to facilitate venous return throughout the leg).

When obtaining anti-embolism stockings for a client, follow the manufacturer's recommendation for measuring and fitting the stockings. See Procedure 44.2.

Sequential Compression/Pneumatic Pressure Devices

Clients who are undergoing surgery or who are immobilized because of illness or injury may benefit from a sequential compression device (SCD) to promote venous return from the legs. SCDs inflate and deflate plastic sleeves wrapped around the legs to promote venous flow. The plastic sleeves are attached by tubing to an air pump that alternately inflates and deflates portions of the sleeve to a specified pressure. The ankle area inflates first, followed by the calf region, and then the thigh area. This sequential inflation and deflation assists the leg muscles in moving blood toward the heart.

Anti-embolism stockings may be worn under the SCD to provide added support and protect the skin from irritation by the plastic. The SCD is removed for ambulation and is usually discontinued when the client resumes activities. SCDs are useful in *preventing* thrombi and edema from venous stasis, but they are not used for clients who have arterial insufficiency, cellulitis, or infection of the extremity. Patients who have ongoing coagulation problems and venous insufficiency may require a sequential compression/pneumatic pressure device for home use. Pressure devices are available for rent or purchase for home use.

Procedure 39.6 outlines how to apply a sequential compression device.

PROCEDURE 39.6 Applying a Sequential Compression Device

PURPOSES

- To facilitate venous return in immobilized clients
- To prevent thrombus formation

Assessment Focus
Cardiovascular status including heart rate and rhythm, peripheral pulses, and capillary refill; colour and temperature of extremities; movement and sensation of feet and lower extremities (for baseline data)

Equipment

- ❑ Measuring tape
- ❑ Anti-embolism stockings
- ❑ Sequential compression device (SCD), including disposable sleeves, air pump, and tubing

INTERVENTION

1. **Verify the physician's orders and check agency policy.**
2. **Prepare the client.**

- Explain the purpose and the procedure for applying the sequential compression device. *The client's cooperation and comfort will be increased by understanding the rationale for applying the SCD.*
- Place the client in a dorsal recumbent or semi-Fowler's position. Provide for privacy, and drape the client appropriately.
- Measure the client's legs as recommended by the manufacturer.
- Apply anti-embolism stockings (see Procedure 44.2 on p. 1241). *Anti-embolism stockings provide added support and reduce skin irritation from the compression sleeve.*

3. **Apply the sequential compression sleeves.**

- Place a sleeve under each leg with the opening at the knee.
- Wrap the sleeve securely around the leg, securing the Velcro tabs (Figure 39.36). Allow two fingers to fit between the leg and the sleeve. *This amount of space ensures that the sleeve does not impair circulation when inflated.*

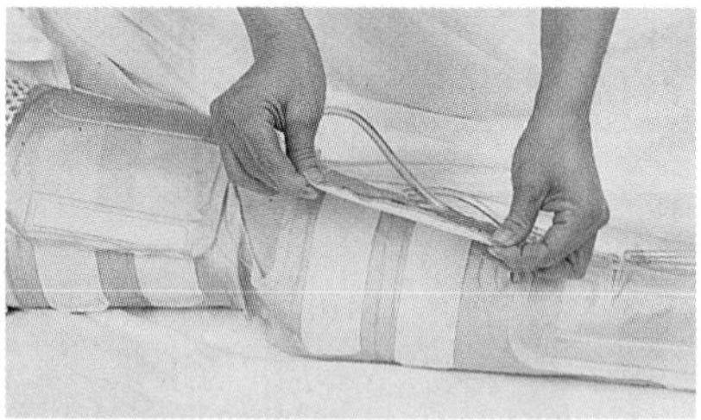

Figure 39.36 Applying a sequential compression device to the leg

4. **Connect the sleeves to the control unit and adjust the pressure, as recommended.**

- Connect the tubing to the sleeves and control unit, ensuring that arrows on the plug and the connector are in alignment and that the tubing is not kinked or twisted. *Improper alignment or obstruction of the tubing by kinks or twists will interfere with operation of the SCD.*
- Turn on the control unit, and adjust the alarms and pressures as needed. The sleeve cooling control and alarm should be "on"; ankle pressure should be set as recommended by the manufacturer. *It is important to have the sleeve cooling control on for comfort and to reduce the risk of skin irritation from moisture under the sleeve. Alarms warn of possible control unit malfunctions.*

5. **Document the procedure.**

- Record baseline assessment data and application of the SCD. Note control unit settings.

PROCEDURE 39.6 Applying a Sequential Compression Device *continued*

- Assess and document skin integrity and neurovascular status regularly according to agency policy while the SCD is in place. Remove the unit and notify the physician if the client complains of numbness and tingling or leg pain. *These may be symptoms of nerve compression.*

Evaluation Focus
Cardiovascular status, including peripheral pulses, skin colour and temperature; skin integrity; neurovascular status, including movement and sensation, capillary refill, colours, and temperature

Cardiopulmonary Resuscitation

Cardiopulmonary resuscitation (CPR) is a combination of oral resuscitation (mouth-to-mouth breathing), which supplies oxygen to the lungs, and external cardiac massage (chest compression), which is intended to re-establish cardiac function and blood circulation. CPR is also referred to as basic life support (BLS).

A **cardiac arrest** is the cessation of cardiac function; the heart stops beating. Often, a cardiac arrest is unexpected and sudden. When it occurs, the heart no longer pumps blood to any of the organs of the body. Breathing then stops, and the person becomes unconscious and limp. Within 20 to 40 seconds of a cardiac arrest, the victim is clinically dead. After four to six minutes, the lack of oxygen supply to the brain causes permanent and extensive damage.

The two cardinal signs of a cardiac arrest are apnea and absence of a carotid pulse. The person's skin and mucous membranes appear pale or greyish and the skin feels cool. The pupils may be dilated. Cyanosis is evident when respiratory function fails prior to heart failure.

A **respiratory arrest** (pulmonary arrest) is the cessation of breathing. It often occurs as a result of a blocked airway, but it can occur following a cardiac arrest and for other reasons. A respiratory arrest may occur abruptly or be preceded by short, shallow breathing that becomes increasingly laboured.

It is vital that all nurses be trained to perform CPR so that resuscitation measures can be initiated immediately when a cardiac or respiratory arrest occurs. Nurses also can be instrumental in increasing community awareness of the need for CPR training and ensuring its availability.

Most health-care agencies have established practices and policies regarding CPR.

Evaluating

Using the goals and desired outcomes identified in the planning stage of the nursing process, the nurse collects data to evaluate the effectiveness of interventions. Examples of outcomes for the goals identified for clients with oxygenation problems are found in Table 39.3.

If outcomes are *not* achieved, the nurse, client, and support person, if appropriate, need to explore the reasons before modifying the care plan. For example, if the outcome "Respirations unlaboured and rate is within expected range" is not met, examples of questions that need to be considered include the following:

- What is the client's perception of the problem?
- Is the client complaining of shortness of breath or difficulty breathing?
- Is the client taking medications or being treated with percussion, vibration, and postural drainage, as prescribed?
- Has the client been exposed to an upper respiratory infection that is affecting breathing?
- Do other factors need to be considered, such as the client's psychological stress level?

Examples of questions to consider if the outcome "Able to complete ADLs without fatigue" is *not* met include the following:

- What other factors may be affecting the client's ability to complete ADLs?
- Is the client getting adequate sleep? If not, what is interfering with the client's rest?
- Are there assistive devices (e.g., a shower chair, clothing that is easy to put on) that could help the client achieve this goal?
- Does the client need help with housework and other ADLs?
- Is the client's diet adequate to meet nutritional needs?

TABLE 39.3 Evaluation Goals and Outcomes: Oxygenation

Goal	Examples of Desired Outcomes
Maintain a patent airway	Unlaboured respirations and rate within expected range Clear lung sounds No stridor or wheezing Expels secretions effectively with coughing
Improve comfort and ease of breathing	Quiet, rhythmic, and effortless breathing pattern Respiratory rate, depth, and rhythm within expected range No dyspnea, shortness of breath (SOB), or orthopnea No restlessness or agitation Uses pursed-lip breathing, as needed
Maintain or improve pulmonary ventilation and oxygenation	Arterial blood gases within normal range SaO_2 is greater than 90 percent Respiratory rate, rhythm, and depth within expected range Symmetrical chest expansion No auscultated adventitious breath sounds No restlessness, agitation, cyanosis, or confusion
Maintain (or promote) cardiac function and output	Blood pressure (systolic and diastolic) within expected range Apical radial heart rate and rhythm within expected range Heart and lung sounds normal Urinary output of 30–50 mL/hr or greater No lethargy or extreme fatigue
Maintain or improve tissue perfusion	Capillary refill is brisk Strong and equal peripheral pulses Skin pink and warm, mucous membranes moist and pink; sensation intact No peripheral edema noted No localized extremity pain or pain with activity
Maintain (or improve) ability to participate in physical activities	Performs usual personal care activities (e.g., bathing, dressing, grooming, toileting) without shortness of breath or fatigue Food and fluid intake adequate to maintain energy level Blood tests within normal range (e.g., hemoglobin, blood gases) Balances rest and activity Adapts lifestyle to energy limitations
Avoid risks associated with oxygenation problems (acid-base imbalances, skin and tissue breakdown, syncope, hopelessness, social isolation)	Skin intact and adequate perfusion Serum electrolytes and blood gases within normal limits Neurological status within normal limits Cognitive status satisfactory (e.g., alert and oriented) Maintains participation in usual social activities Expresses positive future outlook and sense of inner peace

Consider...

What actions would you consider if the client did *not* meet the following outcome criteria?

- "Able to clear secretions effectively with coughing" (Data reveal diminished breath sounds in the right base and coarse rattles present throughout the lung fields.)
- "Alert and oriented, mentation is clear" (Data reveal that the client is agitated, confused, and disoriented to time and place but oriented to person.)

FOCUS ON CRITICAL THINKING

Jerry Markert, 21, was admitted to the acute-care facility following a biking accident in which he received multiple injuries, including a hemothorax. He is receiving 6 L of oxygen, as ordered, by a nasal cannula, has a chest tube connected to a closed drainage system, and is attached to a pulse oximeter that indicates an oxygen saturation level of 98 percent. He is alert, stable, and progressing well.

1. If Mr. Markert is stable and progressing well, why is his oxygen saturation being monitored?
2. Speculate about why Mr. Markert is receiving oxygen by a nasal cannula as opposed to a face mask.
3. Compare and contrast a hemothorax and a pneumothorax.
4. What precautions need to be taken when caring for Mr. Markert while his chest tube is in place?
5. Offer suggestions that would help Mr. Markert, or any person with a respiratory problem, to establish healthy breathing after his chest tube is removed.

See Appendix A for answers to these questions.

CHAPTER HIGHLIGHTS

- Respiration is the process of gas exchange between the individual and the environment.
- The respiratory system contributes to effective respiration through pulmonary ventilation (the movement of air between the atmosphere and the lungs) and the diffusion of oxygen and carbon dioxide across the pulmonary membrane.
- The cardiovascular system transports these gases in the blood to and from the tissues and facilitates the diffusion of gases between the capillaries and body tissues.
- Alveoli and the capillaries that surround them form the respiratory membrane where gas exchange between the lungs and the blood occurs.
- Effective pulmonary ventilation, or breathing, requires clear airways, an intact central nervous system and respiratory centre, an intact thoracic cavity and musculature, and adequate pulmonary compliance (stretch) and recoil.
- Gas exchange occurs by diffusion as gas molecules move from an area of higher concentration to an area of lower concentration. At the respiratory membrane, oxygen moves from the alveolus into the blood, while carbon dioxide moves from the blood into the alveolus.
- Most oxygen (97 percent) is carried to the tissues loosely combined with hemoglobin in red blood cells (RBCs). Anemia, which is too few RBCs or low hemoglobin levels, impairs oxygen transportation.
- Carbon dioxide is transported within RBCs as bicarbonate or combined with hemoglobin, and in blood plasma as carbonic acid.
- The heart and the blood vessels make up the cardiovascular system, which, together with blood, is the major system for transporting oxygen and nutrients to the tissues and waste products away from the tissues for elimination.
- The right side of the heart receives deoxygenated blood from the body and pumps it to the lungs via the pulmonary arteries; the left side receives oxygenated blood from the lungs and pumps it out to the body via the aorta.
- Coronary arteries supply oxygen and nutrients to the heart muscle.
- The cardiac conduction system controls the electrical activity of the heart and the cardiac cycle: systole, contraction of the heart muscle and ejection of blood; and diastole, the relaxation period during which the heart fills with blood.
- Cardiac output depends on the stroke volume, or amount of blood ejected during systole, and the heart rate.
- The systemic blood vessels carry blood to the tissues through a system of arteries, arterioles, and capillaries and return it to the heart through the venules, veins, and venae cavae.
- Heart and respiratory rates normally are highest in neonates and infants, gradually slowing to adult ranges; the blood pressure rises gradually from birth to reach the adult range in adolescence.
- Aging affects both the respiratory and cardiovascular systems: the chest wall becomes more rigid and lungs less elastic; atherosclerosis causes fatty plaque to develop within arteries.

- Other factors affecting oxygenation include the environment, lifestyle, health status, narcotic analgesics, stress and coping, and gender.
- Hypoxia, insufficient oxygen in the tissues, can result from impaired ventilation (hypoventilation) or diffusion, or from impaired oxygen transportation to the tissues because of anemia or decreased cardiac output.
- Normal respirations are quiet and unlaboured; altered respiratory patterns include tachypnea, bradypnea, hyperventilation, hypoventilation, and dyspnea. Shortness of breath is a subjective sensation of not getting enough air.
- Airway obstruction interferes with ventilation. A low-pitched snoring sound, stridor, and abnormal breath sounds may accompany partial airway obstruction. Extreme inspiratory effort with no chest movement indicates complete upper airway obstruction.
- Decreased cardiac output, impaired tissue perfusion, and disorders affecting the blood are the major cardiovascular problems that may affect oxygenation.
- Cardiac output may fall with a myocardial infarction (MI), congestive heart failure (CHF), dysrhythmias, and structural alterations of the heart (e.g., valve deformities).
- The most common cause of impaired blood flow to tissues is atherosclerosis; this can lead to tissue ischemia and pain.
- To assess oxygenation, the nurse conducts a nursing history, performs a complete physical assessment of the client, and reviews relevant diagnostic data.
- The nursing history includes questions about current or past respiratory and cardiovascular problems, including hypertension; about lifestyle; presence of symptoms, such as cough or shortness of breath; smoking and other risk factors; and medications.
- Physical assessment should include a general assessment, as well as specific examination of the respiratory and cardiovascular systems.
- Pulse oximetry is a noninvasive means of assessing the oxygen saturation level, the percentage of hemoglobin that is combined with oxygen.
- Cardiac monitoring is used for continuous observation of the heart rate and rhythm.
- Diagnostic tests that may be performed to assess oxygenation include sputum and throat culture specimens; blood tests, such as the CBC, hemoglobin, and hematocrit, blood chemistries, and arterial blood gases; electrocardiography (ECG) and stress testing; pulmonary function tests; visualization procedures, such as radiography, lung scans, angiography, echocardiography, laryngoscopy, and bronchoscopy; and hemodynamic studies.
- The nurse is responsible for obtaining specimens for diagnostic tests, preparing the client and the support people for diagnostic procedures, monitoring the client's response to certain procedures, and reviewing records and reports of diagnostic tests.
- Nursing diagnoses for the client with problems of oxygenation include ***Ineffective Airway Clearance, Ineffective Breathing Pattern, Impaired Gas Exchange, Altered Peripheral Tissue Perfusion, Decreased Cardiac Output***, and ***Activity Intolerance.*** These problems also may be the etiology for several other nursing diagnoses, including ***Anxiety, Fatigue, Fear, Powerlessness, Sleep Pattern, Disturbed***, and ***Social Isolation.***
- In planning care for clients with problems of oxygenation, the nurse establishes the following goals: maintain a patent airway; improve ease and comfort of breathing; maintain ventilation and oxygenation; ensure tissue perfusion; maintain cardiac output; improve the client's activity tolerance; and prevent risks, such as tissue breakdown and infection.
- In discharge and home care planning, the nurse assesses the client's self-care abilities and need for assistive devices, home environment, compliance with medical regimen, and knowledge level. The ability of the family or support people to provide assistance and financial support and to cope with the changes is also assessed, as are community factors, such as the environment and resources.
- The nurse teaches the client about home care activities to maintain a patent airway and gas exchange, to promote healthy breathing, and to maintain cardiac output and tissue perfusion. Dietary modifications, prescribed medications, and specific procedures also are taught, and the nurse makes referrals to community agencies as needed.
- Nursing interventions to promote oxygenation include promoting healthy breathing and a healthy heart, deep breathing and coughing, and hydration; administering medications; implementing measures to clear secretions (e.g., incentive spirometry, percussion, vibration, and postural drainage); initiating and monitoring oxygen therapy; initiating or assisting with procedures to maintain the airway (e.g., artificial airways and suctioning); providing tracheostomy care; monitoring chest drainage systems; using anti-embolism stockings and sequential compression devices to prevent venous stasis and edema; and administering cardiopulmonary resuscitation.
- The effectiveness of nursing interventions is evaluated by using the goals and desired outcomes identified in the planning stage of the nursing process. If a goal is not met, the nurse asks pertinent questions to assess the reason for not meeting the goal.

READINGS AND REFERENCES

Suggested Readings

Bright, L. D., & Georgi, S. (1994, December). How to protect your patient from DVT. *American Journal of Nursing, 94*(12), 28–32.

This article helps the nurse identify clients who are at low, moderate, and high risk for deep vein thrombosis (DVT) and discusses preventive measures. The pathophysiology of impaired venous return is presented, and tips for using graduated compression stockings and pneumatic compression devices are included.

Leighton, C. (1998, October). A change of heart. *American Journal of Nursing, 98*(10), 33–37.

This article discusses the role of a support group in a wellness program for people with heart disease. A holistic approach is used, moving beyond risk factor management to address basic human needs of participants.

Moser, D. K. (1997, April). Correcting misconceptions about women and heart disease. *American Journal of Nursing, 97*(4), 26–33.

Even though coronary artery disease is the leading cause of death among women in the United States, it often is thought of as a man's disease. Risk factors affect men and women somewhat differently and may be ignored by both the woman and her physician. The presentation of coronary artery disease may differ, and recovery following an MI or revascularization procedure may be more difficult.

Related Research

Higgins, P. A. (1998, May/June). Patient perception of fatigue while undergoing long-term mechanical ventilation: Incidence and associated factors. *Heart & Lung, 27*(3), 177–183.

Lukkarinen, H. (1998, November/December). Quality of life in coronary artery disease. *Nursing Research, 47*(6), 337–343.

Selected References

Ackley, B. J., & Ladwig, G. B. (1997). *Nursing diagnosis handbook: A guide to planning care* (3rd ed.). St. Louis, MO: Mosby-Year Book.

Bright, L. D. (1995, June). Deep vein thrombosis. *American Journal of Nursing, 95*(6), 48–49.

Bright, L. D., & Georgi, S. (1994, December). How to protect your patient from DVT. *American Journal of Nursing, 94*(12), 28–32.

Carpenito, L. (2002) *Nursing diagnosis: Application to clinical practice* (10th ed). Philadephia: Lippincott Williams & Wilkins.

Carroll, P. (1994, May). Safe suctioning prn. *RN, 57*(5), 32–36.

Dabbs, A. D., & Olslund, L. (1994, August). The new alternatives to intubation. *American Journal of Nursing, 94*(8), 42–45.

Dennison, R. D. (1994, August). Making sense of hemodynamic monitoring. *American Journal of Nursing, 94*(8), 24–32.

Dracup, K., Dunbar, S. B., & Baker, D. W. (1995, July). Rethinking heart failure. *American Journal of Nursing, 95*(7), 22–28.

Dumas, M. A. S. (1995, December). Intermittent claudication. *American Journal of Nursing, 95*(12), 34–35.

Galvin, W. F., & Cusano, A. L. (1998, June). Making a clean sweep: Using a closed tracheal suction system. *Nursing 98, 28*(6), 50–51.

Glass, C. A., & Grap, M. J. (1995, May). Ten tips for safer suctioning. *American Journal of Nursing, 95*(5), 51–53.

Gorman, M. (1997, March). Helping patients to quit smoking. *American Journal of Nursing, 95*(3), 64–65.

Griffith, C. J. (1996, May). Evaluation and management of anemia: A cost-effective approach. *Advance for Nurse Practitioners, 4*(5), 29–30, 32–35.

Hahn, M. S. (1996, April). Chronic obstructive pulmonary disease: Understanding this progressive illness. *Advance for Nurse Practitioners, 4*(4), 37–39, 62, 64.

Hanson, M. J. (1997, December). Caring for a patient with COPD: How to help him breathe easier once the damage is done. *Nursing, 27*(12), 39–44.

Harris, A. J., Brown-Etris, M., & Troyer-Caudle, J. (1996, January). Managing vascular leg ulcers: Part 1—Assessment. *American Journal of Nursing, 96*(1), 38–43.

Johanssen, J. (1994, January). Chronic obstructive pulmonary disease: Current comprehensive care for emphysema and bronchitis. *Nurse Practitioner, 19*(1), 59–67.

Johnson, M., & Maas, M. (Eds.). (2000). *Iowa outcomes project: Nursing outcomes classification (NOC).* St. Louis, MO: Mosby.

Kelly, M. (1996, June). Acute respiratory failure. *American Journal of Nursing, 96*(12), 46.

Launius, B. K., & Graham, B. D. (1998, February). Understanding and preventing deep vein thrombosis and pulmonary embolism. *AACN Clinical Issues, 9*(2), 91–99.

Laveau, S. C. (1993). Respiratory problems. In D. L. Carnevali, & M. Patrick (Eds.), *Nursing management for the elderly* (3rd ed.). Philadelphia, PA: J.B. Lippincott.

Leighton, C. (1998, October). A change of heart. *American Journal of Nursing, 98*(10), 33–37.

Marcinelli-Van Atta, J., & Beck, S. L. (1994, October). Endotracheal suctioning: Preventing hypoxemia and hemodynamic compromise. *Nursing, 24*(10), 32.

McCance, K. L., & Huether, S. E. (1998). *Pathophysiology: The biologic basis for disease in adults and children* (3rd ed.). St Louis, MO: Mosby.

McCloskey, J. C., & Bulechek, G. M. (Eds.). (2000). *Iowa intervention project: Nursing interventions classification (NIC)* (3rd ed.). St. Louis, MO: Mosby.

McMahon-Parkes, K. (1997, December 24/January 6). Management of pleural drains. *Nursing Times, 93*(52), 48–52.

Miller, S. K. (1997, June). Congestive heart failure. *Advance for Nurse Practitioners, 5*(6), 16–21, 25–26.

Moser, D. K. (1997, April). Correcting misconceptions about women and heart disease. *American Journal of Nursing, 97*(4), 26–33.

North American Nursing Diagnosis Association. (2001). *Nursing diagnoses: Definitions & classification 2001–2002.* Philadelphia, PA: Author.

O'Hanlon-Nichols, T. (1997, December). The adult cardiovascular system. *American Journal of Nursing, 97*(12), 34–40.

Pagana, K. D., & Pagana, T. J. (1997). *Mosby's diagnostic and laboratory test reference* (3rd ed.). St. Louis, MO: Mosby-Year Book.

Pasero, C., & McCaffery, M. (1994, April). Avoiding opioid-induced respiratory depression. *American Journal of Nursing, 94*(4), 24–30.

Porth, C. M. (2002). *Pathophysiology: Concepts of altered health states* (6th ed.). Philadelphia, PA: Lippincott.

Rokosky, J. M. (1997, January). Misuse of metered-dose inhalers: Helping patients get it right. *Home Healthcare Nurse, 15*(1), 13–21.

Somerson, S. J., Husted, C. W., Somerson, S. W., & Sicilia, M. R. (1996, May). Mastering emergency airway management. *American Journal of Nursing, 96*(5), 24–31.

Strimike, C. (1996, June). New procedures: Understanding intravascular ultrasound. *American Journal of Nursing, 96*(6), 40–44.

West, J. B. (2001). *Pulmonary physiology and pathophysiology: An integrated case based approach.* Philadelphia: Lippincott Williams & Wilkins.

WEBLINKS

Canadian Lung Association
http://www.lung.ca/
This is the umbrella association for the provincial/territorial groups; the Web site provides a variety of educational material for the public and health-care professionals.

Canadian Nurses' Respiratory Society
http://www.lung.ca/resp/news.html
This is a special interest group of nurses. The Web site provides valuable information to its members and to all who are interested in the activities of the society.

Health Canada—Cardiovascular Disease Division
http://www.hc-sc.gc.ca/hpb/lcdc/bcrdd/cardio/
The Cardiovascular Disease Division is one of three divisions within the Bureau of Cardio-Respiratory Diseases and Diabetes of Health Canada. The Web site offers a range of resources and information.

Heart and Stroke Foundation of Canada
www.heartandstroke.ca
This is a national association that provides information and support to the public and health-care professionals.

CHAPTER 40

Fluid, Electrolyte, and Acid-Base Balance

OBJECTIVES

After completing this chapter, you will be able to:

- Discuss the function, distribution, movement, and regulation of fluids and electrolytes in the body.
- Describe the regulation of acid-base balance in the body, including the roles of buffers, the lungs, and the kidneys.
- Identify factors affecting normal body fluid, electrolyte, and acid-base balance.
- Outline the risk factors for and the causes and effects of fluid, electrolyte, and acid-base imbalances.
- Collect assessment data related to the client's fluid, electrolyte, and acid-base balances.
- Select appropriate nursing diagnoses for clients with altered fluid, electrolyte, or acid-base balance.
- Teach client measures to maintain fluid and electrolyte balance.
- Implement measures to correct imbalances of fluids and electrolytes or acids and bases, such as enteral or parenteral replacements and blood transfusions.
- Evaluate the effect of nursing and collaborative interventions on the client's fluid, electrolyte, or acid-base balance.

In physiological homeostasis, a balance of fluids, electrolytes, and acids and bases is maintained in the body. This balance depends on multiple physiological processes that regulate fluid intake and output and the movement of water and the substances dissolved in it among the body compartments.

Almost every illness has the potential to threaten this balance. Even in normal daily living, excessive temperatures or vigorous activity can disturb the balance if adequate water and salt intake is not maintained. Therapeutic measures, such as the use of diuretics or nasogastric suction, can also disturb the body's homeostasis unless water and electrolytes are replaced.

Body Fluids and Electrolytes

In humans, the primary body fluid is water. The proportion of the human body composed of fluid is about 45 to 60 percent of the average adult's weight. This volume of fluid remains relatively constant, and the individual's weight varies by less than 0.2 kg in 24 hours regardless of the amount of fluid ingested.

Water is vital to health and normal cellular function, serving as:

- A medium for metabolic reactions within cells.
- A transporter for nutrients, waste products, and other substances.
- A lubricant.
- An insulator and shock absorber.
- A means of regulating and maintaining body temperature.

Age, gender, and body fat affect total body water. Infants have the highest proportion of water, accounting for 70 to 80 percent of their body weight (Metheny, 1996). The proportion of body water decreases with age. See Table 40.1. Fat tissue is essentially free of water, whereas lean tissue contains a significant amount of water. Water makes up a greater percentage of a lean person's body weight than an obese person's. Women, who have proportionately more body fat than men, have a lower percentage of body water.

TABLE 40.1 Fluid as Percentage of Body Weight (by Age)

Age	Percentage of Fluid*
Full-term newborn	70 to 80
1 year	64
Puberty to 39 years	52 to 60
40 to 60 years	47 to 55
Over 60 years	46 to 52

*Generally, men have a slightly higher percentage of fluid than women.

Source: Adapted from Metheny, N. M. (1996). *Fluid and electrolyte balance: Nursing considerations* (3rd ed.). (p. 5). Philadelphia, PA: Lippincott.

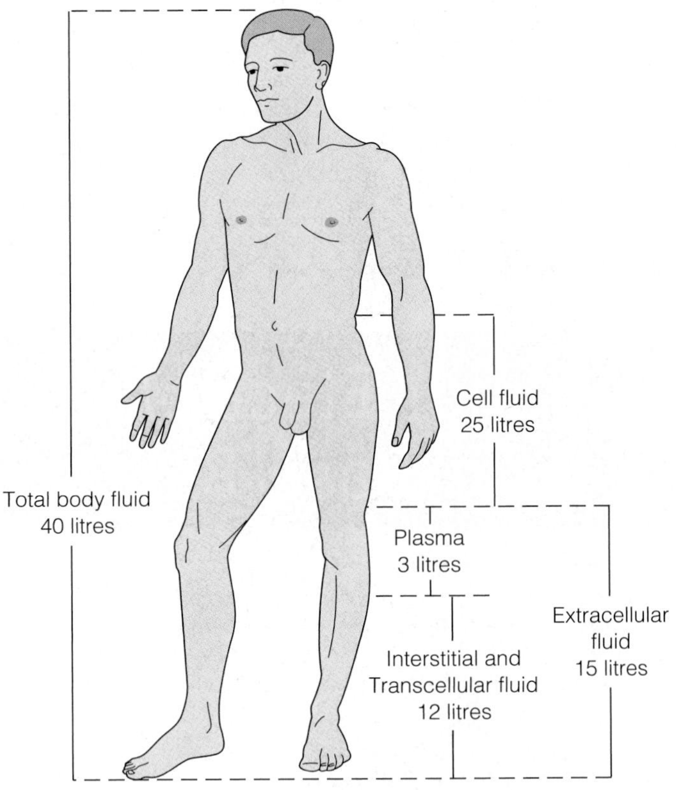

Figure 40.1 Total body fluid represents 40 L in an adult male weighing 70 kg

Distribution of Body Fluids

The body's fluid is divided into two major compartments, intracellular and extracellular. **Intracellular fluid (ICF)** is found within the cells of the body. It constitutes approximately two-thirds of the total body fluid in adults. **Extracellular fluid (ECF)** is found outside the cells and accounts for about one-third of total body fluid. It is subdivided into three compartments: intravascular, interstitial, and transcellular fluid (Figure 40.1). **Intravascular fluid,** or **plasma** is found within the vascular system. **Interstitial fluid** surrounds the cells and includes lymph. **Transcellular fluid,** considered by some as distinct from intracellular and extracellular fluids, includes cerebrospinal, pleural, peritoneal, and synovial fluids.

Intracellular fluid is vital to normal cell functioning. It contains solutes, such as oxygen, electrolytes, and glucose, and it provides a medium in which metabolic processes of the cell take place.

Extracellular fluid provides the transport system that carries nutrients to, and waste products from, the cells. For example, plasma carries oxygen from the lungs and glucose from the gastrointestinal tract to the capillaries of the vascular system. From there, the oxygen and glucose move across the capillary membranes into the interstitial spaces and then across the cellular membranes into the cells. The opposite route is taken for waste products, such as carbon dioxide going from the cells to the lungs and metabolic acid wastes going eventually to the kidneys. Interstitial fluid, which composes three-quarters of the ECF, transports wastes from the cells by way of the lymph system as well as directly into the blood plasma through capillaries.

Composition of Body Fluids

Extracellular and intracellular fluids contain oxygen from the lungs, dissolved nutrients from the gastrointestinal tract, excretory products of metabolism, such as carbon dioxide, and charged particles called **ions.**

Many salts dissociate in water, that is, break up into electrically charged ions. The salt sodium chloride dissociates into one ion of sodium (Na^+) and one ion of chloride (Cl^-). These charged particles are called **electrolytes** because they are capable of conducting electricity. Ions that carry a positive charge are called **cations,** and ions carrying a negative charge are called **anions.** Examples of cations are sodium (Na^+), potassium (K^+), calcium (Ca^{2+}), and magnesium (Mg^{2+}). Anions include chloride (Cl^-), bicarbonate (HCO_3^-), phosphate (HPO_4^{2-}), and sulfate (SO_4^{2-}).

For clinical purposes, the unit of measurement for electrolytes is the mole. A **mole** is defined as 6.02×10^{23} atoms, ions, or molecules of a substance (Silverthorn, 1998). One mole of a substance has the same number of atoms as any other substance. The *weight* of a mole is equal to the atomic mass or molecular weight of a particular substance expressed in grams (also known as the gram molecular weight).

For example, the atomic mass of sodium is 23.0 and the atomic mass of potassium is 39.1; therefore, one mole of sodium weighs 23 grams, whereas one mole of potassium (with the same number of atoms) weighs 39.1 grams. The number of moles of a substance in a one litre solution is known as the **molarity** (commonly abbreviated mol/L). For example, dissolving 40.1 grams of calcium (i.e., its gram molecular weight) in enough water to make one litre would constitute a one molar solution of calcium. In humans, the solutes found in body fluids are usually so dilute that their concentrations are expressed in 1/1,000th of a mole, that is, a millimole (mmol). In clinical practice, common laboratory values are reported in millimoles per litre (mmol/L). For example, the normal ranges for plasma sodium (Na^+) and chloride (Cl^-) are 135 to 145 mmol/L and 95 to 105 mmol/L, respectively.

Laboratory values might be seen being expressed in *equivalents* or *milliequivalents* per litre (mEq/L). An equivalent is obtained by taking the molarity of an electrolyte and multiplying it by the number of charges it carries. Sodium (Na^+) has a charge of +1 and, therefore, has one equivalent per mole. Calcium (Ca^{2+}) with a +2 charge has two equivalents per mole. Similarly, for negatively charged ions, one mole of chloride (Cl^-) has one equivalent per mole. As previously stated, biological solutions may be very dilute, and therefore, their concentrations are expressed in 1/1,000th of an equivalent or *milliequivalents* per litre. It also is important to remember that laboratory tests are usually performed using blood plasma, an extracellular fluid. These results may reflect what is happening in the ECF. Normally, direct measurement of electrolyte concentration within the cell is not done.

The composition of fluids varies from one body compartment to another. In *extracellular fluid,* the principal electrolytes are sodium, chloride, and bicarbonate. Other electrolytes, such as potassium, calcium, and magnesium, are present in much smaller quantities. Plasma and interstitial fluid, the two primary components of ECF, contain similar electrolytes and solutes. Plasma is a protein-rich fluid containing large amounts of albumin; in contrast, interstitial fluid contains very little protein.

The composition of *intracellular fluid* differs significantly from that of ECF. Potassium and magnesium are the primary cations present in ICF, with phosphate and sulfate being the major anions. As in ECF, other electrolytes are present within the cell but in much smaller concentrations.

Maintaining a balance of fluid volumes and electrolyte compositions in the fluid compartments of the body is essential to health. Normal and unusual fluid and electrolyte losses must be replaced if homeostasis is to be maintained.

Other body fluids, such as gastric and intestinal secretions, contain electrolytes. Fluid and electrolyte imbalances can result from excessive loss of electrolytes from the gastrointestinal tract in severe vomiting, diarrhea, and suctioning of gastric secretions.

Movement of Body Fluids and Electrolytes

The body fluid compartments are separated from one another by cell membranes. These membranes are described as **differentially permeable** because substances move across them with varying degrees of ease. Small particles, such as ions, oxygen, and carbon dioxide, easily move across these membranes, but larger molecules, such as glucose and proteins, have more difficulty moving between fluid compartments.

The methods by which electrolytes and other solutes move are osmosis, diffusion, filtration, and active transport.

Osmosis

Osmosis is the passive movement of water across cell membranes from a less concentrated solution to a more concentrated solution (Figure 40.2). In other words, water moves toward the higher concentration of solute. Osmosis is a passive process.

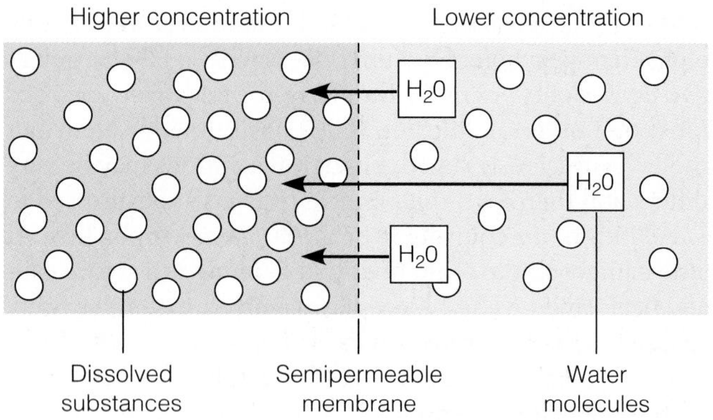

Figure 40.2 Osmosis: Water molecules move from the less concentrated area to the more concentrated area in an attempt to equalize the concentration of solutions on two sides of a membrane

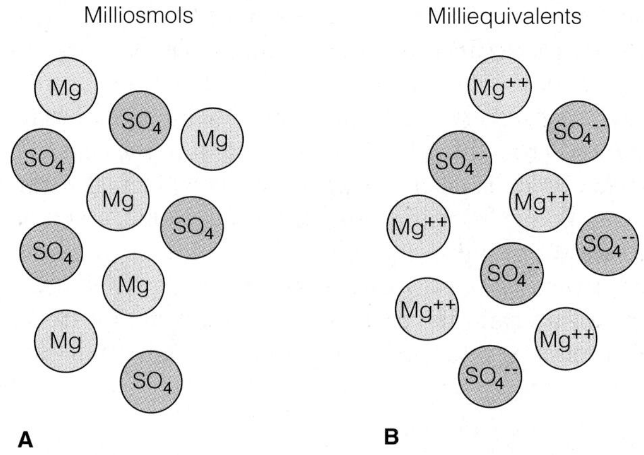

Figure 40.3 Comparison of milliosmols and milliequivalents. *A,* Milliosmols measure osmotic activity as a total of the number of particles present—in this case 10; *B,* Milliequivalents measure the chemical activity as a total of the number of available electrovalent bonds (− −, ++)—in this case, 20.

Solutes are substances dissolved in a liquid. For example, when sugar is added to coffee, the sugar is the solute. Solutes may be **crystalloids** (salts that dissolve readily into true solutions) or **colloids** (substances such as large protein molecules that do not readily dissolve into true solutions). A **solvent** is the component of a solution that can dissolve a solute. In the previous example, coffee is the solvent for the sugar.

In the body, water is the solvent; the solutes include electrolytes, oxygen and carbon dioxide, glucose, urea, amino acids, and proteins. Osmosis occurs when the concentration of solutes on one side of a differentially permeable membrane, such as the capillary membrane, is higher than on the other side. For example, a marathon runner loses a significant amount of water through perspiration, increasing the concentration of solutes in the plasma because of water loss. This higher solute concentration draws water from the interstitial spaces and cells into the vascular compartment to equalize the concentration of solutes in all fluid compartments. Osmosis is an important mechanism for maintaining homeostasis and fluid balance.

The concentration of solutes in body fluids is usually expressed as the **osmolality.** Osmolality is determined by the total solute concentration within a fluid compartment and is measured as parts of solute per kilogram of water (Figure 40.3). Osmolality is reported as milliosmols per kilogram (mOsm/kg). Sodium is by far the greatest determinant of *serum osmolality*, with glucose and urea also contributing. Potassium, glucose, and urea are the primary contributors to the osmolality of intracellular fluid (Toto, 1994). The term *tonicity* may be used to refer to the osmolality of a solution. An *isotonic* solution has the same osmolality as body fluids. Normal saline, 0.9 percent sodium chloride, is an isotonic solution. *Hypertonic* solutions have a higher osmolality than body fluids; 3 percent sodium chloride is a hypertonic solution.

Hypotonic solutions, such as one-half normal saline (0.45 percent sodium chloride), by contrast, have a lower osmolality than body fluids.

Osmotic pressure is the force of osmotic water movement. It refers to the pressure that has to be applied to prevent osmotic movement across a differentially permeable membrane. When two solutions of different solute concentrations are separated by a differentially permeable membrane, the solution of higher solute concentration exerts a higher osmotic pressure, drawing water across the membrane to equalize the concentrations of the solutions. For example, infusing a hypertonic intravenous solution, such as 3 percent sodium chloride, will draw fluid out of red blood cells, causing them to shrink. On the other hand, a hypotonic solution administered intravenously will cause the RBCs to swell as water is drawn into the cells by their higher osmotic pressure. In the body, plasma proteins exert an osmotic draw called **colloid osmotic pressure** or **oncotic pressure,** pulling water from the interstitial spaces into the vascular compartment. This is an important mechanism in maintaining vascular volume.

Diffusion

Diffusion is the continual intermingling of molecules in liquids, gases, or solids brought about by the random movement of the molecules. For example, two gases become mixed by the incessant motion of their molecules. The process of diffusion occurs even when two substances are separated by a thin membrane. In the body, diffusion of *water, electrolytes,* and *other substances* occurs through capillary membranes.

That rate of diffusion of substances varies according to (1) the size of the molecules, (2) the concentration of the solution, and (3) the temperature of the solution. Larger molecules move less quickly than smaller ones because they require more energy to move about. With diffusion, the molecules move from a solution of higher concentration to a solution of lower concentration (Figure 40.4). Increases in temperature increase the rate of motion of molecules and, therefore, the rate of diffusion.

Filtration

Filtration is a process whereby fluid and solutes move together across a membrane from one compartment to another. The movement is from an area of higher pressure to one of lower pressure. An example of filtration is the movement of fluid and nutrients from the capillaries of the arteries to the interstitial fluid around the cells. The difference between the net hydrostatic pressure in the capillaries and the net colloid osmotic pressure is known as the **filtration pressure. Hydrostatic pressure** is the pressure exerted by a fluid within a closed system. The hydrostatic pressure of blood is the force exerted by blood against the vascular walls (e.g., the artery walls). The principle involved in hydrostatic pressure is that fluids move from the area of greater pressure to the area of lesser pressure. Using the example of the blood vessels, the plasma proteins in the blood exert a colloid osmotic pressure that opposes the hydrostatic pressure and holds the fluid in the vascular compartment to maintain the vascular volume. When the hydrostatic pressure is greater than the osmotic pressure, the fluid filters out of the blood vessels. The *filtration pressure* in this example is the difference between the hydrostatic pressure and the osmotic pressure (Figure 40.5).

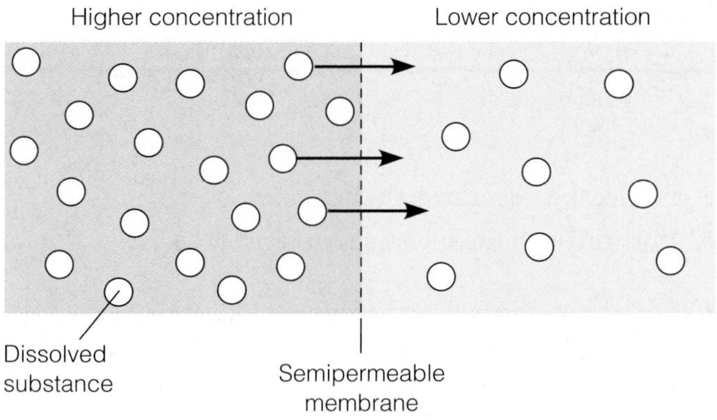

Figure 40.4 Diffusion: The movement of molecules through a semipermeable membrane from an area of higher concentration to an area of lower concentration

Active Transport

Substances can move across cell membranes from a less concentrated to a more concentrated solution by active transport (Figure 40.6). This process differs from diffusion and osmosis in that metabolic energy is expended. In **active transport,** a substance combines with a carrier on the outside surface of the cell membrane, and they move to the inside surface of the cell membrane. Once inside, they separate, and the substance is released to the inside of the cell. A specific carrier is required for each substance, and enzymes are required for active transport.

This process is of particular importance in maintaining the differences in sodium and potassium ion concentrations of extracellular and intracellular fluid. Under normal conditions, sodium concentrations are higher in the extracellular fluid, and potassium concentrations are higher inside the cells. To maintain these proportions, the active transport mechanism (the sodium-potassium pump) is activated, moving sodium from the cells and potassium into the cells.

Regulating Body Fluids

In a healthy person, the volumes and chemical composition of the fluid compartments stay within narrow limits. Normally, fluid intake and fluid loss are balanced. Illness can upset this balance, causing the body to have too little or too much fluid.

Fluid Intake

During periods of moderate activity at moderate temperature, the average adult drinks about 1,500 mL per day but needs 2,500 mL per day, an additional 1,000 mL. This added volume is acquired from foods and from the oxidation of these foods during metabolic processes. Interestingly, the water content of food is relatively large, contributing about 750 mL per day. The water content of fresh vegetables is approximately 90 percent, of fresh fruits, about 85 percent, and of lean meats, around 60 percent.

Figure 40.5 Schematic of filtration pressure changes within a capillary bed. On the arterial side, arterial blood pressure exceeds colloid osmotic pressure, so water and dissolved substances move out of the capillary into the interstitial spaces. On the venous side, venous blood pressure is less than colloid osmotic pressure, so water and dissolved substances move into the capillary.

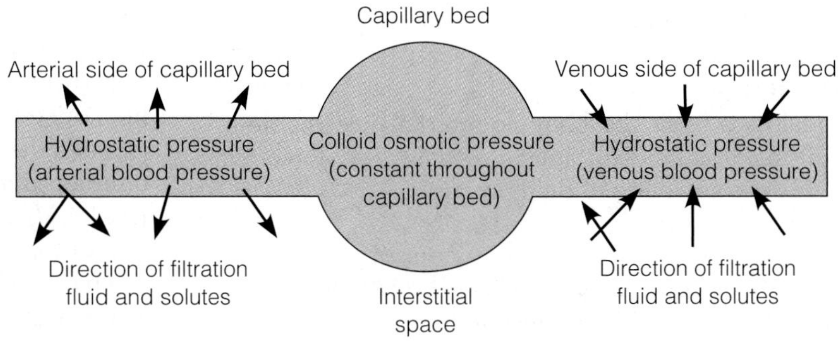

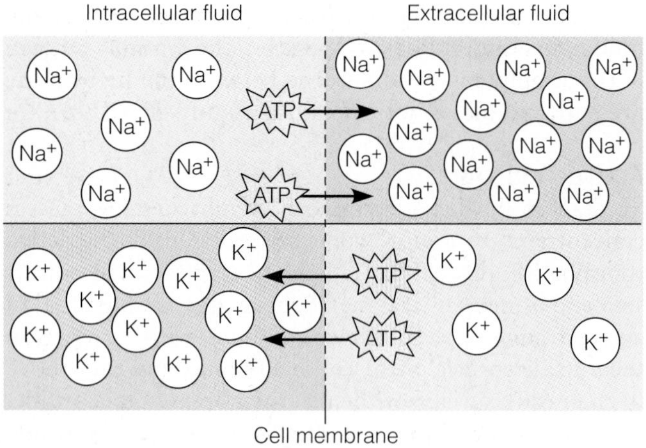

Figure 40.6 An example of active transport. Energy (ATP) is used to move sodium ions and potassium ions across a semipermeable membrane against sodium's and potassium's concentration gradients (i.e., from areas of lesser concentration to areas of greater concentration).

Water as a byproduct of food metabolism accounts for most of the remaining fluid volume required. This quantity is approximately 200 mL per day for the average adult.

The thirst mechanism is the primary regulator of fluid intake. The thirst centre is located in the brain. A number of stimuli trigger this centre, including the osmotic pressure of body fluids, vascular volume, and angiotensin II (a hormone released in response to decreased blood flow to the kidneys). For example, a long-distance runner loses significant amounts of water through perspiration and rapid breathing during a race, increasing the concentration of solutes and the osmotic pressure of body fluids. This increased osmotic pressure stimulates the thirst centre, causing the runner to experience the sensation of thirst and the desire to drink to replace lost fluids.

Thirst is normally relieved immediately after drinking a small amount of fluid, even before it is absorbed from the gastrointestinal tract. However, this relief is only temporary, and the thirst returns in about 15 minutes. The thirst is again temporarily relieved after the ingested fluid distends the upper gastrointestinal tract. These mechanisms protect the individual from drinking too much because it takes from 30 minutes to one hour for the fluid to be absorbed and distributed throughout the body. See Table 40.2 for average fluid requirements by age and weight.

Fluid Output

Fluid losses from the body counterbalance the adult's 2,500-mL average daily intake of fluid. See Table 40.3. There are four routes of fluid output:

1. Urine
2. Insensible loss through the skin as perspiration and through the lungs as water vapour in the expired air
3. Noticeable loss through the skin
4. Loss through the intestines in feces

TABLE 40.2 Average Daily Fluid Requirements by Age and Weight

Age	Approximate Body Weight (kg)	mL/24 hr
3 days	3.0	250 to 300
1 year	9.51	1,150 to 1,300
2 years	11.8	1,350 to 1,500
6 years	20.0	1,800 to 2,000
10 years	28.7	2,000 to 2,500
14 years	45.0	2,200 to 2,700
18 years (adult)	54.0	2,200 to 2,700

Source: Behrman, R. E. (1992). *Nelson textbook of pediatrics.* (p. 107). Philadelphia, PA: Saunders. Reproduced with permission.

TABLE 40.3 Average Daily Fluid Output for an Adult

Route	Amount (mL)
Urine	1,400 to 1,500
Insensible losses	
Lungs	350 to 400
Skin	350 to 400
Sweat	100
Feces	100 to 200
Total	2,300 to 2,600

Urine Urine formed by the kidneys and excreted from the urinary bladder is the major avenue of fluid output. Normal urine output for an adult is 1,400 to 1,500 mL per 24 hours, or at least 30 to 50 mL per hour. In healthy people, urine output may vary noticeably from day to day. Urine volume automatically increases as fluid intake increases. If fluid loss through perspiration is large, however, urine volume decreases to maintain fluid balance in the body. For further information about urine formation, see Chapter 36.

Insensible Losses **Insensible fluid loss** occurs through the skin and lungs. It is called *insensible* because it is usually not noticeable and cannot be measured. Insensible fluid loss through the skin occurs in two ways. Water is lost through diffusion and perspiration (which is noticeable but not measurable). Water losses through diffusion are not noticeable but normally account for 300 to 400 mL per day. This loss can be significantly increased if the protective layer of the skin is lost as with burns or large abrasions. Perspiration varies depending on such factors as environmental temperature and metabolic activity. Fever and exercise increase metabolic activity and heat production, thereby increasing fluid losses through the skin.

Another type of insensible loss is the water in exhaled air. In an adult, this is normally 300 to 400 mL per day. When the respiratory rate accelerates, for example due to exercise or elevated body temperature, this loss can increase.

Feces The chyme that passes from the small intestine into the large intestine contains water and electrolytes. The volume of chyme entering the large intestine in an adult is normally about 1,500 mL per day. Of this amount, all but about 100 mL is absorbed in the proximal half of the large intestine.

Obligatory Fluid Losses Certain fluid losses are required to maintain normal body function. These are known as **obligatory losses.** Approximately 500 mL of fluid *must* be excreted through the kidneys of an adult each day to eliminate metabolic waste products from the body. Water lost through respirations, through the skin, and in feces also are obligatory losses, necessary for temperature regulation and elimination of waste products. The total of all these losses is approximately 1,300 mL per day.

Homeostasis The volume and composition of body fluids is regulated through several homeostatic mechanisms. A number of body systems contribute to this regulation, including the kidneys, the endocrine system, the cardiovascular system, the lungs, and the gastrointestinal system. Hormones, such as antidiuretic hormone (ADH; also known as arginine vasopressin or AVP), the renin-angiotensin-aldosterone system, and atrial natriuretic factor are involved, as are mechanisms to monitor and maintain vascular volume.

Kidneys The kidneys are the primary regulator of body fluids and electrolyte balance. They regulate the volume and osmolality of extracellular fluids by regulating water and electrolyte excretion. The kidneys adjust the reabsorption of water from plasma filtrate and ultimately the amount excreted as urine. Although 135 to 180 L of plasma per day is normally filtered in an adult, only about 1.5 L of urine is excreted (Metheny, 1996). Electrolyte balance is maintained by selective retention and excretion by the kidneys. The kidneys also play a significant role in acid-base regulation, excreting hydrogen ion (H^+) and retaining bicarbonate.

Antidiuretic Hormone Antidiuretic hormone, which regulates water excretion from the kidney, is synthesized in the anterior portion of the hypothalamus, is secreted by the posterior pituitary, and acts on the collecting ducts of the nephrons. When serum osmolality rises, ADH is produced, causing the collecting ducts to become more permeable to water. This increased permeability allows more water to be reabsorbed into the blood. As more water is reabsorbed, urine output falls and serum osmolality decreases because the water dilutes body fluids. Conversely, if serum osmolality decreases, ADH is suppressed, the collecting ducts become less permeable to water, and urine output increases. Excess water is excreted, and serum osmolality returns to normal. Other factors also affect the production and release of ADH, including blood volume, temperature, pain, stress, and some drugs, such as opiates, barbiturates, and nicotine (Toto, 1994).

Renin-Angiotensin-Aldosterone System Specialized receptors in the juxtaglomerular apparatus of the kidney nephrons respond to changes in renal perfusion. If blood flow or pressure to the kidney decreases, renin is released. Renin causes the conversion of angiotensinogen to angiotensin I, which is then converted to angiotensin II by angiotensin-converting enzyme. Angiotensin II acts directly on the nephrons to promote sodium and water retention. In addition, it stimulates the release of aldosterone from the adrenal cortex. Aldosterone also promotes sodium, and, therefore water, retention in the distal nephron (Preston, 1997). The net effect of the renin-angiotensin-aldosterone system is to restore blood volume (and renal perfusion) through sodium and water retention.

Atrial Natriuretic Factor Atrial natriuretic factor (ANF) is released from cells in the atrium of the heart in response to excess blood volume and stretching of the atrial walls. Acting on the nephrons, ANF promotes sodium wasting and acts as a potent diuretic, thus reducing vascular volume. ANF also inhibits thirst, reducing fluid intake (Toto, 1994).

Regulating Electrolytes

Electrolytes, charged ions capable of conducting electricity, are present in all body fluids and fluid compartments. Just as maintaining the fluid balance is vital to normal body function, so is maintaining electrolyte balance. Although the concentration of specific electrolytes differs between fluid compartments, a balance of cations (positively charged ions) and anions (negatively charged ions) always exists. Electrolytes are important for the following:

- Maintaining fluid balance
- Contributing to acid-base regulation
- Facilitating enzyme reactions
- Neuromuscular reactions

Most electrolytes enter the body through dietary intake and are excreted in the urine. Some electrolytes, such as sodium and chloride, are not stored by the body and must be consumed daily to maintain normal levels. Potassium and calcium, on the other hand, are stored in the cells and bone, respectively. When serum levels drop, ions can shift out of the storage "pool" into the blood to maintain adequate serum levels for normal functioning. The regulatory mechanisms and functions of the major electrolytes are summarized in Table 40.4. Normal serum levels of electrolytes are shown in the box on page 1096.

TABLE 40.4 Regulation and Functions of Electrolytes

Electrolyte	Regulation	Function
Sodium (Na^+)	■ Renal reabsorption or excretion ■ Aldosterone increases Na^+ reabsorption in collecting duct of nephrons	■ Regulating ECF volume and distribution ■ Maintaining blood volume ■ Transmitting nerve impulses and contracting muscles
Potassium (K^+)	■ Renal excretion and conservation ■ Aldosterone increases K^+ excretion ■ Movement into and out of cells ■ Insulin helps move K^+ into cells; tissue damage and acidosis shift K^+ out of cells into ECF	■ Maintaining ICF osmolality ■ Transmitting nerve and other electrical impulses ■ Regulating cardiac impulse transmission and muscle contraction ■ Skeletal and smooth muscle function ■ Regulating acid-base balance
Calcium (Ca^{2+})	■ Re-distribution between bones and ECF ■ Parathyroid hormone and calcitriol increase serum Ca^{2+} levels; calcitonin decreases serum levels	■ Forming bones and teeth ■ Transmitting nerve impulses ■ Regulating muscle contractions ■ Maintaining cardiac pacemaker (automaticity) ■ Blood clotting ■ Activating enzymes, such as pancreatic lipase and phospholipase
Magnesium (Mg^{2+})	■ Conservation and excretion by kidneys ■ Intestinal absorption increased by vitamin D and parathyroid hormone	■ Intracellular metabolism ■ Operating sodium-potassium pump ■ Relaxing muscle contractions ■ Transmitting nerve impulses ■ Regulating cardiac function
Chloride (Cl^-)	■ Excreted and reabsorbed along with sodium in the kidneys ■ Aldosterone increases chloride reabsorption with sodium	■ HCl production ■ Regulating ECF balance and vascular volume ■ Regulating acid-base balance ■ Buffer in oxygen–carbon dioxide exchange in RBCs
Phosphate (PO_4^-)	■ Excretion and reabsorption by the kidneys ■ Parathyroid hormone decreases serum levels by increasing renal excretion ■ Reciprocal relationship with calcium: increasing serum calcium levels decreases phosphate levels; decreasing serum calcium increases phosphate	■ Forming bones and teeth ■ Metabolizing carbohydrate, protein, and fat ■ Cellular metabolism; producing ATP and DNA ■ Muscle, nerve, and RBC function ■ Regulating acid-base balance ■ Regulating calcium levels
Bicarbonate (HCO_3^-)	■ Excretion and reabsorption by the kidneys ■ Regeneration by kidneys	■ Major body buffer involved in acid-base regulation

Sodium (Na^+)

Sodium is the most abundant cation in extracellular fluid and a major contributor to serum osmolality. Sodium functions largely in controlling and regulating water balance. When sodium is reabsorbed from the kidney tubules, chloride and water are reabsorbed with it, thus maintaining ECF volume. Sodium is found in many foods, such as bacon, ham, processed cheese, and table salt.

Potassium (K^+)

Potassium is the major cation in intracellular fluids, with only a small amount found in plasma and interstitial fluid. Just as sodium helps maintain ECF water balance, potassium is important in maintaining ICF water balance. Potassium is a vital electrolyte for skeletal, cardiac, and smooth muscle activity. It is involved in maintaining acid-base balance as well, and it contributes to intracellular enzyme reactions (Porth, 1998). Potassium is found in many fruits and vegetables, meat, fish, and other foods. See the accompanying box below.

Potassium-Rich Foods

Vegetables
Avocado
Raw carrot
Baked potato
Raw tomato
Spinach

Meats and Fish
Beef
Cod
Pork
Veal

Fruits
Dried fruits (e.g., raisins and dates)
Banana
Apricot
Cantaloupe
Orange

Beverages
Milk
Orange juice
Apricot nectar

Calcium (Ca^{2+})

The vast majority of calcium in the body is in the skeletal system, with a relatively small amount in extracellular fluid. Although this calcium outside the bones and teeth amounts to only about 1 percent of the total calcium in the body, it is vital in regulating muscle contraction and relaxation, neuromuscular function, coagulation, and cardiac function. ECF calcium is regulated by a complex interaction of parathyroid hormone, calcitonin, and calcitriol, a metabolite of vitamin D. When calcium levels in the ECF fall, parathyroid hormone and calcitriol cause calcium to be released from bones into the ECF and increase the absorption of calcium in the intestines, thus raising serum calcium levels. Conversely, calcitonin stimulates the deposition of calcium in bone, reducing the concentration of calcium ions in the blood.

With aging, the intestines absorb calcium less effectively and more calcium is excreted via the kidneys. Calcium shifts out of the bone to replace these ECF losses, increasing the risk of osteoporosis and fractures of the wrists, vertebrae, and hips. Lack of weight-bearing exercise (which helps keep calcium in the bones) and a vitamin D deficiency because of inadequate exposure to sunlight contribute to this risk (Lee et al., 1996).

Milk and milk products are the richest sources of calcium, with other foods, such as dark green leafy vegetables and canned salmon, containing smaller amounts. Older clients and small-boned women benefit from calcium supplements. A diet high in calcium also has been shown to reduce the blood pressure, although the mechanism of action is not clear (Metheny, 1996).

Magnesium (Mg^{2+})

Magnesium is primarily found in the skeleton and in intracellular fluid. It is important for intracellular metabolism, being particularly involved in the production and use of ATP (Metheny, 1996). Magnesium also is necessary for protein and DNA synthesis within the cells (Porth, 1998). Only about 1 percent of the body's magnesium is in ECF. Magnesium is involved in regulating neuromuscular and cardiac function. Cereal grains, nuts, dried fruit, legumes, and green leafy vegetables are good sources of magnesium in the diet, as are dairy products, meat, and fish (Lee et al., 1996).

Chloride (Cl^-)

Chloride is the major anion of ECF. Chloride functions with sodium to regulate serum osmolality and blood volume. The concentration of chloride in ECF is regulated secondarily to sodium; when sodium is reabsorbed in the kidney, chloride usually follows (Lee et al., 1996). Chloride is a major component of gastric juice as hydrochloric acid (HCl) and is involved in regulating acid-base balance. It also acts as a buffer in the exchange of oxygen and carbon dioxide in red blood cells. Chloride is found in the same foods as sodium.

Phosphate (PO_4^-)

Phosphate is the major anion of intracellular fluids. It also is found in ECF, bone, skeletal muscle, and nerve tissue. Children have much higher phosphate levels than adults, with that of a newborn nearly twice that of an adult (Lee et al., 1996). Higher levels of growth hormone and a faster rate of skeletal growth probably account for this difference. Phosphate is involved in many chemical actions of the cell; it is essential for functioning of muscles, nerves, and red blood cells. It is also involved in the metabolism of protein, fat, and carbohydrate. Phosphate is absorbed from the intestine, and is found in many foods, such as meat, fish, poultry, milk products, and legumes.

Bicarbonate (HCO_3^-)

Bicarbonate is present in both intracellular and extracellular fluids. Its primary function is regulating acid-base balance as an essential component of the carbonic acid–bicarbonate buffering system. Extracellular bicarbonate levels are regulated by the kidneys. Bicarbonate is excreted when too much is present; if more is needed, the kidneys both produce and reabsorb bicarbonate ions. Unlike other electrolytes that must be consumed in the diet, adequate amounts of bicarbonate are produced through metabolic processes to meet the body's needs.

Acid-Base Balance and pH

An important part of regulating the chemical balance or homeostasis of body fluids is regulating their acidity or alkalinity. An **acid** is a substance that releases hydrogen ions (H^+) in solution. Strong acids, such as hydrochloric acid, release nearly all their hydrogen ions; weak acids, such as carbonic acid, release some hydrogen ions. **Bases**, or *alkalis*, have a low hydrogen ion concentration and can accept hydrogen ions in solution. The relative acidity or alkalinity of a solution is measured as pH. The "pH" symbol is taken to mean the hydrogen ion (H^+) concentration of a solution. The scale ranges from 1 to 14. The numbers in the pH scale actually refer to the negative log of the hydrogen ion concentration expressed in moles per litre.

A pH of 7 indicates neutrality of a solution, that is, there are equal amounts of H^+ and hydroxyl (OH^-) ions. In one litre of pure, distilled water there is 0.0000001 moles of hydrogen ions and the same number of hydroxide ions. So, we can say that the *concentration* of hydrogen ions in our 1 litre of distilled water is 0.0000001 moles per litre. This can be written as follows:

$[H^+] = 1 \times 10^{-7}$ mol/L
The square brackets around the name of a substance (in this case hydrogen) mean, "The concentration of…".

Thus, $[H^+] = 1 \times 10^{-7}$ mol/L would be stated as, "The concentration of hydrogen ions equals one times ten to the minus seven moles per litre."

The negative log of 0.0000001 is 7. The hydrogen ion concentration can be expressed in a shorthand way, rather than writing all the zeros out every time. The hydrogen ion concentration of distilled water is: $[H^+] = 1 \times 10^{-7}$ and the shorthand way of stating this is to say the pH is 7. It is important to remember that the pH scale of hydrogen ion concentration is logarithmic: this means the concentration of H^+ changes by a factor of 10 for each unit of the scale. For example, a pH of 7 has a H^+ concentration 10 times that of a pH of 8.

In other words, a substance with a hydrogen ion concentration or pH of 7 has 10 times more hydrogen ions (in moles per litre) than a substance with a pH of 8.

A pH of less than 7 indicates acidity, whereas a pH greater than 7 indicates alkalinity. A *decrease* in the pH number indicates an *increase* in acidity, that is, H^+ concentration and vice versa.

For example, pH 1.7 (***low*** number, ***high*** acidity); pH 10.8 (***high*** number, ***low*** acidity)

The pH of our internal environment continually fluctuates with absorption of acids and bases from foods and from catabolism. Despite these substances, our pH is kept remarkably constant. Apart from the extreme acidity of the stomach (pH 1 to 3), the pH of our blood, cells, and certain tissue fluids tends to be around a neutral pH of 7.

Regulation of Acid-Base Balance

Body fluids are maintained within a narrow range that is slightly alkaline. The normal pH of arterial blood is between 7.35 and 7.45 (Figure 40.7). Acids are continually produced during metabolism. Several body systems, including buffers, the respiratory system, and the renal system, are actively involved in maintaining the narrow pH range necessary for optimal function. Buffers help maintain acid-base balance by neutralizing excess acids or bases. The lungs and the kidneys help maintain a normal pH by either excreting or retaining acids and bases.

Buffers

Buffers prevent excessive changes in pH by removing or releasing hydrogen ions. If excess hydrogen ion is present in body fluids, buffers bind with the hydrogen ion, minimizing the change in pH. When body fluids become too alkaline, buffers can release hydrogen ion, again minimizing the change in pH. The action of a buffer is immediate but is limited in its capacity to maintain or restore normal acid-base balance.

The major buffer system in extracellular fluids is the bicarbonate (HCO_3^-) and carbonic acid (H_2CO_3) system. When a strong acid, such as hydrochloric acid (HCl), is

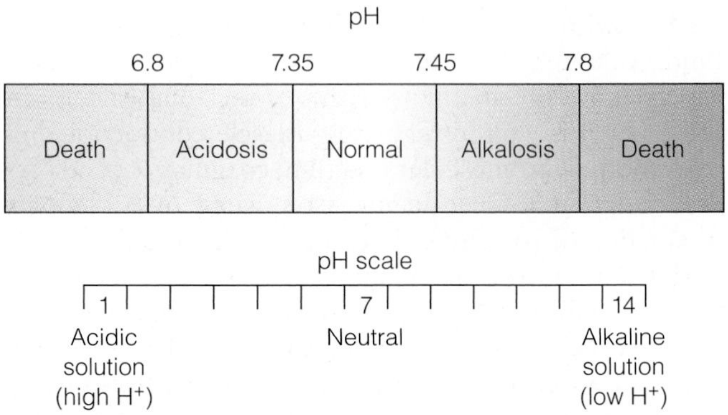

Figure 40.7 Body fluids are normally slightly alkaline, between a pH of 7.35 and 7.45

added, it combines with bicarbonate and the pH drops only slightly. A strong base, such as sodium hydroxide, combines with carbonic acid, the weak acid of the buffer pair, and the pH remains within the narrow range of normal. The amounts of bicarbonate and carbonic acid in the body vary; however, as long as a ratio of 20 parts of bicarbonate to one part of carbonic acid is maintained, the pH remains within its normal range of 7.35 to 7.45 (Figure 40.8). Adding a strong acid to ECF can change this ratio, as bicarbonate is depleted in neutralizing the acid. When this happens, the pH drops, a condition called **acidosis.** The ratio can also be upset by adding a strong base to ECF; in this case, the pH rises, and the client has **alkalosis.**

In addition to the bicarbonate–carbonic acid buffer system, plasma proteins, hemoglobin, and phosphates also function as buffers in body fluids.

Respiratory Regulation

The lungs help regulate acid-base balance by eliminating or retaining carbon dioxide (CO_2). Carbon dioxide and water combine in the presence of the enzyme carbonic anhydrase to form carbonic acid ($CO_2 + H_2O \rightarrow H_2CO_3$). This chemical reaction is reversible; carbonic acid dissociates into carbon dioxide and water. Working together with the bicarbonate–carbonic acid buffer system, the lungs regulate acid-base balance and pH by altering the rate and depth of respirations. Although not instantaneous, the response of the respiratory system to changes in pH is rapid, occurring within minutes.

Carbon dioxide is a powerful stimulator of the respiratory centre. When blood levels of carbonic acid and carbon dioxide rise, the respiratory centre is stimulated, and the rate and depth of respirations increase. Carbon dioxide is excreted, and carbonic acid levels fall. By contrast, when bicarbonate levels are excessive, the rate and depth of respirations are reduced. This allows carbon dioxide to be retained, carbonic acid levels rise, and the excess bicarbonate is neutralized.

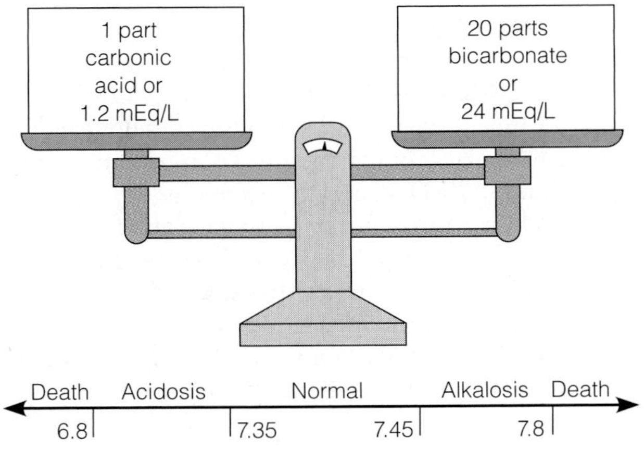

Figure 40.8 Carbonic acid–bicarbonate ratio and pH

Carbon dioxide levels in the blood are measured as the partial pressure of the dissolved gas (PCO_2) in the blood. PCO_2 refers to the pressure of carbon dioxide in *venous* blood. $PaCO_2$ refers to the pressure of carbon dioxide in *arterial* blood. The normal $PaCO_2$ is 35 to 45 mm Hg.

Renal Regulation

Although buffers and the respiratory system can compensate for changes in pH, the kidneys are the ultimate long-term regulators of acid-base balance. They are slower to respond to changes, requiring hours to days to correct imbalances, but their response is more permanent and selective than those of the other systems (Lee et al., 1996).

The kidneys maintain acid-base balance by selectively excreting or conserving bicarbonate and hydrogen ions. When excess hydrogen ion is present and the pH falls (acidosis), the kidneys reabsorb and regenerate bicarbonate and excrete hydrogen ion. In the case of alkalosis and a high pH, excess bicarbonate is excreted, and hydrogen ion is retained. The normal serum bicarbonate level is 24 to 28 mmol/L.

Factors Affecting Body Fluid, Electrolytes, and Acid-Base Balance

Age

Infants and growing children have much greater fluid turnover than have adults because their higher metabolic rate increases fluid loss. Infants lose more fluid through the kidneys because immature kidneys are less able to conserve water than are adult kidneys. In addition, infants' respirations are more rapid, and the body surface area is proportionately greater than an adults, increasing insensible fluid losses. The more rapid turnover of fluid plus the losses produced by disease can create critical fluid imbalances in children much more rapidly than in adults.

In elderly people, the normal aging process may affect fluid balance. The thirst response often is blunted. Antidiuretic hormone (ADH) levels remain normal or may even be elevated, but the nephrons become less able to conserve water in response to ADH. Increased levels of atrial natriuretic factor seen in older adults may also contribute to this impaired ability to conserve water (Miller, 1995). These normal changes of aging increase the risk of dehydration. When combined with the increased likelihood of heart disease, impaired renal function, and multiple drug regimens, the older adult's risk for fluid and electrolyte imbalance is significant.

Gender and Body Size

Total body water also is affected by gender and body size. Because fat cells contain little or no water and lean tissue has a high water content, people with a higher percentage of body fat have less body fluid. Women have proportionately more body fat and less body water than men. Water accounts for approximately 60 percent of an adult male's weight, but only 52 percent for an adult female. In an obese individual, this may be even less, with water responsible for only 30 to 40 percent of the person's weight.

Environmental Temperature

People with an illness and those participating in strenuous activity are at risk for fluid and electrolyte imbalances when the environmental temperature is high. Fluid losses through sweating are increased in hot environments as the body attempts to dissipate heat. These losses are even greater in people who have not been acclimatized to the environment.

Salt and water are lost through sweating and both need to be replaced. The person who is salt depleted may experience fatigue, weakness, headache, and gastrointestinal symptoms, such as anorexia and nausea. The risk of adverse effects is even greater if lost water is not replaced. Body temperature rises, and the person is at risk for heat exhaustion or heatstroke. Heatstroke may occur in older adults or ill people during prolonged periods of heat; it can also affect athletes and labourers when their heat production exceeds the body's ability to dissipate heat (Metheny, 1996).

Consuming adequate amounts of cool liquids, particularly during strenuous activity, reduces the risk of adverse effects from heat. Balanced electrolyte solutions and carbohydrate-electrolyte solutions, such as sports drinks, may be recommended because they replace both water and electrolytes lost through sweat.

Lifestyle

Other factors, such as diet, exercise, and stress, affect fluid, electrolyte, and acid-base balance.

The intake of fluids and electrolytes is affected by diet. People with anorexia nervosa or bulimia are at risk for severe fluid and electrolyte imbalances because of inadequate intake or purging regimens (e.g., induced vomiting, using diuretics and laxatives). Seriously malnourished people have decreased serum albumin levels and may develop edema because the osmotic draw of fluid into the vascular compartment is reduced. When calorie intake is not adequate to meet the body's needs, fat stores are broken down and fatty acids are released, increasing the risk of acidosis.

Regular weight-bearing physical exercise, such as walking, running, or bicycling, has a beneficial effect on calcium balance. The risk of osteoporosis is somewhat reduced in postmenopausal women and older men who get regular exercise as the rate of bone loss is decreased.

Stress can increase cellular metabolism, blood glucose concentration, and catecholamine levels. In addition, stress can increase production of ADH, which, in turn, decreases urine production. The overall response of the body to stress is to increase the blood volume.

Other lifestyle factors can also affect fluid, electrolyte, and acid-base balance. Heavy alcohol consumption affects electrolyte balance, increasing the risk of low calcium, magnesium, and phosphate levels. The risk of acidosis associated with breakdown of fat tissue also is greater in the person who drinks large amounts of alcohol (Metheny, 1996).

Disturbances in Fluid Volume, Electrolyte, and Acid-Base Balances

A number of factors, such as illness, trauma, surgery, and medications, can affect the body's ability to maintain fluid, electrolyte, and acid-base balance. Clients who are confused or unable to communicate their needs are at risk for inadequate fluid intake. Vomiting, diarrhea, or nasogastric suction can cause significant fluid and electrolyte losses. Tissue trauma, such as burns, causes fluid and electrolytes to be lost from damaged cells. Decreased blood flow to the kidneys due to impaired cardiac function stimulates the renin-angiotensin-aldosterone system, causing sodium and water retention. Medications, such as diuretics, can cause abnormal losses of electrolytes and fluid. Diseases, such as diabetes mellitus or chronic obstructive lung disease, may affect acid-base balance.

Fluid Imbalances

Fluid imbalances are of two basic types: isotonic and osmolar. Isotonic imbalances occur when water and electrolytes are lost or gained in equal proportions so that the osmolality of body fluids remains constant. Osmolar imbalances involve the loss or gain of *only* water so that the osmolality of the serum is altered. Thus, four categories of fluid imbalances may occur: (1) an isotonic loss of water and electrolytes, (2) an isotonic gain of water and electrolytes, (3) a hyperosmolar loss of only water, and (4) a hypo-osmolar gain of only water. These are referred to, respectively, as fluid volume deficit, fluid volume excess, dehydration, and overhydration.

Fluid Volume Deficit

Isotonic **fluid volume deficit** (FVD) occurs when the body loses both water and electrolytes from the ECF in similar proportions. In FVD, fluid is initially lost from the intravascular compartment, so it often is called **hypovolemia.** FVD generally occurs as a result of (1) abnormal losses through the skin, gastrointestinal tract, or kidney; (2) decreased intake of fluid; (3) bleeding; or (4) movement of fluid into a **third space.** See the section on third space syndrome that follows.

The risk factors, clinical signs, and nursing interventions related to fluid volume deficit are given in Table 40.5.

Third Space Syndrome In **third space syndrome,** fluid shifts from the vascular space into an area where it is not

TABLE 40.5 Isotonic Fluid Volume Deficit

Risk Factors	Clinical Manifestations	Nursing Interventions
Loss of water and electrolytes from: ■ Vomiting ■ Diarrhea ■ Excessive sweating ■ Polyuria ■ Fever ■ Nasogastric suction ■ Abnormal drainage or wound losses ■ Bleeding Insufficient intake due to: ■ Anorexia ■ Nausea ■ Inability to access fluids ■ Impaired swallowing ■ Confusion, depression	Complaints of weakness and thirst Weight loss: ■ 2% loss = mild FVD ■ 5% loss = moderate ■ 8% loss = severe Fluid intake less than output Decreased tissue turgor Dry mucous membranes, sunken eyeballs, decreased tearing Subnormal temperature Weak, rapid pulse Decreased blood pressure Postural (orthostatic) hypotension (significant drop in BP when moving from lying to sitting or standing position) Flat neck veins, decreased capillary refill Decreased central venous pressure (CVP) Decreased urine volume (<30 mL/h) Increased specific gravity of urine (>1.030) Increased hematocrit Increased blood urea nitrogen (BUN)	Assess for clinical manifestations of FVD. Monitor weight and vital signs, including temperature. Assess tissue turgor. Assess breath sounds. Monitor fluid intake and output. Monitor laboratory findings. Administer oral and intravenous fluids, as indicated. Provide frequent mouth care. Implement measures to prevent skin breakdown. Provide for safety, for example, provide assistance to a client rising from bed.

readily accessible as extracellular fluid. This fluid remains in the body but is essentially unavailable for use, causing an isotonic fluid volume deficit. Fluid may be sequestered in the bowel, in the interstitial space as edema, in inflamed tissue, or in potential spaces, such as the peritoneal or pleural cavities (Metheny, 1996).

The client with third space syndrome has an isotonic fluid deficit but may not manifest apparent fluid loss or weight loss. Careful nursing assessment is important in order to effectively identify and intervene with clients experiencing third spacing. After a period of time, the fluid may return from the third space to the vascular compartment, and consequently, the nurse should assess the client for fluid volume excess.

Fluid Volume Excess

Fluid volume excess (FVE) occurs when the body retains both water and sodium in similar proportions to normal ECF. This is commonly referred to as *hypervolemia* (increased blood volume). Because both water and sodium are retained, the serum sodium concentration remains essentially normal. FVE is always secondary to an increase in the total body sodium content (Metheny, 1996). Specific causes of FVE include (1) excessive intake of sodium chloride; (2) administering sodium-containing infusions too rapidly, particularly to clients with impaired regulatory mechanisms; and (3) disease processes that alter regulatory mechanisms, such as congestive heart failure, renal failure, cirrhosis of the liver, and Cushing's syndrome.

The risk factors, clinical manifestations, and nursing interventions for FVE are summarized in Table 40.6.

Edema In fluid volume excess, both intravascular and interstitial spaces have an increased water and sodium content. Excess interstitial fluid is known as **edema.** Edema typically is most apparent in areas where the tissue pressure is low, such as around the eyes, and in dependent tissues (known as *dependent edema*) where hydrostatic capillary pressure is high.

Edema can be caused by several different mechanisms. It may be due to FVE that increases capillary pressures, pushing fluid into the interstitial tissues. This type of edema is often seen in dependent tissues, such as the feet, hands, ankles, and sacrum, because of the effects of gravity. Low levels of plasma proteins from malnutrition or liver or kidney diseases can reduce the plasma oncotic pressure so

TABLE 40.6 Fluid Volume Excess

Risk Factors	Clinical Manifestations	Nursing Interventions
Excess intake of sodium-containing intravenous fluids Excess ingestion of sodium in diet or medications (e.g., sodium bicarbonate antacids, such as Alka-Seltzer, or hypertonic enema solutions, such as Fleet's) Impaired fluid balance regulation related to: ■ Heart failure ■ Renal failure ■ Cirrhosis of the liver	Weight gain: ■ 2% gain = mild FVE ■ 5% gain = moderate ■ 8% gain = severe Fluid intake greater than output Moist mucous membranes Full, bounding pulse; tachycardia Increased blood pressure and central venous pressure (CVP) Distended neck and peripheral veins; slow vein emptying Moist crackles (rales) in lungs; dyspnea, shortness of breath Mental confusion Peripheral edema	Assess for clinical manifestations of FVE. Monitor weight and vital signs. Assess for edema. Assess breath sounds, dyspnea. Monitor fluid intake and output. Monitor laboratory findings. Place client in Fowler's position. Administer diuretics, as ordered. Restrict fluid intake, as ordered. Restrict dietary sodium, as ordered. Implement measures to prevent skin breakdown.

that fluid is not drawn into the capillaries from interstitial tissues, causing edema. With tissue trauma and some disorders, such as allergic reactions, capillaries become inflamed and have increased permeability. Excess fluid leaks from the capillaries into the interstitial spaces. Excess fluid in the tissue spaces during an inflammatory response is known as *exudate*. Obstructed lymph flow impairs the movement of fluid from interstitial tissues back into the vascular compartment, resulting in edema.

Pitting edema is edema that leaves a small depression or pit after finger pressure is applied to the swollen area. The pit is caused by movement of fluid to adjacent tissue, away from the point of pressure (Figure 40.9). The pit normally disappears within 10 to 30 seconds.

Dehydration

Dehydration, or *hyperosmolar imbalance,* occurs when water is lost from the body without significant loss of electrolytes. Because water is lost while electrolytes, particularly sodium, are retained, the serum osmolality and serum sodium levels increase. Water is drawn into the vascular compartment from the interstitial spaces and cells, resulting in cellular dehydration. Older adults are at particular risk for dehydration because of decreased thirst sensation. This type of water deficit also can affect clients who are hyperventilating or have prolonged fever, in diabetic ketoacidosis, and those receiving enteral feedings with insufficient water intake.

Overhydration

Overhydration, also known as *hypo-osmolar imbalance* or *water intoxication,* occurs when water is gained in excess of electrolytes, resulting in low serum osmolality and low serum sodium levels. Water is drawn into the cells, causing them to swell. In the brain, this can lead to cerebral edema and impaired neurological function. Water intoxication often occurs when both fluid and electrolytes are lost, for example, through excessive sweating, but only water is replaced. It can also result from the syndrome of inappropriate antidiuretic hormone (SIADH), a disorder that can occur with some malignant tumours, acquired immune deficiency syndrome (AIDS), head injury, or administration of certain drugs, such as barbiturates or anesthetics.

Electrolyte Imbalances

Sodium

Sodium (Na^+), the most abundant cation in the extracellular fluid, not only moves into and out of the body but also moves in careful balance among the three fluid compartments. It is found in most body secretions, for example, saliva, gastric and intestinal secretions, bile, and pancreatic fluid. Therefore, continuous excretion of any of these fluids, such as via intestinal suction, can result in a sodium deficit. Because of its role in regulating water balance, sodium imbalances usually are accompanied by water imbalance.

Hyponatremia is a sodium deficit, or serum sodium level of less than 135 mmol/L. Because of sodium's role in determining the osmolality of ECF, hyponatremia typically results in a low serum osmolality. Water is drawn out of the vascular compartment into interstitial tissues and the cells (Figure 40.10, *A*), causing the clinical manifestations associated with this disorder.

Hypernatremia is excess sodium in ECF, or a serum sodium of greater than 145 mmol/L. Because the osmotic pressure of extracellular fluid is increased, fluid moves

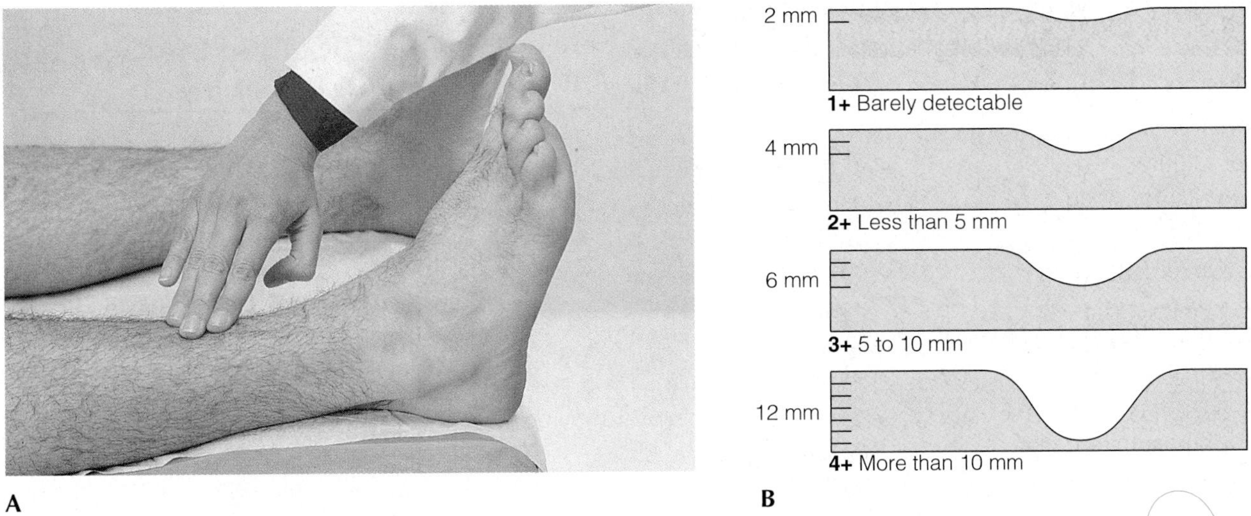

Figure 40.9 Evaluation of edema: *A,* Palpate for edema over the tibia as shown here and behind the medial malleolus and over the dorsum of each foot; *B,* Four-point scale for grading edema

out of the cells into the ECF (Figure 40.10, *B*). As a result, the cells become dehydrated.

See Table 40.7 on page 1086 for risk factors, clinical signs, and nursing interventions for hyponatremia and hypernatremia.

Potassium

There is a small amount of potassium (K^+) in extracellular fluid; however, it is vital to normal neuromuscular and cardiac function. Potassium is usually excreted by the kidneys. The kidneys do not regulate potassium excretion as effectively as sodium excretion. Therefore, an acute potassium deficiency can develop rapidly.

Hypokalemia is a potassium deficit or a serum potassium level of less than 3.5 mmol/L. Gastrointestinal losses of potassium through vomiting and gastric suction are common causes of hypokalemia, as is the use of potassium-wasting diuretics, such as thiazide diuretics or loop diuretics (e.g., furosemide).

Hyperkalemia is a potassium excess or a serum potassium level greater than 5.0 mmol/L. Hyperkalemia is less common than hypokalemia and rarely occurs in clients with normal renal function. Both hyperkalemia and hypokalemia are dangerous and can lead to cardiac arrest.

See Table 40.7 on page 1086 for the risk factors, clinical signs, and nursing interventions for hypokalemia and hyperkalemia.

Calcium

Levels of calcium (Ca^{2+}) in the body can be affected by many factors.

Hypocalcemia is a calcium deficit, or a total serum calcium level of less than 2.1 mmol/L and an ionized calcium level of less than 1.05 mmol/L. Severe depletion of calcium can cause *tetany* and paresthesias and can lead to convulsions. Clients at greatest risk for hypocalcemia are those whose parathyroid glands have been removed. This is frequently associated with total thyroidectomy or bilateral neck surgery for cancer (Metheny, 1996). Low serum magnesium levels (hypomagnesemia) and chronic alcoholism also increase the risk of hypocalcemia.

Hypercalcemia, or serum calcium levels greater than 2.75 mmol/L, occurs when calcium is mobilized from the bony skeleton. This may be due to malignancy or prolonged immobilization.

The risk factors, clinical manifestations, and nursing interventions related to calcium imbalances are found in Table 40.7 on page 1088.

Magnesium

The majority of magnesium (Mg^{2+}) is found intracellularly. Many organs, including nerves and muscles, depend on magnesium. Imbalances may go unrecognized in hospitalized clients. **Hypomagnesemia** occurs more frequently than hypermagnesemia. Chronic alcoholism is the most

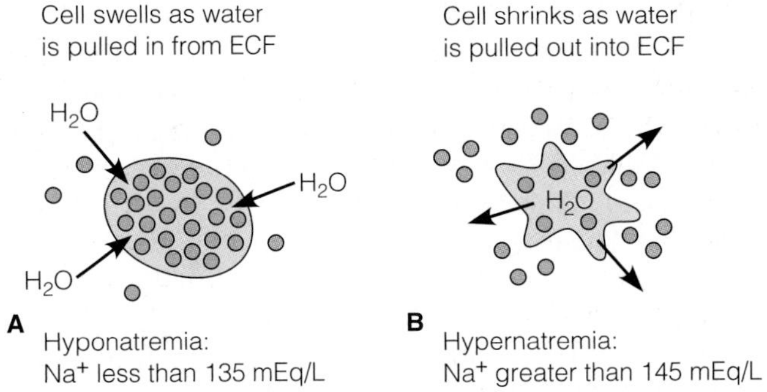

Figure 40.10 The extracellular sodium level affects cell size: *A,* in hyponatremia, cells swell; *B,* in hypernatremia, cells shrink in size

TABLE 40.7 Electrolyte Imbalances

Risk Factors	Clinical Manifestations	Nursing Interventions
Hyponatremia		
Loss of sodium: ▪ Gastrointestinal fluid loss ▪ Sweating ▪ Use of diuretics Gain of water: ▪ Hypotonic tube feedings ▪ Drinking water ▪ Excess IV D5W (dextrose in water) administration Syndrome of inappropriate ADH (SIADH): ▪ Head injury ▪ AIDS ▪ Malignant tumours	Lethargy, confusion, apprehension Muscle twitching Abdominal cramps Anorexia, nausea, vomiting Headache Seizures, coma *Laboratory findings:* Serum sodium below 135 mmol/L Serum osmolality below 280 mOsm/kg	Assess clinical manifestations. Monitor fluid intake and output. Monitor laboratory data (e.g., serum sodium). Assess client closely if administering hypertonic saline solutions. Encourage food and fluid high in sodium, if permitted (e.g., table salt, bacon, ham, processed cheese). Limit water intake, as indicated.
Hypernatremia		
Loss of fluids: ▪ Insensible water loss (hyperventilation or fever) ▪ Diarrhea Water deprivation Excess salt intake: ▪ Parenteral administration of saline solutions ▪ Hypertonic tube feedings without adequate water ▪ Excessive use of table salt (1 tsp or 5 mL contains 2,300 mg of sodium) Conditions, such as: ▪ Diabetes insipidus ▪ Heatstroke	Thirst Dry, sticky mucous membranes Tongue red, dry, swollen Weakness Postural hypotension, dyspnea Severe hypernatremia: ▪ Fatigue, restlessness ▪ Decreasing level of consciousness ▪ Disorientation ▪ Convulsions *Laboratory findings:* Serum sodium above 145 mmol/L Serum osmolality above 300 mOsm/kg	Monitor fluid intake and output. Monitor behaviour changes (e.g., restlessness, disorientation). Monitor laboratory findings (e.g., serum sodium). Encourage fluids, as ordered. Monitor diet, as ordered (eg., restrict intake of salt and foods high in sodium).

common cause of hypomagnesemia. Magnesium deficiency also may aggravate the manifestations of alcohol withdrawal, such as delirium tremens (DTs). **Hypermagnesemia** often is iatrogenic, that is, a result of overzealous magnesium therapy.

See Table 40.7 on page 1089 for risk factors, manifestations, and nursing interventions for clients with altered magesium balance.

Chloride

Because of the relationship between sodium ions and chloride ions (Cl^-), imbalances of chloride often occur in conjunction with sodium imbalances.

Hypochloremia usually is related to excess losses of chloride ions through the gastrointestinal tract, kidneys, or sweating. Hypochloremic clients are at risk for alkalosis and may experience muscle twitching, tremors, or tetany.

Conditions that cause sodium retention can lead to **hyperchloremia.** Excess replacement of sodium or potassium chloride can lead to high serum chloride levels. The manifestations of hyperchloremia include acidosis, weakness, and lethargy, with a risk of dysrhythmias and coma.

Phosphate

The phosphate anion (PO_4^-) is found in intracellular and extracellular fluid. Most of the phosphorus in the body exists as PO_4^-.

Phosphate imbalances frequently are related to therapeutic interventions for other disorders. Glucose and insulin

TABLE 40.7 Electrolyte Imbalances *continued*

Risk Factors	Clinical Manifestations	Nursing Interventions
Hypokalemia		
Loss of potassium: ▪ Vomiting and gastric suction ▪ Diarrhea ▪ Heavy perspiration Use of potassium-wasting drugs (e.g., diuretics) Poor intake of potassium (as with debilitated clients, clients with alcoholism, clients with anorexia) Hyperaldosteronism	Muscle weakness, leg cramps Fatigue, lethargy Anorexia, nausea, vomiting Decreased bowel sounds, decreased bowel motility Cardiac dysrhythmias Depressed deep-tendon reflexes *Laboratory findings:* Serum potassium below 3.5 mmol/L Arterial blood gases (ABGs) may show alkalosis T wave flattening and ST segment depression on ECG	Monitor heart rate and rhythm and ECG. Monitor clients receiving digitalis (e.g., digoxin) closely because hypokalemia increases risk of digitalis toxicity. Administer oral potassium, as ordered, with food or fluid to prevent gastric irritation. Administer diluted IV potassium solutions at a rate no faster than 10–20 mmol/hr; never administer undiluted potassium intravenously. For clients receiving IV potassium, monitor for pain and inflammation at the injection site. Teach client about potassium-rich foods. Teach clients how to prevent excessive loss of potassium (e.g., through avoiding abuse of diuretics and laxatives).
Hyperkalemia		
Decreased potassium excretion: ▪ Renal failure ▪ Hypoaldosteronism ▪ Potassium-conserving diuretics High potassium intake: ▪ Excessive use of potassium-containing salt substitutes ▪ Excessive or rapid IV infusion of potassium Potassium shift out of the tissue cells into the plasma (e.g., infections, burns, acidosis)	Gastrointestinal hyperactivity, diarrhea Irritability, apathy, confusion Cardiac dysrhythmias or arrest Muscle weakness, areflexia (absence of reflexes) Paresthesias and numbness in extremities *Laboratory findings:* Serum potassium above 5.0 mmol/L Peaked T wave, widened QRS on ECG	Closely monitor cardiac status and ECG. Administer diuretics and other medications, such as glucose and insulin, as ordered. Hold potassium supplements and potassium-conserving diuretics as ordered. Monitor serum K^+ levels carefully; a rapid drop may occur as potassium shifts into the cells. Teach clients to avoid foods high in potassium and salt substitutes.

administration and total parenteral nutrition can cause phosphate to shift into the cells from extracellular fluid compartments, leading to **hypophosphatemia.** Alcohol withdrawal, acid-base imbalances, and using antacids, such as Gelusil, Maalox, or Mylanta that bind with phosphate in the gastrointestinal tract, are other possible causes of low serum phosphate levels. Manifestations of hypophosphatemia include paresthesias, muscle weakness and pain, mental changes, and possible seizures.

Hyperphosphatemia occurs when phosphate shifts out of the cells into extracellular fluids (e.g., due to tissue trauma or chemotherapy for malignant tumours), in renal failure, or when excess phosphate is administered or ingested. Infants who are fed cow's milk are at risk for hyperphosphatemia, as are people using Fleet's phospho-soda as an enema solution or laxative (Metheny, 1996). Clients who have high serum phosphate levels may experience numbness and tingling around the mouth and in the fingertips, muscle spasms, and tetany.

Acid-Base Imbalances

Acid-base imbalances generally are classified as *respiratory* or *metabolic*. Carbonic acid levels are normally regulated by the lungs through the retention or excretion of carbon dioxide. For example, retention of CO_2 (e.g., in chronic

TABLE 40.7 Electrolyte Imbalances *continued*

Risk Factors	Clinical Manifestations	Nursing Interventions
Hypocalcemia		
Surgical removal of the parathyroid glands Conditions, such as: ■ Hypoparathyroidism ■ Acute pancreatitis ■ Hyperphosphatemia ■ Thyroid carcinoma Inadequate vitamin D intake Malabsorption Hypomagnesemia Alkalosis Sepsis Alcohol abuse	Numbness, tingling of the extremities and around the mouth Muscle tremors, cramps; if severe, can progress to tetany and convulsions Cardiac dysrhythmias; decreased cardiac output Positive Trousseau's and Chvostek's signs (see Table 40.9) Confusion, anxiety, possible psychoses Dyspnea; laryngospasm Blood clots Bone fractures ECG changes *Laboratory findings:* Serum calcium less than 2.1 mmol/L (total) or 1.05 mmol/L (ionized)	Closely monitor respiratory and cardiovascular status. Take precautions to protect a confused client. Take seizure precautions. Have equipment for intubation available. Administer oral or parenteral calcium supplements as ordered. When administering intravenously, closely monitor cardiac status and ECG during infusion. Teach clients at high risk for osteoporosis about: ■ Dietary sources rich in calcium ■ Recommendation for 1,000–1,200 mg of calcium per day ■ Calcium supplements as ordered ■ Regular exercise ■ Estrogen replacement therapy for postmenopausal women as ordered Monitor respiratory and cardiovascular status.
Hypercalcemia		
Prolonged immobilization Conditions, such as: ■ Hyperparathyroidism ■ Malignancy of the bone ■ Paget's disease	Lethargy, weakness Depressed deep-tendon reflexes Anorexia, nausea, vomiting Constipation Polyuria, hypercalciuria Flank pain secondary to urinary calculi Dysrhythmias, possible heart block Bone pain, fractures ECG changes *Laboratory findings:* Serum calcium greater than 2.75 mmol/L (total)	Increase client movement and exercise. Encourage oral fluids, as permitted, to maintain a dilute urine. Teach clients to limit intake of food and fluid high in calcium. Encourage ingestion of fibre to prevent constipation. Protect a confused client; monitor for pathological fractures in clients with long-term hypercalcemia. Encourage intake of acid-ash fluids (e.g., prune or cranberry juice) to counteract deposits of calcium salts in the urine.

obstructive pulmonary disease[COPD]) may lead to a *respiratory acidosis*, whereas "blowing off CO_2" (e.g., in hyperventilation) can lead to a *respiratory alkalosis*. Bicarbonate and hydrogen ion levels are regulated by the kidneys, and problems of regulation lead to *metabolic acidosis* or *alkalosis*. In health, the body will attempt to correct acid-base imbalances primarily through the respiratory and urinary systems, a process known as compensation.

Respiratory Acidosis

Hypoventilation and carbon dioxide retention cause carbonic acid levels to increase and the pH to fall below 7.35, a condition known as **respiratory acidosis.** Serious lung diseases, such as asthma and COPD, are common causes of respiratory acidosis. Central nervous system depression due to anesthesia or a narcotic overdose can sufficiently slow the respiratory rate so that carbon dioxide is retained.

TABLE 40.7 Electrolyte Imbalances *continued*

Risk Factors	Clinical Manifestations	Nursing Interventions
Hypomagnesemia		
Excessive loss from the gastrointestinal tract (e.g., from nasogastric suction, diarrhea, fistula drainage) Long-term use of certain drugs (e.g., diuretics, aminoglycoside antibiotics) Conditions, such as: ■ Chronic alcoholism ■ Pancreatitis ■ Burns	Neuromuscular irritability with tremors Increased reflexes, tremors, convulsions Positive Chvostek's and Trousseau's signs (see Table 40.9) Tachycardia, elevated blood pressure, dysrhythmias Disorientation and confusion Vertigo, anorexia, nausea *Laboratory findings:* Serum magnesium below 0.8 mmol/L ECG showing prolonged QT intervals, widened QRS, flat T wave; ST depression	Monitor repiratory and cardiovascular status. Assess clients receiving digitalis for digitalis toxicity. Hypomagnesemia increases the risk toxicity. Take protective measures when there is a possibility of seizures. ■ Assess the client's ability to swallow water prior to initiating oral feeding. ■ Initiate safety measures to prevent injury during seizure activity. ■ Carefully administer magnesium salts as ordered. Encourage clients to eat magnesium-rich foods, if permitted (e.g., whole grains, meat, seafood, and green leafy vegetables). Refer clients to alcohol treatment programs, as indicated.
Hypermagnesemia		
Abnormal retention of magnesium, as in: ■ Renal failure ■ Adrenal insufficiency Treatment with magnesium salts	Peripheral vasodilation, flushing Nausea, vomiting Muscle weakness, paralysis Hypotension, bradycardia Depressed deep-tendon reflexes Lethargy, drowsiness Respiratory depression, coma Respiratory and cardiac arrest, if hypermagnesemia is severe *Laboratory findings:* Serum magnesium above 1.2 mmol/L ECG showing prolonged PR and QT interval; an atrioventricular (AV) block may occur	Monitor repiratory and cardiovascular status. Monitor vital signs and level of consciousness when clients are at risk. If patellar reflexes are absent, notify the physician. Advise clients who have renal disease to contact their care provider before taking over-the-counter drugs.

When respiratory acidosis occurs, the kidneys retain bicarbonate to restore the normal carbonic acid to bicarbonate ratio. Recall, however, that the kidneys are relatively slow to respond to changes in acid-base balance, so this compensatory response may require hours to days to restore the normal pH.

Respiratory Alkalosis

When a person hyperventilates, more carbon dioxide than normal is exhaled, carbonic acid levels fall, and the pH rises to greater than 7.45. Psychogenic or anxiety-related hyperventilation is a common cause of **respiratory alkalosis.** Other causes include fever and respiratory infections. In respiratory alkalosis, the kidneys will excrete bicarbonate to return the pH to within the normal range. However, if the cause of the hyperventilation is eliminated, the pH returns to normal before renal compensation takes effect.

Metabolic Acidosis

When bicarbonate levels are low in relation to the amount of carbonic acid in the body, the pH falls and **metabolic acidosis** develops. One cause of metabolic acidosis is renal

TABLE 40.8 Acid-Base Imbalances

Risk Factors	Clinical Manifestations	Nursing Interventions
Respiratory Acidosis Acute lung conditions that impair alveolar gas exchange (e.g., pneumonia, acute pulmonary edema, aspiration of foreign body, near-drowning) Chronic lung disease (e.g., asthma, cystic fibrosis, or emphysema) Overdose of narcotics or sedatives that depress respiratory rate and depth Brain injury that affects the respiratory centre	**Acute:** Increased pulse and respiratory rates, dysrythmias Headache, dizziness Confusion, decreased level of consciousness (LOC) Convulsions Warm, flushed skin **Chronic:** Weakness Headache *Laboratory findings:* Arterial blood pH less than 7.35 $PaCO_2$ above 45 mm Hg HCO_3^- normal or slightly elevated in acute; above 28 mmol/L in chronic	Frequently assess respiratory status and lung sounds. Monitor airway and ventilation; insert artificial airway and prepare for mechanical ventilation, as necessary. Administer pulmonary therapy measures, such as inhalation therapy, percussion and postural drainage, bronchodilators, and antibiotics as ordered. Monitor fluid intake and output, vital signs, and arterial blood gases (ABGs). Administer narcotic antagonists, as indicated. Maintain adequate hydration (2–3 L of fluid per day), unless contraindicated.
Respiratory Alkalosis Hyperventilation due to: ■ Extreme anxiety ■ Elevated body temperature ■ Overventilation with a mechanical ventilator ■ Hypoxia ■ Salicylate overdose	Complaints of shortness of breath, chest tightness Light-headedness with circumoral paresthesias and numbness and tingling of the extremities Difficulty concentrating Tremulousness, blurred vision *Laboratory findings (in uncompensated respiratory alkalosis):* HCO_3^- normal Arterial blood pH above 7.45 $PaCO_2$ less than 35 mm Hg	Monitor vital signs and ABGs. Assist client to breathe more slowly. Help client breathe into a paper bag or apply a rebreather mask (to inhale CO_2). Treat underlying problem as ordered.

failure and the inability of the kidneys to excrete hydrogen ion and produce bicarbonate. Metabolic acidosis may also occur when too much acid is produced in the body, e.g., in diabetic ketoacidosis or starvation when fat tissue is broken down for energy. Metabolic acidosis stimulates the respiratory centre, and the rate and depth of respirations increase. Carbon dioxide is eliminated and carbonic acid levels fall, minimizing the change in pH. This respiratory compensation occurs within minutes of the pH imbalance.

Metabolic Alkalosis

In **metabolic alkalosis,** the amount of bicarbonate in the body exceeds the normal 20 to 1 ratio. Ingestion of bicarbonate of soda as an antacid is one cause of metabolic alkalosis. Another cause is prolonged vomiting with loss of hydrochloric acid from the stomach. The respiratory centre is depressed in metabolic alkalosis, and respirations slow and become more shallow. Carbon dioxide is retained, and carbonic acid levels increase, helping balance the excess bicarbonate.

The risk factors, manifestations, and nursing interventions for acid-base imbalances are listed in Table 40.8.

Assessing

Assessing clients for fluid, electrolyte, and acid-base balance and imbalance is an important nursing care function. Components of the assessment include (1) the nursing history, (2) physical assessment of the client, (3) clinical measurements, and (4) review of laboratory test results.

Nursing History

The nursing history is particularly important for identifying clients who are at risk for fluid, electrolyte, and acid-base imbalances. An accurate assessment will identify

TABLE 40.8 Acid-Base Imbalances *continued*

Risk Factors	Clinical Manifestations	Nursing Interventions
Metabolic Acidosis		
Conditions that increase nonvolatile acids in the blood (e.g., renal impairment, diabetes mellitus, starvation) Conditions that decrease bicarbonate (e.g., prolonged diarrhea) Excessive infusion of chloride-containing IV fluids (e.g., NaCl)	Kussmaul's respirations (deep, rapid respirations) Lethargy, confusion Headache Weakness Nausea and vomiting *Laboratory findings:* Arterial blood pH below 7.35 Serum bicarbonate less than 24 mmol/L $PaCO_2$ less than 35 mm Hg with respiratory compensation	Monitor ABG values, intake and output, LOC, and respiratory status. Administer IV sodium bicarbonate carefully, if ordered. Treat underlying problem, as ordered. Assess cardiovascular status.
Metabolic Alkalosis		
Excessive acid losses due to: ■ Vomiting ■ Gastric suction Excessive use of potassium-losing diuretics Excessive adrenal corticoid hormones due to: ■ Cushing's syndrome ■ Hyperaldosteronism Excessive bicarbonate intake from: ■ Antacids ■ Parenteral $NaHCO_3$	Decreased respiratory rate and depth Dizziness Circumoral paresthesias, numbness and tingling of the extremities Hypertonic muscles, tetany *Laboratory findings:* Arterial blood pH above 7.45 Serum bicarbonate greater than 28 mmol/L $PaCO_2$ higher than 45 mm Hg with respiratory compensation	Monitor intake and output closely. Monitor vital signs, especially respirations, LOC, and intake and output. Administer ordered IV fluids carefully. Treat underlying problem as ordered. Assess cardiovascular status.

such conditions as chronic lung disease or diabetes mellitus that can disrupt normal balances. Medications prescribed to treat acute or chronic conditions (e.g., diuretic therapy for hypertension) may place the client at risk for altered homeostasis. Functional, developmental, and socioeconomic factors must be considered in assessing the client's risk. Older people and very young children, clients who must depend on others to meet their needs for food and fluid intake, and people who cannot afford or do not have the means to cook food for a balanced diet (e.g., homeless people) are at greater risk for fluid and electrolyte imbalances. Common risk factors are listed in the box on page 1092.

When obtaining the nursing history, the nurse needs to not only recognize risk factors but also elicit data about the client's food and fluid intake, fluid output, and the presence of signs or symptoms suggestive of altered fluid and electrolyte balance. The box on page 1092 provides examples of interview questions to elicit information regarding fluid, electrolyte, and acid-base balance.

Physical Assessment

Physical assessment to evaluate a client's fluid, electrolyte, and acid-base status focuses on the skin, the oral cavity and mucous membranes, the eyes, the cardiovascular and respiratory systems, urinary and gastrointestinal systems, and neurological status. Data from this physical assessment are used to expand and verify information obtained in the nursing history. The focused physical assessment is summarized in Table 40.9; refer to Tables 40.5 through 40.8 for possible abnormal findings related to specific imbalances discussed in this chapter.

Clinical Measurements

Three simple clinical measurements that the nurse can initiate are daily weights, vital signs, and fluid intake and output.

Daily Weights

Daily weight measurements provide a relatively accurate assessment of a client's fluid status. Significant changes in

Common Risk Factors for Fluid, Electrolyte, and Acid-Base Imbalances

Chronic Diseases and Conditions

- Chronic lung disease (COPD, asthma, emphysema, cystic fibrosis)
- Heart failure
- Kidney disease
- Diabetes mellitus
- Cushing's syndrome or Addison's disease
- Cancer
- Malnutrition, anorexia nervosa, bulimia
- Ileostomy

Acute Conditions

- Acute gastroenteritis
- Bowel obstruction
- Head injury or decreased level of consciousness
- Trauma, such as burns or crushing injuries
- Surgery
- Fever, draining wounds, fistulas

Medications

- Diuretics
- Corticosteroids
- Nonsteroidal anti-inflammatory drugs (NSAIDs)
- Antibiotics
- Magnesium salts
- Antacids
- Laxatives
- Potassium

Treatments

- Chemotherapy
- IV therapy and total parenteral nutrition (TPN)
- Nasogastric suction
- Enteral feedings
- Mechanical ventilation

Other Factors

- Diet
- Age: very old or very young
- Inability to access food and fluids independently

weight over a short time (e.g., days to a week or two) are indicative of *acute* fluid changes. Each kilogram of weight gained or lost is equivalent to 1 L of fluid gained or lost. Such fluid gains or losses indicate changes in total body

ASSESSMENT INTERVIEW

Fluid, Electrolyte, and Acid-Base Balance

Current and Past Medical History

- Are you currently seeing a health-care provider for treatment of any chronic diseases, such as kidney disease, heart disease, high blood pressure, diabetes insipidus, or thyroid or parathyroid disorders?
- Have you recently experienced any acute conditions, such as gastroenteritis, severe trauma, head injury, or surgery? If so, describe them.

Medications and Treatments

- Are you currently taking any medications on a regular basis, such as diuretics, steroids, potassium supplements, salt substitutes, or antacids?
- Have you recently undergone any treatments, such as dialysis, parenteral nutrition, or tube feedings, or been on a ventilator? If so, when, and why?

Food and Fluid Intake

- How much and what type of fluids do you drink each day?
- Describe your diet for a typical day. (Pay particular attention to the client's intake of foods high in sodium content, of protein and of whole grains, fruits, and vegetables.)
- Have there been any recent changes in your food or fluid intake, for example, as a result of following a weight-loss program?
- Are you on any type of restricted diet?
- Has your food or fluid intake recently been affected by changes in appetite, nausea, or other factors, such as pain or difficulty breathing?

Fluid Output

- Have you noticed any recent changes in the frequency or amount of urine output?
- Have you recently experienced any problems with vomiting, diarrhea, or constipation? If so, when, and for how long?
- Have you noticed any other unusual fluid losses, such as excessive sweating?

Fluid, Electrolyte, and Acid-Base Imbalances

- Have you gained or lost weight in recent weeks?
- Have you recently experienced any symptoms, such as excessive thirst, dry skin or mucous membranes, dark or concentrated urine, or low urine output?
- Do you have problems with swelling of your fingers, hands, feet, or ankles? Do you ever have difficulty breathing, especially when lying down or at night? How many pillows do you use to sleep?
- Have you recently experienced any of the following symptoms: difficulty concentrating or confusion; dizziness or feeling faint; muscle weakness, twitching, cramping, or spasm; excessive fatigue; abnormal sensations, such as numbness, tingling, burning, or prickling; abdominal cramping or distention; heart palpitations?

TABLE 40.9 Focused Physical Assessment for Fluid, Electrolyte, or Acid-Base Imbalances

System	Assessment Focus	Technique	Possible Abnormal Findings
Skin	Colour, temperature, moisture	Inspection, palpation	Flushed, warm, very dry Moist or diaphoretic Cool and pale
	Turgor	Gently pinch up a fold of skin over sternum or inner aspect of thigh for adults, on the abdomen or medial thigh for children	Poor turgor: Skin remains tented for several seconds instead of immediately returning to normal position
	Edema	Inspect for visible swelling around eyes, in fingers, and in lower extremities	Skin around eyes is puffy, lids appear swollen; rings are tight; shoes leave impressions on feet
		Compress the skin over the dorsum of the foot, around the ankles, over the tibia, in the sacral area	Depression remains (pitting): see scale for describing edema in Figure 40.9
Mucous membranes	Colour, moisture	Inspection	Mucous membranes dry, dull, pale in appearance; tongue dry and cracked; edema
Eyes	Firmness	Gently palpate eyeball with lid closed	Eyeball feels soft to palpation
Fontanelles (infant)	Firmness, level	Inspect and gently palpate anterior fontanelle	Fontanelle bulging, firm Fontanelle sunken, soft
Cardiovascular system	Heart rate	Auscultation, cardiac monitor	Tachycardia, bradycardia; ECG changes; dysrhythmias
	Peripheral pulses	Palpation	Weak and thready; bounding; absent
	Blood pressure	Auscultation of Korotkoff's sounds	Hypotension; hypertension
		BP assessment lying and standing	Postural hypotension
	Capillary refill	Palpation	Slowed capillary refill
	Venous filling	Inspection of jugular veins and hand veins	Jugular venous distention; flat jugular veins; poor venous refill
Respiratory system	Respiratory rate and pattern	Inspection	Increased or decreased rate and depth of respirations; use of accessory muscles
	Lung sounds	Auscultation	Crackles or moist rales
Neurological	Level of consciousness (LOC)	Observation, stimulation Glasgow coma scale (GCS)	Decreased LOC, lethargy, stupor, or coma, change in GCS score
	Orientation, cognition	Questioning	Disoriented, confused; difficulty concentrating
	Motor function	Strength testing	Weakness, decreased motor strength
	Reflexes	Deep tendon reflex (DTR) testing	Hyperactive or depressed DTRs
	Abnormal reflexes	Chvostek's sign: Tap over facial nerve about 2 cm anterior to tragus of ear	Facial muscle twitching including eyelids and lips on side of stimulus
		Trousseau's sign: Inflate a blood pressure cuff on the upper arm to 20 mm Hg greater than the systolic pressure, leave in place for two to five minutes	Carpal spasm: contraction of hand and fingers on affected side

→

TABLE 40.9 Focused Physical Assessment for Fluid, Electrolyte, or Acid-Base Imbalances *continued*

System	Assessment Focus	Technique	Possible Abnormal Findings
Urinary and gastrointestinal systems	Intake/output	Measurement of intake of oral/parenteral fluids	Fluid intake or urinary output less than normal
		Output: urine, liquid stool, vomit, drainage from a wound, or operative site, drainage from a nasogastric tube	Excess losses from a surgical drain or vomiting
		Auscultate bowel sounds	High-pitched bowel sounds or absent bowel sounds
		Palpate bladder and abdomen	Firm bladder indicating possible distention

fluid volume, rather than in any specific compartment, such as the intravascular compartment. Rapid losses or gains of 5 to 8 percent of total body weight indicate moderate to severe fluid volume deficits or excesses.

To obtain accurate weight measurements, the nurse should balance the scale before each use and weigh the client (1) at the same time each day (e.g., before breakfast and after the first void), (2) wearing the same or similar clothing, and (3) on the same scale. The type of scale (i.e., standing, bed, chair) should be documented.

Regular assessment of weight is particularly important for clients in the community and extended-care facilities who are at risk for fluid imbalance. For these clients, measuring intake and output may be impractical because of lifestyle or problems with incontinence. Regular weight measurement, either daily, every other day, or weekly, provides valuable information about the client's fluid volume status.

Vital Signs

Changes in the vital signs may indicate, or in some cases precede, fluid, electrolyte, and acid-base imbalances. For example, elevated body temperature may be a result of dehydration or a cause of increased body fluid losses.

Tachycardia is an early sign of hypovolemia. Pulse volume will decrease in FVD and increase in FVE. Irregular pulse rates may occur with electrolyte imbalances. Changes in respiratory rate and depth may cause respiratory acid-base imbalances or act as a compensatory mechanism in metabolic acidosis or alkalosis.

Blood pressure, a sensitive measure to detect blood volume changes, may fall significantly with FVD and hypovolemia or increase with FVE. *Postural,* or *orthostatic, hypotension* may also occur with FVD and hypovolemia.

To assess for orthostatic hypotension, measure the client's baseline blood pressure and pulse in a supine position, then repeat the measurements with the client sitting and then standing. For a client who is too dizzy or weak to stand, assess supine and then sitting with legs dangling. A drop of 10 to 15 mm Hg in the systolic blood pressure with a corresponding drop in diastolic pressure and an increased pulse rate (by 10 or more beats per minute) is indicative of orthostatic or postural hypotension.

Fluid Intake and Output

The measurement and recording of all fluid intake and output (I & O) during a 24-hour period provides important data about the client's fluid and electrolyte balance. Generally, intake and output are measured for hospitalized at-risk clients (see the first box on p. 1092).

The unit used to measure intake and output is the millilitre (mL). To measure fluid intake, nurses convert household measures, such as a glass, cup, or soup bowl, to metric units. Most agencies provide conversion tables since the sizes of dishes vary from agency to agency. Such a table is often provided on or with the bedside I & O record. Examples of equivalents are given in the accompanying box.

Most agencies have a form for recording I & O, usually a bedside record on which the nurse lists all items measured and their quantities per shift (Figure 40.11). Some agencies have another form for recording the specifics of intravenous fluids, such as the type of solution, additives, time started, amounts absorbed, and amounts remaining per shift.

It is important to inform clients, family members, and all caregivers that accurate measurements of the client's fluid intake and output are required, explaining why and emphasizing the need to use a bedpan, urinal, commode, or in-toilet collection device (unless a urinary drainage system is in place). Instruct the client not to put toilet tissue into the container with urine. Clients who wish to be involved in recording fluid intake measurements need to be taught how to compute the values and what foods are considered fluids.

To measure *fluid intake,* the nurse records on the I & O form each fluid item taken (if the client has not already done so) and specifies the time and type of fluid. All of the following fluids need to be recorded:

INTAKE AND OUTPUT RECORD

PATIENT LABEL

PATIENT NAME ____________________

PATIENT # ____________________

PHYSICIAN ____________________

INTAKE						OUTPUT					
TOTAL IV	INTRAVENOUS			TUBE FEED	ORAL	TIME	URINE	NG	EMESIS	BM	MISC.
					Date:						
						6-2					
						2-10					
						10-6					
						24°					
					Date:						
						6-2					
						2-10					
						10-6					
						24°					

Figure 40.11 A sample 24-hour fluid intake and output record

Commonly Used Fluid Containers and Sample Volumes

Water glass	200 mL
Juice glass	120 mL
Cup	180 mL
Soup bowl	
Adult	180 mL
Child	100 mL
Teapot	240 mL
Creamer	
Large	90 mL
Small	30 mL
Water pitcher	1,000 mL
Jello, custard dish	100 mL
Ice cream dish	120 mL
Paper cup	
Large	200 mL
Small	120 mL

N.B.: Measurements vary with agencies.

- *Oral fluids.* These include water, milk, juice, soft drinks, coffee, tea, cream, soup, and any other beverages. Include water taken with medications. To assess the amount of water taken from a water pitcher, measure what remains and subtract this amount from the volume of the full pitcher. Then, refill the pitcher.
- *Ice chips.* Record these as fluids at approximately one half their volume.
- *Foods that are or tend to become liquid at room temperature.* These include ice cream, sherbet, custard, and gelatin (Jello). Do *not* measure foods that are pureed because purees are simply solid foods prepared in a different form.
- *Tube feedings.* Remember to include the water instilled as a rinse at the end of intermittent feedings or during continuous feedings.
- *Parenteral fluids.* The exact amount of intravenous fluid administered is to be recorded, since some fluid containers may be overfilled. Blood transfusions are included.
- *Intravenous medications.* Intravenous medications that are prepared with such solutions as normal saline (NS) and are administered as an intermittent or continuous infusion must also be included (e.g., tobramycin sulfate 80 mg in 100 mL of sterile NS). Most intravenous medications are mixed in 50 to 100 mL of solution.

- *Catheter or tube irrigants.* Fluid used to irrigate urinary catheters, nasogastric tubes, and intestinal tubes must be measured and recorded, if not immediately withdrawn.

To measure *fluid output*, measure the following fluids (remember to observe appropriate infection control precautions):

- *Urinary output.* Following each voiding, pour the urine into a measuring container, observe the amount, and record it and the time of voiding on the I & O form. For clients with retention catheters, empty the drainage bag into a measuring container at the end of the shift (or at prescribed times, if output is to be measured more often). Note and record the amount of urine output. In intensive-care areas, often, urine output is measured hourly.

  If the client is incontinent of urine, estimate and record these outputs. For example, for an incontinent client, the nurse might record "Incontinent × 3" or "Drawsheet soaked in 30-cm diameter." A more accurate estimate of the urine output of infants and incontinent clients may be obtained by first weighing diapers or incontinent pads that are dry, and then subtracting this weight from the weight of the soiled items. Each gram of weight left after subtracting is equal to 1 mL of urine. If urine is frequently soiled with feces, the number of voidings may be recorded, rather than the volume of urine.
- *Vomitus and liquid feces.* The amount and type of fluid and the time need to be specified.
- *Tube drainage*, such as gastric or intestinal drainage.
- *Wound drainage* and *draining fistulas.* Wound drainage may be recorded by documenting the type and number of dressings or linen saturated with drainage or by measuring the exact amount of drainage collected in a vacuum drainage (e.g., Hemovac) or gravity drainage system.

Fluid intake and output measurements are totaled at the end of the shift (every eight to 12 hours), and the totals are recorded in the client's permanent record. In intensive-care areas, the nurse may record intake and output more frequently. Usually, the nurses on night shift total the amounts of I & O recorded for each shift and record the 24-hour total.

To determine whether the fluid output is proportional to fluid intake or whether there are any changes in the client's fluid status, the nurse (1) compares the total 24-hour fluid output measurement with the total fluid intake measurement, and (b) compares both with previous measurements. Urinary output is normally equivalent to the amount of fluids ingested; the usual range is 1,500 to 2,000 mL in 24 hours, or 30 to 50 mL in one hour. Clients whose output substantially exceeds intake are at risk for fluid volume deficit. By contrast, clients whose intake substantially exceeds output are at risk for fluid volume excess. In assessing the client's fluid balance, it is important to consider additional factors that may affect intake and output. The client who is extremely diaphoretic or who has rapid, deep respirations has fluid losses that cannot be measured but must be considered in evaluating fluid status.

When there is a significant discrepancy between intake and output or when fluid intake or output is inadequate (for example, a urine output of less than 500 mL in 24 hours or less than 30 mL per hour in an adult), this information should be reported.

Laboratory Tests

Many laboratory studies are conducted to determine the client's fluid, electrolyte, and acid-base status. Some of the more common tests are discussed here.

Serum Electrolytes

Serum electrolyte levels are often routinely ordered for any client admitted to hospital as a screening test for electrolyte and acid-base imbalances. Serum electrolytes also are routinely assessed for clients at risk in the community, for example, clients who are being treated with a diuretic for hypertension or congestive heart failure. The most commonly ordered serum tests are for sodium, potassium, chloride, and bicarbonate ions. Normal values of commonly measured electrolytes are shown in the accompanying box.

Normal Electrolyte Values for Adults*

Venous blood	
Sodium	135–145 mmol/L
Potassium	3.5–5.0 mmol/L
Chloride	95–105 mmol/L
Calcium (total)	2.1–2.55 mmol/L
Calcium (ionized)	1.05–1.30 mmol/L
Magnesium	0.8–1.2 mmol/L
Phosphate (phosphorus)	0.84–1.45 mmol/L
Serum osmolality	280–300 mmol/kg water

*Normal laboratory values vary from agency to agency.

Complete Blood Count (CBC)

A basic screening test known as a complete blood count (CBC) provides information about the hematocrit. The **hematocrit** measures the volume (percentage) of whole blood that is composed of red blood cells (RBCs). Because the hematocrit is a measure of the volume of cells in relation to plasma, it is affected by changes in plasma volume. Thus, the hematocrit increases with severe dehydration and decreases with severe overhydration. Normal hematocrit values are 40 to 54 percent (males) and 37 to 47 percent (females).

Osmolality

Serum osmolality is a measure of the solute concentration of the blood. The solutes included are sodium ions, chloride, bicarbonate, proteins, glucose, and blood urea nitrogen (BUN). Serum osmolality can be estimated by doubling the serum sodium because sodium and its associated chloride ions are the major determinants of serum osmolality. Serum osmolality values are used primarily to evaluate fluid balance. Normal values are 280 to 300 mmol/kg. An increase in serum osmolality indicates a fluid volume deficit; a decrease reflects a fluid volume excess.

Urine osmolality is a measure of the solute concentration of urine. The particles included are nitrogenous wastes, such as creatinine, urea, and uric acid. Normal values are 500 to 800 mmol/kg. An increased urine osmolality indicates a fluid volume deficit; a decreased urine osmolality reflects a fluid volume excess.

Urine pH

Measurement of urine pH may be obtained by laboratory analysis or by using a dipstick on a freshly voided specimen. Because the kidneys play a critical role in regulating acid-base balance, assessment of urine pH can be useful in determining whether the kidneys are responding appropriately to acid-base imbalances. Normally, the pH of the urine is relatively acidic, averaging about 6, but a range of 4.6 to 8 is considered normal. In metabolic acidosis, urine pH decreases as the kidneys excrete hydrogen ions; in metabolic alkalosis, the pH increases.

Urine Specific Gravity

Specific gravity is an indicator of urine concentration that can be performed quickly and easily. Normal specific gravity ranges from 1.005 to 1.030 (usually 1.010 to 1.025). When the concentration of solutes in the urine is high, the specific gravity rises; in very dilute urine with few solutes, it is abnormally low.

Arterial Blood Gases

Arterial blood gases (ABGs) are performed to evaluate the client's acid-base balance and oxygenation. Arterial blood is used because it provides a truer reflection of gas exchange in the pulmonary system. Blood gases may be drawn by laboratory technicians, respiratory therapy personnel, or nurses with specialized training. Because a high-pressure artery is used to obtain blood, it is important to apply pressure to the puncture site for at least five minutes after the procedure to reduce the risk of bleeding or bruising.

Six measurements are commonly performed in arterial blood gas tests:

1. pH, a measure of the relative acidity or alkalinity of the blood
2. PaO_2, the partial pressure exerted by oxygen dissolved in the plasma of arterial blood; an indirect measure of blood oxygen content
3. $PaCO_2$, the partial pressure of carbon dioxide in arterial plasma; the respiratory component of acid-base determination
4. Bicarbonate (HCO_3^-), a measure of the metabolic component of acid-base balance
5. Base excess (BE), a calculated value of bicarbonate levels, also reflective of the metabolic component of acid-base balance
6. Oxygen saturation (SaO_2), the percentage of hemoglobin saturated (combined) with oxygen

Normal ABG values are listed in the box below. When evaluating ABG results to determine acid-base balance, it is important to use a systematic approach. Changes seen in common acid-base imbalances are summarized in Table 40.10. Note that SaO_2 is important for assessing respiratory status, but it does not provide useful information for assessing acid-base balance and is not included in this table.

Nurses need to assess each measurement individually and then look at the interrelationships to determine what type of acid-base imbalance may be present.

Normal Values of Arterial Blood Gases (ABGs)*

pH	7.35–7.45
PaO_2	80–100 mm Hg
$PaCO_2$	35–45mm Hg
HCO_3^-	24–28 mmol/L
Base excess	−2 to +2 mmol/L
O_2 saturation	95–98%

*Normal laboratory values vary from agency to agency.

Diagnosing

NANDA (2001) nursing diagnoses that relate to fluid and acid-base imbalances include the following:

- ***Fluid Volume Deficient:*** The state in which an individual who is not NPO experiences or is at risk of experiencing decreased intravascular, interstitial, and/or intracellular dehydration. This refers to dehydration—water loss alone without a change in sodium.
- ***Fluid Volume Excess:*** The state in which an individual experiences or is at risk of experiencing intracellular or interstitial fluid overload.
- ***Risk for Fluid Volume Imbalance:*** A state in which an individual is at risk of a decrease, increase, or rapid shift from one to the other of intravascular, interstitial, and/or intracellular fluid.
- ***Impaired Gas Exchange:*** Excess or deficit in oxygenation and/or carbon dioxide elimination at the alveolar-capillary membrane.

TABLE 40.10 Step Guide: What Is the Acid-Base Imbalance?

Respiratory Disturbances

Four-step guide to determine the respiratory disturbance based on laboratory findings
Ask the following questions:

Questions	Examples	General Rule
1. What is the pH? pH < 7.35 indicates acidosis pH > 7.45 indicates alkalosis 2. What is the $PaCO_2$? $PaCO_2$ > 45 indicates acidosis $PaCO_2$ < 35 indicates alkalosis 3. What is the HCO_3? HCO_3^- < 24 indicates acidosis HCO_3^- > 28 indicates alkalosis 4. Check the terms that are the same.	**Example 1** pH 7.34 → **acidosis √** $PaCO_2$ 50 → **acidosis √** HCO_3^- 29 → alkalosis **Respiratory acidosis √** **Example 2** pH 7.49 → **alkalosis √** $PaCO_2$ 30 → **alkalosis √** HCO_3^- 22 → acidosis **Respiratory alkalosis √**	General Rule When the pH indicates: **acidosis,** and it is checked against **$PaCO_2$,** the condition is **respiratory acidosis** **alkalosis,** and it is checked against **$PaCO_2$,** the condition is **respiratory alkalosis**

Metabolic Disturbances

Four-step guide to determine the metabolic disturbance based on laboratory findings
Ask the following questions:

Questions	Examples	General Rule
1. What is the pH? pH < 7.35 indicates acidosis pH > 7.45 indicates alkalosis 2. What is the $PaCO_2$? $PaCO_2$ > 45 indicates acidosis $PaCO_2$ < 35 indicates alkalosis 3. What is the HCO_3? HCO_3^- < 24 indicates acidosis HCO_3^- > 28 indicates alkalosis 4. Check the terms that are the same.	**Example 1** pH 7.26 → **acidosis √** $PaCO_2$ 34 → alkalosis HCO_3^- 22 → **acidosis √** **Metabolic acidosis √** **Example 2** pH 7.48 → **alkalosis √** $PaCO_2$ 46 → acidosis HCO_3^- 30 → **alkalosis √** **Metabolic alkalosis √**	General rule When the pH indicates: **acidosis,** and it is checked against **HCO_3^-,** the condition is **metabolic acidosis** **alkalosis,** and it is checked against **HCO_3^-,** the condition is **metabolic alkalosis**

Note: In clinical practice, the values may not be quite as clear as in the examples above. This is because compensation may be taking place in an attempt to correct the abnormal values caused by the primary condition.

Source: Adapted from Rankin, J. A. (2000). Unit 6. Fluid and electrolytes. In: J. A. Rankin, M. A. Reimer & K. L. Then (Eds.), *Nursing: 461 Pathophysiology Module*. Faculty of Nursing, University of Calgary.

Clinical applications of these diagnoses are shown in Table 40.11.

Fluid, electrolyte, and acid-base imbalances affect many other body areas and, as a consequence, may be the etiology of many other nursing diagnoses, such as:

- ***Impaired Oral Mucous Membrane*** related to fluid volume deficit
- ***Impaired Skin Integrity*** related to dehydration and/or edema
- ***Decreased Cardiac Output*** related to hypovolemia
- ***Altered Tissue Perfusion*** related to decreased cardiac output secondary to fluid volume deficit
- ***Altered Tissue Perfusion*** related to edema
- ***Decreased Cardiac Output*** related to cardiac dysrhythmias secondary to electrolyte imbalance (K^+)
- ***Activity Intolerance*** related to hypervolemia
- ***Risk for Injury*** related to calcium shift out of bones into extracellular fluids
- ***Acute Confusion*** related to electrolyte imbalance

TABLE 40.11 Clinical Application: Assessment Data Clusters and Related Nursing Diagnoses

Data Cluster	Nursing Diagnosis
Merlyn Chapman, a 27-year-old salesclerk, reports weakness, malaise, and flu-like symptoms for three to four days. Although thirsty, she is unable to tolerate fluids because of nausea and vomiting, and she has liquid stools two to four times per day. Physical findings indicate dry oral mucosa, furrowed tongue, cracked lips, mild fever (38.6°C), and scanty concentrated urine output (specific gravity 1.035).	***Fluid Volume Deficient*** related to poor fluid intake, vomiting, and diarrhea for three to four days
Luella Fisher, a frail 93-year-old with congestive heart failure, uses a daily diuretic (furosemide). She has recently had a stroke that impairs her swallowing. A gastric tube and urinary catheter are in place. Appetite is poor.	***Risk for Fluid Volume Deficient*** related to inadequate fluid intake and diuretic therapy
Tom Bricker, a 67-year-old pensioner who has a history of heart disease, has experienced a weight gain of 4 to 5 kg over the past month. He states his rings are too tight to remove, his ankles are swollen, his heart pounds at times, he gets breathless with exertion, and he feels bloated. Physical findings reveal jugular vein distention above 3 cm, delayed emptying of hand veins, bounding pulse (86), pitting edema in feet, ankles, and lower legs, and moist lung sounds (rales).	***Fluid Volume Excess*** related to sodium and water retention secondary to decreased cardiac output
Fred Boysniak was admitted to emergency after being found with an empty bottle of morphine tablets by his bed. He appears very lethargic and stuporous; pulse is 120, respirations 12 and very shallow. Blood gases reveal pH of 7.28, $PaCO_2$ 49 mm Hg, and HCO_3^- 25 mmol/L.	***Impaired Gas Exchange*** related to hypoventilation secondary to overdose of respiratory depressant drug

HOME CARE ASSESSMENT

Fluid, Electrolyte, and Acid-Base Balance

Client

- *Risk factors for imbalances:* The client's age, medications required, such as diuretic therapy or corticosteroids, and presence of chronic diseases, such as diabetes mellitus, heart disease, lung disease, or dementia (see " Risk Factors" on p. 1092)
- *Self-care abilities for maintaining food and fluid intake:* Mobility; ability to chew and swallow, to access fluids and respond to thirst, to purchase food and prepare a balanced diet
- *Current level of knowledge (as appropriate) about:* Prescribed diet, any fluid restrictions, activity restrictions, actions and side effects of prescribed medications, regular weight monitoring, gastric tube care and enteral feedings, central line or PICC catheter care, and parenteral fluids and nutrition

Family

- *Caregiver availability, skills, and responses:* Availability and willingness to assume responsibility for care, knowledge and ability to provide assistance with preparing food and maintaining adequate intake of food and fluids, knowledge of risk factors and early warning signs of problems
- *Family role changes and coping:* Effect on financial status, parenting and spousal roles, social roles
- *Alternative potential primary or respite caregivers:* For example, other family members, volunteers, church members, paid caregivers or housekeeping services; available community care (e.g., adult day care), senior centres

Community

- *Current knowledge of and experience with community resources:* Home care agencies, organizations that offer financial assistance or assistance with food preparation, Meals-on-Wheels or meal services (e.g., at senior centres, homeless shelters), pharmacies, home intravenous services, respiratory care services

Planning

When planning care, the nurse identifies nursing interventions that will assist the client to achieve these broad goals:

- Maintain or restore normal fluid balance
- Maintain or restore normal balance of electrolytes in the intracellular and extracellular compartments
- Maintain or restore pulmonary ventilation and oxygenation
- Prevent associated risks (tissue breakdown, decreased cardiac output, confusion, other neurological signs)
- Maintain or repair renal function

Obviously, goals will vary according to the diagnosis and defining characteristics for each individual. Examples of desired outcomes related to these goals, although established in the planning phase, are shown in Table 40.16 in the "Evaluating" section of this chapter.

Examples of Nursing Interventions Classification (NIC) related to fluid, electrolyte, and acid-base balance include (McCloskey & Bulechek, 2000) the following:

- Acid-base management
- Electrolyte management
- Fluid monitoring
- Hypovolemia management
- Intravenous (IV) therapy

Specific nursing activities associated with each of these interventions can be selected to meet the individual needs of the client. A sample care plan using NIC interventions and activities is provided on page 1127.

Nursing activities to meet goals and outcomes related to fluid, electrolyte, and acid-base imbalances are discussed in the next section. These include (1) monitoring fluid intake and output, cardiovascular and respiratory status, and results of laboratory tests; (2) assessing the client's weight; location and extent of edema, if present; skin turgor and skin status; specific gravity of urine; level of consciousness and mental status; (3) fluid intake modifications; (4) dietary changes; (5) parenteral fluid, electrolyte, and blood replacement; and (6) other appropriate measures, such as administering prescribed medications and oxygen, providing skin care and oral hygiene, positioning the client appropriately, and scheduling rest periods.

Planning for Home Care

To provide for continuity of care, the client's needs for assistance with care in the home need to be considered. Home care planning includes assessment of the client's and family's resources and abilities for care, and the need for referrals and home health services. The box on page 1099 describes the specific assessment data required to establish a home care plan. On the basis of the data gathered in assessment of the home situation, the nurse individualizes the teaching plan for the client and family (see the Wellness Teaching box and also the Home Care Teaching Guide box that follow).

Implementing

Promoting Wellness

Most people rarely think about their fluid, electrolyte, or acid-base balance. They know it is important to drink adequate fluids and consume a balanced diet, but they may not understand the potential effects when this is not done. Nurses can promote clients' health by providing wellness teaching that will help them maintain fluid and electrolyte balance. See the following box for wellness teaching related to fluid and electrolyte balance.

Enteral Fluid and Electrolyte Replacement

Fluids and electrolytes can be provided orally in the home and hospital if the client's health permits, that is, if the client is not vomiting, has not experienced an excessive fluid loss, and has an intact gastrointestinal tract and gag and swallow reflexes. Clients who are unable to ingest solid foods may be able to ingest fluids.

WELLNESS TEACHING

Promoting Fluid and Electrolyte Balance

- Consume 2000 to 2500 mL of water daily, unless contraindicated.
- Avoid excess amounts of foods or fluids high in salt, sugar, and caffeine.
- Eat a well-balanced diet. Include adequate amounts of milk or milk products to maintain bone calcium levels.
- Limit alcohol intake as it has a diuretic effect.
- Increase fluid intake before, during, and after strenuous exercise, particularly when the environmental temperature is high, and replace lost electrolytes from excessive perspiration, as needed, with commercial electrolyte solutions.
- Maintain normal body weight.
- Learn about and monitor side effects of medications that affect fluid and electrolyte balance (e.g., diuretics) and ways to handle side effects.
- Recognize possible risk factors for fluid and electrolyte imbalance, such as prolonged or repeated vomiting, frequent watery stools, or inability to consume fluids because of illness.
- Seek prompt professional health care for noticeable signs of fluid imbalance, such as sudden weight gain or loss, decreased urine volume, swollen ankles, shortness of breath, dizziness, or confusion.

HOME CARE TEACHING GUIDE

Fluid, Electrolyte, and Acid-Base Balance

Monitoring Fluid Intake and Output

- Teach the client and family, as appropriate, how to monitor fluid intake and output, including using a commode or collection device ("hat") in the toilet, emptying and measuring urinary catheter drainage, or counting or weighing diapers.
- Instruct the client and family to monitor weight on a regular basis at the same time of day, using the same scale, and with the client wearing the same amount of clothing after voiding.
- Inform the client and family when to contact a health-care professional, such as in the cases of a significant change in urine output; any change of 2.5 kg or more in a one- to two-week period; prolonged episodes of vomiting, diarrhea, or inability to eat or drink; dry, sticky mucous membranes; extreme thirst; swollen fingers, feet, ankles, or legs; difficulty breathing, shortness of breath, rapid heartbeat; and changes in behaviour or mental status.

Maintaining Food and Fluid Intake

- Instruct the client and family about any diet or fluid restrictions, such as a low-sodium diet. Contact a dietitian to provide appropriate teaching.
- Teach family members the importance of offering fluids regularly to clients who are unable to meet their own needs because of age, impaired mobility or cognition, or other conditions.
- If the client is on enteral or intravenous fluids (parenteral) and feeding at home, teach caregivers about proper administration and care. Contact a home care or home intravenous service to provide services and teaching.

Safety

- Instruct the client to change positions slowly, if appropriate, especially when moving from a supine to a sitting or standing position.
- Inform the client and family about the importance of good mouth and skin care. Teach the client to change positions frequently and to elevate the feet on a stool when sitting for a long period.
- Teach the client and family how to care for intravenous access sites or gastric tubes. Include instructions about what to do if tubes become dislodged.

Medications

- Emphasize the importance of taking medications as prescribed.
- Instruct clients taking diuretics to take the medication in the morning. If a second daily dose is prescribed, they should take it in the late afternoon to avoid disrupting sleep in order to urinate.
- Inform clients about any expected side effects of prescribed medications and how to handle them (e.g., if a potassium-depleting diuretic is prescribed, increase intake of potassium-rich foods; if taking a potassium-sparing diuretic, avoid excess potassium intake, such as using salt substitute).
- Teach clients when to contact their primary-care provider, for example, if they are unable to take a prescribed medication or have signs of an allergic or toxic reaction to a medication.

Measures Specific to Client's Problem

- Provide instructions specific to the client's fluid, electrolyte, or acid-base imbalance, such as:
  a. Fluid volume deficit
  b. Risk for fluid volume deficit (See Table 40.5)
  c. Fluid volume excess (See Table 40.6)

Referrals

- Make appropriate referrals to home care or community social services for assistance with resources, such as meal preparation and food, intravenous infusions and access, enteral feedings, and homemaker or home health aide services to help with ADLs.

Community Agencies and Other Sources of Help

- Provide information about companies or agencies that can provide durable medical equipment, such as commodes, lift chairs, or hospital beds, for purchase, for rental, or free of charge.
- Provide a list of sources for supplies, such as catheters and drainage bags, measuring devices, tube feeding formulas, and electrolyte replacement drinks.
- Suggest additional sources of information and help, such as the local hospital dietician.

Fluid Intake Modifications

Increased fluids (ordered as "push fluids") are often prescribed for clients with actual or potential fluid volume deficits arising, for example, from mild diarrhea or mild to moderate fevers. Guidelines for helping clients increase fluid intake are shown in the box below.

Restricted fluids may be necessary for clients who have fluid retention (fluid volume excess) as a result of renal failure, congestive heart failure, syndrome of inappropriate antidiuretic hormone (SIADH), or other disease processes. Fluid restrictions vary from "nothing by mouth" to a precise amount ordered by a physician. The restriction of fluids can be difficult for some clients, particularly if they are experiencing thirst. Guidelines for helping clients restrict fluid intake are shown in the box below.

Dietary Changes

Specific fluid and electrolyte imbalances may require simple dietary changes. For example, clients receiving potassium-depleting diuretics need to be informed about foods with a high potassium content (e.g., bananas, oranges, and leafy greens). Some clients with fluid retention need to avoid foods high in sodium. Most healthy clients can benefit from foods rich in calcium.

CLINICAL GUIDELINES

Facilitating Fluid Intake

- Explain to the client the reason for the required intake and the specific amount needed. This provides a rationale for the requirement and promotes compliance.
- Establish a 24-hour plan for the client for ingesting the fluids. For the hospitalized or long-term care client, half the total volume is given during the day shift, and the other half is divided between the evening and night shifts, with most of that ingested during the evening shift. For example, if 2,500 mL is to be ingested in 24 hours, the plan may specify 7–3 (1,250 mL); 3–11 (1,000 mL); and 11–7 (250 mL). The client should try to avoid the ingestion of large amounts of fluid immediately before bedtime to prevent the need to urinate during sleeping hours.
- Set short-term outcomes that the client can realistically meet. Examples include ingesting a glass of fluid every hour while awake or a pitcher of water by 12 noon.
- Identify fluids the client likes, and make available a variety of those items, including fruit juices, soft drinks, and milk (if allowed). Remember that such beverages as coffee and tea have a diuretic effect, so their consumption should be limited.
- Help clients to select foods that tend to become liquid at room temperature (e.g., gelatin, ice cream, sherbet), if these are allowed.
- For clients who are confined to bed, supply appropriate cups, glasses, and straws to facilitate appropriate fluid intake and keep the fluids within easy reach.
- Make sure fluids are served at the appropriate temperature: hot fluids hot, and cold fluids cold.
- Encourage clients, when possible, to participate in maintaining the fluid intake record. This helps them evaluate the achievement of desired outcomes.
- Be alert for the cultural implications of food and fluids. Some cultures may restrict certain foods and fluids and view others as having healing properties.

CLINICAL GUIDELINES

Helping Clients Restrict Fluid Intake

- Explain the reason for the restricted intake and how much and what types of fluids are permitted orally. Many clients need to be informed that ice chips, gelatin, and ice cream, for example, are considered fluid.
- Help the client decide the amount of fluid to be taken with each meal, between meals, before bedtime, and with medications. For the hospitalized or long-term care client, half the total volume is scheduled during the day shift when the client is most active, receives two meals, and takes most oral medications. A large part of the remainder is scheduled for the evening shift to permit fluids with meals and while having visitors during the evening.
- Identify fluids or fluidlike substances the client likes, and make sure that these are provided, unless contraindicated. A client who is allowed only 200 mL of fluid for breakfast, for example, should receive the type of fluid the client favours.
- Set short-term goals that make the fluid restriction more tolerable. For example, schedule a specified amount of fluid at one- or two-hourly intervals between meals. Some clients may prefer fluids only between meals if the food provided at mealtime helps relieve thirst.
- Place allowed fluids in small containers, such as a 120-mL juice glass to allow the perception of a full container.
- Periodically offer the client ice chips as an alternative to water because ice chips, when melted, are approximately half the frozen volume.
- Provide frequent mouth care and rinses to reduce the thirst sensation.
- Instruct the client to avoid ingesting or chewing salty or sweet foods (hard candy or gum) because these foods tend to produce thirst. Sugarless gum may be an alternative for some clients.
- Encourage the client, when possible, to participate in maintaining the fluid intake record.

TABLE 40.12 Selected Intravenous Solutions

Type/Examples	Comments/Nursing Implications
Isotonic Solutions	
0.9% NaCl (normal saline) Lactated Ringer's (a balanced electrolyte solution)	Isotonic solutions, such as NS and lactated Ringer's, initially remain in the vascular compartment, expanding vascular volume. Assess clients carefully for signs of hypervolemia, such as bounding pulse and shortness of breath.
5% dextrose in water (D5W)	D5W is isotonic on initial administration but provides free water when dextrose is metabolized, expanding intracellular and extracellular fluid volumes. D5W is avoided in clients at risk for increased intracranial pressure (IICP) because it can increase cerebral edema.
Hypotonic Solutions	
0.45% NaCl (half normal saline) 0.33% NaCl (one-third normal saline)	Hypotonic solutions are used to provide free water and treat cellular dehydration. These solutions promote waste elimination by the kidneys. Do not administer to clients at risk for IICP or third-space fluid shift.
Hypertonic Solutions	
5% dextrose in normal saline (D5NS) 5% dextrose in 0.45% NaCl (D5 1/2NS) 5% dextrose in lactated Ringer's (D5LR)	Hypertonic solutions draw fluid out of the intracellular and interstitial compartments into the vascular compartment, expanding vascular volume. Do not administer to clients with kidney or heart disease or clients who are dehydrated. Watch for signs of hypervolemia.

Oral Electrolyte Supplements

Clients can benefit from oral supplements of electrolytes, particularly when a medication that affects electrolyte balance is prescribed. Supplements may also be used when dietary intake is inadequate for a specific electrolyte or when fluid and electrolyte losses are excessive as a result of excessive perspiration.

Corticosteroids and many diuretics can cause too much potassium to be eliminated through the kidneys. For clients taking these medications, potassium supplements may be prescribed. Instruct clients taking oral potassium supplements to take the medication with juice to mask the unpleasant taste and reduce the possibility of gastric distress.

Emphasize the importance of taking the medication as prescribed and seeing their primary-care provider on a regular basis. Because hyperkalemia can have serious cardiac effects, clients should never increase the amount of potassium being taken without a physician's order to do so. In addition, inform clients that most salt substitutes contain a salt of potassium, so it is important to consult with the primary-care provider before using salt substitutes.

People who ingest insufficient milk and milk products benefit from calcium supplements. The recommended daily allowance for calcium is 1,000 to 1,500 mg (Metheny, 1996). A supplement of 1,000 mg per day may be ordered for some clients, such as postmenopausal women, to reduce the risk of osteoporosis. Long-term use of corticosteroid drugs can also cause calcium loss from the bone, and calcium supplements may help reduce this loss. Clients who are predisposed to developing renal calculi and who take supplemental calcium need to maintain a fluid intake of at least 2,500 mL per day (unless contraindicated) to reduce the risk of kidney stones.

Although routine supplements for other electrolytes generally are not recommended, clients who have poor dietary habits, who are malnourished, or who have difficulty accessing or eating fresh fruits and vegetables may benefit from electrolyte supplements. A daily multiple vitamin with minerals may achieve the desired goal. People who engage in activities that result in excessive perspiration need to replace the water and electrolytes that are lost. Water and electrolytes can be replaced by consuming commercial sports drinks.

Parenteral Fluid and Electrolyte Replacement

Intravenous (IV) fluid therapy is essential when clients are unable to take food and fluids orally. It is an efficient and effective method of supplying fluids directly into the intravascular fluid compartment and replacing electrolyte losses.

Intravenous Solutions

Intravenous solutions can be classified as isotonic, hypotonic, or hypertonic. Most IV solutions are *isotonic*, having the same concentration of solutes as blood plasma. Isotonic solutions are often used to restore vascular volume. *Hypertonic* solutions have a greater concentration of solutes than plasma; *hypotonic* solutions have a lesser concentration of solutes. Table 40.12 provides examples of IV solutions and nursing implications.

IV solutions can also be categorized according to their purpose. *Nutrient solutions* contain some form of carbohydrate and water. Water is supplied for fluid requirements and carbohydrate for calories and energy. For example, 1 L of 5 percent dextrose provides 170 calories. Nutrient solutions are useful in preventing dehydration and ketosis but do not provide sufficient calories to promote wound healing, weight gain, or normal growth in children. Common nutrient solutions are 5 percent dextrose in water (D5W) and 5 percent dextrose in 0.45 percent sodium chloride (dextrose in half-strength saline).

Electrolyte solutions contain varying amounts of cations and anions. Normal saline (0.9 percent sodium chloride), Ringer's (contains sodium, chloride, potassium, and calcium), and lactated Ringer's (contains sodium, chloride, potassium, calcium, and lactate) are solutions that are commonly used for fluid and electrolyte replacement. Lactate is metabolized in the liver to form bicarbonate (HCO_3^-). Saline and balanced electrolyte solutions are used to restore vascular volume. They also may be used to replace fluid and electrolytes for clients with continuing losses, for example, because of gastric suction or wound drainage.

Lactated Ringer's solution is an *alkalinizing solution* that may be given to treat metabolic acidosis. *Acidifying solutions*, in contrast, are administered to counteract metabolic alkalosis. Examples of acidifying solutions are 5 percent dextrose in 0.45 percent sodium chloride and 0.9 percent sodium chloride solution.

CLINICAL GUIDELINES

Vein Selection

- Use distal veins of the arm first.
- Use the client's nondominant arm, whenever possible.
- Select a vein that is
  - Easily palpated and feels soft and full
  - Naturally splinted by bone
  - Large enough to allow adequate circulation around the catheter
- Avoid using veins that are
  - In areas of flexion (e.g., the antecubital fossa)
  - Highly visible, because they tend to roll away from the needle
  - Damaged by previous use, phlebitis, infiltration, or sclerosis
  - Continually distended with blood, or knotted or tortuous
  - In a surgically compromised or injured extremity (e.g., following a mastectomy) because of possible impaired circulation and discomfort for the client

Volume expanders are used to increase the blood volume following severe loss of blood (e.g., from hemorrhage) or loss of plasma (e.g., from severe burns, which draw large amounts of plasma from the bloodstream to the burn site). Examples of volume expanders are dextran, plasma, and human serum albumin.

Venipuncture Sites

The site chosen for venipuncture varies with the client's age, the length of time the infusion is to run, the type of solution used, and the condition of veins. For adults, veins in the hand and arm are commonly used; for infants, veins in the scalp and dorsal foot are often used. Larger veins are preferred for infusions that need to be given rapidly and for solutions that could be irritating (e.g., certain medications).

The metacarpal, basilic, and cephalic veins are commonly used for intermittent or continuous infusions (Figure 40.12, *B*). The ulna and radius act as natural splints at these sites, and the client has greater freedom of arm movements for activities, such as eating. Although the basilic and median cubital veins in the antecubital space are convenient sites for venipuncture, they are usually used for obtaining blood samples, bolus injections of medication, and insertion sites for a peripherally inserted central catheter (PICC) line (see Figure 40.12, *A*). See the previous box for clinical guidelines for vein selection.

When long-term IV therapy or parenteral nutrition is anticipated, or the client is receiving IV medications that are damaging to vessels (e.g., chemotherapy), a **central venous catheter** may be inserted. Central venous catheters usually are inserted into the subclavian or jugular vein, with the distal tip of the catheter resting in the superior vena cava just above the right atrium (Figure 40.13). They may be inserted at the client's bedside or for longer-term access, surgically inserted. Subclavian central venous catheters permit freedom of movement for ambulation; however, there is a risk of pneumothorax on **catheter insertion.** Assess the client closely for manifestations, such as shortness of breath, chest pain, cough, hypotension, tachycardia, and anxiety, after the insertion procedure.

With a **peripherally inserted central venous catheter (PICC),** the catheter is inserted in the basilic or cephalic vein just above or below the antecubital space of the right arm. The tip of the catheter rests in the superior vena cava. The risk of pneumothorax is eliminated with PICC. These catheters frequently are used for long-term intravenous access when the client will be managing IV therapy at home.

Implantable venous access devices or *ports* (Figure 40.14) are used for clients with chronic illness who require long-term IV therapy (e.g., intermittent medications, such as chemotherapy, total parenteral nutrition, and frequent blood samples). The device is designed to provide repeated access to the central venous system, avoiding the trauma and complications of multiple venipunctures. Using local anesthesia, implantable ports are surgically placed into a

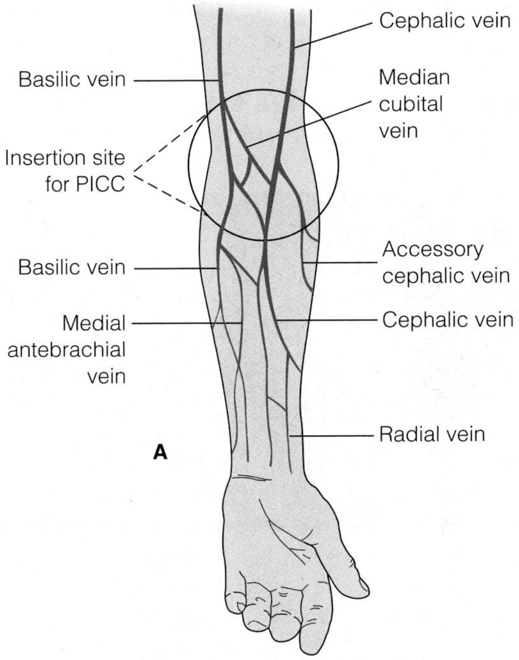

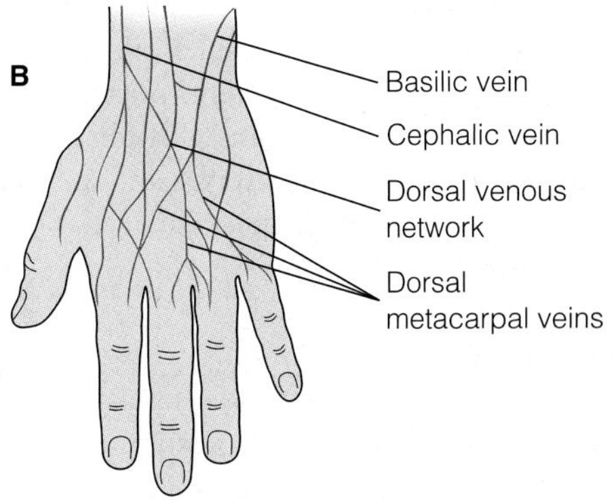

Figure 40.12 Commonly used venipuncture sites: *A,* arm; *B,* hand
A, also shows the site used for a peripherally inserted central catheter (PICC)

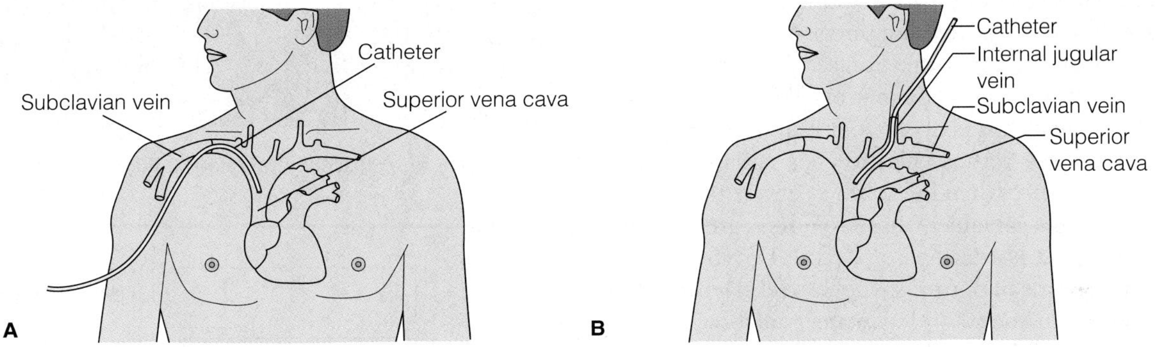

Figure 40.13 Central venous lines: *A,* subclavian vein insertion; *B,* left jugular insertion

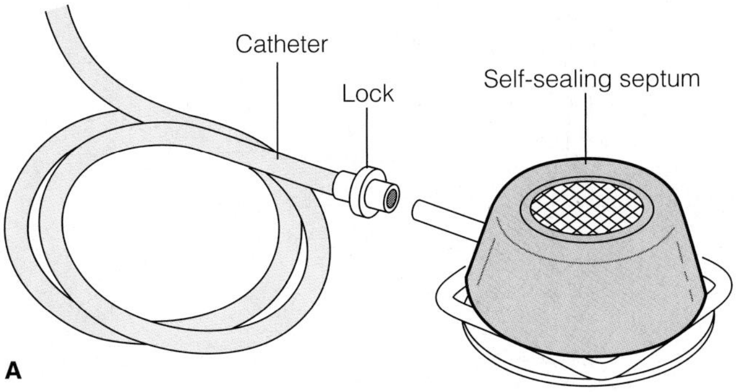

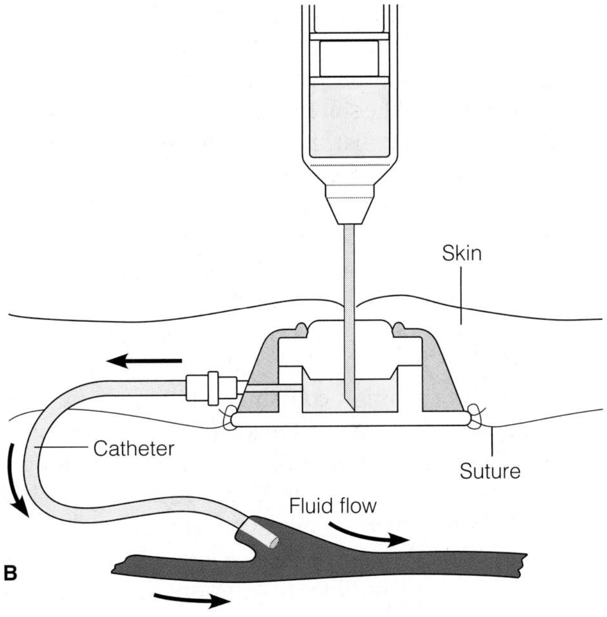

Figure 40.14 An implantable venous access device:
A, components; *B,* the device in place

small subcutaneous pocket, usually on the upper chest. The distal end of the catheter is placed in the subclavian or jugular vein. *Peripheral access system ports (PAS ports)* also may be used for long-term venous access. These ports are implanted in the antecubital area. A special angled needle is used to access both central and peripheral ports.

Special precautions need to be taken with all central lines and venous access ports to ensure asepsis and catheter patency. Nursing care of clients with these devices is outlined in the box opposite.

Intravenous Equipment

Because equipment varies according to the manufacturer, the nurse must become familiar with the equipment used in each particular agency.

Solution containers are available in various sizes (50, 100, 250, 500, or 1,000 mL); the smaller containers are often used to administer medications. Most solutions are dispensed in plastic bags (Figure 40.15). However, glass containers may need to be used if the medications to be administered are incompatible with plastic. Glass containers require an air vent so that air can replace the fluid that enters the client's vein. Some have a tube inside the bottle that serves as a vent; other containers without air vents require a vent on the administration set. Air vents usually have filters to prevent contamination from the air that enters the container. Air vents are not required for plastic solution containers because plastic bags collapse under atmospheric pressure when the solution enters the vein.

Avoid selecting a container whose volume is greater than the volume ordered. For example, if 750 mL D5NS (750 mL of 5 percent dextrose in normal saline) has been *ordered*, the nurse should obtain one 500-mL container and one 250-mL container, which total 750 mL. Do not obtain a 1,000-mL container with the intention of stopping the solution after 750 mL has been administered. Too often, the incorrect amount can be instilled unless an electronic device is used to regulate the volume. If a 1,000-mL solution container *must* be used, remove 250 mL before starting the infusion.

It is essential that the solution be sterile and appear clear. Cloudiness, evidence that the container has been opened previously, or leaks indicate possible contamination. Always check the expiry date on the label. Return any questionable or contaminated solutions to the pharmacy.

Infusion sets usually include an insertion spike, a drip chamber, a roller valve or screw clamp, tubing with secondary ports, and a protective cap over the needle adapter (Figure 40.16). The insertion spike is kept sterile and inserted into the solution container when the equipment is set up and ready to start. The drip chamber permits a predictable amount of fluid to be delivered. A commonly used drip chamber is the macrodrip, which delivers 10 to 20 drops per millilitre of solution. This information is found on the package. There are also microdrip sets, which deliver 60 drops per millilitre of solution. The roller valve or screw clamp, which compresses the lumen of the tubing, controls the rate of the flow. The protective cap over the needle adapter maintains the sterility of the end of the tubing so that it can be attached to a sterile needle or catheter inserted in the client's vein.

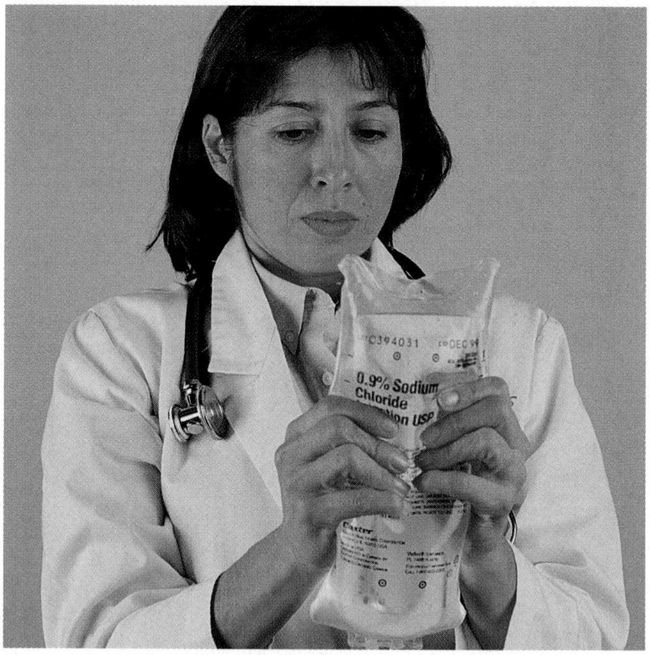

Figure 40.15 A plastic intravenous fluid container

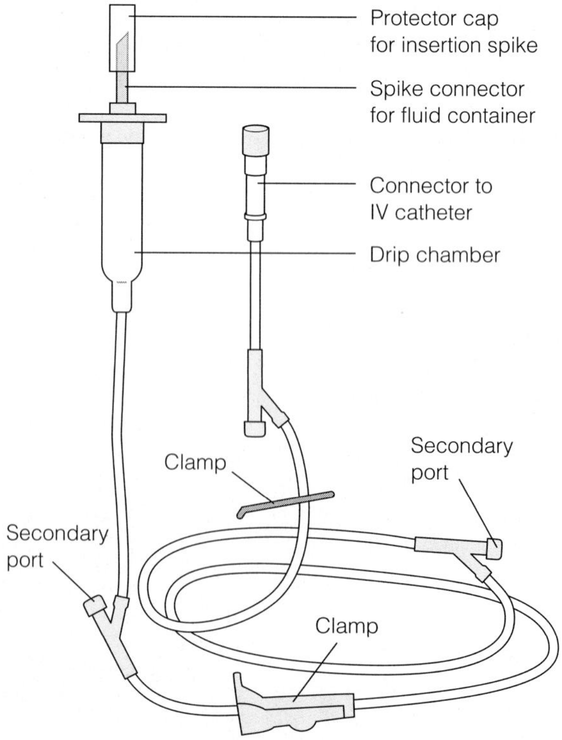

Figure 40.16 A standard IV administration set

CLINICAL GUIDELINES

Caring for Clients with a Venous Access Device

- This procedure is a specialized nursing function and requires certification by the employing agency.
- On insertion, document the date; the site; the brand, gauge, and catheter length; the location of the catheter tip (verified by x-ray); the length of the external segment; and client teaching.

Site Care

- Use strict aseptic technique when caring for central lines and long-term venous access devices.
- The frequency of dressing changes may vary from every three to seven days, depending on the site, physician's orders, and agency policies. Dressings also should be changed when loose or soiled after the initial dressing is changed.
- Assess the site for any redness, swelling, tenderness, or drainage. Compare the length of the external portion of the catheter with its documented length to assess for possible displacement. If displacement is suspected, obtain an order for a chest x-ray to determine the catheter tip's position. Report and document any position changes or signs of infection.
- Follow agency protocol for cleaning solutions and types of dressings.
- Before accessing the port, clean an area 5 cm in diameter around the site with a recommended cleansing solution on a sterile cotton swab. Start at the centre of the port site, moving outward with a firm, circular motion. Follow with povidone-iodine solution if required by agency policy. Allow the site to air dry.
- Secure the catheter, and cover the entry site and external portion of the catheter with an occlusive dressing.
- Provide routine care of the incision site for the implant device according to agency policy.

Catheter Care and Flushing

- Change the catheter cap, as indicated by protocol, usually every three to seven days.
- Using a 10-mL syringe, flush the catheter with a solution of 10 units of heparin after each use. The frequency of flushes between uses may vary from every 12 hours to once a week or less, depending on the type of catheter.
- Remember to flush all lumens for multiple-lumen catheters.
- Use a specially designed needle to access an implanted port. A needle with a 90-degree angle is generally used for infusions because it is easier to stabilize and more comfortable for the client. Stabilizing the port between the thumb and index finger of the nondominant hand, insert the needle through the centre of the port until the resistance of the platform is felt.
- Flush the port with normal saline or as agency protocol recommends for the specific type of port being used. After infusing medications or solutions, again flush the port with saline before using heparinized saline.
- To remove the needle after a treatment, again stabilize the port, and use even pressure to withdraw the needle. Maintain positive pressure by withdrawing the needle as the last millilitre of flush solution is being instilled.
- Flush idle ports with heparinized saline, in accordance with agency protocol or at least every eight weeks.

Teaching

Provide clients with the following instructions:

- Do not allow anyone to take a blood pressure on the arm in which a PICC line or PAS port is inserted.
- Wear a Medic-Alert tag or bracelet if the device is to be in place for a long period.
- For a PICC, you do not need to restrict activities, except do not immerse the arm in water. Showering is allowed if the site and catheter are covered by an occlusive dressing.
- For an implanted venous port, there are no activity restrictions, but remember that the port or catheter tip can become dislodged. Signs of a dislodged catheter tip include pain in the neck or ear on the affected side, swishing or gurgling sounds, or palpitations. Free movement of the port, swelling, or difficulty accessing the port may indicate port dislodgement. Notify the physician should any of these occur or if symptoms of infection develop.

Sources: Information adapted from Sansivero, G. E. (1995, July). Why pick a PICC: What you need to know. *Nursing, 25*(7), 35–41; and D. Christianson. (1994, November). Caring for a patient who has an implanted venous port. *American Journal of Nursing, 94*, 40–44.

Most infusion sets include one or more injection ports for administering IV medications or secondary infusions. Needleless systems reduce the risk of needle-stick injury and contamination of the intravenous line. With a needleless system, a blunt cannula is inserted into a special injection port or adapter on the IV tubing to administer medications or secondary infusions (Figure 40.17). Many infusion sets include an inline filter to trap air, particulate matter,

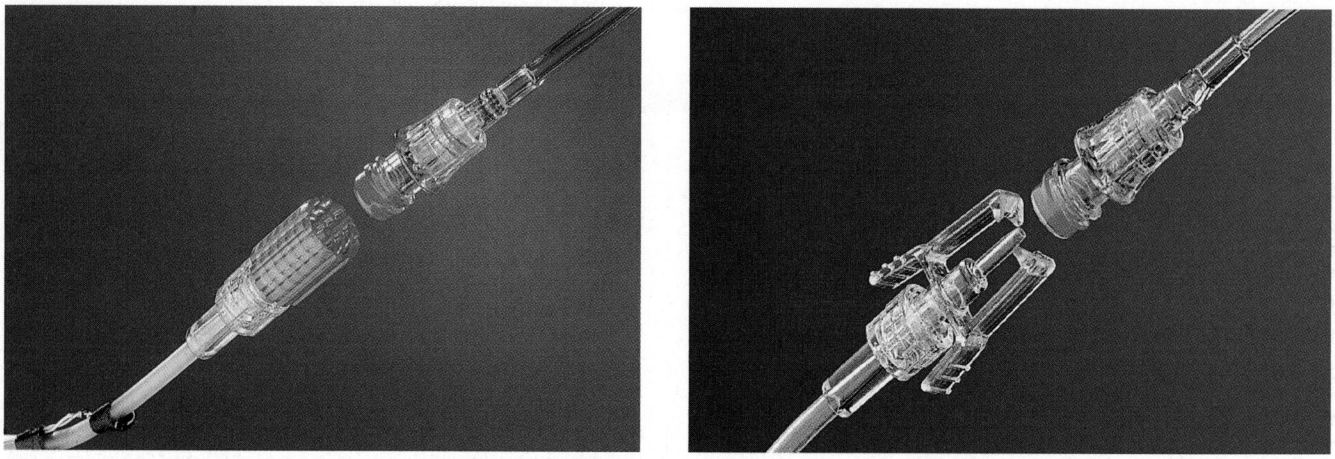

Figure 40.17 Cannulae used to connect the tubing of additive sets to primary infusions: *A,* threaded-lock cannula; *B,* lever-lock cannula

and microbes. A special infusion set may be required if the IV flow rate will be regulated by an infusion pump.

Catheters and *needles* are used for intravenous infusions. Over-the-needle catheters, also known as angiocaths, are commonly used for adult clients. The plastic catheter fits over a needle used to pierce the skin and vein wall (Figure 40.18). Once inserted into the vein, the needle is withdrawn and discarded, leaving the catheter in place. Intravenous catheters allow the client more mobility and rarely *infiltrate*, that is, become dislodged from the vein and allow fluid to flow into interstitial spaces.

Butterfly, or wing-tipped, *needles* with plastic flaps attached to the shaft are sometimes used (Figure 40.19). The flaps are held tightly together to hold the needle securely during insertion; after insertion, they are flattened against the skin and secured with tape.

Intravenous poles are used to hang the solution container. Some poles are attached to hospital beds; others stand on the floor or hang from the ceiling. The height of most poles is adjustable. In the home, plant hangers, robe hooks, kitchen cabinet knobs, or an S-hook over the top of a door may be used to hang solution containers. The higher the solution container, the greater the force of the solution as it enters the client and the faster the rate of flow.

Starting an Intravenous Infusion

Although the physician is responsible for precribing IV therapy for clients, nurses initiate, monitor, and maintain the infusion. This is true not only in hospitals and long-term care facilities but increasingly in community-based settings, such as clinics and clients' homes. Nurses may be required to be certified for initiation of intravenous theraphy by their employing agencies.

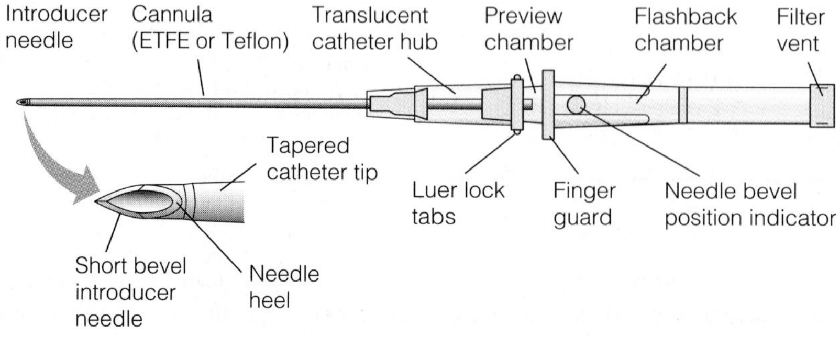

Figure 40.18 Schematic of an over-the-needle catheter

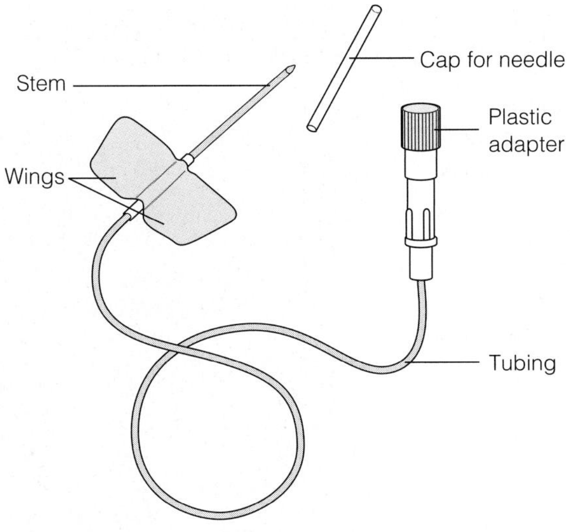

Figure 40.19 Schematic of a butterfly needle with adapter

Before starting an infusion, the nurse determines the following:

- The type and amount of solution to be infused
- The exact amount (dose) of any medications to be added to the solution
- The rate of flow or the time over which the infusion is to be completed

If solutions are prepared by the pharmacy or another department, the nurse must verify that the solution supplied exactly matches that which the physician prescribed.

Understanding the purpose for the infusion is as important as assessing the client. For example, the nurse may question an order for 5 percent dextrose in water (D5W) at 150 mL/hr if the client has peripheral edema and other signs of fluid overload.

To perform venipuncture and start an intravenous infusion, see Procedure 40.1.

PROCEDURE 40.1 Starting an Intravenous Infusion

Before preparing the infusion, the nurse first verifies the physician's prescription indicating the type of solution; the amount to be administered; the rate of flow of the infusion; and any client allergies (e.g., to tape, povidone-iodine, or latex). Agency policy should be checked.

PURPOSES

- To supply fluid when clients are unable to take an adequate volume of fluids by mouth
- To provide salts needed to maintain electrolyte balance
- To provide glucose (dextrose), the main fuel for metabolism
- To provide water-soluble vitamins and medications
- To establish a route of medications in life-threatening situations

Assessment Focus
Vital signs (pulse, respiratory rate, and blood pressure) for baseline data; skin turgor; allergy to tape, iodine, or latex; bleeding tendencies; disease or injury to extremities and status of veins to determine appropriate venipuncture site

Equipment

- ❑ Infusion set
- ❑ Container of sterile parenteral solution
- ❑ IV pole
- ❑ Adhesive or nonallergenic tape
- ❑ Tourniquet
- ❑ Antiseptic swabs
- ❑ Antiseptic ointment, such as povidone-iodine (optional)
- ❑ Intravenous catheter; see Variation at the end of this procedure for a butterfly (winged-tip) needle
- ❑ Disposable gloves
- ❑ Sterile gauze dressing or transparent occlusive dressing
- ❑ Arm splint, if required
- ❑ Towel or pad
- ❑ Electronic infusion device or pump, as necessary

INTERVENTION

1. Prepare the client.

- Explain the procedure to the client. A venipuncture can cause discomfort for a few seconds, but there should be no discomfort while the solution is flowing. Use a doll to demonstrate for children, and explain the procedure to the parents. Clients often want to know how long they will have an infusion. The physician's prescription may specify the length of time of the infusion, for example, 3,000 mL over 24 hours.

PROCEDURE 40.1 Starting an Intravenous Infusion *continued*

- Unless initiating IV therapy is urgent, provide any scheduled care before establishing the infusion to minimize movement of the affected limb during the procedure.
- Make sure that the client's clothing or gown can be removed over the IV apparatus. Some agencies provide special gowns that open over the shoulder and down the sleeve for easy removal.
- Wash hands.

2. Open and prepare the infusion set.

- Remove tubing from the container, and straighten it out.
- Slide the tubing clamp along the tubing until it is just below the drip chamber to facilitate its access.
- Close the clamp.
- Leave the ends of the tubing covered with the plastic caps until the infusion is started. *This will maintain the sterility of the ends of the tubing.*

3. Spike the solution container.

- Remove the protective cover from the entry site of the bag.
- See Procedure 28.7 for adding medications to an intravenous fluid container.
- Remove the cap from the spike, and insert the spike into the insertion site of the bag or bottle (Figure 40.20). Follow manufacturer's instructions.

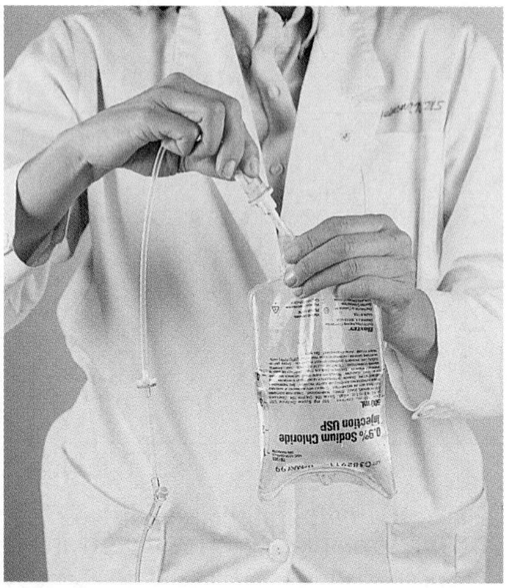

Figure 40.20 Inserting the spike

4. Apply a medication label to the solution container if a medication was added. Follow agency policy.

- In many agencies, medications and labels are applied in the pharmacy; if they are not, apply the label on the container (see Figure 28.44).

5. Apply a timing label on the solution container.

- The timing label may be applied at the time the infusion is started. Follow agency practice. See discussion of regulating infusion flow rates and Figure 40.27 on page 1113.

6. Hang the solution container on the pole.

- Adjust the pole so that the container is suspended about 1 m above the client's head. *This height is needed to enable gravity to overcome venous pressure and facilitate flow of the solution into the vein.*

7. Partially fill the drip chamber with solution.

- Squeeze the chamber gently until it is one-third to one-half full of solution (Figure 40.21).

8. Prime the tubing.

- Remove the protective cap, and hold the tubing over a container. Maintain the sterility of the end of the tubing and the cap.
- Release the clamp, and let the fluid run through the tubing until all bubbles are removed. Tap the tubing, if necessary, with your fingers to help the bubbles move. *The tubing is primed to prevent the introduction of air into the client. Ensure air is removed from secondary line access ports by inverting and tapping ports.*
- Reclamp the tubing, and replace the tubing cap, maintaining aseptic technique.
- For caps with air vents, do not remove the cap when priming this tubing. The flow of solution through the tubing will cease when the cap is moist with one drop of solution.
- If an infusion control pump, electronic device, or controller is being used, follow the manufacturer's directions for inserting the tubing and setting the infusion rate.

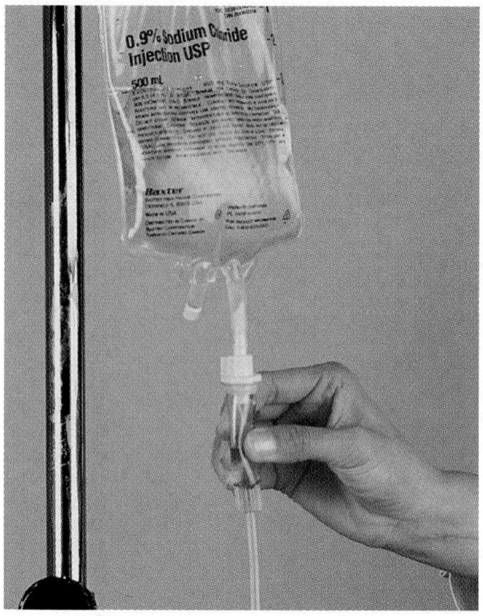

Figure 40.21 Squeezing the drip chamber

9. Wash your hands.

10. Select the venipuncture site.

- Unless contraindicated, use the client's nondominant arm. Identify possible venipuncture sites by looking for veins that are relatively straight, not sclerotic or tortuous. Consider the catheter length; look for a site sufficiently distal to the wrist or elbow that the tip of the catheter will not be at a point of flexion. *Sclerotic veins may make initiating and maintaining the IV difficult. Joint flexion increases the risk of irritation of vein walls by the catheter.*
- Check agency protocol about shaving, if the site is very hairy.
- Place a towel or bed protector under the extremity to protect linens (or furniture, if in the home).

11. Dilate the vein.

- Place the extremity in a dependent position (lower than the client's heart). *Gravity slows venous return and distends the veins. Distending the veins makes it easier to insert the needle properly.*

PROCEDURE 40.1 Starting an Intravenous Infusion *continued*

- Apply a tourniquet firmly 15 to 20 cm above the venipuncture site (Figure 40.22). Explain that the tourniquet will feel tight. The tourniquet must be tight enough to obstruct venous flow but not so tight that it occludes arterial flow. *Obstructing arterial flow inhibits venous filling.* If a radial pulse can be palpated, the arterial flow is not obstructed.
- If the vein is not sufficiently dilated:
  - **a.** Massage or stroke the vein distal to the site and in the direction of venous flow toward the heart. *This action helps fill the vein.*
  - **b.** Encourage the client to clench and unclench the fist. *Contracting the muscles compresses the distal veins, forcing blood along the veins and distending them.*
- If the preceding steps fail to distend the vein so that it is palpable, remove the tourniquet and apply a warm towel to the entire extremity for 10 to 15 minutes. *Warmth dilates superficial blood vessels, causing them to fill.* Then repeat step 11.

12. Put clean gloves on. *Gloves protect the nurse from contamination by the client's blood.*

- Clean the skin at the site of entry with a topical antiseptic alcohol swab, and then an anti-infective solution, such as povidone-iodine if recommended by agency policy.
- Use a circular motion, moving from the centre outward for several centimetres. *This motion carries microorganisms away from the site of entry.*
- Permit the solution to dry on the skin. *Allowing the solution to air dry will increase effectiveness.*

13. Insert the catheter, and initiate the infusion.

- Use the nondominant hand to pull the skin taut below the entry site. *This stabilizes the vein and makes the skin taut for needle entry. It can also make initial tissue penetration less painful.*
- Holding the over-the-needle catheter at a 15- to 30-degree angle with bevel up, insert the catheter through the skin and into the vein in one movement. Sudden lack of resistance is felt as the needle enters the vein.
- Once blood appears in the lumen of the needle or you feel the lack of resistance, reduce the angle of the catheter until it is almost parallel with the skin, and advance the needle and catheter approximately 0.5 to 1 cm further. Holding the needle portion steady, advance the catheter until the hub is at the venipuncture site. *The catheter is advanced to ensure that it, and not just the metal needle, is in the vein.* The exact technique depends on the type of catheter used.
- Release the tourniquet.
- Remove the protective cap from the distal end of the tubing, hold it ready to attach to the catheter, and maintain sterility.
- Remove the needle and attach the end of the infusion tubing to the catheter hub.
- Adjust the roller clamp to start running the infusion.

14. Tape the catheter.

- Tape the catheter by the "U" method or according to manufacturer's instructions. Using three strips of adhesive tape, each about 7.5 cm long:
  - **a.** Place one strip, sticky side up, under the catheter's hub.
  - **b.** Fold each end over so that the sticky sides are against the skin (Figure 40.23).
  - **c.** Place second strip, sticky side down, over catheter hub.
  - **d.** Place third strip, sticky side down, over tubing hub.

15. Dress and label the venipuncture site and tubing according to agency policy.

- In some agencies, the nurse puts a small amount of antiseptic ointment, such as povidone-iodine, over the venipuncture site, then a gauze square. In other agencies, a sterile transparent occlusive dressing is applied. *This permits assessment of the site without disturbing the dressing. This type of dressing can be left on for 48 to 72 hours, then changed.*
- Remove soiled gloves and discard appropriately.
- Discard needle in sharps container.
- Loop the tubing, and secure it with tape. *Looping and securing the tubing prevent the weight of the tubing or any movement from pulling on the needle or catheter.*
- Label the dressing with the date and time of insertion, type and gauge of needle or catheter used, and your initials (Figure 40.24).

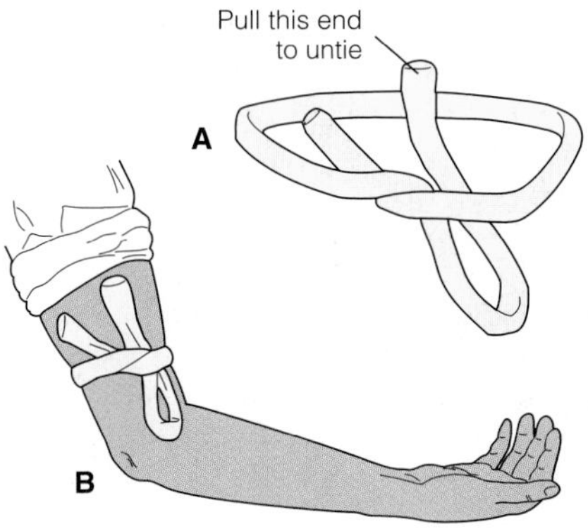

Figure 40.22 Applying a tourniquet

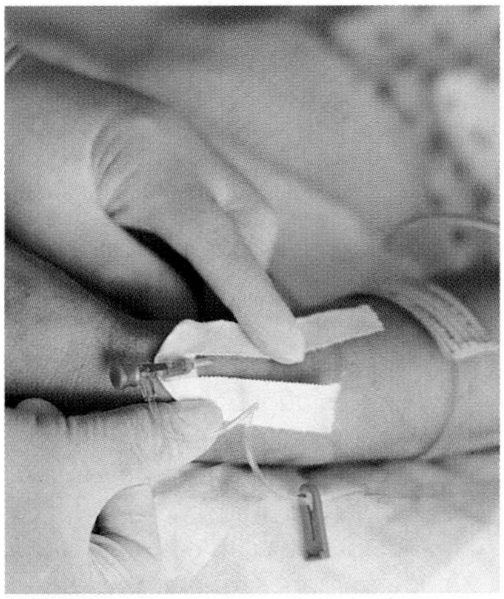

Figure 40.23 Taping an intravenous catheter by the "U" method

PROCEDURE 40.1 Starting an Intravenous Infusion *continued*

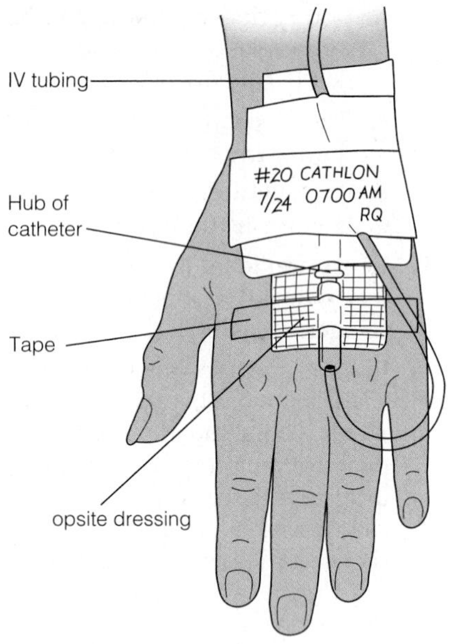

Figure 40.24 Labelled tape for a venipuncture dressing

16. Ensure appropriate infusion flow.

- Apply a padded arm board to splint the joint, as needed.
- Adjust the infusion rate of flow according to the prescription.

17. Label the IV tubing.

- Label the tubing with the date and time of attachment and your initials (Figure 40.25). This labelling may also be done when the infusion is started. *The tubing is labelled to ensure that it is changed at regular intervals (i.e., every 24 to 72 hours according to agency policy).*

18. Document relevant data, including assessments.

- Record the start of the infusion on the client's chart. Some agencies provide a special form for this purpose. Include the date and time of the venipuncture; amount and type of solution used, including any additives (e.g., kind and amount of medications); container number; flow rate; type and gauge of the needle or catheter; venipuncture site; and the client's general response.

Variation: Inserting a Butterfly (Winged-Tip) Needle

- Hold the needle, pointed in the direction of the blood flow, at a 30-degree angle, with the bevel up, and pierce the skin beside the vein about 1 cm below the site planned for piercing the vein.
- Once the needle is through the skin, lower the needle so that it is almost parallel with the skin. *Lowering the needle reduces the chances of puncturing both sides of the vein.* Follow the course of the vein, and pierce one side of the vein. Sudden lack of resistance can be felt as blood enters the needle.
- When blood flows back into the needle tubing, insert the needle to its hub.
- Release the tourniquet, attach the infusion, and initiate flow as quickly as possible. *Attaching the tubing quickly prevents blood from clotting and obstructing the needle.*

Securing a Butterfly Needle

- Tape the butterfly needle securely by the crisscross (chevron) method (Figure 40.26). Place a small gauze square under the needle, if required. *The gauze keeps the needle in position in the vein.*

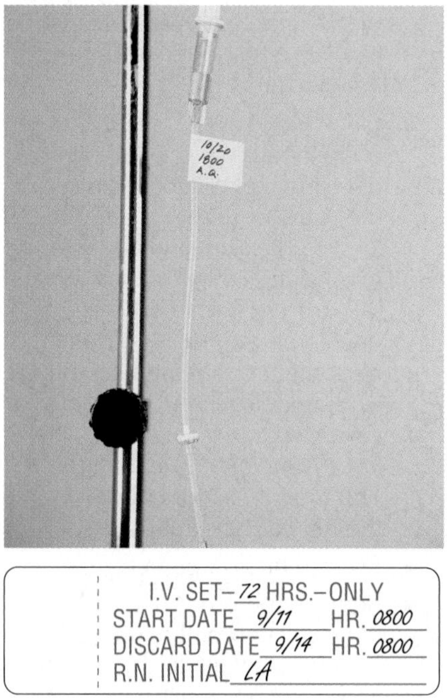
10/20
1800
A.Q.
I.V. SET–72 HRS.–ONLY
START DATE 9/11 HR. 0800
DISCARD DATE 9/14 HR. 0800
R.N. INITIAL LA

Figure 40.25 Tubing labelled with date, time of attachment, and nurse's initials; also shown is a preprinted label

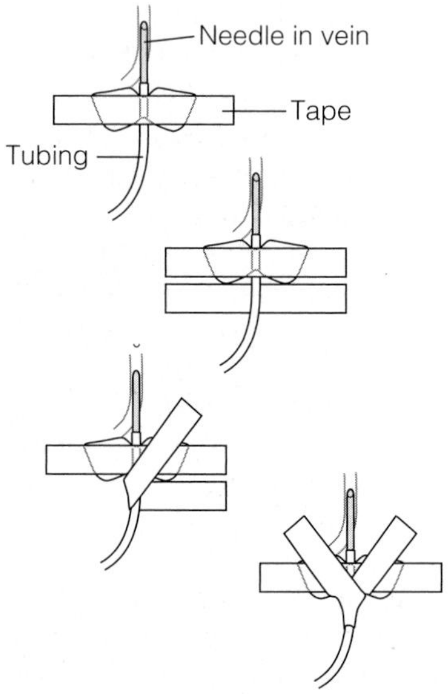

Figure 40.26 Taping the butterfly needle by the chevron method

Evaluation Focus

Skin status at IV site (warm temperature and absence of pain, redness, and draining); status of dressing; IV flow rate consistent with that prescribed; ability to perform self-care activities; understanding of any mobility limitations; vital signs compared with baseline level

Regulating and Monitoring Intravenous Infusions

Prescriptions for IV infusions may take several forms: for example, "3,000 mL over 24 hours"; "1,000 mL every 8 hours × 3 bags"; "125 mL/hr until oral intake is adequate." The nurse initiating the IV calculates the correct flow rate, regulates the infusion, and monitors the client's responses. Unless an infusion control device is used, the nurse manually regulates the drops per minute of flow using the roller clamp to ensure that the prescribed amount of solution will be infused in the correct time span. If the flow is incorrect, such problems as hypervolemia, hypovolemia, or inadequate medication administration can result. It is recommended that an infusion control device be used whenever possible, particularly with administration of medications.

The number of drops delivered per millilitre of solution varies with different brands and types of infusion sets. This rate, called the **drop,** or **drip factor,** generally is printed on the package of the infusion set. Macrodrops commonly have drop factors of 10, 12, 15, or 20 drops/mL; the drop factor for microdrip is 60 drops/mL.

To calculate flow rates, the nurse must know the volume of fluid to be infused and the specific time for the infusion. Two commonly used methods of indicating flow rates are designating the number of millilitres to be administered in one hour (mL/hr) and the number of drops to be given in one minute (gtt/min).

Millilitres per Hour Hourly rates of infusion can be calculated by dividing the total infusion volume by the total infusion time in hours. For example, if 1,000 mL is to be infused in eight hours, the number of millilitres per hour is

$$\frac{1{,}000 \text{ mL (total infusion volume)}}{8 \text{ hr (total infusion time)}} = 125 \text{ mL/hr}$$

Nurses need to check infusions at least every hour to ensure that the indicated millilitres per hour have infused. A strip of adhesive marking the exact time and/or amount to be infused may be taped to the solution container. Some agencies make premarked labels available (Figure 40.27).

Drops per Minute The nurse initiating and monitoring an infusion must regulate the drops per minute to ensure that the prescribed amount of solution will infuse. Drops per minute are calculated by the following formula:

$$\text{Drops per minute} = \frac{\text{Total infusion volume} \times \text{drop factor}}{\text{Total time of infusion in } \textit{minutes}}$$

Using our previous example, if the requirements are 1,000 mL in eight hours and the drip factor is 20 drops/mL, the drops per minute should be

$$\frac{1{,}000 \text{ mL} \times 20 \text{ gtt/mL}}{8 \text{ hr} \times 60 \text{ min/hr}} = 41.66 \text{ gtt/min}$$

Approximating this rate as 42 drops/min, the nurse regulates the drops per minute by tightening or releasing the IV tubing clamp and counting the drops for 15 seconds, then multiplying that number by 4 (e.g., 10 to 11 drops/15 sec).

A number of factors influence flow rate. See the box on the following page.

Devices to Control Infusions A number of devices are used to control the rate of an infusion. *Electronic infusion devices* (EIDs) regulate the infusion rate at preset limits. They also have an alarm that is triggered when the solution in the IV bag is low, when there is air in the tubing, or when the tubing is not high enough. The *Dial-A-Flo* inline device (Figure 40.28) is a regulator that controls the amount of fluid to be administered. It is preset at the volume to be infused and can be attached at the time the infusion is set up or when the tubing is changed. Another variation is a *volume-control set,* or Volutrol, which is used if the volume of fluid administered is to be carefully controlled. The set, which holds a maximum of 100 mL of solution, is attached below the solution container, and the drip chamber is placed below the set. Volume-control sets are frequently used in pediatric settings, where the volume administered is critical.

An *infusion pump* (Figure 40.29) delivers fluids intravenously by exerting positive pressure on the tubing or on the fluid. In situations where the fluid flow is unrestricted, the pump pressure is comparable with that of gravity flow.

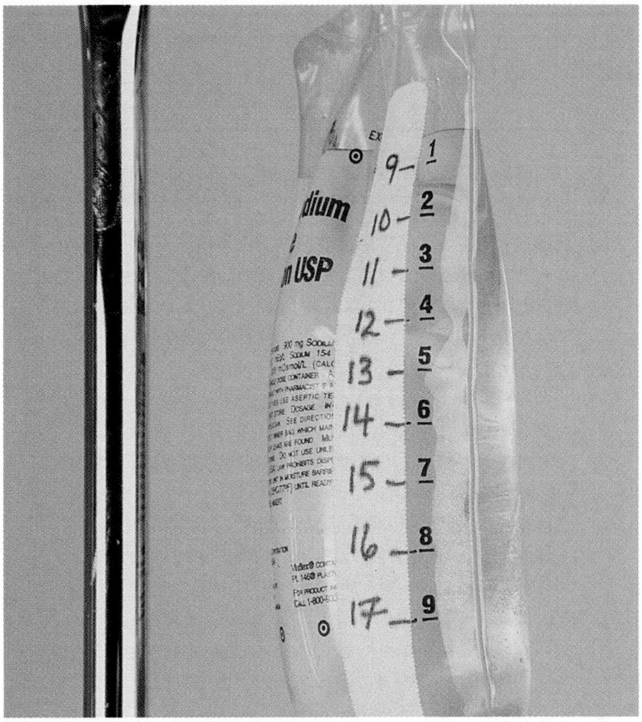

Figure 40.27 Timing label on an intravenous container. The first time marked (0900 hours) would be correct for a bag hung at 0800 hours with a rate of 100 mL per hour.

However, if restrictions develop (increased venous resistance), the pump can maintain the fluid flow by increasing the pressure applied to the fluid.

A *controller*, by contrast, operates solely by gravitational force. The delivery pressure depends on the height of the container in relation to the venipuncture site. The container must be at least 76 cm above the venipuncture site for a controller to work. A controller does not have the ability to add pressure to the line and to overcome resistance to fluid flow.

Procedure 40.2 outlines the steps involved in monitoring an intravenous infusion.

Changing Intravenous Containers, Tubing, and Dressings for Peripheral Intravenous Sites

Intravenous solution containers are changed when a small amount of fluid remains in the neck of the container and fluid still remains in the drip chamber. However, all IV bags should be changed every 24 hours, regardless of how much solution remains, to minimize the risk of contamination. IV tubing is changed every 48 to 72 hours, depending on agency protocol and manufacturer's recommendations, as is the site dressing. Procedure 40.3 provides guidelines for changing an IV solution container, tubing, and the IV site dressing. A peripheral intravenous site is changed every 48 to 72 hours, according to agency policy.

When an IV infusion is no longer necessary to maintain the client's fluid intake or to provide a route for medication administration, the infusion is either discontinued and the catheter removed, or the catheter is left in place and converted to a saline or heparin lock. Guidelines for discontinuing an IV infusion or converting the catheter to a lock are outlined in Procedures 40.4 and 40.5.

Factors Influencing Flow Rates

- *The position of the forearm.* Sometimes, a change in the position of the client's arm decreases flow. Slight pronation, supination, extension, or elevation of the forearm on a pillow can increase flow.
- *The position and patency of the tubing.* Tubing can be obstructed by the client's weight, a kink, or a clamp closed too tightly. The flow rate also diminishes when part of the tubing dangles below the puncture site.
- *The height of the infusion bottle.* Elevating the height of the infusion bottle a few centimetres can speed the flow by creating more pressure.
- *Possible infiltration or fluid leakage.* Swelling, a feeling of coldness, and tenderness at the venipuncture site may indicate infiltration.
- *Relationship of the size of the angiocath to the vein.* A catheter that is too large may impede the infusion flow.

Figure 40.28 The Dial-A-Flo inline device

Blood Transfusions

Intravenous fluids can be effective in restoring intravascular (blood) volume; however, they do not affect the oxygen-carrying capacity of the blood. When red and white blood cells, platelets, or blood proteins are lost because of hemorrhage or disease, it may be necessary to replace these components to restore the blood's ability to transport oxygen and carbon dioxide, to clot, to fight infection, and to keep extracellular fluid within the intravascular compartment. A blood transfusion is the introduction of whole blood or blood components into the venous circulation.

Blood Groups

Human blood is commonly classified into four main groups (A, B, AB, and O). The surface of an individual's red blood cells contains a number of proteins known as **antigens** that are unique for each person. Many blood antigens have been identified, but the antigens A, B, and Rh are the most important in determining blood group or type. Because antigens promote agglutination or clumping of blood cells, they are also known as **agglutinogens.**

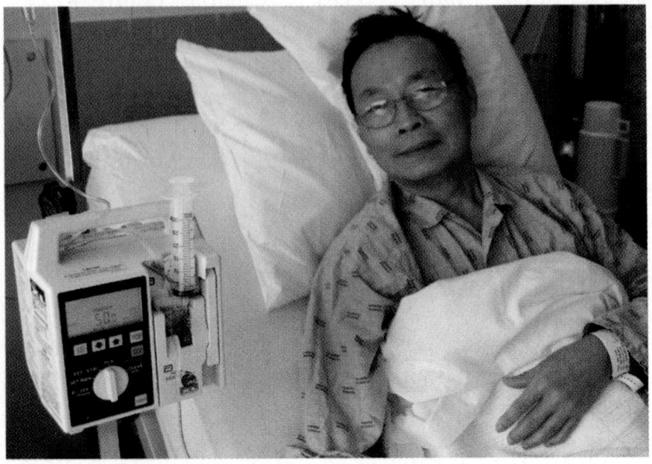

Figure 40.29 An intravenous infusion pump

PROCEDURE 40.2 Monitoring a Peripheral Intravenous Infusion

PURPOSES

- To maintain the prescribed flow rate
- To prevent complications associated with IV therapy

Assessment Focus
Appearance of infusion site; patency of system; type of fluid being infused and rate of flow; response of the client

INTERVENTION

1. Gather the pertinent data.

- From the physician's prescription, determine the type and sequence of solutions to be infused, determine the rate of flow and infusion schedule (should be included in physician's prescription).

2. Ensure that the correct solution is being infused.

- If the solution in incorrect, slow the rate of flow to a minimum to maintain the patency of the catheter. (If patient is at risk for developing an adverse reaction, infusion must be stopped.) *Stopping the infusion may allow a thrombus to form in the IV catheter. If this occurs, the catheter must be removed and another venipuncture performed before the infusion can be resumed.*
- Change the solution to the correct one. Document and report the error according to agency protocol.

3. Observe the rate of flow every hour.

- Compare the rate of flow regularly, for example, at least every hour, against the infusion schedule. *Infusions that are off schedule can be harmful to a client.*
- If the rate is *too fast,* check agency policy. *Solution administered too quickly may cause a significant increase in circulating blood volume (which is about 6 L in an adult). Hypervolemia may result in pulmonary edema and cardiac failure.* Assess the client for manifestations of hypervolemia and its complications, including dyspnea; rapid, laboured breathing; cough; crackles (rales) in the lung bases; tachycardia; and bounding pulses.
- If the rate is *too slow,* check agency practice. Adjustments may require a physician's prescription. *Solution that is administered too slowly can supply insufficient fluid, electrolytes, or medication for a client's needs.*
- If the rate of flow is 150 mL/hr or more, check the rate of flow more frequently, for example, every 15 to 30 minutes.

4. Inspect the patency of the IV tubing and needle.

- Observe the position of the solution container. If it is less than 1 m above the IV site, readjust it to the correct height. Recheck the rate of flow any time the height of the solution container is changed. *If the container is too low, the solution may not flow into the vein because there is insufficient gravitational pressure to overcome the pressure of the blood within the vein.*
- Observe the drip chamber. If it is less than half full, squeeze the chamber to allow the correct amount of fluid to flow in.
- Open the drip regulator, and observe for a rapid flow of fluid from the solution container into the drip chamber. Then, partially close the drip regulator to re-establish the prescribed rate of flow. *Rapid flow of fluid into the drip chamber indicates patency of the IV line. Closing the drip regulator to the prescribed rate of flow prevents fluid overload.*
- Inspect the tubing for pinches or kinks or obstructions to flow. Arrange the tubing so that it is lightly coiled and under no pressure. Sometimes, the tubing becomes caught under the client's arm and the weight of the arm blocks the flow.
- Observe the position of the tubing. If it is dangling below the venipuncture, coil it carefully on the surface of the bed. *The solution cannot flow upward into the vein against the force of gravity.*
- If there is leakage, locate the source. If the leak is at the catheter connection, tighten the tubing into the catheter. If the leak cannot be stopped, slow the infusion as much as possible without stopping it, and replace the tubing with a new sterile set. Estimate the amount of solution lost.

5. Inspect the insertion site for fluid infiltration at least every hour.

- When an IV needle becomes dislodged from the vein, fluid flows into interstitial tissues, causing swelling. This is known or as *infiltration* and is manifested by localized swelling, coolness, pallor, and discomfort at the IV site.
- If an infiltration is present, stop the infusion and remove the catheter. Restart the infusion at another site.
- Apply a warm compress to the site of the infiltration. *Warmth promotes comfort and vasodilation, facilitating absorption of the fluid from interstitial tissues.*

6. Inspect the insertion site for phlebitis (inflammation of a vein).

- Inspect and palpate the site every hour. Phlebitis can occur as a result of injury to a vein, for example, because of mechanical trauma or chemical irritation. Chemical injury to a vein can occur from electrolytes (especially potassium and magnesium) and some medications. The clinical signs of phlebitis are redness, warmth, and swelling at the intravenous site and burning pain along the course of a vein.

→

PROCEDURE 40.2 Monitoring a Peripheral Intravenous Infusion *continued*

- If phlebitis is detected, discontinue the infusion, and apply warm compresses to the venipuncture site as ordered and according to agency policy. Do not use this injured vein for further infusions.

7. Inspect the intravenous site for bleeding.

- Oozing or bleeding into the surrounding tissues can occur while the infusion is freely flowing but is more likely to occur after the needle has been removed from the vein.
- Observation of the venipuncture site is extremely important for clients who bleed readily, such as those receiving anticoagulants.

8. Teach the client ways to maintain the infusion system, for example:

- Avoid sudden twisting or turning movements of the arm with the needle or catheter.
- Avoid stretching or placing tension on the tubing.
- Try to keep the tubing from dangling below the level of the needle.
- Notify a nurse, if
  - **a.** The flow rate suddenly changes or the solution stops dripping.
  - **b.** The solution container is nearly empty.
  - **c.** There is blood in the IV tubing.
  - **d.** Discomfort or swelling is experienced at the IV site.

9. Document all relevant information.

Evaluation Focus
Amount of fluid infused according to the schedule; intactness of IV system; appearance of IV site (e.g., dry, tissue infiltration, discomfort); urinary output compared with intake; tissue turgor; specific gravity of urine; vital signs and lung sounds compared with baseline data

PROCEDURE 40.3 Changing an Intravenous Container, Tubing, and Dressing

PURPOSES

- To maintain the flow of required fluids
- To maintain sterility of the IV system and decrease the incidence of phlebitis and infection
- To maintain patency of the IV tubing
- To prevent infection at the IV site and the introduction of microorganisms into the bloodstream

Assessment Focus
Presence of fluid infiltration, bleeding, or phlebitis at IV site; allergy to tape, latex, or iodine; infusion rate and amount absorbed; blockages in IV system; appearance of the dressing for integrity, moisture, and need for change; the date and the time of the previous dressing change

Equipment

- ❑ Container with the correct kind and amount of sterile solution, according to physician's orders
- ❑ Administration set, including sterile tubing and drip chamber
- ❑ Timing label
- ❑ Receptacle (e.g., a basin) for discarded fluid
- ❑ Sterile gauze square for positioning the needle

For the Dressing

- ❑ Disposable gloves
- ❑ Sterile gauze or transparent opsite dressing
- ❑ Adhesive remover
- ❑ Povidone-iodine swabs (optional)
- ❑ Cleansing solution as recommended by the agency (for example, normal saline)
- ❑ Optional: Antiseptic ointment (e.g., povidone-iodine or other recommended by the agency)
- ❑ Tape
- ❑ Towel

INTERVENTION

1. Obtain the correct solution container.

- Verify the physician's order.
- Read the label of the new container.
- Verify that you have the correct solution, correct client, correct additives (if any), and correct dose (number of bags or total volume ordered).

PROCEDURE 40.3 Changing an Intravenous Container, Tubing, and Dressing *continued*

- Check clarity of solution and expiry date.

2. **Wash your hands.**
3. **Set up the intravenous equipment with the new container, and label them.**

- See Procedure 40.1, steps 1 to 8.
- Apply a timing label to the container.
- Prime the tubing.
- Label the tubing as shown in Figure 40.25, earlier.

4. **Prepare the IV needle or catheter tape and the dressing equipment.**

- Prepare strips of tape as needed for the type of needle or catheter. For the butterfly needle, two or three strips of 7.5-cm tape are needed. For a catheter, three strips of 7.5-cm tape are needed. *These will be used later to secure the needle or catheter without covering the insertion site.*
- Hang the pieces of tape from the edge of a table. *This places the tape in readiness for use without disrupting the adhesive.*
- Open all equipment: povidone-iodine solution or swabs, dressing and adhesive bandage, and ointment. *This facilitates access to supplies.*
- Place a towel under the extremity. *This prevents soiling of bed linens.*
- Put gloves on.

5. **Remove the soiled dressing and all tape, except the tape holding the catheter or IV needle in place.**

- Remove tape and gauze from the old dressing one layer at a time. *This prevents dislodgement of the catheter or needle in case tubing becomes entangled between layers of dressing.*
- Remove adhesive dressings in the direction of the client's hair growth when possible. *This minimizes discomfort when adhesive is removed from the skin.*
- Discard the used dressing materials in the appropriate container.

6. **Assess the IV site.**

- Inspect the IV site for the presence of infiltration or inflammation. *Inflammation or infiltration necessitates removal of the IV needle or catheter to avoid further trauma to the tissues.*
- Go to step 7, or discontinue and relocate the IV site, if indicated. See Procedures 40.1 and 40.4.

7. **Disconnect the used tubing.**

- Place a sterile swab under the hub of the catheter. *This absorbs any leakage that might occur when the tubing is disconnected.*
- Clamp the tubing.
- Holding the hub of the catheter with the nondominant hand, loosen the tubing with the dominant hand, using a twisting, pulling motion. *Holding the catheter firmly but gently maintains its position in the vein.*
- Remove the used IV tubing.
- Place the end of the tubing in the basin or other receptacle.

8. **Connect the new tubing, and re-establish the infusion.**

- Continue to hold the catheter, and grasp the new tubing with the dominant hand.
- Remove the protective tubing cap, and maintaining sterility, insert the tubing end securely into the needle hub. Twist it to secure it.
- Open the clamp to start the solution flowing.

9. **Clean the IV site.**

- Start with adhesive remover to remove adhesive residue. *Removal of adhesive residue facilitates adherence of the new dressing.*
- Then, using the solution recommended by the agency policy, clean the site, beginning at the catheter or needle and cleaning outward in a 5-cm diameter. *Cleaning in this manner prevents contamination of the IV site from bacteria on the peripheral skin areas. Antiseptics reduce the number of microorganisms present at the site, thus reducing the risk of infection.*

10. **Apply antiseptic ointment or solution if indicated and apply the dressing.**

- Place povidone-iodine ointment or solution at the entry site in accordance with agency protocol. *This reduces skin bacteria and risk of infection.* Solution is preferred to ointment when transparent dressings are used because the former facilitates the dressing's adherence. However, solution can traumatize the skin.
- Apply a sterile gauze or transparent dressing over the site.

11. **Label the dressing, and secure IV tubing.**

- Place the date and time of the dressing change and your initials either on the label provided or directly over the top of the dressing.
- Secure IV tubing with additional tape, as required.

12. **Regulate the rate of flow of the solution according to the order on the chart.**
13. **Document all relevant information.**

- Record the change of the solution container, tubing, and/or dressing in the appropriate place on the client's chart. Also record the fluid intake according to agency practice. Record the number of the container, if the containers are numbered at the agency. Also record your assessments.

Evaluation Focus
Status of IV site; patency of IV system; accuracy of flow

PROCEDURE 40.4 Discontinuing a Peripheral Intravenous Infusion

Assessment Focus
Appearance of the venipuncture site; any bleeding from the infusion site; amount of fluid infused; appearance of IV catheter

Equipment

- ❑ Clean gloves
- ❑ Dry or antiseptic-soaked swabs, according to agency practice
- ❑ Small sterile dressing and tape

INTERVENTION

1. Validate physician's orders and check agency policy.

2. Prepare the equipment.

- Wash hands.
- Clamp the infusion tubing. *Clamping the tubing prevents the fluid from flowing out of the needle onto the client or bed.*
- Loosen the tape at the venipuncture site while holding the needle firmly and applying countertraction to the skin. *Movement of the needle can injure the vein and cause discomfort to the client. Countertraction prevents pulling the skin and causing discomfort.*
- Put gloves on. Hold a sterile gauze above the venipuncture site.

3. Withdraw the needle or catheter from the vein.

- Withdraw the needle or catheter by pulling it out along the line of the vein. *Pulling it out in line with the vein avoids injury to the vein.*
- Immediately apply firm pressure to the site using sterile gauze for two to three minutes. *Pressure helps stop the bleeding and prevents hematoma formation.*
- Hold the client's arm or leg above the body if any bleeding persists. *Raising the limb decreases blood flow to the area.*

4. Examine the catheter removed from the client.

- Check the catheter to make sure it is intact. *If a piece of tubing remains in the client's vein it could move centrally (toward the heart or lungs) and cause serious problems.*
- Report a broken catheter to the nurse in charge or physician immediately.
- If the broken piece can be palpated, apply a tourniquet above the insertion site. Application of a tourniquet decreases the possibility of the piece moving until a physician is notified.

5. Cover the venipuncture site.

- Apply the sterile dressing. *The dressing continues the pressure and covers the open area in the skin, preventing infection.*
- Note amount of solution remaining in IV solution container. Discard the IV solution container, and discard the used supplies appropriately.

6. Document all relevant information.

- Record the amount of fluid infused on the intake and output record and on the chart, according to agency practice. Include the container number, type of solution used, time of discontinuing the infusion, and the client's response.

Evaluation Focus
Appearance of the venipuncture site; pulse; respirations, skin colour, edema, sputum, cough, and urine output; and how the person feels physically and psychologically

PROCEDURE 40.5 Changing a Peripheral Intravenous Catheter to an Intermittent Infusion Lock

PURPOSE

- To permit IV administration of medications or fluids on an intermittent basis

Assessment Focus
Patency of the IV catheter, appearance of the site (evidence of inflammation or infiltration)

PROCEDURE 40.5 Changing an Intravenous Catheter to an Intermittent Infusion Lock *continued*

Equipment

- ❑ Intermittent infusion cap or device
- ❑ Clean gloves
- ❑ Sterile 2 × 2 or 4 × 4 gauze
- ❑ Sterile saline for injection (without preservative) or heparin flush solution (use caution in selecting correct concentration of heparin solution) using a 3-mL syringe with a #25 gauge needle, or a needleless infusion device
- ❑ Isopropyl alcohol wipe
- ❑ Tape
- ❑ Clean emesis basin

INTERVENTION

1. **Verify the order and check agency policy.**
   - A specific order may be written to convert an intravenous access to a heparin or saline lock. The order also may be implied, for example, if IV fluids are to be discontinued but the client has orders for an IV antibiotic every six hours or is receiving analgesics intravenously.
2. **Prepare the client and equipment.**
   - Explain the procedure to the client and the reason for leaving the IV catheter in place. Changing an IV to a heparin or saline lock should cause no discomfort other than that associated with removing tape from the IV tubing.
   - Wash your hands.
   - Assess the IV site (if visible) and determine the patency of the catheter (see Procedure 40.2, steps 4 to 8). If the catheter is not fully patent or there is evidence of phlebitis or infiltration, discontinue the catheter and establish a new IV site.
   - Expose the IV catheter hub, and loosen any tape that is holding the IV tubing in place or it will interfere with insertion of the intermittent infusion plug into the catheter.
   - Clamp the IV tubing to stop the flow of IV fluid.
   - Open the gauze pad, and place it under the IV catheter hub.
   - Open the intermittent infusion plug, leaving the plug in its sterile package.
3. **Remove the IV tubing and insert the intermittent infusion plug into the IV catheter.**
   - Don clean gloves.
   - Stabilize the IV catheter with your nondominant hand, and use the little finger to place slight pressure on the vein *above* the end of the catheter. Twist the IV tubing adapter to loosen it from the IV catheter, and remove it, placing the end of the tubing in a clean emesis basin.
   - Pick up the intermittent infusion plug from its package, and remove the protective sleeve from the male adapter, maintaining its sterility. Insert the plug into the IV catheter, twisting it to seat it firmly, or engage the Luer lock.
4. **Instill saline or heparin solution per agency policy.** *Saline or heparin is used to maintain patency of the IV catheter when fluids are not infusing through the catheter.*
5. **Tape the intermittent infusion plug in place using the chevron or U method.** *Tape provides added security to prevent the infusion plug from coming out of the intravenous catheter. It also promotes comfort, preventing the plug from catching on clothing or bedding.*
6. **Teach the client how to maintain the lock.**
   - Avoid manipulating the catheter or infusion plug and protect it from catching on clothing or bedding. A gauze bandage, such as Kerlix or Kling, may be wrapped over the plug to protect it when it is not in use.
   - Cover the site with an occlusive dressing when showering; avoid immersing the site.
   - Flush the catheter with saline or heparin solution, as directed.
   - Notify the nurse or primary-care provider if the plug or catheter comes out, if the site becomes red, inflamed, or painful, or if any drainage or bleeding occurs at the site.
7. **Document all relevant information.**

Evaluation Focus
Patency of the catheter, appearance of the site; ease of flushing

The A antigen or agglutinogen is present on the RBCs of people with blood group A; the B antigen is present in people with blood group B; and, both A and B antigens are found on the RBC surface in people with blood group AB. Neither antigen is present in people with blood group O.

Preformed antibodies to RBC antigens are present in the plasma (these antibodies are also known as **agglutinins**).

Individuals with blood group A have B antibodies, and those with blood group B have A antibodies. People with blood group O have antibodies to both A and B antigens. Those individuals with blood group AB do not have antibodies to either A or B antigens (see Table 40.13).

TABLE 40.13 The Blood Groups with Their Constituent Agglutinogens and Agglutinins

Blood Type	RBC Antigens (Agglutinogens)	Plasma Antibodies (Agglutinins)
A	A	B
B	B	A
AB	A and B	—
O	—	A and B

Rhesus (Rh) Factor

The Rh factor antigen is present on the RBCs of approximately 85 percent of people. Blood that contains the Rh factor is known as Rh-positive (Rh^+); when it is not present, the blood is said to be Rh-negative (Rh^-). In contrast to the ABO blood groups, Rh^- blood does not naturally contain Rh antibodies. However, when individuals are exposed to Rh factor, they develop Rh antibodies. Rh factor exposure may occur, for example, when an Rh^- mother is pregnant with an Rh^+ fetus, or if an Rh^- client is transfused with Rh^+ blood. *Subsequent* exposure to Rh^+ blood places the client at risk for an antigen-antibody reaction resulting in hemolysis of RBCs.

Blood Typing and Cross-Matching

In order to avoid transfusing incompatible red blood cells, both blood donor and recipient are typed, and their blood is cross-matched. *Blood typing* is done to determine the ABO blood group and Rh factor status. This test is also performed on pregnant women and neonates to assess for possible intrauterine exposure of the mother or baby to an incompatible blood type (particularly Rh factor incompatibilities).

Because blood typing only determines the presence of the major ABO and Rh antigens, *cross-matching* also is necessary prior to transfusion to identify possible interactions of minor antigens with their corresponding antibodies. RBCs from the donor blood are mixed with serum from the recipient; a reagent (Coombs' serum) is added, and the mixture is examined for visible agglutination. If the recipient's serum does not contain antibodies to the donor's RBCs, agglutination does not occur, and the risk of a transfusion reaction is small (Pagana & Pagana, 1997).

Selection of Blood Donors

Screening of blood donors is rigorous, using criteria established to protect the donor from possible ill effects of donation and to protect the recipient from exposure to diseases transmitted through the blood. Most blood donors are unpaid volunteers. Potential donors may be declined if they have a history of hepatitis, convulsions, human immundeficiency virus (HIV) infection (or risk factors for HIV infection), heart disease, most cancers, severe asthma, or bleeding disorders. Donation may be deferred for people with malaria or who have been exposed to malaria or hepatitis, or with pregnancy, surgery, anemia, high or low blood pressure, and certain drugs.

Blood and Blood Products for Transfusion

Not all clients require transfusion of whole blood; many times, transfusion of a particular blood component is more appropriate. Table 40.14 lists some of the common blood products that may be transfused.

Transfusion Reactions

Transfusion of ABO or Rh incompatible blood can result in a **hemolytic transfusion reaction** with destruction of the transfused RBCs and subsequent risk of kidney damage or failure. Other forms of transfusion reaction may occur, including febrile, allergic, circulatory overload, and sepsis. Because the risk of an adverse reaction is high when blood is transfused, clients must be frequently and carefully assessed before and during transfusion. Many reactions become evident within 30 minutes of initiating the transfusion; clients are closely monitored during this period. Stop the transfusion immediately if signs of a reaction develop. Possible transfusion reactions, their clinical signs, and nursing implications are listed in Table 40.15.

Administering Blood

Special precautions are necessary when administering blood. When a transfusion is ordered, obtain the blood from the blood bank just before starting the transfusion. Do not store the blood in the refrigerator on the nursing unit; lack of temperature control may damage the blood. Follow agency policies for verifying that the unit of blood is correct for the client.

Blood is administered through a #18- or #19-gauge intravenous needle or catheter; using a smaller needle may slow the infusion and damage blood cells (although a smaller gauge needle may be necessary for small children or clients with small, fragile veins). A Y-type blood transfusion set with an inline or add-on filter is used when administering blood (Figure 40.30). One arm of the administration

TABLE 40.14 Blood Products for Transfusion

Product	Use
Whole blood	Primarily used for cardiac surgery or acute hemorrhage. Replaces blood volume and all blood products: RBCs, plasma, plasma proteins, fresh platelets, and other clotting factors.
Red blood cells	Used to increase the oxygen-carrying capacity of blood in anemias, surgery, disorders with slow bleeding. One unit raises hematocrit by approximately 4 percent.
Autologous red blood cells	Used for blood replacement following planned elective surgery. Clients donate their own blood four to five weeks prior to surgery for autologous transfusion.
Platelets	Replaces platelets in clients with bleeding disorders or platelet deficiency. Fresh platelets are most effective.
Plasma	Expands blood volume and provides clotting factors. Does not need to be cross-matched (contains no RBCs). ABO compatibility must be confirmed.
Albumin	Blood volume expander; provides plasma proteins.
Clotting factors and cryoprecipitate	Used for clients with clotting factor deficiencies. Each provides different factors involved in the clotting pathway; cryoprecipitate also contains fibrinogen.

Source: Adapted from LeMone, P. & Burke, K. M. (1996). *Medical-surgical nursing: Critical thinking in client care.* Menlo Park, CA: Addison Wesley Nursing.

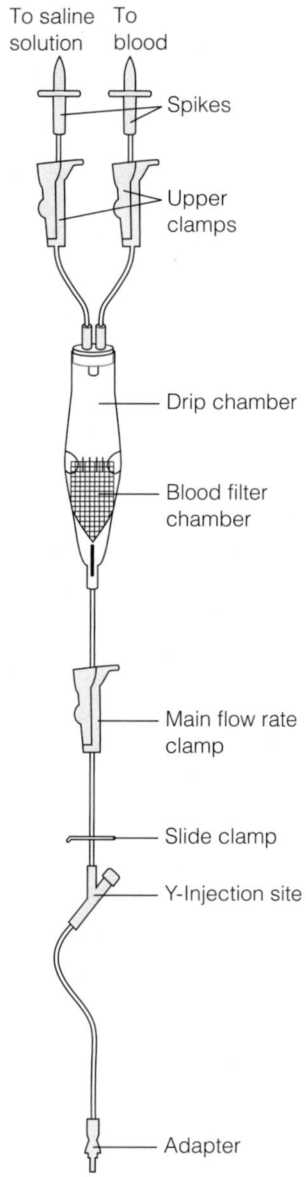

Figure 40.30 Schematic of a Y-set for blood administration

set connects to the blood, and normal saline (0.9 percent NaCl) is attached to the other arm of the Y-type set. Saline is used to prime the set and flush the needle before administering blood. It also provides a means to keep the vein open should a transfusion reaction occur. No other IV solutions should be administered with blood as they may cause the blood cells to clump or cause clotting. Whole blood or packed RBC transfusions should be completed within four hours of initiation according to physician's orders and agency policy. The risk of sepsis increases if blood hangs for a longer period. Blood tubing is changed with each subsequent unit transfused. New intravenous tubing is used following a transfusion.

To start, maintain, and terminate a blood transfusion, see Procedure 40.6.

Evaluating

Using the overall goals identified in the planning stage of maintaining or restoring fluid balance, maintaining or restoring pulmonary ventilation and oxygenation, maintaining or restoring normal balance of electrolytes, and

TABLE 40.15 Transfusion Reactions

Reaction: Cause	Clinical Signs	Nursing Intervention*
Hemolytic reaction: incompatibility between client's blood and donor's blood	Chills, fever, headache, backache, dyspnea, cyanosis, chest pain, tachycardia, hypotension	1. Discontinue the transfusion immediately. 2. Keep the vein open with normal saline, or according to agency protocol. 3. Send the remaining blood, a sample of the client's blood, and a urine sample to the laboratory. This should be done for all reactions, according to doctor's orders and agency policy. 4. Notify the physician immediately. 5. Monitor vital signs. 6. Monitor fluid intake and output.
Febrile reaction: sensitivity of the client's blood to white blood cells, platelets, or plasma proteins	Fever; chills; warm, flushed skin; headache; anxiety; muscle pain	1. Discontinue the transfusion immediately. 2. Give antipyretics, as ordered. 3. Notify the physician immediately.
Allergic reaction (mild): sensitivity to infused plasma proteins	Flushing, itching, urticaria, bronchial wheezing	1. Stop or slow the transfusion, depending on agency protocol. 2. Notify the physician. 3. Administer medication (antihistamines), as ordered.
Allergic reaction (severe): antibody-antigen reaction	Dyspnea, chest pain, circulatory collapse, cardiac arrest	1. Stop the transfusion. 2. Keep the vein open with normal saline. 3. Notify the physician immediately. 4. Monitor vital signs. Administer cardiopulmonary resuscitation (CPR), if needed. 5. Administer medications and/or oxygen, as ordered.
Circulatory overload: blood administered faster than the circulation can accommodate	Cough, dyspnea, crackles (rales), distended neck veins, tachycardia, hypertension	1. Place the client upright with feet dependent. 2. Administer diuretics and oxygen, as ordered. 3. Notify the physician immediately. 4. Stop or slow the transfusion.
Sepsis: contaminated blood administered	High fever, chills, vomiting, diarrhea, hypotension	1. Stop the transfusion. 2. Send the remaining blood to laboratory. 3. Notify the physician immediately. 4. Obtain a blood specimen from the client for culture. 5. Administer IV fluids, antibiotics, as ordered.

*Nurses should follow agency's protocol regarding interventions. These may vary among agencies.

PROCEDURE 40.6 Initiating, Maintaining, and Terminating a Blood Transfusion Using a Y-Set

PURPOSES

- To restore blood volume after severe hemorrhage
- To restore the capacity of the blood to carry oxygen
- To provide plasma factors, such as antihemophilic factor (AHF) or factor VIII, or platelet concentrates to prevent or treat bleeding

Assessment Focus
Clinical signs of reaction (e.g., sudden chills, fever, nausea, itching, rash, low back pain, dyspnea); manifestations of hypervolemia; status of infusion site; vital signs; any unusual symptoms

Equipment

- ❑ Unit of whole blood or packed RBCs
- ❑ Blood administration set
- ❑ 250 mL normal saline for infusion
- ❑ IV pole
- ❑ Venipuncture set containing a #18- or #19-gauge needle or catheter (if one is not already in place) or, if blood is to be administered quickly, a #15-gauge needle or a larger catheter (e.g., #14)
- ❑ Povidone-iodine solution or scrub pad (optional)
- ❑ Alcohol swabs
- ❑ Tape
- ❑ Gloves

INTERVENTION

1. **Verify client consent and obtain baseline data before the transfusion.**

- Verify that a signed consent form was obtained.
- Assess vital signs for baseline data, including blood pressure, pulse, respiratory rate and depth, and temperature.
- Determine any known allergies or previous adverse reactions to blood.
- Note specific signs related to the client's pathology and the reason for the transfusion. For example, for an anemic client, note the hemoglobin and hematocrit levels.

2. **Prepare the client.**

- Explain the procedure and its purpose to the client. Instruct the client to report promptly any sudden chills, nausea, itching, rash, dyspnea, back pain, or other unusual symptoms.
- If the client has an intravenous solution infusing, check whether the needle and solution are appropriate to administer blood. The needle should be #18 or #19 gauge, and the solution must be normal saline. Dextrose (which causes lysis of RBCs), Ringer's solution, medications and other additives, and hyperalimentation solutions are incompatible. See step 7 if the infusing solution is not compatible.
- If the client does not have an IV solution infusing, check agency policies. In some agencies, an infusion must be running before the blood is obtained from the blood bank. In this case, you will need to perform a venipuncture on a suitable vein (see Procedure 40.1) and start an IV infusion of normal saline.

3. **Obtain the correct blood component for the client.**

- Check the physician's order with the requisition.
- Check the requisition form and the blood bag label with a laboratory technician or according to agency policy. Specifically, check the client's name, identification number, blood type (A, B, AB, or O) and Rh group, the blood donor number, and the expiry date of the blood. Observe the blood for abnormal colour, RBC clumping, gas bubbles, and extraneous material. Return outdated or abnormal blood to the blood bank.
- Compare the laboratory blood record with a registered nurse (or according to agency policy) for:
  - **a.** The client's name and identification number
  - **b.** The number on the blood bag label
  - **c.** The ABO group and Rh type on the blood bag label
- If any of the information does not match *exactly,* notify the charge nurse and the blood bank. Do not administer blood until discrepancies are corrected or clarified.
- Sign the appropriate form and complete documentation with the other nurse, according to agency policy.
- Make sure that the blood is left at room temperature for no more than 30 minutes before starting the transfusion (check agency policy). *RBCs deteriorate and lose their effectiveness after two hours at room temperature. Lysis of RBCs releases potassium into the bloodstream, causing hyperkalemia.* Agencies may designate different times at which the blood must be returned to the blood bank if it has not been used. *As blood components warm, the risk of bacterial growth also increases.* If the start of the transfusion is unexpectedly delayed, return the blood to the blood bank. Do not store blood in the unit refrigerator. *The temperature of unit refrigerators is not precisely regulated, and the blood may be damaged.*

→

PROCEDURE 40.6 Initiating, Maintaining, and Terminating a Blood Transfusion Using a Y-Set *continued*

4. Verify the client's identity (two nurses required).

- Wash your hands.
- Ask the client's full name.
- Check the client's arm band for name and ID number. Do not administer blood to a client who does not have an arm band.

5. Set up the infusion equipment.

- Ensure that the blood filter inside the drip chamber is suitable for whole blood or the blood components to be transfused. Attach the blood tubing to the blood filter, if necessary. Blood filters have a surface area large enough to allow the blood components through easily but are designed to trap clots.
- Put on gloves.
- Close all the clamps on the Y-set: the main flow rate clamp and both Y-line clamps.
- Hang the container on the IV pole about 1 m above the planned venipuncture site.
- Using a twisting motion, insert the piercing pin (spike) into a container of 0.9 percent saline solution.

6. Prime the tubing.

- Open the upper clamp on the normal saline tubing, and squeeze the drip chamber until it covers the filter and one-third of the drip chamber above the filter.
- Tap the filter chamber to expel any residual air.
- Remove the adapter cover at the tip of the blood administration set.
- Open the main flow rate clamp, and prime the tubing with saline.
- Close both clamps.

7. Start the saline solution.

- If an IV solution incompatible with blood is infusing, stop the infusion, and discard the solution and tubing according to agency policy.
- Attach the blood tubing primed with normal saline to the intravenous catheter.
- Open the saline and main flow rate clamps, and adjust the flow rate. Use only the main flow rate clamp to adjust the rate.
- Allow a small amount of solution to infuse to make sure there are no problems with the flow or with the venipuncture site. *Infusing normal saline before initiating the transfusion also clears the IV catheter of incompatible solutions or medications.*

8. Prepare the blood bag.

- Invert the blood bag gently several times to mix the cells with the plasma, according to agency policy. *Rough handling can damage the cells.*
- Expose the port on the blood bag by pulling back the tabs (Figure 40.31).
- Insert the remaining Y-set spike into the blood bag.
- Suspend the blood bag.
- Open the upper clamp on the Y-set arm to the blood, and prime the tubing.

9. Establish the blood transfusion.

- Close the upper clamp below the IV saline solution container. Open the upper clamp below the blood bag. The blood will run into the saline-filled drip chamber. If necessary, squeeze the drip chamber to re-establish the liquid level with drip chamber one-third full. (Tap the filter to expel any residual air within the filter.)
- Re-adjust the flow rate with the main clamp.

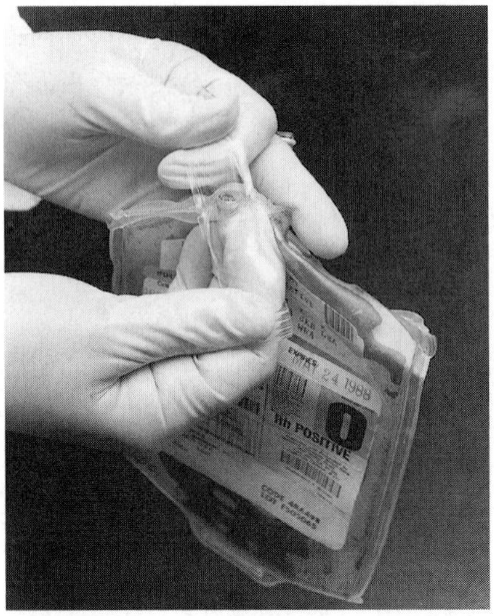

Figure 40.31 Exposing the port on the blood bag by pulling back the tabs

10. Observe the client closely for the first five to 10 minutes, remaining with the client. Assess frequently for the first 30 minutes following.

- Run the blood slowly for the first 15 minutes.
- Note adverse reactions, such as chilling, nausea, vomiting, skin rash, tachycardia, or change in vital signs. *The earlier a transfusion reaction occurs, the more severe it tends to be. Identifying such reactions promptly helps minimize the consequences.*
- Remind the client to tell a nurse immediately if any unusual symptoms are felt during the transfusion.
- If any of these reactions occur, report these to the nurse in charge, and take appropriate nursing action. See Table 40.15 on page 1122.
- Change IV administration set or flush IV administration line and normal saline thoroughly (according to agency policy) between units of blood products.

11. Document relevant data.

- Record initiation of the blood transfusion, including vital signs, type of blood, blood unit number, sequence number (e.g., no. 1 of three ordered units), site of the venipuncture, size of the needle, and drip rate.

12. Monitor the client.

- Fifteen minutes after initiating the transfusion, check the vital signs of the client. If there are no signs of a reaction, establish the required flow rate. Follow physician's orders and agency policy regarding length of time for transfusion. Do not transfuse a unit of blood for longer than four hours.

PROCEDURE 40.6 Initiating, Maintaining, and Terminating a Blood Transfusion Using a Y-Set *continued*

- Assess the client, including vital signs, every 30 minutes or more often, depending on the client's health status, until one hour post transfusion. If the client has a reaction and the blood is discontinued, send the blood bag to the laboratory for investigation of the blood.

13. Terminate the transfusion.

- Wash your hands.
- Put on clean gloves.
- If no infusion is to follow, clamp the blood tubing, and remove the needle.
- If the primary IV is to be continued, flush the maintenance line with saline solution. Disconnect the blood tubing system, and re-establish the intravenous infusion using new tubing. Adjust the drip to the desired rate. *Often, a normal saline or other solution is kept running in case of delayed reaction to the blood.*
- Discard the administration set according to agency practice. Needles should be placed in a labelled, puncture-resistant container designed for such disposal. Blood bags and administration sets should be bagged and labelled before being sent for decontamination and processing. See agency policy.
- Remove gloves.
- Again monitor vital signs.

14. Follow agency protocol for appropriate disposition of the blood bag.

- On the requisition attached to the blood unit, fill in the time the transfusion was completed and the amount transfused.
- Attach one copy of the requisition to the client's record and another to the empty blood bag.
- Return the blood bag and requisition to the blood bank.

15. Document relevant data.

- Record completion of the transfusion, the amount of blood absorbed, the blood unit number, and the vital signs and any signs and symptoms noted. If the primary intravenous infusion was continued, record connecting it. Also record the transfusion on the IV flow sheet and I & O record.

Evaluation Focus
Changes in vital signs or health status; presence of chills, nausea, vomiting, or skin rash (See table 40.15)

preventing associated risks of fluid, electrolyte, and acid-base imbalances, the nurse collects data to evaluate the effectiveness of interventions. Examples of desired outcomes for the identified goals are found in Table 40.16.

If desired outcomes are not achieved, the nurse, client, and support person, if appropriate, need to explore the reasons before modifying the care plan. For example, if the outcome "Urine output is greater than 1,300 mL per day and within 500 mL of intake" is not achieved, questions to be considered might include the following:

- Have other outcome measures for the goal of achieving fluid balance been met?
- Does the client understand and comply with planned fluid intake?
- Is all urinary output being measured?
- Are unusual or excessive amounts of fluid being lost by another route (e.g., gastric suction, excessive perspiration, fever, rapid respiratory rate, wound drainage)?
- Are prescribed medications being taken or administered as ordered?

Consider...

What actions would you take if the client did not meet the following outcome criteria?

- "Lung sounds are clear." (Data reveal a cough productive of yellow sputum and coarse crackles in both lung bases.)
- "Alert; oriented to person, place, and time; speech clear." (Data reveal the client is alert, rousing easily, but is disoriented to time and place, and speech is confused.)

TABLE 40.16 Evaluation Goals and Outcomes: Fluid, Electrolyte, and Acid-Base Balances

Goal	Examples of Expected Outcomes
Maintain or restore normal fluid balance	Vital signs, including blood pressure, pulse, respirations, temperature, and central venous pressure, are within expected ranges
	Lung sounds are clear
	Urine output is greater than 1,300 mL per day and within 500 mL of intake
	Skin turgor is elastic; tongue and mucous membranes are moist
	No edema is evident
	Absence of thirst
	Weight is within normal range for client
	Laboratory values within normal range (serum osmolality, serum sodium, hematocrit, urine specific gravity)
	Explains measures to prevent or treat fluid volume deficit or excess and symptoms that need to be reported to health-care provider
Maintain or restore normal balance of electrolytes in the intracellular and extracellular compartments	Vital signs are stable and within expected ranges
	Alert; oriented to person, place, and time; speech clear
	Muscle strength is normal
	Absence of abnormal sensations, such as numbness, tingling around mouth or distal extremities
	Laboratory values within normal range (serum sodium, potassium, calcium, chloride, magnesium)
	Verbalizes measures to prevent future imbalances, including diet, medications
Maintain or restore pulmonary ventilation and oxygenation	Respiratory rate within normal range, no dyspnea or shortness of breath
	Demonstrates effective cough
	Lung sounds are clear
	Identifies specific factors leading to impaired airway clearance
Prevent associated risks (tissue breakdown, decreased cardiac output, confusion, other neurological signs)	Skin and mucous membranes are intact
	Skin is warm and pink
	Capillary refill is less than three seconds
	Lung sounds are clear
	Alert and oriented; no confusion evident

FOCUS ON CRITICAL THINKING

Mr. Sam, 74, was admitted to the hospital with a diagnosis of acute gastroenteritis following a three-day episode of fever and severe diarrhea. He is 178 cm tall and weighs 78 kg. His oral temperature is 38.7°C; pulse 98 and regular; respirations 32, and BP 106/86. His skin is flushed and diaphoretic. His lungs are clear to auscultation. His abdomen is tender throughout, and bowel sounds are hyperactive in all quadrants. His urine output is scanty and concentrated. He has an intravenous infusion of lactated Ringer's solution infusing at 125 mL/hr via an infusion pump.

1. Predict the possible consequences of Mr. Sam's fever, diarrhea, and diaphoresis on his fluid and electrolyte status.
2. Why do you think the physician ordered lactated Ringer's solution for Mr. Sam rather than another type of fluid replacement, such as 5 percent dextrose in water?
3. Why is it important to monitor Mr. Sam's intake and output?
4. Is it correct to assume that Mr. Sam's intravenous infusion does not need to be monitored since it is being administered by an infusion pump? Why, or why not?
5. How would you know if Mr. Sam was developing an acid-base imbalance related to his severe diarrhea?

See Appendix A for answers to these questions.

SAMPLE CARE PLAN FOR FLUID VOLUME DEFICIT

ASSESSMENT DATA

Nursing Assessment

Mrs. Joan O'Brien is a 46-year-old waitress who underwent extensive surgery yesterday for pancreatic cancer. History includes indigestion for several months, vague pain and tenderness in the upper right abdomen, severe nausea and vomiting, anorexia, and weight loss. Mrs. O'Brien returned from surgery with a nasogastric tube connected to low intermittent suction and a T-tube to gravity drainage. She is NPO and is receiving total parenteral nutrition via a central line at 100 mL/hr. Her skin and mucous membranes are dry.

Physical Examination

Height: 160 cm
Weight: 56.2 kg
Temperature: 38.1°C
Pulse: 96 BPM
Respirations: 28/minute
Blood pressure: 110/70 mm Hg
Diminished skin turgor, skin dry and mucous membranes dry/sticky; dark amber urine; intake 1800 mL, output 600 mL in eight-hour period

Diagnostic Data

Chest x-ray negative; serum sodium 155 mmol/L; serum osmolality 310 mmol/kg; serum potassium 3.2 mmol/L; urine specific gravity 1.035, serum albumin 19 g/L.

Nursing Diagnosis

Fluid Volume Deficit related to nausea, vomiting, nasogastric suctioning (as evidenced by decreased skin turgor, dry skin and mucous membranes, decreased urinary output, elevated urine specific gravity, elevated serum osmolality, hypernatremia)

Client Goal(s)

Mrs. O'Brien will achieve normal hydration and electrolyte balance.

Desired Outcomes

1. Demonstrates no signs and symptoms of dehydration
2. Maintains a urine specific gravity and serum osmolality within normal range
3. Maintains serum sodium levels within normal range

*Nursing Interventions and Selected Activities with Rationale *[in italics]*

Fluid/Electrolyte Management

- Monitor laboratory results relevant to fluid balance (e.g., hematocrit, BUN, serum osmolality, and urine specific gravity levels).
  These serum laboratory values reflect hydration status. Urine specific gravity measures the kidneys' ability to concentrate urine; serum osmolality reflects sodium and water concentration; hematocrit can become diluted or concentrated in direct relation to total body water.
- Maintain intravenous solution containing electrolyte(s) at constant flow rate, as appropriate.
  Electrolyte replacement must be done cautiously so as not to overload the client and create adverse complications. For example, potassium deficit or excess can cause cardiac irregularities.
- Assess Mrs. O'Brien's buccal membranes, sclera, and skin for indications of altered fluid and electrolyte balance (e.g., dryness).
  Skin turgor and hydration of mucous membranes depend partially on interstitial fluid volume. In a client with fluid volume deficit, the skin may remain elevated when pinched and oral mucous membranes may be dry and even sticky.
- Consult physician if signs and symptoms of fluid or electrolyte imbalance persist or worsen.
  For optimal care, the nurse must work closely with the physician in the detection and treatment of fluid and electrolyte imbalances, which can be life-threatening.

Electrolyte Management: Hypernatremia

- Obtain laboratory specimens for analysis of altered sodium levels (e.g., serum and urine sodium, serum and urine chloride, urine osmolality, and urine specific gravity), as appropriate.
  Urinary analysis provides information about retention or loss of sodium and the ability of the kidneys to concentrate or dilute urine in response to fluid alterations.
- Monitor for indications of dehydration (e.g., decreased sweating, decreased urine, decreased skin turgor, and dry mucous membranes).
  Close monitoring for manifestations of low fluid volume will assist in early treatment and prevention of severe fluid and electrolyte imbalances.
- Provide frequent oral hygiene.
  Oral mucous membranes become dry and sticky due to loss of fluid in the interstitial spaces.

→

SAMPLE CARE PLAN FOR FLUID VOLUME DEFICIT *continued*

- Monitor for neurological and neuromuscular manifestations of hypernatremia (e.g., lethargy, irritability, seizures, coma, muscle rigidity, tremors, and hyperreflexia).

Hypernatremia as a result of low fluid volume creates a hypertonic vascular space, which causes water to move out of the cells, including brain cells. This accounts for neurological symptoms.

- Monitor for cardiac manifestations of hypernatremia (e.g., tachycardia, orthostatic hypotension, and flat neck veins).

Hypernatremia, as in this case, is a result of fluid volume deficit, which makes the serum sodium level appear elevated. The heart responds to a loss of fluid from the intravascular space by increasing the heart rate to compensate with an increase in cardiac output. Lowered fluid volume leads to a fall in blood pressure and flat neck veins.

Total Parenteral Nutrition (TPN) Administration

- Monitor the central line for infiltration and infection.

TPN is a glucose-rich solution that invites bacteria. Therefore, the central line should be carefully monitored for infiltration and infection.

- Check the TPN solution to ensure that the correct nutrients are included, as ordered.

TPN is characteristically composed of multiple electrolytes and nutrients, including amino acids, multivitamins, and zinc. Often, these ingredients are adjusted frequently on the basis of the client's serum values, so they should be checked closely before hanging each bottle.

- Use an infusion pump for delivery of TPN solutions.

Because TPN is a hypertonic solution made up of glucose and numerous electrolytes, careful administration is necessary to avoid creating fluid and electrolyte imbalances.

- Monitor daily weight and intake and output.

Weight and I & O are good indicators of fluid volume status. In addition, weight should be monitored in clients receiving TPN as a nutritional supplement.

- Monitor serum albumin, total protein, electrolyte and glucose levels, and chemistry profile.

Because TPN is composed of amino acids, electrolytes, glucose, and other elements, laboratory values that reflect serum levels of these substances should be closely monitored to achieve appropriate outcomes.

- Administer insulin, as ordered, to maintain serum glucose levels in the designated range, as appropriate.

Clients receiving glucose-rich TPN are at risk for hyperglycemia, so blood sugars are monitored approximately q6h for possible insulin administration on a sliding-scale regimen.

Evaluation

Goal met. On the fourth postoperative day, Mrs. O'Brien's skin has normal turgor, and her mucous membranes are moist. The nasogastric tube has been removed, and she is taking sips of water. Her 24-hour fluid intake has been 2,000 mL and her urinary output 1,500 mL. Lab values are within normal range (serum osmolality 285 mmol/kg, serum sodium 138 mmol/L, and urine specific gravity 1.020).

---

*Interventions and activities selected are only a sample of those suggested in the *Nursing interventions classification (NIC)* and should be individualized for each client.

Source: McCloskey, J. C., & Bulechek, G. M. (2000). *Iowa intervention project: Nursing interventions classification (NIC)* (3rd ed.). St. Louis, MO: Mosby.

CHAPTER HIGHLIGHTS

- A balance of fluids, electrolytes, acids, and bases in the body is necessary for health and life.
- The body fluid is divided into two major compartments: the intracellular fluid (ICF) inside the cells and extracellular fluid (ECF) outside the cells.
- Extracellular fluid is subdivided into two compartments: intravascular (plasma) and interstitial. ECF constitutes about 38 percent of total body fluid.
- ECF is in constant motion throughout the body. It is the transport system that carries nutrients to, and waste products from, the cells.
- The percentage of total body fluids varies according to the individual's age, body fat, and gender. The younger the person, the higher the proportion of water in the body. The less body fat present, the greater the proportion of body fluid. Post-adolescent females have a smaller percentage of fluid in relation to total body weight than do men.
- There are two types of electrolytes (ions): positively charged ions (cations) and negatively charged ions (anions).
- The principal ions of ECF are sodium and chloride; the principal ions of ICF are potassium and phosphate.
- Fluids and electrolytes move among the body compartments by osmosis, diffusion, filtration, and active transport.
- The major fluid pressures exerted as part of the movement of fluid and electrolytes from one compartment to another are osmotic pressure and hydrostatic pressure.
- The three sources of body fluid are fluids taken orally, food ingested, and the oxidation of food. Fluid intake is regulated by the thirst mechanism.
- Fluid output occurs chiefly through excretion of urine, although body fluid is also lost through sweat, feces, and insensible vapour loss.
- In healthy adults, measurable fluid intake and output should balance (about 1,500 mL per day). The output of urine normally approximates the oral intake of fluids. Water from food and oxidation is balanced by fluid loss through the skin, respiratory process, and feces.
- A number of body systems and organs are involved in regulating the volume and composition of body fluids: the kidneys, the endocrine system, the cardiovascular system, the lungs, and the gastrointestinal system. The kidneys are the primary regulator of fluid and electrolyte balance.
- Hormones, such as antidiuretic hormone, the renin-angiotensin-aldosterone system, and the atrial natriuretic factor are also involved in maintaining fluid balance.
- Fluid imbalances include:
  - Fluid volume deficit (FVD), also referred to as hypovolemia
  - Fluid volume excess (FVE), also referred to as hypervolemia
  - Dehydration, a deficit in water only
  - Overhydration, an excess of water only
- The most common electrolyte imbalances are deficits or excesses in sodium, potassium, and calcium.
- The pH of body fluids is maintained within a precise range of 7.35 to 7.45.
- Acid-base balance is regulated by buffers that neutralize excess acids or bases; the lungs, which eliminate or retain carbon dioxide, a potential acid; and the kidneys, which excrete or conserve bicarbonate and hydrogen ions.
- Acid-base imbalance occurs when the normal 20-to-1 ratio of bicarbonate to carbonic acid is upset. Imbalances may be either respiratory or metabolic in origin; either can result in acidosis or alkalosis.
- Factors that influence an individual's fluid, electrolyte, and acid-base balance include age, gender, body size, environmental temperature, and lifestyle. Illness, trauma, surgery, and certain medications can place individuals at risk for fluid, electrolyte, and acid-base imbalances.
- Fluid, electrolyte, and acid-base imbalance is most accurately determined through laboratory examination of blood plasma.
- Assessment relative to fluid, electrolyte, and acid-base balances includes (1) a nursing history; (2) physical examination; (3) measurement of body weight, vital signs, and fluid intake and output; and (4) various diagnostic studies of blood and urine.
- A nursing history includes data about the client's fluid and food intake; fluid output; signs of fluid, electrolyte, and acid-base imbalances; and medications, therapies, or disease processes that may disrupt these balances.
- NANDA-approved nursing diagnoses that relate specifically to fluid, electrolyte, and acid-base imbalances include ***Fluid Volume Deficient, Fluid Volume Excess, Risk for Fluid Volume Imbalance***, and ***Impaired Gas Exchange.***

  Other diagnoses that may be relevant are ***Impaired Oral Mucous Membrane, Impaired Skin Integrity, Decreased Cardiac Output, Altered Tissue Perfusion, Activity Intolerance, Risk for Injury***, and ***Acute Confusion.***
- In many instances, fluids and electrolytes are provided orally to clients who are experiencing or at risk of developing fluid deficits. The nurse needs to

establish with the client a 24-hour plan for ingesting the necessary fluids and to respect the client's fluid preferences.

- For clients with fluid retention, fluids may need to be restricted; a schedule and short-term goals that make the fluid restriction more tolerable need to be developed.
- For clients experiencing excessive fluid losses, the administration of fluids and electrolytes intravenously is necessary. Meticulous aseptic technique is required when caring for clients with intravenous infusions.
- Preventing complications, such as infiltration, phlebitis, hypervolemia (circulatory overload), and infection, is an important aspect of intravenous therapy.
- The administration of blood transfusions involves accurately matching and identifying the blood for the individual, correctly identifying the recipient, and monitoring the client throughout the procedure for transfusion reactions.

READINGS AND REFERENCES

Suggested Readings

Cohen, P. (1997, April 9). Intravenous therapy at home. *Nursing Times, 93*(15), 42, 44.
In this article, the benefits and challenges of home intravenous therapy are reviewed. Situations in which home IV therapy may be appropriate are presented, and the need for ongoing assessment and communication is emphasized.

Tasota, F. J., & Wesmiller, S. W. (1994, May). Assessing ABGs: Maintaining the delicate balance. *Nursing, 24*(5), 34–44.
This article reviews arterial blood gases and presents a systematic method for evaluating ABG results and assessing oxygenation and acid-base balance. Four case studies are included.

Vonfrolio, L. G. (1995, June). Back to basics: Would you hang these IV solutions? *American Journal of Nursing, 95*(6), 37–39.
This article reviews isotonic, hypotonic, and hypertonic intravenous solutions and asks the nurse to assess IV orders for clients in different situations.

Zerwekh, J. V. (1997, March). Do dying patients really need IV fluids? *American Journal of Nursing, 97*(3), 26–30.
In this article, the author challenges the assumption that dying clients need to be hydrated for comfort. Studies are reviewed that support the idea that some physiological effects of dehydration actually relieve suffering in the dying client.

Related Research

Meyer, F., Bar-Or, O., MacDougall, D., & Heigenhauser, G. J. F. (1995, June). Drink composition and the electrolyte balance of children exercising in the heat. *Medicine and Science in Sports and Exercise, 27*, 882–887.

Selected References

Abraham, W. T., & Schrier, R. W. (1994). Body fluid volume regulation in health and disease. *Advances in Internal Medicine, 39*, 23–43.

Ackley, B. J., & Ladwig, G. B. (1997). *Nursing diagnosis handbook: A guide to planning care.* St. Louis, MO: Mosby-Year Book.

Belcaster, A. (1997, April). Venous air embolism. *Nursing, 27*(4), 33.

Bove, L. A. (1994, August). How fluids and electrolytes shift after surgery. *Nursing, 24*(8), 34–39.

Carpenito, L. (2002). *Nursing diagnosis: Application to clinical practice* (10th ed.). Philadelphia: Lippincott Williams and Wilkins.

Cirolia, B. (1996, February). Understanding edema: When fluid balance fails. *Nursing, 26*(2), 66.

Claton, K. (1997, May). Cancer-related hypercalcemia: How to spot it, how to manage it. *American Journal of Nursing, 97*(5), 42–48.

Finlay, T. (1997, January 8). Making sense of ... parenteral nutrition in adult patients. *Nursing Times, 93*(2), 35–36.

Frey, A. M. (1997, September). IV rounds: Tips for pediatric IV insertion. *Nursing 97, 27*(9), 32.

Frey, A. M. (1998, April). IV rounds: When a child needs peripheral IV therapy, use these suggestions to choose the right site. *Nursing 98, 28*(4), 18.

Gabriel, J. (1997, March 5). Fibrin sheaths in vascular access devices. *Nursing Times, 93*(10), 56–57.

Galsworthy, T. D., & Wilson, P. L. (1996, June). Osteoporosis: It steals more than bone. *American Journal of Nursing, 96*(6), 27–33.

Grisolfi, C. V. (1996, April). Fluid balance for optimal performance. *Nutrition Reviews, 54*(4), S159–S167.

Hadaway, L. (1999). Choosing the right vascular access device, part I. *Nursing, 29*(2), 28.

Hadaway, L. (1999). Choosing the right vascular access device, part II. *Nursing, 29*(7), 28.

Houston, C. J. (1996, March). Hemolytic transfusion reaction. *American Journal of Nursing, 96*(3), 47.

Johnson, M., & Maas, M. (Eds.). (2000). *Iowa outcomes project: Nursing outcomes classification (NOC).* St. Louis, MO: Mosby.

Josephson, D. L. (1999). *Intravenous infusion therapy for nurses: Principles and practice.* Albany, NY: Delmar.

Lee, C. A. B., Barrett, C. A., & Ignatavicius, D. D. (1996). *Fluids and electrolytes: A practical approach* (4th ed.). Philadelphia, PA: F. A. Davis.

Mack, G. W., Weseman, C. A., Langhans, G. W., Scherzer, H., Gillen, C. M., & Nadel, E. R. (1994, April). Body fluid balance in dehydrated healthy older men: Thirst and renal osmoregulation. *Journal of Applied Physiology, 76*, 1615–1623.

Masoorli, S., Angeles, T., & Barbone, M. (1998, September). Danger points: How to prevent nerve injuries from venipuncture. *Nursing 98, 28*(9), 35–39.

McCloskey, J. C., & Bulechek, G. M. (Eds.). (2000). *Iowa intervention project: Nursing interventions classification (NIC).* St. Louis, MO: Mosby.

McEntee, M. A. (Ed.). (1997). *Fluids and electrolytes.* Albany, NY: Delmar.

Metheny, N. M. (1996). *Fluid and electrolyte balance: Nursing considerations* (3rd ed.). Philadelphia, PA: Lippincott.

Meyer, F., & Bar-Or, O. (1994, January). Fluid and electrolyte loss during exercise: The paediatric angle. *Sports Medicine, 18*(1), 4–9.

Miller, M. (1995, June). Hormonal aspects of fluid and sodium balance in the elderly. *Endocrinology and Metabolism Clinics of North America, 24*(2), 233–250.

North American Nursing Diagnosis Association. (2001). *NANDA nursing diagnoses: Definitions and classification, 2000–2001.* Philadelphia, PA: Author.

Nursing. (1996, April). Blood transfusions: Playing it safe. *Nursing, 26*(4), 50–52.

Nursing. (1996, October). Intravenous therapy handbook. *Nursing, 26*(10), 40–51.

O'Donnell, M. E. (1995, November). Assessing fluid and electrolyte balance in elders. *American Journal of Nursing, 95*(11), 40–45.

Pagana, K. D., & Pagana, T. J. (1997). *Mosby's diagnostic and laboratory test reference* (3rd ed.). St. Louis, MO: Mosby-Year Book.

Peterson, K. L. (1996, August). Performing under pressure. *Nursing, 26*(8), 52–55.

Phillips, L. D. (2001). *Manual of IV therapeutics* (3rd ed.). Philadelphia, PA: F. A. Davis.

Porth, C. M. (1998). *Pathophysiology: Concepts of altered health states* (4th ed.). Philadelphia, PA: Lippincott.

Preston, R. A. (1997). *Acid-base, fluids, and electrolytes made ridiculously simple.* Miami, FL: MedMaster.

Radke, K. J. (1994, June). The aging kidney: Structure, function, and nursing practice implications. *ANNA Journal, 21*(4), 181–190.

Rankin, J. A. (2000). Unit 6: Fluid and electrolytes. In: J. A. Rankin, M. A. Reimer, & K. L. Then (Eds.). *Nursing 461 Pathophysiology Module*. Faculty of Nursing, University of Calgary.

Roper, M. (1996, August). Assessing orthostatic vital signs. *American Journal of Nursing, 96*(8), 43–46.

Scmid. M. (2000). Risks and complications of peripherally and centrally inserted intravenous catheters. *Critical Care Nursing Clinics of North America, 12*(2), 164–174.

Sheahan, S. L. (1996, June). The role of orthostatic vital signs in assessing patients with diarrhea and vomiting. *ADVANCE for Nurse Practitioners, 4*(6), 37–38, 60.

Silverthorn, D.U. (1998). *Human physiology: An integrated approach*. New Jersey, NJ: Prentice Hall.

Thibodeau, G. A., & Patton, K. T. (2003). *Anatomy and physiology* (5th ed.). St. Louis, MO: Mosby.

Toto, K. H. (1994, December). Regulation of plasma osmolality: Thirst and vasopressin. *Critical Care Nursing Clinics of North America, 6*(4), 661–674.

Vander, A. Sherman, J., & Luciano, P. (2001). *Human physiology: The mechanisms of body function* (8th ed.). Boston: McGraw-Hill.

Vander, A. J. (1995). *Renal physiology* (5th ed.). New York: McGraw-Hill.

Vonfrolio, L. G. (1995, June). Back to basics: Would you hang these IV solutions? *American Journal of Nursing, 95*(6), 37–39.

Watkins, S. L. (1995, January). The basics of fluid and electrolyte therapy. *Pediatric Annals, 24*(1), 16–22.

White, V. M. (1997, June). Hyperkalemia. *American Journal of Nursing, 97*(6), 35.

Wilkinson, J. M. (2000). *Nursing diagnosis and intervention guide* (7th ed.). Menlo Park, CA: Addison-Wesley Nursing.

Young, J. (1998, October). A closer look at IV fluids: Learn how to avoid complications by choosing the right fluid for your patient's condition. *Nursing 98, 28*(10), 52–55.

WEBLINKS

Canadian Association of Nephrology Nurses and Technologists
http://www.cannt.ca/cannt_overview.htm
This is a group of health-care professionals with a commitment to specialized care of nephrology patients. The association promotes the dissemination of knowledge among those involved in the care of patients with renal disease.

The Kidney Foundation of Canada
http://www.kidney.ca/index-eng.html
The foundation is a national volunteer organization dedicated to improving the health and quality of life of people living with kidney disease. The organization funds research and related clinical education, provides services for special needs of individuals, and actively promotes the awareness of organ donation.

CHAPTER 41

Sensory Perception

OBJECTIVES

After completing this chapter, you will be able to:

- Discuss anatomical and physiological components of the sensory-perceptual process.
- Describe factors influencing sensory function.
- List factors that place a client at risk for sensory disturbances.
- Outline essential components in assessing a client's sensory-perceptual function.
- Identify clinical signs and symptoms of sensory overload and deprivation.
- Develop nursing diagnoses and outcome criteria for clients with impaired sensory function.
- Discuss nursing interventions to promote and maintain sensory function.
- Describe strategies to promote and maintain orientation to person, place, time, and situation for the client who is disoriented.
- Identify community resources for clients with chronic sensory disturbances.

An individual's senses are essential for growth, development, and survival. Sensory stimuli give meaning to events in the environment. Any alteration in people's sensory functions can affect their ability to function within the environment. For example, many clients have impaired sensory functions that put them at risk in the health-care setting; nurses can help them find ways to function safely in this often confusing environment.

Components of the Sensory Experience

Reception and Perception

The sensory process involves two components: reception and perception. **Sensory reception** is the process of receiving stimuli or data. These stimuli are either external or internal to the body. External stimuli are **visual** (sight), **auditory** (hearing), **olfactory** (smell), **tactile** (touch), and **gustatory** (taste). Gustatory stimuli can be internal as well. Other types of internal stimuli are kinesthetic or visceral. **Kinesthetic** refers to awareness of the position and movement of body parts. For example, a person walking is aware of which leg is forward. A related sense is **stereognosis,** the awareness of an object's size, shape, and texture by touch. For example, a person holding a tennis ball is aware of its size, round shape, and soft surface without seeing it. **Visceral** refers to any large organ within the body. Visceral organs may produce stimuli that make a person aware of them (e.g., a full stomach). **Sensory perception** involves the conscious organization and translation of the data or stimuli into meaningful information.

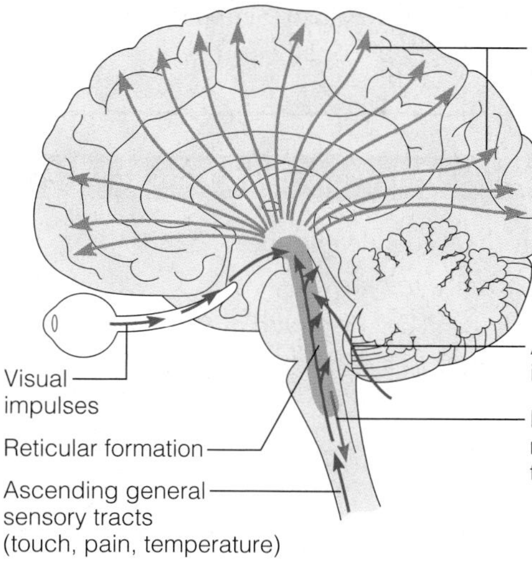

Figure 41.1 The nerve impulses run along the ascending sensory tracts to reach the reticular activating system (RAS); then certain impulses reach the cerebral cortex, where they are perceived

Source: Marieb, E. N. (2003). *Human anatomy and physiology.* 7th ed. Copyright © 2003 by Benjamin Cummings Publishing Company. Reprinted by permission.

For an individual to be aware of the surroundings, four aspects of the sensory process must be present: a stimulus, a receptor, impulse conduction, and perception.

- *Stimulus.* An agent or act that stimulates a nerve receptor.
- *Receptor.* A nerve cell acts as a receptor by converting the stimulus to a nerve impulse. Most receptors are specific, that is, sensitive to only one type of stimulus, such as visual, auditory, or touch.
- *Impulse conduction.* The impulse travels along nerve pathways to the spinal cord or directly to the brain (Figure 41.1). For example, auditory impulses travel to the organ of Corti in the inner ear. From there, the impulses travel along the eighth cranial nerve to the temporal lobe of the brain.
- *Perception.* Perception, or awareness and interpretation of stimuli, takes place in the brain where specialized brain cells interpret the nature and the quality of the sensory stimuli. The level of consciousness affects the perception of the stimuli.

Arousal Mechanism

For the person to receive and interpret stimuli, the brain must be alert. The *reticular activating system* (RAS) in the brain stem is thought to mediate the arousal mechanism. There are two components of the reticular activating system: the *reticular excitatory area* (REA) and the *reticular inhibitory area* (RIA). See Figure 41.1. The reticular excitatory area is responsible for stimulus arousal and wakefulness.

People have their own zone of optimum arousal, the level at which the person feels comfortable. *Sensoristasis* is the term used to describe optimum arousal for an individual. Beyond this comfort zone, people must adapt to the increased or decreased sensory stimuli.

The brain has the capacity to adapt to most sensory stimuli. For example, a person living in a city may not notice traffic noises that someone from a rural area finds loud and disturbing. Not all sensory stimuli are acted on; some are stored by the memory to be used at a later date. *Cognition* is cerebral functioning. It involves such processes as conscious thought, reality orientation, problem solving, judgement, and comprehension.

Awareness is the ability to perceive environmental stimuli and body reactions and to respond appropriately through thought and action. The normal, alert person can assimilate many kinds of information at one time. There are several states of awareness. See Table 41.1.

Sensory Alterations

People become accustomed to certain sensory stimuli, and when these change markedly, the individual may experience discomfort. For example, when clients enter a hospital, they

TABLE 41.1 States of Awareness

State	Description
Full consciousness	Alert; oriented to time, place, person; understands verbal and written words
Disoriented	Not oriented to time, place, or person
Confused	Reduced awareness, easily bewildered; poor memory, misinterprets stimuli; impaired judgement
Somnolent	Extreme drowsiness but will respond to stimuli
Semicomatose	Responds to painful stimuli only
Coma*	No purposeful response to stimuli; may still react to deep pain but only with atypical posturing

*See Glasgow Coma Scale, Table 27.12.

usually experience stimuli that differ in quantity and quality. These changes may cause clients to become confused and disoriented. See Table 41.1.

Nurses should be aware of behaviours that result from different stimuli. Colour, sound, privacy, and social interaction for clients can be modified to more closely resemble those in the home environment. Factors that contribute to alterations in behaviour include sensory deprivation, sensory overload, and sensory deficits.

Sensory Deprivation

Sensory deprivation is generally thought of as a decrease in or lack of meaningful stimuli. When a person experiences sensory deprivation, the balance in the reticular activating system (RAS) is disturbed. The RAS is unable to maintain normal stimulation to the cerebral cortex. Because of this reduced stimulation, a person becomes more acutely aware of the remaining stimuli and often perceives these in a distorted manner. Thus, the person often experiences alterations in perception, cognition, and emotion. See the accompanying box for the clinical signs of sensory deprivation.

Clinical Signs of Sensory Deprivation

- Excessive yawning, drowsiness, sleeping
- Decreased attention span, difficulty concentrating, decreased problem solving
- Impaired memory
- Periodic disorientation, general confusion, or nocturnal confusion
- Preoccupation with somatic complaints, such as palpitations
- Hallucinations or delusions
- Crying, annoyance over small matters, depression
- Apathy, emotional lability

Sensory Overload

Sensory overload generally occurs when a person is unable to process or manage the amount or intensity of sensory stimuli. Three factors contribute to sensory overload:

- Increased quantity or quality of internal stimuli, such as pain, dyspnea, anxiety
- Increased quantity or quality of external stimuli, such as a noisy health-care setting, intrusive diagnostic studies, contacts with many strangers
- Inability to disregard stimuli selectively, perhaps as a result of nervous system disturbances or medications that stimulate the arousal mechanism

Sensory overload can limit the brain's capability to filter or respond to specific stimuli. Because of the many stimuli, the individual has difficulty perceiving the environment in a way that makes sense. As a result, the individual's thoughts race in many directions, and restlessness occurs. The person may feel overwhelmed and out of control. It is important for nurses to remember that the sights and sounds that are familiar to them often represent overload to clients. People who have sensory overload may appear fatigued. They may not be able to internalize new information. Such factors as pain, lack of sleep, and worry can also contribute to sensory overload. See the box below for common signs of sensory overload.

Clinical Signs of Sensory Overload

- Complaints of fatigue, sleeplessness
- Irritability, anxiety, restlessness
- Periodic or general disorientation
- Reduced problem-solving ability and task performance
- Increased muscle tension
- Scattered attention and racing thoughts

Sensory Deficits

A **sensory deficit** is impaired reception, perception, or both, of one or more of the senses. Blindness and deafness are sensory deficits. When only one sense is affected, other senses may become more acute to compensate for the loss. However, sudden loss of eyesight can result in disorientation.

When there is a gradual loss of sensory function, individuals often develop behaviours to compensate for the loss; sometimes, these behaviors are unconscious. For example, a person with gradual hearing loss in the right ear may unconsciously turn the left ear toward a speaker. When the loss is sudden, however, compensatory behaviour often takes days or weeks to develop.

Some neurological diseases cause changes in the kinesthetic sense and tactile perception. Diseases of the inner ear, for example, can cause loss of kinesthetic sense.

Clients with sensory deficits are at risk of both sensory deprivation and sensory overload. Persons with visual problems may be unable to read, watch television, or recognize nurses by sight. An unfamiliar environment can add to their confusion. Blind people often have highly structured home environments, and the diversity and unfamiliarity of the hospital environment can create sensory overload. At the same time, impaired vision often results in an inability to move around readily or socialize with others.

Factors Affecting Sensory Function

A number of factors affect the amount and quality of sensory stimulation, including a person's developmental stage, culture, level of stress, medications and illness, and lifestyle.

Developmental Stage

Perception of sensation is critical to the intellectual, social, and physical development of infants and children. As children grow, they learn that certain sensations provide cues for behaviours already learned, for example, stopping and looking both ways before crossing a street. Adults have many learned responses to sensory cues. The sudden loss or impairment of any sense, therefore, has a profound effect on both the child and adult. The diminishing of sensory perception that often comes with chronic disease or aging is gradual. It may be accompanied by decreased ability to handle multiple, rapid stimuli. Presbycusis, a type of inner ear hearing loss, is common with aging. The ability to hear high frequency sounds and distinguish from background sounds is most affected.

Culture

An individual's culture often determines the amount of stimulation that a person considers usual or "normal." For example, a child raised in a large, active Italian family may be accustomed to more stimulation than an only child raised in an English Canadian family. In addition, the normal amount of stimulation associated with ethnic origin, religious affiliation, and income level, for example, also affects the amount of stimulation an individual desires and believes to be meaningful. A sudden change in cultural surroundings experienced by immigrants or visitors to a new country, especially where there are differences in language, dress, and cultural behaviours, may also result in sensory overload or culture shock.

Cultural deprivation or **cultural care deprivation** is "a lack of culturally assistive, supportive, or facilitative acts" (Kloosterman, 1991, p. 121). It is important that nurses be sensitive to what stimulation is culturally acceptable to a client. For example, in some cultures, touching is comforting, whereas in others, it is offensive. Some clients find the presence of cultural or religious symbols reassuring and their absence a source of anxiety. Nurses should encourage clients who want to have culturally related symbols with them and to follow practices that they are comfortable with, provided that these practices do not endanger health. Ethical and legal implications of cultural practices need to be considered (for example, relating to blood transfusions). The ability to manage a high volume of verbal stimuli may be compromised for people less familiar with the dominant language.

Stress

During times of increased stress, people may find their senses already overloaded and, thus, seek to decrease sensory stimulation. For example, a client dealing with physical illness, pain, hospitalization, and diagnostic tests may wish to have only close support people visiting them. In addition, the client may need the nurse's help to decrease unnecessary stimuli (e.g., noise) as much as possible. On the other hand, clients may seek sensory stimulation during times of low stress in order to maintain cortical arousal.

Medications and Illness

Certain medications can alter an individual's awareness of environmental stimuli. Narcotics and sedatives, for example, can decrease awareness of stimuli. Some medications increase sensitivity to light (e.g., tetracyline). Decreased hearing or tinnitus (ringing in the ears) can be a sign of drug toxicity (e.g., acetylsalicylic acid).

Many diseases affect sensory reception or perception. Direct sensory organ damage may occur, for example, as a result of the following:

- A complication of diabetes mellitus is diabetic retinopathy, in which tiny hemorrhages in the retina can lead to blindness.
- Glaucoma, which is characterized by increased intraocular pressure, can cause temporary or permanent visual changes, eventually causing permanent damage to the optic nerve.
- Cataracts, which are an opacity of the lens of the eye, cause blurred vision.
- Recurrent ear infections may damage the tympanic membrane and, thus, contribute to hearing loss.

Trauma or disease affecting sensory pathways may interfere with conduction (e.g., spinal cord injury, multiple sclerosis, acoustic neuroma). Central nervous system conditions may alter perception. Stroke, for example, may cause loss of part of the visual field (e.g., inability to see and interpret stimuli from one half of the visual field), loss of the ability to interpret speech (known as receptive aphasia), or loss of the ability to identify objects by touch (known as astereognosis). People experiencing these specific sensory impairments are also more vulnerable to sensory overload or deprivation because of their reduced ability to receive and interpret stimuli.

Lifestyle and Personality

Lifestyle influences the quality and quantity of stimulation which an individual is accustomed to. A client who is employed in a large company may be accustomed to many diverse stimuli, whereas a client who is self-employed and works in the home is exposed to fewer, less diverse stimuli. People's personalities also differ in terms of the quantity and quality of stimuli which they are comfortable with. Some people delight in constantly changing stimuli and excitement, whereas others prefer a more structured life with few changes.

Assessing

Nursing assessment of sensory-perceptual functioning includes six components: (1) nursing history, (2) mental status examination, (3) physical examination, (4) identification of clients at risk, (5) the client's environment, and (6) social support network.

Nursing History

In taking a client history, the nurse assesses risk factors, present sensory perceptions, usual functioning, sensory deficits, and potential problems. In some instances, significant others can provide data the client cannot. For example, support people may reveal signs of recent changes in the client's hearing ability, such as inattention to others, recent mood swings, difficulty following clear instructions, frequent requests to have something repeated, and unusually loud radio or television volumes. Examples of interview questions to elicit data about the client's sensory-perceptual functioning are shown in the accompanying box.

To assess for risk of sensory loss, the nurse should inquire about family history (e.g., glaucoma, diabetes), occupational or recreational exposures (e.g., noise), and self-care practices (e.g., ear wax).

ASSESSMENT INTERVIEW

Sensory-Perceptual Functioning

Visual

How would you rate your vision (excellent, good, fair, or poor)? Do you wear eyeglasses or contact lenses? Describe any recent changes in your vision. Do you have any difficulty seeing near or far objects? Do you have any difficulty seeing at night? Have you ever experienced blurred vision, double vision, spots moving in front of your eyes, blind spots, light sensitivity, flashing lights, or halos around objects? When did you last visit an eye doctor?

Auditory

How would you rate your hearing (excellent, good, fair, or poor)? Do you wear a hearing aid? Describe any recent changes in your hearing. Can you locate the direction of sounds and distinguish various voices? Do you experience any dizziness or vertigo? Do you experience any ringing, buzzing, humming, or crackling noises, or fullness in the ears?

Gustatory

Have you experienced any changes in taste (e.g., difficulty in differentiating sweet, sour, salty, and bitter tastes)? Do you enjoy the taste of foods as much as you did previously?

Olfactory

Have you experienced any changes in smell? Do things (foods, flowers, perfumes, and so on) smell the same as they did? Can you distinguish foods by their odours and tell when something is burning? Have you experienced any changes in appetite? (Changes in appetite may be related to an impaired sense of smell.)

Tactile

Are you experiencing any pain or discomfort? Have you experienced any decrease in your ability to perceive heat, cold, or pain in your limbs? Do you have any numbness or tingling in your extremities?

Kinesthetic

Have you noticed any difficulty in perceiving the position of parts of your body?

Mental Status

Mental status is critical to any evaluation of the sensory-perceptual process. Usually, data on mental status, including level of consciousness, orientation, memory, and attention span, can be obtained during nursing history taking. Details of these assessments are discussed in Chapter 27.

Physical Examination

Physical assessment determines whether the senses are impaired. During the physical examination, the nurse assesses vision and hearing, and the olfactory, gustatory, tactile, and kinesthetic senses. The examination should reveal the client's specific visual and hearing abilities; perception of heat, cold, light touch, and pain in the limbs; and awareness of the position of the body parts. Specific sensory tests include the following:

- *Visual acuity*, using a Snellen chart or other reading material, such as a newspaper, and *visual fields*
- *Hearing acuity*, by observing the client's conversation with others and by performing the whisper test and the Weber and Rinne tuning fork tests
- *Olfactory sense*, by having the client identify specific aromas
- *Gustatory sense*, by identifying three tastes such as lemon, salt, and sugar
- *Tactile sense*, by testing light touch, sharp and dull sensation, two-point discrimination, hot and cold sensation, vibration sense, position sense, and stereognosis

These tests are described in detail in Chapter 27. The nurse should also determine whether sensory adaptive devices that the client uses, such as eyeglasses or hearing aids, function properly.

Clients at Risk for Sensory Deprivation or Overload

Clients at risk for sensory-perceptual alterations need to be identified to ensure that preventive measures can be initiated. The accompanying box describes clients at risk.

Client Environment

The nurse assesses the client's environment for quantity, quality, and type of stimuli. The client's environment may produce insufficient stimuli, placing the client at risk for sensory deprivation, or excessive stimuli, placing the client at risk for sensory overload. Nonstimulating environments include those that (1) severely restrict physical activity, and (2) limit social contact with family and friends. Because appropriate or meaningful stimuli decrease the incidence of sensory deprivation, the nurse must consider the client's health-care environment for the presence of the following stimuli:

Clients at Risk for Sensory Deprivation and Overload

Sensory Deprivation

- Clients confined in a nonstimulating or monotonous environment in the home or health-care agency
- Clients who have impaired vision or hearing
- Clients with mobility restrictions, such as quadriplegia, paraplegia with bed rest, traction apparatus
- Clients who are unable to process stimuli (e.g., clients who have brain damage or who are taking medications that affect the central nervous system)
- Clients on isolation precautions
- Clients who have emotional disorders (e.g., depression) and withdraw within themselves
- Clients who have limited social contact with family and friends (e.g., clients from a different culture, clients living in isolated locations)

Sensory Overload

- Clients who have pain or discomfort
- Clients who are acutely ill and have been admitted to an acute-care facility
- Clients who are being closely monitored in an intensive-care unit (ICU) (Figure 41.2) and have intrusive tubes such as IVs, catheters, or nasogastric or endotracheal tubes
- Clients who have decreased cognitive ability (e.g., head injury)

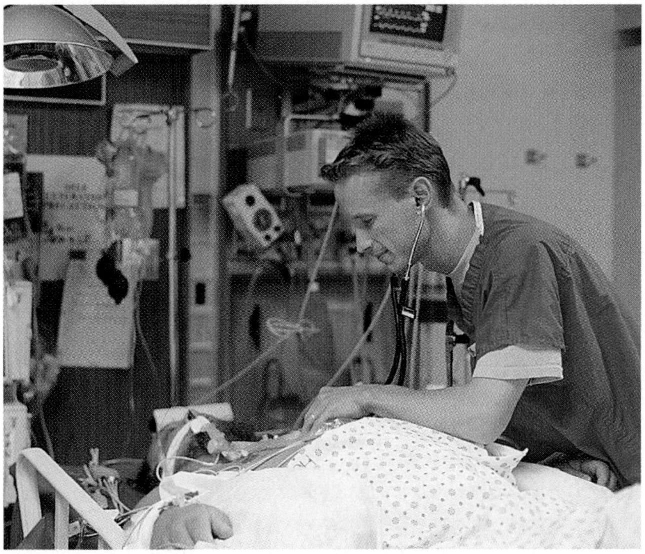

Figure 41.2 A client in an intensive-care unit (ICU) may experience sensory overload

- Radio or other auditory device (e.g., cassette player), television
- Clock or calendar
- Reading material (or toys for children)
- Number and compatibility of roommates
- Number of visitors in home or care facility

In the client's home, the nurse may also note the presence of a videocassette recorder, pets, bright colours, adequacy of lighting, and so on.

To assess a health-care environment that produces excessive stimuli, the nurse considers, for example: bright light, noise, therapeutic measures, and frequency of assessments and procedures.

Social Support Network

The degree of isolation a person feels is significantly influenced by the quality and quantity of support from family members and friends. The nurse assesses (1) whether the client lives alone, (2) who visits and when, (3) any signs indicating social deprivation, such as withdrawal from contact with others to avoid embarrassment or dependence on others, negative self-image, reports of lack of meaningful communication with others, and absence of opportunities to discuss fears or concerns.

Diagnosing

Sensory-Perceptual Problem as the Diagnostic Label

The North American Nursing Diagnosis Association (NANDA, 2001) includes the following diagnostic labels for sensory-perceptual problems:

- ***Sensory-Perceptual, Disturbed:*** A state in which the individual or group experiences or is at risk of experiencing a change in the amount, pattern, or interpretation of incoming stimuli.
- ***Acute Confusion:*** The abrupt onset of a cluster of global, transient changes and disturbances in attention, cognition, psychomotor activity level of consciousness, and/or sleep/wake cycle.
- ***Chronic Confusion:*** An irreversible, longstanding, and/or progressive deterioration of intellect and personality characterized by decreased ability to interpret environmental stimuli, decreased capacity for intellectual thought processes, and manifested by disturbances of memory, orientation, and behaviour.
- ***Impaired Memory:*** The state in which an individual experiences the inability to remember or recall bits of information or behaviour skills. Impaired memory may be attributed to pathophysiological or situational causes that are either temporary or permanent.

Gordon (1997) categorizes sensory-perceptual alterations as follows:

- ***Sensory Deprivation:*** Reduced environmental and social stimuli relative to habitual (or basic orienting) level.
- ***Sensory Overload:*** Environmental stimuli greater than habitual level or input and/or monotonous environmental stimuli.
- ***Uncompensated Sensory Loss:*** Uncompensated decrease in visual, hearing, touch, smell, or kinesthetic acuity (specify degree of loss).

Clinical examples of assessment data clusters and related nursing diagnoses are shown in Table 41.2.

TABLE 41.2 Clinical Application: Assessment Data Clusters and Related Nursing Diagnoses for Clients with Sensory-Perceptual Alterations

Data Cluster	Nursing Diagnosis
Anthony Broom, a 52-year-old lawyer, has multiple sclerosis. Muscle strength and tactile sensation have declined over the past two years. He uses a motorized wheelchair to move about. He reports loss of sensation in his lower limbs and fingers and inability to discern temperature differences. His wife assists with bathing and grooming.	***Risk for Injury*** related to decreased tactile sensation secondary to neurological impairment
Emma Chu, an 84-year-old Chinese Canadian widow, lives alone in her apartment. She can hear words spoken clearly and close to the left ear but cannot hear any sounds with the right ear. She says she spends her time listening to the television and radio (at loud volume). She tends to speak loudly and shout when talking with others and nods and smiles when others speak. Her daughter, who visits, says she refuses to wear a hearing aid (Ms. Chu says it does not help and is uncomfortable). Her daughter has recently noted that her mother has become withdrawn, appears absorbed in her own thoughts, and talks and laughs to herself.	***Sensory-Perceptual, Disturbed*** *(Hearing deficit)* related to neurological impairment associated with aging ***Social Isolation*** related to declining auditory function associated with aging ***Impaired Communication*** related to sensory-perception alteration (hearing deficit)

Sensory-Perceptual Problem as the Etiology

Depending on the data obtained, alterations in sensory-perceptual function may affect other areas of human functioning and indicate other diagnoses. In these instances, the sensory-perceptual problem becomes the etiology.

Examples of nursing diagnoses for which sensory/perceptual alterations are the etiology include the following:

- ***Risk for Injury*** related to sensory/perceptual alterations (specify). For example:
  a. Visual impairment (e.g., decreased depth perception)
  b. Reduced tactile sensation secondary to neurological or circulatory alterations
  c. Decreased sense of smell
  d. Hearing impairment
  e. Decreased kinesthetic sense
- ***Impaired Home Maintenance*** related to sensory/perceptual alterations (declining visual abilities)
- ***Risk for Impaired Skin Integrity*** related to sensory/perceptual alterations (reduced tactile sensation)
- ***Impaired Verbal Communication*** related to sensory/perceptual alterations (specify). For example:
  a. Altered level of consciousness
  b. Hearing impairment
  c. Sensory overload
  d. Sensory deprivation
- ***Self-Care Deficit: Bathing/Hygiene*** related to sensory-perceptual alterations (specify). For example:
  a. Visual impairment
  b. Diminished kinesthetic sense
- ***Social Isolation*** related to sensory/perceptual alterations (specify). For example:
  a. Impaired vision
  b. Impaired hearing

Planning

The overall goals for clients with sensory-perceptual alterations are to:

- Compensate for sensory loss or change.
- Maintain the function of existing senses.
- Develop an effective communication mechanism.
- Prevent injury.
- Prevent sensory overload or deprivation.
- Reduce social isolation.
- Perform activities of daily living independently and safely.
- Reduce risk of damage to sensory organs.

Examples of desired outcomes related to these goals are provided in Table 41.3 in the "Evaluating" section later in this chapter.

Examples of nursing interventions for clients with sensory-perceptual alterations are as follows:

- Increase, reduce, or eliminate environmental stimuli to achieve appropriate sensory input.
- Identify and implement appropriate safety precautions.
- Ensure access to and use of assistive devices, such as eyeglasses and hearing aids.
- Provide teaching regarding use and care of assistive devices.
- Promote the use of existing senses.
- Provide methods for meaningful communication through touch, writing implements, or other methods, as indicated.
- Encourage social interaction with family, friends, and other components of the client's social support network.
- Provide information about social services, community resources, occupational therapy, and other appropriate resources, as indicated.
- Teach risk reduction strategies.

Nursing activities for these interventions are discussed in the "Implementing" section of this chapter.

The Nursing Interventions Classification (NIC) developed by the Iowa Intervention Project can be a guide when planning care (McCloskey & Bulechek, 2000). Appropriate nursing activities may be selected from the following nursing interventions:

- Communication enhancement: hearing deficit
- Communication enhancement: visual deficit
- Coping enhancement
- Environmental management
- Fall prevention
- Health education
- Home maintenance assistance
- Presence
- Support system enhancement
- Surveillance: safety

Planning for Home Care

To provide for continuity of care, the nurse should consider the client's needs for assistance with care in the home or residential treatment setting. Some clients with severe alterations in sensory-perceptual functioning may be discharged to an assisted living facility that provides the specific support the client requires. Discharge planning incorporates a reassessment of the client's abilities for self-care, the availability and skills of support people, financial resources, and the need for referrals and home health services. The box below outlines a home care assessment with regard to sensory-perceptual alterations and confusion. A major aspect of discharge planning involves the instructional needs of the client and family. See methods to support visual and auditory function and maintain a safe environment in the next section.

Implementing

Nurses can assist clients with sensory alterations by promoting healthy sensory function, by adjusting environmental stimuli, and by helping clients to manage acute sensory deficits.

Promoting Healthy Sensory Function

Detecting sensory problems early is one step toward preventing serious problems. The arousal mechanism for sensation is normally present at birth; however, it is undifferentiated. The special senses are also present at birth, although some changes in function occur during the growth process.

Early screening to detect problems in the visual and hearing functions is essential. For example, children with chronic ear infections and people who live or work in an environment where there is a high noise level should receive routine auditory testing. Women who are considering pregnancy should be advised of the importance of testing for syphilis and rubella, which can cause hearing impairments in newborns. Periodic vision screening of all newborns and children is recommended to detect congenital blindness, strabismus, and refractive errors.

Healthy sensory function can be promoted with environmental stimuli that provide appropriate sensory input. This input should vary and be neither excessive nor too limited. As many senses as possible should be stimulated. Various colours, sounds, textures, smells, and body positions can provide various sensations. Nurses can teach parents to stimulate infants and children and teach family members to stimulate an elderly person. Social activities often help stimulate the mind and the senses.

Nurses should also teach clients at risk of sensory loss how to prevent the loss and should teach general health measures, such as getting regular eye examinations and controlling chronic diseases, such as diabetes. See the box opposite for client teaching.

Adjusting Environmental Stimuli

Preventing Sensory Overload

For clients who are at risk of overstimulation, nurses should reduce the number and type of environmental stimuli. The nurse can counteract sensory overload by blocking stimuli and by helping the client organize the stimuli and alter responses to the stimuli.

Dark glasses can partially block light rays, and a window shade or drape can reduce visual stimulation. Earplugs reduce auditory stimuli, as do soft background music and earphones. The odour from a draining wound can be minimized by keeping the dressing dry and clean and using a room deodorizer.

Another method of blocking stimuli is to reduce novelty and surprise and provide rest intervals free of interruptions. Sometimes, the number of visitors and the length of visits must be restricted. Also, if the nurse carries out several nursing measures together, the client can have a scheduled quiet period before the next activity.

By explaining sounds in the environment, the nurse can help the client organize them mentally: a bell signals a change of shift; a buzzer, a change of IV. When clients understand their meaning, stimuli are frequently less confusing and more easily ignored. People can also learn to alter their responses to the stimuli. Clients can employ relaxation techniques to reduce anxiety and stress despite continual senory stimulation. Chapter 47 provides additional information on reducing stress. See the box opposite for nursing measures for clients with sensory overload.

HOME CARE ASSESSMENT

Sensory-Perceptual Alterations

Client and Environment

- *Self-care abilities:* Ability to care for self while adapting to sensory impairment
- *Safety:* Physical safety of client's environment, including lighting, noise, access, lack of clutter or obstructions, use of stairs, assistive devices with respect to sensory impairment, such as flashing fire alarms or telephones for hearing impaired
- *Level of knowledge:* Assistive devices available; ways to maximize use of other senses; local, regional, or national organizations that may provide education, training, support, or other assistance, such as the Canadian National Institute for the Blind (www.cnib.ca) and Canadian Hard of Hearing Association (www.chha.ca/)

CLIENT TEACHING

Preventing Sensory Impairments

- Have regular health examinations.
- Have regular eye examinations, as recommended by the physician or pediatrician, to screen for eye problems. For clients aged 40 years and over, a medical eye examination is generally recommended every one to two years or more frequently if there is a family history of glaucoma.
- Seek early medical attention (1) if signs suggesting visual impairment arise (e.g., failure to react to light or reduced eye contact from an infant), (2) if the child complains of an earache or has an ear infection, and (3) for persistent eye redness, discharge or increased tearing, growths on or near the eye, pupil asymmetry or other irregularity, or any pain or discomfort.
- Obtain regular immunizations of children against diseases capable of causing hearing loss (e.g., rubella, mumps, and measles).
- Avoid giving infants and toddlers toys with long pointed handles, and keep pointed instruments (e.g., scissors and screwdrivers) out of reach. Supervise preschoolers when they use scissors.
- Make sure that toddlers do not walk or run with a pointed object in hand; teach preschoolers to walk carefully when carrying such objects as sticks or toy weapons.
- Teach school-age children and adolescents the proper use of sports equipment (e.g., helmets) and power tools.
- Wear protective eye goggles when using power tools, riding motorcycles, spraying chemicals, and so on.
- Wear ear protectors when working in an environment with high noise levels or brief loud impulse noises (e.g., blasting).
- Wear dark glasses to avoid damage from ultraviolet rays, and never look directly at the sun.
- Keep the volume of radios and other entertainment equipment to a level that still allows the sound of a normal speaking voice to be heard.

Preventing Sensory Overload

- Minimize unnecessary light, noise, and distraction. Provide dark glasses and earplugs, as needed.
- Control pain, as indicated.
- Introduce yourself by name, and address the client by name.
- Provide orienting cues, such as clocks, calendars, equipment, and furniture in the room.
- Limit visitors, if necessary.
- Plan care to allow for uninterrupted periods of rest or sleep of at least two hours at a time if possible.
- Schedule a routine of care so the client knows when and what to expect (post the schedule for the client wherever possible).
- Speak in a low tone of voice and in an unhurried manner.
- Provide new information gradually to enable the client to process the meaning. When providing information, ask the client to repeat it so that there are no misunderstandings.
- Describe any tests and procedures to the client beforehand.
- Reduce noxious odours. Empty a commode or bedpan immediately after use; keep wounds clean and covered; use a room deodorizer when indicated; and provide good ventilation.
- Take time to discuss the client's problems and to correct misinterpretations.
- Assist the client with stress-reducing techniques.

Preventing Sensory Deprivation

For clients who are at risk for sensory deprivation, nurses can increase environmental stimuli in a number of ways. For example, newspapers, books, and television can stimulate the visual and auditory senses. Providing objects that are pleasant to touch, such as a pet to stroke, can provide tactile and interactive stimulation. Clocks that

Preventing Sensory Deprivation

- Encourage the client to use eyeglasses and hearing aids.
- Address the client by name and touch the client while speaking if this is not culturally offensive.
- Communicate frequently with the client, and maintain meaningful interactions (e.g., discuss current events).
- Provide a telephone, radio, and/or TV, clock, and calendar.
- Provide murals, pictures, sculptures, and wall hangings. Many libraries and museums will lend artwork free of charge, or a local school may provide art projects developed by the students.
- Have family and friends bring freshly cut flowers and plants.
- Consider having a resident pet, such as fish, a cat, or a bird, or make arrangements for pets to visit on a regular basis.
- Include different textured objects to feel, such as a sheepskin pillow, silk scarf, soft blanket, or other inanimate objects.
- Increase tactile stimulation through physical care measures, such as back massages, hair care, and foot soaks.
- Encourage social interaction through activity groups or visits by family and friends.
- Encourage the use of crossword puzzles or games to stimulate mental function.
- Encourage environment changes, such as a walk through a mall or, for an immobilized client, sitting near a window or at a place on the nursing unit where the client can watch local traffic.
- Encourage the use of self-stimulation techniques, such as singing, humming, whistling, or reciting.

differentiate night from day by colour can help orient a client to time. The olfactory sense can be stimulated by the presence of fresh flowers or plants.

Arrangements should also be made for people to visit and talk with the client regularly. Many church and community groups provide visitors to "shut-ins," that is, people who are confined to their homes or who reside in nursing homes. See the box above for measures to prevent sensory deprivation.

Managing Acute Sensory Deficits

When assisting clients who have a sensory deficit, the nurse needs to (1) encourage the use of sensory aids to support residual sensory function, (2) promote the use of other senses, (3) communicate effectively, and (4) ensure client safety.

Sensory Aids

Many sensory aids are available for clients who have visual and hearing deficits. Examples are shown in the box below.

Sensory Aids for Visual and Hearing Deficits

Visual

- Eyeglasses of the correct prescription, clean and in good repair
- Adequate room lighting, including night lights
- Sunglasses or shades on windows to reduce glare
- Bright contrasting colours in the environment
- Magnifying glass
- Phone dialer with large numbers
- Clock and wristwatch with large numbers
- Colour code or texture code on stoves, washer, medicine containers, and so on
- Coloured or raised rims on dishes
- Reading material with large print
- Watch that allows touch to determine time or gives audible time
- Braille or recorded books
- Seeing-eye dog

Hearing

- Hearing aid in good order
- Lip reading
- Extra batteries on hand
- Sign language
- Amplified telephones
- Telecommunication device for the deaf (TDD)
- Amplified telephone ringers and doorbells
- Flashing alarm clocks
- Flashing smoke detectors
- Pen and paper available

Sensory aids can be used in the health-care setting as well as in the home. In all situations, the assistance of support people needs to be enlisted, whenever possible, to help the client deal with the deficit.

Promoting the Use of Other Senses

When one sense is lost, the nurse can teach the client to use other senses to supplement the loss. This stimulation is similar to that provided to prevent sensory deprivation, discussed earlier. However, the type of stimulation needs to be adapted in accordance with the client's specific deficit. For example, for the visually impaired client, stimulation of hearing, taste, smell, and touch can be encouraged. A radio, audiotapes of music or books, clocks that chime, music boxes, and wind chimes can be used for auditory stimulation. Diets that include a variety of flavours, temperatures, and textures can be planned to stimulate the taste buds. Taking sips of water between foods and eating foods separately can emphasize the taste sensation. Fresh flowers, room fragrances, brewing coffee, and baking can stimulate the sense of smell. Clients can also be encouraged to remember pleasant or familiar odours, such as the perfume of sweet peas. Such measures as providing a hug, massage, hair brushing, grooming, different textures in clothing and upholstery fabrics, and pets can be used to stimulate touch receptors.

Communicating Effectively

Communication with clients who have sensory deficits should convey respect, enhance the person's self-esteem, and ensure the exchange of correct information. A person with a hearing impairment has to concentrate more than other people and, therefore, tires more readily. Fatigue compounded by an illness can further reduce the person's ability to hear. A person with a visual impairment is unable to observe most nonverbal cues during communication and relies largely on the spoken word and tone of voice. Guidelines for communicating with people who are visually or hearing impaired are shown in the box below.

Ensuring Client Safety

Nurses should implement safety precautions in health-care settings for clients with sensory deficits and teach them special precautions to ensure their safety at home.

Communicating with Clients Who Have a Visual or Hearing Deficit

Visual Deficit

- Always announce your presence when entering the client's room, and identify yourself by name.
- Stay in the client's field of vision if the client has a partial vision loss.
- Speak in a warm and pleasant tone of voice. Some people tend to speak louder than necessary when talking to a blind person.
- Always explain what you are about to do before touching the person.
- Explain the sounds in the environment.
- Indicate when the conversation has ended and when you are leaving the room.

Hearing Deficit

- Before initiating conversation, convey your presence by moving to a position where you can be seen or by gently touching the person.
- Decrease background noises (e.g., radio) before speaking.
- Talk at a moderate rate and in a normal tone of voice. Shouting does not make your voice more distinct and, in some instances, makes understanding more difficult.
- Address the person directly. Do not turn away in the middle of a remark or story. Make sure the person can see your face easily and that it is in good light.
- Avoid talking when you have something in your mouth, such as chewing gum. Avoid covering your mouth with your hand.
- Keep your voice at about the same volume throughout each sentence, without dropping the voice at the end of each sentence.
- Always speak as clearly and accurately as possible. Articulate consonants with particular care. Use other words when client has difficulty hearing phrases.
- Do not "overarticulate"; mouthing or overdoing articulation is just as troublesome as mumbling. Pantomime or write ideas, or use sign language or finger spelling, as appropriate.
- Use simple words and short sentences. Word choice is important: "Fifteen cents" and "fifty cents" may be confused, but "half a dollar" is clear.
- Pronounce every name with care. Make a reference to the name for easier understanding, for example, "Joan, the girl from the office" or "Sears, the big downtown store."
- Change to a new subject at a slower rate, making sure that the person follows the change to the new subject. A key word or two at the beginning of a new topic is a good indicator.

SAMPLE CARE PLAN FOR SENSORY-PERCEPTUAL ALTERATION

ASSESSMENT DATA

Nursing Assessment

Julia Hagstrom is an 80-year-old widow who has recently become a resident of an extended-care facility. Just prior to her admission, she underwent surgery for the removal of cataracts and also experienced more difficulty with hearing. Her children were concerned about her physical safety and lack of socialization and urged her to enter a nursing home. Mrs. Hagstrom had cared for herself independently for 15 years in her own home. Three days after admission, the nurse finds the client somewhat confused and disoriented to person, place, and time. She appears restless, withdrawn, and her syntax is sometimes inappropriate. She states, "I'm afraid of all of these strange creatures in this orphanage."

Physical Examination

Height: 160 cm
Weight: 55.3 kg
Temperature: 37°C
Pulse: 72 BPM
Respirations: 18/minute
Blood Pressure: 128/74 mm Hg
Rinne Test: negative

Diagnostic Data

Chest x-ray, CBC, and urinalysis all within normal ranges

Nursing Diagnosis

Sensory-perceptual alterations (sensory overload) related to change in environment, hearing loss (as evidenced by disorientation to time, place, person; restlessness; and altered behaviour)

Client Goal(s):

The client will demonstrate (1) decreased symptoms and increased level of orientation to reality; and (2) improved ability to communicate.

Desired Outcomes

1. Is oriented to place, month, and year when questioned by day 3
2. Identifies one or two caregivers by name by day 4
3. Communicates needs effectively with care provider by day 5

---

*Nursing Interventions and Selected Activities with Rationale [*in italics*]

Reality Orientation

■ Provide a consistent physical environment and a daily routine.	*Routine eliminates the element of surprise, overstimulation, and further confusion.*
■ Provide caregivers who are familiar to Mrs. Hagstrom.	*Familiarity with caregivers helps reduce confusion and facilitates establishment of rapport.*
■ Provide a low-stimulation environment for Mrs. Hagstrom because disorientation may be increased by overstimulation.	*A disruption in the quality or quantity of incoming stimuli can affect a person's cognitive status. Sensory overload blocks out meaningful stimuli.*
■ Provide for adequate rest, sleep, and daytime naps.	*Reduces overstimulation and fatigue, which may be contributing factors to confusion.*
■ Use a calm and unhurried approach when interacting with Mrs. Hagstrom.	*Promotes communication that enhances the person's sense of dignity.*
■ Speak to the client in a slow, distinct manner with appropriate volume.	*The client who has difficulty hearing will be better able to lip-read and comprehend speech.*
■ Engage Mrs. Hagstrom in concrete "here and now" activities (that is, ADLs) that focus on something outside the self that is concrete and reality oriented.	*Assists the individual to differentiate between own thoughts and reality.*

Communication Enhancement: Hearing Deficit

■ Facilitate use of hearing aids, as appropriate.	*Hearing can be enhanced if the volume is appropriate and the hearing aid is consistently used.*
■ Listen attentively.	*Effective listening is essential in a nurse-client relationship. Poor listening skills can undermine trust and block therapeutic communication.*
■ Use simple words and short sentences, as appropriate.	*Using simple terms and short sentences facilitates understanding and minimizes anxiety.*

SAMPLE CARE PLAN FOR SENSORY-PERCEPTUAL ALTERATION *continued*

■ Obtain Mrs. Hagstrom's attention through touch.	*Gaining the attention of a client with a hearing impairment is an essential first step toward effective communication. However, the client's personal space should be respected and permission to touch should be obtained.*

Evaluation

Goal met. Mrs. Hagstrom identifies her primary nurse by sight and name on the third day. She is aware that Christmas is 3 weeks away and is anxious to go shopping with the group. She bathes herself each morning and makes her own bed. Her daughter has brought new batteries for her hearing aid, which she wears during the day.

*Interventions and activities selected are only a sample of those suggested in the *Nursing interventions classification (NIC)* and should be individualized for each client.

Source: McCloskey, J. C., & Bulechek, G. M. (2000). *Iowa intervention project: Nursing interventions classification* (NIC) (3rd ed.). St. Louis, MO: Mosby-Year Book.

Impaired Vision For clients with visual impairments, nurses need to do the following in a health-care setting:

- Orient the client to the arrangement of room furnishings and maintain an uncluttered environment.
- Keep pathways clear.
- Do not rearrange furniture without orienting the client. Ensure that housekeeping personnel are informed about this.
- Organize self-care articles within the client's reach, and orient the client to their location.
- Keep the call light within easy reach, and place the bed in the low position.
- For a client who does not require physical support during ambulation, assist with ambulation by standing to the client's side, walking about 30 cm ahead, and allowing the person to grasp your arm. Confirm whether the client prefers grasping your arm with the dominant or nondominant hand.

Impaired Hearing Clients with hearing impairments who are unable to hear the alarms of IV pumps and cardiac monitors need to be assessed frequently. They can be taught to use their visual sense to identify kinks in the IV tubing or a loose ECG lead, and so on. For home safety, clients with impaired hearing need to obtain devices that either amplify sounds, respond with flashing lights to such sounds as a doorbell or smoke detector, a baby crying, or a burglar alarm. The sounds of doorbells and alarm clocks may be amplified or changed to a lower frequency or buzzerlike sound. These devices can be obtained from hearing aid dealers, telephone companies, and appliance stores.

Impaired Olfactory Sense Clients with an impaired sense of smell need to be taught about the dangers of cleaning with chemicals, such as ammonia. Because a gas leak can go undetected, clients need to keep gas stoves and heaters in good working order. Strong chemicals, such as ammonia, used in confined spaces, such as a bathroom, may affect the client before they are smelled. Food poisoning is a concern with clients who have difficulty detecting spoiled meat or dairy products. These clients need to carefully inspect food for freshness (check its colour and texture) and check expiry dates on food packages. Installing a smoke detector near the stove is particularly important as is taking care to not leave the stove unattended.

Impaired Tactile Sense Clients with an impaired sense of touch may not be aware of hot temperatures, which can cause burns, or pressure on bony prominences, which can produce pressure ulcers. Clients with decreased sensation to temperature should have the temperature adjusted on their hot water heater and test water temperature with a thermometer before bathing. Clients with decreased sensation to pressure must change their position frequently. Avoid use of heating pads and hot water bottles as burns may result.

The Confused Client

Confusion can occur in clients of all ages, but it is most commonly seen in older people. The causes of confusion can be physiological or situational. The most common causes of confusion are the following:

- *Drug effects,* such as potentiating effects of multiple drug use and drug intoxication
- *Physiological disturbances,* such as hypoxia, dehydration, metabolic or fluid imbalances, neurological disorders, infectious processes, and nutritional deficiencies
- *Abrupt loss* of a significant person or persons
- *Multiple losses* in a short time span

RESEARCH NOTE

Does a Telephone Follow-Up Program Make a Difference for Patients Recently Discharged from an Ophthalmic Unit?

This randomized clinical trial was designed to evaluate a nurse-initiated Telephone Reassurance Program (TRP), in which experienced unit nurses phoned the intervention group (n = 143) three to six days after discharge following treatment for cataracts, glaucoma, and retinal or corneal disorders. Both the intervention and control (n = 154) groups were followed up at seven and 30 days after discharge with a mailed questionnaire that included measures of informational needs, uncertainty, emotional complaints, and functional limitations. No differences were found between groups, except that those in the intervention group reported that they were managing better with housekeeping. The researchers concluded by offering several interpretations of their findings. They noted that similar trials on TRP in other populations have found no or only modest effect, suggesting that there may be no statistically significant difference. However, the lack of difference could also be attributed to a type 1 error, that is, lack of sufficient sample size to detect a real difference. It could also be attributed to lack of sensitivity of the outcome measures. They did find that 89 percent of the patients in the intervention group wanted to be called again, and only 6 percent considered the call unnecessary.

Implications: Telephone follow-up for patients who have received ophthalmic treatment has not been shown to make a difference in measureable outcomes but is valued by patients.

Source: Excerpt from Boter, H., Mistiaen, P., & Groenewegen, I. (2000). A randomized trial of a Telephone Reassurance Programme for patients recently discharged from an ophthalmic unit. *Journal of Clinical Nursing, 9*,199–207.

- *A move* to a radically different environment (Ebersole & Hess, 1998)

Clients who are confused often know something is wrong and want help. See the box on the right for nursing interventions to help orient the confused person to time, place, person, and situation.

Promoting Orientation to Time, Place, Person, and Situation

- Wear a readable name tag.
- Address the person by name and introduce yourself frequently: "Good morning, Mr. Richards. I am Betty Brown. I will be your nurse today."
- Identify time and place as indicated: "Today is December 5, and it is 8:00 in the morning."
- Ask the client, "Where are you?" and orient the client to place (e.g., nursing home), if indicated.
- Place a calendar and clock in the client's room. Mark holidays with ribbons, pins, or other means.
- Provide a means of marking current date.
- Speak clearly and calmly to the client, allowing time for your words to be processed and for the client to give a response.
- Provide frequent face-to-face contact.
- Provide clear, concise explanations of each treatment procedure or task.
- Reinforce reality by interpreting unfamiliar sounds, sights, and smells; correct any misconceptions of events or situations.
- Schedule activities (e.g., meals, bath, activity and rest periods, treatments) at the same time each day to provide a sense of security. If possible, assign the same caregivers.
- Keep familiar items in the client's environment (e.g., photographs), and keep the environment uncluttered. A disorganized, cluttered environment increases confusion.
- Encourage the client to wear familiar or personal clothing and to arrange personal hygiene articles in order of use, as needed.
- Encourage participation in familiar activities or hobbies to emphasize the client's strengths rather than problems.
- Tell the client when you are leaving and when you will return.

The Unconscious Client

The person who is unconscious and unable to respond to the spoken word nevertheless can often hear what is spoken. It is, therefore, important that nurses talk to the client as though they were understood, using a normal tone of voice and speaking before touching the client. Nurses should also try to keep the environmental noises at a minimum so that the client can focus on words. The following are some additional measures nurses can take in caring for the unconscious client:

- Orient the unconscious client to person, time, situation, and place.
- Explain what you are going to do.
- Listen carefully to the support person's concerns. Often, they simply want to express them.
- Maintain the same schedule each day. Routine gives the client a sense of security.
- Touch and stroke the unconscious client.
- Talk about things that previously interested the client (e.g., sports, music).

FOCUS ON CRITICAL THINKING

Mrs. Dodd is a 51-year-old client who is being cared for in the critical care unit following an automobile accident in which she suffered extensive traumatic injuries. Mrs. Dodd is connected to several monitoring devices, has an intubation tube and ventilator to assist her with respirations, and is receiving various pain and other medications.

1. Identify factors that place Mrs. Dodd at risk for the development of sensory deprivation or overload.
2. What assessment findings would alert you to Mrs. Dodd experiencing sensory overload as opposed to sensory deprivation?
3. How can you intervene to reduce Mrs. Dodd's risk for disturbed sensory perception during this stressful event?
4. How might the care of a client in the home setting differ from the care of a client such as Mrs. Dodd who is receiving care in a critical care unit?

See Appendix A for answers to these questions.

TABLE 41.3 Evaluation Goals and Outcomes: Sensory-Perceptual Alternations

Goal	Examples of Desired Outcomes
Maintain or promote sensory functioning	Uses protective devices (e.g., protective eyewear and ear protectors) appropriately
	Identifies hazards to sensory organs
or	Demonstrates effective use of assistive devices (specify)
Prevent sensory deprivation or overload	Experiences a three- to four-hour uninterrupted sleep period in 24 hours (sensory overload)
	Oriented to time, place, and person
	Reports increased energy and reduced feelings of anxiety (sensory overload)
	Reports decreased boredom and depression (sensory deprivation)
	Demonstrates increased attention span (sensory deprivation)
Maintain or improve communication	Demonstrates appropriate emotional responses
	Uses assistive devices for communication (e.g., hearing aid, writing implements, large print)
	Expresses thoughts and feelings about sensory deficits or unusual sensory experiences
Prevent injury	Identifies factors that increase risk for injury
	Makes appropriate use of sensory aids
	Alters home environment and practices to prevent injury
Reduce social isolation	Identifies factors or behaviours that produce social isolation
	Formulates a plan to become more involved with others
	Identifies community resources that will assist in decreasing social isolation

- To the support persons, explain what is happening, and encourage them to talk to and touch the client as though the client were conscious. This auditory and tactile stimulation supports the client and may restore some degree of consciousness.
- Always address the client by name, and explain beforehand the care to be provided. Unconscious clients require bathing, skin care, turning, feeding, and assistance with elimination needs.

Evaluating

Using the measurable desired outcomes developed during the planning stage as a guide, the nurse collects data needed to judge whether client goals and outcomes have been achieved. Examples of client goals and related outcomes are shown in Table 41.3.

If outcomes are not achieved, the nurse and client, and support people if appropriate, need to explore the reasons before modifying the care plan.

CHAPTER HIGHLIGHTS

- The sensory experience consists of two components: sensory reception and sensory perception.
- Sensory stimuli can be either external or internal. Visual, auditory, olfactory, tactile, and gustatory stimuli orient a person to the *external* environment. Kinesthetic and visceral stimuli orient the person to the *internal* environment. Kinesthetic stimuli make the person aware of the position and movement of body parts.
- Sensory perception involves the awareness and interpretation of stimuli into meaningful information. This process occurs in the cerebral cortex.
- The reticular activating system (RAS), with its many ascending and descending connections to other areas of the brain, monitors and regulates incoming stimuli. The RAS maintains, enhances, or inhibits cortical arousal.
- The normal, alert person can assimilate many kinds of information at one time and respond appropriately through thought and action.
- Sensory deprivation occurs when a person receives decreased sensory input or monotonous or meaningless sensory input.
- Sensory overload occurs when a person experiences excessive sensory input and is unable to process or manage the stimuli. The person feels overwhelmed and not in control.
- Responses to both sensory deprivation and sensory overload include perceptual changes (e.g., mild distortions or hallucinations), cognitive changes (e.g., decreased concentration and problem-solving ability), and affective changes (e.g., apathy, anxiety, anger, depression, and rapid mood swings).
- Clients at risk for sensory deprivation include (1) those who are homebound or institutionalized, (2) those on bed rest or isolation precautions, (3) those with sensory deficits, (4) those who come from a different culture, (5) those with certain affective disorders or disturbances of the nervous system, and (6) those on certain medications that affect the central nervous system.
- Clients at risk for sensory overload include (1) those in pain, (2) those in intensive-care units, (3) those with intrusive and uncomfortable monitoring or treatment equipment, and (4) those with disturbances of the nervous system.
- Factors affecting sensory stimulation include developmental stage, culture, stress, medications, illness, and lifestyle and personality.
- Assessment for sensory-perceptual alterations includes (1) a nursing history to identify sensory deficits, (2) physical examination, (3) mental status, (4) identification of clients at risk, (5) immediate environment, (6) presence of clinical signs of sensory deprivation or overload.
- NANDA nursing diagnoses related to a client's sensory-perceptual impairments are ***Sensory/Perceptual Disturbances: Visual, Auditory, Gustatory, Olfactory, Tactile, Kinesthetic; Acute Confusion; Chronic Confusion; Impaired Memory; Social Isolation; Impaired Communication; Risk for Impaired Skin Integrity; Self-Care Deficit: Bathing/Hygiene; Impaired Home Maintenance;*** and ***Risk for Injury.***
- Goals for persons with sensory-perceptual alterations include (1) maintaining or promoting the function of existing senses, (2) maintaining or improving communication, (3) preventing injury, (4) avoiding sensory deprivation or overload, (5) reducing social isolation, (6) maintaining or restoring ability to function safely in the environment and to perform self-care, and (7) reducing risk of damage to sensory organs.
- Interventions to prevent or modify sensory deprivation, sensory overload, and sensory deficits include promoting healthy sensory function, adjusting environmental stimuli, and managing sensory deficits.
- Clients with sensory deficits need instruction about sensory aids available to support residual sensory function, ways to promote the use of other senses, and methods to ensure safety from bodily harm.
- Nurses and support persons need to devise and implement effective communication mechanisms for clients who have visual and hearing impairments.
- Confused clients and unconscious clients need care that is directed to promoting their orientation to time, place, person, and situation.

READINGS AND REFERENCES

Suggested Readings

Kelly, M. (1996, March/April). Medications and the visually impaired elderly. *Geriatric Nursing, 17*(2), 60–62.

This article discusses the problem of medication compliance for visually impaired older adults. The article provides guidelines for medication usage that could be appropriate for visually impaired clients of any age.

Larsen, P. D., Hazen, S. E., & Hoot Martin, J. L. (1997). Assessment and management of sensory loss in elderly patients. *AORN Journal, 65*, 432–437.

This article reviews the sensory changes associated with the aging process and identifies suggested interventions especially appropriate for the elderly client who will be undergoing surgery. Interventions are divided into the three phases of the perioperative process: preoperative, intraoperative, and postoperative.

Lucas, L. J., & Matthews-Flint, L. J. (2001). Sound advice about hearing aids. *Nursing 2001, 31*(2), 59–61.
This photo guide illustrates insertion and removal and also provides tips about helping a learning-impaired client.

Related Research

Fioravanti, M., Zacattini, G., & Buckely, A. E. (1996). Quality of life in chronic diseases of the aged: The importance of cognitive deterioration. *Archives of Gerontology and Geriatrics, 22*(3), 195–205.

Stumer, J., Hickson, L., & Worrall, L. (1996). Hearing impairment, disability and handicap in elderly people living in residential care and in the community. *Disability and Rehabilitation, 18*(2), 76–82.

Selected References

Allen, M. N., Knight, C., Falk, C., & Strang, V. (1992). Effectiveness of a preoperative teaching program for cataract patients. *Journal of Advanced Nursing, 17*, 303–309.

Boter, H., Mistiaen, P., & Groenegen, I. (2000). A randomized trial of a Telephone Reassurance Programme for patients recently discharged from an ophthalmic unit. *Journal of Clinical Nursing, 9*, 199–207.

Carpenito, L. J. (2000). *Nursing diagnosis: Application to clinical practice* (8th ed.). Philadelphia, PA: Lippincott.

Ebersole, P., & Hess, P. (1998). *Toward healthy aging: Human needs and nursing response.* (5th ed.) St. Louis, MO: Mosby.

Fioravanti, M., Zacattini, G., & Buckely, A. E. (1996). Quality of life in chronic diseases of the aged: The importance of cognitive deterioration. *Archives of Gerontology and Geriatrics, 22*(3), 195–205.

Gordon, M. (1997). *Manual of nursing diagnoses 1997–98.* St. Louis, MO: Mosby-Year Book.

Hall, G. R., & Wakefield, B. (1996). Confusion in the elderly. *Nursing 96, 26*(7), 32–37.

Hancock, C. K., Munjas, B., Berry, K., & Jones, J. (1994). Altered thought processes and sensory-perceptual alterations: A critique. *Nursing Diagnosis, 5*(1), 26–30.

Hewawasam, L. (1996, May). Floor patterns limit wandering of people with Alzheimer's. *Nursing Times, 92*(23), 41–44.

Jarvis, C. (2003). *Physical examination and health assessment* (4th ed.). Philadelphia, PA: Saunders.

Johnson, M., & Maas, M. (Eds.). (2000). *Iowa outcomes project: Nursing outcomes classification (NOC).* St. Louis, MO: Mosby.

Kloosterman, N. D. (1991, Fall). Cultural care: The missing link in severe sensory alteration. *Nursing Science Quarterly, 4*, 119–122.

Larsen, P. D., Hazen, S. E., & Hoot Martin, J. L. (1997). Assessment and management of sensory loss in elderly patients. *AORN Journal, 65*(2), 432–437.

Lusk, S. L., Ronis, D. L., & Hogan, M. M. (1997). Test of the health promotion model as a causal model of construction workers' use of hearing protection. *Research in Nursing & Health, 20*(3), 183–194.

Marieb, E. N. (2003). Human anatomy and physiology, (7th ed.). San Francisco: Benjamin Cummings.

McCloskey, J. C., & Bulechek, G. M. (Eds.). (2000). *Iowa intervention project: Nursing interventions classification (NIC)* (3rd ed.). St. Louis, MO: Mosby.

McConnell, E. A. (1996, May). Caring for a patient who has a vision impairment. *Nursing 96, 26*(5), 28.

Meredith, C., & Edworthy, J. (1995). Are there too many alarms in the intensive care unit? An overview of the problems. *Journal of Advanced Nursing, 21*(1), 15–20.

Mirr, M. P. (2001). Abnormally increased behavioral arousal. In C. Stewart-Amidai & J. A. Kunkel (Eds.), *AANN's neuroscience nursing* (2nd ed.). (pp. 119–136). Philadelphia, PA: Saunders.

North American Nursing Diagnosis Association. (2001). *NANDA Nursing diagnoses: Definitions and classification 2001–2002.* Philadelphia, PA: Author.

Trummer, K. H., Foster, B. B., Hartman, L., Lewis-Vais, C., & Sullivan, H. (1996, July). Protecting confused patients from falls. *American Journal of Nursing, 96*(7), 16R–16X.

WEBLINKS

Canadian National Institute for the Blind
www.cnib.ca/
This site provides information related to the visually impaired.

Canadian Association of the Deaf
www.cad.ca/
This site provides information related to the deaf and hearing impaired in Canada.

Canadian Hard of Hearing Association
www.chha.ca/
A nonprofit association that is operated by those with hearing deficits; its role is to promote the interests of its members, and to inform.

The Canadian Hearing Society
www.chs.ca/
The society provides services that augment the independence of deaf, deafened, and hard of hearing people and that encourage prevention of hearing loss.

CHAPTER 42

Rest and Sleep

OBJECTIVES

After completing this chapter, you will be able to:

- Explain the physiology and the functions of sleep.
- Identify the characteristics of NREM and REM sleep.
- List the four stages of NREM sleep.
- Describe variations in sleep patterns throughout the life span.
- Explain factors that affect normal sleep.
- Describe common sleep disorders.
- Outline the components of a sleep pattern assessment.
- Develop nursing diagnoses related to sleep problems.
- Discuss interventions that promote normal sleep.
- Create a nursing care plan for a client with sleep pattern disturbance.

Rest and sleep are essential for health. People who are ill frequently require more rest and sleep than normal. Often, debilitated people expend unusual amounts of energy just to regain health or maintain the activities of daily living. As a result, such people experience increased and frequent fatigue and, thus, need more rest and sleep than usual. Providing a restful environment for clients is an important function of nurses.

The meaning of rest and the need for rest vary among individuals. **Rest** implies calmness, relaxation without emotional stress, and freedom from anxiety. Therefore, rest does not always imply inactivity; in fact, some people find certain activities, such as walking in fresh air, restful. When rest is prescribed for a client, both nurse and client must know whether the client is to be inactive and whether that inactivity involves the whole body or a body part (e.g., an arm).

Rest restores a person's energy, allowing the individual to resume optimal functioning. When people are deprived of rest, they are often irritable, depressed, and tired, and they may have poor control over their emotions.

Sleep is a basic human need. Historically, sleep was considered to be a state of unconsciousness. More recently, **sleep** has come to be considered an altered state of consciousness in which the individual's perception of and reaction to the environment are decreased. Sleep is characterized by minimal physical activity, variable levels of consciousness, changes in the body's physiological processes, and decreased responsiveness to external stimuli. Some environmental stimuli, such as a smoke detector alarm, will usually awaken a sleeper, whereas other noises will not. Individuals respond to meaningful stimuli while sleeping and selectively disregard unmeaningful stimuli.

Physiology of Sleep

The cyclic nature of sleep is controlled by centres located in the lower part of the brain. These centres actively inhibit wakefulness, thus causing sleep. This active inhibitory process replaces an earlier theory that the brain, including the reticular activating system (RAS), simply became fatigued and sleep resulted (Guyton & Hall, 1996).

Circadian Rhythms

Biorhythms (rhythmic biological clocks) exist in plants, animals, and humans. In humans, these are controlled from within the body and are synchronized with environmental factors, such as light and darkness, gravity, and electromagnetic stimuli. The most familiar biorhythm is the *circadian rhythm.* The term *circadian* is from the Latin *circa dies,* meaning "about a day." The human circadian cycle is actually closer to 25, rather than 24 hours, making it relatively easy to get off-schedule by staying up late and not following a set schedule.

Sleep is a complex biological rhythm. When a person's biological clock coincides with sleep-wake patterns and light-dark cycles, the person is said to be in **circadian synchronization;** that is, the person is awake when the physiological and psychological rhythms are most active and is asleep when the physiological and psychological rhythms are most inactive.

Circadian regularity approaching that of adults begins by the third week of life. Babies are awake most often in the early morning and the late afternoon. After four months of age, infants enter a 24-hour cycle in which they sleep mostly during the night. By the end of the fifth or sixth month, infants' sleep-wake patterns are almost like those of adults.

Canadian Society Notes

Fact	Implications for Nursing Practice
Given Canada's northern latitudes, daylight length varies markedly across the year. The farther north one is located, the more variation there is. These variations in the light-dark cycle affect the secretion of melatonin, which peaks during the hours of darkness. The prolonged darkness of northern winters contributes to sleep disturbances associated with seasonal affective disorder, particularly in individuals who do not spend time outdoors in natural light.	Going to bed earlier is less effective as the child or adult may have difficulty getting to sleep, whereas the earlier rising is under voluntary control.
Conversely, the long hours of daylight in the summer evenings exacerbate the effects of the natural 25-hour circadian cycle. This effect is compounded by evening social and sports activities so that by the end of summer break or vacation, children and adults find it difficult to re-adjust to fall school and work schedules.	Nurses can help parents and other adults make this adjustment more smoothly by coaching them to establish earlier rising times in the week before the end of vacation.

Stages of Sleep

The **polysomnogram (PSG)** provides information on stages of sleep and objective physiological evidence useful in the diagnosis of sleep disorders (see Diagnostic Studies, p. 1161). The three basic indicators of sleep stages are:

- brain wave activity (detected by **electroencephalogram [EEG]** in which scalp electrodes record electrical activity of the cerebral cortex),
- eye movements (recorded by **electrooculogram [EOG]** from electrodes placed on either side of the eyes), and
- muscle tone (recorded by **electromyogram [EMG]** from electrodes placed on the chin).

The EEG provides a good picture of what occurs during sleep. Electrodes are placed on various parts of the sleeper's scalp. The electrodes transmit electric energy from the cerebral cortex to pens that record the **brain waves** (fluctuations in energy) on graph paper.

For diagnostic purposes, a PSG also usually includes the following:

- Recording of cardiac activity (detected by **electrocardiogram [ECG]** from electrodes on the chest)
- Oxygen saturation (detected by an oximeter attached to the earlobe or a finger)
- Air exchange (detected by a thermistor at the nose)
- Respiratory movements (detected by bands around the chest and abdomen)
- Snoring (detected by a small microphone often placed on the chest)
- Leg movements (detected by EMG from electrodes placed bilaterally on the anterior tibialis muscles)

Two types of sleep have been identified: **NREM** (non-REM) sleep and **REM** (rapid eye movement) sleep.

NREM Sleep

NREM sleep is characterized by slowed brain activity, reduced muscle tone, decreased metabolic rate, and decreased vital signs.

NREM sleep is divided into four stages. *Stage I* is the stage of very light sleep. During this stage, the person feels drowsy and relaxed, the eyes roll from side to side, and the heart and respiratory rates drop slightly. The sleeper can be readily awakened.This stage lasts only a few minutes.

Stage II is the stage of light sleep during which body processes continue to slow down. The eyes are generally still, the heart and respiratory rates decrease slightly, and body temperature falls. Stage II lasts only about 10 to 15 minutes at a time.

During *Stage III*, the heart and respiratory rates, as well as other body processes, slow further because of the domination of the parasympathetic nervous system. The sleeper becomes more difficult to arouse. The person is not disturbed by sensory stimuli; the skeletal muscles are very relaxed; reflexes are diminished; and snoring may occur.

Stage IV signals deep sleep, called *delta sleep.* The sleeper's heart and respiratory rates drop 20 to 30 percent below those exhibited during waking hours. The sleeper is very relaxed, rarely moves, and is difficult to arouse. Stage IV is thought to restore the body physically. During this stage, the eyes usually roll, and some dreaming occurs. See Table 42.1 for the characteristics of NREM sleep.

REM Sleep

REM sleep constitutes about 25 percent of the sleep of a young adult. It usually recurs about every 90 minutes and lasts five to 30 minutes. REM sleep is not as restful as NREM sleep, and most dreams occur during REM sleep. Furthermore, these dreams are usually remembered; that is, they are consolidated in the memory.

During REM sleep, the brain is highly active, and brain metabolism may increase as much as 20 percent. This type of sleep is also called *paradoxical sleep* because it seems a paradox that sleep can take place simultaneously with this type of brain activity. During REM sleep, the muscle tone is greatly reduced. Breathing is primarily dependent on the diaphragm. See the following box for the characteristics of REM sleep. When a person is very tired, the duration of each REM sleep is very short or even absent. As the person becomes more rested through the night, the duration of the REM sleep increases.

TABLE 42.1 Characteristics of NREM Sleep

Stage	Characteristics
Stage I	Relaxed and drowsy Profound restfulness Usually lasts only a few minutes Floating sensation Eyes roll from side to side
Stage II	Lightly asleep Easily aroused Constitutes 40–45 percent of total sleep time
Stage III	Less easily aroused Medium-depth sleep Muscles relaxed Blood pressure lowers Body temperature lowers
Stage IV	Deepest sleep stage Rarely moves Muscles completely relaxed Difficult to arouse Occurs 30–40 minutes following sleep onset

Characteristics of REM Sleep

- Active dreaming occurs, and dreams are more likely to be remembered.
- May be difficult to arouse or may wake spontaneously.
- Muscle tone is depressed.
- Heart and respiratory rate are often irregular.
- Rapid eye movements occur.
- The brain is very active.

Source: Adapted from Guyton, A. C. & Hall, J. E. (1996). *Textbook of medical physiology* (9th ed.). (p. 762). Philadelphia, PA: Saunders.

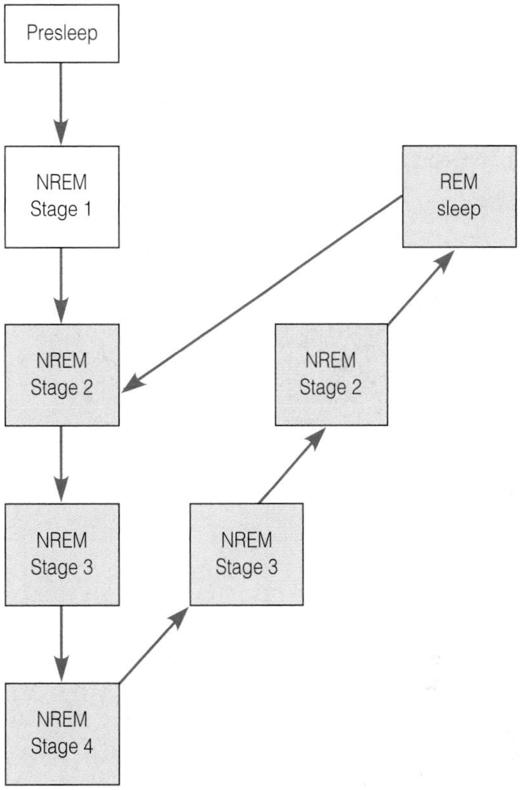

Figure 42.1 The adult sleep cycle. The shaded areas are repeated four or five times during a night's sleep.

Sleep Cycles

During a sleep cycle, a sleeper passes from stage I NREM sleep through stages II and III to stage IV in about 20 to 30 minutes. Stage IV may last about 30 minutes. These stages are then followed by stages III and II, in that order. Thereafter, the first REM stage occurs, lasting about 10 minutes. This sequence completes the first sleep cycle (Figure 42.1). The usual sleeper experiences four to six cycles of sleep during seven to eight hours. Each cycle lasts about 90 minutes.

The sleeper who is awakened during any stage usually begins anew at stage I NREM sleep and proceeds through all the stages to REM sleep.

The duration of NREM stages and REM sleep varies throughout the eight-hour sleep period. As the night progresses, the sleeper spends less time in stages III and IV of NREM sleep. REM sleep increases, and dreams tend to lengthen. If the sleeper is very tired, REM cycles are often short. Before sleep ends, periods of near-wakefulness occur, and stages I and II NREM sleep and REM sleep predominate.

The ratio of NREM to REM sleep varies with age (Figure 42.2).

Functions of Sleep

Sleep exerts physiological effects on both the nervous system and other body structures. Sleep, in some way, restores normal levels of activity and normal balance among parts of the nervous system. The effects of sleep on the body are not understood, but it is known that the activity of the sympathetic nervous system is greater while the person is awake. During sleep, however, the activity of the parasympathetic nervous system increases, causing physiological changes such as lower arterial blood pressure, decreased pulse rate, dilated peripheral blood vessels, occasional increased activity of gastrointestinal tract, relaxed skeletal muscles, and decreased BMR (10–30 percent).

It has been suggested that maintaining a regular sleep-wake rhythm is more important than the number of hours actually slept. Some people, for example, can function well on as little as five hours of sleep each night. Assisting the client to re-establish the sleep-wake cycle (e.g, after the disruption because of surgery) is an important aspect of nursing.

Normal Sleep Patterns and Requirements

Newborns

Newborns sleep 16 to 18 hours a day, usually divided into about seven sleep periods. Quiet sleep (NREM with not yet fully differentiated sleep stages) is characterized by regular respirations, closed eyes, and the absence of body and eye movements. Active sleep (REM sleep) has rapid eye movements that are observable through closed lids, body movement, and irregular respirations. Most of the sleep time is spent in stages III and IV of NREM sleep. Nearly 50 percent of sleep is REM.

Infants

Some infants sleep as long as 22 hours a day, others 12 to 14 hours a day. About 50 percent of sleep is REM sleep, with sleep cycles lasting about 50 to 60 minutes. At first,

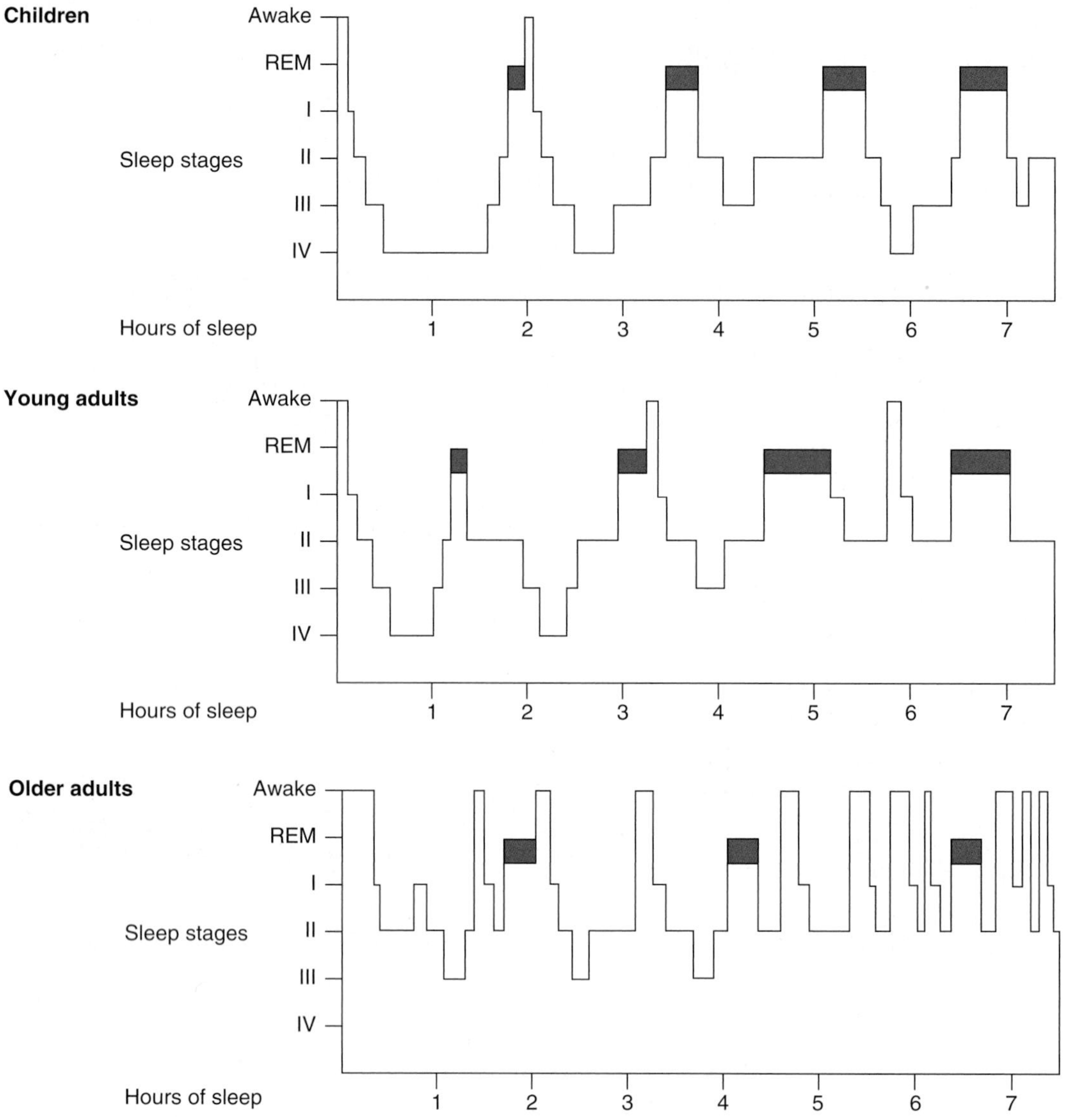

Figure 42.2 Normal sleep cycles of children, young adults, and older adults. Children and young adults show early preponderance of NREM stages III and IV, progressive lengthening of the first three REM periods, and infrequent awakenings. In older adults, there is little or no NREM stage IV sleep, REM periods are fairly uniform in length, and awakenings are frequent and often lengthy.

Source: Kales, A. (1968, May). Sleep and dreams: Recent research in clinical aspects. *Annals of Internal Medicine, 68*, 1078. Used with permission.

infants usually awaken every three or four hours, eat, and then go back to sleep. Periods of wakefulness gradually increase during the first months. By four months, most infants sleep through the night and establish a pattern of daytime naps that varies among individuals. They generally awaken early in the morning, however. At the end of the first year, an infant usually takes one or two naps per day and sleeps about 14 of every 24 hours.

Much of the infant's sleep time is spent in light sleep. During light sleep, the infant exhibits a great deal of activity, such as movement, gurgles, and coughing. Parents need to ascertain that infants are truly awake before picking them up for feeding and changing. Many infants begin waking up again in the middle of the night between five and nine months of age. For parents who find this behaviour a problem, the nurse needs to assess the infant's total sleep pattern and compare it with the parents' sleep schedule. Parents need reassurance that there is no one correct way to handle this situation. The best solution is one that provides a continuous healthy environment for both the infant and the parents.

Toddlers

The sleep requirements of toddlers decrease to 10 to 12 hours per day. About 30 percent is REM sleep. Most still need an afternoon nap, but the need for midmorning naps gradually decreases. The toddler's normal sleep-wake cycle is usually established by age two or three years. The toddler may exhibit a great deal of resistance to going to bed. Parents need assurance that if the child has had adequate attention from them during the day, maintaining a consistent approach with respect to bed-time will promote good sleep habits for the entire family. The toddler may awaken at night afraid of the dark or experiencing night terrors or nightmares.

Preschoolers

The preschool child usually requires 11 to 12 hours of sleep per night, particularly if the child is in preschool. Sleep needs fluctuate in relation to activity and growth spurts. Many children of this age dislike bedtime and resist by requesting another story, game, or television program. The four- to five-year-old may become restless and irritable if sleep requirements are not met. A nap or quiet time during the day may be needed to restore energy levels.

Children in this age group benefit from bedtime rituals. Parents can help children who resist bedtime by warning them that bedtime is approaching and by continuing to use the same firm and consistent approach suggested for the toddler. Preschool children wake up frequently at night. REM sleep is still 20 to 30 percent, higher than for adults; however, stage I sleep is less.

School-Age Children

The school-age child sleeps between eight and 12 hours a night without daytime naps. The eight-year-old requires at least 10 hours of sleep each night. As the child approaches 11 or 12 years of age, less sleep is required, and bedtime may be as late as 10 p.m. The REM sleep of children at this age is reduced to about 20 percent. Although some children still experience night awakenings due to nightmares, this problem continues to decrease with age.

Adolescents

Most adolescents require eight to 10 hours of sleep each night to prevent undue fatigue and susceptibility to infections. A change in sleep pattern is common in adolescence. Children who once were early risers begin to sleep late in the mornings and occasionally take afternoon naps. The reason for daytime sleeping is not fully understood, but it is possibly a result of physical maturity and reduced nocturnal sleep. Sleep at this age is about 20 percent REM.

During adolescence, boys begin to experience **nocturnal emissions** (orgasm and emission of semen during sleep), known as "wet dreams," several times each month. Boys need to be informed about this normal development to prevent embarrassment and fear.

Young Adults

The sleep-wake cycle is very important to young adults. They usually have an active lifestyle, and are thought to require seven to eight hours of sleep each night but may do well on less. The percent of time spent in stage I NREM sleep changes very little throughout life.

Middle-Aged Adults

Middle-aged adults generally maintain the sleep pattern established at a younger age. They usually sleep six to eight hours every night. About 20 percent is REM sleep. The number of arousals from sleep increases, and the amount of stage IV sleep begins to decrease.

Older Adults

The older adult sleeps about six hours a night. About 20 to 25 percent is REM sleep. Stage IV sleep is markedly decreased and, in some instances, absent, especially in men. The first REM period is longer.

Many older adults awaken more often during the night, and it often takes them longer to go back to sleep. They may compensate with a daytime nap.

Factors Affecting Sleep

Both the quality and the quantity of sleep are affected by a number of factors. *Quality of sleep* means the individual's ability to stay asleep and to get appropriate amounts of REM and NREM sleep. *Quantity of sleep* is the total time the individual sleeps.

Age

Age is probably one of the most important factors affecting a person's sleep and rest needs. See the previous section, "Normal Sleep Patterns and Requirements," for sleep pattern variations that occur with age.

Illness

Illness that causes pain or physical distress can result in sleep problems. People who are ill require more sleep than normal, and the normal rhythm of sleep and wakefulness is often disturbed. People deprived of REM sleep subsequently spend more sleep time than normal in this stage.

Respiratory conditions can disturb an individual's sleep. Shortness of breath often makes sleep difficult, and people who have nasal congestion or sinus drainage may have trouble breathing and hence a difficult sleep.

People who have gastric or duodenal ulcers may find their sleep disturbed because of pain, often a result of the increased gastric secretions that occur during REM sleep. Certain endocrine disturbances can also affect sleep. Hyperthyroidism lengthens presleep time, often making it difficult for a client to fall asleep. Hypothyroidism, conversely, decreases stage IV sleep. Elevated body temperatures can cause some reduction in stages III and IV NREM sleep and REM sleep.

The need to urinate during the night (nocturia) also disrupts sleep, and people who awaken at night to urinate sometimes have difficulty getting back to sleep.

Environment

Environment can promote or hinder sleep. Any change—for example, in the noise level in the environment—can inhibit sleep. The absence of usual stimuli or the presence of unfamiliar stimuli can prevent people from sleeping. The level of noise that interferes with sleep depends upon the stage of sleep of the person. Stage I sleep is the lightest and stages III and IV the deepest; as a result, louder noises are needed to awaken a person in stages III and IV. The relevance of the noise is important. However, over time, people can become habituated to a noise so that the level has less effect.

Ventilation and environmental temperature can also affect sleep. Light levels can be another factor. A person accustomed to darkness while sleeping may find it difficult to sleep in the light.

Fatigue

It is thought that a person who is moderately fatigued usually has a restful sleep. Fatigue can also affect a person's sleep pattern. The more tired the person is, the shorter is the first period of paradoxical (REM) sleep. As the person rests, the REM periods become longer.

Lifestyle

Moderate exercise usually is conducive to sleep, but excessive exercise can delay sleep, especially if undertaken shortly before going to bed. The person's ability to relax before retiring is an important factor affecting the ability to fall asleep.

Sleep-Wake Schedule

People who have an irregular sleep-wake schedule are more likely to experience poor quality sleep. Shiftwork and travel across time zones disrupt the normal circadian rhythm. Some hormones, such as growth hormone, are closely tied to the actual sleep cycle, whereas other hormones, such as melatonin, are more closely linked to the light-dark cycle. Thus, with shift work and travel, there may be desynchronization, contributing to difficulty sleeping, fatigue, and reduced alertness during work hours. People who sleep in late on days off or maintain an irregular schedule are also more likely to experience poorer quality sleep. Generally, those individuals who tend to be morning people need a more regular sleep schedule than do night hawks.

The impact of shiftwork is of particular interest to nurses. Research has shown that nurses working 12-hour shifts during their first year of practice generally had lower observed performance when compared with nurses working eight-hour shifts, a finding that may be attributed to greater fatigue with the longer shift (Fitzpatrick, While, & Roberts, 1999). Thurston, Tanguay, and Fraser (2000a, 2000b) have offered a number of useful, research-based tips for nurses doing shift work.

Emotional Stress

Anxiety and depression frequently disturb sleep. A person preoccupied with personal problems may be unable to relax sufficiently to get to sleep. Anxiety increases the norepinephrine levels in the blood through stimulation of the sympathetic nervous system. This chemical change results in less stage IV NREM and REM sleep and more stage changes and awakenings.

People who are depressed typically have disturbed sleep, manifested either as insomnia or excessive sleeping. They may report difficulty getting to sleep, frequent wakenings with inability to get back to sleep, or early morning wakening. Sleep disturbance may precede the onset of other symptoms of depression. This association may be physiological, through neurotransmitter imbalance, as well as psychological, through worry and negative thoughts.

Alcohol and Stimulants

People who drink an excessive amount of alcohol often find their sleep disturbed. Excessive alcohol disrupts REM sleep although it may hasten the onset of sleep. While making up for lost REM sleep after some of the effects of the alcohol have worn off, people often experience nightmares. Tolerance to alcohol also affects sleep; the alcohol-tolerant person may be unable to sleep well and may become irritable as a result.

Caffeine-containing beverages act as stimulants of the central nervous system, thus interfering with sleep.

Diet

Weight loss and weight gain have been thought to affect sleep. Weight loss has been associated with reduced total sleep time as well as interrupted sleep and earlier awakening.

Weight gain, on the other hand, seems to be associated with an increase in total sleep time, less interrupted sleep, and later waking.

The amino acid L-tryptophan is a precursor to serotonin, one of the main neurotransmitters necessary for sleep. Dietary L-tryptophan—found, for example, in cheese and milk—may induce sleep, a fact that might explain why warm milk helps some people get to sleep.

Smoking

Nicotine has a stimulating effect on the body, and smokers often have more difficulty falling asleep than nonsmokers. Smokers are usually easily aroused and often describe themselves as light sleepers. By refraining from smoking after the evening meal, the person usually sleeps better; moreover, many former smokers report that their sleeping patterns improved once they stopped smoking.

Motivation

The desire to stay awake can often overcome a person's fatigue. For example, a tired person can probably stay alert while attending an interesting concert. By contrast, when a person is bored and does not have the motivation to stay awake, sleep often readily ensues.

Medications

Some medications affect the quality of sleep. Hypnotics can interfere with stages III and IV NREM sleep and suppress REM sleep. Beta blockers have been known to cause insomnia and nightmares. Narcotics, such as meperidine hydrochloride (Demerol) and morphine, are known to suppress REM sleep and to cause frequent awakenings and drowsiness. Tranquilizers interfere with REM sleep. Amphetamines and antidepressants decrease REM sleep abnormally. A client withdrawing from any of these drugs gets much more REM sleep than usual and, as a result, may experience upsetting nightmares. See the box right for drugs that can disrupt sleep.

Drugs That Disrupt Sleep

These drugs may cause some of the following sleep problems: disrupted REM sleep, delayed onset of sleep, decreased sleep time, nightmares, increased daytime drowsiness.

- Alcohol
- Amphetamines
- Antidepressants
- Beta blockers
- Bronchodilators
- Caffeine
- Decongestants
- Narcotics
- Steroids
- Thyroid supplements

Common Sleep Disorders

A knowledge of common sleep disorders helps nurses obtain and recognize pertinent data. Sleep disorders may be categorized as primary disorders, secondary disorders, and the parasomnias. **Primary sleep disorders** are those in which the person's sleep problem is the main disorder. These disorders include insomnia, hypersomnia, narcolepsy, sleep apnea, and parasomnias. **Secondary sleep disorders** are sleep disturbances caused by another clinical disorder, such as thyroid dysfunction, depression, or alcoholism.

Insomnia

Insomnia, the most common sleep problem, is the inability to obtain an adequate amount or quality of sleep. People suffering from insomnia do not feel refreshed on arising. There are three types of insomnia:

1. Difficulty in falling asleep (initial insomnia)
2. Difficulty in staying asleep because of frequent or prolonged waking (intermittent or maintenance insomnia)
3. Early morning or premature waking (terminal insomnia)

Some insomniacs have been observed to fall asleep and obtain more sleep than they say they do. This type of insomnia is referred to by some as *sleep state misperception.* Such a condition is no less distressing than the other types of insomnia and may lead to increased wakefulness.

Insomnia can result from physical discomfort but, more often, is a result of mental overstimulation due to anxiety. People sometimes become anxious because they think they might not be able to sleep. People who become habituated to drugs or who drink large quantities of alcohol are likely to have insomnia.

Insomnia is often characterized by predisposing, precipitating, and perpetuating factors. *Predisposing* factors include hyperarousal, predisposition to depression, and tendency to be a night hawk. *Precipitating* factors may include periods of stress or grief, loss of a loved one, a new job, becoming a parent, or perceived need for increased vigilance. *Perpetuating* factors include fear that one will not be able to sleep, irregular sleeping patterns to try to "catch up," and association of the bedroom with the struggle to sleep. Treatment for insomnia frequently requires the client to develop new behaviour patterns that induce sleep. Short-term use of hypnotics during periods of stress may be helpful in reducing the impact of a precipitating event, but they should not be relied upon for long-term use.

Hypersomnia

Hypersomnia, the opposite of insomnia, is excessive sleep, particularly in the daytime. The afflicted person often sleeps until noon and takes many naps during the day. Hypersomnia can be caused by medical conditions, for example, central nervous system damage and certain kidney, liver, or metabolic disorders, such as diabetic acidosis and hypothyroidism. In some instances, a person uses hypersomnia as a coping mechanism to avoid facing the responsibilities of the day.

Narcolepsy

Narcolepsy—from the Greek *narco,* meaning "numbness," and *lepsis,* meaning "seizure"—is a sudden wave of overwhelming sleepiness that occurs during the day; thus, it is referred to as a "sleep attack." Its cause is unknown, although it is believed to be a genetic defect of the central nervous system in which REM sleep cannot be controlled. In narcolepsy, sleep starts with early-onset REM. People with narcolepsy may experience several sleep "attacks" a day in spite of adequate nighttime sleep. Planned naps may help but not eliminate daytime sleepiness. Narcolepsy is often controlled by central nervous system stimulants, such as amphetamine. Other medications may be used to reduce accompanying symptoms, such as cataplexy (sudden weakness associated with intense emotion).

Sleep Apnea

Sleep apnea is the periodic cessation of breathing during sleep. This disorder needs to be assessed by a sleep specialist, but it is often suspected when the person has loud snoring, frequent nocturnal awakenings, excessive daytime sleepiness, insomnia, morning headaches, intellectual deterioration, irritability or other personality changes, and physiological changes, such as hypertension and cardiac arrhythmias. It is most frequent in men over 50 years and in postmenopausal women.

The periods of apnea, which last from 10 seconds to two minutes, occur during REM or NREM sleep. Frequency of episodes ranges from 50 to 600 per night. These apneic episodes drain the person of energy and lead to excessive daytime sleepiness.

Three common types of sleep apnea are obstructive apnea, central apnea, and mixed apnea. *Obstructive apnea* occurs when the structures of the pharynx or oral cavity collapse, blocking the flow of air. The person continues to try to breathe; that is, the chest and abdominal muscles move. Decreased oxygen levels lead to partial arousal, thus opening the airway. Obesity, enlarged tonsils, a deviated nasal septum, and nasal polyps predispose the client to obstructive apnea.

Central apnea is thought to involve a defect in the respiratory centre of the brain. All actions involved in breathing, such as chest movement and airflow, cease. Clients who have brain stem injuries and muscular dystrophy, for example, often have central sleep apnea. *Mixed apnea* is a combination of central apnea and obstructive apnea.

An episode of sleep apnea begins with snoring; thereafter, breathing ceases, followed by marked snorting as breathing resumes. Toward the end of each apneic episode, decreased oxygen levels in the blood cause the client to wake up. The use of a nasal continuous positive airway pressure (CPAP) device at night is effective as it helps keep the upper airway open. Surgical procedures to remove tonsils, re-align the mandible, or open the upper airway are effective for some people. Oral appliances may also be used.

Sleep apnea profoundly affects a person's work or school performance. In addition, prolonged sleep apnea can cause a sharp rise in blood pressure and may also lead to cardiac arrest. Over time, apneic episodes can cause cardiac arrhythmias, pulmonary hypertension, and subsequent left-sided heart failure. Research has shown that nurses can make an important difference in effective CPAP use and outcomes of therapy through education and support (Hoy, Vennelle, Kingshott, Engleman, & Douglas, 1999).

Periodic Limb Movements

Periodic limb movements are repetitive jerky movements, usually of the lower limbs, during sleep that may contribute to frequent partial arousals and excessive daytime sleepiness. People who experience periodic limb movements during sleep often experience **restless legs syndrome** (crawling, aching sensations) when they are resting or trying to fall asleep. Many medications, such as antidepressants, antihistamines, and caffeine, may make the conditions worse. Medications similar to those used in treating Parkinson's disease can bring relief in severe cases.

Parasomnias

Parasomnia is a kind of behaviour that may interfere with sleep. The following box describes four kinds of parasomnia. Most parasomnias are more frequent during times of stress.

Sleep Deprivation

A prolonged disturbance results in decreases in amount, quality, and consistency of sleep and can lead to a syndrome referred to as **sleep deprivation.** This is not a sleep disorder in itself but a result of sleep disturbances. It produces a variety of physiological and behavioural symptoms,

Parasomnias

- **Somnambulism.** Somnambulism (sleepwalking) occurs during stages III and IV of NREM sleep. It is episodic and usually occurs one to two hours after falling asleep. Sleepwalkers tend not to notice dangers (e.g., stairs) and often need to be protected from injury.
- **Sleeptalking.** Talking during sleep occurs during NREM sleep before REM sleep. It rarely presents a problem to the person unless it becomes troublesome to others.
- **Nocturnal enuresis.** Bed wetting that occurs during sleep in children over three years old. More males than females are affected. It often occurs one to two hours after falling asleep when rousing from NREM stages III to IV.
- **Bruxism.** Usually occurring during stage II NREM sleep, this clenching and grinding of the teeth can eventually erode dental crowns and cause teeth to come loose.

the severity of which depends on the degree of the deprivation. There is growing concern as to the prevalence of chronic sleep deprivation in our busy 24-hour society.

Assessing

Assessment relative to a client's sleep and rest includes a sleep history, a sleep diary, a physical examination, and a review of diagnostic studies.

Sleep and Rest History

A brief general sleep and rest history should be obtained for all clients entering a health-care facility or being seen in the community. This enables the nurse to incorporate the client's needs and preferences in the plan of care. A general sleep and rest history often includes the following:

- Usual sleeping pattern, specifically sleeping and waking times; length of time to fall asleep; hours of undisturbed sleep; quality of or satisfaction with sleep (e.g., effect on energy level for daily functioning); and time and duration of naps and rest periods
- Bedtime rituals performed to help the person fall asleep (e.g., a glass of hot milk, reading or other method of relaxing, and special equipment or positioning aids)
- Use of sleep medication and other drugs. Sleep can be disturbed by a variety of drugs, such as stimulants or steroids, if they are taken close to bedtime. Hypnotics and sedating antidepressants may cause excessive daytime sleepiness.
- Preferred sleep environment (e.g., dark room, cool or warm temperature, noise level, night-light)
- Preferred ways to rest
- Recent changes in sleep and rest patterns or difficulties in sleeping

If the client indicates a recent pattern change or difficulties in sleeping, a more detailed history is required. This detailed history should explore the exact nature of the problem and its cause, when it first began and its frequency, how it affects daily living, what the client is doing to cope with the problem, and whether these methods have been effective. Questions the nurse might ask the client with a sleeping disturbance are shown in the following box. Information from the bed partner on snoring, breathing patterns, leg movements, sleeptalking, and sleepwalking is also important in detecting sleep disorders.

Sleep Diary

Sometimes, clients with a sleeping problem can provide more precise information if they keep a written record of their sleep pattern and the habits associated with it. Such a sleep diary or log can be kept by clients who are sleeping at home and should be maintained for at least one week. A sleep diary may include all of the following information or selected aspects of it that pertain to the client's specific problem:

- Total number of sleep hours per night
- Number and length of naps
- Activities performed two to three hours before bedtime (type, duration, and time)
- Bedtime rituals (e.g., ingestion of food, fluid, or medication) before going to bed
- (1) Time of going to bed, (2) approximate time to fall asleep after light out, (3) any instances of waking up and duration of these periods, (4) final time of waking during the night, and (5) time out of bed
- Worries that the client believes may affect sleep
- Factors that the client believes have a positive or negative effect on sleep

From the sleep diary, the nurse can help the client detect such patterns as an irregular sleep schedule and the effect of napping on nighttime sleep. Sleep efficiency can be calculated by dividing the actual time spent asleep by the total time in bed multiplied by 100. Clients who have a sleep efficiency of less than 85 percent should be encouraged to reduce their time in bed by not going to bed until sleepy and getting up at the same time every morning.

Physical Examination

Examination of the client includes observation of the client's facial appearance, behaviour, and energy level. Darkened areas around the eyes, puffy eyelids, reddened conjunctiva, glazed or dull-appearing eyes, and limited

ASSESSMENT INTERVIEW

Sleep Disturbances

Questions	Comments
A. Understanding the problem from the client's perspective	
■ What is the biggest problem with sleep at this time?	Helps client focus
■ When did you first notice this problem?	Determine if acute or chronic, may probe as to what was happening in the client's life about the time the problem started (e.g., change in job, weight gain)
■ How often does it occur?	(e.g., every night, only when overtired)
■ Who else has noticed this problem?	(e.g., bed partner)
■ What makes it worse?	(e.g., alcohol makes sleep apnea worse)
■ What have you found that helps deal with this sleep problem?	(e.g., sleeping in front of the sleep television or away from home suggests the bedroom has become associated with the struggle to sleep)
■ What do you think might be causing or contributing to the problem?	Clients often aware of probable etiologies
■ How is this problem affecting you? Others in your family and workplace?	Sleep disorders often affect others (e.g., snoring, worry about safety)
B. Understanding the problem from the bed partner's perspective	
■ What concerns do you have about your partner's sleep?	The bed partner can provide valuable information about behaviours during sleep as well as waking hours
■ What have you noticed that seems to make it better? Worse?	
C. Screening questions to assist in planning care and determining need for referral	
■ What do you do to prepare for sleep?	Listen for rituals, tendency to be busy right up to bedtime
■ Do you have difficulty getting to sleep?	Probe as to length of time to go to sleep (10 to 30 minutes is within normal range)
■ Do you have difficulty with wakening during the night and being unable to get back to sleep?	If yes, probe as to what the client does if awake for long periods (e.g., racing thoughts)
■ Do you have difficulty by wakening earlier in the morning than you would like?	Particularly common with depression
■ How do you feel when you wake up in the morning?	Morning headaches and feeling unrefreshed are common symptoms of sleep apnea
■ Do you sleep more than usual? Less than usual?	Inquire regarding family or work pressures, fatigue
■ Do you have periods of overwhelming tiredness? If yes, when does this happen? Do you ever feel suddenly weak when laughing or upset?	A positive response may suggest narcolepsy, especially if the client also has symptoms of cataplexy
■ Has anyone every told you that you snore, stop breathing in your sleep? Sleepwalk? Sleeptalk?	Snoring and apneas suggest sleep apnea; parasomnias, such as somnabulism, are uncommon in adults, may be worsened by stress
D. Additional Information	
■ Collect data on current medications (include over-the-counter, street drugs), time and amount of caffeine use, smoking.	Many medications and other substances affect sleep
■ Explore lifestyle regarding shift work, frequent travel across time zones.	Note circadian effects

facial expression are indicative of sleep insufficiency. Such behaviours as irritability, restlessness, inattentiveness, slowed speech, slumped posture, hand tremor, yawning, rubbing the eyes, withdrawal, confusion, and uncoordination are also suggestive of sleep problems. Lack of energy may be noted by observing whether the client appears physically weak, lethargic, or fatigued.

In addition, the nurse assesses whether the client has a deviated nasal septum, has a thick neck, or is obese. These findings may be associated with obstructive sleep apnea or snoring.

Diagnostic Studies

Sleep is measured objectively by **polysomnography,** in which EEG, EMG, and EOG are recorded simultaneously. This simultaneous recording divides sleep into REM and NREM sleep. Electrodes are placed on the scalp to record brain waves (EEG), on the outer canthus of each eye to record eye movement (EOG), and on the chin muscles to record the structural electromyogram (EMG). The following may also be monitored, depending on findings of the initial interview: respiratory effort and airflow, ECG, leg movements, and oxygen saturation. Oxygen saturation is determined by monitoring arterial blood or with an *oximeter*; a light-sensitive electric cell that attaches to the ear or a finger. Oxygen saturation and ECG assessments are of particular importance if sleep apnea is suspected. Through polysomnography, the client's activity (movements, struggling, noisy respirations) during sleep can be assessed. Such activity of which the client is unaware may be the cause of arousal during sleep.

Diagnosing

Sleep Pattern Disturbance, the NANDA nursing diagnosis given to clients with sleep problems, is the state in which the individual experiences a time-limited disruption in the amount or quality of sleep causing discomfort or interference with desired lifestyle. This diagnosis is usually made more explicit with such descriptions as "difficulty falling asleep" or "difficulty staying asleep" (Carpenito, 2002).

Various factors or etiologies may be involved and should be specified for the individual. These include physical discomfort or pain; anxiety about actual or anticipated loss of a loved one, loss of a job, or worry about a family member's behaviour or illness; frequent changes in sleep time due to shift work or overtime; and changes in sleep environment or bedtime rituals (e.g., noise or overstimulation of hospital environment; alcohol or other drug dependency; drug withdrawal; misuse of sedatives prescribed for insomnia; and effects of medications, such as steroids or stimulants).

Examples of assessment data clusters and related nursing diagnoses for sleep pattern disturbances are shown in Table 42.2.

TABLE 42.2 Clinical Application: Assessment Data Clusters and Related Nursing Diagnoses for Clients with Sleep Problems

Data Cluster	Nursing Diagnosis
Gillian Rinningwood, 51, states she has a problem falling asleep since her mastectomy two months ago. She says fears of prognosis become prominent when she is not active and busy. She has tried reading or watching TV, but neither make her sleepy or relaxed. She appears agitated and restless.	***Sleep Pattern Disturbance:*** insomnia (difficulty falling asleep) related to fear of prognosis and difficulty relaxing
Joseph Mintz, 83, was admitted to a four-bed room in the extended care unit three days ago. He states he falls asleep about 10 p.m. but is awakened by roommate's snoring. He states, "At home I used to have a hot cup of Ovaltine whenever I awakened."	***Sleep Pattern Disturbance:*** insomnia (difficulty staying asleep) related to change in sleep environment and sleep-time rituals
Plooney Larsh states he was fired from his job because of alcohol abuse. He has joined Alcoholics Anonymous but has been unable to get any work for the past two years. He states, "Every day I wake up at 4 a.m. (full of self-reproach and self-punitive thinking) and can't get back to sleep."	***Sleep Pattern Disturbance:*** insomnia (early morning waking) related to low self-esteem secondary to loss of job and inability to obtain employment
Marny Closky, a high school student whose parents recently divorced, broke up with her boyfriend two weeks ago. She states she does not have the energy to get up in the morning and just wants to sleep all the time. She has Grade 12 examinations next week.	***Sleep Pattern Disturbance:*** related to inability to cope with multiple stresses
Thomas Strep states that recent shortage of firefighters has resulted in extensive overtime and frequent "double shifts" and rotations from his usual two-weekly 7–3 and 3–7 shifts. He states, "All I want to do is go to sleep when I get home, but I can't. I guess I'm too riled up."	***Sleep Pattern Disturbance:*** altered sleep-wake pattern related to frequent changes in sleep time

Sleep pattern disturbances may also be stated as the etiology of another diagnosis, in which case, the nursing interventions are directed toward the sleep disturbance itself. Examples include the following:

- ***Risk for Injury*** related to somnambulism
- ***Ineffective Individual Coping*** related to insufficient quality and quantity of sleep

- ***Fatigue*** related to insomnia
- ***Risk for Impaired Gas Exchange*** related to sleep apnea
- ***Disturbed Thought Process*** related to chronic insomnia
- ***Activity Intolerance*** related to sleep deprivation

Planning

The major goal for clients with sleep disturbances is to maintain (or develop) a sleeping pattern that provides sufficient energy for daily activities. The nurse plans specific nursing interventions based on the etiology of each nursing diagnosis. These interventions may include reducing environmental distractions; promoting bedtime rituals; providing comfort measures; scheduling nursing care to provide for uninterrupted sleep periods; and teaching stress reduction, relaxation techniques, or ways to develop good sleep habits. If the sleep disturbance is the etiology of the nursing diagnosis, the nurse plans specific strategies to relieve insomnia and deal with sleep deprivation.

The Iowa Intervention Projects Nursing Interventions Classification (NIC) system is a tool for planning nursing interventions (McCloskey & Bulechek, 2000). Examples of NIC interventions to assist clients with sleep disturbances include the following:

- Anxiety reduction
- Environmental management: comfort
- Sleep enhancement
- Simple massage
- Simple relaxation therapy

Specific nursing activities associated with each of these interventions can be selected to meet the individual needs of the client. See the accompanying Sample Care Plan for Rest and Sleep that uses NIC interventions and selective activities.

Implementing

Nursing interventions to enhance the quantity and quality of clients' sleep involve largely nonpharmacological measures. These involve health teaching about sleep habits; support of bedtime rituals; the provision of a restful environment; specific measures to promote comfort and relaxation; and essential considerations about the use of sleep medications.

For hospitalized clients, sleep problems are often related to the hospital environment or their illness. Assisting the client to sleep in such instances can be challenging to a nurse, often involving scheduling activities, administering analgesics, and providing a supportive environment.

Client Teaching

Healthy individuals need to learn the importance of rest and sleep in maintaining active and productive lifestyles. They need to learn (1) the conditions that promote sleep and those that interfere with sleep; (2) safe use of sleep medications (see "Enhancing Sleep with Medications" later in this chapter); (3) effects of other prescribed medications on sleep; and (4) effects of their disease states on sleep. Client teaching for promoting sleep is shown in the box on page 1164.

Supporting Bedtime Rituals

Most people are accustomed to bedtime rituals or presleep routines that are conducive to comfort and relaxation. Altering or eliminating such routines can affect a client's sleep. Common prebedtime activities of adults include an evening stroll, listening to music, watching television, taking a soothing bath, and praying. Children, too, are socialized into presleep routines, such as a bedtime story, holding onto a favourite toy or blanket, and kissing everyone goodnight. Sleep is also usually preceded by hygienic routines, such as washing the face and hands (or bathing), brushing the teeth, and voiding.

In institutional settings, nurses can provide similar bedtime rituals—assisting with a hand and face wash, providing a massage or hot drink, plumping of pillows, and providing extra blankets, as needed. Conversing about accomplishments of the day or enjoyable events, such as visits from friends, can also help relax clients and bring peace of mind.

Creating a Restful Environment

All people need a sleeping environment with minimal noise, a comfortable room temperature, appropriate ventilation, and appropriate lighting. Although most people prefer a darkened environment, a low light source may provide comfort for children or those in a strange environment. Infants and children need a quiet room usually separate from the parents' room, covering with a light or warm blanket, as appropriate, and a location away from open windows or drafts.

Environmental distractions, such as bright lighting and noise, are particularly troublesome for hospitalized clients. There are three general types of noises in the hospital setting: environmental noises, procedural noises, and staff communication noises. Environmental noises include the sound of paging systems, telephones, and call lights; doors slamming; and pieces of furniture squeaking. Procedural noises include those associated with emptying catheter bags, distributing fluids, and wheeling drug or linen carts through corridors. Staff communication is a major factor creating noise, particularly at change of shift.

To create a restful environment, the nurse needs to reduce environmental distractions, reduce sleep interruptions, ensure a safe environment, and provide a room temperature that is satisfactory to the client. Some interventions to reduce environmental distractions, especially noise, are listed in the box on page 1165.

SAMPLE CARE PLAN FOR REST AND SLEEP

ASSESSMENT DATA

Nursing Assessment

Jack Harrison is a 36-year-old police officer assigned to a high-crime police precinct. One week ago, he received a surface bullet wound to his arm. Today, he arrives at the outpatient clinic to have the wound redressed. While speaking with the nurse, Mr. Harrison mentions that he has recently been promoted to the rank of detective and has assumed new responsibilities. He states that since his promotion, he has experienced increasing difficulty falling asleep and sometimes staying asleep. He expresses concern over the danger of his occupation and his desire to do well in his new position. He complains of waking up feeling tired and irritable.

Physical Examination

Height: 185.4 cm
Weight: 85.7 kg
Temperature: 37°C
Pulse: 80 BPM
Respirations: 18/minute
Blood pressure: 144/88 mm Hg
Pale, drawn, with dark circles under eyes.

Diagnostic Data

X-ray left arm: evidence of superficial soft tissue injury

Nursing Diagnosis

Sleep Pattern Disturbance related to anxiety and overstimulation (as evidenced by difficulty falling and remaining asleep, fatigue, irritability, drawn facial appearance, dark circles under eyes)

Client Goal(s):

The client will (1) establish a satisfactory sleep and rest pattern and awaken feeling rested; (2) identify sources of anxiety and coping strategies.

Desired Outcomes

1. Describes one or two factors that contribute to insomnia
2. Identifies two or three measures that induce sleep
3. Verbalizes decreased irritability and a greater sense of well-being by day 21
4. Recognizes his coping patterns by day 7
5. Identifies effective new and old coping strategies by day 10

*Nursing Interventions and Selected Activities with Rationale *[in italics]*

Sleep Enhancement

- Determine the client's sleep and activity pattern. *The amount of sleep an individual needs varies with lifestyle, health, and age.*
- Encourage Mr. Harrison to establish a bedtime routine to facilitate transition from wakefulness to sleep. *Rituals and routines induce comfort, relaxation, and sleep.*
- Encourage him to stop working on projects or other stressful activities at least one hour before bedtime. *Stress interferes with a person's ability to relax, rest, and sleep.*
- Teach Mr. Harrison and significant others about factors (e.g., physiological, psychological, lifestyle, frequent work shift changes, excessively long work hours, and other environmental factors) that contribute to sleep pattern disturbances. *Knowledge of predisposing factors can enable the client to begin to control factors that inhibit sleep.*
- Discuss with Mr. Harrison and his family comfort measures, sleep-promoting techniques, and lifestyle changes that can contribute to optimal sleep. *Knowledge of factors that affect sleep enables the client to implement changes in lifestyle and prebedtime activities.*
- Monitor bedtime food and beverage intake for items that facilitate or interfere with sleep. *Milk and protein foods contain tryptophan, a precursor of serotonin, which is thought to induce and maintain sleep. Stimulants should be avoided because they inhibit sleep.*

Security Enhancement

- Discuss specific situations or individuals that threaten Mr. Harrison or his family. *Fear is reduced when the reality of a situation is confronted in a safe environment. Awareness of factors that cause intensification of fears enhances control.*
- Help Mr. Harrison and his family identify what factors increase their sense of security. *Stress and anxiety can increase a person's risk of stress-related illness. If unable to remove the stressor, the individual can be taught to change ways of responding.*
- Assist him to use coping responses that have been successful in the past. *Feelings of safety and security increase when an individual identifies previously successful ways of dealing with anxiety-provoking or fearful situations.*

→

SAMPLE CARE PLAN FOR REST AND SLEEP *continued*

Anxiety Reduction

■ Create an atmosphere that facilitates trust.	*Trust is an essential first step in the therapeutic relationship.*
■ Seek to understand Mr. Harrison's perspective of a stressful situation.	*Anxiety is a feeling aroused by a vague, nonspecific threat. Identifying the client's perspective will facilitate planning for the best approach to anxiety reduction.*
■ Encourage verbalization of feelings, perceptions, and fears.	*Open expression of feelings facilitates identification of specific emotions, such as anger or helplessness, distorted perceptions, and unrealistic fears.*
■ Help Mr. Harrison identify situations that precipitate anxiety.	*Describing what the person experienced immediately prior to feeling anxious, and identifying associated events, will enable the client to prevent or recognize his anxiety in order to initiate problem solving.*
■ Determine the client's decision-making ability.	*Maladaptive coping mechanisms are characterized by an inability to make decisions and choices.*

Evaluation

Goal met. Mr. Harrison acknowledges his insomnia is a somatic expression of his anxiety regarding job promotion and fear of failing. He states that talking with the police department counsellor has been helpful. He is practising relaxation techniques each night and sleeps an average of seven hours a night. Mr. Harrison expresses a greater sense of well-being.

*Interventions and activities selected are only a sample of those suggested in the *Nursing Interventions Classification (NIC)* and should be individualized for each client.
Source: McCloskey, J. C., & Bulechek, G. M. (2000). *Iowa intervention project: Nursing interventions classification (NIC)* (3rd ed.). St. Louis, MO: Mosby.

WELLNESS TEACHING

Promoting Rest and Sleep

Sleep Pattern

- Establish a regular bedtime and wake-up time for all days of the week to prevent disruptions in your biological rhythm. Eliminate lengthy naps, or if a daytime nap is necessary, take it at the same time each day and limit the time to 30 minutes, preferably once a day.
- Get adequate exercise during the day to reduce stress, but avoid excessive physical exertion two hours before bedtime.
- Avoid dealing with office work or family problems before bedtime.
- Establish a regular routine before sleep, such as reading, listening to soft music, taking a warm bath, or doing some other quiet activity you enjoy.
- When you are unable to sleep, pursue some relaxing activity until you feel drowsy.
- If you have trouble falling asleep, get up and pursue nonstrenuous activity until you feel sleepy.
- Use the bed mainly for sleep so that you associate it with sleep.

Environment

- Ensure appropriate lighting, temperature, and ventilation.
- Keep noise to a minimum; block out extraneous noise, as necessary, with soft music.

Diet

- Avoid heavy meals three hours before bedtime.
- Avoid alcohol and caffeine-containing foods and beverages (coffee, tea, chocolate) at least four hours before bedtime.
- Decrease fluid intake two to four hours before sleep, if necessary, to avoid the need to use the bathroom during sleeping hours.
- If a bedtime snack is necessary, consume only light carbohydrates or a milk drink. Heavy or spicy foods can cause gastrointestinal upsets that disturb sleep.

Medications

- Use sleeping medications only as a last resort. Take them judiciously (e.g., three times a week). Use over-the-counter medications sparingly because many contain antihistamines that cause daytime drowsiness.
- Take analgesics 30 minutes before bedtime to relieve aches and pains, if necessary.
- Consult with your health-care provider about adjusting other medications that may cause insomnia.
- Take diuretics and stimulating medications early in the day.

The environment must also be safe so that the client can relax. People who are unaccustomed to narrow hospital beds may feel more secure with side rails.

Additional safety measures include the following:

- Placing beds in low positions
- Using night-lights
- Placing call bells within easy reach

Promoting Comfort and Relaxation

Comfort measures are essential to help the client fall asleep and stay asleep, especially if the effects of the person's illness interfere with sleep. A concerned, caring attitude, along with the following interventions, can significantly promote client comfort and sleep:

- Provide loose-fitting nightwear.
- Assist clients with hygienic routines.
- Make sure the bed linen is smooth, clean, and dry.
- Assist or encourage the client to void before bedtime.
- Offer to provide a back massage before sleep (see Procedure 42.1).
- Position dependent clients appropriately to aid muscle relaxation, and provide supportive devices to protect pressure areas.
- Schedule medications, especially diuretics, to prevent nocturnal awakenings.

Reducing Environmental Distractions in Hospitals

- Close window curtains if street lights shine through.
- Close curtains between clients in semiprivate and larger rooms.
- Reduce or eliminate overhead lighting; provide a night-light at the bedside or in the bathroom.
- Close the door of the client's room.
- Adhere to agency policy about times to turn off communal televisions or radios.
- Lower the ring tone of nearby telephones.
- Discontinue use of the paging system after a certain hour (e.g., 2100 hours), or reduce its volume.
- Keep required staff conversations at low levels; conduct nursing reports or other discussions in a separate area away from client rooms.
- Wear rubber-soled shoes.
- Ensure that all cart wheels are well oiled.
- Perform only essential nursing tasks during sleeping hours.
- Pair patients with frequent nocturnal needs in the same room to minimize disturbances for other patients.

Helping Older Clients Keep Warm in Bed

- Provide a prewarmed bath blanket, if possible.
- Use cotton flannel sheets, if possible, for warmth. Alternatively, apply thermal blankets between the sheet and bedspread.
- Encourage the client to wear own clothing, such as a flannel nightgown or pajamas, loose-fitting jogging suit, thermal socks, leg warmers, long underwear, sleeping cap (if scalp hair is sparse), a sweater, or use a favourite quilt or blanket.

- For clients who have pain, administer analgesics 30 minutes before sleep, or apply warm or cool applications or supportive dressings or splints to painful areas.
- For clients who have breathing problems, administer prescribed medications, such as bronchodilators, before bedtime, and position clients appropriately (e.g., semi-Fowler's position) to facilitate breathing.
- Listen to the client's concerns, and deal with problems as they arise.

People of any age, but especially older adults, are unable to sleep well if they feel cold. Changes in circulation, metabolism, and body tissue density reduce the older person's ability to generate and conserve heat. To compound this problem, hospital gowns have short sleeves and are made of thin fabric. Bedsheets also are often made of polyester, rather than a warm fabric, such as cotton flannel. Interventions to keep elderly clients warm during sleep are shown in the box above.

Emotional stress obviously interferes with a person's ability to relax, rest, and sleep, and inability to sleep further aggravates feelings of tension. Sleep rarely occurs until a person is relaxed. Relaxation techniques can be encouraged as part of the nightly routine. Slow, deep breathing for a few minutes followed by slow, rhythmic contraction and relaxation of muscles can alleviate tension and induce calm. Imagery, meditation, and yoga can also be taught. These techniques are discussed in Chapter 11.

Enhancing Sleep with Medications

Sleep medications often prescribed on a prn (as needed) basis for clients include the sedative-hypnotics, which induce sleep, and antianxiety drugs or tranquilizers (benzodiazepines), which decrease anxiety and tension. When prn sleep medications are ordered in institutional settings, the nurse is responsible for making decisions with the client about when to administer them. These medications should be administered only with complete knowledge of their actions and effects and only when indicated. Whenever possible, nonpharmacological interventions to induce and maintain sleep, discussed earlier, are the preferred

PROCEDURE 42.1 Providing a Back Massage

PURPOSES

- To relieve muscle tension
- To promote physical and mental relaxation
- To relieve insomnia

Assessment Focus
Vital signs; signs of stress (e.g., muscle tension); receptivity of the client to a massage

Equipment

- ❑ Lotion or oil

INTERVENTION

1. **Select an appropriate time free of interruptions and distractions.**
   - Provide massage following the bath, before sleeping, and at other times as necessary to achieve relaxation and comfort for the client.
   - Assist the client to a prone or lateral position in bed. Remove the client's gown, or open the back of the gown.
2. **Warm the massage lotion or oil before use.**
   - Warm the lotion or oil by pouring and holding it in your hands or placing the container in warm water before applying it to the client's back. *Cold lotion may startle the client and increase discomfort.*
3. **Massage the entire back.** See the centre box for types of massage strokes.
   - Place your hands on either side of the lower spine. Using your palms and fingers, slowly massage using a circular motion and moving upward to the neck, gradually decreasing pressure as you get close to the neck. Use the circular motion over the shoulder blades, and then slowly move down the lateral surface of the back. See Figure 42.3. *Effleurage has a relaxing, sedative effect if slow movement and light pressure are used.*

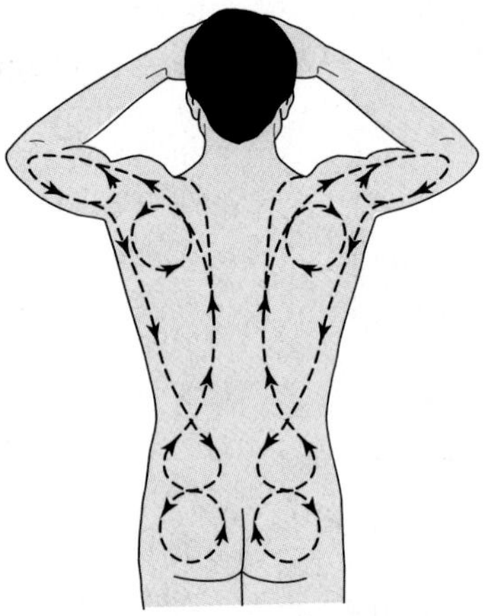

Figure 42.3 A back rub pattern

Types of Massage Strokes

- *Effleurage:* stroking the body
- *Petrissage:* kneading or gently grasping tissues of the skin, subcutaneous tissue, and muscle between fingers

   - Repeat this massage pattern for three to four minutes.
   - Maintain contact with the skin during the massage.
   - Use your thumbs to apply friction strokes (strong circular motions).
4. **Optional: Petrissage the back and shoulders of the client. Use with caution with clients who have bleeding disorders or who are on anticoagulant therapy.**
   - Petrissage first up the vertebral column and then over the entire back. *Petrissage is stimulating, especially if done quickly and with firm pressure.*
   - Observe the client carefully to ensure that petrissage does not cause pain or discomfort. If the client grimaces or withdraws from the touch, ease the kneading pressure.
   - End the massage with long movements, and tell the client you are finishing.
5. **Optional: Effleurage and petrissage the upper back and shoulders.** *This area often experiences the most tension.*
6. **Assist the client to a position of comfort.**
7. **Document the massage and your observations.**

interventions. These medications are contraindicated in pregnant women because of their associated risk of congenital anomalies and in nursing mothers because the medication could be excreted in breast milk.

Both nurses and clients need to be aware of the actions, effects, and risks of the specific medication prescribed. Although medications vary in their activity and effects, considerations include the following:

- Sedative-hypnotic medications produce a general central nervous system (CNS) depression and an unnatural sleep; REM or NREM sleep is altered to some extent and daytime drowsiness and a morning hangover effect may occur.
- Antianxiety medications decrease levels of arousal by facilitating the action of neurons in the central nervous system that suppress responsiveness to stimulation.

- Sleep medications vary in their onset and duration of action and will impair waking function as long as they are chemically active. Some medication effects can last many hours beyond the time that the client's perception of daytime drowsiness and impaired psychomotor skills have disappeared. Clients need to be cautioned about such effects and about driving or handling machinery while the drug is in their system.
- Sleep medications affect REM sleep more than NREM sleep. Clients need to be informed that one or two nights of increased dreaming (REM rebound) is usual after the drug is discontinued.
- Initial doses of medications should be low and increases added gradually, depending on the client's response. Older adults, in particular, are susceptible to side effects because of their metabolic changes; they need to be closely monitored for changes in mental alertness and coordination. Clients need to be instructed to take the smallest effective dose and then only for a few nights or intermittently as required.
- Regular use of any sleep medication can lead to tolerance over time (e.g., four weeks) and a rebound insomnia. In some instances, this may lead clients to increase the dosage or complement the drug with alcohol. Clients must be cautioned about developing a pattern of drug dependency or alcohol abuse.
- Abrupt cessation of *barbiturate* sedative-hypnotics can create withdrawal symptoms, such as restlessness, tremors, weakness, insomnia, increased heart rate, seizures, convulsions, and even death. Long-term users need to taper withdrawal by about 25 to 30 percent weekly, according to physician's orders.

Evaluating

Using data collected during care and the desired outcomes developed during the planning stage as a guide, the nurse judges whether client goals and outcomes have been achieved. Data collection may include (1) observations of the duration of the client's sleep and the presence of signs of REM and NREM sleep, and (2) questions about how the client feels on awakening, or about the effectiveness of specific interventions, such as the use of relaxation techniques, adherence to a consistent sleep-wake cycle, or the ingestion of milk products before bedtime. Examples of client goals and related outcomes are shown in Table 42.3.

If the desired outcomes are *not* achieved, the nurse, client, and support people, if appropriate, should explore the reasons, which may include answers to the following questions:

- Were etiological factors correctly identified?
- Has the client's physical condition or medication therapy changed?
- Did the client comply with instructions about establishing a regular sleep-wake pattern?

TABLE 42.3 Evaluation Goals and Outcomes: Sleep Pattern Disturbances

Goal	Examples of Desired Outcomes
Develop a sleep-wake pattern that ensures sufficient energy for daily activities	Identifies possible causes of sleeping problem
	Identifies stress-relieving measures that enhance ability to fall asleep
	Uses planned relaxation techniques before bedtime
	Falls asleep within 20 to 30 minutes of going to bed
	Sleeps specified number of hours per night or for longer intervals between nursing care functions
	Reports feelings of being rested or refreshed after waking
Decrease signs of sleep deprivation	Absence of signs of sleep deprivation, such as excessive yawning, circles under eyes, and slow responses
	Demonstrates more motivation for activity and animation in activity
Increase physical and psychological comfort level before and during sleep	Reports satisfaction with pain control measures and positioning techniques
	Reports satisfaction with physical surroundings
	Reports effectiveness of bedtime rituals and relaxation techniques (e.g., backrubs, soft music, warm soothing bath) in reducing anxiety

- Did the client avoid ingesting caffeine?
- Were all possible measures taken to provide a restful environment for the client?
- Were bedtime rituals supported?
- Were the comfort and relaxation measures effective?

Consider...

What actions would you take if the client did *not* meet the following outcome criterion?

- "Absence of signs of sleep deprivation" (Data reveal client has dark circles under the eyes, yawns excessively throughout the day, and is not motivated for any activity.)

FOCUS ON CRITICAL THINKING

While making rounds at 1:00 a.m., you note that Jane Marsh, a 23-year-old woman recovering from surgery, is awake and watching television. Concerned that Ms. Marsh may be experiencing too much pain to sleep, you question her about how she is feeling. She states that she is not having pain, she just cannot sleep. Upon further questioning, you learn that she has a pattern of sleepless nights. She explains that she usually goes to bed by 11:00 p.m. after exercising but frequently has difficulty falling asleep. Sometimes, she listens to the radio or watches TV until she is able to sleep. She usually has a soft drink at bedtime but avoids coffee or tea because it keeps her awake. Ms. Marsh admits that she is frequently sleepy during the day and has considered getting a prescription for a sleeping pill from her doctor so that she can develop a better sleep routine.

1. Explain why keeping a sleep diary might be beneficial for Ms. Marsh.
2. What further information would be helpful to obtain from her about her sleep problem?
3. What suggestions can you make that may help her develop better sleep habits when she returns home?
4. What evidence suggests that Ms. Marsh is experiencing a primary, as opposed to a secondary, sleep disorder?
5. What are the most common problems that interfere with clients' ability to sleep while hospitalized?

See Appendix A for answers to these questions.

CHAPTER HIGHLIGHTS

- Sleep is a naturally occurring altered conscious state in which a person's perception and reaction to the environment are decreased.
- The sleep cycle is controlled by specialized areas in the brain stem and is affected by the individual's circadian rhythm.
- Rest and sleep are restorative, protective, and energy-conserving.
- During a normal night's sleep, an adult has four to six sleep cycles, each with NREM (quiet) and REM (rapid eye movement) sleep.
- NREM sleep consists of four stages, progressing from stage I, very light sleep, to stage IV, deep sleep. NREM sleep constitutes most of a sleep cycle.
- REM sleep recurs about every 90 minutes and is often associated with dreaming.
- The ratio of NREM to REM sleep varies with age.
- Many factors can affect sleep, including age, illness, environment, lifestyle, sleep-wake patterns, emotional stress, alcohol and stimulants, diet, smoking, motivation, and medications.
- Common sleep disorders include insomnia, hypersomnia, narcolepsy, sleep apnea, periodic limb movements, and parasomnias, such as somnambulism, talking during sleep, nocturnal enuresis, and bruxism.
- Assessment of a client's sleep includes obtaining a sleep history, reviewing a sleep diary, and conducting a physical examination to detect signs of sleep deprivation.
- Nursing responsibilities to help clients sleep include (1) teaching clients ways to enhance sleep and rest, (2) supporting bedtime rituals, (3) creating a restful environment, (4) promoting comfort and relaxation, and (5) using prescribed sleep medications.
- Nonpharmacological interventions to induce and maintain sleep are the preferred interventions.

READINGS AND REFERENCES

Suggested Readings

Beck-Little, R., & Weinrich, S. P. (1998, April). Assessment and management of sleep disorders in the elderly. *Journal of Gerontological Nursing, 24*(4), 21–29.
The authors explain that sleep disorders are rarely diagnosed in the elderly. They can affect falling asleep or maintaining sleep or cause excessive sleepiness in the daytime. The authors explain three types of disorders: dyssomnias, parasomnias, and medical-psychiatric sleep disorders. Assessment and interventions are also included.

McDowell, J. A, Mion, L. C., Lydon, T. J., & Inouye, S. K. (1998). A nonpharmacologic sleep protocol for hospitalized older patients. *Journal of the American Geriatrics Society, 46*, 700–705.

To test a protocol for improving sleep and reducing use of sedative-hypnotic drugs (SHD) among patients 70 years and older on an acute medical unit, the investigators implemented a protocol in which any patient reporting difficulty initiating sleep or asking for a SHD was offered a back rub, warm drink, and relaxation tapes. They found that these nursing interventions did reduce SHD use with at least two of the three interventions being more effective than one alone. However, patients who habitually used SHD were least likely to accept the other interventions.

Rogers, A. E. (1997, December). Nursing management of sleep disorders Part I–Assessment; Part 2–Behavioural interventions. *American Nephrology Nurses Association Journal, 24*(6), 666–675.

The author explains the assessment of insomnia and hypersomnia. Sleep interventions include pharmacological, psychotherapy, and behavioural approaches. Part 2 also describes the types of insomnia and several behavioural therapies.

Selected References

American Sleep Disorders Association. (1997). *International classification of sleep disorders, revised: Diagnostic and coding manual.* Rochester, MN: Author.

Carpenito, L. J. (2000). *Nursing diagnosis: Application to clinical practice.* (8th ed.). Philadelphia, PA: Lippincott.

Cohen, F. L., Nehring, W. M., & Cloninger, L. (1996). Symptom description and management in narcolepsy. *Holistic Nursing Practice, 10*(4), 44–53.

Driver, H. S., & Taylor, S. R. (2000). Exercise and sleep. *Sleep Medicine Reviews, 4*(4), 387–402.

Evans, J. C., & French, D. G. (1995). Sleep and healing in intensive care settings. *Dimensions of critical care nursing, 14*(4), 189–199.

Fitzpatrick, J. M., While, A. E., & Roberts, J. D. (1999). Shift work and its impact upon nurse performance: Current knowledge and research issues. *Journal of Advanced Nursing, 29*(1), 18–27.

Grandjean, C. K., & Gibbons, S. W. (2000). Assessing ambulatory geriatric sleep complaints. *The Nurse Practitioner, 25*(9), 25–36.

Guyton, A. C., & Hall, J. E. (1996). *Textbook of medical physiology* (9th ed.). Philadelphia, PA: Saunders.

Hoy, C. J., Vennelle, M., Kingshott, R. N., Engleman, H. M., & Douglas, N. J. (1999). Can intensive support improve continuous positive airway pressure use in patients with sleep apnea/hypopnea syndrome? *American Journal of Respiratory and Critical Care Medicine, 159*, 1096–1100.

Humphreys, J. C., Lee, K. A., Neylan, T. C., & Marmar, C. R. (1999). Sleep patterns of sheltered battered women. *Image: Journal of Nursing Scholarship, 31*(2), 139–143.

Johnson, M., & Maas, M. (Eds.). (2000). *Iowa outcomes project: Nursing Outcomes Classification (NOC).* St. Louis, MO: Mosby.

Kales, A. (1968, May). Sleep and dreams: Recent research in clinical aspects. *Annals of Internal Medicine, 68*, 1078.

Kryger M. H., & Dement,W. C. (Eds). (2000). *Principle and practice of sleep medicine* (3rd ed.). Philadelphia, PA: Saunders.

Lee, K. A. (1997, December). An overview of sleep and common sleep problems. *ANNA Journal, 24*(6), 614–676.

Lorrain, D., & De Konick, J. (1998). Sleep position and sleep stages: Evidence of their independence. *Sleep, 21*, 335–340.

McCloskey, J. C., & Bulechek, G. M. (Eds.). (2000). *Iowa intervention project: Nursing Interventions Classification (NIC)* (3rd ed.). St. Louis, MO: Mosby.

Meek, S. S. (1993, Spring). Effects of slow stroke back massage on relaxation in hospice clients. *Image: Journal of Nursing Scholarship, 25*, 17–20.

Mimeault, V., & Morin, C. M. (1999). Self-help treatment for insomnia: Bibliotherapy with and without professional guidance. *Journal of Clinical and Consulting Psychology, 67*(4), 511–519.

Morin, C. M., Colecchi, C., Stone, J., Sood, R., & Brink, D. (1999). Behavioral and pharmacological therapies for late-life insomnia: A randomized controlled trial. *Journal of American Medical Association, 281*(11), 991–999.

Morin, C. M., Hauri, P. J., Espie, C. A., Spielman, A. J., Buysse, D. J., & Bootzin, R. R. (1999). Nonpharmacologic treatment of chronic insomnia. *Sleep, 22*(8), 1134–1156.

Mornhinweg, G. C., & Voignier, R. R. (1996). Rest. *Holistic Nursing Practice, 10*(4), 54–60.

North American Nursing Diagnosis Association. (2001). *NANDA nursing diagnoses: Definitions and classification 2001–2002.* Philadelphia, PA: Author.

Thurston, N. E., Tanguay, S. M., & Fraser, K. L. (2000). Sleep and shiftwork I. *Canadian Nurse, 96*(9), 35–36.

Thurston, N. E., Tanguay, S. M., & Fraser, K. L. (2000). Sleep and shiftwork II. *Canadian Nurse, 96*(10), 31–32.

WEBLINKS

Canadian Sleep Society
www.css.to/sleep/index.htm
This is an organization for health-care professionals and researchers in sleep and circadian rhythms.

Canadian Lung Association
www.lung.ca
This Web site provides an interesting section on sleep apnea.

Alberta Sleep Apnea Society
www.sleep-apnea.ab.ca
This is a site for people wanting to learn more about sleep apnea and to join a support/advocacy group.

National Sleep Foundation (U.S.)
www.sleepfoundation.org
The site includes general sleep information for the lay public such as self-assessment guides.

CHAPTER 43

Activity and Exercise

OBJECTIVES

After completing this chapter, you will be able to:

- Describe four basic elements of normal movement.
- Differentiate isotonic, isometric, isokinetic, aerobic, and anaerobic exercises.
- Compare the effects of exercise and immobility on body systems.
- Identify factors influencing a person's body alignment and activity.
- Assess activity-exercise pattern, alignment, mobility capabilities and limitations, activity tolerance, and potential problems related to immobility.
- Develop nursing diagnoses related to activity and exercise problems.
- Use proper body mechanics when positioning, moving, lifting, and ambulating clients.
- Plan, implement, and evaluate nursing care related to a client's mobility problems.

An **activity-exercise pattern** refers to a person's routine of exercise, activity, leisure, and recreation. It includes (1) activities of daily living (ADLs) that require energy expenditure, such as hygiene, cooking, shopping, eating, working, and home maintenance; and (2) the type, quality, and quantity of exercise, including sports (Gordon, 1994).

Mobility, the ability to move freely, easily, rhythmically, and purposefully in the environment, is an essential part of living. People must move to protect themselves from trauma and to meet their basic needs. Mobility is vital to independence; a fully immobilized person is as vulnerable and dependent as an infant.

People often define their health and physical fitness by their activity because mental well-being and the effectiveness of body functioning depend largely on their mobility status. For example, when a person is upright, the lungs expand more easily, intestinal activity (peristalsis) is more effective, and the kidneys are able to empty completely. In addition, motion is essential for the proper functioning of bones and muscles.

The ability to move also influences self-esteem and body image, both components of self-concept. For most people, self-esteem depends on a sense of independence and a feeling of usefulness or being needed. People with mobility impairments may feel helpless and burdensome to others. Body image can be altered by paralysis, amputations, or any motor impairment. The reaction of others to impaired mobility can also alter self-esteem and body image significantly.

Normal Movement

Normal movement and stability are the result of an intact musculoskeletal system, an intact nervous system, and intact inner ear structures responsible for equilibrium.

Body movement requires coordinated muscle activity and neurological integration. It involves four basic elements: body alignment (posture), joint mobility, balance (stability), and coordinated movement.

Alignment and Posture

Proper body alignment and posture bring body parts into line in a manner that promotes optimal balance and maximal body function in whatever position the client assumes: standing, sitting, or lying down. The line of gravity and the body's centre of gravity influence standing alignment and balance. A person maintains balance as long as the **line of gravity** (an imaginary vertical line drawn through the body's centre of gravity) passes through the **centre of gravity** (the point at which all of the body's mass is centred) and the **base of support** (the foundation on which the body rests). In humans, the usual *line of gravity* begins at the top of the head and falls between the shoulders, through the trunk, slightly anterior to the sacrum, and between the weight-bearing joints and base of support (Figure 43.1). For a person in the upright position, the *centre of gravity* is located in the centre of the pelvis approximately midway between the umbilicus and the symphysis pubis. For greatest balance and stability, a standing adult must centre body weight symmetrically along the line of gravity. Greater stability and balance are provided in the sitting or lying position than in the standing position. The feet of the chair or bed form a considerably wider base of support, the centre of gravity is lower, and the line of gravity is less mobile.

When the body is well aligned, strain on the joints, muscles, tendons, or ligaments is minimized and the internal structures and organs are supported. People are usually unaware of the functions of the skeletal muscles that maintain body posture. These muscles function almost continuously, making tiny adjustments that enable an erect or seated posture despite the endless downward pull of gravity. Sustained contraction of the muscles supporting this upright position is called **postural tonus.** The extensor muscles, often referred to as the *antigravity* muscles, carry the major load. Pressure against the sole of the foot by the ground elicits a reflexive contraction of the extensor muscles of the lower legs.

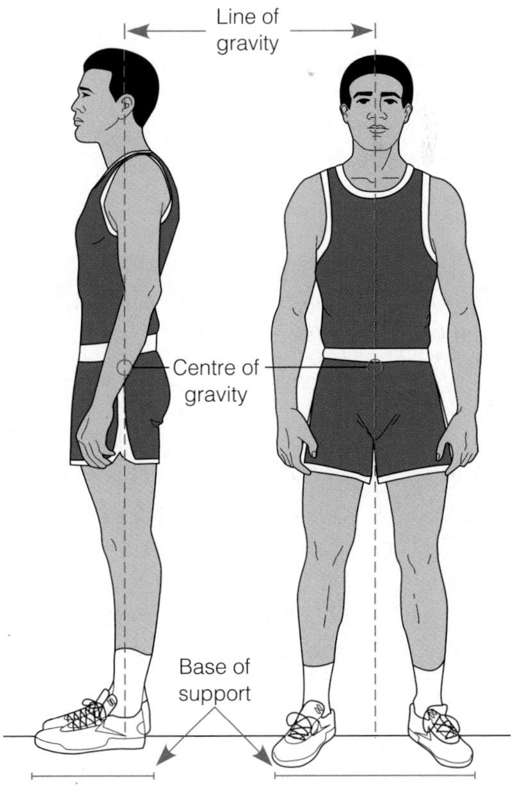

Figure 43.1 The centre of gravity and the line of gravity influence standing alignment

Proper body alignment enhances lung expansion and promotes efficient circulatory, respiratory, renal, and gastrointestinal functions. Conversely, poor body alignment detracts from a pleasing appearance and affects an individual's health adversely. A person's posture is one criterion for assessing general health, physical fitness, and attractiveness. Posture reflects the mood, self-esteem, and personality of an individual.

Joint Mobility

Joints are the functional units of the musculoskeletal system. The bones of the skeleton articulate at the joints and most of the skeletal muscles attach to the bones at the joint. Muscles are categorized according to the type of joint movement they produce on contraction. Muscles are, therefore, called flexors, extensors, internal rotators, and the like. The flexor muscles are stronger than the extensor muscles. Thus, when a person is inactive, the joints are pulled into a flexed (bent) position. If this tendency is not counteracted with exercise and position changes, the muscles permanently shorten, and the joint becomes fixed in a flexed position as a flexion contracture. The types of synovial joint movement are shown in Table 43.1.

The **range of motion (ROM)** of a joint is the maximum movement that is possible for that joint. Joint range of motion varies from individual to individual and is determined by genetic makeup, developmental patterns, the presence or absence of disease, and the amount of physical activity in which the person normally engages. Table 43.2 shows the various joint movements and the usual ranges of motion.

Balance

The mechanisms involved in maintaining balance and posture are complex and beyond the scope of this book. Mechanisms of equilibrium (sense of balance) respond, frequently without our awareness, to various head movements. The equilibrium sense depends on informational inputs from the *labryinth* (inner ear), vision (vestibulo-ocular input), and from stretch receptors of muscles and tendons (proprioceptors and vestibulospinal input). The labyrinth consists of the cochlea, vestibule, and semicircular canals. The cochlea is concerned with hearing and the vestibule and semicircular canals with equilibrium. Under normal conditions, the equilibrium receptors in the semicircular canals and vestibule, collectively called the *vestibular apparatus*, send signals to the brain that initiate reflexes needed to make required changes in position. The receptors (hairlike cells) respond to displacement of the head in any direction. When the head moves, the fluid flow within the vestibule and semicircular canals stimulates sensory hair cells. Information from these balance receptors goes directly to reflex centres in the brain stem rather than to the cerebral cortex as with other special senses. This enables fast reflexive responses to body imbalance.

Coordinated Movement

Balanced, smooth, purposeful movement is the result of proper functioning of the cerebral cortex, cerebellum, and basal ganglia. The cerebral cortex initiates voluntary motor activity; the cerebellum coordinates the motor activities of movement; and the basal ganglia maintain posture. The *cerebral cortex* operates in terms of movements, not muscles. The cortex, for example, may direct the arm to pick up a cup of coffee.

TABLE 43.1 Types of Synovial Joint Movements

Movement	Action	Movement	Action
Flexion	Decreasing the angle of the joint (e.g., bending the elbow)	Eversion	Turning the sole of the foot outward by moving the ankle joint
Extension	Increasing the angle of the joint (e.g., straightening the arm at the elbow)	Inversion	Turning the sole of the foot inward by moving the ankle joint
Hyperextension	Overextension or straightening of a joint (e.g., bending the head backward)	Pronation	Moving the bones of the forearm so that the palm of the hand faces downward when held in front of the body
Abduction	Movement of the bone away from the midline of the body	Supination	Moving the bones of the forearm so that the palm of the hand faces upward when held in front of the body
Adduction	Movement of the bone toward the midline of the body	Protraction	Moving a part of the body forward in the same plane parallel to the ground
Rotation	Movement of the bone around its central axis	Retraction	Moving a part of the body backward in the same plane parallel to the ground
Circumduction	Movement of the distal part of the bone in a circle while the proximal end remains fixed		

TABLE 43.2 Selected Joint Movements

Body Part—Type of Joint/Movement	Normal Range	Illustration
Neck—Pivot Joint		
Flexion. Move the head from the upright midline position forward so that the chin rests on the chest (Figure 1).	45° from midline	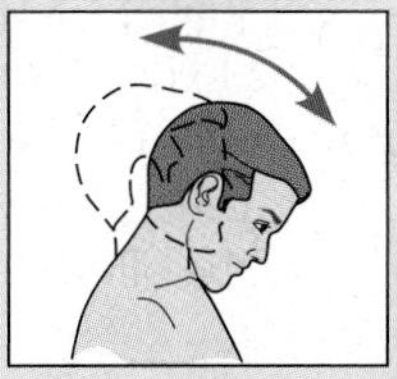 Figure 1
Extension. Move the head from the flexed position to the upright position (Figure 1).	45° from midline	
Hyperextension. Move the head from the upright position back as far as possible.	10°	
Lateral flexion. Move the head laterally to the right and left shoulders (Figure 2).	40° from midline	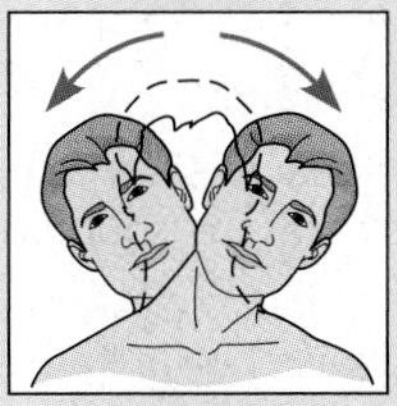 Figure 2
Rotation. Turn the face as far as possible to the right and left (Figure 3).	70° from midline	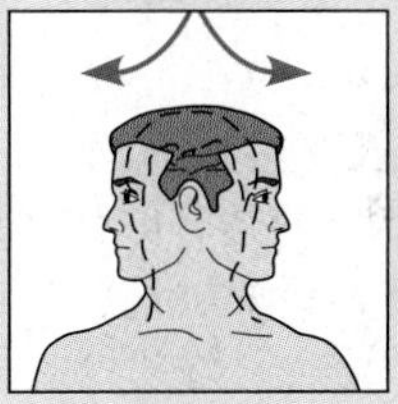 Figure 3
Shoulder—Ball-and-Socket Joint		
Flexion. Raise each arm from a position by the side forward and upward to a position beside the head (Figure 4).	180° from the side	 Figure 4
Extension. Move each arm from a vertical position beside the head forward and down to a resting position at the side of the body (Figure 4).	180° from vertical position beside the head	
Hyperextension. Move each arm from a resting side position to behind the body (Figure 4).	50° from side position	
Abduction. Move each arm laterally from a resting position at the sides to a side position above the head, palm of the hand away from the head (Figure 5).	180°	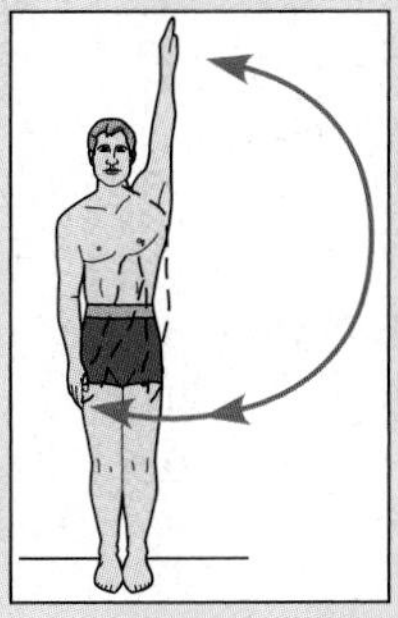 Figure 5
Adduction (anterior). Move each arm from a position beside the head downward laterally and across the front of the body as far as possible (Figure 5).	230°	
Circumduction. Move each arm forward, up, back, and down in a full circle (Figure 6).	360°	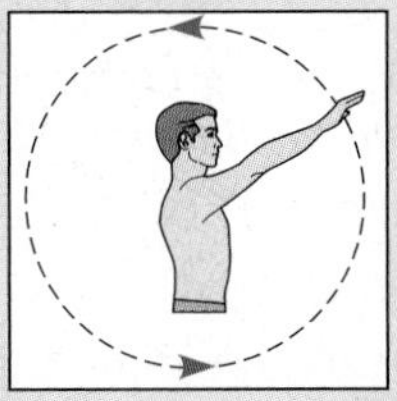 Figure 6

TABLE 43.2 Selected Joint Movements *continued*

Body Part—Type of Joint/Movement	Normal Range	Illustration
External rotation. With each arm held out to the side at shoulder level and the elbow bent to a right angle, fingers pointing down, move the arm upward so that the fingers point up (Figure 7).	90°	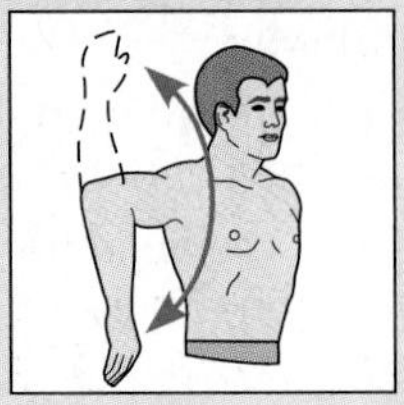 Figure 7
Internal rotation. With each arm held out to the side at shoulder level and the elbow bent to a right angle, fingers pointing up, bring the arm forward and down so that the fingers point down (Figure 7).	90°	
Elbow—Hinge Joint		
Flexion. Bring each lower arm forward and upward so that the hand is at the shoulder (Figure 8).	150°	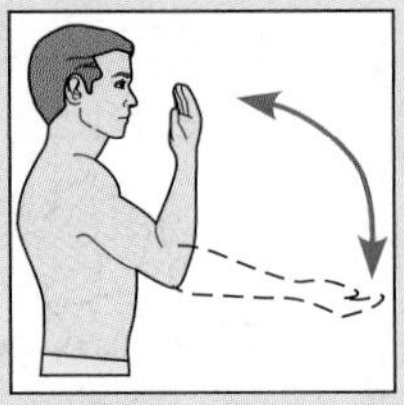 Figure 8
Extension. Bring each lower arm forward and downward, straightening the arm (Figure 8).	150°	
Rotation for supination. Turn each hand and forearm so that the palm is facing upward (Figure 9).	70° to 90°	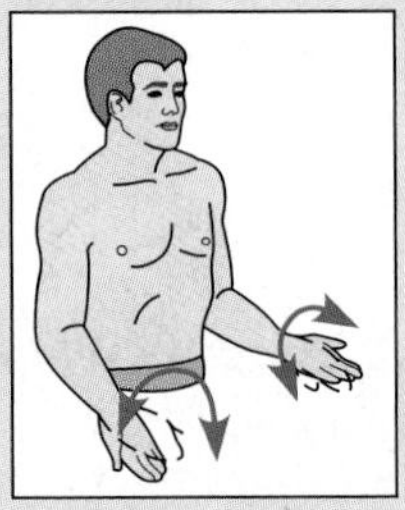 Figure 9
Rotation for pronation. Turn each hand and forearm so that the palm is facing downward (Figure 9).	70° to 90°	
Wrist—Condyloid Joint		
Flexion. Bring the fingers of each hand toward the inner aspect of the forearm (Figure 10).	80° to 90°	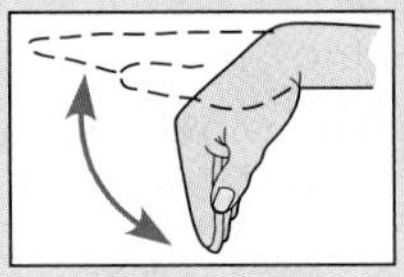 Figure 10
Extension. Straighten each hand to the same plane as the arm (Figure 10).	80° to 90°	
Hyperextension. Bend the fingers of each hand back as far as possible (Figure 11).	70° to 90°	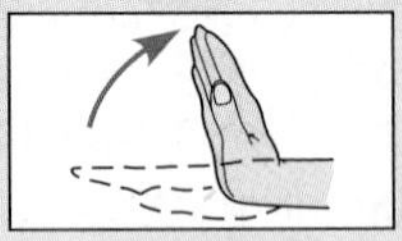 Figure 11
Radial flexion (abduction). Bend each wrist laterally toward the thumb side with hand supinated (Figure 12).	0° to 20°	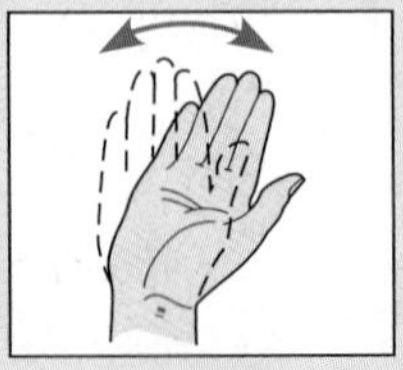 Figure 12
Ulnar flexion (adduction). Bend each wrist laterally toward the fifth finger with the hand supinated (Figure 12).	30° to 50°	
Hand and Fingers: Metacarpophalangeal Joints—Condyloid; Interphalangeal Joints—Hinge		
Flexion. Make a fist with each hand (Figure 13).	90°	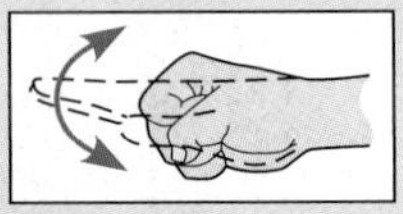 Figure 13
Extension. Straighten the fingers of each hand (Figure 13).	90°	
Hyperextension. Bend the fingers of each hand back as far as possible.	30°	

TABLE 43.2 Selected Joint Movements *continued*

Body Part—Type of Joint/Movement	Normal Range	Illustration	
Abduction. Spread the fingers of each hand apart (Figure 14).	20°	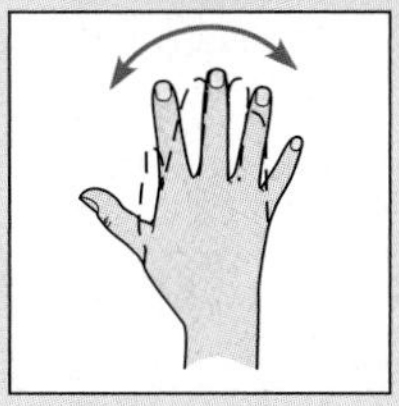	Figure 14
Adduction. Bring the fingers of each hand together (Figure 14).	20°		
Thumb—Saddle Joint			
Flexion. Move each thumb across the palmar surface of the hand toward the fifth finger (Figure 15).	90°	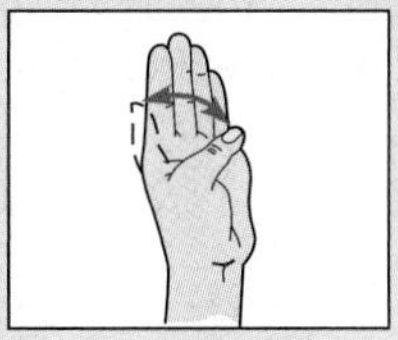	Figure 15
Extension. Move each thumb away from the hand.	90°		
Abduction. Extend each thumb laterally (Figure 16).	30°	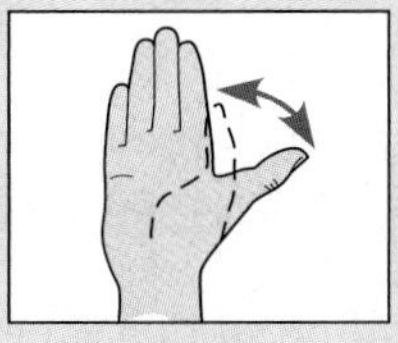	Figure 16
Adduction. Move each thumb back to the hand (Figure 16).	30°		
Opposition. Touch each thumb to the top of each finger of the same hand. The thumb joint movements involved are abduction, rotation, and flexion (Figure 17).		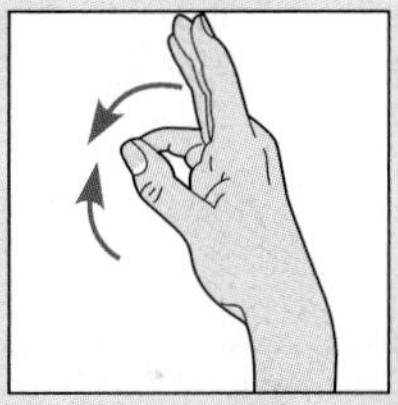	Figure 17
Hip—Ball-and-Socket Joint			
Flexion. Move each leg forward and upward. The knee may be extended or flexed (Figure 18).	Knee extended, 90°; knee flexed, 120°	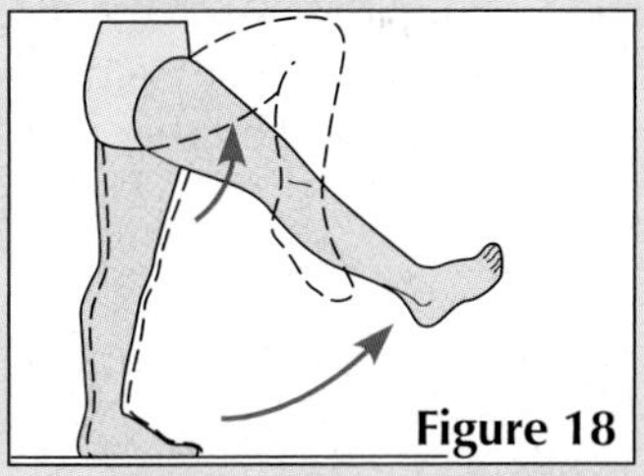	Figure 18
Extension. Move each leg back beside the other (Figure 19).	90° to 120°	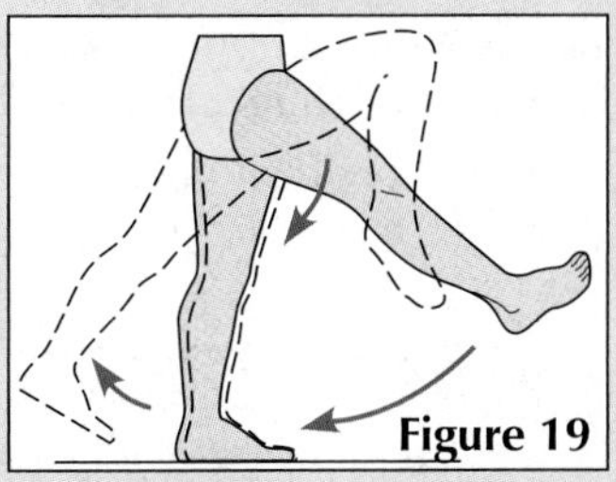	Figure 19
Hyperextension. Move each leg back behind the body (Figure 19).	30° to 50°		

TABLE 43.2 Selected Joint Movements *continued*

Body Part—Type of Joint/Movement	Normal Range	Illustration
Abduction. Move each leg out to the side (Figure 20).	45° to 50°	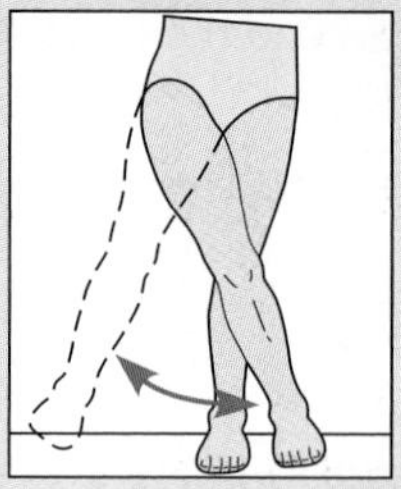 Figure 20
Adduction. Move each leg back to the other leg and beyond in front of it (Figure 20).	20° to 30° beyond other leg	
Circumduction. Move each leg backward, up, to the side, and down in a circle (Figure 21).	360°	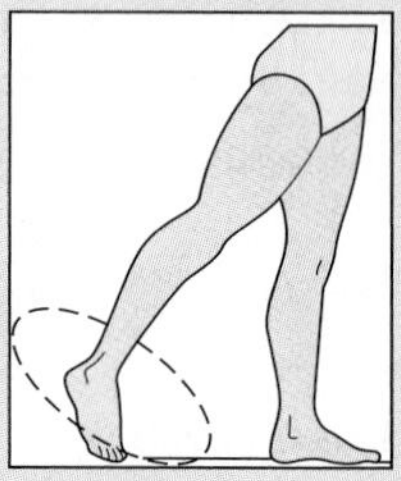 Figure 21
Internal rotation. Turn each foot and leg inward so that the toes point as far as possible toward the other leg (Figure 22).	90°	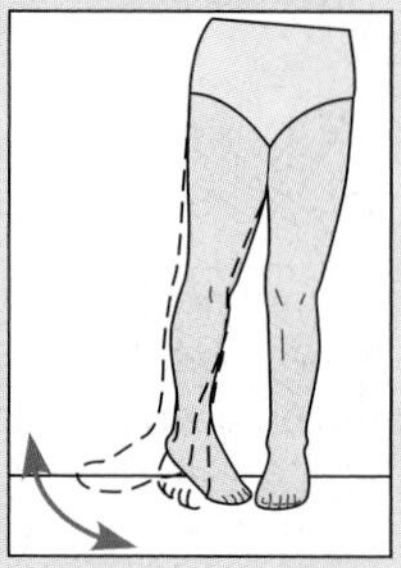 Figure 22
External rotation. Turn each foot and leg outward so that the toes point as far as possible away from the other leg (Figure 22).	90°	
Knee—Hinge Joint		
Flexion. Bend each leg, bringing the heel toward the back of the thigh (Figure 23).	120° to 130°	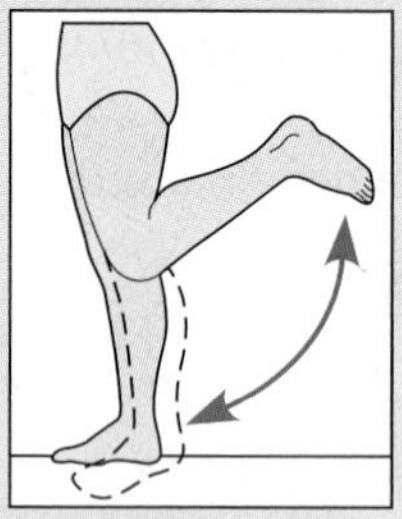 Figure 23
Extension. Straighten each leg, returning the foot to its position beside the other foot (Figure 23).	120° to 130°	
Ankle—Hinge Joint		
Extension (plantar flexion). Point the toes of each foot downward (Figure 24).	45° to 50°	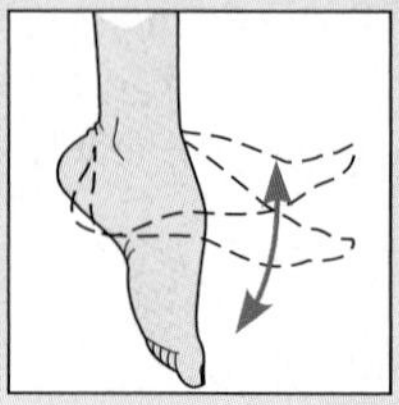 Figure 24
Flexion (dorsiflexion). Point the toes of each foot upward (Figure 24).	20°	

TABLE 43.2 Selected Joint Movements *continued*

Body Part—Type of Joint/Movement	Normal Range	Illustration
Foot—Gliding		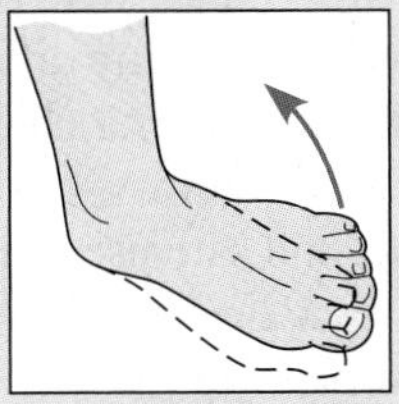 Figure 25
Eversion. Turn the sole of each foot laterally (Figure 25).	5°	
Inversion. Turn the sole of each foot medially.	5°	
Toes: Interphalangeal Joints—Hinge; Metatarsophalangeal Joints—Hinge; Intertarsal Joints—Gliding		
Flexion. Curl the toe joints of each foot downward.	35° to 60°	
Extension. Straighten the toes of each foot.	35° to 60°	
Abduction. Spread the toes of each foot apart.	0° to 15°	
Adduction. Bring the toes of each foot together.	0° to 15°	
Trunk—Gliding Joint		
Flexion. Bend the trunk toward the toes (Figure 26).	70° to 90°	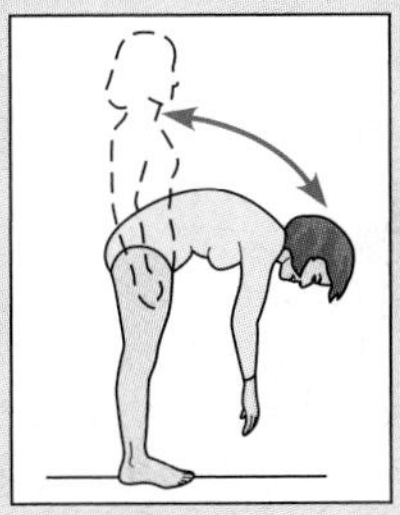 Figure 26
Extension. Straighten the trunk from a flexed position (Figure 26).	70° to 90°	
Hyperextension. Bend the trunk backward.	20° to 30°	
Lateral flexion. Bend the trunk to the right and to the left (Figure 27).	35° on each side	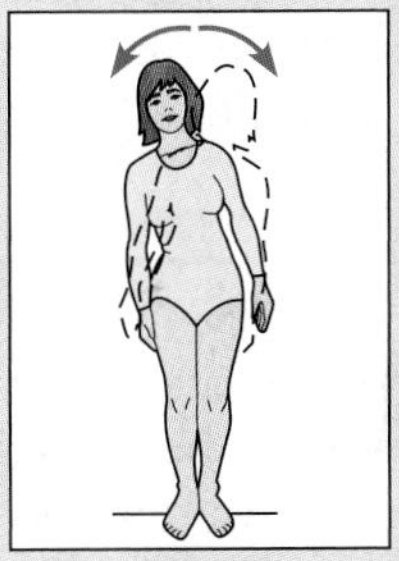 Figure 27
Rotation. Turn the upper part of the body from side to side (Figure 28).	30° to 45°	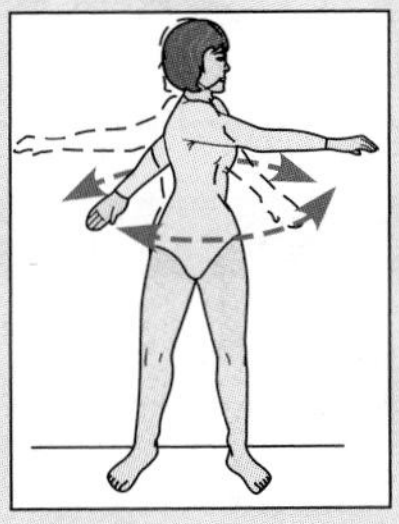 Figure 28

The *cerebellum*, which operates below the level of consciousness, blends and coordinates the muscles involved in voluntary movement. It does not direct the movement but translates the "instructions" from the cerebral cortex into detailed actions by the many different muscles in the hand, arm, and shoulder. When a client's cerebellum is injured, movements become clumsy, unsure, and uncoordinated.

The efficient and safe use of the body to move, lift, and ambulate clients is discussed in the section "Using Body Mechanics" on page 1195.

Exercise

- **Physical activity** is bodily movement produced by skeletal muscles that requires energy expenditure and produces progressive health benefits.
- **Exercise** is a type of physical activity defined as a planned, structured, and repetitive bodily movement done to improve or maintain one or more components of physical fitness.

People are increasingly participating in exercise programs to decrease risk factors for cardiovascular disease and to increase their health and well-being. Therapeutic exercise is used extensively in the health-care arena.

Activity tolerance is the type and amount of exercise or daily living activities an individual is able to perform.

Types of Exercise

Exercise involves the active contraction and relaxation of muscles. Exercises can be classified according to the type of muscle contraction (isotonic, isometric, or isokinetic) and according to the source of energy (aerobic or anaerobic).

Isotonic (dynamic) exercises are those in which the muscle shortens to produce muscle contraction and active movement. Most physical conditioning exercises—running, walking, swimming, cycling, and other such activities—are isotonic, as are activities of daily living (ADLs) and *active* ROM exercises (those initiated by the client). Examples of isotonic *bed* exercises are pushing or pulling against a stationary object, using a trapeze to lift the body off the bed, lifting the buttocks off the bed by pushing with the hands against the mattress, and pushing the body to a sitting position.

Isotonic exercises increase muscle tone, mass, and strength and maintain joint flexibility and circulation. During isotonic exercise, both heart rate and cardiac output quicken to increase blood flow to all parts of the body. Little or no change in blood pressure occurs.

Isometric (static or setting) exercises are those in which there is a change in muscle tension but there is no change in muscle length and no muscle or joint movement. These exercises are useful for strengthening abdominal, gluteal, and quadriceps muscles used in ambulation; for maintaining strength in immobilized muscles in casts or traction; and for endurance training.

Isometric exercises produce a moderate increase in heart rate and cardiac output but no appreciable increase in blood flow to other parts of the body.

Isokinetic (resistive) exercises involve muscle contraction or tension against resistance; thus, they can be either isotonic or isometric. During isokinetic exercises, the person moves (isotonic) or tenses (isometric) against resistance. Special machines or devices provide the resistance to the movement. These exercises are used in physical conditioning and are often done to build up certain muscle groups; for example, the pectorals (chest muscles) may be increased in size and strength by lifting weights.

Guidelines for Physical Activity

Activity Group	Benefit	Frequency	Type of Exercise
Endurance	helps the heart, lungs, and circulatory system	4–7 days per week	walking cycling tennis continuous swimming
Flexibility	helps movement, keeps muscles relaxed and joints mobile	4–7 days per week	gardening mopping the floor yard work stretching exercises
Strength	keeps bones and muscles strong, improves posture, and prevents some diseases	2–4 days per week	heavy yard work climbing stairs weight training routines

Source: *Canada's Physical Activity Guide to Healthy Active Living*, Health Canada, 2000 © Reproduced with the permission of the Minister of Public Works and Government Services Canada.

Aerobic exercise is an activity in which the amount of oxygen taken into the body is greater than or equal to the amount the body requires. Aerobic exercises use large muscle groups, are performed continuously, and are rhythmic in nature. Examples are walking, jogging, running, bicycling, dancing, cross-country skiing, jumping rope, rowing, swimming, and skating. Aerobic exercises improve cardiovascular conditioning and physical fitness. Assessment of physical fitness is discussed in Chapter 27. The box on page 1178 describes the benefit, frequency, and type of exercise recommended for healthy adults.

Intensity of exercise can be measured in three ways:

1. *Target heart rate.* With this system, the goal is to work up to and sustain a target heart rate during exercise based on the person's age. To determine the target heart rate, first calculate the person's *maximum* heart rate by subtracting her or his current age in years from 220. Then, obtain the *target* heart rate by taking 60 to 85 percent of the maximum. At least 60 percent of maximum heart rate is the recommended intensity. Because heart rates are so variable among individuals, the tests that follow are replacing this measure.
2. *Talk test.* This test is easier to implement and keeps most people at 60 percent of maximum heart rate or more. When exercising, the person should be able to carry on a conversation with some laboured breathing. However, exercise intensity should be increased if the person can carry on with unlimited unlaboured discussion.
3. *Borg scale of perceived exertion* (Borg, 1980). This scale measures "how difficult" the exercise feels to the person in terms of heart and lung exertion. The scale progresses as follows:
   - Very, very light
   - Very light
   - Fairly light
   - Somewhat hard
   - Hard
   - Very hard
   - Very, very hard

"Very, very hard" corresponds closely to 100 percent of maximum heart rate. "Very light" is close to 40 percent. Most people need to strive for the "Somewhat hard" level, which corresponds to 75 percent of maximum heart rate.

Anaerobic exercise involves activity in which the muscles cannot draw out enough oxygen from the bloodstream, and anaerobic pathways are used to provide additional energy for a short time. This type of exercise is used in endurance training for athletes.

Benefits of Exercise

Regular exercise is essential for healthy functioning of major body systems. The benefits of exercise on these systems follow.

Musculoskeletal System

The size, shape, tone, and strength of skeletal and cardiac muscles are maintained with mild exercise and increased with strenuous exercise. With strenuous exercise, muscles **hypertrophy** (enlarge), and the efficiency of muscular contraction increases. Hypertrophy is commonly seen in the arm muscles of a tennis player, the leg muscles of a skater, the arm and hand muscles of a carpenter, and the body muscles of weight lifters.

Exercise increases joint flexibility and range of motion. Bone density is maintained through weight bearing by maintaining a balance between *osteoblasts* (bone-building cells) and *osteoclasts* (bone-resorption and breakdown cells).

Cardiovascular System

Adequate exercise increases the heart rate, the strength of heart muscle contraction, and the blood supply to the heart and muscles. Cardiac output (the amount of blood pumped by the heart) increases due to the re-direction of the blood flow. Normal cardiac output is 5 L/min. Exercise can increase cardiac output to 30 L/min (Guyton & Hall, 2000).

Respiratory System

Ventilation (the amount of air taken into and out of the lungs) increases. Normal ventilation is about 5 or 6 L/min. In strenuous exercise, the intake of oxygen increases to as much as 20 times normal intake (Guyton & Hall, 2000). Adequate exercise also prevents pooling of secretions in the bronchi and bronchioles, decreases breathing effort, and improves diaphragmatic excursion.

Gastrointestinal System

Exercise improves the appetite and increases gastrointestinal tract tone, improving digestion and elimination.

Metabolic System

Exercise elevates the metabolic rate, thus increasing the production of body heat and waste products. During strenuous exercise, the metabolic rate can increase to as much as 20 times the normal rate. Lying in bed and eating an average diet utilizes 1,850 calories per day (Guyton & Hall, 2000). Exercise also increases the use of triglycerides and fatty acids, resulting in a reduced level of serum triglycerides and cholesterol.

Urinary System

Because adequate exercise promotes efficient blood flow, the body excretes wastes more effectively, thus preventing urinary stasis.

Psychoneurological System

Exercise produces a sense of well-being and improves tolerance to stress. It may also improve self-concept by reducing depression and improving one's body image. Energy level increases and quality of sleep is enhanced.

Factors Affecting Body Alignment and Activity

A number of factors affect an individual's body alignment, mobility, and daily activity level. These include growth and development, physical health, mental health, nutrition, personal values and attitudes, and certain external factors.

Growth and Development

A person's age and musculoskeletal and nervous system development affect posture, body proportions, body mass, body movements, and reflexes. *Newborn* movements are reflexive and random. All extremities are generally flexed but can be passively moved through a full range of motion. The feet are usually *inverted* (toes pointed inward) but can be passively *everted* (toes pointed outward). As the neurological system matures, control over movement progresses during the first year. Gross motor development precedes fine motor skills. Gross motor development occurs in a head-to-toe fashion, that is, progression from head control, to crawling, to pulling up to a standing position, to standing, and to walking, usually after the first birthday. Initially, walking involves a wide stance and unsteady gait, thus the term *toddler*. From ages one to five years, both gross and fine motor skills are refined. For example, preschoolers master riding a tricycle, dancing, running, jumping, using crayons to draw, fastening or using zippers, and brushing their teeth. For more details, see the "Motor Development" sections for infants, toddlers, and preschoolers in Chapter 20.

From six to 12 years, refinement of motor skills continues and exercise patterns for later life are generally determined. Many schools provide some physical education and competitive sports programs to enhance physical activity. Posture in school-age children is excellent, often the best during one's lifetime. In adolescence, growth spurts may result in awkwardness that can be manifested in poor posture. Postural habits formed during adolescence often persist into adulthood.

Adults between 20 and 40 years of age generally have few physical changes affecting mobility, with the exception of pregnant women. Pregnancy alters centre of gravity, affects balance, and reduces exercise tolerance. As age advances, muscle tone and bone density decrease, joints lose flexibility, reaction time slows, and bone mass decreases, particularly in women who have osteoporosis. **Osteoporosis** is a condition in which the bones become brittle and fragile due to calcium depletion. Osteoporosis is common in older women and primarily affects the weight-bearing joints of the lower extremities and the back, causing compression fractures of the vertebrae and hip fractures. All these changes affect older adults' posture, gait, and balance. Posture becomes forward-leaning and stooped, which shifts the centre of gravity forward. To compensate for this shift, the knees flex slightly for support and the base of support is widened. Gait becomes wide-based, short-stepped, and shuffling.

Physical Health

Mobility and activity tolerance are affected by any disorder that impairs the ability of the nervous system, musculoskeletal system, and vestibular apparatus. Congenital problems, such as hip dysplasia, spina bifida, cerebral palsy, and the muscular dystrophies, affect motor functioning. Disorders of the nervous system, such as Parkinson's disease, multiple sclerosis, central nervous system tumours, cerebrovascular accidents (strokes), infectious processes (e.g., meningitis), and head and spinal cord injuries, can leave muscle groups weakened, paralyzed, **spastic** (with too much muscle tone), or **flaccid** (without muscle tone). Musculoskeletal disorders affecting mobility include strains, sprains, fractures, joint dislocations, amputations, and joint replacements. Inner ear infections and dizziness can impair balance.

Many other acute and chronic illnesses that limit the supply of oxygen and nutrients needed for muscle contraction and movement can seriously affect activity tolerance. Examples include chronic obstructive lung disease, anemia, congestive heart failure, and angina.

Mental Health

Mental or affective disorders, such as depression or chronic stress, may affect a person's desire to move. The depressed person may lack enthusiasm for taking part in any activity and may even lack energy for usual hygiene practices. Lack of visible energy is seen in a slumped posture with head bowed. By contrast, happy, confident people usually stand erect. Chronic stress can deplete the body's energy reserves to the point that fatigue discourages the desire to exercise even though exercise can energize the person and facilitate coping.

Nutrition

Both undernutrition and overnutrition can influence body alignment and mobility. Poorly nourished people may have muscle weakness and fatigue. Vitamin D deficiency causes bone deformity during growth. Inadequate calcium intake increases the risk of osteoporosis. Obesity can distort movement, and an obese person usually expends extra energy to move. In addition, obesity can adversely affect posture and balance.

Personal Values and Attitudes

Whether people value regular exercise is often the result of family influences. In families that incorporate regular exercise in their daily routine or spend time together in physical endeavours (baseball, hiking, swimming), children learn to value physical activity. Sedentary families, on the other hand, participate in sports only as spectators, watching the ball game or hockey game on television, and this lifestyle is often transmitted to their children. Values about physical appearance also influence some people's participation in regular exercise. People who value a muscular build or physical attractiveness may participate in regular exercise programs to produce the appearance they desire. Choice of physical activity or type of exercise is also influenced by values. Choices may be influenced by geographic location and cultural role expectations.

External Factors

Many external factors affect a person's mobility. Excessively high temperature and high humidity discourage activity, whereas comfortable temperature and humidity are conducive to activity, such as a brisk walk or a game of tennis. The availability of recreational facilities also influences activity; for example, lack of money may prohibit a client from joining an exercise group or swimming in an indoor pool. Neighbourhood safety promotes outdoor activity, whereas an unsafe environment discourages people from going outdoors.

Prescribed Limitations

Limitations to movement may be medically prescribed for some health problems. To promote healing, such devices as casts, braces, splints, and traction are often used to immobilize body parts. Clients who are short of breath may be advised not to walk up stairs. Bed rest may be the therapeutic choice for certain clients, for example, to relieve edema, to reduce metabolic and oxygen needs, to promote tissue repair, or to decrease pain.

The term **bed rest** varies in meaning to some extent. In some agencies, bed rest means strict confinement to bed *or complete bed rest.* Others may allow the client to use a bedside commode. Nurses need to familiarize themselves with the meaning of the term "bed rest" in their practice setting.

Effects of Immobility

Individuals who have inactive lifestyles or who are faced with inactivity because of illness or injury are at risk for many problems that can affect major body systems. Whether immobility will cause problems often depends on the duration of the inactivity, the client's health status, and the client's sensory awareness. Potential effects of immobility on body systems follow. Nurses need to understand these risks and encourage client movement as much as possible. Early ambulation after illness or surgery is an essential preventive measure. See also Table 43.3 for desired outcomes and nursing interventions to prevent problems of immobility, and Table 43.4 on page 1191 for assessing problems of immobility.

Musculoskeletal System

The most obvious signs of prolonged immobility are often manifested in the musculoskeletal system. Clients experience a significant decrease in muscular strength whenever they do not maintain a moderate amount of physical activity. Common musculoskeletal problems resulting from prolonged immobility include the following:

- *Disuse osteoporosis.* Without the stress of weight-bearing activity, the bones demineralize. They are depleted chiefly of calcium, which gives the bones strength and density. Regardless of the amount of calcium in a person's diet, the demineralization process, known as osteoporosis, continues with immobility. The bones become spongy and may gradually deform and fracture easily.
- *Disuse atrophy.* Unused muscles **atrophy** (decrease in size), losing most of their strength and normal function.
- *Contractures.* When the muscle fibres are not moved, eventually a **contracture** (permanent shortening of the muscle) forms, limiting joint mobility. This process eventually involves the tendons, ligaments, and joint capsules; it is often irreversible except by surgical intervention. Joint deformities, such as foot drop (Figure 43.2) and external hip rotation, occur when a stronger muscle dominates the opposite muscle.
- *Stiffness and pain in the joints.* Without movement, the collagen (connective) tissues at the joint become **ankylosed** (permanently immobile). In addition, as the bones demineralize, excess calcium may deposit in the joints, contributing to stiffness and pain.

Cardiovascular System

- *Diminished cardiac reserve.* Prolonged immobility weakens the cardiovascular system, which cannot fully meet the demands placed on it. Decreased mobility creates an imbalance in the autonomic nervous system, resulting in a preponderance of sympathetic activity over cholinergic activity that increases heart rate.

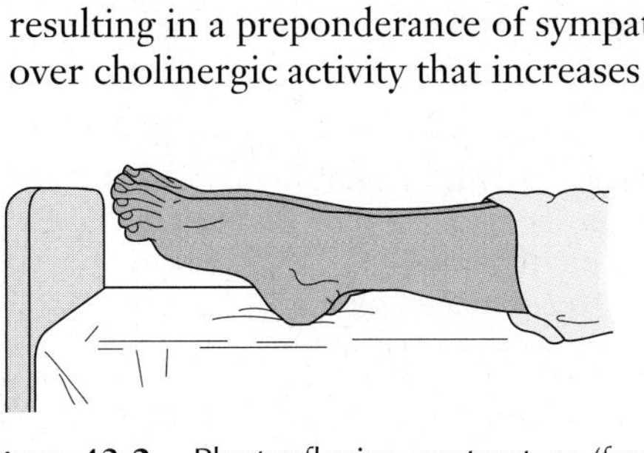

Figure 43.2 Plantar flexion contracture (foot drop)

TABLE 43.3 Desired Outcomes and Nursing Interventions to Prevent the Problems of Immobility (Disuse Syndrome)

Desired Outcome	Nursing Interventions	Rationale
Maintains **normal musculoskeletal function,** as evidenced by usual range of motion in all body joints and maintenance of baseline muscle mass and strength	Implement appropriate exercise program (isometric, isotonic, or passive exercises) at least every two hours as indicated. See p. 1178.	Isotonic exercises prevent contractures and muscle atrophy. Isometric exercises maintain muscle tone. Passive exercises maintain joint mobility.
	Encourage active participation in self-care activities.	Self-care activities involve active movement of joints and muscles.
	Compare muscle size and strength to baseline data and on each side of body daily. See Procedure 27.16 for details about testing and grading muscle strength.	Early detection of muscle atrophy or decreased strength facilitates early intervention to correct the problem.
	Position clients in good alignment.	Good alignment prevents contractures and maintains structural integrity of muscles and joints.
	Ambulate client, as tolerated, or assist to stand at bedside.	Weight bearing prevents disuse osteoporosis.
Experiences **minimal cardiovascular alterations,** as evidenced by maintenance of baseline vital signs and signs of adequate venous blood flow (absence of edema, calf pain, inflammation, venous distention, skin changes)	Monitor vital signs according to client needs and agency protocol (e.g., b.i.d or t.i.d).	Regular monitoring enables the nurse to detect alterations early.
	Instruct client how and when to avoid the Valsalva maneuver.	The Valsalva maneuver increases the stress on the heart.
	Apply anti-embolism stockings as indicated (see Procedure 44.2).	Use of anti-embolism stockings prevents thrombus formation, venous engorgement, dependent edema, and orthostatic hypotension.
	Elevate legs several times each day for 20 minutes.	Elevation increases peripheral venous circulation.
	Implement measures to prevent postural hypotension (see p. 1218).	
	Assess skin of lower limbs, and measure calf circumferences, as indicated.	Regular inspection and measurement enable the nurse to detect changes.
	See also interventions for musculoskeletal function.	These interventions also stimulate blood circulation and prevent cardiovascular complications.
Maintains **normal respiratory function,** as evidenced by normal breath sounds during auscultation; normal chest expansion; and absence of chest pain, fever, or other respiratory signs indicative of pulmonary infarction, emboli, or atelectasis	Assess breath sounds and chest expansion at least every four hours.	This allows the nurse to detect onset of abnormal breath sounds and inadequate chest expansion.
	Teach clients to take five deep breaths and to cough every waking hour.	Deep breaths and coughing increase alveolar expansion, prevent stasis of secretions, promote adequate gaseous exchange, and maintain a patent airway.
	Establish a position schedule, and alter client's position at least every two hours. Ambulate client, if possible, or place client in chair.	Changes in position allow previously dependent lung areas to expand and promote movement and subsequent removal of secretions by coughing.
Maintains **appropriate nutritional and fluid pattern,** as evidenced by maintenance of baseline weight, adequate tissue turgor, balanced fluid intake and output, and normal serum protein values	Monitor the client's weight, tissue turgor, fluid intake and output, and serum protein values.	Normal or baseline findings of these assessments indicate adequate hydration and nutritional intake.

TABLE 43.3 Desired Outcomes and Nursing Interventions to Prevent the Problems of Immobility (Disuse Syndrome) *continued*

Desired Outcome	Nursing Interventions	Rationale
Maintains **normal elimination pattern,** as evidenced by clear amber urinary output of at least 1,500 mL per day; urine specific gravity of 1.010 to 1.030; an acidic urine; absence of signs of urinary retention, calculi, or infection; and excretion of formed semisolid stool at least every two or three days	Monitor colour, clarity, amount, acidity, and specific gravity of urine; colour and characteristics of feces; and frequency of defecation. Ask whether client has pain when urinating.	Decreased urinary output, cloudy urine, and painful urination are indicative of urinary retention and infection. Alkaline urine increases the risk for calculi. Constipation is associated with immobility. Increase fluid to increase urinary output to decrease incidence of renal calculi.
	Refer to Chapter 35 for interventions to prevent constipation. Teach clients to select high-fibre foods.	High-fibre foods promote intestinal peristalsis and defecation. See Chapter 38 for foods high in fibre.
	See "Preventing Pressure Ulcers" in Chapter 37.	
Maintains **intact integument,** as evidenced by clean, intact, well-hydrated skin and absence of pressure signs (pallor, redness, increased warmth or tenderness) over pressure areas		
Maintains **social, emotional, and intellectual well-being,** as evidenced by actively participating in and making decisions about care, verbalizing concerns, maintaining positive relationships with others, and performing satisfying activities	Encourage the client to make as many decisions as possible, such as placement of personal items, daily plan of activities, clothes to wear.	Decision making enhances self-esteem.
	Plan time to be available to the client other than task-oriented time.	Making oneself available for the client may encourage open expression of feelings.
	Explore diversional activities of interest to the client, and develop a daily activity plan.	A satisfying daily activity prevents boredom and gives the client something to look forward to.

Resting heart rate increases approximately 0.5 beat/minute for each day of immobilization (Kottke et al., 1990).

During immobility, the rapid heart rate reduces diastolic pressure, coronary blood flow, and the capacity of the heart to respond to any metabolic demands above the basal levels. Because of this diminished cardiac reserve, the immobilized person may experience tachycardia and angina with even minimal exertion.

- *Increased use of the Valsalva maneuver.* The **Valsalva maneuver** refers to holding the breath and straining against a closed glottis while moving. For example, clients tend to hold their breath when attempting to move up in a bed or sit on a bedpan. This builds up sufficient pressure on the large veins in the thorax to interfere with the return blood flow to the heart and coronary arteries. When the client exhales and the glottis again opens, pressure is suddenly released, and a surge of blood flows to the heart. Tachycardia and cardiac arrhythmias can result if the client has cardiac disease.
- *Orthostatic (postural) hypotension.* Orthostatic hypotension is a common sequela of immobilization. Under normal conditions, sympathetic nervous system activity causes automatic vasoconstriction in the blood vessels in the lower half of the body when a mobile person changes from a horizontal to a vertical posture. Vasoconstriction prevents pooling of the blood in the legs and effectively maintains central blood pressure to ensure adequate perfusion of the heart and brain. During any prolonged immobility, this reflex becomes dormant. When the immobile person attempts to sit or stand, this reconstricting mechanism fails to function properly in spite of increased adrenalin output. The blood pools in the lower extremities, and central blood pressure drops. Cerebral perfusion is seriously compromised, and the person feels dizzy or lightheaded and may even faint. This sequence is usually accompanied by a sudden and marked increase in heart rate, the body's effort to protect the brain from an inadequate blood supply.
- *Venous vasodilation and stasis.* The skeletal muscles of an active person contract with each movement, compressing the blood vessels in those muscles and helping to pump the blood back to the heart against gravity. The tiny valves in the leg veins, which remain constricted,

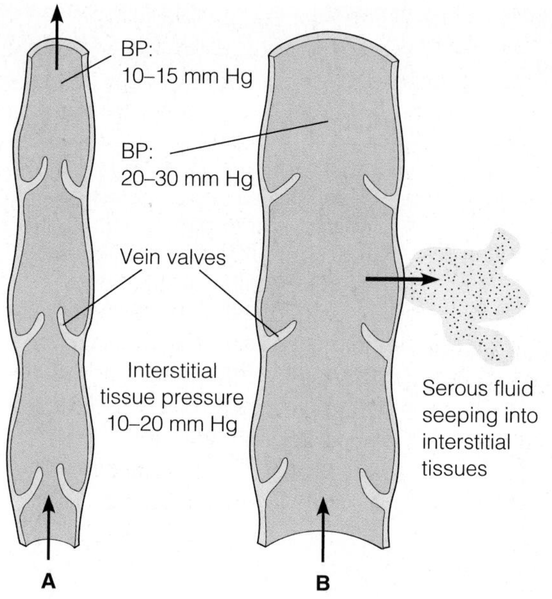

Figure 43.3 Leg veins: *A,* in a mobile person; *B,* in an immobile person

aid in venous return to the heart by preventing backward flow of blood and pooling. In an immobile person, the skeletal muscles do not contract sufficiently, and the muscles atrophy. The skeletal muscles can no longer assist in pumping blood back to the heart against gravity. Blood pools in the leg veins, causing vasodilation and engorgement. The valves in the veins can no longer work effectively to prevent backward flow of blood and pooling (Figure 43.3). This phenomenon is known as *incompetent valves.* As the blood continues to pool in the veins, its greater volume increases venous blood pressure, which can become much higher than that exerted by the tissues surrounding the vessel.

- *Dependent edema.* When the venous pressure is sufficiently great, some of the serous part of the blood is forced out of the blood vessel into the interstitial spaces surrounding the blood vessel, causing edema. Edema is most common in parts of the body positioned below heart level and maintained in that position. Dependent edema is most likely to occur around the sacrum or heels of a client who sits up in bed or in the feet and lower legs of a client who sits on the side of the bed. Edema further impedes venous return of blood to the heart, causing more pooling and more edema. Edematous tissue is uncomfortable and more susceptible to injury than normal tissue.
- *Thrombus formation.* Three factors, known as *Virchow's triad,* collectively predispose a client to the formation of a **thrombophlebitis** (a clot that is loosely attached to an inflamed vein wall). These are impaired venous return to the heart, hypercoagulability of the blood, and injury to a vessel wall.

A thrombus is particularly dangerous if it breaks loose from the vein wall and enters the general circulation as an **embolus** (a clot that has moved from its place of origin, causing obstruction to circulation elsewhere). Large emboli that enter the pulmonary circulation may occlude the vessels that nourish the lungs and cause an infarcted (dead) area of the lung. If the infarcted area is large, pulmonary function is seriously compromised, and death may ensue. Emboli travelling to the coronary vessels or brain can produce a similarly dangerous outcome.

Respiratory System

- *Decreased respiratory movement.* In a recumbent, immobile client, ventilation of the lungs is passively altered. The rigid bed presses against the body and curtails chest movement. The abdominal organs push against the diaphragm, further restricting chest movement and making it difficult to expand the lungs fully. An immobile recumbent person rarely sighs, partly because overall muscle atrophy also affects the respiratory muscles and partly because there is no need to do so without the stimulus of activity. Without these periodic stretching movements, the cartilaginous intercostal joints may become fixed in an expiratory phase of respiration, further restricting the potential for maximal ventilation. These changes produce shallow respirations and reduce vital capacity significantly. **Vital capacity** is the maximum amount of air that can be exhaled after a maximum inhalation. An immobile, paralyzed client can lose as much as 25 to 50 percent of normal vital capacity (Kottke et al., 1990).
- *Pooling of respiratory secretions.* Secretions of the respiratory tract are normally expelled by changing posture and by coughing. Inactivity allows secretions to pool by gravity (Figure 43.4), interfering with the normal diffusion of oxygen and carbon dioxide in the alveoli. The ability to cough up secretions may also be hindered by loss of respiratory muscle tone, dehydration (which thickens secretions), or sedatives that depress the cough reflex. Poor oxygenation and retention of carbon dioxide in the blood may result in respiratory acidosis.
- *Atelectasis.* When ventilation is decreased, pooled secretions may accumulate in a dependent area of a bronchiole and effectively block it. As a result of changes in regional blood flow, bed rest decreases the amount of surfactant produced. (Surfactant enables the alveoli to remain open.) The combination of decreased surfactant and blockage of a bronchiole with mucus can cause atelectasis (the collapse of a lobe or of an entire lung) distal to the mucous blockage. Immobile, elderly, postoperative clients are at greatest risk of atelectasis.

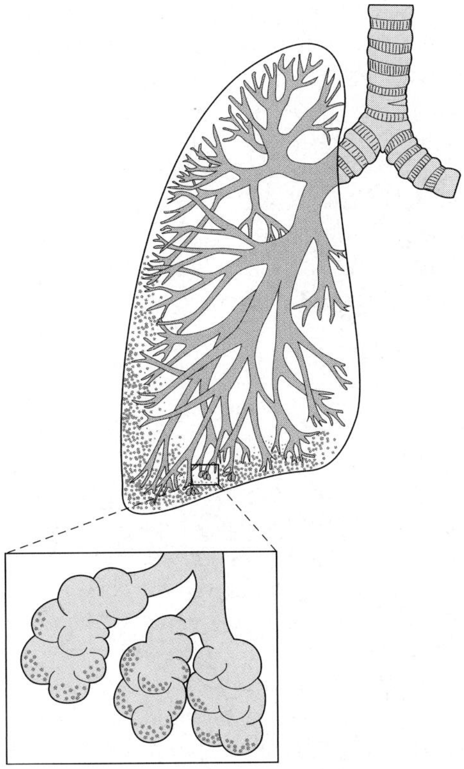

Figure 43.4 Pooling of secretions in the lungs of an immobile person

- *Hypostatic pneumonia.* Pooled (hypostatic) secretions provide excellent media for bacterial growth. Under these conditions, a minor upper respiratory infection can evolve rapidly into a severe infection of the lower respiratory tract. Hypostatic pneumonia caused by static respiratory secretions can severely impair oxygen–carbon dioxide exchange in the alveoli and is a fairly common cause of death among weakened, immobile persons, especially heavy smokers.

Metabolic System

- *Decreased metabolic rate.* **Metabolism** refers to the sum of all the physical and chemical processes by which living substance is formed and maintained and by which energy is made available for use by the body. **Basal metabolism** is the minimal energy expended for the maintenance of these processes. The metabolic rate is the rate of basal metabolism expressed in calories per hour per square metre of body surface. In immobile clients, the basal metabolic rate decreases as the energy requirements of the body decrease. Gastrointestinal motility and secretions of various digestive glands are also reduced.
- *Negative nitrogen balance.* In an active person, there is a balance between protein synthesis **(anabolism)** and protein breakdown **(catabolism).** Immobility creates a marked imbalance, and the catabolic processes exceed the anabolic processes. Over time, more nitrogen is excreted than is ingested, producing a negative nitrogen balance. Catabolized muscle mass is the source of this excreted nitrogen. Excessive amounts are excreted in the urine, reaching peak levels at about the sixth to 10th day of immobilization (Kottke et al., 1990). The negative nitrogen balance represents a depletion of protein stores that are essential for building muscle tissue and for wound healing.
- *Anorexia.* Loss of appetite **(anorexia)** occurs as a result of the decreased metabolic rate and the increased catabolism that accompany immobility. Reduced caloric intake is usually a response to the decreased energy requirements of the inactive person. If protein intake is reduced, the nitrogen imbalance may become more pronounced, sometimes so severely that malnutrition ensues.
- *Negative calcium balance.* A negative calcium balance occurs as a direct result of immobility. Greater amounts of calcium are extracted from bone than can be replaced. The absence of weight bearing and of stress on the musculoskeletal structures is the direct cause of the calcium loss from bones. Weight bearing and stress are also required for calcium to be replaced in bone. A similar process occurs with the body's stores of phosphate causing a negative phosphate balance during immobility.

Urinary System

- *Urinary stasis.* In a mobile person, gravity plays an important role in the emptying of the kidneys and the bladder. The shape and position of the kidneys and active kidney contractions are important in completely emptying the urine from the calyces, renal pelvis, and ureters (Figure 43.5, *A*). The shape and position of the urinary bladder (the detrusor muscle) and active bladder contractions are also important in achieving complete emptying (Figure 43.6, *A*).

  When the person remains in a horizontal position, gravity impedes the emptying of urine from the kidneys and the urinary bladder. To urinate, the person who is supine (in a back-lying position) must push upward, against gravity (Figures 43.5, *B*, and 43.6, *B*). The renal pelvis may fill with urine before it is pushed into the ureters. Emptying is not as complete, and **urinary stasis** occurs after a few days of bed rest. Because of the overall decrease in muscle tone during immobilization, including the tone of the detrusor muscle, bladder emptying is further compromised.
- *Renal calculi.* In a mobile person, calcium in the urine remains dissolved because calcium and citric acid are balanced in an appropriately acid urine. With immobility

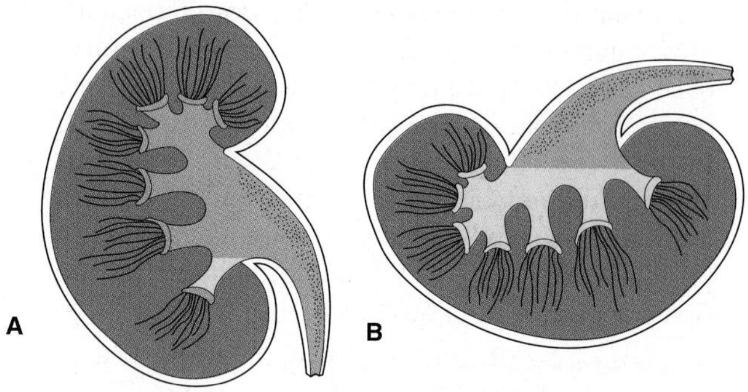

Figure 43.5 Pooling of urine in the kidney: *A,* the client is in an upright position; *B,* the client is in a back-lying position

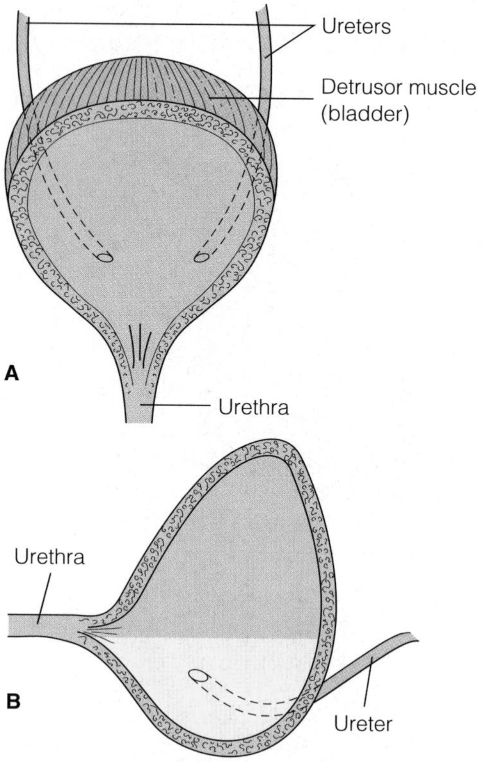

Figure 43.6 Pooling of urine in the urinary bladder: *A,* the client is in an upright position; *B,* the client is in a back-lying position

and the resulting excessive amounts of calcium (and phosphate) in the urine, this balance is no longer maintained. The urine becomes more alkaline, and the calcium salts precipitate out as crystals to form renal **calculi** (stones). In an immobile person in a horizontal position, the renal pelvis filled with stagnant, alkaline urine is an ideal location for calculi to form. The stones usually develop in the renal pelvis and pass through the ureters into the bladder. As the stones pass along the long, narrow ureters, they cause extreme pain and bleeding and can sometimes obstruct the urinary tract.

- *Urinary retention.* The immobile person may suffer from **urinary retention (accumulation of urine in the bladder),** bladder distention, and occasionally **urinary incontinence** (involuntary urination). The decreased muscle tone of the urinary bladder inhibits its ability to empty completely, and the immobilized person is unable to relax the perineal muscles sufficiently to urinate. The discomfort of using a bedpan or urinal, the embarrassment and lack of privacy associated with this function, and the unnatural position for urination combine to make it difficult for the client to relax the perineal muscles sufficiently to urinate while lying in bed.

  When urination is not possible, the bladder gradually becomes distended with urine. The bladder may stretch excessively, eventually inhibiting the urge to void. When bladder distention is considerable, some involuntary urinary "dribbling" may occur **(retention with overflow).** This does not relieve the urinary distention because most of the stagnant urine remains in the bladder.
- *Urinary infection.* Static urine provides an excellent medium for bacterial growth. The flushing action of normal, frequent urination is absent, and urinary distention often causes minute tears in the bladder mucosa, allowing infectious organisms to enter. The increased alkalinity of the urine caused by the hypercalcuria supports bacterial growth. The organism most commonly causing urinary tract infections is *Escherichia coli,* which normally resides in the colon. The normally sterile urinary tract may be contaminated by improper perineal care, the use of an indwelling urinary catheter, or occasionally, **urinary reflux** (backward flow). During reflux, contaminated urine from an overly distended bladder backs up into the renal pelvis to contaminate the kidney pelvis as well.

Gastrointestinal System

Constipation is a frequent problem for immobilized people because of decreased peristalsis and colon motility. The overall skeletal muscle weakness affects the abdominal and perineal muscles used in defecation. When the stool becomes very hard, more strength is required to expel it. The immobile person may lack this strength.

The bedfast person's unnatural and uncomfortable position on the bedpan does not facilitate elimination. The backward-leaning posture does not promote effective use of the muscles used in defecation. Some people are reluctant to use the bedpan in the presence of others. The embarrassment, lack of privacy, dependence on others to assist with the bedpan, and disruption of normal bowel habits may cause the individual to postpone or ignore the urge for elimination. Repeated postponement eventually suppresses the urge and weakens the defecation reflex.

Some persons may make excessive use of the Valsalva maneuver by straining in an attempt to expel the hard stool. This effort dangerously increases intra-abdominal and intrathoracic pressures and places undue stress on the heart and circulatory system. Some clients may exhibit cardiac dysfunction with straining.

Integumentary System

- *Reduced skin turgor.* The skin can atrophy as a result of prolonged immobility. Shifts in body fluids between the fluid compartments can affect the consistency and health of the dermis and subcutaneous tissues in dependent parts of the body, eventually causing a gradual loss in skin **turgor** (elasticity).
- *Skin breakdown.* Normal blood circulation relies on muscle activity. Immobility impedes circulation and diminishes the supply of nutrients to specific areas. As a result, skin breakdown and formation of pressure ulcers can occur. See Chapter 37.

Psychoneurological System

People who are unable to carry out the usual activities related to their roles (e.g., as breadwinner, husband, mother, or athlete) become aware of an increased dependence on others. These factors lower the person's self-esteem. Frustration and the decrease in self-esteem may, in turn, provoke exaggerated emotional reactions. Emotional reactions vary considerably. Some individuals become apathetic and withdrawn; some regress; and some become angry and aggressive.

Because the immobilized person's participation in life becomes much narrower and the variety of stimuli decreases, the person's perception of time intervals deteriorates. Problem-solving and decision-making abilities often deteriorate as a result of lack of intellectual stimulation and the stress of the illness and immobility. In addition, the loss of control over events can cause anxiety.

ASSESSMENT INTERVIEW

Activity and Exercise

Daily Activity Level

- What activities do you usually carry out during a routine day?
- Are you able to carry out the following tasks of daily life independently?
  a. Eating
  b. Dressing/grooming
  c. Bathing
  d. Toileting
  e. Ambulating
  f. Using a wheelchair
  g. Transferring (1) from bed to chair, (2) in and out of bath, and (3) in and out of car
  h. Cooking
  i. Home maintenance
  j. Shopping
- Where problems exist in your ability to carry out such tasks:
  a. What do you have to depend on family or friends to do for you?
  b. How is the task achieved (by family, friend, agency, or use of specialized equipment)?

Activity Tolerance

- How much and what types of activities make you tired?
- Do you ever experience dizziness, shortness of breath, marked increase in respiratory rate, or other problems following mild or moderate activity?

Exercise

- What type of exercise do you carry out to enhance your physical fitness?
- What is the frequency and length of this exercise session?
- Do you believe exercise is beneficial to health? Explain.

Factors Affecting Mobility

Environmental factors. Do stairs, lack of railings or other assistive devices, or an unsafe neighbourhood impede your mobility or exercise regimen?

Health problems. Do any of the following physical or mental health problems, past or current, affect your muscle strength or endurance: heart disease, lung disease, stroke, cancer, neuromuscular problems, musculoskeletal problems, visual or mental impairments, trauma, or pain?

Financial factors. Are your finances adequate to obtain equipment or other aids that you require to enhance your mobility?

Lifestyle variables. Do cultural, leisure, or employment practices influence activity and mobility patterns?

Immobility can impair the social and motor development of young children.

Assessing

Assessment relative to a client's activity and exercise includes a nursing history and a physical examination of body alignment, gait, appearance and movement of joints, capabilities and limitations for movement, muscle mass and strength, activity tolerance, problems related to immobility, and physical fitness.

The nurse collects information from the client, from other nurses, and from the client's records. The examination and history are important sources of information about disabilities affecting the client's mobility and activity status, such as contractures, edema, pain in the extremities, or generalized fatigue.

Nursing History

An activity and exercise history is usually part of the comprehensive nursing history form and includes daily activity level, activity tolerance, type and frequency of exercise, and factors affecting mobility. If the client indicates a recent pattern change or difficulties with mobility, a more detailed history is required. This detailed history should include the specific nature of the problem, when it first began and its frequency, its causes, if known, how the problem affects daily living, what the client is doing to cope with the problem, and whether these methods have been effective. Examples of interview questions to elicit this data are shown in the box on the previous page.

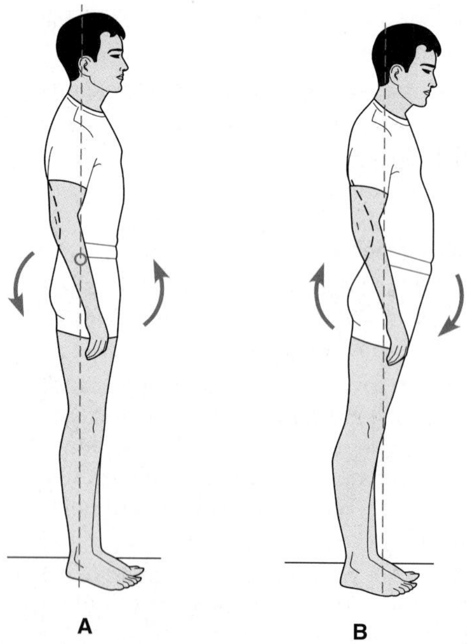

Figure 43.7 A standing person with *A*, good trunk alignment; *B*, poor trunk alignment. The arrows indicate the direction in which the pelvis is tilted.

Physical Examination

Body Alignment

Assessment of body alignment includes an inspection of the client if the client is able to stand. The purpose of body alignment assessment is to identify the following:

- Normal developmental variations in posture
- Poor posture and learning needs to maintain good posture
- Factors contributing to poor posture, such as fatigue or low self-esteem
- Muscle weakness or other motor impairments

To assess alignment, the nurse views the client from lateral, anterior, and posterior perspectives.

The "slumped" posture (Figure 43.7, *B*) is the most common problem that occurs when people stand. The neck is flexed far forward, the abdomen protrudes, the pelvis is thrust forward to create lordosis (an exaggerated curvature of the lumbar spine), and the knees are markedly hyperextended. Lower back pain and fatigue occur quickly in people with poor posture.

From the anterior and posterior views, the nurse should observe the following:

- The shoulders and hips are level.
- The toes point forward.
- The spine is straight, not curved to either side.

Gait

The characteristic pattern of a person's **gait** (walk) is assessed to determine the client's mobility and risk for injury due to falling. Two phases of normal gait are stance and swing (Figure 43.8). In the *stance phase*, (1) the heel of the right foot strikes the ground, and (2) body weight is spread over the ball of the right foot, while the left heel pushes off and leaves the ground. In the *swing phase*, the leg from behind moves in front of the body. When one leg is in the swing phase, the other is in the stance phase.

The nurse assesses gait as the client walks into the room or asks the client to walk a distance of 3.5 m down a hallway and observes for the following:

- Head is erect, gaze is straight ahead, and vertebral column is upright.
- Heel strikes the ground before the toe.
- Feet are dorsiflexed in the swing phase.
- Arm opposite the swing-through foot moves forward at the same time.
- Gait is smooth, coordinated, and rhythmic, with even weight borne on each foot; it produces minimal body swing from side to side and directs movement straight ahead; and it starts and stops with ease.

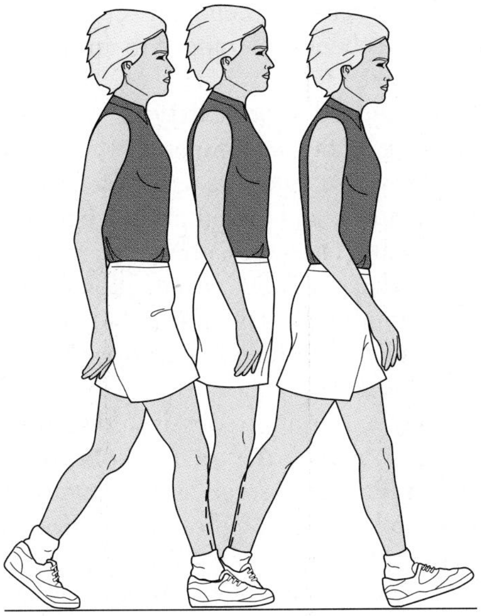

Figure 43.8 The stance and swing phases of a normal gait

The nurse may also assess **pace** (the number of steps taken per minute). A normal walking pace is 70 to 100 steps per minute. The pace of an older person may slow to about 40 steps per minute.

The nurse should also note the client's need for a prosthesis or assistive device, such as a cane or walker. For a client who uses assistive aids, the nurse assesses gait without the device and compares the assisted and unassisted gaits.

Appearance and Movement of Joints

Physical examination of the joints involves inspection; palpation; assessment of range of active motion; and, if active motion is not possible, assessment of range of passive motion. The following joints may be given special attention: neck, shoulder, elbow, wrist, hip, knee, and ankle.

The nurse should assess the following:

- Any joint swelling or redness, which could indicate the presence of an injury or inflammation
- Any deformity, such as a bony enlargement or contracture, and symmetry of involvement
- The muscle development associated with each joint and the relative size and symmetry of the muscles on each side of the body
- Any reported or palpable tenderness
- Crepitation (palpable or audible crackling or grating sensation produced by joint motion)
- Increased temperature over the joint. Palpate the joint using the backs of the fingers and compare the temperature with that of the symmetric joint.
- The degree of joint movement. Ask the client to move selected body parts as shown in Table 43.2 earlier. As indicated, measure the amount of movement by a goniometer, a device that measures the angle of the joint in degrees. See Figure 27.75.

Assessment of range of motion should not be unduly fatiguing, and the joint movements need to be performed smoothly, slowly, and rhythmically. No joint should be forced. Uneven, jerky movement and forcing can injure the joint and its surrounding muscles and ligaments.

Capabilities and Limitations for Movement

The nurse needs to obtain data that may indicate hindrances or restrictions to the client's movement and the need for assistance, including the following:

- How the client's illness influences the ability to move and whether the client's health contraindicates any exertion, position, or movement
- Encumbrances to movement, such as an intravenous line in place or a heavy cast on one leg
- Mental alertness and ability to follow directions. Check whether the client is receiving medications that hinder the ability to walk safely (e.g., narcotics, sedatives, tranquilizers, and some antihistamines cause drowsiness, dizziness, weakness, and orthostatic hypotension).
- Balance and coordination, if the client is to be transferred from the bed
- Presence of orthostatic hypotension before transfers. Specifically, assess for any increase in pulse rate, marked fall in blood pressure, dizziness, lightheadedness, and dimming of vision when the client moves from a supine to a vertical posture.
- Degree of comfort. People who have pain may not want to move and require an analgesic before they are moved.
- Vision: Is it adequate to prevent falls?

The nurse also assesses the amount of assistance the client requires for the following:

- Moving in the bed. In particular, observe for the amount of assistance the client requires for turning:
  a. From a supine position to a lateral position
  b. From a lateral position on one side to a lateral position on the other
  c. From a supine position to a sitting position in bed
- Rising from a lying position to a sitting position on the edge of the bed. Healthy people can normally rise without support from the arms.
- Rising from a chair to a standing position. Normally, this can be done without pushing with the arms.
- Range of motion of joints needed to complete transfer movements (see previous section).
- Coordination and balance. Determine the client's abilities to hold the body erect, to bear weight and keep

balance in a standing position on one or both legs, to take steps, and to push off from a chair or bed.

Muscle Mass and Strength

Before the client undertakes a change in position or attempts to ambulate, it is essential that the nurse assess the client's strength and ability to move. Providing appropriate assistance lowers the risk of muscle strain and body injury to both the client and nurse. Assessment of upper extremity strength is especially important for clients who use ambulation aids, such as walkers and crutches. For information on how to determine muscle mass and strength in lower and upper extremities, see Chapter 27.

Activity Tolerance

By determining an appropriate activity level for a client, the nurse can predict whether the client has the strength and endurance to participate in activities that require similar expenditures of energy. This assessment is useful in encouraging increasing independence in people who (1) have a cardiovascular or respiratory disability, (2) have been completely immobilized for a prolonged period, (3) have decreased muscle mass or a musculoskeletal disorder, (4) have experienced inadequate sleep, (5) have experienced pain, or (6) are depressed, anxious, or unmotivated.

The most useful measures in predicting activity tolerance are heart rate, strength, and rhythm; respiratory rate, depth, and rhythm; and blood pressure. These data are obtained at the following times:

- Before the activity starts (baseline data) while the client is at rest
- During the activity
- Immediately after the activity stops
- Three minutes after the activity has stopped and the client has rested

The activity should be stopped immediately in the event of any physiological change indicating the activity is too strenuous or prolonged for the client. These changes include the following:

- Sudden facial pallor
- Feelings of dizziness or weakness
- Heart rate or respiratory rate that significantly exceeds baseline or pre-established levels
- Change in heart or respiratory rhythm from regular to irregular
- Weakening of the pulse
- Dyspnea, shortness of breath, or chest pain
- Diastolic blood pressure change of 10 mm Hg or more

If, however, the client tolerates the activity well, and if the client's heart rate returns to baseline levels within three minutes after the activity ceases, the activity is considered safe. This activity, then, can serve as a standard for predicting the client's tolerance for similar activities.

Problems Related to Immobility

When collecting data pertaining to the problems of immobility, the nurse uses the assessment methods of inspection, palpation, and auscultation; checks results of laboratory tests; and takes measurements, including body weight, fluid intake, and fluid output. Specific techniques for assessing immobility problems and abnormal assessment findings related to the complications of immobility are listed in Table 43.4.

It is extremely important to obtain and record baseline assessment data soon after the client first becomes immobile. These baseline data serve as the standard against which all data collected throughout the period of immobilization are compared.

Because a major nursing responsibility is to prevent the complications of immobility, the nurse needs to identify clients at risk of developing such complications before problems arise. Clients at risk include those who (1) are poorly nourished, (2) have decreased sensitivity to pain, temperature, or pressure, (3) have existing cardiovascular, pulmonary, or neuromuscular problems, and/or (4) are unconscious.

Diagnosing

Mobility Problem as the Diagnostic Label

NANDA includes the following nursing diagnostic labels for activity and exercise problems:

- ***Activity Intolerance*** (specify level): Reduced physiological or psychological capacity to endure or complete required or desired daily activities. Gordon (1997) delineates four levels that can be used after the diagnostic label:

  Level I: Walk, regular pace, on level ground indefinitely; climb one flight of stairs or more but more short of breath than normal

  Level II: Walk one city block 160 m on level ground; climb one flight slowly without stopping

  Level III: Walk no more than 16 m on level ground without stopping; unable to climb one flight of stairs without stopping

  Level IV: Dyspnea and fatigue at rest
- ***Risk for Activity Intolerance:*** Presence of risk factors for experiencing insufficient physiological or psychological energy to endure or complete required or desired daily activities
- ***Impaired Physical Mobility*** (specify level): Limitation of ability for independent physical movement. Gordon (1997) delineates four levels that can be used after the diagnostic label:

TABLE 43.4 Assessing Problems of Immobility

Assessment	Problem	Assessment	Problem
Musculoskeletal System		**Metabolic System**	
Measure arm and leg circumferences	Decreased circumference due to decreased muscle mass	Measure height and weight	Weight loss due to muscle atrophy and loss of subcutaneous fat
Palpate and observe body joints	Stiffness or pain in joints	Take anthropometric measurements	Loss of body muscle and subcutaneous fat
Take goniometric measurements of joint ROM	Decreased joint ROM, joint contractures	Palpate body skin	Generalized edema due to low blood protein levels
Cardiovascular System		**Urinary System**	
Auscultate the heart	Increased heart rate	Measure intake and output	Dehydration
Measure blood pressure	Orthostatic hypotension	Observe urine output	Cloudy, dark urine, high specific gravity
Palpate and observe sacrum, legs, and feet	Peripheral dependent edema, increased peripheral vein engorgement	Palpate urinary bladder	Distended urinary bladder due to urinary retention
Palpate extremity pulses	Weak peripheral pulses	**Gastrointestinal System**	
Check capillary refill	Decreased peripheral circulation	Observe stool	Hard, dry, small stool
Measure calf muscle circumferences	Edema; thrombus formation	Auscultate bowel sounds	Decreased bowel sounds due to decreased intestinal motility
Observe calf muscle for redness, tenderness, and swelling	Thrombophlebitis	**Integumentary System**	
		Observe skin for intactness, redness, pallor, warmth, tenderness	Break in skin integrity, pressure areas
Respiratory System		**Psychosocial System**	
Observe chest movements	Asymmetric chest movements, dyspnea	Observe for participation in care, verbalization of feelings about immobility	Withdrawing from participation in care
Auscultate chest	Diminished breath sounds, crackles, wheezes, and increased respiratory rate		

Level I: Requires use of equipment or device

Level II: Requires help from another person(s): assistance, supervision, or teaching

Level III: Requires help from another person(s) and equipment or device

Level IV: Is dependent and does not participate in movement

There are additional diagnoses as follows (Doenges, 2003):

a. ***Impaired bed mobility***
b. ***Impaired walking***
c. ***Impaired wheelchair mobility***
d. ***Impaired transfer ability***

- ***Risk for Disuse Syndrome:*** Risk for deterioration of body systems (see the discussion of complications of immobility earlier) as a result of prescribed or unavoidable musculoskeletal inactivity (Carpenito, 2002)

Clinical examples of assessment data clusters and related nursing diagnoses are shown in Table 43.5.

Mobility Problems as the Etiology

Depending on the data obtained, problems with mobility often affect other areas of human functioning and indicate other diagnoses. In these instances, the mobility problem becomes the etiology. Examples in which ***Impaired Physical Mobility*** is the etiology follow. The etiology needs to be described more explicitly in terms such as reduced ROM, neuromuscular impairment or musculoskeletal impairment of upper and lower extremities, or joint pain.

- ***Fear*** (of falling)
- ***Risk for Injury*** (falls)
- ***Powerlessness***
- ***Self-Care Deficit***

- ***Self-Esteem, Chronic Low***
- ***Ineffective Coping***

When problems associated with prolonged *immobility* arise, many other diagnoses may be necessary. Examples include, but are not limited to, the following:

- ***Ineffective Airway Clearance*** if there is stasis of pulmonary secretions
- ***Risk for Infection*** if there is stasis of urinary or pulmonary secretions
- ***Risk for Injury*** if orthostatic hypotension is present

Planning

Positioning, transferring, and ambulating clients are almost always independent nursing functions. The physician usually orders specific body positions only after surgery, anesthesia, or trauma involving the nervous and musculoskeletal systems. All clients should have an activity order written by their physician when they are admitted to the agency for care and following surgery and diagnostic procedures (any change in cause of treatment or health status).

As part of planning, the nurse is responsible for identifying those clients who need assistance with body alignment and determining the degree of assistance they need. The nurse must be sensitive to the client's need to function as independently as possible yet provide assistance when the client needs it. Clients who are not very mobile and can help themselves only minimally may also have low energy levels.

Most clients require some nursing guidance and assistance to learn about, achieve, and maintain proper body mechanics. The nurse should also plan to teach clients applicable skills. For example, a client with a back injury needs to learn how to get out of bed safely and comfortably; a client with an injured leg needs to learn how to transfer from bed to wheelchair safely; and a client with a newly acquired walker needs to learn how to use it safely. Nurses often teach family members or caregivers safe moving, lifting, and transfer techniques in the home setting.

The goals established for clients will vary according to the diagnosis and defining characteristics related to each individual. Examples of overall goals for clients with actual or potential problems related to mobility or activity follow:

- Increase tolerance for physical activity.
- Restore or improve the capability to ambulate and/or participate in ADLs.
- Avoid injury from falling or improper use of body mechanics.
- Improve physical fitness.
- Avoid any complications associated with immobility.
- Maintain or enhance social, emotional, and intellectual well-being.

TABLE 43.5 Clinical Application: Data Clusters and Related Nursing Diagnoses

Data Cluster	Nursing Diagnosis
Ivy Snowfield, a frail-appearing 82-year-old, has an unsteady gait and increasing difficulty maintaining her balance. Pace is slow (20 steps per minute). Posture is stooped. Leg and arm muscle strength is symmetric but weak. She has difficulty rising from a sitting to a standing position. No mechanical assistive devices are used.	***Impaired Physical Mobility*** related to decreased motor agility and muscle weakness associated with advanced age
Peter Chan, a 69-year-old accountant being treated for congestive heart failure, states he has dyspnea with mild activity. ("I cannot climb a flight of stairs without stopping and resting and become breathless even when walking on level ground.") Rales are present in both lungs. ECG reveals an enlarged heart. He prefers the orthopneic position.	***Activity Intolerance*** (Level III) related to imbalance between oxygen supply and demand secondary to decreased cardiac output
Florence Grayson was admitted to hospital with a cerebrovascular accident two days ago. She weighs 46 kg, is stuporous, is anorexic and malnourished, has flaccid paralysis of her left arm and leg, and is incontinent of urine. She is unable to move without help.	***Risk for Disuse Syndrome*** related to neuromuscular impairment (hemiplegia), altered level of consciousness, and inactivity
Tim Cherry, a 93-year-old widower, has chronic obstructive lung disease. States, "I can't breathe properly when I move about. I cannot maintain the house the way my wife did. All I can do is feed myself. Luckily, I have a nice neighbour who shops for me every week."	***Impaired Home Maintenance*** related to chronic debilitating disease, activity intolerance, and lack of familiarity with neighbourhood resources

SAMPLE CARE PLAN FOR ACTIVITY AND EXERCISE

ASSESSMENT DATA FOR KEVIN ANDREWS

Nursing Assessment

Several weeks ago, Kevin Andrews, a 17-year-old high school gymnast, fell from the parallel bars and fractured his left femur. Kevin has been on bed rest in skeletal traction since the accident. He is depressed and bored with the hospital routine of care. Because of painful muscle spasms, he often refuses to be turned or to move voluntarily. His appetite is poor, and he often refuses his hospital meals. He needs encouragement from the nursing staff to cough and deep breathe.

Physical Examination

Height: 175.3 cm
Weight: 70 kg on admission
Temperature: 37°C
Pulse rate: 80 BPM
Respirations: 16/minute
Blood pressure: 114/70 mm Hg

Diagnostic Data

Chest x-ray negative, urinalysis negative, Hgb 13.3 g/L, Hct 37%

Nursing Diagnosis

Risk for Disuse Syndrome related to depression and reluctance to move secondary to painful muscle spasms

Client Goal(s):

The client will (1) regain use and strength of upper and lower limb muscles; and (2) avoid potential complications of immobility and traction (e.g., infection and thrombophlebitis).

Desired Outcomes

1. Performs activities of daily living within limitation of skeletal traction
2. Performs range-of-motion exercises of upper limbs and unaffected lower limb q2h
3. Uses overhead trapeze q3h to strengthen muscles in upper limbs by day 3
4. Traction site remains free of drainage and odour
5. No evidence of thrombophlebitis

---

*Nursing Interventions and Selected Activities with Rationale *(in italics)*

Traction/Immobilization Care

- Maintain proper position in bed to enhance traction.
  Improper body alignment can alter the correct line of pull and degree of traction being placed on the bone and may cause a nonuniting fracture. Proper alignment of the fractured bone is necessary for proper reduction of the fracture and healing.
- Ensure that the pull of ropes and weights remains along the axis of the fractured bone.
  Reduction of the fracture is required to promote normal repair and involves maintaining normal anatomical alignment so that the weight exerts a direct, constant, longitudinal pull. Improper alignment will delay healing or allow improper healing to occur with possible deformity.
- Monitor pin insertion sites.
  A break in the skin's protective barrier increases the risk for invasion of infectious organisms leading to skin and bone infection.
- Perform pin insertion site care.
  Regular care of pin sites using aseptic technique and antibacterial agents reduces the chance of infection.
- Monitor circulation, movement, and sensation of affected extremity.
  To prevent complications from immobility, it is important to assess neurovascular integrity on a routine basis.
- Monitor for complications of immobility.
  There are multiple potential hazards of immobility and bed rest including venous stasis, thrombophlebitis, dependent edema, constipation, negative nitrogen balance, urinary retention, and skin breakdown.
- Administer appropriate skin care at friction points.
  Friction from components of the traction apparatus, such as a splint, creates a condition for skin breakdown.

SAMPLE CARE PLAN FOR ACTIVITY AND EXERCISE *continued*

- Provide trapeze for movement in bed.

An overhead trapeze facilitates movement by allowing the client to use the arms to help lift the body during repositioning. Use of the trapeze also encourages isotonic exercises that help maintain muscle strength and mass.

- Instruct Kevin on the importance of adequate nutrition for bone healing.

Proteins and vitamins are necessary for positive nitrogen balance and bone healing.

Exercise Therapy: Joint Mobility

- Determine Kevin's motivation level for maintaining or restoring joint movement in unaffected joints.

Knowledge of the client's degree of motivation and understanding provides a basis for beginning an exercise program that may require teaching, motivational strategies, and interventions for psychosocial issues, such as depression.

- Explain to Kevin and his family the purpose and plan for joint exercises.

An understanding of the potential risks posed by prolonged immobility, especially for this high school gymnast, is fundamental to a successful exercise program.

- Initiate pain control measures before beginning joint exercise.

Activities and exercises will be enhanced if the client's pain is under control and perceived as tolerable.

- Assist Kevin to the optimal body position for each passive or active joint movement.

Proper body positioning during exercise is necessary to avoid injury and promote full range of motion.

- Encourage active range-of-motion exercises in unaffected joints according to a regular schedule.

ROM exercises improve or maintain joint mobility and help prevent contractures. Joints begin to stiffen within 24 hours of disuse, therefore exercises should be initiated as soon as possible and performed at least three times a day.

- Collaborate with a physical therapist in developing and executing an exercise program.

Incorporating the expertise of a physical therapist will strengthen the plan of care. The therapist may have other creative ideas on how to help motivate and encourage the client with the exercise program.

Circulatory Precautions

- Perform a comprehensive appraisal of peripheral circulation (e.g., check peripheral pulses, edema, capillary refill, colour, and temperature of extremity, sensation, and movement).

Immobility and traction place the client at risk for neurovascular complications, including thrombophlebitis and reduced peripheral perfusion.

- Maintain adequate hydration to prevent increased blood viscosity.

Increased blood viscosity places the immobile client at risk for clot formation. Adequate hydration maintains the extracellular fluid compartment and normal viscosity of the blood.

- Monitor extremities for areas of heat, redness, pain, swelling.

Early detection of signs of impaired tissue perfusion can help prevent serious circulatory complications, such as deep vein thrombosis.

Evaluation

Goal partially met. Kevin performs active ROM exercises only once a day and refuses the other two sessions. He uses the overhead trapeze when repositioning frequently throughout the day but is reluctant to bathe and states "Just leave me alone for a while." His appetite has not improved and he eats approximately 40 to 50 percent of each meal. The skin surrounding the pin site remains odourless, dry, and intact. Pulses are strong bilaterally.

*Interventions and activities selected are only a sample of those suggested in the *Nursing Interventions Classification (NIC)* and should be individualized for each client.

Source: McCloskey, J. C., & Bulechek, G. M. (2000). *Iowa intervention project: Nursing interventions classification (NIC)* (3rd ed.). St. Louis, MO: Mosby.

Examples of desired outcomes, although established in the planning phase, are provided in Table 43.12 in the "Evaluating" section of this chapter (page 1225). See also Table 43.3 on page 1182 for outcomes and nursing interventions related to potential immobility problems.

The Iowa Nursing Project's Nursing Interventions Classification (NIC) and Nursing Outcomes Classification (NOC) are tools in planning care (McCloskey & Bulechek, 2000; Johnson & Maas, 2000). Examples of *NIC interventions* are as follows:

- Bed rest care
- Energy management
- Teaching: prescribed activity/exercise
- Body mechanics promotion
- Exercise promotion
- Exercise therapy: ambulation/balance/joint mobility/muscle control
- Positioning

Specific nursing activities associated with each of these interventions can be selected to meet the individual needs of the client. A sample nursing care plan using NIC interventions and selected activities is provided on pages 1193 and 1194.

Examples of *NOC outcomes* are as follows:

- Endurance
- Energy conservation
- Self-care: activities of daily living
- Ambulation: walking/wheelchair
- Circulation status
- Respiratory status
- Mobility level
- Immobility consequences
- Joint movement
- Transfer performance

Specific indicators for these outcomes can be selected for the individual.

Planning for Home Care

Clients who have been hospitalized for activity or mobility problems often need continued care in the home. In preparation for discharge, the nurse needs to determine the client's actual and potential health problems, strengths, and resources. The accompanying box describes the specific assessment data required before establishing a discharge plan for clients with mobility or activity problems. A major aspect of discharge planning involves instructional needs of the client and family. See the Home Care Teaching Guide box on page 1196 and the Wellness Teaching and Client Teaching boxes later in this chapter.

Using Body Mechanics

Body mechanics is the term used to describe the efficient, coordinated, and safe use of the body to move objects and carry out the activities of daily living. The major purpose of body mechanics is to facilitate the safe

HOME CARE ASSESSMENT

Mobility and Activity Problems

Client and Environment

- *Capabilities or tolerance for required and desired activities:* Self-care (feeding, bathing, toileting, dressing, grooming, home maintenance, shopping, cooking); recreational activities
- *Mobility aids required:* Cane, walker, crutches, wheelchair, transfer boards
- *Equipment required if immobilized:* Special bed, side rails, pressure-reducing mattress
- *Current level of knowledge:* Body mechanics for use of mobility aids; specific exercises prescribed
- *Home mobility hazard appraisal:* Adequacy of lighting; presence of handrails; safety of pathways and stairs; congested areas; unanchored rugs, mats, or electrical cords; and any other obstacles to safe movement (see "Home Hazard Appraisal" in Chapter 17); structural adjustments needed for wheelchair access

Family or Caregiver

- *Caregiver availability, skills, and willingness:* Primary people able to assist client with self-care, movement, shopping, and so on; physical and emotional status to assist with care; learning needs
- *Family role changes and coping:* Effect on financial status, parenting and spousal roles, social roles
- *Availability of caregiver support:* Other support people available for occasional duties, such as shopping, transportation, housekeeping, cooking, budgeting, respite care

Community

- *Resources:* Availability and familiarity with sources of medical equipment, financial assistance, homemaker services, hygienic care, and other services; Meals on Wheels; religious counsellors and visitors; sources of respite for caregiver and efficient use of appropriate muscle groups to maintain balance, reduce the energy required, reduce fatigue, and decrease the risk of injury. Good body mechanics is essential to both clients and nurses. This section focuses on body mechanics used by nurses when moving and turning clients in bed and transferring clients between beds, wheelchairs, and stretchers.

Body mechanics involves the concepts of centre of gravity, line of gravity, and base of support that were discussed earlier in relation to body alignment and balance. When the person moves, the centre of gravity shifts continuously in the direction of the moving body parts. Balance depends on the interrelationship of the centre of gravity, the line of gravity, and the base of support. When a person moves, the closer the line of gravity is to the centre of the base of support, the greater the person's stability (Figure 43.9, *A*). Conversely, the closer the line of gravity is to the edge of the base of support, the more precarious the balance (Figure 43.9, *B*). If the line of gravity falls outside the base of support, the person falls (Figure 43.9, *C*).

The broader the base of support and the lower the centre of gravity, the greater the stability and balance. Body balance, therefore, can be greatly enhanced by (1) widening the base of support, and (2) lowering the centre of gravity, bringing it closer to the base of support. The base of support is easily widened by spreading the feet farther apart. The centre of gravity is readily lowered by flexing the hips and knees until a squatting position is achieved. The importance of these alterations cannot be overemphasized for nurses.

Two movements to avoid because of their potential for causing back injury are twisting (rotation) of the thoracolumbar spine and acute flexion of the back with hips and knees straight (stooping). Undesirable twisting of the back can be prevented by squarely facing the direction of movement, whether pushing, pulling, or sliding, and moving the object directly toward or away from one's centre of gravity.

Lifting

When a person lifts or carries an object, for example, a suitcase, the weight of the object becomes part of the person's body weight. This weight affects the location of the

HOME CARE TEACHING GUIDE

Activity and Exercise

Maintaining Musculoskeletal Function

- Teach the systematic performance of passive or assistive ROM exercises to maintain joint mobility.
- As appropriate, demonstrate the proper way to perform isotonic, isometric, or isokinetic exercises to maintain muscle mass and tone (collaborate with the physician and physical therapist on these). Incorporate ADLs into exercise program, if appropriate.
- Provide a written schedule for the type, frequency, and duration of exercises; encourage the use of a progress graph or chart to facilitate adherence with the therapy.
- Offer an ambulation schedule, as appropriate.
- Instruct in the availability of assistive ambulatory devices and correct use of them. See also adaptive feeding aids in Chapter 38.
- Discuss pain control measures required before exercise, as appropriate.

Preventing Injury

- Teach safe transfer and ambulation techniques.
- Discuss safety measures to avoid falls (e.g., locking wheelchairs, wearing appropriate footwear, using rubber tips on crutches, keeping the environment safe, and using mechanical aids, such as raised toilet seat, grab bars, urinal, bedpan or commode, to facilitate toileting).
- Teach the use of proper body mechanics as needed (see the Wellness Teaching box on page 1198).
- Teach ways to prevent postural hypotension (see the box on page 1218).

Managing Energy to Prevent Fatigue

- Discuss activity and rest patterns and develop a plan, as indicated; intersperse rest periods with activity periods.
- Discuss ways to minimize fatigue, such as performing activities more slowly and for shorter periods, resting more often, and using more assistance, as required.
- Provide information about available resources to help with ADLs and home maintenance management.
- Teach ways to increase energy (e.g., increasing intake of high-energy foods, ensuring adequate rest and sleep, controlling pain).
- Teach techniques to monitor activity tolerance as appropriate. See "Activity Tolerance" in the "Assessing" section on page 1190.

Referrals

Provide appropriate information about accessing community resources: home care agencies, sources of equipment, and so on.

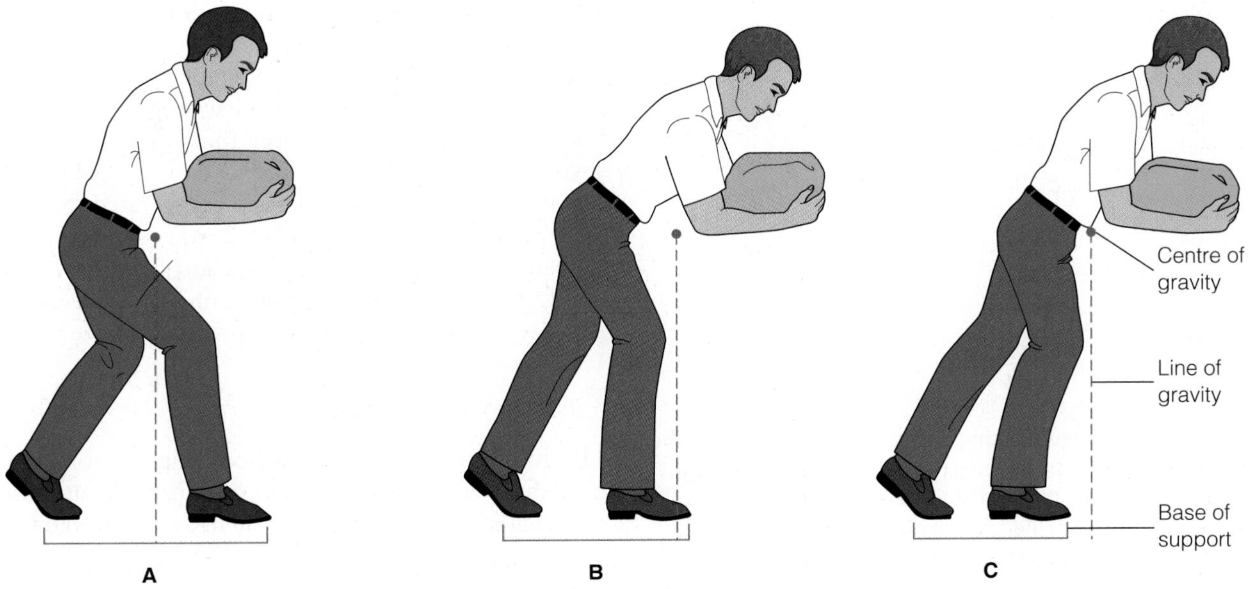

Figure 43.9 *A,* Balance is maintained when the line of gravity falls close to the base of support; *B,* Balance is precarious when the line of gravity falls at the edge of the base of support; *C,* Balance cannot be maintained when the line of gravity falls outside the base of support

person's centre of gravity, which is displaced in the direction of the added weight. To counteract this potential imbalance, body parts (e.g., arm and trunk) move in a direction away from the weight. In this way, the centre of gravity is maintained over the same point in the base of support. By holding the lifted object as close as possible to the body's centre of gravity, the lifter avoids undue displacement of the centre of gravity and achieves greater stability. Agency guidelines for maximum lifting of weights must be followed.

People can lift more weight when they use a lever than when they do not. In the body, the bones of the skeleton act as levers, a joint is a *fulcrum* (fixed point about which a lever moves), and the muscles exert the force (Figure 43.10). Use of the arms as levers is often applied in clinical practice when the nurse needs to raise a client's head off the bed, for example, or give back care to a client in traction.

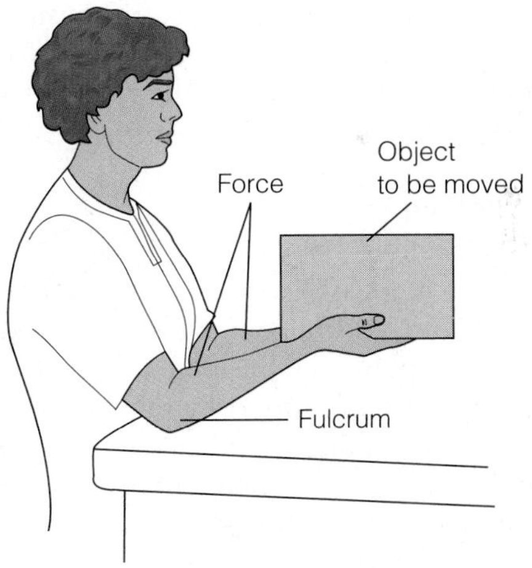

Figure 43.10 Using the arm as a lever

Because lifting involves movement against gravity, the nurse must use major muscle groups of the thighs, knees, upper and lower arms, abdomen, and pelvis to prevent back strain. The nurse can increase overall muscle strength by synchronized use of as many muscle groups as possible during an activity. For instance, when the arms are used in an activity, dividing the work between the arms and legs helps prevent back strain.

Another technique based on the principle of leverage can be used when lifting objects from the floor to waist level. In this technique, the back and knees are flexed until the load is at thigh level, at which point the knees remain flexed to provide thrust as the back begins to straighten (Figure 43.11). This technique provides for better balance, leverage, and synchronized use of muscles, which help avoid back pain and injury. When one lifts an object to knee level, the shoulder and arm muscles pull, the abdominal and pelvic muscles contract for leverage and pull, and the thigh and leg muscles exert the upward thrust to bring the object off the floor. When one lifts an object from midthigh to waist level, force is provided essentially by the leg and thigh muscle groups, but the back and pelvic muscles remain contracted.

Figure 43.11 Stages in lifting an object from the floor to the waist: *A,* Start the lift by keeping the back flexed while the knees begin to straighten so that the leg muscles can exert an upward thrust; *B,* Keep the back and knees in a less flexed, but not straight, position (Owen, 2000)

In all positions, it is important to maintain a distance of shoulder width (and depth) between the feet and to keep the load close to the body (over base of support) (Owen, 1985). Before attempting the lift, the nurse must ensure that there are no hazards on the floor, that there is a clear path for moving the object, and that the nurse's base of support is secure.

Pulling and Pushing

When pulling or pushing an object, a person maintains balance with least effort when the base of support is enlarged in the direction in which the movement is to be produced or opposed. For example, when pushing an object, a person can enlarge the base of support by moving the front foot forward. When pulling an object, a person can enlarge the base of support by moving the rear leg back as the person is facing the object. It is easier and safer to pull an object toward one's own centre of gravity than to push it away, as the person can exert more control of the object's movement when pulling it.

Pivoting

Pivoting is a technique in which the body is turned in a way that avoids twisting of the spine. To pivot, place one foot ahead of the other, raise the heels very slightly, and put the body weight on the balls of the feet. When the weight is off the heels, the frictional surface is decreased and the knees are not twisted when turning. Keeping the body aligned, turn (pivot) about 90 degrees in the desired direction. The foot that was forward will now be behind.

A summary of principles and guidelines related to body mechanics is shown in Table 43.6.

Preventing Back Injury

Many factors increase the potential for lower back injuries. A major contributor is habitually poor standing and sitting posture, which produces an exaggerated curvature of the lumbar spine, called **lordosis.** Overweight individuals who carry their extra weight over their abdomen, pregnant women, and women who consistently wear high-heeled shoes are at risk because of the exaggerated lumbar curvature these situations produce. Sedentary persons are at greater risk because of weak back and abdominal muscles.

Lower back injuries are preventable. Some guidelines for preventing back injuries are presented in the box below.

Positioning Clients

Positioning a client in good body alignment and changing the position regularly and systematically are essential aspects of nursing practice. Clients who can move easily

WELLNESS TEACHING

Preventing Back Injuries

- Become consciously aware of your posture and body mechanics.
- When standing for a period of time, periodically flex one hip and knee and rest your foot on an object, if possible.
- When sitting, keep your knees slightly higher than your hips.
- Use a firm mattress that provides good body support at natural body curvatures.
- Exercise regularly to maintain overall physical condition; include exercises that strengthen the pelvic, abdominal, and lumbar muscles.
- Avoid exercises that cause pain or require spinal flexion with straight legs (e.g., toe-touching and sit-ups) or spinal rotation (twisting).
- When moving an object, spread your feet apart to provide a wide base of support.
- When lifting an object, distribute the weight between large muscles of the legs and arms.
- Wear clothing that allows you to use good body mechanics and comfortable low-heeled shoes that provide good foot support and will not cause you to slip, stumble, or turn your ankle.
- Follow agency guidelines for maximum lifting weights.
- Follow zero lift policies set by agencies.
- Use mechanical lifting devices when lifting of clients is required.

TABLE 43.6 Summary of Guidelines and Principles Related to Body Mechanics

Guidelines	Principles
Plan the move or transfer carefully. Free the surrounding area of obstacles and move required equipment near the head or foot of the bed.	Appropriate preparation prevents potential falls and injury and safeguards the client and equipment.
Obtain the assistance of other people or use mechanical devices to move objects that are too heavy. Encourage clients to assist as much as possible by pushing or pulling themselves to reduce your muscular effort. Use arms as levers, whenever possible, to increase lifting power. Follow agency guidelines for maximum lifting weights.	The heavier an object, the greater the force needed to move the object.
Adjust the working area to the level of centre of gravity, and keep the body close to the area. Elevate adjustable beds and overbed tables or lower the side rails of beds to prevent stretching and reaching.	Objects that are close to the centre of gravity are moved with the least effort.
Provide a firm, smooth, dry bed foundation before moving a client in bed or use a pull sheet.	Less friction between the object moved and the surface on which it is moved requires less energy.
Always face the direction of the movement.	This uses major muscle groups and prevents twisting or rotating of the spine.
Start any body movement with proper alignment. Stand as close as possible to the object to be moved. Avoid stretching, reaching, and twisting, which may place the line of gravity outside the base of support.	Balance is maintained and muscle strain is avoided when the line of gravity passes through the base of support.
Before moving an object, increase your stability by widening your stance and flexing your knees, hips, and ankles.	The wider the base of support and the lower the centre of gravity, the greater is the stability.
Before moving an object, contract your gluteal, abdominal, pelvic, leg, and arm muscles to prepare them for action.	The greater the preparatory isometric tensing, or contraction of muscles, before moving an object, the less the energy required to move it, and the less the likelihood of musculoskeletal strain and injury.
Avoid working against gravity. Pull, push, roll, or turn objects instead of lifting them. Lower the head of the client's bed before moving the client up in bed if not contraindicated.	Moving an object along a level surface requires less energy than moving an object up an inclined surface or lifting it against the force of gravity.
Use your gluteal and leg muscles, rather than the sacrospinal muscles of your back, to exert an upward thrust when lifting. Distribute the work load between both arms and legs to prevent back strain.	The synchronized use of as many large muscle groups as possible during an activity increases overall strength and prevents muscle fatigue and injury.
When *pushing* an object, enlarge the base of support by moving the front foot forward. When *pulling* an object, enlarge the base of support by moving the rear leg while facing the object.	Balance is maintained with minimal effort when the base of support is enlarged in the direction in which the movement will occur.
When moving or carrying objects, hold them as close as possible to your centre of gravity.	The closer the line of gravity to the *centre* of the base of support, the greater the stability.
Use the weight of the body as a force for pulling or pushing by rocking on the feet or leaning forward or backward.	Body weight adds force to counteract the weight of the object and reduces the amount of strain on the arms and back.
Alternate rest periods with periods of muscle use to help prevent fatigue.	Continuous muscle exertion can result in muscle strain and injury.

automatically reposition themselves for comfort. Such people generally require minimal positioning assistance from nurses other than guidance about ways to maintain body alignment and to exercise their joints. However, people who are weak, frail, in pain, paralyzed, or unconscious rely on nurses to provide or assist with position changes. For all clients, it is important to assess the skin and provide skin care before and after a position change.

Any position, correct or incorrect, can be detrimental if maintained for a prolonged period. Frequent change of position helps to prevent muscle discomfort, undue pressure resulting in pressure ulcers, damage to superficial nerves and blood vessels, and contractures. Position changes also maintain muscle tone and stimulate postural reflexes.

When the client is not able to move independently or assist with moving, the *preferred method is to use a mechanical lift to move the client. Two or more people may be needed to turn a client.* Appropriate assistance reduces the risk of muscle strain and body injury to both the client and nurse.

When positioning clients in bed, the nurse can do a number of things to ensure proper alignment and promote client comfort and safety.

- Make sure the mattress is firm and level yet has enough give to fill in and support natural body curvatures. A sagging mattress, a mattress that is too soft, or an underfilled water bed used over a prolonged period can contribute to the development of hip flexion contractures and low back strain and pain. *Bed boards* made of plywood and placed beneath a sagging mattress are increasingly recommended for clients who have back problems or are prone to them. Some bed boards are hinged across the middle so that they will bend as the head of the bed is raised. It is particularly important in the home setting to inspect the mattress for support.
- Ensure that the bed is clean and dry. Wrinkled or damp sheets increase the risk of pressure ulcer formation. See Chapter 37. Make sure extremities can move freely, whenever possible. For example, the top bedclothes need to be loose enough for the client to move the feet.
- Place support devices in specified areas according to the client's position. See the box right for commonly used support devices. Use only those support devices needed to maintain alignment and to prevent stress on the client's muscles and joints. If the person is capable of movement, too many devices limit mobility and increase the potential for muscle weakness and atrophy. Common alignment problems that can be corrected with support devices include the following:
  a. Flexion of the neck
  b. Internal rotation of the shoulder
  c. Adduction of the shoulder
  d. Flexion of the wrist
  e. Anterior convexity of the lumbar spine
  f. External rotation of the hips
  g. Hyperextension of the knees
  h. Plantar flexion of the ankle
- Avoid placing one body part, particularly one with bony prominences, directly on top of another body part. Excessive pressure can damage veins and predispose the client to thrombus formation and decubitus ulcers. Pressure against the popliteal space may damage nerves and blood vessels in this area. Place a folded towel or pillow between the parts.
- Plan a *systematic 24-hour schedule* for position changes.
- Sometimes, a person who appears well aligned may be experiencing real discomfort. Both appearance, in relation to alignment criteria, and comfort are important in achieving effective alignment.

Fowler's Position

Fowler's position, or a semisitting position, is a bed position in which the head and trunk are raised 45 degrees.

Support Devices

- *Pillows*. Different sizes are available. They are used for support or elevation of a body part (e.g., an arm). Specially designed dense pillows can be used to elevate the upper body.
- *Mattresses*. There are two types of mattresses: ones that fit on the bed frame (e.g., standard bed mattress) and those that fit *on* the standard bed mattress (e.g., egg-crate mattress). Mattresses should be evenly supportive. See Chapter 37 for additional information and Table 37.5 for devices that reduce pressure on body parts.
- *Bed boards*. The boards are usually made of wood and are placed under the mattress to provide support.
- *Chair beds*. These beds can be placed into the position of a chair for clients who cannot move from the bed but require a sitting position.
- *Foot boot*. These are made of a variety of substances. They usually have a firm exterior and padding of foam to protect the skin. They provide support to the feet in a natural position and keep the weight of covers off the toes. Without support, an immobilized client's feet assume a plantar flexion position *(foot drop)*. Prolonged assumption of this position results in permanent contracture of the gastrocnemius muscle and tendon.
- *Footboard*. This is a flat panel often made of plastic or wood. It keeps the feet in dorsiflexion to prevent plantar flexion.
- For additional supportive devices, see Chapter 37.

In **low-Fowler's,** or **semi-Fowler's position,** the head and trunk are raised 30 degrees; in **high-Fowler's position,** the head and trunk are raised 90 degrees. See Table 43.7. In this position, the knees should be slightly flexed. Nurses need to clarify the meaning of the term *Fowler's position* in a particular agency.

Fowler's position is the position of choice for people who have difficulty breathing and for some people with heart problems. When the client is in this position, gravity pulls the diaphragm downward, allowing greater chest expansion and lung ventilation. It is not the position of choice if the client is at risk for developing decubitus ulcers (because of the shearing force).

A common error nurses make when aligning clients in Fowler's position is placing an overly large pillow or more than one pillow behind the client's head. These errors promote the development of neck flexion contractures.

Orthopneic Position

An adaptation of high-Fowler's position is the **orthopneic position.** The client sits either in bed or on the side of the bed with an overbed table across the lap (Figure 43.13). This position facilitates respiration by allowing maximum chest expansion. It is particularly helpful to clients who have problems exhaling because they can press the lower part of the chest against the edge of the overbed table.

Dorsal Recumbent Position

In the **dorsal recumbent** (back-lying) **position,** the client's head and shoulders are slightly elevated on a small pillow. In some agencies, the terms *dorsal recumbent* and *supine* are used interchangeably; strictly speaking, however, in the **supine** or **dorsal position** the head and shoulders are not elevated. In both positions, the client's forearms may be elevated on pillows or placed at the client's sides. Supports are similar in both positions, except for the head pillow. See Table 43.8. The dorsal recumbent position is used to provide comfort and to facilitate healing following certain surgeries or administration of anesthetics (e.g., spinal).

Prone Position

In the **prone position,** the client lies on the abdomen with the head turned to one side. The hips are not flexed. Both children and adults often sleep in this position, sometimes with one or both arms flexed over their heads. This position has several advantages. It is the only bed position that allows full extension of the hip and knee joints. When used periodically, the prone position helps prevent flexion contractures of the hips and knees, thereby counteracting a problem caused by all other bed positions. The prone position also promotes drainage from the mouth and is especially useful for unconscious clients or those clients recovering from surgery of the mouth or throat. See Table 43.9.

TABLE 43.7 Fowler's Position

Unsupported Position	Problem to Be Prevented	Corrective Measure*
Bed-sitting position with upper part of body elevated 45° commencing at hips	Posterior flexion of lumbar curvature	Pillow at lower back (lumbar region) to support lumbar region if needed
Head rests on bed surface	Hyperextension or hyperflexion of neck	Pillows to support head, neck, and upper back
Arms fall at sides	Shoulder muscle strain, possible dislocation of shoulders, edema of hands and arms with flaccid paralysis, flexion contracture of the wrist	Pillow under forearms to eliminate pull on shoulder and assist venous blood flow from hands and lower arms
Legs lie flat and straight on lower bed surface	Hyperextension of knees	Small pillow under thighs to flex knees
Legs are externally rotated	External rotation of hips	Trochanter roll lateral to femur (Figure 43.12)
Heels rest on bed surface	Pressure on heels	Small pillow under ankle
Feet are in plantar flexion	Plantar flexion of feet (foot drop)	Footboard or rolled pillow to provide support for dorsal flexion

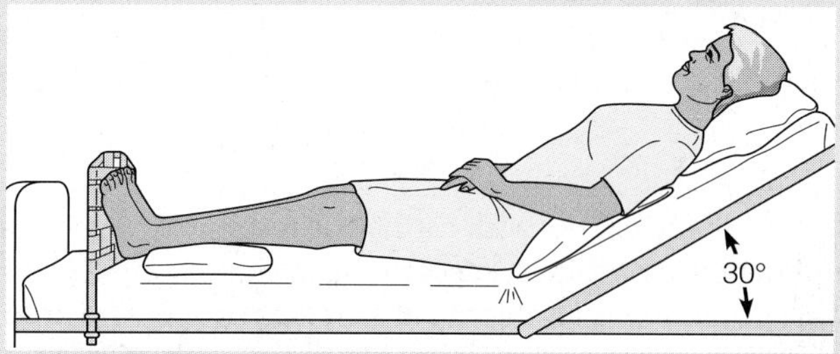

Low-Fowler's (semi-Fowler's) position (supported)
Note that arm support is omitted in this instance.

*The amount of support depends on the needs of the individual client.

The prone position poses some distinct disadvantages. The pull of gravity on the trunk produces a marked lordosis in most people, and the neck is rotated laterally to a significant degree. For this reason, the prone position may not be recommended for people with problems of the cervical or lumbar spine. This position also causes plantar

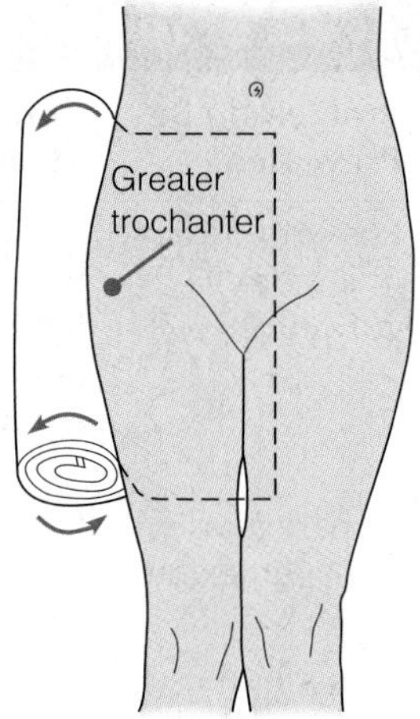

Figure 43.12 Making a trochanter roll: (1) Fold the towel in half lengthwise. (2) Roll the towel tightly, starting at one narrow edge and rolling within approximately 30 cm of the other edge. (3) Invert the roll. Then, palpate the greater trochanter of the femur and place the roll with the centre at the level of the greater trochanter; place the flat part of towel under the client; then roll the towel snugly against the hip.

Figure 43.13 Orthopneic position

TABLE 43.8 Dorsal Recumbent Position

Unsupported Position	Problem to Be Prevented	Corrective Measure*
Head is flat on bed surface	Hyperextension of neck in thick-chested person	Pillow of suitable thickness under head and shoulders, if necessary, for alignment
Lumbar curvature of spine is apparent	Posterior flexion of lumbar curvature	Roll or small pillow under lumbar curvature
Legs may be externally rotated	External rotation of legs	Roll or sandbag placed laterally to trochanter of femur
Legs are extended	Hyperextension of knees	Small pillow under thigh to flex knee slightly
Feet assume plantar flexion position	Plantar flexion (foot drop)	Footboard or rolled pillow to support feet in dorsal flexion
Heels on bed surface	Pressure on heels	Small pillow under ankles

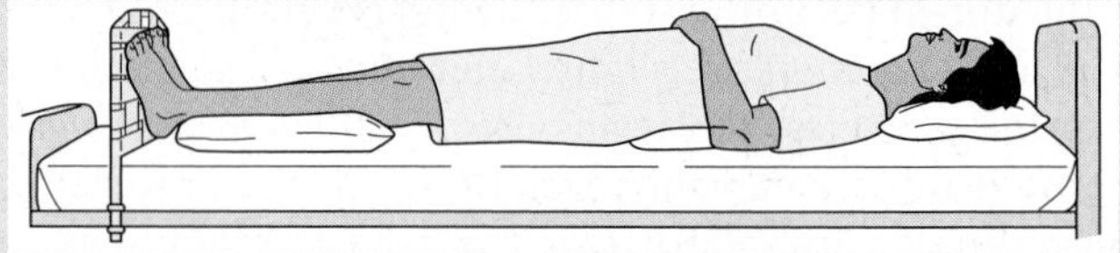

Dorsal recumbent position (supported)

*The amount of support depends on the needs of the individual client.

flexion. Some clients with cardiac or respiratory problems find the prone position confining and suffocating because chest expansion is inhibited during respirations. The prone position should be used only when the client's back is correctly aligned, only for short periods, and only for people with no evidence of spinal abnormalities.

Lateral Position

In the **lateral** (side-lying) **position,** the person lies on one side of the body. Flexing the top hip and knee and placing this leg in front of the body creates a wider, triangular base of support and achieves greater stability. The greater the flexion of the top hip and knee, the greater the stability and balance in this position. This flexion reduces lordosis and promotes good back alignment. For this reason, the lateral position is good for resting and sleeping clients. The lateral position helps relieve pressure on the sacrum and heels in people who sit for much of the day or who are confined to bed and rest in Fowler's or dorsal recumbent positions much of the time. In the lateral position, most of the body's weight is borne by the lateral aspect of the lower scapula, the lateral aspect of the ilium, and the greater trochanter of the femur. People who have sensory or motor deficits on one side of the body usually find that lying on the uninvolved side is more comfortable. See Table 43.10. The left lateral position is commonly used for administering rectal medications.

Sims' Position

In **Sims'** (semiprone) **position,** the client assumes a posture halfway between the lateral and the prone positions. The lower arm is positioned behind the client, and the upper arm is flexed at the shoulder and the elbow. Both legs are

TABLE 43.9 Prone Position

Unsupported Position	Problem to Be Prevented	Corrective Measure*
Head is turned to side and neck is slightly flexed	Flexion or hyperextension of neck	Small or no pillow under head, unless contraindicated because of promotion of mucous drainage from mouth
Body lies flat on abdomen, accentuating lumbar curvature	Hyperextension of lumbar curvature; difficulty breathing; pressure on breasts (women); pressure on genitals (men)	Small pillow or roll under abdomen just below diaphragm
Toes rest on bed surface; feet are in plantar flexion	Plantar flexion of feet (foot drop)	Allow feet to fall naturally over end of mattress, or support lower legs on a pillow so that toes do not touch the bed

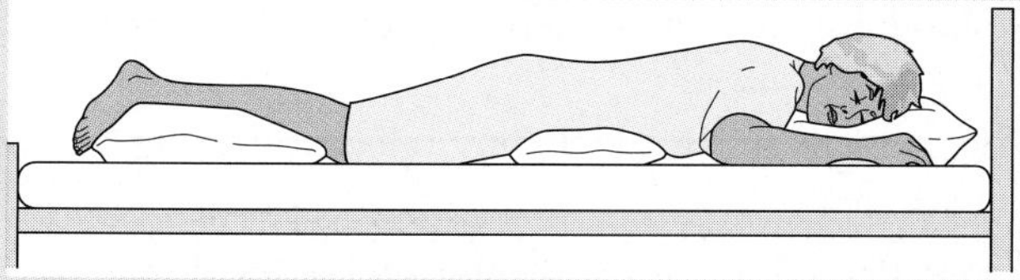

Prone position (supported)

*The amount of support depends on the needs of the individual client.

TABLE 43.10 Lateral Position

Unsupported Position	Problem to Be Prevented	Corrective Measure*
Body is turned to side, both arms in front of body, weight resting primarily on lateral aspects of scapula and ilium	Lateral flexion and fatigue of sternocleidomastoid muscles	Pillow under head and neck to provide good alignment
Upper arm and shoulder are rotated internally and adducted	Internal rotation and adduction of shoulder and subsequent limited function; impaired chest expansion	Pillow under upper arm to place it in good alignment; lower arm should be flexed comfortably
Upper thigh and leg are rotated internally and adducted	Internal rotation and adduction of femur; twisting of the spine	Pillow under leg and thigh to place them in good alignment; shoulders and hips should be aligned

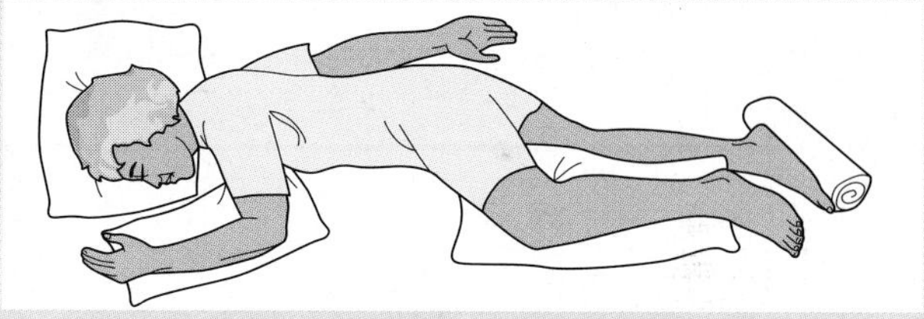

Sims' position (supported)

*The amount of support depends on the needs of the individual client.

flexed in front of the client. The upper leg is more acutely flexed at both the hip and the knee than the lower one is.

Sims' position is occasionally used for unconscious clients because it facilitates drainage from the mouth and prevents aspiration of fluids. It is also used for paralyzed (paraplegic or hemiplegic) clients because it reduces pressure over the sacrum and greater trochanter of the hip. It can be used for clients undergoing examinations or treatments of the perineal area. Many people, especially pregnant women, find Sims' position comfortable for sleeping. People with sensory or motor deficits on one side of the body usually find that lying on the uninvolved side is more comfortable. See Table 43.11.

Moving and Turning Clients in Bed

Although healthy people usually take for granted that they can change body position and go from one place to another with little effort, ill people may have difficulty moving even in bed. How much assistance clients require depends on their own ability to move and their health status. In general, nurses should be sensitive to both the need of people to function independently and their need for assistance to move.

When a nurse assists a person to move, correct body mechanics need to be employed so that the nurse is not injured. Correct body alignment for the client must also be maintained so that undue stress is not placed on the musculoskeletal system.

Actions and rationales applicable to moving and positioning clients include these:

- Before moving a client, assess the degree of exertion permitted, the client's physical abilities (e.g., muscle strength, presence of paralysis), ability to understand instructions, degree of comfort or discomfort when moving, client's weight, presence of orthostatic hypotension

TABLE 43.11 Sims' (Semiprone) Position

Unsupported Position	Problem to Be Prevented	Corrective Measure*
Head rests on bed surface; weight is borne by lateral aspects of cranial and facial bones	Lateral flexion of neck	Small pillow supports head, maintaining it in good alignment, unless drainage from the mouth is required
Upper shoulder and arm are internally rotated	Internal rotation of shoulder and arm; pressure on chest, restricting expansion during breathing	Pillow under upper arm to prevent internal rotation
Upper leg and thigh are adducted and internally rotated	Internal rotation and adduction of hip and leg	Pillow under upper leg to support it in alignment
Feet assume plantar flexion	Foot drop	Sandbags to support feet in dorsal flexion

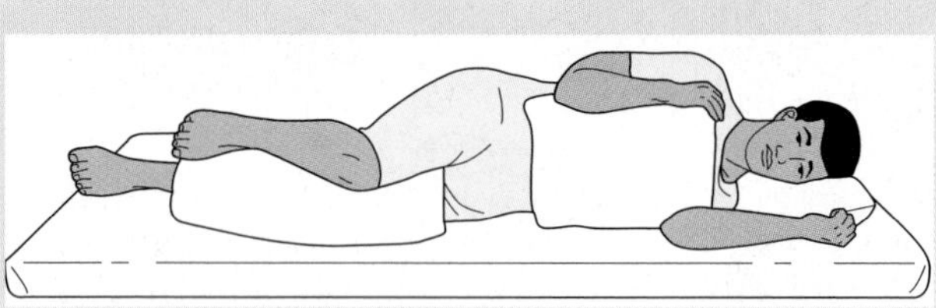

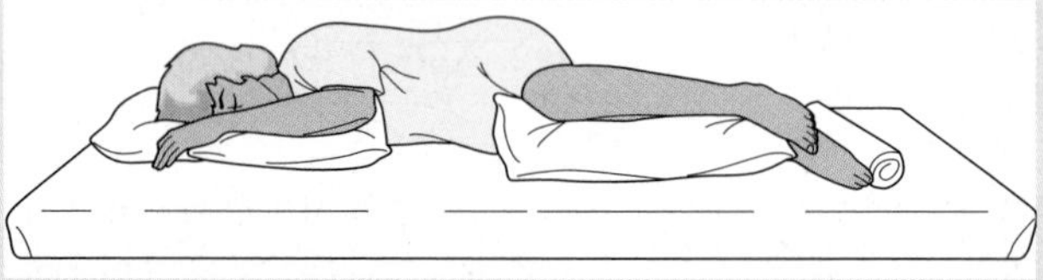

Lateral position (supported)

*The amount of support depends on the needs of the individual client.

(particularly important when client will be standing), and your own strength and ability to move the client.

- Prepare supportive equipment, that is, pillows, trochanter roll, supportive, nonslip footwear, and so on. See Figure 43.12.
- Obtain required assistance. Use mechanical lift device when weight exceeds agency policy maximum lift weight guidelines.
- Explain the procedure to the client and listen to any suggestions the client or support people have.
- Provide privacy.
- Wash hands.
- Raise siderails to ensure safety.
- Raise the height of the bed to bring the client close to your centre of gravity.
- Lock the wheels on the bed, and lower the rail on the side of the bed where you are standing.
- Face in the direction of the movement to prevent spinal twisting.
- Assume a broad stance to increase stability and provide balance.
- Incline your trunk slightly forward, and flex your hips, knees, and ankles to lower your centre of gravity, increase stability, and ensure use of large muscle groups during movements.
- Tighten your gluteal, abdominal, pelvic, leg, and arm muscles to prepare them for action and to prevent injury. When more than one person is lifting, a counting cadence should be raised (1, 2, 3, lift) to ensure that lifting is simultaneous.
- Rock from the front leg to the back leg when pulling or from the back leg to the front leg when pushing to overcome inertia, counteract the client's weight, and help attain a balanced, smooth motion.
- After moving the client, determine the client's comfort, body alignment, tolerance of the activity (e.g., check pulse rate, respirations, oxygen saturation, blood pressure), and safety precautions required (e.g., side rails).
- Document activity, including relevant nursing assessments.

See Procedures 43.1 through 43.4 on moving and turning clients in bed and helping them sit up on the edge of the bed.

Transferring Clients

Many clients require some assistance in transferring between bed and chair or wheelchair, between wheelchair and toilet, and between bed and stretcher. Before transferring any client, however, the nurse must determine the client's physical and mental capabilities to participate in the transfer technique. The client's weight must also be known in order to determine if the transfer can be safely performed with one or more persons assisting or if a mechanical lift needs to be used. In addition, the nurse must mentally analyze and organize the activity. General guidelines for transfer techniques include these:

- Plan what to do and how to do it. Determine the space in which the transfer is maneuvered (bathrooms, for instance, are usually cramped); the number of assistants (one or two) needed to accomplish the transfer safely; the skill of the nurse(s) if a mechanical lift is required; and the client's capabilities.

PROCEDURE 43.1 Moving a Client up in Bed

Clients who have slid down in bed from the Fowler's position or have been pulled down by traction often need assistance to move up in bed.

1. **Adjust the bed and the client's position.**
- Adjust the head of the bed to a flat position if not contraindicated or as low as the client can tolerate. *Moving the client upward against gravity requires more force and can cause back strain.*
- Raise both side rails. Lock wheels of bed.
- Raise the bed to just below your centre of gravity.
- Lock bed brakes. Place a lift sheet under client's trunk.
- Remove all pillows, then place one against the head of the bed. *This pillow protects the client's head from inadvertent injury against the top of the bed during the upward move.*

2. **Elicit the client's help in lessening your workload.**
- Ask the client to flex the hips and knees and position the feet so that they can be used effectively for pushing. Have client flex neck, moving chin to chest if possible. *Flexing the hips and knees keeps the entire lower leg off the bed surface, preventing friction during movement, and ensures use of the large muscle groups in the client's legs when pushing, thus increasing the force of movement.*
- Ask the client to
  - **a.** Raise the upper part of the body on the elbows, and push with the hands and forearms during the move.

  or

  - **b.** Grasp the overhead trapeze with both hands, and lift and pull during the move. *Client assistance provides additional power to overcome inertia and friction during the move. These actions also keep the client's arms partially off the bed surface, reducing friction during movement, and make use of the large muscle groups of the client's arms to increase the force during movement.*

3. **Position yourselves appropriately, and move the client.**
- Face the direction of the movement, and then assume a broad stance with the foot nearest the bed behind the forward foot and weight on the forward foot. Incline your trunk slightly forward from the hips. Flex hips, knees, and ankles.
- A turn sheet should be used to move a client up in bed. *A turn sheet distributes the client's weight more evenly, decreases friction, and exerts a more even force on the client during the move. In addition, it prevents injury of the client's skin because the friction created between two sheets when one is moved is less than that created by the client's body moving over the sheet.*
- Place a drawsheet or a full sheet folded in half under the client, extending from the shoulders to the thighs. Each of you rolls up or fanfolds the turn sheet close to the client's body on either side.
- Both of you then grasp the sheet close to the shoulders and buttocks of the client. *This draws the weight closer to the nurses' centres of gravity and increases the nurses' balance and stability, permitting a smoother movement.*

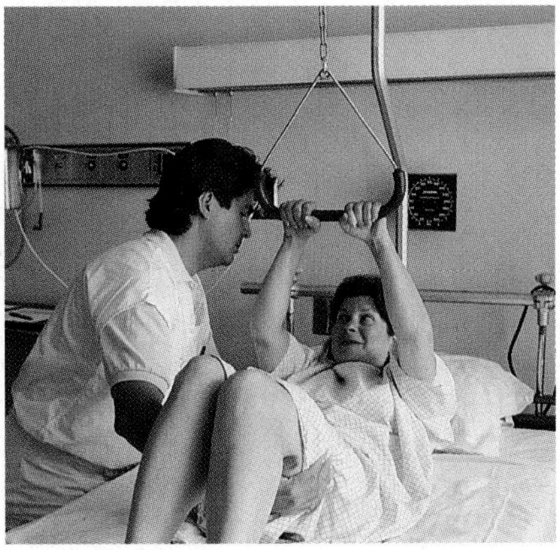

Figure 43.14 Moving a client up in bed

- Tighten your gluteal, pelvic, abdominal, leg, and arm muscles, and rock weight from the back leg to the front leg and back again. *Using the counting cadence, both nurses* shift weight to the front leg as the client pushes with the heels (or lifts with the trapeze) so that the client moves toward the head of the bed.

4. **Ensure client comfort.**
- Elevate the head of the bed, and provide appropriate support devices for the client's new position. Assess client's response. Document.
- See the sections on positioning clients earlier in this chapter.

Variation: A Client Who Has Limited Strength of the Upper Extremities

- Assist the client to flex the hips and knees as in step 2. Place the client's arms across the chest. *This keeps them off the bed surface and minimizes friction during movement.* Ask the client to flex the neck during the move and keep the head off the bed surface.

PROCEDURE 43.2 Turning a Client to a Lateral or Prone Position in Bed

Movement to a lateral (side-lying) position may be necessary when placing a bedpan beneath the client, when changing the client's bed linen, or when repositioning the client.

1. **Position yourself and the client appropriately before performing the move.**

- Wash hands.
- Raise side rails. Ensure bed brakes are on.
- Lower head of bed if not contraindicated.
- Raise bed to working height. Lower side rail on side where you are standing.
- Move the client closer to the side of the bed opposite the side the client will face when turned. *This ensures that the client will be positioned safely in the centre of the bed after turning.* Use a pull sheet beneath the client's trunk and thighs to pull the client to the side of the bed. Roll up the sheet as close as possible to the client's body, and pull the client to the side of the bed, moving the trunk first, then hips, and then the lower legs. Adjust the client's head, and reposition the legs appropriately.
- While standing on the side of the bed nearest the client, place the client's near arm across the chest. Abduct the client's far shoulder slightly from the side of the body. *Pulling the one arm forward facilitates the turning motion. Pulling the other arm away from the body prevents that arm from being caught beneath the client's body during the roll.*
- Place the client's near ankle and foot across the far ankle and foot. *This facilitates the turning motion. Making these preparations on the side of the bed closest to the client helps prevent unnecessary reaching.*
- Raise the side rail next to the client before going to the other side of the bed. *This ensures that the client, who is close to the edge of the mattress, will not fall.*
- Position yourself on the side of the bed toward which the client will turn, directly in line with the client's trunk and as close to the bed as possible.
- Incline your trunk forward from the hips. Flex your hips, knees, and ankles. Assume a broad stance with one foot forward and the weight placed upon this forward foot.

2. **Pull or roll the client to a lateral position.**

- Place one hand on the client's far hip and the other hand on the client's far shoulder (Figure 43.15, *A*). *This position of the hands supports the client at the two heaviest parts of the body, providing greater control in movement during the roll.*
- Tighten your gluteal, pelvic, abdominal, leg, and arm muscles; rock backward, shifting your weight from the forward to the backward foot; and roll the client onto the side of the body to face you (Figure 43.15, *B*).
- Place pillows to maintain the client's lateral position.

Variation: Turning the Client to a Prone Position

To turn a client to the prone position, follow the preceding steps, except:

- Roll the client completely onto the abdomen. *It is essential to move the client as close as possible to the opposite edge of the bed before the turn so that the client will be lying on the centre of the bed after rolling.* Never pull a client across the bed while the client is in the prone position. *Doing so can injure a woman's breasts or a man's genitals.*

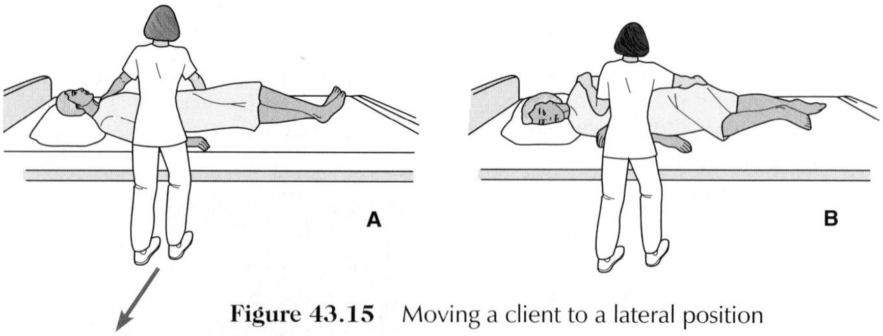

Figure 43.15 Moving a client to a lateral position

PROCEDURE 43.3 Logrolling a Client

Logrolling is a technique used to turn a client whose body must at all times be kept in straight alignment (like a log). An example is the client with a spinal injury. Considerable care must be taken to prevent additional injury. This technique requires at least three nurses or, if the client is large, additional nurses are required. *For the client who has a cervical injury, one nurse must maintain the client's head and neck alignment.*

1. **Position yourselves and the client appropriately before the move.**
   - Raise height of bed to working height. Ensure that bed brakes are on.
   - Stand on the same side of the bed, and assume a broad stance with one foot ahead of the other.
   - Place the client's arms across the chest. *Doing so ensures that they will not be injured or become trapped under the body when the body is turned and maintains alignment during turn.*
   - Incline your trunk, and flex your hips, knees, and ankles.
   - Place your arms under the client as shown in Figure 43.16 or Figure 43.17, depending on the client's size. *Each staff member then has a major weight area of the client centred between the arms.*
   - Tighten your gluteal, pelvic, abdominal, leg, and arm muscles.

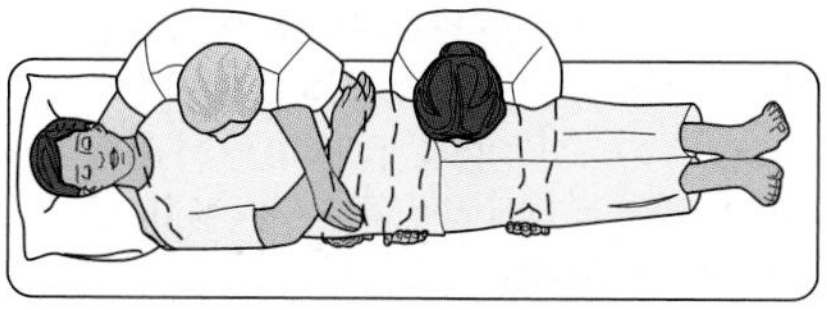

Figure 43.16 Correct arm placement for moving a client to the side of the bed: two nurses

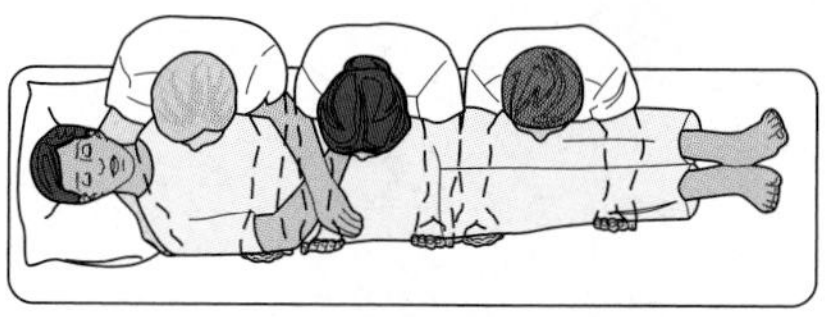

Figure 43.17 Correct arm placement for moving a client to the side of the bed: three nurses

2. **Pull the client to the side of the bed.**
   - One nurse counts, "One, two, three, go." Then, at the same time, all staff members pull the client to the side of the bed by shifting weight to the back foot. *Moving the client in unison maintains the client's body alignment.*
   - Elevate the side rail on this side of the bed. *This prevents the client from falling while lying so close to the edge of the bed.*
3. **Move to the other side of the bed, and place supportive devices for the client when turned.**
   - Place a small pillow where it will support the client's head after the turn. *The pillow prevents lateral flexion of the neck and ensures alignment of the cervical spine.*
   - Place one or two pillows between the client's legs to support the upper leg when the client is turned. *This pillow prevents adduction of the upper leg, keeps the legs parallel and aligned, and prevents twisting of the spine.*
4. **Roll and position the client in proper alignment.**
   - All nurses flex the hips, knees, and ankles and assume a broad stance with one foot forward.

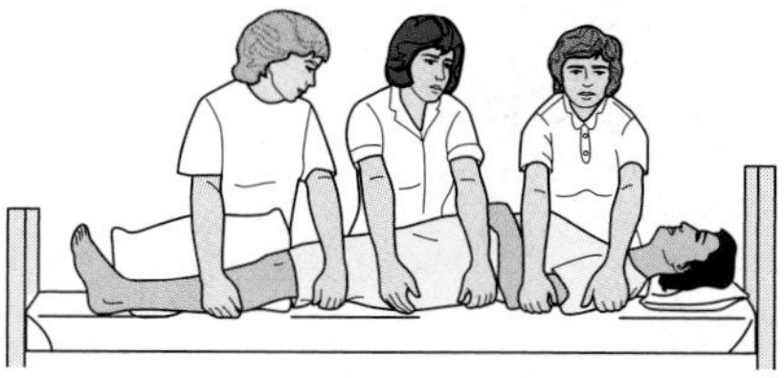

Figure 43.18 Correct hand placement for logrolling a client

   - All nurses reach over the client and place hands as shown in Figure 43.18. *Doing so centres a major weight area of the client between each nurse's arms.*
   - Tighten your gluteal, pelvic, abdominal, leg, and arm muscles.
   - One nurse counts, "One, two, three, lift." Then, at the same time, all nurses roll the client to a lateral position.
   - Place pillows to maintain the client's lateral position. See the discussion of the lateral position on page 1202.

Variation: Using a Turn or Lift Sheet

- Use a turn sheet to facilitate logrolling. First, all staff members stand on the same side of the bed. Assume a broad stance with one foot forward, and grasp half of the fanfolded or rolled edge of the turn sheet. On a signal, pull the client toward both of you (Figure 43.19).

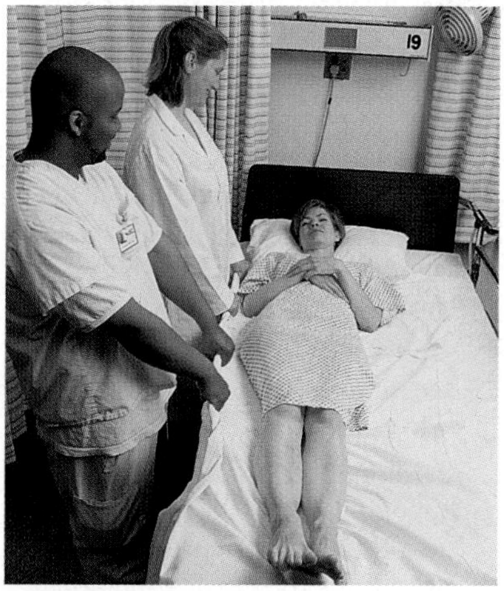

Figure 43.19 Using a turn sheet, the nurses pull the sheet with the client on it to the edge of the bed

PROCEDURE 43.3 Logrolling a Client *continued*

- Before turning the client, place pillow supports for the head and legs, as described in step 3. This helps maintain the client's alignment when turning. Raise side rails, then, go to the other side of the bed (farthest from the client), and assume a stable stance. Reaching over the client, grasp the far edges of the turn sheet, and roll the client toward you. The second nurse (behind the client) helps turn the client and provides pillow supports to ensure good alignment in the lateral position.

PROCEDURE 43.4 Moving a Client to a Sitting Position on the Edge of the Bed

The client assumes a sitting position on the edge of the bed before walking, moving to a chair or wheelchair, eating, or performing other activities.

1. Position yourself and the client appropriately before performing the move.

- Assist the client to a lateral position facing you.
- Raise the head of the bed slowly to a low Fowler's position if not contraindicated. *This decreases the distance that the client needs to move to sit up on the side of the bed.*
- Position the client's feet and lower legs at the edge of the bed. *This enables the client's feet to move easily off the bed during the movement, and the client is aided by gravity into a sitting position.*
- Stand beside the client's hips and face the far corner of the bottom of the bed (the angle in which movement will occur). Assume a broad stance, placing the foot nearest the client forward. Incline your trunk slightly forward from the hips. Flex your hips, knees, and ankles (Figure 43.20, *A*).

2. Move the client to a sitting position.

- Place one arm around the client's shoulders and the other arm beneath both of the client's thighs near the knees (Figure 43.20, *A*). *Supporting the client's shoulders prevents the client from falling backward during the movement. Supporting the client's thighs reduces friction of the thighs against the bed surface during the move and increases the force of the movement.*
- Tighten your gluteal, pelvic, abdominal, leg, and arm muscles.
- Instruct the client to push up with the hand closest to you on the count of three.
- Lift the client's thighs slightly. *This reduces the friction of the client's thighs and the nurse's arm against the bed surface.*
- Pivot on the balls of your feet in the desired direction facing the foot of the bed while pulling the client's feet and legs off the bed (Figure 43.20, *B*). *Pivoting prevents twisting of the nurse's spine. The weight of the client's legs swinging downward increases downward movement of the lower body and helps make the client's upper body vertical.*
- Encourage the client to take a couple of deep breaths.
- Keep supporting the client until the client is well balanced and comfortable. *This movement may cause some clients to faint.*
- Assess vital signs (e.g., pulse, respirations, and blood pressure) as indicated by the client's health status.

Variation: Teaching a Client How to Sit on the Side of the Bed Independently

A client who has had recent abdominal surgery or who is weak may have too much abdominal pain or too little strength to sit straight up in bed. This person can be taught to assume a "dangle" position without assistance. Instruct the client to do the following:

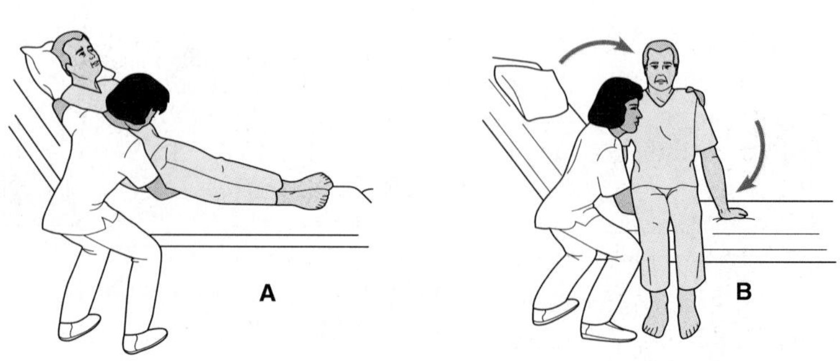

Figure 43.20 Assisting a client to a sitting position on the edge of the bed

PROCEDURE 43.4 Moving a Client to a Sitting Position on the Edge of the Bed *continued*

- Roll to the side and lift the far leg over the near leg (Figure 43.21, *A*).
- Grasp the mattress edge with the lower arm and push the fist of the upper arm into the mattress (Figure 43.21, *B*).
- Push up with the arms as the heels and legs slide over the mattress edge (Figure 43.21, *B*).
- Maintain the sitting position by pushing both fists into the mattress behind and to the sides of the buttocks.

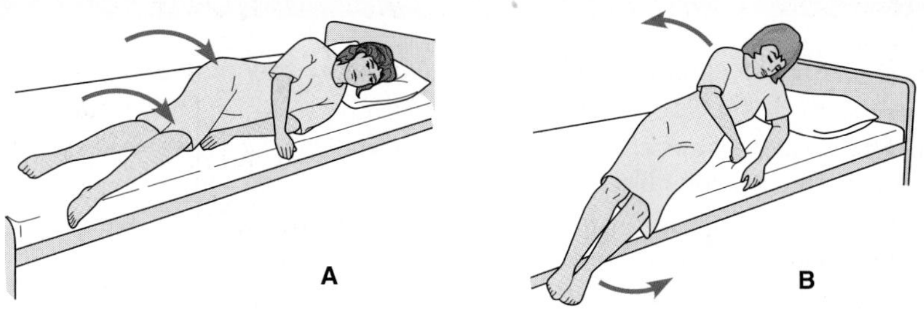

Figure 43.21 Moving to a sitting position independently

- Check physician's orders and agency policies.
- Obtain essential equipment before starting (e.g., transfer belt, wheelchair), and check its function.
- Remove obstacles from the area used for the transfer.
- Explain the transfer to the client, including what the client should do.
- Explain the transfer to the nursing personnel who are helping; specify who will give directions (one person needs to be in charge).
- Place equipment to allow client to move toward stronger side.
- Always support or hold the client rather than the equipment.
- During the transfer, explain step-by-step what the client should do, for example, "Move your right foot forward."
- Make a written plan of the transfer, including the client's tolerance (e.g., pulse and respiratory rates, blood pressure, and oxygen saturation).

Because wheelchairs and stretchers are unstable, they can predispose the client to falls and injury. Guidelines for the safe use of wheelchairs and stretchers are shown in the two boxes that follow.

Transfer (walking) belts provide the greatest safety. This belt may have a handle that allows the nurse to control movement of the client during the transfer. Most health-care agencies require personnel to use the transfer belt to ambulate or move clients. See Procedure 43.5 for transferring a client between a bed and a chair and Procedure 43.6 for transferring a client between a bed and a stretcher.

CLINICAL GUIDELINES

Wheelchair Safety

- Always lock the brakes on both wheels of the wheelchair when the client transfers in or out of it. Locks should be used at all times, except when the client is being moved.
- Remove (if possible) or raise the footplates before transferring the client into the wheelchair.
- Lower the footplates after the transfer, and place the client's feet on them.
- Ensure the client is positioned well back in the seat of the wheelchair.
- Ensure body alignment is maintained. Protect extremities when transporting client (for example, through doorways).
- Use a seat belt. Seat belts that fasten behind the wheelchair protect confused clients from falls.
- Back the wheelchair into or out of an elevator, rear large wheels first.
- Place your body between the wheelchair and the bottom of an incline.
- Use the tipping levers to maneuver up or down curbs.

CLINICAL GUIDELINES

Safe Use of Stretchers

- Lock the wheels of the bed and stretcher before the client transfers in or out of them.
- Fasten safety straps across the client on a stretcher, and raise the side rails.
- Never leave a client unattended on a stretcher unless the wheels are locked and the side rails are raised on both sides and/or the safety straps are securely fastened across the client.
- Always push a stretcher from the end where the client's head is positioned. This position protects the client's head in the event of a collision.
- If the stretcher has two swivel wheels and two stationary wheels:
  a. Always position the client's head at the end with the stationary wheels.

  and

  b. Push the stretcher from the end with the stationary wheels. The stretcher is maneuvered more easily when pushed from this end.
- Maneuver the stretcher when entering the elevator so that the client's head goes in first.

PROCEDURE 43.5 Transferring a Client between a Bed and a Chair

A client may need to be transferred between the bed and a wheelchair or chair, the bed and the commode, or a wheelchair and the toilet. There are numerous variations of the technique. Which variation the nurse selects depends on a number of factors: the client's disabilities, body size, and weight, the technique with which the client is familiar, the client's tolerance for activity, the client's level of cognition (understanding), the space in which the transfer is maneuvered (bathrooms, for instance, are usually cramped), the number of assistants needed to accomplish the transfer safely, and the skill of the nurse(s).

Equipment

- ❑ Transfer (walking) belt
- ❑ Nonslip footwear for client

INTERVENTION

1. Position the equipment appropriately.

- Lower the bed to its lowest position so that the client's feet will rest flat on the floor. Lock the wheels of the bed.
- Place the wheelchair parallel to the bed as close to the bed as possible (Figure 43.22). The wheelchair should be placed at the end of the bed next to the client's unaffected arm (if applicable). This way, the client can use the wheelchair armrest (if not removed) to help support self during transfer. Lock the wheels of the wheelchair, and remove, if possible, or raise the footplate. Remove the arm of the wheelchair closest to the bed, if necessary.

2. Prepare and assess the client.

- Assist the client to a sitting position on the side of the bed. See Procedure 43.4.

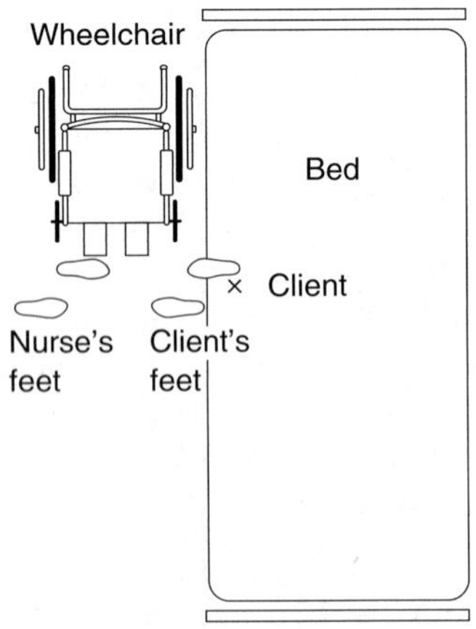

Figure 43.22 The wheelchair is placed parallel to the bed as close to the bed as possible. Note that placement of the nurse's feet mirrors that of the client's feet.

- Assess the client for orthostatic hypotension before moving the client from the bed.
- Assist the client in putting on a bathrobe and nonskid slippers or shoes.
- Place a transfer belt snugly around the client's waist. Check to be certain that the belt is securely fastened.

3. Give explicit instructions to the client. Ask the client to do the following:

- Move forward and sit on the edge of the bed. *This brings the client's centre of gravity closer to the nurse's.*
- Lean forward slightly from the hips. *This brings the client's centre of gravity more directly over the base of support and positions the head and trunk in the direction of the movement.*
- Place the foot of the stronger leg beneath the edge of the bed, and put the other foot forward. *In this way, the client can use the stronger leg muscles to stand and power the movement. A broader base of*

PROCEDURE 43.5 Transferring a Client between a Bed and a Chair *continued*

support makes the client more stable during the transfer.

- Place the client's hands on the bed surface or on your waist so that the client can push while standing. *This provides additional force for the movement and reduces the potential for strain on the nurse's back.* The client should not grasp your neck or shoulders for support. *Doing so can injure the nurse.*

4. Position yourself correctly.

- Stand directly in front of the client. Incline the trunk slightly forward from the hips. Flex the hips, knees, and ankles. Assume a broad stance, placing one foot forward and one back. Mirror the placement of the client's feet, if possible. *This helps prevent loss of balance during the transfer.*
- Encircle the client's waist with your arms, and grasp the transfer belt at the client's back (Figure 43.23) with thumbs pointing downward. *The belt provides a secure handle for holding onto the client and controlling the movement. Downward placement of the thumbs prevents potential wrist injury as the nurse lifts. By supporting the client in this manner, you keep the client from tilting backward during the transfer.*
- Tighten your gluteal, pelvic, abdominal, leg, and arm muscles.

5. Assist the client to stand, and then move together toward the wheelchair.

- On the count of three:
  - **a.** Ask the client to stand.
  - **b.** You push with the forward foot, rock to the back foot, extend the joints of the lower extremities, and pull the client (directly toward your centre of gravity) into a standing position.
- Support the client in an upright standing position for a few moments. *This allows the nurse and the client to extend the joints and provides the nurse with an opportunity to ensure that the client is all right before moving away from the bed.*

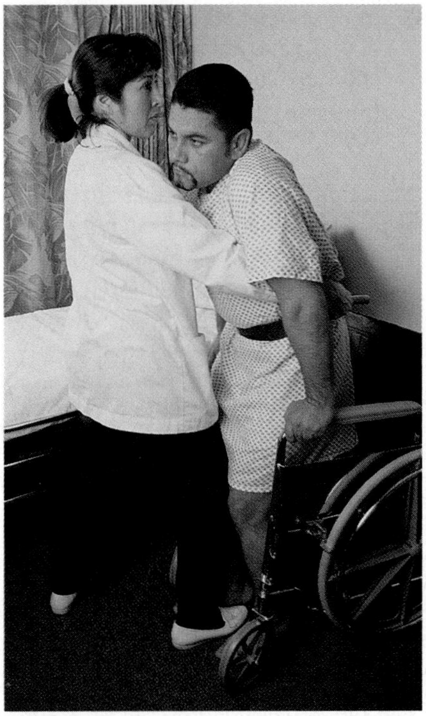

Figure 43.23 Using a transfer (walking) belt

- Together, pivot toward the wheelchair.

6. Assist the client to sit.

- Ask the client to
  - **a.** Back up to the wheelchair and place the legs against the seat. *Having the client place the legs against the wheelchair seat minimizes the risk of the client's falling when sitting down.*
  - **b.** Place the foot of the stronger leg slightly behind the other. *This supports body weight during the movement.*
  - **c.** Keep the other foot forward. *This provides a broad base of support.*
  - **d.** Place both hands on the wheelchair arms. *This increases stability and lessens the strain on the nurse.*
- Stand directly in front of the client. Place one foot forward and one back.
- Tighten your grasp on the transfer belt, and tighten your gluteal, pelvic, abdominal, leg, and arm muscles.
- On the count of three:
  - **a.** Have the client shift the body weight by rocking to the back foot, lower the body onto the edge of the wheelchair seat by flexing the joints of the legs and arms, and place some body weight on the arms, while
  - **b.** You shift your body weight by stepping back with the forward foot and pivoting toward the chair while lowering the client onto the wheelchair seat.

7. Ensure client safety.

- Ask the client to push back into the wheelchair seat. *Sitting well back on the seat provides a broader base of support and greater stability and minimizes the risk of falling from the wheelchair. A wheelchair can topple forward when the client sits on the edge of the seat and leans far forward.*
- Lower the footplates, and place the client's feet on them.
- Apply a seat belt as required. This also maintains body alignment.

Variation: Transferring without a Belt

- If a transfer belt is not available, a client who needs minimal assistance may be supported during transfer by having the nurse place the hands against the sides of the client's chest (not at the axillae) during the transfer (Figure 43.24). Avoid placing hands or pressure on the axillae, especially for clients who have upper extremity paralysis or paresis. It is advisable to use a transfer belt for all clients who require assistance in transferring.
- Follow the steps described previously.

Variation: Transferring with a Belt and Two Nurses

- When the client is ready to stand, position yourselves on both sides of the client, facing the same direction as the client. Flex your hips, knees, and ankles; grasp the

PROCEDURE 43.5 Transferring a Client between a Bed and a Chair *continued*

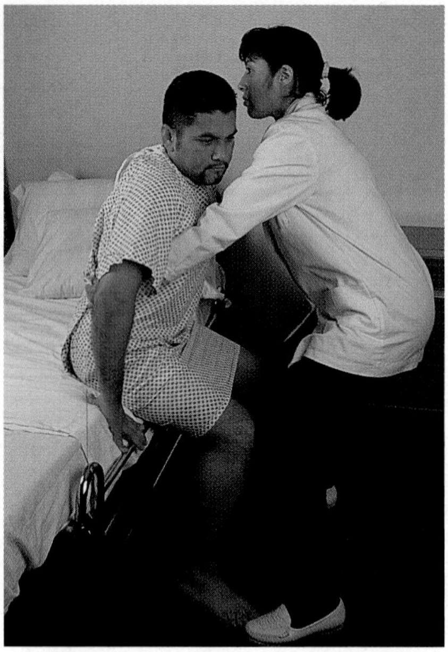

Figure 43.24 Transferring without a belt

client's transfer belt at the back with the hand closest to the client; and with the other hand, support the client's elbows.

- Coordinating your efforts, all three of you stand simultaneously, pivot, and move to the wheelchair. Reverse the process to lower the client onto the wheelchair seat.

Variation: Transferring a Client with an Injured Lower Extremity or Hemiparesis

When the client has an injured lower extremity, movement should always occur toward the client's unaffected (strong) side. For example, if the client's right leg is injured and the client is sitting on the edge of the bed preparing to transfer to a wheelchair, position the wheelchair on the client's left side. *In this way, the client can use the unaffected leg most effectively and safely.*

Variation: Using a Sliding Board

Have a client who cannot stand use a sliding board to move without nursing assistance. This method not only promotes the client's sense of independence but preserves your energy (Figure 43.25).

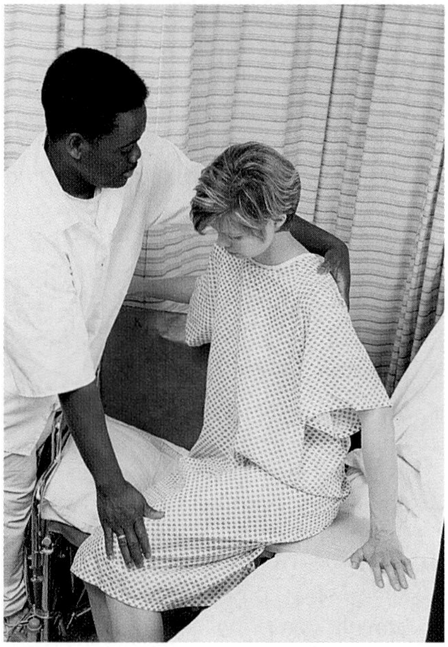

Figure 43.25 Using a sliding board

PROCEDURE 43.6 Transferring a Client between a Bed and a Stretcher

The stretcher, or gurney, is used to transfer supine clients from one location to another. Whenever the client is capable of accomplishing the transfer from bed to stretcher independently, either by lifting onto it or by rolling onto it, the client should be encouraged to do so. If the client cannot move onto the stretcher independently, at least two nurses are needed to assist with the transfer; more may be needed or a mechanical lift should be used if the weight being lifted exceeds agency policy for maximum lift weight.

Equipment

- ❑ Stretcher
- ❑ Roller bar, long board, or slider sheet (sliding board)
- ❑ Lift sheet
- ❑ Mechanical lift may be required

INTERVENTION

1. Adjust the client's bed in preparation for the transfer.

- Lower the head of the bed until it is flat or as low as the client can tolerate.
- Raise the bed so that it is slightly higher than the surface of the stretcher. *It is easier for the client to move down an incline.*
- Ensure that the wheels on the bed are locked.
- Pull the drawsheet out from both sides of the bed.

PROCEDURE 43.6 Transferring a Client between a Bed and a Stretcher *continued*

2. **Move the client to the edge of the bed, and position the stretcher.**
- Roll the drawsheet as close to the client's side as possible.
- Pull the client to the edge of the bed, and cover the client with a sheet or bath blanket to maintain comfort.
- Place the stretcher parallel to the bed, next to the client, and lock its wheels.
- Fill the gap that exists between the bed and the stretcher loosely with the glider or roller.

3. **Transfer the client securely to the stretcher.**
- Using the counting cadence in unison with the other staff members, press your body tightly against the stretcher. *This prevents the stretcher from moving.*
- Roll the pull sheet tightly against the client. *This achieves better control over client movement.*
- Flex your hips, and pull the client on the pull sheet in unison directly toward you and onto the stretcher. *Pulling downward requires less force than pulling along a flat surface.*
- Ask the client to flex the neck during the move, if possible, and place arms across the chest. *This prevents injury to these body parts.*
- A slider sheet may be used to decrease friction between the bed and client, facilitating easier movement.

4. **Ensure client comfort and safety.**
- Make the client comfortable, unlock the stretcher wheels, and move the stretcher away from the bed.
- Immediately raise the stretcher side rails and fasten the safety straps across the client. *Because the stretcher is high and narrow, the client is in danger of falling unless these safety precautions are taken.*

Variation: Using a Roller Bar During the Transfer

A roller bar is a metal frame covered with longitudinal rollers. Place the bar over the gap between the bed and the stretcher. Using a pull sheet, pull the client onto the roller bar, and roll the client easily onto the stretcher.

Variation: Using a Long Board

The long board, which may be referred to as the Smooth Mover or Easyglide, is a lacquered or smooth polyethylene board measuring 45 to 55 cm by 182 cm with handholds along its edges. This device may be used by two nurses alone or up to four nurses together. Turn the client to a lateral position away from you, position the board close to the client's back, and roll the client onto the board. Pull the client and board across the bed to the stretcher. Safety belts may be placed over the chest, abdomen, and legs. Place client in lateral position to remove board.

Variation: Using a Three-Person Carry (Use Caution)

Three people of about equal height stand side-by-side facing the client.

Recommendations vary as to which staff member lifts a specific area of the client. Often, the strongest person supports the heaviest part of the client or the tallest person with the longest reach supports the head and shoulders. The stretcher or bed to which the client will be moved is placed at a right angle at the foot of the bed. The wheels of the bed and stretcher are locked. Each person flexes the knees and places the foot nearest to the stretcher slightly forward.

The arms of the lifters are put under the client at the head and shoulders, hips and thighs, and upper and lower legs. The lifters then, on the count of three, roll the client onto their chests and step back in unison. They then pivot around to the stretcher and lower the client by flexing their knees and hips until their elbows are on the surface of the stretcher. The client is then released on the stretcher surface and is aligned and covered, and the stretcher side rails are raised.

PROCEDURE 43.7 Using a Hydraulic (Electronic Operated) Lift to Transfer Clients from Bed to Chair

The nurse considers several factors in deciding when a mechanical lift is most appropriate to transfer a client from bed to chair. The nurse assesses the client's weight and level of mobility to safely transfer from bed to chair. The nurse should know that lifting an object weighing greater than 35 percent of their own body weight is unsafe. Other factors to consider are: the patient's ability to comprehend instructions, the ability to assist during the move, and the client's degree of comfort. In doubtful cases, the nurse should request the assistance of another nurse or use a mechanical lift.

Using a mechanical lift requires specialized training on the specific lift and use of proper body mechanics. The nurse should be familiar with the agency policy that may require yearly recertification.

PROCEDURE 43.7 Using a Hydraulic (Electronic Operated) Lift to Transfer Clients from Bed to Chair *continued*

INTERVENTION

1. **Identify specific mobility restrictions and explain the procedure to the client. Assess as discussed above.**
2. **Prepare the client and surroundings.**
   - Clear the environment so that the lift can be brought to the bedside.
   - With a nurse on each side of the bed (bed flat), roll the patient onto his/her side and place the support sling under the client to ensure that the client's weight is evenly distributed over the fabric (from shoulders to knees).
3. **Position the hydraulic lift so that the frame is centred over the client.**
   - Have the client's chair nearby.
   - Lower horizontal bar to support the sling using the handset.
   - Attach the support sling to the frame, adhering to the manufacture's instructions.
   - Elevate head of bed and fold client's arms over chest.
   - Warn the client that he/she will be lifted from the bed.
   - Raise the client off the bed.
   - Use steering handle to pull lift from the bed and manoeuvre to chair.
   - Lower client into the chair.
   - Align client in chair and remove straps and frame away from the bed.
   - The sling remains in place under the client and is reattached to the frame when the client is moved back to bed.

Providing ROM Exercises

When people are ill, they often need to perform ROM exercises until they regain their normal activity levels. **Active ROM exercises** are isotonic exercises in which the client moves each joint in the body through its complete range of movement, maximally stretching all muscle groups within each plane over the joint. These exercises maintain or increase muscle strength and endurance and help maintain cardiorespiratory function in an immobilized client. They also prevent deterioration of joint capsules, ankylosis, and contractures. Instructions for the client performing active ROM exercises are shown in the accompanying box.

Full ROM does not occur spontaneously in the immobilized individual who independently achieves ADLs, independently moves about in bed, independently transfers between bed and wheelchair or chair, or independently ambulates a short distance because only a few muscle groups are maximally stretched during these activities. Although the client may successfully achieve some active ROM movements of the upper extremities while combing the hair, bathing, and dressing, the immobilized client is very unlikely to achieve any active ROM movements of the lower extremities when these are not used in the normal functions of standing and walking about. For this reason, most wheelchair and many ambulatory clients need active ROM exercises until they regain their normal activity levels.

At first, the nurse may need to teach the client to perform the needed ROM exercises; eventually, the client may be able to accomplish these independently.

During **passive ROM exercises,** another person moves each of the client's joints through its complete range of movement, maximally stretching all muscle groups within each plane over each joint. Because the client does not contract the muscles, passive ROM exercises are of no value in maintaining muscle strength but are useful in maintaining joint flexibility. For this reason, passive ROM exercises should be performed only when the client is unable to accomplish the movements actively.

Passive ROM exercises should be accomplished for each movement of the arms, legs, and neck *that the client is unable to achieve actively.* As with active ROM exercises, passive ROM exercises should be accomplished to the point of slight resistance, but not beyond, and never to the point of discomfort. The movements should be systematic, and the same sequence should be followed during each exercise session. Each exercise should consist of three repetitions, and the series of exercises should be done at least three times daily.

CLIENT TEACHING

Active ROM Exercises

- Perform each ROM exercise as taught to the point of slight resistance, but not beyond, and never to the point of discomfort.
- Perform the movements systematically, using the same sequence during each session.
- Perform each exercise three times.
- Perform each series of exercises at least three times daily.
- Emphasize that ROM exercise is also achieved while client carries out ADLs, such as walking, dressing, combing hair, showering, and preparing a meal.

CLINICAL GUIDELINES

Providing Passive ROM Exercises

- Ensure that the client understands the reason for doing ROM exercises.
- If there is a possibility of hand swelling, make sure rings are removed.
- Clothe the client in a loose gown, and cover the body with a bath blanket.
- Use correct body mechanics when providing ROM exercise to avoid muscle strain or injury to both yourself and the client.
- Position the bed at an appropriate height.
- Expose only the limb being exercised to avoid embarrassing the client.
- Support the client's limbs above and below the joint as needed to prevent muscle strain or injury (Figure 43.26). This may also be done by cupping joints in the palm of your hand or cradling limbs along your forearm (Figure 43.27). If a joint is painful (e.g., arthritic), support the limb in the muscular areas above and below the joint.
- Use a firm, comfortable grip when handling the limb.
- Move the body parts smoothly, slowly, and rhythmically. Jerky movements cause discomfort and, possibly, injury. Fast movements can cause *spasticity* (sudden, prolonged involuntary muscle contraction) or *rigidity* (stiffness or inflexibility).
- Avoid moving or forcing a body part beyond the existing range of motion. Muscle strain, pain, and injury can result. This is particularly important for people with flaccid (limp) paralysis, whose muscles can be stretched and joints dislocated without their awareness.
- If muscle spasticity occurs during movement, stop the movement temporarily, but continue to apply slow, gentle pressure on the part until the muscle relaxes; then proceed with the motion.
- If a contracture is present, apply slow firm pressure, without causing pain, to stretch the muscle fibres.
- If rigidity occurs, apply slight pressure against the rigidity, and continue the exercise slowly if possible.

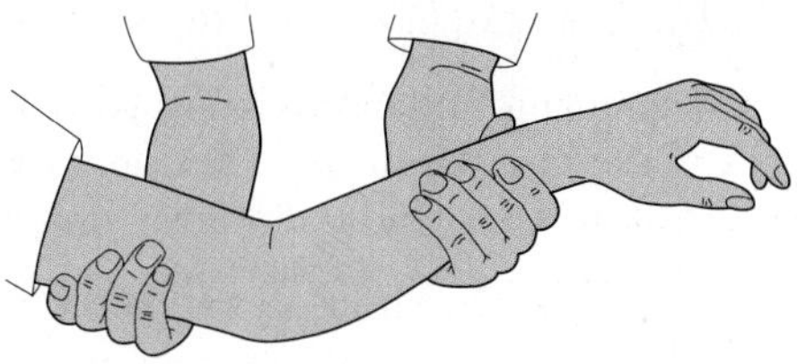

Figure 43.26 Supporting a limb above and below the joint for passive exercise

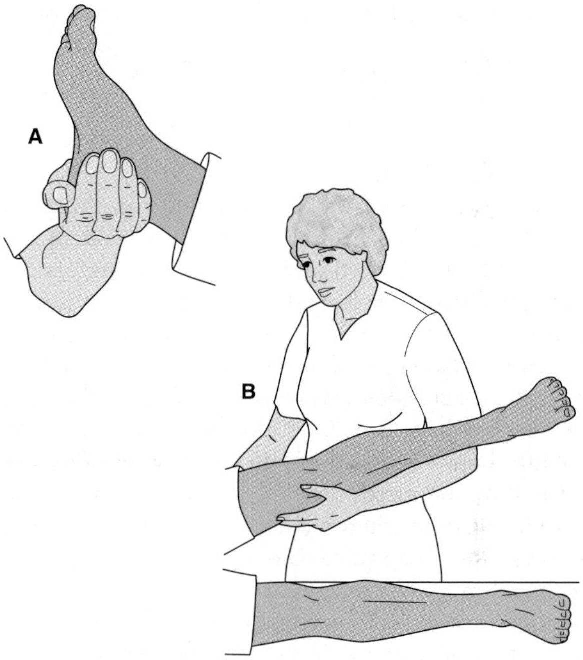

Figure 43.27 Holding limbs for support during passive exercise: *A,* cupping; *B,* cradling

Performing one series of exercises along with the bath is helpful. Passive ROM exercises are accomplished most effectively when the client lies supine in bed.

General guidelines for providing passive exercises are shown in the box above.

During **active-assistive ROM exercises,** the client uses a stronger, opposite arm or leg to move each of the joints of a limb incapable of active motion. The client learns to support and move the weak arm or leg with the strong arm or leg as far as possible. Then, the nurse continues the movement passively to its maximal degree. This activity increases active movement on the strong side of the client's body and maintains joint flexibility on the weak side. Such exercise is especially useful for stroke victims who are hemiplegic (paralyzed on one half of the body). Some clients who begin with passive ROM exercises after a disability progress to active-assistive ROM exercises and, finally, to active ROM exercises.

Functional joint flexibility is also maintained in the performance of activities of daily living (ADLs). The following are examples:

- Eating, shaving, grooming, and bathing exercise the elbow (flexion and extension) and shoulder (abduction).
- Activities requiring fine motor skills, such as writing and eating, exercise the fingers (flexion, extension, adduction, abduction) and the thumb (opposition).
- Walking exercises the shoulders (flexion, extension), hip (flexion, extension, hyperextension), knee (flexion, extension), and ankle (plantar flexion and dorsiflexion).
- Reaching for articles exercises the shoulders (flexion, extension, and perhaps slight abduction or adduction).
- Dressing involves many joint movements.

Ambulating Clients

Ambulation (the act of walking) is a function that most people take for granted. However, when people are ill they are often confined to bed and are thus nonambulatory. The longer clients are in bed, the more difficulty they have walking.

Even one or two days of bed rest can make a person feel weak, unsteady, and shaky when first getting out of bed. A client who has had surgery, is elderly, or who has been immobilized for a longer time will feel more pronounced weakness. The potential problems of immobility are far less likely to occur when clients become ambulatory as soon as possible. The nurse can assist clients to prepare for ambulation by helping them become as independent as possible while in bed. Nurses should encourage clients to perform ADLs, maintain good body alignment, and carry out active range-of-motion exercises to the maximum degree possible yet within the limitations imposed by their illness and recovery program.

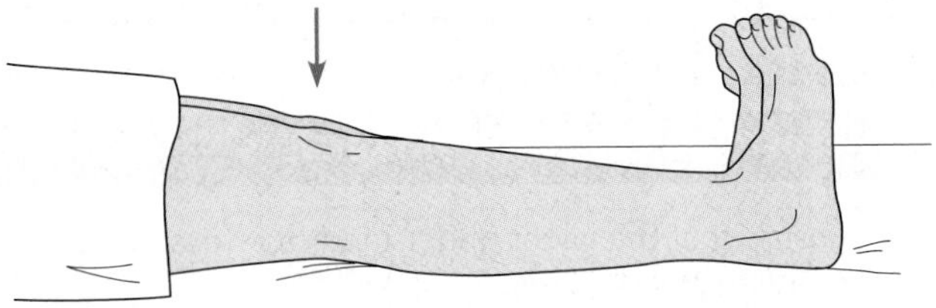

Figure 43.28 Tensing the quadriceps femoris muscles before ambulation

Preambulatory Exercises

Clients who have been in bed for long periods often need a plan of isometric exercises to strengthen the muscles used for walking before attempting to walk. A physician's order may be required. One of the most important muscle groups is the quadriceps femoris, which extends the knee and flexes the thigh. This group is also important for elevating the legs, for example, for walking upstairs. These exercises are frequently called *quadriceps drills* or *sets*. To strengthen these muscles, the client consciously tenses them, drawing the kneecap upward and inward. The client pushes the popliteal space of the knee against the bed surface, relaxing the heels on the bed surface (Figure 43.28). On the count of 1, the muscles are tensed; they are held during the counts of 2, 3, 4; and they are relaxed at the count of 5. The exercise should be done within the client's tolerance, that is, without fatiguing the muscles. Carried out several times an hour during waking hours, this simple exercise significantly strengthens the muscles used for walking.

Assisting Clients to Ambulate

Clients who have been immobilized for even a few days may require assistance with ambulation. The amount of assistance will depend on the client's condition, including age, health status, cognition, and length of inactivity. Assistance may mean walking alongside the client while providing physical support (see Procedure 43.8) or providing instruction to the client about the use of assistive devices such as a cane, walker, or crutches (see the next section).

PROCEDURE 43.8 Assisting a Client to Walk

Equipment

❑ Walking belt

INTERVENTION

1. Prepare the client for ambulation.

- Apply elastic (anti-embolisim) stockings as required. See Procedure 44.2.
- Take baseline vital signs.
- Assist the client to sit on the edge of the bed.
- Assess the client carefully for signs and symptoms of orthostatic hypotension (dizziness, lightheadedness, pallor, or a sudden increase in blood pressure and heart rate) prior to leaving the bedside.
- Ensure that the client is appropriately dressed to walk and wears shoes or slippers with nonskid soles. *Proper attire and footwear prevent chilling and falling.*

PROCEDURE 43.8 Assisting a Client to Walk *continued*

- Assist the client to stand by the side of the bed until the client feels secure.
- Plan the length of the walk with the client in light of the nursing or physician's orders. Be prepared to shorten the walk according to the person's activity tolerance.

One Nurse

2. Ensure client safety while assisting the client to ambulate.

- Encourage the client to ambulate independently if the client is able, but walk to the side of the client, slightly behind.
- Remain physically close to the client in case assistance is needed at any point.
- Make sure the transfer belt is pulled snugly around the client's waist and fastened securely. Grasp the belt at the client's back, and walk behind and slightly to one side of the client (Figure 43.29). The client's forearm can be supported with the other hand. If more support is needed, the nurse can grasp the transfer belt towards the front of the client with the other hand.
- If it is the client's first time out of bed following surgery, injury, or an extended period of immobility, or if the client is quite weak or unstable, have an assistant follow you and the client with a wheelchair in case it is needed quickly.
- Two persons may need to assist the client by each grasping the transfer belt at the client's back and supporting the client from the opposite side.
- If the client is very weak and unstable, grasp the transfer belt at the back with your near arm, and with your other arm support the client's near arm at the elbow. Walk on the client's stronger side.
- Encourage the client to assume a normal walking stance and gait as much as possible.

3. Protect the client who begins to fall while ambulating.

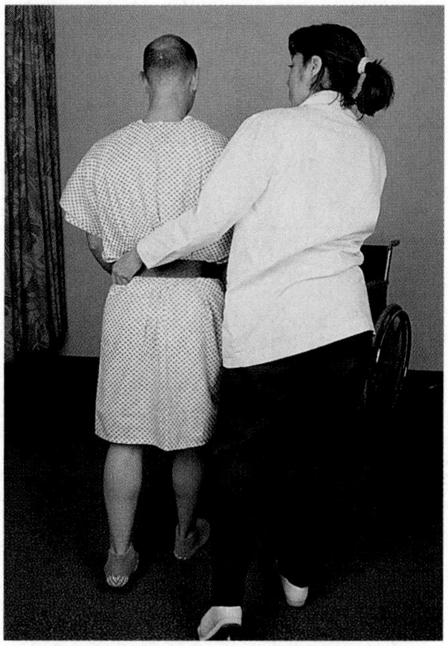

Figure 43.29 Using a transfer (walking) belt to support the client

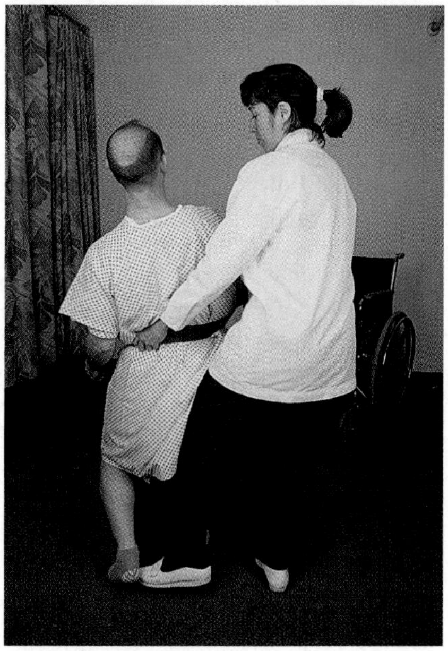

Figure 43.30 Lowering a fainting client to the floor

- If a client begins to experience the signs and symptoms of orthostatic hypotension or extreme weakness, quickly assist the client into a nearby wheelchair or other chair, and help the client to lower the head between the knees if not contraindicated. *Lowering the head facilitates blood flow to the brain.*
- Stay with the client. *A client who faints while in this position could fall, head first, out of the chair.*
- When the weakness subsides, assist the client back to bed.
- If a chair is not close by, assist the client to a horizontal position on the floor before fainting occurs (Figure 43.30). *A vertical position may increase feelings of faintness.*
  - **a.** Assume a broad stance with one foot in front of the other. *A broad stance widens the nurse's base of support for stability. Placing one foot behind the other allows the nurse to rock backward and use the femoral muscles when supporting the client's weight and lowering the centre of gravity (see step b), thus preventing back strain.*
  - **b.** Bring the client backward so that your body supports the person. *Clients who do faint or start to fall and cannot regain their strength or balance usually drop straight downward or pitch slightly forward because of the momentum of ambulating; thus, their head, hips, and knees are most vulnerable to injury. Bringing the client's weight backward against the nurse's body allows gradual movement to the floor without injury to the client.*
  - **c.** Allow the client to slide down your leg, and lower the person gently to the floor, making sure the client's head does not hit any objects.

Two Nurses

4. Prepare the client.

- See step 1.

5. Ensure client safety.

- After the client stands, assume a position with one nurse at either side.

PROCEDURE 43.8 Assisting a Client to Walk *continued*

- Place a walking belt around the client's waist. Each nurse grasps the side handle (or transfer belt at the back of patient) with the near hand and the lower aspect of the client's upper arm with the other hand.
- Walk in unison with the client, using a smooth, even gait at the same speed and with steps the same size as the client's. *This gives the client a greater feeling of security.*
- If the client starts to fall and cannot regain strength or balance, each nurse widens the base of support, grasps the transfer belt with both hands (or one hand on each forearm; one hand on the back of the transfer belt), and together the nurses lower the person gently to the floor or to a nearby chair (Figure 43.32). *Placing the nurses' hands on the transfer belt balances the client's weight between the two nurses, preventing injury to both the nurses and the client.*

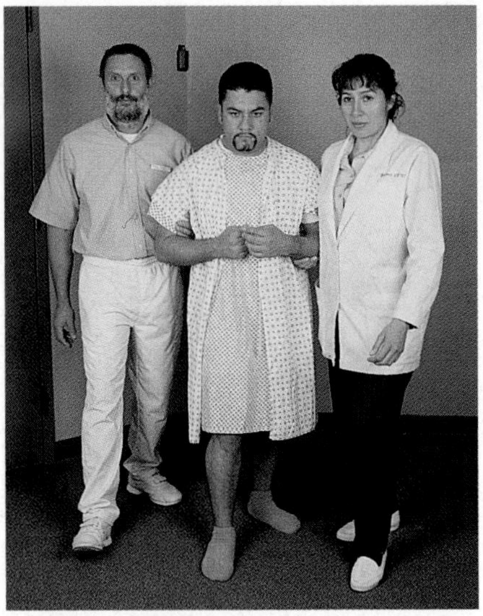

Figure 43.31 Two nurses supporting an ambulatory client

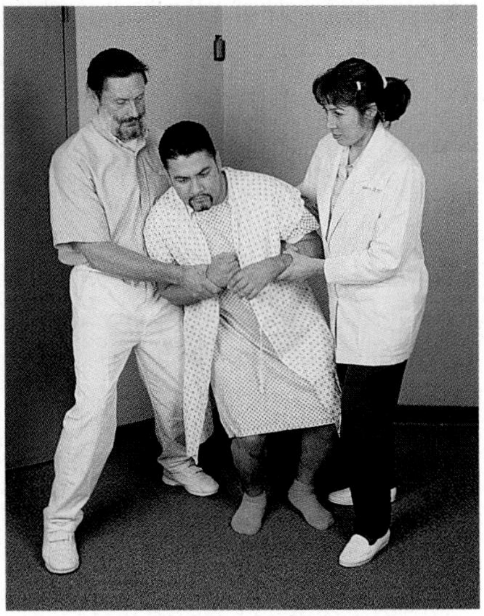

Figure 43.32 Two nurses lowering a fainting client to the floor

6. Document all relevant information.

- Document the time of the walk, the distance walked or time taken, and all nursing assessments, including activity tolerance (e.g., blood pressure, pulse, respirations before, during, and after activity, oxygen saturation).

CLIENT TEACHING

Controlling Postural Hypotension

- Sleep with the head of the bed elevated 20–30 degrees. This position makes the position change on rising less severe.
- Avoid sudden changes in position. Arise from bed in three stages:
  a. Sit up in bed for at least one minute (or until symptoms subside).
  b. Sit on the side of the bed with legs dangling for at least one minute.
  c. Stand with care, holding onto the edge of the bed or another nonmovable object for at least one minute. Gradual changes in position stimulate renin (a kidney enzyme that has a role in regulating blood pressure), which prevents a dramatic drop in pressure.
- Never bend down all the way to the floor or stand up too quickly after stooping. Baroreceptors (sensory nerve endings in the walls of blood vessels) cannot accommodate rapid change.
- Postpone activities, such as shaving and hair grooming, for at least one hour after rising. Baroreceptor reflexes are slow to respond after a night of recumbency during sleep.
- Wear elastic stockings at night to inhibit venous pooling in the legs.
- Be aware that the symptoms of hypotension are most severe at the following times:
  a. 30 to 60 minutes after a heavy meal
  b. One to two hours after taking an antihypertension medication
- Get out of a warm bath very slowly because warm temperatures can lead to venous pooling. Avoid hot water for bathing.
- Use a rocking chair to improve circulation in the lower extremities. Even mild leg conditioning can strengthen muscle tone and enhance circulation.
- Refrain from any strenuous activity that results in holding the breath and bearing down. This Valsalva maneuver slows the heart rate, leading to subsequent lowering of blood pressure.

Some clients experience postural (orthostatic) hypotension on assuming a vertical position from a lying position and may need information about ways to control this problem (see the previous box). The client may exhibit some or all of the following symptoms: pallor, diaphoresis, nausea, tachycardia, and dizziness. If any of these are present, the client should be assisted to a supine position in bed and closely assessed.

Using Mechanical Aids for Walking

Canes

Three types of canes are used today: the standard straight-legged cane; the tripod or crab cane, which has three feet; and the quad cane, which has four feet and provides the most support (Figure 43.33). Cane tips should have rubber caps to improve traction and prevent slipping. The standard cane is 91 cm long; some aluminum canes can be adjusted from 56 to 97 cm. The length should permit the elbow to be slightly flexed. Clients may use either one or two canes depending on how much support they require. The box right provides instructions for clients regarding the use of a cane.

Walkers

Walkers are mechanical devices for ambulatory clients who need more support than a cane provides. There are many types of walkers of different shapes and sizes, with devices suited to individual needs. The standard type is made of polished aluminum. It has four legs with rubber tips and plastic hand grips (Figure 43.34). Many walkers have adjustable legs.

The standard walker needs to be picked up to be used. The client, therefore, requires partial strength in both hands and wrists; strong elbow extensors, such as triceps brachii; and strong shoulder depressors, such as the pectoralis minor. The client also needs the ability to bear at least partial weight on both legs.

Four-wheeled and two-wheeled models of walkers (roller walkers) do not need to be picked up to be moved, but they are less stable than the standard walker. They are used by clients who are too weak or unstable to pick up and move the walker with each step. Some roller walkers have a seat at the back so the client can sit down to rest when desired. An adaptation of the standard and four-wheeled walker is one that has two tips and two wheels. This type provides more stability than the four-wheeled model yet still permits the client to keep the walker in contact with the ground at all time. The client tilts the walker toward the body, lifting the tips while the wheels remain on the ground, then pushes the walker forward.

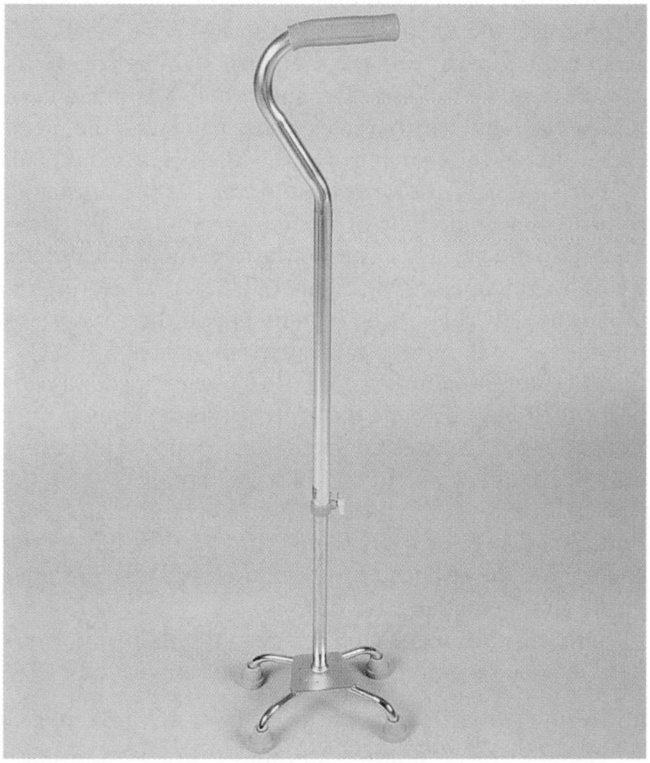

Figure 43.33 A quad cane

CLIENT TEACHING

Using Canes

- Hold the cane with the hand on the stronger side of the body to provide maximum support and appropriate body alignment when walking.
- Position the tip of a standard cane (and the nearest tip of other canes) about 15 cm to the side and 15 cm in front of the near foot, so that the elbow is slightly flexed.

When Maximum Support Is Required

- Move the cane forward about 30 cm, or a distance that is comfortable, while the body weight is borne by both legs.
- Then, move the affected (weak) leg forward to the cane while the weight is borne by the cane and stronger leg.
- Next, move the unaffected (stronger) leg forward ahead of the cane and weak leg while the weight is borne by the cane and weak leg.
- Repeat the steps. This pattern of moving provides at least two points of support on the floor at all times.

As You Become Stronger and Require Less Support

- Move the cane and weak leg forward at the same time while the weight is borne by the stronger leg.
- Move the stronger leg forward while the weight is borne by the cane and the weak leg.

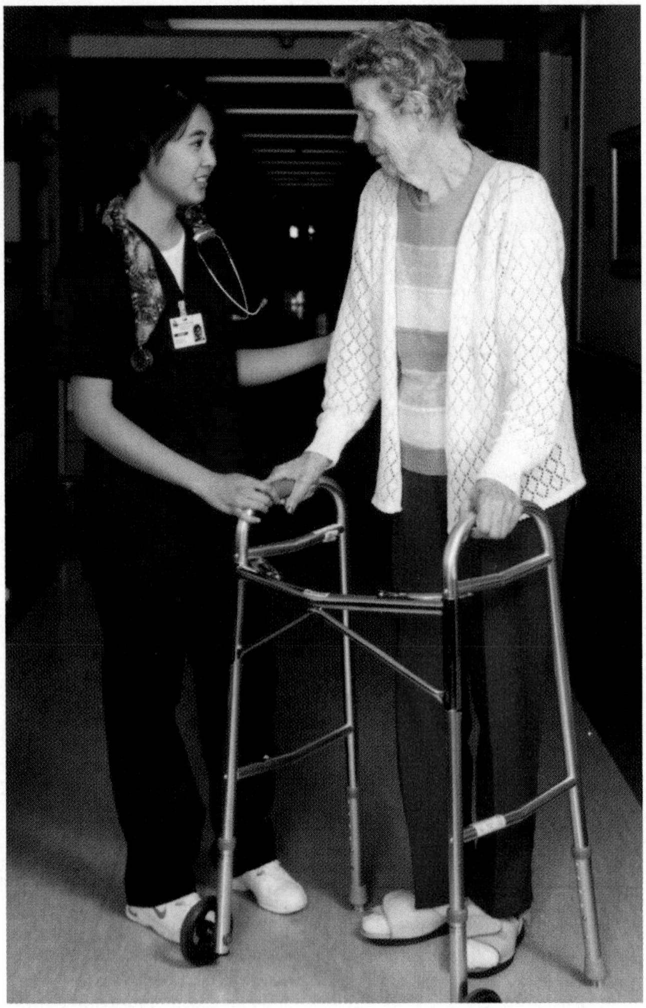

Figure 43.34 A standard walker

The nurse may need to adjust the height of a client's walker so that the hand bar is just below the client's waist and the client's elbows are slightly flexed. This position helps the client assume a more normal stance. A walker that is too low causes the client to stoop; one that is too high makes the client stretch and reach. Instructions for using walkers are provided in the box above right.

Crutches

Crutches may be a temporary need for some people and a permanent one for others. Crutches should enable a person to ambulate independently; therefore, it is important to learn to use them properly. Clients confined to bed are often unaware of weakness that becomes apparent when they try to stand or walk. Clients realize that they can no longer take balance for granted when they must cope with the weight of a heavy cast or a paralyzed limb. Frequently, progress may be slower than the client anticipated.

Encouragement from the nurse and the setting of realistic goals are especially important.

CLIENT TEACHING

Using Walkers

When Maximum Support Is Required

- Move the walker ahead about 15 cm while your body weight is borne by both legs.
- Then, move the right foot up to the walker while your body weight is borne by the left leg and both arms.
- Next, move the left foot up to the right foot while your body weight is borne by the right leg and both arms.

If One Leg Is Weaker Than the Other

- Move the walker and the weak leg ahead together about 15 cm while your weight is borne by the stronger leg.
- Then, move the stronger leg ahead while your weight is borne by the affected leg and both arms.

There are several kinds of crutches. The most frequently used are the underarm crutch, or *axillary crutch*, with hand bars, and the *Lofstrand*, or *forearm crutch*, which extends to the forearm. The underarm crutch can be extended. It has double uprights, an underarm bar, and a hand bar (Figure 43.35, *A*). The Lofstrand crutch is a single adjustable tube of aluminum to which are attached a curved piece of steel, a rubber-covered hand bar, and a metal forearm cuff (Figure 43.35, *B*). This type of crutch is most useful as a substitute for a cane. The metal cuff around the forearm and the metal bar stabilize the wrists and, thus, make walking safer and easier. The person can release the hand bar to use his or her hand, and the metal cuff will hold the crutch in place, while a cane would fall.

The *Canadian*, or *elbow extensor crutch*, like the Lofstrand, is made of a single tube of aluminum with lateral attachments, a hand bar, and a cuff for the forearm, but it also has a cuff for the upper arm (Figure 43.35, *C*). This crutch is usually used by clients who require support for weak extensor muscles of the arm (e.g., weak triceps brachii).

All crutches require suction tips, usually made of rubber, which help prevent the crutches from slipping on a floor surface. Suggested client instructions for using crutches are provided in the following box.

Exercises for Crutch Walking In crutch walking, the client's weight is borne by the muscles of the shoulder girdle and the upper extremities.

Before beginning crutch walking, the following exercises may be recommended (if not contraindicated):

- Flexing and extending the arms in several directions.
- Moving from a supine position to a sitting position by flexing the elbows and pushing the hands against the

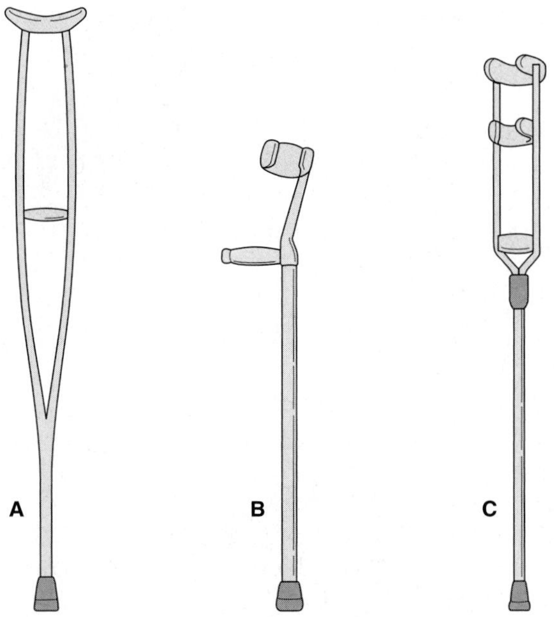

Figure 43.35 Three types of crutches: *A,* axillary crutch; *B,* Lofstrand crutch; *C,* Canadian, or elbow extensor, crutch

bed surface (Figure 43.36). This exercise strengthens the flexor and extensor muscles of the arms and the muscles that dorsiflex the wrists.

- Lifting the body off the bed surface by pushing down with the hands and extending the elbows (Figure 43.37). This exercise is particularly useful in strengthening the extensor muscles of the arms.
- Tensing the quadriceps femoris muscles (Figure 43.28, p. 1216).
- Straight leg exercises. The client lies supine with one knee bent and the other leg straight. The client tightens the quadriceps muscle in the straight leg and slowly raises it until it is parallel with the flexed leg. The client holds the leg in this position for the count of five, then slowly lowers the leg. This is repeated with the opposite leg and is done five times.
- Squeezing a rubber ball or a gripper with the hands. This exercise strengthens the flexor muscles of the fingers.

Measuring Clients for Crutches When nurses measure clients for axillary crutches, it is most important to obtain the correct length for the crutches and the correct placement of the hand piece. There are two methods of measuring crutch length:

1. The client lies in a supine position, and the nurse measures from the anterior fold of the axilla to the heel of the foot and adds 2.5 cm.

CLIENT TEACHING

Using Crutches

- Follow the plan of exercises developed for you to strengthen your arm muscles before beginning crutch walking.
- Have a health-care professional establish the correct length for your crutches and the correct placement of the handpieces. Crutches that are too long force your shoulders upward and make it difficult for you to push your body off the ground. Crutches that are too short will make you hunch over and develop an improper body stance.
- The weight of your body should be borne by the arms, rather than the axillae (armpits). Continual pressure on the axillae can injure the radial nerve and eventually cause *crutch palsy,* a weakness of the muscles of the forearm, wrist, and hand. There should be 3 to 5 cm between the axilla and shoulder rest.
- Maintain an erect posture as much as possible to prevent strain on muscles and joints and to maintain balance.
- Each step taken with crutches should be a comfortable distance for you. It is wise to start with a small, rather than a large, step.
- Inspect the crutch tips regularly, and replace them if they become worn.
- Keep the crutch tips dry and clean to maintain their surface friction. If the tips become wet, dry them well before use.
- Wear a tie shoe with a low heel that grips the floor.

2. The client stands erect and positions the crutch as shown in Figure 43.38. The nurse makes sure the shoulder rest of the crutch is at least three finger widths, that is, 3 to 5 cm, below the axilla.

   To determine the correct placement of the hand bar:

1. The client stands upright and supports the body weight by the hand grips of the crutches.
2. The nurse measures the angle of elbow flexion. It should be about 30 degrees. A goniometer may be used to verify the correct angle.

Crutch Gaits The crutch gait is the gait a person assumes on crutches by alternating body weight on one or both legs and the crutches. Five standard crutch gaits are the four-point gait, three-point gait, two-point gait, swing-to gait, and swing-through gait. The gait used depends on the following individual factors: (1) the ability to take steps, (2) the ability to bear weight and keep balance in a

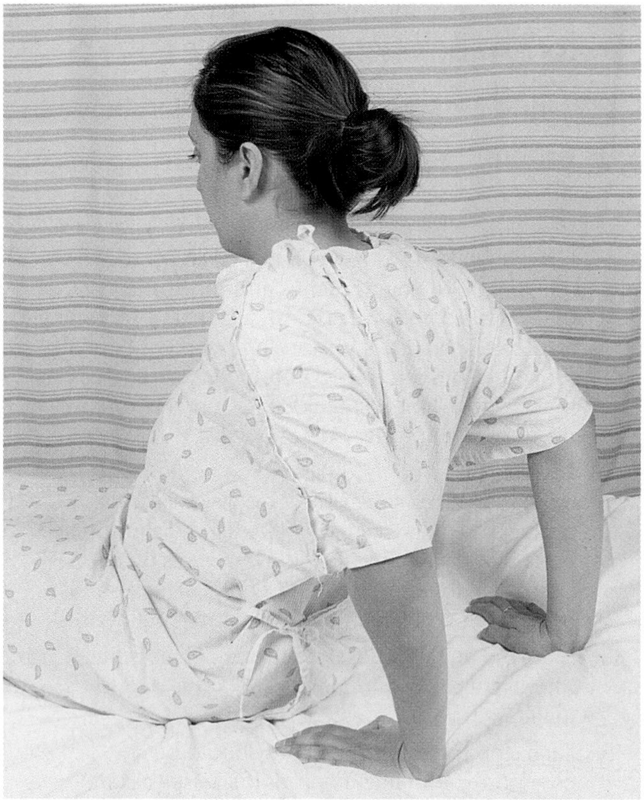

Figure 43.36 Strengthening the flexor and extensor muscles of the arms and the muscles that dorsiflex the wrist

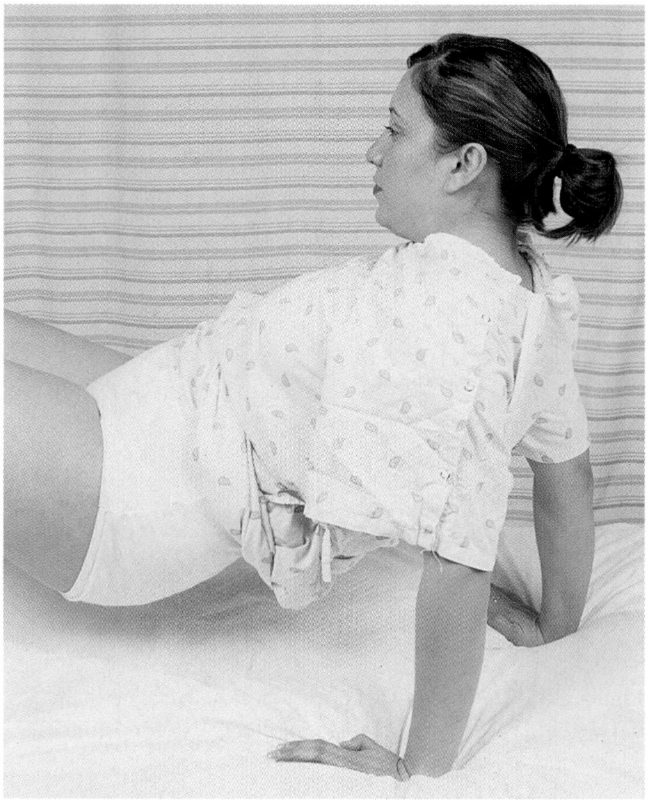

Figure 43.37 Strengthening the extensor muscles of the arms in preparation for crutch walking

standing position on both legs or only one, and (3) the ability to hold the body erect.

Clients also need instruction about how to get into and out of chairs and go up and down stairs safely. All these crutch skills are best taught before the client is discharged and preferably before the client has surgery. The crutch gait may be ordered by the physician or physiotherapist.

Crutch Stance (Tripod Position) Before crutch walking is attempted, the client needs to learn facts about posture and balance. The proper standing position with crutches is called the **tripod (triangle) position** (Figure 43.39). The crutches are placed about 15 cm in front of the feet and out laterally about 15 cm, creating a wide base of support. The feet are slightly apart. A tall person requires a wider base than a short person. Hips and knees are extended, the back is straight, and the head is held straight and high. There should be no hunch to the shoulders and, thus, no weight borne by the axillae. The elbows are extended sufficiently to allow weight bearing on the hands. If the client is unsteady, the nurse places a walking belt around the client's waist and grasps the belt at the back from above, not from below. A fall can be prevented more effectively if the belt is held from above.

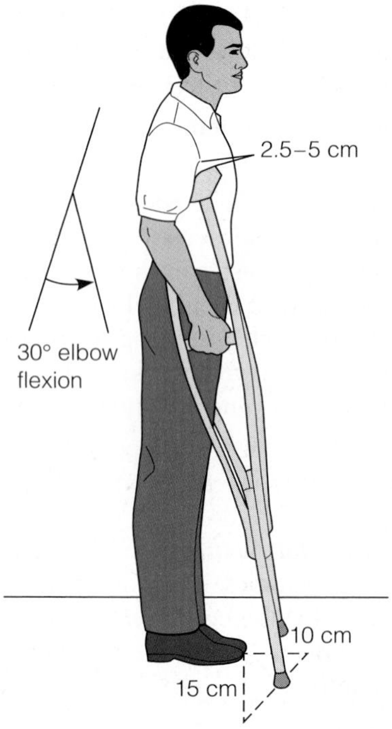

Figure 43.38 The standing position for measuring the correct length for crutches

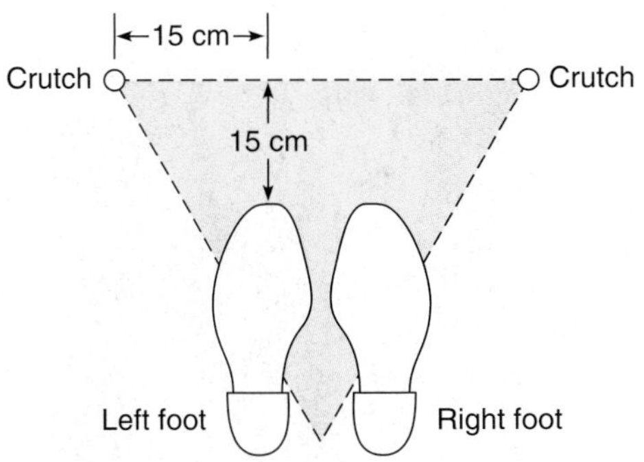

Figure 43.39 The tripod position

Four-Point Alternate Gait This is the most elementary and safest gait, providing at least three points of support at all times, but it requires coordination. Clients can use it when walking in crowds because it does not require much space. To use this gait, the client needs to be able to bear weight on both legs (Figure 43.40, *A*). The nurse asks the client to do the following:

1. Move the right crutch ahead a suitable distance, such as 10 to 15 cm.
2. Move the left front foot forward, preferably to the level of the left crutch.
3. Move the left crutch forward.
4. Move the right foot forward.

Three-Point Gait To use this gait, the client must be able to bear the entire body weight on the unaffected leg. The two crutches and the unaffected leg bear weight alternately (Figure 43.40, *B*). The nurse asks the client to do the following:

1. Move both crutches and the weaker leg forward.
2. Move the stronger leg forward.

Two-Point Alternate Gait This gait is faster than the four-point gait. It requires more balance because only two points support the body at any one time; it also requires at least partial weight bearing on each foot. In this gait, arm movements with the crutches are similar to the arm movements during normal walking (Figure 43.40, *C*). The nurse asks the client to do the following:

1. Move the left crutch and the right foot forward together.
2. Move the right crutch and the left foot ahead together.

Swing-To Gait The swing gaits are used by clients with paralysis of the legs and hips. Prolonged use of these gaits results in atrophy of the unused muscles. The swing-to gait is the easier of these two gaits. The nurse asks the client to do the following:

1. Move both crutches ahead together.
2. Lift body weight by the arms and swing to the crutches.

Swing-Through Gait This gait requires considerable skill, strength, and coordination. The nurse asks the client to do the following:

1. Move both crutches forward together.
2. Lift body weight by the arms and *swing through and beyond* the crutch.

Getting into a Chair Chairs that have armrests and are secure or braced against a wall are essential for clients using crutches. For this procedure, the nurse instructs the client to do the following:

1. Stand with the back of the unaffected leg centred and against the chair. The chair helps support the client during the next steps.
2. Transfer the crutches to the hand on the affected side, and hold the crutches by the hand bars. Grasp the arm of the chair with the hand on the unaffected side (Figure 43.41). This allows the client to support the body weight on the arms and the unaffected leg.
3. Lean forward, flex the knees and hips, and lower into the chair.

Getting out of a Chair For this procedure, the nurse instructs the client to do the following:

1. Move forward to the edge of the chair and place the unaffected leg slightly under or at the edge of the chair. This position helps the client stand up from the chair and achieve balance since the unaffected leg is supported against the edge of the chair.
2. Grasp the crutches by the hand bars in the hand on the affected side, and grasp the arm of the chair by the hand on the unaffected side. The body weight is placed on the crutches and the hand on the armrest to support the unaffected leg when the client rises to stand.
3. Push down on the crutches and the chair armrest while elevating the body out of the chair.
4. Assume the tripod position before moving.

Going up Stairs For this procedure, the nurse stands behind the client and slightly to the affected side if needed. (Use a transfer belt.) The nurse instructs the client to do the following:

1. Assume the tripod position at the bottom of the stairs.
2. Transfer the body weight to the crutches and move the unaffected leg onto the step (Figure 43.42).
3. Transfer the body weight to the unaffected leg on the step, and move the crutches and affected leg up to the step. The affected leg is always supported by the crutches.
4. Repeat steps 2 and 3 until you reach the top of the stairs.

Going down Stairs For this procedure, the nurse stands one step below the client on the affected side if needed. (Use transfer belt.) The nurse instructs the client to do the following:

1. Assume the tripod position at the top of the stairs.
2. Shift the body weight to the unaffected leg, and move the crutches and affected leg down onto the next step (Figure 43.43).
3. Transfer the body weight to the crutches, and move the unaffected leg to that step. The affected leg is always supported by the crutches.
4. Repeat steps 2 and 3 until you reach the bottom of the stairs.

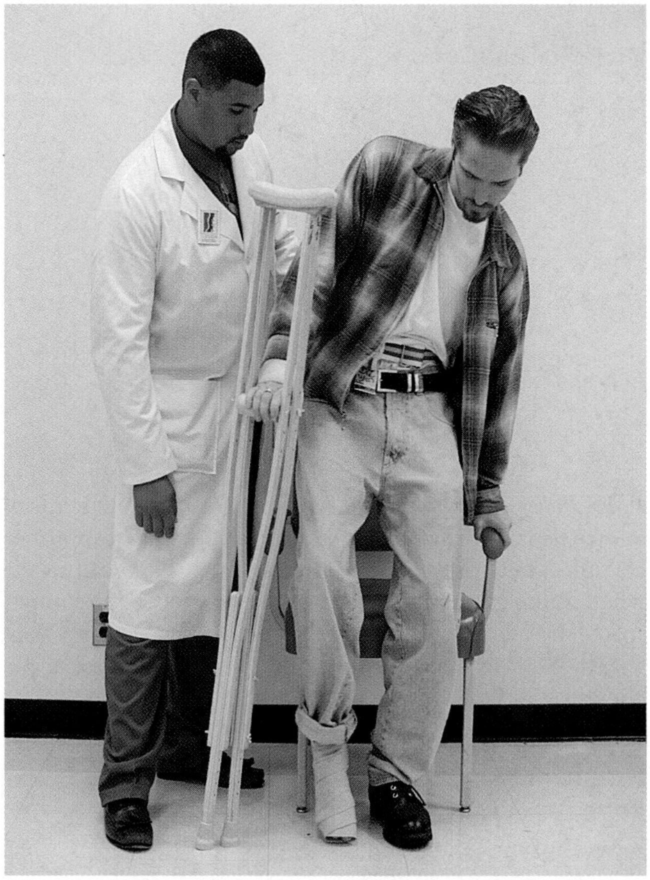

Figure 43.41 A client using crutches to get into a chair

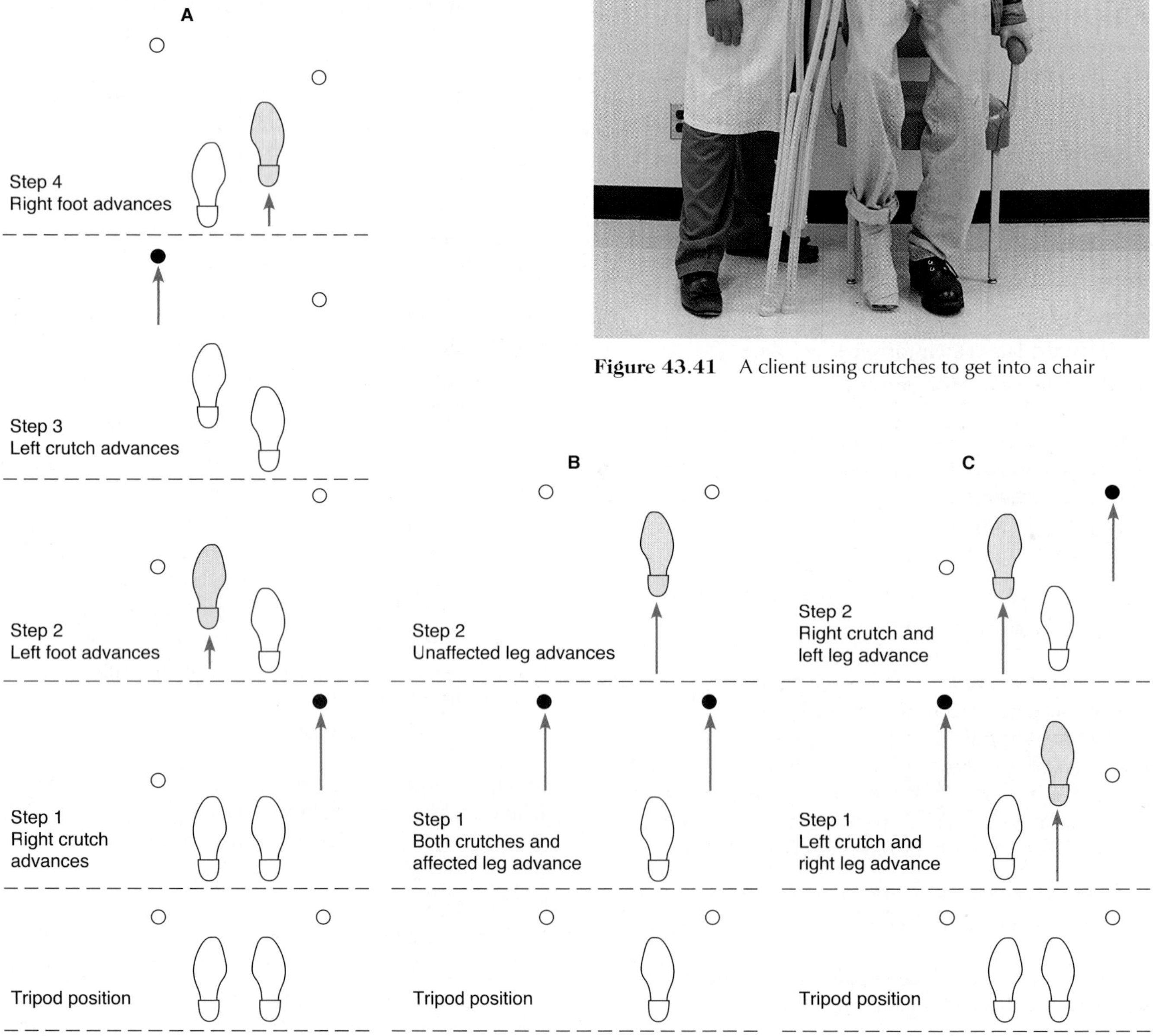

Figure 43.40 *A,* The four-point alternate crutch gait; *B,* The three-point crutch gait; *C,* The two-point alternate crutch gait (Read from bottom to top)

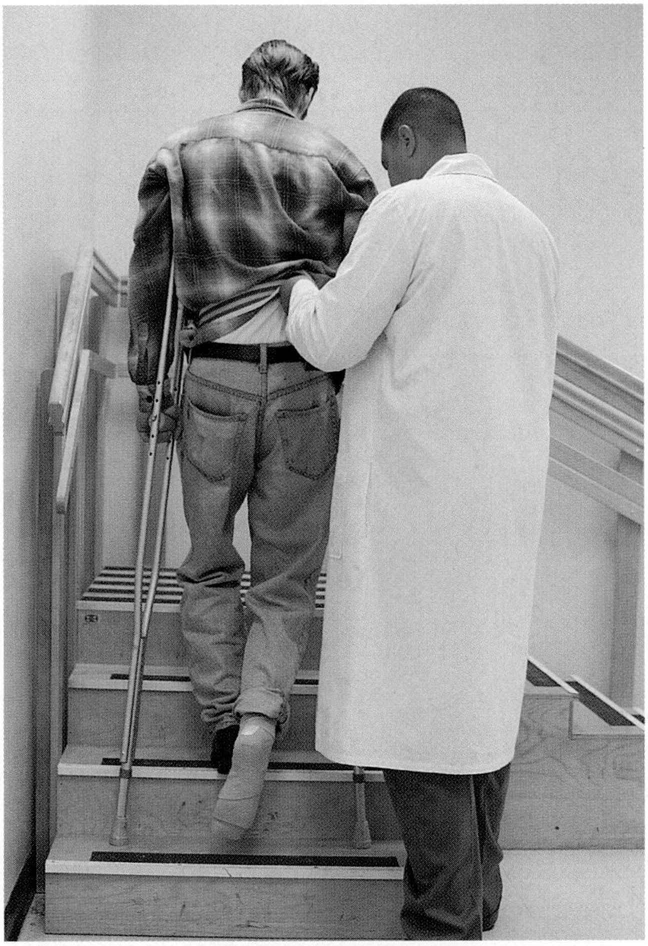

Figure 43.42 Climbing stairs: placing weight on the crutches while first moving the unaffected leg onto a step

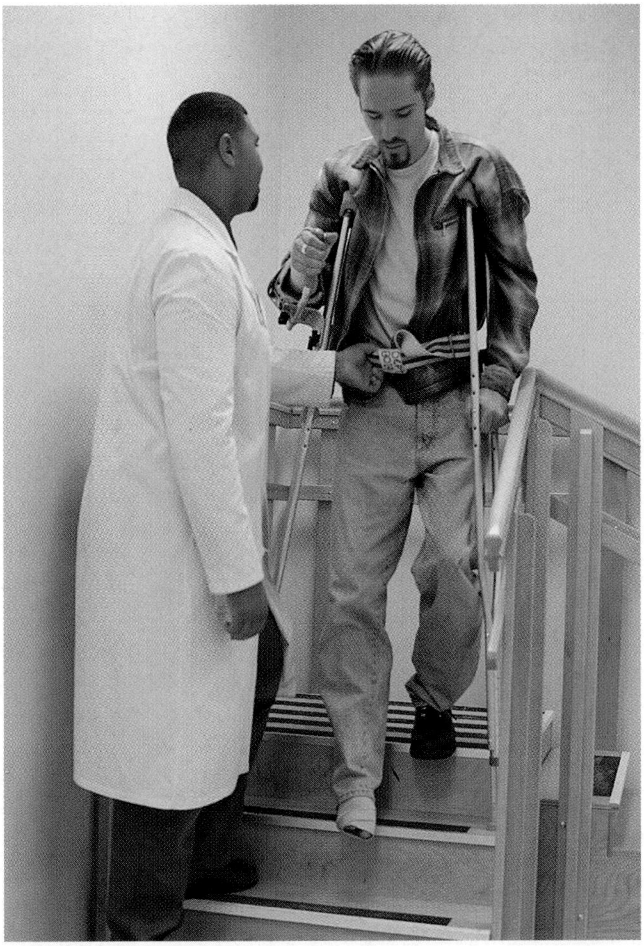

Figure 43.43 Descending stairs: moving the crutches and affected leg to the next step

Evaluating

The goals established during the planning phase are evaluated according to specific desired outcomes also established in that phase. Examples of these are shown in Table 43.12.

If outcomes are *not* achieved, the nurse, client, and support person, if appropriate, need to explore the reasons before modifying the care plan. For example, the following questions may be considered if an immobilized client fails to maintain muscle mass and tone and joint mobility:

- Has the client's physical or mental condition changed motivation to perform required exercise?
- Were appropriate range-of-motion exercises implemented?
- Was the client encouraged to participate in self-care activities as much as possible?
- Was the client encouraged to make as many decisions as possible when developing a daily activity plan and to express concerns?
- Did the nurse provide appropriate supervision and monitoring?
- Was the client's diet adequate to provide appropriate nourishment for energy requirements?

Consider...

What actions would you take if the client did *not* meet the following outcome criterion?

- "Full active ROM of all joints" (Data reveal complaints of stiffness and pain in the joints and reluctance to move.)

TABLE 43.12 Evaluation Goals and Outcomes: Mobility and Activity

Goal	Examples of Desired Outcomes
Avoid any complications associated with immobility	Skin intact
	Muscle size within preimmobility range
	Full active ROM of all joints
	Chest expansion symmetrical
	Depth of respirations within expected range
	Absence of adventitious breath sounds
	Abnormal heart rate, heart sounds, and dysrhythmia not present
	Skinfold measurements within preimmobility range
	Urinary amount, colour, and odour within expected range
	Regular elimination
Restore ability to ambulate	Walks with effective gait with walker
	Walks up and down stairs with assistance of support person
Avoid injury from falling or improper use of body mechanics	Transfers safely to and from bed and chair and from chair to chair *or* to and from wheelchair
	Demonstrates use of good body mechanics when moving and lifting objects
	Wears appropriate footwear
	Alters home environment to eliminate hazards
	Implements measures to avoid postural hypotension
Increase tolerance for physical activity	Balances activity and rest periods
	Adapts lifestyle to energy level
	Recognizes energy limitation
	Maintains adequate nutrition

FOCUS ON CRITICAL THINKING

Mrs. Gomez, 71, underwent surgery two days ago for repair of a fractured hip she suffered in a fall. She has an incision over her left hip area that is free of redness with well-approximated edges. She experiences pain upon movement even though she is being adequately medicated for pain. The physician has ordered daily physical therapy and that Mrs. Gomez be ambulated three times daily. Mrs. Gomez does not want to get out of bed because she does not want to experience another fall.

1. Why is it essential to maintain proper body alignment when turning Mrs. Gomez or helping her out of bed to ambulate?
2. What assessment findings would alert you that Mrs. Gomez is developing problems associated with her current state of decreased mobility?
3. Cite examples of exercises you can recommend for Mrs. Gomez that will reduce her risk for disuse syndrome during her recovery.
4. What are some of the factors you should consider prior to moving Mrs. Gomez to a sitting position on the edge of the bed in preparation for ambulation?
5. Mrs. Gomez will be using a walker to assist her with ambulation when she goes home. What teaching should be done prior to Mrs. Gomez's discharge from the hospital in regard to use of a walker?

See Appendix A for answers to these questions.

CHAPTER HIGHLIGHTS

- The ability to move freely, easily, and purposefully in the environment is essential for people to meet their basic needs.
- Purposeful coordinated movement of the body relies on the integrated functioning of the musculoskeletal system, the nervous system, and the vestibular apparatus of the inner ear.
- Body movement involves four basic elements: body alignment, joint mobility, balance, and coordinated movement.
- People maintain alignment and balance when the *line of gravity* passes through the *centre of gravity* and the *base of support.*
- The broader the base of support and the lower the centre of gravity, the greater is the stability and balance achieved.
- Exercise is physical activity performed to maintain muscle tone and joint mobility, to enhance physiological functioning of body systems, and to improve physical fitness. *Activity tolerance* is the type and amount of exercise or daily living activities an individual is able to perform.
- Exercise is classified as isotonic, isometric, or isokinetic and aerobic or anaerobic. *Isotonic exercises* increase muscle mass, tone, and strength, joint flexibility, and body circulation. *Isometric exercises* increase muscle mass, tone, and strength, and circulation to the exercised part but do not involve joint mobility.
- Many factors influence body alignment and activity. These include growth and development, physical health, mental health, personal values and attitudes, and prescribed limitations to movement.
- Immobility affects almost every body organ and system adversely; complications also include psychosocial problems. Exercise, by contrast, provides many benefits to the same body organs and systems.
- Problems of immobility include disuse osteoporosis and atrophy; contractures; diminished cardiac reserve; orthostatic hypotension; venous stasis, edema, and thrombus formation; decreased respiratory movement and pooling of secretions; decreased metabolic rate and negative nitrogen balance; urinary stasis, retention, and infection; constipation; and varying emotional reactions.
- The nurse has responsibilities (1) to prevent the complications of immobility and reduce the severity of any problems resulting from immobility, and (2) to design exercise programs that promote wellness in clients.
- Assessment relative to a client's activity and exercise includes a nursing history and physical examination of body alignment, gait, joint appearance and movement, capabilities and limitations for movement, muscle mass and strength, activity tolerance, and problems related to immobility.
- An activity and exercise history includes daily activity level, activity tolerance, type and frequency of exercise, and factors affecting mobility.
- NANDA nursing diagnoses that relate to activity and mobility problems include ***Activity Intolerance, Risk for Activity Intolerance, Impaired Physical Mobility,*** and ***Risk for Disuse Syndrome.*** Other relevant diagnoses are ***Self-Care Deficit; Risk for Injury; Fear*** (of falling); ***Powerlessness; Self-Esteem Chronic, Low/Situational, Low; Ineffective Coping;*** and, if the client is immobilized, many other potential problems, such as ***Ineffective Airway Clearance*** and ***Risk for Infection.***
- *Body mechanics* is the efficient, coordinated, and safe use of the body to move objects and carry out the activities of daily living.
- Nurses must use good body mechanics in their daily work and especially when moving and turning clients in bed and assisting clients to make transfers. Falls and back injuries are the most common and serious consequences of improper body mechanics.
- Positioning a client in good body alignment and changing the position regularly and systematically are essential aspects of nursing practice.
- Before positioning dependent clients, the nurse should plan a systematic 24-hour schedule for position changes, including positions that provide for full extension of the neck, hips, and knees. The nurse also uses appropriate supportive devices to maintain alignment and prevent strain on the client's muscles and joints.
- Before moving, turning, or transferring a client, the nurse must consider the client's health status, degree of exertion permitted, physical ability to assist, ability to comprehend instruction, degree of discomfort, client's weight, and the nurse's own skill.
- Assistance from others or the use of mechanical lifting aids is essential for clients who are too heavy for the nurse to move or lift safely. Agency policy for maximum lift weights must be followed.
- Safety measures must always be employed when the nurse uses a wheelchair or stretcher to move and transfer clients.
- Ambulating techniques that facilitate normal walking gait yet provide needed support are most effective. The nurse can assist clients to prepare for ambulation by helping them become as independent as possible while in bed.

- Preambulatory exercises that strengthen the muscles for walking are essential for clients who have been immobilized for a prolonged period.
- Clients need specific instructions about appropriate use of canes, walkers, and crutches.

READINGS AND REFERENCES

Suggested Readings

Goodridge, D., & Laurila, B. (1997, August). Minimizing transfer injuries. *Canadian Nurse, 93*(7), 38–40.
Health-care agencies are beginning to recognize the ineffectiveness of a strictly educational approach to reducing staff injuries. Recent innovations have included ergonomic interventions—altering the design of the workplace or the job to fit the worker. One ergonomic intervention gaining widespread acceptance in health-care agencies is the transfer assessment program. This article reports a study of the impact of a transfer assessment program on staff injuries related to client-handling tasks at a 319-bed, long-term care facility.

Jones, J. M., & Jones, K. D. (1997, July). Healthy people 2000. Promoting physical activity in the senior years. *Journal of Gerontological Nursing, 23*(7), 43–48.
These authors (1) describe the benefits of physical activity in older adults, (2) report data from the Health Evaluation Risk Survey (HERS) on exercise in older women and, more importantly, (3) supply health-care providers with tips for integrating physical activity promotion in their practice. Addresses and phone numbers are provided for 10 national activity resources that clients can contact. A four-tiered activity pyramid offers creative ways to enhance activity.

Related Research

Love, C. (1996). Injury caused by lifting: A study of the nurse's viewpoint. *Nursing Standard, 10*(46), 34–39.

Melillo, K. D., Williamson, E., Futrell, M., & Chamberlain, C. (1997, June). A self-assessment tool to measure older adults' perceptions regarding physical fitness and exercise activity. *Journal of Advanced Nursing, 25*, 1220–1226.

Selected References

Aronson, L., Carlon-Wolfe, W., & Schiener, S. (1991, March/April). Pressures that fall on rising: Ways to control postural hypotension. *Geriatric Nursing, 12*, 67.

Barnett-Damewood, M., & Carlson-Catalano, J. (2000). Physical activity deficit: A proposed nursing diagnosis. *Nursing Diagnosis, 11*(1), 24–31.

Borg, G. A. V. (1980). Psychophysical bases of perceived exertion. *Medicine and Science in Sports and Exercise, 14*, 377–381.

Braun, L. T. (1991, March). Exercise physiology and cardiovascular fitness. *Nursing Clinics of North America, 26*, 135–147.

Carpenito, L. J. (2002). *Handbook of nursing diagnosis* (9th ed.). Philadelphia, PA: Lippincott.

Doenges, M., & Moorehouse, M. (2003) *Application of nursing process and nursing diagnosis: An interactive text for diagnostic reasoning*. Philadelphia: F.A. Davis.

Gebhardt, K. S., Bliss, M. R., Glasziou, P., & De Mar, A. (1999). Bedrest ... A potentially harmful treatment needing more careful evaluation. *Lancet, 354*, 1229–1233.

Gordon, M. (1994). *Nursing diagnosis: Process and application* (3rd ed.). St. Louis, MO: Mosby.

Gordon, M. (1997). *Manual of nursing diagnosis: 1997–1998*. St. Louis, MO: Mosby.

Guyton, A. C., & Hall, J. E. (2000). *Textbook of medical physiology* (10th ed.). Philadelphia, PA: Saunders.

Haigh, C., & Peacok, L. (1998, February). Dilemmas in moving and handling patients. *Community Nurse, 4*(1), 26–28.

Hummer, A. (1993, June). Get your patient moving. *RN, 56*(6), 34–37.

Johnson, M., & Maas, M. (Eds.). (2000). *Iowa outcomes project: Nursing outcomes classification (NOC)*. St. Louis, MO: Mosby.

Kottke, F., Stillwell, G., & Lehmann, J. (Eds.). (1990). *Krusen's handbook of physical medicine and rehabilitation* (4th ed.). Philadelphia, PA: Saunders.

McCloskey, J. C., & Bulechek, G. M. (Eds.). (2000). *Iowa intervention project: Nursing interventions classification (NIC)* (3rd ed.). St. Louis, MO: Mosby.

McConnell, E. (1992, October). Using a stationary walker. *Nursing 92, 22*(10), 75.

McConnell, E. (1994, September). Logrolling a patient safely. *Nursing 94, 24*(9), 16.

Mobily, P. R., & Kelly, L. S. (1991, September). Iatrogenesis in the elderly: Factors of immobility. *Journal of Gerontological Nursing, 17*, 5–11.

Nazarko, L. (1996, October). Power to the people. *Nursing Times, 92*(4), 48–49.

O'Hanlon-Nichols, T. (1998). Basic assessment series: Adult musculoskeletal system. *American Journal of Nursing, 98*(6), 48–52.

Olson, E. V., Johnson, B. J., & Thompson, L. E. (1990, March). The hazards of immobility. *American Journal of Nursing, 90*, 43–44, 46–48. (Classic.)

Owen, B. D. (2000). Teaching students safer methods of patient transfers. *Nurse Education, 25*(6), 288–293.

Schuldenfrei, P. (1998, September). No heavy lifting. *American Journal of Nursing, 98*(9), 46–48.

Sheehan, J. (1999). If you injure your back on the job. *RN, 62*(8), 63–65.

Sobezak, J. (1998, February). Exercising for better health and mobility. *Community Nurse, 4*(1), 20–22.

Thompson L. V. (2001). *Physical activity and exercise: Identification of benefits*. Orthopaedic Physical Therapy Clinics of North America. 10(2), 193–211.

WEBLINKS

Health Canada
http://www.hc-sc.gc.ca/hppb/fitness/index.html
This site identifies the federal programs and initiatives related to fitness in Canada.

Canadian Health Network
http://www.canadian-health-network.ca/customtools/homee.html
The network provides accurate, up-to-date health promotion information by drawing upon the Web documents of numerous local, provincial/territorial, and national associations.

Canadian Fitness and Lifestyle Institute
http://64.26.159.200/cflri/pa/surveys/88survey.html
The mission of the institute is to enhance the well-being of Canadians through research and communication of information about physically active lifestyles to the public and private sectors.

Active Living Alliance for Canadians with a Disability
http://www.ala.ca/
The alliance promotes inclusion and active living lifestyles of Canadians with disabilities by facilitating communication and collaboration among organizations, agencies, and individuals.

Physical Activity Guide—Health Canada
http://www.hc-sc.gc.ca/hppb/paguide/
The site provides the physical activity guide developed by Health Canada.

CHAPTER 44

Clients Having Surgery: Promoting Healthy Recovery

OBJECTIVES

After completing this chapter, you will be able to:

- Describe the phases of the perioperative period.
- Discuss various types of surgery according to degree of urgency, degree of risk, and purpose.
- Identify essential aspects of preoperative assessment.
- Outline nursing responsibilities in planning perioperative nursing care.
- Describe essential preoperative teaching, including pain control, moving, leg exercises, and coughing and deep-breathing exercises.
- List essential aspects of preparing a client for surgery, including skin preparation.
- Compare various types of anesthesia.
- Identify essential nursing assessments and interventions during the immediate postanesthetic phase.
- Demonstrate ongoing nursing assessments and interventions for the postoperative client.
- Discuss potential postoperative complications and describe nursing interventions to prevent them.
- Identify essential aspects of managing gastrointestinal suction.
- Describe appropriate wound care for a postoperative client.
- Evaluate the effectiveness of perioperative nursing interventions.

Surgery is a unique experience of a planned physical alteration encompassing three phases: preoperative, intraoperative, and postoperative. These three phases are together referred to as the **perioperative period.**

The **preoperative phase** begins when the decision to have surgery is made and ends when the client is transferred to the operating table. The nursing activities associated with this phase include assessing the client, identifying potential or actual health problems, planning specific care based on the individual's needs, and providing preoperative teaching for the client and support people.

The **intraoperative phase** begins when the client is transferred to the operating table and ends when the client is admitted to the postanesthesia care unit (PACU), also called the postanesthetic recovery room (PARR) or recovery room (RR). The nursing activities related to this phase include a variety of specialized procedures designed to create and maintain a safe therapeutic environment for the client and the health-care personnel.

The **postoperative phase** begins with the admission of the client to the postanesthesia area and ends when healing is complete. During the postoperative phase, nursing activities include assessing the client's response (physiological and psychological) to surgery, performing interventions to facilitate healing and prevent complications, teaching and providing support to the client and support people, and planning for home care. The goal is to assist the client to achieve the most optimal health status possible.

Traditionally, clients entered the hospital for three to 10 days during which the three phases of care occurred. Today, more than half of all surgeries are performed in an outpatient setting (Brockway, 1997). The client comes to the hospital the day of surgery, has the operation, and leaves the same day. In these instances, the three phases of the perioperative period are shortened, and the postoperative phase continues at home. The nurse's role in assessing, teaching, and following up is vital to successful outcomes for the client who undergoes day surgery.

Types of Surgery

Surgical procedures are commonly grouped according to (1) purpose, (2) degree of urgency, and (3) degree of risk.

Purpose

Surgical procedures may be categorized according to their purpose; see the accompanying box.

Degree of Urgency

Surgery is classified by its urgency and necessity to preserve the client's life, body part, or body function. **Emergency surgery** is performed immediately to preserve function or the life of the client. Surgery to control internal hemorrhage or repair a fracture are examples of emergency surgeries. **Urgent surgery** occurs when the surgical problem requires attention within 24 to 48 hours. For example, to remove a kidney stone that is not likely to be passed naturally by the individual. **Elective surgery** is performed when surgical intervention is the preferred treatment for a condition that is not imminently life threatening (but may ultimately threaten life or well-being) or to improve the client's life. Examples of elective surgeries include laproscopic cholecystectomy for chronic gallbladder disease, hip replacement surgery, and plastic surgery procedures, such as breast reduction surgery.

Degree of Risk

Surgery is also classified as major or minor according to the degree of risk to the client. **Major surgery** involves a high degree of risk, for a variety of reasons: it may be complicated or prolonged; large losses of blood may occur; vital organs may be involved; or postoperative complications may be likely. Examples are organ transplant, open heart surgery, and removal of a kidney. In contrast, **minor surgery** normally involves little risk, produces few complications, and is often performed in a "day surgery." Examples are breast biopsy, removal of tonsils, and knee surgery.

Certain individuals are more vulnerable and are at a higher risk for developing complications during and after surgery. Such factors as the individual's age, general health, medication history, and psychological health affect the ability to recover and heal from surgery.

Age

Very young and elderly clients are greater surgical risks than children and adults. Age and developmental status affect children's ability to cope with the physiological and psychological stresses of surgery. The physiological response

Purposes of Surgical Procedures

Diagnostic	Confirms or establishes a diagnosis; e.g., biopsy of a mass in a breast
Palliative	Relieves or reduces pain or symptoms of a disease; it does not cure; e.g., resection of nerve roots
Ablative or curative	Removes a diseased body part; e.g., removal of a gallbladder (cholecystectomy)
Constructive	Restores function or appearance that has been lost or reduced; e.g., breast implant
Transplant	Replaces malfunctioning structures; e.g., hip replacement

of an infant to surgery is substantially different from an adult's. The blood volume in an infant is small, and its fluid reserves limited. This increases the risk of volume depletion during surgery, resulting in inadequate oxygenation of body tissues. Because of the infant's relatively large body surface area and immature temperature regulatory mechanisms, the risk of hypothermia during surgery is significant. Other organ systems, such as the kidneys, liver, and immune system, also have not achieved maturity in the infant, affecting their ability to metabolize and eliminate drugs and resist infection.

Toddlers and older children are better able to withstand surgery physiologically, but they often fear separation from their parents, painful events (e.g., "shots"), and either not waking up after surgery or waking up during surgery and feeling what is happening (Williams, 1997). The parent-child relationship, the parents' coping abilities, and preoperative teaching and support will affect how well the child is able to deal with these fears and the level of anxiety the child experiences.

The older adult often has fewer physiological reserves to meet the extra demands caused by surgery. Because of a lower percentage of body water, decreased kidney function, and a decreased thirst response, elderly clients are at greater risk for fluid and electrolyte imbalances. The older adult may be poorly nourished, which can impair healing. Declines in sensory function (hearing in particular) or the presence of dementia make it more difficult to understand directions and teaching. In addition, the older adult is more likely to have a chronic disease, such as cardiovascular disease, chronic lung disease, or diabetes, that affects healing and responses to medication and surgery.

General Health

Surgery is least risky when the client's general health is good. Any infection or pathophysiology increases the risk. Of particular concern are upper respiratory tract infections, which, together with a general anesthetic, can adversely affect respiratory function. Where there is a high risk of infection, antibiotics may be administered parenterally within one hour of surgery and continued for 24 to 72 hours. This practice allows time for drugs to reach therapeutic levels in the tissues but does not permit bacterial resistance to develop. Common health problems that increase surgical risk and may lead to the decision to postpone or cancel surgery are listed in the accompanying box.

Health Problems that Increase Surgical Risk

- *Malnutrition* can lead to delayed wound healing, infection, and reduced energy. Protein and vitamins are needed for wound healing; vitamin K is essential for blood clotting.
- *Obesity* leads to hypertension, impaired cardiac function, and impaired respiratory ventilation. Obese clients are also more likely to have delayed wound healing and wound infection because adipose tissue impedes blood circulation and delivery of nutrients, antibodies, and enzymes required for wound healing.
- *Cardiac conditions,* such as angina pectoris, recent myocardial infarction, hypertension, and congestive heart failure, weaken the heart. Well-controlled cardiac problems generally pose minimal operative risk.
- *Blood coagulation disorders* may lead to severe bleeding, hemorrhage, and subsequent shock.
- *Upper respiratory tract infections or chronic obstructive lung diseases,* such as emphysema, adversely affect pulmonary function, especially when exacerbated by the effects of general anesthesia. They also predispose the client to postoperative lung infections.
- *Renal disease or insufficiency* impairs regulation of the body's fluids and electrolytes and excretion of drugs and other toxins.
- *Diabetes mellitus* predisposes the client to wound infection and delayed healing.
- *Liver disease* (e.g., cirrhosis) impairs the liver's ability to detoxify medications used during surgery, produce the prothrombin necessary for blood clotting, and metabolize nutrients essential for healing.
- *Uncontrolled neurological disease,* such as epilepsy, may result in seizures during surgery or recovery.

Medication History

The regular use of certain prescribed and over-the-counter medications can increase surgical risk. The following medications have the potential to affect physiological functions of the body and interact with anesthesia, causing serious problems.

- *Anticoagulants* increase blood coagulation time and, thus, increase the risk of hemorrhaging. They should be discontinued at least 48 hours before surgery. Aspirin, ibuprofen, and common medications can alter clotting mechanisms.
- *Antidepressants*, particularly monoamine oxidase inhibitors (MAOs) and St. John's Wort, a herbal product, increase the hypotensive action of anesthesia.
- *Antihypertensives* interact with anesthetic agents and may cause bradycardia, hypotension, and impaired circulation.
- *Tranquilizers* may cause seizures if withdrawn too quickly.
- *Insulin* may need to be adjusted after surgery to account for the rise in blood sugar associated with the stress of surgery.
- *Diuretics*, particularly thiazides, may affect fluid and electrolyte balance (particularly potassium) after surgery.

- *Corticosteroids*, with prolonged use, decrease the anti-inflammatory effect and may delay wound healing and increase the risk of infection.

Clients may be unaware of the potential adverse interactions of medications and may fail to report the use of medications for conditions unrelated to the indication for surgery. The nurse who collects a preoperative history should ask the client and family about the use of commonly prescribed medications and over-the-counter preparations that the client takes.

Psychological Health

Disorders that affect cognitive function, such as mental illness, mental retardation, or developmental delay, affect the client's ability to understand and cope with the stresses of surgery. These clients also may require medication, such as anticonvulsants or antipsychotic drugs, that can interact with anesthetic and analgesic medications used during and after surgery.

Clients with dementia may have difficulty understanding proposed surgical procedures and may respond unpredictably to anesthetics. Manifestations of dementia, such as confusion, disorientation, and agitation, also may be aggravated by the change of environment in the hospital, interfering with the client's ability to cooperate with pre- and postoperative care.

Extreme anxiety also increases surgical risk and interferes with the client's ability to process information and respond appropriately to instructions. In some instances, professional counselling is indicated prior to surgery. It is also important to determine whether clients have coping skills and support systems to help them.

Preoperative Phase

Preoperative Consent

Prior to any surgical procedure, clients must sign a consent form, which is generally supplied by the agency. This requirement protects the individual's autonomy and ensures that they have a clear understanding about the surgery, the benefits, and the risks. It also protects the hospital and the health personnel from a claim by the client or family that permission was not granted. The consent form becomes a part of the client's record and goes to the operating room with the client.

The surgeon maintains legal responsibility for ensuring that the client is giving *informed* consent and ensuring that the client understands the procedure to be performed. If it is not clear that the client understands and consents to the surgery, the nurse has the responsibility of contacting the surgeon before surgery proceeds.

Preoperative informed consent should include the following:

- Nature and intention of the surgery
- Name and qualifications of the person performing the surgery
- Risks, including tissue damage, disfigurement, or even death
- Chances of success
- Possible alternative measures
- The right of the client to refuse consent or later withdraw consent

Informed consent is only possible when the patient understands the information being provided, that is, speaks the language and is conscious, mentally competent, and not under the influence of sedatives. The patient must also be legally capable. In Canada, depending on the province/territory, a minor under a certain age may not legally give consent (Keatings & Smith, 2000). Nurses must be aware of their responsibilities regarding consents and of the particular hospital policies. See Chapter 8 for further information about informed consent.

Assessing

Preoperative assessment includes collecting and reviewing specific client data to determine the client's needs both pre- and postoperatively.

Nursing History

The nursing history obtained before surgery provides client data that help the nurse plan preoperative and postoperative care. The nurse completes a history according to agency form/policy (see the box on the following page).

Physical Assessment

Preoperatively, the nurse performs a brief but complete physical assessment, paying particular attention to systems that could affect the client's response to anesthesia or surgery. Increased attention by the nurse is often given to oxygen, circulation, nutrition, and elimination needs. The patient's lungs are carefully assessed. Chronic lung conditions, such as emphysema, asthma, and bronchitis, increase operative risk because of the impaired gas exchange in the alveoli, predisposing the patient to postoperative pulmonary conditions. Assessment includes examining for the presence of shortness of breath, wheezing, clubbing of fingers, chest pain, cyanosis, and coughing. History of lifestyle, including smoking habits, exposure to second-hand smoke, and other environmental hazards related to occupation, are important. Also important is the patient's history of allergies and infections. Notification of the physician of any respiratory distress is imperative for successful postoperative recovery.

Nursing History

- *Current health status.* Essential information includes general health status and the presence of any chronic diseases, such as diabetes or asthma, that may affect the client's response to surgery or anesthesia. Note any physical limitations that may affect the client's mobility or ability to communicate after surgery, as well as any prostheses, such as hearing aids or contact lenses.
- *Allergies.* Include allergies to prescription and non-prescription drugs, food allergies, and allergies to tape, latex, soaps, or antiseptic agents. Some food allergies may indicate a potential reaction to drugs or substances used during surgery or diagnostic procedures; for example, an allergy to seafood alerts the nurse to a potential allergy to iodine-based dyes commonly used in radiological procedures.
- *Medications.* List all current medications. It may be vital to maintain a blood level of some medications (e.g., anticonvulsants) throughout the surgical experience; others, such as anticoagulants or aspirin, increase the risks of surgery and anesthesia and need to be discontinued several days prior to surgery.
- *Anesthetic history.* Determine previous history of complications to anesthesia (general and local), such as cardiac arrest or malignant hyperthermia crisis.
- *Previous surgeries.* Previous surgical experiences may influence the client's physical and psychological responses to surgery or may reveal unexpected responses to anesthesia.
- *Mental status.* The client's mental status and ability to understand and respond appropriately can affect the entire perioperative experience. Note any developmental disabilities, mental illness, history of dementia, or excessive anxiety related to the procedure.
- *Understanding of the surgical procedure and anesthesia.* The client should have a good understanding of the planned procedure and what to expect during and after surgery as well as the expected outcome of the procedure.
- *Smoking.* Smokers may have more difficulty clearing respiratory secretions after surgery, increasing the risk of postoperative complications, such as pneumonia and atelectasis.
- *Alcohol and other mind-altering substances.* Use of substances that affect the central nervous system, liver, or other body systems can affect the client's response to anesthesia, and surgery, and postoperative recovery.
- *Coping.* Clients with a healthy self-concept who have successfully employed appropriate coping mechanisms in the past are better able to deal with the stressors associated with surgery.
- *Social resources.* Determine the availability of family or other caregivers as well as the client's social support network. These resources are important to the client's recovery, particularly for the client undergoing same-day or short-stay surgery.
- *Cultural considerations.* Culture influences the client's response to surgery; respecting cultural beliefs and practices can reduce preoperative anxiety and improve recovery.

A thorough assessment of the circulatory system and fluid and electrolytes is essential. All cardiac conditions can lead to decreased tissue perfusion with potential for impairment of surgical wound healing. Noted are existing problems, such as chronic heart conditions, high blood pressure, varicose veins, peripheral circulatory disorders, and diabetes. The circulatory system is assessed in relation to the reserve capacity of the heart and blood vessels. Shortness of breath on minor exertion, presence of chest pain, irregularities of the pulse, and notable deviations of the patient's "normal" blood pressure should be reported to the physician. Pulse oximetry is often used preoperatively to assess gross levels of tissue oxygenation.

Important factors to consider in relation to the patient's nutritional status are body weight, recent weight loss or gain, and hemoglobin. Any history of malnutrition or prolonged nausea and vomiting increases the risk of poor surgical outcome. This is particularly important if the patient is sensitive to anesthesia resulting in nausea and vomiting. To make food more appealing, it is also important to document food and fluid preferences, any food allergies, or diet-related restrictions, such as a sodium-reduced diet. The overweight individual also faces risks postoperatively, such as pulmonary complications. Adipose (fatty) tissue is less vascular and more prone to postoperative infection, incisional hernias, and evisceration or dehiscence.

Kidney and bowel functions are carefully assessed preoperatively. Adequate urine output (approximately 30 mL/hr) usually indicates adequate renal function and cardiac output. Urinary function is assessed in relation to the individual's normal pattern of voiding and any problems that currently exist. If a routine urinalysis is done, it is the nurse's responsibility to teach the patient the proper technique of collecting the sample or to assist with the collection if the client is unable to. Assessing the patient's "normal" bowel routine is important preoperatively. If the patient is prone to constipation, this should be noted as anesthesia and narcotics used for pain control contribute to the problem of constipation. Preoperative enemas till clear may be ordered if the patient is having gastrointestinal surgery because this helps prevent the possible intraoperative spillage of bowel contents, which could lead to peritonitis.

A brief or "mini" mental status examination provides valuable baseline data for evaluating the client's mental status and alertness after surgery. It is also important to evaluate the client's ability to understand what is happening. Assessment of hearing and vision help guide teaching postoperatively.

Screening Tests

The physician orders preoperative diagnostic tests and examinations. Abnormalities may warrant treatment prior to surgery. The nurse's responsibility is to check the orders carefully, to see that they are carried out, and to ensure that the results are obtained and entered into the client's record prior to surgery. See Table 44.1 for preoperative screening tests. The type of preoperative screening tests that are seen as "routine" varies within institutions. In addition to these tests, diagnostic tests directly related to the client's disease are usually appropriate (e.g., gastroscopy to clarify the pathological condition before gastric surgery).

Assessing Preoperative Concerns Two concerns that often exist for the individual who faces the surgical experience are the need for knowledge about preoperative procedures and protocols and knowledge about what is to be expected postoperatively. Surgery may be viewed as a stressful event that threatens the patient's security and self-esteem. The promotion of comfort, security, and well-being of the patient preoperatively is largely due to the trust and confidence that is built in the nurse-patient relationship. Providing emotional support and promoting an understanding of procedures greatly facilitates this process. The family and significant others, whenever possible, should be included in the explanation of surgical procedures. The overall goal in the preoperative period is to ensure that the client is mentally and physically prepared for surgery. Examples of nursing practices to meet this goal are discussed in the "Planning and Implementing" section that follows.

TABLE 44.1 Routine Preoperative Screening Tests

Test	Rationale
Complete blood count (CBC)	RBCs, hemoglobin (Hgb), and hematocrit (Hct) are important to the oxygen-carrying capacity of the blood; WBCs are an indicator of immune function
Blood typing and cross-matching	Determined in case blood transfusion is required during or after surgery
Serum electrolytes (Na^+, K^+, Ca^{2+}, Mg^{2+}, Cl^-, HCO_3^-)	To evaluate fluid and electrolyte status
Fasting blood glucose	High levels may indicate undiagnosed diabetes mellitus
Blood urea nitrogen (BUN) and creatinine	To evaluate renal function
ALT, AST, LDH, and bilirubin	To evaluate liver function
Serum albumin and total protein	To evaluate nutritional status
Urinalysis	To determine urine composition and possible abnormal components (e.g., protein or glucose) or infection
Chest x-ray	To evaluate respiratory status and heart size
Electrocardiogram (ECG)	To identify pre-existing cardiac problems or disease

Planning and Implementing

Preoperative Teaching

Preoperative teaching is a vital part of nursing care. Studies have shown that preoperative teaching reduces clients' anxiety and postoperative complications, as well as increasing their satisfaction with the surgical experience. Good preoperative teaching also facilitates the client's return to work and other activities of daily living. Four dimensions of preoperative teaching have been identified as important to clients:

- Information, including what will happen to the client, when, and what the client will experience, such as expected sensations and discomfort. The nurse needs to listen carefully and attentively to the client to identify specific concerns and fears. Typical questions are: What will happen during surgery? How will I feel after the operation? What will the surgeon find? How long will I be in the hospital?
- Psychosocial support to reduce anxiety. The nurse provides support by actively listening and providing accurate information. It is important to rectify any misperceptions the client may have.
- The roles of the client and support people in preoperative preparation, the surgical procedure, and during the postoperative phase. Understanding his or her role during the perioperative experience increases the client's sense of control and reduces anxiety. This includes what will be expected of the client, desired behaviours, self-care activities, and what the client can do to facilitate recovery.

- Skills training, for example, moving, deep breathing, coughing, splinting incisions with the hands or a pillow, and using an incentive spirometer.

If the client is scheduled for same-day surgery, preoperative teaching is often provided at a preoperative assessment clinic (PAC) before the day of surgery using some combination of videos and verbal and written instructions. The client will have an appointment with day-surgery staff (usually scheduled to coincide with preoperative diagnostic testing) to discuss preoperative concerns, or teaching may be completed by a nurse working with the surgeon. Written instructions are provided, especially when surgery is scheduled several days or weeks hence. Teaching is then reinforced on admission to the surgery unit, and immediate or continuing concerns are addressed.

When the client is a child, addressing the fears and anxieties of both the child and the family is vital. Parents need to know what to expect and to be able to express their concerns. Parents should be considered members of the perioperative team and be allowed to participate in providing as much care as possible. Separation from parents often is the child's greatest fear; the time of separation should be minimized and parents should be allowed to interact with the child both immediately preceding and following the surgery. Teaching of the child (both timing and content) should be geared to the child's developmental level and cognitive abilities. Use of simple terms will help the child understand ("You will have a sore tummy"). Play is an effective teaching tool with children; the child can put a bandage on an "incision" on a doll.

Preoperative instructions for all clients are summarized in the box below. Procedure 44.1 provides guidelines for teaching clients about moving, leg exercises, deep breathing, and coughing.

Preoperative Instructions

Preoperative Regimen

- Explain the need for preoperative tests (e.g., laboratory, x-ray, ECG).
- Discuss bowel preparation, if required.
- Discuss skin preparation, including operative area and preoperative bath or shower. The physician may instruct the operative site to be marked with an X.
- Discuss preoperative medications, if ordered.
- Explain individual therapies ordered by the physician, such as intravenous therapy, the insertion of a urinary catheter or nasogastric tube, use of a spirometer, or anti-embolism stockings.
- Discuss the visit by the anesthetist.
- Explain the need to restrict food and oral fluids at least eight hours before surgery.
- Provide a general timetable for perioperative events, including the time of surgery.
- Discuss the need to remove jewellery, make-up, and all prostheses (e.g., eyeglasses, hearing aids, complete or partial dentures, wig) immediately before surgery. In some cases, the surgeon may leave instructions for the client to leave hearing aids and eye glasses on to enable better communication.
- Inform client about the preoperative holding area, and give the location of the waiting room for support people.
- Teach deep-breathing and coughing exercises, leg exercises, ways to turn and move (see Procedure 44.1), and splinting techniques.
- Complete the preoperative checklist.
- Implement other preoperative measures as ordered by the physician.

Postoperative Regimen

- Discuss the postanesthesia recovery room's routines and emergency equipment.
- Review type and frequency of assessment activities.
- Discuss pain management.
- Explain usual activity restrictions and precautions related to getting up for the first time postoperatively.
- Describe usual dietary alterations.
- Discuss postoperative dressings and drains.
- Provide an explanation and tour of intensive care unit if client is to be transferred there postoperatively.

Day-Surgery Clients

- Confirm place and time of surgery, including when to arrive (e.g., 1 to $1\frac{1}{2}$ hours before scheduled surgery) and where to register (e.g., reception desk).
- Discuss what to wear (e.g., clients having hand surgery should wear a garment with large sleeve openings to fit over a bulky dressing; all clients need to leave valuables at home).
- Explain the need for a responsible adult to drive or accompany the client home, and arrange a place for them to meet.
- Discuss medications, including specific preoperative medications and the client's current medication regimen.
- Review with the client any tests ordered and the need for a urine specimen the morning of surgery.
- Communicate by telephone the evening before surgery to confirm time of surgery and arrival time, and call again the evening after surgery to assess progress.

PROCEDURE 44.1 Teaching Moving, Leg Exercises, Deep Breathing, and Coughing

Before commencing to teach moving, leg exercises, deep-breathing exercises, and coughing, determine (1) the type of surgery, (2) the time of the surgery, (3) the name of the surgeon, (4) the preoperative orders, (5) the agency's policies for preoperative care, and (6) the learning needs of the client. Also, verify that the physician has completed the medical history and physical examination and that the consent form has been signed by the client or the family.

PURPOSES

Moving

- To maintain blood circulation
- To stimulate respiratory function
- To decrease stasis of gas in the intestine
- To facilitate early ambulation

Leg Exercises

- To stimulate blood circulation, thereby preventing thrombophlebitis and thrombus formation

Deep Breathing and Coughing

- To facilitate lung aeration, thereby preventing atelectasis and pneumonia

Assessment Focus
Vital signs; discomfort; peripheral pulses, capillary refill; sensation and movement; temperature and colour of feet and legs; breath sounds; presence of dyspnea or cough; oxygen saturation

INTERVENTION

1. Show the client ways to turn in bed and to get out of bed.

- Instruct a client who will have a right abdominal incision or a right-sided chest incision to turn to the left side of the bed and sit up as follows:
  - **a.** Flex the knees.
  - **b.** Splint the wound by holding the left arm and hand or a small pillow against the incision.
  - **c.** Turn to the left while pushing with the right foot and grasping a partial side rail on the left side of the bed with the right hand.
  - **d.** Come to a sitting position on the side of the bed by using the right arm and hand to push down against the mattress and swinging the feet over the edge of the bed.
- Teach a client with left abdominal or left-sided chest incision to perform the same procedure but splint with the right arm and turn to the right.
- For clients with orthopedic surgery (e.g., hip surgery), use special aids, such as a trapeze, to assist with movement.

2. Teach the client the following three leg exercises.

- Alternate dorsiflexion and plantar flexion of the feet. (See Figure 24 in Table 43.2 on page 1176.) *This exercise is sometimes referred to as calf pumping because it alternately contracts and relaxes the calf muscles, including the gastrocnemius muscles.* See Figure 44.1.

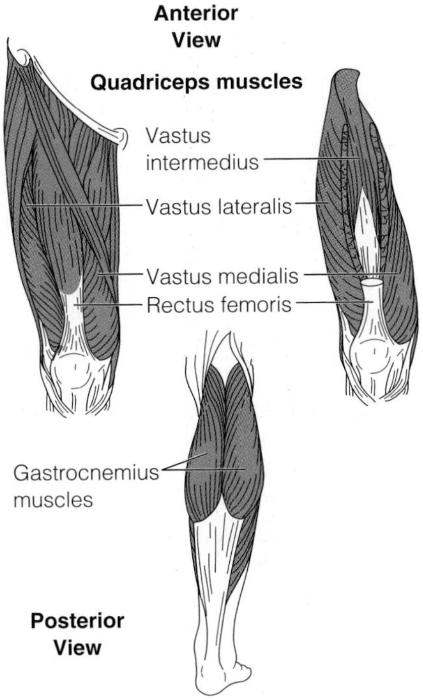

Figure 44.1 Leg muscles: anterior and posterior views

- Flex and extend the knees, and press the backs of the knees into the bed while dorsiflexing the feet (Figure 44.2). Instruct clients who cannot raise their legs to do isometric exercises that contract and relax the muscles.

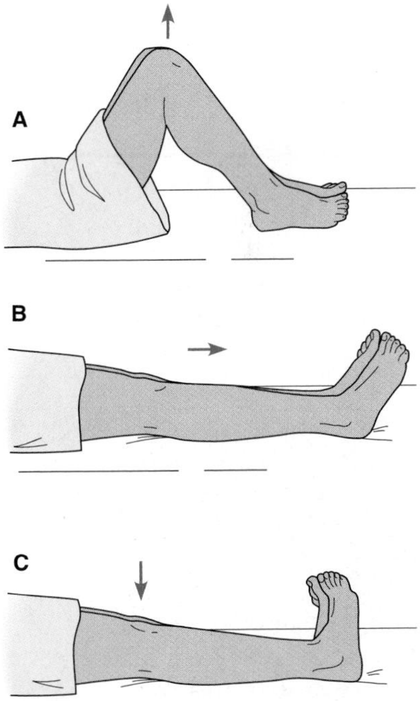

Figure 44.2 Flexing and extending the knees

- Raise and lower the legs alternately from the surface of the bed. Flex the knee of the stable leg and extend the knee of the

PROCEDURE 44.1 Teaching Moving, Leg Exercises, Deep Breathing, and Coughing *continued*

moving leg (Figure 44.3). *This exercise contracts and relaxes the quadriceps muscles.*

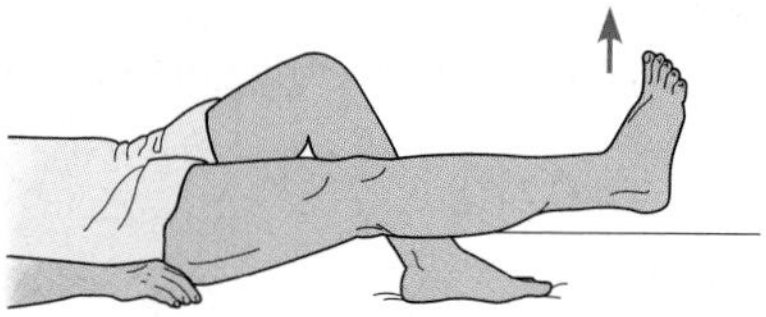

Figure 44.3 Raising and lowering the legs

3. **Demonstrate deep-breathing (diaphragmatic) exercises as follows:**

- Place your hands palms down on the border of your rib cage, and inhale slowly and evenly through the nose until the greatest chest expansion is achieved (Figure 44.4).
- Hold your breath for two to three seconds.

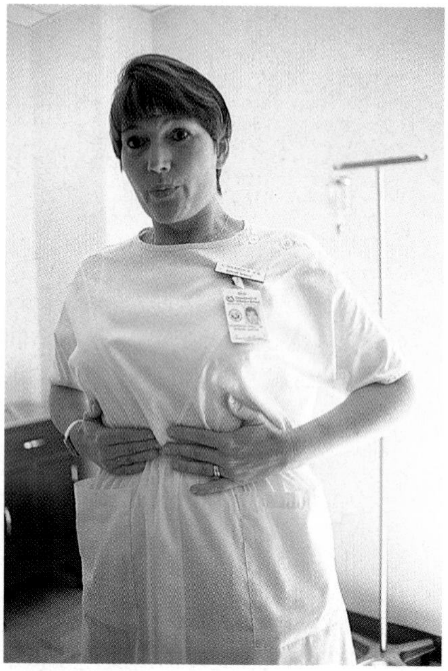

Figure 44.4 Demonstrating deep breathing

- Then, exhale slowly through the mouth.
- Continue exhalation until maximum chest contraction has been achieved.

4. **Help the client perform deep-breathing exercises.**

- Ask the client to assume a sitting position.
- Place the palms of your hands on the border of the client's rib cage to assess respiratory depth.
- Ask the client to perform deep breathing, as described in step 3.

5. **Instruct the client to cough voluntarily after a few deep inhalations.**

- Ask the client to inhale deeply, hold the breath for a few seconds, and then cough once or twice.
- Ensure that the client coughs deeply and does not just clear the throat.

6. **Demonstrate ways to splint the abdomen when coughing if the incision will be painful when the client coughs.**

- Show the client how to support the incision by placing the palms of the hands on either side of the incision site or directly over the incision site, holding the palm of one hand over the other. *Coughing uses the abdominal and other accessory respiratory muscles. Splinting the incision may reduce pain while coughing if the incision is near any of these muscles.*
- Show the client how to splint the abdomen with clasped hands and a firmly rolled pillow held against the client's abdomen (Figure 44.5).

7. **Inform the client about the expected frequency of these exercises.**

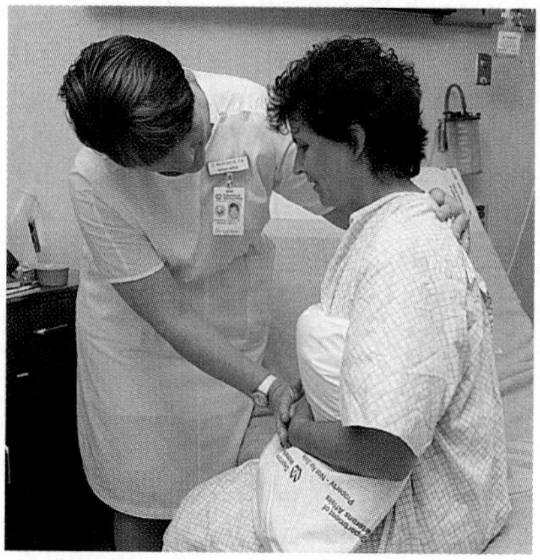

Figure 44.5 Splinting an incision with a pillow while coughing

- Instruct the client to start the exercises as soon after surgery as possible.
- Encourage clients with abdominal or chest surgery to carry out deep breathing and coughing at least every two hours, taking a minimum of five breaths at each session. Note, however, that the number of breaths and frequency of deep breathing varies with the client's condition. People who are susceptible to pulmonary problems may need deep-breathing exercises every hour. People with chronic respiratory disease may need special breathing exercises (e.g., pursed-lip breathing, abdominal breathing, exercises using various kinds of incentive spirometers). See Chapter 39.

8. **Document the teaching and all assessments.**

Evaluation Focus
Client's demonstrated ability to perform moving, leg exercises, deep-breathing, and coughing exercises

Physical Preparation

Preoperative preparation includes the following areas: nutrition and fluids, elimination, hygiene, medications, rest, care of valuables and prostheses, special orders, and surgical skin preparation. In many agencies, a preoperative checklist is used on the day of surgery. The nurse checks the agency's forms and follows appropriate recording procedures. It is essential that (1) all pertinent records (laboratory records, x-ray films, consents) be assembled and completed so that operating and recovery room personnel can refer to them, and (2) all physical preparation is completed to ensure client safety.

Nutrition and Fluids

Adequate hydration and nutrition promote healing. Nurses need to record any signs of malnutrition or fluid imbalance. If the client is on intravenous fluids or on measured fluid intake and output, nurses must ensure that the fluids are carefully measured.

Because anesthetics depress gastrointestinal functioning and because there is a danger the client may vomit and aspirate vomitus during administration of a general anesthetic, the client usually fasts at least six to eight hours before surgery, although in some instances, clear liquids, such as water, apple juice, and black coffee, are permitted up to two hours before surgery. Surgical clients and their support people need to understand the necessity of fasting. Usually, the nurse removes food and fluids from the bedside and places a fasting sign at the bed the evening before surgery. The client can use a mouthwash if the mouth feels dry but must not swallow any. If the client ingests food or fluids during the fasting period, the nurse must notify the surgeon.

Elimination

Enemas before surgery are no longer routine, but cleansing enemas may be ordered if bowel surgery is planned. The enemas help prevent postoperative constipation and contamination of the surgical area by feces. After surgery involving the intestines, peristalsis often doesn't return for 24 to 48 hours.

Prior to surgery, a retention catheter may be ordered to ensure that the bladder remains empty. This helps prevent inadvertent injury to the bladder, particularly during pelvic surgery. If the client does not have a catheter, it is important to empty the bladder prior to receiving preoperative medications. The bladder must be empty during the operation.

Hygiene

In some settings, clients are asked to bathe or shower the evening or morning of surgery (or both). The purpose of hygienic measures is to reduce the risk of wound infection. The bath includes a shampoo, whenever possible.

The client's nails should be trimmed and free of polish and all cosmetics should be removed so that the nail beds, skin, and lips are visible when circulation is assessed during and following surgery.

Surgical caps may be donned the day of surgery by clients in some hospitals. The surgical caps contain the client's hair and any microorganisms on the hair and scalp.

Immediately before surgery, the nurse removes, or asks the client to remove, all hair pins and clips; these may cause pressure or accidental damage to the scalp when the client is unconscious. The client also removes personal clothing and puts on a hospital gown.

Medications

The anesthetist or anesthesiologist may temporarily discontinue routinely taken medications the day of surgery. In some settings, preoperative medications are given after the client goes to the operating room; otherwise, they are given on the hospital unit. The use and number of preoperative medications today has certainly decreased in number, related to improved anesthetic agents and increasing numbers of patients who have day surgery procedures. When preoperative medications are used, common medications include:

- *Sedatives and tranquilizers*, such as lorazepam (Ativan) and diazepam (Valium), to reduce anxiety and ease anesthetic induction
- *Narcotic analgesics*, such as morphine and meperidine (Demerol), to provide client sedation and reduce the required amount of anesthetic
- *Anticholinergics*, such as atropine, scopolamine, and glycopyrrolate (Robinul), to reduce oral and pulmonary secretions and prevent laryngospasm
- *Histamine-receptor antagonists*, such as cimetidine (Tagamet) and ranitidine (Zantac), to reduce gastric fluid volume and gastric acidity
- *Neuroleptanalgesic agents*, such as innovar (Droperidol or Fentalyl), to induce general calmness and sleepiness

Preoperative medications must be given at a scheduled time or "on call," that is, when the operating room notifies the nurse to give the medication.

Rest and Sleep

Nurses should do everything to help the client sleep the night before surgery. Often, a sedative is ordered. Adequate rest helps the client manage the stress of surgery and helps healing.

Valuables

Valuables, such as jewellery and money, should be labelled and placed in safekeeping if the client's support people cannot take them home. If a client wishes not to remove a wedding band, the nurse can tape it in place. Wedding bands must be removed, however, if there is danger of the fingers swelling after surgery. Situations warranting removal include surgery on or cast application to an arm and a mastectomy that involves removal of the lymph nodes. (Mastectomies may cause edema of the arm and hand.)

Prostheses

All prostheses (artificial body parts, such as partial or complete dentures, contact lenses, artificial eyes, and artificial limbs), as well as eyeglasses, wigs, and false eyelashes, must be removed before surgery. Hearing aids are often left in place and the operating room personnel notified.

In some hospitals, dentures are placed in a locked storage area; in others, they are placed in labelled containers and kept at the client's bedside. Partial dentures can become dislodged and obstruct an unconscious client's breathing. The nurse also checks for the presence of chewing gum or loose teeth, a common problem with five- or six-year-olds undergoing tonsillectomy. Loose teeth can become dislodged and be aspirated during anesthesia.

Special Orders

The nurse checks the surgeon's orders for special requirements (e.g., the insertion of a nasogastric tube prior to surgery, the administration of medications, such as insulin, the application of anti-embolism stockings, or the applicatin of SCD's [sequential compression devices]). For the technique of inserting a nasogastric tube, see Procedure 38.1.

Skin Preparation

In most agencies, skin preparation begins during the preoperative phase.

Preoperative Skin Preparation

The Association of Operating Room Nurses (1996) recommends the following skin preparation practices to reduce the risk of postoperative wound infections:

- Clean the surgical site and surrounding areas. This can be accomplished before the surgical prep by having the client shower and shampoo or wash the surgical site before arriving in the surgical setting, or by washing the surgical site in the surgical setting immediately before applying an antimicrobial agent.
- Assess the surgical site before skin preparation. The nurse assesses the site for moles, warts, rashes, or other skin conditions, such as pustules, abrasions, or exudate, and documents their presence before skin preparation.
- Remove hair from the surgical site only when necessary or according to physician's orders or institutional policies and procedures. Personnel skilled in hair removal should remove hair using techniques that preserve skin integrity. Electric clippers or a depilatory cream should be used to reduce the risk of traumatizing the skin during hair removal. If a depilatory is used, hypersensitivity testing is performed prior to applying it to the surgical site. Skin trauma and abrasions increase the risk of microorganisms colonizing the surgical site. If hair is to be removed, it is done as close to the time of surgery as possible (near the room where the surgical procedure will be performed) to reduce the time for microbial growth.
- Prepare the surgical site and surrounding area with an antimicrobial agent when indicated. A nontoxic antimicrobial agent with a broad range of germicidal action is used to inhibit the growth of microorganisms during and following the surgical procedure. The agent selected depends on the client's history of hypersensitivity reactions, the location of the surgical site, and the skin condition. An area large enough to accommodate extension of the incision and any potential drain sites or additional incisions is prepared.
- Document surgical skin preparation in the client's record. Documentation should include the skin condition, including any growths, abrasions, or rashes; hair removal and the techniques used, if performed; the skin preparation, including cleansing and antimicrobial agent applied; who performed the preoperative skin preparation; and any adverse or hypersensitivity responses noted.

Vital Signs

Assess and record vital signs for baseline data. Report any abnormal findings, such as elevated blood pressure or elevated temperature.

Anti-Embolism Stockings

Anti-embolism (elastic) stockings are firm elastic hose that compress the veins of the legs and thereby facilitate the return of venous blood to the heart. They also improve arterial circulation to the feet and prevent edema of the legs and feet. These stockings are frequently applied preoperatively as well as postoperatively.

There are several types of stockings. One type extends from the foot to the knee and another from the foot to midthigh. These stockings usually have a partial foot that exposes the heel or toes so that extremity circulation can be assessed. Elastic stockings usually come in small, medium, and large sizes. See Procedure 44.2 on applying anti-embolism stockings.

Sequential Compression Devices

Clients who are undergoing surgery may benefit from a sequential compression device (SCD) to promote venous return from the legs. SCDs inflate and deflate plastic sleeves wrapped around the legs to promote venous flow. SCDs are discussed in Chapter 39. Procedure 39.6 outlines how to apply a sequential compression device. Application for SCDs needs to follow physician's orders and agency policy.

PROCEDURE 44.2 Applying Anti-Embolism Stockings

Before applying anti-embolism stockings, determine any potential or present circulatory problems and the surgeon's orders involving the lower extremities.

Assessment Focus
Sensation and movement; rates, volumes, and rhythms of posterior tibial and dorsalis pedis pulses; skin colour (note pallor, cyanosis, or other pigmentation); skin temperature; presence of distended veins or gross edema; skin condition (e.g., thickened, shiny, taut); Homans' sign, (pressure zones, decreased circulation (numbness, tingling, pain)

PURPOSES

- To facilitate venous return from the lower extremities
- To prevent venous stasis and venous thrombosis
- To reduce peripheral edema

Equipment

- ❑ Tape measure
- ❑ Clean anti-embolism stockings of appropriate size and type ordered
- ❑ Talcum powder

INTERVENTION

1. **Take measurements as needed to obtain the appropriate size stockings.**
   - Measure the length of both legs from the heel to the gluteal fold (for thigh-length stockings) or from the heel to the popliteal space (for knee-length stockings).
   - Measure the circumference of each calf and each thigh at the widest point.
   - Compare the measurements to the size chart to obtain stockings of correct size. Obtain two sizes if there is a significant difference. *Stockings that are too large for the client do not place adequate pressure on the legs to facilitate venous return and may bunch, increasing the risk of pressure and skin irritation. Stockings that are too small may impede blood flow to the feet and cause discomfort.*
2. **Select an appropriate time to apply the stockings.**
   - Apply stockings in the morning, if possible, before the client rises. *In sitting and standing positions, the veins can become distended so that edema occurs; the stockings should be applied before this happens.*
   - Assist the client who has been ambulating to lie down and elevate the legs for 15 to 30 minutes before applying the stockings. *This facilitates venous return and reduces swelling.*
3. **Prepare the client.**
   - Assist the client to a lying position in bed.
   - Wash and dry the legs, as needed.
   - Dust the ankles with talcum powder. *This eases application.*
4. **Apply the stockings.**
   - Reach inside the stocking from the top, and grasping the heel, turn the upper portion of the stocking inside out over the foot portion. *Firm elastic stockings are easier to fit over the foot and calf when inverted in this manner, rather than bunching the stocking up.*
   - Ask the client to point the toes, and position the stocking on the client's foot, taking care to place the toe and heel portions of the stocking appropriately (Figure 44.6). *Pointing the toes makes application easier.*

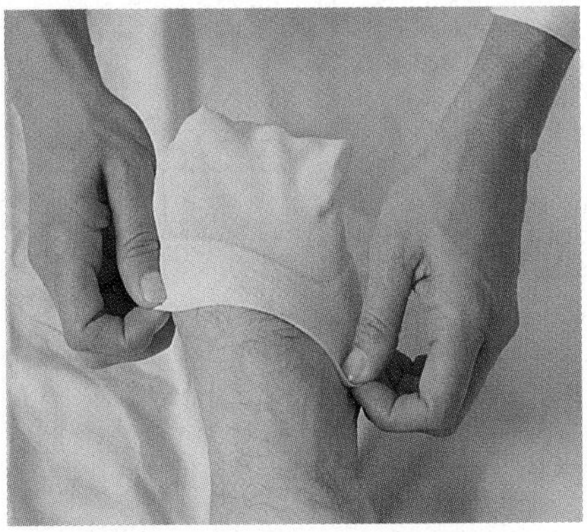

Figure 44.6 Applying the inverted stocking over the toes

   - Grasp the upper edge of the stocking and gently pull the stocking over the leg, turning it right side out in the process (Figure 44.7).
   - Inspect the client's leg and stocking, smoothing any folds or creases. Ensure that the stocking is not rolled down or bunched at the top or ankle. *Folds and creases can cause skin irritation under the stocking; bunching of the stocking can further impair venous return.*
   - Reassess peripheral circulation in 15 to 30 minutes. Then at least q4 h. Remove stockings if any decrease in peripheral circulation is noted.

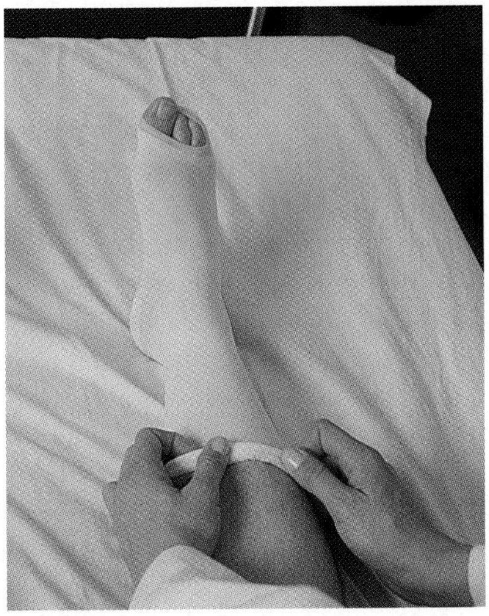

Figure 44.7 Pulling the stocking snugly over the leg

PROCEDURE 44.2 Applying Anti-Embolism Stockings *continued*

- Remove the hose for 30 minutes every eight hours, inspecting the legs and skin while the hose are off.
- Soiled hose may be laundered by hand with warm water and mild soap. Hang to dry.

5. Document the procedure.

- Record the procedure, your assessment data, and when the stockings are removed and reapplied.

Evaluation Focus
Appearance of the legs and skin; any edema; peripheral pulses; skin colour and temperature

Evaluating

The goals established during the planning phase are evaluated according to specific desired outcomes also established in that phase. See Table 44.2 for examples.

Consider...

What actions you would take if the client did *not* meet the following outcome criteria?

- "Stable vital signs" (Data reveal a body temperature of 39.1°C.)
- "Skin intact" (Data reveal a fine maculopapular red rash on the back.)

TABLE 44.2 Evaluation Goals and Outcomes: Preoperative Clients

Goal	Examples of Desired Outcomes
Physically prepared for surgery	Stable vital signs
	Nutritional status within normal limits
	Skin intact and clean
	Laboratory tests (specify) within expected range
Psychologically prepared for surgery	Describes proposed surgery, the reason for surgery, and the anticipated length of stay
	Verbalizes understanding of events that will occur during the perioperative period (e.g., transfer to PAR or ICU, monitoring equipment, infusions)
	States reasons for preoperative and postoperative procedures (e.g., skin prep, bowel prep) and practices (e.g., deep breathing, coughing, turning, leg exercises)
	Demonstrates deep breathing, coughing, splinting, leg exercises, and moving techniques as taught
	Demonstrates correct use of incentive spirometer
	Seeks information to reduce anxiety
	Uses effective coping strategies to control anxiety
	Seeks help, as appropriate
	Reports adequate sleep

Intraoperative Phase

The intraoperative nurse is a vital member of the surgical team, advocating for the client, maintaining safety, and continually assessing the needs of the client and the team.

Types of Anesthesia

Anesthesia is classified as *general* or *regional.* Anesthetic agents are administered by an anesthesiologist. **General anesthesia** is the loss of all sensation and consciousness. Under general anesthesia, protective reflexes, such as cough and gag reflexes, are lost. A general anesthetic acts by blocking awareness centres in the brain so that amnesia (loss of memory), analgesia (insensibility to pain), hypnosis (artificial sleep), and relaxation (rendering a part of the body less tense) occur. General anesthetics are usually administered by intravenous infusion or by inhalation of gases through a mask or through an endotracheal tube inserted into the trachea.

General anesthesia has certain advantages. Because the client is unconscious, rather than awake and anxious, respiration and cardiac function are readily regulated. Also, the anesthesia can be adjusted to the length of the operation and the client's age and physical status. Its chief disadvantage is that it depresses the respiratory and circulatory systems. Some clients become more anxious about a general anesthetic than about the surgery itself. Often, this is because they fear losing the capacity to control their own bodies.

Regional anesthesia is the temporary interruption of the transmission of nerve impulses to and from a specific area or region of the body. The client loses sensation in an area of the body but remains conscious. Several techniques are used.

- **Topical (surface) anesthesia** is applied directly to the skin and mucous membranes, open skin surfaces, wounds, and burns. The most commonly used topical agents are lidocaine (Xylocaine) and benzocaine. Topical anesthetics are readily absorbed and act rapidly.
- **Local anesthesia** (infiltration) is injected into a specific area and is used for minor surgical procedures, such as suturing a small wound or performing a biopsy. Lidocaine may be used.
- A **nerve block** is a technique in which the anesthetic agent is injected into and around a nerve or small nerve group that supplies sensation to a small area of the body. Major blocks involve multiple nerves or a *plexus* (e.g., the brachial plexus anesthetizes the arm); minor blocks involve a single nerve (e.g., a facial nerve).
- An **intravenous block (Bier block)** is used most often for procedures involving the arm, wrist, and hand. An occlusion tourniquet is applied to the extremity to prevent infiltration and absorption of the injected intravenous agent beyond the involved extremity.
- **Spinal anesthesia** is also referred to as **subarachnoid block (SAB).** It requires a lumbar puncture through one of the interspaces between lumbar disc 2 (L_2) and the sacrum (S_1). An anesthetic agent is injected into the subarachnoid space surrounding the spinal cord. Spinal anesthesia is often categorized as a low, mid, or high spinal. *Low spinals* (saddle or caudal blocks) are primarily used for surgeries involving the perineal or rectal areas. *Mid spinals* (below the level of the umbilicus—T_{10}) can be used for hernia repairs or appendectomies, and *high spinals* (reaching the nipple line—T_4) can be used for surgeries, such as cesarean sections.
- **Epidural (peridural) anesthesia** is an injection of an anesthetic agent into the epidural space, the area inside the spinal column but outside the dura mater.

Conscious sedation may be used alone or in conjunction with regional anesthesia for some diagnostic tests and surgical procedures. **Conscious sedation** is defined as minimal depression of the level of consciousness in which the client retains the ability to consciously maintain a patent airway and respond appropriately to verbal and physical stimuli (Kost, 1999). Intravenous narcotics, such as morphine or fentanyl (Sublimaze), and antianxiety agents, such as diazepam (Valium) or midazolam (Versed), are commonly used to induce and maintain conscious sedation. Conscious sedation increases the client's pain threshold and induces a degree of amnesia but allows for prompt reversal of its effects and a rapid return to normal activities of daily living. Such procedures as endoscopies, incision and drainage of abscesses, and even balloon angioplasty may be performed under conscious sedation.

Assessing

On the client's admission to the surgical suite or procedure room, the perioperative nurse confirms the client's identity and assesses the client's physical and emotional status. The nurse verifies the information on the preoperative checklist and evaluates the client's knowledge about the surgery and events to follow. The client's response to preoperative medications is assessed, as well as the placement and patency of tubes, such as IV lines, nasogastric tubes, and urinary catheters.

Assessment continues throughout surgery as the nurse and the anesthetist continuously monitor the client's vital signs (including blood pressure, heart rate, respiratory rate, and temperature), ECG, and oxygen saturation. Fluid intake and urinary output are monitored throughout surgery, and blood loss is estimated. In addition, arterial and venous pressures, pulmonary artery pressures, and laboratory values, such as blood glucose, hemoglobin, hematocrit, serum electrolytes, and arterial blood gases, may be evaluated during surgery. Continual assessment is necessary to rapidly identify adverse responses to surgery or anesthesia and intervene promptly to prevent complications.

During the intraoperative period, the nurse is aware of potential problems that could occur. These problems are likely related to the position of the patient, the effects of the anesthesia, equipment used and potential hazards, disruption of tissue perfusion during surgery, and the incision. The nurse also considers that complications that may occur are hemorrhage, surgical site infection, and neuromuscular injury.

Planning

The overall goals of care in the intraoperative period are to maintain the client's safety and to maintain homeostasis. Examples of nursing practices to achieve these goals include the following:

- Position the client appropriately for surgery
- Perform preoperative skin preparation
- Assist in preparing and maintaining the sterile field
- Open and dispense sterile supplies during surgery
- Provide medications and solutions for the sterile field
- Monitor and maintain a safe, aseptic environment
- Manage catheters, tubes, drains, and specimens
- Perform sponge, sharp, and instrument counts
- Document nursing care provided and the client's response to interventions

During surgery, nurses function as *circulating nurses* and *scrub nurses*. Circulating nurses assist scrub nurses and the surgeons. They help position the client for the operation and often position any needed equipment. During the surgery, circulating nurses obtain additional supplies, as needed, arrange lighting, and so on. Scrub nurses assist the surgeons. They wear sterile gowns, gloves, caps, and so on. Their responsibilities include draping the client with sterile drapes and handling sterile instruments and supplies. They also account for used sponges, needles, and instruments. A surgeon should not close, that is, suture, an incision until the scrub nurse can account for all sponges and instruments. This precaution avoids leaving any supplies inside the client.

Intraoperative Surgical Skin Preparation

Surgical skin preparation involves cleaning the surgical site, removing hair only if necessary, and applying an antimicrobial agent. In most surgery centres, skin preparation is done by surgery personnel close to the time of surgery. The purpose of a surgical skin preparation is to reduce the risk of postoperative wound infection. This is done in the following ways:

- Removing soil and transient microbes from the skin
- Reducing the resident microbial count to subpathogenic amounts in a short time and with the least amount of tissue irritation
- Inhibiting rapid rebound growth of microbes

Positioning

Proper positioning of the client during surgery is an important responsibility shared by the nurse, surgeon, and anesthetist. The ideal intraoperative client position provides the following:

- Optimal visualization of and access to the surgical site
- Optimal access for assessing and maintaining anesthesia and vital functions (vital signs, respirations, cardiovascular function)
- Protection of the client from harm

Positioning is performed after anesthesia is induced and before surgical draping of the client. The client is lifted into position to prevent shearing forces on the skin from sliding or rolling.

The exact position for the client depends on the operation, that is, the surgical approach. For example, a lithotomy position is usually used for vaginal surgery. See Table 27.2.

Positions on the operating table are maintained by straps, and body prominences are frequently padded. The position should consider normal joint range of motion and good body alignment, thereby avoiding strain or injury to muscles, bones, and ligaments.

Documentation Throughout the intraoperative phase, the nurse documents client care activities, such as IV fluid infusions, positioning, gastric suction, and urinary catheterization.

Postoperative Phase

Nursing during the postoperative phase is especially important for the client's recovery. Anesthesia impairs the ability of clients to respond to environmental stimuli and to help themselves, although the degree of consciousness of clients will vary. Moreover, surgery itself traumatizes the body by disrupting protective mechanisms and homeostasis.

Immediate Postanesthetic Phase

Recovery nurses have specialized skills to care for clients recovering from anesthesia and surgery. Once the health status has stabilized, the client is returned to the nursing unit or, in the case of a day-surgery client, to the day-surgery area before discharge. Assessment of the client in the immediate postanesthetic period is summarized in the accompanying box.

During the immediate postanesthetic stage, an unconscious client is positioned on the side with the face slightly down. A pillow is not placed under the head. In this position, gravity keeps the tongue forward, preventing occlusion of the pharynx and allowing drainage of mucus or vomitus out of the mouth rather than down the respiratory tree.

The nurse ensures maximum chest expansion by elevating the client's upper arm on a pillow. The upper arm is supported because the pressure of an arm against the chest reduces chest expansion potential. An artificial airway is maintained in place, and the client is suctioned, as needed, until cough and swallowing reflexes return. Generally, the client spits out an oropharyngeal airway when coughing returns. Endotracheal tubes are not removed until clients are awake and able to maintain their own airway. The client is then helped to turn, cough, and take deep breaths provided that vital signs are stable. When spinal anesthesia is used, the client may be required to remain flat for a specified period. See Chapter 39 for information about artificial airways.

The return of the client's reflexes, such as swallowing and gagging, indicates that anesthesia is wearing off. Time of recovery from anesthesia varies with the kind of anesthetic agent used, its dosage, and the individual's response to it. Nurses should arouse clients by calling them by name, and, in a normal tone of voice, repeatedly telling them that the surgery is over and that they are in the PARR.

Once the health status has stabilized, the client is returned to the nursing unit or, in the case of a day-surgery client, to the day-surgery area.

Clients are usually discharged from the PARR when the following occur:

CLINICAL ASSESSMENT

Immediate Postanesthetic Phase

- Adequacy of airway
- Oxygen saturation
- Adequacy of ventilation
  - Respiratory rate, rhythm, and depth
  - Use of accessory muscles
  - Breath sounds
- Cardiovascular status
  - Heart rate and rhythm
  - Peripheral pulse amplitude and equality
  - Blood pressure
  - Capillary filling
- Level of consciousness
  - Not responding
  - Arousable with verbal stimuli
  - Fully awake
  - Oriented to time, person, and place
- Temperature
- Presence of protective reflexes (e.g., gag, cough)
- Activity, ability to move extremities
- Skin colour (pink, pale, dusky, blotchy, cyanotic, jaundiced)
- Fluid status
  - Intake and output
  - Status of IV infusions (type of fluid, rate, amount in container, patency of tubing)
  - Signs of dehydration or fluid overload (see Chapter 40)
- Condition of operative site
  - Status of dressing
  - Drainage (amount, type, and colour)
- Patency of and character and amount of drainage from catheters, tubes, and drains
- Discomfort (i.e., pain) (type, location, and severity), nausea, vomiting
- Safety (i.e., necessity for side rails, call bell within reach)

- They are conscious and oriented.
- They are able to maintain a clear airway and deep breathe and cough freely.
- Vital signs have been stable or consistent with preoperative vital signs for at least 30 minutes.
- Protective reflexes (e.g., gag, swallowing) are active.
- They are able to move four extremities.
- Intake and urinary output is adequate (at least 30 mL/hr).
- They are afebrile or a febrile condition has been attended to.
- Dressings are dry and intact; there is no overt drainage.

Preparing for Ongoing Care of the Postoperative Client
While the client is in the operating room, the client's bed and room are prepared for the postoperative phase. In some agencies, the client is brought back to the unit on a stretcher and transferred to the bed in the room. In other agencies, the client's bed is brought to the surgery suite, and the client is transferred there. In the latter situation, the bed needs to be made with clean linens as soon as the client goes to surgery so that it can be taken to the operating room when needed. In addition, the nurse must obtain and set up any special equipment, such as an intravenous pole, suction, oxygen equipment, and orthopedic appliances (e.g., traction). If these are not requested on the client's record, the nurse should consult with the perioperative nurse or surgeon.

Return to the Nursing Unit: Immediate Postoperative Care

Assessing

As soon as the client returns to the nursing unit, the nurse conducts an initial assessment. The sequence of these activities varies with the situation. For example, the nurse may need to check the physician's stat orders before conducting the initial assessment; in such a case, nursing interventions to implement the orders can be carried out at the same time as assessment.

The nurse consults the surgeon's postoperative orders to learn the following:

- Food and fluids permitted by mouth
- Intravenous solutions and intravenous medications
- Position in bed
- Medications ordered (e.g., analgesics, antibiotics)
- Laboratory tests
- Intake and output, which in some agencies are monitored for all postoperative clients
- Activity permitted, including ambulation

The nurse also checks the OR and PARR record for the following data:

- Operation performed
- Presence and location of any drains
- Anesthetic used
- Postoperative diagnosis

- Estimated blood loss
- Medications administered in the recovery room

Many hospitals have postoperative protocols for regular assessment of clients. In some agencies, assessments are made every 15 minutes until vital signs stabilize, every hour for the next four hours, then every four hours for the next two days. It is important that the assessments be made as often as the client's condition requires. The nurse assesses the following:

- *Level of consciousness.* Assess orientation to time, place, and person. Most clients are fully conscious but drowsy when returned to their unit. Assess reaction to verbal stimuli and ability to move extremities. Assess ease of arousal.
- *Vital signs.* Take the client's vital signs (pulse, respiration, blood pressure, and oxygen saturation level) every 15 minutes until stable or in accordance with agency protocol. Vital signs may need to be taken more frequently based on client's condition. Compare initial findings with PARR data. In addition, assess the client's lung sounds and assess for signs of common circulatory problems, such as postoperative hypotension, hemorrhage, or shock. Hypovolemia due to fluid losses during surgery is a common cause of postoperative hypotension. Hemorrhage can result from insecure ligation of blood vessels or disruption of sutures. Massive hemorrhage or cardiac insufficiency can lead to shock postoperatively. Common postoperative complications with their manifestations and preventive measures are listed in Table 44.3.
- *Skin colour and temperature,* particularly that of the lips and nail beds. The colour of the lips and nail beds is an indicator of **tissue perfusion** (passage of blood through the vessels). Pale, cyanotic, cool, and moist skin may be a sign of circulatory problems.
- *Comfort.* Assess pain with the client's vital signs and, as needed, between vital sign measurements. Assess the location, type, and intensity of the pain. Do not assume that reported pain is incisional; other causes may include muscle strains, flatus, and angina. Ask the client to rate the pain on a scale of 0 to 10, with 0 being no pain and 10 the worst pain imaginable. Evaluate the client for objective indicators of pain: pallor, perspiration, muscle tension, and reluctance to cough, move, or ambulate. Determine when and what analgesics were last administered, and assess the client for any side effects of medication, such as nausea and vomiting.
- *Fluid balance.* Assess the type and amount of intravenous fluids, flow rate, and infusion site. Monitor the client's fluid intake and output. In addition to watching for shock, assess the client for signs of circulatory overload, and monitor serum electrolytes. Anesthetics and surgery affect the hormones regulating fluid and electrolyte balance (aldosterone and ADH in particular), placing the client at risk for decreased urine output and fluid and electrolyte imbalances. Assess presence of nausea and vomiting.
- *Dressings and bedclothes.* Inspect the client's dressings and bedclothes underneath the client. Excessive sanguineous drainage on dressings or bedclothes, often appearing underneath the client, can indicate hemorrhage. The amount of drainage on dressings is recorded by describing the diameter of the stains or by denoting the number and type of dressings saturated with drainage.
- *Drains and tubes.* Determine colour, consistency, and amount of drainage from all tubes and drains. All tubes should be patent, and tubes and suction equipment should be functioning. Drainage bags must be hanging properly.

Document the client's time of arrival and all assessments. Many agencies have progress flow records for this purpose. Alter the frequency, parameters, and priorities to meet the individual needs of the client.

Planning for Recovery Postoperatively Postoperative care planning and discharge planning begin in the preoperative phase when preoperative teaching is implemented. Client goals during the postoperative period include the following:

- Maintain comfort
- Promote healing
- Prevent associated risks, such as respiratory or cardiovascular complications, infection, and other common problems associated with surgery
- Restore the highest possible level of wellness

Planning for Home Care

To provide for continuity of care for the surgical client after discharge, the nurse needs to consider the client's needs for assistance with care in the home setting. Discharge planning for both the day-surgery client and the client who has been hospitalized for several days following surgery incorporates an assessment of the client's and family's abilities for self-care, financial resources, and the need for referrals and home health services. The box on page 1250 outlines a home care assessment for a surgical client; however, it is important to remember that surgical clients have diverse needs, and additional assessment data may be required.

TABLE 44.3 Potential Postoperative Problems

Problem	Description	Cause	Clinical Signs	Preventive Interventions
Respiratory				
Pneumonia	Inflammation of the alveoli	Infection, toxins, or irritants causing inflammatory process	Elevated temperature, cough, expectoration of blood-tinged or purulent sputum, dyspnea, chest pain	Deep-breathing exercises and coughing, moving in bed, early ambulation
Infectious pneumonia	May be limited to one or more lobes (lobar) or occur as scattered patches throughout the lungs (bronchial); also can involve interstitial tissues of lungs	Common organisms include *Streptococcus pneumoniae, Haemophilus influenzae,* and *Staphylococcus aureus*	Decreased oxygen saturation, increased respiratory rate and pulse	
Hypostatic pneumonia		Immobility and impaired ventilation result in atelectasis and promote growth of pathogens		
Aspiration pneumonia	Inflammatory process caused by irritation of lung tissue by aspirated material, particularly hydrochloric acid (HCl) from the stomach	Aspiration of gastric contents, food, or other substances; often related to loss of gag reflex		Positioning to prevent aspiration (e.g., Sims' position)
Atelectasis	A condition in which alveoli collapse and are not ventilated	Mucous plugs blocking bronchial passageways, inadequate lung expansion, analgesics, immobility	Dyspnea, tachypnea, tachycardia; diaphoresis, anxiety; pleural pain, decreased chest wall movement; dull or absent breath sounds; decreased oxygen saturation (SaO_2)	Deep-breathing exercises and coughing, moving in bed, early ambulation
Pulmonary embolism	Blood clot that has moved to the lungs and blocks a pulmonary artery, thus obstructing blood flow to a portion of the lung	Stasis of venous blood from immobility, venous injury from fractures or during surgery, use of oral contraceptives high in estrogen, pre-existing coagulation or circulatory disorder	Sudden chest pain, shortness of breath, cyanosis, shock (tachycardia, low blood pressure)	Turning, ambulation, anti-embolism stockings, sequential compression devices (SCDs)

TABLE 44.3 Potential Postoperative Problems *continued*

Problem	Description	Cause	Clinical Signs	Preventive Interventions
Circulatory				
Hypovolemia	Inadequate circulating blood volume	Fluid deficit, hemorrhage	Tachycardia, decreased urine output, decreased blood pressure	Early detection of signs; fluid and/or blood replacement
Hemorrhage	Internal or external bleeding	Disruption of sutures, insecure ligation of blood vessels	Overt bleeding (dressings saturated with bright blood; bright, free-flowing blood in drains or chest tubes), increased pain, increasing abdominal girth, swelling or bruising around incision	Early detection of signs; fluid and/or blood replacement; pressure dressings as ordered
Hypovolemic shock	Inadequate tissue perfusion resulting from markedly reduced circulating blood volume	Severe hypovolemia from fluid deficit or hemorrhage	Rapid weak pulse, dyspnea, tachypnea; restlessness and anxiety; urine output less than 30 mL/hr; decreased blood pressure; cool, clammy skin, thirst, pallor	Maintain blood volume through adequate fluid replacement; prevent hemorrhage; early detection of signs
Thrombophlebitis	Inflammation of the veins, usually of the legs and associated with a blood clot	Slowed venous blood flow due to immobility or prolonged sitting; trauma to vein, resulting in inflammation and increased blood coagulability	Aching, cramping pain; absent peripheral pulse, edema, cool extremity, decreased sensation; affected area is swollen, red, and hot to touch; vein feels hard	Early ambulation, leg exercises, anti-embolism stockings, SCDs, adequate fluid intake
Thrombus	Blood clot attached to wall of vein or artery (most commonly the leg veins)	As for thrombophlebitis for venous thrombi; disruption or inflammation of arterial wall for arterial thrombi	Venous: same as thrombophlebitis Arterial: pain and pallor of affected extremity; decreased or absent peripheral pulses	Venous: same as thrombophlebitis Arterial: maintaining prescribed position; early detection of signs
Embolus	Foreign body or clot that has moved from its site of formation to another area of the body (e.g., the lungs, heart, or brain)	Venous or arterial thrombus; broken intravenous catheter, fat, or amniotic fluid	In venous system, usually becomes a pulmonary embolus (see pulmonary embolism); signs of arterial emboli may depend on the location	As for thrombophlebitis or thrombus; careful maintenance of IV catheters

TABLE 44.3 Potential Postoperative Problems *continued*

Problem	Description	Cause	Clinical Signs	Preventive Interventions
Urinary				
Urinary retention	Inability to empty the bladder, with excessive accumulation of urine in the bladder	Depressed bladder muscle tone from narcotics and anesthetics; handling of tissues during surgery on adjacent organs (rectum, vagina)	Fluid intake larger than output; inability to void or frequent voiding of small amounts, bladder distention, suprapubic discomfort, restlessness	Monitoring of fluid intake and output, interventions to facilitate voiding, urinary catheterization, as needed
Urinary tract infection	Inflammation of the bladder, ureters, or urethra	Immobilization and limited fluid intake, instrumentation of the urinary tract	Burning sensation when voiding, urgency, cloudy urine, lower abdominal pain, urgency, frequency	Adequate fluid intake, early ambulation, aseptic straight catheterization only as necessary, good perineal hygiene
Gastrointestinal				
Nausea and vomiting		Pain, abdominal distention, ingesting food or fluids before return of peristalsis, certain medications, anxiety	Complaints of feeling sick to the stomach, retching or gagging	IV fluids until peristalsis returns; then clear fluids, full fluids, and regular diet, as ordered; antiemetic drugs, if ordered; analgesics for pain, as ordered
Constipation	Infrequent or no stool passage for abnormal length of time (e.g., within 48 hours after solid diet started)	Lack of dietary roughage, analgesics (decreased intestinal motility), immobility, anasthetic, decreased fluid intake	Absence of stool elimination, abdominal distention, and discomfort	Adequate fluid intake, high-fibre diet as ordered, early ambulation
Tympanites	Retention of gases within the intestines	Slowed motility of the intestines due to handling of the bowel during surgery and the effects of anesthesia	Obvious abdominal distention, abdominal discomfort (gas pains), absence of bowel sounds	Early ambulation; avoid using a straw, provide ice chips or water at room temperature
Postoperative ileus	Intestinal obstruction characterized by lack of peristaltic activity	Handling the bowel during surgery, anesthesia, electrolyte imbalance, wound infection	Abdominal pain and distention; constipation; absent bowel sounds; vomiting	IV fluids until peristalsis returns; gradual reintroduction of oral feeding, as ordered; early ambulation
Wound				
Wound infection	Inflammation and infection of incision or drain site	Poor aseptic technique; laboratory analysis of wound swab identifies causative microorganism	Purulent exudate, redness, tenderness, elevated body temperature, wound odour	Keeping wound clean and dry, surgical aseptic technique when changing dressings
Wound dehiscence	Separation of a suture line before the incision heals	Malnutrition (emaciation, obesity), poor circulation, excessive strain on suture line	Increased incision drainage, tissues underlying skin become visible along parts of the incision	Adequate nutrition, appropriate incisional support and avoidance of strain

→

TABLE 44.3 Potential Postoperative Problems *continued*

Problem	Description	Cause	Clinical Signs	Preventive Interventions
Wound evisceration	Extrusion of internal organs and tissues through the incision	Same as for wound dehiscence	Opening of incision and visible protrusion of organs	Same as for wound dehiscence
Psychological				
Postoperative depression	Mental disorder characterized by altered mood	Weakness, surprise nature of emergency surgery, news of malignancy, severely altered body image, or other personal matter; may be a physiological response to some surgeries	Anorexia, tearfulness, loss of ambition, withdrawal, rejection of others, feelings of dejection, sleep disturbances (insomnia, excessive sleeping)	Adequate rest, physical activity, opportunity to express anger and other negative feelings; client teaching

HOME CARE ASSESSMENT

Surgical Clients

Client

- *Self-care abilities:* Ability to manage hygiene and other self-care, to perform wound care, as needed, to manage tubes and stomas, and to manage prescribed medications
- *Supplies required:* Wound care supplies, such as dressings, hypoallergenic tape, cleansing solutions, binders or slings, elastic wraps, irrigating syringe and solution
- *Assistive devices required:* Walker, cane, raised toilet seat, commode, overhead trapeze, grab bars
- *Current level of knowledge:* Postoperative pain management, wound care, dressing changes, urinary catheters or other drains, activity restrictions, dietary prescriptions, prescribed exercises (e.g., range-of-motion, postmastectomy exercises), infection control measures, such as hand-washing, medications

Family

- *Caregiver availability, skills, and responses:* Willingness and ability to assume responsibility for care, as needed (e.g., wound care, catheter and tube management, meal preparation, assistance with ADLs, shopping, transportation to and from appointments), other available caregivers
- *Family role changes and coping:* Effect on parenting and spousal roles, sexuality, social roles, financial status
- *Financial resources:* Ability to purchase necessary supplies and equipment; other sources of funding or financial assistance (e.g., private insurance, Blue Cross—see Chapter 15)

Community

- Available community resources, such as equipment and supply companies, support and educational organizations and groups (e.g., ostomy clubs and Reach for Recovery), home health-care agencies or providers, access to pharmacy services, transportation services for medical care, Meals on Wheels, and other charitable support organizations

Implementing

Nursing interventions designed to promote client recovery and prevent complications include (1) pain management; (2) appropriate positioning; (3) incentive spirometry and deep-breathing and coughing exercises; (4) leg exercises; (5) early ambulation; (6) adequate hydration; (7) diet; (8) promoting urinary elimination; (9) suction maintenance; and (10) wound care.

Pain Management
Although pain is a sensory and emotional experience that serves to alert us to harm and initiate responses to avoid or minimize harm, pain in the surgical client has little protective value. It can, in fact, have detrimental effects, leading to stimulation of the sympathetic nervous system, tachycardia, shallow breathing, atelectasis, altered gas exchange, immobility, and immunosuppression (Van Keuren & Eland, 1997). See Chapter 45 for a more in-depth discussion of pain and pain management.

Pain is usually greatest 12 to 36 hours after surgery, decreasing after the second or third postoperative day. During the initial postoperative period, patient-controlled analgesia (PCA) or continuous analgesic administration through an intravenous catheter is often prescribed. The nurse monitors the infusion or amount of analgesic administered by PCA, assesses the client's pain relief, and notifies the physician if the client is experiencing unacceptable side effects or inadequate pain relief. "PRN" parenteral or oral analgesics should be administered on a routine basis (every two to six hours, depending on the drug, route, and dose) for the first 24 to 36 hours depending on physician's orders. When routine analgesic administration is no longer necessary, the prescribed analgesic is generally given before scheduled activities and rest periods.

An anti-inflammatory agent, such as ibuprofen or ketorolac (Toradol), is often administered in conjunction with a narcotic analgesic to enhance pain relief. Clients need to be reminded that analgesics are most effective when taken on a regular basis or before pain becomes severe. Because muscle tension increases pain perception and responses, nurses need to use nonpharmacological measures in addition to prescribed analgesia. These include ensuring that the client is warm and providing back rubs, position changes, diversional activities, and adjunctive measures, such as imagery.

Positioning
Position the client as ordered. Clients who have had spinal anesthetics usually lie flat for eight to 12 hours. An unconscious or semiconscious client is placed on the side with no pillow and no elevation of head in a position that allows fluids to drain from the mouth. Unless contraindicated, elevation of affected extremities (e.g., following foot surgery) with the distal extremity higher than the heart promotes venous drainage and reduces swelling. Unaffected joints should be positioned to maintain body alignment (see Chapter 43).

Deep-Breathing and Coughing Exercises
Deep-breathing exercises help remove mucus, which can form and remain in the lungs due to the effects of general anesthetic and analgesics. These drugs depress the action of both the cilia of the mucous membranes lining the respiratory tract and the respiratory centre in the brain. By increasing lung expansion and preventing the accumulation of secretions, deep breathing helps prevent pneumonia and **atalectasis** (collapse of the alveoli), which may result from stagnation of fluid in the lungs.

An incentive spirometer is often ordered for the postoperative client to encourage deep breathing. This device measures the flow of air inhaled through a mouthpiece. See Chapter 39. The client is instructed to breathe in through the mouthpiece until a certain level is achieved (usually measured by a ball within an enclosed chamber). Inhalation and ventilation are enhanced using the incentive spirometer.

Deep breathing frequently initiates the coughing reflex. Voluntary coughing in conjunction with deep breathing facilitates the movement and expectoration of respiratory tract secretions. Coughing may be contraindicated postoperatively depending on the type of surgery (e.g. craniostomy, eye surgery).

Encourage the client to do deep-breathing and coughing exercises hourly, or at least every two hours, during waking hours for the first few days. Assist the client to a sitting position in bed or on the side of the bed. The client can splint the incision with a pillow when coughing, or the nurse can splint the incision for the client to reduce discomfort.

Leg Exercises
Encourage the client to do leg exercises taught in the preoperative period every one to two hours during waking hours, according to agency policy and physician's orders. Muscle contractions compress the veins, preventing the stasis of blood in the veins, a cause of **thrombus** formation and subsequent **thrombophlebitis** and **emboli.** Contractions also promote arterial blood flow.

Moving and Ambulation
Encourage and assist the client to turn from side to side at least every two hours. Turning alternates which lung can achieve maximum expansion because it is uppermost. Avoid placing pillows or rolls under the client's knees because pressure on the popliteal blood vessels can interfere with blood circulation to and from the lower extremities. Clients who practise turning before surgery usually find it easier to do after surgery.

The client should ambulate as soon as possible after surgery in accordance with the surgeon's orders. Generally, clients begin ambulation the evening of the day of surgery or the first day after surgery unless contraindicated. Early ambulation prevents respiratory, circulatory, urinary, and gastrointestinal complications. It also prevents general muscle weakness. Schedule ambulation for periods after the client has taken an analgesic or when the client is comfortable. Ambulation should be gradual, starting with the client sitting on the bed and dangling the feet over the side. A client who cannot ambulate is periodically assisted to a sitting position in bed, if allowed, and turned frequently. The sitting position permits the greatest lung expansion.

Hydration

Maintain intravenous infusions, as ordered, to replace body fluids lost either before or during surgery. When oral intake is permitted, initially offer only small sips of water. Large amounts of water can induce vomiting because anesthetics and narcotic analgesics temporarily inhibit the motility of the stomach. The client who cannot take fluids by mouth *may* be allowed by the surgeon's orders to suck ice chips. Provide mouth care. Postoperative clients often complain of thirst and a dry, sticky mouth. These discomforts are a result of the preoperative fasting period, preoperative medications (such as atropine), and loss of body fluid.

Measure the client's fluid intake and output for at least two days or until fluid balance is stable without an intravenous infusion. Ensuring adequate fluid balance is important. Sufficient fluids keep the respiratory mucous membranes and secretions moist, thus facilitating the expectoration of mucus during coughing. Also, an adequate fluid balance is important to maintain renal and cardiovascular function.

Nutrition

The surgeon orders the client's postoperative diet. Depending on the extent of surgery and the organs involved, the client may be allowed nothing by mouth for several days or may be able to resume oral intake when nausea is no longer present. When "diet as tolerated" is ordered, offer clear liquids initially. If the client tolerates these with no nausea, the diet can often progress to full liquids and then to a regular diet provided that gastrointestinal functioning is normal. Assess the return of peristalsis by auscultating the abdomen (see Chapter 27). Gurgling and rumbling sounds indicate peristalsis. Anesthetic agents, narcotics, handling of the intestines during abdominal surgery, fasting, and inactivity all inhibit peristalsis. Therefore, bowel sounds should be carefully assessed every four to six hours. Oral fluids and food are usually started after the return of peristalsis. Assist very weak clients to eat.

Observe the client's tolerance of the food and fluids ingested and note and report the passage of flatus, abdominal distention, bowel movements, and eructation.

Urinary Elimination

Provide measures that promote urinary elimination. For example, help male clients stand at the bedside, or female clients to a bedside commode, if allowed, and ensure that fluid intake is adequate. Determine whether the client has any difficulties voiding and assess the client for bladder distention (see Figure 27.74). Report to the surgeon if a client does not void within eight hours following surgery, unless another time frame is specified.

Anesthetic agents temporarily depress urinary bladder tone, which usually returns within six to eight hours after surgery. Surgery in the pubic area, vagina, or rectum, during which the surgeon may manipulate the bladder, often causes urinary retention. If all measures to promote voiding fail, a urinary catheterization is often ordered. See Chapter 36. Measure the fluid intake and output (I & O) of all new postoperative clients. Generally, I & O records are kept for at least two days or until the client re-establishes fluid balance without an IV or catheter in place.

Suction

Some clients return from surgery with a gastric or intestinal tube in place and orders to connect the tube to suction. For more information about gastrointestinal tubes, see Chapter 38. The suction ordered can be continuous or intermittent. Intermittent suction is applied when a single-lumen gastric tube is used to reduce the risk of damaging the mucous membrane near the distal port of the tube. Continuous suction may be applied if a double-lumen tube is in place. Fluids and electrolytes must be replaced intravenously when gastric suction or continuous drainage is ordered. Nasogastric tubes may be irrigated if the lumen becomes clogged. They are generally irrigated before and after tube feedings or the instillation of medications. Nasogastric irrigation may require a physician's order, particularly following gastrointestinal surgery. Agency policy for irrigations must be followed. Procedure 44.3 describes the management of gastrointestinal suction.

Suction may also be applied to other drainage tubes, such as chest tubes or a wound drain. The type and amount of suction is ordered by the physician. Most agencies have *wall suction units* available. A suction regulator with a drainage receptacle connects to a wall outlet that provides negative pressure. Check the receptacle frequently to prevent excess drainage from interfering with the suction apparatus; empty or change the receptacle according to agency policy. *Portable electric suction units* or *pumps* (e.g., the Gomco pump) may be used in the home or when wall suction is not available.

Wound Care

Most clients return from surgery with a sutured wound covered by a dressing, although in some cases the wound may be left unsutured. Dressings are inspected regularly to ensure that they are clean, dry, and intact. Excessive drainage may indicate hemorrhage, infection, or an open wound.

When dressings are changed, the nurse assesses the wound for appearance, size, drainage, swelling, pain, and the status of drains or tubes. Details about these assessments are outlined in the box on page 1256.

Because surgical incisions heal by primary intention, the nurse can expect the following sequential signs of healing:

1. *Absence of bleeding and the appearance of a clot binding the wound edges.* The wound edges are well approximated and bound by fibrin in the clot within the first few hours after surgical closure.

PROCEDURE 44.3 Managing Gastrointestinal Suction

Before initiating gastric suction, determine (1) whether the suction is continuous or intermittent; (2) the ordered suction pressure (a low suction pressure is between 80 and 100 mm Hg, and a high pressure is between 100 and 120 mm Hg); (3) whether there is an order to irrigate the gastrointestinal tube, and if so, the type of solution to use and; (4) agency policy and physician's orders.

PURPOSES

- To relieve abdominal distention
- To maintain gastric decompression after surgery
- To remove blood and secretions from the gastro-intestinal tract (to rest gastrointestional tract)
- To relieve discomfort (e.g., when a client has a bowel obstruction)
- To maintain the patency of the nasogastric tube

Assessment Focus
Presence of abdominal distention on palpation; auscultated bowel sounds; abdominal discomfort; vital signs for baseline data; nausea, vomiting

Equipment

Initiating Suction

- ❑ Gastrointestinal tube in place in the client
- ❑ Basin
- ❑ 50-mL syringe with an adapter
- ❑ Stethoscope
- ❑ Suction device for either continuous or intermittent suction
- ❑ Connector and connecting tubing
- ❑ Disposable gloves

Maintaining Suction

- ❑ Graduated container as required to measure gastric drainage
- ❑ Basin of water
- ❑ Cotton-tipped applicators
- ❑ Ointment or lubricant
- ❑ Disposable gloves

Irrigation

- ❑ Disposable gloves
- ❑ Stethoscope
- ❑ Disposable irrigating set containing a sterile 50-mL syringe, moisture-resistant pad, basin, and graduated container
- ❑ Sterile normal saline (500 mL) or the ordered solution

INTERVENTION

Initiating Suction

1. Position the client appropriately.

- Assist the client to a semi-Fowler's position if it is not contraindicated. *In semi-Fowler's position, the tube is not as likely to lie against the wall of the stomach and will, therefore, suction most efficiently. Semi-Fowler's position also prevents reflux of gastric contents, which could lead to aspiration.*

2. Confirm that the tube is in the stomach.

- Don gloves.
- Aspirate stomach contents and check their acidity using a pH test strip.
- Insert air into the tube with the syringe, and listen with a stethoscope over the stomach (just below the xiphoid process) for a swish of air.
- Use other methods in accordance with agency protocol. See Chapter 38.

3. Set and check the suction.

- Connect the appropriate suction regulator to the wall suction outlet and the collection device to the regulator. *Intermittent suction regulators* generally are used with single-lumen tubes and apply suction for a set interval (15 to 60 seconds), followed by an interval of no suction. Intermittent suction is set at 80 to 100 mm Hg (check agency policy) or as ordered by the physician. Check the suction level by occluding the drainage tube and observing the regulator dial during a suction cycle. *Continuous suction regulators* are used with double-lumen (e.g., Salem sump) nasogastric tubes. Set continuous suction as ordered by the physician, or at 60 to 120 mm Hg (check agency policy).
- If using a portable suction machine, turn on the machine and regulate the suction as above. The Gomco pump has two settings: low intermittent for single-lumen tubes, and high for double-lumen tubes.
- Test for proper suctioning by occluding the tube.

4. Establish gastric suction.

- Connect the gastrointestinal tube to the suction tubing by using the connector.
- If a Salem sump tube is in place, connect the larger lumen to the suction equipment. This double-lumen tube has a smaller tube running inside the primary suction tube. *The smaller tube provides a continuous flow of atmospheric air through the drainage tube at its distal end and prevents excessive suction force on the gastric mucosa at the drainage outlets. Damage to the gastric mucosa is thus avoided.*
- Always keep the air vent tube of a Salem sump tube open and above the level of the stomach when

PROCEDURE 44.3 Managing Gastrointestinal Suction *continued*

suction is applied. *Closing the vent would stop the sump action and cause mucosal damage. Keeping the end of the air vent tube higher than the stomach prevents reflux of gastric contents into the air lumen of the tube.*

- After suction is applied, watch the tubing for a few minutes until the gastric contents appear to be running through the tubing into the receptacle. A Salem sump tube makes a soft, hissing sound when it is functioning correctly.
- If the suction is not working properly, check that all connections are tight and that the tubing is not kinked.
- Anchor the tubing to the patient's gown so that it does not loop below the suction bottle. *If the tubing falls below the suction bottle, the suction may be obstructed because of the pressure required to push the fluid against gravity.*

5. **Assess the drainage.**

- Observe the amount, colour, odour, and consistency of the drainage. Normal gastric drainage has a mucoid consistency and is either colourless or yellow-green because of the presence of bile. A coffee-grounds colour and consistency may indicate bleeding.
- Test the gastric drainage for pH and blood (by using Hematest), when indicated. A person who has had gastrointestinal surgery can be expected to have some blood in the drainage.

MAINTAINING SUCTION

6. **Assess the client and the suction system regularly.**

- Assess the client every 30 minutes until the system is running effectively and then every two hours, or as the client's health indicates, to ensure that the suction is functioning properly. If the client complains of fullness, nausea, or epigastric pain, or if the flow of gastric secretions is absent in the tubing or in the collection bottle, ineffective suctioning or blockage of the nasogastric tube is likely.
- Inspect the suction system for patency of the system (e.g., kinks or blockages in the tubing) and tightness of the connections. *Loose connections can permit air to enter and thus decrease the effectiveness of the suction by decreasing the negative pressure.*

7. **Relieve blockages, if present.**

- Don gloves.
- Check the suction equipment. To do this, disconnect the nasogastric tube from the suction over a collecting basin (to collect gastric drainage), and then, with the suction on, place the end of the suction tubing in a basin of water. If water is drawn into the drainage bottle, the suction equipment is functioning properly, but the nasogastric tube is either blocked or positioned incorrectly.
- Reposition the client (e.g., to the other side) if permitted. *This may facilitate drainage.*
- Rotate the nasogastric tube, and reposition it. This step is contraindicated for clients with gastric surgery. *Moving the tube may interfere with gastric sutures.*
- Irrigate the nasogastric tube as agency protocol states or on the order of the physician. Irrigating the nasogastric tube may also be contraindicated if the client has had gastric or intestinal surgery. See steps 11 to 13.

8. **Prevent reflux into the vent lumen of a Salem sump tube.** *Reflux of gastric contents into the vent lumen may occur when stomach pressure exceeds atmospheric pressure. In this situation, gastric contents follow the path of least resistance and flow out the vent lumen rather than the drainage lumen. To prevent reflux, do the following:*

- Place the vent tubing higher than the client's stomach.
- Keep the drainage collection container below the level of the client's stomach, and do not allow it to become overfull. *A collection device placed above the level of fluid in the stomach or one that is too full may interfere with drainage, allowing reflux of gastric contents into the air lumen.*
- Keep the drainage lumen free of particulate matter that may obstruct the lumen. See steps 11 to 13 for irrigating a nasogastric tube.

9. **Ensure client comfort.**

- Clean the client's nostrils, as needed, using the cotton-tipped applicators and water. Apply a water-soluble lubricant or ointment.
- Provide mouth care every two hours and as needed. Some post-operative clients are permitted to suck ice chips or a moist cloth to maintain the moisture of the oral mucous membranes. A physician's order is required.

10. **Empty the drainage receptacle according to agency policy or physician's order.**

- Clamp the nasogastric tube, and turn off the suction.
- Don gloves.
- If the receptacle is graduated, determine the amount of drainage.
- Disconnect the receptacle.
- If the receptacle is not graduated, empty the contents into a graduated container and measure.
- Inspect the drainage carefully for colour, consistency, and presence of substances (e.g., blood clots).
- Discard and replace receptacle, or rinse the receptacle with cool water and reattach it to the suction. Check agency policy.
- Turn on the suction, and unclamp the nasogastric tube.
- Observe the system for several minutes to make sure function is re-established.
- Go to step 14.

IRRIGATING A GASTROINTESTINAL TUBE

11. **Prepare the client and the equipment.**

- Verify physician's orders and agency policy.

PROCEDURE 44.3 Managing Gastrointestinal Suction *continued*

- Place the moisture-resistant pad under the end of the gastrointestinal tube.
- Turn off the suction.
- Don gloves.
- Disconnect the gastrointestinal tube from the connector.
- Determine that the tube is in the stomach. See step 2 above and Chapter 38. *This ensures that the irrigating solution enters the client's stomach.*

12. Irrigate the tube.

- Draw up the ordered volume of irrigating solution into the syringe; 30 mL of solution per instillation is usual, but up to 50 mL may be given per instillation, if ordered.
- Attach the syringe to the nasogastric tube, and slowly inject the solution.
- Gently aspirate the solution if indicated by agency policy. *Forceful withdrawal could damage the gastric mucosa.*
- If you encounter difficulty in withdrawing the solution, inject 20 mL of air, and aspirate again, and/or reposition the client or the nasogastric tube. *Air and repositioning may move the end of the tube away from the stomach wall.* If aspirating difficulty continues, reattach the tube in intermittent low suction, and notify the nurse in charge or the physician.
- Repeat the preceding steps until the ordered amount of solution is used.
- Note: A Salem sump tube can also be irrigated through the vent lumen without interrupting suction. However, only small quantities of irrigant can be injected via this lumen compared with the drainage lumen.
- After irrigating a Salem sump tube, inject 10 to 20 mL of air into the vent lumen while applying suction to the drainage lumen. *This tests the patency of the vent and ensures sump functioning.*

13. Re-establish suction.

- Reconnect the nasogastric tube to suction.
- If a Salem sump tube is used, inject the air vent lumen with 10 to 20 mL of air after reconnecting the tube to suction.
- Observe the system for several minutes to make sure it is functioning.

14. Document all relevant information.

- Record the time suction was started. Also, record the pressure established, the colour and consistency of the drainage, and nursing assessments.
- During maintenance, record assessments, supportive nursing measures, and data about the suction system.
- When irrigating the tube, record verification of tube placement; the time of the irrigation; the amount and type of irrigating solution used; the number of times irrigated; the amount, colour, and consistency of the returns; the patency of the system following the irrigation; and nursing assessments.
- Record client response and teaching.

Evaluation Focus

Relief of abdominal distention or discomfort; bowel sounds; character and amount of gastric drainage; integrity of nares; hydration of oral mucous membranes; patency of tube; system functioning; relief of nausea and vomiting

Home Care Considerations

Instruct the caregiver to do the following:

- Maintain suction, as ordered; do *not* increase or decrease the suction without instructions from the nurse or the physician.
- Offer mouth care every two hours.
- Avoid tension and pulling on the tube by securing it to the gown.
- Check the patency of the tube if nausea or vomiting occur.
- Report an increasing amount of or bloody drainage.

2. *Inflammation (redness and swelling) at the wound edges for one to three days.*
3. *Reduction in inflammation when the clot diminishes*, as granulation tissue starts to bridge the area. The wound is bridged and closed within seven to 10 days. Increased inflammation associated with fever and drainage is indicative of wound infection; the wound edges then appear brightly inflamed and swollen.
4. *Scar formation.* Collagen synthesis starts four days after injury and continues for six months or longer.
5. *Diminished scar size* over a period of months or years. An increase in scar size indicates keloid formation.

See Chapter 37 for information about wound drainage, cleaning wounds, wound irrigation, hot and cold applications, and supporting and immobilizing wounds.

Surgical Dressings Not all surgical dressings require changing. Sometimes, surgeons in the operating room apply a dressing that remains in place until the sutures are removed, and no further dressings are required. In many situations,

CLINICAL GUIDELINES

Assessing Surgical Wounds

Appearance

- Inspect colour of wound (e.g., for bruising and/or redness) and surrounding area and approximation of wound edges. Note security of sutures.

Size

- Note size and location of dehiscence, if present.

Drainage

- Observe location, colour, consistency, odour, and degree of saturation of dressings. Note number of gauzes saturated or diameter of drainage on gauze.

Swelling

- Observe the amount of swelling; minimal to moderate swelling is normal in early stages of wound healing.

Pain

- Expect severe to moderate postoperative pain for three to five days; persistent severe pain or sudden onset of severe pain may indicate internal hemorrhaging or infection. Note specific areas of incision which cause pain when cleansed/dressed.

Drains or Tubes

- Inspect drain security and placement, amount and character of drainage, and functioning of collecting apparatus, if present. Note method of security (e.g., sutures, safety pin).

RESEARCH NOTE

Can Staff Nurses Prevent Postoperative Tape Blisters?

Using a nursing process framework, a clinical study was conducted to develop a protocol for treating postoperative tape blisters. Preliminary data were collected as nurses were implementing care and the data were evaluated in an ongoing manner. From that data, it was theorized that a lack of stretch in the tape might be causing the blisters. Five types of stretch tape were then put into use on clients in the operating room and on nursing units. After evaluating the tapes for ease in removing the backing, handling, application, flexibility, and adhesion, the preferred tape was selected. In the three years after putting that tape into routine use, no further blisters were noted.

Implications: Bedside nurses can make important contributions toward evaluating and improving specific nursing interventions.

Source: Faller, N. A., Lawrence, K. G., Kantorski, L., Morgan, B., & Keller, B. (1995). Using the nursing process to solve a problem: Post-op tape blisters. *Ostomy Wound Management, 41*(1), 68–70.

however, surgical dressings are changed regularly to prevent the growth of microorganisms.

In some instances, a client may have a Penrose drain inserted (see the next section). In this situation, the main surgical incision is considered cleaner than the surgical stab wound made for the drain insertion because there is usually considerable drainage. The main incision is, therefore, cleaned first, and *under no circumstances are materials that were used to clean the stab wound used subsequently to clean the main incision.* In this way, the main incision is kept free of the microorganisms around the stab wound. Cleaning a wound and applying a sterile dressing are detailed in Procedure 44.4.

Wound Drains and Suction Surgical drains, for example a **Penrose drain,** are inserted to permit the drainage

PROCEDURE 44.4 Cleaning a Sutured Wound and Applying a Sterile Dressing

Before changing a dressing, determine any specific orders about the wound or dressing. The use of sterile gloves is not required (unless agency policy) for cleaning a wound and applying a simple dressing as long as aseptic technique is followed.

Assessment Focus
Allergies to wound cleaning agents, latex, and tape; the appearance and size of the wound; the amount and character of exudate; complaints of discomfort; the time of the last pain medication; signs of systemic infection (e.g., elevated body temperature, diaphoresis, malaise; leukocytosis); presence of sutures, drains, materials used to dress the wound previously; client response to postoperative recovery

PURPOSES

- To promote wound healing by primary intention
- To prevent infection
- To assess the healing process
- To protect the wound from mechanical trauma

PROCEDURE 44.4 Cleaning a Sutured Wound and Applying a Sterile Dressing *continued*

Equipment

- ❑ Bath blanket (if necessary)
- ❑ Moistureproof bag
- ❑ Mask (optional)
- ❑ Acetone or another solution (if necessary, to loosen adhesive)
- ❑ Disposable gloves
- ❑ Sterile gloves
- ❑ Sterile dressing set; if none is available, gather the following sterile items from a central supply cart:
  - ❑ Drape or towel
  - ❑ Sterile gauze squares
  - ❑ Container for the cleaning solution
  - ❑ Cleaning solution (e.g., normal saline)
  - ❑ Antiseptic solution for cleansing table surface
  - ❑ Two pairs of sterile forceps (thumb or artery)
  - ❑ Sterile gauze dressings and surgipads
- ❑ Additional supplies required for the particular dressing (e.g., extra gauze dressings and ointment, if ordered)
- ❑ Tape, tie tapes, or binder

INTERVENTION

1. Prepare the client, and assemble the equipment.

- Validate the physician's order and check agency policy.
- Wash hands.
- Acquire assistance for changing a dressing on a restless or confused adult. *The person might move and contaminate the sterile field or the wound.*
- Assist the client to a comfortable position in which the wound can be readily exposed. Expose only the wound area, using a bath blanket to cover the client, if necessary. *Undue exposure is physically and psychologically distressing to most people.*
- Make a cuff on the moistureproof bag for disposal of the soiled dressings, and place the bag within reach. It can be taped to the bedclothes away from the sterile field. *Making a cuff helps keep the outside of the bag free from contamination by the soiled dressings and prevents subsequent contamination of the nurse's hands or of sterile instrument tips when discarding dressing or sponges. Placement of the bag within reach prevents the nurse from reaching across the sterile field and the wound and potentially contaminating these areas.*
- Clean table surface for the sterile field with antiseptic solution.
- Put on a face mask, if required. *Some agencies require that a mask be worn for surgical dressing changes to prevent contamination of the wound by droplet spray from the nurse's respiratory tract.*

2. Remove binders and tape.

- Remove binders, if used, and place them aside. Untie tie tapes, if used.
- If adhesive tape was used, remove it by holding down the skin and pulling parallel to the skin and toward the dressing. *Pressing down on the skin provides countertraction against the pulling motion. Tape is pulled toward the incision to prevent strain on the sutures or wound.*
- Use a solvent to loosen tape, if required. *Moistening the tape with acetone or a similar solvent lessens the discomfort of removal, particularly from hairy surfaces.*

3. Remove and dispose of soiled dressings appropriately.

- Put on clean disposable gloves, and remove the outer abdominal dressing or surgipad.
- Lift the outer dressing so that the underside is away from the client's face. *The appearance and odour of the drainage may be upsetting to the client. Note any drainage.*
- Place the soiled dressing in the moistureproof bag without touching the outside of the bag. *Contamination of the outside of the bag is avoided to prevent the spread of microorganisms to the nurse and subsequently to others. Then, remove your gloves.*
- Remove the *under* dressings with a sterile forceps, taking care not to dislodge any drains. If the gauze sticks to the drain, support the drain with the forceps, and remove the gauze with the other hand.
- Assess the location, type (colour, consistency), and odour of wound drainage and the number of gauzes saturated or the diameter of drainage collected on the dressings.
- Discard the soiled dressings in the bag as before.

4. Set up the sterile supplies using aseptic technique.

- Open the sterile dressing set using surgical aseptic technique.
- Place the sterile drape beside the wound.
- Open the sterile cleaning solution, and pour it over the gauze sponges in the plastic container. Alternate action: pour solution over each separate gauze as cleansing wound or drain site.

5. Clean the wound, if indicated.

- Clean the wound using your forceps and gauze swabs moistened with cleaning solution.
- Keep the forceps tips lower than the handles at all times. *This prevents their contamination by fluid travelling up to the handle and nurse's wrist and back to the tips.*
- Use the cleaning methods illustrated and described in Figure 44.8 or one recommended by agency protocol.
- Use a separate swab for each stroke, and discard each swab after use. *This prevents the introduction of microorganisms to other wound areas.*
- Dry wound, if required, in same manner as cleaning wound.

→

PROCEDURE 44.4 Cleaning a Sutured Wound and Applying a Sterile Dressing *continued*

- If a drain is present, clean it next, taking care to avoid reaching across the cleaned incision. Clean the skin around the drain site by swabbing in half or full circles from around the drain site outward, using separate swabs for each wipe (Figure 44.8, *B*).
- Support and hold the drain erect while cleaning around it. Clean as many times as necessary to remove the drainage. Clean the drain, cleansing at the stab wound and then up the drain away from skin.
- Dry the drain area with dry gauze swabs, as required, in same manner as cleaning the drain area.

6. **Apply dressings to the incision and drain site using the aseptic technique.**

- Apply dry sterile dressings to incision or wound site first. Then, place a precut 4×4 gauze snugly around the drain (Figure 44.9), or open a 4×4 gauze to 4×8, fold it lengthwise to 2×8, and place the 2×8 around the drain so that the ends overlap. *This dressing absorbs the drainage and helps prevent it from excoriating the skin. Using precut gauze or folding it as described, instead of cutting the gauze, prevents any threads from coming loose and getting into the wound where they could cause inflammation and provide a site for infection.*

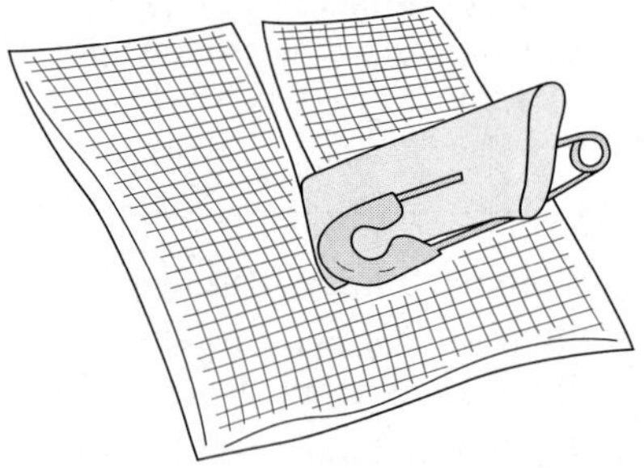

Figure 44.9 Precut gauze in place around a drain

- Apply the sterile dressings one at a time over the drain site. Place the bulk of the dressings over the drain area and below the drain, depending on the client's usual position. *Layers of dressings are placed for best absorption of drainage, which flows by gravity.*
- Apply the final surgipad or abdominal pad over the entire site. Secure the dressing with tape or ties.

7. **Document the procedure and all nursing assessments.**

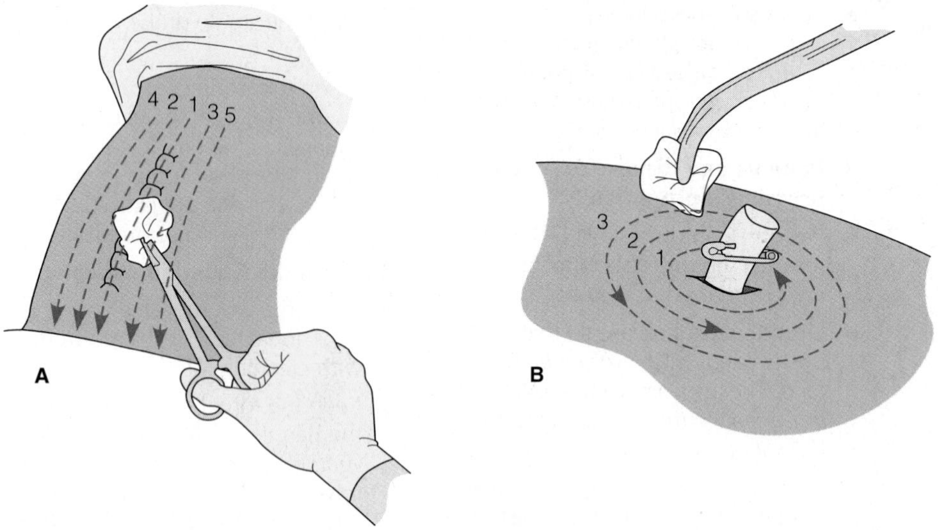

Figure 44.8 Methods of cleaning surgical wounds: *A*, cleaning the wound from top to bottom, starting at the centre; *B*, cleaning around a drain site. For both methods, a clean sterile swab is used for each stroke.

Evaluation Focus

Amount of granulation tissue or degree of healing; amount of drainage and its colour, consistency, and odour; presence of inflammation; degree of discomfort associated with the incision or drain site; bruising; approximation; client response and learning/teaching; security of sutures and drain

PROCEDURE 44.4 Cleaning a Sutured Wound and Applying a Sterile Dressing *continued*

Home Care Considerations

Instruct caregivers to do the following:

- Provide pain medication approximately 30 minutes before the procedure if the wound care causes pain or discomfort.
- Wash hands thoroughly and dry prior to handling wound care supplies and providing wound care.
- Clean and wipe dry a flat surface for the sterile field.
- Keep pets out of the area when setting up for and performing sterile procedures.
- Acquire all needed supplies before starting a *sterile* procedure.
- Maintain sterile or clean technique as instructed.
- Handle all *sterile* supplies from the outside of the wrapper or the edges.
- Do not touch the parts of supplies or equipment that will touch the patient.
- Avoid skin injury by using paper tape or Montgomery tie tapes instead of adhesive tape.
- Report any increasing wound drainage, pain, redness, increasing swelling, or opening or gaping of wound edges.
- Place any soiled dressing materials in a waterproof bag and dispose of it according to public health recommendations.

CLINICAL GUIDELINES

Shortening a Drain

- Remove dressings, put on sterile gloves, and clean the incision (Procedure 44.4).
- Clean the drain site appropriately (Figure 44.8, *B*). Assess the amount and character of drainage, including odour, thickness, and colour.
- If the drain has *not* been shortened before, cut and remove the suture holding it in place. The drain is sutured to the skin during surgery to keep it from slipping into the body cavity.
- Firmly grasp the drain by its full width at the level of the skin with a forcept, and pull the drain out the required length. Grasping the full width of the drain ensures even traction.
- Insert a sterile safety pin through the base of the drain as close to the skin as possible by holding the drain tightly against the skin edge and inserting the pin above your fingers (Figure 44.10). The pin keeps the drain from falling back into the incision. Holding the drain securely in place at the skin level and inserting the pin above the fingers prevents the nurse from pulling the drain further out or pricking the client during this step. The nurse must take care to avoid pricking self.
- With the sterile scissors, cut off the excess drain so that about 2.5 cm remains above the skin (Figure 44.11). Discard the excess in the waste bag.
- Apply dressings to the drain site and the incision.

of excessive serosanguineous fluid and purulent material and to promote healing of underlying tissues. These drains may be inserted and sutured through the incision line, but they are most commonly inserted through stab wounds a few centimetres away from the incision line so that the incision itself may be kept dry. Without a drain, some wounds would heal on the surface and trap the discharge inside, and an abscess might form.

Drains vary in length and width. The length can be 25 to 35 cm and the width 1.25 to 4 cm. To facilitate drainage and healing of tissues from the inside to the outside, the physician may order that the drain be pulled out or shortened 2.5 to 5 cm each day. When a drain is completely removed, the remaining stab wound usually heals within a day or two. Shortening the drain is usually done when the dressing is changed. Steps involved in shortening a drain are shown in the accompanying box.

A *closed wound drainage system* consists of a drain connected to either an electric suction or a portable drainage suction, such as a Hemovac (Figure 44.12) or Jackson-Pratt. The closed system reduces the possible entry of microorganisms into the wound through the drain. The drainage tubes are sutured in place and connected to a reservoir. For example, the Jackson-Pratt drainage tube is connected to a reservoir that maintains constant low suction. These portable wound suctions also provide for accurate measurement of the drainage and prevent leakage of drainage over the incision site.

The surgeon inserts the wound drainage tube during surgery. Generally, the suction is discontinued from three to five days postoperatively or when the drainage is minimal.

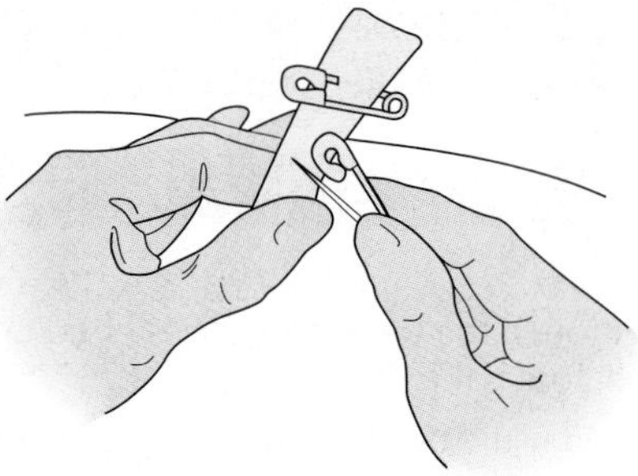

Figure 44.10 Pinning a drain with sterile gloved hands

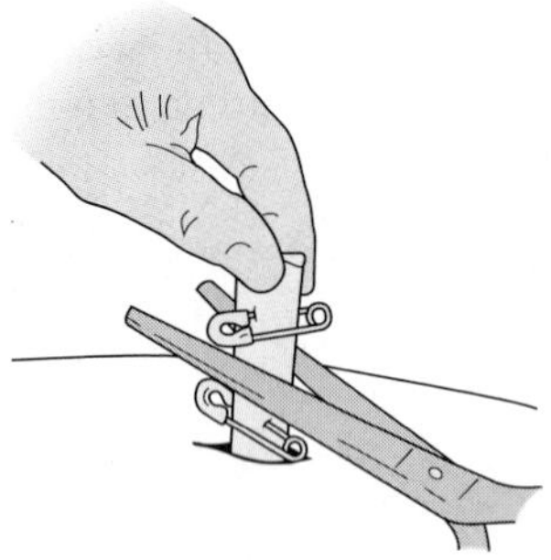

Figure 44.11 Shortening a drain with sterile gloved hand

CLINICAL GUIDELINES

Removing and Emptying a Jackson-Pratt Drain

- Remove dressings, put on sterile gloves, and clean the incision (Procedure 44.4).
- Clean the drain site appropriately (Figure 44.8, *B*, p. 1258) as for Penrose drains. Assess the amount and character of drainage, including odour, thickness, and colour.
- Prior to removing the drain, the nurse releases the suction and empties the contents into a graduated mini cup and leaves the suction bulb decompressed.
- The nurse then removes the suture around the drain and communicates with the client that she/he will now be removing the drain, pulling with an even tension. Encourage client to perform relaxation techniques, such as slow, deep breathing.
- The nurse applies a clean dressing over the drain site and teaches the client to keep the drain site clean and dry.
- Discard the drainage tube and suction bulb in the waste bag.

Nurses are responsible for maintaining the wound suction, which hastens the healing process by draining excess exudate that might otherwise interfere with the formation of granulation tissue.

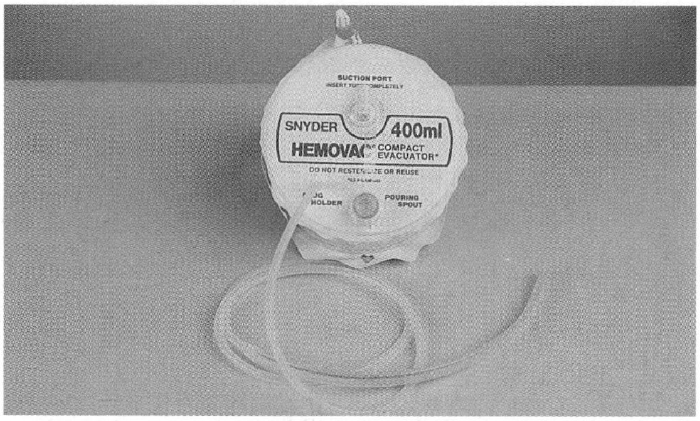

Figure 44.12 Closed wound drainage system (Hemovac)

Other nursing measures include ensuring maintenance of continuous suction, periodic emptying of collection reservoir, securing tubing/reservoir to prevent dislodgement (e.g., by pinning to gown), and keeping the reservoir lower than the insertion site.

Closed wound drainage systems have directions for use printed on the drainage container. When emptying the container, the nurse should wear gloves and avoid touching the drainage port.

Sutures **Sutures** are threads used to sew body tissues together. Sutures used to attach tissues beneath the skin are often made of an absorbable material that disappears in several days. Skin sutures, by contrast, are made of a variety of nonabsorbable materials, such as silk, cotton, linen, wire, nylon, and Dacron (polyester fibre). Silver wire clips or staples are also available. Usually, skin sutures are removed seven to 10 days after surgery.

There are various methods of suturing. Skin sutures can be broadly categorized as either *interrupted* (each stitch is tied and knotted separately) or *continuous* (one thread runs in a series of stitches and is tied only at the beginning and at the end of the run). Common methods of suturing are illustrated in Figure 44.13.

Retention sutures are very large sutures used in addition to skin sutures for some incisions (Figure 44.14). They attach underlying tissues of fat and muscle as well as skin and are used to support incisions in obese individuals or when healing may be prolonged. They are frequently left in place longer than skin sutures (14 to 21 days) but, in some instances, are removed at the same time as the skin sutures. To prevent these large sutures from irritating the incision, the surgeon may place rubber tubing over them or a roll of gauze under them extending down the incision line.

The physician orders the removal of sutures. In some agencies, only physicians remove sutures; in others, registered nurses and nursing students with appropriate supervision may do so. Agency policies about removal of retention sutures vary. The nurse should verify whether they are to be removed and who may remove them.

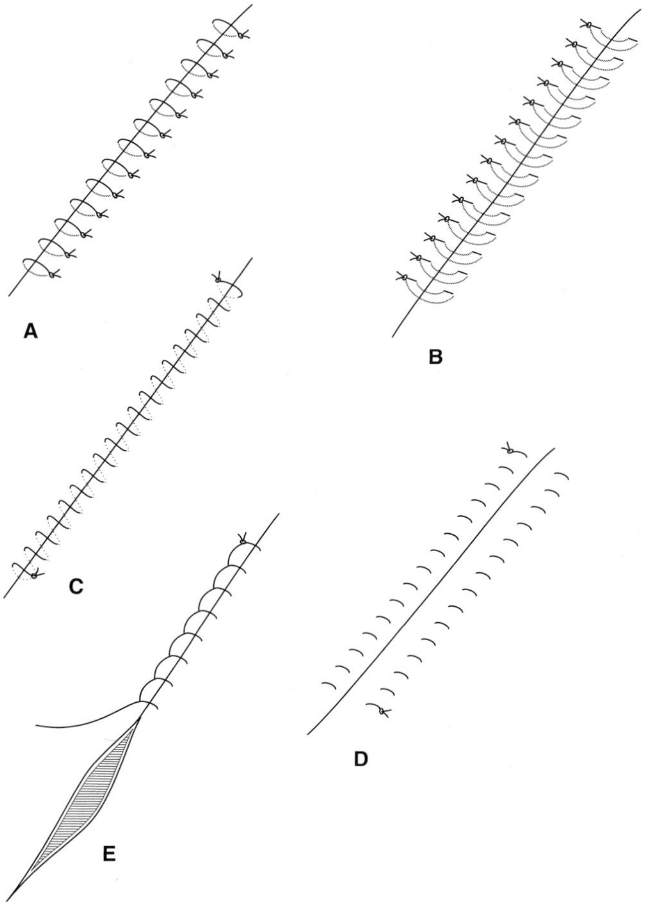

Figure 44.13 Common sutures: *A,* plain interrupted; *B,* mattress interrupted; *C,* plain continuous; *D,* mattress continuous; *E,* blanket continuous

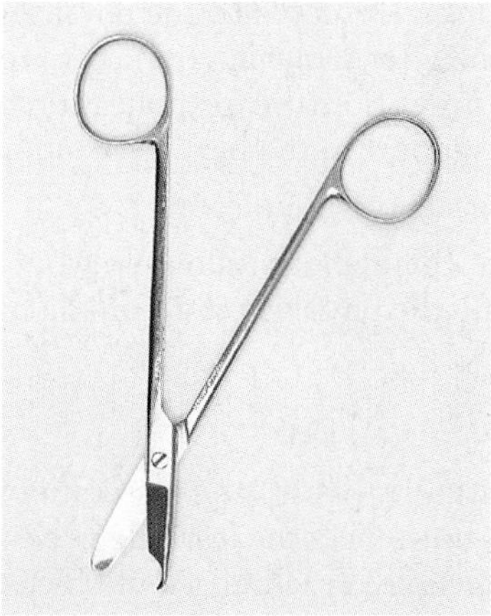

Figure 44.15 Suture scissors

Sterile technique and special suture scissors are used in suture removal. The scissors have a short, curved cutting tip that readily slides under the suture (Figure 44.15). Wire clips or staples are removed with a special instrument that

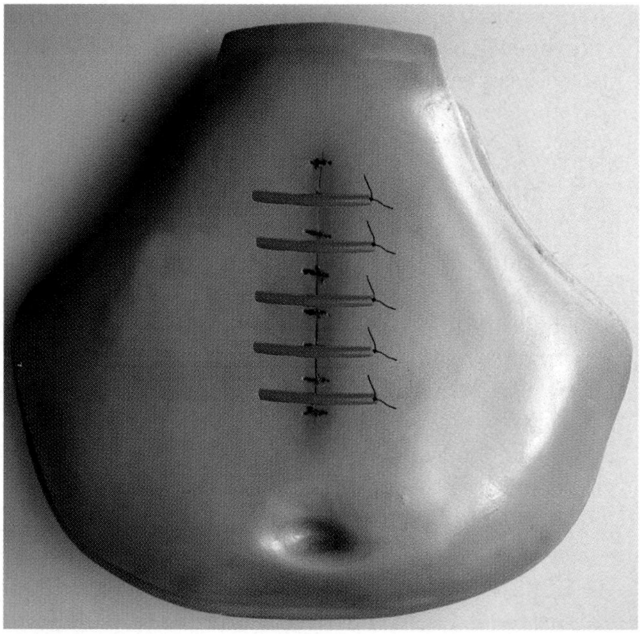

Figure 44.14 A surgical incision with retention sutures

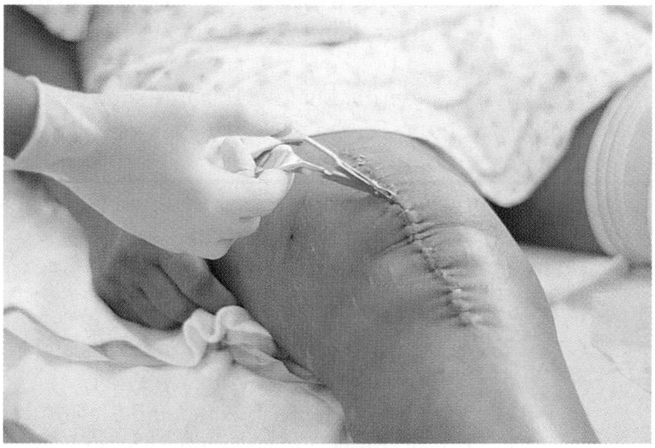

Figure 44.16 Removing surgical clips

squeezes the centre of the clip to remove it from the skin (Figure 44.16). Guidelines for removing sutures follow:

- Before removing skin sutures, verify (1) the orders for suture removal (in many instances, only *alternate* interrupted sutures are removed one day, and the remaining sutures are removed a day or two later); and (2) whether a dressing is to be applied following the suture removal. Some physicians prefer no dressing; others prefer a small, light gauze dressing to prevent friction by clothing.
- Inform the client that suture removal may produce slight discomfort, such as a pulling or stinging sensation, but should not be painful.

- Remove dressings and clean the incision in accordance with agency protocol. Cleaning the suture line with normal saline before and after suture removal may help prevent infection.
- Remove *plain interrupted sutures* as follows:
  a. Grasp the suture at the knot with a pair of forceps.
  b. Place the curved tip of the suture scissors under the suture as close to the skin as possible, either on the side opposite the knot (Figure 44.17) or directly under the knot. Cut the suture. Sutures are cut as close to the skin as possible on one side of the visible part because the suture material that is visible to the eye is in contact with resident bacteria of the skin and must not be pulled beneath the skin during removal. Suture material that is beneath the skin is considered free from bacteria.
  c. With the forceps, pull the suture out in one piece. Inspect the suture carefully to make sure that all suture material is removed. Suture material left beneath the skin acts as a foreign body and causes inflammation.
- Remove *mattress interrupted sutures* as follows:
  a. When possible, cut the visible part of the suture close to the skin at *A* and *B* in Figure 44.18, opposite the knot, and remove this small visible piece. Discard it as described below. In some sutures, the visible part opposite the knot may be so small that it can be cut only once.
  b. Grasp the knot *(C)* with forceps. Remove the remainder of the suture beneath the skin by pulling out in the direction of the knot.
- Remove continuous sutures as follows:
  a. Continuous suturing, as the name implies, is a series of sutures with one knot at each end of the incision line. The knots are grasped and the suture is cut as close to the skin as possible, the top knot first, then the bottom knot.
  b. All sutures are removed remembering the principle of never pulling the visible portion of a suture through underlying tissue.
- Discard the suture onto a piece of sterile gauze or into the moistureproof bag, being careful not to contaminate the forceps tips.
- Continue to remove *alternate* sutures (except for continuous sutures where all sutures are removed), that is, the third, fifth, seventh, and so forth if no dehiscence occurs. Alternate sutures are removed first so that remaining sutures keep the skin edges in close approximation and prevent any dehiscence from becoming large.
- If no dehiscence occurs, remove the remaining sutures. If dehiscence does occur, do not remove the remaining sutures, and report the dehiscence to the nurse in charge.

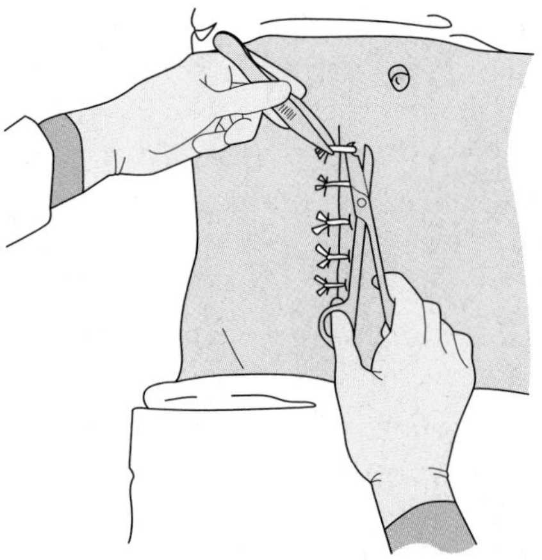

Figure 44.17 Removing a plain interrupted skin suture

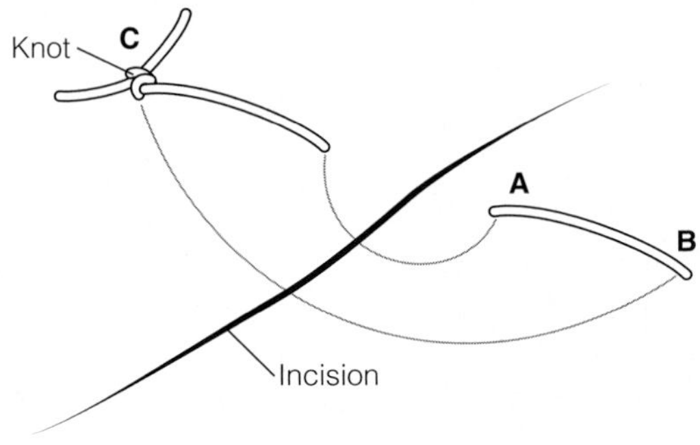

Figure 44.18 Mattress interrupted sutures

- If Steri-Strips are ordered by the physician, apply them to the wound after removing the sutures or clips. Some physicians order Steri-Strip application to provide additional support to the healing wound.
- Reapply a dressing, if indicated.
- Instruct the client about follow-up wound care, such as contacting the physician if wound discharge appears.

Home Care Teaching

To ensure continuity of care and restoration of the client's health, nurses must meet the learning needs of clients and their support people. Teaching should focus on actions to maintain comfort, to promote healing and restore wellness, and to make use of appropriate community agencies and other sources of help.

Maintaining Comfort

- Instruct the client to use pain medications as ordered, not allowing pain to become severe before taking the prescribed dose.

- If not contraindicated, discuss the use of over-the-counter analgesics, such as acetaminophen, as postoperative pain becomes less severe or if the client is reluctant to use prescription drugs due to side effects.
- Teach the client to avoid using alcohol or other central nervous system depressants while taking narcotic analgesics.
- Discuss the importance of gradually resuming activities and avoiding overexertion.
- Emphasize the importance of paying attention to increasing pain or discomfort. Instruct the client to contact the physician if pain increases after a period of decreasing discomfort.
- Teach the client to use nonpharmacological measures to help manage pain, such as conscious relaxation, distraction, meditation, or visualization.

Promoting Healing

- If indicated, teach the client how to change wound dressings and perform wound care.
- Emphasize the importance of hygiene and hand washing to prevent infections.
- Instruct the client to report promptly to the physician any increasing redness, swelling, pain, or discharge from the incision or drain sites.
- Discuss any prescribed activity restrictions, such as avoiding lifting.
- Discuss the importance of keeping follow-up appointments to monitor healing and recovery after surgery.

Restoring Wellness

- Discuss the relationship of increasing activities to restoring wellness and promoting a sense of well-being.
- Teach the client that surgery and stressors can depress immune function and to avoid exposure to illness (e.g., crowded areas and people with upper respiratory illnesses) whenever possible.
- Emphasize the importance of adequate rest for healing and immune function.
- If appropriate, discuss lifestyle changes to promote wellness, such as smoking cessation, increasing activity level, reducing stress, and consuming a healthy diet high in fruits, vegetables, and whole grains with adequate protein to promote healing.

Community Agencies and Other Sources of Help

- Provide information about where durable medical equipment can be purchased, rented, or obtained free of charge; how to access home health care and other services; and where to obtain supplies, such as dressings or nutritional supplements.
- Suggest additional sources of information, such as the Canadian Association of Wound Care, Reach to Recovery, United Ostomy Association of Canada, and so on.

Referrals

The nurse needs to consider appropriate referrals for the client, such as the following:

- Home health agencies for wound care and assessment and for assistance with ADLs, if necessary
- Community social services for assistance in obtaining medical and assistive equipment
- Respiratory, physical, or occupational therapy services, as indicated

Evaluating

Using the goals developed during the planning stage—maintaining comfort, promoting healing, restoring wellness, and preventing risks associated with surgery—the nurse collects data to evaluate whether the identified goals and desired outcomes have been achieved. Examples of client goals and related outcomes are shown in Table 44.4.

If the desired outcomes are not achieved, the nurse, client, and support people need to explore the reasons before modifying the care plan. For example, if the goal "Maintain comfort" is *not* met, questions to be considered include the following:

- What is the client's perception of the problem?
- Does the client understand how to use PCA?
- Is the prescribed analgesic dose adequate for the client?
- Is the client allowing pain to become intense prior to requesting medication or using PCA?
- Where is the client's pain? Could it be due to a problem unrelated to surgery (e.g., chronic arthritis, anginal pain)?
- Is there evidence of a complication that could cause increased pain (an infection, abscess, or hematoma)?

Consider...

What actions would you take if the client did *not* meet the following outcome criteria?

- "Lungs clear with good breath sounds throughout" (Data reveal diminished breath sounds in the right base, respiratory rate 24/min.)
- "Participates actively in postoperative care" (Data reveal that the client refuses to look at or touch the incision, turning his face to the wall during dressing changes.)

TABLE 44.4 Evaluation Goals and Outcomes: Postoperative Clients

Goal	Examples of Desired Outcomes
Maintain comfort	Verbalizes satisfaction with pain control measures
	Absence of nonverbal indications of pain (e.g., protective body position, restlessness, facial expressions of pain)
	Absence of physiological indications of pain (e.g., muscle tension; perspiration; change in blood pressure, heart rate, respiratory rate, and pupil size; loss of appetite)
	Moves and ambulates with minimal difficulty
	Rests for extended periods
Promote healing	Incision clean, dry, and intact
	Wound edges approximated well
	Balanced fluid intake and output
	Tolerating diet rich in fibre, protein, and vitamins A and C
	Active bowel sounds within 48 hours
	Normal defecation within three days following ingestion of food
	Hemoglobin, hematocrit, and serum electrolytes within normal limits
Prevent risks associated with surgery	Performs deep breathing, coughing, and incentive spirometry, as instructed
	Normal auscultated breath sounds
	Adequate respiratory excursion (depth)
	Performs leg exercises, as instructed
	Walks increasing distances (specify) each day
	Stable vital signs
	Strong and equal peripheral pulses in all four extremities
Restore highest possible level of wellness	Increasingly participates in self-care activities (specify)
	Asks pertinent questions concerning ongoing care
	Seeks help, as appropriate
	Demonstrates ability to care for incision
	Reports ability to manage ongoing care

FOCUS ON CRITICAL THINKING

Mr. Teng is a 77-year-old client with a history of chronic obstructive pulmonary disease. Currently, his respiratory condition is being controlled with medications, and he is free of infection. He has just been transferred to the post-anesthesia care unit following a hernia repair performed under spinal anesthesia. His blood pressure is 132/88, pulse 84, respirations 28, and tympanic temperature is 36.8°C. He is awake and stable.

1. What factors place Mr. Teng at increased risk for the development of complications during and after surgery?
2. Speculate about why Mr. Teng's surgeon and anesthesiologist decided to perform Mr. Teng's surgery under regional anesthesia as opposed to general anesthesia?
3. What preparations were taken during the preoperative period in order to protect Mr. Teng from possible complications during and after his surgery?
4. How will Mr. Teng's postoperative assessments differ from a person who received general anesthesia?
5. What postoperative precautions are especially important to Mr. Teng in view of his chronic lung condition?

See Appendix A for answers to these questions.

CHAPTER HIGHLIGHTS

- Surgery is a unique experience that creates stress and necessitates physical and psychological changes.
- The perioperative period includes three phases: preoperative, intraoperative, and postoperative.
- Surgical procedures are categorized by degree of urgency, purpose, and degree of risk.
- Such factors as age, general health, nutritional status, medication history, and psychological health affect a client's risk during surgery.
- Clients must agree to surgery and sign an informed consent.
- Nursing history and physical assessment data are important sources for planning preoperative and postoperative care.
- The overall goal of nursing care during the preoperative phase is to prepare the client mentally and physically for surgery.
- Preoperative teaching includes situational information and psychosocial support, the role of the client throughout the perioperative period, expected sensations and discomfort, and training for the postoperative period.
- Preoperative teaching should include moving, leg exercises, and coughing and deep-breathing exercises. Many aspects of preoperative teaching are intended to prevent postoperative complications.
- Physical preparation includes the following areas: nutrition and fluids, elimination, hygiene, rest, medications, care of valuables and prostheses, special orders, and surgical skin preparation.
- Anti-embolism stockings or sequential compression devices may be ordered for some clients to facilitate venous return.
- A preoperative checklist provides a guide to and documentation of a client's preparation before surgery.
- Maintaining the client's safety is the overall goal of nursing care during the intraoperative phase.
- Anesthesia may be general or regional. Regional anesthesia includes topical, local, nerve block, intravenous block, spinal anesthesia (subarachnoid block), and epidural.
- A surgical skin preparation should be carried out as close to the time of surgery as possible and is commonly performed during the intraoperative phase.
- Positioning of the client during surgery is important to reduce the risk of tissue and nerve damage.
- Immediate postanesthetic care focuses on assessment and monitoring parameters to prevent complications from anesthesia or surgery.
- Initial and ongoing assessment of the postoperative client includes level of consciousness, vital signs, oxygen saturation, skin colour and temperature, comfort, fluid balance, dressings, drains, and tubes.
- The overall goals of nursing care during the postoperative period are to promote comfort and healing, restore the highest possible level of wellness, and prevent associated risks, such as infection or respiratory and cardiovascular complications.
- Ongoing postoperative nursing interventions include (1) managing pain, (2) appropriate positioning, (3) encouraging incentive spirometry and deep-breathing and coughing exercises, (4) promoting leg exercises and early ambulation, (5) maintaining adequate hydration and nutritional status, (6) promoting urinary elimination, (7) continuing gastrointestinal suction, and (8) providing wound care.
- Surgical aseptic technique (sterile technique) is used when changing dressings on surgical wounds to promote healing and reduce the risk of infection.
- Penrose drains and Hemovac drainage systems are examples of drains that may be placed in or near surgical wounds to promote drainage of excess serosanguineous or purulent exudate.
- Sutures, wire clips, or staples are used to approximate skin and underlying tissues after surgery. These are generally removed seven to 10 days after surgery.

READINGS AND REFERENCES

Suggested Readings

Butcher, L. (1999). Teaching Pre-operative. In M. Bulechek, & J. McCloskey (Eds.), *Nursing interventions: Effective nursing treatments* (3rd ed.). (p. 224–234). Philadelphia, PA: W.B. Saunders.
This chapter provides an overview of the intervention of preoperative teaching, including a review of the pertinent research literature and a discussion on effective intervention tools for preoperative teaching.

Fox, V. J. (1998, May). Postoperative education that works. *AORN Journal*, *67*(5), 1010, 1012–1017.
Perioperative nurses have acquired greater responsibility for clients' and family members' postoperative education. Recent nursing research indicates that clients may not be getting specific information about dealing with the everyday practical matters they encounter while recovering at home from their surgical procedures. This article addresses some of these issues (e.g., food, sex, driving,

bathing, wound care, return to work, limits on activities). The author answers questions most often asked by clients and their family members.

Operating Room Nurses Association of Canada. (1998). *Standards for Peri-operative Nursing Practice*. Halifax: Author. This document provides an overview of knowledge of surgical principles and methods to improve the care of surgical clients. The standards outline the scope of responsibility of the perioperative nurse.

Vernon, S., & Pfeifer, G. M. (1997, September). Are you ready for bloodless surgery? *American Journal of Nursing, 97*(9), 40–47. In this article, the authors discuss bloodless surgery and its risks and benefits for clients. Certain religious faiths, such as Jehovah's Witness, forbid the use of blood transfusions. Techniques used to improve the safety and outcome of surgeries for clients of these beliefs are changing the way many surgeries are performed and the use of blood and blood products during and after surgery. All clients stand to benefit, as using fewer transfusions reduces the risks of transfusion reactions and infections, such as hepatitis B and human immunodeficieny virus (HIV).

Related Research

Brumfield, V. C., Kee, C. C., & Johnson, J. Y. (1996, December). Preoperative patient teaching in ambulatory surgery settings. *AORN Journal, 64*(6), 941–952.

Crenshaw, J. (1999). Research for Practice: New guidelines for pre-operative fasting. *American Journal of Nursing, 99*(4), 49.

Faller, N. A., Lawrence, K. G., Kantorski, L., Morgan, B., & Keller, B. (1995). Using the nursing process to solve a problem: Post-op tape blisters. *Ostomy Wound Management, 41*(1), 68–70.

Law, M. L. (1997). A telephone survey of day-surgery eye patients. *Journal of Advanced Nursing, 25*, 355–363.

Lookirland, S., & Pool, M. (1998, January). Study on effect of methods of preoperative education in women. *AORN Journal, 67*(1), 203–206, 208, 210–213.

Schultz, A., Bien, M., Dumond, K., Brown, K., & Myers, A. (1999). Etiology and incidence of pressure ulcers in surgical patients. *AORN, 70*(3), 434–449.

Selected References

Algren, C. L., & Algren, J. T. (1997, March). Pediatric sedation: Essentials for the perioperative nurse. *Nursing clinics of North America, 32*(1), 17–30.

Association of Operating Room Nurses (AORN). (1996, November). Recommended practices for skin preparation of patients. *AORN Journal, 64*(5), 813–816.

Association of Operating Room Nurses. (2000). *AORN Standards, recommended practices and guidelines.* Denver, CO: Author.

Bailies, B. K. (2000). Perioperative care of the elderly surgical patient. *AORN Journal, 72*, 186–207.

Berg, M. (1998). An introduction to anesthesia-related medications. *Journal of Perianesthesia Nursing, 13*(4), 239–242.

Brockway, P. M. (1997, June). The ambulatory surgical nurse: Evolution, competency, and vision. *Nursing Clinics of North America, 32*(2), 387–394.

Brumfield, V. C., Kee, C. C., & Johnson, J. Y. (1996, December). Preoperative patient teaching in ambulatory surgery settings. *AORN Journal, 64*(6), 941–952.

Davidhizar, R., Dowd, S. B., & Bowen, M. (1998, July/ August). Global issues: The educational role of the surgical nurse with the multicultural patient and family. *Today's Surgical Nurse, 20*(4), 20–24.

DeFazio-Quinn, D. M. (1997, June). Ambulatory surgery: An evolution. *Nursing Clinics of North America, 32*(2), 377–386.

Dougherty, J. (1996, July–August). Same-day surgery: The nurse's role. *Orthopaedic Nursing, 15*(4), 15–18.

Doughery, J. (1996). Same-day surgery: The nurse's role. *Orthopaedic Nursing, 15*(4), 15–18.

Ferrara-Love, R. (1997, June). Laparoscopic surgery. *Nursing Clinics of North America, 32*(2), 429–440.

Ferrara-Love, R. (1997, June). Laparoscopic surgery. *Nursing Clinics of North America, 32*(2), 429–440.

Germaine, E., Isman, C., Price, J., & Ross, E. (1996). Surgical pre-admission clinics in Canada: The expanding need with changing technologies. *Seminars in Perioperative Nursing, 5*(4), 199–202.

Gordon, D. B., & Ward, S. E. (1995, July). Correcting patient misconceptions about pain. *American Journal of Nursing, 95*(7), 43–45.

Grossman, D. (1996, July). Cultural dimensions in home health nursing. *American Journal of Nursing, 96*(7), 33–36.

Katz, J. R. (1997, May). Back to basics: Providing effective patient teaching. *American Journal of Nursing, 97*(5), 33–36.

Keatings, M., & Smith, O. (2000). Consent to treatment. In M. Keatings, & O. Smith (Eds.), *Ethical and legal issues in Canadian nursing* (2nd ed.). (p. 187). Toronto: W.B. Saunders.

Keller, C. (1999). The obese patient as surgical risk. *Seminars in Perioperative Nursing, 8*(3), 109–117.

Kost, M. (1999, April). Conscious sedation: Guarding your patient against complications. *Nursing 99, 29*(4), 34–40.

Lancaster, K. A. (1997a, June). Care of the pediatric patient in ambulatory surgery. *Nursing Clinics of North America, 32*(2), 441–455.

Lancaster, K. A. (1997b, June). Patient teaching in ambulatory surgery. *Nursing Clinics of North America, 32*(2), 417–427.

Law, M. L. (1997). A telephone survey of day-surgery eye patients. *Journal of Advanced Nursing, 25*, 355–363.

Lindaman, C. (1995, January). Talking to physicians about pain control. *American Journal of Nursing, 95*(1), 36–37.

Litwack, K. (1997, June). Care of the special needs patient. *Nursing Clinics of North America, 32*(2), 457–468.

Metheny, N. M. (1996). *Fluid and electrolyte balance: Nursing considerations* (3rd ed.). Philadelphia, PA: Lippincott.

Metzler, D. J., & Harr, J. (1996, March). Positioning your patient properly. *American Journal of Nursing, 96*(3), 33–37.

Moseley, M. J. (1997, January). Perioperative problems: Nutrition and electrolytes in the elderly. *Seminars in Perioperative Nursing, 6*(1), 21–30.

Nash, P. L., & O'Malley, M. (1997, March). Streamlining the perioperative process. *Nursing Clinics of North America, 32*(1), 141–151.

Noble, R. R., Micheli, A. J., Hensley, M. A., & McKay, N. (1997, March). Perioperative considerations for the pediatric patient: A developmental approach. *Nursing Clinics of North America, 32*(1), 1–16.

Norman, E. M. (1997). Critical care extra positioning patients to promote oxygenation. *American Journal of Nursing, 97*(8), 16.

Patton, C. M. (1999). Preoperative nursing assessment of the adult patient. *Seminars in Perioperative Nursing, 8*(1), 42–47.

Skewes, S. M. (1996, October). Skin care rituals that do more harm than good. *American Journal of Nursing, 96*(10), 33–35.

Stoller, J. K., & Kester, L. (1998). Respiratory care protocols in postanesthesia care. *Journal* Of *of Perianesthesia Nursing, 13*(6), 349–357.

Swan, B. A. (1996, November–December). Perspectives in ambulatory care: Classifying quality nursing care initiatives: Framework for ambulatory surgery nursing practice. *Nursing Economics, 14*(6), 368–371.

Tusek, D., Church, J. M., & Fazio, V. W. (1997, October). Guided imagery as a coping strategy for perioperative patients. *AORN Journal, 66*(4), 644–649.

Van Keuren, K., & Eland, J. A. (1997, March). Perioperative pain management in children. *Nursing Clinics of North America, 32*(1), 31–44.

Vernon, S., & Pfeifer, G. M. (1997, September). Are you ready for bloodless surgery? *American Journal of Nursing, 97*(9), 40–47.

Williams, G. D. (1997, June). Preoperative assessment and health history interview. *Nursing Clinics of North America, 32*(2), 395–416.

Willins, J. S. (1994, February). Giving fentanyl for pain outside the OR. *American Journal of Nursing, 94*(2), 24–28.

WEBLINKS

The Canadian Anaesthesiologists Society
http://www.cas.ca
The Canadian Anaesthesiologists Society (CAS) is a not-for-profit voluntary organization, and this Web site provides current information and guidelines for the practice of anaesthesia and patient information about anaesthesia.

Operating Room Nurses Association of Canada
http://www.ornac.ca
This Web site provides information related to the history, mission, values, and standards of practice of operating room nurses.

CHAPTER 45

Pain Management

OBJECTIVES

After completing this chapter, you will be able to:

- Identify types and categories of pain according to location, etiology, and duration.
- Differentiate pain threshold from pain tolerance.
- Describe pain transmission, perception, interpretation, and modulation.
- Discuss the gate control theory and its application to nursing care.
- Outline subjective and objective data to collect and analyze when assessing pain.
- List examples of nursing diagnoses for clients with pain.
- State outcome criteria by which to evaluate a client's response to interventions for pain.
- Identify barriers to effective pain management.
- Discuss pharmacological interventions for pain.
- Define tolerance, dependence, and addiction.
- Describe the World Health Organization's step-ladder approach to cancer pain.
- Identify rationales for using various analgesic delivery routes.
- Outline nonpharmacological pain control interventions.

Canada has a rich history in the study and treatment of pain. Melzack (1965; 1999), in addition to his strong humanitarian commitment to caring for patients suffering from pain, paved the way for other exceptional Canadian researchers to understand the mechanism of pain. Recently, the Canadian Consortium on Pain Mechanisms, Diagnosis, and Management was formed with broad representation from universities across Canada, with a mandate, through a number of task forces, to promote pain research, diagnosis, and management by linking expertise with new initiatives.

Pain is a highly unpleasant and very personal sensation that cannot be shared with others. It can occupy all a person's thinking, direct all activities, and change a person's life. Yet, pain is a difficult concept for a client to communicate. A nurse can neither feel nor see a client's pain.

No two people experience pain in exactly the same way. In addition, the differences in individual pain perception and reaction, as well as the many causes of pain, present the nurse with a complex situation when developing a plan to relieve pain and provide comfort. Effective pain management is an important aspect of care.

The last three decades have seen a gradual shift in focus toward pain control and pain management independent of the cause of the pain. Severe pain is now being viewed as an emergency situation deserving anticipation and prompt treatment. Pain is more than a symptom of a problem; it is a high-priority problem in itself. Pain presents both physiological and psychological dangers to health and recovery. Pain increases morbidity and mortality. According to Bocchino (1992, p. 167), "Actual physical damage can result from unresolved pain, and ineffective pain management can inhibit recovery, prolong hospitalization, and contribute to increased health care costs." St. Marie (1991, p. 334) adds, "Driving this greater preoccupation with pain and its suppression is the recognition that pain is not just a side effect of other physiological problems: it can directly impair health and prolong recovery from surgery, disease, and trauma, all of which are accompanied by pain."

The Nature of Pain

Although pain is a universal experience, its exact nature remains a mystery. There are a number of definitions of pain. It has been defined as "an unpleasant sensory and emotional experience associated with actual or potential damage or described in terms of such damage" (International Association for the Study of Pain, 1979). It is known that pain is highly subjective and individual and that it is one of the body's defence mechanisms indicating that there is a problem. McCaffery (1979, p. 11) defines pain as "whatever the experiencing person says it is, existing whenever he (or she) says it does." Basic to this definition is the care provider's willingness to believe that the client is experiencing pain and that the client is the real authority about that pain.

TABLE 45.1 Comparison of Acute and Chronic Pain

Acute Pain	Chronic Pain
Mild to severe	Mild to severe
Sympathetic nervous system responses: Increased pulse rate Increased respiratory rate Elevated blood pressure Diaphoresis Dilated pupils	Parasympathetic nervous system responses: Vital signs normal Dry, warm skin Pupils normal or dilated
Related to tissue injury; resolves with healing	Continues beyond healing
Client appears restless and anxious	Client appears depressed and withdrawn
Client reports pain	Client often does not mention pain, unless asked
Client exhibits behaviour indicative of pain: crying, rubbing area, holding area	Pain behaviour often absent

Types of Pain

Pain may be described in terms of the duration, location, or etiology. When pain lasts only through the expected recovery period, it is described as acute pain whether it has a sudden or slow onset and regardless of the intensity.

Chronic pain lasts beyond the usual course for recovery (Bonica, 1990). Many clinicians use the interval of six months' duration to define pain as chronic. Chronic pain can be further classified as chronic malignant pain, when associated with cancer or other life-threatening conditions, or as chronic nonmalignant pain, when the etiology is a nonprogressive disorder. When chronic pain is extremely difficult to relieve despite therapeutic interventions, it is classified as intractable (Salerno & Willens, 1996). Acute and chronic pains result in different physiological and behavioural responses, as shown in Table 45.1.

Pain can be categorized according to its origin as cutaneous, deep somatic, or visceral. **Cutaneous pain** originates in the skin or subcutaneous tissue. A paper cut

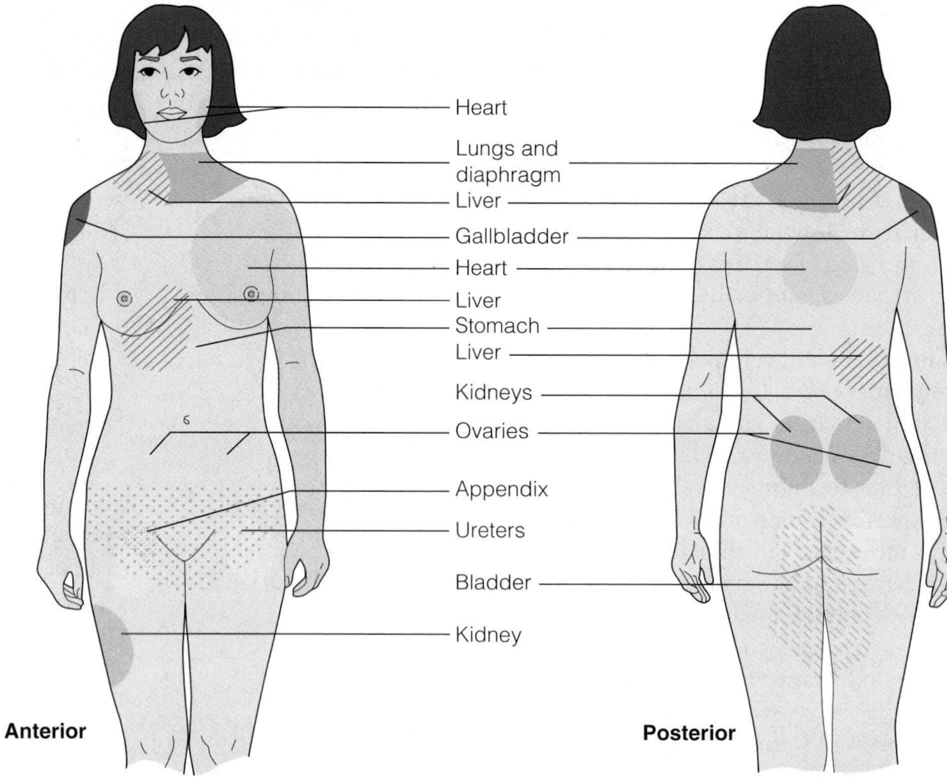

Figure 45.1 Common sites of referred pain from various body organs

causing a sharp pain with some burning is an example of cutaneous pain. **Deep somatic pain** arises from ligaments, tendons, bones, blood vessels, and nerves. It is diffuse and tends to last longer than cutaneous pain. An ankle sprain is an example of deep somatic pain. **Visceral pain** results from stimulation of pain receptors in the abdominal cavity, cranium, and thorax. Visceral pain tends to appear diffuse and often feels like deep somatic pain, that is, burning, aching, or a feeling of pressure. Visceral pain is frequently caused by stretching of the tissues, ischemia, or muscle spasms. For example, an obstructed bowel will result in visceral pain.

Pain may also be described according to where it is experienced in the body. **Radiating pain** is perceived at the source of the pain and extends to nearby tissues. For example, cardiac pain may be felt not only in the chest but also along the left shoulder and down the arm. **Referred pain** is pain felt in a part of the body that is considerably removed from the tissues causing the pain. For example, pain from one part of the abdominal viscera may be perceived in an area of the skin remote from the organ causing the pain (Figure 45.1).

Intractable pain is pain that is highly resistant to relief. One example is the pain from an advanced malignancy. Often, nurses are challenged to use a number of methods, such as imagery and patient-controlled analgesia (PCA), to provide a client with pain relief.

Neuropathic pain is the result of a disturbance of the peripheral or central nervous system that results in pain which may or may not be associated with an ongoing tissue damaging process (Stanton-Hicks, 1995). A number of distinct mechanisms can contribute to the development and continuation of neuropathic pain (Fields & Rowbotham, 1994). Neuropathic pain is described as shooting or stabbing and is often severe. In acquired immunodeficiency syndrome (AIDS), it has been found that as many as 95 percent of clients have evidence of peripheral nerve disease and about 50 percent of these individuals experience severe neuropathic pain (Henderson, 1996).

Phantom pain, which is a painful sensation perceived in a body part that is missing (e.g., an amputated leg) or paralyzed by a spinal cord injury, is also an example of neuropathic pain. This can be distinguished from phantom sensation, that is, the feeling that the missing body part is still present. The incidence of phantom pain can be reduced when analgesics are administered via epidural catheter prior to the amputation.

Pain Syndromes

Certain major pain syndromes have been identified to describe conditions associated with prolonged or severe pain. Common pain syndromes include peripheral pain syndromes, central pain syndromes, and pain with underlying pathology syndromes. See the accompanying box.

Common Pain Syndromes

Peripheral Pain Syndromes

- *Postherpetic neuralgia.* An episode of herpes has two phases: a vesicular eruption and neuralgical pain that often encircles the body. The pain ranges from mild to severe. In the postherpetic syndrome, severe pain persists for months or years with lightning-like pain in the area of the original eruption.
- *Phantom limb pain.* Can occur in anyone who has a body part amputated. The pain varies and may be burning, severe, crushing, or a cramping sensation.

Central Pain Syndromes

- *Trigeminal neuralgia.* This is an intense stablike pain that is distributed by one or more branches of the trigeminal (fifth cranial) nerve. The pain is usually experienced in parts of the face and head; for example, gums, cheek, and surface of the head.

Pain with Underlying Pathology Syndromes

- *Headache.* This common somatic pain can be caused by either intracranial or extracranial problems. To establish a plan to prevent or treat headache, the nurse needs to assess the quality, location, onset, duration, and frequency of the pain, as well as any signs and symptoms that precede the headache.
- *Cancer pain syndrome.* These syndromes can result from the progression of the disease or from efforts to cure or control the disease.
- *Myofascial pain syndrome.* This pain occurs in the muscles and fascia. The pain is frequently severe. It is characterized by muscle spasm, tenderness, stiffness, limitation of movement, and weakness. The pain is often described as dull or aching, and the intensity varies from severe and disabling to mild.

Concepts Associated with Pain

When an individual perceives pain from injured tissue, the pain threshold is reached. An individual's **pain threshold** is the amount of pain stimulation a person requires in order to feel pain. A person's pain threshold is generally fairly uniform; however, it can change. For example, the same stimulus that once produced mild pain can at another time produce intense pain. Excessive sensitivity to pain is called *hyperalgesia.*

Two additional terms used in the context of pain are pain sensation and pain reaction. **Pain sensation** can be considered the same as pain threshold; **pain reaction** includes the autonomic nervous system and behavioural responses to pain. The autonomic nervous system response is the automatic reaction of the body that often protects the individual from further harm, for example, the automatic withdrawal of the hand from a hot stove. The behavioural response is a learned response used as a method of coping with the pain.

Pain tolerance is the maximum amount and duration of pain that an individual is willing to endure. Some clients are unable to tolerate even the slightest pain, whereas others are willing to endure severe pain rather than be treated for it. Thus, pain tolerance varies greatly among people and is widely influenced by psychological and sociocultural factors. Pain tolerance appears to increase with age.

Physiology of Pain

How pain is transmitted and perceived is still incompletely understood. Whether pain is perceived and to what degree depend on the interaction between the body's analgesic system and the nervous system's transmission and interpretation of stimuli.

Peripheral Mechanisms

The peripheral nervous system includes primary sensory neurons specialized to detect tissue damage and to evoke the sensation of touch, heat, cold, pain, and pressure. The receptors that transmit pain sensation are called **nociceptors,** and the physiological processes related to pain perception are described as nociception. These pain receptors or nociceptors can be excited by mechanical, thermal, or chemical stimuli (Table 45.2). When there is a sufficiently noxious stimulus, biochemical mediators are released that sensitize or activate the nociceptors. These mediators include serotonin, histamine, potassium, bradykinin, and substance P (Bonica, 1990). Bradykinin causes direct activation of the nociceptors, the release of inflammatory chemicals, such as histamine, and vasodilation and increased capillary permeability, resulting in reddened and tender tissue. Bradykinin also stimulates the release of prostaglandins. These compounds sensitize the pain receptors and enhance the effect of bradykinin and histamine. Substance P acts on blood vessels in the damaged area to release chemicals that contribute to the conduction of nociception, and like prostaglandins, it increases the inflammatory response. Substance P also serves as a neurotransmitter, enhancing the movement of impulses across the nerve synapse from the primary afferent neuron to the second-order neuron in the dorsal horn of the spinal cord. (See Figure 45.2.)

Nociceptors rarely adapt to a noxious or painful stimulus. In fact, a mechanism described as peripheral sensitization occurs that reduces the threshold of pain receptors at a point where tissue is damaged (Bonn, 1996). The amount of stimulus that results in the sensation of pain will be less once the receptors are sensitized.

TABLE 45.2 Types of Pain Stimuli

Stimulus Type	Physiological Basis of Pain
Mechanical	
1. Trauma to body tissues (e.g., surgery)	Tissue damage; direct irritation of the pain receptors; inflammation
2. Alterations in body tissues (e.g., edema)	Pressure on pain receptors
3. Blockage of a body duct	Distention of the lumen of the duct
4. Tumour	Pressure on pain receptors; irritation of nerve endings
5. Muscle spasm	Stimulation of pain receptors (also see chemical stimuli)
Thermal	
Extreme heat or cold (e.g., burns)	Tissue destruction; stimulation of thermosensitive pain receptors
Chemical	
1. Tissue ischemia (e.g., blocked coronary artery)	Stimulation of pain receptors because of accumulated lactic acid (and other chemicals, such as bradykinin and enzymes) in tissues
2. Muscle spasm	Tissue ischemia secondary to mechanical stimulation (see above)

Pain impulses are transmitted via two types of fibres. The A-delta fibres have a relatively large diameter, are myelinated, and rapidly conduct the impulse. These fibres are associated with the sensation of sharp, pricking pain. The other set of nociceptive fibres is the small-diameter, unmyelinated C fibres. The C fibres transmit the impulse more slowly and mediate long-lasting, burning pain. Nociception is conducted on the A-delta and C fibres to the spinal cord via both the dorsal and ventral roots.

Central Mechanisms

The terminals of these neurons end in the dorsal horn of the spinal cord (Figure 45.3). The fast A fibres primarily conduct impulses from mechanical and thermal pain. They synapse with second-order neurons (long fibres) that cross immediately to the opposite side of the spinal cord and enter the neospinothalamic tract and ascend to the brain. A few fibres terminate in the reticular areas of the brain stem, but most terminate in the thalamus. From there, signals are sent to the basal areas of the brain and to the somatic sensory cortex (Figure 45.4). The slow, type C fibres conduct impulses from mechanical, thermal, and chemical stimuli. These impulses often pass through one or more additional short neurons before travelling up to the brain by the paleospinothalamic tract.

A secondary mechanism, central sensitization, results from increased excitability of spinal neurons by the release at spinal synapses of long-acting neurotransmitters. This produces an exaggerated response and enhances the excitability of spinal neurons, thus maintaining the perception of pain after the painful stimuli have been removed (Bonn, 1996). This phenomenon has motivated clinicians to provide pre-emptive analgesia before surgery or procedures to prevent this hypersensitivity.

Recent research has also found that with the presence of chronic pain there are a number of complex changes in nociceptive pathways. These include alterations in the nerve cells, receptor sites, and transmitters, which can affect the response to pain management interventions (Dray, Urban, & Dickenson, 1994).

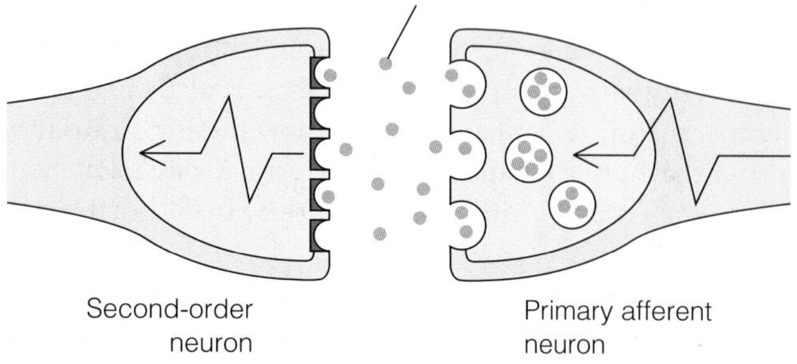

Figure 45.2 Substance P assists the transmission of impulses across the synapse from the primary afferent neuron to a second-order neuron

Pain Perception and Modulation

Nociception continues through the reticular formation, the thalamus, the limbic system, and the cortex. Conscious perception of the pain probably occurs initially at the brain stem and thalamic level. Interpretation, localization, and monitoring of the sensation take place in the cortex (Hall, 1994). This perception will be modulated by a variety of factors (see "Factors Affecting the Pain Experience" later in this chapter).

As pain impulses stimulate regions of the midbrain, descending nerve fibres conduct impulses from the brain

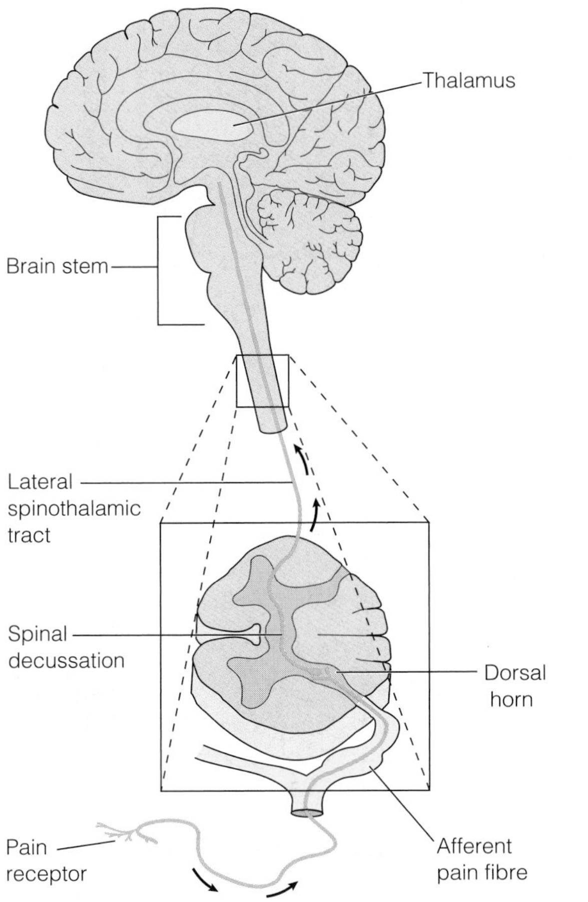

Figure 45.3 The pain impulse is transmitted along a primary afferent pain fibre to the dorsal horn of the spinal cord. The fibre synapses with a second-order neuron, which crosses over at the other side of the spinal cord and ascends to the thalamus.

to the spinal cord where ascending impulses are inhibited at the first synapse in the dorsal horn by the release of endogenous opioids. The three classes of endogenous opioids are enkephalins, dynorphins, and beta endorphins. These substances bind to opiate receptor sites in the central and peripheral nervous system, decreasing or blocking any pain impulse. The opiate binding sites are identified as mu, kappa, and delta and are the same sites where exogenous opioid analgesics (e.g., morphine) bind to provide pain relief.

Gate Control Theory

In 1965, Melzack and Wall proposed the gate control theory (1999). According to this theory, peripheral nerve fibres carrying pain to the spinal cord can have their input modified at the spinal cord level before transmission to the brain. Synapses in the dorsal horns act as gates that close to keep impulses from reaching the brain or open to permit impulses to ascend to the brain.

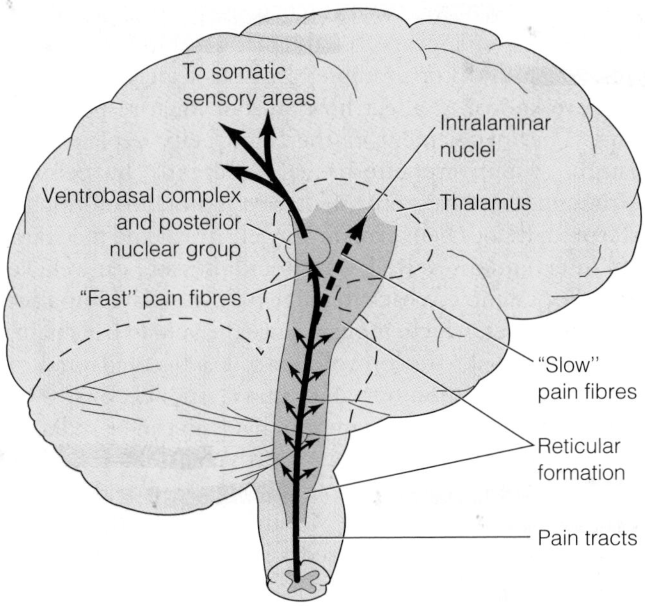

Figure 45.4 The transmission of pain signals to the higher brain centres

According to the gate control theory, small-diameter nerve fibres carry pain stimuli through a gate, but large-diameter nerve fibres going through the same gate can inhibit the transmission of those pain impulses—that is, close the gate (Figure 45.5). The gate mechanism is thought to be situated in the substantia gelatinosa cells in the dorsal horn of the spinal cord. Because a limited amount of sensory information can reach the brain at any

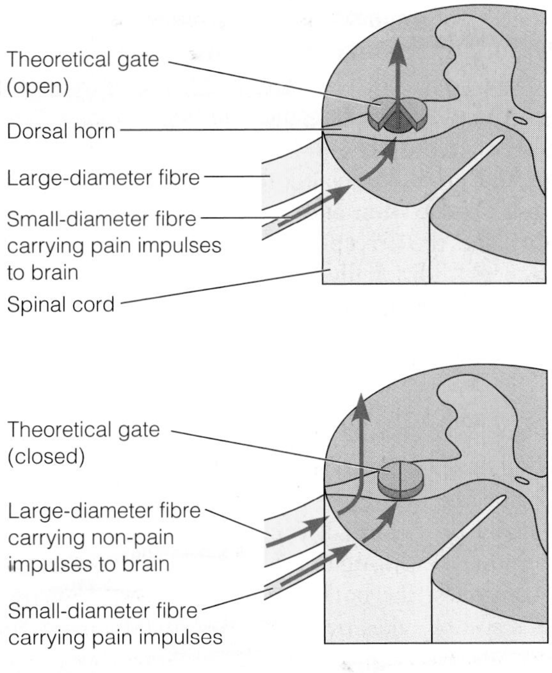

Figure 45.5 A schematic illustration of the gate control theory

given time, certain cells can interrupt the pain impulses. The brain also appears to influence whether the gate is open or closed. For example, previous experiences with pain are known to affect how an individual responds to pain. The involvement of the brain helps explain why painful stimuli are interpreted differently by people. Although the gate control theory is not unanimously accepted, it does help explain why electrical and mechanical interventions as well as heat and pressure can relieve pain. For example, a back massage may stimulate impulses in large nerves, which, in turn, close the gate to back pain.

The original gate control theory has been adapted to encompass new findings and clinical applications. The theory has led to the recognition that pain can be reduced or modulated at four points: (1) the peripheral site of pain, (2) the spinal cord, (3) the brain stem, and (4) the cerebral cortex (Herr & Mobily, 1992). The theory remains incomplete but is used as the basis for many pain management interventions.

Ascending Modulation

The pain gate in the spinal cord can be shut through both ascending and descending modulation. Ascending modulation can occur with the stimulation of large-diameter sensory fibres through massage, heat and cold application, or the use of a transcutaneous electrical nerve stimulation (TENS) unit, with which electrical stimulation is applied to the skin. The administration of opioid analgesics will also inhibit pain impulses by binding to the receptor sites within the peripheral and central nervous system (Salerno & Willens, 1996).

Descending Modulation

The release of endorphins and enkephalins provides the biochemical descending inhibition of pain impulses, as previously described. The cognitive and affective response to pain can provide a descending modulation of the pain impulse when anxiety and fear are relieved through education and emotional support (Dane & Kessler, 1994). The use of relaxation and guided imagery interventions can also alter the perception or interpretation of the pain experience. Additionally, activities that provide a distraction from the pain, such as watching TV or listening to music, can modulate and inhibit the pain perception.

Responses to Pain

The body's response to pain is a complex process rather than a specific action. It involves physiological and psychosocial aspects. Initially, the sympathetic nervous system responds, resulting in the fight-or-flight response. As pain continues, the body adapts as the parasympathetic nervous system takes over, reversing many of the initial physiological responses. This adaptation to the pain occurs after several hours or days of pain. The actual pain receptors adapt very little and continue to transmit the pain message. This serves the purpose of keeping the person continually aware of the damaging stimuli causing the pain (Guyton & Hall, 2000). The person may learn to cope with the pain through cognitive and behavioural activities, such as diversions, imagery, and excessive sleeping. The individual may respond to pain by seeking out physical interventions to manage the pain, such as analgesics, massage, and exercise.

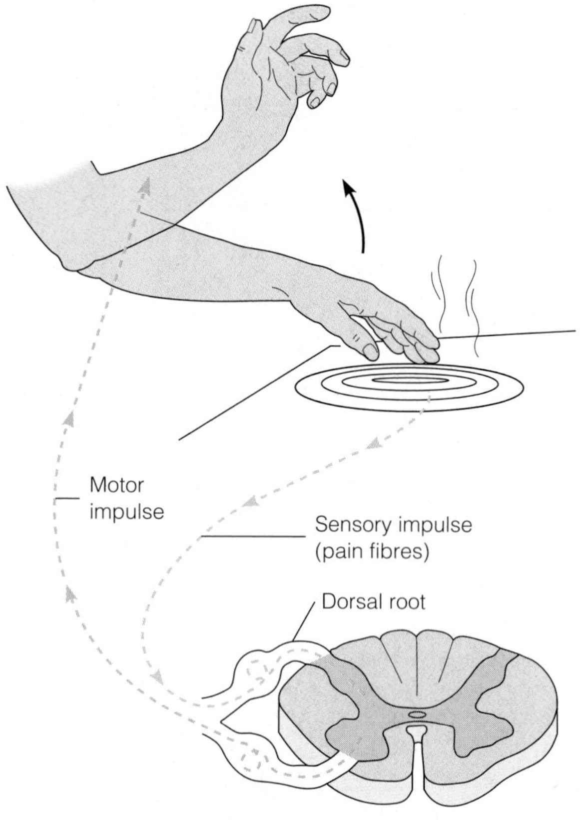

Figure 45.6 Proprioceptive reflex to a pain stimulus

A proprioceptive reflex also occurs with the stimulation of pain receptors. Impulses travel along sensory pain fibres to the spinal cord. There, they synapse with motor neurons, and the impulses travel back via motor fibres to a muscle near the site of the pain (Figure 45.6). The muscle then contracts in a protective action. For example, when a person touches a hot stove, the hand reflexively draws back from the heat even before the person is aware of the pain.

Factors Affecting the Pain Experience

Numerous factors can affect a person's perception of and reaction to pain. These include the person's ethnic and cultural values, developmental stage, environment and support people, previous pain experiences, the meaning of the current pain, as well as anxiety and stress.

Ethnic and Cultural Values

Ethnic background and cultural heritage have long been recognized as factors that influence both a person's reaction to pain and the expression of that pain. Behaviour related to pain is a part of the socialization process.

Although there appears to be little variation in pain threshold, cultural background can affect the level of pain that an individual is willing to tolerate. In some Middle Eastern and African cultures, self-infliction of pain is a sign of mourning or grief. In other groups, pain may be anticipated as part of the ritualistic practices, and therefore, tolerance of pain signifies strength and endurance. Additionally, there are significant variations in the expression of pain. Studies have shown that individuals of northern European descent tend to be more stoic and less expressive of their pain than individuals from southern European backgrounds. One study showed that even the descriptors of pain used varied by cultural group (Andrews & Boyle, 1995).

Developmental Stage

The age and developmental stage of a client are important variables that will influence both the reaction to and the expression of pain. Age variations and related nursing interventions are presented in Table 45.3.

The field of pain management for infants and children has grown significantly. It is now accepted that anatomical, physiological, and biochemical elements necessary for pain transmission are present in newborns regardless of their gestational age (Johnston, Stevens, Yang, & Horton, 1995). Physiological indicators may vary in infants, so behavioural observation is recommended for pain assessment (Hudson, 1997). Children may be less able to articulate their experience or needs related to pain than an adult, which often results in their pain being undertreated (Carr et al., 1992; Stevens, 1999; Brennan Hould, 2003).

Older adults constitute a major portion of the individuals within the health-care system. The prevalence of pain in the older population is generally higher due to both acute and chronic disease conditions. Pain threshold does not appear to change with aging, although the effect of analgesics may increase due to physiological changes related to drug metabolism (Carr et al., 1992).

Environment and Support People

A strange environment, such as a hospital with its noises, lights, and activity, can compound pain. In addition, the lonely person who is without a support network may perceive pain as severe, whereas the person who has supportive people around may perceive less pain. Some people prefer to withdraw when they are in pain, whereas others prefer the distraction of people and activity around them. Family caregivers can be a significant support for a person in pain. With the increase in outpatient and home care, families are assuming an increased responsibility for the management of pain. Education related to the assessment and management of pain can positively affect the perceived quality of life for both clients and their caregivers (Ferrell et al., 1995).

Some clients use pain to acquire secondary gains, that is, special attention from support people and nurses. If the situation becomes difficult for the support people, the nurse can intervene and discuss the problem before the support people become angry and avoid the client.

Expectations of significant others can affect a person's perceptions of and responses to pain. In some situations, for example, girls may be permitted to express pain more openly than boys. Family role can also affect how a person perceives or responds to pain. For instance, a single mother supporting three children may ignore pain because of her need to stay on the job. The presence of support people often changes a client's reaction to pain. For example, toddlers often tolerate pain more readily when supportive parents or nurses are nearby.

Past Pain Experiences

Previous pain experiences alter a client's sensitivity to pain. People who have personally experienced pain or who have been exposed to the suffering of someone close are often more threatened by anticipated pain than people without a pain experience. In addition, the success or lack of success of pain relief measures influence a person's expectations for relief. For example, a person who has tried several pain relief measures without success may have little hope about the helpfulness of nursing interventions.

Meaning of Pain

Some clients may accept pain more readily than others, depending on the circumstances and the client's interpretation of its significance. A client who associates the pain with a positive outcome may withstand the pain amazingly well. For example, a woman giving birth to a child or an athlete undergoing knee surgery to prolong his career may tolerate pain better because of the benefit associated with it. These clients may view the pain as a temporary inconvenience rather than a potential threat or disruption to daily life.

By contrast, clients with unrelenting chronic pain may suffer more intensely. They may respond with despair, anxiety, and depression because they cannot attach a positive significance or purpose to the pain. In this situation, the pain may be looked upon as a threat to body image or lifestyle and as a sign of possible impending death.

Anxiety and Stress

Anxiety often accompanies pain. Threat of the unknown and the inability to control the pain or the events surrounding it often augment the pain perception. Fatigue also reduces a person's ability to cope, thereby increasing pain perception. When pain interferes with sleep, fatigue

TABLE 45.3 Age Variations in the Pain Experience

Age Group	Pain Perception and Behaviour	Selected Nursing Interventions
Infant	Perceives pain	Give a glucose pacifier.
	Responds to pain with increased sensitivity	
	Older infant tries to avoid pain; for example, turns away and physically resists	Use tactile stimulation. Play music or tapes of a heartbeat.
Toddler and preschooler	Develops the ability to describe pain and its intensity and location	Distract the child with toys, books, pictures. Involve the child in blowing bubbles as a way of "blowing away the pain."
	Often responds with crying and anger because child perceives pain as a threat to security	Appeal to the child's belief in magic by using a "magic" blanket or glove to take away pain.
	Reasoning with child at this stage is not always successful	Hold the child to provide comfort.
	May consider pain a punishment	Explore misconceptions about pain.
	Feels sad	
	May learn there are gender differences in pain expression	
	Tends to hold someone accountable for the pain	
School-age child	Tries to be brave when facing pain	Use imagery to turn off "pain switches."
	Rationalizes in an attempt to explain the pain	Provide a behavioural rehearsal of what to expect and how it will look and feel.
	Responsive to explanations	
	Can usually identify the location and describe the pain	
	With persistent pain, may regress to an earlier stage of development	Provide support and nurturing.
Adolescent	May be slow to acknowledge pain	Provide opportunities to discuss pain.
	Recognizing pain or "giving in" may be considered weakness	Provide privacy.
	Wants to appear brave in front of peers and not report pain	Present choices for dealing with pain. Encourage music or TV for distraction.
Adult	Behaviours exhibited when experiencing pain may be gender-based behaviours learned as a child	Deal with any misconceptions about pain.
	May ignore pain because to admit it is perceived as a sign of weakness or failure	Focus on the client's control in dealing with the pain.
	May use pain for secondary gain, for example, to get attention	
	Fear of what pain means may prevent some adults from taking action	Allay fears and anxiety, when possible.
Older adult	May perceive pain as part of the aging process	Spend time with the client, and listen carefully.
	May have decreased sensations or perceptions of the pain	
	Lethargy, anorexia, and fatigue may be indicators of pain	
	May withhold complaints of pain because of fear of the treatment, of any lifestyle changes that may be involved, or of becoming dependent	Clarify misconceptions. Encourage independence, whenever possible.
	May describe pain differently, that is, as "ache," "hurt," or "discomfort"	
	May consider it unacceptable to admit or show pain	

and muscle tension often result and increase the pain; thus, a cycle of pain, fatigue, pain develops. People in pain who believe that they have control of their pain have decreased fear and anxiety, which decreases their pain perception. A perception of lacking control or a sense of helplessness tends to increase pain perception. The expression of pain to an attentive listener and the participation in pain management decisions can increase the sense of control, which decreases pain perception (Dane & Kessler, 1994).

Assessing

Accurate pain assessment is essential for effective pain management. Because pain is subjective and experienced uniquely by each individual, nurses need to assess all factors affecting the pain experience—physiological, psychological, behavioural, emotional, and sociocultural.

The extent and frequency of the pain assessment varies according to the situation. For clients experiencing acute or severe pain, the nurse may focus only on location, quality, severity, and early intervention. Clients with less severe or chronic pain can usually provide a more detailed description of the experience. Frequency of pain assessment usually depends on the pain control measures being used and the clinical circumstances. For example, in the initial postoperative period, pain is often assessed whenever vital signs are taken, which may be as often as every 15 minutes and then extended to every two to four hours. Following pain management interventions, pain intensity should be reassessed at an interval appropriate for the intervention. For example, following the intravenous administration of morphine, the severity of pain should be reassessed in 20 to 30 minutes.

Because it has been found that many people will not voice their pain unless asked about it, pain assessments *must* be initiated by the nurse. Some of the many reasons clients may be reluctant to report pain are listed in the accompanying box. It is also essential that nurses listen to and rely on the client's perceptions of pain. Believing the person who is experiencing and conveying the perceptions is crucial in establishing a sense of trust.

Pain assessments consist of two major components: (1) a pain history to obtain facts from the client, and (2) direct observation of behavioural and physiological responses of the client. The goal of assessment is to gain an objective understanding of a subjective experience.

Why Clients May Be Reluctant to Report Pain

- Unwillingness to trouble staff who are perceived as busy
- Fear of the injectable route of analgesic administration—children in particular
- Belief that pain is to be expected as part of the recovery process
- Belief that pain is a normal part of aging or a necessary part of life—older adults in particular
- Belief that expressions of pain reveal weakness
- Difficulty expressing personal discomfort
- Concern about risks associated with opioid drugs (e.g., addiction)
- Fear about the cause of pain or that reporting pain will lead to further tests and expenses
- Concern about unwanted side effects, especially of opioid drugs
- Concern that use of drugs now will render the drug inefficient if or when the pain becomes worse

Pain History

While taking pain histories, the nurse must provide an opportunity for clients to express in their own words how they view the pain and the situation. This will help the nurse understand what the pain means to the client and how the client is coping with it. Remember that each person's pain experience is unique and that the client is the best interpreter of the pain experience. This history should be geared to the specific client: for example, questions asked of an accident victim would be different from those asked of a postoperative client or one suffering from chronic pain. The initial pain assessment for someone in *severe acute pain* may consist of only a few questions before intervention occurs. In addition, the nurse may focus on the following:

- Previous pain treatment and effectiveness
- When and what analgesics were last taken
- Other medications being taken
- Allergies to medications

For the person with *chronic pain*, the nurse may focus on the client's coping mechanisms, effectiveness of current pain management, and ways in which the pain has affected activities of daily living (ADLs).

Data that should be obtained in a comprehensive pain history include pain location, intensity, quality, patterns, precipitating factors, alleviating factors, associated symptoms, effect on ADLs, past pain experiences, meaning of the pain to the person, coping resources, and affective responses. Questions to elicit this data are shown in the following box.

Location

To ascertain the specific location of the pain, ask the individual to point to the site of the discomfort. A chart consisting of drawings of the body can assist in identifying pain locations. The client marks the location of pain on the chart. This tool can be especially effective with clients who have more than one source of pain.

When assessing the location of a child's pain, the nurse needs to understand the child's vocabulary. For example,

ASSESSMENT INTERVIEW

Pain History

- *Location:* Where is your pain?
- *Intensity:* On a scale of 0 to 10 (with 1 representing the lowest pain level), how would you rate the degree of discomfort you are having?
- *Quality:* Tell me what your pain feels like.
- *Pattern*
  a. *Time of onset:* When did or does the pain start?
  b. *Duration:* How long have you had it, or how long does it usually last?
  c. *Constancy:* Do you have pain-free periods? When? And for how long?
- *Precipitating factors:* What triggers the pain or makes it worse?
- *Alleviating factors:* What measures or methods have you found helpful in lessening or relieving the pain? What pain medications do you use?
- *Associated symptoms:* Do you have any other symptoms (e.g., nausea, dizziness, blurred vision, shortness of breath) before, during, or after your pain?
- *Effects on activities of daily living:* How does the pain affect your family life (e.g., eating, working, sleeping, and social and recreational activities)?
- *Past pain experiences:* Tell me about past pain experiences you have had and the effectiveness of pain relief measures.
- *Meaning of pain:* How do you interpret your pain? What outcomes (implications) do you anticipate from this pain? What do you fear most about your pain?
- *Coping resources:* What do you usually do to help cope with pain?
- *Affective response:* How does the pain make you feel? Anxious? Depressed? Frightened? Tired? Burdensome?

tummy might refer either to the abdomen or to part of the chest. Asking the child to point to the pain helps clarify the child's word usage to identify location. Again, the use of figure drawings can assist in identifying pain locations. Parents can also be helpful in interpreting the meaning of a child's words.

When documenting pain location, the nurse may use various body landmarks. Further clarification is possible with the use of such terms as *proximal, distal, medial, lateral,* and *diffuse.*

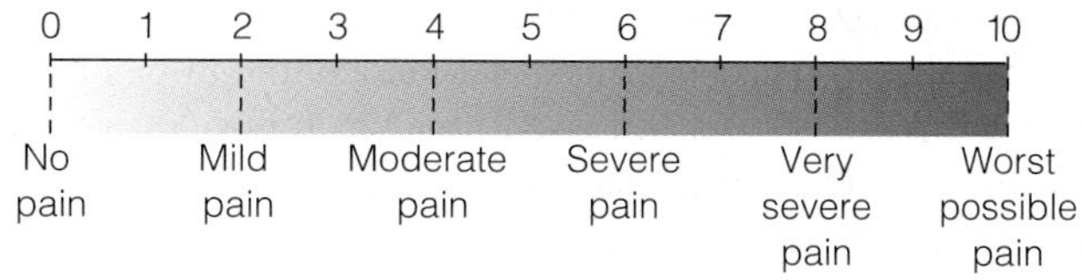

Figure 45.7 A 10-point pain intensity scale with word modifiers

Intensity

The single most important indicator of the intensity of pain is the client's report of pain. Studies have shown that health-care providers may underrate or overrate the pain intensity. The inaccuracy of nurse rating of client's pain tends to be even greater when the pain is severe (Pasero, 1996). The use of pain intensity scales is an easy and reliable method of determining pain intensity. Such scales provide consistency for nurses to communicate with the client and other health-care providers. Most scales use either a 0 to 5 or 0 to 10 range with 0 indicating "no pain" and the highest number indicating the "worst pain possible" for that individual. A 10-point rating scale is shown in Figure 45.7. The inclusion of word modifiers on the scale can assist some clients who find it difficult to apply a number level to their pain. The client is asked to indicate the scale point that best represents the pain intensity.

When noting pain intensity, it is important to determine any related factors that may be affecting the pain. When the intensity changes, the nurse needs to consider the possible cause. For example, the abrupt cessation of acute abdominal pain may indicate a ruptured appendix. Several factors affect the perception of intensity: (1) the amount of distraction or the client's concentration on another event; (2) the client's state of consciousness; (3) the level of activity; and (4) the client's expectations.

Not all clients can understand or relate to numerical pain intensity scales. These include children who are unable to communicate discomfort verbally, elderly clients with impairments in cognition or communication, and people who do not speak English. For these clients the Wong/Baker Faces Rating Scale (Figure 45.8) may be easier to use (Pasero, 1997b). The face scale includes a number scale in relation to each expression so that the pain intensity can be documented. When it is not possible to use any kind of rating scale with a client, the nurse must rely on observation of behaviour and the physiological cues discussed later in this section. The input of the client's significant others, such as parents or caregivers, can assist the nurse in interpreting the observations. An objective description of the behaviour and physiological data is then documented.

For effective use of pain rating scales, clients need to not only understand the use of the scale but also be educated about how the information will be used to determine changes in their condition and the effectiveness of pain management interventions. Clients should also be asked to indicate what level of comfort is acceptable so that they can perform specific activities. This will ensure that adequate pain management is achieved (Pasero, 1997a).

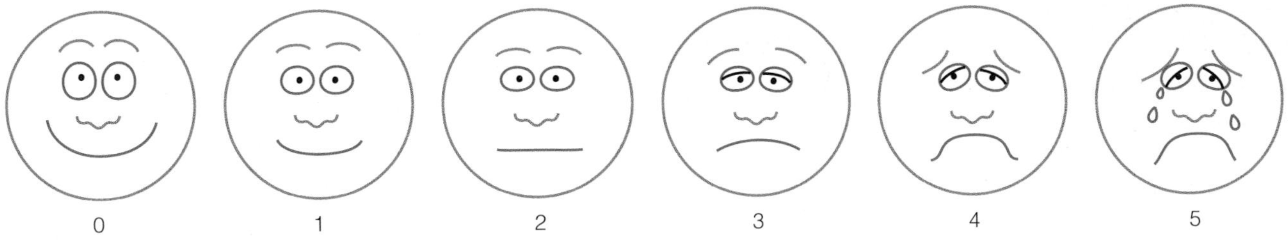

1. Explain to the child that each face is for a person who feels happy because he or she has no pain (hurt, or whatever word the child uses) or feels sad because he or she has some or a lot of pain.

2. Point to the appropriate face and state, "This face..." :
   0—"is very happy because he (or she) doesn't hurt at all."
   1—"hurts just a little bit."
   2—"hurts a little more."
   3—"hurts even more."
   4—"hurts a whole lot."
   5—"hurts as much as you can imagine, although you don't have to be crying to feel this bad."

3. Ask the child to choose the face that best describes how he or she feels. Be specific about which pain (e.g., "shot" or incision) and what time (e.g., Now? Earlier before lunch?).

Figure 45.8 The Wong/Baker Faces Rating Scale

Source: Wong, D. L. (1993). *Whaley and Wong's Essentials of pediatric nursing* (4th ed.). (p. 597). St. Louis, MO: Mosby. Reprinted with permission.

The use of a pain rating scale together with a pain flowsheet (see Figure 45.12) has been shown to result in nurses giving a greater percentage of the analgesic doses available and in client's self-report of pain being lower (Brown, 1992). Documentation can be completed by the nurse, the client, or a caregiver and can be used in acute, outpatient, and home care settings.

Quality

Descriptive adjectives help people communicate the quality of pain. A headache may be described as "hammerlike" or an abdominal pain as "piercing like a knife." Sometimes, clients have difficulty describing pain because they have never experienced any sensation like it. This is particularly true of children and of adults who have pain originating within the nervous system. Some of the terms commonly used to describe pain are listed in Table 45.4.

Nurses need to record the exact words clients use to describe pain. A client's words are more accurate and descriptive than an interpretation in the nurse's words. Exact information can be significant in both the diagnosis of the pain etiology and in the treatment choices made. For example, pain described as hot, electrical, and sharp tends to be neuropathic in origin and will be more responsive to anticonvulsants (e.g., Tegretol) than an opioid (e.g., morphine).

Pattern

The pattern of pain includes time of onset, duration, and recurrence or intervals without pain. The nurse, therefore, determines when the pain began; how long the pain lasts; whether it recurs and, if so, the length of the interval without pain; and when the pain last occurred.

Precipitating Factors

Certain activities sometimes precede pain, for example, physical exertion may precede chest pain, or abdominal pain may occur after eating. These observations can help prevent pain and determine its cause.

Environmental factors, such as extreme cold or heat and extremes of humidity, can affect some types of pain. For example, sudden exercise on a hot day can cause muscle spasm.

Physical and emotional stressors can also precipitate pain. Emotional tension frequently brings on a migraine headache. Intense fear or physical exertion can cause angina.

Alleviating Factors

Nurses must ask clients to describe anything that they have done to help alleviate the pain, (e.g., home remedies, such as herbal teas, or medications, rest, applications of heat or cold, prayer, or distractions like watching TV). It is important to explore the effect any of these measures had on the pain, whether or not relief was obtained, or whether the pain became worse.

Associated Symptoms

Also included in the clinical appraisal of pain are other associated symptoms, such as nausea, vomiting, dizziness, and diarrhea. These symptoms may relate to the onset of the pain or they may result from the presence of the pain.

TABLE 45.4 Commonly Used Pain Descriptors

Short-Form McGill Pain Questionnaire
Ronald Melzack (1987)

Patient's Name: Date:

	None	Mild	Moderate	Severe
Throbbing	0)	1)	2)	3)
Shooting	0)	1)	2)	3)
Stabbing	0)	1)	2)	3)
Sharp	0)	1)	2)	3)
Cramping	0)	1)	2)	3)
Gnawing	0)	1)	2)	3)
Hot-Burning	0)	1)	2)	3)
Aching	0)	1)	2)	3)
Heavy	0)	1)	2)	3)
Tender	0)	1)	2)	3)
Splitting	0)	1)	2)	3)
Tiring-Exhausting	0)	1)	2)	3)
Sickening	0)	1)	2)	3)
Fearful	0)	1)	2)	3)
Punishing-Cruel	0)	1)	2)	3)

No pain Worst Possible Pain

PPI (Point Pain Intensity)
0 No Pain
1 Mild
2 Discomforting
3 Distressing
4 Horrible
5 Excruciating

Source: Melzack, R. (1975). McGill Pain Questionnaire. *Pain, 30,* 277–299. Reproduced with permission.

Effect on Activities of Daily Living

Knowing how activities of daily living (ADLs) are affected by *chronic* pain helps the nurse understand the client's perspective on the pain's severity. The nurse asks the client to describe how the pain has affected the following aspects of life:

- Sleep
- Appetite
- Concentration
- Work/school
- Interpersonal relationships
- Marital relations/sex
- Home activities
- Driving/walking
- Leisure activities
- Emotional status (mood, irritability, depression, anxiety)

A rating scale of none, a little, or a great deal or another range can be used to determine the degree of alteration.

Coping Resources

Each individual will exhibit personal ways of coping with pain. Strategies may relate to past pain experiences or the specific meaning of the pain; some may reflect religious or cultural influences. Nurses can encourage and support the client's use of methods known to have helped in modifying pain. Strategies may include withdrawal, use of distraction, prayer or other religious practices, and support from significant others.

Affective Responses

Affective responses vary according to the situation, the degree and duration of pain, the interpretation of it, and many other factors. The nurse needs to explore the client's feelings, for example, anxiety, fear, exhaustion, depression, or a sense of failure. Because many people with chronic pain become depressed and potentially suicidal, it may also be necessary to assess the client's suicide risk. In such situations, the nurse needs to ask the client, "Do you ever feel so bad that you want to die? Do you feel that way now?"

Observation of Behavioural and Physiological Responses

There are wide variations in nonverbal responses to pain. For clients who are very young, aphasic, confused, or disoriented, nonverbal expressions may be the only means of communicating pain. Facial expression is often the first indication of pain, and it may be the only one. Clenched teeth, tightly shut eyes, open somber eyes, biting of the lower lip, and other facial grimaces may be indicative of pain. Vocalizations like moaning and groaning or crying and screaming are also associated with pain.

Immobilization of the body or a part of the body may also indicate pain. The client with chest pain often holds the left arm across the chest. A person with abdominal pain may assume the position of greatest comfort, often with the knees and hips flexed, and moves reluctantly.

Purposeless body movements can also indicate pain—for example, tossing and turning in bed or flinging the arms about. Involuntary movements, such as a reflexive jerking away from a needle inserted through the skin, indicate pain. An adult may be able to control this reflex; however, a child may be unable or unwilling to do so.

Rhythmic body movements or rubbing may indicate pain. An adult or child may assume a fetal position and rock back and forth when experiencing abdominal pain. During labour, a woman may massage her abdomen rhythmically with her hands.

It is important to note that behavioural responses can be controlled and so may not be very revealing. When pain is chronic, there are rarely overt behavioural responses as the individual develops personal coping styles for dealing with pain, discomfort, or suffering.

Physiological responses vary with the origin and duration of the pain. Early in the onset of acute pain, the sympathetic nervous system is stimulated, resulting in increased blood pressure, pulse rate, respiratory rate, pallor, diaphoresis, and pupil dilation. Although the nociceptors do not adapt to painful stimuli, the sympathetic nervous system does adapt, making the physiological responses less evident or even absent. With visceral pain, signs of parasympathetic stimulation may be observed, such as decreased blood pressure and pulse rate, pupil constriction, and warm dry skin. Physiological responses are most likely to be absent in people with chronic pain because of CNS adaptation.

Daily Pain Diary

For clients who experience chronic pain, a daily diary may help the client and nurse identify pain patterns and factors that exacerbate or mediate the pain experience. In home care, the family or other caregiver can be taught to complete the diary. The record can include time or onset of pain, activity before pain, pain-related positions or behaviours, pain intensity level, use of analgesics or other relief measures, duration of pain, and time spent in relief activities. Recorded data can provide the basis for developing or modifying the plan for care. For this tool to be effective, it is important that the nurse educate the client and family about the value and use of the diary in achieving effective pain control. Determining the client's abilities to use the diary is essential.

Diagnosing

The North American Nursing Diagnosis Association (NANDA, 2003) includes the following diagnostic labels for clients experiencing pain or discomfort:

- ***Pain:*** The state in which an individual experiences and reports the presence of severe discomfort or an uncomfortable sensation lasting from one second to less than six months.
- ***Chronic Pain:*** The state in which an individual experiences pain that is persistent or intermittent and lasts for more than six months.
- ***Comfort:*** The state in which an individual experiences an uncomfortable sensation in response to a noxious stimulus.

When writing the diagnostic statement, the nurse should specify the location (e.g., right ankle pain, or left frontal headache). Etiological factors and precipitating factors, when known, must also be part of the diagnostic statement. In addition to the injurious agent, etiological factors may include knowledge deficit of pain management techniques, fear of drug tolerance or addiction, or other factors cited in the box on page 1277. Precipitating factors were discussed earlier in the "Assessing" section. Clinical examples of assessment data clusters and associated nursing diagnoses are shown in Table 45.5.

Because the presence of pain can affect so many facets of a person's functioning, pain may be the etiology of other nursing diagnoses. Examples of such nursing diagnoses follow:

TABLE 45.5 Clinical Application: Assessment Data Clusters and Related Nursing Diagnoses for Clients Experiencing Pain

Data Cluster	Nursing Diagnosis
Mrs. Robin Wilson, the mother of two children, recently separated from her husband. She works as bank clerk full time. She is worried about her finances and the responsibilities for her children. "Pounding" frontal headaches occur in the late afternoon and evening. At the interview, she holds the palm of her hand across her forehead. Brow is furrowed, and facial muscles tense.	***Pain, acute:*** recurrent headaches related to emotional stress
Mary Anderson, 75, fell and broke her right hip while shopping. She had surgery yesterday to repair the fracture. She rates her pain in the surgical site as 6 on a 0–10 scale and states the pain goes up to 9 when she is repositioned in bed. Morphine 10 mg q4h prn is ordered. She received a dose five hours ago. States, "I try to hold out as long as I can before asking for a pain killer."	***Pain, acute*** related to surgical repair of right hip fracture and movement ***Knowledge Deficit*** related to lack of information or misinformation regarding pain treatment strategies
Lan Nguyen, 51, was diagnosed with breast cancer three years ago and had a metastatic lung tumour removed six months ago. She describes prolonged post-thoracotomy pain as "hot, stabbing, and unbearable." Lan states that although she loves sewing and needlepoint, she is unable to participate in these activities currently because of the pain.	***Chronic Pain*** related to nerve damage and sustained pain sensation ***Self-Concept Disturbance*** related to inability to participate in sewing and needlepoint

- ***Ineffective Airway Clearance*** related to postoperative incisional chest pain
- ***Anxiety*** related to past experiences of poor control of pain and to anticipation of pain
- ***Ineffective Individual Coping*** related to prolonged continuous back pain, ineffective pain management, and inadequate support systems
- ***Ineffective Health Maintenance*** related to chronic pain and fatigue
- ***Knowledge Deficient*** (pain control measures) related to lack of exposure to information resources
- ***Impaired Physical Mobility*** related to arthritic pain in knee and ankle joints
- ***Sleep Pattern Disturbance*** related to increased pain perception at night

Planning

Although the established goals will vary according to the diagnosis and its defining characteristics, individual examples include the following:

- Modify or minimize pain to enable partial or complete resumption of daily activities
- Enhance abilities to control pain
- Demonstrate actions to control pain and associated symptoms

Examples of desired outcomes for each of these goals, although established in the planning phase, are provided in Table 45.8 in the "Evaluating" section of this chapter.

Examples of NIC interventions to assist clients experiencing pain include (McCloskey & Bulechek, 2000) the following:

- Acupressure
- Analgesic administration
- Distraction
- Heat/cold applications
- Music therapy
- Pain management
- Patient-controlled analgesia (PCA) assistance
- Progressive muscle relaxation
- Transcutaneous electrical nerve stimulation (TENS)
- Simple guided imagery
- Simple massage
- Simple relaxation therapy

Specific nursing activities associated with each of these interventions can be selected to meet the individual needs of the client. See the "Implementing" section of this chapter for details. A sample nursing care plan using NIC interventions and selected activities is provided on pages 1294–1295.

When planning, nurses need to choose pain relief measures appropriate for the client based on the assessment data and input from the client or support persons. Nursing interventions may include a variety of pharmacological and nonpharmacological interventions. Developing a plan that incorporates a wide range of strategies is usually most effective. Whether in acute care or in home care, it is important for everyone involved in pain management to understand the plan of care. The plan should be documented in the client's record; in home care, a copy needs to be made available to the client, support persons, and caregivers. Involvement of the client and support persons is essential in pain management.

When the client's pattern and level of pain can be anticipated or is already known, regular or scheduled administration of analgesics can provide a therapeutic plasma level. The importance and meaning of a stable drug level in pain management should be explained to the patient. With acute pain, this may be possible in the first 24 to 48 hours following surgery when the client is likely to have pain requiring opioid analgesics. Frequency of administration can be adjusted to prevent pain from recurring (Carr et al., 1992). When persistent cancer-related pain exists, analgesics should be given around the clock with additional "break through" doses available (Jacox et al., 1994). Nonpharmacological interventions should also be regularly scheduled. The additional advantage of scheduling measures is that the client spends less time in pain and does not experience the anxiety or fear of the pain recurring.

Planning for Home Care

In preparation for discharge, the nurse needs to determine the client's and family's needs, strengths, and resources. The box opposite describes the specific assessment data required when establishing a discharge plan. Using the assessment data, the nurse tailors a teaching plan for the client and family (see the Home Care Teaching Guide that follows).

Implementing

Pain management is the alleviation of pain or a reduction in pain to a level of comfort that is acceptable to the client. It includes two basic types of nursing interventions: pharmacological and nonpharmacological interventions. Nursing management of pain consists of both independent and collaborative nursing actions. In general, noninvasive measures may be performed as an independent nursing function, whereas administration of analgesic medications requires a physician's order. However, the decision to administer the prescribed medication is frequently the nurse's, often requiring judgement as to the dose to be given and the time of administration.

Generally speaking, a combination of strategies is best for the client in pain. Sometimes strategies need to be

HOME CARE ASSESSMENT

Pain

Client

- *Level of knowledge:* Pharmacological and non-pharmacological pain relief measures selected; adverse effects and measures to counteract these effects; warning signs to report to health-care provider
- *Self-care abilities for analgesic administration:* Ability to use analgesics appropriately (e.g., to prepare correct dosages of analgesics and adhere to scheduled administration); physical dexterity to take pills or to administer intravenous medications and to store medications safely; and ability to obtain prescriptions or over-the-counter medications at the pharmacy

Family

- *Caregiver availability, skills, and willingness:* Primary and secondary persons able and willing to assist with pain management; shopping if the client has restricted activity; ability to comprehend selected therapies (e.g., infusion pumps, imagery, massage, positioning, and relaxation techniques) and perform them or assist the client with them, as needed
- *Family role changes and coping:* Effect on financial status, parenting and spousal roles, sexuality, social roles

Community

- *Resources:* Availability of and familiarity with resources, such as supplies, home care aid, or financial assistance

tried and changed until the client obtains effective pain relief. See the box on page 1285 for individualizing care for clients with pain.

Barriers to Pain Management

Misconceptions and biases can affect pain management. Some of these involve attitudes of the nurse or the client as well as knowledge deficits. Clients respond to pain experiences on the basis of their culture, personal experiences, and the meaning the pain has for them. For many people, pain is expected and accepted as a normal aspect of illness. Clients and families may lack knowledge of the adverse effects of pain and may have misinformation regarding the use of analgesics. Clients may not report pain because they expect nothing can be done, they think it is not severe enough, or they feel it would distract or prejudice the health-care provider (Salerno & Willens, 1996). Other common misconceptions are shown in Table 45.6.

Key Factors in Pain Management

Acknowledging and Accepting

Basic to all strategies for reducing pain is that nurses convey to clients that they believe the client is having pain. Four ways of communicating this belief follow:

1. Verbally acknowledge the presence of the pain. "I understand your leg is very painful. How do you feel about the pain?"
2. Listen attentively to what the client says about the pain.
3. Convey that you are assessing the client's pain to understand it better, *not* to determine whether the pain is real, for example, "How does your pain feel now?" or "Tell me how it feels compared with an hour ago."
4. Attend to the client's needs promptly.

Assisting Support Persons

Support persons often need assistance to respond positively to the client experiencing pain. Nurses can help by giving them accurate information about the pain and providing opportunities for them to discuss their emotional reactions, which may include anger, fear, frustration, and feelings of inadequacy. Enlisting the aid of support persons in the provision of pain relief to the client, such as massaging the client's back, may diminish their feelings of helplessness and foster a more positive attitude toward the client's pain experience. Support persons also may need the nurse's verbal recognition of their concern and participation in the client's care.

Reducing Misconceptions about Pain

Reducing a client's misconceptions about the pain and its treatment will often avoid intensifying the pain. The nurse should explain to the client that pain is a highly individual experience and that it is only the client who really experiences the pain, although others can understand and empathize. Misconceptions are also dealt with when nurse and client discuss why the pain has increased or decreased at certain times. For example, a client whose pain increases in the evening may mistakenly think this is the result of eating dinner, rather than fatigue.

HOME CARE TEACHING GUIDE

Monitoring Pain

- Teach client to keep a pain diary to monitor pain onset, activity before pain, pain intensity, use of analgesics or other relief measures, and so on.
- Instruct client to contact a health-care professional if planned pain control measures are ineffective.

Pain Control

- Teach the use of preferred and selected nonpharmacological techniques, such as relaxation, guided imagery, distraction, music therapy, massage, and so on (see "Nonpharmacological Pain Management" on page 1291).
- Discuss the actions, side effects, dosages, frequency, and route of administration of prescribed analgesics.
- Suggest ways to handle side effects of medications (see the box on page 1287).
- Provide accurate information about tolerance, physical dependence, and addiction if opioid analgesics are prescribed and these topics are of concern.
- Instruct the client to use pain control measures *before* the pain becomes severe.
- Inform the client of the effects of untreated pain.
- Demonstrate and have the client or caregiver redemonstrate appropriate skills to administer analgesics (e.g., skin patches, injections, infusion pumps, or patient-controlled analgesia [PCA]). See "Routes for Opiate Delivery" on page 1288. For example, if a home infusion pump is being used, caregivers need to be able to do the following:
  a. Demonstrate stopping and starting the pump
  b. Change the medication cartridge and tubing
  c. Adjust the delivery dose
  d. Demonstrate site care
  e. Identify signs indicating the need to change an injection site
  f. Describe care of the pump and insertion site when the client is ambulatory, bathing, sleeping, or travelling
  g. Perform problem solving for pumps when alarms are activated
  h. Change the battery

Resources

- Provide appropriate information about how to access community resources, home care agencies, and associations that offer self-help groups and educational materials. Examples of these are Victoria Order of Nurses (www.von.ca); Canadian Cancer Society (www.cancer.ca); North American Pain Association of Canada (www.chronicpaincanada.org/index.html).

Reducing Fear and Anxiety

It is important to help relieve the emotional component, that is, anxiety or fear, associated with the pain. When clients have no opportunity to talk about their pain and associated fears, their perceptions and reactions to the pain can be intensified. The client may become angry or complain about the nurse's care when the problem really is a belief that the pain is not being attended to. If the nurse is honest and sincere and promptly attends to the client's needs, the client is much more likely to know that the nurse does believe the client is in pain.

By providing accurate information, the nurse can also reduce many of the client's fears, such as a fear of addiction or a fear that the pain will always be present. It also helps many clients to have privacy when they are experiencing pain.

Preventing Pain

A preventive approach to pain management involves the provision of measures to treat the pain before it occurs or before it is severe. *Preemptive analgesia* is the administration of analgesics prior to an invasive or operative procedure. Treating clients preoperatively with local infiltration of an anesthetic or parenteral administration of an opioid reduces postoperative pain and decreases the development of chronic pain (Goldstein, 1995). Nurses can also use a preemptive approach by providing analgesic around-the-clock (ATC), rather than as needed (PRN).

Pharmacological Pain Management

Pharmacological pain management involves the use of opioids (narcotics), nonopioids/NSAIDs (nonsteroidal anti-inflammatory drugs), and adjuvants, or coanalgesic drugs. See the box on page 1286.

Opioid Analgesics

Opioid (narcotic) analgesics include opium derivatives, such as morphine and codeine. Narcotics relieve pain and provide a sense of euphoria largely by binding to opiate receptors and activating endogenous pain suppression in

CLINICAL GUIDELINES

Individualizing Care for Clients with Pain

- *Establish a trusting relationship.* Convey your concern, and acknowledge that you believe that the client is experiencing pain. A trusting relationship promotes expression of the client's thoughts and feelings and enhances effectiveness of planned pain therapies.
- *Consider the client's ability and willingness to participate actively in pain relief measures.* Some clients who are excessively fatigued, are sedated, or have altered levels of consciousness are less able to participate actively. For example, a client with an altered level of consciousness or altered thought processes may not be able to deal with patient-controlled analgesia (PCA). In contrast, a fatigued client may express a willingness to use pain-relief measures that require little effort, such as listening to music or performing relaxation techniques.
- *Use a variety of pain relief measures.* It is thought that using more than one measure has an additive effect in relieving pain. Two measures that should always be part of any pain relief plan are (1) establishing a client-nurse relationship, and (2) client teaching. Because a client's pain may vary throughout a 24-hour period, different types of pain relief are often indicated during that time.
- *Provide measures to relieve pain before it becomes severe.* For example, providing an analgesic before the onset of pain is preferable to waiting for the client to complain of pain, when a larger dose may be required.
- *Use pain-relieving measures that the client believes are effective.* It has been recognized that clients are usually the authorities about their own pain. Thus, incorporating the client's measures into a pain relief plan is sensible, unless they are harmful.
- *Base the choice of pain relief measure on the client's report of the severity of the pain.* If a client reports mild pain, an analgesic, such as acetominophen, may be indicated, whereas a client who reports severe pain often requires a more potent relief measure.
- *If a pain relief measure is ineffective, encourage the client to try it once or twice more before abandoning it.* Anxiety may diminish the effects of a pain measure, and some approaches, such as distraction strategies, require practice before they are effective.
- *Maintain an unbiased attitude (open mind) about what may relieve the pain.* New ways to relieve pain are continually being developed. It is not always possible to explain pain relief measures; however, measures should be supported, unless they are harmful.
- *Keep trying.* Do *not* ignore a client because pain persists in spite of measures. In these circumstances, reassess the pain, and consider other relief measures.
- *Prevent harm to the client.* Pain therapy should not increase discomfort or harm the client. Some pain relief measures may have adverse untoward effects, such as fatigue, but they should not disable the client.
- *Educate the client and support people about pain.* Clients and support people need to be informed about possible causes of pain, precipitating and alleviating factors, and alternatives to drug therapy. Misconceptions also need to be corrected.

the central nervous system. There are several types of opiate receptors, including mu, delta, and kappa receptors. The mu receptor is most commonly associated with pain relief. Changes in mood and attitude and feelings of well-being make the person feel more comfortable even though the pain persists. These drugs must be ordered by a physician. The nurse requires knowledge of maximum daily dose limits.

There are three primary types of opioids:

1. *Full agonists.* These pure opioid drugs bind tightly to mu receptor sites, producing maximum pain inhibition, an agonist effect. Full **agonist analgesics** include morphine, codeine, meperidine (Demerol), propoxyphene (Darvon), and hydromorphine (Dilaudid). There is no ceiling on the dose of full agonists as the client builds tolerance to them.
2. *Mixed agonists-antagonists.* **Agonist-antagonist analgesic** drugs can act like opioids and relieve pain (agonist effect) when given to a client who has not taken any pure opioids. However, they can block or inactivate other opioid analgesics when given to a client who has been taking pure opioids (antagonist effect). These drugs include dezocine (Dalgan), pentazocine hydrochloride (Talwin), butorphanol tartrate (Stadol), and nalbuphine hydrochloride (Nubain). They block the mu receptor site and activate a kappa receptor site. If a client has been receiving a mu agonist, such as morphine, for pain, the administration of a mixed agonist-antagonist will result in the inactivation of the morphine effect and increase pain. These drugs also have a ceiling dose level. They are not recommended for use in terminally ill clients.
3. *Partial agonists.* Partial agonists have a ceiling effect. These drugs, such as buprenophrine (Buprenex), block the mu receptors or are neutral at that receptor but bind at a kappa receptor site.

When administering any analgesic, the nurse must review side effects. All opioids result in some initial drowsiness when first administered, but with regular administration,

TABLE 45.6 Common Misconceptions about Pain

Misconception	Correction
Clients experience severe pain only when they have had major surgery.	Even after minor surgery, clients can experience intense pain.
The nurse or other health-care professionals are the authorities about a client's pain.	The person who experiences the pain is the only authority about its existence and nature.
Administering analgesics regularly for pain will lead to addiction.	Clients are unlikely to become addicted to an analgesic provided to treat pain.
The amount of tissue damage is directly related to the amount of pain.	Pain is a subjective experience, and the intensity and duration of pain vary considerably among individuals.
Visible physiological or behavioural signs accompany pain and can be used to verify its existence.	Even with severe pain, periods of physiological and behavioural adaptation can occur.

this side effect tends to decrease. Opioids also may cause nausea, vomiting, constipation, and respiratory depression. Opioids must be used cautiously in clients with respiratory problems.

If the client experiences significant respiratory depression (e.g., a drop from 18 to 12) or is overly sedated, the dosage is excessive. *Before* administering narcotics, the nurse needs to assess a client's level of alertness and vital signs for baseline data. An increasing sedation level can be an early warning sign of impending respiratory depression (Pasero, 1994). Agency policy regarding respiratory depression as a result of narcotics administration must be followed. (i.e. withholding medication when respiration decreases to a certain level.) See the sedation rating scale in the box on the right. Often, clients will manifest an increase in sedation *before* they manifest a decrease in respiratory rate and depth. The nurse should assess and document the client's level of sedation at the same time that respiratory status is checked. Early recognition of an increasing level of sedation or respiratory depression will enable the nurse to implement appropriate measures promptly (e.g., obtaining an order to decrease the opioid dosage). The box on page 1287 provides suggested measures to prevent side effects of opioid analgesics.

Equianalgesic Dosing

When individualizing the analgesic regimen, it is sometimes beneficial to adjust the dose and time interval of the doses as well as the route of administration and the exact medication. An equianalgesic chart can be used to help provide doses of approximate equal ability to relieve pain. It is important that doses and intervals between doses are titrated accord-

Categories and Examples of Analgesics

Narcotic Analgesics

- Butorphanol tartrate (Stadol)
- Transdermal fentanyl
- Fentanyl citrate (Duragesic)
- Hydromorphone hydrochloride (Dilaudid)
- Meperidine hydrochloride (Demerol)
- Methylmorphine phosphate (codeine, Tylenol 3)
- Morphine sulfate (morphine)
- Propoxyphene napsylate (Darvon-N)

Non-Narcotic Analgesics/NSAIDs

- Acetaminophen (Tylenol)
- Acetylsalicylic acid (aspirin)
- Choline magnesium trisalicylate (Trilisate)
- Diclofenac sodium (Voltaren)
- Ibuprofen (Motrin, Advil)
- Indomethacin sodium trihydrate (Indocin)
- Naproxen (Naprosyn)
- Naproxen sodium (Anaprox)
- Piroxicam (Feldene)
- Tolmetin sodium (Tolectin)
- Celecoxib (Celebrex)

Adjuvant Analgesics

- Amitriptyline (Elavil)
- Chlorpromazine (Largactil)
- Diazepam (Valium)
- Hydroxyzine hydrochloride (Atarax)

Sedation Rating Scale

S = sleeping, easily aroused; requires no action
1 = awake and alert; requires no action
2 = occasionally drowsy, easy to arouse; requires no action
3 = frequently drowsy, arousable, drifts off to sleep during conversation; decrease the opioid dose
4 = somnolent, minimal or no response to stimuli; discontinue opioid, and consider use of naloxone (Narcan)

Source: McCaffery, M., & Pasero, C. (1999). *Pain clinical manual* (p. 267). St. Louis, MO: Mosby. Reprinted by permission.

Common Opioid Side Effects and Preventive Measures

Constipation

- Increase fluid intake (e.g., to eight glasses daily).
- Increase fibre and bulk-forming agents in the diet (e.g., fresh fruits and vegetables).
- Increase exercise regimen.
- Administer stool softeners, and if necessary, provide a mild laxative.

Nausea and Vomiting

- Inform client that tolerance to this emetic effect generally develops after several days of opiate therapy.
- Provide an antiemetic, as required.
- Change the analgesic, as indicated.

Sedation

- Inform client that tolerance usually develops over three to five days.

Respiratory Depression

- Administer an opioid antagonist, such as naloxone hydrochloride (Narcan), until respirations return to an acceptable rate. Follow agency policy for administration and monitoring.
- If the client is receiving intravenous patient-controlled analgesia (PCA), stop or slow the infusion.

Pruritus

- Apply cool packs, lotion, and diversional activity.
- Administer an antihistamine (e.g., diphenhydramine hydrochloride [Benadryl] as ordered).
- Inform the client that tolerance also develops to pruritus.

Urinary Retention

- The nurse may need to catheterize client.
- Administer narcotic antagonist (naloxone hydrochloride [Narcan] as ordered according to agency policy).

RESEARCH NOTE

Can Nurses Assist Clients with Pain Relief and a Sense of Control Postoperatively?

In this study, the nurse researchers interviewed 16 hospitalized, frail women, aged 75 to 93 years, who had abdominal surgery and could discuss their postoperative pain experience. The study used a phenomenological methodology with open-ended, unstructured interviews asking about what brought them to the hospital and their pain following the surgery. The results were analyzed for particular themes. The uniqueness of the women's pain experiences and the difficulty they had in sharing them showed the importance of taking adequate time to assess older adults' pain. Control was a theme that extended from the preoperative to the postoperative experiences. The doubts about the return of mobility and functional status postoperatively were significant as various strategies were used to achieve a sense of control and pain relief.

Implications: Nurses can facilitate recovery from surgery by exploring the significance that pain may have for a client and individualizing care to support the client's unique strength and needs.

Source: Lieb Zalon, M. & Pieper, B. (1997). Pain in frail, elderly women after surgery. *Image: Journal of Nursing Scholarship, 29*(1), 21–26.

ing to individual responses. It is important that the nurse check the policy of the agency and physicians' orders regarding equianalgesic dosing.

Nonopioids/NSAIDs

Nonopioids (non-narcotic analgesics) include **nonsteroidal anti-inflammatory drugs (NSAIDs),** such as aspirin and ibuprofen. These analgesics have anti-inflammatory, analgesic, and antipyretic effects. Acetaminophen has only analgesic and antipyretic effects. They relieve pain by acting on peripheral nerve endings at the injury site and decreasing the level of inflammatory mediators generated at the site of injury. They may also decrease prostaglandin release at the injury site (American Pain Society, 1992). In addition, several combinations of analgesic drugs are available, for example, a narcotic and non-narcotic, such as Tylenol #3, which combines acetaminophen with 30 mg of codeine.

Individual drugs in this category vary widely in their analgesic properties, metabolism, excretion, and side effects. In addition, the analgesic activity of these drugs has a *ceiling effect*—the level at which increasing the dose results in no further increase in analgesia (Ferrell & Ferrell, 1995).

The most common side effect of nonopioid analgesics is indigestion, which can be prevented by taking the medication with antacid or food. Stomach ulcers and gastric bleeding have also been reported. NSAIDs reduce the dose of opioids needed when the drugs are given together and provide better pain relief than use of either type separately. These drugs must be ordered by the physician; they all have a maximum daily dose limit.

Pharmacological management of mild to moderate pain should begin with NSAIDs unless there is a specific contraindication (Agency for Health Care Policy and Research 1992a). NSAIDs are contraindicated, for example, in clients with impaired blood clotting, gastrointestinal bleeding or ulcer risk, renal disease, thrombocytopenia, and possibly infection (because NSAIDs will obscure fever).

Adjuvant Analgesics

Adjuvant analgesics are medications that were developed for uses other than analgesia but have been found to reduce certain types of chronic pain in addition to their primary action. For example, mild sedatives or tranquilizers, such as diazepam (Valium), may help reduce painful muscle spasms as well as reduce anxiety, stress, and tension so that the client can obtain a good night's sleep. Antidepressants, such as amitriptyline hydrochloride (Elavil), are used to treat underlying depression or mood disorders but may also enhance other pain strategies. Anticonvulsants, such as carbamazepine (Tegretol) and depakene (Valproic Acid), usually prescribed to treat seizures, can be useful in controlling painful neuropathies, such as herpes zoster (shingles) and diabetic neuropathies.

WHO Three-Step Ladder Approach

The World Health Organization (WHO) recommends a sequential or three-step ladder approach to manage cancer pain (Figure 45.9). This approach may also apply to pain resulting from causes other than cancer. Therapy begins with a nonopioid/NSAID (step 1). If the client receives the maximum recommended dose of nonopioids and continues to experience pain, a weak opioid is given (step 2). The dose of the weak opioid is increased until the ceiling dose is reached. If the client continues to experience pain, a stronger opioid is given (step 3). Adjuvant drugs may also be given at any stage of therapy.

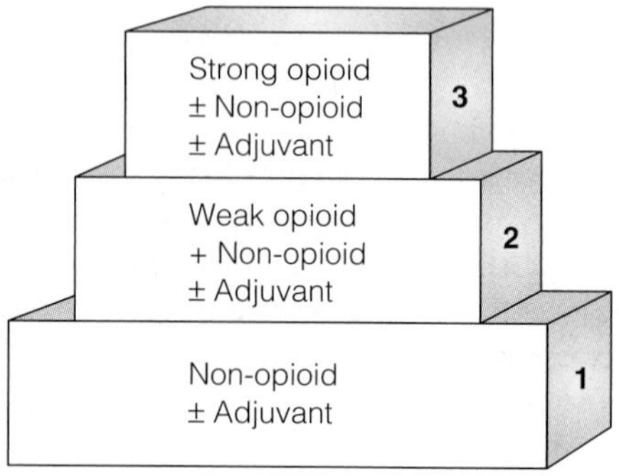

Figure 45.9 The analgesic ladder for cancer pain management proposed by the World Health Organization

Sources: World Health Organization. *Cancer pain relief.* Geneva, Switzerland: Author, 1986; and *Cancer pain relief and palliative care.* Geneva, Switzerland: Author, 1990.

Administration of Placebos

A **placebo** is an inert substance that is "used in research or clinical practice to determine effects attributable to the administration of the placebo rather than to the pharmacologic properties of a legitimate drug or treatment" (McCaffery, Ferrell, & Turner, 1996). The use of placebos to assess the presence or nature of pain raises serious ethical questions and challenges the nurse in relation to the ANA Code of Ethics (Brown et al., 1997). A positive response to a placebo dose is not indicative of a lack of real pain but only of the reality of the placebo response, which can be expected in 30 percent or more of any population (Turner et al., 1994). Because placebos fail to relieve pain for many people, it is recommended that the deceptive use of placebos be considered unacceptable in the management of pain (American Pain Society, 1992; Jacox et al., 1994; McCaffery, Ferrell, & Turner, 1996).

Routes for Opiate Delivery

Opioids have traditionally been administered by oral, subcutaneous, intramuscular, and intravenous routes. In addition, newer methods of delivering opiates have been developed to circumvent potential obstacles that occur with these traditional routes. Examples are transnasal and transdermal drug therapy, continuous subcutaneous infusions, and intraspinal infusion.

Oral

Oral administration of opiates remains the preferred route of delivery because of ease of administration. Because the duration of action of most opiates is approximately four hours, people with chronic pain have had to awaken several times during the night to medicate themselves for pain. To circumvent this problem, *long-acting* forms of morphine with a duration of eight or more hours have been developed. Two examples of long-acting morphine are MS Contin and Oramorph SR. Clients receiving long-acting morphine also may need prn rescue doses of immediate-release analgesics (e.g., short-acting morphine) for acute breakthrough pain.

Another new method of oral opiate delivery is high-concentration *liquid morphine.* This formulation enables clients who can swallow only small amounts to continue taking the drug orally.

Nasal

Transnasal administration has the advantage of rapid action of the medication because of direct absorption through the vascular nasal mucosa. A commonly used agent is the mixed agonist-antagonist butorphanol (Stadol) for acute headaches.

Transdermal

Transdermal drug therapy is advantageous in that it delivers a relatively stable plasma drug level and is noninvasive. Fentanyl (Duragesic) is an opioid currently available as a skin patch with various dosages. It provides drug delivery for up to 72 hours.

Rectal

Several opiates are now available in suppository form. The rectal route is particularly useful for clients who have dysphagia (difficulty swallowing) or nausea and vomiting.

Subcutaneous

Although the subcutaneous (SC) route has been used extensively to deliver opioids, a new technique uses subcutaneous catheters and infusion pumps to provide *continuous subcutaneous infusion* (CSCI) of narcotics. CSCI is particularly helpful for clients (1) whose pain is poorly controlled by oral medications, (2) who are experiencing dysphagia or gastrointestinal obstruction, or (3) who have a need for prolonged use of parenteral narcotics. CSCI involves the use of a small, light, battery-operated pump that administers the drug through a 23- or 25-gauge butterfly needle. The needle can be inserted into the anterior chest, the subclavicular region, the abdominal wall, the outer aspects of the upper arms, or the thighs. Client mobility is maintained with the application of a shoulder bag or holster to hold the pump (Figure 45.10). The frequency of site change ranges from three to seven days.

Because family caregivers must operate the pump and also change and care for the injection site, the nurse needs to provide appropriate instruction. Caregivers need to be able to do the following:

- Describe the basic parts and symbols of the system
- Identify ways to determine whether the pump is working
- Change the battery
- Change the medication
- Demonstrate stopping and starting the pump
- Demonstrate tubing care, site care, and changing of the injection site
- Identify signs indicating the need to change an injection site

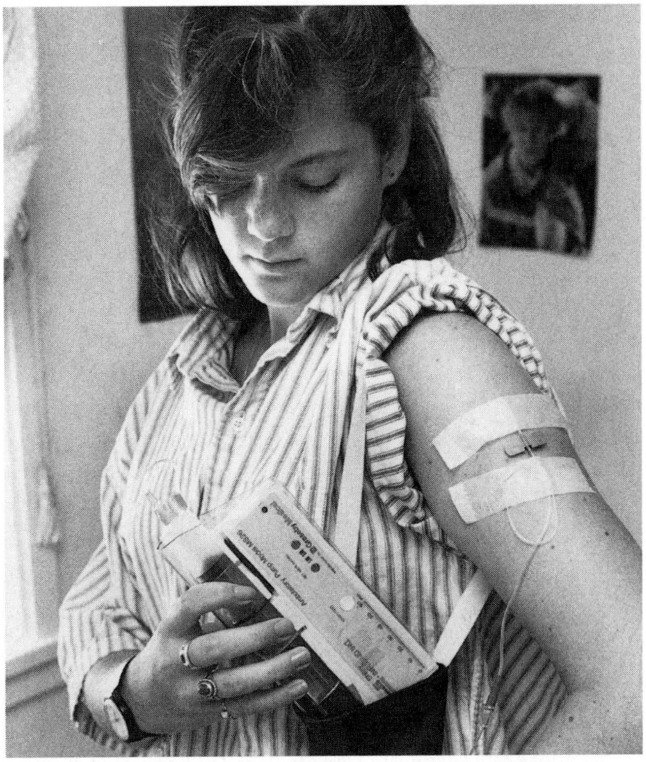

Figure 45.10 A continuous subcutaneous PCA infusion device

- Describe general care of the pump when the client is ambulatory, bathing, sleeping, or travelling
- Identify actions to take to solve problems when the alarm signals

Intramuscular

The intramuscular (IM) route is the least desirable route for opioid administration because of variable absorption, pain involved with administration, and the need to repeat administration every three to four hours.

Intravenous

The intravenous (IV) route provides rapid and effective pain relief with few side effects. The analgesic can be administered by IV bolus or by continuous infusion controlled by the client using a patient-controlled analgesia (PCA) machine at the bedside (see the discussion of PCA later in this chapter).

Intraspinal

Another recent method of delivery is the infusion of opiates into the **epidural** or intrathecal (subarachnoid) space. Intraspinal analgesics act directly on opiate receptors in the dorsal horn of the spinal cord. Two commonly used medications are preservative-free morphine sulfate and

TABLE 45.7 Nursing Interventions for Clients Receiving Analgesics through an Epidural Catheter

Nursing Goal	Interventions
Maintain client safety	Label the tubing, the infusion bag, and the front of the pump with tape marked EPIDURAL to prevent confusion with similar looking IV lines.
	Post sign above client's bed indicating epidural is in place.
	Secure all connections with tape.
	If there is no continuous infusion, apply tape over all injection ports on the epidural line to avoid the injection of substances intended for IV administration into the epidural catheter.
	Do not use alcohol in any care of catheter or insertion site as it can be neurotoxic.
Maintain catheter placement	Secure temporary catheters with tape.
	When bolus doses are used, gently aspirate prior to medication administration to determine that catheter has not migrated into the subarachnoid space. (Expect <1 mL of fluid return in syringe.)
	Assist client in repositioning or moving out of bed.
	Assess insertion site for leakage with each bolus dose or at least every 8–12 hours.
Prevent infection	Use strict aseptic techniques with all epidural related procedures.
	Maintain sterile occlusive dressing over insertion site.
	Assess insertion site for signs of infection.
Maintain urinary and bowel function	Monitor intake and output. Assess for bowel and bladder distention.
Prevent respiratory depression	Assess sedation level and respiratory status q1h for the first 24 hours and q4h thereafter.
	Do not administer other opioids or central nervous system depressants, unless ordered.
	Keep an ampule of naloxone hydrochloride (0.4 mg) at the bedside.
	Notify the clinician in charge if the respiratory rate falls below 8 per minute or if the client is difficult to rouse.

fentanyl. The major benefit of intraspinal drug therapy is that it exerts a lesser sedative effect than systemic opiates. The epidural space is most commonly used because the dura mater acts as a protective barrier against infection, including meningitis.

When the epidural space, rather than the intrathecal space, is used, a higher dosage of medication is required to achieve the same degree of analgesia. Because the intrathecal space contains cerebrospinal fluid (CSF) and directly surrounds the spinal cord, opiates act quickly on the dorsal horn. Very little drug is absorbed by blood vessels into the systemic circulation. In contrast, the epidural space is separated from the spinal cord by the dura mater, which acts as a barrier to drug diffusion. In addition, it is filled with fatty tissue and an extensive venous system. With this diffusion delay, some medication from the epidural space enters the systemic circulation via the venous plexus. Thus, a higher dose of opiate is required to create the desired effect.

Intraspinal catheters, which are inserted by physicians, allow either intermittent bolus injections or continuous drug delivery when attached to electronic infusion pumps. Totally implanted systems are also available for clients with chronic pain.

Temporary catheters are usually connected to tubing positioned along the spine and over the client's shoulder for the nurse to access. The entire catheter and tubing are taped securely to prevent dislodgement. Permanent catheters may be tunnelled subcutaneously through the skin and exit at the client's side. Nursing care of clients with intraspinal infusions is summarized in Table 45.7.

Patient-Controlled Analgesia

Noncancer Chronic Pain

A consensus statement from the Canadian Pain Society outlines the guidelines for the use of opioids for noncancer chronic pain unresponsive to other forms of analgesia (Jovey, 1998).

Patient-controlled analgesia (PCA) is the self-administration of an analgesic by a client who has been instructed regarding the process (Carr et al., 1992). The oral route for PCA is most common, but the subcutaneous, intravenous, and epidural routes are increasingly being used. The physician prescribes the analgesic dose, route, and frequency, with the client administering the medication. With the parenteral routes, an infusion pump is used to deliver the medication. Whether in an acute-care hospital setting, an ambulatory clinic, or in home care, the nurse is responsible for the initial instruction regarding use of the PCA and for the ongoing monitoring of the therapy. The client's pain must be assessed at regular intervals and analgesic use documented in the client's record.

PCA can be effectively used for clients with acute pain related to a surgical incision, traumatic injury, or labour and delivery, and for chronic pain as with cancer. In some settings, PCAs are used even if the client is unable to initiate a dose by pushing the button as long as a caregiver is willing to accept the responsibility; for example, when the client is an infant or toddler or is physically or cognitively impaired (Pasero & McCaffery, 1996). The benefits of this mode of administration include the following:

- Self-control over pain relief
- More stable analgesic blood level for sustained pain relief
- Tendency for the client to need less medication for pain relief

PCA pumps usually have a chamber or cartridge that contains the analgesic, a mechanism for setting the ordered dose, and a control for client activation (see Figure 45.10). When clients want a dose of analgesic, they can push a button attached to the infusion pump and the preset dose is delivered. A programmable lockout interval (usually 10 to 15 minutes) follows the dose, when an additional dose cannot be given even if the client activates the button. It is also possible to program the maximum dose that can be delivered over a period of hours (usually four). Many pumps are capable of delivering a low continuous infusion, or basal rate, to provide sustained analgesia during times of rest and sleep. Refer to agency policy for pain management methods for patients with a PCA pump.

Nonpharmacological Pain Management

Nonpharmacological pain management consists of a variety of physical and cognitive-behavioural pain management strategies. Physical interventions include cutaneous stimulation, immobilization, transcutaneous electrical nerve stimulation (TENS), and acupressure. Mind-body (cognitive-behavioural) interventions include distraction activities, relaxation techniques, imagery, meditation, biofeedback, hypnosis, and therapeutic touch. Several physical interventions and distraction are discussed next. For information about the other mind-body interventions and acupressure, see Chapter 11. Some of these interventions require additional education and/or certification.

Physical Interventions

The goals of physical intervention are the following (Carr et al., 1992):

- Provide comfort
- Correct physical dysfunction
- Alter physiological responses
- Reduce fears associated with pain related immobility or activity restriction

Cutaneous Stimulation

Cutaneous stimulation can provide effective temporary pain relief. It distracts the client and focuses attention on the tactile stimuli, away from the painful sensations, thus reducing pain perception. Cutaneous stimulation is also believed to (1) create the release of **endorphins** that block pain stimuli transmission, and (2) stimulate large-diameter A-beta sensory nerve fibres, thus decreasing the transmission of pain impulses through the smaller A-delta and C fibres. Cutaneous stimulation techniques include the following:

- Massage
- Application of heat or cold
- Acupressure
- Contralateral stimulation

Cutaneous stimulation can be applied directly to the painful area, proximal to the pain, distal to the pain, and contralateral (opposite side) to the pain.

Massage

Massage is a comfort measure that can aid relaxation and decrease muscle tension and may ease anxiety as the physical contact communicates caring (Salerno & Willens, 1996). Massage can also decrease pain intensity by increasing superficial circulation to the area. Massage can involve the back and neck, hands and arms, or feet (techniques are discussed in Chapters 11 and 42). The use of ointments or liniments may provide localized pain relief with joint or muscle pain.

Heat and Cold Applications

A warm bath, warm pads, ice bags, ice massage, warm or cold compresses, and warm or cold sitz baths, in general, relieve pain and promote healing of injured tissues.

Acupressure

Acupressure developed from the ancient Chinese healing system of acupuncture. The therapist applies finger pressure to points that correspond to many of the points used in acupuncture. See Chapter 11 for further information.

Contralateral Stimulation

Contralateral stimulation can be accomplished by stimulating the skin in an area opposite to the painful area (e.g., stimulating the left knee if the pain is in the right knee).

The contralateral area may be scratched for itching, massaged for cramps, if appropriate, or treated with cold packs or analgesic ointments. This method is particularly useful when the painful area cannot be touched because it is hypersensitive, inaccessible by a cast or bandages, or when the pain is felt in a missing part (phantom pain).

Immobilization

Immobilizing or restricting the movement of a painful body part (e.g., arthritic joint, traumatized limb) may help to manage episodes of acute pain. Splints or supportive devices should hold joints in the position of optimal function and should be removed regularly in accordance with agency protocol to provide range-of-motion exercises, if not contraindicated. Prolonged immobilization can result in joint contracture, muscle atrophy, and cardiovascular problems. Therefore, clients should be encouraged to participate in self-care activities and remain as active as possible (Jacox et al., 1994).

Transcutaneous Electrical Nerve Stimulation (TENS)

TENS is a method of applying low-voltage electrical stimulation directly over identified pain areas, at an acupressure point, along peripheral nerve areas that innervate the pain area, or along the spinal column. The TENS unit consists of a portable, battery-operated device with lead wire and electrode pads that are applied to the chosen area of skin (Figure 45.11). Cutaneous stimulation from the TENS unit is thought to activate large-diameter fibres that modulate the transmission of the nociceptive impulse in the peripheral and central nervous system (closing the pain "gate"), resulting in pain relief. This stimulation may also cause a release of endorphins from the central nervous system centres.

Distraction

Distraction draws the person's attention away from the pain and lessens the perception of pain. In some instances, distraction can make a client completely unaware of pain. For example, a client recovering from surgery may feel no pain while watching a football game on television, yet feel pain again when the game is over. Different types of distractions are shown in the box above.

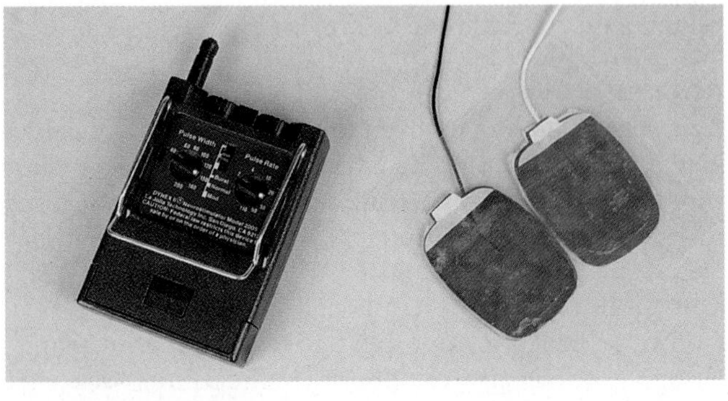

Figure 45.11 A transcutaneous electrical nerve stimulator (TENS)

Types of Distraction

Visual Distraction
- Reading or watching TV
- Watching a baseball game
- Guided imagery

Auditory Distraction
- Humour
- Listening to music

Tactile Distraction
- Slow, rhythmic breathing
- Massage
- Holding or stroking a pet or toy

Intellectual Distraction
- Crossword puzzles
- Card games (e.g., bridge)
- Hobbies (e.g., stamp collecting, writing a story)

Nonpharmacological Invasive Therapies

A **nerve block** is a chemical interruption of a nerve pathway, effected by injecting a local anesthetic into the nerve. Nerve blocks are widely used during dental work. The injected drug blocks nerve pathways from the painful tooth, thus stopping the transmission of pain impulses to the brain. Nerve blocks are often used to relieve the pain of whiplash injury, lower-back disorders, bursitis, and cancer. Sometimes, alcohol blocks are used. These, however, destroy nerve fibres and, as a result, are generally used only for peripheral blocks because peripheral nerve fibres regenerate.

Pain conduction pathways can be interrupted surgically. Because this disruption is permanent, surgery is performed only as a last resort, generally for intractable pain. Several surgical procedures may be performed. A **cordotomy** obliterates pain and temperature sensation below the level of the spinothalamic portion of the anterolateral tract severed and is usually done for pain in the legs and trunk. **Rhizotomy** interrupts the anterior or posterior nerve root between the ganglion and the cord. Interruption of anterior *motor* nerve roots stops spasmodic movements that accompany paraplegia. Interruption of posterior *sen-*

sory nerve roots eliminates pain in areas innervated by that specific nerve root. Rhizotomies are generally performed on cervical nerve roots to alleviate pain of the head and neck from cancer or neuralgia.

In **neurectomy,** peripheral or cranial nerves are interrupted to alleviate localized pain, such as pain in the lower leg or foot arising from a vascular occlusion. In a **sympathectomy,** pathways of the sympathetic division of the autonomic nervous system are severed. This procedure eliminates vasospasm, improves peripheral blood supply, and, thus, is effective in treating painful vascular disorders, such as angina and Raynaud's disease.

Spinal cord stimulation (SCS) is used with nonmalignant pain that has not been controlled with less invasive therapies. SCS involves the insertion of a cable that allows the placement of an electrode directly on the spinal cord. The cable is attached to a device that sends electric impulses to the spinal cord to control pain.

Evaluating

Using the desired outcomes established during the planning stage as a guide, the nurse and client determine whether client goals and outcomes have been achieved. Examples of client goals and related outcomes are shown in Table 45.8.

To assist in the evaluation process, flowsheet records or a client diary may be helpful. See Figure 45.12 for an example of a flowsheet to evaluate the effectiveness of an analgesic. A weekly log or diary can be structured in a similar fashion for the individual client. For example, columns including day, time, onset of pain, activity before pain, pain relief measure, and duration of pain can be devised to help the client and nurse determine the effectiveness of pain relief strategies.

If outcomes are *not* achieved, the nurse and client need to explore the reasons before modifying the care plan. The following are some questions the nurse might consider:

- Is adequate analgesic being given? Would the client benefit from a change in dose or in the time interval between doses?
- Were the client's beliefs and values about pain therapy considered?
- Did the client understate the pain experience for some reason?
- Were appropriate instructions provided to allay misconceptions about pain management?
- Did the client and support people understand the instructions about pain management techniques?
- Is the client receiving adequate support from significant others?
- Has the client's physical condition changed, necessitating modifications in interventions?
- Should selected intervention strategies be re-evaluated?

The use of a formal pain assessment tool and patient flowsheet has been shown to improve documentation in all areas of pain relief measures (Huber, Fesert, & Hughes, 1999).

TABLE 45.8 Evaluation Goals and Outcomes: Pain

Goal	Examples of Desired Outcomes
Modify or minimize pain to enable partial or complete resumption of daily activities	Reports pain relief at level of (specify) or less, on a scale of 0 to 10; or expresses feelings of reasonable comfort
	Reports decreased frequency and length of pain episodes and/or decreased fear and anxiety
	Absence of nonverbal pain responses, such as restlessness, muscle tension, protective body position, facial grimacing (specify)
	Reports increase in mobility and physical activity, in hours of uninterrupted sleep at night, and in quality of life
Enhance abilities to control pain	Identifies factors that precipitate or intensify the pain experience
	Identifies both pharmacological and nonpharmacological pain management techniques
	Identifies ways to prevent side effects of drugs
Demonstrate actions to control pain and associated symptoms	Reduces or eliminates factors that precipitate or intensify the pain experience
	Uses a pain diary to monitor pain pattern and effectiveness of pain measures
	Uses planned nonpharmacological pain relief measures (specify)
	Uses analgesics appropriately

SAMPLE CARE PLAN FOR ACUTE PAIN

ASSESSMENT DATA

Nursing Assessment

Mr. Lee Chin is a 57-year-old Chinese Canadian businessman who was admitted to the surgical unit for treatment of a possible strangulated inguinal hernia. Two days ago, he had a partial bowel resection. Post-operative orders include NPO, intravenous infusion of D5NS at 125 mL/hr left arm, nasogastric tube to low intermittent suction. Mr. Chin is in a dorsal recumbent (supine) position and is attempting to draw up his legs. He appears restless and is complaining of pain (7 on a scale of 1–10).

Physical Examination

Height: 167 cm
Weight: 77 kg
Temperature: 37°C
Pulse: 90 BPM
Respirations: 24/minute
Blood pressure: 158/82 mm Hg
Skin pale and moist, pupils dilated
Midline abdominal incision, sutures dry and intact

Diagnostic Data

Chest x-ray and urinalysis negative
WBC 12.0 × 10^9/L

Nursing Diagnosis

Pain, acute related to surgical incision stimulation of mechanosensitive receptors (as evidenced by restlessness; pallor; elevated pulse, respirations, and systolic blood pressure; and dilated pupils)

Client Goal(s):

The client will experience minimal abdominal pain and discomfort.

Desired Outcomes

1. States postoperative discomfort is relieved within 20 to 30 minutes of verbalized pain
2. Practises one relaxation technique for relief of pain by end of second postop day
3. Turns, coughs, and deep breathes with a minimum of discomfort by second postop day

---

*Nursing Interventions and Selected Activities with Rationale *[in italics]*

Pain Management

- Perform a comprehensive assessment of pain to include location, characteristics, onset, duration, frequency, quality, intensity or severity, and precipitating factors of pain.
  Pain is a subjective experience and must be described by the client in order to plan effective treatment.
- Consider cultural influences on Mr. Chin's pain response *(e.g., cultural beliefs about pain may result in a stoic attitude).*
  Each person experiences and expresses pain in an individual manner using a variety of sociocultural adaptation techniques.
- Reduce or eliminate factors that precipitate or increase Mr. Chin's pain experience (e.g., fear, fatigue, monotony, and lack of knowledge).
  Personal factors can influence pain and pain tolerance. Those factors that may be precipitating or augmenting pain should be reduced or eliminated to enhance the overall pain management program.
- Teach the use of nonpharmacological techniques (e.g., relaxation, guided imagery, music therapy, distraction, and massage) before, after, and, if possible, during painful activities; before pain occurs or increases; and along with other pain relief measures.
  The use of noninvasive pain relief measures can increase the release of endorphins and enhance the therapeutic effects of pain relief medications.
- Provide Mr. Chin optimal pain relief with prescribed analgesics.
  Each client has a right to expect maximum pain relief. Optimal pain relief using analgesics includes determining the preferred route, drug, dosage, and frequency for each individual.
- Medicate before an activity to increase participation, but evaluate the hazard of sedation.
  Turning and ambulation activities will be enhanced if pain is controlled or tolerable. Assessing level of consciousness should precede the activity because many analgesics cause sedation and could compromise safety.
- Evaluate the effectiveness of the pain control measures used through ongoing assessment of Mr. Chin's pain experience.
  Research shows that the most common reason for unrelieved pain is failure to routinely assess pain and pain relief. Many clients silently tolerate pain if not specifically asked about it.

SAMPLE CARE PLAN FOR ACUTE PAIN *continued*

Analgesic Administration

- Check the medical order for drug, dose, and frequency of analgesic prescribed.

  Ensures that the nurse has the right drug, right route, right dosage, right client, right frequency.
- Determine analgesic selections (narcotic, non-narcotic, or NSAID) based on type and severity of pain.

  Various types of pain (e.g., acute, chronic, neuropathic, arthritic) require different analgesic approaches. Some types of pain respond to nonopioid drugs alone while others can be relieved by combining a low-dose opioid with the nonopioid.
- Institute safety precautions, as appropriate, if Mr. Chin receives narcotic analgesics.

  Side effects of opioid narcotics include drowsiness and sedation.
- Instruct Mr. Chin to request prn pain medication before the pain is severe.

  Severe pain is more difficult to control and increases the client's anxiety and fatigue. The preventive approach to pain management can reduce the total 24-hour analgesic dose.
- Evaluate the effectiveness of analgesic at regular, frequent intervals after each administration and especially after the initial doses, also observing for any signs and symptoms of untoward effects (e.g., respiratory depression, nausea and vomiting, dry mouth, and constipation).

  The analgesic dose may not be adequate to raise the client's pain threshold or may be causing intolerable or dangerous side effects or both. Ongoing evaluation will assist in making necessary adjustments for effective pain management.
- Document Mr. Chin's response to analgesics and any untoward effects.

  Documentation facilitates pain management by communicating effective and noneffective pain management strategies to the entire health-care team.
- Implement actions to decrease untoward effects of analgesics (e.g., constipation and gastric irritation).

  Constipation is a common side effect of opioid narcotics and a treatment plan to prevent occurrence should be instituted at the beginning of analgesic therapy.

Simple Relaxation Therapy

- Consider Mr. Chin's willingness and ability to participate, preference, past experiences, and contraindications before selecting a specific relaxation strategy.

  The client must feel comfortable trying a different approach to pain management. To avoid ineffective strategies, the client should be involved in the planning process.
- Elicit behaviours that are conditioned to produce relaxation, such as deep breathing, yawning, abdominal breathing, or peaceful imaging.

  Relaxation techniques help reduce skeletal muscle tension, which will reduce the intensity of the pain.
- Create a quiet, nondisruptive environment with dim lights and comfortable temperature, when possible.

  Comfort and a quiet atmosphere promote a relaxed feeling and permit the client to focus on the relaxation technique, rather than external distraction.
- Individualize the content of the relaxation intervention (e.g., by asking for suggestions about what Mr. Chin enjoys or finds relaxing).

  Each person may find different images or approaches to relaxation more helpful than others.
- Demonstrate and practice the relaxation technique with Mr. Chin.

  Return demonstrations by the participant provide an opportunity for the nurse to evaluate the effectiveness of teaching sessions.
- Evaluate and document his response to relaxation therapy.

  Conveys to the health-care team effective strategies in reducing or eliminating pain.

Evaluation

Goal partially met. The client verbalizes pain and discomfort, requesting analgesics at onset of pain. States "the pain is a 2" (on a scale of 1–10) 30 minutes after analgesic administration. Practises rhythmic breathing q 3–4 hours during the day and requests analgesic 30 minutes before ambulation. Remains hesitant to cough and deep breathe even following analgesic administration on second postop day.

*Interventions and activities selected are only a sample of those suggested in the *Nursing Interventions Classification (NIC)* and should be individualized for each client.

Source: McCloskey, J. C., & Bulechek, G. M. (2000). *Iowa intervention project: Nursing interventions classification (NIC)* (3rd ed.). St. Louis, MO: Mosby.

CRHA
Calgary Regional Health Authority

☐ BVC ☐ FH ☐ RGH
☐ CBH ☐ PLC

PAIN FLOW SHEET

ROUTE:
PCA = Patient Controlled Analgesia
EA = Epidural Analgesia
PNB = Peripheral Nerve Blockade
I.M. = Intramuscular
PO = Oral

SEDATION LEVEL:
0 = Alert
1 = Sometimes Drowsy
2 = Frequently Drowsy, Easy to Arouse
3 = Somnolent, Difficult to Arouse
S = Normal Sleep, Easy to Arouse

SITE ASSESSMENT:
√ = Nothing Abnormal Detected
R = Red
T = Tender
L = Leaking
SW = Swelling
X = Catheter Disconnected

DATE											
TIME											
MEDICATION: • Name • Concentration • Comments											
ROUTE											
Infusion Rate per hour											
PCA Dose											
PCA Lockout Interval											
Breakthrough or Loading Dose											
Doses Received / Attempts											
Accummulated dose since last recording											
PAIN SCALE (Worst Pain) 10											
9											
8											
7											
6											
5											
4											
3											
2											
1											
(No Pain) 0											
Sedation Level											
Respiratory Rate / min.											
Block Level											
O_2 Sats											
Nausea & Vomiting / Treatment Required											
Pruritis / Treatment Required											
Urine Retention / Treatment Required											
Other / Treatment Required											
Intervention											
Site Assessment											
Initials											

PAIN SCALE
R = Rest
M = Moving

10 (Worst Pain)
9
8
7
6
5
4
3
2
1
0 (No Pain)

BLOCK LEVEL

LEVELS OF PRINCIPAL DERMATOMES

C 3-4	"Cape" area of shoulders
C 3-5	Phrenic nerve & diaphragm
C5-T1	Surface of the arms
C6	Thumb
C6-7-8	Hand
T4	Nipples
T10	Umbilicus
T12-L1	Groin

PROBLEMS / OTHER
MY = myoclonus
CO = constipation
CF = confusion

INTERVENTIONS
H = Heat
D = Distraction
I = Imagery

Figure 45.12 Pain flowsheet

Source: Calgary Regional Health Authority.

FOCUS ON CRITICAL THINKING

Mrs. Lundahl underwent abdominal surgery approximately six hours ago. She has a 15-cm midline incision that is covered with a dry and intact surgical dressing. Upon assessing Mrs. Lundahl, you note that she is perspiring, lying in a rigid position, holding her abdomen, and grimacing. Her blood pressure is 150/90, heart rate 100, and respiratory rate 32. When asked to rate her pain on a scale of 1 to 10, Mrs. Lundahl rates her pain as 5.

1. What conclusions, if any, can be drawn about Mrs. Lundahl's pain status?
2. Does Mrs. Lundahl's rating of her pain as 5 mean that she is not experiencing pain severe enough to warrant intervention?
3. What type of pain is Mrs. Lundahl experiencing?
4. What interventions, in addition to pain medication, may be useful in reducing Mrs. Lundahl's pain?
5. How will you know if your interventions have been effective in reducing Mrs. Lundahl's pain?

See Appendix A for answers to these questions.

CHAPTER HIGHLIGHTS

- Pain is a subjective sensation to which no two people respond in the same way. It can directly impair health and prolong recovery from surgery, disease, and trauma.
- Pain can be categorized according to its origin as cutaneous, deep somatic, or visceral; or according to its cause as acute pain, chronic malignant pain, or chronic nonmalignant pain.
- Pain threshold is similar in all people, but pain tolerance and response vary considerably.
- For pain to be perceived, nociceptors must be stimulated. Three types of pain stimuli are mechanical, thermal, and chemical.
- The precise mechanism of pain transmission and perception is unknown. Type A-delta fibres are associated with fast, sharp pain; type C fibres are associated with slow, aching pain.
- The body's analgesia system contains neuromodulators that release endogenous opioids to modulate pain transmission and perception. These endogenous opioids include enkephalins, endorphins, and dynorphins, which are morphinelike in their actions.
- According to the gate control theory, peripheral nerve fibres carrying pain to the spinal cord can have their input modified at the spinal cord level before transmission to the brain. This theory is the basis of many pain intervention strategies.
- Numerous factors influence a person's perception and reaction to pain: ethnic and cultural values, age, environment and support people, and anxiety and stress.
- Pain is subjective, and the most reliable indicator of the presence or intensity of pain is the client's self-report. Assessment of a client who is experiencing pain should include a comprehensive pain history.
- Although the nursing diagnosis given to clients suffering pain is ***Pain*** or ***Chronic Pain,*** the pain itself may be the etiology of many other nursing diagnoses.
- Overall client goals include preventing, modifying, or eliminating pain so that the client is able to partially or completely resume usual daily activities and to cope more effectively with the pain experience.
- When planning, nurses need to choose pain relief measures appropriate for the client. Nursing interventions may include a variety of pharmacologic and nonpharmacologic interventions. Selecting several strategies from both broad categories is usually most effective.
- Scheduling measures to *prevent* pain is far more supportive of the client than trying to deal with pain once it is established.
- Pain management includes two basic types of nursing interventions: pharmacological and nonpharmacological.
- Major nursing functions for all clients are to acknowledge and convey belief in the client's pain, assist support people, reduce misconceptions about pain, and reduce fear and anxiety associated with the pain.
- Pharmacological interventions, ordered by the physician, include the use of opioids, nonopioids/NSAIDs, and adjuvant drugs.
- The nurse assesses the client's pain needs, administers the ordered analgesics, and evaluates the client's response to analgesics provided.
- Analgesic medication can be delivered through a variety of routes and methods to meet the specific needs of the client. These routes include oral, nasal, rectal, transdermal, topical, subcutaneous or intravenous with a continuous infusion or a bolus dose, and intraspinal.
- Patient-controlled analgesia (PCA) enables the client to exercise control and minimize feelings of helplessness.

- Physical nonpharmacological pain interventions include such cutaneous stimulation as warm and cold applications, massage, acupressure, and contralateral stimulation; transcutaneous electrical nerve stimulation (TENS); and immobilization.
- Cognitive-behavioural interventions include distraction techniques, relaxation techniques, and guided imagery.
- Evaluation of the client's pain therapy includes the response of the client, the changes in the pain, and the client's perceptions of the effectiveness of the therapy. Ongoing verbal or written feedback from the client and family is integral to this process.

READINGS AND REFERENCES

Suggested Readings

Bral, E. E. (1998, April). Caring for adults with chronic cancer pain. *American Journal of Nursing, 98*(4), 27–32.
The author describes the essential aspects of nursing care for clients who have chronic cancer pain. This includes the caring aspect of care, the essentials of pain management, and pharmacological and nonpharmacological strategies.

Brown, R. I., & Sullivan, E. (1996, June). Helping families of chronic pain cancer patients to cope. *American Journal of Nursing Supplement, 96*, 22–28.
This article describes the process of coping and how it relates to families. Five strategies that nurses can use to enhance family coping are discussed.

Shipton, E. A. (1999). *PAIN: Acute and Chronic* (2nd ed.). Don Mills, Ontario: Oxford University Press.
This introductory text examines all aspects of the assessment and management of pain, including physiology, pathology, clinical manifestations of different types of pain, and interventions.

Related Research

Dufault, M. A., Bielecki, C., Collins, E., & Willey, C. (1995). Changing nurses' pain assessment practice: A collaborative research utilization approach. *Journal of Advanced Nursing, 21*(4), 634–645.

Francke, A. L., Luiken, J. B., de Schepper, A. M., Abu-Saad, H. H., & Grypdonck, M. (1997). Effects of a continuing education program on nurses' pain assessment practices. *Journal of Pain and Symptom Management, 13*(2), 90–97.

Horgas, A. L., & Tsai, P. F. (1998, July/August). Analgesic drug prescription and use in cognitively impaired nursing home residents. *Nursing Research, 47*(4), 235–242.

Selected References

American Pain Society. (2003). *Principles of analgesic use in the treatment of acute pain and cancer pain* (4th ed.). Skokie, IL: Author.

Andrews, M. M., & Boyle, J. S. (2002). *Transcultural concepts in nursing care* (4th ed.). Philadelphia, PA: Lippincott.

Back, I. N., & Finlay, I. (1995). Analgesic effect of topical opioids on painful skin ulcers. *Journal of Pain and Symptom Management, 10*(7), 493.

Berde, C. B. (1997, January/February). New and old anticonvulsants for management of pain. *International Association for the Study of Pain (IASP) Newsletter*, 3–4.

Berkowitz, C. (1997, August). Epidural pain control—your job too. *RN, 60*(8), 22–27.

Bocchino, C. A. (1992, May/June). An interview with Daniel Carr and Ada Jacox. *Nursing Economics, 10*, 165–175.

Bonica, J. J. (1990). *The management of pain* (2nd ed.). Philadelphia, PA: Lea & Febiger.

Bonn, D. (1996). Exploring central issues in analgesia. *The Lancet, 347*(9000), 530.

Bral, E. E. (1998, April). Caring for adults with chronic cancer pain. *American Journal of Nursing, 98*(4), 27–33.

Brennan-Hould, A. L. (2001). Children's Pain: A mandate for change. *Pain Research and Management, 6*, 29–39.

Brown, J. (1992). Nurses' analgesic choices and postoperative patients' perceived pain: The effect of a pain flow sheet. *American Journal of Pain Management, 2*(4), 192–197.

Brown, J., Moore, D. E., Potter, D., & Stewart, R. (1997). Placebos and the need for good communication: The case of George Hunter. *Orthopaedic Nursing, 16*(3), 61–65.

Carpenito, L. J. (2002). *Handbook of nursing diagnosis* (9th ed.). Philadelphia, PA: Lippincott.

Carr, D. B., Jacox, A. K., Chapman, C. R., Ferrell, B., Fields, H. L., Heidrich, G., Hester, N. K., Hill, C. S., Lipman, A. R., McGarvery, C. L., Miaskowski, C., Mulder, D. S., Payne, R., Schecter, N., Shapiro, B. S., Smith, R. S., Tsou, C. V., & Vecchiarelli, L. (1992). *Acute pain management: Operative or medical procedures and trauma. Clinical practice guidelines.* AHCPR Pub. No. 92-0032. Rockville, MD: Agency for Health Care Policy and Research, PHS, USDHHS.

Carr, E. (1997a, September 17). Assessing pain: A vital part of nursing care. *Nursing Times, 93*(38), 16–18.

Carr, E. (1997b, September 24). Factors influencing the experience of pain. *Nursing Times, 93*(39), 53–54.

Carr, E. (1997c, October 1). Myths and fears about pain-relieving drugs. *Nursing Times, 93*(40), 50–51.

Compton, P. (1997). Pain control: When does "drug-seeking" behaviour signal addiction? *American Journal of Nursing, 97*(5), 17–18.

Coyne, P. (1997, September). Controlling pain. Relieving AIDS-related pain. Responding when traditional strategies don't work. *Nursing 97, 27*(9), 25.

Dane, J. R., & Kessler, R. S. (1994). A matrix model for the psychological assessment and treatment of acute pain. In R. J. Hamill, & J. C. Rowlingson (Eds.), *Handbook of critical care pain management* (pp. 53–81). New York: McGraw-Hill.

Dray, A., Urban, L., & Dickenson, A. (1994). Pharmacology of chronic pain. *Trends in Pharmacological Sciences, 15*(6), 190–198.

Dunbar, P. J., Buckley, P., Gavrin, J. R., et al. (1995). Use of patient-controlled analgesia for pain control for children receiving bone marrow transplant. *Journal of Pain and Symptom Management, 10*(8), 604–611.

Eisenach, J. C., DuPen, S., Dubois, M., Miguel, R., & Allin, D. (1995). Epidural clinidine analgesia for intractable cancer pain. *Pain, 61*, 391–399.

Faries, J. (1998, June). Easing your patient's post-operative pain. *Nursing 98, 28*(6), 58–60.

Ferrell, B. A., Ferrell, B. R., & Rivera, L. (1995). Pain in cognitively impaired nursing home patients. *Journal of Pain and Symptom Management, 10*(8), 591–598.

Ferrell, B. R., Grant, M., Chan, J., Ahn, C., & Ferrell, B. A. (1995). The impact of cancer pain education on family caregivers of elderly patients. *Oncology Nurse Forum, 22*(8), 1211–1217.

Fields, J. L., & Rowbotham, M. C. (1994). Multiple mechanisms of neuropathic pain. In G. F. Gebhart, K. L. Hammond, & T. S. Jensen (Eds.), *Proceedings of the 7th World Congress on Pain, Progress in Pain Research and Management, Vol. 2.* Seattle, WA: IASP Press.

Fins, J. J. (1997, March). Public attitudes about pain and analgesics: Clinical implications. *Journal of Pain and Symptom Management, 13*(3), 169–171.

Flor, H., & Birbaumer, N. (1994). Basic issues in the psychobiology of pain. In G. F. Gebhart, K. L. Hammond, & T. S. Jensen (Eds.), *Proceedings of the 7th World Congress on Pain, Progress in Pain Research and Management, Vol. 2.* Seattle, WA: IASP Press.

Fulmer, T. T., Mion, L. C., Bottrell, M. M., & NICHE Faculty. (1996, September/October). Pain management protocol. *Geriatric Nursing, 17*(5), 222–227.

Goldstein, F. J. (1995, July). Preemptive analgesia: A research review. *MedSurg Nursing, 4*(4), 305–308.

Gordon, D. B. (1996, April). Critical pathways: A road to institutionalizing pain management. *Journal of Pain and Symptom Management, 11*(4), 252–259.

Guyton, A., & Hall, J. E. (2000). *Textbook of medical physiology* (10th ed.). Philadelphia, PA: Saunders.

Hall, J. L. (1994). Anatomy of pain. In C. D. Tollison, J. R. Satterthwaite, & J. W. Tollison (Eds.), *Handbook of pain management* (2nd ed.). (pp. 11–17). Baltimore, MD: Williams & Wilkins.

Harkins, S. W. (1997, March/April). Sans pain? *American Pain Society Bulletin,* 7(2). http://www.ampainsoc.org/pub/bulletin/mar97/qanda.htm.

Henderson, C. (1996, March 25). SNX-111 in treatment of neuropathic pain caused by AIDS. *AIDS Weekly Plus,* 27.

Herr, K. A., & Mobily, P. R. (1991, April). Complexities of pain assessment in the elderly: Clinical considerations. *Journal of Gerontological Nursing, 17*, 12–19.

Herr, K. A., & Mobily, P. R. (1992, June). Interventions related to pain. *Nursing Clinics of North America, 27*, 347–369.

Hudson, D. C. (1997). Pain management in the hospitalized infant. *Journal of the Society of Pediatric Nurses, 2*(2), 93–97.

Huber, S., Fesert, L., Hughes, D., et al. (1999). A collaborative approach to pain: The Calgary experience. *Canadian Nurse, 95*(8), 22–26.

International Association for the Study of Pain (IASP) Subcommittee on Taxonomy. (1979). Pain terms: A list with definitions and notes on usage. *Pain, 6*(2), 249.

Jacox, A., Carr, D. B., Payne, R., Berde, C. B., Breitbart, W., Cain, J. M., Chapman, C. R., Cleeland, C. S., Ferrell, R. R., Finley, R. S., Hester, N.O., Hill, C. S., Leak, W. D., Lipman, A. G., Logan, C. L., McGarvey, C. L., Miaskowski, C. A., Mulder, S., Stover, J., Tsou, C. V., Vecchiarelli, L., & Weissman, D. E. (1994). Management of cancer pain: Clinical practice guideline. AHCPR Pub. No. 94-0592. Rockville, MD: Agency for Health Care Policy and Research, PHS, USDHHS.

Johnson, M., & Maas, M. (Eds.) (2000). *Iowa outcomes project: Nursing outcomes classification (NOC)*. St. Louis, MO: Mosby.

Johnston, C. C., Stevens, B. J., Yang, F., & Horton, L. (1995). Differential response to pain by very premature neonates. *Pain, 61*, 471–479.

Jovey, R. D., Ennis, J., & Nix, J. (1998). Use of opioid analgesics for the treatment of chronic noncancer pain—A consensus statement and guidelines from the Canadian Pain Society. *Pain Research and Management, 3*, 197–208.

Kanjhan, R. (1995). Opioids and pain. *Clinical and Experimental Pharmacology and Physiology, 22*(6–7), 397–403.

Kettleman, K. (1998, July). Controlling pain. Making a smooth switch from I.V. analgesia: Your patient's postoperative pain is under control—What's the next step? *Nursing 98, 28*(7), 26.

McCaffery, M. (1979). *Nursing management of the patient with pain* (2nd ed.). Philadelphia, PA: Lippincott. (Classic.)

McCaffery, M. (1997a). Letter to the editor. *Orthopaedic Nursing, 16*(2), 12.

McCaffery, M. (1997b). Pain management handbook: Practical tips for relieving your patient's pain. *Nursing 97, 27*(4), 42–45.

McCaffery, M. (1998, August). How to make the most of nonopioid analgesics. *Nursing 98, 28*(8), 54–55.

McCaffery, M., Ferrell, B. R., & Turner, M. (1996). Ethical issues in the use of placebos in cancer pain management. *Oncology Nursing Forum, 23*(10), 1587–1593.

McCaffery, M., & Pasero, C. L. (1998, March). Pain control. Talking with patients and families about addiction. *American Journal of Nursing, 98*(3), 18–21.

McCaffery, M., & Pasero, C. (1999). *Pain: Clinical manual.* (2nd ed.). St. Louis, MO: Mosby.

McCloskey, J. C., & Bulechek, G. M. (Eds.) (2000). *Iowa intervention project: Nursing interventions classification (NIC)* (3rd ed.). St. Louis, MO: Mosby.

McQuay, H. J., & Moore, R. A. (1997). Antidepressants and chronic pain: Effective analgesia in neuropathic pain and other syndromes. *British Medical Journal, 314* (7083), 763–764.

Melzack, R., & Wall, P. D. (1965, November). Pain mechanisms: A new theory. *Science, 150*, 971–979. (Classic.)

Melzack, R. (1990). The tragedy of needless pain. *Scientific American, 262*, 27–33.

Millar, W. J. (1996). Chronic Pain, Statistics Canada. *Health Report,* 7, 47–53.

Moulin, D. E. Opioid therapy for chronic noncancer pain—lessons learned from clinical trials. Presentation at 2001 Annual Conference of the Canadian Pain Society.

North American Nursing Diagnosis Association. (2003). *NANDA nursing diagnoses: Definitions and classification 2003–2004.* Philadelphia, PA: Author.

Pasero, C. (1994, February). Pain control. *American Journal of Nursing, 94*, 22–23.

Pasero, C. (1996). Mismatch: When nurses rate patients' pain. *American Journal of Nursing, 96*(5), 21.

Pasero, C. (1997a). Pain ratings: The fifth vital sign. *American Journal of Nursing, 97*(2), 15–16.

Pasero, C. (1997b). Using the face scale to assess pain. *American Journal of Nursing, 97*(7), 19.

Pasero, C., & McCaffery, M. (1996). Alternative use of PCA. *American Journal of Nursing, 96*(10), 66–67.

Ronk, L. L. (1996). Spinal cord stimulation for chronic, nonmalignant pain. *Orthopaedic Nursing, 15*(5), 53–58.

Rook, J. L. (1996). Wound care pain management. *Advances in Wound Care: The Journal for Prevention and Healing, 9*(6), 24–32.

Salerno, E., & Willens, J. (1996). *Pain management handbook: An interdisciplinary approach.* St. Louis, MO: Mosby.

Stanton-Hicks, M. (1995). Rationale and management of chronic pain. *Pain Digest, 5,* 135–139.

St. Marie, B. (1991, September/October). Narcotic infusions: A changing scene. *Journal of Intravenous Nursing, 14,* 334–344.

Stevens, B. (1999). Pain in Infants. In M. McCaffery, & C. Pasero (Eds.), *PAIN: Clinical Manual* (pp. 626–673). St. Louis, MO: Mosby Inc.

Turner, J. A., Deyo, R. A., Loeser, J. D., VonKorff, M., & Fordyce, W. E. (1994). The importance of placebo effects in pain treatment and research. *The Journal of the American Medical Association, 271*(20), 1609–1614.

Wall, P. D., & Melzack, R. (1999). *Textbook of pain* (4th ed.). Edinburgh: Churchill Livingstone.

Ward, S. (1996, May). Pain control. Mismatch: When nurses rate nurses' pain. *American Journal of Nursing, 96*(5), 21.

World Health Organization. (1986). *Cancer pain relief.* Geneva, Switzerland: Author.

WEBLINKS

The Canadian Pain Society
www.canadianpainsociety.ca
The Canadian Pain Society, incorporated in 1982 as a chapter of the International Association for the Study of Pain, includes as members a variety of people interested in pain. The site provides information on the society and its services.

World Institute of Pain
http://wipain.org/
The site provides an overview of the institute and its goal of developing links among international pain centres for patient consultation, physician training, research, protocol development, and pain therapy certification.

International Association for the Study of Pain
www.iasp-pain.org
The association is the largest multidisciplinary not-for-profit international association in the field of pain. Its goal is to advance research on pain and improve the care of patients with pain. The site provides an overview of the association and its activities.

University of Toronto Pain Research Group
www.utoronto.ca/pain
Described on the site is the Centre for the Study of Pain, which is a partnership involving the Faculties of Dentistry, Medicine, and Nursing.

Institute for the Study of Pain
www.istop.org
A Canadian nonprofit society that focuses on resources required for those with soft tissue injuries. Information about the society and treatment options for these types of injuries are presented on the site.

Canadian Consortium on Pain Mechanisms, Diagnosis and Management
http://www.curepain.ca
The site provides an overview of the work done by a MRC/CIHR-funded consortium of Canadian pain researchers.

North American Chronic Pain Association of Canada
http://www.chronicpaincanada.org
The site provides information about this national association of self-help groups dedicated to providing support to people in chronic pain, founded 1986. It also provides a directory of Canadian pain clinics and pain specialists.

CHAPTER 46

Self-Concept

OBJECTIVES

After completing this chapter, you will be able to:

- Identify four personal and social dimensions of self-concept.
- Give Erikson's explanation of the effects of psychosocial crises on self-concept and self-esteem.
- Describe the four components of self-concept.
- Outline common stressors affecting self-concept and coping strategies.
- List important assessment data to be included when identifying clients' stressors and coping strategies.
- Describe the essential aspects of assessing role relationships.
- Identify nursing diagnoses related to altered self-concept.
- Describe nursing actions designed to achieve identified goals for clients with altered self-concept.
- Explain ways to enhance the self-esteem of individuals across the life span.

A positive self-concept is essential to a person's mental and physical health. Individuals with a positive self-concept are better able to develop and maintain interpersonal relationships and resist psychological and physical illness. Research has shown that an individual possessing a strong self-concept will be better able to accept or adapt to changes that may occur over the life span (Moore & Katz, 1996). How we view ourselves affects our interaction with others.

Nurses have a responsibility not only to identify people with a negative self-concept but also to identify the possible causes in order to help people develop a more positive view of themselves. Individuals who have a poor self-concept may view the world and their surroundings differently. They may express feelings of worthlessness, self-dislike, or even self-hatred, which may be projected to others. Individuals with a poor self-concept may feel sad or hopeless and may state they lack energy to perform even the simplest of tasks (Burger, 1992).

A nurse's own self-concept is also important. Nurses who understand the different dimensions of themselves are better able to understand the needs, desires, feelings, and conflicts of their clients. Nurses who feel positive about themselves are better able to help clients meet their needs.

Self-Concept

Self-concept is one's mental image of oneself. It involves all the self-perceptions, that is, appearance, values, and beliefs that influence behaviour and that are referred to when using the words "I" or "me." Self-concept is a complex idea that influences the following:

- How one thinks, talks, and acts
- How one sees and treats another person
- Choices one makes
- Ability to give and receive love
- Ability to take action and to change things

Four dimensions of self-concept are as follows:

- *Self-knowledge:* the knowledge that one has about oneself, including insights into one's abilities, nature, and limitations
- *Self-expectation:* what one expects of oneself; may be a realistic or unrealistic expectation
- *Social self:* how a person is perceived by others and society
- *Social evaluation:* the appraisal of oneself in relationship to others, events, or situations

People who value "how I perceive me" above "how others perceive me" can be termed "me-centred." They try hard to live up to their own expectations and compete only with themselves, not others. In contrast, "other-centred" people have a high need for approval from others and try hard to live up to the expectations of others, constantly comparing, competing, and evaluating themselves in relation to others. They tend not to deal with their personal shortcomings, are unable to assert themselves, and continually fear disapproval. The positive self-concept, therefore, is me-centred and is formed without reference to others' opinions. Research has also shown that people from cultural or ethical backgrounds outside the mainstream who have different philosophical views and a stronger sense of self tend to have less need for approval from others (Burger, 1992).

Formation of Self-Concept

A person is not born with a self-concept; rather, it develops as a result of social interactions with others. Chapter 19 discusses the development of self-concept, including Erikson's stages of development, Piaget's cognitive developmental stages that Havighurst's developmental tasks.

According to Erikson (1963), throughout life, people face certain developmental tasks associated with eight psychosocial stages that provide a convenient and familiar theoretical framework. The success with which a person copes with these developmental crises largely determines the development of self-concept. Inability to cope results in self-concept problems at the time and, often, later in life. See Table 46.1 for behaviours indicating successful and unsuccessful resolution of these developmental crises.

There are three broad steps in the development of one's self-concept:

- The infant learns that the physical self is separate and different from the environment.
- The child internalizes others' attitudes toward self.
- The child and adult internalize the standards of society.

The term **global self** refers to the collective beliefs and images one holds about oneself. It is the most complete description that individuals can give of themselves at any one time. It is also a person's frame of reference for experiencing and viewing the world. Some of these beliefs and images represent statements of fact, for example, "I am a woman"; "I am a mother"; "I am short." Others refer to less tangible aspects of self, for instance, "I am competent"; "I am shy."

Each separate image and belief one holds about oneself has a bearing on self-concept. However, self-concept is not simply a sum of its parts, for the various images and beliefs people hold about themselves are not given equal weight and prominence. Each person's self-concept is like a collage. At the centre of the collage are the beliefs and images that are most vital to the person's identity. They constitute **core self-concept.** For example: "I am competent/incompetent"; "I am male/female." Images and beliefs that are less important to the person are on the periphery. For example: "I am left-/right-handed"; "I am athletic/unathletic."

TABLE 46.1 Examples of Behaviours Associated with Erikson's Stages of Psychosocial Development

Stage: Developmental Crisis	Behaviours Indicating Positive Resolution	Behaviours Indicating Negative Resolution
Infancy: Trust vs. mistrust	Requesting assistance and expecting to receive it Expressing belief of another person Sharing time, opinions, and experiences	Restricting conversation to superficialities Refusing to provide a person with information Being unable to accept assistance
Toddlerhood: Autonomy vs. shame and doubt	Accepting the rules of a group but also expressing disagreement when it is felt Expressing one's own opinion Easily accepting deferment of a wish fulfillment	Failing to express needs Not expressing one's own opinion when opposed Overconcern about being clean
Early childhood: Initiative vs. guilt	Starting projects eagerly Expressing curiosity about many things Demonstrating original thought	Imitating others, rather than developing independent ideas Apologizing and being very embarrassed over small mistakes Verbalizing fear about starting a new project
Early school years: Industry vs. inferiority	Completing a task once it has been started Working well with others Using time effectively	Not completing tasks started Not assisting with the work of others Not organizing work
Adolescence: Identity vs. role confusion	Asserting independence Planning realistically for future roles Establishing close interpersonal relationships	Failing to assume responsibility for directing one's own behaviour Accepting the values of others without question Failing to set goals in life
Early adulthood: Intimacy vs. isolation	Establishing a close, intense relationship with another person Accepting sexual behaviour as desirable Making a commitment to that relationship, even in times of stress and sacrifice	Remaining alone Avoiding close interpersonal relationships
Middle-aged adults: Generativity vs. stagnation	Being willing to share with another person Guiding others Establishing a priority of needs, recognizing both self and others	Talking about oneself instead of listening to others Showing concern for oneself in spite of the needs of others Being unable to accept interdependence
Older adults: Integrity vs. despair	Using past experience to assist others Maintaining productivity in some areas Accepting limitations	Crying and being apathetic Not accepting changes Demanding unnecessary assistance and attention from others

People are thought to base their self-concept on how they perceive and evaluate themselves in these areas:

- Vocational performance
- Intellectual functioning
- Personal appearance and physical attractiveness
- Sexual attractiveness and performance
- Being liked by others
- Ability to cope with and resolve problems
- Independence
- Particular talents

Maintaining and evaluating one's self-concept is an ongoing process. Events or situations may change the level of self-concept over time. It has been established that by the time people reach maturity, their basic self-concept is relatively well established. Having a *basic* self-concept includes how we perceive self, which is how we see ourselves and how we are seen by others. There is also the **ideal self,** which is how we should be or would prefer to be. According to Carpenito (2000), the ideal self is the individual's perception of how one should behave based upon certain personal standards, aspirations, goals, and

RESEARCH NOTE

Understanding the Persistence of Self

The purpose of this study was to identify whether the sense of self persists in individuals with middle to late Alzheimer's disease. The sample consisted of 23 residents of two long-term care facilities. An analysis of conversations conducted with these residents was done. Use of the first person and awareness of the changes happening to oneself were sought in the transcripts of the conversations. The researchers found that the use of first person was frequently and coherently used. While the residents were aware of the cognitive changes happening to them, none identified the cause as Alzheimer's disease. The researchers stated that evidence suggests that the self persists throughout the disease process.

Implications: Nurses need to ensure that residents are informed of their diagnosis and given opportunities to promote a sense of self.

Source: Tappen, R. M., Williams, C., Fishman, S., & Touhy, T. (1999). Clinical scholarship: Persistence of self in advanced Alzheimer's disease. *Image–the Journal of Nursing Scholarship, 31*, 121–125.

values. By the time people reach adulthood, they have some idea about their perceived self; that is, how they see themselves and how they are seen by others. In addition, they have an idea about their ideal self. Sometimes, this ideal self is realistic; sometimes it is not. When the perceived self is close to the ideal self, people do not wish to be much different from what they believe they already are. A discrepancy between the ideal self and the perceived self can be an incentive to self-improvement. However, when the discrepancy is great, low self-esteem can result.

Components of Self-Concept

There are four components of self-concept: body image, role performance, personal identity, and self-esteem.

Body Image

The image of physical self, or **body image,** is how a person perceives the size, appearance, and functioning of the body and its parts. Body image has both cognitive and affective aspects. The cognitive is the knowledge of the material body and its attachments; the affective includes the sensations of the body, such as pain, pleasure, fatigue, and physical movement. Body image is the sum of these attitudes, conscious and unconscious, that a person has toward the body.

Body image encompasses the functioning of the body and its parts. It includes clothing, make-up, hairstyle, jewellery, and other things intimately connected to the person. It also includes body prostheses, such as artificial limbs, dentures, and hairpieces, as well as devices required for functioning, such as wheelchairs, canes, and eyeglasses. Past as well as present perceptions are part of one's body image.

A person's body image develops partly from others' attitudes and responses to that person's body and partly from the individual's own exploration of the body. For example, body image develops in infancy as the parents or caregivers respond to the child with smiles, holding, and touching, and also as the child explores its own body sensations during breast-feeding, thumb sucking, and the bath. Cultural and societal values also influence a person's body image.

The various information and entertainment media have played a part over the years in how individuals view themselves and others. During adolescence, "concerns related to body image are of paramount concern." The "ideal" person portrayed by the media is really an unrealistic goal for many (Sides & Korchek, 1998).

If a person's body image closely resembles one's body ideal, the individual is more likely to think positively about the physical and nonphysical components of the self. The body ideal is greatly influenced by cultural standards. For example, currently in North America, the fit, well-toned body is admired.

Another aspect of body image is the understanding that different parts of the body have different values for different people. For example, large breasts may be highly important to one woman and unimportant to another, or the occurrence of grey hair may be traumatic to one person and barely noticed by another.

A person with a healthy body image will normally show concern for both health and appearance. This person will seek help if ill and will include health-promoting practices in daily activities. A person who has an unhealthy body image is likely to be overly concerned about minor illness and to neglect such activities as sleep and a healthy diet that are important to health.

The individual who has a body image disturbance may hide or not look at or touch a body part that is significantly changed in structure by illness or trauma. Some individuals may also express feelings of helplessness, hopelessness, powerlessness, and vulnerability and may exhibit self-destructive behaviour, such as over- or undereating or suicide attempts.

Role Performance

Throughout life, people undergo numerous role changes. A **role** is a set of expectations about how the person occupying one position behaves toward a person occupying another position. **Role performance** relates what a person does in a particular role to the behaviours expected of that role. **Role mastery** means that the person's behaviours meet social expectations. Expectations, or standards of behaviour of a role, are set by society, a cultural group, or a smaller group to which a person belongs. Each person usually has several roles, such as husband, parent, brother, son, employee, friend, golf club member. Some roles are assumed for only limited periods, such as client, student, and ill person. **Role development** involves socialization into a particular role. For example, nursing students are socialized into nursing through exposure to their instructors, clinical experience, classes, laboratory simulations, and seminars (Day et al., 1995; Reutter et al., 1997).

To act appropriately, people need to know who they are in relation to others and what society expects for the positions they hold. **Role ambiguity** occurs when expectations are unclear and people do not know what to do or how to do it and are unable to predict the reactions of others to their behaviour. This creates confusion and stress. To relate or interact appropriately with others, people also need to know the role positions that others occupy. Failure to master a role creates frustration and feelings of inadequacy, often with consequent lowered self-esteem.

Self-concept is also affected by role strain and role conflicts. People undergoing **role strain** are frustrated because they feel or are made to feel inadequate or unsuited to a role. Role strain is often associated with gender role stereotypes. For example, women in occupations traditionally held by men might be assumed to have less knowledge and competence than men in the same roles. As a result, these women feel the need to surpass the level expected for role mastery by male counterparts.

Role conflicts arise from opposing or incompatible expectations. In an *interpersonal conflict*, different people have different expectations about a particular role. For example, a mother's parents may have different expectations than she does about how she should care for her children. In an *inter-role conflict*, one person's or group's role expectations differ from the expectations of another person or group. For example, a woman who has little flexibility in her full-time job schedule has a role conflict if her husband expects her to handle all child care problems. In a *person-role conflict*, role expectations violate the beliefs or values of the role occupant. For example, a woman who values her right to choose abortion will have a conflict if this right is denied. Role conflict, if not resolved, can lead to "increase[s] in tension, decrease[s] in self-esteem, and an increased sense of threat or embarrassment as [an] individual['s] needs for achievement, independence, and recognition go unmet" (Sims & Napholz, 1996, p. 117).

Personal Identity

A person's personal identity is the conscious sense of individuality and uniqueness that is continually evolving throughout life. People often view their identity in terms of name, gender, age, race, ethnic origin or culture, occupation or roles, talents, and other situational characteristics (e.g., marital status and education).

Personal identity also includes a person's beliefs and values, personality, and character. For instance, is the person outgoing, friendly, reserved, generous, selfish? Personal identity, thus, encompasses both the tangible and factual, such as name and gender, and the intangible, such as values and beliefs. In brief: identity is what distinguishes self from others.

It is important to know whether clients are comfortable with their perceived identities. A person with a strong sense of identity has integrated body image, role performance, and self-esteem into a complete self-concept. This sense of identity provides a person with a sense of continuity and a unity of personality. Furthermore, the individual sees himself or herself as a unique person.

Self-Esteem

Self-esteem is one's judgement of one's own worth, that is, how that person's standards and performances compare to others and also to one's ideal self. If a person's self-concept does not match with the ideal self, then low self-esteem results.

There are two types of self-esteem: global and specific. **Global self-esteem** is how much one likes one's perceived self as a whole. **Specific self-esteem** is how much one approves of a certain part of oneself. Global self-esteem is influenced by specific self-esteem. For example, if a person values looks, then how the person looks will strongly affect global self-esteem. By contrast, if a person places little value on cooking skills, then how well or badly the person cooks will have little influence on global self-esteem.

Self-esteem is basically derived from self and others. In infancy, self-esteem is related to the caregiver's evaluations and acceptances. Later, the child's self-esteem is affected by competition with others. As an adult, a person who has high self-esteem or self-worth has feelings of significance, of competence, of the ability to cope with life, and of control over one's destiny.

Basic self-esteem refers to the foundation for self-esteem that is established during early life experiences, usually within the family structure. However, an adult's functional level of overall self-esteem may change markedly from day to day and moment to moment. *Functional self-esteem* is a result of the person's ongoing evaluation of interactions with people and objects. Functional self-esteem can exceed basic self-esteem, or it can regress to a level below that of basic self-esteem. Severe stress—for example, stress related to prolonged illness or unemployment—can substantially lower a person's basic self-esteem. In ongoing evaluation, people frequently focus on their negative aspects and spend less time on their positive aspects. It is important that both strengths and weaknesses be identified during self-evaluation.

Factors That Affect Self-Concept

Many factors affect a person's self-concept. Major factors are development, family and culture, stressors, resources, history of success and failure, and illness.

Development

As an individual develops, the factors that affect the self-concept change. For example, whereas an infant requires a supportive, caring environment, a child requires freedom to explore and learn.

Family and Culture

A young child's values are largely influenced by the family and culture. Later on, peers influence the child and thereby affect the sense of self. When the child is confronted by differing expectations from family, culture, and peers, the child's sense of self is often confused. For example, a child may realize that his parents expect he will not drink alcohol and that he will attend religious services each Saturday evening. At the same time, his peers drink beer and encourage him to spend Saturday evenings with them.

Stressors

Stressors encountered can result in strengthening the self-concept as an individual copes successfully with problems. On the other hand, stressors can cause maladaptive responses including substance abuse, withdrawal, and anxiety. The ability of a person to handle stressors will largely depend on personal resources.

Resources

An individual's resources may be internal and external. Internal resources, such as confidence and values, can affect the self-concept. External resources, such as a support network, sufficient finances, and organizations, can also influence self-concept. Generally, the greater the number of resources a person has and uses, the more positive the effect on the self-concept.

History of Success and Failure

People who have a history of failures come to see themselves as a failure, whereas people with a history of successes will have a more positive self-concept, making more successes likely.

Illness

Illness and trauma can also affect the self-concept. A woman who has a mastectomy may see herself as less attractive and the loss may affect how she acts and values herself. People respond to illness and aging in a variety of ways: acceptance, denial, withdrawal, and depression are common reactions.

Figure 46.1 Nurses have a responsibility to help people develop a more positive view of themselves

Assessing

A thorough assessment should include a psychosocial assessment of the client and the family or support person, as this provides clues to actual or potential problems that may exist. With any assessment, nurses use all their observational skills to detect any clues. The nurse assessing self-concept focuses on four areas: (1) personal identity, (2) body image, (3) self-esteem, and (4) role performance and relationships.

Before conducting a psychosocial assessment, the nurse must establish trust and a working relationship with the client. Gorman, Sultan, and Raines (1996) provide guidelines for conducting a psychosocial assessment, including the following:

- Create a quiet, private environment.
- Minimize interruptions, if possible.
- Maintain appropriate eye contact.
- Sit at eye level with the client.
- Ask open-ended questions to encourage the client to talk.
- Avoid writing a lot of notes during the interview.
- Demonstrate an interest in the client's concerns.
- Indicate acceptance of the client by not criticizing, frowning, or demonstrating shock.
- Avoid asking more personal questions than are actually needed.

Stressors Affecting Self-Concept

Identity Stressors
- Change in physical appearance (e.g., facial wrinkles)
- Declining physical, mental, or sensory abilities
- Inability to achieve goals
- Relationship concerns
- Sexuality concerns
- Unrealistic ideal self
- Membership in a minority group
- Cultural dissonance

Body-Image Stressors
- Loss of body parts (e.g., due to amputation, mastectomy, hysterectomy)
- Loss of body functions (e.g., from heart disease, renal disease, spinal cord injury, cerebrovascular accident, neuromuscular disease, arthritis, declining mental or sensory abilities)
- Disfigurement (e.g., through pregnancy, severe burns, facial blemishes, colostomy, ileostomy, tracheostomy, laryngectomy)

Self-Esteem Stressors
- Lack of positive feedback from significant others
- Repeated failures
- Unrealistic expectations
- Inability to cope with life stressors
- Abusive relationship
- Loss of financial security

Role Stressors
- Loss of parent, spouse, child, or close friend
- Change or loss of job
- Retirement
- Divorce or separation
- Illness
- Hospitalization
- Ambiguous role expectations
- Conflicting role expectations
- Inability to meet role expectations

- Determine whether the family can provide additional information.
- Maintain confidentiality.
- Be aware of your own biases and discomforts that could influence the assessment.

This assessment can be used in either the acute care or home care environment. Most individuals display some or all of the following responses to illness: altered self-esteem, altered body image, powerlessness, loss, hopelessness, guilt, and anxiety (Gorman et al., 1996).

It is the nurse's responsibility to use therapeutic communication and to remain sensitive to the effect that cultural influences will have on the client's behaviours and needs. Cultural background is not only assessed directly but is also considered as a factor in the areas of self-perception, role relationships, major stressors, and coping strategies. In the area of behaviours that may suggest low self-esteem, nurses need to ask themselves the following question: Is this really a behaviour that would suggest a low self-esteem, or is it part of the cultural behaviour(s) of the client? See Chapters 5 and 14 for additional information. It is also important that the nurse identifies any stressors that may affect aspects of the self-concept. See the box above for examples of stressors that may place a client at risk for problems with self-concept.

When stressors are identified, the nurse needs to determine how the client perceives the stressor. A positive, growth-oriented perception of stressful events reinforces self-worth; a negative, hopeless, defeatist perception leads to decreased self-esteem. The nurse should also identify the client's coping style and determine whether this style is effective by asking the client such questions as the following:

- When you have a problem or face a stressful situation, how do you usually deal with it?
- Do these methods work?

Personal Identity

When assessing self-concept, the information the nurse first needs is about the client's personal identity. This involves who the client believes he or she is. See the next box for examples of questions to ask.

Body Image

If there are indications of a body image disturbance, the nurse should assess the client carefully for possible functional or physical problems.

The disturbance may be a result of a present deformity or malfunction or an anticipated one. In addition to the

ASSESSMENT INTERVIEW

Personal Identity

- How would you describe your personal characteristics? *Or,* how do you see yourself as a person?
- What do you like about yourself?
- How do others describe you as a person?
- What do you do well?
- What are your personal strengths, talents, and abilities?
- What would you change about yourself if you could?
- Does it bother you a great deal if you think someone does not like you?
- Is it difficult for you to say no when you want to say no?

Behaviours Associated with Low Self-Esteem

- Avoids eye contact
- Stoops in posture and moves slowly
- Is poorly groomed and has an unkempt appearance
- Is hesitant or halting in speech
- Is overly critical of self (e.g., "I'm no good," "I'm ugly," or "People don't like me")
- May be overly critical of others
- Is unable to accept positive remarks about self
- Encourages reprimands from others to punish self
- Apologizes frequently
- Verbalizes feelings of hopelessness, helplessness, and powerlessness, such as "I really don't care what happens," "I'll do whatever anyone wants," "Whatever is destined will happen"

stated responses about the problem, it is important to assess related behaviour. See the box below for examples of questions to ask about body image.

Self-Esteem

A nurse can ask the following questions to determine a client's self-esteem:

- Are you satisfied with your life?
- How do you feel about yourself?
- Are you accomplishing what you want?
- What goals in life are important to you?

Some behaviours that might reflect low self-esteem are listed in the box above right. It is important that the nurse determine the client's cultural background first in order to not misinterpret specific behaviours.

ASSESSMENT INTERVIEW

Body Image

- Is there any part of your body you would like to change?
- Are you comfortable discussing your surgery?
- Do you feel different or inferior to others?
- How do you feel about your appearance?
- What changes in your body do you expect following your surgery?
- How have significant others in your life reacted to changes in your body?

Role Relationships

The nurse assesses the client's satisfactions and dissatisfactions associated with role responsibilities and relationships: family roles, work roles, student roles, social roles. Family roles are especially important to people because family relationships are particularly close. Relationships can be supportive and growth producing or, at the opposite extreme, highly stressful if violence and abuse permeate relationships. Assessment of family role relationships may begin with structural aspects, such as the number in the family group, ages, and residence location. To obtain data related to the client's family relationships and satisfaction or dissatisfaction with work roles and social roles, the nurse might ask some of the questions shown in the box opposite, keeping in mind, however, that questions need to be tailored to the individuals and their age and situation.

Diagnosing

The NANDA nursing diagnostic labels relating specifically to self-concept include the following (NANDA, 2001):

- ***Body Image Disturbance:*** Negative feelings or perceptions about characteristics, functions, or limits of body or body part
- ***Self-Esteem, Chronic Low:*** Negative self-evaluation or feelings about self or self capabilities that may be directly or indirectly expressed
- ***Chronic Low Self-Esteem:*** Long-standing negative self-evaluation or feelings about self or capabilities that may be directly or indirectly expressed
- ***Situational Low Self-Esteem:*** Negative self-evaluation or feelings about self or self capabilities in response to

ASSESSMENT INTERVIEW

Role Relationships

Family Relationships

- Tell me about your family.
- What is home like?
- Who are you closest to in the family?
- Who are you most distant from in the family?
- What are your relationships like with your other relatives?
- What are your responsibilities in the family?
- How well do you feel you accomplish what is expected of you?
- What about your role or responsibilities would you like changed?
- Do you see yourself as frequently getting the short end of things and coming out second best?
- Are you proud of your family members?
- Do you feel your family members are proud of you?
- Tell me how you spend your time each day.

Work Roles and Social Roles

- Do you like your work?
- How do you get along at work?
- What about your work would you like to change if you could?
- How do you spend your free time?
- Are you involved in any community groups?
- Are you most comfortable alone, with one other person, or in a group?
- Who is most important to you?
- Whom do you seek out for help?

TABLE 46.2 Clinical Application: Assessment Data Clusters and Related Nursing Diagnoses for Clients with Self-Concept and Role Problems

Data Cluster	Nursing Diagnosis
Frank Sawyers had a permanent colostomy seven days ago for cancer of the sigmoid colon. When the nurse was changing the colostomy appliance, Frank said, "My wife will be repulsed by this." He avoided looking at the stoma and put his arm over his eyes.	***Body Image Disturbance*** related to recent surgery
Sofie Ferraro, a 73-year-old with right-sided (dominant) hemiplegia, says, "Although the rehabilitation centre taught me so much about how to manage in my home, my poor husband has to do a lot to help me with cooking meals and cleaning the house."	***Role Performance, Ineffective*** related to change in physical capacity
George Kawazi, a first-year college student, is studying liberal arts and the sciences. George states that even though he attends all his classes and studies every day and on weekends, his grades do not please his father, who expects straight A's. "I've always had trouble measuring up to Father's expectations. He never thought I was as good as my older brother."	***Chronic Low Self-Esteem*** related to unrealistic parental expectations

a situation or event; previous self-evaluation was positive (e.g., loss or change)

- ***Role Performance, Ineffective*** (specify): Change, conflict, denial of role responsibilities or inability to perform role responsibilities

Defining characteristics and etiologies of these diagnoses are discussed earlier in this chapter. Clinical applications of some of these diagnoses are shown in Table 46.2.

Additional nursing diagnoses that may apply to clients with problems of self-concept include the following:

- ***Identity Disturbed, Personal***
- ***Anxiety*** related to changed physical appearance (e.g., amputation, mastectomy)
- ***Adjustment, Impaired*** to changed physical functioning or appearance
- ***Coping, Ineffective*** with role change related to death of spouse
- ***Grieving, Anticipatory*** or ***Grieving, Dysfunctional*** related to change in physical appearance
- ***Hopelessness***
- ***Powerlessness***
- ***Conflict, Parental Role***
- ***Rape-Trauma Syndrome***
- ***Sleep Pattern, Disturbed***
- ***Social Isolation***
- ***Spiritual Distress***
- ***Thought Processes, Disturbed***

Some of these nursing diagnoses are discussed in other chapters of this book.

Planning

The nurse develops plans in collaboration with the client and support people when possible, according to the client's state of health, level of anxiety, support resources, coping mechanisms, and sociocultural and religious affiliation. The nurse who has little experience in intervening with clients with altered self-concept may wish to consult with a clinical specialist or a more experienced nurse to develop effective plans. The nurse and client set goals to enhance the client's self-concept.

The goals established will vary according to the diagnoses and defining characteristics related to each individual. Examples of overall goals are as follows:

- Develop a realistic and positive perception of body appearance and function
- Increase feelings of self-worth
- Perform new roles responsibly and capably

Examples of desired outcomes, although established in the planning phase, are provided in Table 46.3 in the "Evaluating" section.

The Iowa Intervention Project's Nursing Interventions Classification (NIC) system can be used as a resource for planning nursing interventions (McCloskey & Bulechek, 2000).

NIC interventions to enhance body image, self-esteem, and role performance include the following:

- Active listening
- Presence
- Body image enhancement
- Coping enhancement
- Decision-making support
- Emotional support
- Parent education: childbearing and childrearing
- Role enhancement
- Self-awareness enhancement
- Self-esteem enhancement
- Socialization enhancement
- Support system enhancement

Specific nursing activities associated with each of these interventions can be selected to meet the individual needs of the client. A critical pathway may also be used as a plan of care. See the critical pathway below for an example of a plan of care for a client undergoing a total mastectomy.

Implementing

Nursing interventions to promote a positive self-concept include helping a client to identify areas of strength and to maintain a sense of self. In addition, for clients who have an altered self-concept, nurses should establish a therapeutic relationship and assist clients to evaluate themselves and make behavioural changes.

Identifying Areas of Strength

Healthy people often perceive their problems and weaknesses more clearly than their assets and strengths. People with low self-esteem tend to focus even more on their limitations and to be aware of fewer strengths and many more problems. When a client has difficulty identifying personality strengths and assets, the nurse needs to provide the client with a set of guidelines or a framework that includes the following: interests, abilities, past accomplishments, and experiences. See the box on page 1313 for a framework for identifying personality strengths.

CRITICAL PATHWAY FOR CLIENT FOLLOWING TOTAL MASTECTOMY

ASSESSMENT DATA

Nursing Assessment for Helen Morton

Mrs. Helen Morton, 36 years old, was admitted for a right mastectomy. She had a positive biopsy for breast cancer two weeks prior to admission. On admission to ambulatory surgery, Mrs. Morton asked the nurse, "Will I ever look normal again?" She also told the nurse, "I don't want any visitors after surgery; I don't want anyone to see how I look." The day following surgery, Mrs. Morton states, "I don't want to look at it," when the physician starts the dressing change.

Physical Examination

Height: 167.6 cm
Weight: 65 kg
Temperature: 37°C
Pulse rate: 76 BPM
Respirations: 20/minute
Blood pressure: 120/80 mm Hg
Skin warm, dry, pink, and pale
Mastectomy incision clean, dry, and well approximated

Diagnostic Data

RBC: 4.2×10^{12}/L
Hgb: 102 g/L
Hct: 0.39
Urine: negative

EXPECTED LENGTH OF STAY: 2 to 3 days

CRITICAL PATHWAY FOR CLIENT FOLLOWING TOTAL MASTECTOMY *continued*

	Date ____ First 24 hours postoperative	Date ____ 48 hours postoperative	Date ____ 2–3 days postoperative
Daily outcomes	Client will ■ Be afebrile. ■ Have clean, dry dressing. ■ Recover from anesthesia, as evidenced by vital signs returning to baseline; being awake, alert, and oriented. ■ Verbalize understanding and demonstrate cooperation with turning, coughing, deep breathing, and splinting. ■ Tolerate ordered diet without nausea and vomiting. ■ Verbalize control of incisional pain. ■ Verbalize ability to cope.	Client will ■ Be afebrile. ■ Have clean, dry wound with edges well approximated, healing by first intention. ■ Demonstrate cooperation with turning, coughing, deep breathing, and splinting. ■ Tolerate ordered diet without nausea and vomiting. ■ Ambulate four times a day in hallway. ■ Verbalize control of incisional pain. ■ Verbalize beginning ability to cope with changes in body image. ■ Verbalize ability to cope. ■ Verbalize beginning understanding of home care instructions.	Client will ■ Be afebrile. ■ Have clean, dry wound with edges well approximated, healing by first intention. ■ Manage pain with oral medications and/or non-pharmacological measures. ■ Be independent in self-care. ■ Be fully ambulatory. ■ Have resumed preadmission urine and bowel elimination pattern. ■ Verbalize home care instructions. ■ Tolerate usual diet. ■ Verbalize ability to cope with changes in body image and ongoing stressors. ■ Demonstrate progressive upper extremity exercises that include external rotation and abduction of the affected shoulder when the stitches are removed seven to 10 days after surgery.
Tests and treatments	Vital signs and O_2 saturation, neurovascular assessment, dressing and wound drainage assessment q15min × 4; q30min × 4; q1h × 4 and then q4h if stable NO BLOOD PRESSURES OR VENIPUNCTURE ON AFFECTED ARM Assess respiratory status q4h and prn Incentive spirometer q2h Intake and output q shift Assess voiding—if unable to void, try suggestive voiding techniques or catheterize q8h or prn	Vital signs and dressing and wound drainage assessment q4h NO BLOOD PRESSURES OR VENIPUNCTURE ON AFFECTED ARM Assess respiratory status q4h Incentive spirometer q2h until fully ambulatory Intake and output q shift Assess voiding pattern q shift. Dressing change by surgeon as ordered	Vital signs and dressing and wound drainage assessment q4h–8h NO BLOOD PRESSURES OR VENIPUNCTURE ON AFFECTED ARM Assess respiratory status q4h–8h Assess wound and apply dry sterile dressing q day and prn
Knowledge deficit	Orient to room and surroundings. Provide simple, brief instructions. Review preoperative preparation, including hospital and specific postoperative care: turning, coughing, deep breathing, incentive spirometer, mobilization, intravenous infusions, pain management.	Review plan of care and importance of early mobilization. Begin discharge teaching regarding wound care/dressing change, diet, and activity. Review written discharge instructions with client and support person.	Complete discharge teaching to include wound care, diet, follow-up care, signs and symptoms to report, activity, and medication: frequency, dose, route, and side effects. Provide client with written discharge instructions, including upper arm and shoulder exercises for affected arm.
Diet	Clear to full liquids, as tolerated	Full liquids to usual diet to tolerance	Usual diet to tolerance

→

CRITICAL PATHWAY FOR CLIENT FOLLOWING TOTAL MASTECTOMY *continued*

	Date ______ First 24 hours postoperative	Date ______ 48 hours postoperative	Date ______ 2–3 days postoperative
Activity	Provide safety precautions. Ambulate four times in room. Encourage finger, wrist, and elbow movement and use of affected arm for ADLs and personal hygiene.	Fully ambulatory in room. Walk in hall four to six times per day. Encourage finger, wrist, and elbow movement and use of affected arm for ADLs and personal hygiene. Instruct client in progressive upper arm exercises.	Fully ambulatory. Encourage finger, wrist, and elbow movement and use of affected arm for ADLs and personal hygiene. Reinforce instructions regarding progressive exercises.
Medications	IM or IV/PCA analgesics IV antibiotics IV fluids	PO, IM, or IV/PCA analgesics IV antibiotics Intermittent IV device	PO analgesics Discontinue IV device
Body image	Establish a trusting relationship with client. Encourage client and significant others to verbalize their feelings about the mastectomy. Listen to client and significant others and show interest and concern, rather than giving advice. Allow the client to respond to loss of body part and changed body image with denial, shock, anger, depression, and other grieving behaviours. Support the client's strengths and assist her to look at herself in totality.	Maintain trusting relationship with client. Encourage client and significant others to verbalize their feelings about the mastectomy. Listen to client and significant others and show interest and concern, rather than giving advice. Allow the client to respond to loss of body part and changed body image with denial, shock, anger, depression, and other grieving behaviours. Support the client's strengths and assist her to look at herself in totality.	Provide opportunities to verbalize ongoing concerns regarding changes in body image and self-concept. Encourage and provide opportunities for self-care of wound and dressing. Provide opportunity for client to meet with volunteer from Canadian Cancer Society Support Services. Assist client to obtain temporary breast prosthesis. Answer questions and provide information on breast reconstruction.
Psychosocial	Assess coping status. Use active listening. Provide a nonthreatening environment. Determine support people and resources available to the client. Assess responses of support people. Allow for client's input regarding sequence of care. Be supportive of client's effective coping behaviours.	Assess coping status. Use active listening. Provide a nonthreatening environment. Assist client to identify and develop support system and resources. Assess responses of support people. Allow for client's input regarding sequence of care. Be supportive of client's effective coping behaviours.	Assess coping status. Use active listening. Provide a nonthreatening environment. Determine support people and resources available to the client. Assess responses of support people. Allow for client's input regarding sequence of care. Be supportive of client's effective coping behaviours.
Transfer/ discharge plans	Determine discharge needs with client and support people. Begin home care instructions.	Review progress toward discharge goals. Finalize discharge plans. Refer to Canadian Cancer Society Support Services.	Complete discharge instructions.

> **Framework for Identifying Personality Strengths**
>
> Note past, present, and anticipated future participation in
>
> - Hobbies and crafts
> - Expressive arts, such as writing, painting, sketching, or music appreciation
> - Sports and outdoor activities, including spectator sports
> - Education, training, and related areas (including self-education)
> - Work, vocation, job, or position
>
> In addition, determine
>
> - *Sense of humour* and the ability to laugh at oneself and take kidding
> - *Health status,* including healthy aspects of body function and good health maintenance practices
> - *Special aptitudes,* such as sales or mechanical ability; a "green thumb"; ability to recognize and enjoy beauty; ability to solve problems; a liking for adventure or pioneering; having stick-to-itiveness, perseverance, and the drive or will needed to get things done
> - *Relationship strengths,* including the ability to make people feel comfortable, the capacity to enjoy being with people, being aware of people's needs and feelings, being able to listen
> - *Emotional strengths,* including the capacity to give and receive warmth, affection, and love; the ability to "take" anger and to feel and express a wide range of emotions; the capacity for empathy
> - *Spiritual strengths,* such as religious faith or love of a higher power, membership and participation in spiritual and related activities

Many personal strengths can reveal a fundamentally positive self-concept and be used to reinforce the positive view in a time of stress. Some of these strengths include strong values, a healthy body and good health maintenance practices, good communication, a sense of purpose and meaning in life, a strong social support system, a sense of humour, and the capacity to give warmth and affection.

Nurses can employ the following specific strategies to help clients identify personal strengths:

- Stress positive thinking rather than self-negation.
- Notice and verbally reinforce client's strengths.
- Encourage the setting of attainable goals.
- Acknowledge goals that have been attained.
- Provide honest, positive feedback.

Maintaining a Sense of Self

Sometimes, people who are ill not only are unaware of their strengths but also are separated from a sense of self. Nurses can use these techniques to help clients maintain a sense of self:

- Communicate worth nonverbally and through touch.
- Respect the client's privacy and sensitivities.
- Provide a simple explanation before starting a procedure.
- Listen attentively to the client's concerns.
- Recognize the client's individuality by addressing the client by name.
- Accept the client's responses.

Nursing Interventions for Altered Self-Concept

Nurses assisting clients who have an altered self-concept must establish a therapeutic relationship. To do this, the nurse must have self-awareness and effective communication skills. The following nursing interventions may help clients analyze the problem and change the self-concept:

- Encourage clients to appraise the situation and express their feelings.
- Encourage clients to ask questions.
- Provide accurate information.
- Become aware of distortions, inappropriate or unrealistic standards, and faulty labels in clients' speech.
- Explore clients' positive qualities and strengths.
- Encourage clients to express positive self-evaluation more than negative self-evaluation.
- Avoid criticism.
- Teach clients to substitute negative self-talk ("I can't walk to the store anymore") with positive self-talk ("I can walk half a block each morning"). Negative self-talk reinforces a negative self-concept.

Enhancing Self-Esteem

People who have relatively high self-esteem appear to be adjusted, happy, and competent. Children build strong self-esteem if they develop five basic attitudes: (1) security and trust, (2) identity, (3) belonging, (4) purpose, and (5) personal competence.

Key ingredients for helping children develop high self-esteem are love, acceptance, firmness, consistency, and the establishment of expectations. Love and acceptance indicate to the child that parents, teachers, and caregivers care and want the best for the child. Adults can demonstrate love and acceptance by taking time to be with the child, to listen, to read, to play, or just to be there. Physical contact—such as a hand on the shoulder or a hug—usually conveys warmth and caring more effectively than words.

Firmness and consistency provide the rules and the consequences for breaking them. Such limits provide a safe and predictable world in which to live. Establishing high but reasonable expectations for the child indicates confidence in the child's abilities. As the child succeeds in meeting those expectations, self-confidence increases. Rules or standards need to be reasonable and broad enough to serve as general guidelines in new situations, such as in a neighbour's house, a friend's yard, or school classroom. Standards need to be established for the treatment of others, respect for the property of others, the value of honesty, and routines, such as getting ready for school in the morning, doing homework, completing chores, and going to bed at night.

Children need positive feedback from the people of greatest significance to them: parents, grandparents, older siblings, teachers, and close friends. The kind of feedback given can be more significant than the child's actual level of performance. Positive feedback enhances a child's sense of identity and self-concept.

A sense of purpose provides direction for children and a basis for success, fulfillment, and, therefore, a positive self-concept. Adults can help a child develop a sense of purpose by setting reasonable expectations, by helping the child set realistic goals, by conveying faith and confidence in the child's ability to achieve the goals, and by helping the child expand interests, talents, and abilities.

Individuals who grow up in families whose members value each other are likely to feel good about themselves. If adults help children to accomplish goals that are important to them, children are more likely to develop a sense of personal competence and independence.

Older adults who become increasingly dependent can develop low self-esteem. Old age is frequently accompanied by changes, such as reduced income, decline in physical health, loss of friends and family, and retirement. Nurses can use the following techniques to help elderly adults enhance their self-esteem:

- Encourage clients to participate in planning their own care.
- Listen carefully to their concerns.
- Assist clients to identify and use their own strengths.
- Encourage them to participate in activities in which they can be successful.
- Communicate that the client is valued. Use the client's name, and ask for advice.

Evaluating

The goals discussed in the planning phase are evaluated according to specific desired outcomes, also established in that phase. Examples of these outcomes are shown in Table 46.3.

To determine whether client outcomes have been achieved, the nurse uses data collected during interactions with the client and significant others. To elicit such data, the nurse requires communication and interviewing skills, such as listening attentively and asking open-ended questions. Observation skills are also essential for evaluating changes in behaviour and appearance. If outcomes are not achieved, the nurse should explore the reasons, considering questions, such as the following:

FOCUS ON CRITICAL THINKING

Craig is a 20-year-old male college student who was involved in an automobile accident three days ago, suffering a traumatic amputation of his left lower leg. Craig's mother has remained with him since the accident and is very supportive. His father is grief stricken and is having difficulty dealing with Craig's condition because Craig was captain of his college basketball team and had aspirations of becoming a professional basketball player. Craig's condition is stable and he is being placed into a rehabilitation program immediately. Soon, he will be fitted for a leg prosthesis. Usually an outgoing individual, Craig is somber and noncommunicative. He does not look at his leg when dressings are being changed, and he refuses to discuss his rehabilitation program.

1. Given Craig's age, speculate how Craig's self-concept is at risk of being adversely affected by his disability.
2. What data suggest that Craig's self-esteem is, or is at risk of, being negatively impacted by his amputation?
3. What factors are likely to affect Craig's adaptation to his amputation and rehabilitation?
4. How would your interventions differ for a client who was 70 years old?
5. What other groups of clients, in addition to those with amputations, are at risk for the development of altered self-esteem or body image?

See Appendix A for answers to these questions.

TABLE 46.3 Evaluation Goals and Outcomes: Self-Concept

Goal	Examples of Desired Outcomes
Body Image Develop a realistic and positive perception of body appearance and function	Acknowledges changes in physical appearance or functioning (i.e., looks at and touches body part) Integrates changes in physical health status, appearance, and function into adapted lifestyle Uses strategies to enhance appearance Verbalizes realistic understanding of and satisfaction with body appearance or functioning
Self-Esteem Increase feelings of self-worth	Acknowledges limitations Maintains grooming Accepts positive feedback from others Consistently expresses positive feelings about self and capabilities Verbalizes success in school, work, and social groups
Role Performance Perform new role responsibilities capably	Verbalizes feelings about role changes Verbalizes accurate knowledge of role expectations and requirements Demonstrates role competence Verbalizes satisfaction with role performance

- Have old situations recurred, triggering feelings or behaviours associated with low self-esteem?
- Have new stressful situations occurred which the client feels unable to cope with, resulting in continuing or recurrent low self-esteem?
- Are new or additional roles causing increased stress in adapting?
- Are significant others supporting the client adequately in attempts to improve self-esteem?
- Did the client follow through on referrals to appropriate agencies? Did the agencies provide the expected services?
- Were the client's expectations too high in relation to the time needed for successful resolution of self-esteem problems?

The nurse, client, and significant others need to understand that to change beliefs, feelings, and behaviours affecting self-esteem requires time and ongoing effort. Unlike many physical problems (e.g., wounds) where healing can be quickly observed, improving one's self-concept can be a continuing concern and is not so easily evaluated. New crises can cause clients to doubt themselves and revert to former feelings of inadequacy. People can learn from each new situation and gain new strategies for feeling satisfied with themselves.

CHAPTER HIGHLIGHTS

- A positive self-concept is essential to a person's physical and psychological well-being.
- A person's self-perception can differ from the person's perception of how others see the person and from the ideal self, or how the person would like to be.
- Components of self-concept include body image, role performance, personal identity, and self-esteem.
- From birth, interactions with significant others create the conditions that influence self-concept throughout life.
- When individuals are able to conceptualize the self, they begin a lifelong process of deciding whether and to what extent they are valuable and worthy.
- Individuals who grow up in families whose members value each other are likely to feel good about themselves.
- If adults help children to accomplish goals that are important to them, children are more likely to develop a sense of personal competence and independence.
- Adults base their self-concept on how they perceive and evaluate their performance in the areas of work, intellect, appearance, sexual attractiveness, interpersonal interactions, ability to cope and to resolve problems, independence, and particular talents.
- Because a positive self-concept is basic to health, one of the nurse's major responsibilities is to assist clients whose self-concept is disturbed to develop a more positive and realistic image of themselves.
- A trusting client-nurse relationship is essential for the effective assessment of a client's self-concept, for providing help and support, and for motivating client behaviour change.

READINGS AND REFERENCES

Suggested Readings

Norris, J. (1992, April/June). Nursing interventions for self-esteem disturbances. *Nursing Diagnosis, 23*(3), 48–53.
In 1988, the broad diagnosis of Self-Esteem Disturbance was refined into three distinct problems: Defensive Coping, Situational Low Self-Esteem, and Chronic Low Self-Esteem. The rationale for this refinement is discussed and distinct nursing interventions are proposed that differ by type of self-esteem problem and nursing expertise.

Reutter, L., Field, P., Campbell, I., & Day, R. (1997). Socialization into nursing: Nursing students as learners. *Journal of Nursing Education, 36*, 149–155.
This qualitative longitudinal exploratory study looked at the professional socialization and self-concept in baccalaureate nursing students. This article looked at how nursing students evolved from "first year: learning the ideals" to "the fourth year: extending beyond the reality of student practice."

Related Research

Arthur, D. (1995). Measurement of the professional self-concept of nurses: Developing a measurement instrument. *Nurse Education Today, 15*, 328–335.

Cook, D. L., & Barber, K. R. (1997, Spring). Relationship between social support, self-esteem and codependency on the African American female. *Journal of Cultural Diversity, 4*(1), 32–38.

Jenks, J. M., Morin, K. H., & Tomaselli, N. (1997, November). The influence of ostomy surgery on body image in patients with cancer. *Applied Nursing Research, 10*(4), 174–180.

Tappen, R. M., Williams, C., Fishman, S., & Touhy, T. (1999). Clinical scholarship: Persistence of self in advanced Alzheimer's disease. *Image–the Journal of Nursing Scholarship, 31*, 121–125.

Selected References

Balzer-Riley, J. (1996). *Communications in nursing: Communicating assertively & responsibly in nursing: A guidebook* (3rd ed.). St. Louis, MO: Mosby.

Belenky, M. F., Clinchy, B. M., Goldberger, N. R., & Tarule, J. M. (1986). *Women's ways of knowing: The development of self, voice, and mind.* New York: Basic Books.

Bjorklund, P. (2000). Assessing ego strength: Spinning straw into gold. *Perspectives in Psychiatric Care, 36*(1), 14–23.

Burger, J. M. (1992). *Desire for control: Personality, social and clinical perspectives.* New York: Plenum.

Carpenito, L. J. (2000). *Nursing diagnosis: Application to clinical practice* (8th ed.). Philadelphia, PA: Lippincott.

Czuchta, D. M., & Johnson, B. A. (1998). Reconstructing a sense of self in patients with chronic mental illness. *Perspectives in Psychiatric Care, 34*(3), 31–36.

Davidhizar, R. E., & Schearer, R. (1996). Increasing self-confidence through self-talk. *Home Healthcare Nurse, 14*, 119–122.

Day, R. A., Field, P. A., Campbell, I. E., & Reutter, L. (1995). Student's evolving beliefs about nursing: From entry to graduation in a four-year baccalaureate programme. *Nurse Education Today, 15*, 357–364.

Dweck, C. S. (2000). *Self-theories: Their role in motivation, personality, and development.* Philadelphia, PA: Psychology Press.

Edelman, C. L., & Mandle, C. L. (1998). *Health promotion throughout the life span* (4th ed.). St. Louis, MO: Mosby.

Erikson, E. H. (1963). *Childhood and society* (2nd ed.). New York: Norton. (Classic.)

Gorman, L. M., Sultan, D. F., & Raines, M. L. (1996). *Davis's manual of psychosocial nursing for general patient care.* Philadelphia, PA: F. A. Davis.

Holmberg, S. K., Scott, L. L., Alexy, W., & Fife, B. L. (2001). Relationship issues of women with breast cancer. *Cancer Nursing, 24*(1), 53–60.

Johnson, M., & Maas, M. (Eds.). (2000). *Iowa outcomes project: Nursing outcomes classification (NOC).* St. Louis, MO: Mosby.

McCloskey, J. C., & Bulechek, G. M. (Eds.). (2000). *Iowa intervention project: Nursing interventions classification (NIC)* (3rd ed.). St. Louis, MO: Mosby.

Moore, S., & Katz, B. (1996). Home health nurses: Stress, self-esteem, social intimacy, and job satisfaction. *Home Healthcare Nurse, 14,* 963–969.

North American Nursing Diagnosis Association. (2001). *NANDA Nursing diagnoses: Definitions and classification 2001–2002.* Philadelphia, PA: Author.

Reutter, L., Field, P., Campbell, I., & Day, R. (1997). Socialization into nursing: Nursing students as learners. *Journal of Nursing Education, 36,* 149–155.

Sides, M. B., & Korcheck, N. (1998). Nurse's guide to scientific test taking (2nd ed.). Philadelphia: Lippincott.

Sims, O. V., & Napholz, L. (1996). What are some African American working women's expressed experiences of role conflict? *Journal of Cultural Diversity, 3,* 116–121.

Tappen, R. M., Williams, C., Fishman, S., & Touhy, T. (1999). Clinical scholarship: Persistence of self in advanced Alzheimer's disease. *Image–the Journal of Nursing Scholarship, 31,* 121–125.

WEBLINKS

Canadian Health Network
http://www.canadian-health-network.ca/customtools/homee.html
This site is funded by Health Canada and provides accurate, current, health-promotive material drawn from an extensive network of associations and government sites.

Canada–U.S.A. Women's Health Forum
http://www.hc-sc.gc.ca/canusa/papers/advocate.htm
This site provides a series of commissioned papers related to women.

ERIC Digest
http://www.ed.gov/databases/ERIC_Digests/ed389962.html
This search site permits the user to access journal articles within the digest.

CHAPTER 47

Stress and Coping

OBJECTIVES

After completing this chapter, you will be able to:

- Differentiate the concepts of stress as a stimulus, as a response, and as a transaction.
- Describe the three stages of Selye's general adaptation syndrome.
- Identify physiological, psychological, and cognitive indicators of stress.
- Differentiate four levels of anxiety.
- Outline behaviours related to specific ego defence mechanisms.
- Discuss types of coping and coping strategies.
- Identify essential aspects involved in assessing a client's stress and coping patterns.
- Explain nursing diagnoses related to stress.
- Describe interventions to help clients minimize and manage stress.

Stress is a universal phenomenon. All people experience it. Parents refer to the stress of raising children; working people talk of the stress of their jobs; and students at all levels talk of the stress of school. Stress can result from both positive and negative experiences. For example, a bride preparing for her wedding or a graduate preparing to start a new job may have stress reactions to these positive experiences, and a husband concerned about caring for his wife and family following a diagnosis of cancer may experience similar stress reactions.

The concept of stress is important because it provides a way of understanding the person as a unified being who responds in totality (mind, body, and spirit) to a variety of changes that take place in daily life.

TABLE 47.1 Selected Stressors Associated with Developmental Stages

Developmental Stage	Stressors
Child	Resolving conflict between independence and dependence
	Beginning school
	Establishing peer relationships and adjustments
	Coping with peer competition
Adolescent	Accepting changing physique
	Developing relationships involving sexual attraction
	Achieving independence
	Choosing a career
Young adult	Getting married
	Leaving home
	Managing a home
	Getting started in an occupation
	Continuing one's education
	Rearing children
Middle adult	Accepting physical changes of aging
	Maintaining social status and standard of living
	Helping teenage children to become independent
	Adjusting to aging parents
Older adult	Accepting decreasing physical abilities and health
	Accepting changes in residence
	Adjusting to retirement and reduced income
	Adjusting to death of spouse and friends

Concept of Stress

Stress is a condition in which the human being responds to changes in its normal balanced state. A **stressor** is any event or stimulus that causes an individual to experience stress. When a person faces stressors, responses are made. Those responses are often referred to as **coping responses** or **coping mechanisms.**

Sources of Stress

There are many sources of stress. They can be broadly classified as internal or external stressors, or developmental or situational stressors. *Internal stressors* originate within a person, for example, cancer or feelings of depression. *External stressors* originate outside the individual, for example, a move to another city, a death in the family, or pressure from peers. *Developmental stressors* occur at predictable times throughout an individual's life. Within each developmental stage, certain tasks must be achieved to prevent or reduce stress. Examples of these tasks are shown in Table 47.1. *Situational stressors* are unpredictable and may occur at any time during life. Situational stress may be positive or negative. Examples of this type of stress include the following:

- Death of a family member
- Marriage or divorce
- Birth of a child
- New job
- Illness

The degree to which any of these events has positive or negative effects can depend to some degree upon an individual's developmental stage. For example, the death of a parent may be more stressful for a 12-year-old than for a 40-year-old.

Effects of Stress

Stress can have physical, emotional, intellectual, social, and spiritual consequences. Usually the effects are mixed because stress affects the whole person. Physically, stress can threaten a person's physiological homeostasis. Emotionally, stress can produce negative or nonconstructive feelings about the self. Intellectually, stress can influence a person's perceptual and problem-solving abilities. Socially, stress can alter a person's relationships with others. Spiritually, stress can challenge one's beliefs and values. Many illnesses have been linked to stress (Figure 47.1).

Models of Stress

Models of stress assist nurses to identify the stressor operating in a particular situation and to predict the individual's responses. Nurses can use the knowledge of these

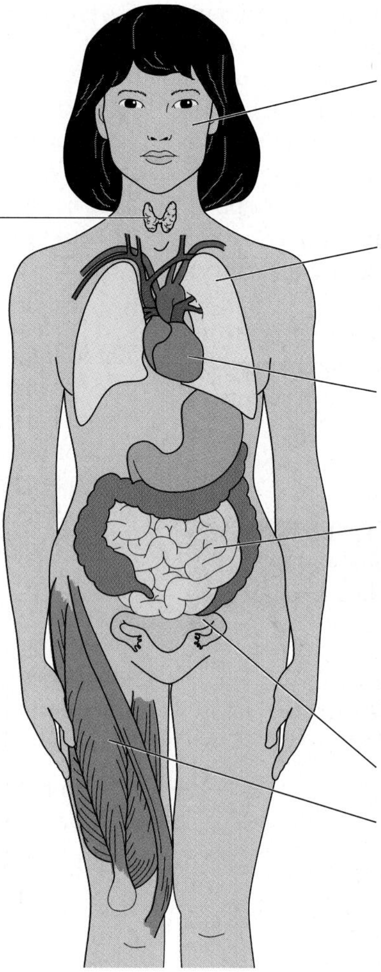

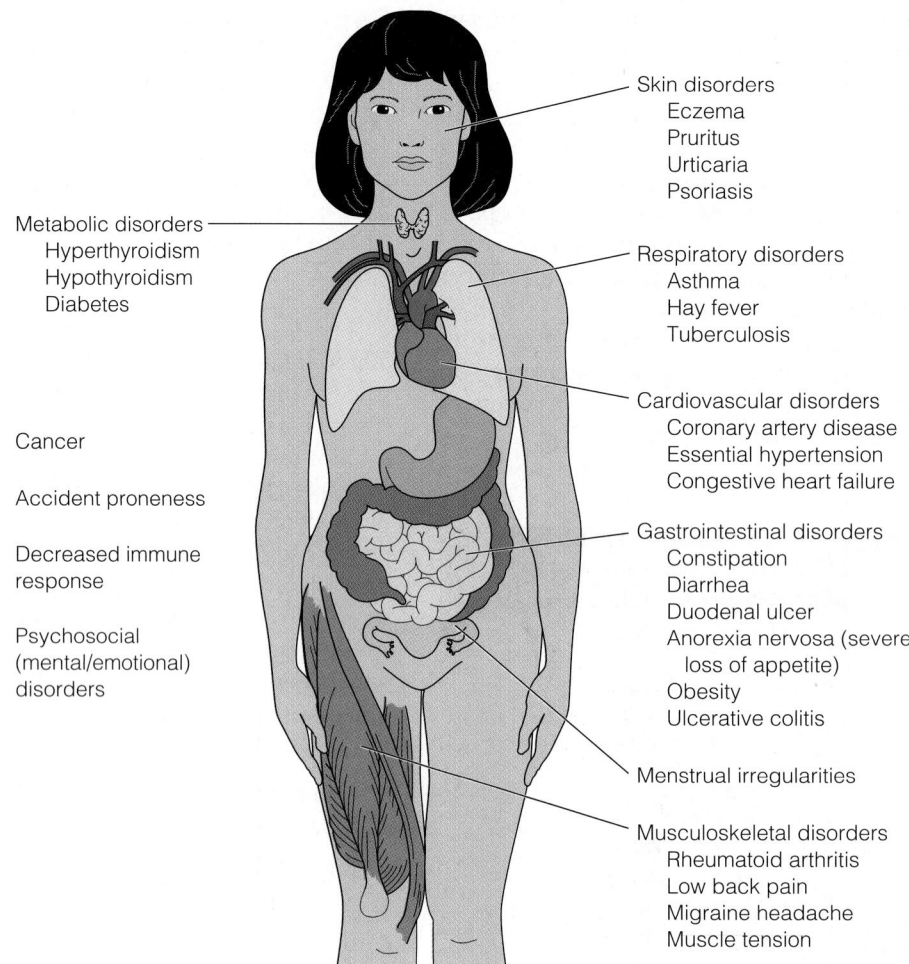

Figure 47.1 Some disorders that can be caused or aggravated by stress

Source: Adapted from Edlin, G. & and Golanty, E. (1992). *Health and wellness: A holistic approach* (4th ed.). (p. 210). Boston, MA: Jones and Bartlett.

models to assist clients in strengthening healthy coping responses and in adjusting unhealthy, unproductive responses. Three main models of stress are stimulus based, response based, and transaction based.

Stimulus-Based Models

In **stimulus-based stress models,** stress is defined as a stimulus, a life event, or a set of circumstances that arouses physiological and/or psychosocial reactions that may increase the individual's vulnerability to illness. Holmes and Rahe (1967) assigned a numerical value to 43 life changes or events. The scale of stressful life events is used to document a person's relatively recent experiences, such as divorce, pregnancy, and retirement. In this view, both positive and negative events are considered stressful.

Similar scales have since been developed, but all such scales require caution because the degree of stress an event presents can be highly individual. For example, a divorce may be highly traumatic to one person and cause relatively little anxiety to another.

Still, whatever the source of stress, research has shown that people who have a high level of stress are often more prone to illness and have a lowered ability to cope with an illness and subsequent stress.

Response-Based Models

Stress may also be considered as a response. This definition was developed and described by Selye (1956, 1976) as "the nonspecific response of the body to any kind of demand made upon it" (1976, p. 1). Schafer (1992, p. 9) defined stress as the "arousal of mind and body in response to demands made upon them."

Regardless of the cause, circumstances, or psychological interpretation of a demanding situation, Selye's stress response is characterized by the same chain or pattern of physiological events. This nonspecific response is called the **general adaptation syndrome (GAS)** or *stress syndrome*.

To differentiate the cause of stress from the response to stress, Selye created the term *stressor* (1976) to denote any factor that produces stress and disturbs the body's equilibrium. Because stress is a state of the body, it can be observed only by the changes it produces in the body. This response of the body, the stress syndrome or general adaptation syndrome, occurs with the release of certain adaptive hormones and subsequent changes in the structure and chemical composition of the body. Body organs affected by stress are the gastrointestinal tract, the adrenal glands, and the lymphatic structures. With prolonged stress, the adrenal glands enlarge considerably and the lymphatic structures, such as the thymus, spleen, and lymph nodes, atrophy (shrink). In addition to adapting globally, the body can also react locally; that is, one organ or a part of the body reacts alone. This is referred to as the **local adaptation syndrome (LAS).** One example of the LAS is inflammation. See the section on the inflammatory response in Chapter 37. Selye proposed that both the GAS and the LAS have three stages (1976): alarm reaction, resistance, and exhaustion (Figure 47.2).

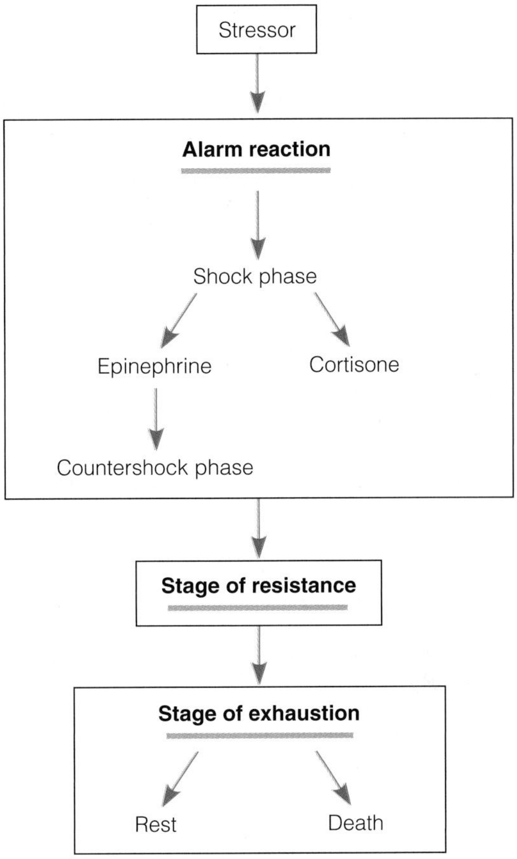

Figure 47.2 The three stages of adaptation to stress: the alarm reaction, the stage of resistance, and the stage of exhaustion

Alarm Reaction

The initial reaction of the body is the **alarm reaction (AR),** which alerts the body's defences against the stressor whether the stressor is heat, bacteria, or a verbal or physical attack from someone. Selye divided this stage into two parts: the shock phase and the countershock phase.

During the **shock phase,** the stressor may be perceived consciously or unconsciously by the person. In any case, the autonomic nervous system reacts, and large amounts of epinephrine (adrenaline) and cortisone are released into the body. The person is then ready for "fight or flight." This primary response is short lived, lasting from one minute to 24 hours.

The second part of the alarm reaction is called the **countershock phase.** During this time, the changes produced in the body during the shock phase are reversed. Thus, a person is best mobilized to react during the shock phase of the alarm reaction.

Stage of Resistance

The second stage in the GAS and LAS syndromes, the **stage of resistance (SR),** occurs when the body's adaptation takes place. In other words, the body attempts to cope with the stressor and to limit the stressor to the smallest area of the body that can deal with it.

Stage of Exhaustion

During the third stage, the **stage of exhaustion (SE),** the adaptation that the body made during the second stage cannot be maintained. This means that the ways used to cope with the stressor have been exhausted. If adaptation has not overcome the stressor, the stress effects may spread to the entire body. At the end of this stage, the body may either rest and return to normal, or death may be the ultimate consequence. The end of this stage depends largely on the adaptive energy resources of the individual, the severity of the stressor, and the external adaptive resources that are provided, such as oxygen.

Selye's general adaptation syndrome encompasses a range of *physiological* responses to stressors in the body as a whole (Figure 47.3). Stressors stimulate the sympathetic nervous system, which, in turn, stimulates the hypothalamus. The hypothalamus releases corticotropin-releasing hormone (CRH), which stimulates the anterior pituitary gland to release adrenocorticotropin hormone (ACTH). During times of stress, the adrenal medulla, which is functionally related to the sympathetic nervous system, secretes epinephrine and norepinephrine in response to sympathetic stimulation. Significant body responses to epinephrine include the following:

1. Increased myocardial contractility, which increases cardiac output and blood flow to active muscles
2. Bronchial dilation, which allows increased oxygen intake

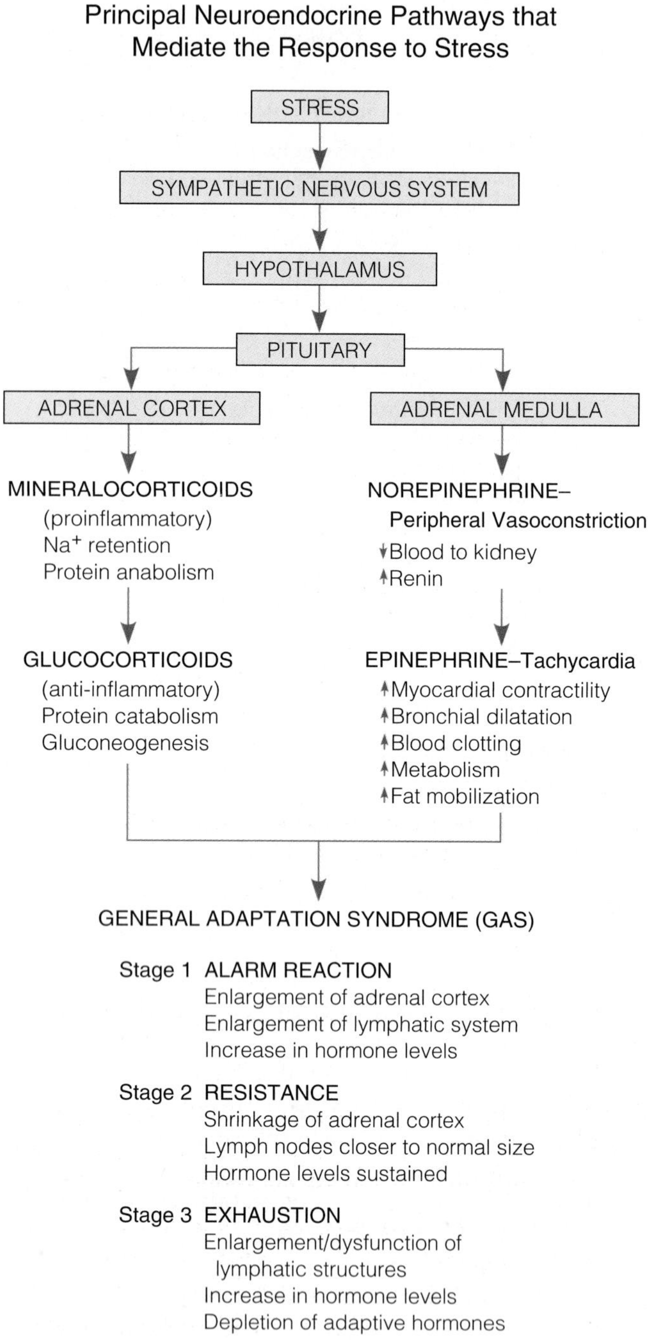

A stress syndrome, termed the General Adaptation Syndrome (GAS) by Hans Selye, evolves in three stages. Stages 1 and 2 are continuously repeated throughout a lifetime cycle. If resistance cannot be sustained, exhaustion (Stage 3), with its altered psychophysiological functioning, occurs.

Figure 47.3 Physiological response to stress: general adaptation syndrome

Source: Smith, M. J. & Selye, H. (1979, November). Stress: Reducing the negative effects of stress. *American Journal of Nursing, 79*(11),1954. Used by permission.

3. Increased blood clotting
4. Increased cellular metabolism
5. Increased fat mobilization to make energy available and to synthesize other compounds needed by the body

The principal effect of norepinephrine is decreased blood to the kidneys and increased secretion of renin. *Renin* is an enzyme that hydrolyzes one of the blood proteins to produce *angiotensin*. Angiotensin tends to increase the blood pressure by constricting arterioles. The sum of all these adrenal hormonal effects permits the person to perform far more strenuous physical activity than would otherwise be possible.

Transaction-Based Models

Transactional theories of stress are based on the work of Lazarus (1966), who states that the stimulus theory and the response theory do not consider individual differences. Neither theory explains which factors lead some people and not others to respond effectively, nor interprets why some people are able to adapt for longer periods than others. According to Lazarus, "Stimulus definitions focus on events in the environment, such as natural disasters, illness, or termination of employment. This approach assumes that certain situations are normally stressful but does not allow for individual differences in the evaluation of events. Response definitions refer to a state of stress; the person is spoken of as reacting with stress, being under stress, and so on. Stimulus and response definitions have limited utility because a stimulus gets defined as stressful only in terms of a stress response" (Lazarus & Folkman, 1984, p. 21).

Although Lazarus recognizes that certain environmental demands and pressures produce stress in substantial numbers of people, he emphasizes that people and groups differ in their sensitivity and vulnerability to certain types of events, as well as in their interpretations and reactions. For example, in terms of illness, one person may respond with denial, another with anxiety, and still another with depression. To explain variations among individuals under comparable conditions, the Lazarus model takes into account cognitive processes that intervene between the encounter and the reaction, and the factors that affect the nature of this process. In contrast to Selye, who focuses on physiological responses, Lazarus includes mental and psychological components or responses as part of his concept of stress.

The Lazarus **transactional stress theory** encompasses a set of cognitive, affective, and adaptive (coping) responses that arise out of person-environment transactions. The person and the environment are inseparable; each affects and is affected by the other. Stress "refers to any event in which environmental demands, internal demands, or both tax or exceed the adaptive resources of an individual, social system, or tissue system" (Monat & Lazarus, 1991, p. 3). The individual responds to perceived environmental changes by adaptive or coping responses. See the section "Coping" later in this chapter.

Indicators of Stress

Indicators of an individual's stress may be physiological, psychological, or cognitive.

Physiological Indicators

Responses to stress vary depending on the individual's perception of events. The physiological signs and symptoms of stress result from the activation of the sympathetic and neuroendocrine systems of the body. See the accompanying box for physiological indicators of stress.

> **Physiological Indicators of Stress**
>
> - Pupils dilate to increase visual perception when serious threats to the body arise.
> - Sweat production (diaphoresis) increases to control elevated body heat due to increased metabolism.
> - The heart rate increases, which leads to an increased pulse rate to transport nutrients and byproducts of metabolism more efficiently.
> - Skin is pallid because of constriction of peripheral blood vessels, an effect of norepinephrine.
>   a. Constriction of vessels in blood reservoirs, such as the skin, kidneys, and most large interior organs
>   b. Increased secretion of renin, an effect of norepinephrine
>   c. Increased sodium and water retention due to release of mineralocorticoids, which results in increased blood volume
>   d. Increased cardiac output
> - The rate and depth of respirations increase because of dilation of the bronchioles, promoting hyperventilation.
> - Urinary output decreases.
> - The mouth may be dry.
> - Peristalsis of the intestines decreases, resulting in possible constipation and flatus.
> - For serious threats, mental alertness improves.
> - Muscle tension increases to prepare for rapid motor activity or defence.
> - Blood sugar increases because of release of glucocorticoids and gluconeogenesis.

Psychological Indicators

Psychological manifestations of stress include anxiety, fear, anger, and depression. Some of these coping patterns are helpful; others are a hindrance, depending on the situation and the length of time they are used or experienced. Indeed, anxiety is often considered to be a response to a stressful event rather than a coping mechanism, inasmuch as it may impede action to remove the stressor.

Anxiety

A common reaction to stress is anxiety, a state of mental uneasiness, apprehension, dread, or foreboding or a feeling of helplessness related to an impending or anticipated unidentified threat to self or significant relationships. Anxiety can be experienced at the conscious, subconscious, or unconscious levels. It differs from fear in four ways:

1. The source of anxiety may not be identifiable; the source of fear is identifiable.
2. Anxiety is related to the future, that is, to an anticipated event. Fear is related to the present.
3. Anxiety is vague, whereas fear is definite.
4. Anxiety is the result of psychological or emotional conflict; fear is the result of a discrete physical or psychological entity.

All people experience anxiety to some degree most of the time. Mild or moderate anxiety is needed to accomplish developmental tasks and motivate goal-directed behaviour. In this sense, anxiety is an effective coping strategy. For example, mild anxiety motivates students to study. Excessive anxiety, however, often has destructive effects.

Anxiety may be manifested at four levels:

1. *Mild anxiety* produces a slight arousal state that enhances perception, learning, and productive abilities. Most healthy people experience mild anxiety, perhaps as a feeling of mild restlessness that prompts a person to seek information and ask questions.
2. *Moderate anxiety* increases the arousal state to a point where the person expresses feelings of tension, nervousness, or concern. Perceptual abilities are narrowed. Attention is focused more on a particular aspect of a situation than on peripheral activities.
3. *Severe anxiety* consumes most of the person's energies and requires intervention. Perception is further decreased. The person, unable to focus on what is really happening, focuses on only one specific detail of the situation generating the anxiety.
4. *Panic* is an overpowering, frightening level of anxiety causing the person to lose control. It is less frequently experienced than other levels of anxiety. The perception of a panicked person can be altered to the point where the person distorts events.

See Table 47.2 for indicators of these levels.

TABLE 47.2 Indicators of Levels of Anxiety

	Level of Anxiety			
Category	**Mild**	**Moderate**	**Severe**	**Panic**
Verbalization changes	Increased questioning	Voice tremors and pitch changes	Communication difficult to understand	Communication may not be understandable
Motor activity changes	Mild restlessness Sleeplessness	Tremors, facial twitches, and shakiness Increased muscle tension	Increased motor activity, inability to relax Fearful facial expression	Increased motor activity, agitation Unpredictable responses Trembling, poor motor coordination
Perception and attention changes	Feelings of increased arousal and alertness Uses learning to adapt	Narrowed focus of attention Able to focus but selectively inattentive Learning slightly impaired	Inability to focus or concentrate Easily distracted Learning severely impaired	Perception distorted or exaggerated Unable to learn or function
Respiratory and circulatory changes	None	Slightly increased respiratory and heart rates	Tachycardia, hyperventilation	Dyspnea, palpitations, choking, chest pain or pressure
Other changes	None	Mild gastric symptoms, e.g., "butterflies in the stomach"	Headache, dizziness, nausea	Feeling of impending doom Paresthesia, sweating

Sources: Carpenito, L. J. (2000). *Nursing diagnosis: Application to clinical practice* (8th ed.). Philadelphia, PA: Lippincott; and Fontaine, K. L., & Fletcher, J. S. (1999). *Essentials of mental health nursing,* (4th ed.). Menlo Park, CA: Addison-Wesley.

Fear

Fear is an emotion or feeling of apprehension aroused by impending or seeming danger, pain, or other perceived threat. The fear may be in response to something that has already occurred, in response to an immediate or current threat, or of something the person believes will happen. The object of fear may or may not be based in reality. For example, the beginning nursing student may be fearful in anticipation of the first experience in a client care setting. The student may fear that the client will not want to be cared for by the student or that the student might inadvertently harm the client. Although the feeling of fear is real and may elicit a stress response, the instructor arranges the student's first client assignment so that the student's feared outcomes are unlikely to occur.

Anger

Anger is an emotional state consisting of a subjective feeling of animosity or strong displeasure. Many people feel guilty when they feel anger because they have learned that to feel angry is wrong. In fact, anger, hostility, violence, and aggression differ. Anger can be expressed in a nonalienating verbal manner; it is then considered a positive emotion and a sign of emotional maturity because growth and beneficial interactions result from it.

Anger is commonly manifested in altered voice tone as a communication to desist from some action or other. A verbal expression of anger can, therefore, be considered a signal to others of one's internal psychological discomfort and a call for assistance to deal with perceived stress. In contrast, *hostility* is usually marked by overt antagonism and harmful or destructive behaviour; *aggression* is an unprovoked attack or a hostile, injurious, or destructive action or outlook; and *violence* is the exertion of physical force to injure or abuse. Verbally expressed anger differs from hostility, aggression, and violence, but it can lead to destructiveness and violence if the anger persists unabated.

A clearly expressed verbal communication of anger, when the angry person tells the other person about the anger and

TABLE 47.3 Defence Mechanisms

Defence Mechanism	Example(s)	Use/Purpose
Compensation Covering up weaknesses by emphasizing a more desirable trait or by overachievement in a more comfortable area.	A high school student too small to play football becomes the star long-distance runner for the track ream.	Allows a person to overcome weakness and achieve success.
Denial An attempt to screen or ignore unacceptable realities by refusing to acknowledge them.	A woman, though told her father has metastatic cancer, continues to plan a family reunion 18 months in advance.	Temporarily isolates a person from the full impact of a traumatic situation.
Displacement The transferring or discharging of emotional reactions from one object or person to another object or person.	A husband and wife are fighting, and the husband becomes so angry he hits a door instead of his wife. A student gets a C on a paper and goes home and yells at the family.	Allows for feelings to be expressed through or to less dangerous objects or people.
Identification An attempt to manage anxiety by imitating the behaviour of someone feared or respected.	A student nurse imitating the nurturing behaviour she observes one of her instructors using with clients.	Helps a person avoid self-devaluation.
Intellectualization A mechanism by which an emotional response that normally would accompany an uncomfortable or painful incident is evaded by the use of rational explanations that remove from the incident any personal significance and feelings.	The pain over a parent's sudden death is reduced by saying, "He wouldn't have wanted to live disabled."	Protects a person from pain and traumatic events.
Introjection A form of identification that allows for the acceptance of others' norms and values into oneself, even when contrary to one's previous assumptions.	A seven-year-old tells his little sister, "Don't talk to strangers." He has introjected this value from the instructions of parents and teachers.	Helps a person avoid social retaliation and punishment; particularly important for the child's development of superego.
Minimization Not acknowledging the significance of one's behaviour.	A person says, "Don't believe everything my wife tells you. I wasn't so drunk I couldn't drive."	Allows a person to decrease responsibility for own behaviour.
Projection A process in which blame is attached to others or the environment for unacceptable desires, thoughts, shortcomings, and mistakes.	A mother is told her child must repeat a grade in school, and she blames this on the teacher's poor instruction. A husband forgets to pay a bill and blames his wife for not giving it to him earlier.	Allows a person to deny the existence of shortcomings and mistakes; protects self-image.

carefully identifies the source, is constructive. This clarity of communication gets the anger out into the open so that the other person can deal with it and help alleviate it. The angry person "gets it off the chest" and prevents an emotional buildup.

Depression

Depression is a common *reaction* to events that seem overwhelming or negative. Depression affects 2.5 million Canadians over the age of 18 years annually (9 percent of the population) (Canadian Mental Health Association, 1998). The signs and symptoms of depression and the severity of the problem vary with the client and the significance of the precipitating event. Emotional symptoms can include feelings of tiredness, sadness, emptiness, or numbness. Behavioural signs of depression include irritability, inability to concentrate, difficulty making decisions, loss of sexual desire, crying, sleep disturbance, and social withdrawal. Physical signs of depression may include loss of appetite, weight loss, constipation, headache,

TABLE 47.3 Defence Mechanisms *continued*

Defence Mechanism	Example(s)	Use/Purpose
Rationalization Justification of certain behaviours by faulty logic and ascription of motives that are socially acceptable but did not, in fact, inspire the behaviour.	A mother spanks her toddler too hard and says it was all right because he could not feel it through the diapers anyway.	Helps a person cope with the inability to meet goals or certain standards.
Reaction Formation A mechanism that causes people to act exactly opposite to the way they feel.	An executive resents the bosses for calling in a consulting firm to make recommendations for change in the department but verbalizes complete support of the idea and is exceedingly polite and cooperative.	Aids in reinforcing repression by allowing feelings to be acted out in a more acceptable way.
Regression Resorting to an earlier, more comfortable level of functioning that is characteristically less demanding and responsible.	An adult throws a temper tantrum. A critically ill client allows the nurse to do the bathing and feeding.	Allows a person to return to a point in development when nurturing and dependency were needed and accepted with comfort.
Repression An unconscious mechanism by which threatening thoughts, feelings, and desires are kept from becoming conscious; the repressed material is denied entry into consciousness.	A teenager seeing his best friend killed in a car accident becomes amnesic about the circumstances surrounding the accident.	Protects a person from a traumatic experience until he or she has the resources to cope.
Sublimation Displacement of energy associated with more primitive sexual or aggressive drives into socially acceptable activities.	A person with excessive, primitive sexual drives invests psychic energy into a well-defined religious value system.	Protects a person from behaving in irrational, impulsive ways.
Substitution The replacement of a highly valued, unacceptable, or unavailable object by a less valuable, acceptable, or available object.	A woman wants to marry a man exactly like her dead father and settles for someone who looks a little bit like him.	Helps a person achieve goals and minimizes frustration and disappointment.
Undoing An action or words designed to cancel some disapproved thoughts, impulses, or acts in which the person relieves guilt by making reparation.	A father spanks his child and the next evening brings home a present for him. A teacher writes an exam that is far too easy, then constructs a grading curve that makes it difficult to earn a high grade.	Allows a person to appease guilty feelings and atone for mistakes.

Source: Fontaine, K. L., & Fletcher, J. S. (1999). *Essentials of mental health nursing* (4th ed.). (p. 9–10). Menlo Park, CA: Addison-Wesley Longman. Reprinted with permission.

and dizziness. Many people may experience short periods of depression in response to overwhelming stressful events, such as the death of a loved one or loss of a job; prolonged depression, however, is a cause for concern and may require treatment.

Unconscious Ego Defence Mechanisms

Unconscious ego defence mechanisms are psychological defensive (adaptive) mechanisms or, in the words of Sigmund Freud (1946), mental mechanisms that develop as the personality attempts to defend itself, establish compromises among conflicting impulses, and allay inner tensions. Defence mechanisms are the unconscious mind working to protect the person from anxiety. They can be considered precursors to conscious cognitive coping mechanisms that will ultimately solve the problem. Like some verbal and motor responses, defence mechanisms release tension. Table 47.3 describes these mechanisms and lists examples of their adaptive and maladaptive use.

Cognitive Indicators

Cognitive indicators of stress are thinking responses that include problem solving, structuring, self-control or self-discipline, suppression, and fantasy. *Problem solving* involves thinking through the threatening situation using specific steps similar to those of the nursing process to arrive at a solution. The person assesses the situation or problem, analyzes or defines it, chooses alternatives, carries out the selected alternative, and evaluates whether the solution was successful.

Structuring is the arrangement or manipulation of a situation so that threatening events do not occur. For example, a nurse can structure or control an interview with a client by asking only direct, closed questions. This strategy avoids information or questions that may be threatening to the nurse's knowledge or values. Structuring, however, can be productive in certain situations. A person who schedules a dental examination semiannually to prevent severe dental disease is using productive structuring.

Self-control (discipline) is assuming a manner and facial expression that convey a sense of being in control or in charge, no matter what the situation is. When self-control prevents panic and harmful or nonproductive actions in a threatening situation, it is a helpful response that conveys strength. Self-control carried to an extreme, however, can delay problem solving and prevent a person from receiving the support of others, who may perceive the person as handling the situation well, as cold, or as unconcerned.

Suppression is consciously and willfully putting a thought or feeling out of mind: "I won't deal with that today. I'll do it tomorrow." This response relieves stress temporarily but does not solve the problem. A person who keeps ignoring a toothache, pushing it out of mind fearing the pain of having a filling, will not relieve symptoms or find the solution.

Fantasy or *daydreaming* is likened to make-believe. Unfulfilled wishes and desires are imagined as fulfilled, or a threatening experience is reworked or replayed so that it ends differently from reality. Experiences can be relived, everyday problems solved, and plans for the future made. The outcome of current problems may also be fantasized. For example, a client who is awaiting the results of a breast biopsy may fantasize the surgeon as saying, "You do not have cancer." Fantasy responses can be helpful if they lead to problem solving. For example, the client awaiting breast biopsy results might say to herself, "Even if the doctor says, 'You have cancer,' as long as the doctor also says it can be treated, I can accept that." Fantasies can be destructive and nonproductive if a person uses them to excess and retreats from reality.

Factors Influencing the Effectiveness of Coping

- The number, duration, and intensity of the stressors
- Past experiences of the individual
- Support systems available to the individual
- Personal qualities of the person

Coping

Coping may be described as dealing with problems and situations or contending with them successfully. A **coping strategy (coping mechanism)** is an innate or acquired way of responding to a changing environment or specific problem or situation. According to Folkman and Lazarus (1991, p. 210), coping is "the cognitive and behavioural effort to manage specific external and/or internal demands that are appraised as taxing or exceeding the resources of the person."

Short-term coping strategies can temporarily reduce stress to a tolerable limit but are, in the long run, ineffective ways to deal with reality. They may even have a destructive or detrimental effect on the person. Examples of short-term strategies are using alcoholic beverages or drugs, daydreaming and fantasizing, relying on the belief that everything will work out, and giving in to others to avoid anger.

Coping strategies vary among individuals and are often related to the individual's perception of the stressful event. Schafer (1992) describes three approaches to coping with stress: alter the stressor, adapt to the stressor, or avoid the stressor. A person's coping strategies often change with a reappraisal of a situation. There is never only one way to cope. Some people choose avoidance; others confront a situation as a means of coping. Still others seek information or rely on religious beliefs as a means of coping.

Coping can be adaptive or maladaptive. Adaptive coping helps the person to deal effectively with stressful events and minimizes distress associated with them. Maladaptive coping can result in unnecessary distress for the person and others associated with the person or stressful event (Schafer, 1992). In nursing literature, effective and ineffective coping are often differentiated. *Effective coping* results in adaptation; *ineffective coping* results in maladaptation. Although coping behaviour may not always seem appropriate, the nurse needs to remember that coping is always purposeful.

The effectiveness of an individual's coping is influenced by a number of factors, listed in the accompanying box. If the duration of the stressors is extended beyond the coping powers of the individual, that person becomes exhausted and may develop increased susceptibility to health problems. Reaction to long-term stress is seen in family members who undertake the care of a person in the home for a long period. This stress is called **caregiver**

TABLE 47.4 Examples of the Effects of Stress on Basic Human Needs

Need	Example
Physiological	Altered elimination pattern
	Change in appetite
	Altered sleep pattern
Safety and security	Expresses nervousness and feelings of being threatened
	Focuses on stressors and inattention to safety measures
Love and belonging	Isolated and withdrawn
	Becomes overly dependent
	Blames others for own problems
Self-esteem	Fails to socialize with others
	Becomes a workaholic
	Draws attention to self
Self-actualization	Preoccupied with own problems
	Shows lack of control
	Unable to accept reality

burden and produces such responses as chronic fatigue, sleeping difficulties, and high blood pressure. Prolonged stress can also result in mental illness. As coping strategies or defence mechanisms (see Table 47.3) become ineffective, the individual may have interpersonal problems, work difficulties, and a significant decrease in abilities to meet basic human needs. See Table 47.4.

ASSESSMENT INTERVIEW

Stress and Coping Patterns

- On a scale of 1 to 10, how would you rate the stress you are experiencing in the following areas?
  a. Home
  b. Work or school
  c. Finance
  d. Recent illness or loss of loved one
  e. Your health
  f. Family responsibilities
  g. Ethnic or cultural group
  h. Religion
  i. Relationships with friends
  j. Relationship with parents or children
  k. Relationship with partner
  l. Recent hospitalization
  m. Other (specify)
- How long have you been dealing with these stressor(s)?
- How do you usually handle stressful situations?
  a. Cry
  b. Get angry
  c. Become verbally abusive
  d. Talk to someone (Who?)
  e. Withdraw from the situation
  f. Structure and control others or situation
  g. Go for a walk or physical exercise
  h. Try to arrive at a solution
  i. Pray for wisdom and courage
  j. Laugh, joke, or use some other expression of humour
  k. Meditate or use some other relaxation technique, such as yoga or guided imagery
- How well does your usual coping strategy work?

Assessing

Nursing assessment of a client's stress and coping patterns includes (1) nursing history, and (2) physical examination of the client for indicators of stress (e.g., nail biting, nervousness, weight changes) or stress-related health problems (e.g., hypertension, dyspnea). When obtaining the nursing history of any client, the nurse poses questions about client-perceived stressors or stressful incidents, manifestations of stress, and past and present coping strategies. During the physical examination, the nurse observes for verbal, motor, cognitive, or other physical manifestations of stress. Remember, however, that clinical signs and symptoms may not occur when cognitive coping is effective. See the sections on "Indicators of Stress" and "Coping" earlier in this chapter. In addition, the nurse should be aware of expected developmental transitions (predictable tasks that must be accomplished if the person is to grow psychologically as well as physically; see Chapters 19–21). This knowledge helps the nurse identify additional stressors that are present and the client's response to them. Table 47.1, on page 1319, provides an overview of developmental stressors. Questions to elicit data about the client's stress and coping patterns are shown in the box above.

Diagnosing

The North American Nursing Diagnosis Association (NANDA) includes several diagnostic labels related to stress, adaptation, and coping. These include the following (NANDA, 2001):

- ***Anxiety***: Feelings of uneasiness (apprehension) and activation of the autonomic nervous system in response to a vague, nonspecific threat
- ***Coping, Ineffective***: An inability or risk of inability to manage internal and external stressors because of inadequate physical, psychological, behavioural, or cognitive resources

- ***Coping, Defensive***: Repeatedly presenting falsely positive self-evaluation as a defence against underlying perceived threats to positive self-regard
- ***Denial, Ineffective:*** Minimizing or disavowing symptoms or a situation to the detriment of one's health
- ***Adjustment, Impaired:*** Unable to modify lifestyle or behaviour in a manner consistent with a change in health status
- ***Conflict, Decisional:*** Uncertainty about a course of action when the choice involves risk, loss, or challenge
- ***Fear:*** Feeling of physiological or emotional disruption related to an identifiable source that is perceived as dangerous
- ***Post-Trauma Syndrome:*** A sustained painful response for more than one month to one or more overwhelming traumatic events that have not been assimilated
- ***Relocation Stress Syndrome:*** Physiological and psychosocial disturbances as a result of transfer from one environment to another
- ***Caregiver Role Strain:*** Physical, emotional, social, or financial stress related to caring for another
- ***Coping, Disabled Family:*** Destructive behaviour or risk of such behaviours by family member in response to an inability to manage internal or external stressors because of inadequate resources
- ***Coping, Compromised Family:*** Provision of insufficient, ineffective, or compromised support, comfort, assistance, or encouragement by primary support person, which may be needed by client to manage or master adaptive tasks related to health challenge

Defining characteristics and etiologies of these diagnostic labels are discussed earlier under manifestations of stress. Clinical examples of assessment data clusters and related nursing diagnoses (***Anxiety*** and ***Ineffective Individual Coping***) are shown in Table 47.5.

TABLE 47.5 Clinical Application: Assessment Data Clusters and Related Nursing Diagnoses: Stress and Coping Abilities

Data Cluster	Nursing Diagnosis
Darryl Johnson, a 47-year-old accountant, was admitted to the emergency department with a heart attack. He says, "I'm scared about this. My dad died of a heart attack when he was 48 years old." He appears restless, questions everything that is going on, and is hyperventilating.	***Anxiety*** related to change in health status and threat of dying
Sonia Park, a 33-year-old mother of three, returned to nursing after taking a refresher course. She says, "I'm so tired since I started work. I'm not keeping up with housekeeping the way I should, and I'm not spending as much time with the kids. I'm too tired to shop and go to my son's baseball game. Tom and all the kids are helping out and not complaining, but I just keep thinking they wish I still baked cookies and played more with them. I'm sure not sleeping well, and I'm having awful headaches."	***Coping, Ineffective*** related to work overload and unrealistic expectations

Planning

The nurse develops plans in collaboration with the client and significant support people, when possible, according to the client's state of health (e.g., ability to return to work), level of anxiety, support resources, coping mechanisms, and sociocultural and religious affiliation. The nurse who has little experience intervening with clients undergoing stress may wish to consult with a clinical specialist or a more experienced nurse to develop effective plans. The nurse and client set goals to change the existing client responses to the stressor or stressors.

The overall client goals for persons experiencing stress-related responses are to:

- Decrease or resolve anxiety
- Increase ability to manage or cope with stressful events or circumstances
- Improve role performance

Examples of specific desired outcomes, although established in this phase, are provided in Table 47.6 in the "Evaluating" section of this chapter.

Examples of NIC interventions include the following:

- Anxiety reduction
- Body image enhancement
- Caregiver support
- Coping enhancement
- Crisis intervention
- Decision-making support
- Role enhancement
- Security enhancement
- Support system enhancement

Specific nursing activities related to each of these interventions can be selected to individualize client care. A sample nursing care plan using NIC interventions and selected activities is provided on the next page.

SAMPLE CARE PLAN FOR INEFFECTIVE INDIVIDUAL COPING

ASSESSMENT DATA

Nursing Assessment

Amanda Crosby, a 42-year-old mother of three children, is hospitalized with breast cancer. She is scheduled for a modified radical mastectomy. Amanda was relatively healthy until she found a lump in her right breast one week ago. She and her husband are extremely anxious about the surgery. Amanda confides to the admitting nurse, "I can't stand the idea of having one of my breasts cut off; I don't know how I'm going to be able to even look at myself." Mr. Crosby informs the nurse that Amanda has been abusing alcohol since her diagnosis and neglecting her responsibilities as a mother. She is tearful and does not see how she will be able to continue her work as a dress designer.

Physical Examination

Height: 164 cm
Weight: 58 kg
Temperature: 37°C
Pulse rate: 88 BPM
Respirations: 16/minute
Blood pressure: 142/88 mm Hg

Diagnostic Data

Chest x-ray negative, CBC and urinalysis within normal limits

Nursing Diagnosis

Ineffective Individual Coping related to personal vulnerability secondary to mastectomy (as evidenced by verbalization of inability to cope, substance abuse, inability to meet role expectations)

Client Goal(s):

The client will demonstrate effective coping strategies.

Desired Outcomes

1. Participates in activities of daily living postoperatively
2. Identifies personal strengths that may promote effective coping before discharge
3. Accepts support through the nursing relationship by day 2
4. Verbalizes positive statements about self before discharge

*Nursing Interventions and Selected Activities with Rationale *(in italics)*

Coping Enhancement

- Provide an atmosphere of acceptance. — *Establishing rapport is essential to a therapeutic relationship and supports the client in self-reflection. Recognizing problems and sharing feelings is best brought about in an atmosphere of warmth and trust.*
- Provide factual information concerning the diagnosis, treatment, and prognosis. — *Factual information serves as a foundation for the individual in exploring feelings and alternative coping strategies. Clients who are experiencing stress often misunderstand facts and require frequent clarification so that appropriate conclusions can be drawn. Having valid information helps relieve stress.*
- Appraise Amanda's adjustment to changes in body image. — *Alteration in body image may be a major issue for Amanda and should be explored to facilitate therapeutic intervention. Coping strategies often change with a reappraisal of the situation.*
- Seek to understand Amanda's perspective of the stressful situation. — *Expressing emotions can decrease the perceived intensity of the stressor and serves as a basis for therapeutic interaction between the client and caregiver.*
- Discourage decision making during this time of stress. — *Stress can often have physiological and psychological manifestations that may interfere with cognitive ability and clear thinking.*
- Arrange situations that encourage her autonomy. — *Enhances a sense of control, personal achievement, and self-esteem.*
- Explore with her previous methods of dealing with life problems. — *Present and past coping status assists both the client and caregiver in capitalizing on successful methods, identifying ineffective strategies, and developing new skills more appropriate to the present situation. Also determines risk for inflicting self-harm.*
- Encourage verbalization of feelings, perceptions, and fears. — *Open, nonthreatening discussions facilitate the identification of causative and contributing factors.*
- Encourage Amanda to identify her own strengths and abilities. — *Assists the client to develop appropriate strategies for coping based on personal strengths and previous experiences. Improves self-concept and sense of ability to manage stress.*

SAMPLE CARE PLAN FOR INEFFECTIVE INDIVIDUAL COPING *continued*

■ Encourage Amanda to realistically describe changes in her role.	*Individuals experiencing stress may have unrealistic perceptions or reality distortions. Helping Amanda clearly describe her role would be beneficial in developing realistic goals for role achievement.*
■ Foster constructive outlets for anger and hostility.	*Assists the individual in channelling potentially harmful emotions and physical energy into constructive behaviour.*
■ Support the use of appropriate defence mechanisms.	*Some defence mechanisms, such as denial, can be temporarily therapeutic in helping the individual cope and relieve tension. After a time, however, denial and other defence mechanisms, such as projecting blame, are counterproductive.*
Body Image Enhancement	
■ Assist Amanda to separate physical appearance from feelings of personal worth.	*Physical appearance in modern society is often a major defining component of self-worth, especially for women. Detaching physical appearance from her definition of self will promote a more positive self-image.*
■ Assist her to discuss changes caused by the surgery.	*Open discussion of actual changes and perceived effects will assist Amanda in facing reality and dealing with her feelings.*
■ Monitor whether Amanda can look at her chest.	*The ability to look at the mastectomy site provides objective data about Amanda's level of acceptance and self-perception.*
■ Determine the client's and family's perceptions of the alteration in body image versus reality.	*Providing accurate information reduces misconceptions, diminishes fears, and promotes adaptation to change in appearance. Involvement of significant others in care shows acceptance of the client and enhances self-worth.*
■ Identify means of reducing the impact of any disfigurement through clothing.	*Assists the client in identifying ways in which she can enhance her physical attributes and minimize the physical alteration (e.g., prostheses).*
■ Facilitate contact with individuals with similar changes in body image.	*Meeting another person who has successfully adjusted to a mastectomy can lower the client's stress and anxiety.*
Support System Enhancement	
■ Identify the degree of family support.	*Assessing family interaction serves as a basis for identifying Amanda's support systems or lack thereof.*
■ Determine barriers to using support systems.	*Although adequate support systems may be available, Amanda may not be using them or may be using them ineffectively.*
■ Involve husband, family, and friends in the care and planning.	*Supporting Amanda in acknowledging changes in her appearance conveys acceptance and provides a foundation for her to begin to adjust.*
■ Discuss with concerned others how they can help.	*Family and friends are often willing but unsure how to help. Identifying specific strategies, such as praise and encouragement, during rehabilitation and healing will promote acceptance of change.*
■ Refer Amanda to a community-based breast cancer support group.	*Community support is beneficial in helping to meet unresolved needs, decreasing feelings of social isolation, and facilitating a positive self-image.*

Evaluation

Goal not met. Following surgery, Amanda was withdrawn. During bathing, she would not assist and turned her head away when the dressing was removed. She refused to learn how to manage the wound drain. Amanda was discharged with her family, and a community nurse was consulted to care for and help her to work through her changed body image.

*Interventions and activities selected are only a sample of those suggested in the *Nursing Interventions Classification (NIC)* and should be individualized for each client.

Source: McCloskey, J. C., & Bulechek, G. M. (2000). *Iowa intervention project: Nursing interventions classification (NIC)* (3rd ed.). St. Louis, MO: Mosby.

HOME CARE ASSESSMENT

Stress and Coping

Client

- *Knowledge:* Client's understanding of the nature of the stressors
- *Current coping strategies:* Effectiveness of current coping strategies and willingness to learn new stress management techniques
- *Self-care abilities:* Physical, emotional, social, and financial ability to minimize associated stressors
- *Role expectations:* Client's perception of the need to return to prior roles and possible stressors associated with these roles

Family

- *Knowledge:* Family members' and significant others' understanding of the nature of the client's stressors and their own relationship with client stressors
- *Family coping strategies:* Effectiveness of family members' and significant others' coping strategies and willingness to learn new stress management techniques
- *Role expectations:* Family members' and significant others' perception of the need for the client to return to family and work roles
- *Support people's availability and skills:* Family and significant others' sensitivity to the client's emotional and physical needs and ability to provide a supportive environment

Community

- *Resources:* Availability of and familiarity with possible sources of assistance for stress management, such as massage therapists, religious or spiritual centres, physical care providers, support groups, and so on

Planning for Home Care

Clients who are experiencing stress may require ongoing nursing support or referral to community agencies that can provide support to meet client needs and enhance client coping. The determination of how much and what type of planning and home care follow-up is based in great part on the nurse's knowledge of how the client and family have coped with previous stressors and the nature of the present stressor. The accompanying box describes data to be gathered for home care or follow-up assessment.

Implementing

Although stress is part of daily life, it is also highly individual; a situation that to one person is a major stressor may not affect another. Some methods to help reduce stress will be effective for one person; other methods will be appropriate for a different person. A nurse who is sensitive to clients' needs and reactions can choose those methods of intervention that will be most effective for each individual.

Encouraging Health-Promotion Strategies

Several health-promotion strategies are often appropriate as interventions for clients with stress-related nursing diagnoses. Among these are physical exercise, optimal nutrition, adequate rest and sleep, and time management.

Exercise

Regular exercise promotes both physical and emotional health. Physiological benefits include improved muscle tone, increased cardiopulmonary function, and weight control. Psychological benefits include relief of tension, a feeling of well-being, and relaxation. In general, health guidelines recommend exercise at least three times a week for 30 to 45 minutes. See Chapter 43 for more detailed information.

Nutrition

Optimal nutrition is essential for health and in increasing the body's resistance to stress. To minimize the effects of a stress response (e.g., irritability, hyperactivity, anxiety), people need to avoid excesses of caffeine, salt, sugar, and fat, and deficiencies in vitamins and minerals. Guidelines for a well-balanced, healthy diet are detailed in Chapter 38.

Rest and Sleep

Rest and sleep restore the body's energy levels and are an essential aspect of stress management. To ensure adequate rest and sleep, clients may need help to attain comfort (such as pain management) and to learn techniques that promote peace of mind and relaxation. (See "Using Relaxation Techniques" later in this chapter.)

Time Management

People who manage their time effectively usually experience less stress because they feel more in control of their circumstances. Clients who feel overwhelmed often need help to prioritize tasks and to consider whether modifications can be made to decrease role demands. Some working mothers, for example, may need to consider delegating more tasks to family members or hiring part-time help. Controlling the demands of others is also an important aspect of effective time management because all requests made by others cannot always be met. Clients may need to learn to develop an awareness of which requests they can meet without undue stress, which ones can be negotiated, and which ones need to be declined. Feelings of control can also be enhanced when clients schedule a daily or weekly period of time to deal with specific tasks. Time management must address both what is important to the client and what can realistically be achieved. For example, clients may need to consider whether a clean house and time spent with the children can both be accomplished satisfactorily and, if not, which is more important. Often, clients who are feeling overwhelmed need to re-examine the "should, ought, and must" approach to their actions and develop more realistic self-expectations.

Minimizing Anxiety

Nurses have always carried out measures to minimize clients' anxiety and stress. For example, nurses encourage clients to take deep breaths before an injection, explain procedures before they are implemented, including sensations likely to be experienced during the procedure, administer a back or neck rub to help the client relax, and offer support to clients and families during times of illness. General guidelines for helping clients who are stressed and feeling anxious are outlined in the accompanying box.

Minimizing Stress and Anxiety

- Help clients to
  a. Determine situations that precipitate anxiety and identify signs of anxiety.
  b. Verbalize feelings, perceptions, and fears as appropriate. Some cultures discourage the expression of feelings.
  c. Identify personal strengths.
  d. Recognize usual coping patterns and differentiate positive from negative coping mechanisms.
  e. Identify new strategies for managing stress (e.g., exercise, massage, progressive relaxation).
  f. Identify available support systems.
- Listen attentively; try to understand the client's perspective of the situation.
- Provide an atmosphere of warmth and trust; convey a sense of caring and empathy.
- Provide factual information, as needed, to prepare clients for tests, treatments, and so on.
- Encourage clients to participate in the plan of care; give them choices about appropriate aspects of care.
- Stay with clients as needed to promote safety and feelings of security and to reduce fear.
- Teach clients about
  a. The importance of adequate exercise, a balanced diet, and rest and sleep to energize the body and enhance coping abilities.
  b. Support groups available, such as Alcoholics Anonymous, Weight Watchers, or Overeaters Anonymous, and parenting and child abuse support groups.
  c. Educational programs available, such as time management, assertiveness training, and meditation groups.

Mediating Anger

Often, nurses find clients' anger difficult to handle. Caring for the client who is angry is difficult for two reasons:

- Clients rarely state, "I feel angry or frustrated," and rarely indicate the reason for their anger. Instead, they may refuse treatment, become verbally abusive or demanding, threaten violence, or become overly critical. Their complaints rarely reflect the cause of their anger.
- Anger from clients can elicit fear and anger in the nurse, who may respond in a manner that intensifies the client's anger, even to the point of violence. The majority of nurses respond in a way that reduces their own stress, rather than the client's stress.

Fontaine and Fletcher (1999) recommend the following strategies for dealing with clients' anger:

- Know and understand your own response to the feelings and expressions of anger.
- Accept the client's right to be angry; feelings are real and cannot be discounted or ignored.
- Try to understand the meaning of the client's anger.
- Ask the client in what way you may have contributed to the anger.
- Help clients "own" the anger—do not assume responsibility for their feelings.
- Let clients talk about their anger.
- Listen to the client, and act as calmly as possible.
- After the interaction is completed, take time to process your feelings and your responses to the client with your colleagues.
- Always consider safety for both the client and nurse as priority.

Relaxation Techniques*

- Breathing exercises
- Massage
- Progressive relaxation
- Imagery
- Biofeedback
- Yoga
- Meditation
- Therapeutic touch
- Music therapy
- Humour and laughter

*See Chapter 11 for details about these techniques.

Common Characteristics of Crises

- All crises are experienced as sudden. The person is usually not aware of a warning signal, even if others could "see it coming." The individual or family may feel that they have little or no preparation for the event or trauma.
- The crisis is often experienced as ultimately life threatening, whether this perception is realistic or not.
- Communication with significant others is often decreased or cut off.
- There may be perceived or real displacement from familiar surroundings or loved ones.
- All crises have an aspect of loss, whether actual or perceived. The losses can include an object, a person, a hope, a dream, or any significant factor for that individual.

Using Relaxation Techniques

Several relaxation techniques can be used to quiet the mind, release tension, and counteract the fight-or-flight responses of GAS discussed earlier in this chapter. Nurses can teach these techniques to clients and then encourage clients to use them to control stress throughout life. Nurses can also encourage hospitalized clients to use these techniques when they encounter stressful situations in a hospital setting. Examples of these situations are (1) during childbirth, (2) postoperatively to cope with pain, and (3) before and during a painful procedure. Many agencies now have relaxation tapes available that the client can purchase, if desired. Some clients make their own recordings. Specific relaxation techniques that may be used are discussed in Chapter 11 (Holistic Healing Modalities) but are listed in the accompanying box above.

Crisis Intervention

A **crisis** is an acute, time-limited state of disequilibrium resulting from situational, developmental, or societal sources of stress. A person in crisis is temporarily unable to cope with or adapt to the stressor by using previous methods of problem solving. People in crisis generally have a distorted perception of the event, do not have adequate situational support, and do not have adequate coping mechanisms. Common characteristics of crises are shown in the accompanying box.

Crisis intervention is a short-term helping process of assisting clients to (1) work through a crisis to its resolution, and (2) restore their pre-crisis level of functioning. It is a process that includes not only the client in crisis but also various members of the client's support network. Crisis intervention is not the specialty of any one professional group. People who intervene in crises come from the fields of nursing, medicine, psychology, social work, and theology. Police officers, teachers, school guidance counsellors, and rescue workers, among others, are often on the spot in moments of crisis.

Because a state of disequilibrium is so uncomfortable, a crisis is self-limiting. However, a person experiencing a crisis alone is more vulnerable to unsuccessful negotiation than a person working through a crisis with help. Working with another person increases the likelihood that the person in crisis will resolve it in a positive way. Often, a state of crisis offers the individual or family great potential for growth and change.

The traditional steps of the nursing process correspond closely to the steps of crisis intervention. *Assessment* is the first phase of crisis intervention. The nurse or helper must focus on the person and the problem, collecting data about the client, the client's coping style, the precipitating event, the situational supports, the client's perception of the crisis, and the client's ability to handle the problem. This is an essential and critical step of crisis intervention. This information is the basis for later decisions about how and when to intervene and whom to call. An individual's perception of the event and personal response will determine the nursing diagnoses. The most common nursing diagnoses for people in crisis are similar to those cited earlier in this chapter. In addition, such diagnoses as ***Risk for Violence: Self-Directed, Risk for Violence: Directed at Others, Rape Trauma Syndrome,*** and ***Hopelessness*** may be appropriate.

Effective *planning* for crisis intervention must be based on careful assessment and developed in active collaboration with the person in crisis and the significant people in that person's life.

Implementation involves crisis counselling and home crisis visits. **Crisis counselling** focuses on solving immediate problems and it involves individuals, groups, or families.

Crisis intervention centres rely heavily on telephone counselling by volunteers who have professional consultation available to them. Also known as hotlines and often available around the clock, they allow callers to remain anonymous and test what it feels like to ask for assistance. The volunteers usually work within a protocol that indicates what information they need from the client to assess the crisis. Their goal is to plan steps to provide immediate relief and then long-term follow-up, if necessary.

Home visits are made when telephone counselling does not suffice or when the crisis workers need to obtain additional information by direct observation or to reach a client who is unobtainable by telephone. Home visits are appropriate when crisis workers need to initiate contacts rather than waiting for clients to come to them; for example, when a telephone caller is assessed to be highly suicidal or when a concerned neighbour, physician, or clergy member informs the agency of clients in potential crisis.

Nurses in acute care or short-term care settings may not see the long-term effects of their interventions. Typically, nurses in these settings need to assess the crisis, set up the plan, and begin implementing it.

RESEARCH NOTE

Use of a Projective Technique to Assess Young Children's Appraisal and Coping Responses to a Venipuncture

The authors describe a study to examine the appraisal and emotional and coping responses of 45 children four to nine years of age regarding venipuncture. Data were obtained using a projective technique using black-and-white drawings and interviews with the children. The children described each phase of the venipuncture as a threat, a benefit, or a threat/benefit. Children as young as four years of age identified cognitive and behavioural strategies for coping. Almost all the children provided suggestions about what the woman in the picture could say to help the children through the venipuncture.

Implications: Nurses can ask even young children for their appraisal of a stressful situation and how they manage. Nurses can give the children information to correct misconceptions and validate efforts to cope with the situation.

Source: Caty, S., Ellerton, M. L., & Ritchie, J. (1997). Use of a projective technique to assess young children's appraisal and coping responses to a venipuncture. *Journal of the Society of Pediatric Nurses, 2*(2), 83–92.

Stress Management for Nurses

Nurses, like clients, are susceptible to experiencing anxiety and stress. Nursing practice involves many stressors related to both clients and the work environment—understaffing and increasing client care assignments, adjusting to various work shifts, being expected to assume responsibilities for which one does not feel prepared, inadequate support from supervisors and peers, visiting homes that are depressing, caring for dying clients, and so on. Four categories of work overload that nurses have described are (1) simultaneous demands, (2) new or unfamiliar procedures and not enough time to do what they like to do, (3) heavy patient loads, and (4) being responsible for safe patient care of their own and other patients (Gaudine, 2000). The theme that was central to these categories was the lack of control the nurses had in their work situations. Although most nurses cope effectively with the physical and emotional demands of nursing, in some situations, nurses become overwhelmed and develop **burnout,** a complex syndrome of behaviours that can be likened to the exhaustion stage of the general adaptation syndrome. The nurse with burnout manifests physical and emotional depletion, a negative attitude and self-concept, and feelings of helplessness and hopelessness.

Nurses can prevent burnout by using the techniques to manage stress discussed for clients. Nurses must first recognize their stress and become attuned to such responses as feelings of being overwhelmed, fatigue, angry outbursts, physical illness, and increases in coffee drinking, smoking, or other substance abuse. Once attuned to stress and personal reactions, it is necessary to identify which situations produce the most pronounced reactions so that steps may be taken to reduce the stress. Suggestions follow:

- Plan a daily relaxation program with meaningful quiet times to reduce tension (e.g., read a novel, listen to music, soak in a hot tub, or meditate).
- Establish a regular exercise program to direct energy outward (e.g., jog, play badminton, or join an aerobics dance class).
- Develop assertiveness techniques to overcome feelings of powerlessness in relationships with others. Learn to say no.
- Learn to accept failures—your own and others—and make it a constructive learning experience. Recognize that most people do the best they can. Learn to ask for help, to show your feelings with colleagues, and to support your colleagues in times of need.
- Accept what cannot be changed. There are certain limitations in every situation. Get involved in constructive change efforts if organizational policies and procedures cause stress.
- Develop collegial support groups to deal with feelings and anxieties generated in the work setting.

Evaluating

Using the desired outcomes developed during the planning stage as a guide, the nurse collects data needed to determine whether client goals and outcomes have been achieved. Examples of client goals and related outcomes are shown in Table 47.6.

If outcomes are not achieved, the nurse, client, and support people, if appropriate, need to explore the reasons before modifying the care plan. For example, if the goals "to reduce anxiety" and "improve coping" are not met, questions, such as the following, need to be considered:

- How does the client perceive the problem?
- Is there an underlying problem that has not been identified?
- Have new stressors occurred that interfere with successful coping?
- Were existing coping strategies sufficient to meet intended outcomes?
- How does the client perceive the effectiveness of new coping strategies?
- Did the client implement new coping strategies properly?
- Did the client access and use available resources?
- Have family members and significant others provided effective support?

TABLE 47.6 Evaluation Goals and Outcomes: Stress and Coping

Goal	Examples of Desired Outcomes
Decrease or resolve anxiety	Describes causes and level of anxiety Eliminates causes of anxiety, as appropriate Verbalizes feelings related to anxiety Decreases external stimuli when experiencing anxiety Verbalizes an increase in emotional and physical comfort
Improve ability to manage or cope with stressful events	Describes usual coping patterns Identifies personal strengths Develops new coping strategies for managing stress Plans coping strategies for stressful situations Uses effective coping strategies in managing anxiety Verbalizes a sense of control Reports decreased stress
Improve role performance	Describes realistic personal role expectations Reports strategies for role change, as appropriate Maintains role performance Performs family roles Performs effective work or school role Maintains social relationships

FOCUS ON CRITICAL THINKING

Ms. Levitt is a 37-year-old divorced mother of three children ages 8, 11, and 14 years. In addition to her full-time job, she transports her children to numerous school and extracurricular activities, is active in her synagogue, and is attending school part-time in order to obtain a better-paying job. Ms. Levitt's ex-husband left the province years ago and does not financially assist with the care of the children. Because of her hectic lifestyle, Ms. Levitt and her family primarily eat fast foods, which has resulted in her gaining 10 kg over the last year. Ms. Levitt has recently consulted with her primary-care physician regarding frequent feelings of nausea, her heart "pounding," headaches, and unusual fatigue. The physician ordered several diagnostic tests, but all were normal.

1. Speculate about the stressors that Ms. Levitt is experiencing.
2. From the data provided, how do you think Ms. Levitt is responding to the stressors you identified?
3. Explore anger as a possible cause of Ms. Levitt's symptoms.
4. What cues would alert you that Ms. Levitt is adapting to the stressors in her life in a positive and healthy manner?
5. As a nurse, there will be situations or events that will increase your anxiety and stress. What can you do to help you deal in a positive manner with those situations or events?

See Appendix A for answers to these questions.

CHAPTER HIGHLIGHTS

- Stress is a state of physiological and psychological tension that affects the whole person—physically, emotionally, intellectually, socially, and spiritually.
- Three models view stress as a stimulus, stress as a response, and stress as a transaction.
- Physiological responses to stress are described by the general adaptation syndrome (GAS) and the local adaptation syndrome (LAS).
- GAS is a multisystem response to stress and involves three steps: alarm reaction, stage of resistance, and stage of exhaustion.
- LAS is a localized physiological response that also expresses the three stages of GAS. An example of LAS is the inflammatory response.
- There are physiological, psychological, and cognitive indicators of stress. Physiological indicators are the result of increased activity of the sympathetic and neuroendocrine systems.
- Common psychological indicators are anxiety, fear, anger, and depression. Anxiety, the most common response, has four levels: mild, moderate, severe, and panic. Unconscious ego defence mechanisms, such as denial, rationalization, compensation, and sublimation, protect individuals from anxiety.
- Cognitive indicators or thinking responses to stress include problem solving, structuring, self-control (discipline), suppression, and fantasy.
- Coping strategies to deal with stress vary significantly among individuals. Strategies may be problem focused or emotion focused; long term or short term; and effective or ineffective.
- The effectiveness of individual coping depends on the number, duration, and intensity of the stressors; past experience; support systems available; and the personal qualities of the person.
- Prolonged stress and ineffective coping interfere with the meeting of basic needs and can affect physical and mental health.
- Nursing assessment of a client experiencing stress involves a nursing history to identify perceptions of and duration of stressors and coping strategies and a physical examination for physical indicators of stress.
- Nursing interventions for clients who are stressed are aimed at encouraging health-promotion strategies (exercise, balanced diet, adequate rest, and time management), minimizing anxiety, mediating anger, teaching about specific relaxation techniques, and implementing crisis interventions, as needed.
- Because nursing practice involves many stressors related to both clients and the work environment, nurses are susceptible to anxiety and, in some cases, burnout. Like clients, they need to implement stress-reduction measures.

READINGS AND REFERENCES

Suggested Readings

Keenan, J. (1996). The Japanese tea ceremony and stress management. *Holistic Nursing Practice, 10*(2), 30–37.
The author discusses the calming effect that people describe after attending a Japanese tea ceremony. The ritualizing of the tea ceremony enables the participants to transform tension-producing details of everyday life into moments of beauty, meaningfulness, and tranquillity.

La Forge, R. (1997). Mind–body fitness: Encouraging prospects for primary and secondary prevention. *Journal of Cardiovascular Nursing, 11*(3), 53–65.
The author discusses incorporating approaches such as mind-body exercise with existing health promotion and cardiac rehabilitation services to improve self-efficacy and long-term adherence to healthy behaviours, as well as to improve personal stress management skills. Mind-body exercise integrates muscular or physical activity with an internally directed focus so that the client enters a temporary self-contemplative or meditative mental state.

Zook, R. (1998). Learning to use positive defense mechanisms. *American Journal of Nursing, 98*(3), 16B, F.H.
The author describes how people use defence mechanisms. These mechanisms are described as existing on a continuum from healthy adaptive approaches to stress, to minimal, moderate, and high levels of distortion. Zook states that the best-known defence mechanism is denial. Included with the article is a glossary of defence mechanisms categorized from highly adaptive to maladaptive (high distortion). Also included is information about recognizing maladaptive behaviours and suggestions on how nurses can help clients drop negative defence mechanisms.

Related Research

Balneaves, L. G., & Long, B. (1999). An embedded decisional model of stress and coping: implications for exploring treatment decision making by women with breast cancer. *Journal of Advanced Nursing, 30*(6), 1321–1331.

Bryla, C. M. (1996). The relationship between stress and the development of breast cancer: A literature review. *Oncology Nursing Forum, 23*(3), 441–448.

McCain, N. L., Zeller, J. M., Cella, D. F., Urbanski, P. A., & Novak, R. M. (1996). The influence of stress management training in HIV disease. *Nursing Research, 45*(4), 246–253.

Provencher, H. L., Fournier, J. P., Perreault, M., & Vezina, J. (2000). The caregiver's perception of behavioral disturbance in relatives with schizophrenia: A stress-coping approach. *Community Mental Health Journal, 36*(3), 293–306.

Rozman, D., Whitaker, R., Beckman, T., & Jones, D. (1996). A pilot intervention program that reduces psychological symptomatology in individuals with human immunodeficiency virus (HIV). *Complementary Therapies in Medicine, 4*(4), 226–232.

Selected References

Achterberg, J., Dossey, B., & Kolkmeier, L. (1994). *Rituals of healing: Using imagery for health and wellness.* New York: Bantam Books.

Admi, H. (1997). Nursing students' stress during the initial clinical experience. *Journal of Nursing Education, 36*(7), 323–327.

Black, J. M., & Matassarin-Jacobs, E. (2001). *Medical-surgical nursing: Clinical management for continuity of care* (6th ed.). Philadelphia, PA: Lippincott.

Bryla, C. M. (1996). The relationship between stress and the development of breast cancer: A literature review. *Oncology Nursing Forum, 23*(3), 441–448.

Burgess, A. W., & Lazare, A. (1976). *Community mental health: Target populations.* Englewood Cliffs, NJ: Prentice Hall.

Byrne, M. L., & Thompson, L. F. (1978). *Key concepts for the study and practice of nursing.* St. Louis, MO: Mosby. (Classic.)

Canadian Mental Health Association. (1998). *Statistics.* Retrieved February 11, 2001 from http://www.cmha.ab.ca/education/stts.htm

Canadian Nurses Association. (March, 2002). *Position statement on Violence*. Ottawa: Author.

Cannard, G. (1996). The effect of aromatherapy in promoting relaxation and stress reduction in a general hospital. *Complementary Therapies in Nursing & Midwifery, 2*(2), 38–40.

Carpenito, L. J. (2000). *Nursing diagnosis: Application to clinical practice* (8th ed.). Philadelphia, PA: Lippincott.

Caty, S., Ellerton, M. L., & Ritchie, J. (1997). Use of a projective technique to assess young children's appraisal and coping responses to a venipuncture. *Journal of the Society of Pediatric Nurses, 2*(2), 83–92.

Chitty, K. K. (1996). Clients with mood disorders. In H. S. Wilson, & C. R. Kneisl (1996). *Psychiatric nursing* (5th ed.). Menlo Park, CA: Addison-Wesley.

Dossey, B. M. (1997). Complementary and alternative therapies for our aging society. *Journal of Gerontological Nursing, 23*(9), 45–51.

Dossey, B. M., Keegan, L., Gizzetta, C. E., & Kolkmeier, L. G. (1995). *Holistic nursing: A handbook for practice* (2nd ed.). Gaithersburg, MD: Aspen.

Folkman, S., & Lazarus, R. S. (1991). Coping and emotion. In A. Monat, & R. S. Lazarus, *Stress and coping.* New York: Columbia University Press.

Folkman, S. (1997). Positive psychological states and coping with severe stress. *Social Science and Medicine, 45*, 1207–1221.

Fontaine, K. L. (2000). *Healing practices: Alternative therapies for nursing*. Upper Saddle River, NJ: Prentice Hall.

Fontaine, K. L., & Fletcher, J. S. (1999). *Essentials of mental health nursing* (4th ed.). Menlo Park, CA: Addison-Wesley.

Freud, S. (1946). *The ego and the mechanisms of defense.* New York: International Universities Press. (Classic.)

Gaudine, A. P. (2000). What do nurses mean by workload and work overload? *Canadian Journal of Nursing Leadership, 13*(2), 22–27.

Holmes, T. H., & Rahe, R. H. (1967, August). The social re-adjustment rating scale. *Journal of Psychomatic Research, 11*, 213–218.

International Council of Nurses. (1999). *Guidelines on coping with violence in the workplace*. Geneva: Author.

Johnson, M., & Maas, M. (Eds.) (2000). *Iowa outcomes project: Nursing outcomes classification (NOC).* St. Louis, MO: Mosby.

Keegan, L. (1994). *The nurse as healer.* Albany, NY: Delmar.

Keenan, J. (1996). The Japanese tea ceremony and stress management. *Holistic Nursing Practice, 10*(2), 30–37.

Krieger, D. (1979). *The therapeutic touch: How to use your hands to help or heal.* Englewood Cliffs, NJ: Prentice Hall.

LaForge, R. (1997). Mind–body fitness: Encouraging prospects for primary and secondary prevention. *Journal of Cardiovascular Nursing, 11*(3), 53–65.

Lazarus, R. S. (1966). *Psychological stress and the coping process.* New York: McGraw-Hill.

Lazarus, R. S., & Folkman, S. (1984). *Stress, appraisal, and coping.* New York: Springer.

LeMone, P., & Burke, K. M. (2000). *Medical-surgical nursing: Critical thinking in client care* (2nd ed.). Menlo Park, CA: Addison-Wesley.

McCain, N. L., Zeller, J. M., Cella, D. F., Urbanski, P. A., & Novak, R. M. (1996). The influence of stress management training in HIV disease. *Nursing Research, 45*(4), 246–253.

McCloskey, J. C., & Bulechek, G. M. (2000). *Nursing interventions classification* (3rd ed.). St. Louis: Mosby.

Monat, A., & Lazarus, R. S. (Eds.) (1991). *Stress and coping* (3rd ed.). New York: Columbia University Press.

Mulloney, S., & Wells-Federman, C. (1996). Therapeutic touch: A healing modality. *Journal of Cardiovascular Nursing, 10*, 27.

North American Nursing Diagnosis Association. (2001). *Nursing diagnoses: Definitions and classification 2001–2002.* Philadelphia, PA: Author.

Roth, B., & Creaser, T. (1997). Mindfulness meditation-based stress reduction: Experience with a bilingual inner-city program. *Nurse Practitioner: American Journal of Primary Health Care, 22*(3), 150, 152, 154.

Rowe, M. A. (1996). The impact of internal and external resources on functional outcomes in chronic illness. *Research in Nursing & Health, 19*(6), 484–497.

Rozman, D., Whitaker, R., Beckman, T., & Jones, D. (1996). A pilot intervention program that reduces psychological symptomatology in individuals with human immunodeficiency virus (HIV). *Complementary Therapies in Medicine, 4*(4), 226–232.

Schafer, W. (1992). *Stress management for wellness* (2nd ed.). Philadelphia, PA: Harcourt Brace Jovanovich.

Selye, H. (1956). *The stress of life.* New York: McGraw-Hill. (Classic.)

Selye, H. (1976). *The stress of life* (revised ed.). New York: McGraw-Hill. (Classic.)

Volicer, B. J., & Burns, M. W. (1975, September/October). A hospital stress rating scale. *Nursing Research*, *24*, 358.

Webb, C. (1996). Caring, curing, coping: Towards an integrated model. *Journal of Advanced Nursing*, *23*, 960–968.

Wilson, H. S., & Kneisl, C. R. (1996). *Psychiatric nursing* (5th ed.). Menlo Park, CA: Addison-Wesley.

WEBLINKS

Canadian Mental Health Association
www.cmha.ca
This Canadian Mental Health Association (CMHA) Web site contains educational information, links to multiple Canadian and international mental health sites, information regarding CMHA provincial locations, and a discussion site.

Health Canada
www.canadian-health-network.ca
This Web site is funded by Health Canada and contains information on multiple health issues on a variety of topics.

Centre for Addiction and Mental Health
www.camh.net
The Centre for Addiction and Mental Health site contains information on addictions, community health and education, mental health, and research at the centre.

CHAPTER 48

Loss, Grieving, and Death

OBJECTIVES

After completing this chapter, you will be able to:

- Describe types and sources of losses.
- Discuss the experience of grief as a response to loss that is individually experienced and expressed.
- Outline factors affecting grief responses.
- Identify measures that facilitate the journey of grief.
- List clinical signs of impending and actual death.
- Discuss the nurse's legal responsibilities regarding client death and such issues as advance directives and do-not-resuscitate orders.
- Describe guidelines for helping clients die with dignity.
- List nursing measures for care of the body after death.
- Analyze the role of the nurse in working with families or caregivers of dying clients.

Loss, grieving, and death are experienced by everyone at some time during their life. People may suffer the loss of valued relationships through life changes, such as moving from one city to another, separation, divorce, or the death of a parent, spouse, or friend. People may grieve changing life roles as they watch grown children leave home or when they retire from their lifelong work. The loss of valued material objects through theft or natural disaster can evoke feelings of grief and loss. When people's lives are affected by civil or national strife, they may grieve the loss of valued ideals, such as safety, freedom, and democracy.

In the clinical setting, the nurse encounters clients who may be experiencing grief related to declining health, loss of a body part, terminal illness, or the impending death of self or a significant other. The nurse may also work in community settings with clients who are grieving losses related to personal crises (e.g., divorce, separation) or natural disasters (earthquakes, floods, or hurricanes). Therefore, it is important that the nurse understand the significance of loss and develop the ability to assist clients in their experiences of grief.

Nurses may interact with dying clients and their families or caregivers in a variety of settings, from the demise of a fetus, to that of an adolescent victim of an accident, to that of an elderly client who finally succumbs to a chronic illness. Nurses must recognize the various influences on the dying process—legal, ethical, religious and spiritual, biological, and personal—and be prepared to provide sensitive, skilled, and supportive care to all those affected.

Loss and Grief

Loss is an actual or potential situation in which something that is valued is changed, no longer available, or gone. People can experience the loss of body image, a significant other, a sense of well-being, a job, personal possessions, beliefs, or a sense of self. Illness and hospitalization often produce losses.

Death is a fundamental loss, both for the dying person and for those who survive. Although death is inevitable, it is an experience that each person ultimately faces alone. Yet, death, like loss, can stimulate people to grow in their understanding of themselves and others. Death can be viewed not simply as loss of life but as the dying person's final opportunity to experience life in ways that bring meaning and fulfillment.

Types and Sources of Loss

There are two general types of loss, actual and perceived. Both losses can be anticipatory. An **actual loss** can be identified by others and can arise either in response to or in anticipation of a situation. For example, a woman whose husband is dying may experience actual loss in anticipation of his death. A **perceived loss** is experienced by one person but cannot be verified by others. Psychological losses are often perceived losses in that they are not directly verifiable. For example, a woman who leaves her employment to care for her children at home may perceive a loss of independence and freedom. An **anticipatory loss** is experienced before the loss actually occurs. Loss can be viewed as situational or developmental. The loss of one's job, the death of a child, or the loss of functional ability as a result of acute illness or injury, for example, are unexpected situational losses. Losses that occur in the process of normal development—such as the departure of grown children from the home, retirement from a career, and the death of aged parents—are developmental losses that can, to some extent, be anticipated and prepared for. How individuals deal with loss is closely related to their life stages and past experiences, personal and family resources, social support systems, and their beliefs about the loss itself.

There are many sources of loss: (1) loss of an aspect of oneself—a body part, a physiological function, or a psychological attribute, (2) loss of an object external to oneself, (3) separation from an accustomed environment, and (4) loss of a loved or valued person.

Aspect of Self

The loss of an aspect of self changes a person's body image, even though the loss may not be obvious to others. A face scarred from a burn is generally obvious to people; loss of part of the stomach or loss of ability to feel emotion may not be as obvious. The degree to which these losses affect a person largely depends on the integrity of the person's body image (part of self-concept). Any change that the person perceives as negative in the way the person relates to the environment can be considered a loss of self. It should be noted that self is a culturally influenced concept, and therefore, experiences of self-loss are particular to individuals and their particular cultural and personal influences.

Such losses as divorce can have a considerable impact. A divorce may mean loss of financial security, a home, daily routines, and one's role as spouse. Therefore, even when the divorce was desired, the sense of loss can be substantial.

During old age, changes occur in physical and mental capabilities. Again the self-image is vulnerable. Old age is when people usually experience many losses: of employment, of usual activities, of independence, of health, of friends, and of family.

External Objects

Loss of external objects includes (1) loss of inanimate objects that have importance to the person, such as the loss of money or the burning down of a family's house, and (2) loss of animate objects, such as pets that provide love and companionship.

Familiar Environment

Separation from an environment and people who provide security can result in a sense of loss. The six-year-old is likely to feel loss when first leaving the usual environment to attend school. The university student who moves away from home for the first time also experiences a sense of loss.

Loved Ones

The loss of a loved one or valued person through illness, separation, or death can, among other experiences, create suffering. In some illnesses, a person may undergo personality changes that make friends and family feel they have lost that person.

The death of a loved one is a permanent and complete loss. In primitive societies, death was considered a normal, natural event, and life was seldom long. In contemporary North American society, death is often denied. People may be uncomfortable talking about death and being around people who are dying. Sometimes, in an effort to escape the finality of death, there is a tendency to use extraordinary measures that prolong and preserve life.

The Experience of Grief

Grief has been explained as a process involving progression through a series of stages or phases requiring work or particular tasks that result in a final resolution of grief feelings (Cowles & Rodgers, 1991; Engel, 1964; Rando, 1984; Schneider, 1984; Worden, 1991). Out of this explanation, stage model theories, some of which are based on Kubler-Ross's (1969) work on death and dying, have provided one template for understanding the experience of grief. A critique of stage model theories is that although they may provide some understanding, recognition, and language for the experience of grief, they may also serve to obscure unique and individual experiences of grief (Moules, 1998). They can narrowly focus on psychological responses while overlooking social, spiritual, familial, and physical domains of the experience of grief. To understand grief as a staged experience can mistakenly invite the belief that grief occurs passively in expected sequences that disregard individual experiences and that fail to resonate with the experiences people actually undergo in grieving.

Martocchio (1985) discussed five clusters of grief, which exemplify common experiences in the grief response. These include shock and disbelief; yearning and protest; anguish, disorganization, and despair; identification in bereavement; and reorganization and restitution. Within these common experiences, however, there is no single correct way or timetable. Whether a person can successfully integrate the loss and how this is accomplished are related to that person's individual development and personal makeup. Individuals responding to the very same loss cannot be expected to follow the same pattern and schedule or reach the same outcome.

Another popularization of the experience of grief is that there is a normal grief reaction and an abnormal or unhealthy one. Grief that does not follow a predictable or expected course is often described as abnormal, complicated, pathological, unresolved, chronic, morbid, prolonged, dysfunctional, exaggerated, or disenfranchised. This pathologizing view of any divergence of expected and typical responses to loss can serve to intensify the suffering of grief, and add, in addition to the experience of loss, a sense of personal failure and incompetence (Moules, 1998).

Furthermore, socially sanctioned notions about grief invite the idea that the "work" of grief resolution is to find a way to let go of the person who is lost and to say goodbye. Alternatively, White (1989) and Moules (1998) suggested that when people lose a loved one, they continue to feel in relationship to the person, and although the relationship is necessarily changed and altered through physical absence, it continues in their emotional and spiritual life. Grief then becomes the process of learning how to live with this new and changed relationship in such a way that it offers aspects of connection and comfort, rather than pain and suffering. Grief is an unwanted visitor that arrives within the context of the experience of loss. It sweeps into every domain of one's life—biological, psychological, social, emotional, and spiritual. Grief endures in a way that shifts over time, eventually creating a mutable or changing and evolving, but, most often, a lifetime relationship with the loss. Unwanted or not, this visitor, grief, takes up residence in lives.

In nursing work with the bereaved, the challenge then is to co-evolve a way to assist people in making room for grief in their lives in ways that open space for other experiences than suffering and in inviting people to remember their lost other and say hello to a new and changed relationship (Moules, 1998).

Experiences of grief can become complicated and can have potentially devastating effects on health. Among the symptoms that can accompany grief are anxiety, depression, weight loss, difficulties in swallowing, vomiting, fatigue, headaches, dizziness, fainting, blurred vision, skin rashes, excessive sweating, menstrual disturbances, palpitations, chest pain, dyspnea, and infection. The bereaved may also experience alterations in libido, concentration, and patterns of eating, sleeping, activity, and communication.

Although bereavement can threaten health, there can be concurrent experiences within grief that can enrich the individual with new insights, values, challenges, openness, and sensitivity. For some, the pain of loss, though diminished, recurs for the rest of their lives. For some, the pain shifts into a continuing experience of remembrance, connection, and even celebration of a life well lived and loved.

A complication that can result from the intense experience of grief is a continuing experience of only sadness, loss, or even depression that is not relieved over time and is not buffered with other experiences of a return to life and joy. Another source of conflict might stem from a held belief that all people experience grief in a similar way. This belief might lead family members into expectations of each other that cannot be fulfilled and may invite a sense of alienation, isolation, or even conflict among those people who are expected to provide comfort and connection for each other. There is some suggestion in the literature that gender differences play out in a family's experience of grief and that men and women experience, express, and have differing expectations of themselves and each other in the experience of grief and loss (Attig, 1996; DeFrain, 1991; Hughes & Page-Lieberman, 1989; Moore, Gilliss, & Martinson, 1988; Moules, 1998; Parkes, 1988; Rosen, 1990; Shapiro, 1994).

Complicating an individual's experience of grief might be ambivalence, unresolved issues, or pre-existing conflict with the lost person; a pervasive and unrelenting sense of guilt or responsibility; past experiences of loss; and the type, timing, and context of the loss (Herz Brown, 1989). Certain kinds of losses that are not synchronous with life stage expectations, such as the loss of a child as opposed to an elderly parent, can (but do not necessarily) generate more intense experiences of grief (Cowles & Rodgers, 1991; Rolland, 1991) and have the potential for more complications in the experience.

RESEARCH NOTE

What Factors Account for Bereavement Outcome Among Spouses and Children of People Who Have Died from Cancer?

The family members of 115 adults who died from cancer in Australia were interviewed three times: six weeks, six months, and 13 months after the death. In addition to open-ended interviews, the spouse and available children also completed instruments that measured thoughts and feelings about the person who had died: depression, psychological symptoms, and social functions. The data were analyzed for correlations. The researchers found that the spouse's rating of "overall family coping" consistently correlated with grief intensity, psychological distress, depression, and social adjustment. That is, the better the family coping was viewed, the less was the grief, distress, and depression, and better adjustments were reported. The authors were able to classify families into five groups: supportive, conflict resolving, sullen, hostile, and intermediate. It is possible that the latter three groups are at greater risk for dysfunctional grieving and coping.

Implications: This research supports the importance of considering the functioning of the entire family when assessing the needs of dying clients and their significant others. It suggests that there are characteristics of families that may help identify them as being at higher risk for developing ineffective grieving and coping strategies.

Source: Kissane, D. W., Bloch, S., & McKenzie, D. P. (1997, May). Family coping and bereavement outcome. *Palliative Medicine, 11,* 191–201.

Factors Influencing the Loss and Grief Responses

A number of factors affect a person's response to a loss or death. These factors include age, significance of the loss, culture, spiritual beliefs, gender, socioeconomic status, support systems, and the cause of the loss or death. Nurses can learn general concepts about the influence of these factors on the grieving experience, but the constellation of these factors and their significance will vary from individual to individual.

Age

Age affects a person's understanding of and reaction to loss. With experience, people usually increase their understanding and acceptance of life, loss, and death.

People do not usually experience the loss of loved ones at regular intervals. As a result, preparation for these experiences is difficult. Coping with other losses in life, such as the loss of a pet, the loss of a friend, the loss of a job, and the loss of youth, can prepare people to anticipate the more severe loss of death.

Childhood Children differ from adults not only in their understanding of loss and death but also in how they are affected by the loss of others. The child's patterns progress rapidly; adult patterns of growth and development are generally stable. The loss of a parent or other significant person can threaten the child's ability to develop, and regression sometimes results. Assisting the child with the grief experience includes helping the child regain the normal continuity and pace of emotional development.

Some adults may assume that children do not have the same need as an adult to grieve the loss of others. In situations of crisis and loss, children are sometimes pushed aside or protected from the pain. They can feel afraid, abandoned, and lonely. Careful work with bereaved children is especially necessary because experiencing a loss in childhood can have serious effects later in life.

Early and Middle Adulthood As people grow, they come to experience loss as part of normal development. By middle age, for example, the loss of a parent through death seems a normal occurrence compared with the death of a younger person. Coping with the death of an aged parent has even been viewed as a necessary developmental task of the middle-aged adult.

The middle-aged adult can experience losses other than death. For example, losses resulting from impaired health or body function and losses of various role functions can be difficult for the middle-aged adult. How the middle-aged adult responds to such losses is influenced by previous experiences with loss, the person's sense of self-esteem, and the strength and availability of support.

Late Adulthood Losses experienced by older adults include loss of health, loss of mobility, loss of independence, and loss of work role. Limited income and the need to change one's living accommodations can also lead to feelings of loss and grieving.

For older adults, the loss through death of a longtime mate is profound. Although individuals differ in their ability to deal with such a loss, research suggests that health problems for widows and widowers increase during the first year following the death of the spouse (Richter, 1984). Because the majority of deaths occur among elderly people and because the number of elderly people is increasing in North America, nurses will need to be especially alert to the potential problems of older grieving adults.

Significance of the Loss

The significance of a loss depends on the perceptions of the individual experiencing the loss. One person may experience a great sense of loss over a divorce; another may find it only mildly disrupting. A number of factors affect the significance of the loss:

- Value placed on the lost person, object, or function
- Degree of change required because of the loss
- The person's beliefs and values

For older people who have already encountered many losses, an anticipated loss, such as their own death, may not be viewed as a highly negative loss, and they may be apathetic about it instead of reactive. More than fearing death, some may fear loss of control or becoming a burden.

Culture

Culture influences an individual's reaction to loss. How grief is expressed is often determined by the customs of the culture. In the United States and Canada, unless an extended family structure exists, grief is handled by the nuclear family. The death of a family member in a typical nuclear North American family leaves a great void because the same few individuals fill most of the roles. In cultures where several generations and extended family members either reside in the same household or are physically close, the impact of a family member's death may be softened because the roles of the deceased are quickly filled by other relatives.

Many North Americans appear to have adopted the belief that grief is a private matter to be endured internally. Therefore, feelings tend to be repressed and may remain unidentified. People who have been socialized to "be strong" and "make the best of the situation" may not express deep feelings or personal concerns when they experience a serious loss.

Some cultural groups value social support and the expression of loss. In some groups, the expression of grief through wailing, crying, physical prostration, and other outward demonstrations are acceptable and encouraged. Other groups may frown on this demonstration as a loss of control, favouring a quieter and more stoic expression of grief. In cultural groups where strong kinship ties are maintained, physical and emotional support and assistance are provided by family members.

Spiritual Beliefs

Spiritual beliefs and practices greatly influence both a person's reaction to loss and subsequent behaviour. Most religious groups have practices related to dying, and these are often important to the client and support people. For additional information, see Chapter 13. To provide support at a time of death, nurses need to understand the client's particular beliefs and practices. A part of one's spirituality is represented in, and influences, the way one makes meaning of the experience of loss. Asking questions of a spiritual nature is within the domain of nursing practice (Moules, 1999; Wright, 1997; 1999).

Gender

As mentioned earlier, the gender roles into which many people are socialized in the United States and Canada affect their reactions at times of loss. Men are frequently expected to "be strong" and show very little emotion during grieving, whereas it is acceptable for women to show grief by crying.

Gender roles also affect the significance of body image changes to clients. A man might consider his facial scar to be "macho," but a woman might consider hers ugly. Thus, the woman, but not the man, would see it as a loss.

Socioeconomic Status

The socioeconomic status of an individual often affects the support system available at the time of a loss. A pension plan or insurance, for example, can offer a widowed or disabled person a choice of ways to deal with a loss. A person who loses a hand and can no longer carry out work-related tasks may be able to pursue vocational re-education; a wealthy person whose spouse has died may decide to take a cruise or visit relatives in Europe. Conversely, a person who is confronted with both severe loss and economic hardship may not be able to cope with either.

Support System

The people closest to the grieving individual are often the first to recognize and provide needed emotional, physical, and functional assistance. However, because many people are uncomfortable or inexperienced in dealing with losses, the usual support people may instead withdraw from the grieving individual. Also, support may be available when the loss is first recognized, but as the support people return to their usual activities, the need for ongoing support may be unmet. Sometimes, the grieving individual is unable or unready to accept support when it is offered.

Cause of Loss or Death

Individual and societal views on the cause of a loss or death may significantly influence the grief response. Some diseases are considered "clean," such as cardiovascular disorders, and engender compassion, whereas others may be viewed as repulsive and less unfortunate. A loss or death that is beyond the control of those involved may be more acceptable than one that is preventable, such as a drunk driving accident. Injuries or deaths occurring during respected activities, such as "in the line of duty," are considered honourable, whereas those occurring during illicit activities may be considered the individual's just rewards.

Assessing

Nursing assessment of the client and family experiencing a loss includes three major components: (1) nursing history, (2) assessment of personal coping resources, and (3) physical assessment. During the routine health assessment of every client, the nurse poses questions regarding previous and current losses. The nature of the loss and the meaning of such losses to the client must be explored.

If there is a current or recent loss, greater detail is needed in the assessment. Because clients do not always associate physical ailments with emotional responses, such as grief, the nurse may need to probe to identify possible loss-related stresses. If the client reports significant losses, it is important to examine how the client usually copes with loss and what resources are available to assist the client in coping. Data regarding general health status; other personal stressors; cultural and spiritual traditions, rituals, and beliefs related to loss and grieving; and the person's support network will be needed in order to determine a plan of care (see the Assessment Interview box below). In assessing the client's response to a current loss, the nurse may identify complications of grief that may be best treated by a health-care professional who is expert in assisting such clients. If the nursing assessment reveals severe physical or psychological signs and symptoms, the client should be referred to an appropriate care provider. Such complications may include clinical depression, extensive social isolation and withdrawal, severe physiological symptoms, suicidal thoughts or urges, or unrelenting and oppressive sorrow that persists for prolonged periods of time and is not balanced by any relief or joy-filled experiences.

Implementing

The skills most relevant to situations of loss and grief are attentive listening, silence, open and closed questioning,

ASSESSMENT INTERVIEW

Loss and Grieving

Previous Losses

- Have you ever lost someone or something very important to you?
- Have you or your family ever moved your home?
- What was it like for you when you first started school? Moved away from home? Got a job? Retired?
- Are you physically able to do all the things you like to do? Used to do?
- Has anyone important or close to you died?
- Do you think there will be any losses in your life in the near future?

Previous Grieving

- Tell me about (the loss). What was losing ________ like for you?
- Did you have trouble sleeping? Eating? Concentrating?
- What kinds of things did you do to make yourself feel better when something like that happened?
- Are there spiritual or cultural practices you observed when you had a loss like that?
- Whom did you turn to if you were very upset about (the loss)?
- How long did it take you to feel more like yourself again and go back to your usual activities?

Current Loss

- What have you been told about (the loss)? Is there anything else you would like to know or do not understand?
- What changes do you think this (illness, surgery, problem) will cause in your life? What do you think it will be like without (the lost object)?
- Have you ever experienced a loss like this before?
- Can you think of anything good that might come out of this?
- What kind of help do you think you will need? Who is going to be helping you with this loss?
- Are there any people or organizations in your community that might be able to help?

Current Grieving

- Are you having trouble sleeping? Eating? Concentrating? Breathing?
- Do you have any pain or other new physical problems?
- Are you taking any drugs or medications to help you cope with this loss?
- What are you doing to help you deal with this loss?

Canadian Society Notes

Fact	Implications for Nursing Practice
The Canadian Hospice Palliative Care Association (CHPCA) is the recognized national organization for leadership in palliative care. The mission of CHPCA is to promote palliative care awareness, education, and research, advocating at a national level for policy development, resource allocation, and support for caregivers.	Nurses need to be aware of the policy papers on nursing care of the dying that have been accepted by each professional association, in accordance with CHPCA standards.
Each province and territory has a provincial palliative care association that is linked to the CHPCA.	Nurses interested in palliative care may want to consider membership in these associations.
The CNA Board of Directors has awarded palliative care the designation of specialty, making it the 12th discipline to become a specialty. Over the next two years, at least 60 palliative care nurses from across the country will be involved in the development of competencies and item writing for the certification examination. It is hoped that the first palliative care nursing certification examination will be offered in 2004.	This is a tremendous achievement for palliative care nursing in Canada, and it is expected that this initiative will lead to the enhancement of palliative care for all Canadians.

paraphrasing, clarifying and reflecting feelings, and summarizing. Less helpful to clients are responses that give advice and evaluation, those that interpret and analyze, and those that give unwarranted reassurance. The offering of platitudes is often a temptation to those trying to comfort someone who is suffering a loss. Though well intended and often arising out of a loss for words, such platitudes as "It must have happened for a reason; you need to accept it," "Time heals all wounds," "Try not to think about it," "You'll get over it in time," or "Now you've got a little angel in heaven" serve only to contribute to messages that a visible grief is unhealthy and that grief is time limited (Moules & Amundson, 1997). These messages deny the right and need of the bereaved to fully experience, acknowledge, and express grief as a part of incorporating loss into their lives. What the nurse says or does is always best guided by the client and in response to the client's needs. Sometimes, a simple statement of "I am sorry for your loss," or a silent presence is what is most needed. To ensure effective communication, the nurse must make an accurate assessment of what is appropriate for the client.

Communication with grieving clients needs to be relevant to meeting clients at the point of *their* needs, not the needs of the nurse. To determine the point of a client's need, the nurse has to be willing to listen to the client's pain and suffering and not be drawn to the temptation to try to take the pain away or heal it, even if such a thing were possible.

In addition to effective communication skills, there are specific ways that a nurse can support and care for a client experiencing loss. Of these, probably the most important is that the nurse "make room for grief" (Moules, 1998). By this, we mean that the nurse accepts, facilitates, and normalizes the experience and expression of grief. This can be done in several actions and attitudes portrayed by the nurse.

- Be present, be comfortable with silence, offer touch if the person indicates that would be comforting.
- Acknowledge pain and suffering.
- Encourage talking about the loss and the loved one, but accept if clients cannot or do not wish to do so.
- Explore and respect clients' racial, cultural, religious, personal, and family values in their expression of grief.
- Explore their support system and personal resources. Who is available to be with them? Who would be most helpful right now? Who can help them take care of practical arrangements and details?
- Assist clients/families in understanding that grief is expressed differently by different people and individuals cannot be expected to adhere to others' expectations of appropriate responses to grief.
- If children are involved, encourage family members to be truthful and to allow the child to participate in the grieving activities of others.
- Though maybe not at the time of the immediate loss, support clients in exploring the meaning they have made of their loss, how they have come to understand it or live with it, and how they have come to make room for a relationship with grief in their lives.
- Provide resource and support information, such as local grief support groups or counselling.

Nursing and Grief "To enter the world of one who is grieving, we must choose to listen to the pain behind the words" (Gibbons, 1993, p. 599). To nurse clients who are suffering with loss and who are experiencing grief is not a painless practice. It is, however, a vital part of nursing. As people, we are not immune to experiences of loss and grief. These experiences are inescapable in the human condition. As such, nurses play a fundamental and important role in helping people move through these experiences with grace, support, dignity, and kindness.

Gyulay (1989) suggested that grief is a journey that is often blurred and muddy. This journey is a journey of relationship—relationship with the lost person, with oneself, with remaining people, with health-care professionals, and ultimately with grief itself. People struggle to make sense of loss and search for ways to stay in a changed relationship with the lost person. They move through the volatile, changing, unpredictable experience of grieving, sorrowing, celebrating, and change. In this movement, people come to their own methods of finding a way to make room for grief in their lives. People feel grief when a loss is significant. Grief, then, in some regards, might be seen as the act and emotion of sorrowing and celebrating the space that was made for another in love. Nurses often have the privilege of walking alongside clients for a part of this journey of relationship, and they have an obligation to do it with integrity and human compassion.

Dying and Death

The concept of death is developed over time, as the person grows, experiences various losses, and reflects on concrete and abstract concepts. In general, humans move from a childhood belief in death as a temporary state, to adulthood in which death is accepted as very real but also very frightening, and to older adulthood in which death may be viewed as more desirable than living with a poor quality of life. Table 48.1 describes some of the specific beliefs common to different age groups. The nurse's knowledge of these developmental stages helps in understanding some of the client's responses to a life-threatening situation.

Responses to Dying and Death

Understanding responses to death and dying begin with the recognition that dying individuals exist within a family system. The nurse considers the impact of the dying individual's illness on the whole family and the family's responses that affect the patient. Caring for the dying individual's family involves understanding family in the broadest sense. Family may include spouses and children, or those the dying individual defines as a "significant other" who functions in supportive ways offering emotional, spiritual, and socioeconomic companionship and, possibly, intimate bonds (Gilliss, Highly, & Roberts, 1989).

TABLE 48.1 Development of the Concept of Death

Age	Beliefs/Attitudes
Infancy to 5 years	Does not understand concept of death
	Infant's sense of separation forms basis for later understanding of loss and death
	Believes death is reversible, a temporary departure, or sleep
	Emphasizes immobility and inactivity as attributes of death
5 to 9 years	Understands that death is final
	Believes own death can be avoided
	Associates death with aggression or violence
	Believes wishes or unrelated actions can be responsible for death
9 to 12 years	Understands death as the inevitable end of life
	Begins to understand own mortality, expressed as interest in afterlife or as fear of death
12 to 18 years	Fears a lingering death
	May fantasize that death can be defied, acting out defiance through reckless behaviours (e.g., dangerous driving, substance abuse)
	Seldom thinks about death, but views it in religious and philosophic terms
	May seem to reach "adult" perception of death but be emotionally unable to accept it
	May still hold concepts from previous developmental stages
18 to 45 years	Has attitude toward death influenced by religious and cultural beliefs
45 to 65 years	Accepts own mortality
	Encounters death of parents and some peers
	Experiences peaks of death anxiety
	Death anxiety diminishes with emotional well-being
65+ years	Fears prolonged illness
	Encounters death of family members and peers
	Sees death as having multiple meanings (e.g., freedom from pain, reunion with already deceased family members)

Both the client who is dying and the family members grieve as they recognize the loss. Nurses and other health-care professionals must strive to understand the meaning of the grief experience to the dying individual and the family. Grieving may include such emotions as fear, inability to focus, hopelessness without a sense of moving beyond the death, powerlessness, losing control over one's emotions, and feelings of despair and depression. There may also be many physical symptoms, including increased pulse and respirations, dry mouth, anorexia, difficulty sleeping, and nightmares. If meaningful care is to be provided to the dying individuals and their families, the nurse must understand their beliefs and values related to the experience, how the relationships fit together, and that many factors impact their experience of dying and illness.

Caregivers, both professionals and support people, also are impacted by the impending death. The ongoing responsibilities for providing physical, economic, psychological, and social support to a dying person can create extreme stress for the provider. Often, the length of time between a terminal diagnosis and when death will occur is unknown and the people supporting the dying person become fatigued, depressed, and feel empty. There may be anger due to loss of time and resources for personal activities or attention to other people. The impending death can pose a challenge to family roles and day-to-day functioning. In this situation, the family may be unable to meet the physical, emotional, or spiritual needs of the members and may have difficulty communicating and problem solving.

Nurses who have developed a close relationship with the dying individual and family may themselves experience a sense of loss and suffer with them as they care for them in the journey of dying (Raffin, 2002). Nurses who spend many hours, even days, with the dying individual and family "do not simply care for the dying individual's physical bodies, they also tend to their spirit, gently, respectfully, and knowingly" (Moules, 2000, p. 4). The very nature of palliative care nursing is such that, every day, practitioners face some of the most fundamental and poignant issues confronting humanity (Perry, 1998). Nurses are invited to share in the intimate journey of living and dying where suffering is present. This sharing often entails a commitment of developing a meaningful relationship as a way to know and understand the dying experience. The relationship, although rewarding, often places the nurse in a vulnerable position. Nurses are affected by this position (Raffin, 2001).

People in North America are socialized to think of death as the worst occurrence in life. They, therefore, do their best to avoid thinking or talking about death—especially their own. Nurses are not immune to such attitudes. They need to take time to analyze their own feelings about death before they can effectively help others with terminal illnesses. Nurses who are unconsciously uncomfortable with dying clients tend to impede the clients' attempts to discuss dying and death in these ways:

- Changing the subject (e.g., "Let's think of something more cheerful," or "You shouldn't say things like that")
- Offering false reassurance (e.g., "You are doing very well")
- Denying what is happening (e.g., "You don't really mean that," or "You're going to live until you're a hundred")
- Being fatalistic (e.g., "Everyone dies sooner or later")
- Blocking discussion (e.g., "I don't think things are really that bad"), conveying an attitude that stops further discussion of the subject
- Being aloof and distant or avoiding the client
- "Managing" the client's care and making the client feel increasingly dependent and powerless

Caring for the dying and the bereaved is one of the nurse's most complex and challenging responsibilities, bringing into play all the skills needed for care of the whole person—mind, body, and spirit. To care for the whole person, nurses must be aware of and comfortable with their own values and beliefs about death, dying, and suffering, as this will surely impact the care they are able to give others.

Legalities Related to Death

Many legal issues surround the event of death, including a legal definition as to when a person is considered clinically dead. Few jurisdictions in Canada or the United States provide a legislative definition of the moment of death. Historically, physicians, until well into the 20th century, concurred that a person was dead when all vital signs (pulse, respiration) have ceased. In the last half of the century, medical technology has allowed physicians to sustain the lives of seriously ill individuals by means of artificial support to sustain blood circulation. As well, the advances of medical transplant technology have made possible transplantation of viable organs from deceased individuals to living recipients.

It has become apparent that the traditional medical criteria for determining the fact of death have become inadequate. In 1975, the province of Manitoba became the first (and, so far, the only) province to enact a legal definition of death. The Manitoba Vital Statistics Act suggests that "the death of a person takes place at the time at which irreversible cessation of all that person's brain function occurs." This definition conforms to the accepted medical practice. With this definition, the client still may be able to breathe but is irreversibly unconscious. People who support this definition of death believe that the cerebral cortex—which holds the capacity for thought, voluntary action, and movement—*is* the individual.

Advance Directives (Living Wills)

Any individuals receiving health care may worry, in the event of becoming incapacitated and unable to express their wishes, that they will be "hooked up to machines" and receive treatment that they do not wish. Advance directives have been suggested as one way to address this problem. The Canadian Nurses Association (CNA, 1998b) and other sponsors produced a Joint Statement on Advance Directives for nurses' use in practice. Advance directives are "the means used to document and communicate a person's preferences regarding life-sustaining treatment in the event that they become incapable of expressing those wishes for themselves" (CNA, 1998b, p. 1). Advance directives are commonly expressed in two ways: an instruction directive, or living will, which identifies what life-sustaining treatment a person wishes in certain situations; or a proxy directive, which explains who is to make health-care decisions if the person becomes incompetent. A proxy directive is often referred to as a power of attorney for personal care (CNA, 1998b). A routine part of any admission to a hospital now includes inquiry about the client's advance directives; if they exist, they are included as part of the medical directives.

It has become necessary for nurses to be aware of the legal status of all types of advance directives in their province or territory. As outlined by the CNA (1998b), some provinces and territories only recognize proxy directives as legally binding, while others recognize both proxy and instructional directives. In addition, nurses need to become familiar with laws and documents regarding a person's competence to consent, issues regarding cardiopulmonary resuscitation (CPR), and issues at the end of life as these are closely related to advance directives (Figure 48.1).

Health-care professionals, including nurses, are responsible for ensuring that advance directives are addressed, not only as an admission duty, but rather as a part of the ongoing communication among all members providing and receiving care. A significant part of this process is to discuss and obtain a statement of the individual's personal values. This inquiry highlights the person's value system and beliefs about health, well-being, choice, and dignity. Identification of the person's values will enable the nurse to approach the hospital experience in a more holistic manner.

Euthanasia

The act of euthanasia can mean different things to different people. The word *euthanasia* comes from Greek words meaning "good death." The term is often used synonymously with the term "mercy killing," a concept that has drawn much controversy over the years. There are two forms of euthanasia: *active* and *passive*. These terms are meant to convey the difference between committing an act that causes death and omitting to take a life-sustaining act, allowing death to ensue.

The issue is an ethical one that remains unsettled. It revolves around two fundamental beliefs: the right of individuals to decide their own time and means of dying, and the equally strong argument that all measures must be tried before death is accepted as inevitable. Often, it becomes a matter of "to treat or not to treat."

A legal distinction, however, is made between acting and omitting to act. An action deliberately causing the death of another person is homicide, whereas omitting treatment when it is futile or refused is not. The withholding or withdrawing of treatments and the provision of compassionate palliative care, even when life is shortened, is considered to be good and ethical medical practice (Lowy, Sawyer, & Williams, 1993). A discussion between the physician and family members to determine when treatment should be stopped or withdrawn is ethical and common practice. Patients and family members may request that a dying individual not be subjected to resuscitative measures in the event of death, in which case the physician should write "do-not-resuscitate (DNR) order" in the patient's chart.

Individuals who argue against euthanasia base their reasoning on the principle of sanctity of life and on the traditional rules and laws prohibiting the taking of life except in situations of self-defence or war. Many are also concerned for the potential abuse of society if euthanasia were to become legal. They see the potential of this law "slipping" (slippery slope argument) to extend to such others as the chronically ill, the elderly, and the demented.

Those individuals who support euthanasia believe that there are situations in life where life is not worth living. They believe that competent individuals should be given the right to end their life when it is burdened with physical, emotional, and psychological pain that is no longer possible to eliminate. These individuals believe that sanctity of life is not an absolute principle and can be overridden out of respect for individual autonomy and for the dignity of human life.

Assisted suicide, on the other hand, means helping someone to commit suicide. It differs from euthanasia in that the person choosing to die takes the action that directly causes death, rather than having a second person commit the act. The *Criminal Code of Canada* (*CCC*) prohibits intentional killing, regardless of the person's consent or desires, and this also applies to assisted suicide. Section 14 of the *CCC* states that "no person can consent to have death inflicted on him." And, according to section 241 of the *CCC*, it is an offence to "aid a person to commit suicide, whether suicide ensues or not."

Do-Not-Resuscitate Orders

Technological advances have raised a number of troubling ethical dilemmas. These dilemmas are complicated by the following issues: health-care team conflicts, unresolved family issues, and the shortage of nurses and other resources.

Physicians may order "no code" or **"do not resuscitate" (DNR)** for clients who are in a stage of terminal, irreversible illness or expected death. A DNR order is generally written when the client or surrogate has expressed the wish for no

Personal Directive

I, ________________________________, of __________________, Alberta, do hereby: Appoint ________________________________, as my Agent; pursuant to the Personal Directives Act of Alberta. If (s)he predeceases me or is unavailable or unwilling to act, then I appoint ________________________________, to be my Alternate Agent. Any Agent appointed by me shall have full authority to interpret all personal and medical decisions, and the instructions below, even if they have no bearing upon the actual situation, should I be unable to make these decisions for myself.

Primary Agent	**Alternate Agent**
Agent's name: ____________________	Agent's name: ____________________
Agent's address: ____________________	Agent's address: ____________________
____________________	____________________
Home phone: ____________________	Home phone: ____________________
Work number: ____________________	Work number: ____________________

If at such a time the situation arises in which there is **no reasonable expectation of my recovery from severe physical or mental disability** to a state of meaningful interaction with loved ones, family and friends, I would like the following directions to be followed:

1. Measures of artificial life-support, in the above stated situation, that I refuse are:
   a. Cardiopulmonary resuscitation and admittance into an intensive care unit.
   b. Mechanical respiration when I cannot breathe by myself.
   c. Prolonged gastric tube or intravenous feeding when I an indefinitely unable to eat through my mouth.
   d. Antibiotic medication to treat or prevent infection.
   e. Other: ________________________________
2. I request to live my last days at home rather than a hospital, if my family agrees.
3. If any of my tissues or organs are healthy and useful for other people I give permission for all such donation, or as specified *during my life*:
4. I do wish to have medication mercifully administered to me in order to stop suffering even though this may shorten remaining life.

Dated at ____________________ in the Province of Alberta, this ________________ day of ________________, 20_______.

________________________________ ________________________________

WITNESS'S SIGNATURE **MAKER'S SIGNATURE**

Figure 48.1 Sample advanced directive appointing an agent and stating instructions

Source: The Alberta Health Ethics Network

resuscitation in the event of a respiratory or cardiac arrest. Many physicians are reluctant to write such an order if there is any conflict between the client and family members or among family members. A "supportive care only" order is written to indicate that the goal of treatment is a comfortable, dignified death and that further life-sustaining measures are not indicated.

The Canadian Association of Registered Nurses (CNA, 1995) developed a joint policy statement to provide guidance for developing policies on the appropriate use of CPR. The following guiding principles are integral to the development of the CPR policy:

1. Good health care requires open communication, discussion, and sensitivity to cultural and religious differences among caregivers, potential recipients of care, their family members, and significant others.
2. A person must be given sufficient information about the benefits, risks, and likely outcomes of all treatment options to enable him or her to make informed decisions.
3. A competent person has the right to refuse, or withdraw consent to, any clinically indicated treatment, including life-saving or life-sustaining treatment. Competence can be difficult to assess because it is not always a constant state. A person may be competent to make decisions regarding some aspects of life but not others; as well, competence can be intermittent; a person may be lucid and oriented at certain times of the day and not at others. The legal definition and assessment of competence are governed by the provinces or territories. Facilities should be aware of the laws (e.g., capacity to consent and age of consent) regarding the assessment and documentation of incompetence.
4. When a person is incompetent, treatment decisions must be based on his or her wishes, if these are known. The person's decision may be found in an advance directive or may have been communicated to the physician, other members of the health-care team, or other relevant people. In some jurisdictions, legislation specifically addresses the issue of decision making about medical treatment for incompetent people; the legislative requirements should be followed.
5. When an incompetent person's wishes are not known, treatment decisions must be based on the person's best interests, taking the following into account:
   i. The person's known values and preferences
   ii. Information received from those who are significant in the person's life and who could help in determining his or her best interests
   iii. Aspects of the person's culture and religion that would influence a treatment decision
   iv. The person's diagnosis and prognosis

   In some jurisdictions, legislation specifies who should be recognized as designated decision makers (proxies) for incompetent people; this legislation should be followed. The term "proxy" is used broadly to identify: (1) people who make a treatment decision based on the decision a person would have made for himself or herself (substitute decision maker), (2) people who help in determining what decision would be in the person's best interests, and (3) people who, under territorial/provincial legislation, are deemed an appropriate choice for making treatment decisions.
6. There is no obligation to offer a person futile or nonbeneficial treatment. Futile and nonbeneficial treatments are controversial concepts when applied to CPR. Policy makers should determine how these concepts should be interpreted in the policy on resuscitation, in light of the facility's mission, the values of the community it serves, and ethical and legal developments. For the purposes of this document and in the context of resuscitation, "futile" and "nonbeneficial" are understood as follows. In some situations, a physician can determine that a treatment is "medically" futile or nonbeneficial because it offers no reasonable hope of recovery or improvement or because the person is permanently unable to experience any benefit. In other cases, the utility and benefit of a treatment can only be determined with reference to the person's subjective judgement about his or her overall well-being. As a general rule, a person should be involved in determining futility in his or her case. In exceptional circumstances, such discussions may not be in the person's best interests. If the person is incompetent, the principles for decision making for incompetent people should be applied.

Health-care professionals should frequently revisit their policies regarding interventions such as CPR, especially in the context of a changing societal environment that recognizes the autonomy of the individual and encourages increased public discussion and participation in these issues. Decisions about CPR as an appropriate treatment option should be clearly identified on a patient's record to make sure that all the involved health-care professionals are aware of these decisions (CNA, 1995).

Death-Related Religious and Cultural Practices

Various cultural and religious traditions and practices associated with death, dying, and the grieving process help people cope with these experiences. Nurses are often present through the dying process and at the moment of death. Knowledge of the client's religious and cultural heritage helps nurses provide individualized care to clients and their families, even though they may not participate in the rituals associated with death.

Dying in solitude is generally unacceptable in most cultures. In many cultures, people prefer a peaceful death at home rather than in the hospital. Members of some ethnic groups may request that health-care professionals not reveal the prognosis to dying clients. They believe the person's last days should be free of worry and pain. People in other cultures prefer that a family member (preferably a male in some cultures) be told the diagnosis so that the client can be tactfully informed by a family member in gradual stages or not be told at all. Nurses also need to determine whom to call, and when, as the impending death draws near.

Beliefs and attitudes about death, its cause, and the soul also vary among cultures. Unnatural deaths, or "bad deaths," are sometimes distinguished from "good deaths." Also, the death of a person who has behaved well in life may be considered less threatening based on the belief that the person will be reincarnated into a good life.

Beliefs about preparation of the body, autopsy, organ donation, cremation, and prolonging life are closely allied to the person's religion. *Autopsy*, for example, may be prohibited, opposed, or discouraged by Eastern Orthodox religions, Muslims, Jehovah's Witnesses, and Orthodox Jews. Some religions prohibit the removal of body parts and dictate that all body parts be given appropriate burial. *Organ donation* is prohibited by Jehovah's Witnesses and Muslims, whereas Buddhists in North America consider it an act of mercy and encourage it. *Cremation* is discouraged, opposed, or prohibited by the Mormon, Eastern Orthodox, Islamic, and Jewish faiths. Hindus, in contrast, prefer cremation and cast the ashes in a holy river. *Prolongation of life* is generally encouraged; however, some religions, such as Christian Science, are unlikely to use medical means to prolong life, and the Jewish faith generally opposes prolonging life after irreversible brain damage. In hopeless illness, Buddhists may permit euthanasia.

Nurses also need to be knowledgeable about the client's death-related rituals, such as last rites and administration of Holy Communion, chanting at the bedside, and other rituals, such as special procedures for washing, dressing, positioning, and shrouding the dead. For example, certain cultures may wish to practise their native customs in which family members of the same sex wash and prepare the body for burial and cremation. Muslims also customarily turn the body toward Mecca. Nurses need to ask family members about their preference and verify who will carry out these activities. Burial clothes and other cultural or religious items are often important symbols for the funeral. For example, faithful Mormons are often dressed in their "temple clothes." Some Native Americans may be dressed in elaborate apparel and jewellery and wrapped in new blankets with money. The nurse must ensure that any ritual items present in the health-care agency be given to the family or to the funeral home.

Assessment During the Transition of Active Dying Through the process of coming to know the dying individual and family's beliefs, desires, and needs in the journey of dying, the nurse through continued conversation/assessment collects a complete patient/family history which includes physical, emotional, social, and spiritual dimensions. In this relationship, the nurse becomes aware of the living/dying transitions that the dying individual and family experience. Knowing the dying individual and family allows the nurse to respond in a way that best supports their state of awareness, beliefs, and values about the dying journey. Glaser and Strauss (1965) described four types of awareness of impending death: closed awareness, suspected awareness, mutual pretense, and open awareness.

In **closed awareness,** the dying individual, and perhaps the family, is unaware of impending death. They may not completely understand why the client is ill, and they believe the client will recover. The physician may believe it is best not to communicate a diagnosis or prognosis to the dying individual. Nurses are confronted with an ethical situation that they must work through. While the intention is to protect the dying individual, difficulties result for the family and the nurse. Families and patients do not have the opportunity to communicate openly and to freely express their feelings, share the burden of grief, and plan realistically for the future. Nurses in this situation express a feeling of ethical burden as they are not able to communicate openly and freely and potentially do not uphold moral values of veracity, or dignity.

In **suspected awareness,** dying individuals do not remain unaware for long. Their deteriorating state of health, changes in physical appearance, and altered behaviours of family members and health-care professionals lead to suspected awareness. The dying individual senses that the information given may not be the truth. Feeling like their trust has been undermined, they choose not to voice what they are sensing, and thus, communication becomes even more difficult.

With **mutual pretense,** the dying individual, family, and health-care personnel know that the prognosis is terminal but do not talk about it and make an effort not to raise the subject. Sometimes, the dying individual refrains from discussing death to protect the family from distress. The client may also sense discomfort on the part of health-care personnel and, therefore, does not bring up the subject. Mutual pretense permits the client a degree of privacy and dignity, but it places a heavy burden on the dying person who then has no one in whom to confide fears.

With **open awareness,** the dying individual and people around know about the impending death and feel comfortable discussing it, even though it is difficult. This awareness provides the client an opportunity to finalize affairs and even participate in planning funeral arrangements.

Not all people can handle open awareness. Some believe that terminal clients acquire knowledge of their condition

Signs of Impending Clinical Death

Loss of Muscle Tone

- Relaxation of the facial muscles (e.g., the jaw may sag)
- Difficulty speaking
- Difficulty swallowing and gradual loss of the gag reflex
- Decreased activity of the gastrointestinal tract, with subsequent nausea, accumulation of flatus, abdominal distention, and retention of feces, especially if narcotics or tranquilizers are being administered
- Possible urinary and rectal incontinence due to decreased sphincter control
- Diminished body movement

Slowing of the Circulation

- Diminished sensation
- Mottling and cyanosis of the extremities
- Cold skin, first in the feet and later in the hands, ears, and nose (the client, however, may feel warm because of elevated body temperature)
- Decelerated and weaker pulse
- Decreased blood pressure

Changes in Respirations

- Rapid, shallow, irregular, or abnormally slow respirations; Cheyne-Stokes respirations; noisy breathing, referred to as the *death rattle,* due to collection of mucus in the throat; mouth breathing, which leads to dry oral mucous membranes

Sensory Impairment

- Blurred vision
- Impaired sense of taste and smell

even if they are not directly informed. Others believe that many clients remain unaware of their condition until the end. It is difficult, however, to distinguish what clients know from what they are willing to accept.

Nursing care and support for the dying client and family include making an accurate assessment of the physiological signs of approaching death. In addition to signs related to the client's specific disease, certain other physical signs are indicative of impending death. The four main characteristic changes are loss of muscle tone, slowing of the circulation, changes in respirations, and sensory impairment. See the box above for indications of impending clinical death.

Various consciousness levels occur just before death. Some clients are alert, whereas others are drowsy, stuporous, or comatose. Hearing is thought to be the last sense that is lost.

ASSESSMENT GUIDELINES

The Dying Individual

Ask the spouse, partner, or significant others:

- Have you ever been close to someone who was dying?
- What have you been told about what may happen when death occurs?
- Do you have questions about what may happen at the time of death?
- Do you have questions about how we are caring for _______ during these last days?
- How do you think you would like to say goodbye?
- How are you taking care of yourself during these times?
- Who can you turn to for help at this time?
- Is there anyone you would like us to contact now or when death occurs?

As death approaches, the nurse assists the family and other significant people to prepare themselves. Depending, in part, upon knowledge of the person's state of awareness, the nurse asks questions that help identify ways the nurse can provide support during the period before and after death. In particular, the nurse needs to know what the family expects to happen when the person dies so accurate information can be given at the appropriate depth. See the box above for sample interview questions. When the family members know what to expect, they are better able to support the dying person and others who are grieving. In addition, they may be able to make certain decisions about events surrounding the death, such as whether they will want to view the body after death.

Planning a Peaceful Death Major desires of dying individuals are (1) maintaining physiological and psychological comfort, and (2) achieving a dignified and peaceful death, which includes maintaining personal control and accepting declining health status. When planning care with these clients, the Dying Person's Bill of Rights can be a useful guide (see the next box).

Examples of specific desired outcomes, although established in the planning phase, are provided in Table 48.4 entitled "Goals in Fostering a Peaceful Death" later in this chapter.

Examples of nursing interventions for the dying individual include the following:

- Helping individuals die with dignity
- Meeting physiological needs
- Providing spiritual support
- Supporting the family
- Providing postmortem care

The Dying Person's Bill of Rights

I have the right to be treated as a living human being until I die.

I have the right to maintain a sense of hopefulness, however changing its focus may be.

I have the right to be cared for by those who can maintain a sense of hopefulness, however changing this might be.

I have the right to express my feelings and emotions about my approaching death in my own way.

I have the right to participate in decisions concerning my care.

I have the right to expect continuing medical and nursing attention even though "cure" goals must be changed to "comfort" goals.

I have the right not to die alone.

I have the right to be free from pain.

I have the right to have my questions answered honestly.

I have the right not to be deceived.

I have the right to have help from and for my family in accepting my death.

I have the right to die in peace and dignity.

I have the right to retain my individuality and not be judged for my decisions which may be contrary to beliefs of others.

I have the right to discuss and enlarge my religious and/or spiritual experiences, whatever these may mean to others.

I have the right to expect that the sanctity of the human body will be respected after death.

I have the right to be cared for by caring, sensitive, knowledgeable people who will attempt to understand my needs and will be able to gain some satisfaction in helping me face my death.

Source: Barbus, A. J. (1975, January). The dying person's bill of rights, © 1975, American Journal of Nursing Company. Reprinted with permission from the *American Journal of Nursing, 75*, 99.

Planning for Home Care

A major factor in determining whether a person will die in a health-care facility or at home is the availability of willing and able caregivers. If the dying person wishes to be at home, and family or others can provide care to maintain symptom control, the nurse should facilitate a referral to hospice services. Hospice staff and nurses will then conduct a full assessment of the home and care providers' skills.

The major nursing responsibility for clients who are dying is to assist the individual to a peaceful death. More specific responsibilities are the following:

- To provide relief from loneliness, fear, and depression
- To maintain the client's sense of security, self-confidence, dignity, and self-worth
- To maintain hope
- To help the client accept losses
- To provide physical comfort

People facing death need help facing the fact that they will have to depend on others. Some dying clients require only minimal care and can be cared for at home; others need continuous attention and the services of a hospital and its staff. People need help, well in advance of death, in planning for the period of dependence. They need to consider what will happen and how and where they would like to die.

Helping Individuals Die with Dignity

Dignity may be defined as the ability to function as a significant and integrated person. True dignity comes from within. Generally, dependence on others and loss of control over oneself and interactions with the environment are associated with loss of dignity. Nurses need to ensure that the client is treated with dignity, that is, with honour and respect. Dying clients often feel they have lost control over their lives and over life itself. By introducing options available to the client and significant others, nurses can restore and support feelings of control. Some choices that individuals can make are the location of care (e.g., hospital, home, or hospice), times of appointments with health-care professionals, activity schedule, use of health-care resources, and times of visits from relatives and friends.

Most clients interviewed about dying indicate that they want to be able to manage the events preceding death so they can die peacefully. Nurses can help individuals to find meaning and completeness and to determine their own physical, psychological, and social priorities. Dying people often strive for self-fulfillment more than for self-preservation, and they need to find meaning in continuing to live while suffering. Part of the nurse's challenge, then, is to help maintain, day to day, the client's will and hope.

Often, nurses have difficulty discussing death with clients who are dying. Although it is natural for people to be uncomfortable discussing death, steps can be taken to make such discussions easier for both the nurse and the client. Callanan (1994) lists the following strategies:

- Identify personal feelings about death and how they may influence interactions with clients. Acknowledge personal fears about death, and discuss them with a friend or colleague.
- Focus on the client's needs. The client's fears and beliefs may be different from the nurse's. It is important that the nurse avoid imposing personal fears and beliefs on the client or family.

- Understand the client and how the client copes. Talk to the client or the family about how the client usually copes with stress. Clients will use their usual coping strategies for dealing with impending death. For example, if they are usually quiet and reflective, they will become quieter and more withdrawn when facing terminal illness.
- Establish a communication relationship that shows concern for and commitment to the client. Communication strategies that let the client know you are available to talk about death include the following:
  a. Describe what you see, for example, "You seem sad. Would you like to talk about what's happening to you?"
  b. Clarify your concern, for example, "I'd like to know better how you feel and how I may help you."
  c. Acknowledge the client's struggle, for example, "It must be difficult to feel so uncomfortable. I care about you and would like to help you be more comfortable."
  d. Provide a caring touch. Holding the client's hand or offering a comforting massage can encourage the client to verbalize feelings.
- Determine what the client knows about the illness and prognosis.
- Respond with honesty and directness to the client's questions about death.
- Make time to be available to the client to provide support, listen, and respond.

Hospice/Palliative Care

Hospice or palliative care has emerged as a specialized field only within the past 30 years (Billings, 1998). The term *hospice* has sometimes been used interchangeably with the term *palliative care*, but more recently, the terms have come to have different meanings (Vachon, 2001). In the United Kingdom, a hospice is a building where dying persons are cared for, but many of these individuals are discharged home and followed up by home care programs. In the United States, the term refers to a specific programmatic model for delivering palliative care. In Canada, hospices are often community-based, volunteer-driven programs providing care in the home or in a free-standing hospice (Vachon, 2001).

Regardless of location or type of program, hospice care is based on the principles of providing care to improve the dying individual's quality of life, rather than aim for cure. The care is patient and family centred, focusing on needs and concerns that are most important to them. A hallmark of palliative/hospice care since Cicely Saunders founded the modern hospice movement has been the combination of scientific rigour with personal concern. By opening the St. Christopher's Hospice, Saunders developed an education program for palliative care which embraced three broad areas: (1) the science and techniques of pain management and symptom control, (2) knowledge of psychosocial, social, and spiritual aspects of dying and grieving; (3) self-knowledge on the part of caregivers, especially related to personal beliefs about death and loss (Barnard, Boston, Towers, & Lambrinidou, 2000). Hospice/palliative care is always provided by a multidisciplinary team of primarily physicians, nurses, social workers, and chaplains.

Meeting Physiological Needs of the Dying Individual

The physiological needs of people who are dying are related to a slowing of body processes and to homeostatic imbalances. Interventions include providing personal hygiene measures; controlling pain; relieving respiratory difficulties; assisting with movement, nutrition, hydration, and elimination; and providing measures related to sensory changes. See also Table 48.2.

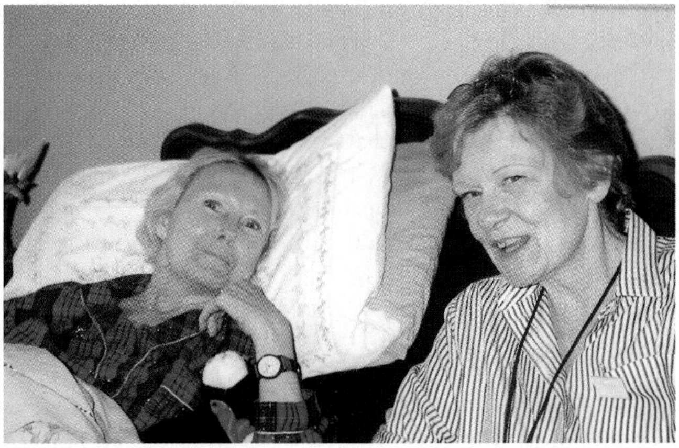

Figure 48.2 The patient/family are the "unit of care" in hospice palliative care

Figure 48.3 Hospice care is based on the principles of providing care to improve the dying individual's quality of life

TABLE 48.2 Physiological Needs of Dying Persons

Problem	Nursing Interventions
Ineffective airway clearance	30° Fowler's position: conscious clients Lateral, throat suctioning: conscious clients Sims', 30° lateral, and lateral position: unconscious clients
Self-care deficit: bathing/hygiene	Frequent baths and linen changes, if diaphoretic Mouth care, as needed, for dry mouth
Impaired physical mobility	Assist client out of bed periodically, if client is able Regularly change bedridden client's position Support client's position with pillows, blanket rolls, or towels, as needed Elevate client's legs when sitting up to prevent pooling of blood
Imbalanced nutrition: less than body requirements	Antiemetics or small amount of alcoholic beverage to stimulate appetite Encourage liquid foods, as tolerated
Constipation	Dietary fibre, as tolerated Laxatives, as needed, to prevent constipation
Impaired urinary elimination	Skin care in response to incontinence of urine or feces Bedpan, urinal, or commode chair within easy reach Call light within reach for assistance onto bedpan or commode Absorbent pads placed under incontinent client; linen changed as often as needed Catheterization, if necessary Keep room as clean and odour free as possible
Disturbed sensory perception: visual, tactile	Clients prefer a well-lit room Hearing is *not* diminished; speak clearly and do not whisper Touch is diminished, but client will feel pressure of touch

Sensory Perceptual Needs

Changes in the level of consciousness may be the first symptom, occurring over a period of weeks or days. Changes may include cloudiness of thought, drowsiness, stupor or unresponsiveness, coma, and, in some individuals, confusion or agitation. Consciousness is an integral aspect of being human; the ability to relate to others and the environment allows the individual an important sense of control. Even though individuals may have mentally accepted the fact that they are dying, the actual process of losing consciousness and the awareness of death may be a frightening experience. The fatigue and exhaustion of illness may prompt a wish of "falling asleep and not waking up." Others may struggle to continue to live and, thus, be very restless and unsettled until death. As the client's body slows down, the nurse must use the knowledge of normal physiological changes to prepare the client for death and lessen anxiety (see Table 48.3).

Pain Management

One of the greatest fears of dying individuals is that they will experience intense unbearable pain. In a study of cancer patients near the end of life, pain occurred in 54 percent and 34 percent at four weeks and one week prior to death, respectively (Coyle, Adelhardt, & Foley, 1990). In other studies of patients admitted to palliative care units, pain is often the dominant symptom along with fatigue and dyspnea (Jenkins, Taube, Ken, Hanson, & Bruera, 1998; Ng & von Gunten, 1998). Pain control is essential because pain alters sleep, appetite, mobility, energy levels, and psychological functioning. Barriers to good pain relief are numerous and pervasive. Often, due to lack of education, misconceptions, and attitudinal issues, these barriers prevent many individuals from receiving adequate pain relief (Parageon & Hailey, 1999).

Most nurses are educated in the observation and assessment of acute pain, which is very different from chronic pain. The dramatic signs and symptoms of acute pain warrant fast and immediate action. Outward signs of chronic pain are not as obvious and, therefore, may go untreated. Lack of expression does not mean lack of pain. Comprehensive assessment of pain is imperative. This must be conducted initially, regularly throughout treatment, and during any changes in the patient's experience of pain. Performing an

TABLE 48.3 State of Consciousness in Dying Patients

A. Consciousness: To be fully conscious is to be aware of one's self and the surrounding environment. There are two aspects:

1. *Content.* The sum of mental processes, including the ability to discriminate among both the sensory inputs and the internal cognitive aspects.

2. *Arousal.* A state of wakefulness or alertness to external and internal processes.

B. Clouding of Consciousness: Defined as a reduced state of wakefulness or awareness.

1. *Mild Clouding.* For the terminal patient, fatigue and periods of drowsiness are not uncommon. After a period of rest, the patient remains fully conscious. Several other features may not be observed or appreciated by caregivers in the early part of this phase. These features include the following:

- Excitability and irritability, which alternate with drowsiness
- Startled by minor stimuli
- Easily distracted
- Misjudges sensory perception, especially visual
- Cannot think clearly or quickly

These features may be intermittent and mistaken for anxiety.

2. *Advanced or subacute confusional state.* In this phase, the intensity and persistence of the symptoms is increased. The patient is "confused."

- Stimuli are more consistently misinterpreted.
- Attention span is shortened.
- The patient is bewildered and has difficulty following commands.
- There is some disorientation to time and sometimes to place and person.
- Memory is faulty.
- Drowsiness is often prominent (may alternate with nighttime agitation).

3. *Delirium.* The next "lower" level of consciousness is delirium. Although defined and used here in the classical sense, the term is not consistently used in all practice settings where care of the dying is provided. The word has a connotation of being "crazy" and is inappropriate in working with dying patients. The next phases are referred to as lower levels of consciousness.

Symptoms at this level include the following:

- Intensified disorientation
- Misinterpretation of stimuli; often visual hallucinations
- Lucid periods that often alternate with delirium
- Delusions
- Loud, talkative, offensive, suspicious, or agitated behaviour

4. *Stupor.* Stupor is defined as a state in which the patient is unresponsive but briefly arousable, only during vigorous and repeated stimuli, and then immediately drifts back to unresponsiveness.

In this stage, the patient may moan or be briefly restless when being turned or when given skin care. Staff need to ascertain whether this "moaning" is due to insufficient pain control or simply being partially roused from a deeper level.

This is not a "withdrawn" state in which the patient, lying in a fetal position, is conscious but does not respond to people. In this type of case, the patient will initially appear to be in a stupor but is, in fact, conscious and just not responding to family or caregivers. Management (and prognosis) of this state is very different from that for the truly stuporous patient.

5. *Coma.* This is the true comatose state, defined as complete unarousable unresponsiveness or "the absence of any psychologically understandable response to external stimuli or inner need."

This is exemplified in a patient who is breathing on his own but is totally unarousable by any physical stimulus, such as pinching, heat or cold, and yelling or sudden noise. There is no intake by the patient.

Source: Victoria Hospice Society, 1998.

individualized pain assessment is the first step to ensuring baseline data and continued treatment resulting in an improved quality of life for the dying individual.

Once the individual's pain has been assessed, a choice of analgesic medication to control the pain is selected (opioid or nonopioid analgesics). The World Health Organization (1990) recommends the use of an analgesic ladder to assist with analgesic selection. With chronic pain, analgesics are generally most effective if administered regularly (or around the clock) rather than on an as-needed basis. Frequently, when patients receive a regular dose of medication, pain may "break through" and require additional doses to keep it under control. Opioid or controlled narcotic substances are used for managing moderate to severe pain. For primarily historical reasons, morphine is the strong opioid of choice. Nonopioid medications are commonly used to ease pain and lower fever. They are generally used for managing mild to moderate pain. Medications for pain management are not limited to analgesics. Medications can include corticosteroids, antidepressants, anticonvulsants, and anxiolytics, determined by the type of pain assessed. Other than medications for the control of pain, there are therapeutic comfort measures performed by the nurse, such as helping the patient relax, providing music, giving warm soothing baths or a massage, providing distraction, and using peripheral nerve stimulators. (See Chapter 45.) The presence of the nurse to ensure support, conversation, and genuine concern is most important and assists in the process of reducing pain and promoting comfort.

Breathing Needs

Shortness of breath (dyspnea) is an uncomfortable awareness of breathing. Like pain, dyspnea is a subjective sensation involving both the perception of breathlessness and the individual's reaction to it. The prevalence of dyspnea varies according to the disease. Approximately 50 percent of the general outpatient cancer population experiences some breathlessness, with this number rising to 45 to 70 percent in the terminal phase of the disease (Dudgeon, Kristjanson, Sloan, & Lertzman, 1999; Fainsinger, MacEachern, Hanson, Miller, & Bruera, 1991).

Dyspnea, like pain, is multidimensional in nature, with not only physical symptoms but also affective components which are shaped by an individual's past experience with dyspnea. Dyspnea, like pain, may not always be evident to the observer. The nurse should inquire specifically about shortness of breath. Occasionally, dying individuals may have physical signs of tachypnea and appear to be in distress; however, they may not feel dyspneic or distressed. The opposite may also occur where individuals who are not tachypneic or in apparent respiratory distress may describe feeling very short of breath. The extent of breathlessness experienced by a patient may or may not be related to the oxygen saturation level. Therefore, the patient's own assessment of level of dyspnea may be a more reliable indicator than the oxygen saturation level. Dyspnea is, thus, a symptom that needs to be reported by the dying individual.

The nurse provides many comfort measures to help relieve, decrease the perception of, and comfort the experience of dyspnea, including (1) the administration of medications, such as opioids, bronchodilators, and diuretics, (2) creating a therapeutic environment where the individual engages in distraction therapy, relaxation exercises, is allowed to rest, or be with family, (3) assisting the individual to a position that makes breathing easier (usually a high sitting position is best), and offering a fan to reduce the perception of breathlessness, (4) offering fluids and using a humidifier to loosen mucus so coughing is easier, and (5) administering oxygen therapy by mask or nasal cannula. If hypoxic, maintain oxygen saturation above 90 percent. The nurse has to be cautious in offering oxygen to a patient with chronic obstructive pulmonary disease (COPD); in these individuals, oxygen saturation should be kept around 90 percent or as ordered by the physician (Pereira & Bruera, 1999). It is important that the nurse offer these interventions early in the experience of dyspnea to reduce anxiety and improve quality of life.

The importance of teaching the dying individual and family cannot be overlooked. Strategies to relieve the acute experience of dyspnea include (1) positioning and structured relaxation techniques, (2) signs and symptoms of an impending exacerbation, (3) techniques to conserve energy and prioritize activities, and (4) ways to maximize the effectiveness of taking medications, such as using a spacer with inhaled drugs and taking an additional dose of the medications prior to activity, as ordered.

Acknowledging and Strengthening Spirituality

Spirituality is an inherent, integrating, and, often, extremely valued dimension of the journey of dying for individuals and their families. Spiritual distress or "soul pain" is a common experience in those who are dying and, sometimes, an experience that is not addressed or understood. The experiences are complex, varied, and individual, and if left unaddressed, they may stifle the opportunity for growth, heighten the loss of a sense of meaning and purpose, and contribute to poorly controlled symptoms (Raffin, 2002).

Often, the experience of suffering prompts people, whether or not they see themselves to be religious, to ask deeply spiritual questions and turn to God or a spiritual guide for solace. Even in the case of those who are avowedly religious, suffering can lead to questioning of fundamental beliefs (Anderson, 1989). To appreciate individual responses to suffering, it is imperative that the nurse attempt to understand the religious/spiritual views of the sufferer.

The compassionate nurse, in a relationship with dying individuals who are suffering, creates space and time in which the nurse considers the dying individual's expression of spirituality. The nurse embraces the experience of the dying individual's loneliness, anxiety, the need to incorporate a transcendent dimension into one's life (faith or religion), the need for relatedness, and/or the need to search for meaning in suffering (Raffin, 2002). For many nurses, this begins with a self-exploration of spirituality that may or may not reveal an inner strength related to a belief in and a sense of interconnectedness with a greater being. Such an exploration brings the nurse face to face with existential questions, such as the inevitability and finality of death. Personal exploration often leads to a spiritual search for faith and/or other religious resources or questions (Raffin, 2002).

Spirituality delves into the nature of humanity and the deep mysteries of life. Spirituality, as related to nurses in a relationship with dying individuals, encompasses values, meaning, and purpose; turning inward to the human traits of honesty, love, caring, wisdom, and compassion; helping others to search for a higher authority, guiding spirit, or transcendence that is mystical; and helping create healing of body, mind, and spirit that may or may not

ping others find
an open inter-
to be divine or

oose their own
to respond to
ckground and
ortant in help-
oing a sense of

ating expres-
, and discus-
adviser. It is
e interdisci-
ecialists. For
Chapter 13.
d groups are

during the
ligation to
client but
eir wishes,
important
than have
members
profound
experience of watching a loved one die.

The most important thing a nurse can do to care for family members is to acknowledge them and include them. If the nurse shifts her thinking from considering the dying individual as the client to accepting the entire family as the client, then care becomes focused on the very significant event that is happening not just to the person but to the entire family system. Acknowledging family members includes consulting the family in terms of care of client and honouring their wisdom and knowledge of the dying individual. It involves a collaborative evolution of ways in which the family needs to be involved and ways in which they prefer the nurse to assume care. For example, some family members want to be involved in physical care, whereas other family members are more comfortable with the nurse assuming these caring practices. It is important, in asking the family members' preferences, to not imply that the nurse has an expectation that they assume these acts, but rather that the nurse respects the members' level of comfort. One way to approach this delicate establishment of roles and involvement would be to say to the family: "Sometimes family members like to be involved in the physical care of their ill members, other times they prefer the nurse to assume these things. What would be most comfortable for you in this area?" At times, family members want other kinds of involvement, rather than physical care, but are unsure of how to offer this. The nurse can help guide family members in knowing that it may be soothing to dying individuals to speak to them, read to them, hold their hands, or simply be present.

A part of what a nurse offers a family is a caring and compassionate presence. Compassion is defined as "suffering with." Though the nurse is not suffering as the family is, the nurse has in some ways entered the world of the family's suffering. "In entering the world of the one who is suffering, we do have to open space to where we listen to the pain, where we see, touch, and feel the pain" (Moules, 1999). Nurses create a context where family members feel as though they can be open about their pain, suffering, and grief. Nurses can offer information about the process of what is occurring and thereby walk alongside the family in understanding this experience.

When the individual dies, family members should be invited to spend time with the body as this important ritual can serve as a significant event in making room for grief and grieving. Some people ask for mementos, such as locks of hair or other bodily reminders. Children should not be discouraged from being involved in this important ritual of viewing the body, and at times, nurses may offer encouragement or even permission to families that it is appropriate to include children. Family members may have specific desires to participate in some care of the body, as in the case of a mother who asked to bathe her child one last time and dress him in special clothes. The nurse, in this instance, helped prepare clean towels and a basin for the mother, showing sensitivity in commenting that the water needed to be warmer, and then returning with warm water. The mother later reported that this simple act of kindness was of great comfort to her. In a health-care system that is often pushed for beds, the nurse may, at times, need to act as an advocate for families to ensure that they have all the time they need to spend with the body to begin saying goodbye to the physical presence of this person in their lives.

Postmortem Care

Rigor mortis is the stiffening of the body that occurs abut two to four hours after death. It results from a lack of adenosine triphosphate (ATP), which is not synthesized because of a lack of glycogen in the body. ATP is necessary for muscle fibre relaxation. Its lack causes the muscles to contract, which, in turn, immobilizes the joints. Rigor mortis starts in the involuntary muscles (heart, bladder, and so on), then progresses to the head, neck, and trunk, and finally reaches the extremities.

Because the deceased person's family often wants to view the body and because it is important that the deceased appear natural and comfortable, nurses need to position the body, place dentures in the mouth, and close the eyes and mouth *before* rigor mortis sets in. Rigor mortis usually leaves the body about 96 hours after death.

Algor mortis is the gradual decrease of the body's temperature after death. When blood circulation terminates and the hypothalamus ceases to function, body temperature falls about 1°C per hour until it reaches room temperature. Simultaneously, the skin loses its elasticity and can easily be broken when removing dressings and adhesive tape.

After blood circulation has ceased, the red blood cells break down, releasing hemoglobin, which discolours the surrounding tissues. This discolouration, referred to as **livor mortis,** appears in the lowermost or dependent areas of the body.

Tissues after death become soft and eventually liquefied by bacterial fermentation. The hotter the temperature, the more rapid the change. Therefore, bodies are often stored in cool places to delay this process. Embalming prevents the process through injection of chemicals into the body to destroy the bacteria.

Nursing personnel may be responsible for care of a body after death. Postmortem care should be carried out according to the policy of the hospital or agency. Because care of the body may be influenced by religious law, the nurse should check the client's religion and make every attempt to comply. If the deceased's family or friends wish to view the body, it is important to make the environment as clean and pleasant as possible and to make the body appear natural and comfortable. All equipment, soiled linen, and supplies should be removed from the bedside. Some agencies require that all tubes in the body remain in place; in other agencies, tubes may be cut to within 2.5 cm of the skin and taped in place; in others, all tubes may be removed. Legal issues surrounding the death (e.g., coroner's case) may necessitate that all tubes remain in place.

Normally, the body is placed in a supine position with the arms either at the sides, palms down, or across the abdomen. One pillow is placed under the head and shoulders to prevent blood from discolouring the face by settling in it. The eyelids are closed and held in place for a few seconds so they remain closed. Dentures are usually inserted to help give the face a natural appearance. The mouth is then closed.

Soiled areas of the body are washed; however, a complete bath is not necessary because the body will be washed by the **mortician** (also referred to as an **undertaker**), a person trained in care of the dead. Absorbent pads are placed under the buttocks to take up any feces and urine released because of relaxation of the sphincter muscles. A clean gown is placed on the client, and the hair is brushed and combed. The top bed linens are adjusted neatly to cover the client to the shoulders. Soft lighting and chairs are provided for the family.

In the hospital, after the body has been viewed by the family, additional identification tags are applied. The body is wrapped in a **shroud,** a large piece of plastic or cotton material used to enclose a body after death. Identification is then applied to the outside of the shroud. The body is taken to the morgue if arrangements have not been made to have a mortician pick it up from the client's room.

FOCUS ON CRITICAL THINKING

Mrs. Govinda was a 75-year-old female who was admitted to the hospital after repeated episodes of pneumonia. Despite aggressive antibiotic therapy, Mrs. Govinda's condition rapidly deteriorated and she died unexpectedly one week after being admitted to the hospital. Mrs. Govinda's oldest son, who lived nearby and frequently cared for his mother, made arrangements for the funeral and visited with relatives. He misses his mother and cries occasionally, but he managed to return to work the following week. The youngest son had difficulty attending the funeral, has been unable to sleep or eat, cannot concentrate at work, and cannot believe that his mother is dead. The middle son did not weep at the funeral and had little to say to his brothers or other relatives. He returned home to another province and has remained distant. He is back at work but feels very fatigued and apathetic.

1. From the data provided, describe the phase of bereavement being experienced by each of the three sons.
2. What factors may have affected how each of the brothers reacted to the death of their mother?
3. What cues, other than physical signs, might have indicated that Mrs. Govinda was dying even though her death was unexpected?
4. What is the primary factor to consider when trying to make the decision to administer or withhold pain medication when a client is dying?
5. Explore your own feelings about death, and consider how those feelings may affect the care you provide to the dying client.

See Appendix A for answers to these questions.

Evaluating the Process of Care To evaluate the achievement of client goals, the nurse collects data in accordance with the desired outcomes established in the planning phase. Evaluation activities may include the following:

- Listening to the client's reports of feeling in control of the environment surrounding death, such as control over pain relief, visitation of family and support people, or treatment plans
- Observing the client's relationship with significant others
- Listening to the client's thoughts and feelings related to hopelessness or powerlessness

Examples of desired outcomes are shown in Table 48.4.

TABLE 48.4 Goals in Fostering a Peaceful Death

Goal	Examples of Desired Outcomes
Maintain personal control over present situation	Identifies areas of personal control
	Participates in self-care activities in accordance with health status
	Makes choices related to care and treatment
	Expresses sense of control over the present situation
Maintain comfort	Maintains physiological comfort
	Maintains psychological comfort
	Skin and oral tissues hydrated
	Absence of constipation or urinary retention
	Absence of restlessness
Accept declining health status	Shares values and personal meaning of life
	Verbalizes acceptance of situation
	Accepts limitations and seeks help, as needed

CHAPTER HIGHLIGHTS

- Nurses help clients deal with all kinds of losses, including loss of body image, loss of a loved one, loss of a sense of well-being, and loss of a job.
- Loss, especially loss of a loved one or a valued body part, can be viewed as either a situational or a developmental loss and either an actual or a perceived loss (both of which can be anticipatory).
- Grieving is a normal, subjective emotional response to loss; it is essential for mental and physical health. Grieving allows the bereaved person to cope with loss gradually and to accept it as part of reality.
- Knowledge of different stages or phases of grieving and factors that influence the loss reaction can help the nurse understand the responses and needs of clients.
- How an individual deals with loss is closely related to the individual's stage of development, personal resources, and social support system.
- Caring for the dying and the bereaved is one of the nurse's most complex and challenging responsibilities.
- Nurses' attitudes about death and dying directly affect their ability to provide care.
- Nurses must consider the entire family as requiring care in situations involving loss, especially death.
- Nurses must be knowledgeable about their responsibilities in regard to legal issues surrounding death: advance directives, euthanasia, and do-not-resuscitate orders.
- Dying clients require open communication, physical help, and emotional and spiritual support to ensure a peaceful and dignified death. They need to maintain a sense of control in managing the events preceding death.

READINGS AND REFERENCES

Suggested Readings

Canadian Nurses Association, Canadian Medical Association, Canadian Health Care Association, Catholic Health Association of Canada, Canadian Bar Association. (1995). *Joint statement on resuscitative interventions*. Ottawa: Authors.

Canadian Nurses Association. (1998b). *Advance directives: The nurse's role*. Ottawa: CNA.
The Canadian Nurses Association (CNA), as part of its mandate to address ethical issues affecting the practice of registered nurses, has prepared this joint statement in collaboration with other national health-related organizations. In considering the range of issues related to end-of-life treatment, the CNA recommends that policy development be guided by this Joint Statement on Resuscitative Interventions and by the Joint Statement on Advance Directives (1994). Technological advance has raised a number of troubling ethical dilemmas. The principles identified in these documents form the basis of decision making about bioethical issues and will be helpful as facilities review their cardiopulmonary resuscitation policies.

Johns, J. L. (1996). Advance directives and opportunities for nurses. *Image: Journal of Nursing Scholarship, 29*, 149–153.
The author reviewed the literature describing the role nurses have taken in the processes of advance directives. Both positive and negative outcomes of the process are described. Positive outcomes include increased discussions with clients regarding end-of-life decisions and greater ability to comply with clients' preferences. Negative outcomes involve the possible misinterpretation of advance directives as indicating that less care should be provided to the client who elects do-not-resuscitate status. Johns found few research studies on the effectiveness of advance directives and proposes a variety of potentially fruitful research questions.

Northcott, H., & Wilson, D. (2001). *Dying and death in Canada*. Aurora: Garamond Press.
This book focuses on Canada and Canadian work in the area of dying and death. The book is written for students who wish to learn about dying and death, for practitioners who work with the dying, and for the dying and bereaved themselves as well as the general public. The book explores the causes of deaths in Canada both historically and at present. It also examines the societal and cultural responses to death and dying. Most importantly, the book includes personal points of view of the dying and the bereaved.

Schut, H. A., Stroebe, M. S., van den Bout, J., & de Keijser, J. (1997, February). Intervention for the bereaved: Gender differences in the efficacy of two counselling programs. *British Journal of Clinical Psychology, 36*, 63–72.
The research found that widows benefited most from problem-focused interventions and widowers benefited most from emotion-focused interventions.

Related Research

Kissane, D. W., Bloch, S., & McKenzie, D. P. (1997, May). Family coping and bereavement outcome. *Palliative Medicine, 11*, 191–201.

Selected References

Anderson, E. G. (1997, September). Grief recovery: Helping those who've had to say goodbye. *Geriatrics, 52*, 103–104.
Anderson, H. (1989). After the diagnosis: An operational theology for the terminally ill. *Journal of Pastoral Care, 43*, 141–150.
Attig, T. (1996). *How we grieve: Relearning the world*. New York: Oxford University Press.
Barnard, D., Towers, A., Boston, P., & Lambrinidou, Y. (2000). *Crossing over: Narratives of palliative care*. New York: Oxford University Press.
Billings, J. (1998). What is palliative care? *Journal Of Palliative Medicine, 1*(1), 73–81.
Brent, N. J. (1997). *Nurses and the law*. Philadelphia, PA: Saunders.
Callanan, M. (1994, January). Dealing with death: Breaking the silence. *American Journal of Nursing, 94*, 22–23.
Canadian Medical Association. (1992). Advance directives for resuscitation and other life-saving sustaining measures. *Canadian Medical Association Journal, 146*, 1072A.
Canadian Nurses Association. (1998b). *Advance directives: The nurse's role*. Ottawa: CNA.
Coyle, N., Adelhardt, J., & Foley, K., et al. (1990). Character of terminal illness in the advanced cancer patient: Pain and other symptoms during the last four weeks of life. *Journal of Pain and Symptom Management, 5*, 83–93.
Cowles, K.V., & Rodgers, B.L. (1991). The concept of grief: A foundation for nursing research and practice. *Research in Nursing & Health, 14*(2), 119–127.
Czerwiec, M. (1996, May). When a loved one is dying: Families talk about nursing care. *American Journal of Nursing, 96*, 32–36.
DeFrain, J. (1991). Learning about grief from normal families: SIDS, stillbirth, and miscarriage. *Journal of Marital and Family Therapy, 17*(3), 215–232.
De Raeve, L. (1996, April/June). Dignity and integrity at the end of life. *International Journal of Palliative Nursing, 2*, 71–76.
Dudgeon, D., Kristjanson, L., Sloan, J., & Lertzman, M. (2001). Dyspnea in cancer patients: Prevalence and associated factors. *Journal of Pain and Symptom Management, 21*(2), 95–102.
Duffield, P. (1998, April). Advance directives in primary care (Nurse Practitioner Extra). *American Journal of Nursing, 98*, (4), 16CCC–16DDD.
Engel, G. L. (1964). Grief and grieving. *American Journal of Nursing, 64*, 93–98.
Esposito, L., Buckalew, P., & Chukunta, T. (1996, June). Cultural diversity in grief. *Home Health Care Management and Practice, 8*, 23–29.
Evans, M. (1996, July/September). Teenagers and loss. *International Journal of Palliative Nursing, 2*, 126–130.
Fainsinger, R., MacEachern, T., Hanson, J., Miller, M., & Bruera, E. (1991). Symptom control during the last week of life on a palliative care unit. *Journal of Palliative Care, 7*, 5–11.
Faulkner, K. W. (1997, June). Talking about death with a dying child. *American Journal of Nursing, 97*, 64, 66, 68–69.
Gates, M. F., Schins, I., & Smith, A. S. (1996). Applying advance directives regulations in home care agencies. *Home Healthcare Nurse, 14*, 127–133.
Gibbons, M. B. (1993). Listening to the lived experience of loss. *Pediatric Nursing, 19*(6), 597–599.

Gilliss, C., Highly, B., & Roberts, B. (1989). *Toward a science of family nursing*. Menlo Park, CA: Addison-Wesley Publishing Co.

Glaser, B., & Strauss, A. (1965). *Awareness of dying*. Chicago, IL: Aldine.

Green, D. B. (1997, January). How to deliver tragic news with compassion. *Nursing 97, 27*, 64.

Gyulay, J. (1989). Grief responses. *Issues in Comprehensive Pediatric Nursing, 12*(1), 1–31.

Haisfield-Wolfe, M. E. (1996, July). End-of-life care: Evolution of the nurse's role. *Oncology Nursing Forum, 23*, 931–935.

Hawley, R. (1997, February). Seasons of grief. *Nursing Times, 93*, 24–26.

Herz Brown, F. (1989). The impact of death and serious illness on the family life cycle. In B. Carter & M. McGoldrick (Eds.), *The changing family life cycle* (2nd ed.). (pp. 457–482). Needham Heights, MA: Allyn & Bacon.

Horowitz, M. J., Siegel, G., Holen, A., Bonanno, G. A., Milbrath, C., & Stinson, C. J. (1997, July). Diagnostic criteria for complicated grief disorder. *American Journal of Psychiatry, 154*, 904–910.

Hughes, C. B., & Page-Leiberman, J. (1989). Fathers experiencing a perinatal loss. *Death Studies, 13*, 537–556.

Jenkins, C., Taube, A., Ken, T., Hanson, J., & Bruera, E. (1998). Initial demographic, symptom, and medication profiles in patients admitted to palliative care units. *Journal of Pain and Symptom Management, 16*, 163–170.

Johns, J. L. (1996, Summer). Advance directives and opportunities for nurses. *Image: Journal of Nursing Scholarship, 28*, 149–153.

Johnson, M., & Maas, M. (Eds.) (2000). *Iowa outcomes project: Nursing outcomes classification (NOC)*. St. Louis, MO: Mosby.

Krigger, K. W., Lippman, S. B., & McNeely, J. D. (1997, March). Dying, death, and grief: Helping patients and their families. *Postgraduate Medicine, 101*, 263–270.

Kowalski, S. D. (1996). Assisted suicide: Is there a future? Ethical and nursing considerations. *Critical Care Nursing Quarterly, 19*(1), 45–54.

Kübler-Ross, E. (1969). *On death and dying*. New York: Macmillan. (Classic.)

Lowy, F., Sawyer, D., Williams, J. (1993). *Canadian physicians and euthanasia*. Ottawa: Canadian Medical Association.

Martocchio, B. C. (1985, June). Grief and bereavement: Healing through hurt. *Nursing Clinics of North America, 20*, 327–341.

Matzo, M. L. (1996, March). Oncology nurses' experiences and actions in response to requests for assisted suicide and euthanasia. *Oncology Nursing Forum, 23*, 348.

McIntyre, M. R. (1997). Understanding living with dying. *Canadian Nurse, 93*, 19–25.

Moore, I. M., Gilliss, C. L., & Martinson, I. (1988). Psychosomatic symptoms in parents two years after the death of a child with cancer. *Nursing Research, 37*, 101–107.

Moules, N. J. (1998). Legitimizing grief: Challenging beliefs that constrain. *Journal of Family Nursing, 4*(2), 142–166.

Moules, N. J. (1999). Suffering together: Whose words were they? *Journal of Family Nursing, 5*(3), 251–258.

Moules, N. J. (2000). Postmodernism and the sacred: Reclaiming connection in our greater-than-human worlds. *Journal of Marital and Family Therapy, 26*(2), 229–240.

Moules, N. J. (2000). Funerals, families and family nursing: Lessons of love and practice. *Journal of Family Nursing, 6*(1), 3–8.

Moules, N. J., & Amundson, J. K. (1997). Grief—An invitation to inertia: A narrative approach to working with grief. *Journal of Family Nursing, 3*(4), 378–393.

Ng, K., & von Gunten, C. (1998). Symptoms and attitudes of 100 consecutive patients admitted to an acute hospice/palliative care unit. *Journal of Pain and Symptom Management, 16*, 307–316.

Nishimoto, P. (1996, July). Venturing into the unknown: Cultural beliefs about death and dying. *Oncology Nursing Forum, 23*(6), 889–894.

North American Nursing Diagnosis Association. (2001). *Nursing diagnoses: Definitions and classification 1999–2000*. Philadelphia, PA: Author.

Parageon, K., & Hailey, B. (1999). Barriers to effective cancer pain management: A review of the literature. *Journal of Pain and Symptom Management, 18*, 358–368.

Parkes, C. M. (1988). Research: Bereavement. *Omega: Journal of Death and Dying, 18*, 365–377.

Perry, B. (1998). *Moments in time: Images of exemplary nursing care*. Ottawa: Canadian Nurses Association.

Peuriera, J., & Bruera, E. (1999). *Palliative care resource book*. Edmonton: Author.

Plum, F., & Posner, J. (1980). *The diagnosis of stupor and coma*. (3rd ed.). Philadelphia, PA: F.A. Davis.

Provincial Health Ethics Network. (1997). *Sample directive of appointing an agent and stating instructions*. Edmonton, Alberta: Author.

Raffin, S. (2002). *Accompanying the dying: Nurses create a moral space for suffering*. Unpublished doctoral dissertation, University of Alberta, Edmonton, Alberta, Canada.

Rando, T. A. (1984). *Grief, dying, and death*. Champaign, IL: Research.

Reese, C. D. (1996). Please cry with me: Six ways to grieve. *Nursing 96, 26*, 56.

Richter, J. M. (1984, July). Crisis of mate loss in the elderly. *American Nursing Society, 6*(4), 45–54.

Rolland, J. S. (1991). Helping families with anticipatory loss. In F. Walsh & M. McGoldrick (Eds.), *Living beyond loss: Death in the family* (pp. 144–163). New York: Norton.

Rosen, E. J. (1990). *Families facing death: Family dynamics of terminal illness*. Boston, MA: Lexington Books.

Ross, M. M. (1998, September). Palliative care. An integral part of life's end. *Canadian Nurse, 94*(9), 28–31.

Sabatino, C. O. (1993, January/February). Surely the wizard will help us, Toto? Implementing the Patient Self-Determination Act. *Hastings Center Report, 23*, 12–16.

Schneider, J. (1984). *Stress, loss and grief: Understanding their origins and growth potential*. Baltimore, MD: University Park Press.

Shapiro, E. R. (1994). *Grief as a family process: A developmental approach to clinical practice*. New York: Guildford.

Strauss, A. L., & Glasser, B. G. (1970). Awareness of dying. In B. Schoenberg, A. C. Carr, D. Peretz, & A. J. Kutcher, (Eds.), *Loss and grief*. New York: Columbia University Press. (Classic.)

Task Force to Improve the Care of the Terminally Ill Oregonians. (1998). *The Oregon Death with Dignity Act: A guidebook for health care providers*. Portland, OR: Center for Ethics in Health Care, Oregon Health Sciences University.

Ufema, J. Monthly column: Insights on death and dying. *Nursing 96*, December 1995, January, February, March, May, September, October, 1996.

Vachon, M. (2001). The nurse's role: The world of palliative care. In B. Ferrell & N. Coyle (Eds.), *Textbook of palliative nursing* (pp. 647–662). New York: Oxford University Press.
Victoria Hospice Society. (1998). Hospice Resource Manual. Volume 1: *Medical care of the dying* (3rd ed.). Victoria: Author.
Wheeler, S. R. (1996, July). Helping families cope with death and dying. *Nursing 96, 26*, 25–31.
White, M. (1989). Saying hello again: The incorporation of the lost relationship in the resolution of grief. In M. White, *Selected papers* (pp. 29–36). Adelaide, Australia: Dulwich Centre.
Wilson, D. M. (1996). Highlighting the role of policy in nursing practice through a comparison of "DNR" policy influences and "no CPR" decision influences. *Nursing Outlook, 44*, 272–279.
Wood, L. C., & DelPapa, L. A. (1996). Nurses' attitudes, ethical reasons, and knowledge of the law concerning advance directives. *Image: Journal of Nursing Scholarship, 28*, 371.
Worden, J.W. (1991). *Grief counseling and grief therapy: A handbook for the mental health practitioner.* New York: Springer.
World Health Organization. (1990). *Cancer pain relief and palliative care.* Report of a WHO expert committee. Geneva, Switzerland: WHO Technical Series #804.
Wright, L. M. (1997). Suffering and spirituality: The soul of clinical work with families. *Journal of Family Nursing, 39*(1), 3–14.
Wright, L. M. (1999). Spirituality, suffering, and beliefs: The soul of healing with families. In F. Walsh (Ed.), *Spiritual resources in families and family therapy* (pp. 61–75). New York: Guilford Press.
Wright, L. M., Watson, W. L., & Bell, J. M. (1996). *Beliefs: The heart of healing in families and illness.* New York: Basic Books.

WEBLINKS

Caregiver Network Inc.
http://www.caregiver.on.ca:80/index
Caregiver Network Inc. (CNI), the first of its kind in Canada, is a resource centre created to help caregivers of the elderly and ill. The goal of the network is to make caregivers' lives easier by providing information on the Internet and in a newsletter (see CNI Services); education through the 13-part TV/video series "Caregiving with June Callwood"; the Canadian Aging and Caregiving Resource Guide; and personal assistance and support through seminar series, Care Management Consulting Service, the Caregiver Club, and Care Across the Border.

The Canadian Hospice Palliative Care Association
http://www.cpca.net/about_us/mission_statement.htm
The Canadian Hospice Palliative Care Association (CHPCA) is the national association providing leadership in hospice/palliative care in Canada. CHPCA will strive to achieve its mission through collaboration and representation, increased awareness, knowledge and skills related to hospice palliative care of the public, health-care providers and volunteers; development of national standards of practice for hospice palliative care in Canada; support of research on hospice palliative care; advocacy for improved hospice palliative care policy, resource allocation, and supports for caregivers towards the pursuit of excellence in care for persons approaching death so that the burdens of suffering, loneliness, and grief are lessened.

The University of Ottawa Institute of Palliative Care
http://www.pallcare.org/english.htm
The University of Ottawa Institute of Palliative Care opened in 1993. The pioneers of palliative care development in Ottawa anticipated a growing burden of suffering caused by such diseases as cancer and AIDS in the National Capital Region, and they had the foresight to call for the creation of Canada's first university institute for research and education in palliative care. Since its opening, the institute has offered increased access to information and services in palliative care to patients/clients and health-care professionals.

The Hospice Association of Ontario Life-Line
http://www.hospicelifeline.com
The Hospice Association of Ontario Life-Line provides information about a wide range of hospice/palliative care services and such resources as hospice/palliative care programs, hospice/palliative care units, community-based services, pain and symptom management, bereavement support services, and palliative care education.

CBC

Canadian Case Study — How Does Jackie View Her Role as a Registered Nurse?

Recently, while working on a busy surgical floor during the 3:15 pm to 11:15 pm shift, Jackie, an RN, expressed the view that the ratio of registered nurses to patients was inadequate. On Jackie's unit there were 48 beds divided into three sections, with 16 patients per each. Four registered nurses and three licensed practical nurses were working that evening. Within the first three hours of the shift, two new admissions arrived on the floor as well as three patients who returned from the recovery room. Jackie felt that nursing care was compromised. She felt that the presence of more complex and acutely ill patients in a hospital setting requires more staff. Laschinger and Sabiston (2000) have suggested that massive downsizing in the Canadian health-care system has created a sense of disempowerment and stress among nurses.

Mr. R. was one of Jackie's patients. She had first cared for Mr. R. when he was admitted directly post surgery to the unit two days earlier. He had exploratory surgery to remove a large abdominal mass. The surgery had proven to be of no benefit because of the location of the mass and its interrelationship with several of the abdominal organs. His prognosis was poor. He was extremely uncomfortable despite being medicated. To complicate his recovery, it was felt that he had experienced a small heart attack on the operating room table. He was continually attempting to disconnect himself from his intravenous line and oxygen.

On the day shift, staff had restrained Mr. R's hands. Jackie felt that he was probably feeling helpless and frightened. He kept begging to be put out of his misery, but morally the staff could do nothing. He said to Jackie, "Just let me go, it is my time." The resident had spoken to the family and had written the order "Do not resuscitate" on the chart. Jackie would have liked to spend more time with him so that she could untie his hands but she was too busy. His wife expressed concern that maybe surgery had not been the right decision for her husband and wondered if it was worth the effort. She said to Jackie, "Perhaps he would have lived longer if he did not have the surgery. He certainly would not be in the misery that he is now." Jackie felt frustrated and had wondered the same thing and was not sure what to say to Mr. R's wife.

Jackie felt that some of the staff believed that the morale on the unit was low, and what they felt was systemic and reflective of health care downsizing across the country. Some staff even talked of strike action. Their hesitancy in acting rested, in part, upon their belief that their actions may place patients at risk because resources would be scarce (Forchuk, Fibson, & Best, 1999). They did realize that the administration might well have a srike contingency plan in place.

Jackie recognized that administration was making efforts to empower the nurses on the unit. Possible empowering activities included participating in organizational committees, agency task forces, and development programs; and fostering relationships outside one's immediate work area (Laschinger & Sabiston, 2000).

QUESTIONS

1. Are there any care situations where it may be appropriate to withhold some information from the client? Relate this discussion to Mr. R. and his wife.
2. Relate concepts of professional nursing practice to the care of Mr. R.
3. What elements of nursing practice energize you?
4. What elements of nursing practice de-energize you?
5. What consideration goes into the decision to call a nurses' strike?

VIDEO RESOURCES:

Series Title:	The National
Segment Title:	Patient No More
Telecast Date:	May 3, 1999
Running Time:	11:53
Series Title:	The Health Show
Segment Title:	Informed Consent
Show Number:	85
Telecast Date:	February 15, 1996
Running Time:	7:41
Series Title:	The Health Show
Segment Title:	Palliative Care (Dying at Home)
Show Number:	130
Telecast Date:	March 19, 1997
Running Time:	8:49

Sources: Forchuk, C., Gibson, D., & Best, H. (1999). Strike contingency planning. *The Canadian Nurse, 95*(1), 33–37; Hardingham L. (2001). Ethics in the workplace. Nurses and informed consent: Lessons from the Winnipeg inquest. *Alberta RN, 57*(2), 22–23, 26; Laschinger, H. K. S., & Sabiston, J. A. (2000). Staff nurse empowerment and workplace behaviours. *The Canadian Nurse*, 96(2), 18–22.

APPENDIX A Critical Thinking Possibilities

CHAPTER 1: HISTORICAL AND CONTEMPORARY NURSING PRACTICE

1. How does the Canadian Nurses Association (CNA) influence national health-care policy?

- The CNA lobbies the federal government to examine the determinants of health and to address factors that have the potential to negatively influence health.
- It develops policies and position statements regarding factors that affect the health of Canadians.
- It educates its members regarding health-care needs and suggests individual political action to them.

Activity
Compare the mandate of provincial and territorial associations with that of the CNA. Speculate how individual nurses may influence the activities of these associations.

2. What is the role of an individual nurse within the mandate of the CNA?

- The individual nurse needs to keep informed of the issues that influence the health of Canadians through reading as well as through critique of the literature.
- Attendance at provincial and territorial and national meetings of nurses can inform the nurse.
- Responding to the invitation of nursing associations for input into policy development

3. What changes are occurring across Canada that influence the discipline of nursing?

- Clients are being discharged from acute-care facilities into the community at higher acuity levels.
- Consumers are becoming increasingly aware of the costs of health care.

CHAPTER 2: NURSING EDUCATION IN CANADA

1. Identify the major components of basic nursing education that will prepare graduates to work as registered nurses. Provide reasons for your answer.

- Communication skills are an essential element of any nursing role to communicate with clients, those important to them, and with health-care colleagues.
- Psychomotor skills provide intervention strategies to help address a client's health-care needs.
- Relational skills are important in promoting the therapeutic relationship between clients and nurses.
- Leadership and management skills will support the nurse in working with colleagues and paraprofessional staff.
- Biological and social sciences provide content that will support the nurse's understanding of clients, their needs, and the context of professional practice.

2. Explain why the Canadian Nurses Association has recommended the baccalaureate as entry level for professional practice degree.

- Exposure to evidence-based practice through the exploration and valuing of research is more commonly associated with a university education.
- Students are exposed to a broad foundation in the sciences and humanities as well as to nursing.
- Increasing responsibilities that registered nurses are expected to assume in response to changing health care require a strong knowledge base.

Activity
Compare the stance of the CNA regarding undergraduate degrees with your knowledge of other professional disciplines, for example, medicine, social work, or education.

3. Identify the difference between an undergraduate and graduate degree in nursing.

- A graduate degree increases the research involvement of the nurse.
- The degree provides an opportunity for in-depth exploration of a specialized area of nursing knowledge in comparison to the generalist education gained at the undergraduate degree level.
- The graduate degree provides for increased employment opportunities for registered nurses at managerial levels.

CHAPTER 3: NURSING RESEARCH IN CANADA

1. Identify responsibilities of beginning nurses in relation to nursing research.

- To think analytically about the situations that they encounter in practice and seek out research results that might positively influence nursing care
- To help researchers acquire data

- To share knowledge gained through a critical appraisal of the nursing research

2. What questions might Jamie ask of the researchers as he explores his possible interest in the study?

- What ethical approval has been obtained?
- How might the study benefit patients?
- What is expected of patients who participate in this study?
- How might he contribute, as a student nurse, to this study?

Activity
Identify the approval process for research studies within a local health-care agency.

3. How might Jamie ensure that he protects the rights of his patients if they decide to participate in the study?

- He should read the information about the study provided to his patients by the researchers.
- If the patient has any questions, he should ensure that the researcher is informed.
- He should provide information to the patients as to how they might contact the researchers or withdraw from the study if they wish.

CHAPTER 4: NURSING PHILOSOPHIES, THEORIES, CONCEPTS, FRAMEWORKS, AND MODELS

1. Thinking *philosophically* has changed the way nurses think about their practice. What do we mean by philosophical thought? Give at least three examples of how philosophical thought has influenced the evolution of nursing knowledge.

- Philosophical thought occurs when we reflect on the truth of an observation in our practice and/or try to determine what the best course of action might be in that situation. Philosophical thinking encourages us to consider our assumptions and beliefs that inform our thinking and influence what we say and do, clarifies how concepts are used and how they have meaning, and assesses arguments made to defend or critique particular ways of thinking.

2. A *concept* is another word for an idea. Nurses make use of concepts to highlight the ideas that are important to the discipline. Discuss at least four concepts that you would consider central to the discipline and give your reasons for each concept you select.

- Concepts important to the discipline are: nursing, person, health, and environment.
- *Nursing*. How we view nursing, its purpose, and the goals (nature) of nursing is the foundation for the care that we give.
- *Person* is the recipient of the nurses' care. It is important to consider our values and assumptions about how we view persons as that will affect the type of care that we give.
- *Health* is considered to be the focus of our care and it is important to see how we have come to believe what health is and help the clients to consider the meaning of health in their experiences.
- *Environment* is not only the external factors that impact the patient's experience of health, but also includes the person's inner thoughts and feelings and relationships with others that can influence health.

Activity
A conceptual framework, viewed simply, is a cluster of related concepts around a particular topic. Identify at least one conceptual framework for nursing. Discuss the fit of the concepts within this framework for nursing. What is the goal for nursing practice of the conceptual framework that you have selected?

A conceptual model is a diagram or illustration showing graphically how concepts within a particular cluster are positioned in relationship to each other. Identify a model for nursing practice. How does this model help explain the relationship between the concepts it contains?

CHAPTER 5: THE INDIVIDUAL—THE CLIENT OF CARE

1. What type of assessment data might you collect?

- Physiological variables, e.g., ability to sleep and nutritional intake
- Psychological factors, e.g., client's perceptions of coping skills, past experiences with illness, anticipation of the future
- Support systems
- Employment patterns
- Spiritual beliefs

2. When dealing with Linda's physical problem, why must the nurse be concerned about the other issues occurring in Linda's life?

- The nurse must keep in mind how Linda, as a whole person rather than a physical part, is affected. Her inability to maintain psychological homeostasis, as evidenced by financial problems, fears, and family role strain, will have an adverse effect on her ability to achieve physiological homeostasis.

Activity
Compare physiological homeostasis and psychological homeostasis, noting the relationship between the two.

3. Explore Linda's situation from the perspective of Maslow.
- Basic needs (physiological) take precedence over others.
- Linda may move back and forth between levels.
- Linda's self-esteem may be influenced by her financial situation and prevent self-actualization.

4. What suggestions might you give to Linda to help her cope with her condition?
- Consider talking to a social worker in the presence of someone she trusts.
- Phone the local arthritis society to identify their services.
- Perhaps talk to other individuals with similar conditions to identify coping strategies.
- Consider attending a support group.

CHAPTER 6: NURSING CARE OF FAMILIES

1. How would you engage this family to foster a more productive and collaborative relationship?
- Acknowledge that they have legitimate concerns about the difficulty in coming to a definitive medical diagnosis.
- Commend their devotion and concern for Mr. Black. The wife and son have obviously spent a great deal of time in the hospital trying to be supportive to him.

2. How would you attempt to address their concerns?
- Ask them to identify the questions that are most pressing for them today, and offer to obtain whatever information it is possible to ascertain.
- Arrange for the family to be present during the physician's visit so that they can have other questions answered directly.

3. What is the relationship between the health problem and the family members?
- The uncertainty of the medical diagnosis may be contributing to a great deal of emotional distress and frustration for other family members.
- Asking questions that seem like "interrogation" may be the only way that the family has been able to feel that they have some influence over the situation.

CHAPTER 7: ETHICS, MORALITY, AND VALUES

1. How can the nurse best help the Smithers make this decision?
- They need to articulate an ethically prudent course of action. You might help them to answer such questions as: What is the issue? Who is involved? What resources are available to help them make this decision? How much time is available to make the decision? What are the consequences of the decision?

Activity
Review the CNA Code of Ethics.

2. How would the nurse resolve the ethical problem in the situation?
- Review the CNA Code of Ethics.
- Seek the advice of the agency's ethics board, if they have one.

CHAPTER 8: LEGAL ASPECTS OF NURSING

1. How can you be certain that Mrs. Jiminez has given informed consent for this invasive procedure?
- Mrs. Jiminez may be able to verbalize the purpose of the treatment, including both the benefit of the procedure and the risks involved, what she can expect to feel during the procedure, and the advantages and disadvantages of alternative treatments.
- You may witness the exchange of information between Mrs. Jiminez and her physician.

Activity
Look for data that indicate or refute that Mrs. Jiminez has given informed consent for the procedure.

2. What is the difference between informed consent and signing a consent form?
- Informed consent means that the client has been fully informed about the medical treatment, including all possible risks and benefits. The consent form is a record of the informed consent. In this case, Mrs. Jiminez has not been fully informed about the procedure but is being encouraged to sign the form.

Activity
Discuss the consequences of Mrs. Jiminez signing the form without being fully informed.

3. Evaluate the nurse's approach to Mrs. Jiminez in regard to this invasive procedure.
- The nurse seemed to be pressuring Mrs. Jiminez into signing the consent form, which is inappropriate.

- The nurse explained the benefits of the procedure to Mrs. Jiminez but failed to explain the possible risks.
- The nurse failed to recognize and acknowledge Mrs. Jiminez's fear and did not explain what Mrs. Jiminez could expect to feel during the procedure.
- It would have been appropriate for the nurse to question the physician about whether or not Mrs. Jiminez had been informed about the risks of the procedure.

Activity
Discuss the pros and cons of the physician delegating informed consent to the nurse. Discuss alternative approaches to providing information to Mrs. Jiminez.

4. When obtaining informed consent for a nursing treatment, such as insertion of a subclavian catheter for administration of total parenteral nutrition, what factors must the nurse consider in order to assure informed consent from the client?

- Language barriers, age (minor vs. adult), mental competency, mental state (confused, disoriented, or sedated), level of consciousness

Activity
Discuss the impact of Mrs. Jiminez's physical state and the possibility that she is receiving pain medications on her ability to understand and give informed consent.

5. How is performing an invasive procedure without informed consent similar to battery?

- They are the same inasmuch as performing an invasive procedure on a client without informed consent *is* battery. If the procedure is performed on Mrs. Jiminez, it may be considered battery even though she may have signed a procedure consent form.

Activity
Discuss the concept of "battery." Discuss situations in which "implied consent" does not constitute battery. Apply the concepts to Mrs. Jiminez's case.

CHAPTER 9: HEALTH, WELLNESS, AND ILLNESS

1. How does Jerry's psychological dimension of health status differ from Joe's?

- Jerry has a positive outlook and views himself as "well," whereas Joe has a negative outlook and views himself as "ill."

Activity
Compare the biological dimensions (genetic makeup, race, gender, age) and the psychological dimensions of health (self-concept, mind-body interaction, "emotional" response to health). Identify and compare data representative of the psychological dimension for both clients. Speculate about how their differences in perception may affect their continuing recovery process.

2. Both Jerry and Joe have heart disease. Jerry considers himself "well," whereas Joe considers himself "ill." Explain this phenomenon based on the health locus of control model.

- Jerry is most likely an "internal" because he has taken charge of his own health by changing his diet, initiating an exercise program, and attempting to lower his stress.
- Joe is more likely an "external" because he has been unable to take control of his health. Joe may believe that his health is largely controlled by outside forces and is beyond his control.

Activity
Review the health locus of control model, and discuss the characteristics of internal versus external locus of control.

3. What external factors may have influenced Jerry's decision to implement positive health behaviours?

- A work environment may provide support; family members may influence smoking reduction.

Activity
Discuss the effect of external variables (geography, environment, lifestyle, standards of living, family and cultural beliefs, and social support networks).

4. What factors may have prevented Joe from developing the same positive outlook and actions that Jerry was able to take in regard to his illness?

- Joe's perception of his illness and, thus, his ability to respond in a positive manner may be affected by a family history of heart disease and his perception that he is at high risk and that there is nothing he can do to change his pattern of health.
- Jerry's wife is pleased about the changes in her husband's behaviour. Joe worries that his condition is an indication that he will die from heart disease as his father did.
- Joe may have perceived barriers to action (cost, time, lack of social support). Perhaps the benefit of assuming the sick role outweighs the benefit of recovery.

Activity
Discuss Rosenstock's and Becker's health belief models, including individual perceptions.

5. What nursing interventions would be most beneficial to Joe in regard to his smoking problem?

- Specific nursing interventions may include, but are not limited to, the following:

- Verifying that Joe values the planned outcome achieved from smoking cessation
- Verifying Joe's knowledge about the effects of smoking and providing needed information or correcting misconceptions
- Demonstrating genuine concern for Joe and positively reinforcing positive changes that Joe does make.
- Allowing Joe to make his own decisions, thereby demonstrating trust and cooperation

Activity
Discuss the implications of client noncompliance and various nursing actions to encourage compliance.

CHAPTER 10: HEALTH PROMOTION

1. On the basis of the limited data provided, speculate whether Mrs. Chu's activities represent health promotion, health prevention, or both.

- Categorization of Mrs. Chu's activities depends on her motivation for doing them. She is concerned about developing the same diseases suffered by her father, and thus, many of her activities are designed for disease avoidance (primary prevention).
- Secondary prevention behaviours are also present (early detection of disease) as evidenced by her regular exams. Her intent to control her weight and engage in an exercise program may be both health promoting and health preventing, as they will result in an increase in her level of well-being as well as a decrease in the probability of disease development.

Activity
Compare and contrast the definitions for health promotion, primary prevention, secondary prevention, and tertiary prevention.

2. What additional activities could you suggest to Mrs. Chu that are "health-promoting"?

- Activities may include a stress reduction program, developing sleep habits that promote adequate sleep, assessing safety risks, attending informational sessions on disease control or nutritional awareness, and participating in environmental control programs within her community.

Activity
Consider the spectrum of activities that promote health and well-being. Examine your own activities that enhance your well-being. Would they be appropriate for Mrs. Chu?

3. What evidence is there that Mrs. Chu will achieve and maintain the lifestyle changes she wants to make?

- Evidence includes, but is not limited to, the following: Mrs. Chu participates in health-preventing and health-promoting behaviours already, she is seeking new information, she considers herself healthy, and she recognizes the benefits of lifestyle changes.
- The above activities support the high value Mrs. Chu places on health and health maintenance; they will be strong motivational factors for achieving and maintaining her goal.

Activity
Review the components of Pender's health promotion model, including cognitive-perceptual factors and cues to action.

4. In what ways might you (the nurse) be able to assist Mrs. Chu?

- In general, the nurse may advocate for, consult with, refer, educate, or coordinate services for individuals or groups. The nurse can also assist clients with lifestyle assessments and plan appropriate lifestyle changes.
- You may be able to assess Mrs. Chu's nutritional status and help her plan a better balanced diet, teach her about factors that contribute to hypertension and diabetes, plan an appropriate exercise program or refer her to a physical fitness centre, help her identify ways to decrease her stress at work, or refer her to community resources.

Activity
Contemplate the nurse's role within the community as well as with individual clients.

5. Devise a plan to intervene with a client who is knowledgeable about the benefits of healthful behaviours and wants to make behavioural changes but has been unable to do so.

Activitiy
Review assessing health-care beliefs and enhancing behaviour change. Consider habits that you would like to change, know how to change, but have not been able to change. What could another nurse do or say to help you make those changes?

- Recognize that the client's motivation is the basis for all behaviour change, whether or not it is positive.
- Assess the situation for barriers to the client's success or motivation.
- Avoid labelling the client as unmotivated.
- Serve as a role model of wellness.
- Focus on factors that do motivate the client.

CHAPTER 11: HOLISTIC HEALING MODALITIES

1. What are your attitudes toward methods of healing that are different from Western contemporary medicine?

- It is important that nurses consider the cultural context of complementary therapies as an integral part of client care.
- We are so socialized to believe in the benefits of contemporary Western medicine that we are sometimes intolerant or judgmental about alternative forms of healing from other cultures.
- You might want to discuss your feelings with others, both in your work place and with family and friends.

2. How would you find out if the herbal teas were effective or detrimental to Mr. Chou's present condition?

- You will need to know whether the herbs offered to Mr. Chou would be contraindicated in any way with his prescribed medications.
- Find out more about the ingredients of the herbal tea—perhaps access the Internet or a natural pharmacist for more information.
- Ascertain if the tea is manufactured by a reputable company or is mixed on-site by the herbalist.

3. What do you know about the benefits of acupuncture?

- Find out if any evidence-based research exists on the use of acupuncture for Mr. Chou's condition.
- Talking to the acupuncturist may be of benefit.

4. How would you deal with this situation with Mr. Chou? With the family? With the agency?

- You should be aware of the hospital policy on the use of alternative therapies while a patient is in the hospital.
- Dialogue with the patient, family, and physician would then be in order to determine a mutually agreeable solution.

CHAPTER 12: SEXUALITY AND SEXUAL HEALTH PRACTICES

1. Speculate about Mr. Curry's reluctance to discuss his sexual concerns.

- Many people are uncomfortable discussing such a private matter with a stranger (such as their nurse) unless they are made to feel that sexuality is normal and okay. They need to be given permission to openly discuss their concerns without fear of being belittled or ridiculed.

Activity
Discuss the benefits of "permission giving." Think about how comfortable you would be discussing your own sexuality with your nurse. What reactions from the nurse would make it easier for you? What factors would inhibit you from discussing such matters?

2. What factors influence nurses' ability to discuss sexual concerns with their clients?

- Factors involved are the following: nurses' knowledge and comfort with their own sexuality; recognition and acceptance of sexuality as a normal and important human function; understanding of how health impacts sexuality; and nurses' ability to communicate in general.

Activity
Think about how you will react when your client begins talking about sexual concerns.

3. What is the relationship between health and sexual function?

- There is a direct relationship between health and ability to function sexually in that the healthier you are, the more likely you are to have the desire and ability to function sexually.
- Both physical and mental status affect the ability to function sexually. Such diseases as heart disease, hypertension, diabetes, renal failure, spinal cord injury, or pain can lessen both sexual desire and ability. Mental disorders, such as depression, can decrease libido.

Activity
Review the effects of disease on sexual function.

4. How can you best intervene to help Mr. Curry?

- You will need to complete a sexual health assessment to provide baseline data.
- Two primary problems need to be addressed: his fear of resuming sexual activity and his antihypertensive medication.
- Specific interventions may include, but are not limited to, the following: providing information; correcting misconceptions; and reassurance that resuming sex is safe and suggesting alternative positions for sex that require less energy expenditure if sexual activity causes him fatigue.
- Consult with Mr. Curry's primary-care provider regarding antihypertensive medications that are less likely to produce sexual dysfunction.

Activity
Review assessing sexual health and the sexual health history.

CHAPTER 13: SPIRITUALITY

1. Terry stated that he was "not very religious." Does that mean that he is not spiritual? Explain.

- Being religious means being part of an organized system of worship, such as a church or a synagogue. Terry may mean that he no longer attends the United Church or participates in organized religion.
- Spirituality refers to belief in or relationship with some higher power, creative force, divine being, or infinite source of energy, such as God or Allah.
- Clients can be deeply spiritual without belonging to an organized system of worship. Terry admits that he is not very religious; however, there are no data to suggest that he is not spiritual. In fact, Terry's statement that he is being punished is evidence that he believes in a higher power who is punishing him for not going to church.

Activity
Discuss the differences among spirituality, religion, and faith.

2. What data suggest that Terry may be experiencing spiritual distress?

- He states, "I can't see any reason for going on." "I know I'm being punished."
- Terry's spiritual distress is related to both his physiological situation as well as his concern over not being religious.

Activity
Compare and contrast spiritual well-being and spiritual distress.

3. How might illness affect one's spiritual beliefs? Religious beliefs?

- Spiritual beliefs and religious beliefs can assume greater importance during times of illness.
- Many persons will return to their religious roots during times of illness in hopes that they will be cured through divine intervention.

Activity
Discuss how religion directs the health-care seeking behaviours of some individuals (e.g., Jehovah's Witnesses, Christian Scientists). Discuss your own feelings about religion, spirituality, and illness.

4. How would you feel and respond if Terry were to ask you to pray with him?

- Perhaps you would be pleased that he sought your support, or distressed because you are of a different religion or faith.
- In responding, express support for Terry's decision to pray.
- Acknowledge Terry's attempts to address his spiritual needs.

Activity
Discuss the concept of prayer and its perceived benefits. Discuss the differences between seven types of prayer: petition, intercession, confession, lamentation, invocation, adoration, and thanksgiving.

5. How might a spiritual assessment be of benefit to both you and Terry?

- A spiritual assessment will help both you and Terry by providing information relative to his spirituality, his religion, and his degree of spiritual distress so that appropriate interventions can be planned and implemented.
- Possible benefits may include, but are not limited to, the following: helping Terry draw on inner resources more effectively to deal with his present physical and emotional situation; helping him find meaning in living and hope for the future even though he is presently very ill; and providing appropriate spiritual resources, such as a minister or priest.

Activity
Discuss aspects of spiritual assessment (history, environment, behaviour, verbalizations, affect, interpersonal relationships) and any spiritual assessment guides that are available (e.g., Fish & Shelly; Stroll; O'Brien).

CHAPTER 14: CULTURE AND ETHNICITY

1. Differentiate between Rachel's culture, ethnicity, and race.

- Rachel's culture (values, beliefs, norms, and life practices that guide thinking, decisions, and actions) is mixed and can be referred to as "bicultural" because she has integrated practices and values from both her mother and father who were of different cultural backgrounds.
- Rachel's ethnicity is most strongly associated with her Jewish background (consciousness of belonging to a group that is differentiated from others by symbolic markers) as evidenced by her return to the Jewish religion as an adult and by her obvious connection with this group.
- Rachel is Jewish by race (shared biological characteristics, genetic markers, or features) because she was born to Jewish parents.

2. How may Rachel's mixed cultural background pose a dilemma for you as her nurse or for her family?

- Cultural values often determine interactions between and roles of family members; identify who will have the "authority" to make decisions on the client's behalf, and dictate the extent of family involvement in the client's care. Without clear guidelines regarding which cultural practices Rachel adheres to, it may be difficult or impossible to provide culturally sensitive care during this important period of Rachel's life.

Activity
Review the concepts of culture and biculturalism and discuss the concept of culturally sensitive care.

3. How may Rachel's culture affect her approach to death and the care of her body following her death?

- Rachel's beliefs and values will strongly affect her approach to death and the way her family reacts toward her prior to and during the death process.
- Rachel's culture will dictate whether or not she dies with family members present, any rites or rituals performed, whether she dies at home or in the hospital, and whether or not she is informed about her impending death.
- Rachel's religion is more likely to influence the care of her body following her death than is her culture and will provide guidelines for postmortem care and burial.

Activity
Discuss death and dying practices, and compare your own cultural practices regarding death with those of fellow students.

4. Of what benefit would a cultural assessment be to Rachel or her family since she is dying?

- A cultural assessment is especially important to Rachel at this time in order to assure her that her death is congruent with her beliefs and traditions.
- It is also important to determine Rachel's primary support systems, preserve or maintain her cultural and religious preferences, and offer support to both Rachel and her family in a sensitive and competent manner.

5. How could nurses' race, culture, or religion influence their care of clients who are racially or culturally different?

- Nurses may not understand the practices or behaviours of clients with diverse backgrounds.
- Nurses may not demonstrate culturally sensitive care.

CHAPTER 15: HEALTH-CARE DELIVERY SYSTEMS

1. What is meant by continuum of health-care service delivery?

- Delivery of services to the client that flow smoothly from one setting to another; uninterrupted care from one care setting to another

2. How might Rebecca's family and friends provide health-care services to her?

- They could provide informal support services, such as grocery shopping, child care support, and transportation to appointments.

Activity
Search the Internet to find at least three local or provincial/territorial health-care services that may be of help to Rebecca if she lived in your area.

3. How would the nurse provide health care to her?

- Initiate home care services for care of the drain.
- Demonstrate to Rebecca how to care for the drain by herself.
- Provide a list of possible community agencies to Rebecca that may help with child care.

CHAPTER 16: COMMUNITY-BASED NURSING

1. Review the principles and components of primary health care. What gaps do you identify?

- Consideration of ethnic and cultural factors might be emphasized to a greater degree; spiritual components of health are not as strongly acknowledged.

2. What specific skills are required to intervene at the community level that might differ from those needed at the individual level?

- Community nursing requires knowledge of group dynamics and conflict resolution; group process skills; group teaching skills; and community assessment strategies.

3. What is the role of environmental factors in promoting the health of individuals?

- The environment can contribute to health through promotive factors, such as a good food supply and clean water; but environmental contaminants and environmental products can pollute and reduce the quality of food products.

Activity
Review the Canadian Nurses Association Position Statement: *The Environment is a Determinant of Health*.

CHAPTER 17: HOME CARE

1. How will the nurse's role differ when delivering care in the home environment as opposed to the acute-care environment?

- Many of the tasks will be similar (e.g., intravenous therapy, central lines, and dressing changes).

The home care nurse will, however, have an expanded role, which includes collaborating with physicians and other health-care providers.

- Home care nurses serve as client advocate, direct care provider, educator, and case manager/coordinator.
- In the home, the client's family is considered a secondary client as they are often associated with caregiving and have a major impact on the client's wellness status. This aspect of home care nursing differs significantly from that of the acute-care nurse.

Activity
Review the role of the nurse in the acute-care setting and discuss how that role changes when the nurse enters a client's private home setting.

2. What rights does the client have when being cared for at home that may not be afforded him while institutionalized?

- The client has the right to be provided with information about the purpose of the home visits, the number of home visits, the time of the visits, and any specific treatments that will be performed.
- The person at home has the right to accept or reject care suggestions offered.

Activity
Compare the rights of hospitalized clients with those of the home-bound client.

3. What obligations to Mr. Yao does the nurse have when visiting him at home?

- Pre-entry obligations: Review referral information, contact the client by telephone, provide information about the visit, schedule the visit, establish rapport, determine what supplies will be needed, and obtain directions.
- Entry obligations: Continue to develop rapport, assess the client and client situation, discuss the plan of care and desired outcomes, explain the nurse's role during home visits, differentiate between the home care nurse's role and that of a private duty nurse, identify other health-care providers that may be needed, and determine the frequency of home visits.
- Include a discussion on maintaining privacy and sensitivity to culture/traditions.

Activity
Discuss the stages of the home care relationship (pre-entry and entry).

4. What factors could negatively impact the care of Mr. Yao in his own home?

- Safety issues: anything that could cause Mr. Yao to fall or become injured, such as improper use of equipment, unsecured area rugs, lack of rails on bathtub or shower
- Lack of medical-alert or alarm systems
- Infection control issues: improper disposal of foot dressings, lack of prevention of wound infection, improper hand-washing technique
- Caregiver support issues: caregiver role strain, lack of assistance for caregiver, and caregiver sleep deprivation

Activity
Discuss the need to protect the nurse's equipment from contamination. Explore other factors that are not covered in the text that could impact the outcomes of care, either positively or negatively.

5. Speculate about the financial savings derived from caring for a patient at home rather than in a hospital or other institution.
   Note: This topic is not specifically covered in the chapter.

- Reduced costs related to reducing contact time with health care staff
- Meals provided and paid for by client
- Medications in hospital paid by health care system; client pays for medications if at home
- Laundry needs done by client

Activity
Discuss the cost of nursing care in an acute-care setting versus a daily home care visit. Investigate the costs of nursing service provided by agencies in their area as well as the cost of supplies (e.g., surgical dressings). Compare the daily hospital charge with the costs of home assistance (e.g., housekeepers or respite care), taking into account such factors as the decreased risk for nosocomial infections in the home setting.

CHAPTER 18: RURAL HEALTH CARE

1. What issues should the nurse discuss with Mr. Donaldson to assist him in choosing his treatment options?

- Distance and the cost of travelling between home and the facility are key factors in all rural and remote health-care delivery. How will Mr. Donaldson be able to travel to and from the hospital? Will someone accompany him?
- Rest is integral to safe and effective treatment. Consideration must be given to what conditions would affect the amount of rest Mr. Donaldson would be able to achieve at home or in the hospital.
- The stresses that would affect any decision include whether there is a family member or friends who can take over the operation of the farm, current

economic realities on farms, the time of year, and the activities required on the farm, for example, calving, haying, seeding, or harvest.

Activity
Discuss current economic concerns of rural residents within your geographical region. Are there particular issues that are affected by globalization?

2. How might the patient's regime vary from that in an urban setting?

- If Mr. Donaldson opts to return regularly for treatment, the nurse would take into account optimal times that would not conflict with necessary farm chores.
- The availability and accessibility of home care treatment may differ depending on where the patient resides.

3. How might Mr. Donaldson's occupation influence his recovery?

- As a self-employed farmer, Mr. Donaldson would not have access to Worker's Compensation and worry about income may affect his recovery. This may cause him to return to work earlier than is recommended.
- Farmers who are self-reliant often will not ask for assistance from family and neighbours who they recognize as being as busy as they are and may return to work themselves against medical advice.

4. What health-care delivery issues common to rural and remote residents affect Mr. Donaldson's treatment?

- Difficulties in transportation between home and treatment facilities and timing of treatments that do not adversely affect his occupation considering the distances involved may affect his treatment.
- Depending on the region of the country where persons reside and the season of the year, access to treatment facilities, such as hospitals, health-care centres, and nursing stations may require medical evacuation or extensive travel over difficult terrain.
- The personal knowledge the nurse has of Mr. Donaldson, his family, where he lives, his current occupational demands, and the resources available to him will be integrated into his care plan.

Activity
On the basis of your geographical location and the primary industry, what factors would be involved in seeking health care following an injury? List the resources available in your region to assist in the recovery and care of a person injured in a remote area.

CHAPTER 19: CONCEPTS OF GROWTH AND DEVELOPMENT

1. What conclusions can you draw about the child's growth and development on the basis of the data provided?

- He appears to be developing within normal parameters.
- At this age, babies will nap morning and afternoon.
- His uncoordinated movements and fisted hands will gradually develop into smoother motions, reaching and grasping, shaking things, and passing objects from hand to mouth.
- John is happier being close to people and has begun to express squeals of joy and babbling sounds to get his mother's attention.

Activity
Review Erikson's or another theorist's stages of childhood development.

2. What contextual factors might influence the client's future development?

- The child's support system
- Presence of parents
- Presence of disease pathology
- Opportunities to play
- Cultural practices

3. What suggestions would you make to his mother to support John's growth and development?

- The simple approach is to build on everyday activities that are part of her daily routine.
- Play hide and seek.
- Cuddle with John.
- Provide him with opportunities to play with objects considered safe for his age.

Activity
Think about your own growth and development compared with that of a sibling. What were some of the major influences upon it?

4. What attitude and cognitive critical thinking skills did you use to answer the questions pertaining to this case?

- Divergent thinking
- Reasoning
- Basic support
- Cultural awareness

CHAPTER 20: DEVELOPMENT FROM CONCEPTION THROUGH ADOLESCENCE

1. How would you help Billy's mother reassure him?
- She might explain that she will pick him up at a certain time.
- She might give him a small trinket of hers for him to hold until she returns.

Activity
Compare Billy's feelings with those of other young children that you might know who have entered the school system for the first time this year.

2. On the basis of his age, what strategies might you use to teach Billy and his classmates about health promotion?
- Use drawing with crayons.
- Use actual food samples to talk about nutrition needs.
- Ask questions about current practices: What do you do after you have gone to the bathroom? When do you brush your teeth?

CHAPTER 21: DEVELOPMENT FROM YOUNG THROUGH OLDER ADULTHOOD

1. What is an adequate knowledge base for a nurse to make decisions about the care required by an older adult?
- Knowledge areas include physiological needs, safety and security, self-esteem and independence, and ability to communicate, in addition to knowledge of normal aging changes.

Activity
Review the Canadian government Web sites for statistics related to the health of older adults and suggest ways that this information may inform nursing practice.

2. What assessment data would you deem important to collect regarding Mrs. Drinkwater's ability to remain within her own home?
- Client's views about her ability, including her reasons for wanting to stay
- Support systems, both informal and formal
- Safety of home environment
- Knowledge and use of available health-care resources, e.g., Meals on Wheels
- Client's ability to perform the activities of daily living

3. Why is Mrs. Drinkwater's input and feedback important in nursing practice?
- Compliance with prescribed treatment regime is often based upon understanding of its goals.
- Her input will contribute to identification of success or need for changes in nursing actions.

CHAPTER 22: CRITICAL THINKING

1. Compare and contrast critical thinking in nursing with critical thinking in daily life situations.
- In nursing, decisions made influence the lives of clients.
- A moral and ethical dimension is present in such thinking.

2. How does your level of nursing knowledge and experience influence your ability to think critically in the clinical setting?
- The depth of nursing knowledge, largely gained from experiences in a variety of settings and with different client groups, provides opportunities to apply theory and skills to real life situations, and this enhances the ability to think critically.
- Expert practitioners have a greater repertoire of information to draw upon in nursing situations.
- Students who are developing their abilities have limited knowledge of suspected problems and, therefore, they question and collect data on a more superficial level than registered nurses with several years of experience.

CHAPTER 23: THE NURSING PROCESS

1. What is the role of the nursing process in providing care to Mr. Frank Reynolds?
- It provides a mechanism to ensure that all relevant data are collected; seeks input of the client; promotes communication among nurses; and provides for evaluation of nursing care.

2. What elements of Mr. Reynold's life are important to include in your assessment?
- His physical, psychosocial, and social status; relationships with his family; ability to perform activities of daily living; available support services

3. What strategies might you use to gain Mr. Frank Reynolds's participation in a plan of care?
- Ask him what his goals and his preferences for care are; seek his participation in his plan of care; involve him in decision making.

CHAPTER 24: DOCUMENTING AND REPORTING

1. Using DARP charting, what would your documentation focus on postoperatively?
- The initial postoperative assessment would focus on key physiological data related to the surgical procedure, vaginal hysterectomy. The focus would be post-op assessment.

Activity

Using DARP charting, chart your initial post-op assessment.

1800/RN/ D) Patient returned from PARR, drowsy but responds to verbal stimuli. Colour pale, skin warm and dry. O_2 on at 3l nasal prongs. Abdominal dressing intact with sanguineous drainage noted covering 2 × 2 inches. JP drain patent and approximately half full with sanguineous drainage. Vaginal flow red, soaking half of one pad. Foley catheter in place draining clear urine.

A) Vital signs: BP 98/60, P. 88 & regular, Respiration 20 & shallow, O_2 sat. 92%.

R) While checking her perineal pad, patient grimaced and clutched her abdomen.

2. Which flowsheets would you use?

- Graphic sheet to chart the vital signs
- Interdisciplinary notes sheet to record detailed postoperative observations
- Intake/output fluid balance sheet to record IV intake, oral intake, urinary and JP drain output
- Checklist to record basic care
- Medication record

3. Legally, what would be most pertinent for you to consider in this situation?

- The nurse must chart the standard postoperative care expected in this agency as it relates to Mrs. Chase.
- Accurate, descriptive postoperative assessments according to agency standards
- A chronology of actions/events that occur during the postoperative period

CHAPTER 25: NURSING INFORMATICS

1. Discuss the privacy, confidentiality, data, integrity, and security implications of this situation from the viewpoints of you, the nurse, the patient, and the coworker.

Patient's Viewpoint:

- Privacy was violated as the patient did not give consent for someone not directly involved in his care to view the record.
- Confidentiality was violated because the patient's information was not protected by the organization holding it when the lab report was left up on the screen.
- The accuracy of the patient's data was upheld by including a correction to the original lab result.
- Security of the patient's data was violated when others were able to access the information without the use of a mechanism, such as a password.

Nurse's Viewpoint:

- The nurse upheld the patient's right to privacy and confidentiality by not discussing information from the electronic health record with her co-worker.
- The nurse is not at liberty to correct the co-worker's belief about the patient's condition. The integrity of the data has been preserved with the correction to accurately reflect the patient's condition.
- Security measures, such as password use, are only effective when people follow procedures, such as always closing a health record before leaving the computer screen.

Co-worker's Viewpoint:

- The co-worker violated the patient's expectation of privacy that his health information would only be shared with those directly involved in his care.
- The co-worker violated confidentiality guidelines by discussing what she had seen with the nurse and others at the lunch table.
- The co-worker did not read the entire report and so did not see that the record had been amended. The integrity of the data had been maintained, but the co-worker did not read the complete record.
- The co-worker accessed the client record without the use of a password. This is not a computer security failure but, rather, a human failure in that the person using the record left it visible on the computer screen.

CHAPTER 26: NURSE-PATIENT RELATIONSHIP

1. Interpret Mrs. Manasovitz's nonverbal behaviour in response to the news about her husband's surgery.

- Mrs. Manasovitz's nonverbal behaviour may include changes in posture, facial expression, lack of verbal expression, and so on.
- Mrs. Manasovitz's nonverbal communication most likely represents fear, disappointment, loss, anxiety, devastation, and so on.

Activity

Compare and contrast verbal and nonverbal communication manifestations. Discuss the importance of accurate interpretation of nonverbal communication.

2. Evaluate the nurse's response towards Mrs. Manasovitz on the basis of the concepts of caring and comforting.

- The nurse conveyed the following caring actions: sitting with Mrs. Manasovitz, listening to her, and giving her undivided attention.
- The nurse conveyed comforting actions: using a soothing voice, reassuring, touching, offering presence,

and offering a cup of coffee. The nurse's actions did communicate caring and comforting as evidenced by Mrs. Manasovitz's willingness to share her feelings.

Activity
Define and discuss the concepts of caring and comforting, and describe how each applies to the nurse's role.

3. Why is it important for the nurse to effectively communicate with Mrs. Manasovitz at this time?
- It is important to provide essential information and establish a trusting relationship during emotionally stressful times.
- Other advantages of effective communication are helping families with stress reduction, helping them understand treatment options, and helping them with decision making.

Activity
Discuss the concepts of communication and therapeutic communication.

4. The nurse was described as listening attentively to Mrs. Manasovitz. Cite actions that portray attentive listening.
- The nurse conveyed attentive listening by sitting with Mrs. Manasovitz, paying attention to both her verbal and nonverbal language, remaining silent, and focusing solely on Mrs. Manasovitz.
- Other examples may include not interrupting the client, noting the congruency between verbal and nonverbal language, encouraging the client to talk, and thinking before responding.

5. Think about your past experiences when you or a family member had been ill. What relationship characteristics did you most value on the part of the nurse caring for you?

Activity
Discuss aspects of the helping relationship and the impact of the nurse's values and attitudes on that relationship. Consider such characteristics as the nurse's willingness to listen to your feelings, not imposing personal values or beliefs on you, ability to empathize with your situation, and not giving the appearance of being too busy to care for you.

CHAPTER 27: HEALTH ASSESSMENT

1. How would you respond to this patient?
- It would be important for the nurse to begin with an acknowledgement of her discomfort and to check to find out if she was feeling physical pain or discomfort or a feeling of embarrassment in having to be exposed and touched by another person she did not know.

Activity

2. How would you develop nursing interventions to put patients at ease for an invasive procedure that has a vital role in physical assessment?
- Always begin with their understanding of the situation (why they have come to clinic).
- Provide an explanation of what you will be doing prior to beginning the exam.
- Ensure the patients that you will keep them as draped as possible, and encourage them to voice any concerns or discomforts at any time during the procedure.

3. How will you address patients in a manner likely to gain their trust and cooperation?
- Professional and ethical knowledge and comportment are inherent in the nurse's practice. Addressing the patient as a person, understanding the reason for the visit, discussing fears and expectations of the visit and any concerns, respecting beliefs and cultural values that the patient would like to share with you will help gain trust and cooperation.

CHAPTER 28: MEDICATIONS

1. It is always possible that a person receiving antibiotic drugs may experience side effects or an allergic reaction to the drug. How does an allergic reaction differ from a drug side effect?
- Side effects are not related to an allergic reaction and do not produce the same symptoms as produced by allergies. Allergic reactions have a distinct pattern of reaction (e.g., skin rash, pruritus, angioedema, rhinitis, tearing, nausea, vomiting, wheezing, dyspnea, or diarrhea).
- A severe reaction called anaphylaxis can produce respiratory and cardiovascular collapse if emergency treatment is not immediately instituted. Drug hypersensitivity or drug allergy is often listed as a systemic side effect in drug handbooks.

Activity
Review the various effects of drugs, including the therapeutic effect, side effect, drug toxicity, drug allergy, drug tolerance, and drug interaction.

2. Predict the possible consequences of not obtaining a medication history from Mr. Ketron despite the fact that he will be receiving antibiotics and pain medication.
- Mr. Ketron may have allergies to either of the drugs; he may be on another prescribed drug, tobacco, alcohol, or nonprescription drug that interferes with or potentiates one of the prescribed drugs; he may have a medical condition that limits the kinds of drugs he can take safely; he could be allergic to penicillin, and so on.

Activity
Review the purpose of and the information obtained from a medication history. Think about your own medication history. What information would be important for your health-care provider to know if you were about to undergo surgery?

3. Mr. Ketron is complaining of pain and you have prepared his intramuscular injection of morphine. How will you select the best site to give the morphine injection?

- The appropriate injection site depends on such factors as Mr. Ketron's body weight, the healthiness of the muscle tissue, the ease of access to the site, the frequency with which the site has been used for previous injections, the condition of the skin over the site, and Mr. Ketron's preference.
- The ventrogluteal site is generally preferred because the area contains no large nerves or blood vessels and has less fat than the buttock area.

Activity
Consider the primary intramuscular sites and note the advantages of one site over the other. Which site poses the least amount of risk for nerve injury?

4. What precautions should you take prior to administering Mr. Ketron's intravenous antibiotic?

- All the same precautions should be taken with intravenous medications as with other medications; correct client, correct dose, correct route, and so on.
- Additional precautions include, but are not limited to, the following: confirming that the antibiotic is compatible with the intravenous fluid infusing, verifying sterility of the system and integrity of the medication bag, verifying that there is no air in the system, cleaning the port prior to placing a needle, and reviewing Mr. Ketron's medication history for possible allergies.

5. Mr. Ketron will be placed on the oral antibiotic when he can tolerate food and oral fluids. What difference, if any, does it make if this drug is given before or after meals?

- Some drugs are better absorbed when given on an empty stomach, whereas others cause gastrointestinal irritation and should be given with meals or after meals.

Activity
Discuss factors that influence drug action, such as genetics, gender, illness or disease, and time of drug administration. Read about the drug Suprax (sefixeem) in a drug handbook or pharmacology text. Are there specific directions about when to take the drug (e.g., prior to or after meals)?

CHAPTER 29: TEACHING

1. How would you evaluate Mrs. Marcos' readiness to learn?

- Mrs. Marcos seems preoccupied, so this may not be the ideal time to proceed with teaching. She needs time to adjust to the news that has been given to her and to come to terms with how her heart condition is going to affect her life. When she is ready to learn, she will give you her full attention, ask questions, talk to others, and show interest.

Activity
Review the indicators of a person's readiness to learn, such as physical readiness, emotional readiness, cognitive readiness, and motivation.

2. Of what benefit would a learning needs assessment be inasmuch as Mrs. Marcos is obviously a well-educated client?

- A needs assessment provides information about numerous factors that affect learning, not just cognitive ability. Do not assume that well-educated persons have all the information they need to make decisions about their health or that persons who are not so well-educated do not have the capacity to understand.
- A needs assessment would provide such information as Mrs. Marcos' baseline knowledge of cardiac disease, any health beliefs or cultural factors that may impact her acceptance or rejection of needed changes, the method of learning she prefers to use, and the support systems available to her.

Activity
Review and discuss the learning needs assessment interview.

3. You recognize that you have a great deal of information to deliver to Mrs. Marcos and you are concerned that you will not be able to teach it all. What can you do to help Mrs. Marcos and still feel that you have accomplished your teaching goals?

- Using your learning needs assessment, consider how Mrs. Marcos prefers to learn.
- Consider leaving material for Mrs. Marcos to read or videos for her to view.
- Schedule short learning sessions rather than overwhelming long sessions, use teaching aids, repeat information often, allow active learning. Allow Mrs. Marcos to set the pace.

Activity
Discuss the guidelines for teaching. Examine your own learning needs, asking yourself such questions as, "How

do I feel when I have a lot of information to learn?", "How do I go about organizing my learning?" Apply your strategies to your client teaching.

4. How will you know if your teaching is effective?

- If Mrs. Marcos is able to accurately select foods in accordance with her prescribed plan, is able to accurately plan an exercise program, and can offer suggestions for stress reduction, your teaching has most likely been effective.
- Do not confuse the client's lack of compliance with ineffective teaching. Clients may choose not to follow a prescribed regimen even though they have thorough knowledge of the regimen.

Activity
Review your learning objectives; they can serve as outcome criteria for evaluating the effectiveness of your teaching.

5. How might your teaching differ if you were teaching Mrs. Marcos at home rather than in a hospital or acute-care setting?

- Teaching strategies may differ depending on the availability of equipment; however, the principles of teaching would be similar.
- A learning needs assessment would still be useful, the person's learning readiness and motivation remain important, and learning objectives would continue to serve as evaluation criteria.
- The client and family would be more in control of the teaching setting, including scheduling, time limits, and pace.

Activity
Discuss the advantages and disadvantages of home teaching.

CHAPTER 30: LEADING, MANAGING, AND INFLUENCING CHANGE

1. On the basis of the brief data provided, speculate about the leadership style of each of these nurse managers.

- Mr. Caruso has characteristics of democratic or participative leadership: he is complimentary of his staff's ability to set goals and make decisions and encourages your input and ideas.
- Mrs. Turner has characteristics of the autocratic leader: she explains her expectations and speaks of implementing her programs.

Activity
Compare and contrast the various leadership styles: charismatic, authoritarian, democratic, laissez-faire, situational, and transformational.

2. Think about managers (or leaders) you have known and admired. What characteristics did they have that you would like to integrate into your own management style?

Activity
Consider the various leadership styles, characteristics of effective leaders, and effective nurse managers. Recall persons whom you felt were good leaders and list their traits. Compare their traits with the characteristics of effective leaders. Recall persons you felt were not good leaders. Identify effective leadership traits you feel they were lacking. Speculate about how leadership style may affect nurses' motivation and productivity.

3. Both nurse managers spoke of changes that were taking place in their facility. As a nurse, how can you assist your peers who are unhappy and seem to resist change even when it is positive?

- Specific strategies for dealing with change may include acknowledging that some resistance to change is normal, serving as a change agent yourself, identifying reasons for resistance to change, developing a positive outlook, forming a support group during the change process, and following steps in the change process.

Activity
Compare positive and negative change; planned and unplanned change. Review characteristics of effective change agents. Identify steps in the change process.

4. What factors should you consider before making a decision about accepting a position in a "team nursing" environment as opposed to a "primary nursing" environment?

- When making a decision, research the differences between team and primary nursing, consider your own values and what you hope to accomplish as a nurse, as well as the physical and time demands of each.
- Consider such questions as: "Do I want to manage my own group of clients, or do I want to share responsibilities with other health-care providers?" "Do I want to be responsible for providing care for only eight hours (one shift), or am I willing to take responsibility for a number of clients for 24 hours a day, 7 days a week?" "Do I mind working with persons less prepared than I?" "Do I wish to provide total care to my clients?"

CHAPTER 31: VITAL SIGNS

1. How might you interpret these values?

- You would compare them with previous baseline values preoperatively and in the recovery room.

2. What variables might have influenced this assessment data?

- Noting the elevated blood pressure, pulse, and respiration, you would check to see if the patient was in pain or was anxious. You would also check if there is a history of cardiovascular problems.

3. How would you proceed?

- You would also complete your assessment and check that the hip dressing is dry and intact.

CHAPTER 32: ASEPSIS

1. Mrs. Cortez's primary-care provider suspects that Mrs. Cortez has pneumonia, a serious respiratory infection. What data support Mrs. Cortez's increased risk for such an infection?

- Specific data may include, but are not limited to, the following: Mrs. Cortez is 76 years old and, thus, has reduced immune defences; she is dehydrated and has a nutritional deficit, therefore, her body is less able to synthesize antibodies to resist infection and disease; and she had a recent, prolonged respiratory infection which placed her at increased risk for other infections, such as pneumonia.

Activity
Consider how immune defences work and the factors that make the host susceptible to disease. Think about the risk factors for infection, especially age, nutritional status, stressors, and disease.

2. What other information or assessment data would be helpful to you when planning care for Mrs. Cortez?

- Review the assessment interview and physical health data. Useful data may include, but are not limited to, the following: Is she up-to-date on immunizations, such as influenza and pneumonia? Does she have any chronic illnesses? Is she taking any prescribed or over-the-counter medications that could increase her susceptibility to infection (e.g., steroids or cancer drugs)? Does she have any allergies? Is she under greater stress at this time than in the past? Does she have a history of frequent colds or upper respiratory infections? Does she have a history of urinary problems? Is she experiencing urinary frequency or pain on urination? What is the colour of her sputum?
- Assess for intact skin and oral mucous membranes, assess skin turgor, note signs of infection (e.g., fever, increased pulse, and respiratory rate).

3. You recognize that standard precautions are instituted for all hospitalized clients. Explain why the use of such precautions may not prevent the spread of Mrs. Cortez's respiratory infection to others.

- Use of standard precautions alone will not prevent the transmission of Mrs. Cortez's respiratory infection to other clients. Standard precautions are designed to prevent the transmission of blood-borne pathogens and do not apply to sputum, nasal secretions, or urine, unless contaminated with blood.

4. What can you do to prevent the spread of Mrs. Cortez's infection to other hospitalized clients and, at the same time, prevent Mrs. Cortez from getting infections from other clients?

- Depending on the type of organism infecting Mrs. Cortez, she may have to be placed on specific isolation precautions.
- Interventions that will protect all clients from the spread of disease include, but are not limited to, the following: consistent and thorough hand washing using antimicrobial agents prior to and after providing care; encouraging clients to cover their mouth with tissues when sneezing or coughing and disposing of soiled tissues in a bedside receptacle; making sure that reusable equipment is cleaned and reprocessed correctly; handling soiled linens to prevent contamination of your clothing; using a private room for infected persons when possible.

Activity
Compare and contrast the various types of isolation: body substance isolation, standard precautions for all hospitalized persons, contact isolation, droplet precautions, and barrier precautions.

5. You note that the housekeeping aide is leaving Mrs. Cortez's room. The aide stops to wash her hands, soaping them and rubbing them together under running water for about five seconds. She then turns off the water and proceeds with drying her hands. Should you intervene, and if so, what should you do?

- Compare the hand washing routine used by the aide with that suggested in your text and decide what aspects of good hand washing technique are missing.
- Consider congratulating the aide on washing her hands but tactfully correct her procedure. Emphasize the importance of washing both the palms of her hand and fingers for a minimum of 10 seconds each, thoroughly drying the hands, and then turning off the water using a paper towel to grasp the hand-operated control.

Activity
Have someone time your own hand washing to determine if you wash your hands for the recommended 20 seconds.

CHAPTER 33: SAFETY

1. While hospitalized, Mr. Moore experienced some mild confusion during the night, but his nurses decided not to restrain him. What are the best reasons for avoiding the use of restraints for some clients such as Mr. Moore?

- Restraints should only be used as a last resort. Some of the reasons include, but are not limited to, the following: research has not proven that restraining clients prevents falls or injury; they lessen the client's movement and independence, which infringes on their rights; the restraints can cause injury (pressure ulcers, skin tears, or death); restraints can interfere with the client's treatment; restraints can potentiate health problems such as poor circulation; restraints can be embarrassing to both client and family members.

Activity
Discuss the various types of restraints and consider the legal implications regarding their use.

2. What are some of the factors that may affect Mr. Moore's safety after he returns home?

- Several factors that could affect Mr. Moore's safety include, but are not limited to, the following: he is older than age 65 years; he has a history of falls; recent surgery for a hip fracture may impair his mobility; he may be weaker now than before his surgery.
- Mr. Moore may resume normal activities before he is strong enough.
- Mr. Moore may not be able to meet his nutritional needs as he will be preparing all but one meal per day. He is at greater risk for injury while preparing his own food.
- Mr. Moore may not understand the precautions necessary to protect his own safety.

3. What do you need to assess in regard to Mr. Moore's safety, and what suggestions can you make for enhancing his safety?

- You need to perform a home hazard appraisal. Suggestions for safety enhancement follow:
  - Because the majority of older adult injuries stem from falls, caution Mr. Moore about using area rugs and to be aware of where his pets are when he is up moving about.
  - Use grip handles in the bathtub and toilet.
  - All rooms should be well lit. Use night lights.
  - Carpets should be in good condition, and hardwood floors should not be waxed.
  - The house should have smoke alarms, and telephones should be easily accessible in case of emergency.

4. What strengths do you note about Mr. Moore that may protect him from injury when he returns home?

- He has been physically and socially active and independent; he has a strong family support system (his son will visit daily); he has access to community resources; his rooms are situated at one level and his house is small; he has pets to decrease his loneliness; and he has no other chronic illnesses that would interfere with his healing process.

Activity
Think about factors that would serve as a strength to you if you were in your own home recovering from an accident or surgery.

CHAPTER 34: HYGIENE

1. Support or contradict the use of the nursing diagnosis ***Self-Care Deficit: Bathing/Hygiene*** as an appropriate nursing diagnosis for Mrs. Baptista.

- There is little data to support that Mrs. Baptista actually has an impaired ability to perform her own bathing and hygiene. She has been providing for her own needs, has been ambulating, has no complaints of pain, and has no physical impairments.

Activity
Review the defining characteristics and related factors for the nursing diagnosis ***Self-Care Deficit: Bathing/Hygiene***.

2. Explain why it would be in Mrs. Baptista's best interests for you to assist her with hygienic care even though she doesn't feel she needs a bath.

- In general, bathing and personal care are essential for maintenance of skin integrity and mucous membranes; decreasing potential for infections; enhancing comfort; fostering a feeling of well-being; enhancing relaxation; minimizing odour; and increasing circulation.
- Benefits of personal care to Mrs. Baptista include, but are not limited to, the following: decreasing her risk of surgical wound infection, enhancing her comfort and ability to relax, cleaning her teeth to decrease the risk for infection and enable her to enjoy her food.

3. What factors should you consider before you attempt to persuade Mrs. Baptista that she needs to attend to her personal care?

- The following factors influence an individual's hygienic practices: culture, religion, environment, developmental level, health and energy, and personal preference.

- Assess Mrs. Baptista for fatigue, embarrassment, cultural beliefs, or personal preferences that may affect her decision to omit her personal care.
- Suggested questions for Mrs. Baptista: "Are you more tired today than yesterday?" "Do you want to wait until you go home?"

Activity
Think about factors that influence your decision to bathe or perform hygienic care when you are ill.

4. What approaches might you use if you feel that Mrs. Baptista does need her hair shampooed and needs to have her personal care attended to?

- Offer Mrs. Baptista several explanations regarding the benefits of proceeding with her bath and personal care, emphasizing the need to prevent infections.
- Offer to assist her and seek her input on where she wants to bathe (e.g., at the bedside or in the bathroom); gather her toiletries and provide for privacy.
- Make sure she has warm water and clean linens.

5. What advantages does performing baths and personal hygiene for clients offer the nurse?

- You can gather information and perform assessments during the bathing process.
- You can convey to clients that you have the time and the interest to make them feel better.

Activity
Think about conversations you have had with clients while bathing them. Did those conversations enhance your relationship with the client? What assessments did you make that would have been more difficult if you were not bathing the client?

CHAPTER 35: FECAL ELIMINATION

1. What conclusions, if any, can be drawn about Mr. Jakes' abdominal distress, diarrhea, and flatulence?

- Depending on the frequency and amount of stool he is having each day, he may be experiencing diarrhea.
- He may have a fecal impaction and is leaking liquid stool around the impaction.
- More information is needed before a definitive conclusion can be drawn.

Activity
Review common fecal elimination problems, especially constipation, diarrhea, and fecal impaction.

2. You learn that Mr. Jakes' stools have been liquid, in very small amounts, and at infrequent intervals, generally occurring when he feels the urge to defecate. What additional data is important to obtain from him?

- Ask Mr. Jakes about the number and amount of stool he is having in order to determine if he is actually having diarrhea or has an impaction.
- Assess his usual diet, his daily fluid intake, the amount of fibre in his diet, his daily activities, any medications that may be causing bowel disturbances, or other factors that could be contributing to constipation and possible impaction.

Activity
Discuss factors that affect defecation, such as age, activity, diet, fluid intake, and so on.

3. What nursing intervention is most appropriate prior to making suggestions to correct the problem he is experiencing?

- A digital examination may be performed to verify or rule out the presence of a fecal impaction.
- Other interventions may include administering an oil retention enema followed by a cleaning enema, suppositories, or stool softeners.
- If all else fails, manual removal of the fecal impaction may be necessary.

Activity
Review assessment and management of a client with a fecal elimination problem, especially constipation and fecal impaction.

4. What suggestions can you give Mr. Jakes about maintaining a regular bowel pattern?

- Consider interventions to promote regular defecation, such as increasing daily intake of fluids, especially liquids or prune juice; adding fibre to the diet; increasing daily activity; maintaining a regular schedule for defecation; and paying attention to the urge to defecate.

5. Explain why cathartics and laxatives are generally contraindicated for people in Mr. Jakes' situation.

- Because Mr. Jakes has some functional disability, he is at increased risk for the development of constipation.
- The chronic use of laxatives will actually make Mr. Jakes more prone to constipation and fecal impaction because he will lose muscle tone.
- Increased dietary fibre, use of fruits and vegetables, and other natural ways of dealing with constipation are safer and more appropriate.

Activity
Discuss laxative use among older clients. Provide research evidence to support your response.

CHAPTER 36: URINARY ELIMINATION

1. Is it correct to assume that Mrs. Kennedy is experiencing incisional pain? Why, or why not?

- It is not correct to assume that Mrs. Kennedy is experiencing incisional pain. Other possibilities may include, but are not limited to, the following: bladder distention from a full urinary bladder; pain from her femur fracture; or positional discomfort. Further assessments are necessary before drawing conclusions about Mrs. Kennedy's pain status.

Activity
Review Mrs. Kennedy's data and draw conclusions about possible causes of her pain.

2. What actions should be taken prior to administering pain medication to Mrs. Kennedy?

- Because Mrs. Kennedy has a distended abdomen, her bladder should be palpated for fullness and the catheter should be checked for patency.
- If the catheter is not patent, it should be repositioned and/or irrigated to re-establish patency, or the collection bag should be lowered to allow for free flow of urine. The presence of urine in the catheter bag does not guarantee catheter patency.

Activity
Consider all possible causes of Mrs. Kennedy's discomfort.

3. What precautions should be taken when collecting a urine sample from a client with an indwelling urinary catheter, and why?

- Because the physician has ordered the urine collection for culture and sensitivity, the presence of infection is suspected.
- Specific precautions involve wearing disposable gloves; maintaining sterility of the aspiration needle and urine collection cup; disinfecting the needle insertion site; avoiding puncture of the tube leading to the catheter balloon; avoiding contamination and possible entry of microorganisms into the client's bladder; and delivering the urine sample to the laboratory in a timely manner to prevent growth of bacteria.

Activity
Review the indications and the procedure for collecting a urine sample.

4. What measures can be taken to prevent Mrs. Kennedy from developing a urinary tract infection, if it is not already present?

- Maintaining absolute sterility when inserting the catheter; assuring patency of the drainage system; increasing fluid intake; performing frequent pericare; avoiding contamination of the catheter with stool when cleaning the site; maintaining the closed drainage system, and so on

Activity
Discuss care of the client with an indwelling urinary catheter.

5. What interventions may be useful in helping Mrs. Kennedy establish a normal urinary pattern following the removal of her catheter?

- Such interventions as clamping Mrs. Kennedy's catheter for specified intervals for a few days prior to catheter removal may help her regain muscle tone; increasing fluid intake will help prevent infections; sitting in a tub of warm water may assist with the urge to void; and activity will assist in regaining muscle control.
- Palpate Mrs. Kennedy's bladder at regular intervals to assess for urinary retention until normal urinary patterns develop.

Activity
Review procedure for removing retention catheters and address the factors that alter urinary elimination.

CHAPTER 37: SKIN INTEGRITY AND WOUND CARE

1. What data suggest that Mr. Johns is particularly vulnerable to pressure sore development?

- Mr. Johns' age (74 years), his decreased activity and mobility, his decreased sensation on the right, his incontinence, his nutritional status (thin for height)
- He has evidence of stage I pressure ulcer formation over his hips and coccyx.

Activity
Discuss factors that contribute to skin alterations and pressure sore development and why those factors place clients like Mr. Johns at risk. Consider clients you have cared for recently who have one or more of these risk factors.

2. What additional information do you need in order to use the Braden scale to determine Mr. Johns' potential for pressure sore development?

- The degree of sensation loss on his right side, his ability to recognize when he is incontinent, the frequency of his urinary incontinence, how often he ambulates and his capacity for ambulation, his serum protein as a measure of his nutritional status, his ability to move about and attend to his own needs

Activity
Review each section of the Braden scale.

3. What independent measures can you take to protect Mr. Johns' skin from further breakdown?

- Specific interventions may include, but are not limited to, the following: providing nutritious, protein-rich, and well-balanced meals and snacks; monitoring Mr. Johns' intake; assisting him to intake an adequate amount of food, if necessary; changing his position at least every two hours; avoiding shearing when moving or turning him; keeping his skin clean and dry; cleaning him of incontinent urine as soon as possible; using protective barriers (creams/ointments) and protective pressure relieving devices (e.g., gel flotation pad); encouraging ambulation with assistance; monitoring current reddened areas for skin breakdown or return to normal colour.

Activity
Consider nursing interventions that can prevent or reduce each of the risk factors that contribute to pressure ulcer development.

4. Considering that Mr. Johns does have impaired skin integrity, why is it important to institute treatment for pressure sores at this time?

- Mr. Johns has a stage I pressure ulcer. Therefore, treatment should be instituted immediately to prevent further skin breakdown and superficial ulcer development. The earlier the process can be reversed, the more likely Mr. Johns is to experience complete recovery. Mr. Johns' nutritional status should be addressed, and localized treatment should be instigated so that he has adequate protein for healing to occur.

Activity
Review and discuss the stages of pressure sore development.

CHAPTER 38: NUTRITION

1. How does Mrs. Lee's age and health status impact her nutritional needs?

- Older adults may need fewer calories but they maintain their need for nutrients. Mrs. Lee's weight loss may be interpreted as inadequate nutrient and/or caloric intake to meet the increased metabolic demands placed by a chronic illness.
- Continual weight loss will result in decreased immune function as well as decreased strength and stamina.

Activity
Review dietary modifications and nutritional requirements for older adults. Consider the demands placed on the body when illness is present.

2. What further information do you need regarding Mrs. Lee's present diet?

- Helpful information may include, but is not limited to, the following: Mrs. Lee's food preferences, current daily food intake, and food allergies; laboratory data, such as hemoglobin and hematocrit, serum albumin, white blood count; accessibility to food; support of family members; financial barriers, and so on.

Activity
Discuss factors that affect food intake. Review daily food and nutrient requirements for older adults. Consider *Canada's Food Guide to Healthy Living*.

3. What alternatives can you offer while Mrs. Lee is unable to tolerate meat?

- The most important aspect of eliminating meat from the diet is to assure adequate protein intake.
- Eggs, cheese, milk, grains, legumes, nuts, soy, and seeds can be combined to provide complete proteins.
- Iron, calcium, and vitamin supplements may be necessary until Mrs. Lee can resume her normal dietary intake.

Activity
Discuss alternatives to meat.

4. Offer suggestions for ways to enhance Mrs. Lee's intake during this period of decreased appetite.

- Strategies that may help Mrs. Lee include small frequent meals as opposed to large meals; use of dietary supplements, such as Ensure; soliciting the assistance of relatives to prepare food so that Mrs. Lee does not have to see or smell the food before eating; planning meals around foods that Mrs. Lee usually enjoys.

Activity
Consider how you feel when you are ill. What foods or techniques are effective in helping you eat when you know it is necessary?

5. Do you think that Mrs. Lee is a good candidate for a feeding tube? Why, or why not?

- Tube feedings are indicated for those clients who are unable to eat by mouth or are unable to swallow without risk of aspiration. At present, Mrs. Lee is able to eat and swallow without fear of aspiration; therefore, she is not a good candidate for a feeding tube.
- Her problem relates to her appetite, not her ability to eat or swallow.

Activity
Discuss the advantages and disadvantages of alternative feeding methods.

CHAPTER 39: OXYGENATION

1. If Mr. Markert is stable and progressing well, why is his oxygen saturation being monitored?

- Mr. Markert is at risk for respiratory complications related to his chest trauma and hemothorax. The pulse can detect changes in oxygen status, such as hypoxemia, before clinical manifestations develop, thus signalling complications early in their development so that actions can be taken before progression of the problem.

Activity
Examine respiratory conditions that affect breathing patterns and discuss interventions to reduce problems. Discuss implications for oxygen saturation monitoring.

2. Speculate about why Mr. Markert is receiving oxygen by nasal cannula as opposed to a face mask.

- Because Mr. Markert is stable and his pulse oximeter indicates an oxygen saturation level of 98 percent, low levels of oxygen are sufficient for his needs, making the nasal cannula the best choice. It is comfortable, inexpensive, and delivers adequate levels of oxygen. Should Mr. Markert become unstable and require more oxygen delivery, a mask would be a better choice.

Activity
Review oxygen delivery systems.

3. Compare and contrast a hemothorax with a pneumothorax.

- Hemothorax and pneumothorax are similar in that they can both be caused by trauma, result in a loss of negative pressure within the pleural cavity, and are treated by insertion of a chest tube. Both cause a decrease in adequate oxygen concentration that leads to patient distress. Pneumothorax can also just occur spontaneously.
- They differ in that a pneumothorax is the accumulation of air within the pleural cavity, whereas a hemothorax is the accumulation of blood and fluid in the pleural cavity.

Activity
Review the definitions of hemothorax and pneumothorax.

4. What precautions need to be taken when caring for Mr. Markert while his chest tube is in place?

- Important nursing care involves frequently monitoring Mr. Markert's respiratory and cardiac status and his oxygen saturations; monitoring the patency of his drainage system; maintaining the integrity of his water seal drainage; never raising the draining system above his chest; implementing emergency measures should an air leak develop; and providing Mr. Markert with information and reassurance.

Activity
Review care of a client with a chest tube and drainage system.

5. Offer suggestions that would help Mr. Markert, or any person with a respiratory problem, to establish healthy breathing after his chest tube is removed.

- Mr. Markert would benefit from sitting or lying in a position that enhances respirations, engaging in keep breathing exercises, ambulating or exercising, and maintaining adequate fluid intake.

CHAPTER 40: FLUID, ELECTROLYTE, AND ACID-BASE BALANCE

1. Predict the possible consequences of Mr. Sam's fever, diarrhea, and diaphoresis on his fluid and electrolyte status.

- Mr. Sam is suffering fluid losses from two primary sources, diarrhea and perspiration. Because diarrhea causes loss of electrolytes, the most likely consequences of his symptoms are hypovolemia electrolyte imbalance, especially sodium imbalance. If he suffered no electrolyte losses, he would become dehydrated but would not suffer an electrolyte imbalance.

Activity
Address the body's regulation of fluid volume and the factors that affect fluid and electrolyte balance.

2. Why do you think the physician ordered lactated Ringer's solution for Mr. Sam rather than another type of fluid replacement, such as 5 percent dextrose in water?

- Mr. Sam is suffering an electrolyte and fluid deficit; therefore, both should be replaced. Lactated Ringer's solution contains electrolytes, such as sodium, potassium, and chloride as well as fluid. Five percent dextrose in water provides fluid and nutrients but no electrolytes.

Activity
Consider the various types of fluid replacements and their therapeutic values.

3. Why is it important to monitor Mr. Sam's intake and output?

- Mr. Sam has several risk factors for fluid and electrolyte imbalance. When output exceeds intake, fluid volume deficit occurs. When intake exceeds output, fluid volume overload occurs. It is important to compare the volume of fluid excreted over a 24-hour period. Intake should approximate output.

Activity
Review the indications for monitoring fluid intake and output.

4. Is it correct to assume that Mr. Sam's intravenous infusion does not need to be monitored because it is being administered by an infusion pump? Why or why not?

- It is incorrect to assume that Mr. Sam's intravenous infusion does not need to monitored. A pump assists with delivering an infusion at a specified rate and may provide warnings about air in the line or the IV battery being low, but provides no information about the IV and subsequent loss of bicarbonate.

Activity
Discuss assessment of and complications associated with intravenous infusions.

5. How would you know if Mr. Sam was developing an acid-base imbalance related to his severe diarrhea?

- Mr. Sam is at risk for the development of metabolic acidosis because of his severe diarrhea and subsequent loss of bicarbonate. Clinical signs may include a fruity odour to his breath, lethargy, headache, weakness, and disorientation. Many of these symptoms can be present with gastroenteritis, so it is important to monitor blood gas results for indications of imbalance.

Activity
Review common acid-base imbalances and their associated clinical manifestations.

CHAPTER 41: SENSORY PERCEPTION

1. Identify factors that place Mrs. Dodd at risk for the development of sensory deprivation or overload.

- Mrs. Dodd is at increased risk for sensory overload due to her environment (critical care unit). She is being bombarded by the noise of her monitors and ventilator, which may be distorted and meaningless due to the sedation she is receiving. Her pain and inability to communicate also contribute to her sensory overload as they contribute to her feelings of being overwhelmed and out of control.

Activity
Consider factors that place the client at risk for either sensory deprivation or sensory overload.

2. What assessment findings would alert you to Mrs. Dodd experiencing sensory overload as opposed to sensory deprivation?

- Signs of sensory overload may include, but are not limited to, the following: restlessness, agitation, confusion, disorientation, hallucinations, or inability to sleep or rest. Signs of sensory deprivation may include apathy, emotional detachment, depression, and so on. Many times, the signs of sensory deprivation and overload are similar, consequently the nurse should assess the client for factors that may be contributing to one problem over the other.

Activity
Review the clinical signs of sensory overload and deprivation.

3. How can you intervene to reduce Mrs. Dodd's risk for disturbed sensory preception?

- Interventions include, but are not limited to, the following: reducing lights; decreasing noise to the degree possible (close doors or curtains); providing comfort measures; explaining procedures; orienting the client to person, place, and time; speaking in a soft, unhurried manner; limiting visitors; and reducing interruptions.

Activity
Review nursing interventions for clients experiencing sensory overload.

4. How might the care of a client in the home setting differ from the care of a client, such as Mrs. Dodd, who is receiving care in a critical care unit?

- Clients cared for at home may experience either sensory deprivation or overload depending on the environment. If it is a busy, active environment with several family members, they may experience overload. If clients live alone, have few supportive family members, experience high noise levels, or are seldom contacted, they are more likely to experience social isolation and become withdrawn or uncommunicative and lose interest in their usual activities.

  Interventions for home care or ICU clients are similar and adapted to the specific needs of the client, regardless of setting.

Activity
Review factors that contribute to sensory deprivation or sensory overload.

CHAPTER 42: REST AND SLEEP

1. Explain why keeping a sleep diary might be beneficial for Ms. Marsh.

- A sleep diary would help Ms. Marsh identify factors that may be interfering with her ability to establish and maintain good sleep habits. Many times, people are unaware of the relationship between what they do at bedtime and their ability to sleep.

- A sleep diary would help Ms. Marsh better estimate the actual amount of sleep she is or is not getting.

Activity
Discuss the benefits of keeping written records of sleep patterns and bedtime habits associated with sleep.

2. What further information would be helpful to obtain from her about her sleep problem?

- Other data that would be helpful may include, but are not limited to, the following: activities or bedtime habits; the degree of noise in Ms. Marsh's home environment; whether she feels stressed or anxious at nighttime; what foods she consumes prior to attempting sleep; if she uses over-the-counter medications to help her sleep; if she has a regular or irregular pattern of arising; whether or not she is a smoker, and so on.

Activity
Review factors that affect sleep.

3. What suggestions can you make that may help her develop better sleep habits when she returns home?

- Suggest that Ms. Marsh exercise earlier in the day, as exercise is a stimulant; read a book or pursue another quiet activity rather than watch TV; maintain regular nighttime and waking hours to develop a pattern; and encourage use of relaxation or meditation techniques to relax before going to bed.

Activity
Discuss interventions to decrease environmental distractions and create a restful environment. Which of your own sleep patterns are beneficial to you in inducing sleep? Which habits do you avoid because you know they will keep you from sleeping?

4. What evidence suggests that Ms. Marsh is experiencing a primary, as opposed to a secondary, sleep disorder?

- Ms. Marsh has a history of insomnia, most likely due to her bedtime habits: this supports her having a primary sleep disorder. If her postoperative pain or medication was keeping her from sleeping, she would be experiencing a secondary sleep disorder.

Activity
Review the difference between primary and secondary sleep disorders. (Primary disorders refer to specific sleep disorders, such as insomnia or narcolepsy.)

5. What are the most common problems that interfere with clients' ability to sleep while hospitalized?

- Some of the common problems are different nighttime routines; too much light or noise; different bed and pillow; unfamiliar immediate environment; the possibility of rooming with a stranger; interruptions for medications or treatments, and so on.

Activity
If you were hospitalized, what factors would interfere with your ability to sleep?

CHAPTER 43: ACTIVITY AND EXERCISE

1. Why is it essential to maintain proper body alignment when turning Mrs. Gomez or helping her out of bed to ambulate?

- Maintaining body alignment will reduce the stress and strain on Mrs. Gomez's joints and muscles, thereby preventing increased pain; enhance lung expansion for better oxygenation; promote efficient circulation; decrease the potential for injury; and maintain her centre of gravity, thereby reducing her chances of falling.

Activity
Explore the concepts of body alignment, balance, and joint mobility and apply the concepts to Mrs. Gomez's situation.

2. What assessment findings would alert you that Mrs. Gomez is developing problems associated with her current state of decreased mobility?

- Adverse signs and symptoms associated with immobility may include, but are not limited to, the following: decreased energy and muscular strength, painful or stiff joints, weakness, muscular atrophy, orthostatic hypotension, dependent edema, cough related to pooling of respiratory secretions, hypostatic pneumonia, and so on.

Activity
Review the effects of immobility and exercise on body systems.

3. Cite examples of exercises you can recommend for Mrs. Gomez that will reduce her risk for disuse syndrome during her recovery.

- Exercises may include actively participating in self-care activities, such as bathing, combing her hair, and so on; active range of motion or isometric exercises every four hours until ambulatory; deep breathing exercises; passive range of motion, if she is unable to actively participate in exercises; ambulation, and so on.

Activity
Consider exercises that maintain joint and skin integrity and can be performed while in bed or sitting in a chair.

4. What are some of the factors you should consider prior to moving Mrs. Gomez to a sitting position on the edge of the bed in preparation for ambulation?

- Factors may include, but are not limited to, the following: Mrs. Gomez's weight and her ability to assist you; her pain status or potential for pain; the number of people available to assist; the need for or availability of equipment, such as a cane or walker; Mrs. Gomez's symptoms when assisted to a sitting position (e.g., hypotension); whether this is Mrs. Gomez's first time up; her state of mental alertness and ability to follow instructions.

Activity
Consider safety factors that are important to both client and nurse.

5. Mrs. Gomez will be using a walker to assist her with ambulation when she goes home. What teaching should be done prior to Mrs. Gomez's discharge from the hospital regarding use of a walker?

- Teach Mrs. Gomez the proper use of the walker, including how and when to move the walker. (Walkers with wheels may be less steady than walkers without wheels but are easier to move.)
- Caution Mrs. Gomez about the use of area rugs or pets that might get under foot when she goes home.
- Advise Mrs. Gomez to rest when she feels fatigued.

Activity
Consider the energy required for use of a walker and possible safety hazards at home.

CHAPTER 44: CLIENTS HAVING SURGERY: PROMOTING HEALTHY RECOVERY

1. What factors place Mr. Teng at increased risk for the development of complications during and after surgery?

- Factors that may increase Mr. Teng's risk may include, but are not limited to, the following: Mr. Teng is 77 years old, placing him at greater risk than younger adults; his respiratory status is compromised, and he runs a greater risk for developing postoperative atelectasis or lung infection; he may be taking medications that will slow healing, such as corticosteroids, and so on.

Activity
Discuss surgical risk factors (age, nutritional status, fluid and electrolyte status, general health, medications, and the client's mental health and attitude). Consider clients you have cared for in the past. What factors may have placed those clients at increased risk for surgical complications?

2. Speculate about why Mr. Teng's surgeon and anesthesiologist decided to perform Mr. Teng's surgery under regional anesthesia as opposed to general anesthesia.

- A major disadvantage of general anesthesia is that it depresses the respiratory and circulatory systems, so the surgeon and anesthesiologist probably chose not to further complicate Mr. Teng's respiratory status. A client's preference for a particular anesthesia is also considered when selecting the type of anesthesia to use.

Activity
Review the various types of anesthesia, including general and regional, and consider the advantages and disadvantages of each type. If you had to have an operation, which type anesthesia would you prefer if given an option?

3. What preparations were taken during the preoperative period in order to protect Mr. Teng from possible complications during and after his surgery?

- Mr. Teng's preoperative preparation most likely included, but was not limited to, the following: preoperative teaching regarding preparation for surgery; what to expect following surgery; deep breathing, coughing, and leg exercises; how to splint his abdomen when moving or coughing; fluid and nutritional support; a bath or shower; anti-embolism stockings; and medications to enhance rest the night prior to the scheduled surgery.

Activity
Consider the physical and psychological preparation of clients for surgery. If you were scheduled for surgery, what information do you think would be helpful to you?

4. How will Mr. Teng's postoperative assessments differ from those of a person who received general anesthesia?

- Even though Mr. Teng had spinal anesthesia and is awake, the same general assessments will be made to detect actual or potential problems. He will not go through the stages of anesthesia arousal or experience altered gag reflexes. He will be assessed for return of feeling to his lower extremities to evaluate remaining spinal anesthesia effect. His postoperative monitoring will not differ from that of other clients.

Activity
Review and discuss recovery room assessments.

5. What postoperative precautions are especially important to Mr. Teng in view of his chronic lung condition?

- Specific precautions may include, but are not limited to, the following: promoting adequate hydration to replace fluids lost during surgery or fluid limitations prior to surgery; early movement and ambulation to foster maximum lung expansion and prevent lung infection; deep breathing exercises to remove mucus and prevent stasis of lung secretions; pain control so that he can ambulate and cough more effectively; leg exercises to prevent thrombophlebitis, and so on.

Activity
Review interventions designed to promote recovery.

CHAPTER 45: PAIN MANAGEMENT

1. What conclusions, if any, can be drawn about Mrs. Lundahl's pain status?
- There is subjective data (rating her pain as 5) and objective data (vital signs, position, holding abdomen, lying in rigid position) to support that Mrs. Lundahl is experiencing pain; however, no conclusions can be drawn about the intensity, location, quality, or pattern of Mrs. Lundahl's pain.

Activity
Review the pain assessment interview.

2. Does Mrs. Lundahl's rating of her pain as 5 mean that she is not experiencing pain severe enough to warrant intervention?
- It would be incorrect to assume that Mrs. Lundahl needs no interventions for her pain. People rate their pain differently on the basis of their past pain experiences, their pain tolerance, their ethnic/cultural values, and so on. Mrs. Lundahl should be asked if she needs pain intervention.

Activity
Review the factors that impact a person's perception of pain.

3. What type of pain is Mrs. Lundahl experiencing?
- Mrs. Lundahl is most likely experiencing acute pain from her surgery. Depending on the amount of manipulation of bowel, blood vessels, and so on, within her abdomen, she may also be experiencing visceral pain.

Activity
Contrast the various types of pain: cutaneous, deep, somatic, visceral, acute, chronic, radiating, and referred.

4. What interventions, in addition to pain medication, may be useful in reducing Mrs. Lundahl's pain?
- Numerous interventions may be helpful, for example, changing her body position, a back massage, use of a cutaneous stimulator, and distraction (e.g., soft music).

Activity
Review the various types of nonpharmacological pain management.

5. How will you know if your interventions have been effective in reducing Mrs. Lundahl's pain?
- The most reliable method of determining that Mrs. Lundahl's pain has been relieved is her telling you that her pain has been relieved.
- Mrs. Lundahl resting quietly or sleeping; pink colour, absence of nausea or perspiration; relaxed facial expression, and so on indicate pain relief. Changes in blood pressure and pulse rate are not always a reliable indicator of the presence or absence of pain.

Activity
Review subjective and objective indicators of pain.

CHAPTER 46: SELF-CONCEPT

1. Given Craig's age, speculate about how Craig's self-concept is at risk of being adversely affected by his disability.
- Because of his age, Craig's basic self-concept may be fairly well set; thus, it is not likely to be adversely altered. Components of his self-concept (body image and self-esteem) may, however, be adversely affected by his amputation. His body image is at risk because his amputation will alter the way he views his body. His personal identity is at risk because he visualizes himself as a basketball player.

Activity
Review the concepts of self-concept and self-esteem. Consider whether this disability will alter the way Craig "sees" himself or "feels about" himself. Discuss the components of self-concept, including body image, role performance, personal identity, and self-esteem.

2. What data suggest that Craig's self-esteem is, or is at risk of being, negatively impacted by his amputation?
- Craig's mood, his inability to view his amputated stump, and his unwillingness to discuss his rehabilitation program are all behaviours associated with low self-esteem. If they continue, and other such behaviours develop, it will be very suggestive of negative alteration of his self-esteem. Craig's father is also having difficulty accepting his son's loss; therefore, he may not be able to adequately support Craig throughout his hospitalization and rehabilitation.

Activity
Review common behaviours associated with low self-esteem and self-esteem assessment parameters.

3. What factors are likely to affect Craig's adaptation to his amputation and rehabilitation?

- Many factors will impact Craig's adaptation process, including, but not limited to, the following: the positive or negative attitude demonstrated by his nurses, the rehabilitation team and primary-care provider; the support of family and friends; his ability to positively integrate his artificial limb into his body image; his ability to revise his personal and professional goals; and his ability to accept and make use of resources that are available to him.

Activity
Discuss how to assist the client with identification of strengths, changing language patterns, and encouraging positive self-evaluation.

4. How would your interventions differ for a client who was 70 years old?

- Older clients fear dependence more than younger clients do; therefore, the loss of a limb places them at greater risk for lowered self-esteem. A 70-year-old would not physically progress as rapidly as a 20-year-old and would, thus, need more time to accomplish rehabilitation goals. A younger person may adapt to a prosthesis more quickly than an older person who may have had mobility problems prior to the loss of a limb. Care would be similar for both age groups: encouraging participation in their plan of care; encouraging them to participate in their own care; identifying personal strengths, and so on.

5. What other groups of clients, in addition to those with amputations, are at risk for the development of altered self-esteem or body image?

- Clients with chronic illnesses (e.g., schizophrenia, diabetes mellitus, renal failure), socially unacceptable diseases (e.g., AIDS, obesity, STDs), disfigurement (burns, colostomy, birth defects)

Activity
Review stressors affecting self-concept and self-esteem. Consider the physical or mental changes that could affect one's self-esteem. Think of a characteristic that you would change about yourself. Do you think that characteristic affects your self-image or self-esteem?

CHAPTER 47: STRESS AND COPING

1. Speculate about the stressors that Ms. Levitt is experiencing.

- Ms. Levitt's stressors may include, but are not limited to, the following: the sole responsibility of three children; the lack of financial assistance from her husband; the demands being placed on her by her job, school, and community activities; the lack of an emotional support system; possible financial problems; weight gain; or not having adequate time for rest or leisure activities.

Activity
Compare stress as a stimulus with stress as a response. Analyze your own lifestyle and daily routines. What are your primary stressors or potential stressors?

2. From the data provided, how do you think Ms. Levitt is responding to the stressors you identified?

- Ms. Levitt seems to have predominantly physiological manifestations of stress—physical problems with no apparent cause.

Activity
Consider the physiological, psychological, and cognitive manifestations that may be associated with stressors and apply them to Ms. Levitt's situation. Think of your own responses to stress. How do you know when you are anxious or feeling stressed?

3. Explore anger as a possible cause of Ms. Levitt's symptoms.

- There are no data to support that Ms. Levitt is angry; however, she may not be expressing her anger. Any of her stressors could provoke anger, and suppression of that anger could result in physical signs and symptoms.

Activity
Compare constructive anger with destructive anger. How do you feel when you are angry? What do you do to resolve your anger?

4. What cues would alert you that Ms. Levitt is adapting to the stressors in her life in a positive and healthy manner?

- Some of the changes that would serve as cues to positive adaptation may include decreased frequency or absence of symptoms produced by stress; lifestyle changes, such as decreased activities; change in diet, balancing leisure with work, and taking time for herself.

Activity
Think about the various modes of adapting to stress and the characteristics associated with the adaptive response. Think of changes that you have made or want to make to reduce stress in your own life.

5. As a nurse, there will be situations or events that will increase your anxiety and stress. What can you do to help youself deal in a positive manner with those situations or events?

- Being able to recognize your own stress is an important first step in dealing with clients' stress.

Activity
Review all the possible interventions for dealing with stress, including techniques for nurses. Think about how those interventions may be helpful for reducing your own stress.

CHAPTER 48: LOSS, GRIEVING, AND DEATH

1. From the data provided, describe the phase of bereavement being experienced by each of the three surviving sons.

- The eldest son most nearly approximates the "awareness of loss" phase. He is experiencing the loss but is able to resume normal activities.
- The middle son has characteristics of the "conservation/withdrawal" phase. He has a need to be alone and is experiencing both physical and psychological symptoms of bereavement.
- The younger son is experiencing "shock." He is having difficulty believing that his mother is dead and is experiencing several physical symptoms.

Activity
Consider the phases of bereavement.

2. What factors may have affected how each of the brothers reacted to the death of their mother?

- Factors may have included the amount of conflict or closeness each brother felt toward the mother; the amount of time and/or caring each was able to provide; the significance of the loss to each; the spiritual beliefs and practices of each; the amount of guilt each may be experiencing related to ability to provide for the mother's needs during her later years or recent illness.

Activity
Consider the impact of age on loss, and review the factors that influence a loss reaction.

3. What cues, other than physical signs, might have indicated that Mrs. Govinda was dying even though her death was unexpected?

- Cues may have included, but are not limited to, the following: wanting to talk about death, reminiscing or reviewing one's life; emotionally withdrawing or becoming quiet and pensive; allowing others to assume responsibility for physical care; voicing a sense of urgency about seeing loved ones; and so on.

Activity
Consider care of the dying client in terms of the three stages of living fully until death.

4. What is the primary factor to consider when trying to make the decision to administer or withhold pain medication when a client is dying?

- All clients have the right to pain control. The primary factor to consider is the client's desire to be pain free or as pain free as possible during the dying process.
- Consider also the clients' ability to seek pain control; if they cannot verbalize their need for pain control, you must be alert for the outward signs that the client is in pain, such as restlessness, moaning, and so on.

Activity
Consider the dying person's bill of rights, and review interventions to meet the physiological needs of the dying client.

5. Explore your own feelings about death, and consider how those feelings may affect the care you provide to the dying client.

Activity
Think about losses you have experienced in your own life. Were those losses expected or unexpected? Who was most supportive to you during your loss? What helped you deal with your grief? How will that experience benefit you when caring for dying clients or their families?

GLOSSARY

24-hour food recall record of food and fluid intake for a 24-hour period

Abdominal breathing respirations in which the abdomen moves out while the diaphragm descends

Abdominal paracentesis removal of fluids from the peritoneal cavity

Abduction movement of a bone away from the midline of the body

Abortion termination of a pregnancy before the fetus reaches the stage of viability, may be accidental, spontaneous, or induced

Abrasion wearing away of a structure, such as the skin or teeth

Abscess a localized collection of pus and disintegrating body tissues

Acapnia a decreased level of carbon dioxide in the blood

Accommodation (Piaget) a process of change whereby cognitive processes mature sufficiently to allow a person to solve problems that were previously unsolvable

Accountable (accountability) being responsible for one's actions and accepting the consequences of one's behaviour

Accreditation the process by which a voluntary organization or governmental agency appraises and grants accredited status to institutions, programs, or services that meet predetermined criteria

Acculturation (assimilation) (of a group) the blending of attitudes and beliefs; process by which members of a foreign culture learn the values and behaviours of a culture to which they have immigrated

Acholic clay coloured and free from bile

Acid a substance which yields hydrogen ions in solution and from which hydrogen may be displaced by a metal to form a salt

Acidosis (acidemia) a condition that occurs with increases in blood carbonic acid or with decreases in blood bicarbonate; blood pH below 7.35

Acne an inflammatory condition of the sebaceous glands

Active assistive range-of-motion (ROM) exercise the client with the nurse's assistance uses a stronger, opposite arm or leg to move each of the joints of a limb incapable of active motion

Active euthanasia actions that directly bring about the client's death with or without consent

Active immunity a resistance of the body to infection in which the host produces its own antibodies in response to natural or artificial antigens

Active range-of-motion (ROM) exercise isotonic exercise in which the client moves each joint in the body through its complete range of movement, maximally stretching all muscle groups within each plane, over the joint

Active transport movement of substances across cell membranes against the concentration gradient

Activity/exercise pattern refers to a person's pattern of exercise, activity, leisure, and recreation

Activity theory describes the best way to age as staying physically active during these years

Activity tolerance the type and amount of exercise or daily activities an individual is able to perform

Actual loss can be identified by others and can arise either in response to or in anticipation of a situation

Acupuncture a Chinese practice of piercing specific superficial nerves with needles, often to treat pain

Acute sharp or severe; describing a severe condition with a sudden onset and short course (as opposed to chronic)

Acute illness rapidly occurring illness that runs its course and the individual then returns to previous level of functioning

Adaptation the process of modifying to meet new, changing, or different conditions

Adaptive behaviour the responses by which the whole person copes with internal and external environmental stimuli

Adaptive mechanisms learned behaviours that assist an individual to adjust to the environment

Addiction a psychological dependence characterized by craving for and compulsive use of opioids for an effect other than pain relief

Adduction movement of a bone toward the midline of the body

Adenosine triphosphate (ATP) a compound with high-energy bonds that store energy for later use in performing cellular functions

Adherent (cohesive) sticking together, clinging

Adhesion a fibrous band or structure by which parts are abnormally held together

Adipose fat; of a fatty nature

Adjuvant analgesic medication that may enhance the effects of other analgesics or have its own analgesic properties

ADLs, activities of daily living the tasks of daily life, such as eating, bathing, and dressing

Adsorbent substance that attracts other particles or materials to its surface

Advance medical directive a statement the client makes prior to receiving health care specifying the client's wishes regarding health-care decisions

Adventitious breath sounds abnormal or acquired breath sounds

Advocacy pleading and supporting clients' rights by respecting client decisions and enhancing client autonomy

Advocate an individual who pleads the cause of another or argues or pleads for a cause or proposal

Aerobic requiring oxygen

Aerobic exercise any activity during which the body takes in more or an equal amount of oxygen than it expends

Afebrile absence of a fever

Affect feelings, emotions

Affective learning acquired knowledge that includes feelings, emotions, interests, attitudes, and appreciations

Agglutination the process of clumping together

Agglutinin a specific antibody formed in the blood

Agglutinogen a substance that acts as an antigen and stimulates the production of agglutinins

Agnostic a person who doubts the existence of God or a supreme being or believes the existence of God has not been proved

Agonist a drug that interacts with a receptor to produce a response

Agonist-antagonist analgesic act like opioids to relieve pain

AIDS (acquired immune deficiency syndrome) an immunodeficiency syndrome which is caused by the human immunodeficiency virus (HIV)

Air-borne precautions practices initiated to prevent the spread of air-borne microorganisms

Air-borne transmission air currents transport the microorganism

Alarm reaction initial stage of the adaptation syndrome described by Selye

Albinism the complete or partial lack of melanin in the skin, hair, and eyes

Albumin the main protein found in the blood, also found in breast milk

Albuminuria the presence of albumin in the urine

Algor mortis the gradual decrease of the body's temperature after death

Alignment (posture) the proper relationship of body segments to one another

Alkalosis (alkalemia) a condition that occurs with increases in blood bicarbonate or decreases in blood carbonic acid; blood pH above 7.45

Alopecia the loss of scalp hair (baldness) or body hair

Alveolar-capillary membrane formed by the alveolar and capillary walls where gas exchange occurs

Alzheimer's disease a progressive, chronic, organic mental disorder

AMA (against medical authority) when a client leaves the agency without permission of the physician

Amblyopia reduced visual acuity in one eye

Ambu bag (resuscitation bag) a device used to provide oxygen to a client when they are unable to breathe for themselves

Ambulation the act of walking

Ampule a small glass container for individual doses of liquid medications

Anabolism a process in which simple substances are converted by the body cells into more complex substances (e.g., building tissue, positive nitrogen balance)

Anaerobe an organism that does not require oxygen to live

Anaerobic not requiring oxygen to live

Anaerobic exercise involves activity in which the muscles cannot draw out enough oxygen from the bloodstream; used in endurance training

Analgesic a medication used to alter the perception and interpretation of pain

Anal intercourse penis is inserted into the anus and rectum of the sexual partner

Anaphylaxis (anaphylactic shock, anaphylactic reaction) a severe allergic reaction

Andragogy the art and science of helping adults learn

Anemia a condition in which the blood is deficient in red blood cells or hemoglobin

Aneroid containing no liquid

Anesthesia loss of sensation or feeling; induced loss of the sense of pain

Aneurysm dilation or outpouching of the wall of an artery or vein

Anger subjective emotional state of strong displeasure

Angiography a diagnostic procedure enabling X-ray visual examination of the vascular system after injection of a radiopaque dye

Angle of Louis the junction between the body of the sternum and the manubrium; the starting point for locating the ribs anteriorly

Anilingus oral-anal stimulation

Anion ion which carries a negative charge; chloride, bicarbonate, phosphate, sulfate

Anisocoria unequal pupils

Ankylosis permanent fixation of a joint

Anorexia lack of appetite

Anorexia nervosa a disease characterized by a prolonged inability or refusal to eat, rapid weight loss, and emaciation in persons who continue to believe they are fat

Anoscopy visual examination of the anal canal using an anoscope (a lighted instrument)

Anoxemia (hypoxemia) a condition in which the level of oxygen in the blood is below normal

Anoxia systemic absence or reduction of oxygen in the body tissues below physiological levels

Answer (legal) a written response made by the defendant

Antagonist a drug that interferes with a cell receptor without stimulating it and blocks the action of an agonist

Antecubital fossa or space the point on the arm located in front of the elbow

Anterior toward, or at the front of

Anthropometric measurements indicators of the size and composition of the body (e.g., height, weight, skinfold)

Antibiotic a natural or synthetic substance that has the capacity to inhibit the growth of or kill other microorganisms

Antibody (immunoglobulin) a protective protein substance produced in the body to counteract antigens

Anticipatory loss the state in which an individual or group experiences reactions in response to an expected significant loss

Antidiuretic hormone (ADH) a hormone that is stored and released by the posterior pituitary gland and that controls water reabsorption from the kidney tubules; also referred to as vasopressin

Antigen a substance capable of inducing the formation of antibodies

Antihelix the semicircular ridge on the anterior of the ear and parallel to the helix

Antimicrobial destructive to or preventing the development of microorganisms

Antipyretic a substance that is effective in relieving fever

Antiseptic an agent that inhibits the growth of some microorganisms

Anuria the failure of the kidneys to produce urine, resulting in a total lack of urination or output of less than 100 mL per day in an adult

Anxiety a state of mental uneasiness, apprehension, or dread producing an increased level of arousal caused by an impending or anticipated threat to self or significant relationships

Apathy lack of interest or feeling

Apex the pointed end of a cone-shaped part

Apgar a scoring system to assess newborn babies

Aphasia inability to communicate through speech, writing, or signs, caused by dysfunction of brain centre

Apical pulse a central pulse located at the apex of the heart

Apical-radial pulse measurement of the apical beat and the radial pulse at the same time

Apnea a complete absence of respirations

Apocrine glands increase secretions and become fully functioning during puberty; release sweat in response to emotional stimuli

Apothecary a system of medication measurement that derives from old England

Approximate (referring to wound or incision edges) to bring close together

Aquathermia to treat with warm water

Arcus senilis partial or complete glossy, white circle around the periphery of the cornea; appears later in life

Areflexia absence of reflexes

Arm muscle circumference (AMC) considered an index of the body's protein reserves, calculated from the triceps skinfold and mid-upper-arm circumference

Arrhythmia (dysrhythmia) a pulse with an abnormal rhythm

Arterial blood gases oxygen and carbon dioxide concentrations (PO_2, PCO_2), hydrogen ion concentration ($_pH$), and oxygen saturation of the hemoglobin in arterial blood; also describe the laboratory tests that measure these levels

Arterial blood pressure the measure of the pressure exerted by the blood as it pulsates through the arteries

Arteriosclerosis a condition in which the elastic and muscular tissues of the arteries are replaced with fibrous tissue

Ascites the accumulation of fluid in the abdominal cavity

Asepsis freedom from infection or infectious material

Asphyxia inadequate intake of oxygen

Aspirate to remove gases or fluids from a cavity by using suction

Assault an attempt or threat to touch another person unjustifiably

Assertiveness standing up for one's rights using direct, honest communication without impeding the rights of others

Assessing the process of collecting, organizing, validating, and recording data (information) about a client's health status

Assimilation (of a group) see *Acculturation*

Assisted suicide a form of active euthanasia in which clients are given the means to kill themselves

Assumptions statements of fact or suppositions that people accept as the underlying theoretical foundation for conceptualizations about a phenomenon

Astigmatism an uneven curvature of the cornea that prevents horizontal and vertical rays from focusing on the retina

Astringent an agent that causes contraction or shrinkage of tissue; usually applied topically

Ataxia impaired muscle coordination

Atelectasis a condition that occurs when ventilation is decreased and pooled secretions accumulate in a dependent area of a bronchiole and block it

Atheist one who denies the existence of God

Athlete's foot a fungal infection of the foot caused by tinea pedis

Atomizer a device that produces large droplets for inhalation

Atony lack of normal muscle tone

Atrophic vaginitis vaginal atrophy characterized by thinning and drying of the vaginal wall, loss of elasticity, and decreased lubrication

Atrophy wasting away; decrease in size of organ or tissue (e.g., muscle)

Attentive listening using all the senses and body positioning to listen to the client

Attitude mental stance that is composed of many different beliefs; usually involving a positive or negative judgment toward a person, object, or idea

Audit (nursing) a process in which the nursing interventions are monitored and measured against established standards

Auditory related to or experienced through hearing

Auricle (pinna) flap of the ear

Auscultation the process of listening to sounds produced within the body

Auscultatory gap the temporary disappearance of sounds normally heard over the brachial artery when the sphygmomanometer cuff pressure is high and the sounds reappear at a lower level

Authority the power given by an organization to direct the work of others; the right to act

Autoantigen an antigen that despite being a constituent of normal tissue is the target of a cell-mediated response

Autocratic (leadership) an authoritarian style of leadership in which the leader makes decisions for the group

Autonomy the state of being independent and self-directed without outside control, to make one's own decisions

Autopsy (postmortem examination) an examination of the body after death to determine the cause of death and to learn more about a disease process

Awareness the ability to perceive environmental stimuli and body reactions and to respond appropriately through thought and action

Axillary line an imaginary line extending vertically from the anterior fold of the axilla

Axillary tail of Spence a projection of breast tissue into the axilla

Babinski (plantar) reflex in infants up to one year, the normal fanning out of toes and dorsiflexion of the big toe elicited by stroking the sole of the foot; after one year the normal flexing of the toes at this stroking

Bacteremia bacteria in the blood

Bacteria infection-causing agents

Bactericide (bactericidal) an agent capable of killing some microorganisms (bacteria)

Bacteriocin substance produced by certain bacteria that kills other strains of bacteria

Bacteriostatic agent an agent that prevents the growth and reproduction of some microorganisms

Bacteriuria bacteria in the urine

Barium a metallic element commonly used in solution as a contrast medium for X-ray filming of the gastrointestinal tract

Barrel chest a variation of chest shape where the ratio of the anteroposterior to lateral diameter is 1:1

Barrier technique (reverse isolation) interventions used to protect clients who are highly susceptible to infection (e.g., clients with AIDS, burns)

Basal metabolic rate (BMR) the rate of energy utilization in the body required to maintain essential activities, such as breathing

Basal metabolism the minimal energy expended for the maintenance of all physical and chemical processes

Base sometimes used to refer to the upper portion of the heart (both atria)

Baseline data all information known about a client when the client first enters the health-care agency

Base of support the area on which an object rests

Bases the nonacid part of a salt; a substance that combines with acids to form salts

Battery the willful or negligent touching of a person (or the person's clothes or even something the person is carrying), which may or may not cause harm

Beau's lines transverse white lines or grooves in the nail resulting from severe injury or illness

Bed pan a vessel used for urination or defecation by patients confined to bed

Bed rest restriction of a patient's activities, either partially or completely

Behavioural effect questions explores the effect of one family member's behaviour on another

Behaviourism a psychological theory based on objective, observable, and measurable data, rather than on subjective phenomena (e.g., emotions)

Belief (opinion) interpretations or conclusions that one accepts as true

Beneficence the moral obligation to do good or to implement actions that benefit clients and their support persons

Bereavement a subjective response of a person who has experienced the loss of a significant other through death

Bicultural is used to describe a person who crosses two cultures, lifestyles, and sets of values

Bilateral affecting two sides

Bilirubin orange pigment in the bile

Binder a type of bandage applied to large body areas (abdomen or chest) or for a specific body part (arm sling); used to provide support

Binocular vision ability to focus on images with both eyes

Bioethics ethical rules or principles that govern right conduct concerning life

Biofeedback a stress management technique that brings under conscious control bodily processes normally thought to be beyond voluntary command

Biological sex refers to an individual's chromosomal makeup, external and internal genitalia, secondary sex characteristics, and hormonal states

Biomedical health belief is based upon belief that life and life processes are controlled by physical and biochemical processes that can be manipulated by humans

Biopsy the removal and examination of tissue from the living body

Biorhythm an inner rhythm that appears to control a variety of biological processes

Biot's respirations shallow breaths interrupted by apnea

Biotransformation process by which a drug is converted to a less active form; also called detoxification

Bisexual one who is sexually attracted to persons of both sexes

Bladder training a program designed to assist patients experiencing difficulty in controlling the flow of urine

Blanch test a test during which the client's fingernail is temporarily pinched to assess capillary refill and peripheral circulation

Bleb (wheal) a small, smooth, slightly raised area on the skin, usually filled with fluid

Blood pressure the pressure of the blood against the walls of the blood vessels

Blood urea nitrogen (BUN) a measure of blood level of urea, the end product of protein metabolism

Blood volume expanders solutions used to increase the volume of blood following severe loss of blood

Body image how a person perceives the size, appearance, and functioning of their body and its parts

Body language nonverbal communication using gestures, body movements, touch, and physical appearance

Body mass index (BMI) indicates whether weight is appropriate for height

Body mechanics the efficient and coordinated use of the body to produce motion and maintain balance during activity

Body temperature the balance between the heat produced by the body and the heat lost from the body

Bottle mouth syndrome describes the decay of the infant's teeth caused by constant contact with the sweet liquid in a bottle

Boundary the real or imaginary line that differentiates one system from another system or a system from its environment

Bowel diversion the surgical creation of an ostomy to enable the excretion of fecal waste while at the same time rerouting the feces away from a specific segment of the intestine

Bowel incontinence (fecal incontinence) refers to loss of voluntary ability to control fecal and gaseous discharges through the anal sphincter

Bowman's capsule the central capsule of each nephron

Brachial pulse a pulse located on the inner side of the biceps muscle just below the axilla; usually palpated medially in the antecubital space

Bradycardia abnormally slow pulse rate, less than 60 per minute

Bradykinin an amino acid chain that causes powerful vasodilation, increased capillary permeability, smooth muscle contraction, and stimulation of pain receptors

Bradypnea abnormally slow respiratory rate, usually less than 10 respirations per minute

Brain waves the electrical signals that can be recorded from the brain, either directly or through the scalp by an EEG

Brand name (trademark) the name given by the drug manufacturer

Breast bud onset of breast development in females; a small mound of breast and nipple develops; areola widens

Breast self-examination an examination done by the woman to identify breast lumps; a possible indicator of cancer

Bromhidrosis foul-smelling perspiration

Bronchial sounds normal loud, harsh, hollow blowing sounds heard by auscultation over the trachea and main bronchi

Bronchodilator an agent that dilates the bronchi of the lungs

Bronchogram an X-ray film of the bronchial tree taken after injection of an iodized oil dye as a contrast medium

Bronchophony an increase in vocal resonance; an abnormal voice sound heard on auscultation of the chest wall

Bronchopneumonia an infection that originates in the bronchi and involves patches of lung tissue

Bronchoscope a lighted instrument used to visualize the bronchi of the lungs

Bronchoscopy visual examination of the bronchi using a bronchoscope

Bronchovesicular sounds combination of bronchial and vesicular sounds heard by auscultation over parts of the chest where a bronchus is near lung tissue

Bruit a blowing or swishing sound created by turbulence of blood flow

Bruxism grinding of the teeth during sleep

Buccal pertaining to the cheek

Buffer an agent or system that tends to maintain constancy or that prevents changes in the chemical concentration of a substance

Bulimia an uncontrollable compulsion to eat large amounts of food and then expel it by self-induced vomiting or by taking laxatives

Bunion lateral deviation of the big toe with swelling or callus formation over the metatarsophalangeal joint

Burden of proof the duty of proving an assertion

Bureaucratic leadership a style of leadership in which the leader is impersonal and inflexible; policies, procedures, and rules serve as the bases for decision making

Burn injury to tissue caused by contact with dry or moist heat

Burnout a complex syndrome of behaviours that can be likened to the exhaustion stage of the general adaptation syndrome; an overwhelming feeling that can lead to physical and emotional depletion, a negative attitude and self concept, and feelings of helplessness and hopelessness

Cafe-au-lait spots patchy pigmentation of skin, usually light brown in colour

CAI computer-assisted instruction

Calculus a stone composed of minerals that is formed in the body (e.g., a renal calculus formed in the kidney)

Calipers an instrument used to measure the thickness of folds of skin or to measure electrocardiogram wave forms

Callus (bone) early bone, formed following fracture of a bone, normally ultimately replaced by hard bone

Callus (skin) a thickened portion of the skin

Caloric value the amount of energy that nutrients or foods supply to the body

Calorie (C, Cal, kcal) a unit of heat energy equivalent to the amount of heat required to raise the temperature of 1 kg of water 1°C

calorie see *Small calorie*

Canadian Charter of Rights and Freedoms federal legislation included within the Canadian constitution

Canadian Nurses Association (CNA) national nursing association of Canada

Cannula a tube with a lumen (channel) that is inserted into a cavity or duct and is often fitted with a trocar during insertion

Canthus the angle formed by the upper and lower eyelids; each eye has an inner and an outer canthus

Carbohydrate a nutrient composed of carbon, hydrogen, and oxygen (e.g., starches and sugars)

Carbonic acid the compound formed when carbon dioxide combines with water

Cardiac arrest the cessation of heart function

Cardiac monitoring continuous observation of the client's cardiac rhythm

Cardiac output the amount of blood ejected by the heart with each ventricular contraction

Cardiopulmonary resuscitation (CPR) artificial stimulation of the heart and lungs; also referred to as basic life support (BLS)

Caregiver burden strain placed upon informal care providers, usually family members, because of the care required by an individual

Caries (dental) tooth cavities

Carina the ridge or junction where the main bronchi meet the trachea

Caring approach (ethics) an approach to ethics that, in judging the rightness or wrongness of an action, focuses on individual care and responsibility in promoting and maintaining relationships

Carminative an agent that promotes the passage of flatus from the colon

Carrier a person or animal that harbours a specific infectious agent and serves as a potential source of infection, yet does not manifest any clinical signs of disease

Case management a method for delivering nursing care in which the nurse is responsible for a case load of clients across the health-care continuum

Catabolism a process in which complex substances are broken down into simpler substances (e.g., breakdown of tissue)

Cataracts opacity of the lens or capsule of the eye

Cathartic (laxative) a drug that induces evacuation of feces from the large intestine

Catheter a tube of rubber, plastic, metal, or other material used to remove or inject fluids into a cavity, such as the bladder

Cation ion that carries a positive charge; sodium, potassium, calcium, magnesium

Caudal anesthetic an anesthetic injected into the caudal canal, below the spinal cord

CD-ROM compact disc with read-only memory

Cell-mediated defence (cellular immunity) occurs through the T-cell system

Cellulitis inflammation of cellular tissue

Celsius (Centigrade) a thermometer scale used to measure heat; the freezing point of water is 0°C and the boiling point is 100°C

Cementum bony tissue covering the root of the tooth that is embedded in the jaw

Central venous catheter venous access device commonly introduced into the subclavian or internal jugular veins and passed to the superior vena cava just above the right atrium

Central venous line a catheter inserted into a large vein located centrally in the body (e.g., the superior vena cava, right atrium)

Central venous pressure (CVP) the measurement of the pressure of the blood, in millimetres of water, within the vena cava or the right atrium of the heart

Centre of gravity the point at which the mass (weight) of the body is centred

Cephalocaudal proceeding in the direction from head to toe

Cerebral death the higher brain centre or cerebral cortex is irreversibly destroyed

Certification the voluntary practice of validating that an individual nurse has met minimum standards of nursing competence in a specialty area

Cerumen the wax-like substance secreted by glands in the external ear canal

Chancre a papular lesion (sore) occurring at the entry of infection in some diseases; the primary lesion of syphilis

Change process of modifying or altering something

Change agent a person (or group) who initiates changes or who assists others in making modifications in themselves or in the system

Change-of-shift report report usually given to nurses starting the next shift

Chaplain one who serves the spiritual needs of clients

Charismatic leadership a contemporary theory of leadership that suggests that charming individuals evoke strong feelings of commitment to the leader and the leader's cause and beliefs

Chart the clinical record

Charting keeping of a clinical record of the facts about a patient and the progression of an illness

Charting by exception a documentation system in which only significant findings or exceptions to norms are recorded

Chemical name the name by which a chemist knows the drug; describes the constituents of the drug precisely

Chemical restraints medications used to control socially disruptive behaviour

Chemical thermogenesis the stimulation of heat production in the body through increased cellular metabolism caused by increases in thyroxine output

Chemoreceptor a receptor that is sensitive to chemical substances

Chemosensitive sensitive to changes in chemical composition

Chemotaxis the action by which leukocytes are attracted to injured cells

Cheyne-Stokes respirations rhythmic waxing and waning of respirations from very deep breathing to very shallow breathing with periods of temporary apnea, often associated with cardiac failure, increased intracranial pressure, or brain damage

Cholesterol a lipid that does not contain fatty acid but possesses many of the chemical and physical properties of other lipids

Chronic persisting for a long time

Chronic illness sickness that lasts for an extended period of time, usually greater than six months

Chronological charting recording of data in sequence as time moves forward

Chvostek's sign an indication of tetany, spasm of facial muscles in response to a tap over the facial nerve

Chyme digested products that leave the stomach through the small intestine and then pass through the ileocecal valve

Cicatrix scar

Circadian synchronization rhythmic repetition of certain phenomena each 24 hours

Circa dies about a day

Circulatory overload a state in which the intravascular fluid compartment contains more fluid than normal

Circumcision surgical removal of part or all of the foreskin of the penis; usually performed during infancy

Circumduction movement of the distal part of the bone in a circle while the proximal end remains fixed

Circumference the outer measurement or perimeter (e.g., the distance around the chest)

Civil action deals with the relationship between individuals in society

Civil law legislative rules that regulate relationships among people

Clapping (percussion, cupping) (in physiotherapy) the forceful striking of the chest with cupped hands to loosen secretions in the lungs

Clean free of potentially infectious agents

Clergy priests, rabbis, ministers, church elders, deacons, and other spiritual advisors

Client a person who engages the advice or services of another person who is qualified to provide this service

Client advocate an individual who pleads the cause of clients' rights

Climacteric the point in development when reproduction capacity in the female terminates (menopause) and the sexual activity of the male decreases (andropause)

Clinical guidelines are systematically developed statements of recommended methods of treatment for specific conditions under specific clinical circumstances

Clinical pharmacist a specialist who may guide the physician in prescribing drugs

Closed awareness of impending death; dying individual and perhaps the family are unaware

Closed questions restrictive questions requiring only a short answer

Closed system a system that does not exchange energy, matter, or information with its environment

Clubbing (of a nail) elevation of the proximal aspect of the nail and softening of the nail bed

Coagulate to clot

Cochlea a seashell-shaped structure found in the inner ear; essential for sound transmission and hearing

Code of Ethics a formal statement of a group's ideals and values; a set of ethical principles shared by members of a group, reflecting their moral judgments and serving as a standard for professional actions

Coercive power influence based on a fear of retribution or withholding of rewards

Cognition cerebral functioning; involves such processes as conscious thought, reality orientation, problem solving, judgment, and comprehension

Cognitive dissonance a theory that holds that the mind rejects ideas that are not congruent with previously held concepts, resulting in "dissonance"

Cognitive skills referring to intellectual processes, such as remembering, thinking, perceiving, abstracting, and generalizing

Cohabiting (communal) family a family made up of unrelated individuals or families living under one roof

Cohesive (adherent) sticking together, clinging

Co-insurance an insurance plan where the client pays a percentage of the payment and some other group (e.g., employer, government) pays the additional percentage

Coitus (copulation) a type of genital intercourse in which the penis is inserted into the vagina

Coitus interruptus withdrawal of the penis before ejaculation

Collaboration a collegial working relationship with another health-care provider in the provision of client care

Collaborative intervention (action) those activities performed either jointly with another member of the health-care team or as a result of a joint decision by the nurse and another health-care team member

Collaborative problem physiological complications that nurses monitor to detect the onset of changes in client status, but for which nurses cannot independently initiate definitive treatment

Collaborative relational stance is one that values the multiple ideas and perspectives that are encountered within a family

Collagen a protein found in connective tissue; a whitish protein substance that adds tensile strength to a wound

Collective bargaining the formalized decision-making process between representatives of management and representatives of labour to negotiate wages and conditions of employment

Colloid substances, such as large plasma protein molecules, that do not readily dissolve in true solution

Colloid osmotic pressure (oncotic pressure) a pulling force exerted by colloids that help maintain the water content of blood

Colloids translucent, yellowish, gelatinous substance that results from colloid degeneration

Colonization the presence of organisms in body secretions or excretions in which strains of bacteria become resident flora but do not cause illness

Colonoscope a lighted instrument used to visualize the interior of the colon

Colonoscopy visual examination of the interior of the colon with a colonoscope

Colostomy an opening into the colon (large bowel)

Comatose a state of unconsciousness in which the person shows no response to maximum painful stimuli, absence of reflexes, and absence of muscle tone in the extremities

Combustible able to burn; flammable

Comedo a blackhead or whitehead; a plug of dried sebum in a sebaceous gland

Comforting a group of nursing interventions based on clients' cues of distress, with the goal of achieving client comfort

Commendations statements of praise or support

Commode a portable, chairlike structure used as a toilet

Common law the body of principles that evolves from court decisions

Communicable disease (infectious disease) a disease that can spread from one person to another

Communication a two-way process involving the sending and receiving of messages

Community a collection of people who share some attribute of their lives

Community-based health care a system that provides health-related services within the context of people's daily lives; that is, in places where people spend their time in the community

Community-based nursing (CBN) nursing care directed toward a specific population or group within the community; primary, secondary, or tertiary care may be provided to individuals or groups

Community health nursing the synthesis of nursing and public health practice as applied to promoting and preserving the health of populations

Compensation defence mechanism in which a person substitutes an activity for one that they would prefer doing or cannot do

Compensatory counterbalancing

Complaint (legal) a document filed by the plaintiff

Complementary proteins combination of two or more proteins which contribute to a balanced ratio of essential amino acids

Complete proteins proteins that contain all of the essential amino acids as well as many nonessential ones

Compliance (of arteries) the distensibility of the arteries (i.e., their ability to contract and expand)

Compliance (client) the extent to which an individual's behaviour coincides with medical or health advice

Compress a moist gauze dressing applied frequently to an open wound, sometimes medicated

Compromised host any person at increased risk for an infection

Computed tomography (CT) see *Tomography*

Computerized axial tomography (CAT) see *Tomography*

Concave hollowed or rounded inward

Concept abstract idea or mental image of phenomena or reality

Conceptual framework a group of related concepts

Conceptual model a graphic illustration of the relationships between concepts

Conceptualization the intellectual process of forming a concept

Concurrent evaluation/audit the evaluation of practices as they occur or while the client is still in the institution

Conditioning behavioural response to a stimulus that causes the response or behaviour

Condom a sheath or cover, usually made of rubber or plastic, worn over the penis during coitus to prevent conception or infection; urinary condoms are used to catch urine

Conduction the transfer of heat from one molecule to another in direct contact

Conduction hearing loss a form of hearing loss in which sound is inadequately conducted through the external or middle ear to the sensorineural apparatus of the inner ear

Confer to consult another person or persons for advice, information, ideas, or instructions

Confidentiality the right of a client or research subject that any information revealed by that individual will not be made public or available to others

Conflict the consequence of real or perceived differences in mutually exclusive goals, values, ideas, attitudes, beliefs, feelings, or actions

Conformity actions in accordance with specified standards

Confusion a mental state in which a person appears bewildered and may make inappropriate statements and answers to questions

Congenital existing at, and often before, birth

Congestion excessive accumulation of blood or fluid in a part of the body

Congruence (congruent) in communication, when words and behaviour coincide or are unified

Conjunctivitis inflammation of the bulbar and palpebral conjunctiva

Connective leadership promotes collaboration and teamwork

Conscious sedation a minimal depression of level of consciousness during which the client retains the ability to consciously maintain a patent airway and respond appropriately to verbal and physical stimuli

Consciousness a person's normal state of awareness of the environment, self, and others

Consensual reaction (eyes) a reaction in which one pupil constricts quickly in response to a bright light and the other pupil constricts also, but more slowly

Consent permission given voluntarily by a person in his or her right mind; informed consent requires that the individual is knowledgeable about the consent and understands it

Consequence-based ethics approach (teleological) the ethics of judging whether an action is moral

Consequence-based theories examine the outcome of an action in judging whether that action is right or wrong

Constant fever a state in which the body temperature fluctuates minimally but always remains above normal

Constipation passage of small, dry, hard stool or passage of no stool for an abnormally long time

Constitution the supreme law of a country, it establishes the general organization of the federal government, grants certain powers, and places limits on what federal and state or provincial governments may do

Construct a concept that has been invented to suit a special purpose

Consultation a process in which two or more people deliberate with one another to seek advice or clarification

Consumer an individual, a group of people, or a community that uses a service or commodity

Contact precautions taken to prevent the possibility of illnesses easily transmitted by direct contact

Continuity of care coordination of services provided to individuals before, during, and after entry into a health-care facility

Continuity theory a belief that people maintain their values, habits, and behaviours in old age

Continuum a grid or graduated scale

Contraception the prevention of fertilization of the ovum by any method

Contract a written or verbal agreement between two or more people to do or not do some lawful act

Contract law the enforcement of agreements among private individuals or the payment of compensation for failure to fulfill the agreement

Contraction an intermittent tightening and shortening of uterine muscle fibres which cause cervical dilation and effacement during labour

Contractual obligation the duty of care established by the presence of an expressed or implied contract

Contractual relationships a legal agreement between two or more partners

Contracture permanent shortening of a muscle and subsequent shortening of tendons and ligaments

Contraindicate not indicated or inappropriate

Controlling is the process of ensuring that plans are carried out and evaluating outcomes

Contusion a closed wound that occurs as a result of a blow from a blunt instrument; a bruise

Convection the dispersion of heat by air currents

Conversion a defence mechanism in which a mental conflict is converted into a physical symptom

Convex curved or rounded like the external surface of a sphere

Coping the process through which the individual manages the demands of the person-environment relationship that are appraised as stressful

Coping behaviour behaviour learned in response to stress; immediate response to a threatening situation

Coping responses (mechanisms) physical or emotional adaptive or defensive abilities

Coping strategy any mechanism directed towards stress management

Copulation heterosexual genital intercourse

Cordotomy (chordotomy) surgical severing of the spinothalamic portion of the anterolateral tract of the spinal cord, usually for the purpose of relieving pain

Core self-concept the beliefs and images that are most central to the person's identity

Core temperature the temperature of the deep tissues of the body (e.g., thorax, abdominal cavity); relatively constant at 37°C

Corn a conical, circular, painful, raised area on the toe or foot

Coroner a public official, not necessarily a physician, appointed or elected to inquire into the causes of death

Corticoid a term applied to hormones of the adrenal cortex or substances with similar activity

Cortiosone a hormone produced by the adrenal cortex that has anti-inflammatory properties and is involved in the metabolism of glycogen to glucose

Costal breathing (thoracic breathing) breathing involving the external intercostal muscles and other accessory muscles, such as the sternocleidomastoid muscles

Costovertebral angle the angle formed by a rib and the spine

Counselling the process of helping a client to recognize and cope with stressful psychological or social problems, to develop improved interpersonal relationships, and to promote personal growth

Countershock part of the alarm phase described by Selye

Covert data (symptoms, subjective data) information (data) apparent only to the person affected that can be described or verified only by that person

CPR see *Cardiopulmonary resuscitation*

CPU the central processing unit of a computer

Crackles (rales) bubbling or rattling sounds audible by ear or stethoscope on inhalation; they are a result of fluid in the lungs

Creatinine a nitrogenous waste that is excreted in the urine

Creatinine clearance test uses 24-hour urine and serum creatinine levels to identify the glomerular filtration rate

Creative thinking thoughts that result in the development of new ideas and products

Credé's maneuver manual exertion of pressure on the bladder to force urine out

Credentialling the process of determining and maintaining competence in practice; includes licensure, registration, certification, and accreditation

Crepitation a dry, crackling sound like that of crumpled cellophane, produced by air in the subcutaneous tissue or by air moving through fluid in the alveoli of the lungs; a crackling, grating sound produced by bone rubbing against bone

Crime an act committed in violation of public (criminal) law and punishable by a fine and/or imprisonment

Criminal action deals with disputes between an individual and the society as a whole

Criminal law deals with actions against the safety and welfare of the public

Crisis an acute, time-limited state of disequilibrium resulting from situational, developmental, or societal sources of stress

Crisis intervention problem-solving technique to promote adaptation and improve future coping

Criterion a standard or model that can be used in judging

Critical analysis a set of questions one can apply to a particular situation or idea to determine essential information and ideas and discard superfluous information and ideas

Critical pathways multidisciplinary guidelines for client care based on specific medical diagnoses designed to achieve predetermined outcomes

Critical thinking a cognitive process that includes creativity, problem solving, and decision making

Cross contamination the transfer of microorganisms from one surface to another

Crown the exposed part of the tooth which is outside the gum

Crutch palsy a weakness of the muscles of the forearm, wrist, and hand caused by prolonged pressure of the crutch on the axillary nerve

Cryptorchidism failure of the testes to descend from the abdominal cavity to the scrotal sacs

Crystalloid salts that dissolve readily in true solutions

Cue(s) any piece of information or data that influences decisions

Cultural awareness conscious and informed recognition of the differences and similarities between different cultural or ethnic groups

Cultural care deprivation lack of culturally assistive, supportive, or facilitative acts

Cultural competence possessing the required knowledge, skill, and ability to provide safe and effective health care regardless of population or setting

Cultural heritage values and beliefs unique to a particular culture that influence the family's structure, methods of interaction, health-care practices, and coping mechanisms

Cultural identity the characteristics of the group which gives the person a sense of identity

Cultural sensitivity respect and appreciation for cultural behaviours based upon an understanding of the other person's perspective

Culture a world view and set of traditions used and transmitted from generation to generation by a particular group, includes related attitudes and institutions

Culture-specifics those values, beliefs, and patterns of behaviour that tend to be unique to a designated culture

Culture shock feelings, usually negative, experienced by a person when placed in a different cultural group

Culture-universals commonalities of values, norms of behaviour, and life patterns among different cultures

Cumulative effect occurs when the body cannot metabolize a drug before additional dosages are administered

Cunnilingus oral stimulation of the female genitals

Cutaneous pain discomfort that originates in the skin or subcutaneous tissue

Cyanosis bluish discolouration of the skin and mucous membranes caused by reduced oxygen in the blood

Cyst an enclosed cavity or sac lined by epithelium and containing liquid or semisolid material

Cystectomy removal of the bladder

Cystitis inflammation of the urinary bladder

Cystocele protrusion of the urinary bladder through the vaginal wall

Cystoscope a lighted instrument used to visualize the interior of the urinary bladder

Cystoscopy visual examination of the urinary bladder with a cystoscope

Cytology the study of the origin, structure, function, and pathology of cells

Dacryocystitis inflammation of the lacrimal sac

Dandruff a dry or greasy, scaly material shed from the scalp

Data information

Data warehousing the accumulation of large amounts of data that are stored over time

Database (baseline data) all information about a client, includes nursing health history and physical assessment, physician's history and physical examination, laboratory and diagnostic test results

Death when a living thing's life has ended; indications of death in a human are: total lack of response to external stimuli; no muscular movement, especially breathing; no reflexes; and a flat encephalogram

Debilitated having lost strength

Débridement removal of infected and necrotic tissue

Deceased dead; a person who is dead

Deciduous teeth temporary teeth that are shed

Decision (legal) outcome made by a judge

Decision-focused ethical problems ethical problems in which it is difficult to decide the right action to take

Decision making the process of establishing criteria by which alternative courses of action are developed and selected

Decode relate the communication message to the receiver's storehouse of information and experiences

Decubitus ulcer see *Pressure sores*

Deductive reasoning making specific observations from a generalization

Deep somatic pain discomfort that arises from ligaments, tendons, bones, blood vessels, and nerves

Defamation (legal) a communication that is false, or made with careless disregard for the truth, and results in injury to the reputation of another

Defecation expulsion of feces from the rectum and anus

Defence (adaptive) mechanisms any reaction that serves to protect against something physically or psychologically harmful

Defendant (legal) person against whom the plaintiff files a complaint

Defervescence the stage of abatement of a fever

Defining characteristics client signs and symptoms that must be present to validate a nursing diagnosis

Dehiscence the partial or total rupturing of a sutured wound; usually involves an abdominal wound in which the layers below the skin also separate

Dehydration insufficient fluid in the body

Delayed closure an anatomically precise closure that is delayed for a few days but undertaken before granulation tissue becomes evident

Delegating care directs the practice of care to another health-care professional

Delegation assigning responsibility and authority for performing specific tasks to another

Delirious experiencing mental confusion, restlessness, and incoherence

Demand feeding the infant is fed when hungry

Dementia a global impairment of cognitive function that usually is progressive and may be permanent, interferes with normal social and occupational activities

Demineralization excessive loss of minerals or inorganic salts

Demise death

Democratic leadership a participative style of leadership in which the leader encourages group discussion and decision making

Demography the study of population, including statistics about distribution by age and place of residence, mortality, and morbidity

Demulcent a drug that coats the intestine, thus protecting the lining

Denial a defence mechanism in which painful or anxiety-producing aspects of reality are blocked out of consciousness

Dental caries tooth decay

Dental plaque deposits on the teeth that serve as a medium for bacterial growth

Dentifrice a paste or powder used to clean or polish the teeth

Dentin chief substance of the teeth

Dentures a natural or artificial set of teeth; usually the term designates artificial replacements for natural teeth

Denver Developmental Screening Test (DDST) a screening test used to assess children from birth to six years of age

Deontology an approach to moral theory which proposes that the morality of a decision is not determined by the consequences; it emphasizes duty, rationality, and obedience to rules

Dependence (drug) a physiological process during which the body adapts to the presence of an opioid, and its abrupt withdrawal or cessation results in physical symptoms

Dependent edema edema of the lowest or most dependent parts of the body

Dependent nursing intervention (action, function) those activities carried out on the order of the physician, under the physician's supervision, or according to specified routines

Dependent variable the behaviour, characteristic, or outcome that the researcher wishes to explain or predict

Depilatory a cream used to remove body hair

Depression feelings of sadness and dejection, often accompanied by physiological change, such as a decreased functional activity

Dermatitis inflammation of the skin

Dermatological preparation a medication applied to the skin

Descriptive statistics procedures that summarize large volumes of data; used to describe and synthesize data, showing patterns and trends

Desire wish, longing, or want

Desired outcome specific observable criteria or indicators used to evaluate whether a goal has been met

Detrusor muscle the collective smooth muscle layers of the bladder

Development an individual's increasing capacity and skill in functioning, related to growth

Developmental crisis a crisis that occurs as a result of stressors related to development

Developmental stressors stressors that occur at predictable times throughout an individual's life

Developmental tasks skills and behaviour patterns learned during stages of development

Deviance behaviour that goes against social norms

Diagnosing the process that results in a diagnostic statement or nursing diagnosis that provides the basis for the selection of nursing interventions for the client

Diagnosis a statement or conclusion concerning the nature of some phenomenon

Diagnostic label (problem statement) title used in writing a nursing diagnosis; taken from the North American Nursing Diagnosis Association's (NANDA) standardized taxonomy of terms

Diagnostic related groups (DRGs) a Medicare payments system to hospitals and physicians which establishes fees according to diagnosis

Dialyzing membrane a membrane that permits water molecules and crystalloids in true solution to move through it but not particles in a colloid dispersion

Diapedesis the movement of blood corpuscles through a blood vessel wall

Diaphoresis profuse perspiration

Diaphragmatic breathing (abdominal breathing) breathing that involves the contraction and relaxation of the diaphragm

Diarrhea defecation of liquid feces and increased frequency of defecation

Diastole the period during which the ventricles relax

Diastolic blood pressure the pressure of the blood against the arterial walls when the ventricles of the heart are at rest

Diet history comprehensive assessment of a client's food intake, usually by a dietitian or nutritionist

Dietitian has specialized knowledge about the diets required to maintain health and to treat disease

Difference questions explore differences among people, relationships, or ideas

Differentially permeable permeability varies based upon the substance

Diffusion the mixing of molecules or ions of two or more substances as a result of random motion

Dignity ability to function as a significant and integrated person

Dilemma a situation involving a choice between equally satisfactory or unsatisfactory alternatives or a difficult problem that seems to have no satisfactory solution

Diplopia double vision

Directing a management function that involves communicating the task to be completed and providing guidance and supervision

Directive interview a highly structured interview that uses closed questions to elicit specific information

Dirty denotes the likely presence of microorganisms, some of which may be capable of causing infection

Disaccharides sugars that are composed of double molecules

Discharge planning the process of anticipating and planning for client needs after discharge

Discovery (legal) pretrial activities to gain all the facts of the situation

Discrimination the differential treatment of individuals or groups based on categories such as race, ethnicity, gender, social class, age, or exceptionality

Discussion specific dialogue or interaction between people

Disease an alteration in body function resulting in a reduction of capacities or shortening of the normal lifespan

Disenfranchised grief occurs when a person is unable to acknowledge to other persons a socially unacceptable loss

Disengagement any withdrawal from usual social patterns

Disengagement theory aging involves mutual withdrawal between an older adult and others within that person's environment

Disequilibrium a disturbed state of equilibrium (balance), either mental or physical

Disinfectant agent that destroys all microorganisms

Disorientation a state of mental confusion; loss of bearings, time, and place

Displacement a defence mechanism in which an emotional reaction is transferred from one object to another less threatening object

Distal farthest from the point of reference

Distention (abdominal) see *Tympanites*

Distraction a mechanism for relieving pain where the person's attention is drawn away from the pain

Diuresis (polyuria) the production of abnormally large amounts of urine by the kidneys without an increased fluid intake

Diuretic an agent that increases urine secretion

Diurnal pertaining to the daytime

Diversity differences, often used in reference to cultural groups and people

DNR (do not resuscitate, no code) a physician's order that requires that no effort be made to resuscitate the client with terminal or irreversible illness in the event of a respiratory or cardiac arrest

Documenting written recording of pertinent information related to the patient

Dorsal toward, or at the back of

Dorsal flexion (dorsiflexion) movement of the ankle so that the toes are pointing upward

Dorsal (supine) position back-lying position without a pillow

Dorsal recumbent position a back-lying position with the head and shoulders slightly elevated

Douche vaginal irrigation; washing of the vagina by a liquid at a low pressure

Drain a substance or appliance that assists in the discharge of serosanguineous fluid and purulent material from a wound and promotes healing of underlying tissues

Drainage a discharge from a wound or cavity

Drawsheet (half sheet) a special sheet, made of cotton, plastic, or rubber, that is placed across the centre of the foundation of the bed and used to facilitate moving bed-bound clients

Dressing a material used to cover and protect a wound

Drip factor (drop factor) the number of drops per millilitre of solution delivered for a particular drip chamber before calculating the drip rate

Droplet nuclei residue of evaporated droplets that remains in the air for long periods of time

Droplet precautions practices initiated to prevent the spread of large particle microorganisms

Drug (medication) a chemical compound taken for disease prevention, diagnosis, cure, or relief or to affect the structure or function of the body

Drug abuse excessive intake of a substance either continually or periodically

Drug allergy an immunological reaction to a drug

Drug dependence inability to keep the intake of a drug or substance under control

Drug habituation a mild form of psychological dependence on a drug

Drug interaction the beneficial or harmful interaction of one drug with another drug

Drug misuse improper use of common medications in ways that can lead to acute and chronic toxicity

Drug tolerance a condition in which successive increases in the dosage of a drug are required to maintain a given therapeutic effect

Drug toxicity the quality of a drug that exerts a deleterious effect on an organism or tissue

DT diphtheria vaccine and tetanus toxoid

DTP (DPT) Diphtheria toxoid, tetanus toxoid, and pertussis vaccine

Dullness (of sound) a thudlike sound produced during percussion by dense tissue of body organs, such as the liver, spleen, or heart

Duodenocolic reflex a mass peristaltic movement of the colon stimulated by the presence of chyme in the duodenum

Duration (of sound) the length of time that a sound is heard

Dynamic equilibrium tendency of the body to maintain a state of balance or equilibrium while continually changing

Dynorphins compounds found in the pituitary gland, hypothalamus, and spinal cord that seem to have an analgesic effect

Dysfunctional grieving the state in which an individual or group experiences prolonged, unresolved grief and engages in detrimental activities

Dysmenorrhea painful menstruation

Dyspareunia pain experienced by a woman during intercourse

Dyspepsia indigestion

Dysphagia difficulty or inability to swallow

Dysphasia difficulty speaking

Dyspnea difficult or laboured breathing

Dysrhythmia (arrhythmia) a pulse with an irregular rhythm

Dysuria painful or difficult voiding

Ecchymosis A bruise that changes in colour from blue-black to greenish brown or yellow

Eccrine glands produce sweat; found over most of the body

Echocardiogram a record of the recording of the position and motion of the heart walls or interior structures

Ecology the study of the relationship of humans with the environment

Ecomap an assessment tool identifying the family's relationship to the environment

Ectoderm the outer layer of tissue formed in the second week of life

Ectropion eversion or outturning of the eyelid

Edema the presence of excess interstitial fluid in the body

Edentulous without teeth

Effectiveness the ability to produce a specific result

Efferent conveying away from the centre

Efficiency a measurement of competency

Effleurage a stroking massage technique

Effluent urine or feces discharged through a stoma

Egg crate mattress a specialized foam rubber mattress designed to provide support while relieving pressure on the body's bony prominences

Ego includes consciousness and memory which serves to mediate between primitive instinctual drives (id), internal social prohibitions (superego), and reality

Egocentricity concern about oneself

Ego integrity feeling satisfied with one's lifestyle and accepting the inevitability of one's life cycle

Egophony a type of bronchophony in which the voice has a nasal, bleating quality

Ejaculation expulsion of seminal fluid and sperm

Ejaculatory incompetence the inability to ejaculate into the vagina or a delayed ejaculation

Elastic recoil (elasticity) the ability to resume normal shape after distortion

Elasticity of the arterial wall the ability to expand and contract

Elective surgery performed when surgical intervention is the preferred treatment for a condition that is not imminently life-threatening or to improve the client's life

Electrocardiogram (ECG, EKG) a graph of the electrical activity of the heart

Electroencephalogram (EEG) a graph of the electrical activity of the brain

Electrolyte a chemical substance that develops an electric charge and is able to conduct an electric current when placed in water; an ion

Electromyogram (EMG) a record of the electrical potential created by the contraction of a muscle

Electro-oculogram (EOG) the tracings made while moving the eyes a constant distance between two fixation points

Electron a negatively charged electric particle

Emaciated excessively thin

Embolus a blood clot (or a substance, such as air) that has moved from its place of origin and is causing obstruction to circulation elsewhere (plural: emboli)

Embryonic phase the stage during which the fertilized ovum develops into an organism with most of the features of the human

Emergency surgery operation that is performed immediately to preserve function or the life of the client

Emigration movement, e.g., of individuals from one country to another; of leukocytes through blood vessel wall into affected tissue

Emmetropic normal refraction so that the eyes focus images on the retina

Emollient an agent that soothes and softens skin or mucous membrane; often an oily substance

Empathy the ability to discriminate what the other person's world is like and to communicate to the other this understanding in a way that shows that the helper understands the client's feelings and the behaviour and experience underlying these feelings

Emphysema a chronic pulmonary condition in which the alveoli are dilated and distended

Empirical by observation or experience

Empirical data information collected from the observable world

Empiricist tradition suggests that there is a single reality that exists independent of our knowledge of it

Emulsion a preparation in which one liquid is distributed throughout another

Enamel the white, compact, and hard substance covering the crown of a tooth

Encoding involves the selection of specific signs or symbols to transmit message during communication

Endemic present in a community all the time

Endoderm (entoderm) the inner layer of tissue formed in the second week of life

Endogenous developing from within

Endogenous opioids chemical regulators in the body that may modify pain

Endorphins a polypeptide found throughout the body that is thought to relieve pain

Endoscope an instrument used for examining the interior of a hollow organ (e.g., the bladder, rectum, stomach, or bronchi)

Endotracheal tube a tube which is inserted through the mouth or nose into the trachea

Enema a solution introduced into the rectum and sigmoid colon to remove feces and/or flatus

Engorgement excessive fullness of an organ or passage

Enkephalins a pentapeptide naturally occurring in the brain that has opiate-like effects

Enteral through the gastrointestinal system

Enteric referring to the intestines

Enteric-coated tablets and capsules surrounded with a special coating that prevents release of the drug until it is in the intestines

Enteric feeding a feeding administered directly into the gastrointestinal tract through a tube

Enteritis inflammation of the small intestine

Enterocele any hernia of the intestine through the vaginal mucosa

Enterostomal therapist a person who specializes in ostomy care

Enterostomy an opening through the abdominal wall into the intestines

Entoderm (endoderm) the inner layer of tissue formed in the second week of life

Entropion inversion or inturning of the eyelid

Enuresis bedwetting; involuntary passing of urine in children after bladder control is achieved

Environment all the conditions, circumstances, and influences surrounding and affecting the development of an organism or person

Enzyme a biological catalyst that speeds up chemical reactions

Epidemic the occurrence of a disease in many people at the same time or in rapid succession in an area

Epidemiology the study of the occurrence and distribution of disease

Epidural into the epidural space

Epidural anesthesia the injection of an anesthetic agent into the epidural space (the area inside the spinal column but outside the dura mater)

Epidural/peridural block means of providing analgesic injection through catheter inserted into mid-lumbar region of epidural space

Episodic learning activities the learning activities that are distinct and separate from formal or planned education

Epispadias opening of the urethra on the upper side of the penis

Epistaxis nose bleed

Epistemology investigates the nature of knowledge

Equilibrium a state of balance

Erectile dysfunction (impotence) the inability to achieve or maintain an erection sufficient for sexual satisfaction for the self and/or partner

Erogenous sexually sensitive

Erotic pertaining to sexual desire

Eructation belching; the expulsion of swallowed gases through the mouth

Erythema a redness associated with a variety of skin rashes

Erythrocyte red blood cell

Erythropoiesis the formation of red blood cells

Eschar thick necrotic tissue produced by burning, by a corrosive application, or by death of tissue associated with loss of vascular supply, bacterial invasion, and putrefaction

Esophagoscopy visual examination of the interior of the esophagus with a lighted instrument

Essential amino acids amino acids that cannot be manufactured in the body and must be supplied as part of the protein ingested in the diet

Essential fatty acids required in the diet

Ethical theories value systems that present a rational approach to moral decision making

Ethics the rules or principles that govern right conduct

Ethnic (Ethnicity) belonging to a specific group of individuals who share a common social and cultural heritage

Ethnic group shares a common social and cultural heritage that is passed on

Ethnic identity a person's subjective perspective of his or her heritage

Ethnocentrism the belief that one's own culture is superior to all others

Ethnorelativity ability to appreciate and respect the viewpoints of other cultures

Ethnoscience the systematic study of the way of life of a designated cultural group to obtain accurate data regarding behaviour, perceptions, and interpretations of the universe

Etiology the causal relationship between a problem and its related or risk factors

Eupnea normal, quiet breathing

Eustachian tube the part of the middle ear that connects the middle ear to the nasopharynx; stabilizes air pressure between the external atmosphere and the middle ear

Euthanasia (mercy killing) the act of painlessly putting to death persons suffering from incurable or distressing disease

Evaluation a planned, ongoing, purposeful activity in which client and health-care professionals determine the client's progress toward goal achievement and the effectiveness of the nursing care plan

Evaporation conversion of a liquid into a vapour

Eversion turning the sole of the foot outward by moving the ankle joint

Evisceration extrusion of the internal organs

Exacerbation the period during a chronic illness when symptoms reappear after remission

Excise to cut off or out

Excoriation loss of the superficial layers of the skin

Excretion elimination of a waste product produced by the body cells from the body

Exercise a type of physical activity; a planned, structured, and repetitive bodily movement done to improve or maintain one or more components of physical fitness

Exhalation (expiration) the movement of gases from the lungs to the atmosphere

Exogenous developing from without

Exophthalmus a protrusion of the eyeballs with elevation of the upper eyelids, resulting in a startled or staring expression

Exotoxin a toxic substance formed by bacteria and found outside the bacterial cell

Expectorate to cough and spit up mucus or other materials

Expert power authority attained through respect for one's abilities, knowledge, and/or skills

Expert witness one who has special training, experience, or skill in a relevant area and is allowed by the court to offer an opinion on some issue within that area of expertise

Expiration (exhalation) the outflow of air from the lungs to the atmosphere

Expiratory reserve volume the maximum amount of air exhaled after a normal exhalation

Expired dead

Expressed consent an oral or written agreement

Extended family includes the relatives of the nuclear family (e.g., grandparents, aunts, uncles)

Extension increasing the angle of a joint

External auditory meatus the entrance to the ear canal

External cardiac massage rhythmic massage of the heart muscle over the sternum during resuscitation

External respiration the interchange of oxygen and carbon dioxide between the alveoli of the lungs and the pulmonary blood

Extinction the failure to perceive touch on one side of the body when two symmetric areas of the body are touched simultaneously

Extracellular outside the cell

Extracellular fluid (ECF) fluid found outside the body cells

Extrapolating inferring facts or data from known facts or data

Extrathecal outside the sheath (e.g., outside the spinal canal)

Extravasation the escape of blood from a vessel into the body tissues

Exudate material, such as fluid and cells, that has escaped from blood vessels during the inflammatory process and is deposited in tissue or on tissue surfaces

Fad a widespread but short-lived interest, or a practice followed with considerable zeal

Fahrenheit a thermometer scale used to measure heat; the freezing point of water is 32°F and the boiling point is 212°F

Failure-to-thrive syndrome delayed infant development without any physical cause; the infant is often malnourished and fails to gain weight and grow normally

Faith an active "mode of being-in-relation" to another or others in which we invest commitment, belief, love, and hope

False imprisonment the unlawful restraint or detention of another person against his or her wishes

Family nursing refers to those relational practices, which involve family members in care

Family support form of social support which helps to buffer stress

Fantasy an adaptive mechanism in which wishes and desires are imagined as fulfilled

Fasciculation an abnormal contraction or shortening of a bundle of muscle fibres

Fasting abstinence from eating

Fat a lipid that is solid at room temperature

Fat embolism fat globules that are released into the blood circulation from bone marrow and from local tissue trauma

Fat-soluble vitamins A, D, E, and K vitamins that the body can store

Fatty acid the basic structural unit of most lipids; made up of carbon chains and hydrogen

Fear an emotional response to an actual, present danger

Febrile pertaining to a fever; feverish

Fecal impaction a mass or collection of hardened, puttylike feces in the folds of the rectum

Fecal incontinence (bowel incontinence) loss of voluntary ability to control fecal and gaseous discharges through the anal sphincter

Feces (stool) body wastes and undigested food eliminated from the rectum

Feedback (homeostasis) the mechanism by which some output of a system is returned to the system as input

Feedback (communication) the response or message that the receiver returns to the sender during communication

Fellatio oral stimulation of the penis by licking and sucking

Felony a crime of a serious nature, such as murder, punishable by a term in prison

Fenestrated drape a drape with an opening in its centre

Fetal phase of prenatal development; characterized by rapid growth of fetus

Fetus the unborn offspring in the postembryonic stage of development

Fever elevated body temperature

Fibre an indigestible carbohydrate derived from plants

Fibrillation involuntary contractions of a muscle; cardiac arrhythmia characterized by extremely rapid, irregular, and ineffective contractions of the atria or ventricles

Fibrin an insoluble protein formed from fibrinogen during the clotting of blood

Fibrinogen a plasma protein that is converted to fibrin when it is released into the tissues and, together with thromboplastin and platelets, forms an interlacing network making a barrier to wall off an area

Fibrous tissue common connective tissue composed of elastic and collagen fibres

Fidelity a moral principle which obligates the individual to be faithful to agreements and responsibilities one has undertaken

Filter needle used to withdraw medications from ampules and vials

Filtration passage through a material that restricts or prevents passage of certain molecules

Filtration pressure the stress or strain exerted during the passage through a filter

FiO_2 fraction of inspired oxygen

First intention healing primary wound healing; occurs when tissue surfaces have been approximated

First-level manager a manager responsible for the work of nonmanagerial personnel and the day-to-day activities of a specific work group or groups

Fissure a cleft or groove

Fistula an abnormal communication or passage usually between two organs or between an organ and the body surface

Fixation (psychological) immobilization or the inability of the personality to proceed to the next developmental stage because of anxiety

Flaccid weak or lax

Flaccid paralysis impaired muscle function with loss of muscle tone

Flaccidity weak or soft, especially in relation to muscles

Flail chest the ballooning out of the chest wall through fractured rib spaces during exhalation

Flatness (of sound) an extremely dull sound produced, during percussion, by very dense tissue, such as muscle or bone

Flatulence the presence of excessive amounts of gas in the stomach or intestines

Flatus gas or air normally present in the stomach or intestines

Flexion decreasing the angle of a joint (between two bones); the act of bending

Flora collective vegetation in a given area

Flowsheet a record of the progress of specific or specialized data, such as vital signs, fluid balance, or routine medications; often charted in graph form

Fluid volume deficit (hypovolemia) an abnormal reduction in blood volume

Fluid volume excess (hypervolemia) an abnormal increase in the body's blood volume; circulatory overload

Fluoroscopy An examination using a fluoroscope, which views internal structures using X-rays

Flushing (of the skin) transient redness of the skin, often of the face and neck; it may be generalized or restricted to a particular area

Foam swabs equipment used to clean mouths of dependent clients

Focus charting a method of charting that uses key words or foci to describe what is happening to the client

Fomite an inanimate object other than food that can harbour disease producing microorganisms and transmit an infection

Fontanelle an unossified membranous gap in the bone structure of the skull of a newborn that makes molding of the head possible

Food diary a detailed record of measured amounts of all food and fluid consumed during a specific period of time

Food-frequency record a checklist which indicates how often general food groups or specific foods are eaten

Footdrop plantar flexion of the foot with permanent contracture of the gastrocnemius (calf) muscle and tendon

Forceps an instrument with two blades and a handle used to grasp sterile supplies and to compress or grasp tissues

Foreplay (precoital stimulation) physical stimulation used as a prelude to intercourse

Formal leader an appointed leader selected by an organization and given official authority to make decisions and act

Formal nursing care plan usually a written guide to direct the efforts of nurses as they work with patients to achieve mutually agreed upon goals

Formulary a collection or list of prescriptions and formulas

Fowler's position a bed sitting position with the head of the bed raised to 45 degrees

Fracture a break in the continuity of a bone

Frail elderly describes the older adult who has significant physiological functional impairment

Fremitus vibrations felt through the chest wall by palpation

Frenulum a midline fold connecting the undersurface of the tongue to the floor of the mouth

Frequency (of urination) voiding at more frequent intervals than usual

Friction rubbing; the force that opposes motion

Fulcrum the fixed point of a lever

Full disclosure all information required by the client will be provided prior to participation in a research study

Functional nursing a model for delivering nursing care which focuses on the tasks to be completed

Functional residual capacity volume of air remaining in the lungs after a normal expiration

Fungi infection-causing microorganisms that include yeasts and moulds

Funnel chest (pectus excavatum) a congenital defect of the chest where the sternum is depressed, narrowing the anteroposterior diameter

Gait the way a person walks

Gastric pertaining to the stomach

Gastrocolic reflex increased peristalsis of the colon after food has entered the stomach

Gastroenteritis inflammation of the stomach and the intestines

Gastroscopy visual examination of the stomach with a lighted instrument (gastroscope)

Gastrostomy an opening through the abdominal wall into the stomach

Gastrostomy feeding the instillation of liquid nourishment via a tube that enters the stomach through a surgical opening in the abdominal wall

Gastrostomy tube a tube inserted through the abdominal wall into the stomach

Gavage administration of nourishment to the stomach through a nasogastric or orogastric tube; tube feeding

Gender indicates biological male or female status

Gender behaviour behaviour with masculine or feminine connotations

Gender identity a person's sense of being masculine or feminine, as distinct from being male or female

Gender role the outward expression of a person's sense of maleness or femaleness, the expression of what is perceived as gender-appropriate behaviour

General adaptation syndrome (GAS, stress syndrome) (Selye) a general arousal response of the body to a stressor that is characterized by certain physiological events and that is dominated by the sympathetic nervous system

General anesthesia sedative drugs that produce relation of skeletal muscles, and reduced or absent reflex action

Generativity (Erikson) concern for establishing and guiding the next generation

Generic name (of drug) a drug name not protected by trademark and usually describing the chemical structure of the drug

Genogram a concise visual depiction of family structure; an assessment tool for family nursing

Genupectoral position kneeling position with torso at a 90-degree angle to hips

Geriatrics the branch of medicine pertaining to elderly people

Germicidal possessing the ability to kill microorganisms

Gerontology the study of all aspects of the aging process, including biological, psychological, and sociological

Gingiva the gum tissue

Gingivitis red, swollen gingiva (gums)

Glaucoma a disturbance in the circulation of aqueous fluid; causes an increase in intraocular pressure

Global self refers to the collective beliefs and images one holds about oneself; the most complete description that individuals can give of themselves at any one time

Global self-esteem how much one likes one's perceived self as a whole

Glomerulus collection of capillary vessels within the kidney involved in the initial formation of urine

Glossitis inflammation of the tongue

Glycemia the presence of glucose in the blood

Glycemic index This index measures how much the blood glucose increases in the two or three hours after one eats

Glyceride a simple lipid; the most common form of lipid, consisting of a glycerol molecule with up to three fatty acids attached

Glycogen the chief carbohydrate stored in the body, particularly in the liver and muscles

Glycosuria the presence of glucose in the urine; glucosuria

Goals or desired outcomes; often identified in relation to nursing diagnosis

Goniometer a device used to measure the angle of a joint in degrees

Good Samaritan health-care practitioner who provides aid to a person in an emergency

Governance the establishment and maintenance of social, political, and economic arrangements by which practitioners control their practice, self-discipline, working conditions, and professional affairs

Granulation tissue young connective tissue with new capillaries formed in the wound healing process

Graphesthesia ability to recognize a figure traced on the skin with the tip of a finger, blunt pencil, or similar object

Grief emotional suffering often caused by bereavement

Grievance any dispute, difference, controversy, or disagreement arising out of the terms and conditions of employment

Grieving a state in which an individual or family experiences a natural human response involving psychosocial and physiological reactions to an actual or perceived loss (person, object, function, status, relationship)

Gross negligence involves extreme lack of knowledge, skill, or decision making that the person clearly should have known would put others at risk for harm

Ground (electrical) to transmit electric current from an object or surface to the ground

Group two or more people with shared purposes and goals

Group dynamics (process) forces that determine the behaviour of the group and the relationships among the group members

Group process a developmental process of group maturation

Growth physical change and increase in size

Guaiac test a test performed for occult (hidden) blood to detect gastrointestinal bleeding not visible to the eye

Guided imagery a relaxation technique using self-chosen positive images to achieve specific health-related goals (i.e., stress reduction, pain control)

Guilt the painful emotion associated with transgression of moral-ethical beliefs

Gurgles see *Rhonchi*

Gustatory referring to the sense of taste

Gynecology the branch of medicine that deals with processes of the female reproductive tract

Habit training (schedule toileting) attempt to keep clients dry by having them void at regular intervals

Half-life (of a drug) the time interval required for the body's elimination processes to reduce the concentration of the drug in the body by one-half

Halitosis bad breath

Hallucinate to perceive through the senses something unreal; such as hearing voices or seeing things that do not exist

Hallucinogens drugs that cause distortion of the sensory perception

Hangnail a shred of epidermal tissue at either side of the nail

Hardware (computer) the physical parts of the computer

Haustra pouches within the large intestine

Haustral churning (shuffling) the movement of the chyme back and forth within the haustra, in the large intestine

Haustrum a saclike formation of a part of the colon, produced by contraction of both the longitudinal and the circular muscles (plural: haustra)

Health a state of being physically fit, mentally stable, and socially comfortable; it encompasses more than the state of being free of disease

Health behaviour the action a person takes to understand his or her health state, maintain an optimal state of health, prevent illness and injury, and reach his or her maximum physical and mental potential

Health beliefs concepts about health that an individual believes are true

Health-care proxy a legal statement that appoints a proxy to make medical decisions for the client in the event the client is unable to do so

Health-care system the totality of services offered by all health disciplines

Health-care team health-care personnel from different disciplines who coordinate their skills to assist a client and/or support persons, commonly includes nurses, physicians, pharmacists, dietitians, physiotherapists

Health hazard appraisal an assessment and educational tool that identifies a client's risk for disease or injury

Health practice an activity that a person carries out as a result of his or her health beliefs and definition of health

Health problem any condition or situation in which a client requires help to promote, maintain, or regain a state of health or to achieve a peaceful death

Health promotion any activity undertaken for the purpose of achieving a higher level of health and well-being

Health risk appraisal (HRA) tool that indicates a client's risk of diseases or injury over time by comparing the client with a large national sample with similar demographic data

Health status the health of a person at a given time

Heart failure inability of the heart to maintain a circulation sufficient to meet the body's needs

Heart-lung death occurs with cessation of the apical pulse, respirations, and blood pressure

Heat balance the state a person is in when the amount of heat produced by the body exactly equals the amount of heat lost

Heave an abnormal lateral movement of the chest related to enlargement of the left ventricle

Height measurement from the top to the base; of a standing person from head to toe

Heimlich maneuver subdiaphragmatic abdominal thrusts used to clear an obstructed airway

Helix the posterior curve of the flap of the ear

Helping relationship a growth-facilitating process in which one person assists another to solve problems and to face crisis in the direction the assisted person chooses

Hemangioma a large, persistent, bright red or dark purple vascular area of the skin

Hematemesis the vomiting of blood

Hematocrit the proportion of red blood cells (erythrocytes) to the total blood volume

Hematoma a collection of blood in a tissue, organ, or space due to a break in the wall of a blood vessel

Hematuria the presence of blood in the urine

Hemiplegia loss of movement on one side of the body

Hemodynamics the study of the movements of the blood

Hemoglobin the red pigment in red blood cells that carries oxygen

Hemoglobinuria the presence of hemoglobin in the urine

Hemolysis rupture of red blood cells

Hemolytic transfusion reaction occurs when incompatible blood is transfused into a patient that should have been given blood of a different blood type

Hemopneumothorax a collection of blood and air or gas in the pleural cavity

Hemoptysis the presence of blood in the sputum

Hemorrhage excessive loss of blood from the vascular system

Hemorrhoids distended veins in the rectum

Hemostasis cessation of bleeding

Hemostat (artery forceps) a small pair of forceps used to constrict blood vessels

Hemothorax a collection of blood in the pleural cavity

Heparin a substance that prevents coagulation of blood

Heparin lock (saline lock) the airtight cap covering the end of a client's intravenous or central venous tubing

Herbalist one who prescribes herbs for treating people

Hering-Breuer reflex a reflex that inhibits inspiration

Hernia a protrusion of the intestine through the inguinal canal

Hesitancy (of urination) delay and difficulty initiating voiding

Heterosexual a person whose primary sexual orientation is to a member of the opposite sex

High-Fowler's position a bed-sitting position in which the head of the bed is elevated 90 degrees

Hirsutism abnormal hairiness, particularly in women

HIS hospital information system

Holism (holistic) all living organisms are seen as interacting, unified wholes that are more than the sums of their parts

Holistic health a model of health based on the belief that the whole is more than the sum of its parts

Holistic health belief holds that forces of nature must be maintained in balance or harmony

Holistic health care a system that considers all the components of health: health promotion, health maintenance, health education and illness prevention, and restorative–rehabilitative care

Holistic nursing nursing practice that has as its goal the healing of the whole person

Holy day a day set aside for special religious observance

Homans' sign calf pain produced by dorsiflexion of the foot

Homeodynamics the continual exchange of energy between humans and the external environment

Homeopathy an alternative therapy based on the theory that the cure for the disease lies in the disease itself; thus, treatment is with highly diluted amounts of substances that at a higher concentration would produce the same symptoms as the disease

Homeostasis the tendency of the body to maintain a state of balance or equilibrium while continually changing; a mechanism in which deviations from normal are sensed and counteracted

Homogeneity a high degree of likeness of attitudes and beliefs among members of a group

Homosexual a person whose primary sexual orientation is to a member of the same sex

Hope a multidimensional concept that includes perceiving realistic expectations and goals, having motivation to achieve goals, anticipating outcomes, establishing trust and interpersonal relationships, relying on internal and external resources, having determination to endure, and being oriented to the future

Hordeolum (sty) a redness, swelling, and tenderness of the hair follicle and glands that empty at the edge of the eyelids

Horizontal recumbent back-lying position with legs extended; small pillow under the head

Hospice the delivery of care for terminally ill clients either in health-care facilities or in the client's home

Hospice care based on holistic concepts that emphasize care to improve the quality of life, rather than cure

Hospital Information System (HIS) a tool used to manage client care data

Hot pack (foment) hot, moist cloth applied to an area of the body

Human needs physiological or psychological conditions that an individual must meet to achieve a state of health or well being

Humanism (learning) learning that focuses on the feelings and attitudes of learners, the importance of the individual in identifying learning needs and taking responsibility for them, and the self-motivation of the learners to work toward self-reliance and independence

Humidifier a device that adds water vapour to inspired air

Humidity the amount of moisture in the air, expressed as a percentage

Humoral immunity antibody-mediated defence; resides ultimately in the B lymphocytes and is mediated by the antibodies produced by B cells

Hydration the act of combining or being combined with water

Hydrolysis the process of splitting a molecule in the presence of digestive enzymes with the addition of water

Hydrometer (urinometer) an instrument used to measure the specific gravity of urine

Hydrostatic pressure the pressure a liquid exerts on the sides of the container that holds it; also called filtration force

Hygiene the science of health and its maintenance

Hyperalgesia extreme sensitivity to pain

Hyperalimentation (Total Parenteral Nutrition, TPN) see *Total Parenteral Nutrition*

Hypercalcemia an excess of calcium in the blood plasma

Hypercalciuria excessive calcium in the urine

Hypercapnea (hypercarbia) accumulation of carbon dioxide in the blood

Hyperchloremia an excess of chloride in the blood plasma

Hyperemia increased blood flow to an area

Hyperesthesia greater than normal sensation

Hyperextension further extension between two bones or stretching out of a joint

Hyperglycemia an excessive concentration of sugar in the blood

Hyperhidrosis excessive perspiration

Hyperkalemia an excess of potassium in the blood plasma

Hyperlipidemia elevated concentration of lipids in the plasma

Hypermagnesia an excess of magnesium in the blood plasma

Hypernatremia an excess of sodium in the blood plasma

Hyperopia (farsightedness) abnormal refraction in which light rays focus behind the retina

Hyperopic farsightedness

Hyperphosphatemia an excess of phosphate in the blood plasma

Hyperplasia an abnormal increase in the number of cells in a tissue or an organ

Hyperpnea an abnormal increase in the rate and depth of respirations

Hyperpyrexia see *Hyperthermia*

Hyperreflexia an exaggeration of the reflexes

Hyperresonance an abnormal booming sound produced during percussion of the lungs

Hypersensitivity an exaggerated response of the body to a foreign substance

Hypersomnia excessive sleep

Hypertension an abnormally high blood pressure; over 140 mm Hg systolic and/or 90 mm Hg diastolic

Hyperthermia (hyperpyrexia) an extremely high body temperature (e.g., 41° C [105.8° F])

Hypertonicity excessive muscle tone or activity

Hypertonic solution a fluid possessing a greater concentration of solutes than plasma

Hypertrophy enlargement of a muscle or organ

Hyperventilate abnormally prolonged and deep breathing

Hyperventilation very deep, rapid respirations

Hypervolemia an abnormal increase in the body's blood volume; circulatory overload

Hypnotic (drug) a drug that induces sleep

Hypoalbuminemia reduction in the level of albumin in the blood

Hypocalcemia deficiency of calcium in the blood plasma

Hypocarbia (hypocapnia) depressed level of carbon dioxide in the blood plasma

Hypochloremia deficiency of chloride in the blood plasma

Hypodermic (subcutaneous) under the skin

Hypodermoclysis the introduction of fluid in the subcutaneous tissues

Hypoesthesia (hypesthesia) less than normal sensation

Hypoglycemia a reduced amount of glucose in the blood

Hypokalemia deficiency of potassium in the blood plasma

Hypomagnesia deficiency of magnesium in the blood plasma

Hyponatremia deficiency of sodium in the blood plasma

Hypophosphatemia deficiency in phosphate in the blood plasma

Hypopnea low rate of alveolar ventilation

Hypoproteinemia small amounts of protein in the blood plasma

Hypospadias opening of the urethra on the underside of the penis

Hypostatic pneumonia an infection of lung tissue resulting from poor circulation or stagnation of secretions

Hypotension an abnormally low blood pressure; less than 100 mm Hg systolic in an adult

Hypothalmic integrator the centre in the brain that controls the core temperature; located in the preoptic area of the hypothalamus

Hypothermia a core body temperature below the lower limit of normal

Hypotheses statements of the relationship between two or more concepts (singular: hypothesis)

Hypothetical/future-oriented questions explore family options and alternative actions or implications in the future

Hypotonicity decreased muscle tone

Hypotonic solution a fluid possessing a lesser concentration of solutes than plasma has

Hypoventilation very shallow respirations

Hypovolemia an abnormal reduction in blood volume

Hypovolemic shock a state of shock caused by a reduction in the volume of circulating blood

Hypoxemia see *Anoxemia*

Hypoxia insufficient oxygen anywhere in the body

Iatrogenic caused by the physician or medical therapy

Iatrogenic disease usually an infection that is acquired as a result of treatment or diagnostic procedure

Id the source of instinctive and unconscious psychological urges

Ideal body weight the weight recommended for optimal health

Ideal image the picture of oneself that one would wish to have; may differ from the actual image

Ideal self how we would prefer to be; the individual's perception of how one should behave based upon certain personal standards, aspirations, goals, or values

Identification perceiving one's self as similar to and behaving like another person

Idiosyncratic effect a different, unexpected or individual effect from the normal one usually expected from a medication; the occurrence of unpredictable and unexplainable symptoms

Ileal conduit most commonly used urinary diversion procedure

Ileostomy an opening into the ileum (small bowel)

Illicit drug a drug that is sold illegally; a street drug

Illness a highly personal state in which the person feels unhealthy or ill, may or may not be related to disease

Illness behaviour the course of action a person takes to define the state of his or her health and pursue a remedy

Illness narratives seek understanding of the person/family's experience of illness in experiences of daily life

Illusion a false interpretation of some stimulus

Imagery the internal experience of memories, dreams, fantasies, and visions that serve as a bridge connecting body, mind, and spirit

Imagination ability to fantasize

Imitation copying the behaviours and attitudes of another person

Immobility prescribed or unavoidable restriction of movement in any area of a person's life

Immunity a specific resistance of the body to infection; it may be natural, or resistance developed after exposure to a disease agent

Immunization the process of becoming immune or rendering someone immune

Immunoglobulin (immune bodies, antibodies) a part of the body's plasma proteins

Immunologic reaction (allergic reaction) production of antibodies in response to an antigen

Impaction a condition of being firmly wedged or lodged; in reference to feces, a collection of hardened puttylike feces in the folds of the rectum

Impaired gas exchange diminished passage of oxygen and carbon dioxide across the alvelolar capillary membrane; nursing diagnosis category

Impaired home maintenance management the state in which an individual or family is unable to maintain independently a safe, growth-promoting environment

Impaired nurse a nurse whose practice has deteriorated because of chemical abuse

Imperforate abnormally closed; used to describe an opening, such as the anus or the hymen, that is not open

Implementing the phase of the nursing process in which the nursing care plan is put into action

Implied consent permission that is assumed in an emergency when consent cannot be obtained from the client or a relative

Implied contract a contract that has not been explicitly agreed to by the parties but that the law nevertheless considers to exist

Impotence (erectile dysfunction) the inability to achieve or maintain an erection sufficient for sexual satisfaction for the self and/or partner

Incentive spirometer (sustained maximal inspiration device, SMI) a device that measures the flow of air through a mouthpiece

Incident report an agency record of an accident or incident

Incision a cut or wound that is intentionally made (e.g., during surgery)

Incomplete proteins proteins that lack one or more essential amino acids; usually derived from vegetables

Incontinence involuntary urination

Incubation period the time between entrance of microorganism into the body and the onset of symptoms of the infection

Incus middle of the three ossicles of the ear

Independent capable of functioning in an autonomous manner

Independent functions are those areas of health care that are unique to nursing

Independent nursing action (intervention or function) an activity that the nurse is licensed to initiate as a result of the nurse's own knowledge and skills

Independent variable is the behaviour, characteristic, or outcome that a researcher wants to explain

Indicator pointer; identifies desired outcome

Indigestion lack or failure of the digestive system

Individualized care plans tailored to meet the needs of a specific client

Inductive reasoning making generalizations from specific data

Induration quality of being hard

Inertia inactivity; inability to move spontaneously

Infarct a localized area of necrosis (dead cells) usually owing to obstructed arterial blood flow to the part

Infection the disease process produced by microorganisms

Inferences interpretation or conclusions made based on cues or observed data

Inferior situated below

Infestation invasion of the body by insects, mites, or ticks

Infiltration the diffusion or deposition into tissue of substances that are not normal to it

Inflammation local and nonspecific defensive tissue response to injury or destruction of cells

Influence an informal strategy used to gain the cooperation of others without exercising formal authority

Informal care plan an unwritten plan of action to address a client health problem

Informal leader an individual selected by the group as its leader because of seniority, age, special abilities, or charisma

Informed consent a client's agreement to accept a course of treatment or a procedure after receiving complete information, including the risks of treatment and facts relating to it, from the physician

Infradian rhythm a biorhythm that cycles monthly, such as the human menstrual cycle

Infrared heat a radiant type of heat capable of penetrating body tissues to a depth of 10 mm; sources include heat lamps and incandescent light bulbs

Infusion the introduction of fluid into vein or part of the body

Infusion controller a device used with intravenous infusions to control the infusion rate by using gravitational force

Infusion pump a device used with intravenous fluids to deliver a desired infusion rate by exerting positive pressure on the tubing or on the fluid

Ingestion the act of taking in food or medication

Ingrown nails aberrant growth of a nail; growing inward of the nail into the soft tissues around it

Inhalation (inspiration) the act of breathing in; the intake of air or other substances into the lungs

Inhalation (aerosol) therapy deliverance of droplets of medication or moisture suspended in a gas, such as oxygen, by inhalation through the nose or mouth

Inorganic substances matter not derived from hydrocarbons and not of organic origin

Input consists of information, material, or energy that enters a system

Inquest a legal inquiry into the cause or manner of a death

Insensible fluid loss fluid loss that is not perceptible to the individual

Insensible heat loss heat loss that occurs from evaporation (vaporization) of moisture from the respiratory tract, mucosa of the mouth, and the skin

Insensible perspiration unnoticeable sweating that evaporates immediately once it reaches the surface of the skin

In-service education teaching that is designed to upgrade the knowledge or skills of employees

In situ in place; localized

Insomnia inability to obtain a sufficient quality or quantity of sleep

Inspection visual examination

Inspiration see *Inhalation*

Inspiratory capacity the maximum amount of air inhaled after a normal expiration

Inspiratory reserve volume the maximum amount of air inhaled after a normal inspiration

Instillation application of a medication into a body cavity or orifice

Insulin resistance the sensitivity to insulin by the cell's receptors is decreased

Integrity-preserving moral compromise the settling of differences in which concessions are made and the conflicting values of all parties are respected

Integumentary system the skin, hair, and nails

Intellectualization a combination of reason, imagination, judgment, and memory

Intensity (amplitude) the loudness or softness of a sound

Intention tremor an involuntary trembling when one attempts voluntary movement

Intercostal between the ribs

Intercostal retractions indrawing between the ribs

Intermittent evaluation evaluation performed at specific intervals

Intermittent (quotidian) fever a body temperature that alternates at regular intervals between periods of fever and periods of normal temperature

Intermittent positive pressure breathing (IPPB) delivery of oxygen into the lungs at positive pressure and release of the pressure passively during expiration

Internal respiration the interchange of oxygen and carbon dioxide between the circulating blood and the cells of the body tissues

Internal rotation a turning toward the midline (e.g., rotation of the hip joint)

Internal stressors factors that originate within a person

Internet a worldwide computer network

Interpersonal skills all the verbal and nonverbal activities people use when communicating directly with one another

Interpretive tradition suggests that there is no single fixed reality against which knowledge can be measured

Interstitial between the cells of the body's tissues

Interstitial fluid liquid that surrounds the cells, includes lymph

Intervertebral between the vertebrae, as in intervertebral disks

Interview a planned communication; a conversation with a purpose

Intra-arterial into an artery

Intra-articular into a joint

Intracardiac into the heart muscle

Intracellular within a cell or cells

Intracellular fluid (ICF) fluid found within the body cells, also called cellular fluid

Intractable pain pain that is resistant to cure or relief

Intradermal (intracutaneous) under the epidermis; into the dermis

Intrafamily communication communication within a family; plays a significant role in the development of self-esteem

Intralipid therapy the infusion of essential fatty acids or fat emulsions through a central venous line

Intramuscular into the muscle

Intraoperative period the phase during surgery; begins when the client is transferred to the operating room and ends when the client is admitted to the recovery room

Intraosseous into the bone

Intrapleural within the pleural cavity

Intrapleural pressure pressure within the pleural cavity

Intrapulmonary pressure pressure within the lungs

Intraspinal (intrathecal) into the spinal canal

Intrauterine within the uterus

Intravascular within a blood vessel

Intravascular fluid plasma

Intravenous within a vein

Intravenous block (Bier block) anesthesia procedure used for the arm, wrist, hand

Intravenous cholangiogram an X-ray film of the bile ducts after a contrast dye has been administered intravenously

Intravenous lock see *Heparin lock*

Intravenous push (IVP, bolus) the direct intravenous administration of a medication that cannot be diluted or that is needed in an emergency

Intravenous pyelography (IVP); intravenous urography (IVU) X-ray filming of the kidney and ureters after injection of a radiopaque material into the vein

Introjection the assimilation of the attributes of others

Intubation the insertion of a tube

Invasion of privacy release of personal information without the individual's consent

Inversion a turning inward

Ion an atom or group of atoms that carry a positive or negative electric charge; an electrolyte

Iron-deficiency anemia a form of anemia caused by inadequate supply of iron for synthesis of hemoglobin

Irradiation exposure to penetrating rays, such as X-rays, gamma rays, infrared rays, or ultraviolet rays

Irrational confused as to time, place, or person

Irrigation (lavage) a flushing or washing-out of a body cavity, organ, or wound with a specified solution

Ischemia deficiency of blood supply caused by obstruction of circulation to the body part

Isokinetic exercise involves muscle contraction or tension against resistance

Isolation practices that prevent the spread of infection and communicable disease

Isometric (static, setting) exercise tensing of a muscle against an immovable outer resistance, which does not change muscle length or produce joint motion

Isotonic (dynamic) exercise exercise in which muscle tension is constant and the muscle shortens to produce muscle contraction and active movement

IV filters devices attached to intravenous infusion tubing to filter or remove air, particulate matter, and microbes

Jaundice a yellowish colour of the sclera, mucous membranes, and/or skin

Jejunostomy an opening through the abdominal wall into the jejunum

Jejunostomy feeding the instillation of liquid nourishment via a tube that enters the jejunum through a surgical opening into the abdominal wall

Justice process that distributes fairly risks, benefits, and costs

JVD jugular venous distention

Kaleidoscopic societies changing societies that consist of many diverse groups

Kardex® the trade name for a method that makes use of a series of cards to concisely organize and record client data and instructions for daily nursing care—especially care that changes frequently and must be kept up-to-date

Kegel's exercises pelvic floor or perineal muscle tightening exercises

Keloid a hypertrophic scar containing an abnormal amount of collagen

Keratotic spots horny growths, such as warts or calluses

Ketone any compound containing the carbonyl group, CO, and having hydrocarbon groups attached to the carbonyl group

Ketone bodies products of incomplete fat metabolism which appear in the urine

Ketosis a condition in which excessive ketones are formed in the body

Kilocalorie see *Calorie*

Kilogram a unit of weight equal to 1,000 grams or approximately 2.2 pounds

Kilojoule (kJ) a metric measurement referring to the amount of energy required when a force of one newton (N) moves one kilogram of weight one metre distance

Kinesiology the study of the motion of the human body

Kinesthesia the ability to perceive extent, direction, or weight of movement

Kinesthetic sense refers to awareness of the position and movement of body parts

Knee-chest position see *Genupectoral position*

Koilonychia the condition in which the nail curves upward from the nailbed

Koplick's spots red spots on the buccal mucosa; associated with measles

Korotkoff's sounds a series of five sounds produced by blood within the artery with each ventricular contraction

Kosher acceptable or prepared according to Jewish law

Kussmaul breathing (Kussmaul-Kien respiration) deep rapid breathing; a dyspnea occurring in paroxysms often preceding diabetic coma; air hunger

Kwashiorkor a condition occurring in children, after weaning, as a result of protein and calorie malnutrition; evidenced by growth failure, potbelly, edema, and mental apathy

Kyphosis excessive convex curvature of the thoracic spine

Laboured breathing breathing with decided effort

Lacerate to tear, rather than cut, a body tissue

Lacrimation tearing of the eyes

Laissez-faire leadership a nondirective style of leadership in which the leader assumes a "hands-off" approach, allowing group members to perform tasks in their area of expertise while the leader acts as a resource person

LAN local area (computer) network

Lanugo the fine, woolly hair or down on the shoulders, back, sacrum, and earlobes of the unborn child that may remain for a few weeks after birth

Large calorie see *Calorie*

Laryngeal stridor a harsh, crowing sound heard during expiration when there is a laryngeal obstruction

Laryngoscopy visual examination of the larynx with a laryngoscope

Lateral to the side, away from the midline

Lateral position a side-lying position

Lavage an irrigation or washing of a body organ, such as the stomach

Laws rules made by humans that regulate social conduct in a formally prescribed and binding manner

Lawsuit legal action within a court of law

Laxative a medication that stimulates bowel activity

Leader a person who influences others to work together to accomplish a specific goal

Leading questions questions that influence the client to give a particular answer

Learning a change in human disposition or capability that persists over a period of time and cannot be solely accounted for by growth

Learning need a desire or requirement to know something that is presently unknown

Legitimate power power related to the authority associated with a specific position or role

Lentigo senilus small brown areas that appear on the hands and arms of an older client

Lesion the traumatic or pathological interruption of a tissue or the loss of function of a body part

Lethargy drowsiness; sleeping much of the time when not stimulated

Leukocyte white blood cell

Leukocytosis an increase in the number of white blood cells

Leukoplakia white patches or spots on the mucous membrane of the tongue or cheek

Lever a rigid bar that moves on a fixed axis called a fulcrum

Levin tube a single-lumen nasogastric tube

Liable being legally responsible to account for one's obligations and actions and to make financial restitution for wrongful acts

Liability legal responsibility for one's action or inaction

Libel defamation by means of print, writing, or pictures

Libido (sexual desire) urge or desire for sexual activity

Lice parasitic insects that infest mammals

Licence a legal permit granted to individuals to engage in the practice of a profession and to use a particular title

Licensed practical nurse (LPN), also referred to as a registered practical nurse (RPN), is an autonomous practitioner who cares for clients with less complex needs and more predictable outcomes

Lifestyle the values and behaviours adopted by a person in daily life

Lifestyle assessment appraisal of the personal lifestyle and habits of the client as they affect health

Lift an abnormal anterior movement of the chest related to enlargement of the right ventricle

Light diet a food plan designed for postoperative and other clients who are not ready for a regular diet; contains foods that are plainly cooked

Line of gravity an imaginary vertical line running through the centre of gravity

Liniment a topical liquid applied to the skin frequently to stimulate circulation or to relieve pain

Lipid an organic substance that is greasy and insoluble in water

Lipoproteins water-soluble substances that are the form in which lipids are transported in the blood (e.g., high-density lipoproteins [HDL])

Lithotomy position a back-lying position in which the feet are supported in stirrups

Litigation the action of a lawsuit

Living will a document that states medical treatments the client chooses to omit or refuse in the event that the client is unable to make these decisions

Livor mortis discolouration of the skin caused by breakdown of the red blood cells; occurs after blood circulation has ceased; appears in the dependent areas of the body

Lobule small segment or lobe

Local adaptation syndrome (LAS) the reaction of one organ or body part to stress

Local anesthesia an anesthetic agent that is injected into a specific area; used for minor surgical procedures

Local infection an infection that is limited to the specific part of the body where the microorganisms remain

Locus of control (LOC) a concept about whether clients believe their health status is under their own or other's control

Longevity life expectancy

Long-term memory the repository for information stored for very long periods

Lordosis an exaggerated concavity in the lumbar region of the vertebral column

Loss an actual or potential situation in which a valued ability, object, or person is inaccessible or changed so that it is perceived as no longer valuable

Lotion a liquid that often carries an insoluble powder

Louse a parasitic insect that infests mammals (plural: lice)

Low-Fowler's (semi-Fowler's) position a bed-sitting position in which the head of the bed is elevated between 15 and 45 degrees, with or without knee flexion

Lumbar puncture (LP, spinal tap) insertion of a needle into the subarachnoid space at the lumbar region

Lumen a channel within a tube

Lung compliance expansibility of the lung

Lung recoil the tendency of lungs to collapse away from the chest wall

Lung scan an image of the lung produced using a detector or a moving beam of radiation

Lymphocyte mononuclear leukocyte formed chiefly by lymphoid tissue

Lysis (of a fever) the gradual reduction of an elevated body temperature to normal

Lysozyme an enzyme in saliva and tears that functions as an antibacterial agent

Maceration the wasting away or softening of a solid as if by the action of soaking; often used to describe degenerative changes and eventual disintegration

Macrocephaly abnormally large head circumference

Macrominerals the minerals that people require daily in amounts over 100 mg

Macronutrients energy-producing nutrients (carbohydrates, fats, and proteins)

Macrophage a large phagocytic cell that destroys microorganisms or harmful cells

Magico-religious health belief system a belief system in which people attribute the fate of the world and those in it to the actions of God, the gods, or other supernatural forces for good or evil

Major surgery operation that involves a high degree of risk for a variety of reasons; it may be complicated or prolonged; large losses of blood may occur; vital organs may be involved; postoperative complications may occur

Malaise a general feeling of being unwell

Malignancy abnormal tissue with a tendency to grow and invade other tissues

Malingering pretending to be ill, rather than facing something unpleasant

Malleus largest of the three ossicles of the ear

Malnutrition a disorder of nutrition; insufficient nourishment of the body cells

Malpractice the negligent acts of persons engaged in professions or occupations in which highly technical or professional skills are employed

Malocclusion malposition and imperfect contact of the mandibular and maxillary teeth

Mammography X-ray study of breast tissue

Managed care a method of organizing care delivery that emphasizes communication and coordination of care among all health-care team members

Management Informations system (MIS) a tool designed to help manage large data bases

Manager one who is appointed to a position in an organization which gives the power to guide and direct the work of others

Manometer an instrument used to measure the pressure of fluids or gases

Manubrium uppermost portion of the sternum

Margination the aggregating or lining up of substances along a surface or edge (e.g., the lining up of white blood cells against the wall of a blood vessel during the inflammatory process)

Mass peristalsis involves a wave of powerful muscular contraction that moves over large areas of the colon; usually occurs after eating

Mastication the act of chewing

Masturbation manual self-stimulation of the genital organs or other erogenous areas

Material culture refers to objects such as dress or eating utensils and the ways that they are used

Matriarchy a system of social organization in which the mother is the head of the house or family

Matrilineal relating to descent through the female line

Maturation the process of becoming mature or fully developed; development of inherited traits

Maturity the state of maximal function and integration; the state of being fully developed

Mean a measure of central tendency, computed by summing all scores and dividing by the number of subjects; commonly symbolized as X or M

Mean blood pressure the midway point between the systolic and diastolic pressures

Measures of central tendency measures that describe the centre of a distribution of data, denoting where most of the subjects lie; include the mean, median, and mode

Measures of variability measures that indicate the degree of dispersion or spread of the data; include range, variance, and standard deviation

Meatus an opening, passage, or channel

Meconium the first fecal material passed by the newborn, normally up to 24 hours after birth

Medial toward the middle or midline

Median a measure of central tendency, representing the exact middle score or value in a distribution of scores; the median is the value above and below which 50 percent of the scores lie

Medicaid in the United States, a federal public assistance program paid out of general taxes and administered through the individual states to provide health care for those who require financial assistance

Medical asepsis all practices intended to confine a specific microorganism to a specific area, limiting the number, growth, and spread of microorganisms

Medical directive a proxy and a guideline to physicians regarding clients' health-care wishes when they are unable to communicate them directly

Medical examiner a physician who usually has advanced education in pathology or forensic medicine who determines causes of death

Medical narratives provide information related to the nature and onset of physical symptoms, diagnosis, and treatment of a disease process

Medication (drug) a substance administered for the diagnosis, cure, treatment, mitigation, or prevention of disease

Medication history includes information about the drugs the client is taking currently or has taken recently

Meditation mental exercise that directs the mind to think inwardly by closing the sense organs to external stimulation

Melanin the pigment that gives colour to the skin

Menarche onset of menstruation

Meniscus the crescent-shaped upper surface of a column of fluid

Menopause cessation of menstruation

Menses menstrual flow

Menstruation the monthly discharge of blood through the vagina occuring in nonpregnant women from puberty to menopause

Mentor a person who serves as an experienced guide, adviser, or advocate and assumes responsibility for promoting the growth and professional advancement of a less experienced individual

Mesoderm the middle layer of tissue formed in the third week of life

Message an expression of thoughts or feelings with verbal or nonverbal communication

Metabolic acidosis a condition characterized by a deficiency of bicarbonate ions in the body in relation to the amount of carbonic acid in the body, in which the pH falls to less than 7.35

Metabolic alkalosis a condition characterized by an excess of bicarbonate ions in the body in relation to the amount of carbonic acid in the body; the pH rises to greater than 7.45

Metabolism the sum of all the physical and chemical processes by which living substance is formed and maintained and by which energy is made available for use by the organism

Metabolites end products or enzymes

Metacarpal referring to the part of the hand between the wrist and the fingers

Metaparadigm a specific relationship among the four major abstract concepts related to nursing

Metered-dose inhaler (MDI) a handheld nebulizer that can be used by clients to self-administer an aerosol medication

Microcephaly abnormally small head circumference

Microminerals the minerals that people require daily in amounts less than 100 mg

Micronutrients vitamins and minerals

Microorganism minute living body visible only under a microscope

Micturition see *Urination*

Midclavicular line an imaginary line that runs inferiorly and vertically from the centre of the clavicle

Middle-level manager a manager who supervises a number of first-level managers and is responsible for the activities in the departments supervised

Midlife crisis realization that half of one's life has been reached, and personal goals may not have been achieved

Midsternal line an imaginary line that runs vertically through the middle of the sternum

Midwife a female who practises the art of aiding in the delivery of infants; may be a nurse who has received special training in obstetrics and is qualified to deliver infants

Milaria rubra a prickly heat rash of the face, neck, trunk, or perineal area of infants

Milk, milking (a tube) the compression and movement of fingers along the length of a tube in order to move its contents toward an opening for removal

Milliequivalent (mEq) one-thousandth of an equivalent, which is the chemical combining power of a substance

Millilitre (mL) a unit of volume in the metric system approximating one cubic centimetre

Millimol one-thousandth of a mol

Minerals found in organic compounds, as inorganic compounds and as free ions

Minim the basic unit of measure in the apothecary system, equal to 0.0616 mL

Minor surgery operation that involves little risk, produces few complications, and is often performed in a "day surgery" facility

Miosis constricted pupils

MIS management information system

Misdemeanor a legal offence usually punishable by a fine or a short-term jail sentence, or both

Mitre a method of folding the bedclothes at the corners to secure them in place while the bed is occupied

Mixed hearing loss a combination of conduction and sensorineural loss

MMR combined measles, mumps, and rubella vaccine

Mobility ability to move about freely, easily, and purposefully in the environment

Mode the score or value that occurs most frequently in a distribution of scores

Modelling observing the behaviour of people who have successfully achieved a goal that one has set for oneself and, through observing, acquiring ideas for behaviour and coping strategies

Mol (Mole) is the unit of measurement for electrolytes

Molarity the number of moles of a solute per litre of solution

Mongolian spots blue-gray areas of discolouration of the skin of the lower back, thighs, and sometimes shoulders of the infant and small children; more often seen in nonwhite children

Monocyte mononuclear leukocyte formed in the bone marrow

Monosaccharides sugars that are composed of single molecules

Monotheism belief in the existence of one God

Monounsaturated fatty acids fatty acids with one double bond

Montgomery straps tie tapes used to hold dressings in place

Moral aspect of ethics; concerned with what constitutes right action

Moral agency an individual's ability to effect or convey moral decisions and actions

Moral behaviour the way an individual perceives and responds to requirements for people living together within a society

Moral development pattern of change in moral behaviour with age

Moral dilemma a decision-focused problem in which two moral principles or actions apply equally, such that an important value must be sacrificed

Moral distress feelings associated with an action-focused ethical problem in which one knows the right course of action to take but cannot carry it out because of institutional policies or other constraints

Morality a doctrine or system denoting what is right and wrong in conduct, character, or attitude

Morbidity incidence of disease

Mores values of members in a group

Morgue a place where dead bodies are temporarily kept before release to a mortician

Moro's reflex the startle reflex of infants, in which the arms and legs are extended outward and retracted in response to a sudden stimulus, such as a loud noise

Mortality death rate

Mortician a person trained in the care of the dead; also called an undertaker

Motivation the desire to learn

Mourning the process through which grief is eventually resolved or altered

Mucous membrane epithelial tissue that forms mucus, concentrates bile, and secretes or excretes enzymes

Mucus the lubricating, free slime of the mucous membranes

Multilumen catheter a catheter which has more than one channel, each channel or lumen has a separate port located along or at the catheter tip

Multiparous two or more pregnancies

Murmurs (cardiac) an adventitious or abnormal sound heard on auscultation of the heart during systole and diastole

Mutual pretense dying individual, family, and health-care professional are aware of impending death but do not talk about it

Mydriasis enlarged pupils

Mydriatic a medication that dilates the pupils of the eyes

Myelogram (myelography) an X-ray film of the spinal cord, nerve roots, and vertebrae after injection of a contrast medium into the subarachnoid space

Myocardial infarction cardiac tissue necrosis owing to obstruction of bloodflow to the heart

Myopia (nearsightedness) abnormal refraction in which light rays focus in front of the retina

Myopic nearsightedness

Myotonia increased muscle tension

Myxedema (hypothyroidism) underactivity of the thyroid

Narcolepsy a condition in which an individual experiences an uncontrollable desire for sleep or attacks of sleep during the day

Narcotic a strong analgesic

Narcotic agonist-antagonist a drug with properties that simulate a narcotic and with properties that act against the effects of a narcotic

Narrative charting a descriptive record of client data and nursing interventions, written in sentences and paragraphs

Nasal cannula (nasal prongs) a device used to administer low-flow oxygen

Nasoenteric tube a long tube that is inserted through one nostril and down into the upper small intestine

Nasogastric tube a plastic or rubber tube inserted through the nose into the stomach for the purpose of feeding or irrigating the stomach

Naturopath a nonmedical practitioner who uses such things as light, heat, and water in therapy, but not drugs

Nausea the urge to vomit

Nebulization the conversion of a fine mist or spray from a liquid

Nebulizer a device which produces a fine mist; atomizer or sprayer

Necrosis death of tissue cells caused by inadequate blood supply

Negative feedback see *Homeostasis*

Negative nitrogen balance a nitrogen output that exceeds nitrogen intake

Negligence failure to behave in a reasonable and prudent manner; an unintentional tort

Neoplasm any growth that is new and abnormal

Nephritis inflammation of a kidney

Nerve block chemical interruption of a nerve pathway effected by injecting a local anesthetic

Network linkages; system

Networking a process by which people develop linkages throughout the profession to communicate, share ideas and information, and offer support and direction to each other

Neurectomy surgery in which peripheral or cranial nerves are interrupted to alleviate localized pain

Neurogenic bladder interference with the normal mechanisms of urine elimination in which the client does not perceive bladder fullness and is unable to control the urinary sphincters; the result of impaired neurological function

Neurological pertaining to the nervous system

Neuromuscular pertaining to the nerves and muscles

Neuropathic pain the result of a disturbance of the peripheral or central nervous system that results in pain that may or may not be associated with an ongoing tissue-damaging process

Neuropeptides amino acid messenger molecules produced at various sites throughout the body

Neutral questions queries that do not direct or pressure a client to answer in a certain way

NIC (Nursing Interventions Classification) a taxonomy of standardized nursing interventions

NOC (Nursing Outcomes Classification) a taxonomy of standardized nurse-sensitive client outcomes

Nociceptor a pain receptor

Nocturia (nycturia) increased frequency of urination at night that is not a result of increased fluid intake

Nocturnal pertaining to night

Nocturnal enuresis involuntary urination at night

Nocturnal frequency the need for older adults to arise during the night to urinate

Noncompliance failure to follow the prescribed treatment plan

Nondirective interview an interview using open-ended questions and empathetic responses to build rapport and learn client concerns

Nonessential amino acids amino acids that the body can manufacture

Nonmaleficence the duty to do no harm

Nonmaterial culture refers to beliefs, customs, languages, and social institutions

Nonopioids non-narcotic analgesics; includes acetaminophen (Tylenol) and nonsteroidal anti-inflammatory drugs

Nonproductive cough a dry, harsh cough without secretions

Non–rapid-eye-movement sleep see *NREM sleep*

Nonspecific defences bodily defences that protect a person against all microorganisms, regardless of prior exposure

Nonverbal communication (body language) communication other than words, including gestures, posture, and facial expressions

Norm an ideal or fixed standard; an expected standard of behaviour of group members

Normal saline an isotonic concentration of salt (NaCl) solution

Normocephalic normal head size

Normocephaly normal head circumference at birth; usually 35 cm

Nosocomial referring to or originating in a hospital or similar institution (e.g., a nosocomial infection)

NREM (non–rapid-eye-movement) sleep a deep restful sleep state; also called slow wave sleep

NSAIDs (nonsteroidal anti-inflammatory drugs) drugs that relieve pain by acting on the peripheral nerve endings to inhibit the formation of the prostaglandins that tend to sensitize nerves to painful stimuli; have analgesic, antipyretic, and anti-inflammatory effect; include aspirin and ibuprofen

Nuclear family a family of parents and their offspring

Nulliparous a female who has never given birth

Nursing diagnosis the nurse's clinical judgment about individual, family, or community responses to actual and potential health problems/life processes to provide the basis for selecting nursing interventions to achieve outcomes for which the nurse is accountable

Nursing ethics ethical issues that occur in nursing practice

Nursing informatics the science of using computer information systems in the practice of nursing

Nursing intervention any treatment that the nurse performs based on clinical knowledge to enhance client care

Nursing Interventions Classification (NIC) *see* NIC

Nursing orders instructions written on the care plan to direct the specific nursing activities that help the client achieve desired outcomes/goals

Nursing Outcomes Classification (NOC) *see* NOC

Nursing practice acts legislation that regulates the practice of nursing

Nursing practice standards provide guidelines for determining the quality of nursing care that a patient or client receives

Nursing process a systematic rational method of planning and providing nursing care

Nursing standards optimum levels of nursing care against which actual performance of a nurse is compared

Nutrient an organic or inorganic substance found in food; nutrients are digested and absorbed in the gastrointestinal tract and then used in the body's metabolic processes

Nutrition the sum of the process of taking in, assimilating, and using nutrients

Nutritionist a person who has specialized knowledge about nutrition and food

Nutritive value the nutrient content of a specified amount of food

Nystagmus involuntary rapid movement of the eyeball

Obese (obesity) body weight greater than 20 percent of the ideal for height and frame

Objective data (signs, overt data) information (data) that is detectable by an observer or can be tested against an accepted standard; can be seen, heard, felt, or smelled

Obligatory heat the heat produced by the body as a result of the metabolism of food

Obligatory loss the essential fluid loss required to maintain body functioning

Obstetrics the branch of medicine dealing with the birth process and related events that precede and follow it

Obtunded difficult to arouse from sleep; requiring shaking or a painful stimulus to awaken

Obturator a disc or instrument that closes an opening (e.g., the obturator of a tracheostomy set fits inside and closes off the end of the outer tube)

Occlusive closed

Occult hidden

Occult blood presence of blood that is undetectable to the naked eye

Occupational therapist one who assists clients with impaired function to gain the skills required to perform activities of daily living

Official name (of drug) the name under which a drug is listed in one of the official publications (e.g., the *Canadian Formulary*)

Oils lipids that are liquid at room temperature

Olfactory referring to the sense of smell

Oliguria production of abnormally small amounts of urine by the kidney

Oncotic pressure pulling force exerted by colloids that help maintain the water content of blood

One-/two-point discrimination the ability to sense whether one or two areas of the skin are being stimulated by pressure

Ongoing evaluation is done while or immediately on implementing a nursing order

Online connected to a computer network

Ontology investigates the nature of being

Opaque not admitting the passage of light

Open awareness dying individual and surrounding people know about the impending death and feel comfortable in talking about it

Open-ended questions queries that specify only the broad topic to be discussed and invite clients to discover and explore their thoughts and feelings about the topic

Open system a system in which energy, matter, and information move into and out of the system through the system boundary

Ophthalmic referring to the eye

Ophthalmoscope an instrument used to examine the interior of the eye

Opioids naturally occurring or synthetic narcotic analgesics

Opportunistic pathogen a microorganism causing disease only in a susceptible individual

Oral referring to the mouth

Organic referring to an organ or organs; in chemistry, referring to compounds containing carbon; arising from an organism

Organizing to systematize, or to provide structure

Orgasm climax of sexual excitement

Orgasmic dysfunction the inability of a woman to achieve orgasm

Orientation awareness of time, place, and person

Orifice an external opening of a body cavity

Orthopnea ability to breathe only when in an upright position (sitting or standing)

Orthopneic position a sitting position to relieve respiratory difficulty in which the client leans over and is supported by an overbed table across the lap

Orthostatic (postural) hypotension decrease in blood pressure related to positional or postural changes from lying to sitting or standing positions

Osmol the number of particles in 1 gram molecular weight of a disassociated solute

Osmolarity (osmolality) the concentration of solutes in solution; the osmolar concentration of a solution expressed in osmols per litre of solution

Osmosis passage of a solvent through a semipermeable membrane from an area of lesser solute concentration to one of greater solute concentration

Osmotic pressure pressure exerted by the number of nondiffusable particles in a solution; the amount of pressure needed to stop the flow of water across a membrane

Ossicles small bones

Osteoarthritis noninflammatory degenerative joint disease

Osteoporosis demineralization of the bone

Ostomy a suffix denoting the formation of an opening or outlet, such as an opening on the abdominal wall, for the elimination of feces or urine

Otic referring to the ear

Otoscope an instrument used to examine the ears

Outcome evaluation focuses on demonstrable changes in clients' health status as a result of nursing care

Output energy, matter, or information from a system given out by the system as a result of its processes

Outward rotation a turning away from the midline

Overhydration excess of water in the extracellular fluid

Overt data see *Objective data*

Over-the-counter drug a drug that is available to a consumer without a prescription

Oxidation a chemical process by which a substance combines with oxygen; energy is released, and other substances are formed

Oxygen analyzer a device used to measure the concentration of oxygen being received by the client

Oxygen saturation (SaO_2) the amount of hemoglobin fully saturated with oxygen; given as a percent value

Oxyhemoglobin hemoglobin combined with molecular oxygen for transportation in blood

Pace number of steps taken per minute or the distance taken in one step when walking

Pack an unsterile hot or cold moist cloth applied to an area of the body

Packing filling an open wound or cavity with a material, such as gauze

$PaCO_2$ partial pressure of carbon dioxide (arterial blood)

Pain management the alleviation of pain or a reduction to a level of comfort

Pain reaction the autonomic nervous system and behavioural responses to pain

Pain sensation see *pain threshold*

Pain threshold (pain sensation) the amount of pain stimulation a person requires before feeling pain

Pain tolerance the maximum amount and duration of pain that an individual is willing to endure

Palliative affording relief but not cure

Palliative nursing care provided to reduce or alleviate uncomfortable symptoms but not to produce a cure

Pallor the absence of underlying red tones in the skin and may be most readily seen in the buccal mucosa

Palmar grasp baby's fingers curl around an object

Palpation the examination of the body using the sense of touch

Pandemic an epidemic disease that is widespread

PaO_2 partial pressure of oxygen (arterial blood)

Pap (Papanicolaou) test/smear a method of taking a sample of cervical cells for microscopic examination to detect malignancy

Papule a superficial, circumscribed elevation of the skin

Paracentesis the insertion of a needle into a cavity (usually the abdominal cavity) to remove fluid

Paradigm (or world view) is a particular way of thinking based on a specific set of beliefs, values, assumptions

Paradoxical breathing the ballooning out of the chest wall during expiration and depression or sucking inward of the chest wall during inspiration

Parallax a distortion in the measurement of blood pressure resulting from the angle of viewing

Paralysis the impairment or loss of motor function of a body part

Paramedical having a connection with medicine

Paraphrasing (restating) actively listening for the client's basic message and then repeating those thoughts and/or feelings in similar words

Paraplegia paralysis of the lower part of the body (including the legs) affecting both motor function and sensation

Parasite a microorganism that lives in or on another from which it obtains nourishment

Parasomnia a cluster or pattern of waking behaviour that appears during sleep, such as somnambulism (sleepwalking), sleep talking, and enuresis (bedwetting)

Parenteral drug administration occurring outside the alimentary tract; injected into the body through some route other than the alimentary canal (e.g., intramuscularly)

Paresis paralysis

Paresthesia an abnormal sensation of burning or prickling

Paronychia infection of the tissue surrounding the nail

Parotitis inflammation of the parotid salivary gland

Paroxysm a sudden attack or sharp recurrence; a spasm

Partial pressure the pressure exerted by each individual gas in a mixture according to its percentage concentration in the mixture

Partially complete proteins proteins that contain less than the required amount of one or more essential amino acids; cannot alone support continued growth

Passive euthanasia allowing a person to die by withholding or withdrawing measures to maintain life

Passive immunity a resistance of the body to infection in which the host receives natural or artificial antibodies produced by another source

Passive range-of-motion (ROM) exercise exercise in which another person moves each of the client's joints through their complete range of movement, maximally stretching all muscle groups within each plane over each joint

Passivity lethargy; receptivity to outside influence; lack of energy or will

Patent open, unobstructed; not closed

Paternalism an action that is based upon what a parent would do

Pathogenic capable of producing disease

Pathogenicity ability to produce pathologic changes or disease

Pathological fractures break resulting from weakened bone tissue; often caused by neoplasms or osteoporosis

Patient a person who is waiting for or undergoing medical treatment and care

Patient-controlled analgesia (PCA) a pain management technique that allows the client to take an active role in managing pain

Patient-focused care a delivery model that brings all services and care providers to the client

Patient Self-Determination Act (PSDA) legislation requiring that every competent adult be informed in writing upon admission to a health-care institution about his or her rights to accept or refuse medical care and to use advance directives

Patriarchy a social system in which the father is the head of the household or family

Patrilineal relating to descent through the male line

PC personal computer

PCO_2 partial pressure of carbon dioxide (venous blood)

Peak plasma level (of drug) the concentration of a drug in the blood plasma that occurs when the elimination rate equals the rate of absorption

Pectoriloquy exaggerated bronchophony

Pedagogy the discipline concerned with helping children to learn

Pediculosis infestation with head lice

Pedophilia sexual acts with children

Peer groups collection of individuals of equal status

Penrose drain a flexible rubber drain

Perceived loss the loss experienced by a person that cannot be verified by others

Perception the ability to interpret the environment through the senses

Perceptor an experienced staff member facilitates and guides a new staff member, sometimes a student

Percussion (clapping, cupping) (in physiotherapy) the forceful striking of the chest with cupped hands to loosen secretions in the lungs

Percussion (in assessment) a method in which the body surface is struck to elicit sounds that can be heard or vibrations that can be felt

Percutaneous the route of absorption of topical medications through the skin

Percutaneous endoscopic gastrostomy (PEG) a procedure in which a PEG catheter is inserted into the stomach through the skin and subcutaneous tissues of the abdomen; used as a feeding tube

Percutaneous endoscopic jejunostomy (PEJ) see percutaneous endoscopic gastrostomy; inserted into jejunum

Perfusion passage of blood constituents through the vessels of the circulatory system

Perineum the area between the anus and the posterior (back) aspect of the genitals

Periodontal disease (pyorrhea) disorder of the supporting structures of the teeth

Perioperative period refers to the three phases of surgery: preoperative, intraoperative, and postoperative

Periorbital around the eye socket

Peripheral at the edge or outward boundary

Peripheral pulse a pulse located in the periphery of the body (e.g., foot, wrist)

Peripheral vascular resistance (PVR) is the resistance to blood flow within the vascular system

PICC peripherally inserted central venous catheter

Peristalsis wavelike movements produced by circular and longitudinal muscle fibres of the intestinal walls; it propels the intestinal contents onward

Peristomal around a stoma

Peritoneal dialysis the instillation and drainage of a solution (dialysate) from the peritoneal cavity

Personal identity the conscious sense of individuality and uniqueness that is continually evolving throughout life

Personal space the distance people prefer in interactions with others

Personal values standards internalized from the society or culture in which one lives

Personality the outward expression of the inner self

Person-in-context of the family the individual is viewed as the primary focus of nursing care and the family is viewed as a contextual influence

Perspiration the fluid secreted by the sweat glands for excreting waste products and cooling the body

PES format the three essential components of nursing diagnostic statements including the terms describing the problem, the etiology of the problem, and the defining characteristics or cluster of signs and symptoms

Petechiae pinpoint red areas in the skin

Petrissage a massage technique consisting of kneading or large, quick pinches of the skin, subcutaneous tissue, and muscle

pH a measure of the relative alkalinity or acidity of a solution; a measure of the concentration of hydrogen ions

Phagocyte a white blood cell; it ingests microorganisms, other cells, and foreign particles

Phagocytosis the process by which cells engulf microorganisms, other cells, or foreign particles

Phantom pain pain that remains after the perceived location has been removed, such as pain perceived in a foot after the leg has been amputated

Pharmacist a person licensed to prepare and dispense drugs and prescriptions

Pharmaco-anthropology the study of how ethnicity and culture may contribute to differences in responses to medications

Pharmacodynamics study of the actions of drugs

Pharmacokinetics the study of the absorption, distribution, biotransformation, and excretion of drugs

Pharmacology the scientific study of the actions of drugs on living animals and humans

Pharmacopoeia a book containing a list of drug products used in medicine, including their descriptions and formulas

Pharmacy the art of preparing, compounding, and dispensing drugs; also refers to the place where drugs are prepared and dispensed

Pharmacy assistant a person who works under the direction of a pharmacist

Pharmacy technician a member of the health-care team who sometimes administers drugs to clients

Pharmadynamics the process by which a drug alters cell physiology

Phlebitis inflammation of a vein

Phlebotomy opening a vein to remove blood

Photophobia intolerance to light

Photosensitive sensitive to light

Phrenic referring to the diaphragm

Physical dependence (of drug) a physiological process in which the body adapts to the presence of an opioid such that its abrupt withdrawal or cessation results in physical symptoms

Physical restraints any manual method or physical or mechanical device, material, or equipment attached to the client's body that restrict the client's movement

Physician-initiated treatments are activities performed under the order or supervision of a physician

Physiological dependence biochemical changes occurring in the body as a result of excessive use of a drug

Physiological homeostasis the internal environment of the body is relatively stable and constant

Pica a craving for unnatural foods, often during pregnancy, some psychological conditions, or extreme malnutrition

PIE an acronym for a charting model that follows a recording sequence of *p*roblems, *i*nterventions, and *e*valuation of the effectiveness of the interventions

Pigeon chest (pectus carinatum) a permanent deformity of the chest characterized by a narrow transverse diameter, an increased anteroposterior diameter, and a protruding sternum

Pitch the frequency or number of the vibrations heard during auscultation

Pitting edema edema in which firm finger pressure on the skin produces an indentation (pit) that remains for several seconds

Placebo any form of treatment (eg, medication) that produces an effect in the client because of its intent, rather than its chemical or physical properties

Placenta a flat, disc-shaped organ that is highly vascular and normally forms in the upper segment of the endometrium of the uterus; exchanges nutrients and gases between the fetus and the mother

Plaintiff a person claiming infringement of legal rights by one or more persons

Planned change an intended, purposive attempt to make something different

Planning an ongoing process that includes assessment of the client and establishment of a plan of care

Plantar flexion movement of the ankle so that the toes point downward

Plantar reflex see *Babinski reflex*

Plantar wart a wart on the sole of the foot

Plaque an invisible soft film consisting of bacteria, molecules of saliva, and remnants of epithelial cells and leukocytes that adheres to the enamel surface of teeth

Plasma the fluid portion of the blood in which the blood cells are suspended

Pleadings a statement of claim and defence as within the legal system

Pleural rub (friction rub) a coarse, leathery, or grating sound produced by the rubbing together of the pleura

Pleural space the potential space between the pleura layers of the lungs

Pleximeter in percussion, the middle finger of the dominant hand placed firmly on the client's skin

Plexor in percussion, the middle finger of the non-dominant hand or a percussion hammer used to strike the pleximeter

Plexus a network (e.g., of nerves or veins)

Plumbism lead poisoning

Pneumonia inflammation of the lung tissue

Pneumothorax accumulation of gas or fluid in the pleural cavity

PO_2 partial pressure of oxygen (venous blood)

Point of maximal impulse (PMI) the point where the apex of the heart touches the anterior chest wall

Policies principles or rules that set standards of behaviour

Polydipsia excessive thirst

Polypnea abnormally fast respirations

Polysaccharides branched chains of dozens, sometimes hundreds, of glucose molecules; starches

Polysomnography electroencephalographic recording of activity (movements, struggling, noisy respirations) during sleep

Polytheism the belief in more than one God

Polyunsaturated fatty acids fatty acids with more than one double bond (or many carbons not bonded to a hydrogen atom)

Polyuria (diuresis) the production of abnormally large amounts of urine by the kidneys without an increased fluid intake

POMR (POR) see *Problem-oriented medical record*

Population used in research to describe all possible members of the group who meet the inclusion criteria for the study

Port (portal) an opening or entrance

Portal of entry in communicable disease, the opening through which infectious organisms invade the body (e.g., urinary tract, respiratory tract, open wound)

Positive feedback stimulates change

Positive nitrogen balance nitrogen input exceeding nitrogen output

Positive reinforcement giving rewards such as praise for a learner's achievements

Postanesthesia care unit (PACU) a type of surgical recovery area

Posterior toward, or at the back of

Postformal operations thinkers possess an understanding of the temporal or relative nature of knowledge

Postoperative period begins with the admission of the client to the postanesthesia area and ends when healing is complete

Postural drainage the drainage, by gravity, of secretions from various lung segments

Postural hypotension See *Orthostatic hypotension*

Postural tonus sustained contraction of the muscles supporting the body's upright position

Posture the bearing and position of the body; the relative arrangements of the various parts of the body

Power capacity to influence another person in some way or to produce change

Powerlessness perceived lack of control over events

Prayer appeal to a higher power; spiritual or religious context

Preceptor an experienced nurse who assists the novice nurse in improving nursing skill and judgment

Precordium an area of the chest overlying the heart

Preferred provider organization (PPO) a group of physicians or a hospital that provides companies with health services at a discounted rate

Preformed antibodies derived from the blood serum of previously infected people or animals

Prejudice a strongly held option about some topic or group of people

Premature closure the acceptance of assumptions as fact; drawing a conclusion without enough thought or data

Premature ejaculation occurs when a man is unable to delay ejaculation long enough to satisfy his partner

Preoperative period the period before an operation; begins when the decision for surgery has been made and ends when the client is transferred to the operating room bed

Presbycusis loss of hearing related to aging

Presbyopia loss of elasticity of the lens and thus loss of ability to see close objects as a result of the aging process

Prescription the written direction for the preparation and administration of a drug

Pressure sores (decubitus ulcers, bedsores, distortion sores) reddened areas, sores, or ulcers of the skin occurring over bony prominences

Primary (source) data or information which is obtained directly from the client

Primary health care the point of entry into the health-care system at which initial health care is given

Primary intention healing (primary union, first intention healing) healing that occurs in a wound in which the tissue surfaces are or have been approximated and there is minimal or no tissue loss; it is characterized by the formation of minimal granulation tissue and scarring

Primary memory short-term memory

Primary prevention activities directed toward the protection from or avoidance of potential health risks

Primary sexual characteristics relate to the organs necessary for reproduction

Primary skin lesions appear in response to some change in the external or internal environment of the skin

Primary sleep disorders the person's main problem is a sleep disorder

Principled reasoning a process during which individuals perceive a conflict with society's rules or laws, and judge according to their own principles

Principles-based ethical approaches (deontologic) ethical approaches or frameworks that emphasize duties, obligations, principles, and rationality in judging whether an action is right or wrong

Priority setting the process of establishing a preferential order for nursing strategies

Privacy a deserved degree of social retreat that provides a comfortable feeling

Private (civil) law the body of law that deals with relationships between private individuals

Privileged communication information given to a professional who is forbidden by law from disclosing the information in a court without the consent of the person who provided it

PRN an order which enables the nurse to give a medication or treatment when, in the nurse's judgment, the client needs it

Problem-oriented medical record (POMR or POR) data about the client are recorded and arranged according to the client's problems, rather than according to the source of the information

Problem solving process of recognizing, defining, and solving a problem

Procedure a series of steps by which a desired result is obtained

Process a series of actions directed toward a particular result; in anatomy, a prominence or projection (e.g., of a bone)

Process evaluation focuses on how care is given

Process recording the verbatim (word-for-word) account of a conversation

Proctoscopy visual examination of the interior of the rectum with a lighted instrument (proctoscope)

Proctosigmoidoscopy visual examination of the rectum and the sigmoid colon with a lighted instrument (proctosigmoidoscope)

Prodromal period the time from the onset of nonspecific symptoms to the appearance of specific symptoms

Productivity a measure of performance

Profession an occupation that requires extensive education or a calling that requires special knowledge, skill, and preparation

Professional socialization the process in which the knowledge, skills, and attitudes characteristic of a profession are acquired

Professional values beliefs that are acquired during socialization into nursing

Professionalism a set of attributes, a way of life that implies responsibility and commitment

Professionalization the process of becoming professional; acquiring characteristics considered to be professional

Prognosis the medical opinion about the outcome of a disease

Progress notes chart entries made by a variety of methods and by all health-care professionals involved in a client's care for the purpose of describing a client's problems, treatments, and progress toward desired outcomes

Progress summary a brief narrative report of a client's health status and needs, nursing care received, and client outcomes and responses during a certain—sometimes extended—period of time

Progressive relaxation a formalized relaxation technique designed to reduce stress and chronic pain

Projection a defence mechanism by which a person attributes his or her own undesired characteristics to another

Proliferation rapid reproduction of parts or cells

Prompted voiding clues provided to patient to support urination

Pronation moving the bones of the forearm so that the palm of the hand faces downward when held in front of the body

Prone position face-lying position, with or without a small pillow

Prophylaxis preventive treatment; prevention of disease

Proprioceptor a sensory receptor that is sensitive to movement and the position of the body

Prostatectomy the removal of the prostate

Prosthesis an artificial part (e.g., a glass eye, an artificial limb, or dentures)

Prostration extreme exhaustion

Protein-calorie malnutrition a serious nutritional deficiency; associated with starvation

Proteinuria the presence of protein in the urine

Protocol a predetermined and preprinted plan specifying the procedure to be followed in a particular situation

Protraction moving a part of the body forward in the same plane parallel to the ground

Proxemics the study of distance between people in their interactions

Proximal closest to the point of reference

Pruritis itching

Psychological dependence (on a drug) a state of emotional reliance on a drug to maintain one's well being; a feeling of need or craving for a drug

Psychological homeostasis emotional or psychological balance or state of mental well being

Psychomotor referring to motor actions, such as hand and finger movements

Psychosomatic concerning the mind and the body; emotional disturbances manifested by physiological symptoms

Ptosis eyelids that lie at or below the pupil margin

Ptyalism excessive secretion of saliva

Puberty the first stage of adolescence in which sexual organs begin to grow and mature

Public law refers to the body of law that deals with relationships between individuals and the government and governmental agencies

Pulmonary capacities the combinations of two or more pulmonary volumes

Pulmonary embolus a blood clot that has moved to the lungs

Pulp cavity the centre of the tooth which contains the blood vessels and nerves

Pulse the wave of blood within an artery that is created by contraction of the left ventricle of the heart

Pulse blood pressure the difference between the systolic and the diastolic blood pressure

Pulse deficit (deficiency) the difference between the apical pulse and the radial pulse

Pulse oximeter a noninvasive device that measures the arterial blood oxygen saturation by means of a sensor attached to the finger

Pulse pressure the difference between the systolic and diastolic blood pressure

Pulse rate the number of pulse beats per minute

Pulse rhythm the pattern of the beats and intervals between the beats

Pulse tension the elasticity of the arteries

Pulse volume the strength or amplitude of the pulse, the force of blood exerted with each heart beat

Puréed diet food which has been blended to a semisolid consistency

Pursed-lip breathing exhalation of air against resistance after a deep inhalation; performed by clients with chronic obstructive lung disease; carried out by forming a small "O" with the lips and exhaling slowly

Purulent containing pus

Purulent exudate an exudate consisting of leukocytes, liquefied dead tissue debris, and dead and living bacteria

Pus a thick liquid associated with inflammation and composed of cells, liquid, microorganisms, and tissue debris

Pustule a visible collection of pus within the epidermis

Putrid rotten

Pyelogram an X-ray film of the kidney and ureter, showing the pelvis of the kidney

Pyogenic pus-producing

Pyogenic bacteria bacteria that produce pus

Pyorrhea purulent periodontal disease

Pyrexia (hyperthermia) a body temperature above the normal range; fever

Pyrogen a substance that produces a fever

Pyuria the presence of pus in the urine

Quality (of sound) a subjective description of a sound (e.g., whistling, gurgling)

Quality assurance (program) the evaluation of nursing services provided and the results achieved against an established standard

Quality improvement an organizational commitment and approach used to continuously improve all processes in the organization with the goal of meeting and exceeding customer expectations and outcomes; also known as total quality management (TQM) and continuous quality improvement (CQI)

Race classification of people according to shared biological characteristics and physical features

Racism assumption of inherent racial superiority or inferiority and the consequent discrimination against certain races

Radial pulse the pulse point located where the radial artery passes over the radius of the arm

Radiating pain pain perceived at the source and in surrounding or nearby tissues

Radiation the transfer of heat from the surface of one object to the surface of another without contact between the two objects

Radiopaque able to block the passage of radiant energy, such as X-rays

Rales (crackles) bubbling or rattling sounds, audible by ear or stethoscope on inhalation; they are a result of fluid in the lungs

RAM random access (computer) memory

Range the difference between the lower and upper range of a variable

Range of motion (ROM) the degree of movement possible for each joint

Rapport a relationship between two or more people of mutual trust and understanding

Rationale the scientific reason for selecting a specific action

Rationalization the attempt to justify behaviour by logical reasoning and explanation

Reaction formation a defence mechanism in which one behaves exactly opposite to the way one is feeling

Reactive hyperemia a bright red flush on the skin occurring after pressure is relieved

Readiness behaviours or cues that reflect a learner's motivation to learn at a specific time

Rebound phenomenon (thermal) the time when the maximum therapeutic effect of a hot or cold application is achieved and the opposite effect begins

Recent memory information held in the brain for a few hours

Receptor (sensor) the terminal of a sensory nerve that is sensitive to specific stimuli

Reciprocity mutual; to each other

Reconstitution the technique of adding a solvent to a powdered drug to prepare it for injection

Record a written communication providing formal, legal documentation of a client's progress

Recording (charting) the process of making written entries about a client on the medical record

Rectal referring to the distal portion of the large intestine

Rectocele (proctocele) a protrusion of part of the rectum into the vagina

Referent power the power associated with the admiration and respect for the leader because of the leader's charisma and success

Referred pain discomfort perceived to be in one area but whose source is another area

Referring the transfer of a client's care to another person

Reflective questions are nursing interventions because they can facilitate change

Reflex an automatic response of the body to a stimulus

Reflexology a treatment based on massage of the feet to relieve symptoms in other parts of the body

Reflux backward flow

Refractory period a time period; not readily responding to a stimuli

Regeneration (tissue) renewal, regrowth, the replacement of destroyed tissue cells by cells that are identical or similar in structure and function

Regimen a regulated pattern of activity

Regional anesthesia the temporary interruption of the transmission of nerve impulses to and from a specific area or region of the body; the client loses sensation in an area of the body but remains conscious

Registered nurse (RN) health-care professional who has completed an approved body of study and has passed an examination administered by the Canadian Nurses Association Testing Service

Registration the listing of an individual's name and other information on the official roster of a governmental or nongovernmental agency

Regression a defence mechanism in which one adapts behaviour that was comforting earlier in life to overcome the discomfort and insecurity of the present situation

Regulatory or administrative licensing a central body responsible for the licensing of individuals within a specific profession

Regurgitation the spitting up or backward flow of undigested food

Rehabilitation the process of restoring clients to useful function in physical, mental, social, economic, and vocational areas of their lives

Relapsing fever the occurrence of short febrile periods of a few days interspersed with periods of one or two days of normal temperature

Relational ethics theories (ethics of care) suggest that individuals have a moral obligation to each other

Relational stance the thoughtful and purposeful choices that nurses make in clinical practice about the ways that they will interact with families

Reliability the degree to which an instrument produces consistent results on repeated use

Religion an organized system of worship

Remission a period during a chronic illness when there is a lessening of severity or cessation of symptoms

Remittent fever the occurrence of a wide range of temperature fluctuations (more than 2°C [3.6°F]) over the 24-hour period, all of which are above normal

REM sleep (paradoxical sleep) sleep during which the person experiences rapid eye movements

Renal relating to the kidney

Renal calculi calcium crystals or stones in the renal system

Renal dialysis a process in which blood flows from an artery through an artificial membrane that removes impurities; the blood then returns to the client through a vein

Renal ultrasonography a noninvasive test that uses reflected sound waves to visualize the kidneys

Renin a substance secreted by the kidneys when blood sodium levels are low; it controls aldosterone secretion

Report a prepared account of an event for formal presentation

Repression a defence mechanism in which painful thoughts, experiences, and impulses are removed from awareness

Research process a series of steps or phases that are dynamic, flexible, and expandable, aimed toward generating useful knowledge

Reservoir a source of microorganisms

Resident flora microorganisms that normally reside on the skin, mucous membranes, and inside the respiratory and gastrointestinal tracts

Residual urine the amount of urine remaining in the bladder after a person voids

Residual volume (air) the amount of air remaining in the lungs after a person exhales both tidal and expiratory reserve volumes

Resistive exercise exercise in which the client contracts a muscle against an opposing force (e.g., a weight)

Resonance a low-pitched, hollow sound produced over normal lung tissue when the chest is percussed

Respiration the act of breathing; transport of oxygen from the atmosphere to the body cells and transport of carbon dioxide from the cells to the atmosphere

Respiratory acidosis (hypercapnia) a state of excess carbon dioxide in the body

Respiratory alkalosis a state of excessive loss of carbon dioxide from the body

Respiratory arrest the sudden cessation of breathing

Respiratory excursion (chest expansion) the amount of chest expansion or movement from full expiration to full inspiration

Respiratory quality (character) refers to those aspects of breathing that are different from normal, effortless breathing, includes the amount of effort exerted to breathe and the sounds produced by breathing

Respiratory rhythm (pattern) refers to the regularity of the expirations and the inspirations

Respite care temporary relief services for the primary care provider of a dependent adult

Respondeat superior a legal term meaning "let the master answer"; the employer assumes responsibility for the conduct of the employee and can also be held responsible for malpractice by the employee

Responsibility an obligation to complete a task

Rest repose after exertion

Resting energy expenditure baseline number of calories required to support involuntary body functions without a previous 12-hour fasting period

Resting tremor a tremor that is apparent when the client is at rest and diminishes with activity

Restitution an adaptive mechanism in which one performs restorative acts to relieve guilt

Restless leg syndrome unpleasant deep discomfort within calves when sitting or lying

Restraints protective devices used to limit physical activity of the client or a part of the client's body

Resuscitate to restore life; to revive

Resuscitation bag (Ambu bag) a device used to provide oxygen to a client when they are unable to breathe for themselves

Retarded ejaculation the inability to ejaculate into the vagina, or a delayed ejaculation of semen

Retching the involuntary attempt to vomit without producing emesis

Retention (urinary) the accumulation of urine in the bladder and the inability of the bladder to empty itself

Retention reflux a backward or return flow

Retention sutures (stay sutures) large sutures used in addition to skin sutures to attach underlying tissues of fat and muscle as well as skin; used to support incisions in obese individuals or when healing may be prolonged

Retention with overflow leakage of urine because of a full bladder

Retraction (mobility) moving a part of the body backward in same plane parallel to the ground

Retrograde pyelography an X-ray film taken after a contrast medium is injected through ureteral catheters into the kidneys

Retroperitoneal behind the peritoneum

Retrospective evaluation the evaluation of client outcomes and/or nursing care after the client has been discharged from the agency; frequently uses chart review and client interviews

Reverse Trendelenburg's position a position with the head of the bed raised and the foot lowered, while the bed foundation remains unbroken

Reward power power based on the incentives a leader can offer

Rhinitis inflammation of the mucous membrane of the nose

Rhizotomy interruption of the anterior or posterior nerve root between the ganglion and the cord; generally performed on cervical nerve roots to alleviate pain of the head and neck

Rhonchi (gurgles) coarse, dry, wheezy, or whistling sounds, more audible during exhalation, as the air moves through tenacious mucus or a constricted bronchus

Right of self-determination subjects in research studies should feel free of undue influence to participate in a study

Rights privileges that individuals possess unless revoked by law or given up voluntarily

Rights- or duties-based theories frameworks based upon something that is due to someone by law or role

Rigidity stiffness or inflexibility of a muscle

Rigor mortis the stiffening of the body that occurs after death

Rinne test a hearing test that compares bone and air conduction of sound

Risk factors features that cause a client to be vulnerable to developing a health problem

Risk of harm exposure to the possibility of injury going beyond everyday situations

Roentgenogram a film produced by photography with X-rays

Role the set of expectations about how a person occupying a specific position behaves

Role ambiguity unclear role expectations; people do not know what to do or how to do it and are unable to predict the reactions of others to their behaviour

Role conflict a clash between the beliefs or behaviours imposed by two or more roles fulfilled by one person

Role development socialization into a specific role

Role mastery performance of role behaviours that meet social expectations

Role performance what a person does in a particular role in relation to the behaviours expected of that role

Role strain a generalized state of frustration or anxiety experienced with the stress of role conflict and ambiguity

ROM read-only (computer) memory

Romberg's sign inability to maintain balance while standing with the feet together

Rooting when the baby's check is touched, the head turns towards that side

Rotation movement of the bone around its central axis either toward the midline of the body (internal rotation) or away from the midline of the body (external rotation)

Rules of civil procedure the rules which control the beginning actions of a lawsuit

S_1 the first heart sound, which occurs when the atrioventricular valves (mitral and tricuspid) close

S_2 the second heart sound which occurs when the semilunar valves (aortic and pulmonic) close

Sadomasochistic bondage heterosexual or homosexual activities that involve inflicting pain or experiencing pain during sexual stimulation

Safety syringes have retractable needles that lock and seal inside the syringe barrel; designed to protect health-care workers

Salem sump tube a double-lumen nasogastric tube

Sample portion of a larger group of subjects in a research study

Sanguineous containing blood

Sanguineous exudate an exudate containing large amounts of red blood cells

Satiety a feeling of fullness as a result of satisfying the desire for food

Saturated fatty acid a fat whose molecular structure is saturated with hydrogen, such as fats in meat, butter, and eggs

Scabies a contagious skin infestation caused by an arachnid, the itch mite

Scald a burn caused by hot liquid or vapour

Scan a noninvasive type of X-ray procedure capable of distinguishing minor differences in the radiodensity of soft tissues

Scar (cicatrical) tissue defence fibrous tissue derived from granulation tissue

Scientific method a logical, systematic approach to solving problems

Sclerosis a process of hardening that occurs from inflammation and disease of the interstitial substance; the term is used to describe hardening of nervous tissues and arterioles

Scoliosis an abnormal lateral deviation of the spine

Screening examination (review of systems) a brief review of essential functioning of various body parts or systems

Sebaceous glands minute glands in the skin that secrete fluid through hair follicles

Seborrheic dermatitis a chronic disease of the skin, characterized by scaling and crusted patches on various body areas (e.g., the scalp)

Sebum the oily, lubricating secretion of glands in the skin called sebaceous glands

Secondary care health care focusing on preventing complications of disease conditions

Secondary data data or information that is obtained from a source other than the client (e.g., family, friends, medical records)

Secondary intention healing (secondary union) healing that occurs in a wound in which the tissue surfaces are not approximated and there is extensive tissue loss; it is characterized by the formation of excessive granulation tissue and scarring

Secondary memory long-term memory

Secondary prevention activities designed for early diagnosis and treatment of disease or illness

Secondary sexual characteristics physical characteristics that differentiate the male from the female but do not relate directly to reproduction

Secondary skin lesions a lesion that does not appear initially but results from modifications, such as chronicity, trauma, or infection of the primary lesion

Secondary sleep disorders sleep disturbances caused by another clinical disorder

Sedative an agent that tends to calm or tranquilize

Self-actualization (Maslow) the highest level of personality development in which people reach their full potential

Self-care activities performed by individuals in their own behalf to maintain health and well being

Self-concept the collection of ideas, feelings, and beliefs one has about oneself

Self-determination the right of clients to feel free from undue influence

Self-esteem the value one has for oneself; self-confidence

Self-expectancy (self-ideal) what a person wants to become; the power a person perceives he or she has to meet self-expectations

Self-identity the conscious sense of individuality and uniqueness that evolves throughout life

Self-image a person's perception of self at a specific time or over a period of time

Self-regulation the homeostatic mechanisms that come into play automatically in a healthy person

Semicircular canals the passages in the inner ear

Semi-Fowler's (low-Fowler's) position a bed-sitting position in which the head of the bed is elevated 15 to 45 degrees, with or without knee flexion

Semiprone position (Sims' position) side-lying position with lowermost arm behind the body and uppermost leg flexed

Senescence the process of growing old

Sensitivity quick response, often referring to the response of microorganisms to an antibiotic

Sensorineural hearing loss is the result of damage to the inner ear, the auditory nerve, or the hearing centre in the brain

Sensoristasis the need for sensory stimulation

Sensory adaptation ability of sensory receptors to adapt partially or completely to a repeated stimulus

Sensory deficit partial or complete impairment of any sensory organ

Sensory deprivation (input deficit) insufficient sensory stimulation for a person to function

Sensory memory momentary perception of stimuli by the senses

Sensory overload an overabundance of sensory stimulation

Sensory perception the organization and translation of stimuli into meaningful information

Sensory reception process of receiving environmental stimuli

Separation anxiety the fear and frustration experienced by young children that comes with parental absences

Sepsis the presence of pathogenic organisms or their toxins in the blood or body tissues

Septic produced by putrefaction or decomposition

Septicemia (blood poisoning) a systemic disease associated with presence of pathogenic microorganisms or their toxins in the blood

Serosanguineous composed of serum and blood

Serous of or like serum

Serous exudate inflammatory material composed of serum (clear portion of blood) derived from the blood and serous membranes of the body, such as the peritoneum, pleura, pericardium, and meninges; watery in appearance and has few cells

Serum (blood) the clear liquid portion of the blood that does not contain fibrinogen

Sex play physical stimulation used for sexual pleasure

Sexual health the integration of the somatic, emotional, intellectual, and social aspects of sexuality, in ways that are positively enriching and that enhance personality, communication, and love

Sexual identity (core-gender identity; sexual identification) a person's inner feeling or sense of being male or female; more commonly indicates a person's sexual orientation

Sexual orientation the preference of a person for one sex or the other

Sexuality the collective characteristics that mark the differences between the male and female, the constitution and life of the individual as related to sex

Sexually transmitted (venereal) disease a disease that can be passed on through intercourse with an infected person

Shaken body syndrome deliberately inflicted; whiplash-shaking; often present without external evidence of head injury

Shared leadership a contemporary theory of leadership that recognizes the leadership capabilities of each member in a professional group and assumes that appropriate leadership will emerge in relation to the challenges that confront the group

Shearing force a combination of friction and pressure which when applied to the skin results in damage to the blood vessels and tissues

Shiatsu (acupressure) form of massage in which firm, gentle pressure is applied to the acupuncture points of the body

Shock acute circulatory failure

Shock phase second stage of the adaptation syndrome described by Selye

Short-term memory information held in the brain for a few minutes

Shroud a large piece of plastic or cotton material that wraps a body after death

Sick role behaviour actions directed at getting well taken by a person who considers himself or herself ill

Side effect (of drug) the secondary effect of a drug that is unintended; usually predictable and may be either harmless or potentially harmful

Side rails (safety rails) movable rails attached to the sides of hospital beds and stretchers designed to decrease the risk of client falls

Sigmoidoscopy visual examination of the interior of the sigmoid colon with a lighted instrument (sigmoidoscope)

Signs (overt data) objective finding perceived by an examiner

Sims' position (semiprone position) side-lying position with lowermost arm behind the body and uppermost leg flexed

Single order a one-time order, e.g., medication

Singultus hiccups

Situational leadership a contemporary theory of leadership that proposes leaders adopt their style of leadership based on the readiness and willingness of the group

Situational stressors unpredictable stressors that can occur at any time during life

Skinfold measurement an indicator of the amount of body fat, the main form of stored energy

Slander defamation by the spoken word, stating unprivileged (not legally protected) or false words by which a reputation is damaged

Sleep a period of rest for the body and mind in which bodily functions are partially suspended

Sleep apnea periodic cessation of breathing during sleep

Sleep deprivation a syndrome caused by decreases in amount, quality, and consistency of sleep; produces a variety of physiological and behavioural symptoms, the severity of which depend on the degree of deprivation

Small calorie (c, cal) the amount of heat required to raise the temperature of 1 g of water 1°C

Soak refers to immersing a body part in a solution or wrapping the part in gauze dressings and then saturating the dressing with a solution

SOAP an acronym for a charting method that follows a recording sequence of *s*ubjective data, *o*bjective data, *a*ssessment, and *p*lanning

Socialization a process by which a person learns the ways of a group or society in order to become a functioning participant

Social support network others outside the immediate family unit who provide strength, encouragement, and assistance to the family, especially during a crisis

Sociogram a diagram of the flow of verbal communication within a group during a specified period

Socratic questioning a technique one can use to look beneath the surface, recognize and examine assumptions, search for inconsistencies, examine multiple points of view, and differentiate what one knows from what one merely believes

Soixante-neuf simultaneous oral-genital stimulation by two persons

Solute a substance dissolved in a liquid

Solvent the liquid in which a solute is dissolved

Somatic referring to the body, referring to the structures of the body wall in contrast to the viscera

Somnambulism sleepwalking

Sordes accumulation of foul matter (food, microorganisms, and epithelial elements) on the teeth and gums

Source-oriented narrative charting a record in which each person or department makes notations in a separate section or sections of the client's chart

Souffle a blowing sound heard by auscultation

Spastic describing the sudden, prolonged involuntary muscle contractions of clients with damage to the central nervous system

Spasticity continuous resistance to stretching of a muscle due to abnormally increased tension

Specific gravity the weight or degree of concentration of a substance compared with that of an equal volume of another, such as distilled water, taken as a standard

Specific immune defence protect the individual against identifiable microorganisms

Specific immunity pertaining to the affinity of antigen for the corresponding antibody

Specific self-esteem how much an individual approves of a certain part of oneself

Spectrophotometry a means of measuring the amount of red and infrared light absorbed by oxygenated and deoxygenated hemoglobin in arterial blood, used in the pulse oximetry

Speculum a funnel-shaped instrument used to widen and examine canals of the body (e.g., the vagina or nasal canal)

Spermicide a substance which kills sperm

Sphygmomanometer an instrument used to measure blood pressure

Spinal anesthesia anesthesia produced by injecting an anesthetic agent into the subarachnoid space surrounding the spinal cord; also referred to as subarachnoid block (SAB)

Spinal cord stimulation nonpharmacological invasive therapy to manage pain; insertion of a cable that allows placement of an electrode directly onto the spinal cord

Spiritual distress a disturbance in or a challenge to a person's belief or value system that provides strength, hope, and meaning to life

Spiritual health (well being) a feeling of inner peace and of being generally alive, purposeful, and fulfilled; the feeling is rooted in spiritual values and/or specific religious beliefs

Spirituality belief in or relationship with some higher power, creative force, driving being, or infinite source of energy

Spirometry the measurement of pulmonary volumes and capacities using a spirometer

Splint a rigid bar or appliance used to stabilize or immobilize a body part

Splinter hemorrhages (nails) red or brown longitudinal streaks in the nail

Spore a round or oval structure enclosed in a tough capsule

Sprain injury of the ligaments and associated structure of a joint by wrenching or twisting; associated structures include tendons, muscles, nerves, and blood vessels

Sputum the mucous secretion from the lungs, bronchi, and trachea

Stage of exhaustion third phase of Selye's adaptation syndrome

Stage of resistance second phase of Selye's adaptation syndrome

Stance the manner in which a person stands

Standard (norm) a generally accepted rule, model, pattern, or measure

Standard deviation the most frequently used measure of variability, indicating the average to which scores deviate from the mean; commonly symbolized as *SD* or *S*

Standardized care plans preprinted guides for giving nursing care of clients with common needs (e.g., a nursing diagnosis)

Standards (of clinical nursing practice) descriptions of the responsibilities for which nurses are accountable

Standards of care detailed guidelines describing the minimal nursing care that can reasonably be expected to ensure high quality care in a defined situation (e.g., a medical diagnosis or a diagnostic test)

Standing order written and approved document containing rules, policies, procedures, regulations and orders for the conduct of patient care in various identified clinical settings

Stapes the stirrups-shaped bone of the middle ear

Stasis stagnation or stoppage of flow of body fluids, such as intestinal fluids, urine, or blood

Stasis dermatitis inflammation of the skin in the lower extremities caused by poor venous circulation

STAT indicates an order that is to be carried out immediately and only once

Statement of claim the initiation of a lawsuit through the submission of a document which identifies how a person's rights might have been infringed upon

Statement of defence the response of the person to a statement of claim made against one

Station (mobility) the way a person stands

Statutes laws enacted by any legislative body

STD (sexually transmitted disease) infectious diseases transmitted through sexual contact

Stereognosis the ability to recognize objects by touching and manipulating them

Stereotyping assuming that all members of a culture or ethnic group are alike

Sterile free from microorganisms, including spores

Sterile field a specified area that is considered free from microorganisms

Sterilization a process that destroys all microorganisms, including spores

Sternum breastbone

Stertor snoring or sonorous respiration, usually due to a partial obstruction of the upper airway

Stethoscope an instrument used to listen to various sounds inside the body, such as the heartbeats

Stimulus-based stress models frameworks in which stress is perceived as a stimulus that may trigger an individual's vulnerability to illness

Stoma an artificial opening in the abdominal wall; it may be permanent or temporary

Stomatitis inflammation of the oral mucosa

Stool (feces) waste products excreted from the large intestine

Strabismus squinting or crossing of the eyes; uncoordinated eye movements

Strain (of a muscle) overexertion or overstretching of a muscle or part of a muscle

Stress (as a stimulus) an event or set of circumstances causing a disrupted response; the disruption caused by a noxious stimulus or stressor

Stressor any factor that produces stress or alters the body's equilibrium

Striae skin streaked with reddish or whitish lines on various parts of the body (e.g., breasts, abdomen, thighs, upper arms) as a result of skin stretching from pregnancy, obesity, tumour, or edema

Stricture a narrowing of a passageway or canal

Stridor a harsh, crowing sound made on inhalation caused by constriction of the upper airway

Stroke volume the amount of blood ejected from the heart with each ventricular contraction

Structure evaluation focus on the setting in which care is given

Stupor a condition of partial or nearly complete unconsciousness; stuporous clients are never fully awakened even when painfully stimulated

Stylet a metal or plastic probe inserted into a needle or cannula to render it stiff and to prevent occlusion of the needle by particles of tissue

Subarachnoid block *see Spinal anesthesia*

Subcostal below the ribs

Subculture a group whose members share characteristics not common to the larger cultural group

Subcutaneous (hypodermic) beneath the layers of the skin

Subjective data (covert data, symptoms) data that are apparent only to the person affected; can be described or verified only by that person

Sublimation the channelling of sexual and aggressive desires into socially acceptable forms of behaviour

Sublingual under the tongue

Suborbital beneath the cavity or orbit

Subscapular below the scapula

Substance P a neurotransmitter in the dorsal horn of the spinal cord that enhances transmission of pain impulses

Substernal retractions indrawing beneath the breastbone

Substitution replacing one thing with another; an adaptive mechanism in which unattainable or unacceptable goals are replaced with ones that are attainable or acceptable

Suctioning the aspiration of secretions by a catheter connected to a suction machine or wall outlet

Sudoriferous glands a gland of the dermis that secretes sweat

Sulcular technique (Bass method) a technique of brushing the teeth under the gingival margins

Superego the conscience of personality; the source of feelings of guilt, shame, and inhibition

Supination moving the bones of the forearm so that the palm of the hand faces upward when held in front of the body

Supine (dorsal) position a back-lying position; lying on the back with the face upward without support for the head and shoulders

Support system the people and activities that can assist a person at a time of stress

Suppository a solid, cone-shaped, medicated substance inserted into the rectum, vagina, or urethra

Suppression the willful exclusion of a thought or feeling from consciousness; the sudden stoppage of a secretion or an excretion (e.g., urine)

Suppuration the formation of pus

Supraclavicular retractions indrawing above the clavicles

Suprapubic above the pubic arch

Surface temperature the temperature of the skin, the subcutaneous tissue, and fat; variable in response to environmental temperature changes

Surfactant a surface-active agent (e.g., soap or a synthetic detergent); in pulmonary physiology, a mixture of phosopholipids secreted by alveolar cells into the alveoli and respiratory air passages that reduces the surface tension of pulmonary fluids and, thus, contributes to the elastic properties of pulmonary tissue

Surgical asepsis (sterile technique) those practices that keep an area or object free of all microorganisms

Surrogate substitute

Susceptibility the degree to which an individual can be affected; the likelihood of an organism causing an infection in that person

Susceptible host any person who is at risk for infection

Suspected awareness dying individual, family, and health-care professionals suspect awareness of death

Sutures (of the skull) junction lines of the skull bones

Sutures (wound) the surgical stitches used to close accidental or surgical wounds, can also refer to the material used to sew the wound

Symbolization an adaptive mechanism by which objects are used to represent ideas or emotions too painful for a person to express; the creation of a mental image to stand for something

Symmetry correspondence in shape, size, and relative position of parts on opposite sides of a body

Sympathectomy severence of the pathways of the sympathetic division of the autonomic nervous system; eliminates vasospasm, improves peripheral blood supply, and is effective in treating painful vascular disorders

Symptoms (covert data) indication of disease expressed by the patient

Synapse the junction between two neurons, where nerve impulses are transmitted from one to another

Syncope faintness

Syndrome a group of signs and symptoms resulting from a single cause and constituting a typical clinical picture (e.g., the shock syndrome)

Synergist an agent that enhances the action of another so that their combined effect is greater than the effect of either

Synergistic effect the effect when one agent enhances the actions of another

Synthesis putting together the parts into the whole

Syringe an instrument used to inject or withdraw liquids

System a set of interacting identifiable parts or components

Systemic infection pertaining to an infection that affects the body as a whole

Systole the period during which the ventricles contract

Systolic blood pressure the pressure of the blood against the arterial walls when the ventricles of the heart contract

Tachycardia an abnormally rapid pulse rate, greater than 100 beats per minute

Tachypnea abnormally fast respirations, usually more than 24 respirations per minute

Tactile related to touch

Tactile (vocal) fremitus vibrations, palpable with the palms of the hands originating in the larynx and transmitted to the chest wall during speech

Tartar a visible, hard deposit of plaque and dead bacteria that forms at the gum lines

Taxonomy a classification system or set of categories, such as nursing diagnoses, arranged on the basis of a single principle or consistent set of principles

Td combined tetanus and diphtheria toxoid used for people over six years of age; has less diphtheria toxoid than DT

Teaching planned method of instruction to an individual or group

Team nursing a group of nurses organized to do a task together

Technical skills "hands-on" skills, such as those required to manipulate equipment, administer injections, and move or reposition patients

Telemedicine technology used to transmit electronic medical data about clients to persons at distant locations

Telenursing the sharing of nursing information using electronic means, such as a telephone or the Internet, to answer consumers' questions

Tenacious sticky, adhesive

Tenesmus straining; painful, ineffective straining during defecation or urination

TENS (Transcutaneous electric nerve stimulation) a noninvasive, nonanalgesic pain control technique that allows the client to assist in the management of acute and chronic pain

Tension the elasticity of the arteries

Terminal evaluation indicates the client's condition at the time of discharge

Territoriality a concept of the space and things that individuals consider their own

Tertiary care rehabilitation or long-term care

Tertiary prevention activities designed to restore disabled individuals to their optimal level of functioning

Testicular self-examination (TSE) a means of early identification of testicular cancer done by the male himself

Tetany a syndrome manifested by muscle twitching, cramps, convulsions, and sharp flexion of the wrist and ankle joints

Theory a system of ideas that is proposed to explain a given phenomenon (e.g., theory of gravity)

Therapeutic healing; supportive of health

Therapeutic communication an interactive process between nurse and client that helps the client overcome temporary stress, to get along with other people, to adjust to the unalterable, and to overcome psychological blocks which stand in the way of self-realization

Therapeutic effect (of drug) the primary effect intended of a drug; reason the drug is prescribed

Therapeutic touch (TT) a process by which energy is transmitted or transferred from one person to another with the intent of potentiating the healing process of one who is ill or injured

Therapy remedial treatment

Thermic effect of food energy required by the body to digest, absorb, transport, store and metabolize food

Thermography the use of an infrared camera to photograph the surface of the body, thus indicating surface temperatures

Third space a shift of body fluid into a space from which it is not easily obtained

Thoracentesis (thoracocentesis) insertion of a needle into the pleural cavity for diagnostic or therapeutic purposes

Thrill a vibrating sensation over a blood vessel which indicates turbulent bloodflow

Throat culture a specimen collected from the mucosa of the oropharynx and tonsillar regions using a culture swab

Thrombocytopenia an abnormal reduction in the number of platelets in the blood

Thrombophlebitis inflammation of a vein followed by formation of a blood clot

Thrombosis the development of a blood clot

Thrombus a solid mass of blood constituents in the circulatory system; a clot (plural: thrombi)

Throughput the process of moving from input to output within an open system

Tic a repetitive twitching of the muscles, often of the face or upper trunk

Tick a parasite that bites into tissue and sucks blood

Tidal volume the volume of air that is normally inhaled and exhaled

Tinea pedis (Athlete's foot) a fungal infection of the foot

Tinnitus a ringing or buzzing in the ears that is purely subjective

Tissue perfusion passage of fluid (e.g., blood) through a specific organ or body part

Tolerance the ability to endure without ill effects; the term is often used with reference to taking medications

Tolerance (of drugs) a physiological process resulting in a larger dose of medication being required to obtain the same effect

Tomography (computerized axial tomography, CAT) a scanning procedure during which a narrow X-ray beam passes through the body part from different angles; see also *Scan*

Tonic neck reflex when the baby is supine and the head is turned to one side, the arm and leg on the opposite side flex

Tonicity the normal condition of tension or tone (e.g., of a muscle)

Tonometer an instrument used to assess the pressure inside the eye

Tonus the slight, continual contraction or tension of muscles

Topical applied externally (e.g., to the skin or mucous membranes)

Topical medications pertaining to a medication applied to the surface of the skin

Topical/surface anesthesia temporary interruption of the transmission of nerve impulses to and from a specific area of the body; applied directly to the skin and mucous membranes

TOPV trivalent oral polio vaccine

Torsion twisting

Tort a civil wrong committed against a person or a person's property

Tort law law that defines and enforces duties and rights among private individuals that are not based on contractual agreements

Tortuous twisted

Total lung capacity the maximum volume to which the lungs can be expanded

Total Parenteral Nutrition (TPN, hyperalimentation) is the intravenous infusion of water, protein, carbohydrates, electrolytes, minerals, and vitamins through a central vein

Tourniquet a device (e.g., a rubber strip) that is wrapped around a body extremity to compress the blood vessels

Toxemia a generalized intoxication due to the absorption of toxins in the body

Toxin a poison produced by some microorganisms, animals, and plants

Toxoid a modified exotoxin that is no longer toxic but still has the ability to stimulate the production of antibodies

Tracheotomy incision of the trachea through the skin and muscles of the neck

Tracheostomy creation of an opening into the trachea through the neck

Tracheostomy tube a tube inserted into the trachea through a surgical incision

Tradename the name given by the drug manufacturer

Traditional medicine refers to ways of protecting and restoring health that existed before the arrival of western health-care practices

Tragus the cartilaginous protrusion at the entrance to the ear canal

Transabdominal through or across the abdomen or abdominal wall

Transactional leadership a contemporary theory of leadership in which resources are exchanged as an incentive for loyalty and performance

Transactional stress theory a theory that encompasses a set of cognitive, affective, and adaptive (coping) responses that arise out of person–environment transactions; the person and the environment are inseparable and affect each other

Transcellular fluid is a set of fluids that are outside of the normal compartments

Transcultural having the traits and characteristics of other than the dominant culture

Transcultural nursing nursing practice that focuses upon how the values and beliefs of cultural groups influence health behaviours

Transdermal a method of medication administration in which medication is absorbed through the skin

Trans-fats also known as trans-fatty acids, are made during partial hydrogenation of vegetable oils. Usually the hydrogen atoms at a double bond are positioned on the same side of the carbon chain. However, partial hydrogenation reconfigures some double bonds and the hydrogens end up on different sides of the chain

Transferrin a blood protein that binds with iron and transports it throughout the body

Transformational leadership a contemporary theory of leadership in which the leader inspires and empowers others to share in a goal

Transfusion (blood) the introduction of whole blood or its components into the venous circulation

Transsexual a person of a certain biological gender who has the feelings of the opposite sex; the person feels usually trapped within the body of the wrong gender

Transvestite a person who desires to wear the clothes or take on the role of the opposite sex

Trapeze bar a triangular handgrip suspended from an overbed frame, used by the client

Trauma injury

Tremor an involuntary trembling of a limb or body part

Triadic questions posed to a third person about the relationship between the other two

Trial the period during which all the relevant facts are presented to a jury or judge

Triangular fossa a depression of the antihelix

Triglycerides substances that have three fatty acids; they account for over 90 percent of the lipids in food and in the body

Trigone a triangular area at the base of the bladder marked by the ureter openings at the posterior corners and the opening of urethra at the anterior corner

Trimester the three-month period during pregnancy marking certain landmarks for developmental changes in mother and the fetus; three trimesters during pregnancy

Tripod position the proper standing position with crutches; the crutches are 15 cm in front of the feet and 15 cm out laterally

Trocar a sharp pointed instrument that fits inside a cannula and is used to pierce body tissues

Trochanter roll a rolled towel support placed against the hips to prevent external rotation of the legs

Trousseau's sign an indicator of tetany; muscular spasm that results when pressure is applied to nerves and vessels of the upper arm

Tuning fork an instrument shaped like a two-pronged fork and made of metal; the prongs vibrate when struck

Turgor normal fullness and elasticity

Tympanic membrane the eardrum

Tympanites (distension) when the presence of excessive flatus leads to stretching and inflation or distention of the intestines

Tympany a musical or drumlike sound produced during percussion over an air-filled stomach and abdomen

Ulcer a localized open sore or lesion characterized by sloughing of tissue or mucous membrane

Ultradian rhythm a biological cycle completed in minutes or hours

Ultrasonography the use of ultrasound to produce an image of an organ or tissue

Ultrasound a noninvasive diagnostic technique that uses sound waves to measure the acoustic density of tissues

Ultraviolet radiation radiation having wavelengths shorter than violet rays and longer than X-rays; has powerful chemical properties

Uncompensated sensory loss an uncompensated decrease in visual, hearing, touch, smell, or kinesthetic acuity (specific degree of loss)

Unconscious incapable of responding to sensory stimuli; insensible

Unconscious ego defence mechanisms psychological defensive (adaptive) mechanisms or mental mechanisms that develop as the personality attempts to defend itself; establish compromises among conflicting impulses and allay inner tensions

Unconscious mind the mental life of a person of which the person is unaware

Undoing to return to a previous state; to restore

Unilateral affecting one side

Unit standard of care are detailed guidelines that represent the predicted care indicated in a specific situation

Unlicensed assistive personnel such personnel as certified nursing assistants, hospital attendants, nurse technicians, and orderlies, who work in health-care settings and are responsible for nursing activities requiring less technical skill (e.g., bathing, feeding, specimen collection, hygiene) and that do not require nursing judgment

Unpalatable distasteful, unpleasant to the taste

Unplanned change haphazard change that occurs without control by any person or group

Unprofessional conduct one of the grounds for action against the nurse's licence; includes incompetence or gross negligence, conviction of practising without a licence, falsification of client records, and illegally obtaining, using, or possessing controlled substances

Unsaturated fatty acid a fatty acid that could accommodate more hydrogen atoms than it currently does

Unsterile containing microorganisms

Untoward adverse, undesirable

Upper-level managers organizational executives who are primarily responsible for establishing goals and developing strategic plans

Urban relating to or constituting a city

Urea a substance found in urine, blood, and lymph; the main nitrogenous substance in blood

Ureterostomy an opening into the ureter

Urethritis inflammation of the urethra

Urgency (of urination) the feeling that one must urinate

Urgent surgery strong or immediate need for surgical intervention

Urinal a receptacle used to collect urine

Urinalysis laboratory analysis of the urine

Urinary diversion the surgical rerouting of the urine produced in the kidneys to a site other than the bladder

Urinary frequency the need to urinate often

Urinary hesitancy a delay and difficulty in initiating voiding; often associated with dysuria

Urinary incontinence a temporary or permanent inability of the external sphincter muscles to control the flow of urine from the bladder

Urinary pH the measurement of the concentration of hydrogen ions in the urine which indicates its acidity or alkalinity

Urinary reflux backward flow of urine

Urinary retention the accumulation of urine in the bladder and inability of the bladder to empty itself

Urinary stasis stagnation of urinary flow

Urinary suppression the sudden stoppage of urine secretion or excretion

Urinary urgency the need to urinate with urgency

Urination (micturition, voiding) the process of emptying the bladder

Urine the fluid of water and waste products excreted by the kidneys

Urinometer (hydrometer) an instrument used to measure the specific gravity of urine

Urography X-ray of any part of the urinary tract after the introduction of a radiopaque dye

Urostomy (ureterostomy) see *Urinary diversion*

Urticaria an allergic reaction marked by smooth, reddened, slightly elevated patches of skin and intense itching

Usual body weight the amount that an individual usually weighs

Uterine prolapse a displacing of the uterus as it pulls downward through the vaginal orifice

Utilitarianism a specific, consequence-based, ethical theory that judges as right the action that does the most good and least amount of harm for the greatest number of persons

Vaccine a suspension of killed, attenuated, or living microorganisms administered to prevent or treat an infectious disease

Vacutainer a device used in the collection of blood specimens that allows the collection of multiple specimens with one needle stick

Vaginismus the irregular and involuntary contraction of the muscles around the outer third of the vagina when coitus is attempted

Validate to use logic, authority, or other data to determine the degree of support for one's data or conclusions

Validation the determination that the diagnosis accurately reflects the problem of the client, that the methods used for data gathering were appropriate, and that the conclusion or diagnosis is justified by the data

Validity the degree to which an instrument measures what it is intended to measure

Valsalva maneuver forceful exhalation against a closed glottis, which increases intrathoracic pressure and, thus, interferes with venous blood return to the heart

Value something of worth; a belief held dearly by a person

Value conflict situation in which two or more values are incongruent

Values clarification a process by which individuals define their own values

Value set all the values (e.g., personal, professional, religous) that a person holds

Value system the organization of a person's values along a continuum of relative importance

Values personal beliefs about the worth of a given idea or behaviour

Vaporization continuous evaporation of moisture from the respiratory tract and from the mucosa of the mouth and from the skin

Variable data information (data) which changes over time (e.g., blood pressure, temperature)

Variance a variation or deviation from a critical pathway; goals not met or interventions not performed according to the time frame

Varicose veins (varicosities) enlarged, twisted superficial veins, most commonly seen in the lower extremities

Vasocongestion congestion of the blood vessels

Vasoconstriction a decrease in the calibre (lumen) of blood vessels

Vasodilation an increase in the calibre (lumen) of blood vessels

Vasopressor an agent that causes the blood pressure to rise

Vasospasm spasm or constriction of the blood vessels

Vasovagal syncope a sudden fainting caused by hypotension induced by the response of the nervous system to abrupt vagal stimulation

Vector an insect or other animal that transfers microorganisms from a reservoir to a host

Vector-borne transmission an animal or insect that serves an intermediate means to transport an infectious agent into a susceptible host

Vehicle-borne transmission a substance that serves an intermediate means to transport an infectious agent into a susceptible host

Vellus fine, nonpigmented body hair

Venipuncture puncture of a vein for collection of a blood specimen or for infusion of therapeutic solutions

Ventilation the movement of air in and out of the lungs; the process of inhalation and exhalation

Ventral toward, or at the front of; anterior

Ventriculogram an X-ray film of the ventricles of the brain taken after the introduction of an opaque medium

Ventriculography radiological examination of the ventricles of the brain following the insertion of air or a radiopaque medium

Veracity a moral principle that holds that one should tell the truth and not lie

Verbal communication use of verbal language to send and receive messages

Verdict the outcome made by a jury

Vermin external animal parasites (e.g., ticks, lice, and fleas)

Vernix caseosa a protective covering that develops over the unborn fetus' skin; a white, cheese-like substance that adheres to the skin and can become .32 cm thick by birth

Vertex the top of the head

Vertigo dizziness

Vesicular sounds normal, quiet, rustling or swishing respiratory sounds heard over the terminal bronchioles and alveoli during auscultation

Vestibule contains the organs of equilibrium; found in the inner ear

Vial a glass medication container with a sealed rubber cap, for single or multiple doses

Vibration a series of vigorous quiverings produced by hands that are placed flat against the chest wall to loosen thick secretions

Virtue of good character

Virulence ability to produce disease

Virus minute infectious agents smaller than bacteria

Visceral referring to viscera

Visceral pain results from stimulation of pain receptors in the abdominal cavity, cranium, and thorax

Viscosity the physical property that results from friction of molecules in a fluid, the greater the viscosity, the "thicker" the fluid

Viscous thick, sticky

Vision the mental image of a possible and desirable future state

Visual related to sight

Visual acuity the degree of detail the eye can discern in an image

Visual fields the area an individual can see when looking straight ahead

Vital capacity the maximum amount of air that can be exhaled after a maximum inhalation

Vital signs (cardinal signs) measurements of physiological functioning, specifically temperature, pulse, respiration, and blood pressure

Vitamin an organic compound that cannot be manufactured by the body and is needed in small quantities to catalyze metabolic processes

Vitiligo patches of hypopigmented skin, caused by the destruction of melanocytes in the area

Vocal resonance vibrations of the larynx transmitted during speech through the respiratory system to the chest wall

Voiding see *Urination*

Volume-control set (intravenous) a small fluid container attached below the primary infusion container used to administer intermittent intravenous medications

Volume expanders given to replace volume when a patient has lost a lot of body fluids but does not need red blood cells

Vomitus material vomited; emesis

Voyeurism seeking sexual arousal by observing the body of another

Vulvodynia a chronic vulvar discomfort or pain

Waist circumference the measurement of the waist

Waist-hip ratio the ratio of the waist and the hip measurements

WAN wide area (computer) network

Water-soluble vitamins water-soluble vitamins that the body cannot store, so people must get a daily supply in the diet; include C and B-complex

Weber's test a test that assesses lateralization of bone conduction of sound

Weight the heaviness of a body; its relative mass

Weight change comparison of usual and ideal body weight

Well being a subjective perception of balance, harmony, and vitality

Wellness a state of well being; engaging in attitudes and behaviours that enhance quality of life and maximize personal potential

Wellness diagnosis a clinical judgment about a client that is in transition from a specific level of wellness to a higher level

Wellness nursing diagnosis clinical judgment that identifies transition towards a higher state of wellness; may relate to individual, family, or group and relates to health processes; and forms the basics of nursing interventions

Wheal see *Bleb*

Wheezing a rasping or whistling sound in breathing caused by constriction in the upper airway

Will a written declaration by a person about how the person's property is to be disposed of after death

Wound a break in the continuity of a body tissue

Wound dehiscence separation of a suture line before the incision heals

Wound evisceration extrusion of internal organs and tissues through the incision

Xerography type of X-ray procedure used in examining different body tissues (e.g., breast tissue)

X-ray examination electromagnetic radiation with extremely short wavelengths produces an image

Yoga a type of meditation that is a system of exercises for attaining bodily or mental control and well being

PHOTOGRAPHIC CREDITS

Chapter 1 1.1 – Hôtel Dieu, Quebec. From Gibson, J., Mathewson, M. (1947). *Three Centuries of Canadian Nursing*. Toronto: McMillian; 1.2 – Victorian Order of Nurses; 1.3 – From Gibson, J., Mathewson, M. (1947).*Three Centuries of Canadian Nursing*. Toronto: McMillian; 1.4 – The Bettman Archive; 1.5 – © Elena Dorfman/Addison Wesley.

Chapter 3 3.1 – Faculty of Nursing, The University of Calgary.

Chapter 5 5.2 – (Top left) © Anne W. Krause/CORBIS/MAGMA; (Bottom left) Kevin Kornemann/Taxi; (Right) Digital Vision.

Chapter 7 7.1 – Faculty of Nursing, The University of Calgary.

Chapter 8 8.1 – Faculty of Nursing, The University of Calgary.

Chapter 11 11.1 – Comstock.com.

Chapter 12 12.5 – © Elena Dorfman/Addison Wesley.

Chapter 14 14.4 – (Left and Right) © Elena Dorfman/Addison Wesley.

Chapter 15 15.1 – Faculty of Nursing, The University of Calgary.

Chapter 16 16.1 – Faculty of Nursing, The University of Calgary.

Chapter 18 18.2 – Meg McDonagh and Elizabeth Thomlinson.

Chapter 20 20.1, 20.2 – © Elena Dorfman/Addison Wesley; 20.4 – Jane Wattenburg/Addison Wesley; 20.5 – © Michael Newman, PhotoEdit; 20.6 – © Elena Dorfman/Addison Wesley; 20.7 – © Elena Dorfman/Addison Wesley; 20.8 – © Elena Dorfman/Addison Wesley.

Chapter 21 21.1, 21.2, 21.3, 21.4 (Left and Right) – © Elena Dorfman/ Addison Wesley; 21.5 – © Adam Smith Productions/Weslight.

Chapter 24 24.4 – © Elena Dorfman/Addison Wesley.

Chapter 25 25.1 – Comstok.com.

Chapter 26 26.2 – © Alain McLaughlin/Addison Wesley; 26.3 – © Elena Dorfman/Addison Wesley; 26.4 – © Alain McLaughlin/Addison Wesley; 26.5 – Faculty of Nursing, The University of Calgary.

Chapter 27 Box Photos: © SPL/Custom Medical Stock Photo, Inc.; Table photos – © Elena Dorfman/Addison Wesley; 27.1, 27.2, 27.3 © Richard Tauber/Addison Wesley; 27.4 – © Elena Dorfman/Addison Wesley; 27.5 – © Richard Tauber/Addison Wesley; 27.10 A – Unknown; 27.10 B – Faculty of Nursing, The University of Calgary; 27.11, 27.12, 27.13, 27.14, 27.15, 27.17, 27.22, 27.23, 27.24, 27.25, 27.26 – © Richard Tauber/Addison Wesley; 27.28 – © Elena Dorfman/ Addison Wesley; 27.31, 27.32, 27.33, 27.34, 27.38, 27.39, 27.42, 27.43, 27.51, 27.55, 27.67, 27.68, 27.69, 27.70, 27.71, 27.72, 27.73, 27.74, 27.75, 27.76, 27.77; 27.78; 27.82 – © Elena Dorfman/ Addison Wesley.

Chapter 28 28.9, 28.10 A and B, 28.15, 28.16 A-C, – © Elena Dorfman/Addison Wesley; 28.18 – © Richard Tauber/Addison Wesley; 28.19, 28.20 – © Elena Dorfman/Addison Wesley; 28.21, 28.22 – © Jenny Thomas Photography/Addison Wesley; 28.23, 28.24, 28.25, 28.31 – © Elena Dorfman/Addison Wesley; 28.41 – © Jenny Thomas Photography/Addison Wesley; 28.42, 28.43, 28.44 – © Elena Dorfman/Addison Wesley; 28.46 A and B – Courtesy of Becton Dickinson; 28.47 – © Elena Dorfman/Addison Wesley; 28.48, 28.49, 28.50 – © Jenny Thomas Photography/Addison Wesley; 28.51– © Elena Dorfman/Addison Wesley; 28.52, 28.53 – © Jenny Thomas Photography/Addison Wesley; 28.55 – © Jenny Thomas Photography/ Addison Wesley 28.61, 28.62 – © Christopher Burke Photography/ Addison Wesley.

Chapter 29 29.1– © Alain McLaughlin/Addison Wesley; 29.2 – © Elena Dorfman/Addison Wesley; 29.3 – © Photo Researchers.

Chapter 30 30.1 A-C – © Alain McLaughlin/Addison Wesley; 29.2 – © Elena Dorfman/Addison Wesley.

Chapter 31 31.4, 31.5 – © Elena Dorfman/Addison Wesley; 31.7, 31.8, 31.9 – © Jenny Thomas Photography/Addison Wesley; 31.11, 31.12, 31.15 – © Elena Dorfman/Addison Wesley; 31.16 A-G – © Richard Tauber/Addison Wesley; 31.17 A and B, 31.18, 31.22 A and B – © Elena Dorfman/Addison Wesley; 31.24 – © Jenny Thomas Photography/Addison Wesley; 31.25 – © Elena Dorfman/Addison Wesley; 31-26 – Faculty of Nursing, The University of Calgary.

Chapter 32 32.2, 32.3, 32.4, 32.5 – © Alain McLaughlin/Addison Wesley; 32.6, 32.12 – © Alain McLaughlin/Addison Wesley; 32.17, 32.18 – © Elena Dorfman/Addison Wesley; 32.19, 32.20, 32.21 – © Alain McLaughlin/Addison Wesley; 32.29, 32.30, 32.31, 32.32, 32.33.

Chapter 33 33.1 – © Alain McLaughlin/Addison Wesley; 33.2 - The City of Calgary, Emergency Medical Services; 33.3 © 2002 Hill-Rom Services, Inc. Reprinted with permission. All rights reserved; 33.5 – © Elena Dorfman/Addison Wesley; 33.6, 33.7– © Jenny Thomas Photography/Addison Wesley; 33.9, 33.13 – © Jenny Thomas Photography/Addison Wesley.

Chapter 34 34.1, 34.2, 34.4 – © Jenny Thomas Photography/ Addison Wesley; 34.20, 34.21 – © Elena Dorfman/Addison Wesley; 34.22, 34.23, 34.24 – © Jenny Thomas Photography/Addison Wesley; 34.26, 34.27 – © William Thompson/Addison Wesley; 34.36, 34.37 – © Alain McLaughlin/Addison Wesley.

Chapter 35 35.11A – Faculty of Nursing, The University of Calgary 35.11B, 35.12 – © Elena Dorfman/Addison Wesley; 35.13 – © Jenny Thomas Photography/Addison Wesley; 35.14, 35.18 – © Elena Dorfman/Addison Wesley; 35.20, 35.21, 35.22 – © William Thompson/Addison Wesley.

Chapter 36 36.5 – © Jenny Thomas Photography/Addison Wesley; 36.7, 36.8, 36.9 – © William Thompson/Addison Wesley.

Chapter 37 37.2D – Caliendo/Custom Medical Stock Photo, Inc.; 37.5, 37.6 – © Elena Dorfman/Addison Wesley; 37.7 – © Jenny Thomas Photography/Addison Wesley; 37.11, 37.12 – © Elena Dorfman/ Addison Wesley; 37.19, 37.20 – © Richard Tauber/Addison Wesley.

Chapter 38 38.2, 38.3 – © Elena Dorfman/Addison Wesley; 38.5, 38.6 – © Jenny Thomas Photography/Addison Wesley; 38.7, 38.10 – © Elena Dorfman/Addison Wesley; 38.12 – © William Thompson/ Addison Wesley.

Chapter 39 39.3 – © Jenny Thomas Photography/Addison Wesley; 39.4 – © Elena Dorfman/Addison Wesley; 39.7, 39.8, 39.9 – © Richard Tauber/Addison Wesley; 39.10, 39.12 – © Jenny Thomas Photography/Addison Wesley; 39.13 – © Elena Dorfman/Addison Wesley; 39.14 – © Richard Tauber/Addison Wesley; 39.15 – © Elena Dorfman/Addison Wesley; 39.16 – © Richard Tauber/Addison Wesley; 39.17 – © William Thompson/Addison Wesley; 39.23 – © Elena Dorfman/Addison Wesley; 39.24, 39.27, 39.29, 39.32, 39.33, 39.34 – © Jenny Thomas Photography/Addison Wesley; 39.35 – © Elena Dorfman/Addison Wesley; 39.36 – © Jenny Thomas Photography/ Addison Wesley.

Chapter 40 40.9A – © Richard Tauber/Addison Wesley; 40.15 – © Elena Dorfman/Addison Wesley; 40.17 A and B – Courtesy of Becton Dickinson; 40.20, 40.21 – © Elena Dorfman/Addison Wesley; 40.23 – © Richard Tauber/Addison Wesley; 40.25, 40.27, 40.28 – © Elena Dorfman/Addison Wesley; 40.29 – M. Kalab 2002/Custom Medical Stock Photo; 40.31– © William Thompson/Addison Wesley.

Chapter 41 41.2 – © Richard Tauber/Addison Wesley.

Chapter 43 43.14 – © Richard Tauber/Addison Wesley; 43.19 – © Jenny Thomas Photography/Addison Wesley; 43.23, 43.24 – © Elena Dorfman/Addison Wesley; 43.25 – © Jenny Thomas Photography/Addison Wesley; 43.29, 43.30, 43.31, 43.32 – © Elena Dorfman/Addison Wesley; 43.33 – © Jenny Thomas Photography/ Addison Wesley; 43.34 – The Faculty of Nursing, The University of Calgary; 43.36, 43.37 – © Jenny Thomas Photography/Addison Wesley; 43.41, 43.42, 43.43– © Richard Tauber/Addison Wesley.

Chapter 44 44.4, 44.5 44.6 44.7 44.12 – © Elena Dorfman/Addison Wesley; 44.14 - Faculty of Nursing, The University of Calgary; 44.15 – © Richard Tauber/Addison Wesley.

Chapter 45 45.10 – Dr Michael English/Custom Medical Stock Photo, Inc; 45.11– © Jenny Thomas Photography/Addison Wesley.

Chapter 46 46.1 – Faculty of Nursing, The University of Calgary.

Chapter 48 48.2, 48.3 – Courtesy Hill House Hospice, Richmond Hill, Ontario.

ART CREDITS

Chapter 4 4.1, 4.2, 4.3 – ArtPlus Ltd.

Chapter 5 5.1 – Kristin Mount; 5.3, 5.4, 5.5 – Nea Hanscomb.

Chapter 6 6.1, 6.2, 6.3, 6.4, 6.5, 6.6, 6.7 – ArtPlus Ltd.

Chapter 7 page 99 – ArtPlus Ltd.

Chapter 9 9.2 – Matt Perry; 9.3 – ArtPlus Ltd.; 9.5 – Matt Perry; 9.6 – Nea Hanscomb; 9.7 – ArtPlus Ltd.

Chapter 10 10.1 – ArtPlus Ltd.; 10.2 – Matt Perry; 10.3 – GTS Graphics.

Chapter 11 11.2 – Matt Perry.

Chapter 12 page 198 – ArtPlus Ltd.

Chapter 14 14.1, 14.2, 14.3 – ArtPlus Ltd; 14.5 – Nea Hanscomb.

Chapter 15 15.1 – GTS Graphics.

Chapter 17 17.1 – ArtPlus Ltd.

Chapter 18 18.1 – ArtPlus Ltd.

Chapter 20 20.3 – Kristin Mount.

Chapter 22 22.1 – Matt Perry.

Chapter 23 23.1 – Matt Perry; 23.2 – GTS Graphics; 23.3 – Nea Hanscomb; 23.4 – GTS Graphics.

Chapter 24 24.1 – GTS Graphics and ArtPlus Ltd.; 24.2, 24.5 – Laura Murray; 24.6, 24.7 – GTS Graphics; 24.8 – Nea Hanscomb.

Chapter 26 26.1 – Nea Hanscomb.

Chapter 27 Table art – Precision Graphics; 27.6, 27.7, 27.8, 27.9 – Christopher Burke; 27.18, 27.19 – Romaine Lo Prete/Matt Perry; 27.20 – Matt Perry; 27.21; 27.27; 27.30 – Christopher Burke; 27.35 – Romaine Lo Prete; 27.36 – Christopher Burke; 27.37 – Kristin Mount; 27.40 – Kristin Mount; 27.41 – Romaine Lo Prete; 27.44 – Precision Graphics; 27.45 – Romaine Lo Prete; 27.46 – Romaine Lo Prete/Matt Perry; 27.47 A-C, 27.48 A-C – Romaine Lo Prete; 27.49, 27.50 A, B – Kristin Mount; 27.52, 27.53, 27.54 – Romaine Lo Prete; 27.56, 27.57, 27.58 – Kristin Mount; 27.59 – Romaine Lo Prete; 27.60 – Nea Hanscomb; 27.61 – Christopher Burke; 27.62 – Matt Perry; 27.63, 27.64 – Christopher Burke; 27.65 – Romaine Lo Prete; 27.66 – Kristin Mount; 27.79 – Romaine Lo Prete; 27.80, 27.81, 27.83 A-C – Kristin Mount; 27.84, 27.85 – Christopher Burke; 27.86, 27.87 – Kristin Mount.

Chapter 28 28.1 – Nea Hanscomb; 28.3 – Precision Graphics; 28.4 – GTS Graphics; 28.5 – ArtPlus Ltd.; 28.7 – GTS Graphics; 28.8, 28.11 – Linda Harris; 28.12, 28.13, 28.14, 28.17, 28.26 – Nea Hanscomb; 28.27, 28.28, 28.29 – Precision Graphics; 28.30, 28.32, 28.33, 28.34, 28.35, 28.36, 28.37, 28.38, 28.39, 28.40 – Christopher Burke; 28.45 A, B – Nea Hanscomb; 28.54, 28.56, 28.57, 28.58, 28.59, 28.60 – Christopher Burke; 28.63 A-D – Nea Hanscomb.

Chapter 31 31.1, 31.2, 31.3, 31.6 – Nea Hanscomb; 31.10, 31.13, 31.14 – Romaine Lo Prete; 31.19, 31.20 – Kristin Mount; 28.22 A, B – Linda Harris; 31.23, 31.27 – Matt Perry; 31.28, 31.29 – Linda Harris.

Chapter 32 32.1 – Nea Hanscomb; 32.7 – ArtPlus Ltd.; 32.8, 32.9, 32.10 – Linda Harris; 32.11 – Precision Graphics; 32.13, 32.14, 32.15, 32.16, 32.22, 32.23, 32.24, 32.25, 32.26, 32.27, 32.28 – Linda Harris.

Chapter 33 page 795 – ArtPlus Ltd.; 33.8 – Linda Harris; 33.10 – Precision Graphics; 33.11 A,B,C; 33.12 A-E – Nea Hanscomb; 33.14 – Precison Graphics/Matt Perry.

Chapter 34 34.3 A,B – Linda Harris; 34.5 – Precision Graphics/ Matt Perry; 34.6, 34.7 – Christopher Burke; 34.8, 34.9 – Linda Harris; 34.10, 34.11, 34.12, 34.13, 34.14 – Precision Graphics; 34.15, 34.16, 34.17 – Linda Harris; 34.18, 34.19, 34.25, 34.28, 34.29 – Precision Graphics; 34.30, 34.31, 34.32 A-E, 34.33, 34.34, 34.35: Nea Hanscomb.

Chapter 35 35.1, 35.2 – Christopher Burke; 35.3 A-C – Nea Hanscomb; 35.4 A, B – Christopher Burke; 35.5, 35.6 – Linda Harris; 35.7, 35.8, 35.9, 35.10 – Matt Perry; 35.15 – Linda Harris; 35.16 – Christopher Burke; 35.18 – Matt Perry; 35.23 – Linda Harris.

Chapter 36 36.1, 36.2, 36.3, 36.4 – Christopher Burke; 36.6 – Linda Harris; 36.10 A, B, 36.11, 36.12 – Nea Hanscomb; 36.13, 36.14 – Precision Graphics; 36.15 A, B – Christopher Burke; 36.16, 36.17 – Precision Graphics; 36.19 – Nea Hanscomb; 36.19 – Kristin Mount; 36.20, 36.21 – Christopher Burke.

Chapter 37 37.1 – Christopher Burke; 37.3 – GTS Graphics; 37.4 B-D – Precision Graphics; 37.8, 37.9, 37.10 – Precision Graphics; 37.13 A-C, 37.14, 37.15, 37.16, 37.17, 37.18 – Linda Harris.

Chapter 38 Table 38.7 – ArtPlus Ltd.; 38.4 – Nea Hanscomb; 38.8 – Christopher Burke; 38.9, 38.11 – Precision Graphics.

Chapter 39 39.1 A,B – Matt Perry; 39.2 – Romaine Lo Prete; 39.5 – Christopher Burke; 39.6 – Nea Hanscomb; 39.11 A,B, 39.18, 39.19, 39.20, 39.21 – Precision Graphics; 39.22 – Nea Hanscomb; 39.26 A-E – Linda Harris; 39.28 – Nea Hanscomb; 39.30, 39.31 – Linda Harris.

Chapter 40 40.1, 40.2, 40.3 A, B, 40.4, 40.5, 40.6, 40.7, 40.8 – Nea Hanscomb; 40.9B – Romaine Lo Prete; 40.10 A,B – Nea Hanscomb; 40.11 – GTS Graphics; 40.12 A,B – Linda Harris; 40.13 A, B - Precision Graphics; 40.14 A, B – Nea Hanscomb; 40.16, 40.18 – Matt Perry; 40.19 – Nea Hanscomb; 40.22 A,B, 40.24 – Linda Harris; 40.25, 40.26 – Nea Hanscomb.

Chapter 41 41.1 – Precision Graphics.

Chapter 42 42.1 – GTS Graphics; 42.2 – Nea Hanscomb; 42.3 – Matt Perry.

Chapter 43 Table art – Precision Graphics; 43.1 – Precision Graphics; 43.2 – Linda Harris; 43.3 A, B, 43.4, 43.5 A, B, 43.6, A, B – Romaine Lo Prete; 43.7 A, B, 43.8, 43.9 A-C, 43.10, 43.11, 43.12 – Precision Graphics; 43.13 – Linda Harris; 43.15 A, B, 43.16, 43.17, 43.18, 43.19, 43.20 A, B, 43.21 A, B – Precision Graphics; 43.22 – Nea Hanscomb; 43.26 – Linda Harris; 43.27 A, B – Precision Graphics; 43.28, 43.35 A-C – Linda Harris; 43.38 – Precision Graphics; 43.39, 43.40 – Nea Hanscomb.

Chapter 44 44.1 – Christopher Burke; 44.2 A-C, 44.3, 44.8 A, B, 44.9, 44.10, 44.11 – Linda Harris; 44.13 A-E, 44.17 – Nea Hanscomb; 44.18 – Precision Graphics.

Chapter 45 45.1 – Precision Graphics; 45.2, 45.3, 45.4, 45.5 – Christopher Burke; 45.6 – Linda Harris; 45.7 – Matt Perry; 45.8, 45.9 – Nea Hanscomb; 45.12 – ArtPlus Ltd.

Chapter 47 47.1, 47.2, 47.3 – Richard Tauber.

Chapter 48 48.1 – ArtPlus Ltd.

INDEX

Numbers/Symbols

24-hour fluid balance record, 453
24-hour food recall, 990

A

abbreviations, usage, 461
Abdellah, Faye, 33
abdomen
    auscultation of, 578–579
    contour and symmetry, 577–578
    landmarks, 575–576
    paplation of, 581–582
    percussion of, 580
    quadrants, 513, 575, 577
    regions, 577
    skin integrity, inspection for, 577–578
abdominal breathing, 1026, 1043
aboriginal peoples, 224
    See also First Nations people
abortion, 197
    ethical issue of, 100
abrasion, 944
abuse
    of elderly, 368
    of women, 351
acceptance, in interpersonal relationships, 490
accessibility
    principle of, 10, 247, 250, 266, 267
    role of nurses, 10
accident prevention
    bike or sports injuries, 794–795
    carbon monoxide poisoning, 794
    falls, 790–792
    fires, 790
    planning, 785
    poisoning, 792–793
    suffocating or choking, 794
accidents
    adolescents, 788–789
    agricultural injuries, 294, 296
    children in rural regions, 296
    drownings, 295
    eye injuries, 298
    home hazard appraisal, 284
    infants, 785
    middle-aged adults, 355, 789
    motor vehicle collisions, 297, 299, 350
    negligence in, 120, 121
    older adults, 366, 789
    past history data, 392
    preschoolers, 335, 786
    primary industry injuries, 294, 296
    responding to, 125
    school-age children, 786–788
    toddlers, 332, 790
    young adults, 350, 789
accommodation
    in cognitive development, 315
accountability, 697
accreditation, 111–112
acculturation, 229
Achieving Health for All. See Epp Report
achilles reflex, 589
acid-base balance
    buffers and, 1080–1081
    electrolytes, 1081–1082
    factors affecting, 1081–1082
    and pH, 1080
    regulation of, 1080–1081
    renal regulation and, 1081
    respiratory regulation and, 1081
acid-base balance assessent. *See* fluid assessment
acidifying Ringer's solution, 1104
acid imbalances, 1086–1091
    metabolic acidosis, 1089–1090
    respiratory acidosis, 1088–1089
    respiratory alkalosis, 1089
acquired immune deficiency
    syndrome (AIDS), 200, 351
acrochordons, 524
actinic keratoses, 525
action plans. *See* critical pathways
action stage, in behavioural change, 153
active imagery, 170
active immunity, 749
active transport, 1075
activity-exercise assessment, 1188–1190
    activity tolerance, 1190
    capabilities and limitations of movement, 1189
    gait, 1188–1189
    immobility, problems related to, 1190–1191
    muscle mass and strength, 1190
    nursing history, 1187–1188
activity-exercise pattern, 1171
activity intolerance, 406, 407
activity theory, 361
activity tolerance, 1178, 1190
acts, 110
    See also nurse practice acts
actual nursing diagnosis, 406, 414
acupressure, 169
acupuncture, 175
acute-care services, 27
acute illness, 139
acute infection, 745
acute wounds, 935, 944–945
adaptation
    to altered health and function, 668
    in cognitive development, 315
    health assessment model (Roy), 399, 402
    health model, 135
    individual as biopsychosocial system, 52, 53
    and nursing, 135
    in verbal communication, 486
adaptive mechanisms, 312, 334
administration, nursing
    budget and finance, 475
    facilities management, 475
    hospital information system (HIS), 474
    human resources, 474
    managment information system (MIS), 474
    medical records management, 474–475
    quality assurance, 475
    utilization review, 475
administrative law, 110
adolescence, 339
adolescent growth spurt, 339
adolescents
    biological maturation, 183
    breast development, 558
    cognitive development, 342
    defecation, 860
    developmental assessment guidelines, 343
    female genitals assessment, 596
    hair, 835
    health problems, 343
    health promotion, 344
    health resources for, 319
    life skills and knowledge, 343
    moral development, 342
    nutrition, 982–983
    oral health, 829–855
    physical development, 339–340, 343
    psychosocial development, 340–341, 343
    sexuality, 183–184, 187, 341
    social interactions, 344
    spiritual development, 209, 342–343
adult development
    developmental tasks of middle age (Peck), 312–314, 354
    in developmental task theory (Havighurst), 311, 352
    stage model (Gould), 314–315
adulthood
    alternative lifestyles, 349
    criteria, 348
    and maturity, 348
    midlife crisis, 353
    phases of, 348
adult respiratory distress syndrome, 1021
advance directive. *See* living will
adventitious breath sounds, 561, 1029
advertising, and nutrition, 980
advice
    telephone advice, 125
advocate
    defined, 102
    See also client advocate
aerobic exercise, 1179
aerosol spray, 654
affective domain, 670
affiliative faith, 319
afterload, 1024
age
    and blood pressure, 732
    and body temperature, 711
    and fluid balance, 1081
    and health assessment, 154
    and learning needs, 676
    and pulse rate, 719
    as risk factor, 156

and safety, 783–784
and sleep, 1155
and susceptibility to infection, 750
See also demography
ageism, 232
agency fires, 790
agent
of illness, 136
agglutinins, 1120
agglutinogens, 1114, 1120
aging
activity theory, 361
cardiovascular system and, 360–361
and chronic conditions, 366
climacteric, 352
and cognition, 364
continuity theory, 361
developmental phases in, 314–315
developmental stressors, 356
developmental tasks in, 313–314, 352–354, 361, 362
disengagement theory, 361
gastrointestinal system and, 361
integumentary system and, 358
and memory, 364
menopause, 352
and mental health, 366–367
in middle years, 352–353
midlife crisis, 353
physical changes, 352–353, 358–359
pulmonary system and, 360
reproductive system and, 361
and self-esteem, 363
sensory/perceptual changes, 360
and sexual expression, 184
theories of, 357
urinary function and, 361
agnostic, 208
agonist, 613
agricultural injuries, 296
air-borne transmission, 747
Alberta Association of Registered Nurses, 444
Alberta Association of Registered Nurses (AARN), 110, 112
Alberta Foundation for Nursing Research, 33
albinism, 520
alcohol
excessive use of, 355, 980
misuse of, 299
and sexual function, 195
and sleep, 1156
See also substance misuse and chemical dependency
Alcoholics Anonymous, 254
Allen, Moyra, 35, 55
allergy
drug allergy, 611
Alma-Alta Declaration, 266
alopecia, 525, 836
alpha-linoleic acid, 974
Altered Oral Mucous Membrane, 416
Altered Parenting, 408
altered sexual function. *See* PLISSIT model
alternative medicine
acupuncture, 11–175
chiropractic therapy, 176
herbal medicine, 176–177
homeopathy, 177
naturopathy, 177
providers of, 256
public consumption of, 176
See also healing; holism
altruism, value of, 92
alveolar-capillary membrane, 1020
amblyopia, 331
amblyopia strabismus, 331
ambulation, 846–850
assisting clients to ambulate, 1216–1225
canes, 1169–1219
crutches, 1169–1220
preambulatory exercises, 1216
walkers, 1169–1219
ambulatory care centres, 251
American Association of Colleges of Nursing (AACN), 92, 97
American Nurses Association, 97
amino acids, 974
amniotic fluid, 323–324
amphetamines, and sexual function, 187
ampules, 633, 635
anabolism, 973
anaerobic exercise, 1179
anal canal, 858
anal intercourse, 188
anal phase, of development, 330
analysis
of diagnostic data, 408–410
function, 408
analysis, critical, 375–376
anaphylactic reaction, 611
Anderson, M.A, 272
andragogy, 669
Andrews, H.A., 135, 399
andropause, 184352
anemia, 1026, 1027
aneroid sphygmomanometers, 733
anesthesia, 590
angina pectoris, 1030
angle of Louis, 560
anilingus, 188
anions, 1073
anisocoria, 530
ankle restraint, 801
Annon, J., 198
anorexia, 987, 1185
anorexia nervosa, 983
antagonist, 613
anterior axillary line, 558
anterosuperior iliac spine, 575
anthropometric measurements, 991
antibiotic enemas, 877
antibodies, 749
antibody mediated defences, 749–750
antiseptics, 760
anticipated recovery plans. *See* critical pathways
antidiarrheal medication, 874–876
antidiuretic hormone (ADH), 892, 1077
anti-embolic stockings, 1063
antiflatulent medications, 874
antigens, 749, 1114
antihelix, 537
antimicrobial soap, 757
antrial natriuretic factor, 1077
anuria, 896
anus
inspection, 604
anxiety, 412, 421, 427, 436
aortic pulmonic tricuspid area, of precordium, 570
aortic valve, 568
apex, of heart, 568
apgar scoring, 328
aphasias, 586
apical area, of precordium, 570
apical pulse, 719, 720
apical pulse assessment, 724–726
assessment focus, 724
equipment, 725
evaluation focus, 726
home care considerations, 726
intervention, 725–726
purposes, 724
apical-radial pulse assessment, 726–727
assessment focus, 726
equipment, 726
evaluation focus, 727
intervention, 726–727
one-nurse technique, 727
purpose, 726
two-nurse technique, 727
apnea, 728, 1029
apneusis, 1029
apocrine glands, 340, 808
apothecaries' system, 621
appetite, improving, 999–1000
Apple, D., 135
arcus senilis, 358
aromatherapy, 173–174
Aroskar, M., 103
arrhythmia, 721
arterial blood gasses, 1097
arterial blood pressure, 731
arterial circulation, 1025
arteriosclerosis, 732
artificial airways, 1052–1054
endotracheal tubes, 1053–1054
oropharyngeal and nasopharyngeal airways, 1052
tracheotomy/tracheostomy, 1053–1054
asanas, 171
asepsis, 662, 744
aseptic practices, 284
medical asepsis, 744–745
sterile field, 768–774
sterile gloves, 770–775
sterile gowns, 770–777
sterile technique, 768
surgical asepsis, 745, 770
Asepto syringe, 662
Ashtanga yoga, 171
as-need care, 807
assault, 121
assessment, assessing
assessment errors, 121
of client's communication, 501–502
communication style, 502
components of, 389

in context, 388
data collection, 391
data-collection methods, 394–399
data organization, 399–403
diagnostic analysis, 408–414
documentation, 404–405
informatics, use of, 469
by observation, 394–395
physical examination, 398–405
in progress notes, 448
types of, 391
validation of data, 403–404
See also health history, nursing; physical health assessment
assimilation
in cognitive development, 315
of culture, 229
assisted-living centres. *See* retirement centres
assistive personnel, supervision of, 433
assumptions
challenging, 373, 378–379, 384
critiquing, 46
defined, 373, 378
role of, 46
asthma, 294, 1026
astigmatism, 528
asymptomatic (subclinical) infection, 744
asynchronous development, 309
atelectasis, 1021, 1184
atheist, 208
athlete's foot, 822
atrioventricular (A-V) valves, 568
at-risk aggregate, 156
atrophy, 584
attention span assessment, 587
attentive listening, 490
audiometric evaluations, 537
audit
nursing audit, 438–439
quality of care, 445
auditory aphasia, 586
auditory stimuli, 1133
auricle (pinna), 537, 538
auscultatory gap, 736
auscultation, 518
authority, 697
autoantigen, 749
autocratic leaders, 693, 694
autonomic nervous system
effects of, 166
and homeostatic regulation, 61
autonomy
illness and, 139
of the individual (bioethic principle), 93
professional, 16
and self-esteem, 363
in toddlers, 330, 331
autopsy
and religion, 238
awareness, 1133–1134
axillary temperature, 714, 715, 718

B

Babinski's (plantar) reflex, 326, 589–590, 595
baccalaureate programs, 24, 25
back
injury, 1198
stress on, 1198
bacteremia, 745
bacteria, 745
bactericidal action, of sebum, 807
bacteriocins, 744
bag bath, 814
bag techniques. *See* asepsis
balance, 1172
balance tests. *See* gross motor and balance tests
Balzer-Riley, J.W., 238
bandages and binders
bandaging, 961
basic turns, 961–963
purposes, 960–961
scultetus binders, 963–964
straight abdominal binders, 963–964
t-binders, 963
triangular arm binder (sling), 962–963
types and uses, 961
Bandura, A., 669
Banks, C., 233
Banks, J., 233
Barnes, D., 266, 271
barriers, perceived
to health-promoting behaviours, 153
Bartholin's glands, 597, 598
basal metabolic rate (BMR), 709, 976, 977
basal metabolism, 1185
base, of heart, 568
base of support, 1171
bathing
cleaning purposes, 813–814
effects of, 812–813
home care considerations, 817
lifespan considerations, 817
perineal-genital care, 817–819
procedure, 814–817
therapeutic baths, 814
bathing/hygiene, 421
battery, 117, 121
B cells, 749–750
beard and mustache, 841
Beau's lines, 526
Beck, C.T., 36, 37
Becker, M.H., 137
bed baths, 813, 815–816
bed cradles, 848
bed making, 848–853
clinical guidelines, 848
occupied bed, 851–853
unoccupied bed, changing, 849–851
bedpans, 872, 875
bed rest, 1181
beds
hospital, 847–848
for wound healing, 951, 952
bedsores. *See* pressure ulcers
behavioural effect questions, 83
behaviourism, 669, 670
beliefs
about food, 978–979
beliefs, 92
Bell, Janice, 75
belt restraint, 798, 800
beneficence, 94
Benner, P., 381
Bennis, W.G., 695
bereavement, 363–364
biceps reflex, 589
bike or sports injuries, 794–795
bilateral jugular vein distention (JVD), 569
Bill 22, 226
Bill 101, 226
bill of rights, patient's, 112
binders. *See* bandages and binders
bioethics
autonomy, 93
beneficence, 94
and decision making, 93–94
fidelity, 94
justice, 94
nonmaleficence, 94
biofeedback, 179
biographical data, in health history, 389
biologic system, 68
biomedical health belief. *See* scientific health belief
biotransformation, 613
Biot's (cluster) respirations, 1029
birth
religious beliefs, 212
birth defects
alcohol and drugs, effects of, 324, 350
increase in body temperature and, 324
Bishop, A., 48
bladder cancer, 355
bladder irrigation, 924
bladder training, 906, 911, 912
blanch test, 526
Blaxter, M., 134
blended families, 76, 77
blood, 1025–1026
blood-borne pathogens, exposure to, 778
blood pressure, 1025
and aging, 361
auscultatory method of assessment, 736–737
blood viscosity and, 732
blood volume and, 732
determinants of, 731–732
diastolic and systolic pressure, 731
direct measurement, 735
elasticity of artries and, 732
factors affecting, 732
heart action and, 731
hypertension, 732–733
hypotension, 361, 733, 1183
palpatory method of assessment, 736
peripheral vascular resistance and, 731–732
blood pressure assessment
equipment, 733–734
methods, 735–736
sites, 735
blood pressure cuffs, 734
blood pressure measurement
assessment focus, 737
common errors in, 736–737
with electronic indirect monitoring device, 739
equipment, 737
evaluation focus, 739

intervention, 738–739
purposes, 737
thigh blood pressure, 739
blood tests, 1035
blood transfusions, 1114–1125
administering blood, 1120–1125
blood groups, 1114–1120
blood products for transfusion, 1120–1121
hemolytic transfusion reactions, 1120–1122
selection of donors, 1120
blood urea nitrogen (BUN), 904
Bloom, B., 669, 670
body alignment
physical examination, 1188
and posture, 1171–1172
body defences, against infection, 748–750
nonspecific defences, 748–749
specific responses, 747–749
body image, 187
body mass index (BMI), 520, 991–992
body mechanics, 1195–1199
lifting, 1196–1198
pivoting, 1198
pulling and pushing, 1198
bodymind healing, 165–166
body odours, 520, 808, 812, 822
body posture, 237
body size, and fluid balance, 1081–1082
body substance isolation (BSI) system, 761
body surface area, 344–622
body systems model, 402–403
body temperature
age and, 711
alterations in, 711–713
core temperature, 709
diurnal variations (circadian rhythms), 711
exercise and, 711
and heat loss, 710
heat production, 709–710
regulation of, 710
and stress, 711
surface temperature, 709
body temperature assessment, 716–719
assessment focus, 716
axillary temperature, 714, 715, 718
with electronic therometer, 717
equipment, 716
evaluation focus, 718–719
with glass (mercury) therometer, 717–718
oral temperature, 713, 715, 717
rectal temperature, 713, 715, 718
safety precautions, 719
sites, measurement, 713–742
tympanic membrane, 714
with tympanic therometer, 716–717
body transcendence, 313, 361
boiling water, 761
bones, assessment of, 584
Borg scale of perceived exertion, 1179
bottle mouth syndrome, 981
boundary, of system, 67
bowel (fecal) incontinence, 863
bowel sounds, 579
Bowman's capsule, 892
brachial pulse site, 720
brachioradialis reflex, 589
Braden Scale for Predicting Pressure Sore Risk, 938, 939–940
bradycardia, 721
bradypnea, 728, 1029
brain waves, 1152
brand name, of drug, 609
breast bud, 340
breast cancer, 356, 368
breast self-examination (BSE), 196–198, 356
screening guidelines for, 512
breasts and axillae assessment, 554–558
breast health guidelines, 554
discolourations, 555
lymph nodes, 556
nipples, 556
palpation of breasts, 556–557
skin retraction, 555
symmetry and contour, 554
tumours, 554
breast self-examination (BSE), 196–198, 351
breath control techniques, 171
breathing. *See* respirations; ventilation
breath sounds, 560–561
adventitious breath sounds, 561
normal sounds, 561
Brenner, P., 16
Brimbecom, Gail, 217
British North America Act, 246
British Pharmacopoeia, 609
brokerage model. *See* service management model
bromhidrosis, 520
bronchial tree, 1019
bronchoscopy, 1037
Browning, Robert, 362
brucellosis, 296
bruit, 569
brushing and combing hair, 837–838
brushing and flossing, 829
assessment focus, 830
equipment, 830
evaluation focus, 831
intervention, 830–831
purposes, 830
bruxism, 1159
buccal administration, 615
Buddhism, 211
Buerger's test, 574
buffers, 1080–1081
bulbar conjunctiva, 530
bulimia, 983
bulla, 522
burden of proof, 114
bureaucratic leaders, 694
burns. *See* scalds and burns
burping, 981
Bushy, A., 301
Butler, Robert, 361
Byrd, Randolf, 175

C

calcium, 1079, 1085
calculation ability assessment, 587
Calgary Family Assessment Model, 75
Calgary Family Intervention Model, 75
callus, 820
Calnan, R., 695
caloric theory approach, to energy balance, 976
caloric value, 976
calorie, 976
Cameron, B., 48
Campbell, M., 51
Canada
cultural diversity, 60, 222
demographic profile, 222–223
ethnic origins, 223–224, 226
European colonization, 222
federal-provincial division of powers, 246
immigration, 222–223
refugees, 223
religion, 217, 226
rural population, 292
See also First Nations people
Canada Health Act, 147, 246
national standards, 9–10, 246–247
Canada Institutes of Health, 251
Canada Pension Plan (CPP), 246
Canada Prenatal Nutrition Program, 342
Canada's Food Guide to Healthy Eating, 984–986
Canadian Agricultural Injury Surveillance Program (CAISP), 296
Canadian Association for Nursing Research (CANR), 35
Canadian Association of Schools of Nursing (CASN), 24, 27, 373
Canadian Association of Wound Care, 936
Canadian Charter of Rights and Freedoms, 101, 112
Canadian Classification of Health Interventions (CCI), 146, 471
Canadian Council of Health Services Accreditation (CCHSA), 444
Canadian Food and Drugs Act, 609
Canadian Formulary, 609
Canadian Foundation for Innovation (CFI), 35
Canadian Health Services Research Foundation (CHSRF), 27–35, 35
Canadian Holistic Nurses Association, 164
Canadian Home Care Association (CHCA), 288
Canadian Human Rights Act, 101
Canadian Institute for Health Information (CIHI), 450, 470, 471
Canadian Institutes of Health Research (CIHR), 35, 41
Canadian Journal of Nursing, 35
Canadian Journal of Nursing Administration, 40
Canadian Journal of Nursing Research, 40
Canadian Narcotic Control Act, 610
Canadian Nurses Association (CNA), 9, 11, 12, 15, 18, 24, 27–28, 29, 32, 35, 41, 111, 239, 265, 469, 472, 476, 668, 796
code of ethics, 97, 101, 112, 388
education and training of nurses, 27
Canadian Nurses Foundation, 35
Canadian Nurse Specialists Association (CNSA), 18
Canadian Nurses Protective Society (CNPS), 122
Canadian Nursing Knowledge Network (CNKN), 35

Canadian Public Health Association (CPHA), 265
Canadian Registered Nurses Examination (CRNE), 24, 28
Canadian Research Information Database (CRID), 40
cancer
  cervical cancer, 351, 512
  colorectal cancer, 512
  incidences and types of, 355, 368
  among middle-aged adults, 355
  among older adults, 368
  prostate cancer, 512, 600
  religious response to, 217
  among rural residents, 295
  screeings for, 356, 512
  testicular cancer, 196, 197, 351, 600
  uterine cancer, 512
  among young adults, 351
  See also breast cancer; testicular self-examination
canes, 1169–1219
Cannon, W.B., 61
cannula, 1049–1050
capacity, 117, 118
capillary refill test, 574
carbohydrates
  digestion, 973
  metabolism, 973
  types of, 973
carbon monoxide poisoning, 794
cardiac arest, 1065
cardiac monitoring, 1033–1034
cardiac output, 731, 1022, 1024
cardinal signs. *See* vital signs
cardiopulmonary resuscitation (CPR), 1065
cardiovascular alterations, 1029–1030
  blood alterations, 1030
  decreased cardiac output, 1029–1030
  impaired tissue perfusion, 1030
cardiovascular assessment
  central vessels, 569–571, 572
  children, 573
  heart, 567–569, 571
  older adults, 573
cardiovascular system, 1023–1026
  arterial circulation, 1025
  blood, 1025–1026
  blood vessels, 1025
  cardiac conduction system, 1024
  cardiac output, 1024
  coronary circulation, 1024
  developmental changes, 1026
  exercise and, 1179
  factors affecting, 1026–1028
  heart, 1023
  immobility and, 1181–1184
  venous return, 1025
caring
  attitude, 489
  attributes of, 55, 481, 494
  caregiving function, 12
  for the dying, 9
  environmental context and, 388
  ethic of care, 316–317, 349
  human caring model (Watson), 52, 53
  as moral ideal, 481
  in nursing practice, 8, 481, 913
  outcomes of, 481–482
  relational practices, 75–76
  virtue of, 94
  See also comforting
Carlson, J., 677
carminative enemas, 877
carotid arteries
  assessment of, 569, 571–572
carotid pulse site, 720
carrier, 746
Carson, V.B., 365
case management, 258–259
  case managers, 256, 259
  critical pathways tool, 259
  documentation system, 451
  home care, 283
  models, 268
  uses, 258–259
case method, 261
case study, 38
catabolism, 973
cataracts, 360, 529
category-specific isolation precautions, 761
cathartics, 874
cations, 1073
Cavillo, E.R., 238
cellular immunity, 750
cementum, 825
Centers for Disease Control and Prevention (CDC), 761
central tendency, measures of, 38, 39
Centre for Nursing Research, 33
centre of gravity, 1171
cephalocaudal growth and development, 309
cephalocaudal (head-to-toe) physical examination, 399, 510
cerebellum
  and motor function, 590
cerebral cortex
  and hearing, 537
certification, 27, 111
cerumen, 537, 845
cervical cancer
  risk factors, 351, 512
cervix
  inspection, 603
change
  in community, 702
  driving forces of, 701
  models of, 700–701
  resistance to, 701
  restraining forces of, 701
  stages in acceptance of, 701
  theories of, 700
  types of, 699–700
  in workplace, 702
change agents
  characteristics of, 699
  nurses as, 13, 699
change-of-shift report, 462–463
chaplains, 256
charismatic leadership, 694
chart, 448
  See also client records
charting, 444
  See also documentation systems
charting by exception, 449, 450
chemical dependency. *See* substance misuse and chemical dependency
chemical disposable thermometer, 715
chemical name, of drug, 609
chemical restraints, 797
chemical thermogenesis, 710
chemotaxis, 749
chest pain, 421
chest tubes and drainage systems, 1062–1063
Cheyne-Stokes respirations, 1029
chief executive nurses (CEN), 13
child abuse, 327
children
  abdomen assessment, 583
  breasts, 558
  childhood illnesses data, 392
  complementary therapy for cancer, 176
  drug administration, 624–625
  health resources for, 319
  heart assessment, 573
  immunization schedule, 759
  motor function assessment, 595
  mouth and oropharynx assessment, 549
  musculoskeletal system assessment, 585
  neck assessment, 553
  nose assessment, 544
  oral administration, 629
  peripheral vascular system, 575
  sexuality, 183
  skin assessment, 524
  spiritual development, 209
  teaching tools for, 684
  thorax and lungs assessment, 567
  weighing and measuring of, 519
  See also infants; preschoolers; school-age children; toddlers
chiropractic therapy, 176
chlamydia, 195, 200
chloride, 1079, 1086
choking. *See* suffocating or choking
cholesterol, 975
Christianity, 210, 211, 212
chronic illness, 139
chronic infection, 745
chronic wounds, 935, 944
chyme, 857
cicatrix tissue, 749
circadian rhythms, 1151
circadian synchronization, 1151
circular turns, 961–962
citizenship, rights and obligations of, 115–116
civil law system, 109
civil (private) law, 113
  court action in, 113–114
  defendant, nurse as, 114
  expert witnesses, 114
clarity and brevity, in verbal communication, 485
Clark, E.G., 136, 149
Clark, J., 270
clean-catch (midstream) specimen, 901–902
clean-contaminated wounds, 935
clean voided specimen, 901

clean wound, 935–936
client advocate
  role of nurses, 12, 102–103
client care assessment flowsheet, 448
client-centred model, 268
client contracting (teaching strategy), 684
client records, 444
  access to, 444
  communication purposes, 444
  confidentiality safeguards, 444
  documentation in, 444
  as educational tool, 445
  planning purposes, 445
  quality assurance purposes, 445
  as research sources, 445
  sources of data, 393–394
  standards for reporting, 444
clients, 8
  externally controlled persons, 137
  homeless populations, 257–258
  inappropriate sexual behaviour, 188, 201–202
  as individuals, 60
  internally controlled persons, 137
  in nursing metaparadigm, 49
  public participation of, 10, 149, 250
  responsibility for own actions, 498
  rights of, 248–250
  rural health-care needs, 257
  See also nurse-client interaction
client teaching
  breast examination, 196–200
  controlled and huff coughing, 1043–1044
  crutches, 1221
  fluid, electrolyte, and acid-base balance, 1101
  foot care, 823–824
  home nutrition therapy, 1012–1013
  incentive spirometry, 1045
  injury prevention, 1196
  maintaining musculoskeletal function, 1196
  managing energy and preventing fatigue, 1196
  metred-dose inhaler, use of, 660–661
  pursed-lip breathing, 1043–1044
  rest and sleep, 1164
  role of, 673
  ROM exercises, 1214
  skin problems, 817–820
  testicular self-examination, 200
  walkers, using, 1169–1220
  See also teaching
climacteric, 352
  See also andropause
clinical graph record, 453–454
clinical guidelines, 419
clinical model of health, 136
clinical nurse specialist (CNS), 13–15, 14–1260
Clinical Nursing Research, 40
clinical pharmacist, 609
clinics, general, 251
cliques, adolescent, 340
clitoris, 596
closed catheter irrigation, 924–925
closed questions, 395, 396
closed system, 81
clubbing, 526
clustering, data, 409–410
coalitions, community, 268
cocaine, and sexual function, 187
cochlea, 537
code of ethics, 16, 41, 91
  American Nurses Association, 97
  Canadian Nurses Association, 97
  International Council of Nurses, 96
  purposes, 95
coercive power, 695
cognition, 1133
cognitive development
  of infants, 327
  of preschoolers, 334
  of school-age children, 337
  of toddler, 331
cognitive development, theory of
  age, 316
  phases and stages, 316
  significant behaviour, 316
cognitive impairments, and communication, 502
cognitivism, 669–670
coitus, 188
colic, infant, 327
collaboration, 271, 272
  with clients, 273
  collaborative relational stance, 82
  in decision making, 272
  defined, 271
  effective communication and, 272
  in ethical decision making, 103
  with legislators, 273
  mutual respect and trust, 272
  with other health professionals, 273
  with peers, 273
  and professionalism, 271
  with professional nursing organizations, 273
collaborative interventions, 425
collaborative problems, 407–409, 414–415
collagen, 941
collective agreement, 116
collective bargaining, 116
College of Nurses of Ontario, 110
colloid oncotic pressure, 1074
colloids, 1074
colon, 857–858
colonization, 745
colorectal cancer, 368
  screening guidelines for, 512
colostomy, 864, 865
colostomy irrigation, 882–886
comforting
  comfort measures, 482–483
  comfort needs, 482
  communication strategies for, 483
  concept of, 482
  desired outcome, 482
  intensity (type) of comfort, 482
  process, 482
  See also caring
commendations, 84–85
commitment
  ethics of, 97
  in professional caring, 55
commode, 872
common-law system, 109
common-law unions, 76
communication
  barriers to, 491–496
  collaborative health care, 272
  documenting, 444
  evaluation, 503–506
  face-to-face process, 484–485
  factors influencing, 488–490
  family conferences, 274
  group communication, 498–501
  health-team conferences, 274
  impairments, 502–508
  interpersonal communication, 483–484
  in interviews, 398
  intrapersonal, 484
  medication order, 618–621
  modes of, 485–487
  nonverbal communication, 236–237, 486–487
  nurse-managers and, 698
  in nursing practice, 12
  therapeutic communication, 490–491
  verbal communication, 485–486
  See also nurse-client interaction; questions
communication problems
  language deficits, 501
  nursing diagnoses, 502
  nursing interventions, 503
  paralysis, and communication, 502
  sensory deficits, 501–502
  structural deficits, 502
  verbal communication, 502
community action research, 141
community-based care
  collaboration in, 270
  community nursing centres, 268–269
  competencies for, 271–272
  components of, 270
  continuity of care, 267, 272
  defined, 267
  group-focused system, 267
  health promotion, 267, 271
  holistic nature of, 267
  home care, 270
  nurse case manager in, 271
  nursing practice, 270–271
  nursing services, 268–270
  occupational health settings, 269
  parish nursing, 269
  preventive care, 270
  school health services, 269
  telehealth services, 270
  wellness programs, 269
  See also collaboration
community care, 27
  McGill Model of Nursing, 55
community care centres, 251
community college, nursing programs, 24, 25
community health centres, 248, 251
community outreach centres, 269
compassion, 55
  in collaborative stance, 82
  ethics of, 97

and personal presence, 214
and spirituality, 210
compensatory homeostatic mechanism, 61
competence
accreditation, 111–112
certification, 27, 111
credentialling, 110
as legal safeguard, 123–124
licensure and registration, 24, 110–111
in professional caring, 55, 114
provincial legislation, 111
competent adult, 117
complete blood count, 1096
complete proteins, 974
compliance, 668
of arteries, 719
comprehensiveness, Canada Health Act, 9, 246–247
compromised hosts, 748
computed tomography (CT), 904
computer-assisted instruction, 685
computerized care plans, 419
computerized documentation, 450–451
computerized patient record (CPR), defined, 469
computer-mediated distance education, 28, 468–473
concentrative meditation, 171
concepts, 46, 49
defined, 49
conceptual framework/model, 50
See also nursing theories; theory
Conceptual Model for Cultural Competence, 232
concrete operations phase, in cognitive development, 316, 337
concurrent audit, 439
conditioning, 669
condoms, use of, 188, 196
conduction, 710
conduction hearing loss, 537
conferences, nursing care, 464
conferring
nursing rounds, 464–465
nursing care conferences, 464
confidence
in professional caring, 55
confidentiality
defined, 470
professional obligation, 116
right of client, 42, 112
safeguarding computerized records, 444
confrontation, in helping relationships, 496
congenital heart defects, 1026, 1030
congestive heart failure, 1030
connective leadership, 695
conscience, 55
consciousness, level of, 587
consent
capacity, 117, 118
disclosure, 117
expressed consent, 117
implied consent, 117
and incompetent adult patient, 118
informed consent, 41, 117
for medical and surgical treatments, 117
of minor, 118
for nursing procedures, 117
obtaining consent, 117
types of, 117
voluntariness, 117
consequence-based ethical theories, 93
constipation, 359, 862
constipation management, 873–874
Constitution Act (1982), 112
consumer, 8
consumer informatics, 471
health-care demands, 17
Consumers' Association of Canada, 248
contact lens care, 843–844
contaminated wound, 935
contemplative stage, in behavioural change, 153
contextual awareness, 378–379
continent urinary diversion, 928
continent vesicostomy, 928
contingency theory, 694
continuing education, 12, 29, 34
continuity of care, 272, 445
continuity theory, 361
continuous quality improvement (CQI). *See* quality of care, quality improvement
contractility, 1024
contract law, 113
contractor for service, 115
contracts. *See* employment contracts
control
and coping, 64
perception of, 152
controlled and huff coughing, 1043–1044
Controlled Drugs and Substances Act, 610
controlling function, 697
convection, 710
conventional level, of moral development, 317, 338, 342, 364
co-ordinated movement, 1172–1178
coping
and cognitive development, 315
coping mechanisms, 63–64
ineffective individual coping, 214
copulation, 188
CORE, 450
core body temperature, 709
core competencies
in nursing practice, 14
corn, 820
corneal sensitivity (reflex) test, 532
coronary angiography, 1036
coronary heart disease
risk factors, 355
screenings, 351
Corpus Juris Civilis, 109
corrective biologic imagery, 170
costal margins, 575
costal (thoracic) breathing, 727
co-transcendence, in human becoming theory, 53
cough reflex, 1019–1020
counselling
for altered sexual function, 198–201
health behaviour change, 158
role of nurses, 12
counting fingers (C/F), vision test, 536
courts, 109
Cousins, N., 173
covert data. *See* subjective data
cranial accessory nerves, 551
cranial nerves, 587–588
creams
dermatologic preparations, 654
vaginal cream, 659
creatinine, 904
creatinine clearance test, 904
creation spirituality, 52
See also faith
creative thinking, 374–375
credentialling, 110
credibility, in communication, 486
crepitations (rales), 561
crime
reporting, 125–126
Criminal Code, 112
criminal law, 113
crisis centres, 253–254
critical paths. *See* critical pathways
critical pathways, 259, 419, 451–452
critical thinking, 697
affective dimension of, 376–378, 382–384
characteristics of, 374
cognitive skills in, 375–376, 382–384
confidence in reasoning, 378
contextual awareness, 378–379
and creative thought, 374–375
curiosity and, 378
dissonance and ambiguity, tolerating, 383
egocentricity, insight into, 377
elements of, 378
fair-mindedness and, 377
independence of thought and, 377
intellectual courage and, 377
intellectual humility and, 377
intellectual integrity and, 377
in nursing practice, 373
and nursing process, 380
in nursing process, 390
perseverance and, 377
self-assessment and, 383
skill development in, 382–384
sociocentricity, insight into, 377
standards of, 379
supportive environment for, 384
underlying feelings, exploring, 378
See also problem solving
critiquing
assumptions, 46
research, 40–41
research article, 42
crown, of tooth, 825
crutches, 1220–1225
crutch stance, 1222
exercises for crutch walking, 1220–1222
four-point gait, 1223
gaits, 1222
getting into a chair, 1223
getting out of a chair, 1223
going down stairs, 1224
kinds of, 1220
measuring clients for, 1221

swing-through gait, 1223
swing-to gait, 1223
three-point gait, 1223
two-point alternate gait, 1223
crying, of infants, 327
crystalloids, 1074
cues
data clustering, 409–410
defined, 404
significant cues, 409
standards and norms, comparison with, 410
cues to action
and health-promotion behaviours, 153
health-protecting behaviours, 137
cultural assessment, 239
assessment tools, 239
open questions, 240
process of assessment, 239
cultural care deprivation, 1135
Cultural Diversity Practice Model (Felder), 232
culturally competent care
and community resources, 241
cultural assessment data, 239
cultural care preservation, 239, 240
family care, 241
negotiation, cultural care, 240–241
verbal and nonverbal communication in, 239
culturally sensitive care
barriers to cultural sensitivity, 232–233
conveying cultural sensitivity, 233
courtesy and respect in, 233, 235
death and dying practices, 238–239
hospital visitations, 234–235
improving sensitivity, 232
nonverbal communication, 236–237, 486
nutritional patterns, 237–238
pain responses, 238
and religious values, 230
and sexuality, 185
space orientation, 237
subculture, 228
and time orientation, 237
translators, use of, 235–236
verbal communication, 235–236
culture
and sensory stimulation, 1135
culture
and adolescence, 339
bicultural, defined, 228
Canadian cultural mosaic, 60, 222
characteristics of, 230
and clinical application ethics, 105
communication style, 235–237
cultural care diversity and universality care theory, 53, 230–232
cultural competence, 229
cultural identity, 228
cultural sensitivity, 229
culture awareness, 229
culture shock, 230
culture-specifics, 228
culture-universals, 228
defined, 223, 228
and diversity, 228
and family patterns, 234–235
forms and expressions of, 230
and health beliefs, 64
and health belief views and practices, 233–234
and health status, 11
material culture, 228
non-material, 228
and nutrition, 977
cumulative effect, 612
Cumulative Index to Nursing and Allied Health Literature (CINAHL), 40
cunnilingus, 188
curing, idea of, 164
curiosity, and critical thinking, 378
cutaneous tags, 524
cyanosis, 520, 1028
cyst, 521
cystic fibrosis, 1026
cystocele, 598
cystoscope, 904
cystoscopy, 904

D

daily nursing care record, 455–456
Dalhousie Outpost Nursing (OPN) Program, 301
Dalhousie University, 28
dandruff, 836
Daniluk, J., 184
data
collection of, 34, 38, 391, 434–435, 475–476
concept of, 468
data analysis, 38–39, 475–476
documentation, 404–405
gaps and inconsistencies in, 410
sources of, 392–394
types of, 391–394
validation, 403–404
database
assessing, 438
client database, 391
incomplete database, 438
of nursing research, 40
of problem-oriented medical record, 447
data-collection methods, 38
interviewing, 395
observing, 394–395
physical examination, 398–399
data integrity, 470
data organization
adaptation model (Roy), 399, 402
assessment frameworks, 399
body systems approach, 399, 400, 403
functional health pattern framework (Gordon), 399–403, 403
Maslow's hierarchy of needs, 403
non-nursing models, 402–403
wellness models, 402
See also health history, nursing; recordkeeping tools
Davidhizar, R.E., 234, 236, 237
Davis, A., 103
day-care centres, 253
deafness, and communication, 501
death, and dying
care for the dying, 9
cultural traditions and practices, 238–239
hospice movement, 253
older adults and, 363–364
religious beliefs, 212
termination of life-sustaining treatment, 100–101
debridement, 953
decisional conflict, 214
decision making
bioethics and, 93–94
in care situations, 98
client's values and, 97
collaboration in, 103, 272
defined, 382
ethical framework for, 98–99, 100
ethical obligations, 98
ethics in, 95–99
nurse's values and, 95–97
in nursing practice, 383
in nursing process, 390
and nursing process compared, 383
rights of client, 10, 149, 250
seven-step process, 382
strategies for, 103
decoding, 485
decubitus ulcers. *See* pressure ulcers
deductive reasoning, 376, 410
deep palpation, 516, 581
deep tendon reflex (DTR), 589
defecation
activity and, 861, 871–872
anesthesia and surgery and, 861
bowel training program, 881
developmental factors, 860
diagnostic procedures and, 861
diet and, 860
fluid intake and, 861, 870–871
habits, 861
medications and, 861
nutrition and, 870–871
pain, 861
pathological conditions and, 861
physiology of, 857–858, 859
positioning, 872
privacy, 870
psychological factors, 861
regularity, 860, 870–872
timing, 870
See also fecal elimination assessment
defence mechanisms, 312
defendants, 113, 114
deficient knowledge, 405
defining characteristics, 406
dehiscence, 943
dehydration, 1084
delegating leader, 694
delegation of care
and legal liability, 114
role of nurse in, 432–433
delta sleep, 1152
deltoid site, 644
demand feeding, 981
dementia, 368

democratic leaders, 694
Democratic Rights, 112
demography
Canadian characteristics, 75, 222
ethnic diversity, 223–224
First Nations people, 224–225
languages, 226
and nursing practice, 18
as perception modifying variable, 137, 153
population distribution, 222, 223
religion, 226
seniors, 356
See also ethnicity; visible minorities
dental assessments, 332, 336, 339, 344, 351, 356
dental caries, 331, 335, 339, 828
dentin, 825
dentists, 255
dentures, 829
assessment, 547
cleaning, 831–833
Denver Developmental Screening Test (DDST), 328
Denver Developmental Screening Test II, 595
deontological theories, 93
Department of Indian Affairs and Northern Development (DIAND), 287
dependent edema, 1184
dependent variable, 37
dermatologic preparations, 654
deTornyay, R., 267
detoxification, 613
detrusor muscle, 893
Deutsch, F., 353
development. *See* growth and development
developmental assessment
data organization, 403
guidelines, 328
ongoing nursing assessment, 328
screening tests, 328
developmental factors
and body movement, 1180
and communication, 487
and drug action, 614
and health and wellness, 140
and health risks, 64
and nutrition, 977
and safety, 783–784
and sensory stimulation, 1135
developmental stage theories, 67
See also growth and development theories
developmental tasks
age periods and, 311
developmental task, defined, 311
developmental task theory (Havighurst), 310–311
learning, role of, 310
middle-aged adults, 352, 354
task achievement models, 310–311, 312
dharana, 171
dhayana, 171
diabetes, 994
diabetes mellitus
non-insulin-dependent diabetes mellitus, 299
and sexual function, 186
diagnosis, diagnosing
avoiding errors in, 413–414
collaborative problems and, 407–409
communication problems, 502
cues, 408–410, 409–410, 411–412
defining characteristics, 406
diagnostic labels, 405, 406–407
diagnostic report, 409–412
infection, 752
NANDA components, 406–408
nursing diagnosis, 405
nursing diagnosis *vs.* medical diagnoses, 407
in nursing process, 388
practice in clinical settings, 415
problems, determining, 410–413
related factors, 406, 414
review of, 438
role of nurse in, 405
strengths, determining, 413
types of, 405–406
wellness diagnosis, 405
diagnostic process
components of, 389, 408
data analysis, 408–410
formulating diagnostic statements, 414–416
identifying health problems, risks, and strengths, 410–414
steps in, 408
diagnostic statements
collaborative problems, diagnostic label for, 414–415
incorrect and/or ambiguous statements, 416
three-part statements, 414
two-part statements, 414
writing guidelines, 415–416
diapedesis, 749
diaphragmatic (abdominal) breathing, 727
diaphragmatic excursion, 564
diarrhea, 863, 872
diastolic blood pressure, 731
DiCiccio, L., 135
DiClemente, C., 153
diet
advertising and, 613
alcohol abuse and, 613
Canada's Food Guide to Healthy Eating, 984–986
clear liquid diet, 997, 1000
cultural patterns, 237–238, 977
and defecation, 860
dietary standards, 985–986
diet as tolerated, 998
and drug action, 611–612, 614
food beliefs and, 978
full liquid diet, 998, 1000
gender and, 977
health status and, 979
lifestyle and, 979
nothing per ora, 997
personal perferences, 978–979
psychological factors and, 613
reducing dietary fat, 985
religious beliefs, 211–212, 974
and sleep, 1156
soft diet, 998, 1000
therapies and, 979
vegetarian diets, 986–987
See also nutrition
diet history, 990
dietitians, 255
difference questions, 83
differentially permeable cell membranes, 1073
differentiated care, 261
differentiated development, 309
diffusion, 1021, 1074–1075
digestion
and aging, 361
of carbohydrates, 973
of fats, 975
of proteins, 974
diphtheria pertussis-tetanus (DPT), immunization against, 329, 332
directing function, 697
direct inguinal hernia, 600, 602
directive interview, 395
direct percussion, 517
direct transmission, 747
disabilities, persons with
care of, 77
disaccharides, 973
discharge note, 455
discharge planning, 272–275, 416
assessment parameters, 274, 275
components of, 274
in home care, 282
in hospital setting, 273
teaching self-care activities, 274
disclosure
invasion of privacy, 122
in obtaining consent, 117
discovery, 114
discovery/problem solving, 685
discrimination, 233
discussion, 444
disease
and blood pressure, 732
and causation, 138
classification, 139
communicable disease, 744
effect on body functions, 138, 744
as failure in adaptation, 135
individual perceptions of, 67–68
infectious diseases, 744
and susceptibility to infection, 751
disease-specific isolation precautions, 761
disengagement theory, 361
disinfectants, 760
disturbed sleep pattern, 399–402, 411, 421
diuresis, 896
diurnal enuresis, 898
diurnal variations (circadian rhythms)
and blood pressure, 732
and body temperature, 711
divided colostomy, 865
divorce, 76, 78
doctorate, 14, 29
documentation, documenting
abbreviations and terminology, 459–461
accuracy, 460
change-of-shift reports, 462–463

completeness of, 460–462
conciseness in, 462
correct spelling, 455–460
defined, 444
frequency of documenting, 459
home care, 459
ink, use of, 459
legal prudence in, 462
legibility, 459
long-term care, 455
narrative charting, 446
nursing activities, 451–459
nursing discharge/referral summaries, 455
for nursing process, 453
in nursing practice, 444
recording guidelines, 459–462
relevant information, 460
sequence in, 460
signing of, 460
of telephone orders, 463–464
of telephone reports, 463
documentation systems
case management, 451
charting by exception, 449, 450
computerized documentation, 450–451
CORE, 450
FACT, 450
Focus Charting, 448–449
outcome documentation, 450
PIE, 448
problem-oriented medical record, 446–448
source-oriented record, 446
See also recordkeeping tools
Donahue, P., 482
Doppler ultrasound stethoscope (DUS), 721, 724, 734
dorsal recumbent position, 1201–1202
dorsogluteal site, 643–644
Dossey, Barbara, 165
Dossey, Larry, 164–165, 211
double-barrellel colostomy, 865
Dowe, M.C., 677
dress, and religious beliefs, 212
Dreyfus, H.L., 16
Dreyfus, S.E., 16
droplet nuclei, 747
drug abuse. *See* substance misuse and chemical dependency
drug action, 614
biotransformation, 613
cultural, ethnic, and genetic factors and, 614
developmental factors and, 614
diet and, 614
distribution, 613
environment and, 614
gender and, 614
illness and disease and, 615
onset of action, 613
peak plasma level, 612, 613
plateau, 613
psychological factors and, 615
time of administration and, 615
drug administration
buccal administration, 615
five "rights" in, 624–625
by gastrostomy tube, 630, 631
to infants and children, 624–625
intradermal injections, 639
intravenous medications, 647–653
legal responsibility, 120, 610
by nasogastric tubes, 630, 631
to older adults, 625–626
oral administration, 615
oral medications, 626–629
parenteral administration, 617, 630–647
process, 623–624
routes of administration, 615–617
safe practice in, 623–624
subcutaneous injections, 639–642
sublingual administration, 615–616
topical application, 617, 653–663
drug allergy, 611
drug dependency, 612
drug interaction, 612
drug measurement
apothecaries' system, 621
calculating dosages, 344–622
conversion of weights and measures, 621, 622
dosages for children, 344–622
household system, 621
metric system, 621
drug orders
communication, 619–621
essential parts of, 617–619
drugs
and cardiovascular system, 1027
control systems, 610
drug standards, 609
effects of, 610–612
government regulation of, 609, 610
half-life of, 612, 613
illicit drugs, 612
kinds of name for, 609
misuse of, 612
and nursing practice, 610
psychological dependency, 612
term in common usage, 608
therapeutic action of, 611
types of preparation, 608–609
See also medication
drug tolerance, 612
drug toxicity, 611
dullness (sound), 517
Dunbar, F., 164
duration, of auscultated sound, 518
duty-based theories, 93
Duvall, E.M., 362
dyspareunia, 191
dysphagia, 987
dyspnea, 359, 1029
dysrhythmia. *See* arrhythmia
dysuria, 898

E

ear, 537
care, 845–847
cleaning, 845
See also hearing appliances
ear irrigation, 662–663
early adulthood
in developmental task theory (Havighurst), 311
early morning care, 807
ease, 482
eccrine glands, 340, 808
echinacea, 177
echocardiography, 1037
ecomap, 79
economic factors
and access to health care, 257–258
and health and wellness, 131, 141, 142
in health-care reform, 265, 266, 268
in home health care, 280, 281
illness, 139
and nursing practice, 17
strain on health-care system, 256–257, 262
in Sunrise Model, 232
See also poverty
ectoderm, 323
edema, 520, 523, 937, 994, 1083–1085, 1184
education
client education, 668
and employment, 349
health promotion, 8–151
and health status, 142
home care clients, 282, 285–286
informatic applications, 473–474
public awareness campaigns, 297, 299
self-care, of clients in, 154, 274, 280
See also teaching
education and training
academic attainment of Canadian nurses, 24
accreditation, 111–112
baccalaureate programs, 24, 25
CASN and, 27
changing health-care needs and, 27
CNA, influence of, 27
community college programs, 24, 25
computer-mediated distance education, 28, 473–474
continuing competence programs, 12, 29
credentialling, 110
demographic changes among students, 28
doctoral programs, 26
early years, 260
entry-to-practice requirements, 27–28, 29
graduate studies, 25–26
hospital-based diploma programs, 25
in-service programs, 29
licensed practical nursing programs, 26
master's programs, 26
for patient-focused care, 259
purposes of nursing theories in, 50
RN licensure, 24, 110–111
for rural nursing practice, 301
Edwards, S., 48
Egan, G., 490
ego
body preoccupation, 313, 319
ego differentiation, 313
ego integrity *versus* despair (Erikson), 361
ego preoccupation, 314
ego transcendence, 314, 320

Erikson and, 312
in Freudian theory, 312
egocentricity, insight into, 377
e-health, 471, 476
ejaculation, 187, 339
ejaculatory incompetence. *See* retarded ejaculation
elastic recoil (elasticity), 1021
elbow restraint, 799, 801
elder care
elder care centres, 253
Electra complex, 333
electrocardiogram (ECG), 1152
electrolyte assessment. *See* fluid assessment
electrolyte imbalance, 1084–1087
calcium, 1085
chloride, 1086
phosphate, 1086–1087
potassium, 1085
sodium, 1084–1085
electrolytes, 1073
bicarbonate, 1080
calcium, 1079
chloride, 1079
factors affecting, 1081–1082
magnesium, 1079
phosphate, 1079
potassium, 1079
regulation and functions of, 1077–1080
sodium, 1079
electromyogram (EMG), 1152
electronic health record
data protection, 470
defined, 469
electronic sphygmomanometers, 734
electronic thermometer, 715, 717
electrooculogram (EOG), 1152
elimination
fetus, 323
infants, 329
preschoolers, 336
school-age children, 339
toddlers, 332
See also defecation; fecal elimination assessment; urination
elimination problems
bowel (fecal) incontinence, 863
constipation, 862
diarrhea, 863
fecal impaction, 862–863
flatulence, 863–864
embryonic phase, 323
emergency assessment, 391
emergency safety measures, 283
emigration, 749
emmetropia, 333
emotions
in infants, 326
negative emotions, dealing with, 378
and therapeutic communication, 490
empathy, 496
emphysema, 1023
empiricism, 47
employment contracts
collective agreement, 116
contractual obligations, 114, 115
contractual relationships, 115
existence of contract, 114
verbal form, 81
written form, 115
employment insurance, 246
empowerment, 147, 149, 267
enamel, 825
endocrine system
and homeostatic regulation, 61
endoderm, 323
end-of-life care. *See* death, and dying
endorphins, 173
end-state imagery, 170
enemas, 874–880
antibiotic enemas, 877
assessment focus, 877–913
carminative enemas, 877
cleansing enemas, 875–877
equipment, 877, 878
evaluation focus, 880
incontinent client, 880
intervention, 878–880
large-volume enemas, 878
lifespan considerations, 880
oil retention enemas, 877
return-flow enemas, 877, 880
small-volume enemas, 878
types of, 874–877
energy balance, 975–978
caloric theory approach, 976
glycemic index approach, 976–978
enkephalins, 173
enteral nutrition, 1002–1012
access devices, 1002
aspirating gastrointestinal secretions, 1005
aspiration, clients at-risk of, 1002
closed systems, 1007
continuous-drip feeding, 1010
continuous feedings, 1007
cyclic feedings, 1007
feeding bag (open system), 1008–1009
gastrostomy and jejunostomy devices, 1002
gastrostomy or jejunostomy feeding, 1010, 1011
open systems, 1007
pedriatric considerations, 1010
percutaneous endoscopic gastrostomy (PEG), 1005
percutaneous endoscopic jejunostomy (PEJ), 1005, 1011
prefilled bottle with drip chamber (closed system), 1009
testing feeding tube placement, 1005, 1007
tube feeding, administering, 1010
See also nasogastric tube
enuresis, 898
enviroment
temperature and fluid balance, 1082
environment
and cardiovascular system, 1027
chemical contaminants, 295
in clinical model, 136
as consideration of caring, 388
and drug action, 614
in ecological approach to health, 140
environmental theory (Nightingale), 51
and health and wellness, 142–143, 148
in health field concept, 140, 147
hygenic environment, 847
leaching, 295
and learning, 672
in nursing metaparadigm, 49
physical environment, 143
and safety, 784
and sleep, 1156
social environment, 142–143
in UBC Model of Nursing, 54
working conditions, 142
environmental comfort needs, 482
environmental protection
environmental control programs, 151
health-care service, 248
enzymes, 974
epidural, route of administration, 617
epinephrine, 710
epistemology, 46, 49
Epp Report, 140–141, 147, 148–149
equality, value of, 92
Equality Rights, 112
equilibrium
physiologic, 61
erectile dysfunction, 188–189
Erikson, Erik H., 326, 333, 337, 352, 353, 361
eight stages of development, 312
erotic stimuli, 187
errors, in nursing care
assessment errors, 121
intervention errors, 121
medication errors, 120, 610
planning errors, 121
erythema, 520
erythrocytes, 1022
eschar, 942
essential amino acids, 974
essential fatty acids, 974
essential oils, 174
esthetics, value of, 92
ethical theories
bioethics, 93–94
relational ethics, 94–95
role of, 92
types of, 92–93
ethic of care, 316–317, 349
ethics
of abortion, 100
of client advocacy, 102–103
code of ethics, 16, 18, 91
in common usage, 91
coping with ethical issues, 91
critique of, 41
and end-of-life care, 100–107
ethical decision making, 95–99
ethics committees, 99, 103
ethics rounds, 103
of euthanasia, 100
and human rights, 101
and law, 91
and nurse-client relationship, 91
in nursing practice, 100–102
philosophical inquiry, 46, 49

in research, 32
of resource allocation, 100
rights of human subjects, 41–42
values and, 92
ethmoid sinus, 658
ethnicity
aboriginal peoples, 224
British origin, 224
and culture, 226–227
defined, 223, 228
ethnic group, 228
ethnic identity, 229
French origin, 224
health-care implications, 226–227
and nutrition, 977
visible minorities, 224–226
See also culture
ethnocentrism, 232
ethnography, 38
ethnorelativity, 232
etiology, 138
eudaimonistic model, 134–135
eupnea, 728
eustachian tube, 537
evaluation, evaluating, 434–439
client communication, 503–504
of client responses, 434
of comforting measures, 483
data collection, 434–435
direct outcomes, identifying, 434
evaluation statement, 435
Internet information, 479
of learning, 687–688
nurse communication, 504–506
nursing actions, 435
nursing care plan, 437–438
and nursing process, 434
outcomes, determining, 435
problem status, drawing conclusions about, 435–437
in progress notes, 448
quality of nursing care, 438–439
sexual health goals, 201–202
of teaching, 688
types of, 434
evening care, 807
evidence, types of, 34
See also data, collection of; data, data analysis
evidence-based decision making, 32, 34
evisceration, 943
exacerbation, 139
excoriations, 944
excretion, 614
exercise
for adolescents, 344
benefits of, 1179–1180
and blood pressure, 732
and body temperature, 711
cardiovascular system, 1179
and defecation, 871–872
defined, 1178
gastrointestinal system, 1179
and health promotion, 149
intensity of, 1179
for middle-aged adults, 356
and musculoskeletal system, 1179
for older adults, 367
psychoneurological system, 1180
and pulse rate, 719
respiratory system, 1179
types of, 1178–1179
and urinary elimination, 895
urinary system, 1179
exhalation. *See* expiration
experience faith, 319
experiential time, 172
experimental design, 37
expert power, 695
expert witness, 38
expiration, 727, 1021
exploitation phase, in interpersonal relations model (Peplau), 51
expressed consent, 117
expressive aphasia. *See* motor aphasia
extended-care facilities, 252–253
external auditory meatus, 537
external respiration, 727
external stimuli, 1133
extinction phenomenon, 590, 595
extracellular fluid, 1072, 1073
exudate, 942
exudate production, 749
eye care, 18–841
artificial eyes, 844–845
assessment, 841
for comatose client, 842
contact lens care, 843–844
diagnoses, 841
eyeglass care, 842–843
eye safety, 842
general care, 844–845
planning, 841
See also vision assessment
eye charts, 529
eye contact, 487, 491
eyes
external eye structures, 530
eye irrigation, 662–663
ophthalmic instillations, 654–656
See also vision (sight)

F

face. *See* skull and face, assessment of
face and skull, assessment of, 527–528
face mask, 1048–1050
face tent, 1050
facial expression, in nonverbal communication, 487
FACT, 450
facts, 376
fads, 978–979
failure-to-thrive syndrome, 327
fair-mindedness, 377
faith
defined, 208, 318
evolution of, 208
nursing practice and, 52, 53
See also religion; spirituality
fale imprisonment, 122
falls, accidental, 120, 121
home hazards, 284
prevention of, 790–792
false light, putting person in, 122
family
abuse of women in, 351
communication and cultural values, 234
in critical care setting, 74
and culturally competent care, 241
and cultural values, 234–235
defining characteristics, 72
disabilities, care for persons with, 77
discord, 340, 341
expectations for involvement, 74, 75
family unit as system, 68
hospital care and, 74
illness, effect on, 80
incomes, 76
marriage and divorce rates, 76
in maternal and pediatric care setting, 74
and medical management at home, 74–75
mobility, 76
new structures, 17
as secondary clients, 283
seniors, providing assistance to, 77
strength and capabilities, 84–85
structural organization, 76
Family Allowance Act, 246
family caregivers
pressures of, 79, 286
signs of strain, 284–285
as sources of data, 392–393
support for, 267
family nursing
Canadian contributions to, 75
clinical practice, evaluation of, 79–80
commendations, 84–85
defined, 72
ecomap, 79
family access, to inpatient practice settings, 83–84
family conflict, handling, 86
family situation, understanding, 77–79
family support, offering, 86
genogram inquiry, 78–79
illness, family responses to, 80
illness narratives, 84
information, providing, 85–86
medical narratives, 84
reflective questions, 83
relational practices, 81–82
role of family in health-care encounter, 72–73
systems-focused nursing, 73
fasciculation, 583
fasting, 210
fasting blood glucose level, 994
fatigue, and sleep, 1156
fat-soluble vitamins, 975
Fawcett, J., 133
fear, 213
feasibility, of research problem, 37, 38
feasting, 210
fecal elimination assessment
diagnoses, 868–870
lab tests, 867–868
planning care for, 870, 879–1144

fecal impaction, 862–863
digital removal of, 880–881
fecal incontinence pouch, 882
feces, 857, 859–860
collecting specimens, 867
fluid output, 1077
occult blood, 867–868
feedback
in communication process, 485
in homeostasis, 61
in systems theory, 68
feelings, exploring, 378, 496–498
Felder, E., 305
fellatio, 188
female circumcision, 185
female genitals and inguinal lymph nodes assessment
adolescent girls, 596
external genitals, 596–597
focus of examination, 596
internal genitals, 597–599
newborns, assessment of, 597
older adults, 597
preparing the client, 596, 597, 599
role of generalist nurse in, 595, 599
speculum examination, 598
female urongenital system, 893
femoral hernia, 600, 602
femoral pulse site, 720
fetal phase, 323–374
fever, 710
and pulse rate, 719
fibre, 973
fibrin, 941
fibrous (scar) tissue, 749
fidelity, 94
figure-eight turn, 962–963
filter needle, 634
filtration, 1075
fire protection, 284
fires, 790
first-level managers, 696
First Nations people
bands, 223
demography, 75
growth rate, 224
health issues, 299
high infant morbidity and mortality rates, 299
and hospital experience, 229
migration to North America, 222, 223
nursing education for, 28
population distribution, 225
First World War, 6
fissures, 822
Fitzgerald, William, 168
fixation, 312
flaccidity, 584
Flaskerud, J.H., 192
flatness (sound), 517
flatulence, 863–864, 871
decreasing, 881
flossing. *See* brushing and flossing
flowsheets, 448, 449, 451, 453
fluid assessment
arterial blood gasses, 1097
clinical measurements, 1091–1096
complete blood count, 1096
daily weight measurement, 1091–1094
fluid intake and output, 1094–1096
laboratory tests, 1096–1098
nursing history, 1090–1092
osmolality, 1097
physical assessment, 1091–1093
serum electrolytes, 1096
urine pH, 1097
urine specific gravity, 1097
vital signs, 1094
fluid care evaluation, 1125
fluid care intervention
enteral fluid and electrolyte replacement, 1100
fluid intake modification, 1102
intravenous equipment, 1106–1108
oral electrolyte supplements, 1103
parenteral fluid and electrolyte replacement, 1103–1104
promoting wellness, 1100
venipuncture sites, 1104–1106
See also intravenous infusion
fluid care planning, 1099–1101
fluid diagnoses, 1097–1098
fluid imbalances, 1082–1084
dehydration, 1084
edema, 1083–1085
fluid volume deficit, 1082–1083
fluid volume excess, 1083–1085
fluids, body
composition of, 1073
distribution of, 1072–1073
fluid intake, 1075–1076
fluid output, 1076–1077
movement of, 1073–1075
regulation of, 1075–1077
water, role of water, 1072
fluid volume deficient, 411, 416, 421, 426–427
fluoride supplements, 329, 332
foam, vaginal, 659
foam swabs, 829–831
Focus Charting, 448–449
Foley catheter. *See* retention catheter
fontanelles, 324, 528
food diary, 990
food-frequency record, 990
food labels, 986
foods
glycemic indices of selected foods, 978
potassium-rich foods, 1079
footboard, 848
foot care, 819–824
assessment focus, 821
client's history and, 819
diagnoses, 823
equipment, 821
evaluation focus, 821
hygiene, 822
intervention, 821
physical assessment, 820–822
planning, 823
purposes, 821
Foothills Hospital School of Nursing, 301
foreplay, 187
formal leader, 693
formal nursing care plan, 417
formal operations phase, in cognitive development, 316, 342
formula, baby, 981
Foucault, Michel, 49
Fowler, J.W., 208, 315, 318, 331, 335, 338, 349, 365
Fowler's position, 936, 1200–1202
frail elderly, 357
freedom, value of, 92
French, J.R.P., 695
Freud, Sigmund, 173, 312, 327, 330, 333, 337
friction, 936
Friedemann, M., 73
frontal sinus, 658
fructose, 973
full disclosure, right to, 42–43
functional health pattern framework (Gordon), 399
functional nursing model, 261
Fundamental Freedoms, 112
fungi, 745

G

Gadow, S., 49, 481
gait
physical examination, 1188–1189
and posture, 487
galactose, 973
gas, 761
gastrocolic reflex, 860
gastrointestinal system
and exercise, 1179
and homeostatic regulation, 61
gastrostomy, 864
gas wells, emissions, 295
gauz dressings, 955–957
Gebbie, Kristine, 405
gender
and blood pressure, 732
and cardiovascular system, 1028
and communication, 488
cultural-role behaviour, 234
and fluid balance, 1081–1082
and moral development, 316–318
and nutrition, 977
and pulse rate, 719
as risk factor, 64
and self-concept, 333
general systems theory, 67–68
generation gap, 341
generativity, 352
generic name, of drug, 609
genetics
and drug action, 614
See also heredity
genogram, 78
genuineness, 496, 498
geragory intervention, 625
gestures
cultural meaning of, 237
in nonverbal communication, 487

Giger J.N., 234, 236, 237
Gilligan, Carol, 316–318, 349
gingiva, 825
gingivitis, 826
gingko biloba, 177
ginseng, 177
Glasgow Coma Scale, 587
glaucoma, 528, 529
Glennon, T.K., 695
glomerulus, 892
glucose, 973
glycemia, 976
glycemic index approach, to energy balance, 976–978
goals/desired outcomes
- client responses and, 434
- components of, 424
- evaluating nursing actions and, 435
- for impaired physical mobility, 422
- for ineffective airway clearance, 422
- long-term/short-term goals, 422–423
- nursing diagnoses and, 423
- Nursing Outcomes Classification (NOC), 422
- purpose of, 422
- review of, 438
- statements, 423–424
- terminology, 422
- writing guidelines, 424–425

gonorrhea, 195
Good Friday, 210
Good Samaritans, 123
Gordon, M., 399
Gould, Roger, 314–315
gowns
- changing clients receiving intravenous therapy, 813
- isolation practices, 765–766
- sterile gowns, 770–777

grants, research, 476
granulation tissue, 749, 942
graphic (clinical) record, 453–454
grievance, 116
Grimm, P.M., 208
gross motor and balance tests, 591
grounded theory, 38
groups
- defined, 499
- group dynamics, 499
- health-care groups, 499–501
- self-awareness/growth groups, 501
- self-help groups, 499–501
- task groups, 499
- teaching groups, 499
- therapy groups, 501
- work-related social support groups, 501

group teaching, 684–685
growth and development
- and caring, 310
- components of, 309
- development, defined, 309
- environmental influences on, 309
- genetics and, 309
- glandular changes, 336, 340
- growth, defined, 309
- interrelated processes of, 309
- motor development, 310, 325, 326, 330, 332, 333, 335, 337, 338
- musculoskeletal system, 336, 340
- principles of, 309
- reflexes, 325, 326
- sensory development, 325, 328, 330, 333, 336–746

growth and developmental stages
- prenatal development, 323–324
- neonates, 324–329
- infants, 329–333
- toddlers, 329–332
- preschoolers (4 and 5 years), 331–336
- school age children (6 to 12 years), 335–342
- adolescents (12 to 18 years), 339–344
- developmental changes, 309–310

growth and development theories
- application of, 320
- cognitive development (Piaget), 315
- developmental task theory (Havighurst), 310–311
- limitations of, 319
- moral development, 315–318
- psychosocial theories, 311–315
- spiritual development, 318–319

growth spurt, adolescent, 339
guided imagery, 170
gustatory stimuli, 1133

H

Haber, J., 38
habit training, 911
Haemophilus influenzae type B, immunization against, 329, 332
Hahnemann, Samuel, 177
hair care
- for African Canadians, 838
- assessment, 525, 809–837
- beard and mustache, 841
- brushing and combing, 837–838
- dandruff, 836
- diagnoses, 837
- hair loss, 836
- hirsutism, 525, 837
- pediculosis, 339, 836
- planning, 837
- scabies, 836
- shampooing, 839–840
- ticks, 836

half-life, of drug, 612, 613
hand movements (H/M), vision test, 536
hand washing
- clinical guidelines, 757–758
- in infection control, 284, 757–758
- soaps, 757

hantavirus, 296
harm
- in negligence lawsuit, 120
- risk of, 41

Hartrick, G., 489
Hatha yoga, 171
haustra, 857
haustral churning, 858
Havelock, R., 700
Havighurst, Robert, 310, 311, 352
head and circumference
- assessment, 527–528
- of infants, 324, 325
- of toddlers, 330

head-to-toe assessment. *See* cephalocaudal (head-to-toe) physical examination
healing
- bodymind healing, 165–166
- concepts of, 164–165
- mind-body therapies, 169–174
- nurses as healers, 166
- and nursing practice, 164
- touch therapies, 167–169
- transpersonal therapies, 174–175
- *See also* alternative medicine

Healing Touch, 175
health and safety
- and accident prevention, 296
- and health-care environment, 795–796
- nursing functions, 269, 1392
- occupational health clinics, 251–252
- wellness programs, 269

health and wellness, 8
- and ability to function in social role, 135
- behavioural approach, 140
- caring and, 52
- concepts of wellness, 133
- culture and, 64, 233–234
- defining health, 133
- determinants of, 131, 148
- developmental factors, 64, 143
- ecological approach, 140
- genetic endowment, 143
- health, in nursing metaparadigm, 49
- and human ecological system, 131
- humanistic concept of, 134–135
- income, social status, and education, 142
- personal definition of health, 132, 143
- personal health practices, 143
- physical environments, 143
- popular notions of, 131
- public participation, 140, 141, 149
- relational practice and, 489
- social environments, 142–143
- WHO definition, 140

health appraisal, 62
- *See also* health assessment

health assessment
- families and communities, 159
- health care beliefs, 156
- health history and physical examination, 154
- health risk appraisal, 154–156
- life stress review, 157
- lifestyle, 154–155
- validation of data, 157
- *See also* health history, nursing; physical health assessment

health behaviour change
- commitment and motivation, 158, 159–160
- cyclical nature of, 153
- education prgrams, 158
- evaluation, 159
- facilitators and barriers to change, 158
- health care goals, 157
- health promotion plans, 157
- implementation of plan, 158–159

outcomes, desired, 157
role models, 160
self-responsibility, 157, 158
stage model, 153
support, nonjudgmental, 158
time frame, 158
See also health-promoting behaviours
health belief models, 137–138
Becker model, 137
health locus of control model, 137
Rosenstock model, 137–138
Health Canada, 251
health-care groups, 499–501
health-care law
advice, providing, 122, 125
betrayal of client's confidence, 116
breach, in standard of care, 120
causation, of harm, 120
contractual terms, fulfillment of, 115
countersuit against nurse, 122
delegation of care, 114
duty, incurrence of, 120
failure to act, 115, 120, 121
falls, accidental, 120, 121
Good Samaritans, 123
harm in, 120
liability protection, 112, 115, 116
malpractice, 120–121
medical records, 124, 462
negligence, 120, 121, 122, 124–125
nursing service outside employment, providing, 122
physician's orders, 123, 610
potential liability situation, role of nurse in, 115
questionable orders, following, 114
responsibility for errors, determining, 120
standards of care, 114
students, legal responsibilities of nursing, 126
treating patient without consent, 117, 121
uncertain competence, 121
witness, nurse as, 114, 117, 119
See also consent; errors, in nursing care
health-care providers
alternative care providers, 256
case managers, 256
dentists, 255
dietitians, 255
nurses, 254
nutritionists, 263
occupational therapists, 66–255
paramedical technologists, 255
pharmacists, 255
physicians, 254
physiotherapists, 263
records of, 393–394
respiratory technologists, 255
social workers, 255–256
spiritual support persons, 256
unlicenced assistive personnel, 254
verbal reports, 394
health-care reform
Canadian Nurses Association and, 265
Canadian Public Health Association and, 265
case management models, 268
community-based care, 267
consumer demands and, 266
and future health-care delivery, 267
integrated health-care system, 268
managed care, 268
nursing agenda, 265
outreach programs, 268
reasons for, 265
shift to community-based care, 265–266
health-care services
access, problems of, 257–258
acute care, 248
demographic changes and, 256
diagnosis and treatment, 248
early detection and treatment, 248
Epp Report, 141
escalating costs and, 256–257, 262
in health field concept, 140, 148
health promotion and illness prevention, 246–248
levels of health care, 248
palliative care, 248
rehabilitation and health restoration, 248
right to equal access, 250
secondary emergency care, 248
technological advances and, 256
tertiary long-term care, 248
uneven distribution of, 257
women's movement and, 257
health-care settings
clinics, 251
community health centres, 251
crisis centres, 253–254
day-care centres, 253
extended-care facilities, 252–253
general clinics, 251
home health-care agencies, 253, 281
hospice services, 253
hospitals, 250–251, 252
occupational health clinics, 251–252
physician's office, 251
rehabilitation centres, 253
retirement and assisted-living centres, 253
rural primary-care hospitals, 253
telehealth, 254
health-care systems
defined, 246
evolution of, 258
indigenous health-care system, 230
integrated systems, 268
professional health-care system, 230
See also health-care reform
health education, 248
health field concept, 140
health hazard appraisal (HHA). *See* health risk appraisal
health history, nursing, 62
biographical data, 392
chief concern/reason for visit, 392
components of, 393
family history of illness, 392
history of present illness, 392
lifestyle data, 392–393
past history, 392
patterns of health care, 393
and physical examination, 154
psychological data, 393
social data, 393
See also data organization; health assessment
health models, 133–138
adaptive model, 135
clinical model, 136
eudaimonistic model, 134–135
role performance model, 135
Health on the Net (HON) Foundation, 471
health policy
Commission on the Future of Health Care, 258
Epp Report, 140–141, 147, 148–149
Lalonde Report, 140, 147–148
Ottawa Charter, 140, 274
Standing Senate Committee on Social Affairs, Science, and Technology, 258
health professionals. *See* health-care providers
health-promoting behaviours
cognitive-perceptual factors, 151–153
cues to action, 153
modifying factors, 153
nurse as role model, 154
See also health behaviour change
health promotion, 10
for adolescents, 366–369
client education, 668
concept of, 149
environmental control programs, 151
gender and, 152
health risk appraisal, 150
for infants, 329
information dissemination programs, 150, 151
lifestyle and behaviour change programs, 151
for middle-aged adults, 356
for older adults, 149
practices, 147
for preschoolers, 335–336
prevention programs, 151
public policy, 140, 147, 150
role of nurse, 154
for school-age children, 339
school programs, 151
strategies, 148–149, 246–248
for toddlers, 331–332
types of programs, 146–150
wellness assessment program, 150
worksite programs, 151, 152
for young adults, 351
Health Promotion Lifestyle Profile (HPLP), 152
health promotion model (Pender). *See* health-promoting behaviours
health promotion orders, 428
health promotion planning
process, 157–158
role of nurse, 157
support resources, 158
Health Promotions and Programs Branch, 251
health-protecting behaviours
barriers to action, 138
individual beliefs, 63

individual perceptions, 137
perception modifying factors, 137
health risk appraisal (HRA), 150, 154–156
Health Self-Determination Index (HSDI), 156
health status
and cardiovascular system, 1027
and nutrition, 979
and safety, 784
health status, perceived
and health-promoting behaviours, 153
Health Summit Working Group, 471
hearing
and aging, 358, 360
impairment, 501–502
of infants, 325
risks of loss, 297
sound transmission and, 537
hearing appliances
cleaning, 845–847
types of, 845
hearing screenings
audiometric evaluations, 537
for preschoolers, 333
for school-age children, 336
for toddlers, 330, 332
tuning fork tests, 540–541
watch tick test, 540
for young adults, 351
heart, 1023
assessment, 567–569
auscultation, 530–531
fetal heart beat, 323
heart sounds, 568–569, 571
location of, 568
sounds, 568, 569
heart assessment. *See* cardiovascular assessment
heart attack. *See* myocardial infarction
heart disease
and sexual function, 186
See also coronary heart disease
heart failure, 1030
heart rate, 1024
heat balance, 709
heave. *See* lift and heave
height
of adolescents, 340
of preschoolers, 333
of school-age children, 336
of toddlers, 330
See also length, of infants
height, measuring, 520
Heimlich maneuver, 794–795
helix, 537
helping relationships. *See* nurse-client relationships
hematocrit, 732, 1022
hemodynamics, 1037
hemoglobin, 1022, 1026
hemorrhage
and pulse rate, 720
hemorrhage, 942
hemorrhoids, 604, 858
hemostasis, 941
Henderson, Virginia, 7, 51, 52
Henry Street Visiting Nurses, 147
hepatitis B vaccine, 329, 332
herbal medicine, 176–177
heredity
in health field concept, 140, 147
and health status, 143
and perceived susceptibility, 137
and physical growth, 340
and risks factors, 64
and susceptibility to infection, 750
hernias, 600, 602
herpes simplex virus (HSV), 195
heterosexism, 182
Hinduism, 211
Hippocrates, 167
hirsutism, 525, 837
history, of nursing
development of nursing practice, 11, 260
family nursing, 73–75
health promotion, 147
nursing diagnoses, development of, 405
nursing research, 32–33
public health care, 246
role of women, 260
theoretical approaches to history, 260
HIV. *See* acquired immune deficiency syndrome (AIDS)
HIV postexposure protocol, 778
holism
concept of, 60–61, 164, 233–234
holistic health, 164
holistic health care, 164
holistic nursing, 164
underlying beliefs, 165
See also healing
Holmes, T.H., 157
holy days, 210
Homans' sign, 574
home care, 270
bathing, 817
catheterization, 919
definitions of, 280
emergency safety measures, 283
enemas, 880
environmental management, 753
fecal elimination assessment, 869, 870–871
fluid, electrolyte, and acid-base balance, 1099–1100
future of, 287
growth of, 280
hand washing, 757
home hazards, 283–284
home setting, 280
hygiene, 807–809
medication instructions, 629
mobility problems, 1195–1196
nurse safety, 283
nutritional care, 995
ostomy appliances, disposable, 886
oxygenation needs, 1038–1042
preventing infections, 753–754
providers of, 281, 282
research, areas of research, 287
sensory-perceptual alterations, 1140
services, 281
sterile field, 770–774
unique aspects of, 280–281
urinary elimination care, 906–910
wound prevention and care, 947–948
home care clients, 280
caregiving demands on, 281
diversity of, 283
elderly, 282, 287
health care cuts and, 287
in long-term care, 284
primary and secondary clients, 280, 283
home care nursing practice
advocacy in, 282
assessing client's needs, 285
caregiver support, 284–285
caregiving in, 282
client safety, 283
coordinating function in, 283
diagnoses for, 285–286
discharge planning in, 282
evaluating and documenting outcomes, 286
independence and autonomy in, 280
infection control, 283–284
nursing roles in, 282–283
objectives of, 280
planning and implementing phases, 285–286
teaching function in, 282
home care programs
eligibility criteria, 287
funding and delivery of, 286–287, 288
referral process, 282
reimbursement and user fees, 281
treatment plans, 281
home fires, 790
home health-care agencies, 253
medical equipment companies, 281
private duty agencies, 281
services, 281
types of, 281
homeless populations, 257–258
homeopathy, 177
homeostasis
defined, 61
feedback system, 61
and fluid loss, 1077
physiologic homeostasis, 61–1364
psychologic homeostasis, 61–62
self-regulation, 61
homophobia, 182
homosexuality
adolescents, 184
sexual identification, 341
hope, 208
hormonal replacement therapy (HRT), 184
hospice services, 253
hospital attendants, 254
hospital diploma program, 24–25
hospital information system (HIS), 474
hospitals
centralized care in, 4
classification of, 252
clinics, 251
and community initiatives, 268
cross-cultural care, 229
health-care services, 250–251, 252
health-promotion programs, 151
religious observances, 210

religious support, 216
rural primary-care facilities, 253
visitations, 234–235
worksite health promotion programs, 151
host
in clinical model, 136
hot-cold theory, of illness, 234
hour of sleep (HS) care, 807
Hultsch, D.F., 353
human caring theory (Watson), 53–68
human dignity, value of, 92
human field, 174
humanism, 139, 670
humanistic leadership, 695–696
human rights, 101
human spirit, 165
human subjects
full-disclosure, 41–42
informed consent, 41
privacy and confidentiality, 42
rights of, 41–42
risk of harm, 41
self-determination, 42
human systems theories, 68
humidifiers, 1043
humoral (circulating) immunity, 749–750
humour
as a caring skill, 173
in communication, 486
Hungler, B.P., 30, 36
Hunt, R., 265, 269, 270
hydrocolloid dressings, 957–959
hydrogenation, 975
hydrotherapy, 177
hygiene
bathing, 812–813
ears, 845–847
environment, 847
etiologies of self-care deficits, 807–810
feet, 822
hair care, 834–841
home care, 807–809
nose, 847
oral hygiene, 827, 829, 835
perineal-genital care, 817–819
personal hygiene, 807
skin care, 809–810
and susceptibility to infection, 758
hypercalcemia, 1085
hypercarbia, 1028
hyperchloremia, 1086
hyperemia, 748
hyperesthesia, 590
hyperglycemia, 976
hyperhidrosis, 520
hyperkalemia, 1085
hypermagnesemia, 1086
hyperopia, 333, 528
hyperosmolar nonketonic syndrome (HHNS), 994
hyperphosphatemia, 1087
hyperpigmentation, 520
hyperresonance (sound), 517
hypersomnia, 1158
hypertension, 732–733
hypertonic solutions, 876
hypertrophy, 584, 1179
hyperventilation, 727, 1028, 1029
hypervolemia, 1030
hypnosis, 173
hypocalcemia, 1085
hypochloremia, 1086
hypoesthesia, 590
hypokalemia, 1085
hypomagnesemia, 1086
hypophosphatemia, 1087
hypopigmentation, 520
hypoproteinemia, 937
hypostatic pneumonia, 1185
hypothermia, 366, 711–713
hypothesis (research question), 37
hypothetical/future-oriented questions, 83
hypoventilation, 727, 1028, 1029
hypoxemia, 1028
hypoxia, 1023, 1028

I

iatrogenic infections, 745
iatrongenic disease, 612
id, 312
ideal body weight (IBW), 987
identification, 334
identification phase, in interpersonal relations model (Peplau), 51
idiosyncratic effect, 612
ileal conduit, 928
ileostomy, 864
illicit drugs, 612
illness
classification, 139
client, impact on, 60, 139
effect of family on, 80
effects of, 139
family, impact on, 139
family history data, 392
hot-cold theory, 234
and sensory stimulation, 1135–1136
and sleep, 1155–1156
subjective nature of, 138
See also disease
illness narratives, 84
imagery, 170
imagination, 334
imbalanced nutrition, 405, 411, 421
imitation, 669
immediate recall, 587
immigration
and ethnic diversity, 223–224
major waves of, 223
refugees, 223
and settlement patterns, 222, 223
immobility
assessment of problems, 1190–1191
cardiovascular system and, 1181–1184
effects of, 1181–1188
and gastrointestinal system, 1186–1187
and integumentary system, 1187
and musculoskeletal system, 1181
and pressure ulcers, 937
and respiratory system, 1184–1185
and urinary system, 1185–1186
immune system
and mind modulation, 166
immunity, 749–750
acquired immunity, 750
humoral (circulating) immunity, 749–750
types of, 749
immunizations, 329, 332, 339, 344, 356, 750
for adults, 760
for children, 759
immunoglobulins. *See* antibodies
impaired gas exchange, 406
impaired home maintenance management, 286
impaired physical mobility, 422
impaired skin integrity, 416
impetigo, 339
implementation, implementing, 431–434
components of, 431
delegating and supervising, 432–433
documenting nursing action, 433
effective communication plan, 503
needed skills in, 431–432
nurse's need for assistance, determining, 432
of nursing orders, 432
and nursing process, 431
nursing strategies, 432–433
process, 432–433
reassessing the client, 432
review of, 438
implied consent, 117
impotence. *See* erectile dysfunction
inadequate nutrition, and pressure ulcers, 937
incentive spirometry, 1045
incident reports, 125
incomplete proteins, 974
inconsistencies, 410
incontinence drawsheets, 913
incus, 537
independence of thought, 377
independent functions, 407
independent interventions, 425
independent variable, 37
indexes, print-based, 40
Index Medicus, 40
indigenous health-care system, 230
indirect inguinal hernia, 600, 602
indirect percussion, 517
indirect transmission, 747
individual health
assessment of, 62–64
within context of family, 73
coping mechanisms, 63–64
cultural beliefs and, 64
developmental stage and, 64
gender and, 64
health beliefs of individual, 63
health-care beliefs, 156
health history, 62, 154
heredity and, 64
individuality, concept of, 60
individualized care, in nursing practice, 60
lifestyle factors, 64–65
race and, 64
risk assessment, 64
sociologic factors, 64

individualized care plans, 417
individual reflexive stage, in spiritual development, 318
individuating-reflective period, 349
inductive reasoning, 376, 410
indwelling catheter, 916–923, 920–923
ineffective airway clearance, 411, 412, 421, 422, 426
ineffective coping, 405
infancy and early childhood
in developmental task theory (Havighurst), 311
infants and neonates
bathing, 812
cognitive development, 327
defecation, 860
feet, 819
head and circumference, 324
head moulding, 325, 528
health examinations, 329
health problems, 327
health promotion guidelines for, 329
length of, 324
life skill and knowledge, 328
moral development, 327
motor development, 325, 326
nutrition, 981
oral health, 828–829
physical development, 324–325
psychosocial development, 28–326
skin assessment, 524
urinary elimination, 894
weight of, 324
infected wound, 935, 942
infection
body defences, 748–750
chain of, 745–748
diagnosing, 752
endogenous source, 745
etiologic agent, 746
exogenous sources, 745
infectious agents, 745
insufficient handwashing and, 745
microorganisms and, 744
nosocomial infections, 745–746
portal of entry, 747
portal of exit, 746
reservoir, 746–747
respiratory infections, 360
susceptibility to, 758–759
transmission, mechanisms of, 746–747
types of, 745
urinary tract infection, 906–910
infection assessment
at-risk clients, 751
laboratory data, 751–752
physical assessment, 751
susceptible host, 747–748, 750–751
infection control
assessment of, 758
for health care workers, 770–777
in home care, 283–284, 753–754
planning, 752–753
respiratory tract and ear infections, 331
infection control nurse, 777–778
infection prevention
breaking chain of infection, 755
cleaning, 760
disinfecting, 760
fluid intake, adequate, 758
hygiene, 758
immunization, 759
nosocomial infections, 753–759
nutrition, 758
rest and sleep, adequate, 758
sterilizing, 760–761
stress reduction, 758
See also isolation
inference, 410
inferences, 376, 404
inflammation
causes, 748
defensive function, 748
exudate production, 749
reparative phase, 749
vascular and cellular responses, 748–749
inflammatory phase, of wound healing, 941
influence, 695
informal leader, 693
informal nursing care plan, 417
informatics, nursing
access and storage of data, 471
assessment application, 469
bedside data entry, 469
in client care, 468–472
and client monitoring, 469
consumer access, 471
in co-ordination of care, 471
data protection, 470
data standardization and classification, 470–471
defined, 468
electronic health records, 469–470
and evidence-based decision-making, 472
in nursing administration, 474–475
in nursing education, 473–474
in nursing research, 475–476
online journals, 472
in practice management, 472–473
search tools, 473
telehealth, 471–472
tracking client status, 471
information
concept of, 468
health-promotion program information, 150, 151
on Internet, 479
information transduction, 166
informed consent, 41, 117
right of human subjects, in research, 41
infrared thermometer, 714, 715
Ingham, Eunice, 168
ingrown nail, 822
inguinal ligaments (Poupart's ligaments), 575
inhalation. *See* inspiration
initial assessment, 391
initial planning, 415
injection caps, 651
inpatients, 251
inputs, 68
insensible heat loss, 710
insensible losses, 1077
insomnia, 1157–1158
inspection, 515
inspiration, 727, 1021
Institute for Philosophical Nursing Research, 48, 49
insulin resistance, 977
insulin syringes, 631
insurance, professional liability, 122
integrated health care system, 268
integrated team model. *See* provider-driven model
integrity
and aging, 361
and critical thinking, 377
integument
aging and, 358
hair, 525
immobility and, 1187
nails, 526–527
skin, 520–525
intellectual capacity
compontnet of, 364
intellectual courage, 377
intellectual humility, 377
intensity, of auscultated sound, 518
intentional tremor, 583
intercessory prayer, 175, 211
interdependence response mode, 53
interdisciplinary plans. *See* critical pathways
intermittent evaluation, 434
intermittent intravenous infusions, 649
intermittent self-catheterization, 924–925
internal respiration, 727
internals, in health locus of control model, 137
internal stimuli, 1133
International Classification of Nursing Practice, 470
International Council of Nurses (ICN), 12, 19, 96, 470
International Journal of Nursing Studies, 40
International Nursing Index, 40
International Parish Nurse Resourses, 269
International System of Units, 715
interpersonal communication
attitudes and, 489–490
congruence in, 489
developmental factors and, 487
environment and, 489
gender and, 488
in nursing practice, 483–484
personal space and, 488
roles and relationships in, 488–489
territoriality and, 488
values and perceptions in, 488
interpersonal relationships. *See* nurse-client relationships
Interpersonal Relations Model (Paplau), 51
interpretation
critique of, 41
translators, use of, 235–236
interpretive tradition, 47, 48
interstitial fluid, 1072
intervention. *See* implementation; nursing intervention
intervention errors, 121
interviews, interviewing

body of interview, 397–398
closing, 398
communicating in, 398
directive interview, 395
interview stages, 397–398
introduction, 397
planning, 397
purpose of, 395
rapport, 395, 397
setting, 397
intestines
large intestines, 857–858
intimate distance, 488
intonation, in verbal communication, 485
intra-arterial, route of administration, 617
intra-articular, route of administration, 617
intracardiac, route of administration, 617
intracellular fluid, 1072, 1073
intradermal injections, 639
intramuscular injections
assessment of client, 645
deltoid site, 644
dorsogluteal site, 643–644
equipment, 645
evaluate effects, 647
injection technique, 644–647
intervention, 645–647
major considerations, 642
rectus femoris site, 644
vastus lateralis site, 643
ventrogluteal site, 642–643
intraosseous, route of administration, 617
intrapleural, route of administration, 617
intrapleural pressure, 1021
intrapulmonary pressure, 1021
intraspinal, route of administration, 617
intrathecal, route of administration, 617
intrauterine development. *See* prenatal development
intravascular fluid, 1072
intravenous equipment, 1106–1108
intravenous hyperalimentation (IVH). *See* parenteral nutrition
intravenous infusion
changing containers, tubing, and dressing, 1114–1116
discontinuing infusion, 1118–1119
monitoring infusion, 1113–1116
starting infusion, 1108–1112
intravenous medications
assessment focus, 651
intermittent injection ports, 651
intermittent intravenous infusions, 649
intravenous push (IVP), 651–653
large volume infusions, 647–649
methods, 647
procedure, 647
volume-control infusions, 649–651
intravenous push (IVP)
assessment focus, 651
equipment, 652
evaluation focus, 653
intervention, 652–653
purpose, 651
intravenous pyelography (IVP), 904
intravenous rods, 848
intravenous solutions, 1103–1104
introjection, 334
intuition, 381
intuitive-projective stage, in spiritual development, 318, 335
intuitive thought phase, in cognitive development, 316, 334
Inuit, 224
invasion of privacy, 122
ions, 1073
Iowa Intervention Project, 428, 906, 907–908
iron deficiency anemia, 981
irrigation, 955
irrigations, 662–663, 924
ischemia, 936, 1030
Islam, 210, 211, 212, 238
isokinetic (resistive) exercises, 1178
isolation
airborne precautions, 762, 763
compromised clients, 762
contact precautions, 762, 763–764
defined, 761
droplet precautions, 762, 763
guidelines, historical development of, 761–762
psychosocial needs of clients in, 768
standard precautions, 762–763
transmission-based precautions, 762–763
two-tiered system, 762
isolation practices, 762–768
disposable gloves, removing, 765
for eyewear, 766–767
for face masks, 765–766
for gowning, 765–766
gowns, 765
protective equipment, removal of, 767
soiled equipment and supplies, disposal of, 767–768
transporting clients, 768
isotonic solutions, 877

J

Jacobsen, E., 169
jaundice, 520
jejunostomy, 864
jelly, vaginal, 659
job market, for nurses, 6–260
nursing shortage, 28
Johnson, Dorothy, 68
Johnson, J.A., 48
Johnson, V.E., 181
joint disease, and sexual function, 186
joint mobility, 1172–1177
joints, 583, 584
assessment of, 1189
mobility, 1172–1177
Journal of Family Nursing, 75
judgements, 376
Judaism, 210, 211, 212, 238
jugular veins, 569, 572
justice
principle of, 94
value of, 92
justice, ethic of, 317

K

Kalish, Richard, 66
Kardexes®, 453
Keegan, L., 164
Keen, S., 208, 365
Kegel exercise, 191, 194, 906, 912–913
keloid, 942
Keyserling, T.C., 677
keytone bodies, 904
kidneys, 892–893, 1077
Ki energy, 169, 175
Kikuchi, J., 48
kilojoule, 976
kinesthetic sensation, assessment of, 594
King, I.M., 135
kinship
in Sunrise Model, 232
Kirby, Michael, 258
Kittler, P.G., 232
knowledge, nursing
assumptions, 46
concept of, 150, 151
conceptual framework, 46
empiricism, 47
foundation of, 49
integration of, 468
interpretive tradition, 47
metaparadigm of nursing, 49
philosophical thought and, 49–50
theories and conceptual models, 50
knowledge deficit, 285
knowledge deficit, diagnostic label, 678
Kohlberg, Lawrence, 315, 317, 331, 354
koilonychia, 526
Kolcaba, K.Y., 482
Kolodny, R.C., 181
Korotkoff's sounds, 736–737
kosher food, 211
Krasnansky, S., 269
Krieger, Delores, 174
KUB, 904
Kübler-Ross, Elisabeth, 253
Kundalini yoga, 171
Kushner, C., 266
Kussmaul's breathing, 1029
kyphosis, 360

L

labia, 596
Labonte, R., 134–135, 149, 271
Laboratory Centre for Disease Control (LCDC), 251, 744, 761, 777
laboratory records, 394
laboratory technologists, 255
lacrimal gland assessment, 531–532
lactated Ringer's solution, 1104
laissez-faire leaders, 694
Lalonde Report, 140, 147, 148
Lamberton, Eleanor, 261
language
cross-cultural communication, 235
culturally sensitive language, 233
language barriers, 235
language deficits, 501
and mental status, 586

lanugo, 323, 835
large calorie, 976
large volume infusions, 647–649
laryngoscopy, 1037
larynx, 1019
latency stage, 337
lateral position, 1202–1203
later maturity
in developmental task theory (Havighurst), 311
laughter, as a caring skill, 173
Lavin, Mary Ann Lavin, 405
law
authority, sources of, 109–110
constitution, 112
defined, 109
and ethics, 91
functions of, 109
lawsuits, 113–114
legal role of nurses, 114–116
and nursing practice, 113
religious laws, 210
sources of, 109
in Sunrise Model, 232
types of, 112–113
See also health-care law
Lawler, J., 49
Lawrence, P.A., 677
laxatives, 860, 861, 874, 877
leaching, 295
leadership
characteristics of, 692
effectiveness, 695–696
nurse leader, 692
role of nurses, 13
theories, 693–695
leading question, 396
lead poisoning, screening for, 332
LEARN, mnemonic device, 103
learning
active involvement and, 671
aging and, 672
attributes of, 668
barriers to learning, 672–673
client support system, 676
complexity of material and, 671
cultural factors and, 675, 676
defined, 668
economic factors and, 676
emotional barriers, 672
environment and, 672
evaluation of, 687–688
feedback and, 671
health beliefs and practices and, 675, 676
learning need, 668, 669
motivation and, 670, 677
nonjudgemental support and, 671
physical exmination data and, 676
psychological barriers, 672
psychomotor skills and, 673
readiness and, 670, 676–677
reading level and, 677–678
relevance and, 671
repetition and, 671
style of, 675, 676
theories, 669–670
timing and, 671
learning needs
diagnosis, 677–679
diagnostic labels, 677–678
knowledge deficit, 678–679
reading level, 677–678
Leavell, H.R., 136, 149
left lower lobe (lung), 560
left upper lobe (lung), 560
legislative authority, 110
legitimate power, 695
Leininger, M.M., 53, 229, 230, 239, 481
Sunrise Model, 230–232
length, of infants, 324
lesions, skin, 521–523, 524
leukocytes, 749
leukocytosis, 749
level of consciousness (LOC), 587
Lewin, K., 157, 669, 700
liability, 114
criminal acts, 115
legal protection in employee-employer relationship, 115
vicarious liability, 115
Liaschenko, J., 49
libido
Freudian concept, 312
sex drive, 187
lice. *See* pediculosis
licensed practical nurse (LPN), 24, 26, 254
licensing, 110–111
Life-Change Index, 157
lifestyle
adjustments due to illness, 139
assessment of, 154–155
and behaviour change programs, 151
and cardiovascular system, 1027
and fluid balance, 1082
and health, 64, 143
health behaviour change, 153
in health field concept, 140
health history data, 392–393
and nutrition, 979
retirement, 362
and safety, 783
and sensory stimulation, 1136
single, 349
and sleep, 1156
wound healing, 943
lift and heave (pulsations), 568
lifting, 1197–1198
light palpation, 581
light perception, vision test, 536
light-touch sensation, assessment of, 593–594
limb restraint, 799
line of gravity, 1171
linoleic acid, 974
lipids, 974–975
lipoprotein, 975
Lippit, R., 700
listening. *See* attentive listening
literature review, 37, 394, 475
literature searching, 472–479, 473
liver
palpation of, 582
percussion of, 580
living will, 30
LoBiondo-Wood, G., 38
lobule, 537
local infection, 745
locus of control (LOC), 137
Loeb Centre for Nursing and Rehabilitation, 261
long-term memory, 364
loop colostomy, 865
lordosis, 1198
love and belonging needs, 65
lung, lobes of, 559–560
See also thorax and lungs assessment
lung cancer, 355, 368
lung compliance, 1021
lymph nodes, 549–550, 551, 552–553
lymphocyte count, 994
lysergic acid diethylamide (LSD)
and sexual function, 187

M

Mack Training School (St. Catharine's, Ontario), 25
macrominerals, 975
macrophages, 748
macule, 521, 524
magico-religious health belief view, 233
magnesium, 1079
male genitals and inguinal area assessment
children, 603
hernias, 600, 602
older adults, 603
penis, 599, 600–601
pubic hair, 599, 600
testes/scrotum, 599, 601–602
male urongenital system, 893
malleus, 537
malnutrition, 987–988, 990
malpractice lawsuit, 114
failure to observe, 121
falls, 120
mamograms, 198
managed care, 259, 261, 268
management
and cultural diversity, 703
functions, 697
levels of, 696
management information system (MIS), 474
manager
levels of responsibility, 696
nurse as, 13, 692–693
role of, 692, 696
Manitoba Association of Registered Nurses, 110
manubrium, 560
margination, 749
marijuana, 610
and sexual function, 187
Maslow, Abraham, 65, 66, 134, 403, 670
massage
back massages, 1165–1166
calming effect of, 847
therapeutic massage, 167–168
mass peristalsis, 858
Master, W.H., 181

mastoid, 537
masturbation, 187–188, 195, 313
Maticaka-Tynsdale, E., 183
matresses, 848
maturation phase, of wound healing, 942
maturity, 348
maxillary sinus, 658
McGill Model of Nursing, 55
McGill University, 33, 35
McWhorter, L., 184
McWilliam, C.L., 274
mean, 38, 39
mean arterial pressure (MAP), 1025
measles-mumps-rubella (MMR), immunization for, 329, 332
meconium, 860
medecine (practice)
  eras of, 164–165
  mind-body medicine, 165
  nonlocal/transpersonal medicine, 165
  physical medicine, 165
median, 38, 39
medical asepsis, 744–745
medical diagnoses, 407
medical equipment companies, 281
medical narratives, 84
medical orders, 425
medical records, 393
  proper recordkeeping, 124
  right to review, 250
medical therapies, and susceptibility to infection, 751
medicare. *See* Canada Health Act
medication
  bronchodilators, 1044
  and defecation, 861
  expectorants, 1044
  flowsheets, 453
  home safety measures, 284
  medication error, 120
  medication instructions, 625
  mixing medications in one syringe, 637–638
  and nutrition, 979–980
  over-the-counter (OTC) drugs, 367
  and pulse rate, 719
  and sensory stimulation, 1135–1136
  and sexual function, 186–187, 191–192
  and sleep, 1157
  sleep medications, 1165–1167
  and susceptibility to infection, 751
  and urinary elimination, 895
  wound healing, 943
  See also drug action; drug administration; drugs; prescriptions
medication administration record (MAR), 626, 627, 628, 635
meditation, 171–172, 211
Medline, 40
melanin, 520
melanotic freckles, 528
memory
  aging and, 364
  assessment, 586–587
  in middle age, 354
  short-term and long-term, 364
menarche
  mean age of, 183
  puberty, 338, 340
meniscus, 1364
menopause
  and sexual activity, 184
  symptoms, 352
mental health and illness
  and body movement, 1180
  homosexual adolescents, 184
  rural regions, 298
mentoring, 698
mercury-in-glass thermometer, 714
mercury sphygmomanometers, 734
meridians, 169, 175
mesoderm, 323
message, in communication process, 484
metabolic acidosis, 1089–1090
metabolism, 613, 973
  carbohydrates, 973
  exercise and, 1179
  fat, 975
  process, 976
  proteins, 974
  rate of, 976
metabolsm
  immobility and, 1185
metaparadigm, 49
  of nursing, 49
methodology, critique of, 41
metred-dose inhaler (MDI), 660–661
Metropolitan School of Nursing, 27
microminerals, 975
microorganisms, 744, 745
  See also infection
midaxillary line, 558
midclavicular line, 558
middle-aged adults
  cognitive development, 353–354
  developmental assessment guidelines, 355
  health problems, 354–356
  health promotion, 356
  moral development, 354
  nutrition, 983
  physical development, 352, 355
  psychosocial development, 352–353, 355
  spiritual development, 354
middle childhood
  in developmental task theory (Havighurst), 311
middle-level managers, 696
midlife crisis, 353
midline, 575
midsternal line, 558
midstream specimen. *See* clean-catch (midstream) specimen
midwife. *See* nurse-midwife
milk, breast, 981
milk thistle, 177
Miller, K.L., 481
mind-body medicine, 165
mind-body therapies
  aromatherapy, 173–174
  biofeedback, 169
  humour and laughter, 172–173
  hypnosis, 173
  imagery, 170
  meditation, 171–172
  music therapy, 172
  prayer, 172
  progressive relaxation, 169
  yoga, 171
"mindfulness" meditation, 172
mind modulation, 166
minerals, 975
minors
  consent of, 41, 118
miosis, 530
mitral valve, 568
mitt restraint, 799, 801
mixed hearing loss, 537
mobility
  external factors and, 1181
  and health, 1171
  See also activity-exercise assessment; movement, body
mobility problems
  care plan, 1192–1196
  diagnoses, 1190–1192
  as etiology, 1191–1192
Mobility Rights, 112
mode, 38, 39
Model for Developing Cultural Sensitivity, 232
modelling, 159, 334, 341, 669
modified scientific method, 381
moist heat (steam), 1364
molarity, 1073
mole, 1073
monosaccharides, 973
monotheism, 208
Montgomery straps, 960
moral development
  of infants, 327
  of toddlers, 331
  of preschoolers, 334
  of school-age children, 338
  of adolescents, 342
  defined, 92, 315
  Gilligan's theory of, 316–318
  Kohlberg's theory of, 315–317
  of preschoolers, 334
morality
  defined, 91
  and ethical theories, 92–94
  moral behaviour, 315
  and values, 92
  See also ethics
morning care, 807
moro reflex, 326
motivation
  and behaviour change, 160
  and sleep, 1157
motor aphasia, 586
motor development, 310
  in infants, 325, 326
  in preschoolers, 333, 335
  in school-age children, 337, 338
  in toddlers, 330, 332
motor function assessment, 590–592
  children, 595
  fine motor tests for lower extremities, 592

fine motor tests for upper extremities, 592
gross motor and balance tests, 591
motor vehicle collisions, 297, 299
mouth, 825–835
common problems, 826–855
and oropharynx assessment, 544–549
periodontal disease, 825–826
teeth, 825
mouth care
clients at risk, identifying, 826–827
client's history, 826
for debilitated or unconscious clients, 831–834
diagnoses, 827–828
evaluation focus, 833–834
implementing, 828
physical assessment, 826–855
planning, 827
See also brushing and flossing; dentures
movement, body
alignment and posture, 1171–1172
balance, 1172
capabilities and limitations, assessment of, 1189
co-ordinated movement, 1172–1178
growth and development and, 1180
joint mobility, 1172–1177
mental health and, 1180
normal movement, 1171–1178
nutrition and, 1180
physical health and, 1180
prescribed limitations, 1181
See also activity-exercise assessment; exercise; mobility
multiculturalism, 226, 384
Multidimensional Health Locus of Control Scale, 137, 156
multi-dose vial, 634
multiparous women, pelvic musculature of, 598
mummy restraint, 799, 800–801
Murphy, B., 269
Murphy, M.M., 159
muscosal epithelium, 748
musculoskeletal system assessment
bones, 584
focus of examination, 584
joints, 584
muscles, 584
strength test, 585, 1190
music therapy, 172
Mussallem, Helen, 695
mutual support and self-help groups, 254, 499–501
mydriasis, 530
myocardial infarction, 1030
myocardial ischemia, 1030
myopia, 333, 528
myotonia, 188
mythic-literal stage, in spiritual development, 318, 338

N

nails, 824–825
assessment, 526–527, 825–855
diagnoses, 824
planning of care, 824–825
trimming, 825
naming systems, 235
Napoleonic Code, 109
narcolepsy, 1158
narcotics, 624
narrative charting, 446
nasal instillations, 657–658
nasal passage, defensive function of, 748
nasal speculum, 543–544
nasoenteric tube, 1002
uses, 1002
nasogastric tube
insertion procedure, 1002–1003
pediatric considerations, 1005
removal procedure, 1002–1003
nasolacrimal duct, 524–532
National Clearinghouse, 254
National Formulary (United States), 609
National Forum on Health, 265, 288
nationalism, Quebec, 226
National Nosocomial Infection Surveillance (NNIS) System, 745
naturopathy, 177
neck assessment, 548–553
needles-stick injuries, preventing, 633
needs theory
characteristics of basic needs, 66–67
Kalish's hierarchy of needs, 65–66
Maslow's hierarchy of needs, 59–1364, 403
negative calcium balance, 1185
negative feedback, 61
negative nitrogen balance, 1185
negative resolution, indicators of, 314
negligence, 117
countersuit against nurse, 122
defined, 120
elements of, 120
exposing, 125–126
falls, accidental, 120, 121
and Good Samaritan laws, 123
students, caused by, 126
telephone advice, 125
negotiation
in ethical decision making, 103
neonates. *See* infants and neonates
nephrons, 892
networking, 698
networks. *See* mutual support and self-help groups; social support networks
neurogenic bladder, 898
neurologic system
assessment considerations, 586
attention span assessment, 587
cranial nerves, 587–588
focus of physical assessment, 586
level of consciousness, 587
memory assessment, 586–587
mental status assessment, 586–587
motor function assessment, 590–592
reflex response assessment, 589–590
sensory function assessment, 590–595
neuropeptides, 166
neutral question, 396
A New Perspective on the Health of Canadians. See Lalonde Report
Newman, M.A., 164
nicotine, 1157
Nightingale, Florence, 7, 25, 32, 51
Nightingale model of nursing, 260
Nightingale Training School for Nurses, 25
Nisbet, R., 135
niyama, 171
nocturia, 897
nocturnal emissions, 1155
nocturnal enuresis, 894, 898, 1159
Noddings, N., 481
nodule, 521
noise, 847
noncompliance, 406, 678
noncontact therapeutic touch, 174–175
nondirective interview, 395
nonessential amino acids, 974
nonexperimental design, 38
nonmaleficence, 94
nonspecific defences, 748–749
anatomical and physiological barriers, 748
inflammatory responses, 748–749
nonverbal communication, 236–237, 486–487
nonviolence, in ethic of care, 317
norepinephrine, 710
norm, 409
normocephalic size, 527
normocephaly, 324
North American Nursing Diagnosis Association (NANDA), 157, 213, 405
Taxonomy II domains, 406
Taxonomy II multiaxial system, 406–407
northern nursing practice. *See* rural, remote, and northern nursing practice
Norton's Pressure Area Risk Assessment Form Scale, 939, 941
nose and sinuses assessment, 542–544
nosocomial infections, 745–746
nothing by mouth (NPO), 626, 630, 631
nothing per ora, 997
NPO. *See* nothing by mouth (NPO)
NREM (non-REM) sleep, 1152
nuclear medicine technologists, 255
nulliparous women, pelvic musculature of, 598
Nunavut Arctic College, 28
nurse-administrator, 14
nurse aides, 254
nurse-client interaction
address, formal style of, 233
courtesy and respect in, 233, 235
culturally-sensitive language, 233
families, relational practices with, 85–86
inappropriate sexual behaviour, 188
intervention errors, 121
physician's orders, carrying out, 123
planning errors, 121
sexual harassment, 201–202
sexuality, discussion of, 182
subjective realities in, 60
nurse-client relationships
characteristics of helping relationship, 491
development phases, 494–498
factors influencing, 491
goals, 491
introductory phase, 494

preinteraction phase, 494
tasks and skills for developing, 497, 498
termination phase, 496
working phase, 494–498
nurse-educator, 14
nurse-managers
communication, 698
critical thinking, 697
delegation, 698–699
enhancing employee performance, 698
evaluation function, 698
managing resources, 698
team-building and managing, 698
nurse-midwife, 14
nurse-physician interaction
physician's orders, 114, 123
questionable orders, 114
nurse practice acts, 11–12, 111
nurse-practitioner, 14
nurse-researcher, 14
nurse technicians, 254
nursing actions
documentation, 402
evaluation of, 435
guidelines for implementing, 432–433
and range of activities, 432
See also nursing intervention; Nursing Interventions Classification
nursing audit, 438–439
nursing care plan
for anxiety, 427, 436
collaborative care plans, 419
computerized care plans, 419
for fluid volume deficient, 426–427
functions, 417
for ineffective airway clearance, 426
nursing orders, 427–428
in problem-oriented medical record, 448
purpose of, 417
reviewing and modifying care plan, 437–438, 448
standardized plans, 453
student care plans, 419
traditional plans, 453
writing guidelines, 419–420
See also planning
nursing diagnosis, 405
See also diagnosis, diagnosing
nursing homes, 363
See also extended-care facilities
nursing intervention
for communication problems, 503
defined, 425
in progress notes, 448
for sexual health, 194
for spiritual distress, 215
strategies, 425–427
types of, 392
See also nursing care plan
Nursing Interventions Classification (NIC)
benefits, 431
and NANDA nursing diagnoses, 399–402
purpose, 428
taxonomy, 429
touch intervention, ????–430
nursing models
case method, 259–261
differential practice, 261
functional method, 261
partners in practice, 261
primary nursing, 10, 261
team nursing, 261
See also case management; patient-focused care
nursing orders
components of, 428
problem status and, 428
review of, 438
Nursing Outcomes Classification (NOC), 422
Nursing Papers, 35
nursing practice
caring in, 52, 53, 481–482
centralized care, 4
clinical guidelines, as legal precautions, 124
definitions of, 7–9, 13, 51–52
downstream thinking, 132
economic factors and, 17
ethical issues, coping with, 91
goal of, 10
healing and, 164
independent functions, 407
influences on, 17–18
nursing diagnosis in clinical settings, use of, 415
in nursing metaparadigm, 49
paradigms, 260
in physician's office, 251
purpose of theories in, 50
research-based practice, 32, 34, 388
in retirement centres, 253
roles and function of nurses, 12–15, 51–52, 53, 54
scope of, 8–9, 34
settings, 9, 251
sexual health, 182–183
See also profession, nursing
nursing process
assessing, 391–405
characteristics of, 390, 439
client-centred process, 390
components of, 388–390
critical thinking in, 390
cyclic and dynamic nature of, 390
defined, 388
diagnosing, 405–416
evaluating, 434–439
planning, 415–431
and problem solving, 381
purpose, 388
vs. decision making process, 383
Nursing Research, 40
nursing rounds, 464–465
Nursing Sisters, 260
nursing theories
adaptation model (Roy), 52
attributes of professional caring, 55
cultural care diversity and universality care theory, 53
environmental theory (Nightingale), 51
human becoming theory (Parse), 53
human caring theory (Watson), 52, 53
interpersonal relations model (Peplau), 51
McGill Model of Nursing, 55
purposes of, 50
role performance (King), 135
UBC Model of Nursing (Campbell), 54–55
unique function of nursing (Henderson), 51–52
nutrients
defined, 973
macronutrients, 973–975
micronutrients, 975
nutrition
for adolescents, 344, 982–983
and body movement, 1180
cultural patterns and, 237–238
and energy, 973
factors affecting, 977–980
for fetus, 323
for infants, 329, 981
for middle-aged adults, 983
nutritional assessment, 154
for older adults, 367, 983–985
for preschoolers, 336, 982
for school-age children, 339, 982
and skin sensitivity, 812
and susceptibility to infection, 750, 758
for toddlers, 332, 981–982
and wound healing, 943, 949–950
for young adults, 351, 983
nutritional care
appetite, improving, 999–1000
assisting with meals, 1000–1002
dietary data, 990
health history, 990–991
lab data and, 993–994
nursing interventions, 995
nutritional assessment, 988
nutritional screening, 989
physical examination, 989–990
planning, 995, 997–999
special community services, 1001
special diets, 914–995
temporary consistency modification, 997–998
nutritive value, 973
nystagmus, 534

O

obesity, 355, 983
and blood pressure, 732
objective data, 392, 394, 448
obligatory fluid losses, 1077
observation, observing, 394–395
observation orders, 428
obstructive pulmonary disease (COPD), 558
occult blood, testing for, 867–868, 904
occupational exposure, 777
occupational health and safety team, 795
occupational health clinics, 251–252
occupational health nurses, 252
occupational therapists (OTs), 255
odours, skin, 520
Oedipus complex, 333
official name, of drug, 609

oil-based lotions, dermatologic preparations, 654
oil retention enemas, 877
ointments, dermatologic preparations, 654
Old Age Security, 246
older adults
 abdomen assessment, 583
 breasts, 558
 catheterization, 919
 cognitive development, 364
 defecation, 860
 developmental assessment guidelines, 365–366
 drug administration, 625–626
 feet, 819
 female genitals assessment, 597–599
 hair, 525, 835
 health problems, 365–368
 health promotion, 367
 heart assessment, 573
 medication instructions, 625
 mental function, changes in, 587
 moral development, 364–365
 mouth and oropharynx assessment, 549
 musculoskeletal system assessment, 585
 nails, 527
 neurologic assessment, 595
 nose assessment, 544
 nutrition, 983–985
 peripheral vascular system, 575
 physical assessment of, 511
 physical changes, 30–361
 psychosocial development, 361–364
 skin assessment, 524–525
 spiritual development, 365
 thorax and lungs assessment, 567
 urinary elimination, 894
 vision, 536
 wound healing, 943
olfactory stimuli, 1133
oliguria, 896
Omega-3 fatty acids, 974
oncotic pressure, 1074
one-point tactile discrimination, 590, 594
ongoing evaluation, 434
ongoing nursing assessment, 328, 431
ongoing planning, 416
online full-text journals, 472
ontology, 46
open-ended questions, 395, 396
open method of catheter irrigation, 926
open system
 nature of, 81
 workings of, 68
ophthalmic instillations, 654–656
 assessment focus, 654
 equipment, 655
 evaluation focus, 656
 intervention, 655–656
 purposes, 654
opinions, 376, 444
opportunistic pathogen, 744
oral administration, 615
 assessment of client, 626–1049
 disposal, proper practice, 629
 documentation, 629
 equipment, 626
 evaluate effects, 629
 infants and children, 629
 liquid medication, 627–628
 medication instructions, 629
 mishandling errors, preventing, 628
 oral narcotics, 628
 preparation of medication, 627–628
 procedure, 626–629
 tablets or capsules, 627
 time of administration, 628–629
 verification procedure, 627
oral permission, 41
oral poliovirus vaccine (OPV), 329, 332
oral temperature, 717
oral thermometers, 714
orderlies, 254
Order of Nurses of Quebec, 141
orders
 physician's orders, 123, 448, 450, 610
 prescriptions, 617–621
 prevention orders, 428
 telephone orders, 463–464
 treatment orders, 428
 See also nursing orders
organ donation, 238
organizing function, 697
orgasm, 187, 195
orgasmic dysfunction, 191
orientation phase, in interpersonal relations model (Peplau), 51
oropharynx, 8–548
orthopnea, 1029
orthopneic position, 1201–1202
orthostatic hypotension, 361, 1183
osmolality, 1074
osmosis, 1073–1074
osmotic pressure, 1074
ossicles, 537
osteoporosis, 184, 360, 983, 1180
ostomies, 864–865
 anatomic location, 864
 construction of stoma, 864–865
 disposable ostomy appliances, 882–886
 stoma assessment, 882–883
 types, 864
 and types of injuries, 864
ostomy appliances, disposable, 882–886
 assessment focus, 883
 changing, procedure for, 882–886
 equipment, 883
 evaluation focus, 883–886
 intervention, 883–886
 purposes, 883
otic instillations
 assessment focus, 656
 equipment, 656
 evaluation focus, 657
 intervention, 657
 purposes, 656
otoscope, 537
Ottawa Charter for Health Promotion, 140, 147, 148, 274
outcome documentation, 450
outcome evaluation, of quality of care, 438
outpatients, 251
outputs, 68
outreach programs, 268
overhydration, 1084
overinvolvement, 167
overlay mattress, 951
overt data. *See* objective data
over-the-counter (OTC) drugs, 367
owned faith, 319
oxygen, 1019
oxygen analyzer, 1052
oxygenation assessment
 angiography, 1036
 blood tests, 1035
 cardiac monitoring, 1033–1034
 echocardiography, 1037
 electrocardiography, 1035
 hemodynamic studies, 1037
 laryngoscopy, 1037
 lung scan, 1036
 nursing history, 1030–1031
 physical assessment, 1032
 pulmonary function tests, 1035–1036
 pulse oximetry, 1032–1033
 sputum specimens, 1034
 x-ray examination, 1036
oxygenation care evaluation, 1065
oxygenation care plan, 1037–1038
oxygenation diagnoses, 1037
oxygenation interventions
 deep breathing and coughing, 1043
 percussion, 1045–1046
 postural drainage, 1046–1047
 promoting healthy breathing, 1043
 promoting healthy heart, 1043
 vibration, 1046
oxygen delivery systems, 1048
oxygen therapy, 1047–1070
 chronic obstructive pulmonary disease, for clients with, 1047, 1048
 safety precautions, 1047
oxyhemogloblin, 1022

P

pace, walking, 1189
pace and intonation, in verbal communication, 485
pain
 cultural responses, 238
 diagnostic label, 411, 416
 nursing priority for, 421
 sensory assessment, 593
 and sexual function, 186
pain management
 accupuncture, 191
 in home care, 287
palates, 548
palliative care, 248, 280
pallor, 520
palmar grasp reflex, 326, 595
Palmer, D.D., 176
palpation, 515–517, 556–557
palpebral conjunctiva, 531
Panel for the Prediction and Prevention of Pressure Ulcers in Adults, 936
Papanicolaou (Pap) test, 351, 596, 598

papule, 521
paradigm, 46
paradoxical-consolidative stage, in spiritual development, 318, 354
paradoxical sleep, 1152
parallax, 734
paralysis, and communication, 502
paramedical technologists, 255
parasites
 and infections, 745
 inspection for, 596
parasomnias, 1158–1159
parenteral administration, 617
 ampules, preparing medications from, 635
 equipment, 630–633
 intramuscular injections, 642–647
 intravenous medications, 647–653
 needles, 632–633
 needle-stick injuries, preventing, 633
 preparation of medication, 633–637
 syringes, 630–632
 vials, preparing medications from, 635–637
parenteral nutrition, 1012–1014
parenting
 and cultural values, 234
 mother-infant interaction, 326
 preschool children, 334
 preschoolers, 334
paresthesia, 590
parish nursing, 218, 269
parliament. *See* legislative authority
paronychia, 526
Parse, R.R., 164, 373
Parsons, T., 135
partial bath, 813
partially complete proteins, 974
partial pressure, 1022
partners-in-practice system, 261
passive immunity, 749
pastes, dermatologic preparations, 654
pastors, 256
Patanjali, 171
patch, 521
patellar reflex, 589
paternalism, 94
pathogenicity, 744
pathologic fractures, 360
patient, 8
patient-focused care, 259
Patient Position Monitor, 790–793
Paul, R., 376, 379
Pavlov, I., 669
peak plasma level, 612, 613
Peck, Robert, 312–314, 353, 361
pedagogy, 669
pedal pulse site, 720
pediculosis, 836
pediculosis (lice), 339
pedophilia, 188
peer groups, 337, 341
 See also cliques, adolescent
pelvic exercises, 912
pelvic musculature, 598
Pender, N.J., 138, 149
 health promotion model, 151–153
Peplau, H.E., 51
perception
 defined, 488
 values and, 488
perceptor, 698
percussion, 517, 1045–1046
percutaneous endoscopic gastrostomy (PEG), 1005
percutaneous endoscopic jejunostomy (PEJ), 1005
perfusion, 573, 574
perfusion scan (Q scan), 1036
perineal-genital care, 817–819
 assessment focus, 818
 equipment, 818
 intervention, 818–819
 for men, 818, 819
 preparing the client, 817
 purposes, 818
 for women, 818, 819
periodic limb movement, 1158
periodontal disease, 825–826
periorbital edema, 528
peripherally inserted central venous catheter, 1104
peripheral pulse assessment, 722–724
 assessment focus, 722
 equipment, 722
 evaluation focus, 724
 home care considerations, 724
 intervention, 723–724
 purposes, 722
peripheral pulses, 573, 719
peripheral vascular resistance (PVR), 1025
peripheral vascular systems, assessment of, 573–575
peripheral veins, 574
peristalsis, 858
perseverance, and critical thinking, 377
persistent quality improvement (PQI). *See* quality of care, quality improvement
person. *See* clients
personal appearance, in nonverbal communication, 486
personal digital assistants (PDAs), 473
personal distance, 488
personal health practices, 143, 152
 health behaviour change, 153
 health-promoting behaviours, 64
 perceived benefits of health-promoting behaviours and, 153
 personal definition of health and, 153
 primary motivational mechanisms, 151–153
personality, 311–312
 and sensory stimulation, 1136
 See also psychosocial development theories
personal meaning, in human becoming theory, 53
personal preferences, and nutrition, 978–979
personal space, and communication, 488
personal values, 92
 and physical activity, 1181
Pert, C.B., 166
pet care, 287
Pew Health Professions Commission, 267, 272
pH, 1080
phagocytes, 748
phagocytosis, 941
phallic stage, of development, 333
pharmacist, 609
pharmacists, 255
pharmaco-anthropology, 614
pharmacodynamics, 613
pharmacokinetics, 613–614
pharmacology, 609
pharmacopoeia, 609
pharmacy, 609
pharmacy assistants, 255
phenomenology, 38, 48
phenylketonuria (PKU), screening for, 329
philosophy
 areas of inquiry, 46
 of life, 348
 in nursing, 47–48
 philosophical thought, 46
 as scientific discipline, 46
 See also ethical theories
philosophy, in nursing
 areas of inquiry, 48–49
 role of, 47
phosphate, 1079, 1086–1087
phospholipids, 975
physical activity, 1178
 personal values and attitudes and, 1181
physical comfort needs, 482
physical examination. *See* physical health assessment
physical health assessment, 351, 356
 abdomen, 575–583
 appearance, 518–519
 behaviour, 519
 breasts and axillae, 554–558
 cardiovascular system, 567–573
 cephalocaudal (head-to-toe) approach, 399, 510
 client, preparing the, 511
 ears and hearing, 537–542
 environment, preparing the, 511
 eyes and vision, 528–536
 female genitals and inguinal lymph nodes, 386–599
 general survey, 518–606
 head, 527–528
 height and weight, 519, 520
 instrumentation, 514–515
 integument, 520–527
 male genitals and inguinal area, 599–603
 mental status, 519, 586–587
 mouth and oropharynx, 544–549
 musculoskeletal system, 583–585
 neck, 549–553
 neurologic system, 586–595
 nose and sinuses, 542–544
 peripheral vascular system, 573–575
 positioning, 511–513, 603
 purposes, 398, 510
 rectum, anus, and prostate, 603–605
 screening examinations, 399
 sequence of assessessment, 510
 in specific client situations, 510–511
 thorax and lungs, 558–567
 vital signs, 519

physical health assessment methods, 514–518
inspection, 515
palpation, 515–517
percussion, 517
physical medicine, 165
physician-initiated treatment. *See* medical orders
physicians
specialists, 254
physiologic needs, 65
physiologic response mode, 53
physiotherapists (PTs), 255
Piaget, Jean, 315, 327, 331, 334, 337, 349, 669
Picot, J., 472
PIE charting model, 448
Pilch, J.J., 208
pilot study, 38
pinna (auricle), 537, 538
piston bulb syringe, 662
pitch, of auscultated sound, 518
pitting edema, 1084
pivoting, 1198
placenta, 323
planning
care plans, 416–420, 448
client records and, 445
collaboration in, 415
for effective communication, 503
goals/desired outcomes, 422–425, 438
health-promotion plans, 157–158
initial planning, 415
integration of nursing functions, 417
interventions and activities, 425–431
nature of, 415
nursing interventions and activities, 425–427
ongoing planning, 416
priorities, 420
sexual health goals, 193–194
standardized approaches to, 417–419
See also discharge planning
planning errors, 121
avoidance of, 413–414
plantar (Babinski) reflex, 326, 589–590, 595
plantar warts, 822
plaque, 521, 826
plasma, 1072
play
infants, 329
preschoolers, 336
school-age children, 339
tddlers, 332
pleadings, 114
pleximeter, 517
plexor, 517
PLISSIT model, 198–201
intensive therapy, 201
limited information, 199–200
permission giving, 199
specific suggestions, 200
point of maximal impulse (PMI), 568, 570
policy, 417
See also health policy
Polit, D.F., 36, 37
polydipsia, 896
polypnea. *See* tachypnea
polysaccharides, 973
polysomnogram (PSG), 1152
polysomnography, 1161
polyunsaturated fats, 974
popliteal pulse site, 720
population, 38
See also demography
population health
strategies, 141–142
portability, Canada Health Act, 10, 246
positioning
physical health assessment, 511–513, 603
thorax and lungs assessment, 561
and wound healing, 950, 951
positioning clients, 1198–1209
client with limited strength of upper extremeties, 1205
dorsal recumbent position, 1201–1202
Fowler's position, 1200–1201
lateral position, 1202–1203
by logrolling, 1207
moving a client up in bed, 1205
moving and turning clients in bed, 1203–1209
orthopneic position, 1201–1202
prone position, 1201–1203
Sim's position, 1202–1204
sitting position, moving a client to a, 1208–1209
support devices for, 1200
turning a client to a lateral or prone position, 1206
turn sheet, using, 1207
See also transferring clients
positive feedback, 61
positive resolution, indicators of, 314
postconventional level, of moral development, 317, 342, 349
posterior axillary line, 558
posterior tibial pulse site, 720
postformal operations thinkers, 349
postural drainage, 1046–1047
postural tonus, 1171
posture, 491
in meditation, 172
"of involvement," 491
in relaxation techniques, 169
in yoga, 171
posture and gait, 487
Post-White, J., 208
potassium, 1079, 1085
"Potential Complication" (PC), diagnostic label, 414–415
Potential for Enhanced Spiritual Well Being, diagnostic label, 213
Poupart's ligament (inguinal ligaments), 575
poverty
and access to health-care services, 257
female single-parent families, 76
and health problems, 148
in rural regions, 294
power, 695
power pudding, 877
pranayama, 171
pratyahara, 171
prayer, 172
forms of, 211
intecessory prayer, 175
nursing assistance with, 216
purpose of, 211
precoital stimulation, 187
preconceptual phase, in cognitive development, 316, 331
precontemplation state, in behavioural change, 153
preconventional level, of moral development, 317, 331, 364
precordium, 568, 570
preformed antibodies, 1120
pregnancy
adolescenct pregnancy, 342
breasts during, 558
health promotion during, 323–324
periodontal disease, 825
and sexual desire, 187
sexual intercourse during, 184
trimesters, 323
prejudice, 232
preload, 1024
premature closure, 404
premature ejaculation, 190
prenatal development
duration of, 323
elimination, 323
embryonic phase, 323
fetal circulation, 323
fetal phase, 323
nutrition and fluids, 323
rest and activity of fetus, 323
temperature maintenance and, 324
preparation stage, in behavioural change, 153
prepubertal changes, 336
presbycusis, 358, 360
presbyopia, 358, 528
preschoolers
cognitive development, 334
developmental assessment guidelines, 335
health examinations, 336
health problems, 335
health promotion, 335–336
moral development, 334
nutrition, 982
oral health, 829
physical development, 331–333
psychosocial development, 333–334
spiritual development, 335
urinary elimination, 894
Prescott, P.A., 271
prescriptions, 609
common abbreviations in, 617–618
parts of, 619
policy of agency, 617
types of, 617
See also drug orders
presence, personal, 167, 214
pressure ulcers
etiology of, 936
prevalence of, 936
risk assessment tools, 937–941
risk factors, 937
stages of formation, 937
treatment of, 952–953

prevention, of illness
    client education, 668
    Epp Report, 141
    health-care service, 248
    levels of, 149–150
    prevention, concept of, 149
    See also health promotion
prevention orders, 428
priests, 256
primary care, 10, 266
    characteristics of, 267
primary health care, 10, 27
    characteristics of, 267
    defined, 10, 265
    origins of, 265, 266
    population-focused services, 266
    principles of, 265
    promotion of health, 10–11
    role of nurses in, 10
    scope of, 10
primary health promotion, 248
primary hypertension, 732
primary nursing, 10, 261
primary prevention, 149, 150
primary sexual characteristics, 340
primary skin lesions, 521–522
primary sleep disorders, 1157
primary sources, 392
principled reasoning, 349
priority setting
    assigning priorities, 416–420
    defined, 420
    factors in, 390–420
    Maslow's hierarchy of needs and, 420
privacy
    defined, 470
    invasion of, 122
    during physical health assessment, 514, 596, 603
    See also confidentiality
private duty nurses, 73
private facts, public disclosure of, 122
private law. *See* civil (private) law
PRN adapters, 651
prn order, 617
probability, 39
problem-focused assessment, 391
problem list, 447
problem-oriented medical record, 446–448
problem solving, 32
    approaches, 381
    defined, 381
    intuition, 381
    modified scientific method, 381
    nursing process, 381
    research process, 381
    trial and error, 381
    See also critical thinking
procedures, 417
process, defined, 388
process evaluation, of quality of care, 438
process imagery, 170
process recording, 504–506
Procheska, J., 153
profession
    criteria of, 15–16
    defined, 15
    professsional organizations, 16
    socialization, 16–17
profession, nursing
    career roles, 13–15
    certification, 27, 111
    conduct, professional, 111
    credentialling, 110
    history, 3–7
    knowledge-based practice, 112
    nursing shortage, 28
    professional designations, 24
    professional organizations, 18–20
    and provincial law, 24, 28, 110, 111
    registration and licensure, 24, 110–111
    self-regulation, 11–12, 15, 110
    service orientation, 16
    socialization, professional, 16–17
    standards and scope of practice, 12, 18, 112
    values, internalization of, 17, 92
    women and, 260
    women's movement and, 18
professional health-care system, 230
professional values, 17, 92
progressive relaxation, 169
progress notes (POR)
    DAR (data, action and response), 448
    formats, 455
    narrative recording, 446
    in PIE charting model, 448
    SOAP data, 448
proliferative phase, of wound healing, 941–942
prologation of life, 238
promotion of health, 10–11
prompted voiding, 911
prone position, 1201–1203
proprioception, 590
proprioceptors, 590
prosocial behaviour, 334
prostate cancer, 368, 600
prostate gland, assessing, 605
protein-calorie malnutrition, 987, 994
prothesis, 844–845
protocol order, 617
protocols, 417
provider-driven model, 268
proxemics, 488
    See also personal space, and communication
psychological dependency, on drugs, 612
psychological factors, and nutrition, 980
psychologic and social systems, 68
psychologic homeostasis, 61–62
psychomotor domain, 670
psychosexual development, 310
psychosocial development
    of infants, 326
    of preschoolers, 333–334
    of school-age children, 337, 338
    of toddlers, 330–331
psychosocial development theories
    of Erikson, 312
    of Freud, 312
    of Gould, 314–315
    of Peck, 312–314
psychospiritual comfort, 482, 493
puberty
    physical development, 339, 340
    rites, 185
pubic hair, 835
    and aging, 597
    development of, 596, 599
    growth in men, 600
    growth in women, 596
public administration, Canada Health Act, 10, 246
public distance, 488
public health care, 246
    client education and, 668
    emergence of, 246, 260
    government agencies, 251
    state sponsorship, 260
public law, 113
public participation, of clients, 10
    in implementing nursing actions, 433
    role of nurses, 10
pulling and pushing, mechanics of, 1198
pulmonary angiography, 1036
pulmonary edema, 1030
pulmonary function tests, 1035–1036
pulmonary ventilation, 1021
pulmonic valve, 568
pulp cavity, 825
pulse assessment
    apical pulse, 724–726
    apical-radial pulse, 726–727
    elasticity of arterial wall, 722
    methods of, 721
    peripheral pulse, 722–724
    pulse rhythm, 721
    pulse volume, 722
pulse oximetry, 1032–1033
pulse pressure, 731
pulses, 569
    cardiac output, 719
    and heartbeat, 719
    pulse rate, 719–720, 721
    pulse sites, 720–721
    waves, 719
puncture injuries, avoiding, 633
pureed diet, 998
Purkis, M.E., 49
Purnell, L., 232
purosanguineous exudate, 942
pursed-lip breathing, 1043–1044
purulent exudate, 942
pus, 942
pustule, 522
pyorrhea, 826
pyrogenic bacteria, 942

Q

qualitative research, 31–37
    data analysis, 39
    design, 38
    informatic analysis programs, 475–476
quality, of auscultated sound, 518
quality of care
    audit, 445
    evaluation of, 438–439

nursing audit, 438–439
outcome evaluation, 438
process evaluation, 438
quality-assurance (QA) program, 438
quality improvement, 438
structure evaluation, 22
quantitative research, 35–36
data analysis, 38–39
pilot study, 38
research design, 37–38
quasi-experimental design, 38
questions
closed questions, 395, 396
in critical analysis, 375–376
cultural assessment, 240
heteronomative bias, reducing, 182
illness narrative, eliciting, 84
leading questions, 396
medical narrative, eliciting, 84
neutral questions, 396
open-ended questions, 395, 396
reflective questions, 83
sexual health, 192
spiritual matters, asking about, 213
See also communication

R

rabbis, 256
rabies, 296
race
and blood pressure, 732
as risk factor, 64
race, defined, 229
Rachlis, M., 266
racism, 233
radial pulse site, 720, 721
radiation, 761
radiology technologists, 255
Rahe, R.H., 157
rales (crepitations), 561
Ramadan, 210
range, 38, 39
range of movement, 1172
rapport building, 395, 397
rationale, 419, 436
rationality, in critical thinking, 30
Raven, B., 695
reaction time, and aging, 360
reactive hyperemia, 936
readability assessment, 677–678
readiness to learn, 676–677
rebound effect, 657
receiver, of message, 485
recent memory, 364, 587
receptive aphasia. *See* sensory (receptive) aphasia
reciprocity, in family support, 86
reconstitution, 633
recording, 444
See also documentation, documenting
recordkeeping tools
clinical graphic record, 453–454
daily care record, 455–456
flowsheets, 453
informatics, 469–470
Kardexes®, 453
medication record, 453
progress notes, 455
24-hour balance record, 453
rectal examination, 603–605
rectal instillations, 660
rectal prolapse, 604
rectal temperature, 718
rectocele, 598
rectum, 858
referrals, 274, 455
reflective questions, 83
reflexes
achilles reflex, 589
assessment, 589–590
biceps reflex, 589
brachioradialis reflex, 589
deep tendon reflex (DTR), 589
infant reflexes, 325, 326, 595
motor function assessment, 595
patellar reflex, 589
plantar (Babinski) reflex, 589–590
triceps reflex, 589
reflexology, 168
reflux, 893, 1186
refractory period, 190
refugees, 223
regeneration, 749
regional health authority (RHA), 300
registered dietitians (RDs). *See* dietitians
Registered Nurses Association of British Columbia, 134
registered nursing assistant (RNA), 24
See also licensed practical nurse
registered psychiatric nurse (RPN), 24
registration, 110–111
regression, 330
regulatory law. *See* administrative law
regurgitation, 981
rehabilitation, 248
rehabilitation centres, 253
Reiki, 175
related factors, 406, 414
relational ethics theories, 94–95
relational practice, 489–490
relational stance, 81
relationship-oriented leader, 694
relaxation, progressive, 169
relief, from discomfort, 482
religion
affiliation, 226
and births, 22–212
in Canadian life, 217
and death, 212, 238
defined, 207
and diet, 21–22, 238
and dress, 212
holy days, 210
and nutrition, 979
prayer, 211
religious development, 207–208
ritual feasting and fasting, 210
sacred symbols, 211
sacred writings, 210–211
and sexuality, 185
remission, 139
remote memory, 587
REM (rapid eye movement) sleep, 1152–1153
renal calculi, 1186
renal system
and homeostatic regulation, 61
renal ultrasonography, 904
renin-angiotensin-aldosterone system, 1077
reports
change-of-shift report, 462–463
defined, 444
telephone orders, 463–464
telephone report, 463
repression, 334
research
dissemination of, 476
grants, 476
informatics applications in, 475–476
research, nursing
application, practice, and theory, 33
approaches, 32, 35–37
critique of, 40–41
data collection, 34, 38
development of research activity, 32–33
evidence, 34
funding, 33–35
nursing theories in, 50
published sources, 40
purposes of theories in, 50
qualitative approach, 31–37
quantitative approach, 35–36
research, defined, 36
research process, 36–39
rights of human subjects, 41–42
role of nurses, 32
researchability, of research problem, 37
research articles, 42
research-based nursing practice, 32, 34, 40, 388
research consumer, 13
research design, 37–38, 475
Research Ethics Board (REB), 41
research process, 36–39
data analysis, 38–39
hypothesis, 37
implication of findings, 39
interpretation of findings, 39
literature review, 37
pilot study, 38
population, sample, setting, 38
purpose, defining, 37
research design, 37–38
research problem, 37
sharing the results, 39, 40
vs. modified scientific method, 381
reservoirs, of infection, 746–747
resident flora, 744
residual urine, 900
resistive behaviours, 494
resolution of conflicts, in cognitive development, 312
resolution phase
in interpersonal relations model (Peplau), 51
resonance (sound), 517
respect
in collaboration, 272
conveying respect, 398
in interpersonal relationships, 490
right of client, 250

respirations
  abdominal breathing, 1026
  altered breathing patterns and sounds, 729, 1029
  body position and, 730
  breathing, 727
  components of, 1019
  defined, 727
  depth of, 729
  homeostatic regulation, 61
  mechanics and regulation of breathing, 727–728
  respiratory rate, 728–729
respirations assessment, 728–731
  assessment focus, 730
  equipment, 730
  evaluation focus, 731
  home care considerations, 731
  intervention, 730–731
  purposes, 730
respiratory acidosis, 1088–1089
respiratory alkalosis, 1089
respiratory alterations, 1028–1029
  altered breathing patterns, 1029
  hypoxia, 1028
  obstructed airway, 1029
respiratory arrest, 1065
respiratory distress syndrome, 1021
respiratory excursion, 562
respiratory inhalation, 660–661
respiratory movement, decreased, 1184
respiratory problems
  immobility and, 1184–1185
  in rural regions, 294
respiratory process
  alveolar gas exchange, 1021–1022
  pulmonary ventilation, 1021
  transport of respiratory gasses, 1022
respiratory quality (character), 730
respiratory rhythm (pattern), 730
respiratory secretions, pooling of, 1184–1185
respiratory system
  exercise and, 1179
  function of, 1019
  regulation of, 1022–1023
  respiratory centre, 728, 1021
  structure of, 1019–1020
respiratory technologists (RTs), 255
respite care, 87
respondent superior, 115, 126
response, in communication process, 485
responsibilities
  of citizenship, 115
  and managers, 697
rest
  function of, 1151
resting energy expenditure (REE), 976
resting tremor, 583
restoring health
  client education for, 668
  nursing activities in, 8
restraints
  alternatives to, 797
  application of, 799–800
  chemical restraints, 797
  kinds of, 798–799
  legal implications, 797–798
  purpose of, 797
  safety considerations, 797
  selection of, 798
retarded ejaculation, 190
retention catheter, 915, 916
reticular activiting system (RAS), 1133
retirement
  financial circumstances, 362
  lifestyle, 361–362
  living arrangements, 363
  and relocation, 363
retirement centres, 253
retrograde pyelography (IVP), 904
return-flow enemas, 877, 880
review of systems. *See* screening examinations
revision, of care plan, 448
reward power, 695
rhesus factor (Rh) factor, 1120
rhythmicity phase, in human becoming theory, 53
ribs, 560, 606
right lower lobe (lung), 560
right middle lobe (lung), 560
rights
  of citizenship, 115, 116
  confidentiality, 42, 112
  constitutional rights, 112
  of health-care consumers, 248–250
  human rights, 101
  of human subjects, in research, 41–42
  patient's bill of rights, 112
  See also consent
rights-based theories, 93
right upper lobe (lung), 560
Rinne test, 541
risk assessment
  health risk appraisal, 154–156
  individual health, 64
  risk nursing diagnosis, 406
risk factors, 8, 406
risk for impaired skin integrity, 416
risk for ineffective airway clearance, 416
risk for infection, 406
risk for interrupted family processes, 412, 421
risk management
  incident report, 125
RN (registered nurse), 11–141, 24
  licensure, 24, 111
  research role, 32
  role of, 254
Roach, Simone, 51, 55
Rodney, P., 103
Rogers, Carl, 377, 670
Rogers, E., 700
Rogers, Martha, 164
role function response mode, 53
role performance health model, 135
Romanow, Roy, 258
Romberg Test, 591
ROM exercises, 1214–1216
  active-assistive exercises, 1215
  active exercises, 1214
  passive exercises, 1214–1215
Rondeau, K.V., 490
rooting reflex, 326, 595
Rosenstock I.M., 137
Rosh Hashanah, 210
Roy, Callista, 51, 52, 53, 135, 399
rubber bulb syringe, 662
rule of civil procedures, 113
rural, remote, and northern nursing practice
  characterics of, 300, 301
  education for, 301
  multiple practice settings and roles in, 300
  recruitment and retention, problems of, 301
rural health issues
  agricultural injuries, 296
  cancer, 295
  chemicals, 295
  eyesight, loss of, 298
  health-care delivery, 253, 299–300
  hearing loss, 297
  mental health, 298
  motor vehicle collisions, 297, 299
  primary industry injuries, 296
  regionalization of administration and services, 300
  respiratory problems, 294
  rural primary-care hospitals, 253
  safe play areas, 296
  shortage of health professionals, 257
  stress, 298–299
  substance abuse, 299
  suicide, 299
  water safety, 295
  zoonoses, 296
rural regions
  demography, 293, 294
  industries, 294
  occupations, 294
  population decline, 292, 293
  problem of definition, 292
  rural/northern distinction, 292, 293
  Statistics Canada definition, 292
Ryan, Y., 269
RYB colour code, 952–953

S

sacred symbols, 207
sacred writings, 210–211
sadomasochistic bondage, 188
safety
  ability to communicate and, 784
  age and development and, 783–784
  cognitive awareness and, 784
  emotional state and, 784
  environmental factors and, 784
  eye safety, 842
  factors affecting, 783–784
  lifestyle and, 783
  mobility and health status and, 784
  safety awareness and, 784
  sensory-perceptual alterations and, 784
  See also accident prevention
safety and security needs, 65
safety belt. *See* belt restraint
safety measures and practices
  for adolescents, 344, 788
  for infants, 329, 787

for middle-aged adults, 356, 788
for older adults, 367, 788
for preschoolers, 336, 787
for school-age children, 339, 787
for toddlers, 332, 787
for young adults, 351, 788
safety risk assessment
diagnosis, 785–786
home hazard appraisal, 785
nursing history and physical examination, 785
tools for, 785
Saint Louis University School of Nursing and Allied Health Professions, 405
St. John's wort, 177
St. Thomas's School, 25
saliva, defensive function of, 748
salivary glands, 548
Salsberry, P., 48
samadhi, 171
sample, 38
sanguineous (hemorrhagic) exudate, 942
sanitation, in nursing practice, 51
SAS (Statistical Analysis System), 476
saturated fatty acids, 974
Saunders, Craig, 253
scabies, 339, 836
scalds and burns, 789–790
scapular lines, 558
Scharff, J.E., 300
Scholarly Inquiry for Nursing Practice, 40
school-age children
cognitive development, 337
defecation, 860
developmental assessment guidelines, 338
health examinations, 339
health promotion, 339
moral development, 338
nutrition, 982
oral health, 829–855
physical development, 336–337
psychosocial development, 337, 338
spiritual development, 338
urinary elimination, 894
schools
health services, 269
school health-promotion programs, 151
science and technology
and health-care delivery, 256, 471–472
in home care, 287
and nursing practice, 17–18
scientific health belief, 233
scientific inquiry, 47, 49
scientific method, 47
See also research process
screening examinations, 399
Scudder, J., 48
scultetus binders, 963–964
sebaceous cysts, 528
sebaceous glands, 340
seborrheic keratosis, 524
sebum, 340, 807
secondary hypertension, 732
secondary prevention, 149, 150
secondary sexual characteristics, 340
secondary skin lesions, 521, 523
secondary sleep disorders, 1157
secondary sources, 392
Second World War, 260
security, of data, 470
self-actualization, 65, 66, 152
self-assessment, and critical thinking, 383
self-awareness/growth groups, 501
self-care, 148, 154
skin problems, 817–820
self-concept
of adolescents, 341
of preschoolers, 333
of school-age children, 331–337
of toddlers, 330
self-concept response mode, 53
self-determination, right to, 42, 250
See also autonomy
self-efficacy, perceived
and health-promoting behaviours, 153
self-esteem
development of, 330, 337, 341
older persons, 363
self-esteem disturbances, 214
self-esteem needs, 65
self-examination
breast examination, 196–198, 351, 356
testicular examination, 200, 351, 356, 600
self-healing methods, for nurses, 167
self-help bed bath, 813
self-help groups. *See* mutual support and self-help groups
self-identity
of client, 60
development of, 340
self-image, 519
self-managed care model. *See* client-centred model
self-regulation, homostatic mechanism, 61
self-talk, 484
Selye, Hans, 164
semicircular canals, 537
sender, of message, 484
senile lentigines, 528
sensorimotor phase, in cognitive development, 316, 327
sensorineural hearing loss, 537
sensory deficits
and behaviour, 1134–1135
and communication, 501–502
sensory deprivation, 1134
sensory function assessment, 590–595
equipment for, 590
light touch sensation, 593–594
pain sensation, 593
position (kinesthetic) sensation, 594
tactile discrimination, 594–595
temperature sensation, 594
sensory memory, 364
sensory overload, 1134
sensory perception
arousal mechanism, 1133–1134
sensory alterations, 1133–1135
sensory process, 1133
sensory-perceptual assessment
at-risk clients, 1137
client environment, 1137–1138
mental status, 1137
nursing history, 1136
physical examination, 1137
social support network, 1138
sensory-perceptual care plan, 1139–1140, 1143–1144
sensory-perceptual diagnoses
diagnostic labels, 1138
sensory problems as etiology, 1139
sensory-perceptual nursing interventions
client safety, ensuring, 1143–1145
communication, effective, 1143
confused client, 1145–1146
healthy sensory functioning, promoting, 1140–1141
promoting use of other senses, 1143
sensory aids, 1142
sensory deprivation, preventing, 1141–1142
sensory overload, preventing, 1140–1141
unconscious client, 1146–1147
sensory-perceptual outcome evaluation, 1146–1147
sensory reception, 1133
sensory (receptive) aphasia, 586
sensory stimulation, for infants, 329
separation anxiety, 330–331
sepsis, 745
septicemia, 745
sequential compression/pneumatic pressure devices, 1063–1065
serosanguineous exudate, 942
serous exudate, 942
serum electrolytes, 1096
serum osmolality, 1097
service management model, 268
sex education
adolescents and, 183, 194
anatomy and physiologic changes, 194
breast health, 196–198
breast self-examination, 196–198
common sexual misconceptions, 194–195
contraception, 197
menstruation, 183
parents and, 194
STI prevention, 195–196
testicular self-examination, 200
unplanned pregnancies, prevention of, 195–197
sex play, 187
sexual arousal
erotic stimuli, 187
hormonal changes and, 187
libido, 187
physical stimulation, 187–188
physiologic changes, 188–190
sexual counselling
acknowledging client's needs and concerns, 199
altered sexual function, 198–201
intensive therapy, 201
in nursing practice, 201
sharing information, 199–200
specific suggestions, offering, 200
sexual dysfunctions
female dysfunctions, 191

male dysfunctions, 188–190
medications, effects of, 186–187, 191–192
sexual expression
alternative forms of, 188
biological changes and, 184
heterosexual intercourse, 188
heterosexual sex play, 187–188
masturbation, 187
successful intimate relationships, 184
sexual health
clients at risk, identifying, 193–194
diagnosis, 193
dysfunctions, 188–191
nomative attitudes and, 182
nonjudgemental nursing approach, 182
in nursing assessments, 192
nursing interventions, 194
organizational culture and, 200
physical examination, 192–193
planning goals, 193–194
sexual history, assessing, 192
sexuality
adolescence, 183–184, 341
adulthood, 184
childhood, 183
concept of, 181
culture and, 185
developmental level and, 183–184
gender, concept of, 181
in health and illness situations, 186–187
personal ethics and, 185–186
psychosexual development, 310
sex, concepts of, 181
sexual characteristics, 339, 340
sexual desire, 187
sexual identification, 341
sexual orientation, 181–182
sexually transmitted infections (STIs)
clinically signs of, 196
nursing functions, 351
prevention of, 195–196
and sexual function, 186
shaken baby syndrome (SBS), 327
Shamian, Judith, 695, 795, 796
shampooing, hair, 839–840
assessment focus, 839
equipment, 839
evaluation focus, 840
intervention, 840
lifespan consideration, 840
purposes, 839
shared leadership, 695
shaving, facial hair, 841
shearing force, 936
S1 (heart sound), 568
S2 (heart sound), 568
Sheehy, Gail, 353
shiatsu, 169
shift work, and sleep, 1156
short-term memory, 364
shower, 814, 816–817
side effect, 611
side rails, 848
Sigma Theta Tau, 19
signature, 460
significance, of research problem, 37
signs. *See* objective data
Sikhism, 211
Simmons, H., 48
simplicity, in verbal communication, 485
Sim's position, 513, 603, 1203–1204
single-dose vial, 634
single order, 617
single-parent families, 76, 258
sinus infections, 658
situational leadership, 694
Skene's (paraurethral) glands, 597, 598
skepticism, 374
skill acquisition
five-stage model (Brenner), 16
general model (Dreyfus), 16
skin
and aging, 808
assessment, 523–525
children, 524
colour, 520, 522–523
defensive function of, 748
dermatologic applications, 654
effect of incontinence on, 912–913
focus of examination, 522
function of, 807, 935
lesions, 521–523, 524
odours, 520, 808, 812
older adults, 524–525
temperature, 516, 524
skin care
assessment interview, 809–810
common agents used, 812–813
common problems, 808–809
data clusters of skin problem, 810
excessive bathing, 812
physical assessment, 808–809
planning, 807
principles of, 811–812
self-care deficits, 808–809, 810
self-care practices, assessment of, 808
stoma and, 882–883
and wound healing, 948–949
skin integrity
advanced age and, 937–971
assessment of, 943
common pressure sites, 944
decreased mental status and, 937
decreased sensation and, 937
excessive body heat and, 937
fecal and urinary incontinence and, 937
friction and, 936
hard support surfaces and, 937
incorrect positioning and, 937
physical assessment, 943
poor lifting techniques and, 937
skin maceration, 937
Skinner, B.F., 610, 669
skin trauma, avoiding, 950–951
skull and face, assessment of, 527–528
sleep
adolescents, 1155
circadian rhythms, 1151
common disorders, 1157–1159
factors affecting, 1155–1157
fetus, 323
function of, 1153
and health promotion, 149
infants, 329, 1153–1154
middle-age adults, 1155
NREM sleep, 1152
older adults, 1155
physiology of, 1151
preschoolers, 336, 1155
REM sleep, 1152–1153
sleep cycles, 1153
sleep-wake schedule and, 1156
stages of, 1152–1153
toddlers, 332, 1155
young adults, 1155
sleep apnea, 1158
sleep assessment
assessment interview, 1160
diagnoses, 1161–1162
diagnostic studies, 1161
physical examination, 1159–1161
sleep and rest history, 1159
sleep diary, 1159
sleep care evaluation, 1167
sleep care interventions, 1162–1167
back massages, 1165–1166
bedtime rituals, supporting, 1162
comfort and relaxation, promoting, 1165
rest and sleep, promoting, 1164
restful environment, creating, 1162–1165
sleep medications, 1165–1167
sleep care plan, 1162–1164
sleep deprivation, 1158–1159
sleep pattern disturbance, 214
sleeptalking, 1159
small calorie, 976
smell (sense)
of infants, 325
toddlers, 330
Smith, J.A., 133, 135
Smith, M., 48
SMOG index, 677, 678
smoking, 350
and sleep, 1157
Smuts, Jan, 61, 164
Snellen eye charts, 529
SOAP. *See* progress notes
social comfort needs, 482
social construction, of gender, 181
social distance, 488
socialization
adolescents, 340–341
and moral development, 92
in nursing, 16–17
shool-age children, 337
social learning theory, 137
social programs
emergence of, 246
rising costs, 246
universal programs, 246
Social Sciences and Humanities Research Council (SSHRC), 35, 41
social support networks, 142, 158, 167
social workers, 255–256
sociocentricity, insight into, 377
sociopsychologic variables, in health belief model, 137
Socrates, 375

Socratic questioning, 375–376
sodium, 1079, 1084–1085
soixante-neuf, 188
solutes, 1074
solvent, 1074
somnambulism, 1159
source-oriented record, 446
sources of data
  client, 392
  client records, 393–394
  health-care professionals, 394
  literature, 394
  support people, 392–393
Sparbel, K.J.H., 272
spasticity, 584
specific gravity of urine, 903
speech development
  in infants, 326
  in preschoolers, 334
sphenoid sinus, 658
sphygmomanometers, 733–735
spinal cord injury
  and sexual function, 186
spiral reverse turns, 962
spiral turns, 961–962
spiritual caring
  care plan, sample, 215
  evaluation of, 218
  planning phase, 214
  prayer, assising with, 216
  providing "presence," 214
  religious support, 214, 216
  spiritual counselling referrals, 217
  spiritual support, 214–217, 215, 216
spiritual development
  of toddlers, 331
  of preschoolers, 335
  of school-age children, 338
  of adolescents, 342–343
  Fowler's theory of, 318
  of preschoolers, 335
  of school-age children, 338
  Westerhoff's theory of, 318–319
spiritual distress, 416
  assessment data clusters, 214
  defined, 210
  as diagnostic label, 213
  as etiology, 213–214
  manifestations of, 210
  nursing assessment, 215
  nursing interventions, 215, 217
spiritual health
  characteristics of, 207
  clinical assessment, 213
  defined, 208
  spiritual assessment, 213
  spiritual wellness, 22
spirituality
  characteristics of, 207–208
  defined, 207
  diety, relationship with, 207
  faith and, 208
  and hope, 208
  nature, relationship with, 207
  others, relationship with, 207
  and religion, 207–208
  self-relationship with, 207
  spiritual development, 208
  See also faith; human spirit; religion
sports injuries. *See* bike or sports injuries
SPSS (Statistical Package for the Social Sciences), 476
sputum specimens, 1034
Staggers, N.T., 468
standard
  defined, 409
  diagnostic data, interpreting, 410
standard deviation, 38, 39
standardized care plans, 417
standardized client outcomes, 388–389
standard of care, 114, 417
standing order, 417, 617
starches, 973
stare decisis, 109
Starzomski, R., 103
statement of claim, 113
statement of defence, 114
Statistics Canada, 292
stat order, 617
statutory laws, 110
steam. *See* moist heat
stepping reflex, 326
stereognosis, 336, 590, 595
stereotyping, 232
sterile field
  commercially prepared package, opening, 772
  drapes, establishing a sterile field with, 772
  establishing and maintaining, 768–774
  home care, 770–774
  wrapped package on a surface, opening, 771
  wrapped package while holding it, opening, 771–775
  wrapped supplies, adding, 772–774
sterile gloves, 770–775
sterile gowns, 770–777
sterile technique, 768
sterilization, 760–761
sternocleidmastoid muscle, 549, 551
sternum, 560
sterols, 975
stethoscope, 518
  See also Doppler ultrasound stethoscope (DUS)
stimulation needs, 66
stoma. *See* ostomies
stool, 857
  See also feces
strabismus, 331, 534
Strader, M., 374, 375, 381, 382
straight catheter, 915
strapes, 537
strength-oriented diagnoses. *See* Wellness nursing diagnoses
stress
  and blood pressure, 732
  and body temperature, 711
  and cardiovascular system, 1027–1028
  instruments for assessing, 157
  and middle-aged adults, 355, 356
  and pulse rate, 720
  research, 164
  rural residents, 298–299
  and sensory stimulation, 1135
  and sleep, 1156
  and susceptibility to infection, 750
  women and, 142
stress management
  basic skills and techniques of, 167
  for infants, 327
  relaxation techniques and, 169
  See also mind-body therapies
stretchers, 1210
stridor, 1029
structural deficits, and communication, 502
structural evaluation, of quality of care, 22
structural variables, in health belief model, 137
student care plan, 419
subclinical) infection. *See* asymptomatic (subclinical) infection
subcutaneous injections
  assessment of client, 640
  common sites for, 639, 640
  equipment, 640
  evaluate effect, 642
  heparin injection, 641–642
  impaired vision, clients with, 642
  insulin injection, 640
  intervention, 640–641
  needle length, determining, 640
subjective data, 392, 394, 448
Subjective Global Assessment (SGA), 989
sublingual administration, 615–616
substance misuse and chemical dependency, 118–119
  causes, 118
  commonly abused substances, 299
  drug abuse, 612
  drug misues, 612
  indicators of substance dependency, 119
  older adults and, 367
  prevention of, 118
  school-age children and, 339
  workplace policies and programs, 118–119
  young adults and, 350
Sucher, K.P., 232
sucking reflex, 326
suctioning, 1057
  oropharyngeal and nasopharyngeal cavities, 1057–1060
  tracheostomy or endotracheal tube, 1060–1062
sudden infant death syndrome (SIDS), 327
sudorferous (sweat) glands, 808
suffocating or choking, 794
sugars, 973
suicide
  in First Nations communities, 299
  among older men, 367
  prevention of, 350
  among rural populations, 299
  among young adults, 350
sulcular technique, 829
Sunrise Model (Leininger), 230–232
superego, 312
superior margin of the pubic symphysis, 575
supervising, role of nurse in, 432–433

support group
health behaviour change, 157
work-related social support group, 501
suppository, 659, 874
suppuration, 942
suprapubic catheter care, 929
surface body temperature, 709
surfactant, 1021
surgical asepsis, 745, 770
surgical procedures
and sexual function, 186
surgical site infections (SSIs), 942
susceptible host, 747–748
factors of susceptibility, 750–751
sutured wounds, 943
sutures, 324
symptoms. *See* subjective data
synovial joint movement, 1172
synthetic-conventional stage, in spiritual development, 318, 342
syphilis, 195
syringes, 630–632
for irrigation, 662
kinds of, 630–631
mixing medications in one syringe, 637–638
safety syringes, 633
systemic infection, 745
systems theories, 67–68
biologic system, 68
and nursing process, 390
subsystem, 67
suprasystems, 67
system, defined, 67
systolic blood pressure, 731

T

tachycardia, 721
tachypnea, 728, 1029
tactile discrimination, assessment of, 594–595
tactile stimuli, 1133
talk test, 1179
Tanner, C., 381
target heart rate, 1179
tartar, 826
task groups, 499
task-oriented leader, 694
taste (sense)
newborns, 325
preschoolers, 333
taxonomy, 405
See also North American Nursing Diagnosis Association (NANDA)
t-binders, 963
T-cell system, 750
teaching
assessment of learning needs, 675
cognition-based strategies, 162
community health programs, 674
differing clientele, 673–674
evaluation of, 688
guidelines, 674–675, 682–684
health personnel, 674
in nursing practice, 12
objective, 674
teacher-learner rapport, 674
teaching process, 673
transcultural teaching, 685–687
See also client teaching; learning
teaching groups, 499
teaching plan, 679–680
teaching priorities
content, 681
learning objectives, 677–681
ordering learning experiences, 682
teaching strategies, 681–683
teaching tools, 682
teaching strategies
behaviour modification, 685
client contracting, 684
computer-assisted instruction, 685
discovery/problem solving, 685
group teaching, 684–685
team nursing, 261
tears, defensive function of, 748
technologic factors
in Sunrise Model, 232
See also science and technology
teeth
anatomic parts, 825
brushing and flossing, 829, 830–831
developmental variations, 825
oral health, promoting, 829–855
tooth decay, preventing, 829–855
telangiectasias, 525
telecounselling, 472
telehealth, 254, 270, 471–472
telephone advice, 125
telephone counselling, 158
telephone orders, 463–464
temperature sensation, assessment of, 594
temperature-sensitive tape, 715
temper tantrums, 330
temporal pulse site, 720
tertiary prevention, 149, 150
terminal evaluation, 434
temperature scales, 715–716
territoriality, 488
Terry, R.W., 695
testicular cancer, 351, 600
testicular self-examination (TSE), 196, 197, 356, 600
theory, 38, 46
critique of, 41
defined, 50
See also ethical theories; nursing theories
therapeutic communication
attentive listening, 490
and client's emotions, 490
physical attending, 490–491
techniques, 494
therapeutic effect, 611
therapeutic massage, 167–168
therapeutic touch, noncontact, 174–175
therapies, and nutrition, 979
thermic effect of food, 976
thermometers, 714–715, 716
third space syndrome, 1083
third thoracic vertebra (T-3), 560
thirst mechanism, 1076
Thompson, C.B., 468
thorax and lungs assessment
anterior thorax, 565–566
breath sounds, 560–561
chest landmarks, 558–560
chest shape and size, 560
instrumentation, 562
positioning, 561
posterior thorax, 562–565
trachea, 567
Thorndike, Edward, 669
thrill, 569
throat culture, 1034
thrombophlebitis, 1184
throughputs, 68
thyroid gland, 515–552
thyroxine, 710
ticks, 836
tidal volume, 729, 1021
timed urine specimen, 903
time-lapsed assessment, 391
timing and relevance, in verbal communication, 485–486
tinea pedis, 822
toddlers
cognitive development, 331
defecation, 860
developmental assessment guidelines, 332
health examinations, 332
health problems, 331
health promotion guidelines, 331–332
living skills and knowledge, 335
moral development, 331
nutrition, 981–982
oral health, 828–829
physical development, 329–330, 332
psychosocial development, 330–331, 332
spiritual development, 331
toileting, assisting with, 906
tongue assessment, 547
tonic neck reflex, 326, 595
tonometry, 356
tonsils, 548
topical application, 617
ophthalmic instillations, 654–656
otic instillations, 656–657
percutaneous absorption, 653
rectal instillations, 660
skin preparations, 654
topical medications, 653
vaginal instillations, 658–660
tort law, 113
intentional torts, 121–122
tort, defined, 119
unintentional torts, 120
total care, in nursing practice, 60
total character, of client, 60
total parenteral nutrition (TPN). *See* parenteral nutrition
total quality improvement (TQI). *See* quality of care, quality improvement
touch, touching
and caring, 485
cultural significance, 236
inappropriate sexual behaviour, 18, 201
NIC intervention, 430
touch (sense)
infants, 325
toddlers, 330

touch therapies, 167–169
  acupressure, 169
  reflexology, 168
  therapeutic massage, 167–168
towel bath, 813–814
toys, 329, 330, 332
trachea, 551
tracheostomy, 1053–1057
traditional medicine, 305
tragus, 537
training. *See* education and training
transactional leadership, 695
transcellular fluid, 1072
transcendence, 482
transcultural nursing, 229
  See also culturally competent care
transcultural teaching, 685–687
transdermal delivery system, 653
transdermal patches, 654
transferring clients, 1204–1213
  between a bed and a chair, 1210–1212
  between a bed and a stretcher, 1213
  guidelines, 1204–1209
  walking belts, 1209
transformational leadership, 695
transient ischemic attach (TIA), 1030
transparent wound barriers, 957–958
transpersonal medicine, 165
transpersonal therapies
  intercessory prayer, 175
  noncontact therapeutic touch, 174–175
  Reiki, 175
transtracheal oxygen delivery, 1052
treatment orders, 428
tremor, 583
triadic questions, 83
trial and error, 381
triangular arm binder (sling), 962–963
triangular fossa, 537
triceps reflex, 589
trichinellosis, 296
Tri-Council Policy Statement on Ethical Conduct for Research Involving Humans, 41
tricuspid valve, 568
triglycerides, 974, 975
trigone, 893
trimesters, 323
trust
  in client-nurse relationship, 280, 494
  in collaborative health care, 272
  and mothering behaviour, 326
  trust *vs.* mistrust stage (Erikson), 326
truth, value of, 92
Tschikota, S., 382
tub bath, 814, 816–817
tuberculin syringes, 631
tuberculosis, screening for, 329, 332
tularemia, 296
tumour, 521
tuning fork tests, 540–541
turgor, skin, 524
Twaddle, A., 135

T

two-point tactile discrimination, 590, 594
tympanic membrane, 537, 540
tympanic therometer, 716–717
typmpany (sound), 517

U

UBC Model of Nursing (Campbell), 54–55
unauthorized use of client's name/likeness, 122
undifferentiated stage, in spiritual development, 318, 331
unemployment, 294
union contracts, 115
unitary theories. *See* holism
United Nations Children's Fund (UNICEF), 185
United States
  drug legislation, 610
unit standards of care, 417
universal access, 250, 266, 267
universal coverage, 9, 246
universalizing stage, in spiritual development, 318
universal precautions (UP), 761
University of Alberta, 48, 49
University of British Columbia, 25, 33
unlicensed assistive personnel (UAPs), 254
unreasonable intrusion, 122
unsaturated fatty acids, 974, 975
Upanishads, 171
upper-level managers, 696
upstream thinking, 132
urea, 904
uretereostomy, 864
ureters, 893
urethra, 893–894
urethral orifice, 596
urgency, 897
urinal, 872
urinary assessment
  factors influencing elimination, 899
  physical examination, 898
  urinary creatinine, 994–995
  urinary diversion ostomy, 899
  urinary urea nitrogen, 994–995
  voiding pattern, 899
urinary bladder, 893
  palpation of, 582
urinary catheterization
  changing catheter and tubing, 916–923
  client teaching, 923
  closed catheter irrigation, 924–925
  dietary measures and, 916
  female catheterization (straight catheter), 916–919
  fluid intake and, 916
  indwelling catheter, 916, 921–924
  infections, preventng, 923–924
  intermittent self-catheterization, 924–925
  male catheterization (straight catheter), 919–920
  nursing interventions for clients on, 916
  open method of catheter irrigation, 926
  perineal care and, 916
  removing retention catheter, 923–924
  suprapubic catheter care, 929
urinary diversions, 925–929
urinary drainage devices, external, 913–914
urinary frequency, 897
urinary hesitancy, 898
urinary incontinence (UI), 898
  bladder training, 911, 912
  habit training, 911
  immobility and, 1186
  Kegel exercises, 912–913
  nursing inteventions, 911–913
  pelvic exercises, 912
  prompted voiding, 911
urinary infections, 1186
urinary meatus, 893
urinary reflux, 1186
urinary retention (UR), 898, 1186
  urinary catheterization, 915–916
urinary tract infection, preventing, 906–910
urination
  and aging, 359, 361
  altered urine elimination, 897–898
  altered urine production, 896
  developmental factors, 894–895
  diagnoses, 904–933
  factors affecting voiding, 894–896
  food and fluid intake and, 895
  maintaining normal elimination, 906–911
  medications and, 895
  muscle tone and, 895
  nocturnal frequency, 352, 680
  pathological conditions and, 896
  planning care, 905–908
  process of, 894
  psychosocial factors, 894–895
  retention of residual urine, 352, 361
  surgical and diagnostic procedures and, 896
  urgency and frequency, with age, 361
urine
  assessment, 898–900, 899
  characteristics of normal and abnormal urine, 898–900
  clean-catch (midstream) specimen, 901–902
  clean voided specimen, 901
  fluid output, 1076
  indwelling catheter specimen, 903
  residual urine, measuring, 900–901
  specimens, collecting, 901–903
  timed urine specimen, 903
  urinary output, measuring, 898–900
urine osmolality, 1097
urine pH, 1097
urine specific gravity, 1097
urine testing
  diagnostic tests, 904
  glucose, 904
  ketones, 904
  occult blood, 904
  protein, 904
  specific gravity, 903
  urinary pH, 904
urongenital systems, 893
uterine cancer
  risk factors, 512

utilitarianism, 93
uvula, 548

V

vaginal instillations
assessment focus, 658
equipment, 658
evaluation focus, 657–660
intervention, 659–660
purposes, 658
vaginal speculum examination, 598
vaginismus, 191
validation, 403–404
Valsalva maneuver, 1183
values
defined, 92
in ethical decision making, 95–98
and perception, 488
personal values, 92
professional values, 92
value set, 92
value system, 92
Valuing Literacy in Canada, 668
vaporization, 710
Vardey, L., 207
variability, measures of, 38, 39
variance
documentation, 452
statistical variance, 38, 39
unattained goals, 451
varicella vaccine, 329
vasocongestion, 188
vastus lateralis site, 642–643
vector-borne transmission, 747
vegetarian diets, 986–987
vehicle-borne transmission, 747
venous stasis
immobility and, 1184
prevention of, 1063
ventilation (breathing), 727
pulmonary ventilation, 1021
ventilation (room), 847
ventilation scan (V scan), 1036
ventrogluteal site, 642–643
veracity, 93, 94
verbal communication, 485–486
verbal contracts, 115
vernix caseosa, 323
vertebral line, 558
vesicle, 522
vestibules, 537
vest restraint, 800
Veterans Affairs Canada, 287
vials, 633, 635–637
vibration, 1046
vicarious liability, 115
See also respondent superior
Victorian Order of Nurses, 147, 274, 669
violence, workplace, 796
virtue, 94
virulence, of microorganism, 744
viruses, 745
visible minorities, 224–226
places of origin, 226
population distribution, 224
vision assessment
anterior eye chamber assessment, 532–533
corneal sensitivity (reflex) test, 532
distance vision, 535
functional vision testing, 535–536
nasolacrimal duct, 531–532
peripheral visual field, 533, 534
pupil reactions, 533–534
reaction to accommodation, 533
screenings, 331, 351
upper eyelid, everting, 531
visual acuity, 534
vision (foresight), 695
vision (sight)
of adolescents, 344
and aging, 358, 360
of children, 536
direct and consensual reaction to light, 533
impairments, 333
of infants, 325, 536
lacrimal gland, 531–532
of middle-aged adults, 356
ocular movements, 534, 535
of older adults, 536
of preschoolers, 333, 536
problems, 331
of school-age children, 336
screenings, 356, 528
of toddlers, 330
visual acuity, 528
visual fields, 528
visual aphasia, 586
visual stimuli, 1133
vital capacity, 1026, 1184
vital signs
assessment times, 709
blood pressure, 731–739
body temperature, 709–714
and fluid assessment, 1094
monitoring, 709
pulse, 719–727
respiration, 727–731
variations by age, 709
vitamins, 975
vitiligo, 520, 524
vocal (tactile) fremitus, 563, 566, 567
volume-control infusions, 649–651
volume expanders, 1104
voluntariness, 117
voyeurism, 188
vulvodynia, 191

W

waist circumfrance (WC), 993
waist hip ratio (WHR), 993
Wald, Lillian, 147
walkers, 1169–1219
walking belt, 1210–1212
watch tick test, 540
waterless hand scrub, 757
water-soluble vitamins, 975
water supply, safe, 295
Watson, J., 53, 55, 92, 164, 481
Web-based instruction, 474
Weber's test, 541
Weed, Lawrence, 446
weight
of adolescents, 340
anthropometric measurements, 991
of neonates, 324
of preschoolers, 333
of school-age children, 336
of toddlers, 329
weighing, 519–520
weight loss, calculating percentage of, 526
wellness, 8
See also health and wellness
wellness assessment programs, 150
wellness diagnosis, 405, 406
wellness models, 402–403
Wellness nursing diagnoses, 157
wellness programs, 269
Westerhoff. J., 208, 318–319, 828
Western Journal of Nursing Research, 40
wet-to-damp dressing, 957
wheal, 522
wheelchairs, 1209, 1211
whistle-blowing, 125–126
WHMIS (Workplace Hazardous Materials Information System), 795
whole-brain thinking, 164
Wilkinson, J.M., 103
wills, 119
witnesses, 114
obtaining consent, 117
women
abuse of, 351
age of first marriages, 78
care for elderly family members, 77
female single-parent families, 76
labour market participation, 60
and nursing, 260
stress, 142, 356
victims of violence, 143
women's health
health-care services, 257
worker's compensation, 246
working conditions, 142
workplace health. *See* health and safety
work-related social support group, 501
work-role preoccupation, 313
worksite wellness programs, 151, 152
World Health Organization (WHO), 140, 148, 181, 185, 246, 265, 274, 744
world views. *See* paradigm
wound drainage, 942
specimen, obtaining, 947
wound dressing
gauze dressings, 955–957
hydrocolloid dressings, 957–959
purposes, 955
securing dressing, 960
transparent wound barriers, 957–958
types of, 955
wound healing, 939–942
complications, 942–943
evaluation of, 964
factors affecting, 943
phases of, 941–942
supportive devices, 951
types of, 941

wound management, 951
  cleaning wounds, 953
  dressing wounds, 953–960
  infection, preventing, 952
  RYB colour code, 952–953
  supporting and mobilizing wounds, 960–964
  wound irrigation and packing, 955
  See also pressure ulcers
wounds
  acute wounds, 935, 944–945
  assessment of, 943–947
  care plan, 945–948
  chronic wounds, 935, 944
  classification of, 935–936
  diagnoses, 945–947
  evaluation focus, 947
  lab data of, 945
  nursing interventions, 947–949
  prevention strategies, 948–951
  sutured wounds, 943
wrist restraint, 801
writ of summons, 113
written contracts, 115

X

xiphoid process of the sternum, 575
x-ray examination, 1036

Y

yama, 171
ying-yang, concept of, 234
yoga, 171
Yom Kippur, 210
young adults
  cognitive development, 349
  developmental assessment guidelines, 350
  health problems, 350–351
  health promotion, 351
  moral development, 349
  nutrition, 983
  oral health, 829–855
  physical development, 348, 350
  psychosocial development, 348–349, 350
  spiritual development, 349

Z

zoonoses, 296
Zoroastrianism, 211

"AS IS" LICENSE AGREEMENT AND LIMITED WARRANTY

READ THIS LICENSE CAREFULLY BEFORE OPENING THIS PACKAGE. BY OPENING THIS PACKAGE, YOU ARE AGREEING TO THE TERMS AND CONDITIONS OF THIS LICENSE. IF YOU DO NOT AGREE, DO NOT OPEN THE PACKAGE. PROMPTLY RETURN THE UNOPENED PACKAGE AND ALL ACCOMPANYING ITEMS TO THE PLACE YOU OBTAINED THEM. THESE TERMS APPLY TO ALL LICENSED SOFTWARE ON THE DISK EXCEPT THAT THE TERMS FOR USE OF ANY SHAREWARE OR FREEWARE ON THE DISKETTES ARE AS SET FORTH IN THE ELECTRONIC LICENSE LOCATED ON THE DISK:

1. GRANT OF LICENSE and OWNERSHIP: The enclosed computer programs <<and any data>> ("Software") are licensed, not sold, to you by Pearson Education Canada Inc. ("We" or the "Company") in consideration of your adoption of the accompanying Company textbooks and/or other materials, and your agreement to these terms. You own only the disk(s) but we and/or our licensors own the Software itself. This license allows instructors and students enrolled in the course using the Company textbook that accompanies this Software (the "Course") to use and display the enclosed copy of the Software for academic use only, so long as you comply with the terms of this Agreement. You may make one copy for back up only. We reserve any rights not granted to you.

2. USE RESTRICTIONS: You may not sell or license copies of the Software or the Documentation to others. You may not transfer, distribute or make available the Software or the Documentation, except to instructors and students in your school who are users of the adopted Company textbook that accompanies this Software in connection with the course for which the textbook was adopted. You may not reverse engineer, disassemble, decompile, modify, adapt, translate or create derivative works based on the Software or the Documentation. You may be held legally responsible for any copying or copyright infringement which is caused by your failure to abide by the terms of these restrictions.

3. TERMINATION: This license is effective until terminated. This license will terminate automatically without notice from the Company if you fail to comply with any provisions or limitations of this license. Upon termination, you shall destroy the Documentation and all copies of the Software. All provisions of this Agreement as to limitation and disclaimer of warranties, limitation of liability, remedies or damages, and our ownership rights shall survive termination.

4. DISCLAIMER OF WARRANTY: THE COMPANY AND ITS LICENSORS MAKE NO WARRANTIES ABOUT THE SOFTWARE, WHICH IS PROVIDED "AS-IS." IF THE DISK IS DEFECTIVE IN MATERIALS OR WORKMANSHIP, YOUR ONLY REMEDY IS TO RETURN IT TO THE COMPANY WITHIN 30 DAYS FOR REPLACEMENT UNLESS THE COMPANY DETERMINES IN GOOD FAITH THAT THE DISK HAS BEEN MISUSED OR IMPROPERLY INSTALLED, REPAIRED, ALTERED OR DAMAGED. THE COMPANY DISCLAIMS ALL WARRANTIES, EXPRESS OR IMPLIED, INCLUDING WITHOUT LIMITATION, THE IMPLIED WARRANTIES OF MERCHANTABILITY AND FITNESS FOR A PARTICULAR PURPOSE. THE COMPANY DOES NOT WARRANT, GUARANTEE OR MAKE ANY REPRESENTATION REGARDING THE ACCURACY, RELIABILITY, CURRENTNESS, USE, OR RESULTS OF USE, OF THE SOFTWARE.

5. LIMITATION OF REMEDIES AND DAMAGES: IN NO EVENT, SHALL THE COMPANY OR ITS EMPLOYEES, AGENTS, LICENSORS OR CONTRACTORS BE LIABLE FOR ANY INCIDENTAL, INDIRECT, SPECIAL OR CONSEQUENTIAL DAMAGES ARISING OUT OF OR IN CONNECTION WITH THIS LICENSE OR THE SOFTWARE, INCLUDING, WITHOUT LIMITATION, LOSS OF USE, LOSS OF DATA, LOSS OF INCOME OR PROFIT, OR OTHER LOSSES SUSTAINED AS A RESULT OF INJURY TO ANY PERSON, OR LOSS OF OR DAMAGE TO PROPERTY, OR CLAIMS OF THIRD PARTIES, EVEN IF THE COMPANY OR AN AUTHORIZED REPRESENTATIVE OF THE COMPANY HAS BEEN ADVISED OF THE POSSIBILITY OF SUCH DAMAGES. SOME JURISDICTIONS DO NOT ALLOW THE LIMITATION OF DAMAGES IN CERTAIN CIRCUMSTANCES, SO THE ABOVE LIMITATIONS MAY NOT ALWAYS APPLY.

6. GENERAL: THIS AGREEMENT SHALL BE CONSTRUED AND INTERPRETED ACCORDING TO THE LAWS OF THE PROVINCE OF ONTARIO. This Agreement is the complete and exclusive statement of the agreement between you and the Company and supersedes all proposals, prior agreements, oral or written, and any other communications between you and the company or any of its representatives relating to the subject matter.

Should you have any questions concerning this agreement or if you wish to contact the Company for any reason, please contact in writing: Customer Service, Pearson Education Canada, 26 Prince Andrew Place, Don Mills, Ontario M3C 2T8.

GUIDELINES FOR THE PROCEDURES

The nursing actions listed below underlie safe, competent nursing and therefore should be considered as part of every procedure in the book.

- Before implementing any interventions, refer to the agency's specific protocols for further information and recommendations.
- Many agencies require a signed, informed consent for certain invasive procedures. Please refer to specific agency policies for this information.
- Wash the hands before gathering any clean or sterile supplies, before gloving, before implementing a procedure, after contact with a client, and after removing gloves to avoid transmission of microorganisms to clients and others.
- Implement appropriate standard and/or transmission-based precautions.
- Identify the client appropriately by reading the client's wrist band and asking the client his or her name.
- Explain the procedure to the client and, in some instances, to support persons, adjusting your explanation to their needs. Explaining what you plan to do reassures people by letting them know what to expect. Specific explanations are provided in some procedures.
- Provide privacy for the client when any aspect of the procedure could be embarrassing to the client or others and as an indication of respect even when the client is not conscious.
- Elevate the client's bed to a working level and lower the near side rail before starting a procedure. These actions help the nurse maintain good body mechanics.
- Recheck an abnormal reading or measurement (eg, blood pressure) and if it is still abnormal, report and record it immediately.
- Procedures pertinent to intravenous therapy may include the use of needles. In many agencies, use of a "needleless" system has replaced traditional needles. Familiarize yourself with an agency's policies and practices regarding the use and disposal of needles during IV therapy.
- Following a procedure, lower the bed and raise the near side rail for clients requiring these precautions. These actions are taken for the client's safety.
- Ensure that the client is comfortable following the procedure.
- Dispose of used and unused supplies according to agency practice. This step includes cleaning and/or disinfecting equipment as necessary.